한영불교사전
韓英佛教辭典
KOREAN-ENGLISH BUDDHIST DICTIONARY
WITH SANSKRIT AND ENGLISH EQUIVALENTS

Edited by

고 영 섭
Ko, Young-Seop

황 남 주
Hwang, Nam-Ju

신아사

韓英불교사전을 내면서 Editors' Preface

우리나라가 서양세계에 문을 연 지 백 사십 여년이 되었습니다. 당시 서양인들에게 비친 우리의 모습은 유교문화와 불교문화 일색이었습니다. 서양인들은 도산서원과 병산서원 등 안동 일대의 유교문화와 유점사와 정양사, 장안사와 표훈사 등 금강산 일대의 불교사찰을 보고 감탄의 소리를 쏟아내었습니다. 그들은 동아시아 문명국의 하나였던 조선문명의 독창성을 보고 조선에 대한 이해를 심화시킬 수 있었습니다. 이후 그들은 한국불교가 조선문명의 중심부에 있다는 사실을 확신하기 시작했습니다.

그 사이 한국 불교계의 몇몇 수행자들이 영미권에 유학을 떠났습니다. 해서 한국불교의 존재감은 스리랑카와 인도를 비롯하여 독일과 프랑스 등지에 전해졌습니다. 점차 미국과 영국 등지로까지 이어지면서 한국불교의 존재감은 새롭게 인식되기 시작했습니다. 당시까지만 해도 그들 일부는 한국불교를 중국불교 혹은 일본불교의 연장 혹은 연속 위에서 바라보고 있었습니다. 그 뒤 한국의 위상이 점차 알려지면서 한국의 전통사상인 한국불교에 대해 새롭게 이해하려고 노력했습니다.

한국전쟁 이후 국내의 몇몇 불교 수행자들이 해외 포교에 나서면서 한국불교는 비로소 서구인들에 의해 타자화되고 객관화되었습니다. 서구에서 한국인들은 인도불교, 중국불교, 일본불교와 다른 한국불교의 정체성과 인식틀의 제시를 요구받았습니다. 그 과정에서 한국인들은 몸에 익지 않은 채로나마 영어 표현을 통해 한국불교를 전했습니다. 이러한 과정을 통해 한국불교의 영어 표현 수요가 급증하였고 공급이 확대되었습니다. 그리고 한국불교 수행에 관심이 있던 몇몇 외국인들의 국내 입국으로 영어의 지형은 보다 확산되었습니다.

우리나라는 1988년에 국제올림픽을 치른 뒤 많은 외국인들을 받아들였습니다. 개방화가 본격화된 1990년대에 들어서면서 국제화와 세계화가 본격화되기 시작했습니다. 더욱이 사찰체험을 비롯하여 사찰음식에 대한 수요가 확대되면서 한국불교에 대한 인식이 바뀌기 시작했습니다. 하지만 이렇게 변화된 상황 아래서도 한문으로 된 한국불교의 성취를 영어로 소개하는 것은 여전히 쉽지 않았습니다. 아울러 한국불교 용어의 개념 통일은 지극히 어려운 일이었습니다.

하여 평소 한영불교사전의 편찬을 발원해온 우리는 당시에 구해볼 수 있었던 수트힐 교수와 호더스 교수가 정리해 놓은 『중국불교용어집』(중영불학사전)에 주목하게 되었습니다. 두 교수는 나름대로 열정과 끈기를 갖고 영어권에서 처음으로 『중국불교용어집』을 만들었습니다. 우리는 이들의 작업을 '원용'하면서 우리식으로 '변용'을 꾀하기로 했습니다. 아직 과도기인 한국 불교영어 지형으로 볼 때 그것은 현실가능한 작업이라고 판단하였습니다.

먼저 두 교수의 작업을 한글 표제어 순으로 바꾸고 여러 차례 교정을 보았습니다. 동시에 한국불교에 관한 새로운 표제어 300여개를 작성하고 영역하여 보충했습니다. 그 과정에서 『한영불교사전』은 점차 한국적인 부분의 보완을 실감했습니다. 외국어인 영어로 모국어인 한국어를 옮겨내는 일이 쉬운 일이 아니듯 한국불교를 영어로 옮겨내는 일 역시 쉬운 일이 아님을 우리는 잘 알고 있습니다. 하지만 우리는 이 사전편찬 작업이 한국불교를 외화시키는 일로 여기며 최선을 다했습니다.

이 『한영불교사전』은 불교철학, 불교사상, 불교문화, 불교인명 등에 관련된 표제어 약 1만 여개를 담아 수록하였습니다. 이 사전을 편찬하면서 우리는 국제화와 세계화 시대에 우리의 정체성 확립과 인식틀 확보가 무엇보다도 중요하다는 사실을 자각하게 되었습니다. 해서 한국불교를 해외에 널리 알릴 수 있는 지름길은 전문성과 대중성을 갖춘 『한국불교통사』의 영역출간과 더불어 『한영불교사전』의 편찬이라는 생각을 더욱 더 하게 되었습니다.

『한영불교사전』은 지난 1990년대 초부터 2010년까지 약 20여 년 간에 걸쳐 이루어졌습니다. 한동안 중단된 적도 있었지만 오늘에 이르러 이렇게 간행해 놓고 보니 감개가 무량합니다. 최근 전통 한국불교 전적과 스님들의 법문집 영역 사업이 본격화되면서 이 사전의 사용도가 더욱 더 높아지리라고 생각합니다. 우리는 앞으로도 여력이 되는대로 이 사전을 보충할 생각입니다. 여러 전문가들의 많은 조언과 질정을 부탁드립니다.

2010. 6. 14.

편저자　고영섭, 황남주

차례 CONTENTS

편저자 서문 Editors' Preface
일러두기 Notes for Readers
한글-한문-영어 불교용어사전 KOREAN-ENGLISH BUDDHIST DICTIONARY

ㄱ 1
ㄴ 71
ㄷ 82
ㄹ 117
ㅁ 127
ㅂ 162
ㅅ 234
ㅇ 372
ㅈ 514
ㅊ 563
ㅋ 590
ㅌ 591
ㅍ 598
ㅎ 618

찾아보기 Index 649

일러두기 NOTES for Readers

1. Order of entries: all entry words are in order of Hangeul alphabet as follows:

   Consonants: ㄱ ㄲ ㄴ ㄷ ㄸ ㄹ ㅁ ㅂ ㅃ ㅅ ㅆ ㅇ ㅈ ㅉ ㅊ ㅋ ㅌ ㅍ ㅎ
   Vowels: ㅏ ㅐ ㅑ ㅒ ㅓ ㅔ ㅕ ㅗ ㅘ ㅙ ㅚ ㅛ ㅜ ㅝ ㅞ ㅟ ㅠ ㅡ ㅢ ㅣ

2. Compound words: compound words with the same root are in consecutive order. In addition, they are arranged in index for easy search.

3. A limited number of abbreviations have been used, which are self-evident, e.g. tr. for translation, translator, etc.; translit. for transliteration, transliterate, etc.; abbr. for abbreviation; intp. for interpreted or interpretation; u.f. for used for; q.v. for quod vide (=which see). "Eitel" refers to Dr. Eitel's Handbook of Chinese Buddhism; "M.W." to Monier-Williams' Sanskrit-English Dictionary; "Keith" to Professor A. Berriedale Keith's Buddhist Philosophy; "Getty" to Miss Alice Getty's The Gods of Northern Buddhism; B.D. to the 佛學大辭典; B.N. to Bunyiu Nanjio's Catalogue.

4. Where characters are followed by others in brackets, they are used alone or in combination; e.g. in 十善(正法) the term 十善 may be used alone or in full 十善正法.

5. In the text a few variations occur in the romanization of Sanskrit and other non-Chinese words. In this Dictionary it was hard to follow the principle of inserting hyphens between the members of Sanskrit compound words.

<ㄱ>

가 또는 **하** 또는 **할** 訶 To blame, reprove, scold ; ridicule ; translit. *ha*, *ka*, *kha*, *ga*, and similar sounds. 가불매조 訶佛罵祖 To scold a Buddha and abuse an elder. 하리 訶利 ; 하리 訶梨 ; 할리 噶里 Hari, tawny, a lion. 하리지 訶利底 Hāritī, also 하리제 訶利帝 or 訶哩帝 ; 가리지 呵利底 ; 가리제 呵利帝 or 가리타 呵利陀 ; 아리지 阿利底 Aritī ; intp. as captivating, charming ; cruel ; dark green, yellow, etc. ; mother of demons, a rākṣasī who was under a vow to devour the children of Rājagṛha, but was converted by the Buddha, and became the guardian of nunneries, where her image, carrying a child and with children by her, is worshipped for children or in children's ailments. 하리지모 訶利底母 or 하리지남 訶利底南 idem. 하리기사 訶利枳舍 ; 할리계사 噶里鷄舍 Harikeśa, yellow-haired, lion's mane, name of a yakṣa. 하실다 訶悉多 Hasta, an arm, a hand. 하리륵 訶梨勒 Harītakī, the yellow Myrobalan tree and fruit, used for medicine ; also 하리달계 訶梨怛鷄 or 하리득지 訶梨得枳, 하자 訶子, etc. 하리발마 訶梨跋摩 Harivarman, tawny armour, and 사자개 師子鎧 lion armour ; a Brahman who, "900 years" after the Nirvāṇa, appeared in Central India and joined the Sarvāstivādin and Satyasiddhi school by the publication of the Satyasiddhi śāstra (tr. as the 성실론 成實論 by Kumārajīva, 407-418). 하라하라 訶羅訶羅 Halāhala, Hālāhala, etc., a deadly poison.

가 街 A street (especially with shops), a market. 가방 街方 The busy mart of life.

가 加 Add, added ; increase ; put on. 가력 加力 Added strength or power (by the Buddhas or bodhisattvas) ; aid. 가시 加尸 ; 가사 加私 ; 가시 迦尸 Kāśa, visibility, splendour ; a species of grass, *Saccharum spontaneum*. [M. W.] 가지 加持 ; 지슬미낭 地瑟娓曩 Adhiṣṭhāna, to depend upon, a base, rule. It is defined as dependence on the Buddha, who 가 加 confers his strength on all (who seek it), and 지 持 upholds them ; hence it implies prayer, because of obtaining the Buddha's power and transferring it to others ; in general it is to aid, support. 가지공물 加持供物 To repeat tantras over offerings, in order to prevent demons from taking them or making them unclean. 가지성불 加持成佛 By the aid of Buddha to enter Buddhahood. 가지장 加持杖 A wand (made of peach wood) laid on in driving out demons, or in healing disease, the painful place being beaten. Tantras are repeated while the wand is used on the patient. 가지신 加持身 The body which the Buddha depends upon for his manifestation, i.e. the nirmāṇakāya. 가사 加沙 ; 가사 迦沙 ; 가사 袈裟 Kaṣāya, a colour composed of red and yellow, i.e. brown, described as a mixed colour, but 가사야 加沙野 is defined as 적 赤 red. 가란가 加蘭伽 Kalaviṅka, v. 가 迦. 가행 加行 Prayoga. Added progress, intensified effort, earnest endeavour. 가행위 加行位 The second of the four stages of the 유식종 唯識宗 known also as 사가행 四加行. 가행선 加行善 ; 수득선 修得善 ; 방편선 方便善 Goodness acquired by earnest effort, or "works", as differentiated from 생득선 生得善 natural goodness. 가피 加被 ; 가우 加祐 ; 가비 加備 ; 가호 加護 Divine or Buddha aid or power bestowed on the living, for their protection or perfection.

가 柯 Axe-handle ; agent ; translit. *k*, v. 가 呵, 가 迦, 가 哥, etc. 가시비여 柯尸悲與 The Kāśyapīyāḥ school.

가 哥 Elder brother. 가대 哥大 Skandha, v. 색 塞. 가(리)왕 哥(利)王 cf. 가 迦. 가라라 哥羅羅 Kalala. The womb, uterus ; an embryo shortly after conception.

가 家 Family ; home ; school, sect ; genus. 가세국 家世國 v. 달 呾 Takṣaśilā, Taxila. 가주 家主 Kulapati, the head of a family. 가구 家狗 A domestic dog, i.e. trouble, whichever dogs one steps.

가 嘉 Good, excellent, praiseworthy, to commend. 가회 嘉會 ; 가집 嘉集 Delightful assembly, an excellent meeting.

가 呵 Ho, k'o. Breathe out, yawn, scold ; ha, laughter ; used for 하 訶 and 아 阿. 가야달나 呵也怛那 Āyatana, an organ of sense, v. 육입 六入. 가리타 呵利陀 or 아리타 阿梨陀 Hāritī, the demon-mother ; also Harita, Haridrā, tawny, yellow, turmeric. 가타가 呵咤迦 or 하타가 訶咤迦 Hāṭaka ; gold, thorn-apple. 가파파 呵婆婆 Hahava, or Ababa, the fourth and 가라라 呵羅羅 Aṭaṭa the third of the eight cold hells, in which the sufferers can only utter these sounds. 가책건도 呵責犍度 The eleventh of the twenty rules for monks, dealing with rebuke and punishment of a wrongdoer.

가 伽 Interchanged with 가 迦 q.v. ; translit. *ga, gha, ka, khya, g,* and in one case for *ha.* 가미니 伽彌尼 Gamini, a king whom the Buddha is said to have addressed, v. sūtra of this name. 가비 伽憊 idem 노가비 路伽憊 Lokavid. 가리 伽梨 Abbrev. for 승가리 僧伽梨 saṅghāṭī, robe. 가범 伽梵 ; 가바 伽婆 Abbrev. for Bhagavān, see 바가범 婆伽梵. A Western Indian monk who tr. a work on 관자재 觀自在 was 가범달마 伽梵達摩 Bhagavaddharma. 가범파제 伽梵波提 ; 가방파제 伽傍簸帝 Gavāṁpati. 우주 牛主 Lord of cattle, name of an arhat ; v. 교 憍. 가비려 伽毗黎 Kapilavastu, v. 겁 劫. 가라 伽羅 Abbrev. for 다가라 多伽羅 Tagara, putchuk, incense. 가라야차 伽羅夜叉 Kālaka, a yakṣa who smote Śāriputra on the head while in meditation, without his perceiving it. 가라니 伽羅尼 ; 갈라나 羯羅拏 Ghrāṇa, smell ; scent. 가라타 伽羅陀 (1) Kharādīya, the mountain where Buddha is supposed to have uttered the 지장십륜경 地藏十輪經, the abode of Ti-tsang ; other names for it are 거라타 佉羅陀, 거라제 佉羅帝 or 거라제야 佉羅提耶. (2) A Bodhisattva stage attained after many kalpas. 가야 伽耶 ; 가사 伽邪 ; 가사 伽闍 Gayā. (1) A city of Magadha, Buddhagayā (north-west of present Gayā), near which Śākyamuni became Buddha. (2) Gaja, an elephant. (3) 가야산 伽耶山 Gajaśīrṣa, Elephant's Head Mountain ; two are mentioned, one near "Vulture Peak," one near the Bo-tree. (4) Kāya, the body. 가야사다 伽耶舍多 or 가사사다 伽邪舍多 Gayaśāta (? Jayata), the eighteenth Indian patriarch, who laboured among the Tokhari. 가야가섭 伽耶迦葉 Gayākāśyapa, a brother of Mahākāśyapa, originally a fire-worshipper, one of the eleven foremost disciples of Buddha, to become Samantaprabhāsa Buddha. 가지 伽胝 Abbrev. for Saṅghāṭī, robe ; v. 승가지 僧伽胝. 가람 伽藍 ; 승가람마 僧伽藍摩 ; 승람 僧藍 Saṅghārāma or Saṅghāgāra. (1) The park of a monastery. (2) A monastery, convent. There are eighteen 가람신 伽藍神 guardian spirits of a monastery. 가란타 伽蘭他 Grantha, a treatise, section, verse ; the scriptures of the Sikhs. 가차제 伽車提 Gacchati, goes, progresses. 가나 伽那 Gaṇa, Ghana ; close, solid, thick. 가가나비려차나 伽伽那卑麗叉那 or 가가나필리기나 伽伽那必利綺那 Gaganaprekṣaṇa, beholding the sky, or looking into space. 가나제바 伽那提婆 Kāṇadeva, i.e. Āryadeva, fifteenth patriarch, disciple of Nāgārjuna, v. 가 迦. 가나복력인 伽那馥力刃 A name of Nāgārjuna. 가타 伽陀 ; 가타 伽他 (1) Gātha = song ; gāthā, a metrical narrative or hymn, with moral purport, described as generally composed of thirty-two characters, and called 고기송 孤起頌 a detached stanza, distinguished from geya, 중송 重頌 which repeats the ideas of preceding prose passages. (2) Agada as adjective = healthy ; as noun = antidote. (3) Gata, arrived at, fallen into, or "in a state."

가 可 May, can, able. 가한 可汗 Khan. A Turkish term for "prince". 가루(자) 可漏(子) A case for books or writings, likened to the shell of an egg (각루 殼漏). 가하돈 可賀敦 Khatun. A Turkish term for "queen" or "princess".

가 假 To borrow, pretend, assume, suppose ; unreal, false, fallacious. In Buddhism it means empirical ; nothing is real and permanent, all is temporal and merely phenomenal, fallacious, and unreal ; hence the term is used in the sense of empirical, phenomenal, temporal, relative, unreal, seeming, fallacious, etc. The three fundamental propositions or 삼제 三諦 are 공가중 空假中 the void, or noumenon ; the empirical, or phenomenal ; and the mean. 가합 假合 ; 가화합 假和合 Phenomena, empirical combinations without permanent reality. 가합지신 假合之身

The empirical body. 가명 假名 Unreal names, i.e. nothing has a name of itself, for all names are mere human appellations. 가명세간 假名世間 The world of unreal names, i.e. the phenomenal world of sentient beings. 가명유 假名有 Things which exist only in name, i.e. all things are combinations of other things and are empirically named. 가명보살 假名菩薩 One who may be called a bodhisattva because he has attained the 십신 十信 q.v. 가실 假實 False and true, unreal and real, empirical and real, etc. 가아 假我 The empirical ego of the five skandhas. 가유 假有 The phenomenal, which in reality no more exists than turtle's hair or rabbit's horns. 가색 假色 Invisible, or internal form, i.e. spiritual form. 가관 假觀 The meditations on relative truth, or phenomenal and therefore illusory existence, in comparison with 공 空 and 중 中 q.v. 가설 假設 Prajñapti ; ordinary teaching, doctrines derived from the phenomenal. 가문 假門 The sects which rely on externals, i.e. on "works" for salvation, in contrast with faith in Amitābha.

가 歌 To sing ; a song ; translit. *ka* ; cf. 가 迦, 갈 羯. 가게 歌偈 Verses for singing ; to sing verses. 가리 歌利 Kali, the present evil age. 가리왕 歌利王 v. 갈 羯 Kalirāja. 가패 歌唄 ; 가탄 歌嘆 ; 가영 歌咏 ; 가송 歌頌 To sing, chant. 가율지가 歌栗底迦 Kārttika, the month October-November. 가무 歌舞 To sing and dance. 가라(분) 歌羅(分) v. 가 迦 Kalā, a fraction. 가라라 歌羅邏 Kalala, an embryo, the womb. 가라빈가 歌羅頻迦 v. 가 迦, Kalaviṅka. 가성 歌聲 The sound of singing, the singing of Kinnaras, cf. 긴 緊.

가 謌 To sing ; song. 가무 謌舞 To sing and dance ; same as 가무 歌舞, see 가 歌.

가 跏 To sit cross-legged 가부좌 跏趺坐, v. 결 結.

가 迦 Translit. *ka, kā* ; cf. 가 伽 ; 각 各 ; 알 嘎 ; 게 揭 ; 가 柯 ; 개 箇 ; 감 紺 ; 갈 羯.

가 珂 White jade shell ; translit. k, khr. 가단니 珂但尼 ; 거타 佉陀 or 거자니 佉闍尼 Khādanīya, food that can be masticated, or eaten. 가돌라 珂咄羅 Kotlan, "an ancient kingdom west of the Tsung-ling, south of the Karakal lake, in Lat. 39° N., Long. 72° E." [Eitel]. 가월 珂月 The jade-like or pearly moon. 가패 珂貝 Jade (or white quartz) and shells (cowries), used as money in ancient times. 가설 珂雪 Snow-white as jade (or white quartz).

가가 迦迦 Kāka, Kākala ; a crow, also 가가가 迦迦迦 ; 가가라 迦迦羅. 가가라충 迦迦羅蟲 is said to be Kākala, a black insect or worm. 가가루다 迦迦婁多 Kākaruta. A crow's caw. 가가바가빈사라 迦迦婆迦頻闍邏 Perhaps kapiñjala, a francolin, partridge, or pheasant. 가가나 迦迦那 Gagana, the firmament, space.

가나가모니 迦那伽牟尼 Kanakamuni, v. 구 拘. 가나제바 迦那提婆 Kāṇadeva, a disciple of Nāgārjuna and fifteenth patriarch, a native of South India, of the Vaiśya caste ; said to have only one eye, hence Kāṇa his name ; known also as Devabodhisattva.

가니(색)가 迦膩(色)伽 Kaniṣka, king of 월지 月支 the Yüeh-chih, i.e. of Tukhāra and the Indo-Scythians, ruler of Gandhāra in northern Punjab, who conquered northern India and as far as Bactria. He Became a patron of Buddhism, the greatest after Aśoka. His date is variously given ; [Keith] says "probably at the close of the first century A.D." It is also put at A.D. 125-165. He convoked "the third (or fourth) synod" in Kashmir, of 500 leading monks, under the presidency of 세우 世友 Vasumitra, when the canon was revised and settled ; this he is said to have had engraved on brass and placed in a stūpa.

가니가 迦尼迦 Kanaka, or Kanika ; a tree or plant, probably a kind of sandal-wood.

가담파 迦曇波 or 迦曇婆 Kadamba, a tree or plant with fragrant flowers ; the *Nauclea cadamba* ; the mustard plant.

가라 迦羅 Kalā, 가라 哥羅 ; 가라 歌羅 ; a minute part, an atom ; the hundredth part lengthwise of a human hair ; also a sixteenth part of anything. Also Kāla (and 가라 迦攞), a definite time, a division of time ; the time of work, study, etc., as opposed to leisure time. Kāla, among other meanings, also means black, for which 가라가 迦羅迦 Kālaka is sometimes used, e.g. the black nāga. 가라비라 迦羅毘囉 Karavīra, a fragrant oleander ; tr. as 양척촉 羊躑躅 a plant whose leaves on pressure exude juice. 가라비가 迦羅毘迦 Probably an incorrect form of Kapilavastu, v. 가비라 迦毘羅. 가(라)사예 迦(羅)沙曳 or 가(라)사야 迦(羅)沙野 or 가(라)사이 迦(羅)沙異 Kaṣāya, a monk's dyed robe, in contrast with white lay garb. 가라비나가 迦羅臂拏迦 Kālapināka, a "city of Magadha, 20 li south-east of Kulika, south of the present city of Behar." [Eitel]. 가라월 迦羅越 Kulapati, the head of a clan, or family. 가라가타 迦羅迦吒 The crab in the zodiac. 가라라 迦羅邏 Karāla, "having projecting teeth, formidable," "epithet of the Rākṣasas, of Śiva, of Kāla, of Viṣṇu," etc. [M. W.] 가라진두 迦羅鎭頭 Kālaka and tinduka, the first a poisonous fruit, the second non-poisonous, similar in appearance ; a simile for bad and good monks. 가라구타 迦羅鳩馱 Krakucchanda, v. 구류손 拘留孫 ; also Kakuda-Kātyāyana, v. 가전 迦旃.

가라가 迦邏迦 Kāra(ka), one who does, or causes ; an agent.

가란다 迦蘭陀 Karaṇḍa, Karaṇḍaka. (1) A bird which flies in flocks and has a pleasant note ; also, a squirrel which awakened Bimbisāra to warn him against a snake. (2) The Karaṇḍa-veṅuvana, a garden belonging to an elder called Karaṇḍa, used by a Nirgrantha sect, then presented by King Bimbisāra to Śākyamuni. Other forms : 가란다이 迦蘭陀夷 ; 가란타 迦蘭馱 ; 가란다가 迦蘭多迦 ; 가람타 迦藍陀 ; 가린 伽隣 ; 갈란탁가 羯蘭鐸迦 or 갈란타가 羯蘭馱迦.

가루라 迦樓羅 Garuḍa ; "a mythical bird, the chief of the feathered race, the enemy of the serpent race, the vehicle of Viṣṇu." [M. W.] Tr. as golden-winged, with an expanse of 3,360,000 li, carrying the ju-i pearl or talisman on its neck ; among other accounts one says it dwells in great trees and feeds on snakes or dragons. Also 가루라 迦婁羅 ; 가류라 迦留羅 ; 가루다 迦嘍荼 ; 가루라 伽樓羅 ; 게로다 揭路荼 ; 아로나 誐嚕拏 or 벽로나 蘗嚕拏. The association of the garuḍa, like the phoenix, with fire makes it also a symbol of flame 가루라염 迦樓羅炎. 가루나 迦樓那 ; 가로나 迦盧拏 Karuṇā, pitying, pity.

가류다이 迦留陀夷 Kālodāyin, also called 오다이 烏陀夷 Udāyin or Black Udāyin, but there are other interpretations ; said to have been schoolmaster to Śākyamuni when young and one of the early disciples ; also to have been murdered.

가릉(빈)가 迦陵(頻)伽 Kalaviṅka. A bird described as having a melodious voice, found in the valleys of the Himalayas. M. W. says "a sparrow." It may be the Kalandaka, or Kokila, the cuckoo. It "sings in the shell" before hatching out. Other forms are 가란(빈)가 迦蘭(頻)伽 or 가란비가 迦蘭毘伽 ; 가비가(라) 迦毘伽(羅) ; 가미라 迦尾羅 ; 갈라(빈)가 羯羅(頻)伽 ; 갈비가라 羯毘伽羅 or 갈필가라 鶡鵯伽羅, etc. 가빈자라 迦頻闍羅 or 迦賓闍羅 ; 자고 鷓鴣 Kapiñjala, a francolin, partridge, or pheasant. 가빈자라왕 迦頻闍羅王 or 迦賓闍羅王 Kapiñjalarāja, a previous incarnation of Śākyamuni as a pheasant.

가리 迦利 Kali, strife, striver ; ill-born ; also 가리 迦梨 ; 가리 迦棃 ; 가람부 迦藍浮 ; 가라부 迦羅富 ; 가릉가왕 迦陵伽王 ; 가리 哥利 or 歌利 ; 갈리 羯利 Kalirāja, Kaliṅgarāja, a king of Magadha noted for his violence ; it is said that in a former incarnation he cut off the ears, nose, and hands of the Buddha, who bore it all unmoved ; cf. Nirvāṇa sūtra, 31. 가리사(나) 迦利沙(那) Karṣa, Karṣaṇa ; dragging, pulling, ploughing ; a weight, intp. as half a Chinese ounce. 가리사바나 迦利沙波拏 Kārṣāpaṇa, tr. as 400 candareens, but the weights vary ; also 가리사반나 迦利沙般拏 or 가리사바나 迦利沙婆拏 or 가리사발나 迦利沙鉢拏 ; 갈리사발나 羯利沙鉢那 or 羯利沙鉢拏 ; 계리사반 罽利沙盤.

가리사사니 迦梨沙舍尼 Karṣaṇīya ; to be drawn, attracted, conciliated ; intp. as forgiveness. 가리가 迦梨迦 or 가라가 迦羅迦 Kālīyaka, a nāga inhabiting the Yamunā (Jumna), slain by Kṛṣṇa ; intp. as a black dragon. Also Kālikā, a garment of diverse colours.

가마 迦摩 Kāma, desire, love, wish. A hungry spirit. 가마랑가 迦摩浪迦 Kāmalaṅkā, an ancient country "probably part of the present Chittagong opposite the mouth of the Ganges." [Eitel]. 가마라 迦摩羅 or 가말라 迦末羅 Kāmalā, jaundice. 가마루파 迦摩縷波 Kāmarūpa, now Kamrup ; "an ancient kingdom formed by the western portion of Assam." [Eitel]. 가마타도 迦摩馱都 Kāmadhātu ; the realm of desire, of sensuous gratification ; this world and the six devalokas ; any world in which the elements of desire have not been suppressed.

가비라 迦比羅 or 迦毘羅 Kapila, tawny, brown, red ; intp. as red head, or yellow head ; name of the founder of the Sāṅkhya philosophy ; also 가비리 迦毘梨 ; 겁비라 劫毘羅 ; cf. 승겁 僧劫 and 수 數. Kapilavastu, v. 겁 劫 or 각 却 ; also written in a dozen varieties, e.g. 가비라(파) 迦毘羅(婆) or 迦比羅(婆) ; 가비라파솔도 迦毘羅皤率都 ; 가유(라열) 迦維(羅閱) or 가유(라월) 迦維(羅越).

가비마라 迦毘摩羅 Kapimala, of Patna, second century A.D., converted by Aśvaghoṣa 마명 馬鳴 ; he himself is said to have converted Nāgārjuna ; he was the thirteenth Patriarch.

가사 袈裟 Kaṣāya, the monk's robe, or cassock. The word is intp. as decayed, impure (in colour), dyed, not of primary colour, so as to distinguish it from the normal white dress of the people. The patch-robe, v. 이십오조 二十五條. A dyed robe "of a colour composed of red and yellow" [M. W.] ; it has a number of poetic names, e.g. robe of patience, or endurance. Also 가(라)사예 迦(邏)沙曳.

가사 迦奢 Kāśa, a species of grass, used for mats, thatch, etc. ; personified as one of Yama's attendants. [M. W.] Eitel says a broom made of it and used by Śākyamuni "is still an object of worship." 가사포라 迦奢布羅 Kāśapura, a city which Eitel locates between Lucknow and Oudh.

가사 迦師 Kṛsara, "rice and peas boiled together" ; "grain and sesamum." [M. W.] It is intp. as a wheat porridge.

가섭(파) 迦葉(波) Kāśyapa, 가섭(파) 迦攝(波) *inter alia* "a class of divine beings similar to or equal to Prajāpati" ; the father "of gods, demons, men, fish, reptiles, and all animals" ; also "a constellation." [M. W.] It is intp. as "drinking light," i.e. swallowing sun and moon, but without apparent justification. (1) One of the seven or ten ancient Indian sages. (2) Name of a tribe or race. (3) Kāśyapa Buddha, the third of the five Buddhas of the present kalpa, the sixth of the seven ancient Buddhas. (4) Mahākāśyapa, a brahman of Magadha, who became one of the principal disciples of Śākyamuni, and after his death became leader of the disciples, "convoked and directed the first synod, whence his title Ārya Sthavira (상좌 上坐, lit. chairman) is derived." [Eitel]. He is accounted the chief of the ascetics before the enlightenment ; the first compiler of the canon and the first patriarch. (5) There were five Kāśyapas, disciples of the Buddha, Mahā-Kāśyapa, Uruvilvā-Kāśyapa, Gayā-Kāśyapa, Nadī-Kāśyapa, and Daśabala-Kāśyapa ; the second, third, and fourth are said to have been brothers. (6) A bodhisattva, whose name heads a chapter in the Nirvāṇa sūtra. (7) 가섭마등 迦葉摩騰 Kāśyapa Mātaṅga, the monk who with Gobharana, or Dharmarakṣa, i.e. Chu Fa-lan 축법란 竺法蘭, according to Buddhist statements, brought images and scriptures to China with the commissioners sent by Ming Ti, arriving in Lo-yang A.D. 67. 가섭유 迦葉遺 Kāśyapīyāḥ, a school formed on the division of the Mahāsāṅghika into five schools a century after the Nirvāṇa. [Keith] gives the southern order, in the second century after the Nirvāṇa, as Theravāda (Sthavira), Mahīśāsaka, Sarvāstivādin, Kāśyapīyāḥ. Other forms : 가섭비 迦葉毘 ; 가섭유 迦葉維 ; 가섭파 迦葉波 ; 가섭비야 迦葉臂耶 ; 가시비여 柯尸悲與.

가습미라 迦濕彌羅 Kāśmīra, Kashmir, formerly known in Chinese as 계빈 罽賓 Chi-pin ("the Kophen of the Greeks, the modern Kabul," Kubhā) ; under Kaniṣka the seat of the final synod for determining the Canon. Other forms are 가섭미라 迦葉彌羅 ; 갈습미라 羯濕弭羅.

가시 迦尸 Kāśī 가사 迦私, a place said to be so called because its bamboos were good for arrows, north of Kośala ; but it is also given by [M. W.] as Benares.

가야 迦耶 Kāya, the body ; an assemblage ; cf. Trikāya.

가자 迦柘 Kāca, glass, crystal ; tr. as a precious stone.

가전(연자) 迦旃(延子) Kātyāyana ; Mahākātyāyana ; Mahākātyanīputra ; one of the ten noted disciples of Śākyamuni. The foundation work of the Abhidharma philosophy, viz. the Abhidharma-jñāna-prasthāna-śāstra, has been attributed to him, but it is by an author of the same name 300 to 500 years later. Other forms are 가다연나 迦多衍那 ; 가다연니자 迦多衍尼子 or 迦多演尼子 ; 가지야야나 迦底耶夜那 ; 가전연(니자) 迦氈延(尼子). There are others of the same name ; e.g. the seventh of the ten non-Buddhist philosophers, perhaps Kakuda-Kātyāyana, associated with mathematics, but spoken of as "a violent adversary of Śākyamuni." [M. W.]

가지라 軻地羅 Khadira, the *Acacia catechu* ; the mimosa ; also 가리라 軻梨羅 ; 가지라 珂地羅 ; 걸지라 朅地羅 ; 거다라 佉陀羅 or 거달라 佉達羅 ; 거제가 佉提迦 ; 걸달라 朅達羅. 가지라산 軻地羅山 The Khadira circle of mountains, the fifth of the seven concentric mountain chains of a world. 가리 軻梨 ; 걸지락가 朅地洛迦 or 걸달락가 朅達洛迦 Khadiraka, idem.

가차말니 迦遮末尼 or **가자말니** 迦柘末尼 Kācamaṇi, crystal, quartz. 가차린지 迦遮鄰地 Kācalindikāka, or Kācilindi, also 가차린지가 迦遮鄰底迦 or 가진린지가 迦眞鄰底迦 ; 가전린제 迦旃鄰提 or 가전린타 迦旃鄰陀 ; 가지율나 迦止栗那 ; 가린제 迦鄰提 or 가린타 迦鄰陀 A sea bird, from whose feathers robes are made.

가치나 迦絺那 Kaṭhina, 가제 迦提 ; 갈치나 羯絺那 hard, inflexible, unyielding ; a robe of merit. 가치나월 迦絺那月 Kārttika-māsa, the month in October-November, intp. as the month after the summer retreat, when monks received the "kaṭhina" rove of merit ; the date of the month is variously given, but it follows the summer retreat ; also 가제월 迦提月 ; 가률지가월 迦慄底迦月 or 갈률지가월 羯慄底迦月 ; 가리지가월 迦利邸迦月 ; 가리지가마세 迦哩底迦麽洗 or 가날지가마세 迦剌底迦麽洗.

가타부단나 迦吒富單那 Kaṭapūtana, 갈타포달나 羯吒布怛那 Pretas, or demons, of remarkably evil odour.

가파리 迦波釐 Kāpālikas, followers of Śiva who wore skulls.

가포당 迦逋唐 v. 가포 迦布.

가포덕가 迦布德迦 Kapotaka, 가포당 迦逋唐 a dove, pigeon. 가포덕가가람 迦布德迦伽藍 ; 합원 鴿園 Kapotaka-saṅghārāma, a monastery of the Sarvāstivāda school, so called because the Buddha in a previous incarnation is said to have changed himself into a pigeon and to have thrown himself into the fire in order to provide food for a hunter who was prevented from catching game because of Buddha's preaching. When the hunter learned of Buddha's power, he repented and attained enlightenment.

가필시 迦畢試 Kapiśā, an ancient kingdom, south of the Hindukush, said to be 4,000 li around, with a capital of the same name 10 li in circumference ; formerly a summer resort of Kaniṣka.

각 閣 A pavilion, temple building ; chamber, council, cabinet.

각 覺 Bodhi, from bodha, "knowing, understanding," means enlightenment, illumination ; 각 覺 is to awake, apprehend, perceive, realize ; awake, aware ; (also, to sleep). It is illumination, enlightenment, or awakening in regard to the real in contrast to the seeming ; also, enlightenment in regard to moral evil. Cf. 보리 菩提 and 불 佛.

각 刻 Cut, carve, engrave ; oppress ; a quarter of an hour, instant. 각장 刻藏 to engrave the canon.

각 却 Decline, reject ; but, yet. 각입생사 却入生死 To leave his perfect life to enter into round of births and deaths, as a Bodhisattva does.

각 各 Each, every. 각종 各種 Each kind, every sort.

각 脚 Foot, leg. 각포 脚布 A bath towel, foot-towel.

각 殼 Husk, shell. 각루자 殼漏子 or 가루자 可漏子 A leaking husk or shell, i.e. the body of a man.

각 角 Viṣāṇa ; a horn, a trumpet ; also a corner, an angle ; to contend. 각타 角駄 Perverted doctrines and wrong thoughts, which weigh down a monk as a pack on an animal.

각견 覺堅 Firm, or secure, enlightenment.

각관 覺觀 Awareness and pondering, acts of intellectuation, later called 심사 尋伺, both of them hindrances to abstraction, or dhyāna. They are described as 추 麤 and 세 細, general and particular, respectively.

각도 覺道 The way of enlightenment, also 각로 覺路. 각도(지) 覺道(支) The 칠각 七覺 and 팔정도 八正道 q.v.

각료 覺了 Completely and clearly enlightened ; clearly to apprehend.

각모 覺母 Mother of enlightenment, a title of Mañjuśrī as the eternal guardian of mystic wisdom, all Buddhas, past, present, and future, deriving their enlightenment from him as its guardian ; also 불모 佛母.

각분 覺分 Bodhyaṅga, the seven 보리분 菩提分 q.v. ; also applied to the thirty-seven Bodhipākṣika, 삼십칠도품 三十七道品, q.v.

각산 覺山 The mountain of enlightenment, i.e. Buddha-truth.

각상 覺相 Sambhogakāya, v. 삼신 三身 ; 삼보 三寶, etc.

각성 覺性 The enlightened mind free from all illusion. The mind as the agent of knowledge, or enlightenment. Also used for Dharmakāya, v. 삼신 三身 ; 삼보 三寶, etc.

각성 覺城 The walled city of enlightenment, into which illusion cannot enter. Gayā, where the Buddha attained enlightenment.

각수 覺樹 The tree of knowledge, or enlightenment, the pippala under which the Buddha attained enlightenment, also called Bodhidruma and *Ficus religiosa*. To plant virtue in order to attain enlightenment.

각심 覺心 The mind of enlightenment, the illuminated mind, the original nature of man.

각안 覺岸 The shore of enlightenment, which Buddha has reached after crossing the sea of illusion.

각여 覺如 idem 각진여 覺眞如 v. 진여 眞如.

각오 覺悟 To awake, become enlightened, comprehend spiritual reality. 각오지 覺悟智 Enlightened wisdom ; wisdom that extends beyond the limitations of time and sense ; omniscience.

각왕 覺王 The king of enlightenment, the enlightened king, Buddha ; also 각제 覺帝.

각용 覺用 Nirmāṇakāya, v. 삼신 三身 ; 삼보 三寶, etc.

각웅 覺雄 The lord, or hero, of enlightenment, Buddha ; also 세웅 世雄.

각원 覺苑 Garden of enlightenment, a Pure Land, or Paradise ; also the mind.

각위 覺位 The stage of perfect enlightenment, that of Buddha.

각인 覺人 An enlightened man who has apprehended Buddha-truth.

각일 覺日 Timelessness, eternity, changelessness, the bodhi-day which has no change. Also 각시 覺時.

각자 覺者 An enlightened one, especially a Buddha, enlightening self and others, 자각각타 自覺覺他.

각지 覺支 The various branches or modes of enlightenment ; for the seven 각지 覺支 v. 칠보리분 七菩提分.

각책 覺策 To awaken and stimulate the mind against illusion and evil.

각타 覺他 To awaken others ; to enlighten others.

각해 覺海 The fathomless ocean of enlightenment, or Buddha-wisdom.

각행 覺行 The procedure, or discipline, of the attainment of enlightenment for self and others.

각화 覺華 The flower of enlightenment, which opens like a flower.

각훈 覺訓 Gak-hun, Goryeo monk who compiled the 해동고승전 海東高僧傳 "Lives of Eminent Korean Monks" in 1215.

간 間 A crevice, interval, space, room ; separate, intermission ; between, during, in ; to divide, interfere, intervene. 간단 間斷 To interrupt, interfere and stop. 간색 間色 Intermediate colours, i.e. not primary colours. 간격 間隔 Interval, intermission, but it is chiefly used for during, while, the period of an event. Cf. 무간 無間 Avīci.

간 干 A shield ; a stem, or pole ; to offend ; to concern ; to seek. 간률타 干栗馱 ; 간률태 干栗太 ; 건률타 乾栗馱 ; 흘리다 訖利多 Hṛd, hṛdaya, the physical heart. 간사나 干闍那 ; 건절나 建折那 Kāñcana, golden ; i.e. a tree, a shrub of the same type, with golden hue, described as of the leguminous order ; perhaps the Kuñjara. Wrongly written 우사라 于闍羅 or 나사라 那闍羅 and 천사나 千闍那.

간 簡 A tablet, memorandum ; to abridge ; appoint ; examine ; abrupt, concise, direct. 간별 簡別 To select, or differentiate.

간 看 Look, see ; watch over. 간방편 看方便 To fix the mind or attention, a Ch'an(Zen) term. 간병 看病 To nurse the sick ; also to attend a patient medically.

간 慳 Matsara ; lobha ; grudging, sparing, stingy, avaricious. 간심 慳心 ; 간석 慳惜 A grudging, mean heart. 간법 慳法 Mean and grudging of the Truth to others, unwillingness to part with it. 간빈 慳貧 Grudging and greed.

간 諫 To admonish. 간왕 諫王 To admonish a king.

간 揀 To pick, choose, select. 간택 揀擇 To choose, select. 간사 揀師 One chosen to be a teacher, but not yet fit for a full appointment.

간경 看經 To read a sūtra silently. It's original meaning is different from 독경 讀經 which means reading a sūtra like chanting. But it is changed to mean the same thing as 독경 讀經.

간경파 看經派 Textual study track ; section of seminary 강원 講院. See 사집과 四集科, 사교과 四教科, 대교과 大教科, 수의과 隨意科. Cf. 독서파 讀書派.

갈 褐 Coarse serge, hence poverty. 갈랄리 褐刺縭 ; 갈뢰리 褐賴襬 Harali, cloth woven of fine hair. 갈려(벌다) 褐麗(伐多) Revata, name of several persons, v. 리 利, 리 離.

갈 竭 Exhaust, used up, finished ; utmost. 갈차 竭叉 A place said to be in the Karakoram mountains, where according to Fa-hsien formerly great assemblies were held under royal patronage and with royal treatment. Eitel gives it as Khaśa, and says "an ancient tribe on the Paropamisus, the Kasioi of Ptolemy" ; others give different places, e.g. Kashmir, Iskardu, Kartchou. 갈지 竭支 v. 승지지 僧祇支. 갈아 竭誐 Khaḍga (sometimes in error Khaṅga), a sword, a rhinoceros' horn, a rhinoceros. 갈타라 竭陀羅 Khadira, the *Acacia catechu* ; khadira, the *Mimosa pudica*. [M. W.] A hard wood, also Karavīra.

갈 葛 The rambling, or creeping bean. 갈등 葛藤 Creepers, trailers, clinging vines, etc., i.e. the afflicting passions ; troublesome people ; talk, words (so used by the Intuitional School). 갈리마 葛哩麻 Karma, v. 업 業. 갈야 葛耶 Kāya, body, v. 신 身.

갈 羯 To castrate ; deer-skin ; translit. *ka, gha*. Cf. 가 迦, 구 拘, 가 軻, 걸 揭, 갈 竭, etc.

갈 渴 Tṛṣṇā. Thirst, thirsty ; translit. *kha*. 갈앙 渴仰 To long for as one thirsts for water. 갈가 渴伽 Khaḍga, a rhinoceros. 갈지옥 渴地獄 The thirst-hell, where red-hot iron pills are administered. 갈애 渴愛 Thirsty desire or longing ; the will to live. 갈수라 渴樹羅 Kharjūra, a date, the wild date, the Persian date. 갈법 渴法 To thirst for the truth, or for the Buddha-way. 갈록 渴鹿 The thirsty deer which mistakes a mirage for water, i.e. human illusion.

갈 喝 또는 **할** 喝 To shout, bawl, call, scold ; to drink. 갈한 喝捍 Gahan, an ancient kingdom, also called 동안국 東安國, i.e. Eastern Parthia, west of Samarkand, now a district of Bukhara.

갈나복 羯拏僕 Kaṇabhuj ; Kaṇāda 건니타 蹇尼陀, founder of the Vaiśeṣika school of Indian philosophy.

갈니(가) 羯尼(迦) Kanaka, gold ; name of several yellow plants, e.g. thorn apple ; *Butea frondosa* ; a species of sandalwood, etc.

갈달라 羯達羅 Khadira 갈타라 羯陀羅 ; v. 갈 竭.

갈라나소벌랄나 羯羅拏蘇伐剌那 Karṇasuvarṇa. "An ancient kingdom in Gundwana, the region about Gangpoor, Lat. 21° 54 N., Long. 84° 30 E." [Eitel]. 갈라사 羯羅舍 Kalaśa, a water-pot, pitcher, jar, dish, also 가라사 迦羅舍 ; 갈라사 羯攞賖. 갈라빈가 羯羅頻迦 cf. 갈릉 羯陵. For Krakucchanda, v. 가 迦.

갈라람 羯邏藍 Kalala, the human embryo during the first seven days ; the womb ; also 갈라람 羯羅藍, 가라라 歌羅邏, etc.

갈락가손타 羯洛迦孫馱 Krakucchanda, v. 가 迦.

갈란탁가 羯蘭鐸迦 Kalandaka, "a species of bird" [M. W.] ; cf. 가 迦.

갈랍바 羯臘婆 ; **갈랍박** 羯臘縛 Karaphu, or Kalahu, "a particularly high number" [M. W.], 10 quintillions ; 대갈랍파 大羯臘婆 100 quintillions ; cf. 낙차 洛叉.

갈릉가 羯陵伽 Kaliṅga, also 갈릉가 羯餧伽. An ancient kingdom south-east of Kosala, a nursery of heretical sects, the present Kalingapatnam. [Eitel]. Also with 갈라빈가 羯羅頻迦 used for Kalaviṅka, v. 가 迦.

갈리왕 羯利王 Kalirāja, a former incarnation of Kauṇḍinya, when as king he cut off the hands and feet of Kṣānti-ṛṣi because his concubines had strayed to the hermit's hut. Converted by the hermit's indifference, it was predicted that he would become a disciple of Buddha. 갈리사발 羯利沙鉢 Kārṣāpaṇa, a coin weighing *ca.* 176 grains.

갈마 羯磨 Karma ; action, work, deed, performance, service, "duty" ; religious action, moral duty ; especially a meeting of the monks for the purpose of ordination, or for the confession of sins and absolution, or for expulsion of the unrepentant. There are numerous kinds of karma, or assemblies for such business, ordinarily requiring the presence of four monks, but others five, ten, or twenty. Cf. 업 業 for definition of Karma, deeds or character as the cause of future conditions ; also 오온 五蘊 for karma as the fourth skandha. 갈마승 羯磨僧 A monastic assembly ; also a monk on duty, e.g. in meditation. 갈마인 羯磨印 An image showing the symbol of a bodhisattva's activity. 갈마회 羯磨會 An assembly for monastic duty ; also the central group of the Vajradhātu maṇḍala. 갈마신 羯磨身 An image, a term used by the esoterics. 갈마타나 羯磨陀那 Karmadāna, i.e. the 유나 維那 or director of duties.

갈마 羯摩 Karma, v. 업 業 and cf. 갈마 羯磨.

갈비(가라) 羯毘(迦羅) Kalaviṅka, v. 가 迦.

갈상나 羯霜那 Kaśanna. "An ancient kingdom 300 li south-west of Kharismiga on the Oxus, the present Koorshee," Karshi. [Eitel].

갈승게라 羯蠅揭羅 Kajinghara, Kajangala, or Kajūghira, a kingdom whose ruling family was extinct in A.D. 400. "The ruins of the capital are situated at the village of Kadjéri near Farakhabad (Lat. 27° 24 N., Long. 79° 27 E.) in the province of Agra." [Eitel]. Also 갈수올기라 羯殊嗢祇羅.

갈야국사 羯若鞠闍 Kanyākubja, "hump-backed maidens." An ancient city and kingdom of Central India. In antiquity this city ranks next to Ayodhyā in Oudh. It is known to classical geography as Canogyza. The etymology refers to the legend of the hundred daughters of Kuśanābha its king, who refused the licentious desires of Vāyu (Mahāvṛkṣa 대수선 大樹仙) and were turned by him into hunchbacks. [M. W.] Eitel says "the modern Canouge."

갈지락가 羯地洛迦 Khadiraka, the third of the seven circles around Meru. Cf. 거 佉.

갈치나 羯耻那 Khaṭṭika. Lictors in hades ; possibly from the root khād, to devour ; also 갈치라 羯耻羅 ; 가치나 伽絺那 ; it is also defined as "dog-cookers," butchers, hunters, those who live by killing and selling animals, persons of very low caste.

갈타포달나 羯吒布怛那 Kaṭapūtana, a kind of ill-smelling demon, a preta in the lower regions. [M. W.]

갈포라 羯布羅 Karpūra, dragon-brain scent, camphor.

감 減 ; 감 減 Diminish, decrease, abate, reduce, abbreviate ; opp. 증 增. 감겁 減劫 The decreasing kalpas in which the period of life is gradually reduced, as the 증겁 增劫 are the kalpas of increase ; together they form twenty kalpas, ten diminishing and ten increasing ; but there are other definitions. 감비 減費 To cut down one's personal expenditure (for the sake of charity).

감 鑑 A mirror 명감 明鑑 ; to note, survey, 감찰 鑑察.

감 龕 A shrine ; a cabinet, box ; a coffin (for a monk) ; to contain. 감탑 龕塔 A pagoda with shrines.

감 紺 A violet or purplish colour, a blend of blue and red, also called 감청 紺靑 and 감유리 紺瑠璃, the colour of the roots. 감발 紺髮 or 감정 紺頂 of the Buddha's hair. 감우 紺宇 ; 감원 紺園 ; 감방 紺坊 ; 감전 紺殿 Names for a Buddhist monastery. 감첩 紺睫 The Buddha's violet or red-blue eyebrows. 감포 紺蒲 Kamboja, described as a round, reddish fruit, the Buddha having something resembling it on his neck, one of his characteristic marks. 감포국 紺蒲國 The country of Kamboja.

감 甘 Sweet, agreeable, willing ; Kansu. 감단 甘丹 Dgaḫ-ldan, the monastery of the yellow sect 30 miles north-east of Lhasa 납살 拉薩, built by Tsoṅ-kha-pa. 감주이 甘珠爾 Kanjur, one of the two divisions of the Tibetan canon, consisting of 180 chüan, each chüan of 1,000 leaves ; a load for ten yaks. 감보(자) 甘菩(遮) ; 감포 紺蒲 ; 검포 劍蒲 Kamboja, one of the "sixteen great countries of India", noted for its beautiful women. 감자 甘蔗 Sugar-cane, symbol of many things. A tr. of Ikṣvāku, one of the surnames of Śākyamuni, from a legend that one of his ancestors was born from a sugar-cane. 감자왕 甘蔗王 ; 의사마 懿師摩 ; 일차구왕 一叉鳩王 King of the sugar-cane ; Ikṣvāku Virūḍhaka, said to be one of the ancestors of Śākyamuni, but the name is claimed by others.

감 堪 To bear, sustain, be adequate to. 감인 堪忍 Sahā ; to bear, patiently endure. 감인세계 堪忍世界 The sahā world of endurance of suffering ; any world of transmigration. 감인지 堪忍地 The stage of endurance, the first of the ten bodhisattva stages. 감능 堪能 Ability to bear, or undertake.

감 敢 To dare, venture. 감만 敢曼 Kambala, a woollen or hair mantle ; a loin cloth.

감 感 To influence, move. 감응 感應 Response to appeal or need ; Buddha moved to respond. 감과 感果 The result that is sought. 감진 感進 To move to zeal, or inspire to progress.

감 勘 To investigate, examine, collate. 감변 勘辨 To examine and define.

감 監 To survey, examine ; a palace-eunuch ; the Academy ; to superintend, oversee ; warden of a jail, warder, jail. 감사 監寺 ; 감원 監院 ; 감수 監收 The warden, or superintendent of a monastery, especially the one who controls its material affairs.

감 減 v. 감 減.

감로 甘露 ; **아밀리다** 阿密哩多 ; **아밀리달** 啞密哩達 Amṛta, sweet dew, ambrosia, the nectar of immortality ; tr. by 천주 天酒 deva-wine, the nectar of the gods. Four kinds of ambrosia are mentioned — green, yellow, red, and white, all coming from "edible trees" and known as 소타 蘇陀 sudhā, or 소마 蘇摩 soma. 감로법 甘露法, or 감로우 甘露雨 The ambrosial truth, or rain, i.e. the Buddha truth. 감로법문 甘露法門 The method of the ambrosial truth. 감로멸 甘露滅 The nectar of nirvāṇa, the entrance is the 감로문 甘露門, and nirvāṇa is the 감로성 甘露城 or 감로계 甘露界 nectar city, or region. 감로왕 甘露王 Amṛta, intp. in its implication of immortality is a name of Amitābha, and connected with him are the 감로주 甘露咒, 감로다라니주 甘露陀羅尼咒, 십감로주 十甘露咒 ; 십감로명 十甘露明, 감로경 甘露經, etc. 감로군다리명왕 甘露軍荼利明王 ; 감로(왕)존 甘露(王)尊 Amṛtakuṇḍalin, one of the five 명왕 明王 Ming Wang, who has three forms, vajra, lotus, and nectar. 감로반 甘露飯 ; 아미도단나 阿彌都檀那 Amṛtodana. The king whose name was "ambrosia-rice", a prince of Magadha, father of Anuruddha and Bhadrika, and paternal uncle of Śākyamuni. 감로고 甘露鼓 The ambrosial drum, the Buddha-truth.

갑 甲 Scale, mail ; the first of the ten "celestial stems". 갑주인 甲冑印 A digital or manual sign, indicating mail and helmet. 갑마 甲馬 A picture, formerly shaped like a horse, of a god or a Buddha, now a picture of a horse.

강 綱 A net rope, bond, social nexus, constant obligation, the restraints of society. 강유 綱維 The controller of a monastery.

강 江 A river ; the River, the Yangtsze. 강천사 江天寺 The River and Sky monastery on Golden Island, Chinkiang, Kiangsu. 강호 江湖 Kiangsi and Hunan, where and whence the 선 禪 Ch'an(Zen) or Intuitive movement had its early spread, the title being applied to followers of this cult. 강서 江西 A title of 마조 馬祖 Ma-tsu, who was a noted monk in Kiangsi, died 788. 강가섭 江迦葉 River-kāśyapa or Nadī-kāśyapa, one of the three Kāśyapa brothers: v. 삼가섭 三迦葉.

강 康 At ease, in repose ; undisturbed ; well, hale. 강거 康居 Samarkand, or Soghdiana, cf. 서역기 西域記 1. 강승개 康僧鎧 or 강승회 康僧會 Saṅghavarman, also said to be Saṅghapāla ; an Indian monk supposed to be of Tibetan descent ; but Saṅghapāla is described as the eldest son of the prime minister of Sogdiana, and is probably a different person. Saṅghavarman tr. at the White Horse Temple, Loyang, in A.D. 252 ; *inter alia* the 무량수경 無量壽經 is accredited to him, but a more reliable tradition of the Canon ascribes the tr. to Dharmarakṣa A.D. 308.

강 薑 Ginger. 강갈라 薑羯羅 Kaṅkara, "a high number, 100 niyutas." M. W.

강 僵 Stiff, rigid ; prostrate. 강사락 僵娑洛 Saṁsāra, course, transmigration, v. 산 散 and 생사 生死.

강 强 Strong, forceful, violent ; to force ; to strengthen. 강가 强伽 The Ganges, v. 항 恒.

강 彊 Strong, violent ; to force ; idem 강 强.

강 講 To talk, explain, preach, discourse. 강하 講下 Descend the pulpit, end the discourse. 강당 講堂 The preaching hall, lecture hall. 강종 講宗 The preaching sects, i.e. all except the Ch'an, or intuitional, and the Vinaya, or ritual sects. 강사 講師 An expounder, or teacher. 강연 講演 ; 강설 講說 To expound, discourse, preach. 강경 講經 To expound the sūtras.

강 降 Descend, send down ; degrade. 강세 降世 To descend to earth from above, as recorded of the Buddha. 강생 降生 To descend into the world, as the Buddha is said to have done from the Tuṣita heaven. 강신 降神 The descent of Buddha's spirit into Māyā's womb ; also to bring down spirits as does a spiritualistic medium. 강태 降胎 The descent into Māyā's womb. 강림 降臨 To descend, draw near from above, condescend, e.g. the Buddha, the spirits, etc. 강탄 降誕 The anniversary of the descent, i.e. the Buddha's birthday, not the conception.

강원 講院 Seminary ; lecture hall ; monk's academy.

개 蓋 A cover, anything that screens, hides, or hinders ; to build ; then, for. The passions which delude the real mind so that it does not develop. A hat, or umbrella, or any cover. The canopy over a Buddha. 개전 蓋纏 Cover and bonds, i.e. the passions which stunt growth and hold in bondage.

개 皆 All. 개공 皆空 All is empty and void.

개 鎧 Armour, mail. 개갑 鎧甲.

개 箇 Each, every. 개개원상도 箇箇圓常道 Every single thing is the complete eternal Tao.

개 疥 Itch, the itch, scabby. 개라야간 疥癩野干 A scabby dog, or jackal.

개 介 Scales, mail ; important ; resolute, firm ; an attendant ; petty, small. 개이 介爾 A transient thought, see kṣaṇa 찰 刹.

개 改 To change, correct. 개종 改宗 To change one's cult, school of thought, or religion. 개회 改悔 To repent and reform.

개 開 To open, begin, institute, unfold, disclose ; dismiss ; write out ; unloose ; to heat, boil.

개각 開覺 To arouse, awaken ; to allow the original Buddha-nature to open and enlighten the mind.

개감로문 開甘露門 To open the ambrosial door, i.e. provide for hungry ghosts.

개광 開光 Introducing the light, the ceremony of "opening the eyes" of an image, i.e. painting or touching in the pupil ; also 개안 開眼.

개구 開具 To make an inventory.

개도자 開道者 The Way-opener, Buddha ; anyone who opens the way, or truth.

개발 開發 To start, begin, send forth.

개백 開白 To start from the bare ground ; to begin a ceremony.

개법 開法 To found a sect or teaching, e.g. as Buddha founded Buddhism ; the method of opening, or beginning.

개본 開本 To commence ; the very beginning ; at the beginning ; to explain the beginning.

개사 開士 The hero who is enlightened, or who opens the way of enlightenment, an epithet of the bodhisattva ; also applied to monks.

개산 開山 To establish a monastery ; to found a sect.

개삼현일 開三顯一 To explain the three vehicles, and reveal the reality of the one method of salvation, as found in the Lotus Sūtra.

개시오입 開示悟入 The four reasons for a Buddha's appearing in the world : to open up the treasury of truth ; to indicate its meaning ; to cause men to apprehend it ; and to lead them into it.

개심 開心 To open the heart ; to develop the mind ; to initiate into truth.

개연 開演 To lecture, explain at length, expound.

개오 開悟 To awaken, arouse, open up the intelligence and bring enlightenment.

개원 開元 The K'ai-yüan period of the T'ang emperor Hsüan Tsung, A.D 713-741 ; during which the monk 지승 智昇 Chih-shêng in 730 issued his "complete list of all the translations of Buddhist books into the Chinese language from the year A.D. 67 up to the date of publication, embracing the labours of 176 individuals, the whole amounting to 2,278 separate works, many of which, however, were at that time already lost." [Wylie]. Its title was 개원석교록 開元釋教錄. He also issued the 개원석교록약출 開元釋教錄略出, an abbreviated version.

개자 芥子 Sarṣapa, 살리찰파 薩利刹跋 ; 사리사파 舍利沙婆 Mustard seed. (1) A measure of length, 10,816,000th part of a yojana, v. 유순 由旬. (2) A weight, the 32nd part of a 뇌제 賴提 or 초자 草子 raktikā, $2\frac{3}{16}$ grains. (3) A trifle. (4) On account of its hardness and bitter taste it is used as a symbol for overcoming illusions and demons by the esoteric sects. (5) The appearance of a Buddha is as rare as the hitting of a needle's point with a mustard-seed thrown from afar. 개자겁 芥子劫 A mustard-seed kalpa, i.e. as long as the time it would take to empty

ㄱ ㄴ ㄷ ㄹ ㅁ ㅂ ㅅ ㅇ ㅈ ㅊ ㅋ ㅌ ㅍ ㅎ 찾아보기

a city 100 yojanas square, by extracting a seed once every century. 개석 芥石 Mustard-seed kalpa and rock kalpa, the former as above, the latter the time required to rub away a rock 40 li square by passing a soft cloth over it once every century.

개재 開齋 To break the fast, breakfast.

개정 開靜 To break the silence, i.e. rouse from sleep.

개조 開祖 The founder of a sect, or clan.

개차 開遮 1. The adversatives, permit 개 開 or prohibit 차 遮 ; also 개폐 開廢. 2. Lit. "opening and closing". To break the rules when the situation calls for. For example, one lies to a hunter when he asks which way the deer went, because it is better in this case to lie than to contribute to the killing of an animal.

개침 開枕 To display the pillows, i.e. retire to bed.

개폐 開廢 idem 개차 開遮.

개해 開解 To expound, explain.

개현 開顯 To open up and reveal ; to expose the one and make manifest the other. It is a term used by T'ien-t'ai, i.e. 개권현실 開權顯實, to expose and dispose of the temporary or partial teaching, and reveal the final and real truth as in the Lotus Sūtra.

개화 開化 To transform the character by instruction ; to teach.

개훈 開葷 ; **개소** 開素 To abandon vegetarianism, as is permitted in case of sickness.

객 客 A guest, visitor, traveller, outsider, merchant. 객사 客司 Guest room ; reception of guests. 객산 客山 The guest hill, or branch monastery, in contrast with the 주산 主山 chief one. 객진 客塵 Āgantu-kleśa, the foreign atom, or intruding element, which enters the mind and causes distress and delusion ; the mind is naturally pure or innocent till the evil element enters ; v. 번뇌 煩惱.

갹차 噱叉 Vākṣu, the Oxus, v. 박 縛.

거 居 Dwell, reside ; be. 거사 居士 ; 구라발저 俱欏鉢底 ; 가라월 迦羅越 Kulapati. A chief, head of a family, squire, landlord. A householder who practises Buddhism at home without becoming a monk. The female counterpart is 여거사 女居士. The 거사전 居士傳 is a compilation giving the biography of many devout Buddhists. 거륜 居倫 ; 거린 居隣 or 구린 俱隣 ; 구륜 拘輪 idem Ājñāta-Kauṇḍinya, v. 교 憍.

거 去 Go, go away ; gone, past ; depart, leave ; to remove, dismiss ; the 거 去 tone. 거래 去來 Go and come. 거래금 去來今 Past, future, present. 거래실유종 去來實有宗 The heretical sect which believed in the reality of past and future as well as the present. 거차가라니시차계라니 去叉迦羅尼尸叉罽羅尼 or 식차가라니시차계라니 式叉迦羅尼尸叉罽羅尼 ; 돌길라 突吉羅 Śikṣākaraṇīya. "A young Brahman studying with his preceptor." [M. W.] Studies, students. Also interpreted as "evil deeds". Also "a section of the Vinaya called 중학법 衆學法 ... consisting of a series of 100 regulations with reference to the conduct of novices". [Eitel].

거 巨 Great ; translit. *ko, kau, go.* 거익 巨益 Great benefit. 거마 巨磨 Gomaya, cow-dung. 거상미 巨賞彌 Kauśāmbī, (Pali) Kosambi, Vatsa-pattana. Also written 구섬미 俱睒彌 ; 구상미 俱賞彌 ; 구사미 俱舍彌 ; 구섬미 拘睒彌 or 拘剡彌 ; 구염 拘鹽 ; 구심 拘深 ; 구라구 拘羅瞿 ; 구익 拘翼 ; 교상미 憍賞彌 ; 교섬미 憍閃彌. The country of King Udayana in "Central India", described as 6,000 li in circuit, soil rich, with a famous capital, in which the 서역기 西域記 5 says there was a great image of the Buddha. Eitel says : It was "one of the most ancient cities of India, identified by some with Kasia near Kurrah (Lat. 25° 41 N., Long. 81° 27 E.), by others with the village of Kosam on the Jumna 30 miles above Allahabad". It is identified with Kosam.

거 呿 To gape ; translit. *kha.*

거 據 To lay hold of, tangible, evidential, according to. 거사 據事 According to fact.

거 擧 To raise (a thing, matter, subject, etc.) ; conduct ; the whole, all. 거일폐제 擧一蔽諸 To raise, or refer to, one point and include all others. 거인 擧人 One who has taken his second degree, an M. A. 거동 擧動 Conduct, movements. 거가 擧家 The whole family.

거 踞 To squat. 거지사자 踞地獅子 A crouching lion.

거 佉 Translit. *kha* ; also *khya, ga, gha, khu, khi* ; cf. 거 呿, 객 喀, 흘 吃, 가 呵, 가 珂, 각 恪, 감 轗 ; it is used to represent 허공 虛空 space, empty. Skt. kha *inter alia* means "sky," "ether." 거가 佉加 ; 갈가 渴伽 Khaḍga, a rhinoceros. 거륵가 佉勒迦 Khārī, a measure (or hamper) of grain ; khārīka, equal to a khārī. 거타가 佉吒迦 Khaṭaka ; a manual sign, wrists together, fingers half-closed ; [M. W.] says "the half-closed hand ; the doubled fist of wrestlers or boxers." 거조라 佉啁羅 Khaṭvā, a bed, couch, cot ; a long, narrow bed. 거제라(가) 佉提羅(迦) ; 거득라가 佉得羅柯 ; 거타라 佉陀羅 ; 걸지락(가) 朅地洛(迦) or 걸달락(가) 朅達洛(迦) ; 걸나리고 朅那里酤 ; 갈지라 羯地羅 ; 가리라 可梨羅 ; 가리라 軻梨羅 ; Khadiraka, or Karavīka. One of the seven concentric ranges of a world ; tr. by Jambu timber, or wood ; also by 공파 空破 bare, unwooded. Its sea is covered with scented flowers, and in it are four islands. It is also a tree of the Acacia order. 거리 佉梨 Khāri, or khārī. A 곡 斛, i.e. bushel, or measure of about ten 두 斗 ; v. 거로 佉盧 ; 거륵 佉勒. 거루 佉樓 ; 거로(풍타) 佉盧(風吒) ; 거로슬타 佉路瑟吒 Kharoṣṭhī, tr. by "Ass's lips" ; name of an ancient ṛṣi, perhaps Jyotīrasa. Also, "the writing of all the northerners," said to have been introduced by him, consisting of seventy-two characters. 거사 佉沙 Kashgar, a country in E. Turkestan, east of the Pamirs, S. of T'ien-shan ; the older name, after the name of its capital, is sometimes given as 소륵 疏勒 or 실리흘률다저 室利訖栗多底 Śrīkrītati. 거로 佉盧 Khāra ; said to be a 두 斗, the tenth of a 거리 佉梨 ; also Khara, the name of a ṛṣi. For Kharoṣṭhī, v. above. 거라타 佉羅陀, or 제 帝, etc. ; v. 가 伽. 거라건타 佉羅騫馱 Kharakaṇṭha ; kings of demons, kings of asuras present when Buddha preached the Lotus Sūtra ; also described as rumbling like thunder, or stirring up the waves of the ocean. 거하라부아 佉訶囉嚩阿 Kha, ha, ra, va, a, the five 종자 種子 roots, or seed-tones of the five elements, space, wind, fire, water, earth respectively. 거타니 佉陀尼 or 거사니 佉闍尼 ; 가단니 珂但尼 Khādanīya, to be chewed ; edible ; a food ; defined as edibles not included in regulation meals.

건 犍 A gelded bull, an ox ; a creature half man, half leopard. 건불남 犍不男 A eunuch by castration, cf. paṇḍaka. 건지 犍地 v. 건치 犍稚 *infra.* 건도 犍度 Khaṇḍa, a piece, fragment, portion, section, chapter ; a collection ; the rules, monastic rules ; also used for skandha, v. 새 塞. There are categories of eight, and twenty subjective divisions for the eight, v. the Abhidharma 팔건도론 八犍度論 [B.N.] 1273. 건덕 犍德 ; 건척(마) 犍陟(馬) Kaṇṭhaka, name of the steed on which Śākyamuni rode away from home. 건답 犍沓 Gandharva, v. 건 乾. 건치 犍稚 Ghaṇṭā, also 건지 犍地 ; 건추 犍椎 ; 건퇴 犍槌 ; 건지 犍遲 ; a bell, gong, or any similar resonant article. 건다 犍陀 Skandha, v. 새 塞 ; 건다라 犍陀羅 ; 건다아 犍陀衙 ; 건다하 犍陀訶 ; 건다라 犍馱邏 Gandhāra ; v. 건 乾. 건황문 犍黃門 Palace eunuchs.

건 乾 Dry, dried up, clean ; heaven, male, masculine, enduring, continual. Translit. gan and h. 간시궐 乾屎橛 A stick used in India as "toilet paper," in China paper, straw, or bamboo. 간혜지 乾慧地 The dry or unfertilized stage of wisdom, the first of the ten stage. 건율타야 乾栗陀耶 ; 건율타 乾栗馱 Hṛdaya, heart, soul, mind, core. 건(달)성 乾(達)城 Gandharva city, infra. 건달바

乾闥婆 ; 건답파 乾沓婆 or 건답화 乾沓和 ; 건달바 健達婆 or 健闥婆 ; 건달박 犍達縛, 건다라 犍陀羅, 언달박 彦達縛 Gandharva or Gandharva Kāyikās, spirits on Gandhamādana 향산 香山 the fragrant or incense mountains, so called because the Gandharvas do not drink wine or eat meat, but feed on incense or fragrance and give off fragrant odours. As musicians of Indrá, or in the retinue of Dhṛtarāṣṭra, they are said to be the same as, or similar to, the Kinnaras. They are, or according to [M. W.], Dhṛtarāṣṭra is associated with soma, the moon, and with medicine. They cause ecstasy, are erotic, and the patrons of marriageable girls ; the Apsaras are their wives, and both are patrons of dicers. 건달바성 乾闥婆城 A Gandharva city, i.e. a mirage city. 건달바왕 乾闥婆王 The king of the Gandharvas, named Citraratha [M. W.], but tr. as Druma, a tree. 건다 乾陀 Yugaṁdhara, cf. 유 踰, the first of the concentric mountains of a world ; also name of a tree. 건다라 乾陀羅 or 건다월 乾陀越 or 건다위 乾陀衛 or 건다바나 乾陀婆那 Gandhāra, an ancient kingdom in the north of the Punjab, "Lat. 35° 5 N., Long. 71° 16 E." [Eitel] ; famous as a centre of Buddhism. Śākyamuni, in a former life, is said to have lived there and torn out his eyes to benefit others, "probably a distortion of the story of Dharmavivardhana, who as governor of Gandhāra was blinded by order of a concubine of his father, Aśoka." [Eitel]. M. W. associates Gandhāra with Kandahar. Also, name of a fragrant tree, and of a yellow colour. 건달하제 乾闥訶提 Gandhahastī, "fragrant elephant," name of a Bodhisattva.

건 蹇 Halt, lame ; unfortunate ; proud ; translit. *ka, kha, ska.* 건니타 蹇尼陀 Kaṇāda, 건나복 蹇拏僕 Kaṇabhuj, atom-eater, Kaṇāda's nickname, the reputed founder of the Vaiśeṣika school. 건다 蹇荼 Khaṇḍa, candy, broken bits.

건 健 Sturdy, strong, hard, bold ; unwearied ; translit. *ga, gha.* 건용좌 健勇座 The heroic posture of the Buddha with his feet on his thighs soles upward. 건남 健南 Ghana, a mass, also 건남 健男 ; 건남 鍵南 or 蹇南 or 갈남 羯南 ; it is intp. as a hard, solid lump, the human embryo formed from the fourth to the seventh day. 건나표하 健拏驃訶 Gandha-vyūha, tr. by 화엄 華嚴 q.v. 건다 健陀 ; 건두 健杜 ; 건달 健達 Gandha, smell, scent ; a tree producing incense ; the first and last also mean (as do 건다 乾陀 and 건다 乾馱) kaṣāya, a colour composed of red and yellow, the monk's robe, but the sounds agree better with kanthā, the patch-robe. Also used for skandha, v. 새 塞, the five constituents ; also for gandharva, v. 건 乾. 건다구지 健陀俱知 Gandhakuṭī, the house of scent, or incense, a temple. 건다마다마라 健陀摩陀摩羅 Gandhamādanamāla, the hill of intoxicating perfume. 건달박 健達縛 Gandharva, v. 건 乾. 건다리 健馱梨 Gandhāri, a spell that gives power to fly. 건다라 健馱羅 Gandhāra, v. 건 乾.

건 鍵 The bolt of a lock ; to lock ; translit. *gha.* 건남 鍵南 Ghana, also 가가나 伽訶那, solid, compact, firm, viscid, mass ; a foetus of forty-seven days. 건용 鍵鎔 A bowl, small almsbowl ; also 건자 鍵鎡 ; 건자 犍茨 ; 건지 健支 ; 건자 建鎡.

건 建 To found, set up, establish, build. 건타가 建佗歌 Kaṇṭhaka, the horse on which Śākyamuni rode when he left home. 건지보라 建志補羅 ; 건지성 建志城 Kāñcīpura, capital of Draviḍa, the modern Conjevaram, about 48 miles south-west of Madras. 건립 建立 To found (a school of thought or practice) ; to set up ; e.g. samāropa, assertion, postulation, theory, opp. of 비방 誹謗 apavāda, refutation.

건달바 揵達婆 Gandharva, v. 건 乾.

걸 朅 To and fro ; translit. *kha* ; cf. 갈 竭 ; 가 軻. 걸가 朅伽 ; 걸아 朅誐 Khaḍga, a sword, rhinoceros' horn, rhinoceros. 걸가비사나 朅伽毘沙拏 ; 걸가파사 朅伽婆沙 Khaḍga-viṣāṇa, a rhinoceros' horn. 걸지락가 朅地洛迦 Khadiraka, the Acacia, or Acacia mountain, i.e. 걸달라 朅達羅 one of the seven concentric mountains around Sumeru.

걸 乞 To beg ; 걸면 乞丐 a beggar. 걸사 乞士 A bhikṣu, mendicant monk, or almsman. 걸율쌍제찬 乞㗚雙提贊 Khri-srong-lde-btsan, king of Tibet (A.D. 743-798). In 747 he brought to Tibet "the real founder of Lamaism" (Eliot), Padmasaṁbhava 연화생상사 蓮華生上師, a Buddhist of Swat (Urgyan), who introduced a system of magic and mysticism (saturated with Śivaism) which found its way into Mongolia and China. The king was converted to Buddhism by his mother, a Chinese princess, and became a powerful supporter of it. He encouraged the translation of the Buddhist canon which was completed by his successors. He is worshipped as an incarnation of Mañjuśrī. 걸쇄 乞灑 ; 걸찰 乞察 ; 걸차 乞叉 ; 흘쇄 吃灑 ; 갈차 葛叉 ; 글쇄 訖灑 ; 차 差 ; 차 叉 ; 찰 刹 ; Kṣaya, used in the sense of omega, implying finality, or nirvāṇa. 걸안바라문 乞眼婆羅門 The Brahman who begged one of Śāriputra's eyes in a former incarnation, then trampled on it, causing Śāriputra to give up his efforts to become a bodhisattva and turn back to the Hīnayāna. 걸식 乞食 To beg for food, one of the twelve dhūtas prescribing outward conduct of the monk ; mendicancy is the 정명 正命 right livelihood of a monk, to work for a living is 사명 邪命 an improper life ; mendicancy keeps a monk humble, frees him from the cares of life, and offers the donors a field of blessedness ; but he may not ask for food. 걸식사분 乞食四分 The four divisions of the mendicant's dole ; to provide for (1) fellow religionists, (2) the poor, (3) the spirits, (4) self.

걸 桀 Vitasti, a span ; the 32,000th part of a yojana.

걸망 Monk's knapsack. = 바랑.

검 檢 A case ; rule ; to collate ; compose ; pick up. 검교 檢校 To check, compare.

검 劍 A sword, a two-edged sword. 검마사제 劍摩舍帝 A spirit or demon, Aniruddha, the unobstructed, the ungovernable, son of Kāma (Love, Lust). 검림지옥 劍林地獄 ; 검수지옥 劍樹地獄 Asipattra, the hell of the forest of swords, or sword-leaf trees. 검파 劍波 Kampa, Bhū-kampa ; deva of earthquakes. 검륜법 劍輪法 A system of revolving swords for subduing demons.

검 劍 A sword, two-edged sword. 검산 劍山 ; 검수지옥 劍樹地獄 Asipattra. The hill of swords, or sword-leaf trees hell, one of the sixteen hells ; also called 도인로 刀刃路.

검 撿 To check, revise, gather. 검교 撿挍 To check, tally.

겁 劫 or 刧 A kalpa, aeon, age ; also translit. *ka* ; "a fabulous period of time, a day of Brahmā or 1,000 Yugas, a period of four hundred and thirty-two million years of mortals, measuring the duration of the world ; (a month of Brahmā is supposed to contain thirty such kalpas ; according to the Mahābhārata twelve months of Brahmā constitute his year, and one hundred such years his lifetime ; fifty years of Brahmā are supposed to have elapsed ...)." [M. W.] An aeon of incalculable time, therefore called a 대시절 大時節 great time-node. v. 겁파 劫波.

겁구 劫具 v. 겁파사 劫波娑.

겁비(라) 劫比(羅) Kapila ; also 겁필라 劫畢羅 ; 가비라 迦比羅 or 迦毗羅 The meaning is "brown," but it is chiefly used for "the sage Kapila, founder of the classical Sāṅkhya" philosophy and the school of that name. 겁비(라)천 劫比(羅)天 ; 금비라천 金比羅天 ; 구국라천 俱鞠羅天 A deva, or demon, called Kapila, or Kumbhīra, or Kubera.

겁비나 劫比拏 idem 겁빈나 劫賓那.

겁비라벌솔도 劫比羅伐窣堵 or 劫比羅伐窣都 Kapilavastu, 겁비라국 劫比羅國 ; 가비라위 迦毘羅衛 ; 가비라소도 迦毗羅蘇都 or 가비라파솔도 伽毗羅皤窣都 ; 가라 迦羅 or 가이 迦夷 or 가유 迦維 ; 가비려 伽毗黎, etc. Capital of the principality occupied by the Śākya clan ; destroyed during Śākyamuni's life, according to legend ; about 100 miles due north of Benares, north-west of present Gorakhpur ; referred to in 서역기 西域記.

겁비사야 劫比舍也 Said to be 계빈 罽賓 Kashmir.

겁비타 劫比他 Kapittha. (1) An ancient kingdom of Central India, also called 승거시 僧佉尸 Sāṅkāśya. (2) A Brahman of Vṛji who ill-treated the Buddhists of his time, was reborn as a fish, and was finally converted by Śākyamuni. [Eitel].

겁빈나 劫賓那 Kapphiṇa ; also 겁비나왕 劫比拏王 ; 겁비나 劫庀那 or 劫比那 or 劫譬那 ; or Kampilla, 금비라 金毗羅 ; whose monastic name was Mahā-kapphiṇa ; intp. as 방수 房宿 (born) under the constellation Scorpio ; he is said to have understood astronomy and been king of Southern Kosala ; he became a disciple of Śākyamuni and is to be reborn as Samantaprabhāsa Buddha.

겁소 劫燒 idem 겁화 劫火.

겁수 劫水 The flood in the kalpa of destruction, v. 삼재 三災.

겁염 劫焰 Kalpa-flames, idem 겁화 劫火.

겁재 劫災 The calamity of fire, wind, and water, during the 괴겁 壞劫 kalpa of destruction.

겁지라 劫地羅 Khadira, v. 갈 竭.

겁초 劫初 The beginning of the kalpa of formation ; the kalpa of creation ; also 성겁 成劫.

겁탁 劫濁 The impure or turbid kalpa, when the age of life is decreasing and all kinds of diseases afflict men.

겁파 劫簸 idem 겁파 劫波.

겁파 劫波 Kalpa ; also 겁파 劫簸 ; 겁파 劫跛 ; v. 겁 劫. Aeon, age. The period of time between the creation and recreation of a world or universe ; also the kalpas of formation, existence, destruction, and non-existence, which four as a complete period are called mahākalpa 대겁 大劫. Each great kalpa is subdivided into four asaṅkhyeya kalpas (아승기야 阿僧企耶 i.e. numberless, incalculable) ; (1) kalpa of destruction 괴겁 壞劫 saṁvarta ; (2) kalpa of utter annihilation, or empty kalpa 증멸겁 增滅劫 ; 공겁 空劫 saṁvartasiddha ; (3) kalpa of formation 성겁 成劫 vivarta ; (4) kalpa of existence 주겁 住劫 vivartasiddha ; or they may be taken in the order 성주괴공 成住壞空. Each of the four kalpas is subdivided into twenty antarakalpas, 소겁 小劫 or small kalpas, so that a mahākalpa consists of eighty small kalpas. Each small kalpa is divided into a period of 증 增 increase and 감 減 decrease ; the increase period is ruled over by the four cakravartīs in succession, i.e. the four ages of iron, copper, silver, gold, during which the length of human life increases by one year every century to 84,000 years, and the length of the human body to 8,400 feet. Then comes the kalpa of decrease divided into periods of the three woes, pestilence, war, famine, during which the length of human life is gradually reduced to ten years and the human body to 1 foot in height. There are other distinctions of the kalpas. A small kalpa is represented as 16,800,000 years, a kalpa as 336,000,000 years, and a mahākalpa as 1,334,000,000 years. Three are many ways of illustrating the length of a kalpa, e.g. pass a soft cloth over a solid rock 40 li in size once in a hundred years, when finally the rock has been thus worn away a kalpa will not yet have passed ; or a city of 40 li, filled with mustard seeds, one being removed every century till all have gone, a kalpa will not yet have passed. Cf. 성겁 成劫. 겁파파 劫波婆 or 겁파육 劫波育 or 겁파라 劫波羅 or 겁파살 劫波薩 ; 겁파라 劫婆羅 ; 겁구(사) 劫具(娑) Kārpāsa is cotton, Gossypium Herbaceum ; but this refers especially to Kārpāsī, the cotton tree. 겁파배 劫波杯 Kapāla, a bowl, skull ; the drinking bowl of Śiva, a skull filled with blood. 겁파수 劫波樹 Kalpataru. A tree in Indra's garden bearing fruit according to the seasons. 겁파라 劫波羅 Kapāla, a skull ; also Kārpāsa, see 겁파사 劫波娑. 겁파라천 劫波羅天 Yama, as ruler of time, 시분천 時分天.

겁파겁파야제 劫跛劫跛夜帝 Kalpa-kalpāyati, perhaps connected with klṛp, intp. as 이분별 離分別 or 무분별 無分別 indiscriminate, undifferentiate.

겁파라수 劫婆羅樹 v. 겁파수 劫波樹 and 겁사파사 劫沙波娑 or 겁구 劫具, for both of which it is used.

겁파타 劫婆吒 ; 겁박나 劫縛拏 Kaparda, a shell, cowrie, small coin.

겁포달나 劫布呾那 or 劫布咀那 or **겁포저나** 劫布咀那 or **겁포조나** 劫布組那 Kapotana, or Kebudhana ; an ancient kingdom, the modern Kebud or Keshbūd, north of Samarkand.

겁포라 劫布羅 Karpūra, camphor, described as 용뇌향 龍腦香 dragon-brain scent.

겁해 劫海 The ocean of kalpas, i.e. their great number.

겁화 劫火 The fire in the kalpa of destruction ; also 겁진화 劫盡火 ; 겁염 劫焰 ; 겁소 劫燒 v. 삼재 三災.

겁회 劫灰 Kalpa-ash, the ashes after the fire kalpa of destruction.

게 偈 Gāthā, metrical hymn or chant, often occurring in sūtra, and usually of 4, 5, or 7 words to the line. Also 게타 偈他 cf. 가타 伽陀. 게찬 偈讚 To sing in verse the praises of the object adored. 게송 偈頌, 게타 偈陀 Hymn, chant ; to hymn.

게 揭 To lift up, or off, uncover ; make known, stick up, publish ; translit. *g, ga, kha.* 게리가발지 揭利呵跋底 Gṛhapati, an elder, householder, proprietor, landlord. 게지 揭底 Gati, "a particular high number" [M. W.], 10 sextillions ; 대게지 大揭底 100 sextillions, v. 락차 洛叉 lakṣa. 게반타 揭盤陀 Khavandha, an ancient kingdom and city, "modern Kartchou" south-east of the Sirikol Lake. [Eitel]. 게직 揭職 Gachi, an ancient kingdom between Balkh and Bamian, about Rui. [Eitel]. 게로다 揭路荼 Garuḍa, the mythical bird on which Viṣṇu rides, v. 가루라 迦樓羅.

격 格 A rule, line, pattern ; reach, research, science. 격외 格外 Extraordinary.

격 隔 To divide off, separate, part. 격숙 隔宿 Separated by a night, i.e. the previous day. 격생 隔生 Divided by birth ; on rebirth to be parted from all knowledge of a previous life. 격력 隔歷 Separate, distinct. 격력삼제 隔歷三諦 To differentiate and apprehend the three distinctive principles 공가중 空假中 noumenon, phenomenon, and the mean.

견 見 Darśana, 날나사낭 捺喇捨囊 ; also dṛṣṭi ; seeing, discerning, judgment, views, opinions ; it is thinking, reasoning, discriminating, selecting truth, including the whole process of deducing conclusions from premises. It is commonly used in the sense of wrong or heterodox views or theories, i.e. 사견 邪見 or 유견 有見, especially such as viewing the seeming as real and the ego as real. There are groups of two, four, five, seven, ten, and sixty-two kinds of 견 見.

견 堅 Dṛḍha, sthira ; firm, firmly fixed, reliable. 견고 堅固 Firm and sure. 견고의 堅固意 Firm-willed, name of a bodhisattva in the Garbhadhātu. 견고혜 堅固慧 Strong in wisdom, ditto. 견(고)림 堅(固)林 The grove of Śāla trees, in which Śākyamuni died. 견뢰 堅牢 Firm and stable ; that which is stable, the earth. 견뢰지신 堅牢地神 or 견뢰지천 堅牢地天 or 견뢰지기 堅牢地祇 The earth-goddess, or deity, or spirits. 견실 堅實 Firm and solid. 견실심 堅實心 With firm heart. 견의 堅意 ; 견혜 堅慧 Sthiramati, of firm mind, or wisdom. An early Indian monk of the Mahāyāna ; perhaps two monks. 견지 堅智 Firm knowledge, or wisdom, a name of Vajrapāṇi. 견법 堅法 The three things assured to the faithful (in reincarnation) — a good body, long life, and boundless wealth. 견만보살 堅滿菩薩 Dhṛtiparipūrṇa, the firm and complete Bodhisattva, who is to be Buddha Padma-vṛṣabha-vikramin, attending on Padmaprabha. 견서사자 堅誓師子 The firmly vowing lion, i.e. Śākyamuni in a previous incarnation.

견 甄 Mould, influence, discern ; translit. *kiṁ, kin.* 견숙가 甄叔迦 Kiṁśuka, the tree *Butea frondosa,* with beautiful red blossoms ; a red stone, perhaps a ruby. 견가라 甄迦羅 Kiṁkara, 10,000,000,000. 견타 甄陀 Kinnara, v. 긴 緊.

견 羂 Pāśa. A noose, bird-net ; to hang, or bind. 견색 羂索 A noose, or net for catching birds ; a symbol of Buddha-love in catching and saving the living.

견 肩 Shoulder ; 견자 肩茨 ; 견하 肩下 ; 하견 下肩 shoulder by shoulder, one next to another.

견 牽 To haul, drag, influence, implicate. 견인인 牽引因 Sarvatraga-hetu, "omnipresent causes, like false views which affect every act." [Keith]. 견도팔도행성 牽道八道行城 To advance on the city from all sides as in chess 파라새 波羅塞 prāsaka, i.e. to employ the omnipresent dharmas (sarvatraga) for salvation.

견 遣 To send ; to drive away. 견환 遣喚 To send, and to call.

견결 見結 The bond of heterodox views, which fastens the individual to the chain of transmigration, one of the nine attachments ; v. 견박 見縛.

견대 見大 Visibility (or perceptibility) as one of the seven elements of the universe.

견도 見道 The way or stage of beholding the truth (of no reincarnation), i.e. that of the śrāvaka and the first stage of the Bodhisattva. The second stage is 수도 修道 cultivating the truth ; the third 무학도 無學道 completely comprehending the truth without further study.

견독 見毒 The poison of wrong views.

견루 見漏 The illusion of viewing the seeming as real, v. 사루 四漏.

견망 見網 The net of heterodox views, or doctrines.

견문 見聞 Seeing and hearing, i.e. beholding Buddha with the eyes and hearing his truth with the ears.

견박 見縛 The bond of the illusion of heterodox opinions, i.e. of mistaking the seeming for the real, which binds men and robs them of freedom ; v. 견결 見結.

견불 見佛 Beholding Buddha ; to see Buddha. Hīnayāna sees only the nirmāṇakāya or body of incarnation, Mahāyāna sees the spiritual body, or body in bliss, the sambhogakāya.

견비견 見非見 The visible and invisible ; phenomenal and noumenal.

견사 見思 Views and thoughts, in general 견혹사혹 見惑思惑 illusory or misleading views and thoughts ; 견 見 refers partly to the visible world, but also to views derived therefrom, e.g. the ego, with the consequent illusion ; 사 思 to the mental and moral world also with its illusion. The 삼혹 三惑 three delusions which hinder the 삼제 三諦 three axioms are 견사 見思, 진사 塵沙, and 무명 無明 q.v. Hīnayāna numbers 88 kinds and the Mahāyāna 112 of 견혹 見惑, of 사혹 思惑 10 and 16 respectively.

견상 見相 The state or condition of visibility, which according to the 기신론 起信論 Awakening of Faith arises from motion, hence is also called 전상 轉相.

견성 見性 To behold the Buddha-nature within oneself, a common saying of the Ch'an(Zen) or Intuitive School.

견수 見修 Views and practice ; heterodoxy ; cf. 견사 見思.

견애 見愛 Views and desires, e.g. the illusion that the ego is a reality and the consequent desires and passions ; the two are the root of all suffering.

견왕재 見王齋 The service on the third day when the deceased goes to see King Yama.

견장 見障 The obstruction of heterodox views to enlightenment.

견쟁 見諍 Wrangling on behalf of heterodox views ; striving to prove them.

견전도 見顚倒 To see things upside down ; to regard illusion as reality.

견정 見正 Seeing correctly ; said to be the name of a disciple of the Buddha who doubted a future life, to whom the Buddha is said to have delivered the contents of the 견정경 見正經.

견제 見諦 The realization of correct views, i.e. the Hīnayāna stage of one who has entered the stream of holy living ; the Mahāyāna stage after the first Bodhisattva stage.

견지 見地 The stage of insight, or discernment of reality, the fourth of the ten stages of progress toward Buddhahood, agreeing with the 예류과 預流果 of Hīnayāna.

견진 見眞 To behold truth, or ultimate reality.

견처 見處 The state of wrong views, i.e. the state of transmigration, because wrong views give rise to it, or maintain it.

견취 見取 Clinging to heterodox views, one of the four 취 取 ; or as 견취견 見取見, one of the 오견 五見 q.v. 견취사 見取使 The trials of delusion and suffering from holding to heterodox doctrines ; one of the ten sufferings or messengers. 견취견 見取見 Dṛṣtiparāmarśa ; to hold heterodox doctrines and be obsessed with the sense of the self, v. 오견 五見.

견탁 見濁 Dṛṣṭi-kaṣāya. Corruption of doctrinal views, one of the five final corruptions.

견혜 見慧 The wisdom of right views, arising from dhyāna meditation.

결 缺 Broken ; deficient, lacking ; a vacancy, a post. 결루 缺漏 A breach and leakage, a breach of the discipline.

결 潔 Clean, pure. 결재 潔齋 To purify a monastery, cleanse away all immorality and impropriety ; a pure establishment.

결 結 Knot, tie, bond ; bound ; settle, wind up ; to form. The bond of transmigration. There are categories of three, five, and nine bonds ; e.g. false views, the passions, etc.

결 決 To divide, decide ; decidedly ; cut off, execute. 결료 決了 Decided, defined, and made clear. 결정 決定 Fixed and settled, determined. 결택 決擇 Deciding and choosing ; that which decides and gives reason, i.e. the truth of the saints, or Buddhism. 결의 決疑 To resolve doubts, doubts solved ; definite.

결가(부좌) 結跏(趺坐) The Buddha's sitting posture with legs crossed and soles upward, left over right being the attitude for subduing demons, right over left for blessing, the hands being placed one above the other in similar order. Also, said to be paryaṅka-bandha, or utkuṭukāsana, sitting on the hams like ascetics in meditation.

결강 結講 Concluding an address, or the addresses, i.e. the final day of an assembly.

결경 結經 The end of a sūtra ; also its continuation.

결계 結界 A fixed place, or territory ; a definite area ; to fix a place for a monastery, or an altar ; a determined number, e.g. for an assembly of monks ; a limit. It is a term specially used by the esoteric sects for an altar and its area, altars being of five different shapes.

결계 結戒 Bound by the commandments.

결루 結漏 Bondage and reincarnation because of the passions.

결박 結縛 To tie and knot, i.e. in the bondage of the passions, or delusion.

결병 結病 The disease of bondage to the passions and reincarnation.

결사 結使 The bondage and instigators of the passions.

결생 結生 The bond of rebirth.

결업 結業 The karma resulting from the bondage to passion, or delusion.

결연 結緣 To form a cause or basis, to form a connection, e.g. for future salvation. 대통결연 大通結緣 The basis or condition laid 84,000 kalpas ago (by Mahābhijñā-jñānābhibhu 대통지승불 大通智勝佛 in his teaching of the Lotus scriptures to 16 disciples who became incarnate as 16 Buddhas) for the subsequent teaching of the Lotus scriptures by Śākyamuni, the last of the 16 incarnations, to his disciples. 결연중 結緣衆 The company or multitude of those who now become Buddhists in the hope of improved karma in the future.

결원 結願 Concluding the vows, the last day of an assembly.

결인 結印 A binding agreement sealed as a contract, employed by the esoteric sects.

결적 結賊 Binders and robbers, the passions, or delusion.

결제 結制 Enter into the retreat season ; meditation season.

결주 結冑 To make the sign of the vajra armour and helmet, i.e. of Vairocana, in order to control the spirits — a method of the esoteric sects.

결집 結集 The collection and fixing of the Buddhist canon ; especially the first assembly which gathered to recite the scriptures, Saṅgīti. Six assemblies for creation or revision of the canon are named, the first at the Pippala cave at Rājagṛha under Ajātaśatru, the second at Vaiśālī, the third at Pāṭaliputra under Aśoka, the fourth in Kashmir under Kaniṣka, the fifth at the Vulture Peak for the Mahāyāna, and the sixth for the esoteric canon. The first is sometimes divided into two, that of those within "the cave," and that of those without, i.e. the intimate disciples, and the greater assembly without ; the accounts are conflicting and unreliable. The notable three disciples to whom the first reciting is attributed are Kāśyapa, as presiding elder, Ānanda for the Sūtras and the Abhidharma, and Upāli for the Vinaya ; others attribute the Abhidharma to Pūrṇa, or Kāśyapa ; but, granted the premises, whatever form their work may have taken, it cannot have been that of the existing Tripiṭaka. The fifth and sixth assemblies are certainly imaginary.

결탄 結嘆 A sigh of praise at the close of a passage of a sūtra.

결하 結夏 The end of the summer retreat.

결하 結河 The river of bondage, i.e. of suffering or illusion.

결해 結解 Bondage and release ; release from bondage.

겸 鎌 A sickle. 겸자 鎌子.

겸 兼 Both ; also ; to unite, join, comprehend. 겸리 兼利 Mutual benefit ; to benefit self and others. 겸단대대 兼但對帶 The first four of the five periods of Buddha's teaching are also defined by T'ien-t'ai as : (1) 겸 兼 Combined teaching ; including 원교 圓教 and 별교 別教 doctrine, the period of the Avataṁsaka-sūtra. (2) 단 但 Sole ; i.e. 장 藏 or Hīnayāna only, that of the Āgamas. (3) 대 對 Comparative ; all four forms of doctrines being compared. (4) 대 帶 Inclusive, that of the 반야 般若 Prajñā, when the perfect teaching was revealed as the fulfilment of the rest.

경 經 A warp, that which runs lengthwise ; to pass through or by, past ; to manage, regulate ; laws, canons, classics. Skt. Sūtras ; threads, threaded together, classical works. Also called 계경 契經 and 경본 經本. The sūtras in the Tripiṭaka are the sermons attributed to the Buddha ; the other two divisions are 율 律 the Vinaya, and 논 論 the śāstras, or Abhidharma ; cf. 삼장 三藏. Every sūtra begins with the words 여시아문 如是我聞 "Thus did I hear", indicating that it contains the words of Śākyamuni.

경 磬 A piece of flat stone or metal, used as a gong, or for musical percussion.

경 徑 A short cut, a diameter. 경산 徑山 A monastery at Ling-an Hsien, Chekiang.

경 鯨 A whale. 경어 鯨魚 Makara, sea-monster, whale. 경음 鯨音 A reverberating sound, like that of a bell, or gong.

경 庚 Age ; change ; west ; to reward ; the seventh of the ten celestial stems. 경신회 庚申會 An assembly for offerings on the night of Kêng-shên to an image in the form of a monkey, which is the shên symbolical animal ; a Taoist rite adopted by Buddhism.

경 慶 Felicity, felicitous, felicitate. 경참 慶懺 ; 경찬 慶讚 A service of felicitation, e.g. on the dedication of an image, temple, etc.

경 硬 Hard, obstinate. 경연 硬軟 Hard and soft.

경 輕 Light ; frivolous ; to slight. 경안 輕安 Not oppressed, at ease. 경만 輕慢 To despise ; the pride of thinking lightly of others. 경모 輕毛 As light as a hair, as unstable as a feather. 경중 輕重 Light and heavy.

경 景 Prospect, view, circumstances. 경명일 景命日 The day of the king's accession, when services were conducted monthly on that day for his welfare. 경교 景教 The Luminous Religion, i.e. Nestorian Christianity.

경 敬 Reverence, respect. 경애 敬愛 Reverence and love ; reverent love. 경전 敬田 The field of reverence, i.e. worship and support of the Buddha, Dharma, and Saṅgha as a means to obtain blessing. 경례 敬禮 Vandanī, paying reverence, worship.

경 更 To change ; a night watch ; again ; the more. 경약 更藥 Medicines that should be taken between dawn and the first watch, of which eight are named, v. 백일갈마 百一羯磨 5.

경 謦 To speak softly ; to clear the throat. It is in contrast with 해 咳 to speak loudly, etc. ; the two together indicate laughter.

경 警 To warn. 경각 警覺 To warn, arouse, stimulate. 경책 警策 A switch to awaken sleepers during an assembly for meditation.

경 驚 Uttras- ; santras- ; alarm, startle, arouse. 경각 驚覺 Arouse, stimulate.

경 境 Viṣaya ; artha ; gocara. A region, territory, environment, surroundings, area, field, sphere, e.g. the sphere of mind, the sphere of form for the eye, of sound for the ear, etc. ; any objective mental projection regarded as reality. 경지 境智 The objective world and the subjective mind, or knowledge of the objective sphere. 경계 境界 Sphere, region, realm, as above. 경계상 境界相 The external, or phenomenal world, the third aspect referred to in the Awakening of Faith ; the three are blind or unintelligent action, the subjective mind, and the objective illusory world. 경계반야 境界般若 External world prajñā, or wisdom of all things ; prajñā is subjective, all things are its objective.

경 鏡 Ādarśa. A mirror. 경상 鏡像 The image in a mirror, i.e. the transient. 경곡 鏡谷 Mirror and gully, reflection and echo, i.e. the response of the Buddhas to prayers.

경(량)부 經(量)部 Sautrāntika, an important Hīnayāna school, which based its doctrine on the sūtras alone, cf. Keith, 151, *et al.*

경가 經家 One who collected or collects the sūtras, especially Ānanda, who according to tradition recorded the first Buddhist sūtras.

경계 經戒 Sūtras and commandments ; the sūtras and morality, or discipline. The commandments found in the sūtras. The commandments regarded as permanent and fundamental.

경교 經教 The teaching of the sūtras, cf. 경량부 經量部.

경궤 經軌 Sūtras and regulations (of the esoteric sects).

경도 經道 The doctrines of the sūtras.

경론 經論 The sūtras and śāstras.

경법 經法 The doctrines of the sūtras as spoken by the Buddha.

경사 經笥 A case for the scriptures, bookcase or box, also 경상 經箱 *et al.* 유각경사 有脚經笥 A walking bookcase, a learned monk.

경사 經師 A teacher of the sūtras, or canon in general.

경생 經生 To pass through life ; also a copier of classical works.

경수 經手 A copier of classical works ; also called 경생 經生.

경율론 經律論 Sūtras, Vinaya, Abhidharma śāstras, the three divisions of the Buddhist canon.

경의 經衣 The garment with sūtras in which the dead were dressed, so called because it had quotations from the sūtras written on it ; also 경유자 經帷子.

경자 經者 One who expounds the sūtras and śāstras ; one who keeps the teaching of the Lotus Sūtra.

경장 經藏 The sūtra-piṭaka.

경전 經典 The discourses of Buddha, the sūtra-piṭaka.

경종 經宗 The sūtra school, any school which bases its doctrines on the sūtras, e.g. the T'ien-t'ai, or Hua-yen, in contrast to schools based on the śāstras, or philosophical discourses.

경탑 經塔 A pagoda containing the scriptures as relics of the Buddha, or having verses on or in the building material.

경패 經唄 Intoning the sūtras.

경행 經行 To walk about when meditating to prevent sleepiness ; also as exercise to keep in health ; the caṅkramaṇa was a place for such exercise, e.g. a cloister, a corridor.

경허 성우 鏡虛惺牛 Gyeong-heo Seong-u(1846-1912). A monk of the late Joseon dynasty in Korea. A contemporary leader in Seon community.

경흥 憬興 Gyeong-heung(620?-700?). A monk of the Silla dynasty in Korea. An authority in the Maitreya and Pure Land. Two kinds of books are present.

계 罽 A fishing net (of hair) ; translit. *k, c, r*. 계리사반 罽利沙盤 cf. 가 迦 Kārṣāpaṇa. 계라다 罽羅多 Kirāta. A tribe north-west of the Himalayas, with invaded Kashmir during the Han dynasty. 계니타왕 罽膩吒王 Caṇḍa-Kaniṣka, 타왕 吒王 the Scythian king, conqueror of northern India and Central Asia, noted for violence, the seizure of Aśvaghoṣa, and, later, patronage of Buddhism. 계빈 罽賓 Kubhā, Kubhāna ; the Kōphēn of the Greeks ; also a Han name for Kashmir ; modern Kabul ; cf. Hupian 호필나 護苾那. 계나시기불 罽那尸棄佛 v. 시기 尸棄 Ratnaśikhin. 계요이 罽饒夷 Kanyākubja, Kanauj, in Central India, cf. 갈 羯.

계 契 A tally, covenant, bond ; to agree with ; devoted to ; adopted (by). 계타 契吒 Kakṣa ; Kacha ; Kach ; ancient kingdom of Mālava, now the peninsula Cutch. 계회 契會 To meet, rally to, or unite in the right or middle path, and not in either extreme. 계범 契範 The covenants and rules, or standard contracts, i.e. the sūtras. 계선 契線 ; 계경 契經 the sūtras, because they tally with the mind of man and the laws of nature.

계 薊 A thistle. 계리야 薊利耶 Sūrya, the sun, the sun-god, v. 소 蘇.

계 誡 Commandment, precept, prohibition, warning, rule. 계벌 誡罰 To warn and punish ; to punish for breach of the commandments or rules. 계권 誡勸 Prohibitions from evil and exhortations to good. See 계 戒.

계 係 Connect, bind, involve ; is, are. 계념 係念 To think of, be drawn to.

계 界 Dhātu. 타도 馱都 Whatever is differentiated ; a boundary, limit, region ; that which is contained, or limited, e.g. the nature of a thing ; provenance ; a species, class, variety ; the underlying principle ; the root or underlying principles of a discourse.

계 稽 Investigate ; delay ; to prostrate oneself. 계수 稽首 Vandana ; vandi. To make obeisance by prostration. 계강나 稽薑那 Kikaṇa. "A people in Afghanistan (east of Kandahar, south of Ghazna) ruled A.D. 630 by independent chieftains, perhaps identical with the Kykānān of Arabic chroniclers." [Eitel].

계 雞 Kukkuṭa, a cock, fowl, chicken, hen ; translit. *ku, ke, go*. 계원 雞園 Kukkuṭa-ārāma, a monastery on the 계족산 雞足山 built by Aśoka ; also called 계두마사 雞頭摩寺 ; 계두말사 雞頭末寺 ; 계작사 雞雀寺. 계독 雞毒 India, Hindu, idem 연독 身毒. 계구계 雞狗戒 Cock or dog discipline, e.g. standing on one leg all day, or eating ordure, like certain ascetics. 계윤부 雞胤部 The Gokulikas ; Kukkulikas ; Kukkuṭikas ; Kaukkuṭikas ; a branch of the Mahāsāṅghikāḥs which early disappeared ; also 굴거 窟居 ; 고구리하 高拘梨訶 ; 교구지 僑矩胝. 계살라 雞薩羅 Kesara, hair, mane (of a lion, etc.), curly, name of a gem. 계귀 雞貴 Honouring, or reverencing the cock, said to be tr. of Kukkuṭeśvara, a name for Korea. 계족산 雞足山 Kukkuṭapāda, cock's foot mountain, in Magadha, on which Kāśyapa entered into nirvāṇa, but where he is still supposed to be living ; also 계봉 雞峯 ; 계령랑적산 雞嶺狼跡山 Wolf-track, or 존족산 尊足山 Buddha's foot mountain, Gurupada.

계 繼 To continue, inherit, adopt, 상계 相繼 ; 계사 繼嗣.

계 繫 To fasten, attach to, connect ; think of, be attached to, fix the thoughts on. 계념 繫念 To fix the mind, attention, or thought on. 계주 繫珠 A pearl fastened in a man's garment, yet he, in ignorance of it, is a beggar. 계박 繫縛 To fasten, tie ; tied to, e.g. things, or the passions ; 계연 繫緣 and 계착 繫著 are similar.

계 啓 To open, begin, inform, 계백 啓白 idem 표백 表白 To inform, make clear, especially to inform the Buddha.

계 計 To reckon, count (on) ; scheme ; add to, annex ; translit. *ke* ; cf. 계 髻, 계 鷄. 계명자상 計名字相 The stage of giving names (to seeming things, etc.), v. 육추 六麤. Cf. Awakening of Faith 기신론 起信論. 계탁 計度 Tarka ; vitarka, conjecture, reckon, calculate, differentiate. 계아실유종 計我實有宗 The sect that reckons on, or advocates, the reality of personality. 계사라 計捨羅 ; 계살라 計薩羅 or 鷄薩羅 Kesara, hair, filament, intp. as stamens and pistils. 계착 計着 To maintain determinedly, bigotedly, on the basis of illusory thinking. 계도 計都 ; 계부 計部 ; 계도 鷄都 or 계두 鷄兜 Ketu, any bright appearance, comet, ensign, eminent, discernment, etc. ; the name of two constellations to the left and right of Aquila.

계 髻 Topknot, tuft, the hair coiled on top. 계주 髻珠 ; 계보 髻寶 The precious stone worn in it ; a king's most prized possession in the Lotus sūtra parable. 계리길라 髻利吉羅 ; 계리지라 計利枳攞 ; 계리계라 計里計羅 Kelikila, the attendant of a deva ; one of the Vajrapāṇis.

계 鷄 v. 계 雞 Eighteen Strokes.

계 戒 Śīla, 시라 尸羅. Precept, command, prohibition, discipline, rule ; morality. It is applied to the five, eight, ten, 250, and other commandments. The five are : (1) not to kill ; (2) not to steal ; (3) not to commit adultery ; (4) not to speak falsely ; (5) not to drink wine. These are the commands for lay disciples ; those who observe them will be reborn in the human realm. The Sarvāstivādins did not sanction the observance of a limited selection from them as did the 성실종 成實宗 Satyasiddhi School. Each of the five precepts has five guardian spirits, in all twenty-five, 오계이십오신 五戒二十五神. The eight for lay disciples are the above five together with Nos. 7, 8, and 9 of the following ; the ten commands for the ordained, monks and nuns, are the above five with the following ; (6) not to use adornments of flowers, nor perfumes ; (7) not to perform as an actor, juggler, acrobat, or go to watch and hear them ; (8) not to sit on elevated, broad, and large divans (or beds) ; (9) not to eat except in regulation hours ; (10) not to possess money, gold or silver, or precious things. The 구족계 具足戒 full commands for a monk number 250, those for a nun are 348, commonly called 500. Śīla is also the first of the 오분법신 五分法身, i.e. a condition above all moral error. The Sūtra of Brahma's Net has the following after the first five: (6) not to speak of the sins of those in orders ; (7) not to vaunt self and depreciate others ; (8) not to be avaricious ; (9) not to be angry ; (10) not to slander the Triratna.

계구 戒垢 The source of defiling the commandments, i.e. woman.

계0 戒禁 Prohibitions arising out of the fundamental rules ; by-laws. 계금취견 戒禁取見 v. 계취 戒取.

계급승완 戒急乘緩 Zealous for the discipline rather than for knowledge, e.g. Hīnayāna ; 승급계완 乘急戒緩 one who is zealous for knowledge rather than the discipline, e.g. Vimalakīrti 유마 維摩 ; 승계구급 乘戒俱急 one who emphasizes both, the bodhisattva ; 승계구완 乘戒俱緩 one who is indifferent to both.

계기 戒器 A utensil fit to receive the rules, i.e. one who is not debarred from entering the Order, as is a eunuch, slave, minor, etc.

계내 界內 Within the region, limited, within the confines of the 삼계 三界, i.e. the three region of desire, form, and formlessness, and not reaching out to the infinite. 계내사교 界內事敎 T'ien-t'ai's term for the Tripiṭaka school, i.e. Hīnayāna, which deals rather with immediate practice, confining itself to the five skandhas, twelve stages, and eighteen regions, and having but imperfect ideas of 공 空 the illimitable. 계내리교 界內理敎 T'ien-t'ai's 통교 通敎, which is considered to be an advance in doctrine on the last, partially dealing with the 공 空 and advancing beyond the merely relative. Cf. 계외 界外. 계내교 界內敎 The above two schools. 계내혹 界內惑 Illusion of these two schools ; illusion of, or in, the above three realms which gives rise to rebirths. 계분 界分 Any region or division, especially the regions of desire, form, and formlessness. 계외 界外 The pure realms, or illimitable "spiritual" regions of the Buddhas outside the three limitations of desire, form, and formlessness. 계외사교 界外事敎 T'ien-t'ai's term for the 별교 別敎, which concerned itself with the practice of the bodhisattva life, a life not limited to three regions of reincarnation, but which had not attained to its fundamental principles. 계내리교 界內理敎 T'ien-t'ai's 원교 圓敎 the school of the complete Buddha-teaching, i.e. that of T'ien-t'ai, which concerns itself with the Śūnya doctrines of the infinite, beyond the realms of reincarnation, and the development of the bodhisattva in those realms. 계외교 界外敎 The above two schools. 계여 界如 The 십계 十界 and 십여 十如 q.v. 계계 界繫 The karma which binds to the finite, i.e. to any one of the three regions. 계취 界趣 The three regions (desire, form, and formlessness) and the six paths (gati), i.e. the spheres of transmigration.

계단 戒壇 The altar at which the commandments are received by the novice ; the 방등계단 方等戒壇 is the Mahāyāna altar.

계덕 戒德 The power of the discipline.

계랍 戒臘 The number of years a monk has been ordained. 납 臘 is the name of an offering made at the end of the year in ancient times. Also 계랍 戒蠟 or 戒臈 ; 승랍 僧臘.

계력 戒力 The power derived from observing the commandments, enabling one who observes the five commandments to be reborn among men, and one who observes the ten positive commands 십선 十善 to be born among devas, or as a king.

계문 戒門 The way or method of the commandments or rules ; obedience to the commandments as a way of salvation.

계바라밀 戒波羅蜜 Moral precepts, the second of the six pāramitās.

계바리 戒婆離 Upāli, a śūdra, disciple of Śākyamuni, famous for his knowledge of the Vinaya ; v. 우바리 優婆離.

계본 戒本 The Prātimokṣa 바라제목차 波羅提木叉 or 婆羅提木叉 q.v. The 계본경 戒本經 is the latter half of the 범망경 梵網經.

계사 戒師 The teacher of the discipline, or of the commandments (to the novice) ; also 계화상 戒和尙.

계사오덕 戒師五德 The five virtues of the teacher of the discipline : obedience to the rules, twenty years as monk, ability to explain the vinaya, meditation, ability to explain the abhidharma.

계상 戒相 The commandments or rules in their various forms ; also the commandments as expressions for restraining evil, etc.

계선 戒善 The good root of keeping the commandments, from which spring the power for one who keeps the five to be reborn as a man ; or for one who keeps the ten to be reborn in the heavens, or as a king.

계슬 戒膝 The "commandments' knee," i.e. the right knee bent as when receiving the commandments.

계율 戒律 Śīla and Vinaya. The rules. 계율장 戒律藏 The Vinaya Piṭaka, the second main division of the Buddhist Canon.

계인 戒忍 Patience acquired by the observance of the discipline ; the first of the ten kṣānti.

계장 戒場 The place where monks are given the commandments.

계장 戒藏 The Vinaya Piṭaka ; the collection of rules.

계정혜 戒定慧 Discipline, meditation, wisdom ; discipline wards off bodily evil, meditation calms mental disturbance, wisdom gets rid of delusion and proves truth.

계주 戒珠 The commandments, or rules, are like pure white pearls, adorning the wearer.

계첩 戒牒 ; **계험** 戒驗 ; **도첩** 度牒 Certificate of ordination of a monk.

계체 戒體 The embodiment of the commandments, in the heart of the recipient. v. 무표 無表 ; also the basis, or body, of the commandments.

계촉 戒躅 The rut or way of the commandments ; the rules.

계취 戒取 Clinging to the commandments of heterodox teachers, e.g. those of ultra-asceticism, one of the four attachments, 사취 四取 catuḥ-parāmarśa. 계취사 戒取使 The delusion resulting from clinging to heterodox commandments. 계취견 戒取見 ; 계금취견 戒禁取見 Clinging to heterodox ascetic views ; one of the five darśana 오견 五見.

계품 戒品 The different groupings or subjects of the commandments, or discipline ; i.e. the 5, 10, 250, etc.

계학 戒學 The study of the rules or discipline ; one of the three departments 삼학 三學, the other two being meditation and philosophy.

계해 戒海 The rules are pure and purify like the waters of the ocean.

계향 戒香 The perfume of the commandments, or rules, i.e. their pervading influence.

계험 戒驗 see **계첩** 戒牒.

계현 戒賢 Śīlabhadra, see 시 尸.

고 鼓 A drum. 고락현가 鼓樂絃歌 Drum-music and singing with stringed instruments. 고음 鼓音 The rolling of drums. 고천 鼓天 The drum-deva, thunder.

고 皐 A marsh, pool, bank ; high ; the fifth month. 고제 皐諦 Kuntī, name of one of the rākṣasī, a female demon.

고 古 Ancient, antique, old ; of old. 고금 古今 Ancient and modern.

고 苦 Duḥkha, 두거 豆佉 bitterness ; unhappiness, suffering, pain, distress, misery ; difficulty. There are lists of two, three, four, five, eight, and ten categories ; the two are internal, i.e. physical and mental, and external, i.e. attacks from without. The four are birth, growing old, illness, and death. The eight are these four along with the pain of parting from the loved, of meeting with the hated, of failure in one's aims, and that caused by the five skandhas ; cf. 사제 四諦.

고 膏 Fat, oil, unguent. 고명 膏明 Oil and light, oil being right conduct, with the resultant shining before men.

고 估 Guess, estimate. 고의 估衣 To estimate the value of a deceased monk's personal possessions, and 고창 估唱 to auction them to the other monks.

고 高 High, lofty, eminent. 고사 高士 Eminent scholar ; old tr. for Bodhisattva. 고세야 高世耶 ; 교사야 憍奢耶 ; 교시 憍尸 Kauśeya, thin silk, lustering ; wild silk-worms. 고승 高僧 Eminent monks. 고창 高昌 ; 고차 高車 Karakhodjo, the ancient town Kao-ch'ang, which lay 30 li east of Turfān in Turkestan, formerly an important Buddhist centre, whence came scriptures and monks to China. 고조 高祖 A founder of a sect or school. 고살라 高薩羅 v. 교 憍 Kośala. 고족 高足 Superior pupils or disciples. 고려 高麗 Korea. 고려장 高麗藏 The Korean canon of Buddhism, one of the three collections which still exists in the 해인사 海印寺 in 639 cases, 1521 부 部 and 6589 권 卷.

고 故 Old, of old ; from of old ; cause ; purposely ; to die ; tr. pūrva. 고이 故二 Pūrva-dvitīya, the former mate or wife of a monk. 고사업 故思業 or 고작업 故作業 The karma produced by former intention. 고의 故意 Intentionally. 고의방행위 故意方行位 The third to the seventh of the 십지 十地 ten bodhisattva stages of development. 고지 故紙 Old or waste paper. 고고 故苦 Old suffering ; also the suffering resulting from prolongation, e.g. too much lying, standing, walking, at first a joy, becomes wearying. 고골 故骨 Old bones, bones of a former incarnation or generation.

고 孤 Orphan, solitary. 고산 孤山 An isolated hill ; a monastery in Kiangsu and name of one of its monks. 고(독)지옥 孤(獨)地獄 Lokāntarika, solitary hells situated in space, or the wilds, etc. 고(독)원 孤(獨)園 ; 급원 給園 ; 기원 祇洹 ; 서다림 逝多林 Jetavana, the seven-storey abode and park presented to Śākyamuni by Anāthapiṇḍika, who bought it from the prince Jeta. It was a favourite resort of the Buddha, and "most of the sūtras (authentic and suppositious) date from this spot." [Eitel]. 고독원 孤獨園 is also a term for an orphanage, asylum, etc. 고락가 孤落迦 A fruit syrup. 고조 孤調 Self-arranging, the Hīnayāna method of salvation by individual effort.

고 姑 Paternal aunt, husband's sister, a nun ; to tolerate ; however ; leave. 고시초 姑尸草, 구사 矩奢 Kuśa grass, grass of good omen for divination. 고장 姑藏 Ku-tsang, formerly a city in Liangchow, Kansu, and an important centre for communication with Tibet.

고 藁 Straw. 고간 藁幹 The farmer farms for grain, not for straw, but also gets the latter, a parable.

고 酤 To deal in spirits, or alcoholic liquor. 고주계 酤酒戒 The commandment against it.

고 告 To inform ; plead ; accuse. 고향 告香 To inform by offering incense.

고 敲 To knock, beat, pound, e.g. a drum, gong, or gate.

고 庫 Treasury ; storehouse. 고륜 庫倫 K'urun, Urga, the Lamaistic centre in Mongolia, the sacred city. 고차 庫車 K'u-ch'ê, or Karashahr, v. 굴 屈.

고 枯 Wither, decay. 고목 枯木 Withered timber, decayed, dried-up trees ; applied to a class of ascetic Buddhists, who sat in meditation, never lying down, like 석상고목 石霜枯木 petrified rocks and withered stumps. 고목당 枯木堂 The hall in which they sat. 고벌라사 枯筏羅闍 1,000 sextillions, cf. 락 洛.

고깔 Peaked hat worn by monks when performing the monk's dance 승무 僧舞.

고고 苦苦 Duḥkha-duḥkhatā. The pain or painfulness of pain ; pain produced by misery or pain ; suffering arising from external circumstances, e.g. famine, storm, sickness, torture, etc.

고공 苦空 Misery and unreality, pain and emptiness.

고과 苦果 The physical and mental suffering resulting from evil conduct (chiefly in previous existences).

고뇌 苦惱 Misery and trouble ; distress.

고도 苦道 The path of suffering ; from illusion arises karma, from karma suffering, from suffering illusion, in a vicious circle.

고래실유종 古來實有宗 idem 거래실유종 去來實有宗.

고류지 苦類智 The wisdom which releases from suffering in all worlds. 고류(지)인 苦類(智)忍 One of the eight forms of endurance arising out of the above, v. 팔인 八忍.

고륜 苦輪 The wheel of suffering, i.e. reincarnation.

고망 苦網 The net of suffering.

고박 苦縛 The bond of suffering.

고법지 苦法智 The knowledge of the law of suffering and the way of release, one of the 팔지 八智. 고법지인 苦法智忍 One of the 팔인 八忍 q.v.

고본 苦本 The root of misery, i.e. desire.

고성 苦性 The nature of misery ; a sorrowful spirit.

고성제 苦聖諦 Duḥkha-āryā-satyam. The first of the four dogmas, that of suffering ; v. 고집 苦集.

고승전 高僧傳 "Lives of Eminent Monks." Fourteen Sections. A work on the biographies, verses and anecdotes of famous monks from the later Han Dynasty to the Liang Dynasty. Compiled by Hui-k'o.

고액 苦厄 The obstruction caused by pain, or suffering.

고언 苦言 Bitter words, words of rebuke.

고업 苦業 The karma of suffering.

고여 苦餘 Remains of suffering awaiting the Hīnayāna disciple who escapes suffering in this world, but still meets it in succeeding worlds.

고역 苦域 The region of misery, i.e. every realm of reincarnation.

고온 苦蘊 The bundle of suffering, i.e. the body as composed of the five skandhas.

고운사 孤雲寺 Go-un-sa. A temple located in Gugye-dong Danchon-myeon Uiseong-gun Gyeongsangbuk-do in Korea. The 16th parish headquarters of Korean Jogye Order.

고음 苦陰 The body with its five skandhas 오음 五陰 enmeshed in suffering.

고인 苦因 The cause of pain.

고제 苦際 The limit of suffering, i.e. entrance to nirvāṇa.

고제 苦諦 Duḥkha-āryā-satyam. The first of the four dogmas, that of suffering ; v. 고집 苦集.

고지 苦智 The knowledge or understanding of the axiom of suffering.

고진 苦津 The deep ford or flood of misery which must be crossed in order to reach enlightenment.

고집 苦集 Samudaya, arising, coming together, collection, multitude. The second of the four axioms, that of "accumulation," that misery is intensified by craving or desire and the passions, which are the cause of reincarnation. 고집멸도 苦集滅道 The four axioms or truths: i.e. duḥkha, pain ; samudaya, as above ; nirodha, the extinguishing of pain and reincarnation ; mārga, the way to such extinction ; cf. 사제 四諦.

고참 古參 Old contemplative ; an experienced member of the meditation hall.

고하 苦河 Misery deep as a river.

고해 苦海 The ocean of misery, its limitlessness.

고행 苦行 Duṣkara-caryā, undergoing difficulties, hardships, or sufferings ; also Tapas, burning, torment ; hence asceticism, religious austerity, mortification. 고행림 苦行林 ; 목과림 木瓜林 Uruvilvā-kāśyapa, the forest near Gayā where Śākyamuni underwent rigorous ascetic discipline ; v. 우 優.

곡 谷 A gully. 곡고고 谷呱呱 Ku-wa-wa, the cry of a ghost, made in proof of its existence to one who had written a treatise on the non-existence of 귀 鬼 ghosts.

곡 曲 Bent, crooked, humpbacked ; to oppress ; ballads. 곡녀성 曲女城 The city of hunchback women, said to be Kanyākubja, an ancient kingdom and capital of Central India, "Canouge Lat. 27° 3 N., Long. 79° 50 E." [Eitel]. The legend in the 서역기 西域記 Record of Western Lands is that ninety-nine of King Brahmadatta's daughters were thus deformed by the ṛṣi Mahāvṛkṣa whom they refused to marry. 곡록 曲彔 ; 곡록 曲錄 ; 곡록 曲祿 ; 곡록 曲緑 A bent chair used in monasteries. 곡치 曲齒 ; 구타단저 矩吒檀底 Kūṭadantī, or Mālākuṭadantī, name of a rākṣasī.

곡 斛 Droṇa, a tub, or wooden vessel ; a measure of capacity. A square wooden vessel, a bushel, a picul. 곡반 斛飯 Droṇodana, cf. 도 途.

곡 穀 Grain ; rice unhulled. 곡두 穀頭 The monk in charge of the grain.

곡 哭 To weep. 곡읍 哭泣 To weep. 곡제 哭啼 To weep and wail.

곤륜 崑崙 K'un-lun, or Pulo Condore Island, or islands generally in the southern seas, hence 곤륜자 崑崙子 or 곤륜노 崑崙奴 is a native of those islands of black colour, and 곤륜국 崑崙國 is described as Java, Sumatra, etc. 곤륜산 崑崙山 The K'un-lun range north of Tibet, the 향산 香山 Gandhamādana.

곤륵 昆勒 Piṭaka, also 곤륵 蜫勒 defined as the Śāstras. 곤 昆 is a misprint for 비 毘. See 비륵 毘勒.

골 骨 Bone ; bones, relics. 골인 骨人 Skeleton. 골불 骨佛 A bone-buddha, a corpse. 골탑 骨塔 A dagoba for the ashes of the dead. 골목 骨目 the bones and eyes, the essentials. 골신 骨身 The bones of the body, the śarīra or remains after cremation. 골쇄천 骨鏁天 The bone-chain deva 상갈라 商羯羅 Śaṅkara, i.e. Śiva.

공 孔 A hole ; surname of Confucius ; great, very ; a peacock. 공작 孔雀 Mayūra, 마유라 摩裕羅 a peacock ; the latter form is also given by Eitel for Mauriya as "an ancient city on the north-east frontier of Matipura, the residence of the ancient Maurya (Morya) princes. The present Amroudh near Hurdwar". 공작성 孔雀城 Mathurā, or Kṛṣṇapura ; modern Muttra ; 마도라 摩度羅 ; 마투라

摩偷羅 ; 마돌라 摩突羅 ; 마두라 摩頭羅 ; 말토라 秣免羅 an ancient city and kingdom of Central India, famous for its stūpas, reputed birthplace of Kṛṣṇa. 공작명왕 孔雀明王 "Peacock king," a former incarnation of Śākyamuni, when as a peacock he sucked from a rock water of miraculous healing power ; now one of the mahārāja bodhisattvas, with four arms, who rides on a peacock ; his full title is 불모대금요공작명왕 佛母大金曜孔雀明王. There is another 공작왕 孔雀王 with two armcase-record ; a cause ; public laws, regulations ; case-law. Problems set by Ch'an(Zen) masters, upon which thought is concentrated as a means to attain inner unity and illumination. 공계 公界 A public place ; in public.

공 供 Pūjā ; to offer (in worship), to honour ; also to supply ; evidence. 공불 供佛 To offer to Buddha. 공구 供具 ; 공물 供物 Offerings, i.e. flowers, unguents ; water, incense, food, light. 공천 供天 ; 천공 天供 The devas who serve Indra. 공봉 供奉 To offer ; the monk who serves at the great altar. 공장 供帳 The T'ang dynasty register, or census of monks and nuns, supplied to the government every three years. 공장운 供帳雲 The cloud of Bodhisattvas who serve the Tathāgata. 공양 供養 To make offerings of whatever nourishes, e.g. food, goods, incense, lamps, scriptures, the doctrine, etc., any offering for body or mind.

공 恭 Respect, reverence. 공어타 恭御陀 Konyodha, a kingdom mentioned by Hsüan-tsang as a stronghold of unbelievers ; it is said to be in south-east Orissa, possibly Ganjam as suggested in [Eitel] ; there is a Konnāda further south. 공경 恭敬 Reverence, worship. 공경시 恭敬施 Worship as an offering, one of the three forms of giving, 공반다 恭畔茶 Kumbhāṇḍa, a demon, v. 구 鳩. 공건나보라 恭建那補羅 Koṅkaṇapura, "An ancient kingdom on the West Coast of India," including Konkan, Goa, and "North Canara, between Lat. 14° 37 N. and Lat. 18° N," [Eitel].

공 貢 Tribute ; best. 공고 貢高 Elevated, proud.

공 工 Work, a period of work, a job. 공부 工夫 Time, work, a term for meditation ; also 공부 功夫. 공교명 工巧明 Śilpasthāna-vidyā. 교업명 巧業明 One of the five departments of knowledge dealing with the arts, e.g. the various crafts, mechanics, natural science (yin-yang), calculations (especially for the calendar and astrology), etc. 공기아 工伎兒 Naṭa, a dancer ; the skilful or wily one, i.e. the heart or mind.

공 空 Śūnya, empty, void, hollow, vacant, non-existent. Śūnyatā, 순야다 舜若多, vacuity, void, emptiness, non-existence, immateriality, perhaps spirituality, unreality, the false or illusory nature of all existence, the seeming 가 假 being unreal. The doctrine that all phenomena and the ego have no reality, but are composed of a certain number of skandhas or elements, which disintegrate. The void, the sky, space. The universal, the absolute, complete abstraction without relativity. There are classifications into 2, 3, 4, 6, 7, 11, 13, 16, and 18 categories. The doctrine is that all things are compounds, or unstable organisms, possessing no self-essence, i.e. are dependent, or caused, come into existence only to perish. The underlying reality, the principle of eternal relativity, or non-infinity, i.e. śūnya, permeates all phenomena making possible their evolution. From this doctrine the Yogācārya school developed the idea of the permanent reality, which is Essence of Mind, the unknowable noumenon behind all phenomena, the entity void of ideas and phenomena, neither matter nor mind, but the root of both.

공가중 空假中 Unreality, reality, and the middle or mean doctrine ; noumenon, phenomenon, and the principle or absolute which unifies both. 공 空 Unreality, that things do not exist in reality ; 가 假 reality, that things exist though in "derived" or "borrowed" form, consisting of elements which are permanent ; 중 中 the "middle" doctrine of the Mādhyamika School, which denies both positions in the interests of the transcendental, or absolute. 공이파일체법 空以破一切法, 가이립일체법 假以立一切法, 중이묘일체법 中以妙一切法 Śūnya (universality) annihilates all relativities, particularity establishes all relativities, the middle path transcends and unites all relativities. T'ien-t'ai asserts that there is no contradiction in them and calls them a unity, the one including the other 즉공즉가즉중 卽空卽假卽中.

공거천 空居天 Devas dwelling in space, or the heavenly regions, i.e. the devalokas and rūpalokas.

공겁 空劫 The empty kalpa, v. 겁 劫.

공견 空見 The heterodox view that karma and nirvāṇa are not real, v. 공유 空有.

공경 空經 The sūtras of unreality or immateriality, e.g. the Prajñāpāramitā Sūtra.

공계 空界 The realm of space, one of the six realms, earth, water, fire, wind, space, knowledge. The 공계색 空界色 is the visible realm of space, the sky, beyond which is real space.

공공 空空 Unreality of unreality. When all has been regarded as illusion, or unreal, the abstract idea of unreality itself must be destroyed. 공공적적 空空寂寂 Void and silent, i.e. everything in the universe, with form or without form, is unreal and not to be considered as real.

공과 空果 Empty fruit ; also fruit of freedom from the illusion that things and the ego are real.

공관 空觀 v. 공유이관 空有二觀.

공교 空敎 The teaching that all is unreal. The 법상종 法相宗 Dharmalakṣaṇa School divided Buddha's teaching into three periods : (1) the Hīnayāna period, teaching that 법유 法有 things are real ; (2) the 반야 般若 Prajñā period, that 법공 法空 things are unreal ; (3) the Hua-yen and Lotus period of the middle or transcendental doctrine 중도교 中道敎.

공권 空拳 Riktamuṣṭi ; empty fist, i.e. deceiving a child by pretending to have something for it in the closed hand ; not the Buddha's method.

공대 空大 Space, one of the five elements (earth, water, fire, wind, space) ; v. 오대 五大.

공륜 空輪 The wheel of space below the water and wind wheels of a world. The element space is called the wheel of space.

공리 空理 The śūnya principle, or law, i.e. the unreality of the ego and phenomena.

공마 空魔 The demons who arouse in the heart the false belief that karma is not real.

공무 空無 Unreality, or immateriality, of things, which is defined as nothing existing of independent or self-contained nature. 공무아 空無我 Unreal and without ego. 공무변처 空無邊處 v. 공처 空處.

공문 空門 (1) The teaching which regards everything as unreal, or immaterial. (2) The school of unreality, one of the four divisions made by T'ien-t'ai. (3) The teaching of immateriality, the door to nirvāṇa, a general name for Buddhism ; hence 공문자 空門子 are Buddhist monks.

공법 空法 (1) To regard everything as unreal, i.e. the ego, things, the dynamic, the static. (2) The nirvāṇa of Hīnayāna.

공변처 空徧處 idem 공일체처 空一切處.

공삼매 空三昧 The samādhi which regards the ego and things as unreal ; one of the 삼삼매 三三昧.

공상 空想 Thinking of immateriality. Also, vainly thinking, or desiring.

공상 空相 Void, emptiness, space, the immaterial, that which cannot be expressed in terms of the material. The characteristic of all things is unreality, i.e. they are composed of elements which disintegrate. v. 공 空.

공색 空色 Formless and with form ; noumena and phenomena.

공생 空生 The one who expounded vacuity or immateriality, i.e. Subhūti, one of the ten great pupils of the Buddha.

공성 空聖 A saint who bears the name without possessing the character.

공성 空性 Śūnyatā, v. 공 空, the nature of the Void, or immaterial, the Bhūtatathatā, the universal substance, which is not 아법 我法 ego and things, but while not Void is of the Void-nature.

공시교 空始教 The initial teaching of the undeveloped Mahāyāna doctrines is the second of the five periods of Śākyamuni's teaching as defined by the Hua-yen School. This consists of two parts : 공시교 空始教 the initial doctrine of śūnya, the texts for which are the 반야 般若, 삼론 三論, etc. ; and 상시교 相始教, the initial doctrine of the essential nature as held by the esoterics ; intp. in the 심밀 深密 and 유가 瑜伽 texts.

공심 空心 An empty mind, or heart ; a mind meditating on the void, or infinite ; a mind not entangled in cause and effect, i.e. detached from the phenomenal.

공여래장 空如來藏 The Bhūtatathatā in its purity, or absoluteness.

공왕 空王 The king of immateriality, or spirituality, Buddha, who is lord of all things. 공왕불 空王佛 Dharmagahanābhyudgata-rāja. A Buddha who is said to have taught absolute intelligence, or knowledge of the absolute, cf. Lotus sūtra 9.

공유 空有 Unreal and real, non-existent and existent, abstract and concrete, negative and positive. 공유이집 空有二執 or 공유이견 空有二見. The two (false) tenets, or views, that karma and nirvāṇa are not real, and that the ego and phenomena are real ; these wrong views are overcome by the 공유이관 空有二觀 meditating on the unreality of the ego and phenomena, and the reality of karma and nirvāṇa 공유이종 空有二宗 The two schools 공 空 and 유 有 in Hīnayāna are given as 구사 俱舍 Kośa for 유 有 and 성실 成實 Satyasiddhi for 공 空, in Mahāyāna 법상 法相 for 유 有 and 삼론 三論 for 공 空.

공인 空忍 Patience attained by regarding suffering as unreal ; one of the 십인 十忍.

공일체처 空一切處 Universal emptiness, or space ; the samādhi which removes all limitations of space ; also 공변처 空徧處.

공적 空寂 Immaterial ; a condition beyond disturbance, the condition of nirvāṇa.

공점 空點 The dot over the *ṁ* or *ṅ* in Sanskrit, symbolizing that all things are empty or unreal ; used by the Shingon sect with various meanings.

공정 空定 The meditation which dwells on the Void or the Immaterial ; it is divided into 내도 內道, i.e. the 삼삼매 三三昧, and 외도 外道, the latter limited to the four dhyānas 사공정 四空定 q.v., except the illusion that things have a reality in themselves, as individuals 법아 法我 q.v.

공제 空際 The region of immateriality, or nirvāṇa. Also called 실제 實際, the region of reality.

공제 空諦 The doctrine of immateriality, one of the three dogmas of T'ien-t'ai, that all things animate and inanimate, seeing that they result from previous causes and are without reality in themselves, are therefore 공 空 or not material, but "spiritual."

공조 空鳥 The bird that cries 공공 空空, the cuckoo, i.e. one who, while not knowing the wonderful law of true immateriality (or spirituality), yet prates about it.

공종 空宗 The Śūnya sects, i.e. those which make the unreality of the ego and things their fundamental tenet.

공즉시색 空卽是色 The immaterial is the material, śūnya is rūpa, and vice versa, 색불이공 色不異空.

공진 空塵 Śūnya as sub-material, ghostly, or spiritual, as having diaphanous form, a non-Buddhist view of the immaterial as an entity, hence the false view of a soul or ego that is real.

공집 空執 v. 공유이집 空有二執.

공처 空處 ; 공무변처 空無邊處 Ākāśānantyāyatana ; the abode of infinite space, the formless, or immaterial world 무색계 無色界 the first of the Arūpaloka heavens, one of the four Brahmalokas. 공(무변)처정 空(無邊)處定 The dhyāna, or meditation connected with the above, in which all thought of form is suppressed.

공취 空聚 (1) An empty abode or place. (2) The body as composed of the six skandhas, which is a temporary assemblage without underlying reality.

공한처 空閑處 A tr. of 아란야 阿蘭若 araṇya, i.e. "forest." A retired place, 300 to 600 steps away from human habitation, suitable for the religious practices of monks.

공해 空海 Like sky and sea ; like space and the ocean for magnitude.

공해 空解 The interpretation (or doctrine) of ultimate reality. 공해탈문 空解脫門 The gate of salvation or deliverance by the realization of the immaterial, i.e. that the ego and things are formed of elements and have no reality in themselves ; one of the three deliverances.

공행 空行 The discipline or practice of the immaterial, or infinite, thus overcoming the illusion that the ego and all phenomena are realities.

공혜 空慧 The wisdom which beholds spiritual truth.

공화 空華 or 空花 Khapuṣpa, flowers in the sky, spots before the eyes, *Muscœ volitantes* ; illusion. The Indian Hīnayānists style Mahāyānists 공화외도 空華外道 Śūnyapuṣpa, sky-flower heretics, or followers of illusion.

과 科 A class, lesson, examination. 과문 科文 A set portion of a book, a lesson. 과의 科儀 The rule of the lesson.

과 鍋 A pan. 과두 鍋頭 The one who attends to the cooking-stoves, etc., in a monastery.

과 戈 A spear. 과추 戈追 idem 구지 俱胝 q.v. Koṭī.

과 瓜 Gourd, melon, etc. 과피 瓜皮 Melon rind.

과 果 Phala, 파라 頗羅 fruit ; offspring ; result, consequence, effect ; reward, retribution ; it contrasts with cause, i.e. 인과 因果 cause and effect. The effect by causing a further effect becomes also a cause.

과 過 To pass ; past ; gone ; transgression, error. 과거 過去 Passed, past. 과거세 過去世 The past, past time, past world or age. 과거칠불 過去七佛 The seven past Buddhas : Vipaśyin, Śikhin, Viśvabhū (of the previous 장엄 莊嚴 kalpa), and Krakucchanda, Kanakamuni, Kāśyapa, and Śākyamuni (of the 현 賢 or present kalpa). 과거성령 過去聖靈 The spirit of the departed. 과하 過夏 To pass the summer, or the summer retreat. 과도 過度 To pass from mortal life. 과만 過慢 The pride which among equals regards self as superior and among superiors as equal ; one of the seven arrogances. 과목교 過木橋 To cross over the single log bridge, i.e.

only one string to the bow. 과현미 過現未 Past, present, future. 과오 過惡 Dauṣṭhulya. Surpassing evil ; extremely evil.

과 跨 To straddle, bestride, pass over. 과절 跨節 To interpret one sūtra by another, a T'ien-t'ai term, e.g. interpreting all other sūtras in the light of the Lotus sūtra.

과계원현 果界圓現 In the Buddha-realm, i.e. of complete bodhi-enlightenment, all things are perfectly manifest.

과과 果果 The fruit of fruit, i.e. nirvāṇa, the fruition of bodhi. 과과불성 果果佛性 The fruit of the fruit of Buddhahood, i.e. parinirvāṇa, one of the 오불성 五佛性.

과극 果極 Fruition perfect, the perfect virtue or merit of Buddha-enlightenment. 과극법신 果極法身 The dharmakāya of complete enlightenment.

과단 果斷 To cut off the fruit, or results, of former karma. The arhat who has a "remnant of karma," though he has cut off the seed of misery, has not yet cut off its fruits.

과덕 果德 The merits nirvāṇa, i.e. 상락아정 常樂我淨 q.v., eternal, blissful, personal (or autonomous), and pure, all transcendental.

과두 果頭 The condition of retribution, especially the reward of bodhi or enlightenment, idem 과상 果上 hence 과두불 果頭佛 is he who has attained the Buddha-condition, a T'ien-t'ai term.

과만 果滿 The full or complete fruition of merit ; perfect reward.

과명 果名 ; **과호** 果號 Attainment-name, or reward-name or title, i.e. of every Buddha, indicating his enlightenment.

과박 果縛 Retribution-bond ; the bitter fruit of transmigration binds the individual so that he cannot attain release. This fruit produces 자박 子縛 or further seeds of bondage. 과박단 果縛斷 Cutting off the ties of retribution, i.e. entering nirvāṇa, e.g. entering salvation.

과보 果報 ; **이숙** 異熟 Retribution for good or evil deeds, implying that different conditions in this (or any) life are the variant ripenings, or fruit, of seed sown in previous life or lives. 과보토 果報土 The realm of reward, where bodhisattvas attain the full reward of their deeds, also called 실보무장애토 實報無障礙土, one of the 사토 四土 of T'ien-t'ai. 과보사상 果報四相 The four forms of retribution — birth, age, sickness, death.

과분 果分 The reward, e.g. of ineffable nirvāṇa, or dharmakāya.

과불성 果佛性 Fruition of the Buddha-enlightenment, its perfection, one of the five forms of the Buddha-nature.

과상 果上 In the stage when the individual receives the consequences of deeds done.

과상 果相 Reward, retribution, or effect ; especially as one of the three forms of the ālaya-vijñāna.

과수 果遂 The fruit follows. 과수원 果遂願 The assurance of universal salvation, the twentieth of Amitābha's forty-eight vows.

과숙식 果熟識 The ālaya-vijñāna, i.e. storehouse or source of consciousness, from which both subject and object are derived.

과순 果脣 Fruit lips, Buddha's were "red like the fruit of the Bimba tree."

과원 果圓 Fruit complete, i.e. perfect enlightenment, one of the eight T'ien-t'ai perfections.

과위 果位 The stage of attainment, or reward as contrasted with the cause-stage, i.e. the deed.

과유식 果唯識 The wisdom attained from investigating and thinking about philosophy, or Buddha-truth, i.e. of the sūtras and abhidharmas ; this includes the first four under 오종유식 五種唯識.

과인 果人 Those who have obtained the fruit, i.e. escaped the chain of transmigration, e.g. Buddha, Pratyeka-buddha, Arhat.

과지 果地 The stage of attainment of the goal of any disciplinary course.

과해 果海 The ocean of bodhi or enlightenment.

곽 藿 Greens, bean-stalks, etc. ; bishopwort, a kind of mint ; the Tamāla, 다마라(발) 多摩羅(跋) *Xanthochymus pictorius, Laurus cassia,* and other odoriferous shrubs. 곽향 藿香 A scent from the above.

곽 霍 Quickly, suddenly. 곽한 霍罕 ; 포한 怖悍 Ferghana, "a mountainous province and city in Turkestan on the upper Jaxartes." Eitel.

곽 or **확** 廓 Wide, spacious, open, vacant. 확연대오 廓然大悟 Widely to have a great apprehension of the truth.

관 棺 a coffin 관재 棺材.

관 管 A pipe, tube ; to rule, control. 관현강 管絃講 Pipes, strings, and preaching, an "accompanied" service in India.

관 官 Official, public. 관난 官難 In danger from the law ; official oppression.

관 關 To shut, a closed place, barrier, frontier ; to include, concern, involve. 관제 關帝 Kuan Ti, the god of War, a deified hero of the Three Kingdoms, a protector of Buddhism.

관 貫 To string, thread, pass through. 관화 貫花 A string of flowers, a term for the gāthās in sūtras, i.e. the prose recapitulated in verse. 관수 貫首 ; 관정 貫頂 A superintendent, head.

관 灌 To water, sprinkle, pour ; to flow together, or into, accumulate. 관불 灌佛 ; 욕불 浴佛 To wash a Buddha's image with scented water, which is a work of great merit and done with much ceremony. 관실 灌室 The building in which the esoterics practise the rite of baptism. 관세 灌洗 To wash a Buddha's image. 관랍 灌臘 The washing of a Buddha's image at the end of the monastic year, the end of summer. 관정 灌頂 Abhiṣecana ; mūrdhābhiṣikta ; inauguration or consecration by sprinkling, or pouring water on the head ; an Indian custom on the investiture of a king, whose head was baptized with water from the four seas and from the rivers in his domain ; in China it is administered as a Buddhist rite chiefly to high personages, and for ordination purposes. Amongst the esoterics it is a rite especially administered to their disciples ; and they have several categories of baptism, e.g. that of ordinary disciples, of teacher, or preacher, of leader, of office-bearer ; also for special causes such as relief from calamity, preparation for the next life, etc. 관정주 灌頂住 The tenth stage of a bodhisattva when he is anointed by the Buddhas as a Buddha.

관 觀 Vipaśyanā ; vidarśanā. To look into, study, examine, contemplate ; contemplation, insight ; a study, a Taoist monastery ; to consider illusion and discern illusion, or discern the seeming from the real ; to contemplate and mentally enter into truth. 각 覺 is defined as awakening, or awareness, 관 觀 as examination or study. It is also an old tr. of the word Yoga ; and cf. 선 禪. Kuan is especially a doctrine of the T'ien-t'ai school as shown in the 지관 止觀 q.v.

관공 觀空 To regard all things as unreal, or as having no fundamental reality.

관념 觀念 To look into and think over, contemplate and ponder.

관달 觀達 To penetrate to reality through contemplation.

관도 觀道 Contemplation, meditation, insight.

관무량수경 觀無量壽經 An important sūtra relating to Amitāyus, or Amitābha, and his Pure Land, known also as 불설관무량수불경 佛說觀無量壽佛經. There are numerous commentaries on it. The title is commonly abbreviated to 관경 觀經.

관문 觀門 Contemplation or meditation as one of the two methods of entry into truth, i.e. instruction and meditation ; also one of the 육묘문 六妙門. 관문십법계 觀門十法界 cf. 십 十 and 법 法.

관문사 觀門寺 Gwan-mun-sa. A large temple located in Umyeon-dong Seocho-gu Seoul in Korea. It belongs to Korean Cheontae Order.

관법 觀法 Methods of contemplation, or obtaining of insight into truth, cf. 육관법 六觀法 and 지관 止觀.

관불 觀佛 To contemplate, or meditate upon, Buddha. 관불삼매 觀佛三昧 A samādhi on the characteristic marks of a Buddha.

관상 觀象 Describing an elephant from sight rather than 모상 摸象, as would a blind man, from feeling it ; i.e. immediate and correct knowledge.

관상 觀想 To meditate and think. 관상염불 觀想念佛 To contemplate Buddha (especially Amitābha) in the mind and repeat his name.

관상염불 觀像念佛 To contemplate the image of (Amitābha) Buddha and repeat his name.

관선 觀禪 Contemplation and meditation, to sit in abstract trance.

관세음 觀世音 Regarder of the world's sounds, or cries, the so-called Goddess of Mercy ; also known as 관음 觀音 ; 관세음보살 觀世音菩薩 ; 관(세)자재 觀(世)自在 ; 관윤 觀尹 ; 광세음 光世音 (the last being the older form). Avalokiteśvara, v. 아 阿 8. Originally represented as a male, the images are now generally those of a female figure. The meaning of the term is in doubt ; it is intp. as above, but the term 관(세)자재 觀(世)自在 accords with the idea of Sovereign Regarder and is not associated with sounds or cries. Kuan-yin is one of the triad of Amida, is represented on his left, and is also represented as crowned with Amida ; but there are as many as thirty-three different forms of Kuan-yin, sometimes with a bird, a vase, a willow wand, a pearl, a "thousand" eyes and hands, etc., and, when as bestower of children, carrying a child. The island of P'u-t'o (Potala) is the chief centre of Kuan-yin worship, where she is the protector of all in distress, especially of those who go to sea. there are many sūtras, etc., devoted to the cult, but its provenance and the date of its introduction to China are still in doubt. Chapter 25 of the Lotus sūtra is devoted to Kuan-yin, and is the principal scripture of the cult ; its date is uncertain. Kuan-yin is sometimes confounded with Amitābha and Maitreya. She is said to be the daughter of king Śubhavyūha 묘장왕 妙莊王, who had her killed by "stifling because the sword of the executioner broke without hurting her. Her spirit went to hell ; but hell changed into paradise. Yama sent her back to life to save his hell, when she was miraculously transported on a Lotus flower to the island of Poo-too." [Eitel]. 관세음모 觀世音母 Tārā, the śakti, or female energy of the masculine Avalokiteśvara.

관수 觀樹 Contemplating the tree (of knowledge, as Śākyamuni is said to have done after his enlightenment).

관심 觀心 Contemplation of the mind, mental contemplation, contemplation of all things as mind.

관음 觀音 v. 관세음 觀世音.

관음사 觀音寺 Gwan-eum-sa. A temple located in Jeju-si in Korea. The 23rd parish headquarters of Korean Jogye Order.

관음전 觀音殿 Hall of the Avalokiteśvara, Bodhisattva of Compassion.

관재살타 觀在薩埵 Idem Kuan-yin Bodhisattva, v. 관세음 觀世音.

관정삼매 觀頂三昧 The samādhi of the summit of contemplation, i.e. the peak whence all the samādhis may be surveyed.

관조 觀照 To be enlightened (or enlighten) as the result of insight, or intelligent contemplation. 관조반야 觀照般若 The prajñā or wisdom of meditative enlightenment on reality.

관지 觀智 Wisdom obtained from contemplation.

관찰 觀察 Pravicaya ; investigation ; meditation on and inquiry into ; vibhāvana, clear perception. 관찰문 觀察門 Contemplation of the joys of Amitābha's Pure Land, one of the 오념문 五念門.

관해 觀解 To contemplate ultimate reality and unravel or expound it.

관행 觀行 Contemplation and (accordant) action ; method of contemplating. 관행불 觀行佛 ; 관행즉 觀行即 The third of the 육즉 六即, the bodhisattva or disciple who has attained to the 오품 五品 stage of Buddhahood.

관혜 觀慧 The wisdom which penetrates to ultimate reality.

광 光 ; 광명 光明 Prabhā, light, brightness, splendour, to illuminate.

광 狂 Deranged, mad, wild. 광난왕생 狂亂往生 Saved out of terror into the next life ; however distressed by thoughts of hell as the result of past evil life, ten repetitions, or even one, of the name of Amitābha ensures entry into his Paradise. 광혜 狂慧 Foolish wisdom ; clever but without calm meditation. 광구 狂狗 A mad dog. 광화 狂華 Muscæ volitantes, dancing flowers before the eyes ; 광상 狂象 a mad elephant, such is the deluded mind.

광 誑 Imposition, deception, lying.

광 曠 Spacious, extensive ; waste ; wilderness ; far, long, wide. 광겁 曠劫 A past kalpa ; the part of a kalpa that is past. 광야 曠野 A wilderness, wild, prairie.

광 廣 Vipula. Broad, wide, extensive, spacious ; extended, enlarged, expanded ; for vaipulya v. 방광 方廣, for which 광 廣 is also used alone to indicate Vaipulya sūtras, etc. 광박 廣博 Wide and spacious, extensively read, very learned. 광박신 廣博身 The one whose body fills space, Vairocana. 광엄성 廣嚴城 Vaiśālī, broad ornate city, cf. 비 毘. 광대 廣大 Broad and great. 광대지 廣大智 The vast wisdom of Buddha beyond measure. 광대회 廣大會 The centre where vast virtues meet, a term for Amitābha. 광혜 廣慧 Vipulaprajña, or Vipulamati, vast wisdom, an epithet of a Buddha, one able to transform all beings. 광교 廣教 Full or detailed teaching by the Buddha about the duties of the order, in contrast with 략교 略教 general or summarized teaching ; the detailed teaching resulting from errors which had crept in among his disciples. 광과천 廣果天 Bṛhatphala, the twelfth Brahmaloka, the third of the eight heavens of the fourth dhyāna realm of form. 광협 廣狹 Broad and narrow. 광목천 廣目天 The wide-eyed deva, virūpākṣa, diversely-eyed, having deformed eyes, an epithet of Śiva, as represented with three eyes ; name of one of the four Mahā-rājas, he who guards the west. 광장설 廣長舌 A broad and long tongue, one of the thirty-two marks of a Buddha, big enough to cover his face ; it is also one of the "marvels" in the Lotus sūtra.

광강 光降 The honoured one descends, i.e. the Buddha or bodhisattva who is worshipped descends.

광기 光記 The above-mentioned 구사론기 俱舍論記 in 30 chüan by 보광 普光 P'u-kuang, v. 광보 光寶.

광덕국 光德國 Avabhāsa, the kingdom of light and virtue, or glorious virtue, in which Mahākāśyapa is to be reborn as a Buddha, under the name of 광명 光明 Raśmiprabhāsa.

광망동자 光網童子 Jālinīprabhakumāra, 야리영발라바구마라 惹哩寧鉢囉婆俱摩羅 ; one of the eight attendants on Mañjuśrī ; he is the youth with the shining net.

광명 光明 v. 광덕국 光德國. 광명토 光明土 The glory land, or Paradise of Amitābha. 광명단 光明壇 The fire altar. 광명대범 光明大梵 Jyotiṣprabha, the great illustrious Brahman, whose Buddha-realm "is to contribute some Bodhisattvas for that of Amitābha." [Eitel]. 광명사 光明寺 ; 광명대사 光明大師 or 광명화상 光明和尙. Kuang-ming ssŭ, temple and title of 선도 善導 Shan-tao, a noted monk of the T'ang dynasty under Kao Tsung. 광명산 光明山 The shining hill, or monastery, a name for the abode of Kuan-yin, said to be in India, and called Potala. 광명심전 光明心殿 The temple of the bright or shining heart ; the seat of Vairocana, the sun Buddha, in the Vajradhātu maṇḍala. 광명왕 光明王 One of the twenty-five bodhisattvas who, with Amitābha, welcomes to Paradise the dying who call on Buddha. 광명진언 光明眞言 A dhāraṇī by whose repetition the brightness or glory of Buddha may be obtained, and all retribution of sin be averted.

광목녀 光目女 The bright-eyed (or wide-eyed) daughter, a former incarnation of 지장 地藏 Kṣitigarbha.

광보 光寶 Two noted monks of 대자은 大慈恩 T'zŭ-en monastery under the T'ang dynasty, 보광 普光 P'u-kuang and 법보 法寶 Fa-pao, the first author of 구사론기 俱舍論記, the second of a commentary 소 疏 on the same śāstra, each in 30 chüan.

광서 光瑞 The auspicious ray sent from between the Buddha's eyebrows before a revelation.

광세음 光世音 idem 관세음 觀世音.

광염왕불 光燄王佛 The royal Buddha of shining flames, or flaming brightness, Amitābha, with reference to his virtues.

광음천 光音天 Ābhāsvara, light and sound, or light-sound heavens, also styled 극광정천 極光淨天, the heavens of utmost light and purity, i.e. the third of the second dhyāna heavens, in which the inhabitants converse by light instead of words ; they recreate the universe from the hells up to and including the first dhyāna heavens after it has been destroyed by fire during the final series of cataclysms ; but they gradually diminish in power and are reborn in lower states. The three heavens of the second dhyāna are 소광 少光, 무량광 無量光, and 광음 光音. 광음궁 光音宮 Ābhāsvara-vimāna, the Ābhāsvara palace, idem.

광조여래상 光照如來相 Vairocana-raśmi-pratimaṇḍita-dhvaja ; "a Bodhisattva, disciple of Śākyamuni, who was in a former life Vimaladattā." [Eitel].

광좌 光座 Prabhā-maṇḍala ; the halo and throne (of a Buddha) ; also 광부 光趺.

광취불정 光聚佛頂 One of the five 불정 佛頂 q.v.

광택 光宅 Kuang-chai, name of the temple where 법운 法雲 Fa-yün early in the sixth century wrote his commentary on the Lotus sūtra, which is known as the 광택소 光宅疏 ; 광택 光宅 became his epithet. He made a division of four yāna from the Burning House parable, the goat cart representing the śrāvaka, the deer cart the pratyeka-buddha, the ox-cart the Hīnayāna bodhisattva, and the great white ox-cart the Mahāyāna bodhisattva ; a division adopted by T'ien-t'ai.

광통 光統 Kuang the general supervisor, i.e. the monk 혜광 慧光 Hui-kuang, sixth century, who resigned the high office of 통 統 and tr. the 십지경론 十地經論.

광호 光毫 The ūrṇā, or curl between the Buddha's eyebrows whence streams light that reveals all worlds, one of the thirty-two characteristics of a Buddha.

괘 罣 A snare ; impediment ; cause of anxiety, anxious. 괘념 罣念 To be anxious about. 괘애 罣礙 hindrance, impediment.

괘 掛 To hang, suspend. 괘자 掛子 A peg for a garment. 괘탑 掛搭 ; 괘답 掛褡 ; 괘단 掛單 One who hangs up all his possessions, i.e. a wandering monk who stays for the night in a monastery. 괘진 掛眞 To hang up a picture (of a Buddha, etc.). 괘락 掛絡 ; 괘락 掛落 ; 괘라 掛羅 A short garment, or cover ; a waistcoat. 괘석 掛錫 To hang up one's staff, similar to 괘탑 掛搭 ; to dwell in a place.

괴 愧 Ashamed, intp. as ashamed for the misdeeds of others. v. 참 慚.

괴 傀 Gigantic, monstrous, part man part devil ; a puppet. 괴뢰자 傀儡子 A puppet, marionette.

괴 壞 To go to ruin, decay, perish, destroy, spoil, worn out, rotten, bad. 괴겁 壞劫 Saṁvarta, v. 겁 劫 7, the periodical gradual destruction of a universe, one of its four kalpas, i.e. 성겁 成劫 Vivarta, formation ; 주겁 住劫 Vivarta-siddha ; abiding, or existence ; 괴겁 壞劫 Saṁvarta, decay, or destruction ; 멸겁 滅劫 Saṁvarta-siddha, final annihilation. 괴산 壞山 As the hills wear down, so is it with man. 괴법 壞法 Any process of destruction, or decay ; to burn the bones of a deceased person so that they may not draw him to rebirth. 괴상 壞相 The aspect, or state of destruction or decay. 괴색 壞色 Kaṣāya, cf. 가 袈 a brown colour ; but it is described as a neutral colour through the dyeing out of the other colours, i.e. for the monk's 괴색의 壞色依 or 괴납 壞納 rag-robe. 괴고 壞苦 The suffering of decay, or destruction, e.g. of the body, reaction from joy, etc. 괴견 壞見 Corrupt, or bad views ; the advocacy of total annihilation. 괴도 壞道 To destroy the truth, or the religion, e.g. by evil conduct. 괴려거 壞驢車 A worn-out donkey cart — i.e. Hīnayāna.

굉 宏 Vast, spacious. 굉지 宏智 Hung-chih, posthumous name of a monk of 천동 天童 T'ien-t'ung monastery, Ningpo, early in the twelfth century.

교 橋 A bridge ; cross-beam ; curved ; lofty. 교량 橋梁 A bridge, trampled on by all but patiently bearing them, a synonym for patience, endurance.

교 憍 Boastful, bragging ; self-indulgent ; indulgent ; translit, *ko, kau, go, gau* ; cf. 구 瞿, 구 俱, 구 拘, 거 巨. 교갱 憍坑 The pit of pride and arrogance. 교사야 憍奢耶 Kauśeya, also 교사야 憍舍耶 ; 고세야 高世耶 cloth made of wild silk. 교시 憍尸 Idem. 교시가 憍尸迦 ; 교지가 憍支迦 Kauśika, of the family of Kuśika, family name of Indra ; one account says Amitābha was of the same family name. 교만 憍慢 Arrogance and pride. 교담미 憍曇彌 ; 교답미 憍答彌 ; 구담미 俱曇彌 Gautamī, feminine of the patronymic Gautama, the family name of Śākyamuni. Gautamī is a name for Mahāprajāpatī, his aunt and nurse, who in the Lotus sūtra is predicted to become Buddha. 교범(바제) 憍梵(波提) Gavāṁpati, also 교범발제 憍梵鉢提 ; 가범바제 迦梵波提 ; 급방발지 笈房鉢底 intp. as chewing the cud ; lord of cattle, etc. A man who became a monk, born with a mouth always ruminating like a cow because of former oral sin. 교살라 憍薩羅 Kosala, Kośala ; also 거살라 居薩羅 ; 구살라 拘薩羅 ; 구사라 拘娑羅, i.e. Northern Kosala, or Uttarakosala, an ancient kingdom, the modern Oude ; also Southern Kosala, or Dakṣiṇakosala, an ancient kingdom, part of the present Central Provinces. 교상미 憍賞彌 Kauśāmbī, also 교섬미 憍閃彌 or 憍睒彌 ; 구섬미 俱睒彌 ; "an ancient city on the Ganges in the lower part of the Doab." [M. W.] It has been identified by some with Kusia near Kurrah ; but is the village of Kosam on the Jumna, 30 miles above Allahabad. Cf. 거 巨. 교진여 憍陳如 ; 교진나 憍陳那 Kauṇḍinya ; also 아야구린 阿若拘隣 ; 아야교진나 阿若憍陳那 Ājñāta-Kauṇḍinya. (1) A prince of Magadha, uncle and first disciple of Śākyamuni. (2) A grammarian mentioned in the Prātiśākhya sūtras. (3) Vyākaraṇa-Kauṇḍinya, who was told by the Buddha that a Buddha is too spiritual to leave any relics behind. [Eitel].

교 校 Compare, collate, compared with, similar to 교 較. 교량 校量 To compare, or collate, and measure ; comparative. 교식 校飾 To adorn, ornament.

교 膠 Glue, gum. 교분자 膠盆子 A glue-pot, referring to running handwriting. 교향 膠香 Incense of the liquidambar tree.

교 交 Interlock, intersect ; crossed ; mutual ; friendship ; to hand over, pay. 교대 交代 ; 교부 交付 to hand over, entrust to. 교당 交堂 To hand over charge of a hall, or monastery. 교로 交蘆 ; 속로 束蘆 A tripod of three rushes or canes — an illustration of the mutuality of cause and effect, each cane depending on the other at the point of intersection. 교로 交露 A curtain festooned with jewels, resembling hanging dewdrops. 교점 交點 To hand over and check (as in the case of an inventory).

교 絞 Intertwine, twist, intermingle. 교식 絞飾 Adorned or robed in grey, a mixture of black and yellow.

교 喬 Lofty. 교답마 喬答摩 Gautama ; 교답미 喬答彌 Gautamī ; v. 구 瞿.

교 教 Pravacana, to teach, instruct, inculcate ; śāśana, teaching, precept, doctrine ; āgama, sect, school, church.

교 巧 Skillful, clever. 교묘지 巧妙智 ; 교지혜 巧智慧 is 일체지지 一切智智 q.v. 교명 巧明 v. 공교론 功巧論.

교관 教觀 Teaching and meditation ; the Buddha's doctrine and meditation on it ; also 교관이문 教觀二門.

교내 教內 Within instruction ; in the sect or church ; especially those who receive normal instruction from the written canon, opposite of 교외 教外.

교도 教導 To instruct and lead.

교도 教道 To teach a way, or religion ; a taught way contrasted with an intuitional way ; the way of teaching.

교령 教令 To instruct, command ; the commands of a sect or school.

교리 教理 The fundamental principles of a religion ; its doctrines, or dogmas, e.g. the four truths, the twelve nidānas, the eightfold noble path. 교리행과 教理行果 The fruit or results arising from the practice of a religion.

교망 教網 The teaching (of Buddha) viewed as a net to catch and save mortals.

교문 教門 A religion, a sect, different religious teachings.

교상 教相 The particular teaching of a sect.

교수 教授 To instruct, give instruction. 교수사 教授師 ; 교수아사리 教授阿闍梨 An ācārya, or instructor, preceptor.

교어 教語 The words of Buddhism ; words of instruction.

교외 教外 Outside the sect, or school, or church ; also not undergoing normal instruction, i.e. the intuitive school which does not rely on texts or writings, but on personal communication of its tenets, either oral or otherwise, including direct contact with the Buddha or object of worship, e.g. "guidance."

교의 教義 The meaning of a teaching, or doctrine.

교적 教迹 The vestiges, or evidences of a religion ; e.g. the doctrines, institutions, and example of the teachings of Buddha and the saints.

교전 教典 The sacred books of a religion, or sect.

교주 教主 The founder of a religion, e.g. the Buddha.

교증 教證 Teaching and evidence, doctrine and its evidential results, or realization.

교체 教體 The body, or corpus of doctrine ; the whole teaching.

교칙 教勅 The commands of a master or father.

교판 教判 The various divisions of teaching or doctrine, such as the T'ien-t'ai theory of the five periods of Śākyamuni's life, the four classes of doctrine, the four styles of teaching, etc.

교행 教行 Instruction and conduct ; teaching and practice ; also the progress of the teaching, or doctrine. 교행증 教行證 Teaching, practice and its realization, its evidential results.

교화 教化 To transform by instruction ; teach and convert ; to cause another to give alms.

교회 教會 An assembly for instruction ; a congregation ; a church.

구 矩 A carpenter's square, a rule ; translit. *ku*, cf. 고 姑, 구 拘, 구 鳩. 구사게라보라 矩奢揭羅補羅 Kuśāgrapura, v. 길상 吉祥 and cf. 구시나 拘尸那. 구랍파 矩拉婆 Kuravaḥ or Uttarakuru, v. 울 鬱 the northern of the four great continents. 구구타 矩矩吒 Kukkuṭa, a cock, fowl. 구구타예설라 矩矩吒翳設羅 Kukkuṭeśvara, Korea.

구 狗 A dog. 구심 狗心 A dog's heart, satisfied with trifles, unreceptive of Buddha's teaching. 구계 狗戒 Dog-rule, dog-morals, i.e. heretics who sought salvation by living like dogs, eating garbage, etc. 구법 狗法 Dog-law, fighting and hating, characteristics of the monks in the last days of the world. 구림정폐 狗臨井吠 Like the dog barking at its own reflection in the well. 구저사자피 狗箸獅子皮 The dog in the lion's skin — all the dogs fear him till he barks.

구 鳩 A dove ; to collect ; translit. *ku, gu, ko, ki* ; cf. 구 瞿, 구 拘, 구 俱, 구 矩. 구원 鳩垣 Kupana, 구원 鳩洹 ; 구환 仇桓 ; an asura who swells with anger. 구이라 鳩夷羅 Kokila, the cuckoo ; or 구나라 鳩那羅 Kuṇāla, cf. 구 拘. There are other forms beginning with 구 拘, 구 俱, 구 瞿. 구마(라) 鳩摩(羅) Kumāra, a child, youth, prince. 구마라 鳩摩羅 ; 구마라집(바) 鳩摩羅什(婆) ; 구마라시바 鳩摩羅時婆 ; 구마라기바 鳩摩羅耆婆 ; 라집 羅什 Kumārajīva, one of the "four suns" of Mahāyāna Buddhism, of which he was the early and most effective propagator in China. He died in Ch'ang-an about A.D. 412. His father was an Indian, his mother a princess of Karashahr. He is noted for the number of his translations and commentaries, which he is said to have dictated to some 800 monastic scribes. After cremation his tongue remained "unconsumed." 구마라가 鳩摩羅伽 Kumāraka, idem Kumāra. 구마라가지 鳩摩羅伽地 Kumāraka-stage, or 구마라부다 鳩摩羅浮多 Kumāra-bhūta, youthful state, i.e. a bodhisattva state or condition, e.g. the position of a prince to the throne. 구마라염 鳩摩羅炎 Kumārāyaṇa, father of Kumārajīva. 구마라다 鳩摩邏多 ; 구마라다 鳩摩邏陀 Kumāralabdha, also 구 矩 and 구 拘 ; two noted monks, one during the period of Aśoka, of the Sautrāntikāḥ sect ; the other Kumāralabdha, or "Kumarata" [Eitel], the nineteenth patriarch. 구반다 鳩槃茶 Kumbhāṇḍa, a demon shaped like a gourd, or pot ; or with a scrotum like one ; it devours the vitality of men ; also written with initials 궁 弓, 공 恭, 구 究, 구 拘, 구 俱, and 길 吉, also 구만나 鳩滿拏. 구구타 鳩鳩吒 Kukkuṭa, a fowl.

구 勾 A hook, to entangle, inveigle, arrest ; a tick, mark. 구당 勾當 An employee in a monastery, especially of the Shingon sect. In Japan, the second rank of official blind men.

구 鬮 A lot, tally, ballot, ticket, made of wood, bamboo, or paper ; also 구 鬮. To cast lots for good or ill fortune.

구 丘 A mound, a plot ; personal name of Confucius. 구정 丘井 A (dry) well on a hill top, symbolical of old age. 구자 丘慈 ; 굴지 屈支 ; 구자 龜茲 q.v. Kuche, Karashahr.

구 句 A sentence, phrase, clause ; also used for a place. 구구 句句 Sentence by sentence, every word. 구신 句身 Padakāya, perhaps Prātipadika ; an inflected word.

구 枸 A spinous shrub ; translit. *k*. 구소마 枸蘇摩 Kusuma, a flower ; especially the white China-aster. 구소마보라 枸蘇摩補羅 Kusumapura, the city of flowers, Pāṭaliputra, i.e. Patna. 구로사 枸盧舍 Krośa, cf. 구 拘, 구 俱 ; the distance the lowing of an ox can be heard, the eight part of a yojana.

구 衢 A thoroughfare, a way, cf. 구 瞿 18.

구 具 All ; complete ; to present ; implements ; translit. *gh*. 구사라 具史羅 or 瞿史羅 or 劬師羅 Ghoṣira, a wealthy householder of Kauśāmbī, who gave Śākyamuni the Ghoṣiravana park and vihāra. 구수 具壽 Āyuṣmant. Having long life, a term by which a monk, a pupil, or a youth may be addressed. 구계 具戒 idem 구족계 具足戒. 구계방편 具戒方便 The "expedient" method of giving the whole rules by stages. 구계지 具戒地 The second of the bodhisattva ten stages in which all the rules are kept. 구지관정 具支灌頂 One of the three abhiṣeka or baptisms of the 대일경 大日經. A ceremonial sprinkling of the head of a monarch at his investiture with water from the seas and rivers (in his domain). It is a mode also employed in the investiture of certain high officials of Buddhism. 구박 具縛 Completely bound, all men are in bondage to illusion. 구설 具說 To discuss completely, state fully. 구담 具譚 Gautama, v. 구 瞿. 구족 具足 All, complete. 구족계 具足戒 The complete rules or commandments — 250 for the monk, 500 (actually 348) for the nun. 구족덕본원 具足德本願 The forty-fourth of Amitābha's forty-eight vows, that all universally should acquire his virtue.

구 俱 All, every ; translit. *ku, ko* ; cf. 구 拘 ; 구 鳩 ; 구 究 ; 거 居 ; 굴 窟 ; 거 巨.

구 懼 Fear, dread ; translit. *gu*. 구낭 懼曩 Guṇa, a power, quality, v. 구 求.

구 鉤 Hook, barb ; also 구 鈎. 구소법 鉤召法 Vaśīkaraṇa, the method in esoteric practice of summoning and influencing the beneficent powers. 구유 鉤鈕 To knot, tie, e.g. a girdle ; to button. 구보살 鉤菩薩 The bodhisattva guardian with the trident, one of the four with barb, noose, chain or bell.

구 久 Long, for long, long ago ; also 구원 久遠. 구주자 久住者 One who has spent many years in monastic life, or in a particular monastery. 구성정각 久成正覺 Perfect enlightenment long acquired ; Śākya-Tathāgata in ancient kalpas having achieved complete bodhi, transmitted it to Mañjuśrī, Avalokiteśvara, and others, i.e. their enlightenment is the fruit of his enlightenment. 법화경수량품 法華經壽量品. 구원실성 久遠實成 The perfect enlightenment achieved by the Buddha in remote kalpas.

구 垢 Mala. Dust, impurity, dregs ; moral impurity ; mental impurity. Whatever misleads or deludes the mind ; illusion ; defilement ; the six forms are vexation, malevolence, hatred, flattery, wild talk, pride ; the seven are desire, false views, doubt, presumption, arrogance, inertia, and meanness. 구유 垢有 v. 이진여 二眞如. 구염 垢染 Taint of earthly things, or illusion. 구오 垢汙 Defilement (of the physical as type of mental illusion). 구결 垢結 The bond of the defiling, i.e. the material, and of reincarnation ; illusion. 구습 垢習 Habituation to defilement ; the influence of its practice. 구식 垢識 Defiling knowledge, the common worldly knowledge that does not discriminate the seeming from the real.

구 口 Mukha, the mouth, especially as the organ of speech. 신 身, 구 口, 의 意 are the three media of corruption, body or deed, mouth or word, and mind or thought. 구전 口傳 ; 구수 口授 Oral transmission. 구력외도 口力外道 One of the eleven heretical sects of India, which is said to have compared the mouth to the great void out of which all things were produced. The great void produced the four elements, these produced herbs, and these in turn all the living ; or more in detail the void produced wind, wind fire, fire warmth, warmth water, water congealed and formed earth which produced herbs, herbs cereals and life, hence life is food ; ultimately all returns to the void, which is nirvāṇa. 구력논사 口力論師 ; 인력론사 因力論師 Exponents of the above doctrine. 구인 口印 The mouth sign, one of the fourteen symbols of 부중존 不重尊 q.v. 구화 口和 Harmony of mouths or voices, unanimous approval. 구사 口四 The four evils of the mouth, lying, double tongue, ill words, and exaggeration ; cf. 십악 十惡. 구밀 口密 ; 어밀 語密 One of the 삼밀 三密. Secret or magical words, either definite formulas of the Buddha or secret words from his dharmakāya, or spirit. 구인 口忍 Patience of the mouth, uttering no rebuke under insult or persecution ; there are similarly 신인 身忍 and 의인 意忍. 구업 口業 ; 어업 語業 One of the 삼업 三業. (1) The work of the mouth, i.e. talk, speech. (2) The evil karma produced by the mouth, especially from lying, double-tongue, ill words and exaggeration. 구업공양 口業供養 The offering of the praise or worship of the lips ; also 신업공양 身業供養 and 의업공양 意業供養. 구소 口疏 ; 오소 奧疏 Esoteric commentary or explanation of two kinds, one general, the other only imparted to the initiated. 구칭 口稱 Invocation. 구칭삼매 口稱三昧 The samādhi in which with a quiet heart the individual repeats the name of Buddha, or the samādhi attained by such repetition. 구결 口訣 Orally transmitted decisions or instructions. 구륜 口輪 ; 정교륜 正教輪 One of the 삼륜 三輪. The wheel of the mouth, or the wheel of the true teaching ; Buddha's teaching rolling on everywhere, like a chariot-wheel, destroying misery. 구두선 口頭禪 Mouth meditation, i.e. dependence on the leading of others, inability to enter into personal meditation.

구 九 Navan ; nava. Nine.

구 舊 Old, ancient. 구주 舊住 Formerly lived there, dwelt of old. 구경 舊經 Old writings, or versions. 구언 舊言 The vernacular language of Magadha, the country of South Behar, called Māgadhī Prākrit, cf. 파리 巴利 Pāli, which is the language of the Ceylon canon. The Ceylon Buddhists speak of it as Māgadhī, but that was quite a different dialect from Pāli. 구역 舊譯 The older translations, i.e. before the T'ang dynasty ; those of Hsüan-tsang and afterwards are called the new.

구 窶 Rustic, poor ; translit. *ku, gu* ; v. 구 求, 구 瞿, 굴 屈.

구 拘 Seize, take, arrest ; translit. *k* sounds, cf. 거 巨, 구 矩, 구 俱, 교 憍.

구 瞿 The wary look of a bird, anxious ; translit. *ga, kau, gau, ko, go, gho, ku, gu* ; cf. 구 鳩, 구 俱, 구 仇, 구 拘, etc.

구 驅 To drive out or away, expel, urge. 구오 驅烏 Scarecrow, term for an acolyte of from seven to thirteen years of age, he being old enough to drive away crows. 구룡 驅龍 Dragon-expeller, a term for an arhat of high character and powers, who can drive away evil nāgas.

구 究 To go to the bottom of ; inquire into ; end, fundamental, supreme, v. 구 鳩 for 구반다 究槃茶 Kumbhāṇḍa and 구마라 究磨羅 Kumāra ; v. 구시나 拘尸那 for 구시 究施 Kuśinagara. 구구타 究究吒 Kukkuṭa, a cock, or fowl. 구경 究竟 Examine exhaustively ; utmost, final, at the end, a tr. of *uttara*, upper, superior, hence 지극 至極 ultimate, supreme. 구경불 究竟佛 The fundamental, ultimate, or supreme Buddha, who has complete comprehension of truth ; Buddha in his supreme reality. 구경위 究竟位 The supreme class or stage, i.e. that of Buddhahood. The Mahāyāna groups the various stages in the attainment of Buddhahood into five, of which this is the highest. 구경즉 究竟卽 The stage of complete comprehension of truth, being the sixth stage of the T'ien-t'ai School, v. 육즉 六卽. 구경락 究竟樂 The supreme joy, i.e. nirvāṇa. 구경법신 究竟法身 The supreme Dharmakāya, the highest conception of Buddha as the absolute. 구경각 究竟覺 Supreme enlightenment, that of Buddha ; one of the four kinds of enlightenment in the 기신론 起信論 Awakening of Faith.

구 救 To save, rescue, prevent from ill. 구세 救世 To save the world ; a saviour of the world, i.e. 구세자 救世者 or 구세존 救世尊 ; 구세보살 救世菩薩 Buddhas and bodhisattvas as world-saviours, especially 구세관세음 救世觀世音 Kuan-yin, also called 구세원만 救世圓滿 complete saviour of the world. 구세륜 救世輪 The wheel of salvation. 구세천제 救世闡提 The world-saving Icchanti, q.v., the Bodhisattva who defers entry into Buddhahood to fulfill his vow of saving all beings. 구발 救拔 To save and drag out of suffering, e.g. hell. 구탈 救脫 To save and set free ; to be saved and freed. 구고 救苦 To save from suffering, to save the suffering. 구호 救護 To save and protect.

구 求 To seek, beseech, pray. 구부득고 求不得苦 The pain which results from not receiving what one seeks, from disappointed hope, or unrewarded effort. One of the eight sorrows. 구명보살 求名菩薩 The Ch'iu-ming (fame-seeking) bodhisattva, v. Lotus sūtra, a name of Maitreya in a previous life. Also, Yaśaskāma, "A disciple of Varaprabha noted for his boundless ambition and utter want of memory." [Eitel]. 구적 求寂 Seeking nirvāṇa, i.e. the disciple who accepts the ten commandments. 구나 求那 Guṇa, a quality, characteristic, or virtue, e.g. sound, taste, etc. 구나비지 求那毘地 Guṇavṛddhi, 덕진 德進, an Indian monk who came to China 492-5, tr. three works, d. 502. 구나발마 求那跋摩 Guṇavarman, tr. 공덕개 功德鎧, a prince of Kubhā (Cashmere), who refused the throne, wandered alone, reached China, tr. ten works, two of which were lost by A.D. 730. Born in 367, he died in Nanking in A.D. 431. He taught that truth is within, not without, and that the truth (dharma) is of oneself, nor of another. The centre of his work is placed in 양주 揚州 Yang-chou. It is said that he started the order of nuns in China, v. 번역명의 翻譯名義 Fan-i-ming-i. 구나발타라 求那跋陀羅 Guṇabhadra, tr. 덕현 德賢. (1) A follower of the Mahīśāsaka in Kapiśā. (2) A Brāhmaṇa of Central India, tr. into Chinese some seventy-eight works A.D. 435-443 ; b. 394, d. 468.

구 漚 See **우** 漚.

구 嘔 To vomit, spit, disgorge. 구후후 嘔侯侯 Ahaha, or Hahava, the fifth of the cold hells, where the condemned neither stir nor speak, but the cold air passing through their throats produces this sound – a hell unknown to Southern Buddhism.

구 劬 Toil ; translit. *k*, *gh*. 구빈(타) 劬嬪(陀) Kapphiṇa, v. 겁 劫. 구사라 劬師羅 Ghoṣira, v. 구 具. 구비야 劬毗耶 ; 구파 瞿波 Gopā, i.e. Yaśodharā, wife of Śākyamuni, v. 야 耶.

구 龜 Tortoise, turtle. The rareness of meeting a Buddha is compared with the difficulty of a blind sea-turtle finding a log to float on, or a one-eyed tortoise finding a log with a spy-hole through it. 구모 龜毛 The hair on a tortoise, i.e. the non-existent. 구자 龜玆 Kucha, also 고차 庫車 ; 굴지 屈支 ; 굴자 屈茨 ; 구자 丘玆 ; 구지 俱支 An ancient kingdom and city in Eastern Turkestan, 41° 45' N., 83° E. It is recorded as the native place of Kumārajīva. 구장육 龜藏六 The parable of the tortoise and the jackal, the tortoise hiding its six vulnerable parts, symbolizing the six senses, the jackal wailing and starving to death.

구가니 瞿伽尼 Godāna ; Godāniya ; Godhanya, also 구타니 瞿陀尼 ; 구야니 瞿耶尼 ; 구가니 劬伽尼 ; v. 우 牛 The continent west of Sumeru ; also Aparagodāna. 구가리 瞿伽離 Gokālī ; Kokāli ; Kokāliya ; Kokālika 구가리 瞿迦離 ; 구가리 仇伽離 ; 구가리 俱伽離 ; 구가리 俱迦利, etc. The 지도론 智度論 1 says a follower of Devadatta who was sent to hell for accusing Śāriputra and Maudgalyāyana of fornication. Eitel says "the parent of Devadatta."

구갈라 拘羯羅 Cakra, v. 작 斫.

구거 九居 v. 구유정거 九有情居.

구겁 九劫 The nine kalpas ; though Śākyamuni and Maitreya started together, the zeal of the first enabled him to become Buddha nine kalpas sooner ; see 대보적경 大寶積經 111.

구결 九結 The nine bonds that bind men to mortality : — love, hate, pride, ignorance, (wrong) views, possessions (or grasping), doubt, envy, meanness (or selfishness). They are the 육수면 六隨眠 plus grasping, envy, and meanness.

구경 九經 idem 구부경 九部經.

구계(정집) 九界(情執) The nine realms of error, or subjection to the passions, i.e. all the realms of the living except the tenth and highest, the Buddha-realm.

구공 九孔 Also 구입 九入, 구규 九竅, 구루 九漏, 구류 九流, 구창 九瘡 the nine orifices, cavities, entrances, leakages, or suppurations, i.e. the two eyes, two ears, two nostrils, mouth, and two lower organs.

구공 俱空 Both or all empty, or unreal, i.e. both ego and things have no reality.

구구라 俱俱羅 Kukkuṭa is a cock, or fowl ; this is intp. as the clucking of fowls ; cf. 구 究 and 구 拘. The 구구라부 俱俱羅部 Kaukkuṭikāḥ is described as one of the eighteen schools of Hīnayāna ; cf. 구 拘 ; 구 鳩 ; 굴 窟 ; 거 居.

구구인 九句因 A term in Buddhist logic ; the nine possible combinations of like and unlike examples in a syllogism.

구귀 九鬼 The nine classes of ghosts are of three kinds : without means, small means, rich. The first group have 거구 炬口 burning torch-like mouths, or 침구 鍼口 narrow needle mouths, or 취구 臭口 stinking mouths ; the second group have hair like needles, or stinking hair, or tumours ; the rich ghosts haunt sacrifices to the dead, or eat human leavings, or live truculently.

구규 九竅 v. 구공 九孔.

구기(나라) 拘耆(那羅) Kokila, also 구시라 拘翅羅, the cuckoo. [M. W.]

구나(함)모니 拘那(含)牟尼 Kanakamuni, 구나함 拘那含 ; 가낙가모니 迦諾迦牟尼 q.v., lit. 금적 金寂

the golden recluse, or 금선 金仙 golden ṛṣi ; a Brahman of the Kāśyapa family, native of Śobhanavatī, second of the five Buddhas of the present Bhadra-kalpa, fifth of the seven ancient Buddhas ; possibly a sage who preceded Śākyamuni in India.

구나라 拘那羅 Kuṇāla ; also 구나라 拘拏羅 ; 구랑나 拘浪拏 ; 구나라 鳩那羅 a bird with beautiful eyes ; name of Dharmavivardhana (son of Aśoka), whose son Sampadi "became the successor of Aśoka." [Eitel]. Kuṇāla is also tr. as an evil man, possibly of the evil eye. 구나라타 拘那羅陀 or 拘那羅他 ; 구란난타 拘蘭難陀 Guṇarata, name of Paramārtha, who was known as 진제삼장 眞諦三藏, also as Kulanātha, came to China A.D. 546 from Ujjain in Western India, tr. many books, especially the treatises of Vasubandhu.

구나말지 瞿那末底 Guṇamati, a native of Parvata, who lived at Valabhī, a noted antagonist of Brahmanism ; his 수상론 隨相論 was tr. by Paramārtha A.D. 557-569.

구나발라바 瞿拏鉢刺婆 Guṇaprabha, of Parvata, who deserted the Mahāyāna for the Hīnayāna ; author of many treatises. A fanciful account is given of his seeking Maitreya in his heavenly palace to solve his doubts, but Maitreya declined because of the inquirer's self-sufficiency.

구난 九難 v. 구뇌 九惱.

구뇌 九惱 ; also 구난 九難, 구횡 九橫, 구죄보 九罪報 The nine distresses borne by the Buddha while in the flesh, i.e. the two women Sundarā and Caṁścā ; others from Devadatta, Ajātaśatru, etc. ; v. 지도론 智度論 9.

구다니 瞿陀尼 v. 구가니 瞿伽尼.

구담 瞿曇 Gautama, the surname of Buddha's family ; hence a name of Śākyamuni. Also 구담 俱譚 ; 구담 具譚 later 교답마 喬答摩 q.v. 구담선 瞿曇仙 An ancient ṛṣi, said to be one of the founders of the clan. 구담승가제바 瞿曇僧伽提婆 Gautama-saṅghadeva, a native of Kabul, tr. of some seven works, A.D. 383-398. 구담미 瞿曇彌 Gautamī, the feminine of Gautama, especially applied to the aunt and nurse of Śākyamuni, who is also known as Mahāprajāpatī, v. 마 摩. 구담(반야)류지 瞿曇(般若)留支 ; 구담(반야)류지 瞿曇(般若)流支 Gautama-prajñāruci, from Benares, tr. some eighteen works, A.D. 538-543. 구담달마사나 瞿曇達磨闍那 ; 구담법지 瞿曇法智 Gautama-dharmajñāna, son of the last ; tr. 582 a work on karma.

구도 九道 idem 구유정거 九有情居.

구라 俱攞 Kūla, a slope, a shore ; a mound ; a small dagoba in which the ashes of a layman are kept. Kula, a herd, family, household. 구라발지 俱攞鉢底 Kulapati, the head of a family, a householder.

구란타 俱蘭吒 Kuraṇṭa ; yellow amaranth ; intp. as a red flower, among men with 10 leaves, among devas 100, among Buddhas 1,000 ; also as a material thing, i.e. something with resistance. Cf. 구 拘.

구련 九蓮 The paradise of Amitābha, i.e. 구품연대 九品蓮臺.

구로(사) 拘盧(舍) Krośa ; also 구루사 拘樓賒 ; 구루 拘屢 ; 구로사 俱盧舍 ; the distance a bull's bellow can be heard, the eighth part of a yojana, or 5 li ; another less probable definition is 2 li. For 구로 拘盧 Uttarakuru, see 구 俱.

구로사 俱盧舍 Krośa, the distance the lowing of an ox or the sound of a drum can be heard, *circa* 5 li. Cf. 구 拘.

구로절나 瞿盧折那 Gorocanā, 구로자나 瞿嚧者那, a bright yellow pigment prepared from the urine or bile of a cow. 구로륭방 瞿盧隆謗 said to be Grosapam, or Karsana, or Bhagārāma, the ārāma (garden of grove) of the god Bhaga, i.e. the capital of Kapiśā, cf. 가 迦.

구로주 俱盧洲 Kurudvīpa ; Uttarakuru. The northern of the four continents of a world ; cf. 대주 大洲 and 울 鬱.

구류 九流 ; 구루 九漏 idem 구공 九孔.

구류사 拘流沙 Kuru, the country where Buddha is said to have delivered the sūtra 장아함대연방편경 長阿含大緣方便經.

구류생 九類生 The nine kinds of birth ; the four from the womb, egg, moisture, transformation are common to devas, earth, and the hells ; the five others are birth into the heavens of form, of non-form, of thought, of non-thought, and of neither (i.e. beyond either).

구류손 俱留孫 Krakucchanda, fourth of the seven ancient Buddhas, first of the Buddhas of the present age. Cf. 구 拘.

구류손불 拘留孫佛 Krakucchanda ; also 구류진불 拘留秦佛 ; 구루진 拘樓秦 ; 구류손 俱留孫 ; 구루손 鳩樓孫 ; 가라구찬타 迦羅鳩餐陀 or 가라구촌타 迦羅鳩村馱 ; 갈락가손타 羯洛迦孫馱 ; 갈라가촌지 羯羅迦寸地 ; 갈구촌나 羯句忖那, etc. The first of the Buddhas of the present Bhadra-kalpa, the fourth of the seven ancient Buddhas.

구륜 九輪 The nine wheels or circles on the top of a pagoda, also called 공륜 空輪 the wheels in space ; the nine should only be on the stūpa of a Buddha, others are entitled to as many as eight and as few as one.

구리 拘利 ; 구지 拘胝 Koṭī. A million. Also explained by 억 億 100,000 or 100 lakṣa, i.e. ten millions. Also 구리 俱利 or 구지 俱胝.

구리가 拘理迦 Kulika. "A city 9 li south-west of Nālandā in Magadha." [Eitel].

구리가라 俱利伽羅 A kind of black dragon ; also 구력가(라) 俱力迦(羅) ; 구리가 俱哩迦 or 구리검 俱哩劍 ; 고력가 古力迦 ; 가리가 加梨加 : 가라가 迦羅迦 ; 율가 律迦, etc. It is one of the symbols of 부동명왕 不動明王, connected with his sword.

구리태자 俱利太子 Kolita, the eldest son of Droṇodana, uncle of Śākyamuni ; said to be Mahānāma, but others say Mahāmaudgalyāyana. Also 구률 拘栗 ; 구이다 拘肄多.

구린 拘隣 Kauṇḍinya ; also 구륜 拘輪 or 俱輪 ; 구린 俱隣 ; 거린 居隣 or 거륜 居倫. v. 교 憍.

구마(이) 瞿摩(夷) Gomaya, cow-dung. 구마제 瞿摩帝 Gomatī ; abounding in herds of cattle. The river Gumti which "flows into the Ganges below Benares." [Eitel]. A monastery A.D. 400 in Khotan.

구마라 拘摩羅 Kumāra ; also 구마라 矩摩羅 or 鳩摩羅 ; a child, youth, prince, tr. by 동자 童子 a youth. 구마라천 拘摩羅天 ; 구마라가천 鳩摩羅伽天 Kumārakadeva, Indra of the first dhyāna heaven whose face is like that of a youth, sitting on a peacock, holding a cock, a bell, and a flag. 구마라존 拘摩羅尊 Kumārata, v. 구 鳩.

구마라 俱摩羅 Kumāra, a boy, youth ; cf. 구 拘. 구마라천 俱摩羅天 A youthful deva.

구만 九慢 The nine forms of pride — that I surpass, am equal to, not so bad as others ; that others surpass, are as bad as, are inferior to me ; that none surpass, are equal to, or worse than me.

구모다라 瞿摸怛羅 Gomūtra, cow's urine.

구무학 九無學 The nine grades (of arhats) who are no longer learning, having attained their goal. 구무위 九無爲 The nine kinds of, and meditations on, 무위 無爲 q.v. There are two somewhat different groups ; one has 택멸 擇滅, 비택멸 非擇滅, 허공 虛空, 공무변처 空無邊處, 식무변처 識無邊處, 무소유처 無所有處, 비상비비상처 非想非非想處 (v. 구유정처 九有情處), 연기지성 緣起支性, and 성도지성 聖道支性. 구무간도 九無間道 In every universe there are nine realms, in every realm there are nine illusions in practice 수 修, and nine ways of relief ; hence the nine ways of overcoming hindrances ; also there are nine uninterrupted ways of advance from one stage to another of the nine stages of the 삼계 三界 trailokya, by the wisdom of overcoming delusion in each stage ; also 구무애 九無礙 ; and cf. 구해탈도 九解脫道.

구문 九門 v. 구유정거 九有情居.

구물두 拘物頭 Kumuda ; also 구물타 拘物陀 ; 구물도 拘物度 ; 구물두 拘勿頭 or 구물투 拘勿投 ; 구모두 拘牟頭 or 拘某頭 or 구무두 拘貿頭 or 구나두 拘那頭 ; 구모타 拘母陀 ; 구문라 句文羅 ; 구물두 俱勿頭 ; 굴마라 屈摩羅 ; 구모타 究牟陀 a lotus ; an opening lotus ; but kumuda refers especially to the esculent white lotus. [M. W.]

구미타 拘謎陀 Kumidha, "An ancient kingdom on the Beloortagh to the north of Badakshan. The *vallis Comedorum* of Ptolemy." [Eitel].

구박일탈 九縛一脫 The nine states of bondage and the one state of liberation. The nine states are the hells of fire, of blood, of swords ; asuras, men, devas, māras, nirgranthas, form and formless states ; these are all saṁsāra states, i.e. of reincarnation. The one state of freedom, or for obtaining freedom, is nirvāṇa.

구방편 九方便 The nine suitable stages in religious service ; cf. 대일경 大日經 7 ; 작례 作禮 salutation to the universal Triratna ; 출죄 出罪 repentance and confession ; 귀의 歸依 trust (in the Triratna) ; 시신 施身 giving of self (to the Tathāgata) ; 발보리심 發菩提心 vowing to devote the mind to bodhi ; 수희 隋喜 rejoicing (in all good) ; 권청 勸請 beseeching (all Tathāgatas to rain down the saving law) ; 봉청법신 奉請法身 praying for the Buddha-nature in self and others for entry in the Pure Land ; 회향 迴向 demitting the good produced by the above eight methods, to others, universally, past, present, and future. This form of service is generally performed before engaging in esoteric observances. The verses in which these nine stages are presented are of a commendably devotional character. 구방편십바라밀보살 九方便十波羅蜜菩薩 Of the ten pāramitā bodhisattvas, q.v., in the tenth or empyrean court of the Garbhadhātu, the first nine are associated with the above nine progressive steps, the tenth is associated with the last four of the nine.

구범 九梵 The nine heavens of the fourth dhyāna heaven.

구변지 九徧知 The nine forms of complete knowledge of the four axioms and the cutting off of passion, delusion, etc., in the processes of 견 見 and 수 修, as distinct from 무학 無學.

구부(경) 九部(經) Nine of the Hīnayāna twelve classes of sūtras, that is, all except the 방광 方廣, 수기 授記 and 무문자설 無問自說. Generally the term is thus interpreted, but there is also a Mahāyāna division of nine of the twelve sūtras, i.e. all except the 연기 緣起, 비유 譬喩, and 논의 論議. These are : sūtras, the Buddha's sermons ; geyas, metrical pieces ; vyākaraṇas, prophecies ; gāthās, chants or poems ; udānas, impromptu or unsolicited addresses ; ityuktas, or itivṛttakas, narratives ; jātakas, stories of former lives of Buddha, etc. ; vaipulyas, expanded sūtras, etc. ; adbhuta-dharmas, miracles, etc. ; v. 십이부경 十二部經.

구불(극)성 俱不(極)成 All incomplete ; a fallacy in the comparison, or example, which leaves the syllogism incomplete.

구불견 俱不遣 A fallacy in a syllogism caused by introducing an irrelevant example, one of the thirty-three fallacies.

구비다라 俱毘陀羅 Kovidāra, 구비다라 拘鞞陀羅 *Bauhinia variegata* ; also one of the trees of paradise. [M. W.] Said to be the tree of the great playground (where the child Śākyamuni played).

구비라 俱毘羅 (1) Kumbhīra, crocodile ; also 구비라 鳩鞞羅 ; 구미라 俱尾羅 (2) Kuvera, Kubera, the guardian king of the north, v. 비사문 毘沙門 Vaiśravaṇa, the god of wealth.

구비류바차 俱毘留波叉 Defined variously, but indicative of Virūpākṣa, the three-eyed Śiva ; the guardian ruler of the West, v. 비 毘.

구비타라 拘鞞陀羅 Kovidāra, *Bauhinia variegata*, fragrant trees in the great pleasure ground (of the child Śākyamuni).

구사 拘沙 A branch of the Yüeh-chih people, v. 월 月.

구사 瞿沙 Ghoṣa, murmur ; sound of voices, etc., noise, roar ; tr. sound of speaking, and 묘음 妙音 ; 미음 美音 beautiful voice or speech ; name of a famous dialectician and preacher who is accredited with restoration of sight to Dharmavivardhana, i.e. Kuṇāla, son of Aśoka, "by washing his eyes with the tears of people who were moved by his eloquence." [Eitel]. Also author of the Abhidharmāmṛta śāstra, which is called 구사경 瞿沙經.

구사 俱舍 Kośa, 구사 句捨 cask, box, treasury ; translated 장 藏 store, also 초 鞘 sheath, scabbard ; especially the 구사론 俱舍論 Abhidharma-kośa-śāstra, v. 아 阿, composed by Vasubandhu, tr. by Paramārtha and Hsüan-tsang. 구사종 俱舍宗 The Abhidharma of Piṭaka School.

구사라 瞿師羅 Ghoṣira ; 구사라 瞿私羅 ; 구사라 具史羅 ; 구사라 劬史羅 name of the donor of the park of this name to Śākyamuni, "identified by Beal as Gopsahasa, a village near Kosam." [Eitel].

구사생지 九士生地 idem Kuśinagara ; v. 구 拘.

구산팔해 九山八海 The nine cakravāla, or concentric mountain ranges or continents, separated by eight seas, of a universe. The central mountain of the nine is Sumeru 수미 須彌 and around it are the ranges Khadiraka 길제라 佉提羅, Īṣādhara 이사다라 伊沙陀羅, Yugaṁdhara 유건다라 遊乾陀羅, Sudarśana 소달리사나 蘇達梨舍那, Aśvakarṇa 안습박갈나 安濕縛竭拏, Nemiṁdhara 니민다라 尼民陀羅, Vinataka 비나다가 毘那多迦, Cakravāḍa 작가라 斫迦羅 ; v. 칠금산 七金山. The Abhidharma-kośa gives a different order : — Sumeru, Yugaṁdhara, Īṣādhara, Khadiraka, Sudarśana, Aśvakarṇa, Vinataka, Nemiṁdhara, with an "iron-wheel" mountain encompassing all ; there are also differences in the detail.

구살달나 瞿薩怛那 Kustana, i.e. Khotan, v. 우 于.

구상(관) 九想(觀) or 구상 九相 Navasaṁjñā Meditation on a corpse in order to curb desire ; one of the meditations on the unclean : — *vyādhmātakasaṁjñā*, its tumefaction ; *vinīlakasaṁjñā*, its blue, mottled colour ; *vipaḍumakasaṁjñā*, its decay ; *vilohitakasaṁjñā*, its mess of blood, etc. ; *vipūyakasaṁjñā*, its discharges and rotten flesh ; *vikhāditakasaṁjñā*, its being devoured by birds and beasts ; *vikṣiptakasaṁjñā*, its dismembering ; *asthisaṁjñā*, its bones ; *vidagdhakasaṁjñā*, their being burnt and returning to dust.

구상연혹 九上緣惑 The nine kinds of error or illusion in 견 見, i.e. views or mental processes, found also in higher conditions of development.

구생 俱生 Natural, spontaneous, inborn as opposed to acquired. 구생혹 俱生惑 Natural doubt, inborn illusion, in contrast to doubt or illusion acquired, e.g. by being taught. 구생(법) 俱生(法) Spontaneous ideas or things. 구생신 俱生神 The spirit, born at the same time as the individual, which records his deeds and reports to one's good and evil. Another says it is the Ālayavijñāna. 구생기 俱生起 Arising and born with one ; spontaneous.

구선 九禪 v. 구종대선 九種大禪.

구섬미 俱睒彌 Kauśāmbī ; 구상미 俱賞彌 or 구사미 俱舍彌 Vatsapattana, an ancient city of central India, identified with the village of Kosam on the Jumna, 30 miles above Allahabad. These are old forms, as are 구심 拘深 ; 구익 拘翼 ; 구염유 拘鹽惟, and forms with 거 巨 and 구 鳩 ; the newer forms being 교상미 憍賞彌 or 교섬미 憍閃彌.

구섬미 拘睒彌 Kauśāmbī, or Vatsapattana 구섬 拘暹 ; 교상미 憍賞彌 ; a country in Central India ; also called 구라구 拘羅瞿 v. 거 巨.

구세 九世 In past, present, and future worlds, each has its own past, present, and future, hence nine worlds or ages. 구세간 九世間 The nine lower of the ten worlds, the highest or tenth being the Buddha-world ; the nine are always subject to illusion, confused by the senses.

구소마 俱蘇摩 Kusuma, a flower, flowers ; v. 구 拘. 구소마발저 俱蘇摩跋低 Kusumavatī ; name of a Buddha-realm. 구소마마라 俱蘇摩摩羅 Kusumamālā, a wreath, garland. 구소락(가) 俱蘇洛(迦) Kuśūla ; a "bin" skirt, worn by nuns ; also 궐소락가 厥蘇洛迦 ; 기수라 祇修羅 or 구수라 瞿修羅 or 궐수라 厥修羅.

구소마 拘蘇摩 Kusuma, "the white China aster." [Eitel]. 구소마보라 拘蘇摩補羅 Kusumapura, city of flower-palaces ; two are named, Pāṭaliputra, ancient capital of Magadha, the modern Patna ; and Kanyākubja, Kanauj (classical Canogyza), a noted city in northern Hindustan (Persian name of India) ; v. 갈 羯.

구손바 俱孫婆 Kusumbha ; safflower, saffron.

구수라 瞿脩羅 Kuśūla is a place for grain, but is intp. as a nun's skirt, cf. 구 俱.

구슬치라 拘瑟耻羅 Kauṣṭhila, also 구슬지라 俱瑟祉羅 ; an arhat, maternal uncle of Śāriputra, who became an eminent disciple of Śākyamuni.

구시나 拘尸那 Kuśinagara ; 구시나갈 拘尸那竭 or 구시나게라 拘尸那揭羅 ; 구이나갈 拘夷那竭 or 俱夷那竭 ; 구시나 俱尸那 ; 구시 究施 a city identified by Professor Vogel with Kasiah, 180 miles north-west of Patna, "capital city of the Mallas" [M. W.] ; the place where Śākyamuni died ; "so called after the sacred Kuśa-grass." [Eitel]. Not the same as Kuśāgrapura, v. 구 矩.

구식 九識 The nine kinds of cognition or consciousness (vijñāna) ; those of sight, hearing, smell, taste, touch, mind, manas (or 아다나식 阿陁那識 ādāna), i.e. mental perception ; 아뢰야식 阿賴耶識 ālaya, bodhi-consciousness, and 아마라식 阿摩羅識 amala, purified or Buddha-consciousness. There is considerable difference as to the meaning of the last three.

구실릉가 瞿室餕伽 Gośṛṅga, cow's horn, a mountain near Khotan.

구심륜 九心輪 The nine evolutions, or movements of the mind in perception.

구십육술 九十六術 Also 구십육종외도 九十六種外道. Ninety-six classes of non-Buddhists or heretics and their practices, i.e. their six founders and each of them with fifteen schools of disciples ; some say 구십오종외도 九十五種外道.

구십팔사 九十八使 Also 구십팔수면 九十八隨眠 The Hīnayāna ninety-eight tempters, or temptations, that follow men with all subtlety to induce laxity. They are the ninety-eight kleśas, or moral temptations in the realm of 견사 見思 view and thought, or external and internal ideas.

구야라 俱夜羅 Things that go with the almsbowl, e.g. spoon, chopsticks, etc.

구업 九業 The nine kinds of karma, i.e. the desire realm and the form realm each has conduct that causes karma, does not cause karma, or is neutral, making 6 ; in the formless realm there are non-causative deeds, neutrality, and immortality, making 9 ; 성실론 成實論 8.

구역 九域 idem 구지 九地 and 구계 九界.

구연과 俱緣果 Bījapūra, or Bījapūraka ; described as a citron. [M. W.] A fruit held in one of the hands of Kunti Kuan-yin.

구요 九曜 ; 구집 九執 q.v. Navagraha. The nine luminaries : 일 日 Āditya, the sun ; 월 月 Soma, the moon ; the five planets, i.e. 화성 火星 Aṅgāraka, Mars ; 수 水 Budha, Mercury ; 목 木 Bṛhaspati, Jupiter ; 금 金 Śukra, Venus ; and 토 土 Śanaiścara, Saturn ; also 라후 羅睺 Rāhu, the spirit that causes eclipses ; and 계도 計都 Ketu, a comet. Each is associated with a region of the sky and also with a bodhisattva, etc., e.g. the sun with Kuan-yin, Venus with Amitābha, etc.

구유 俱有 Existing together ; all being, existing, or having. 구유의 俱有依 ; 구유근 俱有根 Things or conditions on which one relies, or from which things spring, e.g. knowledge. 구유인 俱有因 Sahabhūhetu, mutual causation, the simultaneous causal interaction of a number of things, e.g. earth, water, fire, and air. 구유법 俱有法 Coexistent, co-operative things or conditions.

구유 九有 The nine realities, states, or conditions in which sentient beings enjoy to dwell, v. next. 구유정거 九有情居 ; 구유정처 九有情處, 구중생거 九衆生居, 구거 九居, 구문 九門, see also 구유 九有, 구지 九地, 선 禪 and 정 定 ; the nine happy abodes or states of sentient beings of the 장아함경 長阿含經 9 ; they are the 칠식주 七識住 seven abodes or stages of perception or consciousness to which are added the fifth and ninth below : — (1) 욕계지인천 欲界之人天 the world and the six deva-heavens of desire in which there is variety of bodies (or personalities) and thinking (or ideas) ; (2) 범중천 梵衆天 the three brahma-heavens where bodies differ but thinking is the same, the first dhyāna heaven ; (3) 극광정천 極光淨天 the three bright and pure heavens where bodies are identical but thinking differs, the second dhyāna heaven ; (4) 변정천 遍淨天 the three universally pure heavens where bodies and thinking are the same, the third dhyāna heaven ; (5) 무상천 無想天 the no-thinking or no-thought heaven, the highest of the four dhyāna heavens ; (6) 공무변처 空無邊處 limitless space, the first of the formless realms ; (7) 식무변처 識無邊處 limitless perception, the second ditto ; (8) 무소유처 無所有處 nothingness, the place beyond things, the third ditto ; and (9) 비상비비상 非想非非想 beyond thought or non-thought, the fourth ditto.

구유 九喩 The nine similes : stars, eye-film, lamp, prestidigitation, dew, bubble, dream, lightning, cloud. There is also another group.

구음 九陰 The five elements together with time, space, mind (*manas*), and soul (*ātman*) according to the teaching of the "heretical" Vaiśeṣika sect ; v. 비 鞞.

구의 九儀 The nine "Indian" ways of showing respect, according to Hsüan-tsang — asking about welfare ; bowing the head ; holding high the hands ; bowing with folded hands ; bending the knee ; kneeling ; hands and knees on the ground ; elbows and knees ditto ; the whole body prostrate.

구이 瞿夷 Gopā ; Gopikā, a name of Yaśodharā, wife of Gautama and mother of Rāhula, cf. 교

憍 Gautamī ; also 구비야 瞿毘耶 ; 구비가 瞿比迦 ; 구파 瞿波 ; 구파 瞿婆.

구인사 救仁寺 Gu-in-sa. A temple located in Baekja-ri Yeongchun-myeon Danyang-gun Chungcheongbuk-do in Korea. The headquarters of Korean Cheontae Order.

구인일과 九因一果 Nine of the 십계 十界 ten dhātu or regions are causative, the tenth is the effect or resultant.

구입 九入 v. 구공 九孔.

구자 九字 The nine magical characters 임병투자개진열재전 臨兵鬪者皆陳列在前 implying that the armed forces are arrayed against the powers of evil. After reciting these words, four vertical and five horizontal lines, forming a grid, are drawn in the air to show that the forces are arrayed. It was used among Taoists and soldiers, and is still used in Japan, especially when going into the mountains. 구자만다라 九字曼荼羅 The nine character maṇḍala, i.e. the lotus, with its eight petals and its centre ; Avalokiteśvara may be placed in the heart and Amitābha on each petal, generally in the shape of the Sanskrit "seed" letter, or alphabetic letter.

구재일 九齋日 The nine kinds of days of abstinence on which no food is eaten after twelve o'clock noon and the commands are observed. They are : every day of the first month, of the fifth month, of the ninth month, and the following six days of each month, 8th, 14th, 15th, 23rd, 29th, and 30th. On these days Indra and the four deva-kings investigate the conduct of men.

구절라 瞿折羅 Gurjara, an ancient tribe and kingdom in Rajputana, which moved south and gave its name to Gujarat. [Eitel].

구제 九諦 The nine truths, or postulates : impermanence ; suffering, voidness (or unreality of things) ; no permanent ego, or soul ; love of existence or possessions, resulting in suffering ; the opposite (or fear of being without them), also resulting in suffering ; the cutting off of suffering and its cause ; nirvāṇa with remainder still to be worked out ; complete nirvāṇa.

구조(상승) 九祖(相承) The succession of nine founders of the T'ien-t'ai School ; v. 천태구종 天台九宗.

구조의 九條衣 ; 구조가사 九條袈裟 The lowest rank of the patch-robe, v. 구품대의 九品大衣.

구존 九尊 The nine honoured ones in the eight-petalled hall of the Garbhadhātu, i.e. Vairocana in the centre of the lotus, with four Buddhas and four bodhisattvas on the petals, the lotus representing the human heart ; v. 오불 五佛.

구종 九宗 The eight sects 팔종 八宗 (q.v.) plus the 선 禪 Ch'an(Zen), or the Pure-land or Jōdō sect.

구종대선 九種大禪 The nine kinds of Mahāyāna dhyāna for bodhisattvas, given in the 보살지지경 菩薩地持經 6 and in other works ; they are associated with the patience 인 忍, pāramitā and with the dhyāna of the super-realms. The nine are meditations — (1) 자성선 自性禪 on the original nature of things, or mind as the real nature, from which all things derive ; (2) 일체선 一切禪 on achieving the development of self and all others to the utmost ; (3) 난선 難禪 on the difficulties of certain dhyāna conditions ; (4) 일체문선 一切門禪 on the entrance to all the (superior) dhyāna conditions ; (5) 선인선 善人禪 on the good ; (6) 일체행선 一切行禪 on all Mahāyāna practices and actions ; (7) 제번뇌선 除煩惱禪 on ridding all sufferers from the miseries of passion and delusion ; (8) 차세타세락선 此世他世樂禪 on the way to bring joy to all people both in this life and hereafter ; (9) 청정정선 清淨淨禪 on perfect purity in the termination of all delusion and distress and the obtaining of perfect enlightenment.

구죄보 九罪報 v. 구뇌 九惱.

구주심 九住心 Nine stages of mental concentration when in dhyāna meditation, viz. 안 安, 섭 攝, 해 解, 전 轉, 복 伏, 식 息, 멸 滅, 성 性, and 지(주심) 持(住心).

구중 九衆 The 칠중 七衆 q.v. plus junior monks and nuns, i.e. novices who have received the eight commandments. 구중생거 九衆生居 v. 구유정거 九有情居.

구지 俱胝 Koṭī, 구치 俱致 ; 구치 拘致 ; a crore, 10 millions ; intp. as 100,000 ; 1,000,000 ; or 10,000,000.

구지 九地 The nine lands, i.e. the 욕계 欲界 realm of desire or sensuous realm ; the four 색계 色界 realms of form or material forms ; and the four 무색계 無色界 formless realms, or realms beyond form ; v. 구유 九有, 구유정거 九有情居, 선 禪 and 정 定. The nine realms are : — (1) 욕계오취지 欲界五趣地, the desire-realm with its five gati, i.e. hells, hungry ghosts, animals, men, and devas. In the four form-realms are : — (2) 이생희락지 離生喜樂地 Paradise after earthly life ; this is also the first dhyāna, or subject of meditation, 초선 初禪. (3) 정생희락지 定生喜樂地 Paradise of cessation of rebirth, 이선 二禪. (4) 이선묘락지 離善妙樂地 Land of wondrous joy after the previous joys, 삼선 三禪. (5) 사념청정지 捨念淸淨地 The Pure Land of abandonment of thought, or recollection (of past delights), 사선 四禪. The four formless, or infinite realms, catur arūpa dhātu, are ; — (6) 공무변처지 空無邊處地 ākāśānantyāyatanam, the land of infinite space ; also the first samādhi, 제일정 第一定. (7) 식무변처지 識無邊處地 vijñānānantyāyatanam, the land of omniscience, or infinite perception, 이정 二定. (8) 무소유처지 無所有處地 ākiñcanyāyatana, the land of nothingness, 삼정 三定. (9) 비상비비상처지 非想非非想處地 naivasaṁjñānā-saṁjñānāyatana, the land (of knowledge) without thinking or not thinking, or where there is neither consciousness nor unconsciousness, i.e. above either ; this is the 사정 四定 Eitel says that in the last four, "Life lasts 20,000 great kalpas in the 1st, 40,000 in the 2nd, 60,000 in the 3rd, and 80,000 great kalpas in the 4th of these heavens." 사정구품사혹 四定九品思惑 v. 팔십일품사혹 八十一品思惑.

구지라 瞿枳羅 The Kokila, or Kalaviṅka bird, cf. 구 鳩.

구집 九執 The nine graha, i.e. "seizers" or up-holders, i.e. luminaries or planets, idem 구요 九曜.

구차제정 九次第定 The samādhi of the nine degrees, i.e. the four dhyānas 사선 四禪, the four realms beyond form 사무색 四無色, and the samādhi beyond sensation and thought 멸수상정 滅受想定 ; see 구유정거 九有情居 and 구지 九地.

구참상당 九參上堂 The nine monthly visits or ascents to the hall for worship, every third day.

구창 九瘡 idem 구공 九孔.

구철 九轍 Kumārajīva's nine divisions of the meaning of the Lotus Sūtra, whence he was styled the 구철법사 九轍法師.

구철 九徹 The nine penetrating flames of the sword of Acala, 부동명왕 不動明王, emblem of the destruction of illusions and hindrances in the nine realms, v. 구지 九地 ; also used for the 구존 九尊 q.v.

구타사마리 拘吒賒摩利 Kūṭaśālmali. Also 거타사마리 居吒奢摩利 or 居吒奢摩離 A fabulous tree on which garuḍas find nāgas to eat ; M. W. describes it as "a fabulous cotton-tree with sharp thorns with which the wicked are tortured in the world of Yama." 구타가 拘吒迦 Kuṭaṅgaka, thatched ; a hut.

구파 瞿波 idem 구이 瞿夷. 구파라 瞿波羅 Gopāla, name of a nāga-king, of a yakṣa, and an arhat.

구폐라 俱吠羅 Kuvera ; Kubera ; the god of riches, Vaiśravaṇa, regent of the north ; having three legs and eight teeth ; in Japan Bishamon (비사문 毘沙門). Also 구걸라 俱乞羅 and numerous other names ; cf. 비 毘.

구품 九品 Nine classes, or grades, i.e. 상상 上上, 상중 上中, 상하 上下 upper superior, middle superior, lower superior, and so on with 중 中 and 하 下. They are applied in many ways, e.g. 상품상생 上品上生, the highest type of incarnate being, to 하품하생 下品下生, the lowest, with corresponding karma ; see 구품정토 九品淨土. Each grade may also be subdivided into nine, thus making a list of eighty-one grades, with similar further subdivision *ad infinitum*. 구품상 九品上 An abbreviation for 상품상생 上品上生, the highest grade in the Pure Land, see 구품정토 九品淨土. 구품대의 九品大衣 The 승가리 僧伽梨 saṅghāṭī. There are nine grades of the monk's patch robe ; the three lowest ranks have 9, 11, and 13 patches, two long patches to one short one ; the three middle 15, 17, 19, three long to one short ; and the three superior 21, 23, 25, four long to one short. 구품안양지화생 九品安養之化生 Those born by transformation from the (heavenly) lotus into the ninefold 안양 安養 Paradise, idem 구품정토 九品淨土. 구품미타 九品彌陀 The nine forms of Amitābha, corresponding to the nine departments of the Pure Land ; chiefly used with reference to the manual signs of his images. 구품왕생 九品往生 The ninefold future life, in the Pure Land, v. 구품정토 九品淨土. It is detailed in the sūtra of this name whose full title is 아미타삼마지집다라니경 阿彌陀三摩地集陀羅尼經. 구품혹 九品惑 Also 구품번뇌 九品煩惱 The four 수혹 修惑, i.e. illusions or trials in the practice of religion, i.e. desire, anger, pride, ignorance ; these are divided each into 구품 九品 q.v. ; hence desire has all the nine grades, and so on with the other three. 구품정토 九品淨土, also 구품정찰 九品淨刹, 구품안양 九品安養, 구품연대 九品蓮臺, 구품왕생 九品往生 The nine grades, or rewards, of the Pure Land, corresponding to the nine grades of development in the previous life, upon which depends, in the next life, one's distance from Amitābha, the consequent aeons that are needed to approach him, and whether one's lotus will open early or late. 구품행업 九品行業 The nine karma to be attained by the conduct or practice through which one may be born into the above Pure Land. 구품각왕 九品覺王 The king or lord of the bodhi of the Pure Land, Amitābha.

구해탈 俱解脫 Complete release, i.e. the freedom of the arhat from moral and meditative hindrances.

구해탈도 九解脫道 In the nine stages of the trailokya 삼계 三界 each has its possible delusions and erroneous performances ; the latter are overcome by the 구무간도 九無間道 q.v.

구화산 九華山 Formerly called 구자산 九子山, which was changed by the T'ang poet Li Po to the above ; it is one of the four sacred mountains of Buddhism, situated in Anhui, and its patron Bodhisattva is Ti-tsang, 지장 地藏

구회(만다라) 九會(曼陀羅) The nine groups in the diamond-realm maṇḍala. 구회(설) 九會(說) The Hua-yen 화엄 華嚴 sūtra in its older sixty chüan version is said to have been delivered at eight assemblies in seven places ; the newer eighty chüan at nine assemblies in seven places ; cf. 구처 九處.

구횡(사) 九橫(死) The nine kinds of irregular death ; there are two groups, one connected with improper food or meals, another with improper medical treatment, law-breaking, drowning, etc. See also 구뇌 九惱. 구횡경 九橫經 A sūtra translated in the later Han dynasty by 안세고 安世高 An Shih-kao.

국 國 A country, a nation ; national. 국승정 國僧正 National superintendent of the clergy, an office which at one time existed. 국토 國土 A country, land, native land, abode of a race, or races. 국토세간 國土世間 The world of countries on which people depend for existence. 국토신 國土身 The Buddha as Buddhakṣetra, or abode of the living ; the world as the body of Vairocana.

국사 國師 Imperial preceptor, a title conferred on certain Buddhist monks, especially on 혜능 慧能 Hui-nêng, q.v. 국왕 國王 A king, prince, i.e. one who has attained to his present high estate consequent on keeping all the ten commandments in a previous incarnation ; and being protected by devas 천 天 he is called 천자 天子 deva son, or Son of Heaven.

국 菊 Chrysanthemum ; aster. 국등 菊燈 A chrysanthemum-shaped lamp used in temples.

국 鞠 To nourish, exhaust, address ; a ball ; translit. *ku, gu.* 국리연나 鞠利衍娜 Kuryana ; Kuvayana ; also 국화연나 鞠和衍娜. "An ancient kingdom south-east of Ferghana, north of the upper Oxus, the present Kurrategeen." [Eitel]. 국다 鞠多 Upagupta, v. 우 優.

군 群 A flock of sheep, herd, multitude, the flock, crowd, all. 군유 群有 All that exists. 군생 群生 All the living, especially all living, conscious beings. 군맹 群萌 All the shoots, sprouts, or immature things, i.e. all the living as ignorant and undeveloped. 군미 群迷 All the deluded ; all delusions. 군류 群類 All classes of living beings, especially the sentient.

군 裙 A skirt. Nivāsana, cf. 니 泥, a kind of garment, especially an under garment.

군 軍 An army ; military ; martial ; translit. *kuṇ,* cf. 군 君. 군지 軍持 Kuṇḍi, Kuan-yin with the vase, also 군지 軍鉾 or 鍕鉾 ; 운지 運攑 ; 군지 君持 ; 군지 君遲 ; also 군치가 君稚迦 or 捃稚迦 for Kuṇḍikā, idem. 군지 軍持 and 군지 君遲 are also used for Kuḍikā, an ascetic's water-bottle. 군다 軍荼 Kuṇḍa, firepot, brazier, or fire-hole used by the esoterics in fire-worship. 군다리 軍荼利 ; 군지 軍遲 Kuṇḍalin, ring-shaped, intp. as a vase, bottle. 군다리명왕 軍荼利明王 Amṛta, v. 아 阿, one of the five ming wang, the ambrosia king, also known as a 야차 夜叉 yakṣa in his fierce form of queller of demons. 군나 軍那 Kunda, a flower, perhaps jasmine, oleander, or *Boswellia thurifera.*

군 君 Prince, noble, ideal man, or woman ; translit. *kun.* 군지 君持 ; 군지 君遲 ; 군지 軍持 ; 군치가 捃稺迦 or 捃稚迦 Kuṇḍa, Kuṇḍikā, a pitcher, waterpot ; washbowl. 군다 君荼 or 軍荼 Kuṇḍa, a hole in ground for the fire at the fire altar ; the homa or fire altar.

군 捃 v. 군 君.

굴 窟 Guhā. A cave. 굴내 窟內 "Within the cave," the assembly of the elder disciples, after Śākyamuni's death, in the cave near Magadha, when, according to tradition, Kāśyapa presided over the compiling of the Tripiṭaka ; while at the same time the 굴외 窟外 disciples "without the cave" compiled another canon known as the 오장 五藏 Pañcapiṭaka. To this separation is ascribed, without evidence, the formation of the two schools of the 상좌부 上座部 Mahāsthavira and 대중부 大衆部 Mahāsāṅghika.

굴 崛 Lofty, distinguished. 굴산 崛山 Vulture peak, abbrev. for 기사굴산 耆闍崛山. 굴다 崛多 Abbrev. for Upagupta, cf. 우 優.

굴 屈 To bend ; oppression, wrong. 굴굴타파타 屈屈吒播陀 or 屈屈吒波陀 Kukkuṭapādagiri ; Cock's foot, a mountain said to be 100 li east of the bodhi tree, and, by [Eitel], 7 miles south-east of Gayā, where Kāśyapa entered into nirvāṇa ; also known as 구로파타산 窶盧播陀山 tr. by 존족 尊足 "honoured foot." The legend is that these three sharply rising peaks, on Kāśyapa entering, closed together over him. Later, when Mañjuśrī ascended, he snapped his fingers, the peaks opened, Kāśyapa gave him his robe and entered nirvāṇa by fire. 굴타아람마 屈吒阿濫摩 Kukkuṭa-ārāma, a monastery built on the above mountain by Aśoka, cf. 서역기 西域記 8. 굴지 屈支 ; 굴자 屈茨 ; 고차 庫車 ; 구자 龜玆 ; 구자 丘玆 Kutche (Kucha). An ancient kingdom and city in Turkestan, north-east of Kashgar. 굴랑나 屈浪那 or 屈浪拏 Kūrān, anciently a kingdom in Tokhāra, "the modern Garana, with mines of lapis lazuli (Lat. 36° 28 N., Long.

71° 2 E.)." [Eitel]. 굴마라 屈摩羅 ; 굴만라 屈滿囉 A lotus bud. 굴헌 屈眴 A cottony material of fine texture. 굴타가아함 屈陀迦阿含 The Pali Khuddakāgama, the fifth of the Āgamas, containing fifteen (or fourteen) works, including such as the Dharmapada, Itivṛttaka, Jātaka, Buddhavaṁsa, etc. 굴상니가 屈想儞迦 Kashanian, a region near Kermina, Lat. 39° 50 N., Long. 65° 25 E. [Eitel]. 굴로다 屈露多 Kulūta. An ancient kingdom in north India famous for its rock temples ; Kulu, north of Kangra.

굴 掘 To dig. 굴륜 掘倫 Kulun, i.e. Pulo Condore, also called 곤륜 崑崙. 굴구라 掘具羅 A kind of western incense.

궁 宮 A palace, mansion ; a eunuch. 궁비라 宮毘羅 Kumbhīra, v. 금비라 金毘羅 a crocodile. 궁태 宮胎 The palace-womb, where those who call on Amitābha but are in doubt of him are confined for 500 years, devoid of the riches of Buddha-truth, till born into the Pure Land ; idem 의성태궁 疑城胎宮.

궁 弓 Dhanus. A bow ; a bow's length, i.e. the 4,000th part of a yojana. Seven grains of wheat 맥 麥 make 1 finger-joint 지절 指節 ; 24 finger-joints make 1 elbow or cubit 주 肘 ; 4 cubits make 1 bow ; or 1 foot 5 inches make 1 elbow or cubit ; 4 cubits make 1 bow ; 300 bows make 1 li ; but the measures are variously given. 궁반다 弓槃荼 Kumbhāṇḍa demons, v. 구 鳩.

궁 窮 Poor, impoverished, exhausted ; to exhaust, investigate thoroughly. 궁자 窮子 The poor son, or prodigal son, of the Lotus sūtra. 궁생사온 窮生死蘊 To exhaust the concomitants of reincarnation, be free from transmigration.

권 眷 Regard, love ; wife ; family ; relatives ; retainers. 권속 眷屬 Retinue, retainers, suite, especially the retinue of a god, Buddha, etc.

권 權 The weight (on a steelyard), weight, authority, power ; to balance, adjudge ; bias, expediency, partial, provisional, temporary, positional ; in Buddhist scriptures it is used like 방편 方便 expediency, or temporary ; it is the adversative of 실 實 q.v. 권화 權化 The power of Buddhas and bodhisattvas to transform themselves into any kind of temporal body. 권대승 權大乘 The temporary, or partial, schools of Mahāyāna, the 통 通 and 별 別, in contrast with the 실대승 實大乘 schools which taught universal Buddhahood, e.g. the Hua-yen and T'ien-t'ai schools. 권실 權實 Temporal and real ; 권 權 referring to the conditional, functional, differential, or temporary, 실 實 to the fundamental, absolute, or real. 권실불이문 權實不二門 The two divisions, the provisional and the perfect, are not two but complementary, v. 권교 權教 and 십불이문 十不二門. 권비 權悲 Pity in regard to beings in time and sense, arising from the Buddhas 권지 權智 *infra*. 권교 權教 Temporary, expedient, or functional teaching, preparatory to the perfect teaching, a distinguishing term of the T'ien-t'ai and Hua-yen sects, i.e. the teachings of the three previous periods 장 藏, 통 通 and 별 別 which were regarded as preparatory to their own, cf. 원교 圓教. 권방편 權方便 Expedients of Buddhas and bodhisattvas for saving all beings. 권지 權智 Buddha-wisdom of the phenomenal, in contrast with 실지 實智 knowledge of the fundamental or absolute. 권현 權現 Temporary, or *ad hoc* manifestations, similar to 권화 權化. 권이 權理 Partial, or incomplete truth. 권자 權者 A Buddha or bodhisattva who has assumed a temporary form in order to aid beings ; also 화자 化者 ; 권화 權化 ; 대권 大權, etc. 권모 權謀 Temporary plans, methods suited to immediate needs, similar to 방편 方便. 권적 權迹 Temporal traces, evidences of the incarnation of a Buddha in human form. 권문 權門 The sects which emphasize 방편 方便, i.e. expediency, or expedients ; the undeveloped school, *supra*.

권 勸 To exhort, persuade, admonish. 권화 勸化 To exhort to conversion, to convert. 권발 勸發 To exhort to start (in the Buddhist way). 권계 勸誡 Exhortation and prohibition ; to exhort and admonish ; exhort to be good and forbid the doing of evil. 권전 勸轉 The second, or exhortation turn of the Buddha's wheel, v. 삼전법륜 三轉法輪, men must know the meaning and cause of suffering, cut off its accumulation, realize that it may be extinguished, and follow the eightfold path to attainment. 권문 勸門 The method of exhortation or persuasion, in contrast with prohibition or command.

궐 厥 A city gate ; a blank, deficiency, wanting, waning ; imperial reserve. 궐문 厥文 A hiatus in a text.

궐 厥 Third personal pronoun ; demonstrative pronoun ; also used instead of 구 俱.

궤 櫃 A counter, cupboard, bureau. 궤두 櫃頭 Bursar, storekeeper.

궤 軌 A rut, rule ; axle. 궤지 軌持 A rule and its observance, intp. as to know the rule or doctrine and hold it without confusion with other rules or doctrines. 궤범 軌範 Rule, mode. 궤범사 軌範師 A teacher of rules, discipline, morals ; an ācārya. 궤의 軌儀 Rule, form.

궤 跪 To kneel. 궤배 跪拜 To kneel and worship, or pay respect. 궤로 跪爐 To kneel and offer incense.

귀 貴 Honourable, dear, precious. 귀천 貴賤 Dear and cheap ; noble and base ; your and my.

귀 皈 idem 귀 歸. 귀의 皈依 To turn to and rely on the Triratna.

귀 鬼 Preta 벽여다 薜荔多, departed, dead ; a disembodied spirit, dead person, ghost ; a demon, evil being ; especially a 아귀 餓鬼 hungry ghost. They are of many kinds. The Fan-i-ming-i classifies them as poor, medium, and rich ; each again thrice subdivided: (1) (a) with mouths like burning torches ; (b) throats no bigger than needles ; (c) vile breath, disgusting to themselves ; (2) (a) needle-haired, self-piercing ; (b) hair sharp and stinking ; (c) having great wens on whose pus they must feed. (3) (a) living on the remains of sacrifices ; (b) on leaving in general ; (c) powerful ones, yakṣas, rākṣasas, piśācas, etc. All belong to the realm of Yama, whence they are sent everywhere, consequently are ubiquitous in every house, lane, market, mound, stream, tree, etc. 귀자모 鬼子母 Hāritī 하리제 訶梨帝 intp. as pleased, or pleasing. A "woman who having vowed to devour all the babies at Rājagṛha was reborn as a Rākṣasī, and gave birth to 500 children, one of which she was to devour every day. Converted by Śākyamuni she entered a convent. Her image is to be seen in all nunneries." [Eitel]. Another account is that she is the mother of 500 demons, and that from being an evil goddess or spirit she was converted to become a protectress of Buddhism. 귀자모신 鬼子母神 A rākṣasī who devours men. 귀성 鬼城 The demon-city, that of the Gandharvas. 귀(법)계 鬼(法)界 The region or realm of demons ; one of the ten regions. 귀화 鬼火 Spirit lights, *ignis fatuus*. 귀병 鬼病 Sickness caused by demons, or ghost. 귀신 鬼神 Ghosts and spirits, a general term which includes the spirits of the dead, together with demons and the eight classes of spirits, such as devas, etc. 귀 鬼 is intp. as 위 威 causing fear, 신 神 as 능 能 potent, powerful. 귀신식시 鬼神食時 The time when they feed, i.e. night. 귀견 鬼見 Demon views, i.e. heterodox teaching. 귀도 鬼道 ; 귀취 鬼趣 The way or destiny of yakṣas, rākṣasas, and hungry ghosts ; 귀도 鬼道 also means in league with demons, or following devilish ways. 귀록 鬼錄 The iron record, containing the sins of men, in Yama's office in Hades. 귀문 鬼門 The north-east corner of a house, or of a city-gate enceinte, through which the spirits can come and go. 귀매 鬼魅 Imps or demons who cause sickness, especially malaria in certain regions.

귀 歸 Return to, give oneself up to ; commit oneself to, surrender ; cf. 삼귀 三歸 Śaraṇa-gamana. 귀앙 歸仰 To turn to in expectancy or adoration, put trust in. 귀의 歸依 To turn to and rely on. 귀의불 歸依佛 ; 귀의법 歸依法 ; 귀의승 歸依僧 To commit oneself to the Triratna, i.e. Buddha,

Dharma, Saṅgha ; Buddha, his Truth and his Church. 귀속 歸俗 To return to lay life. 귀원 歸元 To return to one's origin, enter nirvāṇa, i.e. to die ; also 귀화 歸化 ; 귀적 歸寂 ; 귀본 歸本 ; 귀진 歸眞, etc. 귀입 歸入 To turn to and enter, e.g. a religion, church, society, etc. 귀명 歸命 ; 나무 南無 Namas, namaḥ, namo ; to devote one's life (to the Buddha, etc.) ; to entrust one's life ; to obey Buddha's teaching. 귀성 歸性 To turn from the world of phenomena to that of eternal reality, to devote oneself to the spiritual rather than the material. 귀경 歸敬 To turn to in reverence, put one's trust in and worship.

규 叫 To call, cry. 규환 叫喚 To cry, wail, Raurava, hence the fourth and fifth hot hells. v. 규 叫.

규 窺 To peep, spy ; furtive.

규궁 虯宮 The dragon palace in which Nāgārjuna recited the 화엄경 華嚴經 Hua-yen ching.

규환 叫喚 또는 叫喚 Raurava ; also 호규 號叫 ; 호호 呼呼. The wailing hells, the fourth of the eight hot hells, where the inmates cry aloud on account of pain.

균 均 Equal, in balance, all ; used for Kun in 균제 均提 Kunti, (a) said to be a devoted disciple of Śāriputra ; (b) one of the attendants on Mañjuśrī.

균여 均如 Gyun-yeo(923-973). A monk of the Goryeo dynasty in Korea. He established the foundation for 고려 화엄 高麗華嚴 Korea Hua-yen. He wrote 11 kinds of books, 6 of which are present.

극 隙 a crack, crevice, rift ; translit. *kha*. 극유진 隙遊塵 Motes in a sunbeam ; a minute particle. 극기라 隙棄羅 Khakkhara, a mendicant's staff ; a monk's staff.

극 亟 Haste, urgency. 극박사 亟縛屣 Leather sandals.

극 極 Highest point, apex ; utmost, ultimate, extreme, the limit, finality ; reaching to. 극위 極位 The highest stage of enlightenment, that of Buddha. 극광정천 極光淨天 Pure heaven of utmost light, the highest of the second dhyāna heavens of the form-world ; the first to be re-formed after a universal destruction and in it Brahmā and devas come into existence ; also 극광음천 極光音天 Ābhāsvara. 극희지 極喜地 The stage of utmost joy, the first of the ten stages 십지 十地 of the bodhisattva. 극지 極地 Reaching the ground ; utmost ; fundamental principle ; the highest of all, i.e. Buddha. 극묘 極妙 Of utmost beauty, wonder, or mystery. 극존 極尊 The highest revered one, Buddha. 극미 極微 An atom, especially as a mental concept, in contrast with 색취지미 色聚之微, i.e. a material atom which has a centre and the six directions, as actual but imperceptible atom ; seven atoms make a 미진 微塵 molecule, the smallest perceptible aggregation, called an aṇu 아누 阿耨 or 아나 阿拏 ; the perceptibility is ascribed to the deva-eye rather than to the human eye. There is much disputation as to whether the ultimate atom has real existence or not, whether it is eternal and immutable and so on. 극과 極果 The highest fruit, perfect Buddha-enlightenment. 극락 極樂 Sukhāvatī, highest joy, name of the Pure Land of Amitābha in the West, also called 극락세계 極樂世界 the world of utmost joy. 극열지옥 極熱地獄 Pratāpana ; Mahātāpana ; the hottest hell, the seventh of the eight hells. 극략색 極略色 The smallest perceptible particle into which matter can be divided, an atom. 극성 極聖 The highest saint, Buddha. 극랍 極臘 The oldest monk in orders. 극치 極致 Utmost, ultimate, final point ; reaching to. 극각 極覺 Profound enlightenment, utmost awareness. 극정 極靜 Utmost quiescence, or mental repose ; meditation, trance. 극난승지 極難勝地 The stage in which the bodhisattva has overcome his worst difficulties, the fifth stage.

극 剋 To overcome ; successfully attain to. 극실 剋實 To discover the truth. 극과 剋果 To obtain the fruit of endeavour ; the fruit of effort, i.e. salvation. 극종 剋終 Successful end, certainty of obtaining the fruit of one's action. 극성 剋聖 The certainty of attaining arhatship. 극증 剋證 The assurance of success in attaining enlightenment. 극식 剋識 The certainty of the knowledge (by the spirits, of men's good and evil).

근 斤 An adze ; to chop ; a catty, $1\frac{1}{3}$ lb. ; penetrating, minute. 근두 斤斗 ; 근두 筋斗 ; 건두 巾斗 A somersault.

근 根 Mūla, a root, basis, origin : but when meaning an organ of sense, Indriya, a "power," "faculty of sense, sense, organ of sense." [M. W.] A root, or source ; that which is capable of producing or growing, as the eye is able to produce knowledge, as faith is able to bring forth good works, as human nature is able to produce good or evil karma. v. 오근 五根 and 이십이근 二十二根. 근상하지력 根上下智力 One of a Buddha's ten powers, to know the capacities of all beings, their nature and karma. 근리 根利 Of penetrative powers, intelligent, in contrast with 근둔 根鈍 dull powers. 근력 根力 Organs and their powers, the five organs of sense and their five powers. 근기 根器 Natural capacity, capacity of any organ, or being. 근경 根境 The field of any organ, its field of operation. 근진 根塵 The object or sensation of any organ of sense. 근성 根性 Nature and character ; the nature of the powers of any sense. 근본 根本 Fundamental, basal, radical, original, elemental ; when referring to a fundamental text, 근본경 根本經 mūlagrantha, it indicates to a sūtra supposed to contain the original words of the Buddha. 근본정 根本定 ; 근본선 根本禪 ; 근본등지 根本等至 The stages of dhyāna in the formless or immaterial realm. 근본심 根本心 Root or fundamental mind 근본혹 根本惑 ; 근본번뇌 根本煩惱 The fundamental illusions, passions, or afflictions — desire, hate, delusion (moha), pride, doubt, bad views (or false opinions) ; the first five are the 오둔사 五鈍使 ; the last represents 오리사 五利使 q.v. 근본지 根本智 Fundamental, original, or primal wisdom, source of all truth and virtue ; knowledge of fundamental principles ; intuitive knowledge or wisdom, in contrast with acquired wisdom. 근본무명 根本無明 ; 무시무명 無始無明 or 원시무명 元始無明 Primal ignorance, the condition before discernment and differentiation. 근본설일체유부 根本說一切有部 The Sarvāstivādins, v. 일체유근본식 一切有根本識 Original or fundamental mind or intelligence, a name for the ālayavijñāna. 근패 根敗 Decay of the powers, or senses. 근기 根機 Motive power, fundamental ability, opportunity. 근정 根淨 The purity of the six organs of sense. 근연 根緣 Nature and environment ; natural powers and conditioning environment. 근문 根門 The senses as doors (through which illusion enters). 근궐 根闕 ; 근결 根缺 Defective in any organ of sense, e.g. blind or deaf. 근향 根香 Putchuk, idem 목향 木香.

근 近 Near, near to, approach, intimate, close. 근사 近事 Those who attend on and serve the Triratna, the 근사남 近事男 upāsaka, male servant or disciple, and 근사녀 近事女 upāsikā, female servant or disciple, i.e. laymen or women who undertake to obey the five commandments. 근주 近住 Laymen or women who remain at home and observe the eight commandments, i.e. the 근주율의 近住律儀. 근원 近圓 Nearing perfection, i.e. the ten commands, which are "near to" nirvāṇa. 근동 近童 A devotee, or disciple, idem upāsaka.

근 勤 Vīrya, energy, zeal, fortitude, virility ; intp. also as 정진 精進 one of the pāramitās. 근식 勤息 A tr. of śramaṇa, one who diligently pursues the good, and ceases from evil. 근구 勤求 To seek diligently (after the good). 근고 勤苦 Devoted and suffering, zealously suffering. 근행 勤行 Diligently going forward, zealous conduct, devoted to service, worship, etc.

금 金 Hiraṇya, 이란자 伊爛刺 which means gold, any precious metal, semen, etc. ; or 소벌랄 蘇伐剌 Suvarṇa, which means "of a good or beautiful colour," "golden," "yellow," "gold," "a gold coin," etc. The Chinese means metal, gold, money.

금 今 Now, at present, the present. 금원 今圓 A T'ien-t'ai term indicating the present "perfect" teaching, i.e. that of the Lotus, as compared with the 석원 昔圓 older "perfect" teaching which preceded it. 금가 今家 The present school, i.e. my school or sect.

금 禁 Prohibitions, to forbid, prohibit. 금계 禁戒 Prohibitions, commandments, especially the Vinaya as containing the laws and regulations of Buddhism. 금주장 禁呪藏 The Vidyādharapiṭaka, or Dhāraṇīpiṭaka, the canon of dhāraṇīs, a later addition to the Tripiṭaka.

금(강)침 金(剛)針 The straight vajra, or sceptre ; also v. 금강보살 金剛菩薩.

금강 金剛 Vajra, 벌사라 伐闍羅 ; 발절라 跋折羅 or 발사라 跋闍羅 ; 박왈라 縛曰羅 or 박일라 縛日羅 The thunderbolt of Indra, often called the diamond club ; but recent research considers it a sun symbol. The diamond, synonym of hardness, indestructibility, power, the least frangible of minerals. It is one of the Saptaratna 칠보 七寶. 금강저 金剛杵 The Vajra, or thunderbolt ; it is generally shaped as such, but has various other forms. Any one of the beings represented with the vajra is a 금강 金剛. The vajra is also intp. as a weapon of Indian soldiers. It is employed by the esoteric sects, and others, as a symbol of wisdom and power over illusion and evil spirits. When straight as a sceptre it is 독고 獨股 one limbed, when three-pronged it is 삼고 三股, and so on with five and nine limbs.

금강(위)산 金剛(圍)山 or **금강(륜)산** 金剛(輪)山 The concentric iron mountains about the world ; also Sumeru ; also the name of a fabulous mountain. Cf. 금산 金山.

금강경 金剛經 The "Diamond" Sūtra ; Vajracchedikā-prajñāpāramitā-sūtra 금강능단반야바라밀경 金剛能斷般若波羅蜜經 A condensation of the Prajñāpāramitā ; first tr. by Kumārajīva, later by others under slightly varying titles.

금강계 金剛界 Vajradhātu, 금계 金界 The "diamond," or vajra, element of the universe ; it is the 지 智 wisdom of Vairocana in its indestructibility and activity ; it arises from the Garbhadhātu 태장계 胎藏界 q.v., the womb or store of the Vairocana 리 理 reason or principles of such wisdom, v. 이지 理智. The two, Garbhadhātu and Vajradhātu, are shown by the esoteric school, especially in the Japanese Shingon, in two maṇḍalas, i.e. groups or circles, representing in various portrayals the ideas arising from the two fundamental concepts. Vajradhātu is intp. as the 지 智 realm of intellection, and Garbhadhātu as the 리 理 substance underlying it, or the matrix ; the latter is the womb or fundamental reason of all things, and occupies the eastern position as "cause" of the Vajradhātu, which is on the west as the resultant intellectual or spiritual expression. But both are one as are Reason and Wisdom, and Vairocana (the illuminator, the 대일 大日 great sun) presides over both, as source and supply. The Vajradhātu represents the spiritual world of complete enlightenment, the esoteric Dharmakāya doctrine as contrasted with the exoteric Nirmāṇakāya doctrine. It is the sixth element 식 識 mind, and is symbolized by a triangle with the point downwards and by the full moon, which represents 지 智 wisdom or understanding ; it corresponds to 과 果 fruit, or effect, garbhadhātu being 인 因 or cause. The 금강계오부 金剛界五部 or five divisions of the Vajradhātu are represented by the Five Dhyāni-Buddhas, thus: centre 대일 大日 Vairocana ; east 아축 阿閦 Akṣobhya ; south 보생 寶生 Ratnasaṁbhava ; west 아미타 阿彌陀 Amitābha ; north 불공성취 不空成就 Amoghasiddhi, or Śākyamuni. They are seated respectively on a lion, an elephant, a horse, a peacock, and a garuḍa. v. 오불 五佛 ; also 태 胎.

금강관 金剛觀 The diamond insight or vision which penetrates into reality.

금강구 金剛口 Diamond mouth, that of a Buddha.

금강권 金剛拳 Vajra-fist, the hands doubled together on the breast. 금강권보살 金剛拳菩薩 One of the Bodhisattvas in the Diamond group.

금강동자 金剛童子 Vajrakumāra, 금강사자 金剛使者 a vajra-messenger of the Buddhas or bodhisattvas ; also an incarnation of Amitābha in the form of a youth with fierce looks holding a vajra.

금강력 金剛力 Vajra-power, irresistible strength ; 금강력(사) 金剛力(士) is the 금강신 金剛神 q.v.

금강령 金剛鈴 The diamond or vajra bell for attracting the attention of the objects of worship, and stimulating all who hear it. 금강령보살 金剛鈴菩薩 Vajraghaṇṭā, a Bodhisattva holding a bell in the Vajradhātu maṇḍala.

금강륜 金剛輪 The diamond or vajra wheel, symbolical of the esoteric sects. The lowest of the circles beneath the earth.

금강만다라 金剛曼茶羅 v. 금강계 金剛界.

금강문 金剛門 The diamond door of the Garbhadhātu maṇḍala.

금강밀적 金剛密迹 The deva-guardians of the secrets of Vairocana, his inner or personal group of guardians in contrast with the outer or major group of P'u-hsien, Mañjuśrī, etc. Similarly, Śāriputra, the śrāvakas, etc., are the "inner" guardians of Śākyamuni, the Bodhisattvas being the major group. Idem 금강수 金剛手 ; 금강역사 金剛力士 ; 밀적역사 密迹力士, etc.

금강번 金剛幡 Vajraketu. A flag, hung to a pole with a dragon's head. 금강번보살 金剛幡菩薩 Vajraketu Bodhisattva, the flag-bearer, one of the sixteen in the Vajradhātu group.

금강법계궁 金剛法界宮 The palace or shrine of Vairocana in the Garbhadhātu.

금강보계 金剛寶戒 The Mahāyāna rules according to the 범망 梵網 sūtra. 금강보장 金剛寶藏 The "Diamond" treasury, i.e. nirvāṇa. and the pure bodhi-mind, as the source of the mind of all sentient beings, v. Nirvāṇa sūtra.

금강보살 金剛菩薩 There are many of these Vajra-bodhisattvas, e.g.: 금강인보살 金剛因菩薩 Vajrahetu, 금강수보살 金剛手菩薩 Vajrapāṇi, 금강보보살 金剛寶菩薩 Vajraratna, 금강장보살 金剛藏菩薩 Vajragarbha, 금강침보살 金剛針菩薩 Vajrasūci, 금강장보살 金剛將菩薩 Vajrasena, 금강삭보살 金剛索菩薩 Vajrapāśa, 금강구보살 金剛鉤菩薩 Vajrāṅkuśa, 금강향보살 金剛香菩薩 Vajradhūpa, 금강광보살 金剛光菩薩 Vajratejaḥ, 금강법보살 金剛法菩薩 Vajradharma, 금강리보살 金剛利菩薩 Vajratīkṣṇa, and others.

금강부 金剛部 The various groups in the two maṇḍalas, each having a 주 主 or head ; in the Diamond maṇḍala Akṣobhya, or Vajrasattva, is spoken of as such. 금강부모 金剛部母 ; 망망계 忙莽鷄 Māmakī is "mother" in this group.

금강불 金剛佛 Vajra-buddha. Vairocana, or 대일 大日 the Sun-buddha ; sometimes applied to Śākyamuni as embodiment of the Truth, of Wisdom, and of Purity. 금강불자 金剛佛子 A son of the Vajra-buddha, i.e. of Vairocana, a term applied to those newly baptized into the esoteric sect.

금강불괴(신) 金剛不壞(身) The diamond indestructible (body), the Buddha.

금강삭 金剛索 Vajrapāśa, the diamond lasso, or noose, in the hand of 부동명왕 不動明王 and others. 금강삭보살 金剛索菩薩 Vajrapāśa-bodhisattva in the Vajradhātu maṇḍala, who carries the snare of compassion to bind the souls of the living.

금강살타 金剛薩埵 Vajrasattva(-mahāsattva). 금살 金薩 A form of P'u-hsien (Samantabhadra), reckoned as the second of the eight patriarchs of the 진언종 眞言宗 Shingon sect, also known

ㄱ
ㄴ
ㄷ
ㄹ
ㅁ
ㅂ
ㅅ
ㅇ
ㅈ
ㅊ
ㅋ
ㅌ
ㅍ
ㅎ
찾아보기

as 금강수(비밀왕) 金剛手(秘密王) or 금강수(보살) 金剛手(菩薩) and other similar titles. The term is also applied to all vajra-beings, or vajra-bodhisattvas ; especially those in the moon-circle in the east of the Diamond maṇḍala. Śākyamuni also takes the vajrasattva form. (1) All beings are vajra-sattva, because of their Buddha-nature. (2) So are all beginners in the faith and practice. (3) So are the retinue of Akṣobhya. (4) So is Great P'u-hsien.

금강삼매경론 金剛三昧經論 Exposition of the Adamantine Absorption Sŭtra. Written by 원효 元曉 Won-hyo.

금강쇄 金剛鎖 Vajra-śṛṅkhalā. The vajra chain, or fetter. 금강쇄보살 金剛鎖菩薩 The chain-bearer in the Diamond group.

금강수 金剛水 Diamond or vajra water, drunk by a prince on investiture, or by a person who receives the esoteric baptismal rite ; also 서수 誓水.

금강수 金剛手 Vajrapāṇi, a holder of the vajra, a protector, any image with this symbol ; 금강부 金剛部 Groups of the same in the 금 金 and 태 胎 maṇḍalas. 금강수보살 金剛手菩薩 or 금강수살타 金剛手薩埵 Vajrapāṇi Bodhisattva, especially P'u-hsien 보현 普賢 Samantabhadra.

금강승 金剛乘 Vajrayāna. The diamond vehicle, another name of the 진언 眞言 Shingon.

금강신 金剛身 The diamond body, the indestructible body of Buddha.

금강신 金剛神 The guardian spirits of the Buddhist order ; the large idols at the entrance of Buddhist monasteries ; also 금강수 金剛手 ; 금강역사 金剛力士.

금강심 金剛心 Diamond heart, that of the Bodhisattva, i.e. infrangible, unmoved by "illusion." 금강심전 金剛心殿 The Vajradhātu (maṇḍala), in which Vairocana dwells, also called 불괴금강광명심전 不壞金剛光明心殿 the shrine of the indestructible diamond-brilliant heart.

금강야차 金剛夜叉 or **금강약차** 金剛藥叉 Vajrayakṣa. One of the five 대명왕 大明王, fierce guardian of the north in the region of Amoghasiddhi, or Śākyamuni, also styled the Bodhisattva with the fangs.

금강어언 金剛語言 idem 금강염송 金剛念誦.

금강염 金剛炎 Diamond-blaze, a circle of fire to forbid the entry of evil spirits, also called 금염 金炎 ; 화원(계인) 火院(界印) or 화원(밀봉인) 火院(密縫印).

금강염송 金剛念誦 Silent repetition ; also 금강어언 金剛語言.

금강왕 金剛王 The vajra-king, i.e. the strongest, or finest, e.g. a powerful bull. 금강왕보각 金剛王寶覺 The diamond royal-gem enlightenment, i.e. that of the Buddha. 금강왕보살 金剛王菩薩 One of the sixteen bodhisattvas in the Diamond-realm, one of Akṣobhya's retinue ; also known as 금강구왕 金剛鉤王 the vajra hook king.

금강자 金剛子 Rudrākṣa, a seed similar to a peach-stone used for beads, especially in invoking one of the 금강 金剛. Also a vajra son.

금강장 金剛藏 Vajragarbha, the Bodhisattva in the Laṅkāvatāra-sūtra. 금강장왕 金剛藏王 A form of the next entry ; also Śākyamuni.

금강저 金剛杵 or **금강장** 金剛杖 v. 금강 金剛.

금강정 金剛頂 The diamond apex or crown, a general name of the esoteric doctrines and sūtras of Vairocana. The sūtra 금강정경 金剛頂經 is the authority for the 금강정종 金剛頂宗 sect.

금강정 金剛定 Vajrasamādhi, 금강유정 金剛喩定 ; 금강삼매 金剛三昧 ; 금강멸정 金剛滅定 diamond meditation, that of the last stage of the Bodhisattva, characterized by firm, indestructible knowledge, penetrating all reality attained after all remains of illusion have been cu off.

금강좌 金剛座 or **금강상** 金剛床 Vajrāsana, or Bodhimaṇḍa, Buddha's seat on attaining enlightenment, the "diamond" throne. Also a posture or manner of sitting. [M. W.]

금강중 金剛衆 The retinue of the 금강신 金剛神 Vajradevas.

금강지 金剛智 Vajramati. The indestructible and enriching diamond wisdom of the Buddha. Also the name of an Indian who came to China A.D. 619 ; he is said to have introduced the Yogācāra system and founded the esoteric school, but this is attributed to Amoghavajra, v. 대교 大教. 금강지삼장 金剛智三藏 Vajra-bodhi may be the same person, but there is doubt about the matter, cf. 대교 大教.

금강찰 金剛刹 Vajrakṣetra, a vajra or Buddhist monastery or building.

금강천 金剛天 The vajra-devas twenty in number in the Vajradhātu group.

금강체 金剛體 The diamond body, that of Buddha, and his merits.

금강혜 金剛慧 Diamond wisdom, which by its reality overcomes all illusory knowledge.

금계 金鷄 The golden cock (or fowl), with a grain of millet in its beak, a name for Bodhidharma.

금골 金骨 Golden bones, i.e. Buddha's relics.

금광(명) 金光(明) Golden light, an intp. of suvarṇa, prabhāsa, or uttama. It is variously applied, e.g. 금광명녀 金光明女 Wife of 금천동자 金天童子 ; 금광명고 金光明鼓 Golden-light drum. 금광명경 金光明經 Golden-light sūtra, tr. in the sixth century and twice later, used by the founder of T'ien-t'ai ; it is given in its fullest form in the 금광명최승왕경 金光明最勝王經 Suvarṇa-prabhāsa-uttamarāja sūtra. 금광불찰 金光佛刹 The lowest of the Buddha-kṣetra, or lands.

금구 金口 The golden mouth of the Buddha, a reference *inter alia* to 금강구 金剛口 the diamond-like firmness of his doctrine. 금구상승 金口相承 ; 금구조승 金口祖承 The doctrines of the golden mouth transmitted in "apostolic succession" through generations (of patriarchs).

금구 金龜 The golden tortoise on which the world rests, idem 금륜 金輪.

금당 金堂 Golden hall. Another name of 대웅전 大雄殿 Buddha hall, a main building in a temple where Buddha resides.

금대왕 金大王 Protector of travellers, shown in the train of the 1,000-hand Kuan-yin. see 천 千.

금란의 金襴衣 A kāṣāya or robe embroidered with gold ; a golden robe ; also 금란가사 金襴袈裟 ; 금색의 金色衣.

금륜 金輪 The metal circle on which the earth rests, above the water circle which is above the wind (or air) circle which rests on space. Also the cakra, wheel or disc, emblem of sovereignty, one of the seven precious possessions of a king. 금륜왕 金輪王 A golden-wheel king, the highest in comparison with silver, copper, and iron cakravartin.

금모사자 金毛獅子 The lion with golden hair on which Mañjuśrī (Wên-shu) rides ; also a previous incarnation of the Buddha.

금비라 金毘羅 Kumbhīra, 금비라 金毘邏 ; 금파라 金波羅 ; 금비라 禁毘羅 or 궁비라 宮毘羅 ; a crocodile, alligator, described as 교룡 蛟龍 a "boa-dragon" ; cf. 실 失. A yakṣa-king who was converted and became a guardian of Buddhism, also known as 금비라타(가비라) 金毘羅陀(迦毘羅) ; 금비라신 金毘羅神 ; 금비라대장 金毘羅大將. For 금비라비구 金毘羅比丘 Kampilla, v. 겁 劫.

금사 金沙 Golden-sand (river), an imaginary river in the Nirvāṇa sūtra 10. Also the Hiraṇyavatī, v. 시 尸.

금산 金山 Metal or golden mountain, i.e. Buddha, or the Buddha's body. 금산왕 金山王 Buddha, especially Amitābha. The 칠금산 七金山 are the seven concentric ranges around Sumeru, v. 수 須 ; viz. Yugaṁdhara, Īṣādhara, Khadiraka, Sudarśana, Aśvakarṇa, Vinataka, Nemiṁdhara, v. respectively 유 踰, 이 伊, 갈 竭, 소 蘇, 알 頞, 비 毘, and 니 尼.

금산사 金山寺 Geum-san-sa. A temple located in Geumsan-ri Geumsan-myeon Gimje-gun Jeollabuk-do in Korea. The 17th parish headquarters of Korean Jogye Order.

금색 金色 Golden coloured. 금색세계 金色世界 The golden-hued heaven of Mañjuśrī (Wên-shu). 금색녀 金色女 The princess of Vārāṇaśī, who is said to have been offered in marriage to Śākyamuni because he was of the same colour as herself. 금색공작왕 金色孔雀王 The golden-hued peacock king, protector of travellers, in the retinue of the 1,000-hands Kuan-yin. 금색왕 金色王 A previous incarnation of the Buddha. 금색가섭 金色迦葉 ; 금색존자 金色尊者 ; 금색두타 金色頭陀 Names for Mahākāśyapa, as he is said to have 음광 飮光 swallowed light, hence his golden hue.

금선 金仙 Golden ṛṣi, or immortal, i.e. Buddha ; also Taoist genii.

금성 金星 Śukra, the planet Venus.

금속여래 金粟如來 The golden grain Tathāgata, a title of Vimalakīrti 유마 維摩 in a previous incarnation.

금수 金水 Golden water, i.e. wisdom.

금시조(왕) 金翅鳥(王) Garuḍa, 묘시 妙翅 ; 가루라 迦樓羅 the king of birds, with golden wings, companion of Viṣṇu ; a syn. of the Buddha.

금신 金身 ; 금구 金軀 The golden body or person, that of Buddha.

금언 金言 Golden words, i.e. those of Buddha.

금인 金人 Buddha ; an image of Buddha of metal or gold, also 금불 金佛.

금장 金藏 Golden treasury, i.e. the Buddha-nature in all the living. 금장운 金藏雲 The first golden-treasury cloud when a new world is completed, arising in the 광음천 光音天 ābhāsvara heaven and bringing the first rain.

금장 金杖 The golden staff broken into eighteen pieces and the skirt similarly torn, seen in a dream by king Bimbisāra, prophetic of the eighteen divisions of Hīnayāna.

금제 金蹄 Kaṇṭhaka-aśvarāja, 금니 金泥 ; 건섭구 犍涉駒 name of the steed on which Śākyamuni left his home.

금지 金地 A Buddhist monastery ; v. also 서 逝 Jetavana. 금지국 金地國 Suvarṇabhūmi, said to be a country south of Śrāvastī, to which Aśoka sent missionaries. Also 금출 金出 ; 금전 金田.

금찰 金刹 A "golden" pagoda ; the nine "golden" circles on top of a pagoda.

금태 金胎 idem 금강계 金剛界 and 태장계 胎藏界.

금하 金河 Hiranyavatī, v. 시 尸.

급 笈 A satchel, book-box ; translit. *g*. 급다 笈多 Upagupta, v. 우 優. 급방발지 笈房鉢底 ; 교범바제 憍梵波提 Gavāṁpati, a monk with the feet and cud-chewing characteristic of an ox, because he had spilled some grains from an ear of corn he plucked in a former life.

급 汲 Draw water ; emulate, eager ; the round of reincarnations is like the 급정륜 汲井輪 waterwheel at the well ever revolving up and down.

급 給 Dā. To give. 급고(독) 給孤(獨) To give to orphans and widows ; a benefactor ; almsgiver ; e.g. Anāthapiṇḍika, v. 아나 阿那.

급 急 Haste, urgency ; promptly. 급시 急施 Alms made under stress of urgency. 급시여률령 急施如律令 "Swiftly as Lü-ling runs," used by sorcerers in their incantations.

긍 矜 To pity ; boast ; attend to ; vigorous. 긍애 矜哀 To pity. 긍갈라 矜羯羅 ; 금가라 金伽羅 Kiṁkara, a servant, slave ; the seventh of the eight messengers of 부중명왕 不重明王.

긍 兢 Tremble, quiver, shiver, quake, shake. 긍가 兢伽 v. 항하 恒河. Gaṅgā, the Ganges, 긍가하문 兢伽河門 Gaṅgādvāra, the gate of the Ganges. "A famous devālaya, the object of pilgrimages, the present Hurdwar," or Haridwar. [Eitel].

긍가 殑伽 Gaṅgā, the Ganges ; also 긍하 殑河 v. 달 怛. 긍기 殑耆 Gaṅgā, the goddess of the Ganges.

기 綺 A kind of open-work variegated silk. 기어 綺語 Sexual talk ; improper remarks.

기 期 A set time ; a limit of time ; times, seasons ; to expect. 만기 滿期 The time fulfilled. 과기 過期 Beyond the time. 기망 期望 To look for, expect, hope.

기 妓 A singing-girl, courtesan. 기악 妓樂 Female musicians and performers.

기 器 A vessel, utensil, tool. 기세간 器世間 ; 기세계 器世界 ; 기계 器界 The world as a vessel containing countries and peoples ; the material world, a realm of things. 기계설 器界說 The supernatural power of the Buddha to make the material realm (trees and the like) proclaim his truth. 기량 器量 Capacity.

기 忌 Avoid, tabu, dread ; hate, jealous. 기일 忌日 ; 휘일 諱日 The tabu day, i.e. the anniversary of the death of a parent or prince, when all thoughts are directed to him, and other things avoided.

기 嗜 Fond of, given up to, doting ; translit. *sh*, *j* sounds, e.g. 기나야사 嗜那耶舍 Jinayaśas, a noted monk.

기 饑 Hunger, famine. 기아지옥 饑餓地獄 The hell of hunger. 기근재 饑饉災 The calamity of famine.

기 蟣 Likṣā, a nit ; young louse, the egg of a louse ; a minute measure of weight.

기 耆 Old, 60 years of age, experienced ; translit. *ji*, *g*. 기바 耆婆 ; 기역 耆域 ; 시박가 時縛迦 Jīva, Jīvaka. Son of Bimbisāra by the concubine Āmrapālī. On his birth he is said to have seized the acupuncture needle and bag. He became famed for his medical skill. 기바천 耆婆天 Jīva, the deva of long life. 기바조 耆婆鳥 idem 명명조 命命鳥, also 기바기바(가) 耆婆耆婆(迦) ; 자바기바(기) 闍婆耆婆(耆) A bird of the partridge family ; there is a fable about such a bird having two heads, called 가루다 迦嘍嗏 garuḍa, and 우파가루다 憂波迦嘍嗏 upagaruḍa ; one ate a delicious flower while the other was asleep ; when the latter awoke, it was so annoyed at not sharing it that it ate a poisonous flower and the bird died ; thus there is a Jekyll and Hyde in every one. 기나 耆那 Jina, victor, he who overcomes, a title of every Buddha ; also the name of various persons ; the Jaina religion, the Jains. 기사 耆闍 Gṛdhra, a vulture, also an abbrev. for 기사굴 耆闍崛 ; 이사굴 伊沙堀 ; 게리타라구지 揭梨馱羅鳩胝 ; 길률타라구타 姞栗陀羅矩吒 Gṛdhrakūṭa ; a mountain near Rājagṛha said to be shaped like a vulture's head, or to be famous for its vultures and its caverns inhabited by ascetics, where Piśuna (Māra), in the shape of a vulture, hindered the meditations of Ānanda. It has numerous other names.

기 祇 only ; translit. *j* in 기원정사 祇園精舍 ; 기수급고독원 祇樹給孤獨園 The vihāra and garden Jetavana, bought by Anāthapiṇḍika from prince Jeta and given to Śākyamuni.

기 譏 Ridicule, jeer at ; inspect. 기혐 譏嫌 To hold in contempt ; to satirize.

기 己 Self, personal, own. 기리 己利 Personal advantage, or profit. 기심 己心 One's own heart. 기심법문 己心法門 ; 기심중소행법문 己心中所行法門 The method of the self-realization of truth, the intuitive method of meditation, 지관 止觀 1. 기계 己界 The Buddhakāya, or realm of Buddha in contrast with the realm of ordinary beings. 기증 己證, 자증 自證 Self-attained assurance of the truth, such as that of the Buddha. 기신미타유심정토 己身彌陀唯心淨土 Myself (is) Amitābha, my mind (is) the Pure Land. All things are but the one mind, so that outside existing beings there is no Buddha and no Pure Land. Thus Amitābha is the Amitābha within and the Pure Land is the Pure Land of the mind. It is an expression of Buddhist pantheism, that all is Buddha and Buddha is all.

기 伎 Skill ; 기교 伎巧 ; 기예 伎藝. 기아 伎兒 An actor. 기예천녀 伎藝天女 The metamorphic devī on the head of Śiva, perhaps the moon which is the usual figure on Śiva's head.

기 祇 The Earth-Spirit ; repose ; vast ; translit. *j, g.* 기치반나 祇哆槃那 or 기치반림 祇哆槃林 ; 기원(정사) 祇園(精舍) ; 기수원 祇樹園 ; 기수급고독원 祇樹給孤獨園 ; 기수화림굴 祇樹花林窟 ; 기환림 祇桓林 or 기원림 祇洹林 ; 기타림 祇陀林 or 기타원 祇陀園 ; also 서 逝 or 서다 誓多, etc. Jetavana, a park near Śrāvastī, said to have been obtained from Prince Jeta by the elder Anāthapiṇḍika, in which monasterial buildings were erected, the favourite resort of Śākyamuni. Two hundred years later it is said to have been destroyed by fire, rebuilt smaller 500 years after, and again a century later burnt down ; thirteen years afterwards it was rebuilt on the earlier scale, but a century later entirely destroyed. This is the account given in 법원주림 法苑珠林 39. 기다밀 祇多蜜 Gītamitra, tr. 가우 謌友 "friend of song," who in the fourth century tr. some twenty-five works into Chinese. 기야 祇夜 Geya, singing ; Geyam, a song ; preceding prose repeated in verse ; odes in honor of the saints ; cf. 가타 伽陀 gāthā. 기지 祇支 v. 승기지 僧祇支. 기타 祇陀 Jetṛ ; Jetā ; victor, a prince of Śrāvastī, son of king Prasenajit, and previous owner of the Jetavana.

기 機 The spring, or motive principle, machine, contrivance, artifice, occasion, opportunity ; basis, root or germ ; natural bent, fundamental quality. 기의 機宜 Opportune and suitable ; natural qualification (for receiving the truth). 기성 機性 ; 기근 機根 Natural or fundamental quality, original endowment and nature, suitability, capacity. 기감 機感 Potentiality and response, the potentiality of all to respond to the Buddha ; the response of the Buddha to the good in all the living. 기응 機應 Potentiality and response, similar to last entry. 기교 機教 Potentiality and teaching, opportune teaching, suited to the occasion. 기연 機緣 Potentiality and conditions ; favourable circumstances ; opportunity. 기요 機要 Opportunity, strategical possibility, or point. 기견 機見 Vision according to natural capacity, seeing the Buddha according to natural endowment. 기어 機語 Opportune words ; fundamental words. 기관 機關 Spring, motive force, cause, opportunity, etc.

기 棄 To cast aside, reject, abandon. 기세 棄世 To leave the world ; to die. 자기 自棄 To throw oneself away.

기 寄 To go or put under cover, lodge, confide to, deliver, convey, transfer ; to enter, put in a list. 기고 寄庫 To convey to the treasury, i.e. as paper money or goods are transferred to credit in the next world not only of the dead, but also by the living in store for themselves.

기 紀 To record ; regulate ; a year, a period (of twelve years). 기강료 紀綱寮 The office of the director of duties.

기 記 To remember, to record ; to record as foretelling, prophesy. 기별 記別 ; 기별 記莂 ; 수기 授記 To record and differentiate, the Buddha's foretelling of the future of his disciples to Buddhahood, and to their respective Buddha-kalpas, Buddha-realms, titles, etc. ; see the 기별경 記別經 and 화가라나 和伽羅那 Vyākaraṇa, predictions, one of the twelve divisions of the Canon. 기실 記室 ; 서기 書記 Secretary's office, secretary, writer. 기심 記心 Memory. 기론 記論 Vyākaraṇa, a treatise on Sanskrit grammar, cf. 비가라론 毘伽羅論.

기 騎 To ride, sit astride. 기려멱려 騎驢覓驢 To search for your ass while riding it, i.e. not to recognize the mind of Buddha in one's self.

기 起 To rise, raise, start, begin ; uprising ; tr. utpāda. 기신 起信 the uprise or awakening of faith. 기신론 起信論 Śraddhotpāda Śāstra ; it is one of the earliest remaining Mahāyāna texts and is attributed to Aśvaghoṣa ; cf. 마명 馬鳴 ; two tr. have been made, one by Paramārtha in A.D. 554, another by Śikṣānanda, *circa* 700 ; the first text is more generally accepted, as Chih-i, the founder of T'ien-t'ai, was Paramārtha's amanuensis, and 법장 法藏 Fa-tsang (643-712) made the standard commentary on it, the 기신론의기 起信論義記 though he had assisted Śikṣānanda in his translation. It gives the fundamental principles of Mahāyāna, and was tr. into English by Teitaro Suzuki (1900), also by T. Richard. There are several commentaries and treatises on it. 기신이문 起信二門 Two characteristics of mind in the śāstra, as eternal and phenomenal. 기시귀 起尸鬼 To resurrect a corpse by demoniacal influence and cause it to kill another person ; v. 비 毘 vetāla ; 기사인 起死人 is similar, i.e. to raise the newly dead to slay an enemy. 기지처 起止處 A latrine, cesspool. 기멸 起滅 Rise and extinction, birth and death, beginning and end. 기진 起盡 Beginning and end, similar to the last, . 기자 起者 One who begins, or starts ; one who thinks he creates his own welfare or otherwise. 기행 起行 To start out (for the life to come). 기청 起請 To call on the gods or the Buddhas (as witness to the truth of one's statements).

기 祈 Yācñā. Pray ; prayer is spoken of as absent from Hīnayāna, and only known in Mahāyāna, especially in the esoteric sect. 기도 祈禱 ; 기념 祈念 ; 기청 祈請 To pray, beg, implore, invite. 기우 祈雨 To pray for rain. 기원 祈願 To vow.

기 奇 Āścarya, adbhuta ; wonderful, rare, extraordinary ; odd. 기묘 奇妙 Beautiful, or wonderful beyond compare. 기특 奇特 Wonderful, rare, special, the three incomparable kinds of 신통기특 神通奇特 power to convert all beings, 혜심기특 慧心奇特 Buddha-wisdom, and 섭수기특 攝受奇特 Buddha-power to attract and save all beings. 기이 奇異 Extraordinary, uncommon, rare.

기인 技人 A magician, trickster, conjurer.

기타 唫吒 Kheṭa, name of a preta, or hungry ghost.

기화 己和 Gi-hwa(1376-1433). A monk of the early Joseon dynasty in Korea.

긴 緊 Tight ; to bind tight ; press tight ; pressing, urgent ; translit. *kin.* 긴축가 緊祝迦 Kiṁśuka, v. 견 甄 ruby-colour. 긴요 緊要 Important. 긴나라 緊那羅 ; 긴날라 緊捺羅 ; 긴다라 緊陀羅 ; 견다라 甄陀羅 ; 진다라 眞陀羅 Kinnara ; the musicians of Kuvera, with men's bodies and horses' heads ; they are described as 인비인 人非人 men yet not men, and 의신 疑神 mythical beings ; one of the eight classes of heavenly musicians ; they are also described as horned, as having crystal lutes, the females singing and dancing, and as ranking below gandharvas.

길 姞 Chi, name of the concubine of Huang Ti ; translit. *g*. 길률다(라구다) 姞栗陀(羅矩吒) Gṛdhra, a vulture ; Gṛdhrakūṭa, the Vulture Peak, v. 기 耆.

길 吉 Śrī ; auspicious, lucky, fortunate ; translit. *k, ke, ku, g*. 길리 吉利 ; 길률타 姞栗陀 Gṛdhra, a vulture. 길리라 吉利羅 ; 계리길라 髻離吉羅 One of the honourable ones in the Vajradhātu group. 길서 吉庶 or 길차 吉遮 or 길자 吉蔗 ; 흘리다 訖利多 ; 흘률저 訖栗著 Kṛtyā ; a demon, or class of demons, yakṣa and human ; explained by 기시귀 起尸鬼 a corpse-raising demon ; 길리다 吉利多 is explained by 매득 買得 bought as (a serf or slave). 길경 吉慶 Auspicious, lucky, fortunate. 길일양진 吉日良辰 A lucky day and propitious star. 길반다 吉槃茶 Kumbhāṇḍas, demons of monstrous form, idem 구반다 鳩槃茶. 길하 吉河 The auspicious river, the Ganges, because in it the heretics say they can wash away their sins. 길유라 吉由羅 ; 지유라 枳由邏 ; 기유라 鞿由羅 Keyūra, a bracelet (worn on the upper arm). 길상 吉祥 Auspicious, fortunate, tr. of the name of Lakṣmī, the goddess of fortune. See next, also 실리 室利 and 시리 尸里. 길상천녀 吉祥天女 ; 공덕천 功德天 ; 마하실리 摩訶室利 Mahāśrī, identified with Lakṣmī, name "of the goddess of fortune and beauty frequently in the later mythology identified with Śrī and regarded as the wife of Viṣṇu or Nārāyaṇa," she sprang from the ocean with a lotus in her hand, whence she is also called Padma, and is connected in other ways with the lotus. [M. W.] There is some confusion between this goddess and Kuan-yin, possibly through the attribution of Hindu ideas of Lakṣmī to Kuan-yin. 길상과 吉祥果 The auspicious fruit, a pomegranate, held by Hāritī 귀자모 鬼子母 as the bestower of children. 길상해운 吉祥海雲 The auspicious sea-cloud ; tr. as Śrī-vatsa, the breast mark of Viṣṇu, but defined as the svastika, which is the 불심인 佛心印 symbol on a Buddha's breast. 길상초 吉祥草 or 길상모 吉祥茅 ; 구사 矩奢. Kuśa, auspicious grass used at religious ceremonials, Poa cynosuroides. 길상모국 吉祥茅國 ; 구사게라보라 矩奢揭羅補羅 Kuśāgrapura, "ancient residence of the kings of Magadha, surrounded by mountains, 14 miles south of Behar. It was deserted under Bimbisāra, who built 'New Rājagṛha' 6 miles farther to the west." [Eitel]. The distance given is somewhat incorrect, but v. 왕사성 王舍城. 길라 吉羅 Kṛta idem 돌길라 突吉羅 Duṣkṛta ; one of the grave sins. 길가야 吉迦夜 Kekaya, a noted monk of the Liu-Sung dynasty.

깜냥 Natural capacity, capacity of any organ, or being. Equivalent to 근기 根機.

깨달음 覺 Enlightenment ; illumination ; awakening.

꿇어앉기 Kneeling on one's heels.

끽 喫 To eat. 끽소 喫素 To eat ordinary, or vegetarian food. 끽기라 喫棄羅 Khakkhara, a beggar's staff ; an abbot's staff.

<ㄴ>

나 裸 Naked. 나형외도 裸形外道 Nirgranthas, naked ascetics.

나 拏 Take, lay hold of ; translit. for ḍ, ṇ ; e.g. ḍāmara, to affright (demons) ; v. 다 荼.

나 娜 Translit. *da* and *na*, e.g. 나다 娜多 Danta, tooth, tusk, fang. 나가 娜伽 Naga, mountain, hill. 나야 娜耶 Naya, conduct, course, leading.

나 那 Where? How? what? That. Translit. *na, ne, no, nya* ; cf. 나 娜, 나 拏, 낭 曩.

나가 那伽 Nāga. Snake, dragon, elephant. It is tr. by 용 龍 dragon and by 상 象 elephant. (1) As dragon it represents the chief of the scaly reptiles ; it can disappear or be manifest, increase or decrease, lengthen or shrink ; in spring it mounts in the sky and in winter enters the earth. The dragon is of many kinds. Dragons are regarded as beneficent, bringing the rains and guarding the heavens (again Draco) ; they control rivers and lakes, and hibernate in the deep. Nāga and Mahānāga are titles of a Buddha, (also of those freed from reincarnation) because of his powers, or because like the dragon he soars above earthly desires and ties. One of his former reincarnations was a powerful poisonous dragon which, out of pity, permitted itself to be skinned alive and its flesh eaten by worms. (2) A race of serpent-worshippers. 나가알랄수나 那伽閼剌樹那 or 나가알갈수나 那伽閼曷樹那 Nāgārjuna, 용수 龍樹 the dragon-arjuna tree, or Nāgakrośana, intp. probably wrongly as 용맹 龍猛 dragon-fierce. One of the "four suns" and reputed founder of Mahāyāna (but see 아 阿 for Aśvaghoṣa), native of South India, the fourteenth patriarch ; he is said to have cut off his head as an offering. "He probably flourished in the latter half of the second century A.D." [Eliot]. v. 용수 龍樹. He founded the Mādhyamika or 중 中 school, generally considered as advocating doctrines of negation or nihilism, but his aim seems to have been a reality beyond the limitations of positive and negative, the identification of contraries in a higher synthesis, e.g. birth and death, existence and non-existence, eternal and non-eternal ; v. 중론 中論.

나가정 㑚伽定 The nāga meditation, which enables one to become a dragon, hibernate in the deep, prolong one's life and meet Maitreya, the Messiah.

나게(라할라) 那揭(羅喝羅) Nagara ; Nagarahāra. 낭아라하라 曩哦囉賀囉 "An ancient kingdom and city on the southern bank of the Cabool River about 30 miles west of Jellālabad (Lat. 34° 28 N., Long. 70° 30 E.). The Nagara of Ptolemy." [Eitel].

나라 那羅 Naṭa ; cf. 나타 那吒 ; a dancer or actor 기희 伎戲 ; or perhaps Narya, manly, strong, one definition being 력 力. 나라연(나) 那羅延(那) ; 나라야나 那羅野拏 Nārāyaṇa, "son of Nara or the original man, patronymic of the personified Purusha or first living being, author of the Purusha hymn," [M. W.] He is also identified with Brahmā, Viṣṇu, or Kṛṣṇa ; intp. by 인생본 人生本 the originator of human life ; 견고 堅固 firm and stable ; 역사 力士 or 천계역사 天界力士 hero of divine power ; and 금강 金剛 vajra ; the term is used adjectivally with the meaning of manly and strong. Nārāyaṇa is represented with three faces, of greenish-yellow colour, right hand with a wheel, riding a garuḍa-bird. 나라연천 那羅延天 Nārāyaṇa-deva, idem Nārāyaṇa. His 나라연천후 那羅延天后 śakti or female energy is shown in the Garbhadhātu group. 나라마나 那羅摩那 or 나라마납 那羅摩納 Naramānava, a young Brahman, a descendant of Manu. 나라나리 那羅那里 Nara-nārī, union of the male and female natures. 나라타 那羅陀 Narādhāra, a flower, tr. 인지화 人持花 carried about for its scent.

나락가 那洛迦 Naraka, "hell, the place of torment, ... the lower regions" [M. W.], intp. by 지옥 地獄 q.v.

나란타 那爛陁 Nālandā, a famous monastery 7 miles north of Rājagṛha, built by the king Śakrāditya. Nālandā is intp. as 시무염 施無厭 "Unwearying benefactor," a title attributed to the Nāga which dwelt in the lake Āmra there. The village is identified in [Eitel] as Baragong, i.e. Vihāragrāma. For Nālandā excavations see Archaeological Survey Reports, and cf. Hsüan-tsang's account.

나랄차 那辣遮 Nārāca, an iron arrow, intp. 추 錐 a pointed implement.

나련(제여)야사 那連(提黎)耶舍 Narendrayaśas, a monk of Udyāna, north-west India ; sixth century A.D. ; tr. the Candra-garbha, Sūrya-garbha, and other sūtras.

나리(계)라 那利(薊)羅 Nārikela, Nārikera, 날리라길리 捺唎羅吉唎 The coco-nut. Nārikeladvīpa is described as "an island several thousand li south of Ceylon, inhabited by dwarfs 3 feet high, who have human bodies with beaks like birds, and live upon coco-nuts." [Eitel].

나마 那摩 Namaḥ, Namo, idem 나무 南無.

나마 那摩 Nāman 나마 娜麽 or 담마 曇麽. A name 명 名.

나모 那謨 Namaḥ, Namo, idem 나무 南無 q.v.

나무 南無 Namaḥ ; Pali: Namo ; to submit oneself to, from to bend, bow to, make obeisance, pay homage to ; an expression of submission to command, complete commitment, reverence, devotion, trust for salvation, etc. Also written 남모 南牟 ; 남모 南謨 ; 남망 南忙 ; 나모 那謨 or 那模 or 나마 那麻 ; 납막 納莫 or 납모 納慕 ; 나모 娜母 ; 낭막 曩莫 or 낭모 曩謨 ; 날마 捺麻 or 날모 捺謨, etc. It is used constantly in liturgy, incantations, etc., especially as in Namaḥ Amitābha, which is the formula of faith of the Pure-land sect, representing the believing heart of all beings and Amitābha's power and will to save ; repeated in the hour of death it opens the entrance to the Pure Land. 나무불 南無佛 ; 나무삼보 南無三寶 I devote myself entirely to the Buddha, or Triratna, or Amitābha, etc. 나무사 南無師 Masters of Namaḥ, i.e. Buddhist or Taoist priests and sorcerers.

나바(마리) 那婆(摩利) Nava ; Navamālikā. Variegated or mixed flowers.

나비 那鞞 Nābhi ; navel, nave of a wheel.

나선 那先 Nāgasena 나가서나 那伽犀那. The instructor of the king in the Milindapañha, v. 나선(비구)경 那先(比丘)經.

나아뢰야만다라 那阿賴耶曼荼羅 Nālaya-maṇḍala, the non-ālaya maṇḍala, or the 도량 道場 bodhi-site or seat, which is 무의처 無依處 without fixed place, independent of place, and entirely pure.

나야 那耶 Naya ; leading, conduct, politic, prudent, method ; intp. by 정리 正理 right principle ; 승 乘 conveyance, i.e. mode of progress ; and 도 道 way, or method. 나야수마 那耶修摩 Nāya is a name of Jñātṛ, v. 니 尼 Nirgrantha.

나옹 혜근 懶翁惠勤 Na-ong Hye-geun(1320-1376). A monk of the Goryeo dynasty in Korea. He became a monk when his neighbor friend died and he didn't know where he had gone. He traveled in China (Yüan dynasty) at the age of 28 to 39. He became an national preceptor at 52.

나유타 那由他 Nayuta, 나유다 那庾多 or 那由多 ; 나술 那術 or 那述 a numeral, 100,000 or one million, or ten million.

나율 那律 Aniruddha, v. 아 阿.

나제 那提 Nadī, river, torrent ; name of Puṇyopāya, 포여나제 布如那提, 포언벌야 布焉伐耶 a noted monk of Central India. 나제가섭 那提迦葉, 날지가섭파 捺地迦葉波 Nadīkāśyapa, brother of Mahākāśyapa, to become Samantaprabhāsa Buddha.

나찰(사) 羅刹(娑) Rākṣasa, also 나차사 羅叉娑 ; from rakṣas, harm, injuring. Malignant spirits, demons ; sometimes considered inferior to yakṣas, sometimes similar. Their place of abode was Laṅkā in Ceylon, where they are described as the original inhabitants, anthropophagi, once the terror of shipwrecked mariners ; also described as the barbarian races of ancient India. As demons they are described as terrifying, with black bodies, red hair, green eyes, devourers of men. 나찰사 羅刹私 Rākṣasī, also 나차사 羅叉私 ; 나찰사 羅刹斯 ; 나찰녀 羅刹女 Female demons, of whom the names of eight, ten, and twelve are given, and 500 are also mentioned. 나찰천 羅刹天 The deva controlling these demons, who has his abode in the south-west corner of the heavens. 나찰국 羅刹國 An island in the Indian Ocean, supposed to be Ceylon. 나찰라 羅刹羅 Akṣara, a syllable, word, letter.

나타 那他 Nada, a river.

나타 那吒 Naṭa, said to be the eldest son of Vaiśravaṇa, and represented with three faces, eight arms, a powerful demon-king.

나한전 羅漢殿 Arhat hall. A building in a temple.

나함 那含 ; 나금함 那金含 Anāgāmin, v. 아 阿.

낙 洛 Lo-yang 낙양 洛陽, the ancient capital of China. 낙차 洛叉 or 낙사 洛沙 Lakṣa, a lakh, 100,000. For the series of higher numbers, see 수 數.

낙 諾 To answer ; promise ; yes ; translit. *na, nya.* 낙건나 諾健那 ; 다건나 茶健那 ; 낙가나 諾伽那 Nagna ; naked, a naked mendicant ; a name of Śiva ; a vajra-king. 낙거라 諾詎羅 ; 낙구라 諾矩羅 Nakula, one of the sixteen arhats. 낙구타 諾瞿陀 Nyagrodha. The Indian fig-tree, *Ficus indica,* cf. 니 尼.

난 欄 A rail, handrail ; pen, fold. 난순 欄楯 Barrier, railing.

난 難 Difficult, hard ; distress, adversity ; opposite of 이 易 easy ; translit. *nan, nam.* 난복 難伏 Hard to subdue, or submit ; unconquerable. 난입 難入 Hard to enter, or attain. 난승 難勝 Hard to overcome, or be overcome ; unconquerable ; the fifth of the ten bodhisattva 지 地 stages when all passion and illusion is overcome and understanding of all things attained. 난화 難化 Difficult of conversion, or transformation. 난도 難度 Hard to cross over, to save or be saved. 난도해 難度海 The ocean hard to cross, the sea of life and death, or mortality. 난사 難思 Hard to think of, hard to realize, incredible. 난나 難拏 Daṇḍa, 단나 檀拏 ; a club, mace, Yama's symbol. 난제 難提 Nandi, "the happy one," name of Viṣṇu, Śiva, and of a Buddhist monk ; also said to be a term for stūpa. 난제가 難提迦 Nandika, brother of 조달 調達 Devadatta. 난제가물다 難提迦物多 Nandikāvarta ; nandyāvarta ; joyous, or auspicious turning ; defined as turning to the right, i.e. curling as a Buddha's hair. 난유 難有 Hard to have, similar to 희유 希有, rare. 난타 難陀 ; 난타 難陁 Nanda, "happiness, pleasure, joy, felicity." [M. W.] Name of disciples not easy to discriminate ; one is called Cowherd Nanda, an arhat ; another Sundarananda, to distinguish him from Ānanda, and the above ; also, of a milkman who gave Śākyamuni milk ; of a poor woman who could only offer a cash to buy oil for a lamp to Buddha ; of a Nāga king ; etc. 난타발난타 難陀跋難陀 Nanda Upananda, two nāga brothers, who protected Magadha.

난 暖 Warm ; to warm. 난료 暖寮 ; 난사 暖寺 ; 난동 暖洞 ; 난석 暖席 Presents of tea, fruit, etc., brought to a monastery, or offered to a new arrival.

난 煖 Warm, idem 난 暖. 난법 煖法 The first of the 사가행위 四加行位 ; the stage in which dialectic processes are left behind and the mind dwells only on the four dogmas and the sixteen disciplines.

난생 卵生 Aṇḍaja. Egg-born, one of the four ways of coming into existence, v. 사생 四生.

날 捺 To press down ; a pen-stroke to the right ; translit. *na*. 날지가섭파 捺地迦葉波 Nadī-Kāśyapa, also 나제 那提 a brother of Mahā-Kāśyapa, to be reborn as Buddha Samanta-prabhāsa. 날락가 捺落迦 or 나락가 那落迦 Naraka, hell, the hells, v. 지옥 地獄 ; 날락가 捺落迦 sometimes refers to the place of torment, and 나락가 那落迦 nāraka to the sufferer there. 날모 捺謨 ; 날마 捺麻 Namaḥ, v. 남 南.

남 南 Dakṣiṇā, south ; translit. *nāṁ*, and as a suffix intp. as meaning plural, several, i.e. more than three.

남 男 Male. 남녀 男女 Male and female. 남근 男根 The male organ.

남능북수 南能北秀 v. 남종 南宗.

남돈북점 南頓北漸 v. 남종 南宗.

남라 南羅 Southern Lāra ; Mālava, an ancient kingdom in Central India ; headquarters of heretical sects, in the present Malwa. 북라 北羅 was Valabhī, in Gujarat.

남방 南方 The southern quarter ; south. 남방불교 南方佛教 Southern Buddhism in contrast with 북방 北方 northern Buddhism. 남(방)무구(세계) 南(方)無垢(世界) The Southern Pure Land to which the dragon-maid went on attaining Buddhahood, cf. Lotus Sūtra.

남산 南山 Southern hill, name of a monastery which gave its name to 도선 道宣 Tao-hsüan of the T'ang dynasty, founder of the 사분율 四分律 school.

남섬부주 南贍部洲 ; 남염부제 南閻浮提 Jambudvīpa. One of the four continents, that situated south of Mt. Meru, comprising the world known to the early Indians. Also 남주 南洲 ; 남부 南浮 ; 남부 南部.

남양 南陽 Nan-yang, a noted monk who had influence with the T'ang emperors Su Tsung and Tai Tsung, *circa* 761-775.

남장 南藏 The Southern Collection, or Edition, of the Chinese Buddhist Canon, published at Nanking under the reign of T'ai Tsu, the first emperor of the Ming dynasty, who reigned A.D. 1368-1398.

남전 南泉 Nan-ch'üan, a monk of the T'ang dynasty *circa* 800, noted for his cryptic sayings, inheritor of the principles of his master, Ma-tsu 마조 馬祖.

남종 南宗 The Southern sect, or Bodhidharma School, divided into northern and southern, the northern under 신수 神秀 Shên-hsiu, the southern under 혜능 慧能 Hui-nêng, *circa* A.D. 700, hence 남능북수 南能北秀 ; the southern came to be considered the orthodox Intuitional school. The phrase 남돈북점 南頓北漸 or "Southern immediate, northern gradual" refers to the method of enlightenment which separated the two schools.

남중삼교 南中三教 The three models of Śākyamuni's teaching as expounded by the teachers south of the Yangtze after the Ch'i dynasty A.D. 479-501. (1) The 점교 漸教 gradual method, leading the disciples step by step to nirvāṇa. (2) The 돈교 頓教 immediate method, by which he instructed the bodhisattvas, revealing the whole truth. (3) The 부정교 不定教 undetermined method, by which the teaching is adapted to each individual or group.

남천(축) 南天(竺) Southern India.

남해마라야산 南海摩羅耶山 Malayagiri, "the Malaya mountains in Malabar answering to the western Ghāts ; a district in the south of India." [M. W.] A mountain in Ceylon, also called Laṅkā.

남행 南行 Dakṣiṇāyana. The course or declination of the sun to the south ; the half-year in which it moves from north to south ; a period of six months.

납 納 Offer ; pay, give ; receive, take ; translit. *na* ; cf. 납 衲. 납구 納具 To accept all the commandments, or rules. 납가리 納加梨 v. 납 衲. 납수 納受 ; 납득 納得 To receive, accept. 납모 納帽 A cap made of bits of given material. 납모 納慕 ; 납막 納莫 ; 납모 納謨 v. 나무 南無 Namaḥ. 납계 納戒 To receive or accept the commandments. 납파 納播 A stole worn during teaching. 납박승가람 納縛僧伽藍 Navasaṅghārāma. "An ancient monastery near Baktra, famous for three relics of Śākyamuni (a tooth, basin, and staff)." [Eitel]. 납박제반구라 納縛提婆矩羅 Navadevakula. "An ancient city, a few miles south-east of Kanyākūbdja, on the eastern bank of the Ganges. The present Nobatgang." [Eitel]. 납박파 納縛波 Na-fu-po, Hsüan-tsang's name for a city on the ancient site of I-hsün 이순 伊循, capital of Shan-shan 선선 鄯善 in the Former Han dynasty, afterwards known as Nob or Lop (in Marco Polo). It corresponds to the modern Charkhlik. 납사어통 納蛇於筒 To put a snake into a tube, i.e. meditation able to confine unruly thoughts. 납의 納衣 Garments made of castaway rags, the patch-robe of a monk. 납골 納骨 To bury bones, or a skeleton.

납 衲 To patch, line, pad ; a monk's garment, supposed to be made of rags. 납가리 衲伽梨 The saṅghāṭī, or coat of patches varying from 9 to 25. 납자 衲子 A monk, especially a peripatetic monk. 납의 衲衣 or 納衣 A monk's robe. 납가사 衲袈裟 A monk's robe of seven pieces and upwards. 납중 衲衆 Monks who wear these robes.

납 蠟 Wax. 납인 蠟印 To seal with wax, a wax seal.

낭 囊 A bag, sack, purse ; translit. *na*. 낭모 囊莫 ; 낭모 囊謨 ; v. 남 南 Namaḥ. 낭아라하라 囊哦羅賀羅 Nagarahāra, Nagara, a city on the Kabul river, v. 나 那.

낭 娘 Lady, wife, mother, aunt. 사낭 師娘 A nun.

낭 曩 Of old, ancient ; translit. *na*. 낭막 曩莫 Namaḥ, v. 남 南.

내 柰 Berries of the *Nyctanthes* or musk. Āmra, a mango. 내녀 柰女 or 내씨 柰氏 Āmradārikā, Āmrapālī, a woman who is said to have been born on a mango-tree, and to have given the Plum-garden 내원 柰苑 or 柰園 to the Buddha, cf. 암라 菴羅.

내 耐 To endure, bear. 내원해인 耐怨害忍 The patience which endures enmity and injury. 내말타 耐抹陀 Narmadā, the modern Nerbudda river.

내 內 Within, inner.

내 또는 **나** 奈 Remedy, alternative, how? what? a yellow plum. 내리 奈利 idem 니리 泥梨 Niraya, hell. 내하 奈河 The inevitable river in purgatory to be crossed by all souls. 내하교 奈河橋 The bridge in one of the hells, from which certain sinners always fall. 내치라하라 奈耻羅訶羅 Rudhirāhāra, name of a yakṣa.

내걸 內乞 The bhikṣu monk who seeks control from within himself, i.e. by mental processes, as compared with the 외걸 外乞 the one who aims at control by physical discipline, e.g. fasting, etc.

내계 內界 The realm of mind as contrasted with 외계 外界 that of the body ; also the realm of cognition as contrasted with externals, e.g. the 오계 五界 five elements.

내공 內空 Empty within, i.e. no soul or self within.

내공(봉) 內供(奉) A title for the monk who served at the altar in the imperial palace, instituted in A.D. 756 ; also called 공봉 供奉.

내교 內敎 Buddhism, in contrast with 외교 外敎 other cults.

내기 內記 The clerk, or writer of petitions, or prayers, in a monastery ; also 내사 內史.

내도량 內道場 A place for Buddhist worship in the palace ; v. 내재 內齋 and 내사 內寺.

내명 內明 Adhyātma vidyā, a treatise on the inner meaning (of Buddhism), one of the 오명 五明 q.v.

내무위 內無爲 Inner quiescence, cf. the six 묘문 妙門.

내문전 內門轉 The psychological elements in the 팔식 八識, viz. the seventh and eighth categories.

내범 內凡 The inner or higher ranks of ordinary disciples as contrasted with the 외범 外凡 lower grades ; those who are on the road to liberation ; Hīnayāna begins the stage at the 사선근위 四善根位 also styled 내범위 內凡位 ; Mahāyāna with the 삼현위 三賢位 from the 십주 十住 upwards. T'ien-t'ai from the 상사즉 相似卽 of its 육즉 六卽 q.v.

내법 內法 Buddhism, as contrasted with other religions.

내비 內秘 The inner mystic mind of the bodhisattva, though externally he may appear to be a śrāvaka.

내사 內寺 The Buddhist shrines or temples in the palace, v. 내도량 內道場.

내사 內史 The clerk, or writer of petitions, or prayers, in a monastery ; also 내기 內記.

내숙식 內宿食 Food that has been kept overnight in a monastic bedroom and is therefore one of the "unclean" foods ; v. 내자 內煮.

내식 內識 Internal perception, idem 심식 心識.

내심 內心 The mind or heart within ; the red lotus is used in the 대일경 大日經 as its emblem. 내심만다라 內心曼茶羅 or 비밀만다라 秘密曼茶羅 The "central heart" maṇḍala of the 대일경 大日經, or the central throne in the diamond-realm lotus to which it refers.

내아 內我 The antarātman or ego within, one's own soul or self, in contrast with bahirātman 외아 外我 an external soul, or personal, divine ruler.

내연 內緣 The condition of perception arising from the five senses ; also immediate, conditional, or environmental causes, in contrast with the more remote.

내외 內外 Internal and external ; subjective and objective. 내외겸명 內外兼明 Inner and outer both "ming" ; the first four of the 오명 五明 q.v. are "outer" and the fifth "inner". 내외공 內外空 Internal organ and external object are both unreal, or not material. 내외도 內外道 Within and without the religion ; Buddhists and non-Buddhists ; also, heretics within the religion.

내원 內院 The inner court — of the Tuṣita heaven, where Maitreya dwells and preaches ; also 선법당 善法堂.

내의 內衣 Antaravāsaka, one of the three regulation garments of a monk, the inner garment.

내자 內煮 Cooked food in a monastic bedroom, becoming thereby one of the "unclean" foods ; v. 내숙식 內宿食.

내장 內障 Internal, or mental hindrances, or obstacles.

내재 內齋 Buddhist ceremonies in the palace on the emperor's birthday, v. 내도량 內道場.

내전 內典 Buddhist scriptures ; cf. 외전 外典 non-Buddhist scriptures. There are also divisions of internal and external in Buddhist scriptures.

내종 內種 The seed contained in the eighth 식 識, i.e. ālaya-vijñāna, the basis of all phenomena.

내중 內衆 The inner company, i.e. the monks, in contrast with 외속 外俗 the laity.

내증 內證 The witness or realization within ; one's own assurance of the truth.

내지 乃至 (1) A translation of antaśas meaning "at least" ; and (2) of yāvat, as far as. 내지일념 乃至一念 Even, or at least, a thought. 내왕 乃往 As far as the past (is concerned).

내진 內陣 The inner ranks, i.e. the part of a temple near the altar, where the monks sit.

내진 內塵 The inner, or sixth 진 塵 guṇa associated with mind, in contrast with the other five guṇas, qualities or attributes of the visible, audible, etc.

내태 內胎 The inner garbhadhātu, i.e. the eight objects in the eight leaves in the central group of the maṇḍala.

내학 內學 The inner learning, i.e. Buddhism.

내훈 內薰 Inner censing ; primal ignorance, or unenlightenment ; perfuming, censing, or acting upon original intelligence causes the common uncontrolled mind to resent the miseries of mortality and to seek nirvāṇa ; v. 기신론 起信論 Awakening of Faith.

냉 冷 Cold. 냉난 冷暖 Cold and warm. 냉도 冷淘 Cold swill, a name for 냉면 冷麪 cold dough-strings. 냉하 冷河 The cold river Śītā, v. 사다 私多.

녈 涅 Black mud at the bottom of a pool ; muddy ; to blacken, defile. 열반 涅槃 Nirvāṇa, q.v.

녈리지 涅哩底 Nirṛti, destruction, the goddess of death and corruption, regent of the south-west. 녈리지방 涅哩底方 The south-west quarter.

녈말 涅末 Nimat, or Calmadana, "an ancient kingdom and city at the south-east borders of the desert of Gobi." [Eitel].

녈첩반나 涅疊般那 Niṣṭapana, burning, cremation.

념 念 Smṛti. Recollection, memory ; to think on, reflect ; repeat, intone ; a thought ; a moment. 염력 念力 Smṛtibala, one of the five bala or powers, that of memory, that of thought ; mental power, powers of intense concentration. Also one of the seven bodhyaṅga 칠보리분 七菩提分. 염불 念佛 To repeat the name of a Buddha, audibly or inaudibly. 염불자 念佛者 One who repeats the name of a Buddha, especially of Amitābha, with the hope of entering the Pure Land. 염불종 念佛宗 or 염불문 念佛門. The sect which repeats only the name of Amitābha, founded in the T'ang dynasty by 도작 道綽 Tao-ch'o, 선도 善道 Shan-tao, and others. 염불삼매 念佛三昧

The samādhi in which the individual whole-heartedly thinks of the appearance of the Buddha, or of the Dharmakāya, or repeats the Buddha's name. The one who enters into this samādhi, or merely repeats the name of Amitābha, however evil his life may have been, will acquire the merits of Amitābha and be received into Paradise, hence the term 염불왕생 念佛往生. This is the basis or primary cause of such salvation 염불위본 念佛爲本 or 염불위선 念佛爲先. Amitābha's merits by this means revert to the one who repeats his name 염불회향 念佛廻向 the 염불왕생원 念佛往生願 being the eighteenth of Amitābha's forty-eight vows. 염천 念天 One of the six devalokas, that of recollection and desire. 염정 念定 Correct memory and correct samādhi. 염념 念念 Kṣaṇa of a kṣaṇa, a kṣaṇa is the ninetieth part of the duration of a thought ; an instant ; thought after thought. 염념무상 念念無常 Instant after instant, no permanence, i.e. the impermanence of all phenomena ; unceasing change. 염념상속 念念相續 Unbroken continuity ; continuing instant in unbroken thought or meditation on a subject ; also unceasing invocation of a Buddha's name. 염지 念持 To apprehend and hold in memory. 염근 念根 Smṛtīndriya. The root or organ of memory, one of the five indriya 오근 五根. 염루 念漏 The leakages, or stream of delusive memory. 염주 念珠 To tell beads. 염경 念經 To repeat the sūtras, or other books ; to intone them. 염착 念著 Through perverted memory to cling to illusion. 염처 念處 Smṛtyupasthāna. The presence in the mind of all memories, or the region which is contemplated by memory. 사념처 四念處 Four objects on which memory or the thought should dwell – the impurity of the body, that all sensations lead to suffering, that mind is impermanent, and that there is no such thing as an ego. There are other categories for thought or meditation. 염각지 念覺支 Holding in memory continually, one of the Sapta bodhyaṅga 칠각지 七覺支. 염언 念言 (As) the mind remembers, (so) the mouth speaks ; also the words of memory. 염송 念誦 To recite, repeat, intone, e.g. the name of a Buddha ; to recite a dhāraṇī, or spell.

노 奴 A slave 노복 奴僕 ; 노예 奴隸 . 노비 奴婢 Male and female slaves.

노 弩 Crossbow, bow. 노달라쇄 弩達囉灑 Durdharṣa, hard to hold, or hard to overcome, or hard to behold, guardian of the inner gate in Vairocana's maṇḍala. 노벽제 弩蘖帝 Anvāgati, approaching, arriving.

노 老 Jarā ; old, old age. 노사 老死 Jarā-maraṇa, decrepitude and death ; one of the twelve nidānas, a primary dogma of Buddhism that decrepitude and death are the natural products of the maturity of the five skandhas. 노고추 老古錐 An old awl, an experienced and incisive teacher. 노파 老婆 An old woman ; my "old woman," i.e. my wife. 노자 老子 Lao Tzŭ, or Laocius, the accepted founder of the Taoists. The theory that his soul went to India and was reborn as the Buddha is found in the 제서 齊書 History of the Ch'i dynasty 고환전 顧歡傳. 노숙 老宿 Sthavira, an old man, virtuous elder. 노류추 老榴槌 An old pestle, or drumstick, a baldheaded old man, or monk. 노고 老苦 One of the four sufferings, that of old age.

노적건 笯赤建 Nujkend, or Nujketh in Turkestan, between Taras and Khojend.

녹 漉 To strain, filter. 녹수대 漉水袋 or 녹수낭 漉水囊 A monk's filtering-bag to strain off living creatures.

농 籠 A cage, crate ; to ensnare. 농두 籠頭 Blinkers for a horse's head.

농 農 Farm, farming, agriculture ; an intp. of the śūdra caste.

농 膿 Pus. 농혈지옥 膿血地獄 The hell of pus and blood.

뇌 惱 Vexation, irritation, annoyance, e.g. 오뇌 懊惱 and especially 번뇌 煩惱 kleśa, q.v.

뇨 尿 Urine, urinate. 요상귀자 尿牀鬼子 A urinating ghost ; a term of abuse. 요달 尿闥 A urinal.

능 能 Śak. Able to, can ; capability, power. 능인 能人 An able man, i.e. Buddha as the all-powerful man able to transform the world. 능인 能仁 Mighty in loving-kindness, an incorrect interpretation of Śākyamuni, but probably indicating his character. 능의 能依 Dependent on, that which relies on something else, e.g. vegetation on land ; 소의 所依 is that on which it relies. 능신 能信 Can believe, or can be believed, contrasted with 소신 所信 that which is believed. 능대사 能大師 ; 능행자 能行者 The sixth patriarch 혜능 慧能 Hui-nêng of the Ch'an(Zen) School. 능소 能所 These two terms indicate active and passive ideas, e.g. ability to transform, or transformable and the object that is transformed. 능지 能持 Ability to maintain, e.g. to keep the commandments. 능단금강경 能斷金剛經 Vajracchedikā-sūtra, the "Diamond Sūtra," translated by Hsüan-tsang, an extract from the Prajñāpāramitā-sūtra. 능시태자 能施太子 Prince "Giver," a former incarnation of Śākyamuni, when he obtained the magic dragon-pearl and by its power relieved the needs of all the poor. 능립 能立 A proposition in logic that can be established, or postulated. 능연 能緣 The conditioning power in contrast with the conditioned, e.g. the power of seeing and hearing in contrast with that which is seen and heard.

능가 楞伽 Laṅkā, a mountain in the south-east part of Ceylon, now called Adam's Peak ; the island of Ceylon 석란 錫蘭 ; also 능가 棱伽 ; 능가 駿伽. 능가경 楞伽經 The Laṅkāvatāra-sūtra, a philosophical discourse attributed to Śākyamuni as delivered on the Laṅkā mountain in Ceylon. It may have been composed in the fourth or fifth century A.D. ; it "represents a mature phase of speculation and not only criticizes the Sāṅkhya, Pāśupata and other Hindu schools, but is conscious of the growing resemblance of Mahāyānism to Brahmanic philosophy and tries to explain it". [Eliot]. There have been four translations into Chinese, the first by Dharmarakṣa between 412-433, which no longer exists ; the second was by Guṇabhadra in 443, called 능가아발다라보경 楞伽阿跋多羅寶經 4 chüan ; the third by Bodhiruci in 513, called 입릉가경 入楞伽經 10 chüan ; the fourth by Śikṣānanda in 700-704, called 대승입릉가경 大乘入楞伽經 7 chüan. There are many treatises and commentaries on it, by Fa-hsien and others. See *Studies in the Laṅkāvatāra Sūtra* by Suzuki and his translation of it. This was the sūtra allowed by Bodhidharma, and is the recognized text of the Ch'an(Zen) School. There are numerous treatises on it. 능엄경 楞嚴經 Śūraṅgama sūtra, a Tantric work tr. by Paramiti in 705 ; v. 수능엄경 首楞嚴經 ; there are many treatises under both titles.

니 泥 Mud ; paste ; clogged ; bigoted ; translit. *n* ; v. 니 尼 ; 니인 泥人 A sufferer in niraya, or hell, or doomed to it. 니리저 泥哩底 Nirṛti, one of the rakṣa-kings. 니탑 泥塔 Paste pagoda ; a mediaeval Indian custom was to make a small dagoba (syn. stūpa) five or six inches high of incense, place scriptures in and make offerings to it. The esoterics adopted the custom, and worshipped for the purpose of prolonging life and ridding themselves of sins, or sufferings. 니원 泥洹 Nirvāṇa ; also 니환 泥丸 ; 니왈 泥曰 ; 니환 泥桓 ; 니반 泥畔, v. 열반 涅槃. 니리 泥犁 Niraya, intp. as joyless, i.e. hell ; also 니리(야) 泥梨(耶) ; 니리가 泥梨迦 ; 니려 泥黎 ; 니라야 泥囉耶 ; 니저 泥底 v. 날락가 捺落迦 Naraka. 니로발라 泥盧鉢羅 Nīla-utpala ; the blue lotus, portrayed in the hand of Mañjuśrī. 니로도 泥盧都 One of the sixteen hells. 니박사나 泥縛些那 Nivāsana, a garment, a skirt. Also 니파사 泥婆娑 ; 니벌산나 泥伐散娜 ; 열반승 涅槃僧.

니 尼 To stop ; a nun ; near ; translit. *ni*. When used for a nun it is an abbrev. for 비구니 比丘尼 bhikṣuṇī. 니단 尼壇 The nun's alter ; a convent or nunnery. 니대사 尼大師 An abbess. 니고 尼姑 A nun. 니사 尼寺 A nunnery, or convent. 니계 尼戒 The rules for nuns, numbering 341, to which seven more were added making 348, commonly called the 오백계 五百戒 500 rules. 니비구 尼比丘 A female bhikṣu, i.e. a nun. 니법사 尼法師 A nun teacher ; effeminate. 니중주 尼衆主 The Mistress of the nuns, Gautamī, i.e. Mahāprajāpatī, the foster-mother of Śākyamuni.

니가라 尼迦羅 Niṣkala, the name of a tree, but niṣkala means *inter alia* seedless, barren.

니건 尼犍 Nirgrantha, 니건 尼健 ; 니건(타) 尼乾(陀) ; 니건 尼虔, freed from all ties, a naked mendicant, tr. by 이계불계 離繫不繫, 무결 無結 devotees who are free from all ties, wander naked, and cover themselves with ashes. Mahāvīra, one of this sect, called 야제 若提 Jñāti after his family, and also 니건타야제자 尼乾陀若提子 Nirgranthajñātiputra, was an opponent of Śākyamuni. His doctrines were determinist, everything being fated, and no religious practices could change one's lot. 니건도 尼犍度 Bhikṣuṇī-khaṇḍa, a division of the Vinaya, containing the rules for nuns. 니건타불달라 尼犍陀弗呾羅 Nirgrantha-putra, idem Jñāti.

니건타가 尼建他迦 Niṣkaṇṭaka, 니연타가 尼延他柯 a kind of yakṣa, 무인 無咽 throatless.

니구다 尼拘陀 Nyagrodha, the down-growing tree, Ficus Indica, or banyan ; high and wide-spreading, leaves like persimmon-leaves, fruit called 다륵 多勒 to-lo used as a cough-medicine ; also intp. 양류 楊柳 the willow, probably from its drooping characteristic ; the 용수 榕樹 "bastard banyan", Ficus pyrifolia, takes its place as Ficus religiosa in China. Also written 니구율 尼拘律 ; 니구니타 尼拘尼陀 ; 니구로타 尼拘盧陀 ; 니구류타 尼拘類陀 ; 니구루타 尼拘婁陀 ; 니구루타 尼拘屢陀 ; 니구타 尼瞿陀 ; 니구타 尼俱陀 ; 니구류 尼俱類 ; 낙구타 諾瞿陀.

니근저 尼近底 v. 니연저 尼延底.

니다나 尼陀那 Nidāna, a band, bond, link, primary cause. I. The 십이인연 十二因緣 twelve causes or links in the chain of existence : (1) Jarā-maraṇa 노사 老死 old age and death. (2) Jāti 생 生 (re)birth. (3) Bhāva 유 有 existence. (4) Upādāna 취 取 laying hold of, grasping. (5) Tṛṣṇā 애 愛 love, thirst, desire. (6) Vedanā 수 受 receiving, perceiving, sensation. (7) Sparśa 촉 觸 touch, contact, feeling. (8) Ṣaḍ-āyatana, 육입 六入 the six senses. (9) Nāma-rūpa 명색 名色 name and form, individuality (of things). (10) Vijñāna 육식 六識 the six forms of perception, awareness or discernment. (11) Saṁskāra, 행 行 action, moral conduct. (12) Avidyā 무명 無明 unenlightenment, "ignorance which mistakes the illusory phenomena of this world for realities." [Eitel]. These twelve links are stated also in Hīnayāna in reverse order, beginning with Avidyā and ending with Jarā-maraṇa The Fan-i-ming-i says the whole series arises from 무명 無明 ignorance, and if this can be got rid of the whole process of 생사 生死 births and deaths (or reincarnations) comes to an end. II. Applied to the purpose and occasion of writing sūtras, Nidāna means (1) those written because of a request or query ; (2) because certain precepts were violated ; (3) because of certain events. 니다나목득가 尼陀那目得迦 Nidāna-mātṛkā, two of the twelve divisions of the sūtras, one dealing with the nidānas, the other with 본사 本事 previous incarnations.

니라 尼羅 Nīla, dark blue or green. 니라우담발라 尼羅優曇鉢羅 Nīla-udumbara, v. 우 優. 니라바다라 尼羅婆陀羅 ; 니람바 尼藍婆 Nīlavajra, the blue vajra, or thunderbolt. 니라부다 尼羅浮陀 idem 니랄부다 尼剌部陀. 니라오발라 尼羅烏鉢羅 ; 니라구발라 尼羅漚鉢羅 Nīlotpala, the blue lotus. 니라폐다 尼羅蔽荼 Nīlapiṭa, "the blue collection" of annals and royal edicts, mentioned in 서역기 西域記.

니랄부타 尼剌部陀 or 尼剌浮陀 Nirarbuda, 니라부타 尼羅浮陀 "bursting tumours", the second naraka of the eight cold hells.

니련선(나) 尼連禪(那) Nairañjanā, 니련하 尼連河 ; 희련선 希連禪 ; 희련하 希連河 The Nīlājan that flows past Gayā, "an eastern tributary of the Phalgu." [Eitel].

니루다 尼樓陀 Nirodha, restraint, suppression, cessation, annihilation, tr. by 멸 滅 extinction, the third of the four dogmas 사제 四諦 ; with the breaking of the chain of karma there is left no further bond to reincarnation. Used in Anupūrva-nirodha, or "successive terminations", i.e. nine successive stages of dhyāna. Cf. 니미유다 尼彌留陀.

니마라 尼摩羅 Nirmāṇarati, 수밀다천 須密陀天 devas who "delight in transformations", i.e. 화락천

化樂天 or 낙변화천 樂變化天 ; of the six devalokas of desire they occupy the fifth, where life lasts for 8,000 years.

니미유다 尼彌留陀 Nirodha, tr. as 멸 滅 extinction, annihilation, cessation, the third of the four noble truths, cf. 니루다 尼樓陀.

니민다(라) 尼民陀(羅) Nimindhara, or Nemiṁdhara 니민달라 尼民達羅 maintaining the circle, i.e. the outermost ring of the seven concentric ranges of a world, the 지지산 地持山 the mountains that hold the land. Also the name of a sea fish whose head is supposed to resemble this mountain.

니바라 尼波羅 Nepāla, Nepal, anciently corresponding to that part of Nepal which lies east of the Kāṭhmāṇḍū. [Eitel].

니사단 尼師壇 ; **니사단나** 尼師但那 Niṣīdana ; 녕사나낭 甯史娜曩 A thing to sit or lie on, a mat.

니사불 尼思佛 Sugatacetana, a disciple who slighted Śākyamuni in his former incarnation of 상불경 常不輕 Never despise, but who afterwards attained through him to Buddhahood.

니사다 尼沙陀 Upaniṣad, v. 오 鄔.

니살담 尼薩曇 Defined as an atom, the smallest possible particle ; but its extended form of 우파니살담분 優波尼薩曇分 suggests upaniṣad, esoteric doctrine, the secret sense of the sūtras. 니살기바일제 尼薩耆波逸提 Naiḥsargika-prāyaścittika, intp. by 사 捨 and 타 墮, the sin in the former case being forgiven on confession and restoration being made, in the latter being not forgiven because of refusal to confess and restore. Cf. 이백오십계 二百五十戒.

니야마 尼夜摩 Niyama, restraint, vow ; determination, resolve ; a degree of Bodhisattva progress, i.e. never turning back.

니연지 尼延底 Niyanti, or Niyantr. 니근지 尼近底 tr. as 집취 執取 to restrain, hold, also as 심입 深入 deeply enter, and said to be another term for 탐 貪 to desire, covet.

니위 尼衛 Nivāsana, an inner garment.

니지 尼抵 Nidhi (Praṇidhāna) ; also 니지 尼低 ; 니제 尼提 The Sanskrit is doubtful. The intp. is 원 願 vow, or 원지구만족 願志求滿足 seeking the fulfilment of resolves, or aims.

니제 尼提 ; 니타 尼陀 A scavenger.

님의 침묵 A poem collection ; a masterpiece of 만해 萬海.

<ㄷ>

다 多 Bahu ; bhūri. Many ; all ; translit. *ta*.

다 茶 Tea ; tea-leaves ; translit. *ja, jha*. 다탕 茶湯 Tea and hot water, used as offerings to spirits. 다비 茶毘 v. 다 荼. 다구마 茶矩磨 Fragrant flowers, i.e. 울금 鬱金 from Western or Central Asia for scenting wine, and for calling down the spirits. 다자타 茶闍他 Jaḍatā, coldness, apathy, stupidity.

다 荼 A bitter herb ; weeds ; to encroach ; translit. *ḍa, ḍha, dhya, dhu*. 다길니 荼吉尼 Ḍākinī, also 다지니 荼枳尼 ; 타길니 吒吉尼 ; 나길니 拏吉儞 Yakṣas or demons in general, but especially those which eat a man's vitals ; they are invoked in witchcraft to obtain power. 다비 荼毘 ; 사비 闍毘 or 사유 闍維 or 사비다 闍鼻多 ; also 야유 耶維 ; 야순 耶旬 Jhāpita ; cremation. 다구마 荼矩磨 Kuṅkuma, saffron, or turmeric, or the musk-root.

다게라 多揭羅 Tagara, 목향 木香 ; 근향 根香 putchuck, Aplotaxis auriculata, or Tabernæmontana coronaria, the shrub and its fragrant powder ; also 다가라 多伽羅 or 다가류 多伽留 or 다가루 多伽婁.

다라 多羅 Tārā, in the sense of starry, or scintillation ; Tāla, for the fan-palm ; Tara, from "to pass over," a ferry, etc. Tārā, starry, piercing, the eye, the pupil ; the last two are both Sanskrit and Chinese definitions ; it is a term applied to certain female deities and has been adopted especially by Tibetan Buddhism for certain devīs of the Tantric school. The origin of the term is also ascribed to *tar* meaning "to cross," i.e. she who aids to cross the sea of mortality. Getty, 19-27. The Chinese derivation is the eye ; the tārā devīs, either as śakti or independent, are little known outside Lamaism. Tāla is the palmyra, or fan-palm, whose leaves are used for writing and known as 구다 具多 pei-to, pattra. The tree is described as 70 or 80 feet high, with fruit like yellow rice-seeds ; the Borassus flabelliformis ; a measure of 70 feet. Taras, from to cross over, also means a ferry, and a bank, or the other shore. Also 달라 呾囉. 다라야등육사 多羅夜登陸舍 Trayastriṁśāḥ, v. 삼십삼천 三十三天. 다라수 多羅樹 ; 다라과 多羅果 ; 다라엽 多羅葉 ; 다(라)장 多(羅)掌 Tāla, the Tāla tree, its edible fruit resembling the pomegranate, its leaves being used for writing, their palm-shaped parts being made into fans. 다라보살 多羅菩薩 Tārā Bodhisattva, as a form of Kuan-yin, is said to have been produced from the eye of Kuan-yin.

다라 陀羅 Tārā, star, shining, radiating, a female deity, v. 다 多. 다라니 陀羅尼 or 다라나 陀羅那 ; 다린니 陀隣尼 Dhāraṇī. Able to lay hold of the good so that it cannot be lost, and likewise of the evil so that it cannot arise. Magical formulas, or mystic forms of prayer, or spells of Tantric order, often in Sanskrit, found in China as early as the third century A.D. ; they form a portion of the Dhāraṇīpiṭaka ; made popular chiefly through the Yogācārya 유가 瑜伽 or 밀교 密教 esoteric school. Four divisions are given, i.e. 법 法, 의 義, 주 咒, and 인다라니 忍陀羅尼 ; the 주 咒, i.e. mantra or spell, is emphasized by the 진언 眞言 Shingon sect. There are numerous treatises, e.g. 다라니집경 陀羅尼集經 ; 유가사지론 瑜伽師地論 attributed to Asaṅga, founder of the Buddhist Yoga school. 다라니보살 陀羅尼菩薩 Dhāraṇī-bodhisattva, one who has great power to protect and save. 다라나 陀羅那 Name of a yakṣa. 다라라 陀羅羅 Name of a ṛṣi. 다라표 陀羅驃 Dravya, the nine "substances" in the Nyāya philosophy, earth, water, fire, air, ether 공 空, time, space 방 方, soul 신 神, and mind 의 意. 다나 陀那 Dāna, bestow, alms ; the marks on a scale ; ādāna, another name for the ālaya-vijñāna. 다나바 陀那婆 Dānavat, name of a god. 다나가타 陀那伽他 Dānagāthā, or Dakṣiṇāgāthā, the verse or utterance of the almsgiver.

다나발지 陀那鉢底 or 시주 施主 Dānapati, almsgiver.

다령(로가야폐사야) 多齡(路迦也吠闍也) ; **제이** 帝肄 etc. Trailokyavijaya, one of the 명왕 明王 Ming Wang, the term being tr. literally as 삼세항(명왕) 三世降(明王) the Ming-Wang defeater (of evil) in the three spheres.

다마리제 多摩梨帝 Tāmralipti, or Tāmraliptī ; the modern Tumluk in the estuary of the Hugli ; also 달마률저 呾摩栗底 or 담마률저 躭摩栗底. 다마라발전단향 多摩羅跋旃檀香 Tamālapattra-candana-gandha ; a Buddha-incarnation of the 11th son of Mahābhijñā, residing N.W. of our universe ; also the name of the Buddha-incarnation of Mahāmaudgalyāyana.

다문 多聞 Bahu-śruta ; learned, one who has heard much. 다문제일 多聞第一 The chief among the Buddha's hearers : Ānanda.

다발 多髮 Keśinī, having long hair, intp. as many locks (of hair), name of a rākṣasī, v. 계 髻.

다보(여래) 多寶(如來) Prabhūtaratna, abundant treasures, or many jewels. The Ancient Buddha, long in nirvāṇa, who appears in his stūpa to hear the Buddha preach the Lotus doctrine, by his presence revealing, *inter alia*, that nirvāṇa is not annihilation, and that the Lotus doctrine is the Buddha-gospel ; b. Lotus Sūtra 보탑품 寶塔品.

다생 多生 Many births, or productions ; many reincarnations.

다재귀 多財鬼 Wealthy ghosts.

다족 多足 Many-footed, e.g. centipedes.

다체 多體 Many bodies, or forms ; many-bodied.

다타 多他 ; 다타 多咃 ; 다타 多陀 Tathā ; in such a manner, like, so, true ; it is tr. by 여 如 which has the same meanings. It is also said to mean 멸 滅 extinction, or nirvāṇa.

다타아가타 多陀阿伽陀 Tathāgata, 다타아가타(야) 多他阿伽陀(耶) ; 다타아가타 多他阿伽馱 or 다타아가도 多他阿伽度 ; 다아갈 多阿竭 or 달달아갈 怛闥阿竭 or 달살아갈 怛薩阿竭 ; 달타얼다 怛他蘖多 ; intp. by 여래 如來 Ju-lai, q.v. "thus come," or "so come" ; it has distant resemblance to the Messiah, but means one who has arrived according to the norm, one who has attained the goal (of enlightenment). It is also intp. as 여거 如去 Ju-ch'ü, he who so goes, his coming and going being both according to the Buddha-norm. It is the highest of a Buddha's titles. 다아마라발타라 多阿摩羅跋陀羅 Tamālapattra, cassia, "the leaf of the Xanthochymus pictorius, the leaf of the Laurus Cassia," [M. W.] The Malobathrum of Pliny. Also called 곽엽향 藿葉香 betony, bishopwort, or thyme ; also 적동엽 赤銅葉 copper-leaf.

다탐 多貪 Many desires.

단 or **췌** 揣 To estimate, conjecture, guess ; said also to mean 박 搏 to roll into a ball, roll together. 단식 揣食 The Indian way of eating by first rolling the food into a ball in the hand ; also 단식 團食.

단 檀 A hard wood, translit. *da, dan.* Dāna, a giver ; donation, charity, almsgiving, bestowing. 단규 檀主 Dānapati, lord of charity, a patron. 단중 檀中 Among the patrons. 단신 檀信 The faith of an almsgiver ; almsgiving and faith. 단친 檀嚫 Dakṣiṇā, cf. 달 達, the Deccan. 단가 檀家 A patron, patrons. 단도 檀度 cf. 육도 六度. The pāramitā of charity, or almsgiving. 단사 檀捨 ; 단시 檀施 Almsgiving, bestowing, charity. 단나 檀拏 ; 단다 檀陀 Daṇḍa, also 단다 但茶 a staff, club. 단림 檀林 ; 전단지림 旃檀之林 Forest of sandal-wood, or incense, a monastery. 단바라밀 檀波羅蜜 v. 육도 六度 Dānapāramitā. 단특 檀特 ; 단타 檀陀 ; 탄다락가 彈多落迦 Dantaloka, a mountain "near Varucha," with a cavern (now called Kashmiri-Ghār) where Sudāna (cf. 수須) lived, or as some say the place where Śākyamuni, when Siddhārtha, under-went his ascetic sufferings. 단이 檀耳 v. 전단이 旃檀耳 Candana. 단월 檀越 Dānapati, an almsgiver, patron ; various definitions are given, e.g. one who escapes the karma of poverty by giving. 단나 檀那 ; 다나 陀那 Dāna, to give, donate, bestow, charity, alms. 단나발지 檀那鉢底 Dānapati, v. *supra*. 단다가아란야 檀陁迦阿蘭若 Daṇḍaka-araṇyaka, Daṇḍaka forest hermits, one of the three classes of hermits, intp. as those who live on rocks by the seashore.

단 段 A piece ; a section, paragraph. Piṇḍa, a ball, lump, especially of palatable food, sustenance.

단 蔄 A round grain bin. 단의 蔄衣 A nun's skirt.

단 壇 An altar ; an open altar. In the esoteric cult it also means a maṇḍala, objects of worship grouped together.

단 端 Beginning, coming forth, elementary principles ; a point either beginning or end ; straight, proper. 단엄 端嚴 In strict propriety. 단좌 端坐 To sit straight and proper. 단심정의 端心正意 With a proper mind and regulated will, doing no evil. 단정 端正 Proper, properly ordered, rectitude, integrity.

단 旦 Dawn. 단망 旦望 The new moon and full moon, or first and fifteenth of the moon. 단과승 旦過僧 A wandering monk, who stays for a night. 단과료 旦過寮 A monastery at which he stays.

단 但 Only. 단공 但空 Only non-existence, or immateriality, a term used by T'ien-t'ai to denote the orthodox Hīnayāna system. 부단공 不但空 denotes the 통교 通教 intermediate system between the Hīnayāna and the Mahāyāna ; v. 공 空. 단도 但荼 ; 단나 單拏 Daṇḍa, a staff, club.

단 丹 Red, cinnabar colour ; a remedy, drug, elixir. 단전 丹田 The public region, approximately 2½ inches below the navel.

단 團 Round ; a ball, mass, lump ; a group, company, train-band. 단배 團拜 To kneel, or worship altogether as a company. 단식 團食 To roll rice, etc., into a ball in eating Hindu fashion.

단 單 Single, alone ; only ; the odd numbers ; poor, deficient ; a bill, cheque, etc. ; cf. 단 但. 단위 單位 A single seat, or position ; also a fixed, or listed position, or seat. 단전 單前 In front of one's listed name, i.e. in one's allotted place. 단마 單麻 The single hempseed a day to which the Buddha reduced his food before his enlightenment.

단 煅 To forge metal, work upon, calcine. 단발 煅髮 To burn up the hair of a novice, male or female.

단 斷 Uccheda ; to cut off, end, get rid of, cause to cease ; decide, decidedly. 단칠 斷七 The final seventh, i.e. the forty-ninth day of obsequies for the dead. 단복 斷伏 To cut off and overcome. 단화 斷和 To decide a dispute and cause harmony. 단선근 斷善根 To cut off, or destroy, roots of goodness. 단선천제 斷善闡提 The icchanti, or outcast, who cannot attain Buddhahood, i.e. a man of great wickedness ; or, a bodhisattva who separates himself from Buddhahood to save all beings. 단도 斷屠 To prohibit the butchering of animals — on special occasions. 단상 斷常 End or continuance, annihilation or permanence, death or immortality. 단덕 斷德 The power or virtue of bringing to an end all passion and illusion — one of the three powers of a Buddha. 단혹 斷惑 To bring delusion to an end. 단악 斷惡 To cut off evil, or wickedness. 단말마 斷末摩 Marmacchid, to cut through, wound, or reach vital parts ; cause to die. 단멸 斷滅 The heterodox teaching which denies the law of cause and effect, i.e. of karma. 단결 斷結 To snap the bonds, i.e. of passion, etc. 단육 斷肉 To forbid flesh ; meat was permitted by the Buddha under the Hīnayāna cult, but forbidden in Mahāyāna under the bodhisattva cult, also by Hīnayāna. 단견 斷見 Ucchedadarśana ; the view that death ends life, in contrast with 상견 常見 that body and soul are eternal – both views being heterodox ; also world-extinction and the end of causation. 단도 斷道 The stage in development when illusion is cut off. 단두죄 斷頭罪 The "lop off the head" sins, i.e. adultery, stealing, killing, lying, sins which entail immediate exclusion from the order. 단식 斷食 To fast ; voluntarily to starve oneself.

단청 丹靑 Dan-cheong. Literally "red and blue", the principal colors used. Cinnabar and blue-green style of paint used to decorate the temple eaves.

달 闥 An inner door (especially of the women's rooms) ; a recess, corner ; translit. *da, dha*, etc. 달바 闥婆 Gandharvas, v. 건 乾.

달 怛 Distressed ; pity. Translit. for *t, ta, tan*, etc. 달타 怛他 Tadyathā, 소위 所謂 whereas, as here follows. 달타게다 怛他揭多 or 달타벽다 怛他蘗多 ; 달타갈다 怛陀竭多 ; 달타의다 怛佗議多 ; 달살아갈 怛薩阿竭 or 달달아갈 怛闥阿竭 Tathāgata, v. 다 多. 달리야달라사 怛利耶怛喇舍 or 怛利耶怛喇奢 Trayastriṁśāḥ, the thirty-three heavens of Indra, cf. 다 多. 달찰나 怛刹那 Tṛṇa, a length of time consisting of 120 kṣaṇa, or moments ; or "a wink," the time for twenty thoughts. 달리지벌리가 怛哩支伐離迦 Tricīvaraka, the three garments of a monk. 달라마세 怛囉麽洗 Caitra-māsa, tr. as the 정월 正月 or first month ; [M. W.] gives March-April. 달삭가 怛索迦 Takṣaka, name of a dragon-king. 달박 怛縛 Tvam, thou, you. 달라야야 怛羅夜耶 Traya, three, with special reference to the Triratna. 달다 怛茶 Daṇḍa, cf. 단나 檀拏 a staff. 달나 怛那 idem 단나 檀那 Dāna, alms, giving, charity. 달발나 怛鉢那 Tapana, burning, scorched ; parched grain. 달마 怛麽 Ātman, an ego, or self, personal, permanent existence, both 인아 人我 and 법아 法我 q.v.

달 達 Permeate, penetrate, reach to, transfer, inform, promote, successful, reaching everywhere ; translit. *ta, da, dha*, etc.

달 呾 Ta. Call ; stutter ; translit. *ta*. 달니야타 呾你也他 or 呾儞也他 Tadyathā, i.e. 소위 所謂, as or what is said or meant, it means, i.e. etc. 달찰나 呾刹那 Tatkṣaṇa, "the 2250th part of an hour." [Eitel]. 달라건 呾喇健 Talekān, "an ancient kingdom on the frontiers of Persia," its modern town is Talikhan. 달차시라 呾叉始羅 ; 축찰시라 竺刹尸羅 Takṣaśilā, "ancient kingdom and city, the Taxila of the Greeks, the region near Hoosum Abdaul in Lat. 35° 48 N., Long. 72° 44 E." [Eitel]. 달마률지 呾摩栗底 or 담마률지 躭摩栗底 ; 다마리제 多摩梨帝 Tāmralipti (or Tāmraliptī), the modern Tamluk near the mouth of the Hooghly, formerly "the principal emporium for the trade with Ceylon and China." [Eitel]. 달라사 呾羅斯 Talas, or Taras ; "(1) an ancient city in Turkestan 150 li west of Ming bulak (according to Hiuentsang). (2) A river which rises on the mountains west of Lake Issikoul and flows into a large lake to the north-west." [Eitel]. 달밀 呾蜜 Termed, or Tirmez, or Tirmidh. "An ancient kingdom and city on the Oxus Lat. 37° 5 N., Long. 67° 6 E." [Eitel].

달다 達多 Devadatta, v. 제 提.

달라비다 達羅毘茶 Draviḍa, a district on the east coast of the Deccan.

달뢰라마 達賴喇嘛 Dalai Lama, the head of the Yellow-robe sect of Tibetan Buddhism, and chief of the nation.

달리사야 達梨舍耶 Darśana, seeing, a view, views, viewing, showing ; 견 見 v. above, 달리슬치 達利瑟致 Dṛṣṭi.

달리슬치 達利瑟致 Dṛṣṭi, 견 見 seeing, viewing, views, ideas, opinions ; especially seeing the seeming as if real, therefore incorrect views, false opinions, e.g. 아견 我見 the false idea of a permanent self ; cf. Darśana, 달리사야 達梨舍耶.

달마 達磨 Dharma ; also 달마 達摩 ; 달마 達麼 ; 달이마야 達而麻耶 ; 담마 曇摩 ; 타마 馱摩 tr. by 법 法. Dharma is from dhara, holding, bearing, possessing, etc. ; and means "that which is to be held fast or kept, ordinance, statute, law, usage, practice" ; "anything right." [M. W.] It may be variously intp. as (1) characteristic, attribute, predicate ; (2) the bearer, the transcendent substratum of single elements of conscious life ; (3) element, i.e. a part of conscious life ; (4) nirvāṇa, i.e. the Dharma *par excellence*, the object of Buddhist teaching ; (5) the absolute, the real ; (6) the teaching or religion of Buddha ; (7) thing, object, appearance. Also, Tamo, or Bodhidharma, the twenty-eighth Indian and first Chinese patriarch, who arrived in China A.D. 520, the reputed founder of the Ch'an or Intuitional School in China. He is described as son of a king in southern India ; originally called Bodhitara. He arrived at Canton, bringing it is said the sacred begging-bowl, and settled in Loyang, where he engaged in silent meditation for nine years, whence he received the title of wall-gazing Brahman 벽관바라문 壁觀婆羅門, though he was a kṣatriya. His doctrine and practice were those of the "inner light", independent of the written word, but to 혜가 慧可 Hui-k'o, his successor, he commended the Laṅkāvatāra-sūtra as nearest to his views. There are many names with Dharma as initial : Dharmapāla, Dharmagupta, Dharmayaśas, Dharmaruci, Dharmarakṣa, Dharmatrāta, Dharmavivardhana, etc. 달마종 達磨宗 The Tamo, or Dharma sect, i.e. the 선종 禪宗 Meditation, or Intuitional School. 달마기 達磨忌 The anniversary of Bodhidharma's death, fifth of the tenth month. 달마다도 達磨馱都 Dharmadhātu, tr. 법계 法界 "the element of law or of existence" [M. W.] ; all psychic and non-psychic processes (64 dharmas), with the exception of rūpa-skandha and mano-ayatana (11), grouped as one dharma element ; the storehouse or matrix of phenomena, all-embracing totality of things ; in the Tantric school, Vairocana divided into Garbhadhātu (material) and Vajradhātu (indestructible) ; a relic of the Buddha.

달바 達婆 Gandharva, v. 건 乾.

달수 達水 Also 달지 達池, Anavatapta, v. 아 阿.

달수 達須 Dasyu, barbarians ; demons ; also 달수 達首 ; 달가 達架. Used for Sudarśana, v. 수 須.

달친(나) 達嚫(拏) Dakṣiṇā, a gift or fee ; acknowledgment of a gift ; the right hand (which receives the gift) ; the south. Eitel says it is an ancient name for Deccan, "situated south of Behar" and that it is "often confounded with 대진국 大秦國 the eastern Roman empire." Also 달친 達櫬 or 達親 or 達襯 ; 달친 噠嚫 ; 대친 大嚫 ; 단친 檀嚫.

담 潭 A deep, a pool. 담은 潭恩 Profound grace, or favour.

담 噉 Bite, eat, feed on ; a bite, morsel ; to lure. 담월 噉月 To gnaw the moon.

담 曇 Clouds covering the sun, spreading clouds ; translit. *dh* in dharma 담마 曇摩, 담마 曇磨, 담무 曇無 ; v. 달 達 and 법 法. Dharma is also the initial character for a number of names of noted Indian monks, e.g. 담마국다 曇磨毱多 ; 달마구제 達摩瞿諦 ; 담무덕 曇無德 Dharmagupta, founder of a school, the 담무덕부 曇無德部 which flourished in Ceylon A.D. 400. Also Dharmajātayaśas, Dharmakāla, Dharmākara, Dharmamitra, Dharmanandi, Dharmapriya, Dharmarakṣa, Dharmaruci, Dharmasatya, Dharmayaśas, etc. 담화 曇花 The udumbara tree, v. 우 優.

담 湛 Deep, clear, placid, to soak. 잠연 湛然 Chan-jan, the sixth T'ien-t'ai patriarch, also known as 형계 荊溪 Ching-ch'i ; died A.D. 784 ; author of many books.

담 譚 Gossip, talk ; to boast. 담바 譚婆 Translit. of a term defined as eaters of dog's flesh.

담 擔 To carry, undertake ; a load ; also 단 担. 담보라 擔步羅 ; 탐포라 耽餔羅 Tāmbūla, betel, Piper Betel. Eitel says Djambalā, *Citrus acida*.

담 談 To talk, chat, discuss. 담림 談林 A monastic schoolroom. 담공설유 談空說有 To discuss non-existence and talk of existence ; i.e. to discuss the meaning of reality ; in discussing non-existence to talk of the existing ; it is a phrase expressing confusion of ideas or argument. 담의 談義 To discuss the meaning. 담의 談議 To discuss and consult, or deliberate.

담 憺 Tranquil, content. 담박 憺怕 Tranquil and inactive, retired.

답 答 A bamboo hawser, to draw out, to respond, reply, return thanks. 답향 答香 To stick in incense sticks, as a monk does in acknowledgment of those of worshippers. 답마 答摩 Tamas, darkness, gloom, grief, anger, suffering. 답리마 答哩磨 idem 달마 達磨 dharma. 답말소벌나 答秣蘇伐那 Tāmasavana, a monastery "Dark forest," possibly that of Jālandhara where the "fourth synod" under Kaniṣka held its sessions ; "at the junction of the Vipāśā and Śatadru," i.e. Beas and Sutlej. [Eitel].

답 沓 Ripple, babble ; join. Translit. *t*, *d*, etc., e.g. 답파 沓婆 ; 답파마라 沓婆摩羅 Dravya Mallaputra, an arhat who was converted to the Mahāyāna faith.

답 荅 To undertake ; translit. *ta*, *da*. Tathāgata, v. 다 多. 답섭포밀복라첩슬타제 荅攝蒲密卜羅牒瑟吒諦 Daśabhūmipratiṣṭhite, "Thou who art established in the ten stages" — said to the Tathāgatas in invocations. 답말소벌나 荅秣蘇伐那 Tāmasavana, 암림 闇林 the dark forest. "A monastery situated at the junction of the Vipāśā and Śatadru, 50 li south-east of Tchīnapati. It is probably identical with the so-called Jālandhara monastery in which the IV Synod under Kaniṣka held its sessions." [Eitel].

답 踏 Tread, trample. 답상 踏床 A footstool.

당 幢 Dhvaja ; Ketu. A pennant, streamer, flag, sign. 당번 幢幡 A flag, banner. 당상 幢相 A sign, symbol, i.e. the monk's robe.

당 堂 Prāsāda. A hall, temple, court. 당상 堂上 ; 당두 堂頭 The head of the hall, the abbot of a monastery. 당주 堂主 The head of a hall on specific occasion. 당사 堂司 The controller of the business in a monastery. 당탑 堂塔 Temples and monasteries in general. 당달 堂達 The distributor of the liturgies, etc.

당 唐 Rude, wild ; the T'ang dynasty A.D. 618-907. 당삼장 唐三藏 The T'ang Tripiṭaka, a name for Hsüan-tsang. 당승 唐僧 T'ang monks, especially Hsüan-tsang as the T'ang monk. 당연 唐捐 To cast away as valueless.

당 當 Suitable, adequate, equal to ; to bear, undertake ; ought ; proper ; to regard as, as ; to pawn, put in place of ; at, in the future. 당위즉묘 當位卽妙 According to its place, or application, wonderful or effective ; e.g. poison as poison, medicine as medicine. 당래 當來 That which is to come, the future, the future life, etc. 당분 當分 According to condition, position, duty, etc. 당기 當機 To suit the capacity or ability, i.e. or hearers, as did the Buddha ; or avail oneself of an opportunity. 당기중 當機衆 Those hearers of the Lotus who were adaptable to its teaching, and received it ; one of the 사중 四衆 q.v. 당양 當陽 In the sun, in the light. 당체 當體 The present body, or person ; the body before you, or in question ; in body, or person. 당체즉공 當體卽空 idem 체공 體空 Corporeal entities are unreal, for they disintegrate.

대 帶 A girdle, belt, bandage, tape, appendage ; connect ; implicate ; take along. 대도와 帶刀臥 ; 대도수 帶刀睡 To take one's sword to bed, which being worn on the left side compels the wearer to sleep on the right, or proper side. 대탑존 帶塔尊 ; 대탑덕보살 帶塔德菩薩 Maitreya, bearer of the pagoda.

대 臺 A terrace, platform, stage, look-out ; also written 태 台. 대좌 臺座 A platform, or stage, for an image.

대 代 Instead of, in place of, acting for, for ; e.g. 대향 代香 to offer incense in place of another ; a generation, v. 세대 世代.

대 大 Mahā. 마하 摩訶 ; 마하 麽賀. Great, large, big ; all-pervading, all-embracing ; numerous 다 多 ; surpassing 승 勝 ; mysterious 묘 妙 ; beyond comprehension 불가사의 不可思議 ; omnipresent 체무부재 體無不在. The elements, or essential things, i.e. (a) 삼대 三大 The three all-pervasive qualities of the 진여 眞如 q.v. : its 체 體, 상 相, 용 用 substance, form, and functions, v. 기신론 起信論. (b) 사대 四大 The four tanmātra or elements, earth, water, fire, air (or wind) of the 구사론 俱舍論. (c) 오대 五大 The five, i.e. the last four and space 공 空, v. 대일경 大日經. (d) 육대 六大 The six elements, earth, water, fire, wind, space (or ether), mind 식 識. Hīnayāna, emphasizing impersonality 인공 人空, considers these six as the elements of all sentient beings ; Mahāyāna, emphasizing the unreality of all things 법공 法空, counts them as elements, but fluid in a flowing stream of life, with mind 식 識 dominant ; the esoteric sect emphasizing non-production, or non-creation, regards them as universal and as the Absolute in differentiation. (e) 칠대 七大 The 능엄경 楞嚴經 adds 견 見 perception, to the six above named to cover the perceptions of the six organs 근 根.

대 對 To respond, reply, face, opposite, pair, compare ; the opposite of ; agreeing with. 대고중 對告衆 The intermediary for the Buddha's address to the assembly, especially Ānanda. 대양 對揚 One who drew out remarks or sermons from the Buddha. 대기 對機 To respond to the opportunity, or the capacity of hearers. 대법 對法 The corresponding law, the philosophy in the Buddha's teaching, the Abhidharma ; comparison of cause and effect. 대법종 對法宗 The Abhidharma sect. 대법장 對法藏 The third section of the Tripiṭaka, the śāstras, or Abhidharma. 대치 對治 To respond or face up to and control. 대촉례 對觸禮 To worship, or pay respects, face to face. 대수 對首 Face to face (confession).

대 待 To wait, treat, behave to. 대대 待對 Relationship, in relation with, one thing associated with another.

대 戴 To wear (on the head) ; to bear, sustain. 대탑 戴塔 To have a pagoda represented on the head, as in certain images ; a form of Maitreya, āryastūpamahāśrī, 대탑길상 戴搭吉祥 ; also applied to Kuan-yin, etc.

대가다연나 大迦多衍那 Mahākātyāyana or Kātyāyana 마하가전연 摩訶迦旃延 ; 가연 迦延, v. 마 摩 and 가 迦. (1) A disciple of Śākyamuni. (2) Name of many persons. 대가섭 大迦葉 Mahākāśyapa, v. 마하가섭 摩訶迦葉.

대각 大覺 The supreme bodhi, or enlightenment, and the enlightening power of a Buddha. 대각세존 大覺世尊 The World-honoured One of the great enlightenment, an appellation of the Buddha. 대각모 大覺母 The mother of the great enlightenment, an appellation of Mañjuśrī. 대각금선 大覺金仙 The great enlightened golden ṛṣi, a name given to Buddha in the Sung dynasty.

대감(선사) 大鑑(禪師) The great mirror, posthumous title of the sixth 선 禪 Ch'an(Zen) patriarch, 혜능 慧能 Hui-nêng, imperially bestowed in A.D. 815.

대강 大綱 The main principles of Buddhism, likened to the great ropes of a net.

대거 大車 The great bullock-cart in the parable of the burning house, i.e. Mahāyāna, v. Lotus sūtra.

대겁 大劫 Mahākalpa. The great kalpa, from the beginning of a universe till it is destroyed and another begins in its place. It has four kalpas or periods known as vivarta 성겁 成劫 the creation period ; vivarta-siddha 주겁 住劫 the appearance of sun and moon, i.e. light, and the period of life, human and general ; saṁvarta 괴겁 壞劫 or 멸겁 滅劫 destruction first by fire, then water, then fire, then deluge, then a great wind, i.e. water during seven small kalpas, fire during 56 and wind one, in all 64 ; saṁvartatthāhi 증멸겁 增滅劫 total destruction gradually reaching the void. A great kalpa is calculated as eighty small kalpas and to last 1,347,000,000 years. 대겁보녕 大劫寶寧 Kapphiṇa or Mahākapphiṇa. v. 겁빈나 劫賓那.

대경 大經 The great sūtra, i.e. the 2-chüan 불설무량수경 佛說無量壽經, so-called by the Pure-land sect and by T'ien-t'ai, the Amida sūtra being the 소본 小本 smaller sūtra ; cf. 대본 大本 and 대일경 大日經. 대경권 大經卷 A term for the heart.

대계 大界 The area of a vihāra or monastic establishment. 대계외상 大界外相 Four characters often placed on the boundary stones of monasterial grounds.

대계 大戒 The complete commandments of Hīnayāna and Mahāyāna, especially of the latter.

대고왕 大高王 Abhyudgata-rāja. Great august monarch, name of the kalpa in which Śubha-vyūha 묘장엄왕 妙莊嚴王, who is not known in the older literature, is to be reborn as a Buddha.

대고해 大苦海 The great bitter sea, or great sea of suffering, i.e. of mortality in the six gati, or ways of incarnate existence.

대공 大空 The great void, or the Mahāyāna pari-nirvāṇa, as being more complete and final than the nirvāṇa of Hīnayāna. It is used in the Shingon sect for the great immaterial or spiritual wisdom, with its esoteric symbols ; its weapons, such as the vajra ; its samādhis ; its sacred circles, or maṇḍalas, etc. It is used also for space, in which there is neither east, west, north, nor south.

대공작왕 大孔雀王 The mayūra, or "peacock" 명왕 明王, v. 공작왕 孔雀王. There are seven sets of spells connected with him.

대관정 大灌頂 The greater baptism, used on special occasions by the Shingon sect, for washing away sin and evil and entering into virtue ; v. 관정경 灌頂經.

대광명왕 大光明王 The Great-Light Ming-wang, Śākyamuni in a previous existence, when king of Jambudvīpa, at Benares. There his white elephant, stirred by the sight of a female elephant, ran away with him into the forest, where he rebuked his mahout, who replied, "I can only control the body not the mind, only a Buddha can control the mind." Thereupon the royal rider made his resolve to attain bodhi and become a Buddha. Later, he gave to all that asked, finally even his own head to a Brahman who demanded it, at the instigation of an enemy king. 대광음천 大光音天 Ābhāsvara. The third of the celestial regions in the second dhyāna heaven of the form realm ; v. 사선천 四禪天. 대광보조 大光普照 The great light shining everywhere, especially the ray of light that streamed from between the Buddha's eyebrows, referred to in the Lotus sūtra. 대광명왕관음 大光明王觀音 One of the six forms of Kuan-yin.

대광지삼장 大廣智三藏 He of great, wide wisdom in the Tripiṭaka, a title of Amogha 아목거 阿目佉.

대교 大教 The great teaching. (1) That of the Buddha. (2) Tantrayāna. The mahātantra, yoga, yogācārya, or tantra school which claims Samantabhadra as its founder. It aims at ecstatic union of the individual soul with the world soul, Īśvara. From this result the eight great powers of Siddhi (Aṣṭa-mahāsiddhi), namely, ability to (1) make one's body lighter (laghiman) ; (2) heavier (gariman) ; (3) smaller (aṇiman) ; (4) larger (mahiman) than anything in the world

; (5) reach any place (prāpti) ; (6) assume any shape (prākāmya) ; (7) control all natural laws (īśitva) ; (8) make everything depend upon oneself (vaśitva) ; all at will (v. 여의신 如意身 and 신족 神足). By means of mystic formulas (tantras or dhāraṇīs), or spells (mantras), accompanied by music and manipulation of the hands (mudrā), a state of mental fixity characterized neither by thought nor the annihilation of thought, can be reached. This consists of six-fold bodily and mental happiness (yoga), and from this results power to work miracles. Asaṅga compiled his mystic doctrines *circa* A.D. 500. The system was introduced into China A.D. 647 by Hsüan-tsang's translation or the Yogācārya-bhūmi-śāstra 유가사지론 瑜伽師地論 ; v. 유 瑜. On the basis of this, Amoghavajra established the Chinese branch of the school A.D. 720 ; v. 아목 阿目. This was popularized by the labours of Vajrabodhi A.D. 732 ; v. 금강지 金剛智. 대교경 大教經 idem 대금강정경 大金剛頂經. 대교망 大教網 The net of the great teaching, which saves men from the sea of mortal life.

대교과 大教科 The great teaching studies course in seminary 강원 講院

대구치나 大拘絺那 Mahākauṣṭhila, 마하구치라 摩訶俱絺羅 ; 마하구지라 摩訶俱祉羅, an eminent disciple of Śākyamuni, maternal uncle of Śāriputra, reputed author of the Saṅgītiparyāya śāstra.

대권 大權 The great potentiality ; or the great power of Buddhas and bodhisattvas to transform themselves into others, by which e.g. Māyā becomes the mother of 1,000 Buddhas, Rāhula the son of 1,000 Buddhas, and all beings are within the potency of the dharmakāya. 대권선경 大權善經 is an abbreviation of 혜상보살문대권선경 慧上菩薩問大權善經. 대권수리보살 大權修利菩薩 A bodhisattva – protector of monasteries, depicted as shading his eyes with his hand and looking afar, said to have been a Warden of the Coast under the emperor Aśoka.

대규환지옥 大叫喚地獄 Mahāraurava. The hell of great wailing, the fifth of the eight hot hells. Also 대규 大叫 ; 대호규 大號叫 ; 대호 大呼.

대근용 大勤勇 Greatly zealous and bold – a title of Vairocana.

대기 大機 The great opportunity, or Mahāyāna method of becoming a bodhisattva.

대길상천 大吉祥天 The good-fortune devīs, and also devas, also called 공덕천 功德天, concerning whom there are several sūtras. 대길상금강 大吉祥金剛 idem 금강수 金剛手. 대길상명보살 大吉祥明菩薩 The sixth bodhisattva in the second row of the Garbhadhātu Kuan-yin group. 대길대명보살 大吉大明菩薩 The fifth ditto. 대길상변보살 大吉祥變菩薩 The sixth in the third row.

대나 大拏 Sudāna, 수달나 須達拏 ; 수대나 須大拏 ; 소달나 蘇達拏 ; i.e. Śākyamuni as a prince in a former life, when he forfeited the throne by his generosity.

대단 大壇 A great altar, the chief altar.

대당내전록 大唐內典錄 A catalogue of the Buddhist library in the T'ang dynasty A.D. 664. 대당서역기 大唐西域記 The Record of Western Countries by Hsüan-tsang of the T'ang dynasty ; v. 서 西.

대덕 大德 Bhadanta. 바단타 婆檀陀 Most virtuous, a title of honour of a Buddha ; in the Vinaya applied to monks.

대도사 大度師 Great leader across mortality to nirvāṇa, i.e. Buddha, or Bodhisattva.

대도사 大導師 The great guide, i.e. Buddha, or a Bodhisattva.

대도심 大道心 One who has the mind of or for supreme enlightenment, e.g. a bodhisattva-mahāsattva.

대둔사 大芚寺 Dae-dun-sa. A temple located in Gurim-ri Samsan-myeon Haenam-gun Jeollanam-do in Korea. The 22nd parish headquarters of Korean Jogye Order.

대력왕 大力王 King powerful, noted for his unstinted generosity. Indra to test him appeared as a Brahman and asked for his flesh ; the king ungrudgingly cut off and gave him his arm. Indra was then Devadatta, King Powerful was Śākyamuni ; v. 보살장경하 菩薩藏經下. 대력금강 大力金剛 The mighty "diamond" or Vajra-mahārāja in the Garbhadhātu group, a fierce guardian and servant of Buddhism, see below.

대련화 大蓮華 Puṇḍarīka, 분다리 分陀利 ; 분리 芬利 ; 분다 奔荼 the great white lotus ; the last of the eight cold hells is so called. 대련화법장계 大蓮華法藏界 The great Lotus heaven in the Paradise of the West. 대련화지혜삼마지지 大蓮華智慧三摩地智 The wisdom of the great lotus, samādhi-wisdom, the penetrating wisdom of Amitābha.

대로변생 大路邊生 Born by the highway side, v. 주나 周那 Cunda ; also 순타 純陀.

대론 大論 idem 대지도론 大智度論. 대논사 大論師 Mahāvādin, Doctor of the Śāstras, a title given to eminent teachers, especially of the Sāṅkhya and Vaiśeṣika schools.

대룡권현 大龍權現 The Bodhisattva who, having attained the 대지 大地 stage, by the power of his vow transformed himself into a dragon-king, 서역기 西域記 1.

대루탄경 大樓炭經 A sūtra, also called 기세경 起世經, on Buddhist cosmology, 6 chüan, tr. by 법립 法立 Fa-li and others ; 누탄 樓炭 is a Sanskrit term meaning 성패 成敗 creation and destruction.

대륜금강 大輪金剛 One of the thirty-three bodhisattvas in the 금강수 金剛手 court of the Garbhadhātu group, destroyer of delusion. Also 대륜명왕 大輪明王.

대림사 大林寺 Mahāvana-saṅghārāma 마하벌나가람마 摩訶伐那伽藍摩 "The monastery of the great forest," S. of Moṅgali. 대림정사 大林精舍 The Veṅuvana monastery, called 죽림정사 竹林精舍 or 죽림정사 竹林精寺, and 죽원 竹苑, Veṅuvana vihāra, in the Karaṇḍa-veṅuvana, near Rājagṛha, a favourite resort of Śākyamuni.

대만 大滿 Great, full, or complete ; tr. of mahāpūrṇa, king of monster birds or garuḍas who are enemies of the nāgas or serpents ; he is the vehicle of Viṣṇu in Brahmanism. 대만원의 大滿願義 One of the sixteen bodhisattvas of the southern quarter, born by the will of Vairocana.

대만(다라) 大曼(荼羅) The great maṇḍala ; one of four groups of Buddhas and bodhisattvas of the esoteric school . The esoteric word 아 阿 "a" is styled the great maṇḍala-king.

대멸제금강지 大滅諦金剛智 The first two of the 삼덕 三德 three Buddha-powers ; they are (a) his principle of nirvāṇa, i.e. the extinction of suffering, and (b) his supreme or vajra wisdom.

대명 大命 The great order, command, destiny, or fate, i.e. life-and-death, mortality, reincarnation.

대명왕 大明王 The angels or messengers of Vairocana, v. 명왕 明王. 대명삼장성교목록 大明三藏聖教目錄 The "Great Ming" dynasty catalogue of the Tripiṭaka, made during the reign of the emperor Yung Lo ; it is the catalogue of the northern collection. 대명백신보살 大明白身菩薩 The great bright white-bodied bodhisattva, sixth in the first row of the Garbhadhātu Kuan-yin group. 대명속입장제집 大明續入藏諸集 Supplementary miscellaneous collection of Buddhist books, made under the Ming dynasty A.D. 1368-1644.

대목건련 大目乾連 Mahāmaudgalyāyana ; v. 마하목건련 摩訶目犍連.

대몽 大夢 The great dream, "the dream of life," this life, the world.

대무량수경 大無量壽經 idem 대경 大經 q.v.

대바라문 大婆羅門 The great Brāhmaṇa, applied to the Buddha, who though not of Brahman caste was the embodiment of Brahman virtues. 대바라문경 大婆羅門經 A sūtra dealing with this aspect. 대견고바라문 大堅固婆羅門 The great reliable Brāhmaṇa, i.e. Śākyamuni in a previous life when minister of a country ; there is a sūtra of this name.

대바라밀 大波羅蜜 The great pāramitās, or perfections, of bodhisattvas, i.e. the ten pāramitās above the 팔지 八地.

대반야(경) 大般若(經) The Mahā-prajñā-pāramitā-sūtra. 대반야공양 大般若供養 The worship of a new copy of the sūtra when finished, an act first attributed to Hsüan-tsang. 대반야(바라밀다)경 大般若(波羅蜜多)經 Mahā-prajñā-pāramitā sūtra, said to have been delivered by Śākyamuni in four places at sixteen assemblies, i.e. Gṛdhrakūṭa near Rājagṛha (Vulture Peak) ; Śrāvastī ; Paranirmitavaśavartin, and Veluvana (= Veṅuvana, in Pāli) near Rājagṛha (Bamboo Garden). It consists of 600 chüan as translated by Hsüan-tsang. Parts of it were translated by others under various titles and considerable differences are found in them. It is the fundamental philosophical work of the Mahāyāna school, the formulation of wisdom, which is the sixth pāramitā.

대반열반 大般涅槃 Mahāparinirvāṇa, explained by 대입멸식 大入滅息 the great, or final entrance into extinction and cessation ; or 대원적입 大圓寂入 great entrance into perfect rest ; 대멸도 大滅度 great extinction and passing over (from mortality). It is interpreted in Mahāyāna as meaning the cessation or extinction of passion and delusion, of mortality, and of all activities, and deliverance into a state beyond these concepts. In Mahāyāna it is not understood as the annihilation, or cessation of existence ; the reappearance of Dīpaṃkara 연등 然燈 (who had long entered nirvāṇa) along with Śākyamuni on the Vulture Peak supports this view. It is a state above all terms of human expression. See the Lotus sūtra and the Nirvāṇa sūtra. 대반열반경 大般涅槃經 The Mahā-parinirvāṇa sūtras, commonly called the 열반경 涅槃經 Nirvāṇa sūtras, said to have been delivered by Śākyamuni just before his death. The two Hīnayāna versions are found in the 장아함유행경 長阿含遊行經. The Mahāyāna has two Chinese versions, the northern in 40 chüan, and the southern, a revision of the northern version, in 36 chüan. Fa-hsien's version is styled 대반니원경 大般泥洹經 6 chüan. Treatises on the sūtra are 대반니원경후분 大般泥洹經後分 2 chüan tr. by Jñānabhadra ; 대반니원경소 大般泥洹經疏 33 chüan ; 대반니원경론 大般泥洹經論 1 chüan by Vasubandhu, tr. by Bodhidharma.

대방광 大方廣 Mahāvaipulya ; cf. 대방등 大方等 The great vaipulyas, or sūtras of Mahāyāna. 방광 方廣 and 방등 方等 are similar in meaning. Vaipulya is extension, spaciousness, widespread, and this is the idea expressed both in 광 廣 broad, widespread, as opposed to narrow, restricted, and in 등 等 levelled up, equal everywhere, universal. These terms suggest the broadening of the basis of Buddhism, as is found in Mahāyāna. The Vaipulya works are styled sūtras, for the broad doctrine of universalism, very different from the traditional account of his discourses, is put into the mouth of the Buddha in wider, or universal aspect. These sūtras are those of universalism, of which the Lotus 법화 法華 is an outstanding example. The form Vaitulya instead of Vaipulya is found in some Kashgar MSS. of the Lotus, suggesting that in the Vetulla sect lies the origin of the Vaipulyas, and with them of Mahāyāna, but the evidence is inadequate. 대방광불 大方廣佛 The 본존 本尊 fundamental honoured one of the 화엄경 華嚴經, described as the Buddha who has realized the universal law. 대방광불화엄경 大方廣佛華嚴經 Buddhāvataṁsaka-mahāvaipulya-sūtra ; the Avataṁsaka, Hua-yen, or Kegon sūtra ; tr. by Buddha-bhadra and others A.D. 418-420. The various translations are in 60, 80, and 40 chüan, v. 화엄경 華嚴經. 대방광여래비밀장경 大方廣如來秘密藏經 Tathāgata-garbha-sūtra, tr. A.D. 350-431, idem 대방등여래장경 大方等如來藏經, tr. by Buddhabhadra A.D. 417-420, 1 Chüan.

대방등 大方等 Mahāvaipulya or Vaipulya 대방광 大方廣 ; 비불략 毗佛畧. They are called 무량의경 無量義經 sūtras of infinite meaning, or of the infinite ; first introduced into China by Dharmarakṣa (A.D. 266-317). The name is common to Hīnayāna and Mahāyāna, but chiefly claimed by the latter for its special sūtras as extending and universalizing the Buddha's earlier preliminary teaching. v. 대방광 大方廣 and 방등 方等. 대방등대집경 大方等大集經 Mahāvaipulya-mahāsaṁnipāta-sūtra, tr. A.D. 397-439, said to have been preached by the Buddha "from the age of 45 to 49 ... to Buddhas and bodhisattvas assembled from every region, by a great staircase made between the world of desire and that of form." [B.N.] Another version was made by Jñānagupta and others in A.D. 594 called 대방등대집현호경 大方等大集賢護經. 대방등정왕설경 大方等頂王說經 Vimalakīrti-nirdeśa-sūtra, tr. by Dharmarakṣa A.D. 265-316.

대방편 大方便 Mahopāya ; the great appropriate means, or expedient method of teaching by buddhas and bodhisattvas ; v. 방편 方便.

대백산개불모 大白傘蓋佛母 The "mother of Buddhas" with her great snow-white (radiant) umbrella, emblem of her protection of all beings ; there are two dhāraṇī-sūtras that bear this name and give her description, 불정산개불모 佛頂傘蓋佛母 and 불설산개불모총지다라니경 佛說傘蓋佛母總持陀羅尼經. 대백광신 大白光神 ; 울다라가신 鬱多羅迦神 Uttaraka. The deva of the Himālayas, one of the retinue of the 십이신 十二神. 대백우거 大白牛車 The great white-bullock cart of the Lotus sūtra, the Mahāyāna, as contrasted with the deer-cart and goat-cart of śrāvakas and pratyeka-buddhas, i.e. of Hīnayāna. 대백화 大白華 The great mandāra 만다라 曼陀羅 flower, also called 대백단화 大白團華. 대백의 大白衣 Pāṇḍaravāsinī, the great white-robed one, a form of Kuan-yin all in white, with white lotus, throne, etc., also called 백의관음 白衣觀音 or 백처관음 白處觀音.

대번뇌지법 大煩惱地法 The six things or mental conditions producing passion and delusion : stupidity, excess, laziness, unbelief, confusion, discontent (or ambition) ; v. 구사론 俱舍論 4.

대범 大梵 Mahābrahmāṇas ; the third Brahmaloka, the third region of the first dhyāna. Mahābrahman ; the great Brahma, 대범천 大梵天 ; it is also a title of one of the six Kuan-yin of the T'ien-t'ai sect.

대범천 大梵天 Mahābrahman ; Brahmā ; 발라흡마 跋羅吸摩 ; 파라하마 波羅賀磨 ; 범람마 梵覽摩 ; 범천왕 梵天王 ; 범왕 梵王 ; 범 梵. Eitel says : "The first person of the Brahminical Trimūrti, adopted by Buddhism, but placed in an inferior position, being looked upon not as Creator, but as a transitory devatā whom every Buddhistic saint surpasses on obtaining bodhi. Notwithstanding this, the Saddharma-puṇḍarīka calls Brahmā 'the father of all living beings'" 일체중생지부 一切衆生之父. Mahābrahman is the unborn or uncreated ruler over all, especially according to Buddhism over all the heavens of form, i.e. of mortality. He rules over these heavens, which are of threefold form : (a) Brahmā (lord), (b) Brahma-purohitas (ministers), and (c) Brahma-pāriṣadya (people). His heavens are also known as the middle dhyāna heavens, i.e. between the first and second dhyānas. He is often represented on the right of the Buddha. According to Chinese accounts the Hindus speak of him (1) as born of Nārāyaṇa, from Brahmā's mouth sprang the brahmans, from his arms the kṣatriyas, from his thighs the vaiśyas, and from his feet the śūdras ; (2) as born from Viṣṇu ; (3) as a trimūrti, evidently that of Brahmā, Viṣṇu, and Śiva, but Buddhists define Mahābrahmā's dharmakāya as Maheśvara (Śiva), his sambhogakāya as Nārāyaṇa, and his nirmāṇakāya as Brahmā. He is depicted as riding on a swan, or drawn by swans. 대범여의천 大梵如意天 idem 대범천 大梵天 The term is incorrectly said by Chinese interpreters to mean freedom from sexual desire. He is associated with Vairocana, and with fire. v. also 시기 尸棄. 대범천왕 大梵天王 Mahābrahmā devarāja, king of the eighteen Brahmalokas.

대법 大法 The great Dharma, or Law (of Mahāyāna salvation). 대법만 大法慢 Intellectual pride, arrogance through possession of the Truth. 대법왕 大法王 Sudharma-rāja, King of the Sudharma Kinnaras, the horse-headed human-bodied musicians of Kuvera. 대법라 大法螺 The Great Law conch, or Mahāyāna bugle. 대법고 大法鼓 The Great Law drum ; v. 대법고경 大法鼓經 Mahābherī-hāraka-parivarta ; tr. by Guṇabhadra A.D. 420-479. 대법우 大法雨 The raining, i.e. preaching, of the Mahāyāna.

대변천 大辯天 Sarasvatī 대변재천(녀) 大辯才天(女) ; 대변(재)공덕천 大辯(才)功德天 ; 살라사박지 薩羅娑縛底 ; 살라산지 薩羅酸底 A river, "the modern Sursooty" ; the goddess of it, who "was persuaded to descend from heaven and confer her invention of language and letters on the human race by the sage Bhārata, whence one of her names is Bhāratī" ; sometimes assumes the form of a swan ; eloquence, or literary elegance is associated with her. Cf. M.W. Known as the mother of speech, eloquence, letters, and music. Chinese texts describe this deity sometimes as male, but generally as female, and under several forms. As "goddess of music and poetry" she is styled 묘음천 妙音天 or 미음천 美音天 ; 묘음락천 妙音樂天 ; 묘음불모 妙音佛母. She is represented in two forms, one with two arms and a lute, another with eight arms. Sister of Yama. "A consort of both Brahmā and Mañjuśrī," Getty. In Japan, when with a lute, Benten is a form of Sarasvatī, colour white, and riding a peacock. Tib. sbyaṅs-can-ma, or ṅag-gi-lha-mo ; M. kele-yin iikin tegri ; J. ben-zai-ten, or benten.

대보 大寶 Great Jewel, most precious thing, i.e. the Dharma or Buddha-law ; the bodhisattva ; the fire-altar of the esoteric cult. 대보방 大寶坊 the "great precious region," described in the 대집 大集 sūtra as situated between the world of desire and the world of form. 대보마니 大寶摩尼 The great precious maṇi, or pure pearl, the Buddha-truth. 대보법왕 大寶法王 Mahāratna-dharma-rāja. Title of the reformer of the Tibetan church, founder of the Yellow sect, b. A.D. 1417, worshipped as an incarnation of Amitābha, now incarnate in every Bogdo gegen Hutuktu reigning in Mongolia. He received this title in A.D. 1426. v. 종객파 宗喀巴 Tsong-kha-pa. 대보해 大寶海 The "great precious ocean" (of the merit of Amitābha). 대보적경 大寶積經 Mahāratnakūṭa-sūtra. Collection of forty-nine sūtras, of which thirty-six were translated by Bodhiruci and collated by him with various previous translations. 대보화 大寶華 The great precious flower, a lotus made of pearls. 대보화왕 大寶華王 King of jewel-lotuses, i.e. the finest of such gem-flowers. 대보화왕좌 大寶華王座 A throne of such. 대보장 大寶藏 The great precious treasury, containing the gems of the Buddha-truth.

대보리(심) 大菩提(心) The great bodhi, i.e. Mahāyāna-enlightenment or Buddha-enlightenment, as contrasted with the inferior bodhi of the śrāvaka and pratyeka-buddha. 대보리당 大菩提幢 The banner of great bodhi, an esoteric symbol of Buddha-enlightenment.

대보살 大菩薩 Bodhisattva-mahāsattva, a great Bodhisattva.

대보적경 大寶積經 The sūtra of this name (Mahāratnakūṭa) tr. by Bodhiruci (in abridged form) and others.

대본 大本 The great, chief, or fundamental book or text. T'ien-t'ai takes the 무량수경 無量壽經 as the major of the three Pure-land sūtras, and the 아미타경 阿彌陀經 as the 소본 小本 minor.

대불가기자부 大不可棄子部 Āvantikās. The great school of the son who "could not be abandoned" (a subdivision of the Saṁmatīyas 삼미지 三彌底), whose founder when a newborn babe was abandoned by his parents.

대불선지법 大不善地法 The two great characteristics of the evil state, 무참무괴 無慚無愧 no sense of shame or disgrace, shameless.

대불정 大佛頂 A title of the esoteric sect for their form of Buddha, or Buddhas, especially of Vairocana of the Vajradhātu and Śākyamuni of the Garbhadhātu groups. Also, an abbreviation of a dhāraṇī as is 대불정경 大佛頂經 of a sūtra, and there are other 대불정 大佛頂 scriptures.

대비 大悲 Mahākaruṇā, "great pity" ; i.e. greatly pitiful, a heart that seeks to save the suffering ; applied to all Buddhas and bodhisattvas ; especially to Kuan-yin. 대비삼매 大悲三昧 The samādhi of great pity, in which Buddhas and bodhisattvas develop their great pity. 대비대수고 大悲代受苦 Vicarious suffering (in purgatory) for all beings, the work of bodhisattvas. The same idea in regard to Kuan-yin is conveyed in 대비천수(지)옥 大悲千手(地)獄. 대비주 大悲呪 Another name of the 천수경 千手經 or 천수다라니 千手陀羅尼 containing a spell against lust. 대비단 大悲壇 The altar of pity, a term for the Garbhadhātu maṇḍala, or for the Śākyamuni group. 대비궁 大悲弓 The bow of great pity. Pity, a bow in the left hand ; wisdom 지 智, an arrow in the right hand. 사팔지응 四八之應 The thirty-two or thirty-three manifestations of the All-pitiful Kuan-yin responding to every need. 대비보현 大悲普現 Great pity universally manifested, i.e. Kuan-yin, who in thirty-three manifestations meets every need. 대비생심삼매야 大悲生心三昧耶 The samādhi of Maitreya. 대비경 大悲經 Mahākaruṇā-puṇḍarīka sūtra, tr. by Narendrayaśas and Dharmaprajñā A.D. 552, five books. 대비자 大悲者 The great pitiful one, Kuan-yin. 대비태장 大悲胎藏 The womb — store of great pity, the fundamental heart of bodhi in all ; this womb is likened to a heart opening as an eight-leaved lotus, in the centre being Vairocana, the source of pity. 대비(태장)만다라 大悲(胎藏)曼茶羅 The maṇḍala of the above. 대비태장삼매 大悲胎藏三昧 The samādhi in which vairocana evolves the group, and it is described as the "mother of all Buddha-sons." 대비보살 大悲菩薩 Kuan-yin, the Bodhisattva of great pity. 대비관(세)음 大悲觀(世)音 Kuan-yin, the greatly pitiful regarder of (earth's) cries. 대비개주문 大悲鎧冑門 A degree of samādhi in which Vairocana produced the Bodhisattva Vajrapāla 금강호보살 金剛護菩薩 who protects men like a helmet and surrounds them like mail by his great pity. 대비천제 大悲闡提 The greatly pitiful icchantika, who cannot become a Buddha till his saving work is done, i.e. Kuan-yin, Ti-tsang.

대비구 大比丘 Great bhikṣu, i.e. one of virtue and old age ; similar to 대화상 大和尙.

대비로자나 大毘盧遮那 Mahāvairocana, v. 대일 大日.

대사 大師 1. Great teacher, or leader, one of the ten titles of a Buddha. 2. Grand Master (title follows name, as in '서산대사').

대사 大士 Mahāsattva. 개사 開士 A great being, noble, a leader of men, a bodhisattva ; also a śrāvaka, a Buddha ; especially one who 자리이타 自利利他 benefits himself to help others. 대사첨 大士籤 Bamboo slips used before Kuan-yin when the latter is consulted as an oracle.

대사 大寺 Mahāvihāra. The Great Monastery, especially that in Ceylon visited by Fa-hsien about A.D. 400, when it had 3,000 inmates ; v. 비하라 毘訶羅.

대사(인연) 大事(因緣) For the sake of a great cause, or because of a great matter — the Buddha appeared, i.e. for changing illusion into enlightenment. The Louts interprets it as enlightenment ; the Nirvāṇa as the Buddha-nature ; the 무량수경 無量壽經 as the joy of Paradise.

대사문 大沙門 Mahāśramaṇa. The great shaman, i.e. Buddha ; also any bhikṣu in full orders. 대사문통 大沙門統 A director of the order appointed by Wên Ti of the Sui dynasty, A.D. 581-618.

대사저인 大死底人 One who has swept away completely all illusions, or all consciousness ; also 대휴헐저 大休歇底.

대살차니건자 大薩遮尼犍子 Mahāsatya-nirgrantha. An ascetic who is said to have become a disciple of the Buddha.

대삼말다 大三末多 Mahāsaṁmata. The first of the five kings of the Vivarta kalpa (성겁오왕 成劫五王), one of the ancestors of the Śākya clan.

대상 大相 Mahārūpa ; great form. The kalpa of Mahābhijñā-jñānābhibhu, who is to appear as Buddha in a realm called Saṁbhava.

대상국사 大相國寺 The great aid-the-dynasty monastery at Kaifeng, Honan, founded in A.D. 555, first named 건국 建國, changed *circa* 700 to the above ; rebuilt 996, repaired by the Kin, the Yüan, and Ming emperors, swept away in a Yellow River flood, rebuilt under Shun Chih, restored under Ch'ien Lung. 대상간 大相看 The reception by an abbot of all his monks on the first day of the tenth moon.

대상기 大祥忌 The great propitious anniversary, i.e. a sacrifice every third year.

대상장 大象藏 Great elephant (or nāga) treasure, an incense supposed to be produced by nāgas or dragons fighting.

대생주 大生主 Mahāprajāpatī 마하파사파제 摩訶波闍婆提, great "lady of the living," the older translation being 대애도 大愛道 the great way (or exemplar) of love ; also 중주 衆主 head of the community (of nuns), i.e. Gautamī, the aunt and nurse of Śākyamuni, the first nun. She is to be reborn as a Buddha named Sarvasattvapriyadarśana.

대선 大仙 Maharṣi. Great sages, applied to Buddhist saints as superior to ordinary "immortals" ; also to śrāvakas, and especially to Buddha ; 대선계 大仙戒 are the Buddha's laws or commands. Vasiṣṭha 파사슬차 婆私瑟侘 was one of the seven ṛṣis 대선 大仙 of Brahmanic mythology.

대선 大船 The great ship of salvation — Mahāyāna. 대선사 大船師 Its captain, Buddha.

대선리 大善利 The great benefit that results from goodness, also expressed as 대선대리 大善大利 implying the better one is the greater the resulting benefit. 대선지법 大善地法 The ten mental conditions for cultivation of goodness, being a part of the forty-six methods mentioned in the 구사론 俱舍論 4 ; faith, zeal, renunciation, shame (for one's own sin), shame (for another's sin), no desire, no dislike, no harm, calmness, self-control. v. 대지법 大地法. 대선지식 大善知識 Well acquainted with the good ; great friends.

대섭수 大攝受 The great all-embracing receiver — a title of a Buddha, especially Amitābha.

대성 大成 Mahāsaṁbhava. Great completion. The imaginary realm in which (in turn) appeared 20,000 koṭīs of Buddhas all of the same title, Bhīśma-garjita-ghoṣa-svara-rāja.

대성 大聖 The great sage or saint, a title of a Buddha, or a bodhisattva of high rank ; as also are 대성세존 大聖世尊 and 대성주 大聖主 the great holy honoured one, or lord. For 대성천 大聖天 idem 대성환희천 大聖歡喜天 v. 환희천 歡喜天, on whom there are three works. 대성금강야차 大聖金剛夜叉 one of the five 대명왕 大明王. For 대성묘길상 大聖妙吉祥 and 대성만수실리 大聖曼殊室利 see Mañjuśrī ; there are two works under the first of these titles, one under the second, and one under 대성문수 大聖文殊.

대세(지보살) 大勢(至菩薩) Mahāsthāma or Mahāsthāmaprāpta 마하나발 摩訶那鉢. A Bodhisattva representing the Buddha-wisdom of Amitābha ; he is on Amitābha's right, with Avalokiteśvara on the left. They are called the three holy ones of the western region. He has been doubtfully identified with Maudgalyāyana. Also 세지 勢至. 대세불 大勢佛 The Buddha of mighty power (to heal and save), a Buddha's title.

대소 大召 A temple and its great bell in Lhasa, Tibet, styled 노목랑 老木郎, built when the T'ang princess became the wife of the Tibetan king Ts'an-po and converted Tibet to Buddhism.

대소(명왕) 大笑(明王) Vajrahāsa 발절라타가파 跋折羅吒訶婆 The great laughing Ming-wang, v. 명왕 明王.

대소이승 大小二乘 The two vehicles, Mahāyāna and Hīnayāna ; v. 대승 大乘 and 소승 小乘.

대소자옥 大燒炙獄 v. 대염열 大炎熱 Pratāpana, above.

대수 大樹 Great trees, i.e. bodhisattvas, cf. 삼초 三草. 대수선인 大樹仙人 Mahāvṛkṣa ṛṣi, the ascetic Vāyu, who meditated so long that a big tree grew out of his shoulders. Seeing a hundred beautiful princesses he desired them ; being spurned, he was filled with hatred, and with a spell turned them into hunchbacks ; hence Kanyākubja, v. 갈 羯 or 계 罽 the city of hump-backed maidens ; its king was Brahmadatta(?). v. 서역기 西域記 5. 대수긴나라 大樹緊那羅 The King of the mahādruma Kinnaras, Indra's musicians, who lives on Gandha-mādana. His sūtra is 대수긴나라왕소문경 大樹緊那羅王所問經, 4 chüan, tr. by Kumārajīva.

대수화(재) 大水火(災) Mahāpralaya ; the final and utter destruction of a universe by (wind), flood, and fire.

대승 大僧 A fully ordained monk, i.e. a bhikṣu as contrasted with the śramaṇa. 대승정 大僧正 The Director or Pope of monks ; an office under Wu-ti, A.D. 502-550, of the Liang dynasty, for the control of the monks. Wên Ti, 560-7, of the Ch'ên dynasty appointed a 대승통 大僧統 or Director over the monks in his capital.

대승 大乘 Mahāyāna ; also called 상승 上乘 ; 묘승 妙乘 ; 승승 勝乘 ; 무상승 無上乘 ; 무상상승 無上上乘 ; 불악승 不惡乘 ; 무등승 無等乘 ; 무등등승 無等等乘 ; 마하연 摩訶衍 The great yāna, wain, or conveyance, or the greater vehicle in comparison with the 소승 小乘 Hīnayāna. It indicates Universalism, or Salvation for all, for all are Buddha and will attain bodhi. It is the form of Buddhism prevalent in Tibet, Mongolia, China, Korea, Japan, and in other places in the Far East. It is also called Northern Buddhism. It is interpreted as 대교 大教 the greater teaching as compared with 소교 小教 the smaller, or inferior. Hīnayāna, which is undoubtedly nearer to the original teaching of the Buddha, is unfairly described as an endeavour to seek nirvāṇa through an ash-covered body, an extinguished intellect, and solitariness ; its followers are śrāvakas and pratyeka-buddhas (i.e. those who are striving for their own deliverance through ascetic works). Mahāyāna, on the other hand, is described as seeking to find and extend all knowledge, and, in certain schools, to lead all to Buddhahood. It has a conception of an Eternal Buddha, of Buddhahood as Eternal (Ādi-Buddha), but its especial doctrines are, *inter alia*, (a) the bodhisattvas 보살 菩薩, i.e. beings who deny themselves final Nirvāṇa until, according to their vows, they have first saved all the living ; (b) salvation by faith in, or invocation of the Buddhas or bodhisattvas ; (c) Paradise as a nirvāṇa of bliss in the company of Buddhas, bodhisattvas, saints, and believers. Hīnayāna is sometimes described as 자리 自利 self-benefiting, and Mahāyāna as 자리이타 自利利他 self-benefit for the benefit of others, unlimited altruism and pity being the theory of Mahāyāna. There is a further division into one-yāna and three-yānas ; the triyāna may be śrāvaka, pratyeka-buddha, and bodhisattva, represented by a goat, deer, or bullock cart ; the one-yāna is that represented by the Lotus School as the one doctrine of the Buddha, which had been variously taught by him according to the capacity of his hearers, v. 방편 方便. Though Mahāyāna tendencies are seen in later forms of the older Buddhism, the foundation of Mahāyāna has been attributed to Nāgārjuna 용수 龍樹. "the characteristics of this system are an excess of transcendental speculation tending to abstract nihilism, and the substitution of fanciful degrees of meditation and contemplation (v. Samādhi and Dhyāna) in place of the practical asceticism of the Hīnayāna school." [Eitel 68-9]. Two of its foundation books are the 기신론 起信論 and the 묘법연화경 妙法蓮華經, but a large number of Mahāyāna sūtras are ascribed to the Buddha.

대승경 大乘經 Mahāyāna sūtras, the Sūtra-piṭaka. Discourses ascribed to the Buddha, presumed to be written in India and translated into Chinese. These are divided into five classes corresponding to the Mahāyāna theory of the Buddha's life : (1) Avataṁsaka, 화엄 華嚴, the sermons first preached by Śākyamuni after enlightenment ; (2) Vaipulya, 방등 方等 ; (3) Prajñā Pāramitā, 반야 般若 ; (4) Saddharma Puṇḍarīka, 법화 法華 ; and last (5) Mahāparinirvāṇa, 열반 涅槃. Another list of Mahāyāna sūtras is 반야 般若 ; 보적 寶積 ; 대집 大集 ; 화엄 華嚴 and 열반 涅槃. The sūtras of Hīnayāna are given as the Āgamas 아함 阿含, etc.

대승계 大乘戒 The commands or prohibitions for bodhisattvas and monks, also styled 보살계 菩薩戒 ; 삼취정계 三聚淨戒 ; 원돈계 圓頓戒 and other titles according to the school. The 범망경 梵網經 gives ten weighty prohibitions and forty-eight lighter ones ; v. also 대승계경 大乘戒經.

대승교 大乘教 v. 대승 大乘 ; for 대승교구부 大乘教九部 v. 구부 九部.

대승금강 大勝金剛 Another name for 금륜불정 金輪佛頂, one of the incarnations of vairocana represented with twelve arms, each hand holding one of his symbols. Also 대전륜왕 大轉輪王 ; 금강수 金剛手.

대승기 大乘基 "Mahāyāna-fundament," title of 규기 窺基 K'uei-chi, a noted disciple of Hsüan-tsang ; known also as 대승법사 大乘法師.

대승기신론 大乘起信論 Mahāyāna-śraddhotpāda-śāstra, attributed to Aśvaghoṣa 마명 馬鳴 (without sufficient evidence), tr. by Paramārtha A.D. 553 and Śikṣānanda between 695-700 ; there are nineteen commentaries on it. It is described as the foundation work of the Mahāyāna. Tr. into English by Timothy Richard and more correctly by T. Suzuki as *The Awakening of Faith.*

대승기신론소 大乘起信論疏 "Commentary on the Treatise on the Awakening of Faith." Written by Won-hyo.

대승능가경유식론 大乘楞伽經唯識論 Viṁśatikā-vijñaptimātratāsiddhi-śāstra. A title of one of three treatises by Vasubandhu, tr. A.D. 508-535, 대승유식론 大乘唯識論 tr. 557-569, and 유식이십론 唯識二十論 tr. by Hsüan-tsang in 661 being the other two.

대승론 大乘論 Abhidharma of the Mahāyāna, the collection of discourses on metaphysics and doctrines.

대승묘경 大乘妙經 idem 법화경 法華經 the Louts sūtra.

대승무상법 大乘無上法 The supreme Mahāyāna truth, according to the 능가경 楞伽經, is that of ultimate reality in contrast with the temporary and apparent ; also reliance on the power of the vow of the bodhisattva.

대승무작대계 大乘無作大戒 The Mahāyāna great moral law involving on external action ; a T'ien-t'ai expression for the inner change which occurs in the recipient of ordination ; it is the activity within ; also 대승무작원돈계 大乘無作圓頓戒 ; 무표대계 無表大戒.

대승방등경전 大乘方等經典 The sūtras and scriptures of the Mahāyāna, their doctrines being 방정 方正 square and correct and 평등 平等 for all equally, or universal.

대승법사 大乘法師 a title for 규기 窺基 v. 대승기 大乘基.

대승법상교 大乘法相教 and 대승파상교 大乘破相教 v. 법상교 法相教.

대승사과 大乘四果 The four fruits, or bodhisattva stages in Mahāyāna, the fourth being that of a Buddha : 수다원 須陀洹 śrota-āpanna, 사다함 斯陀含 sakṛdāgāmin, 아나함 阿那含 anāgāmin, and 아라한 阿羅漢 arhan. This is a 통교 通教 category.

대승선근계 大乘善根界 The Mahāyāna good roots realm, a name for the Amitābha Pure-land of the West.

대승순계 大乘純界 The lands wholly devoted to Mahāyāna, i.e. China and Japan, where in practice there in no Hīnayāna.

대승심 大乘心 The mind or heart of the Mahāyāna ; seeking the mind of Buddha by means of Mahāyāna.

대승이종성불 大乘二種成佛 The two Mahāyāna kinds of Buddhahood : (1) that of natural purity, of every one has the inherent nature ; (2) that attained by practice.

대승인 大乘因 Mahāyāna "cause" is variously described as the mind of enlightenment 보리심 菩提心 ; or the reality behind all things 제법실상 諸法實相.

대승장엄경론 大乘莊嚴經論 Mahāyānasūtrālaṁkāra-ṭīkā. An exposition of the teachings of the Vijñāna-vāda School, by Asaṅga, tr. A.D. 630-3 by Prabhākaramitra. 13 chüan.

대승정왕경 大乘頂王經 Vimalakīrti-nirdeśa-sūtra, is the Sanskrit title of a work of which there exist six translations, one made by Upaśūnya A.D. 502-557.

대승종 大乘宗 The school of Mahāyāna, attributed to the rise in India of the Mādhyamika, i.e. the 중관 中觀 or 삼론 三論 school ascribed to Nāgārjuna, and the Yoga 유가 瑜伽 or Dharmalakṣaṇa 법상 法相 school, the other schools being Hīnayāna. In China and Japan the 구사 俱舍 and 성실 成實 are classed as Hīnayāna, the rest being Mahāyāna, of which the principal schools are 율 律, 법상 法相, 삼론 三論, 화엄 華嚴, 천태 天台, 진언 眞言, 정토 淨土, 선 禪 q.v.

대승천 大乘天 "Mahāyāna-deva," a title given to 현장 玄奘 Hsüan-tsang, who was also styled 목차제바 木叉提婆 Mokṣa-deva.

대시태자 大施太子 ; **대시보살** 大施菩薩. The great princely almsgiver, i.e. Śākyamuni in a previous life ; also 능시태자 能施太子 ; 능시보살 能施菩薩. 대시회 大施會 ; 무차대회 無遮大會 Mokṣa-mahā-pariṣad ; a great gathering for almsgiving to all, rich and poor, nominally quinquennial.

대신 大身 The great body, i.e. the nirmāṇakāya, or transformable body 화신 化身 of a Buddha. Also, Mahākāya, a king of garuḍas.

대신(심) 大信(心) Great of firm faith in, or surrender to Buddha, especially to Amitābha. 대신심해 大信心海 A heart of faith great as the ocean.

대신력 大神力 Supernatural or magical powers. 대신주 大神呪 are dhāraṇī spells or magical formulae connected with these powers. 대신왕 大神王 The great deva-king, Mahākāla, the great black one, (1) title of Maheśvara, i.e. Śiva ; (2) a guardian of monasteries, with black face, in the dining hall ; he is said to have been a disciple of Mahādeva, a former incarnation of Śākyamuni.

대심력 大心力 The great mind and power, or wisdom and activity of Buddha. 대심해 大心海 Great mind ocean, i.e. omniscience.

대아 大我 The greater self, or the true personality 진아 眞我. Hīnayāna is accused of only knowing and denying the common idea of a self, or soul, whereas there is a greater self, which is a nirvāṇa self. It especially refers to the Great Ego, the Buddha, but also to any Buddha ; v. 대일경 大日經 1, etc., and 열반경 涅槃經 23.

대악상 大惡象 The great wild elephant, i.e. the untamed heart.

대안달라 大安達羅 Mahendra, or Mahendrī, or Rājamahendrī. A city near the mouth of the Godavery, the present Rājamundry. 대안위 大安慰 The great comforter, or pacifier – a Buddha's title.

대애도 大愛道 Mahāprajāpatī, 마하파사파제 摩訶波闍波提 Gautama's aunt and foster-mother, also styled Gotamī or Gautamī, the first woman received into the order. There are sūtras known by her name. 대애 大愛 is also a name for the sea-god.

대야 大夜 The great night, i.e. that before the funeral pyre of monk is lighted ; also 태야 逮夜 ; 숙야 宿夜.

대어 大魚 Makara 마갈(나) 摩竭(羅) a monster fish.

대역룡 大域龍 Dignāga, or Mahā-Dignāga, also known as 진나 陳那 Jina, founder of the medieval school of Buddhist logic about the fifth century A.D. His works are known only in Tibetan translations. [Winternitz].

대염(불) 大念(佛) Invoking Buddha with a loud voice ; meditating on Buddha with continuous concentration.

대염법 大染法 The great taint, or dharma of defilement, sex-attraction, associated with 애염명왕 愛染明王 Eros, the god of love.

대염열 大炎熱 Pratāpana or Mahātāpana ; the hell of great heat, the seventh of the eight hot hells.

대오 탄문 大悟坦文 Dae-o Tan-mun(900-975). A monk of the Goryeo dynasty in Korea. He was the first royal preceptor.

대왕 大王 Mahārāja 마하라야 摩賀羅惹. Applied to the four guardians of the universe, 사대천왕 四大天王.

대요설 大樂說 Mahāpratibhāna. A bodhisattva in the Lotus sūtra, noted for pleasant discourse. 대요불공 大樂不空 ; 대요금강(살타) 大樂金剛(薩埵) "Unceasing great joy," a Shingon name for the second of its eight patriarchs, P'u-hsien, v. 금강살타 金剛薩埵. There are works under this title.

대용 大勇 Āryaśūra. Also 성용 聖勇. The great brave, or Ārya the brave. An Indian Buddhist author of several works. 대용맹보살 大勇猛菩薩 A guardian ruler in the Garbhadhātu group called Mahānīla, the Great Blue Pearl, or perhaps sapphire, which in some way is associated with him.

대우 大愚 The "greatly ignorant," name of a monastery and title of its patriarch, of the Ch'an(Zen) or intuitive school.

대우거 大牛車 The great ox cart in the Lotus sūtra parable of the burning house, i.e. Mahāyāna. 대우음 大牛音 Krośa ; the distance of the lowing of a great ox, the "eighth" (more correctly fourth) part of a yojana ; v. 구로 狗盧.

대운광명사 大雲光明寺 A monastery for Uigur Manichaeans, ordered to be built by 대종 代宗 A.D. 765.

대웅 大雄 The great hero – a Buddha's title, indicating his power over demons. 대웅봉 大雄峯 Great cock peak, any outstanding peak.

대웅(보)전 大雄(寶)殿 Dae-ung-(bo)-jeon. Buddha Hall ; Main Hall ; Dharma Hall ; Main Buddha Hall ; Main Sanctuary. A main building in a temple where Buddha resides. Literally, "Hall of the Great Hero." Basilica of the Great Hero.

대원 大願 The great vow, of a Buddha, or bodhisattva, to save all the living and bring them to Buddhahood. 대원업력 大願業力 The forty-eight vows and the great meritorious power of Amitābha, or the efficacy of his vows. 대원청정보토 大願淸淨報土 The Pure Reward-Land of Amitābha, the reward resulting from his vows. 대원선 大願船 The great vow boat, i.e. that of Amitābha, which ferries the believer over the sea of mortality to the Pure Land.

대원각 大圓覺 Great and perfect enlightenment, Buddha-wisdom. 대원경지 大圓鏡知 Great perfect mirror wisdom, i.e. perfect all-reflecting Buddha-wisdom. 대원경지관 大圓鏡知觀 A meditation on the reflection of the perfect Buddha-wisdom in every being, that as an image may enter into any number of reflectors, so the Buddha can enter into me and I into him 입아아입 入我我入.

대원수명왕 大元帥明王 The great commander, one of the sixteen 명왕 明王 q.v., named Āṭavika 아타박가 阿吒薄迦 ; 아타박구 阿吒薄倶 ; 아타박개 阿吒薄皆. There are four sūtras, chiefly spells connected with his cult.

대위덕 大威德 Mahātejas. Of awe-inspiring power, or virtue, able to suppress evil-doers and protect the good. A king of garuḍas, v. 가 迦. Title of a 명왕 明王 protector of Buddhism styled 대위덕자 大威德者 ; 대위덕존 大威德尊 ; 대위덕명왕 大威德明王 ; 백광변조왕 百光扁照王 ; there are symbols, spells, esoteric words, sūtras, etc., connected with this title.

대은교주 大恩敎主 The Lord of great grace and teacher of men, Buddha.

대음계입 大陰界入 Four fundamentals, i.e. the 사대 四大, 오음 五陰, 십팔계 十八界, and 십이입 十二入 q.v.

대음광 大飮光 Mahākāśyapa q.v., he who "drank in light" (with his mother's milk), she having become radiant with golden-hued light through obtaining a golden-coloured pearl, a relic of Vipaśyin, the first of the seven former Buddhas ; it is a false etymology.

대응공 大應供 The great worshipful — one of the ten titles of a Buddha.

대의 大意 The general meaning or summary of a sūtra or śāstra. Also, the name of a youth, a former incarnation of the Buddha ; to save his nation from their poverty, he plunged into the sea to obtain a valuable pearl from the sea-god who, alarmed by the aid rendered by Indra, gave up the pearl ; v. 경 經 tr. by Guṇabhadra of Liu Sung dynasty, 1 chüan.

대의 大衣 The monk's patch-robe, made in varying grades from nine to twenty-five patches.

대의왕 大義王 ; **대의성** 大義城 The king, or city, of all ideas, or aims, i.e. the heart as mind.

대의왕 大醫王 Great Lord of healing, an epithet of Buddhas and bodhisattvas.

대인다라좌 大因陀羅座 The throne of Indra, whose throne is four-square to the universe ; also 금강륜좌 金剛輪座. 대인다라단 大因陀羅壇 Indra-altar of square shape. He is worshipped as the mind-king of the universe, all things depending on him.

대인법계 大忍法界 The great realm for learning patience, i.e. the present world.

대인상인 大人相印 Sealed with the sign of manhood, i.e. of the religious life.

대일 大日 Vairocana, or Mahāvairocana 대일여래 大日如來 ; 변조여래 遍照如來 ; (마하)비로자나 (摩訶)毘盧遮那 ; 대일각왕 大日覺王 The sun, "shining everywhere." The chief object of worship of the Shingon sect in Japan, "represented by the gigantic image in the temple at Nara." [Eliot]. There he is known as Dai-nichi-nyorai. He is counted as the first, and according to some, the origin of the five celestial Buddhas (dhyāni-buddhas, or jinas). He dwells quiescent in

Arūpadhātu, the Heaven beyond form, and is the essence of wisdom (bodhi) and of absolute purity. Samanta-bhadra (P'u-hsien) is his dhyāni-bodhisattva. The 대일경 大日經 "teaches that Vairocana is the whole world, which is divided into Garbhadhātu (material) and Vajradhātu (indestructible), the two together forming Dharmadhātu. The manifestations of Vairocana's body to himself — that is, Buddhas and Bodhisattvas — are represented symbolically by diagrams of several circles." [Eliot]. In the 금강계 金剛界 or vajradhātu maṇḍala he is the centre of the five groups. In the 태장계 胎藏界 or Garbhadhātu he is the centre of the eight-leaf (lotus) court. His appearance, symbols, esoteric word, differ according to the two above distinctions. Generally he is considered as an embodiment of the Truth 법 法, both in the sense of Dharmakāya 법신 法身 and Dharmaratna 법보 法寶. Some hold vairocana to be the dharmakāya of Śākyamuni 대일여석가동일불 大日與釋迦同一佛 but the esoteric school denies this identity. Also known as 최고현광안장여래 最高顯廣眼藏如來, the Tathāgata who, in the highest, reveals the far-reaching treasure of his eye, i.e. the sun. 대일대성부동명왕 大日大聖不動明王 is described as one of his transformations. Also, a śramaṇa of Kashmir (contemporary of Padma-saṁbhava) ; he is credited with introducing Buddhism into Khotan and being an incarnation of Mañjuśrī ; the king Vijaya Saṁbhava built a monastery for him. 대일공 大日供 A meeting for the worship of Vairocana. 종 宗 The cult of Vairocana especially associated with the 태장계 胎藏界 Garbhakośadhātu, or phenomenal world. 대일경 大日經 The Vairocana sūtra, styled in full 비로자나성불신변가지경 毘盧遮那成佛神變加持經, tr. in the T'ang dynasty by Śubhākarasiṁha 선무외 善無畏 in 7 chüan, of which the first six are the text and the seventh instructions for worship. It is one of the three sūtras of the exoteric school. Its teaching pairs with that of the 금강정경 金剛頂經. There are two versions of notes and comments on the text, the 대일경소 大日經疏 20 chüan, and 대일경의소 大日經義疏 14 chüan ; and other works, e.g. 대일경의석 大日經義釋 ; 대일경부사의소 大日經不思議疏 ; 대일경의궤 大日經義軌 in four versions with different titles. The cult has its chief vogue in Japan. 대일각왕 大日覺王 Vairocana, the king of bodhi.

대자 大姉 Elder sister, a courtesy title for a lay female devotee, or a nun.

대자 大慈 Great mercy, or compassion. 대자대비 大慈大悲 Great mercy and great pity, characteristics of Buddhas and bodhisattvas, i.e. kindness in giving joy and compassion in saving from suffering. It is especially applied to Kuan-yin. 대자존 大慈尊 The honoured one of great kindness, Maitreya. 대자은사 大慈恩寺 The monastery of "Great Kindness and Grace," built in Ch'ang-an by the crown prince of T'ai Tsung A.D. 648, where Hsüan-tsang lived and worked and to which in 652 he added its pagoda, said to be 200 feet high, for storing the scriptures and relics he had brought from India. 대자은사삼장 大慈恩寺三藏 "Tripiṭaka of the Ta-T'zŭ-En-Ssŭ" is one of his titles.

대자생보살 大慈生菩薩 The director or fosterer of pity among all the living, i.e. the fifth in the 제개장 除蓋障 court of the Garbhadhātu group. Also 대자기 大慈起 ; 자발생 慈發生 ; 자민혜 慈愍慧 ; 자념금강 慈念金剛. His Sanskrit name is translit. 매달리야비수나얼다 昧怛利也毘廋拏蘖多.

대자재 大自在 Īśvara, self-existent, sovereign, independent, absolute, used of Buddhas and bodhisattvas. 대자재천 大自在天 Maheśvara, 마혜수습벌라 摩醯首濕伐羅 or Śiva, lord of the present chiliocosm, or universe ; he is described under two forms, one as the prince of demons, the other as divine, i.e. 비사사 毘舍闍 Piśāca-maheśvara and 정거 淨居 Śuddhāvāsa-maheśvara or Śuddhodana-maheśvara. As Piśāca, head of the demons, he is represented with three eyes and eight arms, and riding on a white bull ; a bull or a liṅga being his symbol. The esoteric school takes him for the transformation body of Vairocana, and as appearing in many forms, e.g. Viṣṇu, Nārāyaṇa (i.e. Brahmā), etc. His wife (śakti) is Bhīmā, or 대자재천부 大自在天婦. As Śuddhāvāsa, or Pure dwelling, he is described as a bodhisattva of the tenth or highest degree, on the point of entering Buddhahood. There is dispute as to whether both are the same being, or entirely different. The term also means the sixth or highest of the six desire-heavens. 대자재궁 大自在宮 The abode of Maheśvara at the apex of the Form-realm. Also, the condition or place from which the highest type of bodhisattva proceeds to Buddhahood, whence it is also styled 정거천 淨居天 the pure abode heaven.

대장(경) 大藏(經) The Tripiṭaka ; the Buddhist canon. 대장일람 大藏一覽 "The Tripiṭaka at a Glance" in 10 chüan by 진실 陳實 Ch'ên Shih of the Ming dynasty. 대장목록 大藏目錄 A catalogue of the Korean canon in 3 chüan.

대장엄 大莊嚴 Mahāvyūha ; great fabric ; greatly adorned, the kalpa or Buddha-aeon of Mahākāśyapa. 대장엄세계 大莊嚴世界 The great ornate world ; i.e. the universe of Ākāśagarbha Bodhisattva 허공장보살 虛空藏菩薩 ; it is placed in the west by the sūtra of that name, in the east by the 대척경 大隻經 12. 대장엄경 大莊嚴經 Vaipulya-mahāvyūha-sūtra, tr. by Divākara, T'ang dynasty, 12 chüan ; in which the Buddha describes his life in the Tuṣita heaven and his descent to save the world. 대장엄경론 大莊嚴經論 or 대장엄논경 大莊嚴論經. Sūtrālaṅkāra-śāstra. A work by Aśvaghoṣa, tr. by Kumārajīva A.D. 405, 15 chüan.

대재(회) 大齋(會) A feast given to monks.

대재해탈복 大哉解脫服 Great! the robe of deliverance — verses in praise of the cassock, from the 선견론 善見論, sung on initiation into the order.

대적정 大寂定 The samādhi which the Tathāgata enters, of perfect tranquillity and concentration with total absence of any perturbing element ; also parinirvāṇa. Also 대적실삼매 大寂室三昧 ; 대적정삼마지 大寂靜三摩地. 대적법왕 大寂法王 The great tranquil or nirvāṇa dharma-king, i.e. Vairocana. 대적멸 大寂滅 Parinirvāṇa ; the great nirvāṇa.

대적화 大赤華 Mahāmañjūṣaka 마하만주사 摩訶曼珠沙 or rubia cordifolia, from which madder is made.

대전 大顚 Ta Tien, the appellation of a famous monk and writer, named 보통 寶通 Pao-t'ung, whom tigers followed ; he died at 93 years of age in A.D. 824 ; author of 반야바라밀다심경 般若波羅蜜多心經 and 금강경석의 金剛經釋義.

대전륜왕 大轉輪王 v. 대승금강 大勝金剛. 대전륜불정 大轉輪佛頂 idem 불정존 佛頂尊.

대정지비 大定智悲 Great insight, great wisdom, great pity, the three virtues 삼덕 三德 of a Buddha by which he achieves enlightenment and wisdom and saves all beings.

대정진보살 大精進菩薩 Śūra, a hero bodhisattva, one of the sixteen in the southern external part of the 금강계 金剛界 group.

대제자 大弟子 Sthavira, a chief disciple, the Fathers of the Buddhist church ; an elder ; an abbot ; a priest licensed to preach and become an abbot ; also 상좌 上坐.

대족왕 大族王 Mihirakula 마혜라구라 摩醯羅矩羅, an ancient Hūna king in the Punjab *circa* A.D. 520 who persecuted Buddhism ; v. 서역기 西域記 4.

대종 大種 The four great seeds, or elements (사대 四大) which enter into all things, i.e. earth, water, fire, and wind, from which, as from seed, all things spring.

대종 大鍾 The great bell in the bell tower of a large monastery.

대주 大洲 A great continent ; one of the four great continents of a world ; v. 사주 四洲.

대주간정중경목록 大周刊定衆經目錄 The catalogue in 14 chüan of the Buddhist scriptures made under the Empress Wu of the T'ang dynasty, the name of which she changed to Chou.

대준제 大准提 Mahā-cundī, a form of Kuan-yin. There are dhāraṇīs beginning with the name Cundī.

대중 大衆 Mahāsaṅgha. The great assembly, any assembly, all present, everybody. 대중인 大衆印 The seal of a monastery. 대중위덕외 大衆威德畏 Stage-struck, awed by an assembly, one of the five 포외 怖畏. 대중부 大衆部 ; 마하승기부 摩訶僧祇部 Mahāsāṅghikāḥ, the school of the community, or majority ; one of the chief early divisions, cf. 상좌부 上坐部 Mahāsthavirāḥ or Sthavirāḥ, i.e. the elders. There are two usages of the term, first, when the sthavira, or older disciples assembled in the cave after the Buddha's death, and the others, the 대중 大衆, assembled outside. As sects, the principal division was that which took place later. The Chinese attribute this division to the influence of 대천 大天 Mahādeva, a century after the Nirvāṇa, and its subsequent five subdivisions are also associated with his name ; they are Pūrvaśailāḥ, Avaraśailāḥ, Haimavatāḥ, Lokottaravādinaḥ, and Prajñapti-vādinaḥ ; v. 소승 小乘.

대지 大地 Great earth, the whole earth, everywhere, all the land, etc. 대지(법) 大地(法) Ten bodhisattva bhūmi, or stages above that of 견도 見道 in the 구사론 俱舍論 4, and the mental conditions connected with them. 대지 大地 is also defined as good and evil, the association of mind with them being by the ten methods of 수 受, 상 想, 사 思, 촉 觸, 욕 欲, 혜 慧, 념 念, 작의 作意, 승해 勝解, 삼마지 三摩地.

대지 大智 Mahāmati ; cf. 대혜 大慧 ; Great Wisdom, Buddha-wisdom, omniscience ; a title of Mañjuśrī, as the apotheosis of transcendental wisdom. 대지도론 大智度論 A śāstra ascribed to Nāgārjuna on the greater Prajñā-pāramitā sūtra ; the śāstra was tr. by Kumārajīva, A.D. 397-415, in 100 chüan. 대지혜문 大智慧門 The Buddha-door of great wisdom, as contrasted with that of his 대비 大悲 great compassion. 대지관정지 大智灌頂地 The stage of the Great Wisdom chrism, or anointing of a Buddha, as having attained to the Great Wisdom, of omniscience ; it is the eleventh stage. 대지장 大智藏 The Buddha-wisdom store.

대지분신 大志焚身 The monk Ta-chih who sacrificed himself on the pyre, and thus caused Yang Ti of the Sui dynasty to withdraw his order for dispersing the monks.

대진사 大秦寺 (1) A monastery of the Manichaean sect, erected in Ch'ang-an during the T'ang dynasty by order of the emperor T'ai Tsung A.D. 627-650 ; also 바사사 波斯寺. (2) A Nestorian monastery mentioned in the Christian monument at Sianfu.

대집경 大集經 Mahāsaṅghāta-sūtra 대방등대집경 大方等大集經 The sūtra of the great assembly of Bodhisattvas from 시방 十方 every direction, and of the apocalyptic sermons delivered to them by the Buddha ; 60 chüan, tr. in parts at various times by various translators. There are several works connected with it and others independent, e.g. 대집수미장경 大集須彌藏經, 대집일장경 大集日藏經 and 대집월장경 大集月藏經, 대집(경)현호 大集(經)賢護, 대집회정법경 大集會正法經, 대집비유왕경 大集譬喩王經, etc. 대집부 大集部 Mahāsaṁnipāta. A division of the sūtrapiṭaka containing avadānas, i.e. comparisons, metaphors, parables, and stories illustrating the doctrines.

대천 大天 Mahādeva. 마하제바 摩訶提婆. (1) A former incarnation of Śākyamuni as a Cakravartī. (2) A title of Maheśvara. (3) An able supporter of the Mahāsāṅghikāḥ, whose date is given as about a hundred years after the Buddha's death, but he is also described as a favourite of Aśoka, with whom he is associated as persecutor of the Sthavirāḥ, the head of which escaped into Kashmir. If from the latter school sprang the Mahāyāna, it may account for the detestation in which Mahādeva is held by the Mahāyānists. An account of his wickedness and heresies is given in 서역기 西域記 3 and in 파사론 婆沙論 99.

대천(세계) 大千(世界) A major chiliocosm, or universe, of 3,000 great chiliocosms, v. 삼천대천 三千大千.

대철위(산) 大鐵圍(山) Mahācakravāla. The great circular "iron" enclosure ; the higher of the double circle of mountains forming the outer periphery of every world, concentric to the seven circles around Sumeru.

대청주 大青珠 Mahānīla. 마하니라 摩訶尼羅 A precious stone, large and blue, perhaps identical with Indranīla-muktā, i.e. the Indra of precious stones, a "sapphire" [M.W.]

대총상법문 大總相法門 The Bhūtatathatā as the totality of things, and Mind 심진여 心眞如 as the Absolute, v. 기신론 起信論.

대치성광 大熾盛光 The great blazing perfect light, a title of 금륜불정존 金輪佛頂尊.

대친 大嚫 Dakṣiṇā, v. 달친 達嚫.

대통 大統 The head of the order, an office instituted by Wên Ti of the Sui dynasty ; cf. 대승정 大僧正.

대통(지승) 大通(智勝) Mahābhijñā-jñānābhibhu. The great Buddha of supreme penetration and wisdom. "A fabulous Buddha whose realm was Saṁbhava, his kalpa Mahārūpa. Having spent ten middling kalpas in ecstatic meditation he became a Buddha, and retired again in meditation for 84,000 kalpas, during which his sixteen sons continued (as Buddhas) his preaching. Incarnations of his sons are," Akṣobhya, Merukūṭa, Siṁhaghoṣa, Siṁhadhvaja, Ākāśapratiṣṭhita, Nityaparivṛtta, Indradhvaja, Brahmadhvaja, Amitābha, Sarvalokadhātūpadravodvegapratyuttīrṇa, Tamāla-pattra-candana-gandha, Merukalpa, Meghasvara, Meghasvararāja, Sarvalokabhayastambhitatva-vidhvaṁsanakāra, and Śākyamuni ; v. Eitel. He is said to have lived in a kalpa earlier than the present by kalpas as numerous as the atoms of a chiliocosm. Amitābha is his ninth son, Śākyamuni his sixteenth, and the present 대중 大衆 or assembly of believers are said to be the reincarnation of those who were his disciples in that former aeon ; v. Lotus Sūtra, chapter 7. 대통화상 大通和尙 Title of 신수 神秀 Shên-hsiu, a disciple of the fifth patriarch.

대품(경) 大品(經) The larger, of fuller edition of a canonical work, especially of the next. 대품반야경 大品般若經 ; 마하반야바라밀경 摩訶般若波羅蜜經 The Mahāprajñā-pāramitā sūtra as tr. by Kumārajīva in 27 chüan, in contrast with the 10 chüan edition.

대풍재 大風災 Great Storms, the third of the three destructive calamities to end the world.

대한림 大寒林 The grove of great cold, śītavana, i.e. burial stūpas, the graveyard.

대해 大海 Mahāsamudra-sāgara 마하삼모날라사아나 摩訶三母捺羅娑誐羅 The Ocean. 대해팔부사의 大海八不思議 The eight marvellous characteristics of the ocean — its gradually increasing depth, its unfathomableness, its universal saltiness, its punctual tides, its stores of precious things, its enormous creatures, its objection to corpses, its unvarying level despite all that pours into it. 대해십상 大海十相 The ten aspects of the ocean, the Hua-yen sūtra adds two more to the above eight, i.e. all other waters lose their names in it ; its vastness of expanse. 대해인 大海印 The ocean symbol, i.e. as the face of the sea reflects all forms, so the samādhi of a bodhisattva reflects to him all truths ; it is also termed 해인삼매 海印三昧. 대해중 大海衆 The great ocean congregation ; as all waters flowing into the sea become salty, so all ranks flowing into the saṅgha become of one flavour and lose old differentiations.

대현 大賢 Ta-hsien (Jap. Daiken), a Korean monk who lived in China during the T'ang dynasty, of the 법상 法相 Dharmalakṣaṇa school, noted for his annotations on the sūtras and styled 고적기 古迹記 the archaeologist.

대혜 大慧 Mahāmati 마하마지 摩訶摩底. (1) Great wisdom, the leading bodhisattva of the Laṅkāvatāra-sūtra. (2) Name of a Hangchow master of the Ch'an school, 종고 宗杲 Tsung-kao of the Sung dynasty, whose works are the 대혜서 大慧書. See 대혜 종고 大慧宗杲. (3) Posthumous title of 일행 一行 I-hsing, a master of the Ch'an school, T'ang dynasty. 대혜도인 大慧刀印 The sign of the great wisdom sword, the same esoteric sign as the 보병인 寶瓶印 and 탑인 塔印. There are two books, the abbreviated titles of which are 대혜어록 大慧語錄 and its supplement the 대혜무고 大慧武庫.

대혜 종고 大慧宗杲 Ta-hui Tsung-kao(1089-1163). A Lin-chi Ch'an monk who entered the Order at the age of sixteen and realized enlightenment under the tutelage of Zen Master Yüan-wu. 'Ta-hui' is a name bestowed later upon him. He is said to have had more than two thousand disciples. He advocated the koan method instead of the method of 'silent illumination.' His teachings can be found in the 'Records of Ta-hui.'

대호규 大號叫 Mahāraurava 대규 大叫 ; 대호 大呼 The hell of great wailing, the fifth of the eight hot hells.

대호인 大護印 The great protective sign, a manual sign, accompanied with a transliterated repetition of "Namaḥ sarva-tathāgatebhyaḥ ; Sarvathā Haṁ Khaṁ Rākṣasī mahābali ; Sarva-tathāgata-puṇyo nirjāti ; Hūṁ Hūṁ Trāta Trāta apratihati svāhā."

대홍련 大紅蓮 Great red lotuses – name of a cold hell where the skin is covered with chaps like lotuses.

대화 大化 The transforming teaching and work of a Buddha in one lifetime.

대화상 大和尙 Great monk, senior monk, abbot ; a monk of great virtue and old age. Buddhoṣingha, 불도징 佛圖澄 Fo-t'u-ch'êng, who came to China A.D. 310, was so styled by his Chinese disciple 석자룡 石子龍 Shih-tzŭ-lung. 대화갈라 大和竭羅 Dīpaṃkara. The Buddha of burning light, the twenty-fourth predecessor of Śākyamuni, a disciple of Varaprabha ; v. 연 燃 and 제 提. In the Lotus sūtra he appears from his nirvāṇa on the Vulture Peak with Śākyamuni, manifesting that the nirvāṇa state is one of continued existence.

대환사 大幻師 Great magician, a title given to a Buddha.

대회 大會 A general assembly. 대회중 大會衆 The general assembly (of the saints).

대휴헐저 大休歇底 Ended, finished ; dead to the world ; also 대휴사저 大休死底.

대흑천 大黑天 Mahākāla 마하가라 摩訶迦羅 ; 마하가라 摩訶謌羅 the great black deva 대흑신 大黑神. Two interpretations are given. The esoteric cult describes the deva as the masculine form of Kālī, i.e. Durgā, the wife of Śiva ; with one face and eight arms, or three faces and six arms, a necklace of skulls, etc. He is worshipped as giving warlike power, and fierceness ; said also to be an incarnation of Vairocana for the purpose of destroying the demons ; and is described as 대시 大時 the "great time"(-keeper) which seems to indicate Vairocana, the sun. The exoteric cult interprets him as a beneficent deva, a Pluto, or god of wealth. Consequently he is represented in two forms, by the one school as a fierce deva, by the other as a kindly happy deva. He is shown as one of the eight fierce guardians with trident, generally blue-black but sometimes white ; he may have two elephants underfoot. Six arms and hands hold jewel, skull cup, chopper, drum, trident, elephant-goad. He is the tutelary god of Mongolian Buddhism . Six forms of Mahākāla are noted : (1) 비구대흑 比丘大黑 A black-faced disciple of the Buddha, said to be the Buddha as Mahādeva in a previous incarnation, now guardian of the refectory. (2) 마하가라대흑녀 摩訶迦羅大黑女 Kālī, the wife of Śiva. (3) 왕자가라대흑 王子迦羅大黑 The son of Śiva. (4) 진타대흑 眞陀大黑 Cintā-maṇi, with the talismanic pearl, symbol of bestowing fortune.

(5) 야차대흑 夜叉大黑 Subduer of demons. (6) 마가라대흑 摩迦羅大黑 Mahākāla, who carries a bag on his back and holds a hammer in his right hand. J., Daikoku ; M., Yeke-gara ; T., Nag-po c'en-po. 대흑비력법 大黑飛礫法 The black deva's flying shard magic : take the twig of a 가 榎 *chia* tree (Catalpa Bungei), the twig pointing north-west ; twist it to the shape of a buckwheat grain, write the Sanskrit letter 나 on each of its three faces, place it before the deva, recite his spell a thousand times, then cast the charm into the house of a prosperous person, saying may his wealth come to me.

대흥선사 大興善寺 The great goodness-promoting monastery, one of the ten great T'ang monasteries at Ch'ang-an, commenced in the Sui dynasty.

덕 德 Virtue, moral excellence, moral power, power ; also translates guṇa ; translit. *ta*. 덕(차)시라 德(叉)尸羅 Takṣaśilā, an ancient kingdom and city, the Taxila of the Greeks. Lat. 35° 8' N., Long. 72° 44' E. 덕차가 德叉迦 Takṣaka, one of the four dragon-kings. 덕사 德士 Virtuous scholar, a term for a monk in the T'ang dynasty. 덕자 德字 The svastika. 덕본 德本 The root of the moral life, or of religious power ; also a name for Amitābha as the root of all virtue. 덕모 德母 The mother of virtue, i.e. faith which is the root of the religious life. 덕해 德海 The ocean-like character and influence of virtue. 덕병 德瓶 The vase or talisman of power, cf. 현병 賢瓶. 덕전 德田 Field of virtue, or of religious power, i.e. the cult of arhats and Buddhas. 덕행 德行 Moral conduct and religious exercises, or discipline ; moral conduct. 덕풍 德風 The wind of virtue, or of religious power. 덕향 德香 The fragrance of virtue.

도 圖 A plan, map ; seal ; to plan, scheme, calculate.

도 途 A road, way, method. 도로(낙)단나 途盧(諾)檀那 Droṇodana, a prince of Magadha, father of Devadatta and Mahānāma, and uncle of Śākyamuni.

도 到 Arrive, reach, to. 도피안 到彼岸 Pāramitā, cf. 파 波 ; to reach the other shore, i.e. nirvāṇa. 도두 到頭 At the end, when the end is reached.

도 忉 Grieved, distressed. 도리천 忉利天 Trayastriṁśās, 달리야달리사 怛唎耶怛唎奢 ; 다라야등릉사 多羅夜登陵舍 ; the heavens of the thirty-three devas, 삼십삼천 三十三天, the second of the desire-heavens, the heaven of Indra ; it is the Svarga of Hindu mythology, situated on Meru with thirty-two deva-cities, eight on each side ; a central city is 선견성 善見城 Sudarśana, or Amarāvatī, where Indra, with 1,000 heads and eyes and four arms, lives in his palace called 선연 禪延 ; 비사연 毘闍延 ; 비선연 毘禪延 Vaijayanta, and "revels in numberless sensual pleasures together with his wife" Śacī and with 119,000 concubines. "There he receives the monthly reports of the" four Mahārājas as to the good and evil in the world. "The whole myth may have an astronomical" or meteorological background, e.g. the number thirty-three indicating the "eight Vasus, eleven Rudras, twelve Ādityas, and two Aśvins of Vedic mythology." [Eitel]. Cf. 인다라 因陀羅.

도 稻 Growing rice. 도간 稻稈 Rice straw.

도 都 Metropolis, imperial city or domain ; a district, ward, territory. All. 도사(다) 都史(多) or 도사(천) 都史(天) the Tuṣita heaven, v. 두 兜. 도타가 都吒迦 Joyful sound, united voices ; (derivation uncertain). 도감사 都監寺 ; 도총 都總 The director or second in command of a monastery. 도시왕 都市王 The ruler of the eighth hot hell. 도솔천 都率天 Tuṣita, see above. 도화라 都貨羅 Tukhāra, the 월지 月支 Yüeh-chih country ; "(1) A topographical term designating a country of ice and frost (tukhāra), and corresponding to the present Badakchan which Arab geographers still call Tokharestan. (2) An ethnographical term used by the Greeks to designate the Tocharoi or Indo-Scythians, and likewise by Chinese writers applied to the Tochari Tartars who driven on by the Huns (180 B.C.) conquered Trans-oxania, destroyed the Bactrian kingdom (대하 大夏) 126 B.C., and finally conquered the Punjab, Cashmere, and the greater part of

India. Their greatest king was Kaniṣka." [Eitel].

도 道 Mārga. A way, road ; the right path ; principle, Truth, Reason, Logos, Cosmic energy ; to lead ; to say. The way of transmigration by which one arrives at a good or bad existence ; any of the six gati, or paths of destiny. The way of bodhi, or enlightenment leading to nirvāṇa through spiritual stages. Essential nirvāṇa, in which absolute freedom reigns. For the eightfold noble path v. 팔성도 八聖道.

도 徒 On foot ; a follower, disciple ; in vain ; banishment. 도제 徒弟 A disciple, neophyte, apprentice. 도중 徒衆 The company of disciples.

도 陶 Pottery, kiln. 도가륜 陶家輪 A potter's wheel.

도 度 Pāramitā, 바라밀 波羅蜜; intp. by 도 渡 to ferry over ; to save. The mortal life of reincarnations is the sea; nirvāṇa is the other shore; v. Pāramitā, 파 波. Also, to leave the world as a monk or nun, such is a 도승 度僧 or 도자 度者. 도일체세간고뇌 度一切世間苦腦 Sarvalokadhātūpadravodvega-pratyuttīrṇa. "One who redeems men from the misery of all worlds. A fictitious Buddha who dwelled west of our universe, an incarnation of the tenth son of Mahābhijñā-jñānābhibhu." [Eitel]. 도세 度世 To get through life ; to pass safely through this life. Also, to save the world. 도옥초 度沃焦 An epithet of Buddha who rescues all the living from being consumed by their desires, which resemble the burning rock in the ocean above purgatory. 도락차 度洛叉 Daśalakṣa, 10 lakhs, a million. 도무극 度無極 To ferry across, or save, without limit. 도생 度生 To save, rescue all beings ; also idem 도세 度世. 도과 度科 The portion of the sūtras supposed to be learned by religious novices as preparation for leaving the world as monks. 도탈 度脫 To give release from the wheel of transmigration ; enlightenment.

도 屠 To butcher, kill ; a butcher. 도고 屠沽 Butcher and huckster ; caṇḍāla is "the generic name for a man of the lowest and most despised of the mixed tribes." [M. W.]

도 倒 To fall, lie down ; to pour ; upside down, inverted, perverted ; on the contrary. 도범 倒凡 Perverted folk, the unenlightened who see things upside down. 도합 倒合 A fallacious comparison in a syllogism. 도현 倒懸 Hanging upside down ; the condition of certain condemned souls, especially for whom the Ullambana (or Lambana, cf. 우 盂) festival is held in the seventh month ; the phrase is used as a tr. of Ullambana, and as such seems meant for Lambana. 도아 倒我 The conventional ego, the reverse of reality. 도견 倒見 Cf. 전 顚 19. Upside-down or inverted views, seeing things as they seem, not as they are, e.g. the impermanent as permanent, misery as joy, non-ego as ego, and impurity as purity. 도리 倒離 The fallacy of using a comparison in a syllogism which does not apply.

도 逃 To flee, escape. 도선 逃禪 To escape in or from meditation or thought.

도 導 To lead, indicate, educe, induce. 도화 導化 To lead and convert, or transform. 도인 導引 To lead. 도사 導師 Nāyaka ; a leader, guide, one who guides men to Buddha's teaching ; applied also to Buddhas and bodhisattvas, and to the leaders of the ritual in Buddhist services ; v. 천인도사 天人道師.

도 覩 To look at, see. 도사다천 覩史多天 The Tuṣita heaven, v. 두 兜. 도화라 覩貨羅 Tukhāra, "the present Badakchan which Arab geographers still call Tokharestan" ; the country of the Indo-Scythians, the Tocharoi of the Greeks, idem 월지 月支.

도 盜 To rob ; a robber, bandit, pirate, e.g. 도적 盜賊, 강적 强賊, 해적 解賊, etc.

도 淘 To scour, swill, wash, cleanse ; tricky, playful. 도태 淘汰 The fourth of the five periods of Buddha's teaching, according to T'ien-t'ai, i.e. the sweeping away of false ideas, produced by appearance, with the doctrine of the Void, or the reality behind the seeming.

도 掉 To shake, change, arrange ; to fall. 도회 掉悔 Discontent and regret, ambition and repining. 도산 掉散 Unsteady in act, word, and thought ; unreliable. 도(거) 掉(擧) Ambitious, unsettled.

도 塗 To smear, rub on. 도할 塗割 To anoint the hand, or cut it off, instances of love and hatred. 도독고 塗毒鼓 A drum smeared with poison to destroy those who hear it. 도회외도 塗灰外道 Pāṁśupatas, perhaps Pāśupatas, followers of Śiva, Śaiva ascetics ; a class of heretics who smeared themselves with ashes. 도족유 塗足油 Oil rubbed on the feet to avoid disease. 도향 塗香 To rub the body with incense or scent to worship Buddha.

도 蹈 To trample, tread on. 도칠보화 蹈七寶華 Saptaratna Padmavikramin, the name of Rāhula as Buddha, he whose steps are on flowers of the seven precious things.

도 荼 See **다** 荼.

도감 都監 (In larger monasteries) Provost.. A monk/nun who coordinates the office jobs. Largely a ceremonial position.

도검 道檢 The restraints, or control, of religion.

도과 道果 The result of the Buddha-way, i.e. nirvāṇa.

도관 道觀 Religious practice (or external influence) and internal vision.

도광 道光 The light of Buddha-truth.

도교 道交 Mutual interaction between the individual seeking the truth and the Buddha who responds to his aspirations ; mutual intercourse through religion.

도교 道敎 Taoism. The teaching of the right way, i.e. of Buddhism.

도구 道舊 An old monastic, or religious, friend.

도구 道具 The implements of the faith, such as garments, begging-bowl, and other accessories which aid one in the Way.

도금 道禁 Whatever is prohibited by the religion, or the religious life ; śīla, the second pāramitā, moral purity.

도기 道器 A vessel of religion, the capacity for Buddhism.

도기 道氣 The breath, or vital energy, of the Way, i.e. of Buddhist religion.

도덕 道德 Religion and virtue ; the power of religion.

도도 刀途 The gati or path of rebirth as an animal, so called because animals are subjects of the butcher's knife.

도락 道樂 The joy of religion.

도량 道場 Truth-plot. Bodhimaṇḍala, circle, or place of enlightenment. The place where Buddha attained enlightenment. A place, or method, for attaining to Buddha-truth. An object of or place for religious offerings. A place for teaching, learning, or practising religion. 도량수 道場樹 The bodhidruma, or tree under which the Buddha attained enlightenment. 도량신 道場神 Tutelary deities of Buddhist religious places, etc.

도력 道力 The power which comes from enlightenment, or the right doctrine.

도류 道流 The stream of Truth ; the flow, or progress, of Buddha-truth ; the spread of a particular movement, e.g. the Ch'an school.

도류지 道類智 The wisdom obtained through insight into the way of release in the upper realms of form and formlessness ; one of the 팔지 八智.

도륜 道倫 Do-ryun(?-?). A monk of the Silla dynasty in Korea. He wrote 성유식요결 成唯識要決 and 유가사지론기 瑜伽師地論記.

도리 道理 Truth, doctrine, principle ; the principles of Buddhism, Taoism, etc.

도문 道門 The gate of the Way, or of truth, religion, etc. ; the various schools of Buddhism.

도반 道伴 Lit. "path friend." A fellow practitioner.

도법 道法 The way or methods to obtain nirvāṇa. 도법지 道法智 The wisdom attained by them ; the wisdom which rids one of false views in regard to mārga, or the eightfold noble path.

도사 道士 A Taoist (hermit), also applied to Buddhists, and to Śākyamuni.

도산 刀山 The hill of swords in one of the hells.

도선 道宣 A celebrated T'ang monk, Tao-hsüan, who assisted Hsüan-tsang in his translations.

도속 道俗 Monks and laymen.

도수 道樹 The bodhi-tree, under which Buddha attained enlightenment ; also as a synonym of Buddhism with its powers of growth and fruitfulness.

도수 道水 The water of Truth which washes away defilement.

도술 道術 The methods, or arts, of the Buddhist religion.

도식 道識 The knowledge of religion ; the wisdom, or insight, attained through Buddhism.

도신 道信 Tao-hsin(580-651). Fourth in the traditional Zen lineage of China.

도심 道心 The mind which is bent on the right way, which seeks enlightenment. A mind not free from the five gati, i.e. transmigration. Also 도의 道意.

도아 道芽 The sprouts, or seedlings, of Buddha-truth.

도안 道眼 The eye attained through the cultivation of Buddha-truth ; the eye which sees that truth.

도업 道業 The karma of religion which leads to Buddhahood.

도요 道要 The fundamentals of Buddhism.

도원 道元 (1) The beginning of right doctrine, i.e. faith. (2) Dōgen (1200-1253). Transmitter of Sōtō Zen to Japan.

도위 道位 The stages in the attainment of Buddha-truth.

도인 道人 One who has entered the way, one who seeks enlightenment, a general name for early Buddhists and also for Taoists.

도자 道者 One who practises Buddhism ; the Truth, the religion.

도제 道諦 Mārga, the dogma of the path leading to the extinction of passion, the fourth of the four axioms, i.e. the eightfold noble path, v. 팔성도 八聖道.

도종성 道種性 The nature possessing the seed of Buddhahood. The stage in which the "middle" way is realized. 도종지 道種智 The wisdom which adopts all means to save all the living ; one of the 삼지 三智.

도중 道衆 Those who practise religion, the body of monks.

도지 道智 Religious wisdom ; the wisdom which understands the principles of mārga, the eightfold path.

도차 道次 The stages of enlightenment, or attainment.

도첩 度牒 See **계첩** 戒牒.

도체 道體 The embodiment of truth, the fundament of religion, i.e. the natural heart or mind, the pure nature, the universal mind, the bhūtatathatā.

도통 道統 Dharma lineage.

도품 道品 Religious or monastic grade, or grades.

도풍 道風 The wind of Buddha-truth, as a transforming power ; also as a prognosis of future events.

도풍 刀風 The wind that cuts all living beings to pieces — at the approach of a world-kalpa's end ; also described as the disintegrating force at death.

도행 道行 Conduct according to Buddha-truth ; the discipline of religion.

도호 道號 The hao, or literary name of a monk.

도화 道化 To transform others through the truth of Buddhism ; converted by the Truth.

독 禿 Bald. 독인 禿人 ; 독거사 禿居士 ; 독노 禿奴 A monk ; a nun, sometimes used as a term of abuse.

독 獨 Only, alone, solitary. 독일법계 獨一法界 The one and only universal dharma-realm, or reality, behind all phenomena. 독원 獨園 v. 급 給 and 아 阿 Anāthapiṇḍika. 독고락가 獨孤洛加 Dukūla is a fine cloth, and may be the origin of this Chinese term, which is intp. as 저 紵 a kind of linen. 독존 獨尊 The alone honoured one, Buddha. 독거 獨居 Dwelling alone, e.g. as a hermit. 독영경 獨影境 Imaginary or illusory conditions, ideal and insubstantial. 독가다 獨柯多 v. 돌 突 Duṣkṛta, offence. 독생독사독거독래 獨生獨死獨去獨來 Alone we are born and die, go and come. 독공 獨空 The one immaterial reality behind all phenomena. 독고저 獨股杵 ; 독고(저) 獨鈷(杵) The single-arm vajra. 독각 獨覺 Pratyeka-buddha, v. 연 緣 one who seeks his own enlightenment. 독각선인 獨角仙人 Ekaśṛṅga-ṛṣi, or Unicorn ṛṣi, cf. 일각 一角, the ascetic who fell through the wiles of a woman. 독두무명 獨頭無明 idem 불공무명 不共無明 q.v.

독 毒 Poison. 독기 毒器 The poison vessel, the body. 독천이고 毒天二鼓 The two kinds of drum : poison-drum, harsh or stern words for repressing evil, and deva-drum, gentle words for producing good ; also, misleading contrasted with correct teaching. The 독고 毒鼓 is likened also to the Buddha-nature which can slay all evil. 독수 毒樹 Poison tree, an evil monk. 독기 毒氣 Poison vapour, emitted by the three poisons, 탐진치 貪瞋痴, desire, hate (or anger), stupor (or ignorance). 독전 毒箭 Poison arrow, i.e. illusion. 독약 毒藥 Poison, cf. the sons who drank their father's poisons in the 보문 普門 chapter of The Lotus Sūtra. 독사 毒蛇 Poisonous snakes, the four elements of the body — earth, water, fire, wind (or air) — which harm a man by their variation, i.e. increase and decrease. Also, gold. 독룡 毒龍 The poisonous dragon, who accepted the commandments and thus escaped from his dragon form, i.e. Śākyamuni in a former incarnation. 지도론 智度論 14.

독 篤 Sincere ; serious ; consolidate. 독진 篤進 Toksun, "a city in Mongolia." [Eitel].

독 讀 To read ; a comma, full stop. 독사 讀師 A reader to an assembly. 독경 讀經 Ditto ; also to read the scriptures. 독송 讀誦 Reading and reciting.

독 犢 Vatsa ; a calf, young animal, offspring, child. 독자 犢子 Vatsa, the founder of the 독자부 犢子部, Vātsīputrīyāḥs (Pali Vajjiputtakas), one of the main divisions of the Sarvāstivāda (Vaibhāṣika) school ; they were considered schismatics through their insistence on the reality of the ego ; "their failure in points of discipline," etc. ; the Vinaya as taught by this school "has never reached China." [Eitel]. For other forms of Vātsīputrīyāḥ, v. 발사 跋私 ; also 파婆 and 불 佛.

독서파 讀書派 Recitation track, section of seminary 강원 講院 that recites the texts aloud. Cf. 간경파 看經派.

돈 敦 Staunch, honest, substantial ; to consolidate ; urge, etc. 돈황 敦煌 or 燉煌 The city in Kansu near which are the 천불동 千佛洞 Cave-temples of the thousand Buddhas ; where a monk in A.D. 1900, sweeping away the collected sand, broke through a partition and found a room full of MSS. ranging in date from the beginning of the 5th to the end of the 10th century, together with block prints and paintings, first brought to light by Sir Aurel Stein.

돈 頓 To fall headlong, prostrate ; at one time, at once ; suddenly ; immediate ; a pause ; to stamp ; make ready ; used chiefly in contrast with 점 漸 gradually. 돈원 頓圓 The immediate and complete way of enlightenment of the T'ien-t'ai Lotus school. 돈돈원 頓頓圓 Instantaneous perfect enlightenment of the Hua-yen, a term used by 징관 澄觀 Ch'êng-kuan, who left the Lotus for the Hua-yen. 돈대 頓大 The immediate school and sūtra of the Mahāyāna, i.e. the Hua-yen. 돈사 頓寫 ; 돈경 頓經 ; 일일경 一日經 To copy the Lotus sūtra at one sitting, 돈오 頓悟 Instantly to apprehend, or attain to Buddha-enlightenment, in contrast with Hīnayāna and other methods of gradual attainment. 돈오보살 頓悟菩薩 A bodhisattva who attains immediately without passing through the various stages. 돈성제행 頓成諸行 The immediate fulfilment of all acts, processes, of disciplines (by the fulfilment of one). 돈교 頓教 The doctrine that enlightenment or Buddhahood may be attained at once ; also immediate teaching of the higher truth without preliminary stages. 돈단 頓斷 To cut off at one stroke all the passions, etc. 돈기 頓機 The capacity, or opportunity, for immediate enlightenment. 돈점 頓漸 Immediate, or sudden, attainment in contrast with gradualness. 돈지 頓旨 The will, or aim, of immediate attainment. 돈법 頓法 The method of immediacy. 돈각 頓覺 Immediate apprehension or enlightenment as opposed to gradual development.

돈오점수 頓悟漸修 Doctrine of sudden enlightenment and gradual cultivation, esp. as advocated by Master Ji-nul 지눌 知訥 q.v.

돌 突 Rush out ; protrude ; rude ; suddenly. 돌바 突婆 Dhūpa, incense, frankincense, fragrant gum ; intp. as 모향 茅香 lemon-grass, perhaps *Andropogen nardus*. 돌길라 突吉羅 ; 돌슬길률다 突膝吉栗多 or 돌실길률다 突悉吉栗多 ; 돌슬궤리다 突瑟几理多 Duṣkṛta (Pali Dukkaṭa), wrong-doing, evil action, misdeed, sin ; external sins of body and mouth, i.e. deed and word. Cf. 길라 吉羅. 돌가 突迦 Durgā, Bhīmā, or Marīci, "the wife of Maheśvara, to whom human flesh was offered once a year in autumn." [Eitel]. 돌로나 突路拏 Droṇa, a Brahman who is said to have divided the cremation remains of the Buddha to prevent strife for them among contending princes.

돌로슬검 咄嚕瑟劍 Turuṣka, olibanum, incense ; also the name of an Indo-Scythian or Turkish race.

동 洞 A hole, cave ; to see through, know. 동산 洞山 Cave hill or monastery in Yün-chou, modern Jui-chou, Kiangsi, noted for its T'ang teacher 오본 悟本 Wu-pên. 동가 洞家 ; 동상 洞上 ; 동하 洞下 refer to the 조동 曹洞 school of 혜능 慧能 Hui-nêng.

동 童 A youth, boy, girl, virgin. 동자 童子 Kumāra, a boy, youth, son ; a prince ; a neophyte ; a bodhisattva as son of the Tathāgata. 동진 童眞 A term for a monk, who should have the child-nature of simplicity. 동진주 童眞住 The stage of youth in Buddhahood, the eighth of the 십주 十住. 동농마 童籠磨 Druma, a tree in general ; a king of the Kinnaras, or Gandharvas, the celestial musicians.

동 冬 Hima ; hemanta ; winter. 동안거 冬安居 The winter retreat, 16th of 10th moon to 15th of 1st. 동야 冬夜 The night before the 동지 冬至 winter solstice. 동조 冬朝 The morning of that day. 동재 冬齋 The observances of that day.

동 動 Move, stir, motion, mutable ; movement arises from the nature of wind which is the cause of motion. 동부동법 動不動法 The mutable and the immutable, the changing and the unchanging, the Kāmadhātu, or realms of metempsychosis and the two higher realms, Rūpadhātu and Arūpadhātu. Cf. 부동 不動.

동 東 Pūrva, East. 동승신주 東勝身洲 ; (불바)비제하 (佛婆)毘提訶 ; 불바제 佛婆提 ; 불우체 佛于逮 ; 포리바 逋利婆 ; 비제하 鼻提賀 ; 포로바 布嚕婆, etc. Pūrvavideha. The eastern of the four great continents of a world, east of Mt. Meru, semicircular in shape. 동사 東司 ; 동정 東淨 ; 동측 東厠 The privy in a monastery. 동토 東土 The eastern land, i.e. China. 동밀 東密 The eastern esoteric or Shingon sect of Japan, in contrast with the T'ien-t'ai esoteric sect. 동산 東山 An eastern hill, or monastery, general and specific, especially the 황매동산 黃梅東山 Huang-mei eastern monastery of the fourth and fifth patriarchs of the Ch'an(Zen) school. 동산부 東山部 ; 불반세라부 佛婆勢羅部 Pūrvaśailāḥ ; one of the five divisions of the Mahāsāṅghikāḥ school. 동산사 東山寺 Pūrvaśaila-saṅghārāma, a monastery east of Dhanakaṭaka. 동옥 東獄 The Eastern Peak, T'ai Shan in Shantung, one of the five sacred peaks ; the god or spirit of this peak, whose protection is claimed all over China. 동암 東庵 The eastern hall of a monastery. 동방 東方 The east, or eastern region. 동만다라 東曼陀羅 The eastern maṇḍala, that of the Garbhadhātu.

동 同 Together, with ; mutual ; same. 동사 同事 Samānārthatā, working together (with and for others) ; one of the 사섭법 四攝法. 동분 同分 ; 동품 同品 ; 동류 同類 Of the same class, or order. 동학 同學 Fellow-students, those who learn or study together. 동생천 同生天 ; 동생신 同生神 ; 동명천 同名天 The first two of these terms are intp. as the guardian deva, or spirit, who is sahaja, i.e. born or produced simultaneously with the person he protects ; the last is the deva who has the same name as the one he protects. 동청이문 同聽異聞 To hear the same (words) but understand differently. 동행 同行 Those who are practising religion together. 동체 同體 Of the same body, or nature, as water and wave, but 동체자비 同體慈悲 means fellow-feeling and compassion, looking on all sympathetically as of the same nature as oneself. 동체삼보 同體三寶 idem 일체삼보 一體三寶.

동 銅 Tāmra. Copper, brass. 동전 銅錢 Copper money, cash. 동라 銅鑼 A gong.

동화사 桐華寺 Dong-hwa-sa. A temple located in Dohak-dong Dong-gu, Daegu-si in Korea. The 9th parish headquarters of Korean Jogye Order.

두 斗 A bushel, i.e. ten Chinese pints. 두장 斗帳 A bushel-shaped curtain, e.g. a state umbrella. 두모 斗姥 Dame of the Bushel ; queen of heaven 천후 天后 or Marīci, 마리지 摩利支. 두부천존 斗父天尊 The husband of 두모 斗姥, a Taoist attribution.

두 逗 Delay, loiter ; skulk ; beguile. 두회 逗會 ; 두기 逗機 Adaptation of the teaching to the taught.

두 兜 Helmet, hood ; pocket, bag ; translit. *tu.* 두야 兜夜 The Tuṣita and the Yama heavens. 두파 兜婆 A stūpa. 두사 兜沙 Tuṣāra, frost. 두모로 兜牟盧 Tumburu, probably gandharvas. 두루파 兜樓婆 ; 투로파 妬路婆 Turuṣka ; olibanum ; Indian incense. 도솔(타) 兜率(陀) or 도솔(치) 兜率(哆) ; 두술 兜術 ; 산도사다 珊都史多 or 珊覩史多 ; 투슬다 鬪瑟多 Tuṣita, from Tuṣ, contented, satisfied, gratified ; name of the Tuṣita heaven, the fourth devaloka in the 욕계 欲界 passion-realm, or desire realm, between the Yama, and Nirmāṇarati heavens. Its inner department is the Pure Land of Maitreya who, like Śākyamuni and all Buddhas, is reborn there before descending to earth as the next Buddha ; his life there is 4,000 Tuṣita years, or (each day there being equal to 400 earth-years) 584 million such years. 도솔천자 兜率天子 The Tuṣita prince, i.e. Śākyamuni, whose light while he was in Tuṣita shone into hell and saved all its occupants to that heaven ; hence he is also called 지옥천자 地獄天子 Prince of Hades. 두라 兜羅 ; 투라 妬羅 or 도라 堵羅 or 두라 蠹羅 Tūla, floss, e.g. willow-floss, wild silk ; cotton, also called 두라면 兜羅綿 or 두라이 兜羅毦 also a tree producing such floss.

두 豆 Māṣa, 마사 摩沙 ; 마쇄 磨灑 Legumes, beans, peas, lentils, etc. 두가람 豆伽藍 Masūra Saṅghārāma, Lentil Monastery, "an ancient vihāra about 200 li southeast of Moṅgali." [Eitel]. 두거 豆佉 Duḥkha, trouble, suffering, pain, defined by 핍뇌 逼惱 harassed, distressed. The first of the four dogmas, or "Noble Truths" 사제 四諦 is that all life is involved, through impermanence, in distress. There are many kinds of 고 苦 q.v.

두 杜 Stop, prevent ; azalea. 두구 杜口 To shut the mouth, render speechless. 두로 杜嚕 Turuṣka olibanum, Indian incense, resin, gum used for incense. It is said to resemble peach resin and to grow in Aṭali. Its leaves resemble the pear's and produce pepper ; it is said to flourish in the sands of Central Asia and its gum to flow out on to the sands. 두다 杜多 ; 두다 杜茶 ; 두타 頭陀 q.v. Dhūta, discipline (to shake off sin, etc.). 두저 杜底 Dūta, a messenger ; dūtī, a female messenger. 두로파발타 杜魯婆跋吒 Dhruvapaṭu, a king of Valabhī, son-in-law of Śīlāditya.

두 頭 The head ; chief, first. 두광 頭光 A halo or nimbus round the head (of an image). 두북면서 頭北面西 Head north face west, the proper attitude in which to sleep, the position of the dying Buddha. 두수 頭袖 Head-sleeve, name for a cap. 두타 頭陀 Dhūta, also 두다 杜多 ; 두다 杜茶 shaken, shaken off, cleansed. To get rid of the trials of life ; discipline to remove them and attain nirvāṇa. There are twelve relating to release from ties to clothing, food, and dwelling : (1) garments of cast-off rags ; (2) only the three garments ; (3) eat only food begged ; (4) only breakfast and the noon meal ; (5) no food between them ; (6) limited amount ; (7) dwelling as a hermit ; (8) among tombs ; (9) under a tree ; (10) under the open sky ; (11) anywhere ; (12) sitting and not lying down. There are other groups. 두면작례 頭面作禮 To bow the head and face in worship or reverence, to fall prostrate in reverence. 두수 頭首 The chief monks in a monastery, known as the western band, in contrast with the eastern band of subordinates. 두구라 頭鳩羅 Dukūla, a species of plant, fine cloth made of the inner bark of this plant, silken cloth.

두 抖 To shake. 두수 抖擻 ; 두수 斗藪 Dhūta ; stirring up to duty ; discipline. v. 두타 頭陀.

두순 杜順 Tu Shun(557-640). Founder of the Hua-yen school.

둔 屯 Collect, mass ; to quarter, camp. To sprout ; very ; stingy. 둔륜마 屯崙摩 Druma, the king of the kinnara, male and female spirits whose music awakened mystics from their trance ; v. 지도론 智度論 17.

둔 鈍 Dull, blunt, stupid. 둔사 鈍使 The five envoys of stupidity, i.e. of the lower passions, in contrast with the higher 오리사 五利使 ; the 사 使 is intp. as 번뇌 煩惱 kleśa, the afflicters, or passions ; the five are 탐 貪, 진 瞋, 치 痴, 만 慢, 의 疑 greed, hate, stupidity, arrogance, doubt. 둔근 鈍根 ; 둔기 鈍機 Of dull capacity, unable to receive Buddha-truth.

둔 遁 To retire, vanish. 둔세 遁世 To retire from the world and become a monk ; also to withdraw from the community and become a hermit.

득 得 Prāp ; prāpta. To get, obtain, attain to ; got, obtained, etc. 득입 得入 To attain entry, e.g. to Buddha-truth. 득승 得勝 To obtain the victory. 득대세 得大勢 ; (대)세지 (大)勢至 Mahāsthāmaprāpta, he who has obtained great power, or stability, who sits on the right of Amitābha, controlling all wisdom. 득도 得度 To obtain transport across the river of transmigration, to obtain salvation ; to enter the monastic life. 득의 得意 To obtain one's desires, or aims ; to obtain the meaning (of a sūtra). 득계 得戒 To obtain the commandments ; to attain to the understanding and performance of the moral law. 득계사미 得戒沙彌 A monk who is restored, or not unfrocked, on confession of his sin. 득과 得果 To obtain the fruit of deeds or life. 득안림 得眼林 Āptanetravana, the forest of recovered eyes. 득승 得繩 The cord, or bond, of attaining ; the bondage of possessing. 득라로가 得羅盧迦 Trailokya, 삼계 三界 q.v. 득장 得藏 Śrīgarbha, idem 정안 淨眼 Vimalanetra. 득탈 得脫 To attain to deliverance (from the miseries of reincarnation). 득도 得道 To obtain the way, or the religion ; by obedience to the commandments, practice of meditation, and knowledge, to attain enlightenment. 득수 得髓 To obtain the marrow, the secret, the essence.

등 橙 A stool, bench, footstool, etc.

등 登 Ascend, advance, start ; attain, ripen ; to note, fix. 등시 登時 At once. 등주 登住 The advance of the bodhisattva to the 십주 十住 q.v. 등지 登地 idem 십지 十地 q.v. 등좌 登座 To ascend the throne, or pulpit, etc.

등 藤 Creepers, canes. 등사 藤蛇 Seeing a cane and thinking it a snake.

등 燈 Dīpa, a lamp, lantern ; cf. 연등 然燈. 등광 燈光 The light of a lamp ; lantern light. 등명 燈明 The lamp hung before a Buddha, etc., as a symbol of his wisdom. 등명불 燈明佛 ; 일월등명불 日月燈明佛 A Buddha mentioned in the Lotus Sūtra. 등멸 燈滅 The extinction of a lamp. 등화 燈火 Dīpapradīpa, lamp-light. 등롱 燈籠 ; 등로 燈爐 A lantern.

등 騰 To mount, rise ; translit. *tang.* 등란 騰蘭 Tang and Ran, i.e. Mātaṅga (Kāśyapa Mātaṅga) and Gobharana, the two monks brought to China, according to tradition, by Ming Ti's emissaries, v. 마 摩, 가 迦, and 축 竺.

등 等 To pair ; parallel, equal, of like order ; a class, grade, rank ; common ; to wait ; sign of plural. In Buddhist writings it is also used for "equal everywhere," "equally everywhere," "universal."

등각 等覺 Samyak-sambodhi ; absolute universal enlightenment, omniscience, a quality of and term for a Buddha ; also the 51st stage in the enlightenment of a bodhisattva, the attainment of the Buddha-enlightenment which precedes 묘각 妙覺.

등공 等空 Equal with space, universal.

등공 等供 Synchronous offering, also 등득 等得, i.e. the simultaneous beginning of a meal when the master of ceremonies cries that the meal is served.

등관 等觀 The beholding of all things as equal, e.g. as 공 空 unreal, or immaterial ; or of all beings without distinction, as one beholds one's children, i.e. without respect of persons.

등려 等侶 Of the same class, or company ; fellows, equals.

등류 等流 Niṣyanda, outflow, regular flow, equal current ; like producing like ; the equality of cause and effect ; like causes produce like effects ; of the same order. 등류과 等流果 Like effects arise from like causes, e.g. good from good, evil from evil ; present condition in life from conduct in previous existence ; hearing from sound, etc. 등류상속 等流相續 Of the same nature, or character ; connected as cause and effect.

등묘 等妙 The two supreme forms of Buddha-enlightenment 등각 等覺 and 묘각 妙覺, being the 51st and 52nd stages of the Mahāyāna 계위 階位. A Buddha is known as 등묘각왕 等妙覺王, king of these two forms of universal and supernatural illumination.

등무간연 等無間緣 Uninterrupted continuity, especially of thought, or time.

등미 等味 Of equal flavour, of the same character.

등신 等身 A life-size image or portrait.

등심 等心 Equal mind ; of the same mental characteristics ; the universal mind common to all.

등원 等願 The universal vows common to Buddhas.

등인 等引 Samāhita, body and mind both fixed or concentrated in samādhi.

등일대거 等一大車 The highest class great cart, i.e. universal salvation ; cf. Lotus Sūtra 3.

등일체제불 等一切諸佛 The third of the 십회향 十迴向 q.v.

등자 等慈 Universal or equal mercy toward all beings without distinction.

등정각 等正覺 Samyak-sambodhi ; complete perfect knowledge ; Buddha-knowledge ; omniscience ; the bodhi of all Buddhas ; cf. 등각 等覺 ; 삼막 三藐.

등제 等諦 Ordinary rules of life ; common morality.

등중생계 等衆生界 The universal realm of living beings.

등지 等至 A name for fixation of the mind, or concentration in dhyāna ; an equivalent of samāpatti.

등지 等智 Common knowledge, which only knows phenomena.

등지 等持 Holding oneself in equanimity, a tr. of samādhi, as also is 삼등지 三等持, i.e. samādhi-equilibrium ; also of samāpatti, v. 삼마발지 三摩鉢底 and 등지 等至.

등활 等活 Saṁjīv. Revive, re-animate ; resurrection. 등활지옥 等活地獄 The first of the eight hot hells, in which the denizens are chopped, stabbed, ground, and pounded, but by a cool wind are brought back to life, to undergo renewed torment. Also 갱활 更活.

<ㄹ>

라 攞 To split ; wipe ; choose ; translit. *la*. 라걸첨나 攞乞尖拏 v. 상 相 Lakṣaṇa. 라도가 攞都迦 Laḍḍuka, a cake, or sweetmeat, identified with the 환희환 歡喜丸 joy-buns, q.v.

라 螺 A conch, snail, spiral, screw. 나계 螺髻 Tuft of hair on Brahmā's head resembling a conch, hence a name for Brahmā. 나계선인 螺髻仙人 A former incarnation of the Buddha, when a bird built its nest in his hair during his prolonged meditation. 나계범(지) 螺髻梵(志) A name for Brahmā, and for the Buddha. 나발 螺髮 The curly hair of the Buddha.

라 羅 A net (for catching birds), gauze, openwork ; sieve ; to arrange in order ; translit. *la* and *ra* sounds, e.g. 남라 南羅 S. Lāra ; Lāḍa ; Lāṭa, in Gujarat ; 북라 北羅 N. Lāra, Valabhī, on the western coast of Gujarat.

라 蘿 Creeping or climbing plants. 나의 蘿衣 Coarse garments worn by ascetics.

라 邏 Patrol ; translit. *la, ra*. 라흘쇄 邏吃灑 ; 라걸주 邏乞酒 Lakṣaṇa, v. 상 相, a distinguishing mark, sign, or characteristic. 라구 邏求 Laghu, light, nimble. 라도 邏闍 Rāja, v. 라 羅.

라 囉 To chatter, translit. *ra* sounds ; cf. 라 羅, 라 邏, 로 嚕 e.g. 라서 囉逝 Rājñī, a queen, a princess. 라야 囉惹 Rāja, a king.

라 剌 To cut, slash ; translit. *la, ra, ya*. 라슬지 剌瑟胝 Yaṣṭi, pole, staff, stick, intp. flagpole. 라갈절 剌竭節 or 려갈절 糲竭節 Laguḍa, a staff, stick. 라나 剌那 cf. 라 囉, 라 羅 Ratna, precious thing, jewel, etc. 라나시기 剌那尸棄 Ratnaśikhin, cf. 시 尸, "the 999th Buddha of the preceding kalpa, the second of the Sapta Buddha." [Eitel]. 라나가라 剌那伽羅 Ratnākara, a "jewel-mine, the ocean" [M. W.], intp. jewel-heap ; name of a Buddha and bodhisattva ; the 112th Buddha of the present kalpa ; also of "a native of Vaiśālī, contemporary of Śākyamuni." 라사 剌闍 ; 라야 囉惹 Rajas, atmosphere, vapour, gloom, dust, dirt, etc. ; intp. dust, minute ; also hatred, suffering.

라곡 羅縠 A gauze-like ethereal garment.

라마 喇嘛 Lama, the Lamaistic form of Buddhism found chiefly in Tibet, and Mongolia, and the smaller Himalayan States. In Tibet it is divided into two schools, the older one wearing red robes, the later, which was founded by Tson-kha-pa in the fifteenth century, wearing yellow ; its chiefs are the Dalai Lama and the Panchen Lama, respectively.

라마 羅摩 Rāma, delightful, joyful ; also the name of a grove, perhaps ārāma, a pleasance, garden. 나마가 羅摩伽 is tr. as 입법계 入法界 entering the realm of the law. 나마인도 羅摩印度 Helmund, a river rising in Afghanistan.

라문 羅門 Brāhmaṇa, v. 바라문 婆羅門.

라바 羅婆 Lava, also 나예 羅預 A division of time, an instant. 나바나 羅婆那 Rāvaṇa, king of Ceylon and ruler of the Rākṣasas, overcome by Rāmacandra, v. the Rāmāyaṇa.

라아 羅誐 Rāga, desire, covetousness.

라야 羅惹 Rājan, Rāja ; king, sovereign, ruler.

라열 羅閱 Rājagṛha, also 라열저(가라) 羅閱祇(迦羅) ; 라열기 羅閱耆 ; 라열게려혜 羅閱揭黎醯 ; 라월

羅越 ; 라야흘리희 囉惹訖哩呬 The capital of Magadha, at the foot of the Gṛdhrakūṭa mountain, first metropolis of Buddhism and seat of the first synod ; v. 왕사 王舍.

라월 羅越 Rājagṛha, v. 나열 羅閱.

라제 羅齊 To collect contributions of food ; an almsbowl.

라집 羅十 Kumārajīva, also 라집 羅什 ; v. 구 鳩.

라타(나) 羅陀(那) Ratna, anything precious, a gem, etc. ; also 라달나 羅怛那 ; 라달낭 羅怛曩 ; 라달낭 羅怛囊. Cf. 보 寶 and 칠보 七寶.

라피나 羅被那 Rāvaṇa, clamorous, demanding.

라한 羅漢 Arhan, arhat ; worthy, worshipful, an arhat, the saint, or perfect man of Hīnayāna ; the sixteen, eighteen, or 500 famous disciples appointed to witness to Buddha-truth and save the world ; v. 아 阿.

라후 羅睺 Rāhu, also 라호 羅護 ; 라호 羅虎 ; "the demon who is supposed to seize the sun and moon and thus cause eclipses." [M. W.] 라후라 羅睺羅 Rāhula, the son of Śākyamuni and Yaśodharā ; also 라후 羅睺 ; 라후라 羅吼羅 ; 라운 羅云 ; 라운 羅雲 ; 갈호라 曷怙羅 ; 하호라 何怙羅 ; 라호라 羅怙羅. He is supposed to have been in the womb for six years and born when his father attained Buddhahood ; also said to have been born during an eclipse, and thus acquired his name, though it is defined in other ways ; his father did not see him till he was six years old. He became a disciple of the Hīnayāna, but is said to have become a Mahāyānist when his father preached this final perfect doctrine, a statement gainsaid by his being recognized as founder of the Vaibhāṣika school. He is to be reborn as the eldest son of every Buddha, hence is sometimes called the son of Ānanda. 라후라다 羅睺羅多 Rāhulata, of Kapila, the sixteenth Patriarch, "who miraculously transported himself to the kingdom of Śrāvastī, where he saw on the Hiraṇyavatī the shadow of five Buddhas" ; a sage, Saṅghānandi, was there in meditation, and him he appointed as his successor. 라후아수라 羅睺阿修羅 Rāhu-asura, the asura who in fighting with Indra can seize sun and moon, i.e. cause eclipses.

락 絡 Continuous ; fibres, veins. 연락 聯絡 Connected, linked.

락 酪 Dadhi, a thick, sour milk which is highly esteemed as a food and as a remedy or preventive. 낙미 酪味 Sour, one of the five tastes. T'ien-t'ai compared the second period of the Hīnayāna with this. 낙경 酪經 T'ien-t'ai term for the Hīnayāna sūtras.

락 落 Falling leaves ; to fall, drop, descend, settle ; translit. *la, na.* 낙차 落叉 A lakh, 100,000, v. 락 洛. 낙흘삽미 落吃澁弭 Lakṣmī, the goddess of fortune, of good auspices, etc. 낙잠 落賺 A humbug, trickster, impostor, deceiver. 낙가 落迦 Naraka, hell, v. 나 那. 낙발 落髮 To cut off the hair of the head, shave, become a monk. 낙발염의 落髮染衣 ; 낙염 落染 To shave the head and dye the clothing, i.e. to dye grey the normal white Indian garment ; to become a monk.

란 亂 Disturb, perturb, confusion, disorder, rebellion. 난승 亂僧 A disorderly monk. 난선 亂善 To disturb the good, confound goodness ; the confused goodness of those who worship, etc., with divided mind. 난심 亂心 A perturbed or confused mind, to disturb or unsettle the mind. 난상 亂想 To think confusedly, or improperly. 난행 亂行 Disorderly conduct.

란 爛 Glittering, as iridescent fish, 난어 爛魚 ; rotten, soft ; pulp.

란 蘭 The epidendrum, orchid ; scented, refined ; pledged, sworn ; translit. *ra, ram, ran* ; abbrev. for 투란차 偸蘭遮 q.v. 난실 蘭室 ; 난야 蘭若 Araṇya, lit. forest, hence hermitage, v. 아 阿 ; a monastery. 난분(회) 蘭盆(會) Ullambana, Lambana, Avalamba, v. 우 盂. The festival of masses for destitute ghosts on the 15th of the 7th month. 난국 蘭菊 Orchid and chrysanthemum, spring and autumn, emblems of beauty. 난사 蘭闍 ; 난사(대) 蘭奢(待) A Mongol or Turkish word implying praise. 난향 蘭香 Orchid fragrance, spring.

람 藍 Blue, indigo ; translit. *ram, lam.* 남발라 藍勃羅 Lambura ; Lambhara, a mountain north of Kabul. 남바 藍婆 Lambā, name of a rākṣasī. 남우 藍宇 A saṅghārāma, monastery, monastery-buildings. 남마 藍摩 ; 남막 藍莫 Rāma ; Rāmagrāma, an ancient kingdom and city of Northern India between Kapilavastu and Kuśinagara. 남풍 藍風 Vairambhavāta, a hostile or fierce storm, v. 비람 毘嵐.

람 嵐 Mountain mist ; vapour. 람비니 嵐毘尼 Lumbinī, the park in which Māyā gave birth to Śākyamuni, 15 miles east of Kapilavastu ; also Limbinī, Lambinī, Lavinī. 람비니 嵐鞞尼 ; 람비니 藍毘尼 or 류비니 留毘尼 or 류비니 流毘尼 or 림비니 林毘尼 or 루비니 樓毘尼 ; 류미니 流彌尼 ; 림미니 林微尼 ; 랍벌니 臘伐尼 ; 룡미니 龍彌你 ; 론민니 論民尼 ; 람분니 藍奔尼.

람 濫 Overflowing, excess. 남파 濫波 Lampā(ka) ; the district of Lamghan.

람 覽 To look at, view ; translit. *raṁ-* ; associated with fire.

람 攬 To seize, hold in the arms, embrace ; monopolize.

랍 臈 ; 臘 The end of a Buddhist year ; a Buddhist year ; v. 랍 臘

랍 臘 Dried flesh ; to sacrifice to the gods three days after the winter solstice ; the end of the year ; a year ; a monastic year, i.e. the end of the annual summer retreat, also called 계랍 戒臘 ; 하랍 夏臘 ; 법랍 法臘. 납팔 臘八 The 8th day of the last month of the year, the 8th of the 12th month, the day of the Buddha's enlightenment. 납차 臘次 In order of years, i.e. of ordination. 납벌니 臘伐尼 v. 람 嵐 Lumbinī. 납불 臘佛 The offerings to Buddha after the summer retreat, maintained on the 15th day of the 7th month ; also All Souls' Day, v. 우 盂 ; the 납병 臘餅 annual cakes are then offered and eaten. 납박 臘縛 Lava, a brief time ; the 900th part of a day and night, or 1 minute 36 seconds.

랑 狼 A wolf ; fierce. 낭적산 狼跡山 Wolf track hill, another name for 계족산 鷄足山 q.v.

래 來 Āgama ; āgama ; āgata. Come, the coming, future. 내세 來世 Future world, or rebirth. 내응 來應 To come in response to an invitation ; to answer prayer (by a miracle). 내과 來果 The fruit or condition of the next rebirth, regarded as the result of the present. 내생 來生 Future rebirth ; the future life. 내영 來迎 The coming of Buddhas to meet the dying believer and bid welcome to the Pure Land ; the three special welcomers are Amitābha, Avalokiteśvara, and Mahāsthāmaprāpta.

량 良 Good, virtuous, beneficial. 양일 良日 ; 길일 吉日 A good, or auspicious, day. 양인 良忍 Ryōnin, founder of the Japanese 융통염불 融通念佛 school. 양분 良賁 Liang-pên, the T'ang monk who assisted Amogha in the translation of the 인왕경 仁王經 Jên Wang Ching. 양복전 良福田 The field of blessedness, cultivated by offerings to Buddha, the Law, and the Order.

량 量 Pramāṇa. Measure, capacity, length, ability ; to measure, deliberate ; a syllogism in logic, v. 비량 比量. A syllogism, consisting of 종 宗 pratijñā, proposition ; 인 因 hetu, reason ; 유 喩 udāharaṇa, example ; but the syllogism varies in the number of its avayava, or members. There are other divisions from 2 to 6, e.g. 현량 現量 and 비량 比量 direct or sense inferences, and comparative or logical inferences ; to these are added 성교량 聖敎量 arguments based on authority ; 비유량 譬喩量 analogy ; 의준 義准 postulation, or general assent ; and 무체 無體 negation, or non-existence. 양과 量果 Conditioned by various external objects, different types of consciousness arise (ālambana-pratyaya). The 법상종 法相宗 held that the percipient mind is conditioned by existing things, and when the two are in conjunction the ultimate consequence of any action may be known. 양등신 量等身 The immanence of the Tathāgata in all things, phenomenal and noumenal, he being the all in all.

려 廬 A hut, shelter, hovel. 려사나 廬舍那 Locana ; illuminating ; one of the forms of the Trikāya, similar to the sambhogakāya. Also used for Vairocana, v. 비 毘.

려 黎 Black, black-haired ; cf. 리 離, 리 利, 리 梨, etc. 여야 黎耶 Ālaya, v. 아 阿.

려 麗 Elegant, beautiful ; to display. 여탑 麗塔 An elegant pagoda. 여체비 麗掣毘 Licchavi, v. 리 離, 리 梨. 여장 麗藏 The Korean Tripiṭaka. 고려 高麗 Korea.

려 驢 Khara, an ass, donkey. 여년 驢年 Donkey-year, i.e. without date or period, because the ass does not appear in the list of cyclic animals. 여순 驢脣 Kharoṣṭha, "donkey lips," name of a sage celebrated for his astronomical knowledge.

려 濾 To strain, filter. 여수낭 濾水囊 ; 여라 濾羅 A filtering bag, or cloth ; cf. 녹 漉 .

력 力 Bala ; power, strength, of which there are several categories : 이력 二力 power of choice and of practice ; 삼력 三力 the power of Buddha ; of meditation (samādhi) and of practice. 오력 五力 Pañcabala, the five powers of faith, zeal, memory (or remembering), meditation, and wisdom. 육력 六力 A child's power is in crying ; a woman's in resentment ; a king's in domineering ; an arhat's in zeal (or progress) ; a Buddha's in mercy ; and a bhikṣu's in endurance (of despite). 십력 十力 q.v. The ten powers of Buddhas and bodhisattvas.

력 歷 To pass through, over or to ; successive ; separated ; calendar, astronomical calculations. 역겁 歷劫 To pass through a kalpa ; in the course of a kalpa. 역연 歷然 Separate(ly). 역연대경 歷緣對境 Passing circumstances and the objects of the senses.

련 憐 Commiserate, pity, sympathize, charitable. 연념 憐念 Sympathetic thoughts. 연애 憐愛 To pity, love, care for. 연민 憐愍 To pity, commiserate.

련 蓮 Puṇḍarīka, the lotus, especially the white lotus, *Nymphœa alba* ; Padma, especially the *Nelumbium speciosum* ; Utpala, the *Nymphœa cœrulea*, the blue lotus ; Kumuda, *Nymphœa esculenta*, white lotus, or *Nymphœa rubra*, red lotus ; Nīlotpala, *Nymphœa cyanea*, a blue lotus. The first four are called white, red, blue, and yellow lotuses ; but the white lotus is generally meant unless otherwise specified. 연찰 蓮刹 Lotus-kṣetra, or Lotus-land, the paradise of Amitābha. 연자 蓮子 Lotus seeds. 연종 蓮宗 The Lotus sect founded by 혜원 慧遠 Hui-yuan *circa* A.D. 390 at his monastery, in which was a 백련지 白蓮池 white lotus pond. It has no connection with the White Lily Secret Society which arose during the Mongol or Yüan dynasty. The Lotus sect is traced to the awakening of Hui-yüan by the reading of the Prajñāpāramitā sūtra. He then turned his attention to calling on the name of Buddha to obtain salvation direct to his Pure Land. The school became that of the Amitābha or Pure-land. The school became that of the Amitābha or Pure-land sect, which in later years developed into the principal Buddhist cult in the Far East. 연궁 蓮宮 Padmavimāna. Lotus-palace, the Pure Land of the Sambhogakāya ; also the eight-leaved lotus of the heart. 연좌 蓮座 The lotus throne on which are seated the images ; Buddha-throne. 연리 蓮理 The mystic doctrine of the Lotus faith. 연안 蓮眼 The eye of the blue lotus, i.e. the wonderful eye of Buddha. 연사 蓮社 The White Lotus sect, idem 연종 蓮宗. 연우 蓮祐 Mutual protectors, or helpers of the Lotus sect, i.e. members. 연경 蓮經 The Lotus Sūtra ; v. 법화 法華. 연태 蓮胎 The Lotus-womb in which the believers of Amitābha are born into his paradise ; it is also described as the believer's heart in embryo. 연화 蓮華 or 蓮花 The lotus flower. 연화국 蓮華國 The pure land of every Buddha, the land of his enjoyment. 연화좌 蓮華坐 Padmāsana ; to sit with crossed legs ; also a lotus throne. 연화자 蓮華子 Disciples, or followers, shown in the 연화부 蓮華部 of the maṇḍalas. 연화수보살 蓮華手菩薩 Padmapāṇi, Kuan-yin holding a lotus flower. 연화지 蓮華智 The lotus or mystic wisdom of Amitābha, one of the five 지 智. 연화안 蓮華眼 The blue-lotus eyes of Kuan-yin. 연화대 蓮華臺 Lotus throne for images of Buddhas and bodhisattvas. 연화장세계 蓮華藏世界 The lotus world or universe of each Buddha for his sambhogakāya. 연화의 蓮華衣 ; 연화복 蓮華服 The lotus-garment, or robe of purity, the robe of the monk or nun. 연방 蓮邦 The Lotus land, the Pure Land, of Amitābha. 연문 蓮門 The Lotus sect, idem 연종 蓮宗.

련 連 To connect, continue ; contiguous ; and, even. 연하 連河 The Nairañjanā river, v. 니 尼 ; 희 希.

련 練 To train, practise, drill, exercise. 연마 練磨 To drill and grind, three bodhisattva conditions for maintaining progress: the fixing of attention on those who have attained enlightenment ; the examination of one's purpose ; and the realization of the power at work in others ; v. 삼퇴굴 三退屈. 연야 練若 Araṇya, hermitage, etc., cf. 아 阿. 연행 練行 Religious training or discipline.

렬 烈 Burning, fierce ; virtuous, heroic. 열사지 烈士池 Tyāgīhrada, Jīvakahrada, the lake of the renouncer, or of the hero, near to the Mṛgadāva.

렵 獵 To hunt. 엽사 獵師 A hunter, e.g. a disguised person, a monk who wears the robe but breaks the commandments.

령 鈴 a hand-bell with a tongue.

령 寧 Repose ; settle ; better than ; rather ; how? 영안 寧安 Reposeful, at ease.

령 靈 Spirit, spiritual, energy, effective, clever. 영공 靈供 Offerings to the spirits who are about the dead during the forty-nine days of masses. 영상 靈像 Spirit-image, that of a Buddha or a god. 영묘 靈妙 Abstruse, mysterious ; clever. 영산 靈山 ; 영악 靈嶽 ; 영취산 靈鷲山 The Spirit Vulture Peak, Gṛdhrakūṭa, v. 기 耆 10 and 취 鷲 23. 영감 靈感 ; 영응 靈應 Spirit-response, efficacious as in response to prayer. 영서화 靈瑞華 The udumbara flower, which appears but once in 3,000 years, a symbol of Buddha ; v. 우담 優曇 17. 영계 靈界 The realm of departed spirits ; the world of spirits. 영신 靈神 The spirit, soul ; an efficacious spirit. 영사 靈祠 Spirit-temple, a monastery. 영지 靈芝 The auspicious plant, emblem of good luck, or long life ; name of 원조 元照 Yüan-chao, q.v. 영골 靈骨 Spirit-bones, Buddha-relics. 영혼 靈魂 A spirit, soul. 영감 靈龕 A coffin.

례 隷 To control ; retainers. 예거 隷車 v. 리 離.

례 禮 Worship, offerings, rites ; ritual, ceremonial, decorum, courtesy, etiquette. 예참 禮懺 Worship and repentance, penitential offering. 예배 禮拜 Vandana ; or, when invoking the name of the object of worship, namas-kāra ; to worship, pay reverence. 예경 禮敬 To worship, reverence, pay respect.

로 盧 A rice-vessel ; a fire-pan ; dram-shop ; black ; translit. *lo, ro, ru* ; cf. 루 樓 ; 로 路 ; 류 流. 노구다바타부 盧倶多婆拖部 Lokottaravādinaḥ, superior to the world, an important sect of the Mahāsāṅghikāḥ. 노히지가목다 盧呬胝訶目多 Lohita-mukta or Rohita(ka)-mukta, rubies or red pearls, one of the seven treasures. 노지나 盧脂那 Rocana, illuminating, bright ; name of a flower ; perhaps also spots before the eyes ; identified with 노자나 盧遮那 v. 비 毘 Vairocana. 노지불 盧至佛 ; 노자불 盧遮佛 v. 루 樓 Rucika. 노사 盧舍 v. 구 俱 Krośa. 노사나 盧舍那 Rocana, illuminating, also v. 비 毘 Vairocana. 노행자 盧行者 Surname and title of 혜능 慧能 Hui-nêng. 노가위사제 盧迦委斯諦 Lokeśvara-rāja, lord of the world, an epithet of Kuan-yin and others. 노혜달가 盧慧呾迦 ; 노혜다가 盧慧多迦 Rohita(ka) ; Lohita(ka) ; red. 노다라야 盧陀羅耶 Rudra, roaring, terrible, a name of Śiva, the Rudras or Maruts, storm-gods, etc.

로 路 A road, way. 로가 路伽 idem 로가 路迦. 로가다 路伽多 Lohita, red, copper-coloured. 로가기야 路伽祇夜 Loka-geya, intp. as repetition in verse, but also as singing after common fashion. 로하 路賀 Loha, copper, also gold, iron, etc. 로가 路迦 Loka, intp. by 세간 世間, the world, a region or realm, a division of the universe. 로가비 路迦憊 or 路伽憊 Lokavit, Lokavid, he who knows, or interprets the world, a title of a Buddha. 로가야지가 路迦耶底迦 ; 로가야(타) 路伽耶(陀) ; 로가야지가 路柯耶胝柯 Lokāyatika, "A materialist, follower of the Cārvāka system, atheist, unbeliever" [M. W.] ; intp. as 순세 順世 worldly, Epicurean, the soul perishes with the body, and the pleasures of the senses are the highest good. 로가나타 路迦那他 intp. 세존 世尊 Lokajyeṣṭha ; Lokanātha, most excellent of the world, lord of the world, epithet of Brahmā and of a Buddha.

로 爐 A stove, fireplace, censer. 노단 爐壇 A fire-altar.

로 露 Dew ; symbol of transience ; to expose, disclose. 노명 露命 Dew-like life ; transient. 노지 露地 Bare ground ; like dew on the ground, dewy ground. 노형 露形 ; 노신 露身 Exposed form, naked, e.g. the Nirgrantha ascetics. 노우 露牛 The great white ox and oxcart revealed in the open, i.e. the Mahāyāna, v. Lotus sūtra.

로 蘆 Reeds, rushes. 노엽달마 蘆葉達磨 Bodhidharma and his rush-leaf boat in which he is said to have crossed the Yangtse.

로 魯 Stupid, vulgar, honest. 로달라 魯達羅 Rudra, roaring, awful, terrible, intp. terribly evil, a name for Śiva ; also 로달라 澇達羅 ; 로날라 嚕捺羅.

로 勞 Toil, labour, trouble ; to reward. 노려 勞侶 Troublesome companions, e.g. the passions. 노원 勞怨 The annoyance or hatred of labour, or trouble, or the passions, or demons. 노결 勞結 The troublers, or passions, those which hold one in bondage.

로 嚕 Translit. *ru, rau.* 노다 嚕多 Ruta, a loud sound, or voice. 노라바 嚕羅婆 The Raurava hell of crying and wailing.

로 嚧 Translit. *ru, ro, lṛ, lo,* v. 로 盧.

록 鹿 Mṛga ; a deer ; as Śākyamuni first preached the four noble truths in the Deer-garden, the deer is a symbol of his preaching. 녹선 鹿仙 Śākyamuni as royal stage: he and Devadatta had both been deer in a previous incarnation. 녹계 鹿戒 Deer morals i.e. to live, as some ascetics, like deer. 녹원 鹿苑 ; 녹야원 鹿野園 Mṛgadāva, known also as 선인원 仙人園, etc., the park, abode, or retreat of wise men, whose resort it formed ; "a famous park north-east of Vārāṇaśī, a favourite resort of Śākyamuni. The modern Sārnāth (Śāraṅganātha) near Benares." [M. W.] Here he is reputed to have preached his first sermon and converted his first five disciples. T'ien-t'ai also counts it as the scene of the second period of his teaching, when during twelve years he delivered the Āgama sūtras. 녹거 鹿車 Deer carts, one of the three kinds of vehicle referred to in the Lotus Sūtra, the medium kind ; v. 삼거 三車.

론 論 To discourse upon, discuss, reason over ; tr. for śāstra, abhidharma, and upadeśa, i.e. discourses, discussions, or treatises on dogma, philosophy, discipline, etc. 논종 論宗 The Mādhyamika school of the 삼론 三論 San-lun (Sanron) ; also the Abhidharma, or Śāstra school ; also the same as 논가 論家 ; 논사 論師 śāstra-writers, or interpreters, or philosophers. 논민 論民 v. 람 嵐 Lumbinī. 논소 論疏 Śāstras with commentary. 논장 論藏 Thesaurus of discussions or discourses, the Abhidharma-piṭaka, one of the three divisions of the Tripiṭaka. It comprises the philosophical works. The first compilation is accredited to Mahā-Kāśyapa, disciple of Buddha, but the work is of a later period. The Chinese version is in three sections : 대승론

大乘論 the Mahāyāna philosophy ; 소승론 小乘論 the Hīnayāna philosophy ; 송원속입장제론 宋元續入藏諸論 The Sung and Yüan Addenda, A.D. 960-1368. 논의 論議 Upadeśa, dogmatic treatises, the twelfth and last section of the Canon.

롱 鑨 A metal chime.

뢰 牢 A gaol, fold, pen ; secure, firm. 뇌관 牢關 A firm barrier, a place shut tight, type of the deluded mind. 뇌총 牢籠 Pen, pit, or fold (for animals) and cage (for birds).

뢰 雷 Garjita, thunder, thundering.

뢰 懶 Lazy, negligent, disinclined. 뇌타 懶惰.

뢰 賴 To rely upon, depend on ; throw the burden on, repudiate. 뇌타(화라) 賴吒(啝羅) Rāṣṭrapāla, protector of a kingdom, king. 뇌야 賴耶 Ālaya, v. 아 阿.

료 寮 A hut, study, monastery ; fellow-student. 요주 寮主 ; 요원 寮元 ; 요장 寮長 The head, or manager of a monastery.

료 療 To heal, cure, 요병 療病.

료 料 To measure (grain), calculate ; control, direct ; materials ; glassware. 요간 料簡 To expound, explain, comment upon ; T'ien-t'ai uses the term for question and answer, catechism.

루 樓 An upper storey, storied building, tower ; one of the eighteen hells. 루이환라 樓夷亙羅 Lokeśvara-rāja, an ancient Buddha, successor to 정광 定光 Buddha. 누탄 樓炭 A tower or pile of charcoal, e.g. the world for conflagration, 루비 樓毘 cf. 람 嵐 Lumbinī. 루유 樓由 ; 루지 樓至 Rucika, also 로지 盧至 ; 로차 盧遮, the last of the 1,000 Buddhas of the present kalpa. 루다(라) 樓陀(羅) Rudra, the howler, or god of tempests. 루려 樓黎 Vaiḍūrya, lapis lazuli, cf. 류 瑠.

루 髏 Kapāla ; a skull. 누만 髏鬘 A chaplet or wreath of skulls, worn by the Kāpālikas, a Śivaitic sect ; kapālī is an epithet of Śiva as the skull-wearer.

루 淚 Tears. 누타 淚墮 Falling tears.

루 累 To tie ; accumulate ; repeatedly ; to implicate, involve. 누칠제 累七齊 The sevenfold repetition of masses for the dead. 누겁 累劫 Repeated, or many kalpas. 누형 累形 The body as involved in the distresses of life. 누장 累障 The hindrances of many vexations, responsibilities or affairs.

루 漏 Āsrava, "flowing, running, discharge ; distress, pain, affliction." [M. W.] It is defined as another term for 번뇌 煩惱 q.v. ; also as the discharge, or outflow, from the organs of sense, wherever those exist, hence it is applied to the passions and their filth ; impure efflux from the mind, v. 욕유 欲有 ; also to the leakage or loss thereby of the 정도 正道 truth ; also to the stream of transmigration. 누영진무소외 漏永盡無所畏 Absolute confidence (of Buddha) that transmigration would cease for ever. 누계 漏戒 To make a leak in the commandments, i.e. break them. 누업 漏業 The deeds of the sinner in the stream of transmigration, which produce his karma. 누무루 漏無漏 Transmigration and nirvāṇa. 누진 漏盡 Āsravakṣaya. The end of the passions, or the exhaustion of the stream of transmigration. 누진명 漏盡明 The realization that the stream of transmigration is ended. 누진의해 漏盡意解 The passions ended and the mind freed, the state of the arhat. 누진지 漏盡智 The wisdom of the arhat. 누진비구 漏盡比丘 The monk who has ended the stream of transmigration, the arhat. 누진증명 漏盡證明 The assurance or realization that the stream of transmigration is ended and nirvāṇa attained. 누진통 漏盡通 The super-natural insight into the ending of the stream of transmigration ; one of the six abhijñās.

류 類 Class, species ; to classify. 유지 類智 Knowledge which is of the same order, e.g. the four fundamental dogmas (사제 四諦 or 법지 法智) applicable on earth which are also extended to the higher realms of form and non-form and are called 유지 類智.

류 流 Flow ; float ; spread ; wander. 유래 流來 Flowed or floated down ; that which has come down from the past. 유래생사 流來生死 Transmigration which has come down from the state of primal ignorance. 유지 流支 An abbreviation for Bodhiruci, v. 보 菩. 류비니 流毘尼 ; 류미니 流彌尼 Lumbinī, cf. 람 嵐. 유수 流水 Flowing water, name of a former incarnation of Śākyamuni. 유사 流沙 Floating or shifting sands. 유주 流注 Continuous flow, ceaseless. 유장 流漿 Liquid broth of molten copper, or grains of red-hot iron, in one of the hells. 유사나 流舍那 Locana, cf. 비 毘. Often regarded as the body of bliss of Vairocana. 유전 流轉 Saṁsāra, transmigration, flowing and returning, flowing back again. 유전문 流轉門 The way of transmigration, as contrasted with 멸문 滅門 that of nirvāṇa. 유전진여 流轉眞如 The bhūtatathatā, or absolute, in transmigratory forms. 유통 流通 Spread abroad ; permeate ; flowing through, or everywhere, without effective hindrance.

류 留 Keep, detain ; hand down. 유나 留拏 Ruṇṇapaṇḍakas, castrated males. 유난 留難 The difficulty of one's good deeds being hindered by evil spirits.

륜 輪 Cakra ; wheel, disc, rotation, to revolve ; v. 작 斫. The three wheels are 혹업고 惑業苦 illusion, karma, suffering, in constant revolution. The five are earth, water, fire, wind, and space ; the earth rests on revolving spheres of water, fire, wind, and space. The nine are seen on the tops of pagodas, cf. 구륜 九輪. 윤위산 輪圍山 Cakravāla, the double concentric circles of mountains forming the periphery of a world. 윤원(구족) 輪圓(具足) A complete maṇḍala showing the Buddhas and others, symbolizing their works ; a magic circle. 윤타 輪埵 Ears round and full, a mark of a Buddha. 윤(다리)화 輪(多梨)華 A precious pearl that purifies ; also a specially fragrant flower. 윤보 輪寶 A cakravartin's wheel, i.e. either gold, silver, copper, or iron, manifesting his rank and power. 윤차 輪差 ; 윤번 輪番 To take turns, used to indicate a rota or rotation of duties. 윤좌 輪座 The throne of a cakravartin, or Buddha. 윤회 輪廻 ; 윤전 輪轉 Saṁsāra, the turning of the wheel, to revolve, i.e. transmigration in the six ways, the wheel of transmigration ; the round of existence. 화륜 火輪 Alātacakra, a wheel of fire, produced by rapidly whirling a fire-brand, a symbol of the unreality of the visible, since such a wheel does not exist. 윤왕 輪王 A cakravartin, "a ruler the wheels of whose chariot roll everywhere without obstruction ; an emperor, a sovereign of the world, a supreme ruler." [M. W.] A Buddha, whose truth and realm are universal. There are four kinds of cakravartin, symbolized by wheels of gold, silver, copper, and iron ; each possesses the seven precious things, 칠보 七寶 q.v. 윤상 輪相 The wheel sign, on the top of a pagoda, or on the feet of a cakravartin, or Buddha. 윤제 輪臍 The navel, or hub of a wheel. 윤장 輪藏 Revolving scriptures, a revolving stand with eight faces, representing the eight directions, each containing a portion of the sacred canon ; a praying-wheel, the revolving of which brings as much merit to the operator as if he had read the whole. 윤복 輪輻 Wheel-spokes. 윤망 輪輞 ; 윤연 輪緣 A felly, or tire.

률 栗 Chestnut: translit. *l*, *hr*. 율첩(바)비 栗呫(婆)毘 Licchavi, v. 리 梨. 율타 栗馱 Hṛd, hṛdaya, the heart, v. 오 汙.

륵 勒 Rein ; extort ; a left stroke ; to draw in. 륵사 勒沙 Lākṣā, lac ; a reddish colour, probably cochineal. 륵사바 勒沙婆 Ṛṣabha, described as one of three famous ṛṣi, before the days of Śākyamuni, of the Nirgrantha type of naked ascetics. 륵나마제 勒那摩提 or 륵나바제 勒那婆提 Ratnamati, a monk from Central India, *circa* A.D. 500, who translated three works of which two remain.

릉 駿 Laṅkā. 능가 駿迦 Ceylon, v. 릉 楞.

릉 棱 A corner, a shaped edge, trimmed timber, corner-like ; intractable, uncertain. V. 릉 楞.

릉 陵 A mound, tomb ; cf. 필릉 畢陵.

릉 楞 Same character as 릉 棱, but used widely for buddhist terms. 능엄경 楞嚴經 The Laṅkāvatāra Sūtra.

리 魑 A mountain demon resembling a tiger ; 매 魅 is a demon of marshes having the head of a pig and body of a man. The two words are used together indicating evil spirits.

리 里 A village, neighbourhood, third of an English mile ; translit. *r* and *ṛ* ; perhaps also for *l* and *lṛ*.

리 利 Paṭu, tīkṣṇa ; sharp, keen, clever ; profitable, beneficial ; gain, advantage ; interest. 이인 利人 To benefit or profit men, idem 이타 利他 parahita ; the bodhisattva-mind is 자리이타 自利利他 to improve oneself for the purpose of improving or benefiting others ; the Buddha-mind is 이타일심 利他一心 with single mind to help others, pure altruism ; 이생 利生 is the extension of this idea to 중생 衆生 all the living, which of course is not limited to men or this earthly life ; 이물 利物 is also used with the same meaning, 물 物 being the living. 이사 利使 The sharp or clever envoy, i.e. the chief illusion of regarding the ego and its experiences and ideas as real, one of the five chief illusions. 이검 利劍 A sharp sword, used figuratively for Amitābha, and Mañjuśrī, indicating wisdom, discrimination, or power over evil. 이지 利智 Keen intelligence, wisdom, discrimination ; pāṭava. 이근 利根 Sharpness, cleverness, intelligence, natural powers, endowment ; possessed of power of the pañca-indryāṇi (faith, etc.) or the five sense-organs, v. 오근 五根. 이락 利樂 Blessing and joy ; the blessing being for the future life, the joy for the present ; or aid (for salvation) and the joy of it. 이락유정 利樂有情 To bless and give joy to the living, or sentient, the work of a bodhisattva. 이파파 利波波 ; 이파다 離波多 ; 여파다 黎波多 ; 힐예벌다 頡隸伐多 Revata ; Raivata. (1) A Brahman hermit ; one of the disciples of Śākyamuni, to be reborn as Samanta-prabhāsa. (2) President of the second synod, a native of Sāṅkāśya. (3) A contemporary of Aśoka, mentioned in connection with the third synod. Cf. [Eitel]. 이익 利益 Benefit, aid, to bless ; hence 이익묘 利益妙 the wonder of Buddha's blessing, in opening the minds of all to enter the Buddha-enlightenment. 이행섭 利行攝 Saṅgraha-vastu, the drawing of all beings to Buddhism through blessing them by deed, word, and will ; one of the 사섭법 四攝法 q.v. 이변 利辯 Sharp and keen discrimination, or ratiocination, one of the seven characteristics 칠종변 七種辯 of the Bodhisattva. 이양 利養 To nourish oneself by gain ; gain ; avarice. 이양박 利養縛 The bond of selfish greed, one of the two bonds, gain and fame.

리 理 Siddhānta ; hetu. Ruling principle, fundamental law, intrinsicality, universal basis, essential element ; nidāna, reason ; pramāṇa, to arrange, regulate, rule, rectify.

리 梨 The pear. 리야 梨耶 v. 아 阿 Ārya. 리차 梨車 ; 려차 黎車 ; 리차 離車 ; 률첩반 栗呫媻 Licchavi, the ancient republic of Vaiśālī, whose people were among the earliest followers of Śākyamuni.

리 離 To leave, part from, apart from, abandon ; translit. *li, le, r, re, rai.* 이거 離佉 Likh, to write ; lekha, writings, documents. 이구 離垢 To leave the impure, abandon the defiling influence of the passions, or illusion. 이구세계 離垢世界 The world free from impurity, the name of Śāriputra's Buddha-realm. 이구지 離垢地 The second of the ten bodhisattva stages in which he overcomes all passion and impurity. 이구안 離垢眼 To abandon the eye of impurity, or contamination, and attain the eye which beholds truth and reality. 이진복 離塵服 The monk's robe, or kaṣāya, freed from the dusty world, i.e. free from the contamination of the senses. 이바다 離婆多 ; 이바다 離波多 ; 이월 離越 ; 이왈 離曰 ; 이바다 梨婆多 Revata ; one of the twenty-eight

ㄱ ㄴ ㄷ ㄹ ㅁ ㅂ ㅅ ㅇ ㅈ ㅊ ㅋ ㅌ ㅍ ㅎ 찾아보기

Indian constellations, corresponding with 실 室 the "house," (a) Markab, (b) Scheat, Pegasus ; name of a disciple of Śākyamuni ; of the leader of the second synod ; of a member of the third synod ; cf. 힐 頡. 이미 離微 Apart from all the phenomenal ; *li* is intp. as spirit, *wei* as its subtle, mysterious functioning ; *li* is also intp. as nirvāṇa in character, *wei* as prajñā, or intelligence, knowledge, discrimination. 이성무별불 離性無別佛 Apart from mind, or the soul, there is no other Buddha, i.e. the 성 性 is Buddha. 이염복 離染服 The monk's robe which separates him from contamination ; also the nun's. 이욕 離欲 To leave, or be free from desire, or the passions. 이생 離生 To leave the chain of rebirth. 이생성 離生性 The true nature of the holy man which leaves the round of mortality. 이생희락지 離生喜樂地 The first dhyāna heaven, where is experienced the joy of leaving the evils of life. 이상 離相 One of the 삼상 三相 q.v. 이상계 離相戒 ; 무상계 無相戒 The inner commands, or observance in the heart, in contrast with external observance or ritual. 이계자 離繫子 The Nirgrantha sect of naked devotees who abandoned all ties and forms. 이개 離蓋 To abandon the 오개 五蓋 q.v. five obscurers, or hindrances to truth. 이언 離言 That which cannot be described in words, e.g. the bhūtatathatā, which is beyond definition. 이차(비) 離車(毘) ; 이사 離奢 ; 이차 利車 ; 이차비 梨車毘 ; 예차 隷車 ; 여창 黎昌 ; 율창 栗唱 ; 율첩바 栗呫婆 ; 율첩비 栗呫毘 Licchavi, the kṣatriyas who formed the republic of Vaiśālī, and were "among the earliest followers of Śākyamuni." [Eitel]. The term is intp. as 피박 皮薄 thin-skinned, or 호 豪 heroic, etc. 이간어 離間語 Talk which causes estrangement between friends ; alienating words ; one of the ten wicked things.

린 隣 Neighbouring, adjacent, near. 인단 隣單 One's neighbouring monks, i.e. in the right and left seats. 인원 隣圓 Near to perfect enlightenment, the stage before it. 인지 隣智 Similar to the last entry. 인진 隣珍 A neighbour's pearls – no aid to me. 인허 隣虛 Next to nothing, the minutest particle, an atom. 인근 隣近 Near to, approaching, adjoining, approximate.

림 林 A grove, or wood ; a band. 림미니 林微尼 or 림비니 林毘尼 ; 람비니 嵐毘尼 ; 룽미니 龍彌你 ; 류미니 流彌你 ; 납벌니 臘伐尼 ; 논민 論民 ; 임비 林毘, etc. Lumbinī, the park in which Śākyamuni was born, "15 miles east of Kapilavastu." [Eitel]. 임장 林葬 Forest burial, to cast the corpse into a forest to be eaten by animals. 임등 林藤 Vegetable food, used by men at the beginning of a kalpa. 임섭 林燮 The trees of the wood turned white when the Buddha died.

림 淋 To drip, sprinkle, soak. 임한 淋汗 Dripping sweat ; to sprinkle or pour water on the body to cleanse it.

림 臨 To regard with kindness ; approach, on the brink of, about to ; whilst. 임종 臨終 Approach the end, dying. 임제 臨濟 A monastery during the T'ang dynasty in 진정부 眞定府 Chên-ting fu, Chihli, from which the founder of the 임제 臨濟 school derived his title ; his name was 의현 義玄 I-hsüan ; cf. 선문 禪門. 임재 臨齋. Approaching the midday meal ; near noon.

립 立 Set up, establish, stand, stand up. 입승수좌 立僧首座 The learned monk who occupies the chief seat to edify the body of monks. 입파 立播 Repa, or repha, a "low" garment, a loin-cloth. 입교 立敎 To establish a "school", sect, or church. 입교개종 立敎開宗 To set up a school and start a sect. 입법 立法 To set up, or state a proposition ; to make a law, or rule. 입파 立破 To state – and confute – a proposition. 입량 立量 To state a syllogism with its 종 宗 proposition, 인 因 reason, and 유 喩 example.

<ㅁ>

마 魔 ; 마라 魔羅 Māra, killing, destroying ; "the Destroyer, Evil One, Devil" [M. W.] ; explained by murderer, hinderer, disturber, destroyer ; he is a deva "often represented with a hundred arms and riding on an elephant." [Eitel]. He sends his daughters, or assumes monstrous forms, or inspires wicked men, to seduce or frighten the saints. He "resides with legions of subordinates in the heaven Paranirmita Vaśavartin situated on the top of the Kāmadhātu." [Eitel]. Earlier form 마 磨 ; also v. 파 波 Pāpīyān. He is also called 타화자재천 他化自在天. There are various categories of māras, e.g. the skandha-māra, passion-māra, etc.

마 瑪 Agate 마노 瑪瑙.

마 馬 Aśva, a horse ; a stallion ; one of the seven treasures of a sovereign. 마승 馬勝 ; 마사 馬師 Aśvajit. Horse-breaker or Horse-master. The name of several persons, including one of the first five disciples. 마명 馬鳴 ; 아습박구사 阿濕縛窶沙 Aśvaghoṣa, the famous writer, whose patron was the Indo-Scythian king Kaniṣka q.v., was a Brahmin converted to Buddhism ; he finally settled at Benares, and became the twelfth patriarch. His name is attached to ten works (v. Hōbōgirin 192, 201, 726, 727, 846, 1643, 1666, 1667, 1669, 1687). The two which have exerted great influence on Buddhism are 불소행찬경 佛所行讚經 Buddha-carita-kāvya-sūtra, tr. by Dharmarakṣa A.D. 414-421, tr. into English by Beal, S.B.E. ; and 대승기신론 大乘起信論 Mahāyāna-śraddhotpāda-śāstra, tr. by Paramārtha, A.D. 554, and by Śikṣānanda, A.D. 695-700, tr. into English by Teitaro Suzuki 1900, and also by T. Richard, v. 기 起. He gave to Buddhism the philosophical basis for its Mahāyāna development. There are at least six others who bear this name. Other forms : 마명비구 馬鳴比丘 ; 마명대사 馬鳴大士 ; 마명보살 馬鳴菩薩, etc. 마할마제 馬曷麻諦 Mahāmati, 대혜 大慧, the bodhisattva addressed in the Laṅkāvatāra Sūtra ; v. 마하마지 摩訶摩底. 마사 馬祀 Aśvamedha, the horse sacrifice, either as an annual oblation to Heaven, or for specific purposes. 마조 馬祖 Ma-tsu, founder of the Southern Peak school of the Ch'an or Intuitional sect in Kiangsi, known as 강서도일 江西道一. 마이산 馬耳山 Aśvakarṇa, v. 알 頞, one of the seven concentric rings around Meru. 마원 馬苑 The horse park, i.e. 백마사 白馬寺 the White Horse Monastery at Loyang in the Later Han dynasty, where, according to tradition, the first missionaries dwelt. 마음장 馬陰藏 A retractable penis, e.g. that of the horse, one of the thirty-two signs of a Buddha. 마두 馬頭 Horse-head. 마두나찰 馬頭羅刹 the horse-head rākṣasa in Hades. 마두관음 馬頭觀音 ; 마두대사 馬頭大士 ; 마두명왕 馬頭明王 Hayagrīva, the horse-neck or horse-head Kuan-yin, in awe-inspiring attitude towards evil spirits. 마맥 馬麥 Horse-grain, Buddha's food when he spent three months with the Brahmin ruler Agnidatta with 500 monks, one of his ten sufferings.

마 麻 Hemp, flax, linen, translit. *ma*, cf. 모 牟, 마 麽, etc. 마차 麻蹉 Matsya, a fish 마두구라 麻豆瞿羅 Madhugola, sweet balls, or biscuits.

마 麽 Interrogative particle ; translit. *ma*, *ba* ; cf. 마 摩. 마야 麽也 Māyā, illusion, hallucination ; also intp. as 체 體 body. 마도라 麽度羅 Mathurā, the modern Muttra. 마라 麽攞 ; 마라 麽羅 Mālā, a head-dress, wreath. 마세 麽洗 Māṣa, a month. 마라유 麽羅庾 Malaya, a kind of incense from the Malaya mountains in Malabar. 마마 麽麽 Mama, my, mine, genitive case of the first personal pronoun. 마마계 麽麽鷄 Māmakī ; 망망계 忙忙鷄 or 忙莽鷄 or 忙莽計 ; 마막지 摩莫枳 ; the Vajra mother, mother of the 금강부 金剛部 or of wisdom in all the vajra group.

마 媽 Nurse, mother. 마합살독하 媽哈薩督呀 Mahāsattva, a great or noble being ; the perfect bodhisattva, greater (mahā) than any other being (sattva) except a Buddha ; v. 마하살타 摩訶薩埵.

마 摩 To feel, handle, rub ; translit. *m, ma, mu, ba* ; cf. 말 末, 마 磨.

마 磨 To grind, rub, polish ; a mill for grinding ; translit. *ma* ; cf. 마 摩. 마다 磨多 Mātā, mātṛ, a mother. 마하 磨下 ; 마사 磨司 ; 마원 磨院 The place in a monastery for grinding corn. 마쇄 磨灑 ; 마사 摩沙 Māṣa, a bean, also a weight of gold valued at 80 Chinese cash ; the stealing of goods to the value of 5 māṣa involved expulsion from the monkhood, as also in India it is said to have involved exile. 마우 磨牛 The ox turning the millstone, a formalist, i.e. a disciple who performs the bodily motions, but without heart in his religion. 마전 磨磚 To grind a brick to make a mirror, useless labour. 마마가라 磨磨迦羅 Mama-kāra, feeling of "mine," of interest to oneself. 마납 磨納 A monk's robe, a Korean term. 마하 磨訶 Mahā, 마혜 磨醯 Mahi ; v. 마 摩. 마두 磨頭 The monk who looks after the mill.

마(파)순 魔(波)旬 Māra-pāpīyān, cf. 파 波.

마가 摩伽 Maghā, an asterism "containing five stars figured like a house, apparently α, γ, ζ, η, ν Leonis" [M. W.] ; intp. as governing the eleventh month ; for which 마거 摩佉 ; 마거 摩袪 are also used. 마가라 摩伽羅 Makara, cf. 마갈 摩竭 a sea monster. 마가다 摩伽陀 Magaḍha, cf. 마갈타 摩竭陀 also used for Māgha, the month January-February.

마가타 摩迦吒 Markaṭa, a monkey ; also 마사타 摩斯吒.

마갈(라) 摩竭(羅) Makara. A sea monster, either in the form of a great fish, e.g. a whale, or a great turtle. Also 마가라 摩伽羅 or 摩迦羅. 마갈타 摩竭陀 Magadha, also 마갈제 摩竭提 ; 마게다 摩揭陀 ; 마가다 摩伽陀 ; 마가다 摩訶陀 "A kingdom in Central India, the headquarters of ancient Buddhism up to A.D. 400 ; the holy land of all Buddhists, covered with vihāras and therefore called Behar, the southern portion of which corresponds to ancient Magadha." [Eitel]. A ṛṣi after whom the country of Southern Behar is said to be called. Name of a previous incarnation of Indra ; and of the asterism Maghā 마가 摩伽.

마게 摩揭 v. 마갈 摩竭.

마계 魔戒 Māra-laws, Māra-rules, i.e. those of monks who seek fame and luxury.

마계 魔界 The realm of the māras ; also 마경 魔境 ; 마도 魔道.

마곡사 麻谷寺 Ma-gok-sa. A temple located in Unam-ri Sagok-myeon Gongju-gun Chungcheongnam-do in Korea. The 6th parish headquarters of Korean Jogye Order.

마군 魔軍 The army of Māra.

마기 摩祇 A medicine that can eradicate poison, and so overpowering that serpents avoid it ; also 마사 摩蛇 ; 마지 摩羝 ; 마혜 摩醯 ; 막기 莫耆.

마나 摩拏 v. 마노사 摩奴沙. 마나라 摩拏羅 Manorhita, or Manorhata, an Indian prince who became disciple and successor to Vasubandhu as 22nd Patriarch. Author of the Vibhāṣā śāstra. "He laboured in Western India and in Ferghana where he died in A.D. 165." [Eitel]. Also 마노라 摩奴羅 ; 말노갈리타 末笯曷利他.

마나타 摩那埵 Mānatta, joy to the penitent and his fellow monks caused by confession and absolution ; also a term for penance, or punishment ; and for offences involving reprimand (Pali). 마나바 摩那婆 v. 마납 摩納 Māṇava. 마나사 摩那斯 ; 마나소바제 摩那蘇婆帝 Mānasa ; Manasvatī. A lake in the Himālayas, one of the four lakes formed when the ocean fell from heaven upon Mount Meru. The dragon who is the tutelary deity of this lake.

마납(바가) 摩納(婆迦) Māṇavaka, a Brahman youth, a youth, a man ; also 마납박(가) 摩納縛(迦) ; 마나반 摩那槃 ; 나라마나 那羅摩那 (naramana). 마납선 摩納仙 Śākyamuni in a previous incarnation.

마녀 魔女 The daughters of Māra, who tempt men to their ruin.

마노사 摩奴沙 or 摩奴闍, v. 말노사 末奴沙 Manuṣya, Mānuṣa, man, any rational being. 마노시야 摩奴是若 Manojña, agreeable to the mind, attractive, at will. 마노말야 摩奴末耶 ; 마누말야 摩笯末耶 Manomaya, "consisting of spirit or mind, spiritual, mental." [M. W.] Intp. as mind-produced body, or form, any appearance produced at will.

마누사 摩笯沙 Manuṣya, 마누사 摩笯奢 ; 마누사 摩笯賖 man, any rational being, v. 말누사 末笯沙, 마노사 摩奴沙.

마니 摩尼 Maṇi ; "a jewel, gem, precious stone (especially a pearl, bead, or other globular ornament)." [M. W.] A bright luminous pearl, symbol of Buddha and his doctrines. Tr. "as wished," or at wish, whoever possesses the pearl receives whatever he desires. One of the seven treasures. With Śivaites a symbol of the Liṅga. Also 말니 末尼. 마니발타(라) 摩尼跋陀(羅) Maṇi-bhadra, one of the eight generals ; "a king of the Yakṣas (the tutelary deity of travellers and merchants, probably another name for Kuvera)." [M. W.] 마니건대룡왕 摩尼犍大龍王 Maṇiskandhanāga. The nāga-king in whose hand is the talismanic pearl.

마다 摩多 Mātṛ, a measurer, maker, former, mother. 마다라가 摩多羅迦 Mātṛkā, cf. 마달 摩怛.

마단 魔檀 Māra-gifts, in contrast with those of Buddha.

마달리 摩怛里 Mātṛ, a mother. 마달리가 摩怛里迦 Mātṛkā, also 마달리가 摩咀里迦 ; 마달리가 摩怛履迦 ; 마득륵가 摩得勒伽 ; 마덕륵가 摩德勒伽 ; 마다라가 摩多羅迦 ; 마질리가 摩侄梨迦 ; 마실리가 摩室里迦 ; 마이 摩夷 ; the Abhidharma-piṭaka, as the mother of Buddhist philosophy.

마답반 摩沓婆 Māthava ; Mādhava ; Madhu. "The Mathai of Megasthenes, a tribe of Indian aborigines who lived north of Kosala in Rohilcund and along the southern frontier of Nepal. They gave the name to Mathurā and Matipura." [Eitel]. The last statement at least is doubtful.

마도 魔道 The māra path, or way, i.e. one of the six destinies.

마도라 摩度羅 Mathurā, modern Muttra, v. 마투 摩偸.

마등 摩騰 Kāśyapa Mātaṅga who, according to tradition, accompanied the first envoys back to China, A.D. 64 ; cf. 가 迦.

마등가 摩鄧伽 Mātaṅga, also 마등가 摩登伽 or 摩燈伽 Elephant, greatest, utmost, lowest caste, outcast, barbarian. 마등지 摩鄧祇 Mātaṅgī. Both words bear a low meaning in Chinese, e.g. low caste. Mātaṅgī is the name of the low-caste woman who inveigled Ānanda. The 마등가주 摩鄧伽咒 spell is performed with blood, etc.

마등가아란야 摩登伽阿蘭若 Mātaṅga-araṅyaka. The second class of hermits (probably called after the lowest caste), living in cemeteries, at a distance of 500 bow-lengths (*circa* 3,000 feet) from a village. 마등가경 摩登伽經 A sūtra on Mātaṅgī, and on the stars. Cf. 마등 摩鄧.

마라 摩羅 Mālā, a wreath, garland, chaplet, head-dress ; also tr. as Māra, a huge fish, cf. 마갈라 摩竭羅 Makara. 마라가타 摩羅伽陀 or 摩羅迦陀 Marakata, the emerald. 마라제 摩羅提 ; 마라야제수 摩羅耶提數 ; 마라야저수 摩羅耶底數 ; 마리 摩離 Malaya-deśa, Malaya country. 마라야 摩羅耶 Malaya, the Malabar hills, noted for their sandalwood, cf. 말 末 ; also 마라정 摩羅廷 ; 마리 摩梨 ; 마리가라야 摩利伽羅耶 ; 마뢰야 摩賴耶.

마라 魔羅 Māra, v. 마 魔 ; also 마라 麽羅 ; for 마라야 魔羅耶 v. 마 摩.

마랍바 摩臘婆 Mālava, or Lāra (Lāṭa). An ancient state in Central India, in the present Gujarat.

마뢰야 摩賴耶 v. 마라야 摩羅耶.

마리 摩利 Mallikā, a fragrant flower variously described as jasmine, aloes, musk, etc. Name of the wife of king Prasenajit, also called 마리실라 摩利室羅 Mālyaśrī. 마리가라야 摩利伽羅耶 Malaya in Malabar, cf. 마라 摩羅. 마리지 摩利支 or 摩梨支 or 摩里支 ; 말리지 末利支 Marīci. Rays of light, the sun's rays, said to go before the sun ; mirage ; also intp. as a wreath. A goddess, independent and sovereign, protectress against all violence and peril. "In Brahmanic mythology, the personification of light, offspring of Brahmā, parent of Sūrya." "Among Chinese Buddhists Maritchi is represented as a female with eight arms, two of which are holding aloft emblems of sun and moon, and worshipped as goddess of light and as the guardian of all nations, whom she protects from the fury of war. She is addressed as 천후 天后 queen of heaven, or as 두모 斗姥 lit. mother of the Southern measure (*μλρσιζ* Sagittarii), and identified with Tchundi" and "with Maheśvarī, the wife of Maheśvara, and has therefore the attribute Mātṛkā," mother of Buddhas. [Eitel]. Taoists address her as Queen of Heaven.

마망 魔網 The net of Māra.

마민 魔民 Mārakāyikās, also 마자마녀 魔子魔女 Māra's people, or subjects.

마박 魔縛 Māra-cords ; Māra-bonds ; also 마계 魔繫.

마범 魔梵 Māra and Brahmā ; i.e. Māra, lord of the sixth desire-heaven and Brahmā, lord of the heavens of form.

마사 魔事 Māra-deeds, especially in hindering Buddha-truth.

마사 摩娑 Māṁsa, flesh. 마사라 摩娑羅 Musāragalva, agate, cf. 모 牟.

마사라 摩沙羅 Musāragalva, v. 모 牟.

마선 魔禪 Māra-dhyāna, evil thoughts, wrong and harmful meditation.

마신다 摩哂陀 Mahendra, younger brother of Aśoka, reputed as founder of Buddhism in Ceylon.

마야 摩耶 Māyā, v. Mahāmāyā, see 마하마야 摩訶摩耶.

마연 魔緣 Māra-circumstance, or environment, or conditioning cause, i.e. hindering the good.

마왕 魔王 The king of māras, the lord of the sixth heaven of the desire-realm.

마원 魔怨 Māra enmity ; Māra, the enemy of Buddha.

마유라 摩由羅 Mayūra, 공작 孔雀 a peacock ; also 마유라 摩裕羅 ; 마수라 摩廋囉.

마유라 摩裕羅 v. 마유라 摩由羅.

마유라가람 摩愉羅伽藍 Masūra Saṅghārāma. An ancient vihāra about 200 li south-east of Moṅgali. [Eitel]. Cf. 두 豆.

마이 摩夷 Mātṛkā, cf. 마달 摩怛.

마인 魔忍 Māra-servitude, the condition of those who obey Māra.

마장 魔障 Māra-hindrances ; also 장 障 is an interpretation of 마 魔.

마정 摩頂 To lay the hand on the top of the head, a custom of Buddha in teaching his disciples, from which the burning of the spots on the head of a monk is said to have originated.

마제 摩提 Mati, understanding ; v. 말저 末底.

마지 摩旨 Maji. Rice offering to the Buddha and Bodhisattva (before the lunch-time service).

마천 魔天 Māra-deva, the god of lust, sin, and death, cf. Māra.

마투 摩偸 Madhu, sweet, an intoxicating liquor. 마투라 摩偸羅 Mathurā ; Madhurā. Ancient kingdom and city, the modern Muttra on the bank of the Jumna ; the reputed birthplace of Kṛṣṇa, one of the seven sacred cities, called Peacock City 공작성 孔雀城 Kṛṣṇapura, famous for its stūpas. The ancient name Madhu is given in 마도 摩度. Other forms are 마돌라 摩突羅 ; 마도라 摩度羅 ; 마두라 摩頭羅 ; 말토라 秣菟羅.

마하 摩訶 Mahā, great, large, very ; also 마혜 摩醯 ; 막하 莫訶.

마하가섭(파) 摩訶迦葉(波) Mahākāśyapa, or Kāśyapa-dhātu 가섭(두타) 迦葉(頭陀) ; a Brahman of Magadha, disciple of Śākyamuni ; accredited with presiding over the first synod, hence known as 상좌 上座 ; also with supervising the first compilation of the Buddha's sermons ; is reckoned as the first Patriarch, v. 이십팔조 二十八祖 and 가 迦. 마하가전연 摩訶迦旃延 Mahākātyāyana, one of the principal disciples of Śākyamuni ; v. 대 大 and 가 迦. 마하가라 摩訶迦羅 Mahākāla, the great black deva, v. 대흑 大黑.

마하교담미 摩訶憍曇彌 Mahāgautamī, aunt and nurse of Śākyamuni. Cf. 교 憍.

마하구치라 摩訶拘絺羅 Mahākauṣṭhila, a disciple of the Buddha ; also 마하구슬치라 摩訶俱瑟耻羅 ; v. 구 拘.

마하나가 摩訶那伽 Mahānāga, the great Nāga, "one of the elephants that support the world." [M. W.] A title of a Buddha, or of an arhat. 마하나마 摩訶那摩 ; 마하남 摩訶男 Mahānāman, one of the first five of Śākyamuni's converts. 마하나발 摩訶那鉢 Mahāsthāmaprāpta, the Bodhisattva 대세지 大勢至 q.v.

마하낙가나 摩訶諾伽那 Mahānagna, "quite naked" [M. W.] ; great naked powerful spirits, cf. 낙 諾.

마하니라 摩訶尼羅 or 摩訶泥羅 Mahānīla, dark-blue, a sapphire ; described as the large blue pearl of Indra, perhaps the Indranīla.

마하단특 摩訶袒特 Mahātantra(dhāraṇī), great spell power for overcoming the evil and cleaving to the good.

마하라 摩訶羅 Mahallakas, old, stupid, ignorant ; also 마가라 摩迦羅 ; 막하락가 莫訶洛迦 ; 막갈락가 莫喝洛迦. 마하라사 摩訶羅闍 Mahārāja, a great or superior king ; a king.

마하랄타 摩訶剌侘 Mahārāṣṭra. "The Mahratta country, an ancient kingdom in the north-west corner of the Deccan, near the upper course of the Godavery." [Eitel].

마하로슬나 摩訶盧瑟拏 Mahāroṣaṇa, the angry deva.

마하마야 摩訶摩耶 Mahāmāyā, intp. by M. W. as "great deceit or illusion, worldly illusion, the divine power of illusion (which makes the material universe appear as if really existing and renders it cognizable by the senses), the Great Illusion (the illusory nature of worldly objects personified and identified with Durgā)." Mahāmāyā was the wife of Śuddhodana, and mother of Śākyamuni. He, Siddhārtha, was born "from her right side," and she died seven days later, her sister Mahāprajāpatī becoming his foster-mother. Also called 마하제비 摩訶第脾 Mahādevī ; 마하부인 摩訶夫人 Lady Māyā, etc.

마하만수사화 摩訶曼殊沙華 Mahāmañjūṣaka, a red flower yielding the madder (munjeeth of Bengal). 마하만다라화 摩訶曼陀羅華 Mahāmandārava, a large white lotus ; cf. 만 曼.

마하목건련 摩訶目犍連 Mahāmaudgalyāyana, v. 목 目, one of the chief disciples of Śākyamuni, at whose left his image is placed, Śāriputra being on the right. Mahāsthāmaprāpta is said to be a form of Maudgalyāyana. 마하목지린타 摩訶目脂隣陀 ; 마하목진린타 摩訶目眞隣陀 Mahāmucilinda, name of a Nāga-king, etc. , v. 목 目.

마하바라 摩訶婆羅 ; **마하사라** 摩訶娑羅 Mahāsāra. "An ancient city in Central India, the present Masar, about 30 miles west of Patna." [Eitel].

마하반열반나 摩訶般涅槃那 Mahāparinirvāṇa, v. 녈 涅, the great complete nirvāṇa, final release, perfect rest. 마하반야 摩訶般若 Mahāprajñā, v. 반 般, great wisdom, great insight into all truth. 마하반야바라밀 摩訶般若波羅蜜 Mahā-prajñāpāramitā, v. 반 般, the great wisdom method of crossing the stream to nirvāṇa, i.e. Buddha-truth.

마하발특마 摩訶鉢特摩 Mahāpadma, defined by M. W. as a great "white" lotus ; but intp. in China as the great red lotus, after which the eighth cold hell is named. As the great white lotus it is a Buddha-throne, of purity and fragrance.

마하보리사 摩訶菩提寺 Mahābodhi-saṅghārāma. The monastery of the great enlightenment, a vihāra near the Bodhidruma at Gayā ; cf. 서역기 西域記 8 and Fa-hsien.

마하비로자나 摩訶毘盧遮那 v. 비 毘. Mahāvairocana. 마하비하라 摩訶毘訶羅 Mahāvihāra. A monastery near Anurādhapura, Ceylon, where Fa-hsien (A.D. 400) found 3,000 inmates. 마하비하라주부 摩訶毘訶羅住部 Mahāvihāravāsinaḥ. "A subdivision of the Mahāsthavira school, which combated the Mahāyāna system." [Eitel].

마하살(타) 摩訶薩(埵) Mahāsattva, "great being," one with great compassion and energy, who brings salvation to all living beings ; a Bodhisattva ; also 마하찰두 摩訶刹頭. 마하살타왕자 摩訶薩埵王子 Mahāsattva-kumāra-rāja, the noble and royal prince, Śākyamuni.

마하승기부 摩訶僧祇部 Mahāsāṅghikāḥ or Mahāsaṅghanikāya ; 대중부 大衆部 one of the four branches of the Vaibhāṣika, said to have been formed after the second synod in opposition to the Sthaviras, marking the first division in the Buddhist church. Followers of Mahākāśyapa. After the third synod this school split into five sects : Pūrvaśaila, Avaraśailāḥ, Haimavatāḥ, Lokottaravādinaḥ, Prajñaptivādinaḥ. 마하승기율 摩訶僧祇律 The great canon of monastic rules, tr. by Buddhabhadra and Fa-hsien in 40 chüan.

마하야나제바 摩訶耶那提婆 Mahāyānadeva, a title given to Hsüan-tsang in India ; cf. 현 玄.

마하연(나) 摩訶衍(那) Mahāyāna, 대승 大乘 q.v. the Great Vehicle, in contrast with Hīnayāna 소승 小乘. Also 마하야나 摩訶夜那 ; 마하야니 摩訶夜泥.

마하인다라 摩訶因陀羅 Mahendra, v. 마신 摩哂.

마하제바 摩訶提婆 Mahādeva, the great deva, Maheśvara, i.e. Śiva ; also a former incarnation of Śākyamuni ; and name of an arhat.

마하질제살타 摩訶質帝薩埵 Mahācittasattva. A great-mind being, a Bodhisattva. Also 마하보리질제살타 摩訶菩提質帝薩埵.

마하파사파제 摩訶波闍波提 Mahāprajāpatī, title of aunt and nurse of Śākyamuni ; reputed as the first abbess ; according to the Lotus she is to become a Buddha, under the title of Sarvasattva-priya-darśana. Also 마하발랄사발저 摩訶鉢剌闍鉢底 ; cf. 교 憍 Gautamī.

마향 魔鄕 Māra-country, i.e. the world.

마혜수라 魔醯首羅 Maheśvara, Śiva. 마혜인다라 魔醯因陀羅 Mahendra, a younger brother of Aśoka. 마혜습라보라 魔醯濕羅補羅 Maheśvarapura, the present Machery in Rajputana. 마혜라구라 魔醯邏矩羅 Mihirakula, king of the Punjab, later of Kashmir, about A.D. 400, a persecutor of Buddhism, v. 마 摩.

마혜인다라 摩醯因陀羅 ; **마하인다라** 摩訶因陀羅 Mahendra, younger brother of Aśoka, who, on repenting of his dissolute life, became an arhat and is said to have founded Buddhism in Ceylon. 마혜사사가 摩醯奢娑迦 Mahīśāsaka, cf. 미 彌, one of the subdivisions of the Sarvāstivāda school. 마혜경벌라 摩醯徑伐羅 ; 마혜수라 魔醯首羅 ; 마혜 魔醯 Maheśvara. Explained by 대자재천 大自在天 great sovereign deva, 천왕 天王 king of devas. Śiva, lord of one great chiliocosm, a deity with eight arms, three eyes, riding on a white bull. Hsüan-tsang says specially worshipped in the Panjab. It is a term also for certain bodhisattvas and certain heavens.

마호락가 摩呼洛迦 Mahoraga, described as large-bellied ; a class of demons shaped like the boa ; a spirit in the retinue of Śākyamuni ; a form taken by Vairocana ; also 막호락가(마) 莫呼洛迦(摩) ; 마후라가 摩睺羅伽 ; 마호라아 摩護囉誐.

마후라 摩睺羅 Muhūrta, a moment. Mahoraga, also 마후륵 摩睺勒 v. 마호 摩呼.

마휴륵 摩休勒 Mahoraga, cf. 마후라 摩睺羅.

막 膜 A membrane. 막배 膜拜 To raise the hands to the head in making obeisance.

막 莫 Not ; none ; no ; do not ; translit. *ma, mu* ; cf. 마 摩. 막가 莫伽 Magha, donation, wealth ; maghā, seven stars ; M. W. says a constellation of five stars $\alpha, \gamma, \zeta, \eta, \nu$ Leonis. 막하 莫訶 Mahā, cf. 마 摩 ; Mahī, or Mahānada, a small river in Magadha, and one flowing into the gulf of Cambay. 막하승기니가야 莫訶僧祇尼迦耶 Mahāsāṅghika-nikāya, cf. 마 摩. 막하파가 莫訶婆伽 The musk deer. 막하연적 莫訶衍磧 The great Shamo (Gobi) desert. 막하정 莫賀廷 The same ; also called "Makhai." [Eitel]. 막혜 莫醯 v. 마 摩 Maheśvara, i.e. Śiva.

만 鬘 A head-dress, coiffure ; a chaplet, wreath, etc. ; idem 말리 末利.

만 曼 Long, prolonged, extended, widespread. 만공 曼供 Offerings of mandārava flowers, cf. *infra*. 만승존 曼勝尊 A title of a Buddha. 만달라 曼怛羅 or 만특라 曼特羅 v. *infra* and 만달라 滿怛羅 are also used for mantra, an incantation, spell, magical formula, or muttered sound. 만수실리 曼殊室利 or 만수시리 曼殊尸利 Mañjuśrī, v. 문수 文殊, and the 만수실리경 曼殊室利經. 만수사 曼殊沙 ; 만수안 曼殊顔 Mañjūṣaka, the "*Rubia cordifolia*, the roots of which yield the madder of Bengal called Munjeeth." [Eitel]. 만다라 曼荼羅 ; 만달라 曼怛羅 ; 만특라 曼特羅 ; 만다라 曼陀羅 ; 만나라 曼拏羅 ; 만다라 蔓陀囉 ; 만다라 滿荼邏 Maṇḍala, a circle, globe, wheel, ring ; "any circular figure or diagram" [M. W.] ; a magic circle ; a plot or place of enlightenment ; a round or square altar on which Buddhas and bodhisattvas are placed ; a group of such, especially the Garbhadhātu and Vajradhātu groups of the Shingon sect ; these were arranged by Kōbō Daishi to express the mystic doctrine of the two dhātu by way of illustration, the Garbhadhātu representing the 리 理 and the 인 因 principle and cause, the Vajradhātu the 지 智 and the 과 果 intelligence (or reason) and the effect, i.e. the fundamental realm of being, and mind as inherent in it ; v. 태 胎 and 금강 金剛. The two realms are fundamentally one, as are the absolute and phenomenal, e.g. water and wave. There are many kinds of maṇḍalas, e.g. the group of the Lotus Sūtra ; of the 관경 觀經 ; of the nine luminaries ; of the Buddha's entering into nirvāṇa, etc. The real purpose of a maṇḍala is to gather the spiritual powers together, in order to promote the operation of the dharma or law. The term is commonly applied to a magic circle, subdivided into circles or squares in which are painted Buddhist divinities and symbols. Maṇḍalas also reveal the direct retribution of each of the ten worlds of beings (purgatory, pretas, animals, asuras, men, devas, the heavens of form, formless heavens, bodhisattvas, and Buddhas). Each world has its maṇḍala which represents the originating principle that brings it to completion. The maṇḍala of the tenth world indicates the fulfilment and completion of the nine worlds. 만다라교 曼荼羅敎 Maṇḍala doctrine, mantra teaching, magic, yoga, the True word or Shingon sect. 타라 陀羅 or 陁羅 ; 만다라 漫陀羅 Mandāra(va), the coraltree ; the *Erythrina indica*, or this tree regarded as one of the five trees of Paradise, i.e. Indra's heaven ; a white variety of *Calotropis gigantea*. Name of a noted monk, and of one called Mandra. 만수 曼首 idem 문수 文殊.

만 萬 Myriad, 10,000 ; all. 만팔천세계 萬八千世界 The 18,000 easterly worlds lighted by the ray from the Buddha's brows, v. Lotus sūtra. 만선 萬善 All goodness, all good works. 만경 萬境 All realms, all regions. 만자 萬字 The sauvastika 만 卍, also styled śrīvatsa-lakṣaṇa, the mark on the breast of Viṣṇu, "a particular curl of hair on the breast" ; the lightning ; a sun symbol ; a sign of all power over evil and all favour to the good ; a sign shown on the Buddha's breast. One of the marks on a Buddha's feet. 만법 萬法 All things, everything that has noumenal or phenomenal existence. 만법일여 萬法一如 The absolute in everything ; the ultimate reality behind everything. 만법일심 萬法一心 Myriad things but one mind ; all things as noumenal. 만물 萬物 All things. 만행 萬行 All procedures, all actions, all disciplines, or modes of salvation.

만 慢 Māna. Pride, arrogance, self-conceit, looking down on others, supercilious, etc. ; there are categories of seven and nine kinds of pride. 만사 慢使 The messenger, or lictor, of pride, cf. 오사 五使. 만갱 慢坑 The pit, or pitfall of pride. 만산 慢山 Pride as high as a mountain. 만당 慢幢 Pride as a banner rearing itself aloft. 만감 慢感 One of the ten great delusions, that of pride. 만상 慢想 Proud arrogant thoughts. 만결 慢結 The bondage of pride. 만거 慢擧 To hold oneself arrogantly. 만견 慢見 Pride, regarding oneself as superior, one of the ten wrong views. 만과견 慢過見 Regarding oneself as superior to superiors.

만 漫 Overflowing, boundless ; translit. *man*, *van* ; cf. 만 曼, 만 滿. 만제 漫提 Vande, "I worship." 만다라 漫荼羅 or 만달라 漫怛羅 or 만다라 漫陀羅 v. 만 曼 Maṇḍala. 만다가 漫荼迦 Maṇḍaka, a cake, pastry.

만 滿 Pūrṇa. Full, whole, complete. 만분계 滿分戒 The whole of the commandments, i.e. of the monk. 만자 滿字 The complete word, i.e. Mahāyāna, as compared with the 반자 半字 half word, or incomplete word of Hīnayāna. 만좌 滿座 A complete, or full assembly ; also the last day of a general assembly. 만달라 滿怛羅 ; 만다라 滿荼羅 v. 만 曼 Maṇḍala. 만자자 滿慈子 ; 만축자 滿祝子 ; 만견자 滿見子 ; 만원자 滿願子 see 부 富 Pūrṇa. 만성 滿成 Fully complete, perfect. 만월존 滿月尊 The full-moon honoured one, Buddha. 만과 滿果 ; 만업 滿業 The fruit, or karma, which fills out the details of any incarnation, as distinguished from 인업 引業 which determines the type, e.g. man, animal, etc., of that incarnation. 만수시리 滿殊尸利 v. 문 文 Mañjuśrī. 만니 滿泥 ; 만제 漫提 Vande, "I worship." 만유 滿濡 ; 만수 曼殊 or 만유 曼乳 Mañju, beautiful, lovely. 만다 滿茶 Maṇḍa, solid, the diamond throne. 만족 滿足 Full, complete ; satisfied.

만 卍 Sauvastika, 색박실저가 塞縛悉底迦 ; also styled 실리말차 室利靺瑳 śrīvatsa, lucky sign, Viṣṇu's breast-curl or mark, tr. by 해운 海雲 sea-cloud, or cirrus. Used as a fancy form of 만 萬 or 만 万 ; and is also written in a form said to resemble a curl. It is the 4th of the auspicious signs in the footprint of Buddha, and is a mystic diagram of great antiquity. To be distinguished from 만卐 svastika, the crampons of which turn to the right.

만 晩 Sunset, evening, twilight ; late. 만참 晩參 The evening service. 만죽 晩粥 The evening gruel, which being against the rule of not eating after midday is styled medicine.

만공 월면 滿空月面 Man-gong(1871-1946). A monk of the late Joseon dynasty in Korea. He succeeded to 경허 鏡虛 Gyeong-heo.

만해 용운 萬海龍雲 Man-hae Yong-un(1879-1944). A monk of the late Joseon dynasty in Korea.

말 末 Branch, twig ; end ; dust ; not ; translit. *ma, va, ba* ; cf. 마 摩.

말 靺 Red socks. 말률사가 靺嘌沙迦 ; 말사가 靺師迦 Vārṣika ; a flower that blooms during the rainy season, described as of a white colour and very fragrant ; the aloe.

말 抹 Rub out or on, efface. 말향 抹香 Powdered incense to scatter over images.

말 襪 Stockings, socks ; also 말 韈.

말 秣 To feed a horse ; translit. *ma.* 말토라 秣免羅 Mathurā, v. 마 摩. 말노야구사 秣奴若瞿沙 Manojñaghoṣa, an ancient bhikṣu. 말지보라 秣底補羅 Matipura, an "ancient kingdom (and city) the kings of which in A.D. 600 belonged to the Śūdra caste, the home of many famous priests, The present Rohilcund (Rohilkhand) between the Ganges and Rāmagaṅgā." 말라사 秣羅娑 Malasa. "A mountain valley in the upper Punjab." 말라구타 秣羅矩吒 Malakūṭa. "An ancient kingdom of Southern India, the coast of Malabar, about A.D. 600 a noted haunt of the Nirgrantha sect." [Eitel].

말가 末伽 Mārga ; track, path, way, the way ; the fourth of the four dogmas 사제 四諦, i.e. 도 道, known as the 팔성도 八聖道, 팔정도 八正道 or 팔정문 八正門, the eight holy or correct ways, or gates out of suffering into nirvāṇa. Mārga is described as the 인 因 cause of liberation, bodhi as its 과 果 result. 말가시라 末伽始羅 Mārgaśiras, M. W. says November-December ; the Chinese say from the 16th of the 9th moon to the 15th of the 10th. 말가리 末伽梨 ; 말가리구사리 末伽梨拘賒梨 or 말가려구사려 末伽黎拘賒黎 ; 말거리구사리 末佉梨劬奢離 Maskari Gośālīputra, one of the six Tīrthikas 외도육사 外道六師. He denied that present lot was due to deeds done in previous lives, and the Laṅkāvatāra-sūtra says he taught total annihilation at the end of this life.

말가타하라타 末迦吒賀邏馱 Markaṭa-hrada ; the Apes' Pool, near Vaiśālī.

말나 末那 Manaḥ ; manas ; intp. by 의 意 mind, the (active) mind. Eitel says : "The sixth of the Chaḍâyatana, the mental faculty which constitutes man as an intelligent and moral being." The 말나식 末那識 is defined by the 유식론 唯識論 4 as the seventh of the 팔식 八識, namely 의 意, which means 사량 思量 thinking and measuring, or calculating. It is the active mind, or activity of mind, but is also used for the mind itself.

말나남 末捺南 Vandana, 례 禮 worship, reverence.

말노갈랄타 末笯曷剌他 Manorhita, or Manoratha, tr. by 여의 如意, an Indian prince who became the disciple and successor of Vasubandhu, reputed author of the 비바사론 毘婆沙論 Vibhāṣā śāstra and the twenty-second patriarch.

말노사 末奴沙 Mānuṣa, Manuṣya ; 마노사 摩奴娑 or 摩努娑 ; 마노사 摩奴闍 ; 마노쇄 摩奴曬 ; 마노사 摩奴史 ; 마누사 摩㝹沙 ; 마누사 摩㝹賒 ; 마누사 摩㝹奢 ; 마누사남 摩㝹舍喃 ; 마누 摩㝹 ; 마나사 摩拏赦 man, human, intp. by 인 人 and 의 意 man and mind or intelligence.

말노시야삽바라 末奴是若颯縛羅 Manojñasvara 여의음 如意音, 악음 樂音 lovely sounds, music ; a king of the Gandharva, Indra's musicians.

말니 末尼 Maṇi 마니 摩尼 ; a jewel, a crystal, a pearl, symbol of purity, therefore of Buddha and of his doctrine. It is used in Oṁ-maṇi-padme-hūṁ. 말니교 末尼教 The Manichean religion, first mentioned in Chinese literature by Hsüan-tsang in his Memoirs, between A.D. 630 and 640. The first Manichean missionary from 대진 大秦 Ta-ch'in reached China in 694. In 732, an imperial edict declared the religion of Maṇi a perverse doctrine, falsely taking the name of Buddhism. It continued, however, to flourish in parts of China, especially Fukien, even to the end of the Ming dynasty. Chinese writers have often confused it with Mazdeism 화요교 火祆教.

말다 末陀 Madya, intoxicating liquor, intoxicating. The two characters are also given as a translation of Madhya, and mean 100,000. 말다마 末陀摩 This is intp. as not in the mean or middle way.

말다리 末多利 One of the divisions of the Sarvāstivādāḥ school, said to be the 북산부 北山部 q.v.

말달나 末達那 Madana ; 마다나 摩陀那 ; 마달나 摩達那 ; 마다라 摩陀羅 a fruit called the intoxication fruit 취과 醉果.

말도가 末度迦 Madhūka 말두가 末杜迦 ; 마두 摩頭 ; [M. W.] Bassia latifolia, tr. as 미과 美果 a fine or pleasant fruit.

말라 末羅 Malla 마라 魔羅 ; a term for inhabitants of Kuśinagara and Pāvā. 말라왕경 末羅王經 The sūtra of the king of this name, whose road was blocked by a rock, which his people were unable to remove, but which the Buddha removed easily by his miraculous powers. 말라갈다 末羅羯多 Marakata, 마라가타 摩羅迦陀 the emerald. 말라유 末羅遊 Malaya, "the western Ghats in the Deccan (these mountains abound in sandal trees) ; the country that lies to the east of the Malaya range, Malabar." [M. W.] Eitel gives 말라구타 秣羅矩咤 Malakūṭa, i.e. Malaya, as "an ancient kingdom of Southern India, the coast of Malabar, about A.D. 600 a noted haunt of the Nirgrantha sect". It is also identified with 시리불서 尸利佛逝 Śrībhoja, which is given as 마래반도 馬來半島 the Malay peninsula ; but v. 마라야 摩羅耶 Malaya.

말랄남 末剌諵 Maraṇa, 사 死 dying, mortal, death.

말려낭 末麗曩 Balin 마라 麽攞 ; strong, strengthening.

말률자 末栗者 Marica, pepper.

말리 末梨 Bali, an asura king.

말리 末利 Mallikā, 마리 摩利 ; 말라 末羅 (1) Jasminum Zambac, M. W., which suggests the 말리화 茉莉花, i.e. the Chinese jasmine ; according to Eitel it is the narrow-leafed nyctanthes (with globular berries 내 柰) ; the flower, now called kastūrī (musk) because of its odour. By the Fan-i-ming-i it is styled the 만화 鬘花 chaplet flower, as its flowers may be formed into a chaplet. (2) A concoction of various fruits mixed with water offered in worship. 말리부인 末利夫人 The wife of Prasenajit, king of Kosala, so called because she wove or wore jasmine chaplets, or came from a jasmine garden, etc. 말리실라 末利室羅 Mālyaśrī, said to be a daughter of the last and queen in Ayodhyā, capital of Kosala.

말마 末摩 Marman ; a vital part, or mortal spot.

말법 末法 The last of the three periods 정법 正法, 상법 像法, and 말법 末法 ; that of degeneration and extinction of the Buddha-law.

말사 末寺 Subsidiary buildings of a monastery.

말상 末上 On the last, at last, finally.

말세 末世 The third and last period of a Buddha-kalpa ; the first is the first 500 years of correct doctrine, the second is the 1,000 years of semblance law, or approximation to the doctrine, and the third a myriad years of its decline and end. Also 말대 末代.

말지 末底 Mati 마제 摩提 ; devotion, discernment, understanding, tr. by 혜 慧 wisdom. 말저승하 末底僧訶 Mati-siṁha, the lion of intelligence, an honorific title.

말전 末田 Madhyāntika, 말전지(나) 末田地(那) ; 말전지가 末田底加 ; 말전제 末田提 ; 말전탁가 末田鐸迦 ; 말탄지 末彈地 ; 말천지 末闡地 or 말제마 末提摩 is also used for 말 末. It is tr. by 중 中 ; 일중 日中, 수중하중 水中河中, and 금지 金地. One of the two chief disciples of Ānanda, to whom he handed down the Buddha's doctrine. He is reputed to have been sent to convert 계빈 罽賓 Kashmir, the other, 상나화수 商那和修 Śāṇakavāsa, to convert 중국 中國 which is probably Central India, though it is understood as China. Another account makes the latter a disciple of the former. Eitel says that by his magic power he transported a sculptor to the Tuṣita heavens to obtain a correct image of Maitreya.

말제제사 末睇提舍 Madhyadeśa, 중국 中國 the central kingdom, i.e. Central India.

말차라 末嗟羅 Matsara, 간 慳 grudging, stingy, greedy.

말화 末化 Buddha transformed into (palm-)branches or leaves ; the transformation of the Buddha in the shape of the sūtras.

망 蟒 A boa, python ; a class of demons resembling such, a mahoraga.

망 忙 Busy, bustling. 망망육도 忙忙六道 Bustling about and absorbed in the six paths of transmigration. 망망계 忙忙鷄 ; 망망계금강 忙莽鷄金剛 or 忙莽計金剛 ; 마마계 麽麽鷄 ; 마막지 麽莫枳 Māmakī, or Māmukhī, tr. as 금강모 金剛母 the mother of all the vajra group, whose wisdom is derived from her ; she is represented in the Garbhadhātu maṇḍala.

망 亡 Gone, lost, dead, ruined ; not. 망오중물 亡五衆物 The things left behind at death by any one of the five orders of monks or nuns ; clothing, etc., being divided among the other monks or nuns ; valuables and land, etc., going to the establishment. 망자 亡者 Dead ; the dead. 망혼 亡魂 The soul of the dead.

망 莽 Jungle ; wild ; rude ; translit. *ma,* cf. 마 摩 ; intp. as 무 無 and 공 空.

망 網 Jāla. A net, a web. 망목 網目 The "eyes," or meshes of a net. For the Brahmajāla sūtra v. 범망경 梵網經.

망 妄 Mithyā ; false, untrue, erroneous, wild. 망집 妄執 False tenets, holding on to false views. 망경계 妄境界 False environment ; the unreal world. 망진 妄塵 The unreal and unclean world. 망심 妄心 A wrong, false, or misleading mind. 망념 妄念 False or misleading thoughts. 망상 妄想 Erroneous thinking. 망염 妄染 ; 망풍 妄風 The spread of lies, or false ideas. 망법 妄法 Bhrānti, going astray, error. 망연 妄緣 The unreality of one's environment ; also, the causes of erroneous ideas. 망견 妄見 False views (of reality), taking the seeming as real. 망언 妄言 ; 망설 妄說 False words, or talk ; lies. 망어 妄語 The commandment against lying, either as slander, or false boasting, or deception ; for this the 지도론 智度論 gives ten evil results on reincarnation: (1) stinking breath ; (2) good spirits avoid him, as also do men ; (3) none believes him even when telling the truth ; (4) wise men never admit him to their deliberations ; etc. 망운 妄雲 Clouds of falsity, i.e. delusion.

망 望 To look at, or for ; expect, hope ; towards ; the full moon. 실망 失望 To lose hope. 반망 盼望 To hope for.

매 魅 An ogre, evil spirit. 매녀 魅女 A young woman used as a medium for such a spirit to injure others.

매 毎 Each, every. 매달리 毎怛里 v. 미륵 彌勒 Maitreya. 매달리말나 毎怛里末那 Maitrīmanas, of kindly mind, tr. by 자비 慈悲 merciful.

매 梅 The plum. 매달리(야) 梅咀利(耶) ; 매달리예나 梅咀利曳那 ; 매달라예니 梅咀囉曳尼 ; 매달려 梅咀黎 ; 매달려약 梅咀麗藥 ; 매달리예 昧怛履曳 v. 미륵 彌勒 Maitreya, friendly, benevolent ; the expected Buddhist Messiah.

매 買 To buy, purchase. 매림 買林 Vikrītavana, a "monastery 200 li north-west of the capital of Cashmere." [Eitel].

매 罵 To curse, scold. 주매 呪罵 To curse.

매 賣 To sell. 매롱 賣弄 To show off, boast.

맥 麦 Yava. 야바 耶婆 Corn, wheat, barley, etc. Corn, especially barley ; a grain of barley is the 2,688,000th part of a yojana.

맹 盲 Blind. 맹명 盲冥 Blind and in darkness, ignorant of the truth. 맹파 盲跛 Blind and lame, an ignorant teacher. 맹룡 盲龍 The blind dragon who appealed to the Buddha and was told that his blindness was due to his having been formerly a sinning monk. 맹구 盲龜 It is as easy for a blind turtle to find a floating log as it is for a man to be reborn as a man, or to meet with a Buddha and his teaching.

맹 孟 Eldest, first ; Mencius ; rude. 맹팔랑 孟八郎 The eight violent fellows, a general term for plotters, ruffians, and those who write books opposed to the truth. 맹파신 孟婆神 The Mêng family dame, said to have been born under the Han dynasty, and to have become a Buddhist ; later deified as the bestower of 맹파탕 孟婆湯 the drug of forgetfulness, or oblivion of the past, on the spirits of the dead.

맹 猛 Fierce, violent ; determined ; sudden. 맹리 猛利 Fierce, sudden. 맹화 猛火 Fierce fire, conflagration.

면 免 Avoid ; remit. 면승 免僧 A monk whose attendance at the daily assembly is excused for other duties.

면 面 Face. 면목 面目 Face and eyes, face, looks. 면문 面門 Forehead, or mouth, or the line across the upper lip. 면수 面授 Personal or face-to-face instruction. 면벽 面壁 To sit in meditation with the face to a wall, as did Bodhidharma for nine years, without uttering a word.

면 眠 To close the eyes, to sleep. 면장 眠藏 A monastic sleeping-room.

멸 篾 Bamboo splints, or strips. 멸례거 篾隸車 Mlecchas, v. 멸 蔑 15.

멸 滅 Extinguish, exterminate, destroy ; a tr. of Nirodha, suppression, annihilation ; of Nirvāṇa, blown out, extinguished, dead, perfect rest, highest felicity, etc. ; and of Nivṛtti, cessation, disappearance. Nirodha is the third of the four axioms: 고 苦, 집 集, 멸 滅, 도 道 pain, its focussing, its cessation (or cure), the way of such cure. Various ideas are expressed as to the meaning of 멸 滅, i.e. annihilation or extinction of existence ; or of rebirth and mortal existence ; or of the passions as the cause of pain ; and it is the two latter views which generally prevail ; cf. 열 涅.

멸 蔑 Without, not ; minute, small. 멸려차 蔑戾車 Mleccha, barbarians, non-Aryan, heathen, frontier tribes. Also 멸 蔑, 미 彌, 필 畢.

멸갈마 滅羯磨 The extinguishing karma, or the blotting out of the name of a monk and his expulsion.

멸겁 滅劫 The saṁvarta-kalpa of world-destruction, cf. 괴겁 壞劫.

멸과 滅果 Nirvāṇa as the fruit of extinction (of desire).

멸관 滅觀 The contemplation of extinction: the destruction of ignorance is followed by the annihilation of karma, of birth, old age, and death.

멸도 滅道 Extinction of suffering and the way of extinction, nirodha and mārga ; v. *supra*.

멸도 滅度 Nirvāṇa ; extinction of reincarnation and escape from suffering.

멸리 滅理 The principle or law of extinction, i.e. nirvāṇa.

멸법 滅法 The unconditioned dharma, the ultimate inertia from which all forms come, the noumenal source of all phenomena. 멸법지 滅法智 The knowledge or wisdom of the dogma of extinction (of passion and reincarnation) ; one of the 팔지 八智 q.v. 멸법지인 滅法智忍 One of the 팔인 八忍, the endurance and patience associated with the last. 멸법계 滅法界 The realm of the absolute, of perfect quiescence.

멸병 滅病 One of the 사병 四病 four sick or faulty ways of seeking perfection, the Hīnayāna method of endeavouring to extinguish all perturbing passions so that nothing of them remains.

멸빈 滅擯 Blotting out the name and the expulsion of a monk who has committed a grievous sin without repentance.

멸상 滅相 Extinction, as when the present passes into the past. Also, the absolute, unconditioned aspect of bhūtatathatā.

멸수상정 滅受想定 A samādhi in which there is complete extinction of sensation and thought ; one of the highest forms of kenosis, resulting from concentration.

멸업 滅業 The work of karma of nirodha, the karma resulting from the extinction of suffering, i.e. nirvāṇa.

멸장 滅場 The plot or arena where the extinction (of the passions) is attained ; the place of perfect repose, or nirvāṇa.

멸정 滅定 idem 멸진정 滅盡定. 멸정지통 滅定智通 The freedom or supernatural power of the wisdom attained in nirvāṇa, or perfect passivity.

멸제 滅諦 Nirodha-āryasatya, the third of the four dogmas, the extinction of suffering, which is rooted in reincarnation, v. 사제 四諦.

멸종 滅種 To destroy one's seed of Buddhahood.

멸지 滅智 The knowledge, or wisdom, of the third axiom, nirodha or the extinction of suffering.

멸진정 滅盡定 idem 멸수상정 滅受想定, also called 멸정 滅定 and 멸진삼매 滅盡三昧.

멸후 滅後 After the Nirvāṇa, after the Buddha's death.

명 鳴 Cry, sound, note of a bird, etc. 명어 鳴魚 To sound the wooden fish to announce a meal time. 명석 鳴錫 A rattling staff shaken to warn the spirits.

명 冥 Darkness, obscurity ; deep, Hades ; used chiefly in the sense of 무지 無知 ignorance, profound, secret, invisible, e.g. as opposed to 현 顯 open, manifest. 명일 冥一 Entire obscurity, pristine darkness. 명사 冥使 Lictors, or messengers of Hades. 명리 冥利 ; 명익 冥益 Invisible benefit, or merit, i.e. within, spiritual. 명초 冥初 The primitive darkness (at the beginning of existence). 명가 冥加 The invisible aid of the spiritual powers. 명관 冥官 The rulers in Hades. 명부 冥府 The palace of darkness, Hades. 명왕 冥往 Going into the shades, death. 명사 冥思 ; 명려 冥慮 The unfathomable thought or care of the Buddhas and bodhisattvas, beyond the realization of men. 명응 冥應 Response from the invisible. 명훈 冥熏 or 내훈 內熏 Fumigation within, inner influence. 명계 冥界 Hades, or the three lower forms of incarnation, i.e. hell, preta, animal. 명복 冥福 The happiness of the dead. 명중 冥衆 The invisible powers – Brahmā, Śakra, Yama ; the spirits in general. 명제 冥諦 ; 명성 冥性 ; 자성 自性 The Sāṅkhya doctrine of primordial profundity, beyond estimation, the original nature out of which all things arose. 명자 冥資 Possessions of or for the dead ; their happiness. 명도 冥道 ; 명도 冥途 ; 명토 冥土 The dark way, or land of darkness, the shades, Hades, pretas, etc. 명통 冥通 Mysterious, supernatural, omnipresent power. 명양회 冥陽會 The assembly (for offerings) of the spirits below and above, pretas, etc. 명현양계 冥顯兩界 The two regions of the dead and of the living.

명 命 Jīvita. Life, vital, length of life, fate, decree. 명광 命光 The light of a life, i.e. soon gone. 명광조 命光鳥 ; 기바기바가 耆婆耆婆迦 Jīvajīvaka ; Jīvaṁjīva, a bird with two heads, a sweet songster ; 생생조 生生鳥 or 공명조 共命鳥 is the same bird. 명보 命寶 The precious possession of life. 명근 命根 A root, or basis for life, or reincarnation, the nexus of Hīnayāna between two life-periods, accepted by Mahāyāna as nominal but not real. 명범 命梵 Life and honour, i.e. perils to life and perils to noble character. 명탁 命濁 One of the 오탁 五濁, turbidity or decay of the vital principle, reducing the length of life. 명종 命終 Life's end ; nearing the end. 명자 命者 The living being ; the one possessing life ; life. 명등 命藤 The rope of life (gnawed by the two rats, i.e. night and day). 명도사문 命道沙門 A śramaṇa who makes the commandments, meditation, and knowledge his very life, as Ānanda did. 명난 命難 Life's hardships ; the distress of living.

명 名 Nāman 나마 娜麼 or 娜摩 ; a name, a term ; noted, famous. 명가 名假 Name unreal ; one of the 삼가 三假 ; names are not in themselves realities. 명리 名利 Fame and gain. 명별의통 名別義通 Different in name but of the same meaning. 명자 名字 Name and description, name. 명자비구 名字比丘 A monk in name but not in reality. 명자보살 名字菩薩 A nominal bodhisattva. 명자사미 名字沙彌 One of an age to be a monk, i.e. 20 years of age and over. 명덕 名德 Of notable virtue. 명목 名目 A name, or descriptive title. 명상 名相 Name and appearance ; everything has a name, e.g. sound, or has appearance, i.e. the visible, v. 명색 名色 ; both are unreal and give rise to delusion. The name under which Subhūti will be reborn as Buddha. 명적 名籍 A register of names. 명의 名義 Name and meaning ; the meaning of a name, or term. 명의불리 名義不離 Connotation ; name and meaning not apart, or differing, they are inseparable or identical, the name having equality with the meaning, e.g. a Buddha, or the terms of a dhāraṇī. 명의 名義 or 명의집 名義集 is an abbreviation for the 번역명의 翻譯名義 Fan-i-ming-i dictionary. 명문 名聞 ; 명성 名聲 Yaśas, renown, fame.

명랍 名臘 A monk of renown and of years. 명색 名色 Nāmarūpa, name-form, or name and form, one of the twelve nidānas. In Brahminical tradition it served "to denote spirit and matter," "the concrete individual," [Keith] ; in Buddhism it is intp. as the 오온 五蘊 five skandhas or aggregates, i.e. a "body," 수 受, 상 想, 행 行, and 식 識 vedanā, saṁjñā, karman, and vijñāna being the "name" and 색 色 rūpa the "form" ; the first-named four are mental and the last material. 색 色 Rūpa is described as the minutest particle of matter, that which has resistance ; the embryonic body or foetus is a nāmarūpa, something that can be named. 명호 名號 A name, or title, especially that of Amitābha. 명납 名衲 A name and robe, i.e. a monk. 명신 名身 A word-group, a term of more than one word. 명체 名體 Name and embodiment ; the identity of name and substance, as in the dhāraṇī of the esoteric sects ; somewhat similar to 명의불리 名義不離 q.v.

명 銘 To engrave, on metal, stone, or the tablets of the heart.

명 明 Vidyā, knowledge. Ming means bright, clear, enlightenment, intp. by 지혜 智慧 or 총명 聰明 wisdom, wise ; to understand. It represents Buddha-wisdom and its revelation ; also the manifestation of a Buddha's light or effulgence ; it is a term for 진언 眞言 because the "true word" can destroy the obscurity of illusion ; the "manifestation" of the power of the object of worship ; it means also dhāraṇīs or mantras of mystic wisdom. Also, the Ming dynasty A.D. 1368-1644. 명료 明了 To understand thoroughly ; complete enlightenment. 무명 無名 Commonly tr. "ignorance," means an unenlightened condition, non-perception, before the stirrings of intelligence, belief that the phenomenal is real, etc.

명달 明達 Enlightenment 명 明 in the case of the saint includes knowledge of future incarnations of self and others, of the past incarnations of self and others, and that the present incarnation will end illusion. In the case of the Buddha such knowledge is called 달 達 thorough or perfect enlightenment.

명도 明道 The bright or clear way ; the way of the mantras and dhāraṇīs.

명도무극 明度無極 An old intp. of Prajñā 명 明 pāramitā 도 度, the wisdom that ferries to the other shore without limit ; for which 명거 明炬 a shining torch is also used.

명득(정) 明得(定) A samādhi in the Bodhisattva's 사가행 四加行 in which there are the bright beginnings of release from illusion. 명득보살 明得菩薩 The Bodhisattva who has reached that stage, i.e. the 난위 煖位.

명리 明利 Clear and keen (to penetrate all mystery).

명명 明冥 The (powers of) light and darkness, the devas and Yama, gods and demons, also the visible and invisible.

명민 明敏 Śīghrabodhi. "A famous priest of the Nālandā monastery." [Eitel].

명법 明法 The law or method of mantras, or magic formulae.

명부전 冥府殿 Hall for the kings of the Hell.

명비 明妃 Another name for dhāraṇī as the queen of mystic knowledge and able to overcome all evil. Also the female consorts shown in the maṇḍalas.

명상 明相 Early dawn, the proper time for the monk's breakfast ; brightness.

명성 明星 Venus 태백 太白 and the 천자 天子 or deva-prince who dwells in that planet ; but it is also said to be Aruṇa, which indicates the Dawn.

명신 明神 The bright spirits, i.e. devas, gods, demons.

명신불지 明信佛智 To believe clearly in Buddha's wisdom (as leading to rebirth in the Pure Land).

명심 明心 The enlightened heart.

명왕 明王 The rājas, ming-wang, or fierce spirits who are the messengers and manifestation of Vairocana's wrath against evil spirits.

명월 明月 The bright moon. 명월주 明月珠 ; 명주 明珠 ; 마니 摩尼 The bright-moon maṇi or pearl, emblem of Buddha, Buddhism, the Buddhist Scriptures, purity, etc. 명월천자 明月天子 The moon-deva, in Indra's retinue.

명장 明藏 The Buddhist canon of the Ming dynasty ; there were two editions, one the Southern at Nanking made by T'ai Tsu, the Northern at Peking by Tai Tsung. A later edition was produced in the reign of Shên Tsung (Wan Li), which became the standard in Japan.

명지 明地 The stage of illumination, or 발광지 發光地 the third of the ten stages, v. 십지 十地.

명처 明處 The regions or realms of study which produce wisdom, five in number, v. 오명(처) 五明(處).

명탈 明脫 Enlightenment (from ignorance) and release (from desire).

명행족 明行足 Vidyā-caraṇa-saṁpanna ; knowledge-conduct-perfect 비치차라나삼반나 婢侈遮羅那三般那. (1) The unexcelled universal enlightenment of the Buddha based upon the discipline, meditation, and wisdom regarded as feet ; one of the ten epithets of Buddha. Nirvāṇa sūtra 18. (2) The 지도론 智度論 2 interprets 명 明 by the 삼명 三明 q.v., the 행 行 by the 삼업 三業 q.v., and the 족 足 by complete, or perfect.

명혜 明慧 The three enlightenments 삼명 三明, and the three wisdoms 삼혜 三慧.

명훈 明熏 The inner light, enlightenment censing and overcoming ignorance, like incense perfuming and interpenetrating.

모 毛 Hair ; feathers ; 모병 毛病 flaw, ailment. 모공 毛孔 Hair-hole, pore, the pores. 모승 毛繩 A hair rope, i.e. tied up by the passions, as with an unbreakable hair rope. 모도 毛道 ; 모두 毛頭 A name for 범부 凡夫 ordinary people, i.e. non-Buddhists, the unenlightened ; the 모 毛 is said to be a translation of vāla, hair or down, which in turn is considered an error for bāla, ignorant, foolish, i.e. simple people who are easily beguiled. It is also said to be a form of Bāla-pṛthag-jana, v. 파 婆, which is intp. as born in ignorance ; the ignorant and untutored in general. 모도생 毛道生 The ignorant people. 모도범부 毛道凡夫 An ignorant, gullible person. 모두 毛頭 idem 모도 毛道 ; also, a barber-monk who shaves the fraternity. 모타가라자 毛馱伽羅子 Maudgalaputra idem Mahāmaudgalyāyana, v. 목련 目連.

모 姥 Matron, dame. 모달라 姥達羅 Mudrā(-bala), 100,000 sextillions ; 대모달라 大姥達羅 a septillion ; v. 락 洛.

모 母 Mātṛ, a mother. 모주 母主 The "mother-lord", or mother, as contrasted with 주 主 and 모 母, lord and mother, king and queen, in the maṇḍala of Vajradhātu and Garbhadhātu ; Vairocana, being the source of all things, has no "mother" as progenitor, and is the 부주 部主 or lord of the maṇḍala ; the other four dhyāni-buddhas have "mothers" called 부모 部母, who are supposed to arise from the pāramitās ; thus, Akṣobhya has 금강바라밀 金剛波羅蜜 for mother ; Ratnasaṁbhava has 보바라밀 寶波羅蜜 for mother ; Amitābha has 법바라밀 法波羅蜜 for mother ; Amoghasiddhi has 갈마바라밀 羯磨波羅蜜 for mother. 모경 母經 ; 마달리가 摩怛理迦 Mātṛkā ; a text, as distinguished from its commentary ; an original text ; the Abhidharma. 모읍 母邑 ; 마달리가라마 摩怛理伽羅摩 Mātṛgrāma, the community of mothers, womankind. 모다마노사 母陀摩奴沙 ; 모나마노사 母那摩奴沙 Mṛta-manuṣya ; a human corpse. 모다라 母陀羅 ; 모나라 母捺羅 or 慕捺羅 ; 목다라 目陀羅 ; 말득라 末得羅 Mudrā, 인 印 a seal, stamp, sign, manual sign. 모다라수 母陀羅手 A manual sign of assurance, hence felicitous. 모타 母馱 ; 무타 毋馱 idem 불타 佛陀, i.e. 불 佛 buddha.

모 謨 Plans, schemes ; counterfeit, forge ; translit. *mo*, *mu*. 모살라 謨薩羅 Musālagarbha, v. 모 牟. 모하 謨賀 Moha, intp. as 치 痴 unconsciousness, delusion, ignorance, foolishness, infatuation.

[M. W.] It is used in the sense of unenlightenment, and is one of the three poisons 탐진치 貪瞋痴, i.e. the ignorant, unenlightened state which is deceived by appearances, taking the seeming for real. Also 모하 慕何.

모 茅 Thatch. 모개두 茅蓋頭 A handful of thatch to cover one's head, a hut, or simple monastery.

모 摸 To feel, grope, e.g. as a blind man. 모상 摸象 The blind man who tried to describe an elephant by feeling it, v. Nirvāṇa Sūtra 32.

모 慕 To long for, hanker after, love ; translit. *mo*, *mu*. 모하 慕何 Moha, v. 모 謨 Unenlightened, stupid. 모나라 慕捺囉 Mudrā a seal, sign, token, hand or finger signs. 모라 慕攞 ; 모라 慕羅 Mūla, root, fundamental, hence mūlagrantha, fundamental works, original texts ; Mūla-sarvāstivādāḥ, the Hīnayāna school of that name.

모 牟 To low (as an ox) ; overpass ; barley ; a grain vessel ; weevil ; eye-pupil ; translit. *mu*, *ma*. 모호률다 牟呼栗多 Muhūrta, the thirtieth part of an ahorātra, a day-and-night, i.e. forty-eight minutes ; a brief space of time, moment ; also (wrongly) a firm mind. 모호락 牟呼洛 Mahoraga, boa-demons, v. 마후 摩睺. 모사(라) 牟娑(羅) or 마사(라) 摩娑(羅) or 목사(라) 目娑(羅) ; 모사락(게파) 牟娑洛(揭婆) ; 마사라 摩沙羅 ; 모살라 謨薩羅 or 모살라 牟薩羅 Musāragalva, a kind of coral, white coral, [M. W.] ; defined as 마노 瑪瑙 cornelian, agate ; and 차거 硨磲 mother of pearl ; it is one of the 칠보 七寶 sapta ratna q.v. 모니(선) 牟尼(仙), 문니 文尼 ; 무니 茂泥 ; (마갈)마니 (馬曷)摩尼 Muni ; Mahāmuni ; 월마니 月摩尼 Vimuni. A sage, saint, ascetic, monk, especially Śākyamuni ; interpreted as 적 寂 retired, secluded, silent, solitary, i.e. withdrawn from the world. See also 백팔마니 百八摩尼. 모니실리 牟尼室利 Muniśrī, name of a monk from northern India in the Liu Sung period (5th cent.). 모니왕 牟尼王 The monk-king, a title of the Buddha. 모진린타 牟眞鄰陀 Mucilinda, v. 마 摩 and 목 目. 모다라 牟陀羅 Mardala, or Mṛdaṅga, a kind of drum described as having three faces.

모 冒 To risk ; rash ; counterfeit ; introduce. 모지 冒地 Bodhi. 모지질다 冒地質多 Bodhicitta, the enlightened mind, idem 보리심 菩提心. 모지살달부 冒地薩怛嚩 Bodhisattva. Cf. 보리 菩提.

모 募 To solicit, call upon, invite ; enroll, enlist, subscribe. 모연 募緣 ; 모화 募化 To raise subscriptions.

목 睦 Amicable, friendly. 화목 和睦 Concord, harmony.

목 目 Cakṣu, the eye ; the organ of vision ; the head or chief ; translit. *ma*, *mu*. 목거 目佉 Mukha, mouth, opening. 목다 目多 Mukta, release, free, released ; muktā, a pearl, jewels in general. 목다가 目多伽 Abbrev. for 이제목다가 伊提目多伽 Itivṛttaka, biographical stories. 목제라 目帝羅 ; 목득라 木得羅 Intp. as mukti, release, emancipation 해탈 解脫, or as the knowledge or experience of liberation. 목지린다 目支隣陀 ; 목지린다 目脂隣陀 ; 목진린다 目眞隣陀 ; 목린 目隣 ; 지린 支隣 ; 모진린다 牟眞隣陀 ; 모진린나 母眞隣那 ; 모지린나 母止隣那 ; 문진린다 文眞隣陀 ; 마하문진린다 摩訶文眞隣陀. Mucilinda, or Mahāmucilinda. A nāga or dragon king who dwelt in a lake near a hill and cave of this name, near Gayā, where Śākyamuni sat absorbed for seven days after his enlightenment, protected by this nāga-king. 목기수양 目機銖兩 The power of the eye to discern trifling differences ; quick discernment. 목건련 目犍連 ; 목련 目連 ; 마하목건련 摩訶目犍連 ; 마하라야나 摩訶羅夜那 ; 대목건련 大目犍連 ; 대목건련 大目乾連 ; 몰특가라자 沒特伽羅子 ; 몰력가라자 沒力伽羅子 ; 목가략 目伽略 (Maha-)Maudgalyāyana, or Maudgalaputra ; explained by Mudga 호두 胡豆 lentil, kidney-bean. One of the ten chief disciples of Śākyamuni, specially noted for miraculous powers ; formerly an ascetic, he agreed with Śāriputra that whichever first found the truth would reveal it to the other. Śāriputra found the Buddha and brought Maudgalyāyana to him ; the former is placed on the Buddha's right, the latter on his left. He is also known as 구률 拘栗 Kolita, and when reborn as Buddha his title is to be Tamāla-patra-candana-gandha.

In China Mahāsthāmaprāpta is accounted a canonization of Maudgalyāyana. Several centuries afterwards there were two other great leaders of the Buddhist church bearing the same name, v. [Eitel]. 목갈람 目竭嵐 Mudgara ; a hammer, mallet, mace. 목족 目足 Eye and foot, knowledge and practice ; eyes in the feet. 목족선 目足仙 Akṣapāda, founder of the Nyāya, or logical school of philosophers. [M. W.]

목 沐 To bathe ; translit. *mu, mo* ; 목백태자 沐魄太子 is 모백 募魄 one of the former incarnations of Śākyamuni.

목 牧 To herd, pastor. 목우 牧牛 Cowherd.

목 木 Wood ; a tree ; kāṣṭha, a piece of wood, wood, timber. 목상좌 木上座 The elder with the tree, or the wooden elder ; the elder's staff. 목불 木佛 A Buddha of wood, i.e. an image of wood. 목거포절나 木佉褒折娜 Mukhaproñchana, or face-wiper, towel, handkerchief, one of the thirteen articles of a monk. 목차 木叉 ; 목사 木蛇 ; 바라제목차 波羅提木叉 Mokṣa, pratimokṣa ; mokṣa is deliverance, emancipation ; prati, "towards," implies the getting rid of evils one by one ; the 250 rules of the Vinaya for monks for their deliverance from the round of mortality. 목차제바 木叉提婆 Mokṣadeva. A title given by the Hīnayānists in India to Mahāyānadeva, i.e. 현장 玄奘 Hsüan-tsang. 목차국다 木叉鞠多 Mokṣagupta. A monk of Karashahr, protagonist of the Madhyamayāna school, "whose ignorance Hsüan-tsang publicly exposed." [Eitel]. 목지 木底 Mukti, 해탈 解脫 deliverance, liberation, emancipation ; the same meaning is given to 목제라 目帝羅 mucira, which has more the sense of being free with (gifts), generosity. 목율승 木律僧 A wooden pettifogging monk ; a rigid formalist. 목득라 木得羅 Mudrā, a seal ; mystic signs with the hands. 목성 木星 ; 물리하사파지 勿哩訶娑跛底 Bṛhaspati ; "Lord of increase," the planet Jupiter. 목요 木曜 Jupiter, one of the 구요 九曜 nine luminaries, q.v. ; on the south of the diamond hall outside the Garbhadhātu maṇḍala. 목환자 木槵子 ; 무환자 無患子 A tree whose wood can exorcise evil spirits, or whose seeds are used as rosary-beads. It is said to be the ariṣṭa 아리슬가자 阿梨瑟迦紫, which means unharmed, secure ; it is the name of the soap-berry and other shrubs. 목란자 木欒子 Seeds used for rosary-beads. 목과림 木瓜林 ; 고행림 苦行林 Papaya forest, i.e. Uruvilvā, 우루빈라 優樓頻螺 the place near Gayā where Kāśyapa, Śākyamuni, and others practised their austerities before the latter's enlightenment ; hence the former is styled Uruvilvā Kāśyapa. 목란색 木蘭色 Brownish colour made from bark, probably cinnamon. 목두 木頭 Block-head, a stupid person, one who breaks the commandments. 목향 木香 ; 근향 根香 ; 훈육향 薰陸香 ; 다가라 多伽羅 Tagara. An incense-yielding tree, putchuk ; *Vangueria spinosa* or *Tabernæmontana coronaria* ; Eitel. 목식 木食 Living on wild fruits, nuts, etc. 목어 木魚 The wooden fish ; there are two kinds, one round for use to keep time in chanting, the other long for calling to meals. The origin of the use of a fish is unknown : one version is that as a fish always has its eyes open day and night, so it is an example to monks to be watchful ; there is no evidence of connection with the Christian *ιχθυς*. 목마 木馬 Wooden horse, a symbol of emancipation.

목어 木魚 Wooden fish. Wooden percussion instrument shaped as fish used in a Buddhist service. Wooden-clacker.

목탁 木鐸 Moktak. A round-shaped 목어 木魚 wooden fish. Koreans call the round-shaped ones as 목탁 木鐸 ; the long-shaped ones as 목어 木魚. Historically, the round-shaped ones are originated from the long-shaped ones.

몰 沒 Sunk, gone ; not ; translit. *m, mu, mo, mau, ma, bu, v*, etc. 몰교섭 沒交涉 No inter-relation. 몰겁 沒劫 Moha, delusion, bewilderment, infatuation, tr. by 우 愚 foolishness ; cf. 모 謨. 몰리지야폐 沒哩底野吠 Derived from mṛtyu, death ; one of Yama's 명왕 明王 or rājas. 몰파비 沒巴鼻 No nose to lay hold of ; no lead, no bases. 몰도 沒度 Buddha, v. 불 佛. 몰률도 沒栗度 Mṛdu, soft, pliant, weak. 몰률다 沒栗多 Vrata, temporary chastity, or observance. 몰예달리슬치 沒曳達利瑟致 Māyādṛṣṭi, illusion-views, intp. by 아견 我見 egoism, the false doctrine that there is a real ego. 몰자미 沒滋味 Tasteless, valueless, useless, e.g. the discussion of the colour of milk by blind people. 몰특가라자 沒特伽羅子 or 몰도가라자 沒刀伽羅子 v. 목(건)련 目(犍)連 Maudgalaputra, or Maudgalyāyana. 몰타 沒馱 Buddha, v. 불 佛.

몰록 At one time, at once ; suddenly ; immediately. Similar to 돈 頓.

몽 夢 A dream, a simile of the things of the world. 몽환 夢幻 Dream and illusion, the characteristics of all phenomena. 몽갈리 夢揭釐 Moṅgali, or Maṅgala, ancient capital of Udyāna, the present Manglavor on the left bank of the Swat, a trans-Indus State west of Kashmir. 몽상 夢想 To "dream" a thing to think of in a dream, to imagine. 몽견 夢見 To see in a dream, to imagine one sees, or has seen.

몽 蒙 To cover ; stupid, ignorant ; receive (from above) ; Mongol. 몽고 蒙古 Mongolia, Mongol. 몽감 蒙感 Stupid and deluded.

묘 廟 A fane, temple, palace ; an intp. of caitya, cf. 지 支.

묘 妙 Su, sat, mañju, sūkṣma. Wonderful, beautiful, mystic, supernatural, profound, subtle, mysterious. Su means good, excellent, surpassing, beautiful, fine, easy. Sat means existing, real, good. Mañju means beautiful, lovely, charming. Intp. in Chinese as 불가사의 不可思議 beyond thought or discussion ; 절대 絶待 special, outstanding ; 무비 無比 incomparable ; 정미심원 精微深遠 subtle and profound.

묘가 妙假 The profound meaning of phenomena of T'ien-t'ai, that they are the bhūtatathatā (e.g. water and wave) as distinguished from the 별교 別教 view ; cf. 묘중 妙中.

묘각 妙覺 The wonderful enlightenment of Mahāyāna, or self-enlightenment to enlighten others. 묘각지 妙覺地 The stage of wonderful enlightenment, Buddhahood. 묘각성 妙覺性 The profound, enlightened nature, that of Buddha, one of the 육성 六性.

묘거 妙車 The wonderful vehicles (mentioned in the Lotus sūtra).

묘견 妙見 The beautiful sight, i.e. Ursa Major, or the Bodhisattva who rules there, styled 묘견대사 妙見大士 or 묘견보살 妙見菩薩, though some say Śākyamuni, others Kuan-yin, others 약사 藥師 Bhaiṣajya, others the seven Buddhas. His image is that of a youth in golden armour.

묘고산(왕) 妙高山(王) The wonderful high mountain, Sumeru ; the king of mountains.

묘과 妙果 Wonderful fruit, i.e. bodhi or enlightenment and nirvāṇa.

묘관 妙觀 The wonderful system of the three T'ien-t'ai meditations ; v. 삼제 三諦, 삼관 三觀.

묘광 妙光 Varaprabha, Wonderful Light, an ancient incarnation of Mañjuśrī. 묘광불 妙光佛 Sūryaraśmi, the 930th Buddha of present kalpa.

묘교 妙教 Admirable, profound teaching ; i.e. that of the Lotuṣ Sūtra.

묘길상 妙吉祥 Wonderful and auspicious, the meaning of Mañjuśrī, 묘 妙 for Mañju and 길상 吉祥 for śrī ; v. 문수 文殊.

묘당 妙幢 Ruciraketu. Name of a Bodhisattva. The 묘당상삼매 妙幢相三昧 Dhvajāgrakeyūra, "the ring on the top of a standard," a degree of ecstatic meditation mentioned in the Lotus sūtra.

묘덕 妙德 Wonderful virtue, title of Mañjuśrī ; also an intp. of the meaning of Kapilavastu, v. 겁비 劫比, etc.

묘명 妙明 Profoundly enlightened heart or mind, i.e. the knowledge of the finality of the stream of reincarnation.

묘무 妙無 Asat, the mystery of non-existence.

묘문 妙門 The wonderful door of dharma ; nirvāṇa ; the six T'ien-t'ai methods leading through meditation to enlightenment and the state of nirvāṇa.

묘법 妙法 Saddharma, 살달(라)마 薩達(剌)摩 The wonderful law or truth (of the Lotus Sūtra). 묘법일승 妙法一乘 The One Vehicle of the wonderful dharma, or perfect Mahāyāna. 묘법당 妙法堂 ; 선법당 善法堂 The hall of wonderful dharma, situated in the south-west corner of the Trayastriṁśāḥ heaven, v. 도 忉, where the thirty-three devas discuss whether affairs are according to law or truth or the contrary. 묘법궁 妙法宮 The palace of the wonderful law, in which the Buddha ever dwells. 묘법등 妙法燈 The lamp of the wonderful Law shining into the darkness of ignorance. 묘법선 妙法船 The bark or boat of wonderful dharma, capable of transpoting men over the sea of life into nirvāṇa. 묘법화 妙法華 idem 묘법연화 妙法蓮華. 묘법장 妙法藏 The treasury of the wonderful dharma. 묘법륜 妙法輪 The wheel of the wonderful Law, Buddha's doctrine regarded as a great cakra or wheel. 묘법연화 妙法蓮華 ; 법화 法華 The wonderful truth as found in the Lotus Sūtra, the One Vehicle sūtra ; which is said to contain 실법 實法 Buddha's complete truth as compared with his previous 권법 權法 or 방편법 方便法, i.e. partial, or expedient teaching, but both are included in this perfect truth. The sūtra is the Saddharmapuṇḍarīka 정법화경 正法華經 or (첨품)묘법연화경 (添品)妙法蓮華經, also known as 살담분다리경 薩曇芬陀利經, of which several translations in whole or part were made from Sanskrit into Chinese, the most popular being by Kumārajīva. It was the special classic of the T'ien-t'ai school, which is sometimes known as the 연종 蓮宗 Lotus School, and it profoundly influenced Buddhist doctrine in China, Japan, and Tibet. The commentaries and treatises on it are very numerous ; two by Chih-i 지의 智顗 of the T'ien-t'ai school being the 묘법연화경문구 妙法蓮華經文句 and the 현의 玄義.

묘비보살 妙臂菩薩 Subāhu-kumāra, the bodhisattva of the wonderful arm ; there is a sūtra of this name.

묘색 妙色 Surūpa, 소루파 蘇樓波. The wonderful form or body, i.e. of a Buddha's sambhogakāya and his Buddha-land. 묘색신여래 妙色身如來 Surūpakāya Tathāgata (Akṣobhya, the Buddha of the East), who is thus addressed when offerings are made to the hungry spirits.

묘선공주 妙善公主 The princess of wonderful goodness, name of Kuan-yin as third daughter of King 장엄 莊嚴 Chuang Yen.

묘심 妙心 The mind or heart wonderful and profound beyond human thought. According to T'ien-t'ai the 별교 別教 limited this to mind 진심 眞心 of the Buddha, while the 원교 圓教 universalized it to include the unenlightened heart 망심 妄心 of all men.

묘악 妙樂 Wonderful music (in the Pure Land). Miao-yo, the sixth T'ien-t'ai patriarch.

묘어장 妙語藏 The storehouse of miraculous words, mantras, dhāraṇī, or magic spells of Shingon.

묘연화 妙蓮華 The wonderful lotus, symbol of the pure wisdom of Buddha, unsullied in the midst of the impurity of the world.

묘유 妙有 The absolute reality, the incomprehensible entity, as contrasted with superficial reality of phenomena ; supernatural existence.

묘음 妙音 Wonderful sound. (1) Gadgadasvara, 묘음보살 妙音菩薩 or 묘음대사 妙音大士 a Bodhisattva, master of seventeen degrees of samādhi, residing in Vairocana-raśmi-pratimaṇḍita, whose name heads cap. 24 of the Lotus sūtra. (2) Sughoṣa, a sister of Kuan-yin ; also a Buddha like Varuṇa controlling the waters 수천덕불 水天德佛, the 743rd Buddha of the present kalpa. (3) Ghoṣa, 구사 瞿沙 an arhat, famous for exegesis, who "restored the eyesight of Dharmavivardhana by washing his eyes with the tears of people who were moved by his eloquence." [Eitel]. 묘음변만 妙音徧滿 Universal wonderful sound, Manojña-śabdābhigarjita, the kalpa of Ānanda as Buddha. 묘음(악)천 妙音(樂)天 Sarasvatī, the wife or female energy of Brahmā. Also called 변재천(녀) 辨才天(女) Jap. Benzaiten, or Benten ; goddess of eloquence, learning, and music, bestower of the Sanskrit language and letters, and the bestower of 재 財 riches ; also the river goddess. Sometimes considered as masculine. Honoured among the seven gods of luck, and often represented as mounted on a dragon or a serpent. 묘음조 妙音鳥 The wonderful-voice bird, the Kalaviṅka.

묘응 妙應 The miraculous response, or self-manifestation of Buddhas and bodhisattvas.

묘의보살 妙意菩薩 Māṇavaka, i.e. Śākyamuni in a previous incarnation as disciple of Dīpaṃkara 연등불 然燈佛.

묘인 妙因 The profound cause, the discipline of the bodhisattva, i.e. chastity, and the six pāramitās, etc., as producing the Buddha-fruit.

묘장(엄)왕 妙莊(嚴)王 Śubhavyūha, the king who is the subject and title of the twenty-seventh chapter of the Lotus sūtra. He is also reputed to be the father of Kuan-yin.

묘전 妙典 The classics of the wonderful dharma, i.e. Mahāyāna.

묘종 妙宗 Profound principles ; the Lotus School.

묘중 妙中 The profound medium (madhya) ; the universal life essence, the absolute, the bhūtatathatā which expresses the unity of all things, i.e. the doctrine held by T'ien-t'ai as distinguished from the 별교 別教 which holds the madhya doctrine but emphasizes the dichotomy of the 공 空 transcendental and 가 假 phenomenal.

묘지 妙智 The wonderful Buddha-wisdom.

묘진여성 妙眞如性 The profound nature of the Bhūtatathatā, the totality, or fundamental nature, of all things.

묘취 妙趣 The wonderful destiny or metempsychosis, i.e. that of Mahāyāna.

묘토 妙土 The wonderful land ; a Buddha's reward-land ; especially the Western paradise of Amitābha.

묘행 妙行 The profound act by which a good karma is produced, e.g. faith ; v. 일행일체행 一行一切行.

묘현 妙賢 Subhadra, 선현 善賢 A monk referred to in the 서역기 西域記 Records of Western Lands.

묘현 妙玄 Wonderful and profound ; an abbreviation for 묘법연화경현의 妙法蓮華經玄義 the T'ien-t'ai commentary on the Lotus Sūtra.

묘현산 妙顯山 The mountain of marvellous appearance, i.e. Sumeru.

묘희세계 妙喜世界 The realm of profound joy, the country of Vimalakīrti 유마거사 維摩居士, who is stated to have been a contemporary of Śākyamuni ; v. 유마힐경 維摩詰經 12. 묘희족천 妙喜足天 The heaven full of wonderful joy, idem Tuṣita, v. 두 兜.

무 茂 Flourishing 무니 茂尼 ; 문니 文尼 ; 모니 牟尼 Muni, a solitary, a recluse, e.g. Śākyamuni, the recluse of the Śākya family ; genii ; intp. as one who seeks solitude, and one who is able to be kind. 무라삼부로 茂羅三部盧 Mūlasthānapura, the modern Multan. 무차 茂遮 Moca, the plantain tree, *Musa sapientum*, associated with the idea of liberation from the passions.

무 無 Sanskrit *A*, or before a vowel *An*, similar to English *un-*, *in-*in a negative sense ; not, no, none, non-existent, v. 불 不, 비 非, 부 否 ; opposite of 유 有. 무일 無一 Not one. 무이무삼 無二無三 Neither two nor three, but only 일승 一乘 one Vehicle.

무 舞 To posture, brandish, play ; urge. 무희 舞戲 To play, perform plays.

무 戊 Wu, Mou ; flourishing ; the fifth of the ten "stems". 무지 戊地 The Fan-i-ming-i describes this as 서안국 西安國, perhaps 안서국 安西國 Parthia is meant. 무달라 戊達羅 A misprint for 수달라 戌達羅 ; 수타 首陁 Śūdra, the caste of farmers and slaves.

무간 無間 Avīci, uninterrupted, unseparated, without intermission. 무간지옥 無間地獄 The avīci hell, the last of the eight hot hells, in which punishment, pain, form, birth, death continue without intermission. 무간업 無間業 The unintermitted karma, or unintermitted punishment for any of the five unpardonable sins ; the place of such punishment, the avīci hell ; also styled ānantarya.

무감 無減 The undiminished powers of a bodhisattva after attaining Buddhahood ; i.e. undiminished power and zeal to save all beings, power of memory, wisdom, nirvāṇa, and insight attained through nirvāṇa ; cf. 지도론 智度論 26 ; also for a list of twenty-two cf. 유식론 唯識論 10.

무개 無蓋 That which cannot be covered or contained, universal ; also that which includes all, a characteristic of the pity of Buddha, hence 무개대비 無蓋大悲, uncontainable, or superlative, pity.

무거무래 無去無來 Neither going nor coming, eternal like the dharmakāya.

무견정상 無見頂相 The uṣṇīṣa, or lump, on Buddha's head, called "the invisible mark on the head," because it was supposed to contain an invisible sign ; perhaps because it was covered.

무공용 無功用 Without effort. 무공덕 無功德 Without merit, or virtue.

무광불 無光佛 An unilluminating Buddha, a useless Buddha who gives out no light.

무구 無垢 Vimala ; amala. Undefiled, stainless ; similar to 무루 無漏, 무구지 無垢地 The stage of undefilement, the second stage of a bodhisattva ; also applied to the final stage before attaining Buddhahood. 무구인 無垢忍 The stage of undefiled endurance, the final stage of a bodhisattva as above. 무구의 無垢衣 The stainless garment, the monastic robe of purity. 무구식 無垢識 Amala, undefiled or pure knowing or knowledge, formerly considered as the ninth, later as the eighth vijñāna.

무극 無極 Limitless, infinite. 무극지체 無極之體 The limitless bodies of those in the Pure Land ; the state of one who has attained nirvāṇa.

무근 無根 Without root ; without organs ; without the organs of sex. 무근신 無根信 Faith produced not of oneself but by Buddha in the heart.

무기 無記 Avyākṛta, or Avyākhyāta. Unrecordable (either as good or bad) ; neutral, neither good nor bad ; things that are innocent or cannot be classified under moral categories. One of 삼성 三性.

무념 無念 Without a thought ; without recollection ; absence of false ideas or thoughts, i.e. correct ideas or thoughts ; apart from thought (nothing exists).

무능 無能 Unable, without power. 무능승 無能勝 Ajita. Invincible, unsurpassable, unconquerable ; especially applied to Maitreya, cf. 아일다 阿逸多 ; also to various others.

무도 無倒 Not upside-down, seeing things right-side up, or correctly, i.e. correct views of truth and things, e.g. not regarding the seeming as real, the temporal as eternal, etc.

무도대적 無刀大賊 A bandit without a sword, e.g. a virtueless monk robbing others of their virtue.

무동 無動 Akṣobha ; imperturbable, calm, serene, unagitated. 무동불 無動佛 Akṣobhya, cf. 아촉바 阿閦婆 and 부동불 不動佛 The unperturbed Buddha, sometimes tr. as motionless, but the reference is to his calmness, serenity, and absence of passion ; he is one of the Five Dhyāni-Buddhas, and generally reigns over the east, his kingdom being Abhirati, realm of mystic pleasure. In the Lotus Sūtra he is named as the first of the sixteen sons of Mahābhijñābhibhū. One of his principal characteristics is that of subduing the passions. 무동존 無動尊 idem 부동명왕 不動明王.

무등 無等 Asama ; unequal, unequalled ; the one without equal, Buddha. 무등등 無等等 Asamasama ; of rank unequalled, or equal with the unequalled, Buddha and Buddhism. 무등등승 無等等乘 The unequalled vehicle, Mahāyāna. 무등각 無等覺 The unequalled enlightenment possessed by Buddhas.

무량 無量 Apramāṇa ; Amita ; Ananta ; immeasurable, unlimited, e.g. the "four infinite" characteristics of a bodhisattva are 자비희사 慈悲喜捨 kindness, pity, joy, and self-sacrifice. 무량광 無量光 Apramāṇābha. Immeasurable, or infinite light or splendour. 무량광불 無量光佛 Amitābha, v. 아 阿. 무량광천 無量光天 The heaven of boundless light, the fifth of the Brahmalokas. 무량광명 無量光明 Amitābha. 무량광명토 無量光明土 His land of infinite light. 무량수 無量壽 Boundless, infinite life, a name for Amitābha, as in 무량수불 無量壽佛 ; 무량수여래 無量壽如來 ; 무량수왕 無量壽王. 무량수경 無量壽經 The Sukhāvatīvyūha-sūtra is tr. as the Amitāyus sūtra, and there are other treatises with similar titles, cf. 관무량수경 觀無量壽經, etc. 무량존 無量尊 The infinite honoured one, Amitābha. 무량혜 無量慧 Infinite wisdom, a term applied to a Buddha. 무량의 無量意 Anantamati, boundless mind, intention, will, or meaning. 무량정(천) 無量淨(天) Apramāṇaśubha, boundless purity, the second of the heavens in the third dhyāna heavens of form. 무량청정불 無量淸淨佛 The Buddha of boundless purity, Amitābha. 무량의 無量義 Infinite meaning, or the meaning of infinity ; the meaning of the all, or of all things. 무량의처삼매 無量義處三昧 The anantanirdeśapratiṣṭhāna samādhi, into which the Buddha is represented as entering before preaching the doctrine of infinity as given in the Lotus Sūtra. 무량각 無量覺 Infinite enlightenment, name of Amitābha.

무량수전 無量壽殿 Mu-ryang-su-jeon. Amitābha hall ; a building in a temple where Amitābha resides.

무루 無漏 Anāsrava. No drip, leak, or flow ; outside the passion-stream ; passionless ; outside the stream (of transmigratory suffering) ; away from the down-flow into lower forms of rebirth. 무루인 無漏因 Passionless purity as a cause for attaining nirvāṇa. 무루실상 無漏實相 Reality as passionless or pure. 무루(최)후신 無漏(最)後身 The final pure or passionless body. 무루혜 無漏慧 ; 무루지 無漏智 Passionless, or pure, wisdom, knowledge, or enlightenment. 무루근 無漏根 The three roots which produce pure knowledge, 삼무루근 三無漏根 q.v. 무루과 無漏果 The result of following the way of 계 戒, 정 定, and 혜 慧, i.e. purity, meditation, and wisdom, with liberation from the passions and from lower incarnation. 무루법 無漏法 The way of purity, or escape from the passions and lower transmigration. 무루법성 無漏法性 The pure, passionless dharma-nature. 무루도 無漏道 The way of purity, or deliverance from the passions, i.e. 계정혜 戒定慧 *supra* ; the fourth of the four dogmas 멸 滅 cessation, or annihilation of suffering. 무루문 無漏門 Āsravakṣaya-jñāna, entry into spiritual knowledge free from all faults, the last of the 육통 六通 q.v.

무명 無明 Avidyā, ignorance, and in some senses Māyā, illusion ; it is darkness without illumination, the ignorance which mistakes seeming for being, or illusory phenomena for realities ; it is also intp. as 치 痴 ignorant, stupid, fatuous ; but it means generally, unenlightened, unillumined. The 기신론 起信論 distinguishes two kinds as 근본 根本 the radical, fundamental, original darkness or ignorance considered as a 무시무명 無始無明 primal condition, and 지말 枝末 "branch and twig" conditions, considered as phenomenal. There is also a list of fifteen distinctions in the Vibhāṣā-śāstra 2. Avidyā is also the first, or last of the twelve nidānas. 무명사 無明使 One of the ten lictors, messengers or misleaders, i.e. of ignorance, who drives beings into the chain of transmigration. 무명주지 無明住地 The fifth of the five 주지 住地, i.e. the fundamental, unenlightened condition ; the source or nucleus of ignorance ; also ignorance as to the nature of things, i.e. of their fundamental unreality. 무명혹 無明惑 The illusion arising from primal ignorance which covers and hinders the truth of the *via media* ; one of the 삼혹 三惑 of T'ien-t'ai ; in the 별교 別教 it is overcome by the bodhisattva from the first 지 地 stage, in the 원교 圓交 in the first 주 住 resting-place. 무명업애 無明業愛 Ajñānakarmatṛṣṇā. Ignorance, karma, desire — the three forces that cause reincarnation. 무명법성일체 無明法性一體 Avidyā and the Bhūtatathatā are of the same nature, as are ice and water ; the ice of avidyā is the water of all things, the source out of which all enlightenment has come. 무명류 無明流 Unenlightenment, or ignorance, the cause of the stream of transmigration. 무명루 無明漏 The stream of unenlightenment which carries one along into reincarnation. 무명훈습 無明熏習 v. 사훈습 四熏習. 무명부 無明父 Ignorance as father and desire as mother produce the ego. 무명결 無明結 The bond of ignorance which binds to transmigration. 무명망 無明網 the snare of ignorance. 무명장 無明藏 The storehouse of ignorance, from which issues all illusion and misery. 무명견 無明見 Views produced by ignorance, ignorant perception of phenomena producing all sorts of illusion.

무명초 無明草 Lit. "weeds of ignorance." Monastic expression for hair, which, in this case, represents secular attachments.

무문 無問 Unasked ; not to ask ; volunteered. 무문자설 無問自說 Udāna, that part of the canon spoken voluntarily and not in reply to questions or appeals ; but Kern defines udāna as "enthusiastic utterances in prose and verse."

무문비구 無聞比丘 A monk who refuses instruction, untutored, self-confident.

무문종 無門宗 The unsectarian, Ch'an or meditative sect, so called because it claimed to derive its authority directly from the mind of Buddha.

무방 無方 No place, nowhere ; unlimited to place or method, i.e. Buddha's power.

무번 無煩 Free from trouble, the thirteenth Brahmaloka, the fifth region of the fourth dhyāna.

무변 無邊 Ananta ; endless, boundless, limitless, infinite, e.g. like space. 무변세계 無邊世界 The infinite world, i.e. space ; also infinite worlds ; the numberless worlds in infinite space. 무변법계 無邊法界 The infinite world of things ; the realm of things infinite in number ; the infinite universe behind all phenomena. 무변신 無邊身 The immeasurable body of the Buddha: the more the Brahman measured it the higher it grew, so he threw away his measuring rod, which struck root and became a forest.

무분별 無分別 Nirvikalpa. Non-discriminating. 무분별심 無分別心 The mind free from particularization, especially from affection and feeling ; passionless ; translates avikalpa ; (a) unconditioned or absolute, as in the 진여 眞如 ; (b) conditioned, as in dhyāna. Particularization includes memory, reason, self-consciousness ; the mind free from particularization is free from these. 무분별지 無分別智 The unconditioned or passionless mind as above. 무분별법 無分別法 The absolute dharma underlying all particular dharmas, the absolute as contrasted with the relative.

무불 無不 A double negative, making a positive ; also 무비 無非 ; 무몰 無沒.

무비 無比 Without comparison, no comparing, incomparable. 무비법 無比法 Incomparable truth or law, an incorrect tr. of abhidharma. 무비신 無比身 The incomparable body (of the Buddha).

무사지 無師智 Self-attained enlightenment, wisdom attained without a teacher, that of Buddha.

무상 無相 Animitta ; nirābhāsa. Without form, or sign ; no marks, or characteristics ; nothingness ; absolute truth as having no differentiated ideas ; nirvāṇa. 무상불 無相佛 Nirlakṣaṇa-buddha ; alakṣaṇa-buddha ; the Buddha without the thirty-two or eighty marks, i.e. Nāgārjuna. 무상호불 無相好佛 Ditto, Upagupta, the fourth patriarch. 무상종 無相宗 ; 무상대승 無相大乘 ; 무상교 無相敎 ; 무상공교 無相空敎 The San-lun or Mādhyamika school because of its "nihilism." 무상복전의 無相福田衣 The garment of nothingness for cultivating the field of blessing, i.e. the robe, which separates the monk from earthly contamination. 무상보리 無相菩提 The enlightenment of seclusion, obtained by oneself, or of nirvāṇa, or nothingness, or immateriality. 무상해탈문 無相解脫門 The nirvāṇa type of liberation, cf. 삼삼매 三三昧.

무상 無相 Mu-sang(684-762). A monk of the Silla dynasty in Korea. The 개조 開祖 opening patriarch of 정중종 淨衆宗 Jeong-jung-jong.

무상 無常 Anitya. Impermanent ; the first of the 삼명 三明 Trividyā ; that all things are impermanent, their birth, existence, change, and death never resting for a moment. 무상의 無常依 The reliance of the impermanent, i.e. Buddha, upon whom mortals can rely. 무상당 無常堂 ; 무상원 無常院 ; 연수당 延壽堂 ; 열반당 涅槃堂 The room where a dying monk was placed, in the direction of the sunset at the north-west corner. 무상경 無常磬 ; 무상종 無常鐘 The passing bell, or gong, for the dying. 무상견 無常鵑 The bird which cries of impermanence, messenger of the shades, the goat-sucker.

무상 無上 Anuttara. Unsurpassed, unexcelled, supreme, peerless. 무상상 無上上 Above the supreme, the supreme of the supreme, i.e. Buddha. 무상상승 無上上乘 The most supreme Vehicle, the Mahāyāna. 무상(양족)존 無上(兩足)尊 The peerless (two-legged) honoured one. 무상사 無上士 The peerless nobleman, the Buddha. 무상묘각 無上妙覺 The supreme mystic enlightenment. 무상인 無上忍 The highest patient equanimity in receiving the truth ; also, to believe the truth of impermanence without doubt, v. 십인 十忍. 무상혜 無上慧 Supreme wisdom, that of Buddha. 무상참괴의 無上慚愧衣 The supreme garment of sensitiveness to the shameful, the monk's robe. 무상복전의 無上福田衣 The supreme garment of the field of blessedness, i.e. good works. 무상정변지 無上正徧智, or 무상정변도 無上正徧道 or 무상정변각 無上正徧覺, the last being the later tr., Anuttara-samyak-sambodhi, supreme perfect enlightenment, or wisdom. 무상법 無上法 The supreme dharma, nirvāṇa. 무상법왕 無上法王 Its lord, Buddha. 무상법륜 無上法輪 Its preaching, or propagation. 무상열반 無上涅槃 The supreme nirvāṇa, that of Mahāyāna in contrast with the inferior nirvāṇa of Hīnayāna. 무상등 無上燈 The supreme lamp, that of nirvāṇa, as dispersing the gloom of passion-illusion. 무상안 無上眼 The supreme eye, able to discern the inward significance of all things. 무상보리 無上菩提 The supreme bodhi or enlightenment, that of Buddha. 무상각 無上覺 Ditto. 무상도 無上道 The supreme way, or truth, that of Buddha.

무상 無想 Without thought, absence of thinking. 무상천 無想天 ; 무상계 無想界 ; 무상처 無想處

Avṛha, the thirteenth Brahmaloka, the fourth in the fourth dhyāna, where thinking, or the necessity for thought, ceases. 무상정 無想定 The concentration in which all thinking ceases, in the desire to enter avṛha, v. above ; such entry is into 무상과 無想果. The 무상문 無想門 is parinirvāṇa.

무색 無色 Arūpa, formless, shapeless, immaterial. 무색유 無色有 Existence in the formless or immaterial realm. 무색계 無色界 Arūpaloka, or Arūpadhātu, the heavens without form, immaterial, consisting only of mind in contemplation, being four in number, which are defined as the 사공천 四空天 Catūrūpabrahmaloka, and given as : 공무변처 空無邊處 Ākāśānantyāyatana, 식무변처 識無邊處 Vijñānānantyāyatana, 무소유처 無所有處 Akiñcanyāyatana, 비상비비상처 非想非非想處 Naivasaṁjñānāsaṁjñānāyatana. 무색탐 無色貪 The desire in the world without form of holding on to the illusion of contemplation.

무생 無生 Not born, without being born or produced ; uncreated ; no rebirth ; immortal ; nirvāṇa as not subject to birth and death, or reincarnation, and which negates them ; the condition of the absolute. 무생지생 無生之生 A life that is without birth, an immortal life, a nirmāṇakāya, or transformation appearance of a Buddha in the world. 무생보국 無生寶國 The precious country beyond birth-and-death, the immortal paradise of Amitābha. 무생인 無生忍 The patient rest in belief in immortality, or no rebirth. 무생지 無生智 The final knowledge attained by the arhat, his release from the chain of transmigration ; cf. 십지 十智. Also, the knowledge of the bodhisattva of the assurance of immortality, or no rebirth. 무생법 無生法 The law of no-birth, or immortality, as the fundamental law of the 진여 眞如 and the embodiment of nirvāṇa. 무생법인 無生法忍 idem 무생인 無生忍. 무생장 無生藏 The scriptures which deal with the absolute, e.g. the 중론 中論 Mādhyamika-śāstra. 무생신 無生身 The immortal one, i.e. the Dharmakāya. 무생문 無生門 The doctrine of reality as beyond birth, or creation, i.e. that of the bhūtatathatā ; the gate or school of immortality. 무생제 無生際 The uncreated, or absolute ; the region of the eternal.

무성 無性 Without a nature, nothing has an independent nature of its own ; cf. 삼무성 三無性. 무성유정 無性有情 Men and devas with passions and devoid of natures for enlightenment, hence destined to remain in the six paths of transmigration ; a doctrine of the 법상종 法相宗 Dharmalakṣaṇa school.

무성루 無聲漏 The silent clepsydra, incense in the shape of ancient characters used to indicate the time.

무소 無所 Nothing, nowhere. 무소불능 無所不能 Nothing (he) cannot do, omnipotent. 무소부지 無所不至 Nowhere (it) does not reach. 무소주 無所住 Apratiṣṭhita. No means of staying, non-abiding. 무소득 無所得 Nowhere, or nothing obtainable, the immaterial universal reality behind all phenomena. 무소유 無所有 Avidyamāna, non-existing ; nothing existing, the immaterial. 무소유처 無所有處 The third region in the realm of formlessness. 무소유처정 無所有處定 Akiñcanāyatana. The contemplation of the state of nothingness, or the immaterial, in which ecstasy gives place to serenity. 무소착 無所著 Not bound by any tie, i.e. free from all influence of the passion-nature, an epithet of Buddha. 무소관 無所觀 The contemplation of the immaterial reality behind all phenomena.

무수 無數 Asaṁkhyeya, numberless.

무승 無勝 Ajita ; invincible, unsurpassed. 무승국 無勝國 The unexcelled land, the Pure Land located west of this universe.

무시 無始 Without beginning, as is the chain of transmigration. 무시광겁 無始曠劫 Transmigration which has existed without beginning through vast kalpas. 무시무명 無始無明 ; 원품무명 元品無明 or 근본무명 根本無明 The period of unenlightenment or ignorance without beginning, primal ignorance, also called 무시간격 無始間隔, the period of transmigration which has no beginning ; since under the law of causality everything has a cause, therefore no beginning is possible ; for if there were a beginning it would be without cause, which is impossible. Also primal ignorance is without beginning ; and the 진여 眞如 is without beginning, the two terms connoting the same idea. 생사 生死 Birth and death, or transmigration are 무시무종 無始無終 also without beginning or end, but about the "end" there is difference of interpretation. 무시무변 無始無邊 The Buddha-truth is without beginning and infinite. 무시공 無始空 Without beginning and unreal, void without beginning, the abstract idea of 무시 無始, i.e. without beginning.

무심 無心 Mindless, without thought, will, or purpose ; the real immaterial mind free from illusion ; unconsciousness, or effortless action. 무심삼매 無心三昧 ; 무심정 無心定 The samādhi in which active thought has ceased. 무심도인 無心道人 The hermit or saint in ecstatic contemplation, as with emptied mind he becomes the receptacle of mystic influences.

무아 無我 Anātman ; nairātmya ; no ego, no soul (of an independent and self-contained character), impersonal, no individual independent existence (of conscious or unconscious beings, anātmaka). The empirical ego is merely an aggregation of various elements, and with their disintegration it ceases to exist ; therefore it has no ultimate reality of its own, but the Nirvāṇa Sūtra asserts the reality of the ego in the transcendental realm. The non-Buddhist definition of ego is that it has permanent individuality 상일지체 常一之體 and is independent or sovereign 유주재지용 有主宰之用. When applied to men it is 인아 人我, when to things it is 법아 法我. Cf. 상무아 常無我.

무앙수겁 無央數劫 Asaṅkhyeya kalpa, a period of numberless kalpas.

무애 無礙 Apratihata. Unhindered, without obstacle, resistless, without resistance, permeating everywhere, all pervasive, dynamic omnipresence which enters everywhere without hindrance like the light of a candle. 무애인 無礙人 The unhindered one, the Buddha, who unbarred the way to nirvāṇa which releases from all limitations ; the omnipresent one ; the one who realizes nirvāṇa-truth. 무애광 無礙光 The all-pervasive light or glory, that of Amitābha. 무애대회 無礙大會 cf. 무개대회 無蓋大會. 무애지 無礙智 The omniscience of Buddha.

무애 無愛 Without love, or craving, or attachment.

무언 無言 Without words, silent, speechless. 무언설도 無言說道 The way, or teaching, without speech ; the school which teaches that speaking of things is speaking of nothing, or the non-existent ; the acquisition of truth through contemplation without the aid of words.

무여 無餘 Aśeṣa. Without remainder, no remnant, final ; applied to the section of the Vinaya regarding expulsion for unpardonable sin from the monkhood ; also to final nirvāṇa without remainder of reincarnation. 무여(의)열반 無餘(依)涅槃 Anupadhiśeṣa, the nirvāṇa state in which exists no remainder of the karma of suffering ; it is also the nirvāṇa of arhat extinction of body and mind, described as 무여회단 無餘灰斷. 무여기 無餘記 Complete or final prediction, e.g. to Buddhahood, as contrasted with partial prediction.

무연 無緣 Causeless, without immediate causal connection, uncaused, underived, independent. 무연삼매 無緣三昧 Anilambha or "unpropped samādhi," in which all mental functions cease to connect with environment and cease to function. 무연승 無緣乘 The vehicle, or method, of the subjective mind, by which all existence is seen as mental and not external. The 무연승심 無緣乘心 is the sixth of the ten 주 住 stages. 무연탑 無緣搭 ; 무연총 無緣塚 A stūpa, or funeral monument not connected with any one person, a general cemetery.

무열 無熱 Anavatapta, heatless. 무열천 無熱天 The Anavatapta, or Atapta heaven, without heat or affliction 열뇌 熱惱 ; the second of the 오정천 五淨天 in the fourth dhyāna heaven. 무열지 無熱池 The lake without heat, or cold lake, called Mānasarovara, or Mānasa-saro-vara, "excellent mānasa lake," or modern Manasarovar, 31°N., 81°3 E., "which overflows at certain seasons and forms one lake with" Rakas-tal, which is the source of the Sutlej. It is under the protection of the nāga-king Anavatapta and is also known by his name. It is said to lie south of the Gandhamādana mountains, and is erroneously reputed as the source of the four rivers Ganges, Indus, Śītā (Tārīm River), and Oxus.

무염족 無厭足 Insatiable, name of a rākṣasī, v. 십나찰녀 十羅刹女.

무영상 無影像 Nirābhāsa, without image of shadow, without semblance or appearance.

무외 無畏 Abhaya. Fearless, dauntless, secure, nothing and nobody to fear ; also Vīra, courageous, bold. 무외산 無畏山 Abhayagiri, Mount Fearless in Ceylon, with an ancient monastery where Fa-hsien found 5,000 monks. 무외수 無畏授 ; 근수 勤授 Vīradatta, "hero-giver," a prominent layman, contemporary with Śākyamuni. 무외시 無畏施 Abhayapradāna. The bestowing of confidence by every true Buddhist, i.e. that none may fear him. 무외장 無畏藏 Storehouse of fearlessness, said of members of the esoteric sect.

무우 無憂 Aśoka, "without sorrow, not feeling or not causing sorrow." [M. W.] 무우왕 無憂王 v. 아 阿 King Aśoka. 무우수 無憂樹 *Jonesia Aśoka* Roxb., the tree under which Śākyamuni is said to have been born. 무우가람 無憂伽藍 Aśokārāma, a vihāra in Pāṭaliputra in which the "third synod was held." [Eitel].

무위 無爲 Non-active, passive ; *laisser-faire* ; spontaneous, natural ; uncaused, not subject to cause, condition, or dependence ; transcendental, not in time, unchanging, eternal, inactive, and free from the passions or sense ; non-phenomenal, noumenal ; also intp. as nirvāṇa, dharma-nature, reality, and dharmadhātu. 무위법 無爲法 Asaṁskṛta dharmas, anything not subject to cause, condition, or dependence ; out of time, eternal, inactive, supra-mundane. Sarvāstivādins enumerate three ; ākāśa, space or ether ; pratisaṁkhyā-nirodha, conscious cessation of the contamination of the passions ; apratisaṁkhyā-nirodha, unconscious or effortless cessation. 무위법신 無爲法身 Asaṁskṛta dharmakāya, the eternal body of Buddha not conditioned by cause and effect. 무위열반(계) 無爲涅槃(界) The realm of the eternal, unconditioned nirvāṇa, the Pure Land. 무위생사 無爲生死 The birth-and-death of saints, i.e. without any action ; transformation. 무위공 無爲空 Asaṁskṛta śūnyatā, the immaterial character of the transcendent. 무위자연 無爲自然 Causeless and spontaneous, a tr. of nivṛtti. 무위사 無爲舍 The nirvāṇa home.

무유 無有 Non-existent and existent ; also, non-existent, have not, there is none, etc.

무의 無意 Absence of objective thought, of will or intention ; absence of idea, the highest stage of dhyāna.

무의 無依 Nothing on which to rely ; unreliable. 무의열반 無依涅槃 Final nirvāṇa, v. 무여 無餘 ; nothing for reincarnation to lay hold of.

무의 無疑 Undoubted, without doubt.

무자성 無自性 Asvabhāva ; without self-nature, without a nature of its own, no individual nature ; all things are without 자연성 自然性 individual nature or independent existence, being composed of elements which disintegrate.

무작 無作 Not creating ; uncreated ; not doing ; inactive, physically or mentally ; independent of action, word, or will, i.e. natural, intuitive. 무작계 無作戒 ; 무표계 無表戒 The intangible, invisible moral law that influences the ordinand when he receives visible ordination ; i.e. the internal spiritual moral law and its influence ; the invisible grace of which the visible ordination is a sign ; v. 무표 無表 avijñapti.

무쟁 無諍 Without strife, debate, or contradiction ; passionless ; abiding in the "empty" or spiritual life without debate, or without striving with others. 무쟁삼매 無諍三昧 The samādhi in which there is absence of debate or disputation, or distinction of self and other.

무제 無際 Unlimited, boundless.

무종성 無種姓 The nature without the seed of goodness and so unable to escape from the stream of transmigration. 무종천제 無種闡提 An icchanti, or evil person without the Buddha-seed of goodness.

무주 無住 Not abiding ; impermanence ; things having no independent nature of their own, they have no real existence as separate entities. 무주삼매 無住三昧 the samādhi which contemplates all things as temporal and evanescent.

무지 無知 Ignorant ; ignorance ; absence of perception. Also, ultimate wisdom considered as static, and independent of differentiation.

무진 無塵 Dustless, without an atom of the material or unclean, immaterial, pure. 무진법계 無塵法界 The immaterial realm out of which all things come.

무진 無盡 Inexhaustible, without limit. It is a term applied by the 권교 權敎 to the noumenal or absolute ; by the 실교 實敎 to the phenomenal, both being considered as infinite. The Hua-yen sūtra 십지품 十地品 has ten limitless things, the infinitude of living beings, of worlds, of space, of the dharmadhātu, of nirvāṇa, etc. 무진의 無盡意 Inexhaustible intention, or meaning, name of Akṣayamati, a bodhisattva to whom Śākyamuni is supposed to have addressed the Avalokiteśvara chapter in the Lotus Sūtra. 무진해 無盡海 The Buddha-truth as inexhaustible as the ocean. 무진등 無盡燈 The one lamp which is yet limitless in the lighting of other lamps ; the influence of one disciple may be limitless and inexhaustible ; also limitless mirrored reflections ; also an altar light always burning. 무진연기 無盡緣起 ; 법계연기 法界緣起 Unlimited causation, or the unlimited influence of everything on all things and all things on everything ; one of the Hua-yen 사종연기 四種緣起. 무진장 無盡藏 The inexhaustible treasury.

무차 無遮 Unconcealing, unconfined ; illimitable. Buddha-grace, Buddha-mercy, or Buddha-love ; cf. 무개 無蓋. 무차(대)회 無遮(大)會 Pañca(vārṣika) pariṣad ; the 오년대회 五年大會 quinquennial assembly, for having all things in common, and for confession, penance, and remission.

무차라 無叉羅 Mokṣala, also 무라차 無羅叉 "A native of Kustana who laboured in China as a translator and introduced there a new alphabet (A.D. 291) for the transliteration of Sanskrit." [Eitel].

무착 無著 Unattached, not in bondage to anything. Name of Asaṅga, brother of Vasubandhu, and others. 무착천친종 無著天親宗 The school of Asaṅga and Vasubandhu, i.e. the 법상종 法相宗 q.v. 무착행 無著行 Unfettered action, power to overcome all obstacles.

무참 無慚 Ahrīka, without shame, shameless.

무치대충 無齒大蟲 A toothless great creature, i.e. a toothless tiger.

무택지옥 無擇地獄 idem 무간지옥 無間地獄 q.v.

무표 無表 Avijñapti. Unconscious, latent, not expressed, subjective, e.g. "the taking of a religious vow impresses on a man's character a peculiar bent," [Keith]. This is internal and not visible to others. It has a "quasi-material" basis styled 무표색 無表色 or 무작색 無作色 which has power to resist evil. It is the Sarvāstivādin view, though certain other schools repudiated the material basis and defined it as mental. This invisible power may be both for good and evil, and may perhaps be compared to "animal magnetism" or hypnotic powers. It means occult power whether for higher spiritual ends or for base purposes. 무표계 無表戒 The inward invisible power received with the commandments during ordination. 무표업 無表業 The invisible power conferred at ordination, cf. 무작업 無作業 *supra*.

무학 無學 Aśaikṣa. No longer learning, beyond study, the state of arhatship, the fourth of the śrāvaka stages ; the preceding three stages requiring study ; there are nine grades of arhats who have completed their course of learning. 무학도 無學道 The way of the arhat, especially his attainment to complete truth and freedom from all illusion, with nothing more to learn.

무학 자초 無學自超 Mu-hak Ja-cho(1327-1405). A monk of the late Goryeo dynasty in Korea.

무후생사 無後生死 No more birth-and-death, the bodhisattva who will not again be subject to the wheel of transmigration.

묵 默 Dark, secret, silent, profound. 묵전 默傳 Silent teaching or propagation, i.e. from mind to mind, without words or writing. 묵빈 默擯 ; 범단 梵壇 Brahmadaṇḍa ; to "send to Coventry" an obnoxious monk, all intercourse with him being forbidden. 묵연 默然 Silent, without words. 묵리 默理 The principle of silence, that the absolute is indefinable, the doctrine of Vimalakīrti. 묵치기 默置記 Answering a foolish or improper question by silence.

묵 墨 Ink ; black ; dyed black, e.g. 묵의 墨衣 black clothes, at one time said to have been the garb of the monk to distinguish him from the ordinary people who wore white. 묵갈제 墨竭提 Magadha, v. 마 摩.

묵언 默言 Maintaining silence ; not speaking.

문 門 A door ; gate ; a sect, school, teaching, especially one leading to salvation or nirvāṇa. 문려 門侶 Disciple, fellow-student. 문사 門師 Preceptor, the monk who is recognized as teacher by any family. 문도 門徒 Disciple. 문파 門派 ; 문류 門流 ; 문엽 門葉 ; 문적 門跡 The followers, or development of any sect. 문장 門狀 ; 참상 參狀 or 참방 參榜 A name paper, card, visiting-card. 문신 門神 ; 문승 門丞 The gate-gods or guardians. 문경 門經 The funeral service read at the house-door. 문태랄 門荅辣 Maṇḍala, see 만 曼. 문수 門首 ; 문주 門主 The controller of a gate, or sect.

문 文 Letters, literature, writing ; refined ; culture ; civil ; a despatch ; veined ; a cash ; to gloss.

문 問 To ask, inquire, question ; to adjudicate, sentence. 문법인 問法印 The manual sign indicating the putting of a question. 문신 問訊 To make inquiry ; ask about another's welfare, orally or by folding the hands ; interrogate ; try a case.

문 聞 To hear ; to make known to ; to smell. 문광력 聞光力 To hear of the power of the light of Amitābha. 문명 聞名 To hear the name of ; fame, famous ; to hear the name of Buddha, or a Buddha. 문혜 聞慧 Hearing the word and becoming wise in it ; wisdom obtained from hearing. 문지 聞持 To hear and keep ; hearing and keeping in mind ; hearing and obeying. 문법 聞法 To hear the doctrine. 문(지)다라니 聞(持)陀羅尼 To hear and keep, hear and remember the teaching, dhāraṇī 다라니 陀羅尼 meaning to hold to, maintain.

문구 文句 Textual explanation or criticism, also termed 장 章 ; 소 疏 ; 술의 述義 ; 기 記, etc. ;

the term applies to works on canonical texts in general, but has particular reference to the Lotus sūtra, i.e. the 묘법연화경문구 妙法蓮華經文句.

문니 文尼 Muni, idem 모니 牟尼 and 무니 茂尼, e.g. Śākyamuni.

문리 文理 The written word and the truth expressed ; written principles, or reasonings ; a treatise ; literary style.

문수(사리) 文殊(師利) Mañjuśrī 만수시리 滿殊尸利 later 만수실리 曼殊室利. 문수 文殊 is also used for Mañjunātha, Mañjudeva, Mañjughoṣa, Mañjuṣvara, et al. T., ḫjam-ḏpal ; J., Monju. Origin unknown ; presumably, like most Buddhas and bodhisattvas, an idealization of a particular quality, in his case of Wisdom. Mañju is beautiful, Śrī — good fortune, virtue, majesty, lord, an epithet of a god. Six definitions are obtained from various scriptures ; 묘수 妙首 or 묘두 妙頭 wonderful (or beautiful) head ; 보수 普首 universal head ; 유수 濡首 glossy head (probably a transliteration) ; 경수 敬首 revered head ; 묘덕 妙德 wonderful virtue (or power) ; 묘길상 妙吉祥 wonderfully auspicious ; the last is a later translation in the 서역기 西域記. As guardian of wisdom 지혜 智慧 he is often placed on Śākyamuni's left, with 보현 普顯 on the right as guardian of law 리 理, the latter holding the Law, the former the wisdom or exposition of it ; formerly they held the reverse positions. He is often represented with five curls or waves to his hair indicating the 오지 五智 q.v. or the five peaks ; his hand holds the sword of wisdom and he sits on a lion emblematic of its stern majesty ; but he has other forms. He is represented as a youth, i.e. eternal youth. His present abode is given as east of the universe, known as 청량산 淸涼山 clear and cool mountain, or a region 보주 寶住 precious abode, or Abode of Treasures, or 보씨 寶氏 from which he derives one of his titles, 보상여래 寶相如來. One of his dhāraṇīs prophesies China as his post-nirvāṇa realm. In past incarnations he is described as being the parent of many Buddhas and as having assisted the Buddha into existence ; his title was 용종상불 龍種上佛 the supreme Buddha of the Nāgas, also 대신불 大身佛 or 신선불 神仙佛 ; now his title is 환희장마니보정불 歡喜藏摩尼寶精佛 The spiritual Buddha who joyfully cares for the jewel ; and his future title is to be 보현불 普現佛 Buddha universally revealed. In the 서품 序品 Introductory Chapter of the Lotus sūtra he is also described as the ninth predecessor or Buddha-ancestor of Śākyamuni. He is looked on as the chief of the Bodhisattvas and represents them, as the chief disciple of the Buddha, or as his son 법왕자 法王子. Hīnayāna counts Śāriputra as the wisest of the disciples, Mahāyāna gives Mañjuśrī the chief place, hence he is also styled 각모 覺母 mother, or begetter of understanding. He is shown riding on either a lion or a peacock, or sitting on a white lotus ; often he holds a book, emblem of wisdom, or a blue lotus ; in certain rooms of a monastery he is shown as a monk ; and he appears in military array as defender of the faith. His signs, magic words, and so on, are found in various sūtras. His most famous centre in China is Wu-t'ai shan in Shansi, where he is the object of pilgrimages, especially of Mongols. The legends about him are many. He takes the place in Buddhism of Viśvakarman as Vulcan, or architect, of the universe. He is one of the eight Dhyāni-bodhisattvas, and sometimes has the image of Akṣobhya in his crown. He was mentioned in China as early as the fourth century and in the Lotus sūtra he frequently appears, especially as the converter of the daughter of the Dragon-king of the Ocean. He has five messengers 오사자 五使者 and eight youths 팔동자 八童子 attending on him. His hall in the Garbhadhātu maṇḍala is the seventh, in which his group numbers twenty-five. His position is northeast. There are numerous sūtras and other works with his name as title, e.g. 문수사리문보리경 文殊師利問菩提經 Gayāśīrṣa sūtra, tr. by Kumārajīva 384-417 ; and its 론 論 or Ṭīkā of Vasubandhu, tr. by Bodhiruci 535, see list in [B.N.] 문수삼매 文殊三昧 The samādhi of Mañjuśrī styled the 무상묘혜 無相妙慧 formless wonderful wisdom, or wonderful wisdom in the realm of that which is beyond form. 문수오사자 文殊五使者 The five messengers of Mañjuśrī, each bearing one of his 오지 五智 five expressions of wisdom ; they are 계설니 髻設尼 ; 우파계설니

優波髻設尼 ; 질다라 質多羅 ; 지혜 地慧, and 청소 請召. 문수팔대동자 文殊八大童子 His eight "pages" are 광망 光網 ; 지혜 地慧 ; 무구광 無垢光 ; 불사혜 不思慧 ; 소청 召請 ; 계설니 髻設尼 ; 구호혜 救護慧, and 우파계설니 鄔波髻設尼 Upakeśinī. 문수회과 文殊悔過 The repentance of Mañjuśrī, i.e. of his former doubting mind, cf. St. Thomas. 문수원 文殊院 The seventh great court of the thirteen in the Garbhadhātu group ; it shows Mañjuśrī in the centre of a group of twenty-five.

문아 원측 文雅圓測 Mun-a Won-cheuk(613-696). A monk of the Silla dynasty in Korea. He went to China at the age of 15, and became a prominent member of 법상종 法相宗 Dharmalakṣaṇa Sect. He was a disciple of Hsüan-tsang. An authority in the Seo-myeong school. He wrote twenty three kinds of books, four of which are present.

문자 文字 The letter ; letters ; literal ; the written word is described as the breath and life of the dharmakāya ; cf. 로 嚕 ruta. 문자인 文字人 A literalist, pedant ; narrow. 문자법사 文字法師 A teacher of the letter of the Law, who knows not its spirit.

문증 文證 The evidence of the written word, or scripture.

문지 文池 The dragon pool by the side of the throne of Vajrapāṇi, called 목진린타 目眞鄰陀 Mucilinda q.v.

문다갈 文陀竭 Mūrdhajāta, Māndhātṛ, i.e. 정생왕 頂生王 born from his mother's head, a reputed previous incarnation of the Buddha, who still ambitious, despite his universal earthly sway, his thousand sons, etc., flew to Indra's heaven, saw the 천상옥녀 天上玉女 celestial devī, but on the desire arising to rule there on Indra's death, he was hurled to earth ; v. 문다갈왕경 文陀竭王經.

문타륵 捫打勒 Maṇḍala, v. 만 曼.

문협 文夾 A portfolio, or satchel for Buddhist books.

물 勿 Not ; do not ; translit, *m* and *v*. 물가 勿伽 Mudga ; "phaseolus Mungo (both the plant and its beans)," [M. W.] ; intp. as 호두 胡豆 and 녹두 綠豆 kidney beans by the Fan-i-ming-i. 물가라자 勿伽羅子 Maudgalyāyana or Maudgalaputra, idem Mahāmaudgalyāyana 목련 目連. 물력가난제 勿力伽難提 Mṛgānandi, or 밀리가라 蜜利伽羅 Mṛgala ; rejoicing deer ; a śramaṇa called 녹장 鹿杖 Lu-chang, who was satisfied with the leavings of other monks ; also a previous incarnation of Śākyamuni, and of Devadatta, who are both represented as having been deer. 물리하사파지 勿哩訶娑跛底 Bṛhaspati, Jupiter-lord, 목성 木星 Jupiter.

물 物 Thing, things in general, beings, living beings, matters ; "substance," cf. 다라표 陀羅驃 Dravya. 물시 物施 One of the three kinds of almsgiving, that of things. 물기 物機 That on which anything depends, or turns ; the motive or vital principle.

미 眉 Eyebrow, the eyebrows. 미간백호상 眉間白毫相 Ūrṇā. The curl of white hairs, between the eyebrows of the Buddha, one of the thirty-two signs of Buddhahood. 미간광 眉間光 The ray of light which issued therefrom lighting up all worlds, v. Lotus sūtra.

미 美 Fine, handsome, beautiful, admirable. Madhurā, sweet, pleasant. 미음 美音 Beautiful sound, a king of the 건달바 乾闥婆 Gandharvas, Indra's musicians. Also, the name of a son of Sudhīra and Sumitra converted by Ānanda. 미음(천녀) 美音(天女) ; 묘음천 妙音天 Sarasvatī, 살라살벌지 薩囉薩筏底 the Muse of India, goddess of speech and learning, hence called 대변재천녀 大辯才天女, goddess of rhetoric ; she is the female energy or wife of Brahmā, and also goddess of the river Sarasvatī.

미 獼 Markaṭa, 미후 獼猴 a monkey, typical of the mind of illusion, pictured as trying to pluck the moon out of the water ; also of the five desires ; of foolishness ; of restlessness. 미후지 獼猴地 ; 미후강 獼猴江 The place in Vaiśālī where Buddha preached.

미 迷 Māyā ; delude, deceive, confuse, mislead ; delusion, illusion, etc. 미사 迷事 Delusive phenomena, or affairs, deluded in regard to phenomena, cf. 미리 迷理 *infra*. 미인주 迷人呪 Incantations to delude or confuse others. 미도 迷倒 Deluded, confused, to delude and upset. 미망 迷妄 Deluded and misled ; deluding and false. 미자 迷子 The deluded son who held a gold coin in his hand while starving in poverty ; such is the man with Buddha-nature who fails to use it, v. 금강삼매경 金剛三昧經. 미안 迷岸 The shore of delusion. 미지리 迷底履 v. 미彌 Maitreya. 미심 迷心 A deluded mind. 미혹 迷惑 Deluded and confused, deceived in regard to reality. 미오 迷悟 Illusion and enlightenment ; 미오일여 迷悟一如 the two are aspects of the one reality, as water and ice are the same substance, 미오불이 迷悟不二 and fundamentally are the same. 미오인과 迷悟因果 In the four axioms, that of "accumulation" is caused by illusion, with suffering as effect ; that of "the way" is caused by enlightenment, with extinction (of suffering) as effect. 미몰 迷沒 Deluded and sunk (in the passions). 미진 迷津 The ford of delusion, i.e. mortality. 미리 迷理 Deluded in regard to the fundamental principle, i.e. ignorant of reality ; cf. 미사 迷事. 미생 迷生 All deluded beings. 미계 迷界 Any world of illusion. 미로 迷盧 v. 소미로 蘇迷盧 Sumeru. 미례야 迷隸耶 or 미려야 迷麗耶 Maireya, a kind of intoxicating drink. 미려마라 迷黎麻羅 (and other forms) Confused sight ; blurred.

미 未 Not yet ; the future ; 1-3 p.m. 미료인 未了因 The karma of past life not yet fulfilled. 미래 未來 ; 당래 當來 Anāgata ; that which has not come, or will come ; the future, e.g. 미래세 未來世 a future life, or lives ; also the future tense, one of the 삼세 三世, i.e. 과 過, 현 現, 미 未 past, present, future. 미수구인 未受具人 A monk who has not yet formally pledged himself to all the commandments. 미부연화 未敷蓮華 A half-opened lotus, such as one of the forms of Kuan-yin holds in the hand. 미증유 未曾有 ; 희유 希有 ; 아부타 阿浮陀 Adbhuta ; never yet been, non-such, rare, marvellous. 미증유경 未曾有經 Adbhuta-dharma-paryāya, one of the twelve divisions of the sūtras 십이부경 十二部經. 미증유정법경 未曾有正法經 A Sung translation of the 아사세왕경 阿闍世王經 Ajātaśatru-kaukṛitya-vinodana. 미생원 未生怨 Having no enemy, tr. of the name of Ajātaśatru 아사세왕 阿闍世王 There is a sūtra of this name describing his murder of his father Bimbisāra. 미지 未至 ; 미도 未到 Not yet arrived, or reached. 미타 未陀 Arbuda, 100 (or 10) millions. 미현진실 未顯眞實 ; 미개현 未開顯 The unrevealed truth, the Truth only revealed by the Buddha in his final Mahāyāna doctrine.

미 味 Rasa. Taste, flavour ; the sense of taste. One of the six sensations. 미진 味塵 Taste-dust, one of the six "particles" which form the material or medium of sensation. 미욕 味慾, 미착 味著 The taste-desire, hankering after the pleasures of food, etc. ; the bond of such desire. 미도 味道 Taste, flavour ; the taste of Buddha-truth, or tasting the doctrine.

미 弭 Stop, put down. 미만차 弭曼差 The Mīmāṁsā system of Indian philosophy founded by Jaimini, especially the Pūrva-mīmāṁsā. It was "one of the three great divisions of orthodox Hindu philosophy." [M. W.] Cf. the Nyāya and Sāṅkhya. 미말하 弭秣賀 Mimaha, "an ancient kingdom about seventy miles east of Samarkand, the present Moughian or Maghīn in Turkestan." [Eitel].

미 微 Sūkṣma. Minute, small, slight ; abstruse, subtle ; disguised ; not ; used in the sense of a molecule seven times larger than 극미 極微 an atom ; translit. *vi, bi*. 미진 微塵 A molecule, v. above. 미진수 微塵數 Numerous as molecules, or atoms ; numberless. 미묘 微妙 Abstruse, recondite, mysterious. 미밀 微密 Mysterious, secret, occult. 미수타 微戍陀 Viśuddha, purified, pure. 미사락기다 微沙落起多 Vibhārakṣita, a form of Tiṣyarakṣitā, Aśoka's queen. 미슬뉴 微瑟紐 Viṣṇu, also 비슬뉴 毘瑟紐 or 비슬노 毘瑟笯 or 毘瑟怒 ; 비뉴 毘紐 ; 비수뉴 毘搜紐 or 毘瘦紐 ; 위뉴 韋紐 ; the second in the Trimūrti, Brahma, Viṣṇu, Śiva ; the "preserver," and all-pervading, or encompassing ; identified with Nārāyaṇa-deva. 미약포뇌가 微若布雷迦 Bījapūraka ; a citron, citron medicus. [M. W.] 미세 微細 Minute, fine, refined, subtle. 미세신 微細身 A refined, subtle body. 미취 微聚 A molecule, the smallest aggregation of atoms. 미행 微行 Minute, refined, or subtle action. 미서야 微誓耶 Vijaya, also 미야야 微惹耶 ; 비사야 毘社耶 the overcomer, Durgā, intp. as the wife, or female manifestation, of Vairocana.

미 尾 Tail ; end. 미니야 尾儞也 Vibhā, to shine, illuminate, tr. by 명 明, a name for the Shingon sect 진언 眞言 because of its power to dispel the darkness of delusion. 미로단걸차 尾嚕博乞叉 Virūpākṣa, epithet for the three-eyed deva, Śiva. See also 비류파차 毘流波叉. 미로도가 尾嚕荼迦 Virūḍhaka idem 비류리 毘瑠璃, one of the four mahārāja-devas.

미 彌 To shoot, reach everywhere, pervade ; complete, universal ; prevent, stop ; more ; long.

미 米 Śāli, rice, i.e. hulled rice. The word śāli has been wrongly used for śarīra, relics, and for both words 사리 舍利 has been used. 미두 米頭 Keeper of the stores. 미려야 米麗耶 Maireya, "a kind of intoxicating drink (extracted from the blossoms of *Lythrum fructicosum* with sugar, etc.)." [M. W.]

미가 彌伽 Megha, a cloud ; name of one of the bodhisattvas renowned as a healer, or as a cloud-controller for producing rain.

미가 彌迦 Mekā, said to be the name of the girl who gave milk congee to Śākyamuni immediately after his enlightenment ; seemingly the same as Sujāta, Senā, or Nandā. 미가라 彌迦羅 ; 미가라 彌呵羅 Mekhalā, a girdle, name of an elder.

미란 彌蘭 King Milinda, v. 나선 那先.

미려거 彌戾車 Mleccha, barbarian, foreigner, wicked ; defined as "ill-looking," a term for a non-Buddhist tribe or people. Also 미리거 彌離車 ; cf. 밀 蜜.

미루 彌樓 Meru, "the Olympus of Hindu mythology." [M. W.] Sumeru, cf. 수 須 ; but there is dispute as to the identity of the two. Meru also refers to the mountains represented by the Himalayas, in this not differing from Sumeru. It also has the general meaning of "lofty."

미륵 彌勒 Maitreya, friendly, benevolent. The Buddhist Messiah, or next Buddha, now in the Tuṣita heaven, who is to come 5,000 years after the nirvāṇa of Śākyamuni, or according to other reckoning after 4,000 heavenly years, i.e. 5,670,000,000 human years. According to tradition he was born in Southern India of a Brahman family. His two epithets are 자씨 慈氏 Benevolent, and Ajita 아일다 阿逸多 "Invincible." He presides over the spread of the church, protects its members and will usher in ultimate victory for Buddhism. His image is usually in the hall of the four guardians facing outward, where he is represented as the fat laughing Buddha, but in some places his image is tall, e.g. in Peking in the Yung Ho Kung. Other forms are 미제이 彌帝肄 ; 미제례 迷諦隸 ; 매저리 梅低梨 ; 매달려(약) 梅怛麗(藥) ; 매달려(사) 梅怛麗(邪) ; 매달리 每怛哩 ; 매달리예 昧怛曬曳 ; 미라 彌羅. There are numerous Maitreya sūtras.

미사색(부) 彌沙塞(部) Mahāśāsakāḥ. One of the divisions of the Sarvāstivāda school ; cf. 마 磨. Also name of the 오분률 五分律 tr. by Buddhajīva A.D. 423-4. Also 미희사사아 彌喜捨娑阿.

미지 彌底 Miti, measure, accurate knowledge, evidential. 삼미지 三彌底 ; 삼밀 三蜜 The Saṁmatīya school.

미차가 彌遮迦 Micchaka or Mikkaka. "A native of Central India, the sixth patriarch, who having laboured in Northern India transported himself to Ferghana where he chose Vasumitra as his successor. He died 'by the fire of samādhi'." [Eitel].

미타 彌陀 Amitābha, v. 아 阿. 미타삼존 彌陀三尊 ; 미타삼성 彌陀三聖 The three Amitābha honoured ones ; Amitābha, whose mercy and wisdom are perfect ; Kuan-yin, Avalokiteśvara, on his left, who is the embodiment of mercy ; Ta Shih Chih, Mahāsthāmaprāpta, on his right, the embodiment of wisdom. 미타산 彌陀山 Mitraśānta, a monk from Tukhāra.

민 敏 Clever, active, ingenious, witty. 민구리 敏俱理 Hiṅgulā, an Indian name doubtfully intp. as Korea. 총민 聰敏 Wise, clever.

민 悶 Depressed, oppressed, sad, melancholy ; to cover, shut down, or in. 우민 憂悶 ; 수민 愁悶 Distress, grief, sadness.

민 愍 idem 민 憫. Grieve for, mourn, sympathize. 민기 愍忌 A day of remembrance for a virtuous elder on the anniversary of his birthday.

민 泯 Vast ; to flow off ; ruin, confusion. 민권귀실 泯權歸實 To depart from the temporary and find a home in the real, i.e. forget Hīnayāna, partial salvation, and turn to Mahāyāna for full and complete salvation.

밀 密 Closed in ; close together ; intimate ; quiet, still ; secret, occult, esoteric ; fine, small ; contrasted with 현 顯 open, exoteric. Cf. 비 秘. 밀부 密付 To pass down esoterically, or by word of mouth. 밀인 密印 The esoteric digital sign of a Buddha or bodhisattva indicative of his vow. 밀주 密呪 A dhāraṇī, or esoteric incantation. 밀호 密號 The esoteric name of Vairocana ; also any "true word" (Shingon) or esoteric spell. 밀엄국 密嚴國 ; 밀엄정토 密嚴淨土 The Pure Land of Vairocana ; also in the Hua-yen sūtra called the 화장 華藏 world ; the doctrine is found in this sūtra. 밀인 密因 The esoteric, occult, recondite cause. 밀자 密字 The esoteric letter of Vairocana, or of a Buddha or bodhisattva. 밀종 密宗 The esoteric, mantra, Shingon, or "True word" sect, especially prevalent in Japan, where its two chief texts are 비로자나성불경 毘盧遮那成佛經 and 금강정경 金剛頂經 ; founded by Kōbō Daishi, it developed the two maṇḍalas of the Garbhadhātu and Vajradhātu, q.v. 밀가 密家 idem the last. 밀교 密教 idem, also esoteric teaching in general ; the two classes are divided into the 밀교 密教 esoteric or Yoga school, and 현교 顯教 the open schools or teaching, comprising all the sects of Buddhism, except the esoteric sect. The 밀교삼장 密教三藏 Tripiṭaka of the esoteric sect are, as its sūtra, the 대비로사나금강정경 大毘盧舍那金剛頂經 ; as its vinaya, the 소파호경근본부 蘇婆呼經根本部 ; as its śāstras, the 장엄보리심경 莊嚴菩提心經, etc., q.v. 밀기 密機 The motive power, or fundamental element, in the esoteric ; the opportunity of learning a mantra. 밀법 密法 Esoteric methods. 밀관 密灌 The baptism of the esoteric sect. 밀경 密經 The foundation texts of the esoteric school, i.e. the 대일경 大日經 and 금강정경 金剛頂經 and various sūtras, especially but not exclusively those with mantras ; another group is the first two and the 소실지경 蘇悉地經. 밀의 密義 Esoteric meaning, or doctrine. 밀장 密藏 The esoteric canon. 밀중 密衆 The followers of the esoteric school. 밀행 密行 Esoteric practice, or discipline, the origin of which is attributed to Rāhula. 밀어 密語 Occult, or esoteric expressions. 밀적 密迹 ; 밀적 密跡 Secret or invisible tracks. 밀적금강력사 密迹金剛力士 Vajrapāṇi, guardian of Buddhas, driving away all yakṣa disturbers, a form of Indra ; his dhāraṇīs have been twice translated into Chinese. [B.N.] The 밀사두 密奢兜 esoteric "Cintya" is a mantra said to have been used by all the seven Buddhas down to and including Śākyamuni.

밀 蜜 Honey ; translit. *m.* 밀리가라 蜜利伽羅 Mṛga ; a deer ; mṛga-rāja, royal stag, Buddha. 밀리차 蜜利車 Mleccha, cf. 미 彌 heathen, non-Buddhist nations, the barbarians. 밀률가실타발나 蜜栗伽悉他鉢娜 Mṛgasthāpana, Mṛgadāva, a famous park north-east of Vārāṇaśī, a favourite resort of Śākyamuni. The modern Sārnāth, near Benares. [Eitel].

<ㅂ>

바 嚩 Translit. *va, ba* ; cf. 박 縛 ; e.g. 바왈라 嚩曰羅 Vajra. 바니 嚩泥 v. 바나 婆那 Vana. 바로기제 嚩盧枳諦 Avalokita, cf. 관 觀 to behold, see. 바로나 嚩嚕拏 Varuṇa, the deva of the sky, and of the waters, of the ocean, etc.

바 婆 A dame, mother, wife, granny, crone ; translit. *pa, ba, va, pha, bha,* and similar labial sounds.

바가 婆伽 Bhāga, a portion, division, fraction. 바가바(제) 婆伽婆(帝) Bhagavat, or 바가범 婆伽梵, 바가반 婆伽伴, 바아종 婆誐鍐, 박가범 薄伽梵, 박아범 薄阿梵 Bhagavān, "fortunate," "excellent," "revered, sacred," "the holy one" [M. W.] ; generally intp. by 세존 世尊 world-honoured, but there are other intps. ; an epithet of a Buddha.

바나 婆那 Vana, a wood, grove ; also 반나 飯那 ; 부니 嚩泥.

바다 婆陀 Baddha, bound, tied, fettered, fixed ; also 박타 縛馱 ; also an abbrev. for 아바다나 阿波陀那 Avadāna.

바단타 婆檀陀 Bhadanta, 대덕 大德, laudable, praiseworthy, blessed, of great virtue — a term of respect for a Buddha, or for monks, especially of the Hīnayāna school.

바라 婆羅 Pāla ; keeper, guardian, warden ; vihārapāla, warden of a monastery. Bala ; power, strength, especially the 오력 五力 five powers, pañca balāni, i.e. 오근 五根 ; also the 십력 十力 daśabala, ten powers. Name of the sister of Ānanda who offered milk to Śākyamuni. Bāla ; "young," "immature," "simpleton, fool," "hair" [M. W.] ; ignorant, unenlightened, see Bālapṛthagjana, *infra.* 바라흡마보라 婆羅吸摩補羅 Brahmapura. "An ancient kingdom of Northern India, the dynastic title of which was entailed upon the female line exclusively" ; hence styled 여국 女國. Said to be Garhwal. 바라사 婆羅奢 Phalaśas, the breadfruit tree ; intp. as a tree with red flowers. 바라필율탁흘나 婆羅必栗託仡那, 바라필리타흘나 婆羅必哩他仡那 ; 바라필리타가자나 婆羅必利他伽闍那 Bālapṛthagjana, low, foolish people ; natural-minded, as children, of common intelligence and ideas, a man in his natural state, unilluminated, unenlightened. 바라사거 婆羅捨佉 ; 발리사거 鉢李奢佉 Praśākhā, a fetus of five to seven days. 바라제목차 婆羅提木叉 Pratimokṣa, v. 파 波. 바라날사 婆羅痆斯 ; 바라날사 婆羅捺寫 Vārāṇaśī, an ancient kingdom and city, noted (A.D. 640) as the headquarters of Śivaism ; Benares ; cf. 파 波. 바라(하) 婆羅(訶) Balāhaka, a king of horses, or possessing horses. 바라하마 婆羅賀磨 or 婆羅賀摩 Brahmā ; 바라하마나 婆羅賀磨拏 ; 바라합말나 婆羅欱末拏 Brāhmaṇa ; v. *infra.* 바라나타 婆羅那馱 Varanāda, a bellowing yakṣa. 바라문 婆羅門 ; 발람마 跋濫摩 ; 몰라감마 沒囉憾摩 Brāhmaṇa ; Brāhmanical ; Brahman ; 정행 淨行 ; 파지 婆志 of pure life or mind ; the highest of the four castes, those who serve Brahma, his offspring, the keepers of the Vedas. 바라문국 婆羅門國 Brāhmaṇarāṣṭra, the realm of the Brahmans, India. 바라문성 婆羅門城 A city of Brahmans, from which the Buddha returned with his begging bowl empty. 바라문서 婆羅門書 Brahman writing ; the alphabet. 바라문읍 婆羅門邑 Brāhmaṇapura, "a city northeast of the capital of Mālava." [Eitel].

바라나(사) 波羅奈(斯) Vārāṇaśī. Ancient kingdom and city on the Ganges, now Benares, where was the Mṛgadāva park. Also 바라날(사) 波羅捺(寫) ; 바라날사 波羅痆斯 ; 바랄나사 波剌那斯.

바라니밀바사발제천 波羅尼密婆舍跋提天 Paranirmita-vaśavartin, "obedient to the will of those who are transformed by others," [M. W.] ; v. 타화자재천 他化自在天.

바라문 波羅門 Brahmin, v. 파 婆.

바라밀다 波羅蜜多 Pāramitā, 파라미다 播囉弭多, derived from parama, highest, acme, is intp. as to cross over from this shore of births and deaths to the other shore, or nirvāṇa. The six pāramitās or means of so doing are ; (1) dāna, charity ; (2) śīla, moral conduct ; (3) kṣānti, patience ; (4) vīrya, energy, or devotion ; (5) dhyāna, contemplation, or abstraction ; (6) prajñā, knowledge. The 십도 十度 ten are the above with (7) upāya, use of expedient or proper means ; (8) praṇidhāna, vows, for bodhi and helpfulness ; (9) bala, strength, purpose ; (10) wisdom. Childers givers the list of ten as the perfect exercise of almsgiving, morality, abnegation of the world and of self, wisdom, energy, patience, truth, resolution, kindness, and resignation. Each of the ten is divisible into ordinary, superior, and unlimited perfection, or thirty in all. Pāramitā is tr. by 도 度 ; 도무극 度無極 ; 도피안 到彼岸 ; 구경 究竟.

바라부 波羅赴 Prabhu, 발리부 鉢唎部 surpassing, powerful ; a title of Viṣṇu "as personification of the sun," of Brahmā, Śiva, Indra, etc. Prabhū, come into being, originate, original.

바라이 波羅夷 Pārājika. The first section of the Vinaya piṭaka containing rules of expulsion from the order, for unpardonable sin. Also 바라사이가 波羅闍已迦 ; 바라시가 波羅市迦. Cf. 사바라이 四波羅夷. There are in Hīnayāna eight sins for expulsion of nuns, and in Mahāyāna ten. The esoteric sects have their own rules. The 바라이사유 波羅夷四喩 four metaphors addressed by the Buddha to monks are : he who breaks the vow of chastity is as a needle without an eye, a dead man, a broken stone which cannot be united, a tree cut in two which cannot live.

바라제(제)사니 波羅提(提)舍尼 Prātideśanīya. A section of the Vinaya concerning public confession of sins. Explained by 향피회죄 向彼悔罪 confession of sins before another or others. Also 파라사니 波羅舍尼 ; 제사니 提舍尼 ; 파지라사니 波胝羅舍尼 ; 발랄저라사니 鉢刺底羅舍尼.

바라제목차 波羅提木叉 Pratimokṣa ; emancipation, deliverance, absolution. Prātimokṣa ; the 250 commandments for monks in the Vinaya, v. 목차 木叉 also 파 婆 ; the rules in the Vinaya from the four major to the seventy-five minor offences ; they should be read in assembly twice a month and each monk invited to confess his sins for absolution.

바랑 Monk's knapsack. = 걸망.

바로기지습벌라 婆盧枳底濕伐羅 Avalokiteśvara, see 관음 觀音.

바루나 婆樓那 Varuṇa, v. 수천 水天.

바루나 波樓那 A fierce wind, hurricane, perhaps Vātyā. 파루사가 波樓沙迦 Parūṣaka(vana), a park in the Trayastriṁśāḥ heaven.

바리 婆利 Vaḍiśa, Valiśa, or Vakrī, a hook, bent. 바리사 婆利師 Varṣās, v. 우 雨, the rainy season of retreat. 바리사(가) 婆利師(迦) ; 바리사가라 婆利史迦羅 v. 바사가 婆師迦. 바리야 婆利耶 Bhārya, a wife. 바리질(다)라 婆利質(多)羅 Pārijāta, v. 파 波, a tree in Indra's heaven. 바리자다가 婆利闍多迦 Pārijātaka, a deva flower.

바리 婆梨 Vāri ; water ; fluid, fluidity ; also 바리 婆利 ; 바리 波利.

바리야 婆哩野 Bhāryā, a dependent, a wife ; also 바리야 婆利耶 or 婆梨耶 ; 바유 婆庾.

바리한 婆里旱 Balin, intp. 역사 力士 a strong man, hero.

바바가리 婆婆伽利 Pāpakārin ; evil-doer, name of a prince.

바부아제 婆嚩誐帝 Bhagavat, v. 바가 婆伽.

바비베가 婆毘吠伽 Bhāvaviveka, a learned monk who retired from the world to await the coming of Maitreya, v. 서역기 西域記 10.

바사 婆沙 v. 비 毘 Vibhāṣā. 바사바 婆沙波 ; 바수 婆數 Bāṣpa, v. 바사바 婆師波.

바사(가) 婆師(迦) Vārṣika, the flower that blooms in the rains, the aloe, Agallochum ; also 바리사(가) 婆利師(迦) q.v. ; 바리사가라 婆利史迦羅 ; 바사가 婆使迦 ; 바사바리 婆師波利 Varṣākāla, Varṣipālī.

바사(타) 婆私(吒) Vasiṣṭha, a Brahman who is said to have denied the eternity of nirvāṇa, and maintained that plants had lives and intelligence ; Nirvāṇa Sūtra 39. One of the seven ancient ṛṣis of Brahmanic mythology, one of the champions in the Ṛgveda of the priesthood. Name of a Brahman whose mother lost her six sons, she became mad, wandered naked, met the Buddha, was restored and became a disciple. Also 바타 婆吒 ; 사사타 私私吒 ; 바사슬체 婆私瑟搋 or 바사슬타 婆私瑟侘.

바사바 婆師波 Vāṣpa, Bāṣpa ; one of the first five disciples, Daśabala-Kāśyapa, identified with Mahā-Kāśyapa ; also 바사바 婆師婆 or 바습바 婆濕婆 ; 바사바 波沙波.

바사바제 波闍波提 Prajāpati, see 파사파제 波闍波提.

바사발제 婆舍跋提 Vaśavartin, the sixth desire heaven, the abode of Māra, the god of lust, sin, and death ; its occupants avail themselves of the merits of others for their own pleasure ; it is also called the abode of Śikhin (Brahma) as lord of fire ; also 타화자재천 他化自在天 and 바라니밀바사발제 婆羅尼蜜婆舍跋提 Paranirmitavaśavartin.

바사사다 婆舍斯多 Basiasita (Skt. Vāsi-Asita) or Naśaśata, the twenty-fifth Patriarch who laboured in Central India ; the date of his death is given as A.D. 325.

바사선 婆斯仙 One of the five devas and his 후 后 wife in the Garbhadhātu group ; perhaps Vasu.

바산바연지 婆珊婆演底 Vasanta-vayantī, spring-weaving, but the description is of a guardian of the night or of sleep.

바성 婆城 A gandharva city, a mirage, an illusion city, v. 건 乾.

바수 婆藪 Vasu 바유 婆萸 ; good ; rich ; sweet ; dry ; according to Monier-Williams, eight personifications of natural phenomena ; eight ; the sun, etc. ; father of Kṛṣṇa ; intp. as the first to offer slain sacrifices to Heaven, to have been cast into hell, but after countless kalpas to have become a disciple of Buddha. Also called Vasudeva. Also name of certain devas, e.g. Viṣṇu ; and other beings whom men serve, e.g. a father. 바수반두 婆藪槃豆 ; 바수반타 婆藪槃陀 ; 바수반두 婆藪盤豆 ; 바수반두 婆修盤頭 ; 벌소반도 伐蘇畔徒 ; 벌소반도 筏蘇畔徒 or 벌소반두 筏蘇盤豆 Vasubandhu, known as 천친 天親 q.v., and 세친 世親 kinsman of devas, or of the world.

바수밀(다) 婆須蜜(多) Vasumitra, v. 벌소밀달라 筏蘇蜜呾羅.

바수발다 波輸鉢多 Pāśupata ; a particular sect of Śivaites who smeared their bodies with ashes.

바아 婆誐 Bhaṅga, breaking, fracture, fragment, broken. Also 바가 婆伽 ; 박가 薄伽.

바야 婆耶 Payas ; liquid, fluid, juice, water.

바유 婆瘐 Vāyu, wind, god of the wind. Also 바유 婆牖 ; 박수 縛叟.

바일제 波逸提 ; 파약치 波藥致 Pātaka. A sin causing one to fall into purgatory. Also 바일지가 波逸底迦 ; 파야제 波夜提 ; 파라일니가 波羅逸尼柯 ; 파(라야)질지가 波(羅夜)質胝迦 ; but there seems to be a connection with prāyaścitta, meaning expiation, atonement, restitution.

바자라파니바리한 婆闍羅波尼婆里旱 Vajrapāṇibalin, the powerful one with the thunderbolt, one of the two gate-guardians. See 바리한 婆里旱.

바자자부 婆雌子部 Vātsīputra, also 바추부라 婆麤富羅, v. 바차 婆蹉 and 독자 犢子.

바제 婆提 Bhadrika, one of the first disciples ; cf. 발 跋. Also Vana, a grove ; or vanī.

바차 婆蹉 Vatsa, a calf, offspring, a term of endearment for a child. The founder of the Vātsīputrīyāḥ school. 바차바 婆蹉婆 A term for Śakra. 바차부(다)라 婆蹉富(多)羅 The above school, a branch of the Sarvāstivādins, v. 독 犢. 바차나바 婆蹉那婆 Vatsanābha, a strong poison, "from the root of a kind of aconite." [M. W.]

바차 婆叉 Vākṣu ; Vaṅkṣu ; the Oxus ; Vaṅkṣu is also a small branch of the Ganges, idem 박추 縛芻.

바차우바차 婆差優婆差 Upāsaka-upāsikā, male and female disciples dwelling at home ; lay disciples.

바치 婆稚 Bandhi, or Bali, the origin and meaning are obscure, defined as "bound" and also as round, full-orbed, complete. Bandhiasura, an asura king. Also 바리 婆梨 ; 발치 跋稚 ; 발지 跋墀 ; 발이 跋移 ; 말리 末利.

바타 波陀 Pada ; a step, footprint, position ; a complete world ; u.f. 아바다나 阿波陀那 avadāna. 파타겁 波陀劫 ; 발달라겁 跋達羅劫 Bhadra-kalpa, v. 현겁 賢劫 and 발 颰.

바파사 婆頗娑 Prabhāsa, light, bright.

바하 婆訶 Vāha ; it means bearing, carrying, a beast of burden, but is used in the sense of a large grain-container of twenty bushels 곡 斛 ; supernatural life, or adbhuta, is compared to a vāha full of hemp seed, from which one seed is withdrawn every century. Also 바하마 婆訶摩.

바할나 婆喝那 Vāhana, 10 quadrillions. 대바할나 大婆喝那 100 quadrillions.

박 縛 Bandha. Tie, attachment, bind, bond, another name for kleśa-afflictions, the passions, etc., which bind men ; the "three bonds" are 탐진치 貪瞋痴 desire, resentment, stupidity ; translit. *pa, ba, va* ; cf. 발 跋, 바 婆, 반 飯. 박가낭 縛伽浪 Baghelān, "the country west of the Bunghee river between Koondooz and Ghoree (about Lat. 36° N., Long. 78° E.)." [Eitel]. 박리사건나 縛利沙鍵拏 v. 벌리 伐里 Vārṣagaṇya. 박갈(라) 縛喝(羅) Baktra, the present Balkh, once a nursery of Buddhism and in A.D. 600 still famous for relics and monuments. [Eitel]. 박니 縛尼 Vana, v. 반 飯 a grove. 박저 縛底 Patnī, a mistress, wife, female. 박마 縛摩 Vāma, the left, contrary, crooked. 박사선 縛斯仙 Vasiṣṭha, "a very celebrated Vedic Rishi or inspired sage," owner of the cow of plenty and able therefore to grant all desires. [M. W.] One of the six fire-devas in the maṇḍala. 박왈라 縛日羅 Vajra, 바왈라 嚩日囉 ; 바일라 嚩馹囉 ; 발일라 跋日羅 ; 발절라 跋折羅 ; 발사라 跋闍羅 ; 발절라 跋折羅 ; 바사라 波闍羅 ; 벌절라 伐折羅 ; 벌사라 伐闍羅 ; intp. as 금강(저) 金剛(杵), a diamond (club). Adamantine, hard. The sceptre of Indra as god of thunder and lightning with which he slays the enemies of Buddhism. Used by monks to indicate spiritual authority, and the all-subduing power of Buddha. 박탈 縛脫 Bonds and freedom, escape from entanglement. 박유 縛臾 Vāyu, air, wind, the god of the wind ; he controls the 박유방 縛臾方 or north-west. 박추 縛芻 Vākṣu ; Vaṅkṣu ; 바추 婆芻 ; 바사 婆槎 ; 바수 婆輸 ; 박차 薄叉 ; 박차 博叉 ; the Oxus 청하 青河 or Blue River, one of the "four great rivers of Jambudvipa," rising in the west of the Anavatapta lake (Tibet) and flowing into the north-west sea, the Caspian ; cf. 서역기 西域記 1. 박살달라 縛薩怛羅 Vastra, cloth, clothes. 박가 縛迦 Vākya, speech, saying, sentence, word. 박야폐 縛野吠 Vāyavī, the deva of the north-west, v. Vāyu above. 박마답 縛馬答 An argument or reply in a "vicious circle," like a horse tethered to a peg.

박 薄 Thin poor, shabby ; to slight, despise ; to reach to ; the herb mint. 박거라 薄佉羅 Bactria (or Bukhara), the country of the Yüeh-chih, described as north-west of the Himalayas. 박건 薄健 v. 습 濕 Wakhan. 박지 薄地 Poor land, i.e. the word, as full of trouble. 박구라 薄拘羅 also 박구라 薄矩羅 ; 박구라 薄俱羅 ; 박라파구라 薄羅婆拘羅 ; 박구라 縛矩羅 ; 파구려 波鳩蠡 Vakula, a disciple who, during his eighty years of life, never had a moment's illness or pain. 박복 薄福 Unfortunate ; poor condition due to poor karma ; ill luck. 박증 薄證 Shallow insight, weak in mystic experience. 박가(범) 薄迦(梵) ; 박가(범) 薄伽(梵) Bhagavan, Bhagavat, 세존 世尊 World-honoured, cf. 파 婆.

박 剝 To peel, flay ; kill. 박피 剝皮 To flay, or peel. In one of the previous incarnations of Śākyamuni he is said to have written a certain gāthā containing the Holy Law on a piece of this own flayed skin with one of his bones split into the shape of a pen, and his blood instead of ink. 지도론 智度論 27.

박 博 Wide, universal ; widely read, versed in ; to cause ; gamble ; barter. 박차 博叉 Vaṅkṣu ; Vākṣu ; v. 박 縛 the Oxus. 박차반다가 博叉般荼迦 ; 박차반택가 博叉半擇迦 Pakṣapaṇḍakās ; partial eunuchs, cf. 반 半. 박흘추 博吃蒭 Pakṣa, half a lunar month ; also used for Māra's army.

박 簿 Notebook, register, etc. 박구라 簿句羅 ; 박구라 簿拘羅 Vakula, an intelligent disciple of Śākyamuni. A demon.

박장 拍掌 ; 박수 拍手 Clapping of hands at the beginning and end of worship, a Shingon custom.

반 班 A class, rank, band ; translit. *pan.* 반선라마 班禪喇嘛 ; 반선알이덕니 班禪額爾德尼 The Tibetan Panchen-lama.

반 盤 A dish, plate ; round, to coil, wind up ; to go about, travel, convey ; to inquire about, interrogate. Translit. *pa, ba, bha, va* ; cf. 반 般, 반 半 etc. 반좌 盤坐 To sit with folded legs. 반다미 盤荼味 Vandanī, praise, adore, v. 화 和.

반 畔 A path between fields, or boundary ; to trespass ; translit. *ban, van, par, pra,* v. 선 船, 반 班, etc. 반첩바 畔喋婆 Vātyā. A great calamitous wind. 반탄남 畔彈南 ; 반제 畔睇 Vandana, v. 화 和.

반 磐 A rock. 반석겁 磐石劫 The rock kalpa. Let a rock 40 li in extent be brushed once in a hundred years by a deva garment ; when brushed away the kalpa is ended.

반 般 A sort, a kind ; translit. *par, pra, pan, pa,* etc.

반 槃 A tray ; a hut ; to turn ; translit. *pan, van, va.* 반담 槃淡 cf. 화 和 Vandana, obeisance, worship. 반특 槃特 ; 반타 槃陀 cf. 반 半 Paṇḍaka, eunuch. 반차 槃遮 Vac, speech, talk. 반두 槃頭 Pāṇḍu, father of Vipaśyin, the 998th Buddha of the last kalpa.

반 伴 Companion, associate ; translit. *pan, ban, van* ; cf. 반 畔. 승 僧 Associate or accompanying monks. 반야 伴夜 ; 반령 伴靈 To watch with the spirit of a departed monk the night before the cremation. 반담 伴談 v. 화남 和南 Vandana. 반다라바자니 伴陀羅縛子尼 or 伴陀羅縛字尼 v. 반 半 Pāṇḍaravāsinī.

반 半 Half. Used as translit. for Pan, pun. 반지가 半只迦 or 半支迦 ; 반지가 般止柯 ; 반사가 般闍迦 ; 산지(가) 散支(迦) ; 덕차가 德叉迦 Pāñcika, the third of the eight great yakṣas, husband of Hāritī 귀자모 鬼子母, 반차노 半嗟笯 ; 반노차 半笯嗟 Punaca or Pañcasattra or Pañcarāṣṭra, an ancient province and city of Kashmir (now Punch). 반천바라문 半天婆羅門 Halfdeva brahmans, a term for hungry ghosts. 반나(사) 半娜(娑) ; 반뇨사 半橠娑 ; 반날바 般捺婆 ; 바나사 波那娑 Panasa, bread-fruit ; 파 婆 is incorrectly used for 사 娑. 반자 半字 "Half a character" ; a letter of the alphabet. Hīnayāna is likened to a 반자 半字, Mahāyāna to a 만자 滿字 complete word ; hence 반자교 半字教 is Hīnayāna. 반나라부실령 半拏囉嚩悉寧 ; 반다라박자니 伴陀羅縛子尼 Pāṇḍaravāsinī ; white-clothed, i.e. the white-clothed Kuan-yin ; also tr. as white abode. 반택가 半擇迦 Paṇḍaka, intp. as 변 變 to change from time to time, a general term for eunuchs ; see 반다가 般荼迦. 반만교 半滿教 The half and the complete doctrines, i.e. Hīnayāna and Mahāyāna. 반자가단니 半者珂但尼 or 반자거단니 半者佉但尼 ; 반자거사니 半者佉闍尼 Pañcakhādanīya, the five "chewing" foods, not regular foods, i.e. roots, stems, leaves, flowers, fruits ; or stems, leaves, flowers, fruits, and their triturations. 반자포선니 半者蒲膳尼 or 반자포사니 半者蒲闍尼 Pañcabhojanīya. The five regular articles of food : the 번역명의 繙譯名義 Fan-i-ming-i gives wheat, rice, parched rice (or cakes), fish, and flesh. Another account is rice, boiled wheat or pulse, parched grain, flesh, cakes. 반탁가 半託迦 or 반타가 半他迦 ; 반타(가) 槃陀(迦) ; 반특 槃特 Panthaka, born on the road ; a road ; two brothers — one born by a main road, the other by a path — who both became arhats. 반초 半超 A deva who by devotion advances by leaps, escaping from one to thirteen of the sixteen heavens of form. 반가(부)좌 半跏(趺)坐 A bodhisattva's form of sitting, different from the completely cross-legged form of a Buddha. 반자라 半遮羅 Pañjara, a basket, or cage. 반재 半齋 Half a day's fast, i.e. fasting all day but eating at night.

반 飯 Rice (cooked) ; food ; to eat. 반경 飯磬 The dinner-gong. 반대자 飯袋子 A rice-bag fellow, a monk only devoted to his food, useless. 반나 飯那 Vana, a grove, a wood. 반두 飯頭 a cook.

반 斑 Spotted, striped, streaked, variegated. 반족왕 斑足王 The king with the marks on his feet, Kalmāṣapāda, said to be the name of a previous incarnation of the Buddha.

반 婆 To and fro, to roll ; translit. *bha, va.* 반비폐가 婆毗吠伽 Bhāvaviveka, a disciple of Nāgārjuna, who retired to a rock cavern to await the coming of Maitreya. 반라서나 婆羅犀那 Varasena (the Aparasvin of the Zend-Avesta), a pass on the Paropamisus, now called Khawak, south of Indarab. 반수천 婆藪天 Vasu-deva, in Brahmanic mythology the father of Kṛṣṇa. 반달라발타 婆達羅鉢陀 Bhādrapada, the last month of summer.

반 攀 To grasp, drag, pull, detain ; climb, clamber. 반연 攀緣 Something to lay hold of, a reality, cause, basis ; used for 연 緣 q.v. 반각 攀覺 Seizing and perceiving, like a monkey jumping from branch to branch, i.e. attracted by externals, unstable.

반 反 To turn over, turn or send back ; contrary ; to rebel. 반출생사 反出生死 One of the seven kinds of mortality, i.e. escape from it into nirvāṇa. 반절 反切 The system of indicating the initial and final sounds of a character by two others, ascribed to Sun Yen 손염 孫炎 in the third century A.D., arising out of the translit. of Sanskrit terms in Buddhist translation. 반차합장 反叉合掌 One of the twelve forms of folded bands, i.e. with interlocking fingers.

반나 般那 Prāṇa, exhalation, breathing out, cf. 아나 阿那. 반나마 般那摩 Padma, lotus, cf. 발 鉢.

반녈반(나) 般涅般(那) Parinirvāṇa ; "quite extinguished, quite brought to an end ; the final extinction of the individual." [M. W.] The death of the Buddha. Nirvāṇa may be attained in this life, parinirvāṇa after it ; for the meaning of "extinction" v. 열반 涅槃. It may also correspond to the suppression of all mental activity. It is also the second of the three grades of nirvāṇa, parinirvāṇa, and mahānirvāṇa, which are later developments and have association with the ideas of Hīnayāna, Madhyamayāna, and Mahāyāna, or the small, middle, and great vehicles ; also with the three grades of bodhi which these three vehicles represent ; and the three classes of śrāvakas, pratyeka-buddhas, and bodhisattvas. Other forms are : 반리열반나 般利涅般那 ; 파리열반나 波利涅般那 ; 반니원 般尼洹.

반니원 般泥洹 Parinirvāṇa ; v. 반녈반(나) 般涅般(那).

반다가 般荼迦 Paṇḍaka. The general name for eunuchs. The five classes with various degrees of sexual impotence: (1) 선체 扇搋 Ṣaṇḍha(paṇḍaka) ; by birth impotent. (2) 류나 留拏 Rugṇa or Ruṇḍa paṇḍaka ; "maimed," i.e. emasculated males. (3) 이리사장나 伊梨沙掌拏 Īrṣyā(paṇḍaka) ; those whose sexual desires are only aroused by jealousy. (4) 반택가 半擇迦 Paṇḍaka are eunuchs in general, but in this category are described as hermaphrodites. (5) 박차 博叉 Pakṣa(pāṇḍaka) ; impotent during one-half of the month. A newer classification distinguishes those with incomplete from those with complete organs ; the incomplete being (1) Ṣaṇḍha, or Jātipaṇḍaka as above ; and (2) emasculated males ; the complete are the others ; the fifth being stimulated when bathing or evacuating. Other forms: 반타 般吒, 반탁 半托 ; 반택가 半擇迦 tr. 황문 黃門. 반다로가법 般荼盧伽法 The Pāṇḍaka and Lohitaka rule is that derived from the conduct of these two disciples in the Vinaya, and is against quarrelling and fighting.

반라삽미 般羅颯迷 Parasmaipada. "The transitive or active verb and its terminations." [M. W.]

반랄밀제 般剌蜜帝 Pramiti, Paramiti, a monk from Central India, tr. the Śūraṅgama sūtra 수능엄경 首楞嚴經 A.D. 705.

반리벌라구가 般利伐羅句迦 Parivrājaka, or Wanderer. "A Śivaitic sect, worshippers of Maheśvara, who wear clothes of the colour of red soil and leave a little hair about the crown of the head, shaving off the rest." [Eitel]. Also 바리달라구가 波利呾羅拘迦 ; 파리바자가 簸利婆闍迦.

반배 半拜 Half-bow (from the waist).

반야 般若 Prajñā, "to know, understand" ; "Wisdom." [M. W.] Intp. 혜 慧 wisdom ; 지혜 智慧 understanding, or wisdom ; 명 明 clear, intelligent, the sixth pāramitā. The Prajñā-pāramitā-sūtra describes it as supreme, highest, incomparable, unequalled, unsurpassed. It is spoken of as the principal means, by its enlightenment, of attaining to nirvāṇa, through its revelation of the unreality of all things. Other forms are 반라야 般羅若 ; 반뢰야 般賴若 ; 발야 鉢若 ; 발자야 鉢剌若 ; 발라지양 鉢羅枳孃 ; 발신양 鉢腎禳 ; 파(뢰)야 波(賴)若 ; 파라양 波羅孃 ; 반야 班若. 반(뢰)야 般(賴)若 Prajñā is also the name of a monk from Kabul, A.D. 810, styled 삼장법사 三藏法師 ; tr. four works and author of an alphabet.

반야경 般若經 The wisdom sūtras, especially the 대반야바라밀다경 大般若波羅蜜多經 tr. by Hsüan-tsang in 600 chüan. A compendium of five wisdom sūtras is 마하반야 摩訶般若 ; 금강반야 金剛般若 ; 천왕문반야 天王問般若 ; 광찬반야 光讚般若 and 인왕반야 仁王般若 ; cf. the last. Another compendium contains eight books.

반야국다 般若毱多 Prajñāgupta. A Hīnayāna monk of southern India, who wrote against the Mahāyāna.

반야다라 般若多羅 Prajñātāra. The 27th patriarch, native of eastern India, who laboured in southern India and consumed himself "by the fire of transformation," A.D. 457, teacher of Bodhidharma.

반야두 般若頭 The monk in charge of the Prajñā sūtras.

반야바라밀(다) 般若波羅蜜(多) Prajñāpāramitā. The acme of wisdom, enabling one to reach the other shore, i.e. wisdom for salvation ; the highest of the six pāramitās, the virtue of wisdom as the principal means of attaining to Nirvāṇa. It connotes a knowledge of the illusory character of everything earthly, and destroys error, ignorance, prejudice, and heresy. For the sūtra of this name see 반야경 般若經.

반야보살 般若菩薩 Prajñā-bodhisattva ; wisdom as a female bodhisattva in the Garbhadhātu group ; also known as 지혜금강 智慧金剛.

반야봉 般若鋒 The spear of wisdom (which is able to cut off illusion and evil).

반야불모 般若佛母 Wisdom, or salvation through wisdom (Prajñā-pāramitā), is the mother or source of all Buddhas. 지도론 智度論 34.

반야선 般若船 The boat of wisdom, the means of attaining nirvāṇa.

반야시 般若時 The prajñā period, the fourth of the (T'ien-t'ai) five periods of the Buddha's teaching.

반야심경 般若心經 The sūtra of the heart of prajñā ; there have been several translations, under various titles, the generally accepted version being by Kumārajīva, which gives the essence of the Wisdom Sūtras. There are many treatises on the 심경 心經.

반야탕 般若湯 The soup of wisdom, a name for wine.

반주 般舟 Pratyutpanna, present ; multiplied. 반주(삼매) 般舟(三昧) Pratyutpannasamādhi, the samādhi in which the Buddhas of the ten directions are seen as clearly as the stars at night. Also called 상행도 常行道 or 상행삼매 常行三昧 the prolonged samādhi, because of the length of time required, either seven or ninety days. Its sūtra is the 반주삼매경 般舟三昧經.

반차 般遮 Pañca, five ; also 반자 半者. 반차자순 般遮子旬 Pāñcika. Described as the gods of music, i.e. the gandharvas, also as 반차순 般遮旬 Pañcābhijñāna, the five supernatural powers. 반차우슬 般遮于瑟 Pañca-vārṣika ; Pañca-pariṣad ; Mokṣa-mahāpariṣad, the great quinquennial assembly instituted by Aśoka for the confession of sins, the inculcation of morality and discipline, and the distribution of charity ; also 반차파슬 般遮婆瑟 ; 반차발슬가 般遮跋瑟迦 ; 반차월사 般遮越師 ; 반차파율가사 般遮婆栗迦史 ; 반차발리사 般遮跋利沙 ; 반자우슬 般闍于瑟.

발 颰 A gale ; translit. *pha, bha* ; cf. 발 跋 and 바 婆. 발타 颰陀 ; 발타화(라) 颰陀和(羅) ; 발타바라 颰陀波羅 Bhadra, 발타라파리 颰陀羅波梨 Bhadrapāla, v. 발 跋. 발타겁 颰陀劫 Bhadra-kalpa, v. 발 跋.

발 鈸 Cymbals.

발 髮 Hair (of the head), locks. 발탑 髮塔 A pagoda over a hair of Buddha's head. 발론 髮論 The śāstra of the non-Buddhist Kapila, the 승론 勝論 q.v.

발 拔 Pull up, or out ; raise. 발파 拔婆 ; 발파 拔波 Vatsa, calf, young child. 발저야 拔底耶 Upādhyāya, a spiritual teacher, or monk 화상 和尙 v. 오 烏. 발제 拔提 -vati, a terminal of names of certain rivers, e.g. Hiraṇyavatī. 발제달다 拔提達多 Bhadradatta, name of a king. 발제 拔濟 To rescue, save from trouble. 발설지옥 拔舌地獄 The hell where the tongue is pulled out, as punishment for oral sins. 발고여락 拔苦與樂 To save from suffering and give joy. 발라마라 拔羅魔囉 Bhrāmara, a kind of black bee. 발사발 拔思發 ; 발합사파 拔合思巴 ; 팔사파 八思巴 Baschpa (Phags-pa), Tibetan Buddhist and adviser of Kublai Khan, v. 팔발(사) 八發(思).

발 鉢 Pātra, a bowl, vessel, receptacle, an almsbowl ; translit. *p, pa, ba.* = 발우.

발 勃 Shooting plants ; a comet. 발사 勃沙 ; 불사 弗沙 Puṣya ; foam ; a lunar mansion, i.e. the three arrow starts in the 귀 鬼 constellation of which δ Cancri is one. 발타 勃陀 ; 발타 勃馱 ; 발탑야 勃塔耶 ; 발타 馞陀 ; 불타 佛陀 Buddha ; intp. by 각 覺 and 불 佛 q.v. 발가이 勃伽夷 Bhagai, "a city south of Khotan with a Buddha-statue which exhibits all the" lakṣaṇāni, or thirty-two signs, "brought there from Cashmere." [Eitel].

발 發 To shoot forth, send, issue ; start, initiate ; expound ; prosper. 발광 發光 To send forth light, radiate. 발심 發心 Mental initiation or initiative, resolve, make up the mind to ; to start out for bodhi, or perfect enlightenment ; to show kindness of heart, give alms. 발심공양 發心供養

To make an offering with pious intent. 발사팔 發思八, v. 팔 八 Bāṣpa. 발의 發意 To resolve on, have a mind to ; similar to 발심 發心. 발계 發戒 To issue to, or bestow the commandments on a disciple. 발생 發生 To produce, grow, initiate, prosper. 발진 發眞 To exhibit the truth, tell the truth ; to manifest the 진여 眞如 or innate Buddha. 발강 發講 To commence expounding, to expound. 발기 發起 To spring up, begin, develop, stimulate. 발로 發露 To reveal, manifest, confess. 발원 發願 To vow, resolve.

발 撥 To spread, open out, scatter, disseminate, detach, uproot. 발무인과 撥無因果 To dispense with, or deny the law of karma, one of the five heresies. 발초첨풍 撥草瞻風 ; 발초참현 撥草參玄 To uproot the weeds (of ignorance) and look for the mystic Buddha-breeze.

발 跋 Trudge, tread on, travel ; heel, base ; a summary ; translit. *pa*, *ba*, *bha*, *va* sounds ; cf. 바 波, 바 婆, 바 簸. 발가선 跋伽仙 or 발가바 跋伽婆 Bhārgava, Bhagava, Bhaga, the ascetic under whom Śākyamuni practised the austere life. 발리사 跋利沙 Varṣās, cf. 우 雨 the rains. 발절라 跋折羅 Vajra, v. 금강 金剛 diamond ; thunderbolt. 발절라타하사 跋折羅吒訶沙 Vajrāṭṭahāsa, i.e. Śiva, one of the guardians, the laughing Mahārāja. 발날라파나 跋捺羅婆娜 Bhādrapada, the sixth Indian month. 발제 跋提 Bhadra, or Bhadrika, v. next ; used also for Vatī, the river Hiraṇyavatī, or Gunduck. 발제리가 跋提梨迦 or 跋提唎迦 Bhadrika, also 바제 婆提 or 바제 婆帝, one of the first five disciples, said to be a son of king Amṛtodana. 발마 跋摩 Harivarman, and his school, v. 하 訶. 발일라 跋日羅 Vajra, v. 금강 金剛. 발거 跋渠 Varga, a class, group, cf. 벌 伐. 발남마 跋濫摩 ; 바라문 婆羅門 Brāhmaṇa, Brahman, the caste, or character, i.e. pure. 발로사 跋盧沙 Varuṣa, now Attock, east of Peshawar. 발록갈첩파 跋祿羯呫婆 Bharukaccha, an ancient state in Gujarat, near Baruch, on the Narbudda. 발록가 跋祿迦 An ancient state in east Turkestan, the present Aksu, [Eitel]. 발사불다라 跋私弗多羅 Vātsīputra, 독자 犢子 founder of the sect of this name, one of the Vaibhāṣika schools. 발솔도 跋窣堵 Vastu, real, substance ; intp. as the Vinaya, or part of it ; may be tr. by 사 事, 물 物, 본 本, 유 有. 발라사타 跋羅娑馱 Prāsāda, a temple, palace, assembly hall. 발라참 跋羅攙 Tallakṣaṇa (Julien), 10 octillions ; a 대발라참 大跋羅攙 is 100 octillions, v. 낙차 洛叉. 발라루지 跋羅縷支 Bhadraruci, a monk of west India, of great subtlety and reasoning power ; he opposed an arrogant Brahman, who, defeated, sank alive into hell. 발람 跋藍 Bala, or Mudrābala, 10 septillions ; 대발람 大跋藍 100 septillions, v. 낙 洛. 발로파다 跋路婆陀 or 발로사다 跋路娑陀 Prāsāda, v. above. 발달라 跋達羅 Bhadra, good, auspicious, gracious, excellent, virtuous ; an epithet for every Buddha ; the present 현겁 賢劫 Bhadra-kalpa. 발라말라기리 跋邏末羅耆釐 Bhramaragiri (Beal), a monastery built by Sadvaha for Nāgārjuna on this mountain, 300 li south-west of Kośala. 발나 跋那 Varaṇa, v. 벌 伐, a province of Kapiśā, v. 장 障. 발피 跋陂 Bhadrapāla, name of 현호 賢護 a bodhisattva. 발다 跋陀 Bhadra, v. above. 발다파 跋陀婆 Bhadrapāla, v. above. 발다라 跋陀羅 Bhādrapadā, the 벽 壁 constellation in Pegasus and Andromeda. Bhadrā, a female disciple of Śākyamuni. Guṇabhadra, v. 구 求, a nāga-king ; a tree. 발다라루지 跋陀羅樓支 Bhadraruci, v. above 발라루지 跋羅縷支. 발다라야니 跋陀羅耶尼 Bhadrayānīyāḥ, v. 소승 小乘, one of the eighteen Hīnayāna sects. 발다라가비리야 跋陀羅迦卑梨耶 Bhadrakapilā, also 발다가비라 跋陀迦毘羅 a female disciple of Śākyamuni. 발사 跋闍 Vṛji, the modern Vraja or Braj, west of Delhi and Agra ; also given as Vaiśālī, cf. 비 毘, where the second assembly met and where the ten unlawful acts permitted by the Vṛjiputra monks were condemned. 발사라 跋闍羅 Vajra, v. 금강 金剛. 발사라파니 跋闍羅波膩 Vajrapāṇi, "thunderbolt handed" [M. W.], v. 금강수 金剛手. 발난다 跋難陀 Upananda, a disciple who rejoiced over the Buddha's death because it freed the disciples from restraint. A nāga king.

발건제 鉢健提 Pākhaṇḍa, i.e. Pāṣaṇḍa, Pāṣaṇḍin, heresy, a heretic, intp. 견고 堅固 firm, stubborn ; name of a deva.

발길제 鉢吉帝 Prakṛti, natural ; woman ; etc. Name of the woman at the well who supplied water to Ānanda, seduced him, but became a nun.

발다(라) 鉢多(羅) Pātra, a bowl vessel, receptacle, an almsbowl ; also 발달라 鉢呾羅 ; 발화라 鉢和羅 ; 발화란 鉢和蘭 ; 파달라 波怛囉 or 播怛囉 ; in brief 발 鉢. The almsbowl of the Buddha is said to have been brought by Bodhidharma to China in A.D. 520.

발담 鉢曇 Pada, v. 발타 鉢陀.

발두마 鉢頭摩 Padma, v. 발특 鉢特.

발라 鉢羅 Pala, a particular measure or weight, intp. as 4 ounces ; also 바라 波羅 ; 파뢰타 波賴他 ; but pala also means flesh, meat, and palāda, a flesh-eater, a rākṣasa ; translit. *pra, para.* 발라폐사 鉢羅吠奢 Praveśa, entrance, 입 入 q.v. 발라사거 鉢羅奢佉 or 鉢羅賒佉 Praśākhā ; praśaka ; the fifth stage of the foetus, the limbs being formed. 발라지야 鉢羅底也 Pratyaya, a concurrent or environmental cause. 발라미 鉢羅弭 Parama ; highest, supreme, first. 발라마보리 鉢羅摩菩提 Parama-bodhi, supreme enlightenment. 발라사나특다 鉢羅斯那特多 ; 발라서나특다 鉢羅犀那特多 ; 파사닉 波斯匿 Prasenajit, a king of Kosala, patron of Śākyamuni, who is reputed as the first to make an image of the Buddha. 발라지양 鉢羅枳孃 ; 발라현양 鉢羅賢禳 v. 반 般 Prajñā. 발라보다라달낭야 鉢羅步多囉怛囊野 or 발라부다라달낭야 鉢羅部多囉怛囊野, i.e. 다보 多寶 q.v. Prabhūtaratna. 발라유타 鉢羅由他 ; 발라유타 鉢羅庾他 ; also 파발라유 波鉢羅由 ; Prayuta ; ten billions ; 대발라유타 大鉢羅由他 100 billions, v. 락 洛. 발라급보리 鉢羅笈菩提 Prāgbodhi. A mountain in Magadha, which Śākyamuni ascended "before entering upon Bodhi" ; wrongly explained by 전정각 前正覺 anterior to supreme enlightenment. 발라야가 鉢羅耶伽 Prayāga, now Allahabad. 발라야 鉢羅若 v. 반 般 Prajñā. 발라살타 鉢羅薩他 Prastha, a weight tr. as a 근 斤 Chinese pound ; a measure.

발라야(발다예) 鉢囉惹(鉢多曳) Prajāpati, "lord of creatures," "bestower of progeny," "creator" ; tr. as 생주 生主 lord of life, or production, and intp. as Brahmā. Also, v. Mahāprajāpatī, name of the Buddha's aunt and nurse.

발라지갈란다 鉢刺底羯爛多 Pratikrānta, following in order, or by degrees. 발라예가불타 鉢刺翳迦佛陀 v. 벽 辟, Pratyeka-buddha. 발라가라 鉢刺迦羅 Prakaraṇa, intp. as 장 章 a section, chapter, etc.

발라지목차 鉢喇底木叉 Pratimokṣa, idem mokṣa, v. 목 木, 바 波, 해 解. Prātimokṣa, a portion of the Vinaya, called the sūtra of emancipation. 발라지제사니 鉢喇底提舍尼 ; 발라지제사나 鉢喇底提舍那 Pratideśanā, public confession ; prātideśanīya, offences to be confessed ; a section of the Vinaya, v. 바 波. 발라특기나 鉢喇特崎拏 Pradakṣiṇa, circumambulation with the right shoulder towards the object of homage.

발로아 鉢露兒 Bolor, a kingdom north of the Indus, south-east of the Pamir, rich in minerals, i.e. Hunza-Nagar ; it is to be distinguished from Bolor in Tukhāra. 발로라 鉢露羅 Polulo, perhaps Baltistan.

발리부 鉢唎部 Prabhu, mighty, intp. by 자재 自在 sovereign, a title of Viṣṇu, Brahmā, and others.

발리살라벌나 鉢里薩囉伐拏 Parisrāvaṇa, a filtering bag, or cloth, for straining water (to save the lives of insects), part of the equipment of a monk.

발리체폐 鉢哩體吠 Pṛthivī, the earth, world, ground, soil, etc.

발마라가 鉢摩羅伽 Padmarāga, lotus-hued, a ruby ; also 발담마라가 鉢曇摩羅伽.

발벌다 鉢伐多 Parvata, crags, mountain range. An ancient city and province of Ṭakka, 700 li north-east of Mūlasthānapura, perhaps the modern Futtihpoor between Multan and Lahore. Also 발라벌다 鉢羅伐多.

발색모 鉢塞莫 Pāśakamālā, dice-chain, i.e. a rosary.

발우 A bowl. = **발** 鉢.

발위 鉢位 Bowl seat, the place each monk occupies at table.

발타 鉢吒 Paṭa, woven cloth or silk. 발타보달라 鉢吒補怛囉 Pāṭaliputra, the present Patna.

발타 鉢陀 Pada, footstep, pace, stride, position ; also 발담 鉢曇 ; 파타 波陀 ; 파타 播陀 ; also tr. as foot ; and stop.

발탁창나 鉢鐸創那 Badakshan, "a mountainous district of Tukhāra" [M. W.] ; also 파달극산 巴達克山 .

발특(마) 鉢特(摩) Padma, or Raktapadma, the red lotus ; one of the signs on the foot of a Buddha ; the seventh hell ; also 발특망 鉢特忙 ; 발두마 鉢頭摩 ; 발노마 鉢弩摩 ; 발담마 鉢曇摩 ; 발납마 鉢納摩 ; 발두마 鉢頭摩 ; 발담마 鉢曇摩.

발화라 鉢和羅 Pravāraṇa. A freewill offering made, or the rejoicings on the last day of the summer retreat. Also described as the day of mutual confession ; also 발화란 鉢和蘭 ; 발라바라나 鉢剌婆剌拏 ; 발화라 盋和羅.

방 榜 A placard, list ; model, example.

방 坊 A place, locality ; a temple, place of assembly, etc.

방 旁 A side, beside, adjoining, near. 방생 旁生 ; 방생 傍生 Rebirth as an animal. In some parts of China 방생 旁生 means the next life.

방 房 House, room. The rooms for monks and nuns in a monastery or nunnery. 방숙 房宿 Scorpio, idem 겁빈나 劫貧那.

방 傍 Near, adjoining, side, dependent. 방생 傍生 Tiryagyoni, "born of or as an animal" [M. W.] ; born to walk on one side, i.e. belly downwards, because of sin in past existence. 방생취 傍生趣 The animal path, that of rebirth as an animal, one of the six gati.

방 方 Square ; place ; correct ; a means, plan, prescription ; then, now, just.

방 放 To let go, release, send out ; put, place. 방하 放下 To put down, let down, lay down, 방광 放光 Light-emitting ; to send out an illuminating ray. 방광삼매 放光三昧 A samādhi in which all kinds and colours of light are emitted. 방광서 放光瑞 The auspicious ray emitted from between the eyebrows of the Buddha before pronouncing the Lotus sūtra. 방등 放燈 Lighting strings of lanterns, on the fifteenth of the first month, a custom wrongly attributed to Han Ming Ti, to celebrate the victory of Buddhism in the debate with Taoists ; later extended to the seventh and fifteenth full moons. 방생 放生 To release living creatures as a work of merit. 방일 放逸 Loose, unrestrained.

방 謗 To slander. 비방 誹謗 To slander, vilify, defame. 방삼보계 謗三寶戒 One of the commandments against speaking falsely of the Three Precious Ones. 방법 謗法 To slander the Truth.

방 防 Ward off, protect, beware ; to counter. 방난 防難 To counter, or solve difficulties, especially difficult questions. 방라 防羅 or 防邏 Warders or patrols in Hades. 방나 防那 Vāna, weaving, sewing ; tr. as a tailoress.

방광 方廣 Vaipulya, 비불략 毘佛略 expansion, enlargement, broad, spacious. 방 方 is intp. by 방정 方正 correct in doctrine and 광 廣 by 광박 廣博 broad or wide ; some interpret it by elaboration, or fuller explanation of the doctrine ; in general it may be taken as the broad school, or wider teaching, in contrast with the narrow school, or Hīnayāna. The term covers the whole of the specifically Mahāyāna sūtras. The sūtras are also known as 무량의경 無量義經 scriptures of measureless meaning, i.e. universalistic, or the infinite. Cf. 방등 方等. 방광대장엄경 方廣大莊嚴經 A vaipulya sūtra, the Lalita-vistara, in 12 chüan, giving an account of the Buddha in the Tuṣita heaven and his descent to earth as Śākyamuni ; tr. by Divākara under the T'ang dynasty ; another tr. is the 보요경 普曜經. 방광도인 方廣道人 Heretical followers of Mahāyāna, who hold a false doctrine of 공 空 the Void, teaching it as total non-existence, or nihilism.

방구식 方口食 Opportunism in obtaining a living, i.e. a monk who makes a living by fawning or by bullying, one of the 사사명 四邪命 four illicit ways of livelihood.

방규 方規 Square-shaped, properly, according to scale.

방등 方等 Vaipulya ; cf. 방광 方廣. 방 方 is interpreted as referring to the doctrine, 등 等 as equal, or universal, i.e. everywhere equally. An attempt is made to distinguish between the two above terms, 방광 方廣 being now used for vaipulya, but they are interchangeable. Eitel says the vaipulya sūtras "are distinguished by an expansion of doctrine and style (Sūtras développées, Burnouf). They are apparently of later date, showing the influence of different schools ; their style is diffuse and prolix, repeating the same idea over and over again in prose and in verse ; they are also frequently interlarded with prophecies and dhāraṇīs" ; but the two terms seem to refer rather to the content than the form. The content is that of universalism. Chinese Buddhists assert that all the sūtras from the 화엄 華嚴 Hua-yen onwards are of this class and therefore are Mahāyāna. Consequently all 방등 方等 or 방광 方廣 sūtras are claimed by that school. Cf. 방편 方便. 방등삼매 方等三昧 One of T'ien-t'ai's methods of inducing samādhi, partly by walking, partly by sitting, based on the 대방등다라니경 大方等陀羅尼經 ; Chih-i delivered the 방등삼매행법 方等三昧行法 to his disciple 관정 灌頂 Kuan-ting who wrote it in one chüan. 방등참(회) 方等懺(悔) One of the subjects of meditation in the above on the hindrances caused by the six organs of sense. 방등(계)단 方等(戒)壇 An open altar at which instruction in the commandments was preached to the people, founded on the Mahāyāna-vaipulya sūtras ; the system began in 765 in the capital under 대종 代宗 Tai Tsung of the T'ang dynasty and continued, with an interim under 무종 武宗 Wu Tsung, till the 선종 宣宗 Hsüan Tsung period. 방등시 方等時 The third of the five periods of T'ien-t'ai 오시교 五時教, the eight years from the twelfth to the twentieth years of the Buddha's teaching, i.e. the period of the 유마 維摩, the 금광명 金光明, and other vaipulya sūtras. 방등부 方等部 The sūtras taught during the 방등시 方等時 last-named period.

방복 方服 A monk's robe 가사 袈裟 said to be so called because of its square appearance ; also 방포 方袍.

방상 方相 Square, four square, one of the five shapes.

방예 方詣 Direction.

방외 方外 Out of the world ; the life of a monk.

방장 方丈 An abbot, 사주 寺主 head of a monastery ; the term is said to arise from the ten-foot cubic dwelling in which 유마 維摩 Vimalakīrti lived, but there seems to be no Sanskrit equivalent.

방장 스님 Chief of the precincts ; Zen Master. This title is reserved for the Zen Masters of the four main training monasteries 총림 叢林.

방전 方典 A term covering the whole of the Mahāyāna sūtras, idem 방등경전 方等經典.

방편 方便 Upāya. Convenient to the place, or situation, suited to the condition, opportune, appropriate ; but 방 方 is interpreted as 방법 方法 method, mode, plan, and 편 便 as 편용 便用

convenient for use, i.e. a convenient or expedient method ; also 방 方 as 방정 方正 and 편 便 as 교묘 巧妙, which implies strategically correct. It is also intp. as 권도지 權道智 partial, temporary, or relative (teaching of) knowledge of reality, in contrast with 반야지 般若智 prajñā, and 진실 眞實 absolute truth, or reality instead of the seeming. The term is a translation of 우화 漚和 upāya, a mode of approach, an expedient, stratagem, device. The meaning is — teaching according to the capacity of the hearer, by any suitable method, including that of device or stratagem, but expedience beneficial to the recipient is understood. Mahāyāna claims that the Buddha used this expedient or partial method in his teaching until near the end of his days, when he enlarged it to the revelation of reality, or the preaching of his final and complete truth. Hīnayāna with reason denies this, and it is evident that the Mahāyāna claim has no foundation, for the whole of its 방등 方等 or 방광 方廣 scriptures are of later invention. T'ien-t'ai speaks of the 삼승 三乘 q.v. or Three Vehicles as 방편 方便 expedient or partial revelations, and of its 일승 一乘 or One Vehicle as the complete revelation of universal Buddhahood. This is the teaching of the Lotus sūtra, which itself contains 방편 方便 teaching to lead up to the full revelation ; hence the terms 체내방편 體內方便 or 동체방편 同體方便, i.e. expedient or partial truths within the full revelation, meaning the expedient part of the Lotus, and 체외방편 體外方便 the expedient or partial truths of the teaching which preceded the Lotus ; see the 방편품 方便品 of that work, also the second chapter of the 유마경 維摩經. 방편 方便 is also the seventh of the ten pāramitās. 방편화신토 方便化身土 An intermediate "land" of the Japanese monk 견진 見眞 Kenshin, below the Pure-land, where Amitābha appears in his transformation-body. 방편토 方便土 Abbreviation for the last and next but one. 방편지 方便智 Upāyajñāna ; the wisdom or knowledge of using skilful means (for saving others). 방편유여토 方便有餘土 One of the T'ien-t'ai 사토 四土 Four Lands, which is temporary, as its occupants still have remains to be purged away. 방편살생 方便殺生 The right of great Bodhisattvas, knowing every one's karma, to kill without sinning, e.g. in order to prevent a person from committing sin involving unintermitted suffering, or to aid him in reaching one of the higher reincarnations. 방편바라밀 方便波羅蜜 Upāya, the seventh pāramitā. 방편바라밀보살 方便波羅蜜菩薩 A bodhisattva in the Garbhadhātu group, the second on the right in the hall of Space. 방편현열반 方便現涅槃 Though the Buddha is eternal, he showed himself as temporarily extinct, as necessary to arouse a longing for Buddha, cf. Lotus, 16. 방편문 方便門 The gates of upāya, i.e. convenient or expedient gates leading into Truth. 방편가문 方便假門 Expedient gates or ways of using the seeming for the real.

배 杯 A cup. 배도 杯度 Pei-tu, a fifth-century Buddhist monk said to be able to cross a river in a cup or bowl, hence his name.

배 背 Back, behind ; turn the back on, go contrary to ; carry on the back. 배념 背念 To turn one's back on the transmigration life and abide quietly in the nirvāṇa-mind. 배사 背捨 To turn the back on and leave (the world). 배정 背正 To turn the back on Buddha-truth. 배회경병 背繪經屛 To mince fish on the back of an image, and paste up the scriptures as a screen from the wind — a man without conscience.

배 裴 Beautifully robed. 배불략 裴弗略 Vaipulya, enlarged, v. 방 方.

배 倍 Double, double-fold, a fold ; to turn from or against, to revolt. 배리 倍離 To turn from and depart from.

배 拜 Pay respect (with the hands), worship ; the forms of bowing and kneeling are meticulously regulated. 배불 拜佛 To worship the Buddhas, etc.

배 陪 To accompany, associated with ; add to, assist. 배식 陪食 To keep one company at meals. 배려 陪臚 ; 배라부 陪囉嚩 Bhairava, the terrible, name of Śiva, also of Viṣṇu and other devas, also of a 금강신 金剛神.

백 柏 Cypress, cedar, *Arbor vitae.*

백 白 White, pure, clear ; make clear, inform.

백 百 Śata ; a hundred, all. 백일 百一 One out of a hundred ; or every one of a hundred, i.e. all.

백계 百界 The ten realms each of ten divisions, so called by the T'ien-t'ai school, i.e. of hells, ghosts, animals, asuras, men, devas, śrāvakas, pratyeka-buddhas, bodhisattvas, and Buddhas. Each of the hundred has ten qualities, making in all 백계천여 百界千如 the thousand qualities of the hundred realms ; this 1,000 being multiplied by the three of past, present, future, there are 3,000 ; to behold these 3,000 in an instant is called 일념삼천(지관법) 一念三千(之觀法) and the sphere envisaged is the 백계천여 百界千如.

백고좌회 百高座會 A dharma service with Hundred High Seats.

백광변조왕 百光遍照王 The king of all light universally shining, i.e. Vairocana.

백구지 百俱胝 100 koṭīs.

백납의 百衲衣 A monk's robe made of patches.

백념(적) 白拈(賊) Robbing with bare hands and without leaving a trace, as 백전 白戰 is fighting without weapons, and 백절 白折 is killing with bare hands.

백단 白檀 White candana, or white sandal-wood.

백련교 白蓮教 The White Lily Society, set up near the end of the Yüan dynasty, announcing the coming of Maitreya, the opening of his white lily, and the day of salvation at hand. It developed into a revolution which influenced the expulsion of the Mongols and establishment of the Ming dynasty. Under the Ch'ing dynasty it was resurrected under a variety of names, and caused various uprisings. 백련채 白蓮菜 The Sung vegetarian school of 모자원 茅子元 Mao Tzŭ-yüan. 백련(화) 白蓮(華) ; 분다리 分陀利 Puṇḍarīka, the white lotus. 백련화좌 白蓮華座 The lotus throne in the first court of the Garbhadhātu. 백련(화)사 白蓮(華)社 ; 백련지교 白蓮之交 ; 연사 蓮社 A society formed early in the fourth century A.D. by 혜원 慧遠 Hui-yüan, who with 123 notable literati, swore to a life of purity before the image of Amitābha, and planted white lotuses in symbol. An account of seven of its succeeding patriarchs is given in the 불조통기 佛祖統紀 26 ; as also of eighteen of its worthies.

백로지 白鷺池 The White Heron Lake in Rājagṛha, the scene of Śākyamuni's reputed delivery of part of the Mahāprajñāpāramitā-sūtra 대반야경 大般若經 chüan 593-600, the last of the "16 assemblies" of this sūtra, which is also called the 백로지경 白鷺池經.

백론 百論 Śataśāstra. One of the 삼론 三論 "three śāstras" of the Mādhyamika school, so called because of its 100 verses, each of 32 words ; attributed to Devabodhisattva, it was written in Sanskrit by Vasubandhu and tr. by Kumārajīva, but the versions differ. There is also the 광백론본 廣百論本 Catuḥśataka-[śāstrakārikā], an expansion of the above.

백마사 白馬寺 The White Horse Temple recorded as given to the Indian monks, Mātaṅga and Gobharaṇa, who are reputed to have been fetched from India to China in A.D. 64. The temple was in Honan, in Lo-yang the capital ; it was west of the ancient city, east of the later city. According to tradition, originating at the end of the second century A.D., the White Horse Temple was so called because of the white horse which carried the sūtras they brought.

백만편 百萬遍 To repeat Amitābha's name a million times (ensures rebirth in his Paradise ; for a seven days' unbroken repetition Paradise may be gained).

백목 百目 An earthenware lantern, i.e. with many eyes or holes.

백미 百味 All the (good) tastes, or flavours.

백반왕 白飯王 Śuklodana-rāja, a prince of Kapilavastu, second son of Siṁhahanu, father of Tiṣya 제사 帝沙, Devadatta 조달 調達, and Nandika 난제가 難提迦. [Eitel].

백법 百法 The hundred divisions of all mental qualities and their agents, of the 유식 唯識 School ; also known as the 오위백법 五位百法 five groups of the 100 modes of "things": (1) 심법 心法 the eight 식 識 perceptions, or forms of consciousness ; (2) 심소유법 心所有法 the fifty-one mental ideas ; (3) 색법 色法 the five physical organs and their six modes of sense, e.g. ear and sound ; (4) 불상응행 不相應行 twenty-four indefinites, or unconditioned elements ; (5) 무위 無爲 six inactive or metaphysical concepts. 백법명문 百法明門 The door to the knowledge of universal phenomena, one of the first stages of Bodhisattva progress. The 백법(명문)론 百法(明門)論 was tr. by Hsüan-tsang in 1 chüan. 백법계 百法界 The realm of the hundred qualities, i.e. the phenomenal realm ; the ten stages from Hades to Buddha, each has ten 여시 如是 or qualities which make up the hundred ; cf. 백계 百界.

백보 白報 Pure reward, or the reward of a good life.

백복 百福 The hundred blessings, every kind of happiness.

백본소주 百本疏主 Lord of the hundred commentaries, title of K'uei-chi 규기 窺基 of the 자은사 慈恩寺 T'zŭ-ên monastery, because of his work as a commentator ; also 백본논사 百本論師.

백부지 百不知 or **백불회** 百不會 To know or perceive nothing, insensible (to surroundings).

백불 白佛 To tell the Buddha.

백사십불공법 百四十不共法 The 140 special, or uncommon, characteristics of a Buddha, i.e. 삼십이상 三十二相 ; 팔십종호 八十種好 ; 사정 四淨 ; 십력 十力 ; 사무외 四無畏 ; 삼념처 三念處 ; 삼불호 三不護 ; 대비 大悲 ; 상불망실 常不忘失 ; 단번뇌습 斷煩惱習 ; 일체지 一切智.

백산불정 白傘佛頂 ; **백개불정** 白蓋佛頂 The white umbrella or canopy over the head of buddha, indicating him as a cakravartī, or wheel-king.

백상 白象 The six-tusked white elephant which bore the Buddha on his descent from the Tuṣita heaven into Māyā's womb, through her side. Every Buddha descends in similar fashion. The immaculate path, i.e. the immaculate conception (of Buddha).

백수성 白水城 White-river town, Isfijab, "in Turkestan, situated on a small tributary of the Jaxartes in Lat. 38°30'N., Long 65°E." [Eitel].

백심 白心 A clear heart or conscience.

백양사 白羊寺 Baek-yang-sa. A temple located in Yaksu-ri Bukha-myeon Jangseong-gun Jeollanam-do in Korea. The 18th parish headquarters of Korean Jogye Order.

백우 白牛 A white ox ; 백우무각 白牛無角 a hornless white ox : a horse.

백운 경한 白雲景閑 Baeg-un Gyeong-han(1299-1374). A monk of the late Goryeo dynasty in Korea.

백운(종) 白雲(宗) A Buddhist school formed in the White Cloud monastery during the Sung dynasty ; its followers were known as the 백운채 白雲菜 White Cloud vegetarians.

백월 白月 Śuklapakṣa 백분 白分 ; the bright, i.e. first half of the month, as contrasted with the 흑분 黑分 kṛṣṇapakṣa, dark or latter half.

백유경 百喩經 The sūtra of the 100 parables, tr. by Guṇavṛddhi, late fifth century ; also 백비경 百譬經.

백의 白衣 White clothing, said to be that of Brahmans and other people, hence it and 백속 白俗 are terms for the common people. It is a name also for Kuan-yin. 백의관음 白衣觀音 ; 백처관음 白處觀音 ; 백의대사 白衣大士 ; 반나라부실녕 半拏囉嚩悉寧 Pāṇḍaravāsinī, the white-robed form of Kuan-yin on a white lotus.

백이십팔근본번뇌 百二十八根本煩惱 The 128 delusions of 견 見 views and 사 思 thoughts ; also called 백이십팔사 百二十八使 v. 사 使.

백일갈마 白一羯磨 ; **백이갈마** 白二羯磨 Jñaptidvitīyā karmavācanā ; to discuss with and explain to the body of monks the proposals or work to be undertaken ; 백사갈마 白四羯磨 is to consult with them on matters of grave moment and obtain their complete assent.

백장 百丈 A hundred fathoms of 10 feet each, 1,000 feet ; the name of a noted T'ang abbot of 백장산 百丈山 Pai Chang Shan, the monastery of this name in 홍주 洪州 Hung-chou.

백족(화상) 白足(和尙) ; **백족아련** 白足阿練 The white-foot monk, a disciple of Kumārajīva.

백중학 百衆學 Śikṣākaraṇīya, what all monks and nuns learn, the offence against which is duṣkṛta, v. 돌 突.

백즉백생 百卽百生 Of 100 who call on the Buddha 100 will be saved, all will live.

백진 白眞 To lay a true information.

백찬 白贊 To speak praises to the Buddha.

백추 白槌 ; **백추** 白椎 The informing baton or hammer, calling attention to a plaint, or for silence to give information.

백파 긍선 白坡亘璇 Baek-pa Geung-seon(1767-1852). A monk of the Joseon dynasty in Korea. He restored the contemporary Seon(Ch'an, Zen) tradition. He wrote several books, such as 정혜결사문 定慧結社文.

백팔 百八 108. 백팔환 百八丸 ; 백팔수주 百八數珠 ; 백팔모니 百八牟尼 108 beads on a rosary. 백팔존 百八尊 The 108 honourable ones in the Vajradhātu. 백팔번뇌 百八煩惱 The 108 passions and delusions, also called 백팔결업 百八結業 the 108 karmaic bonds. 백팔종 百八鍾 The 108 tolls of the monastery bell at dawn and dusk.

백호 白毫 The curl between Śākyamuni's eyebrows ; from it, in the Mahāyāna sūtras, he sends out a ray of light which reveals all worlds ; it is used as a synonym of the Buddha, e.g. 백호지사 白毫之賜 (all that a monk has is) a gift from the White-curled One.

백회 百會 Where all things meet, i.e. the head, the place of centralization ; it is applied also to the Buddha as the centre of all wisdom.

백흑 白黑 White and dark, e.g. 백흑업 白黑業 good and evil deeds, or karma ; 백흑포살 白黑布薩 light and dark uposatha, the observances of the waxing and waning moon, cf. 백월 白月.

번 鑁 Translit. *vaṁ*, associated with water and the ocean ; also, the embodiment of wisdom.

번 翻 ; **번** 繙 To translate, interpret. 번범 翻梵 To translate from Sanskrit. 번경 翻經 To translate the scriptures. 번역 翻譯 To translate, interpret. 번역명의집 翻譯名義集 *Fan i ming i chi*, a dictionary of Buddhist technical terms compiled by 법운 法雲 Fa-yün *circa* A.D. 1150.

번 樊 A cage, fence. 번롱 樊籠 A cage, the cage of karma, or the world with its suffering, etc.

번 番 Barbarian, foreign ; a time, a turn. 번승 番僧 Foreign monk, especially from India or the west ; also a temple warden or watchman.

번 幡 Patākā, a flag, banner.

번 旛 Patākā, a flag, streamer. 기번 旗旛 Banners and flags, flags.

번 煩 Trouble, annoyance, perplexity.

번뇌 煩惱 Kleśa, "pain, affliction, distress", "care, trouble" [M. W.] The Chinese tr. is similar, distress, worry, trouble, and whatever causes them. Keith interprets kleśa by "infection", "contamination", "defilement". The Chinese intp. is the delusions, trials, or temptations of the passions and of ignorance which disturb and distress the mind ; also in brief as the three poisons 탐진치 貪瞋痴 desire, detestation, and delusion. There is a division into the six fundamental 번뇌 煩惱, or afflictions, v. below, and the twenty which result or follow them ; and there are other dual divisions. The six are : 탐진치만의 貪瞋痴慢疑 and 악견 惡見 desire, detestation, delusion, pride, doubt, and evil views, which last are the false views of a permanent ego, etc. The ten 번뇌 煩惱 are the first five, and the sixth subdivided into five. 번뇌 煩惱, like kleśa, implies moral affliction or distress, trial, temptation, tempting, sin. Cf. 사 使.

번뇌니 煩惱泥 The soil or mud of moral affliction, out of which grows the lotus of enlightenment.

번뇌도 煩惱道 The way of temptation, or passion, in producing bad karma.

번뇌림 煩惱林 The forest of moral affliction.

번뇌마 煩惱魔 The māra of the passions who troubles mind and body ; the tempter ; cf. 사 使.

번뇌병 煩惱病 The disease of moral affliction.

번뇌빙 煩惱冰 The ice of moral affliction, i.e. its congealing, chilling influence on bodhi.

번뇌습 煩惱習 The habit or influence of the passions after they have been cut off.

번뇌신 煩惱薪 The faggots of passion, which are burnt up by the fire of wisdom.

번뇌애 煩惱礙 The obstruction of temptation, or defilement, to entrance into nirvāṇa peace by perturbing the mind.

번뇌업고 煩惱業苦 The suffering arising out of the working of the passions, which produce good or evil karma, which in turn results in a happy or suffering lot in one of the three realms, and again from the lot of suffering (or mortality) arises the karma of the passions ; also known as 혹업고 惑業苦, 삼륜 三輪, and 삼도 三道.

번뇌여 煩惱餘 The remnants of illusion after it has been cut off in the realms of desire, form, and formlessness — a Hīnayāna term.

번뇌장 煩惱障 The barrier of temptation, passion, or defilement, which obstructs the attainment of the nirvāṇa-mind.

번뇌장 煩惱藏 The store of moral affliction, or defilement, contained in the five 주지 住地, q.v.

번뇌적 煩惱賊 Temptation, or passion, as a thief injuring the spiritual nature.

번뇌즉보리 煩惱卽菩提 The passions, or moral afflictions, are bodhi, i.e. the one is included in the other ; it is a T'ien-t'ai term, and said to be the highest expression of Mahāyāna thought ; cf. 즉 卽.

번뇌진 煩惱陣 The army of temptations, tempters, or allurements.

번뇌탁 煩惱濁 The impurity, or defiling nature of the passions, one of the five 탁 濁.

번뇌하 煩惱河 The river of moral affliction which overwhelms all beings.

번뇌해 煩惱海 The ocean of moral affliction which engulfs all beings.

번담 煩談 Vandana, obeisance, worship, v. 화 和.

번롱 煩籠 The basket of the troublers, i.e. the passions.

벌 筏 A raft. 벌유 筏喩 Raft parable. Buddha's teaching is like a raft, a means of crossing the river, the raft being left when the crossing has been made. 벌소밀달라 筏蘇蜜呾羅 or 伐蘇蜜呾羅 ; 벌소밀다라 筏蘇蜜多羅 or 伐蘇蜜多羅 ; 바소밀달라 婆蘇蜜呾羅 or 바소밀다라 婆蘇蜜多羅 ; 바수밀 婆須蜜 ; 화수밀다 和須蜜多 ; 세우 世友 Vasumitra, described as a native of northern India, converted from riotous living by Micchaka, "was a follower of the Sarvāstivāda school," became president of the last synod for the revision of the Canon under Kaniṣka, q.v., was seventh patriarch, and "wrote the Abhidharma-prakaraṇa-pāda śāstra" [Eitel]. 벌소반두 筏蘇盤豆 ; v. 파 婆 Vasubandhu. 벌소지 筏蘇枳 Vāsuki, or 화수길 和須吉 ; lord of snakes, or nāgas. 벌차자 筏蹉子 Vātsīputra, founder of the 독자부 犢子部 v. 발 跋.

벌 伐 To cut down, chastise ; a go-between ; to make a display ; translit. *va*. 벌가 伐伽 ; 발거 跋渠 Varga, tr. by 부 部 a class, division, group. 벌랄나 伐剌拏 Varaṇa, "a mountainous province of Kapiśā with city of the same name, probably the country south-east of Wauneh in Lat. 32° 30 N., Long. 69° 25 E." [Eitel]. Perhaps Bannu, v. Lévi, *J. Asiatique*, XI, v, p. 73. Also v. 장 障. 벌지 伐地 Vadi or Vati. "An ancient little kingdom and city on the Oxus, the modern Betik, Lat. 39° 7 N., Long. 63° 10 E." [Eitel]. 벌절라 伐折羅 Vajra. 벌사라 伐闍羅 ; 박왈라 縛曰羅 ; 부왈라 囀曰羅 ; 발왈라 跋曰囉 ; 부일라 囀馹囉 ; 발절라 跋折羅 ; 발사라 跋闍羅 ; 발절다 跋折多 ; 바사라 波闍羅 ; 발사라 髮闍羅, tr. by 금강(저) 金剛(杵) Diamond club ; the thunderbolt, svastika ; recently defined by Western scholars as a sun symbol. It is one of the saptaratna, seven precious things ; the sceptre of Indra as god of thunder and lightning, with which he slays the enemies of Buddhism ; the sceptre of the exorcist ; the symbol of the all-conquering power of Buddha. 벌절라다라 伐折羅陀羅 ; 지금강 持金剛 ; 집금강 執金剛 Vajradhara, the bearer of the vajra. 벌절사부라 伐折闍囀羅 Vajrajvāla, i.e. flame, tr. as 금강광 金剛光 the scintillation of the diamond, the lightning. 벌랑가 伐浪伽 Varāṅga, name of a spirit, or god ; a name of Viṣṇu as beautiful. 벌납비 伐臘毗 Valabhī. Modern Wālā. "An ancient kingdom and city on the eastern coast of Gujerat." [Eitel]. Known also as 북라 北羅 northern Lāṭa. 벌소밀달라 伐蘇蜜呾羅 Vasumitra, v. 벌 筏. 벌소반도 伐蘇槃度 ; 벌소반도 伐蘇畔度 ; 바수반두 婆藪槃豆 Vasubandhu, v. 천친 天親. 벌나바사 伐那婆斯 Vanavāsin, one of the sixteen arhats. 벌리사 伐里沙 Varṣa, rain ; name of a noted Sāṁkhya leader, Vārṣagaṇya. 벌사라불다라 伐闍羅弗多羅 Vajraputra, one of the sixteen arhats.

범 凡 All, everybody, common, ordinary. 범승 凡僧 The ordinary practising monk as contrasted with the 성승 聖僧 the holy monk who has achieved higher merit. 범부 凡夫 ; 파라 波羅 ; 파라필율탁흘나 婆羅必栗託仡那 ; 파라필리타가사나 婆羅必利他伽闍那 Bālapṛthagjana. Everyman, the worldly man, the sinner. Explained by 이생 異生 or 우이생 愚異生 one who is born different, or outside the Law of the Buddha, because of his karma. 범부십중망 凡夫十重妄 The serious misfortunes of the sinful man in whom the Ālaya-vijñāna, the fundamental intelligence, or life force, of everyman, is still unenlightened ; they are compared to ten progressive stages of a dream in which a rich man sees himself become poor and in prison. 범(부)성 凡(夫)性 The common underlying nature of all men ; also called 이생성 異生性. 범소 凡小 Common men, or sinners, also believers in Hīnayāna ; also the unenlightened in general. 범소팔도 凡小八倒 The eight subverted views of common men and Hīnayānists – counting the impermanent as permanent, the non-joy as joy, the non-ego as ego, the impure as pure ; the really permanent as impermanent, the real joy, the true ego, the real purity as non-joy, non-ego, impurity ; cf. 사덕 四德. 범사 凡師 Ordinary, or worldly teachers unenlightened by Buddhist truth. 범정 凡情 Desires or passions of the unconverted. 범우 凡愚 Common, ignorant, or unconverted men. 범려 凡慮 The anxieties of common or unconverted men. 범복 凡福 The ordinary blessedness of devas and men as compared with that of the converted. 범종 凡種 Common seed, ordinary people. 범습 凡習 The practices, good and evil, of common, or unconverted men. 범성 凡聖 Sinners and saints. 범성일여 凡聖一如 ; 범성불이 凡聖不二 Sinners and saints are of the same fundamental nature. 범성동거토 凡聖同居土 This world, where saints and sinners dwell together ; one of the T'ien-t'ai 사토 四土. 범식 凡識 Ordinary knowledge, worldly knowledge, that of the unenlightened by Buddha. 범신 凡身 The common mortal body, the ordinary individual.

범 梵 Brahman (from roots *bṛh, vṛh*, connected with *bṛṁh*), "religious devotion," "prayer," "a sacred text," or mantra, "the mystic syllable *Om*" ; "sacred learning," "the religious life," "the Supreme Being regarded as impersonal," "the Absolute," "the priestly or sacerdotal class," etc. [M. W.] Translit. 범마 梵摩 ; 범람마 梵覽摩 or 梵覽磨 ; 발람마 勃嚂摩 ; 바라하마 婆羅賀摩 ; 몰라감마 沒羅憾摩 ; intp. as Brahmā, see 범천 梵天 ; and brahman, or priest ; it is used both in a noble and ignoble sense, ignoble when disparaging brahman opposition ; it is intp. by 정 淨 pure, also by 이욕청정 離欲清淨 celibate and pure.

범 範 Pattern, rule, method. 범위 範衛 Rule and restraint ; to guard by proper means.

범 犯 To offend against, break (as a law). 범계 犯戒 To offend against or break the moral or ceremonial laws (of Buddhism). 범중 犯重 To break the weightier laws.

범가이 梵迦夷 Brahmakāyikas ; the Brahma-devas ; v. 범천 梵天.

범궁 梵宮 Brahmā's palace ; a Buddhist temple.

범궁 梵宮 The realm of Brahmā ; the first dhyāna heaven of the realm of form.

범난 梵難 The difficulty of maintaining celibacy, or purity.

범녀 梵女 A noble woman, a woman of high character.

범단 梵壇 or **범달** 梵怛 Brahmadaṇḍa, Brahma-staff 범장 梵杖, the Brahma (i.e. religious) punishment (stick), but the derivation is uncertain ; the explanation is "to send to Coventry" a recalcitrant monk, the forbidding of any conversation with him, called also 묵빈 默擯 exclusion to silence.

범덕 梵德 The power, or bliss, of Brahmā.

범도 梵道 The way of purity, or celibacy ; the brahman way.

범륜 梵輪 The brahma-wheel, the wheel of the law, or pure preaching of the Buddha ; his four 범행 梵行 v. 사무량심 四無量心 ; the first sermon at the request of Brahmā ; the doctrine or preaching of the Brahmans.

범마 梵摩 Brahmā ; brahman, etc. v. 범 梵 ; 범천 梵天, etc. 범마삼발 梵摩三鉢 Brahmā-sahāṁpati, or Mahābrahmā-sahāṁpati ; Brahmā, lord of the world. 범마니 梵摩尼 Brahma-maṇi, pure pearl, or the magic pearl of Brahmā. 범마라 梵摩羅 Brahman, i.e. Brahmā ; or Brahmā and Māra ; or both as one. 범마달 梵摩達 Brahmadatta, a king of Kanyākubja. A king of Vārāṇasī, father of Kāśyapa.

범마 梵魔 Brahmā and Māra, the former lord of the realm of form, the latter of desire or passion.

범망 梵網 Brahmajāla ; Brahma-net. 범망종 梵網宗 The sect of Ritsu 율종 律宗, brought into Japan by the Chinese monk 감진 鑑眞 Chien-chên in A.D. 754. 범망경 梵網經 Brahmajāla sūtra, tr. by Kumārajīva A.D. 406, the infinitude of worlds being as the eyes or holes in Indra's net, which is all-embracing, like the Buddha's teaching. There are many treatises on it. 범망계품 梵網戒品 A name for the above, or the next. 범망계본 梵網戒本 ; 보살계경 菩薩戒經 The latter part of the above sūtra.

범면불 梵面佛 A Buddha with Brahma's face, said to be 23,000 years old.

범복 梵服 The kaṣāya or monk's robe ; the garment of celibacy.

범본 梵本 Sūtras in the Indian language.

범부루 梵富樓 Brahmapurohita, the ministers, or assistants of Brahmā ; the second Brahmaloka ; the second region of the first dhyāna heaven of form. Also 범보 梵輔.

범상 梵相 Brahmadhvaja, one of the sons of Mahābhijñā ; his Buddha domain is south-west of our universe.

범석 梵釋 Brahmā, the lord of the form-realm, and Śakra of the desire-realm. 범석사천 梵釋四天 Brahmā, Śakra, and the four Mahārājas.

범성 梵聲 The voice of Buddha.

범세계 梵世界 The Brahmaloka of the realm of form ; also 범세천 梵世天.

범승 梵僧 A monk from India. Also a monk who maintains his purity.

범승 梵乘 The brahmayāna, i.e. the noblest of the vehicles, that of the bodhisattva.

범신 梵身 The pure spiritual body, or dharmakāya, of the Buddha, v. 법신 法身. 범신천 梵身天 The Brahmakāyika, or retinue of Brahmā.

범실 梵室 A dwelling where celibate discipline is practised, a monastery, temple.

범심 梵心 The noble or pure mind (which practises the discipline that ensures rebirth in the realm without form).

범어 梵語 Brahma language, Sanskrit, the Sanskrit alphabet ; "the language of India" ; supposed to come from Brahmā.

범어사 梵魚寺 Beom-eo-sa. A temple located in Cheongryong-dong Geumjeong-gu, Busan-si in Korea. The 14th parish headquarters of Korean Jogye Order.

범연나 梵衍那 Bayana, "an ancient kingdom and city in Bokhara famous for a colossal statue of Buddha (entering Nirvāṇa) believed to be 1,000 feet long." [Eitel]. The modern Bamian.

범왕 梵王 Brahmā, cf. 범천 梵天. The father of all living beings ; the first person of the Brahminical Trimūrti, Brahmā, Viṣṇu, and Śiva, recognized by Buddhism as devas but as inferior to a Buddha, or enlightened man. 범왕궁 梵王宮 The palace of Brahmā.

범우 梵宇 A sacred house, i.e. a Buddhist monastery, or temple.

범원 梵苑 A monastery or any place where celibate discipline is practised.

범음 梵音 (1) Brahma voice, clear, melodious, pure, deep, far-reaching, one of the thirty-two marks of a Buddha. (2) Singing in praise of Buddha.

범자 梵字 Brahma letters ; Saṁskṛtam ; Sanskrit ; also 범서 梵書 The classical Aryan language of India, systematized by scholars, in contradistinction to Prākrit, representing the languages as ordinarily spoken. With the exception of a few ancient translations probably from Pāli versions, most of the original texts used in China were Sanskrit. Various alphabets have been introduced into China for transliterating Indian texts, the Devanāgarī alphabet, which was introduced via Tibet, is still used on charms and in sorcery. Pāli is considered by some Chinese writers to be more ancient than Sanskrit both as a written and spoken language.

범장 梵章 Brahmavastu, a Sanskrit syllabary in twelve parts.

범전 梵典 Buddhist sūtras, or books.

범정 梵廷 Brahmā and Nārāyaṇa.

범종 梵鐘 A temple or monastery bell, especially a large bell located in a bell tower.

범중 梵衆 Monks, so called because of their religious practices. 범중천 梵衆天 Brahmapāriṣadya (or Brahmapārṣadya), belonging to the retinue of Brahmā ; the first Brahmaloka ; the first region of the first dhyāna heaven of form.

범지 梵志 Brahmacārin. "Studying sacred learning ; practising continence or chastity." [M. W.] A Brahmacārī is a "young Brahman in the first āśrama or period of his life" [M. W.] ; there are four such periods. A Buddhist ascetic with his will set on 범 梵 purity, also intp. as nirvāṇa.

범찰 梵刹 Brahmakṣetra, Buddha-land ; a name for a Buddhist monastery, i.e. a place of purity.

범천 梵天 Brahmadeva. Brahmā, the ruler of this world. India. Brahmaloka, the eighteen heavens of the realm of form, divided into four dhyāna regions (sixteen heavens in Southern Buddhism). The first three contain the 범중천 梵衆天 assembly of brahmadevas, i.e. the Brahmakāyika ; the 범보천 梵輔天 Brahmapurohitas, retinue of Brahmā ; and 대범천 大梵天 Mahābrahman, Brahman himself. 범천외도 梵天外道 Brahmadeva heretics ; the Brahmans consider Brahmā to be the Creator of all things and the Supreme Being, which is heresy with Buddhism. 범천후 梵天后 The queen, or wife of Brahmā. 범천녀 梵天女 A devī in the Garbhadhātu group. 범천왕 梵天王 Brahmā, v. above, and cf. 범왕 梵王. 범천계 梵天界 His realm.

범토 梵土 Brahman-land, India.

범패 梵唄 Buddhist hymns, cf. 패 唄. They are sung to repress externals and calm the mind within for religious service ; also in praise of Buddha.

범학 梵學 The study of Buddhism ; the study of Brahmanism.

범행 梵行 Pure living ; noble action ; the discipline of celibacy which ensures rebirth in the Brahmaloka, or in the realms beyond form.

범향 梵響 The sound of Buddha's voice ; his preaching.

범협 梵夾 Palm-leaf scriptures ; also 범협 梵莢 ; 범협 梵篋 ; 범협 梵挾 ; 경협 經夾.

범황 梵皇 The Indian Emperor, Buddha.

법 法 Dharma ; (1) thing, object, appearance ; (2) characteristic, attribute, predicate ; (3) the substantial bearer of the transcendent substratum of the simple element of conscious life ; (4) element of conscious life ; (5) nirvāṇa, i.e. dharma *par excellence* ; (6) the absolute, the truly real ; (7) the teaching, the religion of Buddha. 달마 達磨 ; 담무 曇無 or 담마 曇摩 ; 달마 達摩 or 달모 達謨 Law, truth, religion, thing, anything Buddhist. Dharma is "that which is held fast or kept, ordinance, statute, law, usage, practice, custom" ; "duty" ; "right" ; "proper" ; "morality" ; "character." [M. W.] It is used in the sense of 일체 一切 all things, or anything small or great, visible or invisible, real or unreal, affairs, truth, principle, method, concrete things, abstract ideas, etc. Dharma is described as that which has entity and bears its own attributes. It connotes Buddhism as the perfect religion ; it also has the second place in the Triratna 불법승 佛法僧, and in the sense of 법신 法身 Dharmakāya it approaches the Western idea of "spiritual." It is also one of the six media of sensation, i.e. the thing or object in relation to mind, v. 육진 六塵.

법가 法家 Buddhism ; cf. 법문 法門.

법간 法慳 Meanness in offering Buddha-truth, avariciously holding on to it for oneself.

법거 法炬 The torch of Buddhism.

법검 法劍 The sword of Buddha-truth, able to cut off the functioning of illusion.

법견 法見 Maintaining one tenet and considering others wrong ; narrow-minded, bigoted.

법경 法鏡 The Dharma mirror, reflecting the Buddha-wisdom.

법계 法界 Dharmadhātu, 법성 法性 ; 실상 實相 ; 달마타도 達磨馱都 Dharma-element, -factor, or -realm. (1) A name for "things" in general, noumenal or phenomenal ; for the physical universe, or any portion or phase of it. (2) The unifying underlying spiritual reality regarded as the ground or cause of all things, the absolute from which all proceeds. It is one of the eighteen dhātus. There are categories of three, four, five, and ten dharmadhātus ; the first three are combinations of 사 事 and 리 理 or active and passive, dynamic and static ; the ten are : Buddha-realm, Bodhisattva-realm, Pratyekabuddha-realm, Śrāvaka-realm, Deva-realm, Human-realm, Asura-realm, Demon-realm, Animal-realm, and Hades-realm — a Hua-yen category. T'ien-t'ai has ten for meditation, i.e. the realms of the eighteen media of perception (the six organs, six objects, and six sense-data or sensations), of illusion, sickness, karma, māra, samādhi, (false) views, pride, the two lower Vehicles, and the Bodhisattva Vehicle. 법계일상 法界一相 The essential unity of the phenomenal realm.

법계불 法界佛 The Dharmadhātu Buddha, i.e. the Dharmakāya ; the universal Buddha ; the Buddha of a Buddha-realm. 법계가지 法界加持 Mutual dependence and aid of all beings in a universe. 법계유심 法界唯心 The universe is mind only ; cf. Hua-yen sūtra, Laṅkāvatāra-sūtra, etc. 법계원융 法界圓融 The perfect inter-communion or blending of all things in the Dharmadhātu ; the 무애 無礙 of Hua-yen and the 성구 性具 of T'ien-t'ai. 법계정 法界定 In dharmadhātu meditation, a term for Vairocana in both maṇḍalas. 법계궁 法界宮 The dharmadhātu-palace, i.e. the shrine of Vairocana in the Garbhadhātu. 법계실상 法界實相 Dharmadhātu-reality, or Dharmadhātu is Reality, different names but one idea, i.e. 실상 實相 is used for 리 理 or noumenon by the 별교 別教 and 법계 法界 by the 원교 圓教. 법계성 法界性 idem 법계 法界 and 법성 法性. 법계무애지 法界無礙智 ; 법계불변지 法界佛邊智 The unimpeded or unlimited knowledge or omniscience of a Buddha in regard to all beings and things in his realm. 법계등류 法界等流 The universal outflow of the spiritual body of the Buddha, i.e. his teaching. 법계연기 法界緣起 The Dharmadhātu as the environmental cause of all phenomena, everything being dependent on everything else, therefore one is in all and all in one. 법계장 法界藏 The treasury or storehouse or source of all phenomena, or truth. 법계신 法界身 The Dharmakāya (manifesting itself in all beings) ; the Dharmadhātu as the Buddhakāya, all things being Buddha. 법계체성지 法界體性智 Intelligence as the fundamental nature of the universe ; Vairocana as cosmic energy and wisdom interpenetrating all elements of the universe, a term used by the esoteric sects.

법고 法鼓 The drum of the Law, stirring all to advance in virtue. A temple drum used in ceremonies.

법공 法公 Signior of the Law, a courtesy title of any monk.

법공 法空 The emptiness or unreality of things, everything being dependent on something else and having no individual existence apart from other things ; hence the illusory nature of all things as being composed of elements and not possessing reality. 법공진여 法空眞如 The Bhūtatathatā as understood when this non-individuality or unreality of "things" is perceived. 법공관 法空觀 Meditative insight into the unreality of all things.

법공 法空 Beop-gong(?-540, reign. 514-540). A monk of the Silla dynasty in Korea. He was the twenty-third king of Silla, 법흥 法興 Beop-heung, who later ordained as a monk. His biography can be found in the "Lives of Eminent Korean Monks."

법공양 法供養 Dharmapūjā. Serving the Dharma, i.e. believing, explaining, keeping, obeying it, cultivating the spiritual nature, protecting and assisting Buddhism. Also, offerings of or to the Dharma.

법광정 法光定 Samādhi of the light of Truth, that of the bodhisattva in the first stage.

법교 法教 Buddhism.

법교 法橋 The bridge of Buddha-truth, which is able to carry all across to nirvāṇa.

법구경 法句經 Dharmapada, 담발경 曇鉢經 a work by Dharmatrāta, of which there are four Chinese translations, A.D. 224, 290-306, 399, 980-1001.

법기 法器 Implements used in worship ; one who obeys the Buddha ; a vessel of the Law.

법긴나라왕 法緊那羅王 Druma, king of the Kinnaras.

법념처 法念處 The position of insight into the truth that nothing has reality in itself ; v. 사념처 四念處.

법니 法尼 A nun.

법다라니 法陀羅尼 One of the four kinds of dhāraṇī : holding firmly to the truth one has heard, also called 문다라니 聞陀羅尼.

법당 法堂 Lit. "Dharma Hall." Buddha Hall. The chief temple, so called by the Ch'an(Zen) sect ; amongst others it is 강당 講堂 preaching hall.

법당 法幢 The standard of Buddha-truth as an emblem of power over the hosts of Māra.

법도 法度 Rules, or disciplines and methods.

법동사 法同舍 A communal religious abode, i.e. a monastery or convent where religion and food are provided for spiritual and temporal needs.

법등 法燈 The lamp of dharma, which dispels the darkness of ignorance.

법라 法螺 Conch of the Law, a symbol of the universality, power, or command of the Buddha's teaching. Cf. 상거 商佉 Śaṅkha.

법락 法樂 Religious joy, in contrast with the joy of common desire ; that of hearing the dharma, worshipping Buddha, laying up merit, making offerings, repeating sūtras, etc.

법란 法蘭 Gobharana, 축법란 竺法蘭, companion of Mātaṅga, these two being the first Indian monks said to have come to China, in the middle of the first century A.D.

법랍 法臘 The end of the monk's year after the summer retreat ; a Buddhist year ; the number of 하랍 夏臘 or 계랍 戒臘 summer or discipline years indicating the years since a monk's ordination.

법문 法門 Lit. "dharma-gate." Dharma-talk ; formal lecture (which provides a 'gate' by which the listener may enter the 'dharma'), usually given by a zen master.

법장 法場 Any place set aside for religious practices, or purposes ; also 도량 道場.

법려 法侶 A companion of the Dharma, a disciple.

법력 法力 The power of Buddha-truth to do away with calamity and subdue evil.

법령 法鈴 The dharma-bell ; the pleasing sound of intoning the sūtras.

법뢰 法雷 The thunder of dharma, awakening man from stupor and stimulating the growth of virtue, the awful voice of Buddha-truth. 법전 法電 The lightning of the Truth.

법륜 法輪 Dharma-cakra, the Wheel of the Law, Buddha-truth which is able to crush all evil and all opposition, like Indra's wheel, and which rolls on from man to man, place to place, age to age. 전법륜 轉法輪 To turn, or roll along the Law-wheel, i.e. to preach Buddha-truth.

법률 法律 Laws or rules (of the Order).

법리 法利 The blessing, or benefits, of Buddhism.

법마 法魔 Bemused by things ; the illusion that things are real and not merely seeming.

법멸 法滅 The extinction of the Law, or Buddhism, after the third of the three stages 정상말 政像末.

법명 法名 A monk's name, given to him on ordination, a term chiefly used by the 진 眞 Shin sect, 계명 戒名 being the usual term.

법명 法明 Dharmaprabhāsa, brightness of the law, a Buddha who will appear in our universe in the Ratnāvabhāsa-kalpa in a realm called Suviśuddha 선정 善淨, when there will be no sexual difference, birth taking place by transformation. 법명도 法明道 The wisdom of the pure heart which illumines the Way of all Buddhas. 법명문 法明門 The teaching which sheds light on everything, differentiating and explaining them.

법명 法命 The wisdom-life of the Dharmakāya, intp. as 법신혜명 法身慧命. The age or lifetime of a monk.

법무아 法無我 Dharmanairātmya. Things are without independent individuality, i.e. the tenet that things have no independent reality, no reality in themselves. 법무아지 法無我智 The knowledge or wisdom of the above. 법무애(해) 法無礙(解) or 법무애(지) 法無礙(智) Wisdom or power of explanation in unembarrassed accord with the Law, or Buddha-truth.

법문 法門 Dharmaparyāya. The doctrines, or wisdom of Buddha regarded as the door to enlightenment. A method. Any sect. As the living have 84,000 delusions, so the Buddha provides 84,000 methods 법문 法門 of dealing with them. Hence the 법문해 法門海 ocean of Buddha's methods. 법문신 法門身 A T'ien-t'ai definition of the Dharmakāya of the Trinity, i.e.

the qualities, powers, and methods of the Buddha. The various representations of the respective characteristics of Buddhas and bodhisattvas in the maṇḍalas.

법문 法文 The literature of Buddhism.

법미 法味 The taste or flavour of the dharma.

법밀 法密 Dharmagupta, founder of the school of this name in Ceylon, one of the seven divisions of the Sarvāstivāda.

법바라밀 法波羅蜜 One of the four Pāramitā Bodhisattvas in the Diamond realm.

법박 法縛 idem 법집 法執.

법보 法寶 Dharmaratna. (1) Dharma-treasure, i.e. the Law or Buddha-truth, the second personification in the Triratna 삼보 三寶. (2) The personal articles of monk or nun — robe, almsbowl, etc. 법보장 法寶藏 The storehouse of all law and truth, i.e. the sūtras.

법보화삼신 法報化三身 The Trikāya ; 법신 法身 Dharmakāya, the absolute or spiritual body ; 보신 報身 Sambhogakāya, the body of bliss ; 화신 化身 Nirmāṇakāya, the body of incarnation. In Hīnayāna 법신 法身 is described as the commandments, meditations, wisdom, nirvāṇa, and nirvāṇa-enlightenment ; 보신 報身 is the reward-body of bliss ; 화신 化身 or 응(화)신 應(化)身 is the body in its various incarnations. In Mahāyāna, the three bodies are regarded as distinct, but also as aspects of one body which pervades all beings. Cf. 삼신 三身.

법복 法服 ; 법의 法衣 Dharma garment, the robe.

법본 法本 The root or essence of all things, the bhūtatathatā.

법불 法佛 idem 법신불 法身佛 or 법성불 法性佛.

법비 法譬 Similes or illustrations of the dharma.

법비량 法比量 Inferring one thing from another, as from birth deducing death, etc.

법비법 法非法 Dharmādharma ; real and unreal ; thing and nothing ; being and non-being, etc.

법사 法事 ; **불사** 佛事 Religious affairs, e.g. assemblies and services ; discipline and ritual.

법사 法師 A Buddhist teacher, master of the Law ; five kinds are given — a custodian (of the sūtras), reader, intoner, expounder, and copier.

법사 法沙 Kashgar, "or (after the name of the capital) 소륵 疎勒. An ancient Buddhistic kingdom in Central Asia. The *Casia regis* of the ancients." [Eitel].

법사의 法四依 The four trusts of dharma ; trust in the Law, not in men ; trust in sūtras containing ultimate truth ; trust in truth, not in words ; trust in wisdom growing out of eternal truth and not in illusory knowledge.

법산 法山 Buddha-truth mountain, i.e. the exalted dharma.

법상 法相 The aspects or characteristics of things — all things are of monad nature but differ in form. A name of the 법상종 法相宗 Fa-hsiang or Dharmalakṣaṇa sect (Jap. Hossō), called also 자은종 慈恩宗 Tz'ŭ-ên sect from the T'ang temple, in which lived. 규기 窺基 K'uei-chi, known also as 자은 慈恩. It "aims at discovering the ultimate entity of cosmic existence in contemplation, through investigation into the specific characteristics (the marks or criteria) of all existence, and through the realization of the fundamental nature of the soul in mystic illumination." "An inexhaustible number" of "seeds" are "stored up in the Ālaya-soul ; they manifest themselves in innumerable varieties of existence, both physical and mental." "Though there are infinite varieties ... they all participate in the prime nature of the Ālaya." [Anesaki]. The Fa-hsiang School is one of the "eight schools," and was established in China on the return of Hsüan-tsang, consequent on his translation of the Yogācārya works. Its aim is to understand the principle underlying the 만법성상 萬法性相 or nature and characteristics of all things. Its foundation works are the 해심밀경 解深密經 the 유식론 唯識論, and the 유가론 瑜伽論. It is one of the Mahāyāna realistic schools, opposed by the idealistic schools, e.g. the 삼론 三論 school ; yet it was a "combination of realism and idealism, and its religion a profoundly mystic one." Anesaki. (대승)법상교 (大乘)法相敎 The third of the five periods of doctrinal development as distinguished by 규봉 圭峯 Kuei-fêng.

법서 法誓 A religious vow.

법성 法城 Dharma as a citadel against the false ; the secure nirvāṇa abode ; the sūtras as the guardians of truth.

법성 法性 Dharmatā. Dharma-nature, the nature underlying all things, the bhūtatathatā, a Mahāyāna philosophical concept unknown in Hīnayāna, v. 진여 眞如 and its various definitions in the 법상 法相, 삼론 三論 or 법성 法性, 화엄 華嚴 and 천태 天台 Schools. It is discussed both in its absolute and relative senses, or static and dynamic. In the Mahāparinirvāṇa sūtra and various śāstras the term has numerous alternative forms, which may be taken as definitions, i.e. 법정 法定 inherent dharma, or Buddha-nature ; 법주 法住 abiding dharma-nature ; 법계 法界 dharmakṣetra, realm of dharma ; 법신 法身 dharmakāya, embodiment of dharma ; 실제 實際 region of reality ; 실상 實相 reality ; 공성 空性 nature of the Void, i.e. immaterial nature ; 불성 佛性 Buddha-nature ; 무상 無相 appearance of nothingness, or immateriality ; 진여 眞如 bhūtatathatā ; 여래장 如來藏 Tathāgatagarbha ; 평등성 平等性 universal nature ; 이생성 離生性 immortal nature ; 무아성 無我性 impersonal nature ; 허정계 虛定界 realm of abstraction ; 불허망성 不虛妄性 nature of no illusion ; 불변이성 不變異性 immutable nature ; 부사의계 不思議界 realm beyond thought ; 자성청정심 自性淸淨心 mind of absolute purity, or unsulliedness, etc. Of these the terms 진여 眞如, 법성 法性, and 실제 實際 are most used by the Prajñāpāramitā sūtras. 법성토 法性土 The kṣetra, or region of the dharma-nature, i.e. the bhūtatathatā, or 진여 眞如, in its dynamic relations. 법성종 法性宗 The sects, e.g. 화엄 華嚴 Hua-yen, 천태 天台 T'ien-t'ai, 진언 眞言 Shingon, which hold that all things proceed from the bhūtatathatā, i.e. the Dharmakāya, and that all phenomena are of the same essence as the noumenon. 법성산 法性山 The dharma-nature as a mountain, i.e. fixed, immovable. 법성상락 法性常樂 The eternity and bliss of the dharma-nature, v. 상락아정 常樂我淨. 법성수 法性水 The water of the dharma-nature, i.e. pure. 법성해 法性海 The ocean of the dharma-nature, vast, unfathomable. v. 법수 法水. 법성진여 法性眞如 Dharma-nature and bhūtatathatā, different terms but of the same meaning. 법성신 法性身 idem 법신 法身. 법성수망 法性隨妄 The dharma-nature in the sphere of delusion ; i.e. 법성수연 法性隨緣 ; 진여수연 眞如隨緣 the dharma-nature, or bhūtatathatā, in its phenomenal character ; the dharma-nature may be static or dynamic ; when dynamic it may by environment either become sullied, producing the world of illusion, or remain unsullied, resulting in nirvāṇa. Static, it is likened to a smooth sea ; dynamic, to its waves.

법성취 法成就 Siddhi 실지 悉地 ceremony successful, a term of the esoteric sect when prayer is answered.

법수 法水 Buddha-truth likened to water able to wash away the stains of illusion ; 법하 法河 to a deep river ; 법해 法海 to a vast deep ocean.

법수 法數 The categories of Buddhism such as the three realms, five skandhas, five regions, four dogmas, six paths, twelve nidānas, etc.

법수 法樹 The dharma-tree which bears nirvāṇa-fruit.

법시 法施 The almsgiving of the Buddha-truth, i.e. its preaching or explanation ; also 법보시 法布施.

법식 法食 Dharmāhāra. Diet in harmony with the rules of Buddhism ; truth as food. 법식시 法食時 The regulation time for meals, at or before noon, and not after.

법신 法身 Dharmakāya, embodiment of Truth and Law, the "spiritual" or true body ; essential Buddhahood ; the essence of being ; the absolute, the norm of the universe ; the first of the Trikāya, v. 삼신 三身. The Dharmakāya is divided into 총 總 unity and 별 別 diversity ; as in the noumenal absolute and phenomenal activities, or potential and dynamic ; but there are differences of interpretation, e.g. as between the 법상 法相 and 법성 法性 schools. Cf. 법신체성 法身體性. There are many categories of the Dharmakāya. In the 2 group 이법신 二法身 are five kinds : (1) 리 理 "substance" and 지 智 wisdom or expression ; (2) 법성법신 法性法身 essential nature and 응화법신 應化法身 manifestation ; the other three couples are similar. In the 3 group 삼법신 三法身 are (1) the manifested Buddha, i.e. Śākyamuni ; (2) the power of his teaching, etc. ; (3) the absolute or ultimate reality. There are other categories. 법신불 法身佛 The Dharmakāya Buddha. 법신여래 法身如來 The Dharmakāya Tathāgata, the Buddha who reveals the spiritual body. 법신탑 法身塔 The Pagoda where abides a spiritual relic of Buddha ; the esoteric sect uses the letter ᅲ as such an abode of the dharmakāya. 법신유전 法身流轉 Dharmakāya in its phenomenal character, conceived as becoming, as expressing itself in the stream of being. 법(신)사리 法(身)舍利 ; 법신게 法身偈 The śarīra, or spiritual relics of the Buddha, his sūtras, or verses, his doctrine and immutable law. 법신보살 法身菩薩 ; 법신대사 法身大士 Dharmakāya Mahāsattva, one who has freed himself from illusion and attained the six spiritual powers 육신통 六神通 ; he is above the 초지 初地, or, according to T'ien-t'ai, above the 초주 初住. 법신장 法身藏 The storehouse of the Dharmakāya, the essence of Buddhahood, by contemplating which the holy man attains to it. 법신관 法身觀 Meditation on, or insight into, the Dharmakāya, varying in definition in the various schools. 법신체성 法身體性 The embodiment, totality, or nature of the Dharmakāya. In Hīnayāna the Buddha-nature in its 리 理 or absolute side is described as not discussed, being synonymous with the 오분 五分 five divisions of the commandments, meditation, wisdom, release, and doctrine, 계 戒, 정 定, 혜 慧, 해탈 解脫 and 지견 知見. In the Mahāyāna the 삼론종 三論宗 defines the absolute or ultimate reality as the formless which contains all forms, the essence of being, the noumenon of the other two manifestations of the Triratna. The 법상종 法相宗 defines it as (*a*) the nature or essence of the whole Triratna ; (*b*) the particular form of the Dharma in that trinity. The One-Vehicle schools represented by the 화엄종 華嚴宗, 천태종 天台宗, etc., consider it to be the Bhūtatathatā, 리 理 and 지 智 being one and undivided. The Shingon sect takes the six elements — earth, water, fire, air, space, mind — as the 리 理 or fundamental Dharmakāya and the sixth, mind, intelligence, or knowledge, as the 지 智 Wisdom Dharmakāya.

법신 法臣 Ministers of the Law, i.e. Bodhisattvas ; the Buddha is King of the Law, these are his ministers.

법아 法我 A thing *per se*, i.e. the false notion of anything being a thing in itself, individual, independent, and not merely composed of elements to be disintegrated. 법아견 法我見 The false view as above, cf. 아견 我見.

법아 法芽 The sprout or bud of Buddhism.

법아육 法阿育 Dharmāśoka ; name given to Aśoka on his conversion ; cf. 아육 阿育.

법안 法眼 The (bodhisattva) dharma-eye able to penetrate all things. Name of the founder of the 법안종 法眼宗 Fa-yen sect, one of the five Ch'an(Zen) schools. 법안정 法眼淨 To see clearly or purely the truth ; in Hīnayāna, to see the truth of the four dogmas ; in Mahāyāna, to see the truth which releases from reincarnation.

법애 法愛 Religious love in contrast with 욕애 欲愛 ordinary love ; Dharma-love may be Hīnayāna desire for nirvāṇa ; or bodhisattva attachment to illusory things, both of which are to be eradicated ; or Tathāgata-love, which goes out to all beings for salvation.

법약 法藥 The medicine of the Law, capable of healing all misery.

법어 法語 Dharma-words, religious discourses.

법역 法域 The realm of dharma, nirvāṇa ; also 법성토 法性土.

법연 法然 According to rule, naturally ; also 법이 法爾 ; 자연 自然.

법연 法緣 Dharma-caused, i.e. the sense of universal altruism giving rise to pity and mercy.

법열 法悅 Joy from hearing and meditating on the Law.

법온 法蘊 The Buddha's detailed teaching, and in this respect similar to 법장 法藏.

법왕 法王 Dharmarāja, king of the Law, Buddha. 법왕자 法王子 Son of the Dharma-king, a Bodhisattva.

법요 法要 The essentials of the Truth ; v. 법회 法會.

법우 法宇 Dharma roof, or canopy, a monastery.

법우 法雨 The rain of Buddha-truth which fertilizes all beings.

법운 法雲 Dharmamegha. Buddhism as a fertilizing cloud. 법운지 法雲地 The tenth bodhisattva-stage, when the dharma-clouds everywhere drop their sweet dew. 법운등각 法雲等覺 The stage after the last, that of universal knowledge, or enlightenment.

법운 法雲 Beop-un(534-576, reign. 540-576). A monk of the Silla dynasty in Korea. He was the twenty-fourth king of Silla, 진흥 眞興 Jin-heung. He was a nephew of king Beop-heung, ascended the throne at the age of seven, later became a monk. His biography can be found in the "Lives of Eminent Korean Monks."

법원 法苑 The garden of Dharma, Buddhism.

법위 法位 (1) Dharma-state, the bhūtatathatā. (2) The grade or position of a monk.

법유 法有 The false view of Hīnayāna that things, or the elements of which they are made, are real. 법유아무종 法有我無宗 The Sarvāstivādins who while disclaiming the reality of personality claimed the reality of things.

법유 法乳 The milk of the dharma which nourishes the spiritual nature.

법은 法恩 Dharma-grace, i.e. the grace of the Triratna.

법음 法音 The sound of the Truth, or of preaching.

법의 法依 The religious dress, general name of monastic garments.

법이 法爾 idem 법연 法然.

법인 法忍 Patience attained through dharma, to the overcoming of illusion ; also ability to bear patiently external hardships.

법인 法印 The seal of Buddha-truth, expressing its reality and immutability, also its universality and its authentic transmission from one Buddha or patriarch to another.

법인 탄문 法印坦文 See 대오 탄문 大悟坦文.

법입 法入 ; **법처** 法處 The sense-data of direct mental perception, one of the 십이입 十二入 or 십이처 十二處.

법자 法子 Child of the Dharma, one who makes his living by following Buddhism.

법자상상위인 法自相相違因 One of the four fallacies connected with the reason (인 因), in which the reason is contrary to the truth of the premise.

법자재 法自在 A bodhisattva's complete dialectical freedom and power, so that he can expound all things unimpeded.

법장 法匠 Dharma workman, a teacher able to mould his pupils.

법장 法將 Dharma-generals, i.e. monks of high character and leadership.

법장 法藏 Dharma-store ; also 불법장 佛法藏 ; 여래장 如來藏 (1) The absolute, unitary storehouse of the universe, the primal source of all things. (2) The Treasury of Buddha's teaching, the sūtras, etc. (3) Any Buddhist library. (4) Dharmākara, mine of the Law ; one of the incarnations of Amitābha. (5) Title of the founder of the Hua-yen School 현수법장 賢首法藏 Hsien-shou Fa-tsang.

법재 法財 The riches of the Law, or the Law as wealth.

법재일 法齋日 The day of abstinence observed at the end of each half month, also the six abstinence days, in all making the eight days for keeping the eight commandments.

법전 法典 The scriptures of Buddhism.

법전 法殿 The temple, or hall, of the Law, the main hall of a monastery ; also the Kuan-yin hall.

법정 法定 One of the twelve names for the Dharma-nature, implying that it is the basis of all phenomena.

법제 法弟 A Buddhist disciple.

법제 法帝 Dharma emperor, i.e. the Buddha.

법조 法照 Dharma-shining ; name of the fourth patriarch of the 연종 蓮宗 Lotus sect.

법주 法舟 ; 법선 法船 The bark of Buddha-truth which ferries men out from the sea of mortality and reincarnation to nirvāṇa.

법주 法住 Dharma abode, i.e. the omnipresent bhūtatathatā in all things. Dharmasthititā, continuity of dharma.

법주 法主 Dharma-lord, Buddha.

법주사 法住寺 Beop-ju-sa. A temple located in Mt. Songnisan, Sanae-ri Naesongni-myeon Boeun-gun Chungcheongbuk-do in Korea. The 5th parish headquarters of Korean Jogye Order.

법중 法衆 The Buddhist monkhood ; an assembly of monks or nuns.

법지 法智 Dharma-wisdom, which enables one to understand the four dogmas 사제 四諦 ; also, the understanding of the law, or of things.

법진 法塵 A mental object, any direct mental perception, not dependent on the sense organs. Cf. 육진 六塵.

법집 法執 Holding to things as realities, i.e. the false tenet that things are real.

법집 法集 idem 불회 佛會.

법천 法天 Dharmadeva, a monk from the Nālandā-saṁghārāma who tr. under this name forty-six works, 973-981, and under the name of Dharmabhadra seventy-two works, 982-1001.

법체 法體 Embodiment of the Law, or of things. (1) Elements into which the Buddhists divided the universe ; the Abhidharma-kośa has 75, the 성실론 成實論 Satyasiddhi-śāstra 84, the Yogācārya 100. (2) A monk.

법평등 法平等 Dharmasamatā ; the sameness of truth as taught by all Buddhas.

법하 法夏 Dharma summers, the years or age of a monk ; v. 법랍 法臘.

법현 法顯 Fa-hsien, the famous pilgrim who with fellow-monks left Ch'ang-an A.D. 399 overland for India, finally reached it, remained alone for six years, and spent three years on the return journey, arriving by sea in 414. His 불국기 佛國記 *Records of the Buddhistic Kingdoms* were made, on his information, by 불타발타라 佛陀跋陀羅 Buddhabhadra, an Indian monk in China. His own chief translation is the 승기율 僧祇律, a work on monastic discipline.

법호 法號 The name received by a monk on ordination, i.e. his 계명 戒名 ; also his posthumous title.

법화 法華 The Dharma-flower, i.e. the Lotus Sūtra, the 법화경 法華經 or 묘법연화경 妙法蓮華經 q.v. Saddharmapuṇḍarīka-sūtra ; also the 법화종 法華宗 Lotus sect, i.e. that of T'ien-t'ai, which had this sūtra for its basis. There are many treatises with this as part of the title. 법화법 法華法, 법화회 法華會, 법화강 法華講 ceremonials, meetings, or explications connected with this sūtra. 법화일실 法華一實 The one perfect Vehicle of the Lotus gospel. 법화팔년 法華八年 The last eight years of the Buddha's life, when, according to T'ien-t'ai, from 72 to 80 years of age he preached the Lotus gospel. 법화삼매 法華三昧 The samādhi which sees into the three 제諦 dogmas of 공가중 空假中 unreality, dependent reality, and transcendence, or the noumenal, phenomenal, and the absolute which unites them ; it is derived from the "sixteen" samādhis in chapter 24 of The Lotus. There is a 법화삼매경 法華三昧經 independent of this samādhi.

법화 法化 Transformation by Buddha-truth ; teaching in or by it. 법화생신 法化生身 The nirmāṇakāya, or corporeal manifestation of the spiritual Buddha.

법회 法會 An assembly for worship or preaching. 법회사 法會社 A monastery.

법희 法喜 Joy in the Law, the joy of hearing or tasting dharma. Name of Dharmanandi, v. 담曇. 법희식 法喜食 The food of joy in the Law.

벽 辟 A prince, sovereign, lord ; split ; punish, repress ; perverse ; toady ; quiet. 벽지(가) 辟支(迦) Pratyeka, each one, individual, oneself only. 벽지(가)불(타) 辟支(迦)佛(陀) Pratyeka-buddha, one who seeks enlightenment for himself, defined in the Lotus sūtra as a believer who is diligent and zealous in seeking wisdom, loves loneliness and seclusion, and understands deeply the nidānas. Also called 연각 緣覺 ; 독각 獨覺 ; 구존 俱存. It is a stage above the śrāvaka 성문聲聞 and is known as the 중승 中乘 middle vehicle. T'ien-t'ai distinguishes 독각 獨覺 as an ascetic in a period without a Buddha, 연각 緣覺 as a pratyeka-buddha. He attains his enlightenment alone, independently of a teacher, and with the object of attaining nirvāṇa and his own salvation rather than that of others, as is the object of a bodhisattva. Cf. 필 畢. 벽지불승 辟支佛乘 The middle vehicle, that of the pratyeka-buddha, one of the three vehicles. 벽제 辟除 To suppress, get rid of. 벽뢰 辟雷 To rend as thunder, to thunder. 벽귀 辟鬼 To suppress demons.

벽 壁 A wall, partition-wall, screen. 벽정 壁定 Wall-meditation, i.e. steady, not restless, meditation. 벽관 壁觀 The wall-gazer, applied to Bodhidharma, who is said to have gazed at a wall for nine years. Also a name for the meditation of the Ch'an school.

벽 霹 Crash, rumble. 벽력 霹靂 A thunder-crash.

벽 碧 Jade-green, or blue. 벽안호 碧眼胡 The blue-eyed barbarian, Bodhidharma.

벽 僻 Perverse, base, depraved ; partial, prejudiced ; rustic, secluded. 벽견 僻見 Perverse, incorrect, or depraved views.

벽 闢 To open ; translit. *pi*, v. 비 毘. 벽망 闢妄 To explain, or set free from, illusion. 벽전 闢展 Pidjan, or Pi-chang, near Turfān.

벽 劈 To split, rend, tear. 벽전급 劈箭急 Rapid as an arrow cleaving (the air).

변 邊 A side, edge, margin, border. 변지 邊地 The countries bordering on Jambudvīpa. The border land to Amitābha's Pure Land, where the lax and haughty, cf. 해만 懈慢, are detained for 500 years, also called 태궁 胎宮 womb-palace, and 변계 邊界 border-realm. 변주 邊州 The countries bordering on, or outside of India. 변옥 邊獄 The side hells, or lokāntarika hells. 변죄 邊罪 Sins of expulsion from the order, i.e. sexual intercourse, killing, stealing, lying. 변견 邊見 ; 변집견 邊執見 The two extreme views of annihilation and personal immortality. 변제 邊際 Utmost limit, ultimate, final. 변제지 邊際智 The perfect wisdom of a bodhisattva who has attained complete enlightenment.

변 辨 Discriminate, distinguish ; v. 변 辯 21. 변재천 辨才天 One of the devas, of the gandharva order.

변 變 To change, alter, transmute, transform. 변화 變化 To transform, change, change into, become, especially the mutations of Buddhas and bodhisattvas, e.g. 변화인 變化人 becoming men ; also 변화토 變化土 the land where they dwell, whether the Pure Land or any impure world where they live for its enlightenment. 변화법신 變化法身 The dharmakāya in its power of transmutation, or incarnation. 변화생 變化生 Birth by transformation, not by gestation. 변화신 變化身 The nirmāṇakāya, i.e. transformation-body, or incarnation-body, one of the 삼신 三身 Trikāya, q.v. 변괴 變壞 Destroyed, spoilt, turned bad. 변성 變成 To become, turn into, be transformed into. 변성왕 變成王 Pien-ch'êng Wang, one of the kings, or judges of Hades. 변성남자 變成男子 To be transformed from a female to a male. Every Buddha is supposed to vow to change all women into men. 변역 變易 Change, to change, similar to 변화 變化. 변역생사 變易生死 Mortal changes, or a body that is being transformed from mortality, e.g. 변역신 變易身 bodies that are being transformed in a Pure Land, or transformed bodies.

변 辯 To discuss, argue, discourse. 변재 辯才 Ability to discuss, debate, discourse ; rhetoric. 변재천 辯才天 Sarasvatī, goddess of speech and learning, v. 대변재천 大辯才天. 변무애 辯無礙 Power of unhindered discourse, perfect freedom of speech or debate, a bodhisattva power.

변 辮 To plait, a plait, queue. 변발 辮髮 To plait the hair.

별 瞥 A glance. 별지 瞥地 Instant, quickly.

별 鼈 A turtle, tortoise. 별불신구 鼈不愼口 The tortoise, clinging to a stick with its mouth, being carried in flight, warned not to open its mouth to speak, yet did, fell and perished ; moral, guard your lips.

별 別 Separate, divide, part from, other, different, differentiate, special.

별겁 別劫 Antara-kalpas, small or intermediate kalpas, v. 겁 劫.

별견 別見 Unenlightened, or heterodox, views.

별경 別境 Different realms, regions, states, or conditions. 별경심소 別境心所 Vibhāvana ; the ideas, or mental states, which arise according to the various objects or conditions toward which the mind is directed, e.g. if toward a pleasing object, then desire arises.

별교 別教 The "different" teaching of the 화엄종 華嚴宗 Both the Hua-yen school and the Lotus school are founded on the 일승 一乘 or One Vehicle idea ; the Lotus school asserts that the Three Vehicles are really the One Vehicle ; the Hua-yen school that the One Vehicle differs from the Three Vehicles ; hence the Lotus school is called the 동교일승 同教一乘 unitary, while the Hua-yen school is the 별교일승 別教一乘 Differentiating School.

별리수연 別理隨緣 The 리 理 li is the 진여 眞如 Bhūtatathatā, which one school says is different in operation, while another asserts that it is the same, for all things are the 진여 眞如 chên-ju.

별보 別報 Differentiated rewards according to previous deeds, i.e. the differing conditions of people in this life resulting from their previous lives.

별상 別相 Viśeṣa ; differentiation, difference, one of the 육상 六相 of the Hua-yen school. 별상삼관 別相三觀 The three views of the 별교 別教 in regard to the absolute, the phenomenal, the medial 공가중 空假中 as separate ideas.

별시염불 別時念佛 To call upon Buddha at special times. When the ordinary religious practices are ineffective the Pure Land sect call upon Buddha for a period of one to seven days, or ten to ninety days. Also 여법염불 如法念佛.

별업 別業 Differentiated karma (the cause of different resultant conditions) ; cf. 총업 總業.

별염불 別念佛 To intone the name of a special Buddha.

별원 別願 Special vows, as the forty-eight of Amitābha, or the twelve of 약사불 藥師佛 Yao Shih Fo (Bhaiṣajya), as contrasted with general vows taken by all Bodhisattvas.

별원 別圓 The 별 別 and 원 圓 schools, q.v. and 사교 四教.

별의 別依 Secondary texts or authorities, in contrast with 총의 總依 the principal texts of a school.

별전 別傳 Separately handed down ; oral tradition ; to pass on the teaching from mind to mind without writing, as in the Ch'an(Zen) or Intuitional school. Also 단전 單傳.

별중 別衆 For a monk schismatically or perversely to separate himself in religious duties from his fellow-monks is called duṣkṛta, an offence or wickedness, v. 돌 突.

별청 別請 Special deference paid by singling out or inviting one member of the community ; which procedure is against monastic rules.

별타나 別他那 Veṣṭana, 폐솔노천 吠率怒天, name of a deva ; the second term suggests Viṣṇu, and Veṣṭu might be a conception of Viṣṇu ; the intp. 위 圍 suits both, for Veṣṭana means surrounding, enclosing, and Viṣṇu, pervade, encompass.

별해탈계 別解脫戒 Another name for the commandments, which liberate by the avoidance of evil ; also 별해탈율의 別解脫律儀.

별향원수 別向圓修 The 향 向 of the 별 別, i.e. the Separatist or Differentiating School, is the 수 修 of the 원 圓 or Perfect School ; i.e. when the 별교 別教 Bodhisattva reaches the stage of the 십회향 十回向, he has reached the 수 修 stage of the perfect nature and observance according to the 원교 圓教 or Perfect School.

별혹 別惑 ; **별견** 別見 Delusions arising from differentiation, mistaking the seeming for the real ; these delusions according to the 별교 別教 are gradually eradicated by the Bodhisattva during his first stage.

병 瓶 A bottle, vase, jar, pitcher, etc. 천덕병 天德瓶 The vase of divine virtue, i.e. bodhi ; also a sort of cornucopia. 병사왕 瓶沙王 Bimbisāra, v. 빈 頻. 병솔도파 瓶窣都波 Droṇastūpa, a stūpa said to contain a jar of relics of Śākyamuni's body, surreptitiously collected after his cremation by a Brahman. 병기라 瓶耆羅 Eitel gives this as Viṅgila, Viṅkila, Varaṅgala ; the ancient capital of Andhra, cf. 안 案 ; but it is doubtful.

병 柄 A handle ; authority, power. 병어 柄語 Authoritative or pivotal words.

병 丙 Fire, heat, south ; the third of the ten stems, hence 병정 丙丁 means a junior, or so-and-so. 병정동자 丙丁童子 the boy who attends to the lamps (which are associated with "fire").

병 病 Illness, disease ; to hurt. 병자 病子 Just as a mother loves the sick child most, so Buddha loves the most wicked sinner. Nirvāṇa Sūtra 30.

병 屏 Screen ; to exclude, expel, turn away. 병사 屏莎 Bimbisāra, v. 평 苹.

병 竝 Together, idem 병 並. 병기 竝起 To arise together.

병사 洴舍 Bimbisāra, v. 빈 頻.

병사왕 洴沙王 ; **평사왕** 萍沙王 Bimbisāra, v. 빈 頻.

보 寶 v. 보 寶 20.

보 菩 A kind of fragrant grass.

보 步 Pada ; step, pace. 보타 步他 v. 불 佛 Buddha. 보척금강 步擲金剛 or 명왕 明王 ; 파반낭결사파 播般曩結使波 A form of 보현 普賢 Samantabhadra as a vajra-king.

보 保 Protect, ward, guard ; guarantee. 보경장군 保境將軍 The guardian general of the region.

보 寶 Ratna, precious, a treasure, gem, pearl, anything valuable ; for saptaratna, v. 칠보 七寶. Also maṇi, a pearl, gem.

보 報 Recompense, retribution, reward, punishment, to acknowledge, requite, thank ; to report, announce, tell. 보불 報佛 To thank the Buddha ; also idem 보신 報身 *infra*. 보명 報命 The life of reward or punishment for former deeds. 보인 報因 The cause of retribution. 보토 報土 The land of reward, the Pure Land. 보은 報恩 To acknowledge, or requite favours. 보은시 報恩施 Almsgiving out of gratitude. 보은전 報恩田 The field for requiting blessings received, e.g. parents, teachers, etc. 보응 報應 Recompense, reward, punishment ; also the 보신 報身 and 응신 應身 q.v. 보과 報果 The reward-fruit, or consequences of past deeds. 보사 報沙 Pauṣa, the first of the three Indian winter months, from the 16th of the 10th Chinese month. 보생삼매 報生三昧 A degree of bodhisattva samādhi, in which transcendental powers are obtained. 보연 報緣 The circumstantial cause of retribution. 보신 報身 Reward body, the sambhogakāya of a Buddha, in which he enjoys the reward of his labours, v. 삼신 三身 Trikāya. 보사 報謝 To acknowledge and thank ; also, retribution ended. 보통 報通 The supernatural powers that have been acquired as karma by demons, spirits, nāgas, etc. 보장 報障 The veil of delusion which accompanies retribution.

보 煲 To heat ; a pot. 보첩살독하 煲牒薩督呀 Bodhisattva, v. 보 菩.

보 補 To patch, repair, restore ; tonic ; translit. *pu, po*, cf. 부 富, 불 弗, 불 佛, 포 布. 보가라 補伽羅 Pudgala, *infra*. 보랄나 補刺拏 v. 부 富, intp. by 만 滿 Pūrṇa. 보라부 補囉嚩 Pūrva, in Pūrva-videha, the eastern continent. 보달락가 補怛洛迦 Potaraka, Potala, *infra*. 보사 補沙 Puṣya, the 귀 鬼 asterism, v. 부 富. 보삽파 補澁波 Puṣpa, a flower, a bloom, v. 포 布. 보특가라 補特伽羅 Pudgala, "the body, matter ; the soul, personal identity" [M. W.] ; intp. by man, men, human being, and 중생 衆生 all the living ; also by 취향 趣向 direction, or transmigration ; and 유정 有情 the sentient, v. 불 弗. 보슬치 補瑟置 ; 보슬가 補瑟迦 Pauṣṭika, promoting advancement, invigorating, protective. 보로사 補盧沙 Puruṣa, "man collectively or individually" ; "Man personified" ; "the Soul of the universe" [M. W.] ; intp. by 장부 丈夫 and 인 人 ; v. 포 布 ; also the first form of the masculine gender ; (1) puruṣa 보로사 補盧沙 ; (2) puruṣam 보로삼 補盧衫 ; (3) puruṣeṇa 보로사나 補盧沙拏 ; (4) puruṣāya 보로사야 補盧沙耶 ; (5) puruṣāt 보로사다 補盧沙頞 ; (6) puruṣasya 보로살사 補盧殺沙 ; (7) puruṣe 보로쇄 補盧鎩. 보갈파 補羯婆 Paulkasa, an aboriginal, or the son "of a śūdra father and of a kṣatriyā mother" [M. W.] ; intp. as low caste, scavenger, also an unbeliever (in the Buddhist doctrine of 인과 因果 or retribution). 보처 補處 One who repairs, or occupies a vacated place, a Buddha who succeeds a Buddha, as Maitreya is to succeed Śākyamuni. 보타 補陀 ; 보타 補陁 ; 보타락(가) 補陀落(迦) Potala ; Potalaka. (1) A sea-port on the Indus, the πατάλα of the ancients, identified by some with Ṭhaṭṭha, said to be the ancient home of Śākyamuni's ancestors. (2) A mountain south-east of Malakūṭa, reputed as the home of Avalokiteśvara. (3) The island of Pootoo, east of Ningpo, the Kuan-yin centre. (4) The Lhasa Potala in Tibet ; the seat of the Dalai Lama, an incarnation of Avalokiteśvara ; cf. 보 普 ; also written 보달락가 補怛落迦 ; 보단락가 補但落迦 ; 포다(라) 逋多(羅) ; 포달락가 布呾洛加.

보 普 Viśva ; universal, all ; pervasive, ubiquitous ; translit. *po, pa, pu*, 보광 普光 Universal light, to shine everywhere. 보화 普化 Universal change, or transformation. 보명 普明 Samantaprabhāsa, pervading-light, name of 500 arhats on their attaining Buddhahood. 보법 普法 Universal dharmas, or things ; all things. 보도 普渡 Universally to ferry across ; 보도중생 普渡衆生 to deliver, or save all beings. 보왕 普王 Universal king, title of Yama when he has expiated all his sins. 보현 普現 Universal manifestation, especially the manifestation of a Buddha or bodhisattva in any shape at will. 보지 普知 Omniscience, hence 보지자 普知者 the Omniscient, i.e. Buddha. 보례 普禮 To worship all the Buddhas. 보등 普等 Everywhere alike, universal equality, all equally. 보사 普莎 Puṣya, the asterism Tiṣya, and the month Pauṣa ; blossom, foam, scum ; but intp. as 길상 吉祥 auspicious. 보현 普賢 Samantabhadra, Viśvabhadra ; cf. 삼만 三曼 Universal sagacity, or favour ; lord of the 리 理 or fundamental law, the dhyāna, and the practice of all Buddhas. He and Mañjuśrī are the right-and left-hand assistants of Buddha, representing 리 理 and 지 智 respectively. He rides on a white elephant, is the patron of the Lotus Sūtra and its devotees, and has close connection with the Hua-yen Sūtra. His region is in the east. The esoteric school has its own special representation of him, with emphasis on the sword indicative of 리 理 as the basis of 지 智. He has ten vows. 보통 普通 Universal, reaching everywhere, common to all. 보편 普遍 ; 보편 普徧 Universal, everywhere, on all sides. 보문 普門 Universal door, the opening into all things, or universality ; the universe in anything ; the unlimited doors open to a Buddha, or bodhisattva, and the forms in which he can reveal himself. 보타 普陀 Potala, cf. 보 補, 포 布 ; it is also Pattala, an ancient port near the mouth of the Indus ; the Potala in Lhasa, etc., but in this form especially the sacred island of Pootoo, off Ningpo ; also called 보타낙가산 普陀洛伽山 Potaraka monastery.

보개 寶蓋 A canopy above an image or dais, decorated with gems.

보거 寶車 The precious cart (in the Lotus sūtra), i.e. the one vehicle, the Mahāyāna.

보계 寶界 The saptaratna realm of every Buddha, his Pure Land.

보광천자 寶光天子 Precious light deva, Sūrya-deva, the sun-prince, a manifestation of Kuan-yin. 보광명지 寶光明池 A lake in Magadha, where the Buddha is said to have preached.

보국 寶國 Precious country, the Pure Land.

보길상천 寶吉祥天 Deva of the precious omen, i.e. Candradeva, deva of the moon, a manifestation of Mahāsthāmaprāpta.

보녀 寶女 Kanyā-ratna ; precious maidens, one of the seven treasures of the Cakravartin ; also 옥녀 玉女.

보당 寶幢 Ratnadhvaja ; a banner decorated with gems. A deva in the Tuṣita heaven who presides over music.

보룡 哺嚨 Bhūrom, an exclamation frequently occurring at the beginning of mantras, probably in imitation of Brahmanic mantras, which begin by invoking bhūr earth, bhuvaḥ air, and svar heaven ; or it may be a combination of bhūr, earth, and om, the mystic interjection.

보리 菩提 Bodhi ; from budh ; knowledge, understanding ; perfect wisdom ; the illuminated or enlightened mind ; anciently intp. by 도 道, later by 각 覺 to be aware, perceive ; for Sambodhi v. 삼 三.

보리달마 菩提達磨 Bodhidharma, commonly known as Ta-mo, v. 달 達 ; reputed as the founder of the 선 禪 Ch'an(Zen) or Intuitional or Mystic School. His original name is given as 보리다라 菩提多羅 Bodhitara.

보리도량 菩提道場 Bodhimaṇḍa, the bodhi-site, or plot or seat which raised itself where Śākyamuni attained Buddhahood. It is said to be diamond-like, the navel or centre of the earth ; every bodhisattva sits down on such a seat before becoming Buddha.

보리량 菩提場 A place, plot, or site of enlightenment, especially Śākyamuni's under the bodhi-tree.

보리류지 菩提流志 Bodhiruci, intp. as 각애 覺愛, a monk from southern India whose original name 달마류지 達磨流支 Dharmaruci was changed as above by order of the Empress Wu ; he tr. 53 works in A.D. 693-713. 보리류지 菩提流支 Bodhiruci, intp. as 도희 道希, a monk from northern India who arrived at Loyang in A.D. 508 and tr. some 30 works ; also 보리류지 菩提留支, 보리골로지 菩提鶻露支.

보리문 菩提門 The gate of enlightenment ; name for a cemetery.

보리분 菩提分 Bodhyaṅga, a general term for the thirty-seven 도품 道品, more strictly applied to the 칠각지 七覺支 q.v., the seven branches of bodhi-illumination. Also 보리분법 菩提分法.

보리사 菩提寺 Bodhi-vihāra, temple of or for enlightenment, a name used for many monasteries ; also 보리소 菩提所.

보리살타 菩提薩埵 Bodhisattva, a being of enlightenment ; "one whose essence is wisdom" ; "one who has Bodhi or perfect wisdom as his essence," [M. W.] Also 보리색다 菩提索多 v. 보살 菩薩.

보리수 菩提樹 Bodhidruma, Bodhitaru, Bodhivṛkṣa ; the wisdom-tree, i.e. that under which Śākyamuni attained his enlightenment, and became Buddha. The *Ficus religiosa* is the pippala, or aśvattha, wrongly identified by Fa-hsien as the palm-tree ; it is described as an evergreen, to have been 400 feet high, been cut down several times, but in the T'ang dynasty still to be 40 or 50 feet high. A branch of it is said to have been sent by Aśoka to Ceylon, from which sprang the celebrated Bo-tree still flourishing there. 보리수신 菩提樹神 The goddess-guardian of the Bo-tree.

보리심 菩提心 The mind for or of bodhi ; the awakened, or enlightened mind ; the mind that perceives the real behind the seeming, believes in moral consequences, and that all have the Buddha-nature, and aims at Buddhahood.

보리자 菩提者 Bodhi-seeds, or beads, the hard seeds of a kind of Himalayan grass, also of a tree at T'ien-t'ai, used for rosaries.

보림 寶林 The groves, or avenues of precious trees (in the Pure Land). The monastery of Hui-nêng, sixth patriarch of the Ch'an sect, in 소주전강현 韶州典江縣 Tien-chiang Hsien, Shao Chou, Kwangtung, cf. 혜 慧 15. The 보림전 寶林傳 and supplement contain the teachings of this school.

보림 保任 Common pronunciation of 보임 保任. See 보임 保任.

보망 寶網 Indra's net of gems ; also 제망 帝網 ; 인다라망 因陀羅網.

보방 寶坊 Precious place, or the abode of the Triratna, a monastery. 대보방 大寶坊 is the place between the desire-world and the form-world where Buddha expounded the 대집경 大集經.

보벌 寶筏 The precious raft of Buddha-truth, which ferries over the sea of mortality to nirvāṇa.

보병 寶甁 Kuṇḍikā, a precious vase, vessels used in worship ; a baptismal vase used by the esoteric sects for pouring water on the head.

보사마세 寶沙麽洗 Pauṣamāsa, the tenth Indian month, "beginning on the 16th day of the 12th Chinese month." [Eitel].

보살 菩薩 Bodhisattva, cf. 보리살타 菩提薩埵. While the idea is not foreign to Hīnayāna, its extension of meaning is one of the chief marks of Mahāyāna. "The Bodhisattva is indeed the characteristic feature of the Mahāyāna." [Keith]. According to Mahāyāna the Hinayanists, i.e. the śrāvaka and pratyeka-buddha, seek their own salvation, while the bodhisattva's aim is the salvation of others and of all. The earlier intp. of bodhisattva was 대도심중생 大道心衆生 all beings with mind for the truth ; later it became 대각유정 大覺有情 conscious beings of or for the great intelligence, or enlightenment. It is also intp. in terms of leadership, heroism, etc. In general it is a Mahayanist seeking Buddhahood, but seeking it altruistically ; whether monk or layman, he seeks enlightenment to enlighten others, and he will sacrifice himself to save others ; he is devoid of egoism and devoted to helping others. All conscious beings having the Buddha-nature are natural bodhisattvas, but require to undergo development. The mahāsattva is sufficiently advanced to became a Buddha and enter Nirvāṇa, but according to his vow he remains in the realm of incarnation to save all conscious beings. A monk should enter on the arduous course of discipline which leads to Bodhisattvahood and Buddhahood. 보살승 菩薩乘 One of the "five vehicles," which teaches the observance of the six pāramitās, the perfecting of the two 리 利, i.e. 자리이타 自利利他 the perfecting of self for perfecting others, and the attaining of Buddhahood. 보살오지 菩薩五智 The five-fold knowledge of the Bodhisattva: that of all things by intuition, of past events, of establishing men in sound religious life, of the elements in or details of all things, of attaining everything at will. 보살승 菩薩僧 The Bodhisattvasaṅgha, or monks, i.e. Mahāyāna, though there has been dispute whether Hīnayāna monks may be included. 보살십주 菩薩十住 ; 보살십지 菩薩十地 Ten stages in a Bodhisattva's progress ; v. 십十. 보살대사 菩薩大士 Bodhisattva-Mahāsattva, a great Bodhisattva, e.g. Mañjuśrī, Kuan-yin, etc. v. *infra*. 보살성 菩薩性 Bodhisattva nature, or character. 보살계 菩薩戒 The rules are found in the sūtra of this name, taken from the 범망경 梵網經. 보살마하살 菩薩摩訶薩 Bodhisattva-Mahāsattva. Mahāsattva is the perfected Bodhisattva, greater than any other being except a Buddha. 보살성중 菩薩聖衆 the Bodhisattva saints who have overcome illusion, from the first stage upwards, as contrasted with ordinary bodhisattvas. 보살장 菩薩藏 The Mahāyāna scriptures, i.e. those of the bodhisattva school. 보살행 菩薩行 The way or discipline of the bodhisattva, 자리이타 自利利他, i.e. to benefit self and benefit others, leading to Buddhahood. 보살도 菩薩道 ditto.

보상 寶相 The precious likeness, or image (of Buddha). Ratnaketu, one of the seven Tathāgatas ; a name of Ānanda as a future Buddha ; the name under which 2,000 of Śākyamuni's disciples are to be reborn as Buddhas.

보생 寶生 Ratnasaṁbhava, one of the five Dhyāni-Buddhas, the central figure in the southern "diamond" maṇḍala. The realm of Subhūti on his becoming Buddha.

보성 寶城 The city full of precious things, in the Nirvāṇa sūtra, i.e. the teaching of the Buddha.

보성 寶性 The precious nature, or Tathāgatagarbha, underlying all phenomena, always pure despite phenomenal conditions.

보소 寶所 The place of precious things, i.e. the perfect Nirvāṇa.

보수 寶手 Precious hand, the hand which gives alms and precious things.

보수 寶樹 The jewel-trees (of the Pure Land).

보승 寶勝 Ratnaketu, one of the seven Tathāgatas ; also said to be a name for 보생 寶生 q.v.

보승 寶乘 The precious vehicle of the Lotus sūtra ; the Mahāyāna.

보시 布施 Dāna 단나 檀那 ; the sixth pāramitā, almsgiving, i.e. of goods, or the doctrine, with resultant benefits now and also hereafter in the forms of reincarnation, as neglect or refusal will produce the opposite consequences. The 이종보시 二種布施 two kinds of dāna are the pure, or unsullied charity, which looks for no reward here but only hereafter ; and the sullied almsgiving whose object is personal benefit. The three kinds of dāna are goods, the doctrine, and courage, or fearlessness. The four kinds are pens to write the sūtras, ink, the sūtras themselves, and preaching. The five kinds are giving to those who have come from a distance, those who are going to a distance, the sick, the hungry, those wise in the doctrine. The seven kinds are giving to visitors, travellers, the sick, their nurses, monasteries, endowments for the sustenance of monks or nuns, and clothing and food according to season. The eight kinds are giving to those who come for aid, giving for fear (of evil), return for kindness received, anticipating gifts in return, continuing the parental example of giving, giving in hope of rebirth in a particular heaven, in hope of an honoured name, for the adornment of the heart and life. 구사론 俱舍論 18.

보실저가 寶悉底迦 The precious svastika, or sign on Buddha's breast.

보왕 寶王 The Precious King, or King of Treasures, a title of Buddha ; the ruler of the continent west of Sumeru, also called 보주 寶主 Jewel-lord, or Lord of jewels. 보왕삼매 寶王三昧 The King of Treasures samādhi, achieved by fixing the mind on Buddha.

보우 普愚 Tae-go Bo-u(1301-1382). A monk of the Goryeo dynasty in Korea. He became a 초조 初祖 first patriarch of 동국임제종 東國臨濟宗 and a imperial preceptor of Goryeo.

보운 寶雲 Pao-yün, a monk of 양주 涼州 Liang-chou, who travelled to India, *circa* A.D. 397, returned to Ch'ang-an, and died 449 aged 74.

보인 寶印 Precious seal, or symbol. (1) The second of the Triratna, i.e. 법보 法寶. (2) The three evidences of the genuineness of a sūtra, v. 삼법인 三法印. (3) The symbols of Buddhas, or bodhisattvas. (4) Their magical 종자 種子, i.e. germ-letters, or sounds. 보인삼매 寶印三昧 The ratnamudra samādhi, in which are realized the unreality of the ego, the impermanence of all things, and nirvāṇa.

보임 保任 Keeping it wholly, not losing it (after awakening). Making it of one's own.

보장 寶藏 The treasury of precious things, the wonderful religion of Buddha. 보장여래 寶藏如來 Ratna-garbha ; a Buddha to whom Śākyamuni and Amitābha are said to have owed their awakening.

보저 寶渚 Ratnadvīpa ; precious islet, island of pearls of gems ; synonym for perfect nirvāṇa ; also an old name for Ceylon. [Eitel].

보적 寶積 Ratnarāśi, or ratnakūṭa. Gem-heap ; collection of gems ; accumulated treasures. 보적삼매 寶積三昧 The samādhi by which the origin and end of all things are seen. 보적불 寶積佛 Buddha adorned with heaps of treasures, i.e. powers, truths, etc. 보적경 寶積經 v. 대보적경 大寶積經. 보적장자자 寶積長者子 The sons of the elders of Vaiśālī, who are said to have offered canopies of the seven precious things to Śākyamuni in praise of his teaching.

보전 寶典 The precious records, or scriptures.

보주 寶珠 Maṇi, a precious pearl, or gem ; a talisman ; a symbol of Śāriputra.

보주 寶州 The precious continent, or wonderful land of a Buddha.

보지 寶池 The precious lake of the eight virtuous characteristics in the Pure Land.

보찰 寶刹 The precious kṣetra, or Buddha-realm ; a monastery.

보처삼매 寶處三昧 The samādhi of the precious place, the ecstatic trance of Śākyamuni by which he dispensed powers and riches to all beings.

보취 寶聚 Jewel-collection ; a collection of precious things, e.g. the Buddhist religion.

보타암 寶陀巖 Potalaka, the abode of Kuan-yin, v. 보 補.

보탁 寶鐸 Bells hung on pagodas, etc. ; also 풍탁 風鐸 ; 첨탁 簷鐸.

보탑 寶塔 A stūpa, or fane for precious things, or relics ; a pagoda adorned with gems ; the shrine of 다보 多寶 Prabhūtaratna in the Lotus sūtra.

보협 寶篋 Ratnapiṭaka, or Ratnakaraṇḍaka ; a precious box, or box of precious things.

보호 寶號 Precious name or title, especially that of Buddhas and bodhisattvas.

보화 寶華 Precious flowers, deva-flowers.

복 僕 A servant. 복호선나 僕呼繕那 Bahujanya, intp. 중생 衆生 all the living, all who are born. 복나 僕拏 Intp. as a digital sign ; the fourth of the twelve ways of placing the hands together.

복 福 Blessing, happiness, felicity, good fortune. 복지 福地 A place of blessedness, a monastery. 복보 福報 A blessed reward, e.g. to be reborn as a man or a deva. 복인 福因 That which causes or gives rise to blessing, i.e. all good deeds. 복정 福庭 A court, or hall, of blessedness, a monastery. 복덕 福德 Puṇya. Blessed virtues, all good deeds ; The blessing arising from good deeds. 복덕장엄 福德莊嚴 The adornment of blessedness and virtue, i.e. of good deeds. 복덕자량 福德資糧 The nutriment of blessedness, i.e. deeds of charity. 복덕신 福德身 The Buddhakāya, or body of Buddha, in the enjoyment of the highest samādhi bliss. 복덕문 福德門 The gates of blessedness and virtue, the first five of the six pāramitās. 복혜 福慧 Blessedness and wisdom ; or virtue and wisdom. 복경 福慶 Blessedness and felicity, blessed felicity ; to congratulate on good fortune. 복지 福智 Blessedness and wisdom, the two virtues which adorn. 복과 福果 The reward of blessedness. 복업 福業 The karma of blessedness, a happy karma. 복생 福生 Born of or to happiness. 복생천 福生天 Puṇyaprasava, the tenth brahmaloka, the first region of the fourth dhyāna. 복전 福田 The field of blessedness, i.e. any sphere of kindness, charity, or virtue ; there are categories of 2, 3, 4, and 8, e.g. that of study and that of charity ; parents, teachers, etc. ; the field of poverty as a monk, etc. 복전의 福田衣 The garment of the field of blessing, the monk's robe. 복상법신 福相法身 The Buddha-dharmakāya as blessedness, in contrast with it as wisdom. 복록 福祿 Happiness and emolument, good fortune here or hereafter. 복개 福蓋 The cover, or canopy, of blessing. 복행 福行 The life or conduct which results in blessing, e.g. being reborn as a man or a deva. 복관 福觀 Blessedness and insight, similar to 복혜 福慧 ; 복지 福智. 복족 福足 The feet of blessedness, one consisting of the first five pāramitās, the other being the sixth pāramitā, i.e. wisdom ; happiness replete.

복 複 Double garments, wadded, lined ; double ; repeated.

복 伏 Prostrate ; humble ; suffer, bear ; ambush ; dog-days ; hatch ; it is used for control, under control, e.g. as delusion ; 단 斷 is contrasted with it as complete extirpation, so that no delusive thought arises. 복인 伏忍 The first of the 오인 五忍 five forms of submission, self-control, or patience. 복장 伏藏 To bury, hide away. 복타 伏陀 The Vedas, v. 위 韋. 복타밀다 伏馱蜜多 Buddhamitra, of northern India, the ninth patriarch, a Vaiśya by birth (third caste), author of the 오문선경요용법 五門禪經要用法 Pañcadvāra-dhyāna-sūtra-mahārtha-dharma ; he was styled Mahādhyānaguru.

복 服 Submit, serve ; clothing, to wear ; mourning ; to swallow ; a dose. 복수론사 服水論師 The sect of non-Buddhist philosophers who considered water the beginning and end of all things.

복 腹 The belly. 복중 腹中 Within the belly, the heart, womb, unborn child, etc.

복 卜 To divine, foretell.

복 覆 To throw over, overthrow ; prostrate ; to and fro ; repeated ; to report ; to cover. 부(속)제 覆(俗)諦 The unenlightened inversion of reality, common views of things. 복기 覆器 Things for turning off, e.g. water, as tiles do ; impermeable, resistant to teaching. 복묘 覆墓 To return to or visit a grave on the third day after interment. 복백 覆帛 To throw a coverlet (over an image). 복견 覆肩 To throw a robe over the shoulder. 복강 覆講 To repeat a lesson to a teacher. 복발 覆鉢 The inverted bowl at the top of a pagoda below the nine circles. 복면 覆面 A veil for the face ; to cover the face.

복갈사 卜羯娑 Pukkaśa ; also 보갈사 補羯娑 A degraded caste of sweepers, or scavengers, and bearers of corpses.

본 本 Radical, fundamental, original, principal, one's own ; the Buddha himself, contrasted with 적 蹟 chi, traces left by him among men to educate them ; also a volume of a book.

본각 本覺 Original bodhi, i.e. "enlightenment", awareness, knowledge, or wisdom, as contrasted with 시각 始覺 initial knowledge, that is "enlightenment *a priori* is contrasted with enlightenment *a posteriori*". Suzuki, *Awakening of Faith*, p. 62. The reference is to universal mind 중생지심체 衆生之心體, which is conceived as pure and intelligent, with 시각 始覺 as active intelligence. It is considered as the Buddha-dharmakāya, or as it might perhaps be termed, the fundamental mind. Nevertheless in action from the first it was influenced by its antithesis 무명 無明 ignorance, the opposite of awareness, or true knowledge. See 기신론 起信論 and 인왕경중 仁王經中. There are two kinds of 본각 本覺, one which is unconditioned, and never sullied by ignorance and delusion, the other which is conditioned and subject to ignorance. In original enlightenment is implied potential enlightenment in each being. 본각진여 本覺眞如 The 진여 眞如, i.e. bhūtatathatā, is the 체 體 corpus, or embodiment ; the 본각 本覺 is the 상 相 or form of primal intelligence ; the former is the 리 理 or fundamental truth, the latter is the 지 智, i.e. the knowledge or wisdom of it ; together they form the whole embodiment of the Buddha-dharmakāya.

본거 本據 Mūlagrantha ; the original text, or a quotation from it.

본고적하 本高迹下 The higher (Buddha) manifesting himself in lower form, e.g. as a bodhisattva.

본교 本教 The fundamental doctrine, i.e. of the One Vehicle as declared in the Lotus Sūtra, also 근본지교 根本之教.

본나리가 本拏哩迦 idem Puṇḍarīka, v. 분 奔.

본낭가타 本囊伽吒 Pūrṇaghaṭa, full pitcher, "one of the sixty-five mystic figures said to be traceable on every footprint (śrīpada) of Buddha." [Eitel].

본래 本來 Coming from the root, originally, fundamentally, 무시이래 無始以來 from, or before, the very beginning. 본래성불 本來成佛 All things being of Buddha become Buddha. 본래법이 本來法爾 So from the beginning, interpreted as 자시자연 自始自然. 본래무일물 本來無一物 Originally not a thing existing, or before anything existed — a subject of meditation. 본(래)공 本(來)空 That all things come from the Void, or Absolute, the 진여 眞如.

본말 本末 Root and twigs, root and branch, first and last, beginning and end, etc.

본명 本明 The original light, or potential enlightenment, that is in all beings ; also 원명 元明 ; cf. 본각 本覺.

본명성 本命星 The life-star of an individual, i.e. the particular star of the seven stars of Ursa Major which is dominant in the year of birth ; 본명수 本命宿 is the constellation, or star-group, under which he is born ; 본명원진 本命元辰 is the year of birth, i.e. the year of his birth-star. 본명도량 本命道場 Temple for worship of the emperor's birth-star, for the protection of the imperial family and the state.

본모 本母 Upadeśa ; mātṛkā ; the original "mother" or matrix ; the original sūtra, or work.

본문 本門 v. 본적 本迹. 본문본존 本門本尊 The especial honoured one of the Nichiren sect, Svādi-devatā, the Supreme Being, whose maṇḍala is considered as the symbol of the Buddha as infinite, eternal, universal. The Nichiren sect has a meditation 본문사관 本門事觀 on the universality of the Buddha and the unity in the diversity of all his phenomena, the whole truth being embodied in the Lotus Sūtra, and in its title of five words, 묘법연화경 妙法蓮華經 Wonderful-Law Lotus-Flower Sūtra, which are considered to be the embodiment of the eternal, universal Buddha. Their repetition preceded by 나무 南無 Namaḥ! is equivalent to the 귀명 歸命 of other Buddhists.

본불 本佛 The Buddha-nature within oneself ; the original Buddha.

본불생제 本不生際 The original status of no rebirth, i.e. every man has a naturally pure heart, which 불생불멸 不生不滅 is independent of the bonds of mortality.

본사 本師 The original Master or Teacher, Śākyamuni. 본사화상 本師和尙 Upādhyāya 오파다야 烏波陀耶 an original teacher, or founder ; a title of Amitābha.

본사경 本事經 Itivṛttaka ; ityukta ; one of the twelve classes of sūtras, in which the Buddha tells of the deeds of his disciples and others in previous lives, cf. 본생경 本生經.

본산 本山 Native hill ; a monk's original or proper monastery ; this (or that) monastery ; also 본사 本寺.

본삼매야인 本三昧耶印 The first samaya-sign to be made in worship, the forming of the hands after the manner of a lotus.

본생경 本生經 Jātaka sūtras 사타가 闍陀伽 ; stories of the Buddha's previous incarnations, one of the twelve classes of sūtras. 본생설 本生說 The stories thus told. v. 본사경 本事經.

본서 本誓 Samaya ; the original covenant or vow made by every Buddha and Bodhisattva.

본서 本書 The foundation books of any school ; a book.

본성 本性 The spirit one possesses by nature ; hence, the Buddha-nature ; the Buddha-nature within ; one's own nature.

본시 本時 The original time, the period when Śākyamuni obtained enlightenment ; at that time.

본식 本識 The fundamental vijñāna, one of the eighteen names of the Ālaya-vijñāna, the root of all things.

본신 本身 Oneself ; it also means 본심 本心 the inner self.

본심 本心 The original heart, or mind ; one's own heart.

본연 本緣 The origin or cause of any phenomenon.

본원 本願 Pūrvapraṇidhāna. The original vow, or vows, of a Buddha or bodhisattva, e.g. the forty-eight of Amitābha, the twelve of 약사 藥師, etc. 본원일실대도 本願一實大道 The great way of the one reality of Amitābha's vows, i.e. that of calling on his name and trusting to his strength and not one's own.

본유 本有 Originally or fundamentally existing ; primal existence ; the source and substance of all phenomena ; also the present life ; also the eighth 식 識, i.e. Ālaya-vijñāna. 본유수생 本有修生. The 본유 本有 means that original dharma is complete in each individual, the 진여법성지덕 眞如法性之德 the virtue of the bhūtatathatā dharma-nature, being 구족무결 具足無缺 complete without lack ; the 수생 修生 means the development of this original mind in the individual, whether saint or common man, to the realization of Buddha-virtue ; 유관행지력 由觀行之力, 개발기본유지덕 開發其本有之德, 점점수습이차제개현불덕야 漸漸修習而次第開顯佛德也. 본유가 本有家 A division of the Dharmalakṣaṇa school 법상종 法相宗.

본이 本二 His original second (in the house), the wife of a monk, before he retired from the world.

본적 本迹 The original 본 本 Buddha or Bodhisattva and his 적 迹 varied manifestations for saving all beings, e.g. Kuan-yin with thirty-three forms. Also 본지수적 本地垂迹. 본적이문 本迹二門 A division of the Lotus Sūtra into two parts, the 적문 迹門 being the first fourteen chapters, the 본문 本門 the following fourteen chapters ; the first half is related to the Buddha's earthly life and previous teaching ; the second half to the final revelation of the Buddha as eternal and the Bodhi-sattva doctrines.

본정무루 本淨(無漏) Primal purity.

본존 本尊 Satyadevatā, 사야지제박다 娑也地提縛多. The original honoured one ; the most honoured of all Buddhas ; also the chief object of worship in a group ; the specific Buddha, etc., being served.

본지 本地 Native place, natural position, original body ; also the 본신 本身 ; 본법신 本法身 ; or 본지신 本地身 fundamental person or embodiment of a Buddha or bodhisattva, as distinct from his temporal manifestation. 본지문 本地門 The uncreated dharmakāya of Vairocana is eternal and the source of all things and all virtue.

본질 本質 Original substance, the substance itself ; any real object of the senses.

본초 本初 In the beginning ; originally.

본행 本行 The root of action ; the method or motive of attainment ; (his) own deeds, e.g. the doings of a Buddha or bodhisattva. 본행(집)경 本行(集)經 A sūtra of this title.

본형 本形 Original form, or figure ; the substantive form.

본혹 本惑 The root or origin of delusion ; also 근본혹 根本惑 ; 근본번뇌 根本煩惱.

봉 棒 A stick, cudgel. 방할 棒喝 To bang and bawl, in rebuke of a student.

봉 鋒 The point of a sword, or weapon ; points, bristling ; a knife edge.

봉 鳳 The "phoenix," the auspicious bird. 봉찰 鳳刹 phoenix-kṣetra, a term for a Buddhist temple.

봉 捧 To hold in both hands, offer, receive ; a double handful. 봉물 捧物 To bear or offer gifts in both hands.

봉 奉 To receive respectfully ; honoured by, have the honour to, be favoured by, serve, offer. 봉사 奉事 To carry out orders. 봉가 奉加, 봉납 奉納 To make offerings. 봉행 奉行 To obey and do (the Buddha's teaching).

봉 封 To seal, close (a letter) ; classifier, or numerative of letters, etc. ; to appoint (imperially). 봉체 封體 To seal up a god or Buddha in a body by secret methods.

봉선사 奉先寺 Bong-seon-sa. A temple located in Mt. Unaksan, Bupyeong-ri Jinjeon-eup Namyangju-si Gyeonggi-do in Korea. The 25th parish headquarters of Korean Jogye Order.

봉원사 奉元寺 Bong-won-sa. A temple located in Bongwon-dong Seodaemun-gu Seoul-si in Korea. A large temple of Korean Taego Order.

부 棓 A flail. 부랄나 棓剌拏 Pūraṇa, v. 부 富.

부 部 A group, tribe, class, division, section ; a board, office ; school, sect ; a work in volumes, a heading or section of a work. 부인타 部引陀 or 部引陁 The planet Mercury, i.e. Buddha. 부주 部主 The founder of a sect, or school, or group. 부집 部執 The tenets of a sect, or school. 부다 部多 Bhūta, "been, become, produced, formed, being, existing," etc. [M. W.] ; intp. as the consciously existing ; the four great elements, earth, fire, wind, water, as apprehended by touch ; also a kind of demon produced by metamorphosis. Also, the 진여 眞如 bhūtatathatā. 부교 部教 The sūtras, or canon, and their exposition.

부 夫 A man ; a sage, officer, hero ; a husband, mate ; a fellow ; a particle, i.e. for, so, etc. 부인 夫人 A wife ; the wife of a king, i.e. a queen, devī. 범인 凡人 The common people, the unenlightened, *hoi polloi*, a common fellow.

부 婦 A woman ; a wife. 부인 婦人. "Nothing is so dangerous to monastic chastity as woman" ; she is the root of all misery, hindrance, destruction, bondage, sorrow, hatred, blindness, etc.

부 附 Adjoin, attached to, append, near. 부불법외도 附佛法外道 Heretics within Buddhism.

부 復 Again, return, revert, reply. 부활 復活 To live again, return to life. 부식 復飾 To return to ordinary garments, i.e. to doff the robe for lay life.

부 扶 Aid, support, uphold. 부진근 扶塵根 The external organs, i.e. of sight, etc., which aid the senses ; 부 扶 is also written 부 浮 meaning fleeting, vacuous, these external things having an illusory existence ; the real organs, or indriya, are the 정근 正根 or 승의근 勝義根 which evolve the ideas. 부율담상(교) 扶律談常(敎) The teaching which supports the rules and speaks of the eternal, i.e. the 열반종 涅槃宗 Nirvāṇa Sūtra. 부소 扶疏 "Supporting commentary," another name for the same sūtra, because according to T'ien-t'ai it is an amplification of the Lotus Sūtra. 부살 扶薩 Bodhisattva, idem 보살 菩薩.

부 敷 Diffuse, spread, promulgate, announce. 부구 敷具 The displayed, or promulgating article, i.e. the monk's robe. 부만다라 敷曼荼羅 To spread a magic cloth, or maṇḍala, on the ground.

부 浮 Floating, drifting, unsettled. 부공 浮孔 A hole in a floating log, through which a one-eyed turtle accidentally obtains a glimpse of the moon, the rarest of chances, e.g. the rareness of meeting a Buddha. 부낭 浮囊 A floating bag, a swimming float, a lifebuoy. 부도 浮圖 ; 부타 浮陀 ; 부두 浮頭 ; 부도 浮屠 Buddha ; also a stūpa, v. 불 佛 and 탑 塔. 부진 浮塵 Floating dust or atoms, unstable matter, i.e. phenomena, which hide reality. 부상 浮想 Passing thoughts, unreal fancies. 부목 浮木 A floating log, v. 부공 浮孔. 부(진)근 浮(塵)根 ; 부(진)근 扶(塵)根 Indriya, the organs of sensation, eye, ear, etc., in contrast with 승의근 勝義根 the function or faculty of sensation. 부운 浮雲 A drifting cloud, e.g. this life, the body, etc.

부 賻 Pecuniary aid (for funerals), 부의 賻儀.

부 父 Pitṛ, 비다 比多 Father. 부모 父母 Pitṛ mātṛ, father and mother, parents ; 무명 無明 ignorance is referred to as father, and 탐애 貪愛 desire, or concupiscence, as mother, the two – ignorance and concupiscence – being the parents of all delusion and karma. Samādhi is also referred to as father, and prajñā (wisdom) as mother, the parents of all knowledge and virtue. In the vast interchanges of rebirth all have been or are my parents, therefore all males are my father and all females my mother ; 일체남녀아부모 一切男女我父母 see 심지관경 心地觀經 2. 부성 父城 The paternal of native city, especially Śākyamuni's Kapilavastu.

부 富 Rich, wealthy, affluent, well supplied ; translit. *pu* and *ve* sounds ; cf. 불 不, 포 布, 보 補, 파 婆.

부 腐 Rotten, corrupt, putrid, sloughing. 부란약 腐爛藥 Purgatives, diuretics.

부 副 To aid, assist, second ; a deputy. 부료 副寮 Deputy in a monastery.

부 負 To bear on the back ; turn the back on ; lose. 부문 負門 Positions that have been withdrawn from in argument ; defeated.

부 付 To deliver, hand over to, hand down. 부속 付屬 ; 부촉 付囑 To deliver, entrust to. 부법장(인연전) 付法藏(因緣傳) ; 부법장전 付法藏傳 ; 부법장경 付法藏經. The work explaining the handing down of Śākyamuni's teaching by Mahākāśyapa and the elders, twenty-four in number ; tr. in the Yüan dynasty in six chüan ; cf. 석문정통 釋門正統 4.

부 赴 To go to, or into. 부화외도 赴火外道 Ascetics who burn themselves alive. 부청 赴請 To go in response to an invitation ; go to invite. 부기 赴機 To go or to preach according to the need or opportunity.

부 趺 To sit cross-legged 부좌 趺佐, cf. 가 跏.

부 傅 To superintend, teach ; a tutor ; to paint ; a function ; annex. 부훈 傅訓 The instructions of a teacher ; to instruct.

부 溥 Universal. 부수 溥首 A name of Mañjuśrī, v. 문 文.

부(특)가라 富(特)伽羅 Pudgala, that which has (handsome) form ; body ; soul ; beings subject to metempsychosis. Cf. 불 弗, 보 補.

부나 富那 Puṇya ; Punar ; Pūrṇa. 부나기 富那奇 Name of a preta, or hungry ghost ; and of a monk named Pūrṇeccha. 부나바소 富那婆蘇 Punarvasu ; an asterism, i.e. the 불숙 弗宿 ; name of a monk. 부나야사 富那耶舍 ; 부나(야)사 富那(夜)奢 Puṇyayaśas ; the tenth (or eleventh) patriarch ; a descendant of the Gautama family ; born in Pāṭaliputra, laboured in Vārāṇaśī and converted Aśvaghoṣa. 부나발타 富那跋陀 Pūrṇabhadra, name of a spirit-general.

부단 不斷 Without ceasing, unceasing. 부단광 不斷光 The unceasing light (or glory of Amitābha. 부단광불 不斷光佛 One of the twelve shining Buddhas. 부단상 不斷常 Unceasing continuity. 부단염불 不斷念佛 Unceasing remembrance, or invocation of the Buddha. 부단상응염 不斷相應染 One of the 육염심 六染心. 부단(독)경 不斷(讀)經 Unceasing reading of the sūtras. 부단륜 不斷輪 Unceasing turning of the wheel, as in a monastery by relays of prayer and meditation.

부단공 不但空 "Not only the void" ; or, non-void ; śrāvakas and pratyeka-buddhas see only the "void," bodhisattvas see also the non-void, hence 부단공 不但空 is the 중도공 中道空 the "void" of the "mean". It is a term of the 통교 通教 Intermediate school.

부단나 富單那 or **부타나** 富陀那 Pūtana. A class of pretas in charge of fevers, v. 포 布.

부동 不動 Acala ; niścala ; dhruva. The unmoved, immobile, or motionless ; also 무동 無動 the term is used for the unvarying or unchanging, for the pole-star, for fearlessness, for indifference to passion or temptation. It is a special term of Shingon 진언 眞言 applied to its most important Bodhisattva, the 부동명왕 不動明王 q.v. 부동불 不動佛 ; 부동여래 不動如來 ; 아촉(비) 阿閦(鞞) or 아촉(바) 阿閦(婆) Akṣobhya, one of the 오지여래 五智如來 Five Wisdom, or Dhyāni-Buddhas, viz., Vairocana, Akṣobhya, Ratnasaṃbhava, Amitābha, and Amoghasiddhi. He is especially worshipped by the Shingon sect, as a disciple of Vairocana. As Amitābha is Buddha in the western heavens, so Akṣobhya is Buddha in the eastern heaven of Abhirati, the realm of joy, hence he is styled 선쾌 善快 or 묘희 妙喜, also 무진에 無瞋恚 free from anger. His cult has existed since the Han dynasty, see the Akṣobhya-tathāgatasya-vyūha. He is first mentioned in the Prajñāpāramitā Sūtra, then in the Lotus, where he is the first of the sixteen sons of Mahābhijñā-jñānābhibhu. His dhyāni-bodhisattva is Vajrapāṇi. His appearance is variously described, but he generally sits on a lotus, feet crossed, soles upward, left hand closed holding robe, right hand fingers extended touching ground calling it as witness ; he is seated above a blue elephant ; his colour is pale gold, some say blue ; a vajra is before him. His esoteric word is Hūṁ ; his element the air, his human form Kanakamuni, v. 구 拘. Jap. Ashuku, Fudo, and Mudo ; Tib. mi-bskyod-pa, mi-'khrugs-pa(mintug-pa) ; Mong. ülü küdelükci, v. 부동명왕 不動明王. 부동공 不動供 Offerings to 부동명왕 不動明王. 부동사자 不動使者 His messengers. 부동주 不動咒 ; 부동자구주 不動慈救咒 ; 부동자호주 不動慈護咒 ; 부동다라니 不動陀羅尼 ; 부동사자(다라니)비밀법 不動使者(陀羅尼)秘密法. Prayers and spells associated with him and his messengers. 부동지 不動地 The eighth of the ten stages in a Buddha's advance to perfection. 부동안진법 不動安鎭法 Prayers to 부동명왕 不動明王 to protect the house. 부동정 不動定 The samādhi, or abstract meditation, in which he abides. 부동명왕 不動明王 ; 부동존 不動尊 Āryācalanātha 아사라낭 阿奢羅曩 tr. 부동존 不動尊 and 무동존 無動尊 and Acalacetā, 아사라서타 阿奢囉逝吒 tr. 부동사자 不動使者. The mouthpiece or messenger, e.g. the Mercury, of the Buddhas ; and the chief of the five Ming Wang. He is regarded as the third person in the Vairocana trinity. He has a fierce mien overawing all evil spirits. He is said to have attained to Buddhahood, but also still to retain his position with Vairocana. He has many descriptive titles, e.g. 무량력신통무동자 無量力神通無動者 ; 부동분노왕 不動忿怒王, etc. Five different verbal sings are given to him. He carries a sharp wisdom-sword, a noose, a thunder-bolt. The colour of his images is various — black, blue, purple. He has a youthful appearance ; his hair falls over his left shoulder ; he stands or sits on a rock ; left eye closed ; mouth shut, teeth gripping upper lip, wrinkled forehead, seven locks of hair, full-bodied. A second representation is with four faces and four arms, angry mien, protruding teeth, with flames around him. A third with necklaces. A fourth, red, seated on a rock, flames, trident, etc. There are other forms. He has fourteen distinguishing symbols, and many dhāraṇīs associated with the realm of fire, of saving those in distress, and of wisdom. He has two messengers 이동자 二童子 Kiṁkara 긍갈나 矜羯羅 and Ceṭaka 제타가 制吒迦, and, including these, a group of eight messengers 팔대동자 八大童子 each with image, symbol, word-sign, etc. Cf. 부동불 不動佛. 부동법 不動法 Prayer for the aid of 부동명왕 不動明王 to end calamity and cause prosperity. 부동무위 不動無爲 One of the six 무위 無爲 kinds of inaction, or *laissez-aller*, the state of being unmoved by pleasure or pain. Similarly 부동해탈 不動解脫 liberation from being disturbed (by the illusions of life) ; and 부동아라한 不動阿羅漢 an arhat who has attained to this state. 부동생사 不動生死 Immortality, nirvāṇa. 부동의 不動義 Immobility, one of the ten meanings of the void. 부동강 不動講 An assembly for preaching and praising the virtues of 부동존 不動尊. 부동금강명왕 不動金剛明王 The 부동존 不動尊 as the vajra representative, or embodiment, of Vairocana for saving all sentient beings.

부라 富羅 A translit. for a short-legged, or ornamented boot, as 부유발다라 富維跋陀羅 is boot or shoe ornamentation. 부라 富羅 is also intp. as land, country ; perhaps pura, a city.

부란나 富蘭那 Purāṇas. A class of Brahmanic mythological literature ; also 포자나 布剌拏 or 보자나 補剌拏. 부란나가섭 富蘭那迦葉 ; 포자나 布剌拏 or 布剌那 or 晡剌拏 or 晡剌那 or 부자나 棓剌拏 or 棓剌那 ; 부란 不蘭 ; 보자나 補剌那, etc. Pūraṇa Kāśyapa ; one of the six heretics opposed by Śākyamuni ; he taught the non-existence of all things, that all was illusion, and that there was neither birth nor death ; ergo, neither prince nor subject, parent nor child, nor their duties. 부란다라 富蘭陀羅 Purandara ; stronghold-breaker, fortress-destroyer, a name for Indra as thunder-god.

부루나 富樓那 Pūrṇa ; also 부루나미다라니자 富樓那彌多羅尼子 and other similar phonetic forms ; Pūrṇamaitrāyaṇīputra, or Maitrāyaṇīputra, a disciple of Śākyamuni, son of Bhava by a slave girl, often confounded with Maitreya. The chief preacher among the ten principal disciples of Śākyamuni ; ill-treated by his brother, engaged in business, saved his brothers from shipwreck by conquering Indra through samādhi ; built a vihāra for Śākyamuni ; expected to reappear as 법명여래 法明如來 Dharmaprabhāsa Buddha.

부루사 富樓沙 Puruṣa, v. 포 布 ; a man, mankind. Man personified as Nārāyaṇa ; the soul and source of the universe ; soul. Explained by 신아 神我 the spiritual self ; the Ātman whose characteristic is thought, and which produces, through successive modifications, all forms of existence.

부루사부라 富婁沙富羅 or **부류사부라** 富留沙富羅 Puruṣapura, the ancient capital of Gandhāra, the modern Peshawar, stated to be the native country of Vasubandhu.

부사 富沙 Puṣya. An ancient ṛṣi. A constellation, v. 불 弗.

부사의 不思議 Acintya. 아진제야 阿軫帝也 Beyond thought and words, beyond conception, baffling description, amazing. 부사의승 不思議乘 The ineffable vehicle, Buddhism. 부사의혜동자 不思議慧童子 The youth of ineffable wisdom, one of the eight youths in the Mañjuśrī court of the Garbhadhātu. 부사의지 不思議智 Acintya-jñāna, inconceivable wisdom, the indescribable

Buddha-wisdom. 부사의업상 不思議業相 Inexpressible karma-merit always working for the benefit of the living. 부사의계 不思議界 Acintyadhātu. The realm beyond thought and words, another name for the Bhūtatathatā, 진여 眞如. 부사의진언상도법 不思議眞言相道法 The practice of the presence of the invisible Dharmakāya in the esoteric word. 부사의공 不思議空 ; 제일의공 第一義空 The void beyond thought or discussion, a conception of the void, or that which is beyond the material, only attained by Buddhas and bodhisattvas. 부사의공지 不思議空智 The wisdom thus attained which removes all distresses and illusions. 부사의(해탈)경 不思議(解脫)經 The 화엄경 華嚴經 Hua-yen Sūtra. 부사의훈 不思議薰 The indescribable vāsanā, i.e. suffusion, or "fuming", or influence of primal 무명 無明 ignorance, on the 진여 眞如 bhūtatathatā, producing all illusion. v. 기신론 起信論 Awakening of Faith. 부사의변 不思議變 The indescribable changes of the bhūtatathatā in the multitudinous forms of all things. 부사의변역생사 不思議變易生死 Ineffable changes and transmigrations, i.e. to the higher stages of mortality above the traidhātuka or trailokya 삼계 三界.

부자재 不自在 Not independent, not one's own master, under governance.

부재정 不才淨 Neither clever nor pure — a term of rebuke.

부정 不淨 Unclean, common, vile. 부정분노 不淨忿怒 ; 부정금강 不淨金剛 ; 오추사마명왕 烏樞沙摩明王 or 烏芻沙摩明王 ; 촉금강 觸金剛 Ucchuṣma, a bodhisattva connected with 부동명왕 不動明王 who controls unclean demons. 부정시 不淨施 "Unclean" almsgiving, i.e. looking for its reward in this or the next life. 부정육 不淨肉 "Unclean" flesh, i.e. that of animals, fishes, etc., seen being killed, heard being killed, or suspected of being killed ; Hīnayāna forbids these, Mahāyāna forbids all flesh. 부정행 不淨行 ; 비범행 非梵行 Ignoble or impure deeds, sexual immorality. 부정관 不淨觀 The Meditation on the uncleanness of the human body of self and others, e.g. the nine stages of disintegration of the dead body 구상 九想 q.v. ; it is a meditation to destroy 탐 貪 desire ; other details are : parental seed, womb, the nine excretory passages, the body's component parts, worm-devoured corpse-all unclean. 부정관경 不淨觀經 A Sūtra of Dharmatrāta. 부정설법 不淨說法 ; 사명설법 邪命說法 "Unclean" preaching, i.e. to preach, whether rightly or wrongly, from an impure motive, e.g. for making a living. 부정륜 不淨輪 One of the three 윤 輪 impermanence, impurity, distress 무상 無常, 부정 不淨, 고 苦.

부정 不定 Unfixed, unsettled, undetermined, uncertain. 부정수업 不定受業 One of the "four karma" — aniyata or indefinite karma ; opposite of 정업 定業. 부정지법 不定地法 One of the six mental conditions, that of undetermined character, open to any influence good or evil. 부정(종)성 不定(種)性 Of indeterminate nature. The 법상종 法相宗 Dharmalakṣaṇa School divides all beings into five classes according to their potentialities. This is one of the divisions and contains four combinations : (1) Bodhisattva-cum-śrāvaka, with uncertain result depending on the more dominant of the two ; (2) bodhisattva-cum-pratyeka-buddha ; (3) śrāvaka-cum-pratyeka-buddha ; (4) the characteristics of all three vehicles intermingled with uncertain results ; the third cannot attain Buddhahood, the rest may. 부정성취 不定性聚 ; 부정취 不定聚 One of the three T'ien-t'ai groups of humanity, the indeterminate normal class of people, as contrasted with sages 정정성취 正定性聚 whose natures are determined for goodness, and the wicked 사정성취 邪定性聚 whose natures are determined for evil. 부정교 不定教 Indeterminate teaching. T'ien-t'ai divides the Buddha's mode of teaching into four ; this one means that Buddha, by his extraordinary powers of 방편 方便 upāya-kauśalya, or adaptability, could confer Mahāyāna benefits on his hearers out of his Hīnayāna teaching and vice versa, dependent on the capacity of his hearers. 부정(지)관 不定(止)觀 Direct insight without any gradual process of samādhi ; one of three forms of T'ien-t'ai meditation.

부정식 不正食 Not strict food, not exactly food, things that do not count as a meal, e.g. fruit and nuts.

부좌고광대상 不坐高廣大牀 Anuccaśāyanāmahāśāyana. Not to sit on a high, broad, large bed, the ninth of the ten commandments.

부즉류 不喞噹 Ignorant, rustic ; immature or ignorant.

부즉불리 不卽不離 Neither the thing itself nor something apart, e.g. the water and the wave : similar to 불일불이 不一不異.

부증불감 不增不減 Neither adding nor subtracting ; nothing can be added or taken away. In reference to the absolute 실상지공리 實相之公理 nothing can be added or taken away ; vice versa with the relative. 부증감진여 不增減眞如 the unvarying 진여 眞如 Bhūtatathatā, one of the ten 진여 眞如 ; also the eighth of the 십지 十地.

부처(님) 佛 The Buddha.

북 北 Uttara, North. 북산주부 北山住部 ; 울다세라부 鬱多世羅部 Uttaraśailāḥ. One of the sects organized in the third century after the Nirvāṇa, whose seat is described as north of 제다산 制多山 q.v. 북종 北宗 The northern school of the Ch'an(Zen) sect ; from Bodhidharma 달마 達磨 to the fifth patriarch 홍인 弘忍 Hung-jên the school was undivided ; from 혜능 慧能 Hui-nêng began the division of the southern school, 신수 神秀 Shên-hsiu maintaining the northern ; it was the southern school which prevailed. 북도 北度 The pupil's position in paying respect to his master, i.e. facing the north where the master sits. 북두(칠성) 北斗(七星) Ursa major, the Northern Bushel with its seven stars. 북두당 北斗堂 The hall for its worship. 북방칠요중 北方七曜衆 The seven northern constellations from 위 胃 Wei to 허 虛 Hsü are represented in the Garbhadhātu by their seven devas. Cf. 북진 北辰. 북방불교 北方佛教 Northern Buddhism, i.e. Mahāyāna, in contrast with Southern Buddhism, Hīnayāna. 북본열반경 北本涅槃經 The northern version of the Nirvāṇa sūtra, in forty, in forty chüan. 북침 北枕 The northern pillow, i.e. Śākyamuni, when dying, pillowed his head to the north, pointing the way for the extension of his doctrine. 북주 北洲 ; 북구로주 北拘盧洲 or 北俱盧洲 Uttarakuru, the northern of the four continents surrounding Sumeru ; v. 울 鬱. 북라 北羅 Valabhī. Northern Lāṭa. "An ancient kingdom and city on the Eastern coast of Gujarat." [Eitel]. 북대 北臺 The northern T'ai, i.e. Wu-t'ai-shan in Shansi, the northernmost of the Four famous Buddhist Mountains. 북장 北藏 The northern collection or edition of 1,621 works first published in Peking by order of Ch'êng Tsu (1403-1424), together with forty-one additional works, published by 밀장 密藏 Mi-tsang after thirty years' labour beginning A.D. 1586. Later this edition was published in Japan 1678-1681 by 철안 鐵眼 Tetsugen. 북행 北行 Uttarāyaṇa. The northern ascension of the sun between the winter and summer solstices. 북진보살 北辰菩薩 The Bodhisattva 묘견 妙見 Miao Chien of UrsaMajor.

분 墳 A grave 분묘 墳墓.

분 忿 Anger. 분노 忿怒 Anger, angry, fierce, over-awing ; a term for the 분왕 忿王 or 분노(명)왕 忿怒(明)王 the fierce mahārājas as opponents of evil and guardians of Buddhism ; one of the two bodhisattva forms, resisting evil, in contrast with the other form, manifesting goodness. There are three forms of this fierceness in the Garbhadhātu group and five in the Diamond group. 분노구 忿怒鉤 A form of Kuan-yin with a hook. 분결 忿結 The bond of anger.

분 盆 Bowl, basin, tub. 분회 盆會 The All-Souls anniversary, v. 우 盂.

분 粉 Flour, meal, power. 분골쇄신 粉骨碎身 Bones ground to powder and body in fragments.

분 芬 Fragrant ; confused ; translit. *puṇ* in 분다리 芬陀利 or 芬陁利 Puṇḍarīka, the white lotus, v. 분 分.

분 糞 Ordure, sweepings, garbage. 분소 糞掃 Sweepings, garbage. 분소의 糞掃衣 ; 납의 衲衣 The monk's garment of cast-off rags. 분과 糞果 The āmraka fruit in the midden, or a pearl in the mud, cf. Nirvāṇa sūtra 12. 분제 糞除 To get rid of garbage, scavenge ; cf. Lotus sūtra 4.

분 焚 To burn, consume by fire. 분향 焚香 To burn incense.

분 分 To divide, separate ; a fractional part ; a share ; a duty.

분 奮 To rouse, excite, exert ; impetuous, energetic. 분신 奮迅 Speedy, immediate (samādhi), cf. 사 師.

분 奔 To run ; translit. *pun* and *p*. 분양사라 奔攘舍羅 Puṇyaśālā, almshouse or asylum for sick and poor. 분다(리가) 奔荼(利迦) Puṇḍarīka, the white lotus, v. 분 分 or 분 芬 ; also the last of the eight great cold hells, v. 지옥 地獄. 분나벌전나 奔那伐戰那 Puṇḍra-vardhana, an ancient kingdom and city in Bengal. 분나가 奔那伽 Puṣpanāga, the flowering dragon-tree under which Maitreya is said to have attained enlightenment.

분나가 分那柯 Pūrṇaka, i.e. 만 滿 full ; name of a yakṣa, or demon.

분다리(가) 分陀利(迦) Puṇḍarīka, 분타 芬陀 ; 분다리가 分荼利迦 or 분다리화 奔荼利華 ; 본나리가 本拏哩迦 ; the 백련화 白蓮花 white lotus (in full bloom). It is also termed 백엽화 百葉華 or 팔엽화 八葉華 hundred (or eight) leaf flower. For Saddharma-puṇḍarīka, the Lotus Sūtra, v. (묘법)연화경 (妙法)蓮華經. The eighth and coldest hell is called after this flower, because the cold lays bare the bones of the wicked, so that they resemble the whiteness of this lotus. It is also called 수색화 隨色花 ; when a bud, it is known as 굴마라 屈摩羅 ; and when fading, as 가마라 迦摩羅.

분단 分段 Bhāgya. Lot, dispensation, allotment, fate. 분단생사 分段生死, 분단사 分段死, 분단신 分段身, 분단삼도 分段三道 all refer to the mortal lot, or dispensation in regard to the various forms of reincarnation. 분단동거 分段同居 Those of the same lot, or incarnation, dwelling together, e.g. saints and sinners in this world. 분단윤회 分段輪廻 The wheel of fate, or reincarnation. 분단변역 分段變易 Includes (1) 분단생사 分段生死, the condition and station resulting from good or bad karma in the three realms (desire, form, and formlessness) and in the six paths ; (2) 변역생사 變易生死 the condition and station resulting from good karma in the realms beyond transmigration, including arhats and higher saints.

분별 分別 Vibhajya, or vibhāga ; parikalpana ; vikalpa ; divide, discriminate, discern, reason ; to leave. The 삼분별 三分別 three forms are (1) 자성분별 自性分別 natural discrimination, e.g. of present objects ; (2) 계탁분별 計度分別 calculation discrimination (as to future action) ; (3) 수념분별 隨念分別 discriminating by remembrance of affairs that are past. 분별사식 分別事識 The third of the three kinds of perception 식 識, i.e. real (or abstract), manifest, and reasoned (or inferred) ; it includes all the eight 식 識 except the ālaya-vijñāna. 분별지 分別智 Viveka. Differentiating knowledge, discrimination of phenomena, as contrasted with 무분별지 無分別智 the knowledge of the fundamental identity of all things. 분별지상응염 分別智相應染 The taint on mind following upon the action of discriminating, i.e. one of the six 염심 染心 ; v. Awakening of Faith 기신론 起信論. 분별경 分別經 There are several sūtras and śāstras with various 분별 分別 titles. 분별설삼 分別說三 The One vehicle discriminated as "three" for the sake of the ignorant. 분별설부 分別說部 The Vibhajyavādinaḥs. A school the origin of which is obscure. The meaning of the term, not necessarily limited to this school, is the method of particularization in dealing with questions in debate. It is suggested that this school was established to harmonize the differences between the Sthaviras and Mahāsāṅghikas. The Abhidharma-piṭaka "as we have it in the Pali Canon, is the definite work of this school", Keith, 153. 분별식 分別識 The discriminating perception, i.e. of 의 意 mind, the sixth 근 根 organ. 분별기 分別起 Delusions arising from reasoning and teaching, in contrast with 구생기 俱生起 errors that arise naturally among people.

분산 分散 Visarj. To dismiss, scatter, separate, as an assembly.

분상문 分相門 The doctrine which differentiates the three vehicles from the one vehicle ; as 해섭문 該攝門 is that which maintains the three vehicles to be the one

분석 分析 To divide, separate, leave the world, v. 석 析.

분세 分歲 New Year's eve, the dividing night of the year, also styled 세야 歲夜.

분신 分身 Parturition ; in Buddhism it means a Buddha's power to reproduce himself *ad infinitum* and anywhere.

분위 分位 Avasthā ; defined as 시분 時分 time and 지위 地位 position ; i.e. a state, e.g. the state of water disturbed into waves, waves being also a state of water ; a dependent state.

분위 分衛 Piṇḍapāta, 빈다파다 賓茶波多 ; 빈다야 賓茶夜 food given as alms ; piṇḍapātika means one who lives on alms ; it is also interpreted as 단타 團墮 lumps (of food) falling (into the begging bowl) ; the reference is to the Indian method of rolling the cooked food into a bolus for eating, or such a bolus given to the monks.

분유 分喩 A metaphor only correct in part, e.g. a face like the moon.

분자 鐼子 Hsün-tzŭ, a bowl (or bowls) within an almsbowl. Buddha's bowl consisted of four heavy deva-bowls which he received miraculously one on the other ; they are to be recovered with the advent of Maitreya ; v. 건자 鍵鎡.

분증(즉) 分證(卽) One of the T'ien-t'ai 육즉 六卽 q.v. Also 분진(즉) 分眞(卽).

분진즉 分眞卽 idem 분증즉 分證卽.

불 佛 Buddha, from Budh, to "be aware of," "conceive," "observe," "wake" ; also 불타 佛陀 ; 부도 浮圖 ; 부타 浮陀 ; 부두 浮頭 ; 부탑 浮塔 ; 발타 勃陀 ; 발타 勃馱 ; 몰타 沒馱 ; 모타 母馱 ; 모타 母陀 ; 부타 部陀 ; 휴도 休屠. Buddha means "completely conscious, enlightened," and came to mean the enlightener. The Chinese translation is 각 覺 to perceive, aware, awake ; and 지 智 gnosis, knowledge. There is an Eternal Buddha, see e.g. the Lotus Sūtra, cap. 16, and multitudes of Buddhas, but the personality of a Supreme Buddha, an Ādi-Buddha, is not defined. Buddha is in and through all things, and some schools are definitely Pan-Buddhist in the pantheistic sense. In the Triratna 삼보 三寶 commonly known as 삼보불 三寶佛, while Śākyamuni Buddha is the first "person" of the Trinity, his Law the second, and the Order the third, all three by some are accounted as manifestations of the All-Buddha. As Śākyamuni, the title indicates him as the last of the line of Buddhas who have appeared in this world, Maitreya is to be the next. As such he is the one who has achieved enlightenment, having discovered the essential evil of existence (some say mundane existence, others all existence), and the way of deliverance from the constant round of reincarnations ; this way is through the moral life into nirvāṇa, by means of self-abnegation, the monastic life, and meditation. By this method a Buddha, or enlightened one, himself obtains Supreme Enlightenment, or Omniscience, and according to Mahāyānism leads all beings into the same enlightenment. He sees things not as they seem in their phenomenal but in their noumenal aspects, as they really are. The term is also applied to those who understand the chain of causality (twelve nidānas) and have attained enlightenment surpassing that of the arhat. Four types of the Buddha are referred to: (1) 삼장불 三藏佛 the Buddha of the Tripiṭaka who attained enlightenment on the bare ground under the bodhi-tree ; (2) 통불 通佛 the Buddha on the deva robe under the bodhi-tree of the seven precious things ; (3) 별불 別佛 the Buddha on the great precious Lotus throne under the Lotus realm bodhi-tree ; and (4) 원불 圓佛 the Buddha on the throne of Space in the realm of eternal rest and glory, where he is Vairocana. The Hīnayāna only admits the existence of one Buddha at a time ; Mahāyāna claims the existence of many Buddhas at one and the same time, as many Buddhas as there are Buddha-universes, which are infinite in number.

불 不 No, not, none. (Sanskrit *a*, *aṇ*)

불 弗 Not ; no ; do not. 불우체 弗于逮 ; 불우비바제하 弗于毘婆提訶 idem 포로바 布嚕波 Pūrva-Videha. 불가라 弗伽羅 ; 복가라 福伽羅 ; 부가라 富伽羅 ; 보특가라 補特伽羅 Pudgala ; Pali, puggala. M. W. says "handsome", "having form or property", "the soul, personal identity". Keith uses "person", "personality". Eitel, "a general term for all human beings as subject to metempsychosis. A philosophical term denoting personality." It is tr. by 인 人 man and 중생 衆生 all the living ; later by 수취취 數取趣 those who go on to repeated reincarnations, but whether this means the individual soul in its rebirths is not clear. 불여단 弗如檀 Puṇyādarśa, auspicious mirror, interpreted as 법경 法鏡 mirror of the law ; name of a man. 불바세라 弗婆勢羅 Pūrvaśaila, "the eastern mountain behind which the sun is supposed to rise." [M. W.] The eastern mountain, name of a monastery east of Dhānyakaṭaka (Amarāvatī), the 불바세라승가람 弗婆勢羅僧伽藍 or 불반세리승가람 佛槃勢羅僧伽藍 Pūrvaśaila-saṅghārāma. One of the subdivisions of the Mahāsāṅghikāḥ school. 불바하라 弗婆呵羅 Puṣpāhara, flower-plucker, 식화 食花 flower-eater, name of a yakṣa. 불바제 弗婆提 ; 불바비다제 弗婆鞞陀提 idem 불비제하 弗毘提訶. 불사왕 弗沙王 Vatsarāja. King Vatsa, idem Udayana, v. 우전 優塡. The 불사가왕경 弗沙迦王經 is another name for the 평사왕오원경 萍沙王五願經. 불사 弗沙 ; 발사 勃沙 ; 부사 富沙 ; 포사 逋沙 ; 보사 補沙 ; Puṣya ; "the sixth (or in later times the eighth) Nakshatra or lunar mansion, also called Tishya." [M. W.] 저사 底沙. It is the 귀 鬼 group Cancer $\gamma\delta\eta\theta$, the 23rd of the Chinese twenty-eight stellar mansions. Name of an ancient Buddha. 불사불 弗沙佛 idem 저사불 底沙佛. 불사밀다 弗沙蜜多 Puṣyamitra, descendant of Aśoka and enemy of Buddhism ; possibly a mistake for the next. 불사밀다라 弗沙蜜多羅 Puṣyamitra, the fourth successor of King Aśoka ; asking what he should do to perpetuate his name, he was told that Aśoka had erected 84,000 shrines and he might become famous by destroying them, which he is said to have done, v. 잡아함경 雜阿含經 25. 불률특 弗栗特 Vṛji, or 삼벌시 三伐恃 Saṁvaji. An ancient kingdom north of the Ganges, S.E. of Nepal, the inhabitants, called Saṁvaji, were noted for their heretical proclivities. [Eitel]. 불비제하 弗毘提訶 Pūrva-Videha, or Videha, the continent east of Sumeru, idem 포로바 布嚕波. 불바제 弗波提 ; 불바제 弗把提 Either devapuṣpa, or bhūpadī, the latter being Jasminum Zambæ ; both are interpreted by 천화 天華 deva-flowers. 불야다라 弗若多羅 ; 공덕화 功德華 Puṇyatara, a śramaṇa of Kubhā 계빈국 罽賓國 (Kabul), who came to China and in 404 tr. with Kumārajīva the 십송율 十誦律 Sarvāstivāda-vinaya. "One of the twenty-four Deva-Ārya (천존 天尊) worshipped in China." [Eitel].

불 拂 To rub, wipe, dust. 불자 拂子 A duster, fly brush. 불석 拂石 ; 반석겁 槃石劫 A kalpa as measured by the time it would take to wear away an immense rock by rubbing it with a deva-garment ; cf. 개 芥 and 겁파 劫波. 불적입현 拂迹入玄 To rub out the traces of past impurity and enter into profundity of Buddha.

불가 不可 May not, can not ; unpermissible, forbidden ; unable. 불가득 不可得 Anupalabhya ; Alabhya. Beyond laying hold of, unobtainable, unknowable, unreal, another name for 공 空 the void. 삼세심불가득 三世心不可得 The mind or thought, past, present, future, cannot be held fast ; the past is gone, the future not arrived, the present does not stay. 불가득공 不可得空 One of the eighteen 공 空 ; it is the 언망려절지공 言亡慮絶之空, the "void" that is beyond words or thought. 불가사의 不可思議 Beyond thought or description, v. 부사의 不思議. Pu-k'o, the name of a monk of the 영묘사 靈妙寺 Ling Miao monastery in the T'ang dynasty, a disciple of Śubhākarasiṁha, and one of the founders of 진언 眞言 Shingon. The four indescribables, v. 증일아함경 增一阿含經 18, are the worlds ; living beings ; dragons (nāgas) ; and the size of the Buddha-lands. The five, of the 지도론 智度論 30, are : The number of living beings ; all the consequences of karma ; the powers of a state of dhyāna ; the powers of nāgas ; the powers of the Buddhas. 불가사의존 不可思議尊 ; 불가사의광여래 不可思議光如來 The ineffable Honoured One ; the Tathāgata of ineffable light ; titles of Amitābha. 불가사의(해탈)경 不可思議(解脫)經 A name for the 화엄경 華嚴經 Hua-yen sūtra. The full title is also a name for the 유마경 維摩經 Vimalakīrti sūtra. 불가사의해탈법문 不可思議解脫法門 The samādhi, or liberation of mind, that ensures a vision of the ineffable. 불가유 不可有 The existence of those who do the 불가 不可, or forbidden, i.e. the hells. 불가기 不可棄 Not to be cast-away – said to be the name of the founder of the Mahīśāsaka, or 화지 化地 school, cast into a well at birth by his mother, saved by his father, at first a brahman, afterwards a Buddhist ; v. 문수문경 文殊問經, but probably apocryphal. 불가칭지 不可稱智 The Buddha-wisdom that in its variety is beyond description. 불가견유대색 不可見有對色 ; 불가견무대색 不可見無對色 The first refers to invisible, perceptible, or material things, e.g. sound, smell, etc. ; the second to invisible, imperceptible, or immaterial things. 불가설 不可說 Unmentionable, indefinable ; truth that can be thought but not expressed. 불가설불 不可說佛 Gaṇendra ; the 733rd of the Buddhas of the present kalpa 현겁 賢劫, in which 1,000 Buddhas are to appear, of whom four have appeared. 불가월수호 不可越守護 Two guardians of the Law on the right of Mañjuśrī in the Garbhadhātu maṇḍala, named 난지 難持 and 난승 難勝.

불가 佛家 The school or family of Buddhism ; the Pure Land, where is the family of Buddha. Also all Buddhists from the Śrota-āpanna stage upwards.

불가무창기불왕관청 不歌舞倡伎不往觀聽 Nāṭya-gīta-vāditra-viśūkadarśanād vairamaṇī (virati). The seventh commandment against taking part in singing, dancing, play, or going to watch and hear them.

불각 不覺 Unenlightened, uncomprehending, without "spiritual" insight, the condition of people in general, who mistake the phenomenal for the real, and by ignorance beget karma, reaping its results in the mortal round of transmigration ; i.e. people generally. 불각현행위 不覺現行位 The first two of the 십지 十地 of the saint, in which the illusion of mistaking the phenomenal for the real still arises.

불갱악취원 不更惡趣願 The second of Amitābha's forty-eight vows, that those born in his kingdom should never again enter the three evil lower paths of transmigration.

불견 佛見 The correct views, or doctrines, of the Buddha ; Buddha doctrines.

불경 佛經 Buddhist canonical literature ; also Buddha's image and sūtras, with special reference to those purporting to have been introduced under Han Ming Ti ; sūtras probably existed in China before that reign, but evidence is lacking. The first work, generally attributed to Ming Ti's reign, is known as The Sūtra of Forty-two Sections 사십이장경 四十二章經 but Maspero in *B.E.F.E.O.* ascribes it to the second century A.D.

불경 不輕 Never Despise, 상불경보살 常不經菩薩 a previous incarnation of the Buddha, as a monk whose constant greeting to all he met, that they were destined for Buddhahood, brought him much persecution ; see the chapter of this title in the Lotus Sūtra. 불경행 不輕行 The practice of "Never Despise".

불경 佛境 The (spiritual) region of Buddhas.

불계 佛界 The Buddha realm, the state of Buddha-hood, one of the ten realms, which consist of the six gati together with the realms of Buddhas, bodhisattvas, pratyeka-buddhas, and śrāvakas ; also a Buddha-land ; also the Buddha's country ; cf. 불토 佛土.

불계 佛戒 The moral commandments of the Buddha ; also, the laws of reality observed by all Buddhas.

불고론종 不顧論宗 One of the 인명사종 因明四宗, a philosophical school, whose rule was self-gratification, "not caring for" others.

불고불락수 不苦不樂受 One of the 삼수 三受, the state of experiencing neither pain nor pleasure, i.e. above them. Also styled 사수 捨受 the state in which one has abandoned both.

불골 佛骨 A bone of the Buddha, especially the bone against whose reception by the emperor Hsien Tsung the famous protest of Han Yü was made in 819.

불공 不空 Amogha, Amoghavajra. 불공삼장 不空三藏 ; 지장 智藏 ; 아목거발절라 阿目佉跋折羅 Not empty (or not in vain) vajra. The famous head of the Yogācāra school in China. A Singhalese of northern brahmanic descent, having lost his father, he came at the age of 15 with his uncle to 동해 東海, the eastern sea, or China, where in 718 he became a disciple of 금강지 金剛智 Vajrabodhi. After the latter's death in 732, and at his wish, Eliot says in 741, he went to India and Ceylon in search of esoteric or tantric writings, and returned in 746, when he baptized the emperor Hsüan Tsung. He was especially noted for rain-making and stilling storms. in 749 he received permission to return home, but was stopped by imperial orders when in the south of China. In? 756 under Su Tsung he was recalled to the capital. His time until 771 was spent translating and editing tantric books in 120 volumes, and the Yogācāra 밀교 密教 rose to its peak of prosperity. He died greatly honoured at 70 years of age, in 774, the twelfth year of Tai Tsung, the third emperor under whom he had served. The festival of feeding the hungry spirits 우란승회 盂蘭勝會 is attributed to him. His titles of 지장 智藏 and 불공삼장 不空三藏 are Thesaurus of Wisdom and Amogha Tripiṭaka. 불공공양보살 不空供養菩薩 Āryāmogha-pūrṇamaṇi, also styled 여의금강 如意金剛 "At will vajra" ; in the Garbhadhātu maṇḍala, the fifth on the south of the 실지 悉地 court. 불공여래장 不空如來藏, 불공진여 不空眞如 The realm of phenomena ; in contrast with the universal 진여 眞如 or 법신 法身 dharmakāya, unmingled with the illusion of phenomena. 불공성취여래 不空成就如來 Amoghasiddhi. The Tathāgata of unerring performance, the fifth of the five wisdom or dhyāni-buddhas of the diamond-realm. He is placed in the north ; his image is gold-coloured, left hand clenched, right fingers extended pointing to breast. Also, "He is seated in 'adamantine' pose (legs closely locked)" [Getty], soles apparent, left hand in lap, palm upwards, may balance a double vajra, or sword ; right hand erect in blessing, fingers extended. Symbol, double vajra ; colour, green [Getty] ; word, aḥ! ; blue-green lotus ; element, earth ; animal, garuḍa ; Śakti (female personification), Tārā ; Mānuṣi-Buddha (human or saviour Buddha), Maitreya. T., don-grub ; J., Fukū jō-jū. 불공견삭(관음) 不空羂索(觀音) ; 불공견삭(왕) 不空羂索(王) ; 불공견삭(보살) 不空羂索(菩薩) Amoghapāśa 아모가파사 阿牟伽皤賒. Not empty (or unerring) net, or lasso. One of the six forms of Kuan-yin in the Garbhadhātu group, catching deva and human fish for the bodhi-shore. The image has three faces, each with three eyes and six arms, but other forms have existed, one with three heads and ten arms, one with one head and four arms. The hands hold a net, lotus, trident, halberd, the gift of courage, and a plenipotentiary staff ; sometimes accompanied by "the green Tārā, Sudhana-Kumāra, Hayagrīva and Bhṛkuṭī" [Getty]. There are numerous sūtras, etc. 불공견보살 不空見菩薩 Amoghadarśin, the unerringly seeing Bodhisattva, shown in the upper second place of Ti-tsang's court in the Garbhadhātu ; also 보관금강 普觀金剛. 불공금강보살 不空金剛菩薩 Amoghavajra. 아목길발절라 阿目佶跋折羅 A Bodhisattva in the 소실지 蘇悉地 court of the Garbhadhātu. 불공구관음 不空鉤觀音 Amoghāṅkuśa. 앙구사 央俱捨 Kuan-yin of the "Unerring hook", similar to 불공견삭구사 不空羂索俱捨 ; also styled 청정연화명왕앙구사 淸淨蓮華明王央俱捨 ; in the court of the empyrean.

불공 佛供 An offering to Buddha.

불공 不共 Not in the same class, dissimilar, distinctive, each its own. 불공삼매 不共三昧 Asakṛt-samādhi ; a samādhi in more than one formula, or mode. 불공부정 不共不定 One of the six 부정인 不定因 indefinite statements of a syllogism, where proposition and example do not agree. 불공중공 不共中共 The general among the particulars, the whole in the parts. 불공업 不共業 Varied, or individual karma ; each causing and receiving his own recompense. 불공법 不共法 Āveṇika-buddhadharma. The characteristics, achievements, and doctrine of Buddha which distinguish him from all others. 십팔불공법 十八不共法 the eighteen distinctive characteristics as defined by Hīnayāna are his 십력 十力, 사무외 四無畏, 삼념주 三念住 and his 대비 大悲 ; the Mahāyāna eighteen are perfection of body ; of speech ; of memory ; impartiality or universality ; ever in samādhi ; entire self-abnegation ; never diminishing will (to save) ; zeal ; thought ; wisdom ; salvation ; insight into salvation ; deeds and mind accordant with wisdom ; also his speech ; also his mind ; omniscience in regard to the past ; also to the present ; and to the future. 불공무명 不共無明 Distinctive kinds of unenlightenment, one of the two kinds of ignorance, also styled 독두무명 獨頭無明 ; particular results arising from particular evils. 불공상 不共相 Dissimilarity, singularity, *sui generis*. 불공반야 不共般若 The things special to bodhisattvas in the 반야경 般若經 in contrast with the things they have in common with śrāvakas and pratyeka-buddhas. 불공변 不共變 Varied, or individual conditions resulting from karma ; every one is his own transmigration ; one of the 사변 四變.

불과 佛果 Buddhaphala ; the Buddha fruit, the state of Buddhahood ; the fruition of arhatship, arahattvaphala.

불광 佛光 The light of Buddha, spiritual enlightenment ; halo, glory.

불괴 不壞 Avināśya ; indestructible, never decaying, eternal. 불괴구 不壞句 A term in 진언 眞言 Shingon for the magic word 아 阿 "a", the indestructible embodiment of Vairocana. 불괴사선 不壞四禪 The four dhyāna heavens, where the samādhi mind of meditation is indestructible, and the external world is indestructible by the three final catastrophes. 불괴법 不壞法 Two kinds of arhats practise the 백골관 白骨觀 skull meditation, the dull who consider the dead as ashes, the intelligent who do not, but derive supernatural powers from the meditation. 불괴금강 不壞金剛 Vairocana the indestructible, or eternal. 불괴금강광명필전 不壞金剛光明必殿 The luminous mind-temple of the eternal 대일 大日 Vairocana, the place in the Vajradhātu, or Diamond-realm, of Vairocana as teacher.

불교 佛教 Buddha's teaching ; Buddhism. v. 석교 釋教.

불구 佛具 Articles used on an altar in worship of Buddha.

불구 不久 Not long (in time). 불구예도량 不久詣道場 Not long before he visits the place of enlightenment or of Truth, i.e. soon will become a Buddha.

불구십신 佛具十身 The ten perfect bodies or characteristics of Buddha: (1) 보리신 菩提身 Bodhi-body in possession of complete enlightenment. (2) 원신 願身 Vow-body, i.e. the vow to be born in and from the Tuṣita heaven. (3) 화신 化身 Nirmāṇakāya, Buddha incarnate as a man. (4) 주지신 住持身 Buddha who still occupies his relics or what he has left behind on earth and thus upholds the dharma. (5) 상호장엄신 相好莊嚴身 Sambhogakāya, endowed with an idealized body with all Buddha marks and merits. (6) 세력신 勢力身 or 심불 心佛 Power-body, embracing all with his heart of mercy. (7) 여의신 如意身 or 의생신 意生身 At will body, appearing according to wish of need. (8) 복덕신 福德身 or 삼매신 三昧身 Samādhi body, or body of blessed virtue. (9) 지신 智身 or 성불 性佛 Wisdom-body, whose nature embraces all wisdom. (10) 법신 法身 Dharmakāya, the absolute Buddha, or essence of all life.

불국 佛國 Buddhakṣetra. The country of the Buddha's birth. A country being transformed by a Buddha, also one already transformed ; v. 불토 佛土 and 불찰 佛刹. 불국기 佛國記 Fa-hsien's Record of Buddhist countries.

불국사 佛國寺 Bul-guk-sa. A temple located in Mt. Tohamsan, Jinhyeon-dong Gyeongju-si in Korea. The 11th parish headquarters of Korean Jogye Order.

불기 佛記 Buddha's prediction, his foretelling of the future of his disciples.

불기법인 不起法忍 The stage of endurance, or patient meditation, that has reached the state where phenomenal illusion ceases to arise, through entry into the realization of the Void, or noumenal ; also 무생법인 無生法忍 or 무기법인 無起法忍.

불기어 不綺語 Unrefined, indecent, improper, or smart speech.

불납차 不臘次 or **불랍차** 不臈次 Not in order of age, i.e. clerical age ; disorderly sitting ; taking a seat to which one is not entitled.

불단 佛檀 Buddha-dāna, Buddha-giving contrasted with Māra-giving ; Buddha-charity as the motive of giving, or preaching, and of self-sacrifice, or self-immolation.

불덕 佛德 Buddha-virtue, his perfect life, perfect fruit, and perfect mercy in releasing all beings from misery.

불도 佛道 The way of Buddha, leading to Buddha-hood ; intp. as bodhi, enlightenment, gnosis.

불도징 佛圖澄 or **불도등** 佛圖磴 or 佛圖橙 Fo-t'u-ch'êng, an Indian monk who came to Loyang about A.D. 310, also known as 축불도징 竺佛圖澄, noted for his magic ; his name Buddhacinga, or (Eitel) Buddhochinga, is doubtful ; he is also called 불타승하 佛陀僧訶 Buddhasiṁha.

불란가섭 不蘭迦葉 Pūraṇa-kāśyapa. 부란나가섭 富蘭那迦葉 One of the six heretics, or Tīrthyas, opposed to Śākyamuni.

불랍일 佛臘日 The Buddhist last day of the old year, i.e. of the summer retreat.

불래 不來 Not coming (back to mortality), an explanation of 아나함 阿那含 anāgāmin. 불래불거 不來不去 Anāgamana-nirgama. Neither coming into nor going out of existence, i.e. the original constituents of all 법 法 things are eternal ; the eternal conservation of energy, or of the primal substance. 불래영 不來迎 Without being called he comes to welcome ; the Pure-land sect believes that Amitābha himself comes to welcome departing souls of his followers on their calling upon him, but the 정토진종 淨土眞宗 (Jōdō Shin-shu sect) teaches that belief in him at any time ensures rebirth in the Pure Land, independently of calling on him at death.

불롱 佛隴 Name of a peak at the south-west corner of T'ien-t'ai ; also a name for Chih-i 지의 智顗 q.v.

불료 不了 Not to bring to a finish, not to make plain, not plain, not to understand, incomprehensible. 불료의경 不了義經 Texts that do not make plain the Buddha's whole truth, such as Hīnayāna and 통교 通敎 or intermediate Mahāyāna texts. 불료불지 不了佛智 The incomprehensible wisdom of Buddha.

불루사 佛樓沙 Purushapura, v. 포 布.

불률지살당나 佛栗持薩儻那 Urddhasthāna, Ūrdvasthāna, Vardhasthāna, or Vṛjisthāna, "an ancient kingdom, the country of the Vardaks, the Ortospana of Ptolemy, the region about Cabool (Lat. 34° 32 N., Long. 68° 55 E.)." [Eitel].

불리무시자 不釐務侍者 A nominal assistant or attendant, an attendant who has no responsibilities.

불립문자(교) 不立文字(敎) The 선 禪 Ch'an or intuitive School does "not set up scriptures" ; it lays stress on meditation and intuition rather than on books and other external aids ; cf. Laṅkāvatāra-sūtra.

불립삼매 佛立三昧 A degree of samādhi in which the Buddhas appear to the meditator.

불망선 不忘禪 The meditation against forgetfulness.

불망어 不妄語 Musāvādā-veramaṇī, the fourth commandment, thou shalt not lie ; no false speaking.

불멸 不滅 Anirodha, not destroyed, not subject to annihilation. 불멸불생 不滅不生 Anirodhānutpāda, neither dying nor being reborn, immortal. v. 불생 不生.

불멸(도) 佛滅(度) Buddha's nirvāṇa ; it is interpreted as the extinction of suffering, or delusion, and as transport across the 고해 苦海 bitter sea of mortality, v. 멸 滅.

불명 佛鳴 Buddhaghoṣa, the famous commentator and writer of the Hīnayāna School and of Pali canon. He was "born near the Bo Tree, at Buddha Gayā, and came to Ceylon about A.D. 430." "Almost all the commentaries now existing (in Pali) are ascribed to him." Rhys Davids.

불모 佛母 (1) The mother of the Buddha, Mahāmāyā, 마야 摩耶 Māyā, or Mātṛkā. (2) His aunt who was his foster-mother. (3) The Dharma or Law which produced him. (4) The Prajñā-pāramitā, mother or begetter of all Buddhas. (5) Other "Buddha-mothers," e.g. 준제불모 准提佛母 ; 공작불모 孔雀佛母, etc. Cf. 불안 佛眼. 불모진삼매 佛母眞三昧 The samādhi, meditation, or trance by means of which the Buddhas, past, present, and future, become incarnate.

불무애혜 佛無礙慧 Unhindered, infinite Buddha-wisdom.

불무차별 佛無差別 The identity of all Buddhas, and of their methods and purposes of enlightenment. One of the three identities, of all Buddhas, of all minds, and of all beings.

불문악명원 不聞惡名願 The sixteenth of Amitābha's forty-eight vows, that he would not enter final Buddhahood as long as anyone of evil repute existed.

불바제(하) 佛婆提(訶) Pūrvavideha ; 불제반 佛提槃 ; (불)비제하 (佛)毗提訶 ; 포로바비제하 布嚕婆毗提訶 ; 포리바비제하 逋利婆鼻提賀 ; 불우체 佛于逮 The continent of conquering spirits 승신주 勝神洲 ; one of the four great continents, east of Meru, semi-lunar in shape, its people having faces of similar shape. 불바라부 佛婆羅部 idem 독자부 犢子部 Vātsīputrīyāḥ.

불반니원경 佛般泥洹經 ; 불임열반기법주경 佛臨涅槃記法住經 The Nirvāṇa Sūtra or Mahāparinirvāṇa Sūtra.

불반세라 佛槃勢羅 Pūrvaśailāḥ, or Eastern Hill ; one of the five divisions of the Mahāsāṅghikāḥ school. A monastery east of Dhanakaṭaka, i.e. Amarāvatī, on the R. Godavery.

불방일 不放逸 No slackness or looseness ; concentration of mind and will on the good.

불배 不拜 Lay Buddhists may not pay homage to the gods or demons of other religions ; monks and nuns may not pay homage to kings or parents.

불범일체 佛凡一體 Buddha and the common people are one, i.e. all are of Buddha-nature.

불법 佛法 Buddhadharma ; the Dharma or Law preached by the Buddha, the principles underlying these teachings, the truth attained by him, its embodiment in his being. Buddhism. 불법승 佛法僧 Buddha, Dharma, Saṅgha, i.e. the Buddhist Trinity. 불법수명 佛法壽命 The life or extent of a period of Buddhism, i.e. as long as his commandments prevail. 불법장 佛法藏 The storehouse of Buddha-law, the Bhūtatathatā as the source of all things.

불법 不法 Not in accordance with the Buddha-law, wrong, improper, unlawful.

불변역성 不變易性 Unchanging nature, immutable, i.e. the bhūtatathatā. 불변진여 不變眞如 The immutable bhūtatathatā in the absolute, as compared with 수연진여 隨緣眞如, i.e. in relative or phenomenal conditions. 불변수연 不變隨緣 The conditioned immutable, i.e. immutable as a whole, but not in its parts, i.e. its phenomenal activity.

불보 佛寶, 법보승보 法寶僧寶 Buddha, Dharma, Saṅgha, i.e. Buddha, the Law, the Order ; these are the three Jewels, or precious ones, the Buddhist Trinity ; v. 삼보 三寶.

불본행집경 佛本行集經 Buddhacarita ; a life of Śākyamuni, tr. by Jñānaguptā, A.D. 587.

불부 佛部 The groups in which Buddha appears in the Garbhadhātu and Vajradhātu respectively.

불분별 不分別 The indivisible, or middle way 중도 中道.

불비시식 不非時食 Vikāla-bhojanād vairamaṇī (virati) ; part of the sixth of the ten commandments, i.e. against eating out of regulation hours, v. 불식육 不食肉.

불사 佛舍 A Buddhist temple. 불사리 佛舍利 Buddha's śarīra. Relics or ashes left after Buddha's cremation, literally Buddha's body.

불사 佛使 A messenger of the Tathāgata.

불사 佛事 Buddha's affairs, the work of transforming all beings ; or of doing Buddha-work, e.g. prayers and worship.

불사 不死 Undying, immortal. 불사감로 不死甘露 Sweet dew of immortality, a baptismal water of 진언 眞言 Shingon. 불사약 不死藥 Medicine of immortality, called 사하 娑訶 So-ho, which grows on 설산 雪山 the Himalayas and bestows on anyone seeing it endless and painless life. 불사각 不死覺 One of the eight 각 覺, the desire for long life. 불사문 不死門 The gate of immortality or nirvāṇa, i.e. mahāyāna.

불사서약 不捨誓約 Amitābha's vow of non-abandonment, not to enter Buddhahood till all were born into his Paradise.

불사의 不思議 See 부사의 不思議.

불살생 不殺生 Prāṇātipātād vairamaṇī (virati). The first commandment, Thou shalt not kill the living.

불상 佛像 Buddha's image, or pratimā. There is a statement that in the fifth century A.D. the images in China were of Indian features, thick lips, high nose, long eyes, full jaws, etc., but that after the T'ang the form became "more effeminate."

불상응심 不相應心 The non-interrelated mind, see 기신론 起信論. 불상응행 不相應行 Actions non-interrelated (with mind).

불생 不生 Anutpatti ; anutpāda. Non-birth ; not to be reborn, exempt from rebirth ; arhan is mistakenly interpreted as "not born", meaning not born again into mortal worlds. The "nir" in nirvāṇa is also erroneously said to mean "not born" ; certain schools say that nothing ever has been born, or created, for all is eternal. The Shingon word 아 阿 "a" is interpreted as symbolizing the uncreated. The unborn or uncreated is a name for the Tathāgata, who is not born, but eternal ; hence by implication the term means "eternal". Ādi, which means "at first", "beginning", "primary", is also interpreted as 불생 不生 uncreated. 불생단 不生斷 One of the 삼단 三斷, when illusion no longer arises the sufferings of being reborn in the evil paths are ended. 불생불멸 不生不滅 v. 불멸 不滅 "Neither (to be) born not ended" is another term for 상주 常住 permanent, eternal ; nothing having been created nothing can be destroyed ; Hīnayāna limits the meaning to the state of nirvāṇa, no more births and deaths ; Mahāyāna in its Mādhyamika form extends it universally, no birth and death, no creation and annihilation, see 중론 中論. The 사불생 四不生 are that nothing is produced (1) of itself ; (2) of another, i.e. of a cause without itself ; (3) of both ; (4) of no-cause.

불생일 佛生日 Buddha's birthday, the 4th month, 8th day, or 2nd month, 8th day, the former having preference for celebration of his birthday in China.

불석신명 不惜身命 The bodhisattva virtue of not sparing one's life (for the sake of bodhi).

불선 不善 Not good ; contrary to the right and harmful to present and future life, e.g. 오역십악 五逆十惡. 불선율의 不善律儀 idem 비율의 非律儀, i.e. 불법 不法 or 비선계 非善戒.

불설 佛說 Buddha's preaching ; the Buddha said. Buddha's utterance of the sūtras. There are over 150 sūtras of which the titles begin with these two words, e.g. 불설무량수경 佛說無量壽經 Aparimitāyuḥ Sūtra, tr. by Saṅghavarman A.D. 252.

불설사중과죄계 不說四衆過罪戒 The prohibition of mentioning the errors and sins of other disciples, cleric or lay.

불성 佛性 Buddhatā. The Buddha-nature, i.e. gnosis, enlightenment ; potential bodhi remains in every gati, i.e. all have the capacity for enlightenment ; for the Buddha-nature remains in all as wheat-nature remains in all wheat. This nature takes two forms : 리 理 noumenal, in the absolute sense, unproduced and immortal, and 행 行 phenomenal, in action. While every one possesses the Buddha-nature, it requires to be cultivated in order to produce its ripe fruit. 불성불수라 佛性不受羅 The Buddha-nature does not receive punishment in the hells, because it is 공 空 void of form, or spiritual and above the formal or material, only things with form can enter the hells. 불성상주 佛性常住 The eternity of the Buddha-nature, also of Buddha as immortal and immutable. 불성계 佛性戒 The moral law which arises out of the Buddha-nature in all beings ; also which reveals or evolves the Buddha-nature. 불성진여 佛性眞如 The Buddha-nature, the absolute, as eternally existent, i.e. the Bhūtatathatā.

불세 佛世 Buddha-age ; especially the age when Buddha was on earth. 불세존 佛世尊 Buddha, the World-honoured, or honoured of the worlds, a tr. of Bhagavat, revered. 불세계 佛世界 A Buddha-realm, divided into two categories, the pure and the impure, i.e. the passionless and passion worlds.

불소행찬경 佛所行讚經 Buddhacarita-kāvya-sūtra ; a poetic narrative of the life of Śākyamuni by Aśvaghoṣa 마명 馬鳴, tr. by Dharmarakṣa A.D. 414-421.

불수 佛樹 Bodhidruma ; 도수 道樹 the Bodhi-tree under which Śākyamuni obtained enlightenment or became Buddha, *Ficus religiosa*.

불수 佛壽 Buddha's life, or age. While he only lived to eighty as a man, in his Sambhogakāya he is without end, eternal ; cf. Lotus sūtra, 수량품 壽量品, where Buddha is declared to be eternal.

불수외도 不修外道 One of the ten kinds of "heresies" founded by Sañjayin Vairāṭīputra, v. 산 刪, who taught that there is no need to 구도 求道 seek the right path, as when the necessary kalpas have passed, mortality ends and nirvāṇa naturally follows.

불수일체법 不受一切法 Free from the receptivity, or sensation, of things, emancipated from desire. 불수삼매 不受三昧 In the Lotus sūtra, cap. 25, the bodhisattva 무진의 無盡意 obeying the Buddha's command, offered Kuan-yin a jewel-garland, which the latter refused saying he had not received the Buddha's command to accept it. This attitude is attributed to his 불수 不受 samādhi, the samādhi of 필경공 畢竟空 utter "voidness," or spirituality.

불승 佛乘 The Buddha conveyance or vehicle, Buddhism as the vehicle of salvation for all beings ; the doctrine of the 화엄 華嚴 Hua Yen (Kegon) School that all may become Buddha, which is called 일승 一乘 the One Vehicle, the followers of this school calling it the 원교 圓教 complete or perfect doctrine ; this doctrine is also styled in The Lotus 일불승 一佛乘 the One Buddha-Vehicle. 불승계 佛乘戒 The rules and commandments conveying beings to salvation.

불시해탈 不時解脫 The sixth, or highest of the six types of arhats ; the other five groups have to bide their time and opportunity 시해탈 時解脫 for liberation in samādhi, the sixth can enter immediately.

불식육 不食肉 Vikālabhojanā ; part of the sixth of the ten commandments, i.e. against eating flesh ; v. 불비시식 不非時食.

불신 佛身 Buddhakāya, a general term for the Trikāya, or threefold embodiment of Buddha. There are numerous categories or forms of the Buddhakāya.

불심 不審 A term of greeting between monks, i.e. I do not take the liberty of inquiring into your condition.

불심 佛心 The mind of Buddha, the spiritually enlightened heart. A heart of mercy ; a heart abiding in the real, not the seeming ; detached from good and evil and other such contrasts. 불심인 佛心印 The seal of the Buddha heart or mind, the stamp of the universal Buddha-heart in every one ; the seal on a Buddha's heart, or breast ; the svastika. 불심천자 佛心天子 The Son of Heaven of the Buddha-heart, a name given to Wu Ti of the Liang dynasty, A.D. 502-549. 불심종 佛心宗 The sect of the Buddha-heart, i.e. the Ch'an(Zen) or Intuitive sect of Bodhidharma, holding that each individual has direct access to Buddha through meditation.

불안 佛眼 The eye of Buddha, the enlightened one who sees all and is omniscient. 불안존 佛眼尊 A term of the esoteric cult for the source or mother of all wisdom, also called 불안부모 佛眼部母 ; 불안불모 佛眼佛母 ; 불모신 佛母身 ; 불모존 佛母尊 ; 허공불 虛空佛.

불어 佛語 The words, or sayings, of Buddha. 불어심 佛語心 The Bhūtatathatā, as the mind or storehouse of Buddha's words.

불여밀다 不如蜜多 The twenty-sixth patriarch, said to be Puryamitra [Eitel], son of a king in Southern India, laboured in eastern India, d. A.D. 388 by samādhi.

불여취 不與取 Adattādāna. Taking that which is not given, i.e. theft ; against this is the second commandment.

불열 不悅 Unhappy, uneasy, the disturbing influence of desire.

불염세간법 不染世間法 Unsullied by the things of the world (e.g. the lotus). 불염오무지 不染汚無知 Uncontaminated ignorance. 불염착제법삼매 不染著諸法三昧 The samādhi which is uncontaminated by any (evil) thing, the samādhi of purity ; i.e. Mañjuśrī in samādhi holding as symbol of it a blue lotus in his left hand.

불영 佛影 Buddhachāyā ; the shadow of Buddha, formerly exhibited in various places in India, visible only to those "of pure mind."

불오성 佛五姓 The five surnames of Buddha before he became enlightened : 구담 瞿曇 Gautama, a branch of the Śākya clan ; 감자 甘蔗 Ikṣvāku, one of Buddha's ancestors ; 일종 日種 Sūryavaṁśa, of the sun race ; 사이 舍夷 Śāka ; 석가 釋迦 Śākya, the name of Buddha's clan. This last is generally used in China.

불우체 佛于逮 Pūrvavideha, v. 불바 佛婆, etc.

불원 佛願 The vow of Buddha to save all beings.

불월 佛月 The Buddha-moon, Buddha being mirrored in the human heart like the moon in pure water. Also a meaning similar to 불일 佛日.

불위 佛位 The state of Buddhahood.

불위타 佛圍陀 Buddhaveda, i.e. the Tripiṭaka, the Veda of Buddhism.

불율의 不律儀 Practices not in accord with the rule ; immoral or subverted rules, i.e. to do evil, or prevent good ; heretical rules and practices.

불음욕 不婬慾 Abrahmacariyā-veramaṇī, the third commandment, thou shalt not commit adultery, i.e. against fornication and adultery for the lay, and against all unchastity for the clerics.

불음주 不飮酒 Surā-maireya-madya-pramādasthānād vairamaṇī (virati). The fifth of the ten commandments, i.e. against alcohol.

불의살 不疑殺 Not in doubt that the creature has been killed to feed me, v. 부정육 不淨肉.

불이 不二 Advaya. No second, non-duality, the one and undivided, the unity of all things, the one reality, the universal Buddha-nature. There are numerous combinations, e.g. 선악불이 善惡不二 good and evil are not a dualism ; nor are 유 有 and 공 空 the material and immaterial, nor are 미 迷 and 오 悟 delusion and awareness — all these are of the one Buddha-nature. 불이불이 不二不異 neither plural nor diverse, e.g. neither two kinds of nature nor difference in form. 불이지법 不二之法 The one undivided truth, the Buddha-truth. Also, the unity of the Buddha-nature. 불이법문 不二法門 is similar ; also the cult of the monistic doctrine ; and the immediacy of entering into the truth.

불인 佛因 Buddha-cause, that which leads to Buddhahood, i.e. the merit of planting roots of goodness.

불인 佛印 Buddha-seal, the sign of assurance, see 불심인 佛心印.

불일 佛日 The Buddha-sun which drives away the darkness of ignorance ; the day of Buddha.

불일불이 不一不異 Neither unity nor diversity, or doctrine of the 중론 中論, v. 팔불 八不.

불자 佛子 Son of Buddha ; a bodhisattva ; a believer in Buddhism, for every believer is becoming Buddha ; a term also applied to all beings, because all are of Buddha-nature. There is a division of three kinds: 외자 外子 external sons, who have not yet believed ; 서자 庶子 secondary sons, Hīnayānists ; 진자 眞子 true sons, Mahāyānists.

불장 佛藏 Buddha thesaurus, the sūtras of the Buddha's preaching, etc., also all the teaching of Buddha.

불적 佛跡 ; 불적 佛迹 Buddha's relic ; any trace of Buddha, e.g. the imprint of his foot in stone before he entered nirvāṇa.

불전 佛田 Buddha field, in which the planting and cultivation of the Buddhist virtues ensure a rich harvest, especially the Buddha as an object of worship and the Order for almsgiving.

불전함 佛殿函 Donation box.

불정 佛頂 Śākyamuni in the third court of the Garbhadhātu is represented as the 불정존 佛頂尊 in meditation as Universal Wise Sovereign. The 오불정(존) 五佛頂(尊) q.v. Five Buddhas are on his left representing his Wisdom. The three 불정 佛頂 on his right are called 광대불정 廣大佛頂, 극광대불정 極廣大佛頂, and 무변음성불정 無邊音聲佛頂 ; in all they are eight 불정 佛頂. 불정인 佛頂印 The characteristic sign on a Buddha's head, short curls, topknot, or uṣṇīṣa. 불정주 佛頂呪 ; 능엄주 楞嚴呪 Sitātapatroṣṇīṣa-dhāraṇī ; the white-umbrella dhāraṇī in the 수능엄경 首楞嚴經. 불정골 佛頂骨 Buddhoṣṇīṣa ; the skull or cranial protuberance on the Buddha's head: one of his characteristic marks.

불제자 佛弟子 Disciples of Buddha, whether monks or laymen.

불조 佛祖 The Buddha and other founders of cults ; Buddhist patriarchs ; two of the records concerning them are the 불조통기 佛祖統紀 and the 불조(역대)통재 佛祖(歷代)通載.

불종 佛宗 Buddhism ; principles of the Buddha Law, or dharma.

불종 佛種 The seed of Buddhahood ; bodhisattva seeds which, sown in the heart of man, produce the Buddha fruit, enlightenment.

불종성 佛種姓 Those of the Buddha-clan, Buddhists.

불좌고광대상 不坐高廣大牀 See 부좌고광대상 不坐高廣大牀.

불지 佛智 Anuttara-samyak-sambodhi, Buddha-wisdom, i.e. supreme, universal gnosis, awareness or intelligence ; sarvajñatā, omniscience.

불지 佛地 Buddha-bhūmi. The Buddha stage, being the tenth stage of the 통 通 or intermediate school, when the Bodhisattva has arrived at the point of highest enlightenment and is just about to become a Buddha. 불지라 佛地羅 Bodhila. a native of Kashmir and follower of the Mahāsāṅghikāḥ school, author of the 집진론 集眞論.

불지견 佛知見 The penetrative power of Buddha's wisdom, or vision.

불지제 佛支提 Buddha's Caitya, or Stūpa, v. 지제 支提. A Buddhist reliquary, or pagoda, where relics of the Buddha, 사리 舍利 śarīra, were kept ; a stūpa 탑파 塔婆 was a tower for relics ; such towers are of varying shape ; originally sepulchres, then mere cenotaphs, they have become symbols of Buddhism.

불착지생상금은보물 不捉持生像金銀寶物 Jātarūpa-rajata-pratigrahaṇād vairamaṇī (virati). The tenth commandment, not to take or possess uncoined or coined gold and silver, or jewels.

불착향화만불향도신 不著香華鬘不香塗身 Mālā-gandha-vilepana-dhāraṇa-maṇḍana-vibhūṣaṇa- sthānād vairamaṇī (virati). The eighth commandment against adorning the body with wreaths of fragrant flowers, or using fragrant unguents.

불찰 佛刹 Buddhakṣetra. 불흘차달라 佛紇差怛羅 Buddha realm, land or country ; see also 불토 佛土, 불국 佛國. The term is absent from Hīnayāna. In Mahāyāna it is the spiritual realm acquired by one who reaches perfect enlightenment, where he instructs all beings born there, preparing them for enlightenment. In the schools where Mahāyāna adopted an Ādi-Buddha, these realms or Buddha-fields interpenetrated each other, since they were coexistent with the universe. There are two classes of Buddha-kṣetra: (1) in the Vairocana Schools, regarded as the regions of progress for the righteous after death ; (2) in the Amitābha Schools, regarded as the Pure Land ; v. McGovern, *A Manual of Buddhist Philosophy*, pp. 70-2.

불참거 不懺擧 The excommunication of an unrepentant monk ; one of the 삼거 三擧.

불천 佛天 Buddha as Heaven ; Buddha and the devas.

불청 不請 Not to request ; uninvited ; voluntary. 불청지우 不請之友 The uninvited friend, i.e. the Bodhisattva. 불청법 不請法 Uninvited preaching or offering of the Law, i.e. voluntarily bestowing its benefits.

불취정각원 不取正覺願 Amitābha's vow of not taking up his Buddhahood till each of his forty-eight vows is fulfilled, an affix to each of the vows.

불칙 佛敕 또는 佛勅 Buddha's śāsana or orders, i.e. his teaching.

불타 佛馱 ; 불타 佛馱 Used in certain names for 불타 佛陀 Buddha, e.g. 불타집 佛馱什 Buddhajīva ; 불타사나 佛馱斯那 Buddhasena ; 불타급다 佛馱笈多 Buddhagupta ; 불타야 佛馱耶 Buddhāya ; 불타야사 佛馱耶舍 Buddhayaśas, known as the "red-beard Vibhāṣā" ; 불타발타라 佛馱跋陀羅 Buddha-bhadra.

불타 佛陀 v. 불 佛. There are numerous monks from India and Central Asia bearing this as part of their names, e.g. 불타십 佛陀什 Buddhajīva, who arrived in China from Kashmir or Kabul, A.D. 423 ; 불타승하 佛陀僧訶 Buddhasiṁha, a disciple of Asaṅga, probably fifth century A.D., about whose esoteric practices, lofty talents, and final disappearance a lengthy account is given in the Fan-i-ming-i 번역명의 翻譯名義 ; it is also a title of 불도징 佛圖澄 q.v. 불타다라(다) 佛陀多羅(多) Buddhatrāta of Kashmir or Kabul, was a translator about 650 ; 불타선다 佛陀扇多 Buddhaśānta, of Central India, translator of some ten works from 525-539 ; 불타제바 佛陀提婆 Buddhadeva ; 불타반차 佛陀槃遮 Buddhvaca ; 불타국다 佛陀毱多 Buddhagupta, "a Buddhistic king of Magadha, son and successor of Śakrāditya," [Eitel] ; 불타파리 佛陀波利 Buddha-pāla, came from Kabul to China 676 ; also Buddhapālita, a disciple of Nāgārjuna and founder of the 중론성교 中論性教 ; 불타밀다라 佛陀蜜多羅 Buddhamitra, the ninth patriarch ; 불타발타라 佛陀跋陀羅 Buddhabhadra, of Kapilavastu, came to China *circa* 408, introduced an alphabet of forty-two characters and composed numerous works ; also name of a disciple of Dharmakoṣa, whom Hsüan-tsang met in India, 630-640 ; 불타야사 佛陀耶舍 Buddhayaśas, of Kashmir or Kabul, tr. four works, 408-412 ; 불타난제 佛陀難提 Buddhanandi, of Kāmarūpa, descendant of the Gautama family and eighth patriarch ; 불타타사 佛陀馱沙 Buddhadāsa, of Hayamukha 아야목거 阿耶穆佉, author of the 대비바사론 大毗婆沙論. 불타벌나산 佛陀伐那山 Buddhavanagiri, "a mountain near Rājagṛha famous for its rock caverns, in one of which Śākyamuni lived for a time." [Eitel].

불토 佛土 Buddhakṣetra. 불국 佛國 ; 흘차달라 紇差怛羅 ; 차다라 差多羅 ; 찰달리야 刹怛利耶 ; 불찰 佛刹 The land or realm of a Buddha. The land of the Buddha's birth, India. A Buddha-realm in process of transformation, or transformed. A spiritual Buddha-realm. The T'ien-t'ai Sect evolved the idea of four spheres: (1) 동거지국토 同居之國土 Where common beings and saints dwell together, divided into (a) a realm where all beings are subject to transmigration and (b) the Pure Land. (2) 방편유여토 方便有餘土 or 변역토 變易土 The sphere where beings are still subject to higher forms of transmigration, the abode of Hīnayāna saints, i.e. Śrota-āpanna 수다원 須陀洹 ; Sakṛdāgāmin 사다함 斯陀含 ; Anāgāmin 아나함 阿那含 ; Arhat 아라한 阿羅漢. (3) 실보무장애 實報無障礙 Final unlimited reward, the Bodhisattva realm. (4) 상적광토 常寂光土 Where permanent tranquillity and enlightenment reign, Buddha-parinirvāṇa.

불퇴(전) 不退(轉) Avaivartika, or avinivartanīya. Never receding, always progressing, not backsliding, or losing ground ; never retreating but going straight to nirvāṇa ; an epithet of every Buddha. The 삼불퇴 三不退 are never receding from 위 位 position attained ; from a right course of 행 行 action ; from pursuing a right line of 염 念 thought, or mental discipline. These are duties of every bodhisattva, and have numerous interpretations. 사불퇴 四不退 The

Pure Land sect add another 처 處 place or abode to the above three, i.e. that those who reach the Pure Land never fall away, for which five reasons are given termed 오종불퇴(전) 五種不退(轉). The 법상 法相 Dharmalakṣaṇa sect make their four 신 信, 위 位, 증 證, and 행 行, faith, position attained, realization, and accordant procedure. 불퇴주 不退住 The seventh of the 십주 十住, the stage of never receding, or continuous progress. 불퇴토 不退土 The Pure Land, from which there is no falling away. 불퇴지 不退地 The first of a bodhisattva's 십지 十地 ; it is also interpreted by right action and right thought. 불퇴상 不退相 One of the nine 무학 無學 aśaikṣa, i.e. the stage beyond study, where intuition rules. Name of one of the twenty-seven sages. 불퇴보살 不退菩薩 A never-receding bodhisattva, who aims at perfect enlightenment. 불퇴(전법)륜 不退(轉法)輪 The never-receding Buddha-vehicle, of universal salvation.

불투도 不偸盜 Adinnādāna-veramaṇī ; the second of the ten commandments, Thou shalt not steal.

불학 不學 Aśaikṣa ; no longer studying, graduated, one who has attained.

불해 不害 Ahiṁsā. Harmlessness, not injuring, doing harm to none.

불해 佛海 Buddha's ocean, the realm of Buddha boundless as the sea.

불행이행 不行而行 Without doing yet to do, e.g. 무위이위 無爲而爲.

불허망성 不虛妄性 Not of false or untrue nature ; true, sincere ; also 진실성 眞實性.

불혜 佛慧 Buddha-wisdom.

불화합성 不和合城 Unharmonizing natures, one of the 오법 五法.

불환 不還 Not to return, never returning. Cf. 불퇴불환향 不退不還向 The third of the 사향 四向 four directions or aims, see 아나함 阿那含 anāgāmin, not returning to the desire-world, but rising above it to the 색계 色界 or the 무색계 無色界 form-realm, or even formless realm. 불환과 不還果 The fruits, fruition, or rewards of the last. Various stages in the final life of parinirvāṇa are named, i.e. five, six, seven, eight, nine, or eleven kinds.

불환희일 佛歡喜日 The Buddhist joy-day, the 15th of the 7th month, the last day of the summer retreat.

불활외 不活畏 The fear of giving all and having nothing to keep one alive ; one of the five fears.

불회 不廻 Anāgāmin. He who does not return ; one exempt from transmigration.

불후 佛吼 Buddha's nāda, or roar, Buddha's preaching compared to a lion's roar, i.e. authoritative.

불후보현 佛後普賢 After having attained Buddha-hood still to continue the work of blessing and saving other beings ; also P'u-hsien, or Samantabhadra, as continuing the Buddha's work.

비 羆 A bear. 비보살 羆菩薩 The bodhisattva who appeared as a bear and saved a dying man by providing him with food ; he told hunters of its lair ; they killed it, gave him of its flesh, and he died.

비 鞞 A scabbard ; translit. *vi, ve, vai, vya, bhi, bhya, be* ; cf. 비 毘, 폐 吠, 위 韋. 비세사 鞞世師 ; 비새가 鞞崽迦 The Vaiśeṣika school of philosophy, cf. 위 衛. 비치차라나(삼반나) 鞞侈遮羅那(三般那) ; 비다차라나(삼반나) 毘多遮羅那(三般那) Vidyācaraṅa-saṁpanna, perfect in knowledge and conduct 명행족 明行足, one of the ten epithets of a Buddha. 비로두나 鞞嚧杜那 v. 비 毘 Vairocana. 비사례야 鞞奢隸夜 v. 비 毘 Vaiśālī. 비바시 鞞婆尸 ; 비바사 鞞婆沙 v. 비 毘 Vibhāṣā. 비바하라 鞞婆訶羅 (Eka)vyāvahārika, tr. 일설부 一說部, a branch of the Mahāsāṅghikāḥ. 비실라만낭 鞞室羅懣囊 v. 비 毘 Vaiśravaṇa. 비니 鞞尼 v. 비 毘 Vinaya. 비서바부 鞞恕婆附 v. 비 毘 Viśvabhū. 비살사 鞞殺社 v. 약 藥 Bhaiṣajya, healing, medical, remedial. 비사문 鞞沙門 v. 비 毘 Vaiśravaṇa.

비조리야 鞞稠利夜 ; 비두리 鞞頭梨 v. 비 毘, 폐 吠 Vaiḍūrya. 비삭가 鞞索迦 Vaiśākha, the second month of spring, i.e. Chinese second month 16th to the 3rd month 15th day ; name of a wealthy patroness of Śākyamuni and his disciples. 비뉴바나 鞞紐婆那 Veṅuvana, 죽림 竹林 a park near Rājagṛha, the Karaṇḍa-veṅuvana, a favourite resort of Śākyamuni. 비사(례야) 鞞舍(隸夜) ; 비사(리) 鞞舍(離) v. 비 毘 Vaiśālī. 비사라바나 鞞舍羅婆拏 v. 비 毘 Vaiśravaṇa. 비발치 鞞跋致 Vaivartika ; intp. by 퇴 退 to recede, fall back, backslide. 비타 鞞陀 v. 위 韋 The Vedas. 비타로바 鞞陀路婆 v. 비 毘 Vetāla.

비 碑 A stone tablet, or monument.

비 妃 An imperial concubine ; as implying production, or giving birth, it is used by the esoteric cult for samaya and dhāraṇī.

비 批 An order of a court, rescript ; a contract, lease ; to comment, criticize. 비나 批那 Vīṇā ; the Indian lute.

비 毘 Contiguous ; surrounded ; hemmed in ; liberal ; to aid ; manifest ; translit. *v, vi, vai, vya, ve, pi, bh, bhi.* Cf. 비 鞞, 비 鼻, 폐 吠.

비 肥 Fat. 비자야 肥者耶 Vajradhātrī, the wife or female energy of Vairocana. 비니 肥膩 A grass or herb said to enrich the milk of cattle.

비 鼻 Ghrāṇa. The nose ; one of the five 근 根 indriyas ; the organ of smell ; one of the six vijñānas (육식 六識) or perceptions, the sense of smell ; translit. *vai, vi.* 비입 鼻入 Organ and sense of smell. 비사거 鼻奢佉 Vaiśākha, the second month of spring. 비파사 鼻婆沙 see 비 毘, Vibhāṣā. 비근 鼻根 The organ of smell. 비식 鼻息 The breath of the nostrils ; also the perception of smell. 비류다가 鼻溜荼迦 v. 비 毘 Virūḍhaka. 비하라 鼻訶羅 v. 비 毘 Vihāra. 비식 鼻識 The sensation, or perception of smell. 비로파아차 鼻路波阿叉 Virūpākṣa. One of the Lokapāla, or guardians of the four cardinal points of Mount Sumeru. In China known as 광목 廣目 wide-eyed, red in colour, with a small pagoda in his right hand, and a serpent in his left ; in China worshipped as one of the twenty-four Deva Ārya 천존 天尊. Also, a name for Maheśvara or Rudra (Śiva). Cf. 비 毘 and 비 髀. 비나야 鼻那夜 cf. 비 毘 Vinaya. 비격선사 鼻隔禪師 Dhyāna master with nose (and other organs) shut off from sensation, i.e. a stupid mystic. 비고가 鼻鼓迦 ; 비치가 鼻致迦 Bījaka, a seed, v. 종 種.

비 蜫 Insects, creeping things. 비충작불 蜫蟲作佛 Even insects may attain Buddhahood ; v. 지도론 智度論 93.

비 悲 Karuṇā ; kṛpā. Sympathy, pity for another in distress and the desire to help him, sad. 비심 悲心 A heart of pity, of sympathy, or sadness. 비수 悲手 A pitying hand. 비지 悲智 Pity and wisdom ; the two characteristics of a bodhisattva seeking to attain perfect enlightenment and the salvation of all being. In the esoteric sects pity is represented by the garbhadhātu or the womb treasury, while wisdom is represented by the vajradhātu, the diamond treasury. Pity is typified by Kuan-yin, wisdom by Mahāsthāmaprāpta, the two associates of Amitābha. 비무량심 悲無量心 Infinite pity for all. 비전 悲田 The field of pity, cultivated by helping those in trouble, one of the three fields of blessing. 비관자관 悲觀慈觀 The pitying contemplation for saving beings from suffering, and the merciful contemplation for giving joy to all beings. 비원 悲願 The great pitying vow of Buddhas and bodhisattvas to save all beings 비원반 悲願般 The boat of this vow for ferrying beings to salvation.

비 卑 Low, inferior ; translit. *p, pi, v, vy, m.* 비(하)만 卑(下)慢 The pride of regarding self as little inferior to those who far surpass one ; one of the 칠만 七慢. 비선닉 卑先匿 Prasenajit, v. 파 波. 비제리 卑帝利 Pitṛ, a kind of hungry demon. 비발라 卑鉢羅 Pippala, the bodhidruma, v. 보 菩. 비마라차 卑摩羅叉 Vimalākṣa, the pure-eyed, described as of Kabul, expositor of the

십송율 十誦律, teacher of Kumārajīva at Karashahr ; came to China A.D. 406, tr. two works. 비률차 卑栗蹉 ; 멸려차 蔑戾車 Mlecchas, border people, hence outside the borders of Buddhism, non-Buddhist.

비 非 Not ; un- ; without, apart from ; wrong.

비 痺 Numb. 비발라 痺鉢羅 Pippala, the peepul tree, *Ficus religiosa*, v. 필 畢.

비 秘 Secret, occult, esoteric ; opposite of 현 顯. 비인 秘印 Esoteric signs, or seals. 비오 秘奥 Secret, mysterious. 비종 秘宗 ; 밀교 密敎 The esoteric Mantra or Yogācāra sect, developed especially in 진언 眞言 Shingon, with Vairocana 대일여래 大日如來 as the chief object of worship, and the maṇḍalas of the Garbhadhātu and Vajradhātu. 비밀 秘密 Secret, occult, esoteric, mysterious, profound. 비밀(상)승 秘密(上)乘 The esoteric (superior) vehicle, i.e. the above sect. 비밀주 秘密主 Vajrasattva 금강살타 金剛薩埵, who is king of Yakṣas and guardian of the secrets of Buddhas. 비밀주 秘密咒 The mantras, or incantations of the above sect. 비밀호 秘密號 Its dhāraṇīs. 비밀단 秘密壇 Its altars. 비밀종 秘密宗 The (above) esoteric sect. 비밀계 秘密戒 Its commandments. 비(밀)교 秘(密)敎 Its teaching ; the sect itself ; one of the four modes of teaching defined by the T'ien-t'ai ; a name for the 원교 圓敎. 비밀유가 秘密瑜伽 The yoga rules of the esoteric sect ; also a name for the sect. 비(밀)경 秘(密)經 Its sūtras. 비밀결집 秘密結集 The collection of mantras, dhāraṇīs, etc., and of the Vajradhātu and Garbhadhātu literature, attributed to Ānanda, or Vajrasattva, or both. 비(밀)장 秘(密)藏 The treasury of the profound wisdom, or mysteries, variously interpreted. 비결 秘決 or 비결 秘訣 Secret, magical incantations. 비법 秘法 The mysteries of the esoteric sect. 비요 秘要 The essence, the profoundly important.

비 誹 Slander. 비방 誹謗 Apavāda. Slander, refute, deny. 비방정법 誹謗正法 To slander, or deny, the truth, i.e. Buddhism.

비 臂 The arm ; forearm ; translit. *pi*, cf. 필 畢, 비 毘. 비비리야 臂卑履也 Pipīla(ka), an ant. 비다세라 臂多勢羅 Pitāśilā, "an ancient kingdom and city in the province of Sindh, 700 li north of Adhyavakīla, 300 li south-west of Avaṇḍa. Exact position unknown." [Eitel]. 비사자 臂奢柘 Piśāca, a class of demons.

비 髀 The pelvic bones, the rump. 비로파아흘 髀路波阿迄 Virūpākṣa, the western of the four Mahārājas, v. 비 毘.

비 俾 To cause, enable. 비사자라소 俾沙闍羅所 Bhaiṣajya-rāja, the Buddha of medicine, or king of healing, v. 약사 藥師 19. 비례다 俾禮多 Preta, a hungry ghost, v. 귀 鬼 10.

비 比 To compare ; than ; to assemble, arrive ; partisan ; each ; translit. *pi*, *bhi*, *vi*, v. also 비 毘, 비 毗. 비구 比丘 ; 비호 比呼 ; 필추 苾芻 ; 픽추 煏芻 bhikṣu, a religious mendicant, an almsman, one who has left home, been fully ordained, and depends on alms for a living. Some are styled 걸사 乞士 mendicant scholars, all are 석종 釋種 Śākya-seed, offspring of Buddha. The Chinese characters are clearly used as a phonetic equivalent, but many attempts have been made to give meanings to the two words, e.g. 비 比 as 파 破 and 구 丘 as 번뇌 煩惱, hence one who destroys the passions and delusions, also 희능 悕能 able to overawe Māra and his minions ; also 제근 除饉 to get rid of dearth, moral and spiritual. Two kinds 내걸 內乞 and 외걸 外乞 ; both indicate self-control, the first by internal mental or spiritual methods, the second by externals such as strict diet. 필추 苾芻 is a fragrant plant, emblem of the monastic life. 비구니 比丘尼 ; 필추니 苾芻尼 ; 니고 尼姑 Bhikṣuṇī. A nun, or almswoman. The first woman to be ordained was the Buddha's aunt Mahāprajāpatī, who had nursed him. In the fourteenth year after his enlightenment the Buddha yielded to persuasion and admitted his aunt and women to his order of religious mendicants, but said that the admission of women would shorten the period of Buddhism by 500 years. The nun, however old, must acknowledge the superiority of every monk ; must never scold him or tell his faults ; must never accuse him, though he may accuse her ; and must in all respects obey the rules as commanded by him. She accepts all the rules for the monks with additional rules for her own order. Such is the theory rather than the practice. The title by which Mahāprajāpatī was addressed was applied to nuns, i.e. ārya, or noble, 아이 阿姨, though some consider the Chinese term entirely native. 비구니계 比丘尼戒 The nun's "500 rules" and the eight commanding respect for monks, cf. 오백계 五百戒 and 팔경계 八敬戒 ; also 비구니계본 比丘尼戒本 and other works ; the 비구니승기율바라제목차계경 比丘尼僧祇律波羅提木叉戒經 Bhikṣuṇī-sāṅghika-vinaya-prātimokṣa sūtra was tr. by Fa-hsien and also by Buddhabhadra. 비구회 比丘會 An authoritative assembly of at least four monks ; idem 승가 僧伽. 비타가구사 比吒迦俱舍 Piṭaka-kośa, i.e. 장 藏 a thesaurus, treasury, store. 비마사 比摩寺 A monastery five li west of Khotan where Lao Tzŭ is said to have converted the Huns to Buddhism. 비기타선나 比耆陀羨那 ; 비수타승하 毗戍陀僧訶 Viśuddhasiṁha ; the second form is defined by Eitel as 정사자 淨師子 pure lion, a Mahāyānist, *circa* A.D. 640 ; the first is named in the 현우경 賢愚經 6, but they may be two different persons. 비지 比智 idem 유지 類智 q.v. 비라사락(산) 比羅娑落(山) Pīlusāragiri, 상견산 象堅山 Hill firm as an elephant, a mountain south-west of the capital of Kapiśā, "the tutelary deity of which was converted by Śākyamuni." [Eitel]. Aśoka built a stūpa on its summit. 파 婆 is found in error for 사 娑 and 낙 洛 for 락 落. 비나(다) 比那(多) ; 비나 毗那 Vinata, 불고 不高 A low hill. 비량 比量 Comparison and inference ; it is defined as 비 比 comparison of the known, and 량 量 inference of the unknown. It is the second form in logic of the three kinds of example, 현량 現量, 비량 比量 and 성교량 聖敎量, e.g. the inference of fire from smoke. 비량상위 比量相違 Viruddha. A contradicting example or analogy in logic, e.g. the vase is permanent (or eternal), because of its nature ; one of the nine, in the proposition, of the thirty-three possible fallacies in a syllogism.

비 譬 To compare, allegorize ; like, resembling ; parable, metaphor, simile. 비유 譬喩 A parable, metaphor ; the avadāna section of the canon, v. 아파 阿波 ; there are numerous categories, e.g. the seven parables of the Lotus sūtra, the ten of the Prajña and Vimalakīrti sūtras, etc. 비유(론)사 譬喩(論)師 Reputed founder of the 경량부 經量部 Sautrāntikāḥ school, also known as 일출론자 日出論者. 비유량 譬喩量 The example in Logic.

비 飛 To fly. 비(행)선 飛(行)仙 Flying genii. 비화 飛化 Flying and changing. 비행 飛行 Flying anywhere (at will). 비행야차 飛行夜叉 Flying yakṣas, or demons. 비(행황)제 飛(行皇)帝 Flying ruler, synonym for a sovereign. 비석 飛錫 Flying staff, synonym for a travelling monk.

비 媲 To pair. Small. 비마 媲摩 Bhīmā, terrible, fearful ; name of Śiva's wife. "A city west of Khotan noted for a Buddha-status, which had transported itself thither from Udjyana." [Eitel]. Hsüan-tsang's P'i-mo. v. 비 毗.

비 費 To spend, lavish, waste, squander ; expense ; translit. *vi, ve*, in Vidyā, v. 명 明 ; Vīṇā, a lute, v. 비 批 ; Veda, the Vedas, v. 위 韋.

비가라 毘伽羅 Vyākaraṇa, grammatical analysis, grammar ; "formal prophecy," [Keith] ; tr. 성명기론 聲明記論 which may be intp. as a record and discussion to make clear the sounds ; in other words, a grammar, or sūtras to reveal right forms of speech ; said to have been first given by Brahmā in a million stanzas, abridged by Indra to 100,000, by Pāṇini to 8,000, and later reduced by him to 300. Also 비야갈랄남 毘耶羯剌諵 ; 비하갈리나 毘何羯唎拏 ; in the form of 화가라 和伽羅 Vyākaraṇas q.v. it is prediction.

비거라 毘佉羅 or **비저라** 毘低羅 Vikāra, an old housekeeper with many keys round her waist who had charge of the Śākya household, and who loved her things so much that she did not wish to be enlightened.

비구지 毘俱胝 or 毘俱知 Bhrūkuṭī, knitted brow ; one of the forms of Kuan-yin.

비기 非器 A vessel unfit for Buddha or Buddhism, e.g. a woman's body, which is unclean, v. Lotus Sūtra 제바 提婆 chapter 12.

비나야 毘奈耶 Vinaya, 비나야 毘那耶 ; 비니 毘尼 or 鞞尼 ; 비니가 毘泥迦 or 鞞泥迦 ; 비나야 鼻那夜 Moral training ; the disciplinary rules ; the precepts and commands of moral asceticism and monastic discipline (said to have been given by Buddha) ; explained by 률 律 q.v. ordinances ; 멸 滅 destroying sin ; 조복 調伏 subjugation of deed, word, and thought ; 이행 離行 separation from action, e.g. evil. 비나야장 毘奈耶藏 The Vinayapiṭaka, the second portion of the Tripiṭaka, said to have been compiled by Upāli ; cf. 률 律.

비나야가 毘那夜加 Vināyaka, a hinderer, the elephant god, Gaṇeśa ; a demon with a man's body and elephant's head, which places obstacles in the way. 비나달가 毘那怛迦 ; 비니타가 毘泥吒迦 Vinataka, bowed, stooping, is used with the same meaning, and also for the sixth of the seven concentric circles around Mt. Meru ; any mountain resembling an elephant. Also 비나야가 毘那耶加 ; 빈나야가 頻那也加 ; 비나야달가 毘那耶怛加 ; 폐나야달가 吠那野怛加. For 비나야 毘那耶 v. 비나야 毘奈耶.

비니 毘尼 Vinaya, v. 율 律 and 비나야 毘奈耶.

비다 毘茶 Bhiḍa, or Pañca-nada, an ancient kingdom called after its capital of Bhiḍa ; the present Punjab. [Eitel].

비다수 毘多輸 Vītaśoka, younger brother of Aśoka, v. 아 阿.

비달가 毘怛迦 Vitarka, "initial attention", "cognition in initial application", "judgment", [Keith] ; intp. as 심 尋 search or inquiry, and contrasted with 사 伺 spying out, careful examination ; also as 계탁 計度 conjecture, supposition. Cf. 비차라 毘遮羅 vicāra.

비담 毘曇 v. 아비달마 阿毘達磨 Abhidharma.

비도 非道 Wrong ways, heterodox views, or doctrines.

비두리 毘頭利 Vaiḍūrya, lapis lazuli, one of the seven precious things. A mountain near Vārāṇaśī. Also 비류리 毘瑠璃 or 폐류리 吠瑠璃 ; 비조리야 鞞稠利夜.

비라나갈차바 毘囉拏羯車婆 Vīraṇakacchapa, a tortoise, turtle.

비라산나 毘羅刪拏 Vīrasana. "An ancient kingdom and city in the Doab between the Ganges and the Yamuna. The modern Karsanah." [Eitel].

비람풍 毘嵐風 Vairambha. The great wind which finally scatters the universe ; the circle of wind under the circle of water on which the world rests. Also 비람(바) 毘藍(婆) or 鞞藍婆 ; 폐람(바) 吠藍(婆) ; 비람 鞞嵐 ; 폐람바 吠嵐婆 or 폐람승가 吠嵐僧伽 ; 비루나 毘樓那 ; and 비람바 毘藍婆 which is also Pralambā, one of the rākṣasīs.

비로사야 毘盧舍耶 Vairocana, "belonging to or coming from the sun" [M. W.], i.e. light. The 진신 眞身 q.v. true or real Buddha-body, e.g. godhead. There are different definitions. T'ien-t'ai says Vairocana represents the 법신 法身 dharmakāya, Rocana or Locana the 보신 報身 sambhogakāya, Śākyamuni the 응신 應身 nirmāṇakāya. Vairocana is generally recognized as the spiritual or essential body of Buddha-truth, and like light 변일체처 徧一切處 pervading everywhere. The esoteric school intp. it by the sun, or its light, and take the sun as symbol. It has also been intp. by 정만 淨滿 purity and fullness, or fullness of purity. Vairocana is the chief of the Five Dhyāni Buddhas, occupying the central position ; and is the 대일여래 大日如來 Great Sun Tathāgata. There are numerous treatises on the subject. Other forms are 비로 毘盧 ; 비로차야 毘盧遮耶 or 비로절야 毘盧折耶 ; 폐로차나 吠嚧遮那 ; 비로두나 鞞嚧杜那.

비류리 毘瑠璃 Virūḍhaka. Known as Crystal king, and as 악생왕 惡生王 Ill-born king. (1) A king of Kośala (son of Prasenajit), destroyer of Kapilavastu. (2) Ikṣvāku, father of the four founders of Kapilavastu. (3) One of the four mahārājas, guardian of the south, king of kumbhāṇḍas, worshipped in China as one of the twenty-four deva āryas ; colour blue. Also, 비류왕 毘瑠王 ; 유리왕 流離王 ; (비)누륵왕 (毘)婁勒王 ; (유)누려왕 (維)樓黎王 ; 비로석가왕 毘盧釋迦王 or 비로택가왕 毘盧宅迦王 ; 비류다가 鼻溜荼迦, etc.

비류바차 毘流波叉 Virūpākṣa, "irregular-eyed," "three-eyed like Śiva," translated wide-eyed, or evil-eyed ; one of the four mahārājas, guardian of the West, lord of nāgas, colour red. Also 비류박차 毘流博叉 or 비루박차 毘樓博叉 ; 비류바아차 鼻溜波阿叉 ; 비로바아흘 髀路波阿迄.

비륵 毘勒 Piṭaka 비륵 蜫勒. A T'ien-t'ai term for the 장교 藏教 or Hīnayāna.

비리야 毘梨耶 Vīrya, virility, strength, energy ; "well-doing," [Keith] ; intp. 정진 精進 zeal, pure progress, the fourth of the ten pāramitās. Also 비리야 毘利耶 or 비려야 毘黎耶 or 비리야 毘離耶 ; 미리야 尾唎也.

비리야서나 毘離耶犀那 Vīryasena, an instructor of Hsüan-tsang at the Bhadravihāra, v. 발 跋.

비리차 毘利差 Vṛkṣa means a tree, but as the intp. is "a hungry ghost," vṛka, wolf, seems more correct.

비마 毘摩 Bhīmā. (1) Śiva, also a form of Durgā, his wife (the terrible). (2) A city west of Khotan, possessing a statue of Buddha said to have transported itself thither from Udyāna. [Eitel]. Also used for 비마라 毘摩羅 Vimala, unsullied, pure ; name of a river, and especially of Śiva's wife. 비마라힐 毘摩羅詰 ; 비마라계리제 鼻磨羅鷄利帝 ; 유마힐 維磨詰 ; Vimalakīrti, name of a disciple at Vaiśālī, whom Śākyamuni is said to have instructed, see the sūtra of this name. 비마질다 毘摩質多 ; 폐마질달리 吠摩質呾利 Vimalacitra, a king of asuras, residing at the bottom of the ocean, father of Indra's wife.

비멸 非滅 The Buddha's "extinction" or death not considered as real, v. next.

비목차 毘木叉 v. 비목차 毘目叉.

비목차 毘目叉 Vimokṣa, Vimukti, 비목차 毘木叉 or 비목지 毘木底 liberation, emancipation, deliverance, salvation, tr. 해탈 解脫 q.v. 비목구사 毘目瞿沙 Vimuktaghoṣa, the Buddha's voice of liberation (from all fear) ; also 비목다라 毘目多羅.

비바시 毘婆尸 Vipaśyin. 불사 弗沙 ; 지사 底沙 the first of the seven Buddhas of antiquity, Śākyamuni being the seventh. Also 비바사 毘婆沙 ; 비바사 毘頻沙 ; 비발사 毘鉢沙 or 미발사 微鉢沙 ; 비바사 鞞婆沙 or 鼻婆沙 ; 유위 維衛. 비바사 毘婆沙 Vibhāṣā, option, alternative, tr. 광해 廣解 wider interpretation, or 이설 異說 different explanation. (1) The Vibhāṣā-śāstra, a philosophical treatise by Kātyāyanīputra, tr. by Saṅghabhūti A.D. 383. The Vaibhāṣikas 비바사론사 毘婆沙論師 were the followers of this realistic school, "in Chinese texts mostly quoted under the name of Sarvāstivāda." [Eitel]. (2) A figure stated at several tens of thousands of millions. (3) Vipaśyin, v. above. 비바사나 毘婆舍那 or 비발사나 毘鉢舍那 Vipaśyanā, discernment, intp. as 관 觀 insight, 정견 政見 correct perception, or views, etc. Vipaśyanā-vipaśyanā, thorough insight and perception. 비바사바제 毘婆闍婆提 Vibhajyavādinaḥs, answerers in detail, intp. as 분별설 分別說, discriminating explanation, or particularizing ; a school of logicians. "It is reasonable to accept the view that the *Abhidhamma Piṭaka*, as we have it in the Pali Canon, is the definite work of this school." [Keith].

비발야사 毘跋耶斯 The smṛtyupasthāna 사념처 四念處 or four departments of memory ; possibly connected with Vipaśyanā, v. 비바 毘婆.

비보살 非菩薩 Not bodhisattva, those who have not yet inclined their hearts to Mahāyāna.

비부라 毘富羅 Vipula, 비포라 毘布羅 broad, large, spacious. A mountain near Kuśāgrapura, in Magadha ; v. 비불략 毘佛略.

비불략 毘佛略 Vaipulya, large, spacious, intp. 방광 方廣 q.v., expanded, enlarged. The term is applied to sūtras of an expanded nature, especially expansion of the doctrine ; in Hīnayāna the Āgamas, in Mahāyāna the sūtras of Hua-yen and Lotus type ; they are found in the tenth of the 십이부경 十二部經 twelve sections of the classics. Other forms are 비불략 鞞佛略 or 배불략 裴佛略 ; 비부라 毘富羅.

비비상천 非非想天 or **비비상처** 非非想處 v. 비유 非有.

비사 毘舍 Veśa, entrance, house, adornment, prostitute ; but it is probably Vaiśya, the third caste of farmers and traders, explained by 거사 居士 burghers, or 상고 商賈 merchants ; cf. 폐 吠. 비사거 毘舍佉 Vaiśākha, viśākhā 폐사거 吠舍佉 ; 비사거 鼻奢佉 ; one of the constellations similar to Ti 지 氐, the third of the Chinese constellations, in Libra ; [M. W.] says the first month in the year, the Chinese interpret it as from the middle of their second to the middle of their third month. 비사거모 毘舍佉母 ; 녹모 鹿母 A wealthy matron who with her husband gave a vihāra to Śākyamuni, wife of Anāthapiṇḍika ; v. 아나 阿那. 비사지 毘舍支 or 비사차 毘舍遮 Piśācī. female sprites, or demons, said to inhabit privies. 비사부 毘舍浮 Viśvabhū, the second Buddha of the 31st kalpa. Eitel says: "The last (1,000th) Buddha of the preceding kalpa, the third of the Sapta Buddha 칠불 七佛 q.v., who converted on two occasions 130,000 persons." Also 비사바 毘舍婆 or 비사부 毘舍符 ; 비습바부 毘濕婆部 ; 비서사부 毘恕沙付 ; 비섭라 毘攝羅 ; 비서바부 鞞恕婆附 ; 비사 鞞舍 ; 수엽 隨葉 ; 부사 浮舍. 비사라 毘舍羅 Viśāla, a deity who is said to have protected the image of Buddha brought to Ming Ti of the Han dynasty. 비사사 毘舍闍 Piśācaḥ. Imps, goblins, demons in the retinue of 지국천 持國天 Dhṛtarāṣṭra. Also 비사차 毘舍遮 or 필사지 畢舍支 ; 비사자 辟舍柘 or 譬舍柘. 비사리 毘舍離 ; 폐사리 吠舍離 or 吠舍釐. Vaiśālī, an ancient kingdom and city of the Licchavis, where the second synod was held, near Basarh, or "Bassahar, north of Patna." [Eitel]. Also 비야(사) 毘耶(舍) ; 비성 毘城 ; 비야사 鞞耶舍 ; 비례야 鞞隸夜 ; 유야(리) 維夜(離).

비사나 毘沙拏 Viṣāṇa, a horn. It is used for the single horn of the rhinoceros, as an epithet for a pratyeka-buddha, v. 연각 緣覺, whose aim is his own salvation. 비사문(천왕) 毘沙門(天王) Vaiśravaṇa. Cf. 재 財 and 구 俱. One of the four Mahārājas, guardian of the North, king of the Yakṣas. Has the title 다문 多聞 ; 보문 普聞 ; universal or much hearing or learning, said to be so called because he heard the Buddha's preaching ; but Vaiśravaṇa was son of Viśravas, which is from viśru, to be heard of far and wide, celebrated, and should be understood in this sense. Vaiśravaṇa is Kuvera, or Kubera, the Indian Pluto ; originally a chief of evil spirits, afterwards the god of riches, and ruler of the northern quarter. Hsüan Tsung built a temple to him in A.D. 753, since which he has been the god of wealth in China and guardian at the entrance of Buddhist temples. In his right hand he often holds a banner or a lance, in his left a pearl or shrine, or a mongoose out of whose mouth jewels are pouring ; under his feet are two demons. Colour, yellow. 비사나오동자 毘沙拏五童子 The five messengers of Vaiśravaṇa. Other forms are 비사명 毗捨明 ; 비사라바나 鞞舍羅婆拏 ; 비실라만낭 鞞室羅懣囊.

비사량저 非思量底 According to the orthodox or teaching sects, not to discriminate, or reason out ; according to the Ch'an sect, to get rid of wrong thoughts (by freeing the mind from active operation).

비사밀다라 毘奢蜜多羅 Viśvamitra, name of Śākyamuni's school-teacher.

ㄱ ㄴ ㄷ ㄹ ㅁ ㅂ ㅅ ㅇ ㅈ ㅊ ㅋ ㅌ ㅍ ㅎ 찾아보기

비삼비일 非三非一 Neither three nor one ; a T'ien-t'ai phrase, that the 공가중 空假中 or noumenon, phenomenon, and madhya or mean, are three aspects of absolute truth, but are not merely three nor merely one ; idem the 삼덕 三德 three powers, i.e. dharmakāya, wisdom, and nirvāṇa.

비상 非常 Anitya, 무상 無常 impermanent, transient, illusory, as evidenced by old age, disease, and death. 비상고공비아 非常苦空非我 또는 무상고공비아 無常苦空非我 Impermanent, suffering, empty, non-ego — such is life.

비상 非想 Beyond the condition of thinking or non-thinking, of active consciousness or unconsciousness ; an abbrev. for 비상비비상천 非想非非想天 or 비상비비상처 非想非非想處, v. 비유상 非有想. The 정 定 or degree of meditation of this name leads to rebirth in the arūpa heaven ; which is not entirely free from distress, of which it has 팔고 八苦 eight forms.

비색 非色 Arūpa, formless, i.e. without rūpa, form, or shape, not composed of the four elements. Also the four skandhas. 비색사온 非色四蘊, excluding rūpa or form. 비색비심 非色非心 Neither matter nor mind, neither phenomenal nor noumenal ; the triple division of all things into 색 色, 심 心, and 비색비심 非色非心 phenomenal, noumenal, and neither.

비생비멸 非生非滅 The doctrine that the Buddha was not really born and did not really die, for he is eternal ; resembling Docetism.

비소단 非所斷 Not to be cut off, i.e. active or passive nirvāṇa (discipline) ; one of the 삼소단 三所斷.

비쇄가 毘灑迦 Viśākhā, one of the retinue of Vaiśravaṇa.

비수(갈마) 毘首(羯磨) Viśvakarman, all-doer, or maker, the Indian Vulcan, architect of the universe and patron or artisans ; intp. as minister of Indra, and his director of works. Also 비수갈마 毘守羯磨 ; 비습박갈마 毘濕縛羯磨.

비습바 毘濕婆 or 毘濕波 A wind, said to be a transliteration of Viśva, universal, cf. 비람 毘嵐.

비시 非時 Untimely ; not the proper, or regulation time (for meals), which is from dawn to noon ; hence 비시식 非時食 to eat out of hours, i.e. after noon.

비시사 毘尸沙 Viśeṣa, the doctrine of "particularity or individual essence," i.e. the *sui generis* nature of the nine fundamental substances ; it is the doctrine of the Vaiśeṣika school of philosophy founded by Kaṇāda.

비식 非食 Not to eat out of regulation hours, v. 비시식 非時食.

비심 非心 Apart from mind, without mind, beyond mentation.

비심비불 非心非佛 Apart from mind there is no Buddha ; the positive statement is 시심시불 是心是佛 this mind is Buddha.

비안립 非安立 The unestablished, or undetermined ; that which is beyond terminology. 비안립제 非安立諦 The doctrine of 비안립진여 非安立眞如 the bhūtatathatā, the absolute as it exists in itself, i.e. indefinable, contrasted with the absolute as expressible in words and thought, a distinction made by the 유식론 唯識論.

비야사 毘耶娑 Vyāsa, arranger, compiler ; to distribute, diffuse, arrange ; a sage reputed to be the compiler of the Vedas and founder of the Vedānta philosophy.

비야지 毘若底 Vijñapti, information, report, representation ; intp. as 식 識 knowledge, understanding, hence the 비야지마달랄다 毘若底摩呾剌多 Vijñaptimātra, or 유식 唯識. Reality is nothing but representations or ideas. For 비야남 毘若南 v. 비자나 毘闍那.

비업 非業 Death by accident said not to be determined by previous karma ; a sudden, unnatural, accidental death.

비유 非有 Abhāva. Non-existent, not real. 비유상비무상천 非有想非無想天 or 비유상비무상처 非有想非無想處 Naivasaṁjñānāsaṁjñānāyatana. 비상비비상천 非想非非想天 or 비상비비상처 非想非非想處 The heaven or place where there is neither thinking nor non-thinking ; it is beyond thinking ; the fourth of the 사공천 四空天 four immaterial heavens, known also as the 유정천 有頂天.

비유 非喩 An imaginary and not factual metaphor, one of the eight forms of comparison 팔유 八喩.

비유비공 非有非空 Neither existing nor empty ; neither material nor immaterial ; the characterization of the bhūtatathatā (in the 유식론 唯識論), i.e. the ontological reality underlying all phenomena. In the light of this, though the phenomenal has no reality in itself 비유 非有, the noumenal is not void 비공 非空.

비육생 非六生 Not arising directly from the mind, which is the sixth sense, but from the other senses.

비이취 非二聚 Apart from the two categories of matter and mind ; v. 비색비심 非色非心.

비인 非人 Not-men, not of the human race, i.e. devas, kinnaras, nāgas, māras, rakṣas, and all beings of darkness ; sometimes applied to monks who have secluded themselves from the world and to beggars, i.e. not like ordinary men.

비자나 毘闍那 Vijñāna, 비야남 毘若南 "consciousness or intellect," knowledge, perception, understanding, v. 식 識.

비점반보라 毘苫婆補羅 Vichavapura. "The ancient capital of Sindh." [Eitel].

비정 非情 Non-sentient objects such as grass, wood, earth, stone. 비정성불 非情成佛 The insentient become (or are) Buddha, a tenet of the 원교 圓教, i.e. the doctrine of pan-Buddha.

비제 毘睇 Vidyā, 미지아 尾底牙 knowledge, learning, philosophy, science ; incantation ; intp. 명주 明呪 an incantation to get rid of all delusion. The Vidyādharapiṭaka is a section of incantations, etc., added to the Tripiṭaka.

비제하 毘提訶 Videha, 불제반 弗提婆 ; 불어체 弗於逮. (1) Abbrev. for Pūrvavideha, 불바비제하 弗婆毘提訶 the continent east of Meru. (2) "Another name for Vaiśālī and the region near Māthava." [Eitel].

비지다바다 毘指多婆多 Vijitavat, one who has conquered, conqueror, intp. as the sun.

비차라 毘遮羅 Vicāra, "applied attention," [Keith], cf. 비달가 毘怛迦 intp. as pondering, investigating ; the state of the mind in the early stage of dhyāna meditation.

비천 非天 Not devas, i.e. asuras, v. 아수라 阿修羅.

비타 毘陀 The Vedas ; also 피타 皮陀 ; 위타 圍陀 ; 위타 韋陀. 비타라 毘陀羅 Vetāla, an incantation for raising a corpse to kill another person.

비파 琵琶 The p'i-p'a, a Chinese stringed musical instrument somewhat resembling a guitar.

비파사 毘播奢 Vipāśā, a river in the Punjab, "the Hyphasis of the Greeks," now called the Beas. 비파가 毘播迦 Vipāka, ripeness, maturity, change of state ; another name for the eighth 식 識.

ㄱ ㄴ ㄷ ㄹ ㅁ ㅂ ㅅ ㅇ ㅈ ㅊ ㅋ ㅌ ㅍ ㅎ 찾아보기

비폐가 毘吠伽 Viveka, "discrimination," intp. 청변 淸辯 clear distinction or discrimination. (반)비폐가 (槃)毘吠伽 Bhāvaviveka, a disciple of Nāgārjuna, who "retired to a rock cavern to await the coming of Maitreya." [Eitel].

비하라 毘訶羅 Vihāra, a pleasure garden, monastery, temple, intp. as 유행처 遊行處 place for walking about, and 사 寺 monastery, or temple. Also 비하라 鼻訶羅 ; 비하라 鞞訶羅 ; 미하라 尾賀羅. 비하라바라 毘訶羅波羅 Vihārapāla, the guardian of a monastery. 비하라사미 毘訶羅莎弭 Vihārasvāmin, the patron or bestower of the monastery.

비학자 非學者 Those who do not learn Buddha-truth, hence 비학세자 非學世者 is a world of such.

비흑비백업 非黑非白業 Neither black nor white karma, karma which does not affect metempsychosis either for evil or good ; negative or indifferent karma.

비흘라마아질다 毘訖羅摩阿迭多 Vikramāditya, Valour-sun, intp. as surpassing the sun, a celebrated king who drove out the Sakas, or Scythians, and ruled over northern India from 57 B.C., patron of literature and famous benefactor of Buddhism. Also 필가라마아질다 馝柯羅摩阿迭多.

빈 賓 A guest ; to entertain ; to submit. 빈가라 賓伽羅 Piṅgala, an Indian sage to whom is attributed "the Chandas" [M. W.], i.e. a treatise on metre. 빈타라 賓吒羅 Piṇḍāra, Piṇḍala, one of the painless purgatories. 빈지 賓坻 Piṇḍada, abbrev. for Anāthapiṇḍada, v. 아 阿. 빈발리력차 賓撥利力叉 Pippala, pippala-vṛkṣa, the bodhidruma, or tree under which Śākyamuni obtained insight. 빈파라굴 賓波羅窟 Vaibhāra, the Vaibhāra cavern ; "a rock-cut temple on a mountain near Rājagṛha, now called Baibhargiri. Śākyamuni used to resort thither for meditation." [Eitel]. 빈발라 賓鉢羅 Pippala, v. above. 빈두 賓頭 One of the purgatories, v. above. 빈두로파라타 賓頭盧頗羅墮 Piṇḍola-bhāradvāja, name of the first of the sixteen arhats, who became the old man of the mountains, white hair and beard, bushy eyebrows, one of the genii.

빈 貧 Poor, in poverty. 빈녀 貧女 A poor woman. 빈녀보장 貧女寶藏 The poor woman in whose dwelling was a treasure of gold of which she was unaware, v. Nirvāṇa sūtra 7. Another incident, of a poor woman's gift, is in the 지도론 智度論 8, and there are others. 빈궁 貧窮 Poor, poverty. 빈도 貧道 The way of poverty, that of the monk and nun ; also, a poor religion, i.e. without the Buddha-truth.

빈 邠 The ancient state of Pin, south-west Shensi ; translit. *p*, e.g. in Pūrṇamaitrāyaṇīputra 빈기문타불 邠祁文陀弗, Anāthapiṇḍada 아나빈저 阿那邠抵, etc.

빈 檳 The areca or betel-nut, i.e. 빈랑 檳榔 Pūga, the areca catechu, or betel-nut tree.

빈 擯 To expel. 빈치 擯治 The punishment of expulsion, which is of three orders: (1) 빈출 擯出 expulsion from a particular monastery or nunnery, to which there may be a return on repentance ; (2) 묵빈 默擯 prohibition of any intercourse ; (3) 멸빈 滅擯 entire expulsion and deletion from the order.

빈 頻 Urgent, pressing ; repeated ; translit. *bim, vi, vim, vin.* 빈가 頻伽 Kalaviṅka, v. 가 迦. 빈가병 頻伽甁 The kalaviṅka pitcher, an illustration in the 능엄 楞嚴 sūtra of emptiness or non-existence. 빈가타 頻伽陀 ; 비급마 毘笈摩 Vigata ; vigama ; gone away, disappearance, a medicine which causes diseases to disappear. 빈래과 頻來果 Once more to be reborn, v. 사 斯 Sakṛdāgāmin. 빈바 頻婆 Vimba ; Bimba ; a bright red gourd, *Momordica monadelphia* ; a tree with red fruit ; fruit of the Bimba-tree. 빈바(라) 頻婆(羅) Vimbara, differently stated as ten millions, and 100,000 billions, a 대빈바라 大頻婆羅 as a trillion ; it is also intp. as a king of fragrance, or incense. 빈바사라 頻婆娑羅 Bimbisāra, or Bimbasāra 빈비사라 頻毘娑羅 ; 병사 洴沙 ; 병사 瓶沙

; 병사 萍沙. A king of Magadha, residing at Rājagṛha, converted by Śākyamuni, to whom he gave the Veṅuvana park ; imprisoned by his son Ajātaśatru, and died. 빈나야가 頻那夜迦 Vināyaka (Gaṇeśa), name of a demon or spirit, cf. 비 毘.

빙 氷 Ice ; chaste. 빙게라 氷揭羅 ; 빙가라 氷伽羅 ; 필리잉가 畢哩孕迦 Piṅgala, name of the son of Hāritī, 아리저 阿利底 the mother of demons. She is now represented as a saint holding a child, Piṅgala, as beloved son, in her left arm. The sūtra of his name 빙게라천동자경 氷揭羅天童子經 was tr. by 불공금강 不空金剛 Amoghavajra, middle of the eighth century.

빙 冰 Ice, chaste. 빙가라 冰伽羅 Piṅgala, tawny ; tr. as 창색 蒼色 azure, grey.

<ㅅ>

사 闍 Translit. *c, j, k, g* sounds. 사세 闍世 cf. 아 阿 Ajātaśatru. 사이나 闍伊那 Jaina, the Jains, founded by Jñātṛputra, cf. 약 若, contemporary of Śākyamuni. 사리 闍利 Jala, water. 사부라 闍嚩囉 Jvala, shining ; light. 사다가 闍多伽 Jātaka, stories of previous incarnations of Buddhas and bodhisattvas. 사야 闍夜 Jaya, conquering, a manual sing of overcoming. 사야다 闍夜多 Jayata, twentieth Indian patriarch, teacher of Vasubandhu. 사파례 闍婆隸 Jvāla, flame(-mouth), a class of hungry demons. 사굴산 闍堀山 Gṛdhrakūṭa, cf. 기 耆 Vulture peak. 사제 闍提 Jāti, 생 生 birth, production ; genus ; name of several plants, e.g. marigold. 사제사라 闍提闍羅 Jātijarā, birth and decrepitude. 사제수나 闍提首那 Jātiṣenā, an ancient sage mentioned in the Nirvāṇa sūtra. 사리 闍梨 ; 사려 闍黎 Ācārya, cf. 아 阿, a teacher, instructor, exemplar. 사루 闍樓 Jarāyu, a placenta, an after-birth. 사비 闍毘 idem 다비 荼毘 Jhāpita, 사연제 闍演帝 ; 사연지 闍演底 Jayanta, conqueror, name of Śiva and others. 사란달라 闍爛達羅 Jālandhara, an ancient kingdom and city in the Punjab, the present Jalandar. 사왕 闍王 v. 아 阿 Ajātaśatru. 사유 闍維 A monk's funeral pyre, perhaps jhāpita. 사야인다라 闍耶因陀羅 Jayendra, a monastery of Pravarasenapura, now Srinagar, Kashmir. 사야국다 闍耶麴多 Jayagupta, a teacher of Hsüan-tsang in Srughna. 사야서나 闍耶犀那 ; 사야재나 闍耶宰那 Jayasena, a noted Buddhist scholar of the Vedas. 사야보라 闍耶補羅 Jayapura, "an ancient city in the Punjab, probable the present Hasaurah, 30 miles north-west of Lahore." [Eitel]. 사나굴다 闍那崛多 Jñānaguptā, a native of Gandhāra, tr. forty-three works into Chinese A.D. 561-592. 사나야사 闍那耶舍 Jñānayaśas, a native of Magadha, teacher of Yaśogupta and Jñānaguptā, co-translator of six works, A.D. 564-572. 사다가 闍陀伽 idem 사다가 闍多伽 Jātaka. 사비다 闍鼻多 Jhāpita, idem 다비 荼毘.

사 士 A gentleman, scholar, officer. 사부 士夫 v. 보노사 補盧沙 Puruṣa. 사부견 士夫見 One of the eight heterodox views, i.e. the pride arising from belief in a puruṣa, 보노사 補盧沙 q.v. 사만두 士饅頭 Śmaśāna. A crematory ; a burial place for remains from cremation. A grave ; v. 토만두 土饅頭. The form is doubtful.

사 師 A host, army ; a leader, preceptor, teacher, model ; tr. of upādhyāya, an "under-teacher," generally intp. as a Buddhist monk.

사 獅 A lion ; cf. 사자 師子.

사 辭 A phrase, words, language ; to decline, resign. 사무애지 辭無礙智 Unhindered knowledge of all languages or terms.

사 舍 A shelter, cottage ; used as a term of humility for "my" to lodge ; let go, relinquish.

사 莎 A species of grass, or sedge ; cf. 사 娑. 사게치 莎揭哆 Svāgata 선래 善來 "well come," a term of salutation ; also 선서 善逝 "well departed." It is a title of every Buddha ; also 사가타 莎迦陀 or 莎伽陀 ; 사가타 沙伽陀 or 사갈타 沙竭陀 ; 사바갈다 娑婆羯多 ; 소게다 蘇揭多. 사라수 莎羅樹 The Sala-tree. 사계 莎髻 A crown of grass put on the head of 부동존 不動尊 q.v. as a servant of the Buddhas.

사 詞 An expression, phrase, word. 사무애지 詞無礙智 Pratisaṁvid, v. 사 四.

사 似 Appearance of, seeming as, like, as ; than. 사현량 似現量 A syllogism assuming e.g. that a vase or garment is real, and not made up of certain elements. 사립종 似立宗 A fallacious proposition ; containing any one of the nine fallacies connected with the thesis, or pratijñā, of the syllogism. 사능파 似能破 A fallacious counter-proposition ; containing one of the thirty-three fallacies connected with the thesis (pratijñā 종 宗), reason (hetu 인 因), or example (udāharaṇa 유 喩).

사 事 Artha 왈가타 曰迦他 (가 迦 being an error for 알 遏) ; affair, concern, matter ; action, practice ; phenomena ; to serve. It is "practice" or the thing, affair, matter, in contrast with 리 理 theory, or the underlying principle. 사도 事度 Salvation by observing the five commandments, the ten good deeds, etc.

사 沙 Bālukā. Sand ; sands, e.g. of Ganges 항하 恒河, implying countless ; translit. *s, ś, ṣ,* Cf. 사 莎.

사 四 Catur. Four.

사 思 Cint- 지지 指底. Think, thought ; turn the attention to ; intp. by 심소법 心所法 mental action or contents, mentality, intellection. 사가 思假 Thought or its content as illusion. 사유 思惟 To consider or reflect on an object with discrimination ; thought, reflection. 사혹 思惑 The illusion of thought. 사혜 思慧 The wisdom attained by meditating (on the principles and doctrines of Buddhism). 사택력 思擇力 Power in thought and selection (of correct principles). 사량 思量 Thinking and measuring, or comparing ; reasoning. 사량(능변)식 思量(能變)識 The seventh vijñāna, intellection, reasoning. 사식 思食 Thought-food, mental food ; to desire food.

사 邪 Deflected, erroneous, heterodox, depraved ; the opposite of 정 正 ; also erroneously used for 야 耶.

사 社 Gods of the land ; a village, clan, society. 사가 社伽 Jagat, all the living. 사득가 社得迦 Jātaka, previous births or incarnations (especially of Buddhas or bodhisattvas). 사득가마라 社得迦摩羅 Jātakamālā, a garland of incarnation stories in verse.

사 砂 Gravel, sand. 이사시불 以砂施佛 The legend of Aśoka when a child giving a handful of gravel as alms to the Buddha in a previous incarnation, hence his rebirth as a king.

사 詐 Impose on, deceive, feign, pretend. 간사 奸詐 Fraudulent, crafty, to cheat.

사 死 Maraṇa ; 말랄남 末剌諵 ; mṛta 모타 母陀 ; to die, death ; dead ; also cyuti. 사망 死亡 Dead and gone (or lost). 사도 死刀 The (sharp) sword of death. 사산 死山 The hill of death. 사시 死屍 "Dead corpse," e.g. a wicked monk. 사해 死海 The sea of mortality. 사왕 死王 Yama, 염마 焰魔 as lord of death and hell. 사생 死生 Death and life, mortality, transmigration ; v. 생 生. 사상 死相 The appearance of death ; signs at death indicating the person's good or evil karma. 사선화자 死禪和子 Die! monk ; dead monk! a term of abuse to, or in regard to, a monk. 사고 死苦 The misery, or pain, or death, one of the Four Sufferings. 사적 死賊 The robber death. 사문 死門 ; 사궐 死闕 The gate, or border of death, leading from one incarnation to another. 사령 死靈 The spirit of one who is dead, a ghost. 사풍 死風 The destroying wind in the final destruction of the world.

사 私 Private, secret, selfish, illicit. 사인 私印 A monk's private seal, which should resemble a skull as reminder of the brevity of life. 파타 婆吒 Vasiṣṭha, v. 파 婆. 사파파 私婆婆 Svabhāva, "own state, essential or inherent property, innate or peculiar disposition, natural state or constitution nature" [M. W.], intp. as 자체체 自體體 or 자성성 者性性. 사다 私多 ; 사타 私陀 ; 실타 悉陀 ; 척다 徙多 ; 시다 枲多 Śītā. Described as the "cold" river ; one of the four great rivers flowing from the Anavatapta or Anavadata Lake 아뇩달지 阿耨達池 in Tibet. One account makes it "an eastern outflux" which subsequently becomes the Yellow River. It is also said to issue from the west. Again, "the Ganges flows eastward, the Indus south, Vatsch (Oxus) west, Śītā north." Vatsch = Vākṣu. "According to Hiuentsang, however, it is the northern outflux of the Sirikol (Sarikkol) Lake (Lat. 38° 20' N., Long. 74° E.) now called Yarkand daria, which flows into Lake Lop, thence underneath the desert of Gobi, and reappears as the source of the Hoangho." [Eitel]. According to Richard, the Hwangho "rises a little above two neighbouring lakes of Khchara (Charing-nor) and Khnora (Oring-nor). Both are connected by a channel and are situated at an elevation of 14,000 feet. It may perhaps be at first confounded with Djaghing-gol, a river 110 miles long, which flows from the south and empties into the channel joining the two lakes."

사 徙 Remove, flit. 사다 徙多 v. 사 私 Śītā.

사 蛇 Sarpa, a serpent, snake. 독사 毒蛇 A poisonous snake. 불구사심 佛口蛇心 A Buddha's mouth but a serpent's heart. 사승마 蛇繩麻 The seeming snake, which is only a rope, and in reality hemp. 사약 蛇藥 Snake-medicine, name of the Sarpauṣadhi monastery in Udyāna, where Śākyamuni in a former incarnation appeared as an immense snake, and by giving his flesh saved the starving people from death. 사행 蛇行 To crawl, go on the belly. 사족 蛇足 Snake's legs, i.e. the non-existent.

사 祠 The spring ancestral sacrifice ; the spring ; ancestral temple, tablet, etc. 사당 祠堂 An ancestral temple or hall. 사당은 祠堂銀 An endowment for masses to be said for the departed, also 장생은 長生銀 ; 무진재 無盡財.

사 斯 This, these ; to rive ; forthwith ; translit. *s*. 사리아 斯哩牙 Sūrya, the sun, the sun-deva. 사다함 斯陀含 Sakṛdāgāmin, once more to arrive, or be born ; the second grade of arhatship involving only one rebirth. Cf. 사향 四向 and 사과 四果.

사 賒 To buy or sell on credit ; to borrow ; slow, remiss, shirk. 사내이실절라 賒乃以室折羅 Śanaiścara 토성 土星, Saturn, or its regent. 사다 賒多 Śānta, pacified, at ease, ceased, dead, liberated ; also 사다 奢多.

사 赦 To pardon. 사니사 赦儞娑 The son of Vaiśravaṇa, see 비 毘.

사 娑 To play, careless, idle, easy going ; translit. *s*, *ś*, chiefly *sa*, *sā*. 사야지제바다 娑也地提嚩多 Satyadevatā, intp. as 본존 本尊 the fundamental, or original, or principal honoured one. 사가라 娑伽羅 Sāgara. 사갈라 娑竭羅 The Ocean. The Nāga king of the ocean palace north of Mt. Meru, possessed of priceless pearls ; the dragon king of rain ; his eight-year-old daughter instantly attained Buddhahood, v. the Lotus sūtra. 사가 娑呵 Sahā, a herb in the Himālayas imparting immortality to the finder, v. 사바 娑婆. 사다길리 娑多吉哩 Śatakri, name of one of the yakṣa generals. 사다바(한)나 娑多婆(漢)那 Sadvāhana, Sātavāhana, name of a royal patron of Nāgārjuna. 사바 娑婆 Sahā ; that which bears, the earth, v. 지 地 ; intp. as bearing, enduring ; the place of good and evil ; a universe, or great chiliocosm, where all are subject to transmigration and which a Buddha transforms ; it is divided into three regions 삼계 三界 and Mahābrahmā Sahāṁpati is its lord. Other forms : 사바세계 娑婆世界 ; 사계 娑界 ; 사반 娑槃 ; 사하 娑訶 ; 사하 沙訶 ; 삭하 索訶. 사하루타 娑訶樓陀 Sahālokadhātu, the world. 사바하 娑婆訶 ; 사박하 娑縛賀 Svāhā, an oblation by fire, also Hail! a brahminical salutation at the end of a sacrifice. 사지야 娑底也 Satya, true ; satyatā, truth, a truth. 사도 娑度 Sādhu, good, virtuous, perfect, a sage, saint, tr. 선 善 good. 사비가라 娑毘迦羅 ; 겁비라 劫毘羅 Kapila, possibly Sāṅkhya Kapila, the founder of the Sāṅkhya philosophy. 사마 娑磨 Sāmaveda, the third of the Vedas, containing the hymns. 사라 娑羅 ; 사라 沙羅 Śāla, Sāla ; the Sāl tree, 사라수 娑羅樹 *Shorea robusta*, the teak tree. 사라림 娑羅林 Śālavana, the grove of Sāl trees near Kuśinagara, the reputed place of the Buddha's death. 사라(수)왕 娑羅(樹)王 Śālendra-rāja, a title of a Buddha ; also of Śubhavyūha, father of Kuan-yin. 사라사 娑羅娑 Sārasa, the Indian crane. 사라리불

娑羅梨弗 "Salaribhu, an ancient kingdom or province in India. Exact position unknown." [Eitel]. 사로다라 娑路多羅 ; 수루다 戍縷多 Śrotra, the ear. 사마라 娑麼囉 Smara, recollection, remembrance.

사 瀉 To purge, drain. 사약 瀉藥 Purgatives.

사 使 To send ; cause ; a messenger ; a pursuer, molester, lictor, disturber, troubler, intp. as 번뇌 煩惱 kleśa, affliction, distress, worldly cares, vexations, and as consequent reincarnation. There are categories of 10, 16, 98, 112, and 128 such troublers, e.g. desire, hate, stupor, pride, doubt, erroneous views, etc., leading to painful results in future rebirths, for they are karma-messengers executing its purpose. Also 금강동자 金剛童子 q.v.

사 奢 To spread out ; profuse ; extravagant. 사리 奢利 ; 사리불다라 奢利弗多羅 or 사리부다라 奢利富多羅 ; 사리보단라 奢利補担羅 v. 사 舍 Śāriputra. 사미 奢彌 ; 사미 奢弭 Śamī, a leguminous tree associated with Śiva. 사마타 奢摩他 or 奢摩陀 ; 사마타 舍摩他 Śamatha, "quiet, tranquillity, calmness of mind, absence of passion." [M. W.] Rest, peace, power to end (passion, etc.), one of the seven names for dhyāna. 사갈라 奢羯羅 Śākala, the ancient capital of Ṭakka and (under Mihirakula) of the whole Punjab ; the Sagala of Ptolemy ; Eitel gives it as the present village of Sanga a few miles south-west of Amritsar, but this is doubtful. 사살달라 奢薩怛羅 ; 사살달라 舍薩怛羅 ; 설사달라 設娑怛羅 Śāstra, intp. by 논 論 treatise, q.v. 사타 奢陀 Śāṭhya, knavery, fawning, crooked.

사 嗣 To succeed to, continue, adopt, posterity, follow after. 사법 嗣法 To succeed to the dharma, or methods, of the master, a term used by the meditative school ; 전법 傳法 is used by the esoteric sect.

사 謝 To thank ; return (with thanks), decline ; fall ; apologize ; accept with thanks. 사계 謝戒 To give thanks for being given the commandments, i.e. being ordained.

사 寫 To write. 사경 寫經 To copy the scriptures.

사 捨 Upekṣā, neglect, indifference, abandoning, [M. W.] To relinquish, renounce, abandon, reject, give. One of the chief Buddhist virtues, that of renunciation, leading to a state of "indifference without pleasure or pain" [Keith], or independence of both. V. 사 舍. It is defined as the mind 평등 平等 in equilibrium, i.e. above the distinction of things or persons, of self or others ; indifferent, having abandoned the world and all things, and having no affections or desires. One of the seven bodhyaṅgas. Translit. *sa*, *śa*, *s(r)*. 사라범 捨囉梵 Śarāva, a shard, an earthenware vessel. 사심 捨心 The mind of renunciation. 염청정지 念清淨地 The pure land or heaven free from thinking, the fifth of the nine Brahmalokas in the fourth dhyāna region. 사라타 捨攞馱 Śraddhā, faith, confidence, trust, belief. 사수 捨受 The state of renunciation, or indifference to sensation. 사가기욕 捨家棄欲 To leave home and cast off desire, i.e. to become a monk. 사무량심 捨無量心 Upekṣā, one of the four forms of the unsparing or unlimited mind, complete abandonment, absolute indifference, renunciation of the mental faculties. 사신 捨身 Bodily sacrifice, e.g. by burning, or cutting off a limb, etc.

사 伺 Vicāra, 비차라 毘遮羅 Investigation, consideration, search for truth ; to spy ; wait on.

사 寺 Vihāra, 비하라 毘訶羅 or 鼻訶羅 ; Saṅghārāma 승가람 僧伽藍 ; an official hall, a temple, adopted by Buddhists for a monastery, many other names are given to it, e.g. 정주 淨住 ; 법동사 法同舍 ; 출세사 出世舍 ; 정사 精舍 ; 청정원 淸淨遠 ; 금강찰 金剛刹 ; 적멸도량 寂滅道場 ; 원리처 遠離處 ; 친근처 親近處 "A model vihāra ought to be built of red sandalwood, with 32 chambers, 8 Tāla trees in height, with a garden, park and bathing tank attached ; it ought to have promenades for peripatetic meditation and to be richly furnished with stores of clothes, food, bedsteads, mattresses, medicines and all creature comforts." [Eitel]. 사원 寺院 Monastery grounds and buildings, a monastery.

사가 四家 The schools of 반야 般若, 제 諦, 사번뇌 捨煩惱, and 고청 苦淸 likened by 장안 章安 Chang-an of the T'ien-t'ai to the 사교 四敎, i.e. seriatim : 별 別, 원 圓, 통 通, and 삼장 三藏.

사가행 四加行 v. 사선근 四善根.

사각 四覺 The "four intelligences, or apprehensions" of the Awakening of Faith 기신론 起信論, q.v., viz. 본각 本覺, 상사각 相似覺, 수분각 隨分覺, and 구경각 究竟覺.

사개대승 四箇大乘 The four mahāyānas, i.e. the four great schools : (1) 화엄 華嚴 Hua-yen or Avataṁsaka ; (2) 천태 天台 T'ien-t'ai ; (3) 진언 眞言 Chên-yen, Shingon, or esoteric ; (4) 선 禪 Ch'an(Zen), or intuitive school. Another group is the 법상 法相, 삼론 三論, 천태 天台, and 화엄 華嚴.

사거 四車 The four vehicles 사승 四乘 of the Lotus sūtra 비유품 譬喩品, i.e. goat, deer, bullock, and great white-bullock carts. 사거가 四車家 The Lotus School, which adds to the Triyāna, or Three Vehicles, a fourth which includes the other three, viz. the 일불승 一佛乘 q.v.

사겁 沙劫 Kalpas countless as the sands of Ganges.

사겁 四劫 The four kalpas, or epochs, of a world, 성겁 成劫 that of formation and completion ; 주겁 住劫 existing or abiding ; 괴겁 壞劫 destruction ; and 공겁 空劫 annihilation, or the succeeding void. 구사론 俱舍論 12.

사견 邪見 Heterodox views, not recognizing the doctrine of moral karma, one of the five heterodox opinions and ten evils 오견십악 五見十惡. 사견승 邪見乘 The Hīnayāna, the Vehicle of perverted views. 사견조림 邪見稠林 The thickets of heterodoxy.

사견신 四堅信 The four firm or 사불괴신 四不壞信 indestructible beliefs, in the Buddha, the law, the order, and the commandments.

사결 四結 The four knots, or bonds, saṁyojana, which hinder free development ; they are likened to the 사예 四翳 q.v. four things that becloud, i.e. rain-clouds, resembling desire ; dust-storms, hate ; smoke, ignorance ; and asuras, gain.

사경 四鏡 The four resemblances between a mirror and the bhūtatathatā in the Awakening of Faith 기신론 起信論. The bhūtatathatā, like the mirror, is independent of all beings, reveals all objects, is not hindered by objects, and serves all beings.

사계 四戒 Four stages in moral development : that of release, or deliverance from the world on becoming a monk ; that arising from the four meditations on the realms of form ; that above the stage of 견도 見道 q.v. ; that in which all moral evil is ended and delusion ceases.

사계 四界 The four realms, idem 사대 四大 earth, water, fire, and air. 사계섭지 四界攝持 The four are the substance and upholders of all things.

사계 沙界 Worlds as numerous as the sands of Ganges.

사계성도 四階成道 ; **사계성불** 四階成佛 The four Hīnayāna steps for attaining Buddhahood, i.e. the myriad deeds of the three asaṅkhyeya kalpas ; the continually good karma of a hundred great kalpas ; in the final body the cutting off of the illusions of the lower eight states ; and the taking of one's seat on the bodhi-plot for final enlightenment, and the cutting off of the thirty-four forms of delusive thought.

사고 師姑 A nun ; also 니고 尼姑.

사고 四苦 The four miseries, or sufferings — birth, age, disease, and death.

사고 四股 The four-armed svastika, of thunderbolt.

사고사영 四枯四榮 When the Buddha died, of the eight śālatrees surrounding him four are said to have withered while four continued in full leaf – a sign that the four doctrines of 고 苦 suffering, 공 空 the void, 무상 無常 impermanence, and 무아 無我 impersonality were to perish and those of 상 常 permanence, 락 樂 joy, 아 我 personality, and 정 淨 purity, the transcendent bodhisattva doctrines, were to flourish.

사공(처) 四空(處) ; **사공(천)** 四空(天) Catur-ārūpya (brahma)lokas ; also 사무색계 四無色界 and see 사공정 四空定. The four immaterial or formless heavens, arūpadhātu, above the eighteen brahmalokas : (1) 공무변처 空無邊處 ākāśānantyāyatana, also termed (허)공처 (虛)空處 the state or heaven of boundless space ; (2) 식(무변)처 識(無邊)處 vijñānānantyāyatana, of boundless knowledge ; (3) 무소유처 無所有處 ākiñcanyāyatana, of nothing, or nonexistence ; (4) 비상비비상처 非想非非想處 naivasaṁjñānāsaṁjñānāyatana, also styled 비유상비무상 非有想非無想 the state of neither thinking nor not thinking (which may resemble a state of intuition). Existence in the first state lasts 20,000 great kalpas, increasing respectively to 40,000, 60,000 and 80,000 in the other three. 사공정 四空定 ; 사무색정 四無色定 The last four of the twelve dhyānas ; the auto-hypnotic, or ecstatic entry into the four states represented by the four dhyāna heavens, i.e. 사공처 四空處 *supra.* In the first, the mind becomes void and vast like space ; in the second, the powers of perception and understanding are unlimited ; in the third, the discriminative powers of mind are subdued ; in the fourth, the realm of consciousness (or knowledge) without thought is reached e.g. intuitive wisdom. These four are considered both as states of dhyāna, and as heavens into which one who practises these forms of dhyāna may be born.

사과 四果 The four phala, i.e. fruitions, or rewards – śrota-āpanna-phala, sakṛdāgāmin-phala, anāgāmin-phala, arhat-phala, i.e. four grades of saintship ; see 수다원 須陀洹, 사다함 斯陀含, 아나함 阿那含, and 아라한 阿羅漢. The four titles are also applied to four grades of śramaṇas – yellow and blue flower śramaṇas, lotus śramaṇas, meek śramaṇas, and ultra-meek śramaṇas.

사교 四敎 Four teachings, doctrines, or schools ; five groups are given, whose titles are abbreviated to 광천효원룡 光天曉苑龍 (1) 광택사교 光宅四敎 The four schools or 법운 法雲 Fa-yün of the 광택 光宅 Kuang-chai monastery are the four vehicles referred to in the burning house parable of the Lotus Sūtra, i.e. śrāvaka, pratyeka-buddha, bodhisattva, and the final or one-vehicle teaching. (2) 천태사교 天台四敎 The T'ien-t'ai four are 장교 藏敎, 통교 通敎, 별교 別敎, and 원교 圓敎, v. 팔교 八敎 (3) 효공사교 曉公四敎 The group of 원효 元曉 Won-hyo(C. Yüan-hsiao) of 해동 海東 Hai-tung are the 삼승별교 三乘別敎 represented by the 사제연기경 四諦緣起經 ; 삼승통교 三乘通敎 represented by the 반야심밀경 般若深密經 ; 일승분교 一乘分敎 represented by the 범망경 梵網經 ; and 일승만교 一乘滿敎 represented by the 화엄경 華嚴經. (4) 원공사교 苑公四敎 The group of 혜원 慧苑 Hui-yüan : the schools of unbelievers, who are misled and mislead ; of śrāvakas and pratyeka-buddhas who know only the phenomenal bhūtatathatā ; of novitiate bodhisattvas who know only the noumenal bhūtatathatā ; and of fully developed bodhisattvas, who know both. (5) 용수사교 龍樹四敎 Nāgārjuna's division of the canon into 유 有 dealing with existence, or reality, cf. the 사아함 四阿含 ; 공 空 the Void, cf. 반야경 般若經 ; 역유역공 亦有亦空 both, cf. 심밀경 深密經 ; and 비유비공 非有非空 neither, cf. 중론 中論. 사교삼밀 四敎三密 Now a 진언 眞言 Shingon term ; the 사교 四敎 are the T'ien-t'ai four schools of 현 顯 open or exoteric teaching ; the 삼밀 三密 are the Shingon esoteric teaching in which the three 신구의 身口意 body, mouth, and mind have special functions. 사교삼관 四敎三觀 The T'ien-t'ai four main doctrinal divisions as above and its three kinds of meditation. 사교오시 四敎五時 T'ien-t'ai's doctrine of the four developments of the Buddha's own teaching, v. above, and the five periods of the same, v. 오시교 五時敎. 사교의 四敎儀 A work of 지의 智顗 Chih-i of T'ien-t'ai. 사교지 四敎地 Four stages, as given in the 대일경구연품 大日經具緣品, i.e. 장 藏, 통 通, 별 別, and 원 圓 q.v.

사교 事教 Teaching dealing with phenomena. The characterization by T'ien-t'ai of the Tripiṭaka or Hīnayāna teaching as 계내사교 界內事教 within the three realms of desire, form, and formlessness ; and the 별교 別教 "different teaching" as 계외사교 界外事教 outside or superior to those realms ; the one dealt with the activities of time and sense, the other transcended these but was still involved in the transient ; the 별교 別教 was initial Mahāyāna incompletely developed.

사교과 四教科 Four Studies Course in seminary 강원 講院, consisting of : (1) Book of the Heroic March Samadhi (Su-neung-eom-gyeong, Śūraṅgama sūtra) (2) Awakening of Faith in the Mahayana (3) Perfection of Wisdom Sutra (Diamond sūtra) (4) Book of Consummate Enlightenment (Wongak-gyeong).

사구 四句 The four terms, phrases, or four-line verses, e.g. 사구분별 四句分別 The four terms of differentiation, e.g. of all things into 유 有 the existing ; 공 空 non-existing ; both ; neither ; or phenomenal, noumenal, both, neither. Also, double, single, both, neither ; and other similar applications. 사구집 四句執 The four tenets held by various non-Buddhist schools : (1) the permanence of the ego, i.e. that the ego of past lives is the ego of the present ; (2) its impermanence, i.e. that the present ego is of independent birth ; (3) both permanent and impermanent, that the ego is permanent, the body impermanent ; (4) neither permanent nor impermanent ; that the body is impermanent but the ego not impermanent. 사구성도 四句成道 The swan-song of an arhat, who has attained to the perfect life : —

All rebirths are ended,	아생이진 我生已盡.
The noble life established,	범행이립 梵行已立.
My work is accomplished.	소작이작 所作已作.
No further existence is mine.	(자지) 불수후유 (自知)不受後有.

사구추검 四句推撿 The four-phrase classification that phenomena are 자인 自因 self-caused, 타인 他因 caused by another, 공인 共因 by both, 무인 無因 by neither ; cf. 사불생 四不生.

사구 死句 A dead phrase. A Seon hwadu which still allows intellectualization. Antonym of 활구 活句 q.v.

사근본성죄 四根本性罪 ; **사근본중죄** 四根本重罪 idem 사바라이 四波羅夷.

사금강 四金剛 The four mahārājas, v. 사천왕 四天王.

사기 四記 ; **사답** 四答 The Buddha's four methods of dealing with questions : direct answer, discriminating answer, questioning in return, and silence.

사기 四棄 The four pārājika sins resulting in excommunication, v. 파 波.

사나리가 沙那利迦 Ṣāṇṇagarika, one of the eighteen Hīnayāna sects.

사나신 舍那身 The body or person of Vairocana ; 사나존특 舍那尊特 is defined as Locana ; the 사나 舍那 in both cases seems to be "cana," an abbreviation of Vairocana, or Locana.

사념주 四念住 idem 사념처 四念處. 사념주 四念珠 The four classes of "prayer-beads", numbering 27, 54, 108, or 1,080, styled 하품 下品, 중품 中品, 최승 最勝, and 상품 上品, lower, middle, superior, and most superior. 사념처(관) 四念處(觀) ; 사념주 四念住 Smṛtyupasthāna. The fourfold stage of mindfulness, thought, or meditation that follows the 오정심관 五停心觀 five-fold procedure for quieting the mind. This four-fold method, or objectivity of thought, is for stimulating the mind in ethical wisdom. It consists of contemplating (1) 신 身 the body as impure and utterly filthy ; (2) 수 受 sensation, or consciousness, as always resulting in suffering ; (3) 심 心 mind as impermanent, merely one sensation after another ; (4) 법 法 things in general as being dependent and without a nature of their own. The four negate the ideas of permanence, joy, personality, and purity 상 常, 락 樂, 아 我, and 정 淨, i.e. the four 전도 顚到, but v. 사덕 四德. They are further subdivided into 별 別 and 총 總 particular and general, termed 별상념처 別相念處 and 총상념처 總相念處, and there are further subdivisions.

사다비사 舍多毘沙 Śatabhiṣā, a constellation identified with 위 危 in Aquarius.

사다제바마누사남 舍多提婆魔㝹舍諵 Śāstādevamanuṣyāṇām, intp. as 천인사 天人師 teacher of gods and men, one of the ten titles of a Buddha.

사단 師檀 Teacher and donor, or monk and patron.

사달 四達 Saindhava, 선다바 先陀婆 rock-salt, but intp. as salt, water, a utensil, and a horse, the four necessaries, i.e. water for washing, salt for food, a vessel to contain it, and a horse for progress ; also called 사실 四實.

사대 四大 Mahābhūta, 사계 四界 ; 사대계 四大界. The four elements of which all things are made ; or the four realms ; i.e. earth, water, fire, and wind (or air) ; they represent 견 堅, 습 濕, 난 煖, and 동 動 solid, liquid, heat, and motion ; motion produces and maintains life. As 실 實 active or formative forces they are styled 사(대)계 四(大)界 ; as 가 假 passive or material objects they are 사대 四大 ; but the 성실론 成實論 Satyasiddhi śāstra disputes the 실 實 and recognizes only the 가 假. 사대부조 四大不調 The inharmonious working of the four elements in the body, which causes the 440 ailments ; cf. 사사 四蛇. 사대원무주 四大元無主 The verse uttered by 조법사 肇法師 Chao Fa-shih when facing death under the 요진 姚秦 Yao Ch'in emperor, fourth century A.D. :-

> "No master have the four elements,
> Unreal are the five skandhas,
> When my head meets the white blade,
> 'Twill be but slicing the spring wind."

The "four elements" are the physical body. 사대명산 四大名山 The four famous "hills" or monasteries in China : 보타 普陀 P'u-t'o, for Kuan-yin, element water ; 오대 五臺 Wu-t'ai, Wên-shu, wind ; 아미 峨眉 O-mei, P'u-hsien, fire ; and 구화 九華 Chiu-hua, Ti-tsang, earth. 사대천왕 四大天王 see 사천왕 四天王. The four deva-kings of the four quarters, guardians in a monastery. 사대명왕 四大明王 v. 대명왕 大明王. 사대사 四大師 The four monastic heads imperially appointed during the T'ang dynasty. 사대제자 四大弟子 The four great disciples of the Buddha – Śāriputra, Mahāmaudgalyāyana, Subhūti, and Mahākāśyapa. Another group is Mahākāśyapa, Piṇḍola, Rāhula, and Kauṇḍinya. 사대해 四大海 The four great oceans in a world, around Sumeru, in which are the four great continents ; cf. 구산팔해 九山八海. 사대(부)주 四大(部)洲 The four great continents of a world, v. 사주 四洲. 사대종 四大種 idem 사대 四大. 사대성문 四大聲聞 The four great śrāvakas, idem 사대제자 四大弟子. 사대보살 四大菩薩 The for great Bodhisattvas of the Lotus Sūtra, i.e. Maitreya, Mañjuśrī, Avalokiteśvara, and Samantabhadra. Another list of previous Bodhisattvas is 상행 上行 Viśiṣṭacāritra ; 무변행 無邊行 Anantacāritra ; 정행 淨行 Viśuddhacāritra, and 안립행 安立行 Supratiṣṭhitacāritra. 사대호 四大護 The guardian devas of the four quarters : south 금강무승결호 金剛無勝結護 ; east 무외결호 無畏結護 ; north 괴제포결호 壞諸怖結護 ; and west 난항복결호 難降伏結護. The 사대불호원 四大佛護院 is the thirteenth group of the Garbhadhātu. 사대부경 四大部經 Four great sūtras ; 화엄 華嚴 Hua-yen ; 열반 涅槃 Nirvāṇa ; 보적 寶積 Mahāratnakūṭa, and 반야 般若 Prajñā.

사덕 四德 The four nirvāṇa virtues, or values, according to the Mahāyāna Nirvāṇa sūtra : (1) 상 常 permanence or eternity ; (2) 락 樂 joy ; (3) 아 我 personality or the soul ; (4) 정 淨 purity. These four important terms, while denied in the lower realms, are affirmed by the sūtra in the transcendental, or nirvāṇa-realm. 사덕락방 四德樂邦 ; 사덕바라밀 四德波羅蜜 The joyful realm, or acme of the above four virtues, the nirvāṇa-realm, the abode or dharmakāya of the Tathāgata.

사도 邪道 Heterodox ways, or doctrines.

사도 四倒 The four viparyaya, i.e. inverted or false beliefs in regard to 상 常, 낙 樂, 아 我, 정 淨. There are two groups : (1) the common belief in the four above, denied by the early Buddhist doctrine that all is impermanent, suffering, impersonal, and impure ; (2) the false belief of the Hīnayāna school that nirvāṇa is not a state of permanence, joy, personality, and purity. Hīnayāna refutes the common view in regard to the phenomenal life ; bodhisattvism refutes both views.

사도 四道 The tao or road means the nirvāṇa road ; the "four" are rather modes of progress, or stages in it : (1) 가행도 加行道 discipline or effort, i.e. progress from the 삼현 三賢 and 사선근 四善根 stages to that of the 삼학위 三學位 ,i.e. morality, meditation, and understanding ; (2) 무간도 無間道 uninterrupted progress to the stage in which all delusion is banished ; (3) 해탈도 解脫道 liberation, or freedom, reaching the state of assurance or proof and knowledge of the truth ; and (4) 승진도 勝進道 surpassing progress in dhyāni-wisdom. Those four stages are also associated with those of śrota-āpanna, sakṛdāgāmin, anāgāmin, and arhat.

사도가행 四度加行 Special study of or advancement in the four degrees, a method of the esoterics, formerly extending over 800 or 1,000 days, later contracted to 200. The four "degrees" are 십팔도 十八道, 태장 胎臟, 금강 金剛, and 호마 護摩, but the order varies.

사도견 邪倒見 Heterodoxy ; perverted views or opinions.

사도리교형 四忉利交形 Copulation in the first and in the second devalokas, i.e. 사왕 四王 and 도리 忉利 heavens ; in the third it is by embrace ; in the fourth, by holding hands ; in the fifth, by mutual smiling ; in the sixth by a mutual look.

사독사 四毒蛇 Four poisonous snakes (in a basket), e.g. the four elements, earth, water, fire, and air, or which a man is formed.

사두간 舍頭諫 Śārdūlakarṇa. The original name of Ānanda, intp. 호이 虎耳 tiger's ears.

사등 四等 The four virtues which a Buddha out of his infinite heart manifests equally to all ; also called 사무량 四無量 q.v. They are : 자비희사 慈悲喜捨 maitrī, karuṇā, muditā, upekṣā, i.e. kindness, pity, joy and indifference, or 호 護 protection. Another group is 자어법신 字語法身, i.e. 자 字 that all Buddhas have the same title or titles ; 어 語 speak the same language ; 법 法 proclaim the same truth ; and 신 身 have each the threefold body, or trikāya. A third group is 제법 諸法 all things are equally included in the bhūtatathatā ; 발심 發心 the mind-nature being universal, its field of action is universal ; 도등 道等 the way or method is also universal ; therefore 자비 慈悲 the mercy (of the Buddhas) is universal for all.

사라 沙羅 Sāla, or Śāla, 사라 娑羅 the Sāl tree or Śal tree ; the teak tree ; the Shorea (or Valeria) Robusta ; a tree in general. 사라왕 沙羅王 Sālarāja, a title of the Buddha. 사라나 沙羅那 or 沙羅拏 ; 사랄라왕 娑刺拏王 Śāraṇa (said to be a son of King Udayana) who become a monk. 사라쌍수 沙羅雙樹 The twin trees in the grove 사라림 娑羅林 in which Śākyamuni entered nirvāṇa.

사라 舍羅 Śārikā, Śārī, v. 사리 舍利. Śalākā, bamboo or wooden tallies used in numbering monks. 사라바가 舍羅婆迦 Śrāvaka ; a hearer, disciple, 성문 聲聞 q.v. (1) He who has heard (the voice of Buddha). All the personal disciples of Śākyamuni, the chief disciples being called Mahāśrāvaka. (2) The lowest degree of saintship, the others being Pratyeka-buddha, Bodhisattva, Buddha.

사라마나 舍囉摩拏 Śramaṇa. 실나 室拏 ; 사가만낭 沙迦滿囊 ; 사문 沙門 ; 상문 桑門 ; v. 사문 沙門.

사락가 沙洛迦 "Charaka, a monastery in Kapiśa." [Eitel].

사력 四力 The four powers for attaining enlightenment : independent personal power ; power derived from others ; power of past good karma ; and power arising from environment.

사로 四爐 The four furnaces, or altars of the esoteric cult, each differing in shape : earth, square ; water, round ; fire, triangular ; wind, half-moon shape.

사론 事論 Discussion of phenomena in contrast with 이론 理論.

사론 四論 Four famous śāstras : (1) 중관론 中觀論 Prāṇyamūla-śāstraṭīkā by Nāgārjuna, four chüan ; (2) 백론 百論 Śata-śāstra by Devabodhisattva, two chüan ; (3) 십이문론 十二門論 Dvādaśanikāya (-mukha)-śāstra by Nāgārjuna, one chüan ; (4) 대지도론 大智度論 Mahāprajñāpāramitā-śāstra by Nāgārjuna, 100 chüan. During the Sui dynasty the followers of these four śāstras formed the 사론종 四論宗.

사료간 四料簡 A summary of the 임제 臨濟 Lin-chi school, an offshoot of the Ch'an, in reference to subjective, objective, both, neither.

사류 四流 The four currents (that carry the unthinking along) : i.e. the illusions of 견 見 seeing things as they seem, not as they really are ; 욕 欲 desires ; 유 有 existence, life ; 무명 無明 ignorance, or an unenlightened condition.

사륜 四輪 The four wheels or circles : (1) 대지사륜 大地四輪 the four on which the earth rests, wind (or air), water, metal, and space. (2) Four images with wheels, yellow associated with metal or gold, white with water, red with fire, and black with wind. (3) The four dhyāni-buddhas, 금강륜 金剛輪 Akṣobhya ; 보륜 寶輪 Ratnasaṁbhava ; 법륜 法輪 Amitābha ; 갈마륜 羯磨輪 Amoghasiddhi. (4) Also the four metals, gold, silver, copper, iron, of the cakravartin kings. 사륜왕 四輪王 The four kinds of cakravartin kings.

사륵 舍勒 Śāṭaka, 사타가 舍吒迦 ; 사나 舍那 or 奢那 An inner garment, a skirt.

사리 舍利 (1) Śārī, Śārikā ; a bird able to talk, intp. variously, but M. W. says the maina. Śārikā was the name of Śāriputra's mother, because her eyes were bright and clever like those of a maina ; there are other interpretations. (2) Śarīra(m). 설리라 設利羅 or 실리라 室利羅 ; 실리 實利 ; 섭실람 攝嚟藍 Relics or ashes left after the cremation of a Buddha or saint ; placed in stūpas and worshipped. The white represent bones ; the black, hair ; and the red, flesh. Also called dhātu-śarīra or dharma-śarīra. The body, a dead body. The body looked upon as dead by reason of obedience to the discipline, meditation, and wisdom. The Lotus and other sūtras are counted as relics. Śākyamuni's relics are said to have amounted to 팔곡사두 八斛四斗 84 pecks, for which Aśoka is reputed to have built in one day 84,000 stūpas ; but other figures are also given. Śarīra is also intp. by grains of rice, etc., and by rice as food. 사리탑 舍利塔 Śarīra-stūpa, a reliquary, or pagoda for a relic (of Buddha). 사리사파 舍利娑婆 Sarṣapa, a mustard seed, 개자 芥子 q.v., the 10,816,000th part of a yojana 由旬 q.v. 사리불 舍利佛 ; 사리불(다)라 奢利佛(多)羅 or 사리부(다)라 奢利富(多)羅 ; 사리보단라 奢利補袒羅 ; 사리자 舍利子 Śāriputra. One of the principal disciples of Śākyamuni, born at Nālandāgrāma, the son of Śārikā and Tiṣya, hence known as Upatiṣya ; noted for his wisdom and learning ; he is the "right-hand attendant on Śākyamuni." The followers of the Abhidharma count him as their founder and other works are attributed, without evidence, to him. He figures prominently in certain sūtras. He is said to have died before his master ; he is represented as standing with Maudgalyāyana by the Buddha when entering nirvāṇa. He is to reappear as Padmaprabha Buddha 화광불 華光佛.

사리 事理 Practice and theory ; phenomenon and noumenon, activity and principle, or the absolute

; phenomena ever change, the underlying principle, being absolute, neither changes nor acts, it is the 진여 眞如 q.v. also v. 이 理. For 사리(무애)법계 事理(無礙)法界 v. 사법계 四法界. 사리삼천 事理三千 The three thousand phenomenal activities and three thousand principles, a term of the T'ien-t'ai School. 사리오법 事理五法 v. 오법 五法.

사마 邪魔 Evil demons and spirits, māras. 사마외도 邪魔外道 Māras and heretics.

사마 四馬 Four kinds of horses, likened to four classes of monks : those that respond to the shadow of the whip, its lightest touch, its mild application, and those who need the spur to bite the bone.

사마 舍摩 Śama, calm, quiet, a name for the bodhi tree. For 사마타 舍摩陀 v. 사 奢.

사마(실) 四摩(室) Sīmā. A boundary, a separate dwelling, or dwellings (for monks and/or visitors).

사마사나 舍磨奢那 Śmaśāna, a cemetery or crematorium ; a low mound of stone under which the remains of monks are buried in countries west of China. Also 사마사나 奢磨奢那.

사마제 沙摩帝 Saṁmatīya, 정량부 正量部 one of the eighteen Hīnayāna sects.

사만 邪慢 Mithyāmāna ; perverse or evil pride, doing evil for self-advancement ; to hold to heterodox views and not to reverence the Triratna.

사망 邪網 The net of heterodoxy, or falsity.

사망 四忘 The state of a saint, i.e. beyond, or oblivious of the four conditions of 일이유무 一異有無 unity, difference, existence, non-existence.

사맹월 四孟月 The four senior or prime months, i.e. the first of each season, first, fourth, seventh, and tenth.

사면비로자나 四面毘盧遮那 The four-faced Vairocana, his dharmakāya of Wisdom.

사명 四明 Four Shingon emblems, aids to Yoga-possession by a Buddha or bodhisattva ; they are 구 鉤, 삭 索, 쇄 鏁, 령 鈴, a hook, a cord, a lock, and a bell ; the hook for summoning, the cord for leading, the lock for firmly holding, and the bell for the resultant joy. Also, the four Veda śāstras. 사명산 四明山 A mountain range in Ningpo prefecture where the 사명 四明 are clearly seen, i.e. sun, moon, stars, and constellations. 지례 知禮 Chih-li of the Sung dynasty is known as the 사명존자 四明尊者 honoured one of Ssŭ-ming and his school as the 사명가 四明家 Ssŭ-ming school in the direct line of T'ien-t'ai. In Japan Mt. Hiyei 비예산 比叡山 is known by this title, through Dengyō 전교 傳敎 the founder of the Japanese T'ien-t'ai School.

사명(식) 邪命(食) Heterodox or improper ways of obtaining a living on the part of a monk, e.g. by doing work with his hands, by astrology, his wits, flattery, magic, etc. Begging, or seeking alms, was the orthodox way of obtaining a living. 사명설법 邪命說法 The heterodox way of preaching or teaching, for the purpose of making a living.

사명 유정 四溟惟政 Sa-myeong Yu-jeong(1544-1610). A monk of the Joseon dynasty in Korea. He was a disciple of 휴정 休靜 Hyu-jeong. He rendered distinguished services in Japanese invasion(1592-1598).

사무상게 四無常偈 ; **사비상게** 四非常偈 Eight stanzas in the 인왕경 仁王經, two each on 무상 無常 impermanence, 고 苦 suffering, 공 空 the void, and 무아 無我 non-personality ; the whole four sets embodying the impermanence of all things. 사무(소)외 四無(所)畏 The four kinds of fearlessness, or courage, of which there are two groups : Buddha-fearlessness arises from his omniscience ; perfection of character ; overcoming opposition ; and ending of suffering. Bodhisattva-fearlessness arises from powers of memory ; of moral diagnosis and application of the remedy ; of ratiocination ; and of solving doubts. v. 지도론 智度論 48 and 5. 사무애해 四無礙解 ; 사무애지 四無礙智 ; 사무애변 四無礙辯. Pratisaṁvid, the four unhindered or unlimited bodhisattva powers of interpretation, or reasoning, i.e. in 법 法 dharma, the letter of the law ; 의 義 artha, its meaning ; 사 辭 nirukti, in any language, or form of expression ; 요설 樂說 pratibhāna, in eloquence, or pleasure in speaking, or argument. 사무색 四無色 idem 사공처 四空處, 사공정 四空定. 사무량(심) 四無量(心) Catvāri apramāṇāni ; the four immeasurables, or infinite Buddha-states of mind, also styled 사등 四等 the four equalities, or universals, and 사범행 四梵行 four noble acts or characteristics ; i.e. four of the twelve 선 禪 dhyānas : 자무량심 慈無量心 boundless kindness, maitrī, or bestowing of joy or happiness ; 비무량심 悲無量心 boundless pity, karuṇā, to save from suffering ; 희무량심 喜無量心 boundless joy, muditā, on seeing others rescued from suffering ; 사무량심 捨無量心 limitless indifference, upekṣā, i.e. rising above these emotions, or giving up all things, e.g. distinctions of friend and enemy, love and hate, etc. The esoteric sect has a special definition of its own, connecting each of the four with 보현 普賢 ; 허공장 虛空藏 ; 관자재 觀自在 ; or 허공고 虛空庫.

사문 四門 The four doors, schools of thought, or theories : 유 有 is the phenomenal world real, or 공 空 unreal, or both, or neither? According to the T'ien-t'ai school each of the four schools 사교 四教 in discussing these four questions emphasizes one of them, i.e. 삼장교 三藏教 that it is real, 통교 通教 unreal, 별교 別教 both, 원교 圓教 neither ; v. 유 有 and 공 空, and each of the four schools. In esoteric symbolism the 사문 四門 are four stages of initiation, development, enlightenment, and nirvāṇa, and are associated with E., S., W., and N. ; with the four seasons ; with warmth, heat, coolness and cold, etc. 사문유관 四門遊觀 The four distresses observed during his wanderings by the Buddha when a prince — birth, age, disease, death.

사문 沙門 Śramaṇa. 상문 桑門 ; 사문 娑門 ; 상문 喪門 ; 사문나 沙門那 ; 사라마나 舍羅磨拏 ; 사가만낭 沙迦懣囊 ; 실마나라 室摩那拏 (1) Ascetics of all kinds ; "the Sarmanai, or Samanaioi, or Germanai of the Greeks, perhaps identical also with the Tungusian Saman or Shaman." [Eitel]. (2) Buddhist monks "who 'have left their families and quitted the passions', the Semnoi of the Greeks." [Eitel]. Explained by 공로 功勞 toilful achievement, 근식 勤息 diligent quieting (of the mind and the passions), 정지 淨志 purity of mind, 빈도 貧道 poverty. "He must keep well the Truth, guard well every uprising (of desire), be uncontaminated by outward attractions, be merciful to all and impure to none, be not elated to joy nor harrowed by distress, and able to bear whatever may came." The Sanskrit root is śram, to make effort ; exert oneself, do austerities. 사문과 沙門果 The fruit, or rebirth, resulting from the practices of the śramaṇa. 사문통 沙門統 The national superintendent or archbishop over the Order appointed under the Wei dynasty.

사물 四物 Four things. A general term referring to 법고 法鼓, 운판 雲板, 목어 木魚, 대종 大鐘.

사미 四迷 idem 사집 四執.

사미 四微 The four minutest forms or atoms perceptible to the four senses of sight, smell, taste, or touch ; from these arise the 사대 四大 four elements, from which arise the 오지 五智 five wisdoms, q.v.

사미 四味 The four "tastes" : the T'ien-t'ai definition of the four periods of the Buddha's teaching preliminary to the fifth, i.e. that of the Lotus sūtra ; cf. 오미 五味.

사미 沙彌 Śrāmaṇera, 실라마나락가 室羅摩拏洛迦 ; 실말나이낙가 室末那伊洛迦 ; 실라마니라 室羅摩尼羅 The male religious novice, who has taken vows to obey the ten commandments. The term is explained by 식악행자 息惡行慈 one who ceases from evil and does works of mercy, or lives altruistically ; 근책남 勤策男 a zealous man ; 구적 求寂 one who seeks rest ; 구열반적 求涅盤寂 one who seeks the peace of nirvāṇa. Three kinds are recognized according to age, i.e. 7 to 13 years old, old enough to 구오 驅烏 "drive away crows" ; 14 to 19, called 응법 應法 able to respond to or follow the doctrine ; 20 to 70. 사(미)니 沙(彌)尼 Śrāmaṇerikā 실라마나리가 室羅摩拏理迦. A female religious novice who has taken a vow to obey the ten commandments, i.e. 근책녀 勤策女 a zealous woman, devoted. 사미니계 沙彌尼戒 The ten commandments taken by the śrāmaṇerikā ; not to kill living beings, not to steal, not to lie or speak evil, not to have sexual intercourse, not to use perfumes or decorate oneself with flowers, not to occupy high beds, not to sing or dance, not to possess wealth, not to eat out of regulation hours, not to drink wine. 사미계 沙彌戒 The ten commandments of the śrāmaṇera ; v. 십계 十戒.

사미과 沙彌科 or 치문반 緇文班 The male or female observers of the minor commandments studies course in seminary 강원 講院.

사바 四波 An abbreviation for 사바라밀(보살) 四波羅蜜(菩薩). The four female attendants on Vairocana in the Vajradhātu, evolved from him, each of them a "mother" of one of the four Buddhas of the four quarters ; v. 사불 四佛, etc. 사바라이 四波羅夷 ; 사중 四重 ; 사기 四棄, 사극중감타죄 四極重感墮罪 The four pārājikas, or grievous sins or monks or nuns : (1) abrahmacarya, sexual immorality, or bestiality ; (2) adattādāna, stealing ; (3) vadha(hiṁsā), killing ; (4) uttaramanuṣyadharmapralāpa, false speaking.

사바제 舍婆提 v. 사위 舍衛.

사바하 沙波訶 Svāhā, hail! 사하 娑訶 v. 소 蘇.

사박 四縛 The four bandha, or bonds are (1) desire, resentment, heretical morality, egoism ; or (2) desire, possession (or existence), ignorance, and unenlightened views.

사발 四鉢 The four heavy stone begging-bowls offered to Śākyamuni by the four devas, which he miraculously combined into one and used as if ordinary material.

사방 四方 The four quarters of the compass ; a square, square ; the E. is ruled by Indra, S. by Yama, W. by Varuṇa, and N. by Vaiśramaṇa ; the N.E. is ruled by 이사니 伊舍尼 Īśāna, S.E. by 호마 護摩 Homa, S.W. by 녈리지 涅哩底 Nirṛti, and the N.W. by 부유 嚩庾 Varuṇa. 사방사불 四方四佛 The four Buddhas of the four regions — E. the world of 향적 香積 abundant fragrance where reigns 아촉 阿閦 Akṣobhya ; S. of 환희 歡喜 pleasure, 보상 寶相 Ratnaketu ; W. of 안락 安樂 restfulness, or joyful comfort, 무량수 無量壽 Amitābha ; and N. of 연화장엄 蓮華莊嚴 lotus adornment, 미묘성 微妙聲 Amoghasiddhi, or Śākyamuni. 사방대장 四方大將 The four "generals" or guardians of the Law, of the four directions : N. 산지대장 散脂大將, E. 낙욕대장 樂欲大將, S. 단제대장 檀帝大將, W. 선현대장 善現大將. Each has 500 followers and twenty-eight companies of demons and spirits. Cf. 사천왕 四天王.

사배 四輩 The four grades : (1) bhikṣu, bhikṣuṇī, upāsaka, upāsikā, i.e. monks, nuns, male and female disciples, v. 사중 四衆 ; (2) men, devas, nāgas, and ghosts 귀 鬼.

사백 四百 Four hundred.

사백계 四百戒 The 400 disciplinary laws of a bodhisattva, referred to in the 약사경 藥師經 but without detail.

사백사병 四百四病 The 404 ailments of the body ; each of the four elements — earth, water, fire, and wind — is responsible for 101 ; there are 202 fevers, or hot humours caused by earth and fire ; and 202 chills or cold humours caused by water and wind ; v. 지도론 智度論 65.

사번뇌 四煩惱 The four delusions in reference to the ego : 아치 我痴 ignorance in regard to the ego ; 아견 我見 holding to the ego idea ; 아만 我慢 self-esteem, egotism, pride ; 아애 我愛 self-seeking, or desire, both the latter arising from belief in the ego. Also 사혹 四惑.

사범주 四梵住 The noble state of unlimited 자비희사 慈悲喜捨 love, pity, joy, and indifference. 사범당 四梵堂 Four ways of attaining arhatship, idem 사범주 四梵住, except that the last of the four is 호 護 protection (of others). 사범지 四梵志 The four Brahmacārīs who resolved to escape death each on mountain, sea, in the air, or the market place, and yet failed ; v. 산 山.

사법 邪法 Heterodoxy, false doctrines or methods.

사법 四法 There are several groups of four dharma : (1) 교법 教法 the teaching (of the Buddha) ; 이법 理法 its principles, or meaning ; 행법 行法 its practice ; 과법 果法 its fruits or rewards. (2) Another group relates to bodhisattvas, their never losing the bodhi-mind, or the wisdom attained, or perseverance in progress, or the monastic forest life (araṇyaka). (3) Also 신해행증 信解行證 faith, discernment, performance, and assurance. (4) The Pure-land "True" sect of Japan has a division : 교법 教法, i.e. the 대무량수경 大無量壽經 ; 행법 行法 the practice of the seventeenth of Amitābha's vows ; 신법 信法 faith in the eighteenth ; and 증법 證法 proof of the eleventh, The most important work of Shinran, the founder of the sect, is these four, i.e. 교행신증 教行信證. (5) A "Lotus" division of 사법 四法 is the answer to a question of P'u-hsien (Samantabhadra) how the Lotus is to be possessed after the Buddha's demise, i.e. by thought (or protection) of the Buddhas ; the cultivation of virtue ; entry into correct dhyāna ; and having a mind to save all creatures. 사법삼원 四法三願 idem (4) above ; the three vows are the seventeenth, eighteenth, and eleventh of Amitābha. 사법불괴 四法不壞 The four imperishables — the correctly receptive heart, the diamond, the relics of a Buddha, and the palace of the devas of light and sound, ābhāsvaras. 사법인 四法印 The seal or impression of the four dogmas, suffering, impermanence, non ego, nirvāṇa, see 사법본말 四法本末. 사법성취 四法成就 idem 사종단법 四種檀法. 사법본말 四法本末 The alpha and omega in four laws or dogmas — that nothing is permanent, that all things involve suffering, that there is no personality, and that nirvāṇa is 영적 永寂 eternal rest. 사법시 四法施 The Buddha's gift of the four laws or dogmas, that all things are impermanent, that all (sentient) existence is suffering, that there is no (essential) personality, that all form (or matter) returns to the void. 사법계 四法界 ; 사종법계 四種法界 The four dharma-realms of the Hua-yen School : (1) 사법계 事法界 the phenomenal realm, with differentiation ; (2) 이법계 理法界 noumenal, with unity ; (3) 이사무애법계 理事無礙法界 both 리 理 noumenal and 사 事 phenomenal are interdependent ; (4) 사사무애법계 事事無礙法界 phenomena are also interdependent.

사법계 事法界 The phenomenal world, phenomenal existence. v. 사법계 四法界. 사법신 事法身 The Buddha-nature in practice, cf. 이법신 理法身, which is the Buddha-nature in principle, or essence, or the truth itself.

사병 四兵 Catur-aṅgabalakāya ; the four divisions of a cakravartī's troops — elephant, hastikāya ; horse, aśvakāya ; chariot, rathakāya ; and foot, pattikāya.

사병 四病 The four ailments, or mistaken ways of seeking perfection : 작병 作病 "works" or effort ; 임병 任病 *laissez-faire* ; 지병 止病 cessation of all mental operation ; 멸병 滅病 annihilation (of all desire).

사보살 四菩薩 The four bodhisattvas — Avalokiteśvara, Maitreya, Samantabhadra, and Mañjuśrī. Also, the four chief bodhisattvas in the Garbhadhātu. There are also the 본화사보살 本化四菩薩 of the Lotus sūtra, named 상행 上行, 무변행 無邊行, 정행 淨行, and 안립행 安立行.

사본지관 四本止觀 The four books of T'ien-t'ai on meditation 지관 止觀, i.e. 마하지관 摩訶止觀 ;

선바라밀 禪波羅蜜 ; 육묘문 六妙門 ; and 좌선법요 坐禪法要. 사본상 四本相 The four fundamental states — birth, stay, change, and extinction (or death), v. 사상 四相.

사부 四部 The four classes, e.g. śrota-āpanna, sakṛdāgāmin, anāgāmin, and arhat. v. 사도 四道.

사부경 四部經 The four sūtras of the Pure-land sect, according to 자은 慈恩 Tz'ŭ-ên, i.e. the 무량수경 無量壽經 ; 관무량수경 觀無量壽經 ; 아미타경 阿彌陀經, and 고음성다라니경 鼓音聲陀羅尼經.

사부율 四部律 v. 사율오론 四律五論.

사부중 四部衆 ; **사부제자** 四部弟子 ; **사부승** 四部僧 ; **사중** 四衆 The four divisions of disciples — bhikṣu, bhikṣuṇī, upāsaka, and upāsikā, monks, nuns, and male and female devotees.

사분 四分 The 법상 法相 Dharmalakṣaṇa school divides the function of 식 識 cognition into four, i.e. 상분 相分 mental phenomena, 견분 見分 discriminating such phenomena, 자증분 自證分 the power that discriminates, and 증자증 證自證 the proof or assurance of that power. Another group is : 신 信 faith, 해 解 liberty, 행 行 action, and 증 證 assurance or realization. 사분승계본 四分僧戒本 Extracts from the 사분율 四分律 four-division Vinaya with verses, for use on days when the discipline is recited ; there are other works under a similar title. 사분종 四分宗 idem 율종 律宗. 사분가 四分家 The 법상 法相 school which divides the 식심 識心 cognition-mind into four parts, v. above. 사분율 四分律 The four-division Vinaya or discipline of the Dharmagupta school, divided into four sections of 20, 15, 14, and 11 chüan. The 사분율장 四分律藏 Dharmagupta-vinaya was tr. in A.D. 405 by Buddhayaśas and 축불념 竺佛念 Chu Fo-nien ; the 사분비구니갈마법 四分比丘尼羯磨法 Dharmagupta-bhikṣuṇī-karman was tr. by Guṇavarman in 431 ; and there are numerous other works of this order.

사불 四佛 Four of the Five Dhyāni-Buddhas, i.e. the four regional Buddhas ; they are variously stated. The 금광명경 金光明經 gives E. 아촉 阿閦 ; S. 보상 寶相 ; W. 무량수 無量壽 ; N. 미묘성 微妙聲. The 대일경 大日經 gives E. 보당 寶幢 ; S. 대근용변각화개부 大勤勇遍覺華開敷 ; W. 인승 仁勝 (i.e. 무량수 無量壽) ; N. 불근 不勤, i.e. 고음여래 鼓音如來. The 금강정경 金剛頂經 gives 불근 不勤 ; 보생 寶生 ; 관자재 觀自在, and 불공성취여래 不空成就如來. v. 오지여래 五智如來. 사불토 四佛土 idem 사토 四土. 사불지견 四佛知見 The four purposes of the Buddha's appearing, that the Buddha-knowledge might be 개시오입 開示悟入 revealed, proclaimed, understood, and entered ; v. Lotus 방편품方便品.

사불가득 四不可得 The four unattainables, perpetual youth, no sickness, perennial life, no death. There is a work, the Catur-lābha-sūtra, tr. into Chinese under this title. 사불가사의 四不可思議 The four things of a Buddha which are beyond human conception ; 세계 世界 his world, 중생 衆生 his living beings, 용 龍 his nāgas, and 불토경계 佛土境界 the bounds of his Buddha-realm. 사불가경 四不可輕 The four that may not be treated lightly : a prince though young, a snake though small, a fire though tiny, and above all a "novice" though a beginner, for he may become an arhat. Cf. 아함경 阿含經 46.

사불견 四不見 The four invisibles — water to fish, wind (or air) to man, the nature (of things) to the deluded, and the 공 空 "void" to the 오 悟 enlightened, because he is in his own element, and the Void is beyond conception.

사불괴정 四不壞淨 or **사불괴신** 四不壞信 The four objects of unfailing purity (or faith), i.e. the three precious ones (triratna) and the 계 戒 moral law.

사불기부 四不寄附 The four to whom one does not entrust valuables — the old, for death is nigh ; the distant, lest one has immediate need of them ; the evil ; or the 대력 大力 strong ; lest the temptation be too strong for the last two.

사불생 四不生 That a thing is not born or not produced of itself, of another, of both, of neither ; cf. 사구추검 四句推撿.

사불성 四不成 Four forms of asiddha or incomplete statement, part of the thirty-three fallacies in logic.

사비구 四比丘 v. 사악비구 四惡比丘.

사사 邪私 Depraved and selfish desires, lust.

사사 四蛇 idem 사독사 四毒蛇. The Fan-i-ming-i under this heading gives the parable of a man who fled from the two bewildering forms of life and death, and climbed down a rope (of life) 명근 命根, into the well of impermanence 무상 無常, where two mice, night and day, gnawed the rattan rope ; on the four sides four snakes 사사 四蛇 sought to poison him, i.e. the 사대 四大 or four elements (of his physical nature) ; below were three dragons 삼독룡 三毒龍 breathing fire and trying to seize him. On looking up he saw that two 상 象 elephants (darkness and light) had come to the mouth of the well ; he was in despair, when a bee flew by and dropped some honey (the five desires 오욕 五欲) into his mouth, which he ate and entirely forgot his peril.

사사 四邪 idem 사집 四執.

사사 四捨 The four givings, i.e. of goods, of the Truth, of courage (or fearlessness), and the giving up of the passions and delusions ; cf. dāna-pāramitā, 사 捨.

사사 四事 The four necessaries of a monk — clothing, victuals, bedding, medicine (or herbs). Another set is a dwelling, clothing, victuals, medicine. 사사공양 四事供養 The four offerings or provisions for a monk. There is a sūtra, the 사사경 四事經, or 아난사사경 阿難四事經. For 사사불가사의 四事不可思議 v. 사불가사의 四不可思議. 사사법문 四事法門 Four methods of a bodhisattva's preparation for preaching the Law — entry into meditation ; into wisdom ; into complete moral self-control ; and into clear discernment, or reasoning, 변재문 辯才門.

사사가 舍舍迦 Śaśaka, a hare, rabbit, v. 사지 舍支.

사사유 邪思惟 Heterodox reflection, or thought.

사산 邪山 A mountain of error or heterodox ideas ; such ideas as great as a mountain.

사산 四山 Like four closing-in mountains are birth, age, sickness, and death ; another group is age, sickness, death, and decay (쇠 衰, i.e. of wealth, honours, etc., or 무상 無常 impermanence).

사상 事相 Phenomenon, affair, practice. The practices of the esoterics are called 사상부 事相部 as contrasted with their open teaching called 교상부 教相部. 사상선사 事相禪師 A mystic, or monk in meditation, yet busy with affairs: an epithet of reproach.

사상 四相 The four avasthā, or states of all phenomena, i.e. 생주이멸 生住異滅 birth, being, change (i.e. decay), and death ; also 사유위상 四有爲相. There are several groups, e.g. 과보사상 果報四相 birth, age, disease, death. Also 장식사상 藏識四相 of the "Awakening of Faith" referring to the initiation, continuation, change, and cessation of the Ālaya-vijñāna. Also 아인사상 我人四相 The ideas : (1) that there is an ego ; (2) that man is different from other organisms ; (3) that all the living are produced by the skandhas ; (4) that life is limited to the organism. Also 지경사상 智境四相 dealing differently with the four last headings 아 我 ; 인 人 ; 중생 衆生 ; and 수상 壽相.

사상 四上 The four times a day of going up to worship — daybreak, noon, evening, and midnight.

사생 四生 Catur-yoni, the four forms of birth : (1) 태생 胎生 or 복생 腹生 jarāyuja, viviparous, as with mammalia ; (2) 난생 卵生 aṇḍaja, oviparous, as with birds ; (3) 습생 濕生 or 한열화합생 寒熱和合生 saṁsvedaja, moisture, or water-born, as with worms and fishes ; (4) 화생 化生 aupapāduka, metamorphic, as with moths from the chrysalis, or with devas, or in the hells, or the first beings in a newly evolved world. 사생백겁 四生百劫 A pratyeka-buddha method of obtaining release, by intensive effort, at the shortest in four rebirths, at the longest in a hundred kalpas.

사루가 舍樓伽 Śāluka, esculent lotus roots ; intp. as a kind of cooked liquid food.

사선 邪扇 Heterodox fanning, i.e. to influence people by false doctrines.

사선 四仙 The three genii, or founders of systems, together with 야제자 若提子 Nirgranthajñāti ; v. 이천삼선 二天三仙. 사선피사 四仙避死 The four wise men who sought escape from death : one in the mountains, another in the ocean, another in the air, and a fourth in the market place — all in vain.

사선(천) 四禪(天) The four dhyāna heavens, 사정려(천) 四靜慮(天), i.e. the division of the eighteen brahmalokas into four dhyānas : the disciple attains to one of these heavens according to the dhyāna he observes : (1) 초선천 初禪天 The first region, "as large as one whole universe," comprises the three heavens, Brahma-pāriṣadya, Brahma-purohita, and Mahābrahmā, 범보 梵輔, 범중 梵衆, and 대범천 大梵天 ; the inhabitants are without gustatory or olfactory organs, not needing food, but possess the other four of the six organs. (2) 이선천 二禪天 The second region, equal to "a small chiliocosmos" 소천계 小千界, comprises the three heavens, according to Eitel, "Parīttābha, Apramāṇābha, and Ābhāsvara," i.e. 소광 少光 minor light, 무량광 無量光 infinite light, and 극광정 極光淨 utmost light-purity ; the inhabitants have ceased to require the five physical organs, possessing only the organ of mind. (3) 삼선천 三禪天 The third region, equal to "a middling chiliocosmos" 중천계 中千界, comprises three heavens ; Eitel gives them as Parīttaśubha, Apramāṇaśubha, and Śubhakṛtsna, i.e. 소정 少淨 minor purity, 무량정 無量淨 infinite purity, and 변정 徧淨 universal purity ; the inhabitants still have the organ of mind and are receptive of great joy. (4) 사선천 四禪天 The fourth region, equal to a great chiliocosmos, 대천계 大千界, comprises the remaining nine Brahmalokas, namely, Puṇyaprasava, Anabhraka, Bṛhatphala, Asañjñisattva, Avṛhās, Atapās, Sudṛśa, Sudarśana, and Akaniṣṭha [Eitel]. The Chinese titles are 복생 福生 felicitous birth, 무운 無雲 cloudless, 광과 廣果 large fruitage, 무번 無煩 no vexations, atapās is 무열 無熱 no heat, sudṛśa is 선견 善見 beautiful to see, sudarśana is 선현 善現 beautiful appearing, two others are 색구경 色究竟 the end of form, and 무상천 無想天 the heaven above thought, but it is difficult to trace avṛhās and akaniṣṭha ; the inhabitants of this fourth region still have mind. The number of the dhyāna heavens differs ; the Sarvāstivādins say 16, the 경 經 or Sūtra school 17, and the Sthavira school 18. Eitel points out that first dhyāna has one world with one moon, one meru, four continents, and six devalokas ; the second dhyāna has 1,000 times the worlds of the first ; the third has 1,000 times the worlds of the second ; the fourth dhyāna has 1,000 times those of the third. Within a kalpa of destruction 괴겁 壞劫 the first is destroyed fifty-six times by fire, the second seven by water, the third once by wind, the fourth "corresponding to a state of absolute indifference" remains "untouched" by all the other evolutions ; when "fate (천명 天命) comes to an end then the fourth Dhyāna may come to an end too, but not sooner". 사선팔정 四禪八定 The four dhyānas on the form-realms and the eight concentrations, i.e. four on the form-realms and four on the formless-realms. 사선정 四禪定 The four dhyāna-concentrations which lead to the four dhyāna heavenly regions, see above.

사선근 四善根 Catuṣ-kuśala-mūla, the four good roots, or sources from which spring good fruit or development. In Hīnayāna they form the stage after 총상념주 總相念住 as represented by the 구사 俱舍 and 성실 成實 ; in Mahāyāna it is the final stage of the 십회향 十迴向 as represented by the 법상종 法相宗. There are also four similar stages connected with śrāvaka, pratyeka-buddha, and Buddha, styled 삼품사선근 三品四善根. The four of the 구사종 俱舍宗 are 난법 煖法, 정법 頂法, 인법 忍法, and 세제일법 世第一法. The four of the 성실종 成實宗 are the same, but are applied differently. The 법상종 法相宗 retains the same four terms, but connects them with the four dhyāna stages of the 진유식관 眞唯識觀 in its four first 가행 加行 developments.

사섭법 四攝法 ; **사섭사** 四攝事 Catuḥ-saṁgraha-vastu ; four all-embracing (bodhisattva) virtues : (1) 보시 布施 dāna, giving what others like, in order to lead them to love and receive the truth ; (2) 애어 愛語 priyavacana, affectionate speech, with the same purpose ; (3) 이행 利行 arthakṛtya, conduct profitable to others, with the same purpose ; (4) 동사 同事 samānārthatā, co-operation with and adaptation of oneself to others, to lead them into the truth. 사섭보살 四攝菩薩 ; 사섭중 四攝衆 ; 사섭금강 四攝金剛 The four bodhisattvas in the Vajradhātu with the hook, the rope, the chain, and the bell, whose office is to 화타 化他 convert the living.

사성 四姓 The four Indian "clans" or castes — brāhmaṇa, kṣatriya, vaiśya, śūdra, i.e. (1) priestly, (2) military and ruling, (3) farmers and traders, and (4) serfs ; born respectively from the mouth, shoulders, flanks, and feet of Brahmā.

사성 四聖 The four kinds of holy men — śrāvakas, pratyeka-buddhas, bodhisattvas, and Buddhas. Also, the four chief disciples of Kumārajīva, i.e. 도생 道生 Tao-shêng, 승조 僧肇 Sêng-chao, 도융 道融 Tao-jung, and 승예 僧叡 Sêng-jui. 사성행 四聖行 The four holy ways — wearing rags from dust-heaps, begging for food, sitting under trees, and entire withdrawal from the world. The meaning is similar in 사양약 四良藥 ; 행사의 行四依 ; and 사성종 四聖種. 사성제 四聖諦 The four holy or noble truths, idem 사제 四諦.

사성정(취) 邪性定(聚) The accumulation (of suffering) to be endured in purgatory by one of heterodox nature ; one of the three accumulations 삼취 三聚.

사성행 四性行 The four kinds of conduct natural to a Bodhisattva, that arising from his native goodness, his vow-nature, his compliant nature, i.e. to the six pāramitās, and his transforming nature, i.e. his powers of conversion or salvation.

사세 四世 The period of the Buddha's earthly life, styled 성세 聖世 the sacred period (or period of the sage), is added to the three periods of 정법 正法 correct Law ; 상법 像法 semblance of the Law ; and 말법 末法 decadence of the Law.

사손 師孫 Disciple of a disciple.

사수유 四須臾 The four short divisions of time — a wink ; a snap of the fingers ; 라예 羅預 a lava, 20 finger-snaps ; and 수유 須臾 kṣaṇa, said to be 20 lava ; but a lava is "the sixtieth of a twinkling" [M. W.] and a kṣaṇa an instant.

사순 邪旬 Jhāpita, 순 旬 being erroneously used to represent the syllable *pi*, v. 다 茶.

사술 四術 idem 사집 四執.

사승 四乘 The goat, deer, and ox carts and the great white-bullock cart of the Lotus sūtra, see 사거 四車.

사승의제 四勝義諦 idem 사제 四諦. 사승신 四勝身 The four with victorious bodies, who were transformed independently of normal rebirth ; also styled 해행신 解行身 bodies set free from all physical taint, thus attaining to Buddhahood. The four are the 용녀 龍女 dragon-daughter of the Lotus sūtra, who instantly became a male bodhisattva ; and three others of the 화엄

華嚴 Hua-yen sūtra, i.e. 선재동자 善財童子 ; 도솔천자 兜率天子, and 보장엄동자 普莊嚴童子.

사시 四施 Four benefactions, i.e. pen, ink, sūtras, preaching.

사식 四食 The four kinds of food, i.e. 단식 段食 or 단식 摶食 for the body and its senses ; 촉식 觸食 or 낙식 樂食 for the emotions ; 사식 思食 or 염식 念食 for thought ; and 식식 識食 for wisdom, i.e. the 육식 六識 of Hīnayāna and the 팔식 八識 of Mahāyāna, of which the eighth, i.e. ālayavijñāna, is the chief.

사식시 四食時 The four times for food, i.e. of the devas at dawn, of all Buddhas at noon, of animals in the evening, and of demons and ghosts at night.

사신 四身 The four kāya, or "bodies". The Laṅkāvatāra-sūtra gives 화불 化佛 ; 공덕불 功德佛 ; 지혜불 智慧佛, and 여여불 如如佛 ; the first is the nirmāṇakāya, the second and third sambhogakāya, and the fourth dharmakāya. The 유식론 唯識論 gives 자성신 自性身 ; 타수용신 他受用身 ; 자수용신 自受用身, and 변화신 變化身, the first being 법신 法身, the second and third 보신 報身, and the fourth 화신 化身. The T'ien-t'ai School gives 법신 法身 ; 보신 報身 ; 응신 應身, and 화신 化身. The esoteric sect has four divisions of the 법신 法身. See 삼신 三身.

사신 四信 v. 사종신심 四種信心. 사신오행 四信五行 The four right objects of faith and the five right modes of procedure ; the 진여 眞如 Bhūtatathatā and the 삼보 三寶 Three Precious Ones are the four ; the five are almsgiving, morality, patience, zeal (or progress), and 지관 止觀 meditation.

사신족 四神足 idem 사여의족 四如意足.

사실단 四悉檀 The four siddhānta, v. 실 悉. The Buddha taught by (1) 세계실단 世界悉檀 mundane or ordinary modes of expression ; (2) 각각위인실단 各各爲人悉檀 individual treatment, adapting his teaching to the capacity of his hearers ; (3) 대치실단 對治悉檀 diagnostic treatment of their moral diseases ; and (4) 제일의실단 第一義悉檀 the perfect and highest truth.

사심 沙心 Mind like sand in its countless functionings.

사심 四心 The hearts of kindness, pity, joy, and indifference, idem 사무량심 四無量心.

사심사관 四尋思觀 A study or contemplation of the 법상종 法相宗 Dharmalakṣaṇa sect, on 명 名 the terms used, 의 義 the meanings of the things or phenomena, 자성 自性 the nature of the things, 차별 差別 their differentiation.

사십 四十 Catvāriṁśat ; forty. 사십일위 四十一位 or 사십일지 四十一地 Forty-one of the fifty-two bodhisattva stages (of development), i.e. all except the 십신 十信 and 묘각 妙覺. For this and 사십이위 四十二位 v. 오십이위 五十二位. 사십구승 四十九僧 and 사십구등 四十九燈. The service to 약사 藥師 the Master of Healing, when forty-nine lamps are displayed and forty-nine monks engaged ; seven of his images are used, seven of the lamps being placed before each image. 사십구일 四十九日 The seven times seven days of funeral services ; the forty-ninth day. 사십구중마니전 四十九重摩尼殿 or 사십구중여의전 四十九重如意殿. The Maṇi, or Pearl palace of forty-nine stories above the Tuṣita heaven. 사십이사자 四十二使者 The forty-two messengers, or angels of 부동존 不動尊 q.v. 사십이위 四十二位 The forty-two stages, i.e. all above the 십신 十信 of the fifty-two stages. 사십이품무명 四十二品無明 The forty-two species of ignorance which, according to T'ien-t'ai, are to be cut off seriatim in the above forty-two stages. 사십이자문 四十二字門 The doctrine of the forty-two 실담 悉曇 Siddham letters as given in the 화엄 華嚴 76 and 반야경 般若經 4. They have special meanings, independent of their use among the fourteen vowels and thirty-five consonants, i.e. forty-nine alphabetic signs. The forty-two are supposed by the 지도론 智度論 47 to be the root or basis of all letters ; and each letter has its own specific value as a spiritual symbol ; T'ien-t'ai associates each of them with one of the forty-two 위

位. The letters begin with 아 阿 and end with 다 荼 or 타 佗. 사십이장경 四十二章經 The "Sūtra of Forty-two Sections" generally attributed to Kāśyapa Mātaṅga, v. 가 迦, and Gobharana, v. 축 竺, the first Indian monks to arrive officially in China. It was, however, probably first produced in China in the 진 晉 Chin dynasty. There are various editions and commentaries. 사십위 四十位 The "forty bodhisattva positions" of the 범망경 梵網經. They are classified into four groups : (1) 십발취 十發趣 Ten initial stages, i.e. the minds 심 心 of abandoning things of the world, of keeping the moral law, patience, zealous progress, dhyāna, wisdom, resolve, guarding (the Law), joy, and spiritual baptism by the Buddha. These are associated with the 십주 十住. (2) 십장양 十長養 Ten steps in the nourishment of perfection, i.e. minds of kindness, pity, joy, relinquishing, almsgiving, good discourse, benefiting, friendship, dhyāna, wisdom. These are associated with the 십행 十行. (3) 십금강 十金剛 Ten "diamond" steps of firmness, i.e. a mind of faith, remembrance, bestowing one's merits on others, understanding, uprightness, no-retreat, mahāyāna, formlessness, wisdom, indestructibility ; these are associated with the 십회향 十廻向. (4) The 십지 十地 q.v. 사십팔사자 四十八使者 The forty-eight demon satellites of Āryācalanātha 부동명왕 不動明王 as subduer of demons, etc. 사십팔년 四十八年 The forty-eight years of service demanded by an old physician of his pupil in order to acquire his skill — likened to the slow and difficult methods of Hīnayāna and of early Mahāyāna. 사십팔원 四十八願 The forty-eight vows of Amitābha that he would not enter into his final nirvāṇa or heaven, unless all beings shared it ; the lists vary. 사십여년미현진실 四十餘年未顯眞實 For forty and more years (the Buddha) was unable to unfold the full truth (until he first gave it in the Lotus sūtra).

사아함 四阿含 The four Āgamas 사아급마 四阿笈摩, or divisions of the Hīnayāna scriptures : 장아함 長阿含 dīrghāgamas, "long" works, cosmological ; 중아함 中阿含 madhyamāgamas, metaphysical ; 잡아함 雜阿含 saṁyuktāgamas, general, on dhyāna, trance, etc. ; 증일아함 增一阿含 ekottarikāgamas, numerically arranged subjects.

사악(취) 四惡(趣) ; **사악(도)** 四惡(道) The four apāya, or evil destinies : the hells, as hungry ghosts, animals, or asuras. The asuras are sometimes evil, sometimes good, hence the term 삼악도 三惡道 "three evil destinies" excepts the asuras. 사악비구 四惡比丘 The four wicked bhikṣus who threw over the teaching of their Buddha 대장엄 大莊嚴 Ta Chuang Yen after his nirvāṇa ; these suffered in the deepest hells, came forth purified, but have not been able to attain perfection because of their past unbelief ; v. 불장경왕고품 佛藏經往古品. Also four disobedient bhikṣus who through much purgation ultimately became the Buddhas of the four points of the compass, 아촉 阿閦, 보상 寶相, 무량수 無量壽, and 미묘성 微妙聲.

사안 四眼 The four powers of sight of bodhisattvas, a Buddha has a fifth power ; v. 오안 五眼.

사안락(행) 四安樂(行) The four means of attaining to a happy contentment, by proper direction of the deeds of the body ; the words of the mouth ; the thoughts of the mind ; and the resolve(of the will) to preach to all the Lotus sūtra.

사애생 四愛生 ; **사애기** 四愛起 Four sources of affection : the giving or receiving of clothing, or food, or bedding, or independently of gifts.

사액 四軛 The four yokes, or fetters, i.e. 욕 欲 desire, 유 有 possessions and existence, 견 見 (unenlightened or non-Buddhist) views, 무명 無明 ignorance.

사야팔주 四夜八晝 The four hours of the night 술해자축 戌亥子丑, i.e. 7 to 3, and the eight hours of the day from 인 寅 to 유 酉 3 a.m. to 7 p.m.

사양약 四良藥 The four good physicians, or medicines ; idem 사성행 四聖行.

사여실관 四如實觀 A meditation method on the 사가행위 四加行位 q.v. 사여의족 四如意足 ; 사신족

四神足 Ṛddhipāda ; the third group of the 삼십칠과도품 三十七科道品 bodhipākṣika-dharma ; the four steps to ṛddhi, or supernatural powers, making the body independent of ordinary or natural law. The four steps are said to be the 사종선정 四種禪定 four kinds of dhyāna, but there are several definitions, e.g. 욕신족 欲神足 chanda-ṛddhi-pādaḥ, desire (or intensive longing, or concentration) ; 근신족 勤神足 vīrya-ṛddhi-pādaḥ, energy (or intensified effort) ; 심신족 心神足 citta-ṛddhi-pādaḥ, memory (or intense holding on to the position reached) ; 관신족 觀神足 mīmāṁsā-ṛddhi-pādaḥ, meditation (or survey, the state of dhyāna).

사연 四衍 The four yānas or vehicles, idem 사승 四乘.

사예 四翳 The four films, or things that becloud, i.e. rain-clouds ; dust-storms ; smoke ; and asuras, i.e. eclipses of sun and moon ; emblematic of desire, hate, ignorance, and pride ; cf. 사결 四結.

사왕(천) 四王(天) Catur-mahārāja-kāyikas, the four heavens of the four deva-kings, i.e. the lowest of the six heavens of desire ; v. 사천왕 四天王. 사왕도리 四王忉利 The above four and trayastriṁśāḥ, Indra's heaven.

사요품 四要品 The four most important chapters of the Lotus sūtra, i.e. 방편품 方便品 ; 안락행품 安樂行品 ; 수량품 壽量品, and 보문품 普門品 ; this is T'ien-t'ai's selection ; the Nichiren sect makes 권지품 勸持品 the second and 신력품 神力品 the fourth.

사욕 四欲 The four desires or passions : 정 情 sexual love ; 색 色 sexual beauty or attractiveness ; 식 食 food ; 음 婬 lust.

사우단나 四優檀那 Yu-t'an-na, udāna, the four dogmas : all is impermanent, all is suffering, there is no ego, nirvāṇa.

사우사행살타 四隅四行薩埵 The four female attendants on Vairocana in the Vajradhātu 금 金, 보 寶, 법 法, and 업 業, q.v. ; also 사바 四波.

사운 邪雲 Clouds of falsity or heterodoxy, which cover over the Buddha-mature in the heart.

사운(심) 四運(心) The four stages of a thought : not yet arisen, its initiation, its realization, its passing away, styled 미념 未念, 욕념 欲念, 정념 正念, and 염이 念已.

사원 四園 idem 사원 四苑.

사원 四怨 The four enemies — the passions-and-delusion māras, death māra, the five-skandhas māras, and the supreme māra-king.

사원 四苑 The pleasure grounds outside 선견성 善見城 Sudarśana, the heavenly city of Indra : E. 중차원 衆車苑 Caitrarathavana, the park of chariots ; S. 추악원 麤惡苑 Parūṣakavana, the war park ; W. 잡림원 雜林苑 Miśrakāvana, intp. as the park where all desires are fulfilled ; N. 희림원 喜林苑 Nandanavana, the park of all delights. Also 사원 四園.

사원사 四蚖蛇 idem 사사 四蛇.

사월 四月 Āṣāḍhā, the fourth month. 사월파일 四月八日 The eighth of the fourth moon, the Buddha's birthday.

사위 舍衛 Śrāvastī, 사바제 舍婆提 ; 실라벌(실지) 室羅伐(悉底) ; 시라발제 尸羅跋提 ; 사라바실제야 舍羅婆悉帝耶 ; intp. as 문물 聞物 the city of famous things, or men, or the famous city ; it was a city and ancient kingdom 500 li north-west of Kapilavastu, now Rapetmapet south of Rapti River (M. W. says Sāhet-Māhet). It is said to have been in 북교살라 北憍薩羅 northern Kosala, distinct from the southern kingdom of that name. It was a favourite resort of Śākyamuni, the 기원 祇園 Jetavana being there.

사위(타) 四韋(陀) The four Vedas.

사위의 四威儀 Four respect-inspiring forms of demeanour in walking, standing, sitting, lying.

사유 四維 The four half points of the compass, N.E., N.W., S.E., S.W.

사유 四喩 The four metaphors (of infinity, etc.) : 산근 山斤 the weight of all the mountains in pounds ; 해 海 the drops in the ocean ; 지진 地塵 the atoms of dust in the earth ; 공계 空界 the extent of space.

사유위상 四有爲相 The four functioning forms, i.e. 생 生 birth, 주 住 stay, 이 異 change, and 멸 滅 extinction ; v. 사상 四相.

사율오론 四律五論 The four vinaya and the five śāstras. The four vinaya, or disciplinary regulations, are the 십송율 十誦律 Sarvāstivāda-version tr. in 61 chüan by Puṇyatara, 사분율 四分律 Dharmagupta's version, tr. in 60 chüan by Buddhayaśas ; 승기율 僧祇律 Sāṁghika-version or Mahāsāṅghikāḥ-version, tr. in 40 chüan, by Buddhabhadra ; and 오부율 五部律 Mahīśāsaka- version, tr. in 30 chüan by Buddhajīva and others, also known as Mahīśāsakanikāya-pañcavargavinaya. The five śāstras are 비니모론 毘尼母論 ; 마득륵가론 摩得勒伽論 ; 선견론 善見論 ; 살바다론 薩婆多論 ; and 명료론 明了論. v. 론 論.

사음 邪婬 Adultery.

사의 四依 The four necessaries, or things on which the religious rely. (1) 행사의 行四依 The four of ascetic practitioners — rag clothing ; begging for food ; sitting under trees ; purgatives and diuretics as moral and spiritual means ; these are also termed 사성종 四聖種. (2) 법사의 法四依 The four of the dharma, i.e. the truth, which is eternal, rather than man, even its propagator ; the sūtras of perfect meaning, i.e. of the 중도실상 中道實相 the truth of the "middle" way ; the meaning, or spirit, not the letter ; wisdom 지 智, i.e. Buddha-wisdom rather than mere knowledge 식 識. There are other groups. Cf. 사사 四事. 사의입정 四依入正 The first four above, 행사의 行四依, and the 팔정도 八正道 q.v.

사의단 四意斷 idem 사정근 四正勤.

사이 舍夷 Śākya, one of the five surnames of the Buddha.

사이(계) 四夷(戒) or **사이(죄)** 四夷(罪) v. 사바라이 四波羅夷.

사인관세 四人觀世 The world from four points of view : that of men in general — its pleasures, thoughtlessly ; of śrāvakas and pratyeka-buddhas — as a burning house, uneasily ; of bodhisattvas — as an empty flower ; of Buddhas — as mind, all things being for (or of) intelligent mind.

사일 四日 Catvāraḥsūryās, the four suns, i.e. Aśvaghoṣa, Devabodhisattva, Nāgārjuna, and Kumāralabdha (or -lāta).

사일 四一 The four "ones", or the unity contained (according to T'ien-t'ai) in the 방편품 方便品 of the Lotus Sūtra ; i.e. 교일 敎一 its teaching of one Vehicle ; 행일 行一 its sole bodhisattva procedure ; 인일 人一 its men all and only as bodhisattvas ; 이일 理一 its one ultimate truth of the reality of all existence.

사자 師子 Siṁha, a lion ; also 시가 枲伽 ; idem 사자 獅子 Buddha, likened to the lion, the king of animals, in respect of his fearlessness.

사자광 師子光 Siṁharaśmi. "A learned opponent of the Yogācāra school who lived about A.D. 630." [Eitel].

사자국 師子國 Siṁhala, Ceylon, the kingdom reputed to be founded by Siṁha, first an Indian merchant, later king of the country, who overcame the "demons" of Ceylon and conquered the island.

사자분신 師子奮迅 The lion aroused to anger, i.e. the Buddha's power of arousing awe.

사자상 師子相 Siṁhadhvaja ; "lion-flag," a Buddha south-east of our universe, fourth son of Mahābhijñā.

사자신중충 師子身中蟲 Just as no animal eats a dead lion, but it is destroyed by worms produced within itself, so no outside force can destroy Buddhism, only evil monks within it can destroy it.

사자왕 師子王 The lion king, Buddha.

사자유 獅子乳 Lion's milk, like bodhi-enlightenment, which is able to annihilate countless ages of the karma of affliction, just as one drop of lion's milk can disintegrate an ocean of ordinary milk.

사자유희삼매 師子遊戲三昧 The joyous samādhi which is likened to the play of the lion with his prey. When a Buddha enters this degree of samādhi he causes the earth to tremble, and the purgatories to give up their inmates.

사자음 師子音 Siṁhaghoṣa ; "lion's voice," a Buddha south-east of our universe, third son of Mahābhijñā.

사자존자 師子尊者 ; **사자비구** 師子比丘 Āryasiṁha, or Siṁha-bhikṣu. The 23rd or 24th patriarch, Brahman by birth ; a native of Central India ; laboured in Kashmir, where he died a martyr A.D. 259.

사자좌 師子座 or **사자상** 師子牀 Siṁhāsana. A lion throne, or couch. A Buddha throne, or seat ; wherever the Buddha sits, even the bare ground ; a royal throne.

사자주 師子冑 or **사자개** 師子鎧 Harivarman, to whom the 성실론 成實論 Satyasiddhi-śāstra is ascribed.

사자침 四自侵 The four self-raidings, or self-injuries — in youth not to study from morn till night ; in advancing years not to cease sexual intercourse ; wealthy and not being charitable ; not accepting the Buddha's teaching. 사자재 四自在 The four sovereign powers : 계 戒 the moral law ; 신통 神通 supernatural power ; 지 智 knowledge ; and 혜 慧 wisdom.

사자협옥 師子頰玉 Siṁhahanu. The paternal grandfather of Śākyamuni, a king of Kapilavastu, father of Śuddhodana, Śuklodana, Droṇodana, and Amṛtodana.

사자후 師子吼 Siṁhanāda. The lion's roar, a term designating authoritative or powerful preaching. As the lion's roar makes all animals tremble, subdues elephants, arrests birds in their flight and fishes in the water, so Buddha's preaching overthrows all other religions, subdues devils, conquers heretics, and arrests the misery of life.

사장 事障 Phenomenal hindrances to entry into nirvāṇa, such as desire, etc. ; 이장 理障 are noumenal hindrances, such as false doctrine, etc.

사재일 四齋日 The four fast days, i.e. the quarters of the moon — new, full, 8th, and 23rd.

사적 事迹 Traces of the deeds or life of an individual ; biography.

사전 四田 The four fields for cultivating happiness — animals ; the poor ; parents, etc. ; the religion.

사절 四絶 The four ideas to be got rid of in order to obtain the "mean" or ultimate reality, according to the 중론 中論 : they are that things exist, do not exist, both, neither.

사절 四節 The four monastic annual periods — beginning of summer, end of summer, winter solstice, and the new year.

사정 四定 The four dhyāna heavens of form, and the four degrees of dhyāna corresponding to them. For 사정기 四定記 v. 사기 四記.

사정근 四正勤 Samyakprahāṇa, v. 삼십칠도품 三十七道品 ; the four right efforts — to put an end to existing evil ; prevent evil arising ; bring good into existence ; develop existing good ; 사정단 四正斷 ; 사의단 四意斷 are similar but the third point is the conservation of the good.

사정려(천) 四靜慮(天) v. 사선(천) 四禪(天).

사정정 四淨定 The "pure" dhyāna, i.e. one of the 삼정 三定 three dhyānas ; this dhyāna is in four parts.

사제 四諦 Catvāri ārya-satyāni ; 사성제 四聖諦 ; 사진제 四眞諦. The four dogmas, or noble truths, the primary and fundamental doctrines of Śākyamuni, said to approximate to the form of medical diagnosis. They are pain or "suffering, its cause, its ending, the way thereto ; that existence is suffering, that human passion (taṇhā, desire) is the cause of continued suffering, that by the destruction of human passion existence may be brought to an end ; that by a life of holiness the destruction of human passion may be attained". Childers. The four are 고 苦, 취 聚 (or 집 集), 멸 滅, and 도제 道諦, i.e. duḥkha 두거 豆佉, samudaya 삼모제야 三牟提耶, nirodha 니루타 尼樓陀, and mārga 말가 末加. Eitel interprets them (1) "that 'misery' is a necessary attribute of sentient existence" ; (2) that "the 'accumulation' of misery is caused by the passions" ; (3) that "the 'extinction' of passion is possible" ; (4) mārga is "the doctrine of the 'path' that leads to the extinction of passion". (1) 고 苦 suffering is the lot of the 육취 六趣 six states of existence ; (2) 집 集 is the aggregation (or exacerbation) of suffering by reason of the passions ; (3) 멸 滅 is nirvāṇa, the extinction of desire and its consequences, and the leaving of the sufferings of mortality as void and extinct ; (4) 도 道 is the way of such extinction, i.e. the 팔정도 八正道 eightfold correct way. The first two are considered to be related to this life, the last two to 출세간 出世間 a life outside or apart from the world. The four are described as the fundamental doctrines first preached to his five former ascetic companions. Those who accepted these truths were in the stage of śrāvaka. There is much dispute as to the meaning of 멸 滅 "extinction" as to whether it means extinction of suffering, of passion, or of existence. The Nirvāṇa sūtra 18 says that whoever accepts the four dogmas will put an end to births and deaths 약능견사제즉득단생사 若能見四諦則得斷生死 which does not of necessity mean the termination of existence but that of continued transmigration. v. 멸 滅. 사제경 四諦經 The sūtra of the four dogmas, tr. by 안세고 安世高 An Shih-kao, one chüan.

사제일게 四第一偈 A verse from the 장엄론 莊嚴論 Chuang Yen Lun —

> Health is the best wealth,
> Contentment the best riches,
> Friendship the best relationship,
> Nirvāṇa the best joy.

사조 事造 Phenomenal activities. According to T'ien-t'ai there are 3,000 underlying factors or principles 이구 理具 giving rise to the 3,000 phenomenal activities.

ㄱ ㄴ ㄷ ㄹ ㅁ ㅂ ㅅ ㅇ ㅈ ㅊ ㅋ ㅌ ㅍ ㅎ 찾아보기

사조 師祖 The teacher of one's teacher.

사종 四種 Four kinds ; where phrases containing the 종 種 are not found here, they may occur direct, e.g. 사법계 四法界. 사종삼매(야) 四種三昧(耶) The four samaya, i.e. the four pārājikas – killing, stealing, carnality, lying. 사종신심 四種信心 The four kinds of faith given in the Awakening of Faith, i.e. (1) in the 진여 眞如 q.v. as the teacher of all Buddhas and fount of all action ; (2) in Buddha, or the Buddhas ; (3) in the Dharma ; and (4) in the Saṁgha. 사종근본죄 四種根本罪 The four deadly sins, i.e. the four pārājikas-killing, stealing, carnality, lying. 사종단법 四種壇法 ; 사종실지 四種悉地 ; 사종성취법 四種成就法 The four kinds of altar-worship of the esoteric sect for (1) averting calamities from self and others ; (2) seeking good fortune ; (3) seeking the love and protection of Buddhas ; (4) subduing enemies. 사종사생 四種死生 Four kinds of rebirth dependent on present deeds : from obscurity and poverty to be reborn in the same condition ; from obscurity and poverty to be reborn in light and honour ; from light and honour to be reborn in obscurity and poverty ; from light and honour to be reborn in the heavens. 사종법계 四種法界 v. 사법계 四法界. 사종총지 四種總持 The four kinds of dhāraṇī 다라니 陀羅尼 q.v. 사종행인 四種行人 The four grades of earnest doers, who follow the bodhisattva discipline and attain to the 십주 十住, 십행 十行, 십회향 十迴向, and 십지 十地. 사종관행 四種觀行 The four kinds of examination, a method of repentance as a way to get rid of any sin : study the cause of the sin, which lies in ignorance, or lack of clear understanding, e.g. moth and flame ; study its inevitable effect, its karma ; study oneself, introspection ; and study the Tathāgata in his perfect character, and saving power.

사종 四宗 The four kinds of inference in logic – common, prejudged or opposing, insufficiently founded, arbitrary. Also, the four schools of thought : I. According to 정영 淨影 Ching-ying they are (1) 입성종 立性宗 that everything exists, or has its own nature ; e.g. Sarvāstivāda, in the "lower" schools of Hīnayāna ; (2) 파성종 破性宗 that everything has not a nature of its own ; e.g. the 성실종 成實宗 a "higher" Hīnayāna school, the Satyasiddhi ; (3) 파상종 破相宗 that form has no reality, because of the doctrine of the void, "lower" Mahāyāna ; (4) 현실종 顯實宗 revelation of reality, that all comes from the bhūtatathatā, "higher" Mahāyāna. II. According to 담은 曇隱 T'an-yin of the 대연 大衍 monastery they are (1) 인연종 因緣宗, i.e. 입성종 立性宗 all things are causally produced ; (2) 가명종 假名宗, i.e. 파성종 破性宗 things are but names ; (3) 부진종 不眞宗, i.e. 파상종 破相宗, denying the reality of form, this school fails to define reality ; (4) 진종 眞宗, i.e. 현실종 顯實宗 the school of the real, in contrast with the seeming.

사주 四洲 Catur-dvīpa ; the four inhabited continents of every universe ; they are situated S., E., W., and N. of the central mountain Sumeru ; S. is Jambudvīpa 섬부주 贍部洲 ; E. Pūrva-videha 동비제하 東毘提訶 ; W. Aparagodānīya 우화 牛貨 ; and N. Uttarakuru 구로 瞿盧.

사주 四住 The four abodes or states in the 지도론 智度論 3, i.e. (1) 천주 天住 the devalokas, equivalents of charity, morality, and goodness of heart ; (2) 범주 梵住 the brahmalokas, equivalents of benevolence, pity, joy, and indifference ; (3) 성주 聖住 the abode of śrāvakas, pratyeka-buddhas, and bodhisattvas, equivalent of the samādhi of the immaterial realm, formless and still ; (4) 불주 佛住 the Buddha-abode, the equivalent of the samādhis of the infinite. v. 사주(지) 四住(地).

사주 四主 The four Lords of the world, whose domains were supposed to stretch E., S., W., and N. of the Himalayas ; E. 인주 人主 the lord of men ; S. 상주 象主 of elephants ; W. 보주 寶主 of jewels (or precious things) ; N. 마주 馬主 of horses. 서역기주 西域記主.

사주(지) 四住(地) The four states or conditions found in mortality ; wherein are the delusions of misleading view and desires. They are (1) 견일체주지 見一切住地 the delusions arising from seeing things as they seem, not as they really are. (2) 욕애주지 欲愛住地 the desires in the desire-realm. (3) 색애주지 色愛住地 the desires in the form-realm. (4) 유애주지 有愛住地 the desires in the formless realm. When 무명주지 無明住地 the state of ignorance is added we have the 오주지 五住地 five states. These five states condition all error, and are the ground in which spring the roots of the countless passions and delusions of all mortal beings.

사중 四衆 The four varga (groups, or orders), i.e. bhikṣu, bhikṣuṇī, upāsaka and upāsikā, monks, nuns, male and female devotees. Another group, according to T'ien-t'ai's commentary of the Lotus, is 발기중 發起衆 the assembly which, through Śāriputra, stirred the Buddha to begin his Lotus Sūtra sermons ; 당기중 當機衆 the pivotal assembly, those who were responsive to him ; 영향중 影向衆 the reflection assembly, those like Mañjuśrī, etc., who reflected on, or drew out the Buddha's teaching ; and 결연중 結緣衆 those who only profited in having seen and heard a Buddha, and therefore whose enlightenment is delayed to a future life.

사중(금) 四重(禁) The four grave prohibitions, or sins, 사중죄 四重罪 pārājikas : killing, stealing, carnality, lying. Also four of the esoteric sect, i.e. discarding the truth, discarding the bodhi-mind, being mean or selfish in regard to the supreme law, injuring the living. 사중팔중 四重八重 The four pārājikas for monks and eight for nuns.

사중원단 四重圓壇 ; 사중만다라 四重曼荼羅 The Garbhadhātu maṇḍala of one central and three surrounding courts. The occupants are described as 사중성중 四重聖衆 the sacred host of the four courts.

사지 四持 idem 사종총지 四種總持.

사지 四智 The four forms of wisdom of a Buddha according to the 법상 法相 Dharmalakṣaṇa school : (1) 대원경지 大圓鏡智 the great mirror wisdom of Akṣobhya ; (2) 평등성지 平等性智 the universal wisdom of Ratnaketu ; (3) 묘관찰지 妙觀察智 the profound observing wisdom of Amitābha ; (4) 성소작지 成所作智 the perfecting wisdom of Amoghasiddhi. There are various other groups. 사지인 四智印 Four wisdom symbols of the Shingon cult : 대지인 大智印 or 마하기야물다라 摩訶岐若勿他羅 mahājñāna-mudrā, the forms of the images ; 삼매야인 三昧耶印 samaya-jñāna-mudrā, their symbols and manual signs ; 법지인 法智印 dharma-jñāna-mudrā, the magic formula of each ; 갈마지인 羯摩智印 karma-jñāna-mudrā, the emblems of their specific functions. 사지찬 四智讚 The praise hymns of the four "wisdoms", v. above.

사지 四知 The four who know the workings of one's mind for good or evil — heaven, earth, one's intimates, and oneself.

사지 舍脂 Śacī, 사지 舍支 ; 설시 設施 power of speech and action. Name of Indra's chief consort. Indra is known as 사지발저 舍脂鉢低 Śacīpati.

사지 舍支 Śaśa, 설시 設施 a hare ; Śaśī, or Śaśin, the moon ; Śakti, energy. (1) The hare (which threw itself into the fire to save starving people), transferred by Indra to the centre of the moon. (2) Śakti is the wife or female energy of a deity, cf. 사지 舍脂. (3) The female organ.

사진 四鎭 The four guardians, v. 사천왕 四天王.

사진(제) 四眞(諦) The four noble truths, v. 사(성)제 四(聖)諦, i.e. 고 苦, 집 集, 멸 滅, 도 道 pain, its location, its cessation, the way of cure.

사집 邪執 Heterodox tenets and attachment to them.

사집 四執 The four erroneous tenets ; also 사사 四邪 ; 사미 四迷 ; 사술 四術 ; there are two groups : I. The four of the 외도 外道 outsiders, or non-Buddhists, i.e of Brahminism, concerning the law of cause and effect : (1) 사인사과 邪因邪果 heretical theory of causation, e.g. creation by Maheśvara ; (2) 무인유과 無因有果 or 자연 自然, effect independent of cause, e.g. creation without a cause, or spontaneous generation ; (3) 유인무과 有因無果 cause without effect, e.g. no future life as the result of this. (4) 무인무과 無因無果 neither cause nor effect, e.g. that rewards and punishments are independent of morals. II. The four erroneous tenets of 내외도 內外道 insiders and outsiders, Buddhist and Brahman, also styled 사종 四宗 the four schools, as negated in the 중론 中論 Mādhyamika śāstra : (1) outsiders, who do not accept either the 인 人 jên or 법 法 fa ideas of 공 空 k'ung ; (2) insiders who hold the Abhidharma or Sarvāstivāda tenet, which recognizes 인공 人空 human impersonality, but not 법공 法空 the unreality of things ; (3) also those who hold the 성실 成實 Satyasiddhi tenet which discriminates the two meanings of 공 空 k'ung but not clearly ; and also (4) those in Mahāyāna who hold the tenet of the realists. 사집금강 四執金剛 The four Vajra-rulers of the four elements — earth, water, fire, wind, and of the S.E., S.W., N.W., and N.E.

사집과 四集科 Four studies in seminary 강원 講院.

사창 四唱 The four commanders or leaders ; see Lotus Sūtra 15.

사처십육회 四處十六會 The sixteen assemblies, or addresses in the four places where the 대반야경 大般若經 complete Prajñā-pāramitā is said to have been delivered. 사처문신 四處問訊 To inquire (or worship at) the four places for lighting incense at a monastery.

사천하 四天下 The four quarters or continents of the world. 사천상하 四天上下 In the upper regions there are the four heavens of the four deva-kings ; below are the people of the four continents. 사(대)천왕 四(大)天王 Catur-mahārājās, or Lokapālas ; the four deva-kings. Indra's external "generals" who dwell each on a side of Mount Meru, and who ward off from the world the attacks of malicious spirits, or asuras, hence their name 호세사천왕 護世四天王 the four deva-kings, guardians of the world. Their abode is the 사천왕천 四天王天 catur-mahārāja-kāyikas ; and their titles are : East 지국천 持國天 Deva who keeps (his) kingdom ; colour white ; name Dhṛtarāṣṭra. South 증장천 增長天 Deva of increase and growth ; blue ; name Virūḍhaka. West 광목천 廣目天 The broad-eyed (also ugly-eyed) deva (perhaps a form of Śiva) ; red ; name Virūpākṣa. North 다문천 多聞天 The deva who hears much and is well-versed ; yellow ; name Vaiśravaṇa, or Dhanada ; he is a form of Kuvera, the god of wealth. These are the four giant temple-guardians introduced as such to China by Amogha ; cf. 사천하경 四天下經. 사천왕천 四天王天 Catur-mahārāja-kāyikas ; the four heavens of the four deva-kings.

사취 四取 Catuḥ-parāmarśa, the four attachments, i.e. desire, (unenlightened) views, (fakir) morals, and ideas arising from the conception of the self. Also, the possible delusions of the 사주지 四住地. Also, seeking fame in the four quarters.

사취 四趣 Durgati ; the four evil directions or destinations : the hells, hungry ghosts, animals, asuras ; v. 사악 四惡.

사취 邪聚 The accumulation of misery produced by false views, one of the 삼취 三聚.

사친근 四親近 The four bodhisattvas associated with the five dhyāni-buddhas in the Vajradhātu.

사칠품 四七品 The twenty-eight chapters of the Lotus Sūtra.

사타(락법) 四墮(落法) The four causes of falling from grace and final excommunication of a monk or nun : adultery, stealing, killing, falsity ; v. 사바라이 四波羅夷.

사탑 四塔 The four stūpas at the places of Buddha's birth, Kapilavastu ; enlightenment, Magadha ; preaching, Benares ; and parinirvāṇa, Kuśinagara. Four more are located in the heavens of the Trayastriṁśāḥ gods, one each for his hair, nails, begging-bowl, and teeth, E., S., W., N., respectively.

사토 四土 The four Buddha-kṣetra, or realms, of T'ien-t'ai : (1) 범성거동토 凡聖居同土 Realms where all classes dwell — men, devas, Buddhas, disciples, non-disciples ; it has two divisions, the impure, e.g. this world, and the pure, e.g. the "Western" pure-land. (2) 방편유여토 方便有餘土 Temporary realms, where the occupants have got rid of the evils of 견사 見思 unenlightened views and thoughts, but still have to be reborn. (3) 실보무장애토 實報無障礙土 Realms of permanent reward and freedom, for those who have attained bodhisattva rank. (4) 상적광토 常寂光土 Realm of eternal rest and light (i.e. wisdom) and of eternal spirit (dharmakāya), the abode of Buddhas ; but in reality all the others are included in this, and are only separated for convenience' sake.

사바바슬 沙婆婆瑟 Ṣaḍ-varṣa ; the sexennial assembly.

사판 事判 Lit. "scrutinizer of phenomena." 1. Monastics who work in the office, library, etc. 2. Their duty. Cf. 이판 理判.

사팔상 四八相 The thirty-two marks of a Buddha.

사평가 四評家 The four great scholars (among the 500 arhats) who made the Vibhāṣā-śāstra, a critical commentary on the Abhidharma. Their names are 세우 世友 Vasumitra, 묘음 妙音 Ghoṣa, 법구 法救 Dharmatrāta, and 각천 覺天 Buddhadeva.

사하 沙訶 Sahā, 사하 娑訶 ; 삭사 索訶 the world around us, the present world. Also Svāhā, see 사바하 沙波訶.

사하 四河 The four rivers — Ganges, Sindhu (Indus), Vākṣu (Oxus), and Tārīm, all reputed to arise out of a lake, Anavatapta, in Tibet.

사함 四含 idem 사아함경 四阿含經.

사항 四恒 As the sands of four Ganges.

사해 四海 The four oceans around Mount Sumeru ; cf. 구산팔해 九山八海. 사해론주 四海論主 Honorific title of the monk 경탈 敬脫 Ching-t'o of the Sui dynasty.

사행 邪行 Erroneous ways, the ninety-six heretical ways ; the disciplines of non-Buddhist sects. 사행진여 邪行眞如 The phenomenal bhūtatathatā, from which arises the accumulation of misery.

사행 四行 The four disciplinary processes : enlightenment ; good deeds ; wisdom ; and worship. 사행상 四行相 To meditate upon the implications or disciplines of pain, unreality, impermanence, and the non-ego.

사향 四向 The four stages in Hīnayāna sanctity : śrota-āpanna, sakṛdāgāmin, anāgāmin, and arhan.

사현 師絃 or **사근** 師筋 A tiger's tendons as lute-strings, i.e. bodhi music silences all minor strings.

사혜 四慧 The four kinds of wisdom received : (1) by birth, or nature ; (2) by hearing, or being taught ; (3) by thought ; (4) by dhyāna meditation.

사혹 四惑 idem 사번뇌 四煩惱.

사홍서원 四弘誓願 The four universal vows of a Buddha or bodhisattva : 중생무변서원도 衆生無邊誓願度 to save all living beings without limit ; 번뇌무수서원단 煩惱無數誓願斷 to put an end to all passions and delusions however numerous ; 법문무진서원학 法門無盡誓願學 to study and learn all methods and means without end ; 불도무상서원성 佛道無上誓願成 to become perfect in the supreme Buddha-law. The four vows are considered as arising one by one out of the 사제 四諦 Four Noble Truths.

ㄱ ㄴ ㄷ ㄹ ㅁ ㅂ ㅅ ㅇ ㅈ ㅊ ㅋ ㅌ ㅍ ㅎ 찾아보기

사화 事火 Phenomenal fire, v. 성화 性火 fire as an element ; also, fire-worship.

사화 四花 The four (divine) flowers — mandāra, mahāmandāra, mañjūṣaka, and mahāmañjūṣaka. Also, puṇḍarīka, utpala, padma, and kumuda or white, blue, red, and yellow lotuses.

사화법 四化法 The 사무애변 四無礙辯 q.v. whereby all beings may be saved.

사회 四悔 See 오회 五悔 and omit the first.

삭 or **색** 索 Cord ; to extort, express ; the cord or noose of Kuan-yin by which she binds the good ; the cord of the vajra-king by which he binds the evil ; translit. *sa.* 삭치 索哆 v. 살 薩 Sattva. 삭하 索訶 ; 삭아 索阿 v. 사 娑 Sahā, the world. 삭어 索語 ; 삭화 索話 Express, expression (in words) ; forced statements, a demand or request (e.g. for information).

삭 爍 Bright, glistening, flashing, shining ; translit. *c, ś.* 삭갈라 爍羯囉 Śakra, cf. 사 賒 ; 석 釋 name of Indra. 삭도로 爍覩嚧 cf. 설 設 Śatru, enemy, a demon. 삭가라 爍迦羅 Cakra, a wheel, cf. 작 斫.

삭 鑠 To melt ; bright ; translit. *śa.* 삭지저 鑠枳底 ; 삭흘저 鑠訖底 Śakti, a halberd or lance ; a tally or sign. 삭가라아일다 鑠迦羅阿逸多 Śakrāditya, also 제일 帝日, a king of Magadha, some time after Śākyamuni's death, to whom he built a temple. 삭계모니 鑠雞謀儞 Śākyamuni, v. 석 釋.

삭발 削髮 Getting one's head shaved.

산 刪 v. 승 僧.

산 山 A hill, mountain ; a monastery.

산 訕 Abuse, slander ; translit. *san, śan.* 산지 訕底 v. 선 扇 Śāntika. 산야 訕若 Sañjaya, "entirely vanquishing," name of the founder of one of the ten heretical sects. Also, one of the six Tīrthyas, former teacher of Maudgalyāyana and Śāriputra ; also, a king of yakṣas ; cf. 산 珊.

산 珊 Coral ; translit. for *san, saṁ.* 산니라자 珊尼羅闍 Śanirājā, a river of Udyāna. 산호 珊瑚 Pravāḍa, or prabāla, coral, one of the seven treasures. 산야 珊若 Sañjñā, "a particularly high number," [M. W.] 1,000 septillions, a 대산야 大珊若 is 10,000 septillions. 산야바 珊若婆 A wasting disease. 산사야비라지 珊闍邪毘羅胝 or 珊闍夜毘羅胝 Sañjaya-Vairāṭī, a king of yakṣas ; also the teacher of Maudgalyāyana and Śāriputra before their conversion.

산 刪 Cut, excise ; translit. *s, ś.* 산지열모절나 刪地涅暮折那 Sandhinirmocana, name of the 해심밀경 解深密經. 산제람 刪提嵐 Described as a fabulous world of the past whose name is given as Śāṇḍilya, but this is doubtful. 산사야 刪闍夜 or 산사야비라지자 刪闍耶毗羅胝子 ; 산서이비랄지자 刪逝移毗剌知子 Sañjaya-Vairāṭīputra, or Sañjayin Vairadīputra, one of the six founders of heretical or non-Buddhist schools, whose doctrine was that pain and suffering would end in due course, like unwinding a ball of silk, hence there was no need of seeking the "Way."

산 算 Reckon, count, calculate. 산수 算數 To count numbers, to count, number.

산 散 Viprakṛ. Scatter, disperse, dismiss ; scattered ; broken, powder ; translit. *saṁ, san.* 산란 散亂 Scattered, dispersed, unsettled, disturbed, restless. 산공 散供 To scatter paper money, etc., as offerings. 산선 散善 Goodness cultivated during normal life, not as 정선 定善, i.e. by meditation. 산지 散地 The stage of distraction, i.e. the world of desire. 산심 散心 A distracted or unsettled mind ; inattentive. 산탁라 散拓羅 Saṁsāra, course, passage, transmigration. 산지 散支 ; 산지(가) 散脂(迦) ; 반지가 半只迦 or 半支迦 Pāñcika, one of the eight generals of Vaiśravaṇa, cf. 비 毘. 산일 散日 The dispersing day, the last of an assembly. 산업 散業 The good karma acquired in a life of activity. 산업염불 散業念佛 To repeat the name of Buddha generally and habitually. 산생재 散生齋 Almsgiving in petition for restoration from illness. 산의삼매 散疑三昧 A samādhi free from all doubt. 산화 散花 ; 산화 散華 To scatter flowers in honour of a Buddha, etc. 산전 散錢 To scatter paper money as offerings. 산타나 散陀那 Sandānikā, a kind of flower.

산가 山家 The "mountain school," the "profounder" interpretation of T'ien-t'ai doctrines developed by 사명 四明 Ssŭ-ming.

산근 山斤 The weight of a mountain, or of Sumeru — may be more readily ascertained than the eternity of the Buddha.

산문 山門 The gate of a monastery ; a monastery.

산세 山世 "Mountain world," i.e. monasteries.

산수납 山水衲 "Mountain and water robe," the name of a monastic garment during the Sung dynasty ; later this was the name given to a richly embroidered dress.

산승 山僧 (1) "Hill monk," self-deprecatory term used by monks. (2) A monk dwelling apart from monasteries.

산신 山神 Mountain god. A deity/spirit adopted by Korean Buddhism from Korean Shamanism.

산신각 山神閣 Mountain Spirit Shrine. A building in a temple.

산왕 山王 The king of the mountains, i.e. the highest peak.

산외종 山外宗 A branch of the T'ien-t'ai School founded by 오은 晤恩 Wu Ên (d. A.D. 986) giving the "shallower" interpretation of the teaching of this sect ; called Shan-wai because it was developed in temples away from the T'ien-t'ai mountain. The "profounder" sect was developed at T'ien-t'ai and is known as 산가종 山家宗 "the sect of the mountain family," or home sect.

산해여래 山海如來 Sāgara-varadhara-buddhi-vikrīḍitābhijña. 산해혜자재통왕여래 山海慧自在通王如來 or 山海惠自在通王如來. The name under which Ānanda is to reappear as Buddha, in Anavanāmita-vaijayanta, during the kalpa Manojña-śabdābhigarjita, v. 법화경 法華經. 산해공시 山海空市 "Mountains, seas, the sky, the (busy) market place" cannot conceal one form the eye of 무상 無常 Impermanence, the messenger of death, a phrase summing up a story of four brothers who tried to use their miraculous power to escape death by hiding in the mountains, seas, sky, and market places. The one in the market place was the first to be reported as dead, 법구경 法句經 2.

산호 山毫 Writing brushes as numerous as mountains, or as the trees on the mountains (and ink as vast as the ocean).

살 薩 A character introduced by the Buddhists, used as a translit. of *sa* sounds.

살 殺 To kill, cut down, cut off. 살삼마사 殺三摩娑 Ṣaṭsamāsa, cf. 삼 三. 살업 殺業 The karma resulting from killing. 살생 殺生 To take life, kill the living, or any conscious being ; the taking of human life offends against the major commands, of animal life against the less stringent commands. Suicide also leads to severe penalties. 살자 殺者 The murderer, a name for Māra. 살적 殺賊 Kṣīṇāśrava, thief-destroyer, i.e. conqueror of the passions, an arhat. 살귀 殺鬼 To slay demons ; a ghost of the slain ; a murderous demon ; a metaphor for impermanence.

살 撒 To scatter, set loose, sow. 살마아한 撒馬兒罕 Samakan, Samarkand, v. 삽 颯.

살가야견 薩迦耶見 Satkāyadarśana, the view of the reality of personality.

살다기리 薩多琦梨 Name of a demon king, intp. as a deva of great strength or power.

살다바륜 薩陀波崙 Sadāpralāpa ; ever chattering, or bewailing, name of a Bodhisattva, some say who wept while searching for truth. Also the 상제불 常啼佛 ever-wailing Buddha, name of the final Buddha of the present kalpa.

살다야 薩哆也 Satya, true, genuine, virtuous, etc., tr. 제 諦 a proved, or accepted, truth. Also 살지야 薩底也.

살달다반달라 薩怛多般怛羅 A dhāraṇī, intp. as a large white canopy indicating the purity of the Tathāgata-garbha.

살달라마 薩達喇摩 Saddharma, the good, true, beautiful, or excellent law, tr. by 정법 正法, the right, or correct law, or method ; or by 묘법 妙法 the wonderful law, or method, i.e. the 살달마분다리(가) 薩達磨芬陀利(迦) ; 살달마분다리가 薩達磨奔茶利迦 ; 살담분다리 薩曇分陀利 Saddharma-puṇḍarīka, the Lotus Sūtra, v. 법화경 法華經 and 묘 妙.

살라 薩羅 Sālva, Śālva, a country, a tribe "inhabiting Bhāratavarṣa." [M. W.] 살라륭벌지 薩羅隆伐底 ; 살라바박지 薩羅婆縛底 ; 살라산지 薩羅酸底 Sarasvatī, "the goddess of speech and learning," interpretation of music and of rhetoric.

살리살파 薩利殺跛 Sarṣapa, mustard-seed.

살바 薩婆 Sarva, "all, every ; whole, entire, universal, complete." [M. W.] 살바흘예사 薩婆吃隸奢 Sarvakleśa, all the passions or afflictions. 살바다(부) 薩婆多(部) Sarvāstivāda, the doctrine that all things are real, the school of this name, v. 유 有 and 일체유 一切有. 살바실다 薩婆悉多 ; 살바실달다 薩婆悉達多 ; 살바갈라타실타 薩婆曷剌他悉陀 Sarvārthasiddha, Sarvasiddhārtha, every object (or desire) attained, personal birthname of Śākyamuni ; also 살바알타실타 薩婆頞他悉陀 ; 살박알타실지 薩縛頞他悉地 ; abbrev. to 실달 悉達. 살바신야제바 薩婆愼若提婆 Sarvajñadeva, the omniscient deva, a title of a Buddha. 살바야 薩婆若 Sarvajña, having complete knowledge, omniscience, the perfect knowledge attained by Śākyamuni on attaining Buddhahood ; also 살바야낭 薩婆若囊 ; 살바야나 薩婆若那 ; 살바야다 薩婆若多 ; 살운야 薩云若 ; 살운연 薩云然 ; 살운야 薩雲若 ; 살벌야 薩伐若 ; 살벌야 薩栰若 etc. 살바가마 薩婆迦摩 Sarvakāma, all kinds of desires ; fulfilling all wishes. [M. W.] 살바아사지바타 薩婆阿私底婆拖 Sarvāstivāda, v. *supra.*

살바달 薩縛達 Sarvadā, the all-giving, or all abandoning, a name for the Buddha in a former incarnation.

살부살지 薩裒煞地 Sarpauṣadhi, serpent-medicine, said to have been provided by (the Buddha when he was) Indra, as a python, in giving his flesh to feed the starving. A monastery in Udyāna built on the reputed spot. Also 살부시살 薩裒施殺.

살불답 薩不荅 Sapta, seven ; 살불답라적날 薩不荅羅的捺 Saptaratna, the seven precious things, 칠보 七寶.

살사라사 薩闍羅娑 Sarjarasa ; 살절라사 薩折羅娑 ; resin of the Sal-tree, resin used as scent or incense.

살차니건(련타) 薩遮尼乾(連陀) Jñāti Nirgrantha, v. 니 尼.

살타 薩埵 Sattva, being, existence, essence, nature, life, sense, consciousness, substance, any living or sentient being, etc. [M. W.] Tr. by 정 情 sentient, 유정 有情 possessing sentience, feeling, or consciousness ; and by 중생 衆生 all the living. Abbrev. for Bodhisattva. Also 살다바 薩多婆 ; 살달박 薩怛縛 ; 색타 索埵, etc.

살타니습벌라 薩他泥濕伐羅 Sthāṇvīśvara, "a kingdom and city in Central India. The scene of the battle between the Pandus and Kurus." The modern Thanesar.

삼 森 Dense, forest-like. 삼라만상 森羅萬象 The myriad forms dense and close, i.e. the universe. 삼라만상즉법신 森羅萬象卽法身 The universe in its vast variety is the Dharmakāya, or Buddha-body ; in the esoteric school it is the Vairocana-body.

삼 三 Tri, trayas ; three. 삼일 三一 Trinity ; also 31.

삼가 三假 Prajñapti. The word 가 假 q.v. in Buddhist terminology means that everything is merely phenomenal, and consists of derived elements ; nothing therefore has real existence, but all is empty and unreal, 허망부실 虛妄不實. The three 가 假 are 법 法 things, 수 受 sensations, and 명 名 names. 삼가시설 三假施設 ; 삼섭제 三攝提 The three fallacious postulates in regard to 법 法, 수 受, and 명 名. 삼가관 三假觀 The meditations on the above.

삼가섭 三迦葉 Three brothers Kāśyapa, all three said to be disciples of the Buddha.

삼각 三覺 The three kinds of enlightenment : (1) (a) 자각 自覺 Enlightenment for self ; (b) 각타 覺他 for others ; (c) 각행원만 覺行圓滿 ; 각행궁만 覺行窮滿 perfect enlightenment and accomplishment ; the first is an arhat's, the first and second a bodhisattva's, all three a Buddha's. (2) From the Awakening of Faith 기신론 起信論 (a) 본각 本覺 inherent, potential enlightenment or intelligence of every being ; (b) 시각 始覺, initial, or early stages of such enlightenment, brought about through the external perfuming or influence of teaching, working on the internal perfuming of subconscious intelligence ; (c) 구경각 究竟覺 completion of enlightenment, the subjective mind in perfect accord with the subconscious (or superconscious) mind, or the inherent intelligence.

삼각단 三角壇 A three-cornered altar in the fire-worship of Shingon, connected with exorcism.

삼감 三監 idem 삼종 三從.

삼강 三綱 The three bonds, i.e. directors of a monastery : (a) 상좌 上座 sthavira, elder, president ; (b) 사주 寺主 vihārasvāmin, v. 비 毘 the abbot who directs the temporal affairs ; (c) 유나 維那 karmadāna, v. 갈 羯 who directs the monks. Another meaning : (a) 상좌 上座 ; (b) 유나 維那 ; (c) 전좌 典座 vihārapāla, v. 비 毘 director of worship. The three vary in different countries.

삼거 三擧 The three exposures, i.e. the three sins of a monk each entailing his unfrocking — wilful non-confession of sin, unwillingness to repent, claiming that lust is not contrary to the doctrine.

삼건 三愆 The three misleading things : 탐 貪 desire, 진 瞋 ire, and 사 邪 perverted views. 건 僁 = 건 愆.

삼겁 三劫 The three asaṅkhyeya kalpas, the three countless æons, the period of a bodhisattva's development ; also the past 장엄겁 莊嚴劫, the present 현겁 賢劫, and the future 성수겁 星宿劫 kalpas. There are other groups. 삼겁삼천불 三劫三千佛 The thousand Buddhas in each of the three kalpas.

삼견 三堅 The three sure or certain things are 신 身, 명 命 and 재 財, i.e. the reward of the true disciple is an infinite body or personality, an endless life, and boundless (spiritual) possessions, 무극지신 無極之身, 무궁지명 無窮之命, 무진지재 無盡之財, v. 유마경보살품 維摩經菩薩品.

삼결 三結 The three ties : (a) 견결 見結, the tie of false views, e.g. of a permanent ego ; (b) 계취결 戒取結 of discipline ; (c) 의결 疑結 of doubt. The three are also parts of 견혹 見惑 and used for it.

삼경 三境 v. 삼류경 三類境.

삼경일론 三經一論 The three sūtras and one śāstra on which the Pure Land sect bases its teaching : 불설무량수경 佛說無量壽經 ; 불설관무량수경 佛說觀無量壽經 ; 불설아미타경 佛說阿彌陀經 ; 천친정토론 天親淨土論.

삼계 三戒 The three sets of commandments, i.e. the ten for the ordained who have left home, the eight for the devout at home, and the five for the ordinary laity.

삼계 三季 The "three seasons" of an Indian year — spring, summer, and winter ; a year.

삼계 三契 Three repetitions (of a verse).

삼계 三界 Trailokya or Triloka ; the three realms ; also 삼유 三有. It is the Buddhist metaphysical equivalent for the Brahmanic cosmological bhuvanatraya, or triple world of bhūr, bhuvaḥ, and svar, earth, atmosphere, and heaven. The Buddhist three are 욕 欲, 색 色, and 무색계 無色界, i.e. world of sensuous desire, form, and formless world of pure spirit. (a) 욕계 欲界 Kāmadhātu is the realm of sensuous desire, of 음 婬 and 식 食 sex and food ; it includes the six heavens of desire, the human world, and the hells. (b) 색계 色界 Rūpadhātu is the realm of form, meaning 질애 質礙 that which is substantial and resistant ; it is above the lust-world and contains (so to speak) bodies, palaces, things, all mystic and wonderful — a semi-material conception like that in Revelation ; it is represented in the 사선천 四禪天, or Brahmalokas. (c) 무색계 無色界 Arūpadhātu, or ārūpyadhātu, is the formless realm of pure spirit, where there are no bodies, places, things, at any rate none to which human terms would apply, but where the mind dwells in mystic contemplation ; its extent is indefinable, but it is conceived of in four stages, i.e. 사공처 四空處 the four "empty" regions, or regions of space in the immaterial world, which are 사무색 四無色 the four "formless" realms, or realms beyond form ; being above the realm of form, their bounds cannot be defined. v. 구사론세간품 俱舍論世間品. 삼계구지 三界九地 v. 구지 九地. 삼계유일심 三界唯一心 The triple world is but one mind ; from a verse of the 화엄 華嚴 sūtra ; it proceeds 심외무별법 心外無別法, 심불급중생 心佛及衆生, 시삼무차별 是三無差別 "outside mind there is no other thing ; mind, Buddha, and all the living, these three are not different" ; in other words, there in on differentiating between these three, for all is mind. 삼계존 三界尊 The honoured one of the three worlds, i.e. Buddha. 삼계자부 三界慈父 The kindly father of the triple world — Buddha. 삼계화택 三界火宅 The burning house of the triple world, as in the Lotus Sūtra parable. 삼계상 三界牀 The sick-bed of the trailokya, especially this world of suffering. 삼계안 三界眼 The trailokya eye, i.e. Buddha, who sees all the realms and the way of universal escape. 삼계만영패 三界萬靈牌 The tablet used at the annual ceremonial offerings to "all souls," v. 우란 盂蘭. 삼계장 三界藏 The trailokya-garbha, the womb or storehouse of all the transmigrational. 삼계웅 三界雄 The hero of the trailokya — Buddha.

삼계(불)법 三階(佛)法 The Three Stages School founded by the monk 신행 信行 Hsin-hsing in the Sui dynasty ; it was proscribed in A.D. 600 and again finally in A.D. 725 ; also styled 삼계원 三階院 ; 삼계교 三階敎.

삼고 三鈷 A trident ; emblem of the Garbhadhātu 삼부 三部 ; and of the 삼지 三智, 삼관등 三觀等, and 삼궤 三軌. Also written 삼고 三古 ; 삼호 三胡 ; 삼고 三股.

삼고 三苦 The three kinds of duḥkha, pain, or suffering : 고고 苦苦 that produced by direct causes ; 양고 壞苦 by loss or deprivation ; 행고 行苦 by the passing or impermanency of all things.

삼공 三空 The three voids or immaterialities. The first set of three is (a) 공 空, (b) 무상 無相, (c) 무원 無願, v. 삼삼매 三三昧. The second, (a) 아공 我空, (b) 법공 法空, (c) 구공 俱空 the self, things, all phenomena as "empty" or immaterial. The third relates to charity : (a) giver, (b) receiver, (c) gift, all are "empty." 삼공(관)문 三空(觀)門 idem 삼해탈문 三解脫門.

삼과 三果 The third of the Hīnayāna 사과 四果 four fruits or results, i.e. non-return to mortality.

삼과 三科 The three categories of 오온 五蘊, 십이처 十二處 or 십이입 十二入, and eighteen 계 界.

삼과 三過 Transgressions of body, mouth, mind, i.e. thought, word, deed.

삼관 三觀 The three studies, meditations, or insights. The most general group is that of T'ien-t'ai : (a) 공관 空觀 study of all as void, or immaterial ; (b) 가관 假觀 of all as unreal, transient, or temporal ; (c) 중관 中觀 as the *via media* inclusive of both. The Hua-yen group is 진공관 眞空觀, 이사무애관 理事無礙觀 and 주변함용관 周遍含容觀, see 화엄경법계관 華嚴經法界觀. The 남산 南山 group is 성공관 性空觀, 상공관 相空觀, and 유식관 唯識觀. The 자은 慈恩 group is 유관 有觀, 공관 空觀 and 중관 中觀.

삼광(천) 三光(天) Sun, moon, and stars. Also, in the second dhyāna of the form-world there are the two deva regions 소광천 少光天, 무량광천 無量光天, and 광음천 光音天 q.v. Also 관음 觀音 Avalokiteśvara is styled 일천자 日天子 sun-prince, or divine son of the sun, 대세지 大勢至 Mahāsthāmaprāpta is styled 월천자 月天子 divine son of the moon, and 허공장보살 虛空藏菩薩 the bodhisattva of the empyrean, is styled 명성천자 明星天子 divine son of the bright stars.

삼광사 三光寺 Sam-gwang-sa. A temple located in Busan-si in Korea, belonging to Korean Cheontae Order.

삼교 三敎 The three teachings, i.e. 유 儒, 불 佛 or 석 釋, and 도 道 Confucianism, Buddhism, and Taoism ; or 공 孔, 노 老, 석 釋 Confucianism, Taoism (also known as 신교 神敎), and Buddhism. In Japan they are Shinto, Confucianism, and Buddhism. In Buddhism the term is applied to the three periods of Śākyamuni's own teaching, of which there are several definitions : (1) The Kiang-nan 남중 南中 School describe his teaching as (a) 점 漸 progressive or gradual ; (b) 돈 頓 immediate, i.e. as one whole, especially in the 화엄경 華嚴經 ; and (c) 부정 不定 or indeterminate. (2) 광통 光統 Kuang-t'ung, a writer of the later Wei dynasty, describes the three as (a) 점 漸 progressive for beginners, i.e. from impermanence to permanence, from the void to reality, etc. ; (b) 돈 頓 immediate for the more advanced ; and (c) 원 圓 complete, to the most advanced, i.e. the Hua-yen as above. (3) The 삼시교 三時敎 q.v. (4) The 남산 南山 Southern school deals with (a) the 성공 性空 of Hīnayāna ; (b) 상공 相空 of Mahāyāna ; and (c) 유식원 唯識圓 the perfect idealism. v. 행사초중 行事鈔中 4. T'ien-t'ai accepts the division of 점 漸, 돈 頓, and 부정 不定 for pre-Lotus teaching, but adopts 점 漸 gradual, 돈 頓 immediate, and 원 圓 perfect, with the Lotus as the perfect teaching ; it also has the division of 삼장교 三藏敎, 통교 通敎, and 별교 別敎 q.v. 삼장법사 三藏法師 Master of the Tripiṭaka ; a title of Hsüan-tsang 현장 玄奘.

삼구 三垢 The three defilers — desire, hate, stupidity (or ignorance), idem 삼독 三毒.

삼구 三句 Three cryptic questions of 운문 雲門 Yün-mên, founder of the Yün-mên Ch'an School. They are : (1) 절단중류 截斷衆流 What is it that stops all flow (of reincarnation)? The reply from the 기신론 起信論 is 일심 一心, i.e. the realization of the oneness of mind, or that all is mind. (2) 함개건곤 函蓋乾坤 What contains and includes the universe? The 진여 眞如. (3) 수파축랑 隨波逐浪 One wave following another — what is this? Birth and death 생사 生死, or transmigration, phenomenal existence.

삼구족 三具足 The three essential articles for worship : flower-vase, candlestick, and censer.

삼국토 三國土 idem 사토 四土 omitting 적광토 寂光土.

삼권일실 三權一實 The T'ien-t'ai division of the Schools of Buddhism into four, three termed 권 權 temporary, i.e. 장 藏, 통 通, and 별 別 q.v., the fourth is the 실 實 or 원 圓 real or perfect School of Salvation by faith to Buddhahood, especially as revealed in the Lotus Sūtra, see 일실 一實.

삼궤 三軌 The three rules 삼법(묘) 三法(妙) of the T'ien-t'ai Lotus School : (a) 진성궤 眞性軌 The absolute and real, the 진여 眞如 or bhūtatathatā ; (b) 관조궤 觀照軌 meditation upon and understanding of it ; (c) 자성궤 資成軌 the extension of this understanding to all its workings. In the 삼궤홍경 三軌弘經 the three are traced to the 법사품 法師品 of the Lotus Sūtra and are developed as : (a) 자비실 慈悲室 the abode of mercy, or to dwell in mercy ; (b) 인욕의 忍辱衣 the garment of endurance, or patience under opposition ; (c) 법공좌 法空座 the throne of immateriality (or spirituality), a state of nirvāṇa tranquillity. Mercy to all is an extension of 자성궤 資成軌, patience of 관조궤 觀照軌 and nirvāṇa tranquillity of 진성궤 眞性軌.

삼귀 三皈 idem 삼귀 三歸.

삼귀 三歸 Triśaraṇa, or Śaraṇa-gamana. The three surrenders to, or "formulas of refuge" in, the Three Precious Ones 삼보 三寶, i.e. to the Buddha 불 佛, the Dharma 법 法, the Saṅgha 승 僧. The three formulas are 귀의불 歸依佛 Buddhaṁ śaraṇaṁ gacchāmi, 귀의법 歸依法 Dharmaṁ śaraṇaṁ gacchāmi, 귀의승 歸依僧 Saṅghaṁ śaraṇaṁ gacchāmi. It is "the most primitive formula fidei of the early Buddhists." The surrender is to the Buddha as teacher 사 師, the Law as medicine 약 藥, the Ecclesia as friends 우 友. These are known as the 삼귀의 三歸依. 삼귀수법 三歸受法 The receiving of the Law, or admission of a lay disciple, after recantation of his previous wrong belief and sincere repetition to the abbot or monk of the above three surrenders. 삼귀(오)계 三歸(五)戒 The ceremony which makes the recipient a 우바새 優婆塞 or 우바이 優婆夷 upāsaka or upāsikā, male or female disciple, accepting the five commandments. There are 오종삼귀 五種三歸 five stages of san-kuei ; the first two are as above, at the third the eight commandments are accepted, at the fourth the ten, at the fifth all the commandments. 삼귀 三歸 is also a general term for a Buddhist.

삼극소 三極少 The three smallest things, i.e. an atom as the smallest particle of matter ; a letter as the shortest possible name ; a kṣaṇa, as the shortest period of time.

삼근 三根 The three (evil) "roots" — desire, hate, stupidity, idem 삼독 三毒. Another group is the three grades of good "roots," or abilities 상 上, 중 中, 하 下 superior, medium, and inferior. Another is the three grades of faultlessness 삼무루근 三無漏根.

삼금 三金 The three metals, gold, silver, copper. The esoterics have (a) earth, water, fire, representing the 신밀 身密 mystic body ; (b) space and wind, the 어밀 語密 mystic mouth or speech ; (c) 식 識 cognition, the 의밀 意密 mystic mind.

삼기 三機 v. 삼취 三聚.

삼나삼불 三那三佛 idem 삼막삼불타 三藐三佛陀.

삼난 三難 The three hardships, or sufferings in the three lower paths of transmigration, v. 삼악도 三惡道.

삼념주 三念住 ; **삼념처** 三念處. Whether all creatures believe, do not believe, or part believe and part do not believe, the Buddha neither rejoices, nor grieves, but rests in his proper mind and wisdom, i.e. though full of pity, his far-seeing wisdom 정념정지 正念正智 keeps him above the disturbances of joy and sorrow. 구사론 俱舍論 27.

삼능삼불능 三能三不能 The three things possible and impossible to a Buddha. He can (a) have perfect knowledge of all things ; (b) know all the natures of all beings, and fathom the affairs of countless ages ; (c) save countless beings. But he cannot (a) annihilate causality, i.e. karma ; (b) save unconditionally ; (c) end the realm of the living.

삼다 三多 Much intercourse with good friends, much hearing of the Law, much meditation on the impure. Also, much worship, much service of good friends, much inquiry on important doctrines. There are other groups.

삼다라니 三陀羅尼 The three dhāraṇī, which word from dhāra, "maintaining," "preserving," is defined as the power maintaining wisdom or knowledge. Dhāraṇī are "spells chiefly for personal use" (Eliot), as compared with mantra, which are associated with religious services. The T'ien-t'ai School interprets the "three dhāraṇī" of the Lotus Sūtra on the lines of the 삼제 三諦, i.e. 공 空, 가 假, and 중 中. Another group is 문지다라니 聞持陀羅尼 the power to retain all the teaching one hears ; 분별다라니 分別陀羅尼 unerring powers of discrimination ; 입음성다라니 入音聲陀羅尼 power to rise superior to external praise or blame.

삼단 三斷 The three cuttings off or excisions (of 혹 惑 beguiling delusions, or perplexities). (1) (a) 견소단 見所斷 to cut off delusions of view, of which Hīnayāna has eighty-eight kinds ; (b) 수소단 修所斷 in practice, eighty-one kinds ; (c) 비소단 非所斷 nothing left to cut off, perfect. v. 구사론 俱舍論 2. (2) (a) 자성단 自性斷 to cut off the nature or root (of delusion) ; (b) 연박 緣縛 to cut off the external bonds, or objective causes (of delusions) ; (c) 불생단 不生斷 (delusion) no longer arising, therefore nothing produced to cut off. The third stage in both groups is that of an arhat.

삼단 三檀 The three kinds of dāna, i.e. charity ; giving of goods, of the dharma, of abhaya, or fearlessness. Idem 삼시 三施.

삼달 三達 Three aspects of the omniscience of Buddha : knowledge of future karma, of past karma, of present illusion and liberation ; v. 삼명 三明.

삼대 三大 The three great characteristics of the 진여 眞如 in the 기신론 起信論 Awakening of Faith : (1) 체대 體大 The greatness of the bhūtatathatā in its essence or substance ; it is 중생심지체성 衆生心之體性 the embodied nature of the mind of all the living, universal, immortal, immutable, eternal ; (2) 상대 相大 the greatness of its attributes or manifestations, perfect in wisdom and mercy, and every achievement ; (3) 용대 用大 the greatness of its functions and operations within and without, perfectly transforming all the living to good works and good karma now and hereafter. There are other groups, e.g. 체 體, 종 宗, and 용 用. 삼대부 三大部 Three authoritative works of the T'ien-t'ai School, i.e. the 현의 玄義, 문구 文句, and 지관 止觀, each of ten chüan.

삼덕 三德 The three virtues or powers, of which three groups are given below. (1) (a) 법신덕 法身德 The virtue, or potency of the Buddha's eternal, spiritual body, the dharmakāya ; (b) 반야덕 般若德 of his prajñā, or wisdom, knowing all things in their reality ; (c) 해탈 解脫 of his freedom from all bonds and his sovereign liberty. Each of these has the four qualities of 상 常, 낙 樂, 아 我, 정 淨 eternity, joy, personality, and purity ; v. 열반경 涅槃經. (2) (a) 지덕 智德 The potency of his perfect knowledge ; (b) 단덕 斷德 of his cutting off all illusion and perfecting of supreme nirvāṇa ; the above two are 자리 自利 for his own advantage ; (c) 은덕 恩德 of his universal grace and salvation, which 이타 利他 bestows the benefits he has acquired on others, (3) (a) 인원덕 因圓德 The perfection of his causative or karmaic works during his three great kalpas of preparation ; (b) 과원덕 果圓德 the perfection of the fruit, or results in his own character and wisdom ; (c) 은원덕 恩圓德 the perfection of his grace in the salvation of others.

ㄱ ㄴ ㄷ ㄹ ㅁ ㅂ ㅅ ㅇ ㅈ ㅊ ㅋ ㅌ ㅍ ㅎ 찾아보기

삼도 三道 (1) The three paths all have to tread ; 윤회삼도 輪廻三道, 삼륜 三輪, i.e. (a) 번뇌도 煩惱道 ; 혹도 惑道 ; the path of misery, illusion, mortality ; (b) 업도 業道 the path of works, action, or doing, productive of karma ; (c) 고도 苦道 the resultant path of suffering. As ever recurring they are called the three wheels. (2) 성 聲, 연 緣, 보 菩 Śrāvakas, pratyeka-buddhas, bodhisattvas, cf. 삼승 三乘. 삼도진언 三道眞言 Three magical "true words" or terms of Shingon for self-purification, i.e. 우람락 吽嚂啸 which is the "true word" for 신 身 the body ; 하라학 訶囉鶴 for 어 語 the mouth or speech ; and 남락 嚂啸 for 의 意 the mind.

삼도 三倒 idem 삼전도 三顚倒.

삼도 三塗 The 도 塗 mire is intp. by 도 途 a road, i.e. the three unhappy gati or ways ; (a) 화도 火塗 to the fires of hell ; (b) 혈도 血塗 to the hell of blood, where as animals they devour each other ; (c) 도도 刀塗 the asipattra hell of swords, where the leaves and grasses are sharp-edged swords. Cf. 삼악취 三惡趣.

삼독 三毒 The three poisons, also styled 삼근 三根 ; 삼주 三株 ; they are 탐 貪 concupiscence, or wrong desire, 진 瞋 anger, hate, or resentment, and 치 痴 stupidity, ignorance, unintelligence, or unwillingness to accept Buddha-truth ; these three are the source of all the passions and delusions. They represent in part the ideas of love, hate, and moral inertia. v. 지도론 智度論 19, 31. 삼독시리 三毒尸利 The Śrī (i.e. goddess of Fortune) of the three poisons, a title of Mañjuśrī.

삼등 三等 The three equal and universal characteristics of the one Tathāgata, an esoteric definition : (1) (a) his 신 身 body, (b) 어 語 discourse, (c) 의 意 mind. (2) (a) his life or works 수행 修行 ; (b) spiritual body 법신 法身 ; (c) salvation 도생 度生 ; in their equal values and universality. 삼등류 三等流 Three equal or universal currents or consequences, i.e. 진등류 眞等流 the certain consequences that follow on a good, evil, or neutral kind of nature, respectively ; 가등류 假等流 the temporal or particular fate derived from a previous life's ill deeds, e.g. shortened life from taking life ; 분위등류 分位等流 each organ as reincarnated according to its previous deeds, hence the blind.

삼락 三樂 The three joys — the joy of being born a deva, the joy of meditation, the joy of nirvāṇa.

삼락차 三落叉 The three lakṣa ; a lakṣa is a mark, sign, token, aim, object ; it is also 100,000, i.e. an 억 億. The three lakṣa of the esoteric sects are the 자 字 or magic word, the 인 印 symbol and the 본존 本尊 object worshipped. Other such threes are body, mouth, and mind ; morning, noon, and evening ; cold, heat, and rain, etc.

삼력 三力 The three powers, of which there are various groups : (1) (a) personal power ; (b) tathāgata-power ; (c) power of the Buddha-nature within. (2) (a) power of a wise eye to see the Buddha-medicine (for evil) ; (b) of diagnosis of the ailment ; (c) of suiting and applying the medicine to the disease. (3) (a) the power of Buddha ; (b) of samādhi ; (c) of personal achievement or merit. 삼력게 三力偈 The triple-power verse : —

이아공덕력 以我功德力 In the power of my virtue,
여래가지력 如來加持力 And the aiding power of the Tathāgata,
급여법계력 及與法界力 And the power of the spiritual realm,
주변중생계 周遍衆生界 I can go anywhere in the land of the living.

삼례 三禮 Worship with 신 身, 구 口, 의 意, body, mouth, and mind.

삼론 三論 The three śāstras translated by Kumārajīva, on which the 삼론종 三論宗 Three Śāstra School (Mādhyamika) bases its doctrines, i.e. 중론 中論 Mādhyamaka-śāstra, on "the Mean," A.D. 409 ; 십이문론 十二門論 Dvādaśanikāya-śāstra, on the twelve points, A.D. 408 ; 백론 百論

Śata-śāstra, the hundred verses, A.D. 404. 삼론종 三論宗 The San-lun, Mādhyamika, or Middle School, founded in India by Nāgārjuna, in China by 가상 嘉祥 Chia-hsiang during the reign of 안제 安帝 An Ti, Eastern Tsin, A.D. 397-419. It flourished up to the latter part of the T'ang dynasty. In 625 it was carried to Japan as Sanron. After the death of Chia-hsiang, who wrote the 삼론현의 三論玄義, a northern and southern division took place. While the Mādhyamika denied the reality of all phenomenal existence, and defined the noumenal world in negative terms, its aim seems not to have been nihilistic, but the advocacy of a reality beyond human conception and expression, which in our terminology may be termed a spiritual realm.

삼루 三漏 The three affluents that feed the stream of mortality, or transmigration : 욕 欲 desire ; 유 有 (material, or phenomenal) existence ; 무명 無明 ignorance (of the way of escape). 열반경 涅槃經 22.

삼륙 三六 Eighteen, especially referring to the eighteen sects of Hīnayāna.

삼륙구 三六九 An esoteric objection to three, six, or nine persons worshipping together.

삼륜 三輪 The three wheels : (1) The Buddha's (a) 신 身 body or deeds ; (b) 구 口 mouth, or discourses ; (c) 의 意 mind or ideas. (2) (a) 신통 神通 ; 신변 神變 His super-natural powers, or powers of (bodily) self-transformation, associated with 신 身 body ; (b) 기심륜 記心輪 his discriminating understanding of others, associated with 의 意 mind ; (c) 교계륜 教誡輪 or 정교륜 正教輪 his (oral) powers of teaching, associated with 구 口. (3) Similarly (a) 신족륜 神足輪 ; (b) 설법륜 說法輪 ; (c) 억념륜 憶念輪. (4) 혹 惑, 업 業, and 고 苦. The wheel of illusion produces karma, that of karma sets rolling that of suffering, which in turn sets rolling the wheel of illusion. (5) (a) Impermanence ; (b) uncleanness ; (c) suffering. Cf. 삼도 三道. 삼륜세계 三輪世界 The three-wheel world, i.e. 풍 風, 수 水, and 금륜 金輪. Every world is founded on a wheel of whirling wind ; above this is one of water ; above this is one of metal, on which its nine mountains and eight seas are formed. 삼륜화도 三輪化導 idem 삼종시도 三種示導. 삼륜교 三輪教 The three periods of the Buddha's teaching as defined by Paramārtha : (a) 전법륜 轉法輪 the first rolling onwards of the Law-wheel, the first seven years' teaching of Hīnayāna, i.e. the 사제 四諦 four axioms and 공 空 unreality ; (b) 조법륜 照法輪 illuminating or explaining the law-wheel, the thirty years' teaching of the 반야 般若 prajñā or wisdom sūtras, illuminating 공 空 and by 공 空 illuminating 유 有 reality ; (c) 지법륜 持法輪 maintaining the law-wheel, i.e. the remaining years of teaching of the deeper truths of 공유 空有 both unreality and reality. Also the three-fold group of the Lotus School : (a) 근본법륜 根本法輪 radical, or fundamental, as found in the 화엄 華嚴 sūtra ; (b) 지말법륜 枝末法輪 branch and leaf, i.e. all other teaching ; until (c) 섭말귀본법륜 攝末歸本法輪 branches and leaves are reunited with the root in the Lotus Sūtra, 법화경 法華經. 삼륜상 三輪相 The three-wheel condition — giver, receiver, gift.

삼마 三摩 Sama, level, equal, same, etc. ; cf. 삼매(야) 三昧(耶) and 평등 平等. 삼마반나 三摩半那 Samāpanna, in the state of samādhi, 삼마희다 三摩呬多 Samāhita ; steadfast, tranquil. A degree of meditation. 삼마달타 三摩呾吒 Samataṭa, an ancient kingdom on the left bank of the Ganges, near its mouths, extending to the Hooghly, over 3,000 li in circuit, low and damp, with a hardy people, short and dark. Eitel says : "close to the sea at the mouth of the Brahmaputra." Eliot says : "In the east of Bengal and not far from the modern Burmese frontier," 삼마지 三摩地 ; 삼마제 三摩提 ; 삼마제 三摩帝 ; 삼마지 三摩底 ; 삼마지 三摩踶 Samādhi ; idem 삼매 三昧. 삼마지염송 三摩地念誦 Silent or meditative repetition of the name of Buddha. 삼마사 三摩娑 Samāsa. 살삼마사 煞三摩娑 Ṣaṭ-samāsa, v. 육리합석 六離合釋. 삼마바야 三摩婆夜 Samavāya, coming together, combination ; 이합 利合 advantageous union. 삼마피타 三摩皮陀 ; 착마폐타 縒摩吠陀 ; 사마 沙磨 ; 평론 平論 ; 가영 歌詠 Sāma-veda-saṁhitā. A collection of verses sung at sacrifices, etc. The third of the three Vedas, or four if Atharva-veda is counted, as it was later ; the verses are taken almost wholly from the Ṛgveda. 삼마갈 三摩竭 Sumāgadhā, said to be a daughter of Anāthapiṇḍada of Śrāvastī, who married the ruler of 난국 難國 and converted the ruler and people. 삼마야 三摩耶 ; 삼마예 三摩曳 idem 삼매야 三昧耶 ; but 삼마야 三摩耶 is also explained as a short period, a season of the year. 삼마야도 三摩耶道 A term among the esoterics for the 삼평등 三平等 q.v. 삼마야 三摩若 Sāmānya, generality ; in common ; inclusive ; v. 공 共. 삼마월 三摩越 idem 삼마발지 三摩鉢底. 삼마근리 三摩近離 The public gathering for a festival, lay and cleric, before parting at the end of the summer retreat. 삼마발지 三摩鉢底 ; 삼마발제 三摩鉢提 ; 삼마발제 三摩拔提 ; 삼마발제 三摩跋提 ; 삼마월 三摩越 Samāpatti, attainment, arrival ; defined by 등지 等至 and 등지 等持, which is intp. as complete dhyāna ; similar to 삼마반나 三摩半那 Samāpanna, attainment. Eitel says : "a degree of abstract ecstatic meditation preparatory to the final attainment of samādhi." Clough speaks of eight samāpattis, i.e. attainments — "eight successive states induced by the ecstatic meditation." v. also 삼마월 三摩越. 삼마난달라 三摩難呾囉 Samanantaram, immediately following or contiguous ; 등무간연 等無間緣, i.e. one of the four 연 緣 q.v. ; it means without interval, i.e. an immediate cause.

삼마 三馬 The three horses, one young, strong, and tractable ; another similar but not tractable ; a third old and intractable, i.e. bodhisattvas (or bodhisattva-monks), śrāvakas, and icchantis.

삼마 三魔 The three kinds of evil spirits, of which three groups are given : (1) 번뇌마 煩惱魔, 음마 陰魔, and 타화자재천자마 他化自在天子魔 ; (2) 번뇌마 煩惱魔, 천마 天魔, and 사마 死魔 ; (3) 선지식마 善知識魔, 삼매마 三昧魔, and 보리심마 菩提心魔.

삼만다 三曼多 Samanta ; tr. by 등 等, 보 普, 편 遍 universal, everywhere ; also 삼만다 三曼陀, 삼만다 三滿多. 삼만다건다 三曼陀犍陀 ; 삼만다건제 三萬陀犍提 Samantagandha, 보훈 普熏 universally fragrant. A tree in Paradise ; a title of a Buddha. 삼만(다)발다(라) 三曼(陀)颰陀(羅) ; 삼만발다 三曼跋陀 Samantabhadra, 보현 普賢 P'u-hsien ; v. 삼만 三滿.

삼만다발날라 三滿多跋捺囉 Samantabhadra, interpreted 보현 普賢 P'u-hsien, pervading goodness, or "all gracious," Eliot ; also 편길 徧吉 universal fortune ; also styled Viśvabhadra. The principal Bodhisattva of O-mei shan. He is the special patron of followers of the Lotus Sūtra. He is usually seated on a white elephant, and his abode is said to be in the East. He is one of the four Bodhisattvas of the Yoga school. v. 삼만 三曼.

삼말다 三末多 Saṁmata, intp. as 공허 共許 "unanimously accorded" ; i.e. name of the first king (elected) at the beginning of each world-kalpa.

삼매(야) 三昧(耶) Samaya is variously defined as 회 會 coming together, meeting, convention ; 시 時 timely ; 종 宗 in agreement, of the same class ; 평등 平等 equal, equalized ; 경각 驚覺 aroused, warned ; 제구장 除垢障 riddance of unclean hindrances. Especially it is used as indicating the vows made by Buddhas and bodhisattvas, hence as a tally, symbol or emblem of the spiritual quality of a Buddha or bodhisattva. 삼매야형 三昧耶形 The distinguishing symbol of a Buddha or bodhisattva, e.g. the Lotus of Kuan-yin ; also used for 삼매야신 三昧耶身 q.v. 삼매야계 三昧耶戒 Samaya commandments : the rules to be strictly observed before full ordination in the esoteric sects. 삼매야만다라 三昧耶曼荼羅 Samaya-maṇḍala. One of the four kinds of magic circles in which the saints are represented by the symbols of their power, e.g. pagoda, jewel, lotus, sword. 삼매야지 三昧耶智 Samaya wisdom. In esoteric teaching, the characteristic of a Buddha's or bodhisattva's wisdom, as shown in the maṇḍala 삼매야회 三昧耶會 The Samaya assembly, i.e. the second of the nine maṇḍalas, consisting of seventy-three saints represented by the symbols of their power. 삼매야계 三昧耶界 Samaya world, a general name for the esoteric sect. 삼매야신 三昧耶身 ; 삼매야형 三昧耶形 The embodiment of Samaya, a term of the esoteric sect ; i.e. the symbol of a Buddha or bodhisattva which expresses his inner nature, e.g. the stūpa as one of the symbols of Vairocana 대일 大日 ; the lotus of Kuan-yin, etc. 신 身 is used for a Buddha, 형 形 for a bodhisattva. The exoteric sects associate the term with the 보신 報身 sambhogakāya.

삼매(지) 三昧(地) Samādhi, "putting together, composing the mind, intent contemplation, perfect absorption, union of the meditator with the object of meditation." (M.W.) Also 삼마지(제) 三摩地(提) ; 삼마지(제) 三摩地(帝) ; 삼마지(지) 三摩地(底) ; 삼마지(지) 三摩地(胝). Interpreted by 정 定 or 정정 正定, the mind fixed and undisturbed ; by 정수 正受 correct sensation of the object contemplated ; by 조직정 調直定 ordering and fixing the mind ; by 정심행처 正心行處 the condition when the motions of the mind are steadied and harmonized with the object ; by 식려응심 息慮凝心 the cessation of distraction and the fixation of the mind ; by 등지 等持 the mind held in equilibrium ; by 사마지 奢摩地, i.e. 지식 止息 to stay the breathing. It is described as concentration of the mind (upon an object). The aim is 해탈 解脫, mukti, deliverance from all the trammels of life, the bondage of the passions and reincarnations. It may pass from abstraction to ecstasy, or rapture, or trance. Dhyāna 정 定 represents a simpler form of contemplation ; samāpatti 삼마발지 三摩鉢底 a stage further advanced ; and samādhi the highest stage of the Buddhist equivalent for Yoga, though Yoga is considered by some as a Buddhist development differing from samādhi. The 번역명의 翻譯名義 says : 사전 思專 when the mind has been concentrated, then 지일불분 志一不分 the will is undivided ; when 상적 想寂 active thought has been put to rest, then 기허신랑 氣虛神朗 the material becomes etherealized and the spirit liberated, on which 지 智 knowledge, or the power to know, has free course, and there is no mystery into which it cannot probe. Cf. 지도론 智度論 5, 20, 23, 28 ; 지관 止觀 2 ; 대승의장 大乘義章 2, 9, 13, 20, etc. There are numerous kinds and degrees of samādhi. 삼매불 三昧佛 Samādhi Buddha, one of the ten Buddhas mentioned in the 화엄경 華嚴經. 삼매월륜상 三昧月輪相 ; 월륜삼매 月輪三昧 The candra-maṇḍala, i.e. moon-wheel or disc samādhi ; Nāgārjuna is said to have entered it and taken his departure as a cicada after delivering the Law (or patriarchate) to Kāṇadeva. 삼매화 三昧火 Fire of samādhi, the fire that consumed the body of Buddha when he entered nirvāṇa. 삼매상응 三昧相應 The symbols or offerings should tally with the object worshipped, e.g. a white flower with a merciful or a white image. 삼매문 三昧門 The different stages of a bodhisattva's samādhi ; cf. 지도론 智度論 28. 삼매마 三昧魔 Samādhi-māra, one of the ten māras, who lurks in the heart and hinders progress in meditation, obstructs the truth and destroys wisdom.

삼막삼불타 三藐三佛陀 Samyaksambuddha 삼야삼불(단) 三耶三佛(壇). The third of the ten titles of a Buddha, defined as 정변지 正徧知 ; 정변각 正徧覺, or 정등각 正等覺, etc., one who has perfect universal knowledge or understanding ; omniscient. 삼막삼보리 三藐三菩提 ; 삼막삼모지 三貌糝帽地 ; 삼야삼보 三耶三菩 Samyak-sambodhi. Correct universal intelligence, 정변지(도) 正徧知(道). Correct equal or universal enlightenment (정등각 正等覺). Correct universal perfect enlightenment (정등정각 正等正覺). An epithet of every Buddha. The full term is anuttara-samyak-sambodhi, perfect universal enlightenment, knowledge, or understanding ; omniscience.

삼면대흑 三面大黑 The three-faced great black deva, Mahākāla v. 마 摩, with angry mien, a form of Maheśvara, or Śiva, as destroyer. Another interpretation says he is a union of Mahākāla, Vaiśravaṇa and a Gandharva.

삼명 三明 The three insights ; also 삼달 三達. Applied to Buddhas they are called 삼달 三達, to arhats 삼명 三明. (a) 숙명명 宿命明 Insight into the mortal conditions of self and others in previous lives ; (b) 천안명 天眼明 supernatural insight into future mortal conditions ; (c) 누진명 漏盡明 nirvāṇa. insight, i.e. into present mortal sufferings so as to overcome all passions or temptations. In the 구사론 俱舍論 27 the three are termed 숙주지증명 宿住智證明 ; 사생지증명 死生智證明 and 누진지증명 漏盡智證明. For 삼명경 三明經 v. 장아함 長阿含 16. 삼명(지) 三明(智) Trividyā. The three clear conceptions that (1) all is impermanent 무상 無常 anitya ; (2) all is sorrowful 고 苦 duḥkha ; (3) all is devoid of a self 무아 無我 anātman.

삼모다 三暮多 God of the wind, which is Vāta in Sanskrit.

삼모달라 三慕達羅 Samudra, the sea, an ocean ; also 삼모날라사아라 三母捺羅娑誐羅 samudra-sāgara. Samudra and sāgara are synonyms.

삼모제야 三牟提耶 Samudaya, gather together, accumulate, the 취제 聚諦 or 집제 集諦, i.e. the second of the Four Truths, the aggregation of suffering.

삼목 三目 The three-eyed, a term for Śiva, i.e. Maheśvara ; simile for the dharmakāya, or spiritual body, prajñā, or wisdom, and nirvāṇa emancipation.

삼묘행 三妙行 A muni, recluse, or monk, who controls his body, mouth, and mind 신 身, 구 口, 의 意 Also 삼모니 三牟尼.

삼무 三武 The three emperors Wu who persecuted Buddhism ; 태무 太武 of the Wei dynasty A.D. 424-452 ; 무제 武帝 of the Chou A.D. 561-578 ; 무종 武宗 of the T'ang A.D. 841-7.

삼무차(별) 三無差(別) The three that are without (essential) difference, i.e. are of the same nature ; (a) 심 心 The nature of mind is the same in Buddhas, and men, and all the living ; (b) 불 佛 the nature and enlightenment of all Buddhas is the same ; (c) 중생 衆生 the nature and enlightenment of all the living is the same. The 화엄경 華嚴經 says 심불급중생 心佛及衆生, 시삼무차별 是三無差別. 삼무성 三無性 The three things without a nature or separate existence of their own : (a) 상무성 相無性 form, appearance or seeming, is unreal, e.g. a rope appearing like a snake ; (b) 생무성 生無性 life ditto, for it is like the rope, which is derived from constituent materials ; (c) 승의무성 勝義無性 the 승의 勝義, concept of the 진여 眞如 or bhūtatathatā is unreal, e.g. the hemp of which the rope is made ; the bhūtatathatā is perfect and eternal. Every representation of it is abstract and unreal. The three are also known as 상무성 相無性, 무자연성 無自然性, 법무성 法無性 ; v. 유식론 唯識論 9. 삼무루학 三無漏學 The three studies, or endeavours, after the passionless life and escape from transmigration : (a) 계 戒 Moral discipline ; (b) 정 定 meditation, or trance ; (c) 혜 慧 the resulting wisdom. 삼무루근 三無漏根 The three roots for the passionless life and final escape from transmigration, i.e. the last three of the 이십이근 二十二根 q.v. An older group was 미지욕지근 未知欲知根 ; 지근 知根 ; 지이근 知已根 v. 구사론 俱舍論 3. 지도론 智度論 23. 삼무진장엄장 三無盡莊嚴藏 The treasury of the three inexhaustible adornments or glories, i.e. the 신 身, 구 口, 의 意, deeds, words, and thoughts of a Buddha.

삼묵당 三默堂 The three halls of silence where talk and laughter are prohibited : the bathroom, the sleeping apartment, the privy.

삼문 三門 Trividha-dvāra, the three gates ; a monastery ; purity of body, speech, and thought ; idem 삼해탈문 三解脫門 also 삼업 三業. 삼문삼대시자 三門三大侍者 The three officiators in a monastery — for incense, for writing, and for acting as host.

삼미 三迷 Sama, 등 等, equal, like, same as.

삼미 三味 The three flavours, or pleasant savours : the monastic life, reading the scriptures, meditation.

삼미지여부 三眉底與部 Saṁmatīya, v. 삼미지 三彌底.

삼미차 三彌叉 Samīkṣā, 관찰 觀察 investigation, i.e. the Sāṅkhya, a system of philosophy, wrongly ascribed by Buddhists to 사제수나 闍提首那 Jātiṣenā, or 사야서나 闍耶犀那 Jayasena, who debated the twenty-five Sāṅkhya principles (tattvas) with Śākyamuni, but succumbed, shaved his head and became a disciple, according to the 열반경 涅槃經 39. 삼미지 三彌底 : 미지 彌底 ; 미리지 彌離底 ; 삼밀율지니가야 三密栗底尼迦耶 ; 삼밀율지니가야 三蜜栗底尼迦耶 ; 삼미지여량제자 三眉底與量

弟子 Saṁmitīyanikāya, Saṁmata, or Saṁmitīyas. A Hīnayāna sect, the 정량부 正量部 correctly commensurate or logical school, very numerous and widely spread during the early centuries of our era. The 삼미지부론 三彌底部論 is in the Tripiṭaka. It taught "that a soul exists in the highest and truest sense," "that an arhat can fall from arhatship, that a god can enter the paths of the Order, and that even an unconverted man can get rid of all lust and ill-will" (Eliot, i, 260). It split into the three branches of Kaurukullakāḥ, Āvantikāḥ, and Vātsīputrīyāḥ. 삼미제 三彌提 Saṁmiti is a saint mentioned in the 아함경 阿含經.

삼밀 三密 The three mystic things : the body, mouth (i.e. voice), and mind of the Tathāgata, which are universal, all things being this mystic body, all sound this mystic voice, and all thought this mystic mind. All creatures in body, voice, and mind are only individualized parts of the Tathāgata, but illusion hides their Tathāgata nature from them. The esoterics seek to realize their Tathāgata nature by physical signs and postures, by voicing of 진언 眞言 dhāraṇī and by meditations, so that 입아아입 入我我入 He may enter me and I Him, which is the perfection of siddhi 실지 悉地 ; v. 대일경소 大日經疏 1. 보리심론 菩提心論. 삼밀육대 三密六大 The three mystic things associated with the six elements, i.e. the mystic body is associated with earth, water, and fire ; the mystic words with wind and space ; the mystic mind with 식 識 cognition. 삼밀율지니가야 三密栗底尼迦耶, v. 삼미지 三彌底 Saṁmitīyanikāya. 삼밀상응 三密相應 The three mystic things, body, mouth, and mind, of the Tathāgata are identical with those of all the living, so that even the fleshly body born of parents is the dharmakāya, or body of Buddha : 부모소생지육신즉위불신야 父母所生之肉身卽爲佛身也.

삼박 三縛 The three bonds — desire, anger, stupidity ; idem 삼독 三毒.

삼반야 三般若 The three prajñās, or perfect enlightenments : (a) 실상반야 實相般若 wisdom in its essence or reality ; (b) 관조반야 觀照般若 the wisdom of perceiving the real meaning of the last ; (c) 방편반야 方便般若 or 문자반야 文字般若 the wisdom of knowing things in their temporary and changing condition.

삼발라 三跋羅 Saṁvara. 삼바라 三婆羅 ; 삼부라 三嚩羅 To hinder, ward off, protect from falling into the three inferior transmigrations ; a divine being that fills this office worshipped by the Tantra School. The sixth vijñāna, v. 팔식 八識.

삼발라거치 三鉢羅佉哆 Samprāpta, intp. by 선지 善至, 정지 正至, or 시지 時至 well, properly, or timely arrived. Also written 승발 僧跋 intp. 등시 等施 bestowed equally or universally. It is a word spoken authoritatively, some say before, some say after a common meal ; a "blessing" to ward off evil from the food.

삼발심 三發心 The three resolves of the 기신론 起信論 Awakening of Faith : (a) 신성취발심 信成就發心 to perfect the bodhi of faith, i.e. in the stage of faith ; (b) 해행발심 解行發心 to understand and carry into practice this wisdom ; (c) 증발심 證發心 the realization, or proof of or union with bodhi.

삼발제 三拔諦 idem 삼발치 三拔致.

삼발치 三跋致 ; **삼발제** 三跋諦 Sampatti. To turn out well, prosper, be on the path of success.

삼방편 三方便 A term of the esoterics for body, mouth (speech), and mind, their control, and the entry into the 삼밀 三密 q.v. 대일경소 大日經疏 1.

삼배 三輩 The three ranks of those who reach the Pure Land of Amitābha : superior, i.e. monks and nuns who become enlightened and devote themselves to invocation of the Buddha of boundless age ; medium, i.e. laymen of similar character who do pious deeds ; inferior, i.e. laymen less perfect than the last.

ㄱ ㄴ ㄷ ㄹ ㅁ ㅂ ㅅ ㅇ ㅈ ㅊ ㅋ ㅌ ㅍ ㅎ 찾아보기

삼배 三拜 Three prostrations, performed by a lay-person when formally greeting a monk, by monks when greeting each other, or to the Buddha when one first enters a Buddha Hall.

삼백사십팔계 三百四十八戒 ; **삼백사십일계** 三百四十一戒 The 348 or 341 rules for a nun ; there are also groups of 250 and 500 such rules. 삼백육십회 三百六十會 The reputed and disputed number (360) of Śākyamuni's assemblies for preaching. 삼백유순 三百由旬 The 300 yojanas parable of the Magic City, erected by a leader who feared that his people would become weary and return ; i.e. Hīnayāna nirvāṇa, a temporary rest on the way to the real land of precious things, or true nirvāṇa ; v. 법화화성품 法華化城品.

삼백식 三白食 The three white foods – milk, cream (or curd), and rice (especially upland rice) ; 삼백법 三白法 is the rule of these three.

삼번뇌 三煩惱 v. 삼혹 三惑.

삼벌업 三罰業 The three things that work for punishment – body, mouth, and mind.

삼벌지 三伐持 Saṁvaji ; the heretical people of Vṛji, an ancient kingdom north of the Ganges, southeast of Nepal. [Eitel].

삼범 三梵 The three Brahma heavens of the first dhyāna : that of 범중 梵衆 Brahma-pāriṣadya, the assembly of Brahmā ; 범보 梵輔 Brahma-purohitas, his attendants ; 대범 大梵 Mahābrahmā, Great Brahmā.

삼법 三法 The three dharma, i.e. 교법 敎法 the Buddha's teaching ; 행법 行法 the practice of it ; 증법 證法 realization or experiential proof of it in bodhi and nirvāṇa. 삼법인 三法印 idem 삼인 三印. 삼법인 三法忍 idem 삼인 三忍. For 삼법묘 三法妙 v. 삼궤 三軌.

삼법무차 三法無差 idem 삼무차별 三無差別 q.v. 삼법륜 三法輪 The three law-wheels, or periods of the Buddha's preaching, according to Paramārtha, to 가상 嘉祥 Chia-hsiang of the 삼론 三論 school, and to 현장 玄奘 Hsüan-tsang of the 법상 法相 school.

삼변(토전) 三變(土田) The three transformations of his Buddha-realm made by Śākyamuni on the Vulture Peak – first, his revelation of this world, then its vast extension, and again its still vaster extension. See Lotus Sūtra.

삼병 三病 The three ailments : (1) (a) 탐 貪 lust, for which the 부정관 不淨觀 meditation on uncleanness is the remedy ; (b) 진 瞋 anger, or hate, remedy 자비관 慈悲觀 meditation on kindness and pity ; (c) 치 癡 stupidity, or ignorance, remedy 인연관 因緣觀 meditation on causality. (2) (a) 방 謗 Slander of Mahāyāna ; (b) 오역죄 五逆罪 the five gross sins ; (c) to be a "heathen" or outsider ; the forms recorded seem to be icchantika, ecchantika, and aicchantika. Cf. 삼독 三毒.

삼보 三報 The three recompenses, i.e. 현보 現報 in the present life for deeds now done ; 생보 生報 in the next rebirth for deeds now done ; and 후보 後報 in subsequent lives.

삼보 三寶 Triratna, or Ratnatraya, i.e. the Three Precious Ones : 불 佛 Buddha, 법 法 Dharma, 승 僧 Saṅgha, i.e. Buddha, the Law, the Ecclesia or Order. Eitel suggests this trinity may be adapted from the Trimūrti, i.e. Brahmā, Viṣṇu, and Śiva. The Triratna takes many forms, e.g. the Trikāya 삼신 三身 q.v. There is also the Nepalese idea of a triple existence of each Buddha as a Nirvāṇa-Buddha, Dhyāni-Buddha, and Mānuṣi-Buddha ; also the Tantric trinity of Vairocana as Nirvāṇa-buddha, Locana according to Eitel "existing in reflex in the world of forms," and the human Buddha, Śākyamuni. There are other elaborated details known as the four and the six kinds of triratna 사 四 and 육종삼보 六種三寶, e.g. that the Triratna exists in each member of the trinity. The term has also been applied to the 삼선 三仙 q.v. Popularly the 삼보 三寶 are referred to the three images in the main hall of monasteries. The centre one is Śākyamuni, on his left Bhaiṣajya 약사 藥師 and on his right Amitābha. There are other explanations, e.g. in some temples Amitābha is in the centre, Avalokiteśvara on his left, and Mahāsthāmaprāpta or Mañjuśrī on his right. Table of Triratna, Trikāya, and Trailokya : —

DHARMA	SAṄGHA	BUDDHA
Essential Bodhi	Reflected Bodhi	Practical Bodhi
Dhyāni Buddha	Dhyāni Bodhisattva	Mānuṣi Buddha
Dharmakāya	Sambhogakāya	Nirmāṇakāya
Purity	Completeness	Transformations
4th Buddha-kṣetra	3rd Buddha-kṣetra	1st and 2nd Buddha-kṣetra
Arūpadhātu	Rūpadhātu	Kāmadhātu

삼보물 三寶物 The things appertaining to the Triratna, i.e. to the Buddha — temples and images, etc. ; to the Dharma — the scriptures ; to the Saṅgha — cassock, bowl, etc. 삼보장 三寶藏 The Triratna as the treasury of all virtue and merit ; also the Tripiṭaka, sūtras 경 經, vinaya 율 律, abhidharma 론 論 ; also śrāvakas, pratyeka-buddhas, and bodhisattvas. 삼보의 三寶衣 idem 삼의 三衣. 삼보신 三寶身 v. 삼신 三身.

삼보가 三菩伽 Sambhoga or Sambhūta. An ancient ṛṣi of Mathurā. 삼보가가야 三菩伽迦耶 Sambhogakāya. (1) The "body of enjoyment" or recompense-body of a Buddha ; his 보신 報身 or reward-body, one of the Trikāya, 삼신 三身. (2) The third of the Buddhakṣetra 불토 佛土, the domain in which all respond perfectly to their Buddha.

삼보리 三菩提 Sambodhi, 삼모지 糝帽地 intp. 정등각 正等覺. Perfect universal awareness, perfectly enlightened ; v. 보리 菩提.

삼보종찰 三寶宗刹 Monasteries of the Triratna 삼보 三寶. They are Tongdosa (representing the Buddha 불 佛), Haeinsa (Dharma 법 法), Songgwangsa (Saṅgha 승 僧).

삼보타 三補吒 Sampuṭa. One of the twelve ways of putting the hands together in worship, i.e. bringing the hands together without the palms touching.

삼복 三福 The three (sources of) felicity : (1) The 무량수경 無量壽經 has the felicity of (a) 세복 世福 filial piety, regard for elders, keeping the ten commandments ; (b) 계복 戒福 of keeping the other commandments ; (c) 행복 行福 of resolve on complete bodhi and the pursuit of the Buddha-way. (2) The 구사론 俱舍論 18, has the blessedness of (a) 시류복 施類福 almsgiving, in evoking resultant wealth ; (b) 계류복 戒類福 observance of the 성계 性戒 (against killing, stealing, adultery, lying) and the 차계 遮戒 (against alcohol, etc.), in obtaining a happy lot in the heavens ; (c) 수류복 修類福 observance of meditation in obtaining final escape from the mortal round. Cf. 삼종정업 三種淨業. 삼복업 三福業 The three things that bring a happy lot — almsgiving, impartial kindness and love, pondering over the demands of the life beyond.

삼복팔교 三覆八校 The three reports and eight investigations. 삼복 三覆 denote a day in each of the first, fifth, and ninth months when the recording angels of the four Lokapālas report on the conduct of each individual ; 팔교 八校 are the opening days of the four seasons and the two solstices and two equinoxes during which similar investigations are made. Two angels, 동생 同生 and 동명 同名, observe each individual, the first a female at his right shoulder noting the evil deeds ; the second, a male, at his left shoulder noting the good deeds ; both report on high and in hades six times a month. Thus in each month there are 육재 六齋 and in each year 삼복 三覆 and 팔교 八校.

삼부(대법) 三部(大法) (1) The Garbhadhātu maṇḍala, or pantheon, has the three divisions of 불 佛, 연 蓮, 금 金, i.e. Vairocana, Lotus, and Diamond or Vajra. (2) The teaching of the 태장계 胎藏界, 금강계 金剛界, and 소실지법 蘇悉地法 is said to cover the whole of esoteric Buddhism. 삼부주색 三部主色 the colours of the three divisions : Vairocana, white ; 관세음 觀世音 (as representing) Amitābha, yellow ; and the Diamond Ruler, Śākyamuni, a ruddy yellow. 삼부경 三部經 There are several groups : (1) The Amitābha group, also styled 정토삼부 淨土三部, is 무량수경 無量壽經, 관무량수경 觀無量壽經 and 아미타경 阿彌陀經. (2) The Vairocana group is 대일경 大日經, 금강정경 金剛頂經 and 소실지경 蘇悉地經 ; also called 삼부비경 三部秘經. (3) The Lotus group is the 무량의경 無量義經, 묘법연화경 妙法蓮華經 and 관보현보살행법경 觀普賢菩薩行法經. (4) The Maitreya group is 관미륵보살상생도솔천경 觀彌勒菩薩上生兜率天經, 미륵하생경 彌勒下生經 and 미륵대성불경 彌勒大成佛經.

삼분과경 三分科經 The three divisions of a treatise on a sūtra, i.e. 서분 序分 introduction, 정종분 正宗分 discussion of the subject, 유통분 流通分 application.

삼불 三佛 Trikāya, v. 삼신 三身. Also the three 기 岐 or founders of the 양기 楊岐 branch of the Ch'an(Zen) School, i.e. 혜근 慧勤 Hui-ch'in, 청원 清遠 Ch'ing-yüan, and 극근 克勤 K'o-ch'in. 삼불토 三佛土 The three Buddha-lands, realms, or environment, corresponding to the Trikāya ; v. 삼신 三身 and 불토 佛土. 삼불자 三佛子 All the living are Buddha-sons, but they are of three kinds — the commonalty are 외자 外子 external sons ; the followers of the two inferior Buddhist vehicles, 소승 小乘 and 중승 中乘, are 서자 庶子 secondary sons (i.e. of concubines) ; the bodhisattvas (i.e. mahāyānists) are 도자 道子 true sons, or sons in the truth. 삼불성 三佛性 The three kinds of Buddha-nature : (1) 자성주불성 自性住佛性 the Buddha-nature which is in all living beings, even those in the three evil paths (gati). (2) 인출불성 引出佛性 the Buddha-nature developed by the right discipline. (3) 지득과불성 至得果佛性 the final or perfected Buddha-nature resulting from the development of the original potentiality. 삼불율지 三佛栗底 Saṁvṛti, which means concealed, not apparent, is intp. as common ideas 세속제 世俗諦 or phenomenal truth ; it is also intp. as that which hides reality, or seems to be real, the seeming. 삼불보리 三佛菩提 The bodhi, or wisdom, of each of the Trikāya, 삼신 三身, i.e. that under the bodhi tree, that of parinirvāṇa, that of tathāgatagarbha in its eternal nirvāṇa aspect. 삼불어 三佛語 The Buddha's three modes of discourse — unqualified, i.e. out of the fullness of his nature ; qualified to suit the intelligence of his hearers ; and both. 삼불신 三佛身 idem 삼신 三身. 삼불타 三佛陀 Sambuddha ; the truly enlightened one, or correct enlightenment.

삼불삼신 三不三信 This refers to the state of faith in the worshipper ; the three 불 不 are impure, not single, not constant ; the three 신 信 are the opposite. 삼불선근 三不善根 There bad roots, or qualities — desire, anger, and stupidity 탐 貪, 진 瞋, 치 痴, v. 삼독 三毒. 삼불견법 三不堅法 Three unstable things — the body, length of life, wealth. 삼불실 三不失 The three never lost, idem 삼불호 三不護. 삼부정육 三不淨肉 The three kinds of flesh unclean to a monk, i.e. when he has seen or heard the animal killed or has doubt about it ; v. 삼정육 三淨肉. 삼불능 三不能 v. 삼능 三能. 삼불호 三不護 The three that need no guarding, i.e. the 삼업 三業 of a Buddha, his body, mouth (or lips), and mind, which he does not need to guard as they are above error. 삼불퇴 三不退 The three non-backslidings, i.e. from position attained, from line of action pursued, and in dhyāna.

삼비밀 三秘密 The three mysteries, a term of the esoteric school for 신 身, 구 口, and 의 意 ; i.e. the symbol ; the mystic word, or sound ; the meditation of the mind. The 삼비밀신 三秘密身 is a term for the mystic letter, the mystic symbol, and the image.

삼사 三思 All action and speech have three mental conditions — reflection, judgment, decision.

삼사 三使 The three (divine) messengers — birth, sickness, death ; v. 사 使. Also 삼천사 三天使.

삼사계 三事戒 The commands relating to body, speech, and mind 신 身, 구 口, 의 意. 삼사련마 三事練磨 v. 삼퇴굴 三退屈. 삼사납 三事衲 ; 삼사의 三事衣 A term for a monk's robe of five, seven, or nine patches.

삼사칠증 三師七證 The three superior monks and a minimum of seven witnesses required for an ordination to full orders ; except in outlandish places, when two witnesses are valid.

삼삼매(지) 三三昧(地) The three samādhis, or the samādhi on three subjects ; 삼삼마(지) 三三摩(地) ; 삼정 三定, 삼등지 三等持 ; 삼공 三空 ; 삼치 三治 ; 해탈문 解脫門 ; 삼중삼매 三重三昧 ; 삼중등지 三重等持. There are two forms of such meditation, that of 유루 有漏 reincarnational, or temporal, called 삼삼매 三三昧 ; and that of 무루 無漏 liberation, or nirvāṇa, called 삼해탈 三解脫. The three subjects and objects of the meditation are (1) 공 空 to empty the mind of the ideas of me and mine and suffering, which are unreal ; (2) 무상 無相 to get rid of the idea of form, or externals, i.e. the 십상 十相 which are the five senses, and male and female, and the three 유 有 ; (3) 무원 無願 to get rid of all wish or desire, also termed 무작 無作 and 무기 無起. A more advanced meditation is called the Double Three Samādhi 중삼삼매 重三三昧 which each term is doubled 공공 空空, 무상무상 無相無相, 무원무원 無願無願. The esoteric sect has also a group of its own.

삼상 三想 The three evil thoughts are the last, desire, hate, malevolence ; the three good thoughts are 원상 怨想 thoughts of (love to) enemies, 친상 親想 the same to family and friends, 중인상 中人想 the same to those who are neither enemies nor friends, i.e. to all ; v. 지도론 智度論 72.

삼상 三相 The three forms of positions : 해탈상 解脫相 nirvāṇa ; 이상 離相 no nirvāṇa ; 멸상 滅相 or 비유비무지중도 非有非無之中道 absence of both, or the "middle way" of neither. 삼상속 三相續 The three links, or consequences : (a) the worlds with their kingdoms, which arise from the karma of existence ; (b) all beings, who arise out of the five skandhas ; (c) rewards and punishments, which arise out of moral karma causes.

삼색 三色 The three kinds of rūpa, or form-realms : the five organs (of sense), their objects, and invisible perceptions, or ideas. Cf. 삼종색 三種色.

삼생 三生 The three births, or reincarnations, past, present, future. T'ien-t'ai has (a) 종 種 planting the seed ; (b) 숙 熟 ripening ; (c) 탈 脫 liberating, stripping, or harvesting, i.e. beginning, development, and reward of bodhi, a process either gradual or instantaneous. Hua-yen has (a) 견문생 見聞生 a past life of seeing and hearing Buddha-truth ; (b) 해행생 解行生 liberation it the present life ; (c) 증입생 證入生 realization of life in Buddhahood. This is also called 삼생성불 三生成佛, Buddhahood in the course of three lives. There is also a definition of three rebirths as the shortest term for arhatship, sixty kalpas being the longest. There are other definitions.

삼선 三善 idem 삼시교 三時教 and 삼선근 三善根. 삼선근 三善根 The three good "roots," the foundation of all moral development, i.e. 무탐 無貪, 무진 無瞋, 무치 無痴 no lust (or selfish desire), no ire, no stupidity (or unwillingness to learn). Also, 시 施, 자 慈, 혜 慧 giving, kindness, moral wisdom ; v. 삼독 三毒 the three poisons for which these are a cure. 삼선지식 三善知識 The three types of friends with whom to be intimate, i.e. a teacher (or the Way), a fellow-endeavourer and encourager, and a patron who supports by gifts (dānapati). 삼선도 三善道 ; 삼선취 三善趣 The three good or upward directions or states of existence : 천 天 the highest class of goodness rewarded with the deva life, or heaven ; 인 人 the middle class of goodness with a return to human life ; 아수라 阿修羅 the inferior class of goodness with the asura state. Cf. ; 삼악도 三惡道 : v. 지도론 智度論 30

삼선 三禪 The third dhyāna heaven of form, the highest paradise of form.

삼선이천 三仙二天 The three ṛṣis or wise men and the two devas, i.e. 가비라 迦毘羅 Kapila, founder of the Sāṅkhya philosophy ; 휴류 鵂鶹 or 우루거 優樓佉 Ulūka or Kaṇāda, founder of the 승론종 勝論宗 or Vaiśeṣika philosophy ; and 륵사파 勒沙婆 Ṛṣabha, founder of the Nirgranthas ; with Śiva and Viṣṇu as the two deities.

삼섭제 三攝提 The three prajñapti, v. 삼가시설 三假施設 ; they are the 수 受 and 법 法 and 명가시설 名假施設.

삼성 三聖 The three sages, or holy ones, of whom there are several groups. The 화엄 華嚴 Hua-yen have Vairocana in the centre with Mañjuśrī on his left and Samantabhadra on his right. The 미타 彌陀 Mi-t'o, or Pure-land sect, have Amitābha in the centre, with Avalokiteśvara on his left and Mahāsthāma-prāpta on his right. The T'ien-t'ai use the term for the 장 藏, 별 別, and 원교 圓教, v. 삼교 三教.

삼성 三性 The three types of character 선 善, 악 惡, 무기 無記 good, bad and undefinable, or neutral ; v. 유식론 唯識論 5. Also, 변의원삼성 徧依圓三性 the three aspects of the nature of a thing — partial, as when a rope is mistaken for a snake ; only partly reliable, i.e. incomplete inference, as when it is considered as mere hemp ; all round, or perfect, when content, form, etc., are all considered. 삼성분별 三性分別 The differentiation of the three conditions of good, evil, and neutral.

삼세 三世 The three periods, 과거 過去, 현재 現在, 미래 未來 or 과 過, 현 現, 미 未, past, present, and future. The universe is described as eternally in motion, like a flowing stream. Also 미생 未生, 이생 已生, 후멸 後滅, or 미 未, 현 現, 과 過 unborn, born, dead. The 화엄경 華嚴經 Hua-yen sūtra has a division of ten kinds of past, present, and future, i.e. the past spoken of as past, present, and future, the present spoken of in like manner, the future also, with the addition of the present as the three periods in one instant. Also 삼제 三際. 삼세삼천불 三世三千佛 The thousand Buddhas of each of the three kalpas — of the past, called 장엄 莊嚴 kalpa, the present 현 賢, and the future 성수 星宿. Their names are variously given in several sūtras ; a complete list is in the 삼천불명경 三千佛名經. 삼세불가득 三世不可得 Everything past, present, future, whether mental or material, is intangible, fleeting, and cannot be held ; v. 삼세심 三世心. 삼세요달 三世了達 A Buddha's perfect knowledge of past, present, and future. 삼세불 三世佛 The Buddhas of the past, present, and future, i.e. Kāśyapa, Śākyamuni, and Maitreya. 삼세가실 三世假實 The reality or otherwise of things or events past, present, and future. Some Hīnayāna schools admit the reality of the present but dispute the reality of the past 이유 已有 and the future 당유 當有. Others take different views, all of which have been exhaustively discussed. See Vibhāṣā śāstra 파사론 婆沙論 77, or 구사론 俱舍論 20. 삼세실유법체항유 三世實有法體恒有 The Sarvāstivāda school maintains that as the three states (past, present, future) are real, so the substance of all things is permanent ; i.e. time is real, matter is eternal. 삼세심 三世心 Mind, or thought, past, present or future, is momentary, always moving, unreal and cannot be laid hold of. 삼세성불 三世成佛 idem 삼생 三生. 삼세지 三世智 One of a Tathāgata's ten kinds of wisdom, i.e. knowledge of past, present, and future. 삼세무장애지계 三世無障礙智戒 The wisdom-law or moral law that frees from all impediments, past, present, and future. Also styled 삼매야계 三昧耶戒 ; 자성본원계 自性本源戒 ; 삼평등계 三平等戒 ; 보리심계 菩提心戒 ; 무위계 無爲戒 and 진법계 眞法戒. 삼세각모 三世覺母 A name for Mañjuśrī 문수 文殊 ; as guardian of the wisdom of Vairocana he is the bodhi-mother of all Buddhas past, present, and future. 삼세간 三世間 There are two definitions : (1) The realms of 기 器 matter, of 중생 衆生 life, and 지정각 智正覺 mind, especially the Buddha's mind. (2) The 오음 五陰 psychological realm (mind), 중생 衆生 realm of life, and 국토 國土 or 기 器 material realm.

삼세 三細 The three refined, or subtle conceptions, in contrast with the 육추 六麤 cruder or common concepts, in the Awakening of Faith 기신론 起信論. The three are 무명업상 無明業相 "ignorance," or the unenlightened condition, considered as in primal action, the stirring of the perceptive faculty ; 능견상 能見相 ability to perceive phenomena ; perceptive faculties ; 경계상 境界相 the object perceived, or the empirical world, The first is associated with the 체 體 corpus or substance, the second and third with function, but both must have co-existence, e.g. water and waves. v. 육추 六麤.

삼쇠 三衰 The three deteriorators, idem 삼독 三毒.

삼수 三獸 The three animals — hare, horse, elephant — crossing a stream. The śrāvaka is like the hare who crosses by swimming on the surface ; the pratyeka-buddha is like the horse who crosses deeper than the hare ; the bodhisattva is like the elephant who walks across on the bottom. Also likened to the triyāna. 열반경 涅槃經 23, 27.

삼수 三受 The three states of Vedanā, i.e. sensation, are divided into painful, pleasurable and freedom from both 고 苦, 낙 樂, 사 捨. When things are opposed to desire, pain arises ; when accordant, there is pleasure and a desire for their continuance ; when neither, one is detached or free. 구사론 俱舍論 1. 삼수업 三受業 The karma or results arising from the pursuit of courses that produce pain, pleasure, or freedom from both.

삼수 三修 The three ways of discipline, i.e. three śrāvaka and three bodhisattva ways. The three śrāvaka ways are 무상수 無常修 no realization of the eternal, seeing everything as transient ; 비락수 非樂修 joyless, through only contemplating misery and not realizing the ultimate nirvāṇa-joy ; 무아수 無我修 non-ego discipline, seeing only the perishing self and not realizing the immortal self. The bodhisattva three are the opposite of these.

삼수 三銖 Three twenty-fourths of a tael, the weight of a deva's garments, e.g. featherweight.

삼술 三術 Three devices in meditation for getting rid of Māra-hindrances : within, to get rid of passion and delusion ; without, to refuse or to withdraw from external temptation.

삼승 三乘 Triyāna, the three vehicles, or conveyances which carry living beings across saṁsāra or mortality (births-and-deaths) to the shores of nirvāṇa. The three are styled 소승 小乘, 중승 中乘, and 대승 大乘. Sometimes the three vehicles are defined as 성문 聲聞 Śrāvaka, that of the hearer or obedient disciple ; 연각 緣覺 Pratyeka-buddha, that of the enlightened for self ; these are described as 소승 小乘 because the objective of both is personal salvation ; the third is 보살 菩薩 Bodhisattva, or 대승 大乘 Mahāyāna, because the objective is the salvation of all the living. The three are also depicted as 삼차 三車 three wains, drawn by a goat, a deer, an ox. The Lotus declares that the three are really the One Buddha-vehicle, which has been revealed in three expedient forms suited to his disciples' capacity, the Lotus Sūtra being the unifying, complete, and final exposition. The Three Vehicles are differently explained by different exponents, e.g. (1) Mahāyāna recognizes (a) Śrāvaka, called Hīnayāna, leading in longer or shorter periods to arhatship ; (b) Pratyekabuddha, called Madhyamayāna, leading after still longer or shorter periods to a Buddhahood ascetically attained and for self ; (c) Bodhisattva, called Mahāyāna, leading after countless ages of self-sacrifice in saving others and progressive enlightenment to ultimate Buddhahood. (2) Hīnayāna is also described as possessing three vehicles 성 聲, 연 緣, 보 菩 or 소 小, 중 中, 대 大, the 소 小 and 중 中 conveying to personal salvation their devotees in ascetic dust and ashes and mental annihilation, the 대 大 leading to bodhi, or perfect enlightenment, and the Buddha's way. Further definitions of the Triyāna are : (3) True bodhisattva teaching for the 대 大 ; pratyeka-buddha without ignorant asceticism for the 중 中 ; and śrāvaka with ignorant asceticism for the 소 小. (4) (a) 일승 一乘 The One-Vehicle which carries all to Buddhahood ; of this the 화엄 華嚴 Hua-yen and 법화 法華 Fa-hua are typical exponents ; (b) 삼승법 三乘法 the three-vehicle, containing practitioners of all three systems, as expounded in books of the 심밀반야 深密般若 ; (c) 소승 小乘 the Hīnayāna pure and simple as seen in the 사아함경 四阿含經 Four Āgamas. Śrāvakas are also described as hearers of the Four Truths and limited to that degree of development ; they hear from the pratyeka-buddhas, who are enlightened in the Twelve Nidānas 인연 因緣 ; the bodhisattvas make the 육도 六度 or six forms of transmigration their field of sacrificial saving work, and of enlightenment. The Lotus Sūtra really treats the 삼승 三乘 Three Vehicles as 방편 方便 or expedient ways, and offers a 불승 佛乘 Buddha Vehicle as the inclusive and final vehicle. 삼승가 三乘家 The Dharmalakṣaṇa School of the Three Vehicles, led by the 법상종 法相宗. 삼승진실일승방편 三乘眞實一乘方便 The 삼승가 三乘家 consider the Triyāna as real, and the "one vehicle" of the Lotus School as merely tactical, or an expedient form of expression.

삼승기 三僧祇 idem 삼아승기겁 三阿僧祇劫.

삼시 三時 The three divisions of the day, i.e. dawn, daylight, and sunset ; or morning, noon, and evening ; also the three periods, after his nirvāṇa, of every Buddha's teaching, viz., 정 正 correct, or the period of orthodoxy and vigour, 상 像 semblance, or the period of scholasticism, and 말 末 end, the period of decline and termination. 삼시좌선 三時坐禪 The thrice a day meditation — about 10 a.m. and 4 and 8 p.m. 삼시년한 三時年限 The three periods of Buddhism — 1,000 years of 정법 正法 pure or orthodox doctrine, 1,000 years of 상법 像法 resemblance to purity, and 10,000 years of 말법 末法 decay. Other definitions are 정 正 and 상 像 500 years each, or 정 正 1,000 and 상 像 500, or 정 正 500 and 상 像 1,000. 삼시성 三時性 i.e. 변의원삼성 徧依圓三性 v. 삼성 三性. 삼시교(판) 三時教(判) The three periods and characteristics of Buddha's teaching, as defined by the Dharmalakṣaṇa school 법상종 法相宗. They are : (1) 유 有, when he taught the 실유 實有 reality of the skandhas and elements, but denied the common belief in 실아 實我 real personality or a permanent soul ; this period is represented by the four 아함경 阿含經 āgamas and other Hīnayāna sūtras. (2) 공 空 Śūnya, when he negatived the idea of 실법 實法 the reality of things and advocated that all was 공 空 unreal ; the period of the 반야경 般若經 prajñā sūtras. (3) 중 中 Madhyama, the mean, that mind or spirit is real, while things are unreal ; the period of this school's specific sūtra the 해심밀경 解深密經, also the 법화 法華 and later sūtras. In the two earlier periods he is said to have 방편 方便 adapted his teaching to the development of his hearers ; in the third to have delivered his complete and perfect doctrine. Another division by the 공종 空宗 is (1) as above ; (2) the early period of the Mahāyāna represented by the 심밀경 深密經 ; (3) the higher Mahāyāna as in the 반야경 般若經. V. also 삼교 三教. 삼시업 三時業 The three stages of karma — in the present life because of present deeds ; in the next life because of present actions ; and in future lives because of present actions.

삼시 三施 The three forms of giving : (1) (a) one's goods ; (b) the Law or Truth ; (c) courage, or confidence : 지도론 智度論 11. (2) (a) goods ; (b) worship ; (c) preaching. (3) (a) food ; (b) valuables ; (c) life.

삼식 三識 The three states of mind or consciousness : 진식 眞識 the original unsullied consciousness or Mind, the Tathāgata-garbha, the eighth or ālaya식 ālaya識 ; 현식 現識 mind or consciousness diversified in contact with or producing phenomena, good and evil ; 분별식 分別識 consciousness discriminating and evolving the objects of the five senses. Also 의식 意識 manas, 심식 心識 ālaya, and 무구식 無垢識 amala, v. 식 識.

삼신 三身 Trikāya. 삼보신 三寶身 The threefold body or nature of a Buddha, i.e. the 법신 法身, 보신 報身, and 화신 化身, or Dharmakāya, Sambhogakāya, and Nirmāṇakāya. The three are defined as 자성 自性, 수용 受用, and 변화 變化, the Buddha-body *per se*, or in its essential nature ; his body of bliss, which he "receives" for his own "use" and enjoyment ; and his body of transformation, by which he can appear in any form ; i.e. spiritual, or essential ; glorified ; revealed. While the doctrine of the Trikāya is a Mahāyāna concept, it partly results from the Hīnayāna idealization of the earthly Buddha with his thirty-two signs, eighty physical marks, clairvoyance, clairaudience, holiness, purity, wisdom, pity, etc. Mahāyāna, however, proceeded to conceive of Buddha as the Universal, the All, with infinity of forms, yet above all our concepts of unity or diversity. To every Buddha Mahāyāna attributed a three-fold body : that of essential Buddha ; that of joy or enjoyment of the fruits of his past saving labours ; that of power to transform himself at will to any shape for omnipresent salvation of those who need him. The trinity finds different methods of expression, e.g. Vairocana is entitled 법신 法身, the embodiment of the Law, shinning everywhere, enlightening all ; Locana is 보신 報身 ; cf. 삼보 三寶, the embodiment of purity and bliss ; Śākyamuni is 화신 化身 or Buddha revealed. In the esoteric sect they are 법 法 Vairocana, 보 報 Amitābha, and 화 化 Śākyamuni. The 삼보 三寶 are also 법 法 Dharma, 보 報 Saṅgha, 화 化 Buddha. Nevertheless, the three are considered as a trinity, the three being essentially one, each in the other. (1) 법신 法身 Dharmakāya in its earliest conception was that of the body of the dharma, or truth, as preached by Śākyamuni ; later it became his mind or soul in contrast with his material body. In Mādhyamika, the dharmakāya was the only reality, i.e. the void, or the immaterial, the ground of all phenomena ; in other words, the 진여 眞如, the Tathāgata-garbha, the bhūtatathatā. According to the Hua-yen (Kegon) School it is the 이 理 or noumenon, while the other two are 기 氣 or phenomenal aspects. "For the Vijñānavāda ... the body of the law as highest reality is the void intelligence, whose infection (saṅkleśa) results in the process of birth and death, whilst its purification brings about Nirvāṇa, or its restoration to its primitive transparence" (Keith). The "body of the law is the true reality of everything." Nevertheless, in Mahāyāna every Buddha has his own 법신 法身 ; e.g. in the dharmakāya aspect we have the designation Amitābha, who in his sambhogakāya aspect is styled Amitāyus. (2) 보신 報身 Sambhogakāya, a Buddha's reward body, or body of enjoyment of the merits he attained as a bodhisattva ; in other words, a Buddha in glory in his heaven. This is the form of Buddha as an object of worship. It is defined in two aspects, (a) 자수용신 自受用身 for his own bliss, and (b) 타수용신 他受用身 for the sake of others, revealing himself in his glory to bodhisattvas, enlightening and inspiring them. By wisdom a Buddha's dharmakāya is attained, by bodhisattva-merits his sambhogakāya . Not only has every Buddha all the three bodies or aspects, but as all men are of the same essence, or nature, as Buddhas, they are therefore potential Buddhas and are in and of the Trikāya. Moreover, Trikāya is not divided, for a Buddha in his 화신 化身 is still one with his 법신 法身 and 보신 報身, all three bodies being co-existent. (3) 화신 化身 ; 응신 應身 ; 응화신 應化身 Nirmāṇakāya, a Buddha's transformation, or miraculous body, in which he appears at will and in any form outside his heaven, e.g. as Śākyamuni among men. 삼신삼덕 三身三德 The 삼신 三身 are as above the 법보응 法報應 ; the 삼덕 三德 are 법 法, 반 般, and 해 解, i.e. the virtue, or merit, of the (a) 법신 法身 being absolute independence, reality ; of (b) 보신 報身, being 반야 般若 prajñā or wisdom ; and of (c) 응신 應身, being 해탈덕 解脫德 liberation, or Nirvāṇa. 삼신불성 三身佛性 v. 삼신 三身. 삼신여래 三身如來 v. 삼신 三身. 삼신업 三身業 The three physical wrong deeds — killing, robbing, adultery.

삼심 三心 The three minds, or hearts ; various groups are given : (1) Three assured ways of reaching the Pure Land, by (a) 지성심 至誠心 perfect sincerity ; (b) 심심 深心 profound resolve for it ; (c) 회향발원심 廻向發願心 resolve on demitting one's merits to others. (2) (a) 근본심 根本心 The 8th or ālaya-vijñāna mind, the store-house, or source of all seeds of good or evil ; (b) 의본심 依本心 the 7th or mano-vijñāna mind, the mediating cause of all taint ; (c) 기사심 起事心 the ṣaḍāyatana-vijñāna mind, the immediate influence of the six senses. (3) (a) 입심 入心 (b) 주심 住心 (c) 출심 出心 The mind entering into a condition, staying there, departing. (4) A pure, a single, and an undistracted mind. There are other groups.

삼십 三十 Tridaśa. Thirty ; abbreviation for the thirty-three deities, heavens, etc.

삼십사타 三十捨墮 idem 니살기바일제 尼薩耆波逸提.

삼십삼 三十三 Trayastriṁśāḥ. Thirty-three. 삼십삼천 三十三天 ; 도리천 忉利天 ; 달리천 怛利天, 다라야등릉사 多羅夜登陵舍 ; 달리야등릉사 怛利夜登陵奢 ; 달리야달리사 怛利耶怛利奢 Trayastriṁśās. The Indra heaven, the second of the six heavens of form. Its capital is situated on the summit of Mt. Sumeru, where Indra rules over his thirty-two devas, who reside on thirty-two peaks of Sumeru, eight in each of the four directions. Indra's capital is called 수승 殊勝 Sudarśana, 희견성 喜見城 Joy-view city. Its people are a yojana in height, each one's clothing weighs 육수 六銖 (1/4 oz.), and they live 1,000 years, a day and night being equal to 100 earthly years. Eitel says Indra's heaven "tallies in all its details with the Svarga of Brahminic mythology" and suggests that "the whole myth may have an astronomical meaning," or be connected with "the atmosphere with its phenomena, which strengthens Koeppen's hypothesis explaining the number thirty-three as referring to the eight Vasus, eleven Rudras, twelve Ādityas, and two Aśvins of Vedic mythology." In his palace called Vaijayanta "Indra is enthroned with 1,000 eyes with four arms grasping the vajra. There he revels in numberless sensual pleasures together with his wife Śacī ... and with 119,000 concubines with whom he associates by means of transformation." 삼십삼(존)관음 三十三(尊)觀音 The thirty-three forms in which Kuan-yin is represented : with willow, dragon, sūtra, halo, as strolling, with white robe, as lotus-sleeping, with fishing-creel, as medicine-bestowing, with folded hands, holding a lotus, pouring water, etc. 삼십삼과 三十三過 The thirty-three possible fallacies in the statement of a syllogism, nine in the proposition 종 宗 pratijñā, fourteen in the reason 인 因 hetu, and ten in the example 유 喩 udāharaṇa. 삼십삼신 三十三身 The thirty-three forms in which Avalokiteśvara (Kuan-yin) is said to have presented himself, from that of a Buddha to that of a woman or a rakṣas. Cf. Lotus Sūtra 보문 普門 chapter.

삼십생 三十生 In each of the 십지 十地 ten states there are three conditions, 입 入, 주 住, 출 出, entry, stay, exit, hence the "thirty lives."

삼십오불 三十五佛 The thirty-five Buddhas before whom those who have committed sins involving interminable suffering should heartily repent. There are different lists.

삼십육(부)신 三十六(部)神 The thirty-six departmental guardian divinities given in the 관정...주경 灌頂...咒經. Each is styled 미율두 彌栗頭 mṛdu, benign, kindly, for which 선 善 is used. Their Sanskrit and Chinese names are given in Chinese as follows : (1) 불라파 不羅婆 or 선광 善光 kindly light, has to do with attacks of disease ; (2) 파가파 婆呵婆 or 선명 善明 headaches ; (3) 파라파 婆邏婆 or 선력 善力 fevers ; (4) 항다라 抗陀羅 or 선월 善月 disorders of the stomach ; (5) 타리사 陀利奢 or 선견 善見 tumours ; (6) 아루가 阿婁呵 or 선공 善供 madness ; (7) 가파제 伽婆帝 or 선사 善捨 stupidity ; (8) 실저치 悉抵哆 or 선적 善寂 irascibility ; (9) 보리살 菩提薩 or 선각 善覺 lust ; (10) 제파라 提婆羅 or 선천 善天 devils ; (11) 가파제 呵婆帝 or 선주 善住 deadly injuries ; (12) 불약라 不若羅 or 선복 善福 graves ; (13) 필도가 苾闍伽 or 선술 善術 the four quarters ; (14) 가이파 迦隸婆 or 선제 善帝 enemies ; (15) 나도차 羅闍遮 or 선주 善主 robbers ; (16) 수건타 須乾陀 or 선향 善香 creditors ; (17) 단나파 檀那波 or 선시 善施 thieves ; (18) 지다나 支多那 or 선의 善意 pestilence ; (19) 나파나 羅婆那 or 선길 善吉 the five plagues(? typhoid) ; (20) 발파타 鉢婆馱 or 선산 善山 corpse worms ; (21) 삼마착 三摩捉 or 선조 善調 continuous concentration ; (22) 여체타 戾禘馱 or 선비 善備 restlessness ; (23) 파리타 波利陀 or 선경 善敬 attraction ; (24) 파리나 波利那 or 선정 善淨 evil cabals ; (25) 도가지 度伽地 or 선품 善品 deadly poison ; (26) 비리타 毘梨馱 or 선결 善結 fear ; (27) 지타나 支陀那 or 선수 善壽 calamities ; (28) 가림마 伽林摩 or 선서 善逝 childbirth and nursing ; (29) 아유가 阿留伽 or 선원 善願 the district magistracy ; (30) 도리타 闍利馱 or 선고 善固 altercations ; (31) 아가타 阿伽馱 or 선조 善照 anxieties and distresses ; (32) 아가파 阿訶婆 or 선생 善生 uneasiness ; (33) 파화나 婆和邏 or 선사 善思 supernatural manifestations ; (34) 파리나 波利那 or 선장 善藏 jealousy ; (35) 고타나 固陀那 or 선음 善音 curses ; (36) 위다라

韋陀羅 or 선묘 善妙 exorcism. They have innumerable assistants. He who writes their names and carries them with him can be free from all fear.

삼십육물 三十六物 The thirty-six physical parts and excretions of the human body, all being unclean, i.e. the vile body.

삼십이 三十二 Dvātriṁśat. Thirty-two. 삼십이응 三十二應 ; 삼십이신 三十二身 The thirty-two forms of Kuan-yin, and of P'u-hsien, ranging from that of a Buddha to that of a man, a maid, a rakṣas ; similar to the thirty-three forms named in the Lotus Sūtra. 삼십이상 三十二相 ; 삼십이대인상 三十二大人相 Dvātriṁśadvaralakṣaṇa. The thirty-two lakṣaṇas, or physical marks of a cakravartī, or "wheel-king," especially of the Buddha, i.e. level feet, thousand-spoke wheel-sign on feet, long slender fingers, pliant hands and feet, toes and fingers finely webbed, full-sized heels, arched insteps, thighs like a royal stag, hands reaching below the knees, well-retracted male organ, height and stretch of arms equal, every hair-root dark coloured, body hair graceful and curly, golden-hued body, a 10 foot halo around him, soft smooth skin, the 칠처 七處, i.e. two soles, two palms, two shoulders, and crown well rounded, below the armpits well-filled, lion-shaped body, erect, full shoulders, forty teeth, teeth white even and close, the four canine teeth pure white, lion-jawed, saliva improving the taste of all food, tongue long and broad, voice deep and resonant, eyes deep blue, eyelashes like a royal bull, a white ūrṇā or curl between the eyebrows emitting light, an uṣṇīṣa or fleshy protuberance on the crown. These are from the 삼장법수 三藏法數 48, with which the 지도론 智度論 4, 열반경 涅槃經 28, 중아함경 中阿含經, 삼십이상경 三十二相經 generally agree. The 무량의경 無量義經 has a different list. 무량의경경 無量義經經 The eleventh chapter of the 아함경 阿含經. 무량의경경원 無量義經經願 The twenty-first of Amitābha's vows, v. 무량수경 無量壽經.

삼십칠(조)도품 三十七(助)道品 Bodhipākṣika-dharma. 삼십칠(보리)분법 三十七(菩提)分法, 삼십칠품 三十七品 The thirty-seven conditions leading to bodhi, or Buddha-hood, i.e. 사념처 四念處 smṛtyupasthāna, four states of memory, or subjects of reflection ; 사정근 四正勤 samyakprahāṇa, four proper lines of exertion ; 사여의족 四如意足 ṛddhipāda, four steps towards supernatural power ; 오근 五根 pañca indriyāṇi, five spiritual faculties ; 오력 五力 pañca balāni, their five powers ; 칠각지 七覺支 sapta bodhyaṅga, seven degrees of enlightenment, or intelligence ; and 팔정도 八正道 aṣṭa-mārga, the eight-fold noble path. 삼십칠존 三十七尊 The thirty-seven heads in the Vajradhātu or Diamond-realm maṇḍala. 삼십칠존사대륜 三十七尊四大輪 The four large circles in each of which the thirty-seven are represented, in one all hold the diamond-realm symbol, the vajra ; in another, the symbol relating to the triple realm of time, past, present, future ; in another, the Kuan-yin symbol ; and in another, the symbol of infinite space.

삼아승기겁 三阿僧祇劫 The three great asaṁkhyeya (i.e. beyond number) kalpas — the three timeless periods of a bodhisattva's progress to Buddhahood.

삼악 三惡 The three evil gati, or paths of transmigration ; also 삼악도 三惡道, 삼악취 三惡趣 the hells, hungry ghosts, animals. 삼악각 三惡覺 The three evil mental states : 욕 欲 desire, 진 瞋 hate (or anger), 해 害 malevolence.

삼안거 三安居 The three months of summer retreat, varṣā ; v. 발 跋.

삼야삼불(단) 三耶三佛(壇) v. 삼먁삼불타 三藐三佛陀. 삼야삼보 三耶三菩 v. 삼먁삼보리 三藐三菩提.

삼어 三語 Buddha's three modes of discourse, i.e. without reserve, or the whole truth ; tactical or partial, adapting truth to the capacity of his hearers ; and a combination of both.

삼억가 三億家 The 300,000 families of Śrāvastī city who had never heard of the Buddha's epiphany — though he was often among them.

삼업 三業 Trividha-dvāra. The three conditions, inheritances, or karma, of which there are several groups. (1) Deed, word, thought, 신 身, 구 口, 의 意. (2) (a) present-life happy karma ; (b) present-life unhappy karma ; (c) 부동 不動 karma of an imperturbable nature. (3) (a) Good ; (b) evil ; (c) neutral karma. (4) (a) 누업 漏業 Karma of ordinary rebirth ; (b) 무루업 無漏業 karma of Hīnayāna nirvāṇa ; (c) 비루비무루업 非漏非無漏業 karma of neither, independent of both, Mahāyāna nirvāṇa. (5) (a) Present deeds and their consequences in this life ; (b) present deeds and their next life consequences ; (c) present deeds and consequences after the next life. There are other groups of three. 삼업공양 三業供養 ; 삼업상응 三業相應 To serve or worship with perfect sincerity of body, mouth, and mind ; the second form means that in worship all three correspond.

삼여 三餘 The three after death remainders, or continued mortal experiences, of śrāvakas and pratyekabuddhas, who mistakenly think they are going to 무여열반 無餘涅槃 final nirvāṇa, but will still find 번뇌여 煩惱餘 further passion and illusion, 업여 業餘 further karma, and 과여 果餘 continued rebirth, in realms beyond the 삼계 三界 trailokya.

삼역 三逆 The three unpardonable sins of Devadatta, which sent him to the Avīci hell – schism, stoning the Buddha to the shedding of his blood, killing a nun.

삼연 三緣 The three nidānas or links with the Buddha resulting from calling upon him, a term of the Pure Land sect : (a) 친연 親緣 that he hears those who call his name, sees their worship, knows their hearts and is one with them ; (b) 근연 近緣 that he shows himself to those who desire to see him ; (c) 증상연 增上緣 that at every invocation aeons of sin are blotted out, and he and his sacred host receive such a disciple at death.

삼연 三衍 The three yāna, or vehicles to nirvāṇa, i.e. śrāvaka, pratyekabuddha, and bodhisattva, v. 삼승 三乘.

삼연마 三練磨 v. 삼퇴굴 三退屈.

삼열 三熱 The three distresses of which dragons and dragon-kings are afraid – fiery heat, fierce wind, and the garuḍa-bird which preys on them for food.

삼열반문 三列槃門 The three gates to the city of nirvāṇa, i.e. 공 空, 무상 無相, and 무작 無作 the void (or the immaterial), formlessness, and inactivity ; idem 삼해탈문 三解脫門.

삼온 三蘊 The three kinds of skandhas, aggregations, or combinations, into which all life may be expressed according to the 화지 化地 or Mahīśāsaka school : 일념온 一念蘊 combination for a moment, momentary existence ; 일기온 一期蘊 combination for a period, e.g. a single human lifetime ; 궁생사온 窮生死蘊 the total existence of all beings.

삼욕 三欲 The three lusts, i.e. for 형모 形貌 form, 자태 姿態 carriage or beauty, and 세촉 細觸 refinement, or softness to the touch.

삼원 三猿 The three monkeys, one guarding its eyes, another its ears, a third its mouth.

삼위일진 三僞一眞 The three half-true, or partial revelations of the 소승 小乘, 중승 中乘 and 대승 大乘, and the true one of the Lotus Sūtra.

삼유 三有 The three kinds of bhava, or existence ; idem 삼계 三界 q.v. The three states of mortal existence in the trailokya, i.e. in the realms of desire, of form, and beyond form. Another definition is 현유 現有 present existence, or the present body and mind ; 당유 當有 in a future state ; 중유 中有 antarā-bhava, in the intermediate state. 삼유대 三有對 The three sets of limitation on freedom : (a) direct resistance or opposition ; (b) environment or condition ; (c) attachment. 삼유위법 三有爲法 The three active or functioning dharmas : (1) pratigha, matter or form, i.e.

that which has "substantial resistance" ; (2) mind ; and (3) 비색비심 非色非心 entities neither of matter nor mind ; cf. 칠십오법 七十五法. 삼유위상 三有爲相 The three forms of all phenomena, birth, stay (i.e. life), death ; utpāda, sthiti, and nirvāṇa.

삼응공양 三應供養 The three who should be served, or worshipped — a Buddha, an arhat, and a cakravartī king.

삼의 三疑 The three doubts — of self, of teacher, of the dharma-truth.

삼의 三醫 The three modes of diagnosis : the superior, 청성 聽聲 listening to the voice ; the medium, 상색 相色 observing the external appearance ; the inferior, 진맥 診脈 testing the pulse.

삼의 三衣 The three regulation garments of a monk, 가사 袈裟 kāṣāya, i.e. 승가리 僧伽梨 saṅghāṭī, assembly robe ; 울다라승 鬱多羅僧 uttarāsaṅga, upper garment worn over the 안타회 安陀會 antaravāsaka, vest or shirt. 단삼의 單三衣 The only proper garments of a monk.

삼인 三因 The six "causes" of the Abhidharma-kośa 구사론 俱舍論 as reduced to three in the Satya-siddhi śāstra 성실론 成實論, i.e. 생인 生因 producing cause, as good or evil deeds cause good or evil karma ; 습인 習因 habit cause, e.g. lust breeding lust ; 의인 依因 dependent or hypostatic cause, e.g. the six organs 육근 六根 and their objects 육경 六境 causing the cognitions 육식 六識. 삼인삼과 三因三果 The three causes produce their three effects : (1) 이숙인이숙과 異熟因異熟果 differently ripening causes produce differently ripening effects, i.e. every developed cause produces its developed effect, especially the effect of the present causes in the next transmigration ; (2) 복인복보 福因福報 blessed deeds produce blessed rewards, now and hereafter ; (3) 지인지과 智因智果 wisdom (now) produces wisdom-fruit (hereafter).

삼인 三忍 The three forms of kṣānti, i.e. patience (or endurance, tolerance). One of the groups is patience under hatred, under physical hardship, and in pursuit of the faith. Another is patience of the blessed in the Pure Land in understanding the truth they hear, patience in obeying the truth, patience in attaining absolute reality ; v. 무량수경 無量壽經. Another is patience in the joy of remembering Amitābha, patience in meditation on his truth, and patience in constant faith in him. Another is the patience of submission, of faith, and of obedience.

삼인 三印 The three signs or proofs of a Hīnayāna sūtra — non-permanence, non-personality, nirvāṇa ; without these the sūtra is spurious and the doctrine is of Māra ; the proof of a Mahāyāna sūtra is the doctrine of 일실 一實 ultimate reality, q.v. Also 삼법인 三法印.

삼일재 三日齋 The third day's ceremonies after a death, to gain Yama's favour as the deceased appears before him.

삼자 三子 The three sons, one filial, wise, and competent ; one unfilial but clever and competent ; one unfilial, stupid, and incompetent ; types respectively of bodhisattvas, śrāvakas, and icchantikas, 열반경 涅槃經 33.

삼자 三字 The "three characters," a term for 아미타 阿彌陀 Amitābha.

삼자 三自 Three divisions of the eight-fold noble path, the first to the third 자조 自調 self-control, the fourth and fifth 자정 自淨 self-purification, the last three 자도 自度 self-development in the religious life and in wisdom. Also 자체 自體, 자상 自相, 자용 自用, substance, form, and function.

삼자 三慈 v. 삼종자비 三種慈悲.

삼잡 三帀 The thrice repeated procession around an image ; there is dispute as to which shoulder should be next to the image, v. 우요 右繞.

삼잡염 三雜染 The three kaṣāya, i.e. "mixed dyes" or infections : the passions ; their karma ; reincarnation ; or illusion, karma, and suffering.

삼장 三障 The three vighna, i.e. hinderers or barriers, of which three groups are given : (1) (a) 번뇌장 煩惱障 the passions, i.e. 삼독 三毒 desire, hate, stupidity ; (b) 업장 業障 the deeds done ; (c) 보장 報障 the retributions. (2) (a) 피번뇌장 皮煩惱障 ; (b) 육번뇌장 肉煩惱障 ; (c) 심번뇌장 心煩惱障 skin, flesh, and heart (or mind) troublers, i.e. delusions from external objects, internal views, and mental ignorance. (3) 삼중장 三重障 the three weighty obstructions : (a) self-importance, 아만 我慢 ; (b) envy, 질투 嫉妬 ; (c) desire, 탐욕 貪欲.

삼장 三藏 v. 장 藏. 삼장교 三藏教 A T'ien-t'ai name for Hīnayāna, whose tripiṭaka is ascribed to Mahākāśyapa. 삼장학자 三藏學者 A student of Hīnayāna. 삼장법사 三藏法師 A teacher of the Law ; especially 현장 玄奘 Hsüan-tsang of the T'ang dynasty ; and cf. 반야 般若.

삼장(재)월 三長(齋)月 The three whole months of abstinence, the first, fifth, and ninth months, when no food should be taken after noon, The four deva-kings are on tours of inspection during these months.

삼장엄 三莊嚴 The three adornments, or glories, of a country : material attractions ; religion and learning ; men, i.e. religious men and bodhisattvas.

삼재 三災 The three calamities ; they are of two kinds, minor and major. The minor, appearing during a decadent world-period, are sword, pestilence, and famine ; the major, for world-destruction, are fire, water, and wind. 구사론 俱舍論 12.

삼재월 三齋月 See 삼장(재)월 三長(齋)月.

삼전 三田 The three "fields" of varying qualities of fertility, i.e. bodhisattvas, śrāvakas, and icchantis, respectively producing a hundred-fold, fifty-fold, one-fold. 열반경 涅槃經 33.

삼전(법륜) 三轉(法輪) The three turns of the law-wheel when the Buddha preached in the Deer Park : (a) 시전 示轉 indicative, i.e. postulation and definition of the 사제 四諦 ; (b) 권전 勸轉 hortative, e.g. 고당지 苦當知 suffering should be diagnosed ; (c) 증전 增轉 evidential. e.g. I have overcome suffering, etc. 삼전법륜십이행(상) 三轉法輪十二行(相) The twelve 행 行 processes are the application of the above 시 示, 권 勸, and 증 證 to each of the four postulates. The three "turns" are also applied to the four kinds of knowledge, i.e. 안 眼, 지 智, 명 明, and 각 覺.

삼전도 三顚倒 The three subversions or subverters : (evil) thoughts, (false) views, and (a deluded) mind.

삼절 三節 The three divisions of the 십이인연 十二因緣 twelve nidānas, q.v. : (a) past, i.e. the first two ; (b) present — the next eight ; (c) future — the last two.

삼점 三點 See 이자삼점 伊字三點.

삼점 三漸 The three progressive developments of the Buddha's teaching according to the Prajñā school : (a) the 녹원 鹿苑 initial stage in the Lumbinī deer park ; (b) the 방등 方等 period of the eight succeeding years ; (c) the 반야 般若 prajñā or wisdom period which succeeded.

삼정기 三精氣 The three auras of earth, of the animate, and of the inanimate invoked against demon influences.

삼정육 三淨肉 The three kinds of "clean" flesh — when a monk has not seen the creature killed, has not heard of its being killed for him, and has no doubt thereon.

삼정취 三定聚 idem 삼취 三聚.

삼제 三際 Past, present, future, idem 삼세 三世. 삼제시 三際時 The three Indian seasons, spring, summer, and winter, also styled 열 熱, 우 雨, 한제시 寒際時, the hot, rainy, and cold seasons.

삼제 三諦 The three dogmas. The "middle" school of T'ien-t'ai says 즉공 卽空, 즉가 卽假, 즉중 卽中, i.e. 취시공 就是空, 가 假, 중 中 ; (a) by 공 空 śūnya is meant that things causally produced are in their essential nature unreal (or immaterial) 실공무 實空無 ; (b) 가 假, though things are unreal in their essential nature their derived forms are real ; (c) 중 中 ; but both are one, being of the one 여 如 or reality. These three dogmas are founded on a verse of Nāgārjuna's —

인연소생법 因緣所生法, 아설즉시공 我說卽是空,
역위시가명 亦爲是假名, 역시중도의 亦是中道義.

"All causally produced phenomena, I say, are unreal, Are but a passing name, and indicate the 'mean'." There are other explanations — the 원교 圓教 interprets the 공 空 and 가 假 as 중 中 ; the 별교 別教 makes 중 中 independent. 공 空 is the all, i.e. the totality of all things, and is spoken of as the 진 眞 or 실 實 true, or real ; 가 假 is the differentiation of all things and is spoken of as 속 俗 common, i.e. things as commonly named ; 중 中 is the connecting idea which makes a unity of both, e.g. "all are but parts of one stupendous whole." The 중 中 makes all and the all into one whole, unifying the whole and its parts. 공 空 may be taken as the immaterial, the undifferentiated all, the sum of existences, by some as the Tathāgata-garbha 여래장 如來藏 ; 가 假 as the unreal, or impermanent, the material or transient form, the temporal that can be named, the relative or discrete ; 중 中 as the unifier, which places each in the other and all in all. The "shallower" 산외 山外 school associated 공 空 and 중 中 with the noumenal universe as opposed to the phenomenal and illusory existence represented by 가 假. The "profounder" 산내 山內 school teaches that all three are aspects of the same. 삼제상즉 三諦相卽 The unity of 공 空, 가 假, 중 中, three aspects of the same reality, taught by the 원교 圓教 as distinguished from the 별교 別教 which separates them.

삼조 三照 The three shinings ; the sun first shining on the hill-tops, then the valleys and plains. So, according to T'ien-t'ai teaching of the Hua-yen sūtra, the Buddha's doctrine had three periods of such shining : (a) first, he taught the Hua-yen sūtra, transforming his chief disciples into bodhisattvas ; (b) second, the Hīnayāna sūtras in general to śrāvakas and pratyeka-buddhas in the Lumbinī garden ; (c) third, the 방등 方等 sūtras down to the 열반경 涅槃經 for all the living. See the 육십화엄경 六十華嚴經 35, where the order is five, i.e. bodhisattvas, pratyeka-buddhas, śrāvakas, lay disciples, and all creatures.

삼조연하 三條椽下 Under three rafters — the regulation space for a monk's bed or seat ; in meditation.

삼존 三尊 The three honoured ones : Buddha, the Law, the Ecclesia or Order. Others are : Amitābha, Avalokiteśvara, and Mahāsthāmaprāpta, who, according to the Pure-land sect, come to welcome the dying invoker. Another group is Bhaiṣajya, Vairocana, and Candraprabha ; and another, Śākyamuni, Mañjuśrī, and Samantabhadra. 삼존불 三尊佛 The three honoured Buddhas of the West : Amitābha, Avalokiteśvara, Mahāsthāmaprāpta. Though bodhisattvas, the two latter are called Buddhas when thus associated with Amitābha. 삼존내영 三尊來迎 Amitābha, Avalokiteśvara, Mahāsthāmaprāpta, receive into the western paradise the believer who calls on Amitābha.

삼종 三從 A woman's three subordinations, to father, husband, and son ; stated in several sūtras, e.g. 사십화엄경 四十華嚴經 28.

삼종 三宗 The three Schools of 법상종 法相宗, 파상종 破相宗, and 법성종 法性宗 q.v., representing the ideas of 공 空, 가 假, and 불공가 不空假, i.e. unreality, temporary reality, and neither ; or absolute, relative, and neither.

삼종 三種 Three kinds, sorts, classes, categories, etc.

삼종견혹 三種見惑 Three classes of delusive views, or illusions — those common to humanity ; those of the inquiring mind ; and those of the learned and settled mind.

삼종공양 三種供養 Three modes of serving (the Buddha, etc.) : (a) offerings of incense, flowers, food, etc. ; (b) of praise and reverence ; (c) of right conduct.

삼종관정 三種灌頂 Three kinds of baptism : (1) (a) 마정관정 摩頂灌頂 Every Buddha baptizes a disciple by laying a hand on his head ; (b) 수기관정 授記灌頂 by predicting Buddhahood to him ; (c) 방광관정 放光灌頂 by revealing his glory to him to his profit. (2) Shingon has (a) baptism on acquiring the mystic word ; (b) on remission of sin and prayer for blessing and protection ; (c) on seeking for reward in the next life.

삼종광명 三種光明 The three kinds of light : (a) external — sun, moon, stars, lamps, etc. ; (b) dharma, or the light of right teaching and conduct ; (c) the effulgence or bodily halo emitted by Buddhas, bodhisattvas, devas.

삼종교상 三種教相 The three modes of the Buddha's teaching of the Southern Sects : 돈 頓 immediate, 점 漸 gradual or progressive, and 부정 不定 indeterminate.

삼종단 三種斷 The three kinds of uccheda — cutting-off, excision, or bringing to an end : (1) (a) 자성단 自性斷 with the incoming of wisdom, passion or illusion ceases of itself ; (b) 불생단 不生斷 with realization of the doctrine that all is 공 空 unreal, evil karma ceases to arise ; (c) 연박단 緣縛斷 illusion being ended, the causal nexus of the passions disappears and the attraction of the external ceases. (2) The three śrāvaka or ascetic stages are (a) 견소단 見所斷 ending the condition of false views ; (b) 수행단 修行斷 getting rid of desire and illusion in practice ; (c) 비소단 非所斷 no more illusion or desire to be cut off.

삼종대지 三種大智 The three major kinds of wisdom : (a) self-acquired, no master needed ; (b) unacquired and natural ; (c) universal.

삼종바라밀 三種波羅蜜 The three kinds of pāramitā ideals, or methods of perfection : (a) 세간바라밀 世間波羅蜜 that of people in general relating to this world ; (b) 출세간바라밀 出世間波羅蜜 that of śrāvakas and pratyeka-buddhas relating to the future life for themselves ; (c) 출세간상상바라밀 出世間上上波羅蜜 the supreme one of bodhisattvas, relating to the future life for all ; cf. 삼종지 三種智.

삼종법륜 三種法輪 v. 삼륜교 三輪教.

삼종삼관 三種三觀 The three types of meditation on the principles of the 삼제 三諦 q.v., i.e. the dogmas of 공 空, 가 假, 중 中.

삼종삼세 三種三世 Three kinds of past, present, and future as intp. according to 도리 道理, 신통 神通, and 유식 唯識.

삼종상 三種常 A Buddha in his three eternal qualities : (a) 본성상 本性常 in his nature or dharmakāya ; (b) 부단상 不斷常 in his unbroken eternity, sambhogakāya ; (c) 상속상 相續常 in his continuous and eternally varied forms, nirmāṇakāya.

삼종상 三種相 The three kinds of appearance : (1) In logic, the three kinds of percepts : (a) 표상

標相 inferential, as fire is inferred from smoke ; (b) 형상 形相 formal or spatial, as length, breadth, etc. ; (c) 체상 體相 qualitative, as heat is in fire, etc. (2) (a) 가명상 假名相 names, which are merely indications of the temporal ; (b) 법상 法相 dharmas, or "things" ; (c) 무상상 無相相 the formless — all three are incorrect positions.

삼종색 三種色 Three kinds of rūpa, i.e. appearance or object : (1) (a) visible objects ; (b) invisible objects, e.g. sound ; (c) invisible, immaterial, or abstract objects. (2) (a) colour, (b) shape, (c) quality.

삼종생 三種生 The three sources, or causes of the rise of the passions and illusions : (a) 상생 想生 the mind, or active thought ; (b) 상생 相生 the objective world ; (c) 유주생 流注生 their constant interaction, or the continuous stream of latent predispositions.

삼종선근 三種善根 The three kinds of good roots — almsgiving, mercy, and wisdom.

삼종세간 三種世間 v. 삼세간 三世間.

삼종시도 三種示導 Three ways in which bodhisattvas manifest themselves for saving those suffering the pains of hell, i.e. 신 身 physically, by super-natural powers, change of form, etc. ; 의 意 mentally, through powers of memory and enlightenment ; 구 口 orally, by moral exhortation.

삼종신 三種身 The T'ien-t'ai School has a definition of 색신 色身 the physical body of the Buddha ; 법문신 法門身 his psychological body with its vast variety ; 실상신 實相身 his real body, or dharmakāya. The esoteric sect ascribes a trikāya to each of its honoured ones. v. 삼신 三身. 삼종신고 三種身苦 The three duḥkha or afflictions of the body — old age, sickness, death.

삼종심고 三種心苦 The three kinds of mental distress : desire, anger, stupidity, idem 삼독 三毒.

삼종욕 三種欲 Three kinds of desire — food, sleep, sex.

삼종원융 三種圓融 Three kinds of unity or identity of (a) 사리 事理 phenomena with "substance," e.g. waves and the water ; (b) 사사 事事 phenomena with phenomena, e.g. wave with wave ; (c) 이리 理理 substance with substance, e.g. water with water.

삼종유 三種有 Three kinds of existence : (a) 상대유 相待有 that of qualities, as of opposites, e.g. length and shortness ; (b) 가명유 假名有 that of phenomenal things so-called, e.g. a jar, a man ; (c) 법유 法有 that of the noumenal, or imaginary, understood as facts and not as illusions, such as a "hare's horns" or a "turtle's fur."

삼종인행 三種忍行 Patience or forbearance of body, mouth, and mind.

삼종자비 三種慈悲 ; **삼종연자** 三種緣慈 The three reasons of a bodhisattva's pity — because all beings are like helpless infants ; because of his knowledge of all laws and their consequences ; without external cause, i.e. because of his own nature.

삼종정업 三種淨業 The threefold way of obtaining a pure karma, idem 삼복 三福.

삼종지 三種智 The wisdom of common men, of the heterodox, and of Buddhism ; i.e. (a) 세간지 世間智 normal, worldly knowledge or ideas ; (b) 출세간지 出世間智 other-worldly wisdom, e.g. of Hīnayāna ; (c) 출세간상상지 出世間上上智 the highest other-worldly wisdom, of Mahāyāna ; cf. 삼종바라밀 三種波羅蜜.

삼종지관 三種止觀 Three T'ien-t'ai modes of entering dhyāna : (a) 점차 漸次 gradual, from the shallow to the deep, the simple to the complex ; (b) 부정 不定 irregular, simple, and complex mixed ; (c) 원돈 圓頓 immediate and whole.

삼종지옥 三種地獄 The three kinds of hells — hot, cold, and solitary.

삼종천 三種天 Three definitions of heaven : (a) as a name or title, e.g. divine king, son of Heaven etc. ; (b) as a place for rebirth, the heavens of the gods ; (c) the pure Buddha-land.

삼종천제 三種闡提 The three kinds of icchantika : (a) 일천제가 一闡提迦 the wicked ; (b) 아천제가 阿闡提迦 called 대비천제 大悲闡提 bodhisattvas who become icchantika to save all beings ; (c) 아전저가 阿顚底迦 otherwise 무성천제 無性闡提 those without a nature for final nirvāṇa. Cf. 삼병 三病.

삼종청정 三種淸淨 The three purities of a bodhisattva — a mind free from all impurity, a body pure because never to be reborn save by transformation, an appearance 상 相 perfectly pure and adorned.

삼종향 三種香 Three kinds of scent, or incense, i.e. from root, branch, or flower.

삼종회법 三種悔法 ; **삼종참법** 三種懺法 Three modes of repentance : (a) 무생회 無生悔 to meditate on the way to prevent wrong thoughts and delusions ; (b) 취상회 取相悔 to seek the presence of the Buddha to rid one of sinful thoughts and passions ; (c) 작법참 作法懺 in proper form to confess one's breach of the rules before the Buddha and seek remission.

삼주 三株 The three tree-trunks, or main stems — desire, hate, stupidity ; v. 삼독 三毒.

삼주관월 三舟觀月 v. 일월삼주 一月三舟.

삼중삼매 三重三昧 ; **삼중등지** 三重等持 idem 삼삼매 三三昧. 삼중법계 三重法界 The three meditations, on the relationship of the noumenal and phenomenal, of the 화엄종 華嚴宗 Hua-yen school : (a) 이법계 理法界 the universe as law or mind, that all things are 진여 眞如, i.e. all things or phenomena are of the same Buddha-nature, or the Absolute ; (b) 이사무애법계 理事無礙法界 that the Buddha-nature and the thing, or the Absolute and phenomena are not mutually exclusive ; (c) 사사무애법계 事事無礙法界 that phenomena are not mutually exclusive, but in a common harmony as parts of the whole.

삼즉일 三卽一 The three vehicles (Hīnayāna, Madhyamayāna, Mahāyāna) are one, i.e. the three lead to bodhisattvaship and Buddhahood for all.

삼지 三智 The three kinds of wisdom : (1) (a) 일체지 一切智 śrāvaka and pratyeka-buddha knowledge that all the dharma or laws are 공 空 void and unreal ; (b) 도종지 道種智 bodhisattva-knowledge of all things in their proper discrimination ; (c) 일체종지 一切種智 Buddha-knowledge, or perfect knowledge of all things in their every aspect and relationship past, present, and future. T'ien-t'ai associates the above with 공 空, 가 假, 중 中. (2) (a) 세간지 世間智 earthly or ordinary wisdom ; (b) 출세간지 出世間智 supra-mundane, or spiritual (śrāvaka and pratyeka-buddha) wisdom ; (c) 출세간상상지 出世間上上智 supreme wisdom of bodhisattvas and Buddhas. v. 지도론 智度論 27, 지관 止觀 3, and 능가경 楞伽經 3. Cf. 일심삼지 一心三智.

삼지(비량) 三支(比量) Three members of a syllogism : pratijñā 종 宗 the proposition, hetu 인 因 the reason, udāharaṇa 유 喩 the example ; cf. 인명 因明.

삼지백(대)겁 三祇百(大)劫 The period necessary for a bodhisattva to become a Buddha, i.e. three asaṅkhyeyas 아승지 阿僧祇 to attain the 육도 六度, and 100 kalpas to acquire the thirty-two 상 相 or characteristic marks of a Buddha ; cf. 삼아 三阿.

삼진여 三眞如 Three aspects of the bhūtatathatā, implying that it is above the limitations of form, creation, or a soul. (1) (a) 무상진여 無相眞如 without form ; (b) 무생진여 無生眞如 without creation

; (c) 무성진여 無性眞如 without anything that can be called a nature for comparison ; e.g. chaos, or primal matter. (2) (a) 선법진여 善法眞如 The bhūtatathatā as good ; (b) 불선법진여 不善法眞如 as evil ; (c) 무기법진여 無記法眞如 as neutral, or neither good nor evil.

삼차 三車 Triyāna. 삼승 三乘 or 삼승법문 三乘法門 (1) The three vehicles across saṁsāra into nirvāṇa, i.e. the carts offered by the father in the Lotus Sūtra to lure his children out of the burning house : (a) goat carts, representing śrāvakas ; (b) deer carts, pratyeka-buddhas ; (c) bullock carts, bodhisattvas. (2) The three principal schools of Buddhism — Hīnayāna, Madhyamayāna, Mahāyāna. 삼차가 三車家 idem 삼승가 三乘家.

삼참 三懺 idem 삼종회법 三種悔法.

삼처전심 三處傳心 The three places where Śākyamuni is said to have transmitted his mind or thought direct and without speech to Kāśyapa : at the 영산 靈山 by a smile when plucking a flower ; at the 다자탑 多子塔 when he shared his seat with him ; finally by putting his foot out of his coffin. 삼처목차 三處木叉 The mokṣa of the three places, i.e. moral control over body, mouth, and mind. 삼처아란야 三處阿蘭若 Three classes of araṇyaka or ascetics distinguished by their three kinds of abode — those who dwell in retired places, as in forests ; among tombs ; in deserts ; v. 아란야 阿蘭若.

삼천 三天 The trimūrti — Śiva, Viṣṇu, and Brahmā. 삼천사 三天使 v. 삼사 三使. 삼천사선 三天四仙 v. 이천삼선 二天三仙 and add 구마라 鳩摩羅 Kuveradeva and 야제자 若提子 Nirgrantha, son of Jñātṛ, i.e. of the Jñātṛ clan.

삼천 三千 Trisahasra, three thousand ; a term used by the T'ien-t'ai School for 일체제법 一切諸法, i.e. all things, everything in a chiliocosm, or Buddha-world ; v. 삼천대천세계 三千大千世界. 삼천불 三千佛 idem 삼세 三世. 삼천진점겁 三千塵點劫 The kalpa of the ancient Buddha Mahābhijñābhibhū (대통지 大通智 ; 승불 勝佛), mentioned in the Lotus Sūtra, i.e. a kalpa of incalculable antiquity, e.g. surpassing the number of the particles of a chiliocosm which has been ground to powder, turned into ink, and dropped, drop by drop, at vast distances throughout boundless space. 삼천대천세계 三千大千世界 Tri-sahasra-mahā-sahasra-loka-dhātu, a great chiliocosm ; 삼천 三千 ; 삼천(세)계 三千(世)界. Mt. Sumeru and its seven surrounding continents, eight seas and ring of iron mountains form one small world ; 1,000 of these form a small chiliocosm 소천세계 小千世界 ; 1,000 of these small chiliocosms form a medium chiliocosm 중천세계 中千世界 ; a thousand of these form a great chiliocosm 대천세계 大千世界, which thus consists of 1,000,000,000 small worlds. The 삼천 三千 indicates the above three kinds of thousands, therefore 삼천대천세계 三千大千世界 is the same as 대천세계 大千世界, which is one Buddha-world. 삼천실상 三千實相 The reality at the basis of all things, a T'ien-t'ai doctrine, i.e. the 진여 眞如 or 법성 法性 idem 제법실상 諸法實相. 삼천년일현 三千年一現. The udumbara flower which flowers but once in 3,000 years ; v. 우 優. 삼천위의 三千威儀 A bhikṣu's regulations amount to about 250 ; these are multiplied by four for the conditions of walking, standing, sitting, and sleeping and thus make 1,000 ; again multiplied by three for past, present, and future, they become 3,000 regulations. 삼천세계경 三千世界經 The sūtra of this name.

삼첨 三甜 The three sweet things — cream, honey, curd.

삼청 三請 A request thrice repeated — implying earnest desire.

삼초이목 三草二木 A parable in the Lotus Sūtra ; the small plants representing ordinary men and devas, medium sized plants śrāvakas and pratyeka-buddhas, and 대초 大草, 소수 小樹 and 대수 大樹 tall plants and small and large trees three grades of bodhisattvas. Another definition applies the term to the 오승 五乘 five "vehicles." There are also others.

삼취 三聚 The three groups, i.e. 정정취 正定聚 Those decided for the truth ; 사정취 邪定聚 those who are decided for heresy ; 부정취 不定聚 the undecided. Definitions vary in different schools. 삼취(정)계 三聚(淨)戒 The three cumulative commandments : (a) the formal 5, 8, or 10, and the rest ; (b) whatever works for goodness ; (c) whatever works for the welfare or salvation of living, sentient beings. 삼취원계 三聚圓戒 interprets the above three as implicit in each of the ten commandments, e.g. (a) not to kill implies (b) mercy and (c) protection or salvation.

삼치 三治 idem 삼삼매문 三三昧門 v. 삼해탈 三解脫.

삼칠일사유 三七日思惟 The twenty-one days spent by the Buddha, after his enlightenment, in walking round the bō-tree and considering how to carry his Mahāyāna way of salvation to the world ; v. 법화경방편품 法華經方便品.

삼탈문 三脫門 v. 삼해탈(문) 三解脫(門), but the former is only associated with 무루 無漏, or nirvāṇa.

삼토 三土 idem 삼불토 三佛土.

삼통력 三通力 idem 삼달 三達 and 삼명 三明.

삼퇴굴 三退屈 The three feelings of oppression that make for a bodhisattva's recreancy – the vastness of bodhi ; the unlimited call to sacrifice ; the uncertainty of final perseverance. There are 삼사연마 三事練磨 three modes of training against them.

삼파다 三波多 Samāpta ; finished, ended, perfect ; a term used at the conclusion of Homa or Fire-worship. 삼파라섭제 三波羅攝提 The three prajñapti, 삼가 三假 q.v. 삼파하 三波訶 Sampaha, according to Eitel, Malasa, a valley in the upper Punjab ; but perhaps Śāmbī, a state north of Citral in the Hindukush.

삼팔일 三八日 The eighth, eighteenth, and twenty-eighth days of a moon.

삼평등 三平等 The esoteric doctrine that the three – body, mouth, and mind – are one and universal. Thus in samādhi the Buddha "body" is found everywhere and in everything (pan-Buddha), every sound becomes a "true word," dhāraṇī or potent phrase, and these are summed up in mind, which being universal is my mind and my mind it, 입아아입 入我我入 it in me and I in it. Other definitions of the three are 불 佛, 법 法, 승 僧 the Triratna ; and 심 心, 불 佛, 중생 衆生 mind, Buddha, and the living. Also 삼삼매 三三昧. Cf. 삼밀 三密. v. 대일경 大日經 1. 삼평등지 三平等地 The three universal positions or stages, i.e. the three states expressed by 공 空, 무상 無相, and 무원 無願 ; v. 삼삼매지 三三昧地. idem 삼평등계 三平等戒 idem 삼매야계 三昧耶戒 and 삼세무장애지계 三世無障礙智戒. 삼평등관 三平等觀 idem 삼삼매관 三三昧觀. 삼평등호마단 三平等護摩壇 The three equal essentials of the fire sacrifice, i.e. the individual as offerer, the object of worship, and the altar.

삼품 三品 The general meaning is 상품 上品, 중품 中品, 하품 下品 superior, medium, inferior. 삼품실지 三品悉地 The three esoteric kinds of siddhi, i.e. complete attainment, supreme felicity. They are 상 上 superior, to be born in the 밀엄국 密嚴國 Vairocana Pure-land ; 중 中 in one of the other Pure-lands among which is the Western Paradise ; and 하 下 in the 수라궁 修羅宮 Sun palaces among the devas. Also styled 삼품성취 三品成就. 삼품사미 三品沙彌 The three grades of śrāmaṇera, i.e. 7-13 years old styled 구오사미 駈烏沙彌 ; 14-19 응법사미 應法沙彌 ; and 20 and upwards 명자사미 名字沙彌. 삼품청법 三品聽法 The three grades of hearers, i.e. 상 上 with the 신 神 spirit ; 중 中 with the 심 心 mind ; 하 下 with the 이 耳 ear.

삼학 三學 The "three studies" or vehicles of learning – discipline, meditation, wisdom : (a) 계학 戒學 learning by the commandments, or prohibitions, so as to guard against the evil consequences of error by mouth, body, or mind, i.e. word, deed, or thought ; (b) 정학 定學 by dhyāna, or quietist meditation ; (c) 혜학 慧學 by philosophy, i.e. study of principles and solving of doubts. Also the Tripiṭaka ; the 계 戒 being referred to the 율 律 vinaya, the 정 定 to the 경 經 sūtras, and the 혜 慧 to the 논 論 śāstras.

삼해탈(문) 三解脫(門) The three emancipations, idem 삼공 三空 and 삼삼매 三三昧 q.v. They are 공해탈 空解脫, 무상해탈 無相解脫 and 무작해탈 無作解脫. Cf. 삼열반문 三涅槃門.

삼행 三行 Three lines of action that affect karma, i.e. the ten good deeds that cause happy karma ; the ten evil deeds that cause unhappy karma ; 부동업 不動業 or 무동행 無動行 karma arising without activity, e.g. meditation on error and its remedy.

삼현십성 三賢十聖 ; **삼현십지** 三賢十地. The three virtuous positions, or states, of a bodhisattva are 십주 十住, 십행 十行 and 십회향 十廻向. The ten excellent characteristics of a 성 聖 saint or holy one are the whole of the 십지 十地.

삼협 三篋 idem 삼장 三藏 tripiṭaka.

삼형 三形 idem 삼매야형 三昧耶形.

삼혜 三慧 The three modes of attaining moral wisdom : 개혜 開慧 from reading, hearing, instruction ; 사혜 思慧 from reflection, etc. ; 수혜 修慧 from practice (of abstract meditation).

삼혹 三惑 A T'ien-t'ai classification of the three delusions, also styled 삼번뇌 三煩惱 ; 삼루 三漏 ; 삼구 三垢 ; 삼결 三結 ; trials or temptations, leakages, uncleannesses, and bonds. the first of the following three is common to all disciples, the two last to bodhisattvas. They arise from (a) 견 見, 사 思, 혹 惑 things seen and thought, i.e. illusions from imperfect perception, with temptation to love, hate, etc. ; to be rid of these false views and temptations is the discipline and nirvāṇa of ascetic or Hīnayāna Buddhists. Mahāyāna proceeds further in and by its bodhisattva aims, which produce their own difficulties, i.e. (b) 진사혹 塵沙惑 illusion and temptation through the immense variety of duties in saving men ; and (c) 무명혹 無明惑 the illusions and temptations that arise from failure philosophically to understand things in their reality.

삼화 三火 The three fires — desire, hate, and stupidity ; v. 삼독 三毒.

삼화 三和 The union of the three, i.e. 근 根 indriya, 경 境 ālambana, and 식 識 vijñāna, i.e. organ, object, and cognition.

삽 澁 Acrid, astringent, rough ; 삽촉 澁觸 one of the eight sensations of touch.

삽 颯 In gusts, suddenly. 삽말건 颯秣建 Samakan, the modern Samarkand. [Eitel]. 삽파치가 颯破檄迦 Sphaṭika, see 파 頗.

삽 揷 To insert, stick in. 삽단 揷單 To insert one's slip, or credentials.

삽 馺 v. 소 蘇 Svāhā.

상 祥 Felicitous. 상월 祥月 Felicitous month, an anniversary. 상서 祥瑞 Auspicious. 상초 祥草 The felicitous herb, or grass, that on which the Buddha sat when he attained enlightenment.

상 象 Gaja ; Hastin ; also Nāga ; an elephant ; v. 상 像 14. 상주 象主 The southern division of India, v. 사주 四主. 상견산 象堅山 Pīlusāragiri, a mountain southwest of Kapiśā, on the top of which Aśoka erected a stūpa, the Pīlusāra-stūpa. 상타갱 象墮阬 Hastigarta, "elephant's hold," i.e. the hollow formed by the elephant's fall, when Śākyamuni flung aside a dead elephant put in his path by Devadatta. 상존국 象尊國 The elephant-honouring country, India. 상교

象教 The teaching by images or symbols, i.e. Buddhism, v. 상교 像敎. 상아 象牙 Elephant's tusk, ivory. 상왕 象王 Gajapati, Lord of Elephants, a term for Śākyamuni ; also the fabulous ruler of the southern division of the Jambudvīpa continent. 상군 象軍 Hastikāya, the elephant corps of an Indian army. 상두산 象頭山 Gayāśīrṣa, tr. as elephant-head mountain, name of two mountains, one near Gayā, the other said to be near the river Nairañjanā, 150 li away. 상가 象駕 The elephant chariot, or riding forward, i.e. the eastward progress of Buddhism. 상비 象鼻 Elephant's trunk ; a wrong way of wearing a monk's robe.

상 相 Lakṣaṇa 락걸첨나 攞乞尖拏. Also, nimitta. A "distinctive mark, sign," "indication, characteristic," "designation." [M. W.] External appearance ; the appearance of things ; form ; a phenomenon 유위법 有爲法 in the sense of appearance ; mutual ; to regard. The four forms taken by every phenomenon are 생주이멸 生住異滅 rise, stay, change, cease, i.e. birth, life, old age, death. The Hua-yen school has a six-fold division of form, namely, whole and parts, together and separate, integrate and disintegrate. A Buddha or Cakravartī is recognized by his thirty-two lakṣaṇa, i.e. his thirty-two characteristic physiological marks. 상성 相性 Form and nature ; phenomenon and noumenon.

상 喪 Mourning. To lose ; destroy. 상친 喪襯 Gifts to monks for masses for the dead.

상 桑 Mulberry. 상갈야 桑渴耶 v. 승 僧 Saṅgha. 상문 桑門 v. 사 沙 Śramaṇa.

상 常 Nitya ; śāśvata. Prolonged, constant, always, unceasing, permanent, perpetual, ever, eternal ; normal, ordinary, regular. 상불경 常不輕 Sadāparibhūta, the monk who never slighted others, but assured all of Buddhahood, a former incarnation of Śākyamuni ; Lotus Sūtra 20. 상주 常住 Permanent, always abiding, eternal. 상주일상 常住一相 The eternal unity or reality behind all things. 상광 常光 The unceasing radiance of the Buddha's body, represented as a halo. 상력 常力 Unfailing powers. 상제보살 常啼菩薩 v. 살타 薩陀. 상경 常境 The eternal realm. 상적 常寂 Eternal peace, nirvāṇa. 상적광토 常寂光土 The realm (of spirit) where all are in perpetual peace and glory ; T'ien-t'ai's fourth Buddhakṣetra. 상항 常恒 Constantly. 상념 常念 Always remembering ; always repeating. 상지 常智 Knowledge *sub specie æternitatis*, not conditioned by phenomena, abstract. 상락아정 常樂我淨 The four pāramitās of knowledge: eternity, bliss, personality, purity, the four transcendental realities in nirvāṇa, v. Nirvāṇa Sūtra. 상몰 常沒 Ever drowning in the sea of mortality. 상바라밀 常波羅蜜 The first of the four pāramitās, eternity. 상안 常眼 The ordinary physical eye. 상립승번 常立勝幡 Anavanāmita-vaijayanta. With ever erect victorious banner ; name of Ānanda's future Buddha-realm. 상행 常行 Constantly doing, or practising ; ordinary procedure. 상견 常見 The view that (personality) is permanent. 상신 常身 The eternal Buddha-body, the Dharmakāya. 상도 常途 Regular ways, or methods. 상도 常道 Eternal Tao ; the way of eternity ; regular ways, the regulation path.

상 像 Pratirūpa ; pratirūpaka. Like, similar, resemblance ; semblance ; image ; portrait ; form, formal. 상화 像化 The religion of the image or symbol, Buddhism. Also the second or formal period of the teaching of Buddhism by symbol, v. 상법 像法. 상시 像始 The beginning of the formal period. 상계 像季 The end of that period. 상교 像敎 idem 상화 像化. 상말 像末 The two final stages of Buddhism. 상법 像法 Saddharma-pratirūpaka, the formal or image period of Buddhism ; the three periods are 정상말 正像末, those of the real, the formal, and the final ; or correct, semblance, and termination. The first period is of 500 years ; the second of 1,000 years ; the third 3,000 years, when Maitreya is to appear and restore all things. There are varied statements about periods and dates, e.g. there is a division of four periods, that while the Buddha was alive, the early stage after his death, then formal and the final periods. 상경 像經 Images and sūtras. 상운 像運 The period of formality, or symbolism.

상 商 To consult, arrange ; trade, a merchant ; translit. *śaṅ*, *śām*, *śa*, *śā*. 상거 商佉 ; 상가 商迦

Śaṅkha, 향거 餉佉 or 상거 傷佉 or 승거 勝佉 or 양거 儴佉 or 양거 蠰佉 or 상거 霜佉 ; 승가 勝伽 ; 상기라 商企羅 ; 상기라 償起羅 A conch, shell. 상갈라 商羯羅 Śaṅkara, "auspicious" [M. W.], a name for "Śiva," and intp. as 골쇄 骨鎖 bone-chains ; name of 상갈라아사리 商羯羅阿闍梨 Śaṅkarācārya the celebrated Indian philosopher of the eighth century A.D. who is known as a great opponent of Buddhism. 상낙(가)박사 商諾(迦)縛娑 ; 상나화수 商那和修 ; 사나화수 舍那和修 or 사나바사 舍那波私 Śāṇakavāsa ; Śaṇavāsa ; a younger brother of Ānanda. Also an arhat, whom Eitel gives as the third patriarch, a native of Mathurā, and says: "A Tibetan tradition identifies him with Yaśas, the leader of the II Synod." Because of his name he is associated with a hemp or linen garment, or a covering with which he was born. 상고 商賈 A trader, one of the vaiśya caste. 상량 商量 To consult, discuss together, e.g. as master and pupil.

상 傷 To injure, wound, hurt, harm, distress. A tr. of yakṣa. 상화기 傷和氣 To disturb the harmony. 상명 傷命 Injury to life.

상 償 To repay, compensate ; cf. 상 商.

상 想 To think, meditate, reflect, expect ; a function of mind. 상지옥 想地獄 Sañjīva, idem 등지옥 等地獄 the resurrecting hell. 상념 想念 To think and reflect. 상애 想愛 Thought of and desire for, thought leading to desire. 상온 想蘊 Sañjñā, one of the five skandhas, perception. 상전도 想顚倒 Inverted thoughts or perceptions, i.e. the illusion of regarding the seeming as real.

상 上 Uttara 올달라 嗢呾羅 ; above, upper, superior ; on ; former. To ascend, offer to a superior.

상간 上間 The superior rooms, i.e. on the right as one enters a monastery, the 하간 下間 are on the left.

상강 上綱 The "higher bond" or superior, the 상좌 上座 or Sthavira, among the three directors of a monastery. v. 삼강 三綱.

상견 上肩 Upper shoulder, i.e. the left or superior ; one worthy of respect. 상견순전 上肩順轉 Circumambulation with the superior shoulder to the image ; the left was formerly considered the superior side ; but this is uncertain.

상계천 上界天 The devas of the regions of form and formlessness. v. 색 色.

상공 相空 The unreality of form ; the doctrine that phenomena have no reality in themselves, in contrast with that of Hīnayāna which only held that the ego had no reality.

상공 上供 To offer up an offering to Buddha, or to ancestors.

상구본래 上求本來 Similar to the first half of 상구보리하화중생 上求菩提下化衆生 Above to seek bodhi, below to save all. 본래 本來 means the original or Buddha-nature, which is the real nature of all beings.

상근 上根 A man of superior character or capacity, e.g. with superior organs of sight, hearing, etc.

상당 上堂 To go into the hall to expound the doctrine ; to go to a temple for the purpose of worship, or bearing presents to the monks ; to go to the refectory for meals. 상당패 上堂牌 The tablet announcing the time of worship at a temple or monastery.

상대 相對 Opposite, opposed ; in comparison.

상대 相待 The doctrine of mutual dependence or relativity of all things for their existence, e.g. the triangle depends on its three lines, the eye on things having colour and form, long on short.

상대 相大 The greatness of the potentialities, or attributes of the Tathāgata ; v. the Awakening of Faith 기신론 起信論.

상랍 上臘 The "la" is the end of a summer's retreat, which ends the monastic year, hence 상랍 上臘 are senior, 하랍 下臘 junior monks.

상류(반) 上流(般) Ūrdhvasrotas. The flow upwards, or to go upwards against the stream of transmigration to parinirvāṇa. Also 상류반열반 上流般涅槃.

상륜 相輪 The sign or form of wheels, also 윤상 輪相, i.e. the nine wheels or circles at the top of a pagoda.

상명오법 相名五法 v. 오법 五法.

상모(궁)성 上茅(宮)城 Kuśāgrapura, 구사게라보라 矩奢揭羅補羅 city of Kuśa-grass palaces, or 산성 山城 the mountain city. v. 길상모국 吉祥茅國.

상무성 相無性 Unreal in phenomena, e.g. turtle-hair or rabbit's horns ; the unreality of phenomena, one of the 삼무성 三無性.

상박 相縛 To be bound by externals, by the six guṇas, or objects of sensation. Cf. 상응박 相應縛.

상방 上方 ; 상수 上手 An abbot. 상방 上方 originally meant a mountain monastery.

상배 上輩 Superior, or highest class, idem 상품 上品. 상배관 上輩觀 The fourteenth of the sixteen contemplations of the Amitābha School, with reference to those who seek the Pure Land with sincere, profound, and altruistic hearts.

상번뇌 上煩惱 The severe fundamental trials arising out of the ten great delusions ; also the trials or distresses of present delusions.

상분 相分 An idea, a mental eject ; a form.

상사 相似 Alike, like, similar, identical. 상사불 相似佛 Approximation or identity of the individual and Buddha, a doctrine of T'ien-t'ai ; the stage of 십신 十信. 상사즉(불) 相似卽(佛) One of the six of such identities, similarity in form. 상사각 相似覺 The approximate enlightenment which in the stages of 십주 十住, 십행 十行 and 십회향 十廻向 approximates to perfect enlightenment by the subjection of all illusion ; the second of the four degrees of bodhi in the Awakening of Faith 기신론 起信論.

상사 上士 The superior disciple, who becomes perfect in (spiritually) profiting himself and others. The 중사 中士 profits self but not others ; the 하사 下士 neither.

상상구절종 相想俱絶宗 One of the ten schools, as classified by Hsien-shou of Hua-yen, which sought to eliminate phenomena and thought about them, in favour of intuition.

상속 相續 Santati. Continuity, especially of cause and effect. 상속가 相續假 Illusory ideas continuously succeed one another producing other illusory ideas, one of the three hypotheses of the 성실론 成實論 Satya-siddhi-śāstra. 상속상 相續常 Nodal or successive continuity in contrast with 부단상 不斷常 uninterrupted continuity. 상속심 相續心 A continuous mind, unceasing thought. 상속상 相續相 Continuity of memory, or sensation, in regard to agreeables or disagreeables, remaining through other succeeding sensations, cf. 기신론 起信論 Awakening of Faith. 상속식 相續識 Continuity-consciousness which never loses any past karma or fails to mature it.

상수 上首 President, or presiding elders.

상승 上乘 Mahāyāna ; also 상연 上衍, 대승 大乘 q.v. 상승밀종 上乘密宗 The Mahāyāna esoteric school, especially the 진언 眞言 Shingon. 상승유가 上乘瑜伽 Mahāyāna-yoga, chiefly associated with the last. 상승선 上乘禪 The Mahāyāna Ch'an(Zen) School, which considers that it alone attains the highest realization of Mahāyāna truth. Hīnayāna philosophy is said only to realize the unreality of the ego and not the unreality of all things. The Mahāyāna realizes the unreality of the ego and of all things. But the Ch'an school is pure idealism, all being mind. This mind is Buddha, and is the universal fundamental mind.

상승 相承 Mutually receiving, handing on and receiving, mutually connected.

상연 上衍 Mahāyāna, 상승 上乘 ; v. 대승 大乘.

상원소등 上元燒燈 The lantern festival at the first full moon of the year.

상위인 相違因 Mutually opposing causes ; one of the 십인 十因.

상응 相應 Response, correspond, tally, agreement, yukta, or yoga, interpreted by 계합 契合 union of the tallies, one agreeing or uniting with the other. 상응인 相應因 Corresponding, or mutual causation, e.g. mind, or mental conditions causing mentation, and vice versa. 상응종 相應宗 Yoga, the sect of mutual response between the man and his object of worship, resulting in correspondence in body, mouth, and mind, i.e. deed, word, and thought ; it is a term for the Shingon or 진언 眞言 school. 상응법 相應法 The correspondence of mind with mental data dependent on five correspondences common to both, i.e. the senses, reasoning, process, time, and object. 상응아급마 相應阿笈摩 The Saṁyuktāgamas, or "miscellaneous" āgamas ; v. 아 阿. 상응박 相應縛 The bond (of illusion) which hinders the response of mind to the higher data.

상의 上衣 The superior or outer robe described as of twenty-five patches, and styled the uttara saṅghāṭī.

상인 上人 A man of superior wisdom, virtue, and conduct, a term applied to monks during the T'ang dynasty. 상상인 上上人 A term used in the Pure-land sect for a worshipper of Amitābha.

상입 相入 Mutual entry ; the blending of things, e.g. the common light from many lamps.

상전 上轉 The upward turn : (1) progress upward, especially in transmigration ; (2) increase in enlightenment for self, while 하전 下轉 q.v. is for others.

상제 上祭 To place offerings on an altar ; also 하제 下祭.

상족 上足 A superior disciple or follower.

상종 相宗 idem 법상종 法相宗.

상좌 上座 Sthavira ; or Mahāsthavira. Old man, or elder ; head monk, president, or abbot, the first Buddhist fathers ; a title of Mahākāśyapa ; also of monks of twenty to forty-nine years standing, as 중좌 中座 are from ten to nineteen and 하좌 下座 under ten. The 석씨요람 釋氏要覽 divides presiding elders into four classes, those presiding over monasteries, over assemblies of monks, over sects, and laymen presiding over feasts to monks. 상좌부 上座部 ; 타비리여부 他毘梨與部 ; 타비라부 他鞞羅部 Sthavirāḥ ; Sthaviranikāya ; or Āryasthāvirāḥ. The school of the presiding elder, or elders. The two earliest sections of Buddhism were this (which developed into the Mahāsthavira) and the Mahāsāṅghikāḥ or 대중부 大衆部. At first they were not considered to be different schools, the 상좌부 上座部 merely representing the intimate and older disciples of Śākyamuni and the 대중 大衆 being the rest. It is said that a century later under Mahādeva 대천 大天 a difference of opinion arose on certain doctrines. Three divisions are named as resulting, viz. Mahāvihāravāsinaḥ, Jetavanīyāḥ, and Abhayagiri-vāsinaḥ. These were in Ceylon.

In course of time the eighteen Hīnayāna sects were developed. From the time of Aśoka four principal schools are counted as prevailing : Mahāsāṅghikāḥ, Sthavira, Mūlasarvāstivādāḥ, and Saṁmitīya. The following is a list of the eleven sects reckoned as of the 상좌부 上座部 : 설일체유부 說一切有部 ; 설산 雪山 ; 독자 犢子 ; 법상 法上 ; 현주 賢胄 ; 정량 正量 ; 밀림산 密林山 ; 화지 化地 ; 법장 法藏 ; 음광 飮光 ; and 경량부 輕量部. The Sthaviravādin is reputed as nearest to early Buddhism in its tenets, though it is said to have changed the basis of Buddhism from an agnostic system to a realistic philosophy.

상중하법 上中下法 The three dharmas, systems, or vehicles, 보살 菩薩, 연각 緣覺, and 성문 聲聞 bodhisattva, pratyeka-buddha, and śrāvaka.

상즉 相卽 Phenomenal identity, e.g. the wave is water and water the wave.

상지 相智 Knowledge derived form phenomena.

상착의 上著衣 A monk's outer robe, uttara saṅghāṭī, worn over the shirt or antaravāsaka.

상취 上趣 The higher gati, directions, or transmigrations.

상품 上品 Superior order, grade, or class. 상품상생 上品上生 ; 상품중생 上品中生 ; 상품하생 上品下生 The three highest of the nine stages of birth in the Pure Land, v. 중품 中品, 하품 下品 and 구품 九品. 상품연대 上品蓮臺 The highest stages in the Pure Land where the best appear as lotus flowers on the pool of the seven precious things ; when the lotuses open they are transformed into beings of the Pure Land.

상행보살 上行菩薩 Viśiṣṭa-cāritra Bodhisattva, who suddenly rose out of the earth as Buddha was concluding one of his Lotus sermons ; v. Lotus sūtra 15 and 21. He is supposed to have been a convert of the Buddha in long past ages and to come to the world in its days of evil. Nichiren in Japan believed himself to be this Bodhisattva's reincarnation, and the Nichiren trinity is the Buddha, i.e. the eternal Śākyamuni Buddha ; the Law, i.e. the Lotus Truth ; and the Saṅgha, i.e. this Bodhisattva, in other words Nichiren himself as the head of all living beings, or eldest son of the Buddha.

상호 相好 Lakṣaṇa-vyañjana ; the thirty-two 상 相 or marks and the eighty 호 好 or signs on the physical body of Buddha. The marks on a Buddha's sambhogakāya number 84,000. 상 相 is intp. as larger signs, 호 好 as smaller ; but as they are also intp. as marks that please, 호 好 may be a euphemism for 호 號.

새 賽 Money offerings 새전 賽錢 (to the Buddhas or gods) ; to compete.

새 塞 To stop up, block, gag ; dull ; honest ; a barrier, frontier ; translit. s. 새건다(라) 塞建陀(羅) ; 새건타 塞健陀 Skandha, "the shoulder" ; "the body" ; "the trunk of a tree" ; "a section," etc. [M. W.] "Five psychological constituents." "Five attributes of every human being." [Eitel]. Commonly known as the five aggregates, constituents, or groups ; the pañcaskandha ; under the Han dynasty 음 陰 was used, under the Chin 중 衆, under the T'ang 온 蘊. The five are: 색 色 Rūpa, form, or sensuous quality ; 수 受 Vedanā, reception, feeling, sensation ; 상 想 Sañjñā, thought, consciousness, perception ; 행 行 Karman, or Saṁskāra, action, mental activity ; 식 識 Vijñāna, cognition. The last four are mental constituents of the ego. Skandha is also the name of an arhat, and Skanda, also 새건나 塞健那, of a deva. 새필력가 塞畢力迦 Spṛkkā, clover, lucern. 새박실지가 塞縛悉底迦 Svastika, v. 만 萬. 새파지가 塞頗胝加 Sphaṭika, crystal, quartz, one of the saptaratna, seven treasures.

색 色 Rūpa, outward appearance, form, colour, matter, thing ; the desirable, especially feminine attraction. It is defined as that which has resistance ; or which changes and disappears, i.e. the phenomenal ; also as 현 顯, 형 形 and 표색 表色 colour and quality, form or the measurable, and mode or action. There are divisions of two, i.e. inner and outer, as the organs and objects of sense ; also colour and form ; or three, i.e. the visible object, e.g. colour, the invisible object, e.g. sound, the invisible and immaterial ; of eleven, i.e. the five organs and five objects of sense and the immaterial object ; of fourteen, the five organs and five objects of sense and the four elements, earth, water, fire, air. Rūpa is one of the six Bāhya-āyatana, the 육진 六塵 ; also one of the five Skandhas, 오온 五蘊, i.e. the 색신 色身. Keith refers to Rūpa as "material form or matter which is underived (no-utpādā) and which is derived (utpādā)," the underived or independent being the tangible ; the derived or dependent being the sense, e.g. of hearing ; most of their objects, e.g. sound ; the qualities or faculties of femininity, masculinity, vitality ; intimation by act and speech ; space ; qualities of matter, e.g. buoyancy ; and physical nutriment.

색개 色蓋 The concealing, or misleading, character of the visible or material, the seeming concealing reality.

색경 色境 Visible objects, the realm of vision, or form.

색계 色界 Rūpadhātu, or rūpāvacara, or rūpaloka, any material world, or world of form ; it especially refers to the second of the Trailokya 삼계 三界, the Brahmalokas above the Devalokas, comprising sixteen or seventeen or eighteen "Heavens of Form," divided into four Dhyānas, in which life lasts from one-fourth of a mahākalpa to 16,000 mahākalpas, and the average stature is from one-half a yojana to 16,000 yojanas. The inhabitants are above the desire for sex or food. The Rūpadhātu, with variants, are given as — 초선천 初禪天 The first dhyāna heavens : 범중천 梵衆天 Brahmapāriṣadya, 범보천 梵輔天 Brahmapurohita or Brahmakāyika, 대범천 大梵天 Mahābrahmā. 이선천 二禪天 The second dhyāna heavens : 소광천 少光天 Parīttābha, 무량광천 無量光天 Apramāṇābha, 광음천 光音天 Ābhāsvara. 삼선천 三禪天 The third dhyāna heavens : 소정천 少淨天 Parīttaśubha, 무량정천 無量淨天 Apramāṇaśubha, 변정천 徧淨天 Śubhakṛtsna. 사선천 四禪天 The fourth dhyāna heavens : 무운천 無雲天 Anabhraka, 복생천 福生天 Puṇyaprasava, 광과천 廣果天 Bṛhatphala, 무상천 無想天 Asañjñisattva, 무번천 無煩天 Avṛhās, 무열천 無熱天 Atapās, 선현천 善現天 Sudṛśa, 선견천 善見天 Sudarśana, 색구경천 色究竟天 Akaniṣṭha, 화음천 和音天 Aghaniṣṭha, 대자재천 大自在天 Mahāmaheśvara.

색공외도 色空外道 Heretics who denied material existence (and consequently sought self-control, or nirvāṇa).

색광 色光 Physical light, as contrasted with 심광 心光 light of the mind ; every Buddha has both, e.g. his halo.

색구 色具 Material objects.

색구경천 色究竟天 ; **색정** 色頂 Akaniṣṭha, the highest of the material heavens.

색미 色微 Atoms of things, of form, or colour.

색미 色味 The flavour of sexual attraction, love of women.

색상 色相 The material, material appearance, or external manifestation, the visible. 색상토 色相土 A Buddha's material or visible world.

색성 色聲 The visible and audible.

색신 色身 Rūpa-kāya. The physical body, as contrasted with the 법신 法身 dharma-kāya, the immaterial, spiritual, or immortal body.

색심 色心 Matter and mind, the material and immaterial.

색온 色蘊 The skandha of rūpa, or that which has form, v. 오온 五蘊.

색욕 色欲 Sexual desire, or passion.

색유 色有 Material existence.

색입 色入 ; **색처** 色處 The entrances, or places, where the organs and objects of physical sense meet, ten in all ; cf. 오입 五入. Also, one of the twelve nidānas.

색제 色諦 idem 가제 假諦.

색중 色衆 idem 색온 色蘊, 색음 色陰.

색진 色塵 The quality of form, colour, or sexual attraction, one of the 육진 六塵.

색처 色處 idem 색입 色入.

색포 色泡 ; **색염** 色焰 The material as a bubble, or a flame ; impermanent.

생 生 Jāti 야다 惹多 ; life ; Utpāda means coming forth, birth, production ; 생 生 means beget, bear, birth, rebirth, born, begin, produce, life, the living. One of the twelve nidānas, 십이인연 十二因緣 ; birth takes place in four forms, catur yoni, v. 사생 四生, in each case causing a sentient being to enter one of the 육도 六道 six gati, or paths of transmigration.

생경 生經 Stories of the previous incarnations of the Buddha and his disciples, tr. by Dharmapāla, 5 chüan, third century A.D.

생공 生空 Empty at birth, i.e. 아공 我空, 인공 人空 void of a permanent ego.

생기 生起 Birth and what arises from it ; cause of an act ; the beginning and rise.

생념처보살 生念處菩薩 The second Bodhisattva on the right of the Bodhisattva of Space 허공장 虛空藏 in the Garbhadhātu.

생도 生途 The way or lot of those born, i.e. of mortality.

생령 生靈 The mind or intelligence of the living ; a living intelligent being ; a living soul.

생로병사 生老病死 Birth, age, sickness, death, the 사고 四苦 four afflictions that are the lot of every man. The five are the above four and 고 苦 misery, or suffering.

생맹 生盲 Born blind.

생멸 生滅 Utpādanirodha. Birth and death, production and annihilation ; all life, all phenomena, have birth and death, beginning and end ; the 삼론 三論 Mādhyamika school deny this in the 실 實 absolute, but recognize it in the 가 假 relative. 생멸거래 生滅去來 Coming into existence and ceasing to exist, past and future, are merely relative terms and not true in reality ; they are the first two antitheses in the 중론 中論 Mādhyamika-śāstra, the other two antitheses being 일이단상 一異斷常 unity and difference, impermanence and permanence.

생반 生飯 ; **출반** 出飯 Offerings made before a meal of a small portion of food to ghosts and all the living ; cf. Nirvāṇa sūtra 16, and Vinaya 잡사 雜事 31. 생대 生臺 A board on which the offerings are placed. 생반 生盤 The bowl in which they are contained.

생법 生法 The living and things, i.e. 인법 人法, 아법 我法 men and things, the self and things ; the 유정 有情 sentient, or those with emotions, i.e. the living ; and 비정 非情 those without, i.e. insentient things. 생법이신 生法二身 The physical body and the spiritual body of the Buddha : the Nirmāṇakāya and Dharmakāya.

생보 生報 Life's retribution, i.e. the deeds done in this life produce their results in the next reincarnation.

생불 生佛 Buddha alive ; a living Buddha ; also 생 生, i.e. 중생 衆生 all the living, and 불 佛, i.e. Buddha. 생불일여 生佛一如 ; 생불일체 生佛一體 ; 생불불이 生佛不二 ; 범성일여 凡聖一如 The living and the Buddha are one, i.e. all are the one undivided whole, or absolute ; they are all of the same substance ; all are Buddha, and of the same 법신 法身 dharmakāya, or spiritual nature ; all are of the same 공 空 infinity. 생불부증불멸 生佛不增不滅 The indestructibility of the living and the Buddha ; they neither increase nor decrease, being the absolute. 생불가명 生佛假名 The living and the Buddha are but temporary names, borrowed or derived for temporal indication.

생사 生死 Saṁsāra ; birth and death ; rebirth and redeath ; life and death ; 생사 生死, 사생 死生 ; 생생사사 生生死死 ever-recurring saṁsāra or transmigrations ; the round of mortality. There are two, three, four, seven, and twelve kinds of 생사 生死 ; the two are 분단생사 分斷生死 the various karmaic transmigrations, and 부사의변역생사 不思義變易生死 the inconceivable transformation life in the Pure Land. Among the twelve are final separation from mortality of the arhat, with 무여 無餘 no remains of it causing return ; one final death and no rebirth of the anāgāmin ; the seven advancing rebirths of the śrota-āpanna ; down to the births-cum-deaths of hungry ghosts. 생사즉열반 生死卽涅槃 Mortality is nirvāṇa, but there are varying definitions of 즉 卽 q.v. 생사원 生死園 The garden of life-and-death, this mortal world in which the unenlightened find their satisfaction. 생사(대)해 生死(大)海 The ocean of mortality, mortal life, 윤회 輪廻 saṁsāra, or transmigrations. 생사안 生死岸 The shore of mortal life ; as 생사류 生死流 is its flow ; 생사니 生死泥 its quagmire ; 생사연 生死淵 its abyss ; 생사야 生死野 its wilderness ; 생사운 生死雲 its envelopment in cloud. 생사해탈 生死解脫 Release from the bonds of births-and-deaths, nirvāṇa. 생사륜 生死輪 The wheel of births-and-deaths, the round of mortality. 생사장야 生死長夜 The long night of births-and-deaths. 생사제 生死際 The region of births-and-deaths, as compared with that of nirvāṇa.

생상 生像 ; **생사** 生似 Natural and similar, i.e. gold and silver, gold being the natural and perfect metal and colour ; silver being next, though it will tarnish ; the two are also called 생색 生色 and 가염 可染 i.e. the proper natural (unchanging) colour, and the tarnishable.

생색 生色 Jāta-rūpa ; gold, v. 생상 生像.

생생 生生 Birth and rebirth (without end).

생신 生身 The physical body ; also that of a Buddha in contrast with his 법신 法身 dharmakāya ; also a bodhisattva's body when born into any mortal form. 생신공 生身供 The worship paid to Buddha-relics, 생신사리 生身舍利.

생유 生有 One of the four forms of existence, cf. 유 有.

생인 生忍 Common or ordinary patience, i.e. of 중생 衆生 the masses.

생전 生田 The three regions 삼계 三界 of the constant round of rebirth.

생조융예 生肇融叡 Four great disciples of Kumārajīva, the Indian Buddhajīva or 도생 道生 Tao-shêng and the three Chinese 승조 僧肇 Sêng-chao, 도융 道融 Tao-jung, and 승예 僧叡 Sêng-jui.

생주이멸 生住異滅 Birth, stay, change (or decay), death.

생즉무생, 무생즉생 生卽無生, 無生卽生 To be born is not to be born, not to be born is to be born — an instance of the identity of contraries. It is an accepted doctrine of the 반야 般若 prajñā teaching and the ultimate doctrine of the 삼론 三論 Mādhyamika school. Birth, creation, life, each is but a 가 假 temporary term, in common statement 속제 俗諦 it is called birth, in truth 진제 眞諦 it is not birth ; in the relative it is birth, in the absolute non-birth.

생지 生支 Liṅga ; aṅgajāta ; the male organ, penis.

생진 生津 The ford of life, or mortality.

생천 生天 The heavens where those living in this world can be reborn, i.e. from that of the 사천왕 四天王 to the 비상천 非想天 ; v. 복생천 福生天.

생취 生趣 The 사생 四生 four forms of birth and the 육취 六趣 six forms of transmigration.

생화 生化 ; **화생** 化生 Aupapāduka ; one of the four forms of birth, i.e. by transformation, without parentage, and in full maturity ; thus do bodhisattvas come from the Tuṣita heaven ; the dhyāni-buddhas and bodhisattvas are also of such miraculous origin. 생화이신 生化二身 The physical body of Buddha and his transformation body capable of any form ; the Nirmāṇakāya in its two forms of 응 應 and 화 化.

서 庶 A multitude ; all ; the ; a concubine ; so that ; nearly so. 서류 庶類 The common people.

서 瑞 Auspicious ; a jade token. 서상 瑞像 Auspicious image, especially the first image of Śākyamuni made of sandalwood and attributed to Udayana, king of Kauśāmbī, a contemporary of Śākyamuni. Cf. 서역기 西域記 5. 서응 瑞應 Auspicious response, the name of the Udumbara flower, v. 우 優. 서상 瑞相 Auspicious, auspicious sign, or aspect.

서 書 Likh ; to write ; pustaka, a writing, book ; lekha, a letter, document. 서사 書寫 To write, record ; a recorder. 서기 書記 A record.

서 鼠 Mūṣa ; ākhu ; a mouse, rat. 백흑이서 白黑二鼠 The two mice in the parable, one white, the other black, gnawing at the rope of life, i.e. day and night, or sun and moon. 서즉조공 鼠喞鳥空 Vain discussions, like rat-squeakings and cuckoo-callings.

서 逝 Pass away, depart, die, evanescent. 서다 逝多 Jeta ; Jetṛ ; v. 기 祇. 서궁 逝宮 The transient mansions of Brahmā and of men. Astronomical "mansions." 서슬타 逝瑟吒 The month Jyaiṣṭha (May-June), when the full moon is in the constellation Jyeṣṭhā.

서 西 Paścima, 파실제마 跛室制摩 ; west ; it is largely used in the limited sense of Kashmir in such terms as 서방 西方 the west, or western regions ; but it is also much used for the western heavens of Amitābha ; 서천 西天 is India, the western 천축국 天竺國. 서주 西主 The Lord of the West, Amitābha, who is also the 서천교주 西天教主 load of the cult, or sovereign teacher, of the western paradise. 서건 西乾 A name for India, cf. 서천 西天. 서니가 西儞迦 ; 선니 先尼 Sainika, military. 서광 西光 The light of the western paradise. 서찰 西刹 Kṣetra, land, region, country.

서 棲 Roost, rest. 서광 棲光 To bring his light to rest, the Buddha's nirvāṇa. 서신 棲身 To take one's rest, retire from the world. 서신 棲神 To rest the spirit, or mind, be unperturbed.

서 序 Seriatim ; preface, introduction ; the opening phrase of a sūtra, "Thus have I heard" ; an opening phrase leading up to a subject. 서왕 序王 The introduction by Chin-i to the Lotus sūtra. Introductions are divided into 서 序, 정 正, and 유통 流通, the first relating to the reason for the book ; the second to its method ; and the third to its subsequent history.

서 誓 To swear, vow, engage to, enter into a contract. 서약 誓約 To swear and engage to. 서원 誓願 To swear and vow, e.g. the forty-eight vows of Amitābha to save all beings.

서산대사 西山大師 see 휴정 休靜.

서역구법고승전 西域求法高僧傳 Biographies of famous pilgrims, fifty-six in number, with four added ; it is by I-ching 의정 義淨. 서역기 西域記 ; 대당서역기 大唐西域記 ; 서역전 西域傳 Records of Western countries, by the T'ang dynasty pilgrim 현장 玄奘 Hsüan-tsang, in 12 chüan A.D. 646-8. There was a previous 서역전 西域傳 by 언종 彥琮 Yen-Ts'ung of the Sui dynasty. 서산주부 西山住部 Avaraśailāḥ 아벌라숙라 阿伐羅塾羅 the second subdivision of the Mahāsāṅghikāḥ school. A monastery of this name was in Dhana-kaṭaka, said to have been built 600 B.C., deserted A.D. 600. 서서 西序 ; 서반 西班 The western group, i.e. teaching monks stood on the west of the abbot, while those engaged in practical affairs stood on the east ; this was in imitation of the Court practice in regard to civil and military officials. 서방 西方 The west, especially Amitābha's Western Pure Land 서방정토 西方淨土, Sukhāvatī or Paradise 서방극락세계 西方極樂世界, to which Amitābha is the guide and welcomer 서방접인 西方接引. 서명 西明 Hsi-ming, name of 도선 道宣 Tao-hsüan of the T'ang who founded the Southern Hill school, and also of 문아원측 文雅圓測 Yüan-ts'ê, both of whom were from the 서명사 西明寺 monastery of Western Enlightenment established by Kao Tsung (650-684) at Ch'ang-an, the capital. 서만다라 西曼陀羅 The "western" maṇḍala is that of the Vajradhātu, as the "eastern" is of the Garbhadhātu. 서하 西河 Hsi-ho, a name for 도작 道綽 Tao-ch'o of the T'ang dynasty. 서정 西淨 The western cleanser, the privy, situated on the west of a monastery. 서우화주 西牛貨洲 ; 서구다니 西瞿陀尼 or 서구야니 西瞿耶尼 The western continent of a world, Godānīya, v. 구 瞿, or Aparagodānīya, or Aparagodāna, "western-cattle-giving," where cattle are the medium of exchange, possibly referring to the "pecuniary" barter of the north-west. 서장 西藏 Tibet ; 서장불교 西藏佛教 Tibetan Buddhism, 서장라마교 西藏喇嘛教 Tibetan Lamaism. 서행 西行 Going west ; practices of the Amitābha cult, leading to salvation in the Western Paradise.

석 夕 Evening. 석좌 夕座 The evening service, as 조좌 朝座 is the morning service.

석 昔 Of old, formerly. 석리 昔哩 Śrī, fortunate, idem 실리 室利 or 시리 尸利.

석 錫 Pewter, tin ; to bestow ; a monk's staff. 석장 錫丈 Khakkhara, a monk's staff partly of metal, especially with metal rings for shaking to make announcement of one's presence, and also used for demon expulsion, etc. 석륜 錫崙 Ceylon.

석 石 Stone, rock. 화석 畫石 A painting of a rock ; though the water of the water-colour rapidly disappears, the painting remains. 난석석열 難石石裂 Even a rock meeting hard treatment will split. 석벽경 石壁經 Sūtras cut in stone in A.D. 829 in the 중현사 重玄寺 Ch'ung-hsüan temple, Soo-chow, where Po Chü-i put up a tablet. They consist of 69,550 words of the 법화 法華, 27,092 of the 유마 維摩, 5,287 of the 금강 金剛, 3,020 of the 존승다라니 尊勝陀羅尼, 1,800 of the 아미타 阿彌陀, 6,990 of the 보현행법 普賢行法, 3,150 of the 실상법밀 實相法密, and 258 of the 반야심경 般若心經. 석녀 石女 A barren woman ; a woman incompetent for sexual intercourse. 석녀아 石女兒 Son of a barren woman, an impossibility. 석류 石榴 The pomegranate, symbol of many children because of its seeds ; a symbol held in the hand of 귀자모신 鬼子母神 Hāritī, the deva-mother of demons, converted by the Buddha. 석화 石火 Tinder ; lighted tinder, i.e. of but momentary existence. 석경산 石經山 The hill with the stone sūtras, which are said to have been carved in the Sui dynasty in grottoes on 백대산 白帶山 Pai Tai Shan, west of 착주 涿州 Cho-chou in Shun-t'ien-fu, Chihli. 석밀 石蜜 Stone honey ; a toffee, made of sugar, or sugar and cream (or butter). 석발 石鉢 The four heavy stone begging-bowls handed by the four devas to the Buddha on his enlightenment, which he miraculously received one piled on the other.

ㄱ ㄴ ㄷ ㄹ ㅁ ㅂ ㅅ ㅇ ㅈ ㅊ ㅋ ㅌ ㅍ ㅎ 찾아보기

석 惜 To care for, regard, compassionate, pity ; spare. 석낭 惜囊 To be as careful of (the monastic law as of) the skin-floats when swimming a river.

석 析 To divide, separate, differentiate, explain. 분석 分析 To divide ; leave the world ; separation. 석소 析小 To traverse or expose the fallacy of Hīnayāna arguments. 석미진 析微塵 To subdivide molecules till nothing is reached. 석수 析水 To rinse (the alms-bowl). 석지 析智 Analytical wisdom, which analyses Hīnayāna dharmas and attains to the truth that neither the ego nor things have a basis in reality.

석 釋 To separate out, set free, unloose, explain ; Buddhism, Buddhist ; translit. *śa, śi* ; also *ḍ, ḍh.*

석가 釋家 The Śākya family, i.e. the expounders of Buddhist sūtras and scriptures.

석가 釋迦 Śākya, the clan or family of the Buddha, said to be derived from śāka, vegetables, but intp. in Chinese as powerful, strong, and explained by 능 能 powerful, also erroneously by 인 仁 charitable, which belongs rather to association with Śākyamuni. The clan, which is said to have wandered hither from the delta of the Indus, occupied a district of a few thousand square miles lying on the slopes of the Nepalese hills and on the plains to the south. Its capital was Kapilavastu. At the time of Buddha the clan was under the suzerainty of Kosala, an adjoining kingdom. Later Buddhists, in order to surpass Brahmans, invented a fabulous line of five kings of the Vivartakalpa headed by Mahāsaṁmata 대삼말다 大三末多 ; these were followed by five cakravartī, the first being Mūrdhaja 정생왕 頂生王 ; after these came nineteen kings, the first being Cetiya 사제 捨帝, the last Mahādeva 대천 大天 ; these were succeeded by dynasties of 5,000, 7,000, 8,000, 9,000, 10,000, 15,000 kings ; after which king Gautama opens a line of 1,100 kings, the last, Ikṣvāku, reigning at Potala. With Ikṣvāku the Śākyas are said to have begun. His four sons reigned at Kapilavastu. "Śākyamuni was one of his descendants in the seventh generation." Later, after the destruction of Kapilavastu by Virūḍhaka, four survivors of the family founded the kingdoms of Udyāna, Bamyam, Himatala, and Śāmbī. [Eitel]. 석가(파) 釋迦(婆) Śakra. 석가제바인(다라) 釋迦提婆因(陀羅) ; 석가제환인(다라) 釋迦提桓因(陀羅) Śakra-devendra ; Śakro-devānāmindra ; v. 석제 釋帝, i.e. Indra. 석가존 釋迦尊 The honoured one of the Śākyas, i.e. Śākyamuni. 석가모니 釋迦牟尼 ; 석가문(니) 釋迦文(尼) ; 가문 伽文 Śākyamuni, the saint of the Śākya tribe. Muni is saint, holy man, sage, ascetic, monk ; it is intp. as 인 仁 benevolent, charitable, kind, also as 적묵 寂默 one who dwells in seclusion. After "500 or 550" previous incarnations, Śākyamuni finally attained to the state of Bodhisattva, was born in the Tuṣita heaven, and descended as a white elephant, through her right side, into the womb of the immaculate Māyā, the purest woman on earth ; this was on the 8th day of the 4th month ; next year on the 8th day of the 2nd month he was born from her right side painlessly as she stood under a tree in the Lumbinī garden. For the subsequent miraculous events v. Eitel, also the 신통유희경 神通遊戲經 또는 神通遊戲經 (Lalitavistara), the 석가여래성도기 釋迦如來成道記, etc. Simpler statements say that he was born the son of Śuddhodana, of the kṣatriya caste, ruler of Kapilavastu, and Māyā his wife ; that Māyā died seven days later, leaving him to be brought up by her sister Prajāpati ; that in due course he was married to Yaśodharā who bore him a son, Rāhula ; that in search of truth he left home, became an ascetic, severely disciplined himself, and finally at 35 years of age, under a tree, realized that the way of release from the chain of rebirth and death lay not in asceticism but in moral purity ; this he explained first in his four dogmas, v. 사제 四諦 and eightfold noble way 팔정도 八正道, later amplified and developed in many sermons. He founded his community on the basis of poverty, chastity, and insight or meditation, and it became known as Buddhism, as he became known as Buddha, the enlightened. His death was probably in or near 487 B.C., a few years before that of Confucius in 479. The sacerdotal name of his family is Gautama, said to be the original name of the whole clan, Śākya being that of his branch, v. 구 瞿, 교 喬 ; his personal name was Siddhārtha, or Sarvārthasiddha, v. 실 悉. 석가사자 釋迦獅子 Śākyasiṁha, the lion of the Śākyas, i.e. the Buddha. 석가보살 釋迦菩薩 Śākya-bodhisattva, one of the previous incarnations of the Buddha.

석교 釋敎 Buddhism ; the teaching or school of Śākyamuni.

석궁 釋宮 The Śākya palace, from which prince Siddhārtha went forth to become Buddha.

석녀 釋女 The women of the Śākya clan.

석등 石燈 Stone lantern.

석려 釋侶 Any follower or disciple of the Buddha ; any Buddhist comrade ; Buddhists.

석론 釋論 The Prajñā-pāramitā-sūtra ; also explanatory discussions, or notes on foundation treatises.

석륜 釋輪 Śakra's wheel, the discus of Indra, symbol of the earth.

석마남 釋摩男 Śākya Mahānāma Kulika, one of the first five of the Buddha's disciples, i.e. prince Kulika.

석문 釋門 The school of Śākyamuni, Buddhism.

석범 釋梵 Indra and Brahma, both protectors of Buddhism.

석사 釋師 The Śākya teacher, Buddha. 석사자 釋師子 The lion of the Śākyas, Buddha.

석시(수) 釋翅(搜) Śākyeṣu, defined as a name for Kapilavastu city ; also 석씨수 釋氏度.

석씨 釋氏 The Śākya clan, or family name ; Śākyamuni.

석웅 釋雄 The hero of the Śākyas, Buddha ; also 세웅 世雄.

석의 釋疑 Explanation of doubtful points, solution of doubts.

석자 釋子 Śākyaputrīya, sons of Śākyamuni, i.e. his disciples in general.

석장 釋藏 The Śākya thesaurus, i.e. the Tripiṭaka, the Buddhist scriptures, cf. 장 藏.

석전 釋典 The scriptures of Buddhism.

석제 釋帝 Śakra, Indra, lord of the thirty-three heavens ; also 제석 帝釋 ; 석가(파) 釋迦(婆) q.v.

석제환인 釋提桓因 Śakro-devānāmindra, 석 釋 Śakra 제환 提桓 devānām 인 因 Indra ; Śakra the Indra of the devas, the sky-god, the god of the nature-gods, ruler of the thirty-three heavens, considered by Buddhists as inferior to the Buddhist saint, but as a deva-protector of Buddhism. Also 석라 釋羅 ; 사갈라인다라 賒羯羅因陀羅 ; 제석 帝釋 ; 석제 釋帝 ; v. 석가 釋迦. He has numerous other appellations.

석종 釋種 Śākya-seed ; the Śākya clan ; the disciples of Śākyamuni, especially monks and nuns.

석풍 釋風 The custom of Buddhism ; also its "breeze" or progress.

선 綫 Thread ; a clue, continuation. An intp. of sūtra.

선 仙 ; 선 僊 Ṛṣi, 리시 哩始 an immortal ; 선인 仙人 ; 인선 人仙 the genii, of whom there is a famous group of eight 팔선 八仙 ; an ascetic, a man of the hills, a hermit ; the Buddha. The 능엄경

楞嚴經 gives ten kinds of immortals, walkers on the earth, fliers, wanderers at will, into space, into the deva heavens, transforming themselves into any form, etc. The names of ten ṛṣis, who preceded Śākyamuni, the first being 사제수나 闍提首那 Jātiṣenā ; there is also a list of sixty-eight 대선 大仙 given in the 대공작주왕경 大孔雀咒王經 下. A classification of five is 천선 天仙 deva genii, 신선 神仙 spirit genii, 인선 人仙 human genii, 지선 地仙 earth, or cavern genii, and 귀선 鬼仙 ghost genii. 선인녹야원 仙人鹿野苑 ; 선인녹원 仙人鹿園, 선원 仙苑 The Mṛgadāva, a deer park N.E. of Vārāṇaśī, "a favourite resort of Śākyamuni. The modern Sārnāth (Śāraṅganātha) near Benares." [Eitel]. 선성 仙城 The Ṛṣi's city, i.e. the Buddha's native city, Kapilavastu. 선경 仙經 Taoist treatises on alchemy and immortality. 선음 仙音 The voice of Buddha. 선록왕 仙鹿王 The royal-stag Genius, i.e. Buddha.

선 船 A boat, ship. 선사 船師 Captain, i.e. the Buddha as captain of salvation, ferrying across to the nirvāṇa shore. 선벌 船筏 A boat, or raft, i.e. Buddhism.

선 線 A thread, wire, clue, spy, lead, connection. 선향 線香 Thread or string incense, slow-burning and prolonged.

선 扇 Fan ; door-leaf ; translit. ś, ṣ. 선지가 扇底迦 Śāntika, propitiatory, producing ease or quiet ; a ceremony for causing calamities to cease. 선체 扇搋 ; 선반택가 扇半擇迦 or 선반다가 扇般茶迦 Ṣaṇḍhaka, a eunuch, sexually impotent ; v. 반 般 ; 반 半.

선 先 Fore, before, former, first ; precede. 선세 先世 A previous life, or world. 선철 先哲 ; 선달 先達 One who has preceded (me) in understanding, or achievement. 선니 先尼 ; 서니가 西儞迦 ; 산니 霰尼 Sainika, Senika, martial, a commander ; a class of non-Buddhists, perhaps the Jains ; it may be connected with Śraiṇya, Śreṇika. 선업 先業 Karma from a previous life. 선조고산 先照高山 The rising sun first shines on the highest mountains. 선생 先生 Senior, sir, teacher, master, Mr. ; a previous life. 선진 先進 ; 선배 先輩 Of earlier, or senior rank or achievement. 선타(바) 先陀(婆) Saindhava, interpreted as salt, a cup, water, and a horse ; born or produced in Sindh, or near the Indus ; also a minister of state in personal attendance on the king. 선타객 先陀客 A man of renown, wealth, and wisdom.

선 宣 Proclaim ; spread abroad ; widespread. 선류 宣流 ; 선설 宣說.

선 旋 Revolve, turn round, whirl. 선람 旋嵐 A whirlwind, cyclone. 선화륜 旋火輪 A whirling wheel of fire, a circle yet not a circle, a simile of the seeming but unreal, i.e. the unreality of phenomena. 선다라니 旋陀羅尼 A spell which endows with extensive powers of evolution ; also varied involutions of magical terms.

선 善 Su ; sādhu ; bhadra ; kuśala. Good, virtuous, well, good at ; skilful.

선 詵 Talking, inquiring, buzzing, swarming. 선자 詵遮 Abhiṣecana, to baptize, or sprinkle upon ; also 비선자 毘詵遮.

선 選 To choose ; a myriad. 선우 選友 Śākyamuni's schoolmaster, usually named Viśvamitra, or Kauśika. 선택 選擇 To choose, select.

선 羨 To desire ; praise ; surplus. 선나 羨那 Senā, an army.

선 繕 To repair, put in order, write out, copy. 선마말라남 繕摩末剌諵 Janma-maraṇa, 생사 生死 birth and death. 선도 繕都 Jantu, 중생 衆生 all living beings ; also 선두 禪豆 ; 선두 繕頭 ; 선두 繕兜.

선 禪 To level a place for an altar, to sacrifice to the hills and fountains ; to abdicate. Adopted by Buddhists for dhyāna. 선 禪 or 선나 禪那, i.e. meditation, abstraction, trance. Dhyāna is "meditation, thought, reflection, especially profound and abstract religious contemplation." [M. W.] It was intp: as "getting rid of evil," etc., later as 정려 靜慮 quiet meditation. It is a form of 정 定, but that word is more closely allied with samādhi, cf. 선정 禪定. The term also connotes Buddhism and Buddhist things in general, but has special application to the 선종 禪宗 q.v. It is one of the six pāramitās, cf. 파 波. There are numerous methods and subjects of meditation. The eighteen Brahmalokas are divided into four dhyāna regions "corresponding to certain frames of mind where individuals might be reborn in strict accordance with their spiritual state." The first three are the first dhyāna, the second three the second dhyāna, the third three the third dhyāna, and the remaining nine the fourth dhyāna. See Eitel. According to Childers' *Pali Dictionary*, "The four Jhānas(Jñānas in Sanskrit) are four stages of mystic meditation, whereby the believer's mind is purged from all earthly emotions, and detached as it were from his body, which remains plunged in a profound trance." Seated cross-legged, the practiser "concentrates his mind upon a single thought. Gradually his soul becomes filled with a supernatural ecstasy and serenity," his mind still reasoning: this is the first jhána. Concentrating his mind on the same subject, he frees it from reasoning, the ecstasy and serenity remaining, which is the second jhána. Then he divests himself of ecstasy, reaching the third stage of serenity. Lastly, in the fourth stage the mind becomes indifferent to all emotions, being exalted above them and purified. There are differences in the Mahāyāna methods, but similarity of aim.

선가 禪家 The Ch'an sect, v. 선종 禪宗 ; 선문 禪門.

선가귀감 禪家龜鑑 Lit. "Tortoise Mirror on the Seon School." A book on Buddhists' practice; written by 휴정 休靜.

선거 禪居 A meditation abode ; to dwell in meditation ; a hermitage ; a hermit monk.

선겁 善劫 A good kalpa, bhadra-kalpa, especially that in which we now live.

선견 善見 Sudarśana, good to see, good for seeing, belle vue, etc., similar to 희견 喜見 q.v.

선과 善果 Good fruit from 선인 善因 q.v. ; good fortune in life resulting from previous goodness.

선관 禪觀 Dhyāna-contemplation.

선교 善巧 Clever, skilful, adroit, apt.

선교 禪敎 The teaching of the Ch'an sect. Also, 선 禪 the esoteric tradition and 교 敎 the teaching of the scriptures.

선구 禪毬 A ball of hair used to throw at and awaken those who fell asleep during meditation.

선굴 禪窟 A cell, or cave, for meditation, or retirement from the world.

선권 禪卷 The meditation fist (muṣṭi), the sign of meditation shown by the left first, the right indicating wisdom.

선근 善根 Kuśala-mūla. Good roots, good qualities, good seed sown by a good life to be reaped later.

선나 禪那 Dhyāna abstract contemplation. There are four degrees through which the mind frees itself from all subjective and objective hindrances and reaches a state of absolute indifference and annihilation of thought, perception, and will ; v. 선 禪. The River Jumna.

선남자 善男子 Good sons, or sons of good families, one of the Buddha's terms of address to his disciples, somewhat resembling "gentlemen." 선남신녀 善男信女 Good men and believing women.

선니 禪尼 A nun.

선당 禪堂 Meditation-hall of the Ch'an sect. A common name for the monastic hall.

선락 禪樂 The joy of abstract meditation.

선래 善來 Svāgata, suṣvāgata ; "welcome" ; well come, a title of a Buddha ; v. 선서 善逝.

선려 禪侶 Fellow-meditators ; fellow-monks.

선록 禪錄 The records of the Ch'an sect.

선림 禪林 Grove of meditation, i.e. a monastery. Monasteries as numerous as trees in a forest. Also 선원 禪苑.

선문 禪門 The meditative method in general. The dhyāna pāramitā, v. 육도 六度. The intuitional school established in China according to tradition by Bodhidharma, personally propagated from mind to mind as an esoteric school. 선문오종 禪門五宗 Five Ch'an schools, viz. 임제종 臨濟宗 ; 위앙종 潙仰宗 ; 운문종 雲門宗 ; 법안종 法眼宗, and 조동종 曹洞宗 ; the fourth was removed to Korea ; the second disappeared ; the other three remained, the first being most successful ; in the Sung it divided into the two sects of 양기 楊岐 and 황룡 黃龍. Cf. 릉 楞 13 Laṅkāvatāra-sūtra.

선문답 禪問答 Seon dialogue.

선문정로 禪門正路 A masterpiece of 퇴옹 성철 退翁性徹.

선미 禪味 Meditation-flavour, the mysterious taste or sensation experienced by one who enters abstract meditation.

선방 禪房 Meditation abode, a room for meditation, a cell, a hermitage, general name for a monastery.

선범천 禪梵天 The three Brahmaloka heavens of the first Dhyāna ; cf. 선 禪.

선법 禪法 Methods of mysticism as found in (1) the dhyānas recorded in the sūtras, called 여래선 如來禪 Tathāgata-dhyānas ; (2) traditional dhyāna, or the intuitional method brought to China by Bodhidharma, called 조사선 祖師禪, which also includes dhyāna ideas represented by some external act having an occult indication.

선병 禪病 The ills of meditation, i.e. wandering thoughts, illusions. The illusions and nervous troubles of the mystic.

선본 善本 Good stock, or roots, planting good seed or roots ; good in the root of enlightenment.

선사 禪師 A master, or teacher, of meditation, or of the Ch'an school.

선사 禪思 Meditation thoughts ; the mystic trance.

선삼매 禪三昧 Dhyāna and samādhi, dhyāna considered as 사유 思惟 meditating, samādhi as 정 定 abstraction ; or meditation in the realms of 색 色 the visible, or known, and concentration on 무색 無色 the invisible, or supramundane ; v. 선정 禪定.

선생 善生 Sujāta, "well born, of high birth," [M. W.] Also tr. of Susambhava, a former incarnation of Śākyamuni.

선서 善逝 Sugata, well departed, gone as he should go ; a title of a Buddha ; cf. 선래 善來.

선성 善性 Good nature, good in nature, or in fundamental quality.

선수 禪髓 The marrow of meditation — a term for the Laṅkāvatāra-sūtra.

선숙 善宿 Abiding in goodness, disciples who keep eight commandments, upavasatha, poṣadha.

선습 禪習 The practice of religion through the mystic trance.

선승 禪僧 A monk of the Ch'an sect ; a monk in meditation.

선신 善神 The good devas, or spirits, who protect Buddhism, 8, 16, or 36 in number ; the 8 are also called 선귀신 善鬼神.

선실 禪室 Meditation hall or room ; other similar terms are 선옥 禪屋 ; 선방 禪房 ; 선원 禪院 ; 선당 禪堂 ; 선거 禪居.

선심 善心 A good heart, or mind.

선악 善惡 Good and evil ; good, *inter alia*, is defined as 순리 順理, evil as 위리 違理 ; i.e. to accord with, or to disobey the right. The 십선십악 十善十惡 are the keeping or breaking of the ten commandments.

선암사 仙巖寺 Seon-am-sa. A temple located in Jukhak-ri Seungju-eup Suncheon-si Jeollanam-do in Korea. It is the headquarters of Korean Taego Order. It is also the 20th parish headquarters of Korean Jogye Order.

선열 禪悅 Joy of the mystic trance. 선열식 禪悅食 Its nourishing powers.

선우 善友 Kalyāṇamitra, "a friend of virtue, a religious counsellor," [M. W.] ; a friend in the good life, or one who stimulates to goodness.

선운사 禪雲寺 Seon-un-sa. A temple located in Mt. Dosolsan, Samin-ri Asan-myeon Gochang-gun Jeollabuk-do in Korea. The 24th parish headquarters of Korean Jogye Order.

선원 禪院 Seon center. Meditation precinct ; area around meditation hall. It may be a part of a large temple or it can constitute an independent temple.

선월 善月 Good months, i.e. the first, fifth, and ninth ; because they are the most important in which to do good works and thus obtain a good report in the spirit realm.

선율 禪律 The Ch'an and Lü (Vinaya) sects ; i.e. the Meditative and Disciplinary schools.

선인 善人 A good man, especially one who believes in Buddhist ideas of causality and lives a good life.

선인 禪人 A member of the Ch'an(Zen), i.e. the Intuitional or Meditative sect.

선인 善因 Good causation, i.e. a good cause for a good effect.

선장 禪杖 A staff or pole for touching those who fall asleep while assembled in meditation.

선재 善哉 Sādhu. Good! excellent!

선재동자 善財童子 Sudhana, a disciple mentioned in the 화엄경 華嚴經 34 and elsewhere, one of the 사승신 四勝身 q.v. ; the story is given in Divyāvadāna, ed. Cowell and Neil, pp. 441 seq.

선정 禪定 Ch'an is dhyāna, probably a transliteration ; ting is an interpretation of samādhi. Ch'an is an element in ting, or samādhi, which covers the whole ground of meditation, concentration, abstraction, reaching to the ultimate beyond emotion or thinking ; cf. 선 禪, for which the two words ch'an-ting are loosely used.

선정 禪靜 Dhyāna and its Chinese translation, quieting of thought, or its control, or suppression, silent meditation.

선제 禪齊 idem 선실 禪室.

선종 禪宗 The Ch'an, meditative or intuitional, sect usually said to have been established in China by Bodhidharma, v. 달 達, the twenty-eighth patriarch, who brought the tradition of the Buddha-mind from India. Cf. 릉 楞 13 Laṅkāvatāra-sūtra. This sect, believing in direct enlightenment, disregarded ritual and sūtras and depended upon the inner light and personal influence for the propagation of its tenets, founding itself on the esoteric tradition supposed to have been imparted to Kāśyapa by the Buddha, who indicated his meaning by plucking a flower without further explanation. Kāśyapa smiled in apprehension and is supposed to have passed on this mystic method to the patriarchs. The successor of Bodhidharma was 혜가 慧可 Hui-k'o, and he was succeeded by 승찬 僧璨 Sêng-ts'an ; 도신 道信 Tao-hsin ; 홍인 弘忍 Hung-jên ; 혜능 慧能 Hui-nêng, and 신수 神秀 Shên-hsiu, the sect dividing under the two latter into the southern and northern schools ; the southern school became prominent, producing 남악 南嶽 Nan-yo and 청원 青原 Ch'ing-yüan, the former succeeded by 마조 馬祖 Ma-tsu, the latter by 석두 石頭 Shih-t'ou. From Ma-tsu's school arose the five later schools, v. 선문 禪門.

선좌 禪坐 To sit cross-legged in meditation.

선지 禪智 Meditation and wisdom, cf. 선권 禪卷.

선지 善知 Vibhāvana, clear perception. 선지식 善知識 A good friend or intimate, one well known and intimate.

선진 禪鎭 The meditation-warden, a piece of wood so hung as to strike the monk's head when he nodded in sleep.

선천 禪天 Dhyāna heavens, four in number, where those who practise meditation may be reborn, v. 선 禪.

선파 禪波 Disturbing waves, or thoughts, during meditation. 선바라밀 禪波羅密 The sixth or dhyāna pāramitā, the attainment of perfection in the mystic trance.

선하 禪河 The dhyāna river, i.e. the mystic trance like a river extinguishes the fires of the mind. The 니련선 尼連禪 river Nairañjanā (Niladyan), which flows past Gayā.

선행 禪行 The methods employed in meditation ; the practices, or discipline, of the Ch'an school.

선현 善現 Well appearing, name of Subhūti, v. 소 蘇. 선현천 善現天 or 선현색 善現色 Sudṛśa, the seventh Brahmaloka ; the eighth region of the fourth dhyāna.

선혜 禪慧 The mystic trance and wisdom.

선혜지 善慧地 Sādhumatī, v. 십지 十地.

선화 禪和 Meditation-associates, fellow-monks ; also 선화자 禪和子 ; 선화자 禪和者.

선화 禪化 The transforming character of Ch'an.

설 舌 Jihvā, 시걸바 時乞縛 ; the tongue ; 설근 舌根 the organ of taste ; 설식 舌識 tongue-perception ; v. 육근 六根 ; 육식 六識. 설상 舌相 The broad, long tongue of a Buddha, one of the thirty-two physical signs. 설불란 舌不爛 Tongue-unconsumed, a term for Kumārajīva ; on his cremation his tongue is said to have remained unconsumed.

설 雪 Snow. 설산 雪山 ; 설령 雪嶺 The snow mountains, the Himālayas. 설산대사 雪山大士 ; 설산동자 雪山童子 The great man, or youth of the Himālayas, the Buddha in a former incarnation. 설산부 雪山部 Haimavatāḥ, the Himālaya school, one of the five divisions of the Mahāsāṅghikas.

설 洩 To leak, diminish. 예슬지림 洩瑟知林 Yaṣṭivana, forest of the bamboo staff which took root when thrown away by the Brahman who did not believe the Buddha was 16 feet in height ; but the more he measured the taller grew the Buddha, hence his chagrin. Name of a forest near Rājagṛha.

설 設 To set up, establish, institute ; arrange, spread ; suppose ; translit. *ś*. 설리(라) 設利(羅) Śarīra, relics, remains, see 사 舍. 설리불달라 設利弗怛羅 Śāriputra, v. 사 舍. 설다도로 設多圖盧 Śatadru, "an ancient kingdom of northern India, noted for its mineral wealth. Exact position unknown." [Eitel]. Also, the River Sutlej. 설시 設施 Śacī, Śakti, v. 사 舍. 설도로 設覩嚕 Śatru, an enemy, a destroyer, the enemy, also 설돌로 設咄嚕 ; 설도로 設都嚧 ; 사도로 捨覩嚧 or 삭도로 爍覩嚧 ; 솔도환 窣覩喚 ; 사눌로 娑訥嚕. 설상가 設賞迦 Śaśāṅka. "A king of Karṇasuvarṇa, who tried to destroy the sacred Bodhidruma. He was dethroned by Śīlāditya." [Eitel].

설 說 To speak, say, talk, discourse, expound ; speech, etc. Used for 열 悅 pleased. 설일체유부 說一切有部 v. 일 一 and 유 有 ; the Sarvāstivāda realistic, school. 설가부 說假部 The Prajñaptivādinaḥ school, a branch of the Mahāsāṅghikāḥ, which took the view of phenomenality and reality, founded on the Prajñaptiśāstra. 설출세부 說出世部 The Lokottaravādinaḥ school, a branch of the Mahāsāṅghikāḥ, which held the view that all in the world is merely phenomenal and that reality exists outside it. 설인부 說因部 Hetuvādinaḥ, idem Sarvāstivāda. 설계 說戒 The bi-monthly reading of the prohibitions for the order and of mutual confession. 설법 說法 To tell or expound the law, or doctrine ; to preach. 설시 說示 To tell and indicate. 설경 說經 To expound the sūtras. 설죄 說罪 To confess sin, or wrong-doing. 설전부 說轉部 idem 경(량)부 經(量)部 Sautrāntikāḥ school. 설통 說通 To expound thoroughly, penetration exposition. 설묵 說黙 Speech and silence.

설 薛 Wild hemp ; translit. *p, ve, vai* ; cf. 비 毘, 폐 吠, 폐 閉, etc. 설실라말나 薛室羅末拏 v. 비 毘 Vaiśravaṇa. 설라작갈라 薛攞斫羯羅 Velācakra, a kind of clock. 설복 薛服 Hemp garments, the coarse monastic dress. 설사(리) 薛舍(離) v. 비 毘 Vaiśālī. 설려(다) 薛荔(多) cf. 폐 閉 Preta, intp. as an ancestral spirit, but chiefly as a hungry ghost who is also harmful. 설타 薛陀 Veda, cf. 폐 吠.

설법전 說法殿 Lecture Hall.

섬 閃 Flash ; get out of the way. 섬다 閃多 A demon ; one of Yama's names. 섬전광 閃電光 Lightning-flashing, therefore awe-inspiring.

섬 睒 Glance ; lustrous ; translit. *śa*. 섬미 睒彌 Śamī, a kind of acacia. 섬마 睒摩 Śāmaka, a bodhisattva born to a blind couple, clad in deerskin, slain by the king in hunting, restored to life and to his blind parents by the gods.

섬 譫 Incoherent talk. 섬부주 譫浮洲 Jambudvīpa, v. 섬 贍.

섬 贍 To supply ; supplied, enough ; translit. *jam*. 섬부 贍部 Jambū, "a fruit tree, the rose apple, *Eugenia jambolana*, or another species of Eugenia." M. W. Also 섬부제 贍部提 ; 염부 閻浮 ; 섬부 剡浮 ; 섬부 譫浮 also applied to the next. 섬부주 贍部洲 Jambudvīpa. Name of the southern of the four great continents, said to be of triangular shape, and to be called after the shape of the leaf of an immense Jambu-tree on Mount Meru ; or after fine gold that is found below the tree. It is divided into four parts: south of the Himalayas by the lord of elephants, because of their number ; north by the lord of horses ; west by the lord of jewels ; east by the lord of men. This seems to imply a region larger than India, and Eitel includes in Jambudvīpa the following countries around the Anavatapta lake and the Himalayas. North: Huns, Uigurs, Turks. East : China, Corea, Japan, and some islands. South: Northern India with twenty-seven kingdoms, Eastern India ten kingdoms, Southern India fifteen kingdoms, Central India thirty kingdoms. West: Thirty-four kingdoms. 섬부(금) 贍部(金) Jāmbūnada, the produce of the river Jambūnadī, i.e. gold, hence 섬부광상 贍部光像 is an image of golden glory, especially the image of Śākyamuni attributed to Anāthapiṇḍika. 섬부날타금 贍部捺陀金 Jāmbūnada-suvarṇa, the gold from the Jambūnadī river.

섭 鍱 A thin metal plate. 섭복 鍱腹 The Indian philosopher who is said to have worn a rice-pan over his belly, the seat of wisdom, lest it should be injured and his wisdom be lost.

섭 攝 To collect, gather together, combine, include ; lay hold of ; assist, act for or with ; control, direct, attend to ; translit. *ś*, *śa*. 섭취 攝取, 섭수 攝受 To gather, gather up, receive. 섭리람 攝哩藍 Śarīra, v. 사 舍 relics. 섭박 攝縛 Śava, a corpse (not yet decayed). 섭대승론 攝大乘論 Mahāyāna-saṁparigraha-śāstra, a collection of Mahā-yāna śāstras, ascribed to Asaṅga, of which three tr. were made into Chinese. 섭심 攝心 to collect the mind, concentrate the attention. 섭념산림 攝念山林 The hill-grove for concentrating the thoughts, a monastery. 섭의음악 攝意音樂 Music that calms the mind, or helps to concentration. 섭타필다 攝拖苾馱 Śabda-vidyā, (a śāstra on) grammar, logic. 섭마등 攝摩騰 Kāśyapa Mātaṅga, v. 가 迦, according to tradition the first official Indian monk (along with Gobharana) to arrive in China, *circa* A.D. 67 ; tr. the Sūtra of the Forty-two Sections. 섭중생계 攝衆生戒 ; 접생계 接生戒 The commands which include or confer blessing on all the living. 섭론 攝論 The collected śāstras, v. *supra*. 섭론종 攝論宗 The school of the collected śāstras.

성 城 A city (or defensive) wall ; a city, a walled town. 성황신 城隍神 The city god, protector of the wall and moat and all they contain.

성 成 Complete, finish, perfect, become.

성 省 Look into minutely, inspect, examine ; arouse ; spare, save ; an inspectorate, hence a province. 성행당 省行堂 another name for 연수당 延壽堂.

성 性 Svabhāva, prakṛti, pradhāna. The nature, intp. as embodied, causative, unchanging ; also as independent or self-dependent ; fundamental nature behind the manifestation or expression. Also, the Buddha-nature immanent in all beings, the Buddha heart or mind.

성 誠 Truthful, true, truth ; real ; sincere, sincerity. 성신 誠信 True and trustworthy, true, reliable. 성제 誠諦 Truth, a truth, the true teaching of Buddhism.

성 星 Tārā, a star ; the 25th constellation consisting of stars in Hydra ; a spark. 성수 星宿 The twenty-eight Chinese constellations 이십팔수 二十八宿 ; also the twenty-eight nakṣatras ; the 십이궁 十二宮 twelve rāśi, or zodiacal mansions ; and the 칠요 七曜 seven mobile stars : sun, moon, and five graha or planets ; all which are used as auguries in 성점법 星占法 astrology. A list giving Sanskrit and Chinese names, etc., is given in 불학대사전 佛學大辭典, pp. 1579-1580. 성수겁 星宿劫 A future kalpa of the constellations in which a thousand Buddhas will appear. 성력 星曆 Jyotiṣa, relating to astronomy, or the calendar ; Jyotiṣka 수지색가 殊底色迦 was a native of Rājagṛha, who gave all his goods to the poor. 성제 星祭 ; 성공 星供 To sacrifice, or pay homage to a star, especially one's natal star.

성 聖 Ārya ; sādhu ; a sage ; wise and good ; upright, or correct in all his character ; sacred, holy, saintly. The 성인 聖人 is the opposite of the 범인 凡人 common, or unenlightened man.

성 聲 Śabda. Sound, tone, voice, repute ; one of the five physical senses or sensations, i.e. sound, the 성입 聲入, 성근 聲根, or 성진 聲塵, cf. 육 六 and 십이입 十二入. 성념송 聲念誦 Vocal intonation. 성교 聲敎 Vocal teaching. 성장 聲杖 The sounding or rattling staff, said to have been ordained by the Buddha to drive away crawling poisonous insects. 성명 聲明 Śabdavidyā, one of the 오명 五明 five sciences, the 성명론 聲明論 Śabdavidyā śāstra being a treatise on words and their meanings. 성독 聲獨 ; 성연 聲緣 Śrāvakas and pratyeka-buddhas, cf. next entry and 연각 緣覺. 성문 聲聞 Śrāvaka, a hearer, a term applied to the personal disciples of the Buddha, distinguished as mahā-śrāvaka ; it is also applied to hearers, or disciples in general ; but its general connotation relates it to Hīnayāna disciples who understand the four dogmas, rid themselves of the unreality of the phenomenal, and enter nirvāṇa ; it is the initial stage ; cf. 사 舍. 성문승 聲聞乘 Śrāvakayāna ; the śrāvaka vehicle or sect, the initial stage, Hīnayāna, the second stage being that of pratyeka-buddha, v. above. 성문승 聲聞僧 A Hīnayāna monk. 성문장 聲聞藏 The Hīnayāna canon. 성론 聲論 cf. 성명 聲明, also vyākaraṇa, a treatise on sounds and the structure of Sanskrit.

성각 性覺 Inherent intelligence, or knowledge, i.e. that of the bhūtatathatā.

성겁 成劫 Vivarta kalpa, one of the four kalpas, consisting of twenty small kalpas during which worlds and the beings on them are formed. The others are : 주겁 住劫 Vivarta-siddha kalpa, kalpa of abiding, or existence, sun and moon rise, sexes are differentiated, heroes arise, four castes are formed, social life evolves. 괴겁 壞劫 Saṁvarta kalpa, that of destruction, consisting of sixty-four small kalpas when fire, water, and wind destroy everything except the fourth Dhyāna. 공겁 空劫 Saṁvarta-siddha kalpa, i.e. of annihilation. v. 겁파 劫波. 성유식론 成唯識論 Vidyā-mātra-siddhi śāstra, in 10 chüan, being Vasubandhu's 유식 唯識 in 30 chüan reduced by Hsüan-tsang, also by others, to 10. There are works on it by various authors.

성계 性戒 The natural moral law, e.g. not to kill, steal, etc., not requiring the law of Buddha.

성공 聖供 Holy offerings, or those made to the saints, especially to the Triratna.

성공 性空 The nature void, i.e. the immateriality of the nature of all things. 성공교 性空敎 One of the three 남산 南山 Nan-shan sects which regarded the nature of things as unreal or immaterial, but held that the things were temporally entities. 성공관 性空觀 The meditation of this sect on the unreality, or immateriality, of the nature of things.

성과 聖果 The holy fruit, or fruit of the saintly life, i.e. bodhi, nirvāṇa.

성교 聖敎 The teaching of the sage, or holy one ; holy teaching. 성교량 聖敎量 The argument or evidence of authority in logic, i.e. that of the sacred books.

성구 性具 The T'ien-t'ai doctrine that the Buddha-nature includes both good and evil ; v. 관음현의기 觀音玄義記 2. Cf. 체구 體具 ; 이구 理具 of similar meaning.

성기 性起 Arising from the primal nature, or bhūtatathatā, in contrast with 연기 緣起 arising from secondary causes.

성념처 性念處 Citta-smṛtyupasthāna, one of the four objects of thought, i.e. that the original nature is the same as the Buddha-nature, v. 사념처 四念處.

성덕 性德 Natural capacity for good (or evil), in contrast with 수덕 修德 powers (of goodness) attained by practice.

성도 聖道 The holy way, Buddhism ; the way of the saints, or sages ; also the noble eightfold path. 성도문 聖道門 The ordinary schools of the way of holiness by the processes of devotion, in contrast with immediate salvation by faith in Amitābha.

성득 性得 Natural attainment, i.e. not acquired by effort ; also 생득 生得.

성령 聖靈 The saintly spirits (of the dead).

성망 聖網 The holy jāla, or net, of Buddha's teaching which gathers all into the truth.

성명 聖明 Holy enlightenment ; or the enlightenment of saints.

성명 性命 The life of conscious beings ; nature and life.

성방 聖方 Āryadeśa, the holy land, India ; the land of the sage, Buddha.

성법 聖法 The holy law of Buddha ; the law or teaching of the saints, or sages.

성보장신 聖寶藏神 The deva, or devas, of the sacred treasury of precious things (who bestows them on the living).

성복 聖福 Holy happiness, that of Buddhism, in contrast with 범복 梵福 that of Brahma and Brahmanism.

성분 性分 The nature of anything ; the various natures of various things.

성불 性佛 The Dharmakāya 법성불 法性佛. v. 법신 法身.

성불 成佛 To become Buddha, as a Bodhisattva does on reaching supreme perfect bodhi. 성불득탈 成佛得脫 To become Buddha and obtain deliverance (from the round of mortality).

성사자 聖師子 The holy lion, Buddha.

성상 性相 The nature (of anything) and its phenomenal expression ; hsing being 무위 無爲 non-functional, or noumenal, and hsiang 유위 有爲 functional, or phenomenal. 성상학 性相學 The philosophy of the above, i.e. of the noumenal and phenomenal. There are ten points of difference between the 성상이종 性相二宗, i.e. between the 성 性 and 상 相 schools, v. 이종 二宗.

성색 性色 Transcendent rūpa or form within or of the Tathāgata-garbha ; also 진색 眞色.

성선 性善 Good by nature (rather than by effort) ; naturally good ; in contrast with 성악 性惡 evil by nature. Cf. 성구 性具.

성선 聖仙 The holy ṛṣi, Buddha.

성성 聖性 The holy nature, according to the Abhidharma-kośa 구사론 俱舍論, of the passionless life ; according to the Vijñānamātrasiddhi 유식론 唯識論, of enlightenment and wisdom. 성성리생 聖性離生 The life of holiness apart or distinguished from the life of common unenlightened people.

성승 聖僧 The holy monk, the image in the monks' assembly room ; in Mahāyāna that of Mañjuśrī, in Hīnayāna that of Kāśyapa, or Subhūti, etc.

성식 性識 Natural powers of perception, or the knowledge acquired through the sense organs ; mental knowledge.

성실 成實 Completely true, or reliable, perfect truth, an abbreviation for 성실종 成實宗, 성실론 成實論, 성실사 成實師.

성실종 成實宗 Satyasiddhi sect (Jap. Jōjitsu-shū), based upon the Satyasiddhi śāstra of Harivarman, v. 하 訶, tr. by Kumārajīva. In China it was a branch of the 삼론 三論 San Lun Sect. It was a Hīnayāna variation of the Śūnya 공 空 doctrine. The term is defined as perfectly establishing the real meaning of the sūtras. The 성실론 成實論 tr. as above is in 16 chüan ; there are other works on it. 성취 成就 Siddhi ; accomplishment, fulfilment, completion, to bring to perfection. 성취중생 成就衆生 To transform all beings by developing their Buddha-nature and causing them to obtain enlightenment. 성숙자 成熟者 The ripe ; those who attain ; those in whom the good nature, immanent in all the living, completes their salvation. 성등정각 成等正覺 To attain to perfect enlightenment, become Buddha. 성자연각 成自然覺 To attain to natural enlightenment as all may do by beholding eternal truth 실상 實相 within their own hearts. 성신회 成身會 ; 근본회 根本會 ; 갈마회 羯磨會 The first group in the nine Vajradhātu groups. 성도 成道 To attain the Way, or become enlightened, e.g. the Buddha under the bodhi tree. 성도회 成道會 ; 납팔 臘八 The annual commemoration of the Buddha's enlightenment on the 8th day of the 12th month.

성심 聖心 The holy mind, that of Buddha.

성심 性心 The perfectly clear and unsullied mind, i.e. the Buddha mind or heart. The Ch'an(Zen) school use 성심 性心 or 심성 心性 indifferently.

성아 性我 The Buddha-nature ego, which is apperceived when the illusory ego is banished.

성어 聖語 Āryabhāṣā. Sacred speech, language, words, or sayings ; Sanskrit.

성언 聖言 Holy words ; the words of a saint, or sage ; the correct words of Buddhism.

성연 聖緣 Holy conditions of, or aids to the holy life.

성욕 性慾 Desires that have become second nature ; desires of the nature.

성위 聖位 The holy position, the holy life of Buddhism.

성유식론소 成唯識論疏 A masterpiece of 문아 원측 文雅圓測.

성응 聖應 The influence of Buddha ; the response of the Buddhas, or saints.

성의 聖儀 The saintly appearance, i.e. an image of Buddha.

성자 聖者 Ārya, holy or saintly one ; one who has started on the path to nirvāṇa ; holiness.

성전 聖典 The sacred canon, or holy classics, the Tripiṭaka.

성정 聖淨 The schools of Buddhism and the Pure-land School, cf. 성도 聖道.

성제 聖諦 The sacred principles or dogmas, or those of the saints, or sages ; especially the four noble truths, cf. 사성제 四聖諦.

성제바 聖提婆 Āryadeva, or Devabodhisattva, a native of Ceylon and disciple of Nāgārjuna, famous for his writings and discussions.

성존 聖尊 The holy honoured one, Buddha.

성종 聖種 (1) The holy seed, i.e. the community of monks ; (2) that which produces the discipline of the saints, or monastic community.

성종 性宗 v. 법성종 法性宗.

성종성 性種性 Nature-seed nature, i.e. original or primary nature, in contrast with 습종성 習種性 active or functioning nature ; it is also the bodhisattva 십행 十行 stage. 성종계 性種戒 idem 성계 性戒.

성죄 性罪 Sins that are such according to natural law, apart from Buddha's teaching, e.g. murder, etc.

성주천중천 聖主天中天 The holy lord, deva of devas, i.e. Buddha ; also 성주사자 聖主師子 the holy lion-lord.

성중 聖衆 The holy multitude, all the saints. 성중래영 聖衆來迎 Amitābha's saintly host come to welcome at death those who call upon him.

성지 性地 Spiritual nature, the second of the ten stages as defined by the 통교 通教 Intermediate School, in which the illusion produced by 견사 見思 seeing and thinking is subdued and the mind obtains a glimmer of the immateriality of things. Cf. 십지 十地.

성지 聖智 Ārya-jñāna ; the wisdom of Buddha, or the saints, or sages ; the wisdom which is above all particularization, i.e. that of transcendental truth.

성차 性遮 Natural and conventional sins, i.e. sins against natural law, e.g. murder, and sins against conventional or religious law, e.g. for a monk to drink wine, cut down trees, etc.

성철 性徹 Seong-cheol(1912-1993). A monk of Korea. He was the 8th 종정 宗正 of a Korean Jogye Order.

성태 聖胎 The womb of holiness which enfolds and develops the bodhisattva, i.e. the 삼현위 三賢位 three excellent positions attained in the 십주 十住, 십행 十行 and 십회향 十廻向.

성토 性土 The sphere of the dharma-nature, i.e. the bhūtatathatā, idem 법성토 法性土.

성해 性海 The ocean of the bhūtatathatā, the all-containing, immaterial nature of the Dharmakāya.

성행 聖行 The holy bodhisattva life of 계정혜 戒定慧 the (monastic) commandments, meditation and wisdom.

성화 性火 Fire as one of the five elements, contrasted with 사화 事火 phenomenal fire.

성횡수종 性横修縱 A division of the Triratna in its three aspects into the categories of 횡 横 and 종 縱, i.e. cause and effect, or effect and cause ; a 별교 別教 division, not that of the 원교 圓教.

세 勢 Bala, sthāman. Power, influence, authority ; aspect, circumstances. 세력귀 勢力鬼 A powerful demon. 세라 勢羅 Śaila, craggy, mountainous, mountain. 세지 勢至 He whose wisdom and power reach everywhere, Mahāsthāmaprāpta, i.e. 대세지 大勢至 q.v. Great power arrived (at maturity), the bodhisattva on the right of Amitābha, who is the guardian of Buddha-wisdom.

세 細 Fine, small, minute ; in detail ; careful. 세사상 細四相 The four states of 생주이멸 生住異滅 birth, abiding, change, extinction, e.g. birth, life, decay, death. 세심 細心 Carefully, in detail, similar to 세의식 細意識 the vijñāna of detailed, unintermitting attention. 세골욕 細骨欲 Sexual attraction through softness and smoothness. 세색 細色 Refined appearance. Cf. 미 微.

세 洗 To wash, cleanse. 세정 洗淨 Cleansing, especially after stool.

세 歲 Vatsara, a year ; cf. 납 臘 19 strokes.

세 世 Yuga. An age, 1,000th part of a kalpa. Loka, the world. 세 世 originally meant a human generation, a period of thirty years ; it is used in Buddhism both for Yuga, a period of time ever flowing, and Loka, the world, worldly, earthly. The world is that which is to be destroyed ; it is sunk in the round of mortality, or transmigration ; and conceals, or is a veil over reality.

세(속)지 世(俗)智 Ordinary or worldly knowledge or wisdom.

세간 世間 The world ; in the world ; the finite impermanent world, idem 세계 世界. 세간승 世間乘 The Vehicle, or teaching for the attainment of good fruit in the present life, in contrast with

출세간승 出世間乘 that for attainment in lives outside this world. 세간천 世間天 World-devas, i.e. earthly kings. 세간천원 世間天院 The third court in the Garbhadhātu. 세간지 世間智 Worldly knowledge, i.e. that of ordinary men and those unenlightened by Buddhism. 세간단 世間檀 Worldly dāna, or giving, i.e. with thoughts of possession, meum, tuum, and the thing given, v. 삼애 三礙. 세간법 世間法 The world-law, or law of this world, especially of birth-and-death ; in this respect it is associated with the first two of the four dogmas, i.e. 고 苦 suffering, and 집 集 its accumulated consequences in karma. 세간상상주 世間相常住 World-forms, systems, or states are eternal (as existing in the Absolute, the 진여 眞如). 세간상위 世間相違 Lokaviruddha ; one of the thirty-three logical errors, to set up a premise contrary to human experience. 세간안 世間眼 The Eye of the world, the eye that sees for all men, i.e. the Buddha, who is also the one that opens the eyes of men. Worldly, or ordinary eyes. Also 세안 世眼. 세간경 世間經 A sūtra discussing causality in regard to the first three of the Four Dogmas 고집멸 苦集滅 in the 아함경 阿含經 34. 세간해 世間解 Lokavid, 로가비 路迦憊 tr. as 지세간 知世間 Knower of the world, one of the ten titles of a Buddha. 세간난신첩경 世間難信捷徑 The speedy and straight way to Buddhahood (for all) which the world finds it hard to believe.

세계 世界 Loka 세간 世間 ; the finite world, the world, a world, which is of two kinds : (1) 중생세계 衆生世界 that of the living, who are receiving their 정보 正報 correct recompense or karma ; (2) 기세계 器世界 that of the material, or that on which karma depends for expression. By the living is meant 유정 有情 the sentient. 세계주 世界主 The lord, or ruler over a world or dhyāna heaven, one for each of the four dhyāna heavens. 세계실단 世界悉檀 One of the four siddhāntas : the Buddha's line of reasoning in earthly or common terms to draw men to the higher truth.

세대 世代 A generation, a lifetime ; the world.

세라 世羅 Śaila 세라 勢羅 ; 시라 施羅 ; a crag, a mountain.

세로 世路 The ways, or procedure, of the world ; the phenomenal.

세론 世論 Worldly discussions ; ordinary unenlightened ways of description or definition ; also styled 악론 惡論 evil discussions, especially when applied to the hedonistic Lokāyatika teachings, v. 로가 路迦.

세법 世法 Common or ordinary dharmas, i.e. truths, laws, things, etc.

세복 世福 Earthly happiness, arising from the ordinary good living of those unenlightened by Buddhism, one of the 삼복 三福 ; also, the blessings of this world.

세상 世相 World-state, or condition ; appearances, phenomena.

세선 世善 The pleasures of the world, v. 세복 世福.

세세생생 世世生生 Transmigration after transmigration in the six states of mortal existence.

세속 世俗 Laukika ; common or ordinary things, custom, experiences, common or worldly ways (or views).

세속오계 世俗五戒 Five Commandments for Laymen, as taught by 원광 圓光 Won-gwang. (1) Serve the king with loyalty. (2) Serve and tend parents with filial devotion. (3) Treat friends with sincerity. (4) Do not retreat from battlefields. (5) Be discriminating in the taking of life.

세안 世眼 idem 세간안 世間眼.

세야나살남 世耶那薩喃 Śayanāsana, lying and sitting, couch and seat.

세영 世英 World hero, i.e. a Buddha ; also 세웅 世雄.

세우 世友 Vasumitra ; v. 벌소밀달라 筏蘇蜜呾羅.

세웅양족존 世雄兩足尊 The World-hero and two-legged (or human) honoured one, Buddha, or the honoured among human bipeds.

세의 世依 He on whom the world relies — Buddha.

세자재왕 世自在王 Lokeśvara-rāja, 세요왕 世饒王 a Buddha under whom Amitābha, in a previous existence, entered into the ascetic life and made his forty-eight vows.

세전 世典 Non-Buddhist classical works.

세제 世諦 Ordinary or worldly truth, opposite of 진제 眞諦 truth in reality ; also 속제 俗諦 ; 세속제 世俗諦 ; 부속제 覆俗諦. 세제불생멸 世諦不生滅 Ordinary worldly postulates that things are permanent, as contrasted with the doctrine of impermanence advocated by Hīnayāna ; both positions are controverted by T'ien-t'ai, which holds that the phenomenal world is neither becoming nor passing, but is an aspect of eternal reality.

세제일법 世第一法 The highest of the 사가행위 四加行位 q.v.

세존 世尊 Lokajyeṣṭha, world's most venerable, or Lokanātha, lord of worlds. 로가위사제 盧迦委斯諦 ; 로가나타 路迦那他 World-honoured, an epithet of every Buddha. Also a tr. of Bhagavat, v. 파 婆.

세주(천) 世主(天) The Lord of the world, Brahmā ; Maheśvara ; also the four mahārājas 사천왕 四天王 v. 범천 梵天 ; 대자재천 大自在天.

세친 世親 Vasubandhu, idem 천친 天親 q.v.

소 疏 ; **소** 疎 Open, wide apart ; distant, coarse ; estrange ; lax, careless ; to state, report ; commentary ; also used for 소 蔬 vegetarian food. 소륵 疏勒 Su-lo, a hsien or district in Western Kashgaria and a Han name for Kashgar. 소소연연 疏所緣緣 A distant circumstance, or remote cause, one of the four conditional causes in the 유식 唯識 school. 소두 疏頭 Written incantations, spells, or prayers burnt before the spirits.

소 所 A place ; where, what, that which, he (etc.) who. 소작 所作 That which is done, or to be done, or made, or set up, etc. 소의 所依 Āśraya, that on which anything depends, the basis of the vijñānas. 소별 所別 The subject of the thesis of a syllogism in contrast with 능별 能別 the predicate ; that which is differentiated. 소화 所化 The one who is transformed or instructed. 소인 所引 That which is brought forward or out ; a quotation. 소유 所有 What one has, what there is, whatever exists. 소지의 所知依 That on which all knowledge depends, i.e. the ālayavijñāna, the other vijñānas being derived from it ; cf. 입식 入識. 소지장 所知障 The barrier of the known, arising from regarding the seeming as real. 소립 所立 A thesis ; that which is set up. 소연 所緣 Ālambana ; that upon which something rests or depends, hence object of perception ; that which is the environmental or contributory cause ; attendant circumstances. 소연연 所緣緣 Adhipati-pratyaya. The influence of one factor in causing others ; one of the 사연 四緣. 소전 所詮 That which is expounded, explained, or commented on. 소변계 所遍計 That by which the mind is circumscribed, i.e. impregnated with the false view that the ego and things possess reality. 소량 所量 That which is estimated ; the content of reasoning, or judgment.

소 酥 Curd, butter ; crisp. It is described as produced by churning milk or treating it with herbs. Milk produces 락 酪, then 생소 生酥, then 숙소 熟酥, then 제호 醍醐. 소등 酥燈 A lamp burning butter-oil.

소 少 Few ; also used as a transliteration of Ṣaṭ, six. 소광(천) 少光(天) ; 합천 盧天 Parīttābhās ; the fourth Brahmaloka, i.e. the first region of the second dhyāna heavens, also called 유광수 有光壽. 소실 少室 Shao-shih, a hill on the 숭산 嵩山 Sung shan where Bodhidharma set up his 소림사 少林寺 *infra*. 소실육문집 少室六門集 Six brief treatises attributed to Bodhidharma, but their authenticity is denied. 소강 少康 Shao-k'ang, a famous monk of the T'ang dynasty, known as the later 선도 善導 Shan-tao, his master. 소림사 少林寺 The monastery at 소실 少室 in 등봉 登封 Têng-fêng hsien, Honanfu, where Bodhidharma sat with his face to a wall for nine years. 소림무예 少林武藝 Wu-i, a cook of the Shao-lin monastery, who is said single-handed to have driven off the Yellow Turban rebels with a three-foot staff, and who was posthumously rewarded with the rank of "general" ; a school of adepts of the quarter-staff, etc., was called after him, of whom thirteen were far-famed. 소욕지족 少欲知足 Content with few desires. 소정(천) 少淨(天) Parīttaśubhas. The first and smallest heaven (brahmaloka) in the third dhyāna region of form. 소재귀 少財鬼 Hungry ghosts who pilfer because they are poor and get but little food.

소 消 Melt, disperse, expend, digest, dispose of. 소멸 消滅 To put an end to, cause to cease. 소재 消災 To disperse, or put an end to calamity. 소수복 消瘦服 The monk's robe as putting an end to illusion. 소석 消釋 To solve and explain. 소제 消除 To eradicate.

소 素 Original colour or state ; plain, white ; heretofore, usual ; translit. *su*. 소구 素具 Already prepared. 소바리나 素嚩哩拏 ; 소벌라 蘇伐羅 ; 수발나 修跋拏 Suvarṇa ; v. 금 金 gold. 소의 素意 ; 소회 素懷 Ordinary thoughts, or hopes ; the common purposes of the mind. 소달람 素怛纜 v. 수 修 Sūtra. 소법신 素法身 Possessing the fundamental dharmakāya nature though still in sin, i.e. the beings in the three lowest orders of transmigration. 소견 素絹 Plain silk lustring, thin silk. 소호 素豪 The ūrṇā, or white curl between the Buddha's eyebrows. 소식 素食 ; 소찬 素饌 Vegetarian food.

소 蘇 Refreshing thyme ; revive, cheer ; Soochow ; translit. *su, so, sa, s*. Most frequently it translit. the Sanskrit *su*, which means good, well, excellent, very. Cf. 수 須, 수 修.

소 小 Small, little ; mean, pretty ; inferior.

소 燒 To burn. 소구지옥 燒灸地獄 The burning, blistering hell. 소향 燒香 To burn incense.

소 紹 To continue, hand down. 소륭 紹隆 To continue (or perpetuate) and prosper Buddhist truth, or the Triratna.

소 銷 To melt metal, dissolve, dispel, dissipate, spend, cancel, end. 소석 銷釋 To solve, explain.

소 塑 To model in clay. 이소목조 泥塑木雕 Modelled clay and carved wood, images. 소상 塑像 To model images.

소 逍 To roam, saunter. 소요자재 逍遙自在 To go anywhere at will, to roam where one will.

소 召 To summon, call. 소청 召請 To invite, especially the Buddhas or bodhisattvas to worship. 소청동자 召請童子 ; 아갈라쇄 阿羯囉灑 The inviter, possibly etymologically connected with acchāvāka ; he is the youth fifth on the left of Mañjuśrī in his group of the Garbhadhātu, and is supposed to invite all the living to enlightenment.

소 掃 To sweep. 소지 掃地 To sweep the floor, or ground, an act to which the Buddha is said to have attributed five kinds of merit ; v. 비나야잡사 毘奈耶雜事.

소 騷 Trouble, sad ; poetic, learned ; translit. *su, s*. 소가타 騷伽陁 ; 소게다 騷揭多 Sugata, v. 수 修. 소비라 騷毗羅 Parisrāvaṇa, a filtering cloth or bag, v. 발리 鉢里.

소겁 小劫 Antara-kalpa, or intermediate kalpa ; according to the 구사론 俱舍論 it is the period in which human life increases by one year a century till it reaches 84,000 with men 8,400 feet high ; then it is reduced at the same rate till the life-period reaches ten years with men a foot high ; these two are each a small kalpa ; the 지도론 智度論 reckons the two together as one kalpa ; and there are other definitions.

소게다 蘇揭多 Sugata ; Svāgata ; well come, or well departed, title of a Buddha ; also 소가다 蘇伽多 ; 소가타 蘇伽陁 ; v. 수 修, 사 沙, 사 莎, 색 索.

소경 小經 v. 소본 小本 ; also styled 소미경 小彌經.

소계 小界 A small assembly of monks for ceremonial purposes.

소공 小空 The Hīnayāna doctrine of the void, as contrasted with that of Mahāyāna.

소근 小根 ; 소기 小機 Having a mind fit only for Hīnayāna doctrine.

소념 小念 To repeat Buddha's name in a quiet voice, opposite of 대념 大念.

소달다 蘇達多 Sudatta, v. 수 須 name of Anāthapiṇḍika (Sanskrit Anāthapiṇḍada). 소달나 蘇達拏 Sudāna, name of Śākyamuni as a great almsgiver in a previous incarnation. 소달이사나 蘇達梨舍那 Sudarśana, the fourth of the seven concentric circles around Sumeru ; also 소질리사나 蘇跌里舍那 ; v. 수 修 and 수 須.

소달라 蘇怛羅 Sūtra ; thread ; a classical work 경 經, especially the sermons or sayings of the Buddha, v. 소 素 and 수 修.

소등 蘇燈 A lamp using butter and fragrant oil ; also 소등 酥燈.

소라다 蘇囉多 Surata, enjoyment, amorous pleasures.

소로다파나 蘇盧多波那 Śrota-āpanna 입류 入流 v. 수 須 and 솔 窣.

소루파 蘇樓波 Surūpa, of beautiful form, handsome.

소리야 蘇利耶 Sūrya, the sun, also 소리야 蘇哩耶 ; 수리야 須梨耶.

소마 蘇摩 Soma, to distil, extract, generate ; the moon-plant, hence the moon ; probably wild rhubarb (Stein). The alcoholic drink made from the plant and formerly offered to the Brahminical gods ; tr. 신주 神酒, wine of the gods. Also rendered 향유 香油 a sweet-smelling oil. 소마제바 蘇摩提婆 Soma-deva, i.e. Candra-deva, the moon-deva. 소마사 蘇摩蛇 Sūmasarpa, a former incarnation of Śākyamuni when he gave his body as a great snake to feed the starving people.

소말나 蘇末那 Sumanā. A yellow sweet-smelling flower growing on a bush 3 or 4 feet high, perhaps the "great-flowered jasmine" ; associated by some with the soma plant, saumanā, a blossom ; also 소마나 蘇摩那 ; 소만나 蘇蔓那 ; 수마나 須摩那.

소목련 小目連 The small Maudgalyāyana, one of six of that name, v. 목 目.

소미(로) 蘇迷(盧) Sumeru, "the Olympus of Hindu mythology," [M. W.] It is the central mountain of every world. Also 소미루 蘇彌樓 v. 수 須.

소바하 蘇波訶 Svāhā, Hail! A kind of Amen ; a mystic word indicating completion, good luck, nirvāṇa, may evil disappear and good be increased ; in India it also indicates an oblation, especially a burnt offering ; the oblation as a female deity. Also 소화하 蘇和訶 ; 소바하 蘇婆訶 ; 소가 蘇呵, also with 사 沙, 사 娑, 사 莎, 살 薩, 솔 率, 삽 馺 as initial syllable.

소반다 蘇槃多 Subanta, also 소만다 蘇漫多, the case of a noun. 소반벌솔다 蘇槃伐率多 ; 소바살도 蘇婆薩都 Śubhavastu, the river Swat.

소발다라 蘇跋陀羅 Subhadra, a learned Brahmiṅ, 120 years old, the last convert made by Śākyamuni.

소백화 小白華 One of the four divine flowers, the mandāra-flower, v. 만 曼.

소번뇌지법 小煩惱地法 Upakleśabhūmikāh. The ten lesser evils or illusions, or temptations, one of the five groups of mental conditions of the seventy-five Hīnayāna elements. They are the minor moral defects arising from 무명 無明 unenlightenment ; i.e. 분 忿 anger, 복 覆 hidden sin, 간 慳 stinginess, 질 嫉 envy, 뇌 惱 vexation, 해 害 ill-will, 한 恨 hate, 도 諂 adulation, 광 誑 deceit, 교 憍 pride.

소벌라 蘇伐剌 Suvarṇa, gold, v. 금 金 ; also 소벌라 蘇伐羅 ; 소부라 蘇嚩囉 and v. 소 素. 소벌라나구달라 蘇伐剌拏瞿怛羅 Suvarṇagotra, a matriarchal kingdom, somewhere in the Himālayas, described as the Golden Clan.

소법 小法 The laws or methods of Hīnayāna.

소본 小本 A small volume ; T'ien-t'ai's term for the (소)아미타경 (小)阿彌陀經 ; the large sūtra being the 무량수경 無量壽經.

소부지 蘇部底 Subhūti, also 소보지 蘇補底 ; v. 수 須 and the 반야 般若 sūtra.

소사 小師 A junior monk of less than ten years full ordination, also a courtesy title for a disciple ; and a self-depreciatory title of any monk ; v. 탁 鐸 dahara.

소사 蕭寺 A name for monasteries in the Liang dynasty, A.D. 502-557, because Liang Wu Ti built so many that they were called after his surname 소 蕭 Hsiao.

소사 小使 To urinate ; also 소행 小行. Buddhist monks are enjoined to urinate only in one fixed spot.

소삼 小參 Small group, a class for instruction outside the regular morning or evening services ; also a class in a household ; the leader is called 소삼두 小參頭.

소상기 小祥忌 An anniversary (sacrifice).

소성 小聖 The Hīnayāna saint, or arhat. The inferior saint, or bodhisattva, as compared with the Buddha.

소수 小樹 Small trees, bodhisattvas in the lower stages, v. 삼초이목 三草二木.

소수천석 小水穿石 A little water or "dripping water penetrates stone" ; the reward of the religious life, though difficult to attain, yields to persistent effort.

소승 小乘 Hīnayāna 희나연 希那衍. The small, or inferior wain, or vehicle ; the form of Buddhism which developed after Śākyamuni's death to about the beginning of the Christian era, when Mahāyāna doctrines were introduced. It is the orthodox school and more in direct line with the Buddhist succession than Mahāyānism which developed on lines fundamentally different. The Buddha was a spiritual doctor, less interested in philosophy than in the remedy for human misery and perpetual transmigration. He "turned aside from idle metaphysical speculations ; if he held views on such topics, he deemed them valueless for the purposes of salvation, which was his goal" (Keith). Metaphysical speculations arose after his death, and naturally developed into a variety of Hīnayāna schools before and after the separation of a distinct school of Mahāyāna. Hīnayāna remains the form in Ceylon, Burma, and Siam, hence is known as Southern Buddhism in contrast with Northern Buddhism or Mahāyāna, the form chiefly prevalent from Nepal to Japan. Another rough division is that of Pali and Sanskrit, Pali being the general literary language of the surviving form of Hīnayāna, Sanskrit of Mahāyāna. The term Hīnayāna is of Mahāyānist origination to emphasize the universalism and altruism of Mahāyāna over the narrower personal salvation of its rival. According to Mahāyāna teaching its own aim is universal Buddhahood, which means the utmost development of wisdom and the perfect transformation of all the living in the future state ; it declares that Hīnayāna, aiming at arhatship and pratyekabuddhahood, seeks the destruction of body and mind and extinction in nirvāṇa. For arhatship the 사제 四諦 Four Noble Truths are the foundation teaching, for pratyeka-buddhahood the 십이인연 十二因緣 twelve-nidānas, and these two are therefore sometimes styled the two vehicles 이승 二乘. T'ien-t'ai sometimes calls them the (Hīnayāna) Tripiṭaka school. Three of the eighteen Hīnayāna schools were transported to China : 구사 俱舍 (Abhidharma) Kośa ; 성실 成實 Satyasiddhi ; and the school of Harivarman, the 율 律 Vinaya school. These are described by Mahāyānists as the Buddha's adaptable way of meeting the questions and capacity of his hearers, though his own mind is spoken of as always being in the absolute Mahāyāna all-embracing realm. Such is the Mahāyāna view of Hīnayāna, and if the Vaipulya sūtras and special scriptures of their school, which are repudiated by Hīnayāna, are apocryphal, of which there seems no doubt, then Mahāyāna in condemning Hīnayāna must find other support for its claim to orthodoxy. The sūtras on which it chiefly relies, as regards the Buddha, have no authenticity ; while those of Hīnayāna cannot be accepted as his veritable teaching in the absence of fundamental research. Hīnayāna is said to have first been divided into minority and majority sections immediately after the death of Śākyamuni, when the sthavira, or older disciples, remained in what is spoken of as "the cave," some place at Rājagṛha, to settle the future of the order, and the general body of disciples remained outside ; these two are the first 상좌부 上坐部 and 대중부 大衆部 q.v. The first doctrinal division is reported to have taken place under the leadership of the monk 대천 大天 Mahādeva (q.v.) a hundred years after the Buddha's nirvāṇa and during the reign of Aśoka ; his reign, however, has been placed later than this by historians. Mahādeva's sect became the Mahāsāṅghika, the other the Sthavira. In time the two are said to have divided into eighteen, which with the two originals are the so-called "twenty sects" of Hīnayāna. Another division of four sects, referred to by I-ching, is that of the 대중부 大衆部 (Arya) Mahāsaṅghanikāya, 상좌부 上座部 Āryasthāvirāḥ, 근본설일체유부 根本說一切有部 Mūlasarvāstivādāḥ, and 정량부 正量部 Saṁmatīya. There is still another division of five sects, 오부율 五部律. For the eighteen Hīnayāna sects see below.

소승경 小乘經 The Hīnayāna sūtras, the four sections of the Āgamas 아함경 阿含經, v. 소승구부 小乘九部.

소승계 小乘戒 The commandments of the Hīnayāna, also recognized by the Mahāyāna : the five, eight, and ten commandments, the 250 for the monks, and the 348 for the nuns.

소승구부 小乘九部 The nine classes of works belonging to the Hīnayāna, i.e. the whole of the twelve classes, v. 십이부 十二部, less the Udāna or Voluntary discourses ; the Vaipulya, or broader teaching ; and the Vyākaraṇa, or prophesies.

소승론 小乘論 The Hīnayāna śāstras or Abhidharma 소승아비달마 小乘阿毗達磨 The philosophical canon of the Hīnayāna, now supposed to consist of some thirty-seven works, the earliest of which is said to be the Guṇanirdeśa-śāstra, tr. as 분별공덕론 分別功德論 before A.D. 220. "The date of the Abhidharma" is "unknown to us" (Keith).

소승사문 小乘四門 T'ien-t'ai's division of Hīnayāna into four schools or doctrines : (1) 유문 有門

Of reality, the existence of all phenomena, the doctrine of being (cf. 발지육족론 發智六足論, etc.) ; (2) 공문 空門 of unreality, or non-existence (cf. 성실론 成實論) ; (3) 역유역공문 亦有亦空門 of both, or relativity of existence and non-existence (cf. 비륵론 毘勒論) ; (4) 비유비공 非有非空 of neither, or transcending existence and non-existence (cf. 가전연경 迦旃延經).

소승삼인 小乘三印 The three characteristic marks of all Hīnayāna sūtras : the impermanence of phenomena, the unreality of the ego, and nirvāṇa.

소승십팔부 小乘十八部 A Chinese list of the "eighteen" sects of the Hīnayāna, omitting Mahāsāṅghikāḥ, Sthavira, and Sarvāstivāda as generic schools : I. 대중부 大衆部 The Mahāsāṅghikāḥ is divided into eight schools as follows : (1) 일설부 一說部 Ekavyāvahārika ; (2) 설출세부 說出世部 Lokottaravādinaḥ ; (3) 계윤부 雞胤部 Kaukkuṭikāḥ (Gokulika) ; (4) 다문부 多聞部 Bahuśrutīyāḥ ; (5) 설가부 說假部 Prajñaptivādin ; (6) 제다산부 制多山部 Jetavanīyāḥ, or Caityaśailāḥ ; (7) 서산주부 西山住部 Aparaśailāḥ ; (8) 북산주부 北山住部 Uttaraśailāḥ. II. 상좌부 上坐部 Āryasthāvirāḥ, or Sthaviravādin, divided into eight schools : (1) 설산부 雪山部 Haimavatāḥ. The 설일체유부 說一切有部 Sarvāstivāda gave rise to (2) 독자부 犢子部 Vātsīputrīyāḥ, which gave rise to (3) 법상부 法上部 Dharmottarīyāḥ ; (4) 현주부 賢胄部 Bhadrayānīyāḥ ; (5) 정량부 正量部 Saṁmatīya ; and (6) 밀림산부 密林山部 Ṣāṇṇagarika ; (7) 화지부 化地部 Mahīśāsaka produced (8) 법장부 法藏部 Dharmaguptāḥ. From the Sarvāstivādins arose also (9) 음광부 飮光部 Kāśyapīyāḥ and (10) 경량부 經量部 Sautrāntikāḥ. v. 종륜론 宗輪論. Cf. Keith, 149-150. The division of the two schools is ascribed to Mahādeva a century after the Nirvāṇa. Under I the first five are stated as arising two centuries after the Nirvāṇa, and the remaining three a century later, dates which are unreliable. Under II, the Haimavatāḥ and the Sarvāstivāda are dated some 200 years after the Nirvāṇa ; from the Sarvāstivādins soon arose the Vātsīputrīyāḥs, from whom soon sprang the third, fourth, fifth, and sixth ; then from the Sarvāstivādins there arose the seventh which gave rise to the eighth, and again, nearing the 400th year, the Sarvāstivādins gave rise to the ninth and soon after the tenth. In the list of eighteen the Sarvāstivāda is not counted, as it split into all the rest.

소승외도 小乘外道 Hīnayāna and the heretical sects ; also, Hīnayāna is a heretical sect.

소승이부 小乘二部 The 상좌부 上座部 Sthaviravādin, School of Presbyters, and 대중부 大衆部 Sarvāstivādin, q.v.

소승편점계 小乘偏漸戒 The Hīnayāna partial and gradual method of obeying laws and commandments, as compared with the full and immediate salvation of Mahāyāna.

소식 小食 The small meal, breakfast, also called 점심 點心.

소실지 蘇悉地 Susiddhi, a mystic word of the Tantra School, meaning "may it be excellently accomplished," v. the 소실지경 蘇悉地經 Susiddhi and 소실지갈라경 蘇悉地羯羅經 Susiddhikāra sūtras.

소아사 小阿師 A junior monk ordained less than ten years.

소오조 小五條 The robe of five patches worn by some monks in China and by the 정토종 淨土宗 Jōdō sect of Japan ; v. 괘 掛.

소왕 小王 The small rājas, called 속산왕 粟散王 millet-scattering kings.

소원 小院 A junior teacher.

소원 小遠 The monk 혜원 慧遠 Hui-yüan of the Sui dynasty. There was a 진 晉 Chin dynasty monk of the same name.

소유 蘇油 Ghṛta, ghee, or clarified butter ; scented oil extracted from the sumanā plant.

소율의 小律儀 The rules and regulations for monks and nuns in Hīnayāna.

소적화 小赤華 Mañjūṣaka. 만수사화 曼殊沙華 ; 만수안 曼殊顔 Explained by 유연 柔軟 pliable. Rubia cordifolia, yielding the madder (munjeeth) of Bengal.

소종 小宗 The sects of Hīnayāna.

소천(세계) 小千(世界) A small chiliocosm, consisting of a thousand worlds each with its Mt. Sumeru, continents, seas, and ring of iron mountains ; v. 삼천대천세계 三千大千世界.

소초 小草 Smaller herbs, those who keep the five commandments and do the ten good deeds, thereby attaining to rebirth as men or devas, v. 삼초이목 三草二木.

소투파 蘇偸婆 Stūpa, v. 솔 率.

소품 小品 A summarized version. 소품(반야바라밀)경 小品(般若波羅蜜)經 Kumārajīva's abbreviated version, in ten chüan, of the Mahā-prajñā-pāramitā-sūtra.

소행 小行 The practice, or discipline of Hīnayāna ; also, urination.

속 俗 Common, ordinary, usual, vulgar. 속인 俗人 Gṛhastha, an ordinary householder ; an ordinary man ; the laity. 속진 俗塵 common dust, earthly pollution. 속형 俗形 Of ordinary appearance, e.g. the laity. 속계 俗戒 The common commandments for the laity. 속아 俗我 The popular idea of the ego or soul. i.e. the empirical or false ego 가아 假我, composed of the five skandhas. This is to be distinguished from the true ego 진아 眞我 or 실아 實我, the metaphysical substratum from which all empirical elements have been eliminated ; v. 팔대자재아 八大自在我. 속지 俗智 Common or worldly wisdom, which by its illusion blurs or colours the mind, binding it to reality. 속류 俗流 The common run or flow. 속제 俗諦, 세제 世諦 Common principles, or axioms ; normal unenlightened ideas, in contrast with reality.

속 速 Haste, quick ; speedily, urgent. 속득 速得 Speedily obtain, or ensure. 속성 速成 Speedily completed. 속질귀 速疾鬼 Hurrying demons, rākṣasa. 속향 速香 Quickly burnt inferior incense.

속 粟 Maize, millet. 속산 粟散 Like scattered millet. 속산왕 粟散王 Scattered kings, or rulers who own allegiance to a supreme sovereign, as 속산국 粟散國 means their territories.

속 續 To join on, continue, add, supplementary, a supplement. 속명 續命 (Prayers for) continued life, for which the 속명신번 續命神幡 flag of five colours is displayed.

속 贖 To redeem, ransom. 속명 贖命 To redeem life ; a redeemer of life, said of the Nirvāṇa sūtra.

속려 束慮 To tie reeds together in order to make them stand up, illustration of the interdependence of things and principles.

손 孫 Grandchild ; grandson ; translit. *sun*. 손다리 孫陀利 Sundarī, wife of Sundarananda ; Sundari, name of an arhat ; also a courtesan who defamed the Buddha. 손다라난다 孫陀羅難陀 Sundarananda, or Sunanda, said to be younger brother of Śākyamuni, his wife being the above Sundarī ; thus called to distinguish him from Ānanda.

손 損 To spoil, hurt, damage. 손복단 損伏斷 To spoil, subject and destroy (the passions).

손 遜 To yield, accord ; modest.

솔 率 A net with handle ; to pursue, follow after ; lead on ; suddenly ; generally. 솔도파 率都婆 Stūpa, a mound, v. 탑 塔. 솔록근나 率祿勤那 Srughna. "An ancient kingdom and city near the upper course of the Yamunā, probably the region between" Saharanpur and Srinagar. [Eitel].

솔 窣 Rustle, move, rush ; translit. *s*. 솔누려습벌라 窣耨黎濕伐羅 Sūnurīśvara, ancient capital of Laṅgala, in the Punjab. 솔리 窣利 Suri, "an ancient kingdom to the west of Kachgar, peopled by Turks (A.D. 600)." [Eitel]. 솔리 窣唎 ; 솔라 窣羅 Surī, or Surā, distilled liquor. 솔도파 窣堵波 Stūpa, a tumulus, or building over relics, v. 솔 率. 솔사게치 窣莎揭哆 Suṣvāgata, most welcome (a greeting). 솔로다아반나 窣路多阿半那 Śrota-āpanna, one who has entered the stream of the holy life, cf. 수 須 and 입류 入流. 솔도리혜나 窣都利慧那 Sutriṣṇa, Satruṣṇa, Osrushna, Ura-tepe, "an ancient city in Turkestan between Kojend and Samarcand." [Eitel].

송 頌 Extol, praise. Gāthā hymns, songs, verses, stanzas, the metrical part of a sūtra ; cf. 가타 伽陀.

송 宋 The Sung dynasty, A.D. 960-1280. 송원입장제대소승경 宋元入藏諸大小乘經 Sūtras of the Hīnayāna and Mahāyāna admitted into the canon during the Northern and Southern Sung (A.D. 960-1127 and 1127-1280) and Yüan (A.D. 1280-1368) dynasties. [B.N.] 782-1081. 송제왕 宋帝王 The third of the ten rulers of Hades, who presides over the Kālasūtra, the hell of black ropes.

송 送 To escort, send, give as a present. 송망 送亡 To escort or take the departed to the grave. 송장 送葬 To escort for burial.

송 誦 To murmur, recite, intone, memorize by repeating in a murmur, cf. 염 念. 송경 誦經 To intone sūtras.

송광사 松廣寺 Song-gwang-sa. Lit. "Piny Expanse Monastery". A temple located in Mt. Jogyesan, Sinpyeong-ri Songgwang-myeon Seungju-gun Jeollanam-do in Korea. The 21th parish headquarters of Korean Jogye Order. It is one of the four 총림 叢林.

쇄 碎 Broken, fragments. 쇄신사리 碎身舍利 Relics of a cremated body.

쇄 鎖 Lock, chain. 쇄시 鎖匙 ; 쇄약 鎖鑰 Lock and key ; key.

쇄 曬 To dry in the sun. 쇄계 曬闍 Sukha, delight, joy.

쇄 灑 To sprinkle, translit. *sa*. 쇄수 灑水 To sprinkle water. 쇄정 灑淨 To purify by sprinkling.

쇠 衰 Decay, fade, decline ; frayed, i.e. mourning clothes. 쇠상 衰相 The (five) indications of approaching death, v. 오쇠 五衰. 쇠환 衰患 The calamities of decadence, famine, epidemics, etc.

수 藪 A marsh, reserve, retreat, refuge, lair ; translit. *s*, *su*. 수두파 藪斗婆 v. 탑 塔 13 Stūpa. 수달리사누 藪達梨舍菟 Sudarśana, the fourth circle round Meru, cf. 소 蘇 20.

수 銖 A weight equal to the twenty-fourth part of a tael ; a small ancient coin ; a scruple ; trifles. 수의 銖衣 The gossamer clothing of the devas, or angels.

수 獸 An animal, a brute. 수주 獸主 Paśupati, lord of the animals, or herds ; Śiva ; also name of a non-Buddhist sect. Cf. 축생 畜生 10.

수 嗽 Cough. 수비 嗽卑 Upāsikā, an old form, see 오 烏 a female disciple.

수 垂 Drop, droop, let down, pass down ; regard. 수시 垂示 ; 수어 垂語 To make an announcement. 수적 垂迹 Traces, vestiges ; manifestations or incarnations of Buddhas and bodhisattvas in their work of saving the living.

수 隨 Follow, comply with ; sequent, consequent, after, according to, as ; often used for the prefix *anu*.

수 首 Head. 수도다나 首圖駄那 ; 수두단 輸頭檀 or 열두단 閱頭檀 Śuddhodana, intp. "정반 淨飯 pure food," king of Kapilavastu, husband of Mahāmāyā, and father of Śākyamuni. 수좌 首座 The chief seat, president, chief. 수회 首悔 Voluntary confession and repentance. 수능엄 首楞嚴 ; 수릉가마 首楞伽摩 Śūraṁgama, intp. 건상 健相 heroic, resolute ; the virtue or power which enables a Buddha to overcome every obstacle, obtained in the 수능엄정 首楞嚴定 or 삼매 三昧 Śūraṁgama dhyāna or samādhi ; 수능엄경 首楞嚴經 is the sūtra on the subject, whose full title commences 대불정 大佛頂, etc. 수로(가) 首盧(迦) or 首盧(柯) ; 수로가(바) 輸盧迦(波) or 실로가(바) 室盧迦(波) ; 실로가 室路迦 Śloka, a stanza of thirty-two syllables, either in four lines of eight each, or two of sixteen. 수라(발) 首羅(髮) or 주라(발) 周羅(髮) Cūlaka, Cūḍa ; one of the eight yakṣas, or demons. 수하기나 首訶既那 or 수아기나 首阿既那 Śubhakṛtsna, the ninth brahmaloka, i.e. the third region of the third dhyāna of form. 수다(라) 首陀(羅) ; 수다라 戍陀羅 or 수달라 戍達羅 or 수날라 戍捺羅 Śūdra, the fourth of the four castes, peasants. 수다(사)바 首陀(娑)婆 or 사다(사)바 私陀(娑)婆 Śuddhāvāsa, the five pure abodes, or heavens. 수제 首題 Heading or title (of a sūtra).

수 守 Keep, guard, observe. 수사 守寺 The guardian, or caretaker, of a monastery. 수법 守法 To keep the law. 수호 守護 To guard, protect. 수문천 守門天 or 수문존 守門尊 The deva gate-guardian of a temple.

수 壽 Long life, longevity, age, v. 기바 耆婆 jīva. 수상 壽像 A portrait, or statue of a man of years while still alive. 수명 壽命 Jīvita, life, length of days, age. 수명무유량 壽命無有量 ; 수명무수겁 壽命無數劫 The infinite life of Buddha. 수론 壽論 ; 아유 阿由 The Āyurveda, the medical Vedas, v. 위 韋. 수량품 壽量品 The chapter in the Lotus sūtra where Buddha declares his eternity ; v. also the 무량수경 無量壽經.

수 酬 Pledge, toast, requite. 수환 酬還 To pay a vow, repay.

수 手 Pāṇi ; hasta ; kara ; hand, arm. 수인 手印 Mudrā, mystic positions of the hand ; signet-rings, seals ; finger-prints. 수구의상응 手口意相應 In yoga practices it means correspondence of hand, mouth, and mind, i.e. manual signs, esoteric words or spells, and thought or mental projection. 수집금강저 手執金剛杵 Vajrapāṇi, or Vajradhara, who holds the thunderbolt. 수로 手爐 A portable censer (with handle). 수경 手磬 A hand-chime (or bell) struck with a stick. 수륜 手輪 The lines on the palm and fingers — especially the "thousand" lines on a Buddha's hand.

수 繡 To embroider, embellish. 수불 繡佛 Embroidered pictures of the Buddha, etc. 수리밀다 繡利蜜多 Sūryamitra, the sun-god.

수 須 To expect, wait for, wait on ; necessary, must ; moment, small, translit. for *su* ; cf. 소 蘇. 수야마 須夜摩 Suyāma, also 수염마 須炎摩 or 須燄摩, intp. as Yama, the ruler of the Yama heaven ; and in other similar ways. 수대나 須大拏 Sudāna, *infra.* 수미 須彌 Sumeru, also 수미루 須彌樓 ; 미루 彌樓 ; 소미루 蘇彌樓 ; 수미루 修迷樓 ; later 소미로 蘇迷盧 ; the central mountain of every world, tr. as 묘고 妙高 ; 묘광 妙光, etc., wonderful height, wonderful brilliancy, etc. ; at the top is Indra's heaven, or heavens, below them are the four devalokas ; around are eight circles of mountains and between them the eight seas, the whole forming nine mountains and eight seas. 수미좌 須彌座 ; 수미단 須彌壇 A kind of throne for a Buddha. 수미상 須彌相 Merudhvaja, or Merukalpa, name of the universe of 수미등왕불 須彌燈王佛, in the northwest, twelfth son of Mahābhijñā. 수미정 須彌頂 Merukūṭa, second son of Mahābhijñā, whose name is 수밀라천 須蜜羅天 Abhirati. 수선다 須扇多 Suśānta, a Buddha of this name, "very placid," [M. W.] ; entirely pure ; also 수연두 須延頭 Suyata. 수마제 須摩提 or 須摩題 Sumati, of wonderful meaning, or wisdom, the abode of Amitābha, his Pure Land. 수마나 須摩那 Sumanā, also 수마나 修摩那 or 소마나 蘇摩那 ; 수만나 須曼那 ; a plant 4 or 5 feet high with light yellow flowers, the "great flowered jasmine." [M. W.] 수리야 須梨耶 Sūrya, the sun. 수열밀타 須涅蜜陀 Sunirmita, but suggestive in meaning of nirmāṇarati, heavens or devas of joyful transformation. 수진 須眞 Sucinti, or Sucintā, or Sucitti, name of a deva. 수유 須臾 A kṣaṇa, a moment. 수보리 須菩提 Subhūti, also 수부리 須扶提 ; 수부제 須浮帝 ; 소보지 蘇補底 or 소부지 蘇部底 ; one of ten chief disciples, said to have been the best exponent of Śūnya, or the void 해공제일 解空第一 ; he is the principal interlocutor in the Prajñāpāramitā sūtra. There are two later personages of this name. 수발다(라) 須跋陀(羅) Subhadra ; the last convert of the Buddha, "a Brahman 120 years old." 수달(다) 須達(多) ; 소달다 蘇達多 Sudatta, well-given, intp. as a good giver, beneficent ; known as 급독 給獨 benefactor of orphans, etc. His name was Anāthapiṇḍika, who bestowed the Jetavana vihāra on the Buddha. 수달천 須達天 Sudṛśa, the 선현천 善現天 ; seventh Brahmaloka, eighth of the Dhyāna heavens. 수달나 須達拏 Sudāna, also 수대나 須大拏 ; 수제리나 須提梨拏 ; 소달나 蘇達拏, a previous incarnation of the Buddha, when he forfeited the throne by almsgiving ; it is confused in meaning with 선아 善牙 Sudanta, good teeth. 수달리사나 須達梨舍那 ; 수대 須帶 Sudarśana, the heaven of beautiful appearance, the sixteenth Brahmaloka, and seventh of the fourth Dhyāna. 수다 須陀 Śūdra, the fourth caste, cultivators, etc., cf. 수 首 ; also sudhā, nectar. 수다원 須陀洹 Śrota-āpanna ; also 수다반나 須陀般那 ; 솔로다아반나 窣路多阿半那 or 솔로타아발낭 窣路陀阿鉢囊 ; intp. by 입류 入流, one who has entered the stream of holy living, also 역류 逆流, one who goes against the stream of transmigration ; the first stage of the arhat, that of a śrāvaka, v. 성문 聲聞. 수다(수)마 須陀(須)摩 Sudhāman, a king mentioned in the 지도론 智度論 4.

수 授 To give, confer, deliver, communicate to, hand down. 수사 授事 Karmadāna, the director of duties, the one who gives out the work. 수수 授手 To proffer the hand, to come in person to welcome the dying, as e.g. does Kuan-yin in certain cases. 수결 授決 To give decisions, idem 수기 授記. 수의 授衣 To give out winter garments in the ninth month. 수기 授記 ; 화가라 和伽羅 Vyākaraṇa, Vyākāra ; the giving of a record, prediction ; foretelling ; the prophetic books of the Canon predicting the future glory of individuals and groups of disciples, both final and temporary, and the various stages of progress. There are several classifications, v. 이기 二記 and 팔기 八記. Cf. 교 憍.

수 殊 To kill, exterminate ; different ; very. 수승 殊勝 Rare, extraordinary, surpassing, as the 수승전 殊勝殿 and 수승지 殊勝池 surpassing palace and lake of Indra. 수묘신 殊妙身 Surpassingly wonderful body, i.e. Padmottara, the 729th Buddha of the present kalpa. 수지(색)가 殊底(色)迦 Jyotiṣka, 수지색가 殊底穡迦 ; 취지색가 聚底色迦 ; 수제가 樹提迦 "a luminary, a heavenly body." [M. W.] Name of a wealthy elder of Rājagṛha, who gave all his goods to the poor. 수미가 殊微伽 One of the four kinds of ascetics who dressed in rags and ate garbage. 수치아라바 殊致阿羅婆 Jyotīrasa, tr. as 광미 光味 flavour of light, said to be the proper name of Kharoṣṭha, v. 거 佉.

수 數 To number, count, enumerate, figure out, calculate, reason, reprimand ; numbers, an account, fate, destiny ; flurried. It is also used for 지 智 knowledge, and for mental content or conditions as in 심수 心數. 수인 數人 ; 수법인 數法人 Those of the Sarvāstivāda school, cf. 살 薩, who held that all things are real. 수취취 數取趣 A definition of Pudgala, i.e. all beings subject to transmigration. 수식 數息 To count the breathings in order to calm mind and body for meditation, e.g. 수식관 數息觀 ; 수(식)문 數(息)門 ; cf. 아 阿 Ānāpāna. 수주 數珠 A rosary ; to tell beads, which consist of various numbers, generally 108. 수연진 數緣盡 ; 수멸무위 數滅無爲 idem 택멸 擇滅. 수행번뇌 數行煩惱 The common passions and their consequences. 수론 數論 The śāstras of the Sarvāstivādins ; also Kapila, called 수론외도 數論外道 ; 수론사 數論師 founder of the Sāṅkhya philosophy ; v. 승가 僧伽 ; 겁 劫 and 가 迦. It is an attempt to place all concepts in twenty-five categories, with Puruṣa at the head and the others in ordered progress. *Inter alia* it also teaches "the eternity and multiplicity of souls" [Eitel]. Vasubandhu wrote in criticism of the system.

The series of higher numbers is as follows :

낙차 洛叉 or 낙사 洛沙 Lakṣa 100,000
도락차 度洛叉 a million
조구지 兆俱胝 10 millions 경 京
미타 末陀 100 millions 자 秭
아수다 阿庾多 1,000 millions 해 垓
대아수다 大阿庾多 10,000 millions 양 壤
나수다 那庾多 100,000 millions 구 溝
대나수다 大那庾多 1 billion 간 澗
발라수다 鉢羅庾多 10 billions 정 正
대발라수다 大鉢羅庾多 100 billions 대 戴
긍갈라 矜羯羅 ; 견가라 甄迦羅 1,000 billions
대긍갈라 大矜羯羅 10,000 billions
빈바라 頻婆羅 or 빈발라 頻跋羅 100,000 billions
대빈바라 大頻婆羅 1 trillion
아촉바 阿閦婆 or 아추바 阿芻婆 10 trillions
대아촉바 大阿閦婆 100 trillions
비바하 毘婆訶 1,000 trillions
대비바하 大毘婆訶 10,000 trillions
올층가 嗢蹭伽 100,000 trillions
대올층가 大嗢蹭伽 1 quadrillion
바갈나 婆喝那 10 quadrillions
대바갈나 大婆喝那 100 quadrillions
지치바 地致婆 1,000 quadrillions
대지치바 大地致婆 10,000 quadrillions
혜도 醯都 100,000 quadrillions
대혜도 大醯都 1 quintillion
갈랍박 羯臘縛 or 羯臘縛 10 quintillions
대갈랍박 大羯臘縛 or 大羯臘縛 100 quintillions
인달라 印達羅 1,000 quintillions
대인달라 大印達羅 10,000 quintillions
삼마발탐 三磨鉢耽 100,000 quintillions
대삼마발탐 大三磨鉢耽 1 sextillion
게지 揭底 10 sextillions
대게지 大揭底 100 sextillions
고벌라사 枯筏羅闍 1,000 sextillions
대고벌라사 大枯筏羅闍 10,000 sextillions
모달라 姥達羅 100,000 sextillions
대모달라 大姥達羅 1 septillion
발람 跋藍 10 septillions
대발람 大跋藍 100 septillions
산야 珊若 1,000 septillions
대산야 大珊若 10,000 septillions
비보다 毘步多 100,000 septillions
대비보다 大毘步多 1 octillion
발라참 跋羅攙 10 octillions
대발라참 大跋羅攙 100 octillions
아승기야 阿僧企耶 asaṁkhyeya, innumerable.

수 輸 To pay one's dues, to lose, be beaten, ruined ; translit. *su*, *śu* ; cf. 수 首 ; 실 室 ; 소 蘇. 수구로나 輸拘盧那 Śuklodana, a prince of Kapilavastu, younger brother of Śuddhodana, and father of Tiṣya, Devadatta, and Nandika. 수바가라 輸波迦羅 ; 수바가라 輸婆迦羅 Śubhākarasiṁha, name of 선무외삼장 善無畏三藏 a famous Indian monk. 수라 輸羅 ; 수나 輸那 Śūla, a lance, dart, etc. ; also Śūra, hero, heroic. 수로가(바) 輸盧迦(波) v. 수 首 Śloka. 수달라 輸達羅 Śūdra, the fourth caste, i.e. of slaves, servants, labourers, farmers, etc.

수 修 To put in order, mend, cultivate, observe. Translit. *su*, *sū*. Cf. 수 須 ; 소 蘇.

수 收 To receive ; collect, gather ; withdraw. 수초 收鈔 To collect paper money, i.e. receive contributions. 수골 收骨 To collect the bones, or relics, after cremation.

수 受 To receive, be, bear, intp. of Vedanā, "perception," "knowledge obtained by the senses, feeling, sensation." [M. W.] It is defined as mental reaction to the object, but in general it means receptivity, or sensation ; the two forms of sensation of physical and mental objects are indicated. It is one of the five skandhas ; as one of the twelve nidānas it indicates the incipient stage of sensation in the embryo. 수구 受具 To receive the entire commandments, as does a fully ordained monk or nun. 수상행식 受想行識 The four immaterial skandhas — vedanā, saṁjñā, saṁskāra, vijñāna, i.e. feeling, ideation, reaction, consciousness. 수계 受戒 To receive, or accept, the commandments, or rules ; a disciple ; the beginner receives the first five, the monk, nun, and the earnest laity proceed to the reception of eight, the fully ordained accepts the ten. The term is also applied by the esoteric sects to the reception of their rules on admission. 수지 受持 To receive and retain, or hold on to, or keep (the Buddha's teaching). 수업 受業 Duties of the receiver of the rules ; also to receive the results or karma of one's deeds. 수세 受歲 To receive, or add, a year to his monastic age, on the conclusion of the summer's retreat. 수용 受用 Received for use. 수용신 受用身 The Sambhogakāya 보신 報身 v. 삼신 三身 Trikāya, i.e. the functioning glorious body, 자수용 自受用 for a Buddha's own use, bliss ; 타수용 他受用 for the spiritual benefit of others. 수용토 受用土 The realm of the Sambhogakāya. 수자 受者 A recipient (e.g. of the rules). The illusory view that the ego will receive reward or punishment in a future life, one of the sixteen false views. 수온 受蘊 Vedanā, sensation, one of the five skandhas. 수기 受記 ; 수결 受決 ; 수별 受別 To receive from a Buddha predestination (to become a Buddha) ; the prophecy of a bodhisattva's future Buddhahood. 수수 受隨 To receive the rules and follow them out 수체수행 受體隨行.

수 竪 To stand, erect, upright. 수지사론 竪底沙論 The Jyotiṣa śāstra. 수적 竪敵 Protagonist and antagonist in debate. 수의 竪義 ; 입의 立義 To propound a thesis and defend it. 수자 竪者 One who supplies answers to difficulties.

수 樹 Vṛkṣa, a tree ; to stand, erect, establish. 수제(가) 樹提(伽) ; 수지색가 殊底色迦 Jyotiṣka, "a luminary, a heavenly body" [M. W.] ; tr. asterisms, shining, fire, or fate. A wealthy man of Rājagṛha, who gave all his goods to the poor ; there is a sūtra called after him. 수림 樹林 A grove, a forest. 수경 樹經 Scriptures written on tree-leaves or bark, chiefly on palm-leaves.

수 水 Water ; liquid.

수 睡 Śaya, asleep ; sleep ; śay, to sleep. 수면 睡眠 idem ; also Middha, drowsiness, torpor, sloth. 수면욕 睡眠欲 The lust for sleep, physical and spiritual, hence 수면개 睡眠蓋 sleep, drowsiness, or sloth as a hindrance to progress.

수 宿 A halting-place ; nakṣatra, the constellations. 수요 宿曜 The twenty-eight constellations and seven luminaries.

수가타 修伽陀 Sugata, one who has gone the right way, one of a Buddha's titles ; sometimes

. intp. as well-come (Svāgata). Also 수가다 修伽多 ; 수가도 修伽度 ; 수게다 修揭多 or 소게다 蘇揭多 ; 사파게다 沙婆揭多 ; 사가(타) 莎伽(陀).

수견 修堅 Firmness in observing or maintaining ; established conviction, e.g. of the 별교 別教 bodhisattva that all phenomena in essence are identical.

수경률 隨經律 According to the discipline as described in the sūtras, i.e. the various regulations for conduct in the Sūtra-piṭaka ; the phrase 수율경 隨律經 means according to the wisdom and insight as described in the Vinaya-piṭaka.

수계 水界 The realm of water, one of the 사대 四大 four elements.

수관 水冠 A monk's hat shaped like the character "water" in front.

수관 水觀 also 수상관 水相觀 ; 수상 水想 similar to 수정 水定 q.v.

수구 隨求 According to prayer. Name of a deva who was formerly a wicked monk who died and went to hell, but when dying repented, prayed, and was reborn the deva 수구천자 隨求天子 or 수구즉득천자 隨求卽得天子. Also, a bodhisattva in the Kuan-yin group of the Garbhadhātu, a metamorphosis of Kuan-yin, who sees that all prayers are answered, 수구보살 隨求菩薩.

수기 隨機 According to capacity, capability, or opportunity, e.g. the teaching of the Buddha according with the capacity of everyone.

수기 水器 Water vessel ; a filter used by the esoterics in baptismal and other rites.

수낭 水囊 A water-bag, or filter.

수능 秀能 The two patriarchs 신수 神秀 Shên-hsiu and 혜능 慧能 Hui-nêng, q.v.

수다라 修多羅 Sūtra ; from *siv*, to sew, to thread, to string together, intp. as 정 綎 ; i.e. 선 線 thread, string ; strung together as a garland of flowers. Sūtras or addresses attributed to the Buddha, usually introduced by 여시아문 如是我聞 thus have I heard, Evam mayā śrutam. It is intp. by 경 經 a warp, i.e. the threads on which a piece is woven ; it is the Sūtra-piṭaka, or first portion of the Tripiṭaka ; but is sometimes applied to the whole cannon. It is also intp. 계 契 or 계경 契經 scriptures. Also 수단라 修單羅 ; 수투로 修妬路 ; 수다란 修多闌 ; 수단란다 修單蘭多 ; 소달람 素呾纜 or 素怛纜 ; 소다라 素多羅 or 소달라 素呾羅. A clasp on the seven-piece robe of the 진종 眞宗 Shin sect.

수다리사나 修陀里舍那 Sudarśana, intp. 선견 善見 beautiful, given as the name of a yakṣa ; cf. also 소 蘇.

수단 水壇 The water, or round, altar in the Homa, or Fire ceremonial of the esoterics ; also an altar in a house, which is cleansed with filtered water in times of peril.

수대 水大 The element water, one of the four elements 사대 四大 q.v.

수덕사 修德寺 Su-deog-sa. A temple located in Mt. Deogsungsan, Sacheon-ri Deogsan-myeon Yesan-gun Chungcheongnam-do in Korea. The 7th parish headquarters of Korean Jogye Order.

수도 修道 To cultivate the way of religion ; be religious ; the way of self-cultivation. In the Hīnayāna the stage from anāgāmin to arhat ; in Mahāyāna one of the bodhisattva stages.

수두 水頭 The waterman in a monastery.

수등 水燈 The water-lantern festival in the seventh month.

수라 水羅 A gauze filter.

수라 修羅 Asura, demons who war with Indra ; v. 아수라 阿修羅 ; it is also Sura, which means a god, or deity. 수라군 修羅軍 The army of asuras, fighting on the 수라장 修羅場 asura battlefield against Indra. 수라주 修羅酒 Surā, wine, spirits ; but it is also intp. as asura wine, i.e. the nonexistent. 수라도 修羅道 or 수라취 修羅趣 Asura way, or destiny.

수로학 水老鶴 A bird, very rarely seen, possibly a snow-goose ; also 수백학 水白鶴 ; 수백로 水白鷺 ; 수학 水涸.

수류 隨類 According to class, or type. 수류응동 隨類應同 Buddhas and bodhisattvas reveal themselves in varying forms according to the need or nature of the beings whom they desire to save. 수류생 隨類生 They are also born into the conditions of those they seek to save.

수륙회 水陸會 ; 수륙재 水陸齋 The festival of water and land, attributed to Wu Ti of the Liang dynasty consequent on a dream ; it began with placing food in the water for water sprites, and on land for 귀 鬼 ghosts ; see 석문정통 釋門正統 4.

수륜 水輪 The third of the four "wheels" on which the earth rests — space, wind (or air), water, and metal. 수륜삼매 水輪三昧 The samādhi of the above water "wheel", one of the 오륜삼매 五輪三昧, water is fertilizing and soft, in like manner the effect of this samādhi is the fertilizing of good roots, and the softening or reduction of ambition and pride.

수리 修利 Sūrya, 소리야 蘇利耶 the sun ; also name of a yakṣa, the ruler of the sun.

수만 水滿 Jalāmbara (third son of 유수 流水 Jalavāhana) reborn as Śākyamuni's son Rāhula.

수말포염 水沫泡焰 Spume, bubbles, and flame, e.g. that all is unreal and transient.

수면 隨眠 Yielding to sleep, sleepiness, drowsiness, comatose, one of the kleśa, or temptations ; also used by the Sarvāstivādins as an equivalent for kleśa, the passions and delusions ; by the 유식 唯識 school as the seed of kleśa ; there are categories of 6, 7, 10, 12, and 98 kinds of 수면 隨眠.

수발나 修跋拏 Suvarṇa ; 수월나 修越拏 ; 소벌랄 蘇伐剌 gold.

수방 隨方 According to place ; suitable to the place ; in whatever place ; wherever. 수방비니 隨方毘尼 Vinaya, or rules, suitable to local conditions ; or to conditions everywhere.

수번뇌 隨煩惱 Sequent, or associated kleśa-trials, or evils, either all of them as always dogging the foot-steps ; or, especially those which follow the six 수면 隨眠 q.v. Also called 수혹 隨惑.

수법행 隨法行 Those who follow the truth by reason of intellectual ability, in contrast with the non-intellectual, who put their trust in others. v. 수신행 隨信行.

수분 隨分 According to the part assigned or expected ; according to lot, or duty. 수분각 隨分覺 Partial enlightenment, the third of the 사각 四覺 in the Awakening of Faith 기신론 起信論.

수사리 隨舍利 Vaiśālī ; the Licchavis were the people of "the ancient republic of Vaiśālī who were among the earliest followers of Śākyamuni." Also 수사리 隨邪利 and v. 리 梨.

수사화 水梭花 Water shuttle flowers, i.e. fish.

수상 隨相 The secondary states, i.e. of birth, stay, change, and death, in all phenomena. 수상계 隨相戒 To follow the forms and discipline of the Buddha, i.e. become a monk.

수상포 水上泡 A bubble on the water, emblem of all things being transient.

수색마니 隨色摩尼 A precious stone that takes on the colour of its surroundings.

수생 修生 That which is produced by cultivation, or observance.

수선 修善 To cultivate goodness ; the goodness that is cultivated, in contrast with natural goodness.

수선육묘문 修禪六妙門 The six mysterious gates or ways of practising meditation, consisting mostly of breathing exercises.

수성 修性 To cultivate the nature ; the natural proclivities. 수성불이문 修性不二門 The identity of cultivation and the cultivated.

수소단 修所斷 To cut off illusion in practice, or performance.

수순 隨順 To follow, accord with, obey ; to believe and follow the teaching of another.

수습력 修習力 The power acquired by the practice of all (good) conduct ; the power of habit.

수신행 隨信行 The religious life which is evolved from faith in the teaching of others ; it is that of the 둔근 鈍根 unintellectual type.

수심 隨心 According to mind, or wish.

수심결 修心訣 A masterpiece of 지눌 知訥.

수악 修惡 To cultivate evil ; cultivated evil in contrast with evil by nature.

수연 隨緣 According with, or resulting from conditioning causes, or circumstances, as waves result from wind ; also, sequent conditions ; also, according to circumstances, e.g. 수연화물 隨緣化物 to convert or transform people according to their conditions, or to circumstances in general. 수연불변 隨緣不變 Ever changing in conditions yet immutable in essence ; i.e. the 진여 眞如, in its two aspects of 수연진여 隨緣眞如 the absolute in its phenomenal relativity ; and considered as immutable, the 불변진여 不變眞如, which is likened to the water as opposed to the waves.

수옥 水玉 Sphaṭika, 색파지가 塞頗胝迦 ; 파치가 婆致迦 water crystal, rock crystal.

수요 水曜 The planet Mercury, one of the nine luminaries ; it is shown south of the west door of the diamond court in the Garbhadhātu.

수원 水圓 Water-globule, a tabu term for the more dangerous term 화주 火珠 fire-pearl or ruby, also altered to 주원 珠圓 pearl ball ; it is the ball on top of a pagoda.

수월 水月 Udakacandra ; jalacandra ; the moon reflected in the water, i.e. all is illusory and unreal. 수월관음 水月觀音 Kuan-yin gazing at the moon in the water, i.e. the unreality of all phenomena.

수유 水乳 Water and milk – an illustration of the intermingling of things ; but their essential separateness is recognized in that the rāja-haṁsa (a kind of goose) is said to be able to drink up the milk leaving behind the water.

수의 隨義 According to intention, to meaning, or to the right.

수의 隨宜 As suitable, proper, or needed.

수의 隨意 At will, following one's own wishes.

수의과 隨意科 Following one's own wishes studies course in seminary 강원 講院 ; graduate school course work.

수자 隨自 At one's own will ; voluntary. 수자의어 隨自意語 Voluntary addresses, or remarks volunteered by the Buddha.

수장 水葬 Water-burial, casting a corpse into the water, one of the four forms of burial.

수장 水藏 Water-store, or treasury ; second son of Jalavāhana, born as 구파 瞿波 Gopā, see 수만 水滿.

수재 水災 The calamity of water, or flood ; one of the three final world catastrophes of fire, wind, and water, v. 삼재 三災.

수전(리문) 隨轉(理門) The sects or teaching of adaptable philosophies not revealed by the Buddhas and bodhisattvas, in contrast with 진실(리문) 眞實(理門) the truth as revealed by them.

수전의 水田衣 A monk's robe, because its patches resemble rice-fields ; also 도전의 稻田衣.

수정 水淨 Cleansed by water ; edibles recovered from flowing water are "clean" food to a monk.

수정 隨情 Compliant, yielding to other people's wishes.

수정 水精 Sphaṭika, crystal, idem 수옥 水玉.

수정 水定 The water dhyāna, in which one becomes identified with water, for during the period of trance one may become water ; stories are told of devotees who, having turned to water, on awaking found stones in their bodies which had been thrown into their liquid bodies, and which were only removed during a succeeding similar trance.

수조국 修造局 A workshop (in a monastery).

수중월 水中月 v. 수월 水月.

수진 水塵 An atom of dust wandering freely in water — one of the smallest of things.

수참 修懺 To undergo the discipline of penitence.

수천 水天 Varuṇa, 박로나 縛嚕拏 ; 파루나 婆樓那 *οὐρανός*, the heavens, or the sky, where are clouds and dragons ; the 수신 水神 water-deva, or dragon-king, who rules the clouds, rains, and water generally. One of the 대신 大神 in the esoteric maṇḍalas ; he rules the west ; his consort is the 수천비 水天妃 represented on his left, and his chief retainer 수천권속 水天眷屬 is placed on his right. 수천공 水天供 or 수천법 水天法 is the method of worshipping him for rain. 수천덕불 水天德佛 The 743rd Buddha of the present universe.

수축 隨逐 To attach oneself to and follow, e.g. Buddha.

수파 水波 Waves of water ; the wave and the water are two yet one — an illustration of the identity of differences.

수풍화재 水風火災 The three final catastrophes, see 삼재 三災.

수행 修行 Caryā, conduct ; to observe and do ; to mend one's ways ; to cultivate oneself in right practice ; be religious, or pious. 수행주 修行住 A bodhisattva's stage of conduct, the third of his ten stages.

수형호 隨形好 Excellent in every detail ; the individual excellences of others united in the Buddha.

수혹 修惑 Illusion, such as desire, hate, etc., in practice or performance, i.e. in the process of attaining enlightenment ; cf. 사혹 思惑.

수희 隨喜 To rejoice in the welfare of others. To do that which one enjoys, to follow one's inclination.

숙 叔 A father's younger brother ; translit. *śi, śu.* 숙숙(마)라 叔叔(摩)羅 Śiśumāra, a crocodile. 숙가(바) 叔迦(婆) or 啾迦(婆) Śuka, a parrot. 숙리 叔離 Śukla, or Śukra, white, silvery ; the waxing half of the moon, or month ; one of the asterisms, "the twenty-fourth of the astronomical Yogas," [M. W.] ; associated with Venus.

숙 熟 Ripe. 숙소경 熟酥經 The sūtras of ripe curds or cheese, the Prajñā group.

숙 宿 To pass the night, sojourn, stay ; early, former ; left over. 숙세 宿世 A former existence. 숙작 宿作 The deeds of a former life. 숙작외도 宿作外道 One of the ascetic sects who sought release from penalties for the deeds of a former life by severe austerities now. 숙주 宿住 Pūrvanivāsana, former abidings, or habitations, hence 숙주(수념지증)통 宿住(隨念智證)通, i.e. Buddha-knowledge of the former incarnations of himself and others. 숙채 宿債 The unrepaid debts from, or sins of, former incarnations. 숙합 宿哈 idem 사하 娑訶 Svāhā. 숙명 宿命 Previous life, or lives ; v. 숙주 宿住. 숙명력 宿命力 Buddha-power to know all previous transmigrations. 숙명명 宿命明 The knowledge of the arhat of his own and other previous transmigrations. 숙명(지)통 宿命(智)通 Pūrvanivāsānusmṛti-(jñāna) ; Buddha-knowledge of all forms of previous existence of self and others ; one of the 육(신)통 六(神)通. 숙선 宿善 Good deeds done in previous existence. 숙인 宿因 Good or evil cause in previous existence. 숙집 宿執 The character acquired in a previous existence and maintained. 숙집개발 宿執開發 The present fruition of the meritorious character developed in previous existence. 숙보 宿報 The consequence of deeds done in former existence, 숙야 宿夜 To stay the night ; the previous night, e.g. the night before any special service. 숙기 宿忌 The night before a fast-day. 숙의 宿意 A former intention, or vow. 숙근 宿根 ; 숙식 宿植 The root of one's present lot planted in previous existence. 숙업 宿業 Former karma, the karma of previous existence. 숙왕희 宿王戲 Nakṣatra-rāja-vikrīḍita, the play of the star-king, or king of the constellations, one of the samādhi in the Lotus Sūtra. 숙왕화 宿王華 Nakṣatra-rāja-saṅkusumitābhijña, king of the star-flowers, a bodhisattva in the Lotus. 숙복 宿福 Happy karma from previous existence, 숙연 宿緣 Causation or inheritance from previous existence. 숙습 宿習 The practices, habits, or deeds of or inherited from former existence. 숙원 宿願 The vow made in a former existence. 숙원력 宿願力 The power of an ancient vow.

순 旬 A decade, a period of ten days. 순단 旬單 The ten days' account in a monastery.

순 順 Accord with, comply, yield, obey, agreeable ; v. 역 逆 to resist. 순세 順世 To accord with the world, its ways and customs ; to die. 순상분결 順上分結 The five ties in the higher realm which hold the individual in the realms of form and formlessness: desire for form, desire for formlessness, restlessness, pride, and ignorance. 순하분결 順下分結 The five ties in the lower realm which hold the individual in the realms of desire, i.e. desire, resentment, egoism, false tenets, and doubt. 순분 順分 To follow out one's duty ; to accord with one's calling ; to carry out the line of bodhisattva progress according to plan. 순화 順化 To accord with one's lessons ; to follow the custom ; to die. 순인 順忍 The third of the five bodhisattva stages of endurance, i.e. from the fourth to sixth stages. 순차 順次 According to order or rank, one after another, the next life in Paradise to follow immediately after this without intervening stages. 순류 順流 Going with the stream, i.e. of transmigration, custom, etc. 순아 順牙 Śūnya, v. 공 空. 순역 順逆 To go with, or resist, e.g. the stream to reincarnation, or to nirvāṇa.

순 純 One-coloured, unadulterated, pure, sincere. 순일 純一 Pure, unmixed, solely, simply, entirely. 순진 純眞 Sincere, true ; name of a man who asked the Buddha questions which are replied to in a sūtra. 순다 純陀 Cunda, who is believed to have supplied Śākyamuni with his last meal ; it is said to have been of 전단이 旃檀耳 q.v., but there are other accounts including a stew of flesh food ; also 준순 准純, 순순 淳純, 주나 周那.

순 舜 The legendary Emperor Shun, 2255-2205 B.C. 순야 舜若 Śūnya, empty, unreal, incorporeal, immaterial, 공 空 q.v. 순야다 舜若多 Śūnyatā ; emptiness, unreality, i.e. 공성 空性 of the nature of the void.

순 循 To follow, accord with, according to. 순환 循環 Pradakṣiṇa ; moving round so that the right shoulder is towards the object of reverence. 순신관 循身觀 The meditation which observes the body in detail and considers its filthiness.

순 巡 Wander about, patrol, inspect. 순당 巡當 To patrol, or circumambulate the hall. 순요 巡寮 To inspect all the buildings of a monastery. 순안 巡案 To patrol and receive any complaints. 순경 巡更 To patrol as night-watchman, or 순화 巡火 as guarding against fire. 순석 巡錫 To walk about with a metal staff, i.e. to teach.

순나 諄那 Cūrṇa, powder, flour, dust, sand, etc.

술 述 Narrate, publish ; narration. 술로달라 述嚕怛羅 ; 수루다 戍縷多 Śrotra, the ear.

술 戍 The hour from 7-9 p.m. ; translit. *śū, śu*. 술타 戍陀 ; 술달 戍達 ; 술타라 戍陀羅 or 술날라 戍捺羅 or 술달라 戍怛羅 Śūdra, the fourth or servile caste, whose duty is to serve the three higher castes. 술타전달라 戍陀戰達羅 Śuddhacandra, 정월 淨月 pure moon, name of one of the ten authorities on 유식 唯識 q.v. 술파게라승하 戍婆揭羅僧訶 Śubhākarasiṁha. Propitious lion, i.e. auspicious and heroic ; fearless. 술루다 戍縷多 v. 술 述. 술갈라 戍羯羅 Śukra ; 금성 金星 the planet Venus. 술륜율제 戍輪聿提 Śudhyanti ; clean or pure. It may be an epithet of *vāk* "voice" in the musical sense of "natural diatonic melody." 술가 戍迦 Śuka, a parrot ; an epithet of the Buddha. 술가라박걸사 戍迦羅博乞史 Śuklapakṣa, the waxing period of the moon, 1st to 15th.

술 術 Way or method ; art ; trick, plan. 술바가 術婆迦 Śubhakara, a fisherman who was burnt up by his own sexual love.

숭 崇 Lofty, eminent, honourable ; to reverence, adore. 숭신 崇信 Reverence and faith, to revere and trust. 숭경 崇敬 To reverence and respect.

스님 Seunim. Term of respect for a Buddhist monk or nun. Venerable ; Reverend. The word comes from the contraction of 승 僧 plus Korean honorific suffix 님.

스승 Master ; teacher. See 사 師.

슬 瑟 A lute ; massive. 슬슬 瑟瑟 ; 슬석 瑟石 The stone of which the throne of 부동명왕 不動明王 q.v. consists.

습 習 Repetition, practice, habit, skilled ; u.f. 습기 習氣 intp. vāsanā. 습인습과 習因習果 The continuity of cause and effect, as the cause so the effect. 습기 習氣 Habit, the force of habit ; the uprising or recurrence of thoughts, passions, or delusions after the passion or delusion has itself been overcome, the remainder or remaining influence of illusion. 습멸 習滅 To practise (the good) and destroy (the evil).

습 溼 The class of beings produced by moisture, such as fish, etc. v. 사생 四生.

습 拾 To gather, pick up, arrange ; ten. 습득 拾得 To gather ; gathered up, picked up, a foundling.

습 濕 Wet, humid, moist. 습생 濕生 Moisture-born ; born in damp or wet places ; spawn, etc., one of the four forms of birth, v. 사생 四生.

승 僧 ; **승가** 僧伽 Saṅgha, an assembly, collection, company, society. The corporate assembly of at least three (formerly four) monks under a chairman, empowered to hear confession, grant absolution, and ordain. The church or monastic order, the third member of the Triratna.

The term 승 僧 used alone has come to mean a monk, or monks in general. Also 승법 僧法, 승가 僧加, 승기야 僧企耶. 승가타 僧伽吒 ; 승가다 僧伽多 ; 승가타 僧伽陀 Saṅghāta, an assemblage ; also the final hurricane in the kalpa of destruction. 승가바시사 僧伽婆尸沙 v. 승잔 僧殘. 승가바라 僧伽婆羅 Saṅghapāla ; a monk of 부남국 扶南國 Siam, who tr. ten or eleven works A.D. 506-520. 승가리 僧伽梨 or 승가려 僧伽黎 v. 승가지 僧伽胝 Saṅghāṭī. 승가라 僧伽羅 Siṁhala, Ceylon ; also name of the Buddha in a previous incarnation when, as a travelling merchant, he, along with 500 others, was driven on to the island ; there the rākṣasīs bewitched them ; later the Buddha and his companions (like the Argonauts) escaped, and ultimately he destroyed the witches and founded his kingdom there. 승가지 僧伽胝 Saṅghāṭī. the patch-robe, one of the three garments of a monk reaching from shoulders to the knees and fastened around the waist, made up of nine to twenty-five pieces and so called 중잡의 重雜衣 ; also 대의 大衣 great robe ; also 중 重 in layers and 합 合 composite ; v. 구품 九品. 승가람(마) 僧伽藍(摩) Saṅghārāma, a monastery with its garden or grove ; also 가람 伽藍. 승보라 僧補羅 Siṁhapura. Eitel says "an ancient province and city of Cashmere, probably the modern Simla." 승가발마 僧伽跋摩 Saṅghavarman, an Indian monk who arrived in Nanking A.D. 433, tr. five works in 434, went westward in 442. 승가발다라 僧伽跋陀羅 Ṣaṅghabhadra. "A learned priest of Cashmere, a follower of the Sarvāstivāda school, the author of many philosophical works." [Eitel]. 승가난제 僧伽難提 Saṅghānandi, a prince of Śrāvastī, lived in a cave, was discovered by Rāhulata, became the sixteenth patriarch.

승 勝 Jina, victorious, from *ji*, to overcome, surpass. 승승 勝乘 The victorious vehicle, i.e. Mahāyāna. 승우 勝友 Jinamitra, friend of the Jina, or, having the Jina for friend ; also the name of an eloquent monk of Nālandā, *circa* A.D. 630, author of Sarvāstivāda-vinaya-saṅgraha, tr. A.D. 700. 승사 勝士 Victor, one who keeps the commandments. 승자수 勝子樹 v. 기 祇. The Jeta grove, Jetavana. 승종 勝宗 v. 승론종 勝論宗 *infra*. 승주 勝州 Uttarakuru, v. 울 鬱 the continent north of Meru 승심 勝心 The victorious mind, which carries out the Buddhist discipline. 승응신 勝應身 A T'ien-t'ai term for the superior incarnational Buddha-body, i.e. his compensation-body under the aspect of 타수용신 他受用身 saving others. 승림 勝林 v. 기 祇 The Jeta grove, Jetavana. 승과 勝果 The surpassing fruit, i.e. that of the attainment of Buddhahood, in contrast with Hīnayāna lower aims ; two of these fruits are transcendent nirvāṇa and complete bodhi. 승업 勝業 Surpassing karma. 승신주 勝神州 Pūrvavideha, Videha, the continent east of Meru. 승의 勝義 Beyond description, that which surpasses mere earthly ideas ; superlative, inscrutable. 승의근 勝義根 The surpassing organ, i.e. intellectual perception, behind the ordinary organs of perception, e.g. eyes, ears, etc. 승의법 勝義法 The superlative dharma, nirvāṇa. 승의공 勝義空 Nirvāṇa as surpassingly real or transcendental. 승의제 勝義諦 The superior truth, enlightened truth as contrasted with worldly truth. 승의제론 勝義諦論 Paramārtha-satya-śāstra, a philosophical work by Vasubandhu. 승자 勝者 Pradhāna, pre-eminent, predominant. 승론 勝論 v. 폐 吠 Vaiśeṣika-śāstra, and 승론종 勝論宗 The Vaiśeṣika school of Indian philosophy, whose foundation is ascribed to Kaṇāda (Ulūka) ; he and his successors are respectfully styled 논사 論師 or slightingly 논외도 論外道 ; the school, when combined with the Nyāya, is also known as Nyāya-vaiśeṣika. 승군 勝軍 Prasenajit, conquering army, or conqueror of an army ; king of Kośala and patron of Śākyamuni ; also one of the Mahārājas, v. 명왕 明王. 승만부인 勝鬘夫人 Mālyaśrī, daughter of Prasenajit, wife of the king of Kośala (Oudh), after whom the Śrīmālā-devī-siṁhanāda 승만회 勝鬘會 and 승만경 勝鬘經 are named.

승 承 Receive, succeed to, undertake, serve. 승사 承事 Entrusted with duties, serve, obey, and minister. 승로반 承露盤 or 承露槃 The "dew-receivers," or metal circles at the top of a pagoda.

승 繩 String, cord. 승상 繩床 A string-bed.

승 陞 To ascend ; rise, raise. 승좌 陞座 To ascend the platform to expound the sūtras.

승 乘 To lay hold of, grasp. 승불 乘拂 To hold the fly-brush, or whisk, the head of an assembly, the five heads of a monastery have this privilege. 승지 乘持 To hold firmly (to the discipline, or rules). 승거 乘炬 To carry the torch (for cremation).

승 乘 Yāna 연 衍 ; 야나 野那 a vehicle, wain, any means of conveyance ; a term applied to Buddhism as carrying men to salvation. The two chief divisions are the 소승 小乘 Hīnayāna and 대승 大乘 Mahāyāna ; but there are categories of one, two, three, four, and five shêng 오승 五乘 q.v., and they have further subdivisions. 승진 乘津 The vehicle and ford to nirvāṇa, i.e. Buddha-truth. 승종 乘種 The vehicle-seed, or seed issuing from the Buddha-vehicle.

승가 僧可 Name of 혜가 慧可 Hui-k'o, second patriarch of the Intuitive School.

승가사 僧迦舍 Sāṅkāśya, an ancient kingdom and city in Northern India (v. Kapittha 겁 劫) The modern Samkassam, now a village 45 miles north-west of Kanauj. Also 승가시 僧伽施.

승가자 僧柯者 idem 승가사 僧迦舍. Sāṅkāśya. 승가표다미 僧柯慓多弭 Saṁskṛtam, which means composite, compounded, perfected, but intp. as active, phenomenal, causally produced, characterized by birth, existence, change, and death.

승거 僧佉 Sāṅkhya. 승기야 僧企耶 ; intp. 수 數 number, reckon, calculate ; sāṅkhya, "one of the great divisions of Hindu philosophy ascribed to the sage Kapila and so called as 'reckoning up' or 'enumerating' twenty-five Tattvas or true principles, its object being to effect the final liberation of the twenty-fifth (Purusha, the Soul) from the fetters of the phenomenal creation by conveying the correct knowledge of the twenty-four other Tattvas, and rightly discriminating the soul from them." [M. W.] Cf. 가 迦 and 수 數.

승계 僧戒 The ten prohibitions ; the complete commands for monks.

승관 僧官 Director of monks, an official first appointed by the government in the fourth century A.D. ; then and later the office was called 승정 僧正 ; 승통 僧統 ; 록(사) 錄(司).

승기 僧祇 Sāṅghika, relating to a saṅgha ; a complete set of land and buildings for a monastery. 승기지 僧祇支 Saṅkakṣikā, or Uttarasaṅghāṭī, described as a kind of toga passed over the left shoulder and under the right armpit ; also 승가 僧迦 ; 승갈지 僧竭支 ; 승각기 僧却崎 ; 승각기가 僧脚崎迦 ; 기지 祇支 ; 갈지 竭支. 승기물 僧祇物 Monastic possessions, or things. 승기율 僧祇律 Sāṅghikavinaya, the rules for monks and nuns. 승기부 僧祇部 Sāṅghika, the Mahāsāṅghikāḥ school, v. 대중부 大衆部.

승길이삭 僧吉肄鑠 Saṅkleśa, whatever defiles, e.g. the passions.

승나승열 僧那(僧涅) Sannāha(-sannaddha), girding on armour, intp. as a Buddha's or bodhisattva's great vow.

승니 僧尼 Monks and nuns.

僧朗 Seung-rang(427?-510?). A monk of the Goguryeo dynasty in Korea. He went to China to study 삼론 三論. He established the foundation for 삼론종 三論宗 in China, which was completed by 길장 吉藏.

승려 僧侶 Monastic companions, or company.

승무 僧舞 Monk's dance.

승방 僧坊 ; **승방** 僧房 A vihāra, or saṅghārāma, a monastery ; also a nunnery.

승보 僧寶 Saṅgha, the idealized church, the third member of the Triratna. 승보과 僧寶果 The perfect arhat who has not to be reborn.

승사 僧訶 Siṁha, a lion, also 승가 僧伽.

승색가라 僧塞迦羅 Saṁskāra, impressions resulting from action, the fourth skandha.

승속 僧俗 Monks and the laity.

승야 僧若 Sañjñā ; saṁjñā, the third of the five skandhas, i.e. 상 想 thought, ideation, consciousness.

승오 僧伍 The monastic ranks.

승의 僧儀 The monastic custom, i.e. shaving head and beard, wearing the robe, etc.

승잔 僧殘 Saṅghāvaśeṣa ; Pali, Saṅghādiśeṣa. A sin of an ordained person, requiring open confession before the assembly for absolution, or riddance 잔 殘 ; failing confession, dismissal from the order. Thirteen of these sins are of sexual thoughts, or their verbal expression, also greed, even for the sake of the order, etc.

승중 僧衆 The body or assembly of monks.

승차 僧次 In order of monastic age, according to years of ordination. 승자자일 僧自恣日 The 15th of the 7th month ; the last day of the summer retreat, on which the monks confessed their sins.

시 尸 A corpse ; to manage ; u.f. 시라 尸羅.

시 市 A market, a fair, an open place for public assembly. 시연득가 市演得迦 Jetaka, or 사다파한나 娑多婆漢那 Sadvāhana. A king of southern Kosala, patron of Nāgārjuna.

시 翅 A wing, fin, translit. *ke*. 시이라 翅夷羅 Feather robes. 시유라 翅由邏 ; 지유라 枳由羅 ; 길유라 吉由攞 Keyūra, an armlet, necklace. 시사흠바라 翅舍欽婆羅 Keśakambala, a hair garment or covering ; name of one of the ten heretical Indian schools.

시 矢 An arrow ; to take an oath ; a marshal ; ordure. 시석 矢石 Arrow and rock are two incompatibles, for an arrow cannot pierce a rock.

시 侍 Attend ; wait on ; attendant. 시자 侍者 An attendant, e.g. as Ānanda was to the Buddha ; assistants in general, e.g. the incense-assistant in a temple.

시 厮 Attendant, an attendant, servant ; to serve.

시 始 Beginning, first, initial ; thereupon. 시사 始士 An initiator ; a Bodhisattva who stimulates beings to enlightenment. 시교 始教 According to T'ien-t'ai , the preliminary teaching of the Mahāyāna, made by the Avataṁsaka (Kegon) School ; also called 상시교 相始教 ; it discussed the nature of all phenomena as in the 유식론 唯識論, 공시교 空始教 ; and held to the immateriality of all things, but did not teach that all beings have the Buddha-nature. 시종 始終 Beginning and end, first and last. 시행인 始行人 A beginner. 시각 始覺 The initial functioning of mind or intelligence as a process of "becoming," arising from 본각 本覺 which is Mind or Intelligence, self-contained, unsullied, and considered as universal, the source of all enlightenment. The "initial intelligence" or enlightenment arises from the inner influence 훈 薰 of the Mind and from external teaching. In the "original intelligence" are the four values adopted and made transcendent by the Nirvāṇa-sūtra, viz. 상 常, 락 樂, 아 我, 정 淨, perpetuity, joy, personality, and purity ; these are acquired through the 시각 始覺 process of enlightenment. Cf. 기신론 起信論 Awakening of Faith.

시 屍 Corpse (of a murdered person). v. 시 尸 and 비다라 毘陀羅. 시귀 屍鬼 A corpse-ghost (called up to kill an enemy). 시다림 屍陀林 Śītavana, a cemetery. 시려밀 屍黎密 Śrīmitra, cf. 실 室.

시 施 Dāna 단나 檀那 Alms ; charity. To give, bestow. See also 실 實. 시주 施主 Dānapati ; an almsgiver, a patron of Buddhism. 시승 施僧 To give alms to monks. 시화 施化 To bestow the transforming truth. 시림 施林 To give to the forest, i.e. burial by casting the corpse into the forest. 시무염(사) 施無厭(寺), i.e. 나란다 那爛陀 Nālandā-saṅghārāma, a monastery seven miles north of Rājagṛha, where Hsüan-tsang studied ; built by Śakrāditya ; now "Baragong (i.e. vihāragrāma)." [Eitel]. 시무외 施無畏 Abhayandada ; abhayadāna ; the bestower of fearlessness, a title of Kuan-yin ; a bodhisattva in the Garbhadhātu. 시행 施行 The practice of charity. 시설 施設 To set up, establish, start. 시설론부 施設論部 Kārmikāḥ, the school of Karma, which taught the superiority of morality over knowledge. 시호 施護 Dānapāla, a native of Udyāna who translated into Chinese some 111 works and in A.D. 982 received the title of Great Master and brilliant expositor of the faith. 시개폐 施開廢 A T'ien-t'ai term indicating the three periods of the Buddha's teaching: (1) bestowing the truth in Hīnayāna and other partial forms ; (2) opening of the perfect truth like the lotus, as in the Lotus sūtra ; (3) abrogating the earlier imperfect forms. 시식 施食 To bestow food (on monks), and on hungry ghosts.

시 屎 Excrement. 시담자 屎擔子 A load of night-soil, i.e. the human body that has to be carried about. 시분지옥 屎糞地獄 the excrement hell.

시 柴 Fuel, firewood, brushwood. 시두 柴頭 The one who looks after it in a monastery.

시 視 Look, see, behold. 시나 視那 Jina, victor, idem 기나 耆那.

시 柴 See under Ten Strokes.

시 是 The verb to be, is, are, etc. ; right ; this, these. 시심시불 是心是佛 This mind is Buddha ; the mind is Buddha, cf. 즉 卽. 시처비처력 是處非處力 The power to distinguish right from wrong, one of the ten Buddha-powers.

시 時 Time, hour, period ; constantly ; as kāla, time in general, e.g. year, month, season, period ; as samaya, it means kṣaṇa, momentary, passing ; translit. *ji.* 시걸박 時乞縛 Jihvā, the tongue. 시분 時分 Time-division of the day, variously made in Buddhist works : (1) Three periods each of day and night. (2) Eight periods of day and night, each divided into four parts. (3) Twelve periods, each under its animal, as in China. (4) Thirty hours, sixty hours, of varying definition. 시(산)외도 時(散)外道 The non-Buddhist sect which regarded Time, or Chronos, as creator of all things. 시바시바가 時婆時婆迦 Jīvajīvaka, v. 기 耆. 시미귀 時媚鬼 or 정미귀 精媚鬼 One of the three classes of demons ; capable of changing at the 자 子 tzŭ hour (midnight) into the form of a rat, boy, girl, or old, sick person. 시종 時宗 ; 육시왕생종 六時往生宗 A Japanese sect, whose members by dividing day and night into six periods of worship seek immortality. 시성취 時成就 The third of the six initial statements in a sūtra, i.e. 일시 一時 "at one time" or "once," cf. 육성취 六成就. 시비다가라 時毘多迦羅 Jīvitākāra, name of a spirit described as a devourer of life or length of days. 시박가 時縛迦 Jīvaka, one of the eight principal drugs ; living, making or seeking a living, causing to live, etc. ; an "illegitimate son of king Bimbisāra by Āmradārikā," who resigned his claim to the throne to Ajātaśatru and practised medicine ; a physician. 시처제연 時處諸緣 The conditions or causes of time and place into which one is born. 시중 時衆 The present company, i.e. of monks and laity ; the community in general. 시의 時衣 Garments suited to the time or occasion. 시식 時食 Seasonable or timely food, especially roots used as food in sickness, part of the 오약 五藥, i.e. turnip, onion, arrowroot, radish (or carrot), and a root curing poison.

시 示 To indicate, notify, proclaim. 시교 示教 To point out and instruct, e.g. 시적 示寂 to indicate the way of nirvāṇa. 고시 告示 A proclamation ; to notify.

시 嘶 To neigh ; a crashing noise. 시야나 嘶夜那 Śyena, a hawk, falcon.

시 試 To try, test, attempt ; tempt. 시경 試經 To test or prove the scriptures ; to examine them. 시라 試羅 Śilā, a stone, flat stone, intp. as "probably a coral" (Eitel), also as "mother"-of-pearl.

시가라월 尸迦羅越 Said to be Sujāta, son of an elder of Rājagṛha and the same as 수자타 須闍陀.

시기 尸棄 Śikhin, 식기 式棄 ; 식힐 式詰 ; 시기나 尸棄那 ; 시기불 尸棄佛 ; 계나시기 罽那尸棄 ; crested, or a flame ; explained by 화 火 fire ; 랄나시기 剌那尸棄 Ratnaśikhin occurs in the Abhidharma. In the 본행경 本行經 it is 나계 螺髻 a shell-like tuft of hair. (1) The 999th Buddha of the last kalpa, whom Śākyamuni is said to have met. (2) The second of the seven Buddhas of antiquity, born in Prabhadvaja 광상성 光相城 as a Kṣatriya. (3) A Mahābrahmā, whose name Śikhin is defined as 정계 頂髻 or 화재정 火災頂 having a flaming tuft on his head ; connected with the world-destruction by fire. The Fan-i-ming-i describes Śikhin as 화 火 or 화수 火首 flame, or a flaming head and as the god of fire, styled also 수제 樹提 Śuddha, pure ; he observed the 화정 火定 Fire Dhyāna, broke the lures of the realm of desire, and followed virtue. 시기비 尸棄毘 A deva of music located in the East.

시기니 尸棄尼 Also 식닉 識匿 or 슬닉 瑟匿 or 식닉 式匿. Chavannes accepts the identification with Chighnān, a region of the Pamirs (*Documents sur les Tou-kiue Occidentaux*, p. 162).

시다(림) 尸陀(林) Śītavana, 시림 尸林 ; 시타파 尸陀婆 ; 시다파나 尸多婆那 ; 시타벌나 尸陀伐那 ; 시타 屍陀 cold grove 한림 寒林, i.e. a place for exposing corpses, a cemetery. It is also styled 공비림 恐毘林, 안타림 安陀林, 주암림 晝暗林 ; also v. 시마사나 尸摩賒那 or 심마사나 深摩舍那 śmaśāna.

시다바나 尸多婆那 Śītavana, v. 시다림 尸陀林.

시라 尸羅 Śīla, 시 尸 ; 시달나 尸怛羅 intp. by 청량 清涼 pure and cool, i.e. chaste ; also by 계 戒 restraint, or keeping the commandments ; also by 성선 性善 of good disposition. It is the second pāramitā, moral purity, i.e. of thought, word, and deed. The four conditions of śīla are chaste, calm, quiet, extinguished, i.e. no longer perturbed by the passions. Also, perhaps śilā, a stone, i.e. a precious stone, pearl, or coral. For the ten śīlas or commandments v. 십계 十戒, the first five, or pañca-śīla, are for all Buddhists. 시라불청정 尸羅不清淨 If the śīla, or moral state, is not pure, none can enter samādhi. 시라바라밀 尸羅波羅蜜 Śīlapāramitā. Morality, the second of the pāramitās. 시라당 尸羅幢 A curtain made of chaste precious stones. 시라발다제 尸羅拔陀提 or 시라발타라 尸羅拔陀羅 ; 계현 戒賢(b. 530 - d. 640) Śīlabhadra, a prince mentioned in 현우경 賢愚經 6. 시라청정 尸羅清淨 Moral purity, essential to enter into samādhi. 시라발제 尸羅跋提 Śrāvastī, idem 사위 舍衛. 시라발타라 尸羅跋陀羅 Śīlabhadra. A learned monk of Nālandā, teacher of Hsüan-tsang, A.D. 625. 시라달마 尸羅達磨 Śīla-dharma, a śramaṇa of Khotan. 시라발파 尸羅鉢頗 Śīlaprabha, the Sanskrit name of a learned monk. 시라아질다 尸羅阿迭多 Śīlāditya, son of Pratāpāditya and brother of Rājyavardhana. Under the spiritual auspices of Avalokiteśvara, he became king of Kanyākubja A.D. 606 and conquered India and the Punjab. He was merciful to all creatures, strained drinking water for horses and elephants, was a most liberal patron of Buddhism, re-established the great quinquennial assembly, built many stūpas, showed special favour to Śīlabhadra and Hsüan-tsang, and composed the 팔대영탑범찬 八大靈塔梵讚 Aṣṭama- hāśrī-caitya-saṁskṛta-stotra. He reigned about forty years.

시랑 豺狼 A wolf. 시랑지옥 豺狼地獄 One of the sixteen hells, where sinners are devoured by wolves.

시뢰나벌지 尸賴拏伐底 Hiraṇyavatī, 시리랄나벌지 吚離剌拏伐底 ; 아리라벌지 阿利羅伐底 ; The gold river, a river of Nepal, now called the Gaṇḍakī, near which Śākyamuni is said to have entered nirvāṇa. The river is identified with the Ajitavatī.

시리 尸利 Śrī. 사리 師利 ; 실리 室利 ; 실리 室離 ; 실리 室哩 ; 수리 修利 ; 석리 昔哩, 실리 悉利 (1) Fortune, prosperity ; high rank, success, good fortune, virtues, these four are named as its connotation. (2) The wife of Viṣṇu. (3) An honorific prefix or affix to names of gods, great men, and books. (4) An exclamation at the head of liturgies. (5) An abbreviation for Mañjuśrī. 시리불서 尸利佛逝 Śrībhuja, i.e. Malaya 시리야 尸利夜. Śrīyaśas, a god who bestows good luck. 시리사 尸利沙 ; 시리쇄 尸利灑 ; 사리사 舍利沙 ; 야합수 夜合樹 Śirīṣa. Acacia sirisa. The marriage tree 합혼수 合婚樹. The 시리사 尸利沙 is described as with large leaves and fruit ; another kind the 시리사 尸利駛 with small leaves and fruit. Also called 사라수 沙羅樹. 시리사가 尸利沙迦 Śirīṣaka. Name of a monk. 시리국다 尸利毱多 ; 시리굴다 尸利崛多 ; 실리국다 室利毱多 Śrīgupta, an elder in Rājagṛha, who tried to kill the Buddha with fire and poison ; v. 시리국다장자경 尸利毱多長者經. 시리밀다라 尸利蜜多羅 ; 시려밀 屍黎密 Śrīmitra, an Indian prince who resigned his throne to his younger brother, became a monk, came to China, translated the 관정 灌頂 and other books.

시리가나 尸梨伽那 Śrīguṇa, 후덕 厚德 abundantly virtuous, a title of a Buddha.

시마사나 尸摩舍那 or 尸摩賒那 Śmaśāna, Aśmaśāyana, a cemetery, idem 시다림 尸陀林.

시반시 尸半尸 To kill a person by the 비다라 毘陀羅 vetāla method of obtaining magic power by incantations on a dead body ; when a headless corpse, or some part of the body, is used it is 반시 半尸 ; when the whole corpse it is 시 尸.

시방 十方 The ten directions of space, i.e. the eight points of the compass and the nadir and zenith. There is a Buddha for each direction 시방십불 十方十佛. 시방세계 十方世界 The worlds in all directions. 시방불토 十方佛土 A Buddha-realm, idem 대천세계 大千世界. 시방상주승물 十方常住僧物 ; 시방현전승물 十方現前僧物 see 사종승물 四種僧物.

시비가 尸毘迦 Śivi, 시비가 尸毘伽 ; 시비략 尸毘略 ; also wrongly 습비 濕鞞 ; one of Śākyamuni's former incarnations, when to save the life of a dove he cut off and gave his own flesh to an eagle which pursued it, which eagle was Śiva transformed in order to test him. 지도론 智度論 35.

시성 尸城 Kuśinagara or Kuśigrāmaka. 구시나성 拘尸那城 ; 구시나게라 拘尸那揭羅 ; 구이나갈 拘夷那竭 ; 구시성 拘尸城 Explained by 구사생지 九士生地 the birthplace of nine scholars. An ancient kingdom and city, near Kasiah, 180 miles north of Patna ; the place where Śākyamuni died.

시왕 十王 The ten kings presiding over the ten departments of purgatory.

식 式 Style, shape, fashion, kind. 식기 式棄 ; 식엽 式葉, v. 시 尸. 식차 式叉 Śikṣā ; learning, study. 식차(마나)니 式叉(摩那)尼 Śikṣamāṇa, a female neophyte who from 18 to 20 years of age studies the six rules, in regard to adultery, stealing, killing, lying, alcoholic liquor, not eating at unregulated hours. 식차가라니 式叉迦羅尼 Śikṣākaraṇīya, intp. as study, or should study or be studied, also as duṣkṛta, bad deed, breach of the law. The form meaning is suggestive of a female preceptor.

식 飾 To adorn ; gloss over ; pretend. 장식 裝飾.

식 息 To breathe ; breath ; rest, stop, settle, cease ; produce, interest. 식화 息化 To cease the transforming work (and enter nirvāṇa as did the Buddha). 식심 息心 To set the heart at rest ; a disciple. 식기가미 息忌伽彌 ; 식기다가미 息忌陀伽迷 Sakṛdāgāmin, he who is to be reborn only once before entering nirvāṇa. 식자 息慈 At rest and kind, an old translation of śramaṇa, one who has entered into the life of rest and shows loving-kindness to all. 식재 息災 To cause calamities to cease, for which the esoteric sect uses magical formula, especially for illness, or personal misfortune. 식고 息苦 To put an end to suffering.

식 植 To plant, set up. 식중덕본 植衆德本 To plant all virtuous roots, cultivate all capacities and powers.

식 識 Vijñāna, "the art of distinguishing, or perceiving, or recognizing, discerning, understanding, comprehending, distinction, intelligence, knowledge, science, learning ... wisdom." [M. W.] Parijñāna, "perception, thorough knowledge," etc. [M. W.] It is intp. by 심 心 the mind, mental discernment, perception, in contrast with the object discerned ; also by 요별 了別 understanding and discrimination. There are classifications of 일식 一識 that all things are the one mind, or are metaphysical ; 이식 二識 q.v. discriminating the ālaya-vijñāna or primal undivided condition from the mano-vijñāna or that of discrimination ; 삼식 三識 in the Laṅkāvatāra-sūtra, fundamental, manifested and discriminate ; 오식 五識 q.v. in the 기신론 起信論, i.e. 업 業, 전 轉, 현 現, 지 知, and 상속식 相續識 ; 육식 六識 the perceptions and discernings of the six organs of sense ; also of 8, 9, 10, and 11 식 識. The most important is the eight of the 기신론 起信論, i.e. the perceptions of the six organs of sense, eye, ear, nose, tongue, body (or touch), and mind, together with manas, intp. as 의식 意識 the consciousness of the previous moment, on which the other six depend ; the eighth is the ālaya-vijñāna, v. 아뢰야식 阿賴耶識, in which is contained the seed or stock of all phenomena and which 무몰 無沒 loses none, or nothing, is indestructible ; a substitute for the seventh is ādāna "receiving" of the 유식 唯識, which is intp. as 무해 無解 undiscriminated, or indefinite perception ; there is a difference of view between the 상 相 and the 성 性 schools in regard to the seventh and eighth 식 識 ; and the latter school add a ninth called the amala, or pure vijñāna, i.e. the non-phenomenal 진여식 眞如識. The esoterics add that all phenomena are mental and all things are the one mind, hence the one mind is 무량식 無量識 unlimited mind or knowledge, every kind of knowledge, or omniscience. Vijñāna is one of the twelve nidānas.

식 食 Āhāra, 아하라 阿賀羅 food ; to eat, feed. The rules are numerous, and seem to have changed ; originally flesh food was not improper and vegetarianism was a later development ; the early three rules in regard to "clean" foods are that "I shall not have seen the creature killed, nor heard it killed for me, nor have any doubt that it was killed for me." The five "unclean" foods are the above three, with creatures that have died a natural death ; and creatures that have been killed by other creatures. The nine classes add to the five, creatures not killed for me ; raw flesh, or creatures mauled by other creatures ; things not seasonable or at the right time ; things previously killed. The Laṅkāvatāra and certain other sūtras forbid all killed food. 식전 食前 Before food, i.e. before the principal meal at noon ; but 식후 食後 after food, especially after breakfast till noon. 식당 食堂 or 재당 齋堂 The dining-hall of a monastery. 식시 食時 The time of eating the principal meal, i.e. noon ; nothing might be eaten by members of the Order after noon. 식욕 食欲 The lust for food, one of the four cravings. 식물오과 食物五果 The five kinds of edible fruits and grains : those with stones (or pips), rinds, shells, seeds (e.g. grains), pods. 식랑탕 食莨菪 To eat some kind of poisonous herb. (랑탕 莨菪 is a kind of herb with poison in its leaves and seeds, causing people mad. It is used as an anaesthetic medicine.) 식밀 食蜜 To eat honey, i.e. to absorb the Buddha's teaching. 식경 食頃 The time of a meal, i.e. but a short time.

식계 識界 Vijñāna dhātu, the elements of consciousness, the realm of mind, the sphere of mind, mind as a distinct realm.

식랑 識浪 The waves or nodes of particularized discernment, produced on the bhūtatathatā considered as the sea of mind.

식무변처 識無邊處 The Brahmaloka of limitless knowledge or perception, v. 사공천 四空天 (or 사공처 四空處) and 식처천 識處天. 식무변처정 識無邊處定 The dhyāna corresponding to it. 식무변처해탈 識無邊處解脫 The vimokṣa, or liberation from it to a higher stage.

식변 識變 Mental changes, i.e. all transformations, or phenomenal changes, are mental, a term of the 법상 法相 school.

식숙명통 識宿命通 Pūrvanivāsānusmṛti-jñāna ; knowledge of all forms of previous existence of oneself and others.

식식 識食 Spiritual food, mental food, by which are kept alive the devas of the formless realms and the dwellers in the hells.

식심 識心 The perceptive mind.

식온 識蘊 Vijñāna-skandha, one of the five aggregates or attributes.

식우 識牛 Intellect the motive power of the body, as the ox is of the cart.

식장 識藏 The storehouse of mind, or discernment, the ālaya-vijñāna whence all intelligence or discrimination comes.

식정 識精 Pure or correct discernment or knowledge ; the essence of mind.

식주 識住 That on which perception, or mind, is dependent ; the four 식주 識住 are phenomenon, receptivity, cognition, and reaction ; a further category of seven 식주 識住 is divided into phenomenal and supra-phenomenal.

식주 識主 The lord of the intellect, the mind, the ālaya-vijñāna as discriminator.

식처천 識處天 The heaven of (limitless) knowledge, the second of the catur ārūpya brahmalokas, or four formless havens, also v. *supra*. 식처정 識處定 The dhyāna, or abstract state, which corresponds to the above.

식해 識海 The ocean of mind, i.e. the bhūtatathatā as the store of all mind.

식환 識幻 The illusion of perception, or mind.

신 愼 Careful, cautious, attentive, heedful. 신근 愼謹 ; translit. *ji*, e.g. 신나불달라 愼那弗怛羅 Jinaputra, author of the Yogācāryabhūmi-śāstra-kārikā, tr. by Hsüan-tsang A.D. 654.

신 晨 Dawn, morning. 신조 晨朝 The morning period, the first of the three divisions of the day.

신 薪 Fuel, firewood ; wages. 신진(화멸) 薪盡(火滅) Fuel consumed fire extinguished, a term for nirvāṇa, especially the Buddha's death or nirvāṇa.

신 神 Inscrutable spiritual powers, or power ; a spirit ; a deva, god, or divinity ; the human spirit ; divine, spiritual, supernatural.

신 身 Kāya ; tanu ; deha. The body ; the self. 신입 身入 The sense of touch, one of the 육입 六入 six senses.

신 蜃 Mirage ; sea-serpent ; frog. 신루대 蜃樓臺 A mirage palace, cf. 건 乾.

신 新 New, newly, just, opposite of 구 舊 old. 신계 新戒 One who has newly been admitted ; a novice. 신세 新歲 The new year of the monks, beginning on the day after the summer retreat. 신발의 新發意 One who has newly resolved on becoming a Buddhist, or on any new line of conduct. 신구양역 新舊兩譯 Old and new methods of or terms in translation, the old before, the new with Hsüan-tsang. 신구의 新舊醫 Old and new methods of healing, e.g. Hīnayāna and Mahāyāna, v. Nirvāṇa Sūtra 2.

신 申 To draw out, stretch, extend, expand ; notify, report ; quote. 신일 申日 Candra, the moon ; also the name of an elder. 신독 申毒 ; 연독 身毒 ; 현두 賢頭 Sindhu, Indus, Sindh, v. 인도 印度. 신하 申河 The river Hiraṇyavatī, v. 시뢰 尸賴 ; otherwise said to be the Nairañjanā 니련선하

尼連禪河. 신슬지림 申瑟知林 ; 신노(파)림 申怒(波)林 ; 장림 杖林 Yaṣṭi-vana, grove of staves, said to have grown from the staff with which a heretic measured the Buddha and which he threw away because the more he measured the higher the Buddha grew. 신두라 申頭羅 Sindūra, the trick of the illusionist who disappears in the air and reappears.

신 信 Śraddhā. Faith ; to believe ; belief ; faith regarded as the faculty of the mind which sees, appropriates, and trusts the things of religion ; it joyfully trusts in the Buddha, in the pure virtue of the Triratna and earthly and transcendental goodness ; it is the cause of the pure life, and the solvent of doubt. Two forms are mentioned : (1) Adhimukti, intuition, tr. by self-assured enlightenment. (2) Śraddhā, faith through hearing or being taught. For the Awakening of Faith, Śraddhotpāda, v. 기신론 起信論.

신거 身車 The body as the vehicle which, according with previous karma, carries one into the paths of transmigration.

신견 身見 Satkāyadṛṣṭi ; the illusion that the body, or self, is real and not simply a compound of the five skandhas ; one of the five wrong views 오견 五見.

신계 信戒 Faith and morals, i.e. the moral law, or commandments ; to put faith in the commandments.

신고 信鼓 The drum or stimulant of faith.

신공 神供 Offerings placed before the gods or spirits.

신광 神光 Deva-light, the light of the gods.

신광 身光 The glory shining from the person of a Buddha, or Bodhisattva ; a halo.

신근 身根 Kāyendriya ; the organ of touch, one of the six senses.

신근 神根 The vital spirit as the basis of bodily life.

신근 信根 Śraddhendriya. Faith, one of the five roots or organs producing a sound moral life.

신기 身器 The body as a utensil, i.e. containing all the twelve parts, skin, flesh, blood, hair, etc.

신녀 神女 A devī, a female spirit ; a sorceress.

신녀 信女 Upāsikā. A female devotee, who remains at home. Cf. 우 優.

신덕 信德 The merit of the believing heart ; the power of faith.

신도 信度 Sindhu, Sindh, Scinde, 신두 辛頭 the country of 신도하 信度河 the Indus, one of the "four great rivers." Sindhu is a general name for India, but refers especially to the kingdom along the banks of the river Indus, whose capital was Vichavapura.

신도 神道 The spirit world of devas, asuras, and pretas. Psychology, or the doctrines concerning the soul. The teaching of Buddha. Shintō, the Way of the Gods, a Japanese national religion.

신도 信徒 Lit. "believing/faithful follower." Devotee ; believer ; lay follower ; adherent.

신두 辛頭 The Indus ; Sindh ; idem 신도 信度. 신두파라향 辛頭波羅香 Sindhupāra (? Sindhuvāra), incense or perfume, from a fragrant plant said to grow on the banks(pāra) of the Indus(Sindhu).

신등 身燈 The body as a lamp, burnt in offering to a Buddha, e.g. the Medicine King in the Lotus sūtra.

신락 信樂 To believe and rejoice in the dharma ; the joy of believing.

신력 神力 v. 신통 神通.

신력 信力 Śraddhābala. The power of faith ; one of the five bala or powers.

신련 身蓮 The lotus in the body, i.e. the heart, or eight-leafed lotus in all beings ; it represents also the Garbhadhātu, which is the matrix of the material world out of which all beings come.

신명 身命 Body and life ; bodily life.

신명 神明 The spirits of heaven and earth, the gods ; also the intelligent or spiritual nature.

신모상미상 身毛上靡相 The hairs on Buddha's body curled upwards, one of the thirty-two marks.

신묘 神妙 Mysterious, mystic, occult, recondite, marvellous.

신변 神變 Supernatural influences causing the changes in natural events ; miracles ; miraculous transformations, e.g. the transforming powers of a Buddha, both in regard to himself and others ; also his miraculous acts, e.g. unharmed by poisonous snakes, unburnt by dragon fire, etc. Tantra, or Yogācāra.

신복 信伏 To believe in and submit oneself to.

신사 信士 Upāsaka, 신사남 信事男 a male devotee, who remains in the world as a lay disciple. A bestower of aims. Cf. 우 優.

신삼구사의삼 身三口四意三 The three commandments dealing with the body, prohibiting taking of life, theft, unchastity ; the four dealing with the mouth, against lying, exaggeration, abuse, and ambiguous talk ; the three belonging to the mind, covetousness, malice, and unbelief.

신상 身相 Bodily form ; the body.

신선 神仙 ; 신선 神僊 The genii, immortals, ṛṣi, of whom the five kinds are 천 天, 신 神, 인 人, 지 地, and 귀선 鬼仙, i.e. deva, spirit, human, earth (or cave), and preta immortals.

신성 身城 The body as the citadel of the mind.

신수 信首 Faith as the first and leading step.

신수 信水 Faith pure and purifying like water.

신수 信手 Faith, regarded as a hand grasping the precious truth of Buddha.

신수 信受 The receptivity and obedience of faith ; to believe and receive (the doctrine). 신수봉행 信受奉行 In faith receive and obey, a sentence found at the end of sūtras.

신순 信順 To believe and obey.

신시 信施 Almsgiving because of faith ; the gifts of the faithful.

신식 身識 Kāya-vijñāna. Cognition of the objects of touch, one of the five forms of cognition ; v. 오근 五根.

신식 神識 The intelligent spirit, also called 영혼 靈魂 the soul ; incomprehensible or divine wisdom.

신심 信心 A believing mind, which receives without doubting.

신심 身心 Body and mind, the direct fruit of the previous life. The body is rūpa, the first skandha ; mind embraces the other four, consciousness, perception, action, and knowledge ; v. 오온 五蘊.

ㄱ ㄴ ㄷ ㄹ ㅁ ㅂ ㅅ ㅇ ㅈ ㅊ ㅋ ㅌ ㅍ ㅎ 찾아보기

신아 神我 Puruṣa, or Ātman. The soul, the spiritual ego, or permanent person, which by non-Buddhists was said to migrate on the death of the body. Puruṣa is also the Supreme Soul, or Spirit, which produces all forms of existence.

신암 神闇 The darkened mind without faith.

신앙 信仰 To believe in and look up to.

신업 身業 The karma operating in the body ; the body as representing the fruit of action in previous existence. One of the three karmas, the other two referring to speech and thought.

신여의통 身如意通 Ṛddhividhi-jñāna. Also 신통 身通, 신족통 身足通 ; the power to transfer oneself to various regions at will, also to change the body at will.

신역 神域 The realm of spirit, of reality, surpassing thought, supra-natural.

신운 身雲 The numberless bodies of Buddhas, hovering like clouds over men ; the numberless forms which the Buddhas take to protect and save men, resembling clouds ; the numberless saints compared to clouds.

신인 信忍 Faith-patience, faith-endurance : (1) To abide patiently in the faith and repeat the name of Amitābha. (2) To believe in the Truth and attain the nature of patient faith. (3) According to T'ien-t'ai the 별교 別教 meaning is the unperturbed faith of the Bodhisattvas (that all dharma is unreal)

신인 神人 Gods, or spirits, and men.

신장 信藏 The treasury of faith (which contains all merits).

신전 身田 The body regarded as a field which produces good and evil fruit in future existence.

신족(통) 神足(通) Deva-foot ubiquity. Ṛddhipāda ; ṛddhi-sākṣātkriyā. Also 신경지통 神境智通 ; 여의통 如意通 Supernatural power to appear at will in any place, to fly or go without hindrance, to have absolute freedom ; cf. 대교 大教. 신족월 神足月 The first, fifth, and ninth months, when the devas go on circuit throughout the earth.

신종 信種 The seed of faith.

신좌 神坐 Deva or spirit thrones.

신좌 身座 The body as the throne of Buddha.

신주 信珠 The pearl of faith ; as faith purifies the heart it is likened to a pearl of the purest water.

신주 神咒 Ṛddhi-mantra, or dhāraṇī ; divine or magic incantations.

신지 神智 Spiritual wisdom, divine wisdom which comprehends all things, material and immaterial.

신토 身土 Body and environment. The body is the direct fruit of the previous life ; the environment is the indirect fruit of the previous life.

신통 身通 The power to transfer the body through space at will, one of the marks of the Buddha.

신통(력) 神通(力) Ubiquitous supernatural power, especially of a Buddha, his ten powers including power to shake the earth, to issue light from his pores, extend his tongue to the Brahma-heavens effulgent with light, cause divine flowers, etc., to rain from the sky, be omnipresent, and other powers. Supernatural powers of eye, ear, body, mind, etc. 신통월 神通月 idem 신족월 神足月. 신통승 神通乘 The supernatural or magic vehicle, i.e. the esoteric sect of 진언 眞言 Shingon.

신해 信解 Faith and interpretation, i.e. to believe and understand or explain the doctrine ; the dull or unintellectual believe, the intelligent interpret ; also, faith rids of heresy, interpretation of ignorance. 신해행증 信解行證 Faith, interpretation, performance, and evidence or realization of the fruit of Buddha's doctrine.

신해 信海 The ocean of faith ; the true virtue of the believing heart is vast and boundless as the ocean.

신행 信行 Believing action ; faith and practice. Action resulting from faith in another's teaching, in contrast with 법행 法行 action resulting from direct apprehension of the doctrine ; the former is found among the 둔근 鈍根, i.e. those of inferior ability, the latter among the 이근 利根, i.e. the mentally acute.

신향 信向 To believe in and entrust oneself to the Triratna 삼보 三寶.

신현관 信現觀 Firm faith in the Triratna as revealing true knowledge ; one of the 육현관 六現觀.

신혜 信慧 Faith and wisdom, two of the 오근 五根.

신흥사 神興寺 Shin-heung-sa. A temple located in Mt. Seoraksan, Seorak-dong Sokcho-si Gangwon-do. The 3rd parish headquarters of Korean Jogye Order.

실 室 House, household, abode ; translit. *ś, s, śr, śl.* Cf. 시 尸 ; 사 舍 ; 수 首 ; for 실마 室摩 v. 사문 沙門.

실 悉 Investigate thoroughly ; fully, minutely ; all ; translit. *si, sa, s, śṛ.* 실가라 悉伽羅 Śṛgāla, 야간 野干 a jackal. 실타벽라 悉他薛攞 ; 실체야 悉替耶 Sthavira, an elder, a term applied to a monk of 20-50 years of age and of ten years' standing ; the Sthaviranikāya 실타페라니가야 悉他陛攞尼迦耶, or 상좌부 上坐部 q.v., was one of the four branches of the Vaibhāṣika school. 실리 悉利 idem 실리 室利 q.v. 실지 悉地 Siddhi, accomplishment, complete attainment, perfection, proof, truth, final emancipation, supreme felicity, magical or supernatural powers ; cf. [M. W.] As supernatural power it is used to end calamities, subdue demons, etc. 실다알타 悉多頞他 Siddhārtha, *infra.* 실지 悉底 Siddhi, *supra.* 실달다반달라 悉怛多般怛羅 Sitātapatra, a white umbrella, or canopy. 실담 悉曇 ; 실단 悉檀 ; 실담 悉談 Siddha(m), accomplished, finished, v. Siddhi above ; and next. 실담장 悉曇章 Siddhavastu, the first of twelve chapters of a syllabary attributed to Brahmā, originating the thirty-six letters of the alphabet, later said to be expanded to as many as fifty-two. 실단 悉檀 ; 실담 悉談 Siddhānta, an established conclusion, proved fact, axiom, dogma, a text or authoritative work, cf. [M. W.] ; intp. as 성취 成就 complete, and incorrectly as the Buddha's unstinted gift of the 사법 四法 q.v. 실치라말지 悉耻羅末底 Sthiramati, one of the 유식 唯識 writers. 실달(다) 悉達(多) Siddhārtha, Sarvārthasiddha, also 실다(알타) 悉多(頞他) ; 실타 悉陀 the realization of all aims, prosperous ; personal name of Śākyamuni. 실타 悉阤 idem 사다 私多.

실 實 Real, true, honest, sincere ; solid ; fixed ; full ; to fill ; fruit, kernel, effects ; verily, in fact ; it is used for 진 眞, as in 일실 一實 the supreme fact, or ultimate reality ; also for bhūta.

실 失 To lose, opp. of 득 得 ; to err. 실수마라 失守摩羅 or 失收摩羅 Śiśumāra, "child-killing, the Gangetic porpoise, Delphinus Gangeticus," [M. W.] Tr. by 악 鰐 a crocodile, which is the kumbhīra 금비라 金毘羅. 실념 失念 To lose the train of thought, or meditation ; a wandering mind ; loss of memory. 실라바 失羅婆 Śravaṇā, a constellation identified with the Ox, or 9th Chinese constellation, in Aries and Sagittarius.

실경 實經 The true sūtras as contrasted to the relative or temporary sūtras, a term of the Lotus school.

실공 實空 Absolute śūnya, or vacuity ; all things being produced by cause and environment are unreal.

실교 實敎 The teaching of Reality ; also, the real or reliable teaching.

실대승교 實大乘敎 The real Mahāyāna, freed from temporal, relative, or expedient ideas ; the T'ien-t'ai, Hua-yen, Intuitional, and Shingon schools claim to be such.

실도 實道 The true way, the true religion, absolute Buddha-truth.

실라말니라 室羅末尼羅 Śrāmaṇera, v. 사미 沙彌 ; also for 실라마나락가 室羅摩拏洛迦 or 실라마나리가 室羅摩拏理迦.

실라벌나(마세) 室羅伐拏(磨洗) or **실라바나(마세)** 室羅縛拏(磨洗) Śrāvaṇa(-māsa). The hottest month of summer, July-August (from 16th of 5th moon to 15th of 6th moon)

실라벌실지 室羅伐悉底 Śrāvastī or Śarāvatī, also 실라벌 室羅伐, v. 사위국 舍衛國.

실리 實利 Śarīra, relics, see 사 舍.

실리 室利 Śrī, fortunate, lucky, prosperous ; wealth ; beauty ; name applied to Lakṣmī and Sarasvatī, also used as a prefix to names of various deities and men ; an abbrev. for Mañjuśrī. 실리바새가 室利嚩塞迦 Śrīvāsas, turpentine. 실리밀다라 室利蜜多羅 Śrīmitra, a prince of India, who became a monk and tr. three works in Nanking A.D. 317-322. 실리게바 室利揭婆 Śrīgarbha, Fortune's womb, epithet of Viṣṇu. M. W. also tr. it "a sword," but it is intp. as a precious stone. 실리제바 室利提婆 Śrīdeva, name of 도희 道希 Tao-hsi, a noted monk. 실리국 室利鞠 Śrīgupta, an enemy of Śākyamuni, whom he tried to destroy with a pitfall of fire and a poisoned drink. 실리라 室利羅 Śarīra, relics, v. 사 舍. 실리라다 室利羅多 or 室利邏多 Śrīlabdha, a celebrated commentator, to whom is attributed, *inter alia*, the chief commentary on the 기신론 起信論 Awakening of Faith ; he was called the enlightener of northern India. 실리차달라 室利差呾羅 Śrīkṣetra, "an ancient kingdom near the mouth of the Brahmaputra" ; capital probably "modern Silhet (Śrīhatta)." [Eitel]. 실리흘률다지 室利訖栗多底 Śrīkrītati, ancient name of Kashgar ; [Eitel]. 실리말차 室利靺蹉 Śrīvatsa, the mark of Viṣṇu and Kṛṣṇa, a curl of hair on their breasts, resembling a cruciform flower [M. W.], intp. as resembling the svastika.

실보토 實報土 The land of Buddha-reward in Reality free from all barriers, that of the bodhisattva, the third of the four "lands" of T'ien-t'ai. A Buddha-kṣetra.

실본 實本 Fundamental reality, applied to the teaching of the Lotus sūtra, as opposed to the previous Buddhist teaching.

실상 實相 Reality, in contrast with 허망 虛妄 ; absolute fundamental reality, the ultimate, the absolute ; the 법신 法身, i.e. Dharmakāya, or 진여 眞如 Bhūtatathatā. Other terms are 일실 一實 ; 일여 一如 ; 일상 一相 ; 무상 無相 ; 법증 法證 ; 법위 法位 ; 열반 涅槃 ; 무위 無爲 ; 진제 眞諦 ; 진성 眞性 ; 진공 眞空 ; 실성 實性 ; 실제 實諦 ; 실제 實際, q.v. 실상삼매 實相三昧 The samādhi of reality, in which the unreality of the phenomenal is realized. 실상인 實相印 The seal or witness of reality, which is passed on from Buddha to Buddha. 실상혜 實相慧 Wisdom in regard to reality. 실상지신 實相智身 The body of absolute knowledge, or of complete knowledge of Reality, i.e. that of Vairocana. 실상법계 實相法界 The first half is a Lotus sūtra term for Reality, the latter half a Hua-yen term for the same. 실상위물이신 實相爲物二身 The Dharmakāya or spiritual Buddha, and the Nirmāṇakāya, i.e. manifested or phenomenal Buddha. 실상무상 實相無相 Reality is Nullity, i.e. is devoid of Phenomenal characteristics, unconditioned. 실상화 實相花 ; 실상풍 實相風 The flower, or breeze, of Reality, i.e. the truth, or glory, of Buddhist teaching. 실상관 實相觀 Insight into, or meditation on Reality.

실색신 實色身 The real Buddha-body, or his sambhogakāya in contrast with his nirmāṇakāya.

실성 實性 Real nature, or essence, i.e. the 진여 眞如 bhūtatathatā.

실성 室星 The Revatī constellation in India, that of the "house" or the thirteenth constellation in China.

실쇄 室灑 Śiṣya, a pupil, disciple.

실수마라 室獸摩羅 Śiśumāra, a crocodile ; see 실수마라 失收摩羅.

실아 實我 The true ego, in contrast with the 가아 假我 phenomenal ego.

실안 實眼 An eye able to discern reality, i.e. the Buddha-eye.

실어 實語 True, or reliable words ; words corresponding to reality ; discussions of Reality.

실제 實際 The region of Reality. 실제리지 實際理地 The noumenal universe, the bhūtatathatā.

실제 實諦 A truth ; the true statement of a fundamental principle.

실지 實智 The knowledge or wisdom of Reality, in contrast with knowledge of the 권 權 relative.

실차난타 實叉難陀 Śikṣānanda. A śramaṇa of Kustana (Khotan) who in A.D. 695 introduced a new alphabet into China and translated nineteen works ; the Empress Wu invited him to bring a complete copy of the Hua-yen sūtra to Lo-yang ; sixteen works in the present collection are assigned to him. Also 시걸차난타 施乞叉難陀.

실창 實唱 Reality-proclamation, i.e. to preach the Tathāgata's law of Reality.

실화 實化 The real or noumenal Buddha as contrasted with 권화 權化 the temporal or phenomenal Buddha ; the 실화이신 實化二身 are his 보신 報身 sambhogakāya and his 화신 化身 nirmāṇakāya.

심 深 Deep, profound, abstruse. 심입 深入 Deep entering, or the deep sense, i.e. 빈 貧 desire, covetousness, cupidity. 심오 深奧 ; 심묘 深妙 ; 심밀 深密 ; 심비 深秘 Deep, profound, abstruse. 심갱 深坑 A deep or fathomless pit. 심신 深信 Deep faith. 심심 深心 A mind profoundly engrossed (in Buddha-truth, or thought, or illusion, etc.). 심마사나 深摩舍那 Śmaśāna, v. 시 尸, place for disposing of the dead. 심지 深智 Profound knowledge or wisdom. 심법(문) 深法(門) Profound truth, or method. 심법인 深法忍 Patience, or perseverance, in faith and practice. 심정 深淨 Profoundly pure. 심현 深玄 Deep, abstruse, dark, deep black. 심리 深理 Profound principle, law, or truth. 심경 深經 ; 심장 深藏 The profound sūtras, or texts, those of Mahāyāna. 심행 深行 Deep or deepening progress, that above the initial bodhisattva stage.

심 心 Hṛd, hṛdaya 한률태 汗栗太 ; 한률타 汗栗馱 ; 기리타 紀哩馱 the heart, mind, soul ; citta 질다 質多 the heart as the seat of thought or intelligence. In both senses the heart is likened to a lotus. There are various definitions, of which the following are six instances : (1) 육단심 肉團心 hṛd, the physical heart of sentient or nonsentient living beings, e.g. men, trees, etc. (2) 집기심 集起心 citta, the Ālaya-vijñāna, or totality of mind, and the source of all mental activity. (3) 사량심 思量心 manas, the thinking and calculating mind ; (4) 연려심 緣慮心 ; 요별심 了別心 ; 여지심 慮知心 ; citta ; the discriminating mind ; (5) 견실심 堅實心 the bhūtatathatā mind, or the permanent mind ; (6) 적취정요심 積聚精要心 the mind-essence of the sūtras.

심 尋 To seek ; investigate ; to continue ; usually ; a fathom, 8 Chinese feet. 심사 尋伺 Vitarka and vicāra, two conditions in dhyāna discovery and analysis of principles ; vitarka 비달가 毘怛迦 a dharma which tends to increase, and vicāra 비차라 毘遮羅 one which tends to diminish, definiteness and clearness in the stream of consciousness ; cf. 중간정 中間定. 심상염불 尋常念佛 Normal or ordinary worship of Buddha, in contrast with special occasions.

심 審 To try, judge, examine. 심려사 審慮思 Discriminating thought.

심 甚 What? any ; very, extreme. 심심 甚深 The profundity (of Buddha-truth).

심경 心經 Hṛdaya or "Heart" Sūtra, idem 반야심경 般若心經 ; 반야바라밀다심경 般若波羅蜜多心經 ; styled 신분심경 神分心經 "divinely distributed", when publicly recited to get rid of evil spirits.

심경 心鏡 The heart-mirror, or mirror of the mind, which must be kept clean if it is to reflect the Truth.

심공 心空 Mind-space, or mind spaciousness, mind holding all things, hence like space ; also, the emptied mind, kenosis.

심관 心觀 Contemplation of the mind and its thoughts, v. 일심삼관 一心三觀.

심광 心光 The light from (a Buddha's) mind, or merciful heart, especially that of Amitābha.

심구 心垢 The impurities of the mind, i.e. 번뇌 煩惱 passion and delusion ; the two phrases are used as synonyms.

심귀 心鬼 A perverse mind, whose karma will be that of a wandering ghost.

심극 心極 The pole or extreme of the mind, the mental reach ; the Buddha.

심근 心根 Manas, or the mind-organ, one of the twenty-five tattva 제 諦 or postulates of a universe.

심기 心器 Mind as the receptacle of all phenomena.

심기 心機 The motive power of the mind, the mind the motor.

심념불공과 心念不空過 Pondering on (Buddha) and not passing (the time) in vain.

심등 心燈 The lamp of the mind ; inner light, intelligence.

심량 心量 Mind-measure ; the ordinary man's calculating mind ; also, capacity of mind.

심련 心蓮 The lotus of the mind or heart ; the exoteric school interprets it by original purity ; the esoteric by the physical heart, which resembles a closed lotus with eight petals.

심령 心靈 The mind spirit, or genius ; intelligence ; cf. 심등 心燈.

심로 心路 The mind-road, i.e. the road to Buddha-hood.

심마 心馬 The mind like a horse, that needs breaking in, or stimulating with a whip, cf. 심원 心猿.

심마(적) 心魔(賊) The māra-robbers of the mind, i.e. the passions.

심명 心命 Mind life, i.e. the life, longevity, or eternity of the dharmakāya or spiritual body, that of mind ; also 혜명 慧命. v. 지도론 智度論 78.

심목 心目 Mind and eye, the chief causes of the emotions.

심무소주 心無所住 The mind without resting-place, i.e. detached from time and space, e.g. the past being past may be considered as a "non-past" or non-existent, so with present and future, thus realizing their unreality. The result is detachment, or the liberated mind, which is the Buddha-mind, the bodhimind, 무생심 無生心 the mind free from ideas of creation and extinction, of beginning and end, recognizing that all forms and natures are of the Void, or Absolute.

심박 心縛 The mind in bondage — taking the seeming for the real.

심법 心法 Mental dharmas, ideas — all "things" are divided into two classes 색 色 and 심 心 physical and mental ; that which has 질애 質礙 substance and resistance is physical, that which is devoid of these is mental ; or the root of all phenomena is mind 연기제법지근본자위심법 緣起諸法之根本者爲心法. The exoteric and esoteric schools differ in their interpretation : the exoterics hold that mental ideas or "things" are 무색무형 無色無形 unsubstantial and invisible, the esoterics that they 유색유형 有色有形 have both substance and form. 심법신 心法身 ; 심시법신 心是法身 The mind is dharmakāya, "tathāgata in bonds," 재전여래 在纏如來.

심불 心佛 The Buddha within the heart : from mind is Buddhahood ; the Buddha revealed in or to the mind ; the mind is Buddha. 심불급중생 心佛及衆生, 시삼무차별 是三無差別 The mind, Buddha, and all the living — there is no difference between the three, i.e. all are of the same order. This is an important doctrine of the 화엄경 華嚴經 Hua-yen sūtra, cf. its 야마천궁품 夜摩天宮品 ; by T'ien-t'ai it is called 삼법묘 三法妙 the mystery of the three things.

심불상응(행) 心不相應(行) or 심불상응(행법) 心不相應(行法) The functioning of the mind not corresponding with the first three of the 오법 五法 five laws, of which this is the fourth.

심빙 心冰 The heart chaste as ice ; the mind congealed as ice, i.e. unable to solve a difficulty.

심사 心師 The mind as master, not (like the heretics) mastering (or subduing) the mind 사심 師心.

심상 心相 Heart-shape (of the physical heart) ; manifestation of mind in action ; (the folly of assuming that) mind has shape. 심상응행 心相應行 Actions corresponding with mind, or mind productive of all action.

심상 心想 Thought ; the thoughts of the mind.

심생멸문 心生滅門 The two gates of mind, creation and destruction, or beginning and end.

심성 心性 Immutable mind-corpus, or mind-nature, the self-existing fundamental pure mind, the all, the tathāgata-garbha, or 여래장심 如來藏心 ; 자성청정심 自性淸淨心 ; also described in the 기신론 起信論 Awakening of Faith as immortal 불생불멸 不生不滅. Another definition identifies 심 心 with 성 性, saying 성즉시심심즉시불 性卽是心心卽是佛 the nature is the mind, and mind is Buddha ; another, that mind and nature are the same when 오 悟 awake and understanding, but differ when 미 迷 in illusion ; and further, in reply to the statement that the Buddha-nature is eternal but the mind not eternal, it is said, the nature is like water, the mind like ice, illusion turns nature to mental ice form, awakening melts it back to its proper nature. 심성삼천 心性三千 The universe in a thought ; the mind as a microcosm.

심성 心城 The citadel of the mind, i.e. as guardian over action ; others intp. it as the body, cf. 심정 心亭.

심소(법) 心所(法) Mental conditions, the attributes of the mind, especially the moral qualities, or emotions, love, hate, etc. ; also 심소유법 心所有法, v. 심심 心心.

심수 心數 An older term for 심소 心所 q.v. the several qualities of the mind. The esoterics make Vairocana the 심왕 心王, i.e. Mind or Will, and 심수 心數 the moral qualities, or mental attributes, are personified as his retinue.

심수 心水 The mind as a reflecting water-surface ; also the mind as water, clear or turbid.

심승 心乘 The mind vehicle, i.e. 심관 心觀 meditation, insight.

심식 心識 The mind and cognition ; mind and its contents ; the two are considered as identical in the Abhidharma-kośa, but different in Mahāyāna.

심신 心神 The spirit of the mind, mental intelligence ; mind.

심심 心心 Every mind ; also citta-caitta, mind and mental conditions, i.e. 심 心 and 심소 心所. 심심수 心心數 The mind and its conditions or emotions ; 심수 心數 is an older form of 심소 心所.

심안 心眼 The eye of the mind, mental vision.

심약 心藥 Medicine for the mind, or spirit.

심연 心緣 Mental cognition of the environment ; to lay hold of external things by means of the mind.

심왕 心王 The mind, the will, the directive or controlling mind, the functioning mind as a whole, distinct from its 심소 心所 or qualities. 심왕여래 心王如來 Vairocana as the ultimate mind, the attributes being personified as his retinue. Applied also to the 오불 五佛 and the 구존 九尊. 심왕심소 心王心所 The mind and its qualities, or conditions.

심요 心要 The very core, or essence.

심원 心源 The fountain of the mind ; the thought-welling fountain ; mind as the *fons et origo* of all things.

심원 心猿 The mind as a restless monkey.

심원 心願 The will of the mind, resolve, vow.

심월 心月 Mind (as the) moon, the natural mind or heart pure and bright as the full moon. 심월륜 心月輪 The mind's or heart's moon-revolutions, i.e. the moon's varying stages, typifying the grades of enlightenment from beginner to saint.

심의식 心意識 Mind, thought, and perception (or discernment).

심인 心印 Mental impression, intuitive certainty ; the mind is the Buddha-mind in all, which can seal or assure the truth ; the term indicates the intuitive method of the 선 禪 Ch'an(Zen) school, which was independent of the spoken or written word.

심일경성 心一境性 One of the seven dhyāna 정 定, the mind fixed in one condition.

심자재자 心自在者 He whose mind is free, or sovereign, an arhat who has got rid of all hindrances to abstraction.

심작 心作 The karmaic activity of the mind, the 의업 意業 of the three agents, body, mouth, and mind.

심적 心跡 Footprints, or indications of mind, i.e. the mind revealed by deeds.

심전 心田 The field of the mind, or heart, in which spring up good and evil.

심정 心亭 The pavilion of the mind, i.e. the body ; cf. 심성 心城.

심종 心宗 The intuitive sect, i.e. the Ch'an(Zen) school ; also 불심종 佛心宗 ; 선종 禪宗.

심주 心咒 One of the three classes of spells, idem 일자주 一字咒.

심주 心珠 The mind stuff of all the living, being of the pure Buddha-nature, is likened to a translucent gem.

심증 心證 The inner witness, or assurance, mind and Buddha witnessing together.

심지 心智 Mind and knowledge, or the wisdom of the mind, mind being the organ, knowing the function.

심지 心地 Mind, from which all things spring ; the mental ground, or condition ; also used for 의 意 the third of the three agents — body, mouth, mind.

심진 心塵 Mind dust or dirt, i.e. 번뇌 煩惱 the passions, greed, anger, etc.

심진 心眞 Our mind is by nature that of the bhūtatathatā. 심진여문 心眞如門 The mind as bhūtatathatā, one of the 이문 二門 of the 기신론 起信論 Awakening of Faith.

심취 心趣 The bent or direction of the mind, or moral nature.

심파 心波 Mind waves, i.e. mental activity.

심해 心海 Mind as a sea or ocean, external phenomena being the wind, and the 팔식 八識 eight forms of cognition being the waves.

심행 心行 The activities of the mind, or heart ; also working on the mind for its control ; also mind and action. 심행불리 心行不離 Mind and act not separated, thought and deed in accord, especially in relation to Amitābha.

심향 心香 The incense of the mind, or heart, i.e. sincere devotion.

심혜 心慧 Wisdom, i.e. mind or heart wisdom, e.g. 신계심혜 身戒心慧 controlled in body and wise in mind.

심화 心華 Heart-flower, the heart in its original innocence resembling a flower.

심회연모 心懷戀慕 Heart-yearning (for the Buddha).

십 什 A file of ten ; sundry, what. 십물 什物 Things (in general), oddments. 십조 什肇 The 십 什 is Kumārajīva and the 조 肇 his disciple 승조 僧肇 Sêng-chao. 십마 什麽 idem 심마 甚麽 What? What.

십 十 Daśa, ten, the perfect number.

십감로왕 十甘露王 The king of the ten sweet dews, i.e. Amitābha.

십겁 十劫 The ten kalpas that have expired since Amitābha made his forty-eight vows, or 십겁정각 十劫正覺 attained complete bodhi, hence he is styled 십겁미타 十劫彌陀. These ten kalpas as seen by P'u-hsien are 십겁수유 十劫須臾 but as a moment.

십견 十見 The ten (wrong) views ; see 오견 五見 and add 탐 貪, 혜 慧, 만 慢, 무명 無明 and 의견 疑見 desire, hate, pride, ignorance, and doubt.

십경 十境 The ten objects of or stages in meditation 관 觀 in the T'ien-t'ai school, i.e. 음경 陰境 the five skandhas ; 번뇌경 煩惱境 life's distresses and delusion ; 병환경 病患境 sickness, or duḥkha, its cause and cure ; 업상경 業相境 age-long karmaic influences ; 마사경 摩事境 Māra affairs, how to overthrow their rule ; 선정경 禪定境 the conditions of dhyāna and samādhi ; 제견경 諸見境 various views and doubts that arise ; 만경 慢境 pride in progress and the delusion that one has attained nirvāṇa ; 이승경 二乘境 temptation to be content with the lower nirvāṇa, instead of going on to the greater reward ; 보살경 菩薩境 bodhisattvahood ; see the 지관 止觀 5.

십계 十誡 idem 십계 十戒.

십계 十界 idem 십법계 十法界. 십계개성불 十界皆成佛 The teaching of the Lotus Sūtra of universalism, that all become Buddha. 십계능화보살 十界能化菩薩 Bodhisattvas, above the 초지 初地, who have reached the stage of transforming beings in all the ten kinds of realms.

십계 十戒 Śikṣāpada. The ten prohibitions (in Pāli form) consist of five commandments for the layman : (1) not to destroy life 불살생 不殺生 pāṇātipātā-veramaṇī ; (2) not to steal 불투도 不偸盜 adinnādāna-veramaṇī ; (3) not to commit adultery 불음욕 不婬慾 abrahmacariyā-veramaṇī ; (4) not to lie 불망어 不妄語 musāvādā-veramaṇī ; (5) not to take intoxication liquor 불음주 不飮酒 surāmerayamajjapamādaṭṭhānā-veramaṇī. Eight special commandments for laymen consist of the preceding five plus : (6) not to eat food out of regulated hours 불비시식 不非時食 vikālabhojanā-veramaṇī ; (7) not to use garlands or perfumes 불착화만호향도신 不著華鬘好香塗身 mālāgandha-vilepana-dhāraṇa-maṇḍana-vibhūṣanaṭṭhānā ; (8) not to sleep on high or broad beds (chastity) 부좌고광대상 不坐高廣大牀 uccāsayanā-mahāsayanā-veramaṇī. The ten commandments for the monk are the preceding eight plus : (9) not to take part in singing, dancing, musical or theatrical performances, not to see or listen to such 불가무창기부주관청 不歌舞倡伎不住觀聽 ṇacca-gīta-vādita-visūkadassanā-veramaṇī ; (10) to refrain from acquiring uncoined or coined gold, or silver, or jewels 부득착전금은보물 不得捉錢金銀寶物 jātarūpa-rajata- paṭiggahaṇā-veramaṇī. Under the Mahāyāna these ten commands for the monk were changed, to accord with the new environment of the monk, to the following : not to kill, not to steal, to avoid all unchastity, not to lie, not to slander, not to insult, not to chatter, not to covet, not to give way to anger, to harbour no scepticism.

십공덕(론) 十功德(論) The merits (or powers) commended by the Buddha to his bhikṣus — zealous progress, contentment with few desires, courage, learning (so as to teach), fearlessness, perfect observance of the commands and the fraternity's regulations, perfect meditation, perfect wisdom, perfect liberation, and perfect understanding of it.

십과 十科 ; 십조 十條 The ten rules for translation. v. 번역명의집 翻譯名義集 3.

십과 十過 Ten faults in eating flesh, and ten in drinking intoxicants.

십교 十敎 v. 십종 十宗.

십군 十軍 The ten armies of Māra, which the Buddha attacks and destroys ; the armies are desire, anxiety, hunger and thirst, longing, torpidity, fear, doubt, poison, gain, haughtiness (i.e. disdaining monks).

십근본번뇌 十根本煩惱 idem 십사 十使.

십금강심 十金剛心 Ten characteristics of the "diamond heart" as developed by a bodhisattva : (1) complete insight into all truth ; (2) saving of all creatures ; (3) the glorifying of all Buddha-worlds ; (4) supererogation of his good deeds ; (5) service of all Buddhas ; (6) realization of the truth of all Buddha-laws ; (7) manifestation of all patience and endurance ; (8) unflagging devotion to his vocation ; (9) perfection of his work ; (10) aiding all to fulfil their vows and accomplish their spiritual ends. 화엄경 華嚴經 55. 십금강심향과 十金剛心向果 Ten "fruits" that accrue to the resolute "diamond-heart" of a bodhisattva : faith ; meditation ; reflection on the doctrine ; thoroughness in contemplation ; straightforward progress to Buddhahood ; no retrogression ; the Mahāyāna spirit (of universal salvation) ; freedom from externals (or impressions) ; wisdom ; firm establishment ; v. 범망경심지품 梵網經心地品.

십나찰녀 十羅刹女 The ten rākṣasī, or demonesses mentioned in the Lotus Sūtra 다라니품 陀羅尼品. They are now represented in the temples, each as an attendant on a Buddha or bodhisattva, and are chiefly connected with sorcery. They are said to be previous incarnations of the Buddhas and bodhisattvas with whom they are associated. In their evil state they were enemies of the living, converted they are enemies of evil. There are other definitions. Their names are : (1) 남파 藍婆 Lambā, who is associated with Śākyamuni ; (2) 비남파 毘藍婆 Vilamba, ditto with Amitābha ; (3) 곡치 曲齒 Kūṭadantī, with 약사 藥師 Bhaiṣajya ; (4) 화치 華齒 Puṣpadantī, with 다보 多寶 Prabhūtaratna ; (5) 흑치 黑齒 Makuṭadantī, with 대일 大日 Vairocana ; (6) 다발 多髮 Keśinī, with 보현 普賢 Samantabhadra ; (7) 무염족 無厭足 Acalā, with 문수 文殊 Mañjuśrī ; (8) 지영락 持瓔珞 Mālādharī, with 미륵 彌勒 Maitreya ; (9) 고제 皐帝 Kuntī, with 관음 觀音 Avalokiteśvara ; (10) 탈일체중생정기 奪一切衆生精氣 Sarvasattvāujohārī, with 지장 地藏 Kṣitigarbha.

십념 十念 The ten repetitions of an invocation, e.g. Namo Amitābha. 십념왕생 十念往生 These ten invocations will carry a dying man with an evil karma into the Pure-land. 십념성취 十念成就 similar to the last, but cf. 십성 十聲. 십념처 十念處 A bodhisattva's ten objects of thought or meditation, i.e. body, the senses, mind, things, environment, monastery, city (or district), good name, Buddha-learning, riddance of all passion and delusion. 십념혈맥 十念血脈 The arteries of the "ten invocations," i.e. the teacher's giving and the disciple's receiving of the law.

십뇌란 十惱亂 The ten disturbers of the religious life : a domineering (spirit) ; heretical ways ; dangerous amusements ; a butcher's or other low occupation ; asceticism (or selfish hīnayāna salvation) ; (the condition of a) eunuch ; lust ; endangering (the character by improper intimacy) ; contempt ; breeding animals, etc. (for slaughter).

십대제자 十大弟子 The ten chief disciples of Śākyamuni, each of whom was master of one power or gift. Śāriputra of wisdom ; Maudgalyāyana of supernatural powers ; Mahākāśyapa of discipline ; Aniruddha of 천안 天眼 deva vision ; Subhūti of explaining the void or immaterial ; Pūrṇa of expounding the law ; Kātyāyana of its fundamental principles ; Upāli of maintaining the rules ; Rāhula of the esoteric ; and Ānanda of hearing and remembering. 십대혹 十大惑 idem 십사 十使. 십대원 十大願 The ten vows of P'u Hsien 보현 普賢, or Samantabhadra.

십덕 十德 The ten virtues, powers, or qualities, of which there are several groups, e.g. in the 화엄경십지품 華嚴經十地品 there are 법사십덕 法師十德 the ten virtues of a teacher of the Law, i.e. he should be well versed in its meaning ; able widely to publish it ; not be nervous before an audience ; be untiring in argument ; adaptable ; orderly so that his teaching can be easily followed ; serious and dignified ; bold and zealous ; unwearied ; and enduring (able to bear insult, etc.). The 제자십덕 弟子十德 ten virtues or qualities of a disciple according to the 대일경소 大日經疏 4, are faith ; sincerity ; devotion to the trikāya ; (seeking the) adornment of true wisdom ; perseverance ; moral purity ; patience (or bearing shame) ; generosity in giving ; courage ; resoluteness.

십도 十道 The ten (good) ways for deliverance from mortality — not to kill, steal, act wrongly, lie, be double-tongued, be of evil speech, slander, covet, be angry, look wrongly (or wrong views).

십도 十度 The ten pāramitās or virtues transporting to nirvāṇa ; idem 십바라밀 十波羅蜜 q.v. 십도삼행 十度三行 each of the pāramitās has three forms of observance, e.g. the first, 시 施 dāna or giving has 재시 財施 alms-giving, 법시 法施 truth-giving, and 무외시 無畏施 courage-giving. The three forms differ with each pāramitā.

십락 十樂 v. 십쾌 十快.

십래(게) 十來(偈) The ten rhymes in "lai," a verse which expresses the Buddhist doctrine of moral determinism, i.e. that the position anyone now occupies is solely the result of his character in past lives ; heredity and environment having nothing to do with his present condition, for, whether in prince or beggar, it is the reward of past deeds.

The upright from the forbearing come,
The poor from the mean and greedy come,
Those of high rank from worshippers come,
The low and common from the prideful come,
Those who are dumb from slanderers come,
The blind and deaf from unbelievers come,
The long-lived from the merciful come,
The short-lived from life-takers come,
The deficient in faculties from command-breakers come,
The complete in faculties from command-keepers come.

단정자인욕중래 端正者忍辱中來.
빈궁자간탐중래 貧窮者慳貪中來.
고위자예배중래 高位者禮拜中來.
하천자교만중래 下賤者憍慢中來.
음아자비방중래 瘖啞者誹謗中來.
맹롱자불신중래 盲聾者不信中來.
장수자자비중래 長壽者慈悲中來.
단명자살생중래 短命者殺生中來.
제근불구자파계중래 諸根不具者破戒中來.
육근구족자지계중래 六根具足者持戒中來.

십력 十力 Daśabala. The ten powers of a Buddha, giving complete knowledge of : (1) what is right or wrong in every condition ; (2) what is the karma of every being, past, present, and future ; (3) all stages of dhyāna liberation, and samādhi ; (4) the powers and faculties of all beings ; (5) the desires, or moral direction of every being ; (6) the actual condition of every individual ; (7) the direction and consequence of all laws ; (8) all causes of mortality and of good and evil in their reality ; (9) the end of all beings and nirvāṇa ; (10) the destruction of all illusion of every kind. See the 지도론 智度論 25 and the 구사론 俱舍論 29. 십력교 十力教 The religion of Him who has the ten powers, i.e. Buddhism. 십력(무등)존 十力(無等)尊 The honoured (unequalled) possessor of the ten powers, Buddha. 십력가섭 十力迦葉 Daśabala-Kāśyapa, one of the first five disciples. 십력명 十力明 The ten powers and ten understandings of a Buddha.

십륜 十輪 idem 십종지력 十種智力 ; v. 십력 十力.

십리 十利 There are many groups of ten profitable things or advantages, e.g. ten in regard to edibles, ten to congee, to learning, to study of the Scriptures, to wisdom, to zeal, etc.

십만 十萬 A lakh, i.e. an 억 億 or 낙차 洛叉. 십만억불토 十萬億佛土 The Happy Land, i.e. Amitābha's Paradise in the West, beyond ten thousand million Buddha-realms.

십명 十名 idem 십호 十號.

십묘 十妙 The ten wonders, or incomprehensibles ; there are two groups, the 적 迹 traceable or manifested and 본문 本門 the fundamental. The 적문십묘 迹門十妙 are the wonder of : (1) 경묘 境妙 the universe, sphere, or whole, embracing mind, Buddha, and all things as a unity ; (2) 지묘 智妙 a Buddha's all-embracing knowledge arising from such universe ; (3) 행묘 行妙 his deeds, expressive of his wisdom ; (4) 위묘 位妙 his attainment of all the various Buddha stages, i.e. 십주 十住 and 십지 十地 ; (5) 삼법묘 三法妙 his three laws of 리 理, 혜 慧, and 정 定 truth, wisdom, and vision ; (6) 감응묘 感應妙 his response to appeal, i.e. his (spiritual) response or relation to humanity, for "all beings are my children" ; (7) 신통묘 神通妙 his supernatural powers ; (8) 설법묘 說法妙 his preaching ; (9) 권속묘 眷屬妙 his supernatural retinue ; (10) 이익묘

利益妙 the blessings derived through universal elevation into Buddhahood. The 본문십묘 本門十妙 are the wonder of (1) 본인 本因 the initial impulse or causative stage of Buddhahood ; (2) 본과묘 本果妙 its fruit or result in eternity, joy, and purity ; (3) 국토묘 國土妙 his (Buddha) realm ; (4) 감응묘 感應妙 his response (to human needs) ; (5) 신통묘 神通妙 his supernatural powers ; (6) 설법묘 說法妙 his preaching ; (7) 권속묘 眷屬妙 his supernatural retinue ; (8) 열반묘 涅槃妙 his nirvāṇa ; (9) 수명묘 壽命妙 his (eternal) life ; (10) his blessings as above. Both groups are further defined as progressive stages in a Buddha's career. These "wonders" are derived from the Lotus sūtra.

십무이 十無二 Ten powers only possessed by Buddhas : (1) prediction ; (2) knowing and fulfilling the desires of the living ; (3)-(10) are various forms of omniscience, i.e. (3) of all Buddha-realms and their inhabitants ; (4) their natures ; (5) good roots ; (6) laws ; (7) wisdom ; (8) every moment ; (9) evolving domains, or conditions ; (10) language, words, and discussions. v. 종경록 宗鏡錄 99. 십무진계 十無盡戒 idem 십중(금)계 十重(禁)戒. 십무진장 十無盡藏 The ten boundless treasuries of a bodhisattva : (1) 신 信 belief and faith ; (2) 계 戒 the commandments ; (3) 참 慚 shame of past misdeeds ; (4) 괴 愧 blushing over the misdeeds of others ; (5) hearing and knowledge of the truth ; (6) giving ; (7) wisdom ; (8) memory ; (9) keeping and guarding the sūtras ; (10) powers of expounding them. 화엄경 華嚴經 20. 십무애 十無礙 The ten unhindered transformations and ubiquitous powers of a Buddha.

십문 十問 The ten questions to the Buddha, put into the mouth of Vajrapāṇi, which, with the answers given, form the basis of the 대일경 大日經. What is (or are) (1) the nature of the bodhi-mind? (2) its form or forms? (3) the mental stages requisite to attainment? (4) the difference between them? (5) the time required? (6) the character of the merits attained? (7) the activities or practices necessary? (8) the way of such practices? (9) the condition of the uncultivated and cultivated mind? (10) the difference between it and that of the follower of Yoga?

십문 十門 The ten "doors" or connections between 사 事 and 리 理 ; 사 事 is defined as 현상 現象 form and 리 理 as 본체 本體 substance ; the common illustration of wave and water indicates the idea thus expressed. The 이사무애십문 理事無礙十門 means that in ten ways form and substance are not separate, unconnected entities. (1) 리 理 *li* the substance is always present with 사 事 *shih* the phenomena ; (2) *shih* is always present with *li* ; (3) *shih* depends on *li* for its existence ; (4) the *shih* can reveal the *li* ; (5) the *shih* (mere form, which is unreal) can disappear in the *li* ; (6) the *shih* can conceal the *li* ; (7) the true *li* is the *shih* ; (8) the *shih* is *li* ; (9) the true *li* (or reality) is not the *shih* ; (10) the *shih* is not the (whole) *li* ; v. 화엄대소 華嚴大疏 2. 주변함용관십문 周遍含容觀十門 The fifth of the five 관 觀 meditations of the 화엄종 華嚴宗, i.e. on *li* and *shih* e.g. (1) the *li* is as the *shih* ; (2) the *shih* is as the *li* : 이여사 理如事, 사여리 事如理 and so on. The 지관십문 止觀十門 in the 종경록 宗鏡錄 35, also deals with *li* and *shih* chiefly for purposes of meditation. Another group, the 화엄석경십문 華嚴釋經十門, treats of the Canon and the schools.

십문화쟁론 十門和諍論 "Treatise on Ten Approaches to the Reconciliation of Doctrinal Controversy." Written by Won-hyo.

십바라이 十波羅夷 The ten pārājikas, or sins unpardonable in a monk involving his exclusion from the community ; v. 십중금계 十重禁戒. 십바라밀 十波羅蜜 ; 십바라밀다 十波羅密多 The ten are the six pāramitās with four added. The six are charity (or almsgiving), purity (or morality), patience, zealous progress, meditation, wisdom ; i.e. 시 施, 계 戒, 인욕 忍辱, 정진 精進, 선 禪, 혜 慧. The four additions are 방편 方便 ; 원 願 ; 역 力 and 지 智 upāya, adaptability (or, teaching as suited to the occasion and hearer) ; praṇidhāna, vows ; bala, force of purpose ; and jñāna, knowledge. Also 십도 十度.

십발취심 十發趣心 The ten directional decisions : (1) renouncement of the world ; (2) observance of the commandments ; (3) patience or endurance ; (4) zealous progress ; (5) meditation ; (6) wisdom or understanding ; (7) 원심 願心 the will for good for oneself and others ; (8) 호심 護心 protection (of Buddha, Dharma, Saṅgha) ; (9) 희심 喜心 joy ; (10) 정심 頂心 highest wisdom. v. 범망경심지품 梵網經心地品.

십법 十法 The ten 성취 成就 perfect or perfecting Mahāyāna rules ; i.e. in (1) right belief ; (2) conduct ; (3) spirit ; (4) the joy of the bodhi mind ; (5) joy in the dharma ; (6) joy in meditation in it ; (7) pursuing the correct dharma ; (8) obedience to, or accordance with it ; (9) departing from pride, etc. ; (10) comprehending the inner teaching of Buddha and taking no pleasure in that of the śrāvaka and pratyeka-buddha order. 십법계 十法界 The ten dharma-worlds, or states of existence, i.e. the hells (or purgatories), pretas, animals, asuras, men, devas, śrāvakas, pratyeka-buddhas, bodhisattvas, Buddhas. In the esoteric teaching there is a series of hells, pretas, animals, asuras, men, devas, śrāvakas, bodhisattvas, 권불 權佛 relative Buddhas, 실불 實佛 absolute Buddhas. 십법행 十法行 Ten ways of devotion to the Buddhist sūtras : to copy them ; serve the places where they are kept, as if serving the Buddha's shrine ; preach or give them to others ; listen attentively to their exposition ; read ; maintain ; discourse on them to others ; intone them ; ponder over them ; observe their lessons.

십변처정 十遍處定 v. 십일체처 十一切處.

십보 十寶 The ten precious things ; 십보산 十寶山 the ten precious mountains, or mountain of ten precious things ; v. 십선 十善 and 십선왕 十善王.

십보문 十普門 The ten universals of a bodhisattva : 자비보 慈悲普 universal pity ; 홍서문 弘誓門 vow of universal salvation ; 수행문 修行門 accordant action ; 단혹문 斷惑門 universal cutting off of delusions ; 입법문문 入法門門 freedom of entry into all forms of truth ; 신통문 神通門 universal superhuman powers ; 방편문 方便門 universal accordance with conditions of the receptivity of others ; 설법문 說法門 powers of universal explication of the truth ; 공양제불문 供養諸佛門 power of universal service of all Buddhas ; 성취중생문 成就衆生門 the perfecting of all beings universally.

십분로명왕 十忿怒明王 The ten irate rājas, or protectors, whose huge images with many heads and limbs are seen in temples ; perhaps the ten krodha gods of the Tibetans (Khro-bo) ; their names are 염만득가 焰鬘得迦 Yamāntaka ; 무능승 無能勝 Ajita ; 발납만득가 鉢納鬘得迦 Padmāntaka ; 미관나득가 尾觀那得迦 Vighnāntaka ; 부동존 不動尊 Acala ; 타지 吒枳 Ḍākinī ; 니라난나 儞羅難拏 Nīladaṇḍa ; 대력 大力, 송파 送婆 Śambara ; and 박일라파다라 縛日羅播多羅 Vīrabhadra.

십불 十佛 There are several groups ; that of the Hua-yen sūtra is Kāśyapa, Kanakamuni, Krakucchanda, Viśvabhū, Śikhin, Vipaśyi, Tiṣya (or Puṣya), Tissa, Padma, and Dīpaṃkara. Another group is that of the Amitābha cult, one for each of the ten directions, There are other groups.

십불이문 十不二門 The school of the ten pairs of unified opposites founded by 형계 荊溪 Ching-ch'i on the teaching of the Lotus sūtra. There are several books bearing the name. The unifying principle is that of the identity of contraries, and the ten apparent contraries are matter and mind, internal and external, 수증 修證 practice and proof (or realization), cause and effect, impurity and purity, objective and subjective, self and other, 삼업 三業 action, speech, and thought, 권실 權實 relative and absolute, the fertilizes and the fertilizer (i.e. receiver and giver). There are several treatises on the subject in the Canon. 십불선업 十不善業 ; 십불선도 十不善道 idem 십악(업) 十惡(業). 십불회계 十不悔戒 The ten rules which produce no regrets — not to kill, steal, fornicate, lie, tell of a fellow-Buddhist's sins, deal in wine, praise oneself and discredit others, be mean, be angry, defame the Triratna (Buddha, Law, Fraternity).

십사 十使 ; **십대혹** 十大惑 ; **십근본번뇌** 十根本煩惱 The ten messengers, deluders, fundamental passions ; they are divided into five sharp and five dull ; the five 둔사 鈍使 dull ones are desire, hate, stupidity, pride, and doubt ; the five sharp 이사 利使 are 신견 身見, 변견 邊見, 사견 邪見, 견취견 見取見, 계금견 戒禁見, v. 견 見.

십사 十四 Caturdaśa, fourteen. 십사불국왕생 十四佛國往生 The fourteen other-world realms of fourteen Buddhas, i.e. this realm of Śākyamuni and thirteen others. 십사신구왕 十四神九王 The fourteen devas and nine dragon and other kings, who went in the train of Mañjuśrī to thank the Buddha at the last of his Hua-yen addresses ; for list see 당화엄경 唐華嚴經 61. 십사변화 十四變化 The fourteen transformations that are connected with the four dhyāna heavens. 십사난 十四難 The fourteen difficult questions of the "heretics" to which the Buddha made no reply, for, as it is said, the questions were no more properly put than if one asked "How much milk can you get from a cow's horn?" They are forms of : All is permanent, impermanent, both or neither ; all changes, changes not, both, neither ; at death a spirit departs, does not, both, neither ; after death we have the same body (or personality) and spirit, or body and spirit are different.

십사 十師 The ten monks necessary for a full ordination of a monk, i.e. 삼사칠증 三師七證 three leaders and seven witnesses.

십사공덕 十事功德 The bodhisattva-merit resulting from the attainment of the ten groups of excellences in the southern version of the Nirvāṇa Sūtra 남본열반경 南本涅槃經 19-24. There is an unimportant 십사경 十事經 not connected with the above. 십사비법 十事非法 Ten unlawful things said to have been advocated by the Vaiśālī monks, which led to the calling of the second Council.

십산왕 十山王 The spirit king of each of the ten mountains — Himālaya, Gandhamādana, Vaidharī, 신선 神仙, Yugaṁdhara, Aśvakarṇa, Nemindhara, Cakravāḍa, Ketumatī, and Sumeru.

십삼 十三 Trayodaśa ; thirteen. 십삼불 十三佛 The thirteen Shingon rulers of the dead during the forty-nine days and until the thirty-third commemoration. The thirteen are 부동명왕 不動明王, 석가 釋迦, 문수 文殊, 보현 普賢, 지장 地藏, 미륵 彌勒, 약사 藥師, 관음 觀音, 세지 勢至, 아미타 阿彌陀, 아촉 阿閦, 대일 大日 and 허공장 虛空藏 ; each has his place, duties, magical letter, sings, etc. 십삼력 十三力 The thirteen powers or bodhisattva balas of the Pureland school : 인력 因力, 연력 緣力, 의력 意力, 원력 願力, 방편력 方便力, 상력 常力, 선력 善力, 정력 定力, 혜력 慧力, 다문력 多聞力, 지계인욕정진선정력 持戒忍辱精進禪定力, 정념정관제통명력 正念正觀諸通明力, and 여법조복제중생력 如法調伏諸衆生力. 십삼종 十三宗 The thirteen Buddhist schools of China, v. 종파 宗派.

십선(정법) 十善(正法) The ten good characteristics, or virtues, defined as the non-committal of the 십악 十惡 ten evils, q.v. T'ien-t'ai has two groups, one of ceasing 지 止 to do evil, the other of learning to do well 행 行. 십선위 十善位 ; 십선계력 十善戒力 ; 십선왕 十善王 The position, or power, attained in the next life by observing the ten commandments here, to be born in the heavens, or as rulers of men. 십선교 十善巧 The ten good crafts, of meditations of pratyeka-buddhas, i.e. on the five skandhas, twelve 처 處, eighteen 계 界, twelve 인연 因緣, etc. 십선계 十善戒 The ten commandments (as observed by the laity). 십선업(도) 十善業(道) The excellent karma resulting from practice of the ten commandments. 십선보살 十善菩薩 The bodhisattvas of the 십신위 十信位 q.v.

십선지 十禪支 v. 십일체처 十一切處.

십성 十成 Entirely completed, perfect.

십수승어 十殊勝語 The ten rare or surpassing terms connected with the ten surpassing laws ; they are given in Hsüan-tsang's translation of Vasubandhu's 섭론석 攝論釋.

십승(관) 十乘(觀) A T'ien-t'ai mode of meditation in ten "vehicles" or stages, for the attainment of bodhi. 십승상 十乘床 The comfort or ease of progress produced by the above is compared to a couch or divan. 십승풍 十乘風 The above method like a breeze blows away error and falsity as dust.

십승행 十勝行 The ten pāramitās observed by bodhisattvas, see 십지 十地 and 십주 十住. Hīnayāna has another group, adding to the four 범복 梵福 q.v. the six of sacrificing one's life to save mother ; or father ; or a Buddha ; to become a monk to induce another to become a monk ; to obtain authority to preach.

십신 十身 Ten aspects of the Buddhakāya 불신 佛身 q.v.

십신 十信 The ten grades of bodhisattva faith, i.e. the first ten 위 位 in the fifty-two bodhisattva positions : (1) 신 信 faith (which destroys illusion and results in) (2) 염 念 remembrance, or unforgetfulness ; (3) 정진 精進 zealous progress ; (4) 혜 慧 wisdom ; (5) 정 定 settled firmness in concentration ; (6) 불퇴 不退 non-retrogression ; (7) 호법 護法 protection of the Truth ; (8) 회향 廻向 reflexive powers, e.g. for reflecting the Truth ; (9) 계 戒 the nirvāṇa mind in 무위 無爲 effortlessness ; (10) 원 願 action at will in anything and everywhere.

십심 十心 The ten kinds of heart or mind ; there are three groups. One is from the 지관 止觀 4, minds ignorant and dark ; affected by evil companions ; not following the good ; doing evil in thought, word, deed ; spreading evil abroad ; unceasingly wicked ; secret sin ; open crime ; utterly shameless ; denying cause and effect (retribution) — all such must remain in the flow 유 流 of reincarnation. The second group (from the same book) is the 역류 逆流 the mind striving against the stream of perpetual reincarnation ; it shows itself in devout faith, shame (for sin), fear (of wrong-doing), repentance and confession, reform, bodhi (i.e. the bodhisattva mind), doing good, maintaining the right law, thinking on all the Buddhas, meditating on the void (or, the unreality of sin). The third is the 진언 眞言 group from the 대일경소 大日經疏 3 ; the "seed" heart (i.e. the original good desire), the sprout (under Buddhist religious influence), the bud, leaf, flower, fruit, its serviceableness ; the child-heart, the discriminating heart, the heart of settled judgment (or resolve).

십악 十惡 Daśākuśala. The ten "not right" or evil things are killing, stealing, adultery, lying, double-tongue, coarse language, filthy language, covetousness, anger, perverted views ; these produce the ten resultant evils 십악업(도) 十惡業(道). Cf. 십선 十善 ; 십계 十戒.

십안 十眼 The ten kinds of eyes : (1) 육안 肉眼 eyes of flesh ; (2) 천안 天眼 deva eyes ; (3) 혜안 慧眼 wisdom eyes ; (4) 법안 法眼 dharma eyes ; (5) 불안 佛眼 Buddha eyes ; (6) 지안 智眼 eyes of judgment ; (7) 광명안 光明眼 eyes shining with Buddha-light ; (8) 출생사안 出生死眼 immortal eyes ; (9) 무애안 無碍眼 unhindered eyes ; (10) 일체지안 一切智眼 omniscient eyes.

십야(염불) 十夜(念佛) The ten nights (and days) from the sixth to the fifteenth of the tenth moon, when the Pure-land sect intones sūtras.

십여(시) 十如(是) The ten essential qualities, or characteristics, of a thing, according to the 방편 方便 chapter of the Lotus sūtra : 상여 相如 form ; 성여 性如 nature ; 체여 體如 corpus or embodiment ; 역여 力如 powers ; 작여 作如 function ; 인여 因如 primary cause ; 연여 緣如 environmental cause ; 과여 果如 effect ; 보여 報如 karmaic reward ; 본말구경등 本末究竟等 the inseparability, or inevitability of them all.

십여래지 十如來地 v. 십지 十地.

십연생구 十緣生句 Ten illusions arising from environmental conditions : sleight of hand ; mirage ; dreams ; reflections or shadows ; gandharva cities (or cities of the sirens, seen in the sea-mist) ; echoes ; the moon reflected in water ; floating bubbles ; motes (*muscæ volitantes*) ; fire-wheel (made by revolving a flare). 십연관 十緣觀 ; 십유관 十喩觀 A meditation, or reflection on these ten illusions.

십오 十五 Pañcadaśa, fifteen. 십오존 十五尊 The fifteen honoured ones, with whom certain 진언 眞言 Shingon devotees seek by yoga to become united ; of the fifteen, each represents a part of the whole, e.g. the eyes, ears, mouth, hands, feet, etc. v. 유기경 瑜祇經 in its 금강살타 金剛薩埵, etc., chapter. 십오존관음 十五尊觀音 The fifteen kinds of Kuan-yin's images — normal faces, with thousand hands, horse's head, eleven faces, as Cundā (Marīci), with the 여의 如意 talismanic wheel, net, white robe, leaf robe, moon, willow, fruit, as Tārā, with azure neck, and as Gandharāja. 십오지단 十五智斷 The fifteen days of the waxing moon are likened to the fifteen kinds of increasing wisdom 지 智, and the fifteen waning days to the fifteen kinds of deliverance from evil 단 斷.

십우도(서) 十牛圖(序) The ten ox-pictures, the first, a man looking for an ox, then seeing its tracks, then seeing the ox, catching it, feeding it, riding it home, ox dies man lives, both dead, read, return whence they came, and enter the dust.

십원왕 十願王 The king of the ten vows, P'u Hsien 보현 普賢, or Samantabhadra.

십육 十六 Ṣoḍaśa. Sixteen is the esoteric (Shingon) perfect number, just as ten is the perfect number in the Hua-yen sūtra and generally, see 대일경소 大日經疏 5. 십육심 十六心, i.e. the 팔인 八忍 and 팔지 八智. 십육(대)천 十六(大)天 The sixteen devas are E. Indra and his wife ; S.E. the fire deva and his wife ; S. Yama and his wife ; S.W. Yakṣa-rāja (Kuvera) and wife ; W. the water deva and his nāga wife (Śakti) ; N.W. the wind deva and wife ; N. Vaiśramaṇa and wife ; N.E. Īśāna and wife. 십육사 十六師 The sixteen non-Buddhist "heretical" Indian philosophers. 십육회 十六會 The sixteen lessons of the Prajñā-pāramitā. 십육(심)행 十六(心)行 ; 십육제관 十六諦觀 idem 십육행상 十六行相. The sixteen 행상 行相 of the Four Axioms 사제 四諦, i.e. four forms of considering each of the axioms, associated with 견도 見道. 십육선신 十六善神 Two lists are given, one of sixteen 대장 大將 mahārājas ; another of sixteen 선신 善神 good spirits or gods ; all of them are guardians of the good and enemies of evil. 십육국왕 十六國王 ; 십육대국 十六大國 The sixteen ancient kingdoms of India whose kings are addressed in the 인왕경 仁王經 2 ; i.e. Vaiśālī, Kośala, Śrāvastī, Magadha, Bārāṇasī, Kapilavastu, Kuśinagara, Kauśāmbī, Pañcāla, Pāṭaliputra, Mathurā, Uṣa (Uśīra), Puṇyavardhana, Devāvatāra, Kāśī, and Campā. 십육대력 十六大力 The sixteen great powers obtainable by a bodhisattva, i.e. of will, mind, action, shame (to do evil), energy, firmness, wisdom, virtue, reasoning, personal appearance, physical powers, wealth, spirit, magic, spreading the truth, subduing demons. 십육상관 十六想觀 idem 십육관 十六觀. 십육왕자(불) 十六王子(佛) ; 십육사미 十六沙彌 The sixteen princes in the Lotus Sūtra who became Buddhas after hearing their father preach it. 지견 知見 ; 십육신아 十六神我 The sixteen heretical views on me and mine, i.e. the ego in self and others, determinism or fate, immortality, etc. ; v. 지도론 智度論 25. 십육보살 十六菩薩 ; 십육대사 十六大士 ; 십육정사 十六正士 The sixteen bodhisattvas ; there two groups, one of the 현교 顯教 exoteric, one of the 밀교 密教 esoteric cults ; the exoteric list is indefinite ; the esoteric has two lists, one is of four bodhisattvas to each of the Buddhas of the four quarters of the Diamond Realm ; the other is of the sixteen who represent the body of bodhisattvas in a 현 賢 kalpa, such as the present : E. 미륵 彌勒, 불공 不空, 제우 除憂, 제악 除惡 ; S. 향상 香象, 대정진 大精進, 허공장 虛空藏, 지당 智幢 ; W. 무량광 無量光, 현호 賢護, 망명 網明, 월광 月光 ; N. 무량의(문수) 無量意(文殊), 변적 辨積, 금강장 金剛藏, 보현 普賢. 십육관 十六觀 The sixteen meditations of Amitābha on the setting sun, water (as ice, crystal, etc.), the earth, and so on. 십육자구 十六資具 Sixteen necessaries of a strict observer of ascetic rules, ranging from garments made of rags collected from the dust heap to sleeping among graves.

십은 十恩 Ten kinds of the Buddha's grace : his (1) initial resolve to universalize (his salvation) ; (2) self-sacrifice (in previous lives) ; (3) complete altruism ; (4) his descent into all the six states of existence for their salvation ; (5) relief of the living from distress and mortality ; (6) profound pity ; (7) revelation of himself in human and glorified form ; (8) teaching in accordance with the capacity of his hearers, first hīnayāna, then mahāyāna doctrine ; (9) revealing his nirvāṇa to stimulate his disciples ; (10) pitying thought for all creatures, in that dying at 80 instead of at 100 he left twenty years of his own happiness to his disciples ; and also the tripiṭaka of universal salvation.

십이 十二 Dvādaśa, twelve.

십이(대)원 十二(大)願 or **십이(상)원** 十二(上)願 The twelve vows of the Master of Healing ; v. 약사 藥師.

십이공 十二空 v. 십이진여 十二眞如.

십이광불 十二光佛 Amitābha's twelve titles of light. The 무량수경상 無量壽經上 gives them as 무량광불 無量光佛, etc., i.e. the Buddha of light that is immeasurable, boundless, irresistible, incomparable, yama (or flaming), pure, joy, wisdom, unceasing, surpassing thought, ineffable, surpassing sun and moon. Another list is given in the 구품왕생아미타...경 九品往生阿彌陀...經.

십이궁 十二宮 The twelve zodiacal mansions : east — Gemini 부부 夫婦 or 쌍녀 雙女 ; Aries 양 羊 ; Taurus 우 牛 ; west — Libra 칭 秤 ; Scorpio 갈 蝎 ; Sagittarius 궁 弓 or 인마 人馬 ; south — Aquarius 병 瓶 ; Pisces 어 魚 ; Capricornus 밀우 密牛 ; north — Cancer 방해 螃蟹 ; Leo 사자 獅子 ; Virgo (or twin maidens 쌍녀 雙女). They are used in the vajradhātu group of the Garbhadhātu maṇḍala, E. W. S. N.

십이금 十二禽 idem 십이수 十二獸.

십이등 十二燈 The twelve lamps used in the cult of the Master of Healing 약사 藥師.

십이무위 十二無爲 v. 십이진여 十二眞如.

십이문 十二門 idem 십이인연 十二因緣. 십이문론 十二門論 Dvādaśanikāya Śāstra. One of the 삼론 三論, composed by Nāgārjuna, translated by Kumārajīva A.D. 408. There are several works on it.

십이법인 十二法人 Those who follow the twelve practices of the ascetics : (1) live in a hermitage ; (2) always beg for food ; (3) take turns at begging food ; (4) one meal a day ; (5) reduce amount of food ; (6) do not take a drink made of fruit or honey after midday ; (7) wear dust-heap garments ; (8) wear only the three clerical garments ; (9) dwell among graves ; (10) stay under a tree ; (11) on the dewy ground ; (12) sit and never lie.

십이부경 十二部經 Twelve divisions of the Mahāyāna canon : (1) 수다라 修多羅 sūtra ; (2) 기야 祇夜 geya ; (3) 가타 伽陀 gāthā ; (4) 니다나 尼陀那 nidāna, also 인연 因緣 ; (5) 이제목다 伊帝目多 itivṛttaka ; (6) 사다가 闍多伽 jātaka ; (7) 아부달마 阿浮達摩 adbhuta-dharma, i.e. the 아비달마 阿毘達摩 abhidharma ; (8) 아바다나 阿波陀那 avadāna ; (9) 우바제사 優婆提舍 upadeśa ; (10) 우다나 優陀那 udāna ; (11) 비불략 毘佛略 vaipulya ; (12) 화가라 和伽羅 vyākaraṇa. Cf. 구부경 九部經.

십이분경 十二分經 ; **십이분교** 十二分教 idem 십이부경 十二部經.

십이불 十二佛 The twelve Buddhas of the esoteric sect placed three on the east, one in each of the other seven directions, and one each for zenith and nadir.

십이불율의 十二不律儀 idem 십이악율의 十二惡律儀.

십이수 十二獸 The twelve animals for the "twelve horary branches" with their names, hours, and the Chinese transliterations of their Sanskrit equivalents ; v. 대집경 大集經 23 and 56. There are also the thirty-six animals, three for each hour. The twelve are : Serpent 사사 蛇巳, 9-11 a.m. 가야 迦若 ; Horse 마오 馬午, 11-1 noon 두라 兜羅 ; Sheep 양미 羊未, 1-3 p.m. 비리지가 毘棃支迦 ; Monkey 후신 猴申, 3-5 p.m. 단니비 檀尼毘 ; Cock 계유 鷄酉, 5-7 p.m. 마가라 摩迦羅 ; Dog 견술 犬戌, 7-9 p.m. 구반 鳩槃 ; Boar 시해 豕亥, 9-11 p.m. 미나 彌那 ; Rat 서자 鼠子, 11-1 midnight 미사 彌沙 ; Ox 우축 牛丑, 1-3 a.m. 비리사 毘利沙 ; Tiger (or Lion) 호인 虎寅, 3-5 a.m. 미륜나 彌倫那 ; Hare 토묘 兎卯, 5-7 a.m. 갈가타가 羯迦吒迦 ; Dragon 용진 龍辰, 7-9 a.m. 사아 絲阿.

십이신(명왕) 十二神(明王) The twelve spirits connected with the cult of 약사 藥師 the Master of Healing. Also 십이신장 十二神將. They are associated with the twelve hours of the day, of which they are guardian spirits. Their names are as follows : 궁비라 宮毘羅 ; 금비라 金毘羅 Kumbhīra ; 벌절라 伐折羅 Vajra ; 미기라 迷企羅 Mihira ; 안지라 安底羅 Aṇḍīra ; 알니라 頞儞羅 Anila ; 산지라 珊底羅 Śaṇḍila ; 인다라 因陀羅 Indra ; 파이라 波夷羅 Pajra ; 마호라 摩虎羅 Mahoraga ; 진달라 眞達羅 Kinnara 초두라 招杜羅 Catura ; and 비갈라 毘羯羅 Vikarāla.

십이악률의 十二惡律儀 The twelve bad occupations : sheep-butcher ; poulterer (or hen-breeder) ; pork butcher ; fowler ; fisherman ; hunger ; thief ; executioner ; jailer ; juggler ; dog-butcher ; beater (i.e. hunt servant).

십이약차대장 十二藥叉大將 idem 십이신 十二神.

십이연기 十二緣起 ; 십이륜 十二輪 ; 십이문 十二門 ; idem 십이인연 十二因緣.

십이원왕 十二願王 The twelve-vow king, i.e. Yao Shih 약사 藥師, the Master of Healing.

십이유경 十二遊經 Dvādaśaviharaṇa sūtra. The life of Śākyamuni to his twelfth year, translated by Kālodaka A.D. 392.

십이인연 十二因緣 Dvādaśāṅga pratītyasamutpāda ; the twelve nidānas ; v. 니 尼 and 인 因 ; also 십이연기 十二緣起 ; 십이(유)지 十二(有)支 ; 십이솔련 十二率連 ; 십이극원 十二棘園 ; 십이륜 十二輪 ; 십이중성 十二重城 ; 인연관 因緣觀 ; 지불관 支佛觀. They are the twelve links in the chain of existence : (1) 무명 無明 avidyā, ignorance, or unenlightenment ; (2) 행 行 saṁskāra, action, activity, conception, "dispositions," Keith ; (3) 식 識 vijñāna, consciousness ; (4) 명색 名色 nāmarūpa, name and form ; (5) 육입 六入 ṣaḍāyatana, the six sense organs, i.e. eye, ear, nose, tongue, body, and mind ; (6) 촉 觸 sparśa, contact, touch ; (7) 수 受 vedanā, sensation, feeling ; (8) 애 愛 tṛṣṇā, thirst, desire, craving ; (9) 취 取 upādāna, laying hold of, grasping ; (10) 유 有 bhava, being, existing ; (11) 생 生 jāti, birth ; (12) 노사 老死 jarā-maraṇa, old age, death. The "classical formula" reads "By reason of ignorance dispositions ; by reason of dispositions consciousness," etc. A further application of the twelve nidānas is made in regard to their causation of rebirth : (1) ignorance, as inherited passion from the beginningless past ; (2) karma, good and evil, of past lives ; (3) conception as a form of perception ; (4) nāmarūpa, or body and mind evolving (in the womb) ; (5) the six organs on the verge of birth ; (6) childhood whose intelligence is limited to sparśa, contact or touch ; (7) receptivity or budding intelligence and discrimination from 6 or 7 years ; (8) thirst, desire, or love, age of puberty ; (9) the urge of sensuous existence ; (10) forming the substance, bhava, of future karma ; (11) the completed karma ready for rebirth ; (12) old age and death. The two first are associated with the previous life, the other ten with the present. The theory is equally applicable to all realms of reincarnation. The twelve links are also represented in a chart, at the centre of which are the serpent (anger), boar (ignorance, or stupidity), and dove (lust) representing the fundamental sins. Each catches the other by the tail, typifying the train of sins producing the wheel of life. In another circle the twelve links are represented as follows : (1) ignorance, a blind woman ; (2) action, a potter at work, or a man gathering fruit ; (3) consciousness, a restless monkey ; (4) name and form, a boat ; (5) sense organs, a house ; (6) contact, a man and woman sitting together ; (7) sensation, a man pierced by an arrow ; (8) desire, a man drinking wine ; (9) craving, a couple in union ; (10) existence through childbirth ; (11) birth, a man carrying a corpse ; (12) disease, old age, death, an old woman leaning on a stick. v. 십이인연론 十二因緣論 Pratītya-samutpāda śāstra.

십이종화법 十二種火法 v. 십이화천 十二火天.

십이지 十二地 To the 십지 十地 add 등각 等覺 and 묘각 妙覺 q.v.

십이진여 十二眞如 The twelve aspects of the bhūtatathatā or the ultimate, which is also styled the 십이무위 十二無爲 "inactive" or nirvāṇa-like : and the 십이공 十二空 "void" or immaterial : (1) The *chên-ju* itself ; (2) 법계 法界 as the medium of all things ; (3) 법성 法性 as the nature of all things ; (4) 불허망성 不虛妄性 its reality contra the unreality of phenomena ; (5) 불변이성 不變異性 its immutability contra mortality and phenomenal variation ; (6) 평등성 平等性 as universal or undifferentiated ; (7) 이생성 離生性 as immortal, i.e. apart from birth and death, or creation and destruction ; (8) 법정 法定 as eternal, its nature ever sure ; (9) 법주 法住 as the abode of all things ; (10) 실제 實際 as the bounds of all reality ; (11) 허공계 虛空界 as the realm of space, the void, or immateriality ; (12) 부사의계 不思議界 as the realm beyond thought or expression.

십이천 十二天 The twelve devas (especially of the Shingon sect) : Brahmā ; the deva of earth ; of the moon ; of the sun ; Indra ; of fire ; Yama ; of the rakṣas (or demons) ; of water ; of wind ; Vaiśramaṇa (wealth) ; and Maheśvara (Śiva). Also 십이대천중 十二大天衆.

십이화천 十二火天 The homa-spirits, or fire-spirits ; whose representations, colours, magic words, signs, symbols, and mode of worship are given in the 대일경소 大日經疏 20. Also 십이화존 十二火尊 ; 십이종화법 十二種火法. The twelve fire-spirits are : (1) Indra or Vairocana, the discoverer or source of fire, symbolizing 지 智 knowledge ; (2) the moon 행만 行滿 which progresses to fullness, with mercy as root and enlightenment as fruit, i.e. Buddha ; (3) the wind, represented as a half-moon, fanner of flame, of zeal, and by driving away dark clouds, of enlightenment ; (4) the red rays of the rising sun, rohitaka, his swords (or rays) indicating 혜 慧 wisdom ; (5) 몰률나 沒嘌拏 a form half stern, half smiling, sternly driving away the passions and trials ; (6) 분노 忿怒 irate, bellowing with open mouth, showing four teeth, flowing locks, one eye closed ; (7) 사타라 闍吒羅 fire burning within, i.e. the inner witness, or realization ; (8) 흘쇄야 訖灑耶 the waster, or destroyer of waste and injurious products within, i.e. inner purification ; (9) 의생 意生 the producer at will, capable of all variety, resembling Viśvakarman, the Brahmanic Vulcan ; (10) 갈라미 羯羅微 the fire-eater ; (11) untraceable ; (12) 모하나 謨賀那 the completer, also the subduer of demons.

십일 十一 Ekādaśa, eleven. 십일체처 十一切處 The universals, or modes of contemplating the universe from ten aspects, i.e. from the viewpoint of earth, water, fire, wind, blue, yellow, red, white, space, or mind. For example, contemplated under the aspect of water, then the universe is regarded as in flux and change. Also called 십선지 十禪支, 시변처정 十遍處定. It is one of the 삼법 三法. 십일면관음 十一面觀音 The eleven-faced Kuan-yin, especially connected with tantric performances, ekādaśamukha ; there are three or more sūtras on the subject.

십장 十障 Ten hindrances ; bodhisattvas in the stage of 십지 十地 overcome these ten hindrances and realize the 십진여 十眞如 q.v. The hindrances are : (1) 이생성장 異生性障 the common illusions of the unenlightened, taking the seeming for real ; (2) 사행장 邪行障 common unenlightened conduct ; (3) 암둔장 暗鈍障 ignorant and dull ideas ; (4) 세혹현행장 細惑現行障 the illusion that things are real and have independent existence ; (5) 하승열반장 下乘涅槃障 the lower ideals in Hīnayāna of nirvāṇa ; (6) 조상현행장 粗相現行障 the ordinary ideas of the pure and impure ; (7) 세상현행장 細相現行障 the idea of reincarnation ; (8) 무상가행장 無相加行障 the continuance of activity even in the formless world ; (9) 불욕행장 不欲行障 no desire to act for the salvation of others ; (10) 법미자재장 法未自在障 nonattainment of complete mastery of all things. v. 유식론 唯識論 10.

십장양심 十長養心 The ten kinds of well-nourished heart, essential to entry into the cult of the higher patience and endurance : a heart of kindness ; of pity ; of joy (in progress toward salvation of others) ; renunciation ; almsgiving ; delight in telling the doctrine ; benefiting or aiding others to salvation ; unity, or amity ; concentration in meditation ; wisdom ; v. 범망경심지품 梵網經心地品.

십재(일) 十齋(日) The ten "fast" days of a month are 1, 8, 14, 15, 18, 23, 24, 28, 29 and 30. In certain periods flesh was forbidden on these days, also all killing, hunting, fishing, executions, etc. 십재(일)불 十齋(日)佛 The ten Buddhas or bodhisattvas connected with these days who in turn are 정광 定光, 약사 藥師, 보현 普賢, 아미타 阿彌陀, 관음 觀音, 세지 勢至, 지장 地藏, 비로자나 毘盧遮那, 약왕 藥王, 석가 釋迦.

십전 十纏 The ten bonds that bind men to mortality — to be shameless, unblushing, envious, mean, regretful, torpid, busy, absorbed, angry, secretive (of sin).

십전염왕 十殿閻王 The ten Yama courts, cf. 시왕 十王.

십제자 十弟子 The ten acolytes or attendants on an ācārya, or superior religious teacher, in his ceremonial offices, following the pattern of the ten principal disciples of Śākyamuni.

십종 十宗 The ten schools of Chinese Buddhism : I. The (1) 율종 律宗 Vinaya-discipline, or 남산종 南山宗 ; (2) 구사 俱舍 Kośa, Abhidharma, or Reality (Sarvāstivādin) 유종 有宗 ; (3) 성실종 成實宗 Satya-siddhi sect founded on this śāstra by Harivarman ; (4) 삼론종 三論宗 Mādhyamika or 성공종 性空宗 ; (5) 법화종 法華宗 Lotus, "Law-flower" or T'ien-t'ai 천태종 天台宗 ; (6) 화엄종 華嚴宗 Hua-yen or 법성 法性 or 현수종 賢首宗 ; (7) 법상종 法相宗 Dharmalakṣaṇa or 자은종 慈恩宗 founded on the 유식론 唯識論 ; (8) 심종 心宗 Ch'an(Zen), mind-only or intuitive, v. 선종 禪宗 ; (9) 진언종 眞言宗 (Jap. Shingon) or esoteric 밀종 密宗 ; (10) 연종 蓮宗 Amitābha-lotus or Pure Land (Jap. Jōdō) 정토종 淨土宗. The 2nd, 3rd, 4th, and 9th are found in Japan rather than in China, where they have ceased to be of importance. II. The Hua-yen has also ten divisions into ten schools of thought : (1) 아법구유 我法俱有 the reality of self (or soul) and things, e.g. mind and matter ; (2) 법유아무 法有我無 the reality of things but not of soul ; (3) 법무거래 法無去來 things have neither creation nor destruction ; (4) 현통가실 現通假實 present things are both apparent and real ; (5) 속망진실 俗妄眞實 common or phenomenal ideas are wrong, fundamental reality is the only truth ; (6) things are merely names ; (7) all things are unreal 공 空 ; (8) the bhūtatathatā is not unreal ; (9) phenomena and their perception are to be got rid of ; (10) the perfect, all-inclusive, and complete teaching of the One Vehicle. III. There are two old Japanese divisions : 대승률종 大乘律宗, 구사종 俱舍宗, 성실종 成實宗, 법상종 法相宗, 삼론종 三論宗, 천태종 天台宗, 화엄종 華嚴宗, 진언종 眞言宗, 소승율종 小乘律宗, and 정토종 淨土宗 ; the second list adds 선종 禪宗 and omits 대승율종 大乘律宗. They are the Ritsu, Kusha, Jōjitsu, Hossō, Sanron, Tendai, Kegon, Shingon, (Hīnayāna) Ritsu, and Jōdō ; the addition being Ch'an(Zen).

십종부정 十種不淨 The deluded, e.g. the hīnayānists, because of their refusal to follow the higher truth, remain in the condition of reincarnation and are impure in ten ways : in body, mouth, mind, deed, state, sitting, sleeping, practice, converting others, their expectations. 십종소관법 十種所觀法 Ten meditations on each of the 십주 十住, 십행 十行, 십회향 十廻向, 십지 十地 and

등각 等覺. 십종방편 十種方便 Ten kinds of suitable aids to religious success : almsgiving (or self-sacrifice) ; keeping the commandments ; forbearance ; zealous progress ; meditation ; wisdom ; great kindness ; great pity ; awaking and stimulating others ; preaching (or revolving) the never receding wheel of the Law. 십종지력 十種智力 The ten kinds of wisdom and power, v. 십지 十智 and 십력 十力. 십종지명 十種智明 Ten kinds of bodhisattva wisdom, or omniscience, for the understanding of all things relating to all beings, in order to save them from the sufferings of mortality and bring them to true bodhi. The ten are detailed in the Hua-yen 화엄 華嚴 sūtra in two groups, one in the 십명품 十明品 and one in the 이세간품 離世間品. 십종행원 十種行願 The ten vows of P'u Hsien 보현 普賢. 십종관법 十種觀法 idem 십승관법 十乘觀法. 십종마군 十種魔軍 idem 십군 十軍.

십주 十住 The ten stages, or periods, in bodhisattva-wisdom, prajñā 반야 般若, are the 십주 十住 ; the merits or character attained are the 십지 十地 q.v. Two interpretations may be given. In the first of these, the first four stages are likened to entry into the holy womb, the next four to the period of gestation, the ninth to birth, and the tenth to the washing or baptism with the water of wisdom, e.g. the baptism of a Kṣatriya prince. The ten stages are (1) 발심주 發心住 the purposive stage, the mind set upon Buddhahood ; (2) 치지주 治地住 clear understanding and mental control ; (3) 수행주 修行住 unhampered liberty in every direction ; (4) 생귀주 生貴住 acquiring the Tathāgata nature or seed ; (5) 방편구족주 方便具足住 perfect adaptability and resemblance in self-development and development of others ; (6) 정심주 正心住 the whole mind becoming Buddha-like ; (7) 불퇴주 不退住 no retrogression, perfect unity and constant progress ; (8) 동진주 童眞住 as a Buddha-son now complete ; (9) 법왕자주 法王子住 as prince of the law ; (10) 관정주 灌頂住 baptism as such, e.g. the consecration of kings. Another interpretation of the above is : (1) spiritual resolve, stage of śrota-āpanna ; (2) submission to rule, preparation for Sakṛdāgāmin stage ; (3) cultivation of virtue, attainment of Sakṛdāgāmin stage ; (4) noble birth, preparation for the anāgāmin stage ; (5) perfect means, attainment of anāgāmin stage ; (6) right mind, preparation for arhatship ; (7) no-retrogradation, the attainment of arhatship ; (8) immortal youth, pratyekabuddhahood ; (9) son of the law-king, the conception of bodhisattvahood ; (10) baptism as the summit of attainment, the conception of Buddhahood. 십주심 十住心 Ten stages of mental or spiritual development in the 진언 眞言 Shingon sect, beginning with the human animal and ending with perfect enlightenment ; a category by the Japanese monk 홍법 弘法 Kōhō, founded on the 대일경십심품 大日經十心品. 십주비바사론 十住毘婆沙論 Daśabhūmivibhāṣā śāstra. A commentary by Nāgārjuna on the 십주경 十住經 and the 십지경 十地經, said to contain the earliest teaching regarding Amitābha ; translated by Kumārajīva *circa* A.D. 405.

십중(금)계 十重(禁)戒 The ten pārājika, or a monk's most serious sins ; also 십바라이 十波羅夷 ; 바라사이가 波螺闍已迦. They are killing, stealing, adultery, lying, selling wine, talking of a monk's misdeeds, self-praise for degrading others, meanness, anger at rebuke, vilifying the Triratna. The esoteric sect has a group in regard to giving up the mind of enlightenment, renouncing the Triratna and going to heretical sects, slandering the Triratna, etc. Another group of ten is in the 대일경 大日經 9 and 17 ; cf. 십바라이 十波羅夷.

십중장 十重障 The ten weighty bodhisattva hindrances, according to the 별교 別教, which are respectively overcome by entry into the 십지 十地 ; v. 성유식론 成唯識論 9 ; the first is 이생성 異生性 the natural heart hindering the 성성 聖性 holy heart, etc. ; v. 십장 十障.

십중죄 十重罪 idem 십악 十惡, 십불선 十不善.

십지 十地 Daśabhūmi ; v. 십주 十住. The "ten stages" in the fifty-two sections of the development of a bodhisattva into a Buddha. After completing the 십사향 十四向 he proceeds to the 십지

十地. There are several groups. I. The ten stages common to the Three Vehicles 삼승 三乘 are : (1) 간혜지 乾慧地 dry wisdom stage, i.e. unfertilized by Buddha-truth, worldly wisdom ; (2) 성지 性地 the embryo-stage of the nature of Buddha-truth, the 사선근 四善根 ; (3) 팔인지 八人地 ; 팔인지 八忍地, the stage of the eight patient endurances ; (4) 견지 見地 of freedom from wrong views ; (5) 박지 薄地 of freedom from the first six of the nine delusions in practice ; (6) 이욕지 離欲地 of freedom from the remaining three ; (7) 이변지 已辨地 complete discrimination in regard to wrong views and thoughts, the stage of an arhat ; (8) 벽지불지 辟支佛地 or 지불지 支佛地 pratyekabuddhahood, only the dead ashes of the past left to sift ; (9) 보살지 菩薩地 bodhisattvahood ; (10) 불지 佛地 Buddhahood. v. 지도론 智度論 78. II. 대승보살십지 大乘菩薩十地 The ten stages of Mahāyāna bodhisattva development are : (1) 환희지 歡喜地 Pramuditā, joy at having overcome the former difficulties and now entering on the path to Buddhahood ; (2) 이구지 離垢地 Vimalā, freedom from all possible defilement, the stage of purity ; (3) 발광지 發光地 Prabhākārī, stage of further enlightenment ; (4) 염혜지 焰慧地 Arciṣmatī, of glowing wisdom ; (5) 극난승지 極難勝地 Sudurjayā, mastery of utmost or final difficulties ; (6) 현전지 現前地 Abhimukhī, the open way of wisdom above definitions of impurity and purity ; (7) 원행지 遠行地 Dūraṁgamā, proceeding afar, getting above ideas of self in order to save others ; (8) 부동지 不動地 Acalā, attainment of calm unperturbedness ; (9) 선혜지 善慧地 Sādhumatī, of the finest discriminatory wisdom, knowing where and how to save, and possessed of the 십력 十力 ten powers ; (10) 법운지 法雲地 Dharmamegha, attaining to the fertilizing powers of the law-cloud. Each of the ten stages is connected with each of the ten pāramitās, v. 파 波. Each of the 사승 四乘 or four vehicles has a division of ten. III. The 성문승십지 聲聞乘十地 ten Śrāvaka stages are : (1) 수삼귀지 受三歸地 initiation as a disciple by receiving the three refuges, in the Buddha, Dharma, and Saṅgha ; (2) 신지 信地 belief, or the faith-root ; (3) 신법지 信法地 belief in the four truths ; (4) 내범부지 內凡夫地 ordinary disciples who observe the 오정심관 五停心觀, etc. ; (5) 학신계 學信戒 those who pursue the 삼학 三學 three studies ; (6) 팔인지 八人地 i.e. 팔인지 八忍地 the stage of 견도 見道 seeing the true Way ; (7) 수다원지 須陀洹地 śrota-āpanna, now definitely in the stream and assured of nirvāṇa ; (8) 사다함지 斯陀含地 sakṛdāgāmin, only one more rebirth ; (9) 아나함지 阿那含地 anāgāmin, no rebirth ; and (10) 아라한지 阿羅漢地 arhatship. IV. The ten stages of the pratyeka-buddha 연각승십지 緣覺乘十地 are (1) perfect asceticism ; (2) mastery of the twelve links of causation ; (3) of the four noble truths ; (4) of the deeper knowledge ; (5) of the eightfold noble path ; (6) of the three realms 삼법계 三法界 ; (7) of the nirvāṇa state ; (8) of the six supernatural powers ; (9) arrival at the intuitive stage ; (10) mastery of the remaining influence of former habits. V. 불승십지 佛乘十地 The ten stages, or characteristics of a Buddha, are those of the sovereign or perfect attainment of wisdom, exposition, discrimination, māra-subjugation, suppression of evil, the six transcendent faculties, manifestation of all bodhisattva enlightenment, powers of prediction, of adaptability, of powers to reveal the bodhisattva Truth. VI. The shingon has its own elaborate ten stages, and also a group 십지십심 十地十心, see 십심 十心 ; and there are other groups. 십지품 十地品 The twenty-second chapter of the sixty-chapter version of the 화엄경 華嚴經, the twenty-sixth of the eighty-chapter version. 십지원행 十地願行 The vow of bodhisattvas to attain the 십지 十地 by fulfilling the ten pāramitās, v. 십파 十波. 십지심 十地心 Ten stages of mind, or mental development, i.e. (1) 사무량심 四無量心 the four kinds of boundless mind ; (2) 십선심 十善心 the mind of the ten good qualities ; (3) 명광심 明光心 the illuminated mind ; (4) 염혜심 焰慧心 the mind of glowing wisdom ; (5) 대승심 大勝心 the mind of mastery ; (6) 현전심 現前心 the mind of the open way (above normal definitions) ; (7) 무생심 無生心 the mind of no rebirth ; (8) 부사의심 不思議心 the mind of the inexpressible ; (9) 혜광심 慧光心 the mind of wisdom-radiance ; (10) 수위심 受位心 the mind of perfect receptivity. v. also 십심 十心.

십지 十智 The ten forms of understanding. I. Hīnayāna : (1) 세속지 世俗智 common understanding

; (2) 법지 法智 enlightened understanding, i.e. on the Four Truths in this life ; (3) 유지 類智 ditto, applied to the two upper realms 상이계 上二界 ; (4), (5), (6), (7) understanding *re* each of the Four Truths separately, both in the upper and lower realms, e.g. 고지 苦智 ; (8) 타심지 他心智 understanding of the minds of others ; (9) 진지 盡智 the understanding that puts an end to all previous faith in or for self, i.e. 자신지 自信智 ; (10) 무생지 無生智 nirvāṇa wisdom ; v. 구사론 俱舍論 26. II. Mahāyāna. A Tathāgata's ten powers of understanding or wisdom : (1) 삼세지 三世智 perfect understanding of past, present, and future ; (2) ditto of Buddha Law ; (3) 법계무애지 法界無礙智 unimpeded understanding of the whole Buddha-realm ; (4) 법계무변지 法界無邊智 unlimited, or infinite ditto ; (5) 충만일체지 充滿一切智 of ubiquity ; (6) 보조일체세간지 普照一切世間智 of universal enlightenment ; (7) 주지일체세계지 住持一切世界智 of omnipotence, or universal control ; (8) 지일체중생지 知一切衆生智 of omniscience *re* all living beings ; (9) 지일체법지 知一切法智 of omniscience *re* the laws of universal salvation ; (10) 지무변제불지 知無邊諸佛智 of omniscience *re* all Buddha wisdom. v. 화엄경 華嚴經 16. There are also his ten forms of understanding of the "Five Seas" 오해 五海 of worlds, living beings, karma, passions, and Buddhas.

십지론 十支論 The ten Yoga books, the foundation work being the 유가론 瑜伽論, the other ten are 백법론 百法論, 오온론 五蘊論, 현양론 顯揚論, 섭대승론 攝大乘論, 잡집론 雜集論, 변중변론 辨中邊論, 이십유식론 二十唯識論, 삼십유식론 三十唯識論, 대장엄론 大莊嚴論, and 분별유가론 分別瑜伽論.

십진구퇴 十進九退 The Buddha's teaching is so difficult that of ten who enter it nine fall away.

십진여 十眞如 The ten aspects of the bhūtatathatā or reality attained by a bodhisattva during his fifty-two stages of development, cf. 십지 十地 and 십장 十障, each of which is associated with one of these *chên-ju* : (1) 변행진여 遍行眞如 the universality of the *chên-ju* ; (2) 최승진여 最勝眞如 its superiority over all else ; (3) 승류진여 勝流眞如 its ubiquity ; (4) 무섭수진여 無攝受眞如 its independence or self-containedness ; (5) 무별진여 無別眞如 subjective indifferentiation ; (6) 무염정진여 無染淨眞如 above differences of impurity and purity ; (7) 법무별진여 法無別眞如 objective indifferentiation ; (8) 부증감진여 不增減眞如 in variable, i.e. can be neither added to nor taken from ; (9) 지자재소의 智自在所依 the basis of all wisdom ; (10) 업자재등소의진여 業自在等所依眞如 and of all power. The above are the 별교 別教 group from the 유식론 唯識論 10. Another group, of the 원교 圓教, is the same as the 십여시 十如是 q.v.

십쾌 十快 The ten inexpressible joys of the Pureland ; also 십락 十樂.

십통 十通 Ten supernatural powers, e.g. of seeing, hearing, appearance, etc. ; cf. 오신통 五神通.

십팔 十八 Aṣṭadaśa, eighteen. 십팔불공법 十八不共法 Āveṇikadharma, or Buddhadharma, the eighteen different characteristics of a Buddha as compared with bodhisattvas, i.e. his perfection of body (or person), mouth (or speech), memory, impartiality to all, serenity, self-sacrifice, unceasing desire to save, unflagging zeal therein, unfailing thought thereto, wisdom in it, powers of deliverance, the principles of it, revealing perfect wisdom in deed, in word, in thought, perfect knowledge of past, future, and present. v. 지도론 智度論 26. 십팔원정 十八圓淨 The eighteen perfections of a buddha's sambhogakāya, v. 삼신 三身. Also 십팔원만 十八圓滿. 십팔천 十八天 Brahmaloka, the eighteen heavens of form, rūpadhātu, three of the first dhyāna, 범중천 梵衆天 ; 범보천 梵輔天 ; 대범천 大梵天 ; three of the second, 소광천 少光天 ; 무량광천 無量光天 ; 광음천 光音天 ; three of the third, 소정천 少淨天 ; 무량정천 無量淨天 ; 변정천 徧淨天 ; and nine of the fourth, 무운천 無雲天 ; 복생천 福生天 ; 광과천 廣果天 ; 무상천 無想天 ; 무번천 無煩天 ; 무열천 無熱天 ; 선견천 善見天 ; 선현천 善現天 ; 색구의천 色究意天. "Southern Buddhism knows only sixteen. Those two which Northern Buddhists added are Puṇya-prasava 복생 福生 and Anabhraka 무운 無雲." [Eitel.] 십팔종 十八宗 the eighteen Japanese Buddhist sects, i.e. 삼론 三論 ; 법상 法相 ; 화엄 華嚴 ; 율 律 ; 구사 俱舍 ; 성실 成實 ; 천태 天台 ; 진언 眞言 ; 융통염불 融通念佛 ; 정토 淨土

; 진 眞 ; 일련 日蓮 ; 시 時 ; 임제 臨濟 ; 조동 曹洞 ; 황벽 黃檗 ; 보화 普化 ; and 수험종 修驗宗. 십팔응진 十八應眞 The eighteen arhats. 십팔물 十八物 The eighteen things a monk should carry in the performance of his duties — willow twigs, soap, the three garments, a water-bottle, a begging-bowl, mat, staff, censer, filter, handkerchief, knife, fire-producer, pincers, hammock, sūtra, the vinaya, the Buddha's image, and bodhisattva image or images ; cf. 범망경 梵網經 37. 십팔생처 十八生處 The eighteen Brahmalokas, where rebirth is necessary, i.e. where mortality still exists. 십팔계 十八界 The eighteen dhātu, or realms of sense, i.e. 육근 六根, 육경 六境, 육식 六識 the six organs, their objects or conditions, and their perceptions. 십팔(대)경 十八(大)經 ; 십팔명처 十八明處 The eighteen Indian non-Buddhist classics, i.e. the four vedas, six śāstras, and eight śāstras. 십팔현(성) 十八賢(聖) ; 십팔현(중) 十八賢(衆) ; 십팔경계 十八境界 ; 십팔유학 十八有學 v. 유학 有學. 십팔부 十八部 The eighteen schools of Hīnayāna as formerly existing in India ; v. 소승 小乘. 십팔중지옥 十八重地獄 The eighteen layers of hells, which are described by one writer as the conditions in which the six sense organs, their six objects, and the six perceptions do not harmonize. Another says the eighteen are the hell of knives, the boiling sands, the boiling excrement, the fiery carriage, the boiling cauldron, the iron bed, etc. 십팔도 十八道 In the two maṇḍalas, Vajradhātu and Garbhadhātu, each has nine central objects of worship. The Shingon disciple devotes himself to meditation on one of these eighteen each day.

십행 十行 The ten necessary activities in the fifty-two stages of a bodhisattva, following on the 십신 十信 and 십주 十住 ; the two latter indicate personal development 자리 自利. These ten lines of action are for the universal welfare of others 이타 利他. They are : joyful service ; beneficial service ; never resenting ; without limit ; never out of order ; appearing in any form at will ; unimpeded ; exalting the pāramitās amongst all beings ; perfecting the Buddha-law by complete virtue ; manifesting in all things the pure, final, true reality.

십현(연기) 十玄(緣起) ; 십현문 十玄門 The ten philosophic ideas expressed in two metrical versions, each line ending with 문 門. v. 현문 玄門.

십호 十護 The ten guardians of the law, assistants to the 십대명왕 十大明王.

십호 十號 The titles of a Buddha : 여래 如來 Tathāgata ; 응공 應供 Arhat ; 정변지 正徧知 Samyak-sambuddha ; 명행족 明行足 Vidyācaraṅa-saṁpanna ; 선서 善逝 Sugata ; 세간해 世間解 Lokavid ; 무상사 無上士 Anuttara ; 조어장부 調御丈夫 Puruṣa-damya-sārathi ; 천인사 天人師 Śāstā devamanuṣyāṇām ; 불세존 佛世尊 Buddha-lokanātha, or Bhagavān.

십혹 十惑 idem 십사 十使.

쌍 雙 A pair, couple, twin ; mates, matched. 쌍목 雙木 ; 쌍림 雙林 ; 쌍수 雙樹 Twin trees, the śāla-trees under which the Buddha entered nirvāṇa. 쌍지 雙持 The Yugaṁdhara, v. 유 踰. 쌍류 雙流 The twin streams of teaching and mystic contemplation. 쌍왕 雙王 A term for Yama, v. 야 夜. 쌍신 雙身 Twin-bodied, especially the two bodies of Vaiśramaṇa, v. 비 毘.

쌍계사 雙溪寺 Ssang-gye-sa. A temple located in Mt. Jirisan, Unsu-ri Hwagae-myeon Hadong-gun Gyeongsangnam-do in Korea. The 13th parish headquarters of Korean Jogye Order.

<ㅇ>

아 誐 To intone, hum ; translit. *ga.* 아라나 誐囉娜 Gardabha, defined as an ass. 아로 誐嚕 Garuḍa, v. 가 迦. 아나발씨 誐那鉢氏 Gaṇapati, a leader, Gaṇeśa, the "elephant god" ; it is, however, defined as 환희 歡喜 pleased, joyful.

아 蛾 A moth. 여아취등화 如蛾趣燈火 Like a moth flying into the lamp – is man after his pleasures.

아 阿 A or Ā ; 狅, 狋. It is the first letter of the Sanskrit Siddham alphabet, and is also translit. by 갈 曷, 알 遏, 안 安, 알 頞, 운 韻, 오 噁, etc. From it are supposed to be born all the other letters, and it is the first sound uttered by the human mouth. It has therefore numerous mystical indications. Being also a negation it symbolizes the unproduced, the impermanent, the immaterial ; but it is employed in many ways indicative of the positive. Amongst other uses it indicates Amitābha, from the first syllable in that name. It is much in use for esoteric purposes.

아 啞 Eḍa, dumb ; eḍamūka, deaf and dumb, unable to express oneself ; translit. *a*, v. 아 阿. 아와라고답니야 啞呃囉孤答尼耶 Aparagodāna, the Western continent, see 아 阿. 아자득몽 啞子得夢 A dumb man who has had a dream – but cannot tell it. 아밀리달 啞密哩達 Amṛta, ambrosia, v. 아 阿. 아별석해이 啞撇釋該而 Abhiṣeka, "consecrate me by sprinkling," said in prayer. 아할라아할라마마애유이솔탑라니 啞曷囉啞曷囉馬麻藹由而率塔囉尼 Āhāra āharaṇam āyuḥ-saṁtāraṇe "Give me, give me, old age, oh protector." 아법 啞法 The doctrine of a deaf and dumb person, which he cannot proclaim. 아양(승) 啞羊(僧) A dumb sheep (monk), stupid, one who does not know good from bad, nor enough to repent of sin.

아 峨 High, commanding. 아미산 峨眉山 or 峩眉山 O-mei Shan or Mt. Omi in Szechwan. Two of its peaks are said to be like 아미 蛾眉 a moth's eyebrows, also pronounced O-mei ; the monastery at the top is the 광상사 光相寺 where P'u-hsien (Samantabhadra) is supreme.

아 餓 Hungry, famished, starving. 아귀 餓鬼 Pretas, hungry spirits, one of the three lower destinies. They are of varied classes, numbering nine or thirty-six, and are in differing degrees and kinds of suffering, some wealthy and of light torment, others possessing nothing and in perpetual torment ; some are jailers and executioners of Yama in the hells, others wander to and fro amongst men, especially at night. Their city or region is called 아귀성 餓鬼城 ; 아귀계 餓鬼界. Their destination or path is the 아귀취 餓鬼趣 or 아귀도 餓鬼道. 아귀애 餓鬼愛 Desire as eager as that of a hungry ghost.

아 我 I, my, mine ; the ego, the master of the body, compared to the ruler of a country. Composed of the five skandhas and hence not a permanent entity. It is used for ātman, the self, personality. Buddhism takes as a fundamental dogma 무아 無我, i.e. no 상아 常我, no permanent ego, only recognizing a temporal or functional ego. The errôneous idea of a permanent self continued in reincarnation is the source of all illusion. But the Nirvāṇa sūtra definitely asserts a permanent ego in the transcendental world, above the range of reincarnation ; and the trend of Mahāyāna supports such permanence ; v. 상락아정 常樂我淨.

아 亞 Second, inferior ; used in translit. as 아 阿 "a," e.g. 아략 亞略 Ārya.

아 痾 Sickness, pain ; diarrhoea. 아로기 痾嚕祇 Ārogya, freedom from sickness, healthy ; a greeting from a superior monk, Are you well? or Be you well!

아 俄 Suddenly, on the point of. 아나발저 俄那鉢底 Gaṇapati, v. 아 誐.

아 牙 Tooth, teeth ; toothed ; a broker. 아보살 牙菩薩 The bodhisattva fiercely showing his teeth in defence of the Buddha, also styled 금강약차 金剛藥叉 ; he is east of the Buddha in the Vajradhātu.

아 哦 Translit. *ga* ; cf. 아 我, 아 誐, 가 伽, 알 哳, 흘 疙, 아치야 哦哆也 Gatayaḥ, nominative plural of gati, intp. as going, coming.

아가 阿伽 Arghya, argha, 알가 閼伽 ; 알가 遏伽 ; 알가 遏迦 tr. by water, but it specially indicates ceremonial water, e.g. offerings of scented water, or water containing fragrant flowers. 아가배 阿伽坏 The vase or bowl so used. 아가로 阿伽嚧 ; 아가루 阿伽樓 ; 악게로 惡揭嚕 Agaru, aguru, fragrant aloe-wood, intp. 침향 沈香 the incense that sinks in water, the Agallochum ; "the Ahalim or Ahaloth of the Hebrews." [Eitel]. 아가마 阿伽摩 v. 아함 阿含 Āgama. 아가라가 阿伽羅伽 Aṅgāraka, the planet Mars ; a star of ill omen ; a representation in the Garbhadhātu. 아가다 阿伽陀 ; 아갈다 阿竭陀 ; 아게(다) 阿揭(陀) Agada, free from disease, an antidote, intp. as 보거 普去 a medicine that entirely rids (of disease), elixir of life, universal remedy. 아가담 阿伽曇 Aghana, not solid, not dense.

아가 阿迦 Translit. *aka, agha,* etc. 아가사 阿迦奢 Ākāśa, the sky space, the air, ether, atmosphere. 아가색 阿迦色 Agha, but may be Ākāśa ; it has two opposite interpretations, substantial and unsubstantial, the latter having special reference to the empyrean. 아가낭 阿迦囊 ; 아가 阿迦 ; 아게다 阿揭多 A flash in the east, the lightning god ; the term is defined as 무후 無厚 not solid, liquid, Sanskrit aghana(m). 아가운 阿迦雲 A physician, a healer, probably should be 아가담 阿迦曇 Agadaṁ ; especially Bhaiṣajya-rāja, the King of Medicine, or Healing. 아가니(슬)타 阿迦尼(瑟)吒 Akaniṣṭha, not the least, i.e. the highest, or eighteenth of the heavens of form, or Brahmalokas ; also 아가니사타 阿迦尼沙吒 or 아가니사탁 阿迦尼師託 ; 아가이타 阿迦貳吒 ; 아가니(슬)곽 阿迦尼(瑟)搉 ; 니(사)타 尼(師)吒 ; 이타 二吒.

아갈다 阿竭多 or **아게다** 阿揭多 Agastya, the star Canopus, also intp. as lightning. 아갈다선 阿竭多仙 One of the genii in the Nirvāṇa sūtra, who stopped the flow of the Ganges for twelve years by allowing it to run into one of his ears.

아갈라 阿羯羅 Āgāra, a house, dwelling, receptacle ; tr. 경 境 and used in the sense of an organ, e.g. the ear for sound, etc.

아건다 阿犍多 or 阿揵多 Āgantuka, any visitant, or incident ; a visiting monk ; accidental.

아견 我見 ; **신견** 身見 The erroneous doctrine that the ego, or self, composed of the temporary five skandhas, is a reality and permanent.

아공 我空 ; (중)생공(衆)生空 ; 인공 人空 Illusion of the concept of the reality of the ego, man being composed of elements and disintegrated when these are dissolved. 아공진여 我空眞如 The Hīnayāna doctrine of impersonality in the absolute, that in truth there is no ego ; this position abrogates moral responsibility, cf. 원인론 原人論.

아구 阿歐 Au! An exclamation, e.g. Ho! oh! Ah! Also 아구 阿傴 ; 아구 阿嘔 ; 아구 阿漚 or 아우 阿優. The two letters *a* and *u* fell from the corners of Brahmā's mouth when he gave the seventy-two letters of Kharoṣṭhī, and they are said to be placed at the beginning of the Brahminical sacred books as divine letters, the Buddhists adopting 여시 如是 "Thus" (*Evam*) instead.

아구라가라 阿鳩羅加羅 Ākulakara, disturbing, upsetting ; name of a wind.

아구로사 阿拘盧奢 Ākrośa ; 매 罵 scolding, abusing.

아기니 阿祇儞 or 阿祇尼 Agni, 아기니 阿耆尼 or 아의니 阿擬尼 Fire, the fire-deva.

아기다 阿耆多 Ajita, v. 아일다 阿逸多. 아기다시사흠바라 阿耆多翅舍欽婆羅 or 아기다경사감바라 阿耆多頸舍甘婆羅 ; 아말다 阿末多 Ajita-keśakambali, the unyielding one whose cloak is his hair. One of the six Tīrthyas, or Brahminical heretics, given to extravagant austerities ; his doctrine was that the happiness of the next life is correlative to the sufferings of this life. 아기니 阿耆尼 Agni, fire, v. 아기니 阿祇儞. Also "Agni or Akni, name of a kingdom ... north of lake Lop." [Eitel]. 아기(다)달 阿耆(多)達 or 아기(다)타 阿耆(多)陀 Agnidatta, name of a king. 아기비가 阿耆毘伽 Ājīvika, or Ājīvaka, 사명 邪命 One who lives on others, i.e. by improper means ; an improper livelihood (for one in orders).

아나 阿拏 Aṇu, 아누 阿㝹 ; 아누 阿耨 Minute, infinitesimal, the smallest aggregation of matter, a molecule consisting of 칠미 七微 seven atoms.

아나 阿那 Āna, 안나 安那 inhalation, v. 아나바나 阿那波那. 아나타 阿那他 Anātha, protector-less. 아나타빈저 阿那他賓低 Anāthapiṇḍika, a wealthy elder of Śrāvastī, famous for liberality to the needy, and his gift of the Jetavana with its gardens and buildings to the Buddha, cf. 기 祇. His original name was 수달다 須達多 Sudatta and his wife's 비사거 毘舍佉 Viśākhā. 아나함 阿那含 or 阿那鋡 ; 아나가미 阿那伽迷 or 阿那伽彌 Anāgāmin, the 불래 不來 non-coming, or 불환 不還 non-returning arhat or saint, who will not be reborn in this world, but in the rūpa and arūpa heavens, where he will attain to nirvāṇa. 아나함향 阿那含向 One who is aiming at the above stage. 아나함과 阿那含果 The third of the 사과 四果 four fruits, i.e. the reward of the seeker after the above stage. 아나파루길지수 阿那婆婁吉低輸 Āryāvalokiteśvara, a title of Kuan-yin, v. 아박 阿縛. 아나율 阿那律 ; 아나율도 阿那律徒 or 아나율타 阿那律陀 ; 아누루타 阿㝹樓馱 or 아우루타 阿㝹樓馱 ; 아니로두 阿尼盧豆 or 아누률타 阿㝹律陀 Aniruddha, "unrestrained," tr. by 무멸 無滅 unceasing, i.e. the benefits resulting from his charity ; or 여의무탐 如意無貪 able to gratify every wish and without desire. One of the ten chief disciples of Buddha ; to reappear as the Buddha Samantaprabhāsa ; he was considered supreme in 천안 天眼 deva insight. Cf. 아누 阿耨. 아나(아)바나 阿那(阿)波那 ; 안반 安般 ; 안나반나 安那般那 or 아나반나 阿那般那 Ānāpāna, breathing, especially controlled breathing ; āna is intp. as exhaling and apāna as inhaling, which is the opposite of the correct meaning ; the process is for calming body and mind for contemplation by counting the breathing. 아나기지라 阿那耆智羅 A spell for healing sickness, or charm for preventing it ; others of similar title are for other saving purposes. 아나수라바 阿那藪囉嚩 or 아나리라바 阿那籬攞嚩 Anāsrava, free from mortality and its delusions.

아난 阿難 Ānanda, 아난타 阿難陀 ; intp. by 환희 歡喜 Joy ; son of Droṇodana-rāja, and younger brother of Devadatta ; he was noted as the most learned disciple of Buddha, and famed for hearing and remembering his teaching, hence is styled 다문 多聞 ; after the Buddha's death he is said to have compiled the sūtras in the Vaibhāra cave, v. 필 畢, where the disciples were assembled in Magadha. He is reckoned as the second patriarch. Ānandabhadra and Ānandasāgara are generally given as two other Ānandas, but this is uncertain. 아난타야차 阿難陀夜叉 A yakṣa, called White Teeth. 아난타보라 阿難陀補羅 Ānandapura, a place given by Eitel as north-east of Gujarat ; "the present Bārnagar, near Kurree," which was "one of the strongholds of the Jain sect."

아노모다 阿奴謨柁 Anumoda, concurrence, a term of thanks from a monk to a donor on parting. 아노라타 阿奴邏陀 Anurādhā, the seventeenth of the twenty-eight Nakṣatras, or lunar mansions. [M. W.] The 방 房 constellation in Scorpio.

아누 阿㝹 Aṇu, v. 아나 阿拏. 아누타천제 阿㝹吒闡提 Anuṣṭubh-chandas, a metre of two lines each in 8 + 8 syllables ; also 아누솔도파 阿耨窣都婆.

아누 阿耨 v. 아나 阿拏 Aṇu ; and used for Anavatapta, *infra.* 아누(다라삼막삼)보리 阿耨(多羅三藐三)菩提 Anuttara-samyak-sambodhi ; or Anubodhi. Unexcelled complete enlightenment, an attribute of every Buddha ; tr. by 무상정변지 無上正徧知 ; 무상정등정각 無上正等正覺, the highest correct and complete, or universal knowledge or awareness, the perfect wisdom of a Buddha, omniscience. 아누루타 阿耨樓陀 Anuruddha, son of Amṛtodana, and "cousin german" to Śākyamuni [Eitel] ; not Aniruddha ; cf. 아나 阿那. 아누솔도파 阿耨窣都婆 Anuṣṭubh ; v. 아누 阿耨. 아누관음 阿耨觀音 Anu Kuan-yin, the twentieth of the thirty-three forms of the "Goddess of Mercy," seated on a rock scanning the sea to protect or save voyagers. 아누달 阿耨達 ; 아나바태다 阿那婆答多 or 아나바달다 阿那波達多 Anavatapta, a lake in Jambudvīpa, north of the Himālayas, south of 향산 香山 Gandha-mādana, described as about 800 li in circumference, bordered by gold, silver, precious stones, etc. It is said to be the source of the four great rivers : east, the Ganges out of a silver ox mouth ; south, the Indus out of that of an elephant ; west, the Oxus ; and north, the Śītā, said to be the Yellow River. Eitel has the Brahmaputra, Ganges, Śatadru (or Sutlej), and the Oxus ; but there is confusion in the records. The Dragon-king of this lake became a bodhisattva and is exempt from the distresses of the other seven dragon-kings. The 아누달산 阿耨達山 are the mountains north of the lake.

아누루타 阿㝹樓馱 v. 아나율 阿那律 Aniruddha. 아누라다보라 阿㝹羅陀補羅 Anurādhapura, a northern city of Ceylon, at which tradition says Buddhism was introduced into the island ; cf. Abhayagiri, 아발 阿跋.

아니라가 阿儞囉迦 Ārdraka, raw ginger.

아니지야 阿泥底耶 Āditya, the sons of Aditi, the gods ; Varuṇa ; the sun ; the sky ; son of the sun-deva.

아다라 阿馱囉 Ādara 아다라 阿陀囉 to salute with folded hands, palms together.

아달바나 阿闥婆那 or 阿達婆那 ; **아달바다** 阿達波陀 Ātharvaṇa, v. 아타 阿他 the Atharva Veda.

아덕 我德 Power or virtue of the ego, the ego being defined as 자재 自在 sovereign, master, free ; v. 바라밀 波羅蜜.

아도 我倒 The illusion of an ego, one of the four inverted or upside-down ideas.

아등만 我等慢 Mānātimāna ; the pride of thinking oneself equal to those who surpass us. One of the 구만 九慢.

아라가 阿羅伽 Rāga, desire, emotion, feeling, greed, anger, wrath ; and many other meanings ; derived from to dye, colour, etc. 아라가 阿羅歌 ; 아가 阿迦 or 阿伽 Arka, or white flower, *Asclepias* (M. W. says *Calotropis*) *gigantea.* Cf. 아호 阿呼. 아라파자나 阿羅派遮那 or 阿羅婆遮那 Arapacana, a mystical formula, v. Lévi's article on arapacana, Batavian Society Feestbundel, 1929, II, pp.100 seq. 아라한 阿羅漢 Arhan, arhat, lohan ; worthy, venerable ; an enlightened, saintly man ; the highest type or ideal saint in Hīnayāna in contrast with the bodhisattva as the saint in Mahāyāna ; intp. as 응공 應供 worthy of worship, or respect ; intp. as 살적 殺賊 arihat, arihan, slayer of the enemy, i.e. of mortality ; for the arhat enters nirvāṇa 불생 不生 not to be reborn, having destroyed the karma of reincarnation ; he is also in the stage of 불학 不學 no longer learning, having attained. Also 나한 羅漢 ; 아로가 阿盧伽 ; 아라하 阿羅訶 or 阿羅呵 ; 아리하 阿梨呵 or 아려하 阿黎呵 ; 라하 羅呵, etc. ; cf. 아이 阿夷 ; 아략 阿畧 or 阿略. 아라가향 阿羅伽向 The direction leading to arhatship, by cutting off all illusion in the realms of form and beyond form. 아라가과 阿羅伽果 The fruit of arhat discipline. 아라가하 阿羅伽訶 One of the titles of Buddha, the Arhan who has overcome mortality. 아라마 阿羅磨 Ārāma, garden, grove, pleasance ; hence saṅghārāma, a monastery with its gardens. Also, 아라 阿羅 ; 아라미 阿羅彌 ; 아람마 阿藍麼

or 阿藍摩 ; 아람 阿藍. 아라라 阿羅邏 Ārāḍa Kālāma, v. next. Also the Atata or Hahava cold hells. 아라라가람 阿羅邏迦藍 Ālāra-Kālāma or Ārāḍa-Kālāma, the ṛṣi to whom Śākyamuni went on leaving home ; another was Udraka Rāmaputra ; they had attained to the concept of nothingness, including the non-existence of ideas. Other forms are 아라라가라마 阿羅邏迦羅摩 ; 아라다가라마 阿羅茶迦邏摩 ; 아람가 阿藍迦 ; 아람(가람) 阿藍(伽藍) ; 아란가란 阿蘭迦蘭 ; 라륵가람 羅勒迦藍. 아라사 阿羅闍 Rāja, a king. 아라가계 阿羅伽界 Rāja-dhātu, a dominion ; kingdom.

아락찰파 阿落刹婆 Rākṣasa, 아락가파 阿落迦婆 demons, evil spirits ; rākṣasī are female demons, but are also said to be protectresses, cf. 라차파 羅叉婆.

아란야 阿蘭若 Āraṇya ; from araṇya, "forest" ; 아란야가 阿蘭若迦 āraṇyaka, one who lives there. Intp. by 무쟁성 無諍聲 no sound of discord ; 한정 閑靜 shut in and quiet ; 원리 遠離 far removed ; 공적 空寂 uninhabited and still ; a lonely abode 500 bow-lengths from any village. A hermitage, or place of retirement for meditation. Three kinds of occupants are given : 달마아란야가 達磨阿蘭若迦 Dharma-āraṇyaka., meditators on the principle of inactivity, or letting Nature have its course ; 마제아란야가 摩祭阿蘭若迦 Mātaṅga-āraṇyaka., those who dwell among the dead, away from human voices ; 단타아란야가 檀陀阿蘭若迦 Daṇḍaka-āraṇyaka., those who dwell in sandy deserts and among rocks (as in the ancient Deccan). Other forms are : 아란나 阿蘭那 or 아란양 阿蘭攘 ; 아란타 阿蘭陀 or 阿蘭陁 ; 아련야 阿練若 or 아련여 阿練茹 ; 갈랄예 曷剌羪.

아로나 阿盧那 Aruṇa, 아류나 阿留那 or 아루나 阿樓那 ruddy, dawn-colour, dawn, south, fire, Mars, etc. 아로나화 阿盧那花 Aruṇakamala, the red lotus. 아로나발저 阿盧那跋底 A red-colored incense.

아로파 阿路巴 Rūpya, silver. 아로노 阿路猱 Aruṇa, a mountain in the Punjab said formerly to fluctuate in height.

아록록지 阿轆轆地 The land where all goes smoothly along (a-lu-lu) at will ; idem 전록록지 轉轆轆地.

아뢰야 阿賴耶 Ālaya, an abode, resting-place (hence Himālaya, the storehouse of snow), intp. as 무몰 無沒 non-disappearing, perhaps non-melting, also as 장 藏 store. Other forms are 아리야 阿利耶 or 阿梨耶 or 아려야 阿黎耶 or 아라야 阿羅耶 ; also 뢰 賴 or 리야 利耶. Any of these terms is used in abbreviation for Ālaya-vijñāna. 아뢰야외도 阿賴耶外道 The ālaya heresy, one of the thirty heretical sects named in the 대일경 大日經, 주심 住心, chapter 1, that the ālaya is a sort of eternal substance of matter, creative and containing all forms ; when considered as a whole, it is non-existent, or contains nothing ; when considered "unrolled," or phenomenal, it fills the universe. It seems to be of the nature of materialism as opposed to the idealistic conception of the Ālaya-vijñāna. 아뢰야식 阿賴耶識 Ālaya-vijñāna. "The receptacle intellect or consciousness" ; "the originating or receptacle intelligence" ; "basic consciousness" [Keith]. It is the store or totality of consciousness, both absolute and relative, impersonal in the whole, temporally personal or individual in its separated parts, always reproductive. It is described as 유정근본지심식 有情根本之心識 the fundamental mind-consciousness of conscious beings, which lays hold of all the experiences of the individual life ; and which as storehouse holds the germs 종자 種子 of all affairs ; it is at the root of all experience, of the skandhas, and of things on which sentient beings depend for existence. Mind is another term for it, as it both stores and gives rise to all seeds of phenomena and knowledge. It is called 본식 本識 original mind, because it is the root of all things ; 무몰식 無沒識 inexhaustible mind, because none of its seeds (or products) is lost ; 현식 現識 manifested mind, because all things are revealed in or by it ; 종자식 種子識 seeds mind, because from it spring all individualities, or particulars ; 소지의식 所知依識 because it is the basis of all knowledge ; 이숙식 異熟識 because it produces the rounds of mortality, good and evil karma, etc. ; 집지식 執持識 or 아타나 阿陀那 q.v., that which holds together, or is the seed of another rebirth, or phenomena, the causal nexus ; 제일식 第一識

the prime or supreme mind or consciousness ; 택식 宅識 abode (of) consciousness ; 무구식 無垢識 unsullied consciousness when considered in the absolute, i.e. the Tathāgata ; and 제팔식 第八識, as the last of the eight vijñānas. There has been discussion as to the meaning and implications of the Ālaya-vijñāna. It may also be termed the unconscious, or unconscious absolute, out of whose ignorance or unconsciousness arises all consciousness.

아리(야)다라 阿唎(耶)多羅 Ārya-tārā ; one of the titles of Kuan-yin, Āryāvalokiteśvara 아리야바로갈제삭발라야 阿唎耶婆盧羯帝爍鉢囉耶.

아리니 阿利尼 Alni or Arni ; "a kingdom which formed part of ancient Tukhāra, situated near to the sources of the Oxus." [Eitel].

아리라발제 阿利羅跋提 Ajitavatī, 아특다벌지 阿特多伐底, see 시 尸 Hiraṇyavatī.

아리사 阿利沙 or **아려사** 阿黎沙 Ārṣa, connected with the ṛṣis, or holy men ; especially their religious utterances in verse 아리사게 阿利沙偈 ; also a title of a Buddha ; and 아리사주처 阿利沙住處 is the highest position of achievement, perfection.

아리야 阿利耶 idem 아뢰야 阿賴耶 Ālaya, and 아리야 阿梨耶.

아리의 阿梨宜 Āliṅg- ; to embrace ; āliṅgī, a small drum ; a kind of ecstatic meditation. 아리수 阿梨樹 or 阿黎樹 Arjaka, *Ocymum pilosum*, a tree with white scented flowers, said to fall in seven parts, like an epidendrum, styled also 알두가만절리 頞杜迦曼折利. 아리(슬)타 阿梨(瑟)吒 ariṣṭa(ka), the soap-berry tree, *Sapindus detergens*, 목환자 木槵子, whose berries are used for rosaries. Name of a bhikṣu. 아리야 阿梨耶 Ārya, 아리의 阿利宜 ; 아리의 阿棃宜 ; 아려의 阿黎宜 ; 아리의 阿犁宜 ; 아리의 阿離宜 ; 아리야 阿哩夜 ; 아략 阿略 or 아이 阿夷 ; 리야 梨耶 loyal, honourable, noble, Āryan, "a man who has thought on the four chief principles of Buddhism and lives according to them," intp. by 존 尊 honourable, and 성 聖 sage, wise, saintly, sacred. Also, ulūka, an owl. 아리하 阿梨呵 Arhan, 아라한 阿羅漢 q.v. 아리야벌마 阿梨耶伐摩 Āryavarman, of the Sarvāstivādin school, author of a work on the Vaibhāṣika philosophy. 아리(의)사나 阿梨(宜)斯那 Āryasena, a monk of the Mahāsāṅghika. 아리의타사 阿梨宜駄娑 Āryadāsa, ditto.

아마 阿摩 Ambā, or mother, a title of respect. 아마다다 阿摩爹爹 Mother and father. 아마제 阿摩提 or 阿麽提 ; 아마채 阿摩觟 The 21st of the thirty-three forms of Kuan-yin, three eyes, four arms, two playing a lute with a phoenix-head, one foot on a lion, the other pendent. 아마라 阿摩羅 Amala ; spotless, unstained, pure ; the permanent and unchanging in contrast with the changing ; the pure and unsullied, e.g. saintliness ; the true nirvāṇa. Also 암마라 菴摩羅 ; 아말라 阿末羅 q.v.

아만 我慢 Abhimāna, ātma-mada. Egotism ; exalting self and depreciating others ; self-intoxication, pride.

아말라 阿末羅 Āmra, Āmalaka, Āmrāta. 아마락가 阿摩洛迦 ; 암마락가 菴摩洛迦 or 암마라가 菴摩羅迦 or 암마륵가 菴摩勒迦 Āmra, mango, *Mangifera indica* ; Āmalaka, *Emblic myrobalan*, or *Phyllanthus emblica*, whose nuts are valued medicinally ; Āmrāta, hog-plum, *Spondias mangifera*. Also used for discernment of mental ideas, the ninth of the nine kinds of 심식 心識. 암몰라 菴沒羅 or 암마라 菴摩羅 or 암파라 菴婆羅 should apply to Āmra the mango, but the forms are used indiscriminately. Cf. 아마라 阿摩羅.

아모가 阿牟伽 v. 아목거 阿目佉 Amogha. 아모가파사 阿牟伽皤賒 Amoghapāśa, Kuan-yin with the noose.

아목거(발절라) 阿目佉(跋折羅) Amogha, or Amoghavajra, 아모가 阿牟伽 or 阿謨伽 or 아목가 阿穆伽 intp. 불공(금강) 不空(金剛) a monk from northern India, a follower of the mystic teachings of Samantabhadra. Vajramati 금강지 金剛智 is reputed to have founded the Yogācārya or Tantric school in Chins about A.D. 719-720. Amogha succeeded him in its leadership in 732. From a journey through India and Ceylon, 741-6, he brought to China more than 500 sūtras and śāstras ; introduced a new form for transliterating Sanskrit and published 108 works. He is credited with the introduction of the Ullambana festival of All Souls, 15th of 17th moon, v. 우 盂. He is the chief representative of Buddhist mysticism in China, spreading it widely through the patronage of three successive emperors, Hsüan Tsung, Su Tsung, who gave him the title of 대광지삼장 大廣智三藏 q.v., and Tai Tsung, who gave him the posthumous rank and title of a Minister of State. He died 774.

아미(타) 阿彌(陀) Amita, boundless, infinite ; tr. by 무량 無量 immeasurable. The Buddha of infinite qualities, known as 아미타바 阿彌陀婆 or 아미타불 阿彌陀佛 Amitābha, tr. 무량광 無量光 boundless light ; 아미타유사 阿彌陀庾斯 Amitāyus, tr. 무량수 無量壽 boundless age, or life ; and among the esoteric sects Amṛta 감로(왕) 甘露(王) sweet-dew (king). An imaginary being unknown to ancient Buddhism, possibly of Persian or Iranian origin, who has eclipsed the historical Buddha in becoming the most popular divinity in the Mahāyāna pantheon. His name indicates an idealization rather than an historic personality, the idea of eternal light and life. The origin and date of the concept are unknown, but he has always been associated with the west, where in his Paradise, Sukhāvatī, the Western Pure Land, he receives to unbounded happiness all who call upon his name (cf. the Pure Lands 정토 淨土 of Maitreya and Akṣobhya). This is consequent on his forty-eight vows, especially the eighteenth, in which he vows to refuse Buddhahood until he has saved all living beings to his Paradise, except those who had committed the five unpardonable sins, or were guilty of blasphemy against the Faith. While his Paradise is theoretically only a stage on the way to rebirth in the final joys of Nirvāṇa, it is popularly considered as the final resting-place of those who cry Na-mo A-mi-to-Fo, or Blessed be, or Adoration to, Amita Buddha. The 정토 淨土 Pure-land (Jap. Jōdō) sect is especially devoted to this cult, which arises chiefly out of the Sukhāvatīvyūha, but Amita is referred to in many other texts and recognized, with differing interpretations and emphasis, by the other sects. Eitel attributes the first preaching of the dogma to "a priest from Tokhāra." in A.D. 147, and says that Fa-hsien and Hsüan-tsang make no mention of the cult. But the Chinese pilgrim 혜일 慧日 Hui-jih says he found it prevalent in India 702-719. The first translation of the Amitāyus sūtra, *circa* A.D. 223-253, had disappeared when the K'ai-yüan catalogue was compiled A.D. 730. The eighteenth vow occurs in the tr. by Dharmarakṣa A.D. 308. With Amita is closely associated Avalokiteśvara, who is also considered as his incarnation, and appears crowned with, or bearing the image of Amita. In the trinity of Amita, Avalokiteśvara appears on his left and Mahāsthāmaprāpta on his right. Another group, of five, includes Kṣitigarbha and Nāgārjuna, the latter counted as the second patriarch of the Pure-land sect. One who calls on the name of Amitābha is styled 아미타성 阿彌陀聖 a saint of Amitābha. Amitābha is one of the Five "Dhyāni Buddhas" 오불 五佛, q.v. He has many titles, amongst which are the following twelve relating to him as Buddha of light, also his title of eternal life : 무량광불 無量光佛 B. of boundless light ; 무변광불 無邊光佛 B. of unlimited light ; 무애광불 無礙光佛 B. of irresistible light ; 무대광불 無對光佛 B. of incomparable light ; 염왕광불 燄王光佛 B. of yama or flame-king light ; 청정광불 淸淨光佛 B. of pure light ; 환희광불 歡喜光佛 B. of joyous light ; 지혜광불 智慧光佛 B. of wisdom light ; 부단광불 不斷光佛 B. of unending light ; 난사광불 難思光佛 B. of inconceivable light ; 무칭광불 無稱光佛 B. of indescribable light ; 초일월광불 超日月光佛 B. of light surpassing that of sun and moon ; 무량수 無量壽 B. of boundless age. As Buddha he has, of course, all the attributes of a Buddha, including the Trikāya, or 법보화신 法報化身, about which in *re* Amita there are differences of opinion in the various schools. His esoteric germ-letter is Hrīḥ, and he has specific manual-sings. Cf. 아미타경 阿彌陀經, of which with commentaries there are numerous editions.

아미사 阿尾捨 Āveśa, spiritualistic possession, a youthful medium. Also 아미사 阿尾舍, 아미사 阿尾奢, 아미사 阿尾賒, 아비사 阿毘舍.

아미타단나 阿彌陀檀那 Amṛtodana 감로왕 甘露王. A king of Magadha, father of Anuruddha and Bhadrika, uncle of Śākyamuni.

아밀리다 阿密哩多 Amṛta, 아밀률제 阿密慄帝 ; 아몰률도 阿沒慄都 nectar, ambrosia. 아밀리다군다리 阿密哩多軍荼利 One of the five 명왕 明王 q.v.

아바라밀 我波羅蜜 The ego pāramitā in the four based on the Nirvāṇa sūtra in which the transcendental ego is 자재 自在, i.e. has a real and permanent nature ; the four are 상 常 permanency, 락 樂 joy, 아 我 personality, 정 淨 purity.

아바라하거 阿縛羅訶佉 A-va-ra-ha-kha, a spell uniting the powers respectively of earth, water, fire, air, and space. 아바로기지습벌라 阿縛盧枳低濕伐邏 Avalokiteśvara, 아바로기제습벌라 阿縛盧枳帝濕伐邏 or 아바로다이습벌라 阿縛盧多伊濕伐邏 ; 아바라길제사바라 阿婆羅吉帝舍婆羅 ; 아나바루길저수 阿那婆婁吉低輸 ; 아리야바루길호세 阿梨耶婆樓吉弖稅 also Āryāvalokiteśvara. Intp. as 관세음 觀世音 or 광세음 光世音 "Regarder (or Observer) of the world's sounds, or cries" ; or "Sounds that enlighten the world." Also 관자재 觀自在 The Sovereign beholder, a tr. of īśvara, lord, sovereign. There is much debate as to whether the latter part of the word is svara, sound, or īśvara, lord ; Chinese interpretations vary. Cf. 관음 觀音.

아박건 阿薄健 Avakan, Vakhan, Khavakan ; Wakhan, an ancient kingdom on the borders of the present Afghanistan, described by Hsüan-tsang as 200 li south-east of Badakshan. Also 습박건 濕薄健 ; 겁박건 劫薄健.

아반 阿潘 A-p'an, name of the "first" Chinese Buddhist nun, of Lo-yang in Honan.

아반다라 阿槃陀羅 Avāntara, intermediate, within limits, included.

아발다라 阿跋多羅 Avatāra, descent of epiphany, especially of a deity ; but intp. as 무상 無上 peerless and 입 入 to enter, the former at least in mistake for anuttara. 아발야기리 阿跋耶祇釐 Abhayagiri, Mount Fearless, in Ceylon at Anurādhapura ; in its monastery a broad school of the Sthavirāḥ arose.

아발리구타니 阿鉢唎瞿陀尼 Aparagodāna ; apara, west ; godāna, ox-exchange, where oxen are used as money ; the western of the four continents of every world, circular in shape and with circular-faced people. Also 아와나고답니야 啞啝囉孤答尼耶. Cf. 구 瞿. 아발지발라지제사나 阿鉢底鉢喇底提舍那 Āpatti-pratideśanā, confession, 참회 懺悔. 아발라지하제 阿鉢羅哌訶諦 Apratihata, irresistible, unaffected by. 아발리시다 阿鉢唎市多 Aparājita, name of a yakṣa ; also 아발리이다 阿跋唎爾多 ; 아파라실다 阿波羅實多 ; as a symbol of invincibility it is written 아파라질다 阿波羅質多.

아방 阿傍 ; 아방 阿防 The ox-head tortures in Hades. Also 아방라찰 阿傍羅刹.

아번 阿鑁 Avaṁ. "A" is the Vairocana germ-word in the Garbhadhātu, "Vaṁ" the same in the Vajradhātu, hence Avaṁ includes both. 아번람함흠 阿鑁覽哈欠 A-vaṁ-raṁ-haṁ-khaṁ, is the highest formula of the 진언 眞言 Shingon sect ; it represents all five elements, or composite parts of Vairocana in his corporeal nature, but also represents him in his 법신 法身 or spiritual nature ; cf. 아비 阿卑, etc., and 아라 阿羅 Arapacana.

아벌라세라 阿伐羅勢羅 Avaraśailāḥ, the school of the dwellers in the Western mountains 서산사 西山寺 in Dhanakaṭaka ; it was a subdivision of the Mahāsāṅghika.

아법 我法 Self (or the ego), and things. 아법구유종 我法俱有宗 The school that regards the ego and things as real ; the 독자부 犢子部 Vātsīputrīyāḥ school.

아부담 阿部曇 The Arbuda hell, cf. 알 頞.

아부하나 阿浮呵那 or 阿浮訶那 Āvāhana, or Āpattivyutthāna, the calling of a monk or nun into the assembly for penance, or to rid the delinquent of sin. 아부(타)달마 阿浮(陀)達摩 Adbhuta-dharma, miraculous or supernatural things, a section of the canon recounting miracles and prodigies.

아비 阿毗 Avīci, 비(지) 毘(至) cf. 아비 阿鼻. 아비삼불(타) 阿毗三佛(陀) ; 아유삼불 阿惟三佛 Abhisaṁbuddha, Abhisaṁbodha ; realizing or manifesting universal enlightenment ; fully awake, complete realization. 아비목지 阿毗目底 Abhimukti, probably in error for Adhimukti, implicit faith, conviction. 아비목거 阿毗目佉 or 阿比目佉 Abhimukham, towards, approaching, in presence of, tr. 현전 現前. Abhimukhī, the sixth of the ten stages 십주 十住. 아비사도 阿毗私度 Abhijit, 여숙 女宿 the tenth Chinese stellar mansion, stars in Aquarius. 아비발치 阿毗跋致 ; 아비발치 阿鞞跋致 ; 아유월치 阿惟越致 Avivartin, 불퇴 不退 No retrogression. 아비달마 阿毗達磨 ; 아비담 阿毗曇 ; 아비달마 阿鼻達磨 Abhidharma. The śāstras, which discuss Buddhist philosophy or metaphysics ; defined by Buddhaghoṣa as the law or truth (dharma) which (abhi) goes beyond or behind the law ; explained by 전 傳 tradition, 승법 勝法 surpassing law, 무비법 無比法 incomparable law, 대법 對法 comparing the law, 향법 向法 directional law, showing cause and effect. The 아비달마장 阿毗達磨藏 or 아비달마논장 阿毗達磨論藏 is the Abhidharma-piṭaka, the third part of the Tripiṭaka. In the Chinese canon it consists of 대승론 大乘論 Mahāyāna treatises, 소승론 小乘論 Hīnayāna treatises, and 장제론 藏諸論 those brought in during the Sung and Yüan dynasties. The 아비달마구사론 阿毗達磨俱舍論 Abhidharma-kośa-śāstra, tr. by Hsüan-tsang, is a philosophical work by Vasubandhu refuting doctrines of the Vibhāṣā school. There are many works of which Abhidharma forms part of the title. 아비차라 阿毗遮羅 Abhicāra. A hungry ghost. 아비차로가 阿毗遮嚕迦 ; 아비척류가 阿毗拓嚠迦 or 아비좌류가 阿毗左嚠迦 ; 아비좌라 阿毗左囉 Abhicāraka, exorcism ; an exorciser, or controller (of demons).

아비 阿鼻 Avīci, 아비지 阿鼻旨 ; 아비지 阿鼻脂 ; 아비지 阿鼻至 ; the last and deepest of the eight hot hells, where the culprits suffer, die, and are instantly reborn to suffering, without interruption 무간 無間. It is the 아비(지)지옥 阿鼻(旨)地獄 or the 아비초열지옥 阿鼻焦熱地獄 hell of unintermitted scorching ; or the 아비환지옥 阿鼻喚地獄 hell of unintermitted wailing ; its wall, out of which there is no escape, is the 아비대성 阿鼻大城.

아비다갈라나 阿避陀羯刺拏 Āviddhakarṇa, unpierced ears, name of an ancient monastery near Benares ; "near Yodhapatipura" [Eitel].

아비라흠흠 阿卑羅吽欠 A-vi-ra-hūm-kham or Āḥ-vi-ra-hūm-kham, the Shingon "true word" or spell of Vairocana, for subduing all māras, each sound representing one of the five elements, earth, water, fire, wind (or air), and space (or ether). Also, 아비비라흠 阿毘卑羅吽 or 아미비라검 阿尾卑羅劍 ; 아미라흠흠 阿味囉許欠.

아비발치 阿鞞跋致 Avaivartika, Avivartin, Aparivartya. 불퇴전 不退轉 One who never recedes ; a bodhisattva who, in his progress towards Buddhahood, never retrogrades to a lower state than that to which he has attained. Also 아비발치 阿毘跋致 ; 아유월치 阿惟越致.

아사 我事 My body ; myself ; my affair.

아사가 阿賒迦 A kind of hungry ghost ; connected with Aśanāyuka.

아사바 阿娑嚩 A-sa-va, a formula covering the three sections of the Garbhadhātu — "a" the Tathāgata section, "sa" the Lotus section, and "va" the Diamond section. 아사마보다 阿娑摩補多

Asamāpta, incomplete, unended. 아사마사마 阿娑磨娑摩 or 阿娑摩娑摩 Asamasama, one of the titles of a Buddha ; it is defined as 무등등 無等等 which has various interpretations, but generally means of unequalled rank. 아사미 阿娑弭 has similar meaning. 아사라 阿娑羅 Asaru, a medicine ; a plant, *Blumea lacera* ; or perhaps Asāra, the castor-oil plant, or the aloe. 아사파나가 阿娑頗那伽 Āśvāsa-apānaka, contemplation by counting the breathings ; cf. 아나바나 阿那波那.

아사선 阿私仙 Asita-ṛṣi. 아사타 阿私陀 or 阿斯陀 ; 아씨다 阿氏多 ; 아이 阿夷. (1) A ṛṣi who spoke the Saddharmapuṇḍarīka-sūtra to Śākyamuni in a former incarnation. (2) The aged saint who pointed out the Buddha-signs on Buddha's body at his birth.

아사세 阿闍世 Ajātaśatru, 아사세 阿闍貰 ; 아사다설돌로 阿闍多設咄路 ; 미생원 未生怨 "Enemy before birth" ; a king of Magadha whose father, Bimbisāra, is said to have sought to kill him as ill-omened. When grown up he killed his father and ascended the throne. At first inimical to Śākyamuni, later he was converted and became noted for his liberality ; died *circa* 519 B.C. Also called "Broken fingers" and Kṣemadarśin. His son and successor was Udāyi ; and a daughter was Aśu-dharā. According to a Tibetan legend an infant son of Ajātaśatru was kidnapped, or exposed, and finally became king of Tibet named Ña-khri-btsan-po. 아사리 阿闍梨 Ācārya, ācārin, v. 아차 阿遮.

아사야 阿奢也 v. 아세야 阿世耶. 아사리이 阿奢理貳 or 아사리아 阿奢理兒 Āścarya, rare, extraordinary. Part of the name of an ancient monastery in Karashahr.

아사타 阿沙陀 Āṣāḍhā, 아사다 阿沙荼 ; 알사다 頞沙荼 the fourth month, part of June and July. Name of a monk. Āṣāḍhā, an Indian constellation comprising 기 箕 and 두 斗, stars in Sagittarius. Cf. 아살다 阿薩多.

아살다 阿薩多 Āṣāḍhā is a double nakṣatra (two lunar mansions) associated with 기 箕, stars in Sagittarius ; this form is said to be Pūrva-aṣādhā and is intp. as 진 軫, i.e. stars in Corvus, but these stars are in the Indian constellation Hastā, the Hand, which may be the more correct transliteration ; cf. 아사타 阿沙陀. 아살사 阿薩闍 Asādhya, incurable.

아상 我相 Egoism, the concept of the ego as real. Anyone who believes in 아상 我相, 인상 人相, 중생상 衆生相, 수상 壽相 is not a true bodhisattva, v. 아인사상 我人四相.

아상 我相 The thought that the ego has reality.

아서단사나 阿誓單闍那 or **아시단사나** 阿恃單闍那 Ajitaṁjaya, invincible, a charm for entering the meditation on invincibility. Cf. 아시 阿恃.

아설타 阿說他 Aśvattha, a tree, the *Ficus religiosa*, or bodhi-tree, called also the 무죄수 無罪樹 no-sin tree, because whoever goes around it three times is rid of sin. Also 아습파타 阿濕婆他, 아사파타 阿舍波他 ; 아수타 阿輸他. 아설라부 阿說羅部 Aiśvarikas, a theistic school of Nepāla (presently, Nepal), which set up Ādi-Buddha as a supreme divinity.

아섬지하라 阿剡底訶羅 Name of a demon burnt by the fire it eats.

아세야 阿世耶 Āśaya, 아사야 阿奢也, disposition, mind ; pleased to, desire to, pleasure.

아소 我所 ; **아소유** 我所有 ; **아소사** 我所事 Mine, personal, subjective ; personal conditions, possessions, or anything related to the self. 아소심 我所心 The mind that thinks it is owner of things. 아소견 我所見 The incorrect view that anything is really mine, for all things are but temporal combinations.

아수가 阿輸柯 Younger brother of Aśoka ; he is said to have reigned for seven days and then resigned to Aśoka, but cf. Mahendra under 마 摩.

아수라 阿修羅 Asura, 수라 修羅 originally meaning a spirit, spirits, or even the gods, it generally indicates titanic demons, enemies of the gods, with whom, especially Indra, they wage constant war. They are defined as "not devas," and "ugly," and "without wine." Other forms are 아수라 阿須羅 or 아소라 阿蘇羅 or 阿素羅 ; 아수륜 阿修倫 or 阿須倫 or 阿須輪 ; 아소락 阿素洛 ; 아차 阿差. Four classes are named according to their manner of rebirth — egg-born, womb-born, transformation-born, and spawn-or water-born. Their abode is in the ocean, north of Sumeru, but certain of the weaker dwell in a western mountain cave. They have realms, rulers, and palaces, as have the devas. The 아수라도 阿修羅道 is one of the six gatis, or ways of reincarnation. The 수라장 修羅場 or 수라항 修羅巷 is the battlefield of the asuras against India. The 아수라금 阿修羅琴 are their harps.

아순나 阿順那 Arjuna, white, silvery ; the tree *Terminalia arjuna* ; part of the name of 나가알랄수나 那伽閼剌樹那 Nāgārjuna q.v. Also 아사나 阿闍那 ; 아주다나 阿周陀那 ; 알순나 頞順那 ; 이리순나 夷離淳那.

아술달 阿術達 Āśu-cittā, daughter of Ajātaśatru, king of Magadha, noted for her wisdom at 12 years of age.

아습갈타파력차 阿濕喝咃波力叉 Aśvattha-vṛkṣa ; v. 보리수 菩提樹 the *Ficus religiosa.* 아습파 阿濕婆 Aśva, a horse. 아습갈미타 阿濕喝迷陀 Aśvamedha, the ancient royal horse-sacrifice. 아습마 阿濕摩 or 阿濕麽 or 阿濕魔 Aśman, a stone, rock. 아습갈게파 阿濕喝揭婆 Aśmagarbha ; emerald, tr. by 석장 石藏, but also by 마뇌 馬腦 agate, the idea apparently being derived from another form 아습바게바 阿濕嚩揭波 aśvagarbha, horse matrix. Other forms are 아습갈갈파 阿濕喝碣波 or 아수갈게파 阿輸喝揭波 or 아사갈갈파 阿舍喝竭波 ; 알습갈타파 遏濕喝咃波. 아습비니 阿濕毘儞 Aśvinī. M. W. says it is the first of the twenty-eight Nakshatras ; the eleventh of the Chinese twenty-eight constellations, Hsü, β Aquarii, a Equulei. 아습바 阿濕波 Aśvin, the twins of the Zodiac, Castor and Pollux, sons of the Sun and Aśvinī ; they appear in the sky before dawn riding in a golden carriage drawn by horses or birds. 아습박벌다 阿濕縛伐多 ; 아습파시 阿濕婆恃 ; 아습파(씨다) 阿濕婆(氏多) ; 아습파지 阿濕波持 ; 아설시 阿說示 or 아설지 阿說旨 ; 아수실 阿輸實 ; 알비 頞鞞 Aśvajit 마승 馬勝 "Gaining horses by conquest." [M. W.] Name of one of the first five disciples and a relative of Śākyamuni ; teacher of Śāriputra. 아습박유사 阿濕縛庾闍 ; 아습바유야 阿濕嚩喩若 Aśvayuja. The month in which the moon is in conjunction with Aśvinī, 16th of the 8th moon to 15th of the 9th ; it is the middle month of autumn. 아습박구사 阿濕縛窶沙 or 阿溼縛窶沙 ; 마명 馬鳴 q.v. Aśvaghoṣa. 아습박갈나 阿濕縛羯拏 ; 아수할나 阿輸割那 Aśvakarṇa, 마이 馬耳 the horse-ear mountains, fifth of the seven concentric mountains around Sumeru.

아승(가) 阿僧(伽) Asaṅga, Āryāsaṅga, intp. as 무착 無著 또는 無着 unattached, free ; lived "a thousand years after the Nirvāṇa," probably the fourth century A.D., said to be the eldest brother of 천친 天親 Vasubandhu, whom he converted to Mahāyāna. He was first a follower of the Mahīśāsaka school, but founded the Yogācārya or Tantric school with his Yogācāryabhūmi-śāstra 유가사지론 瑜伽師地論, which in the 삼장전 三藏傳 is said to have been dictated to him by Maitreya in the Tuṣita heaven, along with the 장엄대승론 莊嚴大乘論 and the 중변분별론 中邊分別論. He was a native of Gandhāra, but lived mostly in Ayodhyā (Oudh).

아승기 阿僧祇 Asaṅkhya, Asaṅkhyeya, 아승기야 阿僧企耶 ; 승기 僧祇 intp. 무수 無數 innumerable, countless, said to be 일천만만만만만만만만조 一千萬萬萬萬萬萬萬萬兆 kalpas. There are four asaṅkhya kalpas in the rise, duration, and end of every universe, cf. 겁 劫.

아승만 我勝慢 Adhimāna ; the pride of thinking oneself superior to equals. One of the 구만 九慢.

아시 阿施 Artha, 의 義 reason, sense, purpose. 시 施 is probably a misprint for 타 陁 ; the Hua-yen uses 갈라다 曷攞多 ; also 타 他 is used for 시 施.

아시다벌지 阿恃多伐底 Ajiravatī ; v. 시 尸. The river Hiraṇyavatī, also 아리라발제 阿利羅䟦提 or 아이라발제 阿夷羅拔提 ; 아이라바지 阿夷羅婆底 or 아지라바지 阿脂羅婆底 or 아인라바지 阿寅羅婆底 ; 아이다부지 阿爾多嚩底. It is probable that 아시다 阿恃多, intp. 무승 無勝 unconquered, is Ajita and an error. Cf. 아서 阿誓.

아시라바나 阿尸羅婆那 Śravaṇā, which M. W. gives as "one of the lunar asterisms ... α, β, γ, Aquilae." Śrāvaṇa is the month which falls in July-August.

아실 我室 The ego as the abode (of all suffering).

아실려사 阿失麗沙 Aśleṣā, the 류 柳 or 24th constellation, stars in Hydra ; M. W. says the 9th Nakṣatra containing five stars.

아아소 我我所 I and mine ; the self and its possessions.

아애 我愛 Self-love ; the love of or attachment to the ego, arising with the eighth vijñāna.

아야 阿耶 Āya, approach, drawing near ; 아야라 阿耶羅 Āyāna has the same meaning, but is intp. by 관 觀 to contemplate, to look into. 아야달나 阿耶怛那 or 阿也怛那 Āyatana, seat, abode, intp. by 입 入 or 처 處 entrance, or place, i.e. the ṣaḍāyatanas, six entrances or places of sense-data, or sensation ; v. 육입 六入. 아야게리바 阿耶揭哩婆 or 阿耶揭唎婆 Hayagrīva, the horse-head Kuan-yin. 아야목거 阿耶穆佉 Ayamukha, Hayamukha, an ancient kingdom in Central India.

아야(다) 阿若(多) Ājñāta-Kauṇḍinya, 아야교진여 阿若憍陳如 one of the first five disciples of Śākyamuni, said to be the first to realize the Buddha-truth. Ājñāta, his designation (i.e. recognized of confessed), is intp. as 이지 已知 Having Known and 무지 無知 Not knowing, or knowledge of non-existence. Or perhaps for Ājñātṛ, confessor. Kauṇḍinya, his surname, is said to mean a "fire holder" from "the early fire-worship of the Brahmins."

아야건다 阿夜健多 Ayaḥkāṇḍa, an iron arrow ; also 아야새건나 阿夜塞健那.

아어취 我語取 The attachment to doctrines or statements about the ego. One of the 사취 四取.

아열만 我劣慢 Unamāna ; the pride of thinking myself not much inferior to those who far surpass me. One of the 구만 九慢 q.v.

아예라 阿詣羅 Aṅgiras, one of the seven deva-ṛṣis born from Brahma's mouth, shown in the Diamond Court of the Garbhadhātu, red coloured, holding a lotus on which is a vase ; in Sanskrit the planet Jupiter. A title of the Buddha. Also 여앙가라화 與盎伽羅和.

아왕 鵝王 Rāja-haṁsa, the king-goose, leader of the flight, i.e. Buddha, one of whose thirty-two marks is webbed hands and feet ; also the walk of a Buddha is dignified like that of the goose. 아왕별유 鵝王別乳 A king-goose is reputed to be able to absorb the milk from a mixture of milk and water, leaving the water behind, so with the bodhisattva and truth. 아(왕)안 鵝(王)眼 The eye of the king-goose, distinguishing milk from water, used for the eye of the truth-discerner.

아우 我愚 Ego ignorance, holding to the illusion of the reality of the ego.

아유 我有 The illusion that ego has real existence.

아유 阿由 Āyurveda, one of the Vedas, the science of life or longevity. 아유다 阿由多 or 阿庾多 Ayuta, variously stated as a million or a thousand millions ; and a 대아유다 大阿由多 as ten thousand millions.

아유다 阿庾多 idem 아유다 阿由多.

아유라제 阿維羅提 or **아비라제** 阿比羅提 Abhirati, the eastern Pure Land of Akṣobhya.

아유사 阿踰闍 Ayodhyā, 아유타 阿踰陀 ; 아수사 阿輸闍 capital of Kośala, headquarters of ancient Buddhism, the present Oudh, Lat. 26° N., Long. 82° 4 E.

아육 阿育 Aśoka, 아서가 阿恕伽 ; 아수가 阿輸迦 or 아서가 阿舒迦 or 아숙가 阿叔迦 Grandson of Candragupta (Sandrokottos), who united India and reached the summit of his career about 315 B.C. Aśoka reigned from about 274 to 237 B.C. His name Aśoka, "free from care," may have been adopted on his conversion. He is accused of the assassination of his brother and relatives to gain the throne, and of a fierce temperament in his earlier days. Converted, he became the first famous patron of Buddhism, encouraging its development and propaganda at home and abroad, to which existing pillars, etc., bear witness ; his propaganda is said to have spread from the borders of China to Macedonia, Epirus, Egypt, and Cyrene. His title is Dharmāśoka ; he should be distinguished from Kālāśoka, grandson of Ajātaśatru. Cf. 아육가경 阿育伽經, 아육가전 阿育伽傳, etc. 아육가수 阿育伽樹 The name of a tree under which the mother of the Buddha was painlessly delivered of her son, for which Chinese texts give eight different dates ; the Jonesia aśoka ; it is also called 필리차 畢利叉 Vṛkṣa.

아이 阿夷 Arhan, a worthy, noble, or saintly man ; especially 아사타 阿私陀 Asita, q.v. 아이념 阿夷恬 Ādikarmika, a beginner, neophyte. 아이두 阿夷頭 idem 아기다 阿耆多 Ajita. 아이라화제 阿夷羅和帝 or 아이라바제 阿夷羅婆帝 or 아이라바지 阿夷羅婆底 or 아이라발제 阿夷羅跋提, v. 아시 阿恃 the river Ajiravatī. v. 아라한 阿羅漢.

아인사상 我人四相 The four ejects of the ego in the Diamond Sūtra ; (1) 아상 我相 the illusion that in the five skandhas there is a real ego ; (2) 인상 人相 that this ego is a man, and different from beings of the other paths ; (3) 중생상 衆生相 that all beings have an ego born of the five skandhas ; (4) 수상 壽相 that the ego has age, i.e. a determined or fated period of existence.

아일(다) 阿逸(多) Ajita, 무능승 無能勝 invincible, title of Maitreya ; and of others. Also 아씨다 阿氏多 or 아지다 阿底多 or 아제다 阿啣多 or 아기다 阿嗜多 : 아사타 阿私陀 ; 아이두 阿夷頭.

아전도 我顚倒 The illusion that the ego is real ; also the incorrect view that the Nirvāṇa-ego is non-ego. One of the 사전도 四顚倒.

아전지가 阿顚底迦 Ātyantika, final, endless, tr. by 필경 畢竟 to or at the end, e.g. no mind for attaining Buddhahood ; cf. 아천 阿闡.

아절라 阿折羅 Ācāra, an arhat of the kingdom of Andhra, founder of a monastery.

아점바시라국 阿點婆翅羅國 Atyambakela, an ancient kingdom near Karachi.

아제다 阿制多 Ajita, v. 아일다 阿逸多.

아제불타 阿提佛陀 Ādi-buddha, the primal Buddha of ancient Lamaism (Tib. chos-kyi-daṅ-poḥi-saṅs-rgyas) ; by the older school he is associated with P'u-hsien born of Vairocana, i.e. Kuntu-bzan-po, or Dharmakāya-Samantabhadra ; by the later school with Vajradhara, or Vajrasattva, who are considered as identical, and spoken of as omniscient, omnipotent, omnipresent, eternal, infinite, uncaused, and causing all things. 아제목다(가) 阿提目多(伽) or 아지목다(가) 阿地目多(伽) Adhimukti or atimukti, entire freedom of mind, confidence, intp. by 선사유 善思惟 "pious thoughtfulness," good propensity. Atimuktaka, a plant like the "dragon-lick," suggestive of hemp, with red flowers and bluish-green leaves ; its seeds produce fragrant oil, sesame. Also, a kind of tree. 아제아눅바다 阿提阿耨波陀 Ādyanutpāda, or Ādyanutpanna ; 본초불생 本初不生 the original uncreated letter ā or a.

아주다 阿周陀 The name of 목련 目連 Mahāmaudgalyāyana as a ṛṣi. 아주다나 阿周陀那 Arjuna, v. 아순나 阿順那.

아지리 阿底哩 or **아질리** 阿跌哩 Atri, a devourer ; one of the stars in Ursa Major ; one of the assistants of Agni shown in the Garbhadhātu ; an ancient ṛṣi.

아지목득가 阿地目得迦 Atimuktaka, v. 아제 阿提.

아진타 阿軫䭾 Acintya, beyond conception, v. 부사의 不思議.

아집 我執 Ātma-grāha ; holding to the concept of the ego ; also 인집 人執.

아차리야 阿遮利耶 Ācārya, (아)사려 (阿)闍黎 or (아)사리 (阿)闍梨 ; 아사리 阿舍梨 ; 아지리 阿祇利 or 阿祇梨 spiritual teacher, master, preceptor ; one of 정행 正行 correct conduct, and able to teach others. There are various categories, e.g. 출가아차리 出家阿遮利 one who has charge of novices ; 교수아차리 教授阿遮利 a teacher of the discipline ; 갈마아차리 羯磨阿遮利 of duties ; 수경아차리 授經阿遮利 of the scriptures ; 의지아차리 依止阿遮利 the master of the community. 아차라 阿遮(羅) or 阿遮攞 ; 아사라 阿奢羅 Acala, Immovable, the name of Āryācalanātha 부동명왕 不動明王, the one who executes the orders of Vairocana. Also, a stage in Bodhisattva development, the eighth in the ten stages towards Buddhahood. 아차루 阿遮樓 Name of a mountain.

아차마라 阿叉摩羅 Akṣamālā, a rosary, especially of the seeds of the Eleocarpus. [M. W.] Also a symbol of the ten perfections.

아차말 阿差末 Akṣayamati, unceasing devotion, with an unfailing mind ; name of a bodhisattva.

아천 阿擅 Anātman, 아단 阿檀 ; 아날마 阿捺摩, i.e. 무아 無我 without an ego, impersonality, different from soul or spirit.

아천지(가) 阿闡底(迦) Anicchantika, without desire, averse from, i.e. undesirous of nirvāṇa.

아촉 阿閦 Akṣobhya, 아촉비 阿閦鞞 ; 아촉바 阿閦婆 ; 아추비야 阿芻鞞耶 unmoved, imperturbable ; tr. 부동 不動 ; 무동 無動 also 무노 無怒 ; 무진에 無瞋恚, free from anger, according to his Buddha-vow. One of the Five Buddhas, his realm Abhirati, Delightful, now being in the east, as Amitābha's is in the west. He is represented in the Lotus as the eldest son of Mahābhijñābhibhū 대통지승 大通智勝, and was the Bodhisattva? Jñānākara 지적 智積 before he became Buddha ; he has other appearances. Akṣobhya is also said to mean 100 vivaras, or 1 followed by 17 ciphers, and a 대아촉비 大阿閦鞞 is ten times that figure.

아치 我痴 Ego-infatuation, confused by the belief in the reality of the ego.

아타 阿陀 Agada, v. 아가타 阿伽陀. 아타나 阿陀那 Ādāna, intp. by 집지 執持 holding on to, maintaining ; holding together the karma, good or evil, maintaining the sentient organism, or the germ in the seed or plant. It is another name for the ālaya-vijñāna, and is known as the 아타나식 阿陀那識 ādānavijñāna.

아타리 阿吒利 Aṭāli, 아타리 阿吒釐 a province of the ancient kingdom of Malwa, or Malava ; its people rejected Buddhism. 아타타 阿吒吒 Aṭaṭa ; the third of the four cold hells. 아타파구 阿吒婆拘 ; 아타부가 阿吒嚩迦 ; 아타박구 阿吒薄俱 or 알타박구 遏吒薄俱 Āṭavika, name of a demon-general. 아타벌저 阿吒筏底 Alakavatī, the city of Vaiśravaṇa.

아타바페타 阿他婆吠陀 Atharva-veda, also Ātharvaṇa, the fourth Veda, dealing with sorcery or magic ; also 아달바비타 阿達婆鞞陀 ; 아달바타 阿闥婆陀.

아파 阿婆 Apa, abha, ava, etc. 아파(사)마라 阿婆(娑)摩羅 Apasmāra, epileptic demons, demons of epilepsy. 아바잉가라 阿婆孕迦羅 Abhayaṁkara, giving security from fear, name of a Tathāgata. 아바로길지사바라 阿婆盧吉低舍婆羅 Avalokiteśvara, name of Kuan-yin. 아파마 阿婆磨 Anupama, applied to a Buddha as 무등등 無等等 of unequalled rank, cf. 아사마 阿娑磨.

아파마라 阿波摩羅 Apasmāra, malevolent demons, epilepsy, and the demons who cause it ; also 아파마라 阿婆摩羅 ; 아발마라 阿跋摩羅 ; 아파사마라 阿跛娑摩囉. 아파회 阿波會 ; 아파회 阿婆譮 ; 아파라 阿波羅 Ābhāsvara(-vimāna), the sixth of the Brahmalokas 광음천 光音天 of light and sound (ābhāsvara) and its devas, but it is better intp. as ābhās, shining and vara, ground, or splendid, the splendid devas or heaven ; shown in the Garbhadhātu. Like other devas they are subject to rebirth. Also 아회긍수 阿會亘修 or 아회긍차 阿會亘差 ; 아파최라(서) 阿波嘬羅(庶) ; 아위화라 阿衛貨羅. 아파말가 阿波末加 or 阿婆末加 ; 아파마라아 阿波麼羅誐 Apāmārga, 우슬초 牛膝草 *Achryanthes aspera.* 아파파 阿波波 Ababa, Hahava, the only sound possible to those in the fourth of the eight cold hells. 아파라라 阿波羅囉 ; 아파라라 阿波邏囉 ; 아파라리 阿波邏利 ; 아파파 阿波波 ; 아발마 阿鉢摩 ; and 아라파루 阿羅波樓 Apalāla, "not fond of flesh" [M. W.], a destroyer by flood of the crops ; the nāga of the source of the river Śubhavastu (Swat) of Udyāna, about which there are various legends ; he, his wife 비수니 比壽尼, and his children were all converted to Buddhism. 아파(라)마나(아)파 阿波(羅)摩那(阿)婆 ; 아파마나파 阿婆摩那婆 or 합발마나파 盍鉢摩那婆 ; 아파마나 阿波摩那 ; 파마나 波摩那 Apramāṇābha, intp. as 무량광 無量光 immeasurable light, the fifth of the Brahmalokas. 아파나가지 阿波那伽低 Aparagati, the three evil paths, i.e. animal, hungry ghost, hell, but some say only the path to the hells. 아파다나 阿波陀那 ; 아파타라 阿波陁羅 ; 아파타라 阿波他羅 Avadāna, parables, metaphors, stories, illustrations ; one of the twelve classes of sūtras ; the stories, etc., are divided into eight categories.

아하라 阿賀羅 Āhāra, v. 식 食 9.

아하하 阿呵呵 Ahaha, sound of laughter.

아함 阿含 Āgama, 아함모 阿含暮 ; 아함 阿鋡 ; 아가마 阿伽摩 or 아급마 阿笈摩, the Āgamas, a collection of doctrines, general name for the Hīnayāna scriptures ; tr. 법귀 法歸 the home or collecting-place of the Law or Truth ; 무비법 無比法 peerless Law ; or 취무 趣無 *ne plus ultra,* ultimate, absolute truth. The 사아함경 四阿含經 or Four Āgamas are (1) 장아함 長阿含 Dīrghāgama, "Long" treatises on cosmogony. (2) Madhyamāgama, 중아함 中阿含, "middle" treatises on metaphysics. (3) Saṁyuktāgama, 잡아함 雜阿含 "miscellaneous" treatises on abstract contemplation. (4) Ekottara-āgama 증일아함 增一阿含 "numerical" treatises, subjects treated numerically. There is also a division of Five Āgamas. 아함시 阿含時 The period when the Buddha taught Hīnayāna doctrine in the Lumbinī garden during the first twelve years of his ministry. 아함부 阿含部 Hīnayāna.

아호 阿呼 Ahu! Aho! an interjection, e.g. 기재 奇哉 Wonderful! Also arka, a flash, ray, the sun ; praise ; name of a mountain ; cf. 아라가 阿羅歌. 아호지옥 阿呼地獄 The hell of groaning.

아훔 阿吽 Ahūṁ, the supposed foundation of all sounds and writing, "A" being the open and "hūṁ" the closed sound. "A" is the seed of Vairocana, "hūṁ" that of Vajrasattva, and both have other indications. "A" represents the absolute, "hūṁ" the particular, or phenomenal.

악 樂 Music, that which causes joy, hence joy, joyful, glad, rejoice ; also to find joy in, enjoy. 악건달바 樂乾闥婆 The Gandharvas, Indra's musicians. 낙수 樂受 The sensation, or perception of pleasure. 낙토 樂土 A happy land. 악천 樂天 Deva musicians, see 악건달바 樂乾闥婆 above. 낙시 樂施 Joyful giver, tr. of Sudatta, i.e. Anāthapiṇḍada, v. 아 阿. 낙과 樂果 Joyful fruit, i.e. nirvāṇa. 낙근 樂根 The organs of pleasure — eyes, ears, nose, tongue, and body. 낙욕 樂欲 Desire for the pleasant, or pleasure. 낙법 樂法 Delight in Buddha-truth, or the religion. 낙바라밀 樂波羅蜜 The pāramitā of joy, one of the 사덕바라밀 四德波羅蜜 four transcendent pāramitās q.v., i.e. 상 常, 아 我, and 정 淨. 악신 樂神 Deva musicians, v. 악건달바 樂乾闥婆 above. 낙착 樂著 The bond of pleasure binding to the phenomenal life. 요설 樂說 Joy in preaching, or telling the way of salvation ; joy in that which is preached. It is also called pratibhāna, bold and illuminating discourse, or freedom in expounding the truth with correct meaning and appropriate words, one of the 무애지 無礙智 four pratisaṁvids. 요설변재 樂說辯才 similar to the last. 낙변화천 樂變化天 Sunirmita, the fifth of the six desire-heavens, where every form of joy is attainable at will ; also 화(자)락천 化(自)樂天 ; 묘락화천 妙樂化天. 낙방 樂邦 The joyful country, the paradise of the West. 악음 樂音 The sound of music. 악음수 樂音樹 The trees in Amitābha's paradise which give forth music to the breeze.

악 鰐 A crocodile. 악어 鰐魚 v. 금 金 Kumbhīra.

악 惡 Agha. Bad, evil, wicked, hateful ; to hate, dislike ; translit. *a*, cf. 아 阿.

악각 惡覺 Contemplation or thought contrary to Buddhist principles.

악게로 惡揭嚕 Aguru, Lignum Aloes, v. 침수향 沉水香.

악견 惡見 Evil or heterodox views. 악견처 惡見處 The place in Hades whence the sinner beholds the evil done in life, one of the sixteen special hells.

악과 惡果 Evil fruit from evil deeds.

악구 惡口 Evil mouth, evil speech ; a slanderous, evil-speaking person.

악귀신 惡鬼神 Evil demons and evil spirits, yakṣas, rākṣasas, etc.

악기니 惡祁尼 Agni ; intp. by 화신 火神 the god of fire, cf. 아 阿.

악나야간심 惡癩野干心 A scabby pariah, a phrase describing the evil of mind.

악도 惡道 Evil ways ; also the three evil paths or destinies — animals, pretas, and purgatory.

악로 惡露 Foul discharges from the body ; also evil revealed.

악마 惡魔 Evil māras, demon enemies of Buddhism.

악무과 惡無過 That it is not wrong to do evil ; that there are no consequences attached to an evil life.

악보 惡報 Recompense for ill, punishment.

악사 惡師 An evil teacher who teaches harmful doctrines.

악세계 惡世界 An evil world.

악업 惡業 Evil conduct in thought, word, or deed, which leads to evil recompense ; evil karma.

악연 惡緣 External conditions or circumstances which stir or tempt one to do evil.

악율의 惡律儀 Bad, or evil rules and customs.

악인 惡因 A cause of evil, or of a bad fate ; an evil cause.

악작 惡作 Evil doings ; also to hate that which one has done, to repent.

악지식 惡知識 A bad intimate, or friend, or teacher.

악차 惡叉 Akṣa, "a seed of which rosaries are made (in compound words, like Indrākṣa, Rudrākṣa) ; a shrub producing that seed (*Eleocarpus ganitrus*)." [M. W.] It is called the 악차취 惡叉聚 because its seeds are said to be formed in triplets, and illustrate the simultaneous character of 혹행고 惑行苦 illusion, action, and suffering ; another version is that the seeds fall in clusters, and illustrate numbers, or numerous ; they are also known as 금강자 金剛子.

악찰나 惡察那 or **악찰라** 惡察羅 Akṣara ; imperishable, unalterable ; a syllable ; words ; intp. as an unchanging word, a root word, or word-root. Also 악찰라 惡刹羅 ; 아걸사라 阿乞史羅.

악촉 惡觸 Evil touch ; contaminated as is food by being handled or touched.

악취 惡趣 The evil directions or incarnations, i.e. those of animals, pretas, and beings in purgatory ; to which some add asuras.

악취공 惡取空 To have evil ideas of the doctrine of voidness, to deny the doctrine of cause and effect.

안 雁 A hawk, also used for Haṁsa, a wild goose. 안탑 雁塔 The Wild Goose pagoda, name of a famous monastery. 안자 雁字 A term for a monastery. 안행 雁行 To pass in V-shaped formation like wild geese.

안 案 A judge's desk ; a case at law. 안달라 案達羅 Andhra, a kingdom in southern India, between the Krishna and Godāvarī rivers, whose capital was Veṅgī ; the country south-east of this was known as 대안달라 大案達羅.

안 鴈 A wild goose. 안왕 鴈王 King or leader of the flight, or flock ; Buddha, hence 안문 鴈門 Buddhism.

안 眼 Cakṣu, the eye. 안입 眼入 The eye entrance, one of the twelve entrances, i.e. the basis of sight consciousness. 안지 眼智 Knowledge obtained from seeing. 안근 眼根 The organ of sight. 안계 眼界 The element or realm of sight. 안목 眼目 The eye, eyes. 안식 眼識 Sight-perception, the first vijñāna. 안식계 眼識界 Cakṣurvijñāna-dhātu, the element or realm of sight-perception.

안 岸 Kūla. Shore, bank. 안수 岸樹 A tree on a river's brink, life's uncertainty. 안두 岸頭 The shore of the ocean of suffering. 피안 彼岸 The other shore ; nirvāṇa.

안 安 Peace, tranquil, quiet, pacify ; to put, place ; where? how? 안하 安下 To put down. 안하처 安下處 A place for putting things down, e.g. baggage ; a resting place, a place to stay at. 안명 安名 To give a religious name to a beginner. 안달라바 安呾羅縛 Andarab, a country through which Hsüan-tsang passed, north of Kapiśā, v. 가 迦. 안토지 安土地 To tranquillize the land, or a plot of land, by freeing it from harmful influences. 안거 安居 Tranquil dwelling. Varṣa, Varṣās, or Varṣāvasāna. A retreat during the three months of the Indian rainy season, and also, say some, in the depth of winter. During the rains it was "difficult to move without injuring insect life." But the object was for study and meditation. In Tokhāra the retreat is said to have been in winter, from the middle of the 12th to the middle of the 3rd moon ; in India from the middle of the 5th to the 8th, or the 6th to the 9th moons ; usually from Śrāvaṇa, Chinese 5th moon, to Aśvayuja, Chinese 8th moon ; but the 16th of the 4th to the 15th of the 7th moon has been the common period in China and Japan. The two annual periods are sometimes called 좌하 坐夏 and 좌랍 坐臘 sitting or resting for the summer and for the end of the year. The period is divided into three sections, former, middle, and latter, each of a month. 안지라 安底羅 Aṇḍīra, one of the twelve attendants on 약사 藥師 Bhaiṣajya. 안름 安廩 Anlin, a noted monk *circa* A.D. 500. 안심 安心 To quiet the heart, or mind ; be at rest. 안식 安息 To rest. 안식(국) 安息(國) Parthia, 파사 波斯 modern Persia, from which several monks came to China in the later Han dynasty, such as 안세고 安世高 An Shih-kao, 안현 安玄 An-hsüan, 담무제 曇無諦 T'an Wu-ti, 안법흠 安法欽 An Fa-ch'in, 안청 安淸 An-ch'ing. 안식향 安息香 Persian incense, or benzoin. 안혜 安慧 Settled or firm resolve on wisdom ; established wisdom ; tr. of 실치라말지 悉耻羅末底 Sthiramati, or Sthitamati, one of the ten great exponents of the 유식론 唯識論 Vijñaptimātratāsiddhi-śāstra, a native of southern India. 안명(유)산 安明(由)山 Sumeru, v. 수 須. 안락 安樂 Happy ; ease (of body) and joy (of heart) 신안심락 身安心樂. The 안락국 安樂國 or 안락정토 安樂淨土 is Amitābha's Happy Land in the western region, which is his domain ; it is also called 안양정토 安養淨土 or 정찰 淨刹, Pure Land of Tranquil Nourishment. 안선 安禪 To enter into dhyāna meditation. 안온 安穩 ; 안은 安隱 Body and mind at rest. 안립

安立 To set up, establish, stand firm. 안립행 安立行 Supratiṣṭhita-cāritra ; a Bodhisattva in the Lotus sūtra who rose up out of the earth to greet Śākyamuni. 안선나 安膳那 or 安繕那 or 安禪那 or 안사나 安闍那 An Indian eye medicine, said to be Añjana. 안원 安遠 Two noted monks of the 진 晉 Chin dynasty, i.e. 도안 道安 Tao-an and 혜원 慧遠 Hui-yüan. 안나반나 安那般那 ; 안반 安般 ; 아나(아)파나 阿那(阿)波那 Ānāpāna, expiration and inspiration, a method of breathing and counting the breaths for purposes of concentration ; the 대안반수의경 大安般守意經 is a treatise on the subject. 안타회 安陁會 ; 안달바사 安怛婆沙 or 안달바삼 安怛婆參 or 안다바사 安多婆沙 or 안다바삼 安多婆參 ; 안다발살 安多跋薩 or 안타발살 安陀跋薩 antaravāsaka, antarvāsas ; a monk's inner garment described as a sort of waist-coat. It is also explained by 군 裙 ch'ün which means a skirt. This inner garment is said to be worn against desire, the middle one against hate, and the outer one against ignorance and delusion. It is described as the present-day 락자 絡子 a jacket or vest.

안 按 To place, lay down, lay the hand on ; examine ; accord with. 안지 按指 To make a finger-mark, or sign.

알 斡 A handle for turning a wheel, a wheel, to revolve, circulate. 알자라 斡資羅 Vajra, v. 발 跋 and 금강 金剛.

알 遏 Check, stop. 알부다 遏部多 Adbhuta, the marvellous ; name of a stūpa in Udyāna, north-west India.

알 頞 The root of the nose, the brow ; a saddle ; translit. *a, an, ar,* cf. 아 阿. 알찰타 頞哳吒 Aṭaṭa, one of the cold hells. 알실다 頞悉多 Asta, the western hill behind which the sun sets, sunset, death, home. 안두가 頞杜迦 Andūka, v. 아리 阿梨. 알사다 頞沙茶 Āṣāḍhā, the first month of summer, 16th of 4th Chinese moon to 15th of 5th. 알부타 頞浮陀 ; 알부타 頞部陀 ; 알부담 頞部曇 Arbuda, cf. 아 阿, the first of the eight cold hells, where the cold raises tumours on the skin ; also a foetus of twenty-seven days. 알습박갈나 頞濕縛羯拏 Aśvakarṇa, the fifth of the seven circles round Meru. 알습바유사 頞濕縛庾闍 ; 알습바유사 頞濕婆庾闍 Aśvayuja, the first month of autumn (September-October). 알슬타 頞瑟吒 Aṣṭa, eight, the eight divisions of the 24-hour day. 안나 頞那 Anna, food, but intp. as the name of a mountain. 알비 頞鞞 Upasena, v. 아습 阿濕 one of the first five converts, idem Aśvajit. 알순나 頞順那 v. 아 阿 Arjuna. 알반저 頞飯底 v. 아 阿 Avantī.

알 閼 To obstruct, stop ; hoodwink. 알가 閼伽 Arghya, v. 아가 阿伽 scented water, or flowers in water as an offering, the word arghya meaning primarily some-thing valuable, or presentable ; hence 알가배 閼伽杯, a golden or metal vessel to hold such water ; 알가화 閼伽花 the flowers which float on its surface, etc.

암 巖 A crag, cliff. 암곡 巖谷 Cliffs and gullies.

암 庵 A thatched hut, shelter, place of retirement from the world ; a small temple ; especially a nunnery, hence 암실 庵室 ; 암사 庵寺 generally applies to such, and 암주 庵主 is the abbess.

암 暗 Dark, dim, gloom, dull ; secret, hidden. 암폐 暗蔽 Dark, ignorant. 암증선사 暗證禪師 ; 암증 暗證 ; 암선 暗禪, etc. A charlatan who teaches intuitional meditation differently from the methods of that school ; an ignorant preceptor.

암 菴 Hut, thatched cottage, small temple, nunnery ; translit. *am, ām.* 암마니필멸감 菴乜呢必滅堪 Om-maṇi-padme-hūṁ, cf. 암 唵. 암원 菴園 The Āmravana garden. 암바(라)녀 菴婆(羅)女 Āmradārikā, Āmrapālī, Ambapālī ; the guardian of the āmra tree ; a female who presented to Śākyamuni the Āmravana garden ; another legend says she was born of an āmra tree ; mother of Jīvaka, son of Bimbisāra. 암바라다가 菴婆羅多迦 Āmrātaka, a celestial fruit ; similar to 암라 菴羅.

암바리사 菴婆利沙 Ambarīṣa, name of a king. 암미라 菴弭羅 Āmla ; Amlikā, the tamarisk indica. 암마륵 菴摩勒 Amalā, *Emblica officinalis*, like the betel nut, used as a cure for colds. 암마라 菴摩羅 or 암몰라 菴沒羅 Amala, spotless, stainless, pure, white. Āmra, cf. 아말라 阿末羅 and *infra* ; the term is variously used, sometimes for pure, at others for the amalā, at others for the āmra, or mango. 암마라식 菴摩羅識 Pure knowledge, 진여 眞如 knowledge, v. 아말라식 阿末羅識. 암몰라 菴沒羅 v. *supra*. 암라 菴羅 Āmra, the mango, though its definition in Chinese is uncertain ; v. *supra*. 암라원 菴羅園 or 암수원 菴樹園 or 암위원 菴衛園 Āmravana, Āmrapālī, Āmrāvatī, v. *supra*. 암라녀 菴羅女 Ditto. 암화 菴華 The āmra flower.

암 唵 Om ; aum ; "a word of solemn affirmation and respectful assent (sometimes translated by yes, verily, so be it, and in this sense compared with Amen)." [M. W.] It is "the mystic name for the Hindū triad," and has other significations. It was adopted by Buddhists, especially by the Tantric school, as a mystic spell, and as an object of meditation. It forms the first syllable of certain mystical combinations, e.g. 암마니팔이우 唵嚤呢叭𠺗吽 Om maṇi padme hūṁ., which is a formula of the Lamaistic branch, said to be a prayer to Padmapāṇi ; each of the six syllables having its own mystic power of salvation from the lower paths of transmigration, etc. ; the formula is used in sorcery, auguries, etc. ; other forms of it are 암마니발두미우 唵嚤呢鉢頭迷吽 ; 암마니발눌명우 唵麽抳鉢訥銘吽.

암 闇 To shut ; dark ; retired ; translit. *am*, cf. 암 暗, 암 菴. 암실 闇室 A dark room, a place for meditation. 암밀리제다리 闇密里帝荼利 Amṛtakuṇḍalin, the vase of ambrosia. 암심 闇心 A dark, ignorant, or doubting mind. 암림 闇林 Tāmasavana, see 답 答. 암둔 闇鈍 Ignorant and dull. 암장 闇障 The hindrance of ignorance.

암자 庵子 Hermitage.

압 壓 To press, squeeze, crush ; repress. 압사유 壓沙油 To press oil out of sand, impossible. 압유 壓油 To crush seed for oil. 압유륜죄 壓油輪罪 The sin of the oil-presser, i.e. the killing of insects among the seeds crushed.

앙 盎 A bowl ; abundant ; translit. *ang*. 앙아라가 盎哦囉迦 Aṅgāraka, the planet Mars. 앙구리마라 盎窶利魔羅 Aṅgulimālya ; 지만 指鬘 A wreath, or chaplet, of finger-bones ; a Śivaitic sect which practised assassination as a religious act.

앙 鴦 Hen of mandarin duck, symbolizing conjugal fidelity ; translit. *aṅg*. 앙가 鴦伽 ; 앙굴다라 鴦掘多羅 Aṅga, described as a country north of Magadha. 앙가사치 鴦伽社哆 Aṅgajāta, "produced from or on the body," a son, but intp. as the membrum virile. 앙구사 鴦俱舍 Aṅgūṣa, an arrow, a barbed weapon. 앙아라가 鴦哦囉迦 Aṅgāraka, charcoal ; intp. fire star, the planet Mars. 앙굴(리)마라 鴦崛(利)摩羅 Aṅgulimālya, chaplet of finger-bones ; the Śivaitic sect that wore such chaplets ; also 앙굴마라 鴦堀摩羅 ; 앙굴마라 鴦掘摩羅 ; 앙구리마라 鴦窶利摩羅 v. 앙 央. One converted by the Buddha is known by this name. 앙수벌마 鴦輸伐摩 Aṁśuvarman, a king of ancient Nepal, descendant of the Licchavis, author of the 성명론 聲明論.

앙 仰 Look up, respectful ; lying with the face upward, opposite of 부 俯 ; translit. *ṅ* as in aṅga, cf. 아 我, 아 俄, 아 哦. 앙산 仰山 To look up to the hills ; Yang-shan, name of a noted monk. 앙월점 仰月點 A half-moon on its back, i.e. ⌣, a sign in the esoteric sect.

앙 央 The middle, medial ; to solicit ; ample, vast. 앙굴(마라) 央掘(摩羅) ; 앙구마라 央仇魔羅 ; 앙굴만 央崛鬘 ; 앙굴리마라 盎崛利摩羅 or 鴦崛利摩羅 ; 앙구리마라 盎窶利摩羅 or 鴦窶利摩羅 Aṅgulimālya, Śivaitic fanatics who "made assassination a religious act", and wore finger-bones as a chaplet. One who had assassinated 999, and was about to assassinate his mother for the thousandth, is said to have been then converted by the Buddha.

애 礙 A stumbling-block ; hindrance ; cf. 장 障.

애 哀 Alas! mourn, wail. 애민 哀愍 ; 애련 哀憐 Pity for one in misery. 애아 哀雅 Ai ya! an exclamation of pain, or surprise.

애 愛 Kāma ; rāga. Love, affection, desire ; also used for tṛṣṇā, thirst, avidity, desire, one of the twelve nidānas. It is intp. as 탐 貪 coveting, and 염착 染著 defiling attachment ; also defined as defiling love like that toward wife and children, and undefiling love like that toward one's teachers and elders.

애 藹 Luxuriant, graceful ; translit. *ai.* 애길(지) 藹吉(支) v. 비 毘 ; idem vetāla. 애라벌나 藹羅筏拏 Airāvaṇa, a king of the nāgas ; Indra's elephant ; also elāpattra, v. 이 伊.

애가 愛假 The falseness or unreality of desire.

애갈 愛渴 The thirst of desire, also 갈애 渴愛 thirstily to desire.

애견 愛見 Attachment or love growing from thinking of others. Also, attachment to things 애 愛 and attachment to false views 견 見 ; also emotional and rational.

애견 愛繭 The cocoon of desire spun about beings as a silkworm spins a cocoon about itself.

애견 愛羂 The noose, or net, of desire.

애결 愛結 The tie of love or desire.

애계 愛繫 The bond of love, or desire.

애계 愛界 The realm of desire, or love ; those who dwell in it.

애과 愛果 The fruit of desire and attachment, i.e. suffering.

애귀 愛鬼 The demon of desire.

애근 愛根 The root of desire, which produces the passions.

애독 愛毒 The poison of desire, or love, which harms devotion to Buddha.

애라찰녀 愛羅刹女 The rākṣasī, or female demon, of desire.

애락 愛樂 The joy of right love, i.e. the love of the good.

애론 愛論 Talk of love or desire, which gives rise to improper conversation.

애류 愛流 The flood of desire which overwhelms.

애륜 愛輪 The wheel of desire which turns men into the six paths of transmigration.

애법 愛法 Love for Buddha-truth ; the method of love.

애별리고 愛別離苦 The suffering of being separated from those whom one loves. v. 팔고 八苦.

애석 愛惜 Love and care for ; to be unwilling to give up ; sparing.

애수 愛水 Semen ; also the passion of desire which fertilizes evil fruit.

애신천 愛身天 The heaven of lovely form in the desire-realm, but said to be above the devalokas ; cf. sudṛśa 선현 善現.

애심 愛心 A loving heart ; a mind full of desire ; a mind dominated by desire.

애안 愛眼 The eye of love, that of Buddha.

애어 愛語 Loving speech ; the words of love of a bodhisattva.

애업 愛業 The karma which follows desire.

애에 愛恚 Love and hate, desire and hate.

애연 愛緣 Love or desire as a contributory cause, or attachment.

애연 愛涎 The mouth watering with desire.

애염 愛染 The taint of desire. 애염왕 愛染王 Rāga, one of the 명왕 明王 with angry appearance, three faces and six arms.

애옥 愛獄 The prison of desire.

애욕 愛欲 Love and desire ; love of family. 애욕해 愛欲海 The ocean of desire.

애윤 愛潤 The fertilizing of desire ; i.e. when dying the illusion of attachment fertilizes the seed of future karma, producing the fruit of further suffering.

애자 愛刺 The thorn of love ; the suffering of attachment which pierces like a thorn.

애종 愛種 The seed of desire, with its harvest of pain.

애증 愛憎 Love and hate, desire and dislike.

애집 愛執 The grip of love and desire.

애착 愛著 The strong attachment of love ; the bondage of desire. From this bond of love also arises pity 자비 慈悲, which is fundamental to Buddhism. There is also 애착생사 愛著生死 bondage to rebirth and mortality by love of life, and to be rid of this love is essential to deliverance. 애착미 愛著迷 The delusion of love for and attachment to the transient and perishing.

애하 愛河 The river of desire in which men are drowned.

애해 愛海 The ocean of desire.

애행 愛行 Emotional behaviour, or the emotions of desire, as contrasted with 견행 見行 rational behaviour.

애혹 愛惑 The illusion of love, or desire.

애화 愛火 Love as fire that burns.

액 額 The forehead ; a fixed (number) ; suddenly ; translit. *a* ; v. 아 阿, 안 安, etc. 액상주 額上珠 The pearl on the forehead, e.g. the Buddha-nature in every one.

앵 鸚 Śuka ; a parrot 앵무 鸚鵡. 앵무보 鸚鵡寶 v. 견 甄 14 Kiṁśuka, "a tree with red flowers, said to be the *Butea frondosa*." [Eitel].

야 耶 An interrogative particle ; translit. for *jha, ya* ; 야순 耶旬 ; 야유 耶維 cf. 다비 荼毘 Jhāpita, cremation. 야바 耶婆 Yava, barley ; a barleycorn, the 2,688,000th part of a yojana ; also a measure in general of varying weight and length. 야바제 耶婆提 Yavana, Yavadvīpa, i.e. Java. 야바로길제 耶婆盧吉帝 cf. 관음 觀音 Avalokiteśvara. 야사 耶舍 Yaśas, or 야사다 耶舍陀 Yaśodā. There were two persons of this name ; (1) a disciple of Ānanda ; (2) another who is said to have "played an important part in connection with the second synod." 야수다(라) 耶輸陀(羅) ; 야수다라 耶輸多羅 ; 야수달라 耶戍達羅 Yaśodharā ; the wife of Śākyamuni, mother of Rāhula, who became a nun five years after her husband's enlightenment. She is to become the Buddha Raśmi-śata-sahasra-pari-pūrṇa-dhvaja ; v. Lotus sūtra. Her name was also Gopā, 구파 瞿波 ; 구비야 劬毘耶 is perhaps Gopī.

야 惹 Incite, provoke, irritate ; translit. *j, ja, jña* ; cf. 사 社 ; 사 闍. 야나 惹那 Jñāna, v. 지 智 knowledge, wisdom.

야 夜 Night ; translit. *ya.* 야타발 夜他跋 Yathāvat, suitably, exactly, solid, really. 야차 夜叉 ; 야걸차 夜乞叉 ; 약차 藥叉 ; 열차 閱叉 Yakṣa, (1) demons in the earth, or in the air, or in the lower heavens ; they are malignant, and violent, and devourers (of human flesh). (2) The 팔대장 八大將, the eight attendants on Kuvera, or Vaiśravaṇa, the god of wealth ; those on earth bestow wealth, those in the empyrean houses and carriages, those in the lower heavens guard the moat and gates of the heavenly city. There is another set of sixteen. The names of all are given in 다라니집경 陀羅尼集經 3. See also 라 羅 for rakṣa and 길 吉 for kṛtya. Yakṣa-kṛtya are credited with the powers of both yakṣa and kṛtya. 야마 夜摩 Yama, "originally the Aryan god of the dead, living in a heaven above the world, the regent of the South ; but Brahminism transferred his abode to hell. Both views have been retained by Buddhism." [Eitel]. Yama in Indian mythology is ruler over the dead and judge in the hells, is "grim in aspect, green in colour, clothed in red, riding on a buffalo, and holding a club in one hand and noose in the other": he has two four-eyed watch-dogs. [M. W.] The usual form is 염마 閻摩 q.v. 야마천 夜摩天 Yama deva ; the third devaloka, which is also called 수야마 須夜摩 or 소야마 蘇夜摩, intp. as 시분 時分 or 선시분 善時分 the place where the times, or seasons, are always good. 야마려가 夜摩廬迦 Yamaloka, the realm of Yama, the third devaloka. 야수 夜殊 Yajurveda, "the sacrificial Veda" of the Brahmans ; the liturgy associated with Brahminical sacrificial services.

야 冶 Smelt, melt ; fascinating ; translit. for *ya* in Akṣaya ; also in Yajurveda 야수피타 冶受皮陀 one of the four Vedas.

야 野 The country, wilderness, wild, rustic, uncultivated, rude. 야매니 野寐尼 Yamani, Java. 야보시 野布施 To scatter offerings at the grave to satisfy hungry ghosts. 야간 野干 Śṛgāla ; jackal, or an animal resembling a fox sprite. 야호선 野狐禪 Wild-fox meditators, i.e. non-Buddhist ascetics, heterodoxy in general. 야반승 野盤僧 A roaming monk without fixed abode. 야장 野葬 Burial by abandoning the corpse in the wilds.

약 略 To mark off, define ; abridge, outline, sketch ; summarize in general ; rather, somewhat. 요약 要略 An outline of the important points. 약계 略戒 The first period of general moral law, before the detailed commandments became necessary ; i.e. the first twelve years of the Buddha's ministry.

약 約 Bind, restrain ; agree, covenant ; about. 약기 約機 To avail oneself of opportunity, or suitable conditions. 약교 約教 ; 약부 約部 According to their doctrine or according to their school. 약법 約法 According to the doctrine, or method.

약 若 If ; as, like ; the said ; translit. *j* or *jñ* sounds. 야나 若那 or 야남 若南 ; 야나 惹那 Jñāna, tr. by 지 智 knowledge, understanding, intellectual judgments, as compared with 혜 慧 wisdom, moral judgments ; prajñā is supposed to cover both meanings. 야제자 若提子 Jñātīputra, v. 니 尼 Nirgranthajñāti.

약 藥 Medicine, chemicals. 약상보살 藥上菩薩 Bhaiṣajya-samudgata, bodhisattva of healing, he whose office, together with his brother, is to heal the sick. He is described as the younger of two brothers, the elder of whom is the 약왕 藥王 *infra.* 약차 藥叉 Yakṣa ; also 약걸차 藥乞叉

v. 야 夜. 약사 藥師 Bhaiṣajya-guru-vaiḍūrya-prabhāsa ; 약사유리광여래 藥師琉璃光如來 ; 대의왕불 大醫王佛 ; 의왕선서 醫王善逝, etc. The Buddha of Medicine, who heals all diseases, including the disease of ignorance. His image is often at the left of Śākyamuni Buddha's, and he is associated with the east. The history of this personification is not yet known, but cf. the chapter on the 약왕 藥王 in the Lotus Sūtra. There are several sūtras relating to him, the 약왕유리광 藥王瑠璃光 etc., tr. by Hsüan-tsang *circa* A.D. 650, and others. There are shrines of the 약왕삼존 藥王三尊 the three honoured doctors, with Yao-shih in the middle and as assistants 일광변조 日光邊照 the Bodhisattva Sunlight everywhere shining on his right and 월광변조 月光邊照 the Bodhisattva Moonlight, etc., on his left. The 약왕칠불 藥王七佛 seven healing Buddhas are also all in the east. There are also the 약왕십이신장 藥王十二神將 twelve spiritual generals or protectors of Yao-shin, for guarding his worshippers. 약왕십이서원 藥王十二誓願 The twelve vows of the Buddha of Medicine are: (1) To shine upon all beings with his light ; (2) to reveal his great power to all beings ; (3) to fulfil the desires of all beings ; (4) to cause all beings to enter the Great Vehicle ; (5) to enable all beings to observe all the moral laws ; (6) to heal all those whose senses are imperfect ; (7) to remove all diseases and give perfect health of body and mind and bring all to perfect enlightenment ; (8) to transform women into men (in the next rebirth) ; (9) to enable all beings to escape false doctrines and bonds and attain to truth ; (10) to enable all beings to escape evil kalpas, etc. ; (11) to give superior food to the hungry ; (12) and wonderful garments to the naked. 약왕보살 藥王菩薩 Bhaiṣajya-rāja Bodhisattva, the elder of the two brothers, who was the first to decide on his career as Bodhisattva of healing, and led his younger brother to adopt the same course ; *supra*. They are also styled Pure-eyed and Pure-treasury, which may indicate diagnosis and treatment. He is referred to in the Lotus sūtra as offering his arms as a burnt sacrifice to his Buddha. 약왕수 藥王樹 ; 약수왕 藥樹王 The king of healing herbs and trees. 약수왕신 藥樹王身 The body or form which is taken by this bodhisattva at any time for healing the sick. 약초 藥草 Medicine, herbs.

양 羊 Avi, a sheep, goat, ram. 양모진 羊毛塵 The minute speck of dust that can rest on the tip of a sheep's hair. 양석 羊石 An abbreviation for 갈마 羯磨 karma, from the radicals of the two words. 양각 羊角 A ram's horn is used for 번뇌 煩惱 the passions and delusions of life. 양거 羊車 ; 양승 羊乘 The inferior, or śrāvaka, form of Buddhism, v. Lotus sūtra, in the parable of the burning house.

양 養 Poṣa. Nourish, rear, support.

양 陽 The side on which the sun shines, the sun, heat, this life, positive, masculine, dynamic, etc. 양광 陽光 The sun's light, also idem 양염 陽燄 sun flames, or heat, i.e. the mirage causing the illusion of lakes.

양 癢 To itch. 양화자 癢和子 A back-scratcher ; a term for 여의 如意, a ceremonial sceptre, a talisman.

양 禳 To pray to avert ; e.g. 양일식 禳日蝕 ; 양월식 禳月蝕 to avert the calamity threatened by an eclipse of sun or moon. 양재 禳災 Ceremonies to avert calamity, indicating also the Atharva-veda, and other incantations.

양 兩 Two, a couple, both ; an ounce, or tael. 양권경 兩卷經 The two-chüan sūtra, i.e. the 불설무량수경 佛說無量壽經. 양구(여여) 兩垢(如如) The contaminated and uncontaminated Bhūtatathatā, or Buddha-nature, v. 지관 止觀 2 and 기신론 起信論 Awakening of Faith. 양권 兩權 The two temporary vehicles, Śrāvaka and Pratyeka-buddha, as contrasted with the 실 實 complete Bodhisattva doctrine of Mahāyāna. 양하 兩河 The "two rivers," Nairañjanā, v. 니 尼, where Buddha attained enlightenment, and Hiraṇyavatī, see 시 尸, where he entered Nirvāṇa. 양시 兩翅 The two wings of 정 定 and 혜 慧 meditation and wisdom. 양견신 兩肩神 The two recording spirits, one at each shoulder, v. 동명 同名 and 동좌신 同坐神. 양계 兩界 v. 양부 兩部. 양설 兩舌 Double tongue.

One of the ten forms of evil conduct 십악업 十惡業. 양재 兩財 The two talents, or rewards from previous incarnations, 내 內 inner, i.e. bodily or personal conditions, and 외 外 external, i.e. wealth or poverty, etc. 양족존 兩足尊 The most honoured among men and devas (lit. among two-footed beings), a title of the Buddha. The two feet are compared to the commandments and meditation, blessing and wisdom, relative and absolute teaching (i.e. Hīnayāna and Mahāyāna), meditation and action. 양부 兩部 ; 양계 兩界 Two sections, or classes. 양부만다라 兩部曼荼羅 Maṇḍala of the two sections, i.e. dual powers of the two Japanese groups symbolizing the Vajradhātu and Garbhadhātu, v. 금강계 金剛界 and 태장계 胎藏界. 양서 兩鼠 The two rats (or black and white mice), night and day.

양 楊 Willow ; aspen, poplar, arbutus ; syphilis. 양지 楊枝 Willow branches, or twigs, used as danta-kāṣṭha, i.e. for cleansing the teeth by chewing or rubbing. 양류관음 楊柳觀音 Kuan-yin with the willowbranch. 양엽 楊葉 Willow leaves, e.g. yellow willow leaves given to a child as golden leaves to stop its crying, a parallel to the Buddha's opportune methods of teaching.

양황참 梁皇懺 The litany of Liang Wu Ti for his wife, who became a large snake, or dragon, after her death, and troubled the emperor's dreams. After the litany was performed, she became a devī, thanked the emperor, and departed.

어 醧 A potation, or drinking ; a secret or private drinking ; private. 어망대 醧忘臺 The terrace of the potation of forgetfulness, e.g. the waters of Lethe. Also the birds, animals, fish, and creeping things about to be reincarnated as human beings are taken to this terrace and given the drink which produces oblivion of the past.

어 於 At, in, on, to, from, by, than. 어제 於諦 All Buddha's teaching is "based upon the dogmas" that all things are unreal, and that the world is illusion ; a 삼론 三論 phrase. 어휘 於麾 A name for Ladakh. "The upper Indus valley under Cashmerian rule but inhabited by Tibetans." [Eitel].

어 魚 Matsya. Fish. 어토 魚兎 Like a fish or a hare, when caught the net may be ignored, i.e. the meaning or spirit of a sūtra more valuable than the letter. 어자 魚子 Spawn, vast in multitude compared with those that develop. 어판 魚板 The wooden fish in monasteries, beaten to announce meals, and to beat time at the services. 어모 魚母 The care of a mother-fish for its multitudinous young, e.g. Amitābha's care of all in leading them to his Pure Land. 어고 魚鼓 Similar to 어판 魚板.

어 語 Words, discourse, conversation, speech, language ; to say, speak with ; cf. 로 嚕 ruta. 어업 語業 The karma produced by speech. 어의 語義 Rutārtha, word-meaning ; word and meaning. 어언 語言 Abhidhāna. Words, talk, speech ; naming.

억 億 A number varying from the Chinese 100,000 to a Buddhist 1,000,000, 10,000,000, and 100,000,000.

억 抑 Curb, repress ; or. 억양교 抑揚敎 The third of the five periods of Buddha's teaching, as held by the Nirvāṇa sect of China 열반종 涅槃宗, during which the 유마사익 維摩思益 is a attributed to him. 억지 抑止 To suppress, e.g. 억지악사 抑止惡事 suppress evil deeds. 억지섭취 抑止攝取 The suppression or universal reception of evil beings ; pity demands the latter course.

억 憶 To recall, reflect on. 억념 憶念 To keep in mind. 억지 憶持 To keep in mind, to remember and maintain.

언 彥 Accomplished, refined. 언종 彥琮 Yen-ts'ung, a famous monk, translator and writer, A.D. 557~610. 언종 彥悰 Yen-ts'ung, T'ang monk, translator and writer, date unknown. 언달박 彥達縛 Gandharva, v. 건 乾.

언 言 Words, speech ; to speak. 언의 言依 Word-dependence, i.e. that which can be expressed in words, the phenomenal, or describable. 언구 言句 Sentences. 언전 言詮 Words as explaining meaning ; explanation ; 이언전 離言詮 is beyond explanation. 언교 言教 The teaching of Buddha as embodied in words. 언행 言行 Words and deeds. 언어 言語 ; 언설 言說 Words, speech, verbal expression. 언진 言陳 Set out in words, i.e. a syllogism.

얼 蘖 A shrub, tree stump, etc., translit. *g, ga, gan.* 얼리하 蘖哩訶 ; 얼라하 蘖羅訶 Gṛha ; Graha ; the seizer, name of a demon. 얼라바 蘖喇婆 Garbha, tr. 중심 中心 ; the womb, interior part. 얼로나 蘖嚕拏 v. 가 迦 Garuḍa. 얼다타구타 蘖多馱矩吒 Gandhakuṭī, a temple for offering incense (in the Jetavana monastery and elsewhere).

얼 孽 Retribution ; an illicit son ; son of a concubine. 죄얼 罪孽 Sins, crimes.

엄 嚴 Commanding, strict, awe-inspiring, glorious. For 화엄 華嚴 v. Twelve Strokes. 엄정 嚴淨 Glorious and pure, gloriously pure. 엄왕 嚴王, i.e. 묘장왕 妙莊王 in the Lotus sūtra. 엄식 嚴飾 Gloriously adorned.

엄 掩 To cover (with the hand), screen, shut up. 엄토 掩土 To bury, inter. 엄실 掩室 To shut (oneself) in a room, as did the Buddha for meditation. 엄색 掩色 To cover the form, or face, i.e. the death of the Buddha, or a noted monk, referring to the covering of the face.

엄 頷 Translit. *kam* in 엄발라 頷鉢羅 Kambala, a woollen garment, or blanket.

업 業 Karman, Karma, "action, work, deed" ; "moral duty" ; "product, result, effect." [M. W.] The doctrine of the act ; deeds and their effects on the character, especially in their relation to succeeding forms of transmigration. The 삼업 三業 are thought, word, and deed, each as good, bad, or indifferent. Karma from former lives is 숙업 宿業, from present conduct 현업 現業. Karma is moral action which causes future retribution, and either good or evil transmigration. It is also that moral kernel in each being which survives death for further rebirth or metempsychosis. There are categories of 2, 3, 4, 6, and 10 ; the 육업 六業 are rebirth in the hells, or as animals, hungry ghosts, men, devas, or asuras : v. 육취 六趣.

업감 業感 The influence of karma ; caused by karma.

업견 業羂 The noose of karma which entangles in transmigration.

업결 業結 The bond of karma ; karma and the bond (of the passions).

업경 業鏡 Karma-mirror, that kept in Hades reveals all karma.

업계 業繫 Karma-bonds ; karma-fetters. 업계고상 業繫苦相 The suffering state of karma-bondage.

업고 業苦 Karmaic suffering.

업과 業果 The fruit of karma, conditions of rebirth depending in previous karmaic conduct.

업구 業垢 Karma defilement.

업뇌 業惱 Karmaic distress ; karma and distress.

업도 業道 The way of karma. 업도(신) 業道(神) The gods who watch over men's deeds.

업력 業力 The power of karma to produce good and evil fruit.

업륜 業輪 The wheel of karma which turns men into the six paths of transmigration.

업마 業魔 Karma-māras, the demons who or the karma which hinders and harms goodness.

업망 業網 The net of karma which entangles beings in the sufferings of rebirth.

업박 業縛 Karma-bonds ; the binding power of karma.

업병 業病 Illness as the result of previous karma.

업보 業報 Karma-reward ; the retribution of karma, good or evil. 업보신 業報身 The body of karmaic-retribution, especially that assumed by a bodhisattva to accord with the conditions of those he seeks to save.

업부 業簿 The record, or account book, kept by the rulers of Hades, recording the deeds of all sentient beings.

업상 業相 Action, activity, the karmaic, the condition of karmaic action. The first of the three 상 相 of the Awakening of Faith, when mental activity is stirred to action by unenlightenment.

업성 業性 The nature of karma, its essential being ; idem 업체 業體.

업수 業壽 Life, long or short, as determined by previous karma.

업수 業受 That which is received as the result of former karmaic conduct, e.g. long or short life, etc.

업승 業繩 Karma-cords, the bonds of karma.

업식 業食 Karma as nutritive basis for succeeding existence.

업식 業識 "Activity-consciousness in the sense that through the agency of ignorance an unenlightened mind begins to be disturbed (or awakened)." Suzuki's *Awakening of Faith*, 76.

업액 業厄 The constraints of karma ; i.e. restricted conditions now as resulting from previous lives.

업여 業餘 A remnant of karma after the six paths of existence. v. 삼여 三餘.

업연 業緣 Karma-cause, karma-circumstance, condition resulting from karma.

업영 業影 Karma-shadow, karma dogging one's steps like a shadow.

업유 業有 Reality of karma, idem 행유 行有.

업인 業因 The deed as cause ; the cause of good or bad karma.

업장 業障 Karmāvaraṇa ; the screen, or hindrance, of past karma, hindering the attainment of bodhi. 업장제 業障除 A symbol indicating the cutting away of all karmaic hindrances by the sword of wisdom.

업적 業賊 Robber-karma ; evil karma harms as does a robber.

업전 業田 The field of karma ; the life in which the seeds of future harvest are sown.

업종 業種 Karmabīja ; karma-seed which springs up in happy or in suffering rebirth.

업진 業塵 Karma-dirt, the defilement or remains of evil karma.

업처 業處 Karmasthāna ; a place for working, of business, etc. ; the place, or condition, in which the mind is maintained in meditation ; by inference, the Pure Land, etc.

업천 業天 The karma of heaven, i.e. the natural inevitable law of cause and effect.

업체 業體 idem 업성 業性.

업칭 業秤 The scales of karma, in which good and evil are weighed by the rulers of Hades.

업통 業通 Supernatural powers obtained from former karma ; idem 보통 報通.

업풍 業風 Karma-wind (1) the fierce wind of evil karma and the wind from the hells, at the end of the age ; (2) karma as wind blowing a person into good or evil rebirth.

업해 業海 The vast, deep ocean of (evil) karma.

업행 業行 Deeds, actions ; karma deeds, moral action which influences future rebirth.

업화 業火 The fires of evil karma ; the fires of the hells.

에 恚 Hate, anger, rage. 에로 恚怒 Hate and anger. 에결 恚結 The fetter of hatred binding to transmigration.

여 女 Women, female ; u.f. 여 汝 thou, you.

여 與 Give, grant ; with, associate ; present at, share in ; mark of interrogation or exclamation. 여력 與力 To give strength. 여원 與願 To be willing (or vow) to grant.

여 餘 Remains, remainder, the rest, the other ; surplus. 여종 餘宗 ; 여승 餘乘 Other schools ; other vehicles, i.e. other than one's own. 여념 餘念 Divided thoughts, inattentive. 여감자 餘甘子 Āmrapālī, v. 암 菴. 여습 餘習 The remnants of habit which persist after passion has been subdued ; also called 여기 餘氣 ; 습기 習氣 ; 잔습 殘習.

여 如 Tathā, 다타 多陀 or 多他 ; 단타 但他 or 달타 怛他, so, thus, in such a manner, like, as. It is used in the sense of the absolute, the 공 空 śūnya, which is 제불지실상 諸佛之實相 the reality of all Buddhas ; hence 여 如 ju is 실상 實相 the undifferentiated whole of things, the ultimate reality ; it is 제법지성 諸法之性 the nature of all things, hence it connotes 법성 法性 fa-hsing which is 진실지제극 眞實之際極 the ultimate of reality, or the absolute, and therefore connotes 실제 實際 ultimate reality. The ultimate nature of all things being 여 如 ju, the one undivided same, it also connotes 리 理 li, the principle or theory behind all things, and this 리 理 li universal law, being the 진실 眞實 truth or ultimate reality ; 여 如 ju is termed 진여 眞如 bhūtatathatā, the real so, or suchness, or reality, the ultimate or the all, i.e. the 일여 一如 i-ju. In regard to 여 如 ju as 리 理 li the Prajñāpāramitā makes it the 공 空 śūnya, while the Saddharma-puṇḍarīka makes it the 중 中 chung, neither matter nor nothingness. It is also used in the ordinary sense of so, like, as (cf. yathā), e.g. 여환 如幻 as an illusion, or illusory ; 여화 如化 as if transformed ; 여염 如焰 like smoke ; 여운 如雲 like a cloud ; 여전 如電 like lightning ; 여몽 如夢 like a dream ; 여포 如泡 like a bubble ; 여영 如影 like a shadow ; 여향 如響 like an echo.

여거 如去 Tathāgata means both "so-come" and "so-gone," i.e. into Nirvāṇa ; v. 여래 如來 and 다타 多陀.

여거사 女居士 A lay woman who devotes herself to Buddhism.

여국 女國 The woman-kingdom, where matriarchal government is said to have prevailed, e.g. Brahmapura, v. 파 婆, and Suvarṇagotra, v. 소 蘇.

여근 女根 Yoni. The female sex-organ.

여덕 女德 A woman of virtue, i.e. a nun, or bhikṣuṇī. The emperor Hui Tsung of the Sung dynasty (A.D. 1101-1126) changed the term 니 尼 to 여덕 女德.

여래 如來 Tathāgata, 다타아가타 多陀阿伽陀 q.v. ; 달타게다 怛他揭多 defined as he who comes as do all other Buddhas ; or as he who took the 진여 眞如 chên-ju or absolute way of cause and effect, and attained to perfect wisdom ; or as the absolute come ; one of the highest titles of a Buddha. It is the Buddha in his nirmāṇakāya, i.e. his "transformation" or corporeal manifestation descended on earth. The two kinds of Tathāgata are (1) 재전 在纏 the Tathāgata in bonds, i.e. limited and subject to the delusions and sufferings of life, and (2) 출전 出纏 unlimited and free from them. There are numerous sūtras and śāstras bearing this title of 여래 如來 Ju-lai. 여래승 如來乘 Tathāgatayāna, the Tathāgata vehicle, or means of salvation. 여래사 如來使 Tathāgata-dūta, or Tathāgata-preṣya ; a Tathāgata apostle sent to do his work. 여래광명출이환입 如來光明出已還入 According to the Nirvāṇa sūtra, at the Tathāgata's nirvāṇa he sent forth his glory in a wonderful light which finally returned into his mouth. 여래지 如來地 The state or condition of a Tathāgata. 여래실 如來室 The abode of the Tathāgata, i.e. 자비 慈悲 mercy, or pity. 여래상주 如來常住 The Tathāgata is eternal, always abiding. 여래민보살 如來愍菩薩 ; 달타얼다모예저다 怛他孽多母隷底多 The seventh Bodhisattva to the right of Śākyamuni in the Garbhadhātu group, in charge of the pity or sympathy of the Tathāgata. There are other bodhisattvas in charge of other Tathāgata forms or qualities in the same group. 여래응공정변지 如來應供正徧智 Tathāgata Worshipful Omniscient — three titles of a Buddha. 여래일 如來日 ; 보상일 寶相日 The Tathāgata day, which is without beginning or end and has no limit of past, present, or future. 여래신력품 如來神力品 ; 여래수량품 如來壽量品 Chapters in the Lotus sūtra on Tathāgata powers and eternity. 여래무 如來舞 The play of the Tathāgata, i.e. the exercise of his manifold powers. 여래장 如來藏 Tathāgatagarbha, the Tathāgata womb or store, defined as (1) the 진여 眞如 chên-ju, q.v. in the midst of 번뇌 煩惱 the delusion of passions and desires ; (2) sūtras of the Buddha's uttering. The first especially refers to the chên-ju as the source of all things: whether compatibles or incompatibles, whether forces of purity or impurity, good or bad, all created things are in the Tathāgatagarbha, which is the womb that gives birth to them all. The second is the storehouse of the Buddha's teaching. 여래장심 如來藏心 idem 진여심 眞如心. 여래장성 如來藏性 The natures of all the living are the nature of the Tathāgata ; for which v. the 여래장경 如來藏經, 여래장론 如來藏論, etc. 여래신 如來身 Tathāgatakāya, Buddha-body. 여래부 如來部 The court of Vairocana-Tathāgata in the Garbhadhātu group.

여리사 如理師 A title of the Buddha, the Master who taught according to the truth, or fundamental law.

여범 女犯 The woman offence, i.e. sexual immorality on the part of a monk.

여법 如法 According to the Law, according to rule. 여법치 如法治 punished according to law, i.e. 돌길라 突吉羅 duṣkṛta, the punishments due to law-breaking monks or nuns.

여병 女病 Woman as a disease ; feminine disease.

여색 女色 Female beauty — is a chain, a serious delusion, a grievous calamity. The 지도론 智度論 14 says it is better to burn out the eyes with a red-hot iron than behold woman with unsteady heart.

여쇄 女鎖 Woman as chain, or lock, the binding power of sex. 지도론 智度論 14.

여승 女僧 A nun, or 비구니 比丘尼 bhikṣuṇī, which is abbreviated to 니 尼. The first nunnery in China is said to have been established in the Han dynasty.

여시 如是 Evam ; thus, so ; so it is ; so let it be ; such and such ; (as) ... so. Most of the sūtras open with the phrase 여시아문 如是我聞 or 문여시 聞如是 Thus have I heard, i.e. from the Buddha.

여실 如實 Real, reality, according to reality (yathābhūtam) ; true ; the 진여 眞如 chên-ju, or bhūtatathatā, for which it is also used ; the universal undifferentiated, i.e. 평등불이 平等不二, or the primary essence out of which the phenomenal arises ; 여실공 如實空 is this essence in its purity ; 여실불공 如實不空 is this essence in its differentiation. 여실지 如實智 Knowledge of reality, i.e. of all things whether whole of divided, universal or particular, as distinguished from their seeming ; Buddha-omniscience. 여실지자 如實知者 The knower of reality, a Buddha. 여실지견 如實知見 To know and see the reality of all things as does the Buddha. 여실지자심 如實知自心 To know one's heart in reality.

여어 如語 True words, right discourse.

여여 如如 The 진여 眞如 chên-ju or absolute ; also the absolute in differentiation, or in the relative. The 여여경 如如境 and 여여지 如如智 are the realm or "substance," and the wisdom or law of the absolute.

여의 如意 At will ; according to desire ; a ceremonial emblem, originally a short sword ; tr. of Manoratha 말노갈랄타 末笯曷剌他 successor of Vasubandhu as 22nd patriarch and of Maharddhiprāpta, a king of garuḍas. 여의주 如意珠 Cintāmaṇi, a fabulous gem, the philosopher's stone, the talisman-pearl capable of responding to every wish, said to be obtained from the dragon-king of the sea, or the head of the great fish, Makara, or the relics of a Buddha. It is also called 여의보(주) 如意寶(珠) ; 여의마니 如意摩尼. There is also the 여의병 如意甁 or talismanic vase ; the 여의륜 如意輪 talismanic wheel, as in the case of 여의륜관음 如意輪觀音 Kuan-yin with the wheel, holding the pearl in her hand symbolizing a response to every prayer, also styled 지보금강 持寶金剛 the Vajra-bodhisattva with six hands, one holding the pearl, or gem, another the wheel, etc. There are several sūtras, etc., under these titles, associated with Kuan-yin. 여의족 如意足 Ṛddhipāda, magical psychic powers of ubiquity, idem 신족 神足. 여의신 如意身 Ṛddhi, magic power exempting the body from physical limitations, v. 대교 大敎 and 신족 神足.

여인 女人 Woman, described in the Nirvāṇa sūtra 열반경 涅槃經 9 as the "abode of all evil," 일체여인개시중악지소주처 一切女人皆是衆惡之所住處. The 지도론 智度論 14 says : 대화소인시유가근 大火燒人是猶可近, 청풍무형시역가착 淸風無形是亦可捉, 원사함독유역가촉 蚖蛇含毒猶亦可觸, 여인지심불가득실 女人之心不可得實 "Fierce fire that would burn men may yet be approached, clear breezes without form may yet be grasped, cobras that harbour poison may yet be touched, but a woman's heart is never to be relied upon." The Buddha ordered Ānanda : "Do not look at a woman ; if you must, then do not talk with her ; if you must, then call on the Buddha with all your mind" — an evidently apocryphal statement of 문구 文句 8. 여인육욕 女人六欲 The six feminine attractions ; eight are given, but the sixth and eighth are considered to be included in the others : colour, looks, style, carriage, talk, voice, refinement, and appearance, 여인정 女人定 v. 여자출정 女子出定. 여인왕생원 女人往生願 The thirty-fifth vow of Amitābha that he will refuse to enter into his final joy until every woman who calls on his name rejoices in enlightenment and who, hating her woman's body, has ceased to be reborn as a woman ; also 여인성불원 女人成佛願. 여인배 女人拜 A woman's salutation, greeting, or obeisance, performed by standing and bending the knees, or putting hands together before the breast and bending the body. 여인금제 女人禁制 "Women forbidden to approach," a sign placed on certain altars. 여인권속론사 女人眷屬論師 One of the twenty heretical sects, who held that Maheśvara created the first woman, who begot all creatures.

여자출정 女子出定 The story of a woman named Li-i 리의 離意 who was so deeply in samādhi before the Buddha that Mañjuśrī could not arouse her ; she could only be aroused by a bodhisattva who has sloughed off the skandhas and attained enlightenment.

여적 女賊 Woman the robber, as the cause of sexual passion, stealing away the riches of religion, v. 지도론 智度論 14.

여정 女情 Sexual desire.

여천 女天 Female devas in the desire-realm. In and above the Brahmalokas 색계 色界 they do not exist.

역 or **이** 易 Change ; easy. 이행 易行 Easy progress, easy to do. 변역 變易 To change.

역 亦 Also ; moreover. 역유역공문 亦有亦空門 Both reality and unreality (or, relative and absolute, phenomenal and non-phenomenal), a term for the middle school ; Mādhyamika.

역 域 Frontier, limit ; region ; tomb. 역심 域心 ; 역회 域懷 The limits of the mind, natural endowment. 역룡 域龍 Dignāga, Diṅnāga, a celebrated Buddhist philosopher 진나 陳那 author of a famous treatise on logic.

역 譯 To translate, 번역 繙譯 ; 번역 翻譯. An oral interpreter, 전역 傳譯 ; 역관 譯官.

역 逆 Vāma. To go against, contrary, adverse, reverse, rebellious, oppose, resist. 역수 逆修 ; 예수 豫修 To observe in contrary order ; to observe before death the Buddhist rites in preparation for it. 역화 逆化 (The ability of the Buddhas and bodhisattvas) to convert the heterodox or opponents. 역유 逆喩 Argument by illustration from effect to cause, e.g. the source of the ocean is the river, of the river the streams, of these the ponds. 역류 逆流 To go against the current, i.e. the stream of transmigration, and enter the path of Nirvāṇa, also called 예류 預流, the Śrota-āpanna, or śrāvaka first stage. 역연 逆緣 Resisting accessory-cause ; as goodness is the 순 順 or accordant cause so evil is the resisting cause of the Buddha way. 역관 逆觀 The inverse method in meditation. 역방 逆謗 To resist and abuse. 역로가야타 逆路伽耶陀 Vāma-lokāyata ; the Lokāyata were materialistic and "worldly" followers of the Cārvāka school ; the Vāma-lokāyata were opposed to the conventions of the world. An earlier intp. of Lokāyata is, "Ill response to questions," the sophistical method of Chuang Tzŭ being mentioned as comparison. Vāma-lokāyata is also described as Evil questioning, which is the above method reversed. 역순 逆順 The adversatives, resisting and complying, opposing and according with, reverse or direct, backward or forward.

역무(소)외 力無(所)畏 The 력 力 is intp. as the ten powers of a Buddha, the 무소외 無所畏 are his four qualities of fearlessness.

역바라밀 力波羅蜜 The vīrya-pāramitā. 역바라밀보살 力波羅蜜菩薩 One of the twenty-eight honoured ones in the Garbhadhātu group.

역사 力士 ; **역자** 力者 Vīra. A strong or mighty man, hero, demigod. Used for the Licchavi, also 이차 離車 ; 이차 梨車 ; 여차 黎車 ; 율첩반 栗呫嬖. The terms 역사성 力士城 and 역사생지 力士生地 are defined as Kuśinagara.

역생 力生 Power-born ; one who is born from the Truth, a monk.

역자(법사) 力者(法師) A monk who degrades himself by becoming a fighter (e.g. boxer), or a slave.

연 宴 A banquet ; to repose ; at ease. 연좌 宴坐 To sit in meditation. 연적 宴寂 To enter into rest, to die. 연묵 宴黙 Peaceful and silent.

연 年 A year, years. 연기 年忌 Anniversary of a death, and the ceremonies associated with it. 연계 年戒 The (number of) years since receiving the commandments. 연성 年星 The year-star of an individual. 연만수구 年滿受具 To receive the full commandments, i.e. be fully ordained at the regulation age of 20. 연랍 年臘 The end of a year, also a year. 연소정행 年少淨行 A young Brahman.

연 衍 Overflow, inundate ; abundant ; ample ; superfluous ; fertile ; used in 마하연 摩訶衍 Mahāyāna. 연문 衍門 The ample door, school, or way, the Mahāyāna.

연 緣 Pratyaya means conviction, reliance, but with Buddhists especially it means "a co-operating cause, the concurrent occasion of an event as distinguished from its proximate cause." [M. W.] It is the circumstantial, conditioning, or secondary cause, in contrast with 인 因 hetu, the direct or fundamental cause. Hetu is as the seed, pratyaya the soil, rain, sunshine, etc. To reason, conclude. To climb, lay hold of. The mind 능연 能緣 can reason, the objective is 소연 所緣, the two in contact constitute the reasoning process. The four kinds of causes are 인연 因緣 ; 차제연 次第緣 ; 연연 緣緣, and 증상연 增上緣 q.v.

연 延 Prolong, prolonged, delay ; invite. 연년 延年 ; 연수 延壽 ; 연명 延命 Prolonged life. 연년전수 延年轉壽 Prolonged years and returning anniversaries. 연명법 延命法 Methods of worship of the 연명보살 延命菩薩 life-prolonging bodhisattvas to increase length of life ; these bodhisattvas are 보현 普賢 ; 금강살타 金剛薩埵 ; 지장 地藏 ; 관음 觀音, and others. 연촉겁지 延促劫智 Buddha-wisdom, which surmounts all extending or shrinking kalpas, v. 겁파 劫波. 연수 延壽 Prolonged life, the name of Yen-shou, a noted Hangchow (or Hangzhou) monk of the Sung dynasty. 연수당 延壽堂 The hall or room into which a dying person is taken to enter upon his "long life." 연경사 延慶寺 Yen-ch'ing ssŭ, the monastery in which is the ancient lecture hall of T'ien-t'ai at 사명산 四明山 Ssŭ-ming Shan in Chekiang.

연 椽 Rafters.

연 烟 Smoke ; also tobacco, opium. 연개 烟蓋 Smoke (of incense) like a canopy.

연 煙 Smoke, tobacco, opium. 연개 煙蓋 A smoke cover, i.e. a cloud of incense.

연 輭 Soft, yielding, pliant, supple. 연적 輭賊 Treacherous thieves, i.e. fame and gain, which injure the aspiration of the religious man.

연 軟 Soft, yielding. 연어 軟語 Soft or gentle words adapted to the feelings of men.

연 綖 The threads of beads or gems which hang, front and back, from the ceremonial square cap. 연경 綖經 or 선경 線經 A sūtra, or sūtras.

연 戀 To be fond of, hanker after, cleave to ; 연모 戀慕.

연 然 To burn, simmer ; so, yes ; but, however. 연등불 然燈佛 Dīpaṃkara Buddha, the twenty-fourth predecessor of Śākyamuni, who always appears when a Buddha preaches the gospel found in the Lotus Sūtra, in which sūtra he is an important hearer ; also 정광 錠光 ; 제원갈 提洹竭 or 제화갈 提和竭 ; 대화갈라 大和竭羅.

연 演 To extend, expound, practise, perform. 연창 演暢 To expound and make clear. 연약(달다) 演若(達多) Yajñadatta, "obtained from sacrifice," a crazy man who saw his eyebrows and eyes in a mirror but not seeing them in his own head thought himself bedevilled ; the eyes and head are a symbol of 정성 正性 reality, those in the mirror of 망상 妄相 unreality. 연설 演說 To expound, dilate upon, discourse.

연 燃 To set fire to, light, burn ; idem 연 然 q.v.

연 蠕 Wrigglers, crawlers, e.g. worms. 연동 蠕動 To wriggle, etc.

연각 緣覺 Pratyeka-buddha 벽지불 辟支佛 ; 벽지가불 辟支迦佛 ; 발랄예가(불)타 鉢剌翳伽(佛)陀. In the early translations it was rendered 연각 緣覺, i.e. enlightened through reasoning on the riddle of life, especially as defined in the twelve nidānas. Later it was rendered 독각 獨覺 or individual enlightenment, i.e. one who lives apart from others and attains enlightenment alone, or for himself, in contrast with the altruism of the bodhi-sattva principle. The term pratyeka-buddha is not limited to Buddhists, but is also general for recluses pondering alone over the meaning of life, an illustration being the rhinoceros, which lives in isolation. The non-Buddhist enlightenment is illusion, e.g. from observing the "flying flowers and falling leaves" ; the Buddhist enlightenment arises from pondering over the twelve nidānas. As a degree of saintship it is undefined by early Buddhism, receiving its definition at a later period. 연각승 緣覺乘 The "middle conveyance" period, characterized as that of the pratyeka-buddha, who is enlightened by the twelve nidānas ; it is considered as an advance on the Hīnayāna, cf. śrāvaka, but not yet the standard of the altruistic bodhisattva-vehicle, the Mahāyāna. 연각법계 緣覺法界 The pratyeka-buddha realm, one of the ten T'ien-t'ai categories of intelligent beings. 연각보리 緣覺菩提 The pratyeka-buddha form of enlightenment, for self. 연각신 緣覺身 The pratyeka-buddha or personal appearing of the Buddha.

연관 緣觀 The phenomenal and noumenal, i.e. the observed and the observing, the object and subject.

연기 緣起 Arising from conditional causation ; everything arises from conditions, and not being spontaneous and self-contained has no separate and independent nature ; cf. 연생 緣生. It is a fundamental doctrine of the Hua-yen school, which defines four principal uses of the term: (1) 업감연기 業感緣起 that of the Hīnayāna, i.e. under the influence of karma the conditions of reincarnation arise ; (2) 뢰야연기 賴耶緣起 that of the primitive Mahāyāna school, i.e. that all things arise from the Ālaya, or 장 藏 fundamental store ; (3) 여래장연기 如來藏緣起 that of the advancing Mahāyāna, that all things arise from the Tathāgata-garbha, or bhūtatathatā ; (4) 법계연기 法界緣起 that of complete Mahāyāna, in which one is all and all are one, each being a universal cause. 연기법 緣起法 Pratītya-samutpāda ; idem 십이연기 十二緣起, i.e. the twelve nidānas, cf. 십이인연 十二因緣. 연기게 緣起偈 ; 연기(법)송 緣起(法)頌 The gāthā of three of the four fundamental dogmas of Buddhism ; that all is suffering, that suffering is intensified by desire, and that extinction of desire is practicable. This is found in the 지도론 智度論. It is also called 연기법송 緣起法頌. It is placed in the foundations of pagodas and inside of images of Buddha and so is called 법신게 法身偈 dharmakāya gāthā.

연기 緣機 Conditions opportune ; favourable circumstances ; cause and conditions co-operating for achieving Buddhahood.

연념 緣念 ; 연상 緣想 Thoughts arising from environment, similar to 연심 緣心.

연담 유일 蓮潭有一 Yeon-dam Yu-il(1720-1799). A monk of the Joseon dynasty in Korea.

연독 身毒 Sindhu, Scinde, v. 인도 印度.

연려심 緣慮心 The rational cogitating mind ; also 여지심 慮知心 the cogitating perceiving mind.

연력 緣力 Pratyaya-bala ; the power of the conditioning cause, circumstance, or contributing environment, in contrast with the 인력 因力 direct cause.

연리 緣理 To study, or reason on fundamental principles ; to contemplate ultimate reality, cf. 연사 緣事. 연리단구 緣理斷九 By the consideration of the tenth realm only, i.e. the Buddha-realm, to cut off the illusion of the nine other realms of time and sense.

연불 緣佛 A deceased relative or friend, i.e. a Buddha connected with me.

연비 燃臂 Making a small burn on the arm (done during precept ceremonies).

연사 緣事 To lay hold of, or study things or phenomena, in contrast to principles or noumena, cf. 연리 緣理 ; meditation on the Buddha's nirmāṇakāya and sambhogakāya, in contrast with the dharmakāya.

연상 緣相 Reasoning, mentality, the mind.

연생 緣生 Produced by causal conditions. The twelve nidānas are also called 십이연생 十二緣生. Cf. 연기 緣起.

연성 緣成 The phenomenal, whatever is produced by causal conditions.

연심 緣心 The conditioned mind, the mind held by the phenomenal.

연연 緣緣 The reasoning mind, or the mind reasoning, intelligence in contact with its object ; later termed 소연연 所緣緣, i.e. 소연 所緣 being the object and 연 緣 the mind ; the relationship being like that of form or colour to the eye.

연인 緣因 Developing cause, i.e. development of the fundamental Buddha-nature, cf. 연정 緣正.

연일 緣日 The day of the month on which a particular Buddha or bodhisattva is worshipped, he being in special charge of mundane affairs on that day, e.g. the 5th is Maitreya, 15th Amitābha, 25th Mañjuśrī, 30th Śākyamuni.

연정 緣正 Conditioned and fundamental ; 정 正 refers to the Buddha-nature, the bhūtatathatā 정인불성 正因佛性 ; 연 緣 to the Buddha-nature in all undergoing development 연인불성 緣因佛性.

연중 緣中 The place or idea on which the mind is centralized.

연지 燃指 Burning off a finger to show that one will strive only for enlightenment, disregarding even one's attachment to the body, in Korea. Usually the fourth finger of the left hand.

연진 緣塵 The guṇas, qualities, or sense-data which cause the six sensations of form, sound, odour, taste, touch, and thought.

연화 緣化 To convert or instruct those under influence.

열 涅 ; **열** 湼 Black mud at the bottom of a pool ; muddy ; to blacken, defile ; the first form is more correct, but the second is more common.

열 閱 Examine, inspect, look over. 열장 閱藏 To examine (and dust) the scriptures, or library. 열차 閱叉 Yakṣa, v. 야 夜. 열두단 閱頭檀 Śuddhodana, v. 수 首.

열 劣 Inferior, vicious. 열지 劣智 Inferior wisdom, harmful wisdom.

열 熱 Tap, tapana, tapas. Hot ; to heat. 열뇌 熱惱 Perturbed, feverish, troubled, distressed. 열시염 熱時炎 Mirage, idem 양염 陽炎. 열병 熱病 Fever. 열철지옥 熱鐵地獄 The hell of red-hot iron (pills).

열 悅 To please, pleased. 열중 悅衆 Please all, name for the manager of affairs in a monastery, also called 지사 知事 karmadāna.

열 裂 To rip, split, crack. 열상 裂裳 The torn robe (of Buddhism), i.e. split into eighteen pieces, like the Hīnayāna sects.

열가라 涅迦羅 Niṣkala, without parts ; seedless ; indivisible ; or perhaps niṣkāla, but a short time to live, intp. as 잠시 暫時 a short time, temporary.

열반 涅槃 Nirvāṇa, "blown out, gone out, put out, extinguished" ; "liberated from existence" ; "dead, deceased, defunct." "Liberation, eternal bliss" ; "(with Buddhists and Jainas) absolute extinction or annihilation, complete extinction of individual existence." [M. W.] Other forms are 열반나 涅槃那 ; 니일 泥日 ; 니원 泥洹 ; 니반 泥畔 Originally translated 멸 滅 to extinguish, extinction, put out (as a lamp or fire), it was also described as 해탈 解脫 release, 적멸 寂滅 tranquil extinction ; 무위 無爲 inaction, without effort, passiveness ; 불생 不生 no (re)birth ; 안락 安樂 calm joy ; 멸도 滅度 transmigration to "extinction." The meaning given to "extinction" varies, e.g. individual extinction ; cessation of rebirth ; annihilation of passion ; extinction of all misery and entry into bliss. While the meaning of individual extinction is not without advocates, the general acceptation is the extinction or end of all return to reincarnation with its concomitant suffering, and the entry into bliss. Nirvāṇa may be enjoyed in the present life as an attainable state, with entry into parinirvāṇa, or perfect bliss to follow. It may be (*a*) with a "remainder," i.e. the cause, but not all the effect (karma), of reincarnation having been destroyed ; (*b*) without "remainder," both cause and effect having been extinguished. The answer of the Buddha as to the continued personal existence of the Tathāgata in Nirvāṇa is, in the Hīnayāna cannon, relegated "to the sphere of the indeterminates" [Keith], as one of the questions which are not essential to salvation. One argument is that flame when blown out does not perish but returns to the totality of Fire. The Nirvāṇa Sūtra claims for nirvāṇa the ancient ideas of 상락아정 常樂我淨 permanence, bliss, personality, purity in the transcendental realm. Mahāyāna declares that Hīnayāna by denying personality in the transcendental realm denies the existence of the Buddha. In Mahāyāna final nirvāṇa is transcendental, and is also used as a term for absolute. The place where the Buddha entered his earthly nirvāṇa is given as Kuśinagara, cf. 구 拘. 열반불 涅槃佛 The nirvāṇa-form of Buddha ; also 열반상 涅槃像 the "sleeping Buddha," i.e. the Buddha entering nirvāṇa. 열반승 涅槃僧 Nivāsana, an inner garment, cf. 니 泥. 열반팔미 涅槃八味 The eight rasa, i.e. flavours, or characteristics of nirvāṇa — permanence, peace, no growing old, no death, purity, transcendence, unperturbedness, joy. 열반분 涅槃分 The part, or lot, of nirvāṇa 열반(적정)인 涅槃(寂靜)印 The seal or teaching of nirvāṇa, one of the three proofs that a sūtra was uttered by the Buddha, i.e. its teaching of impermanence, non-ego, nirvāṇa ; also the witness within to the attainment of nirvāṇa. 열반성 涅槃城 The nirvāṇa city, the abode of the saints. 열반당 涅槃堂 The nirvāṇa hall, or dying place of a monk in a monastery. 열반종 涅槃宗 The School based on the 대반열반경 大般涅槃經 Mahāparinirvāṇa Sūtra, first tr. by Dharmarakṣa A.D. 423. Under the 진 陳 Ch'ên dynasty this Nirvāṇa school became merged in the T'ien-t'ai sect. 열반궁 涅槃宮 The nirvāṇa palace of the saints. 열반산 涅槃山 The steadfast mountain of nirvāṇa in contrast with the changing stream of mortality. 열반기 涅槃忌 ; 열반회 涅槃會 The Nirvāṇa assembly, 2nd moon 15th day, on the anniversary of the Buddha's death. 열반월일 涅槃月日 The date of the Buddha's death, variously stated as 2nd moon 15th or 8th day ; 8th moon 8th ; 3rd moon 15th ; and 9th moon 8th. 열반락 涅槃樂 Nirvāṇa-joy or bliss. 열반주 涅槃洲 Nirvāṇa-island, i.e. in the stream of mortality, from which stream the Buddha saves men with his eight-oar boat of truth, v. 팔성도 八聖道. 열반계 涅槃界 Nirvāṇadhātu ; the realm of nirvāṇa, or bliss, where all virtues are stored and whence all good comes ; one of the 삼무위법 三無爲法. 열반첩나 涅槃疊那 Nidhāpana, Nirdahana, cremation. 열반상 涅槃相 The 8th sign of the Buddha, his entry into nirvāṇa, i.e. his death, after delivering "in one day and night" the 대반열반경 大般涅槃經 Mahāparinirvāṇa sūtra 열반경 涅槃經 Nirvāṇa sūtra. There are two versions, one the Hīnayāna, the other the Mahāyāna, both of which are translated into Chinese, in several versions, and there are numerous treatises on them. Hīnayāna : 불반니원경 佛般泥洹經 Mahāparinirvāṇa-sūtra, tr. by Po Fa-tsu A.D. 290-306 of the Western Chin dynasty, [B.N.] 552. 대반열반경 大般涅槃經 tr. by Fa-hsien, [B.N.] 118. 반니원경 般泥洹經 translator unknown. These are different translations of the same work. In the Āgamas 아함 阿含 there is also a Hīnayāna Nirvāṇa sūtra. Mahāyāna : 불설방등반니원경 佛說方等般泥洹經 Caturdāraka-samādhi-sūtra, tr. by Dharmarakṣa of the Western Chin A.D. 265-316, [B.N.] 116. 대반니원경 大般泥洹經 Mahāparinirvāṇa-sūtra, tr. by Fa-hsien, together with Buddhabhadra of the Eastern Chin, A.D. 317 - 420, [B.N.] 120, being a similar and incomplete translation of [B.N.] 113, 114. 사동자삼매경 四童子三昧經 Caturdāraka-samādhi-sūtra , tr. by Jñānagupta of the Sui dynasty, A.D. 589-618, [B.N.] 121. The above three differ, though they are the first part of the Nirvāṇa sūtra of the Mahāyāna. The complete translation is 대반열반경 大般涅槃經 tr. by Dharmarakṣa A.D. 423, [B.N.] 113 ; v. a partial translation of fasc. 12 and 39 by Beal, in his *Catena of Buddhist Scriptures*, pp. 160-188. It is sometimes called 북본 北本 or Northern Book, when compared with its revision, the Southern book, i.e. 남본대반열반경 南本大般涅槃經 Mahāparinirvāṇa-sūtra, produced in Chien-yeh, the modern Nanking, by two Chinese monks, Hui-yen and Hui-kuan, and a literary man, Hsieh Ling-yün, [B.N.] 114 대반열반경후분 大般涅槃經後分 The latter part of the Mahāparinirvāṇa-sūtra, tr. by Jñānabhadra together with Hui-ning and others of the T'ang dynasty, [B.N.] 115, a continuation of the last chapter of [B.N.] 113 and 114. 열반박 涅槃縛 The fetter of nirvāṇa, i.e. the desire for it, which hinders entry upon the Bodhisattva life of saving others ; it is the fetter of Hīnayāna, resulting in imperfect nirvāṇa. 열반성 涅槃聖 Nickname of 도생 道生 Tao-shêng, pupil of Kumārajīva, tr. part of the Nirvāṇa sūtra, asserted the eternity of Buddha, for which he was much abused, hence the nickname. 열반색 涅槃色 Nirvāṇa-colour, i.e. black, representing the north. 열반문 涅槃門 The gate or door into nirvāṇa ; also the northern gate of a cemetery. 열반제 涅槃際 The region of nirvāṇa in contrast with that of mortality. 열반풍 涅槃風 The nirvāṇa-wind which wafts the believer into bodhi. 열반식 涅槃食 Nirvāṇa food ; the passions are faggots, wisdom is fire, the two prepare nirvāṇa as food.

염 拈 To take in the fingers, pluck, pinch. 염우 拈右 ; 염제 拈提 To refer to ancient examples. 염화미소 拈花微笑 "Buddha held up a flower and Kāśyapa smiled." This incident does not appear till about A.D. 800, but is regarded as the beginning of the tradition on which the Ch'an(Zen) or Intuitional sect based its existence. 염의 拈衣 To gather up the garment. 염향 拈香 To take and offer incense. 염어 拈語 To take up and pass on a verbal tradition, a Ch'an(Zen) term.

염 剡 Pointed, sharp. 섬부 剡浮 Jambudvīpa, and Yama, v. 염 閻.

염 閻 A gate, border-gate, hamlet, lane ; translit. *ya, ja* ; cf. 야 夜 ; 염 炎 ; 염 焰 ; 염 燄 ; 염 剡 ; 염 琰. 염파도 閻婆度 A bird in purgatory as large as an elephant, who picks up the wicked, flies with and drops them, when they are broken to pieces. 염마 閻摩 Yama ; v. *infra.* 염마나주국 閻摩那洲國 Yavana, Yamana, the island nation of Java, visited by Fa-hsien and Hsüan-tsang. 염만덕가 閻曼德迦 Yamāntaka, the destroyer ; Śiva, Yama's destroyer ; one of the 명왕 明王 represented with six legs, guardian of the West. 염부 閻浮 ; 첨부 瞻部 Jambu (at present the rose-apple, the *Eugenia jambolana*), described as a lofty tree giving its name to 염부제 閻浮提 Jambudvīpa, "one of the seven continents or rather large islands surrounding the mountain Meru ; it is so named either from the Jambu trees abounding in it, or from an enormous Jambu tree on Mount Meru visible like a standard to the whole continent" ; "the central division of the world" [M. W.] With Buddhists it is the southern of the four continents, shaped like a triangle resembling the triangular leaves of the Jambu tree, and called after a forest of such trees on Meru. 염부단금 閻浮檀金 ; 염부나제금 閻浮那提金 Jāmbūnada-suvarṇa, Jambu-river gold, the golden sand of the Jambu. 염모나 閻牟那 Yamunā, the modern river Jamna. 염왕 閻王 ; 염라 閻羅 ; 염마(왕) 閻魔(王) ; 염마라 閻摩羅 ; 염로 閻老 Yama, also v. 야 夜 ; 염라왕 閻羅王

Yama. (1) In the Vedas the god of the dead, with whom the spirits of the departed dwell. He was son of the Sun and had a twin sister Yamī or Yamunā. By some they were looked upon as the first human pair. (2) In later Brahmanic mythology, one of the eight Lokapālas, guardian of the South and ruler of the Yamadevaloka and judge of the dead. (3) In Buddhist mythology, the regent of the Nārakas, residing south of Jambu-dvīpa, outside of the Cakravālas, in a palace of copper and iron. Originally he is described as a king of Vaiśālī, who, when engaged in a bloody war, wished he were master of hell, and was accordingly reborn as Yama in hell, together with his eighteen generals and his army of 80,000 men, who now serve him in purgatory. His sister Yamī deals with female culprits. Three times in every twenty-four hours a demon pours into Yama's mouth boiling copper (by way of punishment), his subordinates receiving the same dose at the same time, until their sins are expiated, when he will be reborn as Samantarāja 보왕 普王. In China he rules the fifth court of purgatory. In some sources he is spoken of as ruling the eighteen judges of purgatory.

염 炎 Blazing, burning. 염열지옥 炎熱地獄 Tapana, the hell of burning or roasting, the sixth of the eight hot hells, where 24 hours equal 2,600 years on earth, life lasting 16,000 years. 염경 炎經 A name for the Nirvāṇa sūtra, referring to the Buddha's cremation ; also to its glorious teaching. 염점 炎點 Nirvāṇa, which burns up metempsychosis.

염 燄 Flame, blaze ; idem 염 焰 ; 염 爓 q.v. 염구 燄口 Ulkā-mukha. Flaming mouth, a hungry ghost or preta, that is represented as appearing to Ānanda in the 구발염구아귀다라니경 救拔燄口餓鬼陀羅尼經 ([B.N.] 984).

염 焰 Flame, blaze ; nirvāṇa ; translit. *ya*. Cf. 염 炎 ; 염 閻 ; 야 夜. 염혜지 焰慧地 The stage of flaming wisdom, the fourth of the ten Bodhisattva-stages. 염마대화선 焰摩大火仙 Jamadagni, one of the seven ancient sage-ṛṣis. 염마천 焰摩天 Yamadevaloka, the third of the desire-heavens, above the Trayastriṁśas ; also deva Yama, v. 야 夜 ; whose wife is 염마천비 焰摩天妃 in the Yama-maṇḍala. 염왕광불 焰王光佛 The fifth of the twelve shining Buddhas. 염망 焰網 The flaming, or shining net of Buddha, the glory of Buddha, which encloses everything like the net of Indra. 염태 焰胎 The flaming womb, the garbhadhātu which surrounds with light.

염 鹽 Salt ; translit. *ya*. 염천 鹽天 Yama, v. 염 焰. 염모(니)나 鹽牟(尼)那 ; 요우나 搖尤那 The river Yamunā, or Jamna, a tributary of the Ganges. 염향 鹽香 Salt-smell, i.e. non-existent.

염 厭 Satiated ; weary of ; disgusted with. 염세 厭世 Weary of the world ; to renounce the world. 염흔 厭欣 Disgusted with, or rejoicing in. 염구 厭求 Weary of the miseries of earth and seeking deliverance. 염리 厭離 To weary of the world and abandon it. 염매 厭魅 ; 염도귀 厭禱鬼 Vetāla ; a demon appealed to in order to raise a corpse and with it to cause the death of an enemy.

염 染 To dye, infect, contaminate, pollute ; lust. 염구 染垢 ; 염오 染汚 Soiled, contaminated, impure, especially by holding on to the illusory ideas and things of life ; deluded. The kleśas or contaminations of attachment to the pleasures of the senses, to false views, to moral and ascetic practices regarded as adequate for salvation, to the belief in a self which causes suffering, etc. 염심 染心 A mind contaminated (with desire, or sexual passion). 염에치 染恚痴 Lust, anger, stupidity (or ignorance) ; also 음노치 婬怒痴 ; 탐진치 貪瞋痴. 염애 染愛 Polluting desire. 염법 染法 Polluted thing, i.e. all phenomena ; mode of contamination. 염오 染汚 idem 염구 染垢. 염오의 染汚意 A name for the seventh vijñāna, the mind of contamination, i.e. in egoism, or wrong notions of the self. 염정 染淨 Impurity and purity ; the thoughts and things of desire are impure, the thoughts and methods of salvation are pure. 염정불이문 染淨不二門 Impurity and purity as aspects of the total reality and not fundamentally ideas apart, one of the 십불이문 十不二門 q.v. 염정진여 染淨眞如 The bhūtatathatā as contaminated in phenomena and as pure being. 염계 染界 The sphere of pollution, i.e. the inhabited part of every universe, as subject to reincarnation. 염연 染緣 The nidāna or link of pollution, which connects illusion with the karmaic miseries of reincarnation. From the "water" of the bhūtatathatā, affected by the "waves" of this nidāna-pollution, arise the waves of reincarnation.

염마 琰魔 Yama, the lord of Hades ; v. 야 夜. 염마계 琰魔界 Yamaloka, the hells under the earth. 염마왕청 琰魔王廳 Yama's judgment hall. 염마사 琰魔使 His messengers. 염마졸 琰魔卒 His lictors. 염마모나 琰魔母那 ; 염모나 閻牟那 Yamunā, the River Jumna.

염습 染習 Contaminated by bad customs, or habit. 염착 染著 Pollution-bond ; a heart polluted by the things to which it cleaves. 염(색)의 染(色)衣 Dyed garments, i.e. the kaṣāya of the early Indian monks, dyed to distinguish them from the white garments of the laity.

염주 念珠 Prayer beads. Buddhist rosary.

엽 葉 Pattra ; Parṇa ; leaf, leaves. 엽개 葉蓋 A leaf-hat, or cover made of leaves. 엽의관음 葉衣觀音 A form of Kuan-yin clad in leaves to represent the 84,000 merits.

영 瓔 A gem, a necklace. 영락 瓔珞 A necklace of precious stones ; things strung together.

영 榮 Glory, splendour. 영화 榮華 Glory, the glory of life, viewed as transient.

영 迎 Go to meet, receive, welcome. 영접 迎接 To receive, or be received, e.g. by Amitābha into Paradise.

영 嬰 Infant, baby. 영동 嬰童 A child.

영 領 Neck, collar ; lead, direct ; receive. 영납 領納 To receive, accept. 영해 領解 To receive and interpret.

영 永 Perpetual, eternal, everlasting (like the unceasing flow of water). 영겁 永劫 Eternity ; the everlasting aeon. 영생 永生 Eternal life ; immortality ; nirvāṇa is defined as 불생 不生 not being born, i.e. not reborn, and therefore 불멸 不滅 not dying ; 영생 永生 is also perpetual life ; the Amitābha cult says in the Pure Land.

영 影 Shadow, picture, image, reflection, hint ; one of the twelve "colours." 영사 影事 Shadow things, i.e. all things are mere shadows. 영공 影供 Image worship. 영상 影像 Pratibimba. Shadows, reflections, with no real existence or nature of their own. 영향 影向 The coming of a deity, responding, responsive. 영당 影堂 A hall where are the images, or pictures, of objects of worship. 영현 影現 The epiphany of the shadow, i.e. the temporal Buddha. 영호 影護 Like a shadow-guardian, always following like a shadow the substance. 영향중 影響衆 ; 영향중 影向衆 The responsive group in the Lotus sūtra, who came in response to a call, e.g. Mañjuśrī, Kuan-yin, etc.

영서 榮西 Eisai(1141-1215). Founder of the Lin-chi (Jap. Rinzai) Sect of Japan.

예 猊 A fabulous beast like a lion, of extraordinary powers. 예하 猊下 A kind of lion-throne for Buddhas, etc. ; a term of respect like 족하 足下. 예좌 猊座 A lion-throne.

예 翳 A film ; screen ; fan ; hide, invisible ; translit. *e, a.* 예가 翳迦 Eka, one, once, single, unique. 예라발달라 翳羅鉢呾羅 Elāpattra, a nāga who is said to have consulted Śākyamuni about rebirth in a higher sphere ; also, a palm-tree formerly destroyed by that nāga. 예신약 翳身藥 A drug for marking the body invisible.

예 豫 At ease ; beforehand ; prepared, v. 예 預.

예 預 At ease, contented, pleased ; arranged, provided for ; beforehand ; an autumn trip. 예류 預流 According with the stream of holy living, the śrota-āpanna disciple of the śrāvaka stage, who has overcome the illusion of the seeming, the first stage in Hīnayāna. 예미국 預彌國 Yāmī, the land or state of Yama, where is no Buddha.

예 穢 Foul, filthy, unclean, impure. 예거아실지가 穢佉阿悉底迦 v. 색 塞 Svastika. 예토 穢土 ; 예찰 穢刹 ; 예국 穢國 This impure world, in contrast with the Pure Land. 예업 穢業 Impure karma, one of the 삼업 三業 q.v. 예신 穢身 The impure or sinful body. 예적금강 穢迹金剛 The vajra-ruler who controls unclean places. 예식 穢食 Unclean, or contaminated food, e.g. left over, or used by the sick.

예 瞖 Timira, an affection of the eye, eye-film, cataract, dim sight, blindness.

예 瘞 To bury, offer in sacrifice. 예전 瘞錢 Offerings of paper money at the grave.

예 曳 To trail, drag. 예슬지림 曳瑟知林 Yaṣṭivana, v. 장림 杖林.

예불 禮佛 Buddhist services.

오 塢 A bank, wall, entrenchment, dock ; translit. *u*, for which many other characters are used, e.g. 오 烏 ; 우 憂 ; 우 于, etc.

오 伍 A rank of five. 오관왕 伍官王 Wu-kuan Wang, the fourth of the ten rulers of Hades.

오 悟 Awaken to, apprehend, perceive, become aware ; similar to 각 覺, hence 각오 覺悟. 오입 悟入 To apprehend or perceive and enter into (the idea of reality). Name of a Kashmir monk, Sugandhara. 오찰 悟刹 The kṣetra or land of perception or enlightenment. 오인 悟忍 The patience of enlightenment, obtained by Vaidehī, wife of Bimbisāra, "on her vision of Amitābha," also known as Joy-perseverance, or Faith-perseverance ; one of the ten stages of faith. 오도 悟道 To awaken to the truth.

오 晤 Clear ; to meet ; to explain. 오은 晤恩 Wu-ssŭ, founder of the 산외 山外 external school of the T'ien-t'ai, died A.D. 986.

오 汚 Filthy, impure ; to defile. Kleśa ; contamination of attachment to the pleasures of sense, to heretical views, to moral and ascetic practices regarded as adequate to salvation, to the belief in the self, all which cause misery. 오가 汚家 To defile a household, i.e. by deeming it ungrateful or being dissatisfied with its gifts. 오염 汚染 To taint ; taint. 오도사문 汚道沙門 A shameless monk who defiles his religion.

오 午 Noon. 오공 午供 The noon offering (of incense).

오 嗚 Oh! alas! to wail. 오로날라차 嗚嚕捺囉叉 Rudrākṣa, the *Elceocarpus ganitrus*, whose berries are used for rosaries ; hence, a rosary.

오 五 Pañca, five.

오 奧 South-west corner where were the lares ; retired, quiet ; abstruse, mysterious ; blended ; warm ; translit. *au*. 오비가 奧箄迦 Aupayika, proper, fit, suitable.

오 烏 The crow ; black, not ; ah! alas! translit. chiefly *u* ; cf. 우 優 ; 우 盂 ; 울 鬱 ; 우 鄔 ; 오 塢.

오 澳 The south-west corner of a hall where the lares were kept ; secluded, deep, profound, mysterious. 오나 澳那 Kustana, Khotan, v. 우 于.

오 懊 Vexed, distressed ; regret. 오뇌 懊惱 Harassed, uneasy, distressed.

오 汙 또는 汚 Stagnant water, impure ; but it is explained as a torrent, impermanent ; translit. *o* and *u*, and *h*. 오률타 汙栗馱 Hṛd, Hṛdaya, the 심 心 heart, core, mind, soul.

오(종)증상연 五(種)增上緣 ; 오연 五緣 Five excellent causes, e.g. of blessedness : keeping the commandments ; sufficient food and clothing ; a secluded abode ; cessation of worry ; good friendship. Another group is : riddance of sin ; protection through long life ; vision of Buddha (or Amitābha, etc.) ; universal salvation (by Amitābha) ; assurance of Amitābha's heaven.

오(포)외 五(怖)畏 The five fears of beginners in the bodhisattva-way : fear of (1) giving away all lest they should have no means of livelihood ; (2) sacrificing their reputation ; (3) sacrificing themselves through dread of dying ; (4) falling into evil ; (5) addressing an assembly, especially of men of position.

오가(칠종) 五家(七宗) Divisions in China of the 선 禪 Ch'an, Intuitive or Meditative School. It divided into northern and southern schools under 신수 神秀 Shên-hsiu and 혜능 慧能 Hui-nêng respectively. The northern school continued as a unit, the southern divided into five or seven 종 宗, viz. 위앙종 潙仰宗, 임제종 臨濟宗, 조동종 曹洞宗, 운문종 雲門宗, and 법안종 法眼宗 ; the two others are 황룡 黃龍 and 양기 楊岐 or 揚岐. 오가소공 五家所共 What the five classes, i.e. rulers, thieves, water, fire, and prodigal sons, have as their common prey, the wealth struggled for by others.

오각 五覺 The five bodhi, or states of enlightenment, as described in the 기신론 起信論 Awakening of Faith ; see also 오보리 五菩提 for a different group. (1) 본각 本覺 Absolute eternal wisdom, or bodhi ; (2) 시각 始覺 bodhi in its initial stages, or in action, arising from right observances ; (3) 상사각 相似覺 bodhisattva-attainment of bodhi in action, in the 십신 十信 ; (4) 수분각 隨分覺 further bodhisattva-enlightenment according to capacity, i.e. the stages 십주 十住, 십행 十行, and 십회향 十廻向 ; (5) 구경각 究竟覺 final or complete enlightenment, i.e. the stage of 묘각 妙覺, which is one with the first, i.e. 본각 本覺. The 본각 本覺 is bodhi in the potential, 시각 始覺 is bodhi in the active state, hence (2), (3), (4), and (5) are all the latter, but the fifth has reached the perfect quiescent stage of original bodhi.

오간 五慳 The five kinds of selfishness, or meanness : monopolizing (1) an abode ; (2) an almsgiving household ; (3) alms received ; (4) praise ; (5) knowledge of the truth, e.g. of a sūtra.

오간색 五間色 The five compound colours, v. 오색 五色.

오개 五蓋 The five covers, i.e. mental and moral hindrances — desire, anger, drowsiness, excitability, doubt.

오거 五居 idem 오정거천 五淨居天.

오겁사유 五劫思惟 The five kalpas spent by Amitābha thinking out and preparing for his vows.

오견 五見 The five wrong views : (1) 신견 身見 satkāyadṛṣṭi, i.e. 아견 我見 and 아소견 我所見 the view that there is a real self, an ego, and a mine and thine ; (2) 변견 邊見 antargrāha, extreme views, e.g. extinction or permanence ; (3) 사견 邪見 mithyā, perverse views, which, denying cause and effect, destroy the foundations of morality ; (4) 견취견 見取見 dṛṣṭiparāmarśa, stubborn perverted views, viewing inferior things as superior, or counting the worse as the better ; (5) 계금취견 戒禁取見 śīla-vrata-parāmarśa, rigid views in favour of rigorous ascetic prohibitions, e.g. covering oneself with ashes. Cf. 오리사 五利使.

오견고 五堅固 idem 오오백년 五五百年.

오결 五結 The five bonds to mortality : 탐 貪 desire, 에 恚 hate, 만 慢 pride, 질 嫉 envy, 간 慳 grudging. 오결악자 五結樂子 One of Indra's musicians who praised Buddha on a crystal lute ; v. 중아함경 中阿含經 33.

오경 五更 The five night watches ; also the fifth watch.

오경 五境 The objects of the five senses, corresponding to the senses of form, sound, smell, taste, and touch.

오계 五髻 The five cūḍā, topknots or locks, emblems of the 오지 五智 q.v. 오계관 五髻冠 A five-pointed crown with a similar meaning. 오계문수 五髻文殊 Mañjuśrī of the five locks.

오계 五繫 The five suspended corpses, or dead snakes, hanging from the four limbs and neck of Māra as Pāpīyān ; v. Nirmāṇa sūtra 6.

오계(법) 五戒(法) Pañca veramaṇī ; the first five of the ten commandments, against killing, stealing, adultery, lying, and intoxicating liquors. 불살생 不殺生 ; 불투도 不偸盜 ; 불사음 不邪婬 ; 불망어 不妄語 ; 불음주 不飮酒 They are binding on laity, male and female, as well as on monks and nuns. The observance of these five ensures rebirth in the human realm. Each command has five spirits to guard its observer 오계이십오신 五戒二十五神.

오고 五苦 The five forms of suffering : I. (1) Birth, age, sickness, death ; (2) parting with those loved ; (3) meeting with the hated or disliked ; (4) inability to obtain the desired ; (5) the five skandha sufferings, mental and physical. II. Birth, age, sickness, death, and the shackles (for criminals). III. The sufferings of the hells, and as hungry ghosts, animals, asuras, and human beings.

오고(저) 五股(杵) or **오고(금강)** 五股(金剛) ; also 오고 五鈷, 오고 五古, or 오고 五胋 The five-pronged vajra or thunderbolt emblem of the 오부 五部 five groups and 오지 五智 five wisdom powers of the vajradhātu ; doubled it is an emblem of the ten pāramitās. In the esoteric cult the 오고인 五股印 five-pronged vajra is the symbol of the 오지 五智 five wisdom powers and the 오불 五佛 five Buddhas, and has several names 오대인 五大印, 오지인 五智印, 오봉인 五峯印 ; 금강혜인 金剛慧印, 대갈인 大羯印, and 대솔파인 大率婆印, and has many definitions.

오고금강(저) 五鈷金剛(杵) or 오호금강(저) 五胡金剛(杵) or 오고금강(저) 五股金剛(杵) The five-armed vajra, 오지금강저 五智金剛杵 ; 오봉금강저 五峯金剛杵, 오봉광명 五峯光明 ; emblem of the powers of the 오지여래 五智如來 q.v.

오공덕문 五功德門 The five effective or meritorious gates to Amitābha's Pure Land, i.e. worship of him, praise of him, vows to him, meditation on him, willingness to suffer for universal salvation.

오공양 五供養 The five kinds of offerings — unguents, chaplets, incense, food, and lamps (or candles).

오과 五果 The five fruits, or effects ; there are various groups, e.g. I. (1) 이숙과 異熟果 fruit ripening divergently, e.g. pleasure and goodness are in different categories ; present organs accord in pain or pleasure with their past good or evil deeds ; (2) 등류과 等流果 fruit of the same order, e.g. goodness reborn from previous goodness ; (3) 사용과 士用果 present position and function fruit, the rewards of moral merit in previous lives ; (4) 증상과 增上果 superior fruit, or position arising from previous earnest endeavour and superior capacity ; (5) 이계과 離繫果 fruit of freedom from all bonds, nirvāṇa fruit. II. Fruit, or rebirth : (1) 식 識 conception (viewed psychologically) ; (2) 명색 名色 formation mental and physical ; (3) 육처 六處 the six organs of perception complete ; (4) 촉 觸 their birth and contact with the world ; (5) 수 受 consciousness. III. Five orders of fruit, with stones, pips, shells (as nuts), chaff-like (as pine seeds), and with pods.

오관 五官 The five controlling powers, v. 오대사 五大使, birth, old age, sickness, death, and the (imperial) magistrate. 오관왕 五官王 The fourth of the 시왕 十王 judges of the dead, who registers the weight of the sins of the deceased.

오관 五觀 The five meditations referred to in the Lotus 25 : (1) 진관 眞觀 on the true, idem 공관 空觀, to meditate on the reality of the void, or infinite, in order to be rid of illusion in views and thoughts ; (2) 청정관 淸淨觀 on purity, to be rid of any remains of impurity connected with the temporal, idem 가관 假觀 ; (3) 광대지혜관 廣大智慧觀 on the wider and greater wisdom, idem 중관 中觀, by study of the "middle" way ; (4) 비관 悲觀 on pitifulness, or the pitiable condition of the living, and by the above three to meditate on their salvation ; (5) 자관 慈觀 on mercy and the extension of the first three meditations to the carrying of joy to all the living.

오교 五敎 The five divisions of Buddhism according to the Hua-yen School, of which there are two groups. That of 두순 杜順 Tu-shun down to 현수 賢首 Hsien-shou is (1) 소승교 小乘敎 Hīnayāna which interprets nirvāṇa as annihilation ; (2) 대승시교 大乘始敎 the primary stage of Mahāyāna, with two sections the 상시교 相始敎 and 공시교 空始敎 or realistic and idealistic ; (3) 대승종교 大乘終敎 Mahāyāna in its final stage, teaching the 진여 眞如 and universal Buddhahood ; (4) 돈교 頓敎 the immediate, direct, or intuitive school, e.g. by right concentration of thought, or faith, apart from "works" ; (5) 원교 圓敎 the complete or perfect teaching of the Hua-yen, combining all the rest into one all-embracing vehicle. The five are now differentiated into 십종 十宗 ten schools. The other division, by 규봉 圭峯 Kuei-fêng of the same school, is (1) 인천교 人天敎 rebirth as human beings for those who keep the five commandments and as devas those who keep the 십선 十善 q.v. ; (2) 소승교 小乘敎 as above ; (3) 대승법상교 大乘法相敎 as 상시교 相始敎 above ; (4) 소승파상교 小乘破相敎 as 공시교 空始敎 above ; and (5) 일승현성교 一乘顯性敎 the one vehicle which reveals the universal Buddha-nature ; it includes (3), (4), and (5) of the first group. See also 오시교 五時敎. 오교장 五敎章 The work in three chüan by 법장 法藏 Fa-tsang of the T'ang dynasty, explaining the doctrines of the Five Schools.

오구륜 五俱倫 The five comrades, i.e. Śākyamuni's five old companions in asceticism and first converts, v. 오비구 五比丘. Also 오구린 五拘隣.

오구족 五具足 The five complete utensils for worship — two flower vases, two candlesticks, and a censer.

오구파아 烏俱婆誐 Ugra-bhaga, formidable or fierce lord, one of the eight servants of 부동명왕 不動明王 q.v.

오근 五根 Pañcendriyāṇi. (1) The five roots, i.e. the five organs of the senses : eyes, ears, nose, tongue, and body as roots of knowing. (2) The five spiritual organs or positive agents : 신 信 faith, 정진 精進 energy, 염 念 memory, 정 定 visionary meditation, 혜 慧 wisdom. The 오력 五力 q.v. are regarded as negative agents. For 오근색 五根色 see 오색 五色. 오근본 五根本 They are the six great kleśa, i.e. passions, or disturbers, minus 견 見 views, or delusions ; i.e. desire, anger, stupidity (or ignorance), pride, and doubt.

오금 五禁 idem 오계 五戒.

오기 烏耆 Agni, or Akni, an ancient kingdom north of Lop Nor, identified with Karashahr. Also 아기니 阿耆尼 ; 오이 僞夷.

오나함천 五那含天 idem 오정거천 五淨居天.

오납의 五納衣 A monk's garment of patches.

오년대회 五年大會 Pañca (vārṣika) pariṣad, or mokṣa mahā pariṣad, v. 반 般. The ancient quinquennial assembly for confession and exhortation, ascribed by some to Aśoka.

오념문 五念門 The five devotional gates of the Pure-land sect : (1) worship of Amitābha with the 신 身 body ; (2) invocation with the 구 口 mouth ; (3) resolve with the 의 意 mind to be reborn in the Pure-land ; (4) meditation on the glories of that land, etc. ; (5) resolve to bestow one's merits, e.g. works of supererogation, on all creatures.

오다 烏荼 Uḍa, Uḍradeśa, Oḍra, Oḍivisa ; an ancient country of eastern India with a busy port called 절리달라 折利呾羅 Charitrapura (Hsüan-tsang), probably the province of Orissa.

오다연나 烏陀衍那 Udayana, a king of Vatsa, or Kauśāmbī, "contemporary of Śākyamuni," of whom he is said to have had the first statue made.

오단법 五壇法 The ceremonies before the 오대명왕 五大明王.

오대 五大 The five elements – earth, water, fire, wind, and space. v. also 오행 五行 the five agents. In the esoteric cult the five are the physical manifestation, or garbhadhātu, v. 태 胎 ; as being in all phenomena they are called 오륜 五輪 the five evolvers ; their phonetic embryos 종자 種子 are those of the Five Dhyāni-Buddhas of the five directions, v. 오불 五佛. 오대사자 五大使者 ; 오천사자 五天使者 The five dūta, i.e. great lictors, or deva-messengers – birth, old age, disease, death, earthly laws and punishments – said to be sent by Māra as warnings. 오대력보살 五大力菩薩 The five powerful Bodhisattvas, guardians of the four quarters and the centre. 오대존 五大尊 idem 오대명왕 五大明王. 오대형 五大形 The symbols of the five elements – earth as square, water round, fire triangular, wind half-moon, and space a combination of the other four. 오대시 五大施 The five great gifts, i.e. ability to keep the five commandments. 오대명왕 五大明王 The five Dharmapālas, or Law-guardians of the Five Dhyāni-Buddhas, of whom they are emanations or embodiments in two forms, compassionate and minatory. The five kings are the fierce aspect, e.g. Yamāntaka, or the 육족존금강 六足尊金剛 Six-legged Honoured One is an emanation of Mañjuśrī, who is an emanation of Amitābha. The five kings are 부동 不動, 항삼세 降三世, 군다리 軍荼梨, 육족존 六足尊, and 정신 淨身, all vajra-kings. 오대색 五大色 The five chief colours – yellow for earth, white for water, red for fire, black for wind, azure for space (or the sky). Some say white for wind and black for water. 오대관 五大觀 The meditation on the 오대 五大. 오대원 五大院 The fifth of the thirteen great courts of the Garbhadhātu maṇḍala, named 지명원 持明院, the court of the five Dharmapālas. 오대용왕 五大龍王 ; 오류용왕 五類龍王 The five great dragon-kings of India.

오대산 五臺山 Pancaśirsha, Pañcaśikha. Wu-t'ai Shan, near the north-eastern border of Shansi, one of the four mountains sacred to Buddhism in China. The principal temple was built A.D. 471-500. There are about 150 monasteries, of which 24 are lamaseries. The chief director is known as Ch'ang-chia Fo (the ever-renewing Buddha). Mañjuśrī is its patron saint. It is also styled 청량산 淸涼山.

오덕 五德 The five virtues, of which there are various definitions. The five virtues required in a confessor at the annual confessional ending the rainy retreat are : freedom from predilections, from anger, from fear, not easily deceived, discernment of shirkers of confession. Another group is the five virtues for a nurse of the sick, and there are others.

오도 五道 idem 오취 五趣. 오도육도 五道六道 There is difference of statement whether there are five or six gati, i.e. ways or destinies ; if six, then there is added the asura, a being having functions both good and evil, both deva and demon. 오도명관 五道冥官 An officer in the retinue of the ten kings of Hades. 오도장군 五道將軍 A general in the retinue of the ten kings of Hades, who keeps the book of life. 오도전륜왕 五道轉輪王 One of the ten kings of Hades who retries the sufferers on their third year of imprisonment.

오도 五度 The five means of transportation over the sea of mortality to salvation ; they are the five pāramitās 오바라밀 五波羅蜜 – almsgiving, commandment-keeping, patience under provocation, zeal, and meditation.

오도 五刀 The "five swords" or slayers who were sent in pursuit of a man who fled from his king, e.g. the five skandhas.

오동연의식 五同緣意識 One of the four kinds of 의식 意識 q.v. ; the mental concept of the perceptions of the five senses.

오둔사 五鈍使 Pañca-kleśa. 오중체 五重滯 ; 오혹 五惑 The five dull, unintelligent, or stupid vices or temptations : 탐 貪 desire, 진 嗔 anger or resentment, 치 癡 stupidity or foolishness, 만 慢 arrogance, 의 疑 doubt. Overcoming these constitutes the pañca-śīla, five virtues, v. 시라 尸羅 Of the ten 사 使 or agents the other five are styled 이 利 keen, acute, intelligent, as they deal with higher qualities.

오등록 五燈錄 The five Têng-lu are (1) 전등록 傳燈錄 A.D. 1004-8 ; (2) 광등록 廣燈錄 ; (3) 속등록 續燈錄 ; (4) 연등록 聯燈錄, and (5) 보등록 普燈錄 ; the 오등회원 五燈會元 and 오등엄통 五燈嚴統 are later collections.

오락 五樂 The pleasures of the five senses, v. 오욕 五欲.

오락 烏落 Ulak ; Ulag ; a Uigur term meaning horse, indicating relays of post-horses.

오락가전단 烏洛迦旃檀 Uraga(sāra)-candana, serpent-sandal, a kind of sandal wood, used as a febrifuge. 오락가 烏洛迦 ; 오라가 烏羅伽 Uraga, going on the belly, a serpent.

오랄시 烏剌尸 Uraśī, or Uraśā ; anciently in Kashmir, "the region south-west of Serinagur, Lat. 33° 23 N., Long. 74° 47 E." [Eitel]. The Hazāra district.

오력 五力 pañcabalāni, the five powers or faculties — one of the categories of the thirty-seven bodhipākṣika-dharma 삼십칠조도품 三十七助道品 ; they destroy the 오장 五障 five obstacles, each by each, and are : 신력 信力 śraddhābala, faith (destroying doubt) ; 정진력 精進力 vīryabala, zeal (destroying remissness) ; 염력 念力 or 근념력 勤念力 smṛtibala, memory or thought (destroying falsity) ; 정정 正定 samādhibala, concentration of mind, or meditation (destroying confused or wandering thoughts) ; and 혜력 慧力 prajñābala, wisdom (destroying all illusion and delusion). Also the five transcendent powers, i.e. 정력 定力 the power of meditation ; 통력 通力 the resulting supernatural powers ; 차식력 借識力 adaptability, or powers of "borrowing" or evolving any required organ of sense, or knowledge, i.e. by beings above the second dhyāna heavens ; 대원력 大願力 the power of accomplishing a vow by a Buddha or bodhisattva ; and 법위덕력 法威德力 the august power of Dharma. Also, the five kinds of Māra powers exerted on sight, hearing, smell, taste, and touch. 오력명왕 五力明王 idem 오대명왕 五大明王.

오론 五論 idem 오부대론 五部大論.

오류천 五類天 The five kinds of devas : (1) 상계천 上界天 in the upper realms of form and non-form ; (2) 허공천 虛空天 in the sky, i.e. four of the six devas of the desire-realm ; (3) 지거천 地居天 on the earth, i.e. the other two of the six devas, on Sumeru ; (4) 유허공천 遊虛空天 wandering devas of the sky, e.g. sun, moon, stars ; (5) 지하천 地下天 under-world devas, e.g. nāgas, asuras, māras, etc. Cf. 오대명왕 五大明王. 오류성 五類聲 The five groups of five each of the consonants in the syllabary called 실담 悉曇 Siddha. 오류설법 五類說法 The five preachers in the Hua-yen sūtra : the Buddha ; bodhisattvas ; śrāvakas ; the devas in their praise-songs ; and material things, e.g. the bodhi-tree ; v. 오종설인 五種說人.

오륜 五輪 The five wheels, or things that turn : I. The 오체 五體 or five members, i.e. the knees, the elbows, and the head ; when all are placed on the ground it implies the utmost respect. II. The five foundations of the world, first and lowest the wheel or circle of space ; above are those of wind ; of water ; the diamond, or earth ; on these rest the nine concentric circles and eight seas. III. The esoteric sect uses the term for the 오대 五大 five elements, earth, water, fire, wind, and space ; also for the 오해탈륜 五解脫輪 q.v. IV. The five fingers (of a Buddha). 오륜육대 五輪六大 The five are the 오대 五大 five elements, to which the sixth 대 大 is added, i.e. the six elements, earth, water, fire, air and space, and 식 識 intelligence or mind. 오륜(솔)탑파 五輪(率)塔婆 A stūpa with five wheels at the top ; chiefly used by the Shingon sect on graves as indicating the indwelling Vairocana. 오륜관 五輪觀 ; 오륜삼마지 五輪三摩地 A meditation of the esoteric school on the five elements, earth, water, fire, air, and space, with their germ-words, their forms (i.e. square, round, triangular, half-moon, and spherical), and their colours (i.e. yellow, white, red, black, and blue). The five wheels also represent the Five Dhyāni-Buddhas, v. 오지 五智. The object is that 오륜성신 五輪成身 the individual may be united with the five Buddhas, or Vairocana. 오륜제 五輪際 The fifth wheel limit, or world-foundation, i.e. that of space.

오리사 五利使 Five of the ten "runners" or lictors, i.e. delusions ; the ten are divided into five 둔 鈍 dull, or stupid, and five 리 利 sharp or keen, appealing to the intellect ; the latter are 신견 身見, 변견 邊見, 사견 邪見, 견취견 見取見, 계금취견 戒禁取見.

오마 烏摩 Unmada, 우마타 優摩陀 a demon or god of craziness or intoxication. 오마비 烏摩妃 Umā, "flax," "wife of Rudra and Śiva" [M. W.], intp. as wife of Śiva, and as a symbol of 탐 貪 covetousness, desire, Umā being described as trampling Śiva under her left foot.

오명 五明 Pañcavidyā, the five sciences or studies of India : (1) śabda, grammar and composition ; śilpakarmasthāna, the arts and mathematics ; cikitsā, medicine ; hetu, logic ; adhyātma, philosophy, which Monier Williams says is the "knowledge of the supreme spirit, or of ātman", the basis of the four Vedas ; the Buddhists reckon the Tripiṭaka and the 십이부교 十二部敎 as their 내명 內明, i.e. their inner or special philosophy.

오몽 五夢 The five bad dreams of King Ajātaśatru on the night that Buddha entered nirvāṇa — as the moon sank the sun arose from the earth, the stars fell like rain, seven comets appeared, and a great conflagration filling the sky fell on the earth.

오묘 五妙 The five wonders, i.e. of purified or transcendental sight, sound, taste, smell, and touch in the Pure-land. 오묘경계락 五妙境界樂 The joys in the Pure-land as above. 오묘(욕) 五妙(欲) The five creature desires stimulated by the objects of the five earthly senses.

오무량 五無量 The five infinities, or immeasurables — body, mind, wisdom, space, and all the living — as represented respectively by the five Dhyāni-Buddhas, i.e. 보생 寶生, 아촉 阿閦, 무량수 無量壽, 대일 大日, and 불공 不空. 오무간 五無間 The uninterrupted, or no-interval hell, i.e. avīci hell, the worst, or eighth of the eight hells. It is ceaseless in five respects — karma and its effects are an endless chain with no escape ; its sufferings are ceaseless ; it is timeless ; its fate or life is endless ; it is ceaselessly full. Another interpretation takes the second, third, and fifth of the above and adds that it is packed with 죄기 罪器 implements of torture, and that it is full of all kinds of living beings. 오무량업 五無量業 or 오무량죄 五無量罪 The five karma, or sins, leading to the avīci hell, v. 오역 五逆.

오문선 五門禪 idem 오정심관 五停心觀 ; there is also a fivefold meditation on impermanence, suffering, the void, the non-ego, and nirvāṇa.

오미 五味 The five flavours, or stages of making ghee, which is said to be a cure for all ailments ; it is a T'ien-t'ai illustration of the five periods of the Buddha's teaching : (1) 유미 乳味 kṣīra, fresh milk, his first preaching, i.e. that of the 화엄경 華嚴經 Avataṁsaka, for śrāvakas and pratyeka-buddhas ; (2) 낙미 酪味 dadhi, coagulated milk, cream, the 아함경 阿含經 Āgamas, for Hīnayāna generally ; (3) 생소미 生酥味 navanīta, curdled, the 방등경 方等經 Vaipulyas, for the Mahāyāna 통교 通教 ; (4) 숙소미 熟酥味 ghola, butter, the 반야경 般若經 Prajñā, for the Mahāyāna 별교 別教 ; (5) 제호미 醍醐味 sarpirmaṇḍa, clarified butter, ghee, the 법화 法華 Lotus and 열반경 涅槃經 Nirvāṇa sūtras, for the Mahāyāna 원교 圓教 ; see also 오시교 五時教, and v. 열반경 涅槃經 14. Also, the ordinary five flavours — sour, bitter, sweet, pungent, and salty. 오미선 五味禪 Five kinds of concentration, i.e. that of heretics, ordinary people, Hīnayāna, Mahāyāna, and 최상승 最上乘 the supreme vehicle, or that of believers in the fundamental Buddha-nature of all things ; this is styled 여래청정선 如來淸淨禪 : 일행삼매 一行三昧 ; 진여삼매 眞如三昧. 오미죽 五味粥 The porridge of five flavours made on the eighth day of the twelfth moon, the anniversary of the Buddha's enlightenment.

오바라밀 五波羅密 The five pāramitās (omitting the sixth, wisdom), i.e. dāna, almsgiving ; śīla, commandment-keeping ; kṣānti, patience (under provocation) ; vīrya, zeal ; and dhyāna, meditation.

오발도적 五拔刀賊 The five skandhas, idem 오도 五刀.

오방오지 五方五智 The five Dhyāni-Buddhas of the five regions ; see the esoteric 오대 五大. 오방편 五方便 An abbreviation for 오오재편 五五才便, i.e. 이십오방편 二十五方便 ; also the T'ien-t'ai 오방오념불문 五方五念佛門.

오백 五百 Pañcaśata. Five hundred, of which there are numerous instances, e.g. 500 former existences ; the 500 disciples, etc. 오백세 五百世 or 오백생 五百生 500 generations. 오백생무수 五百生無手 A disciple who even passes the wine decanter to another person will be reborn without hands for 500 generations ; v. 범망경 梵網經 下. 오백(대)나한 五百(大)羅漢 500 great arhats who formed the synod under Kaniṣka and are the supposed compilers of the Abhidharma-mahāvibhāṣā-śāstra, 400 years after Buddha entered nirvāṇa (아비달마대비바사론 阿毗達磨大毗婆娑論), tr. by Hsüan-tsang (A.D. 656-9). The 500 Lohans found in some monasteries have various definitions. 오백계 五百戒 The "five hundred" rules for nuns, really 348, viz. 8 바라이 波羅夷, 17 승잔 僧殘, 30 사타 捨墮, 178 단제 單提, 8 제사니 提捨尼, 100 중학 衆學, and 7 멸쟁 滅諍. 오백생 五百生 idem 오백세 五百世. 오백부 五百部 ; 오백소승 五百小乘 ; 오백이부 五百異部 The 500 sects according to the 500 years after the Buddha's death ; 지도론 智度論 63. 오백문(사) 五百問(事) The 500 questions of Mahāmaudgalyāyana to the Buddha on discipline. 오백유순 五百由旬 The 500 yojanas of difficult and perilous journey to the Land of Treasures ; v. the Lotus Sūtra.

오법 五法 Pañcadharma. The five laws or categories, of which four groups are as follows : I. 상명오법 相名五法 The five categories of form and name : (1) 상 相 appearances, or phenomena ; (2) 명 名 their names ; (3) 분별 分別 sometimes called 망상 妄想 ordinary mental discrimination of them — (1) and (2) are objective, (3) subjective ; (4) 정지 正智 corrective wisdom, which corrects the deficiencies and errors of the last ; (5) 여여 如如 the 진여 眞如 Bhūtatathatā or absolute wisdom, reached through the 여리지 如理智 understanding of the law of the absolute, or ultimate truth. II. 사리오법 事理五法 The five categories into which things and their principles are divided : (1) 심법 心法 mind ; (2) 심소법 心所法 mental conditions or activities ; (3) 색법 色法 the actual states or categories as conceived ; (4) 불상응법 不相應法 hypothetic categories, 유식 唯識 has twenty-four, the Abhidharma fourteen ; (5) 무위법 無爲法 has state of rest, or the inactive principle pervading all things ; the first four are the 사 事 and the last the 리 理. III. 이지오법 理智五法 cf. 오지 五智 ; the five categories of essential wisdom : (1) 진여 眞如 the absolute ; (2) 대원경지 大圓鏡智 wisdom as the great perfect mirror reflecting all things ; (3) 평등성지 平等性智 wisdom of the equal Buddha-nature of all beings ; (4) 묘관찰지 妙觀察智 wisdom of mystic insight into all things and removal of ignorance and doubt ; (5) 성소작지 成所作智 wisdom perfect in action and bringing blessing to self and others. IV. 제바오법 提婆五法 The five obnoxious rules of Devadatta : not to take milk in any form, nor meat, nor salt ; to wear unshaped garments, and to live apart. Another set is : to wear cast-off rags, beg food, have only one set meal a day, dwell in the open, and abstain from all kinds of flesh, milk, etc. 오법인 五法人 Followers of the five ascetic rules of Devadatta, the enemy of the Buddha. 오법성신 五法成身 idem 오상성신 五相成身. 오법신 五法身 idem 오분법신 五分法身.

오변 五邊 The five alternatives, i.e. (things) exist ; do not exist ; both exist and non-exist ; neither exist nor non-exist ; neither non-exist nor are without non-existence.

오변행 五遍行 The five universal mental activities associated with every thought – the idea, mental contact, reception, conception, perception, 작의 作意, 촉 觸, 수 受, 상 想, 사 思 ; cf. 오온 五蘊.

오병 五瓶 The five vases used by the esoteric school for offering flowers to their Buddha, the flowers are stuck in a mixture of the five precious things, the five grains and the five medicines mingled with scented water. 오병지수 五瓶智水 The five vases are emblems of the five departments of the Vajradhātu, and the fragrant water the wisdom of the five Wisdom-Buddhas. 오병관정 五瓶灌頂 Baptism with water of the five vases representing the wisdom of these five Buddhas.

오보 五寶 The five precious things, syn. all the precious things. There are several groups, e.g. – gold, silver, pearls, cowries, and rubies ; or, coral, crystal, gold, silver, and cowries ; or, gold, silver, pearls, coral, and amber ; etc.

오보리 五菩提 The five bodhi, or stages of enlightenment : (1) 발심보리 發心菩提 resolve on supreme bodhi ; (2) 복심보리 伏心菩提 mind control, i.e. of the passions and observance of the pāramitās ; (3) 명심보리 明心菩提 mental enlightenment, study, and increase in knowledge and in the prajñāpāramitā ; (4) 출도보리 出到菩提 mental expansion, freedom from the limitations of reincarnation and attainment of complete knowledge ; (5) 무상보리 無上菩提 attainment of a passionless condition and of supreme perfect enlightenment.

오부 五部 The five classes, or groups : I. The 사제 四諦 four truths, which four are classified as 견도 見道 or theory, and 수도 修道 practice, e.g. the eightfold path. II. The five early Hīnayāna sects, see 일체유부 一切有部 or Sarvāstivāda. III. The five groups of the Vajradhātu maṇḍala 오부합단 五部合斷 To cut off the five classes of misleading things, i.e. four 견 見 and one 수 修, i.e. false theory in regard to the 사제 四諦 four truths, and erroneous practice. Each of the two classes is extended into each of the three divisions of past, three of present, and three of future, making eighteen mental conditions. 오부대승경 五部大乘經 The five chief Mahāyāna sūtras according to T'ien-t'ai are : 화엄 華嚴 ; 대집 大集 ; 대품반야 大品般若 ; 법화 法華, and 열반경 涅槃經, i.e. Avataṁsaka, Mahāsaṅghāta, Mahāprajñā, Lotus, and Nirvāṇa sūtras. 오부대론 五部大論 Asaṅga, founder of the Yogācāra school, is said, by command of Maitreya, to have edited the five great śāstras, 유가사지론 瑜伽師地論, 분별유가론 分別瑜伽論, 대승장엄경론 大乘莊嚴經論, 변중변론송 辨中邊論頌, and 금강반야론 金剛般若論. 오부존법 五部尊法 ; 오종단법 五種壇法 ; 오종호마 五種護摩 ; 오종실지 五種悉地. Ceremonials of the esoteric cult for ridding from calamity ; for prosperity ; subduing evil (spirits) ; seeking the love of Buddhas ; calling the good to aid ; cf. 오종수법 五種修法. 오부좌 五部座 The five Dhyāni-Buddhas, v. 오지여래 五智如來. 오부율 五部律 The first five Hīnayāna sects – Dharmagupta, Sarvāstivāda, Mahīśāsaka, Kāśyapīyāḥ, and Vātsīputrīyāḥ ; see 오사 五師. 오부교주 五部教主 The five Dhyāni-Buddhas, v. 오지여래 五智如來. 오부법 五部法 idem 오부존법 五部尊法. 오부정(거염마라) 五部淨(居炎摩羅) Yama as protector in the retinue of the thousand-hand Kuan-yin. 오부비장 五部秘藏 idem 오부존법 五部尊法.

오분 五分 idem 오분법신 五分法身 and 오부대론 五部大論. 오분율 五分律 ; 오분계본 五分戒本 The Mahīśāsaka Vinaya, or five divisions of the law according to that school. 오분법신 五分法身

Pañca-dharmakāya, the five attributes of the dharmakāya or "spiritual" body of the Tathāgata, i.e. 계 戒 that he is above all moral conditions ; 정 定 tranquil and apart from all false ideas ; 혜 慧 wise and omniscient ; 해탈 解脫 free, unlimited, unconditioned, which is the state of nirvāṇa ; 해탈지견 解脫知見 that he has perfect knowledge of this state. These five attributes surpass all conditions of form, or the five skandhas ; Eitel interprets this by exemption from all materiality (rūpa) ; all sensations (vedanā) ; all consciousness (saṁjñā) ; all moral activity (karman) ; all knowledge (vijñāna). The esoteric sect has its own group. See also 오종법신 五種法身. 오분향 五分香 The five kinds of incense, or fragrance, corresponding with the 오분법신 五分法身, i.e. the fragrance of 계향 戒香, 정향 定香, etc., as above.

오분노 五忿怒 The five angry ones, idem 오대명왕 五大明王.

오불 五佛 The Five Dhyāni-Buddhas of the Vajradhātu and Garbhadhātu ; v. 오지여래 五智如來. 오불오신 五佛五身 A Shingon term for the five Buddhas in their five manifestations : Vairocana as eternal and pure dharmakāya ; Akṣobhya as immutable and sovereign ; Ratnasaṃbhava as bliss and glory ; Amitābha as wisdom in action ; Śākyamuni as incarnation and nirmāṇakāya. 오불자 五佛子 Five classes of Buddhists ; also idem 오비구 五比丘 q.v. 오불보관 五佛寶冠 ; 오불관 五佛冠 ; 오지(보)관 五智(寶)冠 ; 오보천관 五寶天冠 ; 보관 寶冠 A Buddha-crown containing the Five Dhyāni-Buddhas. The five Buddhas "are always crowned when holding the śakti, and hence are called by the Tibetans the 'crowned Buddhas'" [Getty]. Vairocana in the Vajradhātu wears a crown with five points indicative of the five qualities of perfect wisdom, etc., as represented by the Five Dhyāni-Buddhas. 오불성 五佛性 The five characteristics of a Buddha's nature ; the first three are the 삼인불성 三因佛性 q.v., the fourth is 과불성 果佛性 the fruition of perfect enlightenment, and the fifth 과과불성 果果佛性 the fruition of that fruition, or the revelation of parinirvāṇa. The first three are natural attributes, the two last are acquired. 오불갈마인 五佛羯磨印 The manual signs by which the characteristic of each of the Five Dhyāni-Buddhas is shown in the Diamond-realm group, i.e. Vairocana, the closed hand of wisdom ; Akṣobhya, right fingers touching the ground, firm wisdom ; Ratnasaṃbhava, right hand open uplifted, vow-making sign ; Amitābha, samādhi sign, right fingers in left palm, preaching and ending doubts ; and Amoghasiddhi, i.e. Śākyamuni, the karma sign, i.e. final nirvāṇa. These mudrā, or manual signs, are from the 유지경 瑜祇經 but other forms are common. 오불정(존) 五佛頂(尊) ; 오정륜왕 五頂輪王 Five bodhisattvas sometimes placed on the left of Śākyamuni, indicative of five forms of wisdom : (1) 백솔(개)불정륜왕 白率(蓋)佛頂輪王 ; 백산불정 白繖佛頂, Sitātapatra, with white parasol, symbol of pure mercy, one of the titles of Avalokiteśvara ; (2) (수)승불정 (殊)勝佛頂 Jaya, with sword symbol of wisdom, or discretion ; (3) (일자)최승불정(륜왕) (一字)最勝佛頂(輪王) ; (최승)금륜불정 (最勝)金輪佛頂 ; 전륜왕불정 轉輪王佛頂 Vijaya, with golden wheel symbol of unexcelled power of preaching ; (4) 화취불정 火聚佛頂 ; 광취불정 光聚佛頂 or 방광불정 放光佛頂 or 화광불정 火光佛頂 ; 고불정 高佛頂 Tejorāśi, collected brilliance, with insignia of authority 여의보 如意寶 or a flame ; (5) 사제불정 捨除佛頂 ; 제장불정 除障佛頂 ; 최쇄불정 摧碎佛頂 ; 제업불정 除業佛頂 ; 제개장불정 除蓋障佛頂 ; 존승 尊勝, etc. Vikīrṇa, scattering and destroying all distressing delusion, with a hook as symbol. 오불정법 五佛頂法 The forms, colours, symbols, etc., of the above. 오불정경 五佛頂經 Abbreviation for 일자불정륜왕경 一字佛頂輪王經. There is also a 오불정삼매다라니경 五佛頂三昧陀羅尼經 translated by Bodhiruci circa A.D. 503. 오불관정 五佛灌頂 Baptism with five vases of perfumed water, symbol of Buddha-wisdom in its five forms.

오불가사의 五不可思議 The five inconceivable, or thought-surpassing things. v. 불가사의 不可思議. 오부정식 五不正食 Five improper things for a monk to eat — twigs, leaves, flowers, fruit, powders. 오불환천 五不還天 idem 오정거천 五淨居天. 오불가과 五不可果 idem 오종아나함 五種阿那含.

오비(밀) 五秘(密) The five esoteric or occult ones, i.e. the five bodhisattvas of the diamond realm, known as Vajrasattva in the middle ; 욕 欲 desire on the east ; 촉 觸 contact, south ; 애 愛 love, west ; and 만 慢 pride, north. Vajrasattva represents the six fundamental elements of sentient existence and here indicates the birth of bodhisattva sentience ; desire is that of bodhi and the salvation of all ; contact with the needy world for its salvation follows ; love of all the living comes next ; pride or the power of nirvāṇa succeeds. 오비(밀)만다라 五秘(密)曼荼羅 or 십칠존만다라 十七尊曼荼羅 The maṇḍala of this group contains seventeen figures representing the five above named, with their twelve subordinates.

오비구 五比丘 The first five of Buddha's converts, also called 오불자 五佛子, Ājñāta-Kauṇḍinya, Aśvajit, Bhadrika, Daśabala-Kāśyapa, and Mahānāma-Kulika, i.e. 교진여 憍陳如 ; 액비 額鞞 ; 발제 拔提 ; 십력가섭 十力迦葉 ; 마남구리 摩男拘利 ; but there are numerous other forms of their names.

오사 五師 The five masters or teachers, i.e. respectively of the sūtras, the vinaya, the śāstras, the abhidharma, and meditation. A further division is made of 이세오사 異世五師 and 동세오사 同世五師. The first, i.e. of different periods, are Mahākāśyapa, Ānanda, Madhyāntika, Śaṇavāsa, and Upagupta ; another group connected with the Vinaya is Upāli, Dāsaka, Śoṇaka, Siggava, and Moggaliputta Tissa. The 동세 同世 or five of the same period are variously stated ; the Sarvāstivādins say they were the five immediate disciples of Upagupta, i.e. Dharmagupta, etc. ; see 오부 五部. 오사자 五師子 The five lions that sprang from the Buddha's five fingers ; 열반경 涅槃經 16.

오사(명) 五邪(命) The five improper ways of gain or livelihood for a monk, i.e. (1) changing his appearance, e.g. theatrically ; (2) advertising his own powers and virtue ; (3) fortune-telling by physiognomy, etc. ; (4) hectoring and bullying ; (5) praising the generosity of another to induce the hearer to bestow presents.

오사망어 五事妄語 The five things fallaciously explained by Mahādeva, as stated in the Kathāvatthu.

오사사 烏沙斯 Uṣas. The dawn, but intp. as the planet Venus.

오사자 五使者 The five messengers of Mañjuśrī, 문수오사자 文殊五使者, 오종금강사 五種金剛使 ; they are shown on his left in his court in the Garbhadhātu group ; their names are (1) Keśinī 계설니 髻設尼 or 計設尼 ; 계실니 繼室尼. (2) Upakeśinī 우파계설니 鄔波計設尼 ; 오파계시니 烏波髻施儞 or 烏波髻施尼 ; 우파계설니 優婆計設尼. (3) Citrā 질다나 質多羅 or 질달나 質怛羅. (4) Vasumatī, tr. 혜 慧 and 재혜 財慧 ; 부소마지 嚩蘇摩底. (5) Ākarṣaṇī, tr. 청소 請召, 조소 鉤召 and 초소 招召 ; 아갈사니 阿羯沙尼.

오산 五山 Five mountains and monasteries : (1) in India, sacred because of their connection with the Buddha : 비파라발노 鞞婆羅跋怒 Vaibhāra-vana ; 살다반나구가 薩多般那求呵 Saptaparṇaguhā ; 인다라세라구가 因陀羅勢羅求呵 Indraśailaguhā ; 살파서혼직가발파라 薩簸恕魂直迦鉢婆羅 Sarpiṣkuṇḍaika-pravara ; 기사굴 耆闍崛 Gṛdhrakūṭa ; (2) in China, established during the Five Dynasties and the Southern Sung dynasty, on the analogy of those in India ; three at Hangchow at 경산 徑山 Ching Shan, 북산 北山 Pei Shan, and 남산 南山 Nan Shan and two at Ningpo at 아육왕산 阿育王山 King Aśoka Shan and 태백산 太白山 T'ai Po Shan. Later the Yüan dynasty established one at 금릉 金陵 Chin Ling, the 천계대룡상척경사 天界大龍翔隻慶寺 which became chief of these under the Ming dynasty.

오삼팔이 五三八二 Five, three, eight, two, a summary of the tenets of the 법상 法相 school, 오법 五法, 삼성 三性, 팔식 八識, and 이무아 二無我 q.v.

오상 五相 idem 오상성신 五相成身 and 오쇠 五衰. 오상성신(관) 五相成身(觀) A contemplation of the five stages in Vairocana Buddhahood — entry into the bodhi-mind ; maintenance of it ; attainment of the diamond mind ; realization of the diamond embodiment ; and perfect attainment of Buddhahood. It refers also to the 오지 五智 of the Vairocana group ; also 오전성신 五轉成身 or 오법성신 五法成身.

오상분결 五上分結 The five higher bonds of desire still existing in the upper realms, i.e. in both the form and formless realms.

오색 五色 The five primary colours, also called 오정색색 五正色色 or 오대색색 五大色色 : 청 靑 blue, 황 黃 yellow, 적 赤 red, 백 白 white, 흑 黑 black. The 오간색 五間色 or compound colours are 비 緋 crimson, 홍 紅 scarlet, 자 紫 purple, 녹 綠 green, 유황 硫黃 brown. The two sects correspond to the cardinal points as follows : east, blue and green ; west, white and crimson ; south, red and scarlet ; north, black and purple ; and centre, yellow and brown. The five are permutated in various ways to represent various ideas. The 오근색 五根色 are : faith, white ; zeal, red ; memory, yellow ; meditation, blue ; and wisdom, black. These are represented *inter alia* in the 오색선 五色線 or 오색루 五色縷 or 오색정 五色綎 or 오색승 五色繩 the five-coloured emblematic cord ; this cord is also a Brahman's sign worn on the shoulder and forbidden by the Buddha.

오생 五生 Five rebirths, i.e. five states, or conditions of a bodhisattva's rebirth : (1) to stay calamities, e.g. by sacrificing himself ; (2) in any class that may need him ; (3) in superior condition, handsome, wealthy, or noble ; (4) in various grades of kingship ; (5) final rebirth before Buddhahood ; v. 유가론 瑜伽論 4.

오선 五善 The five good (things), i.e. the first five commandments.

오선제라 五扇提羅 idem 오천제라 五闡提羅.

오설 五說 idem 오종설인 五種說人.

오섭론 五攝論 A śāstra of Asaṅga 무착 無着, also tr. as the 섭대승론 攝大乘論, giving a description of Mahāyāna doctrine ; Vasubandhu prepared a summary of it ; tr. by 무성 無性 Wu-hsing. Translations were also made by Paramārtha and Hsüan-tsang ; other versions and treatises under various names exist.

오성 五聲 idem 오음 五音.

오성 五性 The five different natures as grouped by the 법상종 法相宗 Dharmalakṣaṇa sect ; of these the first and second, while able to attain to non-return to mortality, are unable to reach Buddhahood ; of the fourth some may, others may not reach it ; the fifth will be reborn as devas or men : (1) śrāvakas for arhats ; (2) pratyeka-buddhas for pratyeka-buddhahood ; (3) bodhisattvas for Buddhahood ; (4) indefinite ; (5) outsiders who have not the Buddha-mind. The 원각경 圓覺經 has another group, i.e. the natures of (1) ordinary good people ; (2) śrāvakas and pratyeka-buddhas ; (3) bodhisattvas ; (4) indefinite ; (5) heretics. 오성종 五性宗 idem 법상종 法相宗.

오성 五星 The five planets, Jupiter, Mars, Saturn, Venus, and Mercury ; also 오집 五執.

오성음고 五盛陰苦 The mental and physical sufferings arising from the full-orbed activities of the skandhas 오음 五陰, one of the eight sufferings ; also 오음성(고) 五陰盛(苦).

오소 五燒 The five burnings, or 오통 五痛 five pains, i.e. infraction of the first five commandments leads to state punishment in this life and the hells in the next.

오소의토 五所依土 The five Buddha-kṣetra, or dependencies, the realms, or conditions of a Buddha. They are : (1) 법성토 法性土 his dharmakāya-kṣetra, or realm of his "spiritual nature", dependent on and yet identical with the 진여 眞如 bhūtatathatā ; (2) 실보토 實報土, i.e. his 자수용토 自受用土 or sambhogakāya realm with its five immortal skandhas, i.e. his glorified body for his own enjoyment ; (3) 색상토 色相土 the land or condition of his self-expression as wisdom ; (4) 타수용토 他受用土 his sambhogakāya realm for the joy of others ; (5) 변화토 變化土 the realm on which his nirmāṇakāya depends, that of the wisdom of perfect service of all, which results in his relation to every kind of condition.

오쇠 五衰 The five signs of decay or approaching death, of which descriptions vary, e.g. uncontrolled discharges, flowers on the head wither, unpleasant odour, sweating armpits, uneasiness (or anxiety) ; Nirvāṇa sūtra 19.

오수 五受 The five vedanās, or sensations ; i.e. of sorrow, of joy ; of pain, of pleasure ; of freedom from them all ; the first two are limited to mental emotions, the two next are of the senses, and the fifth of both ; v. 유식론 唯識論 5.

오순 五旬 Pañcābhijñā. The five supernatural or magical powers ; six is the more common number in Chinese texts, five is the number in Ceylon ; v. 오신통 五神通.

오슬(니사) 烏瑟(膩沙) Uṣṇīṣa, a turban, diadem, distinguishing mark ; intp. as 불정 佛頂 the crown of the Buddha's head ; and 육계 肉髻 fleshy tuft or coif, one of the thirty-two lakṣaṇāni of a Buddha, generally represented as a protuberance on the frontal crown. Also 오슬(니사) 塢瑟(膩沙) ; 오실니사 烏失尼沙 ; 울슬니사 鬱瑟膩沙 or 올슬니사 嗢瑟膩沙.

오승 五乘 The five vehicles conveying to the karma-reward which differs according to the vehicle : they are generally summed up as (1) 인승 人乘 rebirth among men conveyed by observing the five commandments ; (2) 천승 天乘 among the devas by the ten forms of good action ; (3) 성문승 聲聞乘 among the śrāvakas by the four noble truths ; (4) 연각승 緣覺乘 among pratyeka-buddhas by the twelve nidānas ; (5) 보살승 菩薩乘 among the Buddhas and bodhisattvas by the six pāramitās 육도 六度 q.v. Another division is the various vehicles of bodhisattvas ; pratyeka-buddhas ; śrāvakas ; general ; and devas-and-men. Another is Hīnayāna Buddha, pratyeka-buddhas, śrāvakas, the gods of the Brahma-heavens, and those of the desire-realm. Another is Hīnayāna ordinary disciples ; śrāvakas ; pratyeka-buddhas ; bodhisattvas ; and the one all-inclusive vehicle. And a sixth, of T'ien-t'ai, is for men ; devas ; śrāvakas-cum-pratyeka-buddhas ; bodhisattvas ; and the Buddha-vehicle. The esoteric cult has : men, corresponding with earth ; devas, with water ; śrāvakas, with fire ; pratyeka-buddhas, with wind ; and bodhisattvas, with 공 空 the "void". 오승제입 五乘齊入 All the different classes will obtain an entrance into the Pure Land by the vow of Amitābha.

오시팔교 五時八教 A T'ien-t'ai classification of the Buddha's teaching into five periods and eight kinds of doctrine, which eight are subdivided into two groups of four each, 화의사교 化儀四教 and 화법사교 化法四教. 오시(교) 五時(教) The five periods or divisions of Śākyamuni's teaching. According to T'ien-t'ai they are (1) 화엄시 華嚴時 the Avataṁsaka or first period in three divisions each of seven days, after his enlightenment, when he preached the contents of this sūtra ; (2) 녹원시 鹿苑時 the twelve years of his preaching the āgamas 아함 阿含 in the deer park ; (3) 방등시 方等時 the eight years of preaching mahāyāna-cum-hīnayāna doctrines, the vaipulya period ; (4) 반야시 般若時 the twenty-two years of his preaching the prajñā or wisdom sūtras ; (5) 법화열반시 法華涅槃時 the eight years of his preaching the Lotus Sūtra and, in a day and a night, the Nirvāṇa sūtra. According to the Nirvāṇa School (now part of the T'ien-t'ai) they are (1) 삼승별교 三乘別教 the period when the differentiated teaching began and the distinction of the three vehicles, as represented by the 사제 四諦 Four Noble Truths for śrāvakas, the 십이인연 十二因緣 Twelve Nidānas for pratyeka-buddhas, and the 육도 六度 Six Pāramitās for bodhisattvas ; (2) 삼승통교 三乘通教 the teaching common to all three vehicles, as seen in the 반야경 般若經 ; (3) 억양교 抑揚敎 the teaching of the 유마경 維摩經, the 사익범천소문경 思益梵天所問經, and other sūtras extolling the bodhisattva teaching at the expense of that for śrāvakas ; (4) 동귀교 同歸敎 the common objective teaching calling all three vehicles, through the Lotus, to union in the one vehicle ; (5) 상주교 常住敎 the teaching of eternal life, i.e. the revelation through the Nirvāṇa sūtra of the eternity of Buddhahood ; these five are also called 유상 有相 ; 무상 無相 ; 억양 抑揚 ; 회삼귀일 會三歸一 ; and 원상 圓常. According to 유규 劉虯 or 劉虯 Liu Ch'iu of the 진 晉 Chin dynasty, the teaching is divided into 돈 頓 immediate and 점 漸 gradual attainment, the latter having five divisions called 오시교 五時敎 similar to those of the T'ien-t'ai group. According to 법보 法寶 Fa-pao of the T'ang dynasty the five are (1) 소승 小乘 ; (2) 반야 般若 or 대승 大乘 ; (3) 심밀 深密 or 삼승 三乘 ; (4) 법화 法華 or 일승 一乘 ; (5) 열반 涅槃 or 불성교 佛性敎.

오식 五食 The five kinds of spiritual food by which roots of goodness are nourished : correct thoughts ; delight in the Law ; pleasure in meditation ; firm resolve, or vows of self-control ; and deliverance from the karma of illusion.

오식 五識 The five parijñānas, perceptions or cognitions ; ordinarily those arising from the five senses, i.e. of form-and-colour, sound, smell, taste, and touch. The 기신론 起身論 Awakening of Faith has a different set of five steps in the history of cognition : (1) 업식 業識 initial functioning of mind under the influence of the original 무명 無明 unenlightenment or state of ignorance ; (2) 전식 轉識 the act of turning towards the apparent object for its observation ; (3) 현식 現識 observation of the object as it appears ; (4) 지식 知識 the deductions derived from its appearance ; (5) 상속식 相續識 the consequent feelings of like or dislike, pleasure or pain, from which arise the delusions and incarnations.

오신 五身 see 오종법신 五種法身.

오신 五辛 The five forbidden pungent roots, 오훈 五葷 garlic, three kinds of onions, and leeks ; if eaten raw they are said to cause irritability of temper, and if eaten cooked, to act as an aphrodisiac ; moreover, the breath of the eater, if reading the sūtras, will drive away the good spirits.

오신통 五神通 or **오신변** 五神變 Pañcābhijñā ; also 오통(력) 五通(力) the five supernatural powers. (1) 천안(지증)통 天眼(智證)通 divyacakṣus ; deva-vision, instantaneous view of anything anywhere in the form-realm. (2) 천이(지증)통 天耳(智證)通 divyaśrotra, ability to hear any sound anywhere. (3) 타심(지증)통 他心(智證)通 paracitta-jñāna, ability to know the thoughts of all other minds. (4) 숙명(지증)통 宿命(智證)通 pūrvanivāsānusmṛti-jñāna, knowledge of all former existences of self and others. (5) 신통(지증)통 神通(智證)通 ; 신족통 神足通 ; 신여의통 神如意通 ṛddhi-sākṣātkriyā, power to be anywhere or do anything at will. See 지도론 智度論 5. Powers similar to these are also attainable by meditation, incantations, and drugs, hence heterodox teachers also may possess them.

오심 五心 The five conditions of mind produced by objective perception : 졸이심 卒爾心 immediate or instantaneous, the first impression ; 심구심 尋求心 attention, or inquiry ; 결정심 決定心 conclusion, decision ; 염정심 染淨心 the effect, evil or good ; 등류심 等流心 the production therefrom of other causations.

오십공덕 五十功德 idem 오십전전 五十展轉 and 오십전 五十轉.

오십법 五十法 Fifty modes of meditation mentioned in the 대품반야 大品般若 ; i.e. the 삼십칠품 三十七品 bodhi pakṣika dharma, the 삼삼매 三三昧, four 선 禪, four 무량심 無量心, four 무색정 無色定, eight 배사 背捨, eight 승처 勝處, nine 차제정 次第定, and eleven 절처 切處.

오십삼불 五十三佛 Fifty-three past Buddhas, of which the lists vary. 오십삼존 五十三尊 The fifty-three honoured ones of the Diamond group, i.e. the thirty-seven plus sixteen bodhisattvas of the present kalpa. 오십삼지식 五十三智識 ; 오십삼삼 五十三參 The fifty-three wise ones mentioned in the 입법계 入法界 chapter of the Hua-yen Sūtra.

오십소겁 五十小劫 The fifty minor kalpas which, in the 통출 通出 chapter of the Lotus, are supernaturally made to seem as but half a day.

오십악 五十惡 The fifty evils produced by the five skandhas, i.e. 색 色 seventeen, 수 受 eight, 상 想 eight, 행 行 nine, 식 識 eight.

오십오선지식 五十五善知識 similar to 오십삼지식 五十三智識.

오십육억칠천만세 五十六億七千萬歲 The period to elapse between Śākyamuni's nirvāṇa and the advent of Maitreya, 56,070,000,000 years.

오십이위 五十二位 The fifty-two stages in the process of becoming a Buddha ; of these fifty-one are to bodhisattvahood, the fifty-second to Buddhahood. They are : Ten 신 信 or stages of faith ; thirty of the 삼현 三賢 or three grades of virtue, i.e. ten 주 住, ten 행 行, and ten 회향 廻向 ; and twelve of the three grades of 성 聖 holiness, or sainthood, i.e. ten 지 地, plus 등각 等覺 and 묘각 妙覺. These are the T'ien-t'ai stages ; there are others, and the number and character of the stages vary in different schools. 오십이중 五十二衆 ; 오십이류 五十二類 The fifty-two groups of living beings, human and not-human, who, according to the Nirvāṇa sūtra, assembled at the nirvāṇa of the Buddha. 오십이종공물 五十二種供物 The fifty-two kinds of offerings of the 오십이중 五十二衆. 오십이신상 五十二身像 The maṇḍala of Amitābha with his fifty-two attendant Bodhisattvas and Buddhas. Also known as 아미타불오십보살상 阿彌陀佛五十菩薩像 or 오십이존 五十二尊 or 오통만다라 五通曼荼羅 ; said to have been communicated to 오통보살 五通菩薩 in India at the 계두마사 鷄頭摩寺.

오십자문 五十字門 The Sanskrit alphabet given as of fifty letters.

오십전전 五十展轉 The fiftieth turn, i.e. the greatness of the bliss of one who hears the Lotus sūtra even at fiftieth hand ; how much greater that of him who hears at first hand!

오십천공 五十天供 The fifty (or fifty-two) objects of worship for suppressing demons and pestilences, and producing peace, good harvests, etc. ; the lists differ.

오십팔계 五十八戒 The ten primary commands and the forty-eight secondary commands of the 범망경 梵網經.

오아함 五阿含 The five Āgamas, 오아급마 五阿笈摩, i.e. (1) 장아함경 長阿含經 Dīrghāgama ; (2) 중아함 中阿含 Madhyamāgama ; (3) 승육다아함 僧育多阿含 Saṁyuktāgama ; (4) 앙굴다라아함 鴦掘多羅阿含 Ekottarikāgama, and (5) 굴타가아함 屈陀伽阿含 Kṣudrakāgama.

오악 五惡 The five sins — killing, stealing, adultery, lying, drinking intoxicants. Cf. 오계 五戒. 오악견 五惡見 idem 오견 五見. 오악취 五惡趣 idem 오취 五趣 and 오도 五道.

오안 五眼 The five kinds of eyes or vision : human ; deva (attainable by men in dhyāna) ; Hīnayāna wisdom ; bodhisattva truth ; and Buddha-vision or omniscience. There are five more related to omniscience making 십안 十眼 ten kinds of eyes or vision.

오암 烏菴 Om or aum ; cf. 암 唵.

오애 五礙 idem 오장 五障.

오업 五業 The five kinds of karma : of which the groups are numerous and differ.

오여래 五如來 The five Tathāgatas, or Dhyāni-Buddhas, in their special capacity of relieving the lot of hungry ghosts ; i.e. Ratnasaṃbhava, Akṣobhya, Amoghasiddhi, Vairocana, and Śākyamuni ; v. 오지여래 五智如來.

오역 五逆 Pañcānantarya ; 오무간업 五無間業. I. The five rebellious acts or deadly sins, parricide, matricide, killing an arhat, shedding the blood of a Buddha, destroying the harmony of the saṅgha, or fraternity. The above definition is common both to Hīnayāna and Mahāyāna. The lightest of these sins is the first ; the heaviest the last. II. Another group is : (1) sacrilege, such as destroying temples, burning sūtras, stealing a Buddha's or a monk's things, inducing others to do so, or taking pleasure therein ; (2) slander, or abuse of the teaching of śrāvakas, pratyeka-buddhas, or bodhisattvas ; (3) ill-treatment or killing of a monk ; (4) any one of the five deadly sins given above ; (5) denial of the karma consequences of ill deeds, acting or teaching others accordingly, and unceasing evil life. III. There are also five deadly sins, each of which is equal to each of the first set of five : (1) violation of a mother, or a fully ordained nun ; (2) killing a bodhisattva in dhyāna ; (3) killing anyone in training to be an arhat ; (4) preventing the restoration of harmony in a saṅgha ; (5) destroying a Buddha's stūpa. IV. The five unpardonable sins of Devadatta who (1) destroyed the harmony of the community ; (2) injured Śākyamuni with a stone, shedding his blood ; (3) induced the king to let loose a rutting elephant to trample down Śākyamuni ; (4) killed a nun ; (5) put poison on his finger-nails and saluted Śākyamuni intending to destroy him thereby.

오연 五衍 The five Yānas or Vehicles, idem 오승 五乘.

오예 五翳 The five films, or interceptors of the light of sun and moon — smoke, cloud, dust, fog, and the hands of asuras.

오오백년 五五百年 The five periods each of 500 years. In the tenth chapter of the 대집월장경 大集月藏經 the Buddha is reported as saying that after his death there would be five successive periods each of 500 years, strong consecutively in power (1) of salvation, (2) of meditation, (3) of learning, (4) of stūpa and temple building, and finally (5) of dissension. 오오보살 五五菩薩 The twenty-five Bodhisattvas 이십오보살 二十五菩薩.

오온 五蘊 The five skandhas, Pañcaskandha ; also 오음 五陰 ; 오중 五衆 ; 오색건타 五塞犍陀 The five cumulations, substances, or aggregates, i.e. the components of an intelligent being, especially a human being : (1) 색 色 rūpa, form, matter, the physical form related to the five organs of sense ; (2) 수 受 vedanā, reception, sensation, feeling, the functioning of the mind or senses in connection with affairs and things ; (3) 상 想 sañjñā, conception, or discerning ; the functioning of mind in distinguishing ; (4) 행 行 saṁskāra, the functioning of mind in its processes regarding like and dislike, good and evil, etc. ; (5) 식 識 vijñāna, mental faculty in regard to perception and cognition, discriminative of affairs and things. The first is said to be physical, the other four mental qualities ; (2), (3), and (4) are associated with mental functioning, and therefore with 심소 心所 ; (5) is associated with the faculty or nature of the mind 심왕 心王 manas. Eitel gives — form, perception, consciousness, action, knowledge. See also Keith's *Buddhist Philosophy*, 85-91. 오온세간 五蘊世間 or 오음세간 五陰世間 or 오중세간 五衆世間 The worlds in which the five skandhas exist. 오온택 五蘊宅 The abode of the five skandhas — the human body. 오온론 五蘊論 ; 대승오온론 大乘五蘊論 A śāstra by Vasubandhu on the Mahāyāna interpretation of the five skandhas, tr. by Hsüan-tsang ; 1 chüan. Other works are the 오온개공경 五蘊皆空經 tr. by I-ching of the T'ang dynasty. 오온비유경 五蘊譬喻經 tr. by 안세고 安世高 An Shih-kao of the Han dynasty ; both are in the 잡아함경 雜阿含經 2 and 10 respectively ; also 오온론석 五蘊論釋 a commentary by Vinītaprabha. 오온마 五蘊魔 The Māra of the skandhas, v. 오종마 五種魔.

오외 五畏 idem 오포외 五怖畏.

오욕 五欲 The five desires, arising from the objects of the five senses, things seen, heard, smelt, tasted, or touched. Also, the five desires of wealth, sex, food-and-drink, fame, and sleep.

오운 五雲 v. 오장 五障.

오위 五位 The five categories, or divisions ; there are several groups, e.g. (1) Hīnayāna and Mahāyāna have groupings of all phenomena under five heads, i.e. Hīnayāna has 75 법 法 which are 11 색법 色法, 1 심법 心法, 46 심소법 心所法, 14 불상리법 不相離法, and 3 무위법 無爲法 ; Mahāyāna has 100 법 法 which are 8 심법 心法, 51 심소법 心所法, 11 색법 色法, 24 불상인법 不相因法, and 6 무위법 無爲法, (2) The five divisions of 유식 唯識 are 자량위 資糧位, 가행위 加行位, 통달위 通達位, 수습위 修習位, and 구경위 究竟位 or 불위위 佛位位. (3) The five evolutions in the womb are : kalalaṁ, embryo-initiation ; arbudaṁ, after 27 days ; peśī, 37 ; ghana, 47 ; praśākhā, 57 days when form and organs are all complete. (4) Certain combinations of the 팔괘 八卦 Eight Diagrams are sometimes styled 오위군신 五位君臣 five positions of prince and minister. 오위삼매 五位三昧 ; 오종삼매 五種三昧 The five kinds of samādhi : (1) On mortality, the four 선 禪 and eight 정 定 ; (2) śrāvaka on the four axioms ; (3) pratyeka-buddha on the twelve nidānas ; (4) bodhisattva on the six 도 度 and the 만행 萬行 ; (5) Buddha on the one Buddha-vehicle, which includes all others ; v. 오승 五乘.

오유(량) 五唯(量) Pañcatanmātrāṇi, the five subtle or rudimentary elements out of which rise the five sensations of sound, touch, form, taste, and smell. They are the fourth of the twenty-five 제 諦.

오율 五律 The doctrines of the 오부 五部 q.v.

오음 五陰 ; 오중 五衆 see 오온 五蘊. 음 陰 is the older term. 오음세간 五陰世間 idem 오온세간 五蘊世間. 오음(성)고 五陰(盛)苦 idem 오성음고 五盛陰苦. 오음마 五陰魔 idem 오온마 五蘊魔.

오음 五音 The five musical tones, or pentatonic scale – do, re, mi, sol, la ; also 오성 五聲 ; 오조자 五調子.

오의 五衣 The five garments worn by a nun are the three worn by a monk with two others.

오인 五因 The five causes, v. 구사론 俱舍論 7. i.e. (1) 생인 生因 producing cause ; (2) 의인 依因 supporting cause ; (3) 입인 立因 upholding or establishing cause ; (4) 지인 持因 maintaining cause ; (5) 양인 養因 nourishing or strengthening cause. These all refer to the four elements, earth, water, fire, wind, for they are the 인 因 causers or producers and maintainers of the 과 果 infinite forms of nature. Another list from the Nirvāṇa Sūtra 21 is (1) 생인 生因 cause of rebirth, i.e. previous delusion ; (2) 화합인 和合因 intermingling cause, i.e. good with good, bad with bad, neutral with neutral ; (3) 주인 住因 cause of abiding in the present condition, i.e. the self in its attachments ; (4) 증장인 增長因 causes of development, e.g. food, clothing, etc. ; (5) 원인 遠因 remoter cause, the parental seed.

오인 五忍 The five stages of bodhisattva-kṣānti, patience or endurance according to the 별교 別教 : (1) 복인 伏忍 the causes of passion and illusion controlled but not finally cut off, the condition of 십주 十住, 십행 十行, and 십회향 十廻向 ; (2) 신인 信忍 firm belief, i.e. from the 초지 初地 to the 삼지 三地 ; (3) 순인 順忍 patient progress towards the end of all mortality, i.e. 사지 四地 to 육지 六地 ; (4) 무생인 無生忍 patience for full apprehension of the truth of no rebirth, 칠지 七地 to 구지 九地 ; and (5) 적멸인 寂滅忍 the patience that leads to complete nirvāṇa, 십지 十地 to 묘각 妙覺 ; cf. 오위 五位.

오인(도) 五印(度) The five Indias, or five regions of India, idem 오천축 五天竺 q.v.

오인설경 五人說經 v. 오종설인 五種說人.

오자연나 烏闍衍那 Ujjayinī, Ujjain, Oujein, 우선나 優禪那 the Greek Ozēnē, in Avanti (Mālava), one of the seven sacred cities of the Hindus, and the first meridian of their geographers, from which they calculate longitude ; the modern Ujjain is about a mile south of the ancient city. [M. W.]

오작업근 五作業根 The five working organs : the mouth, hands, feet, sex organ, and anus.

오장 五障 The five hindrances, or obstacles ; also 오애 五礙 ; 오운 五雲. I. Of women, i.e. inability to become Brahma-kings, Indras, Māra-kings, Cakravartī kings, or Buddhas. II. The hindrances to the five 역 力 powers, i.e. (self-)deception a bar to faith, as sloth is to zeal, anger to remembrance, hatred to meditation, and discontent to wisdom. III. The hindrances of (1) the passion-nature, e.g. original sin ; (2) of karma caused in previous lives ; (3) the affairs of life ; (4) no friendly or competent preceptor ; (5) partial knowledge. 오장삼종 五障三從 The five hindrances to woman, see above, and her three subordinations, i.e. to father, husband, and son.

오장나 烏仗那 Udyāna, a park or garden ; the park (of Aśoka) ; an "ancient kingdom in the north-west of India, the country along the Śubhavastu ; the Suastene of the Greeks, noted for its forests, flowers, and fruits." [Eitel]. Also 오장나 烏杖那 ; 오장 烏場 ; 오장 烏萇 ; 오손 烏孫 ; 오니야낭 烏儞也曩 ; 오기연나 烏耆延那 said to be the present Yūsufzai.

오전 五箭 The five arrows, i.e. the five desires 오욕 五欲.

오전 五轉 The five evolutions, or developments : (1) resolve on Buddhahood ; (2) observance of the rules ; (3) attainment of enlightenment ; (4) of nirvāṇa ; (5) of power to aid others according to need. 오전성신 五轉成身 idem 오상성신 五相成身. 오전색 五轉色 The above five developments are given the colours respectively of yellow, red, white, black, and blue (or green), each colour being symbolic, e.g. yellow of Vairocana, red of Mañjuśrī, etc.

오전 五專 The five special things, or five devotions, observance of any one of which, according to the Japanese 진 眞 Shin sect, ensures rebirth in the Pure-land ; they are 전례 專禮, 오독 五讀, 오관 五觀, 오명 五名, or 오찬탄 五讚嘆 either worship, reading, meditation, invocation, or praise.

오정 五頂 Pañcaśikha, the five locks on a boy's head ; also used for 오불정존 五佛頂尊 q.v. 오정륜왕 五頂輪王 idem 오불정존 五佛頂尊. 오정산 五頂山 idem Wu-t'ai Shan 오대 五臺.

오정 五情 The feelings, or passions, which are stirred by the 오근 五根 five senses.

오정 五淨 The five "clean" products of the cow, its pañca-gavya, i.e. urine, dung, milk, cream (or sour milk), and cheese (or butter) ; cf. [M. W.] 오정(거천) 五淨(居天), 오불환천 五不還天 Cf. 색계 色界. The five pure-dwelling heavens in the fourth dhyāna heaven, into which arhats are finally born : 무번천 無煩天 Avṛhās, the heaven free from all trouble ; 무열천 無熱天 Atapās, of no heat or distress ; 선현천 善現天 Sudṛśas, of beautiful presentation ; 선견천 善見天 Sudarśanas, beautiful ; and 색구경천 色究竟天 Akaniṣṭha, the highest heaven of the form-realm. 오정식 五淨食, 오종정식 五種淨食 idem 오정식 五正食.

오정사념 五停四念 idem 오정심관 五停心觀 and 사념처 四念處 i.e. the five meditations for settling the mind and ridding it of the five errors of desire hate, ignorance, the self, and a wayward or confused mind ; the five meditations are 부정관 不淨觀, 자비관 慈悲觀, 인연관 因緣觀, 계분별관 界分別觀 and 수식관 數息觀 i.e. the vileness of all things, pity for all, causality, right discrimination, breathing ; some substitute meditation on the Buddha in place of the fourth ; another division puts breathing first, and there are other differences.

오정색 五正色 idem 오색 五色. 오정행 五正行 ; 오종정색 五種正色 The five proper courses to ensure the bliss of the Pure Land : (1) Intone the three sūtras 무량수경 無量壽經, 관무량수경 觀無量壽經, and 아미타경 阿彌陀經 ; (2) meditate on the Pure Land ; (3) worship solely Amitābha ; (4) invoke his name ; (5) extol and make offerings to him. Service of other Buddhas, etc., is styled 오(종)잡행 五(種)雜行. 오정식 五正食 ; 반자포선니 半者蒲膳尼 Pañcabhojanīya. The five foods considered proper for monks in early Buddhism : boiled rice, boiled grain or peas, parched grain, flesh, cakes.

오제 五諦 The five axioms : (1) 인제 因諦 the cause, which is described as 집 集 of the Four Noble Truths ; (2) 과제 果諦 the effect as 고 苦 ; (3) 지제 智諦 or 능지제 能知諦 diagnosis as 도 道 ; (4) 경제 境諦 or 소지제 所知諦 the end or cure as 멸 滅 ; to these add (5) 승제 勝諦 or 지제 至諦 the supreme axiom, i.e. the 진여 眞如 ; v. 사제 四諦.

오조 五祖 The five patriarchs. Those of the Hua-yen (Kegon) sect are 종남 두순 終南杜順 ; 운화 지엄 雲華智儼 ; 현수 법장 賢首法藏 ; 청량 징관 淸涼澄觀, and 규봉 종밀 圭峯宗密. The Pure-land sect five patriarchs are 담난 曇鸞 ; 도작 道綽 ; 선도 善導 ; 회감 懷感, and 소강 小康. The (백)련사 (白)蓮社 Lien-shê sect has 선도 善導 ; 법조 法照 ; 소강 小康 ; 성상 省常, and 종색 宗賾.

오조(가사) 五條(袈裟) The monk's robe of five patches or lengths, also termed 하의 下衣 as the lowest of the grades of patch-robes. It is styled 원내도행잡작의 院內道行雜作衣 the garment ordinarily worn in the monastery, when abroad and for general purposes.

오조자 五調子 idem 오음 五音.

오족여래 五族如來 The five Dhyāni-Buddhas of the Vajradhātu.

오종 五宗 The five great schools of Mahāyāna, i.e. 천태 天台, 화엄 華嚴, 법상 法相, 삼론 三論, and 율종 律宗. There are other classes, or groups.

오종 五種 The five kinds ; but frequently the 종 種 is omitted, e.g. for 오종정식 五種正食 see 오정식 五正食.

오종관정 五種灌頂 The five abhiṣecana baptisms of the esoteric school – for ordaining ācāryas, teachers, or preachers of the Law ; for admitting disciples ; for putting an end to calamities or suffering for sins ; for advancement, or success ; and for controlling (evil spirits) or getting rid of difficulties, cf. 오종수법 五種修法. Also, baptism of light ; of sweet dew (i.e. perfume) ; of the "germ-word" as seed ; of the five baptismal signs of wisdom made on the forehead, shoulders, heart, and throat, indicating the five Dhyāni-Buddhas ; and of the "true word" on the breast.

오종나함 五種那含 v. 오종불환 五種不還.

오종단법 五種壇法 The five kinds of maṇḍala ceremonials, v. 오부존법 五部尊法.

오종령 五種鈴 The five kinds of bells used by the Shingon sect in Japan, also called 금강령 金剛鈴, i.e. 오고령 五鈷鈴, 보령 寶鈴, 일고령 一鈷鈴, 삼고령 三鈷鈴, 탑령 塔鈴 ; the different names are derived from their handles ; the four first named, beginning with the five-pronged one, are placed each at a corner of the altar, the last in the middle.

오종마 五種魔 The five Māras associated with the five skandhas ; also 오온마 五蘊魔 ; 오음마 五陰魔, 오중마 五衆魔.

오종반 五種般 see 오중불환 五種不還.

오종법계 五種法界 The Hua-yen school's five forms of dharmadhātu : (1) 유위법계 有爲法界 or 사법계 事法界 the phenomenal realm ; (2) 무위법계 無爲法界 or 이법계 理法界 the inactive, quiescent, or noumenal realm ; (3) 역유위역무위법계 亦有爲亦無爲法界 or 사리무애법계 事理無礙法界 both, i.e. interdependent and interactive ; (4) 비유위비무위법계 非有爲非無爲法界 neither active nor inactive, but it is also 사리무애법계 事理無礙法界, e.g. water and wave, wave being water and water wave ; (5) 무장애법계 無障礙法界 or 사사무애법계 事事無礙法界 the unimpeded realm, the unity of the phenomenal and noumenal, of the collective and individual.

오종법사 五種法師 The five kinds of masters of the Law, v. Lotus Sūtra, 법사품 法師品 — one who receives and keeps ; reads ; recites ; expounds ; and copies the sūtra.

오종법신 五種法身 The five kinds of a Buddha's dharmakāya. There are four groups. I. (1) 여여지법신 如如智法身 the spiritual body of bhūtatathatā-wisdom ; (2) 공덕법신 功德法身 of all virtuous achievement ; (3) 자법신 自法身 of incarnation in the world ; (4) 변화법신 變化法身 of unlimited powers of transformation ; (5) 허공법신 虛空法身 of unlimited space ; the first and second are defined as sambhogakāya, the third and fourth as nirmāṇakāya, and the fifth as the dharmakāya, but all are included under dharmakāya as it possesses all the others. II. The esoteric cult uses the first four and adds as fifth 법계신 法界身 indicating the universe as pan-Buddha. III. Hua-yen gives (1) 법성생신 法性生身 the body or person of Buddha born from the dharma-nature ; (2) 공덕법신 功德法身 the dharmakāya evolved by Buddha virtue, or achievement ; (3) 변화법신 變化法身 the dharmakāya with unlimited powers of transformation ; (4) 실상법신 實相法身 the real dharmakāya ; (5) 허공법신 虛空法身 the universal dharmakāya. IV. Hīnayāna defines them as 오분법신 五分法身 q.v.

오종보시 五種布施 The five kinds of almsgiving or dānas — to those from afar, to those going afar, to the sick, the hungry, and those wise in Buddhist doctrine.

오종불남 五種不男 The five kinds of 반다가 般荼迦 paṇḍakas, i.e. eunuchs, or impotent males : by birth ; emasculation ; uncontrollable emission ; hermaphrodite ; impotent for half the month ; they are known as 선체 扇搋 Ṣaṇḍha ; 유나 留拏 Ruṇḍa ; 이리사장나 伊梨沙掌拏 Īrṣyāpaṇḍaka ; 반택가 半擇迦 Paṇḍaka ; 박차 博叉 Pakṣapaṇḍaka ; there are numerous subdivisions.

오종불녀 五種不女 The five kinds of sexually incomplete females, 라 螺, 근 筋, 고 鼓, 각 角, and 맥 脉. v. 대장법수 大藏法數 32.

오종불번 五種不翻 The five kinds of terms which Hsüan-tsang did not translate but transliterated — the esoteric ; those with several meanings ; those without equivalent in China ; old-established terms ; and those which would be less impressive when translated.

오종불환 五種不還 The five kinds of anāgāmins 나함 那含, who never return to the desire-realm : (1) 중반 中般 the anāgāmin who enters on the intermediate stage between the realm of desire and the higher realm of form ; (2) 생반 生般 who is born into the form-world and soon overcomes the remains of illusion ; (3) 유행반 有行般 who diligently works his way through the final stages ; (4) 무행반 無行般 whose final departure is delayed through lack of aid and slackness ; (5) 상류반 上流般 who proceeds from lower to higher heavens into nirvāṇa. Also 오종나함 五種那含 and 오종반 五種般, the 반 般 being "parinirvāṇa".

오종비량 五種比量 The five inferences in (Indian) logic : (1) 상 相 from appearance, e.g. fire from smoke ; (2) 체 體 from the corporeal, e.g. two or more things from one ; (3) 업 業 from action, e.g. the animal from its footmark ; (4) 법 法 from recognized law, old age from birth ; (5) 인과 因果 from cause and effect, that a traveller has a destination.

오종산란 五種散亂 The five kinds of mental aberration : (1) the five senses themselves not functioning properly ; (2) external distraction, or inability to concentrate the attention ; (3) internal distraction, or mental confusion ; (4) distraction caused by ideas of me and mine, personality, possession, etc. ; (5) confusion of thought produced by hīnayāna ideas.

오종삼귀 五種三歸 The five modes of triśaraṇa, or formulas of trust in the Triratna, taken by those who (1) 번사 翻邪 turn from heresy ; (2) take the five commandments ; (3) the eight commandments ; (4) the ten commandments ; (5) the complete commandments.

오종설인 五種說人 The five kinds of those who have testified to Buddhism ; also 오인설경 五人說經 ; 오설 五說 ; i.e. the Buddha, his disciples, the ṛṣis, devas, and incarnate beings. Also, the Buddha, sages, devas, supernatural beings, and incarnate beings. Also, the Buddha, bodhisattvas, śrāvakas, men, and things. See 오류설법 五類說法.

오종성 五種性 The five germ-natures, or roots of bodhisattva development : (1) 습종성 習種性 the germ-nature of study of the 공 空 void (or immaterial), which corrects all illusions of time and space ; it corresponds to the 십주 十住 stage ; (2) 성종성 性種性 that of ability to discriminate all the 성 性 natures of phenomena and transform the living ; the 십행 十行 stage ; (3) 도종성 道種性 (the middle-)way germ-nature, which attains insight into Buddha-laws ; the 십회향 十迴向 ; (4) 성종성 聖種性 the saint germ-nature which produces holiness by destroying ignorance ; the 십지 十地, in which the bodhisattva leaves the ranks of the 현 賢 and becomes 성 聖 ; (5) 등각종성 等覺種性 the bodhi-rank germ-nature which produces Buddhahood, i.e. 등각 等覺.

오종수법 五種修法 Five kinds of esoteric ceremonial, i.e. (1) 선지가 扇底迦 śāntika, for stopping calamities ; (2) 포슬징가 布瑟徵迦 or 보슬징가 補瑟徵迦 pauṣṭika, for success or prosperity ; (3) 아외자로가 阿畏遮嚕迦 abhicāraka, for suppressing, or exorcising ; (4) 아갈사니 阿羯沙尼 ākarṣaṇī, for calling, or attracting (good beings, or aid) ; (5) 벌시가라궤 伐施迦囉軌 vaśīkaraṇa, for seeking the aid of Buddhas and bodhisattvas ; also 오부존법 五部尊法 and cf. 오종관정 五種灌頂.

오종악병 五種惡病 Five epidemics in Vaiśālī during the Buddha's lifetime — bleeding from the eyes, pus from the ears, nose-bleeding, lockjaw, and astringent taste of all food.

오종유식 五種唯識 The five kinds of wei-shih, or idealistic representation in the sūtras and śāstras as summed up by Tzŭ-ên 자은 慈恩 of the 법상종 法相宗 Dharmalakṣaṇa school : (1) 경유식 境唯識 wisdom or insight in objective conditions ; (2) 교유식 敎唯識 in interpretation ; (3) 이유식 理唯識 in principles ; (4) 행유식 行唯識 in meditation and practice ; (5) 과유식 果唯識 in the fruits or results of Buddhahood. The first four are objective, the fifth subjective.

오종인 五種印 The signs of the five kinds of vision, v. 오안 五眼.

오종잡행 五種雜行 see 오정행 五正行.

오종장 五種藏 The five "stores", or the five differentiations of the one Buddha-nature ; (1) 여래장 如來藏 the Tathāgata-nature, which is the fundamental universal nature possessed by all the living ; (2) 정법장 正法藏 the source or treasury of all right laws and virtues ; (3) 법신장 法身藏 the storehouse of the dharmakāya obtained by all saints ; (4) 출세장 出世藏 the eternal spiritual nature, free from earthly errors ; (5) 자성청정장 自性清淨藏 the storehouse of the pure Buddha-nature. Another similar group is 여래장 如來藏, 법계장 法界藏, 법신장 法身藏, 출세간상상장 出世間上上藏, and 자성청정장 自性清淨藏.

오종통 五種通 Five kinds of supernatural power : (1) 도통 道通 of bodhisattvas through their insight into truth ; (2) 신통 神通 of arhats through their mental concentration ; (3) 의통 依通 supernatural or magical powers dependent on drugs, charms, incantations, etc. ; (4) 보통 報通 or 업통 業通 reward or karma powers of transformation possessed by devas, nāgas, etc. ; (5) 요통 妖通 magical powers of goblins, satyrs, etc.

오종행 五種行 The acts of the 오종법사 五種法師 q.v. ; also idem 오정행 五正行.

ㄱ ㄴ ㄷ ㄹ ㅁ ㅂ ㅅ ㅇ ㅈ ㅊ ㅋ ㅌ ㅍ ㅎ 찾아보기

오주(지) 五住(地) The five fundamental conditions of 번뇌 煩惱 the passions and delusions : wrong views which are common to the trailokya ; clinging, or attachment, in the desire-realm ; clinging, or attachment, in the form-realm ; clinging, or attachment, in the formless realm which is still mortal ; the state of unenlightenment or ignorance in the trailokya 삼계 三界 which is the root-cause of all distressful delusion. Also 오주지혹 五住地惑.

오주인과 五周因果 The five circuits or areas of cause and effect, i.e. the five main subjects of the Hua-yen sūtra.

오중 五衆 idem 오온 五蘊. Also, the five groups, i.e. monks, nuns, nun-candidates, and male and female novices.

오중세계 五重世界 The five graduated series of universes : (1) 삼천대천세계 三千大千世界 Tri-sahasra-mahā-sahasra-loka-dhātu ; a universe, or chiliocosm ; (2) such chiliocosms, numerous as the sands of Ganges, form one Buddha-universe ; (3) an aggregation of these forms a Buddha-universe ocean ; (4) an aggregation of these latter forms a Buddha-realm seed ; (5) an infinite aggregation of these seeds forms a great Buddha-universe. 지도론 智度論 50. Another division is (1) a world, or universe ; (2) a Buddha-nature universe, with a different interpretation ; and the remaining three are as above, the sea, the seed, and the whole Buddha- universe. 오중체 五重滯 The five heavy blockages, or serious hindrances ; see 오둔사 五鈍使 infra. 오중운 五重雲 The five banks of clouds or obstructions for a woman, see 오장 五障.

오지 五智 The five kinds of wisdom of the 진언 眞言 Shingon School. Of the six elements 육대 六大 earth, water, fire, air (or wind), ether (or space) 공 空, and consciousness (or mind 식 識), the first five form the phenomenal world, or Garbhadhātu, the womb of all things 태장계 胎藏界, the sixth is the conscious, or perceptive, or wisdom world, the Vajradhātu 금강계 金剛界, sometimes called the Diamond realm. The two realms are not originally apart, but one, and there is no consciousness without the other five elements. The sixth element, vijñāna, is further subdivided into five called the 오지 五智 Five Wisdoms : (1) 법계체성지 法界體性智 Dharmadhātu-prakṛti-jñāna, derived from the amala-vijñāna, or pure 식 識 ; it is the wisdom of the embodied nature of the dharmadhātu, defined as the six elements, and is associated with Vairocana 대일 大日, in the centre, who abides in this samādhi ; it also corresponds to the ether 공 空 element. (2) 대원경지 大圓鏡智 Ādarśana-jñāna, the great round mirror wisdom, derived from the ālaya-vijñāna, reflecting all things ; corresponds to earth, and is associated with Akṣobhya and the east. (3) 평등성지 平等性智 Samatā-jñāna, derived from manovijñāna, wisdom in regard to all things equally and universally ; corresponds to fire, and is associated with Ratnasaṃbhava and the south. (4) 묘관찰지 妙觀察智 Pratyavekṣaṇa-jñāna, derived from 의식 意識, wisdom of profound insight, or discrimination, for exposition and doubt-destruction ; corresponds to water, and is associated with Amitābha and the west. (5) 성소작지 成所作智 Kṛtyānuṣṭhāna-jñāna, derived from the five senses, the wisdom of perfecting the double work of self-welfare and the welfare of others ; corresponds to air 풍 風 and is associated with Amoghasiddhi and the north.

These five Dhyāni-Buddhas are the 오지여래 五智如來. The five kinds of wisdom are the four belonging to every Buddha, of the exoteric cult, to which the esoteric cult adds the first, pure, all-reflecting, universal, all-discerning, and all-perfecting. 오지여래 五智如來 ; 오지오불 五智五佛 ; 오불 五佛 ; 오여래 五如來 The five Dhyāni-Buddhas, or Wisdom-Tathāgatas of the Vajradhātu 금강계 金剛界, idealizations of five aspects of wisdom ; possibly of Nepalese origin. The Wisdom-Buddha represents the dharmakāya or Buddha-mind, also the Dharma of the triratna, or trinity. Each evolves one of the five colours, one of the five senses, a Dhyāni-bodhisattva in two forms (one gracious, the other fierce), and a Mānuṣi-Buddha ; each has his own śakti, i.e. feminine energy or complement ; also his own bīja, or germ-sound 종자 種子 or 인 印 seal,

i.e. 진언 眞言 real or substantive word, the five being for 대일 大日 aṁ, for 아축 阿閦 hūṁ, for 보생 寶生 hrīḥ, for 미타 彌陀 aḥ, for 불공 不空 āḥ. The five are also described as the emanations or forms of an Ādi-Buddha, Vajrasattva ; the four are considered by others to be emanations or forms of Vairocana as the Supreme Buddha. The five are not always described as the same, e.g. they may be 약사 藥師 or 약왕 藥王 Bhaiṣajya, 다보 多寶 Prabhūtaratna, Vairocana, Akṣobhya, and either Amoghasiddhi or Śākyamuni.
Below is a classified list of the generally accepted five with certain particulars connected with them, but these differ in different places, and the list can only be a general guide. As to the Dhyāni-bodhisattvas, each Buddha evolves three forms 오불생오보살 五佛生五菩薩, 오금강 五金剛, 오분노 五忿怒, i.e. (1) a bodhisattva who represents the Buddha's dharmakāya, or spiritual body ; (2) a vajra or diamond form who represents his wisdom in graciousness ; and (3) a fierce or angry form, the 명왕 明王 who represents his power against evil. (1) Vairocana appears in the three forms of 전법륜보살 轉法輪菩薩 Vajra-pāramitā Bodhisattva, 변조금강 遍照金剛 Universally Shining Vajrasattva, and 부동명왕 不動明王 Āryācalanātha Rāja ; (2) Akṣobhya's three forms are 허공장 虛空藏 Ākāśagarbha, 여의 如意 complete power, and 군다리명왕 軍荼利明王 Kuṇḍali-rāja ; (3) Ratnasaṃbhava's three forms are 보현 普賢 Samantabhadra, 살타 薩埵 Sattvavajra, and 손파 孫婆 or 항삼세명왕 降三世明王 Trailokyavijayarāja ; (4) Amitābha's three forms are 관세음 觀世音 Avalokiteśvara, 법금강 法金剛 Dharmarāja, and 마두명왕 馬頭明王 Hayagrīva, the horse-head Dharmapāla : (5) Amoghasiddhi's three forms are 미륵 彌勒 Maitreya, 업금강 業金剛 Karmavajra, and 금강야차 金剛夜叉 Vajrayakṣa. The above Bodhisattvas differ from those in the following list : —

	Vairocana 대일 大日	Akṣobhya 아축 阿閦	Ratnasaṃbhava 보생 寶生	Amitābha 미타 彌陀	Amoghasiddhi 불공 不空
Position	centre	east	south	west	north
Element	ether	earth	fire	water	air
Sense	sight	sound	smell	taste	touch
colour	white	blue	yellow	red	green
Germ	aṁ	hūṁ	? aḥ	? hrīḥ	? āḥ
Animal	lion	elephant	horse	goose or eacock	garuḍa
Dhyāni-Bodhisattva	Samantabhadra 보현 普賢	Vajrapāṇi 금강역사 金剛力士	Ratnapāṇi 보수 寶手	Avalokiteśvara 관음 觀音	Viśvapāṇi ?
Buddha	Krakucchanda	Kanakamuni	Kāśyapa	Śākyamuni	Maitreya

오지보관 五智寶冠 idem 오불보관 五佛寶冠. 오지소생삼신 五智所生三身 Each of the Five Dhyāni-Buddhas is accredited with the three forms which represent his 신업 身業 body, 구업 口業 speech, and 의업 意業 mind, e.g. the embodiment of Wisdom is Vairocana, his preaching form is 보현 普賢, and his will form is 부동명왕 不動明王 ; the embodiment 신 身 of the mirror is Akṣobhya, his 구 口 is Mañjuśrī, his 의 意 is 항삼세금강 降三世金剛 ; and so on ; v. above.

오지근 五知根 The five indriyas or organs of perception — eyes, ears, nose, tongue, and skin. v. 오근 五根.

오지다 烏地多 "The king of an unknown country in Northern India who patronized Hsüan-tsang (A.D. 640)." [Eitel].

오지작법 五支作法 or **오분작법** 五分作法 The five parts (avayava) of a syllogism : 입종 立宗 pratijñā, the proposition ; 변인 辯因 hetu, the reason ; 인유 引喩 udāharaṇa, the example ; 합 合 upanaya, the application ; and 결 結 nigamana, the summing up, or conclusion. These are also expressed in other terms, i.e. 입의 立義 ; 인 因 ; 비여 譬如 ; 합비 合譬 ; and 결정 決定. 오지계 五支戒 The five moral laws or principles arising out of the idea of the mahā-nirvāṇa in the 대열반경 大涅槃經 11.

오진 五塵 The objects of the five senses, which being dusty or earthly things can taint the true nature ; idem 오경 五境.

오집 五執 The five planets, see 오성 五星.

오차지옥 五叉地獄 The hell in which the sufferers are dismembered with five-pronged forks.

오참일 五參日 Worship on the four fives, i.e. the fifth, tenth, twentieth, and twenty-fifth days of the month ; also 오참상당 五參上堂.

오처공양 五處供養 The five to be constantly served — father, mother, teacher, religious director, the sick. 오처가지 五處加持 Ceremonial touching of the five places on the body — brow, right and left shoulders, heart, and throat ; 오처진언 五處眞言 has similar reference, v. 오종관정 五種灌頂.

오천(자) 五天(子) Five devas in the Garbhadhātu maṇḍala located in the north-east. Also 오정거천 五淨居天 or 오정거중 五淨居衆 ; 오나함천자 五那含天子. 오천축 五天竺 ; 오천 五天 The five regions of India, north, south, east, west, and central ; v. 서역기 西域記.

오천상만 五千上慢 The five thousand supremely arrogant (i.e. Hīnayāna) monks who left the great assembly, refusing to hear the Buddha preach the new doctrine of the Lotus sūtra ; see its 방편 方便 chapter.

오천제라 五闡提羅 The five ṣaṇḍhilas, i.e. five bad monks who died, went to the hells, and were reborn as ṣaṇḍhilas or imperfect males ; also 오선제라 五扇提羅.

오체 五體 and 오체투지 五體投地 v. 오륜 五輪.

오추슬마 烏芻瑟摩 Ucchuṣma. One of the 명왕 明王 ming wang ; he presides over the cesspool and is described both as "unclean" and as "fire-head" ; he is credited with purifying the unclean. Also 오추사마 烏芻沙摩 ; 오추삽마 烏芻澁摩 ; 오추슬마 烏樞瑟摩 or 오추사마 烏樞沙摩 ; 오소사마 烏素沙摩.

오취 五趣 The five gati, i.e. destinations, destinies : the hells, hungry ghosts, animals, human beings, devas ; cf. 오악취 五惡趣 and 오도 五道. 오취생사륜 五趣生死輪 A series of pictures to show the course of life and death, ascribed in the Sarvāstivāda Vinaya 34 to the Buddha.

오취온 五取蘊 The five tenacious bonds, or skandhas, attaching to mortality.

오침남 烏枕南 Udāna, breathing upwards a solemn utterance, or song of joy, intp. as unsolicited or voluntary statements, i.e. by the Buddha, in contrast with replies to questions ; it is a section of Buddhist literature.

오탁 五濁 ; 오재 五滓 ; 오혼 五渾 The five kaṣāya periods of turbidity, impurity, or chaos, i.e. of decay ; they are accredited to the 주겁 住劫 kalpa, see 사겁 四劫, and commence when human life begins to decrease below 20,000 years. (1) 겁탁 劫濁 the kalpa in decay, when it suffers deterioration and gives rise to the ensuing form ; (2) 견탁 見濁 deterioration of view, egoism, etc., arising ; (3) 번뇌탁 煩惱濁 the passions and delusions of desire, anger, stupidity, pride, and doubt prevail ; (4) 중생탁 衆生濁 in consequence human miseries increase and happiness decreases ; (5) 명탁 命濁 human lifetime gradually diminishes to ten years. The second and third are described as the 탁 濁 itself and the fourth and fifth its results. 오탁증시 五濁增時 The above period of increasing turbidity or decay.

오탁가한다 烏鐸迦漢荼 Uṭabhāṇḍa, or Uḍakhāṇḍa, an ancient city of Gandhāra, on the northern bank of the Indus, identified with Ohind ; Eitel gives it as "the modern Attok."

오통 五痛 idem 오소 五燒.

오통 五通 v. 오신통 五神通. 오통선 五通仙 One who by non-Buddhistic methods has attained to the five supernatural powers. 오통신 五通神 Spirits possessed of the five supernatural powers. They are also identified with five spirits known as the 오성 五聖 or 오현 五顯, of whom there are varying accounts. 오통보살 五通菩薩 The five bodhisattvas of the 계두마 鷄頭摩 monastery in India, who, possessed of supernatural powers, went to the Western Paradise and begged the image of Maitreya, whence it is said to have been spread over India.

오파 烏波 Upādāna, laying hold of, grasp ; hence material, things ; it transliterates bhāva, and is intp. as 유 有 to have, be, exist, things, the resultant or karma of all previous and the cause of all future lives, v. 취 取 and 우 優. 오파사가 烏波斯迦 ; 우바이(사가) 優波夷(賜迦) Upāsikā, female disciples who remain at home. 오파제 烏波提 Upādhi ; a condition ; peculiar, limited, special ; the upādhi-nirvāṇa is the 고 苦 or wretched condition of heretics. 오파국다 烏波毱多 Upagupta, also 우 鄔 and 우 優, a Śūdra by birth, who became the fourth patriarch. 오파제삭 烏波第鑠 ; 우바제삭 鄔波提鑠 ; 우바제사 優波提舍 Upadeśa, a section of Buddhist literature, general treatises ; a synonym for the Abhidharma-piṭaka, and for the Tantras of the Yogācāra school. 오파삭가 烏波索迦 or 오파사가 烏波娑迦 ; 우바새 優婆塞 ; 우바사가 優波娑迦 Upāsaka, lay male disciples who remain at home and observe the moral commandments. 오파다야 烏波陀耶 ; 유파제야야 有波弟耶夜 ; 화상 和尙 or 화자 和闍 or 화암 和闇 Upādhyāya, originally a subsidiary teacher of the Vedāṅgas ; later, through Central Asia, it became a term for a teacher of Buddhism, in distinction from 율사 律師 disciplinists and 선사 禪師 intuitionalists, but as Ho-shang it attained universal application to all masters. 오파난다 烏波難陀 or 塢波難陀 Upananda, a disciple of Śākyamuni ; also one of the eight Nāga-kings in the Garbhadhātu. 오파계사자 烏波髻使者 ; 오파계설니 烏婆計設尼 Upakeśinī, one of the messengers of Mañjuśrī.

오팔 五八 Five eights, i.e. forty. 오팔십구 五八十具 All the five, eight, and ten commandments, i.e. the three groups of disciples, laity who keep the five and eight and monks who keep the ten. 오팔존 五八尊 The forty forms of Kuan-yin, or the Kuan-yin with forty hands ; the forty forms multiplied by the twenty-five 유 有 things make 1,000, hence Kuan-yin with the thousand hands. 오팔식 五八識 The five sense perceptions and the eighth or Ālaya vijñāna, the fecundating principle of consciousness in man.

오포사타 烏逋沙他 Upavasatha (Pali, Uposatha). A fast-day, originally in preparation for the brahminical soma sacrifice ; in Buddhism there are six fast-days in the month.

오품 五品 A division of the disciples, in the Lotus sūtra, into five grades — those who hear and rejoice ; read and repeat ; preach ; observe and meditate ; and transform self and others.

오하분결 五下分結 The five bonds in the lower desire-realms, i.e. desire, dislike, self, heretical ideals, doubt 탐 貪, 진 瞋, 아 我, 사계 邪戒, 의 疑.

오학처 五學處 idem 오계 五戒.

오해 五海 The five "seas" or infinities seen in a vision by P'u-hsien, v. 구화엄경 舊華嚴經 3 viz., (1) all worlds, (2) all the living, (3) universal karma, (4) the roots of desire and pleasure of all the living, (5) all the Buddhas, past, present, and future.

오해탈륜 五解脫輪 The five wheels of liberation, or salvation, i.e. the five maṇḍalas in which are the Five Dhyāni-Buddhas, see 오지여래 五智如來 ; also called 오대월륜 五大月輪 and 오륜탑파 五輪塔婆.

오행 五行 The five lines of conduct. I. According to the 기신론 起信論 Awakening of Faith they are almsgiving ; keeping the commandments ; patience under insult ; zeal or progress ;

meditation. II. According to the 열반경 涅般經 Nirvāṇa sūtra they are saintly or bodhisattva deeds ; arhat, or noble deeds ; deva deeds ; children's deeds (i.e. normal good deeds of men, devas, and Hīnayānists) ; sickness conditions, e.g. illness, delusion, etc. ; — into all these lines of conduct and conditions a Bodhisattva enters. III. The five elements, or tanmātra — wood, fire, earth, mental, and water ; or earth, water, fire, air, and ether (or space) as taught by the later Mahāyāna philosophy ; idem 오대 五大.

오향 五香 The incense composed of five ingredients (sandalwood, aloes, cloves, saffron, and camphor) offered by the esoteric sects in building their altars and in performing their rituals. Cf. 오분향 五分香.

오혹 五惑 The five delusions, idem 오둔사 五鈍使.

오회 五悔 The five stages in a penitential service. T'ien-t'ai gives : (1) confession of past sins and forbidding them for the future ; (2) appeal to the universal Buddhas to keep the law-wheel rolling ; (3) rejoicing over the good in self and others ; (4) 회향 廻向 offering all one's goodness to all the living and to the Buddha-way ; (5) resolve, or vows, i.e. the 사홍서 四弘誓. The 진언 眞言 Shingon sect divides the ten great vows of 보현 普顯 Samantabhadra into five 회 悔, the first three vows being included under 귀명 歸命 or submission ; the fourth is repentance ; the fifth rejoicing ; the sixth, seventh, and eighth appeal to the Buddhas ; the ninth and tenth, bestowal of acquired merit.

오회염불 五會念佛 Five ways of intoning "Amitābha" established by 법조 法照 Fa-chao of the T'ang dynasty, known as 오회법사 五會法師 from his brochure 오회법사찬 五會法師讚.

오훈 五葷 idem 오신 五辛.

옥 屋 A house, a room. 옥리인 屋裏人 The master of the house ; the mind within ; also a wife.

옥 玉 Jade, a gem ; jade-like, precious ; you, your. 옥불 玉佛 A famous jade Buddha recovered while digging a well in Khotan, 3 to 4 feet high. 옥유 玉柔 Pliable jade, i.e. 우육 牛肉 beef. 옥천옥화양종 玉泉玉花兩宗 The two schools of the Jade-fountain and Jade-flower, i.e. 천태 天台 T'ien-t'ai and 법상 法相 Dharmalakṣaṇa, the latter with Hsüan-tsang as founder in China. 옥천 玉泉 Yü-ch'üan was the name of the monastery in Tang-yang 당양 當陽 Hsien, An-lu Fu, Hupeh, where Chih-i, the founder of the T'ien-t'ai School, lived ; 옥화 玉花 Yü-hua, where Hsüan-tsang lived. 옥환 玉環 The Jade ring in one of the right hands of the "thousand-hand" Kuan-yin. 옥야 玉耶 The name of the woman to whom the sūtra 옥야(녀)경 玉耶(女)經 is addressed. 옥화 玉花 The palace 옥화궁 玉花宮 "Yü-hua kung", transformed into a temple for Hsüan-tsang to work in, where he tr. the 대반야경 大般若經 Mahāprajñā-pāramitā sūtra, 600 chüan, etc. Cf. 옥천 玉泉. 옥호 玉豪 ; 옥호 玉毫 The ūrṇā or white curl between the Buddha's eyebrows, from which he sent forth his ray of light illuminating all worlds.

옥 獄 Litigation, law-case ; a prison ; 지옥 地獄 q.v. Earth-prison, the hells.

옥 沃 Wet, wash, enrich. 옥초석 沃焦石 or 옥초산 沃焦山 The rock, or mountain, Pātāla, on the bottom of the ocean, just above the hot purgatory, which absorbs the water and thus keeps the sea from increasing and overflowing. 옥초해 沃焦海 is the ocean which contains this rock, or mountain.

온 蘊 Skandha, v. 색 塞 ; older tr. 음 陰, intp. as that which covers or conceals, implying that physical and mental forms obstruct realization of the truth ; while the tr. 온 蘊, implying an accumulation or heap, is a nearer connotation to Skandha, which, originally meaning the shoulder, becomes stem, branch, combination, the objects of sense, the elements of being or mundane consciousness. The term is intp. as the five physical and mental constituents, which combine to form the intelligent 성 性 or nature ; rūpa, the first of the five, is considered as physical, the remaining four as mental ; v. 오온 五蘊. The skandhas refer only to the phenomenal, not to the 무위 無爲 non-phenomenal. 온락 蘊落 Any unit, or body, consisting of skandhas. 온처계 蘊處界 The five skandhas, twelve 처 處 āyatana or bases, and eighteen 계 界 dhātu or elements. 온식 蘊識 The skandha of intelligence, or intellectuation ; also intp. as 유정 有情 consciousness, or emotion. 온타남 蘊馱南 Udāna, v. 우 優, an expression of joy, or praise ; voluntary addresses (by the Buddha). 온마 蘊魔 The evil spirit (or spirits) that works (or work) through the five skandhas.

온 溫 Warm, mild, bland, gentle ; acquainted with ; to warm. 온실 溫室 Bath-house ; bathroom. 온숙 溫宿 Wên-su, a district in Sinkiang, on the river Aksu. 온다라 溫陀羅 Uttara, cf. 올 嗢.

올 嗢 To clear the throat ; translit. *u*, cf. 울 鬱, 오 烏, 온 溫, 우 優. 올달라 嗢咀羅 or 嗢怛羅 Uttara, tr. by 상 上 superior, predominant, above all. 올달라구로 嗢咀羅矩嚕 Uttarakuru, one of the four continents, that north of Meru. 올달라서나 嗢咀羅犀那 Uttarasena, a king of Udyāna who obtained part of Śākyamuni's relics. 올달라알사다 嗢咀羅頞沙荼 Uttarāṣāḍhā, the nakṣatra presiding over the second half of the 4th month, "the month in which Śākyamuni was conceived." [Eitel]. 올시라 嗢尸羅 Uśīra, fragrant root of *Andropogon muricatus*. 올굴죽가 嗢屈竹迦 ; 올구타 嗢俱吒 Utkuṭukāsana v. 결가 結跏 to squat on the heels. 올슬니사 嗢瑟尼沙 Uṣṇīṣa, the protuberance on the Buddha's head, v. 오 烏. 올층가 嗢蹭伽 Utsaṅga, 100,000 trillions, a 대올층가 大嗢蹭伽 being a quadrillion, v. 락차 洛叉. 올발(라) 嗢鉢(羅) Utpala, the blue lotus ; the 6th cold hell.

옹 癰 A tumour, abscess. 옹창 癰瘡 A tumour of pus, a running sore.

옹 甕 Kumbha, a pitcher, jar, pot. 옹형 甕形 Jar-shaped, pot-shaped ; kumbhāṇḍka, v. 구 鳩.

옹 擁 To crowd, press ; embrace, hug. 옹호 擁護 To hug in the bosom and guard.

와 瓦 Tiles, pottery. 와기금기 瓦器金器 An earthen vessel, i.e. the śrāvaka method, and a golden vessel, the bodhisattva method. 와사 瓦師 The Buddha in a previous incarnation as a potter. 와발 瓦鉢 An earthenware begging bowl.

와 臥 or 卧 Śayana, lying down, sleeping. 와구 臥具 A couch, bed, mat, bedding, sleeping garments, etc. 와불사 臥佛寺 A shrine of the "sleeping Buddha," i.e. of the dying Buddha.

완 頑 Stupid, obstinate. 완석점두 頑石點頭 (Moved by the reciting of the Mahāparinirvāṇa Sūtra,) even the stupid stones nodded their heads.

완 剜 To scoop out. 완등 剜燈 To scoop out (one's body) and turn (it) into a lamp, attributed to Śākyamuni in a former incarnation.

왕 枉 Oppression, wrong ; crooked ; in vain. 왕사 枉死 Wrongly done to death.

왕 王 Rāja, king, prince, royal ; to rule. 왕삼매 王三昧 ; 삼매왕삼매 三昧王三昧 ; 삼매왕 三昧王 The king of samādhis, the highest degree of samādhi, the 수릉엄정 首楞嚴定 q.v. The first is also applied to invoking Buddha, or sitting in meditation or trance. 왕선 王仙 A royal ṛṣi, i.e. a sovereign who retires from the world and attains to the five transcendent powers. 왕고 王古 Wang Ku, name of a President of the Board of Rites during the Sung dynasty, who was also a devout Buddhist, end of eleventh century. 왕일 王日 idem 팔왕일 八王日. 왕일휴 王日休 Wang Jih-hsiu, a 진사 進士 doctor who became a devout and learned follower of Amida and Kuan-yin ; he was of 용서 龍舒 Lung-shu, was also known as 허중 虛中 Hsü-chung, and compiled the 대아미타경 大阿彌陀經 1160-2. 왕갈라사벌탄나 王曷邏闍伐彈那 Rājyavardhana, tr. by 왕증 王增

Wang Tsêng. A brother of Harshavardhana, king of Kanyākubja. 왕법 王法 Royal law, the law by which a king should rule his country. 왕법경 王法經 A sūtra on royal law, tr. by I-ching ; there are other treatises on it. 왕선 王膳 A royal feast referred to in the Lotus sūtra, where the hungry people feared to accept the King's feast till he came himself and called them ; i.e. the feast of Buddhahood and the Buddha's call. 왕사(성) 王舍(城) Rājagṛha. King Bimbisāra is said to have removed his capital here from Kuśāgrapura, v. 구 矩 and 길 吉, a little further eastward, because of fire and other calamities. Rājagṛha was surrounded by five hills, of which Gṛdhrakūṭa (Vulture Peak) became the most famous. It was the royal city from the time of Bimbisāra "until the time of Aśoka". Its ruins are still extant at the village of Rājgir, some sixteen miles S.S.W. of Bihār ; they "form an object of pilgrimages for the Jains". [Eitel]. The first synod is said to have assembled here.

왕 往 To go ; gone, past ; to be going to, future. 왕생 往生 The future life, the life to which anyone is going ; to go to be born in the Pure Land of Amitābha. (1) 왕상회향 往相回向 To transfer one's merits to all beings that they may attain the Pure Land of Amitābha. (2) 환상회향 還相回向 Having been born in the Pure Land to return to mortality and by one's merits to bring mortals to the Pure Land.

왕사 王師 Royal Preceptor.

외 外 Bāhya. Outside, external ; opposite to 내 內 within, inner, e.g. 내증 內證 inner witness, or realization and 외용 外用 external manifestation, function, or use. 외걸 外乞 The mendicant monk who seeks self-control by external means, e.g. abstinence from food, as contrasted with the 내걸 內乞 who seeks it by spiritual methods. 외진 外塵 The external objects of the six internal senses. 외외도 外外道 Outside outsiders, those of other cults. 외학 外學 Study of outside, or non-Buddhist doctrines. 외아 外我 An external Ego, e.g. a Creator or ruler of the world, such as Śiva. 외법 外法 ; 외교 外敎 ; 외전 外典 ; 외집 外執 External doctrines ; rules or tenets non-Buddhist, or heretical. 외해 外海 The sea that surrounds the four world- continents. 외무위 外無爲 Unmoved by externals, none of the senses stirred. 외상 外相 External appearance or conduct ; what is manifested without ; externally. The 십이외상 十二外相 are the hair, teeth nails, etc. 외호 外護 External protection, or aid, e.g. food and clothing for monks and nuns, contrasted with the internal aid of the Buddha's teaching. 외탐욕 外貪欲 Sexual thoughts towards others than one's own wife, or husband. 외도 外道 Outside doctrines ; non-Buddhist ; heresy, heretics ; the Tīrthyas or Tīrthikas ; there are many groups of these : that of the 이천삼선 二天三仙 two devas and three sages, i.e. the Viṣṇuites, the Maheśvarites (or Śivaites), and the followers of Kapila, Ulūka, and Ṛṣabha. Another group of four is given as Kapila, Ulūka, Nirgrantha-putra (Jainas), and Jñātṛ (Jainas). A group of six, known as the 외도육사 外道六師 six heretical masters, is Pūraṇa-Kāśyapa, Maskari-Gośālīputra, Sañjaya-Vairāṭīputra, Ajita-Keśakambala, Kakuda-Kātyāyana, and Nirgrantha-Jñātiputra (Nirgranthajñātiputra) ; there are also two other groupings of six, one of them indicative of their various forms of asceticism and self-torture. There are also groups of 13, 16, 20, 30, 95, and 96 heretics, or forms of non-Buddhist doctrine, the 95 being divided into 11 classes, beginning with the Sāṅkhya philosophy and ending with that of no-cause, or existence as accidental. 외금강부 外金剛部 The external twenty devas in the Vajradhātu group, whose names, many of them doubtful, are given as Nārāyaṇa, Kumāra, Vajragoḍa, Brahmā, Śakra, Āditya, Candra, Vajramāha, Musala, Piṅgala, Rakṣalevatā, Vāyu, Vajravāsin, Agni, Vaiśravaṇa, Vajrāṅkuśa, Yama, Vajrajaya, Vināyaka, Nāgavajra. 외금강부원 外金剛部院 The last of the thirteen courts in the Garbhadhātu group.

요 鐃 A hand-bell, cymbals.

요 了 To end, see through, understand, thoroughly know, make clear, thoroughly, completely, final.

요 妖 An imp ; to bewitch ; magical. 요통 妖通 The power to change miraculously into trees and animals ; v. 오종통 五種通.

요 曜 Brilliant, shining. 칠요 七曜 The sun, moon, and five planets. 요숙 曜宿 These seven and the constellations, the celestial orbs.

요 要 Important, essential, necessary, strategic ; want, need ; about to ; intercept ; coerce ; agree, etc. 요묘 要妙 The essential and mystic nature (of Buddha-truth). 요문 要文 The important text or texts. 요지 要旨 The important meaning or aim. 요진 要津 The essential ford, or road. 요행 要行 The essential mode of action, or conduct. 요언 要言 Important, or essential words. 요문 要門 Essential door, or opening. 요로 要路 ; 요도 要道 The essential or strategic way.

요 瑤 Jasper (green), green crystal. 요화궁 瑤花宮 cf. 옥 玉.

요 饒 Spare ; abundance, surplus ; to pardon. 요왕(불) 饒王(佛) Lokeśvara, "the lord or ruler of the world ; N. of a Buddha" [M. W.] ; probably a development of the idea of Brahmā, Viṣṇu, or Śiva as lokanātha, "lord of worlds." In Indo-China especially it refers to Avalokiteśvara, whose image or face, in masculine form, is frequently seen, e.g. at Angkor. Also 세요왕(불) 世饒王(佛). It is to Lokeśvara that Amitābha announces his forty-eight vows. 요익 饒益 To enrich. 요설 饒舌 A fluent tongue ; loquacious.

요 腰 The waist, middle. 요의 腰衣 A skirt, "shorts," etc. 요백 腰白 A white, or undyed, sash worn in mourning.

요 遶 To go round, revolve around, encompass ; to pay respect by walking around the object of regard. 요불 遶佛 ; 요탑 遶塔 To circumambulate an image of the Buddha, or a pagoda.

요 澆 To sprinkle, to water ; perfidious, infamous. 요계 澆季 The evil period of the world's existence leading to its end.

요 繞 To wind round, go round. 요불 繞佛 To go three times around the Buddha to his right in worship.

요교 了教 A noted disciple named Ājñāta-Kauṇḍinya, v. 아 阿, also known as 구린린 拘鄰隣, 요본제 了本際 and 지본제 知本際. He is described as "a prince of Magadha, maternal uncle of Śākyamuni, whose first disciple he became." He is "to be reborn as Buddha under the name of Samanta-Prabhāsa." [Eitel].

요달 了達 Thorough penetration, clear understanding.

요령 鐃鈴 or 搖鈴 A hand bell. A small bell made of brass, shakable by hands. It is used in Buddhist services.

요료견 了了見 The complete vision obtained when the body is in complete rest and the mind freed from phenomenal disturbance.

요오 了悟 Complete enlightenment, or clear apprehension.

요의 了義 Revelation of the whole meaning, or truth, as 불료의 不了義 is partial revelation adapted (방편 方便) to the capacity of the hearers. 요의교 了義教 Teaching of the whole truth. 요의경 了義經 The sūtras containing it. Mahāyāna counts all Hīnayāna sūtras as 불료의경 不了義經 ; Mahāyāna sūtras are divided into both kinds according to different schools.

요인 了因 A revealing cause, v. 이인 二因, i.e. 생인 生因 a producing or direct cause, e.g. a seed ; and 요인 了因 a revealing "cause," e.g. a light, as indicating the effect ; knowledge or wisdom. 요인불성 了因佛性 The second of the three Buddha-nature "causes," i.e. 정인불성 正因佛性 is the 진여 眞如 as direct cause of attaining the perfect Buddha-nature, associated with the 법신 法身 ; 요인불성 了因佛性 is the revealing or enlightening cause, associated with the Buddha-wisdom ; 연인불성 緣因佛性 is the environing cause, e.g. his goodness and merits which result in deliverance, or salvation.

요지 了知 Parijñāna, thorough knowledge.

요철선정 了徹禪定 The mastery of abstract contemplation

욕 慾 Passion, inordinate desire, lust, v. 욕 欲. 욕애 慾愛 To hanker after, desire.

욕 欲 Rajas, passion. Also Kāma, desire, love. The Chinese word means to breathe after, aspire to, desire, and is also used as 욕 慾 for lust, passion ; it is *inter alia* intp. as 염애진 染愛塵 tainted with the dust (or dirt) of love, or lust. The three desires are for beauty, demeanour, and softness ; the five are those of the five physical senses.

욕 浴 To bathe, wash. 욕주 浴主 ; 지욕 知浴 ; 욕두 浴頭 Bath-controller. 욕실 浴室 A bath-house. 욕고 浴鼓 The bathing-drum, announcing the time for washing in the Ch'an monasteries.

욕불 浴佛 ; **욕상** 浴像 To wash the image of the Buddha ; that is a ceremony on his birthday, 8th of the 4th month.

욕불식 浴佛式 Bathing the Buddha Ceremony, performed on Buddha's Birthday.

욕각 欲覺 Passion-consciousness ; the consciousness of desire.

욕계 欲界 Kāmadhātu. The realm, or realms, of desire for food, sleep, and sex, consisting of souls in purgatory, hungry spirits, animals, asuras, men, and the six heavens of desire, so called because the beings in these states are dominated by desire. The Kāmadhātu realms are given as : 지거 地居 Bhauma. 허공천 虛空天 Antarikṣa. 사천왕천 四天王天 Caturmahārājakāyika [i.e. the realms of 지국천 持國天 Dhṛtarāṣṭra, east ; 증장천 增長天 Virūḍhaka, south ; 광목천 廣目天 Virūpākṣa, west ; 다문천 多聞天 Vaiśramaṇa (Dhanada), north]. 도리천 忉利天 Trayastriṁśāḥ. 도솔천 兜率天 Tuṣita. 화락천 化樂天 Nirmāṇarati. 타화자재천 他化自在天 Paranirmitavaśavartin.

욕고 欲苦 The sufferings of desire, or in desire-realms.

욕구 欲鉤 The hook of desire ; the bodhisattva attracts men through desire, and then draws them to the enlightenment of Buddha.

욕기 欲氣 Desire-breath, passion-influence, the spirit or influence of desire, lust.

욕니 欲泥 The mire of desire, or lust.

욕락 欲樂 The joys of the five desires.

욕루 欲漏 The stream or flow of existence, evoked by desire interpenetrated by unenlightened views and thoughts ; these stimulating desires produce karma which in turn produces reincarnation ; v. 삼루 三漏.

욕류 欲流 The stream of the passions, i.e. the illusions of cupidity, anger, etc., which keep the individual in the realm of desire ; the stream of transmigration, which results from desire.

욕마 欲魔 The evil demon of lust.

욕사행 欲邪行 Adulterous conduct, prohibited in the five commandments.

욕색 欲色 The two realms of desire and form, or the passions and the sensuous.

욕성 欲性 Desire-nature, the lusts.

욕심 欲心 A desirous, covetous, passionate, or lustful heart.

욕애 欲愛 Passion-love ; love inspired by desire, through any of the five senses ; love in the passion-realm as contrasted to 법애 法愛 the love inspired by the dharma. 욕애주지 欲愛住地 One of the five fundamental conditions of the passions, v. 오주(지) 五住(地).

욕염 欲染 The tainting, or contaminating influence of desire.

욕유 欲有 The realm of desire, one of the 삼유 三有. 욕유견무명 欲有見無明 The unenlightened condition of desire ; kāma-bhava-dṛṣṭi-avidyā are the four constituents which produce 루 漏 q.v.

욕자 欲刺 The sharp point of desire.

욕전 欲箭 The arrows of desire, or lust. Also the darts of the Bodhisattva 욕금강 欲金剛, who hooks and draws all beings to Buddha.

욕진 欲塵 The dust, or dirt, or infection of the passions ; the guṇas, or qualities, or material factors of desire regarded as forces. Also the six desires and the five guṇas 육욕오진 六欲五塵.

욕천 欲天 The six heavens of desire or passion, the kāmadhātu. 욕천오음 欲天五婬 The five methods of sexual intercourse in the heavens of desire ; in the heaven of the Four Great Kings and in Trayastriṁśāḥs the method is the same as on earth ; in the Yama-devaloka a mere embrace is sufficient ; in the Tuṣita-heaven, holding hands ; in the Nirmāṇarati heaven, mutual smiles ; in the other heavens of Transformation, regarding each other.

욕탐 欲貪 Desire and coveting, or coveting as the result of passion ; craving.

욕하 欲河 The river of desire, or lust (which drowns).

욕해 欲海 The ocean of desire, so called because of its extent and depth.

욕화 欲火 The fire of desire.

용 龍 A dragon, dragon-like, imperial ; tr. for nāga, which means snake, serpent ; also elephant, elephantine, serpent-like, etc., cf. 나 那.

용 勇 Brave, bold, courageous, fearless. 용맹정진 勇猛精進 Bold advance, or progress. 용시보살 勇施菩薩 Pradhānaśūra, a bodhisattva now in Śākyamuni's retinue.

용 容 Contain ; bear ; allow ; bearing, face, looks ; easy. 용유석 容有釋 or 용유설 容有說 An admissible though indirect interpretation ; containing that meaning.

용 用 To use, to employ ; use, function. 용대 用大 Great in function, the universal activity of the 진여 眞如 bhūtatathatā ; v. 기신론 起信論 ; and cf. 성상용 性相用 inner nature, form and function. 용멸 用滅 Function or activity ceasing ; i.e. matter (or the body 체 體) does not cease to exist, but only its varying functions or activities.

용 涌 To well up, spring up. 용출 涌出 To spring forth. 용천 涌泉 The springing fountain, i.e. the sūtras.

용감 龍龕 Dragon coffins, i.e. those for monks.

용군 龍軍 A tr. of Nāgasena, v. 나선 那先 ; 나가서나 那伽犀那 ; and the 나선비구경 那先比丘經 Milindapañha sūtra.

용궁 龍宮 Dragon palace ; palaces of the dragon kings ; also 용호 龍戶.

용녀 龍女 Nāgakanyā, a nāga maiden. Daughter of Sāgara-nāgarāja, the dragon king at the bottom of the ocean ; she is presented in the Lotus sūtra, though a female and only eight years old, as instantly becoming a Buddha, under the tuition of Mañjuśrī.

용맹 龍猛 Nāgārjuna, v. 나 那.

용맹정진 勇猛精進 Lit. "ferocious effort." Vigilance ; intensive part of a retreat where sleeping is not allowed.

용미니 龍彌你 Lumbinī, v. 람 嵐.

용발 龍鉢 A begging-bowl formerly used by a certain monk for obtaining rain, the dragon descending into his bowl.

용방 龍方 The dragon-quarter, i.e. the north.

용분신삼매 龍奮迅三昧 A samādhi powerful like the dragon ; abstract meditation which results in great spiritual power.

용상 龍象 Dragon elephant, or dragon and elephant, i.e. great saints, Buddhas, bodhisattvas. A large elephant is called a dragon elephant. The term is also one of respect applied to a monk.

용수 龍樹 Nāgārjuna, v. 나 那.

용신 龍神 A dragon-god, or spirit.

용왕 龍王 Nāgarāja, dragon king, a title for the tutelary deity of a lake, river, sea, and other places ; there are lists of 5, 7, 8, 81, and 185 dragon kings.

용장 龍章 Dragon books, i.e. the sūtras, so called because the Sanskrit writing seemed to the Chinese to resemble the forms of snakes an dragons.

용장 龍藏 The Dragon Treasury or library, formerly in the 용흥 龍興 Lung Hsing monastery at Ch'ang-an.

용종(상)존(왕불) 龍種(上)尊(王佛) The Buddha of the race of honourable dragon kings, a title of Mañjuśrī.

용주 龍珠 Dragon-pearl ; pearl below the dragon's jaws ; the sun or moon associated with the dragon and spring.

용주사 龍珠寺 Yong-ju-sa. A temple located in Songsan-ri Taean-eup Hwaseong-gun Gyeonggi-do. The 2nd parish headquarters of Korean Jogye Order.

용천 龍天 Dragon kings and deva ; also Nāgārjuna and Vasubandhu. 용천팔부 龍天八部 Nāgas, devas, rākṣasas, gandharvas, asuras, garuḍas, kinnaras, and mahoragas.

용탕 龍湯 Dragon soup, a purgative concocted of human and animal urine and excrement ; also called 황룡탕 黃龍湯.

용하 龍河 Another name for the river Nairañjanā, cf. 니 尼.

용화수 龍華樹 Nāga-puṣpa ; 분나가 奔那伽 puṣpanāga, the dragon-flower tree, which will be the bodhi-tree of Maitreya, the Buddhist Messiah, when he comes to earth. 용화회 龍華會 His assembly under it for preaching the Buddha-truth. The eighth of the fourth moon has been so called, an occasion when the images are washed with fragrant water, in connection with the expected Messiah.

우 or **구** 漚 To steep, macerate, rot ; bubble ; translit. *u, o*, etc. 우화구사라 漚和俱舍羅 or 傴和拘舍羅 Upāyakauśalya, intp. by 방편선교 方便善巧 expediency and skill, adaptable, suited to conditions, opportunist, the adaptation of teaching to the capacity of the hearer. 우다라승 漚多羅僧 v. 울 鬱 Uttarāsaṅga, a toga worn over the left shoulder. 우파야바라밀 漚婆耶婆羅蜜 Upāya-pāramitā, saving by the method of expedient teaching, v. above. 우발라 漚鉢羅 Utpala, also 올발라 嗢鉢羅 ; 우발라 優鉢羅 ; 오발라 烏鉢羅 the blue lotus ; also a lord of Nāgas and his blue lotus lake.

우 or **오** 鄔 Translit. *u, ū*, cf. 오 烏, 오 塢, 우 優, e.g. 우파니살담 鄔波尼殺曇 Upaniṣad, cf. 우 優 ; variously intp. but in general refers to drawing near (to a teacher to hear instruction) ; the Upanishads. 우자연나 鄔闍衍那 Ujjayinī, Oujein ; cf. 오 烏. 우다연 鄔陀延 ; 오다연나 烏陀衍那 Udayana, king of Kauśāmbī, cf. 오 烏.

우 禺 A monkey ; begin ; the 사 巳 hour, 9-11 a.m. ; 우중 禺中 the middle of that hour, 10 a.m. T'ien-t'ai called the fourth period of Buddha's teaching the 우중 禺中.

우 優 Abundant, excessive ; exceptional, extra ; at ease ; an actor ; chiefly translit. *u* sounds, cf. 울 鬱, 우 憂, 오 烏, etc.

우 偶 An image ; a mate ; unexpectedly. 우상 偶像 An image, an idol.

우 右 Dakṣiṇā. The right hand, on the right, e.g. 우수 右手 right hand, 우선 右旋 right turn, 우요 右繞 pradakṣiṇa, turning or processing with the right shoulder towards an object of reverence.

우 牛 Go, gaus ; ox, bull, bullock, etc. A term applied to the Buddha Gautama as in 우왕 牛王 king of bulls, possibly because of the derivation of his name ; the phrase 기우래우 騎牛來牛 or 기우멱우 騎牛覓牛 to ride an ox, to seek an ox, means to use the Buddha to find the Buddha.

우 愚 Monkey-witted, silly, stupid, ignorant. 우승 愚僧 Ignorant monk. 우부 愚夫 Bāla ; ignorant, immature, a simpleton, the unenlightened. 우혹 愚惑 Deluded by ignorance, the delusion of ignorance. 우법 愚法 Ignorant, or immature law, or method, i.e. that of śrāvakas and pratyeka-buddhas, Hīnayāna. 우치 愚痴 Mūḍha ; ignorant and unenlightened, v. 치 痴. 우둔 愚鈍 Ignorant and dull-witted.

우 憂 Sorrow, grief, melancholy, anxiety ; to mourn, grieve ; translit. *u, yu* ; cf. 우 優, 오 烏. 우세 憂世 The world of trouble and sorrow. 우수 憂受 Sorrow, one of the five emotions. 우바제사 憂婆提舍 Upatiṣya, perhaps a name of Śāriputra. 우화 憂火 The fires of sorrow or distress. 우필차 憂畢叉 Upekṣā, cf. 우 優 indifference attained in abstraction, i.e. "indifference to pain or pleasure, equanimity, resignation, stoicism." [Childers]. "Looking on, hedonic neutrality or indifference, zero point between joy and sorrow, disinterestedness, neutral feeling, equanimity." [*Pali Text Society's Dictionary*]. 우다가 憂陀伽 Udaka, water. 우다나 憂陀那 Udāna, cf. 우 優, 오 烏, etc. Breathing upwards from the throat into the head ; guttural sounds ; the navel, umbilical ; the middle ; volunteered remarks or addresses by the Buddha, sermons that came from within him without external request ; voluntarily to testify.

우 藕 The water-lily root, arrowroot. 우사 藕絲 Lily-root fibres.

우 寓 To dwell, lodge ; appertain, belong to, resemble. 우종 寓宗 A branch sect ; one school appertaining to another. 우전 寓錢 Semblance money, i.e. paper money.

우 雨 Varṣa. Rain ; to rain. 우걸 雨乞 To pray for rain. 우안거 雨安居 ; 우시 雨時 ; 우기 雨期 ; Varṣās ; varṣāvasāna ; the rains, the rainy season, when was the summer retreat, v. 안거

安居. 우화 雨花, 우화 雨華 To rain down (celestial) flowers. 우중 雨衆 The disciples of 벌리사 伐里沙 Varṣya, i.e. Vārṣagaṇya, a leader of the Sāṅkhya school.

우 于 Yü, a preposition, in, at, etc., similar to 어 於. In 우차나마라 于遮那摩羅 and the next it is used in error for 간 干 kan ; Kāñcana-mālā, a hair circlet or ornament of pure gold ; name of the wife of Kuṇāla, noted for fidelity to her husband when he had been disgraced. 우사나 于闍那 ; 우사라 于闍羅 Kuñjara. Name of a tree. 우전 于闐 ; 우둔 于遁 ; 우전 于殿 ; 우전 于塡 ; 계단 谿丹 ; 굴단 屈丹 ; 화전 和闐 ; 오나 澳那 ; 구살달나 瞿薩怛那 Kustana, or Khotan, in Turkestan, the principal centre of Central Asian Buddhism until the Moslem invasion. Buddhism was introduced there about 200 B.C. or earlier. It was the centre from which is credited the spread of Mahāyānism, v. 서역기 西域記 12.

우각 牛角 Ox-horns, a synonym for things that are even, or on a level. 우각일촉 牛角一觸 The ox that by merely touching a monk's robe with its horn was transformed into a deva. 우각사라림 牛角娑羅林 Ox-horns śāla grove, said to be a couple of śāla or teak trees shaped like ox-horns, which grew near Kuśinagara, under which the Buddha preached the Nirvāṇa sūtra. He is reported to have entered nirvāṇa in a grove of eight śāla trees standing in pairs. 우각산 牛角山 v. 우두산 牛頭山.

우거 牛車 Bullock cart, the 백우거 白牛車 white-bullock cart as the one universal vehicle of salvation, v. 화택 火宅.

우계 牛戒 To live as a cow, eating grass with bent head, etc. — as certain Indian heretics are said to have done, in the belief that a cow's next reincarnation would be in the heavens.

우구외도 牛狗外道 Go-vratika, or kukkura-vratika. Heretics who lived as oxen or dogs.

우다라 優多羅 Uttara. Upper, superior, higher, further.

우다이 優陀夷 Udāyin, to rise, shine forth ; a disciple of Śākyamuni, to appear as Buddha Samanta-prabhāsa. 우다연 優陀延 v. *supra* and 우다연 鄔陀延 Udayana. 우다나 優陀那 Udāna(ya), voluntary discourses, a section of the canon.

우단나 優檀那 Uddāna, fasten, bind, seal.

우담(발) 優曇(鉢) The udumbara tree ; supposed to produce fruit without flowers ; once in 3,000 years it is said to flower, hence is a symbol of the rare appearance of a Buddha. The *Ficus glomerata*. Also 우담바라 優曇婆羅 ; 오담발라 烏曇跋羅 ; 우담발라 鄔曇跋羅.

우두 牛頭 The ox-head lictors in the hells. 우두산 牛頭山 or 우각산 牛角山 Gośṛṅga 구실릉가 瞿室餕伽 a mountain 13 li from Khotan. One of the same name exists in Kiangning in Kiangsu, which gave its name to a school, the followers of 법융 法融 Fa-jung, called 우두산법 牛頭山法 Niu-t'ou shan fa, or 우두선 牛頭禪 or 우두종 牛頭宗 ; its fundamental teaching was the unreality of all things, that all is dream, or illusion. 우두대왕 牛頭大王 The guardian deity of the Jetavana monastery, and an incarnation of 약사 藥師 q.v. 우두전단 牛頭栴檀 ; 우단전단 牛檀栴檀 ; 우두향 牛頭香 Gośīrṣa-candana, ox-head sandal-wood, also styled 적전단 赤栴檀 red sandal-wood ; said to come from the Ox-head mountains, and if rubbed on the body to make one impervious to fire, also generally protective against fire, curative of wounds and generally medicinal. "The first image of Śākyamuni was made of this wood." [Eitel]. 서역기西域記 10.

우란(분) 盂蘭(盆) ; **우람바(나)** 烏藍婆(拏) Ullambana 우란 盂蘭 may be another form of Lambana, or Avalamba, "hanging down," "depending," "support" ; it is intp. "to hang upside down," or "to be in suspense," referring to extreme suffering in purgatory ; but there is a suggestion of the dependence of the dead on the living. By some 분 盆 is regarded as a Chinese word, not part of the transliteration, meaning a vessel filled with offerings of food. The term is applied to the festival of All Souls, held about the 15th of the 7th moon, when masses are read by Buddhist and Taoist priests and elaborate offerings made to the Buddhist Trinity for the purpose of releasing from purgatory the souls of those who have died on land or sea. The Ullambanapātra-sūtra is attributed to Śākyamuni, of course incorrectly ; it was first tr. into Chinese by Dharmarakṣa, A.D. 266-313 or 317 ; the first masses are not reported until the time of Liang Wu Ti, A.D. 538 ; and were popularized by Amogha (A.D. 732) under the influence of the Yogācārya School. They are generally observed in China, but are unknown to Southern Buddhism. The "idea of intercession on the part of the priesthood for the benefit of" souls in hell "is utterly antagonistic to the explicit teaching of primitive Buddhism." The origin of the custom is unknown, but it is foisted on to Śākyamuni, whose disciple Maudgalyāyana is represented as having been to purgatory to relieve his mother's sufferings. Śākyamuni told him that only the united efforts of the whole priesthood 시방중회 十方衆會 could alleviate the pains of the suffering. The mere suggestion of an All Souls Day with a great national day for the monks is sufficient to account for the spread of the festival. Eitel says ; "Engrafted upon the native ancestral worship, this ceremonial for feeding the ghosts of deceased ancestors of seven generations obtained immense popularity and is now practised by everybody in China, by Taoists even and by Confucianists." All kinds of food offerings are made and paper garments, etc., burnt. The occasion, 7th moon, 15th day, is known as the 우란(분)회 盂蘭(盆)會 or 우란(분)재 盂蘭(盆)齋 and the sūtra as 우란(분)경 盂蘭(盆)經.

우려이유 牛驢二乳 The milk of cow and ass, the one turns to "curd", the other to "dung", i.e. alike in appearance, but fundamentally different, as is the case with the Buddha's teaching and that of outsiders.

우루(가) 優樓(迦) Ulūka, the owl ; a ṛṣi "800 years" before Śākyamuni, reputed as founder of the Vaiśeṣikaphilosophy. Also 우루거 優婁佉 ; 우류가 憂流迦 ; 구로가 嘔盧伽 ; 구루 漚樓 ; 올로가 嗢露迦.

우루빈라 優樓頻螺 Uruvilvā, papaya tree ; name of the forest near Gayā where Śākyamuni practised austere asceticism before his enlightenment. Also 우루빈려 優樓頻蠡 ; 우루비려 優樓毘蠡 ; 오로빈라 烏盧頻螺 ; 오로빈라 烏盧頻羅 ; 구루빈라 漚樓頻螺. 우루빈라가섭 優樓頻螺迦葉 and other forms ; Uruvilvā Kāśyapa ; "one of the principal disciples of Śākyamuni, so called because he practised asceticism in the Uruvilvā forest," or "because he had on his breast a mark resembling the fruit of the" papaya. He "is to reappear as Buddha Samantaprabhāsa." [Eitel].

우류만타 優流漫陀 Urumuṇḍa, name of a mountain in the Aśoka sūtra.

우모진 牛毛塵 Go-rajas, the amount of dust that can rest on the top of a cow's hair, i.e. seven times that on a sheep's.

우발라 優鉢羅 Utpala, the blue lotus, to the shape of whose leaves the Buddha's eyes are likened ; also applied to other water lilies. Name of a dragon king ; also of one of the cold hells, and one of the hot hells. Also 우발라 優鉢剌 ; 우발라 鄔鉢羅 ; 구발라 漚鉢羅.

우분 牛糞 Gomaya, cow-dung, considered in India as clean and cleansing ; used by the esoterics for "cleansing" altars. 우분종 牛糞種 The first Gautama ancestor of Śākyamuni, who is reputed to have sprung from cow-dung in the Sugar-cane garden, probably a mere tradition that the family sprang from herdsmen.

우선니 優禪尼 Ujjayinī, Oujein, v. 오자 烏闍.

우양(심)안 牛羊(心)眼 Only the eyes (i.e. vision, or insight) of oxen and sheep.

우왕 牛王 The king of bulls, i.e. a Buddha, or bodhisattva ; it is applied to Gautama Buddha, possibly derived from his name. 우왕존자 牛王尊者 ; 우사 牛司 ; 우상 牛相 ; 우적 牛跡 Gavāṁpati, v. 교범바제 憍梵婆提 and 우적비구 牛跡比丘.

우적 牛跡 Ox-tracks, i.e. the teaching of a Buddha the 우왕 牛王 royal bull. 우적비구 牛跡比丘 the bhikṣu Gavāṁpati, 교범바제 憍梵波提 q.v., also styled 우왕(존자) 牛王(尊者), said to have been a disciple of Śākyamuni ; also styled 우사 牛司 ruminating like a cow, and 우상 牛相 cow-faced ; so born because of his previous herdsman's misdeeds.

우전 優塡 Udayana, king of Kauśāmbī and contemporary of Śākyamuni, who is reputed to have made the first image of the Buddha ; also 우다연 優陀延 ; 우전 于闐 ; 우다연나 鄔陀衍那 ; 올다연나벌차 嗢陀演那伐蹉 Udayana Vatsa. Cf. 거 巨 , 구 俱 , 구 拘 , and 불사왕 弗沙王.

우파 優婆 cf. 우파 優波. 우바새 優婆塞 Upāsaka, 우바사가 優婆娑柯 ; 우바사가 優波娑迦 ; 우바색(가) 鄔波塞(加) ; 우바삭가 鄔波索迦 ; 우바소가 鄔波素迦 ; 이포새 伊蒲塞. Originally meaning a servant, one of low caste, it became the name for a Buddhist layman who engages to observe the first five commandments, a follower, disciple, devotee. 우바이 優婆夷 Upāsikā. 우바이 優波夷 ; 우바사 優婆斯 ; 우바사가 優婆私柯 ; 우바사가 優波賜迦 ; 우바사가 鄔婆斯迦 ; 우바사가 鄔波斯迦 Female lay disciples who engage to observe the first five commandments. 우파니사타 優婆尼沙陀 ; 우파니사담 優婆尼沙曇 Upaniṣad, v. 우파 優波. 우바굴다 優婆掘多 v. Upagupta, *infra*. 우바제사 優婆提舍 Upadeśa ; 우바제사 優婆題舍 ; 우바제사 優波提舍 ; 우바체사 優波替舍 ; 우바제삭 鄔波題鑠 ; 우바제삭 鄔波弟鑠. Discourses and discussions by question and answer ; one of the twelve divisions of the Canon ; a synonym for the Abhidharma, also for the Tantras. 우바국다 優婆毱多 Upagupta, 우바국다 優婆鞠多 ; 우바굴다 優婆掘多 ; 우바급다 優波笈多 ; 우바국다 優波毱多 ; 우바국다 鄔波毱多 ; 우바급다 鄔波級多 ; 우바굴다 鄔波屈多 ; 오바국다 烏波毱多. A "Śūdra by birth, who entered upon monastic life when 17 years old." [Eitel]. He was renowned as almost a Buddha, lived under King Aśoka, and is reputed as the fifth patriarch, 200 years after the Nirvāṇa. 우바지사 優婆至沙 ; 우바실사 優婆室沙 Upatiṣya, i.e. Śāriputra, v. 사 舍. 우바리 優婆離 Upāli 우바리 優婆利 ; 우바리 優波利 ; 우바리 優波離 ; 우바리 鄔波離. A barber of śūdra caste, who became a disciple of Śākyamuni, was one of the three sthaviras of the first Synod, and reputed as the principal compiler of the Vinaya, hence his title 지계 持戒 Keeper of the laws. There was another Upāli, a Nirgrantha ascetic. 우바다야 優婆馱耶 Upādhyāya, "a sub-teacher" ; "a spiritual teacher." [M. W.] A general term for monk. There are various names, etc., beginning with 우 優 ; 우 憂 ; 우 鄔 ; 오 塢 ; 욱 郁 , etc.

우파 優波 v. 우파 優婆. 우바사가 優波娑迦 v. 우바새 優婆塞 Upāsaka. 우바바사 優波婆娑 Upavāsa, to dwell in, or by ; fasting, abstinence ; to keep eight of the ten prohibitions. 우파니사토 優波尼沙土 ; 우파니사타 優波尼沙陀 Upaniṣad, also 우파니사담 優婆尼沙曇 ; certain philosophical or mystical writings by various authors at various periods "attached to the Brāhmaṇas, the aim of which is the ascertainment of the secret sense of the Veda (they are more than a hundred in number, and are said to have been the source of the six darśanas, or systems of philosophy)." [M. W.] The best known is the Bṛhad-araṇyaka. 우바교사라 優波憍舍羅 Upāyakauśalya, the seventh pāramitā, cf. 바 波. 우바체(사) 優波替(舍) v. 사 舍 Upatiṣya (son of Tiṣya), i.e. Śāriputra. 우바라참 優波羅懺 ; 우바라차 優婆羅叉 Upalakṣaṇa, a mark or property, tr. as 률 律 the law, or the monastic rules. 우바다 優波陀 v. 우발라 優鉢羅 Utpala. 우파나하 優波那訶 v. 우바다야 優婆馱耶 Upādhyāya. 우바난다 優波難陀 Upananda, a disciple of Śākyamuni ; also a nāga king. 우바리 優波離 Upāli, v. 우파 優婆.

우피 牛皮 Ox hide – mortal happiness injures the wisdom-life of gods and men, just as ox hide shrinks and crushes a man who is wrapped in it and placed under the hot sun.

우필사 優畢捨 ; **우필차** 優畢叉 Upekṣā. The state of mental equilibrium in which the mind has no bent or attachment, and neither meditates nor acts, a state of indifference. Explained by 사 捨 abandonment.

우화주 牛貨洲 Godānīya, 구가니 瞿伽尼 or 구야니 瞿耶尼 or 구다니 瞿陀尼 ; 구조니 俱助尼 ; 우부니 遇嚩柅 ; Aparagodāna, 아발리구다니 阿鉢利瞿陀尼, the western of the four continents into which every world is divided, where oxen are the principal product and medium of exchange.

우황가지 牛黃加持 or **우왕가지** 牛王加持 Cow-bezoar aid, a charm used for childless women to obtain children – the four words should be written with cow bezoar on birch-bark and carried on the person.

욱 郁 Elegant, refined, translit. *y* and *u*. 욱가 郁伽 Yoga, cf. 유 瑜. 욱가지라 郁伽支羅 Ukkacela, is a place unknown. 욱다(라승가) 郁多(羅僧伽) Uttarāsaṅga, the cassock, the seven-patch robe ; for this and Uttarakuru cf. 울 鬱. 욱가 郁迦 Ugra, an elder of Śrāvastī, whose name is given to a sūtra.

운 雲 Megha. Cloud, cloudy, abundant. 운형수제 雲兄水弟 ; 운중수중 雲衆水衆 Brothers or men of the clouds and waters, fellow-monks. 운종 雲宗 idem 백운종 白雲宗. 운당 雲堂 The assembly hall of a monastery, because of the massed congregation. 운심 雲心 Clouded heart, depressed. 운수 雲水 ; 운형수제 雲兄水弟 ; 운납 雲衲 ; 운납 雲納 Homeless or roaming monks. 운해 雲海 Many as the clouds and the waters of the ocean. 운판 雲板 A sort of cloud-shaped gong (made of bronze or metal), struck to indicate the meal times. 운뢰음왕 雲雷音王 Megha-dundubhi-ṣvara-rāja, or 운뢰음숙왕화지 雲雷音宿王華智 Jaladhara-garjita-ghoṣa-susvara-nakṣatra-rāja-saṅkusumitā-bhijña. A Buddha "having a voice musical as the second of the thunder of the clouds and conversant with the appearance of the regents of the nakshatras." [M. W.] A Buddha possessing the wisdom of the Thunder-god and of the flowery stars. 운자재왕 雲自在王 Meghasvara-rāja, ruler of the cloud drums, a son of Mahābhijñābhibhū. 운문 雲門 The Cloud-gate monastery in Kwangtung, from which 문언 文偃 Wên-yen derived his title ; his name was 장설봉 張雪峯 Chang Hsüeh-fêng ; he lived early in the tenth century and founded the 운문(선)종 雲門(禪)宗, v. 삼구 三句. 운집 雲集 Flocking like clouds, a great assembly. 운고 雲鼓 A drum ornamented with clouds for calling to midday meals.

운 運 Revolve ; turn of the wheel, luck ; carry, transport. 운심 運心 Revolve in the mind ; indecision ; to have in mind ; to carry the mind, or thought, towards.

운 殞 To perish, die ; fall ; become extinct.

운 云 To say, speak. 운운 云云 Continuing to speak ; they say, people say ; as follows, and so on, etc. 운하 云何 Why? 운하패 云何唄 The opening stanza of the Nirvāṇa sūtra 3.

울 鬱 Dense, oppressive, anxious ; translit. u sounds ; cf. 욱 郁, 우 優, 올 口㗨, 온 殟, 오 烏. 울다마 鬱多摩 Uttama, highest, chief, greatest. 울다라 鬱多羅 Uttara, upper, higher, superior ; subsequent ; result ; excess ; the north ; also 울달라 鬱怛羅, etc. 울다라승(가) 鬱多羅僧(伽) Uttarāsaṅga, an upper or outer garment ; the seven-patch robe of a monk ; also used for the robe flung toga-like over the left shoulder. 울다라구류 鬱多羅究留 Uttarakuru, also 울다라구루 鬱多羅拘樓 ; 울다라구루 鬱多羅鳩婁 ; 욱다라구루 郁多羅拘樓 ; 울달라구류 鬱怛羅拘瑠 ; 울달라월 鬱怛羅越 ; 울단월 鬱單越, etc. The northern of the four continents around Meru, square in shape, inhabited by square-faced people ; explained by 고상작 高上作 superior to or higher than other continents, 승 勝 superior, 승생 勝生 superior life, because human life there was supposed to last a thousand years and food was produced without human effort. Also, the dwelling of gods and saints in Brahmanic cosmology ; one of the Indian "nine divisions of the world, the country of the northern Kurus, situated in the north of India, and described as the country of eternal beatitude." [M. W.] 울지 鬱持 Uda ; also 울지가 鬱持迦 ; 우다가 優陀伽 ; 오나가 烏娜迦 Udaka ; water. 울슬니사 鬱瑟尼沙 ; 울실니사 鬱失尼沙 v. 오 烏 10 Uṣṇīṣa. 울두람(불) 鬱頭藍(佛) Udra(ka) Rāmaputra ; 울두람자 鬱頭藍子 ; 울다라마자 鬱陀羅摩子 A Brahman ascetic, to whom miraculous powers are ascribed, for a time mentor of Śākyamuni after he left home. 울금 鬱金 Kuṅkuma, saffron ; a plant from which scent is made. 울발라 鬱鉢羅 v. 우 優 17 Utpala, blue lotus. 울타 鬱陀 cf. 우 憂 15 and 울두 鬱頭. 울다나 鬱陀那 v. 우 優 17 Udāna, voluntary addresses. 울비라 鬱鞞羅 Uruvilvā, the forest near Gayā where Śākyamuni was an ascetic for six years ; also defined as a stream in that forest ; cf. 우 優 17.

울력 Harmonious teamwork. The work done by a group of people ; or the power.

웅 熊 A bear. 웅이산 熊耳山 Bear's ear mount, the place where Bodhidharma was buried.

원 苑 A park, imperial park, a collection ; v. Jetavana 기 祇. 원공사교 苑公四教 v. 사교 四教.

원 元 Beginning, first, original, head ; dollar ; Mongol (dynasty). 원길수 元吉樹 The tree of the origin of felicity, i.e. the bodhi-tree or ficus religiosa, also styled 불수 佛樹 ; 도수 道樹, and 보리수 菩提樹. 원품무명 元品無明 Primal ignorance ; the original state of avidyā, unenlightenment, or ignorance ; original innocence. Also 근본무명 根本無明 ; 무시무명 無始無明. 원인 元因 ; 원인 原因 The original or fundamental cause which produces phenomena, e.g. karma, reincarnation, etc. ; every cause has its fruit or consequences. The idea of cause and effect is a necessary condition of antecedent and consequence ; it includes such relations as interaction, correlation, interdependence, coordination based on an intrinsic necessity. 원묘 元妙 The original or fundamental marvel or mystery, i.e. the conception of nirvāṇa. 원시 元始 Prabhū, 파라부 波羅赴 ; 발리부 鉢利部 beginning, in the beginning, primordial. Prabhū is a title of Viṣṇu as a personification of the sun. 원심 元心 The original or primal mind behind all things, idem the 일심 一心 of the 기신론 起信論 Awakening of Faith, the 삼라만상지원 森羅萬象之元 source of all phenomena, the mind which is in all things. 원명 元明 ; 본명 本明 Original brightness or intelligence ; the 진여 眞如 or bhūtatathatā as the source of all light or enlightenment. 원효 元曉 Won-hyo(C. Yüan-hsiao), a famous Korean monk who studied and wrote in Shilla during the T'ang dynasty ; known as 해동사 海東師 Hai-tung Shih. 원조 元照 Name of 잠연 湛然 Chan-jan, the seventh head of the T'ien-t'ai School ; he died 1116. 원조 元祖 The original patriarch, or founder of a sect or school ; sometimes applied to the Buddha as the founder of virtue. 원장 元藏 The Yüan Tripiṭaka, compiled by order of Shih Tsu (Kublai), founder of the Yüan dynasty, and printed from blocks ; begun in 1277, the work was finished in 1290, in 1,422 부 部 works, 6,017 권 卷 sections, 558 함 函 cases or covers. It contained 528 Mahāyānist and 242 Hīnayānist sūtras ; 25 Mahāyāna and 54 Hīnayāna vinaya ; 97 Mahāyāna and 36 Hīnayāna śāstras ; 108 biographies ; and 332 supplementary or general works. In size, and generally, it was similar to the Sung edition. The 원장목록 元藏目錄 or Catalogue of the Yüan Tripiṭaka is also known as 대보령사대장경목록 大普寧寺大藏經目錄. 원진성 元辰星 ; 원신성 元神星 A star that controls the attainment of honours, and the riddance of sickness and distresses. The star varies according to the year star of the suppliant which is one of the seven stars in Ursa Major.

원 鴛 Drake of mandarin duck ; v. next. 원반 鴛班 Paired bands, i.e. to stand facing each other when reciting sūtras.

원 遠 Far, distant, far removed. 원진리구 遠塵離垢 To be far removed from the dust and defilement of the world. 원사 遠師 idem 혜원 慧遠 q.v. 원행지 遠行地 The seventh stage of the bodhisattva, in which he leaves the world of phenomena and enjoys mystic contemplation. 원리 遠離 Vivṛj ; vivarjana ; leave afar off, be far removed ; absolute separation of unconditioned reality from the realm of phenomena. 원리락 遠離樂 The joy of the first dhyāna heaven, in which the defilement of desire is left far behind in mystic contemplation.

원 原 Origin, original. (화엄)원인론 (華嚴)原人論 A treatise on the original or fundamental nature of man, by 종밀 宗密 Tsung-mi, the fifth patriarch of the Hua-yen school, explaining its doctrine, in one chüan.

원 願 Praṇihita ; praṇidhāna ; resolve, will, desire, cf. 서 誓. 원주 願主 The original resolve in a previous existence which incites a man to build a pagoda, copy a sūtra, etc., leading him to become Buddha or reach the Pure Land. 원불 願佛 A Buddha of the vow, who passes through the eight forms of an incarnate Buddha, v. 팔상 八相. 원작 願作 Resolve to be or become, e.g. 원작불 願作佛 resolve to become Buddha. 원력 願力 The power of the vow. 원토 願土 The land of the vow, the Pure Land of Amitābha. 원도 願度 Salvation through trust in the vow, e.g. of Amitābha. 원심 願心 The heart of resolve (of Buddha to save all beings). 원지 願智 Wisdom resulting from the vow. 원바라밀 願波羅蜜 The vow pāramitā, the eighth of the ten pāramitās, a bodhisattva's vow to attain bodhi, and save all beings to the other shore. 원해 願海 The Bodhisattva vow is deep and wide like the ocean. 원선 願船 The Amitābha's vow likened to a boat which ferries all beings to his Pure Land. 원행 願行 To vow and perform the discipline the vow involves. 원신 願身 The resolve of a Buddha to be born in the Tuṣita heaven for the work of saving all beings, also idem 원불 願佛 *supra*. 원륜 願輪 The vow-wheel, which overcomes all opposition ; also the revolving of the bodhisattva's life around his vow. 원식 願食 Vow-food ; to nourish the life by the vow, and thus have strength to fulfil its duties.

원 怨 Resentment, grievance, hatred. 원가 怨家 ; 원적 怨敵 An enemy. 원증회고 怨憎會苦 One of the eight sufferings, to have to meet the hateful. 원결 怨結 The knot of hatred. 원친 怨親 Hate and affection. 원적 怨賊 The robber hatred, hurtful to life and goods. 원령 怨靈 An avenging spirit or ghost.

원 圓 Round, all-round, full-orbed, inclusive, all embracing, whole, perfect, complete.

원 源 Spring, source, origin, *fons et origo*. 원저 源底 The very beginning, source, or basis.

원 寃 To oppress, wrong ; a grievance ; enmity. 원친 寃親 Enmity and friendship. 원친평등심 寃親平等心 A mind that knows neither enmity nor friendship, no discrimination of persons.

원 園 Vihāra ; place for walking about, pleasure-ground, garden, park. 원관 園觀 A garden look-out, or terrace. 원두 園頭 A gardener, or head of a monastery-garden, either for pleasure, or for vegetables.

원 院 Ārāma, pleasance, garden, grove ; a monastery, hall, court. 원주 院主 The abbot of a monastery.

원각 圓覺 Complete enlightenment potentially present in each being, for all have 본각 本覺 primal awareness, or 진심 眞心 the true heart (e.g. conscience), which has always remained pure and shining ; considered as essence it is the 일심 一心 one mind, considered causally it is the Tathāgata-garbha, considered in its result it is 원각 圓覺 perfect enlightenment, cf. 원각경 圓覺經.

원계 圓戒 v. 원돈계 圓頓戒.

원공 圓空 Complete vacuity, i.e. 공공 空空, from which even the idea of vacuity is absent.

원과 圓果 Perfect fruit, nirvāṇa.

원광 圓光 The halo surrounding the head of a Buddha, etc.

원교 圓教 The complete, perfect, or comprehensive doctrine ; the school or sect of Mahāyāna which represents it. The term has had three references. The first was by 광통 光統 Kuang-t'ung of the Later Wei, sixth century, who defined three schools, 점 漸 gradual, 돈 頓 immediate, and 원 圓 inclusive or complete. The T'ien-t'ai called its fourth section the inclusive, complete, or perfect teaching 원 圓, the other three being 삼장 三藏 Hīnayāna, 통 通 Mahāyāna-cum-Hīnayāna, 별 別 Mahāyāna. The Hua-yen so called its fifth section, i.e. 소승 小乘 ; 대승시 大乘始 ; 대승종 大乘終 ; 돈 頓 and 원 圓. It is the T'ien-t'ai version that is in general acceptance, defined as a perfect whole and as complete in its parts ; for the whole is the absolute and its parts are therefore the absolute ; the two may be called noumenon and phenomenon, or 공 空 and 가 假 (or 속 俗), but in reality they are one, i.e. the 중 中 medial condition. To conceive these three as a whole is the T'ien-t'ai inclusive or "perfect" doctrine. The Hua-yen "perfect" doctrine also taught that unity and differentiation, or absolute and relative, were one, a similar doctrine to that of the identity of contraries. In T'ien-t'ai teaching the harmony is due to its underlying unity ; its completeness to the permeation of this unity in all phenomena ; these two are united in the medial 중 中 principle ; to comprehend these three principles at one and the same time is the complete, all-containing, or "perfect" doctrine of T'ien-t'ai. There are other definitions of the all-inclusive doctrine, e.g. the eight complete things, complete in teaching, principles, knowledge, etc. 원교사문 圓教四門 v. 사문 四門.

원구 圓具 Whole and complete, i.e. the whole of the commandments, by the observance of which one is near to nirvāṇa.

원극 圓極 Inclusive to the uttermost ; absolute perfection.

원기 圓機 The potentiality of becoming fully enlightened at once.

원단 圓壇 Round altar ; a complete group of objects of worship, a maṇḍala.

원단 圓斷 The T'ien-t'ai doctrine of the complete cutting off, at one remove, of the three illusions, i.e. 견사 見思 associated with 공 空 ; 진사 塵沙 with 가 假 ; and 무명 無明 with 중 中 ; q.v.

원도 圓道 The perfect way (of the three principles of T'ien-t'ai, v. above).

원돈 圓頓 Complete and immediate, i.e. to comprehend the three principles 공가중 空假中 at one and the same time, cf. 원교 圓教. 원돈일승 圓頓一乘 The complete immediate vehicle, that of T'ien-t'ai. 원돈종 圓頓宗 ; 원돈교 圓頓教 ditto. 원돈계 圓頓戒 The rules of the T'ien-t'ai school, especially for attaining immediate enlightenment as above ; also called 원돈무작대계 圓頓無作大戒 or 원돈보살대계 圓頓菩薩大戒. 원돈(지)관 圓頓(止)觀 as given in the 마하지관 摩訶止觀 is the concentration, or mental state, in which is perceived, at one and the same time, the unity in the diversity and the diversity in the unity, a method ascribed by T'ien-t'ai to the Lotus sūtra ; v. above.

원만 圓滿 Completely full ; wholly complete ; the fulfilling of the whole, i.e. that the part contains the whole. the absolute in the relative. 원만경 圓滿經 The complete, or all-inclusive sūtra, a term applied to the Hua-yen ching.

원묘 圓妙 The mystery of the "perfect" school, i.e. the complete harmony of 공가중 空假中 noumenon, phenomenon, and the middle way.

원밀 圓密 The complete teaching of T'ien-t'ai and the esoteric teaching. Also, the harmony of both as one.

원불 圓佛 The Buddha of the "perfect" school, the perfect pan-Buddha embracing all things in every direction ; the dharmakāya ; Vairocana, identified with Śākyamuni.

원성 圓成 Complete perfection. 원성실성 圓成實性 The perfect true nature, absolute reality, the bhūtatathatā.

원수 圓修 (1) To observe the complete T'ien-t'ai meditation, at one and the same time to comprehend the three ideas of 공가중 空假中 q.v. (2) To keep all the commandments perfectly.

원승 圓乘 The all-complete vehicle, the final teaching of Buddha.

원신 圓信 Complete faith ; the faith of the "perfect" school. A T'ien-t'ai doctrine that a moment's faith embraces the universe.

원실 圓實 Perfect reality ; the T'ien-t'ai perfect doctrine which enables one to attain reality or Buddhahood at once.

원심 圓心 The perfect mind, the mind that seeks perfection, i.e. nirvāṇa.

원오 圓悟 Completely to apprehend the truth. In T'ien-t'ai, the complete apprehension at the same time of noumenon, phenomenon, and the middle way.

원위 圓位 The perfect status, the position of the "perfect" school, perfect unity which embraces all diversity.

원융 圓融 Complete combination ; the absolute in the relative and vice versa ; the identity of apparent contraries ; perfect harmony among all differences, as in water and waves, passion and enlightenment, transmigration and nirvāṇa, or life and death, etc. ; all are of the same fundamental nature, all are bhūtatathatā, and bhūtatathatā is all ; waves are one with waves, and water is one with water, and water and wave are one. 원융삼제 圓融三諦 The three dogmas of 공가중 空假中 as combined, as one and the same, as a unity, according to the T'ien-t'ai inclusive or perfect school. The universal 공 空 apart from the particular 가 假 is an abstraction. The particular apart from the universal is unreal. The universal realizes its true nature in the particular, and the particular derives its meaning from the universal. The middle path 중 中 unites these two aspects of one reality.

원응 圓凝 Complete crystallization, or formation, i.e. perfect nirvāṇa.

원적 圓寂 Perfect rest, i.e. parinirvāṇa ; the perfection of all virtue and the elimination of all evil, release from the miseries of transmigration and entrance into the fullest joy.

원전 圓詮 Exposition of the perfect or all-embracing doctrine, as found in the Hua-yen and Lotus sūtras.

원종 圓宗 The sect of the complete or final Buddha-truth, i.e. T'ien-t'ai ; cf. 원교 圓教.

원종문류 圓宗文類 A masterpiece of 의천 義天 on 화엄 華嚴.

원주 院主 Lit. "master of the monastery." Monastic official in charge of the everyday affairs of the monastery.

원주실 院主室 The room of 원주 院主.

원측 圓測 See 문아 원측 文雅圓測.

원통 圓通 Universally penetrating ; supernatural powers of omnipresence ; universality ; by wisdom to penetrate the nature or truth of all things. 원통삼매 圓通三昧 The various samādhi of supernatural powers of the twenty-five "great ones" of the 능엄경 楞嚴經 Śūraṅgama sūtra, especially of 원통대사 圓通大士 the omnipresent hearer of those who call, i.e. Kuan-yin.

원합 圓合 All-embracing, all inclusive.

원해 圓海 The all-embracing ocean, i.e. the perfection or power of the Tathāgata.

원행 圓行 The conduct or discipline of the T'ien-t'ai "perfect" school.

원효 元曉 Won-hyo(C. Yüan-hsiao)(617-686). A famous Korean monk who studied and wrote in Silla during the T'ang dynasty ; known as 해동사 海東師 Hai-tung Shih. He is regarded as "the dawn of Korean philosophy". He is also known as "the author-monk" for his numerous writings as many as 87 kinds. 23 kinds of them are present.

월 月 Candra, 기달(라) 旃達(羅) ; 기다라 旃陀羅 ; 전달라 戰達羅 ; 전날라 戰捺羅 the moon, called also 소마 蘇摩 soma, from the fermented juice of *Asclepias acida*, used in worship, and later personified in association with the moon. It has many other epithets, e.g. 인도 印度 Indu, incorrectly intp. as marked like a hare ; 창야신 創夜神 Niśākara, maker of the night ; 성수왕 星宿王 Nakṣatranātha, lord of constellations ; 희회지두식 喜懷之頭飾 the crest of Śiva ; 연화왕 蓮華王 Kumuda-pati, lotus lord ; 백마주 白馬主 Śvetavājin, drawn by (or lord of) white horses ; 대백광신 大白光神 Śītāṁśu, the spirit with white rays ; 냉광신 冷光神 Śītamarīci, the spirit with cool rays ; 녹형신 鹿形神 Mṛgāṅka, the spirit with marks or form like a deer ; 야토형신 野兎形神 Śaśī, ditto like a hare.

월 越 To step over, pass over, surpass, exceed ; similar to 초 超, with which it is often connected. 월희삼매 越喜三昧 The samādhi of Yaśodharā, wife of Śākyamuni and mother of Rāhula, which causes all kinds of joy to self and others. 월죄 越罪 Exceeding sin, or transgression of the law, particularly of esoteric law or monastic vows. 월사 越闍 Vajra, cf. 금강 金剛.

월개 月蓋 An elder of Vaiśālī, who at the Buddha's bidding sought the aid of Amitābha, 세지 勢至 (Mahāsthāmaprāpta) and Kuan-yin, especially the last, to rid his people of a pestilence. See Vimalakīrti sūtra.

월광 月光 Candraprabha, 전달라발랄바 戰達羅鉢剌婆 Moonlight. One of the three honoured ones in the Vajradhātu, and in the Mañjuśrī court of the Garbhadhātu, known also as 청량금강 清涼金剛. 월광태자 月光太子 Moonlight prince, name of Śākyamuni in a previous incarnation as a prince, when he split one of his bones to anoint a leper with its marrow and gave him of his blood to drink. 지도론 智度論 12. 월광왕 月光王 The same, called Moonlight king, when he gave his head to a brahman. 월광동자 月光童子 ; 월광아 月光兒 The son of an elder of the capital of Magadha, who listening to heretics and against his son's pleadings, endeavoured to destroy the Buddha in a pitfall of fire, but, on the Buddha's approach, the fire turned to a pool and the father was converted ; the son was then predicted by the Buddha to be king of China in a future incarnation, when all China and the Mongolian and other tribes would be converted, v. 월광동자경 月光童子經. 월광보살 月光菩薩 The bodhisattva Moonlight who attends on 약사 藥師 the Master of Healing ; also in the Mañjuśrī court of the Garbhadhātu ; used for 월광왕 月光王 ; v. 월광보살경 月光菩薩經.

월궁 月宮 The moon-palace of the 월천자 月天子 made of silver and crystal ; it is described as forty-nine yojanas square, but there are other accounts.

월기 月忌 The return of the day in each month when a person died.

월단 月壇 an external altar in temples in the open, i.e. under the moon.

월등삼매 月燈三昧 Candra-dīpa-samādhi, the samādhi said to have been given to 월광동자 月光童子 by Buddha, the sūtra of which is in two translations.

월륜 月輪 The moon's disc, the moon. 월륜관 月輪觀 or 월륜삼매 月輪三昧 The moon contemplation (or samādhi) in regard to its sixteen nights of waxing to the full, and the application of this contemplation to the development of bodhi within, especially of the sixteen kinds of bodhisattva mind of the lotus and of the human heart.

월면불 月面佛 The "moon-face Buddha", whose life is only a day and a night, in contrast with the sun-face Buddha whose life is 1,800 years.

월명보살 月明菩薩 idem 월광보살 月光菩薩 ; there is a 월명보살경 月明菩薩經. Also 월명동자 月明童子 or 월명동남 月明童男.

월미 月眉 New moon eyebrows, i.e. arched like the Buddha's.

월분 月分 Moon and division, a tr. of Candrabhāgā. 전달라파가 旃達羅婆伽 The two rivers Candra and Bhāga joined. The Chenab river, Punjab, the Acesines of Alexander.

월상녀경 月上女經 Candrottarā-dārikā-vyākaraṇa-sūtra of the maid in the moon.

월서 月鼠 The moon rat, one of the two rats, black and white, that gnaw the cord of life, i.e. night and day.

월애삼매 月愛三昧 A Buddha's "moon-love samādhi", in which he rids men of the distresses of love and hate. 월애주 月愛珠 Candrakānta, the moon-love pearl or moonstone, which bestows abundance of water or rain.

월연 月輦 The chariot of 월천자 月天子.

월염존 月黶尊 One of the names of a 명왕 明王 Ming Wang, i.e. "moon-black" or "moon-spots", 항삼세명왕 降三世明王 the mahārāja who subdues all resisters, past, present, and future, represented with black face, three eyes, four protruding teeth, and fierce laugh.

월왕 月王 Moon-king, 설상가 設賞迦 Śaśāṅka, a ruler of Karṇasuvarṇa, who tried to destroy the bodhidruma, Buddha's tree ; dethroned by Śīlāditya.

월요 月曜 Moon-shining, or Moon-effulgence ; a group shown outside the Garbhadhātu group in the Diamond Court.

월정(마니) 月精(摩尼) The pearl or jewel in the fortieth hand of the "thousand hand" Kuan-yin, towards which worship is paid in case of fevers ; the hand is called 월정수 月精手.

월정사 月精寺 Wol-jeong-sa. A temple located in Mt. Odaesan, Dongsan-ri Jinbu-myeon Kangwon-do in Korea. The 4th parish headquarters of Korean Jogye Order.

월종 月種 Candravaṁśa, descendants of the moon, "the lunar race of kings or the second great line of Kṣatriya or royal dynasties in India." [M. W.]

월주 月胄 Candravarma, 전달라벌마 旃達羅伐摩 a learned monk of the Nāgavadana monastery.

월지(국) 月支(國) The Yüeh-chih, or "Indo-Scythians", 월씨(국) 月氏(國) and a country they at one time occupied, i.e. 도화라 都貨羅 Tukhāra, Tokharestan, or Badakshan. Driven out from the northern curve of the Yellow River by the Huns, *circa* 165 B.C., they conquered Bactria 대하 大夏, the Punjab, Kashmir, "and the greater part of India." Their expulsion from the north of Shansi was the cause of the famous journey of Chang Ch'ien of the Han dynasty and the beginning of Chinese expansion to the north-west. Kaniṣka, king of the Yüeh-chih towards the end of the first century A.D., became the great protector and propagator of Buddhism.

월천 月天 Candradeva, or Somadeva. 전달제바 旃達提婆 or 소마제바 蘇摩提婆 The ruler of the moon, to whom the terms under 월 月 *supra* are also applied. 월천자 月天子 The male regent of the moon, named 보길상 寶吉祥, one of the metamorphoses of the bodhisattva 세지 勢至 Mahāsthāmaprāpta ; the male regent has also his queen 월천비 月天妃.

월토 月兎 The hare in the moon.

월파수나 月婆首那 Upaśūnya, 고공 高空 an Indian monk, son of the king of 우선니 優禪尼 Udyāna, who tr. 승가타경 僧伽吒經.

위 韋 A thong ; translit. for *vi, ve, vai* sounds. 위(천)장군 韋(天)將軍 One of the generals under the southern Mahārāja guardian in a temple. 위제(희) 韋提(希) ; 비제희 毘提希 or 폐제희 吠提希 ; 폐제희불다라 吠題呬弗多羅 Vaidehī, wife of Bimbisāra, and mother of Ajātaśatru ; also called Śrībhadra. 위뉴천 韋紐天 ; 위유 韋糅 ; 위뉴 違紐 ; 비뉴 毘紐 ; 비슬뉴 毘瑟紐 ; 위수뉴 韋搜紐 ; 위수뉴 韋廋紐 ; 비슬노 毘瑟怒 or 毘瑟皴 Viṣṇu, all-pervading, encompassing ; "the preserver" in the Trimūrti, Brahmā, Viṣṇu, Śiva, creator, preserver, destroyer ; the Vaiṣṇavas (Vishnuites) are devoted to him as the Śaivas are to Śiva. His wife is Lakṣmī, or Śrī. The Chinese describe him as born out of water at the beginning of a world-kalpa with 1,000 heads and 2,000 hands ; from his navel springs a lotus, from which is evolved Brahmā. 위타 韋陀 ; 위타 圍陀 ; 비타 毘陀 ; 피타 皮陀 ; 폐타 吠陀 or 吠馱 ; 벽타 薜陀 ; 비타 鞞陀 Veda ; knowledge, tr. 명지 明智 or 명분 明分 clear knowledge or discernment. The four Vedas are the Ṛgveda, Yajurveda, Sāmaveda, and Atharvaveda ; they were never translated into Chinese, being accounted heretical. 위타수 韋陀輸 or 韋馱輸 Vītāśoka, Vigatāśoka, younger brother of king Aśoka. 위타라 韋陀羅 Vetāla, v. 비 毘. 위타(천) 韋馱(天) Wei-to, the guardian facing the main hall of a temple. For the origin of Wei-to, see 위타천 韋陀天.

위 僞 False, counterfeit, forged. False or forged sūtras which were produced after the Wei dynasty ; catalogues of these forged sūtras are given in various books.

위 衛 Guard, defend, restrain, an outpost, garrison ; to escort. 위세사 衛世師 Vaiśeṣika ; derived from viśeṣa, characteristic, individuality, particularity or individual essence. [M. W.] Also 비세사 鞞世師 ; 비세사가 鞞世思迦 ; 폐세사가 吠世史迦 ; 승론종 勝論宗 An atomistic school founded by Kaṇāda. Like the Sāṅkhya philosophy it taught a dualism and an endless number of souls, also by its doctrine of particularity or individual essence maintained "the eternally distinct or *sui generis* nature of the nine substances" (see below), "of which the first five including mind are held to be atomic." [M. W.] The interaction of these with the six mentioned below produces cosmic evolution. It chiefly occupied itself, like the orthodox Nyāya philosophy, with the theory of knowledge, but it differed by distinguishing only six categories of cognition 육제 六諦, viz. substance, quality, activity, species, distinction, and correlation, also a seventh of non-existence, and nine substances possessed of qualities, these 구음 九陰 being : the five elements, air, fire, water, earth, ether, together with time, space, spirit (manas), and soul (ātman). Cf. Keith, *Indian Logic and Atomism*, and Dasgupta, *History of Indian Philosophy*.

위 潙 Name of several streams, etc. 위산 潙山 Kuei-shan, a noted mountain, monastery, and T'ang monk in Fukien, by whom the 위앙 潙仰 Kuei-yang branch of the Ch'an school was founded.

위 危 Perilous. 위성 危城 A perilous citadel, i.e. the body.

위 位 Position, seat, throne. 위불퇴 位不退 One of the 삼불퇴 三不退 q.v. three kinds of never receding. 위패 位牌 The board, or record of official position.

위 威 Prabhāva. Awe-inspiring majesty ; also 위력 威力 and 위신력 威神力. 위의 威儀 Respect-inspiring deportment ; dignity, i.e. in walking, standing, sitting, lying. There are said to be 3,000 and also 80,000 forms of such deportment. 위의(법)사 威儀(法)師 ; 위의승 威儀僧 A master of ceremonies. 위덕 威德 Of respect-inspiring virtue ; dignified. 위노 威怒 Awe-inspiring ; wrathful majesty. 위노왕 威怒王 The wrathful Mahārāja guardians of Buddhism. 위신 威神 The awe-inspiring gods, or spirits. 위음왕 威音王 Bhīṣma-garjita-ghoṣa-svara-rāja, the king with the awe-inspiring voice, the name of countless Buddhas successively appearing during the 이쇠 離衰 kalpa ; cf. Lotus Sūtra.

위 圍 Surround, enclose, encircle, go round. 위요 圍繞 To surround, go round ; especially to make three complete turns to the right round an image of Buddha.

위 為 To do ; to make ; to effect ; to be ; because of ; for. 유위무위 有爲無爲 Action and inaction ; active and passive ; dynamic and static ; things and phenomena in general are 유위 有爲 ; nirvāṇa, quiescence, the void, etc., are 무위 無爲. 명위 名爲 Its name is (so-and-so). 위선 爲善 To do good, be good, because of the good, etc. 위리 爲利 For gain, or profit. 위기 爲己 For self. 이위 以爲 To take to be, consider as, etc.

위 違 To oppose, disregard, disobey ; leave, avoid. 위타순자 違他順自 To disregard or oppose others and follow one's own way ; the opposite of 위자순타 違自順他. 위경 違境 To oppose or disregard conditions ; opposing or unfavourable circumstances. 위연 違緣 Opposing or hostile conditions. 위타 違陀 Veda, knowledge, the Vedas, cf. 위 韋, 비 毘. 위순 違順 To oppose, or accord with ; hostile or favourable.

위 委 To throw down, depute ; really ; crooked ; the end. 위순 委順 To die, said of a monk.

위타천 韋陀天 or 韋馱天 Wi-ta-cheon(C. Wei-to). Originally he was a historical general in ancient China ; he became an entrusted general who protects the Dharma. During services in Korea, the congregation faces a picture of this general when chanting the Heart Sūtra, inside of the Main Buddha Hall.

유 柳 A willow. 유지 柳枝 Willow branches put in clean water to keep away evil spirits.

유 維 A carriage-curtain ; a net ; a corner, cardinal point ; to tie or hold together, connect ; a copula, also, but, whereas, now. 유구식 維口食 Improper means of existence by spells, fortune-telling, etc., one of the four cardinal improper ways of earning a livelihood. 유마 維摩 Vimalakīrti, 유마(라)힐 維摩(羅)詰 ; 비마라힐 毘摩羅詰 undefiled or spotless reputation, "a native of Vaiśālī, said to have been a contemporary of Śākyamuni, and to have visited China." [Eitel]. The Vimalakīrti-nirdeśa sūtra 유마힐소설경 維摩詰所說經 is an apocryphal account of "conversations between Śākyamuni and some residents of Vaiśālī," tr. by Kumārajīva ; an earlier tr. was the 유마힐경 維摩詰經, a later was by Hsüan-tsang, and there are numerous treatises. 유야리 維耶離 cf. 비 毘 Vaiśālī. 유위(불) 維衛(佛) cf. 비 毘 Vipaśyin, one of the seven ancient Buddhas. 유월 維越 Avaivartika, cf. 아 阿, one who never reverts to a lower condition. 유나 維那 ; 갈마타나 羯磨陀那 Karmadāna, the duty-distributor, deacon, arranger of duties, second in command of a monastery.

유 猶 A monkey ; doubtful ; if, so ; like, as ; yet, still ; to scheme. 유약 猶若 As if. 유미정 猶未定 Still unsettled, uncertain.

유 儒 A scholar ; learned. Confucian. 유동보살 儒童菩薩 Learned-youth Bodhisattva, i.e. Confucius, he having been sent from India by the Buddha to instruct China! Also a name of Śākyamuni in a previous existence.

유 游 Bhrāmyati ; to ramble, travel ; swim. 유람 游藍 Ambrosia, nectar.

유 遊 Bhrāmyati. Ramble, wander, travel, go from place to place. 유화 遊化 To go about preaching and converting men. 유산 遊山 To go from monastery to monastery ; ramble about the hills. 유증지옥 遊增地獄 The sixteen subsidiary hells of each of the eight hot hells. 유심법계 遊心法界 A mind free to wander in the realm of all things ; that realm as the realm of the liberated mind. 유희 遊戱 Vikrīḍita. To roam for pleasure ; play, sport. 유희신통 遊戱神通 The supernatural powers in which Buddhas and bodhisattvas indulge, or take their pleasure. 유방 遊方 To wander from place to place. 유허공천 遊虛空天 To roam in space, as do the devas of the sun, moon, stars, etc. ; also the four upper devalokas, 유행 遊行 To roam, wander, travel, etc.

유 有 Bhāva ; that which exists, the existing, existence ; to have, possess, be. It is defined as (1) the opposite of 무 無 wu and 공 空 K'ung the non-existent ; (2) one of the twelve nidānas, existence ; the condition which, considered as cause, produces effect ; (3) effect, the consequence of cause ; (4) anything that can be relied upon in the visible or invisible realm. It means any state which lies between birth and death, or beginning and end. There are numerous categories — 3, 4, 7, 9, 18, 25, and 29. The 삼유 三有 are the 삼계 三界 trailokya, i.e. 욕계 欲界, 색계 色界 and 무색계 無色界 the realms of desire, of form, and of non-form, all of them realms of mortality ; another three are 본유 本有 the present body and mind, or existence, 당유 當有 the future ditto, 중유 中有 the intermediate ditto. Other definitions give the different forms or modes of existence.

유 唯 Eva. Affirmative, yes ; to answer, respond ; said to interpret Mātratā, and is defined as discrimination, decision, approval. It is also used for only, alone, but. 유명 唯名 Nāmamātra ; name only. 유경무식 唯境無識 Realism as opposed to 유식무경 唯識無境 Idealism ; implying that the four elements are real and permanent. 유심 唯心 Idealism, mind only, the theory that the only reality is mental, that of the mind. Similar to 유식 唯識 q.v. and v. Laṅkāvatāra-sūtra. 유심게 唯心偈 The eight-line verse of the older 화엄 華嚴 sūtra, which summarizes the idealistic idea. 유색 唯色 All things are matter, because mind and matter are identical, for matter is mind. 유식 唯識 Vijñānamātra-(vāda) ; cittamātra. Idealism, the doctrine that nothing exists apart from mind, 식외무법 識外無法. 유식중도 唯識中道 The madhya, or medial doctrine of idealism as held by the 법상 法相 Dharmalakṣaṇa school, that all things are of mind-evolution, and are neither in themselves real nor unreal. 유식수도오위 唯識修道五位 The five stages of attaining enlightenment in the idealistic sect : stage of reason and speculation ; of asceticism ; of apprehension of truth ; of practice of contemplation from the first to the tenth stage ; of complete comprehension of truth. 유식원교 唯識圓敎 The third of the three divisions of the Buddha's teaching as defined by Tao-hsüan of Nan-shan, the perfect doctrine of idealism. 유식종 唯識宗 The Dharmalakṣaṇa sect 법상종 法相宗, which holds that all is mind in its ultimate nature. Also 유식가 唯識家. 유식관 唯識觀 The three subjects of idealistic reflection : that the ego and things are realities ; that things are produced by cause and circumstance ; that the bhūtatathatā is the only reality. Also called 유식심정 唯識心定 ; 유식삼성관 唯識三性觀, cf. 삼성 三性. 유식론 唯識論 Vijñaptimātratāsiddhi-śāstra, also called the 성유식론 成唯識論 ; 유식이십론 唯識二十論 Vidyāmātrasiddhi-viṃśakakārikā-śāstra ; another is the 유식삼십론 唯識三十論 Vidyāmātrasiddhi-tridaśakārikā-śāstra. There are numerous commentaries and treatises on the subject. See de la Vallée Poussin's version.

유 由 From ; by ; a cause, motive ; to allow, let ; translit. *yo, yu* ; e.g. 유건 由乾 ; 유건다라 由乾陀羅 or 由乾陁羅, Yugaṁdhara, idem 유건달라 踰健達羅. 유순 由旬 ; 유연 由延 ; 유순 兪旬 ; 유순 揄旬 ; 유선나 踰繕那 ; 유사나 踰闍那 ; 유연나 踰延那 Yojana ; described as anciently a royal day's march for the army ; also 40, 30, or 16 li ; 8 krośas 구라사 拘羅舍, one being the distance at which a bull's bellow can be heard ; M. W. says 4 krośas or about 9 English miles, or nearly 30 Chinese li.

유 幽 Hidden, dark, mysterious. 유의 幽儀 The mysterious form, the spirit of the dead. 유명 幽冥 Mysterious, beyond comprehension ; the shades. 유도 幽途 The dark paths, i.e. of rebirth in purgatory or as hungry ghosts or animals. 유령 幽靈 Invisible spirits, the spirits in the shades, the souls of the departed.

유 喩 Illustrate, example ; to know 종인유 宗因喩 q.v. The example (dṛṣṭānta) in a syllogism. 유의 喩依 The subject of the example, e.g. a vase, or bottle ; as contrasted with 유체 喩體 the predicate, e.g. (the vase) is not eternal.

유 瑜 Lustre of gems ; a beautiful stone ; excellences, virtues ; translit. *yu, yo.* 유건타라 瑜乾馱羅 Yugaṁdhara, v. 유 踰, the first of the seven concentric circles around Meru. 유가 瑜伽 Yoga ; also 유아 瑜誐 ; 유가 遊迦 ; a yoke, yoking, union, especially an ecstatic union of the individual soul with a divine being, or spirit, also of the individual soul with the universal soul. The method requires the mutual response or relation of 경 境, 행 行, 리 理, 과 果 and 기 機 ; i.e. (1) state, or environment, referred to mind ; (2) action, or mode of practice ; (3) right principle ; (4) results in enlightenment ; (5) motivity, i.e. practical application in saving others. Also the mutual relation of hand, mouth, and mind referring to manifestation, incantation, and mental operation ; these are known as 유가삼밀 瑜伽三密, the three esoteric (means) of Yoga. The older practice of meditation as a means of obtaining spiritual or magical power was distorted in Tantrism to exorcism, sorcery, and juggling in general. 유가종 瑜伽宗 The Yogācāra, Vijñānavāda, Tantric, or esoteric sect. The principles of Yoga are accredited to Patañjali in the second century B.C., later founded as a school in Buddhism by Asaṅga, fourth century A.D. Cf. 대교 大教. Hsüan-tsang became a disciple and advocate of this school. 유가사 瑜伽師 ; 유가아사리 瑜伽阿闍梨 Yogācāra, a teacher, or master of magic, or of this school. 유가사지론 瑜伽師地論 Yogācāryabhūmi-śāstra, the work of Asaṅga, said to have been dictated to him in or from the Tuṣita heaven by Maitreya, tr. by Hsüan-tsang, is the foundation text of this school, on which there are numerous treatises, the 유가사지론석 瑜伽師地論釋 being a commentary on it by Jinaputra, tr. by Hsüan-tsang. 유가기 瑜伽祇 ; 유기 瑜岐 ; 유기 瑜祁 Yogin, one who practices yoga.

유 乳 Milk, which in its five forms illustrates the T'ien-t'ai 오시교 五時教 five periods of the Buddha's teaching. 유미 乳味 The flavour of fresh milk, to which the Buddha's teaching in the 화엄경 華嚴經 Hua-yen ching is compared. 유목 乳木 Resinous wood (for homa, or fire sacrifice). 유수안 乳水眼 The eye able to distinguish milk from water ; as the goose drinks the milk and rejects the water, so the student should distinguish orthodox from heterodox teaching. 유경 乳經 T'ien-t'ai compares the Avataṁsaka-sūtra 화엄경 華嚴經 to milk, from which come all its other products. 유향 乳香 Kunduruka, *Boswellia thurifera,* both the plant and its resin.

유 油 Oil. 유발 油鉢 A bowl of oil. 지유발 持油鉢 As careful as carrying a bowl of oil.

유 柔 Pliant, yielding, soft. 유화 柔和 Gentle, forbearing, tolerant. 유연 柔輭 (A heart) mild and pliable (responsive to the truth). 유연어 柔輭語 Gentle, persuasive words. 유순인 柔順忍 The patience of meekness, i.e. in meekness to accord with the truth.

유 濡 To dip, wet, soak ; damp ; glossy ; forbearing. 유불 濡佛 An image of Vairocana in the open. 유수 濡首 A faulty tr. of Mañjuśrī, cf. 문 文.

유 揄 To draw out, extol. 유순 揄旬 Yojana, v. 유 由.

유 遺 To leave behind, bequeath, bestow, residue. 유제 遺弟 The disciples left behind by a deceased master. 유형 遺形 Relics of the Buddha. 유교 遺教 ; 유화 遺化 ; 유법 遺法 ; 유훈 遺訓 Doctrine, or transforming teaching, handed down or bequeathed (by a Buddha). 유적 遺跡 Traces, tracks, evidences, examples left behind.

유 逾 To pass over, exceed. 유월 逾越 To pass over. 유시 逾時 To exceed the time. 유건달라 逾健達羅 Yugaṁdhara, v. 유 踰.

유 踰 To pass over, or by ; exceed ; beyond ; translit. *yo, yu*. 유건달라 踰健達羅 ; 유건타라 踰乾陀羅 ; v. 유 瑜 Yugaṅdhara. 유선나 踰繕那 ; 유사(나) 踰闍(那) v. 유 由 Yojana. 유사 踰闍 v. 아 阿 Ayodhyā.

유 惟 To reflect on ; but, only ; verbal particle ; cf. 유 唯. 유자파라 惟子頗羅 or 유간파라 惟干頗羅 Bṛhatphala 광과 廣果, "great fruit," or abundant merits ; the twelfth Brahmaloka, or second region of the fourth dhyāna.

유간 有間 Interrupted, not continuous, not intermingled, opposite of 무간 無間.

유견 有見 The visible, but it is used also in the sense of the erroneous view that things really exist. Another meaning is the 색계 色界 realm of form, as contrasted with the 무견 無見 invisible, or with the formless realms.

유결 有結 The bond of existence, or mortal life.

유계 有界 The realm of existence.

유공 有空 Phenomenal and noumenal ; the manifold forms of things exist, but things, being constructed of elements, have no *per se* reality. 유공불이 有空不二 The phenomenal and the noumenal are identical, the phenomenal expresses the noumenal and the noumenon contains the phenomenon. 유공중 有空中 The three terms, phenomenal, noumenal, and the link or mean, v. 중 中 and 공 空. 유공중삼시 有空中三時 The 법상종 法相宗 Dharma-lakṣaṇa school divides the Buddha's teaching into three periods, in which he taught (1) the unreality of the ego, as shown in the 아함 阿含 Āgamas, etc. ; (2) the unreality of the dharmas, as in the 반야 般若 Prajñāpāramitā, etc. ; and (3) the middle or uniting way, as in the 해심밀경 解深密經 Sandhinirmocana-sūtra, etc., the last being the foundation text of this school.

유교 有教 The realistic school as opposed to the 공교 空教 teaching of unreality ; especially (1) the Hīnayāna teaching of the 구사종 俱舍宗 Abhidharma-kośa school of Vasubandhu, opposed to the 성실종 成實宗 Satya-siddhi school of Harivarman ; (2) the Mahāyāna 법상종 法相宗 Dharma-lakṣaṇa school, also called the 유식종 唯識宗, founded in China by Hsüan-tsang, opposed to the 삼론종 三論宗 Mādhyamika school of Nāgārjuna.

유근신 有根身 The body with its five senses.

유대 有對 Pratigha, sapratigha ; resistance, opposition, whatever is capable of offering resistance, an object ; ṃaterial ; opposing, opposite.

유대 有待 That which is dependent on material things, i.e. the body.

유덕녀 有德女 A woman of Brahman family in Benares, who became a convert and is the questioner of the Buddha in the Śrīmatī-brāhmaṇī-paripṛcchā 유덕녀소문대승경 有德女所問大乘經.

유량 有量 Limited, finite ; opposite of 무량 無量 measureless, boundless, infinite. 유상유량 有相有量 That which has form and measurement is called 추 麤 coarse, i.e. palpable, that which is without form and measurement 무상무량 無相無量 is called 세 細 fine, i.e. impalpable.

유령 有靈 Having souls, sentient beings, similar to 유정 有情 ; possessing magical or spiritual powers.

유루 有漏 Āsrava, means "outflow, discharge" ; "distress, pain, affliction" ; it is intp. by 번뇌 煩惱 kleśa, the passions, distress, trouble, which in turn is intp. as 혹 惑 delusion. Whatever has kleśa, i.e. distress or trouble, is 유루 有漏 ; all things are of this nature, hence it means whatever is in the stream of births-and-deaths, and also means mortal life or births-and-deaths, i.e. mortality as contrasted with 무루 無漏, which is nirvāṇa. 유루세계 有漏世界 or 유루삼계 有漏三界 The world, or worlds, of distress and illusion. 유루선법 有漏善法 or 유루악법 有漏惡法 Good (or evil) done in a mortal body is rewarded accordingly in the character of another mortal body. 유루정토 有漏淨土 A purifying stage which, for certain types, precedes entry into the Pure Land. 유루도 有漏道 or 유루로 有漏路 The way of mortal saṁsāra, in contrast with 무루도 無漏道 that of nirvāṇa.

유류 有流 The mortal stream of existence with its karma and delusion. Cf. 견류 見流.

유륜 有輪 The wheel of existence, the round of mortality, of births-and-deaths.

유무이견 有無二見 Bhāvābhāva. Existence or non-existence, being or non-being ; these two opposite views, opinions, or theories are the basis of all erroneous views, etc. 유무이변 有無二邊 The two extremes of being or non-being. 유무사견 有無邪見 Both views are erroneous in the opinion of upholders of the 중도 中道, the Mādhyamika school.

유법 有法 A thing that exists, not like "the horns of a hare," which are 무법 無法 non-existent things. Also in logic the subject in contrast with the predicate, e.g. "sound" is the 유법 有法 or thing, "is eternal" the 법 法 or law stated.

유변 有邊 The one extreme of "existence," the opposite extreme being 무변 無邊 "non-existence."

유부 有部 ; **일체유부** 一切有部 ; **살바다** 薩婆多 Sarvāstivāda ; the school of the reality of all phenomena, one of the early Hīnayāna sects, said to have been formed, about 300 years after the Nirvāṇa, out of the Sthavira ; later it subdivided into five, Dharmaguptāḥ, Mūlasarvāstivādāḥ, Kāśyapīyāḥ, Mahīśāsaka, and the influential Vātsīputrīyāḥ. v. 일체유부 一切有部. Its scriptures are known as the 유부율 有部律 ; 율서 律書 ; 십송율 十誦律 ; 근본설일체유부비나야 根本說一切有部毘那耶 ; (근본설일체)유부니다나 (根本說一切)有部尼陀那 ; (근본설일체)유부목득가 (根本說一切)有部目得迦 ; 근본살바다부율섭 根本薩婆多部律攝 or 근본살바유부율섭 根本薩婆有部律攝, etc.

유분별 有分別 The sixth sense of mental discrimination, manas, as contrasted with the other five senses, sight, hearing, etc., each of which deals only with its own perceptions, and is 무분별 無分別. 유분식 有分識 Discrimination, another name for the ālaya-vijñāna.

유사 有事 To have affairs, functioning, phenomenal, idem 유위법 有爲法.

유상 有相 To have form, whatever has form, whether ideal or real. 유상업 有相業 Action through faith in the idea, e.g. of the Pure Land ; the acts which produce such results. 유상교 有相教 The first twelve years of the Buddha's teaching, when he treated the phenomenal as real ; v. 유공중 有空中. 유상종 有相宗 v. 법상종 法相宗 and 유부 有部 Sarvāstivāda.

유상 有想 To have thoughts, or desires, opp. 무상 無想.

유상사 有上士 A bodhisattva who has reached the stage of 등각 等覺 and is above the state of being, or the existing, i.e. as conceivable by human minds.

유선다 有善多 Ujjayanta, a mountain and monastery in Surāṣṭra on the peninsula of Gujarat. [Eitel].

유성 有性 "To have the nature," i.e. to be a Buddhist ; have the bodhi-mind, in contrast with the 무성 無性 absence of this mind, i.e. the 천제 闡提 icchanti, or unconverted.

유소연 有所緣 Mental activity, the mind being able to climb, or reach anywhere, in contrast with the non-mental activities, which are 무소연 無所緣.

유수 有手 To have a hand, or hands. Hastin, possessing a hand, i.e. a trunk ; an elephant.

유식 有識 Perceptive beings, similar to 유정 有情 sentient beings.

유야무야 有耶無耶 Existence? non-existence? Material? immaterial? i.e. uncertainty, a wavering mind.

유여 有餘 Something more ; those who have remainder to fulfil, e.g. of karma ; incomplete ; extra, additional. 유여토 有餘土 One of the four lands, or realms, the 방편유여토 方便有餘土 to which, according to Mahāyāna, arhats go at their decease ; cf. next. 유여열반 有餘涅槃 ; 유여의(열반) 有餘依(涅槃) Incomplete nirvāṇa. Hīnayāna holds that the arhat after his last term of mortal existence enters into nirvāṇa, while alive here he is in the state of sopādhiśeṣa-nirvāṇa, limited, or modified, nirvāṇa, as contrasted with 무여열반 無餘涅槃 nirupadhiśeṣa-nirvāṇa. Mahāyāna holds that when the cause 인 因 of reincarnation is ended the state is that of 유여열반 有餘涅槃 incomplete nirvāṇa ; when the effect 과 果 is ended, and 득불지상신 得佛之常身 the eternal Buddha-body has been obtained, then there is 무여열반 無餘涅槃 complete nirvāṇa. Mahāyāna writers say that in the Hīnayāna 무여열반 無餘涅槃 "remainderless" nirvāṇa for the arhat there are still remains of illusion, karma, and suffering, and it is therefore 유여열반 有餘涅槃 ; in Mahāyāna 무여열반 無餘涅槃 these remains of illusion, etc., are ended. 유여설 有餘說 Something further to say, incomplete explanation. 유여사 有餘師 Masters, or exponents, in addition to the chief or recognized authorities ; also spoken of as 유여 有餘 ; 여사 餘師 ; 유제사 有諸師 ; 유인 有人 ; hence 유여사설 有餘師說 refers to other than the recognized, or orthodox, explanations.

유연 有緣 Those who have the cause, link, or connection, i.e. are influenced by and responsive to the Buddha.

유위 有爲 Active, creative, productive, functioning, causative, phenomenal, the processes resulting from the laws of karma, v. 유작 有作 ; opposite of 무위 無爲 passive, inert, inactive, non-causative, laisser-faire. It is defined by 조작 造作 to make, and associated with saṁskṛta. The three active things 삼유위법 三有爲法 are 색 色 material, or things which have form, 심 心 mental and 비색비심 非色非心 neither the one nor the other. The four forms of activity 사유위상 四有爲相 are 생주이멸 生住異滅 coming into existence, abiding, change, and extinction ; they are also spoken of as three, the two middle terms being treated as having like meaning. 유위과 有爲果 The result or effect of action. 유위무상 有爲無常 Activity implies impermanency. 유위생사 有爲生死 The mortal saṁsāra life of births and deaths, contrasted with 무위생사 無爲生死 effortless mortality, e.g. transformation such as that of the Bodhisattva. 유위공 有爲空 The unreality of the phenomenal. 유위전변 有爲轉變 The permutations of activity, or phenomena, in arising, abiding, change, and extinction.

유의 有意 Mati ; matimant ; possessing mind, intelligent ; a tr. of manuṣya, man, a rational being. The name of the eldest son of Candra-sūrya-pradīpa.

유작 有作 ; 유위 有爲 Functioning, effective ; phenomenal, the processes resulting from the law of karma ; later 안립 安立 came into use.

유정 有情 Sattva, 살타 薩埵 in the sense of any sentient being ; the term was formerly tr. as 중생 衆生 all the living, which includes the vegetable kingdom, while 유정 有情 limits the meaning to those endowed with consciousness. 유정거 有情居 The nine abodes, or states of conscious beings, v. 구유정거 九有情居. 유정수 有情數 Among the number, or in the category, of conscious beings. 유정연자 有情緣慈 Sentience gives rise to pity, or to have feeling causes pity.

유정(천) 有頂(天) Akaniṣṭha, 색구경천 色究竟天 the highest heaven of form, the ninth and last of the fourth dhyāna heavens. 유정혹 有頂惑 In that region there still exist the possibilities of delusion both in theory (or views) and practice, arising from the taking of the seeming for the real.

유주물 有主物 Things that have an owner.

유지 有支 To have a branch ; also the category of bhāva, one of the twelve nidānas, v. 유 有.

유지혜 有智慧 Manuṣya, an intelligent being, possessing wisdom, cf. 유의 有意.

유집수 有執受 The perceived, perceptive, perception.

유체 有體 A thing, form, dharma, anything of ideal or real form ; embodied things, bodies ; varying list of 75, 84, and 100 are given.

유탐 有貪 Bhavarāga, the desire for existence, which is the cause of existence ; 구사론 俱舍論 19.

유파제야야 有波第耶夜 Upādhyāya, 오파다야 烏波陀耶 in India a teacher especially of the Vedāṅgas, a term adopted by the Buddhists and gradually applied to all monks. The Chinese form is 화상 和尙, q.v.

유표업 有表業 or **유표색** 有表色 The manifested activities of the 신구의 身口意 body, month, and mind (or will) in contrast with their 무표업 無表業 unmanifested activities.

유학 有學 Śaikṣa ; in Hīnayāna those in the first three stages of training as arhats, the fourth and last stage being 무학 無學 those beyond the need of further teaching or study. There are eighteen grades of śaikṣa.

유해 有解 The intp. of things as real, or material, opposite of 무해 無解 the intp. of them as unreal, or immaterial.

유해 有海 The sea of existence, i.e. of mortality, or births-and-deaths.

육 肉 Māṁsa. Flesh. 육심 肉心 ; 육단심 肉團心 ; 흘리다야 紇利陀耶 Hṛdaya ; the physical heart. 육등 肉燈 ; 육향 肉香 To cremate oneself alive as a lamp or as incense for Buddha. 육안 肉眼 Māṁsacakṣus. Eye of flesh, the physical eye. 육색 肉色 Flesh-coloured, red. 육신 肉身 The physical body. 육신보살 肉身菩薩 One who becomes a bodhisattva in the physical body, in the present life. 육식 肉食 Māṁsabhakṣaṇa, meat-eating. 육계 肉髻 ; 오실니사 烏失尼沙 or 울슬니사 鬱瑟尼沙 ; 오슬니사 烏瑟膩沙 Uṣṇīṣa. One of the thirty-two marks (lakṣaṇa) of a Buddha ; originally a conical or flame-shaped tuft of hair on the crown of a Buddha, in later ages represented as a fleshly excrescence on the skull itself ; interpreted as coiffure of flesh. In China it is low and large at the base, sometimes with a tonsure on top of the protuberance.

육 育 To rear, nurture. 육지 育坻 ; 육저 育抵 Yukti, yoking, joining, combination, plan. 육지화 育坻華 Yuktā, a kind of celestial flower. 육다바제 育多婆提 Yuktabodhi, steps in Yoga wisdom.

육 六 Ṣaṭ, ṣaḍ. Six.

육검 六劍 ; 육전 六箭 The six swords (or arrows), i.e. the six senses, v. 육진 六塵, which are defined as the qualities of sight, sound, smell, taste, touch, and mind.

육결 六結 A cloth or cord tied in six consecutive double loops and knots. The cloth represents the fundamental unity, the knots the apparent diversity. v. 능가경 楞伽經 5.

육결정 六決定 v. 육종결정 六種決定 ; also 칠심신 七深信.

육경 六境 The six fields of the senses, i.e. the objective fields of sight, sound, smell, taste, touch, and idea (or thought) ; rūpa, form and colour, is the field of vision ; sound, of hearing ; scent, of smelling ; the five flavours, of tasting ; physical feeling, of touch ; and mental presentation, of discernment ; cf. 육입 六入 ; 육처 六處 and 육진 六塵.

육계 六界 The six elements : earth , water, fire, air (or wind), space, and mind ; idem 육대 六大. 육계취 六界聚 The (human) body, which is composed of these six.

육고행 六苦行 The heretics of the six austerities are referred to as 육고행외도 六苦行外道 ; v. 육행 六行.

육공구 六供具 The six articles for worship — flowers, a censer, candles, hot liquid, fruits, tea.

육관(법) 六觀(法) Cf. 육종성 六種性 and 육위 六位. 육관음 六觀音 The six kinds of Kuan-yin. There are two groups — I. That of T'ien-t'ai : 대비 大悲 most pitiful ; 대자 大慈 most merciful ; 사자무외 師子無畏 of lion-courage ; 대광보조 大光普照 of universal light ; 천인장부 天人丈夫 leader amongst gods and men ; 대범심원 大梵深遠 the great omnipresent Brahma. Each of this bodhisattva's six qualities of pity, etc., breaks the hindrances 삼장 三障 respectively of the hells, pretas, animals, asuras, men, and devas. II. As thousand-handed ; the holy one ; horse-headed ; eleven-faced ; Cundī (or Marīci) ; with the wheel of sovereign power.

육구(법) 六垢(法) Six things that defile : 광 誑 exaggeration, 첨 諂 flattery, 교 憍 arrogance, 뇌 惱 vexation, 한 恨 hatred, 해 害 malice.

육군비구 六群比丘 The six common-herd bhikṣus, to whose improper or evil conduct is attributed the laying down of many of the laws by Śākyamuni ; also 육중 六衆 ; different lists of names are given, the generally accepted list indicating Nanda, Upananda, Aśvaka, Punarvasu, Chanda, and Udāyin. Udāyin is probably Kālodayin, a name given in other lists.

육근 六根 The six indriyas or sense-organs : eye, ear, nose, tongue, body, and mind. See also 육입 六入, 육경 六境, 육진 六塵, and 육처 六處. 육근오용 六根五用 Substitution of one organ for another, or use of one organ to do the work of all the others, which is a Buddha's power. 육근공덕 六根功德 The powers of the six senses, i.e. the achievement by purification of their interchange of function. 육근참회 六根懺悔 A penitential service over the sins of the six senses. 육근(청)정 六根(淸)淨 The six organs and their purification in order to develop their unlimited power and interchange, as in the case of a Buddha. This full development enables e.g. the eye to see everything in a great chiliocosm form its highest heaven down to its lowest hells and all the beings past, present, and future, with all the karma of each. 육근청정위 六根淸淨位 The state of the organs thus purified is defined by T'ien-t'ai as the 십신위 十信位 of the 별교 別教, or the 상사즉 相似卽 of the 원교 圓教, v. 육즉 六卽.

육나한 六羅漢 The six arhats i.e. Śākyamuni and his first five disciples, cf. 오나한 五羅漢.

육난 六難 The six difficult things — to be born in a Buddha-age, to hear the true Buddha-law, to beget a good heart, to be born in the central kingdom (India), to be born in human form, and to be perfect ; see Nirvāṇa sūtra 23.

육년고행 六年苦行 The six years of Śākyamuni's austerities before his enlightenment.

육념(법) 六念(法) The six thoughts to dwell upon : Buddha, the Law, the Order, the commands, alms-giving, and heaven with its prospective joys. 육념처 六念處 The six stages of the above.

육대 六大 The six great or fundamental things, or elements — earth ; water ; fire ; wind (or air) ; space (or ether) ; and 식 識 mind, or perception. These are universal and creative of all things, but the inanimate 비정 非情 are made only of the first five, while the animate 유정 有情 are of all six. The esoteric cult represents the six elements, somewhat differently interpreted in the garbhadhātu and vajradhātu. Also 육계 六界. 육대법성 六大法性 The unity in variety of the six elements and their products ; ordinary eyes see only the differentiated forms or appearances, the sage or philosopher sees the unity. 육대무애 六大無礙 The six elements unimpeded, or interactive ; or 육대체대 六大體大 the six elements in their greater substance, or whole. The doctrine of the esoteric cult of transubstantiation, or the free interchangeability of the six Buddha elements with the human, like with like, whereby yoga becomes possible, i.e. the Buddha elements entering into and possessing the human elements, for both are of the same elemental nature. 육대번뇌 六大煩惱 The six great kleśa, passions, or distressers : desire, resentment, stupidity, pride, doubt, and false views. 육대신 六大神 The spirits of the six elements. 육대관 六大觀 Meditation on the six elements ; in the esoteric cult, that they are unreal and unclean ; in the exoteric cult, that the Buddha and human elements are of the same substance and interchangeable, see above. 육대적 六大賊 v. 육적 六賊.

육덕 六德 The six characteristics of a Bhagavat, which is one of a Buddha's titles ; sovereign, glorious, majestic, famous, propitious, honoured.

육도 六度 The six things that ferry one beyond the sea of mortality to nirvāṇa, i.e. the six pāramitās 바라밀(다) 波羅蜜(多) : (1) 보시 布施 dāna, charity, or giving, including the bestowing of the truth on others ; (2) 지계 持戒 śīla, keeping the commandments ; (3) 인욕 忍辱 kṣānti, patience under insult ; (4) 정진 精進 vīrya, zeal and progress ; (5) 선정 禪定 dhyāna, meditation or contemplation ; (6) 지혜 智慧 prajñā, wisdom, the power to discern reality or truth. It is the last which carries across the saṁsāra (sea of incarnate life) to the shores of nirvāṇa. The opposites of these virtues are meanness, wickedness, anger, sloth, a distracted mind, and ignorance. The 유식론 唯識論 adds four other pāramitās : (7) 방편 方便 Upāya, the use of appropriate means ; (8) 원 願 praṇidhāna, pious vows ; (9) 력 力 bala, power of fulfilment ; (10) 지 智 jñāna, knowledge. 육도과보 六度果報 The rewards stimulated by the six pāramitās are 부 富 enrichment ; 구색 具色 all things, or perfection ; 력 力 power ; 수 壽 long life ; 안 安 peace (or calmness) ; 변 辯 discrimination, or powers of exposition of the truth. 육도무극 六度無極 The six infinite means of crossing the sea of mortality, i.e. the six pāramitās 육도 六度.

육도 六道 The six ways or conditions of sentient existence ; v. 육취 六趣 ; the three higher are the 상삼도 上三途, the three lower 하삼도 下三途. 육도불보살 六道佛菩薩 The Buddhas and bodhisattvas of the six gati, i.e. the six Ti-tsang 육지장 六地藏 q.v. ; also the 육관음 六觀音 q.v. ; the six Ti-tsang are also styled 육도능화보살 六道能化菩薩 Bodhisattvas who can change the lot of those in the six gati. 육도사생 六道四生 The four modes of the six rebirths — womb, egg, moisture, or transformation. 육도사성 六道四聖 The six ways of rebirth, see above, and the four holy ways of rebirth, the latter being respectively into the realms of śrāvakas, pratyeka-buddhas, bodhisattvas, and Buddhas ; the ten are known as the 십계 十界. 육도집경 六道集經 and 육도가타경 六道伽陀經 Two sūtras dealing with the six ways of rebirth.

육도피안 六到彼岸 The six things that ferry one to the other shore, i.e. the six pāramitās, v. 육도 六度.

육론 六論 The six 외도론 外道論 vedāṅgas, works which are "regarded as auxiliary to and even in some sense as part of the Veda, their object being to secure the proper pronunciation and correctness of the text and the right employment of the Mantras of sacrifice as taught in the Brāhmaṇas". [M. W.] They are spoken of together as the 사피다육론 四皮陀六論 four Vedas and six śāstras, and the six are Śikṣā, Chandas, Vyākaraṇa, Nirukta, Jyotiṣa, and Kalpa.

육륜 六輪 The six kinds of cakravartī, or wheel-kings, each allotted to one of the 육위 六位 ; the iron-wheel king to the 십신위 十信位, copper 십주 十住, silver 십행 十行, gold 십회향 十廻向, crystal

십지 十地, and pearl 등각 等覺.

육리합석 六離合釋 Ṣaṭ-samāsa ; also 육종석 六種釋 or 육합석 六合釋 the six interpretations of compound terms, considered in their component parts or together. (1) 지업석 持業釋 or 동의석 同依釋 karmadhāraya, referring to the equality of dependence of both terms, e.g. 대승 大乘 mahāyāna, "great" and "vehicle", both equally essential to "mahāyāna" with its specific meaning ; (2) 의주석 依主釋 or 의사석 依士釋 tatpuruṣa, containing a principal term, e.g. 안식 眼識 eye-perception, where the eye is the qualifying term ; (3) 유재석 有財釋 or 다재석 多財釋 bahuvrīhi, the sign of possession, e.g. 각자 覺者 he who has enlightenment ; (4) 상위석 相違釋 dvandva, a term indicating two separate ideas, e.g. 교관 教觀 teaching and meditation ; (5) 인근석 隣近釋 avyayībhāva, an adverbial compound, or a term resulting from "neighbouring" association, e.g. 염처 念處 thought or remembering place, i.e. memory ; (6) 대수석 帶數釋 dvigu, a numerative term, e.g. 오온 五蘊 pañcaskandha, the five skandhas. [M. W.] gives the order as 4, 3, 1, 2, 6, and 5.

육만장 六萬藏 The sixty thousand verses of the Buddha-law which Devadatta could recite, and ability which did not save him from the avīci hell.

육망 六妄 The six misleaders, i.e. the six senses.

육면존 六面尊 idem 육족존 六足尊.

육묘행 六妙行 idem 육행관 六行觀.

육무상육비 六無常六譬 v. 육유 六喩.

육물 六物 The six things personal to a monk — saṅghāṭī, the patch robe ; uttara-saṅghāṭī, the stole of seven pieces ; antaravāsaka, the skirt of inner garment of five pieces ; the above are the 삼의 三衣 three garments : pātra, begging bowl ; niṣīdana, a stool ; and a water-strainer : the six are also called the 삼의육물 三衣六物.

육미 六味 The six tastes, or flavours — bitter, sour, sweet, acrid, salt, and insipid.

육반신족 六般神足 The six supernatural signs ; idem 육서 六瑞.

육방 六方 The six directions — E. W. N. S. above and below. 육방례 六方禮 The brahman morning act of bathing and paying homage in the six directions ; observing the "well-born" do this ; the Buddha is said to have given the discourse in the 선생경 善生經. 육방호념 六方護念, 육방증명 六方證明 or 육방증성 六方證誠 The praises of Amitābha proclaimed by the Buddhas of the six directions.

육번뇌 六煩惱 v. 육대번뇌 六大煩惱.

육범 六凡 The six stages of rebirth for ordinary people, as contrasted with the saints 성자 聖者 : in the hells, and as hungry ghosts, animals, asuras, men, and devas.

육법(계) 六法(戒) The six prohibition rules for a female devotee : indelicacy of contact with a male ; purloining four cash ; killing animals ; untruthfulness ; food after the midday meal ; and wine-drinking. 육법 六法 is also a term for 육념 六念.

육부대승경 六部大乘經 The six works chosen by Tz'ŭ-ên 자은 慈恩 as authoritative in the 법상종 法相宗 Dharmalakṣaṇa school, i.e. 대방광불화엄경 大方廣佛華嚴經 of which there are three translations ; 해심밀경 解深密經 4 tr. ; 여래출현공덕장엄경 如來出現功德莊嚴經 untranslated ; 아비달마경 阿毘達磨經 untranslated ; 능가경 楞伽經 3 tr. ; 후엄경 厚嚴經 (also called 대승밀엄경 大乘密嚴經).

육비 六譬 The six metaphors, v. 육중생 六衆生.

육사 六師 The six tīrthikas or heterodox teaches — Pūraṇa-Kāśyapa, Maskarin, Sañjayin, Ajita-keśakambala, Kakuda-Kātyāyana, and Nirgrantha ; see 외도 外道. 육사가왕 六師迦王 Name of the king who, thirteen years after the destruction of the Jetavana vihāra, which had been rebuilt "five centuries" after the nirvāṇa, again restored it.

육사성취 六事成就 The six things which enable a bodhisattva to keep perfectly the six pāramitās — worshipful offerings, study of the moral duties, pity, zeal in goodness, isolation, delight in the law ; these are described as corresponding to the pāramitās seriatim ; v. 장엄경 莊嚴經 12.

육상 六相 The six characteristics found in everything — whole and parts, unity and diversity, entirety and (its) fractions.

육서 六瑞 The six auspicious indications attributed to the Buddha as a preliminary to his delivery of the Lotus Sūtra, see 법화경서품 法華經序品 : (1) his opening address on the infinite ; (2) his samādhi ; (3) the rain of flowers ; (4) the earthquake ; (5) the delight of the beholders ; (6) the Buddha-ray.

육성부 六城部 Ṣāṇṇagarika, 산타나가리가부 山拖那伽梨柯部 ; or 밀림산부 密林山部. One of the twenty Hīnayāna sects, connected with the Vātsīputrīyāḥ 독자부 犢子部.

육성취 六成就 Six perfections (some say five, some seven) found in the opening phrase of each sūtra : (1) "Thus" implies perfect faith ; (2) "have I heard," perfect hearing ; (3) "once," the perfect time ; (4) "the Buddha," the perfect lord or master ; (5) "on Mt. Gṛdhrakūṭa," the perfect place ; (6) "with the great assembly of bhikṣus," the perfect assembly.

육쇠 六衰 The six ruiners, i.e. the attractions of the six senses, idem 육진 六塵, 육적 六賊 q.v.

육수 六受 The six vedanās, i.e. receptions, or sensations from the 육근 六根 six organs. Also 육작 六作.

육술 六術 idem 육종외도 六種外道 ; see 육행 六行.

육시 六時 The six "hours" or periods in a day, three for night and three for day, i.e. morning, noon, evening ; night, midnight, and dawn. Also, the six divisions of the year, two each of spring, summer, and winter. 육시참 六時懺, 육시삼매 六時三昧, 육시부단 六時不斷, 육시예찬 六時禮讚 all refer respectively to the six daily periods of worship, of meditation, of unintermitting devotions, and of ceremonial.

육신통 六神通 The six transcendental, or magical, powers, v. 육통 六通.

육십 六十 Ṣaṣṭi, sixty. 육십이견 六十二見 The sixty-two 견 見 or views, of which three groups are given : The 대품반야경 大品般若經 in the 불모품 佛母品 takes each of the five skandhas under four considerations of 상 常 time, considered as time past, whether each of the five has had permanence, impermanence, both, neither, 5 × 4 = 20 ; again as to their space, or extension, considered as present time, whether each is finite, infinite, both, neither = 20 ; again as to their destination, i.e. future, as to whether each goes on, or does not, both, neither (e.g. continued personality) = 20, or in all 60 ; add the two ideas whether body and mind 신 神 are a unity or different = 62. The T'ien-t'ai School takes 아견 我見, or personality, as its basis and considers each of the five skandhas under four aspects, e.g. (1) rūpa, the organized body, as the ego ; (2) the ego as apart from the rūpa ; (3) rūpa as the greater, the ego the smaller or inferior, and the ego as dwelling in the rūpa ; (4) the ego as the greater, rūpa the inferior, and the rūpa in the ego. Consider these twenty in the past, present, and future = 60, and add 단 斷 and 상 常 impermanence and permanence as fundamentals = 62. There is also a third group. 육십권 六十卷 The 60 rolls : the T'ien-t'ai 삼대부 三大部, or three collections of fundamental texts of that school. 육십사서 六十四書 The sixty-four classes of Indian writing or literature, Brāhmī, Kharoṣṭhī, etc. 육십사범음 六十四梵音 The sixty-four Aryan or noble characteristics of a Buddha's tones or voice, e.g. snigdha 유택성 流澤聲 smooth ; mṛdukā 유연성 柔軟聲 gentle, etc. 육십사안 六十四眼 Eighteen lictors in the avīci hell each with sixty-four eyes. 육십심 六十心 The sixty different mental positions that may occur to the practiser of Yoga, see 대일경주심품 大日經住心品 ; examples of them are desire, non-desire, ire, kindness, foolishness, wisdom, decision, doubt, depression, brightness, contention, dispute, non-contention, the spirit of devas, of asuras, of nagas, of humanity, woman (i.e. lust), mastery, commercial, and so on.

육여 六如 The six "likes" or comparisons, like a dream, a phantasm, a bubble, a shadow, dew, and lightning. v. 육유 六喩.

육염심 六染心 The six mental "taints" of the Awakening of Faith 기신론 起信論. Though mind-essence is by nature pure and without stain, the condition of 무명 無明 ignorance, or innocence, permits of taint or defilement corresponding to the following six phases : (1) 집상응염 執相應染 the taint interrelated to attachment, or holding the seeming for the real ; it is the state of 집취상 執取相 and 명자상 名字相 which is cut off in the final pratyeka and śrāvaka stage and the bodhisattva 십주 十住 of faith ; (2) 부단상응염 不斷相應染 the taint interrelated to the persisting attraction of the causes of pain and pleasure ; it is the 상속상 相續相 finally eradicated in the bodhisattva 초지 初地 stage of purity ; (3) 분별지상응염 分別智相應染 the taint interrelated to the "particularizing intelligence" which discerns things within and without this world ; it is the first 지상 智相, cut off in the bodhisattva 칠지 七地 stage of spirituality ; (4) 현색불상응염 現色不相應染 the non-interrelated or primary taint, i.e. of the "ignorant" mind as yet hardly discerning subject from object, of accepting an external world ; the third 현상 現相 cut off in the bodhisattva 팔지 八地 stage of emancipation from the material ; (5) 능견심불상응염 能見心不相應染 the non-interrelated or primary taint of accepting a perceptive mind, the second 전상 轉相, cut off in the bodhisattva 구지 九地 of intuition, or emancipation from mental effort ; (6) 근본업불상응염 根本業不相應染 the non-interrelated or primary taint of accepting the idea of primal action or activity in the absolute ; it is the first 업상 業相, and cut off in the 십지 十地 highest bodhisattva stage, entering on Buddhahood. See Suzuki's translation, 80-1.

육욕 六欲 The six sexual attractions arising from colour ; form ; carriage ; voice (or speech) ; softness (or smoothness) ; and features. 육욕(천) 六欲(天) The devalokas, i.e. the heavens of desire, i.e. with sense-organs ; the first is described as half-way up Mt. Sumeru, the second at its summit, and the rest between it and the Brahmalokas ; for list v. 육천 六天. Descriptions are given in the 지도론 智度論 9 and the 구사론 俱舍論 8. They are also spoken of as 육욕천음상 六欲天婬相, i.e. as still in the region of sexual desire. The 육욕사선 六欲四禪 are these six heavens where sexual desire continues, and the four dhyāna heavens of purity above them free from such desire.

육위 六位 The six stages of Bodhisattva development, i.e. 십신위 十信位 ; 십주위 十住位 ; 십회향위 十廻向位 ; 십지위 十地位 ; 등각위 等覺位 ; 불지위 佛地位 ; these are from the older Hua-yen ching.

육유 六喩 The six illustrations of unreality in the Diamond Sūtra : a dream, a phantasm, a bubble, a shadow, dew, and lightning. Also 육여 六如.

육의 六依 The six senses on which one relies, or from which knowledge is received ; v. 육정 六情.

육이 六夷 The six pārājikas, v. 바라이 波羅夷.

육인 六因 The six causations of the 육위 六位 six stages of Bodhisattva development, q.v. Also, the sixfold division of causes of the Vaibhāṣikas (cf. Keith, 177-8) ; every phenomenon depends upon the union of 인 因 primary cause and 연 緣 conditional or environmental cause ; and of the 인 因 there are six kinds : (1) 능작인 能作因 Kāraṇahetu, effective causes of two kinds : 여력인 與力因 empowering cause, as the earth empowers plant growth, and 부장인 不障因 non-resistant cause, as space does not resist, i.e. active and passive causes ; (2) 구유인 俱有因 Sahabhūhetu, cooperative causes, as the four elements 사대 四大 in nature, not one of which can be omitted ; (3) 동류인 同類因 Sabhāgahetu, causes of the same kind as the effect, good producing good, etc. ; (4) 상응인 相應因 Samprayuktahetu, mutual responsive or associated causes, e.g. mind and mental conditions, subject with object ; Keith gives "faith and intelligence" ; similar to (2) ; (5) 변행인 遍行因 Sarvatragahetu, universal or omnipresent cause, i.e. of illusion, as of false views affecting every act ; it resembles (3) but is confined to delusion ; (6) 이숙인 異熟因 Vipākahetu, differential fruition, i.e. the effect different from the cause, as the hells are from evil deeds.

육입 六入 Ṣaḍāyatana ; 육아야달나 六阿耶怛那 or 六阿也怛那 the six entrances, or locations, both the organ and the sensation — eye, ear, nose, tongue, body, and mind ; sight, hearing, smell, taste, touch, and perception. The six form one of the twelve nidānas, see 십이인연 十二因緣. The 육근 六根 are the six organs, the 육경 六境 the six objects, and the 육진 六塵 or guṇas, the six inherent qualities. The later term is 육처 六處 q.v.

육자 六字 The six words or syllables, 나무아미타불 南無阿彌陀佛 Namo Amitābha ; 육자명호 六字名號 a name for him. The 육자문수 六字文殊 six-word dhāraṇī of Mañjuśrī 암파계타나마 闇婆髻馱那麽 or 闇婆計陀那麽 ; 암박계담납막 唵縛鷄淡納莫. There are also the esoteric (Shingon) six words connected with the six forms of Kuan-yin and the 육자법 六字法, 육자공 六字供, 육자하림법 六字河臨法, and 육자호마 六字護摩 ceremonials, some connected with Mañjuśrī, and all with Kuan-yin. There are several 육자 六字 dhāraṇīs, e.g. the Ṣaḍakṣara-vidyāmantra. The six words generally associated with Kuan-yin are 안다리반다리 安荼詈般荼詈 or 안다예반다예 安荼隸般荼隸. There is also the six-word Lamaistic charm Oṁ maṇi padme hūṁ 암마니팔미우 唵嚤呢叭㖿吽.

육자재왕 六自在王 The six sovereign rulers, i.e. the six senses, see 육근 六根.

육작 六作 idem 육수 六受.

육재 六裁 The six decisions, i.e. the concepts formed through the mental contact of the six senses ; later called 육촉 六觸.

육재일 六齋日 The six monthly poṣadha, or fast days : the 8th, 14th, 15th, 23rd, 29th, and 30th. They are the days on which the Four Mahārājas 사천왕 四天王 take note of human conduct and when evil demons are busy, so that great care is required and consequently nothing should be eaten after noon, hence the "fast", v. 범왕경 梵王經 30th command. The 지도론 智度論 13 describes them as 악일 惡日 evil or dangerous days, and says they arose from an ancient custom of cutting off the flesh and casting it into the fire.

육적 六賊 The six cauras, or robbers, i.e. the six senses ; the 육근 六根 sense organs are the 매 媒 "matchmakers", or medial agents, of the six robbers. The 육적 六賊 are also likened to the six pleasures of the six sense organs. Prevention is by not acting with them, i.e. the eye avoiding beauty, the ear sound, nose scent, tongue flavours, body seductions, and mind uncontrolled thoughts.

육전 六箭 The six arrows, i.e. the six senses ; v. 육진 六塵.

육정 六情 The emotions arising from the six organs of sense 육근 六根 for which term 육정 六情 is the older interpretation ; v. 육의 六依.

육제 六諦 The six logical categories of the Vaiśeṣika philosophy : dravya, substance ; guṇa, quality ; karman, motion or activity ; sāmānya, generality ; viśeṣa, particularity ; samavāya, inherence : Keith, *Logic*, 179. Eitel has "substance, quality, action, existence, the unum et diversum, and the aggregate".

육조 六祖 The six patriarchs of the Ch'an(Zen) school 선종 禪宗, who passed down robe and begging bowl in succession, i.e. Bodhidharma, Hui-k'o, Sêng-ts'an, Tao-hsin, Hung-jên, and Hui-nêng 달마 達摩, 혜가 慧可, 승찬 僧璨, 도신 道信, 홍인 弘忍, and 혜능 慧能.

육족존 六足尊 The six-legged Honoured One, one of the five 명왕 明王 fierce guardians of Amitābha, i.e. 대위덕 大威悳, who has six heads, faces, arms, and legs ; rides on an ox ; and is an incarnation of Mañjuśrī. The 육족아비담마 六足阿毗曇摩 Jñāna-prasthāna-ṣaṭpādābhidharma is a philosophical work in the Canon.

육종 六宗 The six schools, i.e. 삼론 三論 ; 법상 法相 ; 화엄 華嚴 ; 율 律 ; 성실 成實, and 구사 俱舍 q.v. ; the last two are styled Hīnayāna schools. Mahāyāna in Japan puts in place of them 천태 天台 and 진언 眞言 Tendai and Shingon.

육종결정 六種決定 The six kinds of certainty resulting from observance of the six pāramitās : 재성결정 財成決定 the certainty of wealth ; 생승결정 生勝決定 of rebirth in honourable families ; 불퇴결정 不退決定 of no retrogression (to lower conditions) ; 수습결정 修習決定 of progress in practice ; 정업결정 定業決定 of unfailingly good karma ; 무공용결정 無功用決定 of effortless abode in truth and wisdom. 대승장엄론 大乘莊嚴論 12.

육종교방편 六種巧方便 The six able devices of Bodhisattvas : (1) preaching deep truths in simple form to lead on people gladly to believe ; (2) promising them every good way of realizing their desires, of wealth, etc. ; (3) showing a threatening aspect to the disobedient to induce reform ; (4) rebuking and punishing them with a like object ; (5) granting wealth to induce grateful offerings and almsgiving ; (6) descending from heaven, leaving home, attaining bodhi, and leading all to joy and purity. 보살지지경 菩薩地持經 8.

육종구생혹 六種俱生惑 The six deceivers common to all the living — greed, anger, torpor, ignorance, doubt, and incorrect views.

육종석 六種釋 idem 육리합석 六離合釋.

육종성 六種性 For the first five see 오종성 五種性 ; the sixth is the Buddha stage of 묘각성 妙覺性. The meditation on these is the 육관 六觀. Cf. 육위 六位.

육종외도 六種外道 The six kinds of ascetics ; also 육종고행외도 六種苦行外道 ; 육술 六術 ; v. 육행 六行.

육종인 六種印 The six seals, or proofs, i.e. the six pāramitās, 육도 六度.

육종인 六種因 v. 육인 六因.

육종정행 六種正行 The fifth of the 오종정행 五種正行 q.v. is expanded into six kinds of proper practice : reading and intoning, studying, worshipping, invoking, praising, and making offerings.

육종주 六種住 The six Bodhisattva-stages in the Bodhisattvabhūmi sūtra 보살지지경 菩薩地持經 are : (1) 종성주 種性住 the attainment of the Buddha-seed nature in the 십주 十住 ; (2) 해행주 解行住 of discernment and practice in the 십행 十行 and 십회향 十廻向 ; (3) 정심주 淨心住 of purity by attaining reality in the 초지견도 初地見道 ; (4) 행도적주 行道迹住 of progress in riddance of incorrect thinking, in the 이지 二地 to the 칠지 七地 ; (5) 결정주 決定住 of powers of correct decision and judgment in the eighth and ninth 지 地 ; (6) 구경주 究竟住 of the perfect

Bodhisattva-stage in the tenth 지 地 and the 등각위 等覺位, but not including the 묘각위 妙覺位 which is the Buddha-stage.

육종진동 六種震動 The six earthquakes, or earth-shakings, also 육종동상 六種動相, of which there are three different categories. I. Those at the Buddha's conception, birth, enlightenment, first preaching, when Māra besought him to live, and at his nirvāṇa ; some omit the fifth and after "birth" add "leaving home". II. The six different kinds of shaking of the chiliocosm, or universe, when the Buddha entered into the samādhi of joyful wandering, see 대품반야경 大品般若經 1, i.e. east rose and west sank, and so on with w.e., n.s., s.n., middle and borders, borders and middle. III. Another group is shaking, rising, waving, reverberating, roaring, arousing, the first three referring to motion, the last three to sounds ; see the above 반야경 般若經 ; which in later translations gives shaking, rising, reverberating, beating, roaring, crackling.

육죄인 六罪人 The six kinds of offender, i.e. one who commits any of the 사중(죄) 四重(罪) four grave sins, or destroys harmony in the order, or sheds a Buddha's blood.

육주 六舟 The six boats, i.e. the six pāramitās 육도 六度 for ferrying to the bank beyond mortality.

육주 六住 The sixth of the 십주 十住 q.v.

육중 六衆 idem 육군비구 六羣比丘. 육중생 六衆生 The six senses 육근 六根 are likened to six wild creatures in confinement always struggling to escape. Only when they are domesticated will they be happy. So is it with the six senses and the taming power of Buddha-truth. The six creatures are a dog, a bird, a snake, a hyena, a crocodile (śiśumāra), and a monkey.

육즉 六卽 The six stages of Bodhisattva developments as defined in the T'ien-t'ai 원교 圓教, i.e. Perfect, or Final Teaching, in contrast with the previous, or ordinary six developments of 십신 十信, 십주 十住, 십행 十行, etc., as found in the 별교 別教 Differentiated or Separate school. The T'ien-t'ai six are : (1) 이즉 理卽 realization that all beings are of Buddha-nature ; (2) 명자즉 名字卽 the apprehension of terms, that those who only hear and believe are in the Buddha-law and potentially Buddha ; (3) 관행즉 觀行卽 advance beyond terminology to meditation, or study and accordant action ; it is known as 오품관행 五品觀行 or 오품제자위 五品弟子位 ; (4) 상사즉 相似卽 semblance stage, or approximation to perfection in purity, the 육근청정위 六根淸淨位, i.e. the 십신위 十信位 ; (5) 분증즉 分證卽 discrimination of truth and its progressive experiential proof, i.e. the 십주 十住, 십행 十行, 십회향 十廻向, 십지 十地, and 등각위 等覺位 of the 별교 別教, known also as the 성인 聖因 cause or root of holiness. (6) 구경즉 究竟卽 perfect enlightenment, i.e. the 묘각위 妙覺位 or 성과 聖果 fruition of holiness. (1) and (2) are known as 외범 外凡 external for, or common to, all. (1) is theoretical ; (2) is the first step in practical advance, followed by (3) and (4) styled 내범 內凡 internal for all, and (3), (4), (5), and (6) are known as the 팔위 八位 the eight grades. 육즉불 六卽佛 Buddha in six forms : (1) 이불 理佛 as the principle in and through all things, as pan-Buddha — all things being of Buddha-nature ; (2) 명자불 名字佛 Buddha as a name or person. The other four are the last four forms above.

육지장 六地藏 Six bodhisattvas in the Ti Tsang group of the garbhadhātu, each controlling one of the 육도 六道 or ways of sentient existence. They deal with rebirth in the hells, as hungry ghosts, animals, asuras, men, and devas.

육진 六震 idem 육종진 六種震.

육진 六塵 The six guṇas qualities produced by the objects and organs of sense, i.e. sight, sound, smell, taste, touch, and idea ; the organs are the 육근 六根, 육입 六入, 육처 六處, and the perceptions or discernments the 육식 六識 ; cf. 육경 六境. Dust 진 塵 is dirt, and these six qualities are therefore the cause of all impurity. Yet 육진설법 六塵說法 the Buddha made use of them to preach his law.

육착(심) 六著(心) or 六着(心) The six bonds, or the mind of the six bonds : greed, love, hate, doubt, lust, pride.

육창일원 六窗一猿 Six windows and one monkey (climbing in and out), i.e. the six organs of sense and the active mind.

육처 六處 Ṣaḍāyatana. The six places, or abodes of perception or sensation, one of the nidānas, see 십이인연 十二因緣 ; they are the 육근 六根 or six organs of sense, but the term is also used for the 육입 六入 and 육경 六境 q.v. ; also 육진 六塵.

육천 六天 The six devalokas, i.e. the heavens with sense organs above Sumeru, between the brahmalokas and the earth, i.e. 사왕천 四王天 ; 도리천 忉利天 ; 야마천 夜摩天 ; 도솔천 兜率天 ; 낙변화천 樂變化天 ; and 타화자재천 他化自在天. The sixth is the heaven of Māra, v. 육욕천 六欲天.

육촉 六觸 idem 육재 六裁.

육추 六麤 The six "coarser" stages arising from the 삼세 三細 or three finer stages which in turn are produced by original 무명 無明, the unenlightened condition of ignorance ; v. Awakening of Faith 기신론 起信論. They are the states of (1) 지상 智相 knowledge or consciousness of like and dislike arising from mental conditions ; (2) 상속상 相續相 consciousness of pain and pleasure resulting from the first, causing continuous responsive memory ; (3) 집취상 執取相 attachment or clinging, arising from the last ; (4) 계명자상 計名字相 assigning names according to the seeming and unreal (with fixation of ideas) ; (5) 기업상 起業相 the consequent activity with all the variety of deeds ; (6) 업계고상 業繫苦相 the suffering resulting from being tied to deeds and their karma consequences.

육축 六畜 The six animals likened to the six organs 육근 六根, v. 육중생 六衆生.

육취 六趣 The six directions of reincarnation, also 육도 六道 : (1) 지옥취 地獄趣 naraka-gati, or that of the hells ; (2) 아귀취 餓鬼趣 preta-gati, of hungry ghosts ; (3) 축생취 畜生趣 tiryagyoni-gati, of animals ; (4) 아수라취 阿修羅趣 asura-gati, of malevolent nature spirits ; (5) 인취 人趣 manuṣya-gati, of human existence ; (6) 천취 天趣 deva-gati, of deva existence. The 육취윤회경 六趣輪廻經 is attributed to Aśvaghoṣa.

육친 六親 The six immediate relatives – father and mother, wife and child, elder and younger brothers.

육통 六通 Abhijñā, or ṣaḍabhijñā. The six super-natural or universal powers acquired by a Buddha, also by an arhat through the fourth degree of dhyāna. The "southern" Buddhists only have the first five, which are also known in China ; v. 오신통 五神通 ; the sixth is 누진(지증)통 漏盡(智證)通 āsravakṣaya-jñāna, super-natural consciousness of the waning of vicious propensities.

육파 六波 The six pāramitās, v. 바라밀 波羅蜜.

육팔홍서 六八弘誓 The forty-eight great or surpassing vows of Amitābha, also 육팔초세본원 六八超世本願.

육폐 六蔽 The six sins that smother the six pāramitās : grudging, commandment-breaking, anger, family attachment, confused thoughts, and stupid ignorance.

육합석 六合釋 v. 육리합석 六離合釋.

육해일망 六解一亡 "When the six knots are untied the unity disappears." The six knots represent the six organs 육근 六根 causing mortality, the cloth or cord tied in a series of knots represents nirvāṇa. This illustrates the interdependence of nirvāṇa and mortality. Cf. 육결 六結 ; v. 능가경 楞伽經 5.

육행 六行 Among Buddhists the term means the practice of the 육도 六度 six pāramitās ; it is referred, among outsiders, to the six austerities of the six kinds of heretics : (1) 자아 自我 starvation ; (2) 투연 投淵 naked cave-dwelling (or, throwing oneself down precipices) ; (3) 부화 赴火 self-immolation, or self-torturing by fire ; (4) 자좌 自坐 sitting naked in pubic ; (5) 적묵 寂默 dwelling in silence among graves ; (6) 우구 牛狗 living as animals. 육행관 六行觀 The six meditations, also called 염흔관 厭欣觀 ; 육묘행 六妙行 comparing the 하지 下地 lower realms with the 상지 上地 higher, the six following characters being the subject of meditation : the three lower represent 추 麤 coarseness, 고 苦 suffering, and 장 障 resistance ; these in meditation are seen as distasteful ; while the higher are the 정 靜 calm, 묘 妙 mystic, 이 離 free, which are matters for delight. By this meditation on the distasteful and the delectable the delusions of the lower realms may be overcome.

육혜 六慧 The six kinds of wisdom. Each is allotted seriatim to one of the six positions 육위 六位 q.v. (1) 문혜 聞慧 the wisdom of hearing and apprehending the truth of the middle way is associated with the 십주 十住 ; (2) 사혜 思慧 wisdom of thought with the 십행 十行 ; (3) 수혜 修慧 wisdom of observance with the 십회향 十廻向 ; (4) 무상혜 無相慧 wisdom of neither extreme, or the mean, with the 십지 十地 ; (5) 조적혜 照寂慧 wisdom of understanding of nirvāṇa with 등각혜 等覺慧 ; (6) 적조혜 寂照慧 wisdom of making nirvāṇa illuminate all beings associated with 불과 佛果 Buddha-fruition. They are a 별교 別教 Differentiated School series and all are associated with 중도 中道 the school of the 중 中 or middle way.

육화(경) 六和(敬) The six points of reverent harmony or unity in a monastery or convent : 신화 身和 bodily unity in form of worship, 구화 口和 oral unity in chanting, 의화 意和 mental unity in faith, 계화 戒和 moral unity in observing the commandments, 견화 見和 doctrinal unity in views and explanations, and 이화 利和, 행화 行和, 학화 學和, or 시화 施和 economic unity in community of goods, deeds, studies, or charity. 육화합 六和合 The six unions of the six sense organs with the six objects of the senses, the eye with the object seen, etc.

윤 潤 Moisten, soak, enrich, fertilize, sleek, smooth, profit. 윤업 潤業 Fertilized karma, the original karma fertilized by the passions and distresses of life. 윤생 潤生 The fertilization of the natural conditions which produce rebirth, especially those of the three kinds of attachment in the hour of death, love of body, of home, and of life.

윤 允 Sincere, true ; to assent. 윤감 允堪 Yün-k'an, a famous monk of the Sung dynasty. 윤야 允若 Yün-jo, a famous monk of the Yüan dynasty.

율 律 Vinaya, from Vi-nī, to lead, train ; discipline ; v. 비나야 毘奈耶 ; other names are pratimokṣa, śīla, and upalakṣa. The discipline, or monastic rules ; one of the three divisions of the Canon, or Tripiṭaka, and said to have been compiled by Upāli. 율승 律乘 The Vinaya-vehicle, the teaching which emphasizes the discipline. 율의 律儀 Rules and ceremonies, an intuitive apprehension of which, both written and unwritten, enables the individual to act properly under all circumstances. 율의계 律儀戒 The first of the three 취계 聚戒, i.e. to avoid evil by keeping to the discipline. 율종 律宗 The Vinaya school, emphasizing the monastic discipline, founded in China by 도선 道宣 Tao-hsüan of the T'ang dynasty. 율파 律派 The discipline branch, or school. 율사 律師 Master and teacher of the rules of the discipline. 율참 律懺 Repentance and penance according to the rules. 율법 律法 The laws or methods of the discipline ; rules and laws. 율상 律相 The discipline, or its characteristics. 율선 律禪 The two schools of Discipline and Intuition. 율장 律藏 The Vinaya-piṭaka. 율행 律行 The discipline in practice, to act according to the rules.

ㄱ ㄴ ㄷ ㄹ ㅁ ㅂ ㅅ ㅇ ㅈ ㅊ ㅋ ㅌ ㅍ ㅎ 찾아보기

융 融 Blending, combining ; melting, thawing ; clear, intelligent. 융통 融通 To blend, combine, mix, unite, assemble. 융식 融識 Perspicacity, insight into both the phenomenal and noumenal.

은 慇 Anxious ; 은근 慇懃 zealous, careful.

은 恩 Grace, favour. 은도 恩度 One who graciously saves — a term for a monk. 은애 恩愛 Grace and love ; human affection, which is one of the causes of rebirth. 은애옥 恩愛獄 The prison of affection, which holds men in bondage. 은련 恩憐 Loving-kindness and pity. 은하 恩河 The river of grace. 은해 恩海 The sea of grace. 은전 恩田 The field of grace, i.e. parents, teachers, elders, monks, in return for the benefits they have conferred ; one of the 삼복전 三福田.

은 銀 Rūpya. Silver ; money. 은색 銀色 Silver-colour.

은 隱 To hide, conceal ; obscure, esoteric ; retired. 은밀 隱密 Esoteric meaning in contrast with 현료 顯了 exoteric, or plain meaning. 은형 隱形 ; 은신 隱身 To vanish, become invisible. 은소 隱所 A privy. 은복 隱覆 To hide, conceal ; secret.

은사 恩師 Lit. "beneficient master." Vocation Master, similar to "vocational father" in Catholic tradition. Usually required to have trained 10 years as a monastic, and nominally responsible for the material needs of his disciple(s).

은해사 銀海寺 Eun-hae-sa. A temple located in Mt. Palgongsan, Chi-il-dong Cheongtong-myeon Yeongcheon-si Gyeongsangbuk-do in Korea. The 10th parish headquarters of Korean Jogye Order.

음 吟 Chant, hum, mutter. 음영 吟詠 ; 음풍 吟諷 To intone, repeat.

음 淫 Excess, excessive ; licentious, lewd ; adultery, fornication. 음욕 淫欲 Sexual passion. 음욕화 淫欲火 Its fire, or burning. 음욕병 淫欲病 The (spiritual) disease it causes. 음탕 淫湯 A kind of rice soup, or gruel. 음라 淫羅 The net of passion. Also 음 婬.

음 婬 Licentious, lewd ; adultery, fornication ; similar to 음 淫 q.v. 음노치 婬怒癡 The three poisons of sexual desire, anger, and ignorance (or heedlessness). 음계 婬戒 The commandment against adultery. 음욕 婬欲 Sexual desire. 음화 婬火 The fire of sexual passion. 음라망 婬羅網 Its net.

음 陰 Shade, dark, the shades, the negative as opposed to the positive principle, female, the moon, back, secret. In Buddhism it is the phenomenal, as obscuring the true nature of things ; also the aggregation of phenomenal things resulting in births and deaths, hence it is used as a translation like 온 蘊 q.v. for skandha, the 오음 五陰 being the five skandhas or aggregates. 음입계 陰入界 The five skandhas, the twelve entrances, or bases through which consciousness enters (āyatana), and the eighteen dhātu or elements, called the 삼과 三科. 음경 陰境 The present world as the state of the five skandhas. 음망 陰妄 The skandha-illusion, or the unreality of the skandhas. 음망일념 陰妄一念 The illusion of the skandhas like a passing thought. 음환 陰幻 The five skandhas like a passing illusion. 음계 陰界 The five skandhas and the eighteen dhātu. 음장 陰藏 A retractable penis — one of the thirty-two marks of a Buddha. 음전 陰錢 Paper money for use in services to the dead. 음마 陰魔 The five skandhas considered as māras or demons fighting against the Buddha-nature of men.

음 音 Sound, note, that which is heard. 음교 音教 Vocal teaching, Buddha's preaching. 음목 音木 Sounding block, or board for keeping time or rhythm. 음악 音樂 Music, a musical accompaniment to a service. 음의 音義 Sound and meaning, i.e. a pronouncing dictionary. 음성 音聲 Sound, note, preaching. 음성불사 音聲佛事 Buddha's work in saving by his preaching. 음향인 音響忍 Sound and echo perseverance, the patience which realizes that all is as unreal as sound and echo.

음 飮 to drink, swallow ; to water cattle. 음광 飮光 Drinking light, a tr. of the name of Kāśyapa, v. 가 迦, or his patronymic, possibly because it is a title of Aruṇa, the charioteer of the sun, but said to be because of Kāśyapa's radiant body. 음광부 飮光部 Mahākāśyapīyāḥ, or school of the Mahāsāṅghikāḥ. 음혈지옥 飮血地獄 The hell where they have to drink blood. 음주 飮酒 to drink wine, or alcoholic liquor, forbidden by the fifth of the five commandments ; 10, 35, and 36 reasons for abstinence from it are given. 음식 飮食 Drink and food, two things on which sentient beings depend ; desire for them is one of the three passions ; offerings of them are one of the five forms of offerings.

응 應 Respond, correspond, answer, reply ; ought, should, proper, deserving, worthy of.

응 凝 To congeal, consolidate, form. 응연상 凝然常 Solid, unchanging, immutable.

응가 應伽 Aṅga, a limb, member, body.

응감 應感 The response of Buddhas and spirits (to the needs of men).

응공 應供 Worthy of worship, a tr. of the term arhat ; one of the ten titles of a Tathāgata.

응과 應果 Arhat-fruit, the reward of arhatship.

응기 應器 The pātra, or begging-bowl, the utensil corresponding to the dharma ; the utensil which responds to the respectful gifts of others ; the vessel which corresponds with one's needs ; also 응량기 應量器.

응리(원실)종 應理(圓實)宗 A name of the Dharma-lakṣaṇa school, 법상종 法相宗 q.v.

응문 膺文 Ying Wên ; the grandson of the founder of the Ming dynasty, T'ai Tsu, to whom he succeeded, but was dethroned by Young Lo and escaped disguised as a monk ; he remained hidden as a monk till his 64th year, afterwards he was provided for by the reigning ruler. His name is also given as 응능 膺能 Ying Nêng ; 응현 膺賢 Ying Hsien ; and posthumously as 윤문 允炆 Yün Wên.

응법 應法 In harmony with dharma or law. 응법묘복 應法妙服 The mystic (or beautiful) garment of accordance with Buddha-truth, i.e. the monk's robe. 응법사미 應法沙彌 A novice, preparing for the monkhood, between 14 and 19 years of age.

응병여약 應病與藥 To give medicine suited to the disease, the Buddha's mode of teaching.

응보 應報 Corresponding retribution ; rewards and punishments in accordance with previous moral action.

응불 應佛 idem 응신 應身 q.v.

응송 應頌 Geya, corresponding verses, i.e. a prose address repeated in verse, idem 중송 重頌 ; the verse section of the canon.

응신 應身 Nirmāṇakāya, one of the 삼신 三身 q.v. Any incarnation of Buddha. The Buddha-incarnation of the 진여 眞如 q.v. Also occasionally used for the sambhogakāya. There are various interpretations: (a) The 동성경 同性經 says the Buddha as revealed supernaturally in glory to bodhisattvas is 응신 應身, in contrast with 화신 化身, which latter is the revelation on earth to his disciples. (b) The 기신론 起信論 makes no difference between the two, the 응신 應身 being the Buddha of the thirty-two marks who revealed himself to the earthly disciples. The 금광명경 金光明經 makes all revelations of Buddha as Buddha to be 응신 應身 ; while all incarnations not as Buddha, but in the form of any of the five paths of existence, are Buddha's

화신 化身. T'ien-t'ai has the distinction of 승응신 勝應身 and 열응신 劣應身, i.e. superior and inferior nirmāṇakāya, or supernatural and natural. 응신토 應身土 Any realm in which a Buddha is incarnate.

응용무변 應用無邊 Omnipresent response to need ; universal ability to aid.

응응 應應 Nirmāṇakāya response, its response to the needs of all ; that of the Dharmakāya is called 법응 法應.

응의 應儀 Deserving of respect, or corresponding to the correct, an old tr. of arhat.

응인 應人 Arhat, arhan ; deserving (worship), an old tr. of arhat.

응작 應作 Responsive appearance, revelation, idem 응현 應現.

응적 應迹 Evidential nirmāṇakāya, manifestations or indications of incarnation.

응정변지 應正遍知 The arhat of perfect knowledge, a title of a Buddha.

응진 應眞 A worthy true one, an old tr. of the term arhat. Also, one who is in harmony with truth.

응토 應土 Any land or realm suited to the needs of its occupants ; also called 화토 化土.

응현 應現 Responsive manifestation, revelation through a suitable medium.

응형 應形 The form of manifestation, the nirmāṇa-kāya, idem 응신 應身.

응호 應護 The response and protection of Buddhas and bodhisattvas according to the desires of all beings.

응화 應化 Nirmāṇa means formation, with Buddhists transformation, or incarnation. Responsive incarnation, or manifestation, in accordance with the nature or needs of different beings. 응화이생 應化利生 Revelation or incarnation for the benefit of the living. 응화법신 應化法身 Responsive manifestation of the Dharmakāya, or Absolute Buddha, in infinite forms. 응화성문 應化聲聞 Buddhas or bodhisattvas incarnate as śrāvakas, or disciples. 응화신 應化身 ; 응신 應身 ; 화신 化身 Nirmāṇakāya, the Buddha incarnate, the transformation body, capable of assuming any form (for the propagation of Buddha-truth).

의 矣 A particle of finality, pronounced *i*, used in 의률타 矣栗馱 Hṛd, the heart ; the essence of a thing.

의 蟻 Ant. 의술 蟻術 The duty and mode of saving the lives of ants.

의 衣 Clothes, especially a monk's robes which are of two kinds. the compulsory three garments of five, seven, or nine pieces ; and the permissive clothing for the manual work of the monastery, etc. The 삼의 三衣 or three garments are (1) 안타회의 安陀會衣 antarvāsas, an inner garment ; the five-piece 가사 袈裟 cassock ; (2) 울다라승의 鬱多羅僧衣 Uttarāsaṅga, outer garment, the seven-piece cassock ; (3) 승가리의 僧伽梨衣 Saṅghāṭī, assembly cassock of from nine to twenty-five pieces. The permissive clothing is of ten kinds. 의좌실 衣座室 The robe, throne, and abode of the Tathāgata, see Lotus sūtra 법사품 法師品. 의법 衣法 The robe and the Buddha-truth. 의주 衣珠 ; 의보 衣寶 The pearl in the garment, i.e. a man starving yet possessed of a priceless pearl in his garment, of which he was unaware ; v. Lotus sūtra 오백수기품 五百授記品. 의복천 衣服天 The Vajradeva in the Vajradhātu group who guards the placenta and the unborn child ; his colour is black and he holds a bow and arrow. 의복수념원 衣服隨念願 The vow of Amitābha that all the devas and men in his realm shall instantly have whatever beautiful clothing they wish. 의계 衣裓 A towel, cloth, wrapper, or mantle. 의발 衣鉢 Cassock and almsbowl. 의나 衣那 The umbilical cord.

의 意 Manas, the sixth of the ṣaḍāyatanas or six means of perception, i.e. sight, hearing, smell, taste, touch, and mind. Manas means "mind (in its widest sense as applied to all the mental powers), intellect, intelligence, understanding, perception, sense, conscience, will." [M. W.] It is "the intellectual function of consciousness," [Keith]. In Chinese it connotes thought, idea, intention, meaning, will ; but in Buddhist terminology its distinctive meaning is mind, or the faculty of thought.

의 儀 Manner, mode, style ; ceremony, etiquette. 의식 儀式 ; 의궤 儀軌 Mode, style, manner.

의 義 The right ; proper, righteous ; loyal ; public-spirited, public ; meaning, significance. It is used for the Skt. artha, object, purpose, meaning, etc. ; also for abhidheya. 의례 義例 Meaning and rules, or method, abbrev. for 지관의례 止觀義例 q.v. 의의 義意 Meaning and aim. 의정 義淨 I-ching, A.D. 635-713, the famous monk who in 671 set out by the sea-route for India, where he remained for over twenty years, spending half this period in the Nālandā monastery. He returned to China in 695, was received with much honour, brought back some four hundred works, tr. with Śikṣānanda the Avataṁsaka-sūtra, later tr. many other works and left a valuable account of his travels and life in India, died aged 79. 의무애 義無礙 Unobstructed knowledge of the meaning, or the truth ; complete knowledge. 의소 義疏 Meaning and comments on or explanations. 의상 義相 Truth, meaning ; meaning and form, truth and its aspect. 의변 義辯 One of the seven powers of reasoning, or discourse of a bodhisattva, that on the things that are profitable to the attainment of nirvāṇa. 의취 義趣 The path of truth, the right direction, or objective. 의문 義門 The gate of righteousness ; the schools, or sects of the meaning or truth of Buddhism. 의다라니 義陀羅尼 Truth dhāraṇī, the power of the bodhisattva to retain all truth he hears.

의 擬 To compare, estimate, guess, adjudge, decide, intend. 의죄 擬罪 To judge a case.

의 依 To depend, rely on ; dependent, conditioned ; accord with. 의타 依他 Dependent on or trusting to someone or something else ; trusting on another, not on self or "works." 의타(기)성 依他(起)性 Not having an independent nature, not a nature of its own, but constituted of elements. 의타자성 依他自性 One of the 삼성 三性 dependent on constructive elements and without a nature of its own. 의타심 依他心 The mind in a dependent state, that of the Buddha in incarnation. 의타십유 依他十喩 The unreality of dependent or conditioned things, e.g. the body, or self, illustrated in ten comparisons: foam, bubble, flame, plantain, illusion, dream, shadow, echo, cloud, lightning ; v. 유마힐경 維摩詰經 2. 의원 依圓 Dependent and perfect, i.e. the dependent or conditioned nature, and the perfect nature of the unconditioned bhūtatathatā. 의지 依地 The ground on which one relies ; the body, on which sight, hearing, etc., depend ; the degree of samādhi attained ; cf. 의신 依身. 의보 依報 v. 의정 依正. 의호 依怙 To rely on, depend on. 의과 依果 idem 의보 依報 v. 의정 依正. 의지 依止 To depend and rest upon. 의지심심 依止甚深 The profundity on which all things depend, i.e the bhūtatathatā ; also the Buddha. 의지사 依止師, 의지아사리 依止阿闍梨 The ācārya, or master of a junior monk. 의정 依正 The two forms of karma resulting from one's past ; 정보 定報 being the resultant person, 의보 依報 being the dependent condition or environment, e.g. country, family, possessions, etc. 의법불의인 依法不依人 To rely upon the dharma, or truth itself, and not upon (the false interpretations of) men. 의판 依版 ; 선판 禪版 A board to lean against when in meditation. 의언진여 依言眞如 The bhūtatathatā in its expressible form, as distinguished from it as 이언 離言 inexpressible. 의신 依身 The body on which one depends, or on which its parts depend, cf. 의타 依他. 의통 依通 The magical powers which depend upon drugs, spells, etc., v. 오통 五通.

의 醫 To heal. 의자 醫子 The parable of the healing of his poisoned sons by the doctor in the Lotus Sūtra. 의방 醫方 A prescription. 의왕 醫王 The Buddha as healer of sufferings ; also the Medicine King, v. 약 藥 19. 의라발달라 醫羅鉢呾邏 Elāpattra, the nāga-or dragon-king of this name ; also a place in Taxila.

의 疑 Vicikitsā ; doubt, suspect ; hesitate, be uncertain, fear, surmise. 의사 疑使 The messenger, tempter, or lictor, of doubt. 의자 疑刺 The thorn of doubt. 의성태궁 疑城胎宮 The palace for doubters outside Amitābha's heaven, where all doubters of him are confined for 500 years until fit to enjoy his paradise. 의집 疑執 The holding to doubt. 의심 疑心 A doubting heart, dubious, suspicious. 의감 疑惑 Doubt and delusion, doubt, uncertainty. 의회 疑悔 To repent of doubt. 의결 疑結 The bondage of doubt. 의개 疑蓋 The overhanging cover of doubt. 의견 疑見 Doubtfully to view, doubtful views, doubt.

의견 意見 Thoughts, ideas, concepts, views.

의계 意界 Manodhātu, the realm of mind.

의근 意根 The mind-sense, or indriya, the sixth of the senses ; v. 육처 六處.

의념왕생 意念往生 By thought and remembrance or invocation of Amitābha to enter into his Pure Land.

의락 意樂 Joy of the mind, the mind satisfied and joyful. Manobhirāma, the realm foretold for Maudgalyāyana as a Buddha.

의력 意力 Mental power or intention ; the purpose to attain bodhi or enlightenment.

의마 意馬 The mind as a horse, ever running from one thing to another. 의마심원 意馬心猿 The mind like a horse and the heart like a monkey — restless and intractable.

의분천 意憤天 A deva who sinned and was sent down to be born among men.

의삼 意三 The three evils which belong to intellect — lobha, dveṣa, moha, i.e. desire, dislike, delusion.

의상 義湘 or 義相 Ui-sang(625-702). A Korean monk who studied in China during the T'ang dynasty, then returned to Silla. The founder of 해동화엄종 海東華嚴宗 Hai-tung Hua-yen sect — Korean Hwaeom(C. Hua-yen) School. He wrote 7 kinds of books, 4 of which are present.

의생신 意生身 A body mentally produced, or produced at will, a tr. of manomaya. Bodhisattvas from the first stage 지 地 upwards are able to take any form at will to save the living ; also 의생화신 意生化身 ; 의성신 意成身.

의성 意成 Mentally evolved, or evolved at will. 의성천 意成天 Devas independent of the nourishment of the realms of form and formlessness, who live only in the realm of mind. 의성신 意成身 idem 의생신 意生身 q.v.

의수 意水 The mind or will to become calm as still water, on entering samādhi.

의식 意識 Manovijñāna ; the faculty of mind, one of the six vijñānas.

의안락행 意安樂行 The calmly joyful life of the mind — one of the four in the Lotus sūtra 14 ; v. 사안락행 四安樂行.

의언 意言 Mental words, words within the intellectual consciousness ; thought and words.

의업 意業 The function of mind or thought, one of the 삼업 三業 thought, word, deed.

의원 意猿 The mind as intractable as a monkey.

의지 意地 The stage of intellectual consciousness, being the sixth vijñāna, the source of all concepts.

의차 意車 The mind vehicle, the vehicle of intellectual consciousness, the imagination.

의처 意處 The mind-sense, the mind, the sixth of the six senses ; v. 육처 六處.

의천 義天 Ui-cheon(1055-1101). A monk of the Goryeo dynasty in Korea. He revived 천태종 天台宗 T'ien-t'ai Sect in Goryeo and became a imperial preceptor of Goryeo.

의취 意趣 The direction of the mind, or will.

의학 意學 Mental learning, learning by meditation rather than from books, the special cult of the Ch'an or Intuitional school, which is also called the School of the Buddha-mind.

의해 意解 Intellectual explanation ; liberation of the mind, or thought.

이 犛 A yak 이우 犛牛.

이 已 Already, past ; end, cease. 이금당 已今當 Past, present, future, 과거 過去, 현재 現在, 미래 未來. 이금당왕생 已今當往生 Those born into the "future life" (of the Pure Land) in the past, in the present, and to be born in the future. 이생 已生 ; 부다 部多 Bhūta. Become, the moment just come into existence, the present moment ; being, existing ; a being, ghost, demon ; a fact ; an element, of which the Hindus have five — earth, water, fire, air, ether ; the past. 이지근 已知根 Ājñendriya. The second of the 삼무루근 三無漏根 q.v. One who already knows the indriya or roots that arise from the practical stage associated with the Four Dogmas, i.e. purpose, joy, pleasure, renunciation, faith, zeal, memory, abstract meditation, wisdom. 이달대덕 已達大德 A monk far advanced in religion ; an arhat. 이환 已還 Already returned, or, begun again, e.g. the recommencement of a cycle, or course. 이리욕자 已離欲者 Those who have abandoned the desire-realm ; divided into two classes, 이생 異生 ordinary people who have left desire, but will be born into the six gati ; 성자 聖者 the saints, who will not be reborn into desire-realm ; e.g. non-Buddhists and Buddhists.

이 以 By means of, by using, by ; whereby, in order to. 이심전심 以心傳心 Direct transmission from mind to mind, as contrasted with the written word ; the intuitive principle of the Ch'an(Zen), or intuitive school.

이 二 Dvā, dvau. Two ; dvitīya, second.

이 伊 He, she, it ; that ; translit. *i*, *ai*, *ṛ* ; cf. 일 壹, 이 彝 and 의 意 ; for the long ī the double characters 예이 翳咿 and 이이 伊伊 are sometimes used. 이자삼점 伊字三點 refers to the Sanskrit sign ∴ as neither across nor upright, being of triangular shape, and indicating neither unity nor difference, before nor after. The Nirvāṇa Sūtra applies the three parts to 법신 法身 dharmakāya, 반야 般若 prajñā, and 해탈 解脫 vimokṣa, all three being necessary to complete nirvāṇa. It is also associated with the three eyes of Śiva. When considered across they represent fire, when upright, water. At a later period the three were joined ः in writing.

이 李 Plum. 이원 李園 Āmravana, the wild-plum (or mango) grove, see 암 菴.

이 異 Pṛthak. Different, separate, unlike, not the same ; diverse, diversity ; strange ; heterodox ; extraordinary. 이인 異人 Different person, another. 이구동음 異口同音 Different or many mouths, but the same response, unanimous. 이품 異品 Of different order, or class. 이인 異因 A different cause, or origin. 이집 異執 A different tenet ; to hold to heterodoxy 이학 異學 Different studies ; heterodoxy. 이심 異心 Different mind ; heterodox mind ; amazed. 이혜 異慧 Heterodox wisdom. 이방편 異方便 Extraordinary, or unusual adaptations, devices, or means. 이숙 異熟

Vipāka, different when cooked, or matured, i.e. the effect differing from the cause, e.g. pleasure differing from goodness its cause, and pain from evil. Also, maturing or producing its effects in another life. 이숙인 異熟因 Vipākahetu, heterogeneous cause, i.e. a cause producing a different effect, known as 무기 無記 neutral, or not ethical, e.g. goodness resulting in pleasure, evil in pain. 이숙과 異熟果 Fruit ripening differently, i.e. in another incarnation, or life, e.g. the condition of the eye and other organs now resulting from specific sins or otherwise in previous existence. The 이숙등오과 異熟等五果 are the five fruits of karma ; pañcaphalāni, or effects produced by one or more of the six hetus or causes. They are as follows ; (1) 이숙과 異熟果 Vipāka-phala, heterogeneous effect produced by heterogeneous cause. (2) 등류과 等流果 Niṣyanda-phala, uniformly continuous effect. (3) 사용과 士用果 Puruṣakāra-phala, simultaneous effect produced by the sahabhūhetu and the samprayuktahetu ; v. 육인 六因. (4) 증상과 增上果 Adhipati-phala, aggregate effect produced by the karma-hetu. (5) 이계과 離繫果 Visaṁyoga-phala, emancipated effect produced by all the six causes. 이숙생 異熟生 A difference is made in Mahāyāna between 이숙(식) 異熟(識) which is considered as Ālaya-vijñāna, and 이숙생 異熟生 the six senses, which are produced from the Ālaya-vijñāna. 이생 異生 Pṛthagjana ; bālapṛthagjana, v. 바 婆 ; an ordinary person unenlightened by Buddhism ; an unbeliever, sinner ; childish, ignorant, foolish ; the lower orders. 이생저양심 異生羝羊心 Common "butting goat," or animal, propensities for food and lust. 이상 異相 Difference, differentiation. 이단 異端 Heterodoxy. 이연 異緣 Ālambana-pratyaya, things distracting the attention, distracting thoughts ; the action of external objects conditioning consciousness. 이견 異見 A different view, heterodoxy. 이해 異解 A different, or heterodox, interpretation. 이설 異說 A ditto explanation. 이부 異部 Of a different class, or sect ; heterodox schools, etc.

이 移 To transplant, transpose, transmit, convey, remove. 이산 移山 To remove mountains. 이감 移龕 To remove the coffin to the hall for the masses for the dead on the third day after the encoffinment.

이 貳 Two ; translit. *ni*, e.g. 이타 貳吒 Akaniṣṭha, not the smallest, i.e. the highest of the Brahmalokas, v. 아가 阿迦.

이 爾 You, thou ; so, thus ; used adverbially. 이전 爾前 Before this, formerly, used by T'ien-t'ai to denote the time preceding the Lotus sūtra. 이염 爾燄 ; 이염 爾炎 Jñeya, cognizable, the region or basis of knowledge.

이 耳 Śrotra, the ear, one of the 육근 六根 six organs of sense, hence 이입 耳入 is one of the twelve 입 入, as 이처 耳處 is one of the twelve 처 處. 이근 耳根 Śrotrendriya, the organ of hearing. 이어계 耳語戒 Secret rules whispered in the ear, an esoteric practice. 이식 耳識 Śrotravijñāna. Ear-perception, ear-discernment. 이륜 耳輪 An ear-ring.

이가 二加 The dual aid bestowed by the Buddha, 현가 顯加 manifest or external, in the blessings and powers of this life ; 명가 冥加 invisible, in getting rid of sins, increasing virtue, etc.

이가 二假 Two hypotheses in the 유식론 有識論 1 : — (1) 무체수정가 無體隨情假 the non-substantial hypothesis, that there is no substantial entity or individuality, i.e. no 견분 見分 and 상분 相分, no 실아 實我 and 실법 實法, no real subject and object, but that all is transient emotion ; (2) 유체시설가 有體施設假 the factual hypothesis, that there is entity or individuality, subject and object, etc.

이가바제라나 伊迦波提羅那 A title of a Tathāgata, intp. as 최상천왕 最上天王 the supreme deva-king.

이각 二覺 The two enlightenments : (1) The 기신론 起信論 has two — (a) 본각 本覺 the immanent mind in all things, e.g. "which lighteth every man that cometh into the world," also defined as the 법신 法身 dharmakāya ; (b) 시각 始覺 initial enlightenment or beginning of illumination

; this initiation leads on to Buddhahood, or full enlightenment. (2) (a) 등각 等覺 The fifty-first stage of a bodhisattva's 행위 行位 practice ; (b) 묘각 妙覺 the fifty-second stage, or enlightenment of Buddhahood. (3) (a) 자각 自覺 A Buddha's own or natural enlightenment ; (b) 각타 覺他 his enlightening of all others.

이견 二見 Two (wrong) views : (1) Looking on people grudgingly with regard to almsgiving and preaching the Buddha-truth. (2) (a) 유견 有見 Holding to the real existence of (material) things ; (b) 무견 無見 holding to their entire unreality. (3) (a) 단견 斷見 Holing to the view of total annihilation ; (b) 상견 常見 to that of permanence or immortality.

이경체 二經體 The two bodies or elements in a sūtra : 문 文 and 의 義 the words and the meaning, or ideas.

이계 理界 The realm of *li* in contrast with 지계 智界 ; cf. 이지 理智.

이계 二戒 The two grades of commandments, or prohibitions, e.g. 십계 十戒 and 구족계 具足戒 for monks ; 오계 五戒 and 팔계 八戒 for the laity ; 사계 邪戒 and 정계 正戒, heretical rules and correct rules ; and numerous other pairs.

이고 二苦 Two kinds of suffering : within, e.g. sickness, sorrow ; from without, e.g. calamities.

이공 二空 The two voids, unrealities, or immaterialities ; v. 공 空. There are several antitheses : (1) (a) 인공 人空 ; 아공 我空 The non-reality of the ātman, the soul, the person ; (b) 법공 法空 the non-reality of things. (2) (a) 성공 性空 The T'ien-t'ai division that nothing has a nature of its own ; (b) 상공 相空 therefore its form is unreal, i.e. forms are temporary names. (3) (a) 단공 但空 T'ien-t'ai says the 장 藏 and 통 通 know only the 공 空 ; (b) 부단공 不但空 the 별 別 and 원 圓 have 공 空, 가 假, and 중 中 q.v. (4) (a) 여실공 如實空 The division of the 기신론 起信論 that the 진여 眞如 is devoid of all impurity ; (b) 여실불공 如實不空 and full of all merit, or achievement. 이공관 二空觀 Two kinds of meditation on the "void," or unreality : (a) 무생관 無生觀 the meditation that things are unproduced, having no individual or separate natures, i.e. that all things are void and unreal ; cf. 성공 性空 ; (b) 무상관 無相觀 that they are therefore formless, cf. 상공 相空. Also 인공관 人空觀 and 법공관 法空觀 see above.

이과 二果 Sakṛdāgāmin ; v. 사 娑 and 사 斯. The second "fruit" of the four kinds of Hīnayāna arhats, who have only once more to return to mortality. Also the two kinds of fruit or karma : (a) 습기과 習氣果 The good or evil characteristics resulting from habit or practice in a former existence ; (b) 보과 報果 the pain or pleasure resulting (in this life) from the practices of a previous life.

이관 理觀 The concept of absolute truth ; the concentration of the mind upon reality.

이관 二觀 The two universal bases of meditation : 사관 事觀 the external forms, or the phenomenal, and 이관 理觀 the real or underlying nature, i.e. practice and theory.

이광 二光 The dual lights, i.e. 색광 色光 the halo from a Buddha's body and 심광 心光 the light from his mind. Also 상광 常光 the constant halo from bodies of Buddhas and 신통광 神通光 the supernatural light sent out by a Buddha (e.g. from between his eyebrows) to illuminate a distant world.

이교 二教 Dual division of the Buddha's teaching. There are various definitions : (1) T'ien-t'ai has (a) 현교 顯教 exoteric or public teaching to the visible audience, and (b) 밀교 密教 at the same time esoteric teaching to an audience invisible to the other assembly. (2) The 진언 眞言 Shingon School by "exoteric" means all the Buddha's preaching, save that of the 대일경 大日經 which it counts esoteric. (3) (a) 점교 漸教 and (b) 돈교 頓教 graduated and immediate teaching, terms with various uses, e.g. salvation by works, Hīnayāna, and by faith, Mahāyāna, etc. ; they are applied to the Buddha's method, to the receptivity of hearers and to the teaching itself. (4) T'ien-t'ai has (a) 계내교 界內教 and (b) 계외교 界外教 teachings relating to the 삼계 三界 or realms of mortality and teachings relating to immortal realms. (5) (a) 반자교 半字教 and (b) 만자교 滿字教 Terms used in the Nirvāṇa sūtra, meaning incomplete word, or letter, teaching and complete-word teaching, i.e. partial and complete, likened to Hīnayāna and Mahāyāna. (6) (a) 군수교 捃收教 and (b) 부율담상교 扶律談常教 of the Nirvāṇa sūtra, (a) completing those who failed to hear the Lotus ; (b) "supporting the law, while discoursing on immortality," i.e. that the keeping of the law is also necessary to salvation. (7) T'ien-t'ai's division of (a) 편교 偏教 and (b) 원교 圓教 the partial teaching of the 장 藏, 통 通, and 별 別 schools as contrasted with the perfect teaching of the 원 圓 school. (8) T'ien-t'ai's division of (a) 권교 權教 and (b) 실교 實教 temporary and permanent, similar to the last two. (9) (a) 세간교 世間教 The ordinary teaching of a moral life here ; (b) 출세간교 出世間教 the teaching of Buddha-truth of other-worldly happiness in escape from mortality. (10) (a) 요의교 了義教 the Mahāyāna perfect or complete teaching, and (b) 불료의교 不了義教 Hīnayāna incompleteness. (11) The Hua-yen division of (a) 굴곡교 屈曲教 indirect or uneven teaching as in the Lotus and Nirvāṇa sūtras, and (b) 평도교 平道教 direct or levelled up teaching as in the Hua-yen sūtra. (12) The Hua-yen division of (a) 화교 化教 all the Buddha's teaching for conversion and general instruction, and (b) 제교 制教 his rules and commandments for the control and development of his order.

이구 理具 Wholly noumenal, or all things as aspects of the absolute, a doctrine of the T'ien-t'ai "profounder" school, in contrast with the 사조 事造 of the "shallower" school, which considered all things to be phenomenally produced. 이구삼천 理具三千 The things of a 삼천대천세계 三千大千世界 great chiliocosm considered as noumenal throughout, or all dharmakāya.

이구 二求 The two kinds of seeking : 득구 得求 seeking to get (e.g. pleasure) and 명구 命求 seeking long life.

이구범과 二俱犯過 or 이인구범 二人俱犯 A term applied by T'ien-t'ai in criticism of Hua-yen, which while it is a 원교 圓教 perfect or complete doctrine, yet has the "crudities" of the 별교 別教 and comes short of the really perfect Lotus doctrine.

이구오부 二九五部 The eighteen Hīnayāna sects and the five Vinaya 율 律 sects. 이구운 二九韻 The eighteen 정안치 丁岸哆 tiṅanta, personal endings of the Sanskrit verb.

이근 二根 The two "roots," or natural powers. (1) (a) 이근 利根 keen, able (in the religion) ; (b) 둔근 鈍根 dull. (2) (a) 정근 正根 ; 승의근 勝義根 The power or ability which uses the sense organs to discern the truth ; (b) 부근 扶根 ; 부진근 扶塵根 ; 부진근 浮塵根 the sense organs 오근 五根 as aids. (3) The male and female sexual organs.

이길라 二吉羅 The two duṣkṛta, doing evil and speaking evil ; v. 돌길라 突吉羅.

이녀 二女 The two sisters, one the deva 공덕 功德 "merit" or "achieving," who causes people to acquire wealth ; the other, 흑암녀 黑闇女 the "dark" one, who causes them to spend and waste ; these sisters always accompany each other.

이니연 伊尼延 Aiṇeya(s) ; also 이니연(타) 伊尼延(陀) ; 이리연(타) 伊梨延(陀) ; 인니연 因尼延 ; 예니연 黳尼延 ; 열니연 咽尼延 ; 예니야 翳尼耶 ; 예니야 瑿尼耶 the black antelope ; intp. as 녹(왕) 鹿(王) a deer, or royal stag. 감이니연천상 甘伊泥延腨相 ; 감이니연천상 甘伊泥延踹相 Aiṇeyajaṅgha. The eighth of the thirty-two characteristic signs of a Buddha, knees like those of a royal stag.

이단 二壇 The two dāna 단나 壇那, i.e. kinds of donating, or almsgiving : (a) 세간단 世間壇 ordinary alms, and (b) 출세간단 出世間壇 spiritual, or other-worldly gifts.

이답 二答 Two kinds of reply, one by words, the other by signs.

이덕 二德 The two kinds of power or virtue are 지덕 智德 and 단덕 斷德 ; also 비덕 悲德 and 지덕 智德 ; also 성덕 性德 and 수덕 修德 q.v. and v. 덕 德.

이도 二道 The two Ways : (1) (a) 무애도 無礙道 or 무간도 無間道 The open or unhindered way, or the way of removing all obstacles or intervention, i.e. all delusion ; (b) 해탈도 解脫道 the way of release, by realization of truth. (2) (a) 난행도 難行道 The hard way of "works," i.e. by the six pāramitā and the disciplines. (b) 이행도 易行道 the easy way of salvation, by the invocation of Amitābha. (3) (a) 유루도 有漏道 The way of reincarnation or mortality ; (b) 무루도 無漏道 the enlightened way of escape from the miseries of transmigration. (4) (a) 교도 教道 The way of instruction ; (b) 증도 證道 the way of realization. (5) The two lower excretory organs.

이돈 二頓 The two immediate or direct ways to perfection, as defined by 형계 荊溪 Ching-ch'i of the Hua-yen school ; the gradual direct way of the Lotus ; the direct way of the Hua-yen sūtra, which is called the 돈돈돈원 頓頓頓圓, while that of the Lotus is called the 점돈점원 漸頓漸圓.

이라바나 伊羅婆那 Airāvaṇa ; 이라바나 伊羅婆拏 ; 이라발나 伊羅鉢那 or 이나발나 伊那鉢那 ; 이란 伊蘭 ; 인라 堙羅 or 인나 堙那 q.v. ; 열라파나 堙羅婆那 or 열나파나 堙那婆那 ; 예라엽 黳羅葉 or 의라엽 毉羅葉, etc. Airāvaṇa, come from the water ; Indra's elephant ; a tree, the elāpattra ; name of a park (i.e. Lumbinī, where the Buddha is said to have been born). 이라발제하 伊羅跋提河 Erāvati, Airāvatī, Irāvatī, the river Ravi, also abbrev. to 발제 跋提 Vati. 이라발(다라)용왕 伊羅鉢(多羅)龍王 ; 이라다라 伊羅多羅 or 이라발라 伊羅跋羅 ; 이라바나 伊羅婆那 ; 이나반파룡 伊那槃婆龍 and many other forms, v. *supra*. Elāpattra, Erāpattra, Eḍavarṇa, Erāvarṇa. A nāga, or elephant, which is also a meaning of Airāvaṇa and Airāvata. A nāga-guardian of a sea or lake, who had plucked a herb wrongfully in a previous incarnation, been made into a nāga and now begged the Buddha that he might be reborn in a higher sphere. Another version is that he pulled up a tree which stuck to his head and grew there, hence his name. One form is 이라바나용상왕 伊羅婆那龍象王, which may have an association with Indra's elephant.

이란 伊蘭 Airāvaṇa, Erāvaṇa, 이라 伊羅 and other forms, v. *supra* ; name of a tree with beautiful flowers of nauseous scent which spreads its odour for 40 li ; typifying 번뇌 煩惱 the passions and delusions.

이란나(발벌다) 伊爛拏(鉢伐多) Īriṇa-parvata, or Hiraṇya-parvata. An ancient kingdom noted for a volcano near its capital, the present Monghir, Lat. 25° 16 N., Long. 86° 26 E. [Eitel].

이량 二量 The two "measurings," or parts of a syllogism : (a) 현량 現量 appearance, e.g. smoke ; (b) 비량 比量 inference, e.g. fire from smoke.

이력 二力 Dual powers ; there are three definitions : — (1) 자력 自力 one's own strength, or endeavours, i.e. salvation by cultivating 계 戒, 정 定, and 혜 慧 ; 타력 他力 another's strength, e.g. the saving power of Amitābha. (2) 사택력 思擇力 Power of thought in choosing (right principles) ; 수습력 修習力 power of practice and performance. (3) 유력 有力 and 무력 無力 positive and negative forces ; dominant and subordinate ; active and inert energy.

이론 理論 Reasoning on, or discussion of, principles, or fundamental truth.

이루 二漏 The two conditions relating to the passions and delusions : 유루 有漏 the condition in which they can prevail ; 무루 無漏 that in which they cannot prevail.

이류 二流 The two ways in the current of transmigration : 순류 順流 to flow with it in continual re-incarnation ; 역류 逆流 resist it and seek a way of escape by getting rid of life's delusions, as in the case of the saints.

이류각생 二類各生 The Pure Land will not be limited to those who repeat the name of Amitābha according to his eighteenth vow ; but includes those who adopt other ways (as shown in his nineteenth and twentieth vows). 이류종자 二類種子 v. 이종자 二種子.

이륙 二六 Twelve. 이륙지연 二六之緣 idem 십이인연 十二因緣. 이륙지원 二六之願 the twelve vows of 약사 藥師. 이륙시중 二六時中 during the twelve hours (currently twenty-four hours) of the day.

이륜 二輪 The two wheels of a cart compared by the T'ien-t'ai school to 정 定 (or to its T'ien-t'ai form 지관 止觀) and 혜 慧 meditation and wisdom ; see 지관 止觀 5. Also 식 食 food and 법 法 the doctrine, i.e. food physical and spiritual.

이르다 道曰 Tell out. (ex) "이 공안에 대해서 일러 보시오."

이리 二利 The dual benefits, or profits : benefiting or developing oneself and others ; 자리 自利 in seeking enlightenment in bodhisattvahood, 이타 利他 in saving the multitude. Hīnayāna "seeks only one's own benefit" ; the bodhisattva rule seeks both one's own benefit and that of others, or personal improvement for the improving of others.

이리사반다가 伊梨沙般茶迦 or 伊利沙般茶迦 Īrṣyāpaṇḍaka, also 이리사장나 伊梨沙掌拏 eunuchs, or impotent save when stirred by jealousy, cf. 반 般.

이만다라 理曼陀羅 The noumenal maṇḍala, i.e. the Garbhadhātu in contrast with the 지만다라 智曼陀羅 or Vajradhātu maṇḍala.

이묘 二妙 The dual "marvel" of the Lotus sūtra, the 상대묘 相待妙 or comparative view, i.e. compared with all previous teaching, which is the rough ground-work ; and the 절대묘 絶待妙 or view of it as the perfection of teaching ; hence it is "wonderful" in comparison with all previous doctrine, and absolutely "wonderful" in itself ; cf. 이원 二圓.

이무기 二無記 The two neutrals, or indeterminates which cannot be noted as good or evil.

이무상 二無常 Two kinds of impermanence, immediate and delayed. 염념무상 念念無常 things in motion, manifestly transient ; 상속무상 相續無常 things that have the semblance of continuity, but are also transient, as life ending in death, or a candle in extinction.

이무아 二無我 The two categories of anātman : — 인무아 人無我 no (permanent) human ego, or soul ; 법무아 法無我 no (permanent) individuality in or independence of things, the latter is a Mahāyāna extension of the former, and takes the form of the unreality of the self or of things. 이무아지 二無我智 The wisdom that recognizes the above laws, v. 사제 四諦.

이문 二門 Two doors, entrances, schools, etc. There are many such pairs.

이뭣고 (= 이것이 무엇인고?) Translation of Chinese '是甚磨 shih-shen-ma'. "What is this?" ; "Who am I?" In Korea, '이뭣고' is believed to be the basic question underlying all kōans.

이미 二美 Two excellent things, i.e. meditation and wisdom.

이밀 二密 The two esoteric aspects, i.e. 이밀 理密 and 사밀 事密, the former referring to the doctrine, the latter to the esoteric acts of a Tathāgata.

이반야 二般若 Two kinds of prajñā, or wisdom. (1) (a) 공반야 共般若 That of the three stages of śrāvaka, pratyekabuddha, and imperfect Bodhisattva schools ; (b) 불공반야 不共般若 that of the perfect Bodhisattva teaching — a T'ien-t'ai division. (2) (a) 세간반야 世間般若 Temporal ; (b) 출세간반야 出世間般若 supernatural. (3) (a) 실상반야 實相般若 The first part of the Prajñāpāramitā ; (b) 관조반야 觀照般若 the second part.

이백오십계 二百五十戒 The 250 commandments, or 구족계 具足戒 perfect or complete commandments, which are obligatory on monks and nuns. They are 사바라이 四波羅夷 or 사근본극악 四根本極惡 the four pārājika ; 십삼잔 十三殘 thirteen saṅghāvaśeṣa ; 이부정법 二不定法 two aniyata ; 삼십사수 三十捨隨 thirty naiḥsargikāḥ-pāyattikāḥ ; 구십바일제 九十波逸提 ninety prāyaścittikāḥ ; 사제사니 四提舍尼 four prātideśanīya ; 백중학 百衆學 hundred śikṣākaraṇīya, and 칠멸쟁 七滅諍 seven kinds of vinaya for ending disputes.

이번뇌 二煩惱 The two kinds of kleśa, i.e. passions, delusions, temptations, or trials. (1) (a) 근본번뇌 根本煩惱 The six fundamental kleśas arising from the six senses ; (b) 수번뇌 隨煩惱 the twenty consequent kleśas arising out of the six. (2) (a) 분별기번뇌 分別起煩惱 kleśa arising from false reasoning ; (b) 구생기번뇌 俱生起煩惱 that which is natural to all. (3) (a) 대번뇌지법 大煩惱地法 The six great, e.g. extravagance, and (b) 소번뇌지법 小煩惱地法 ten minor afflictions, e.g. irritability. (4) (a) 수행번뇌 數行煩惱 Ordinary passions, or temptations ; (b) 맹리번뇌 猛利煩惱 fierce, sudden, or violent ditto.

이범 二凡 The two external and internal, or ordinary ranks, 외범 外凡 and 내범 內凡, in the first forty of the fifty-two stages 위 位 ; the 외범 外凡 are ordinary believers who pursue the stages of 십신 十信 ; the 내범 內凡 are the zealous, who are advancing through the next three groups of stages up to the fortieth.

이범 二犯 The two kinds of sin, 지범 止犯 and 작범 作犯 preventing good and doing evil ; also, sins of omission and commission.

이법신 理法身 The Dharmakāya as absolute being, in contrast with 지법신 智法身 the Dharmakāya as wisdom, both according to the older school being 무위 無爲 noumenal ; later writers treat 이법신 理法身 as noumenal and 지법신 智法身 as kinetic or active. 이법계 理法界 One of the 사계 四界, that of the common essence or dharmakāya of all beings.

이법신 二法身 Contrasted types of the Dharmakāya ; five pairs are given, 이법신 理法身 and 지법신 智法身 ; 과극법신 果極法身 and 응화법신 應化法身 ; 자성법신 自性法身 and 응화법신 應化法身 ; 법성법신 法性法身 and 방편법신 方便法身 ; 이법신 理法身 and 사법신 事法身 ; cf. 법신 法身.

이법집 二法執 The two tenets in regard to things ; cf. 이아집 二我執 i.e. 구생법집 俱生法執 the common or natural tendency to consider them as real ; 분별법집 分別法執 the tenet of their reality as the result of false reasoning and teaching.

이변 二邊 The two sides, extremes, or antitheses. (1) (a) 유변 有邊 That things exist ; (b) 무변 無邊 that since nothing is self-existent, things cannot be said to exist. (2) (a) 증익변 增益邊 The plus side, the common belief in a soul and permanence ; (b) 손멸변 損滅邊 the minus side, that nothing exists even of karma. (3) (a) 단변견 斷邊見 and (b) 상변견 常邊見 annihilation and immortality ; v. 견 見.

이보 二報 The dual reward. (1) 의보 依報 or 의과 依果 The material environment on which a person depends, resulting from former karma, e.g. country, house, property, etc. (2) 정보 正報 or 정과 正果 his direct reward, i.e. his body, or person.

이복 二福 The bliss of the gods, and the bliss of the saints 성 聖 ; v. also 복 福. 이복전 二福田 The two fields for the cultivation of happiness : (a) 학인전 學人田 the eighteen Hīnayāna classes of those under training in religion ; (b) 무학인전 無學人田 the nine divisions of those no longer in training, i.e. who have completed their course. Also (a) 비전 悲田 the pitiable, or poor and needy, as the field or opportunity for charity ; (b) 경전 敬田 the field of religion and reverence of the Buddhas, the saints, the priesthood.

이부오부 二部五部 The two are the divisions which took place immediately after the Buddha's death into (a) the elder monks or intimate disciples, and (b) the general body of disciples, styled respectively 상좌 上座 and 대중 大衆 q.v. ; the five are the divisions, which are said to have occurred a century later, into Dharmaguptāḥ 담무덕 曇無德, Mūlasarvāstivādāḥ 살바다 薩婆多, Mahīśāsaka 미사색 彌沙塞, Kāśyapīyāḥ 가섭유 迦葉遺, and Vātsīputrīyāḥ 바추부라 婆麤富羅.

이불 理佛 The fundamental or intrinsic Buddha, i.e. the Dharmakāya ; also the T'ien-t'ai doctrine of Buddha as immanent in all beings, even those of the three lowest orders ; which doctrine is also called 소법신 素法身 the plain, or undeveloped Dharmakāya. 이불성 理佛性 The fundamental Buddha-nature in contrast with 행불성 行佛性 the Buddha-nature in action or development.

이불병좌 二佛竝坐 The two Buddhas sitting together, v. 이세존 二世尊. 이불중문 二佛中門 The period between the nirvāṇa of Śākyamuni and the future advent of Maitreya, i.e. the present period. 이불성 二佛性 Dual aspects of the Buddha-nature, i.e. 이불성 理佛性 the Buddha-nature which is a fundamentally in all sentient beings, and 행불성 行佛性 the functioning Buddha-nature active and effective in some, but not in others, a doctrine of the 법상 法相 school. 이불신 二佛身 v. 이신 二身.

이빈 二貧 The two kinds of poverty : of goods, and of the religion.

이사 理事 Noumena and phenomena, principle and practice, absolute and relative, real and empirical, cause and effect, fundamental essence and external activity, potential and actual ; e.g. store and distribution, ocean and wave, static and kinetic. 이사무애 理事無礙 Unimpeded interaction of noumenon and phenomenon, principle and practice, etc. ; no barrier in either of the two. Cf. 십문 十門.

이사 二師 The two sages, or preceptors in the Lotus Sūtra, Śākyamuni and Prabhūtaratna. Also sages and ordinary preceptors.

이사 伊沙 Īśa, master, lord. 이사 伊沙 is used for 이사나 伊舍那 q.v., but 이사나 伊沙那 Īśāna, possessing, is intp. as 취락 聚落 a settled place, locality, and may be Īśānapura, v. *infra* 이상 伊賞. 이사다라 伊沙陁羅 ; 이사다라 伊沙馱羅 Iṣādhara. A chain of mountains, being the second of the seven concentric circles surrounding Sumeru ; defined as 지축 持軸 holding the axis, or axle, also as 차축 車軸 the axle-tree, or 자재지 自在持 sovereign control. It is made of the seven precious things, and its sea, 42,000 yojanas wide, is filled with fragrant flowers.

이사가 伊師迦 Iṣīkā, an arrow, dart, elephant's eyeball ; Ṛṣigiri, a high hill at Rājagṛha, v. 이사 伊私 ; a type of 아견 我見, 아만 我曼 egoism, etc.

이사기리 伊私耆梨 Ṛṣigiri, 선산 仙山, name of a mountain in Magadha. [M. W.]

이사나(천) 伊舍那(天) Īśāna ; 이사나 伊邪那 or 伊賒那 ; v. 이사 伊沙 "one of the older names of Śiva-Rudra ; one of the Rudras ; the sun as a form of Śiva," [M. W.] Maheśvara ; the deva of the sixth desire-heaven ; head of the external Vajra-hall of the Vajradhātu group ; Śiva with his three fierce eyes and tusks. 이사나후 伊舍那后 Īśānī, wife of Śiva, Durgā.

이삼 二三 The six non-Buddhist philosophers, 이삼사도 二三邪徒.

이상 二相 The two forms, or characteristics, of the bhūtatathatā, universal and particular. The 기신론 起信論 gives (a) 정지상 淨智相 pure wisdom, cf. ālaya-vijñāna, out of whose primary condition arise (b) 부사의용상 不思議用相 inconceivable, beneficial functions and uses. The same śāstra gives also a definition of the 진여 眞如 as (a) 동상 同相 that all things, pure or impure, are fundamentally of the same universal, e.g. clay which is made into tiles ; (b) 이상 異相 but display particular qualities, as affected by pure or impure causes, e.g. the tiles. Another definition, of the 지도론 智度論 31, is (a) 총상 總相 universals, as impermanence ; (b) 별상 別相 particulars, for though all things have the universal basis of impermanence they have particular qualities, e.g. earth-solidity, heat of fire, etc.

이상나보라 伊賞那補羅 Īśānapura. An ancient kingdom in Burma. [Eitel]. Cf. 이사나 伊沙那.

이색신 二色身 The two rūpakāya or incarnation-bodies of a Buddha, his 보신 報身 and 응신 應身 or sambhogakāya and nirmāṇakāya, as distinguished from 법신 法身 the dharmakāya.

이서 二鼠 The black and white rats – night and day.

이서 二序 The two kinds of introductory phrase : (a) the ordinary opening phrase of a sūtra – "Thus have I heard" ; and (b) specific openings referring to the circumstances in which the sūtra was produced.

이선 理禪 The dhyāna of or concentration on absolute truth free from phenomenal contamination.

이선 二善 The two good things, 정선 定善 the good character that arises from meditation or contemplation – especially of the Pure Land ; 산선 散善 the good character attainable when, though not in meditation, one controls oneself in thought, word, and deed. Also 미생선 未生善 and 이생선 已生善 the good character not yet and that already evolved. Also 사리선 事理善 goodness in theory and practice.

이섭파라 伊葉波羅 Īśvara 이습벌라 伊溼伐羅 (1) King, sovereign ; Śiva and others ; intp. by 자재 自在 self-existing, independent ; applied to Kuan-yin and other popular deities. (2) A śramaṇa of the West, learned in the Tripiṭaka, who *inter alia* translated A.D. 426 Saṁyuktābhidharma-hṛdaya-śāstra, lost since A.D. 730. (3) A bhikṣu of India, commentator on 보리자량론 菩提資糧論 attributed to Nāgārjuna, tr. by Dharmagupta, A.D. 590-616.

이성 理性 Absolute nature, immutable reality, fundamental principle or character.

이성 二聖 Śākyamuni and Prabhūtaratna 다보 多寶.

이세 二世 This life and the hereafter. 이세존 二世尊 Śākyamuni and Prabhūtaratna, the Buddha 다보 多寶 in the eleventh chapter of the Lotus Sūtra ; see also 이존 二尊. 이세간 二世間 The two realms of conscious or sentient beings 유정세간 有情世間, and unconscious or material things 기세간 器世間.

이수 二受 The dual receptivity or karma of pleasure and pain, the physical and the mental, i.e. 신 身 and 심 心.

이수 二修 Two kinds of devotion or practice, 전 專 and 잡 雜 sole or single-minded, and miscellaneous or varied, defined as (1) chief or sole duty, and (2) aids thereto or adjunctive observances. Also 연수 緣修 causative devotion of a bodhisattva in former life, and 진수 眞修 its actual manifestation here.

이승 二乘 Dviyāna. The two vehicles conveying to the final goal. There are several definitions : – (1) Mahāyāna and Hīnayāna. (2) 성문 聲聞 and 연각 緣覺 or 성각이승 聲覺二乘. Śrāvaka and Pratyekabuddha. (3) 이승작불 二乘作佛 The Lotus Sūtra teaches that śrāvakas and pratyekas also become Buddhas. (4) 삼일이승 三一二乘 The "two vehicles" of "three" and "one," the three being the pre-Lotus ideas of śrāvaka, pratyeka, and bodhisattva, the one being the doctrine of the Lotus Sūtra which combined all three in one.

이승과 二勝果 The two surpassing fruits, or rewards given by Buddha, i.e. final nirvāṇa and perfect enlightenment.

이시 二始 The two beginnings, i.e. of Hīnayāna, by the preaching of the 아함 阿含 Āgama sūtras ; and of Mahāyāna by the preaching of the 화엄 華嚴 Avataṁsaka-sūtra.

이시 二時 The two times or periods – morning and evening. Also 가라 迦羅 kāla, a regular or fixed hour for meals, and 삼매야 三昧耶 samaya, irregular or unfixed hours or times.

이식 二食 The two kinds of food : (1) (a) The joy of the Law ; (b) the bliss of meditation. (2) (a) The right kind of monk's livelihood – by mendicancy ; (b) the wrong kind – by any other means.

이식 二識 Ālaya-vijñāna and mano-vijñāna ; i.e. 아리야식 阿梨耶識 and 분별사식 分別事識 ; v. 식 識.

이신 二身 Two forms of body ; there are numerous pairs, e.g. (1) (a) 분단신 分段身 The varied forms of the karmaic or ordinary mortal body, or being ; (b) 변역신 變易身 the transformable, or spiritual body. (2) (a) 생신 生身 The earthly body of the Buddha ; (b) 화신 化身 his nirmāṇakāya, which may take any form at will. (3) (a) 생신 生身 his earthly body ; (b) 법신 法身 his moral and mental nature – a Hīnayāna definition, but Mahāyāna takes his earthly nirmāṇakāya as the 생신 生身 and his dharmakāya or that and his sambhogakāya as 법신 法身. (4) 진응이신 眞應二身 The dharmakāya and nirmāṇakāya. (5) (a) 실상신 實相身 The absolute truth, or light, of the Buddha, i.e. the dharmakāya ; (b) 위물신 爲物身 the functioning or temporal body. (6) (a) 진신 眞身 the dharmakāya and sambhogakāya ; (b) 화신 化身 the nirmāṇakāya. (7) (a) 상신 常身 his permanent or eternal body ; (b) 무상신 無常身 his temporal body. (8) (a) 실신 實身 and 화신 化身 idem 이색신 二色身.

이신이토 理身理土 The dharmakāya in the dharmakṣetra, e.g. the spiritual Vairocana in the eternal light.

이심 二心 The two minds, 진심 眞心 the original, simple, pure, natural mind of all creatures, the Buddha-mind, i.e. 여래장심 如來藏心 ; and 망심 妄心 the illusion-mind, which results in complexity and confusion. Also 정심 定心 the meditative mind, or mind fixed on goodness ; and the 산심 散心 the scattered, inattentive mind, or mind that is only good at intervals.

이십 二十 Viṁśati. Twenty.

이십억이 二十億耳 Śroṇakoṭīviṁśa. Defined as the most zealous of Śākyamuni's disciples, who became an arhat. Having lived in a heaven for ninety-one kalpas, where his feet did not touch the ground, he was born with hair on his soles two inches long, an omen which led his father and brothers to endow him with twenty koṭīs of ounces of gold, hence this name. v. 지도론 智度論 22.

이십오조 二十五條 The monk's twenty-five-patch garment, v. 가 袈. 이십오원통 二十五圓通 The twenty-five kinds of perfect understanding of the truth ; they refer to the 육진 六塵, 육근 六根, 육식 六識, and 칠대 七大 ; disciples of the Buddha are said each to have acquired a special knowledge of one of these twenty-five and to have been recognized as its authority, e.g. Kuan-yin of the ear, Dignāga of sound, etc. 이십오방편 二十五方便 T'ien-t'ai's twenty-five aids to meditation, v. 지관 止觀. 이십오유 二十五有 The twenty-five forms of existence, fourteen in the desire realms 욕계 欲界, seven in the realms of form 색계 色界, and four in the formless realms 무색계 無色界, v. 유 有. 이십오신 二十五神 The twenty-five guardian deities who protect any keeper of the commandments, i.e. five for each of the commandments against killing, robbing, adultery, lying, and drinking. 이십오보살 二十五菩薩 The twenty-five bodhisattvas who protect all who call on Amitābha, i.e. 관음 觀音, 대세지 大勢至, 약왕 藥王, 약상 藥上, 보현 普賢, 법자재 法自在, 사자후 師子吼, 다라니 陀羅尼, 허공장 虛空藏, 불장 佛藏, 보장 菩藏, 금장 金藏, 금강장 金剛藏, 산해혜 山海慧,

광명왕 光明王, 화엄왕 華嚴王, 중보왕 衆寶王, 월광왕 月光王, 일조왕 日照王, 삼매왕 三昧王, 정자재왕 定自在王, 대자재왕 大自在王, 백상왕 白象王, 대위덕왕 大威德王 and 무변신보살 無邊身菩薩. 이십오점 二十五點 Each of the five 경 更 night watches is divided into five, making twenty-five tien.

이십유식 二十唯識 The name of the 유식이십론 唯識二十論.

이십이품 二十二品 Twenty-two of the 삼십칠도품 三十七道品 q.v. ; they are 사념처 四念處, 사정근 四正勤, 사여의 四如意, 족오근 足五根 and 오력 五力. 이십이근 二十二根 The twenty-two roots, organs, or powers, v. 근 根. They are : — (1) 안근 眼根 eye, *cakṣurindriya* ; (2) 이근 耳根 ear, *śrotrendriya* ; (3) 비근 鼻根 nose, *ghrāṇendriya* ; (4) 설근 舌根 tongue, *jihvendriya* ; (5) 신근 身根 body, *kāyendriya* ; (6) 의근 意根 mind, *manaïndriya* (the above are the 육근 六根) ; (7) 여근 女根 female organ, *strīndriya* ; 남근 男根 male organ, *puruṣendriya* ; (9) 명근 命根 life, *jīvitendriya* ; (10) 고근 苦根 suffering (or pain), *duḥkhendriya* ; (11) 낙근 樂根 pleasure, *sukhendriya* ; (12) 우근 憂根 sorrow, *daurmanasyendriya* ; (13) 희근 喜根 joy, *saumanasyendriya* ; (14) 사근 捨根 abandoning, *upekṣendriya* (from 10 to 14 they are the 오수 五受) ; (15) 신근 信根 faith, *śraddhendriya* ; (16) 정진근 精進根 zeal, *vīryendriya* ; (17) 염근 念根 memory, *smṛtīndriya* ; (18) 정근 定根 meditation, or trance, *samādhīndriya* ; (19) 혜근 慧根 wisdom, *prajñendriya* (these are the 신등지오근 信等之五根) ; (20) 미지당지근 未知當知根 the power for learning (the Four Noble Truths) *anājñātamājñāsyāmīndriya* ; (21) 이지근 已知根 the power of having learned (them), *ājñendriya* ; (22) 구지근 具知根 the power of perfect knowledge (of them), *ājñātāvīndriya* (these three are called the 무루근 無漏根). 이십이문 二十二門 The Abhidharma-kośa divides the eighteen realms 십팔계 十八界 into twenty-two categories. Also, there are twenty-two modes or processes in the perfect development of a Buddha and his works.

이십지 二十智 The twenty kinds of wisdom or knowledge as defined by T'ien-t'ai, i.e. the Hīnayāna (or 삼장 三藏) with seven kinds, 통교 通教 five, 별교 別教 four, and 원교 圓教 four ; cf. 지 智. 이십건도 二十犍度 The twenty skandhas, intp. as 장편 章篇 sections or chapters, i.e. the thirty-one to the fifty-three chüan of the 사분율 四分律, beginning with 수계건도 受戒犍度 and ending with 잡건도 雜犍度 ; they are twenty sections containing rules for the monastic life and intercourse. 이십부 二十部 The eighteen Hīnayāna sects, together with the two original assemblies of elders.

이십천 二十天 The twenty devas. (1) 대범천왕 大梵天王 (Mahābrahman), (2) 제석존천 帝釋尊天 (Śakra devānām Indra), (3) 다문천왕 多聞天王 (Vaiśravaṇa, 비사문 毘沙門, or Dhanada), (4) 지국천왕 持國天王 (Dhṛtarāṣṭra), (5) 증장천왕 增長天王 (Virūḍhaka), (6) 광목천왕 廣目天王 (Virūpākṣa), (7) 금강밀적 金剛密迹 (Guhyapati), (8) 마혜수라 摩醯首羅 (Maheśvara), (9) 산지(가)대장 散脂(迦)大將 (Pāñcika), (10) 대변재천 大辯才天 (Sarasvatī), (11) 대공덕천 大功德天 (Lakṣmī), (12) 위타천신 韋馱天神 (Skanda), (13) 견뢰지신 堅牢地神 (Pṛthivī), (14) 보리수신 菩提樹神 (Bodhidruma, or Bodhivṛkṣa), (15) 귀자모신 鬼子母神 (Hāritī), (16) 마리지천 摩利支天 (Marīci), (17) 일궁천자 日宮天子 (Sūrya), (18) 월궁천자 月宮天子 (Candra, etc. There are many different names), (19) 사갈용왕 娑竭龍王 (Sāgara), (20) 염마라왕 閻摩羅王 (Yama-rāja).

이십팔천 二十八天 The twenty-eight heavens, or devalokas : six of the desire-world 욕계 欲界, eighteen of the form-world 색계 色界, and four arūpa or formless heavens 무색계 無色界. The heavens of the world of form are sixteen according to the 살바다부 薩婆多部 Sarvāstivāda School, seventeen according to 경부 經部 Sūtra School, and eighteen according to the 상좌부 上座部 Sthavirāḥ. 이십팔수 二十八宿 The twenty-eight nakṣatras or constellations, divided into four mansions of seven each, referred to East, or Spring ; South, Summer ; West, Autumn ; and North, Winter. The month-names derived from them differ slightly in form. E. : 각 角 Citrā, 항 亢 Niṣṭyā (or Svāti), 씨 氐 Viśākhā, 방 房 Anurādhā, 심 心 Rohiṇī, Jyeṣṭhaghnī (or Jyeṣṭhā), 미 尾 Mūlabarhaṇī (or Mūla), 기 箕 Pūrva-Aṣādhā. N. : 두 斗 Uttara-Aṣāḍhā, 우 牛 Abhijit, 여 女 Śravaṇā, 허 虛 Śraviṣṭhā (or Dhaniṣṭhā), 위 危 Śatabhiṣā, 실 室 Pūrva-Proṣṭhapada, 벽

壁 Uttara-Proṣṭhapada. W. : 규 奎 Revatī, 루 婁 Aśvayuj (or Aśvinī), 위 胃 Apabharaṇī (or Bharaṇī), 앙 昴 Kṛttikā, 필 畢 Rohiṇī, 자 觜 Invakā (or Mṛgaśiras), 삼 參 Bāhu (or Ārdrā). S. : 정 井 Punarvasu, 귀 鬼 Tiṣya (or Puṣya), 유 柳 Aśleṣā, 성 星 Maghā, 장 張 Pūrva-Phalgunī, 익 翼 Uttara-Phalgunī, 진 軫 Hastā. 이십팔유 二十八有 ; 이십팔생 二十八生 The twenty-eight forms of existence, or birth. 이십구유 二十九有 the twenty-ninth is the non-existent ; v. 유 有.

이십팔조 二十八祖 The twenty-eight Buddhist patriarchs as stated by the Mahāyānists. The T'ien-t'ai school reckons twenty-three, or twenty-four, with the addition of Śāṇakavāsa, contemporary with his predecessors, but the Ch'an school reckons twenty-eight : — (1) Mahākāśyapa, 마하가섭(파) 摩訶迦葉(波) ; (2) Ānanda, 아난 阿難 ; (3) Śāṇakavāsa, 상나화수 商那和修 ; (4) Upagupta, 우파국다 優婆毱多 ; (5) Dhṛtaka, 제다가 提多迦 ; (6) Mikkaka, or Miccaka, or Micchaka, 미차가 彌遮迦 ; (7) Vasumitra, 파수밀 婆須蜜 ; (8) Buddhanandi, 불타난제 佛陀難提 ; (9) Buddhamitra, 복타밀다 伏馱密多 ; (10) Pārśva, or Pārśvika, 파율습박 波栗溼縛 or 협존자 脇尊者 ; (11) Puṇyayaśas, 부나야사 富那耶舍 ; (12) Aśvaghoṣa, 마명대사 馬鳴大士 ; (13) Kapimala, 가비마라 迦毘摩羅 ; (14) Nāgārjuna, 용수 龍樹 ; (15) Kāṇadeva, 가나제바 迦那提婆 ; (16) Rāhulata, 라후라다 羅睺羅多 ; (17) Saṅghanandi, 승가난제 僧伽難提 ; (18) Gayaśāta, 가야사다 伽耶舍多 ; (19) Kumārata, 구마라다 鳩摩羅多 ; (20) Jayata, 사야다 闍夜多 ; (21) Vasubandhu, 바수반두 婆修盤頭 ; (22) Manorhita, 마나라 摩拏羅 ; (23) Haklena, 학륵나 鶴勒那 ; (24) Āryasiṁha, 사자존자 師子尊者 ; (25) Basiasita, 파사사다 婆舍斯多 ; (26) Puṇyamitra, 불여밀다 不如密多 ; (27) Prajñātāra, 반야다라 般若多羅 ; (28) Bodhidharma, 보리달마 菩提達磨. 이십팔약차 二十八藥叉 the twenty-eight yakṣas. 이십팔부중 二十八部衆 The thousand-hand Kuan-yin has twenty-eight groups of 대선중 大仙衆 great ṛṣis or genii, under the direction of the 공작왕 孔雀王 Peacock king, Mayūrarāja ; also each of the 사천왕 四天王 mahārājas, or guardians of the four regions, has the same provision of demons, known as 귀신중 鬼神衆 company of spirits.

이아(견) 二我(見) The two erroneous views of individualism : (a) 인아견 人我見 The erroneous view that there is an independent human personality or soul, and (b) 법아견 法我見 the like view that anything exists with an independent nature. 이아집 二我執 The two reasons for clinging to the idea of the self : (a) 구생아집 具生我執 the natural, or instinctive cleaving to the idea of a self, or soul ; (b) 분별아집 分別我執 the same idea developed as the result of (erroneous) reasoning. Cf. 이법집 二法執.

이애 二礙 idem 이장 二障.

이애 二愛 The two kinds of love, 욕애 欲愛 ordinary human love springing from desire ; 법애 法愛 bodhisattva or religious love, i.e. desiring to save all creatures.

이어 二語 Double-tongued ; also 이설 二舌.

이엄 二嚴 The dual adornment, that of 지혜 智慧 wisdom and that of 복덕 福德, good deeds, 열반경 涅槃經 27.

이업 二業 Two classes of karma. (1) (a) 인업 引業 leads to the 총보 總報, i.e. the award as to the species into which one is to be born, e.g. men, gods, etc. ; (b) 만업 滿業 is the 별보 別報 or fulfilment in detail, i.e. the kind or quality of being, e.g. clever or stupid, happy or unhappy, etc. (2) (a) 선업 善業 and (b) 악업 惡業 Good and evil karma, resulting in happiness or misery. (3) (a) 조업 助業 Aids to the karma of being reborn in Amitābha's Pure-land, e.g. offerings, chantings, etc. ; (b) 정업 正業 thought and invocation of Amitābha with undivided mind, as the direct method.

이여 二餘 see 여 餘

이여 二如 There are various definitions of the two aspects of the 진여 眞如 bhūtatathatā. (1) (a) 불변진여 不變眞如 The changeless essence or substance, e.g. the sea ; (b) 수연진여 隨緣眞如

its conditioned or ever-changing forms, as in the phenomenal world, e.g. the waves. (2) (a) 이언진여 離言眞如 The inexpressible absolute, only mentally conceivable ; (b) 의언진여 依言眞如 aspects of it expressible in words, its ideal reflex. (3) (a) 공진여 空眞如 The absolute as the void, e.g. as space, the sky, a clear mirror ; (b) 불공진여 不空眞如 the absolute in manifestation, or phenomenal, e.g. images in the mirror ; the womb of the universe in which are all potentialities. (4) (a) 재전진여 在纏眞如 The Buddha-nature in bonds, i.e. all beings in suffering ; (b) 출전진여 出纏眞如 the Buddha-nature set free by the manifestation of the Buddha and bodhisattvas. (5) (a) 유구진여 有垢眞如 The Buddha-nature defiled, as in unenlightened man, etc., e.g. the water-lily with its roots in the mud ; (b) 무구진여 無垢眞如 the pure Buddha-nature, purified or bright as the full moon. (6) 안립 安立 and 비안립진여 非安立眞如 similar to the first definition given above.

이열반 二涅槃 Two Nirvāṇas, v. 이종열반 二種涅槃.

이오 二悟 The two awakenings, or kinds of entry into bodhisattvahood, i.e. 돈 頓 immediate and 점 漸 gradual.

이오(로) 伊吾(盧) I-wu(-lu), the modern Hami, so called during the Han dynasty. Later it was known as I-wu Chün and I-chou. V. *Serindia*, p. 1147.

이오식 二五食 The two groups of food, each of five kinds : *bhojanīya*, v. 포 蒲 cereals, fish, and flesh ; and *khādanīya*, v. 거 佉 fruits and sweetmeats.

이왕 二往 and 재왕 再往 Twice over, a second time.

이왕 二王 The two guardian spirits represented on the temple gates, styled Vajrayakṣa 금강야차 金剛夜叉 or 금강신 金剛神, or 야차신 夜叉神.

이원 二圓 The two perfect doctrines, a term of the T'ien-t'ai School, called 금원 今圓 (also 개현원 開顯圓 and 절대원 絶待圓) and 석원 昔圓 (also 상대원 相待圓). 금원 今圓 is the present really perfect 일실 一實 doctrine arising from the Lotus Sūtra ; 석원 昔圓 the older, or 상대 相待 comparatively speaking perfect doctrine of the pre-Lotus teaching, that of the 장 藏, 통 通, and 별 別 schools ; but the older was for limited salvation and not universal like the 금원 今圓 ; these two are also termed 부원 部圓 and 교원 教圓. The Hua-yen school has a division of the two perfections into 점원 漸圓 and 돈원 頓圓 gradual and immediate perfection.

이응신 二應身 The two kinds of transformation-body of a Buddha, i.e. 승응신 勝應身 his surpassing body as seen by bodhisattvas, and 열응신 劣應身 his inferior human body as seen by ordinary people.

이의 二衣 The two kinds of clothing : (a) 제의 制衣 the regulation three robes for monks and five for nuns, which must be worn ; (b) 청의 聽衣 optional garments.

이의 二義 The two meanings or teachings, partial and complete ; v. 이교 二教.

이이합연 二二合緣 A method of meditation by coupling 법 法 with 신 身, 수 受, 심 心 respectively. Cf. 사념처관 四念處觀.

이익 二翼 A pair of wings : charity and wisdom.

이익 二益 The dual advantages or benefits : profitable to the life which now is, and that which is to come.

이인 二忍 The two patiences or endurances : 중생인 衆生忍 patience towards all under all circumstances ; 무생(법)인 無生(法)忍 calm rest, as a bodhisattva, in the assurance of no (re-)birth, i.e. in immortality. Also 안수고인 安受苦忍 patience under suffering, and 관찰법인 觀察法忍 imperturbable examination of or meditation in the law or of all things. Also, physical and mental patience, or endurance.

이인 二因 Two causes, of which there are various definitions : (1) 생인 生因 The producing cause (of all good things) ; and 요인 了因 the revealing or illuminating cause, i.e. knowledge, or wisdom. (2) 능생인 能生因 The 8th 식 識 q.v. : the cause that is able to produce all sense and perceptions, also all good and evil ; and 방편인 方便因 the environmental or adaptive cause, which aids the 8th 식 識, as water or earth does the seed, etc. (3) 습인 習因 or 동류인 同類因 Practice or habit as cause, e.g. desire causing desire ; and 보인 報因 or 과숙인 果熟因 the rewarding-cause, or fruit-ripening cause, e.g. pleasure or pain caused by good or evil deeds. (4) 정인 正因 Correct or direct cause, i.e. the Buddha-nature of all beings ; and 연인 緣因 the contributory cause, or enlightenment (see 요인 了因 above) which evolves the 정인 正因 or Buddha-nature by good works. (5) 근인 近因 Immediate or direct cause and 원인 遠因 distant or indirect cause or causes.

이입 理入 Entry by the truth, or by means of the doctrine, or reason, as 행입 行入 is entry by conduct or practice, the two depending one on the other, cf. 이입 二入.

이입 二入 The two ways of entering the truth : — 이입 理入 by conviction intellectually, 행입 行入 by (proving it in) practice.

이자 二字 Double-letters, i.e. a monk-because a monk's name consists of two characters. 이자문수 二字文殊 The two-character Mañjuśrī.

이장 理障 The hindrance caused by incorrect views of truth.

이장 二障 The two hindrances : (1) (a) 번뇌장 煩惱障 The passions and delusion which aid rebirth and hinder entrance into nirvāṇa ; (b) 지장 智障 or 소지장 所知障, worldly wisdom, e.g. accounting the seeming as real, a hindrance to true wisdom. (2) (a) 번뇌장 煩惱障 as above ; (b) 해탈장 解脫障 hindrances to deliverance. (3) (a) 이장 理障 hindrances to truth ; (b) 사장 事障 hindrances of the passions, etc.

이장의 二障義 "Meaning of Two Obstructions." Written by Won-hyo.

이장 二藏 The two piṭakas, or tripiṭakas, i.e. the Buddhist canon : (a) 성문장 聲聞藏 the Śrāvaka, or Hīnayāna canon ; (b) 보살장 菩薩藏 the Bodhisattva canon, or Mahāyāna canon.

이재절언 理在絶言 Truth is in eliminating words ; it is independent of words ; it does not require words to express it.

이전 二詮 Two kinds of statement, or definition : 차 遮 latent or negative and 표 表 patent or positive ; e.g. 불생불멸 不生不滅 is a negative statement, 지견각조 知見覺照 is a positive statement.

이제 二際 The two borders, or states : according to Hīnayāna, nirvāṇa and mortality ; according to Mahāyāna the two are one.

이제 二諦 Two forms of statement : (a) 속제 俗諦 Saṁvṛti-satya, also called 세제 世諦, 세속제 世俗諦, 복속제 覆俗諦, 복제 覆諦, meaning common or ordinary statement, as if phenomena were real ; (b) 진제 眞諦 paramārtha-satya, also called 제일제 第一諦, 승의제 勝義諦, meaning the correct dogma or averment of the enlightened. Another definition is 왕법 王法 and 불법 佛法, royal law and Buddha law.

이제목다가 伊帝目多伽 or **이제왈다가** 伊帝曰多伽 or **이제월다가** 伊帝越多伽 Ityuktas, so said, or reported ; Itivṛttaka, so occurring ; the Buddha's discourses arising out of events ; intp. as

본사 本事 q.v. personal events, or Jātaka stories, one of the twelve classes of Buddhist literature, i.e. 십이부경 十二部經 biographical narratives.

이조 二鳥 The drake and hen of the mandarin duck who are always together, typifying various contrasted theories and ideas, e.g. permanence and impermanence, joy and sorrow, emptiness and non-emptiness, etc.

이조(단비) 二祖(斷臂) The second patriarch in China 혜가 慧可 Hui-k'o of the 선 禪 Ch'an(Zen) school who, to induce Bodhidharma to receive him, is said to have cut off his left arm in the snow in order to prove his firmness and determination.

이족 二足 A man's two legs, compared to goodness and wisdom, 복 福 being counted as the first five of the pāramitās, 지 智 as the sixth ; v. 육도 六度. 이족존 二足尊 The honoured one among bipeds or men, i.e. a Buddha ; cf. 양족 兩足.

이존 二尊 The two honoured ones, Śākyamuni and Amitābha. 이존일교 二尊一教 ; 이존일치 二尊一致 The two as one in teaching. 이존이교 二尊二教 The two as teacher and saviour, with reference to the teaching of the way of salvation of the first, and the consequent saving vows of the second ; cf. 이세존 二世尊.

이종 二種 Two kinds or classes. For those not given below see under 이 二, etc., as for instance 이종세간 二種世間 see under 이세간 二世間.

이종 二宗 Two theories or schools stated by the Hua-yen (Kegon) school as 법상종 法相宗 and 법성종 法性宗 q.v., known also as 상종 相宗 and 성종 性宗. There are ten points of difference between them. Another division is the 공종 空宗 and 성종 性宗 q.v.

이종(보)시 二種(布)施 Two kinds of charity : (1) (a) goods ; (b) the saving truth. (2) (a) 정시 淨施 Pure charity, expecting no return ; (b) the opposite.

이종(일)천제 二種(一)闡提 Two kinds of icchantika, q.v. : (a) the utterly depraved, abandoned, and blasphemers of Buddha-truth ; (b) bodhisattvas who refuse to enter upon their Buddhahood in order to save all beings.

이종공양 二種供養 The two forms of service, or offerings : (1) (a) 출전공양 出纏供養 to those who have escaped from the toils, e.g. Buddhas ; (b) 재전공양 在纏供養 to those still living in the toils. (2) (a) 재공양 財供養 offerings of goods ; (b) 법공양 法供養 of the Buddha-truth.

이종관정 二種灌頂 Two forms of esoteric baptism, v. 관 灌.

이종광명 二種光明 The two kinds of light : — (1) (a) 색광명 色光明 physical light ; (b) 지(혜)광명 智(慧)光明 or 심광명 心光明 wisdom or mental light. (2) (a) 마광 魔光 Māra's delusive light ; (b) 불광 佛光 the true light of the Buddha. (3) (a) 상광 常光 The constant or eternal light ; (b) 현기광 現起光 the light in temporary manifestations.

이종병 二種病 Two kinds of sickness : physical and mental or spiritual.

이종보살 二種菩薩 Monastic and lay bodhisattvas. 이종보살신 二種菩薩身 A bodhisattva's mortal and immortal bodies.

이종불경 二種佛境 The two Buddha-domains : (a) 증경 證境 his domain or state of absolute enlightenment ; (b) 화경 化境 the domain that he is transforming.

이종비구 二種比丘 Two classes of monks : 다문비구 多聞比丘 those who hear and repeat many sūtras, but are not devoted doers ; 과천비구 寡淺比丘 those who read and repeat few sūtras but are devoted in their lives.

이종사 二種死 The two kinds of death, 명진사 命盡死 natural, and 외연사 外緣死 violent death, or from external cause.

이종사견 二種邪見 The two false views, one that of a nihilistic school which denied that earthly happiness is dependent on a moral life ; the other a materialistic school which maintained the moral life in the interests of self, sought earthly happiness, and failed to apprehend nirvāṇa.

이종사리 二種舍利 Two kinds of relics — the whole body, or parts of it. Also, the Buddha's physical remains or relics, and the sūtras, which form his spiritual (dharmakāya) remains.

이종성 二種聖 Two classes of saints or preachers : those who preach and those who preach without words.

이종성 二種性 Two kinds of seed-nature, the character of the ālaya seed and its development : (1) (a) 성종자 性種子 The original good seed-nature ; (b) 습종자 習種子 the seed-nature in practice or development. (2) (a) 본성주종성 本性住種性 The immanent abiding original good seed-nature ; (b) 습소성종성 習所成種性 the seed productive according to its ground. (3) (a) 성종성 聖種性 The seed-nature of the saints, by which they attain nirvāṇa ; (b) 우부종성 愚夫種性 the seed-nature in the foolish and ignorant.

이종수기 二種授記 Two classes of Buddha's predictions of a disciple's destiny, 무여수기 無餘授記 prediction in finality, or complete detail ; 유여수기 有餘授記 partial, or incomplete prediction.

이종시 二種施 v. 이종보시 二種布施.

이종심상 二種心相 Two kinds of mind : mind in its inner character and influence ; in its outer manifestations.

이종열반 二種涅槃 Two nirvāṇas : (1) 유여열반 有餘涅槃 also 유여의 有餘依 That with a remnant ; the cause 인 因 has been annihilated, but the remnant of the effect 과 果 still remains, so that a saint may enter this nirvāṇa during life, but have to continue to live in this mortal realm till the death of his body. (2) 무여열반 無餘涅槃 or 무여의 無餘依 Remnantless nirvāṇa, without cause and effect, the connection with the chain of mortal life being ended, so that the saint enters upon perfect nirvāṇa on the death of the body ; cf. 지도론 智度論 31. Another definition is that Hīnayāna has further transmigration, while Mahāyāna maintains final nirvāṇa. "Nothing remaining" is differently interpreted in different schools, by some literally, but in Mahāyāna generally as meaning no further mortal suffering, i.e. final nirvāṇa.

이종인과 二種因果 Two aspects of cause and effect, a division of the 사제 四諦 "four noble truths" : (a) 세간인과 世間因果 in the present life, the 고제 苦諦 being the effect, and the 집제 集諦 the cause ; (b) 출세간인과 出世間因果 in the future life, the 멸제 滅諦, extinction (of passion, or mortality) being the fruit, and the 도제 道諦 the "eightfold noble path" the cause.

이종인욕 二種忍辱 Two kinds of patience, or endurance : (a) of the assaults of nature, heat, cold, etc. ; (b) of human assaults and insults.

이종자 二種子 Two kinds of seed : (1) (a) 본유종자 本有種子 the seed or latent undivided (moral) force immanent in the highest of the eight 식 識, i.e. the ālaya-vijñāna ; (b) 신훈종자 新薰種子 the newly influenced, or active seed when acted upon by the seven other 식 識, thus becoming productive. (2) (a) 명언종자 名言種子 The so-called seed which causes moral action similar to 본유종자 本有種子, e.g. good or evil seed producing good or evil deeds ; (b) 업종자 業種子 karma seed, the sixth 식 識 acting with the eighth.

이종자량 二種資糧 The two kinds of (spiritual) provender : charity and wisdom.

이종적정 二種寂靜 Two kinds of seclusion, or retirement from the world : Bodily withdrawal into seclusion. Spiritual withdrawal from all evil, and into meditation.

이종청정 二種淸淨 Two kinds of purity, according to the Hua-yen sūtra ; 자성청정 自性淸淨 natural purity, i.e. the natural 진여 眞如 purity ; and 이구청정 離垢淸淨 acquired purity through avoiding pollution.

이죄 二罪 The two classes of offence : (a) 성죄 性罪 that which is wrong in itself, e.g. murder, etc. ; (b) 차죄 遮罪 not wrong in itself, e.g. taking alcohol, but forbidden by the Buddha for the sake of the other commandments ; transgression of this is therefore a sin against the Buddha.

이중 二衆 The two groups : the monks, or clergy ; the laity who observe the five and the eight commands.

이즉(불) 理卽(佛) The underlying truth of all things is Buddha ; immanent reason ; Buddhahood ; the T'ien-t'ai doctrine of essential universal Buddhahood, or the undeveloped Buddha in all beings.

이증보살 二增菩薩 The two superior kinds of bodhisattvas, 지증보살 智增菩薩 superior in wisdom (chiefly beneficial to self) ; 비증보살 悲增菩薩 superior in pity for others and devotion to their salvation.

이지 理智 Principle and gnosis (or reason) ; the noumenal in essence and in knowledge ; the truth in itself and in knowledge ; *li* is also the fundamental principle of the phenomenon under observation, *chih* the observing wisdom ; one is reality, the other the knower or knowing ; one is the known object, the other the knower, the knowing, or what is known ; each is dependent on the other, *chih* depends on *li*, *li* is revealed by *chih*. Also knowledge or enlightenment in its essence or purity, free from incarnational influences. 이지오법 理智五法 v. 오법 五法.

이지 二智 The two kinds of wisdom ; there are various pairs. The Hua-yen school uses 여리 如理 and 여량 如量 ; the Fa-hsiang (법상 法相) uses 근본 根本 and 후득 後得 ; the T'ien-t'ai uses 권지 權智 and 실지 實智. (1) (a) 여리지 如理智 or 근본지 根本智, 무분별지 無分別智, 정체지 正體智, 진지 眞智, 실지 實智 is Buddha-wisdom, or Bodhisattva real wisdom ; (b) 여량지 如量智 or 후득지 後得智, 유분별지 有分別智, 속지 俗智, 편지 偏智, the same wisdom in its limitation and relation to ordinary human affairs. (2) (a) 실지 實智 Absolute wisdom and (b) 권편지 權便智 or 방편지 方便智 relative or temporal wisdom. (3) (a) 일체지 一切智 wisdom of the all, (b) 일체종지 一切種智 wisdom of all the particulars. 이지원만 二智圓滿 The two kinds of Tathāgata-wisdom, 실 實 and 권 權 absolute and functional (or relative), both perfect and complete.

이지 二持 The two values of the commandments : (a) 지지 止持 prohibitive, restraining from evil ; (b) 작지 作持 constructive, constraining to goodness.

이진여 二眞如 v. 이여 二如 and 진여 眞如.

이집 二執 The two (erroneous) tenets, or attachments : (1) 아집 我執 or 인집 人執 that of the reality of the ego, permanent personality, the ātman, soul or self. (2) 법집 法執 that of the reality of dharma, things or phenomena. Both are illusions. "All illusion arises from holding to the reality of the ego and of things."

이찰니 伊刹尼 Īkṣaṇi, or Īkṣaṇa, defined as a magic mode of reading another's thoughts.

이처삼회 二處三會 The two places from which the Buddha is supposed to have preached the Lotus Sūtra, i.e. the Vulture Peak, the sky, and again the Vulture Peak ; the three assemblies are

(1) those he addressed from the Peak, chapters 1 to the middle of the eleventh chapter ; (2) those addressed from the sky, to the end of the twenty-second chapter ; and (3) again those on the Vulture Peak, from the twenty-third chapter to the end.

이천 二天 The two devas. (1) 일천 日天 and 월천 月天 Sun-deva and Moon-deva. (2) 동생천 同生天 A deva born simultaneously with the individual, and 동명천 同名天 a deva with the same name as the individual ; both devas have the duty of watching over the individual. (3) 범천 梵天 and 제석천 帝釋天 Brahmā and Indra. 이천삼선 二天三仙 The two devas are Maheśvara and Viṣṇu ; the three ṛṣi are Kapila, Ulūka, and Ṛṣabha ; v. 가 迦, 우 優, and 늑 勒.

이체 理體 The fundamental substance or body of all things.

이초 二超 Two ways of passing over (to bliss) : 수 竪 the lengthwise, or long way (of Hīnayāna) ; and 횡 橫 the crosswise, or short way of Mahāyāna.

이출 二出 The two modes of escape from mortality, 수출 竪出 the long way called the 성도문 聖道門 or 자력교 自力敎, i.e. working out one's own salvation ; and 횡출 橫出 the across or short way of the Pure-land sect or 타력교 他力敎 faith in or invocation of another, i.e. Amitābha.

이토 二土 There are three groups : 성토 性土 and 상토 相土 : 1 the former is the ubiquitous, unadulterated or innocent 법성지리 法性之理 dharma-nature, or essence of things ; the latter is the form-nature, or formal existence of the dharma, pure or impure according to the mind and action of the living. The 정토 淨土 and 예토 穢土 are Pure-land or Paradise ; and impure land, e.g. the present world. In the Pure-land there are also 보토 報土, the land in which a Buddha himself dwells and 화토 化土 in which all beings are transformed. There are other definitions, e.g. the former is Buddha's Paradise, the latter the world in which he dwells and which he is transforming, e.g. this Sahā-world.

이판 理判 Lit. "scrutinizer of principle." A monk who has embarked on his practice career ; a meditator. Cf. 사판 事判.

이팔 二八 The sixteen 관 觀 or meditations, v. 십육관 十六觀.

이포색 伊蒲塞 Upāsaka, a lay member of the Buddhist Church, v. 이우 伊優.

이하백도 二河白道 The two rivers and the white path, i.e. the path leading to life between the rivers of desire and hatred, which are compared to water and fire.

이학 二學 The two kinds of study or learning : (a) reading and reciting, (b) meditation and thought.

이해탈 二解脫 Two kinds of deliverance, mukti or mokṣa : (1) (a) 유위해탈 有爲解脫 Active or earthly deliverance to arhatship ; (b) 무위해탈 無爲解脫 nirvāṇa-deliverance. (2) (a) 성정해탈 性淨解脫 The pure, original freedom or innocence ; (b) 장진해탈 障盡解脫 deliverance acquired by the ending of all hindrances (to salvation). (3) (a) 혜해탈 慧解脫 The arhat's deliverance from hindrances to wisdom ; (b) 구해탈 具解脫 his complete deliverance in regard to both wisdom and vision 혜 慧 and 정 定. (4) (a) 시해탈 時解脫 The dull who take time or are slow in attaining to 정 定 vision ; (b) 불시해탈 不時解脫 the quick or clever who take "no time." (5) (a) 심해탈 心解脫 A heart or mind delivered from desires ; (b) 혜해탈 慧解脫 a mind delivered from ignorance by wisdom.

이행 二行 Two classes of conduct : following wrong views ; following wrong desires, or emotions. There are other pairs.

이현 二現 The two kinds of manifestation, or appearance, 수현 須現 and 불수현 不須現, the necessary appearance in the flesh of the Buddha for ordinary people, and the non-necessity for this to those of spiritual vision.

이협사 二脇士 ; 이협시 二挾侍 The two attendants by the side of Amitābha, i.e. 관음 觀音 Kuan-yin and 대세지 大勢至 Mahāsthāmaprāpta ; also the two by Yao Shih, the Master of Medicine, i.e. 일광 日光 sunlight and 월광 月光 moonlight ; also the two by Śākyamuni, i.e. 문수 文殊 Mañjuśrī and 보현 普賢 Samantabhadra.

이호 二護 The two protectors : the inner, oneself, by studying and following the Law ; the outer, those who supply what is needful for one's body and mind, e.g. supporters.

이혹 理惑 Illusion in regard to fundamental truth, e.g. the reality of the ego and things ; as 사혹 事惑 is illusion in regard to things themselves. Also, fundamental illusion ; reality and illusion.

이혹 二惑 The two aspects of illusion : 견혹 見惑 perplexities or illusions and temptations arise form false views or theories. 사혹 思惑 or 수혹 修惑, ditto from thoughts arising through contact with the world, or by habit, such as desire, anger, infatuation, etc. They are also styled 이혹 理惑 illusions connected with principles and 사혹 事惑 illusions arising in practice ; v. 견사 見思.

이화 二和 The double harmony or unity, i.e. 리 理 and 사 事, indicating those who are united in doctrine and practice, or the saṅgha.

인 刃 A blade, a sword ; to kill. 인엽림 刃葉林 ; 검엽림 劍葉林 Asipattravana ; the forest of swords, where every leaf is a sharp sword, v. 지옥 地獄.

인 因 Hetu ; a cause ; because ; a reason ; to follow, it follows, that which produces a 과 果 result or effect. 인 因 is a primary cause in comparison with 연 緣 pratyaya, which is an environmental or secondary cause. In the 십인십과 十因十果 ten causes and ten effects, adultery results in the iron bed, the copper pillar, and the eight hot hells ; covetousness in the cold hells ; and so on, as shown in the 능엄경 楞嚴經. Translit. *in*, *yin*. Cf. 인 印.

인 仁 Kindness, benevolence, virtue. 인자 仁者 or 인 仁 Kind sir! 인존 仁尊 Benevolent and honoured, or kindly honoured one, i.e. Buddha. 인왕 仁王 The benevolent king, Buddha ; the name Śākya is intp. as 능인 能仁 able in generosity. Also an ancient king, probably imaginary, of the "sixteen countries" of India, for whom the Buddha is said to have dictated the 인왕경 仁王經, a sūtra with two principal translations into Chinese, the first by Kumārajīva styled 인왕반야경 仁王般若經 or 불설인왕반야바라밀경 佛說仁王般若波羅蜜經 without magical formulae, the second by Amogha (불공 不空) styled 인왕호국반야 仁王護國般若, etc., into which the magical formulae were introduced ; these were for royal ceremonials to protect the country from all kinds of calamities and induce prosperity. 인왕공 仁王供 Service of the 인왕회 仁王會 or 인왕강 仁王講 the meeting of monks to chant the above incantations. 인왕주 仁王咒 ; 인왕다라니 仁王陀羅尼 The incantations in the above. 인왕존 仁王尊 The two Vajrapāṇi 아 阿 and 우 吽 who act as door guardians of temples, variously known as 밀적보살 密跡菩薩, 밀수역사 密修力士, 집금강신 執金剛神, and 나라연금강 那羅延金剛.

인 忍 Kṣānti, 찬제 羼提 or 찬지 羼底 ; patience, endurance, (a) in adverse circumstances, (b) in the religious state. There are groups of two, four, five, six, ten, and fourteen, indicating various forms of patience, equanimity, repression, forbearance, endurance, constancy, or "perseverance of the saints," both in mundane and spiritual things. 인불타악취 忍不墮惡趣 The stage of patience ensures that there will be no falling into the lower paths of transmigration. 인선 忍仙 The patient ṛṣi, or immortal of patience, i.e. the Buddha. 인위 忍位 The stage of patience. 인가행 忍加行 The discipline of patience, in the 서가행 西加行 four Hīnayāna disciplines ; also in the Mahāyāna. 인선 忍善 The patient and good ; or patient in doing good ; 인토 忍土 The place of patience or endurance, this world. 인지 忍地 The stage of patience, i.e. of enlightenment separating from the chain of transmigration. 인지 忍智 Patience and wisdom. In the Hīnayāna, patience is cause, wisdom effect ; in Mahāyāna, the two are merged, though patience precedes wisdom. 인수 忍水 Patience in its depth and expanse compared to water. 인법(위) 忍法(位) The method or stage of patience, the sixth of the seven stages of the Hīnayāna in the attainment of arhatship, or sainthood ; also the third of the four roots of goodness. 인바라밀 忍波羅蜜 The patience pāramitā, v. 인욕 忍辱. 인계 忍界 Sahā, or Sahāloka, or Sahālokadhātu. The universe of persons subject to transmigration, the universe of endurance. 인조 忍調 Patiently to harmonize, i.e. the patient heart tempers and subdues anger and hatred. 인욕 忍辱 ; 찬제바라밀다 羼提波羅蜜多 or 찬지바라밀다 羼底波羅蜜多 Kṣānti pāramitā ; patience, especially bearing insult and distress without resentment, the third of the six pāramitās 육도 六度. Its guardian bodhisattva is the third on the left in the hall of space in the Garbhadhātu. 인욕선 忍辱仙 Kṣāntyṛṣi ; the ṛṣi who patiently suffered insult, i.e. Śākyamuni, in a former life, suffering mutilation to convert Kalirāja. 인욕지 忍辱地 The stage of patience. Two kinds are distinguished, patience which endures (1) insults originating in men, such as hatred, or abuse, (2) distresses arising from natural causes such as heat, cold, age, sickness, etc. 인욕태자 忍辱太子 The patient prince, of Vārāṇasī (Benares), who gave a piece of his flesh to heal his sick parents, which was efficacious because he had never given way to anger. 인욕의 忍辱衣 The robe of patience, a patient heart which, like a garment, wards off all outward sin. A general name for the kaṣāya, monk's robe. 인(욕)개 忍(辱)鎧 Patience as armour, protecting against evils ; also the kaṣāya, monk's robe.

인 人 Manuṣya ; nara ; puruṣa ; pudgala. Man, the sentient thinking being in the desire-realm, whose past deeds affect his present condition.

인 印 Mudrā ; seal, sign, symbol, emblem, proof, assurance, approve ; also 인계 印契 ; 계인 契印 ; 인상 印相. Manual signs indicative of various ideas, e.g. each finger represents one of the five primary elements, earth, water, fire, air, and space, beginning with the little finger ; the left hand represents 정 定 stillness, or meditation, the right hand 혜 慧 discernment or wisdom ; they have also many other indications. Also, the various symbols of the Buddhas and Bodhisattvas, e.g. the thunderbolt ; cf. 인 因. 인불 印佛 A Buddha made of incense and burnt, a symbolical Buddha. 인불작법 印佛作法 An esoteric method of seeking spirit-aid by printing a Buddha on paper, or forming his image on sand, or in the air, and performing specified rites. 인광 印光 Illumination from the symbol on a Buddha's or Bodhisattva's breast. 인가 印可 Assuredly can, i.e. recognition of ability, or suitability. 인토 印土 idem 인도 印度 India. 인역 印域 The territory of India. 인도 印度 ; 인특가 印特伽 ; 연독 身毒 ; 현두 賢豆 ; 천축 天竺 Indu (meaning "moon" in Sanskrit), Hindu, Sindhu ; see also 신도 信度 and 염부 閻浮 India in general. In the T'ang dynasty its territory is described as extending over 90,000 li in circuit, being bounded on three sides by the sea ; north it rested on the Snow mountains 설산 雪山, i.e. Himālayas ; wide at the north, narrowing to the south, shaped like a half-moon ; it contained over seventy kingdoms, was extremely hot, well watered and damp ; from the centre eastwards to 진단 震旦 China was 58,000 li ; and the same distance southwards to 금지국 金地國, westwards to 아구차국 阿拘遮國, and northwards to 소향산아녹달 小香山阿耨達. 인도불교 印度佛教 Indian Buddhism, which began in Magadha, now Bihār, under Śākyamuni, the date of whose nirvāṇa was *circa* 486 B.C. V. 불 佛 and 불교 佛教. 인모 印母 Añjali ; the two hands with palms and fingers together — the "mother" of all manual signs. 인치 印治 Approval of a course of action. 인지동시 印紙同時 At one and the same time, like printing (which is synchronous, not like writing which is word by word). 인달라 印達羅 Indra ; a thousand quinquillions. 대인달라 大印達羅 Mahendra ; ten times that amount.

인 麟 The lin, or female unicorn. 기린 麒麟 Male and female unicorns ; the ch'i-lin in general. 인각 麟角 The unicorn with its single horn is a simile for 독각 獨覺 q.v. pratyeka-buddha.

인 認 To recognize 인식 認識 ; to acknowledge, e.g. sin 인죄 認罪.

인 引 To stretch, draw, lead, bring in or on. 인입 引入 To introduce, initiate. 인화 引化 Initiate and instruct. 인출불성 引出佛性 One of the 삼불성 三佛性 q.v., the Buddha-nature in all the living to be developed by proper processes. 인도 引導 To lead (men into Buddha-truth) ; also a phrase used at funerals implying the leading of the dead soul to the other world, possibly arising form setting alight the funeral pyre. 인좌 引座 A phrase used by one who ushers a preacher into the "pulpit" to expound the Law. 인접 引接 ; 인섭 引攝 To accept, receive, welcome — as a Buddha does all who call on him, as stated in the nineteenth vow of Amitābha. 인과 引果 The stage of fruition, i.e. reward or punishment in the genus, as contrasted with 만인 滿引 the differentiated species or stages, e.g. for each organ, or variety of condition. 유식론 唯識論 2. 인업 引業 ; 인인 引因 ; 견인업 牽引業 ; 총보업 總報業 The principal or integral direction of karma, in contrast with 만인 滿引 its more detailed stages ; see last entry. 인정태자 引正太子 Sātavāhana, 사다파한나 沙多婆漢那 a prince of Kośala, whose father the king was the patron of Nāgārjuna ; the prince, attributing his father's unduly prolonged life to Nāgārjuna's magic, is said to have compelled the latter to commit suicide, on hearing of which the king died and the prince ascended the throne. 서역기 西域記 10. 인발인 引發因 One of the 십인 十因 the force or cause that releases other forces or causes. 경 磬 ; 수경 手磬 A hand-bell to direct the attention in services. 인청사리 引請闍梨 A term for the instructor of beginners. 인반대사 引飯大師 The great leader who introduces the meal, i.e. the club which beats the call to meals. 인가대사 引駕大師 One of the 사대사 四大師 of the T'ang dynasty ; it was his duty to welcome back the emperor on his return to the palace, a duty at times apparently devolving on Buddhist monks.

인가 印可 In-ga. 1. Formal recognition received from a Zen master after one awakens to one's true nature. 2. Informal, private recognition by a teacher of a student's potential to finish his practice and ultimately gain enlightenment. Cf. 전법 傳法.

인가람 人伽藍 This is given by Eitel as "Narasaṁghārāma." "An ancient monastery close to the capital of Kapiśā." But this is doubtful.

인공 人空 Man is only a temporary combination formed by the five skandhas and the twelve nidānas, being the product of previous causes, and without a real self or permanent soul. Hīnayāna is said to end these causes and consequent reincarnation by discipline in subjection of the passions and entry into nirvāṇa by the emptying of the self. Mahāyāna fills the "void" with the Absolute, declaring that when man has emptied himself of the ego he realizes his nature to be that of the absolute, bhūtatathatā ; v. 이공 二空. 인공관 人空觀 The meditation on, or insight into the above.

인과 因果 Cause and effect ; every cause has its effect, as every effect arises from a cause. 인과응보 因果應報 Cause and effect in the moral realm have their corresponding relations, the denial of which destroys all moral responsibility. 인과개공종 因果皆空宗 A sect of "heretics" who denied cause and effect both in regard to creation and morals.

인귀 人鬼 Men and disembodied spirits, or demons ; disembodied ghosts.

인길서 人吉庶 Mānuṣa-kṛtya ; demons shaped like men ; domestic slaves, introduced into Kashmir by Madhyāntika ; also intp. as "work to be done by men."

인내(이명) 因內(二明) Reason and authority ; i.e. two of the five 명 明, v. 인명 因明 and 내명 內明 the latter referring to the statements, therefore authoritative, of the Scriptures.

인능변 因能變 The power in a cause to transform itself into an effect ; a cause that is also an effect, e.g. a seed.

인니연 因尼延 Aiṇeya, black antelope, v. 이 伊.

인다라 因陀羅 Indra, 인지 因坻 ; 인제 因提 ; 인제리 因提梨 ; 인달라 因達羅 ; 천제 天帝 ; 천주제 天主帝 ; 제석천 帝釋天 ; originally a god of the atmosphere, i.e. of thunder and rain ; idem Śakra ; his symbol is the vajra, or thunderbolt, hence he is the 금강수 金剛手 ; he became "lord of the gods of the sky," "regent of the east quarter," "popularly chief after Brahmā, Viṣṇu, and Śiva" [M. W.] ; in Buddhism he represents the secular power, and is inferior to a Buddhist saint. Cf. 도리 忉利 and 인 印. 인다라세라구하 因陀羅勢羅窶訶 ; 인다라세라구하 因陀羅世羅求訶 ; 인다라굴 因陀羅窟 ; 인사구 因沙舊 Indraśailaguhā ; explained by 제석석굴 帝釋石窟 Indra's cave ; also by 사신산 蛇神山 the mountain of the snake god, also by 소고석산 小孤石山 the mountain of the small isolated peaks located near Nālandā, where on the south crag of the west peak is a rock cave, broad but not high, which Śākyamuni frequently visited. Indra is said to have written forty-two questions on stone, to which the Buddha replied. 인다라가실다 因陀羅呵悉多 ; 인다라갈실치 因陀羅喝悉哆 ; 인다라하색다 因陀羅訶塞多. Probably Indra-hasta, Indra's hand, "a kind of medicament." [M. W.] Is it the 불수 佛手 "Buddha's hand," a kind of citron? 인다라바다나 因陀羅婆他那 Indravadana, or Indrabhavana. A "name for India proper," [Eitel]. 인다(라)니라(목다) 因陀(羅)尼羅(目多) Indranīla-(muktā). Indra's blue (or green) stone, which suggests an emerald, Indranīlaka [M. W.] ; but according to M. W. Indranīla is a sapphire ; muktā is a pearl. 인다라발제 因陀羅跋帝 Tr. as Indra's city, or Indra's banner, but the latter is Indraketu ; Indravatī.

인다라서다 因陀囉誓多 Indraceṭa, Indra's attendants, or slaves. 인다라달바문불 因陀囉達婆門佛 Indradhvaja, a Buddha-incarnation of the seventh son of the Buddha Mahābhijñābhibhū 대통지승 大通智勝.

인달라대장 因達羅大將 or **인다라대장** 因陀羅大將 Indra as General (guarding the shrine of 약사 藥師 Bhaiṣajya).

인도 因道 The way, or principle, of causation.

인동품 因同品 (The example in logic must be) of the same order as the reason.

인두당 人頭幢 A human head at the top of a daṇḍa or flagpole, used as one of Yama's symbols ; v. 단다 檀茶 ; 단나 檀拏.

인라나 堙羅那 Airāvaṇa, a king of the elephants ; Indra's white elephant, cf. 이 伊. It is also confused with Airāvata in the above senses, and for certain trees, herbs, etc. ; also with Elāpattra, name of a nāga.

인력 因力 The causal force, or cause, contrasted with 연력 緣力 environmental, or secondary forces.

인론 因論 idem 인명론 因明論.

인만다라 因曼陀羅 The Garbhadhātu 태장 胎藏 maṇḍala, which is also east and 인 因, or cause, as contrasted with the Vajradhātu, which is west and 과 果, or effect.

인망사 人莽娑 ; 인마사 人摩娑 Human māṁsa or flesh.

인명 因明 Hetuvidyā, 혜도비타 醯都費陀, the science of cause, logical reasoning, logic, with its syllogistic method of the proposition, the reason, the example. The creation of this school of logic is attributed to Akṣapāda, probably a name for the philosopher Gautama (not Śākyamuni). The 인명론 因明論 or Hetuvidyā-śāstra is one of the 오명론 五明論 pañcavidyā-śāstras, a treatise explaining causality, or the nature of truth and error. 인명입정리론 因明入正理論 Nyāyapraveśa ; a treatise on logic by 상갈라주 商羯羅主 Śaṅkarasvāmin, follower of Dignāga, tr. by Hsüan-tsang in 1 chüan, on which there are numerous commentaries and works. 인명정리문론 因明正理門論 Nyāyadvāratāraka-śāstra, a treatise by 진나 陳那 Dignāga, tr. by I-ching, 1 chüan.

인무아 人無我 Man as without ego, or permanent soul ; cf. 인아 人我 and 이무아 二無我. Other similar terms are 중생무아 衆生無我 ; 생공 生空 ; 인공 人空 and 아공 我空. 인무아지 人無我智 The knowledge, or wisdom, of anātman, cf. above.

인법 人法 Men and things ; also, men and the Buddha's law, or teaching.

인보 人寶 The treasure of men, Buddha.

인분 因分 Cause, as contrasted with effect 과분 果分. 인분가설과분불가설 因分可說果分不可說 The causes (that give rise to a Buddha's Buddhahood) may, in a measure, be stated, that is, such part as is humanly manifested ; but the full result is beyond description.

인비인 人非人 A being resembling but not a human being, i.e. a kinnara.

인사 人師 A leader or teacher of men. 인사자 人師子 ; 인사자 人獅子 Nṛsiṁha. The Lion of men, Buddha as leader and commander.

인상 因相 Causation ; one of the three forms or characteristics of the Ālayavijñāna, the character of the origin of all things.

인선 人仙 The ṛṣi jina, or immortal among men, i.e. the Buddha ; also a name for Bimbisāra in his reincarnation.

인수 因修 The practice of Buddhism as the "cause" of Buddhahood.

인승 人乘 One of the five vehicles, v. 오승 五乘, that of the five commandments, the keeping of which ensures rebirth in the world of men.

인신 人身 The human body, or person. 인신우 人身牛 Cattle in human shape, stupid, ignorant, heedless.

인십사과 因十四過 The fourteen possible errors or fallacies in the reason in a syllogism.

인아 人我 Personality, the human soul, i.e. the false view, 인아견 人我見 that every man has a permanent lord within. 상일주재 常一主宰, which he calls the ātman, soul, or permanent self, a view which forms the basis of all erroneous doctrine. Also styled 인견 人見 ; 아견 我見 ; 인집 人執 ; cf. 이아 二我.

인약왕자 人藥王子 Human-touch healing prince, i.e. Śākyamuni in a previous incarnation, whose touch healed all diseases, as did the application of his powdered bones after his decease in that incarnation.

인업 因業 The work, or operation, of cause, or causes, i.e. the co-operation of direct and indirect causes, of primary and environmental causes.

인연 因緣 Hetupratyaya. Cause ; causes ; 인 因 hetu, is primary cause, 연 緣 pratyaya, secondary cause, or causes, e.g. a seed is 인 因, rain, dew, farmer, etc., are 연 緣. The 십이인연 十二因緣 twelve nidānas or links are "the concatenation of cause and effect in the whole range of existence." 인연의 因緣依 Dependent on cause, or the cause or causes on which anything depends. 인연생 因緣生 Causally-produced. 인연관 因緣觀 A meditation on the nidānas.

인웅사자 人雄師子 idem 인중사자 人中師子.

인원 因源 Cause ; cause and origin.

인원과만 因圓果滿 The cause perfect and the effect complete, i.e. the practice of Buddhism.

인위 因位 The causative position, i.e. that of a Buddhist, for he has accepted a cause, or enlightenment, that produces a changed outlook.

인유 人有 Human bhāva or existence, one of the 칠유 七有.

인이품 因異品 Hetu-viruddha ; in a syllogism the example not accordant with the reason.

인인 因人 Followers of Buddha who have not yet attained Buddhahood, but are still producers of karma and reincarnation.

인인 人因 The causative influences for being reborn as a human being, i.e. a good life. Those in positions of honour have obtained them by former deeds of benevolence, reverence to Buddhas and monks, patience, humility, devotion to the sūtras, charity, morality, zeal and exhortation, obedience, loyalty — hence they have obtained affluence, long life, and are held in high regard. Those in mean condition are thus born because of the opposite characteristics in previous incarnation.

인인본구 人人本具 Every man has by origin the perfect Buddha-nature.

인정 人定 The third beat of the first watch, 9-11 p.m., when men are settled for the night.

인존 人尊 idem 인중존 人中尊.

인중존 人中尊 The Honoured One among or of men, the Buddha. 인(중)분다리화 人(中)分陀利華 A Lotus among men, a Buddha, also applied to all who invoke Amitābha, 인(중)사자 人(中)師子 ; 인사자 人師子 ; 인사자 人獅子 ; 인웅사자 人雄師子 A Lion among men, a Buddha. 인(중)수 人(中)樹 The Tree among men, giving shelter as the bodhi-tree, a Buddha. 인중우왕 人中牛王 The Lord of the herd. These and other similar terms are applied to the Buddha. 인중삼악 人中三惡 The three most wicked among men : the Icchantika ; v. 일천제 一闡提 : the slanderers of Mahāyāna, and those who break the four great commandments.

인지 因地 The causal ground, fundamental cause ; the state of practising the Buddha-religion which leads to the 과지 果地 or resulting Buddhahood.

인집 人執 The (false) tenet of a soul, or ego, or permanent individual, i.e. that the individual is real, the ego an independent unit and not a mere combination of the five skandhas produced by cause and in effect disintegrating ; v. 아집 我執.

인천 人天 Men and devas. 인천승 人天乘 Two of the 오승 五乘 q.v. 인천교 人天敎 Two of the 오교 五敎 q.v. 인천안목 人天眼目 A summary of the teaching of the 선 禪 Ch'an(Zen) sect by 지조 智照 Chih-chao of the Sung dynasty. 인천승묘선과 人天勝妙善果 The highest forms of reincarnation, i.e. those of devas and men.

인취 人趣 ; 인도 人道 The human stage of the six gati, or states of existence.

인행과 因行果 Cause, action, effect ; e.g. seed, germination, fruit.

일 一 Eka. One, unity, monad, once, the same ; immediately on (seeing, hearing, etc.). 일일 一一 One by one, each, every one, severally.

일 日 Sūrya ; the sun ; a day. 소리야 蘇利耶. 일광(보살) 日光(菩薩) ; 소리야바라피자나 蘇利也波羅皮遮那 Sūrya-prabhāsana. Sunlight, and 월광(보살) 月光(菩薩) Moonlight, name of two Bodhisattva assistants of 약사 藥師 the Master of Healing ; Sunlight is the ninth in the Ti-tsang Court of the Garbhadhātu group. 일출론자 日出論者 The sunrise exponents, a title of the founders of the 경부종 經部宗 before the Christian era. 일역 日域 Japan. 일천(자) 日天(子) Sūrya, 소리야 蘇利耶 ; 수리 修利 ; 수야천자 修野天子 or 수의천자 修意天子 ; also 보광천자 寶光天子. The sun-ruler ; one of the metamorphoses of Kuan-yin, dwelling in the sun as palace, driving a quadriga. 일천중 日天衆 The retinue of Indra in his palace of the sun. 일궁 日宮 The sun-palace, the abode of 일천자 日天子 *supra*. 일당화안고 日幢華眼鼓 Five characters taken from the names of, and representing five Buddhas in the Vajradhātu 대일 大日, 보당 寶幢, 화개부 華開敷, 연화안 蓮華眼, and 천고뇌음 天鼓雷音. 일상관 日想觀 Meditation on, and observing of the setting sun, the first of the sixteen meditations in the 관무량수경 觀無量壽經. 일선삼매 日旋三昧 Sūryāvarta samādhi, one of the sixteen samādhi mentioned in the 법화경묘음품 法華經妙音品 ; 일륜삼매 日輪三昧 is an older name for it. 일성수 日星宿. Nakṣatratārā-rājāditya ; a degree of meditation, i.e. the sun, stars and constellations samādhi. 일요 日曜 The sun, one of the nine 요 曜 luminaries ; one of the retinue of 일천 日天 shown in the eastern part of the Garbhadhātu group driving three horses. 일월정명덕 日月淨明德 Candra-vimala-sūrya-prabhāsa-śrī. A Buddha whose realm resembles Sukhāvatī. 일월등명불 日月燈明佛 Candra-sūrya-pradīpa, or Candrārkadīpa. The title of 20,000 Buddhas who succeeded each other preaching the Lotus sūtra, v. 법화경서품 法華經序品. 일본 日本 Japan. Buddhism was introduced there from Korea in the sixth century, and in the seventh from China. 일우중 日禺中 10 a.m. styled by T'ien-t'ai the hour of 반야 般若 wisdom. 일종 日種 Sūryavaṁśa, one of the five surnames of Śākyamuni, sun-seed or lineage, his first ancestors having been produced by the sun from "two stalks of sugar-cane" ; v. Ikṣvāku. 일정마니 日精摩尼 A maṇi, or pearl, crystal-clear as the sun, which gives sight to the blind. 일련 日蓮 Nichiren, the Japanese founder, in A.D. 1252, of the 일련종 日蓮宗 Nichiren sect, which is also known as the 법화종 法華宗 or Lotus sect. Its chief tenets are the three great mysteries 삼대비법 三大秘法, representing the Trikāya : (1) 본존 本尊 or chief object of worship, being the great maṇḍala of the worlds of the ten directions, or universe, i.e. the body or nirmāṇakāya of Buddha ; (2) 제목 題目 the title of the Lotus sūtra 묘법연화경 妙法蓮華經 Myō-hō-ren-gwe kyō, preceded by Namo, or, "Adoration to the scripture of the lotus of the wonderful law," for it is Buddha's spiritual body ; (3) 계단 戒壇 the altar of the law, which is also the title of the Lotus as above ; the believer, wherever he is, dwells in the Pure-land of calm light 적광정토 寂光淨土, the sambhogakāya. 일륜 日輪 The sun's disc, which is the exterior of the sun palace of 일천자 日天子 ; it is said to consist of sphaṭika, or fiery crystal.

일 逸 To get away from ; retire, be at ease, indulgence, excess. 일다 逸多 Ajita, Maitreya, v. 아일다 阿逸多.

일가연 一家宴 A monasterial family party, i.e. when a monk, on becoming head of a monastery, invites its inmates to a feast.

일각선인 一角仙人 Ekaśṛṅga-ṛṣi ; also 독각선인 獨角仙人 The unicorn ṛṣi, an ascetic born of a deer ; ensnared by a woman, he lost his power, and became a minister of state ; he is one of the previous incarnations of Śākyamuni.

일간 一間 Ekavīcika 예가비치가 翳迦鼻致迦 Still one final stage of mortality before nirvāṇa. Also wrongly styled Bījaka 비치가 鼻致迦, a seed 일종 一種 which leads to one more reincarnation. 일간성자 一間聖者 The holy ones who have only one interval, or stage of mortality before nirvāṇa.

일개반개 一個半個 A particle, the very least.

일경 一境 One region, realm, order, or category. 일경삼제 一境三諦 The three axioms in the one category ; the three are 공 空, 가 假, and 중 中, which exist in every universe ; v. 삼제 三諦. It is a principle of the T'ien-t'ai 원교 圓教. 일경사심 一境四心 Four different ways of looking at the same thing. Similar to 일수사견 一水四見, i.e. one and the same reality though seen from different aspects.

일경초 一莖草 A blade of grass — may represent the Buddha, as does his image ; it is a Buddha-centre.

일계 一髻 A topknot. 일계문수 一髻文殊 The one topknot Mañjuśrī ; there are other representations with 5 and 8 ; cf. 일자문수 一字文殊. 일계나찰녀 一髻羅刹女 The female rakṣaḥ styled "Single top-knot," wife of a great rakṣaḥ who dwells by a great ocean ; on scenting blood, she can fly to it in a night 80,000 yojanas. 일계나찰왕보살 一髻羅刹王菩薩 The four-handed, dark-blue rakṣaḥ with the flame of fire coming out of his head, a bodhisattva in the Garbhadhātu maṇḍala.

일공 一空 All is empty, or of the void, non-material.

일광삼존 一光三尊 Three honoured ones in one light or halo — Amitābha, Avalokiteśvara, and Mahāsthāmaprāpta ; or Śākyamuni, Bhaiṣajya the 약왕 藥王 and 약상 藥上 his younger brother.

일구 一九 A Shingon term for Amitābha. 일구지생 一九之生 Future life in the Amitābha Pure Land.

일구 一句 A word, or sentence ; 일구자 一句子 a sub-ordinate or explanatory word or sentence ; 구 句 is also used for 처 處. 일구투화 一句投火 For but one sentence of the Truth willingly to cast oneself into the fire. 일구도진 一句道盡 With one word to make clear the whole Law.

일극 一極 The one ultimate, or finality ; ultimate enlightenment ; the one final truth or way ; the 일실 一實 or Absolute.

일기 一期 A date, fixed time ; a lifetime.

일기 一蟣 A likṣā, a nit, the 131,712,000th part of a yojana, seven times the smallest atom.

일기일경 一機一境 The 기 機 is subjective ; the 경 境 is objective, e.g. smoke is the objective phenomenon, fire the subjective inference.

일념 一念 A kṣaṇa, or thought ; a concentration of mind ; a moment ; the time of a thought, of which there are varying measurements from 60 kṣaṇa upwards ; the Fan-i-ming-i makes it one kṣaṇa. A reading. A repetition (especially of Amitābha's name). The Pure-land sect identify the thought of Buddha with Amitābha's vow, hence it is an assurance of salvation. 일념불생 一念不生 Not a thought arising ; beyond the necessity of thinking, as in the case of a Buddha. 일념삼천 一念三千 In one thought to survey or embrace the 3,000 worlds, or a chiliocosmos with all its forms of existence ; to see the universe as a thought ; it is a T'ien-t'ai mode of meditation. 일념업성 一念業成 At one thought the work completed ; karma complete in one thought. One repetition, or sincere thought of or faith in Amitābha's vow, and entrance into the Pure Land is assured. 일념만년 一念萬年 In a moment's thought to obtain a myriad years and no return to mortality.

일녕 一寧 I-ning, a monk who went to Japan in 1299 ; v. 일산 一山.

일단구 一壇構 The setting up of altars before the Vajradhātu and Garbhadhātu maṇḍalas, each erected and worshipped separately ; also 일단구 一檀構.

일단사 一段事 The unity or continuity in the unbroken processes of nature ; all nature, all being is but one continuous process.

일단식 一揣食 A ball (or handful) of food ; one helping ; a frugal meal, the sixth of the 12 dhūtas ; also called 절량식 節量食 and 일단식 一摶食.

일대 一代 A human lifetime ; especially the lifetime of Śākyamuni on earth. 일대삼단 一代三段 The three sections, divisions, or periods of Buddha's teaching in his lifetime, known as 서분 序分, i.e. the 화엄 華嚴, 아함 阿含, 방등 方等, and 반야 般若 sūtras ; 정종분 正宗分, i.e. 무량의 無量義, 법화 法華, and 보현관 普賢觀 sūtras ; and 유통분 流通分, i.e. the 열반경 涅槃經 ; they are known as introductory, main discourse, and final application. There are other definitions. 일대오시불법 一代五時佛法 The five periods of Buddha's teachings, as stated by Chih-i 지의 智顗 of the T'ien-t'ai School. The five are 화엄 華嚴, 아함 阿含, 방등 方等, 반야 般若, 법화 法華, 열반 涅槃 the last two being the final period. 일대교 一代教 The whole of the Buddha's teaching from his enlightenment to his nirvāṇa, including Hīnayāna and Mahāyāna teaching.

일대삼천세계 一大三千世界 A great chiliocosm or universe of the three kinds of thousands of worlds. The three 천 千 are termed 일천 一千 ; 중천 中千 ; 대천 大千. A great chiliocosm is also termed 삼천대천세계 三千大千世界 q.v. Each world consists of its central mountain Sumeru, surrounded by four continents, its seas being surrounded by s girdle or wall of iron ; 1,000 such worlds make a small chiliocosm ; 1,000 of these make a medium chiliocosm ; 1,000 of these make a great chiliocosm, or 1,000,000,000 worlds. Later Buddhists increased this number to a figure with 4,456,489 digits. It is a Buddha-universe.

일대택 一大宅 The great house, i.e. the burning house (of the world) in the Lotus Sūtra ; also 화택 火宅. 일대차 一大車 The one great salvation vehicle of the Lotus Sūtra, the Mahāyāna. 일대사 一大事 The one great work of a Buddha, universal enlightenment and release ; also a life, or lifetime.

일도 一道 One way, the one way ; the way of deliverance from mortality, the Mahāyāna. I-tao, a learned monk of the Pure-land sect. 일도법문 一道法門 The 아 阿 "A" school (Shingon) which takes A as the alpha (and even omega) of all wisdom ; the way by which all escape mortality. 일도무위심 一道無爲心 Mind apart from all ideas of activity or inactivity. Also styled, or explained, by 여실일도심 如實一道心, 여실지자심 如實知自心, 공성무경심 空性無境心, 일여본정심 一如本淨心. The third of the ten mental resting places of the esoteric school. 일도신광 一道神光 Inner light ; intuitive wisdom.

일도삼례 一刀三禮 In carving an image of Buddha, at each cut thrice to pay homage to the Triratna. 일필삼례 一筆三禮 and 일자삼례 一字三禮 indicate a similar rule for the painter and the writer.

일독승 一禿乘 A bald-pated "vehicle" — an unproductive monk or disciple.

일등 一等 Equal, all equal ; of the first stage ; a grade, rank, step.

일랍 一臈 ; 일랍 一臘 The end of the monastic year at the summer retreat ; a monastic year ; also called 법랍 法臈 or 법세 法歲, the religious year ; cf. 일하 一夏.

일래(향) 一來(向) Sakṛdāgāmin. Only one more return to mortality, v. 사 斯 and 사향 四向. 일래과 一來果 v. 사과 四果.

일련 一蓮 The Lotus-flower of the Pure-land of Amitābha, idem 연대 蓮臺. 일련지실 一蓮之實 The certainty of being born in the Pure-land. 일련탁생 一蓮托生 One lotus bearing all the living, i.e. the Pure-land of Amitābha.

일루일촉 一縷一觸 "A thread, a butt" ; the dragon which snatched a thread of a monk's robe and was consequently protected from a dangerous bird ; the ox which butted a monk's robe and became a monk at its next transmigration ; e.g. the virtue of the robe.

일류 一流 In one, or the same flow ; of the same class.

일마만전 一魔萬箭 One demon a myriad arrows, i.e. to listen to one Māra-temptation opens the way for a myriad Māra-arrows.

일마일미 一麻一米 A hempseed and a grain of rice a day, the scanty diet to which Śākyamuni reduced himself before his enlightenment.

일명 一明 Ming (i.e. bright, clear, illuminating) is the Shingon word for a dhāraṇī, or magical formula ; especially applied to magical acts.

일모단 一毛端 A hair's tip ; the smallest division (of space or time).

일목다가 一目多伽 Itivṛttaka ; stories of the lives of saints, part of the canon ; also 일왈다가 一曰多伽.

일무애도 一無礙道 The one way without barrier, i.e. the end of reincarnations in nirvāṇa ; a meditation on it.

일문 一門 The one door out of mortality into Nirvāṇa, i.e. the Pure-land door. 일문보문 一門普門 The one door is the all-door ; by entering the one door all doors of the faith are opened.

일물부장래 一物不將來 A Ch'an sect idea — not a thing to bring or carry away, empty-handed, i.e. nothingness.

일미 一味 One, or the same flavour, kind or character, i.e. the Buddha's teaching. 일미사병 一味瀉瓶 Completely, exhaustively, e.g. as water can be poured from one bottle to another without loss, so should be a master's pouring of the Law into the minds of his disciples.

일미진 一微塵 A particle of dust ; an atom, the smallest particle, a microcosm of the universe.

일백 一百 Śata. A hundred. 일백팔 一百八 ; 백팔 百八 Aṣṭa-śatam. The 108 kleśa, distresses, disturbing passions, or illusions 번뇌 煩惱 of mankind, hence the 108 beads on a rosary, repetitions of the Buddha's name, strokes of a bell, etc., one for each distress. Also, one of the Mahārājas, with 108 hands, each holding a different implement.

일백삼갈마 一白三羯磨 One announcement, or reading, and three responses, or promises of performance (karman) ; it is the mode of ordaining monks, three responses to the one call of the abbot. Also 백사(갈마) 白四(羯磨).

일법 一法 A dharma, or law ; an ordered something, a thing, a matter. 일법인 一法印 The seal or assurance of the one truth or law, see 일여 一如 and 일실 一實 ; the criterion of Mahāyāna doctrine, that all is bhūtatathatā, as contrasted with the Hīnayāna criteria of impermanence, non-personality, and nirvāṇa. 일법구 一法句 The one-law abode, i.e. the sum of the 29 particular 구 句 or states of perfection in the Pure-land śāstra of Vasubandhu. 일법계 一法界 The bhūtatathatā considered in terms of mind and as a whole ; a law-realm ; a spiritual realm ; a universe. 일법계심 一法界心 A mind universal, above limitations of existence or differentiation.

일변 一遍 Once, one recital of Buddha's name, or of a sūtra, or magic formula ; style of 지진 智眞 Chih-chên, founder of the 시종 時宗 Ji-shū (Japan).

일보 一普 A company ; a general assembly of monks in a monastery.

일보 一寶 The one precious thing, the spirit, or intelligent nature ; the intelligent mind (behind all things).

일부구 一浮漚 floating bubble (on the ocean), a man's life, or body.

일분가 一分家 A school founded by 안혜 安慧 An-hui, teaching 심식지일분설 心識之一分說 that cognition is subjective.

일분보살 一分菩薩 A one-tenth bodhisattva, or disciple ; one who keeps one-tenth of the commandments.

일불세계 一佛世界 A Buddha-cosmos ; a world undergoing transformation by a Buddha. 일불승 一佛乘 The Mahāyāna, or one-Buddha vehicle, especially the teaching of the Lotus Sūtra. 일불(국)토 一佛(國)土 ; idem 일불세계 一佛世界 A Buddha-domain ; or a one-Buddha region ; also the Pure Land. 일불다불 一佛多佛 One Buddha or many Buddhas, i.e. some Hīnayāna Schools say only one Buddha exists in the same aeon ; Mahāyāna says many Buddhas appear in the same aeon in many worlds. 일불정토 一佛淨土 A Buddha's Pure Land, especially that of Amitābha.

일사구게 一四句偈 A four-character line of a gāthā, or verse. 일사천하 一四天下 A world of four great continents surrounding a Mt. Sumeru.

일산 一山 A hill ; a monastery ; I-shan, the name of a Chinese monk who voyaged to Japan in A.D. 1299 and who was also styled 일녕 一寧 I-ning.

일살다생 一殺多生 To kill one that many may live.

일삼매 一三昧 Ekāgra, aikāgrya. Undeflected concentration, meditation on one object ; v. 일행삼매 一行三昧.

일상 一相 Lakṣaṇa. One aspect, form, or side ; ekatva, unity as contrasted with diversity ; monism ; the bhūtatathatā ; the one mind in all things ; cf. 일이 一異. 일상일미 一相一味 The term 일상 一相 is defined as the common mind in all beings, or the universal mind ; the 일미 一味 is the Buddha's Mahāyāna teaching ; the former is symbolized by the land, the latter by the rain fertilizing it. 일상삼매 一相三昧 A state of samādhi in which are repressed hate and love, accepting and rejecting, etc., and in which the mind reaches an undivided state, being anchored in calm and quiet. 일상지 一相智 The wisdom that all is bhūtatathatā and a unity. 일상법문 一相法門 The unitary or monistic method is interpreted in more than a dozen ways ; in general it means to reach a stage beyond differentiation where all is seen as a unity. 일상무상 一相無相 One-ness means none-ness ; in ultimate unity, or the unity of the absolute, there is no diversity.

일색 一色 A colour, the same colour ; the same ; especially a thing, or a form, v. rūpa 색 色 ; minute, trifling, an atom. 일색일향무비중도 一色一香無非中道 An atom or an odour is a complete microcosm of the 중도 中道 middle way or golden mean ; the Mean is found in all things.

일생 一生 All one's life, a whole lifetime. 일생불범 一生不犯 Life-long innocence — especially sexual. 일생입묘각 一生入妙覺 A T'ien-t'ai doctrine that Buddha-enlightenment can be attained by any in one lifetime, i.e. the present life. 일생소계보살 一生所繫菩薩 idem 일생보처보살 一生補處菩薩. 일생과수 一生果遂 In this one life to accomplish the three stages for final entry ; it is associated with the 20th vow of Amitābha ; cf. 삼생과수 三生果遂. 일생보처 一生補處 Eka-jāti-prati-baddha ; a name for Maitreya, who is to be the next Buddha in this world. Another definition is — from one enlightenment to attain to Buddhahood. 일생보처보살상 一生補處菩薩像 A 30-armed image of Maitreya.

일설부 一說部 Ekavyāvahārika 의가비여바하리가 猗柯毘與婆訶利柯 or (Pali) Ekabyohāra 비바하라 鞞婆訶羅 One of the 20 Hīnayāna schools, a nominalistic school, which considered things as nominal, i.e. names without any underlying reality ; also styled 제법단명종 諸法但名宗 that things are but names.

일성일체성 一成一切成 The Hua-yen doctrine that the law of the universal runs through the phenomenal, therefore a speck of dust is a micro-cosmos ; also that with the Tathāgata's enlightenment all beings were enlightened in him ; in the perfection of one all are perfected ; one deed includes all.

일성종 一性宗 Monophysitic or "pantheistic" sects of Mahāyāna, which assert that all beings have one and the same nature with Buddha.

일소겁 一小劫 A small kalpa ; a period of the growth and decay of a universe. See 일증일감 一增一減 and 겁 劫.

일수사견 一水四見 The same water may be viewed in four ways — devas see it as bejewelled land, men as water, hungry ghosts as pus and blood, fish as a place to live in. Cf. 일경사심 一境四心.

일승 一乘 Ekayāna, One Yāna, the One Yāna, the vehicle of one-ness. 일불승 一佛乘 The one Buddha-Yāna. The One Vehicle, i.e. Mahāyāna, which contains the final or complete law of the Buddha and not merely a part, or preliminary stage, as in Hīnayāna. Mahāyānists claim it as the perfect and only way to the shore of parinirvāṇa. It is especially the doctrine of the 법화경 法華經 Lotus Sūtra ; v. 대승 大乘. 일승지주 一乘之珠 The pearl of the One Yāna, i.e. The Lotus Scripture. 일승원종 一乘圓宗. The T'ien-t'ai, or Lotus School of the perfect teaching, or the one vehicle ; v. 천태종 天台宗. 일승가 一乘家 The one-vehicle family or sect, especially the T'ien-t'ai or Lotus School. 일승법(문) 一乘法(門) The one-vehicle method as revealed in the Lotus Sūtra. 일승구경교 一乘究竟教 The One Vehicle in its final teaching, especially as found in the Lotus Sūtra. 일승경 一乘經 ; 일승묘전 一乘妙典 ; 일승묘문 一乘妙文 Another name for the Lotus Sūtra, so called because it declares the one way of salvation, the perfect Mahāyāna. 일승보리 一乘菩提 The one-vehicle enlightenment. 일승현성교 一乘顯性教 One of the five divisions made by 규봉 圭峯 Kuei-fêng of the Hua-yen 화엄 華嚴 or Avataṁsaka School ; v. 오교 五教.

일시 一時 Ekasmin samaye (Pali : ekaṃ samayaṃ) ; "on one occasion," part of the usual opening phrase of a sūtra — "Thus have I heard, once," etc. A period, e.g. a session of expounding a sūtra.

일식 一息 A breath, i.e. inspiration-cum-expiration ; a rest, or cessation. 일식반보 一息半步 half a step at a breathing on arising from meditation.

일식 一食 A meal a day, one of the twelve dhūtas.

일식 一識 One sense or perception ; the one individual intelligence or soul which uses the various senses, likened to a monkey which climbs in and out of the various windows of a house — a Satya-siddhi and Sautrāntika doctrine. Also, a Vairocana maṇḍala. 일식외도 一識外道 Followers of the above heretical view.

일실 一實 The one reality ; the bhūtatathatā ; idem 일여 一如, 일진 一眞. 일실승 一實乘 The one method of salvation, the 일실 一實 School. 일실원승 一實圓乘 The Tathāgata's perfect vehicle, i.e. that of the Lotus Scripture. 일실원종 一實圓宗 The one real and perfect school, i.e. the T'ien-t'ai or Lotus School. 일실경계 一實境界 The state or realm of 일실 一實 ; the realization of the spirituality of all things ; it is the 여래법신 如來法身 the Tathāgata-dharmakāya. 일실상 一實相 The state of bhūtatathatā, above all differentiation, immutable ; it implies the Buddha-nature, or the immateriality and unity of all things ; 진여지리무이무별 眞如之理無二無別, 이제허망지상 離諸虛妄之相 ; it is undivided unity apart from all phenomena. 일실무상 一實無相 The one reality being indivisible is apart from all transient (or empty) forms, and is therefore styled the formless, e.g. the invisible.

일심 一心 With the whole mind or heart ; one mind or heart ; also the bhūtatathatā, or the whole of things ; the universe as one mind, or a spiritual unity. 일심칭명 一心稱名 With undivided mind to call on the name (of Kuan-yin). 일심삼혹 一心三惑 ; 동체삼혹 同體三惑 The T'ien-t'ai "three doubts" in the mind of a bodhisattva, producing fear of illusion, confusion through multiplicity of duties, and ignorance, i.e. 견사 見思 ; 진묘 塵妙 and 무명 無明 q.v. 일심삼지 一心三智 One mind and three aspects of knowledge. The 별교 別教 separates the three aspects into 공 空, 가 假, and 중 中 q.v. ; T'ien-t'ai unifies them into one immediate vision, or regards the three as aspects of the one mind. 일심삼관 一心三觀 The above T'ien-t'ai insight ; also simultaneous vision of past, present, and future ; also called 원융삼관 圓融三觀 ; 불가사의삼관 不可思議三觀. 일심금강보계 一心金剛寶戒 ; 원돈계 圓頓戒 The infrangible-diamond rules of all bodhisattvas and Buddhas, a term of the T'ien-t'ai School, founded on the 범망경 梵網經.

일안지귀 一眼之龜 A sea turtle with only one eye, and that underneath, entered a hollow in a floating log ; the log, tossed by the waves, happened to roll over, whereupon the turtle momentarily saw the sun and moon ; an illustration of the rareness of the appearance of a Buddha ; also of the difficulty of being reborn as a man.

일업 一業 A karma ; a 업인 業因 karma-cause, causative of the next form of existence.

일여 一如 The one Ju, i.e. the bhūtatathatā, or absolute, as the norm and essence of life. The 진여 眞如 true suchness, or true character, or reality ; the 법성 法性 nature of things or beings. The whole of things as they are, or seem ; a cosmos ; a species ; things of the same order. Name of a celebrated monk, I-ju. V. 일진 一眞 ; 일실 一實. 일여관음 一如觀音 One of the 33 representations of Kuan-yin, ascending on the clouds. 일여돈증 一如頓證 Immediate experiential enlightenment by the Tathāgata truth ; the immediate realization that all is 진여 眞如 bhūtatathatā.

일엽 一葉 A leaf ; a palm-leaf or page of a sūtra. 일엽관음 一葉觀音 One of the 33 forms of Kuan-yin, standing on a lotus leaf.

일예 一翳 A film on the eye ; a hindrance to enlightenment.

일왕 一往 One passage, or time, once ; on one superficial going.

일우 一雨 A rain, i.e. a lesson from the Buddha, or his teaching, see Lotus V.

일원건립 一願建立 The one vow, i.e. the 18th of the 48 vows of Amitābha, on which his sect is established.

일월삼주 一月三舟 The one moon represents Buddha, the three boats represent varying ways of viewing him, e.g. according as those in an anchored boat and those in two others sailing in opposite directions see different aspects of the moon, so is it in regard to the Buddha. 일월삼신 一月三身 The allegorical trikāya or three bodies of the moon, i.e. its form as 법신 法身, its light as 보신 報身, its reflection as 응신 應身 ; the Buddha-truth 법 法 has also its 체 體 body, its light of wisdom 지 智, and its application or use 용 用, but all three are one, or a trinity ; see Trikāya, 삼신 三身.

일위일체위 一位一切位 idem 일문보문 一門普門.

일음교 一音教 The one-sound teaching, i.e. the totality of the Buddha's doctrine ; a school founded by Kumārajīva and Bodhiruci.

일이 一異 Unity-cum-differentiation ; monism and pluralism ; one and many ; ekatva-anyatva, oneness and otherness.

일인 一因 A cause ; the cause from which the Buddha-law arises.

일인 一印 A seal, sign, symbol. 일인회 一印會 the sixth of the nine Vajradhātu groups.

일인작허만인전실 一人作虛萬人傳實 One man's untruth is propagated by a myriad men as truth ; famae mendacia.

일일 一日 A sun, or day from sunrise to sunset. 일일일야 一日一夜 Ahorātra. One day one night, a day and night, a division of time. 일일삼시 一日三時 The three divisions of a day, morning, noon, evening. 일일불 一日佛 A one-day Buddha, i.e. he who lives a whole day purely. 일일경 一日經 A sūtra copied in one day (perhaps by many hands) ; also styled 돈사 頓寫.

일자 一字 One word ; a magic or esoteric word. 일자삼례 一字三禮 Three homages at every word one copies of the sūtras. 일자문수 一字文殊 The "Single-word Mañjuśrī," the magic word is 치림 齒臨 ; or 체리희음 體哩呬淫 ; or 질락희염 叱洛呬焰, and is used to avoid difficult parturition and to heal arrow-wounds. The image used is of a youthful smiling Mañjuśrī, wearing the felicitous pearl, with one tress on his head, hence also called 일계문수 一髻文殊. 일자선 一字禪 A cryptic single-word reply to a question, requiring meditation for its apprehension ; it is a Ch'an(Zen) method. 일자금륜(정)법 一字金輪(頂)法 The one word golden-wheel magical method (Shingon), the one word is Bhrūṁ ; also 일자금륜불정법 一字金輪佛頂法.

일장육상 一丈六像 Sixteen "feet" form, or image, said to be the height of the Buddha's body, or "transformation" body ; v. 장륙금신 丈六金身.

일전가 一顚迦 idem 일천제가 一闡提迦.

일전도 一箭道 An arrow's flight, two li.

일전어 一轉語 A turning word ; a fateful word.

일제 一際 Of the same realm or boundary, i.e. the world and nirvāṇa are one.

일제 一諦 The doctrine of fundamental unity ; an abbrev. for 일실제 一實諦 the Mādhyamika fundamental doctrine ; also, generally, in the sense of an axiom, or fundamental truth ; there are varying definitions of the one fundamental truth.

일좌식 一坐食 One meal a day taken before noon and without rising from the seat ; it is the 5th of the 12 dhūtas.

일주 一炷 One burning of incense ; a candle, or lamp

일주기 一周忌 Anniversary of a death ; also 일주관 一周關 and 일회기 一回忌.

일주문 一柱門 Il-ju-mun. Lit. "Single Beam Gate." A gate of temple.

일중 一中 A hall of spread tables ; idem 일보 一普.

일중일체중 一中一切中 One being recognized as "mean" then all is of "the mean" ; the three aspects of reality, noumenon, phenomenon, and madhya, are identical in essence ; v. 지관 止觀 5.

일즉일체일체즉일 一卽一切一切卽一 "One is all and all is one." Expressing the essential unity of all things ; a tenet of the Hua-yen and T'ien-t'ai schools. 일즉삼 一卽三 One is (or includes) three ; especially the one Yāna (the Buddha vehicle) is, or includes the three vehicles, i.e. bodhisattva, pratyekabuddha, and śrāvaka. 일즉십 一卽十 One is ten, or, if one then ten, one being the root or seed of numbers, and containing all the rest. There are many other forms, e.g. 일심즉일체심 一心卽一切心 and so on.

일증일감 一增一減 A kalpa during which a human lifetime increases from ten years to 80,000 years and then decreases back to ten. At the end of the first century the increase is to 11 years ; at the end of the second century to 12 years, and so on till a lifetime lasts 80,000 years ; then decrease follows in the same ratio till 10 is reached. The whole period of accretion and declension covers a small kalpa, i.e. 16,800,000 years ; also called 중겁 中劫.

일지 一持 Adherence to one Buddha and one sūtra.

일지 一地 The one ground ; the same ground ; the Buddha-nature of all living beings, i.e. as all the plants grow out of the one ground, so all good character and works grow from the one Buddha-nature.

일지두선 一指頭禪 The one finger-tip contemplation used by a certain monk to bring to another a conception of the universe. Also a parable in the 능가경 楞伽經 Laṅkāvatāra-sūtra. The Ch'an(Zen) sect 선종 禪宗 regard the sūtras merely as indicators, i.e. pointing fingers, their real object being only attained through personal meditation.

일진 一塵 A grain of dust, an atom, a particle. 일진법계 一塵法界 The whole in an atom, a universe in a grain of dust, one grain of dust is a microcosm of the universal whole.

일진 一眞 The whole of reality, the universe, the all, idem 진여 眞如 ; cf. 일여 一如, 일실 一實 bhūtatathatā. 일진지 一眞地 The state of meditation on the absolute. 일진법계 一眞法界 The dharma realm of the one reality, i.e. of the bhūtatathatā, complete in a speck of dust as in a universe ; such is the dharmakāya, or spiritual body of all Buddhas, eternal, above terms of being, undefinable, neither immanent nor transcendent, yet the one reality, though beyond thought. It is the fundamental doctrine of the 화엄종 華嚴宗. The 법계 法界 is 제불평등법신 諸佛平等法身, 종본이래불생불멸 從本以來不生不滅, 비공비유 非空非有, 이명이상 離名離相, 무내무외 無內無外, 유일진실 惟一眞實, 불가사의 不可思議, 시명일진법계 是名一眞法界 ; see 삼장법수 三藏法數 4. 일진무위 一眞無爲 The 일진법계一眞法界 one reality, or undivided absolute, is static, not phenomenal, it is effortless, just as it is 자연 自然 self-existing.

일차구왕 一叉鳩王 Ikṣvāku Virūḍhaka or Videhaka, translated by 감자왕 甘蔗王 Sugar-cane king, also 일종선생 日種善生 Sūryavaṁśa, an ancient king of Potala and ancestor of the Śākya line.

일찰 一拶 A sudden remark, or question, by a monk or master to test a disciple, a Ch'an(Zen) method.

일찰 一刹 v. 체 掣. A kṣetra, a land, a Buddha-realm or chiliocosm. 일찰나 一刹那 A kṣaṇa, the shortest space of time, a moment, the 90th part of a thought, and 4,500th part of a minute, during which 90 or 100 are born and as many die.

일천 一千 Sahasra ; a thousand. 일천이백 一千二百 1,200. 일천이백공덕 一千二百功德 The 1,200 merits or powers of the organs of eye, tongue, and mind predicted in the Lotus Sūtra, but, generally, the merits therein predicted to all six organs.

일천제(가) 一闡提(迦) Icchantika. Also 일전가 一顚迦, 아천지가 阿闡底迦 One without desire for Buddha-enlightenment ; an unbeliever ; shameless, an enemy of the good ; full of desires ; 단선근자 斷善根者 one who has cut off his roots of goodness ; it is applied also to a bodhisattva who has made a vow not to become a Buddha until all beings are saved. This is called 대비천제 大悲闡提 the icchantika of great mercy.

일체 一切 Sarva. All, the whole ; 보 普, 편 遍, 구 具.

일체 一體 Though externally differing, in nature the same ; the fundamental unity of the universe. 천지여아동근 天地與我同根, 만물여아일체 萬物與我一體 Heaven, earth, and myself have the same root ; all things are one corpus with me. 일체삼분 一體三分 The trinity of 마혜수라 摩醯首羅 Maheśvara (Śiva), 나라연 那羅延 Nārāyaṇa (Viṣṇu), and 범천 梵天 Brahmā. One being in three manifestations. 일체삼보 一體三寶 In the one body of the Saṅgha is the whole Triratna, Buddha, Dharma, and Saṅgha. Also, Mind, Buddha, and the living, these three are without differentiation, 심불급중생시삼무차별 心佛及衆生是三無差別, i.e. are all one. 일체삼신자성불 一體三身自性佛 In one's own body to have the Trikāya of the self-natured Buddha, i.e. by personal surrender to the Buddha. 일체속질력삼매 一體速疾力三昧 A samādhi in which instantaneous powers are acquired.

일체개성불 一切皆成佛 All beings become Buddhas, for all have the Buddha-nature and must ultimately become enlightened, i.e. 일체중생개실성불 一切衆生皆悉成佛. This is the doctrine of developed Mahāyāna, or Universalism, as opposed to the limited salvation of Hīnayāna and of undeveloped Mahāyāna ; 법화경방편품 法華經方便品 ; 약유문법자무일불성불 若有聞法者無一不成佛 if there be any who hear the dharma, not one will fail to become Buddha. 일체개공종 一切皆空宗 The sects which maintain the unreality of all things ; v. 십종 十宗.

일체경 一切經 The Tripiṭaka 대장경 大藏經 or 장경 藏經, i.e. the whole of the Buddhist Canon. The collection was first made in China in the first year of 개황 開皇 A.D. 581. See [B.N.]

일체만법 一切萬法 ; 일체제법 一切諸法 ; 일체물 一切物 All things, idem 일체법 一切法.

일체무장법인명 一切無障法印明 A sign for overcoming all hindrances, i.e. by making the sign of a sword through lifting both hands, palms outward and thumbs joined, saying Hail! Bhagavat! Bhagavat svāhā! 일체무장애 一切無障礙 Absolutely free or unhindered, e.g. like air ; illimitable, universal.

일체법 一切法 ; 일체만법 一切萬法 ; 일체제법 一切諸法 Sarvadharma. All things ; all laws, existences, or beings. 일체법계생인 一切法界生印 One of the three signs in the maṇḍala of the Shingon School — the sign of producing all things or realms. 일체법계결정지인 一切法界決定智印 The "true word" of assurance of Vairocana and of all the eight classes of beings, as the symbol through which all may attain the sure Buddha-wisdom. 일체법계자신표 一切法界自身表 Buddha's self-manifestation to all creation. 일체법공 一切法空 Sarvadharma-śūnyatā, the emptiness or unreality of all things.

일체변지인 一切遍智印 Trikoṇa. A triangle above a white lotus, apex downward, of pure white colour, representing wisdom as a flame which burns up all passion and overcomes all opposition ; the symbol of every Tathāgata. It is specially connected with Vairocana. Also 일체불심인 一切佛心印 ; 제불심인 諸佛心印.

일체보문신 一切普門身 The one who completely fills all the "four realms" (dharmadhātu), a doctrine of the 화엄 華嚴 School.

일체불심인 一切佛心印 Trikoṇa. The sign on a Buddha's breast, especially that on Vairocana's ; the sign of the Buddha-mind ; it is a triangle of flame pointing downwards to indicate power over all temptations ; it is also 일체변지인 一切徧智印 the sign of omniscience.

일체불회 一切佛會 The assembly of all the Buddhas, a term for the two maṇḍalas, or circles ; v. 태장계 胎藏界 and 금강계 金剛界 i.e. the Garbhadhātu and the Vajradhātu.

일체세존최존특신 一切世尊最尊特身 The most honoured of all the world-honoured ; a title of Vairocana ; v. 비 毘.

일체시 一切施 Sarvadā. 살박달 薩縛達 One who gives his all ; all-bestowing.

일체어언부 一切語言部 idem 일체유부 一切有部.

일체여래 一切如來 Sarvatathāgata, all Tathāgatas, all the Buddhas.

일체여래금강서계 一切如來金剛誓誡 The original oath of every Tathāgata, when as with the roar of a lion he declares that all creatures shall become as himself.

일체여래보 一切如來寶 The talismanic pearl of all Buddhas, especially one in the Garbhadhātu maṇḍala who holds a lotus in his left hand and the talismanic pearl in his right.

일체여래안색여명조삼마지 一切如來眼色如明照三摩地 A Vairocana-samādhi, in which the light of the Tathāgata-eye streams forth radiance. Vairocana by reason of this samādhi is accredited with delivering the "true word" which sums up all the principles and practices of the masters.

일체여래정 一切如來定 The highest of the 108 degrees of samādhi practised by bodhisattvas, also called 대공삼매 大空三昧 Śūnyasamādhi, i.e. of the great void, or immateriality, and 금강삼매 金剛三昧 Vajrasamādhi, Diamond samādhi. A samādhi on the idea that all things are of the (same) Buddha-nature.

일체여래제법본성청정연화삼매 一切如來諸法本性淸淨蓮華三昧 A lotus-samādhi of Vairocana from which Amitābha was born. It is a Tathāgata meditation, that the fundamental nature of all existence is pure like the lotus.

일체여래지인 一切如來智印 A sign of the wisdom of all Buddhas, a triangle on a lotus in the Garbhadhātu group.

일체여래필정인 一切如來必定印 The sign of the assurance of attaining Buddhahood.

일체유 一切有 Sarvabhāva. All things or beings ; tr. of the name of Viśvabhū ; v. 비 毘. 일체유정 一切有情 ; 일체중생 一切衆生 All sentient beings. 일체유근본 一切有根本 The Mūlasarvāstivādaḥ, a branch of the Sarvāstivādin sect, which asserted the reality of things. 일체유위 一切有爲 All phenomena, the phenomenal ; all that is produced by causative action ; everything that is dynamic and not static. 일체유부 一切有部 The realistic School, Sarvāstivādaḥ, a branch of the Vaibhāṣika, claiming Rāhula as founder, asserting the reality of all phenomena : 설일체유부 說一切有部 ; 살바다부 薩婆多部 ; 살바아사저바타부 薩婆阿私底婆拖部 ; 일체어언부 一切語言部. It divided, and the following seven schools are recorded, but the list is doubtful : — Mūlasarvāstivādaḥ 일체유근본부 一切有根本部. Kāṣyapīyāḥ 가섭비유 迦葉毘維, also known as Suvarṣakāḥ 소발리가부 蘇跋梨柯部 ; 유리사부 遊梨沙部 ; 소리사부 蘇梨沙部 ; and 선세부 善歲部. Dharmaguptāḥ 법밀부 法密部 ; 법장부 法藏部 ; 법호부 法護部. Mahīśāsakāḥ or Mahīśāsikāḥ. 마혜사바가부 摩醯奢婆迦部 ; 미희사바아부 彌喜捨婆阿部 ; 미사새부 彌沙塞部 ; 화지부 化地部 정지부 正地部. Tāmraṣāṭīyāḥ. Vibhajyavādinaḥ 분별설부 分別說部. Bahuśrutīyāḥ 바수루다가 婆收婁多柯 or 다문부 多聞部.

일체의성 一切義成 Sarvārthasiddha, or Siddhārtha ; all wishes realized, name given to Śākyamuni at his birth ; v. 실 悉, 살 薩.

일체인중존 一切人仲尊 The most honoured among men, especially Vairocana ; v. 비 毘.

일체일심식 一切一心識 That all things are mind, or mental.

일체제불 一切諸佛 All Buddhas.

일체종묘삼매 一切種妙三昧 The samādhi, or trance, which brings every kind of merit for one's adornment. 일체종지 一切種智, see 삼지 三智. 일체종식 一切種識 The 8th of the 팔식 八識 q.v.

일체중생지부 一切衆生之父 The Father of all the living, Brahmā 범왕 梵王. 일체중생희견불 一切衆生喜見佛 Sarvasattva-priya-darśana. The Buddha at whose appearance all beings rejoice. (1) A fabulous Bodhisattva who destroyed himself by fire and when reborn burned both arms to cinders, an act described in the Lotus Sūtra as the highest form of sacrifice. Reborn as Bhaiṣajya-rāja 약왕 藥王. (2) The name under which Buddha's aunt, Mahāprajāpatī, is to be reborn as Buddha. 일체중생정기 一切衆生精氣 Sarvasattvāujohārī. Lit. subtle vitality of all beings ; the quintessence or energy of all living beings. A certain Rākṣasī, wife of a demon. 일체중생이제악취 一切衆生離諸惡趣 Sarvasattva-pāpa-prahāṇa. A samādhi on a world free from all the evil destinies.

일체즉일 一切卽一 v. 일즉일체 一卽一切.

일체지 一切智 Sarvajña ; v. 살 薩, i.e. 불지 佛智 Buddha-wisdom, perfect knowledge, omniscience. 일체지지 一切智地 The state or place of such wisdom. 일체지장 一切智藏 Its thesaurus ; Buddha. 일체지인 一切智人 or 일체지자 一切智者 Buddha. 일체지주 一切智舟 ; 일체지선 一切智船 Its vehicle (Mahāyāna), which carries men to the 일체지지 一切智地. 일체지상 一切智相 Sarvajñatā, omniscience, or the state or condition of such wisdom. 일체지경 一切智經 The 59th chapter of the 중아함경 中阿含經. 일체지지 一切智智 The wisdom of all wisdom, Buddha's wisdom, including bodhi, perfect enlightenment and purity ; 대비 大悲 great pity (for mortals) ; and 방편 方便 tact or skill in teaching according to receptivity. 일체지구 一切智句 The state or abode of all wisdom, i.e. of Buddha ; 구 句 is 주처 住處. 일체지천 一切智天 ; 살바신야제바 薩婆愼若提婆 Sarvajñadeva, the deva (i.e. Buddha) of universal wisdom. 일체지심 一切智心 The Buddha-wisdom mind. 일체지혜자 一切智慧者 The all-wise one, a title of Vairocana ; v. 비 毘.

일체진언주 一切眞言主 All the "true word" rulers, shown in the Garbhadhātu and Vajradhātu groups. 일체진언심 一切眞言心 The first Sanskrit letter "a" ; it is pronounced "an" by the Shingon School and emphasized as the heart of all wisdom. In India "a" is the "name of Viṣṇu (especially as the first of the three sounds in the sacred syllable *om* or *aum*), also of Brahmā, Śiva, and Vaiśvānara (Agni)" M.W.

일체처 一切處 Samanta. Everywhere, universal ; a universal dhyāna. 일체처무불상응진언 一切處無不相應眞言 The Shingon or "True word" that responds everywhere.

일촉 一觸 See 일루 一縷.

일취 一吹 v. 일타 一唾.

일타일취 一唾一吹 A spit or a puff, i.e. as futile as thinking that a man could puff out a burning world and blow it again into complete existence, or could with a spit or a puff put it out.

일토모진 一兎毛塵 An atom of dust on a hare's down (śaśorṇa). A measure, the 22,588,608,000th part of a yojana.

일품(경) 一品(經) Varga 발거 跋渠 ; a chapter, or division (of a sūtra).

일필삼례 一筆三禮 Three salutations at each (use of the) pen, on painting a picture of the Buddha, or copying a scripture ; cf. 일도삼례 一刀三禮. 일필구(소) 一筆勾(銷) "Crossed out" with a stroke of the pen ; expunged ; forgiven.

일하 一夏 The summer retreat in India of 90 days, from the 16th of the 4th moon to the 15th of the 7th ; v. 우 雨.

일하자 一訶子 Harītakī. A fruit of the yellow myrobolan. Also 아여륵과 阿黎勒果 ; 하여륵과 訶黎勒果.

일할 一喝 A call, shout, deafening shout.

일합상 一合相 An organism, a cosmos, or any combined form, e.g. a man, a world.

일항(하사) 一恒(河沙) As one Ganges, i.e. as the sands of one Ganges river.

일행 一行 One act (of body, mouth, or mind) ; holding to one course ; devoted. I-hsing, A.D. 672-717, a celebrated monk whose secular name was 장수 張遂 Chang Sui, posthumous title 대혜선사 大慧禪師 ; he was versed in mathematics and astronomy, a reformer of the Chinese calendar, and author of several works. 일행일체행 一行一切行 In one act to do all other acts ; the act which includes all other acts, e.g. the first step ; the one discipline which embraces all discipline ; the fourth degree of a samādhi. 일행삼매 一行三昧, 진여삼매 眞如三昧, 일상삼매 一相三昧 A samādhi for realizing that the nature of all Buddhas is the same ; the 기신론 起信論 says all Buddhas and all beings. Another meaning is entire concentration of the mind on Buddha.

일향 一向 One direction, each direction ; with single mind, the mind fixed in one direction, undistracted ; e.g. 일향청정무유여인 一向淸淨無有女人 (The land of that Buddha is) everywhere pure ; no women are there. 일향종 一向宗 The 진종 眞宗 Shin or Pure-land Shin Sect founded by Shinran, in Japan, whose chief tenet is unwavering reflection on Amida (by repeating his name). 일향소승사 一向小乘寺 A monastery wholly Hīnayāna. 일향대승사 一向大乘寺 A monastery wholly Mahāyāna. 일향기 一向記 A confirmatory reply to a question, e.g. Do not all die? All die.

일협사사 一篋四蛇 Four snakes in one basket, i.e. the four passions in one body ; cf. 사대 四大.

일형 一形 An appearance, a lifetime, the period of an individual existence, also 일기 一期 and 일생애 一生涯.

일화 一化 The teaching and influence of a Buddha during one Buddha-period ; also the teaching of the whole truth at once ; also an instantaneous reform. 일화오미지교 一化五味之敎 The Five Tastes or periods of the Buddha's teaching as defined by the T'ien-t'ai School, i.e. the 화엄 華嚴 ; 아함 阿含 ; 방등 方等 ; 반야 般若 and 법화열반 法華涅槃 q.v. and v. 오미 五味.

일회기 一回忌 The first anniversary of a death ; any such anniversary ; also 일주기 一周忌.

임 紝 To lay a warp, wind, weave. 임바 紝婆 ; 임바 任婆 Nimba, the Neemb tree, which has a small bitter fruit like the 고동 苦楝 ; its leaves in India are "chewed at funeral ceremonies." [M. W.]

임 任 Bear, endure, let ; office ; it is used to connote laisser-faire ; one of the 사병 四病, as 임운 任運 implies laisser-aller ; it is intp. by let things follow their own course, or by 자연 自然 naturally, without intervention.

입 入 To enter, entry, entrance ; come, bring or take in ; at home ; awaken to the truth ; begin to understand ; to relate the mind to reality and thus evolve knowledge. The "six entries" 육입 六入 ṣaḍāyatana, which form one of the links in the chain of causation, v. 십이인연 十二因緣, the preceding link being 촉 觸 contact, and the succeeding link 식 識 perception. The six are the qualities and effects of the six organs of sense producing sight, hearing, smell, taste, touch, and thought (or mental presentations). v. also 이입 二入.

입감 入龕 Entering, or putting into the casket (for cremation) ; i.e. encoffining a dead monk.

입골 入骨 To inter the bones (of a monk) in a stūpa, or a grave.

입관 入觀 To enter into meditation ; it differs from 입정 入定 as 정 定 means 자심지적정 自心之寂靜 complete stillness of the mind, while 관 觀 means 자관조리 自觀照理 thought and study for enlightenment in regard to truth.

입단 入壇 To go to the altar (for baptism, in the esoteric sect).

입당(오법) 入堂(五法) v. 입중 入衆.

입당팔가 入唐八家 The eight Japanese who came to China in the T'ang dynasty and studied the 밀교 密教 esoteric doctrine.

입도 入道 To become a monk, 출가입도 出家入道 to leave home and enter the Way

입류 入流 Śrota-āpanna, v. 수다원 須陀洹.

입멸 入滅 idem 입적 入寂.

입문해석 入文解釋 The method in expounding scriptures of giving the main idea before proceeding to detailed exposition.

입부라 入嚩羅 Jvāla. Flaming, blazing, glowing.

입불 入佛 The bringing in of an image of a Buddha. 입불공양 入佛供養 The ceremony of bringing in a Buddha's image. 입불평등계 入佛平等戒 The Buddha-law by which all may attain to Buddhahood.

입불이문 入不二門 To enter the school of monism, i.e. that the 일실 一實 one great reality is universal and absolute without differentiation.

입산 入山 Lit. "to enter the mountains." To become a monastic.

입성 入聖 To become an arhat.

입승 立繩 Lit "he who upholds the thread of practice." Head monk in the Sŏn hall ; monk who enforces schedule and regulations of Sŏn hall.

입신 入信 To believe, or enter into belief.

입실 入室 To enter the master's study for examination or instruction ; to enter the status of a disciple, but strictly of an advanced disciple. To receive consecration.

입심 入心 To enter the heart, or mind ; also used for 입지 入地 entering a particular state, its three stages being 입주출 入住出 entry, stay, and exit.

입아아입 入我我入 He in me and I in him, i.e. the indwelling of the Buddha, any Buddha, or the Buddhas.

입왕궁취락의 入王宮聚落衣 The monk's robe, worn equally for a palace, or for begging in town or hamlet.

입적 入寂 To enter into rest, or nirvāṇa ; also, to die. Also 입멸 入滅 or 입적멸 入寂滅.

입정 入定 To enter into meditation by tranquillizing the body, mouth (i.e. lips), and mind, 신구의 身口意.

입주출삼심 入住出三心 Entrance, stay, exit ; v. 입심 入心.

입중 入衆 To enter the assembly (of monks) ; also 교중 交衆. 입중오법 入衆五法 Five rules for the entrant — submission, kindness, respect, recognition of rank or order, and none but religious conversation.

입중현문 入重玄門 To enter again through the dark gate into mortality, e.g. as a bodhisattva does, even into the hells, to save the suffering. Another interpretation is the return of a bodhisattva to common life for further enlightenment.

입출이문 入出二門 The two doors of ingress and egress, i.e. enter the gate of self-purification and adornment, then go forth 출 出 to benefit and save others.

입탑 入塔 To inter the bones or body of a monk in a dagoba ; v. 입골 入骨.

<ㅈ>

자 鷓 A partridge 자고 鷓鴣. 자고반 鷓鴣斑 Spotted like a partridge, a kind of incense.

자 慈 Affection (as that of a mother), mercy, compassion, tenderness ; mother. 자광 慈光 Merciful light, that of the Buddhas. 자력왕 慈力王 Maitrībala-rāja, king of merciful virtue, or power, a former incarnation of the Buddha when, as all his people had embraced the vegetarian life, and yakṣas had no animal food and were suffering, the king fed five of them with his own blood. 자엄 慈嚴 Compassion and strictness, the maternal-cum-paternal spirit. 자자 慈子 Sons of compassion, i.e. the disciples of Maitreya. 자존 慈尊 The compassionate honoured one, Maitreya. 자심 慈心 A compassionate heart. 자인 慈忍 Compassion and patience, compassionate tolerance. 자은 慈恩 Compassion and grace, merciful favour ; name of a temple in Loyang, under the T'ang dynasty, which gave its name to K'uei-chi 규기 窺基 q.v., founder of the 법상 法相 school, known also as the 자은 慈恩 or 유식 唯識 school ; he was a disciple of and collaborator with Hsüan-tsang, and died A.D. 682. 자비 慈悲 Compassion and pity, merciful, compassionate. 자비실 慈悲室 The abode of compassion, the dwelling of Buddha, v. Lotus sūtra. 자비만행 慈悲萬行 Tender compassion in all things, or with compassion all things succeed. 자비의 慈悲衣 Compassionate garment, the monk's robe. 자비관 慈悲觀 The compassion-contemplation, in which pity destroys resentment. 자의 慈意 The mind or spirit of compassion and kindness. 자경 慈敬 Loving reverence. 자명 慈明 Tz'ŭ-ming, a noted monk of the Sung dynasty. 자씨 慈氏 The compassionate one, Maitreya. 자수 慈水 Mercy as water fertilizing the life. 자안 慈眼 The compassionate eye (of Buddha). 자항 慈航 The bark of mercy. 자변 慈辯 To discuss compassionately. 자문 慈門 The gate of mercy, Buddhism. 자운 慈雲 The over-spreading, fructifying cloud of compassion, the Buddha-heart ; also Tz'ŭ-yün, the name of a noted Sung monk. 자주 慈霔 To rain down compassion on men.

자 字 Akṣara, 아걸사라 阿乞使囉 ; 아찰라 阿刹羅 ; a letter, character ; akṣara is also used for a vowel, especially the vowel "a" as distinguished from the other vowels ; a word, words. 자상자의 字相字義 Word-form and word-meaning, differentiated by the esoteric sect for its own ends, 아 阿 being considered the alpha and root of all sounds and words ; the 자 字 among esoteric Buddhists is the 종자 種子 bīja, or seed-word possessing power through the object with which it is associated ; there is also the 자륜 字輪, the wheel, rotation, or inter-change or words for esoteric purposes, especially the five Sanskrit signs adopted for the five elements earth, water, fire, air, space. 자모 字母 The Sanskrit alphabet of 42, 47, or 50 letters, the "Siddham" 실담 悉曇 consisting of 35 체문 體文 consonants and 12 마다 摩多 vowels. The 자모표 字母表 deals with the alphabet in 1 chüan. The 자모품 字母品 is an abbreviation of 문수문경자모품 文殊問經字母品. 자연 字緣 ; 모음 母音 The 12 or 14 Sanskrit vowels, as contrasted with the 35 or 36 consonants, which are 근본 根本 radical or 자계 字界 limited or fixed letters.

자 資 Funds, basis, property, supplies ; fees ; to depend on ; disposition ; expenditure. 자생 資生 Necessaries of life. 자량 資糧 Sambhāra ; supplies for body or soul, e.g. food, almsgiving, wisdom, etc. 자연 資緣 The material necessaries of a monk, clothing, food, and shelter. 자재장 資財帳 Schedule of property (of a monastery).

자 子 Kumāra ; son ; seed ; sir ; 11-1 midnight.

자 赭 Ochre, brown ; translit. *cha.* 자시 赭時 "Tchadj or Tchāseh" ; Kingdom of stone or stones. An ancient place "in Turkestan on the Sir ; the modern Tashkend." [Eitel]. 자갈 赭羯 "Tchakas.

A race of people near Samarkand who furnished excellent soldiers." [Eitel].

자 磁 Porcelain crockery, chinaware. 자석 磁石 A lodestone, magnet.

자 紫 Purple, dark red. 자고 紫姑 The goddess of the cesspool. 자마 紫磨 Pure gold, hence 자마금 紫磨金 ; also 자마인욕 紫磨忍辱 The Buddha's image in attitude of calmness and indifference to pleasure or pain. 자의 紫衣 ; 자가 紫袈 ; 자복 紫服 The purple robe, said to have been bestowed on certain monks during the T'ang dynasty.

자 自 Sva, svayam ; the self, one's own, personal ; of itself, naturally, of course ; also, from (i.e. from the self as central). 자 自 is used as the opposite of 타 他 another, other's, etc., e.g. 자력 自力 (in) one's own strength as contrasted with 타력 他力 the strength of another especially in the power to save of a Buddha or Bodhisattva. It is also used in the sense of Ātman 아달마 阿怛摩 the self, or the soul.

자 煮 To boil, cook. 자사 煮沙 Like boiling sand for food.

자 藉 To rely on, avail oneself of. 자통개도 藉通開導 (The two other schools 별 別 and 원 圓) depended on the T'ung or Intermediate school for their evolution.

자각오심 自覺悟心 A mind independent of externals, pure thought, capable of enlightenment from within. 자각성지 自覺聖智 The uncaused omniscience of Vairocana ; it is also called 법계(체성)지 法界(體性)智 and 금강지 金剛智.

자과 子果 Seed and fruit ; seed-produced fruit is 자과 子果, fruit-produced seed is 과자 果子. The fruit produced by illusion in former incarnation is 자과 子果, which the Hīnayāna arhat has not yet finally cut off. It is necessary to enter Nirvāṇa without remnant of mortality to be free from its "fruit," or karma.

자내증 自內證 Inner witness.

자단 子斷 The seed 종자 種子 cut off, i.e. the seed which produces the miseries of transmigration.

자류인과 自類因果 Cause and effect of the same order.

자리 自利 Ātmahitam, self-profit ; beneficial to oneself. 자리이타 自利利他 "Self-profit profit others," i.e. the essential nature and work of a bodhisattva, to benefit himself and benefit others, or himself press forward in the Buddhist life in order to carry others forward. Hīnayāna is considered to be self-advancement, self-salvation by works or discipline ; Bodhisattva Buddhism as saving oneself in order to save others, or making progress and helping others to progress, bodhisattvism being essentially altruistic.

자만과 子滿果 The fruit full of seeds, the pomegranate.

자박 子縛 The seed bond, or delusion of the mind, which keeps men in bondage

자살 自殺 To commit suicide ; for a monk to commit suicide is said to be against the rules.

자상 自相 Svalakṣaṇa ; individuality, particular, personal, as contrasted with 공상 共相 general or common.

자생 自生 Self-produced, or naturally existing ; also an intp. of bhūta 부다 部多 produced, existing, real ; also demons born by transformation 화생 化生 in contrast to the 야차 夜叉 yakṣa who are born from parents.

자서수계 自誓受戒 To make the vows and undertake the commandments oneself (before the image of a Buddha), i.e. self-ordination when unable to obtain ordination from the ordained.

자선 子璿 A famous learned monk Tzŭ-hsüan, of the Sung dynasty whose style was 장수 長水 Ch'ang-shui, the name of his district ; he had a large following ; at first he specialized on the Śūraṁgama 능엄경 楞嚴經 ; later he adopted the teaching of 현수 賢首 Hsien-shou of the 화엄 華嚴 Hua-yen school.

자성 自性 Own nature ; of (its) own nature. As an intp. of Pradhāna (and resembling 명성 冥性) in the Sāṅkhya philosophy it is "Prakṛti, the Originant, primary or original matter or rather the primary germ out of which all material appearances are evolved, the first evolver or source of the material world (hence in a general acceptation 'nature' or rather 'matter' as opposed to *purusha*, or 'spirit')." [M. W.] As 사발알 莎發斡 svabhāva, it is "own state, essential or inherent property, innate or peculiar disposition, natural state or constitution, nature." [M. W.] The self-substance, self-nature, or unchanging character of anything. 자성삼보 自性三寶 The Triratna, each with its own characteristic, Buddha being wisdom 각 覺 ; the Law correctness 정 正 ; and the Order purity 정 淨.

자성계 自性戒 The ten natural moral laws, i.e. which are natural to man, apart from the Buddha's commands ; also 자성선 自性善.

자손손타 自損損他 To harm oneself and harm others, to harm oneself is to harm others, etc. ; opposite of 자리이타 自利利他.

자수용토 自受用土 The third of the four Buddha-kṣetra or Buddha-domains, that in which there is complete response to his teaching and powers ; v. 불토 佛土. 자수용신 自受用身 One of the two kinds of sambhogakāya, for his own enjoyment ; cf. 사신 四身. 자수법락 自受法樂 The dharma-delights a Buddha enjoys in the above state.

자신자불 自身自佛 One's own body is Buddha.

자심 自心 Svacitta, self-mind, one's own mind.

자애 自愛 Self-love, cause of all pursuit or seeking, which in turn causes all suffering. All Buddhas put away self-love and all pursuit, or seeking, such elimination being nirvāṇa.

자어상위 自語相違 A manifest contradiction, one of the nine fallacies of a proposition, svārtha-viruddha, e.g. "my mother is barren."

자연 自然 Svayambhū, also 자이 自爾 ; 법이 法爾 self-existing, the self-existent ; Brahmā, Viṣṇu, and others ; in Chinese it is "self-so," so of itself, natural, or course, spontaneous. It also means uncaused existence, certain sects of heretics 자연외도 自然外道 denying Buddhist cause and effect and holding that things happen spontaneously. 자연자 自然慈 Intuitive mercy possessed by a bodhisattva, untaught and without causal nexus. 자연오도 自然悟道 Enlightenment by the inner light, independent of external teaching ; to become Buddha by one's own power, e.g. Śākyamuni who is called 자연석가 自然釋迦. 자연성불도 自然成佛道 Svayambhuvaḥ. Similar to the last, independent attainment of Buddhahood. 자연지 自然智 The intuitive or inborn wisdom of a Buddha, untaught to him and outside the causal nexus. 자연허무신 自然虛無身 A Buddha's spiritual of absolute body, his dharmakāya ; also, those who are born in Paradise, i.e. who are spontaneously and independently produced there.

자원 子院 Small courts and buildings attached to a central monastery.

자자 自恣 Pravāraṇa, to follow one's own bent, the modern term being 수의 隨意 ; it means the end of restraint, i.e. following the period of retreat. 자자일 自恣日 The last day of the annual retreat.

자작자수 自作自受 As one does one receives, every man receives the reward of his deeds, creating his own karma, 자업자득 自業自得.

자재 自在 Īśvara, 이습벌라 伊濕伐羅 ; can, king, master, sovereign, independent, royal ; intp. as free from resistance ; also, the mind free from delusion ; in the Avataṁsaka-sūtra it translates vaśitā. There are several groups of this independence, or sovereignty — 2, 4, 5, 8, and 10, e.g. the 2 are that a bodhisattva has sovereign knowledge and sovereign power ; the others are categories of a bodhisattva's sovereign powers. For the eight powers v. 팔대자재아 八大自在我. 자재천 自在天 or 자재왕 自在王 Īśvaradeva, a title of Śiva, king of the devas, also known as 대자재천 大自在天 Maheśvara, q.v. It is a title also applied to Kuan-yin and others. 자재천외도 自在天外道 Śivaites, who ascribed creation and destruction to Śiva, and that all things form his body, space his head, sun and moon his eyes, earth his body, rivers and seas his urine, mountains his faces, wind his life, fire his heat, and all living things the vermin on his body. This sect is also known as the 자재등인종 自在等因宗. Śiva is represented with eight arms, three eyes, sitting on a bull. 자재왕 自在王 is also a title of Vairocana ; and, as Sureśvara, is the name of a mythical king, contemporary of the mythical Śikhin Buddha.

자조자정자도 自調自淨自度 The śrāvaka method of salvation by personal discipline, or "works" ; 자조 自調 self-progress by keeping the commandments ; 자정 自淨 self-purification by emptying the mind ; 자도 自度 self-release by the attainment of gnosis, or wisdom.

자증 自證 The witness within, inner assurance. 자증단 自證壇 or 자증회 自證會 The 성신회 成身會 assembly of all the Buddha and bodhisattva embodiments in the Vajradhātu maṇḍala. 자증성지 自證聖智 Pratyātmāryajñāna, personal apprehension of Buddha-truth. 자증신 自證身 A title of Vairocana, his dharmakāya of self-assurance, or realization, from which issues his retinue of proclaimers of the truth.

자합국 子合國 Kukyar, Kokyar, or Kukejar, a country west of Khotan, 1,000 li from Kashgar, perhaps Yarkand.

자행화타 自行化他 To discipline, or perform, oneself and (or in order to) convert or transform others, v. 자리이타 自利利他.

작 鵲 A magpie ; jay, daw. 작소 鵲巢 A magpie's nest, sometimes applied to a place of meditation. 작원 鵲園 Magpie garden, applied to the Veṅuvana, v. 죽림 竹林.

작 嚼 To chew. 작납 嚼蠟 Chewing wax, tasteless.

작 斫 To chop ; translit. *ca, cha.* 작구가 斫句迦 or 탁구가 拆句迦 or 소구가 所句迦 Chakoka, or Cugopa. "An ancient kingdom and city in Little Bukharia, probably the modern Yerkiang (엽이강 葉爾羌) in Lat. 38° 13 N., Long. 78° 49 E." [Eitel]. Or perhaps Karghalik in the Khotan region. 작(걸)추 斫(乞)芻 Cakṣu(s), the eye, one of the six organs of sense. Cakṣurdhātu is the 안계 眼界 eye-realm, or sight-faculty. There are definitions such as the eye of body, mind, wisdom, Buddha-truth, Buddha ; or human, deva, bodhisattva, dharma, and Buddha vision. 작흘라 斫訖羅 idem 작가라 斫迦羅 or 자가라 柘迦羅 ; 차가라 遮伽羅 or 遮迦羅 ; 사갈라 賒羯羅 Cakra, a wheel, disc, cycle ; the wheel of the sun's chariot, of time, etc. ; like the vajra it is a symbol of sovereignty, of advancing or doing at will ; to revolve the wheel is to manifest power or wisdom. It is a symbol of a 작흘라벌랄지 斫訖羅伐辣底 ; 차가월라 遮迦越羅 ; 전륜(왕) 轉輪(王) Cakravartī (-rāja), sovereign ruler, whose chariot wheels roll everywhere without hindrance ; the extent of his realm and power are indicated by the quality of the metal, iron, copper, silver, or, for universality, gold. The highest cakravartī uses the wheel or thunderbolt as a weapon and "hurls his Tchakra into the midst of his enemies," but the Buddha "meekly turns the wheel of doctrine and conquers every universe by his teaching." [Eitel]. The cakra is one of the thirty-two signs on a Buddha's soles. 작흘라바(가) 斫訖羅婆(迦) Cakravāka, Cakrāhva, "the ruddy goose," "the Brāhmany duck." [M. W.] The mandarin duck. 작흘라산 斫訖羅山 Cakravāla, Cakravāḍa, the circle of iron mountains "forming the periphery of a universe."

작 作 To make, do, act, be ; arise. 작불 作佛 To become or be a Buddha ; to cut off illusion, attain complete enlightenment, and end the stage of Bodhisattva discipline. 작불사 作佛事 To do the works of Buddha ; perform Buddhist ceremonies. 작선 作善 To do good, e.g. worship, bestow alms, etc. 작가 作家 Leader, founder, head of sect, a term used by the 선 禪 Ch'an(Zen) or Intuitive school. 작악 作惡 To do evil. 작의 作意 Cittotpāda ; to have the thought arise, be aroused, beget the resolve, etc. 작계 作戒 Obedience to the commandments, external fulfilment of them ; also called 표색 表色, in contrast with 무작계 無作戒, 무표색 無表色 the inner grace ; moral action in contrast with inner moral character. 작지계 作持戒 Active keeping of the commandments, active law in contrast with 지지계 止持戒 passive, such as not killing, not stealing, etc. v. 지범 持犯. 작범(패) 作梵(唄) The call to order in the assembly. 작업 作業 Karma produced, i.e. by the action of body, words, and thought, which educe the kernel of the next rebirth. 작법 作法 Karma, which results from action, i.e. the "deeds" of body or mouth ; to perform ceremonies. 작법득 作法得 To receive ceremonial ordination as a monk. 작법참(회) 作法懺(悔) One of the three kinds of monastic confession and repentance. 작법계 作法界 The place of assembly for ceremonial purposes. 작범 作犯 Transgression, sin by action, active sin. 작용 作用 Function, activity, act. 작례 作禮 To pay one's respect by worship ; to make an obeisance. 작자 作者 Kartṛ ; a doer, he who does things, hence the ātman, ego, or person within ; the active element, or principle ; one of the sixteen non-Buddhist definitions of the soul. Also kāraṇa, a cause, maker, creator, deity. 작거 作擧 The accusation of sin made against particular monks by the virtuous monk who presides at the pravāraṇa gathering on the last day of the summer's rest. 작원문 作願門 To make a vow to benefit self and others, and to fulfil the vow so as to be born in the Pure Land of Amitābha. The third of the five doors or ways of entering the Pure Land. 작마(생) 作麽(生) How? What? What are you doing?

잔 殘 To spoil, injure ; cruel. 잔과 殘果 Spoiled fruit, i.e. a corpse.

잠 暫 Temporarily, briefly, meanwhile, suddenly. 잠가 暫暇 A brief relief, or leave of absence.

잠 蠶 The silkworm. 잠견 蠶繭 A silkworm's cocoon, simile of the self-binding effects of the passions, etc.

잡 雜 Mixed, variegated, heterogeneous, hybrid, confused, disordered. 잡주계 雜住界 The world of mixed dwellers, i.e. the five species 오취 五趣, v. *infra* ; this or any similar world. 잡함 雜含 The Saṁyuktāgama, tr. by Guṇabhadra. 잡업 雜業 A world of varied karma. 잡염 雜染 All kinds of moral infection, the various causes of transmigration. 잡생세계 雜生世界 A world of various beings, i.e. that of the five destinies, hells, demons, animals, men, and devas. 잡화(경) 雜華(經) A name for the Hua-yen sūtra. 잡장 雜藏 Saṁyuktapiṭaka, the miscellaneous canon, at first said to relate to bodhisattvas, but it contains miscellaneous works of Indian and Chinese authors, collections made under the Ming dynasty and supplements of the northern Chinese canon with their case marks from the southern canon.

장 掌 A palm, a paw ; to grasp, control, administer. 장과 掌果 (As easy to see) as a mango in the hand.

장 章 A section, chapter ; finished, elegant ; essay, document ; rule, according to pattern. 장복 章服 Regulation dress.

장 場 Area, arena, field, especially the bodhi-plot, or place of enlightenment, etc. ; cf. 도량 道場 ; 보리량 菩提場.

장 長 Ch'ang, long ; always ; Chang, to grow, rising, senior. 장걸식 長乞食 Always to ask food as alms, one of the twelve duties of a monk. 장수 長壽 Long life. 장수천 長壽天 Devas of long life, in the fourth dhyāna heaven where life is 500 great kalpas, and in the fourth arūpaloka where life extends over 80,000 kalpas. 장야 長夜 The whole night, the long night of mortality or transmigration. 장일 長日 The long day, or succeeding days prolonged. 장생 長生 Long or eternal life (in Paradise), 장생불사 長生不死, 장생불로 長生不老 long life without death, or growing old, immortality. 장생부 長生符 The charm for immortality, i.e. Buddhism. 장로 長老 Senior, venerable, title for aged and virtuous monks ; also an abbot. 장자 長者 ; 게리가발지 揭利呵跋底 ; 의력하발지 疑叻賀鉢底 Gṛhapati. A householder ; one who is just, straightforward, truthful, honest, advanced in age, and wealthy ; an elder. 장의 長衣 ; 장물 長物 ; 장발 長鉢 Clothes, things, or almsbowls in excess of the permitted number. 장궤 長跪 Kneeling with knees and toes touching the ground and thighs and body erect ; tall kneeling. 장아함경 長阿含經 Dīrghāgama, the long āgamas, cf. 아함 阿含. 장식 長食 Ample supplies of food, i.e. for a long time.

장 葬 Inter, bury. 장송 葬送 ; 송장 送葬 To escort the deceased to the grave.

장 莊 Sedate, serious, proper, stern. 장왕 莊王 v. 묘 妙 Śubhavyūha, reputed father of Kuan-yin. 장엄 莊嚴 Alaṁkāraka. Adorn, adornment, glory, honour, ornament, ornate ; e.g. the adornments of morality, meditation, wisdom, and the control of good and evil forces. In Amitābha's paradise twenty-nine forms of adornment are described, v. 정토론 淨土論. 장엄겁 莊嚴劫 The glorious kalpa to which the thousand Buddhas, one succeeding another, bring their contribution of adornment. 장엄왕 莊嚴王 Vyūharāja, a bodhisattva in the retinue of Śākyamuni. 장엄왕경 莊嚴王經 Vyūharāja sūtra, an exposition of the principal doctrines of the Tantra school. 장엄문 莊嚴門 The gate or school of the adornment of the spirit, in contrast with external practices, ceremonies, asceticism, etc.

장 丈 Ten feet ; an elder ; a wife's parents ; a husband. 장륙 丈六 Sixteen "feet," the normal height of a Buddha in his "transformation body" 화신 化身 nirmāṇa-kāya ; said to be the height of the Buddha when he was on earth. 장륙금신 丈六金身 Ditto ; also a metal or golden image of the Buddha 16 feet high mentioned in the 북사 北史 Northern History. 장부 丈夫 A virile, zealous disciple, a man who presses forward unceasingly. 장부지간 丈夫志幹 A firm-willed man, especially used of a bodhisattva who dauntlessly presses forward. 장부국 丈夫國 The country of virile men, Puruṣapura 부루사부라 富婁沙富羅, ancient capital of Gandhāra, the modern Peshawar ; birthplace of 천친 天親 Vasubandhu.

장 裝 To dress, make up, pretend, pack, load, store ; a fashion. 장상 裝像 To dress an image. 장향 裝香 To put incense into a censer.

장 藏 Treasury, thesaurus, store, to hide ; the Canon. An intp. of piṭaka, a basket. box, granary, collection of writings. The 이장 二藏 twofold canon may be the sūtras and the vinaya ; or the Hīnayāna and Mahāyāna scriptures. The 삼장 三藏 or Tripiṭaka consists of the sūtras, vinaya, and śāstras (Abhidharma). The 사장 四藏 fourfold canon adds a miscellaneous collection. The 오장 五藏 fivefold collection is sūtras, vinaya, abhidharma, miscellaneous, and spells, or, instead of the spells, a bodhisattva collection. There is also an esoteric fivefold canon, the first three being the above, the last two being the Prajñāpāramitā and the Dhāraṇīs. 장주 藏主 Librarian. 장사 藏司 Library ; librarian. 장진 藏塵 The store of dust, i.e. the earthly body of Buddha, his nirmāṇakāya. 장교 藏教 The Piṭaka, i.e. Tripiṭaka school, one of the four divisions 장통별원 藏通別圓 as classified by T'ien-t'ai ; it is the Hīnayāna school of the śrāvaka and pratyeka-buddha type, based on the Tripiṭaka and its four dogmas, with the bodhisattva doctrine as an unimportant side issue. It is also subdivided into four others, 유 有 the reality of things, 공 空 their unreality, both and neither. The bodhisattva of the Piṭaka school is defined as undergoing seven stages, beginning with the four dogmas and ending with complete enlightenment under the bodhi-tree. 장전 藏殿 A library of the scriptures. 장리 藏理 The Tathāgatagarbha, or universal storehouse whence all truth comes. 장경 藏經 The Canon, of which there are catalogues varying in number of contents, the first by Liang Wu Ti of 5,400 chüan ; the K'ai-yüan Catalogue contained 5,048 chüan. The oldest existing canon is believed to be the Korean with 6,467 chüan ; the Sung canon has 5,714 ; the Yüan, 5,397 ; the Japanese, 665 covers ; the Ming, 6,771 chüan, reprinted in the Ts'ing dynasty with supplement ; and a new and much enlarged edition has recently been published in Shanghai, and one in Tokyo ; cf. 삼장 三藏 and 일체경 一切經. 장식 藏識 The Ālayavijñāna, the storehouse of all knowledge, the eighth of the vijñānas, cf. 아 阿 and 팔 八. 장통 藏通 The Tsang and T'ung schools as classified by T'ien-t'ai, v. *supra*.

장 障 Varaṇa ; āvaraṇa ; a screen, barricade, partition, a term for the passions or any delusion which hinders enlightenment. 장애 障礙 Screen and obstruction, i.e. anything that hinders. 장진해탈 障盡解脫 Salvation through the complete removal of the obstruction of illusion.

장림 杖林 Yaṣṭivana, 설슬지림 洩瑟知林 ; the forest in which a Brahman tried to measure Buddha's height with a 16ft. bamboo pole, but the more he measured the higher the body became ; another part of the legend is that the forest grew from the bamboo which he left behind in chagrin.

재 再 Again, a second time, also 재왕 再往.

재 在 At, in, on, present. 재세 在世 In the world, while alive here. 재속 在俗 In and of the world, unenlightened ; in a lay condition 재재처처 在在處處 In every place. 재가 在家 At home, a layman or woman, not 출가 出家, i.e. not leaving home as a monk or nun. 재가이계 在家二戒 The two grades of commandments observed by the lay, one the five, the other the eight, v. 오 五 and 팔계 八戒 ; these are the Hīnayāna rules ; the 재가계 在家戒 of Mahāyāna are the 십선계 十善戒 ten good rules. 재가출가 在家出家 One who while remaining at home observes the whole of a monk's or nun's rules. 재리교 在理教 The Tsai-li secret society, an offshoot of the White Lily Society, was founded in Shantung at the beginning of the Ch'ing dynasty ; the title "In the Li" indicating that the society associated itself with all three religions, Confucianism, Taoism, and Buddhism ; its followers set up no images, burnt no incense, neither smoked nor drank, and were vegetarian. 재전 在纏 In bonds, i.e. the 재전진여 在纏眞如 the Bhūtatathatā in limitations, e.g. relative, v. 기신론 起信論 Awakening of Faith.

재 財 Vasu ; Artha. Wealth, riches. 재주 財主 A wealthy man, rich. 재공양 財供養 ; 재시 財施 Offerings or gifts of material goods. 재간 財慳 Meanness, stinginess. 재욕 財欲 The desire for wealth, one of the five wrong desires. 재신 財神 Kuvera, v. 구 俱 Vaiśravaṇa, v. 비 毘 the god of wealth. 재색 財色 Wealth and beauty (i.e. woman).

쟁 諍 Remonstrate with ; debate, dispute. 쟁론 諍論 Debate, dispute, disputation.

저 猪 A hog, pig. 저두화상 猪頭和尙 Pig-head monk, because of his meditative or dormant appearance.

저 底 Bottom, basis ; translit. *t, d, dh.* 저하 底下 At the bottom, below, the lowest class(of men). 저리 底哩 Tri, three, in Trisamaya, etc. 저언다 底彥多 ; 정안치 丁岸哆 Tiṅanta, Tryanta, described as the singular, dual, and plural endings in verbs. 저률차 底栗車 Tiryagyoni, the animal species, animals, especially the six domestic animals. 저사 底沙 Tiṣya (1) The twenty-third of the twenty-eight constellations 귀숙 鬼宿 $\gamma\delta\eta\theta$ in Cancer ; it has connection with Śiva. (2) Name of a Buddha who taught Śākyamuni and Maitreya in a former incarnation. 저리 底理 The fundamental principle or law.

저 這 This ; these. 저리 這裏 This place, here. 저개 這箇 This.

저 低 To let down, lower. 저라택가 低羅擇迦 or 저라석가 低羅釋迦 Tiladhāka, Tiladaka, or Tilaśākya. “A monastery, three yojanas west of Nālandā, perhaps the modern village of Thelari near Gayā.” [Eitel].

저 著 To manifest, display, publish, fix. See 착 著.

저돌 觝突 To butt against, gore, as an angry bull.

적 or **자** 炙 Broil, burn, roast, dry ; intimate. 자가회 炙茄會 A Ch'an(Zen) School winter festival at which roasted lily roots were eaten.

적 賊 A thief, robber, spoiler ; to rob, steal, etc. 적주 賊住 An unordained person who passes himself off as a monk.

적 積 Accumulate, pile up ; many, long. 적공루덕 積功累德 ; 적루 積累 To accumulate or lay up merit. 적석산 積石山 Aśmakūṭa, stone-heap mountains, the eastern border of the Gobi desert.

적 赤 Kaṣāya 가사야 袈沙野, red, hot ; south ; naked. 적매단 赤梅檀 A tree used for incense. 적백이제 赤白二渧 The “drops” of red and white, i.e. female and male sperm which unite in conception. 적안 赤眼 The red-eye, i.e. a turtle. 적육(단) 赤肉(團) The red flesh (lump), the heart. 적악연나 赤鄂衍那 Chagayana. “An ancient province and city of Tukhāra, the present Chaganian in Lat. 38° 21 N., Long. 69° 21 E.” [Eitel]. 적자비바사 赤髭毘婆沙 The red-moustached (or bearded) Vibhāṣā, a name for 불타야사 佛陀耶舍 Buddhayaśas.

적 寂 Praśama ; vivikta ; śānti. Still, silent, quiet, solitary, calm, tranquil, nirvāṇa. 적광 寂光 Calm and illuminating as are Truth and Knowledge ; the hidden truth illuminating. 적광(토) 寂光(土) The land (of Buddhas) where is calm illumination. 적명지 寂命智 Buddha-knowledge of the transmigratory forms of all beings. 적정 寂定 Tranquil concentration ; contemplation in which disturbing illusion is eliminated. 적안 寂岸 The shore of peace, nirvāṇa. 적상 寂常 Peace eternal, eternal nirvāṇa. 적인 寂忍 Calmness and endurance, quiet patience. 적념 寂念 Calm thoughts ; to calm the mind ; contemplation. 적업사자 寂業師子 The lion of nirvāṇa, Śākyamuni. 적멸 寂滅 Calmness and extinction, nirvāṇa. 적멸인 寂滅忍 Nirvāṇa-patience ; the patience of the nirvāṇa (the suppression of all passion). 적멸법 寂滅法 The nirvāṇa-method. 적멸무이 寂滅無二 Nirvāṇa as absolute without disunity or phenomena. 적멸상 寂滅相 Nirvāṇa considered independently of the phenomenal. 적(멸도)량 寂(滅道)場 The place where a Buddha attains the truth of nirvāṇa, especially where Śākyamuni attained it. 적재 寂災 To quell calamities (by spells, or ceremonies). 적연 寂然 In calmness, quietude, silence ; undisturbed. 적연계 寂然界 The Hīnayāna nirvāṇa-realm or border. 적조 寂照 Nirvāṇa-illumination ; ultimate reality shinning forth. 적조혜 寂照慧 Buddha-wisdom which comprehends nirvāṇa reality and its functioning. 적용담연 寂用湛然 Character (nirvāṇa-like) and function concomitant in the absolute and relative, in being and becoming, etc. 적종 寂種 The nirvāṇa class, i.e. the Hinayanists who are said to seek only their own salvation. 적정 寂靜 Calm and quiet ; free from temptation and distress ; nirvāṇa. 적정법 寂靜法 Ceremonies for restoring peace from calamity. 적정행 寂靜行 Hīnayāna discipline to ensure nirvāṇa. 적정문 寂靜門 Nirvāṇa, or the absolute 일체제법 一切諸法 as the door of release from trouble and suffering. 적묵외도 寂默外道 Ascetics vowed to silence who dwell among tombs or in solitude.

적 適 To go to, reach ; happen ; follow, accord with ; suddenly, now, then. 적화 適化 To adapt teaching to circumstances. 적막 適莫 Pro and con, according or contrary (to wishes).

적 敵 To oppose, compete ; an enemy. 적증 敵證 Opposition and affirmation, negative and positive.

ㄱ ㄴ ㄷ ㄹ ㅁ ㅂ ㅅ ㅇ ㅈ ㅊ ㅋ ㅌ ㅍ ㅎ 찾아보기

적 迹 Traces, footsteps ; external evidences or indications. 적화 迹化 Teaching or lessons derived from external events, i.e. of the Buddha's life and work, shown in the first fourteen sections of the Lotus Sūtra ; the second fourteen sections of that work are called 본화 本化 his direct teaching. The lessons from the external indications are called 적화십묘 迹化十妙 the ten marvellous indications, cf. 십묘 十妙.

적귀 赤鬼 The red demons of purgatory, one with the head of a bull, another with that of a horse, etc.

전 筌 A bamboo fishing-trap. 전어 筌魚 Trap and fish, a difficult passage in a book and its interpretation. 득어망전 得魚忘筌 Having caught the fish, the trap may be forgotten, i.e. it is of secondary importance ; also ingratitude.

전 田 A field, fields ; a place, or state, for the cultivation of meritorious or other deeds ; cf. 복전 福田. 전(상)의 田(相)衣 A patch-robe, its patches resembling the rectangular divisions of fields.

전 旃 A flag on a bent pole ; to warn ; translit. generally *can*, rarely *śan*, *ṣan*, *cin*, *kim*. 전단 旃丹 v. 진 震 China. 전연 旃延 v. 가 迦 abbrev. for Kātyāyana. 전제라 旃提羅 Ṣaṇḍha or Ṣaṇḍhaka, a eunuch. 전단(나) 旃檀(娜) Candana, from cand, to brighten, gladden ; sandal-wood, either the tree, wood, or incense-powder, from southern India ; there are various kinds, e.g. 우두전단 牛頭旃檀 q.v. 전단이 旃檀耳 A fungus or fruit of the sandal tree, a broth or decoction of which is said to have been given to the Buddha at his last meal, by Cunda 순타 純陀 q.v. ; v. 장아함경 長阿含經 3. 전시가 旃簛迦 Campaka, also 첨복 瞻蔔 or 첨박 瞻博 or 첨파 瞻波. A tree with yellow fragrant flowers, *Michelia champaka* ; a kind of perfume ; a kind of bread-fruit tree ; a district in the upper Punjab. 전다라 旃茶羅 Caṇḍāla, v. below. 전달라바가 旃達羅婆伽 ; 월분 月分 Candrabhāgā. "The largest Punjab stream, the Acesines of Alexander, now called Chenab." [Eitel]. 전달라 旃達羅 ; 전달제바 旃達提婆 Candradeva, the moon, the moon-deva, the male ruler of the moon. 전차 旃遮 Ciñcā-Māṇavikā, or Sundarī, also 전자 旃闍, 전차 戰遮 name of a brahmin woman who falsely accused the Buddha of adultery with her, 흥기행경하 興起行經下 q.v. 전다라 旃陀羅 Caṇḍāla, derived from violent, and intp. as a butcher, bad man. 전다리 旃陀利 Caṇḍāla, "an outcast," "a man of the lowest and most despised of the mixed tribes, born from a Śūdra father and Brahman mother." [M. W.] He bore a flag and sounded a bell to warn of his presence. Converts from this class were admitted to ordination in Buddhism. 전다아수가 旃陀阿輸柯 Cāṇḍāśoka, Cruel Aśoka, a name given to Aśoka before his conversion.

전 箋 A tablet, slip. 전서 箋書 Sūtras.

전 殿 A temple, hall, palace ; rearguard. 전주 殿主 ; 전사 殿司 The warden of a temple.

전 全 All, whole, complete. 전분계 全分戒 or 전분수 全分受 Fully ordained by receiving all the commandments. 전가부좌 全跏趺坐 The legs completely crossed as in a completely seated image.

전 箭 An arrow, dart. 전도 箭道 An arrow-shot, or bow-shot, in distance.

전 典 Canon, rule ; allusion ; to take charge of ; mortgage. 전객 典客 or 전빈 典賓 ; 지객 知客 The one who takes charge of visitors in a monastery. 전좌 典座 The verger who indicates the order of sitting, etc. 전람 典攬 Summary of the essentials of a sūtra, or canonical book. 사전 辭典 A dictionary, phrase-book.

전 詮 Explain, expound, discourse upon. 전지 詮旨 To explain the meaning, or import. 전변 詮辯 To explain, comment on.

전 電 Lightning, symbolizes the impermanent and transient. 전광석화 電光石火 Lightning and flint-fire, transient. 전영 電影 Impermanence of all things like lightning and shadow.

전 顚 Overturn, upset, upside down ; the forehead, top. 전도 顚倒 Viparyaya ; error. Upside down, inverted ; contrary to reality ; to believe things to be as they seem to be, e.g. the impermanent to be permanent, the apparent ego to be real ; cf. 칠전도 七顚倒 and 팔전도 八顚倒. 전도망상 顚倒妄想 Upside-down and delusive ideas.

전 前 Pūrva. Before ; former, previous ; in front . 전세 前世 ; 전생 前生 Former life or lives. 전중후 前中後 Former, intermediate, after. 전불 前佛 A preceding Buddha ; former Buddhas who have entered into nirvāṇa. 전당 前堂 The front hall, or its front part. 전진 前塵 Previous impure conditions (influencing the succeeding stage or stages). 전정각산 前正覺山 Prāgbodhi, v. 발 鉢 A mountain in Magadha, reported to have been ascended by Śākyamuni before his enlightenment, hence its name. 전신 前身 The previous body, or incarnation. 전후제단 前後際斷 Discontinuous function, though seemingly continuous, e.g. a "Catherine-wheel," or torch whirled around.

전 專 Single ; special ; solely. 전심 專心 With single mind ; whole-heartedly. 전념 專念 To fix the mind, or attention, upon ; solely to invoke (a certain Buddha). 전상 專想 To think wholly, or only, of or upon. 전정 專精 Solely and purely (to advance in the Way).

전 纏 To bind with cords ; bonds ; another name for 번뇌 煩惱 the passions and delusions, etc. 전보 纏報 The retribution of transmigrational-bondage. 전무명 纏無明 The bondage of unenlightenment. 전박 纏縛 Bondage ; to bind ; also the 십전 十纏 and 사박 四縛 q.v.

전 展 To extend, expand, stretch. 전전력 展轉力 Powers of extension or expansion.

전 塡 To fill up. 전왕 塡王 Udayana, v. 우전 優塡 king of Kauśāmbī. 전릉 塡陵 A raised mound, a stūpa.

전 奠 To settle, offer, condole. 전다 奠茶 To make an offering of tea to a Buddha, a spirit, etc.

전 煎 To simmer, fry. 전점 煎點 To fry cakes.

전 傳 To transmit, pass on, hand down, promulgate, propagate ; tradition ; summon ; interpret ; record ; the Abhidharma. 전심 傳心 To pass from mind to mind, to pass by narration or tradition, to transmit the mind of Buddha as in the Intuitional school, mental transmission. 전계 傳戒 To transmit the commandments, to grant them as at ordination. 전지 傳持 To maintain what has been transmitted ; to transmit and maintain. 전교 傳教 To spread the teaching, or doctrine ; to transmit and instruct. 전법 傳法 To transmit, or spread abroad the Buddha truth. 전등 傳燈 To transmit the light, pass on the lamp of truth. 전의 傳衣 To hand down the mantle, or garments. 전통 傳通 Universal propagation ; unhindered transmission.

전 囀 Translit. *vā*. 전라희 囀羅呬 Vārāhī, tr. as the gods below the earth.

전 轉 Vartana ; pravartana ; vṛtti. Turn, transform, revolve, evolve, change, the process of birth and rebirth ; again, re-.

전 戰 War, hostilities, battle ; alarm, anxiety, terrified ; translit. *can.* 전승림 戰勝林 The grove of victory, v. 서 逝 Jetavana, Jetṛvana. 전달라 戰達羅 ; 전나라 戰捺羅 Candra, shining ; the moon, especially as the moon-deity. 전달라발랄바 戰達羅鉢剌婆 Candraprabha, moonlight, name of Śākyamuni when a king in a former incarnation, who cut off his head as a gift to others.

전격란 轉格欄 The circuit of the central Lhasa temple, made by prostrations every third step, to get rid of evils or obtain blessings.

전경 轉經 To recite a scripture ; to scan a scripture by reading the beginning, middle, and end of each chapter ; cf. 전대 轉大. To roll or unroll a scripture-roll. To copy a scripture. 전장 轉藏 ; 전독 轉讀 are similar in meaning.

전교 轉敎 To teach or preach through a deputy ; to pass on the doctrine from one to another.

전녀성남 轉女成男 To be transformed from, or transform, a female into a male.

전대반야경 轉大般若經 To turn over the leaves of and scan (for acquiring merit) the 600 chüan of the complete Prajñā-pāramitā ; cf. 전경 轉經.

전등록 傳燈錄 "The (Records of the) Transmission of the Lamp." Buddhist chronicles compiled by Tao-yuan, a Ch'an Monk of the Sung Dynasty.

전륜 轉輪 Cakravartī, "a ruler the wheels of whose chariot roll everywhere without hindrance." M. W. Revolving wheels ; to turn a wheel ; also 전륜(성)왕 轉輪(聖)王 ; 윤왕 輪王 ; 전륜성제 轉輪聖帝, cf. 작 斫. The symbol is the cakra or disc, which is of four kinds indicating the rank, i.e. gold, silver, copper, or iron, the iron cakravartī ruling over one continent, the south ; the copper, over two, east and south ; the silver, over three, east, west, and south ; the golden being supreme over all the four continents. The term is also applied to the gods over a universe, and to a Buddha as universal spiritual king, and as preacher of the supreme doctrine. Only a cakravartī possesses the 칠보 七寶 Saptaratna and 1,000 sons. The cakra, or discus, is also a missile used by a cakravartī for overthrowing his enemies. Its origin is probably the sun with its myriad rays.

전물 轉物 To transform things, especially by supernatural power.

전미개오 轉迷開悟 To reject the illusion of the transmigrational worlds and enter into nirvāṇa-enlightenment.

전범륜 轉梵輪 To turn the noble or pure wheel, idem 전법 轉法.

전법 傳法 Formal, public conferment of a master's teaching to someone who has already received in-ga ; official recognition of the student's ability to teach others.

전법륜 轉法輪 To turn the dharma-cakra, or wheel of dharma, to preach, to teach, to explain the religion of Buddha. 전법륜일 轉法輪日 The day when the Buddha first preached, in the Deer Park, i.e. the eighth day of the eighth month. 전법륜상 轉法輪相 The sign of preaching, one of the eight signs that Śākyamuni was a Buddha. 전법륜보살 轉法輪菩薩 The preaching Bodhisattva, especially the Pāramitā (i.e. Prajñā) Bodhisattva.

전변 轉變 Pariṇāma ; change, transform, evolve. 전변무상 轉變無常 Change and impermanence.

전세 轉世 To return to this life.

전식 轉識 (1) Pravṛtti-vijñāna ; knowledge or mind being stirred, the external world enters into consciousness, the second of the five processes of mental evolution in the 기신론 起信論. (2) The seven stages of knowledge (vijñāna), other than the ālaya-vijñāna, of the 유식론 唯識論. (3) Knowledge which transmutes the common knowledge of this transmigration-world into Buddha-knowledge.

전회 轉廻 To return, revolve, be reborn ; idem 윤회 輪廻.

절 (C. 拜) Bow ; prostration. 큰절 means prostration, touching one's forehead to the floor ; 반배 半拜 means bow, bending the body at the waist.

절 (C. 寺) Buddhist temple.

절 截 To cut off, intercept. 절우주 截雨呪 Incantations for the cessation of rain.

절 絶 To cut off, sunder, terminate, end ; decidedly, superlatively. 절대 絶大 Superlatively great. 절학 絶學 To cease study, beyond the need of study, a hint being enough. 절대 絶對 Beyond compare, supreme. 절대 絶待 Final, supreme, special. 절대진여 絶待眞如 Bhūtatathatā as absolute, apart from all phenomena and limiting terms ; or as being, in contrast to the bhūtatathatā as becoming. 절식 絶食 To cut off food, cease to eat.

절 切 To cut, carve ; a whole ; urgent ; the 반절 反切 system of spelling, i.e. the combination of the initial sound of one Chinese word with the final sound of another to indicate the sound of a third, a system introduced by translators of Buddhist works ; v. 반 反. 절승 切勝 A title of Aśvaghoṣa.

절 折 To snap, break ; decide ; compound ; fold. 절복섭수 折伏攝受 To subdue the evil and receive the good ; cf. 억 抑. 절리달라 折利怛羅 or 절리단라 折利但羅 Caritra, 발행성 發行城 "A port on the south-east frontier of Uḍa (Orissa) whence a considerable trade was carried on with Ceylon." [Eitel]. 절구가 折句迦 ; 작구가 斫句迦 or 소구가 所句迦 Cakoka, i.e. Karghalik in Turkestan. 절석 折石 A broken stone, i.e. irreparable. 절로 折蘆 The snapped-off reed on which Bodhidharma is said to have crossed the Yangtsze from Nanking.

점 漸 Gradual, by degrees, to flow little by little, 점차 漸次 step by step, by degrees, gradually. 점교 漸教 The gradual method of teaching by beginning with the Hīnayāna and proceeding to the Mahāyāna, in contrast with 돈교 頓教 q.v. the immediate teaching of the Mahāyāna doctrine, or of any truth directly ; e.g. the Hua-yen school considers the Hua-yen sūtra as the immediate or direct teaching, and the Lotus sūtra as both gradual and direct ; T'ien-t'ai considers the Lotus direct and complete ; but there are other definitions. 점단 漸斷 Gradually to cut off, as contrasted with 돈단 頓斷 sudden or instantaneous excision. 점열 漸熱 Increasing heat ; grīṣma, the two months from middle of May to middle of July.

점 苫 Thatch ; mat ; mourning. 점바라 苫婆羅 ; 담보라 擔步羅 Jambhala, Jambhīra, the citron tree, *Blyxa octandra*. 점말라 苫末羅 Cāmara, name of several plants, āmra, betel-nut, etc. ; the resort of "golden-winged birds."

점 占 To divine, prognosticate. 점찰 占察 A method of divination in the esoteric school by means of the Sanskrit letter "a". 점수나 占戍拏 "Tchañśuna" is the highly doubtful form given by Eitel, who describes it as the ancient capital of Vṛji, an "ancient kingdom N. of the Ganges, S.E. of Nepal".

점 點 To dot, touch, punctuate, light, nod ; the stroke of a clock ; to check off ; a speck, dot, drop, etc. 점화 點化 Touched into activity, or conversion. 점심 點心 A snack, slight repast, not a proper meal. 점등 點燈 To light a lamp. 점석 點石 The stones nodded in approval (when 도생 道生 Tao-shêng read the Nirvāṇa sūtra).

접 接 To receive, take ; join on ; graft. 접인 接引 To receive and lead, to welcome. 접대 接待 To receive and treat, or wait upon. 접생 接生 To receive the living ; also to receive at birth as a midwife does. 접족작례 接足作禮 To embrace the (Buddha's) feet in reverence or pleading, or to extend the arms in that posture.

정 鉦 A small gong struck during the worship, or service. 정고 鉦鼓 Cymbals, or small gongs and drums.

정 井 A well. 정중로월 井中撈月 Like ladling the moon out of the well ; the parable of the monkeys who saw the moon fallen into a well, and fearing there would be no more moonlight, sought to save it ; the monkey-king hung on to a branch, one hung on to his tail and so on, but the branch broke and all were drowned. 정하 井河 "Like the well and the river", indicating the impermanence of life. The "well" refers to the legend of the man who running away from a mad elephant fell into a well ; the "river" to a great tree growing on the river bank yet blown over by the wind. 정화 井華 The flower of the water, i.e. that drawn from the well in the last watch of the night, at which time the water is supposed not to produce animal life.

정 靜 Cessation of strife, peace, calm, quietness, stillness. 정주 靜主 The elder presiding over a company of monks in meditation. 정력 靜力 The power of abstract meditation. 정실 靜室 Abode of peace, the quiet heart. 정사 靜思 Calm thought ; meditation, a meditator, i.e. a monk. 정식 靜息 A tr. of Yama, he who restrains, curbs, controls, keeps in check. 정혜 靜慧 Calm wisdom, insight into the void, or immaterial, removed from the transient. 정려 靜慮 A tr. of dhyāna, calm thought, unperturbed abstraction. 정지 靜智 Calm wisdom, the wisdom derived from quietness, or mystic trance.

정 貞 Chaste, lucky. 정실 貞實 Pure and true.

정 精 Cleaned rice, freed from the husk, pure ; essential, essence, germinating principle, spirit ; fine, best, finest. 정실 精室 ; 정려 精廬 ; 정사 精舍 A place for pure, or spiritual, cultivation, a pure abode, the abode of the celibate, a monastery or nunnery. 정기 精氣 Vitality, virility. 정진 精眞 Pure truth, apprehension of ultimate reality. 정신 精神 Vitality ; also the pure and spiritual, the subtle, or recondite. 정진 精進 Vīrya, one of the seven Bodhyaṅga ; "vigour," "valour, fortitude," "virility" [M. W.] ; "well-doing" [Keith]. The Chinese interpretation may be defined as pure or unadulterated progress, i.e. 근 勤 zeal, zealous, courageously progressing in the good and eliminating the evil. 정진력 精進力 Vīryabala. The power of unfailing progress, one of the five moral powers. 정진궁지혜전 精進弓智慧箭 Zeal as the bow, wisdom the arrow. 정진바라밀 精進波羅蜜 Zeal, energy, or progress as the fourth of the six pāramitās. 정령붕 精靈棚 The booth, or canopy, where the feast of all souls is provided.

정 庭 Court, hall, family ; forehead. 정의 庭儀 The ceremony on entering the hall for service.

정 政 Government, administration, policy, politics. 정교 政教 Political teaching, governmental education ; politics and the church (or religion).

정 正 Right, correct ; just, exact ; chief, principal ; the first month.

정 情 The feelings, passions, desires, affections, sensations ; sentient ; affinities ; affairs, facts. Particular affections, duties, or affairs. 정진 情塵 The six guṇas or objects of sensation of the six organs of sense ; sensation and its data ; sensation-data ; passion-defilement. 정유 情有 The realm of feeling, i.e. any world of sentience or feeling, especially this world as empirically considered ; 유정 有情 is to have consciousness, the conscious, or sentient. 정유리무 情有理無 Empirically or sentiently existing, in essence or reality non-existent. 정욕 情欲 The passions, desires. 정원 情猿 The passions like an ape, never still. 정견 情見 The perverted views produced by passion or affection.

정 定 To fix, settle. Samādhi. "Composing the mind" ; "intent contemplation" ; "perfect absorption of thought into the one object of meditation." [M. W.] Abstract meditation, the mind fixed in one direction, or field. (1) 산정 散定 scattered or general meditation (in the world of desire). (2) 선정 禪定 abstract meditation (in the realms of form and beyond form). It is also one of the five attributes of the Dharmakāya 법신 法身, i.e. an internal state of imperturbability or tranquillity, exempt from all external sensations, 초수음 超受陰 ; cf. 삼마제 三摩提.

정 停 To stop, rest, settle, delay. 정심 停心 To fix or settle the mind in meditation, cf. 오정심관 五停心觀.

정 頂 Top of the head, crown, summit, apex, zenith ; highest ; to rise ; oppose ; an official's "button." 정광 頂光 The halo round the head of an image. 정소 頂巢 Contemplation so profound that a bird may build its nest on the individual's head. 정주 頂珠 The gem in the head-dress, or coiffure ; the protuberance on the Buddha's brow. 정생왕 頂生王 Mūrdhaja-rāja, the king born from the crown of the head, name of the first cakravartī ancestors of the Śākya clan ; the name is also applied to a former incarnation of Śākyamuni. 정상 頂相 The protuberance on the Buddha's brow, one of the thirty-two marks of a Buddha ; also an image, or portrait of the upper half of the body. 정석 頂石 Like a heavy stone on the head, to be got rid of with speed, e.g. transmigration. 정례 頂禮 To prostrate oneself with the head at the feet of the one reverenced. 정륜 頂輪 A wheel or disc at the top, or on the head, idem 금륜불정 金輪佛頂 q.v. 정문안 頂門眼 The middle upstanding eye in Maheśvara's forehead.

정 淨 Vimala. Clean, pure ; to cleanse, purify ; chastity. In Buddhism it also has reference to the place of cleansing, the latrine, etc. Also 정 淨.

정가 淨家 The Pure-land sect.

정각 淨覺 Pure enlightenment.

정각 正覺 Sambodhi, the wisdom or omniscience of a Buddha.

정각지 定覺支 The enlightenment of meditation, the sixth of the Sapta bodhyaṅga 칠보리분 七菩提分 q.v.

정거천 淨居天 The five heavens of purity, in the fourth dhyāna heaven, where the saints dwell who will not return to another rebirth. Also Śuddhāvāsadeva, "a deva who served as guardian angel to Śākyamuni and brought about his conversion." [Eitel].

정견 正見 Samyagdṛṣṭi, right views, understanding the four noble truths ; the first of the 팔정도 八正道 ; "knowledge of the four noble truths." [Keith].

정결오욕 淨潔五欲 The five pure desires, or senses, i.e. of the higher worlds in contrast with the coarse senses of the lower worlds.

정계 淨戒 The pure commandments, or to keep them in purity.

정관 淨觀 Pure contemplation, such as the sixteen mentioned in the 무량수경 無量壽經.

정광 定光 (1) Dīpaṃkara 제원갈 提洹羯 ; 연등불 然燈佛, to whom Śākyamuni offered five lotuses when the latter was 유동 儒童 Ju-t'ung Bodhisattva, and was thereupon designated as a coming Buddha. He is called the twenty-fourth predecessor of Śākyamuni. He appears whenever a Buddha preaches the Lotus sūtra. (2) Crystal, or some other bright stone.

정국 淨國 The pure land, i.e. Buddha-land.

정근 定根 Samādhīndriya. Meditation as the root of all virtue, being the fourth of the five indriya 오근 五根.

정기 正忌 The day of decease.

정념 正念 Samyaksmṛti, right remembrance, the seventh of the 팔정도 八正道 ; "right mindfulness, the looking on the body and the spirit in such a way as to remain ardent, self-possessed and mindful, having overcome both hankering and dejection." [Keith].

정당임마시 正當恁麽時 Just at such and such an hour.

정도 淨道 The pure enlightenment of Buddha.

정두 淨頭 The monk who controls the latrines.

정등각 正等覺 Samyagbuddhi, or Samyagbodhi ; the perfect universal wisdom of a Buddha.

정등정각 正等正覺 idem 정변지 正偏智.

정량부 正量部 Saṁmatīya, Saṁmitīya (삼)미지 (三)彌底 ; the school of correct measures, or correct evaluation. Three hundred years after the Nirvāṇa it is said that from the Vātsīputrīyāḥ school four divisions were formed, of which this was the third.

정려 定侶 Fellow-meditators ; fellow-monks.

정려 淨呂 The company of pure ones, i.e. monks or nuns.

정력 定力 Samādhibala. The power of abstract or ecstatic meditation, ability to overcome all disturbing thoughts, the fourth of the five bala 오력 五力 ; described also as 섭심 攝心 powers of mind-control.

정명 定命 Determined period of life ; fate.

정명 淨命 Pure livelihood, 정명 正命, i.e. that of the monk. Also the life of a pure or unperturbed mind.

정명 正命 Samyagājīva, the fifth of the 팔정도 八正道, right livelihood, right life ; "abstaining from any of the forbidden modes of living."

정문 淨門 Gate of purity to nirvāṇa, one of the 육묘 六妙.

정바라밀 淨波羅密 The fourth pāramitā of the Nirvāṇa sūtra, 상락아정 常樂我淨 v. 상 常.

정반왕 淨飯王 Pure rice king, Śuddhodana, the father of Śākyamuni ; v. 수 首.

정발 淨髮 To cleanse the hair, i.e. shave the head as do the monks.

정방 淨邦 idem 정토 淨土.

정방 淨方 The Pure Land of Amitābha, v. 정토 淨土.

정범왕 淨梵王 Brahmā, as the pure divine ruler. Also 정반왕 淨飯王 q.v.

정법 正法 The correct doctrine of the Buddha, whose period was to last 500, some say 1,000 years, be followed by the 상법시 像法時 semblance period of 1,000 years, and then by the 말법시 末法時 period of decay and termination, lasting 10,000 years. The 정법시 正法時 is also known as 정법수 正法壽. 정법의 正法依 He on whom the Truth depends, a term for a Buddha. 정법명여래 正法明如來 The Tathāgata who clearly understands the true law, i.e. Kuan-yin, who attained Buddhahood in the past. 정법거 正法炬 The torch of truth, i.e. Buddhism. 정법화경 正法華經 The earliest translation of the Lotus sūtra in 10 chüan by Dharmarakṣa, A.D. 286, still in existence.

정법계 淨法界 The realm of pure dharma, the unsullied realm, i.e. the bhūtatathatā.

정변지 正偏智 Samyaksambuddha 삼먁삼불타 三藐三佛陀 ; omniscience, completely enlightened, the universal knowledge of a Buddha, hence he is the 정변해 正偏海 ocean of omniscience. Also 정변각 正偏覺 ; 정등정각 正等正覺.

정보 正報 The direct retribution of the individual's previous existence, such as being born as a man, etc. Also 정과 正果.

정보리심 淨菩提心 Pure bodhi mind, or mind of pure enlightenment, the first stage of the practitioner in the esoteric sect.

정불 淨佛 Pure Buddha, perfect Buddhahood, of the dharmakāya nature.

정비 定妃 The female figures representing meditation in the maṇḍalas ; male is wisdom, female is meditation.

정사 正士 Correct scholar, bodhisattva.

정사유 正思惟 Samyaksaṁkalpa, right thought and intent, the second of the 팔정도 八正道 ; "right aspiration towards renunciation, benevolence and kindness." [Keith].

정산 定散 A settled, or a wandering mind ; the mind organized by meditation, or disorganized by distraction. The first is characteristic of the saint and sage, the second of the common untutored man. The fixed heart may or may not belong to the realm of transmigration ; the distracted heart has the distinctions of good, bad, or indifferent. 정산이선 定散二善 Both a definite subject for meditation and an undefined field are considered as valuable.

정상 定相 Fixity, determined, determination, settled, unchanging, nirvāṇa. The appearance of meditation.

정상말 正像末 The three periods of correct law, semblance law, and decadence, or finality ; cf. 정법 正法.

정성 定性 Fixed nature ; settled mind. A classification of "five kinds of nature" 오종성 五種性 is made by the 법상종 法相宗, the first two being the 정성이승 定性二乘, i.e. śrāvakas and pratyeka-buddhas, whose mind is fixed on arhatship, and not on Buddhahood. The 정성희락지 定性喜樂地 is the second dhyāna heaven of form, in which the occupants abide in surpassing meditation or trance, which produces mental joy.

정성 淨聖 Pure saint, the superior class of saints.

정수 定水 Calm waters ; quieting the waters of the heart (and so beholding the Buddha, as the moon is reflected in still water).

정시 淨施 Pure charity, which does not seek fame or blessing in this world, but only desires to sow nirvāṇa-seed.

정신 淨信 Pure faith.

정신 定身 The Dharmakāya of meditation, one of the 오분법신 五分法身 five forms of the Buddha-dharmakāya.

정심 定心 ; 정의 定意 A mind fixed in meditation. 정심삼매 定心三昧 A fixed mind samādhi, i.e. fixed on the Pure Land and its glories.

정심 淨心 The pure heart or mind, which is the original Buddha-nature in every man. 정심주 淨心住 The pure heart stage, the third of the six resting-places of a bodhisattva, in which all illusory views are abandoned.

정안 淨眼 The clear or pure eyes that behold, with enlightened vision, things not only as they seem but in their reality. Also Vimalanetra, second son of Śubhavyūha in the Lotus Sūtra.

정어 淨語 Pure words ; words that express reality.

정어 正語 Samyagvāk, right speech ; the third of the 팔정도 八正道 ; "abstaining from lying, slander, abuse, and idle talk." Keith.

정업 定業 Fixed karma, rebirth determined by the good or bad actions of the past. Also, the work of meditation with its result. 정업역능전 定業亦能轉 Even the determined fate can be changed (by the power of Buddhas and bodhisattvas).

정업 淨業 Good karma ; also the deeds which lead to birth in the Pure Land.

정업 正業 Samyakkarmānta, right action, purity of body, avoiding all wrong, the fourth of the 팔정도 八正道 ; "right action, abstaining from taking life, or what is not given, or from carnal indulgence." [Keith].

정역 淨域 The pure Lands of all Buddhas.

정예 淨裔 Of pure descent, or line ; a young Brahman ; an ascetic in general.

정옥 淨屋 House of chastity, i.e. a monastery or convent.

정원각심 淨圓覺心 Pure and perfect enlightened mind : the complete enlightenment of the Buddha.

정유리세계 淨瑠璃世界 The pure crystal realm in the eastern region, the paradise of Yao Shih 약사 藥師 Buddha ; it is the Bhaiṣajyaguruvaiḍūrya-prabhāsa.

정육 淨肉 Pure flesh, the kind which may be eaten by a monk without sin, three, five, and nine classes being given.

정의경 正依經 The sūtras on which any sect specially relies.

정인 定忍 Patience and perseverance in meditation.

정인 正因 The true or direct cause, as compared with 연인 緣因 a contributory cause.

정일 正日 Correct day, the day of a funeral.

정장 淨藏 Vimalagarbha, eldest son of Śubhavyūha in the Lotus Sūtra.

정정 正定 Samyaksamādhi, right abstraction or concentration, so that the mind becomes vacant and receptive, the eighth of the 팔정도 八正道 ; "right concentration, in the shape of the Four Meditations." Keith. 정정업 正定業 concentration upon the eighteenth vow of Amitābha and the Western Paradise, in repeating the name of Amitābha.

정정진 正精進 Samyagvyāyāma, right effort, zeal, or progress, unintermitting perseverance, the sixth of the 팔정도 八正道 ; "right effort, to suppress the rising of evil states, to eradicate those which have arisen, to stimulate good states, and to perfect those which have come into being." [Keith].

정제근 淨諸根 Undefiled senses ; i.e. undefiled eye, ear, mouth, nose, body.

정종 淨宗 idem 정토종 淨土宗.

정주 淨住 A pure rest, or abode of purity, a term for a Buddhist monastery.

정주 淨主 The donor of chastity, i.e. of an abode for monks or nuns.

정중 正中 Exactly middle ; midday.

정중 淨衆 Pure assembly, the company of the chaste, the body of monks.

정지 定智 Meditation and wisdom.

정지 淨地 Pure locality, i.e. where a chaste monk dwells.

정지 正智 Samyagjñāna ; correct knowledge ; 성지 聖智 sage-like, or saint-like knowledge.

정지부 正地部 v. 마 磨 Mahīśāsaka.

정직 正直 Correct and straight ; it is also referred to the One Vehicle teaching of T'ien-t'ai. 정직사방편 正直捨方便 The straight way which has cast aside expediency.

정진각 正盡覺 idem 정등각 正等覺.

정찰 淨刹 The pure kṣetra, i.e. Buddha-land.

정천 淨天 Pure heaven, or pure devas ; śrota-āpannas to pratyeka-buddhas are so called. 정천안 淨天眼 The pure deva eye, which can see all things small and great, near and far, and the forms of all beings before their transmigration.

정취 定聚 One of the 삼취 三聚 q.v.

정토 淨土 Sukhāvatī. The Pure Land, or Paradise of the West, presided over by Amitābha. Other Buddhas have their Pure Lands ; seventeen other kinds of pure land are also described, all of them of moral or spiritual conditions of development, e.g. the pure land of patience, zeal, wisdom, etc. 정토종 淨土宗 The Pure-land sect, whose chief tenet is salvation by faith in Amitābha ; it is the popular cult in China, also in Japan, where it is the Jōdō sect ; it is also called 연(화)종 蓮(花)宗 the Lotus sect. Established by Hui-yüan 혜원 慧遠 of the Chin dynasty (317-419), it claims P'u-hsien 보현 普賢 Samantabhadra as founder. Its seven chief textbooks are 무량청정평등각경 無量清淨平等覺經 ; 대아미타경 大阿彌陀經 ; 무량수경 無量壽經 ; 관무량수경 觀無量壽經 ; 아미타경 阿彌陀經 ; 칭찬정토불섭수경 稱讚淨土拂攝受經 ; and 고음성삼다라니경 鼓音聲三陀羅尼經. The 정토진종 淨土眞宗 is the Jōdō Shin-shu, or Shin sect of Japan.

정판 定判 To determine, adjudge, settle.

정학 定學 Learning through meditation, one of the three forms of learning 삼학 三學.

정행 正行 Right deeds, or action, opposite of 사행 邪行. The 정행경 正行經 is an abbreviation of 불설아함정행경 佛說阿含正行經.

정행자 淨行者 One who observes ascetic practices ; one of pure or celibate conduct ; a Brahman ; also 범지 梵志.

정혜 定慧 Meditation and wisdom, two of the six pāramitās ; likened to the two hands, the left meditation, the right wisdom.

정화중 淨華衆 The pure flower multitude, i.e. those who are born into the Pure Land by means of a lotus flower.

제 際 A border, region, juncture, limit ; between ; to join on ; then, since, now. 생사지제 生死之際 Between life and death. 무제 無際 Unlimited. 제사타 際史吒 Jyaiṣṭha, the month in May-June.

제 梯 A ladder, stairs. 제등 梯隥 Ladder rungs, or steps, used for the 점교 漸敎 school of gradual revelation in contrast with the 돈교 頓敎 full and immediate revelation.

제 齊 Even, level, equal, uniform ; complete, perfect ; equalize ; tranquillize ; alike ; all ; at the same time, altogether. 제업신 齊業身 The final body which brings to an end all former karma. 제설제문 齊說齊聞 Speaking and hearing together, or at the same time.

제 除 Get rid of. 제일체악 除一切惡 To get rid of all evil. 제산 除散 Get rid of and scatter away. 제단 除斷 Get rid of completely, cut off. 제재 除災 Get rid of calamity. 제의 除疑 Eliminate doubt. 제개장 除蓋障 To dispose of hindrances. 제각지 除覺支 To get rid of mental effort and produce mental and physical buoyancy. 제근 除饉 He (or she) who puts away want (by receiving alms), an intp. of bhikṣu and bhikṣuṇī.

제 題 Heading, theme, thesis, subject, text ; to state, mention, refer to. 제목 題目 A heading, theme, etc. 입제 立題 To set a subject, state a proposition.

제 第 Number, degree, sign of the ordinals ; only. 제일 第一 The first, chief, prime, supreme. 제일승 第一乘 The supreme vehicle, Mahāyāna. 제일구 第一句 The first and supreme letter, *a*, the alpha of all wisdom. 제일적멸 第一寂滅 The supreme reality, nirvāṇa. 제일의 第一義 The supreme, or fundamental meaning, the supreme reality, i.e. enlightenment. 제일의실단 第一義悉檀 The highest Siddhānta, or Truth, the highest universal gift of Buddha, his teaching which awakens the highest capacity in all beings to attain salvation. 제일의지 第一義智 The highest knowledge, or wisdom. 제일의락 第一義樂 The highest bliss, i.e. nirvāṇa. 제일의공 第一義空 The highest Void, or reality, the Mahāyāna nirvāṇa, though it is also applied to Hīnayāna nirvāṇa. 제일의관 第一義觀 The highest meditation of T'ien-t'ai, that on 중 中 the Mean. 제일의제 第一義諦 The supreme truth, or reality in contrast with the seeming ; also called Veritable truth, sage-truth, surpassing truth, nirvāṇa, bhūtatathatā, madhya, śūnyatā, etc. 제삼선 第三禪 The third dhyāna, a degree of contemplation in which ecstasy gives way to serenity ; also a state, or heaven, corresponding to this degree of contemplation, including the third three of the rūpa heavens. 제삼능변 第三能變 The third power of change, i.e. the six senses, or vijñānas, 능변 能變 means 식 識. 제칠선 第七仙 The seventh "immortal, the last of the seven Buddhas, Śākyamuni. 제칠정 第七情 A seventh sense ; non-existent, like a 십삼입 十三入 thirteenth base of perception, or a 십구계 十九界 19th dhātu. 제이월 第二月 A double or second moon, which is an optical illusion, unreal. 제이선 第二禪 The second dhyāna, a degree of contemplation where reasoning gives way to intuition. The second three rūpa heavens. 제이능변 第二能變 The second power of change, the kliṣṭamano-vijñāna, disturbed-mind, consciousness, or self-consciousness which gives form to the universe. The first power of change is the Ālaya-vijñāna. 제오대 第五大 A fifth element, the non-existent. 제육음 第六陰 A sixth skandha : as there are only five skandhas it means the non-existent. 제팔식 第八識 The eighth, or ālaya-vijñāna, mind-essence, the root and essence of all things. 제십팔원 第十八願 The eighteenth of Amitābha's forty-eight vows, the one vowing salvation to all believers. 제사선 第四禪 The fourth dhyāna, a degree of contemplation when the mind becomes indifferent to pleasure and pain ; also the last eight rūpa heavens. 제야나 第耶那 v. 선 禪 Dhyāna. 제려다할라살타라 第黎多曷羅殺吒羅 Dhṛtarāṣṭra, one of the four mahārājas, the white guardian of the east, one of the lokapālas, a king of gandharvas and piśācas ; cf. 제 提.

제 醍 Oil of butter ; 제호 醍醐 a rich liquor skimmed from boiled butter ; clarified butter ; ghee ; used for the perfect Buddha-truth as found, according to T'ien-t'ai, in the Nirvāṇa and Lotus sūtras. 제비사 醍鞞沙 Dveṣa, hatred, dislike.

제 制 Restrain, govern ; regulations ; mourning. 제다 制多 ; 제저 制底 or 질저 質底 ; 제체 制體 Caitya, a tumulus, mausoleum, monastery, temple, spire, flagstaff on a pagoda, sacred place or thing, idem 지제 支提 or 支帝, cf. 찰 刹. 제다산부 制多山部 Jetavanīyāḥ, a Hīnayāna sect. 제저반제 制底畔睇 or 제저반탄나 制底畔彈那 Caitya-vandana, to pay reverence to, or worship a stūpa, image, etc. 제달라 制怛羅 Caitra, the spring month in which the full moon is in this constellation, i.e. Virgo or 각 角 ; M. W. gives it as March-April, in China it is the first month of spring from the 16th of the first moon to the 15th of the second. Also idem 제다 制多 Caitya. 제계 制戒, 제교 制教 The restraints, or rules, i.e. of the Vinaya. 제문 制門 The way or method of discipline, contrasted with the 화문 化門, i.e. of teaching, both methods used by the Buddha, hence called 화제이문 化制二門.

제 帝 Ruler, sovereign ; translit. *t.* 제리야구유니가 帝利耶瞿榆泥伽 ; 방행 傍行 Tiryagyoni-gati ; the animal path of reincarnation. 제실라차 帝失羅叉 Tiṣya-rakṣitā ; "a concubine of Aśoka, the rejected lover and enemy of Kuṇāla" [Eitel]. M. W. says Aśoka's second wife. 제거 帝居 The abode of Indra. 제심 帝心 Title given to 두순 杜順 Tu Shun, founder of the Hua-yen school, by T'ang T'ai Tsung. 제사 帝沙 Tiṣya ; an ancient Buddha ; also the father of Śāriputra. 제상 帝相 Indra-dhvaja, a Buddha "said to have been a contemporary of Śākyamuni, living south-west of our universe, an incarnation of the seventh son of Mahābhijñā-jñānābhibhu." [Eitel]. 제석 帝釋 Sovereign Śakra ; Indra ; 능천제 能天帝 mighty lord of devas ; Lord of the Trayastriṁśas, i.e. the thirty-three heavens 삼십삼천 三十三天 q.v. ; he is also styled 석가제환인다라 釋迦提桓因陀羅 or 석가제바인달라 釋迦提婆因達羅 ; 석제환인 釋帝桓因 Śakro-devānām-indra. 제(석)궁 帝(釋)弓 ; 천궁 天弓 Indradhanus, the rainbow. 제석암 帝釋巖 ; 제석굴 帝釋窟 Indraśailaguhā, Indra's cave at Nālandā in Magadha, where Indra is supposed to have sought relief for his doubts from the Buddha. 제석병 帝釋瓶 The vase of Indra, from which came all things he needed ; called also 덕상병 德祥瓶 or 현상병 賢祥瓶 or 길상병 吉祥瓶 vase of virtue, or of worth, or of good fortune. 제(석)망 帝(釋)網 Indra-jāla. The net of Indra, hanging in Indra's 궁 宮 hall, out of which all things can be produced ; also the name of an incarnation considered all-powerful. 제예로가야폐사야 帝隸路迦也吠闍耶 Trailokya-vijaya, victor or lord over the 삼세 三世 three realms. 제청 帝青 Indranīla, an emerald.

제 祭 Sacrifice, sacrificial. 제문 祭文 ; 제문 齊文. The prayer or statement read and burnt at a funeral. 제사론 祭祠論 The Yajurveda, v. 위 韋.

제 諸 The diverse kinds, many, the many, all, every ; on, at, in regard to ; a final interrogative particle, also a rhythmic ending ; used for sarva.

제 濟 To cross a stream ; aid ; cause, bring about. 제가 濟家 ; 제하 濟下 The school, or disciples of 임제 臨濟 Lin-chi. 제도 濟度 To ferry the living across the sea of reincarnation to the shore of nirvāṇa.

제 提 To raise, mention, bring forward, summon, lead.

제 齋 To reverence ; abstinence ; to purify as by fasting, or abstaining, e.g. from flesh food ; religious or abstinential duties, or times ; upavasatha (uposatha), a fast ; the ritual period for food, i.e. before noon ; a room for meditation, a study, a building, etc., devoted to abstinence, chastity, or the Buddhist religion ; mourning (for parents). 제칠 齋七 The seven periods of masses for the dead, during the seven sevens or forty-nine days after death. 제주 齋主 The donor of monastic food. 제승 齋僧 To provide a meal for monks. 제당 齋堂 Abstinence hall, i.e. monastic dining-hall. 제장 齋場 Similarly a dining-place. 제석 齋席 A table of food for monks, or nuns. 제계 齋戒 Purification, or abstinential rules, e.g. the eight prohibitions. 제지 齋持 To observe the law of abstinence, i.e. food at the regulation times. 제일 齋日 Days of offerings to the dead, ceremonial days. 제시 齋時 The regulation hours for monastic meals, especially the midday meal, after which no food should eaten. 제월 齋月 The three special months of abstinence and care, the first, fifth, and ninth months. 제회 齋會 An assembly of monks for chanting, with food provided. 제법 齋法 The rule of not eating after noon ; also the discipline of the order, or the establishment. 제연 齋筵 Offerings of food to the Triratna. 제죽 齋粥 The midday and morning meals, breakfast of rice or millet congee, dinner of vegetarian foods. 제파 齋罷 ; 제퇴 齋退 Afternoon, i.e. after the midday meal. 제종 齋鐘 ; 제고 齋鼓 The bell, or drum, calling to the midday meal. 제식 齋食 The midday meal ; not eating after noon ; abstinential food, i.e. vegetarian food, excluding vegetables of strong odour, as garlic, or onions.

ㄱ ㄴ ㄷ ㄹ ㅁ ㅂ ㅅ ㅇ ㅈ ㅊ ㅋ ㅌ ㅍ ㅎ 찾아보기

제 啼 To wail ; crow. 제곡 啼哭 To weep and wail ; to weep. 제곡불 啼哭佛 The ever-wailing Buddha, the final Buddha of the present kalpa ; cf. 살타 薩陀.

제 弟 Younger brother. 제자 弟子 Disciple, disciples.

제 諦 To judge, examine into, investigate, used in Buddhism for satya, a truth, a dogma, an axiom ; applied to the Āryasatyāni, the four dogmas, or noble truths, of 고 苦, 집 集, 멸 滅, and 도 道 suffering, (the cause of its) assembly, (the possibility of its cure, or) extinction, and the way (to extinction), i.e. the eightfold noble path, v. 사제 四諦 and 팔성도 八聖道. There are other categories of 제 諦, e.g. (2) 진 眞 and 속 俗 Reality in contrast with ordinary ideas of things ; (3) 공 空, 가 假 and 중 中 q.v. ; (6) by the 승론종 勝論宗 ; and (8) by the 법상종 法相宗. 제바달도 諦婆達兜 v. 제 提 Devadatta. 체수라시 諦殊羅施 Tejorāśi, the flame-god, one of the five 불정 佛頂 crowned Buddhas.

제견 諸見 All the diverse views ; all heterodox opinions, sixty-two in number.

제관 諦觀 Je-gwan(?-970). A monk of the Goryeo dynasty in Korea. He wrote 천태사교의 天台四教儀 which was annotated by several persons.

제근 諸根 All roots, powers, or organs, e.g. (1) faith, energy, memory, meditation, wisdom ; (2) eyes, ears, nose, tongue, and body.

제나바 提那婆 "Dinabha," or Dineśvara, the sun-god, worshipped by "heretics in Persia." [Eitel].

제다라타 提多羅吒 Dhṛtarāṣṭra, one of the four mahārājas, the yellow guardian eastward of Sumeru ; also 두뢰타 頭賴吒 ; 제려다갈라살타라 第黎多曷羅殺吒羅. 제다가 提多迦 Dhṛtaka ; the fifth patriarch "unknown to Southern Buddhists, born in Magadha, a disciple of Upagupta, he went to Madhyadeśa where he converted the heretic Micchaka and his 8,000 followers." [Eitel].

제라 提羅 One with abnormal sexual organs ; abbreviation of ṣaṇḍhila, cf. 반 般, 반 半.

제명 諸冥 All darkness, i.e. all ignorance.

제바 提波 Deva, v. 제바 提婆.

제바 提婆 Deva. Explained by 천 天 celestial ; also by 범천인 梵天人 inhabitants of the Brahmalokas, or by 천신 天神 celestial spirits. General designation of the gods of Brahmanism, and of all the inhabitants of Devalokas who are subject to metempsychosis. Also 제바 提波 ; 제화 提和 ; 제환 提桓. Used also for Devadatta, infra. 제바지제바 提婆地提婆 Devātideva, the god of gods, Viṣṇu ; also name of the Buddha before he left home. 제바종 提婆宗 The school of Nāgārjuna, so called after Āryadeva, *infra*. 제바서나 提婆犀那 Devasena, celestial host, name of an arhat. 제바보살 提婆菩薩 Devabodhisattva, or Āryadeva, or Kāṇadeva, the one-eyed deva, disciple of Nāgārjuna, and one of the "four sons" of Buddhism ; fourteenth patriarch ; a monk of Pāṭaliputra ; along with Nāgārjuna he is counted as founder of the 삼론종 三論宗 q.v. 제바설마 提婆設摩 Devakṣema, or Devaśarman, an arhat who wrote the 아비달마식신족론 阿毘達磨識身足論 tr. by Hsüan-tsang, A.D. 649, in which he denied the ego. 제바달다 提婆達多 ; 제바 提婆 ; 제바달 提婆達 ; 제바달도 提婆達兜 ; 달도 達兜 ; 지바달다 地婆達多 or 지바달도 地婆達兜 ; 체바달다 禘婆達多 ; 조바달다 調婆達多 Devadatta, son of Droṇodana rāja 곡반왕 斛飯王, and cousin of Śākyamuni, of whom he was enemy and rival cultivating magical powers. For his wicked designs on the Buddha he is said to have been swallowed up alive in hell ; nevertheless, he is predicted to become a Buddha as Devarāja ; he was worshipped as a Buddha by a sect "up to A.D. 400." [Eitel]. 제바마라파패 提婆魔囉播稗 Deva-māra-pāpīyān, Māra, the evil one, king of demons.

제법 諸法 Sarvadharma ; sarvabhāva ; all things ; every dharma, law, thing, method, etc. 제법오위

諸法五位 v. 오위 五位 The five orders of things. 제법적멸상 諸法寂滅相 All things in their nirvāṇa aspect, inscrutable. 제법실상 諸法實相 All things in their real aspect, i.e. the reality beneath all things, the Bhūtatathatā, or Dharmakāya, or Ultimate ; the term also connotes 공 空 śūnya, nirvāṇa, Amitābha, the eight negations of the Mādhyamika school, etc. 제법무아 諸法無我 Nothing has an ego, or is independent of the law of causation. 제법개공 諸法皆空 All things being produced by causes and accessory conditions have no reality, a doctrine differently interpreted in different schools of Buddhism.

제불가 諸佛家 The home of all Buddhas, i.e. the Pure Land. 제불모보살 諸佛母菩薩 v. 허공안 虛空眼 The mother of all Buddhas.

제비 提鞞 Devī. Female devas ; apsaras. 제비사 提鞞沙 Dveṣa, hatred, dislike, enmity, one of the 삼독 三毒 three poisons. 제비파 提鞞波 Dvīpa, an island, or continent ; four dvīpa compose a world, v. 사주 四洲.

제사 提舍 Intp. as preaching to and ferrying people over the stream of transmigration ; also 저사 底沙. 제사니 提舍尼 Prātideśanīya, v. 바 波. 제사나 提舍那 Deśanīya, confession.

제상 諸相 All the differentiating characteristics of things.

제색 諸色 All kinds of things.

제석법왕 諸釋法王 The dharma-king of all the Śākyas, a title of Buddha.

제선 諸仙 All the hermits, mystics, ṛṣi ; a term also applied to the Brahmans.

제수 諸數 All the variety of things, all phenomena.

제수 提樹 The bodhidruma tree, v. 보 菩.

제시 提撕 To arouse or stimulate a student.

제악무작 諸惡無作 "To do no evil, to do only good, to purify the will, is the doctrine of all Buddhas," i.e. "제악무작 諸惡無作, 제선봉행 諸善奉行, 자정기의 自淨其意, 시제불교 是諸佛教." These four sentences are said to include all the Buddha-teaching ; cf. 아함경 阿含經 1.

제연 諸緣 All the accessory conditions, or environmental causes which influence life.

제온 諸蘊 All the skandhas.

제운반야 提雲般若 Devaprajña, a Śramaṇa of Kustana (Khotan) who tr. six works A.D. 689-691 ; in [B.N.] eight works are ascribed to him. Also 제담타야나 提曇陀若那.

제원갈 提洹竭 Dīpaṃkara, cf. 연등 然燈.

제위파리 提謂波利 Trapuṣa and Bhallika, the two merchants who offered Śākyamuni barley and honey after his enlightenment.

제유 諸有 All that exists ; all beings.

제조 提調 To arrange, or manage, as deputy ; a deputy manager or director.

제존 諸尊 All the honoured ones.

제진 諸塵 All the atoms, or active principles of form, sound, smell, taste, touch.

제착 諸著 All attachments : the ordinary man is attached to life, the arhat to nirvāṇa, the bodhisattva to his saving work.

ㄱ ㄴ ㄷ ㄹ ㅁ ㅂ ㅅ ㅇ ㅈ ㅊ ㅋ ㅌ ㅍ ㅎ 찾아보기

제창 提唱 To mention, to deliver oral instruction, or the gist of a subject, as done in the Intuitional School. Also 제강 提綱 ; 제요 提要.

제천 諸天 All the devas.

제취 諸趣 All paths or destinies of sentient existence, i.e. devas, men, asuras, beings in purgatory, pretas, and animals.

제통 諸通 All spiritual or magical powers.

제하 提訶 Deha ; the body. Also v. 팔중주 八中洲.

제한불한 諸閑不閑 All in happy and unhappy conditions of metempsychosis.

제행 諸行 All phenomenal changes ; all conduct or action. 제행무상 諸行無常 Whatever is phenomenal is impermanent.

제화 提和 Deva. 제화갈라 提和竭羅 Dīpaṃkara, v. 연등 然燈.

제환 提桓 Deva, v. 제바 提婆.

조 鳥 A bird. 조적 鳥迹 The tracks left in the air by a flying bird, unreal. 조도 鳥道 The path of the birds, evasive, mysterious, difficult, as is the mystic life. Also a fabulous island only reached by flight. 조서승 鳥鼠僧 A "bat monk," i.e. one who breaks the commandments, with the elusiveness of a creature that is partly bird and partly mouse ; also who chatters without meaning like the twittering of birds or the squeaking of rats.

조 漕 A channel, canal ; transport, especially by the 조하 漕河 Grand Canal. 조구타 漕矩吒 Tsaukūṭa, an "ancient (Arakhotos) kingdom in N.W. India (near Ghuznee)." [Eitel].

조 竈 A kitchen-stove. 조신 竈神 The kitchen-stove god, or kitchen-god who at the end of each year is supposed to report above on the conduct of members of the family.

조 條 A length (of anything) ; a law, order. 조지 條支 The Tajiks anciently settled "near the Sirikol lake." [Eitel]. 조의 條衣 The monk's patch-robe.

조 槽 A trough, manger, channel. 조창 槽廠 A stable.

조 兆 An omen ; a million. 조재영겁 兆載永劫 The perpetual aeon of millions of years, the kalpa beyond numbers.

조 照 Bright, illustrious. 조현사 照玄寺 The bureau for nuns in the fifth century A.D.

조 爪 Claws, talons ; servants. 조(상)토 爪(上)土 The quantity of earth one can put on a toe-nail, i.e. in proportion to the whole earth in the world, such is the rareness of being reborn as a human being ; or, according to the Nirvāṇa Sūtra 33, of attaining nirvāṇa. 조탑 爪塔 A stūpa, or reliquary, for preserving and honouring the nails and hair of the Buddha, said to be the first Buddhist stūpa raised. 조정 爪淨 Nail-"cleaned", i.e. fruit, etc., that can be peeled with the nails, one of the five kinds of "clean" food. 조독 爪犢 The long-nailed ascetic Brahmacārī (or the) Vātsīputrīyāḥ ; it is said that his nails were a treatise and his hair a discourse 조장발론 爪章髮論.

조 曹 Company, class ; used as the plural of pronouns, etc. 조산 曹山 Ts'ao-shan in Kiangsu, where the Ts'ao-tung sect 조동종 曹洞宗, a branch of the Ch'an school, was founded by Tung-shan 동산 洞山 ; Ts'ao-shan was the name of the second patriarch of this sect. 조계 曹溪 Ts'ao-ch'i, a stream, south-east of Shao-chou, Kwangtung, which gave its name to 혜능 慧能 Hui-nêng.

조 造 Create, make, build. Hurried, careless. 조상 造像 To make an image ; the first one made of the Buddha is attributed to Udayana, king of Kauśāmbī, a contemporary of Śākyamuni, who is said to have made an image of him, after his death, in sandalwood, 5 feet high. 조화 造化 To create ; to make and transform. 조서천 造書天 The deva-creator of writing, Brahmā. 조화 造花 To make flowers, especially paper flowers.

조 早 Early ; morning. 조참 早參 The early morning assembly. 조제리 早帝梨 Name of a 귀 鬼 demon.

조 祖 Grandfather ; ancestor ; patriarch ; founder ; origin. See 이십팔조 二十八祖. 조사 祖師 A first teacher, or leader, founder of a school or sect ; it has particular reference to Bodhidharma.

조 助 Help, aid, assist ; auxiliary. 조음 助音 To assist in singing, or intoning. 조업 助業 Auxiliary karma, i.e. deeds or works, e.g. reciting the sūtras about the Pure Land, worship, praise, and offering, as additional to direct karma 정업 正業, i.e. faith in Amitābha, expressed by constant thought of him and calling on his name. 조도 助道 Auxiliary means, e.g. of meditation ; auxiliary discipline ; any aid to faith or virtue.

조 朝 Morning. Court, dynasty ; towards. 조석 朝夕 ; 조모 朝暮 Morning and evening. 조산 朝山 To worship (towards) the hills, pay court to a noted monastery, especially to pay court to the Dalai Lama. 조로 朝露 Morning dew, e.g. man's life as transient. 조선 朝鮮 Korea, Joseon(or Chosŏn).

조 臊 Rancid, rank ; shame ; translit. *su*, in 조타 臊陀 intp. as Śuka, parrot ; more correctly 숙가 叔迦.

조 潮 The tide ; tidal ; damp. 승조 乘潮 To take advantage of the tide.

조 稠 Thick-set as growing grain, dense. 조림 稠林 A dense forest, e.g. the passions, etc.

조 釣 To angle, fish. 조어 釣語 Angling words or questions, to fish out what a student knows.

조 澡 To bathe, wash, cleanse. 조병 澡瓶 ; 조관 澡罐 Kuṇḍikā, a water-pot. 조병천자 澡瓶天子 ; 작병천자 作瓶天子 Śuddhāvāsa-deva, who appeared to Śākyamuni when a prince, leading him to leave home.

조 肇 To begin, initiate. 조법사 肇法師 or 승조 僧肇 Sêng-chao, name of a monk in the fourth century whose treatise is called by this name.

조 調 To harmonize, blend ; regulate, control ; to change about, exchange ; a song, tune. 조복 調伏 To discipline, bring under control, e.g. bring into submission the body, mouth, and will ; control, or subjugate evil spirits, etc. ; it is one of the intp. of vinaya. 조(바)달(다) 調(婆)達(多) v. 제 提 Devadatta. 조도 調度 To arrange, calculate, manage, especially relating to provision for material needs. 조어 調御 To tame and control as a master does a wild elephant or horse, or as the Buddha brings the passions of men under control, hence he is termed 조어장부 調御丈夫 and 조어사 調御師 Puruṣa-damya-sārathi. 조의 調意 To control the will, to subdue its evil. 조직정 調直定 To harmonize the discords of the mind, to straighten its irregularities, and quiet its distractions, an explanation of samādhi given by T'ien-t'ai. 조송 調頌 Hymns and chants, an intp. of gāthā.

조 趙 To hasten to, return ; a long time. 조주 趙州 A prefecture in south-west Chihli, with a monastery, from which the T'ang monk Chao-chou got his pseudonym.

조 照 To shine, illumine ; to superintend ; a dispatch, pass ; as, according to. 조적 照寂 The shining mystic purity of Buddha, or the bhūtatathatā. 조불 照拂 The manager of affairs in a monastery. 조패 照牌 A notice board, especially allotting seats. 조람 照覽 To shine upon and behold ; to survey ; to enlighten. 조경 照鏡 To look at oneself in a mirror, forbidden to monks except for specified reasons.

조강 糟糠 Dregs and chaff, said of a proud monk, or of inferior teaching.

조계사 曹溪寺 Jo-gye-sa. A temple located in Susong-dong Jongno-gu Seoul in Korea. The headquarters of Korean Jogye Order.

조계산 曹溪山 1. Ts'ao-ch'i Mountain, located in Shao-chou, Kwangtung Province. The mountain is famous as the place where 혜능 慧能 Hui-nêng lived. 2. Mt. Jo-gye, the mountains around Songgwangsa in Jeollanam-do, Korea.

조선불교유신론 朝鮮佛教維新論 A masterpiece of 만해 萬海 Man-hae.

조실 祖室 The room where chief Zen Master resides.

조실스님 祖室- Official title of the chief Zen Master who resides in 조실 祖室.

족 足 Foot, leg ; enough, full. 족목 足目 "Eyes in his feet," name of Akṣapāda Gautama, to whom is ascribed the beginning of logic ; his work is seen "in five books of aphorisms on the Nyāya." [Keith].

존 尊 To honour. Ārya ; honoured, honourable. 존칙 尊勅 The honourable commands, Buddha's teaching. 존승 尊勝 Honoured and victorious, the honoured victorious one, one of the five 불정 佛頂, also known as 제장불정 除障佛頂, one of the divinities of the Yoga school. 존숙 尊宿 A monk honoured and advanced in years. 존자 尊者 Ārya, honourable one, a sage, a saint, an arhat. 존기 尊記 The prediction of Buddhahood to his disciples by the Honoured One ; the honourable prediction. 존귀 尊貴 ; 존중 尊重 Honoured, honourable ; to honour.

존 存 To keep, maintain, preserve ; 존생(명) 存生(命) ; 존명 存命 to preserve one's life, to preserve alive ; 존견 存見 to keep to (wrong) views.

졸 拙 Stupid, clumsy. 졸구라 拙具羅 or 구구라 窶具羅 ; 구구라 求求羅 Kukura, Kukkura ; a plant and its perfume. 졸도 拙度 A stupid, powerless salvation, that of Hīnayāna.

종 宗 Ancestors, ancestral ; clan ; class, category, kind ; school, sect ; siddhānta, summary, main doctrine, syllogism, proposition, conclusion, realization. Sects are of two kinds: (1) those founded on principles having historic continuity, as the twenty sects of the Hīnayāna, the thirteen sects of China, and the fourteen sects of Japan ; (2) those arising from an individual interpretation of the general teaching of Buddhism, as the sub-sects founded by Yung-ming 영명 永明 (d. 975), 법상종 法相宗, 법성종 法性宗, 파상종 破相宗, or those based on a peculiar interpretation of one of the recognized sects, as the Jōdō Shin-shu 정토진종 淨土眞宗 founded by Shinran-Shōnin. There are also divisions of five, six, and ten, which have reference to specific doctrinal differences. cf. 종파 宗派.

종 終 End, termination, final, utmost, death, the whole ; opposite of 시 始. 종남산 終南山 Chung-nan Shan, a mountain in Shensi ; a posthumous name for Tu Shun 두순 杜順, founder of the Hua-yen or Avataṁsaka School in China. 종교 終教 The "final teaching," i.e. third in the category of the Hua-yen School, cf. 오교 五教 ; the final metaphysical concepts of Mahāyāna, as presented in the Laṅkāvatāra-sūtra, Awakening of Faith, etc. 종귀어공 終歸於空 All things in the end return to the Void.

종 鐘 Ghaṇṭā, 건치 犍稚 a bell, a chime. 백팔종 百八鐘 The 108 strokes of the temple bell struck at dawn and dusk. 종루 鐘樓 Bell-tower.

종 從 To follow, agree with, obey ; from ; followers, secondary. 종지용출 從地踊出 Springing out of the earth, chapter 15 in the Lotus Sūtra. 종용 從容 Of calm demeanour, easy and natural, unperturbed. 종승 從僧 A "half-monk," a neophyte.

종 種 Vīja ; bīja. Seed, germ ; sort species ; also to sow, plant. 종자 種子 Seed, germ ; the content of the ālayavijñāna as the seed of all phenomena ; the esoterics also have certain Sanskrit letters, especially the first letter ā, seed or germ containing supernatural powers. 종자식 種子識 Ālayavijñāna, the abode or seed-store of consciousness from which all phenomena spring, producing and reproducing momentarily. 종성 種性 Seed nature, germ nature ; derivative or inherited nature. 종지 種智 Omniscience, knowledge of the seed or cause of all phenomena. 종근기 種根器 The three categories of the Ālayavijñāna : (1) the seed, or cause, of all phenomena ; (2) the five organs of sensation ; (3) the material environment on which they depend. 종숙탈 種熟脫 The seed of Buddha-truth implanted, its ripening, and its liberation or harvest. 종종색세계 種種色世界 A world of every kind of thing. 종각 種覺 The insight into all seeds or causes, Buddha-knowledge, omniscience. 종식 種識 The ālayavijñāna.

종각 鐘閣 Bell tower. A pavilion of the temple where the bell is located.

종객파 宗客巴 Sumatikīrti (Tib. Tsoṅ-kha-pa), the reformer of the Tibetan church, founder of the Yellow Sect (황모교 黃帽敎) ; according to the 서장신지 西藏新志 b. A.D. 1417 at Hsining, Kansu. His sect was founded on strict discipline, as opposed to the lax practices of the Red sect, which permitted marriage of monks, sorcery, etc. He is considered to be an incarnation of Mañjuśrī ; others say of Amitābha.

종고루 鐘鼓樓 Bell and drum tower.

종골 宗骨 The "bones" or essential tenets of a sect.

종극 宗極 Ultimate or fundamental principles.

종무소 宗務所 Temple office.

종문 宗門 Originally the general name for sects. Later appropriated to itself by the 선 禪 Ch'an(Zen) or Intuitional school, which refers to the other schools as 교문 敎門 teaching sects, i.e. those who rely on the written word rather than on the "inner light."

종밀 宗密 Tsung-mi, one of the five patriarchs of the Hua-yen (Avataṁsaka) sect, d. 841.

종법 宗法, **종체** 宗體 The thesis of a syllogism consisting of two terms, each of which has five different names : 자성 自性 subject ; 차별 差別 its differentiation ; 유법 有法 that which acts ; 법 法 the action ; 소별 所別 that which is differentiated ; 능별 能別 that which differentiates ; 전진 前陳 first statement ; 후진 後陳 following statement ; 종의 宗依 that on which the syllogism depends, both for subject and predicate.

종설구통 宗說俱通 In doctrine and expression both thorough, a term applied to a great teacher.

종승 宗乘 The vehicle of a sect, i.e. its essential tenets.

종요 宗要 The fundamental tenets of a sect ; the important elements, or main principle.

종용 宗用 Principles and their practice, or application.

종원 宗元 The basic principles of a sect ; its origin or cause of existence.

종의 宗依 That on which a sect depends, v. 종법 宗法.

종의 宗儀 The rules or ritual of a sect.

종의 宗義 The tenets of a sect.

종인유 宗因喩 Proposition, reason, example, the three parts of a syllogism.

종장 宗匠 The master workman of a sect who founded its doctrines.

종정 宗正 The head of a Buddhist sect ; supreme patriarch. He is a spiritual leader of the sect.

종조 宗祖 The founder of a sect or school. 종가 宗家 A name for Shan-tao 선도 善導 (d. 681), a writer of commentaries on the sūtras of the Pure Land sect, and one of its principal literary men ; cf. 염불종 念佛宗.

종지 宗旨 The main thesis, or ideas, e.g. of a text.

종체 宗體 The body of doctrine of a sect. The thesis of a syllogism, v. 종법 宗法.

종치 宗致 The ultimate or fundamental tenets of a sect.

종파 宗派 Sects (of Buddhism). In India, according to Chinese accounts, the two schools of Hīnayāna became divided into twenty sects. Mahāyāna had two main schools, the Mādhyamika, ascribed to Nāgārjuna and Āryadeva about the second century A.D., and the Yogācārya, ascribed to Asaṅga and Vasubandhu in the fourth century A.D. In China thirteen sects were founded: (1) 구사종 俱舍宗 Abhidharma or Kośa sect, representing Hīnayāna, based upon the Abhidharma-kośa-śāstra or 구사론 俱舍論. (2) 성실종 成實宗 Satyasiddhi sect, based on the 성실론 成實論 Satyasiddhi-śāstra, tr. by Kumārajīva ; no sect corresponds to it in India ; in China and Japan it became incorporated in the 삼론종 三論宗. (3) 율종 律宗 Vinaya or Discipline sect, based on 십송율 十誦律, 사분율 四分律, 승기율 僧祇律, etc. (4) 삼론종 三論宗 The three-śāstra sect, based on the Mādhyamika-śāstra 중관론 中觀論 of Nāgārjuna, the Śata-śāstra 백론 百論 of Āryadeva, and the Dvādaśa-nikāya-śāstra 십이문론 十二門論 of Nāgārjuna ; this school dates back to the translation of the three śāstras by Kumārajīva in A.D. 409. (5) 열반종 涅槃宗 Nirvāṇa sect, based upon the Mahāparinirvāṇa-sūtra 열반경 涅槃經 tr. by Dharmarakṣa in 423 ; later incorporated in T'ien-t'ai , with which it had much in common. (6) 지론종 地論宗 Daśabhūmikā sect, based on Vasubandhu's work on the ten stages of the bodhisattva's path to Buddhahood, tr. by Bodhiruci 508, absorbed by the Avataṁsaka school, *infra*. (7) 정토종 淨土宗 Pure-land or Sukhāvatī sect, founded in China by Bodhiruci ; its doctrine was salvation through faith in Amitābha into the Western Paradise. (8) 선종 禪宗 Dhyāna, meditative or intuitional sect, attributed to Bodhidharma about A.D. 527, but it existed before he came to China. (9) 섭론종 攝論宗, based upon the 섭대승론 攝大乘論 Mahāyāna-saṁparigraha-śāstra by Asaṅga, tr. by Paramartha in 563, subsequently absorbed by the Avataṁsaka sect. (10) 천태종 天台宗 T'ien-t'ai, based on the 법화경 法華經 Saddharmapuṇḍarīka Sūtra, or the Lotus of the Good Law ; it is a consummation of the Mādhyamika tradition. (11) 화엄종 華嚴宗 Avataṁsaka sect, based on the Buddhāvataṁsaka-sūtra, or Gandha-vyūha 화엄경 華嚴經 tr. in 418. (12) 법상종 法相宗 Dharmalakṣaṇa sect, established after the return of Hsüan-tsang from India and his trans. of the important Yogācārya works. (13) 진언종 眞言宗 Mantra sect, A.D. 716. In Japan twelve sects are named : Sanron, Hossō, Kegon, Kusha, Jōjitsu, Ritsu, Tendai, Shingon ; these are known as the ancient sects, the two last being styled mediaeval ; there follow the Zen and Jōdō ; the remaining two are Shin and Nichiren ; at present there are the Hossō, Kegon, Tendai, Shingon, Zen, Jōdō, Shin, and Nichiren sects.

종풍 宗風 The customs or traditions of a sect. In the Ch'an sect it means the regulations of the founder.

종학 宗學 The study or teaching of a sect.

좌 坐 Niṣad ; niṣaṇṇa ; sit ; rest ; situated. 좌구 坐具 given as niṣīdana, an article for sitting on, said to be a cloth, or mat. 좌구성로 坐久成勞 To accomplish one's labour by prolonged sitting, as did Bodhidharma. 좌참 坐參 The evening meditation at a monastery (preceding instruction by the abbot). 좌당 坐堂 A sitting-room, the assembly room of the monks. 좌하 坐夏 ; 좌랍 坐臘 Varṣā ; the retreat or rest during the summer rains. 좌하유 坐夏由 A certificate of "retreat" given to a wandering monk. 좌선 坐禪 To sit in dhyāna, i.e. abstract meditation, fixed abstraction, contemplation ; its introduction to China is attributed to Bodhidharma (though it came earlier), and its extension to T'ien-t'ai. 좌선당 坐禪堂 The monks' assembly room. 좌증 坐證 Another term for dhyāna contemplation.

좌 左 The left hand. 좌계 左溪 Tso-ch'i, the eighth T'ien-t'ai patriarch, named Hsüan-lang 현랑 玄朗.

좌 座 Āsana. A seat ; throne ; classifier of buildings, etc. 좌주 座主 ; 상좌 上座 ; 수좌 首座 ; 좌원 座元 A chairman, president ; the head of the monks ; an abbot. 좌광 座光 ; 광좌 光座 The halo behind of the throne of an image ; a halo throne. 좌랍 座臘 The end of the summer retreat ; the monastic end of the year.

죄 罪 That which is blameworthy and brings about bad karma ; entangled in the net of wrong-doing ; sin, crime. 죄구 罪垢 The filth of sin, moral defilement. 죄보 罪報 The retribution of sin, its punishment in suffering. 죄성 罪性 A sinful nature ; the nature of sin. 죄악 罪惡 Sin and evil. 죄근 罪根 The root of sin, i.e. unenlightenment or ignorance. 죄업 罪業 That which sin does, its karma, producing subsequent suffering. 죄복 罪福 Sinfulness and blessedness. 죄복무주 罪福無主 Sinfulness and blessedness have no lord, or governor, i.e. we induce them ourselves. 죄행 罪行 Sinful acts, or conduct. 죄장 罪障 The veil, or barrier of sin, which hinders the obtaining of good karma, and the obedient hearing of the truth.

주 麈 A great deer, whose tail is used as a fly-whip ; the use of which is forbidden to monks.

주 廚 A kitchen ; also a cabinet for an image.

주 拄 A prop, a post. 주장(자) 拄杖(子) A crutch, staff.

주 洲 An islet ; a continent. 주저 洲渚 An island, i.e. cut off, separated, a synonym for nirvāṇa.

주 周 Around, on every side, complete. 주리반타가 周利槃陀加 or 周梨槃陀加 Kṣudrapanthaka ; little (or mean) path. Twin brothers were born on the road, one called Śuddhipanthaka, Purity-path, the other born soon after and called as above, intp. 소로 小路 small road, and 계도 繼道 successor by the road. The elder was clever, the younger stupid, not even remembering his name, but became one of the earliest disciples of Buddha, and finally an arhat. The records are uncertain and confusing. Also, 주리반토 周利般兎, 주치반타가 周稚般他迦, 주리반특(가) 周利槃特(迦) ; 주다반탁가 朱茶半託迦 ; 주타 周陀. 주기 周忌 ; 주관 周關 The first anniversary of a death, when 주기재 周忌齋 anniversary masses are said. 주상 周祥 The anniversary of Buddha's birthday. 주라(발) 周羅(髮) ; 수라 首羅 Cūḍā ; a topknot left on the head of an ordinand when he receives the commandments ; the locks are later taken off by his teacher as a sign of his complete devotion. 주변 周遍 Universal, everywhere, on every side. 주변법계 周遍法界 The universal dharmadhātu ; the universe as an expression of the dharmakāya, the universe ; cf. 법계 法界. 주나 周那 Cundā, said to be the same as 순타 純陀. 주타 周陀 Kṣudra, said to be the same as 주리 周利 *supra.*

주 主 chief, lord, master ; to control. 주사 主事 Vihārasvāmin ; controller, director, the four heads of affairs in a monastery 감사 監寺, 유나 維那, 전좌 典坐, and 직세 直歲. 주반 主伴 Chief and attendant, principal and secondary. 주재 主宰 Lord, master ; to dominate, control ; the lord within, the soul ; the lord of the universe, God. 주방신 主方神 The spirits controlling the eight directions. 주수 主首 The 감사 監寺 or abbot of a monastery.

주 晝 Day, daytime, daylight. 주암림 晝暗林 The grove of daylight darkness, a cemetery.

주 呪 Dhāraṇī 다라니 陀羅尼 ; mantra ; an incantation, spell, oath, curse ; also a vow with penalties for failure. Mystical, or magical, formulae employed in Yoga. In Lamaism they consist of sets of Tibetan words connected with Sanskrit syllables. In a wider sense dhāraṇī is a treatise with mystical meaning, or explaining it. 주저 呪咀 ; 주살 呪殺 ; 주기사귀 呪起死鬼 or 주기시귀 呪起屍鬼 An incantation for raising the vetāla 외타라 畏陀羅 or corpse-demons to cause the death of another person. 주심 呪心 The heart of a spell, or vow. 주장 呪藏 One of the four piṭakas, the thesaurus of dhāraṇīs. 주술 呪術 Sorcery, the sorcerer's arts. 주원 呪願 Vows, prayers, or formulas uttered in behalf of donors, or of the dead ; especially at the All Souls Day's offerings to the seven generations of ancestors. Every word and deed of a bodhisattva should be a dhāraṇī.

주 註 Explain, open up the meaning, define. 주소 註疏 Notes and comments.

주 注 Fix, record ; flow. 주다반탁가 注荼半托迦 Cūḍapanthaka, the sixteenth of the sixteen arhats.

주 肘 Hasta, forearm, the 16,000th part of a yojana ; it varies from 1 ft. 4 in. to 1 ft. 8 in. in length.

주 珠 Maṇi. A pearl ; a bead ; synonym for Buddha-truth. 주리야 珠利耶 Culya, Caula, Cola. "An ancient kingdom in the north-east corner of the present Madras presidency, described A.D. 640 as a scarcely cultivated country with semi-savage and anti-Buddhistic inhabitants." [Eitel].

주 柱 Pillar, post, support. 주탑 柱塔 A pagoda.

주 朱 Red, vermilion. 주리 朱利 Caura, a thief, robber. 주리초 朱利草 Caurī, robber-grass or herb, name of a plant. 주라파리가라 朱羅波梨迦羅 Defined as 잡쇄의 雜碎衣, i.e. cīvara, or ragged clothes.

주 住 Sthiti. To abide, dwell, stay, stop, settle. 생주멸 生住滅 birth, existence, death. 주위 住位 Abiding place, one of the ten stages, resting and developing places or abodes of the Bodhisattva, which is entered after the stage of belief has been passed ; v. 십주 十住 ; 십지 十地 ; 지 地. 주겁 住劫 Vivarta siddha kalpa ; the abiding or existing kalpa ; the kalpa of human existence ; v. 겁 劫. 주지 住地 Dwelling-place ; abiding place in the Truth, i.e. the acquirement by faith of a self believing in the dharma and producing its fruits. 주정 住定 Fixed, certain, firmly settled. 주정보살 住定菩薩 A Bodhisattva firmly fixed, or abiding in certainty. After a Bodhisattva has completed three great asaṁkhyeya kalpas he has still one hundred great kalpas to complete. This period is called abiding in fixity or firmness, divided into six kinds ; certainty of being born in a good gati, in a noble family, with a good body, a man, Knowing the abiding places of his transmigrations, knowing the abiding character of his good works. 주지 住持 To dwell and control ; the abbot of a monastery ; resident superintendent ; to maintain, or firmly hold to (faith in the Buddha, etc.). For 주지신 住持身 v. 불구십신 佛具十身. 주과 住果 Abiding in the fruit ; e.g. śrāvakas and pratyeka-buddhas who rest satisfied in their attainments and do not strive for Buddhahood ; they are known as 주과연각 住果緣覺 or 주과나한 住果羅漢. 주상 住相 Sthiti ; abiding, being, the state of existence, one of the four characteristics of all beings and things, i.e. birth, existence, change (or decay), death (or cessation).

주 酒 Surā ; Maireya ; Madya. Wine, alcoholic liquor ; forbidden to monks and nuns by the fifth commandment.

주 籌 To calculate, devise, plan ; a tally. 주량 籌量 Reckoning, to reckon and measure.

주 走 To walk, go. 주해 走海 To travel by sea.

주지 住持 Chief monk ; abbot. A monastic who holds executive control over the support positions of the monastery.

죽 粥 Congee, gruel. 죽반승 粥飯僧 A rice-gruel monk, or gruel and rice monk, i.e. useless.

죽 竹 Veṇu, bamboo. 죽림(정사) 竹林(精舍) or 竹林(精寺) ; 죽원 竹園 ; 죽원 竹苑 Veṇuvana, "bamboo-grove," a park called Karaṇḍa-veṇuvana, near Rājagṛha, made by Bimbisāra for a group of ascetics, later given by him to Śākyamuni [Eitel], but another version says by the elder Karaṇḍa, who built there a vihāra for him.

죽비 竹篦 Bamboo clapper.

준 準 Correct, exact, a rule. 준제 準提 Candī, or Cundi ; also 준지 准胝 ; 존제 尊提. (1) In Brahmanic mythology a vindictive form of Durgā, or Pārvatī, wife of Śiva. (2) In China identified with Marīci 마리지 摩里支 or 천후 天后 Queen of Heaven. She is represented with three eyes and eighteen arms ; also as a form of Kuan-yin, or in Kuan-yin's retinue. 준타 準陀 ; 순타 純陀 Cunda, a native of Kuśinagara from whom Śākyamuni accepted his last meal.

준 遵 To comply with, accord with, obey ; accordingly. 준수 遵守 To obey and keep, e.g. the rules.

준 准 To permit, grant, acknowledge ; used for 준 準 in 준제 准提 q.v.

중 衆 All, the many ; a company of at least three (monks). At present, 중 衆 refers the monks itself ; 스님 Sunim is being used instead as a term of respect. 중승 衆僧 Saṁgha, all the monks, an assembly of at least three monks. 중합(지옥) 衆合(地獄) ; 중개 衆磕 The third of the eight hot hells, Saṁghāta, where two ranges of mountains meet to crush the sinners. 중원 衆園 ; 중료 衆寮 Saṁghārāma, a monastery, a nunnery ; originally only the surrounding park. 중도 衆徒 The whole body of followers ; also the monks, all the monks. 중회 衆會 An assembly (of all the monks). 중생 衆生 Sattva ; all the living, living beings, older tr. 유정 有情 sentient, or conscious beings ; also many lives, i.e. many transmigrations. 중생세간 衆生世間 The world of beings from Hades to Buddha-land ; also all beings subject to transformation by Buddha. 중생구 衆生垢 The common defilement of all beings by the false view that the ego has real existence. 중생인 衆生忍 Patience towards all living beings under all circumstances. 중생상 衆生想 The false notion that all beings have reality. 중생본성 衆生本性 The original nature of all the living, i.e. the Bhūtatathatā in its phenomenal aspect. 중생근 衆生根 The nature, or root, of all beings, cf. last entry. 중생탁 衆生濁 The fourth of the five periods of decay, sattvakaṣāya, when all creatures are stupid and unclean. 중생무시무종 衆生無始無終 As all beings are part of the 법신 法身 dharmakāya they have neither beginning nor end. 중생계 衆生界 The realm of all the living in contrast with the Buddha-realm. 중생상 衆生相 ; 중생견 衆生見 The concept that all beings have reality. 중우 衆祐 Protector or Benefactor of all, an old intp. of Bhagavat. 중성 衆聖 All saints, all who have realized the Buddha-truth. 중고 衆苦 All the miseries of existence, the sufferings of all. 중도 衆道 The way of all ; all the three yāna, or vehicles of salvation. 중향국토 衆香國土 The country of all fragrance, i.e. the Pure Land, also the Sūtras.

중 重 Heavy, weighty, grave, serious ; to lay stress upon, regard respectfully ; again, double, repeated. 중여 重如 v. 여여 如如 the double ju. 중산 重山 The heavy mountain (of delusion). 중화 重火 To pay respect to the god of fire. 중공 重空 The double space, i.e. the space beyond space, the void beyond the void. 중중 重重 Repeated, again and again, manifold, e.g. 중중제강 重重帝網 The multi-meshed net of Indra. 중관 重關 The grave barriers (to meditation and enlightenment). 중각강당 重閣講堂 The double-storeyed hall at Vaiśālī where the Buddha stayed. 중장 重障 Serious hindrances (to enlightenment), e.g. delusion, sin, retribution (or the results of one's previous lives). 중송 重頌 ; 기야 祇夜 Geya, repetition in verse of a prose section.

중 中 Madhya. Middle, central, medium, the mean, within ; to hit the centre. v. also 삼제 三諦.

중가의 中價衣 Another name for the uttara-saṅghāṭī, the middle garment of price, or esteem.

중간정 中間定 An intermediate dhyāna stage between two dhyāna heavens ; also 중간삼매 中間三昧 ; 중간선 中間禪 ; 중간정려 中間靜慮.

중겁 中劫 Middling kalpa, a period of 336,000,000 years.

중관 中觀 Meditation on the Mean, one of the 삼관 三觀 ; also meditation on the absolute which unites all opposites. There are various forms of such meditation, that of the 법상종 法相宗, the 삼론종 三論宗, the 천태종 天台宗. v. 중론 中論.

중국 中國 Madhyadeśa. 중천(축) 中天(竺) ; 중범 中梵 The middle kingdom, i.e. Central North India, v. 중인 中印.

중근 中根 Medium capacity, neither clever nor dull, of each of the six organs 육근 六根 ; there are three powers of each organ 상 上, 중 中, and 하 下.

중대 中臺 The name of a Buddha in the centre of a lotus. 중대팔엽원 中臺八葉院 The Court of the eight-petalled lotus in the middle of the Garbhadhātu, with Vairocana in its centre and four Buddhas and four bodhisattvas on the eight petals. The lotus is likened to the human heart, with the Sun-Buddha 대일 大日 at its centre. The four Buddhas are E. Akṣobhya, S. Ratnasaṃbhava, W. Amitābha, N. Amoghasiddhi ; the four bodhisattvas are S.E. Samantabhadra, S.W. Mañjuśrī, N.W. Avalokiteśvara, and N.E. Maitreya.

중도 中道 The "mean" has various interpretations. In general it denotes the mean between two extremes, and has special reference to the mean between realism and nihilism, or eternal substantial existence and annihilation ; this "mean" is found in a third principle between the two, suggesting the idea of a realm of mine or sprit beyond the terminology of 유 有 or 무 無, substance or nothing, or, that which has form, and is therefore measurable and ponderable, and its opposite of total non-existence. See 중론 中論. The following four Schools define the term according to their several scriptures : the 법상 法相 School describes it as the 유식 唯識, v. 유식중도 唯識中道 ; the 삼론 三論 School as the 팔불 八不 eight negations, v. 삼론 三論 ; the T'ien-t'ai as 실상 實相 the true reality ; and the Hua-yen as the 법계 法界 dharmadhātu. Four forms of the Mean are given by the 삼론현의 三論玄義. 중도즉법계 中道卽法界 The doctrine of the "mean" is the dharmadhātu, or "spiritual" universe.

중도종 中道宗 The third period of the Buddha's teaching, according to the 법상종 法相宗, giving the via media between the two extremes, the absolute as not confined to the phenomenal or the noumenal ; also called 중도교 中道教. 중도실상 中道實相 The reality of the "mean" is neither 유 有 substance or existent, nor 공 空 void or non-existent, but a reality which is neither, or a mean between the two extremes of materialism and nihilism ; also 중실 中實. 중도응본 中道應本 The "mean" as the basic principle in the 별 別 and 원 圓 Schools of the doctrine of the 응화신 應化身 "transformation body". 중도제일의 中道第一義 The "mean" is the first and chief of all principles, nothing is outside it. 중도관 中道觀 One of the T'ien-t'ai 삼관 三觀 three meditations, i.e. on the doctrine of the Mean to get rid of the illusion of phenomena.

중론 中論 ; 중관론 中觀論 Prāñnyāya-mūla-śāstra-ṭīkā, or Prāṇyamūla-śāstra-ṭīkā ; the Mādhyamika śāstra, attributed to the bodhisattvas Nāgārjuna as creator, and Nīlacakṣus as compiler ; tr.

by Kumārajīva A.D. 409. It is the principal work of the Mādhyamika, or Middle School, attributed to Nāgārjuna. Versions only exist in Chinese and Tibetan ; an English translation by Miyamoto exists and publication is promised ; a German version is by Walleser. The 중론 中論 is the first and most important of the 삼론 三論 q.v. The teaching of this School is found additionally in the 순중론 順中論 ; 반야등론석대승중관석론 般若燈論釋大乘中觀釋論 and 중론소 中論疏. Cf. 중도 中道. The doctrine opposes the rigid categories of existence and non-existence 가 假 and 공 空, and denies the two extremes of production (or creation) and non-production and other antitheses, in the interests of a middle or superior way.

중론성교 中論性教 The Mādhyamika school, which has been described as a system of sophistic nihilism, dissolving every proposition into a thesis and its antithesis, and refuting both ; but it is considered by some that the refuting of both is in the interests of a third, the 중 中 which transcends both.

중류 中流 In the midst of the stream, i.e. of 생사 生死 mortality, or reincarnations.

중반 中般 One of the five kinds of those who never recede but go on to parinirvāṇa, cf. 불환 不還.

중배 中輩 The middle stage of the 삼배 三輩 referred to in the 무량수경 無量壽經, i.e. the middle class of those in the next life ; also 중배생 中輩生 ; the 중배관 中輩觀 is the meditation on this condition.

중범 中梵 Central North India, idem 중국 中國.

중변론 中邊論 A treatise by Vasubandhu, translated by Hsüan-tsang in three chüan and by 진진제 陳眞諦 Ch'ên Chên-ti in two chüan. It is an explanation of the 변중변론송 辨中邊論頌 Madhyānta-vibhāga-śāstra, said to have been given by Maitreya to Asaṅga.

중사 中士 Medium disciples, i.e. śrāvakas and pratyeka-buddhas, who can gain emancipation for themselves, but cannot confer it on other ; cf. 하사 下士 and 상사 上士.

중숙의 中宿衣 A monk's inner garment, i.e. the five-patch garment ; also 중착의 中着衣.

중승 中乘 The middle vehicle to nirvāṇa, includes all intermediate or medial systems between Hīnayāna and Mahāyāna. It also corresponds with the state of a pratyeka-buddha, who lives chiefly for his own salvation but partly for others, like a man sitting in the middle of a vehicle, leaving scarcely room for others. It is a definition made by Mahāyānists unknown to Hīnayāna.

중식 中食 The midday meal, after which nothing whatever may be eaten.

중실 中實 idem 중도실상 中道實相.

중심경 中心經 idem 충심경 忠心經.

중원 中元 The fifteenth of the seventh moon ; the 상원 上元 and 하원 下元 are the fifteenth of the first and tenth moons respectively ; cf. 맹란분 孟蘭盆.

중유 中有 One of the 사유 四有, i.e. the antarā-bhava or intermediate state of existence between death and reincarnation ; hence 중유지려 中有之旅 is an unsettled being in search of a new habitat or reincarnation ; v. 중음 中陰.

중음 中陰 The intermediate existence between death and reincarnation, a stage varying from seven to forty-nine days, when the karma-body will certainly be reborn ; v. 중유 中有. 중음법사 中陰法事 The means used (by the deceased's family) for ensuring a favourable reincarnation during the intermediate stage, between death and reincarnation.

중인 中因 An arrangement by the esoteric sect of the Five Dhyāni-Buddhas, vairocana being the first in position, Akṣobhya east, and so on.

중인 中印 Central India, i.e. of the 오인 五印 Five Indies, as mentioned by Hsüan-tsang in the 서역기 西域記.

중제 中諦 The third of the 삼제 三諦 three postulates of the T'ien-t'ai school, i.e. 공 空, 가 假, and 중 中 q.v.

중존 中尊 The central honoured one — in any group of Buddhas, e.g. 불근존 不動尊 among the five 명왕 明王.

중종 中宗 The school or principle of the mean, represented by the 법상종 法相宗 Dharmalakṣaṇa school, which divides the Buddha's teaching into three periods, the first in which he preached 유 有 existence, the second 공 空 non-existence, the third 중 中 neither, something "between" or above them, e.g. a realm of pure spirit, vide the 심밀경 深密經 Sandhinirmocana sūtra and the Lotus Sūtra.

중주 中洲 Each of the four great continents at the foot of Mount Sumeru has two middling continents.

중천(세)계 中千(世)界 A middling chiliocosm, see 삼천대천세계 三千大千世界.

중천(축) 中天(竺) Central North India, idem 중국 中國. 중천축사 中天竺寺 A monastery on the 비래 飛來 Fei-lai peak at Hangchow.

중체 中體 The central Buddha is a group.

중초 中草 Medium-sized herbs, medium capacity, v. 삼초 三草.

중태(장) 中胎(藏) The central figure of the eight-petalled group of the Garbhadhātu maṇḍala ; i.e. the phenomenal Vairocana who has around him four Buddhas and four bodhisattvas, each on a petal. From this maṇḍala spring the four other great maṇḍalas.

중패 中唄 Chanting of 범패 梵唄 Buddhist hymns is divided into three kinds 초 初, 중 中, and 후 後.

중품 中品 Middle rank or class.

중함 中含 The middle Āgama 아함경 阿含經.

중회 中悔 Repenting or recanting midway, i.e. doubting and falling away.

즉 卽 To draw up to, or near ; approach ; forth-with ; to be ; i.e. *alias* ; if, even if ; 취시 就是. It is intp. as 화융 和融 united together ; 불이 不二 not two, i.e. identical ; 불리 不離 not separate, inseparable. It resembles implication, e.g. the afflictions cr passions imply, or are, bodhi ; births-and-deaths imply, or are, nirvāṇa ; the indication being that the one is contained in or leads to the other. T'ien-t'ai has three definitions : (1) The union, or unity, of two things, e.g. 번뇌 煩惱 and 보리 菩提, i.e. the passions and enlightenment, the former being taken as the 상 相 form, the latter 성 性 spirit, which two are inseparable ; in other words, apart from the subjection of the passions there is no enlightenment. (2) Back and front are inseparables ; also (3) substance and quality, e.g. water and wave.

즉공즉가즉중 卽空卽假卽中 All things are void, or noumenal, are phenomenal, are medial, the three meditations 삼관 三觀 of T'ien-t'ai.

즉득 卽得 Immediately to obtain, e.g. rebirth in the Pure Land, or the new birth here and now.

즉리 卽離 Identity and difference, agreement and disagreement.

즉비 卽非 Identity and difference.

즉사즉리 卽事卽理 The identity of phenomena with their underlying principle, e.g. body and spirit are a unity ; 즉사이진 卽事而眞 approximates to the same meaning that phenomena are identical with reality, e.g. water and wave.

즉상즉심 卽相卽心 Both form and mind are identical, e.g. the Pure Land as a place is identical with the Pure Land in the mind or heart — a doctrine of the Pure-land or Jōdō sect.

즉시 卽時 Immediately, forthwith.

즉신 卽身 The doctrine of the Shingon 진언 眞言 sect that the body is also Buddha ; in other words Buddha is not only 즉심 卽心 mind, but body ; hence 즉신성불 卽身成佛 ; 즉신보리 卽身菩提 the body is to become (consciously) Buddha by Yoga practices.

즉심 卽心 Of the mind, mental, i.e. all things are mental, and are not apart from mind. 즉심즉불 卽心卽佛, 즉심시불 卽心是佛 or 즉심성불 卽心成佛 The identity of mind and Buddha, mind is Buddha, the highest doctrine of Mahāyāna ; the negative form is 비심비불 非心非佛 no mind no Buddha, or apart from mind there is no Buddha ; and all the living are of the one mind. 즉심념불 卽心念佛 To remember, or call upon, Amitābha Buddha within the heart, which is his Pure Land.

즉유즉공 卽有卽空 All things, or phenomena, are identical with the void, or the noumenon.

즉중 卽中 The *via media* is that which lies between or embraces both the 공 空 and the 가 假, i.e. the void, or noumenal, and the phenomenal.

즘 怎 How? What? Why? Anything. 즘생 怎生 How born? How did it arise?

증 贈 A present (at parting), a souvenir ; posthumous honours ; a title patent. 증오중 贈五重 A service of the Pure-land sect, consisting of five esoteric rituals, for admitting the deceased into the lineage of the Buddha to ensure his welfare in the next life. 증별야 贈別夜 The night (of ceremony) before a funeral.

증 憎 Hate, dislike. 증애 憎愛 Hate and love.

증 增 To increase, add, augment, more. 증일아함경 增一阿含經 Ekottara-āgama. The āgama in which the sections each increase by one, e.g. the Aṅguttara Nikāya of the Hīnayāna ; a branch of literature classifying subjects numerically, cf. 아 阿 āgama. 증상 增上 Additional, increase, superior, strengthened. 증상심 增上心 Advancing or improving mind, superior mind. 증상심학 增上心學 The study of increased powers of mind (through meditation). 증상만 增上慢 Arrogance, pride (of superior knowledge) ; e.g. the 5,000 disciples who, in their Hīnayāna superiority, thought they had gained all wisdom and refused to hear the Lotus gospel. 증상과 增上果 Adhipati-phala, v. 이숙과 異熟果, dominant effect ; increased or superior effect, e.g. eye-sight as an advance on the eye-organ. 증상연 增上緣 The cause, condition, or organ of advance to a higher stage, e.g. the eye as able to produce sight. 증겁 增劫 The kalpa of increment, during which human life increases by one year every century, from an initial life of ten years, till it reaches 84,000 (and the body from 1 foot to 8,400 feet in height), in the 감겁 減劫 similarly diminishing. 증식 增息 Increasing (power of prayer for) cessation of calamity. 증비 增悲 Augmented pity of a bodhisattva, who remains to save, though his 증지 增智 advanced knowledge would justify his withdrawal to nirvāṇa. 증계학 增戒學 Advanced or increasing study of the moral law ; the study of the higher moral law. 증익 增益 Increasing, improving. 증진 增進 Advance, progress. 증도손생 增道損生 A bodhisattva's progress in the doctrine with concurrent reduction in reincarnation. 증장 增長 Increasing both broad and long, 증 增 referring to breadth and 장 長 to height, or length. 증장천 增長天 Virūḍhaka, the Mahārāja of the southern quarter. 증장광목 增長廣目 Virūḍhaka and Śiva.

증 證 To prove, witness to, testify, substantiate, attain to ; evidence ; experience ; realize ; assurance, conviction ; v. 아 阿 Abhisaṁbuddha. 증입 證入 Experiential entry into Buddha-truth, (1) partial, as in Hīnayāna and the earlier Mahāyāna ; (2) complete, as in the perfect school of Mahāyāna. 증득 證得 To realize, to attain truth by personal experience. 증대보리 證大菩提 To experience, attain to, realize, or prove, perfect enlightenment. 증덕 證德 Attainment of virtue, or spiritual power, through the four dogmas, twelve nidānas and six pāramitās, in the Hīnayāna and Madhyamayāna. 증오 證悟 Mystic insight ; conviction by thinking, realization, to prove and ponder. 증명 證明 To prove clearly, have the clear witness within. 증지 證智 Adhigamāvabodha. Experiential knowledge ; realization ; the attainment of truth by the bodhisattva in the first stage. 증과 證果 The fruits or rewards of the various stages of attainment. 증각 證覺 To prove and perceive, to know by experience. 증도 證道 The way of (mystic) experience ; to witness to the truth. 교증 教證 The two ways of learning, by teaching or experience.

증 烝 To steam ; advance ; all. 증사작반 烝砂作飯 Like cooking sand for food.

증 蒸 Twigs ; to steam, vapour. 증사 蒸沙 Steaming or cooking sand for food : an impossibility, like Ānanda trying to meditate without cutting off evil conduct.

지 抵 Knock ; arrive ; resist, bear ; substitute. 저미 抵彌 Timi, Timiṅgila, a huge fish, perhaps a whale.

지 支 A branch ; to branch, put off, pay, advance. 지벌라 支伐羅 ; 지박라 至縛羅 Cīvara. A mendicant's garment. 지불 支佛, 벽지불 辟支佛 A pratyeka-buddha, who understands the twelve nidānas, or chain of causation, and so attains to complete wisdom. His stage of attainment is the 지불지 支佛地. 지구 支具 ; 지도 支度 The various articles required for worship. 지제 支提 ; 지제 支帝 ; 지미 支徵 ; 지타 支陀 ; 지제 脂帝. Newer forms are 제다 制多 ; 제저(야) 制底(耶) ; 제지 制地, i.e. 찰 刹, 탑 塔, 묘 廟 Caitya. A tumulus, a mausoleum ; a place where the relics of Buddha were collected, hence a place where his sūtras or images are placed. Eight famous Caityas formerly existed : Lumbinī, Buddha-gayā, Vārāṇaśī, Jetavana, Kanyākubja, Rājagṛha, Vaiśālī, and the Sāla grove in Kuśinagara. Considerable difference of opinion exists as to the exact connotation of the terms given, some being referred to graves or stūpas, others to shrines or temples, but in general the meaning is stūpas, shrines, and any collection of objects of worship. 지제산부 支提山部 ; 지제가부 支提加部 ; 제다산부 制多山部 ; 지저가부 只底舸部 Caityaśaila ; described as one of the twenty sects of the Hīnayāna, and as ascetic dwellers among tombs or in caves. 지루가참 支樓迦讖 ; 지참 支讖 Chih-lou-chia-ch'an, a śramaṇa who came to China from Yüeh-chih A.D. 147 or A.D. 164 and worked at translations till A.D. 186 at Loyang. 지용 支用 To divide, distribute for use, i.e. 분용 分用. 지겸 支謙 Chih-ch'ien ; name of a Yüeh-chih monk said to have come to Loyang at the end of the Han dynasty and under the Wei ; tall, dark, emaciated, with light brown eyes ; very learned and wise. 지나 支那, 지나 指那, 진단 眞丹, 지나 至那, 사나 斯那, 진단 振旦, 진단 震旦, 진나 眞那, 진단 振丹, 지란 脂難, 전단 旃丹 ; 마하지나 摩訶至那 Cīna ; Mahā-cīna. The name by which China is referred to in the laws of Manu (which assert that the Chinese were degenerate Kṣatriya), in the Mahābhārata, and in Buddhist works. This name may have been derived from families ruling in western China under such titles as 진 晉 Chin at Fên-chou in Shansi 1106-376 B.C., 진 陳 Ch'ên in Honan 1122-479 B.C., 진 秦 Ch'in in Shensi as early as the ninth century B.C., and to this latter dynasty the designation is generally attributed. 지나제바구항라 支那提婆瞿恒羅 ; 한천종 漢天種 Cīna-deva-gotra. The "solar deva" of Han descent, first king of Khavandha, born to a princess of the Han dynasty (206 B.C.-A.D. 220) on her way as a bride-elect to Persia, the parentage being attributed to the solar deva. 서역기 西域記 12. 지린타 支隣陀 Mucilinda, v. 목 目 or 마하 摩訶 Maha-m. 지랑 支郎 Chih-lang, formerly a polite term for a monk, said to have arisen from the fame of the three 지 支 Chih of the Wei dynasty 지겸 支謙 Chih-ch'ien, 지참 支讖 Chih-ch'an, and 지량 支亮 Chih-liang.

지 枝 A branch. 지향 枝香 Incense made of branches of trees, one of the three kinds of incense, the other two being from roots and flowers. 지말혹 枝末惑 or 지말무명 枝末無明 Branch and twig illusion, or ignorance in detail, contrasted with 근본무명 根本無明 root, or radical ignorance, i.e. original ignorance out of which arises karma, false views, and realms of illusion which are the "branch and twig" condition or unenlightenment in detail or result. Also, the first four of the 오주지 五住地 five causal relationships, the fifth being 근본무명 根本無明.

지 芝 A felicitous plant ; sesamum. 지원 芝苑 Name for 원조 元照 Yüan-chao of 영지 靈芝 Ling-chih monastery, Hangchow.

지 持 Dhṛ ; Dhara. Lay hold of, grasp, hold, maintain, keep ; control. 지구 持句 One who holds to or retains the words (of the dhāraṇī). 지명 持名 to hold to, i.e. rely on the name (of Amitābha). 지국자 持國者 A sovereign, ruler of a kingdom. 지국천 持國天 or 치국천 治國天 Dhṛtarāṣṭra, one of the four deva-guardians or mahārājas, controlling the east, of white colour. 지지 持地 Dharaṇiṁdhara, holder, or ruler of the earth, or land ; name of a Bodhisattva, who predicted the future of Avalokiteśvara. 지율 持律 A keeper or observer of the discipline. 지념 持念 To hold in memory. 지식념 持息念 The contemplation in which the breathing is controlled, v. Ānāpāna 아나 阿那. 지계 持戒 To keep the commandments, or rules. 지계바라밀 持戒波羅蜜 One of the six pāramitās, morality, keeping the moral law. 지본 持本 Holding to the root, or fundamental ; ruler of the earth, which is the root and source of all things. 지명 持明 The dhāraṇī illuminant, i.e. the effective "true word" or magical term. 지명선 持明仙 The magician who possesses this term. 지명장 持明藏 The canon of the dhāraṇīs ; vidyādhara-piṭaka. 지수 持水 Jātiṁdhara, a physician who adjusted prescriptions and diet to the seasons ; reborn as Śuddhodana. 지법자 持法者 A keeper or protector of the Buddha-law. 지범 持犯 "maintaining and transgressing," i.e. keeping the commandments by 지지 止持 ceasing to do wrong and 작지 作持 doing what is right, e.g. worship, the monastic life, etc. ; transgression is also of two kinds, i.e. 작범 作犯 positive in doing evil and 지범 止犯 negative in not doing good. 지우계 持牛戒 Keepers of the law of oxen, an ascetic sect who ate and acted like oxen. 지영락 持瓔珞 Mālādharī, wearing a chaplet, name of a rākṣasī, or demoness. 지소 持素 To keep to vegetarian diet ; vegetarian. 지축산 持軸山 Īṣādhara, the second of the seven concentric mountains round Mt. Meru, rounded like a hub. 지변산 持邊山 Nemiṁdhara, the outermost of the seven mountain circles around Mt. Meru. 지쌍산 持雙山 Yugaṁdhara ; the first of the seven concentric mountains. 지금강 持金剛 ; 집금강 執金剛 Vajradhara, or Vajrapāṇi, a Bodhisattva who holds a vajra or thunderbolt, of these there are several ; a name for Indra. 지재 持齋 To keep the fast, i.e. not eat after noon.

지 脂 Fat, lard ; gum ; soapstone ; wealth ; translit. *ci, cai* ; see 지 支. 지나 脂那 China ; intp. as the country of culture, with a people clothed and capped ; also as a frontier (of India), a place of banishment. 지제부도 脂帝浮圖 Caitya, a stūpa, a mausoleum, a place or object of worship.

지 指 Finger, toe ; to point, indicate. 지토 指兎 idem 지월 指月 To indicate the hare (in the moon). 지인 指印 To sign by a thumb-mark ; a sign. 지다 指多 ; 질다 質多 Citta, the mind. 지방립상

指方立相 To point to the west, the location of the Pure Land, and to set up in the mind the presence of Amitābha ; to hold this idea, and to trust in Amitābha, and thus attain salvation. The mystics regard this as a mental experience, while the ordinary believer regards it as an objective reality. 지월 指月 To point a finger at the moon: the finger represents the sūtras, the moon represents their doctrines. 지환 指環 ; 초지 草指 ; 지천 指釧 or 초천 草釧 Fingering ; sometimes of grass, used by the esoteric sect. 지절 指節 Aṅguli-parvan ; finger-joint ; a measure, the 24th part of a forearm (hasta). 지복친 指腹親 Related by the betrothal of son and daughter still in the womb. 지난 指難 idem 지나 支那 China. 지만 指鬘 Aṅgulimālya, name of a convert of Śākyamuni, who had belonged to a Śivaitic sect which wore chaplets of finger-bones, and "made assassination a religious act."

지 智 Jñāna 야나 若那 ; 사나 闍那 Knowledge ; wisdom ; defined as 어사리결단야 於事理決斷也 decision or judgment as to phenomena or affairs and their principles, of things and their fundamental laws. There are numerous categories, up to 20, 48, and 77, v. 일지 一智 ; 이지 二智 and others. It is also used as a tr. of prajñā, cf. 지도 智度.

지 只 Only ; a final particle ; translit. *j.* 지저가부 只底舸部 ; 지저여세라부 只底與世羅部 ; 지제가부 支提加部 ; 지제산부 支提山部 ; 제다산부 制多山部 ; 주지제산부 住支提山部 ; 서다림 逝多林 or 서다원 逝多苑 ; 지환 祇桓 Jetavanīyāḥ or Jetīyaśailāḥ. School of the dwellers on Mount Jeta, or 승림부 勝林部 School of Jetṛvana. A subdivision of the Sthavira. Cf. 북 北.

지 紙 Paper. 지엽 紙葉 Palm-leaves. 지의 紙衣, 지관 紙冠, 지전 紙錢 Paper clothing, hats, money, etc., burnt as offerings to the dead.

지 旨 Purport, will ; good. 지귀 旨歸 The purport, aim, or objective.

지 地 Pṛthivī, 발리체미 鉢里體尾 the earth, ground ; Bhūmi, 보미 步弭, the earth, place, situation ; Talima, 탁사마 託史麽 or 탁리마 託吏麽 ground, site ; explained by 토지 土地 earth, ground ; 능생 能生 capable of producing ; 소의 所依 that on which things rely. It is also the spiritual rank, position, or character attained by a Bodhisattva as a result of 주 住 remaining and developing in a given state in order to attain this 지 地 rank ; v. 십주 十住 ; 주위 住位 and 십지 十地.

지 至 Reach, arrive at ; utmost, perfect. 지인 至人 The perfect man, i.e. Śākyamuni. 지심 至心 With the utmost mind, or a perfect mind. 지교 至教 Complete or perfect teaching. 지리 至理 The utmost principle, the fundamental law. 지진 至眞 Perfect truth. 지상존자 至相尊者 The second patriarch of the Hua-yen (Kegon) school 지엄 智儼 Chih-yen. 지언 至言 Perfect words, words of complete explanation. 지나 至那 Cīna, China, hence 지나니 至那儞 Cīnānī, the peach-tree, said to have been imported into India from China. 지나복지 至那僕底 Cīnapati, Lord (from) China, said in the Record of Western Lands 서역기 西域記 to have been appointed by the Han rulers ; a country so-called because the son of 번유질 蕃維質 Fan Wei Chih of 하서 河西 Ho-hsi dwelt (and reigned) there. Eitel says, "A small kingdom in the north-west of India (near Lahore) the inhabitants of which asserted (A.D. 640) that their first kings had come from China." 지나라사불달라 至那羅闍弗呾羅 Cīnarājaputra, "son of the China king," intp. by 한왕자 漢王子 Prince of Han, which was also an Indian name for a pear-tree, said to have been imported from China in the Han dynasty ; v. 서역기 西域記 4. 지사 至沙 ; 제사 帝沙 Tiṣya, an ancient Buddha. The father of Śāriputra. A son of Śuklodana.

지 枳 Thorn, thorns ; translit. *ke, ki.* 지리지리 枳哩枳哩 Kelikila, one of the rājas who subdues demons. 지타 枳吒 ; 지달(나) 枳怛(那) An island which rises out of the sea. 지라소 枳羅蘇 or 지라파 枳羅婆 Kilāsa, white leprosy, tr. as "white" and a "hill."

지 知 To know. Sanskrit root Vid, hence vidyā, knowledge ; the Vedas, etc. 지 知 vijñā is to know, 지 智 is vijñāna, wisdom arising from perception or knowing.

지 誌 To remember, record.

지 祇 To revere, venerate.

지 止 To stop, halt, cease ; one of the seven definitions of 선정 禪定 dhyāna described as 사마타 奢摩他 śamatha or 삼마지 三摩地 samādhi ; it is defined as 정식동심 靜息動心 silencing, or putting to rest the active mind, or auto-hypnosis ; also 심정지어일처 心定止於一處 the mind centred, lit. the mind steadily fixed on one place, or in one position. It differs from 관 觀 which observes, examines, sifts evidence ; 지 止 has to do with 불망 拂妄 getting rid of distraction for moral ends ; it is abstraction, rather than contemplation ; see 지관 止觀. In practice there are three methods of attaining such abstraction : (a) by fixing the mind on the nose, navel, etc. ; (b) by stopping every thought as it arises ; (c) by dwelling on the thought that nothing exists of itself, but from a preceding cause. 지식 止息 To stop, cease ; to stop breathing by self-control ; to bring the mind to rest ; used for 지관 止觀. 지지 止持 Self-control in keeping the commandments or prohibitions relating to deeds and words, which are styled 지지계 止持戒, 지지문 止持門, 지악문 止惡門. 지범 止犯 ; 지지작범 止持作犯 Stopping offences ; ceasing to do evil, preventing others from doing wrong. 지관 止觀 ; 사마타비바사나 奢摩他毗婆舍那 or 사마타비발사나 奢摩他毗鉢舍那 Śamatha-vipaśyanā, which Sanskrit words are intp. by 지관 止觀 ; 정혜 定慧 ; 적조 寂照 ; and 명정 明靜 ; for their respective meanings see 지 止 and 관 觀. When the physical organism is at rest it is called 지 止 Chih, when the mind is seeing clearly it is called 관 觀 Kuan. The term and form of meditation is specially connected with its chief exponent, the founder of the T'ien-t'ai school, which school is styled 지관종 止觀宗 Chih-kuan Tsung, its chief object being concentration of the mind by special methods for the purpose of clear insight into truth, and to be rid of illusion. The T'ien-t'ai work gives ten fields of meditation, or concentration : (1) the five 음 陰, eighteen 계 界, and twelve 입 入 ; (2) passion and delusion ; (3) sickness ; (4) karma forms ; (5) māra-deeds ; (6) dhyāna ; (7) (wrong) theories ; (8) arrogance ; (9) the two Vehicles ; (10) bodhisattvahood. 지관화상 止觀和尙 A name for the T'ang monk Tao-sui 도수 道邃. 지관종 止觀宗 Another name for the T'ien-t'ai school. 지관사 止觀捨 The upekṣā, indifference to or abandonment of both 지 止 and 관 觀, i.e. to rise above both into the universal. 지관현문 止觀玄文 Another name for the 지관론 止觀論. 지관론 止觀論 ; 마하지관론 摩訶止觀論 The foundation work on T'ien-t'ai's modified form of samādhi, rest of body for clearness of vision. It is one of the three foundation works of the T'ien-t'ai School ; was delivered by 지의 智顗 Chih-i to his disciple 장안 章安 Chang-an who committed it to writing. The treatises on it are numerous.

지 志 Will, resolve, 지의 志意 ; 심지 心志 ; also data, records.

지(행)선 地(行)仙 Earth-immortals, or genii, one of the classes of ṛṣis ; i.e. bhūdeva = Brahman.

지가 地珂 Dīrgha, long ; also 지률가 地嘌伽.

지가반바나승가람 地迦縏縛那僧伽藍 Dīrghabhavana-saṁghārāma. A monastery near Khotan 활단 豁旦, with a statue dressed in silk which had "transported itself" thither from Karashahr 고차 庫車. [Eitel].

지객 知客 The director of guests, i.e. the host.

지거 智炬 The torch of wisdom.

지거천 地居天 Indra's heaven on the top of Sumeru, below the 공거천 空居天 heavens in space.

지견 知見 To know, to know by seeing, becoming aware, intellection ; the function of knowing, views, doctrines. 지견바라밀 知見波羅蜜 The Prajñāpāramitā, v. 반야 般若.

지경 智鏡 The mirror of wisdom.

지경 智境 The objects of wisdom, or its state, or conditions.

지계 地界 The realm of earth, one of the four elements, v. 지대 地大.

지계 智界 The realm of knowledge in contrast with 리계 理界 that of fundamental principles or law.

지고 知庫 The bursar (of a monastery).

지고단집 知苦斷集 To know (the dogma of) suffering and be able to cut off its accumulation ; cf. 사제 四諦.

지과 智果 The fruit of knowledge, enlightenment.

지광 智光 Jñānaprabha, Having the light of knowledge ; name of a disciple of Śilabhadra.

지근 知根 The organs of perception. To know the roots, or capacities (of all beings, as does a Bodhisattva ; hence he has no fears).

지눌 知訥 Bo-jo Ji-nul(1158-1210). A monk of the Goryeo dynasty in Korea. He led a group of monks in Mt. Jo-gye. He was an imperial preceptor and his teachings have a great effect on Korean Buddhism up to now.

지단 地壇 A square altar used by the esoteric cult.

지단 智斷 Mystic wisdom which attains absolute truth, and cuts off misery.

지대 地大 Earth as one of the 사대 四大 four elements, 지 地 earth, 수 水 water, 화 火 fire, and 풍 風 air (i.e. air in motion, wind) ; to these 공 空 space (Skt. ākāśa) is added to make the 오대 五大 five elements ; 식 識 vijñāna, perception to make the six elements ; and 견 見 darśana, views, concepts, or reasonings to make the seven elements. The esoteric sect use the five fingers, beginning with the little finger, to symbolize the five elements.

지도 智度 Prajñā-pāramitā, the sixth of the six pāramitās, wisdom which brings men to nirvāṇa. (대)지도론 (大)智度論 The śāstra, or commentary on the Prajñā-pāramitā sūtra ; cf. 반야 般若. It is a famous philosophical Mahāyāna work.

지도자 知道者 The one who knows the path to salvation, an epithet of the Buddha.

지동 地動 Earthquake ; the earth shaken, one of the signs of Buddha-power.

지랍비 地臘脾 Ḍravya, substance, thing, object.

지력 智力 Knowledge and supernatural power ; power of knowledge ; the efficient use of mystic knowledge.

지례 知禮 Knowing the right modes of respect, or ceremonial ; courteous, reverential ; Chih-li, name of the famous tenth-century monk of the Sung dynasty, Ssŭ-ming 사명 四明, so called after the name of his monastery, a follower of the T'ien-t'ai school, sought out by a Japanese deputation in 1017.

지론 知論 A name for the Prajñāpāramitā, v. 반야 般若.

지론 地論 item 십지경론 十地經論.

지료 知寮 Warden of the monasterial abodes.

지륜 地輪 the earth-wheel, one of the 오륜 五輪 five circles, i.e. space, wind, water, earth, and above them fire ; the five "wheels" or umbrellas shown on the top of certain stūpas or pagodas. 지륜단 地輪壇 The earth-altar is four-cornered and used by the esoteric sect.

지모 智母 The mother of knowledge ; wisdom-mother ; v. Mātṛkā 마 摩.

지묘 智妙 Mystic knowledge (which reveals spiritual realities).

지무변제불지 知無邊諸佛智 To have the infinite Buddha-wisdom (of knowing all the Buddha-worlds and how to save the beings in them).

지문 智門 Wisdom gate ; Buddha-wisdom and Buddha-pity are the two gates or ways through which Buddhism expresses itself: the way of enlightenment directed to the self, and the way of pity directed to others.

지바라밀 智波羅蜜 Prajñā-pāramitā, see 지도 智度.

지바하라 地婆訶羅 Divākara, tr. as 일조 日照 Jih-chao, a śramaṇa from Central India, A.D. 676-688, tr. of eighteen or nineteen works, introduced an alphabet of forty-two letters or characters. 지바달다 地婆達多 or 지바달두 地婆達兜 Devadatta, v. 제 提.

지법 知法 To know the Buddha-law, or the rules ; to know things ; in the exoteric sects, to know the deep meaning of the sūtras ; in the esoteric sects, to know the mysteries.

지변 智辯 Wisdom and dialectic power ; wise discrimination ; argument from knowledge.

지비 智悲 All-knowing and all-pitying ; these two with 정 定 "contemplative" make up the 삼덕 三德 three virtues or qualities of a Buddha.

지사 知事 To know affairs. The karmadāna, or director of affairs in a monastery, next below the abbot.

지산 智山 The mountain of knowledge ; knowledge exalted as a mountain.

지상 地上 On the ground ; above the ground ; used for 초지이상 初地以上 the stages above the initial stage of a Bodhisattva's development.

지상 智象 Prajñā, or Wisdom, likened to an elephant, a title of Buddha, famous monks, the Nirvāṇa-sūtra, the Prajñā-pāramitā sūtra, etc.

지상 智相 Wise mien or appearance, the wisdom-light shining from the Buddha's face ; also human intelligence.

지성 智城 The city of mystic wisdom, Buddhahood.

지세간 知世間 Lokavid. He who knows the world, one of the ten characteristics of a Buddha.

지수 智手 The knowing hand, the right hand.

지식 知識 (1) To know and perceive, perception, knowledge. (2) A friend, an intimate. (3) The false ideas produced in the mind by common, or unenlightened knowledge ; one of the 오식 五識 in 기신론 起信論. 지식중 知識衆 A body of friends, all you friends.

지신 智身 Jñānakāya, wisdom-body, the Tathāgata.

지신 地神 The earth-devī, Pṛthivī, also styled 견뢰 堅牢 firm and secure ; cf. 지천 地天.

지심 智心 The mind of knowledge ; a wise mind.

ㄱ ㄴ ㄷ ㄹ ㅁ ㅂ ㅅ ㅇ ㅈ ㅊ ㅋ ㅌ ㅍ ㅎ 찾아보기

지안 智眼 The eye of wisdom ; wisdom as an eye.

지애 智礙 Obstacles to attaining Buddha-wisdom, especially original ignorance.

지엄 智儼 Fourth patriarch of the 화엄 華嚴 Hua-yen school, also called 운화 雲華 Yün-hua, A.D. 600-668.

지옥 地獄 Naraka, 날락가 捺落迦 or 나락가 那落迦 ; Niraya 니리 泥犁 ; explained by 불락 不樂 joyless ; 가염 可厭 disgusting, hateful ; 고구 苦具, 고기 苦器 means of suffering ; 지옥 地獄 earth-prison ; 명부 冥府 the shades, or departments of darkness. Earth-prison is generally intp. as hell or the hells ; it may also be termed purgatory ; one of the six gati or ways of transmigration. The hells are divided into three classes: I. Central, or radical, 근본지옥 根本地獄 consisting of (1) The eight hot hells. These were the original hells of primitive Buddhism, and are supposed to be located under the southern continent Jambudvīpa 섬부주 瞻部州, 500 yojanas below the surface. (a) 등활 等活 or 갱활 更活 Saṁjīv, rebirth, where after many kinds of suffering a cold wind blows over the soul and returns it to this life as it was before, hence the name 등활 等活. (b) 흑승 黑繩 Kālasūtra, where the sufferer is bound with black chains and chopped or sawn asunder. (c) 선합 線合 ; 중합 衆合 ; 퇴압 堆壓 Saṁghāta, where are multitudes of implements of torture, or the falling of mountains upon the sufferer. (d) 호규 號叫 ; 호호 呼呼 ; 규환 叫喚 Raurava, hell of wailing. (e) 대규 大叫 ; 대호규 大號叫 ; 대호 大呼 Mahāraurava, hell of great wailing. (f) 염열 炎熱 ; 소자 燒炙 Tapana, hell of flames and burning. (g) 대열 大熱 ; 대소자 大燒炙 ; 대염열 大炎熱 Pratāpana, hell of molten lead. (h) 무간 無間 ; 하비지 河鼻旨 ; 아유월치 阿惟越致 ; 아비지 阿毗至 ; 아비 阿鼻 ; 아비 阿毗 Avīci, unintermitted suffering, where sinners die and are reborn to suffer without interval. (2) The eight cold hells 팔한지옥 八寒地獄. (a) 알부타지옥 頞浮陀地獄 Arbuda, where the cold causes blisters. (b) 니랄부타 尼剌部陀 Nirarbuda, colder still, causing the blisters to burst. (c) 알찰타 頞哳吒 ; 아타타 阿吒吒 Aṭaṭa, where this is the only possible sound from frozen lips. (d) 학학파 臛臛婆 ; 아파파 阿波波 Hahava or Apapa, where it is so cold that only this sound can be uttered. (e) 호호파 虎虎婆 Hāhādhara or Huhuva, where only this sound can be uttered. (f) 올발라 嗢鉢羅 ; 울발라 鬱鉢羅 or 우발라 優鉢羅 Utpala, or 니라오발라 尼羅烏鉢羅 or 니라구발라 尼羅漚鉢羅 Nīlotpala, where the skin is frozen like blue lotus buds. (g) 발특마 鉢特摩 Padma, where the skin is frozen and bursts open like red lotus buds. (h) 마하발특마 摩訶鉢特摩 Mahāpadma, ditto like great red lotus buds. Somewhat different names are also given. Cf. 구사론 俱舍論 8 ; 지도론 智度論 16 ; 열반경 涅槃經 11, Ⅱ. The secondary hells are called 근변지옥 近邊地獄 adjacent hells or 십육유증지옥 十六遊增地獄 the sixteen progressive, or 십육소지옥 十六小地獄 sixteen inferior hells. Each hot hell has a door on each of its four sides, opening from each such door are four adjacent hells, in all sixteen ; thus with the original eight there are 136. A list of eighteen hells is given in the 십팔니리경 十八泥梨經. Ⅲ. A third class is called the 고(독)지옥 孤(獨)地獄 Lokāntarika, or isolated hells in mountains, deserts, below the earth and above it. Eitel says in regard to the eight hot hells that they range "one beneath the other in tiers which begin at a depth of 11,900 yojanas and reach to a depth of 40,000 yojanas." The cold hells are under "the two Tchakravālas and range shaft-like one below the other, but so that this shaft is gradually widening to the fourth hell and then narrowing itself again so that the first and last hell have the shortest, those in the centre the longest diameter." "Every universe has the same number of hells," but "the northern continent has no hell whatever, the two continents east and west of Meru have only small Lokāntarika hells ... whilst all the other hells are required for the inhabitants of the southern continent." It may be noted that the purpose of these hells is definitely punitive, as well as purgatorial. Yama is the judge and ruler, assisted by eighteen officers and a host of demons, who order or administer the various degrees of torture. "His sister performs the same duties with regard to female criminals," and it may be mentioned that the Chinese have added the

혈분지 血盆池 Lake of the bloody bath, or "placenta tank," for women who die in childbirth. Release from the hells is in the power of the monks by tantric means. 지옥천자 地獄天子 The immediate transformation of one in hell into a deva because he had in a previous life known of the merit and power of the 화엄 華嚴 Hua-yen sūtra. 지옥도 地獄道 or 지옥취 地獄趣 The hell-gati, or destiny of reincarnation in the hells.

지용 地涌 To spring forth, or burst from the earth, a chapter in the Lotus sūtra.

지월 智月 Jñānacandra. Knowledge bright as the moon ; name of a prince of Karashahr who became a monk A.D. 625.

지위 地位 Position, place, state.

지의 智顗 Chih-i, founder of the T'ien-t'ai school, also known as 지자 智者 and 천태(대사) 天台(大師) ; his surname was 진 陳 Ch'ên ; his 자 字 was 덕안 德安 Tê-an ; born about A.D. 538, he died in 597 at 60 years of age. He was a native of 영천 穎川 Ying-ch'uan in Anhui, became a neophyte at 7, was fully ordained at 20. At first a follower of 혜사 慧思 Hui-ssŭ, in 575 he went to the T'ien-t'ai mountain in Chekiang, where he founded his famous school on the Lotus Sūtra as containing the complete gospel of the Buddha.

지인 智刃 The sword of knowledge ; knowledge like a sword.

지일체법지 知一切法智 The Buddha-wisdom of knowing every thing or method (of salvation). 지일체중생지 知一切衆生智 The Buddha-wisdom which knows (the karma of) all beings.

지자 智者 The knower, or wise man ; a name for 지의 智顗 q.v.

지자 知者 The knower, the cognizer, the person within who perceives.

지장 智藏 The treasury of Buddha-wisdom ; posthumous title of Amogha.

지장 地藏 Ti-tsang, J. Jizō, Kṣitigarbha, 걸차저벽사 乞叉底蘗沙 ; Earth-store, Earth-treasury, or Earth-womb. One of the group of eight Dhyāni-Bodhisattvas. With hints of a feminine origin, he is now the guardian of the earth. Though associated with Yama as overlord, and with the dead and the hells, his role is that of saviour. Depicted with the alarum staff with its six rings, he is accredited with power over the hells and is devoted to the saving of all creatures between the nirvāṇa of Śākyamuni and the advent of Maitreya. From the fifth century he has been especially considered as the deliverer from the hells. His central place in China is at Chiu-hua-shan, forty li south-west of Ch'ing-yang in Anhui. In Japan he is also the protector of travellers by land and his image accordingly appears on the roads ; bereaved parents put stones by his images to seek his aid in relieving the labours of their dead in the task of piling stones on the banks of the Buddhist Styx ; he also helps women in labour. He is described as holding a place between the gods and men on the one hand and the hells on the other for saving all in distress ; some say he is an incarnation of Yama. At dawn he sits immobile on the earth 지 地 and meditates on the myriads of its beings 장 藏. When represented as a monk, it may be through the influence of a Korean monk who is considered to be his incarnation, and who came to China in 653 and died in 728 at the age of 99 after residing at Chiu-hua-shan for seventy-five years ; his body, not decaying, is said to have been gilded over and became an object of worship. Many have confused 신라 新羅 part of Korea with 섬라 暹羅 Siam. There are other developments of Ti-tsang, such as the 육지장 六地藏 Six Ti-tsang, i.e. severally converting or transforming those in the hells, pretas, animals, asuras, men, and the devas ; these six Ti-tsang have different images and symbols. Ti-tsang has also six messengers 육사자 六使者 : Yama for transforming those in hell ; the pearl-holder for pretas

; the strong one for animals ; the devī of mercy for asuras ; the devī of the treasure for human beings ; one who has charge of the heavens for the devas. There is also the 연명지장 延命地藏 Yen-ming Ti-tsang, who controls length of days and who is approached, as also may be P'u-hsien, for that purpose ; his two assistants are the Supervisors of good and evil 장선 掌善 and 장악 掌惡. Under another form, as 승군지장 勝軍地藏 Ti-tsang of the conquering host, he is chiefly associated with the esoteric cult. The benefits derived from his worship are many, some say ten, others say twenty-eight. His vows are contained in the 지장(보살)본원경 地藏(菩薩)本願經. There is also the (대승대집)지장십륜경 (大乘大集)地藏十輪經 tr. by Hsüan-tsang in 10 chüan in the seventh century, which probably influenced the spread of the Ti-tsang cult.

지장전 地藏殿 Ji-jang-jeon. Kṣitigarbha hall. A building in a temple where 지장 地藏 Ti-tsang is enshrined.

지저 智杵 The wisdom hammer, the vajra or "diamond club."

지적 智積 Jñānākara. Accumulation of knowledge. Eldest son of Mahābhijñā ; also said to be Akṣobhya. Prajñākūṭa. A Bodhisattva in the retinue of Prabhūtaratna, v. Lotus Sūtra.

지전 地前 The stages of a Bodhisattva before the 초지 初地.

지전 知殿 The warden of a temple.

지정상 智淨相 Pure-wisdom-aspect ; pure wisdom ; wisdom and purity.

지족 知足 Complete knowledge ; satisfaction. 지족(천) 知足(天) Tuṣita, the fourth Devaloka, Maitreya's heaven of full knowledge, where all bodhisattvas are reborn before rebirth as Buddhas ; the inner court is 지족원 知足院.

지종 地種 Earth-seed, or atoms of the element earth.

지중 地中 ; **지내** 地內 Annexes, or subsidiary buildings in the grounds of a monastery.

지즙 智楫 Oar of wisdom, that rows across to nirvāṇa.

지증 智證 Wisdom assurance, the witness of knowledge, the wisdom which realizes nirvāṇa.

지지 智智 Wisdom of wisdom ; Buddha-omniscience.

지지가 地底迦 Dhītika, originally Dhṛtaka, an ancient monk, whose name is tr. by 유괴 有愧 Yu-k'uei, ashamed, shy.

지진 地塵 Earth-dust ; as dust of earth (in number) ; atoms of the earth element.

지천 地天 The earth-devī, Pṛthivī, one of the four with thunderbolts in the Vajradhātu group ; also 지천후 地天后 the earth-devī in the Garbhadhātu group. Cf. 지신 地神.

지치바 地致婆 Tiṭibha, Titilambha, "a particular high mountain," [M. W.] 1,000 quadrillions ; a 대지치바 大地致婆 is said to be 10,000 quadrillions.

지혜 智慧 Jñāna as 지 智 knowledge and prajñā as 혜 慧 discernment, i.e. knowledge of things and realization of truth ; in general, knowledge and wisdom ; but sometimes implying mental and moral wisdom. 지혜력 智慧力 Wisdom, insight. 지혜광불 智慧光佛 Wisdom-light Buddha, i.e. Amitābha. 지(혜)검 智(慧)劍 The sword of wisdom which cuts away passion and severs the link of transmigration. 지혜수 智慧水 The water of wisdom which washes away the filth of passion. 지혜해 智慧海 Buddha-wisdom deep and wide as the ocean. 지혜관 智慧觀 One of the meditations of Kuan-yin, insight into reality. 지혜문 智慧門 The gate of Buddha-wisdom which leads into all truth.

지혜동자 地慧童子 or 持慧童子 ; **재혜동자** 財慧童子 The youth who controls earthly possessions, the fourth on the left of the messengers of Mañjuśrī in the Garbhadhātu group.

지혹 智惑 Wisdom and delusion.

지화 智火 The fire of knowledge which burns up misery.

직 直 Straight, upright, direct ; to arrange. 직전 直傳 Direct information or transmission (by word of mouth). 직당 直堂 The servant who attends in the hall ; an announcer. 직심 直心 Straightforward, sincere, blunt. 직철 直掇 ; 직철 直裰 A monk's garment, upper and lower in one. 직세 直歲 A straight year, a year's (plans, or duties). 직설 直說 Straight or direct speech ; the sūtras. 직도 直道 The direct way (to nirvāṇa and Buddha-land).

직 職 To record, oversee, direct ; office, official duty. 직분 職分 Duty, responsibility.

직지사 直指寺 Jik-ji-sa. A temple located in Unsu-dong Daehang-myeon Gimcheon-si Gyeongsangbuk-do in Korea. The 8th parish headquarters of Korean Jogye Order.

진 振 To shake, rouse, restore. 진지 振地 To shake the earth. 진령 振鈴 To shake or ring a bell.

진 進 Advance, progress, enter. 진구 進具 To reach the age (20) and advance to full ordination. 정진 精進 Vīrya, zeal, unchecked progress.

진 盡 An emptied vessel, all used up ; end, finish, complete, nothing left ; all, utmost, entirely. 진칠일 盡七日 At the end of seven days, seven days being completed. 진시방 盡十方 The entire ten directions, the universe, everywhere. 진미래제 盡未來際 To the end of all time, eternal. 진정허융 盡淨虛融 The identity of the absolute and the empirical, a doctrine of the Prajñāpāramitā.

진 陳 Arrange, marshal, spread, state ; old, stale. 진기약 陳棄藥 ; 부란약 腐爛藥 Purgative medicines. 진나 陳那 Dignāga, Diṅnāga ; a native of southern India, the great Buddhist logician, *circa* A.D. 500 or 550, founder of the new logic, cf. 인명 因明 ; he is known also as 동수 童授 and 역룡 域龍. Also used for Jina, victorious, the overcomer, a title of a Buddha.

진 津 Ford, ferry, place of crossing a stream. 진량 津梁 A bridge or ferry across a stream ; i.e. religion. 진송 津送 To escort to the ferry, either the living to deliverance or more generally the dead ; to bid goodbye (to a guest).

진 塵 Guṇa, in Sanskrit *inter alia* means "a secondary element," "a quality," "an attribute of the five elements," e.g. "ether has śabda or sound for its guṇa and the ear for its organ." In Chinese it means "dust, small particles ; molecules, atoms, exhalations." It may be intp. as an atom, or matter, which is considered as defilement ; or as an active, conditioned principle in nature, minute, subtle, and generally speaking defiling to pure mind ; worldly, earthly, the world. The six guṇas or sensation-data are those of sight, sound smell, taste, touch, and thought. 진찰 塵刹 Guṇakṣetra, "field of qualities," certain sins. 진로 塵勞 The trouble of the world, the passions. 진경 塵境 The environment of the six guṇas or qualities of sight, sound, smell, taste, touch, and thought. 진진삼매 塵塵三昧 The samādhi in which, in a moment of time, entry is made into all samādhis. 진진찰토 塵塵刹土 Numberless lands ; also in every grain, or atom, there is a whole realm. 진망 塵妄 Impure and false, as are all temporal things. 진구 塵垢 Material, or phenomenal defilement ; the defilement of the passions. 진욕 塵欲 The desires connected with the six guṇas. 진사 塵沙 Dust and sand, i.e. numberless as the atoms. T'ien-t'ai uses the term as one of the three illusions, i.e. the trial of the bodhisattva in facing the vast amount of detail in knowledge and operation required for his task of saving the world. 진주 塵洲 Worlds as numerous as atoms. 진(점)겁 塵(點)劫 A period of time as impossible of calculation as the atoms of a ground-up world, an attempt to define the infinite, v. Lotus sūtra 7 and 16. 진루 塵累 The passion-karma which entangles the mind. 진망 塵網 The net of the six guṇas, i.e. those connected with the six senses. 진연 塵緣 The circumstances or conditions environing the mind created by the six guṇas. 진표 塵表 Outside of the secular, i.e. the doctrine of Buddha, 진도 塵道 The dusty path, the phenomenal world, or worlds. 진나라 塵那羅 Dīnāra, a coin, a gold coin, from δηνάριον. 진향 塵鄕 The native place or home of the six guṇas, i.e. that of transmigration.

진 辰 Hour ; time ; the celestial bodies. 진나 辰那 Jina, victorious, applied to a Buddha, a saint, etc. ; forms part of the names of 진나달라다 辰那呾邏多 Jinatrāta ; 진나불다라 辰那弗多羅 Jinaputra ; 진나반다 辰那飯茶 Jinabandhu ; three Indian monks in China, the first and last during the seventh century.

진 瞋 Krodha ; pratigha ; dveṣa ; one of the six fundamental kleśas, anger, ire, wrath, resentment, one of the three poisons ; also called 진에 瞋恚. 진에사 瞋恚使 The messenger, or lictor of anger. 진심 瞋心 ; 진에심 瞋恚心 A heart of anger. 진화 瞋火 The fire of anger. 진번뇌 瞋煩惱 The passion or defilement of anger.

진 珍 Precious ; rare. 진역 珍域 The precious region, or Pure Land of a Buddha. 진보 珍寶 A pearl ; jewel ; precious thing. 진중 珍重 To esteem and treat as precious.

진 秦 The Ch'in state and dynasty, 255-205 B.C. 대진 大秦 Syria, the Eastern Roman Empire. 진광왕 秦廣王 Ch'in-kuang, the first of the ten kings of Hades.

진 鎭 To guard, protect, repress ; a town with a guard, a market town. 진수 鎭守 To protect, watch over. 진두가 鎭頭迦 Tinduka, the *Diospyros embryopteros*, or *glutinosa* ; tr. 시 柹 the persimmon ; the 진두가라 鎭頭迦羅 are two fruits, i.e. 진두 鎭頭 and 가라 迦羅, the former good, the latter poisonous.

진 震 To shake, thunder, tremble, awe, quicken ; translit. *cin*, *ci*. 진동 震動 To shake, agitate. 진다말니 震多末尼 Cintāmaṇi, the philosopher's stone, granting all one's wishes. 진단 震旦 Cīna, name of China in ancient India ; also 진단 振旦 ; 진단 眞旦 ; 신단 神旦 intp. as the place where the sun rises, but a translit. of Cīnasthāna. 진령 震嶺 China. 진월 震越 Cīvara, a garment ; an article for sleeping on, or in.

진 眞 True, real ; verisimilitude, e.g. a portrait. 진단 眞丹 ; 진단 震旦 ; 신단 神丹 An ancient Indian term for China ; v. 지나 支那.

진각 眞覺 The true and complete enlightenment, i.e. the perfect nirvāṇa of the Buddha ; the perception of ultimate truth.

진견도 眞見道 The realization of reality in the absolute as whole and undivided, one of the 견도위 見道位.

진경 眞境 The region of truth or reality.

진공 眞空 (1) The absolute void, complete vacuity, said to be the nirvāṇa of the Hīnayāna. (2) The essence of the bhūtatathatā, as the 공진여 空眞如 of the 기신론 起信論, 유식 唯識, and 화엄 華嚴. (3) The void or immaterial as reality, as essential or substantial, the 비공지공 非空之空 not-void void, the ultimate reality, the highest Mahāyāna concept of true voidness, or of ultimate reality. 진공묘유 眞空妙有 The true void is the mysteriously existing ; truly void, or immaterial, yet transcendentally existing.

진금 眞金 Pure gold. 진금상 眞金像 An image of pure gold ; the body of the Buddha. 진금산 眞金山 A mountain of pure gold, i.e. Buddha's body.

진도 眞道 The Truth ; the true way ; reality.

진리 眞理 Truth, the true principle, the principle of truth ; the absolute apart from phenomena.

진망 眞妄 True and false, real and unreal. (1) That which has its rise in Buddha-truth, meditation, wisdom is true ; that which arises from the influences of unenlightenment is untrue. (2) The essential bhūtatathatā as the real, phenomena as the unreal. 진망이심 眞妄二心 The true and false minds, i.e. (1) The true bhūtatathatā mind, defined as the ninth or amala-vijñāna. (2) The false or illusion mind as represented by the eight vijñānas, 팔식 八識.

진명 眞明 True knowledge or enlightenment (in regard to reality in contrast with appearance).

진묘 眞妙 the mysterious reality ; reality in its profundity.

진무루지 眞無漏智 The true knowledge of the Mahāyāna in its concept of mental reality, in contrast with Hīnayāna concepts of material reality.

진문 眞門 The gateway of truth, or reality ; the Truth ; the school of perfect truth, in contrast with partial truth adapted to the condition of the disciple.

진문 眞文 The writings of Truth, those giving the words of the Buddha or bodhisattvas.

진발명성 眞發明性 The spirit of true enlightenment, i.e. the discipline of the mind for the development of the fundamental spiritual or Buddha-nature.

진법 眞法 The real or absolute dharma without attributes, in contrast to phenomena which are regarded as momentary constructs. 진법계 眞法界 The region of reality apart from the temporal and unreal.

진보현 眞普賢 A true P'u-hsien or Samantabhadra, a living incarnation of him.

진불 眞佛 The real Buddha, i.e. the sambhogakāya, or reward body, in contrast to the nirmāṇakāya, or manifested body. Also the Dharmakāya 법신 法身 q.v. 진불자 眞佛子 A true Buddha son, i.e. one who has attained the first stage of bodhisattvahood according to the 별교 definition, i.e. the unreality of the ego and phenomena.

진상 眞常 True and eternal ; the eternal reality of Buddha-truth.

진색 眞色 The mystic or subtle form of the bhūtatathatā, or absolute, the form of the void, or immaterial, Dharmakāya.

진설 眞說 True speech or teaching ; the words of the Buddha.

진성 眞性 The true nature ; the fundamental nature of each individual, i.e. the Buddha-nature.

진속 眞俗 Truth and convention ; the true view and the ordinary ; reality and appearance. 진 眞 is 공 空, and 속 俗 is 가 假.

진승 眞乘 The true vehicle, i.e. the true teaching or doctrine.

진식 眞識 Buddha-wisdom ; the original unadulterated, or innocent mind in all, which is independent of birth and death ; cf. 능가경 楞伽經 and 기신론 起信論. Real knowledge free from illusion, the sixth vijñāna.

진신 眞身 The true body, corpus of truth, dharmakāya, Buddha as absolute.

진실 眞實 Tattva. Truth, reality ; true, real. 진실명 眞實明 The Truth-wisdom, or Buddha-illumination, i.e. prajñā. 진실지 眞實智 Tattvajñāna, knowledge of absolute truth. 진실제 眞實際 The region of reality, the bhūtatathatā.

진심직설 眞心直說 A masterpiece of 지눌 知訥.

진아 眞我 (1) The real or nirvāṇa ego, the transcendental ego, as contrasted with the illusory or temporal ego. (2) The ego as considered real by non-Buddhists.

진어 眞語 True words, especially as expressing the truth of the bhūtatathatā ; the words of the Tathāgata as true and consistent.

진언 眞言 True words, words of Truth, the words of the Tathāgata, Buddha-truth. The term is used for mantra and dhāraṇī, indicating magical formulae, spells, charms, esoteric words. Buddhas and Bodhisattvas have each an esoteric sound represented by a Sanskrit letter, the primary Vairocana letter, the alpha of all sounds being "a" 아 阿, which is also styled 진언구세자 眞言救世者 the True Word that saves the world. 진언승 眞言乘 The True Word, or Mantra-Vehicle, called also the supernatural vehicle, because of immediate attainment of the Buddha-land through tantric methods. 진언종 眞言宗 The True-word or Shingon sect, founded on the mystical teaching "of all Buddhas," the "very words" of the Buddhas ; the especial authority being Vairocana ; cf. the 대일 大日 sūtra, 금강정경 金剛頂經 ; 소실지경 蘇悉地經, etc. The founding of the esoteric sect is attributed to Vairocana, through the imaginary Bodhisattva Vajrasattva, then through Nāgārjuna to Vajramati and to Amoghavajra, *circa* A.D. 733 ; the latter became the effective propagator of the Yogācāra school in China ; he is counted as the sixth patriarch of the school and the second in China. The three esoteric duties of body, mouth, and mind are to hold the symbol in the hand, recite the dhāraṇīs, and ponder over the word "a" 아 阿 as the principle of the ungenerated, i.e. the eternal. 진언지 眞言智 The mantra wisdom, which surpasses all other wisdom. 진언비밀 眞言秘密 The mystic nature of the mantras and dhāraṇīs ; the esoteric things of Shingon.

진여 眞如 Bhūtatathatā, 부다다타다 部多多他多. The 진 眞 is intp. as 진실 眞實 the real. 여 如 as 여상 如常 thus always, or eternally so ; i.e. reality as contrasted with 허망 虛妄 unreality, or appearance, and 불변불개 不變不改 unchanging or immutable as contrasted with form and phenomena. It resembles the ocean in contrast with waves. It is the eternal, impersonal, unchangeable reality behind all phenomena. Bhūta is substance, that which exists ; tathatā is suchness, thusness, i.e. such is its nature. The word is fundamental to Mahāyāna philosophy, implying the absolute, the ultimate source and character of all phenomena, it is the All. It is also called 자성청정심 自性淸淨心 self-existent pure Mind ; 불성 佛性 Buddha-nature ; 법신 法身 Dharmakāya ; 여래장 如來藏 Tathāgata-garbha, or Buddha-treasury ; 실상 實相 reality ; 법계 法界 Dharma-realm ; 법성 法性 Dharma-nature ; 원성실성 圓成實性 The complete and perfect real nature, or reality. There are categories of 1, 2, 3, 7, 10, and 12 in number : (1) The undifferentiated whole. (2) There are several antithetical classes, e.g. the unconditioned and the conditioned ; the 공 空 void, static, abstract, noumenal, and the 불공 不空 not-void, dynamic, phenomenal ; pure, and affected (or infected) ; undefiled (or innocent), i.e. that of Buddhas, defiled, that of all beings ; in bonds and free ; (3) 무상 無相 Formless ; 무생 無生 uncreated ; 무성 無性 without nature, i.e. without characteristics or qualities, absolute in itself. Also, as relative, i.e. good, bad, and indeterminate. (7, 10, 12) the 7 are given in the 유식론 唯識論 8 ; the 10 are in two classes, one of the 별교 別教, cf. 유식론 唯識論 8 ; the other of the 원교 圓教, cf. 보리심의 菩提心義 4 ; the 12 are given in the Nirvāṇa sūtra.

진여내훈 眞如內熏 The internal perfuming or influence of the bhūtatathatā, or Buddha-spirituality.

진여법신 眞如法身 The absolute as dharmakāya, or spiritual body, all embracing.

진여삼매 眞如三昧 The meditation in which all phenomena are eliminated and the bhūtatathatā or absolute is realized.

진여수연 眞如隨緣 The conditioned bhūtatathatā, i.e. as becoming ; it accords with the 무명염연 無明染緣 unconscious and tainting environment to produce all phenomena.

진여실상 眞如實相 The essential characteristic or mark (lakṣaṇa) of the bhūtatathatā, i.e. reality. 진여 眞如 is bhūtatathatā from the point of view of the void, attributeless absolute ; 실상 實相 is bhūtatathatā from the point of view of phenomena.

진여연기 眞如緣起 The absolute in its causative or relative condition ; the bhūtatathatā influenced by environment, or pure and impure conditions, produces all things, v. 연기 緣起.

진여일실 眞如一實 Bhūtatathatā the only reality, the one bhūtatathatā reality.

진여해 眞如海 The ocean of the bhūtatathatā, limitless.

진영 眞影 A reflection of the true, i.e. a portrait, photograph, image, etc.

진응이신 眞應二身 The Dharmakāya and Nirmāṇakāya ; v. 삼신 三身.

진인 眞人 One who embodies the Truth, an arhat ; a Buddha.

진인 眞因 The true cause ; reality as cause.

진자 眞子 A son of the True One, i.e. the Tathāgata ; a Buddha-son, one who embodies Buddha's teaching.

진적 眞寂 The true Buddha-nirvāṇa as contrasted with that of the Hīnayāna.

진전 眞詮 Commentaries or treatise on reality.

진정 眞淨 The true and pure teaching of the Mahāyāna, in contrast to the Hīnayāna.

진제 眞際 The region of reality, ultimate truth, idem 진실제 眞實際.

진제 眞諦 The asseverations or categories of reality, in contrast with 속제 俗諦 ordinary categories ; they are those of the sage, or man of insight, in contrast with those of the common man, who knows only appearance and not reality. 진제삼장 眞諦三藏 Paramārtha 파라말타 波羅末陀, also called Guṇarata 구나라타 拘那羅陀 or Kulanātha, from Ujjain in western India, who came to China A.D. 546, and is famous as translator or editor, e.g. of the 기신론 起信論.

진종 眞宗 The true sect or teaching, a term applied by each sect to its own teaching ; the teaching which makes clear the truth of the bhūtatathatā. The True Sect, or Shin Sect of Japan, founded by Shinran in A.D. 1224, known also as the Hongwanji sect ; celibacy of priests is not required ; Amida is the especial object of trust, and his Pure Land of hope.

진증 眞證 Real evidence, proof, or assurance, or realization of truth. The knowledge, concept, or idea which corresponds to reality.

진지 眞智 Wisdom or knowledge of ultimate truth, or the absolute, also called 무지 無智 knowledge of the no-thing, i.e. of the immaterial or absolute ; also 성지 聖智 sage wisdom, or wisdom of the sage.

진해탈 眞解脫 Release from all the hindrances of passion and attainment of the Buddha's nirvāṇa, which is not a permanent state of absence from the needs of the living, but is spiritual, omniscient, and liberating.

진화 眞化 The teaching of the 진종 眞宗 True (or Shin) sect. 진화이신 眞化二身 The 진신 眞身 is the dharmakāya and sambhogakāya, and the 화신 化身 the nirmāṇakāya ; v. 삼신 三身.

질 蛭 A leech. 질수 蛭數 idem 저사 底沙 Tiṣya.

질 疾 Sickness, an attack of illness ; haste, speedy ; angry. 질서 疾書 Hasty writing ; a hurried note ; write speedily, or at once.

질 質 Substance, matter ; to substantiate, to con-front ; substantial, honest, sound ; translit. *ci, ce.* 질다(야) 質多(耶) ; 질제 質帝 Citta(m), the heart considered as the seat of intellect ; the thinking, reflecting mind. 질다라 質多羅 Citra, variegated, of mixed colours, not of a primary colour. Citrā, the name of a star, Spica in Virgo. 질저 質底 Ci, to assemble, pile up ; caitya, a funeral pile, or mound. 질직 質直 Substantial and straight ; honestly, firmly, straight without dissemblance. Cf. 화변 火辨.

질 蒺 Thorny bushes, furze. 질려 蒺藜 The calthrop, *Tribulus terrestris.*

질 咥 To laugh ; to bite. Translit. *t.* 질리약지 咥哩若底 Trijāti, the three stages of birth, past, present, future. (마)질리가 (摩)咥哩迦 Mātṛkā, a name for Abhidharma-piṭaka.

질 嫉 Īrṣyā ; envy of other's possessions, jealousy.

집 執 Grah, grabh ; graha. To seize, grasp, hold on to, maintain ; obstinate. 집사 執事 To manage, control ; a manager. 집수 執受 Impressions, ideas grasped and held. 집취상 執取相 Retention of memories of past joys and sorrows as if they were realities and not illusions, one of the 육추 六麤 in the Awakening of Faith. 집사자국 執師子國 Siṁhala, Ceylon. 집심 執心 The mind which clings to (things as real). 집정 執情 The foolish passion of clinging to the unreal. 집지 執持 To hold firmly. 집지식 執持識 Ādāna-vijñāna, a name for the ālaya-vijñāna. 집요 執曜 Graha, the planets, nine or seven. 집착 執著 To cling to things as real ; used for abhiniveśa. 집견 執見 Views obstinately held, with consequent delusion ; bigoted. 집금강신 執金剛神 Vajrapāṇi, vajradhara. Any deva-holder of the vajra. (1) Indra, who in a former incarnation took on oath to defend Buddhism, was reborn as king of the Yakṣas, hence he and his yakṣas carry vajras. (2) Mañjuśrī as the spiritual reflex of the Dhyāni Buddha Akṣobhya. (3) A popular deity, the terror of all enemies of Buddhist believers, specially worshipped in exorcisms and sorcery by the Yoga school. 집장 執障 The holding on to the reality of self and things and the consequent hindrance to entrance into nirvāṇa.

집 集 Samudāya. To assemble, collect together, aggregate, accumulate. 집회 集會 To assemble, an assembly. 집회소 集會所 A place of assembly. 집중 集衆 To assemble all, or everybody. 집제 集諦 Samudaya, the second of the four dogmas, that the cause of suffering lies in the passions and their resultant karma. The Chinese 집 集 "accumulation" does not correctly translate Samudaya, which means "origination." 집기 集起 A term for citta, the mind, and for ālayavijñāna, as giving rise to the mass of things.

징 澄 Clear, limpid. 징관 澄觀 Ch'êng-kuan, a famous monk and author, a follower of 현수 賢首 Hsien-shou and supporter of the Hua-yen school, died A.D. 806.

<ㅊ>

차 또는 **거** 車 A cart, wheeled conveyance. 차야 車也 Chāyā, 음 陰 shade, shadow. 차익 車匿 ; 천탁가 闡鐸迦 Chandaka, the driver of Śākyamuni when he left his home. 차제 車帝 The name of a cave, said to be Śataparṇa, or Saptaparṇaguhā. 차축 車軸 The hub of a cart ; applied to large drops (of rain). 차발라파 車鉢羅婆 Name of a spirit.

차 叉 A fork, forked ; to fold, folded. 차수 叉手 The palms of the hands together with the fingers crossed forming ten. Also, the palms together with the middle fingers crossing each other, an old Indian from of greeting. In China anciently the left hand was folded over the right, but with women the right hand was over the left. In mourning salutations the order was reversed. 차나 叉拏 Kṣaṇa, an instant, a moment ; also 찰나 刹那. 차마 叉磨 kṣamā, v. 참회 懺悔. 차야 叉耶 Kṣaya, diminish, decay, end ; v. 걸 乞.

차 嵯 Irregular, uneven ; translit. *jha*.

차 且 Moreover, yet, meanwhile. 차희 且喜 So be it, granted, a qualified assent.

차 次 Second, secondary ; a turn, next. 차제 次第 In turn, one after another. 차제연 次第緣 ; 무간연 無間緣 Connected or consequent causes ; continuous conditional or accessory cause.

차 此 This, here. 차세 此世 ; 차생 此生 This world, or life. 차토저술 此土著述 Narratives in regard to the present life, part of the 잡장 雜藏 miscellaneous piṭaka. 차토이근리 此土耳根利 Clearness of hearing in this world, i.e. the organ of sound fitted to hear the Buddha-gospel and the transcendental. 차안 此岸 This shore, the present life.

차 借 To borrow, lend. 차화헌불 借花獻佛 To borrow a flower to offer to Buddha, i.e. to serve him with another's gift.

차 遮 To cover, screen, veil, hide, hinder ; translit. *ca, cha, tya*. 차제 遮制 ; 차계 遮戒 A secondary commandment, deriving from the mandate of Buddha, e.g. against drinking wine, as opposed to 성계 性戒 a commandment based on the primary laws of human nature, e.g. against murder, etc. ; cf. 이계 二戒. 차타가 遮吒迦 Cātaka, a sparrow ; the bird *Cuculus melanoleucus*, which is supposed only to drink falling rain. 차성 遮性 The two kinds of commandment mentioned above. 차악 遮惡 ; 차죄 遮罪 The second kind of sin as above, e.g. drinking. 차문다 遮文荼 Cāmuṇḍā, a jealous woman ; angry spirit ; evil demon, one used to call up the dead to slay an enemy. 차단 遮斷 To prevent, suppress, cut off. 차말라 遮末邏 ; 차마라 遮摩羅 Cāmara, name of one of the central parts of the southern continent, Jambudvīpa. 차리야 遮梨夜 ; 차리야 遮唎耶 Caryā, actions, doings, proceedings, course. 차조 遮照 To suppress or to reveal (or illuminate) ; destructive or constructive ; to negate or to affirm. 차유 遮遣 To negate, disprove, dispose of . 차나 遮那 ; 비로자나 毘盧遮那 Vairocana, v. 비 毘. 차난 遮難 Tests for applicants for full orders ; there are sixteen (or ten) 차 遮 and thirteen 난 難, the former relating to general character and fitness, the latter referring to moral conduct.

차 磋 To polish ; translit. *cha* ; cf. 차 車, etc.

차 差 To send ; to differ, err ; translit. *kṣ*. 차별 差別 Pariccheda. Difference, different, discrimination ; opposite of 평등 平等 on a level, equal, identical. 차리니가 差利尼迦 Kṣīriṇikā, sap-bearing, a tree of that kind. 차다라 差多羅 Kṣetra, land, region, country. 차라파니 差羅波尼 Kṣārapāṇīya, alkaline water, caustic liquid ; also said to be a kind of garment.

차 嗟 To sigh. 차탄 嗟嘆 Alas! translit. *cha*.

차가(라) 遮迦(羅) Cakra, a wheel, hence Cakravartī or wheel-king.

차거 硨磲 Musāragalva ; Musālagarbha. One of the saptaratna 칠보 七寶 ; M. W. says coral ; others cornelian, or agate.

착 著 To cover, put on ; cause ; place ; complete ; ought, must ; 착 著 is inter-changed with 착 着. In a Buddhist sense it is used for attachment to anything, e.g. the attachment of love, desire, greed, etc. 착개 著鎧 Put on (the Buddha-)armour. 착심 著心 The mind of attachment, or attached. 착상 著想 The attachment of thought, or desire. 착아 著我 Attachment to the ego, or idea of a permanent self. 착락 著樂 Attachment to bliss, or pleasure regarded as real and permanent. 착법 著法 Attachment to things ; attachment and its object. 착의 著衣 To don clothes. 착의끽반 著衣喫飯 To wear clothes and eat food, i.e. the common things of life.

착 着 See 착 著.

찬 羼 Crowding sheep, confusion ; translit. *kṣan*, *ṣan*. 찬지 羼底 ; 찬제 羼提 Kṣānti, patience, forbearance, enduring shame, one of the six pāramitās. 찬제선인 羼提仙人 Kṣāntyṛṣi, name of Śākyamuni in a previous incarnation, the patient or enduring ṛṣi. 찬저라 羼底羅 ; 찬제라 羼提羅 Śaṇḍila, a sterile woman, cf. 선 扇.

찬 讚 Stotra, hymn, praise. 찬불 讚佛 To praise Buddha. 찬패 讚唄 A hymn in praise (of Buddha). 찬탄 讚嘆 ; 찬탄 讚歎 To praise (Buddha). 찬례 讚禮 To praise and worship. 찬중 讚衆 The assembly of praise-singers, led by the 찬두 讚頭 precentor. 찬송 讚誦 To praise and intone ; to sing praises ; a tr. of Rigveda.

찬 贊 To assist. 찬녕 贊寧 Tsan-ning, a learned Sung monk of the tenth century, author of many works, e.g. 송고승전 宋高僧傳 the biographies of noted monks. 찬나낭 贊那囊 Candana, sandal-wood incense.

찬 鑽 To bore, pierce ; an awl. 찬수구소 鑽水求酥 To churn water to get curd.

찬 撰 To compose, compile. 찬호 撰號 Compiler's name, author's title.

찰 刹 Ch'a ; translit. *kṣ*, 찰토 刹土 ; 걸차 乞叉 ; 걸쇄 乞灑 kṣetra, land, fields, country, place ; also a universe consisting of three thousand large chiliocosms ; also, a spire, or flagstaff on a pagoda, a monastery, but this interprets caitya. cf. 제 制. Other forms are 찰다라 刹多羅 or 제다라 制多羅 or 차다라 差多羅 ; 흘차달라 紇差怛羅. 찰진 刹塵 Lands, countless as the dust. 찰(제)리 刹(帝)利 ; 찰달리야 刹怛利耶 Kṣatriya. The second, or warrior and ruling caste ; Chinese render it as 전주 田主 landowners and 왕종 王種 royal caste ; the caste from which the Buddhas (여래 如來) spring. 찰마 刹摩 Kṣema, a residence, dwelling, abode, land, property ; idem 찰 刹 and 찰간 刹竿. 찰해 刹海 Land and sea. 찰간 刹竿 Yaṣṭi. The flagpole of a monastery, surmounted by a gilt ball or pearl, symbolical of Buddhism ; inferentially a monastery with its land. Also 찰주 刹柱, 금찰 金刹 or 표찰 表刹. 찰나 刹那 Kṣaṇa. An indefinite space of time, a moment, an instant ; the shortest measure of time, as kalpa is the longest ; it is defined as 일념 一念 a thought, but according to another definition 60 kṣaṇa equal one finger-snap, 90 a thought 염 念, 4,500 a minute ; there are other definitions. In each kṣaṇa 900 persons are born and die. 찰나삼세 刹那三世 The moments past, present, future. 찰나무상 刹那無常 Not a moment is permanent, but passes through the stages of birth, stay, change, death. 찰나생멸 刹那生滅 All things are in continuous flow, born and destroyed every instant.

찰 擦 To rub, wipe. 찰한 擦汗 To wipe off sweat.

참 or **삼** 參 Reflect on, counsel, visit superior. An assembly, a gathering for the purpose of meditation, preaching, worship. Read *shên*, the twenty-first constellation, *α, β, γ, δ, ε, ζ, η* and *k* in Orion. 조참 早參 Morning assembly ; 만참 晩參 evening assembly ; 소참 小參 a special meeting ; a discussion following an address. 참전 參前 Before the evening assembly ; 참후 參後 ; 참퇴 參退 after the evening assembly. 참문 參問 To seek instruction-generally as a class. 참당 參堂 The initiation to the services of one newly ordained. 참선 參禪 To inquire, discuss, seek religious instruction. 참예 參詣 To approach the gods or Buddhas in worship. 참청 參請 To request instruction, or discussion. 참두 參頭 One versed in the ceremonies and capable of leading others.

참 懺 Kṣamayati, "to ask pardon" ; to seek forgiveness, patience or indulgence, kṣamā meaning patience, forbearance, tr. as 회과 悔過 repentance, or regret for error ; also as confession. It especially refers to the regular confessional service for monks and for nuns. 참의 懺儀 The rules for confession and pardon. 참회 懺悔 Ch'an is the translit. of Kṣamā, 회 悔 its translation, i.e. repentance ; but also the first is intp. as confession, cf. 제 提 deśanā, the second as repentance and reform. 참마 懺摩 ; 차마 叉磨 Kṣamā, kṣamayati, v. *supra* ; to forbear, have patience with ; ask for consideration, or pardon. 참마의 懺摩衣 Clothing made of kṣauma, i.e. wild flax. 참법 懺法 The mode of action, or ritual, at the confessional ; also the various types of confessional, e.g. that of Kuan-yin, Amitābha, etc. 참제 懺除 Confession and forgiveness.

참 讖 To prognosticate, prophesy ; supplicate, fulfil, a password ; translit. *kṣa*. 참라반니 讖羅半尼 Kṣārapāṇīya, ash-water, also intp. as an ash-coloured garment, v. 차 差 10.

참 慙 or 慚 Shame, ashamed ; i.e. for one's own faults, cf. 괴 愧.

창 瘡 A sore, ulcer. 창문 瘡門 Ulcerating orifices, i.e. the nine orifices in the body which discharge.

창 蒼 Azure ; the heavens ; grey, old. 창룡굴 蒼龍窟 The cave of the azure or green dragon, where it lies curled over the talismanic pearl, which only a hero can obtain.

창 唱 To cry out, sing. 창명 唱名 To cry out names ; to call (on) the name (of Buddha). 창적 唱寂 To cry out nirvāṇa, as the Buddha is said to have done at his death. 창도 唱導 To preach to people and lead them to conversion. 창례 唱禮 To announce the ceremonial duty. 창의 唱衣 To cry for sale the robes of a deceased monk, or person. 창도사 唱道師 A preacher ; the president of a monastic assembly. 창식 唱食 To give the "blessing" at meals.

창 彰 Variegated, adorned ; to display, show, make manifest.

채 蔡 Chāyā, a shadow, reflection ; gnomon, dial. 채화 蔡華 A lotus.

채 採 To pick, gather, choose. 채화 採花 ; 채화 採華 To pick flowers. 채숙씨 採菽氏 Bean-picker, a tr. of the name of Maudgalyāyana, from mudga, kidney-beans.

채 菜 Vegetables. 채소 菜蔬 Vegetarian food. 채두 菜頭 The monk who has charge of this department.

책 策 A treatise, book, memo, tablet, card ; a plan, scheme ; question ; whip ; etc. 책수 策修 To stimulate to cultivation of the good ; to keep oneself up to the mark.

책 柵 Palisades, rails, 책문나 柵門那, idem 산야 訕若 Sañjaya.

처 處 To dwell, abide ; fix, decide, punish ; a place, state. Āyatana, 아야달나 阿耶怛那, also tr. 입 入, place or entrance of the sense, both the organ and the sensation, or sense datum ; hence the 십이처 十二處 twelve āyatana, i.e. six organs, and six sense data that enter for discrimination. 처불퇴 處不退 Not to fall away from the status attained. 처중 處中 To abide in the *via media*, which transcends ideas both of existence and non-existence.

척 踢 To kick. 척도 踢倒 To kick over.

척 擲 To throw, throw away, reject. 척악인 擲惡人 To cast away , or reject, wicked men. 척지다 擲枳多 Chikdha, the modern Chitor, or Chittore, in Central India. Eitel.

천 川 A stream, a mountain stream ; Ssŭ-ch'uan province. 천시아귀 川施餓鬼 Making offerings at the streams to the ghosts of the drowned.

천 天 Heaven ; the sky ; a day ; cf. dyo, dyaus also as 제바 提婆 a deva, or divine being, deity ; and as 소라 素羅 sura, shining, bright. 삼종천 三種天 The three classes of devas : (1) 명천 名天 famous rulers on earth styled 천왕 天王, 천자 天子 ; (2) 생천 生天 the highest incarnations of the six paths ; (3) 정천 淨天 the pure, or the saints, from śrāvakas to pratyeka-buddhas. 지도론 智度論 7. 사종천 四種天 The four classes of devas include (1), (2), (3), above ; and (4) 의천 義天 all bodhisattvas above the ten stages 십주 十住. The Buddhas are not included ; 지도론 智度論 22. 오종천 五種天 The above four with the addition of 제일의천 第一義天 a supreme heaven with bodhisattvas and Buddhas in eternal immutability ; 열반경 涅槃經 23. Cf. 천궁 天宮.

천 祆 Hsien, commonly but incorrectly written 요 祆, a Western Asian name for Heaven, or the 천신 天神 God of Heaven, adopted by the Zoroastrians and borrowed later by the Manicheans ; also intp. as Maheśvara. 천사 祆寺 A Manichean monastery. 천교 祆教 or 말니교 末尼教 The Manichean religion.

천 千 Sahasra. A thousand. 천이백오십인 千二百五十人 The 1,250, i.e. the immediate disciples of Buddha's disciples, all former heretics converted to Buddha's truth. 천이백설공덕 千二百舌功德 ; 천이백이공덕 千二百耳功德 ; 천이백의공덕 千二百意功德 The 1,200 merits of tongue, ear, or mind, in the Lotus Sūtra. 천불 千佛 The thousand Buddhas. Each of the past, present, and future kalpas has a thousand Buddhas ; Śākyamuni is the "fourth" Buddha in the present kalpa. The 천불명경 千佛名經 professes to give their names. 천화 千化 The thousand-petalled lotus on which sits Locana Buddha, each petal a transformation of Śākyamuni ; Locana represents also the Saṅgha, as Vairocana represents the Dharma. 천여시 千如是 The thousand "suchnesses" or characteristics, a term of the T'ien-t'ai sect. In each of the ten realms 십계 十界, from Buddha to purgatory, the ten are present, totalling one hundred. These multiplied by the ten categories of existence make a thousand, and multiplied by the three categories of group existence make 3,000. 천수(천안) 千手(千眼) ; 천수천안대자대비관음보살 千手千眼大慈大悲觀音菩薩 The thousand-hand Kuan-yin, see below. There are various sūtras associated with this title, e.g. 천수경 千手經, an abbreviation of 천수천안관세음보살대...다라니경 千手千眼觀世音菩薩大...陀羅尼經 ; also 천수궤 千手軌 or 궤경 軌經 an abbreviation of 금강정유가천수...의궤경 金剛頂瑜伽千手...儀軌經 ; it is also called 천수다라니 千手陀羅尼 and 천수천안의궤경 千手千眼儀軌經 ; there are many others, e.g. 천수천안관세음보살모다라니신경 千手千眼觀世音菩薩姥陀羅尼身經 and 천수천안광대원만무애대비심다라니경 千手千眼廣大圓滿無礙大悲心陀羅尼經 both idem 천수천비다라니신주 千手千臂陀羅尼神咒, which is the Avalokiteśvara-padma-jāla-mūla-tantra-nāma-dhāraṇī. 천수관음 千手觀音 ; 천수천안관음 千手千眼觀音 ; 천안천비관세음 千眼千臂觀世音 Sahasrabhujasahasranetra. One of the six forms of Kuan-yin with a thousand arms and a thousand eyes. The image usually has forty arms, one eye in each hand ; and forty multiplied by twenty-five is the number of regions in this universe. For the 이십팔부 二十八部 or retinue, the maṇḍala and signs v. 천수경 千手經. 천법명문 千法明門 The gate of understanding of the thousand laws – the second stage of a bodhisattva's study and attainment. 천천 千泉 Bingheul. 병율 屏律 Mingbulak. A lake country 30 li E. of Talas. 천백억신 千百億身 The Buddha Locana seated on a lotus of a thousand petals, each containing myriads of worlds ; in each world is Śākyamuni seated under a bodhi-tree, all such worlds attaining bodhi at the same instant ; see above. 천안천 千眼天 The Deva with 1,000 eyes, epithet of Indra, 제석 帝釋. 천엽대 千葉臺 The throne of a thousand petals, i.e. that of

Locana Buddha ; see above. 천폭륜상 千輻輪相 Sahasrāra ; the thousand-spoked wheel sign, i.e. the wrinkles on the soles of a cakravartī, or Buddha. 천부론사 千部論師 ; 천부론주 千部論主 Master of a thousand śāstras – a title of Nāgārjuna and of Vasubandhu. 천리구 千里駒 The thousand-li colt, a name for Hsüan-tsang.

천 淺 Shallow ; superficial ; light in colour ; simple, easy. 천략 淺略 Superficial, simple, not profound. 천랍 淺臘 Of few years, i.e. youthful in monastic years.

천 穿 To bore, pierce ; to thread ; to don, put on. To bore a well, and gradually discover water, likened to the gradual discovery of the Buddha-nature. 천이승 穿耳僧 Pierced-ear monks, many of the Indian monks wore ear-rings ; Bodhidharma was called 천이객 穿耳客 the ear-pierced guest.

천 遷 To move, remove, improve, promote, dismiss. 천화 遷化 To be taken away, i.e. die.

천 闡 To open, spread, enlarge, expand, expound ; translit. *chan*. 천제 闡提 v. 일천제 一闡提 Icchantika, intp. as unable to become Buddha (a) because of unbelief, or abandoned character ; (b) because of a bodhisattva vow. 천타 闡陀 Chandaka, name of the Buddha's driver when he left home ; he became a monk ; also 천나 闡那 ; 천택가 闡擇迦 ; 천석가 闡釋迦 ; 천탁가 闡鐸迦 ; 차닉 車匿 ; also a form of metre ; poetry ; hymns ; a style of poetic recitation.

천(계)역사 天(界)力士 idem 나라연 那羅延 Nārāyaṇa.

천가로 天迦盧 Devanāgarī, 신자 神字 the usual form of Sanskrit writing, introduced into Tibet, v. 범자 梵字.

천개 天蓋 A Buddha's canopy, or umbrella ; a nimbus of rays of light, a halo.

천계 天界 idem 천도 天道.

천고 天鼓 The deva drum – in the 선법 善法 Good Law Hall of the Trayastriṁśāḥs heavens, which sounds of itself, warning the inhabitants of the thirty-three heavens that even their life is impermanent and subject to karma ; at the sound of the drum Indra preaches against excess. Hence it is a title of Buddha as the great law-drum, who warns, exhorts, and encourages the good and frightens the evil and the demons. 천고뢰음불 天鼓雷音佛 ; 고음여래 鼓音如來 Divyadundubhimeghanirghoṣa. One of the five Buddhas in the Garbhadhātu maṇḍala, on the north of the central group ; said to be one of the dharmakāya of Śākyamuni, his 등류신 等流身 or universal emanation body ; and is known as 부동존 不動尊 corresponding with Akṣobhya, cf. 오지여래 五智如來 and 대일경소 大日經疏 4. 천고음 天鼓音 ; 운자재등왕 雲自在燈王 Dundubhiṣvara-rāja. Lord of the sound of celestial drums, i.e. the thunder. Name of each of 2,000 koṭīs of Buddhas who attained Buddhahood.

천관 天冠 A deva-crown, surpassing human thought.

천구 天口 The mouth of Brahma, or the gods, a synonym for fire, as that element devours the offerings ; to this the 호마 護摩 homa, or fire altar cult is attributed, fire becoming the object of worship for good fortune. Fire is also said to speak for or tell the will of the gods.

천구 天狗 Ulkā, 우류가 憂流迦 the "heavenly dog," i.e. a meteor. Also "a star in Argo," Williams.

천궁 天宮 Devapura ; devaloka ; the palace of devas, the abode of the gods, i.e. the six celestial worlds situated above the Menu, between the earth and the Brahmalokas. v. 육천 六天. 천궁보장 天宮寶藏 A library of the sūtras. The treasury of all the sūtras in the Tuṣita Heaven in Maitreya's palace. Another collection is said to be in the 용궁 龍宮 or Dragon's palace, but is associated with Nāgārjuna.

천궁 天弓 The deva-bow, the rainbow.

천귀 天鬼 Gods and demons ; gati, or reincarnation, among devas and demons.

천근 天根 The phallic emblem of Śiva, which Hsüan-tsang found in the temples of India ; he says the Hindus "worship it without being ashamed."

천기 天機 Natural capacity ; the nature bestowed by Heaven.

천녀 天女 Devakanyā ; apsaras ; goddesses in general ; attendants on the regents of the sun and moon ; wives of Gandharvas ; the division of the sexes is maintained throughout the devalokas 육천 六天.

천당 天堂 The mansions of the devas, located between the earth and the Brahmalokas ; the heavenly halls ; heaven. The Ganges is spoken of as 천당래자 天堂來者 coming from the heavenly mansions. 천당지옥 天堂地獄 The heavens and the hells, places of reward or punishment for moral conduct.

천덕병 天德甁 The vase of deva virtue, i.e. the bodhi heart, because all that one desires comes from it, e.g. the 여의주 如意珠 the talismanic pearl. Cf. 천의수 天意樹.

천도 天道 Deva-gati, or Devasopāna, 천취 天趣. (1) The highest of the six paths 육도 六道, the realm of devas, i.e. the eighteen heavens of form and four of formlessness. A place of enjoyment, where the meritorious enjoy the fruits of good karma, but not a place of progress toward bodhisattva perfection. (2) The Tao of Heaven, natural law, cosmic energy ; according to the Taoists, the origin and law of all things.

천독 天督 T'ien-tu, an erroneous form of 천축 天竺, or 인도 印度 Yin-tu, India.

천동 天童 Divine youths, i.e. deva guardians of the Buddha-law who appear as Mercuries, or youthful messengers of the Buddhas and bodhisattvas. 천동산 天童山 ; 천동산 天潼山 A famous group of monasteries in the mountains near Ningpo, also called 태백산 太白山 Venus-planet mountain ; this is one of the five famous mountains of China.

천라국 天羅國 The kingdom of the king with kalmāṣapāda, i.e. spotted, or striped feet 반정왕 斑定王 ; cf. 인왕경 仁王經.

천룡 天龍 Devas, including Brahmā, Indra, and the devas, together with the nāgas. 천룡팔부 天龍八部 Devas, nāgas, and others of the eight classes : devas, nāgas, yakṣas, gandharvas, asuras, garuḍas, kinnaras, mahoragas. 천 天 ; 용 龍 ; 야차 夜叉 ; 건달바 乾闥婆 ; 아수라 阿修羅 ; 가루라 迦樓羅 ; 견나라 堅那羅 ; 마후라가 摩睺羅迦. 천룡야차 天龍夜叉 Devas, nāgas, yakṣas.

천마 天魔 Deva Māra, 마라 魔羅 one of the four Māras, who dwells in the sixth heaven, Paranirmita-vaśavartin, at the top of the Kāmadhātu, with his innumerable host, whence he constantly obstructs the Buddha-truth and its followers. He is also styled 살자 殺者 the slayer ; also 파순 波旬 explained by 악애 惡愛 sinful love or desire, as he sends his daughters to seduce the saints ; also 파비(야) 波卑(夜) Pāpīyān, the evil one. He is the special Māra of the Śākyamuni period ; other Buddhas suffer from other Māras ; v. 마 魔. 천마외도 天魔外道 Māras and heretics — both enemies of Buddha-truth.

천부 天部 The classes of devas ; the host of devas ; the host of heaven. 천부선신 天部善神 Brahmā, Indra, the four devaloka-rājas, and the other spirit guardians of Buddhism.

천비성 天臂城 Devadarśita or Devadiṣṭa, Deva-arm city, but the Sanskrit means deva (or divinely) indicated. The residence of Suprabuddha, 선각장자 善覺長者 father of Māyā, mother of the Buddha.

천사 天祠 Devālaya, Devatāgāra, or Devatāgṛha. Brahminical temples.

천사 天使 Divine messengers, especially those of Yama ; also his 삼천사 三天使 three messengers, or lictors — old age, sickness, death ; and his 오천사 五天使 or 오대사 五大使, i.e. the last three together with rebirth and prisons or punishments on earth.

천사 天師 Preceptor of the emperor, a title of the monk 일행 一行 I-hsing, and of the so-called Taoist Pope.

천상 天上 The heavens above, i.e. the six devalokas 육욕천 六欲天 of the region of desire and the rūpalokas and arūpalokas, i.e. 색 色 and 무색계 無色界.

천상천하유아독존 天上天下唯我獨尊 The first words attributed to Śākyamuni after his first seven steps when born from his mother's right side : "In the heavens above and (earth) beneath I alone am the honoured one." This announcement is ascribed to every Buddha, as are also the same special characteristics attributed to every Buddha, hence he is the 여래 如來 come in the manner of all Buddhas. In Mahāyānism he is the type of countless other Buddhas in countless realms and periods.

천선 天仙 Deva-ṛṣis, or devas and ṛṣis, or immortals. Nāgārjuna gives ten classes of ṛṣis whose lifetime is 100,000 years, then they are reincarnated. Another category is fivefold ; 천선 天仙 deva-ṛṣis in the mountains round Sumeru ; 신선 神仙 spirit-ṛṣis who roam the air ; 인선 人仙 humans who have attained the powers of immortals ; 지선 地仙 earth ṛṣis, subterranean ; 귀선 鬼仙 pretas, or malevolent ṛṣis.

천수 天授 Heaven-bestowed, a name of Devadatta, v. 제 提.

천수보리 天須菩提 Deva Subhūti, one of three Subhūtis, disciples of the Buddha ; said to have been so called because of his love of fine clothing and purity of life.

천수왕 天樹王 The pārijāta tree 파리질다 波利質多 which grows in front of Indra's palace — the king among the heavenly trees.

천승 天乘 Devayāna. The deva vehicle — one of the 오승 五乘 five vehicles ; it transports observers of the ten good qualities 십희 十喜 to one of the six deva realms of desire, and those who observe dhyāna meditation to the higher heavens of form and non-form.

천식 天識 Natural perception, or wisdom ; the primal endowment in man ; the 진여 眞如 or Bhūtatathatā.

천식 天食 Sudhā, food of the gods, sweet dew, ambrosia, nectar ; blue, yellow, red, and white in colour, white for the higher ranks, the other colours for the lower.

천신 天神 Deva 제바 提婆 or Devatā 이박다 泥縛多. (1) Brahmā and the gods in general, including the inhabitants of the devalokas, all subject to metempsychosis. (2) The fifteenth patriarch, a native of South India, or Ceylon, and disciple of Nāgārjuna ; he is also styled Devabodhisattva 제바보살 提婆菩薩, Āryadeva 성천 聖天, and Nīlanetra 청목 青木 blue-eyed, or 분별명 分別明 clear discriminator. He was the author of nine works and a famous antagonist of Brahmanism. 천신지기 天神地祇 The spirits 천신 天神 are Indra and his retinue ; devas in general ; the 지기 地祇 are the earth spirits, nāgas, demons, ghosts, etc.

천악 天樂 Heavenly music, the music of the inhabitants of the heavens. Also one of the three "joys" — that of those in the heavens.

천안 天眼 Divyacakṣus. The deva-eye ; the first abhijñā, v. 육통 六通 ; one of the five classes of eyes ; divine sight, unlimited vision ; all things are open to it, large and small, near and distant, the destiny of all beings in future rebirths. It may be obtained among men by their human eyes through the practice of meditation 수득 修得 ; and as a reward or natural possession by those born in the deva heavens 보득 報得. Cf. 천이 天耳, etc. 천안력 天眼力 The power of the celestial or deva eye, one of the ten power of a Buddha. 천안명 天眼明 One of the three enlightenments 삼명 三明, or clear visions of the saint, which enables him to know the future rebirths of himself and all beings. 천안지 天眼智 The wisdom obtained by the deva eye. 천안지(증)통 天眼智(證)通 The complete universal knowledge and assurance of the deva eye. 천안지통원 天眼智通願 The sixth of Amitābha's forty-eight vows, that he would not enter the final stage until all beings had obtained this divine vision. 천안통 天眼通 idem 천안 天眼 ; also a term used by those who practice hypnotism.

천애 天愛 Devānāṁpriya. "Beloved of the gods," i.e. natural fools, simpletons, or the ignorant.

천어 天語 The deva language, i.e. that of the Brahman, Sanskrit.

천옥 天獄 The heavens and hells ; devalokas and purgatories.

천왕 天王 Mahārāja-devas ; 사천왕 四天王 Catur-mahārāja. The four deva kings in the first or lowest devaloka, on its four sides. E. 지국천왕 持國天王 Dhṛtarāṣṭra. S. 증장천왕 增長天王 Virūḍhaka. W. 광목천왕 廣目天王 Virūpākṣa. N. 다문천왕 多聞天王 Dhanada, or Vaiśravaṇa. The four are said to have appeared to 불공 不空 Amogha in a temple in Hsi-an-fu, some time between 742-6, and in consequence he introduced their worship to China as guardians of the monasteries, where their images are seen in the hall at the entrance, which is sometimes called the 천왕당 天王堂 hall of the deva-kings. 천왕 天王 is also a designation of Śiva the 대자재 大自在, i.e. Maheśvara 마혜수라 摩醯首羅, the great sovereign ruler. 천왕여래 天王如來 Devarāja-tathāgata, the name by which Devadatta, v. 제 提, the enemy of Śākyamuni, will be known on his future appearance as a Buddha in the universe called 천도 天道 Devasopāna ; his present residence in hell being temporary for his karmaic expurgation.

천유 天有 Existence and joy as a deva, derived from previous devotion, the fourth of the seven forms of existence.

천의 天衣 Deva garments, of extreme lightness. 천의불천세 天衣拂千歲 An illustration of the length of a small kalpa ; if a great rock, let it be one, two, or even 40 li square, be dusted with a deva-garment once in a hundred years till the rock be worn away, the kalpa would still be unfinished.

천의수 天意樹 The tree in each devaloka which produces whatever the devas desire.

천이(통) 天耳(通) Divyaśrotra, deva-ear, celestial ear. 천이지(통) 天耳智(通) ; 천이지증통 天耳智證通 The second of the six abhijñās 육통 六通 by which devas in the form-world, certain arhats through the fourth dhyāna, and others can hear all sounds and understand all languages in the realms of form, with resulting wisdom. For its equivalent interpretation and its 수득 修得 and 보득 報得 v. 천안 天眼. 천이지통원 天耳智通願 The seventh of the forty-eight vows of Amitābha, not to become Buddha until all obtain the divine ear.

천인 天人 Devas and men ; also a name for devas. 천인사 天人師 Śāstā Devamanuṣyāṇām 사다제바마누사남 舍多提婆摩㝹舍喃, teacher of devas and men, one of the ten epithets of a Buddha, because he reveals goodness and morality, and is able to save. 천인산화신상 天人散花身上 The story of the man who saw a disembodied ghost beating a corpse which he said was his body that had led him into all sin, and further on an angel stroking and scattering flowers on a corpse, which he said was the body he had just left, always his friend. 천인도사 天人道師 idem 천인사 天人師.

천자 天子 A son of Heaven. The Emperor-Princes, i.e. those who in previous incarnations have kept the middle and lower grades of the ten good qualities 십선 十善 and, in consequence, are born here as princes. It is the title of one of the four māra, who is 천주 天主 or lord of the sixth heaven of desire ; he is also known as 천자(업)마 天子(業)魔 and with his following opposes the Buddha-truth.

천제 天帝 King, or emperor of Heaven, i.e. 인다라 因陀羅 Indra, i.e. 석(가) 釋(迦) ; 석가바 釋迦婆 ; 제(석) 帝(釋) ; Śakra, king of the devaloka 도리천 忉利天, one of the ancient gods of India, the god of the sky who fights the demons with his vajra, or thunderbolt. He is inferior to the trimūrti, Brahma, Viṣṇu, and Śiva, having taken the place of Varuṇa, or sky. Buddhism adopted him as its defender, though, like all the gods, he is considered inferior to a Buddha or any who have attained bodhi. His wife is Indrāṇī. 천제생려태 天帝生驢胎 Lord of devas, born in the womb of an ass, a Buddhist fable, that Indra knowing he was to be reborn from the womb of an ass, in sorrow sought to escape his fate, and was told that trust in Buddha was the only way. Before he reached Buddha his life came to an end and he found himself in the ass. His resolve, however, had proved effective, for the master of the ass beat her so hard that she dropped her foal dead. Thus Indra returned to his former existence and began his ascent to Buddha. 천제석성 天帝釋城 The city of Śakra, the Lord of devas, called 선견성 善見城 Sudarśana city good to behold, or 희견성 喜見城 city a joy to behold.

천제산 天悌山 The ladder-to-heaven hill or monastery, i.e. 천태산 天台山 T'ien-t'ai mountain in Chekiang.

천존 天尊 The most honoured among devas, a title of a Buddha, i.e. the highest of divine beings ; also used for certain mahārāja protectors of Buddhism and others in the sense of honoured devas. Title applied by the Taoists to their divinities as a counterpart to the Buddhist 세존 世尊.

천주 天主 Devapati, The Lord of devas, a title of Indra. 천주교법 天主教法 Devendra-samaya. Doctrinal method of the lord do devas. A work on royalty in the possession of a son of Rājabalendraketu.

천중 天衆 The host of heaven, Brahma, Indra, and all their host. 천중오상 天衆五相 The five signs of approaching demise among the devas, cf. 오쇠 五衰.

천중천 天中天 Devātideva ; deva of devas. The name given to Siddhārtha (i.e. Śākyamuni) when, on his presentation in the temple of 천왕 天王 Maheśvara (Śiva), the statues of all the gods prostrated themselves before him.

천지경 天地鏡 The mirror of heaven and earth i.e. the Prajñā-pāramitā Sūtra, see 반야 般若.

천진 天眞 Bhūtatathatā, permanent reality underlying all phenomena, pure and unchanging, e.g. the sea in contrast with the waves ; nature, the natural, 천연지진리 天然之眞理, 비인지조작자 非人之造作者 natural reality, not of human creation. 천진불 天眞佛 The real or ultimate Buddha ; the bhūtatathatā ; another name for the Dharmakāya, the source of all life. 천진독랑 天眞獨朗 The fundamental reality, or bhūtatathatā, is the only illumination. It is a dictum of 도수 道邃 Tao-sui of the T'ang to the famous Japanese monk 전교 傳教 Dengyō. The apprehension of this fundamental reality makes all things clear, including the universality of Buddhahood. It also interprets the phrase 일심삼관 一心三觀 that 공중가 空中假 the void, the "mean", the seeming, are all aspects of the one mind.

천축(국) 天竺(國) India ; 죽 竹 Chu is said to have the same sound as 독 篤 tu, suggesting a connection with the 도 度 tu in 인도 印度 Indu ; other forms are 연독 身毒 Sindhu, Scinde

; 현두 賢豆 Hindu ; and 인지가라 印持伽羅. The term is explained by 월 月 moon, which is the meaning of Indu, but it is said to be so called because the sages of India illumine the rest of the world ; or because of the half-moon shape of the land, which was supposed to be 90,000 li in circumference, and placed among other kingdoms like the moon among the stars. Another name is 인다라바다나 因陀羅婆他那 Indravadana, or Indrabhavana, the region where Indra dwells. A hill and monastery near Hangchow. 천축삼시 天竺三時 or 천축삼제 天竺三際. The three seasons of an Indian year : Grīṣma, the hot season, from fist month, sixteenth day, to fifth month, fifteenth ; Varṣākāla, the rainy season, fifth month, sixteenth, to ninth month, fifteenth ; Hemanta, the cold season, ninth month, sixteenth, to first month, fifteenth. These three are each divided into two, making six seasons, or six periods : Vasanta and grīṣma, varṣākāla and śarad, hemanta and śiśira. The twelve months are Caitra, Vaiśākha, Jyaiṣṭha, Āṣāḍhā, Śrāvaṇa, Bhādrapada, Aśvayuja, Kārttika, Mārgaśirṣa, Pauṣa, Māgha, and Phālguna. 천축구의 天竺九儀 The nine forms of etiquette of India : speaking softly, bowing the head, raising the hands high, placing hands together, bending knees, kneeling long, hands and knees touching the ground, bowing the head, lowering arms and bending knees, bringing head, arms, and knees to the ground. 천축오산 天竺五山 The five mountains of India on which the Buddha assembled his disciples : Vaibhāra, Saptaparṇaguhā, Indraśailaguhā, Sarpiṣkuṇḍikā-prāgbhāra, Gṛdhrakūṭa.

천취 天趣 idem 천도 天道.

천친 天親 Vasubandhu, 벌소반도 伐蘇畔度 ; 파수반두 婆藪槃豆 or 婆修槃豆 or 파수반타 婆藪槃陀 "akin to the gods", or 세친 世親 "akin to the world". Vasubandhu is described as a native of Puruṣapura, or Peshawar, by Eitel as of Rājagṛha, born "900 years after the nirvāṇa", or about A.D. 400 ; Takakusu suggests 420-500, Pe'ri puts his death not later than 350. In Eitel's day the date of his death was put definitely at A.D. 117. Vasubandhu's great work, the Abhidharma-kośa, is only one of his thirty-six works. He is said to be the younger brother of Asaṅga of the Yogācāra school, by whom he was converted from the Sarvāstivāda school of thought to that of Mahāyāna and of Nāgārjuna. On his conversion he would have "cut out his tongue" for its past heresy, but was dissuaded by his brother, who bade him use the same tongue to correct his errors, whereupon he wrote the 유식론 唯識論 and other Mahāyānist works. He is called the twenty-first patriarch and died in Ayodhyā.

천태 天台 The T'ien-t'ai (sect). 천태산 天台山 The T'ien-t'ai or Heavenly Terrace mountain, the location of the T'ien-t'ai sect ; its name is attributed to the 삼태 三台 six stars at the foot of Ursa Major, under which it is supposed to be, but more likely because of its height and appearance. It gives its name to a hsien in the Chekiang T'aichow prefecture, south-west of Ningpo. The monastery, or group of monasteries, was founded there by 지의 智顗 Chih-i, who is known as 천태대사 天台大師.

천태구조 天台九祖 The nine patriarchs of the T'ien-t'ai sect : 용수龍樹 Nāgārjuna ; 혜문 慧文 Hui-wên of the 북제 北齊 Northern Ch'i dynasty, 혜사 慧思 Hui-ssŭ of 남악 南岳 Nan-yo ; 지자 智者 or 지의 智顗 Chih-chê, or Chih-i ; 관정 灌頂 Kuan-ting of 장안 章安 Chang-an ; 법화 法華 Fa-hua ; 천궁 天宮 T'ien-kung 좌계 左溪 Tso-ch'i ; and 잠연 湛然 Chan-jan of 형계 荊溪 Ching-ch'i. The ten patriarchs 십조 十祖 are the above nine with 도수 道邃 Tao-sui considered a patriarch in Japan, because he was the teacher of Dengyō Daishi who brought the Tendai system to that country in the ninth century. Some name Hui-wên and Hui-ssŭ as the first and second patriarchs of the school of thought developed by Chih-i at T'ien-t'ai ; v. 천태종 天台宗.

천태대사 天台大師 The actual founder of the T'ien-t'ai "school" 지의 智顗 Chih-i ; his 자 字 was 덕안 德安 Tê-an, and his surname 진 陳 Ch'ên, A.D. 538-597. Studying under 혜사 慧思 Hui-ssŭ of Hunan, he was greatly influenced by his teaching ; and found in the Lotus Sūtra the real interpretation of Mahāyānism. In 575 he first came to T'ien-t'ai and established his school, which in turn was the foundation of important Buddhist schools in Korea and Japan.

천태덕소국사 天台德韶國師 T'ien-t'ai-dé-Shao-Kuo-Shih, a Chekiang priest who revived the T'ien-t'ai sect by journeying to Korea, where the only copy of Chih-i's works existed, copied them, and returned to revive the T'ien-t'ai school. 전숙 錢俶 Ch'ien Shu (A.D. 960-997), ruler of 오월 吳越 Wu Yüeh, whose capital was at Hangchow, entitled him Imperial Teacher.

천태사교 天台四教 The four types each of method and doctrine, as defined by T'ien-t'ai ; see last entry 화의사교 化儀四教.

천태사교의 天台四教儀 A masterpiece of 제관 諦觀 on 천태 天台 philosophies.

천태삼교 天台三教 The three modes of Śākyamuni's teaching as explained by the T'ien-t'ai sect : (1) the sudden, or immediate teaching, by which the learner is taught the whole truth at once 돈교 頓教 ; (2) the gradual teaching 점교 漸教 ; (3) the undetermined or variable method whereby he is taught what he is capable of receiving 부정 不定. Another category is 점 漸 gradual, 돈 頓 direct, and 원 圓 perfect, the last being found in the final or complete doctrine of the 법화경 法華經 Lotus Sūtra. Another is : (1) 삼장교 三藏教 the Tripiṭaka doctrine, i.e. the orthodox Hīnayāna ; (2) 통교 通教 intermediate, or interrelated doctrine, i.e. Hīnayāna-cum-Mahāyāna ; (3) 별교 別教 differentiated or separated doctrine, i.e. the early Mahāyāna as a cult or development, as distinct from Hīnayāna.

천태율 天台律 The laws of the T'ien-t'ai sect as given in the Lotus, and the ten primary commandments and forty-eight secondary commandments of 범망경 梵網經 the sūtra of Brahma's net (Brahmajāla) ; they are ascribed as the 대승원돈계 大乘圓頓戒 the Mahāyāna perfect and immediate moral precepts, immediate in the sense of the possibility of all instantly becoming Buddha.

천태종 天台宗 The T'ien-t'ai, or Tendai, sect founded by 지의 智顗 Chih-i. It bases its tenets on the Lotus Sūtra 법화경 法華經 with the 지도론 智度論 ; 열반경 涅槃經, and 대품경 大品經 ; it maintains the identity of the Absolute and the world of phenomena, and attempts to unlock the secrets of all phenomena by means of meditation. It flourished during the T'ang dynasty. Under the Sung, when the school was decadent, arose 사명 四明 Ssŭ-ming, under whom there came the division of 산가 山家 Hill or T'ien-t'ai School and 산외 山外 the School outside, the latter following 오은 悟恩 Wu-ên and in time dying out ; the former, a more profound school, adhered to Ssŭ-ming ; it was from this school that the T'ien-t'ai doctrine spread to Japan. The three principal works of the T'ien-t'ai founder are called 천태삼부 天台三部, i.e. 현의 玄義 exposition of the deeper meaning of the Lotus ; 문구 文句 exposition of its text ; and 지관 止觀 meditation ; the last was directive and practical ; it was in the line of Bodhidharma, stressing the "inner light."

천태팔교 天台八教 ; 팔교 八教 The 화법사교 化法四教 or four periods of teaching, i.e. 장 藏, 통 通, 별 別, and 원 圓 Hīnayāna, Interrelated, Differentiated, and Complete or Final ; the 화의사교 化儀四教 q.v. are the four modes of teaching, direct, gradual, esoteric, and indefinite.

천행 天行 A bodhisattva's natural or spontaneous correspondence with fundamental law ; one of the 오행 五行 of the 열반경 涅槃經 Nirvāṇa sūtra.

천향 天香 Deva incense, divine or excellent incense.

천화 天華 Deva, or divine, flowers, stated in the Lotus sūtra as of four kinds, mandāras, mahāmandāras, mañjūṣakas, and mahāmañjūṣakas, the first two white, the last two red.

천화 天畫 Deva lines or pictures.

천황 天皇 Deva-king ; the T'ang monk 도오 道悟 Tao-wu of the 천황 天皇 T'ien-huang monastery at 형주 荊州 Ching-chou.

천후 天后 Queen of Heaven, v. 마리지 摩利支.

철 鐵 Iron. 철위산 鐵圍山 Cakravāla, Cakravāḍa. The iron enclosing mountains supposed to encircle the earth, forming the periphery of a world. Mount Meru is the centre and between it and the Iron mountains are the seven 금산 金山 metal-mountains and the eight seas. 철성 鐵城 The iron city, hell. 철찰 鐵札 Iron tablets in Hades, on which are recorded each person's crimes and merits. 철륜 鐵輪 The iron wheel ; also cakravāla, *supra*. 철륜왕 鐵輪王 Iron-wheel king, ruler of the south and of Jambudvīpa, one of the 사륜왕 四輪王. 철발 鐵鉢 Cf. 사발 四鉢. Iron pātra, or almsbowl. 철제 鐵際 The boundary of the cakravāla, v. *supra*.

철 徹 Penetrate, pervious, perspicacious ; throughout ; communal. 철심 徹心 To penetrate or reach the heart or mind.

첨 添 Add, additional, increase. 첨품 添品 Additional chapter, or chapters.

첨 檐 Eaves, v. 섬 贍 20.

첨 諂 To flatter, fawn, cajole, sycophancy. 첨곡 諂曲 Flattery and fawning.

첨 瞻 To look up to, or for ; revere, adore, expect, i.e. 첨앙 瞻仰 ; translit. *ca, ja*. 첨복(가) 瞻匐(迦) Campa, Campaka, a yellow fragrant flower, *Michelia champaka* ; also 첨파 瞻波 ; 첨파 瞻婆 ; 첨박(가) 瞻博(迦) ; 섬파 睒婆 ; 점파 占婆 ; 전파가 旃波迦, etc. 첨파국 瞻波國 ; 첨파성 瞻婆城 The country and city of Campā, given by M. W. as "the modern Bhāgalpur or a place in its vicinity, founded by Campa" ; by Eitel as "a district in the upper Punjab." 첨병 瞻病 To examine a sick person medically. 첨부 瞻部 v. 염 閻 Jambudvīpa. 첨풍 瞻風 To hope for the wind (of Buddha truth or aid).

첩 牒 Tablets, records. 계첩 戒牒 A monk's certificate, useful to a wandering or travelling monk.

첩 貼 To stick, attach to ; make up, add. 첩친 貼嚫 Dakṣiṇā, right-hand, south, dexterity ; donations, offerings, etc.

청 清 Amala. Pure, clear. 청신사 淸身士 or 청신남 淸信男 and 청신녀 淸信女 Upāsaka and Upāsikā, male and female lay devotees. 청양 淸揚 Clear and resonant. 청명 淸明 Clear and bright ; the Chinese spring festival on the 19th of the 2nd moon, when honour is paid to departed spirits. 청범 淸梵 Pure Sanskrit ; Buddha's resonant voice, or pure enunciation. 청량 淸涼 or 淸凉 Clear and cool ; clear, pure. 청량국사 淸涼國師 Pure-minded preceptor of the State, title of the fourth patriarch of the Hua-yen school. 청량사 淸涼寺 A monastery at Wu-t'ai shan. 청량산 淸涼山 A name for Wu-t'ai in north Shansi ; also the abode of Mañjuśrī, north-east of our universe. 청량월 淸涼月 The pure moon, i.e. the Buddha. 청량지 淸涼地 The pure lake, or pool, i.e. nirvāṇa. 청정 淸淨 Pariśuddhi ; viśuddhi. Pure and clean, free from evil and defilement, perfectly clean. 청정인 淸淨人 The pure and clean man, especially the Buddha. 청정광명신 淸淨光明身 The pure, shining body or appearance (of the Buddha). 청정원 淸淨園 Pure garden, or garden of purity, i.e. a monastery or convent. 청정심 淸淨心 A pure mind free from doubt or defilement. 청정지 淸淨智 Undefiled knowledge. 청정본연 淸淨本然 Purely and naturally so, spontaneous. 청정업처 淸淨業處 The state which one who has a pure karma reaches. 청정법 淸淨法 Dharmaviraja, pure truth. 청정법계 淸淨法界 The pure Buddha-truth (realm). 청정법안 淸淨法眼 The pure dharma-eye, with which the Hīnayāna disciple first discerns the four noble truths, and the Mahāyāna disciple discerns the unreality of self and things.

청정진여 淸淨眞如 One of the seven 진여 眞如 Chên-ju, q.v. 청정각해 淸淨覺海 The pure ocean of enlightenment, which underlies the disturbed life of all. 청정해탈삼매 淸淨解脫三昧 A samādhi free from all impurity and in which complete freedom is obtained. 청정식 淸淨識 Amala-vijñāna, pure, uncontaminated knowledge ; earlier regarded as the ninth, later as the eighth or ālaya-vijñāna. 청백 淸白 Pure and white, pure white, as Buddha-truth, or as pure goodness. 청변 淸辯 Bhāvaviveka, a noted Buddhist philosopher *circa* A.D. 600, a follower of Nāgārjuna. 청재 淸齋 Pure observance of monastic rules for food ; to eat purely, i.e. vegetarian food ; fasting.

청 靑 Nīla, blue, dark-coloured ; also green, black, or grey ; clear. 청심 靑心 An unperturbed mind. 청제녀 靑提女 The mother of Maudgalyāyana in a former incarnation, noted for her meanness. 청하 靑河, 청하 淸河 The blue, or clear river, Vaṅkṣu, Vākṣu, the Oxus. 청목 靑目 Blue-eyed. 청련 靑蓮 Utpala, v. 우 優 Blue lotus. 청면금강 靑面金剛 The blue-faced rāja, protector of Buddhism, king of the yakṣas, with open mouth, dog's fangs, three eyes, four arms, wearing skulls on his head, serpents on his legs, etc. 청두 靑頭 ; 청경관음 靑頸觀音 The blue-head, or blue-neck Kuan-yin, the former seated on a cliff, the latter with three faces, the front one of pity, the side ones of a tiger and a pig. 청귀 靑鬼 Blue (or green) demons who abuse the sufferers in Hades. 청룡 靑龍 Blue or Green dragon.

청 請 Request, ask, invite ; please ; engage ; acknowledge, announce. 청불 請佛 To invite a Buddha. 청가 請假 ; 잠가 暫假 To ask for leave of absence, or permission to go out. 청절 請折 To ask for, or reject. 청익 請益 To ask for an increase, for more, for advancement, etc. 청우 請雨 To pray for rain.

청 聽 To hear, listen, hearken ; listen to, obey. 청교 聽教 Those who hear the Buddha's doctrine ; those who obey. 청문 聽聞 To hear ; to hear and obey.

체 體 Body, limbs ; corpus, corporeal ; the substance, the essentials ; to show respect to, accord with. 체내방편 體內方便 ; 체외방편 體外方便 A term of the T'ien-t'ai school indicating that the "expedient" methods of the 방편 方便 chapter of the Lotus sūtra are within the ultimate reality of that sūtra, while those of other schools are without it. 체대 體大 Great in substance, the "greatness of quintessence" or the fundamental immutable substance of all things ; cf. Awakening of Faith 기신론 起信論. 체성 體性 Ātmakatva ; dharmatā ; the essential, or substantial nature of anything, self-substance. 체지 體智 Fundamental wisdom which penetrates all reality. 체비리 體毘履 v. 타 他 Sthavira, elder, president. 체법 體法 The universality of substance and the unreality of dharmas or phenomena, the view of the 통교 通教 as contrasted with that of the 장교 藏教. 체용 體用 Substance, or body, and function ; the fundamental and phenomenal ; the function of any body. 체상 體相 Substance and phenomena or characteristics, substance being unity and phenomena diversity. 체상용 體相用 The three great fundamentals in the Awakening of Faith — substance, characteristics, function. 체공 體空 The emptiness, unreality, or immateriality of substance, the "mind-only" theory, that all is mind or mental, a Mahāyāna doctrine. 체달 體達 The universal fundamental principle all pervasive. 체로 體露 Complete exposure or manifestation.

체 替 Substitute, deputy, on behalf of, for, exchange. 체승 替僧 A youth who becomes a monk as deputy for a new-born prince.

체 逮 To reach, catch up, until, when, wait for. 체야 逮夜 The night previous to a fast day, or to any special occasion.

체 剃 To shave. 체도 剃刀 A razor. 체두 剃頭 To shave the head. 체발 剃髮 To shave the hair, following Śākyamuni, who cut off his locks with a sharp sword or knife signify his cutting himself off from the world.

초 鈔 A voucher, banknote, paper-money, taxes ; to pinch up, take up ; to seize all, sequestrate ; to copy, transcribe, extract.

초 楚 Brambles, spinous ; painful, grievous ; to flog ; clear up ; the Ch'u state. 초강왕 楚江王 King of the grievous river, the second of the ten rulers of Hades.

초 麨 Broken dry rice, grits, crumbled grain.

초 招 Call, beckon, notify, cause ; confess. 초혼 招魂 To call back the spirit (of the dead). 초제 招提 ; 탁투제사 拓鬪提舍 Caturdiśaḥ, the four directions of space ; cāturdiśa, belonging to the four quarters, i.e. the Saṁgha or Church ; name for a monastery.

초 草 Grass, herbs, plants ; rough ; female (of animals, birds, etc.). 초창 草創 Newly or roughly built, unfinished. 초당 草堂 The building in the 초당사 草堂寺 monastery at Ch'ang-an where Kumārajīva translated. 초좌 草座 Mats or cushions to sit on. 초암 草庵 A thatched hut as a monastery or retreat. 초목 草木 Herbs and trees — equally recipients of rain, as all humanity is of the Buddha's truth. 초목성불 草木成佛 Even inanimate things, e.g. grass and trees, are Buddha, all being of the 일여 一如 q.v., a T'ien-t'ai and Chên-yen (Shingon) doctrine. 초환 草環 or 모환 茅環 A grass finger-ring used by the esoteric sect. 초혜 草鞋 Straw shoes. 초반 草飯 A coarse or rough meal.

초 醮 Libations or offerings, especially to ancestors ; the offerings of All Souls' Day, v. 우 盂 8 ; emptied, finished.

초 焦 Scorch, harass. 초열지옥 焦熱地獄 Tapana, the sixth of the eight hot hells ; the 초열대초열 焦熱大焦熱 is the seventh, i.e. Pratāpana.

초 初 To cut cloth for clothes ; beginning, first. 초야 初夜 The first of the three divisions of the night. 초위 初位 The initial stage on the road to enlightenment. 초주 初住 The first of the ten stages, or resting-places, of the bodhisattva. 주 住 is the resting-place or stage for a particular course of development ; 지 地 is the position or rank attained by the spiritual characteristics achieved in this place. 초승기 初僧祇 The first of the three asaṁkhyeya or incalculable kalpas. 초찰나식 初刹那識 The initial kṣaṇa, initial consciousness, i.e. the eighth or ālaya-vijñāna, from which arises consciousness. 초지 初地 The first of the 십지 十地 ten bodhisattva stages to perfect enlightenment and nirvāṇa. 초심 初心 The initial resolve or mind of the novice. 초일분 初日分 The first of the three divisions of the day, beginning, middle, end 초중후 初中後. 초경 初更 The first watch of the night. 초시교 初時教 A term of the 법상종 法相宗 Dharmalakṣaṇa school, the first of the three periods of the Buddha's teaching, in which he overcame the ideas of heterodox teachers that the ego is real, and preached the four noble truths and the five skandhas, etc. 초과 初果 The initial fruit, or achievement, the stage of Śrota-āpanna, illusion being discarded and the stream of enlightenment entered. 초과향 初果向 is the aiming at this. The other stages of Hīnayāna are Sakṛdāgāmin, Anāgāmin, and Arhat. 초환희지 初歡喜地 The first of the ten stages toward Buddhahood, that of joy. 초발심 初發心 The initial determination to seek enlightenment ; about which the 진 晉 Chin dynasty Hua-yen Ching says ; 초발심시변성정각 初發心時便成正覺 at this very moment the novice enters into the status of perfect enlightenment ; but other schools dispute the point. 초선천 初禪天 The first of the four dhyāna heavens, corresponding to the first stage of dhyāna meditation. 초선범천 初禪梵天 Devas in the realms of form, who have purged themselves from all sexuality. 초선정 初禪定 The first dhyāna, the first degree of dhyāna-meditation, which produces rebirth in the first dhyāna heaven. 초능변 初能變 The initiator of change, or mutation, i.e. the ālaya-vijñāna, so called because the other vijñānas are derived from it.

초 超 Vikrama. Leap over, surpass ; exempt from ; to save. 초세 超世 Surpassing the world, superior to anything in the world. 초팔 超八 Surpassing the eight other schools, as does the teaching of the Lotus and Nirvāṇa Sūtras, according to T'ien-t'ai. 초일왕 超日王 Vikramāditya, "a celebrated Hindu king," 57 B.C., who drove out the Śākas or Scythians, ruled all northern India, was one of the wisest of Hindu kings and a great patron of literature. [M. W.] 초월 超越 Surpassing, supreme ; to pass over, be exempt from. 초과 超過 Samatikram, to go beyond, cross over, transgress.

촉 髑 A skull 촉루 髑髏.

촉 囑 To bid, order, tell, enjoin on. 촉루 囑累 To entrust to, lay responsibility upon.

촉 觸 To butt, strike against ; contact. Sparśa, touch, contact, collision, the quality of tangibility, feeling, sensation. M. W. Eleven kinds of sensation are given – hot, cold, hard, soft, etc. Sparśa is one of the twelve nidānas, cf. 십이인연 十二因緣, and of the ṣaḍāyatana, cf. 육입 六入. It is also used with the meaning of 탁 濁 unclean. 촉인 觸因 Touch, or sensation cause, v. 이십오원통 二十五圓通. 촉진 觸塵 The medium or quality of touch. 촉지 觸指 The fourth and fifth fingers of the left hand which in India are used at stool, the unclean fingers. 촉통 觸桶 ; 촉병 觸瓶 A commode, ordure tub, etc. 촉락 觸樂 The pleasure produced by touch. 촉욕 觸欲 Desire awakened by touch. 촉독 觸毒 The poison of touch, a term applied to woman. 촉례 觸禮 To prostrate one's head to a stool, or footstool, in reverence. 촉예 觸穢 To touch anything unclean and become unclean. 촉종 觸鐘 To strike a bell. 촉식 觸食 Food made unclean by being touched, or handled ; any food soiled, or unclean ; the food of sensation, or imagination, mentally conceived.

촌 寸 An inch.

촌사불괘 寸絲不掛 Questioned as to what he did with his day, 육긍일 陸亘日 Lu Hsüan-jih replied "one does not hang things on an inch of thread."

총 叢 A copse, grove, wood ; crowded. 총림 叢林 A thickly populated monastery ; a monastery. 총규 叢規 The rules of the establishment.

총 塚 A tomb, mound, cemetery ; śmaśāna, v. 사 舍.

총 聰 Quick at hearing, sharp, clever, astute, wise, 총명 聰明.

총 總 Sādhāraṇa. Altogether, all, whole, general ; certainly. 총공 總供 A general offering to all spirits in contrast with specific worship. 총별 總別 General and particular. 총보업 總報業 General karma determining the species, race, and country into which one is born ; 별보 別報 is the particular karma relating to one's condition in that species, e.g. rich, poor, well, ill, etc. 총지 總持 Dhāraṇī, cf. 타 陀, entire control, a tr. of the Sanskrit word, and associated with the Yogācārya school ; absolute control over good and evil passions and influences. 총지문 總持門 The esoteric or Tantric sects and methods. 총명론 總明論 A name for the Abhidharma-kośa. 총상 總相 Universal characteristics of all phenomena, in contrast with 별상 別相 specific characteristics. 총상계 總相戒 The general commandments for all disciples, in contrast with the 별상계 別相戒, e.g. the 250 monastic rules. 총원 總願 Universal vows common to all Buddhas, in contrast with 별원 別願 specific vows, e.g. the forty-eight of Amitābha.

총림 叢林 A big monastery in Korea that provide comprehensive training for monastics. The four monasteries in Korea are : Tongdosa (representing the jewel of the Buddha), Haeinsa (representing the jewel of the Dharma), Songgwangsa (representing the jewel of the Saṁgha) and Sudeoksa.

최 最 Most, very, superlative. 최상 最上 Supreme, superlative. 최상승 最上乘 The supreme vehicle, or teaching. 최상대실지 最上大悉地 The stage of supreme siddhi or wisdom, Buddhahood. 최승 最勝 Jina ; vijaya ; conquering, all-conquering, pre-eminent, peerless, supreme. 최승승 最勝乘 The supreme vehicle, Mahāyāna. 최승존 最勝尊 The most honoured one, Buddha. 최(말)후 最(末)後 The last of all, ultimate ; final, finally, at death. 최후십념 最後十念 To call on Amitābha ten times when dying. 최후심 最後心 ; 최후념 最後念 The final mind, or ultimate thought, on entering final nirvāṇa. 최후신 最後身 ; 최후생 最後生 The final body, or rebirth, that of an arhat, or a bodhisattva in the last stage. 최정각 最正覺 Supreme perfect enlightenment, i.e. Buddhahood.

추 雛 A fledgling. 추승 雛僧 A fledgling priest, neophyte.

추 椎 A hammer, especially for a gong, etc. ; idem 추 槌.

추 樞 A pivot, axis. 추요 樞要 The pivot ; principles.

추 鶖 A stork. 추(로)자 鶖(鷺)子 Śāriputra, also 추로자 秋露子 meaning son of Śārī, his mother ; Śārī is a kind of bird "commonly called the Maina." M. W. It is tr. as a stork. Cf. 사 舍.

추 抽 Draw, withdraw, pull out. 추첨 抽籤 To draw lots, seek divine indications, etc. 추탈 抽脫 To go to the latrine.

추 芻 Hay, straw ; translit. *kṣ*. 추마 芻摩 or 蒭摩 ; 수마(가) 須摩(迦) Kṣauma, kṣaumaka, flax, linen, linen garment.

추 蒭 Hay, straw, fodder. 추마 蒭摩 Kṣumā, kṣauma, linen, flax, linen garments ; also 추마가 芻摩迦 ; 추마 菆摩 ; 수마 須摩 ; 소마 蘇摩 ; 참마 讖摩.

추 麤 Sthūla. Coarse, rough, crude, unrefined, immature. 추인 麤人 The immature man of Hīnayāna, who has a rough foundation, in contrast with the mature or refined 세인 細人 man of Mahāyāna. T'ien-t'ai applied 추 麤 to the 장 藏, 통 通, and 별 別 schools, reserving 세 細 for the 원 圓 school. 추악원 麤惡苑 The rough and evil park, one of Indra's four parks, that of armaments and war. 추악어 麤惡語 Coarse, evil, slanderous language. 추상 麤相 The six grosser or cruder forms of unenlightenment or ignorance mentioned in the 기신론 起信論 in contrast with its three finer forms. 추언 麤言 Coarse, crude, rough, immature words or talk ; evil words. Rough, outline, preliminary words, e.g. Hīnayāna in contrast with Mahāyāna. The rough-and-ready, or cruder words and method of 계 誡 prohibitions from evil, in contrast with the more refined method of 권 勸 exhortation to good.

추 墜 To fall, sink, settle, slide. 추개 墜芥 To drop a mustard seed from the Tuṣita heaven on to the point of a needle on the earth, most difficult, rare.

추 追 To pursue, follow after ; to follow the dead with thoughts and services. 추수 追修 To follow the departed with observances. 추복 追福 To pursue the departed with rites for their happiness. 추천 追薦 and 추선 追善 have similar meaning ; also 추엄 追嚴 for a sovereign.

추 推 To push away, recede from, decline, resign, push, put, put off ; investigate. 추공귀본 推功歸本 To put off minor merit for the sake of fundamentals. 추구 推究 To search out, investigate. 추각 推却 To decline.

추 醜 Ugly, shameful, shame, disgraceful. 추목 醜目 ; 추안 醜眼 Virūpākṣa ; ugly-eyed, i.e. Śiva with his three eyes ; also the name of the mahārāja-protector of the West, v. 비 毘. 추루 醜陋 Ugly, vile.

축 竺 Indian. 축토 竺土 ; 천축 天竺 ; 축건 竺乾 India. 축경 竺經 Indian, i.e. Buddhist, sūtras. Several Indians are known by this term, e.g. 축담마라찰 竺曇摩羅察 ; 축법호 竺法護 Dharmarakṣa, or Indu-dharmarakṣa, a native of Tukhāra, who knew thirty-six languages and tr. (A.D. 266-317) some 175 works. 축법란 竺法蘭 Dharmāraṇya, or Indu-dharmāraṇya, to whom with Kāśyapa Mātaṅga the translation of the sūtra of 42 sections is wrongly attributed ; he tr. five works in A.D. 68-70. 축법력 竺法力 Dharmabala, translator A.D. 419 of the larger Sukhāvatī-vyūha, now lost. 축섭마등 竺葉摩騰 or 가섭마등 迦葉摩騰 Kāśyapa Mātaṅga, v. 가 迦. 축찰시라 竺刹尸羅 Takṣaśilā, v. 달 呾.

축 逐 To drive, urge ; expel ; exorcise. 축기돈 逐機頓 Immediate accordance with opportunity ; 축 逐 is used as 수 遂 ; i.e. to avail oneself of receptivity to expound the whole truth at once instead of gradually.

축 祝 To invoke, either to bless or curse. 축성 祝聖 To invoke blessings on the emperor's birthday.

축 畜 To rear, feed, domesticate ; restrain ; cattle. 축생 畜生 Tiryagyoni, 지률거 底栗車 ; 방생 傍生 "Born of or as an animal," rebirth as an animal ; animals in general ; especially domestic animals. 축생인 畜生因 The cause, or karma, of rebirth as an animal. 축생계 畜生界 The animal kingdom. 축생도 畜生道 ; 축생취 畜生趣 The way, destiny, or gati of rebirth as animals, cf. 육도 六道 ; 육취 六趣.

출 出 To go out, come forth, put forth ; exit ; beyond.

출가 出家 Pravraj ; to leave home and become a monk or nun. 출가인 出家人 One who has left home and become a monk or nun. Two kinds are named ; (1) 신출가 身出家 one who physically leaves home, and (2) 심출가 心出家 one who does so in spirit and conduct. A further division of four is : (1) one who physically leaves home, but in spirit remains with wife and family ; (2) one who physically remains at home but whose spirit goes forth ; (3) one who leaves home, body and spirit ; and (4) one who, body and mind, refuses to leave home.

출가행 出假行 A bodhisattva's entry into time and space, or the phenomenal 가 假, for the sake of saving others.

출기 出期 The going forth period, i.e. from the sufferings of mortality ; the appointed time of going forth ; the period of setting forth.

출대 出隊 Outstanding, of outstanding ability, egregious, standing forth. 출대가제 出隊迦提 The public announcement of the distribution of the kaṭhina garment (v. 공덕의 功德衣) in the last month of the rainy season, i.e. of the coming forth of the monks from their retreat.

출도 出道 To leave the world and enter the nirvāṇa way.

출리 出離 To leave, come out from. 출리번뇌 出離煩惱 to leave the passions and delusions of life, an intp. of nirvāṇa.

출불신혈 出佛身血 To shed a Buddha's blood, one of the five grave sins.

출생 出生 To be born ; to produce ; monastic food, superior as bestowed in alms, called 출반 出飯 and 생반 生飯.

출성 出聖 The surpassing sacred truth, or the sacred immortal truth.

출세 出世 (1) Appearance in the world, e.g. the Buddha's appearing. (2) To leave the world ; a monk or nun. (3) Beyond, or outside this world, not of this world ; of nirvāṇa character. 출세대사 出世大事 The great work of the Buddha's appearing, or for which he appeared. 출세심 出世心 The nirvāṇa, or other-world mind. 출세본회 出世本懷 The aim cherished by the Buddha in appearing in the world. 출세과 出世果 The fruit of leaving the world ; the result in another world ; nirvāṇa. 출세업 出世業 The work or position of one who has quitted the world, that of a monk. 출세복 出世服 The garment of one who has left the world. 출세사 出世舍 An abode away from the world, a monastery, hermitage. 출세부 出世部 ; 출세(간)설부 出世(間)說部 or 출세(간)어언부 出世(間)語言部 ; Lokottaravādinaḥ, 노구다바타부 盧俱多婆拖部 an offshoot of the Mahāsāṅghikāḥ division of the eighteen Hīnayāna schools ; the tenets of the school are unknown, but the name, as implied by the Chinese translation, suggests if not the idea of Ādi-Buddha, yet that of supra-mundane nature. 출세간 出世間 To go out of the world ; the world (or life) beyond this ; the supra-mundane ; the spiritual world. 출세간도 出世間道, or 출세간법 出世間法. The way of leaving the world, i.e. of enlightenment, idem 보리도 菩提道 ; the spiritual law.

출식 出息 To breathe out. 출식부대입 出息不待入 Breathing-out not waiting for breathing-in, breathless.

출요경 出曜經 Avadānas, 아바다나 阿波陀那 stories of memorable deeds. The sixth of the twelve sections of the canon, consisting of 비유 譬喩 parables and comparisons.

출전진여 出纏眞如 The unfettered, or free bhūtatathatā, as contrasted with the 재전진여 在纏眞如.

출정 出定 To come out of the state of dhyāna ; to enter into it is 입정 入定.

출진 出塵 To leave the dusty world of passion and delusion.

출진 出陣 To stand out from the class of rank (e.g. to ask a question).

출체 出體 External ; the components of a thing or matter ; to put forth a body.

출출세간 出出世間 Surpassing the supra-mundane ; the stage of Bodhisattvahood above the eighth 지 地 or degree.

출현 出現 To manifest, reveal, be manifested, appear, e.g. as does a Buddha's temporary body, of nirmāṇakāya. Name of Udāyi 우다이 優陀夷 a disciple of Buddha to be reborn as Samantaprabhāsa ; also of a son of Ajātaśatru.

출혜 出慧 The wisdom of leaving mortality, or reincarnations ; the wisdom of leaving the world.

충 虫 Insect, reptile ; any creeping thing ; animal, man as of the animal kingdom.

충 忠 Loyal. 충심 忠心 Loyal, faithful, honest.

충 蟲 The animal kingdom including man, but generally applied to worms, snails, insects, etc. ; also 충 虫 q.v. 충식 蟲食 To eat as do grubs, moth-eat, etc.

취 鷲 A vulture. 취산 鷲山 Gṛdhrakūṭa, Vulture Peak near Rājagṛha, "the modern Giddore, so called because Piśuna (Māra) once assumed there the guise of a vulture to interrupt the meditation of Ānanda" [Eitel] ; more probably because of its shape, or because of the vultures who fed there on the dead ; a place frequented by the Buddha ; the imaginary scene of the preaching of the Lotus sūtra, and called 영취산 靈鷲山 Spiritual Vulture Peak, as the Lotus sūtra is also known as the 취봉게 鷲峯偈 Vulture Peak gāthā. The peak is also called 취봉 鷲峯 ; 취두(산) 鷲頭(山) ; 취대 鷲臺 ; 취악 鷲嶽 ; 취암 鷲巖 ; 영산 靈山 ; cf. 기사굴산 耆闍崛山.

취 趣 Destination, destiny (especially on rebirth) ; v. 오취 五趣, i.e. the hells, pretas, animals, man, devas. 취적 趣寂 The destiny of nirvāṇa, as understood by the Hīnayāna.

취 毳 Down, feathered. 취의 毳衣 A garment wadded with down.

취 醉 Drunk, intoxicated. 취상 醉象 A mad elephant, like evil hard to subdue.

취 聚 Samāsa ; assemble, collect ; an assemblage. 취말 聚沫 The phenomenal world likened to assembled scum, or bubbles. 취제 聚諦 Samudaya, the second of the four dogmas, that of "accumulation," i.e. that suffering is caused by the passions. 취집 聚集 To assemble, flock together.

취 臭 Stink, stinking ; smell. 취구귀 臭口鬼 or 취모귀 臭毛鬼 Demons with stinking breath, or hair.

취 吹 To blow ; puff, praise. 취광 吹光 to blow out a light, a blown-out light. 취모 吹毛 Name of a sharp sword, or Excalibur, that would sever a falling feather ; to blow hair or fur. 취법나 吹法螺 To blow the conch of the Law, the Buddha's preaching.

취 取 Upādāna. To grasp, hold on to, held by, be attached to, love ; used as indicating both 애 愛 love or desire and 번뇌 煩惱 the vexing passions and illusions. It is one of the twelve nidānas 십이인연 十二因緣 or 십이지 十二支 the grasping at or holding on to self-existence and things. 취차어 取次語 Easy, facile, loose talk or explanations. 취상 取相 The state of holding to the illusions of life as realities. 취상참 取相懺 To hold repentance before the mind until the sign of Buddha's presence annihilates the sin. 취여 取與 The producing seed is called 취과 取果, that which it gives, or produces, is called 여과 與果. 취착 取著 To grasp, hold on to, or be held by any thing or idea. 취온 取蘊 The skandhas which give rise to grasping or desire, which in turn produces the skandhas. 견취 見取 v. 견 見.

측 厠 A privy, cesspool ; also called 서정 西淨 ; 동정 東淨 ; 동사 東司 ; 설은 雪隱 ; 후가 後架 ; 기지처 起止處, etc. Ucchuṣma, v. 오 烏, is the guardian spirit of the cesspool.

치 耻 ; 치 恥 Shame ; ashamed. 치소모대 耻小慕大 Ashamed of the small (Hīnayāna) and in love with the great (Mahāyāna).

치 雉 A pheasant ; a parapet. 치구림화 雉救林火 The pheasant which busied itself in putting out the forest on fire and was pitied and saved by the fire-god.

치 緇 Black garments ; at one time black was used for monastic robes. 치도 緇徒 ; 치류 緇流 Monks. 치림 緇林 A monastery. 치의 緇衣 Black robes, monks. 치문 緇門 The black-robe order, monks.

치 熾 Blaze, flame, burn, effulgent. 치성광불 熾盛光佛 Name of a Buddha, noted for effulgence, light streaming from every pore.

치 痴 Moha, "unconsciousness," "delusion," "perplexity," "ignorance, folly," "infatuation," etc. [M. W.] Also, Mūḍha. In Chinese it is silly, foolish, daft, stupid. It is intp. by 무명 無明 unenlightened, i.e. misled by appearances, taking the seeming for real ; from this unenlightened condition arises every kind of kleśa, i.e. affliction or defilement by the passions, etc. It is one of the three poisons, desire, dislike, delusion. 치사 痴使 The messenger, lictor, or affliction of unenlightenment. 치범 痴凡 ; 치자 痴子 The common, unenlightened people. 치취 痴取 The kleśa of moha, held in unenlightenment. 치정 痴定 The samādhi of ignorance, i.e. without mystic insight. 치심 痴心 An unenlightened mind, ignorance darkening the mind. 치혹 痴惑 Unenlightened and deluded, ignorant of the right way of seeing life and phenomena. 치애 痴愛 Ignorance and desire, or unenlightened desire, ignorance being father, desire mother, which produce all affliction and evil karma. 치만 痴慢 Ignorance and pride, or ignorant pride. 치독 痴毒 The poison of ignorance, or delusion, one of the three poisons. 치수 痴水 The turbid waters of ignorance ; also to drink the water of delusion. 치등 痴燈 The lamp of delusion, attracting the unenlightened as a lamp does the moth. 치구 痴狗 Deluded dogs, i.e. the Hīnayāna śrāvakas and pratyeka-buddhas. 치후 痴猴 The deluded monkey seizing the reflection of the moon in the water, e.g. unenlightened men who take the seeming for the real. 치미 痴迷 Unenlightened and led astray. 치망 痴網 The net of delusion, or ignorance. 치박 痴縛 The bond of unenlightenment. 치암 痴闇 The darkness of the unenlightened condition.

치 治 Rule, govern ; prepare ; treat, cure ; repress, punish. 치국천 治國天 or 지국천 持國天 One of the four devas or mahārājas, guarding the eastern quarter. 치지주 治地住 One of the 십주 十住 q.v. 치생 治生 A living, that by which one maintains life.

치 齒 The teeth, especially the front and upper teeth ; toothed, serrated ; age, class. 치인 齒印 A serrated seal, or serrations as evidence. 치목 齒木 Danta-kāṣṭha. A stick for cleaning the teeth.

치 值 To meet ; happen on ; attend to ; worth, valued at. 치우 值遇 To meet, happen on unexpectedly.

치 置 To set up, place, arrange ; set aside, buy. 치답 置答 To reply by ignoring a question.

치 癡 v. 치 痴 13.

치문반 緇文班 or 사미과 沙彌科 The black-robe order course in seminary 강원 講院.

칙 or **즉** 則 Pattern, rule ; then, therefore. 칙극 則劇 To play ; a form of play.

칙 勅 Imperial commands. 칙명 勅命 The sovereign commands of the Buddha.

친 親 Personally related, own, intimate ; family ; a wife, marriage. 부친 父親 ; 모친 母親 Father ; mother. 친우 親友 An intimate friend. 친척 親戚 ; 친권 親眷 Relatives. 친애 親愛 To love, beloved. 친교(사) 親教(師) One's own teacher, a tr. of upādhyāya, v. 우 鄔.

친 嚫 Translit. *kṣi* in dakṣiṇā, which means a donation, gift, e.g. 친시 嚫施 ; 친물 嚫物 ; 친재 嚫財 ; 친자 嚫資 ; 친금 嚫金 ; 친전 嚫錢 cf. 달 噠.

칠 七 Sapta, seven.

칠 漆 Varnish, lacquer. 칠통 漆桶 Varnish tub, a stupid, unseeing fellow.

칠가행 七加行 idem 칠방편 七方便.

칠각분 七覺分 or 칠각지 七覺支, v. 칠보리분 七菩提分.

칠갈마 七羯磨 Karmavācā. 칠치 七治 The seven punishments of a monk.

칠견 七見 The seven heretical views, v. 견 見. They are 사견 邪見, 아견 我見, 상견 常見, 단견 斷見, 계도견 戒盜見, 과도견 果盜見, and 의견 疑見.

칠공 七空 The seven unrealities or illusions, v. 공 空. There are two lists : (1) 상공 相空, 성자성공 性自性空, 행공 行空, 무행공 無行空, 일체법리언설공 一切法離言說空, 제일의성지대공 第一義聖智大空 and 피피공 彼彼空 ; v. Laṅkāvatāra-sūtra 1. (2) 성공 性空, 자상공 自相空, 제법공 諸法空, 불가득공 不可得空, 무법공 無法空, 유법공 有法空 and 무법유법공 無法有法空 ; v. 지도론 智度論 36.

칠구 七垢 The seven defilements — desire 욕 欲, false views 견 見, doubt 의 疑, pride 만 慢, arrogance 교 憍, torpor 수면 隨眠, and 간 慳 stinginess ; cf. 칠사 七使.

칠구지불모존 七俱胝佛母尊 Saptakoṭibuddha-mātṛ. The fabulous mother of seven koṭīs of Buddhas ; i.e. Marīci 마리지 摩利支 ; also 준제 準提 Cuṇḍī, or Cundā ; or 준제관음 準提觀音 Cuṇḍī-Kuanyin, q.v., who is represented as of whitish colour, with eighteen hands and three eyes.

칠궁의왕 七躬醫王 v. 칠불약사 七佛藥師.

칠금산 七金山 The seven concentric mountain ranges which surround Sumeru, the central mountain of a universe, each range separated from the others by a sea ; see 구산팔해 九山八海. Their names are 지쌍 持雙, 지축 持軸, 담목(수) 擔木(樹), 선견 善見, 마이 馬耳, 장애 障礙 or 상비 象鼻, 지지산 持地山 or 지변산 持邊山.

칠난 七難 The seven calamities in the 인왕경수지품 仁王經受持品 during which that sūtra should be recited : sun and moon losing their order (eclipses), constellations irregular, fire, flood, wind-storms, drought, brigands. Another set is — pestilence, invasion, rebellion, unlucky stars, eclipses, too early monsoon, too late monsoon. Another is — fire, flood, rakṣas, misrule, evil spirits, cangue and prison, and robbers.

칠담 七曇 Siddham, idem 실담 悉曇.

칠대 七大 Earth, water, fire, wind, space (or ether), sight, and perception 지 地, 수 水, 화 火, 풍 風, 공 空, 견 見, 식 識 ; cf. 대 大, 오대 五大 and 육경 六境 ; 견대 見大 and 육근 六根 ; 식대 識大 and 육식 六識.

칠등각지 七等覺支 v. 칠보리분 七菩提分.

칠마달리 七摩怛里 Saptamātṛ. The seven "divine mothers, or personified energies of the principal deities" ; they are associated "with the worship of the god Śiva," and attend on "his son Skanda or Kārttikeya, to whom at first only seven Mātṛs were assigned, but in the later mythology an innumerable number, who are sometimes represented as having displaced the original divine mothers" M.W. Their names are given as (1) Cāmuṇḍā 차문다 遮文荼 or 좌문나 左問拏 ; (2) Gaurī 교폐리 嬌吠哩 ; (3) Vaiṣṇavī 폐슬나미 吠瑟拏微 ; (4) Kaumārī 교마리 嬌麼哩 ; (5) Indrāṇī, Aindrī, or Māhendrī 연날리 燕捺利 or 인날리 印捺哩 ; (6) Raudrī 로날리 勞捺哩 ; and (7) Vārāhī 말라희미 末羅呬弭 ; cf. 칠모천 七母天.

칠만 七慢 The seven pretensions or arrogances — 만 慢 asserting superiority over inferiors and equality with equals, 과만 過慢 superiority over equals and equality with superiors, 칠과만 七過慢 superiority over manifest superiors, 아만 我慢 egotism or overweening pride, 증상만 增上慢 vaunting assertion of possessing the Truth, 비만 卑慢 vaunting one's inferiority (or false humility), and 사만 邪慢 vaunting lack of virtue for virtue.

칠멸쟁법 七滅諍法 Saptādhikaraṇa-śamatha. Seven rules given in the Vinaya for settling disputes among the monks. Disputes arise from four causes : from arguments ; from discovery of misconduct ; judgment and punishment of such ; the correctness or otherwise of a religious observance. The seven rules are : — 현전비니 現前毘尼 Saṁmukha-vinaya, face to face evidence, or appeal to the law ; 억념비니 憶念毘尼 Smṛti-vinaya, witness or proof ; 불치비니 不痴毘尼 Amūḍha-vinaya, irresponsibility, e.g. lunacy ; 자언비니 自言毘尼 Tatsvabhāvaiṣīya-vinaya, voluntary confession ; 다어비니 多語毘尼 Pratijñākāraka-vinaya, decision by majority vote ; 죄처소비니 罪處所毘尼 Yadbhūyasikīya-vinaya, condemnation of unconfessed sin by the 백사 白四 or jñapticaturthin method, i.e. to make a statement and ask thrice for judgment, 초복지비니 草覆地毘尼 Tṛṇastāraka-vinaya, i.e. covering the mud with straw, i.e. in protracted disputes the appointment by each side of an elder to spread the straw of the law over the mud of the dispute.

칠모천 七母天 ; 칠자매 七姉妹 The seven divine mothers, also styled the seven sisters ; v. 칠마달리 七摩怛里.

칠몽(경) 七夢(經) Ānanda's seven dreams, and the account of them.

칠무상도 七無上道 idem 칠종무상 七種無上.

칠미 七微 The seven atoms composing an aṇu 아뇩 阿耨, 아나 阿拏, 아토색 阿菟色. Eitel's definition is seven atoms of dust, but the definition is doubtful. This molecule is larger than an "atom," and according to the Sarvāstivāda it is the smallest visible particle. It is also a division of a yojana.

칠방편(위) 七方便(位) (1) The seven "expedient" or temporary attainments or positions of Hīnayāna, superseded in Mahāyāna by the 칠현(위) 七賢(位) or 칠가행(위) 七加行(位) all preparatory to the 칠성(위) 七聖(位). (2) The seven vehicles, i.e. those of ordinary human beings, of devas, of śrāvakas, of pratyeka-buddhas, and of the three bodhisattvas of the three teachings 장 藏, 통 通 and 별 別. (3) Also, 장교지성연이인 藏教之聲緣二人, 통교지성연보삼인 通教之聲緣菩三人, 별교 別教 and 원교지이보살 圓教之二菩薩 ; (2) and (3) are T'ien-t'ai groups.

칠백현성 七百賢聖 The 700 disciples who met in the second synod at Vaiśālī ; also 칠백결집 七白結集.

칠법 七法 The seven (unavoidable) things, v. 칠불가피 七不可避.

칠법재 七法財 The seven riches, or seven ways of becoming rich in the Law : 신 信 faith, 진 進 zeal, 계 戒 moral restraint, 참괴 慚愧 shame, 문 聞 obedient hearing (of the Law), 사 捨 abnegation, and 정혜 定慧 wisdom arising from meditation.

칠보 七寶 Sapta ratna 살불답라적날 薩不荅羅的捺 The seven treasures, or precious things, of which there are varying descriptions, e.g. 금 金 *suvarṇa*, gold ; 은 銀 *rūpya*, silver ; 유리 琉璃 *vaiḍūrya*, lapis lazuli ; 파려 玻瓈 *sphaṭika*, crystal ; 차거 硨磲 *musāragalva*, agate ; 적주 赤珠 *rohita-mukta*, rubies or red pearls ; 마노 瑪瑙 *aśmagarbha*, cornelian. Also the seven royal (*cakravartin*) treasures — the golden wheel ; elephants ; dark swift horses ; the divine pearl, or beautiful pearls ; able ministers of the Treasury ; jewels of women ; and loyal generals. 칠보수림 七寶樹林 The grove of jewel trees, or trees of the seven precious things — a part of the "Pure-land," or Paradise.

칠보리분 七菩提分 Saptabodhyaṅga, also 칠보리보 七菩提寶, 칠각분 七覺分, 칠각지 七覺支, 칠등각지 七等覺支. Seven characteristics of bodhi ; the sixth of the 칠과도품 七科道品 in the thirty-seven categories of the bodhipakṣika dharma, v. 삼십칠보리분 三十七菩提分. It represents seven grades in bodhi, viz. (1) 택법각지 擇法覺支 (or 택법보리분 擇法菩提分 and so throughout), dharmapravicaya-saṁbodhyaṅga, discrimination of the true and the false ; (2) 정진 精進 vīrya-saṁbodhyaṅga, zeal, or undeflected progress ; (3) 희 喜 prīti-saṁbodhyaṅga, joy, delight ; (4) 경안 輕安 or 제 除 praśrabdhi-saṁbodhyaṅga, riddance of all grossness or weight of body or mind, so that they may be light, free, and at ease ; (5) 념 念 smṛti-saṁbodhyaṅga, power of remembering the various states passed through in contemplation ; (6) 정 定 samādhi-saṁbodhyaṅga, power to keep the mind in a given realm undiverted ; (7) 행사 行捨 or 사 捨 upekṣā-saṁbodhyaṅga, or upekṣaka, complete abandonment, autohypnosis, or indifference to all disturbances of the subconscious or ecstatic mind.

칠보사 七步蛇 A snake whose bite brings death before seven steps can be taken.

칠불 七佛 Sapta Buddha. The seven ancient Buddhas, viz. Vipaśyin 비바시 毘婆尸, Śikhin 시기 尸棄, Viśvabhū 비사바 毘舍婆, Krakucchanda 구루손 拘樓孫, Kanakamuni 구나함모니 俱那含牟尼 or 구나함 拘那含, Kāśyapa 가섭 迦葉, and Śākyamuni 석가 釋迦. The last four are said to be of the present kalpa. 칠불약사 七佛藥師 The seven healing Buddhas, also 칠궁의왕 七躬醫王, of whom there are two descriptions, one representing them as at various places in the eastern regions of space ; another gives five in the east and two in the south.

칠불가피 七不可避 The seven unavoidables — rebirth, old age, sickness, death, punishment (for sin), happiness (for goodness), consequences (cause and effect 인연 因緣).

칠비니 七毘尼 The seven vinaya, v. 칠멸쟁법 七滅諍法.

칠사 七使 The seven messengers, agents, or kleśas – desire 욕애 欲愛 ; anger, or hate 진에 瞋恚 ; attachment, or clinging 유애 有愛 ; pride, or arrogance 만 慢 ; ignorance, or unenlightenment 무명 無明 ; false views 견 見 ; and doubt 의 疑.

칠사수신 七事隨身 The seven appurtenances of a monk – the three garments, bowl, censer, duster (or fly-brush), stool (*niṣīdana*), paper, and material for washing.

칠생 七生 idem 칠유 七有.

칠선 七善 The seven excellences claimed for the Buddha's teaching – good in its 시 時 timing or seasonableness, 의 義 meaning, 어 語 expression, 독법 獨法 uniqueness, 구족 具足 completeness, 청정조유 淸淨調柔 pure adaptability, and 범행 梵行 its noble objective, nirvāṇa. There are other similar groups.

칠성 七星 Ursa major. Lit. "seven stars." It is worshipped in Japan as 묘견보살 妙見菩薩 q.v. Wonderful Sight Bodhisattva who protects this world. In Korea a native Shamanistic tradition was incorporated into Korean Buddhism ; as a result 칠성각 七星閣 Chil-seong-gak became a part of the temple.

칠성 七聲 v. 칠전구례 七轉九例.

칠성 七聖 v. 칠현칠성 七賢七聖. 칠성재 七聖財 Saptadhana. The Seven sacred graces, variously defined, e.g. 신 信 faith, 계 戒 observance of the commandments, 문 聞 hearing instruction, 참 慙 shame (for self), 괴 愧 shame (for others) ; 사 捨 renunciation ; and 혜 慧 wisdom. 칠성각 七聖覺 v. 칠보리분 七菩提分.

칠성각 七星閣 Chil-seong-gak. Shrine hall for the Seven Stars (Big Dipper).

칠승 七僧 A monastery is supposed to possess the following seven monks : 주원사 呪願師 invoker ; 도사 導師 leader ; 패사 唄師 intoner, or leader of the chanting ; 산화사 散花師 flower-scatterer ; 범음사 梵音師 master of sacred words, or Sanskrit ; 석장사 錫杖師 shaker of the rings on the metal staff, or crozier ; 당달 堂達 distributor of missals, etc. Another division is 강사 講師 expounder ; 독사 讀師 reader ; 주원사 呪願師 ; 삼례사 三禮師 director of the three ceremonies ; 패사 唄師 ; 산화사 散花師 ; and 당달 堂達. 칠승법회 七僧法會 An assembly of a monasterial fraternity. 칠승재 七僧齋 A "western" term meaning an endowment for a complete monastic fraternity of seven monks.

칠승사 七勝事 The seven surpassing qualities of a Buddha ; v. also 칠종무상 七種無上 ; they are his body, or person, his universal law, wisdom, perfection, destination (nirvāṇa), ineffable truth, and deliverance.

칠식십명 七識十名 The ten names of the seventh vijñāna, v. manas 말나식 末那識.

칠식주 七識住 v. 구유정거 九有情居.

칠심계 七心界 The seven realms of vijñāna, or perception, produced by eye, ear, nose, tongue, body, mind, to which is added thought, 의근 意根 q.v.

칠십 七十 Saptati, seventy. 칠십삼존 七十三尊 The "Diamond world" maṇḍala, or pantheon, of the esoteric sect, containing seventy-three honoured ones.

칠십오 七十五 Pañcasaptati ; 75.

칠십오법 七十五法 The seventy-five dharmas of the Abhidharma-kośa, which classifies all phenomena under seventy-five categories or elements, divided into five groups ; cf. 오근 五根, 오경 五境, 무표색 無表色. (1) Material 색법 色法 Rūpāṇi, 11. (2) Mind 심법 心法 Cittam, 1. (3) Mental qualities 심소유법 心所有法 Cittasamprayuktasaṁskārāḥ, 46. (4) Non-mental 심불상응

행법 心不相應行法 Cittaviprayuktasaṁskārāḥ, 14. These are the seventy-two Sarvāstivādin divisions (v. Keith, B.I., p. 201). (5) In addition there are three unconditioned or non-phenomenal elements 무위법 無爲法 Asaṁskṛta dharma, 3 (v. Keith, p. 160).

칠십이천 七十二天 The seventy-two devas, namely, sixty-nine devas, the lord of T'ai Shan, the god of the five roads, and 대길상천 大吉祥天 Mahāśrī. 칠십이자 七十二字 Brahmā obtained seventy-two words with which to save the world, but failing he swallowed seventy, leaving one at each side of his mouth 아 阿 and 구 漚, i.e. 무 無 and 유 有 things are, things are not, being and non-being. 칠십이세 七十二歲 The age, 72, at which Buddha is reputed to have preached the Lotus Sūtra.

칠여래 七如來 Sapta Tathāgatāḥ. The seven Tathāgatas whose names are inscribed on a heptagonal pillar (칠여래보탑 七如來寶塔) in some Buddhist temples. One list is 아미타 阿彌陀, 감로반왕 甘露飯王, 관음 觀音, 비야사 毘耶娑, 묘색신 妙色身, 나단납단라야 羅担納担羅耶 and 보승 寶勝. Another list gives Amitābha, Kan-lu-wang, 리포외 離怖畏, 광박신 廣博身, Miao-sê-shên, Pao-shêng (Ratnasaṁbhava) and 다보 多寶 (Prabhūtaratna).

칠역(죄) 七逆(罪) The seven rebellious acts, or deadly sins – shedding a Buddha's blood, killing father, mother, monk, teacher, subverting or disrupting monks, killing an arhat. v. 범망경하 梵網經下.

칠엽암 七葉巖 The crag at Rājagṛha on which the "seven-leaf tree" grew, in the cave beneath which the first "synod" is said to have been held after the Buddha's death, to recall and determine his teaching.

칠예구 七例句 v. 칠전구예 七轉九例.

칠요 七曜 The seven brilliant ones – the sun and moon, together with the five planets which are connected with fire, water, wood, metal, and earth. Their essence shines in the sky, but their spirits are over men as judges of their good and evil, and as rulers over good and evil fortune. The following table shows their names in

Chinese	*Sanskrit*
Sun 일 日, 태양 太陽	Āditya 아미저야 阿彌底耶
Moon 월 月, 태음 太陰	Soma 소마 蘇摩
Mars 화성 火星, 형혹 熒惑	Aṅgāraka 앙아라가 盎哦囉迦
Mercury 수성 水星, 진성 辰星	Budha 부타 部陀
Jupiter 목성 木星, 세성 歲星	Bṛhaspati 물리하사파지 勿哩訶娑跛底
Venus 금성 金星, 태백 太白	Śukra 수갈라 戍羯羅
Saturn 토성 土星, 진성 鎭星	Śanaiścara 사내이실절라 賒乃以室折羅

칠유 七有 ; 칠생 七生 The seven stages of existence in a human world, or in any 욕계 欲界 desire-world. Also (1) in the hells, (2) as animals, (3) hungry ghosts, (4) gods, (5) men, (6) karma 업 業, and (7) in the intermediate stage.

칠유 七喩 The seven parables of the Lotus Sūtra.

칠유의복업 七有依福業 The seven grounds for a happy karma through benevolence to the needy – almsgiving to visitors, to travellers, to the sick, to their nurses, gifts of gardens and groves to monasteries, etc., regular provision of food for them, and seasonable clothing and food for their occupants.

칠자 七子 The parable in the Nirvāṇa Sūtra of the sick son whose parents, though they love all their sons equally, devote themselves to him. So does the Buddha specially care for sinners.

The seven sons are likened to mankind, devas, śrāvakas, pratyeka-buddhas, and the three kinds of bodhisattvas of the 장 藏, 통 通 and 별교 別教.

칠장부 七丈夫 also 칠사부취 七士夫趣 ; v. 칠현칠성 七賢七聖.

칠재 七財 v. 칠법재 七法財.

칠재난 七災難 v. 칠난 七難.

칠전구례 七轉九例 The seven Sanskrit cases and nine conjugations. The former are also styled 칠성 七聲 and 칠례 七例 subanta 소만 蘇漫 or 소반다 蘇槃多 ; sometimes with the Vocative called 팔전성 八轉聲. The 구례 九例 or tiṅanta 정언다 丁彥多 are also styled 이구운 二九韻, i.e. nine parasmai and nine ātmane.

칠전도 七顚倒 v. 전도 顚倒 ; viparyaya, the seven inversions, or upside-downs, i.e. contrary or false positions — 상 想, 견 見, 심 心, 상무상 常無常, 고락 苦樂, 정부정 淨不淨, 아무아 我無我.

칠정 七情 The seven emotions : pleasure, anger, sorrow, joy, love, hate, desire.

칠정화 七淨華 see 칠화 七華.

칠조 七祖 The seven founders of the (1) 화엄 華嚴 Hua-yen or Kegon School, whose names are given as 마명 馬鳴 Aśvaghoṣa, 용수 龍樹 Nāgārjuna, 두순 杜順 (i.e. 법순 法順), 지엄 智嚴, 법장 法藏, 징관 澄觀 and 종밀 宗密 ; (2) of the 선 禪 Ch'an(Zen) School, i.e. 달마 達磨 or 보리달마 菩提達磨 Bodhidharma ; 혜가 慧可, 승찬 僧璨, 도신 道信, 홍인 弘忍, 혜능 慧能 and 하택 荷澤 (or 신회 神會) ; (3) of the 정토 淨土 Ching-t'u (Jōdō) or Pure-land School, i.e. Nāgārjuna, 천친 天親 or 세친 世親 Vasubandhu, 담란 曇鸞, 도작 道綽, 선도 善導, 원신 源信 and 원공 源空 (or 법연 法然), whose teaching is contained in the 칠조성교 七祖聖教.

칠조(의) 七條(衣) ; **칠조(가사)** 七條(袈裟) The outer mantle, or toga, of a monk, composed of seven pieces ; the Uttarāsaṅga, v. 울 鬱.

칠종 七宗 The seven Japanese sects of 율 律 Ritsu (or Risshū), 법상 法相 Hossō, 삼론 三論 Sanron, 화엄 華嚴 Kegon, 천태 天台 Tendai, 진언 眞言 Shingon, and 선 禪 Ch'an(Zen).

칠종부정 七種不淨 The seven kinds of uncleanness, derived from the parental seed, parental intercourse, the womb, the pre-natal blood of the mother, birth, one's own flesh, one's own putrid corpse. 칠종보시 七種布施 The seven kinds of almsgiving — to callers, travellers, the sick, their nurses, monasteries, regular food (to monks), general alms ; v. 칠유 七有, etc. 칠종참회심 七種懺悔心 The seven mental attitudes in penitential meditation or worship : shame, at not yet being free from mortality ; fear, of the pains of hell, etc. ; turning from the evil world ; desire for enlightenment and complete renunciation, impartiality in love to all ; gratitude to the Buddha ; meditation on the unreality of the sin-nature, that sin arises from perversion and that it has no real existence. 칠종사 七種捨 Seven abandonments or riddances — cherishing none and nothing, no relations with others, riddance of love and hate, of anxiety about the salvation of others, of form, giving to others (e.g. supererogation), benefiting others without hope of return. Another form is — cherishing nothing, riddance of love and hate, of desire, anger, etc., of anxiety about, etc., as above. 칠종무상 七種無上 The seven peerless qualities of a Buddha : — his body 신 身 with its thirty-two signs and eighty-four marks ; his way 도 道 of universal mercy ; his perfect insight or doctrine 견 見 ; his wisdom 지 智 ; his supernatural power 신력 神力 ; his ability to overcome hindrances 단장 斷障, e.g. illusion, karma, and suffering, and his abiding place 주 住, i.e. Nirvāṇa. Cf. 칠승사 七勝事. 칠종무상 七種無常 Sapta-anitya. The seven impermanences, a non-Buddhist nihilistic doctrine discussed in the 능가경 楞伽經 4. 칠종생사 七種生死 The seven kinds of mortality, chiefly relating to bodhisattva incarnation. 칠종예불 七種禮佛 Seven degrees of worshipping Buddha, ranging from the merely external to the highest grade. 칠종자성 七種自性 The seven characteristics of a Buddha's nature, v. 자성 自性. 칠종반 七種般 v. 불환 不還. 칠종의 七種衣 The seven kinds of clothing, i.e. of hair, hemp, linen, felt, fine linen, wool, or silk. 칠종어 七種語 Buddha's seven modes of discourse : 인어 因語 from present cause to future effect ; 과어 果語 from present effect to past cause ; 인과어 因果語 inherent cause and effect ; 유어 喩語 illustrative or figurative ; 불응설어 不應說語 spontaneous or parabolic ; 세계류어 世界流語 ordinary or popular ; 여의어 如意語 unreserved, or as he really thought, e.g. as when he said that all things have the Buddha-nature. 칠종변 七種辯 The seven rhetorical powers or methods of bodhisattvas : — direct and unimpeded ; acute and deep ; unlimited in scope ; irrefutable ; appropriate, or according to receptivity ; purposive or objective (i.e. nirvāṇa) ; proving the universal supreme method of attainment, i.e. Mahāyāna. 칠종식 七種食 The seven kinds of food or āhāra, sustenance : — sleep for eyes, sound for ears, fragrance for nose, taste for tongue, fine smooth things for the body, the Law for the mind, and freedom from laxness for nirvāṇa.

칠중 七衆 The seven classes of disciples : — (1) 비구 比丘 bhikṣu, monk ; (2) 비구니 比丘尼 bhikṣuṇī, a female observer of all the commandments ; (3) 식차마나 式叉摩那 śikṣamāṇa, a novice, or observer of the six commandments ; (4) 사미 沙彌 śrāmaṇera, and (5) 사미니 沙彌尼 śrāmaṇerikā, male and female observers of the minor commandments ; (6) 우바새 優婆塞 upāsaka, male observers of the five commandments ; and (7) 우바이 優婆夷 upāsikā, female ditto. The first five have left home, the last two remain at home. T'ien-t'ai makes nine groups by dividing the last two into four, two remaining at home, two leaving home and keeping the eight commandments. Others make four groups, i.e. (1), (2), (6), and (7) of the above. T'ien-t'ai also has a four-group.

칠중익수 七衆溺水 The seven types who fall into the waters of this life — the first is drowned, the seventh is a Buddha ; the seven are icchantika, men and devas, ordinary believers, śrāvakas, pratyeka-buddhas, bodhisattvas, and Buddhas ; also called 칠중인 七衆人.

칠중행수 七重行樹 The seven avenues of gem trees in Paradise.

칠증(사) 七證(師) v. 삼사칠증 三師七證.

칠지 七支 The seven (spreading) branches — three sins of the body and four of speech, 신삼 身三 killing, robbing, adultery ; 구사 口四 lying, slander, abuse, double-tongue (or vain conversation). These are the first seven of the ten evils 십악 十惡. 칠지염송 七支念誦 A method of invocation in which only seven kinds of signs and magical words are required. It is explained in the 칠지염송수행법 七支念誦隨行法 part of the Vairocana sūtra. 칠지업 七支業 The karma resulting from the above seven sins.

칠지 七知 The seven knowings — to know the Law, its meaning, the times for all duties, moderation, oneself, the different classes of people, and people as individuals.

칠진 七珍 idem 칠보 七寶.

칠진여 七眞如 The seven aspects of the bhūtatathatā, v. 진여 眞如. One list is 유전진여 流轉眞如, 실상진여 實相眞如, 유식진여 唯識眞如, 안립진여 安立眞如, 사행진여 邪行眞如, 청정진여 清淨眞如, and 정행진여 正行眞如. Cf. 유식론 唯識論 8.

칠차죄 七遮罪 Concealing, or non-confession of, any one of the seven deadly sins 칠역 七逆, for which it is also used.

칠처팔회 七處八會 The eight assemblies in seven different places, at which the sixty sections of the 화엄경 華嚴經 Avataṁsaka-sūtra are said to have been preached ; the same sūtra in eighty sections is accredited to the 칠처구회 七處九會. 칠처평만상 七處平滿相 One of the thirty-two signs on the Buddha's body — the perfection of feet, hands, shoulders, and head.

칠최승 七最勝 The seven perfections, see 유식론 唯識論 9. 안주최승 安住最勝 Perfect rest in the bodhisattva nature. 의지최승 依止最勝 Perfect reliance on, or holding fast to the great bodhi (or, awakened mind). 의과최승 意果最勝 Perfect resultant aim — in pity for all. 사업최승 事業最勝 Perfect in constant performance. 교편최승 巧便最勝 Perfect in able device (for spiritual presentation). 회향최승 廻向最勝 Perfect direction towards the highest bodhi. 청정최승 淸淨最勝 Perfect purity and peace.

칠취 七趣 The seven gati or states of sentient beings — *nārakagati*, in hell, *preta*, hungry ghost ; *tiryagyoni*, animal ; *manuṣya*, man ; *ṛṣi*, a genius or higher spiritual being ; *deva*, god ; *asura*, demon of the higher order.

칠치 七治 Seven forms of punishment for monks, v. 칠갈마 七羯磨.

칠칠 七七 The period of forty-nine days after death, when masses are said every seventh day till the seventh seventh day. 칠칠기 七七忌 The seventh seventh day of the masses for the dead. 칠칠재 七七齋 Masses for the dead on every seventh day for seven times. During this period the deceased is in the antarā-bhava or intermediate state, known as 중유 中有 and 중음 中陰 ; at the end of forty-nine days, judgment having been made, he enters upon his next state. By observing the proper rites, his family may aid him in overcoming his perils and attaining to a happy destiny.

칠팔행 七八行 The practice of the seven bodhyaṅga 칠보리분 七菩提分, and the 팔정도 八正道 eight mārga or noble paths.

칠현(위) 七賢(位) Also 칠방편위 七方便位, 칠가행위 七加行位 The seven grades or steps in virtue preceding the entry into 견도 見道 faultless wisdom, or faultlessness in its first realization. These seven are preliminary to the 칠성(위) 七聖(位). Both are grades of the 구사 俱舍 Kośa school of Hīnayāna. 칠현칠성 七賢七聖 The 칠성 七聖 are seven developments of holiness, which follow the above. In the Hua-yen 화엄 華嚴 school they are called 칠사부 七士夫, 칠대부 七大夫 or 칠성인 七聖人. Cf. 구사론 俱舍論 25.

칠화 七華 The seven flowers of enlightenment, idem 칠보리분 七菩提分. Another version is pure in the commandments, in heart, in views, in doubt-discrimination, in judgment, in conduct, and in nirvāṇa.

침 沈 ; 침 沉 To sink ; heavy. 침명 沈冥 Sunk in the gloom of reincarnations and ignorance. 침단 沈檀 Agaru, or aguru, sandal incense. 침(수)향 沈(水)香 Aguru, the tree and incense of that name. 침공 沈空 To sink into emptiness, or uselessness.

침 針 Sūci ; a needle. 침공 針孔 A needle's eye ; it is as difficult to be reborn as a man as it is to thread a needle on earth by throwing the thread at it from the sky. 침구귀 針口鬼 Needle-mouth ghosts, with mouths so small that they cannot satisfy their hunger or thirst. 침모귀 針毛鬼 Ghosts with needle hair, distressing to themselves and others. 침개 針芥 Needle and mustard seed ; the appearance of Buddha is as rare as hitting the point of a needle on earth by a mustard seed thrown from the sky. 침봉 針鋒 A needle's point, similar to the last.

침 寢 To sleep, rest ; stop ; a retiring room, resting-place. 침당 寢堂 A dormitory.

칭 稱 To call, style, invoke ; to weigh ; a steelyard, scale ; to suit, tally with. 칭불 稱佛 To invoke a Buddha. 칭명 稱名 To invoke the (Buddha's) name, especially that of Amitābha. 칭명잡행 稱名雜行 To worship a variety of Buddhas, etc., instead of cleaving to Amitābha alone. 칭의화 稱意華 The soma plant, suggested by Sir Aurel Stein as possibly wild rhubarb. 칭찬 稱讚 To praise.

<ㅋ>

쾌 快 Glad, joyful ; quick, sharp. 쾌락 快樂 Joyful. 쾌목왕 快目王 The quick-eyed king, Sudhīra, or highly intelligent, who could see through a wall 40 li away, yet who took out his eyes to give as alms ; v. 현우경 賢愚經 6.

큰방 Lit. "big room." Multi-purpose big hall in monastery.

큰스님 Keun-seunim ; great master. Usually a senior and respected monk.

<ㅌ>

타 咃 Translit. *ṭha.*

타 他 Another, other, the other, his, her, it, etc. 타력 他力 Another's strength, especially that of a Buddha, or bodhisattva, obtained through faith in Mahāyāna salvation. 타력종 他力宗 Those who trust to salvation by faith, contrasted with 자력종 自力宗 those who seek salvation by works, or by their own strength. 타력염불 他力念佛 Trusting to and calling on the Buddha, especially Amitābha.

타 佗 He, she, it ; other ; i.e. 타 他 ; translit. *thā*, e.g. in sthāna, sthāman.

타 陁 idem 타 陀.

타 陀 Steep bank, declivity ; translit. *t, th, d, dh, ty, dy, dhy* ; cf. 다 茶, 다 多, 단 檀. 다하 陀呵 Dāha, burning. 다다갈다 陀多竭多 Tathāgata, v. 다 多. 다마 陀摩 Dama, tamed, domiciled, obedient, good. 다력 陀歷 Darada, "the country of the ancient Dardae mentioned by Strabo and Pliny. The region near Dardu Lat. 35° 11N., Long. 73° 54E." [Eitel]. 다비라 陀毘羅 or 다비다 陀毘茶 ; 달라비다 達羅毘茶 or 달라미다 達羅弭茶 Damila, Dravila, probably Draviḍa, or Drāvira, anciently a kingdom in Southern India, "bounded in the South by the Cauveri and reaching northward as far as Arcot or Madras." [Eitel].

타 打 To beat, strike, make, do ; used for many kinds of such action. 타공 打供 To make offerings. 타포 打包 To wrap up or carry a bundle, i.e. a wandering monk. 타좌 打坐 To squat, sit down crosslegged. 타성일편 打成一片 To knock all into one, bring things together, or into order. 타판 打板 To beat the board, or wooden block, e.g. as an announcement, or intimation. 타면의 打眠衣 A monk's sleeping garment. 타청 打聽 To make inquiries. 타정 打靜 To beat the silencer, or beat for silence. 타반 打飯 To eat rice or a meal.

타 咤 To entrust ; translit. *ṭ* or *t*. 타파 咤婆 Something rigid, an obstruction.

타 墮 To fall ; dilapidated ; to fall from a higher to a lower place or condition ; a tr. of Prāyaścitta, expiation, a section in the Vinaya of ninety offences for which atonement is required. 타라발지 墮羅鉢底 Dvārapati or Dvāravatī, "an ancient kingdom on the upper Irawaddy." [Eitel].

타 拖 Tow, tug ; delay ; implicate. 타니대수 拖泥帶水 ; 화니합수 和泥合水 Mud and water hauler, or made of mud and water, a Ch'an(Zen) school censure of facile remarks.

타기 他己 Another and oneself ; both he and I.

타보 他寶 The valuables of another person ; other valuables.

타비리여부 他毘梨與部 ; 타비리 他毘利 ; 제비리 梯毘利 ; 타비라부 他鞞羅部 ; 체비리 體毘履 or 體毘裏 Sthavira ; 상좌 上坐 ; 노숙 老宿 One of the four branches of the Vaibhāṣika School, so called after the Vaibhāṣika śāstra, v. 비 毘 ; the school was reputed as later represented by the Mahāvihāravāsinaḥ, Jetavanīyāḥ, Abhayagiri-vāsinaḥ, in Ceylon ; but the history of the Buddhist sects is uncertain, cf. Tārānāth, *Hist. Buddhism*, tr. pp. 270-.

타생 他生 ; 타세 他世 Another life, or world, either previous to or after this. 타나 他那 ; 타나 吒那 Sthāna, 처 處 a place, state, condition.

타수용토 他受用土 That part of a Buddhakṣetra, or reward land of a Buddha, in which all beings receive and obey his truth ; cf. 자수용토 自受用土.

타승죄 他勝罪 Overcome by specific sin ; i.e. any of the four pārājikas, or sins of excommunication.

타심지 他心智 ; 타심통 他心通 ; 타심지통 他心智通 ; 지타심통 知他心通 Paracittajñāna. Intuitive knowledge of the minds of all other beings. The eighth of the 십지 十智, and the fourth or third of the 육신통 六神通. The eighth of Amitābha's forty-eight vows that men and devas in his paradise should all have the joy of this power.

타화(자재)천 他化(自在)天 Paranirmita-vaśavartin, 바라니밀파사발제천 婆羅尼蜜婆舍跋提天 ; 바나화제 婆那和提 ; 바사발제 波舍跋提 the sixth of the six heavens of desire, or passion-heavens, the last of the six devalokas, the abode of Maheśvara (i.e. Śiva), and of Māra.

탁 鐸 A bell with a clapper ; translit. *da.* 탁갈라 鐸曷攞 Dahara, small, young ; a monk ordained less than ten years.

탁 拓 Carry (on the palm), entrust to, pretext, extend. 탁림라 拓林羅 One of the twelve generals in the Yao-shih (Bhaiṣajya) sūtra.

탁 卓 Lofty, tall, erect. 탁석 卓錫 Tall, or erect staves, i.e. their place, a monastery.

탁 拆 Tear open, break down. 탁마타나 拆摩駄那 Calmadana or 녈말 涅末 Nimat, "An ancient kingdom and city at the south-east borders of the desert of Gobi." [Eitel].

탁 托 To carry on the palm, entrust to. 탁탑천왕 托塔天王 The deva-king who bears a pagoda on his palm, one of the four mahārājas, i.e. 비사문 毘沙門 Vaiśravaṇa. 탁생 托生 That to which birth is entrusted, as a womb, or a lotus in Paradise. 탁태 托胎 A womb ; conception. 탁발 托鉢 An almsbowl ; to carry it.

탁 濁 Turbid, muddy, impure, opposite of 청 淸. An intp. of kaṣāya, especially in reference to the 오탁 五濁 five stages of a world's existence. 탁난 濁亂 Impure and lawless, the reign of evil. 탁세 濁世 An impure world in its five stages, v. 오탁 五濁. 탁겁 濁劫 An impure kalpa, the kalpa of impurity, degenerate, corrupt ; an age of disease, famine, and war. 탁악세 濁惡世 A world of impurity or degeneration, i.e. of the 오탁 五濁 and 십악 十惡. 탁악처 濁惡處 The present contaminated evil world. 탁업 濁業 Contaminated karma, that produced by 탐 貪 desire.

탄 誕 A birthday ; to bear, produce ; wide, boastful. 탄생회 誕生會 An assembly to celebrate a birthday, e.g. the Buddha's on the 8th of the 4th month.

탄 彈 A bullet, shot ; to strum, snap ; repress, impeach ; translit. *dan.* 탄다 彈多 Danta, a tooth. 탄다니슬체 彈多抳瑟搋 Danta-kāṣṭha, a tooth stick, v. 탄 憚. 탄다락가 彈多落迦 Dantalokagiri, a mountain (the montes Daedali of Justinian) near Varuṣa with its cavern (now called Kashmiri-Ghār), where Sudāna lived. 탄택가 彈宅迦 Daṇḍaka, name of a king. 탄택가림 彈宅迦林 The forest of Daṇḍaka, destroyed by a ṛṣi because the king had carried off the ṛṣi's wife, saying a ṛṣi had no need for one. 탄지 彈指 To snap the fingers — in assent, in joy, in warning ; a measure of time equal to twenty winks.

탄 炭 Charcoal, coal. 탄두 炭頭 The fire-tender in a monastery.

탄 憚 Dread ; dislike ; translit. *dan.* 탄다 憚哆 Danta, tooth, teeth ; cf. 탄 彈 and 나 娜. 탄다가슬다 憚哆家瑟多 Danta-kāṣṭha, tooth stick, said to be chewed as a dentifrice ; also, to be the name of a tree grown from a tooth-pick of the Buddha.

탄 歎 To praise ; to sigh. 탄파나 歎波那 Broken rice, v. 초 麨.

탄 嘆 To praise, extol ; to sigh. 탄불 嘆佛 To praise Buddha. 탄덕 嘆德 To praise the virtue of others. 탄령 嘆靈 To praise the spirit of the departed.

탈 奪 Snatch, carry off, take by force ; decide. 탈혼귀 奪魂鬼 A demon that carries off the soul. 탈정귀 奪精鬼 One that carries off the vital breath of the dying.

탈 脫 To take the flesh from the bones ; to strip, undress, doff ; to escape, avoid ; let go, relinquish. 탈진착폐 脫珍著幣 To doff jewels and don rags, as did the Buddha, on leaving home, but it is intp. as a kenosis, the putting off of his celestial body for an incarnate, earthly body. 해탈 解脫 v. 해 解. 탈사 脫闍 Dhvaja, a banner, flag. 탈체 脫體 To strip the body, naked ; to get rid of the body.

탐 貪 Rāga ; colouring, dyeing, tint, red ; affection, passion ; vehement longing or desire ; cf. [M. W.] In Chinese : cupidity, desire ; intp. as tainted by and in bondage to the five desires ; it is the first in order of the 오둔사 五鈍使 pañca-kleśa q.v., and means hankering after, desire for, greed, which causes clinging to earthly life and things, therefore reincarnation. 탐(욕)사 貪(欲)使 The messenger, or temptation of desire. 탐에치 貪恚痴 v. *infra.* 탐석 貪惜 To begrudge ; be unwilling to give. 탐애 貪愛 Desire, cupidity. 탐염 貪染 The taint of desire, or greed. 탐욕 貪欲 Desire for and love of (the things of this life). 탐욕즉시도 貪欲卽是道 Desire is part of the universal law, and may be used for leading into the truth, a tenet of T'ien-t'ai. 탐욕진에우치 貪欲瞋恚愚痴 Rāga, dveṣa, moha ; desire, anger, ignorance (or stupidity), the three poisons. 탐욕개 貪欲蓋 The cover of desire which overlays the mind and prevents the good from appearing. 탐독 貪毒 The poison of desire. 탐수 貪水 Desire is like water carrying things along. 탐탁 貪濁 The contamination of desire. 탐번뇌 貪煩惱 The kleśa, temptation or passion of desire. 탐랑 貪狼 Greedy wolf, wolfish desire or cupidity. 탐진치 貪瞋痴 Rāgadveṣamoha, the three poison, v. *supra.* 탐결 貪結 The bond of desire, binding in the chain of transmigration. 탐박 貪縛 The tie of desire. 탐습 貪習 The habit of desire, desire become habitual. 탐습인 貪習因 Habitual cupidity leading to punishment in the cold hells, one of the 십인 十因. 탐착 貪著 The attachment of desire. 탐견 貪見 The illusions or false views caused by desire.

탐 探 To feel for, explore, investigate, search ; to spy, inquire into. 탐수 探水 To sound the depth of water, the lower part of a staff, i.e. for sounding depth.

탐마율저 耽摩栗底 Tamluk, v. 다 多.

탐마율지 耽摩栗底 Tāmralipti, Tamlook, v. 다마 多摩.

탑 塔 Stūpa ; tope ; a tumulus, or mound, for the bones, or remains of the dead, or for other sacred relics, especially of the Buddha, whether relics of the body or the mind, e.g. bones or scriptures. As the body is supposed to consist of 84,000 atoms, Aśoka is said to have built 84,000 stūpas to preserve relics of Śākyamuni. Pagodas, dagobas, or towers with an odd number of stories are use in China for the purpose of controlling the geomantic influences of a neighbourhood. Also 탑파 塔婆 ; 두파 兜婆 ; 투파 偸婆 ; 수두파 藪斗波 ; 솔도파 窣堵波 ; 솔도파 率都婆 ; 소도파 素覩波 ; 사유파 私鍮簸, etc. The stūpas erected over relics of the Buddha vary from the four at his birthplace, the scene of his enlightenment, of his first sermon, and of his death, to the 84,000 accredited to Aśoka. 탑상 塔像 Stūpas and images. 탑묘 塔廟 Pagodas and temples.

탕 湯 Hot liquid, hot water, soup, etc. 탕두 湯頭 The monk in charge of the kettles, etc.

태 or **타** 馱 or 駄 Translit. *dha, dhya.* 타남 馱南 Dhyāna, also 타(나)연나 馱(那)演那 ; 타연나 馱衍那 tr. by 정 定 and 선 禪 q.v. 타기니 馱器尼 v. 달 達 The Deccan. 타마 馱摩 v. 달 達 Dharma. 타삭가 馱索迦 Dāsaka, a slave, or dāsikā, a female slave. 타박야 馱縛若 Dhvaja, a flag. 타나갈책가

馱那羯磔迦 Dhanakaṭaka, or Amarāvatī, an ancient kingdom in the north-east of the modern Madras presidency. 타도 馱都 Dhātu, intp. by 계 界 field, area, sphere ; 체 體 embodiment, body, corpus ; 성 性 nature, characteristic. It means that which is placed or laid ; a deposit, foundation, constituent, ingredient, element ; also a śarīra, or relic of Buddha. The two dhātus are the conditioned and unconditioned, phenomenal and noumenal ; the three are the realms of desire, of form, and of the formless ; the four are earth, water, fire, and air ; the six add space and intelligence ; the eighteen are the twelve āyatanas, with six sensations added.

태 台 A flat place, platform, plateau, terrace ; an abbrev. for 대 臺 and for 천태 天台 T'ien-t'ai, hence 태악 台岳 the T'ien-t'ai mountain ; 태종 台宗 ; 태가 台家 its "school" ; 태도 台徒 its disciples ; 태교 台教 ; 태도 台道 its doctrine, or way. 태형 台衡 The school of T'ai-Hêng, or T'ai and Hêng ; T'ai is T'ien-t'ai, i.e. Chih-i 지의 智顗 its founder, Hêng is 형악 衡岳 the Hêng-yo monastery, i.e. a term for Hui-ssŭ 혜사 慧思 the teacher of Chih-i.

태 胎 Garbha, the womb, uterus.

태 泰 Prosperous, exalted ; many. 태산 泰山 T'ai Shan in Shantung, the eastern sacred mountain of China.

태 太 Too, very, great. 태자 太子 Kumārarāja. Crown-prince. An epithet of Buddhas, and of Mañjuśrī. 태자화휴경 太子和休經 ; 태자쇄호경 太子刷護經 There are several 태자 太子, etc. 경 經. One named the Subāhu-paripṛcchā was translated under the first title between 256-316 A.D., four leaves ; under the second title by Dharmarakṣa during the same period. 태고위생 太孤危生 Life perilous as the (unscaleable) top of the loneliest peak. 태허공 太虛空 Space, where nothing exists ; also 완공 頑空 ; 편공 偏空. 태추생 太麤生 A ruffian, a rough fellow.

태고 太古 Tae-go(1301-1382). Dharma-name of 보우 普愚 Bo-u, q.v.

태고사 太古寺 Tae-go-sa. A temple located in Seongbug-dong Seongbug-gu Seoul in Korea. The headquarters of Korean Taego Order.

태고집 太古集 Tae-go-jip. The analects of 태고 太古 Tae-go.

태금 胎金 The Garbhadhātu and the Vajradhātu.

태내오위 胎內五位 The five periods of the child in the uterus. 태외오위 胎外五位 Ditto after birth, i.e. infancy, childhood, youth, middle age, old age.

태대일 胎大日 Vairocana in the Garbhadhātu.

태란습화 胎卵濕化 The four yoni or modes of birth — womb-born, egg-born, spawn-born, and born by transformation (e.g. moths, certain deities, etc.).

태생 胎生 Uterine birth, womb-born. Before the differentiation of the sexes birth is supposed to have been by transformation. The term is also applied to beings enclosed in unopened lotuses in paradise, who have not had faith in Amitābha but trusted to their own strength to attain salvation ; there they remain for proportionate periods, happy, but without the presence of the Buddha, or Bodhisattvas, or the sacred host, and do not hear their teaching. The condition is also known as 태궁 胎宮, the womb-palace.

태옥 胎獄 ; 태궁 胎宮 The womb prison, the womb regarded as a prison ; see 태생 胎生.

태장계 胎藏界 Garbhadhātu, or Garbhakośa-(dhātu), the womb treasury, the universal source from which all things are produced ; the matrix ; the embryo ; likened to a womb in which all of a child is conceived — its body, mind, etc. It is container and content ; it covers and nourishes ; and is the source of all supply. It represents the 이성 理性 fundamental nature, both material elements and pure bodhi, or wisdom in essence or purity ; 리 理 being the garbhadhātu as fundamental wisdom, and 지 智 acquired wisdom or knowledge, the vajradhātu. It also represents the human heart in its innocence or pristine purity, which is considered as the source of all Buddha-pity and moral knowledge. And it indicates that from the central being in the maṇḍala, viz. the Sun as symbol of Vairocana, there issue all the other manifestations of wisdom and power, Buddhas, bodhisattvas, demons, etc. It is 본각 本覺 original intellect, or the static intellectuality, in contrast with 시각 始覺 intellection, the initial or dynamic intellectuality represented in the vajradhātu ; hence it is the 인 因 cause and vajradhātu the 과 果 effect ; though as both are a unity, the reverse may be the rule, the effect being also the cause ; it is also likened to 이타 利他 enriching others, as vajradhātu is to 자리 自利 enriching self. Kōbō Daishi, founder of the Yoga or Shingon 진언 眞言 School in Japan, adopted the representation of the ideas in maṇḍalas, or diagrams, as the best way of revealing the mystic doctrine to the ignorant. The garbhadhātu is the womb or treasury of all things, the universe ; the 리 理 fundamental principle, the source ; its symbols are a triangle on its base, and an open lotus as representing the sun and Vairocana. In Japan this maṇḍala is placed on the east, typifying the rising sun as source, or 리 理. The vajradhātu is placed west and represents 지 智 wisdom or knowledge as derived from 리 理 the underlying principle, but the two are essential one to the other, neither existing apart. The material and spiritual ; wisdom-source and intelligence ; essence and substance ; and similar complementary ideas are thus portrayed ; the garbhadhātu may be generally considered as the static and the vajradhātu as the dynamic categories, which are nevertheless a unity. The garbhadhātu is divided into 삼부 三部 three sections representing samādhi or quiescence, wisdom-store, and pity-store, or thought, knowledge, pity ; one is called the Buddha-section, the others the Vajra and Lotus sections respectively ; the three also typify vimokṣa, prajñā, and dharmakāya, or freedom, understanding, and spirituality. There are three heads of these sections, i.e. Vairocana, Vajrapāṇi, and Avalokiteśvara ; each has a mother or source, e.g. Vairocana from Buddha's-eye ; and each has a 명왕 明王 or emanation of protection against evil ; also a śakti or female energy ; a germ-letter, etc. The diagram of five Buddhas contains also four bodhisattvas, making nine in all, and there are altogether thirteen 대원 大院 or great courts of various types of ideas, of varying numbers, generally spoken of as 414. Cf. 금강계 金剛界 ; 대일 大日 ; 양부 兩部.

태현 太賢 or 大賢 Tae-hyeon(680?-760?). A monk of the Silla dynasty in Korea. An authority in 유가학 瑜伽學 Yogācāra, 계율학 戒律學 Vinaya. One book is present.

택 宅 Residential part of a palace, or mansion ; a residence.

택 擇 To select, pick, choose ; used for pravicāra, the second of the seven bodhyaṅga, cf. 각분 覺分 ; dharmapravicaya, discrimination, the faculty of discerning the true from the false. 택유안 擇乳眼 The power to choose and drink the milk out of watered milk, leaving the water, as Haṇsarāja, the "king of geese," is said to do. 택력 擇力 The power of discrimination. 택지 擇地 To select a site. 택법안 擇法眼 ; 택법학지 擇法學支 The bodhyaṅga of discrimination, v. above. 택멸 擇滅 Pratisaṁkhyānirodha. Nirvāṇa as a result of the above discrimination, the elimination of desire by means of mind and will.

토 土 Bhū ; bhūmi ; pṛthivī. Earth, locality, local, vulgar. 토지신 土地神 The local guardian deity of the soil or locality, deus loci ; in the classics and government sacrifices known as 사 社 ; as guardian deity of the grave 후토 后土. The 토지당 土地堂 is the shrine of this deity as ruler of the site of a monastery, and is usually east of the main hall. On the 2nd and 16th of each month a 토지풍경 土地諷經 or reading of a sūtra should be done at the shrine. 토성 土星 ; 사내이실탁라 賒乃以室拆羅 Śanaiścara. Saturn. Śani, the Hindu ruler of the planet, was "identified with the planet itself." [Eitel]. 토파 土波 Tibet. 토사공양 土砂供養 ; 토사가지 土砂加持 The putting of earth on the grave 108 times by the Shingon sect ; they also put it on the deceased's body, and even on the sick, as a kind of baptism for sin, to save the deceased from the hells and base reincarnations, and bring them to the Pure Land. 토라차 土羅遮 ; 투란차 偸蘭遮 Sthūlātyaya. Serious sin. 토만두 土饅頭 An earthen loaf, i.e. a grave ; but v. 사만두 土饅頭. 토초 土麨 Aśoka is said to have become king as a reward for offering, when a child in a previous incarnation, a double-handful of sand as wheat of food to the Buddha.

토 吐 To spit, excrete, put forth. 토루 吐淚 Female and male seminal fluids which blend for conception.

토 兎 Śaśa ; a rabbit ; also a hare. The hare in the moon, hence 회토자 懷兎者 is the moon or śaśin. 토모진 兎毛塵 The speck of dust that can rest on the point of a hare's down, one-seventh of that on a sheep's hair. 토각 兎角 Śaśa-viṣāṇa ; Śaśa-śṛṅga ; a rabbit's horns, i.e. the non-existent ; all phenomena are as unreal as a rabbit's horns.

통 桶 A tub, bucket, barrel. 통두 桶頭 The monk who looks after these things in a large establishment.

통 通 Permeate, pass through, pervade ; perceive, know thoroughly ; communicate ; current ; free, without hindrance, unimpeded, universal ; e.g. 신통 神通 supernatural, ubiquitous powers. There are categories of 오통 五通, 육통 六通, and 십통 十通, all referring to supernatural powers ; the five are (1) knowledge of the supernatural world ; (2) deva vision ; (3) deva hearing ; (4) knowledge of the minds of all others ; (5) knowledge of all the transmigrations of self and all others. The six are the above together with perfect wisdom for ending moral hindrance and delusion. The ten are knowing all previous transmigrations, having deva hearing, knowing the minds of others, having deva vision, showing deva powers, manifesting many bodies or forms, being anywhere instantly, power of bringing glory to one's domain, manifesting a body of transformation, and power to end evil and transmigration.

통교 通教 T'ien-t'ai classified Buddhist schools into four periods 장 藏, 통 通, 별 別, and 원 圓. The 장 藏 Piṭaka school was that of Hīnayāna. The 통 通 T'ung, interrelated or intermediate school, was the first stage of Mahāyāna, having in it elements of all the three vehicles, śrāvaka, pratyekabuddha, and bodhisattva. Its developing doctrine linked it with Hīnayāna on the one hand and on the other with the two further developments of the 별 別 "separate," or "differentiated" Mahāyāna teaching, and the 원 圓 full-orbed, complete, or perfect Mahāyāna. The 통교 通教 held the doctrine of the Void, but not arrived at the doctrine of the Mean.

통달 通達 To pervade, perceive, unimpeded, universal. 통달심 通達心 ; 통달보리심 通達菩提心 To attain to the enlightened mind ; the stage of one who has passed through the novitiate and understands the truth.

통도 通途 Thoroughfare, an open way.

통도사 通度寺 Tong-do-sa. A temple located in Mt. Yeongchu-san, Jisan-ri Habuk-myeon Yangsan-gun Gyeongsangnam-do in Korea. The 15th parish headquarters of Korean Jogye Order.

통력 通力 The capacity to employ supernatural powers without hindrance. Buddhas, bodhisattvas, etc., have 신력 神力 spiritual or transcendent power ; demons have 업력 業力 power acquired through their karma.

통리 通利 Intelligence keen as a blade, able to penetrate truth.

통리원 統理院 Tong-ri-won. The headquarters of Korean Jingak Order, located in Seoul, Korea.

통명혜 通明慧 The six 통 通, three 명 明, and three 혜 慧 q.v.

통별이서 通別二序 The general and specific introductions to a sūtra ; 여시아문 如是我聞 being the 통서 通序 general introduction in every sūtra.

통야 通夜 The whole night, i.e. to recite or intone throughout the night.

통염불 通念佛 To call on the Buddhas in general, i.e. not limited to one Buddha.

통행 通行 The thoroughfare, or path which leads to nirvāṇa.

통혜 通慧 Supernatural powers and wisdom, the former being based on the latter.

통혹 通惑 The two all-pervading deluders 견 見 and 사 思 seeing and thinking wrongly, i.e. taking appearance for reality.

통화 通化 Perspicacious, or influential teaching ; universal powers of teaching.

통회 通會 To harmonize differences of teaching.

퇴 堆 A heap, a pile. 퇴압지옥 堆壓地獄 The hell of crushing, also 중합지옥 衆合地獄 the third great hell in which sinners are crushed to death.

퇴 槌 Hammer, mallet. 퇴침 槌砧 ; 퇴돈 槌墩 Hammer and block, or anvil.

퇴 退 Retire, withdraw, backslide, recede, yield. 퇴대 退大 To backslide from Mahāyāna (and revert to Hīnayāna). 퇴굴 退屈 To yield or recede, as is possible to a Bodhisattva facing the hardships of further progress. 퇴좌 退座 To withdraw from one's seat. 퇴몰 退沒 To be reborn in a lower stage of existence. 퇴전 退轉 To withdraw and turn back, i.e. from any position attained.

퇴척귀 䭔惕鬼 A demon of the nerves who troubles those who sit in meditation. Also 퇴척귀 堆惕鬼 ; 부척귀 埠惕鬼.

투 妬 Jealous, envious. 투불남 妬不男 Īrṣyāpaṇḍaka. Impotent except when aroused by Jealousy, one of the five classes of "eunuchs."

투 偷 Remiss ; to steal ; stealthy. 투파 偷婆 Stūpa, cf. 탑 塔. 투도 偷盜 Steal, rob ; one of the ten sins. 투란(차야) 偷蘭(遮耶), 살투라 薩偷羅 ; 인란 因蘭 Sthūlātyaya, a great transgression, one of the major transgressions of a monk or nun.

투 投 To cast, throw into, surrender, tender. 투자 投子 T'ou-tzŭ, name of a hill and monastery at 서주 舒州 Shu-chou and of 의청 義青 I-ch'ing its noted monk. 투기 投機 To avail oneself of an opportunity ; to surrender oneself to the principles of the Buddha in the search for perfect enlightenment. 투연 投淵 To cast oneself into an abyss (hoping for eternal life). 투화 投華 To cast, or offer flowers in worship. 투신 投身 To cast away, or surrender, one's body, or oneself.

투 鬪 To contest, fight. 투승 鬪勝 To overcome in a contest of any kind. 투쟁 鬪諍 Argument, debate, contention. 투쟁왕 鬪諍王 The fractious king, Kalirāja, v. 갈 羯 15.

특 特 A bull, stallion ; outstanding, special, alone. 특승 特勝 Special, extraordinary. 특존 特尊 The outstanding honoured one. 특의나가타 特欹拏伽陀 Dakṣiṇāgāthā, a song offering, or expression of gratitude by a monk for food or gifts.

<ㅍ>

파 簸 A winnowing fan ; to winnow. 파랍부다 簸臈復多 Prabhūta, abundant, numerous ; a yakṣa. 파리바라사가 簸利婆羅闍迦 Parivrājaka, a Śivaitic sect ; v. 반 般.

파 罷 Cease, stop ; mark of finality. 파참 罷參 To dismiss the assembly.

파 皤 Grey, white. 파리 皤利 Bali, the offering of a portion of a meal to all creatures ; also royal revenue, a sacrifice, etc. 파자자부 皤雌子部 v. 독 犢.

파 帕 Kerchief, veil. 파극사파 帕克斯巴 Bashpa, v. 팔 八 and 파 巴.

파 叵 May not, cannot ; translit. *ph*. 파라우나마세 叵囉虞那麼洗 ; 파륵나 叵勒拏 ; 파라우니 頗攞遇抳 ; 파륵구나 頗勒窶拏 Phālgunamāsa, the twelfth month ; M. W. says February-March, the month, māsa, of the Nakṣatra Phālgunī.

파 頗 Somewhat, quite, very ; partial ; translit. *pha, bha*. Cf. 파 叵. 파륵구나 頗勒具那 or 頗勒窶拏 Phālguna, the twelfth month in India (February-March). 파니다 頗尼多 Phāṇita, the inspissated juice of the sugar cane, raw sugar. 파라 頗羅 Phala, fruit, produce, progeny, profit, etc. 파라타 頗羅墮 or 頗羅陀 Bhāradvāja, descendant of the ancient sage Bhāradvāja, intp. as one of the six (or eighteen) Brahmin surnames, and as meaning 이근 利根 of keen mind, clever. 파지가 頗胝迦 ; 파치가 頗置迦 ; 파려 頗黎 ; 파리 頗梨 Sphaṭika, rock crystal.

파 波 Taraṅga. A wave, waves ; to involve ; translit. *p, b, v* ; cf. 파 婆 ; 반 般 ; 발 鉢, etc.

파 巴 The open hand, palm ; to lay hold of ; to flatter. 파리 巴利 Pali considered by "Southern" Buddhists to be the language of Magadha, i.e. Māgadhī Prākrit, spoken by Śākyamuni ; their Tripiṭaka is written in it. It is closely allied to Sanskrit, but phonetically decayed and grammatically degenerate. 파사파 巴思巴 v. 팔사파 八思巴. 파련불 巴連佛 Pāṭaliputra, v. 파타리 波吒釐. 파능삼전어 巴陵三轉語 The three cryptic sayings of Hao-chien 호감 顥鑑 styled Pa-ling, name of his place in 악주 岳州 Yo-chou. He was the successor of Yün-mên 운문 雲門. "What is the way? The seeing fall into wells. What is the feather-cutting sword (of Truth)? Coral branches (i.e. moonbeams) prop up the moon. What is the divine (or deva) throng? A silver bowl full of snow." 파비 巴鼻 or 把鼻 or 巴臂 Something to lay hold of, e.g. a nose or an arm ; evidence.

파 破 To break, disrupt, destroy, cause schism ; solve, disprove, refute, negate. 파승 破僧 To disrupt a monk's meditation or preaching, also 파화합승 破和合僧 Saṅghabheda, disrupt the harmony of the community of monks, to cause schism, e.g. by heretical opinions. 파지옥 破地獄 To break open the gates of hell, by chants and incantations, for the release of a departed spirit. 파집 破執 To refute (false) tenets, e.g. the belief in the reality of the ego and things. 파괴 破壞 To destroy. 파괴선 破壞善 Destroyer of good, a name for Māra. 파하 破夏 To neglect the summer retreat. 파계 破戒 To break the commandments. 파유 破有 To refute the belief in the reality of things ; to break the power of transmigration as does the Buddha. 파정 破正 That which denies the truth, e.g. heresy. 파정명 破正命 An incorrect or wrong form of livelihood. 파법 破法 To break the (Buddha-)law, e.g. by the adoption of heresy. 파상종 破相宗 The sects established by Yung-ming 영명 永明, Ching-ying 정영 淨影, and Hui-yüan 혜원 慧遠, which held the unreality of all things. 파립 破立 also called 차조 遮照 Refuting and establishing ; by refuting to prove, or to establish, i.e. in refuting the particular to prove the universal, and vice versa.

파살제 破薩提 Upaśānti, tranquillity, calm. 파(사)현(정) 破(邪)顯(正) To break, or disprove the false and make manifest the right. 파문 破門 To break a door, leave a sect. 파암만원 破闇滿願 To destroy darkness or ignorance and fulfil the Buddha-vow, i.e. that of Amitābha. 파안미소 破顔微笑 To break into a smile, the mark of Kāśyapa's enlightenment when Buddha announced on Vulture Peak that he had a teaching which was propagated from mind to mind, a speech taken as authoritative by the Intuitional School. 파마 破魔 To overcome the māras, exorcise demons. 파재 破齋 To break the monastic rule of the regulation food, or time for meals, for which the punishment is hell, or to become a hungry ghost like the kind with throats small as needles and distended bellies, or to become an animal.

파 播 To sow, publish ; reject ; to winnow ; to stir up, cheat ; translit. *pa*, *pā*. 파니 播尼 Pāṇi, the palm of the hand. 파사 播捨 Pāśa, a noose, snare. 파마 播磨 Upamā, a resemblance, simile. 파수발다 播輸鉢多 Pāśupata, followers of the lord of cattle, Śiva, who smeared themselves with ashes, also 파수발다 波輸鉢多.

파(률)습바 波(栗)濕縛 ; **파사** 波奢 Pārśva, the ribs. The tenth patriarch, previously a Brahman of Gandhāra, who took a vow not to lie down until he had mastered the meaning of the Tripiṭaka, cut off all desire in the realms of sense, form and non-form, and obtained the six supernatural powers and the eight pāramitās. This he accomplished after three years. His death is put at 36 B.C. His name is tr. as 협존자 脇尊者 his Worship of the Ribs.

파나사 波那娑 Panasa, 반나사 半那娑 the bread-fruit tree, jaka or jack-fruit.

파날라파날마세 婆捺囉婆捺麼洗 Bhādrapadamāsa, the sixth month, middle of August to middle of September ; the third and fourth Nakṣatras or lunar mansions, Pūrva and Uttara ; also 발날라바나 跋捺囉婆娜 ; 발다나바나 跋陀娜婆娜 ; 바달라발다 婆達羅鉢陀.

파노 波奴 Vidhu, a syn. for the moon.

파니 波尼 ; 파니 波抳 Pāna, drink, beverage ; tr. as water (to drink) ; 파니람 波尼藍 tr. as "water," but may be Pānila, a drinking vessel.

파두마 波頭摩 Padma, 파담마 波曇摩 ; 파모 波暮 ; etc., the red lotus ; v. 발 鉢 ; tr. 화 華 or 연 蓮. 파두마색니 波頭摩色尼 Padmapāṇi, one of the forms of Kuan-yin, holding a lotus.

파라가 波羅伽 Pāraka, carrying over, saving ; the pāramitā boat. 파라가 波羅迦 Pāraga, a title of Buddha who has reached the other shore. 파라가라 波羅伽羅 ; 발라가라 鉢囉迦羅 Prākāra, a containing wall, fence.

파라말타 波羅末陀 Paramārtha, the highest truth, ultimate truth, reality, fundamental meaning, 진제 眞諦. Name of a famous monk from Western India, Guṇarata, v. 구 拘, whose title was 진제삼장 眞諦三藏 ; reached China 547 or 548, but the country was so disturbed that he set off to return by sea ; his ship was driven back to Canton, where he translated some fifty works.

파라사화 波羅奢華 Palāśa ; a leaf, petal, foliage ; the blossom of the *Butea frondosa*, a tree with red flowers, whose sap is used for dye ; said to be black before sunrise, red during the day, and yellow after sunset.

파라월 波羅越 Pārāvata, a dove ; the fifth row of a rock-cut temple in the Deccan, said to resemble a dove, described by Fa-hsien.

파라제비 波羅提毘 or 波羅梯毘 Pṛthivī, the earth. Also 발리체미 鉢里體尾. See 지 地.

파라파바지 波羅頗婆底 Prabhāvatī, younger sister of Aśoka. 파라파가라밀다라 波羅頗迦羅蜜多羅 Prabhākaramitra, enlightener, v. 파파 波頗.

파랑 波浪 Taraṅga, a wave, waves.

파륜 波崙 v. 살타 薩陀.

파리 波利 Pari, round, round about ; complete, all. 파(리)가라 波利伽羅 Parikara, an auxiliary garment, loincloth, towel, etc. 파리파사 波利婆娑 Parivāsa, sent to a separate abode, isolation for improper conduct. 파리질(다)라 波利質(多)羅 ; 파의질구 波疑質姤 ; 파리수 波利樹 Paricitra, a tree in the Trayastriṁśāḥ heavens which fills the heavens with fragrance ; also Pārijāta, a tree in Indra's heaven, one of the five trees of paradise, the coral-tree, Erythina Indica. 파리열박남 波利涅縛南 ; 파리닐박남 波利昵縛喃 Parinirvāṇa, v. 반 般.

파리 玻璃 Sphaṭika. Rock crystal, one of the seven precious things. Also 파리 頗梨 or 파려 頗黎 ; 새파치가 塞頗致迦, etc.

파리 波離 Upāli, v. 우 優.

파리 玻璃 Vaiḍūrya, described as a green indestructible gem, one of the seven precious things. A mountain near Vārāṇaśī. Also 폐파리(야) 吠玻璃(耶) ; 비두리 毘頭梨. 파리왕 玻璃王 Virūḍhaka, cf. 비 毘.

파리나 波夷羅 Vajra, one of the generals of Yao-shih, Bhaiṣajya, the Buddha of Healing.

파리의다라 波里衣多羅 Pāriyātra, "an ancient kingdom 800 li south-west of Śatadru, a centre of heretical sects. The present city of Birat, west of Mathurā." [Eitel].

파미니 波彌尼 or **파니니** 波你尼 Pāṇini, the great Indian grammarian and writer of the fourth century B.C., also known as Śālāturīya.

파미라 波謎羅 Pamira, the Pamirs, "the centre of the Tsung-ling mountains with the Sirikol lake (v. Anavatapta) in Lat. 38° 20 N., Long. 74° E." [Eitel].

파비 波卑 idem 파순 波旬.

파비 波鞞 v. 파순 波旬.

파사 波斯 Pārasī, Persian, Persia. 파시 波嘶 ; 파자사 波剌斯 or 파자사 波剌私 ; 파라실 波羅悉. In its capital of Surasthāna the Buddha's almsbowl was said to be in A.D. 600. [Eitel]. 파사(닉) 波斯(匿) ; 발라서나시다 鉢邏犀那恃多 or 발라사나시다 鉢邏斯那時多 ; 파자사 波剌斯 Prasenajit, king of Śrāvastī, contemporary of the Buddha, and known *inter alia* as (승)광왕 (勝)光王 ; father of Virūḍhaka, who supplanted him.

파사파제 波闍波提 Prajāpati, 파(라)사발제 波(邏)闍鉢提 aunt and nurse of the Buddha, v. 마하 摩訶. 바사라 波闍羅 Vajra, the diamond sceptre, v. 금강저 金剛杵.

파순(유) 波旬(踰) ; 파비 波鞞 Pāpīyān. Pāpīmān. Pāpīmā. Pāpīyān is very wicked. Pāpīyān is a Buddhist term for 악자 惡者 the Evil One ; 살자 殺者 the Murderer ; Māra ; because he strives to kill all goodness ; v. 마 魔. Also 파비면 波卑面 or 파비연 波卑椽 or 파비연 波卑緣.

파술 波戍 Paśu, any animal.

파야 波耶 Payas, water ; in Sanskrit it also means milk, juice, vital force.

파연나 波演那 or 波衍那 Paryayaṇa, suggesting an ambulatory ; intp. as a courtyard.

파제 波帝 Pati, 발지 鉢底 master, lord, proprietor, husband.

파차 波叉 Virūpākṣa, 비류단차 毘留博叉 ; 비류파아차 鼻溜波阿叉 irregular-eyed, a syn. of Śiva ; the guardian king of the West.

파치가 波哆迦 Patākā, a flag.

파치가 婆致迦 Sphaṭika, v. 수옥 水玉.

파타라 波吒羅 Pāṭalī, 발달라 鉢怛羅 a tree scented blossoms, the trumpet-flower, *Bignonia Suaveolens*. A kingdom, i.e. 파타리(자) 波吒釐(子) ; 파타리불 波吒利弗 ; 파타리야 波吒梨耶 ; 파라리불다라 波羅利弗多羅 ; 파련불 巴蓮弗 Pāṭaliputra, originally Kusumapura, the modern Patna ; capital of Aśoka, where the third synod was held.

파파 波頗 Prabhā(kara)mitra, an Indian monk, who came to China in A.D. 626.

파파 波波 Running hither and thither. Also, Pāvā, a place near Rājagṛha. 파파겁겁 波波劫劫 Rushing about for ever. 파파라 波波羅 Pippala, *Ficus religiosa*.

파파리 波波利 or **파화리** 波和利 Pravari, or perhaps Pravara, woollen or hairy cloth, name of a monastery, the 파파리엄파 波波梨奄婆. Also 파파리 波波梨 or 파파리 波波離 name of a maternal aunt of Maitreya.

판 板 A board ; a board struck for calling, e.g. to meals.

판 瓣 A section, or division (of a melon). 판향 瓣香 Incense with sections resembling a melon.

판 判 Divide, judge, decide. 판교 判敎 Division of the Buddha's teaching, e.g. that of T'ien-t'ai, into the five periods and eight teachings, that of Hua-yen into five teachings, etc. 판석 判釋 To divide and explain sūtras ; to arrange in order, analyse the Buddha's teaching.

판 辦 To transact, carry out ; prepare ; punish. 판사 辦事 To transact affairs, attend to, arrange. 판도 辦道 To carry out religious duty or discipline.

팔 八 Aṣṭa, eight. 팔불(중도) 八不(中道) The eight negations of Nāgārjuna, founder of the Mādhyamika or Middle School 삼론종 三論宗. The four pairs are "neither birth nor death, neither end nor permanence, neither identity nor difference, neither coming nor going." These are the eight negations ; add "neither cause nor effect" and there are the 십불 十不 ten negations ; v. 팔미 八迷. 팔불정관 八不正觀 ; 팔불중관 八不中觀 Meditation on the above eight negations. These eight, birth, death, etc., are the 팔미 八迷 eight misleading ideas, or 팔계 八計 eight wrong calculations. No objection is made to the terms in the apparent, or relative, sense 속제 俗諦, but in the real or absolute sense 진제 眞諦 these eight ideas are incorrect, and the truth lies between them ; in the relative, mortality need not be denied, but in the absolute we cannot speak of mortality or immortality. In regard to the relative view, beings have apparent birth and apparent death from various causes, but are not really born and do not really die, i.e. there is the difference of appearance and reality. In the absolute there is no apparent birth and apparent death. The other three pairs are similarly studied. 팔불가월 八不可越 idem 팔경계 八敬戒. 팔부사의 八不思議 The eight inexpressibles, or things surpassing thought, i.e. eight qualities of the ocean (depth, extent, etc.) in illustration of nirvāṇa ; v. 대해 大海. 팔불정견 八不正見 The teaching of the 대집경 大集經 26, on the eight incorrect views in regard to (1) 아견 我見 the existence of a permanent ego ; (2) 중생견 衆生見 the five skandhas as not the constituents of the living ; (3) 수명견 壽命見 fate, or determination of length of life ; (4) 사부견 士夫見 a creator ; (5) 상견 常見 permanence ; (6) 단견 斷見 annihilation ; (7) 유견 有見 the reality of things ; (8) 무견 無見 their unreality. 팔부정 八不淨 The eight things "unclean" to monks, of which there are different groups. One group is — to keep gold, silver, male slaves, female slaves, cattle, stores, or to trade or farm. Another is — to own cultivated lands, to farm, keep supplies of grain and silk, servants, animals or birds, money, cushions and pans, and furniture and gilded beds. 팔불현실 八不顯實 By the eight negations of the Mādhyamika doctrine, the true reality of things is shown.

팔각 八覺 The eight (wrong) perceptions or thoughts, i.e. desire ; hate ; vexation (with others) ; 친리 親里 home-sickness ; patriotism (or thoughts of the country's welfare) ; dislike of death ; ambition for one's clan or family ; slighting or being rude to others. 화엄경 華嚴經 13.

팔건 八乾 The eight skandhas, or sections of the Abhidharma, v. 팔건도 八犍度.

팔건도 八犍度 The eight skandhas or sections of the Abhidharma, i.e. miscellaneous ; concerning bondage to the passions, etc. ; wisdom ; practice ; the four fundamentals, or elements ; the roots, or organs ; meditation ; and views. The 팔건론 八犍論 in thirty sections, attributed to Kātyāyana, is in the Abhidharma,

팔경계 八敬戒 The eight commands giver by the Buddha to his foster-mother, i.e. aunt, when she was admitted to the order, and which remain as commands to nuns : (1) even though a hundred years old a nun must pay respect to a monk, however young, and offer her seat to him ; (2) must never scold a monk ; (3) never accuse, or speak of his misdeeds ; but a monk may speak of hers ; (4) at his hands obtain reception into the order ; (5) confess sin (sexual or other) before the assembly of monks and nuns ; (6) ask the fraternity for a monk as preceptor ; (7) never share the same summer resort with monks ; (8) after the summer retreat she must report and ask for a responsible confessor. Also 팔경법 八敬法 ; 팔불가월법 八不可越法 ; 팔불가과법 八不可過法 ; 팔존중법 八尊重法 ; v. 사분율 四分律 48.

팔계(재) 八戒(齋) The first eight of the ten commandments, see 계 戒 ; not to kill ; not to take things not given ; no ignoble (i.e. sexual) conduct ; not to speak falsely ; not to drink wine ; not to indulge in cosmetics, personal adornments, dancing, or music ; not to sleep on fine beds, but on a mat on the ground ; and not to eat out of regulation hours, i.e. after noon. Another group divides the sixth into two — against cosmetics and adornments and against dancing and music ; the first eight are then called the eight prohibitory commands and the last the 재 齋 or fasting commandment. Also 팔재계 八齋戒 ; 팔관재 八關齋 ; 팔지재 八支齋 ; cf. 팔종승법 八種勝法.

팔고 八苦 The eight distresses — birth, age, sickness, death, parting with what we love, meeting with what we hate, unattained aims, and all the ills of the five skandhas.

팔관재 八關齋 idem 팔계재 八戒齋.

팔교 八憍 The eight kinds of pride, or arrogance, resulting in domineering : because of strength ; of clan, or name ; of wealth ; of independence, or position ; of years, or age ; of cleverness, or wisdom ; of good or charitable deeds ; of good looks. Of these, eight birds are named as types : 치효 鴟梟 two kinds of owl, eagle, vulture, crow, magpie, pigeon, wagtail.

팔교 八教 The eight T'ien-t'ai classifications of Śākyamuni's teaching, from the Avataṁsaka to the Lotus and Nirvāṇa sūtras, divided into the two sections (1) 화법사교 化法四教 his four kinds of teaching of the content of the Truth accommodated to the capacity of his disciples ; (2) 화의사교 化儀四教 his four modes of instruction. (1) The four 화법교 化法教 are : (a) 삼장교 三藏教 The Tripiṭaka or Hīnayāna teaching, for śrāvakas and pratyekabuddhas, the bodhisattva doctrine being subordinate ; it also included the primitive śūnya doctrine as developed in the Satya-siddhi śāstra. (b) 통교 通教 His later "intermediate" teaching which contained Hīnayāna and mahāyāna doctrine for śrāvaka, pratyekabuddha, and bodhisattva, to which are attributed the doctrines of the Dharmalakṣaṇa or Yogācārya and Mādhyamika schools. (c) 별교 別教 His differentiated, or separated, bodhisattva teaching, definitely Mahāyāna. (d) 원교 圓教 His final, perfect, bodhisattva, universal teaching as preached, e.g. in the Lotus and Nirvāṇa sūtras. (2) The four methods of instruction 화의 化儀 are : (a) 돈교 頓教 Direct teaching without reserve of the whole truth, e.g. the 화엄 華嚴 sūtra. (b) 점교 漸教 Gradual or graded, e.g. the 아함

阿含, 방등 方等, and 반야 般若 sūtras ; all the four 화법 化法 are also included under this heading. (c) 비밀교 秘密教 Esoteric teaching, only understood by special members of the assembly. (d) 부정교 不定教 General or indeterminate teaching, from which each hearer would derive benefit according to his interpretation.

팔교도 八交道 The eight roads in the eight directions, bounded with golden cords, mentioned in the Lotus Sūtra as in certain Buddha-realms.

팔구의 八句義 The eight fundamental principles, intuitional or relating to direct mental vision, of the Ch'an(Zen) school, 선종 禪宗 q.v. ; they are 정법안장 正法眼藏 ; 열반묘심 涅槃妙心 ; 실상무상 實相無相 ; 미묘법문 微妙法門 ; 불립문자 不立文字 ; 교외별전 教外別傳 ; 직지인심 直指人心 ; 견성성불 見性成佛.

팔금 八禁 idem 팔계 八戒.

팔기 八棄 idem 팔바라이 八波羅夷.

팔난 八難 The eight conditions in which it is difficult to see a Buddha or hear his dharma : in the hells ; as hungry ghosts ; as animals ; in Uttarakuru (the northern continent where all is pleasant) ; in the long-life heavens (where life is long and easy) ; as deaf, blind, and dumb ; as a worldly philosopher ; in the intermediate period between a Buddha and his successor. Also 팔무가 八無暇.

팔념(법) 八念(法) ; **팔념(문)** 八念(門) Eight lines of thought, in the 지도론 智度論 21, for resisting Māra-attacks and evil promptings during the meditation on impurity, etc. ; i.e. thought of the Buddha, of the Law (or Truth), the fraternity, the commandments, almsgiving, the devas, breathing, and death. There are also the 대인팔념 大人八念, i.e. that truth 도 道 is obtained through absence of desire, contentment, aloneness, zeal, correct thinking, a fixed mind, wisdom, and inner joy. v. 팔념경 八念經.

팔다라수 八多羅樹 As high as eight tāla (palmyra) trees, very high.

팔대(지옥) 八大(地獄) The eight great naraka, or hot hells : (1) sañjīva 등활 等活 hell of rebirth into (2) kālasūtra 흑승 黑繩, i.e. the hell of black cords or chains ; (3) saṅghāta 중합 衆合, in which all are squeezed into a mass between two mountains falling together ; (4) raurava 호규 號叫 hell of crying and wailing ; (5) mahāraurava 대호규 大號叫 hell of great crying ; (6) tapana 염열 炎熱 hell of burning ; (7) pratāpana 대열 大熱 hell of fierce heat ; (8) avīci 무간 無間 unintermitted rebirth into its sufferings with no respite. v. 지옥 地獄 and 팔한지옥 八寒地獄.

팔대관음 八大觀音 The eight Shingon representations of Kuan-yin : as one of the above 팔대명왕 八大明王, as the white-robed one, as a rākṣasī, as with four faces, as with a horse's head, as Mahāsthāmaprāpta 대세지 大勢至, and as Tārā 타라 陀羅.

팔대금강명왕 八大金剛明王 or 팔대금강동자 八大金剛童子 The eight attendants on 부동명왕 不動明王 (cf. 팔대명왕 八大明王). They are 혜광 慧光, 혜희 慧喜, 아뇩달다 阿耨達多, 지덕 指德, 오구파가 烏俱婆迦, 청덕 清德, 긍갈라 矜羯羅, and 제타가 制吒迦.

팔대동자 八大童子 The eight messengers of 부동명왕 不動明王, also known as 팔대금강동자 八大金剛童子 ; Mañjuśrī also has eight.

팔대명왕 八大明王 The eight diamond-kings, or bodhisattva, in their representations as fierce guardians of Vairocana 대일 大日 ; 금강수 金剛手 is represented as 항삼세 降三世 ; 묘길상 妙吉祥 as 대위덕 大威德 ; 허공장 虛空藏 as 대소 大笑 ; 자씨 慈氏 as 대륜 大輪 ; 관자재 觀自在 as 마두 馬頭 ; 지장 地藏 as 무능승명 無能勝明 ; 제개장 除蓋障 as 부동존 不動尊 ; and 보현 普賢 as 보척 步擲.

팔대보살 八大菩薩 see 팔대명왕 八大明王. Another group is given in the 팔대보살만다라경 八大菩薩曼荼羅經 ; another in the 약사경 藥師經 translated by I-ching ; another in the 팔대보살경 八大菩薩經 translated by Fa-hsien ; and there are other groups.

팔대신고 八大辛苦 idem 팔고 八苦.

팔대영탑 八大靈塔 The eight great "spirit" or sacred stūpas erected at (1) Kapilavastu, Buddha's birthplace ; (2) Magadha, where he was first enlightened ; (3) the deer-park Benares, where he first preached ; (4) Jetavana, where he revealed his super-natural powers ; (5) Kanyākubja (Kanauj), where he descended from Indra's heavens ; (6) Rājagṛha, where Devadatta was destroyed and the Saṅgha purified ; (7) Vaiśālī, where he announced his speedy nirvāṇa ; (8) Kuśinagara, where he entered nirvāṇa. There is another slightly variant list.

팔대자재아 八大自在我 The eight great powers of personality or sovereign independence, as one of the four qualities 상락아정 常樂我淨 of nirvāṇa : powers of self-manifolding, infinite expansion, levitation and transportation, manifesting countless forms permanently in one and the same place, use of one physical organ in place of another, obtaining all things as if nothing, expounding a stanza through countless kalpas, ability to traverse the solid as space. v. 열반경 涅槃經 23.

팔도 八倒 v. 팔전도 八顚倒.

팔도(지) 八道(支) ; **팔도(선)** 八道(船) ; **팔도(행)** 八道(行) idem 팔정도 八正道.

팔동자 八童子 idem 팔대금강동자 八大金剛童子.

팔론 八論 The eight śāstras ; there are three lists of eight ; one non-Buddhist ; one by 무착 無着 Asaṅga, founder of the Yoga School ; a third by 진나 陳那 Jina Dignāga. Details are given in the 기귀전 寄歸傳 4 and 해람초 解纜鈔 4.

팔륜 八輪 The eight (spoke)wheel, idem 팔정도 八正道.

팔마 八魔 The eight Māras, or destroyers : 번뇌마 煩惱魔 the māras of the passions ; 음마 陰魔 the skandha-māras, v. 오음 五陰 ; 사마 死魔 death-māra ; 타화자재천마 他化自在天魔 the māra-king. The above four are ordinarily termed the four māras ; the other four are the four Hīnayāna delusions of śrāvakas and pratyekabuddhas, i.e. 무상 無常 impermanence ; 무락 無樂 joylessness ; 무아 無我 impersonality ; 무정 無淨 impurity ; cf. 팔전도 八顚倒.

팔만 八萬 An abbreviation for 팔만사(천) 八萬四(千) The number of atoms in the human body is supposed to be 84,000. Hence the term is used for a number of things, often in the general sense of a great number. It is also the age apex of life in each human world. There are the 84,000 stūpas erected by Aśoka, each to accommodate one of the 84,000 relics of the Buddha's body ; also the 84,000 forms of illumination shed by Amitābha ; the 84,000 excellent physical signs of a Buddha ; the 84,000 mortal distresses, i.e. 84,000 번뇌 煩惱 or 진로 塵勞 ; also the cure found in the 84,000 methods, i.e. 법장 法藏, 법온 法蘊, 법문 法門, or 교문 教門. 팔만십이 八萬十二 An abbreviation for 팔만사천법장 八萬四千法藏 the 84,000 teachings or lessons credited to the Buddha for the cure of all sufferings, and the 십이부경 十二部經 12 sūtras in which they are contained. 팔만위의 八萬威儀 The bodhisattva's 80,000 duties.

팔만 八慢 The eight kinds of pride, māna, arrogance, or self-conceit, 여만 如慢 though inferior, to think oneself equal to others (in religion) ; 만만 慢慢 to think oneself superior among manifest superiors ; 불여만 不如慢 to think oneself not so much inferior among manifest superiors ; 증상만 增上慢 to think one has attained more than is the fact, or when it is not the fact ; 아만 我慢 self-superiority, or self-sufficiency ; 사만 邪慢 pride in false views, or doings ; 교만 憍慢 arrogance ; 대만 大慢 extreme arrogance.

팔무가 八無暇 The eight conditions of no leisure or time to hear a Buddha or his truth, idem 팔난무가애 八難無暇礙 The eight universalized powers of the 육식 六識 six senses, 의근 意根 the mind and the 법계 法界 dharmadhātu.

팔문(이오) 八門(二悟) ; **팔문(양익)** 八門(兩益) Eight kinds of syllogisms in Buddhist logic ; v. 인명팔정리론 因明八正理論. (1) 능립 能立 a valid proposition ; (2) 능파 能破 an invalid proposition ; (3) 사능립 似能立 doubtful, or seemingly valid bur faulty ; (4) 사능파 似能破 seemingly invalid, and assailable ; (5) 현량 現量 manifest, or evidential ; (6) 비량 比量 inferential ; (7) 사현량 似現量 seemingly evidential ; (8) 사비량 似比量 seemingly inferential.

팔미 八迷 The eight misleading terms, which form the basis of the logic of the 중론 中論, i.e. 생 生 birth, 멸 滅 death, 거 去 past, 래 來 future, 일 一 identity, 이 異 difference, 단 斷 annihilation, 상 常 perpetuity (or eternity). The 삼론종 三論宗 regard these as unreal ; v. 팔불중도 八不中道.

팔미 八味 The eight savours (or pleasures) of the Buddha's nirvāṇa : 상주 常住 perpetual abode, 적멸 寂滅 extinction (of distress, etc.), 불로 不老 eternal youth, 불사 不死 immortality, 청정 淸淨 purity, 허통 虛通 absolute freedom (as space), 부동 不動 imperturbability, and 쾌락 快樂 joy.

팔바라이 八波羅夷 or 팔중죄 八重罪 The eight pārājika, in relation to the sins of a nun ; for the first four see 사바라이 四波羅夷 ; (5) libidinous contact with a male ; (6) any sort of improper association (leading to adultery) ; (7) concealing the misbehaviour (of an equal, or inferior) ; (8) improper dealings with a monk.

팔방상하 八方上下 The four quarters, the four 유 維 half-quarters and above and below, i.e. the universe in all directions. 팔방천 八方天 The eight heavens and devas at the eight points of the compass : E., the Indra, or Śakra heaven ; S., the Yama heaven ; W., the Varuṇa, or water heaven ; N., the Vaiśramaṇa, or Pluto heaven ; N.E., the Īśāna, or Śiva heaven ; S.E., the Homa, or fire heaven ; S.W., the Nirṛti, or Rakṣaḥ heaven ; N.W., the Vāyu, or wind heaven. All these may be considered as devalokas or heavens.

팔배 八輩 The eight grades, i.e. those who have attained the 사향 四向 and 사과 四果.

팔배사 八背捨 idem 팔해탈 八解脫.

팔벌 八筏 The eight rafts, idem 팔정도 八正道 The eightfold noble path.

팔법 八法 The eight dharmas, things, or methods. There are three groups : (1) idem 팔풍 八風 q.v. (2) 사대 四大 and 사미 四微 q.v. (3) The eight essential things, i.e. 교 敎 instruction, 리 理 doctrine, 지 智 knowledge or wisdom attained, 단 斷 cutting away of delusion, 행 行 practice of the religious life, 위 位 progressive status, 인 因 producing 과 果 the fruit of saintliness. Of these 교리행과 敎理行果 are known as the 사법 四法.

팔변 八辯 Eight characteristics of a Buddha's speaking : never hectoring ; never misleading or confused ; fearless ; never haughty ; perfect in meaning ; and in flavour ; free from harshness ; seasonable (or, suited to the occasion).

팔변화 八變化 Eight supernatural powers of transformation, characteristics of every Buddha : (1) to shrink self or others, or the world and all things to an atom ; (2) to enlarge ditto to fill all space ; (3) to make the same light as a feather ; (4) to make the same any size or anywhere at will ; (5) everywhere and in everything to be omnipotent ; (6) to be anywhere at will, either by self-transportation, or bringing the destination to himself, etc. ; (7) to shake all things (in the six, or eighteen ways) ; (8) to be one or many and at will pass through the solid or through space, or through fire or water, or transform the four elements at will, e.g. turn earth into water. Also 팔신변 八神變 ; 팔자재 八自在.

팔보살 八菩薩 idem 팔대보살 八大菩薩.

팔복생처 八福生處 The eight happy conditions in which he may he reborn who keeps the five commands and the ten good ways and bestows alms : (1) rich and honourable among men ; (2) in the heavens of the four deva kings ; (3) the Indra heavens ; (4) Suyāma heavens ; (5) Tuṣita heaven ; (6) 화락 化樂 nirmāṇarati heaven, i.e. the fifth devaloka ; (7) 타화 他化 paranirmita-vaśavartin, i.e. the sixth devaloka heaven ; (8) the brahma-heavens. 팔복전 八福田 The eight fields for cultivating blessedness : Buddhas ; arhats (or saints) ; preaching monks (upādhyāya) ; teachers (ācārya) ; friars ; father ; mother ; the sick. Buddhas, arhats, and friars (or monks in general) are termed 경전 敬田 reverence-fields ; the sick are 비전 悲田 compassion-fields ; the rest are 은전 恩田 grace-or gratitude-fields. Another group is : to make roads and wells ; canals and bridges ; repair dangerous roads ; be dutiful to parents ; support monks ; tend the sick ; save from disaster or distress ; provide for a quinquennial assembly. Another : serving the Three Precious Ones, i.e. the Buddha ; the Law ; the order ; parents ; the monks as teachers ; the poor ; the sick ; animals.

팔부(중) 八部(衆) The eight classes of supernatural beings in the Lotus sūtra : 천 天 deva, 용 龍 nāga, 야차 夜叉 yakṣa, 건달바 乾闥婆 gandharva, 아수라 阿修羅 asura, 가루라 迦樓羅 garuḍa, 긴나라 緊那羅 kinnara, 마후라가 摩睺羅迦 mahoraga. Also called 천룡팔부 天龍八部 and 용신팔부 龍神八部. 팔부귀중 八部鬼衆 The eight groups of demon-followers of the four mahārājas, i.e. gandharvas, piśācas, kumbhāṇḍas, pretas, nāgas, pūtanas, yakṣas, and rākṣasas.

팔불 八佛 Eight Buddhas of the eastern quarter.

팔비천 八臂天 The eight-arm deva ; an epithet of Brahma as Nārāyaṇadeva 나라연천 那羅延天 creator of men.

팔사 八邪 The eight heterodox or improper practices, the opposite of the eight correct paths 팔정도 八正道.

팔사 八師 The eight teachers — murder, robbery, adultery, lying, drinking, age, sickness, and death ; v. 팔사경 八師經.

팔사수신 八事隨身 The eight appurtenances of a monk — three garments, bowl, stool, filter, needle and thread, and chopper.

팔사파 八思巴 ; **발사파** 發思巴 Bashpa, Phagspa, Baghcheba, Blo-gros-rgyal-mtshan. A śramaṇa of Tibet, teacher and confidential adviser of Kublai Khan, who appointed him head of the Buddhist church of Tibet A.D. 1260. He is the author of a manual of Buddhist terminology 창소지론 彰所知論 and translated another work into Chinese. In A.D. 1269 he constructed an alphabet for the Mongol language, "adapted from the Tibetan and written vertically," and a syllabary borrowed from Tibetan, known by the name of Ḫkor-yig, for which, however, the Lama Chos-kyi-ḫod-zer 1307-1311 substituted another alphabet based on that of Śākyapaṇḍita.

팔상(성도) 八相(成道) also 팔상시현 八相示現 Eight aspects of the Buddha's life, which the 기신론 起信論 gives as : (1) descent into and abode in the Tuṣita heaven ; (2) entry into his mother's womb ; (3) abode there visibly preaching to the devas ; (4) birth from mother's side in Lumbinī ; (5) leaving home at 19 (or 25) as a hermit ; (6) after six years' suffering attaining enlightenment ; (7) rolling the Law-wheel, or preaching ; (8) at 80 entering nirvāṇa. The 사교의 四教義 group of T'ien-t'ai is slightly different — descent from Tuṣita, entry into womb, birth, leaving home, subjection of Māra, attaining perfect wisdom, preaching, nirvāṇa. See also the two 사상 四相, i.e. 사본상 四本相 and 사수상 四隨相.

팔색번 八色幡 The Amitābha eight pennons of various colours, indicating the eight directions of space.

팔성 八成 idem 팔상성도 八相成道. 팔성립인 八成立因 The eight factors of a Buddhist syllogism.

팔성 八聖 The 사향 四向 and 사과 四果 of śrāvakas. 팔성(도지) 八聖(道支) idem 팔정도 八正道.

팔수 八水 Eight rivers of India — Ganges, Jumna, 살라 薩羅 Sarasvatī, Hiraṇyavatī or Ajiravatī, 마하 摩河 Mahī, Indus, Oxus, and Śītā.

팔승처 八勝處 The eight victorious stages, or degrees, in meditation for overcoming desire, or attachment to the world of sense ; v. 팔해탈 八解脫.

팔시 八時 An Indian division of the day into eight "hours," four for day and four for night.

팔식 八識 The eight parijñāna, or kinds of cognition, perception, or consciousness. They are the five senses of cakṣur-vijñāna, śrotra-vijñāna, ghrāṇa-vijñāna, jihvā-vijñāna and kāya-vijñāna, i.e. seeing, hearing, smelling, tasting, and touch. The sixth is mano-vijñāna, the mental sense, or intellect, v. 말나 末那. It is defined as 의 意 mentality, apprehension, or by some as will. The seventh is styled kliṣṭa-mano-vijñāna 말나식 末那識 discriminated from the last as 사량 思量 pondering, calculating ; it is the discriminating and constructive sense, more than the intellectually perceptive ; as infected by the ālaya-vijñāna, or receiving "seeds" from it, it is considered as the cause of all egoism and individualizing, i.e. of men and things, therefore of all illusion arising from assuming the seeming as the real. The eighth is the ālaya-vijñāna, 아뢰야식 阿賴耶識 which is the storehouse, or basis from which come all "seeds" of consciousness. The seventh is also defined as the ādāna 아다나식 阿陀那識 or "laying hold of" or "holding on to" consciousness. 팔식심왕 八識心王 The eight fundamental powers of the 팔식 八識 and 팔식심소 八識心所 the eight powers functioning, or the concomitant sensations. 팔식체일 八識體一 The eight perceptions are fundamentally a unity, opposed by the 유식 唯識 school with the doctrine 팔식체별 八識體別 that they are fundamentally discrete.

팔신변 八神變 idem 팔변화 八變化.

팔십 八十 Aśīti, eighty. 팔십일품사혹 八十一品思惑 The eighty-one kinds of illusion, or misleading thoughts, arising out of desire, anger, foolishness, and pride — nine grades in each of the nine realms of desire, of form and beyond form. 팔십일법 八十一法 The eighty-one divisions in the Prajñā-pāramitā sūtra 대반야경 大般若經 comprising form 색 色 ; mind 심 心 ; the five skandhas 오음 五陰 ; twelve means of sensation 입 入 ; eighteen realms 계 界 ; four axioms 제 諦 ; twelve nidānas 인연 因緣 ; eighteen śūnya 공 空 ; six pāramitā 도 度, and four jñāna 지 智. Also 팔십일과 八十一科. 팔십종호 八十種好 ; 팔십수형호 八十隨形好 The eighty notable physical characteristics of Buddha ; cf. 삼십이상 三十二相. 팔십화엄경 八十華嚴經 The translation of the Hua-yen 화엄경 華嚴經 in eighty chüan, made by Śikṣānanda in the T'ang dynasty. 팔십송률 八十誦律 The original Vinaya recited by the Buddha's disciple Upāli eighty times during the summer retreat, while the Tripiṭaka was being composed after the Buddha's death.

팔억사천만념 八億四千萬念 The myriads of "thoughts," or moments in a single day and night, each with its consequences of good and evil ; probably 8,400,000,000 is meant.

팔열지옥 八熱地獄 v. 팔대지옥 八大地獄.

팔엽 八葉 The eight lotus-petals, a name for Sumeru. 팔엽원 八葉院 is the central court of the 태장계 胎藏界 with Vairocana as its central figure, also termed 팔엽연대 八葉蓮臺 ; 팔엽연좌 八葉蓮座 An esoteric name for the heart is the eight-petal fleshly heart, and being the seat of meditation it gives rise to the term eight-leaf lotus meditation.

팔예 八穢 Eight things unclean to a monk : buying land for self, not for Buddha or the fraternity ; ditto cultivating ; ditto laying by or storing up ; ditto keeping servants (or slaves) ; keeping animals (for slaughter) ; treasuring up gold, etc. ; ivory and ornaments ; utensils for private use.

팔오삼이 八五三二 The four special characteristics of the 법상 法相 Dharmalakṣaṇa sect, i.e. 팔식 八識, 오법 五法, 삼성 三性, and 이무아 二無我 q.v.

팔왕자 八王子 The eight sons of the last of the 20,000 shining Buddhas 등명불 燈明佛 born before he left home to become a monk ; their names are given in the first chapter of the Lotus sūtra. In Japan there are also eight sons of a Shinto deity, reincarnated as one of the six Kuan-yin. 팔왕일 八王日 The eight royal days, i.e. the solstices, the equinoxes, and the first day of each of the four seasons.

팔원 八圓 Eight fundamental characteristics of a 원교 圓教 complete or perfect school of teaching, which must perfectly express 교 教, 리 理, 지 智, 단 斷, 행 行, 위 位, 인 因, and 과 果.

팔위 八位 The classification or grades of disciples according to the T'ien-t'ai 원교 圓教 perfect teaching, i.e. (1) 관행즉 觀行卽 grade of the five classes, or stages, of lay disciples ; (2) 상사즉 相似卽 grade of the ten classes of ordinary monks and nuns ; above these are the 분진즉 分眞卽 bodhisattva stages of those progressing towards Buddhahood, i.e. (3) 십주 十住, (4) 십행 十行, (5) 십회향 十廻向, (6) 십지 十地, (7) 등각 等覺, and (8) the perfect or Buddha stage 구경즉 究竟卽, i.e. 묘각 妙覺. Cf. 육즉 六卽. 팔위태장 八位胎藏 The eight stages of the human foetus : 갈라람 羯羅藍 kalala, the appearance after the first week from conception ; 액부담 頞部曇 arbuda, at end of second week ; 폐시 閉尸 peśī, third ; 건남 健南 ghana, fourth ; 발라사거 鉢羅奢佉 praśākhā, limbs formed during fifth week ; sixth, hair, nails, and teeth ; seventh, the organs of sense, eyes, ears, nose, and tongue ; and eighth, complete formation.

팔유행 八遊行 idem 팔정도 八正道.

팔유행 八由行, also 팔직행 八直行 ; 팔직도 八直道 idem 팔정도 八正道.

팔음 八音 The eight tones of a Buddha's voice — beautiful, flexible, harmonious, respect-producing, not effeminate (i.e. manly), unerring, deep and resonant.

팔인 八忍 The eight kṣānti, or powers of patient endurance, in the desire-realm and the two realms above it, necessary to acquire the full realization of the truth of the Four Axioms, 사제 四諦 ; these four give rise to the 사법인 四法忍, i.e. 고법인 苦法忍, 집법인 集法忍, 멸법인 滅法忍, 도법인 道法忍, the endurance or patient pursuit that results in their realization. In the realm of form and the formless, they are called the 사류인 四類忍. By patient meditation the 견혹 見惑 false or perplexed views will cease, and the 팔지 八智 eight kinds of jñāna or gnosis be acquired ; therefore 지 智 results from 인 忍 and the sixteen, 팔인팔지 八忍八智 ; 팔인팔관 八忍八觀, are called the 십육심 十六心, i.e. the sixteen mental conditions during the stage of 견도 見道, when 혹 惑 illusions or perplexities of view are destroyed. Such is the teaching of the 유식종 唯識宗. The 팔지 八智 are 고법지 苦法智, 집법지 集法智, 멸법지 滅法智, 도법지 道法智 and, 고류지 苦類智, 집류지 集類智, 멸류지 滅類智, 도류지 道類智.

팔자 八字 The eight leading characters of the 성행 聖行 chapter in the Nirvāṇa sūtra 생멸멸이적멸위락 生滅滅已寂滅爲樂, the teaching of the sūtra is death, or nirvāṇa, as entry into joy. 팔자포자 八字布字 The eight magic words to be placed on eight parts of the body. 팔자문수법 八字文殊法 The eight-word dhāraṇī, esoteric methods connected with Vairocana and Mañjuśrī.

팔자재 八自在 idem 팔변화 八變化 and 팔대자재 八大自在.

팔재(계) 八齋(戒) idem 팔계재 八戒齋.

팔전 八纏 The eight entanglements, or evils : to be without shame ; without a blush ; envious ; mean ; unregretful ; sleepy (or indolent) ; ambitious ; stupid (or depressed).

팔전(성) 八囀(聲) The eight cases of nouns in Sanskrit, termed Subanta, 소만다 蘇漫多, i.e. nirdeśa, upadeśana, kartṛkaraṇa, sampradāna, apādāna, svāmivacana, saṁnidhānārtha, āmantraṇa.

팔전도 八顚倒 The eight upside-down views : heretics believe in 상락아정 常樂我淨 permanence, pleasure, personality, and purity ; the two Hīnayāna vehicles deny these both now and in nirvāṇa. Mahāyāna denies them now, but asserts them in nirvāṇa. Also 팔도 八倒.

팔정 八定 The eight degrees of fixed abstraction, i.e. the four dhyānas corresponding to the four divisions in the heavens of form, and the four degrees of absolute fixed abstraction on the 공 空 or immaterial, corresponding to the arūpadhātu, i.e. heavens of formlessness.

팔정도(분) 八正道(分) Āryamārga. The eight right or correct ways, the "eightfold noble path" for the arhat to nirvāṇa ; also styled 팔도선 八道船, 팔정문 八正門, 팔유행 八由行, 팔유행 八遊行, 팔성도지 八聖道支, 팔도행 八道行, 팔직행 八直行, 팔직도 八直道. The eight are : (1) 정견 正見 Samyag-dṛṣṭi, correct views in regard to the Four Axioms, and freedom from the common delusion. (2) 정사 正思 Samyak-saṁkalpa, correct thought and purpose. (3) 정어 正語 Samyag-vāc, correct speech, avoidance of false and idle talk, (4) 정업 正業 Samyak-karmānta, correct deed, or conduct, getting rid of all improper action so as to dwell in purity. (5) 정명 正命 Samyag-ājīva, correct livelihood or occupation, avoiding the five immoral occupations. (6) 정정진 正精進 Samyag-vyāyāma, correct zeal, or energy in uninterrupted progress in the way of nirvāṇa. (7) 정념 正念 Samyak-smṛti, correct remembrance, or memory, which retains the true and excludes the false. (8) 정정 正定 Samyak-samādhi, correct meditation, absorption, or abstraction. The 정 正 means of course Buddhist orthodoxy, anything contrary to this being 사 邪 or heterodox, and wrong. 팔정도경 八正道經 Buddhabhāṣita-aṣṭāṅga-samyaṅ-mārga sūtra. Tr. by An Shih-kao of the Eastern Han. [B.N.] 659 ; being an earlier translation of the Saṁyuktāgama 잡아함경 雜阿含經.

팔제 八諦 The eight truths, postulates, or judgments of the 법상 法相 Dharmalakṣaṇa school, i.e. four common or mundane, and four of higher meaning. The first four are (1) common postulates on reality, considering the nominal as real, e.g. a pot ; (2) common doctrinal postulates, e.g. the five skandhas ; (3) abstract postulates, e.g. the four noble truths 사제 四諦 ; and (4) temporal postulates in regard to the spiritual in the material. The second abstract or philosophical four are (5) postulates on constitution and function, e.g. of the skandhas ; (6) on cause and effect, e.g. the 사제 四諦 ; (7) on the void, the immaterial, or reality ; and (8) on the pure inexpressible ultimate or absolute.

팔조상승 八組相承 The succession of the eight founders of the esoteric sect, 진언 眞言 or Shingon, i.e. 대일 大日, 금강 金剛, 용맹 龍猛, 용지 龍智, 금강지 金剛智, 불공 不空, 혜과 惠果 and the Japanese 홍법 弘法.

팔존중법 八尊重法 idem 팔경계 八敬戒.

팔종 八宗 or 팔가 八家 Eight of the early Japanese sects : 구사 俱舍 Kusha, 성실 成實 Jōjitsu, 율 律 Ritsu, 법상 法相 Hossō, 삼론 三論 Sanron, 화엄 華嚴 Kegon, 천태 天台 Tendai, 진언 眞言 Shingon. 팔종구종 八宗九宗 ; 팔가구종 八家九宗 The above eight with the Ch'an(Zen) 선 禪 school added. The first four are almost or entirely extinct.

팔종별해탈계 八種別解脫戒 Differentiated rules of liberation for the eight orders — monks ; nuns

; mendicants ; novices male ; and female ; disciples male ; and female ; and the laity who observe the first eight commandments. 팔종승법 八種勝法 The eight kinds of surpassing things, i.e. those who keep the first eight commandments receive the eight kinds of reward – they escape from falling into the hells ; becoming pretas ; or animals ; or asuras ; they will be born among men, become monks, and obtain the truth ; in the heavens of desire ; in the brahma-heaven, or meet a Buddha ; and obtain perfect enlightenment. 팔종죽 八種粥 The eight kinds of congee, or gruel, served by the citizens to the Buddha and his disciples when in retreat in the bamboo-grove of Kāśī ; they were of butter, or fats, or hempseed, milk, peas, beans, sesamum, or plain gruel. 팔종(보)시 八種(布)施 Eight causes of giving – convenience ; fear ; gratitude ; reward-seeking ; traditional (or customary) ; hoping for heaven ; name and fame ; personal virtue. 팔종수기 八種授記 The eight kinds of prediction-made known to self, not to others ; to others not to self ; to self and others ; unknown to self or others ; the near made known but the remote not ; the remote made known but not the intermediate steps ; near and remote both made known ; near and remote both not made known. 팔종법 八種法 idem 팔계 八戒 ; also eight divisions of the 오십법 五十法 q.v. 팔종청풍 八種淸風 Pleasant breezes from the eight directions of the compass.

팔중주 八中洲 Each of the "four continents" has two other continents, i.e. Jambudvīpa has Cāmara and Varacāmara ; Pūrvavideha has Deha and Videha ; Aparagodānīya has Śāṭhā and Uttaramantriṇaḥ ; and Uttarakuru has Kuravaḥ and Kaurava ; v. 사주 四洲.

팔중진보 八重眞寶 The eight weighty and truly precious things, i.e. the eight metals, which depend for evaluation on gold, the highest and greatest, used to illustrate the Buddha as supreme and the other classes in grades beneath him. Also 팔중무가 八重無價, i.e. the eight priceless things.

팔지 八支 idem 팔정도 八正道 ; also the eight sections of the 팔지 八支 śāstra ; also a term for the first eight commandments.

팔지 八智 The 사법지 四法智 and 사류지 四類智 ; see 팔인 八忍.

팔차 八遮 A 삼론 三論 term for 팔불중도 八不中道 q.v.

팔천 八天 The eight devalokas, i.e. four dhyāna devalokas of the region of form, and four arūpalokas ; 사선천 四禪天 and 사공처 四空處.

팔촉 八觸 Eight physical sensations which hinder meditation in its early stages : restlessness, itching, buoyancy, heaviness, coldness, heat, roughness, smoothness. 지관 止觀 8.

팔타 八墮 idem 팔바라이 八波羅夷.

팔탑 八塔 idem 팔대영탑 八大靈塔.

팔풍 八風 The eight winds, or influences which fan the passions, i.e. gain, loss ; defamation, eulogy ; praise, ridicule ; sorrow, joy. Also 팔법 八法.

팔한(빙)지옥 八寒(冰)地獄 The eight cold narakas, or hells : (1) 알부타 頞浮陀 arbuda, tumours, blains ; (2) 니라부타 泥羅浮陀 nirarbuda, enlarged ditto ; 포열 疱裂 bursting blains ; (3) 아타타 阿吒吒 aṭaṭa, chattering (teeth) ; (4) 아파파 阿波波 hahava, or ababa, the only sound possible to frozen tongues ; (5) 구후후 嘔侯侯 ahaha, or hahava, ditto to frozen throats ; (6) 우발라 優鉢羅 utpala, blue lotus flower, the flesh being covered with sores resembling it ; (7) 파두마 波頭摩 padma, red lotus flower, ditto ; (8) 분다리 分陀利 puṇḍarīka, the great lotus, ditto. v. 지옥 地獄 and 팔대지옥 八大地獄.

팔한팔열 八寒八熱 The eight cold and eight hot hells.

팔해 八海 v. 구산팔해 九山八海.

팔해탈 八解脫 Aṣṭa-vimokṣa, mokṣa, vimukti, mukti. Liberation, deliverance, freedom, emancipation, escape, release — in eight forms ; also 팔배사 八背捨 and cf. 해탈 解脫 and 팔승처 八勝處. The eight are stages of mental concentration : (1) 내유색상관외색해탈 內有色想觀外色解脫 Liberation, when subjective desire arises, by examination of the object, or of all things and realization of their filthiness. (2) 내무색상관외색해탈 內無色想觀外色解脫 Liberation, when no subjective desire arises, by still meditating as above. These two are deliverance by meditation on impurity, the next on purity. (3) 정신작증구족주해탈 淨身作證具足住解脫 Liberation by concentration on the pure to the realization of a permanent state of freedom from all desire. The above three "correspond to the four Dhyānas." [Eitel.] (4) 공무변처해탈 空無邊處解脫 Liberation in realization of the infinity of space, or the immaterial. (5) 식무변처해탈 識無邊處解脫 Liberation in realization of infinite knowledge. (6) 무소유처해탈 無所有處解脫 Liberation in realization of nothingness, or nowhereness. (7) 비상비비상처해탈 非想非非想處解脫 Liberation in the state of mind where there is neither thought nor absence of thought. These four arise out of abstract meditation in regard to desire and form, and are associated with the 사공천 四空天. (8) 멸수상정해탈 滅受想定解脫 Liberation by means of a state of mind in which there is final extinction, nirvāṇa, of both sensation, vedanā, and consciousness, saṁjñā.

팔회 八會 The 화엄경 華嚴經 Hua-yen sūtra, as delivered at eight assemblies.

패 梖 Pattra ; 패다엽 梖多葉 the palm-leaves used for writing ; the 패다수 梖多樹 is erroneously said to be the *Borassus flabelliformis,* described as 60 or 70 feet high, not deciduous, the bark used for writing.

패 孛 Po ; plants shooting ; a comet. 패가이 孛伽夷 Bhagai. A city south of Khotan, formerly famous for a statue exhibiting all the thirty-two lakṣaṇas or marks on the body of Buddha.

패 唄 Pāṭha ; pāṭhaka ; read, recite, intone, chant, hymns in praise of Buddha ; 패닉 唄匿 is erroneously said to transliterate the Sanskrit root vi-ne and to be the same as 바척 婆陟 or 바사 婆師, but these are bhāṣā. 패기 唄器 Instruments for keeping time during chanting. 패사 唄士 ; 패사 唄師 Leader of the chanting. 패비구 唄比丘 ; 영성비구 鈴聲比丘 A famous Buddhist singer of old, ugly but with bell-like voice. 패찬 唄讃 To sing hymns of praise.

패 敗 Subvert, defeat, ruin, spoil, destroy. 패괴보살 敗壞菩薩 Bodhisattvas who defeat their proper end of becoming Buddha, and who are reborn in lower positions, e.g. as kings or princes, or as dragon-kings, etc. 패근 敗根 ; 패종 敗種 Spoiled roots, or seed, i.e. Hīnayānists who do not seek Buddhahood, but are content with the rewards of asceticism.

패 稗 Tares, weeds. 패사문 稗沙門 Lazy monks, cumberers of the ground. 패제 稗稊 tares, weeds, only fit to be ploughed up.

패 貝 Śaṅkha ; a shell, cowry, conch ; valuables, riches ; a large trumpet sounded to call the assembly together ; 패종 貝鐘 conch and bell. 패다 貝多 ; 패다라(엽) 貝多羅(葉) ; 패엽 貝葉 Pattra ; palm leaves from the *Borassus flabelliformis,* used for writing material. 패문 貝文 The scriptures written on such leaves. 패지가 貝支迦 Pratyeka, v. 벽지가 辟支迦. 패첩 貝牒 Pattra tablets, sūtras written on them.

편 片 A slice, slip, card ; brief, few. 편선 片禪 A brief samādhi, or meditation.

편 篇 A slip of bamboo, a slip, leaf, page, books. 편목 篇目 A subject or text exposed on a slip ; the publication, e.g., of the name of a wrong-doer. 편취 篇聚 Two divisions of wrong-doing, one called the 오편 五篇 five p'ien, the other the six and seven chü. The five p'ien are: (1) pārājika, v. 파 波, sins demanding expulsion from the order ; (2) saṅghāvaśeṣa, v. 승 僧, sins verging on expulsion, which demand confession before and absolution by the assembly ; (3) prāyaścitta, v. 파일 波逸, sins deserving hell which may be forgiven ; (4) prātideśanīya, v. 파라 波羅 and 제사 提舍, sins which must be confessed ; (5) duṣkṛta, v. 돌 突, light sins, errors, or faults. The six chü are the five above with sthūlātyaya, v. 투 偸, associated with the third, implying thought not developed in action. The seven chü are the above with the division of the fifth into two, action and speech. There are further divisions of eight and nine.

편 便 Convenient, convenience ; then, so ; easy ; cheap. 편리 便利 Convenient and beneficial ; to urinate or evacuate the bowels ; a latrine. 변선 便旋 A mere turn, i.e. immediate and easy. 변선나 便膳那 or 便善那 or 변사나 便社那 ; 편선나 鞭膳那 Vyañjana. "making clear, marking, distinguishing," [M. W.] a "relish" ; intp. by 문 文 a mark, sign, or script which manifests the meaning ; also 미 味 a taste or flavour, that which distinguishes one taste from another.

편 遍 Sarvatraga. Everywhere, universe, whole ; a time. 변의원 遍依圓 The three points of view : 변계 遍計 which regards the seeming as real ; 의타 依他 which sees things as derived ; 원성 圓成 which sees them in their true nature ; cf. 삼성 三性. 변출외도 遍出外道 Ascetics who entirely separate themselves from their fellow-men. 변주 遍周 Universal, everywhere. 변지 遍智 Universal knowledge, omniscience. 변정천 遍淨天 The heaven of universal purity, the third of the third dhyāna heavens. 변법계신 遍法界身 The universal dharmakāya, i.e. the universal body of Buddha, pan-Buddha. 변조여래 遍照如來 The universally shining Tathāgata, i.e. Vairocana. 변지 遍至 Universally reaching, universal. 변행 遍行 Universally operative ; omnipresent. 변계소집성 遍計所執性 The nature that maintains the seeming to be real. 변처 遍處 Everywhere, universal.

편 蝙 The bat. 편복승 蝙蝠僧 A bat monk, v. 조 鳥.

편 偏 To or on one side, deflected, one-sided, biased, partial, prejudiced. 편원 偏圓 Partial and all-embracing, relative and complete, e.g. Hīnayāna and Mahāyāna, also the intermediate schools (between Hīnayāna and Mahāyāna) and the perfect school of T'ien-t'ai. 편집 偏執 To hold firmly to a one-sided interpretation ; bigoted. 편소 偏小 The partial and minor teaching of the Buddha during the first twelve years of his ministry. 편소정 偏小情 The partial or narrower Hīnayāna idea that thought the ego is unreal, things are real. 편교 偏敎 ; 권교 權敎 Partial or relative teaching ; T'ien-t'ai regarded its own teaching as the complete, or final and all-embracing teaching of the Buddha, while that of the 법상 法相, 삼론 三論, etc., was partial and imperfect ; in like manner, the three schools. 장 藏, 통 通, and 별 別, piṭaka, intermediate, and separate, were partial and imperfect. 편진 偏眞, 편공 偏空, 단공 單空 The Hīnayāna doctrine of unreality, a one-sided dogma in contrast with the transcendental reality of Mahāyāna. 편삼 偏衫 The monk's toga, or robe, thrown over one shoulder, some say the right, others the left. 편단 偏袒 Bare on one side, i.e. to wear the toga, or robe, over the right shoulder, baring the other as a mark of respect. 편문 偏門 A side door, one through which offenders are expelled.

편 編 To plait ; enroll ; compile. 편발 編髮 To plait the hair, or roll it into conch-shape.

편 徧 또는 遍 Sarvatraga. On every side, ambit, everywhere, universal, pervade, all, the whole. 변일체처 徧一切處 Pervading everywhere, omnipresent, an epithet for Vairocana. 편길 徧吉 Universally auspicious, a tr. of 보현 普賢 Samantabhadra. 편성 徧成 To complete wholly, fulfil in every detail. 변정 徧淨 Universal purity. 변조 徧照 Universally shining, everywhere illuminating. 변계 徧界 The whole universe. 변행인 徧行因 Sarvatragahetu, "omnipresent causes, like false views which affect every act." [Keith]. 편각 徧覺 The omniscience, absolute enlightenment, or universal awareness of a Buddha. 변계 徧計 Parikalpita. Counting everything as real, the way of the unenlightened. 변계소집성 徧計所執性 The nature of the unenlightened, holding to the tenet that everything is calculable or reliable, i.e. is what it appears to be.

평 評 Criticize, discuss. 평주 評註 Criticize, comment on. 평론 評論 Discuss. 기평 譏評 Censure, criticize.

평 萍 Duckweed ; floating. 평사 萍沙 Bimbisāra, see 빈 頻.

평 平 Even, level, tranquil ; ordinary. 평상 平常 Ordinary, usual, common. 평생 平生 Throughout life ; all one's life. 평등 平等 Sama ; samatā. Level, even, everywhere the same, universal, without partiality ; it especially refers to the Buddha in his universal, impartial, and equal attitude towards all beings. 평등력 平等力 Universal power, or omnipotence, i.e. to save all beings, a title of a Buddha. 평등대혜 平等大慧 "Universal great wisdom", the declaration by the ancient Buddha in the Lotus sūtra, that all would obtain the Buddha-wisdom. 평등심 平等心 An impartial mind, "no respecter of persons," not loving one and hating another. 평등성 平等性 The universal nature, i.e. the 진여 眞如 bhūtatathatā q.v. 평등성지 平等性智 Samatājñāna. The wisdom of rising above such distinctions as I and Thou, meum and tuum, thus being rid of the ego idea, and wisdom in regard to all things equally and universally, cf. 오지 五智. The esoteric school also call it the 관정지 灌頂智 and Ratnasaṁbhava wisdom. 평등교 平等教 One of two schools founded by 인법사 印法師 Yin Fa-shih early in the T'ang dynasty. 평등지 平等智 Samatājñāna, wisdom of universality or sameness, v. *supra*. 평등법 平等法 The universal or impartial truth that all become Buddha, 일체중생평등성불 一切衆生平等成佛. 평등법신 平等法身 Universalized dharmakāya, a stage in Bodhisattva development above the eighth, i.e. above the 팔지 八地. 평등왕 平等王 Yama, the impartial or just judge and awarder. But the name is also applied to one of the Ten Rulers of the Underworld, distinct from Yama. Also, name of the founder of the Kṣatriya caste, to which the Śākya belonged. 평등의 平等義 The meaning of universal, i.e. that the 진여 眞如 q.v. is equally and everywhere in all things. 평등각 平等覺 A Buddha's universal and impartial perception, his absolute intuition above the laws of differentiation. 평등관 平等觀 One of the three T'ien-t'ai meditations, the 가관 假觀 phenomenal being blended with the noumenal or universal. The term is also used for 공관 空觀 meditation on the universal, or absolute.

평가사 平袈裟 A one-coloured robe of seven pieces.

폐 吠 To bark (as a dog) ; translit. *ve*, *vi*, *vai* ; cf. 비 毘 ; 비 鞞 ; 위 衛 ; 별 別. 폐세사 吠世師 ; 폐세사가 吠世史迦 Vaiśeṣika, v. 위 衛. 폐노리야 吠努璃耶 Vaiḍūrya, lapis lazuli. 폐로차나 吠嚧遮那 ; 폐로자나 吠路者那 Vairocana ; v. 비 毘. 폐실라말나 吠室囉末拏 Vaiśravaṇa, v. 비 鞞. 폐람 吠嵐 Vairambha, v. 비 毘. 폐마질달리 吠摩質怛利 Vimalacitra, v. 비 毘. 폐솔노 吠率怒 Veṣṭana, v. 별 別. 폐류리(야) 吠瑠璃(耶) Vaiḍūrya, lapis lazuli. 폐사 吠舍 ; 비폐 鞞吠 or 毘吠 ; 폐사 吠奢 Vaiśya ; the third of the four Indian castes, that of agriculture and trade. 폐사거 吠舍佉 or 설사거 薛舍佉 ; 비사가 鼻奢迦 Vaiśākha ; the second Indian month, from 15th of 2nd to 16th of 3rd Chinese months. 폐사리 吠舍釐 or 吠舍離 Vaiśālī, v. 비 毘. 폐타 吠陀 Veda, v. 위 韋.

폐 閉 To close, stop, block. 폐시 閉尸 Peśī v. 팔위태장 八位胎藏 A piece of flesh ; a mass ; a fetus. 폐로 閉爐 To cease lighting the stove (in spring). 폐관 閉關 To shut in ; to isolate oneself for meditation. 폐려다 閉黎多 Preta, hungry ghost, see 벽 薜.

폐 廢 To fall in ruins ; come to nought ; cast aside, do away with, discard ; spoil, waste. 폐전교 廢前教 The discarding of previous rules in the Nirvāṇa sūtra, e.g. previously monks were allowed the three kinds of clean meat ; in this sūtra all are forbidden. 폐악수선 廢惡修善 To cast aside evil and perform the good. 폐권립실 廢權立實 To set aside the temporary and establish the real and permanent. 폐적현본 廢迹顯本 To set aside the temporal life (of the Buddha) and reveal the fundamental eternal life.

폐 弊 Worn out, reduced to extremities, corrupt, deceptive ; my, mine. 폐욕 弊欲 Corrupt, or base desires.

폐시 蔽尸 Peśī, the embryo in the third of its five stages, a thirty-seven days' foetus, lit. a lump of flesh. 폐시 閉尸 ; 비시 箄尸 ; 비라시 蜱羅尸.

포 泡 A bubble, a blister ; to infuse. 포영 泡影 Bubble and shadow, such is everything.

포 袍 A robe. 포휴라란 袍休羅蘭 Bahularatna, i.e. Prabhūtaratna, abundance of precious things, the 다보 多寶 Buddha of the Lotus sūtra. 포상 袍裳 ; 포복 袍服 Upper and lower garments.

포 逋 Abscond, default, owe ; translit. *po, pu, va,* 포리바비제하 逋利婆鼻提賀 Pūrvavideha, the eastern of the 사대주 四大洲 four continents. 포다(라) 逋多(羅) Potalaka, v. 보 補. 포사 逋沙 Puruṣa, v. 포 布. 포사타 逋沙他 Upavasatha, a fast day. 포로갈지섭벌라 逋盧羯底攝伐羅 Avalokiteśvara, v. 관음 觀音.

포 捕 Arrest, catch. 포갈 捕喝 ; 포포 捕哺 ; 포게 捕揭 Bukhara. The present Bokhara, 39° 47 N., 64° 25 E.

포 布 Cloth, to spread ; translit. *pu, po, pau.*

포 抱 Embrace, enfold, cherish. 포불각 抱佛脚 (Only when old or in trouble) to embrace the Buddha's feet.

포 胞 Placenta, womb ; bladder. 포태 胞胎 Womb, uterine, v. 태생 胎生.

포 飽 Replete, full. 포학 飽學 Replete with learning ; fed full with study.

포 蒲 Rushes, flags, grass. 포단 蒲團 A rush cushion, or hassock. 포새 蒲塞 Upāsaka, 이포색 伊蒲塞 cf. 우 優. 포사니 蒲闍尼 ; 포선니 蒲膳尼 Bhojanīya, to be eaten, edible ; what is suitable as the fare of monks and nuns, proper food ; one list gives wheat, rice (boiled), parched rice, fish, and flesh ; another gives cakes (or loaves), porridge, parched grain, flesh, and boiled rice.

포 褒 To praise ; salutation. Poṣadha, v. 포 布.

포 怖 Uttras- ; santras- ; fear, afraid. 포한 怖捍 ; 곽한 霍罕 Ferghana, in Russian Turkestan. 포외시 怖畏施 Almsgiving to remove one's fears. 포마 怖魔 Scare-demon, a supposed tr. of the term bhikṣu.

포교 布教 To publish, or spread abroad the doctrine.

포니아게 布儞阿偈 Pūti-agada, purgatives.

포다 餔多 Bhūta, a sect of ascetics who smeared themselves with ashes.

포달나 布怛那 Pūtana, 포단나 布單那 ; 부다나 富多那 ; 부단나 富單那 ; 부다나 富陀那 a female demon poisoning or the cause of wasting in a child ; interpreted as a stinking hungry demon, and the most successful of demons.

포달납 布達拉 Potala, 보다라 普陀羅 the monastery of the Dalai Lama in Lhasa ; v. 보 普.

포대화상 布袋和尚 Pu-tai Ho-shang (J. : Hotei Oshō) Cloth-bag monk, an erratic monk 장정자 長汀子 Ch'ang-t'ing-tzŭ early in the tenth century, noted, *inter alia*, for his shoulder bag. Often depicted, especially in Japanese art, as a jovial, corpulent monk, scantily clad and surrounded by children.

포랄나 布剌拏 Pūraṇa-Kāśyapa, v. 부 富. Also Pūrṇa of the 석비바소론 釋毘婆少論 v. 비 毘.

포로나발다라 布嚕那跋陀羅 Pūrṇabhadra, one of the eight yakṣa generals.

포로바비제하 布嚕婆毗提訶 Pūrva-Videha, or Videha. 불바(비)제(하) 弗婆(毗)提(訶) ; 불우비바제하 弗于毗婆提訶 ; 포리바비제하 逋利婆鼻提賀 One of the four great continents east of Sumeru.

포로사 布路沙 Puruṣa, 포로사 布嚕沙 ; 보로사 補盧沙 man, mankind, a man, Man as Nārāyaṇa the soul and origin of the universe, the soul, the Soul, Supreme Being, God, see M. W. ; intp. as 인 人 and 장부 丈夫 man, and an adult man, also by 사부 士夫 master or educated man, "explained by 신아 神我, literally the spiritual self. A metaphysical term ; the spirit which together with nature (자성 自性 Svabhāva), through the successive modifications (전변 轉變) of Guṇa (구나 求那 attributes or qualities), or the active principles (작자 作者), produces all forms of existence (작일체물 作一切物)." [Eitel]. 포로사포라 布路沙布羅 ; 불루사 佛樓沙 Puruṣapura ; the ancient capital of Gandhāra, the modern Peshāwar.

포리가 布利迦 Pūrikā, a kind of cake.

포사 布史 Pauṣa, the 10th month in India.

포살 布薩 Poṣadha, Upavasatha, Upoṣaṇa ; 포사타 布沙他 ; 포쇄타 布灑他 ; 보사타 褒沙陀 Pali : Uposatha ; fasting, a fast, the nurturing or renewal of vows, intp. by 정주 淨住 or 선숙 善宿 or 장양 長養, meaning abiding in retreat for spiritual refreshment. There are other similar terms, e.g. 포살타파 布薩陀婆 ; 우보타파 優補陀婆 ; also 포살건도 布薩犍度 which the Vinaya uses for the meeting place ; 발라제제사야매 鉢囉帝提舍耶寐 prātideśanīya, is self-examination and public confession during the fast. It is also an old Indian fast. Buddha's monks should meet at the new and full moons and read the Prātimokṣa sūtra for their moral edification, also disciples at home should observe the six fast days and the eight commands. The 포살일 布薩日 fast days are 15th and 29th or 30th of the moon. 포살호 布薩護 is a term for the lay observance of the first eight commandments on fast days, and it is used as a name for those commands.

포슬파 布瑟波 Puṣpa, 보삽파 補澀波 a flower 화 華.

포여조벌야 布如烏伐耶 Puṇyopāya, or 나제 那提 Nadī. A monk of Central India, said to have brought over 1,500 texts of the Mahāyāna and Hīnayāna schools to China A.D. 655. In 656 he was sent to 곤륜산 崑崙山 Pulo Condore Island in the China Sea for some strange medicine. Tr. three works, one lost by A.D. 730.

포자관 布字觀 A Shingon meditation on the Sanskrit letter "a" and others, written on the devotee's own body.

포저락가 布咀洛迦 Potala, v. 보 補 and 보 普.

폭 瀑 A torrent, cataract, cascade. 폭류 瀑流 A torrent, the stream of passion, or illusion.

표 幖 A streamer, pennant 표치 幖幟.

표 表 Indicate, manifest, express, expose ; external. 표찰 表刹 The flagpole on a pagoda. 표덕 表德 To manifest virtue, in contrast with 차정 遮情 to repress the passions ; the positive in deed and thought, as expounded by the 화엄종 華嚴宗 Hua-yen school. 표무표계 表無表戒 The expressed and unexpressed moral law, the letter and the spirit. 표백 表白 To explain, expound, clear up. 표시 表示 To indicate, explain. 표색 表色 Active expression, as walking, sitting, taking, refusing, bending, stretching, etc. ; one of the three 색 色 forms, the other two being 현 顯 the colours, red, blue, etc., and 형 形 shape, long, short, etc. 표전 表銓 Positive or open exposition, contrasted with 차전 遮銓 negative or hidden exposition ; a term of the 법상종 法相宗

Dharmalakṣaṇa school.

표 標 Signal, flag, banner ; the troops under a particular banner ; a notice, list, signboard, ticket ; to publish. 표치 標幟 Signals, symbols, especially those used by the Yoga sect. 표월 標月 To indicate the moon. 표령 標領 The leader, chief.

품 稟 To petition, report, request, beg ; to receive (from above) ; endowment. 품구 稟具 To be fully ordained, i.e. receive all the commandments. 품교 稟教 To receive the Buddha's teaching.

품 品 Varga, 발거 跋渠 class, series, rank, character ; a chapter of a sūtra. 상중하품 上中下品 Superior, middle, and lower class, grade, or rank.

풍 豊 Abundant. 풍재 豊財 Wealthy.

풍 諷 To intone ; to satirize. 풍경 諷經 To intone a scripture, especially one suited to the occasion. 풍송 諷誦 To intone, sing. 풍송 諷頌 A gāthā, or hymn, v. 가 伽.

풍 風 Vāyu. Wind, air ; rumour, repute ; custom ; temper, lust. 풍삼매 風三昧 ; 풍분삼매 風奮三昧 A samādhi in which the whole body is conceived of as scattered. 풍(중)등 風(中)燈 ; 풍(중)촉 風(中)燭 ; 풍(전)등 風(前)燈 ; 풍(전)촉 風(前)燭 "As a lamp (or candle) in the wind," such is the evanescence of the world and man. 풍도 風刀 The wind knife, i.e. the approach of death and its agonies. 풍대 風大 Wind or air as one of the four elements. 풍천 風天 The wind deva. 풍계 風界 The realm of wind, or air, with motion as its principle, one of the 사대 四大 q.v. 풍재 風災 The calamity of destruction by wind at the end of the third period of destruction of a world. 풍색 風色 Wind colour, i.e. nonexistent, like a rabbit's horns, tortoise-hair, or scent of salt. 풍륜 風輪 The wheel, or circle, of wind below the circle of water and metal on which the earth rests ; the circle of wind rests on space. 풍(륜)제 風(輪)際 The region of the wind-circle.

풍경 風磬 A fish-shaped chime bell hung under the roof which swings in the wind.

피 皮 ; 피혁 皮革 Leather, skin, hide. 피각루자 皮殼漏子 ; 피가루자 皮可漏子 The body, lit. "skin and shell leaking". 피의 皮衣 Clothing of hides or skins ; a name for a monk's garments, implying their roughness and simplicity. 피대 皮袋 Skin bag, i.e. the body.

피 被 A quilt, coverlet ; to cover ; to suffer ; sign of the passive. 피위 被位 Covered seats for meditation. 피엽의관음 被葉衣觀音 Kuan-yin clad in leaves.

피 避 Avoid, escape, flee. 피사 避死 To avoid death. 피라 避羅 Vimbara, idem 빈바라 頻婆羅.

피 彼 That, the other, in contrast with 차 此 this. 피안 彼岸 ; 파라 波羅 Pāra, yonder shore, i.e. nirvāṇa. The saṁsāra life of reincarnation is 차안 此岸 this shore ; the stream of karma is 중류 中流 the stream between the one shore and the other. Metaphor for an end to any affair. Pāramitā (an incorrect etymology, no doubt old) is the way to reach the other shore. 피다 彼茶 Peṭa, or Piṭaka, a basket.

피 披 To spread open, unroll, thrown on (as a cloak). 피 披 is to wear the garment over both shoulders ; 단 袒 is to throw it over one shoulder. 피체 披剃 The first donning of the robe and shaving of the head (by a novice).

픽 煏 To dry by the fire. 픽추 煏芻 Bhikṣu, v. 비 比.

필 筆 A pen. 필수 筆受 To receive in writing ; to record, write down from dictation.

필 必 Certainly, necessary, must. 필정 必定 Certainly, assuredly ; tr. of 아비발치 阿鞞跋致 Avaivartika, intp. as 불퇴전 不退轉 never receding, or turning back, always progressing, and certainly reaching nirvāṇa. 필률탁흘나 必栗託仡那 Pṛthagjana, interpreted as 독생 獨生, 이생 異生, and 범부 凡夫 ; pṛthak is separately, individually ; with Buddhists the whole term means born an ordinary man ; the common people. 필적가 必椄家 ; 비적가 比摘迦 Piṭaka, a basket, receptacle, thesaurus, hence the Tripiṭaka 삼장 三藏. 필지 必至 Certainly will, certainly arrive at.

필 苾 Fragrant. 필추 苾芻 ; 벽추 煏芻 ; 비구 比丘 q.v. Bhikṣu, a beggar, religious mendicant ; a Buddhist monk. 필추니 苾芻尼 Bhikṣuṇī, a nun. 필추율의 苾芻律儀 The 250 rules for monks.

필 畢 To end, final, complete, all ; translit. *p*, *v* ; 필리차 畢利叉 ; 필락차 畢洛叉 ; 필랄차 畢剌叉 Vṛkṣa is a tree ; here it is described as *the* tree, i.e. the *Jonesia aśoka*, a tree under which the Buddha is said to have been born. 필리다 畢利多 Preta, hungry ghost. 필력가 畢力迦 or 필률가 畢栗迦 Pṛkkā, Spṛkkā, a fragrant plant, said to be the *Trigonella corniculata*. 필륵지지가(불) 畢勒支底迦(佛) ; 필지불 畢支佛 ; 벽지불 辟支佛 ; 발라지가불 鉢攞底迦佛 Pratyeka(-buddha). Cf. 벽 辟. Singly, individually, one "who lives in seclusion and obtains emancipation for himself only." [M. W.] It is intp. as 독각 獨覺 lonely (or alone) enlightenment, i.e. for self alone ; also 연각 緣覺 enlightened in the 십이인연 十二因緣 twelve nidānas ; or 원각 圓覺 completely enlightened, i.e. for self. 필경 畢境 Atyanta, At bottom, finally, at last, fundamental, final, ultimate. 필경의 畢境依 A final trust, ultimate reliance, i.e. Buddha. 필경지 畢境智 Ultimate, or final wisdom, or knowledge of the ultimate. 필경무 畢境無 Never, fundamentally not, or none. 필경공 畢境空 Fundamentally unreal, immaterial, or void, see 공 空. 필경각 畢境覺 The ultimate enlightenment, or bodhi, that of a Buddha. 필사차 畢舍遮 ; 비사차 毘舍遮 ; 비사자 毘舍闍 ; 비사자 臂奢柘 Piśāca, demons that eat flesh, malignant sprites or demons. 필발(라) 畢鉢(羅) Pippala, one of the names of the *Ficus religiosa* ; also the name of Mahā-Kāśyapa. 필릉(가바차) 畢陵(伽婆蹉) Pilindavatsa, who for 500 generations had been a Brahman, cursed the god of the Ganges, became a disciple, but still has to do penance for his ill-temper.

필가 祕柯 Vikramāditya, a king of Śrāvastī and famous benefactor of Buddhism, v. 비 毘.

필수발타 邲輸跋陀 Viśvabhadra, name of 보현 普顯 P'u-hsien, Samantabhadra.

핍 乏 Lacking ; 핍도 乏道 lacking in the right way, shortcoming, poor, — an expression of humility.

핍 逼 To press, constrain, urge, harass. 핍박 逼迫 To constrain, compel, bring strong pressure to bear.

<ㅎ>

하 蝦 A shrimp, prawn ; a frog. 하마선 蝦蟆禪 Frog samādhi, which causes one to leap with joy at half-truths.

하 荷 A small-leaved water-lily, a marshmallow ; to carry, bear. 하력피타 荷力皮陀 v. 폐 吠 The Ṛgveda. 하담 荷擔 To carry, bear on the back or shoulder.

하 下 Hīna, adhara. Below, lower, inferior, low ; to descend, let down, put down.

하 河 River (in north), canal (in south), especially the Yellow River in China and the Ganges 항하 恒河 in India. 하사 河沙 The sands of Ganges, vast in number. 하비지 河鼻旨 Avīci, the hell of uninterrupted suffering, where the sufferers die and are reborn to torture without intermission.

하 夏 Summer. 하중 夏中 During the summer, the middle of the summer ; the rainy season spent by the monks of India in retirement. 하좌 夏坐 ; 좌하 坐夏 ; 하안거 夏安居 The period of the summer retreat for meditation, known as varṣās, the rains. 하말 夏末 ; 하만 夏滿 ; 하경 夏竟 ; 하해 夏解 The end of the summer (retreat), the 15th of the 7th month. 하랍 夏臘 ; 법랍 法臘 The age of a monk as monk, the years of his ordination. 하중 夏衆 The assembly of monks at the summer retreat. 하수 夏首 The first day, or beginning, of the retreat.

하 賀 To make offerings in congratulation ; congratulate ; translit. *h*, cf. 하 訶. 하날파 賀捺婆 Haṁsa, a goose. 하라타 賀羅馱 or 賀邏馱 Hrada, a lake, pool, ray of light. 하야흘리부 賀野紇哩嚩 or 하연흘리부 賀演屹哩嚩 Hayagrīva, the horse-necked one, a form of Viṣṇu and of Kuan-yin.

하 何 Translit. *ha, hai, a, ra, he* ; cf. 하 賀 and 갈 曷. What? How? 하사생 何似生 How does it thus happen? 하이마가 何夷摩柯 Haimaka, a king at the beginning of a kalpa, 금 金 by name. 하리나 何履那 Hariṇa, a deer. 하라호라 何羅怙羅 Rāhula, name of Śākyamuni's son, also of an asura. 하야 何耶 Haya, the horse-head form of Kuan-yin. 하야게리바 何耶揭唎婆 Hayagrīva, Horse-neck, a form of Viṣṇu, name of a 명왕 名王 Ming-wang.

하간 下間 The inferior rooms of a monastery, on the left as one enters.

하계 下界 The lower, or human world 인계 人界.

하구식 下口食 One of the 사사명식 四邪命食 four heterodox means of living, i.e. for a monk to earn his livelihood by bending down to cultivate the land, collect herbs, etc. ; opposite of 앙구식 仰口食, i.e. making a heterodox living by looking up, as in astrology, fortune-telling, etc. 지도론 智度論 3.

하근 下根 Those (born) with base character, or of low capacity.

하당 下堂 To descend from the hall, especially after the morning congee.

하랍 下蠟 Inferior candles. The 상 上 and 하 下 superior and inferior candles are senior and junior monks ; those of longer and shorter service ; but see 상랍 上臘.

하배관 下輩觀 A meditation of the Amitābha sect on the 하품 下品 q.v. ; it is the last of sixteen contemplations, and deals with those who have committed the five rebellious acts 오역 五逆 and the ten evils 십악 十惡, but who still can obtain salvation ; v. 무량수경 無量壽經. 하배하생관 下輩下生觀 idem.

하봉 下棒 To lay on the cudgel, beat ; syn. for the 덕산 德山 Tê Shan monastery, whose Ch'an sect abbot instilled intelligence with his staff.

하삼도 下三途 The three lower paths of the six destinations (gati) 육도 六道, i.e. beings in hell, pretas, and animals.

하생경 下生經 idem 미륵하생경 彌勒下生經.

하승 下乘 The lower yāna, i.e. Hīnayāna ; likened to an old worn-out horse. To alight from (a vehicle, horse, etc.).

하어 下語 To give instruction ; to state a case (as at law).

하열승 下劣乘 The inferior, mean yāna, a scornful term for Hīnayāna.

하의 下衣 The lowest order of a monk's robes, that of five patches ; lower garments.

하전 下轉 The downward turn, in transmigration. Primal ignorance or unenlightenment 무명 無明 acting against the primal, true, or Buddhanature causes transmigration. The opposite is 상전 上轉 when the good prevails over the evil. 하전 下轉 is sometimes used for 하화 下化 to save those below.

하종 下種 To sow the seed ; to preach, or teach. T'ien-t'ai defines three periods : (1) 종 種 when the seed of Buddha's teaching is sown in the heart ; (2) 숙 熟 when it ripens ; (3) 탈 脫 when it is stripped or harvested, i.e. when one abandons all things.

하중 下衆 The seven lower orders of disciples, who with the monks and nuns in full orders make the 구중 九衆.

하지 下地 The lower regions of the 구지 九地 q.v. ; also the lower half of the 십지 十地 in the fifty-two grades of bodhisattva development. 하지추고장 下地麤苦障 To see the lower grade out of which one has migrated, as rough, wretched, and a hindrance ; a brahman form of meditation.

하진 下塵 The lower gati, the hells, hungry ghosts, animals.

하팔지 下八地 The regions in the nine divisions of the trailokya below the 무소유처지 無所有處地 of the arūpadhātu, v. 구지 九地.

하품 下品 The three lowest of the nine classes born in the Amitābha Pure Land, v. 무량수경 無量壽經. These three lowest grades are (1) 하품상생 下品上生 The highest of the three lowest classes who enter the Pure Land of Amitābha, i.e. those who have committed all sins except dishonouring the sūtras. If at the end of life the sinner clasps hands and says "Namo Amitābha," such a one will be born in His precious lake. (2) 하품중생 下品中生 The middle class consists of those who have broken all the commandments, even stolen from monks and abused the law. If at death such a one hears of the great power of Amitābha, and assents with but a thought, he will be received into paradise. (3) 하품하생 下品下生 The lowest class, because of their sins, should have fallen into the lowest gati, but by invoking the name of Amitābha, they can escape countless ages of reincarnation and suffering and on dying will behold a lotus flower like the sun, and, by the response of a single thought, will enter the Pure Land of Amitābha.

하화 下火 ; 하거 下炬 To apply the torch ; syn. for setting alight the funeral pyre of a monk.

하화(중생) 下化(衆生) Below, to transform all beings, one of the great vows of a bodhisattva. 상구보리 上求菩提 above, to seek bodhi. Also 하제중생 下濟衆生.

학 瘧 Fever, ague. 학가지 瘧加持 ; 학병법 瘧病法 Treatment of feverish ailments by tantric measures. 학귀 瘧鬼 Apasmāra, a demon supposed to cause the above.

학 鶴 The crane ; the egret ; translit. *ha, ho.* 학림 鶴林 ; 학수 鶴樹 Crane grove, a name for the place where Śākyamuni died, when the trees burst into white blossom resembling a flock of white cranes. 학륵나야사 鶴勒那夜奢 Haklenayaśas, or Padmaratna, the twenty-third patriarch, born in the palace of the king of Tokhāra. 학실나 鶴悉那 Hosna, or Ghazna, "the capital of Tsaukūṭa, the present Ghuznee" (Ghazni) in Afghanistan. [Eitel]. 학말 鶴秣 Homa, "a city on the eastern frontier of Persia, perhaps the modern Humoon." [Eitel]. 학원 鶴苑 Crane-garden, a term for a monastery. 학살라 鶴薩羅 Hasara, "the second capital of Tsaukūṭa, perhaps the modern Assaia Hazaréh between Ghuznee and Kandahar in Afghanistan." [Eitel].

학 學 Śikṣ ; to study, learn, the process of acquiring knowledge ; learning. 학려 學侶 Fellow-students, the company of monks who are studying. 학회 學悔 Studying to repent, as when a monk having committed sin seeks to repent. 학교성미 學教成迷 To study the Buddha's teaching yet interpret it misleadingly, or falsely. 학법녀 學法女 v. 식 式 Śikṣamāṇa. 학무학 學無學 One who is still learning, and one who has attained : 학 學 is to study religion in order to get rid of illusion ; 무학 無學 begins when illusion is cast off. In Hīnayāna the first three stages, v. 사과 四果, belong to the period of 학 學 ; the arhat to the 무학 無學. In the Mahāyāna, the ten stages of the bodhisattva belong to 학 學 ; the stage of Buddha to 무학 無學. 학생 學生 ; 학인 學人 ; 학장 學匠 ; 학도 學徒 A student, a neophyte. 학자 學者 Śaikṣa ; one still under instruction, who has not yet reached the arhat position ; a student.

한 恨 Hate, annoyed, vexed. 한심 恨心 ; 원한 怨恨 ; 한노 恨怒.

한 限 Limit, boundary, to fix. 한분 限分 limited, e.g. limited culpability by reason of accident, unintentional error.

한 汗 Sweat ; vast. 한율타 汗栗馱 or 간율타 干栗馱 or 건율타 乾栗馱 ; 흘리타야 紇哩陀耶 Hṛd, Hṛdaya, the heart, core, mind, soul.

한 漢 The River Han ; the Han dynasty ; a fine fellow ; China.

한 閑 To bar, a barrier ; to shut out ; trained. 한거십덕 閑居十德 Ten advantages of a hermitage given in verse, i.e. absence of sex and passion ; of temptation to say wrong things ; of enemies, and so of strife ; of friends to praise or blame ; of others' faults, and so of talk about them ; of followers or servants, and so no longing for companions ; of society, and so no burden of politenesses ; of guests, and so no preparations ; of social intercourse, and so no trouble about garments ; of hindrance from others in mystic practice. 한문자 閑文字 ; 한진경 閑塵境 Words, or expressions to be shut out ; unnecessary words. 한처 閑處 A shut-in place, a place of peace, a hermitage, a Buddhist monastery. 한도인 閑道人 One well-trained in the religion ; a practitioner.

한 寒 Śīta. Cold ; in poverty ; plain. 한서 寒暑 Cold and heat. 한림 寒林 The cold forest, where the dead were exposed (to be devoured by vultures, etc.) ; a cemetery ; v. 시 尸 for śītavana and śmaśāna. 한옥 寒獄 The cold hells, v. 지옥 地獄.

할 曷 How? What? Why? Translit. *a, ha, ra, ro.* 할리나 曷利拏 Hariṇa, deer of several kinds. 할리사벌탄나 曷利沙伐彈那 Harṣavardhana, king of Kanyākubja, protector of Buddhism about A.D. 625. 할랄달나게파 曷剌怛那揭婆 Ratnagarbha, jewel treasury, or throne. 할랄예 曷剌梲 Āraṇya, v. 아 阿. 할라호라 曷羅怙羅 Rāhula, v. 라 羅. 할라호 曷羅胡 Rohu, "an ancient city and province of Tukhāra, south of the Oxus." [Eitel]. 할라사길리희 曷羅闍姞利呬 ; 나열성 羅閱城 Rājagṛha, v. 왕사성 王舍城. 할라사보라 曷羅闍補羅 Rājapura, a province and city, now Rajaori in south-west Kashmir. 할부다 曷部多 Adbhuta, remarkable, miraculous, supernatural.

할 瞎 Blind. 할루생 瞎屢生 A blind, stupid man. 할려 瞎驢 A blind or blind-folded donkey, stupid.

할 割 To cut, gash, sever. 할단 割斷 To cut off.

할 喝 Hal (C. Ho, J. Katsu). The shout popularized by 마조 馬祖 Ma-tsu, 임제 臨濟 Lin-chi who used it to prod his disciples towards awakening.

함 函 A box, receptacle ; to enfold ; a letter. 함개상응 函蓋相應 Agreeing like a box and lid.

함 咸 All, entirely. 함동 咸同 All together.

함 鹹 Salty, salted. 함수 鹹水 Salt water.

함 含 To hold in the mouth ; cherish ; restrain. 함중교 含中教 A T'ien-t'ai term for the 통교 通教 which was midway between or interrelated with Hīnayāna and Mahāyāna. 함정 含情 All beings possessing feeling, sentience. 함생 含生 ; 함령 含靈 Living beings, all beings possessing life, especially sentient life. 함화 含華 In the closed lotus flower, i.e. those who await the opening of the flower for rebirth in Paradise. 함식 含識 ; 함류 含類 All sentient beings.

합 盍 A cave. 합천 盍天 Parīttābha, the fourth Brahma-loka, the first region of the second dhyāna. 합루긍 盍樓亘 An early attempt to translate the name of Kuan-yin. 합파(마나) 盍波(摩那) Apramāṇābha, the heaven of infinite light, the second region of the second dhyāna.

합 蛤 Bivalves, clams. 합리관음 蛤啣觀音 One of the thirty-three forms of Kuan-yin, seated on a shell.

합 合 Bring together, unite, unison, in accord. 합십 合十 ; 합조 合爪 ; 합장 合掌 To bring the ten fingers or two palms together ; a monk's salutation ; 합장차수 合掌叉手 to put the hands together and fold the fingers. 합단 合壇 United, or common altar, or altars, as distinguished from 리단 離壇 separate altars. 합혼수 合昏(樹) ; 합환 合歡 ; 시리사 尸利沙 or 시리쇄 尸利灑 Śirīṣa, the acacia sirisa. 합살 合殺 The closing note of a chant or song ; bring to an end. 합용 合用 In accordance with need ; suitable. 합련화 合連華 A closed lotus-flower.

합 鴿 Pārāvata ; kapotaka ; a dove, pigeon. 합원 鴿園 A famous monastery said to be in Kashmir, the Kapotaka-saṁghārāma, v. 가포덕가 迦佈德迦.

합밀 哈密 Hami, "an ancient city and kingdom in Central Asia north-east of lake Lop in Lat. 43° 3 N., Long. 93° 10 E." [Eitel]. From Han to T'ang times known as I-wu 이오 伊吾, now called Kumul by Turkey Mohammadans. For more than 1500 years, owing to its location and supply of water, Hami was a bridgehead for the expansion and control of the outposts of the Chinese empire in Central Asia.

항 恒 Constant ; perseverance, persistence ; translit. *ga, ha.* 항상 恒常 Constant, regular. 항가하 恒伽河 The Ganges, v. 항하 恒河. 항가제바 恒伽提婆 Gaṅgādevī, name of a female disciple of the Buddha. 항가달 恒伽達 Gaṅgādatta, son of a wealthy landowner and disciple of the Buddha. 항사 恒娑 or 긍사 亘娑 Haṁsa, a goose. 항하 恒河 ; 항수 恒水 ; 항가 恒伽 or 긍가 兢伽 or 긍가 殑伽 or 강가 强伽 Gaṅgā, the river Ganges, "said to drop from the centre of Śiva's ear into the Anavatapta lake" [Eitel], passing through an orifice called variously ox's mouth, lion's month, golden elephant's mouth, then round the lake and out to the ocean on the south-east. 항가사 恒伽沙 more commonly 항사 恒沙 Gaṅgā-nadī-vālukā ; as the sands of Ganges, numberless.

항 降 Subdue ; submit. 항삼세 降三世 To subdue the three worlds, as conqueror of them, e.g. 항삼세명왕 降三世明王 Trailokya-vijaya-rāja, Rāja subduing the three realms above, here, below, one of the five great 명왕 明王 q.v. ; the one controlling the east ; subduer of the three realms of desire, resentment, and stupidity ; also of the these three passions in past, present, future.

There are other similar rājas. 항복 降伏 Abhicāraka, exorciser ; magic ; subjugator (of demons). 항염마존 降焰魔尊 Yamāntaka, cf. 염 焰 the fierce mahārāja with six legs who controls the demons of the West. 항마 降魔 To overcome demons, e.g. as the Buddha did at his enlightenment. 항용 降龍 To subdue nāgas, e.g. 항용발 降龍鉢 to compel a nāga to enter an almsbowl as did the Buddha ; 항용복호 降龍伏虎 to subdue nāgas and subjugate tigers.

해 姟 Ten millions, tr. of Ayuta 아유타 阿由他, Nayuta 나유타 那由他 ; but other accounts say 100 millions or more.

해 廨 An official building ; a monastic granary ; 해원주 廨院主 the head of it.

해 害 Hiṁsā ; vihiṁsā ; hurt, harm, injure. 해상 害想 ; 해각 害覺 The wish, or thought, to injure another.

해 懈 Idle, lazy, negligent. 해태 懈怠 Kausīdya, indolent, lazy or remiss (in discipline). 해태적 懈怠賊 The robber indolence, robber of religious progress. 해만국 懈慢國 ; 해만계 懈慢界 A country that lies between this world and the Western Paradise, in which those who are reborn become slothful and proud, and have no desire to be reborn in Paradise.

해 海 Sāgara, the ocean, the sea. 해인 海印 The ocean symbol, indicating the vastness of the meditation of the Buddha, the vision of all things. 해덕 海德 The eight virtues, or powers of the ocean, i.e. vastness, tidal regularity, throwing out of the dead, containing the seven kinds of pearls, absorption of all rivers, of all rain without increase, holding the most mighty fish, universal unvarying saltness. 해회 海會 The assembly of the saints ; also a cemetery. 해조음 海潮音 The ocean-tide voice, i.e. of the Buddha. 해주 海珠 Ocean pearls, things hard to obtain. 해중 海衆 Ocean assembly, i.e. a great assembly of monks, the whole body of monks. 해룡왕 海龍王 The Ocean-nāga, or Dragon King of the Ocean ; hence the 해룡왕경 海龍王經 sūtra of this name.

해 該 To connect, belong to ; proper ; ought, owe ; the said ; the whole. 해라 該羅 ; 해섭 該攝 Containing, inclusive, undivided, whole ; the one vehicle containing the three.

해 解 To unloose, let go, release, untie, disentangle, explain, expound ; intp. by mokṣa, mukti, vimokṣa, vimukti, cf. 해탈 解脫.

해경십불 解境十佛 All existence discriminated as ten forms of Buddha. The Hua-yen school sees all things as pan-Buddha, but discriminates them into ten forms : all the living, countries (or places), karma, śrāvakas, pratyeka-buddhas, bodhisattvas, tathāgatas, 지 智 jñānakāya, dharmakāya, and space ; i.e. each is a 신 身 corpus of the Buddha.

해계 解界 To release or liberate the powers by magic words, in esoteric practice.

해공 解空 To apprehend, or interpret the immateriality of all things.

해동고승전 海東高僧傳 Hae-dong Go-seung Jeon. "Lives of Eminent Korean Monks." Biographies of Korean monks compiled by 각훈 覺訓 Gak-hun in 1215.

해심밀경 解深蜜經 Sandhi-nirmocana-sūtra, tr. by Hsüan-tsang, the chief text of the Dharmalakṣaṇa school, 법상종 法相宗. Four tr. have been made, three preceding that of Hsüan-tsang, the first in the fifth century A.D.

해오 解悟 Release and awareness ; the attaining of liberation through enlightenment.

해인사 海印寺 Hae-in-sa. A temple located in Chiin-ri Gaya-myeon Hapcheon-gun Gyeongsangnam-do in Korea. The 12th parish headquarters of Korean Jogye Order.

해일체중생언어 解一切衆生言語 Sarva-ruta-kauśalya, supernatural power of interpreting all the language of all beings.

해지견 解知見 A Buddha's understanding, or intp. of release, or nirvāṇa, the fifth of the 오분법신 五分法身.

해탈 解脫 Mukti, "loosing, release, deliverance, liberation, setting free, ... emancipation," [M. W.] Mokṣa, "emancipation, deliverance, freedom, liberation, escape, release." [M. W.] Escape from bonds and the obtaining of freedom, freedom from transmigration, from karma, from illusion, from suffering ; it denotes nirvāṇa and also the freedom obtained in dhyāna-meditation ; it is one of the five characteristics of Buddha ; v. 오분법신 五分法身. It is also vimukti and vimokṣa, especially in the sense of final emancipation. There are several categories of two kinds of emancipation, also categories of three and eight. Cf. 비 毘 ; and 팔해탈 八解脫.

해탈계 解脫戒 The commandments accepted on leaving the world and becoming a disciple or a monk.

해탈관 解脫冠 The crown of release.

해탈도 解脫道 The way or doctrine of liberation, Buddhism.

해탈문 解脫門 The door of release, the stage of meditation characterized by vacuity and absence of perception or wishes.

해탈미 解脫味 The flavour of release, i.e. nirvāṇa.

해탈상 解脫相 Liberation ; the mark, or condition, of liberation, release from the idea of transmigration.

해탈신 解脫身 The body of liberation, the body of Buddha released from kleśa, i.e. passion-affliction.

해탈의 解脫衣 The garment of liberation, the robe ; also 해탈당상의 解脫幢相衣 ; 해탈복 解脫服.

해탈이 解脫耳 The ear of deliverance, the ear freed, hearing the truth is the entrance to nirvāṇa.

해탈지견 解脫知見 The knowledge and experience of nirvāṇa, v. 해지견 解知見.

해탈처 解脫處 v. 팔해탈 八解脫.

해탈천 解脫天 Mokṣadeva, a name given to Hsüan-tsang in India.

해탈청정법전 解脫淸淨法殿 The pure dharma-court of nirvāṇa, the sphere of nirvāṇa, the abode of the dharmakāya.

해탈풍 解脫風 The wind of liberation from the fires of worldly suffering.

해탈해 解脫海 The ocean of liberation.

해하 解夏 The dismissing of the summer retreat ; also 해제 解制.

해행 解行 Interpretation and conduct ; to understand and do. 해행지 解行地 The stage of apprehending and following the teaching.

행 行 Go ; act ; do ; perform ; action ; conduct ; functioning ; the deed ; whatever is done by mind, mouth, or body, i.e. in thought, word, or deed. It is used for ayana, going, road, course ; a march, a division of time equal to six months ; also for saṁskāra, form, operation, perfecting, as one of the twelve nidānas, similar to karma, action, work, deed, especially moral action, cf. 업 業.

행각(승) 行脚(僧) A wandering monk.

행건도 行犍度 The saṁskāra skandha, the fourth of the five skandhas. v. 행온 行蘊.

행걸 行乞 To go begging, or asking for alms ; also 행발 行鉢 ; 탁발 托鉢.

행고 行苦 The suffering inevitably consequent on action.

행공양 行供養 The making of offerings, to go to make offerings.

행과 行果 Deed and result ; the inevitable sequence of act and its effect.

행교 行敎 To carry out the vinaya discipline ; the vinaya.

행덕 行德 The virtue of performance, or discipline ; to perform virtuous deeds.

행도 行道 To walk in the way, follow the Buddha-truth ; to make procession round an image, especially of the Buddha, with the right shoulder towards it.

행리 行履 The common acts of daily life – sitting, eating, thinking, etc.

행만 行滿 Hsing-man, a monk of the 불룡사 佛龍寺 Fo-lung monastery, about whom little is known, but who is accredited with supplying Dengyō of Japan with T'ien-t'ai scriptures in the latter part of the eighth century.

행모 行母 Mātṛkā, 마덕리가 摩德理迦 ; the "mother of karma," i.e. the Abhidharma-piṭaka, which shows that karma produces karma, one act producing another.

행상 行相 Activity ; performance ; mental activity.

행상 行像 To take an image (of Buddha) in procession ; it was a custom observed on Buddha's birthday according to the 불국기 佛國記.

행선 行善 To do good ; deeds that are good ; to offer up deeds of goodness.

행수 行樹 Trees in rows, avenues of trees.

행신 行信 Act and faith, doing and believing, acting out one's belief.

행업 行業 That which is done, the activities of thought, word, or deed ; moral action ; karma.

행온 行蘊 The fourth of the five skandhas, saṁskāra, action which inevitably passes on its effects.

행요 行要 The requirements for action ; to do that which is most important.

행우 行雨 To rain, or produce rain ; Varṣākāra, name of a minister of king Bimbisāra.

행원 行願 Action and vow ; act and vow, resolve or intention ; to act out one's vows ; to vow.

행의 行儀 To perform the proper duties, especially of monks and nuns.

행인 行人 A traveller, wayfarer ; a follower of Buddha ; a disciple.

행자 行者 A postulant ; prospective ordinand ; an abbot's attendant ; also ācārin, performing the duties of a disciple. Lit. "one who cultivates." Sometimes it is translated as "novice" but this translation is problematic since 사미 沙彌 Śrāmaṇera is usually translated "novice" and a Śrāmaṇera is senior to a 행자 行者 in the Korean monastic system. 행자기간 行者期間 Postulancy. The term was originally 3 years in duration, reduced to six months after 1945.

행족 行足 As works are the feet (so wisdom is the eye).

행주 行籌 To cast lots, divine (length of life).

행주좌와 行住坐臥 Walking, standing, sitting, lying — in every state.

행증 行證 Action and proof ; knowledge or assurance derived from doing ; practice of religious discipline and the resulting enlightenment.

행측 行厠 To go to the privy ; the privy to which one goes, metaphor of the human body as filthy.

행향 行香 To offer incense.

행화 行化 To go and convert ; also 행교화 行敎化.

행화 行華 To offer flowers.

향 香 Gandha. Fragrance ; incense ; the sense of smell, i.e. one of the ṣaḍāyatana, six senses. Incense is one of the 사 使 Buddha's messengers to stimulate faith and devotion.

향 享 Offer up ; enjoy. 향당 享堂 The hall of offerings, an ancestral hall.

향 響 Pratiśrut. Echo, resonance. 영향 影響 Shadow and echo.

향 餉 Rations, food ; revenue. 향공 餉供 Offerings of food.

향 鄕 The country, rural, village. 향인 鄕人 Country people, people of one's village.

향 向 Towards, to go towards, facing, heretofore. 향상 向上 To trace backwards, as from the later to the earlier, primary, the earliest or first ; upwards. 향하 向下 Downwards ; to trace downwards, i.e. forwards, "from root to branches." 향피회 向彼悔 prātideśanīya 바라제제사니 波羅提提舍尼 sin to be confessed before the assembly.

향(광장)엄 香(光莊)嚴 The one whose mind meditates on Buddha becomes interpenetrated and glorified by Buddha-fragrance (and light). There are several deva-sons and others called Hsiang-yen.

향계 香界 Incense region, a temple.

향로 香爐 A censer ; an incense burner.

향룡뇌 香龍腦 Scented dragon's brains, camphor ; v. 갈포라 羯布羅.

향루 香樓 The fragrant pyre on which the body of Buddha was consumed.

향산 香山 Gandhamādana. Incense mountain, one of the ten fabulous mountains known to Chinese Buddhism, located in the region of the Anavatapta lake in Tibet ; also placed in the Kunlun range. Among its great trees dwell the Kinnaras, Indra's musicians.

향상 香象 Gandhahastī. Fragrant elephant ; one of the sixteen honoured ones of the Bhadra-kalpa ; also a bodhisattva in the north who lives on the 향취산 香聚山 or 香醉山 with Buddha 향적 香積 ; cf. 향집 香集. 향상지문 香象之文 A narrative in the Abhidharma-kośa ; also a title for the Buddhist canon. 향상대사 香象大師 The third patriarch of the Hua-yen school, Fa-tsang 법장 法藏.

향수 香水 Liquid scent, or perfume. 향수전 香水錢 Money given to monks. 향(수)해 香(水)海 The scented ocean surrounding Sumeru.

향식 香食 Fragrance for food ; fragrant food.

향신 香神 ; **향음신** 香音神 The gods of fragrance (and music), i.e. the Gandharvas who live on Gandhamādana ; the musicians of Indra, with Dhṛtarāṣṭra as their ruler.

향실 香室 Gandhakuṭī ; house of incense, i.e. where Buddha dwells, a temple.

향염 香染 Incense-coloured, yellowish-grey, the colour of a monk's robe ; also 향색 香色 ; 향(복)의 香(複)衣.

향왕 香王 Gandharāja, a bodhisattva in whose image the finger tips are shown as dripping ambrosia. There is also a 향왕 香王 Kuanyin.

향욕 香欲 The desire for fragrance, the lust of the nasal organ, one of the five desires.

향입 香入 The sense of smell and its organ, the nose.

향적 香積 Hsiang-chi, the Buddha of Fragrance-land 향국 香國, described in the 유마경 維摩經. The inhabitants live on the odour of incense, which surpasses that of all other lands ; cf. 향상 香象 ; also the kitchen and food of a monastery.

향전 香篆 Incense made in coils and burnt to measure the time ; also 향반 香盤 ; 향인 香印.

향전 香殿 The incense hall, especially the large hall of the Triratna.

향주 香廚 The fragrant kitchen, i.e. a monastery kitchen.

향주 香炷 Thread incense (in coils) ; a lamp or candle giving a fragrant odour ; incense and candles.

향진 香塵 The atom or element of smell, one of the six guṇas.

향집 香集 The name of the western Buddha-land in which Ākāśa Bodhisattva lives, described in the 허공장보살경 虛空藏菩薩經 Ākāśagarbha sūtra ; cf. 향상 香象.

향찰 香刹 An incense kṣetra, i.e. a monastery.

향탕 香湯 A fragrant liquid made of thirty-two ingredients, used by the secret sects in washing the body at the time of initiation.

향풍산 香風山 The abode of the Bodhisattva of fragrance and light.

향화 香火 Incense and candles (or lamps).

향화 香華 Incense and flowers, offerings to Buddha.

향환 香丸 Incense balls.

허 許 Grant, permit, admit, promise ; very. 허가 許可 Grant, permit, admit.

허 虛 Śūnya. Empty, vacant ; unreal, unsubstantial, untrue ; space ; humble ; in vain. 허가 虛假 Baseless, false. 허위 虛僞 Unreal, deceptive. 허당 虛堂 Hsü-t'ang, name of a noted monk of the Sung dynasty. 허망 虛妄 Vitatha. Unreal and false, baseless ; abhūta, non-existent. 허망법 虛妄法 Unreal things or sensations, such as those perceived by the senses. 허망륜 虛妄輪 The unreal wheel of life, or transmigration. 허심 虛心 With humble mind, or heart. 허무 虛無 Empty, non-existent, unreal, incorporeal, immaterial. 허무신 虛無身 The immaterial Buddha-body, the spirit free from all limitations. 허공 虛空 Śūnya ; empty, void, space ; ākāśa, in the sense of space, or the ether ; gagana, the sky, atmosphere, heaven ; kha, space, sky, ether. 허 虛 is defined as that which is without shape or substantiality, 공 空 as that which has no resistance. The immaterial universe behind all phenomena. 허공주 虛空住 Ākāśapratiṣṭhita, abiding in space, the fifth son of Mahābhijñā, a bodhisattva to the south of our universe.

허공천 虛空天 The four heavens of desire above Meru in space, from the Yama heaven upwards. 허공잉 虛空孕 The womb of space, ākāśagarbha, idem 허공장 虛空藏 *infra*. 허공법신 虛空法身 The Dharmakāya as being like space which enfolds all things, omniscient and pure. 허공무위 虛空無爲 Ākāśa, one of the asaṁskṛta dharmas, passive void or space ; two kinds of space, or the immaterial, are named, the active and passive, or phenomenal and non-phenomenal (i.e. noumenal). The phenomenal is differentiated and limited, and apprehended by sight ; the noumenal is without bounds or limitations, and belongs entirely to mental conception. 허공계 虛空界 The visible vault of space. 허공안 虛空眼 The eye of space, or of the immaterial ; name of the mother of Buddhas in the garbhadhātu group. 허공신 虛空神 Śūnyatā, the god of space. 허공화 虛空華 Spots before the eyes, *Muscoe volitantes*. 허공장 虛空藏 Ākāśagarbha, or Gaganagarbha, the central bodhisattva in the court of space in the garbhadhātu group ; guardian of the treasury of all wisdom and achievement ; his powers extend to the five directions of space ; five forms of him are portrayed under different names ; he is also identified with the dawn, Aruṇa, and the 명성 明星 or Venus. 허공신 虛空身 The body which fills space, Vairocana. 허언 虛言 Empty words, baseless talk. 허광어 虛誑語 Untrue or misleading talk, which is against the fourth commandment.

헌 獻 To offer up, present. 헌신 獻身 To offer up one's body as a sacrifice.

헌향 獻香 To offer incense ; to burn the light incense.

험 驗 To examine into, hold an inquest ; to come true, verify. 험생인중 驗生人中 An inquiry into the mode of a person's death, to judge whether he will be reborn as a man, and so on with the other possible destinies, e.g. 험생지옥 驗生地獄 whether he will be reborn in the hells.

혁 革 Skins, hides, pelts ; strip, cut off. 혁총 革蔥 ; 명총 茗葱 Latārka, "green onions" [M. W.], tr. as 산 蒜 garlic.

현 現 Appear, apparent ; manifest, visible ; now ; present ; ready.

현 賢 Bhadra. Wise and virtuous, sage, second in rank to a 성 聖 saint ; good, excellent in character, virtuous. 현인 賢人 A wise and virtuous man. 현겁 賢劫 Bhadra-kalpa, the present period ; the last was 장엄겁 莊嚴劫, the next is to be 성수겁 星宿劫. A Bhadra-kalpa has 1,000 Buddhas, hence its name "the good kalpa," also called 선겁 善劫. There are varied statements in regard to the thousand Buddhas, and variety as to their names. Śākyamuni is the fourth of the present kalpa, Maitreya is to follow and 995 to succeed him. "It is to last 236 million years, but over 151 millions have already elapsed." [Eitel]. Cf. 현겁경 賢劫經 ; 현재현겁천불경 現在賢劫千佛經 and 발발 颰跋 for Bhadra. 현병 賢甁 Bhadra-kumbha ; auspicious jar, magic bottle, from which all good things may be wished. 현자 賢者 A good and wise man, not yet free from illusion or fully comprehending reality ; also anyone occupying a superior position, or a good man in general. 현성 賢聖 Those who are noted for goodness, and those who are also noted for wisdom, or insight ; the 현 賢 hsien are still of ordinary human standard, the 성 聖 shêng transcend them in wisdom and character ; the attainments from 견도 見道 upwards are those of the shêng ; the hsien is on the moral plane, and has not eliminated illusion ; the shêng has cut off illusion and has insight into absolute reality. The Mahāyāna has three stages for the hsien and ten for the shêng ; the Hīnayāna has seven for each. 현호 賢護 Bhadrapāla, a disciple who kept the faith at home at the time of the Buddha. Also, a bodhisattva who with 500 others slighted Śākyamuni in a previous existence, was converted and became a Buddha. An image of Bhadrapāla is kept in the monastic bath-room ; cf. 능엄경 楞嚴經 5. 현두 賢豆 Hindu, India, cf. 인 印. 현수 賢首 Sage head or leader, a term of address to a monk. A bodhisattva in the Hua-yen sūtra. A queen mentioned in the same sūtra, and in the 현수경

賢首經. The third patriarch 법장 法藏 Fa-tsang, of the Hua-yen sect, which is also known by his title 현수종 賢首宗 Hsien Shou Tsung.

현 玄 Dark, sombre, black ; abstruse, obscure, deep, profound ; hence it is used to indicate Taoism, and was afterwards adopted by the Buddhists.

현 顯 Manifest, reveal, open, clear, plain, known, illustrious ; exoteric. 현전 顯典 ; 현경 顯經 The exoteric or general scriptures, as distinguished from the 밀 蜜 esoteric, occult, or tantric scriptures. 현명 顯冥 Open or hidden, external or internal (illumination, or powers). 현종 顯宗 ; 현가 顯家 The exoteric sects, in contrast with the 밀 蜜 esoteric. 현교 顯教 The open, or general teaching ; the exoteric schools. 현명 顯明 Open, manifest ; pure ; to reveal. 현본 顯本 The revelation of his fundamental or eternal life by the Buddha in the Lotus Sūtra. 현정 顯正 To show the truth, reveal that which is correct. 현시 顯示 To reveal, indicate. 현색 顯色 The visible or light colours. 현밀 顯蜜 Exoteric and esoteric ; the 진언 眞言 Shingon, or True-word sect, is the esoteric sect, which exercises occult rites of Yoga character, and considers all the other sects as exoteric. 현식 顯識 Manifest, revealing, or open knowledge, the store of knowledge where all is revealed both good and bad, a name for the ālaya-vijñāna. 현로 顯露 To reveal, disclose.

현 懸 Suspend, hang. 현광 懸曠 Hanging and wide-spread, e.g. sun and sky, the mystery and extensiveness (or all-embracing character of Buddha-truth). 현기 懸記 Prophecy ; to prophesy. 현담 懸談 A foreword, or introduction, to a discourse on a scripture, outlining the main ideas ; also 현담 玄談.

현각 玄覺 Hsüan-chio, a Wenchow monk, also named 명도 明道 Ming-tao, who had a large following ; he is said to have attained to enlightenment in one night, hence is known as 일숙각 一宿覺.

현감거사 玄鑑居士 An Indian, the patron of an Indian monk Dharmapāla, author of the 유식석론 唯識釋論. After his death the patron gave the MS. to Hsüan-tsang.

현경 玄鏡 An abbreviation of 화엄법계현경 華嚴法界玄鏡.

현경 玄景 Hsüan-ching, a monk, d. 606, noted for his preaching, and for his many changes of garments, as 형악 衡岳 Hêng-yo was noted for wearing one garment all his days.

현고 玄高 Hsüan-kao, a famous Shensi monk, influential politically, later killed by order of the emperor Wu Ti, *circa* 400.

현과미 現過未 or **현과당** 現過當 Present, past, and future.

현관 現觀 Insight into, or meditation on, immediate presentations ; present insight into the deep truth of Buddhism.

현기광 現起光 The phenomenal radiance of Buddha which shines out when circumstances require it, as contrasted to his noumenal radiance which is constant.

현당 現當 Present and future (i.e. 당래 當來).

현도 玄道 The profound doctrine, Buddhism.

현도만다라 現圖曼陀羅 The two revealed or revealing maṇḍalas, the Garbhadhātu and Vajradhātu.

현랑 玄朗 Hsüan-lang, a Chekiang monk of the T'ang dynasty, died 854, at 83 years of age, noted for his influence on his disciples and for having remained in one room for over thirty years ; also called 혜명 慧明 Hui-ming and 좌계 左溪 Tso-ch'i.

현량 現量 Reasoning from the manifest, pratyakṣa. (1) Immediate, or direct reasoning, whereby the eye apprehends and distinguishes colour and form, the ear sound, etc. (2) Immediate insight into, or direct inference in a trance (정 定) of all the conditions of the ālayavijñāna. 현량상위 現量相違 A fallacy of the major premiss in which the premiss contradicts experience, e.g. sound is something not heard, this being one of the nine fallacies of the major premiss.

현류 玄流 The black-robed sect of monks.

현문 玄門 The profound school, i.e. Buddhism. Also that of the 화엄 華嚴 Hua-yen (Kegon) which has a division of 십현문 十玄門 or 십현연기 十玄緣起, indicating the ten metaphysical propositions, or lines of thought ; of these there are two or more versions.

현범 玄範 Hsüan-fan, a T'ang monk and editor, said to be a contemporary of Hsüan-tsang, some say his disciple.

현보 現報 Present-life recompense for good or evil done in the present life.

현사 玄沙 Hsüan-sha, a famous Fukien monk who had over 800 disciples, died A.D. 908 ; his chief subjects were the fundamental ailments of men — blindness, deafness, and dumbness.

현상 現相 Manifest forms, i.e. the external or phenomenal world, the 경계상 境界相, one of the 삼세 三細 q.v. of the 기신론 起信論 Awakening of Faith.

현생 現生 The present life. 현생이익 現生利益 Benefits in the present life (from serving Buddha).

현성 現成 Manifest, existing, evident, ready-made, self-evident or self-existing.

현세 現世 The present world.

현소 玄疏 The 현의 玄義, a T'ien-t'ai commentary on the contents and meaning of the Lotus Sūtra, and 소 疏 the critical commentary on the text.

현식 現識 Direct knowledge, manifesting wisdom, another name of the ālayavijñāna, on which all things depend for realization, for it completes the knowledge of the other vijñānas. Also the "representation-consciousness" or perception of an external world, one of the 오식 五識 q.v. of the 기신론 起信論.

현신 現身 The present body. Also the various bodies or manifestations in which the Buddhas and bodhisattvas reveal themselves.

현완 玄琬 Hsüan-yüan, an influential Shensi monk who lived through the persecution of Buddhism in the 북주 北周 Northern chou dynasty into the Sui and T'ang dynasties.

현유 現喩 A comparison consisting of immediate facts, or circumstances.

현응 玄應 Deep, or abstruse response ; also Hsüan-ying, the author in the T'ang dynasty of the 현응음의 玄應音義, i.e. 일체경음의 一切經音義 a Buddhist dictionary in 25 chüan, not considered very reliable.

현의 玄義 The deep meaning ; the meaning of the profound ; it refers chiefly to the T'ien-t'ai method of teaching which was to proceed from a general explanation of the content and meaning of the various great sūtras to a discussion of the deeper meaning ; the method was : (1) 석명 釋名 explanation of the terms ; (2) 변체 辨體 definition of the substance ; (3) 명종 明宗 making clear the principles ; (4) 논용 論用 discussing their application ; (5) 판교 判敎 discriminating the doctrine. V. also 현소 玄疏.

현익 現益 Benefit in the present life.

현일 玄一 Hsüan-i, a commentator of the 법상 法相 Dharmalakṣaṇa school during the T'ang dynasty.

현장 玄奘 Hsüan-tsang, whose name is written variously e.g. Hsüan Chuang, Hiüen-tsang, Hiouen Tsang, Yüan Tsang, Yüan Chwang ; the famous pilgrim to India, whose surname was 진 陳 Ch'ên and personal name 의 禕 Wei ; a native of Honan, A.D. 600-664 (Giles). It is said that he entered a monastery at 13 years of age and in 618 with his elder brother, who had preceded him in becoming a monk, went to Ch'ang-an 장안 長安, the capital, where in 622 he was fully ordained. Finding that China possessed only half of the Buddhist classics, he took his staff, bound his feet, and on foot braved the perils of the deserts and mountains of Central Asia. The date of his setting out is uncertain (629 or 627), but the year of his arrival in India is given as 633 ; after visiting and studying in many parts of India, he returned home, reaching the capital in 645, was received with honour and presented his collection of 657 works, "besides many images and pictures, and one hundred and fifty relics," to the Court. T'ai Tsung, the emperor, gave him the 홍복사 弘福寺 Hung Fu monastery in which to work. He presented the manuscript of his famous 대당서역기 大唐西域記 *Record of Western Countries* in 646 and completed it as it now stands by 648. The emperor Kao Tsung called him to Court in 653 and gave him the 자은사 慈恩寺 T'zŭ En monastery in which to work, a monastery which ever after was associated with him ; in 657 he removed him to the 옥화궁 玉華宮 Yü Hua Kung and made that palace a monastery. He translated seventy-five works in 1335 chüan. In India he received the titles of 마하야나제파 摩訶耶那提婆 Mahāyānadeva and 목차제파 木叉提婆 Mokṣadeva ; he was also known as 삼장법사 三藏法師 Tripiṭaka teacher of Dharma. He died in 664, in his 65th year.

현재 現在 Now, at present, the present. 현재세 現在世 The present world. 현재현겁 現在賢劫 The present bhadra-kalpa. 현재 現在, 과거 過去, 미래 未來 Present, past, and future.

현전 現前 Now present, manifest before one. 현전지 現前地 The sixth of the ten stages of the bodhisattva, in which the bhūtatathatā is manifested to him.

현종 玄宗 The profound principles, or propositions, i.e. Buddhism.

현증 現證 The immediate realization of enlightenment, or nirvāṇa ; abhisamaya, inner realization ; pratyakṣa, immediate perception, evidence of the eye or other organ.

현찬 玄贊 An abbreviation of 법화경현찬 法華經玄贊.

현창 玄暢 Hsüan-ch'ang, a famous Shensi monk, who was invited to be tutor of the heir-apparent, A.D. 445, but refused, died 484.

현행 現行 Now going, or proceeding ; present or manifest activities. 현행법 現行法 Things in present or manifested action, phenomena in general.

혈 血 Blood. 이혈세혈 以血洗血 To wash out blood with blood, from one sin to fall into another. 혈서 血書 Written with (one's own) blood. 혈오지 血汚池 The pool, or lake, of blood in one of the hells. 혈해 血海 The sea of blood, i.e. the hells and lower incarnations. 혈분경 血盆經 The sūtra describing the blood bath for women in Hades ; it is a Chinese invention and is called by Eitel "the placenta tank, which consists of an immense pool of blood, and from this hell, it is said, no release is possible" ; but there are ceremonies for release from it. 혈맥 血脈 The arteries and veins, linked, closely connected. 혈도 血途 The gati or destiny of rebirth as an animal.

협 頰 Cheeks, jaws. 협차 頰車 The cheeks rounded — one of the characteristics of a Buddha.

협 夾 Squeeze, clip, nip ; lined. 협산 夾山 Name of a monastery and monk in 예주 澧州 Li-chou under the T'ang dynasty.

협 脇 The ribs, flanks, sides ; forceful, to coerce. 협시 脇侍 ; 협시 挾侍 ; 협사 脇士 Bodhisattvas, or other images on either side of a Buddha. 협존 脇尊 v. 파 波 Pārśva.

협 挾 To clasp under the arm ; to cherish ; to presume on. 협시 挾侍 ; 협사 脇士 The two assistants of a Buddha, etc., right and left.

형 衡 A cross-bar, crosswise ; a balance ; to weigh, balance, compare, adjust, adjudge, judgment. 형산 衡山 The Hêng mountains in Hunan, where was the 남악 南岳 Southern Peak monastery, from which came 혜사 慧思 Hui-ssŭ, second patriarch of T'ien-t'ai. 형량 衡量 Balancing and measuring, judging.

형 兄 Elder brother. 형제 兄弟 Elder and younger brothers ; brother, brethren, i.e. members of the fraternity.

형 形 Form, figure, appearance, the body. 형상 形像 Pratimā, an image or likeness (of Buddha). 형산 形山 The body, comparable to a mountain. 형모 形貌 Form, appearance. 형모욕 形貌欲 The desire awakened on seeing a beautiful form, one of the 육욕 六慾 six desires. 형색 形色 Saṁsthānarūpa, the characteristics of form – long, short, square, round, high, low, straight, crooked. It is also associated with Rūpāvacara as personal appearance, and as a class of gods in the realm of form.

형 熒 Glitter, twinkle. 형감심 熒感心 or 형감천 熒感天 or 형혹성 熒惑星 Aṅgāraka, the planet Mars ; also 화요일 火曜日 ; it is also described as a nakṣatra, or asterism, and such is represented in feminine form in the Vajradhātu group.

형 荊 Thorns. 형계 荊溪 Ching-ch'i, thorn-stream, name of the ninth T'ien-t'ai patriarch 잠연 湛然 Chan-jan.

혜 惠 Kind, gracious, forbearing, accordant. 은혜 恩惠 Grace, kindness. 시혜 施惠 To bestow kindness, or charity. 혜리 惠利 To show kindness to and benefit others.

혜 醯 Pickle. Translit. *hi, he, hai.* 혜두파타부 醯兜婆拖部 Hetuvādapūrva Sthavira, the first school of the Sthaviras treating of causality, or hetuvāda, the 인론 因論 school ; it was a subdivision of the Sarvāstivāda. 혜마부다 醯摩嚩多 ; 혜마발타 醯摩跋陀 A ruler of the Himālayas, in the retinue of Vaiśravaṇa, v. 비 毘. 혜마발다부 醯摩跋多部 Haimavatāḥ, school of the snow mountains, "a schismatic philosophical school, one of the five subdivisions" of the Mahāsāṅghikāḥ. [Eitel]. 혜라 醯羅 Hiḍḍa, five miles south of Jellālabad. [Eitel]. 혜도 醯都 Hetu, a cause, logical reason. 혜도비타 醯都費陀 Hetuvidyā, 인명 因明, logic. 혜도발라지야 醯都鉢羅底也 Hetupratyaya, primary and secondary cause.

혜 慧 Prajñā ; sometimes Jñāna. Wisdom, discernment, understanding ; the power to discern things and their underlying principles and to decide the doubtful. It is often interchanged with 지 智, though not correctly, for *chih* means knowledge, the science of the phenomenal, while *hui* refers more generally to principles or morals. It is part of the name of many monks, e.g. 혜가 慧可 Hui-k'o ; 혜사 慧思 Hui-ssŭ.

혜가 慧可 Hui-k'o, the successor of Bodhidharma, v. 달 達 ; he previously cut off his arm in appeal to be received as disciple, and finally inherited his mantle and alms-bowl.

혜개 慧愷 Hui-k'ai, a monk and author, also known as 지개 智愷 Chih-k'ai of the sixth century A.D.

혜거 慧炬 The torch of wisdom.

혜검 慧劍 The sword of wisdom which cuts away illusion.

혜견 慧見 Wise views, or insight into wisdom, the views of wisdom.

혜경 慧鏡 The mirror of wisdom.

혜관 慧觀 Hui-kuan, one of Kumārajīva's chief assistants in translation, died 424.

혜근 慧根 The root, i.e. the organ, of wisdom.

혜능 慧能 The power of wisdom. Hui-nêng, name of a noted monk, sixth patriarch of the Intuitional or Meditation sect ; died 713.

혜등 慧燈 The lamp of wisdom. 혜등왕 慧燈王 A king who gave his flesh and blood to save the lives of others.

혜력 慧力 Prajñābala, one of the five powers, that of wisdom.

혜류 慧流 The living stream of wisdom able to cleanse all impurity.

혜림 慧琳 Hui-lin, a disciple of the Indian monk Amogha 불공 不空 ; he made the 혜림음의 慧琳音義 dictionary of sounds and meanings of Buddhist words and phrases, based upon the works of 현응 玄應 Hsüan-ying, 혜원 慧苑 Hui-yüan, 규기 窺基 K'uei-chi, and 운공 雲公 Yün-kung, in 100 chüan, beginning the work in A.D. 788 and ending it in 810. He is also called 대장음의 大藏音義 ; died 820.

혜명 慧命 Wisdom-life, or wisdom as life, wisdom being the basis of spiritual character. A term of address to a monk, also 혜수 慧壽, and to a monk by a superior.

혜목 慧目 The eye of wisdom. 혜안 慧眼 The wisdom-eye that sees all things as unreal.

혜박 慧縛 The bond of ignorance and stupidity which fetters wisdom.

혜사 慧思 Hui-ssŭ, the second patriarch of the T'ien-t'ai school 남악대사 南嶽大師.

혜수 慧數 Mental conditions in contrast to mind itself.

혜신 慧身 Wisdom body, one of the five divisions of the Dharmakāya, which is the embodiment *inter alia* of inherent wisdom.

혜업 慧業 Undertaking and doing ; practical goodness resulting from wisdom.

혜운 慧雲 The clouds of wisdom with which the Tathāgata covers all beings.

혜원 慧苑 Hui-yüan, a noted T'ang monk and lexicographer, author of the 혜원음의 慧苑音義 dictionary of sounds and meanings, cf. 혜림 慧琳.

혜월 慧月 Jñānacandra, author of the non-Buddhist 승종십구의론 勝宗十句義論, Vaiśeṣika-nikāya-daśapadārtha-śāstra, tr. by Hsüan-tsang ; perhaps the same as 지월 智月.

혜의 慧義 The apprehension of the meaning of reality through wisdom.

혜인 慧忍 Wisdom-patience, one of the 십인 十忍.

혜인 慧印 Wisdom-sign, or seal ; also 지인 智印.

혜일 慧日 Wisdom-sun, Buddha-wisdom. Hui-jih, a celebrated T'ang monk and author (disciple of I-ching) who also went on pilgrimage to India and spent thirteen years there, died A.D. 748 ; entitled 자민삼장 慈愍三藏.

혜장 慧藏 Wisdom-store, the Abhidharma-piṭaka, which embodies the science of ascertaining the meaning of the sūtras. Also, the whole of the Tripiṭaka.

혜정 慧淨 Hui-ching, a noted T'ang monk, translator and author, who was commanded to assist Hsüan-tsang in his translations but was unable through failing health.

혜족 慧足 The leg of wisdom, the other being 복족 福足 q.v.

혜초 慧超 Hui-ch'ao, a monk who travelled in India.

혜학 慧學 The study of wisdom, e.g. the Abhidharma.

혜해 慧解 The function of wisdom — to explain all things. 혜해탈 慧解脫 The escape by, or into wisdom, i.e. of the arhat who overcomes the hindrances to wisdom, or insight, but not the practical side of abstraction, etc. ; better able to understand than to do.

혜환 慧幻 Wisdom-illusion, wisdom-conjuring ; the kaleidoscope of wisdom.

호 互 Interlock, dovetail, mutual. 호용죄 互用罪 The fault of transferring from one object of worship over to another a gift, or duty, e.g. using gilt given for an image of Śākyamuni to make one for Maitreya ; or "robbing Peter to pay Paul". 호궤 互跪 Kneeling with both knees at once, as in India ; in China the left knee is first placed on the ground ; also 호궤 互跪. 호사가람 互娑伽藍 Haṁsa saṁghārāma, "Wild goose monastery," on Mount Indraśailaguhā, whose inmates were once saved from starving by the self-sacrifice of a wild goose ; also 승사가람 僧娑伽藍 or 승응가람 僧鷹伽藍.

호 狐 A fox ; seems to be used also for a jackal.

호 湖 A lake. 호남 湖南 The province of Hunan.

호 呼 Call ; breathe out. 호호 呼呼 The raurava or fourth hot hell. 호도극도 呼圖克圖 or 호토극도 胡土克圖 Hutuktu, a chief Lama of Mongolian Buddhism, who is repeatedly reincarnated. 호마 呼摩 ; 호마 護摩 Homa, an oblation by fire.

호 瑚 Coral. 호연 瑚璉 A sacrificial grain-vessel ; described as a precious stone.

호 毫 Down, soft hair ; minute, trifling, tiny. 호미 毫眉 The white hair between Buddha's eyebrows, the 호상 毫相 i.e. one of the thirty-two signs of a Buddha.

호 好 Good, well ; to like, be fond of, love. 호조 好照 Good at shining, a mirror. 호생 好生 Love of life ; love of the living. 호상 好相 A good appearance, omen, or sign. 호성조 好聲鳥 or 호음조 好音鳥 A bird with a beautiful note, the Kokila, or Kalaviṅka, some say Karaṇḍa(ka).

호 胡 How? Why? Hun ; Turk ; random ; hemp ; long-lived ; pepper, etc. ; translit. *go, hu.* 호란 胡亂 Disorderly, without order. 호로차나 胡嚧遮那 Gorocanā, "a bright yellow pigment prepared from the urine or bile of a cow." [M. W.] 호자 胡子 Hun, or Turk, a term applied to the people west and north of China ; a nickname for Bodhidharma. 호종족 胡種族 Of West Asian race, a term applied to the Buddha, as the sūtras were also styled 호경 胡經 Hun classics and 노호 老胡 Old Hun was also a nickname for the Buddha. 호소다 胡蘇多 A charm, or incantation against evil vapours, etc. 호궤 胡跪 The Hun way of kneeling, right knee on the ground, left knee up. 호도인 胡道人 Monks from Central Asia or India. 호실건 胡實健 Hujikan, "an ancient kingdom south-west of Balkh ... in Lat. 35° 20' N., Long. 65° E." [Eitel].

ㄱ ㄴ ㄷ ㄹ ㅁ ㅂ ㅅ ㅇ ㅈ ㅊ ㅋ ㅌ ㅍ ㅎ 찾아보기

호 護 To protect, guard, succour. 호세자 護世者 The four Lokapālas, each protecting one of the four quarters of space, the guardians of the world and of the Buddhist faith. 호명 護命 Protection of life. 호국 護國 The four Lokapālas, or Rāṣṭrapālas, who protect a country. 호사 護寺 Vihārapāla, guardian deity of a monastery. 호념 護念 To guard and care for, protect and keep in mind. 호계신 護戒神 The five guardian-spirits of each of the five commandments, cf. 이십오신 二十五神. 호마 護摩 Homa, also 호마 護磨 ; 호마 呼麽 ; described as originally a burnt offering to Heaven ; the esoterics adopted the idea of worshipping with fire, symbolizing wisdom as fire burning up the faggots of passion and illusion, and therewith preparing nirvāṇa as food, etc. ; cf. 대일경 ; 大日經 ; four kinds of braziers are used, round, semi-circular, square, and octagonal ; four, five, or six purposes are recorded, i.e. Śāntika, to end calamities ; Pauṣṭika (or Puṣṭikarman) for prosperity ; Vaśīkaraṇa, "dominating," intp. as calling down the good by means of enchantments ; Abhicāraka, exorcising the evil ; a fifth is to obtain the loving protection of the Buddhas and bodhisattvas ; a sixth divides Puṣṭikarman into two parts, the second part being length of life ; each of these six has its controlling Buddha and bodhisattvas, and different forms and accessories of worship. 호명대사 護明大士 Prabhāpāla ; guardian of light, or illumination, name of Śākyamuni when in the Tuṣita heaven before earthly incarnation. 호법 護法 To protect or maintain the Buddha-truth ; also name of Dharmapāla q.v. 호법신 護法神 The four lokapālas, seen at the entrance to Buddhist temples, v. *supra*. 호동자법 護童子法 Method of protecting the young against the fifteen evil spirits which seek to harm them. 호부 護符 A charm used by the esoterics. 호필나 護苾那 Hupian, "the capital of Vṛjisthāna, probably in the neighbourhood of the present Charekoor ... to the north of Cabool." [Eitel]. 호신 護身 Protection of the body, for which the charm last named is used, and also other methods.

호 號 To roar, call, cry, scream ; sign, mark, designation. 호규지옥 號叫地獄 Raurava ; the hell of wailing.

호 浩 Vast, great. 호묘 浩妙 Vast and mysterious.

호 虎 Vyāghra, 미야갈라 弭也竭羅 a tiger. 호구산 虎丘山 Huch'iu Shan, a monastery at Soochow, which gave rise to a branch of the Ch'an(Zen) school, founded by 소륭 紹隆 Shao-lung. 호호파 虎虎婆 Hahava, the fifth hell. For 호이 虎耳 v. 사두 舍頭.

호박 琥珀 Amber ; intp. of aśmagarbha, v. 아 阿 one of the saptaratna ; cf. 칠보 七寶.

혹 惑 Moha. Illusion, delusion, doubt, unbelief ; it is also used for kleśa, passion, temptation, distress, care, trouble. 혹인 惑人 A deluded person, to delude others. 혹염 惑染 The taint of delusion, the contamination of illusion. 혹업고 惑業苦 Illusion, accordant action, and suffering ; the pains arising from a life of illusion. 혹착 惑著 The bond of illusion, the delusive bondage of desire to its environment. 혹취 惑趣 The way or direction of illusion, delusive objective, intp. as deluded in fundamental principles. 혹장 惑障 The hindrance, or obstruction of the delusive passions to entry into truth.

혼 惛 Confused, stupefied. 혼침 惛沈 Sunk in stupor.

혼 昏 Dusk, dull, confused. 혼성 昏城 The dim city, the abode of the common, unenlightened man. 혼식 昏識 Dull, or confused, knowledge. 혼취 昏醉 Matta, drunk, intoxicated. 혼종 昏鐘 ; 혼고 昏鼓 The bell, or drum, at dusk. 혼묵다 昏默多 Kandat, the capital of Tamasthiti, perhaps the modern Kunduz, but Eitel says. "Kundoot about 40 miles above Jshtrakh, Lat. 36° 42 N., Long. 71° 39 E."

혼 魂 The mind, the soul, conscious mind, vijñāna ; also 혼신 魂神. 혼백 魂魄 Animus and anima ; the spiritual nature or mind, and the animal soul ; the two are defined as mind and body or mental and physical, the invisible soul inhabiting the visible body, the former being celestial, the latter terrestrial.

혼 混 Turbid, intermingled, confused, chaotic. 혼돈 混沌 Mixed, confused, in disorder.

홀 忽 Suddenly ; hastily ; a millionth. 홀름 忽懍 Khulm, an ancient kingdom and city between Balkh and Kunduz. 홀로마 忽露摩 Shadumān, "a district of ancient Tukhāra, north of the Wakhan." [Eitel].

홍 紅 Aruṇa, rakta ; red. 홍교 紅教 ; 홍의파 紅衣派 The red sect, i.e. the Zva-dmar, or Shamar, the older Lamaistic sect of Tibet, who wear red clothes and hats. 홍련화 紅蓮花 Padma, the red lotus, after which the 홍련지옥 紅蓮地獄 red lotus hell is called, the seventh of the eight cold hells, where the flesh of the sufferers bursts open like red lotuses.

홍 弘 Vast, great ; to enlarge, spread abroad ; e.g. 홍선 弘宣 ; 홍교 弘教 ; 홍법 弘法 ; 홍통 弘通 widely to proclaim the Buddhist truth ; 홍인 弘忍 ; 홍법 弘法 Hung-jên and Hung-fa, names of noted monks ; 홍서 弘誓 ; 홍(서)원 弘(誓)願 vast or universal vows of a Buddha, or Bodhisattva, especially Amitābha's forty-eight vows.

화 花 ; 화 華 Puṣpa, a flower, flowers ; especially the lotus, and celestial flowers. 화좌 花座 The lotus throne on which Buddhas and Bodhisattvas sit. 화거 花筥 ; 화롱 花籠 ; 화혈 花血 Flower baskets for scattering lotus flowers, or leaves and flowers in general.

화 畫 Draw, paint, picture, sketch ; devise, fix. 화수 畫水 Like drawing a line across water, which leaves no trace, unlike 화석 畫石 sculpture in stone, which remains. 화병 畫餅 ; 화중지병 畫中之餅 Pictured biscuits, a term of the Intuitive School for the scriptures, i.e. useless as food in the picture. 화상 畫像 Portraits, painting of images, maṇḍalas.

화 火 Fire, flame. Śikhin 시기 尸棄 ; 식기 式棄, which means fire in the sense of flame, is the name of the 999th Buddha of the kalpa preceding this.

화 貨 Goods, wares. 화리습미가 貨利習彌迦 Khārismiga, an "ancient kingdom on the upper Oxus, which formed part of Tukhāra, the Kharizm of Arabic geographers." [Eitel].

화 禾 Growing grain. 화산 禾山 Ho-shan, a monastery in 길주 吉州 Chi-chou, and its abbot who died A.D. 960.

화 和 Harmony, peace ; to blend, mix ; with, unite with ; respond, rhyme, e.g. 화순 和順 harmonious and compliant ; 화회 和會 to blend, unite. 화가라(나) 和伽羅(那) ; 화가나 和伽那 ; 화라나 和羅那 Vyākaraṇa, grammar, analysis, change of form ; intp. as 수기 授記 prediction, i.e. by the Buddha of the future felicity and realm of a disciple, hence Kauṇḍinya is known as Vyākaraṇa-Kauṇḍinya. 화남 和南 ; 파남 婆南 ; 반담 伴談 or 반제 伴題 ; 반제 畔睇 ; 반탄남 畔彈南 ; 반담 槃淡 ; 반나매 槃那寐 ; 반다미 盤荼味 ; 번담 煩淡 Vandana. Obeisance, prostration, bowing the head, reverencing, worshipping. 화합 和合 To blend, unite, be of one mind, harmonize. 화(합)승 和(合)僧 ; 화(합)중 和(合)衆 A saṁgha 승가 僧伽, a monastery. 화합해 和合海 A monastery where all are of one mind as the sea is of one taste. 화상 和尙 A general term for a monk. It is said to be derived from Khotan in the form of 화사 和闍 or 화사 和社 or 오사 烏社 which might be a translit. of *Vandya* (Tibetan and Khotanī *ban-de*), "reverend." Later it took the form of 화상 和尙 or 화상 和上. The 율종 律宗 use 화상 和上, others generally 화상 和尙. The Sanskrit term used in its interpretation is 오파타야 烏波陀耶 Upādhyāya, a "sub-teacher" of the Vedas, inferior to an ācārya ; this is intp. as 역생 力生 strong in producing (knowledge), or in begetting strength in his disciples ; also by 지유죄지무죄 知有罪知無罪 a discerner of sin from not-sin, or the sinful from the not-sinful. It has been used as a synonym for 법사 法師 a teacher of doctrine, in distinction from 율사 律師 a teacher of the vinaya, also from 선사 禪師 a teacher of the Intuitive school. 화이라 和夷羅 Vajra, 화이라원열차 和夷羅洹閱叉 ; 발사라파니 跋闍羅波膩 Vajrapāṇi, the 금강수 金剛手 Bodhisattva holding the sceptre or thunderbolt, or 금강신 金剛神 one of the names of Indra, as a demon king and protector of Buddhism. 화전 和闐 Khotan, Kustana, cf. 우 于. 화수길 和須吉 Vāsuki, lord of nāgas, name of a "dragon-king," with nine heads, hydra-headed ; also 화수길 和修吉. 화수밀(다) 和須蜜(多) Vasumitra. A distinction is made (probably in error) between Vasumitra, noted as a libertine and for his beauty, and Vasumitra 벌소밀달라 筏蘇蜜呾羅 q.v., a converted profligate who became president of the synod under Kaniṣka. 화향환 和香丸 A pill compounded of many kinds of incense typifying that in the one Buddha-truth lies all truth.

화 華 Kusuma ; puṣpa ; padma ; a flower, blossom ; flowery ; especially the lotus ; also 화 花, which also means pleasure, vice ; to spend, waste, profligate. 화 華 also means splendour, glory, ornate ; to decorate ; China.

화 化 To transform, metamorphose : (1) conversion by instruction, salvation into Buddhism ; (2) magic powers 통력 通力 of transformation, of which there are said to be fourteen mental and eight formal kinds. It also has the meaning of immediate appearance out of the void, or creation 무이홀기 無而忽起 ; and of giving alms, spending, digesting, melting, etc.

화 禍 Woe, calamity, misfortune.

화 話 Words, language, talk. 화칙 話則 Word-norm, the spoken words of the Buddha ; the norm of conduct.

화개 華蓋 A flowery umbrella, a canopy of flowers.

화객 火客 The monk who attends to the fire ; also 화반 火伴 ; 화전 火佃.

화갱 火坑 The fiery pit (of the five desires 오욕 五欲) ; also that of the three ill destinies — the hells, animals, hungry ghosts.

화경 化境 The region, condition, or environment of Buddha instruction or conversion ; similar to 화토 化土.

화계 火界 The realm of fire, one of the realms of the four elements 사대 四大, i.e. earth, water, fire, and wind. Cf. 화원 火院. 화계주 火界咒 A dhāraṇī of 부동존 不動尊 q.v. 화계정 火界定 Agni-dhātu-samādhi ; the meditation on the final destruction of the world by fire.

화공귀기 化功歸己 The merit of converting others becomes one's own (in increased insight and liberation) ; it is the third stage of merit of the T'ien-t'ai five stages of meditation and action 관행오품위 觀行五品位.

화광 火光 Fire-light, flame. 화광정 火光定 The flame dhyāna by which the body is self-immolated. 화광삼매 火光三昧 The flame samādhi, also styled the fourth dhyāna. 화광존 火光尊 idem 화천 火天.

화광 華光 Padmaprabha, Lotus-radiance, the name by which Śāriputra is to be known as a Buddha. 화광대제 華光大帝 The Chinese god of fire, Aśvakarṇa, see 아 阿, "mentioned in a list of 1,000 Buddhas" and who "is reported to have lived here in his first incarnation." [Eitel].

화교 化教 see 화행이교 化行二教.

화구 火狗 The fiery dogs — which vomit fire on sinners in hell.

화궁전 化宮殿 The magical palace, or, palace of joy, held in the fortieth left hand of Kuan-yin of the thousand hands ; the hand is styled 화궁전수 化宮殿手 or 보전수 寶殿手.

화니 化尼 The power of a Buddha, or bodhisattva, to be transformed into a nun.

화단 火壇 Fire altar, connected with homa or fire worship ; also 노단 爐壇.

화단 化壇 The altar of transformation, i.e. a crematorium.

화대 火大 The element fire, one of the 사대 四大 four elements.

화대 華臺 The lotus dais, seat, or throne.

화덕보살 華德菩薩 Padmaśrī, Lotus-brilliance Bodhisattva, tr. as Lotus-virtue, name of Śubha-vyūha, v. 묘 妙, when incarnated as a member of Śākyamuni's retinue.

화덕성군 火德星君 The ruler over the fire-star, Mars, whose tablet hangs in the south side of a temple and whose days of worship, to prevent conflagrations, are the fourth and eighteenth of each moon ; he is identified with the ancient emperor 염제 炎帝 Yen Ti.

화도 化道 The way of conversion, transformation, or development ; also 교도 敎道.

화도 化度 To convert and transport, or save.

화도 化導 To instruct and guide ; the 삼륜화도 三輪化導 or three sovereign powers for converting other are those of 신변 神變 supernatural transformation (i.e. physical 신 身) ; 기심 記心 memory or knowledge of all the thoughts of all beings (i.e. mental 의 意) ; and 교계 敎誡 teaching and warning (i.e. oral 구 口). 화도력 化導力 Power to instruct and guide, one of the 삼력 三力.

화도 火塗 or 火道 The fiery way, i.e. the destiny of the hot hells, one of the three evil destinies.

화두 火頭 A monastery cook. 화두금강 火頭金剛 One of the Ming Wang 명왕 明王 v. 오추슬마 烏芻瑟摩.

화두 話頭 Hwadu. A koan's "critical phrase" ; the "punch-line" of a koan. According to the folk etymology, the term literally means the "head of speech" but this is wrong ; 頭 is merely a grammatical particle. Cf. 활구 活句 & 사구 死句 q.v.

화라 火羅 Horā, hour, hours, time ; astrologically a horoscope ; said to be the country where 일행 一行 I-hsing studied astronomy.

화락천 化樂天 Nirmāṇarati, 낙변화천 樂變化天 the fifth of the six desire-heavens, 640,000 yojanas above Meru ; it is next above the Tuṣita, or fourth devaloka ; a day is equal to 800 human years ; life lasts for 8,000 years ; its inhabitants are eight yojanas in height, and light-emitting ; mutual smiling produces impregnation and children are born on the knees by metamorphosis, at birth equal in development to human children of twelve — hence the "joy-born heaven."

화령 火鈴 Fire-bell — in warning to be careful of fire.

화로 火爐 ; 화려 火鑪 The homa or fire altar of the esoterics.

화륜 火輪 Whirling fire, e.g. fire whirled in a circle, the whole circle seeming to be on fire, emblem of illusion ; a fire wheel. 화륜인 火輪印 A sign made by putting the doubled fists together and opening the index fingers to form the fire-sign, a triangle.

화리 化理 The law of phenomenal change — which never rests.

화만 華鬘 Kusuma-mālā, a wreath, or chaplet of flowers.

화목 華目 Eyes like the blue lotus, i.e. pure.

화미 化米 Rice obtained by monastic begging and the offering of exhortation or instruction, similarly 화탄 化炭 charcoal and 화다 化茶 tea ; sometimes used with larger connotation.

화반 火伴 The fire-tender in a monastic kitchen.

화방 華方 The flowery region, the south.

화범 華梵 China and India.

화법 化法 Instruction in the Buddhist principles, as 화의 化儀 is in practice. T'ien-t'ai in its 화법사교 化法四教 divides the Buddha's teaching during his lifetime into the four periods of 장 藏, 통 通, 별 別, and 원 圓 Piṭaka, Interrelated, Differentiated, and Complete, or All-embracing.

화법 火法 The homa or fire service of the esoterics.

화변 火辨 Citrabhānu, 질달라바나 質呾羅婆拏 described as one of the ten great writers of the Indian 법상종 法相宗 Dharmalakṣaṇa school, a contemporary and colleague of Vasubandhu ; but the description is doubtful.

화보 華報 Flower recompense, i.e. flowers to him who cultivates them, and fruit corresponding to the seed sown, i.e. retribution for good or evil living.

화보살 化菩薩 A Buddha or bodhisattva transformed into a (human) bodhisattva ; or a bodhisattva in various metamorphoses.

화분지옥 火焚地獄 The scorching hell, where sinners are burnt up.

화불 化佛 Nirmāṇabuddha, an incarnate, or metamorphosed Buddha ; Buddhas and bodhisattvas have universal and unlimited powers of appearance, v. 신통력 神通力.

화사 火舍 A kind of censer, made in two superimposed circles with a cover.

화사 火蛇 Fire-vomiting serpents in the hells.

화사법 火祠法 The directions for the fire sacrifices in the Atharvaveda, the fourth Veda ; the esoteric sect has also its 화법 火法 for magical purposes.

화산 華山 Mt. Hua in Shensi, one of the Five Sacred Mountains of China ; v. also 구화산 九華山.

화상 化相 The transformation form or body (in which the Buddha converts the living). 화상삼보 化相三寶 The nirmāṇakāya Buddha in the Triratna forms ; in Hīnayāna these are the human 16-foot Buddha, his dharma as revealed in the four axioms and twelve nidānas, and his saṅgha, or disciples, i.e. arhats and pratyeka-buddhas.

화색(신) 化色(身) A Buddha's or bodhisattva's metamorphoses of body, or incarnations at will.

화생 化生 Aupapādaka, or aupapāduka. Direct metamorphosis, or birth by transformation, one of the 사생 四生, by which existence in any required form is attained in an instant in full maturity. By this birth bodhisattvas residing in Tuṣita appear on earth. Dhyāni Buddhas and Avalokiteśvara are likewise called 화생 化生. It also means unconditional creation at the beginning of a kalpa. Bhūta 부다 部多 is also used with similar meaning. There are various kinds of 화생 化生, e.g. 불보살화생 佛菩薩化生 the transformation of a Buddha or bodhisattva, in any form at will, without gestation, or intermediary conditions ; 극락화생 極樂化生 birth in the happy land of Amitābha by transformation through the Lotus ; 법신화생 法身化生 the dharmakāya, or spiritual body, born or formed on a disciple's conversion.

화생삼매 火生三昧 A flame-emitting samādhi, the power to emit flames from the body for auto-holocaust, or other purposes. It is especially associated with 부동존 不動尊 q.v. and Shingon practice of the yoga which unites the devotee to him and his powers.

화성 火星 Aṅgāraka, 앙아라가 鴦哦囉迦 the planet Mars.

화성 化城 The magic, or illusion city, in the Lotus Sūtra ; it typifies temporary or incomplete nirvāṇa, i.e. the imperfect nirvāṇa of Hīnayāna.

화소 化疏 A subscription list, or book ; an offering burnt for ease of transmission to the spirit-realm.

화속 化屬 The converted followers — of a Buddha, or bodhisattva.

화속결연 化俗結緣 For the sake of converting the people.

화수 華手 The hands folded lotus-fashion.

화식 火食 Burnt offerings, as in the homa worship.

화신 化身 Nirmāṇakāya, 응(화)신 應(化)身 ; 변화신 變化身 The third characteristic or power of the Trikāya 삼신 三身, Buddha's metamorphosic body, which has power to assume any shape to propagate the Truth. Some interpret the term as connoting pan-Buddha, that all nature in its infinite variety is the phenomenal 불신 佛身 Buddha-body. A narrower interpretation is his appearance in human form expressed by 응신 應身, while 화신 化身 is used for his manifold other forms of appearances. 화생 化生 q.v. means direct "birth" by metamorphosis. It also means the incarnate avatāra of a deity. 화신팔상 化身八相 The eight forms of a Buddha from birth to nirvāṇa, v. 팔상 八相.

화신 火神 The gods of fire, stated as numbering forty-four in the Vedic pantheon, with Mahābrahmā as the first ; of these the Vairocana sūtra takes twelve, i.e. 대인다라 大因陀羅 ; 행만 行滿 ; 마로다 摩嚕多 ; 노혜다 盧醯多 ; 몰률나 沒嘌拏 ; 분노 忿怒 ; 사타라 闍吒羅 ; 흘쇄야 吃灑耶 ; 의생 意生 ; 갈라미 羯攞微 ; (11th unknown) ; 모하나 謨賀那. Cf. 화존 火尊 ; 화천 火天.

화심 化心 The mind in the transformation body of a Buddha or bodhisattva, which apprehends things in their reality.

화씨성 華氏城 Kusumapura, Puṣpapura ; the city of flowers, or of the palace of flowers, also known as Pāṭaliputra, the modern Patna. It was the residence of Aśoka, to whom the title of 화씨 華氏 is applied. He there convoked the third synod.

화야 火夜 Hāva ; to call, invoke ; also 하바 訶婆.

화엄 華嚴 Avataṁsa, a garland, a ring-shaped ornament, [M. W.] ; the flower-adorned, or a garland ; the name of the Hua-yen sūtra, and the Hua-yen (Jap. Kegon) school ; cf. 건 健. 화엄일승 華嚴一乘 The one Hua-yen yāna, or vehicle, for bringing all to Buddhahood. 화엄삼매 華嚴三昧 The Buddha-samādhi of an eternal spiritual realm from which all Buddha-activities are evolved. 화엄삼왕 華嚴三王 The three Hua-yen kings, Vairocana in the centre with Samantabhadra and Mañjuśrī left and right. 화엄종 華嚴宗 The Hua-yen (Kegon) school, whose foundation work is the Avataṁsaka-sūtra ; founded in China by 제심 두순 帝心杜順 Ti-hsin Tu-shun ; he died A.D. 640 and was followed by 운화 지엄 雲華智嚴 Yün-hua Chih-yen ; 현수 법장 賢首法藏 Hsien-shou Fa-tsang ; 청량 징관 淸涼澄觀 Ch'ing-liang Ch'êng-kuan ; 규봉 종밀 圭峯宗密 Kuei-fêng Tsung-mi, and other noted patriarchs of the sect ; its chief patron is Mañjuśrī. The school was imported into Japan early in the T'ang dynasty and flourished there. It held the doctrine of the 법성 法性 Dharma-nature, by which name it was also called. 화엄시 華嚴時 The first of the "five periods" as defined by T'ien-t'ai, according to which school this sūtra was delivered by Śākyamuni immediately after his enlightenment ; but accounts vary as to whether it was on the second or third seventh day ; all these claims are, however, devoid of evidence, the sūtra being a Mahāyāna creation. 화엄경 華嚴經 Avataṁsaka-sūtra, also 대방광불화엄경 大方廣佛

華嚴經. Three tr. have been made: (1) by Buddhabhadra, who arrived in China A.D. 406, in 60 chüan, known also as the 진경 晉經 Chin sūtra and 구경 舊經 the old sūtra ; (2) by Śikṣānanda, about A.D. 700, in 80 chüan, known also as the 당경 唐經 T'ang sūtra and 신경 新經 the new sūtra ; (3) by Prājña about A.D. 800, in 40 chüan. The treatises on this sūtra are very numerous, and the whole are known as the 화엄부 華嚴部 ; they include the 화엄음의 華嚴音義 dictionary of the Classic by 혜원 慧苑 Hui-yüan, about A.D. 700.

화엄사 華嚴寺 Hwa-eom-sa. A temple located in Hwangjeon-ri Masan-myeon Gurye-gun Jeollanam-do in Korea. The 19th parish headquarters of Korean Jogye Order.

화엄일승교분기원통초 華嚴一乘敎分記圓通抄 A masterpiece of 균여 均如 Gyun-yeo.

화엄일승법계도기 華嚴一乘法界圖記 A masterpiece of 의상 義湘 or 義相 Ui-sang.

화엄일승법계도원통기 華嚴一乘法界圖圓通記 A masterpiece of 균여 均如 Gyun-yeo.

화연 化緣 The cause of a Buddha's or bodhisattva's coming to the world, i.e. the transformation of the living ; also, a contribution to the needs of the community.

화염삼매 火燄三昧 A samādhi entered into by the Buddha, in which he emitted flames to overcome a poisonous dragon. Also 화광삼매 火光三昧 ; 화생삼매 火生三昧 q.v.

화예 華翳 Flowery films, motes, specks, *muscae volitantes*.

화완포가사 火浣布袈裟 An asbestos cassock ; also a non-inflammable robe said to be made of the hair of the 화서 火鼠 fire-rat.

화왕세계 華王世界 The world of the lotus-king, that of Vairocana.

화요 火曜 Mars, one of the nine luminaries, shown south of the Diamond hall in the Garbhadhātu.

화원 化源 The fount of conversion, or salvation, the beginning of the Buddha's teaching.

화원 火院 The "fire-court", a kind of contemplation, in which the devotee sees himself encircled by fire after circumambulating three times to the right while making the fire-sign. Also 화계 火界 ; 금강염 金剛炎.

화유 化誘 To convert and entice (into the way of truth).

화의 化儀 The rules or methods laid down by the Buddha for salvation ; T'ien-t'ai speaks of 화의 化儀 as transforming method, and 화법 化法 q.v. as transforming truth ; its 화의사교 化儀四敎 are four modes of conversion or enlightenment : 돈 頓 direct or sudden, 점 漸 gradual, 비밀 秘密 esoteric, and 부정 不定 variable.

화인 化人 A deva or Buddha transformed into human shape ; 화녀 化女 is the same in female form.

화인 火印 The fire sign, for which a triangle pointing upwards is used ; a triangular arrangement of fingers of the right hand with the left.

화일체처 火一切處 Universal conflagration — one of the ten universals, and one of the meditations on the final destruction of all things by fire.

화작 化作 To transform (into), create, make.

화장 火葬 Jhāpita, 다비 荼毘 ; 사유 闍維 cremation, the relics 사리 舍利 being buried.

화장 華藏 Lotus-treasury. 화장(세)계 華藏(世)界 The lotus-store, or lotus-world, the Pure Land of Vairocana, also the Pure Land of all Buddhas in their sambhogakāya, or enjoyment bodies. Above the wind or air circle is a sea of fragrant water, in which is the thousand-petal lotus with its infinite variety of worlds, hence the meaning is the Lotus which contains a store of myriads of worlds ; cf. the T'ang Hua-yen sūtra 8, 9, and 10 ; the 범망경 梵網經 ch. 1, etc. 화장팔엽 華藏八葉 The maṇḍala of the Garbhadhātu. 화장여극락 華藏與極樂 The Lotus-world and that of Perfect Joy (of Amitābha and others) ; they are the same.

화장 火帳 The kitchen account of the rice cooked and persons served.

화재 火災 The conflagration catastrophe, for world destruction, v. 삼재 三災.

화적 化迹 The traces or evidences of the Buddha's transforming teaching ; also 교적 敎迹.

화전 化前 In the Amitābha cult the term means before its first sūtra, the 관무량수경 觀無量壽經, just as 이전 爾前 in the Lotus School means "before the Lotus". 화전서 化前序 the preface to the 관경소 觀經疏 by 선도 善導 Shan-tao of the T'ang dynasty. 화전방편 化前方便 All the expedient, or partial, teaching suited to the conditions before the above Wu-liang-shou-ching.

화전 化轉 To transform, convert (form evil to good, delusion to deliverance).

화정 火淨 Purified, food made "clean" by fire, or cooking.

화정 火定 The fire dhyāna, v. 화생 火生.

화정산 火頂山 A peak near T'ien-t'ai, where the founder of that school overcame Māra.

화제이교 化制二敎 The twofold division of the Buddha's teaching into converting or enlightening and discipline, as made by the Vinaya School, v. 화행 化行.

화존 火尊 i.e. 화신 火神 q.v.

화종거사 火種居士 Brahmans, servers of the sacred fire.

화좌 華座 The lotus throne.

화주 火珠 Fire-pearl, or ruby ; the ball on top of a pagoda, see 수원 水圓.

화주 化主 The lord of transformation, or conversion, i.e. a Buddha ; also one who exhorts believers to give alms for worship ; also an almsgiver.

화지부 化地部 Mahīśāsaka, 마혜사사가부 磨醯奢娑迦部 ; 미희사사아 彌喜捨娑阿 ; 미사색부 彌娑塞部, 정지부 正地部 an offshoot from the 설일체유부 說一切有部 or Sarvāstivāda school, supposed to have been founded 300 years after the nirvāṇa. The name Mahīśāsaka is said to be that of a ruler who "converted his land" or people ; or 정지 正地 "rectified his land." The doctrines of the school are said to be similar to those of the 대중부 大衆部 Mahāsāṅghika ; and to have maintained, *inter alia*, the reality of the present, but not of the past and future ; also the doctrine of the void and the non-ego ; the production of taint 염 染 by the five 식 識 perceptions ; the theory of nine kinds of non-activity, and so on. It was also called 법무거래종 法無去來宗 the school which denied reality to past and future.

화차 火車 The fiery chariot (belonging to the hells) ; there is also the 화차지옥 火車地獄 hell of the fire-chariot, and the fire-pit with its fiery wheels ; the sufferer first freezes, then is tempted into the chariot which bursts into flames and he perishes in the fire pit, a process each sufferer repeats daily 90 kotis of times.

ㄱ ㄴ ㄷ ㄹ ㅁ ㅂ ㅅ ㅇ ㅈ ㅊ ㅋ ㅌ ㅍ ㅎ 찾아보기

화천 火天 The fire devas shown as the 12th group in the diamond court of the Garbhadhātu ; v. 화신 火神.

화천 華天 The Hua-yen and T'ien-t'ai Schools.

화첨 火㮇 Fire-tongs, made of wood, themselves burnt up before all brushwood is used up, a simile of a bodhisattva who so far forgot his vow to save all the living as to enter nirvāṇa before completing his work.

화취 火聚 Accumulated fires (of hell) ; accumulating one's own hell-fires ; the body as a heap of fire, i.e. to be feared ; the fires of angry passions. 화취선 火聚仙 This genius and his wife are shown above Vaiśramaṇa in the Garbhadhātu. 화취불정 火聚佛頂 ; 광취불정 光聚佛頂 ; 방광 放光 or 방광불정 放光佛頂 One of the five 불정 佛頂, i.e. one of the incarnations of Śākyamuni, whose Indian name is given as 제취라작갈라박리지 帝聚羅斫羯羅縛哩底 Tejorāśi-cakravartī, called by Shingon 신통금강 神通金剛 ; this incarnation is placed fourth on Śākyamuni's left in the Garbhadhātu.

화치 華齒 Puṣpadantī. Flowery or ornate teeth, name of a rākṣasī.

화타 化他 To save others. 화타수 化他壽 A Buddha's long or "eternal" life spent in saving others, implying his powers of unlimited salvation.

화탕 火湯 The hell of liquid fire.

화태 華胎 The lotus womb in which doubters and those of little virtue are detained in semi-bliss for 500 years before they can be born into the Pure Land by the opening of the lotus.

화택 火宅 The parable of the burning house ; one of the "seven parables" in the Lotus Sūtra 비유품 譬喩品, that of the burning house from which the owner tempts his heedless children by the device of the three kinds of carts — goat, deer, and bullock, especially a white-bullock cart, i.e. Mahāyāna. 화택승 火宅僧 Monks in a burning house, i.e. married monks.

화토 化土 One of the 삼토 三土 three kinds of lands, or realms ; it is any land or realm whose inhabitants are subject to reincarnation ; any land which a Buddha is converting, or one in which is the transformed body of a Buddha. These lands are of two kinds, pure like the Tuṣita heaven, and vile or unclean like this world. T'ien-t'ai defines the hua-t'u or the transformation realm of Amitābha as the Pure-land of the West, but other schools speak of hua-t'u as the realm on which depends the nirmāṇakāya, with varying definitions.

화판 火版 The "fire-board", or wooden plaque, hung in the kitchen, the striking of which warns the monks that the meal is ready.

화행(이교) 化行(二教) The two lines of teaching : i.e. in the elements, for conversion and admission, and 행교 行教 or 제교 制教 in the practices and moral duties especially for the Order, as represented in the Vinaya ; cf. 화제 化制.

화현 化現 Metamorphosis and manifestation ; the appearance or forms of a Buddha or bodhisattva for saving creatures may take any form required for that end.

화혈도 火血刀 The hells, animals, and hungry ghosts, i.e. the fiery, bloody, and knife-sharp destinies, the 삼악도 三惡道.

확 鑊 Caldron, rice pan. 확사 鑊沙 ; 오쇄 烏鎩 Ōsh, or Ūsh, "an ancient kingdom north of the Śītā, probably the present Ingachar" ; possibly Uch-Turfān or Yangishahr, 의내 依耐 or 영길사이 英吉沙爾. 확탕지옥 鑊湯地獄 The purgatory of caldrons of molten iron.

확확파 臛臛婆 The third of the cold hells, where the sinner's tongue is so cold that he can only utter the word Ho-ho-p'o or Apapa. Also 학학파 嚯嚯婆, 아파파 阿波波.

환 鐶 A metal ring ; a ring. 환천 鐶釧 Finger-rings and armlets.

환 槵 A species of Sapindus, or soap-berry tree, whose seeds 환자 槵子 are used for rosaries.

환 桓 A tree whose hard, black seeds are used for beads ; a pillar, post, tablet. 환인 桓因 Indra, abbrev. for 석제환인 釋提桓因.

환 幻 Māyā. Illusion, hallucination, a conjurer's trick, jugglery, i.e. one of the ten illustrations of unreality. 환인 幻人 or 환사 幻士 An illusionist, a conjurer. 환력 幻力 His powers. 환화 幻化 Illusion and transformation, or illusory transformation. 환구 幻垢 Illusory and defiled, i.e. body and mind are alike illusion and unclean. 환사 幻師 An illusionist, a conjurer. 환심 幻心 The illusion mind, or mind is unreal. 환감 幻惑 Illusory ; to delude. 환일왕 幻日王 Bālāditya, 파라아질다 婆羅阿迭多 the morning sun (lit. mock-sun) king, *circa* A.D. 191. 환 幻 probably should be 유 幼 : a king of Magadha, who fought and captured Mihirakula, the king of 책가 磔迦 Ceka, or the Hūnas, who was an opponent of Buddhism. 환유 幻有 Illusory existence. 환법 幻法 Conjuring tricks, illusion, methods of Bodhisattva transformation, 환상 幻相 Illusion, illusory appearance. 환자 幻者 The illusory ; anything that is an illusion ; all things, for they are illusion. 환신 幻身 The illusion-body, i.e. this body is not real but an illusion. 환야 幻野 The wilderness of illusion, i.e. mortal life. 환문 幻門 The ways or methods of illusion, or of bodhisattva transformation.

환 歡 Nanda. Pleased, glad. 환희 歡喜 Pleased, glad ; pleasure, gladness. 환희환 歡喜丸 ; 환희단 歡喜團 Joy-buns, a name for a kind of honey-cake. 환희광불 歡喜光佛 Buddha of joyful light, Amitābha. 환희국 歡喜國 ; 묘희국 妙喜國 Abhirati, the happy land, or paradise of Akṣobhya, east of our universe. 환희원 歡喜苑 ; 환락원 歡樂園 ; 희림원 喜林苑 Nandana-vana. Garden of joy ; one of the four gardens of Indra's paradise, north of his central city. 환희지 歡喜地 Pramuditā. The bodhisattva's stage of joy, the first of his ten stages (bhūmi). 환희천 歡喜天 ; 대성환희천 大聖歡喜天 ; (대)성천 (大)聖天 The joyful devas, or devas of pleasure, 'represented as two figures embracing each other, with elephants' heads and human bodies ; the two embracing figures are interpreted as Gaṇeśa (the eldest son of Śiva) and an incarnation of Kuan-yin ; the elephant-head represents Gaṇeśa ; the origin is older than the Kuan-yin idea and seems to be a derivation from the Śivaitic linga-worship. 환희일 歡喜日 The happy day of the Buddha, and of the order, i.e. that ending the "retreat," 15th day of the 7th (or 8th) moon ; also every 15th day of the month. 환희회 歡喜會 The festival of All Souls, v. 우 盂.

환 喚 To call, summon. 환종 喚鐘 ; 반종 半鐘 or 飯鐘 The dinner bell or gong.

환 還 To return ; repay ; still, yet. 환년약 還年藥 A drug to return the year and restore one's youth. 환속 還俗 To return to lay life, leave the monastic order. 환상 還相 To return to the world, form the Pure Land, to save its people ; i.e. one of the forms of 회향 廻向 q.v. 환멸 還滅 To return to nirvāṇa and escape from the backward flow to transmigration. 환원 還源 To return to the source, i.e. abandon illusion and turn to enlightenment. 환생 還生 To return to life ; to be reborn in this world ; to be reborn form the Hīnayāna nirvāṇa in order to be able to attain to Mahāyāna Buddhahood ; also, restoration to the order, after repentance for sin. 환례 還禮 ; 환배 還拜 ; 환향 還香 Return of courtesy, of a salute, of incense offered, etc. 환문 還門 One of the six 묘문 妙門, i.e. to realize by introspection that the thinker, or introspecting agent, is unreal.

환향 丸香 Incense balls made of various kinds of ingredients ; typifying the aggregation of mortal suffering, and its destruction by the fires of wisdom.

활 闊 Broad, wide, spacious ; well-off, liberal. 활실다 闊悉多 Khusta, "a district of ancient Tukhara, probably the region south of Talikhan, Lat. 36° 42 N., Long. 69° 25 E." [Eitel]. But it may be Khost in Afghanistan, south-west of Peshawar.

활 活 Jīva, jīvaka ; alive, living, lively, revive, movable. 활국 活國 Ghūr, or Ghori, name of an ancient country in Turkestan, which Eitel gives as Lat. 35° 41 N., Long. 68° 59 E., mentioned in Hsüan-tsang's *Records of Western Countries*, 12. 활불 活佛 A living Buddha, i.e. a reincarnation Buddha, e.g. Hutuktu, Dalai Lama, etc. 활아자 活兒子 A name for the bodhi-tree. 활명 活命 Life, living ; to revive.

활 豁 Open, clear ; intelligent. 활단 豁旦 Kustana ; Khoten ; v. 우 于, 구 瞿.

활구 活句 Living phrase. A Seon hwadu that does not leave the practitioner anything to grasp. An antonym of 사구 死句 q.v.

황 荒 Wild, waste ; wilds ; empty ; famine ; reckless ; to nullify ; an angry appearance. 황야 荒野, 황교 荒郊 A Wilderness, uncultivated. 황공 荒空 Empty, deserted.

황 黃 Yellow. 황로 黃壚 A grave, idem 황답 黃沓. 황번 黃幡 Yellow paper streamers hung a grave. 황교 黃敎 ; 황모교 黃帽敎 The yellow sect of Lamaism, founded in 1417 by 종객파 宗喀巴 Tsoṅ-kha-pa, Sumatikīrti, who overthrew the decadent sect, which wears red robes, and established the sect that wears yellow, and which at first was noted for the austere life of the monks ; it is found chiefly in Tibet, Mongolia, and Ili. 황혼 黃昏 Evening. 황양목선 黃楊木禪 The yellow poplar meditation. The yellow poplar grows slowly, and in years with intercalary months is supposed to recede in growth ; hence the term refers to the backwardness, or decline of stupid disciples. 황벽 黃檗 Huang-po, *Phallodendron amurense*, a tree which gave its name to a monastery in Fukien, and to a sect founded by 희운 希運 Hsi-yün, its noted abbot of the T'ang dynasty. 황천 黃泉 The yellow springs, the shades. 황엽 黃葉 Yellow willow leaves, resembling gold, given to children to stop their crying ; the evanescent joys of the heavens offered by Buddha to curb evil. 황의 黃衣 Yellow robes (of the monks), but as yellow is a prime colour and therefore unlawful, the garments are dyed a mixture, yellowish-grey. 황금 黃金 The yellow metal, i.e. gold. 황금택 黃金宅 Golden abode, i.e. a monastery, so called after the Jetavana vihāra, for whose purchase the site was "covered with gold." 황문 黃門 Eunuchs, paṇḍakas, v. 반 般 10. 황면 黃面 The yellow-faced Lao Tzŭ, i.e. Buddha, because his images are gold-colour. 황룡사 黃龍寺 Huang-lung, the Yellow Dragon monastery in Kiangsi after which 혜남 慧南 Hui-nan was called.

회 回 ; 회 囘 To turn, revolve, return. 회호 回互 Interchange, intermutation. 회광반조 回光返照 To turn the light inwards on oneself, concern oneself with one's own duty. 회향 回向 ; 회향 廻向 Pariṇāmanā. To turn towards ; to turn something from one person or thing to another ; transference (of merit) ; the term is intp. by 전취 轉趣 turn towards ; it is used for works of supererogation, or rather, it means the bestowing on another, or others, of merits acquired by oneself, especially the merits acquired by a bodhisattva or Buddha for the salvation of all, e.g. the bestowing of his merits by Amitābha on all the living. There are other kinds, such as the turning of acquired merit to attain further progress in bodhi, or nirvāṇa. One definition is 회사향리 回事向理 to turn (from) practice to theory ; 회자향타 回自向他 from oneself to another ; 회인향과 回因向果 from cause to effect. Other definitions include 회세이향출세 回世而向出世 to turn from this world to what is beyond this world, from the worldly to the unworldly. 회소향대 回小向大 To turn from Hīnayāna to Mahāyāna. 회심 回心 ; 회심참회 回心懺悔 To turn the mind from evil to good, to repent. 회심계 回心戒 Commandments bestowed on the converted, or repentant. 회오 回悟 To turn and apprehend ; be converted. 회례 回禮 To return, or acknowledge a courtesy or gift. 회재 回財 ; 회제 回祭 Payment by a donor of sums already expended at his request by a monastery. 회취 回趣 To turn from other things to Buddhism.

회 灰 Ash ; lime ; lot or fiery as ashes. 회인 灰人 An image of ashes or lime made and worshipped seven times a day by a woman whose marriage is hindered by unpropitious circumstances. 회산주부 灰山住部 Sect of the Limestone hill dwellers, one of the twenty Hīnayāna schools ; the Gokulikas, v. 계 鷄, 회사 灰沙 Ascetics who cover themselves with ashes, or burn their flesh. 회하 灰河 A river of lava or fire, reducing all to ashes. 회신멸지 灰身滅智 Destruction of the body and annihilation of the mind — for the attainment of nirvāṇa. 회두토면 灰頭土面 To put ashes on the head and dust on the face.

회 會 Meet, assemble, collect, associate, unite ; assembly, company ; communicate ; comprehend, skilled in, can, will ; a time, moment. 회삼귀일 會三歸一 To unite the three vehicles in one, as in the Lotus sūtra. 회하 會下 The lower, or junior members of an assembly, or company. 회득 會得 To comprehend, understand ; to meet with. 회식 會式 The manners, customs, or rules of an assembly, or community. 회역 會繹 To assemble and explain the meaning ; to comprehend and explain. 회중 會衆 To assemble the community, or company ; to meet all. 회통 會通 To compare and adjust ; compound ; bring into agreement ; solve and unify conflicting ideas.

회 悔 Regret, repent. 회참법 悔懺法 The rules for repentance and confession. 회과 悔過 To repent of error.

회 回 Return, turn back, a turn. 회기 回忌 The days on which the day of death is remembered. 회가솔탑파 回駕窣塔婆 Nivartana-stūpa, erected on the spot where Śākyamuni sent back his horse after quitting home.

회 廻 Return, turn back, turn to, give back ; a turn. 회대입일 廻大入一 To turn to and enter One Vehicle of Mahāyāna. 회심 廻心 To turn the mind or heart towards (Mahāyāna). 회향 廻向 The goal or direction of any discipline such as that of bodhisattva, Buddha, etc. ; to devote one's merits to the salvation of others ; works of supererogation ; 회시 廻施 is similar ; cf. 회향 回向 ; 십회향 十廻向 ; 오회 五悔 ; 삼심 三心 ; 구방편 九方便.

회 繪 Silk pongee ; an arrow, dart. 회개 繪蓋 A large embroidered canopy of silk.

회 晦 The last day of the moon ; night ; dark, obscure ; unlucky. 혼회 昏晦 Obscure, dark.

회 懷 To carry in the bosom, mind, or heart ; to embrace, cherish ; the bosom. 회토 懷兎 Śaśa-dhara, the i.e. the hare-bearer, or in Chinese the hare-embracer, moon. 회령 懷靈 Spirit-enfolders, i.e. all conscious beings.

회 廻 v. 회 回 6.

회 迴 v. 회 廻.

회이 偽彝 Uighurs, 회호 偽胡 ; 회골 回鶻 ; 고차 高車 ; 고창 高昌. A branch of the Turks first heard of in the seventh century in the Orkhon district where they remained until A.D. 840, when they were defeated and driven out by the Kirghiz ; one group went to Kansu, where they remained until about 1020 ; another group founded a kingdom in the Turfān country which survived until Mongol times. They had an alphabet which was copied from the Soghdian. Chingis Khan adopted it for writing Mongolian. A.D. 1294 the whole Buddhist canon was translated into Uighur.

획 獲 To catch, seize, obtain, recover, 획득 獲得.

횡 橫 A crossbar, crosswise, athwart, across, per-verse, arrogant ; unexpected, i.e. lucky or unlucky. 횡출 橫出 By discipline to attain to temporary nirvāṇa in contrast with 횡초 橫超 happy salvation to Amitābha's paradise through trust in him. 횡절 橫截 To thwart, intercept, cut off, e.g. to end reincarnation and enter Paradise. 횡수 橫竪 Crosswise and upright, to lay across or to stand upright. 횡종 橫縱 Across and direct, crosswise and lengthwise.

효 曉 Dawn, shining, clear ; to know, to make known. 효료 曉了 To make clear. 효공 曉公, i.e. 원효 元曉 Won-hyo(C. Yüan-hsiao), the author-monk. 효고 曉鼓 The reveillé drum at dawn.

효 孝 Filial, obedient. 효자 孝子 A filial son. 효복 孝服 Mourning clothes for parents. 효순 孝順 Obedient.

후 後 After, behind, later, posterior. 후세 後世 The life after this ; later generations or ages. 후오(백년) 後五(百年) or 후오(백세) 後五(百歲) The pratirūpaka 상법 象法 or 像法 symbol, formal, or image period, to begin 500 years after the Nirvāṇa ; also the last of the periods of 500 years when strife would prevail. 후광 後光 The halo behind an image. 후패 後唄 The third of the three chants in praise of Buddha. 후보 後報 The retribution received in further incarnation (for the deeds done in this life). 후야 後夜 The third division of the night. 후득지 後得智 ; 분별지 分別智 Detailed, or specific, knowledge or wisdom succeeding upon or arising from 근본지 根本智 fundamental knowledge. 후유 後有 Future karma ; the person in the subsequent incarnation ; also, the final incarnation of the arhat, or bodhisattva. 후법 後法 ; 상법 像法 The latter, or symbol, age of Buddhism ; see above. 후생 後生 The after condition of rebirth ; later born ; youth. 후설 後說 Spoken later, or after ; the predicate of the major premise of a syllogism. 후신 後身 The body or person in the next stage of transmigration.

후 猴 The monkey ; 3-5 p.m. 미후 獼猴 The larger monkey, mischievous, restless, like the passions.

훈 薰 A fragrant plant which expels noxious influences ; vāsanā, perfume, fumigate, becloud. 훈습 薰習 Fumigation, influence, "perfuming" ; defiling, the inter-perfuming of bhūtatathatā, v. 진여 眞如, of ignorance (avidyā), of the empirical mind, and of the empirical world. 훈육향 薰陸香 Kunduruka, "the resin of the plant *Boswellia thurifera*." [M. W.]

훈 葷 Strongly smelling vegetables, e.g. onions, garlic, leeks, etc., forbidden to Buddhist vegetarians ; any non-vegetarian food. 훈신 葷辛 Strong or peppery vegetables, or foods. 훈주 葷酒 Non-vegetarian foods and wine.

훈 熏 To smoke, fumigate, cense, perfume, exhale ; fog, becloud. 훈습 熏習 To fumigate, perfume, i.e. the influence of unenlightenment, ignorance, or blind fate, on the unconditioned producing the conditioned, v. 훈 薰.

훈 訓 To teach. 교훈 敎訓 ; 훈회 訓誨 To teach, instruct.

훼 毁 To break down, destroy, abolish, defame. 훼자 毁呰 To defame, vilify. 훼석 毁釋 To slander the Buddha or Buddhism.

휴 休 Desist, give up ; resign ; divorce ; blessing, favour. 휴도 休屠 Lit. "Desist from butchering," said to be the earliest Han term for 부도 浮屠 ; 불도 佛圖, etc., Buddha. The 한무고사 漢武故事 says that the King of Vaiśālī 비사 毘邪 killed King 휴도 休屠 (or the non-butchering kings), took his golden gods, over 10 feet in height, and put them in the 감천궁 甘泉宮 Sweet-spring palace ; they required no sacrifices of bulls or rams, but only worship of incense, so the king ordered that they should be served after their national method.

휴 鵂 Ulūka, an owl. 휴류 鵂鶹 Ulūka, i.e. Kaṇāda, a celebrated philosopher, said to have lived "800 years" before Śākyamuni.

휴정 休靜 Cheong-heo Hyu-jeong(1520-1604). A monk of the Joseon dynasty in Korea. He is also called 서산 대사 西山大師. He was the master of 유정 惟政 and rendered distinguished services in Japanese invasion(1592-1598). He wrote 선가귀감 禪家龜鑑 and led hundreds of disciples.

흉 胸 The breast. 흉자 胸字 The svastika on Buddha's breast, one of the thirty-two marks. 흉행 胸行 Creatures that crawl on their bellies, like snakes.

흑 黑 Kāla ; kṛṣṇa ; black ; dark. 흑분 黑分 ; 흑월 黑月 Kṛṣṇapakṣa, the darkening, or latter half of the month, the period of the waning moon. 흑야신 黑夜神 Kālarātri, also 흑야천 黑夜天 ; 흑암천 黑闇天 ; 암야천 闇夜天 ; one of the three queens of Yama, who controls midnight. 흑천 黑天 Mahākāla, the black deva, a title of Śiva, the fierce Ṛudra, a black or dark-blue deity with eight arms and three eyes. 흑업 黑業 Black karma, or evil deeds, which produce like karmaic results. 흑칠통 黑漆桶 Black varnish tub, blank ignorance. 흑백 黑白 Black and white, evil and good ; also the two halves of the month, the waning and waxing moon. 흑승 黑繩 Kālasūtra, the black-rope or black-bonds hell. 흑원 黑蚖 The black adder, or venomous snake, i.e. kleśa, passion, or illusion. 흑의 黑衣 ; 흑가 黑袈 Black, or dark monastic garments. 흑암 黑闇 Black, dark, secluded, shut off ; in darkness, ignorant. 흑풍 黑風 Black wind, i.e. a dark storm. 흑치 黑齒 Maṭutacaṇḍī, black teeth, name of one of the rākṣasī.

흔 忻 Delight, joy.

흔 欣 Joyful, elated, elevated. 흔구 欣求 To seek gladly. 흔계 欣界 The joyful realm (of saints and sages).

흘 仡 Strong, valiant ; suddenly. 흘나 仡那 ; 선마 繕摩 Jāuman, 생 生 Jāti, birth, production ; rebirth as man, animal, etc. ; life, position assigned by birth ; race, being ; the four methods of birth are egg, womb, water, and transformation.

흘 紇 Tassels ; the Uigur tribe ; a knot. 흘리타야 紇利陀耶 ; 흘리구 紇利俱 ; 흘리타야 紇哩陀耶 or 흘리내야 紇哩乃耶 or 흘리나야 紇哩娜耶 ; 흘리타야 訖利馱耶 ; 흘리타 釳利陀 ; 한율타 汗栗馱 ; 간율대 肝栗大 Hṛdaya, the heart, the mind ; some forms are applied to the physical heart, others somewhat indiscriminately to the tathāgata-heart, or the true, natural, innocent heart ; 흘리(구) 紇哩(俱) or 紇利(俱) ; 힐리 纈利 Hrīḥ is a germ-word of Amitābha and Kuan-yin 흘차달라 紇差怛羅 Kṣetra, a land, country, especially a Buddha-realm, cf. 찰 刹. 흘로실니 紇露悉泥 Hrosminkan or Semenghān, an ancient kingdom near Khulm and Kunduz. "Lat. 35° 40 N., Long. 68° 22 E." [Eitel].

흘 吃 To eat ; to stutter. 흘률다 吃栗多 Kṛtyā ; a 천인 賤人 low or common fellow.

흘 訖 To finish, end, stop, to reach (an end) ; until ; entirely ; translit. *k*. 흘리다 訖利多 Kṛta, Kṛtya, v. 길 吉 ; a slave, serf, bought or hired worker. 흘리다왕 訖利多王 King Kṛta of Kashmir, whose descendants were opposed to Buddhism ; they were dethroned by Kaniṣka, who restored Buddhism ; but later the royal line regained the throne and drove out the Buddhist monks. 흘리슬나 訖里瑟拏 Kṛṣṇa, black, dark, dark blue ; Krishna, the hero-god of India, "with Buddhists he is chief of the black demons, who are enemies of Buddha and the white demons." [M. W.]

흠 吽 or 䛘 Translit. for *Hūṁ*, which is interpreted as the bodhi, or omniscience, of all Buddhas. 흠흠 吽吽 The lowing of oxen. 흠가라신 吽迦囉身 Hūṁkāra, P'u-hsien 보현 普賢 Samantabhadra in his minatory aspect against demons.

흠 欽 Imperial ; to respect, reverence. 흠바라 欽婆羅 Kambala, a woollen or hair mantle, v. 감 敢 12.

흠 欠 To owe ; debt ; deficient ; to bend, bow, yawn, etc. ; the Sanskrit sign 𑖏 said to imply 대공불가득 大空不可得 space, great and unattainable or immeasurable.

흡 吸 To suck up, inhale ; 호흡 呼吸 exhale and inhale.

흥 興 Abhyudaya. Rise, begin ; prosper ; elated. 흥세 興世 The raising, or beginning of the salvation, of the world, i.e. the birth of Buddha. 흥거 興渠 ; 흥구 興舊 ; 흥의 興宜 ; 형구 刑具 Hiṅgu. Asafoetida, 아위 阿魏 ; there are other interpretations. 흥성 興盛 Prosper, successful. 흥행 興行 Prospering and progressing.

희 戲 Khelā, krīḍā. Play, sport, take one's pleasure ; theatricals, which are forbidden to a monk or nun. 희망(염)천 戲忘(念)天 One of the six devalokas of the desire-heavens, where amusement and laughter cause forgetfulness of the true and right. 희론 戲論 Prapañca. Sophistry ; meaningless argument ; frivolous or unreal discourse.

희 熙 Light, bright, splendid, prosperous. 희련 熙連 The river Hiraṇyavatī, see 시 尸.

희 嬉 Play, pleasure. 희희 嬉戲 To play, perform.

희 喜 Prīti ; ānanda. Joy ; glad ; delighted, rejoice ; to like. 희수 喜受 The sensation, or receptivity, of joy ; to receive with pleasure. 희인 喜忍 The "patience" of joy, achieved on beholding by faith Amitābha and his Pure Land ; one of the 삼인 三忍. 희열 喜悅 ; 희환 喜歡 ; 희락 喜樂 Pleased, delighted. 희사 喜捨 Joyful giving. 희림원 喜林苑 Joy-grove garden, a name for Indra's garden or paradise. 희견 喜見 Priyadarśana. Joyful to see, beautiful, name of a kalpa. 희견성 喜見城 Sudarśana, the city beautiful, the chief city, or capital, of the thirty-three Indra-heavens ; also 선견성 善見城. 희견천 喜見天 The Trayastriṁśāḥ, or thirty-three devas or gods of Indra's heaven, on the summit of Meru. 희견보살 喜見菩薩 The Bodhisattva Beautiful, an incarnation of 약왕 藥王. 희각지 喜覺支 The third bodhyaṅga, the stage of joy on attaining the truth.

희 希 Rare, seldom, few ; to hope for. 희기 希奇 Rare and extraordinary. 희천시 希天施 ; 희구시 希求施 Giving in hope of heaven, or bliss ; one of the 팔종보시 八種布施. 희유 希有 Rare, extraordinary, uncommon, few. 희유인 希有人 There are few, a sad exclamation, indicating that those who accept Buddha's teaching are few, or that those who do evil and repent, or give favours and remember favours, etc., are few. 희법 希法 Adbhuta-dharma ; supernatural things, prodigies, miracles, a section of the twelve classical books. 희사귀 希祀鬼 Ghosts that hope for sacrificial offerings (from their descendants). 희련하 希連河 ; 희련선 希連禪 The river Nairañjanā, v. 니 尼. 희린음의 希麟音義 The dictionary compiled by Hsi-lin of the T'ang dynasty, supplementing the 혜림음의 慧琳音義 Hui-lin-yin-i. Sound and meaning accord with Hui-lin, and terms used in translations made subsequent to that work are added.

희랄나벌지 呬剌拏伐底 v. 아시다벌지 阿恃多伐底 Hiraṇyavatī, Hiraṇya, Ajitavatī, the river near which Śākyamuni entered into Nirvāṇa ; the Gunduck (Gandak), flowing south of Kuśinagara city.

희마달라 呬摩呾羅 Himatala 설산하 雪山下. "An ancient kingdom ruled in A.D. 43 by a descendant of the Śākya family. Probably the region south of Kundoot and Issar north of Hindukush near the principal source of the Oxus." [Eitel]. 서역기 西域記 3.

힐 黠 Smart, clever, intelligent. 힐혜 黠慧 Worldly wisdom, cleverness, intelligence.

찾아보기

(1)
1,200 507
10,000,000 55
108 177
108 beads 177
108 kleśa 502

(2)
250 481

(5)
500 416
500 yojanas 416

(7)
700 disciples 584
72 586
75 585

(8)
84,000 604
84,000 kalpas 105
84,000 stūpas 604

(A)
A 379
a-lu-lu 376
A-p'an 379
a-sa-va 380
A-va-ra-ha-kha 379
A-vaṁ-raṁ-haṁ-khaṁ 379
A-vi-ra-hūm-kham 380
ababa 2, 386, 610
abbot 173, 298, 299, 542
abha 385
abhaya 154, 269
abhayadāna 341
Abhayagiri 154, 375, 379
Abhayagiri-vāsinaḥ 299, 591
abhayandada 341
abhayapradāna 154
Abhayaṁkara 385
Abhicāra 380
abhicāraka 380, 429, 622, 634
Abhidharma 15, 23, 88, 98, 142, 227, 243, 277, 324, 342, 364, 367, 380, 416, 419, 519, 523, 540, 602, 633
  philosophy 6
Abhidharma of Piṭaka School 51
Abhidharma sect 88
Abhidharma-jñāna-prasthāna-śāstra 6
Abhidharma-kośa 51, 191, 287, 316, 485, 572, 577, 585, 625
  心識, the mind and cognition 354
Abhidharma-kośa school 456
Abhidharma-kośa-śāstra 51, 380, 540
Abhidharma-mahāvibhāṣā-śāstra 416
Abhidharma-piṭaka 122, 129, 380, 433, 562, 624, 633
  分別 209
Abhidharma-prakaraṇa-pāda śāstra 179
Abhidharmāmṛta śāstra 51
abhidheya 473
Abhidhāna 395
Abhijit 380, 485
abhijñā 123, 468, 569, 570
abhimukham 380
Abhimukhī 369, 380
abhimukti 380
abhimāna 377
abhiniveśa 562
Abhirati 149, 205, 328, 383, 385, 643
abhisamaya 630
Abhisaṁbodha 380
Abhisaṁbuddha 380, 548
abhiṣecana 37, 308
abhiṣecana baptisms 427
abhiṣeka 372
abhyudaya 648
Abhyudgata-rāja 89
abhāva 231
Abode of Treasures 157
abrahmacariyā-veramaṇī 356
Abrahmacariyād vairamaṇī, 220
abrahmacarya 246
Absolute 201, 292, 500, 505
Acacia sirisa 343
acacia sirisa 621
Acala 55, 205, 360, 385
Acalacetā 205
Acalā 357, 369
acchāvāka 321
accumulate 274
accumulation
  samudaya, the second of the four axioms 31
Acesines of Alexander 522
acintya 206, 385
acintya-jñāna 206
acintyadhātu 207
action 222
activity 466
adamantine 165
Adam's Peak 79
adattādāna 219, 246
adbhuta 69, 159, 165, 389, 620
adbhuta-dharma 50, 364, 380, 648
Adbhuta-dharma-paryāya 159
add 1
adhara 618
adhigamāvabodha 548
adhimukti 346, 380, 384
adhimāna 382
adhipati-phala 476, 547
adhipati-pratyaya 320
Adhiṣṭhāna 1
Adhyavakīla 225
adhyātma 415
Adhyātma vidyā 76
adinnādāna-veramaṇī 223, 356
adultery 220
advaya 220
adze 61
aeon 17

Afghanistan 25, 379, 620, 644
agada 2, 373, 385
Agadaṁ 373
Agallochum 164, 373
agaru 373, 589
Agastya 373
agate 127
age
old age, 丘井 44
世, 1,000th part of a kalpa 318
aggregation of suffering 274
aggregations 286
agha 373, 387
aghana(m) 373
Aghaniṣṭha 301
Agni 374, 385, 387, 412, 436, 510
agni 374
Agni-dhātu-samādhi 636
Agnidatta 374
agreeable 11
aguru 373, 387, 589
ahaha 46, 386, 610
Ahalim 373
Ahaloth 373
Ahiṁsā 223
Aho 386
ahorātra 143
ahrīka 155
Ahu 386
ahūṁ 386
aicchantika 276
aikāgrya 503
ailments 246, 276
Aindrī 583
air 552
Airāvata 479, 496
Airāvatī 479
Airāvaṇa 391, 479, 496
aiśvarikas 381
aiṇeya(s) 478, 496
aiṇeyajaṅgha 478
Ajiravatī 383, 384, 607
Ajita 149, 152, 160, 360, 374, 383, 384
Ajita-keśakambala 436, 463
Ajita-keśakambali 374
Ajitavatī 342, 377, 648
ajitaṁjaya 381
ajñānakarmatṛṣṇā 150
Ajātaśatru 22, 48, 159, 233, 234, 341, 381, 382, 384, 415, 452, 580
Ajātaśatru-kaukṛitya-vinodana 159
Akaniṣṭha 250, 301, 373, 426, 458, 476
akiñcanyāyatana 152
akiñcanāyatana 152
Akni 412
Aksu 435
akṣa 387
akṣamālā 385
Akṣapāda 144, 496
Akṣapāda Gautama 538
akṣara 73, 387, 514
Akṣaya 393
Akṣayamati 385
akṣobha 149
Akṣobhya 62, 63, 64, 105, 142, 146, 149, 157, 205, 243, 378, 383, 385, 418, 424, 431, 544, 546, 556, 562, 567, 643
four regions 246
大圓鏡智 259
Akṣobhya-tathāgatasya-vyūha 205
Akṣobhya's retinue 64
Akṣobhya's three forms 431
Alabhya 211
Alakavatī 385
alakṣaṇa-buddha 151
Alaṁkāraka 519
alchemy, Taoist treatises on, 仙經 308
alcoholic liquor 542
all 175
All Buddhas 509
All things 508
Allahabad 15, 42, 52, 171
almsgiver 341
almsgiving 198, 357, 416
almsman, 비구 比丘 225
almswoman, 비구니 比丘尼 225
Alni 377
aloes 434
altruistic 515
alātacakra 124
amala 52, 148, 282, 377, 390, 574
amala-vijñāna 430, 559, 575
amalā 390
amaranth 48
Amarāvatī 107, 216, 594
Ambapālī 389
Ambarīṣa 390
ambrosia 11, 372, 390, 453, 569
ambrosia king 57
ambrosia-rice 11
ambrosial drum 11
ambrosial truth 11
ambā 377
Amen 390
Amida 38, 511, 561
Amida sūtra 89
Amita 149, 378
Amita Buddha 378
Amitābha 11, 38, 39, 41, 48, 53, 54, 56, 62, 68, 94, 96, 99, 101, 105, 119, 141, 142, 149, 152, 153, 156, 161, 190, 201, 205, 212, 215, 243, 275, 277, 278, 280, 283, 287, 289, 315, 348, 355, 357, 363, 364, 368, 378, 400, 410, 418, 427, 430, 434, 450, 479, 480, 484, 489, 492, 493, 498, 500, 501, 503, 505, 509, 539, 540, 544, 586, 589, 604, 607, 619, 643, 644
a sharp sword 125
four regions 246
guardians of, 466
praises of, proclaimed by the Buddhas of the six directions 462
seventh of the forty-eight vows 570
the western heavens 304
vow that all in his realm shall have beautiful clothing 472
Western Pure Land 305
他力念佛 591
妙觀察智 259
Amitābha Buddha 547
Amitābha cult 360, 408

Amitābha group 278
Amitābha School 221, 298
Amitābha-lotus 367
Amitābha's forty-eight vows 216, 635
Amitābha's heaven 410
Amitābha's name 176, 500
Amitābha's Paradise 358
Amitābha's three forms 431
Amitābha's vow 202, 217, 285, 500
Amitāyus 38, 283, 378
Amitāyus sūtra 149, 378
Amlikā 390
Amogha 89, 119, 213, 377, 378, 443, 493, 555, 570, 632
Amogha Tripiṭaka 213
Amoghadarśin 213
Amoghapāśa 213, 377
Amoghasiddhi 62, 64, 142, 205, 213, 243, 418, 424, 430, 431, 544
  four regions 246
  three forms 431
  成所作智 259
Amoghavajra 65, 90, 213, 233, 377, 560
Amoghāṅkuśa 213
Amritsar 237
Amroudh 31
Amūḍha-vinaya 583
Amṛta 11, 57, 378
amṛta 11, 372, 379
Amṛtakuṇḍalin 11
amṛtakuṇḍalin 390
Amṛtodana 11, 170, 256, 375, 379
An Fa-ch'in 388
An Shih-kao 56, 257, 388, 424, 609
An Ti 271
An-ch'ing 388
An-hsüan 388
An-hui 502
An-lu Fu 434
Anabhraka 250, 301, 370
ananta 149, 150
Anantacāritra 241
Anantamati 149
anantanirdeśapratiṣṭhāna samādhi 149
Anavadata Lake 235
Anavanāmita-vaijayanta 263
anavanāmita-vaijayanta 296
Anavatapta 86, 153, 154, 165, 235, 314, 375, 600, 621, 625
  four rivers 261
ancient 28
Andarab 388
Andhra 194, 384, 388
Andromeda 170
andūka 389
anger 276
Angkor 437
Anhui 56, 555
anicchantika 385
Anila 365
anilambha 153
anima 634
Animal-realm 183
animitta 151
animus 634
Anirodha 216
Anirodhānutpāda 216
Aniruddha 17, 73, 357, 374, 375
anitya 151, 230, 273
aniyata 207, 481
Anlin 388
Anna 389
annihilation 81
antara-kalpa 18, 193, 322
antaravāsaka 77, 287, 300, 389, 462
antargrāha 410
Antarikṣa 438
antarvāsas 389, 472
antarā-bhava 286, 545, 589
antarātman 76
antaśas 77
antecedent 446
antique 28
Anu Kuan-yin 375
Anubodhi 375
Anuccaśāyanāmahāśāyana 208
anumoda 374
anupadhiśeṣa 153
Anupalabhya 211
Anupama 385
Anupūrva-nirodha 80
Anuruddha 11, 375, 379
Anurādhapura 132, 375, 379
Anurādhā 374, 485
Anutpatti 217
anutpāda 217
anuttara 151, 371
anuttara-samyak-sambodhi 151, 221, 273, 375
Anuṣṭubh 375
Anuṣṭubh-chandas 374
Anvāgati 78
Anāgamana-nirgama 215
Anāgata 159
anāgāmin 73, 98, 215, 222, 223, 303, 332, 368, 369, 374, 428, 576
  four stages 242
  四向 261
  四部 248
anāgāmin-phala
  四果 239
anājñātamājñāsyāmīndriya 485
anāsrava 149, 374
Anātha 374
Anāthapiṇḍada 232, 272, 322, 386
Anāthapiṇḍika 29, 67, 68, 111, 229, 314, 322, 329, 374
anātmaka 153
anātman 153, 274, 385, 480, 497
apa 385
Apabharaṇī 486
Apalāla 386
Apapa 643
apara 379
Aparagati 386
Aparagodāna 47, 305, 372, 379, 445
Aparagodānīya 258, 305, 610
Aparasvin 167
Aparaśailāḥ 325
Aparimitāyuḥ Sūtra 218
Aparivartya 380
Aparājita 379
Apasmāra 385, 386, 620
apavāda 16, 225

Apes' Pool 135
aphrodisiac 422
Aplotaxis auriculata 82
appear 580
Apramāṇa 149
Apramāṇaśubha 149, 250, 301
Apramāṇābha 149, 250, 301, 386, 621
apratihata 153, 379
apratihati 106
apratisaṁkhyā-nirodha 154
apratiṣṭhita 152
apsaras 16, 535, 568
apādāna 609
Apāmārga 386
apāya 253
Aquarius 241, 364, 380
Aquila 26
arahattvaphala 214
Arakhotos 536
arapacana 375, 379
araṇya 35, 118, 121, 376
araṇyaka 247, 293
arbuda 159, 389, 554, 608, 610
arbuda hell 380
arbudaṁ 425
Archaeological Survey Reports 72
archaeologist 105
Arciṣmatī 369
areca catechu 232
argha 373
arghya 373, 389
Argo 567
Argonauts 338
arhan 98, 118, 375, 377, 384
  四向 261
arhat 2, 36, 37, 50, 118, 222, 323, 371, 375, 420, 475, 576, 606, 609
  four stages 242
  Hīnayāna 515
  six 460
  四部 248
arhat-phala 239
arhatship 279, 281, 324, 492
arhat's deliverance 492
Aries 349, 364
ariṣṭa(ka) 144, 377
Arjaka 377
Arjuna 382, 384, 389
arka 375, 386
Arni 377
around 541
arrogance 460
  ten fields of meditation 551
arrow 340, 482
artha 24, 235, 245, 382, 473, 520
arthakṛtya 251
arts and mathematics 415
Aruṇa 141, 376, 471, 627, 635
Aruṇakamala 376
Arya 324
Aryan language 182
arūpa 152, 230, 374, 485
arūpadhātu 102, 113, 152, 239, 266, 277, 609, 619
arūpaloka 35, 152, 519, 569
arūpalokas 610
Asafoetida 648
Asakṛt-samādhi 214
asama 149
asamasama 149, 381
asamāpta 381
Asaru 381
Asañjñisattva 250, 301
asaṁkhyeya 152, 285, 576
asaṁskṛta 627
asaṁskṛta dharma 154, 586
asaṁskṛta dharmakāya 154
asaṁskṛta śūnyatā 154
Asaṅga 82, 90, 99, 155, 222, 314, 382, 417, 420, 455, 540, 545, 572, 604
Asaṅkhya 382
asaṅkhyeya 265, 292, 382
asaṅkhyeya kalpa 153
asaṅkhyeya-kalpa 18
asbestos cassock 640
ascetics
  six kinds 466
ash 645
Ashuku 205
asiddha
  fallacies in logic 249
asipattra 17, 270
Asipattravana 493
Asita 384
Asita-ṛṣi 381
Assaia Hazaréh 620
Assam 5
asta 389
asthisaṁjñā 51
astrology 314
asura 50, 253, 333, 360, 382, 413, 414, 424, 462, 568, 589, 606, 610
asura battlefield 333
asura king 136, 165
asura wine 333
asura-gati 468
asura-realm 183
asvabhāva 154
asādhya 381
Asāra 381
Atapta heaven 153
Atapās 250, 301, 426
Atata 376
Atharva Veda 375
Atharva-veda 271, 385, 394
Atharvaveda 452, 638
atimuktaka 384, 385
atimukti 384
atom 245, 502, 507
Atri 385
attachments, four 260
attainment 272
Atyambakela 384
Atyanta 617
aum 390, 423
aupapādaka 638
aupapāduka 250, 304, 638
aupayika 409
Aurel Stein 112
auspicious 70
ava 385
Avabhāsa 40
avadāna 104, 162, 165, 364, 386, 580
Avaivartika 222, 380, 453, 616
Avakan 379
Avalamba 119, 442
Avalokita 162
Avalokiteśvara 38, 45, 54, 96, 119, 155, 163, 195, 241, 267, 277, 280, 284, 289, 342, 357, 378, 379, 385, 392, 418, 431,

437, 500, 544, 595, 614
four chief bodhisattvas 247
Avanti 426
Avantī 389
Avaraśailāḥ 104, 132, 305, 379
avasthā 210, 249
Avataṁsa 639
Avataṁsaka 92, 98, 415, 417, 602
Avataṁsaka school 504, 540
Avataṁsaka sect 539, 540
Avataṁsaka-sūtra 23, 455, 473, 484, 588, 639
avatāra 379, 639
avayava 431
Avaṁ 379
Avaṇḍa 225
avi 394
avidyamāna 152
avidyā 80, 150, 365, 446, 646
avijñapti 156
avikalpa 151
avinivartanīya 222
Avināśya 214
avivartin 380
avyayībhāva 462
Avyākhyāta 148
Avyākṛta 148
avāntara 379
avīci 8, 148, 380, 554, 603, 618
avīci hell 148, 286, 415, 462, 464
avṛha 152
avṛhā 250, 301
Awakening of Faith 20, 46, 77, 98, 207, 265, 269, 275, 281, 298, 333, 346, 350, 353, 394, 410, 433, 446, 464, 575
axioms
five 427
Ayamukha 383
ayana 623
ayaḥkāṇḍa 383
Ayodhyā 10, 136, 384, 456, 572
Ayodhyā (Oudh) 382
Ayuta 383, 622
Añjali 494
Añjana 389
aśaikṣa 156, 223
Aśanāyuka 380
aśeṣa 153
Aśleṣā 383, 486
aśmagarbha 382, 584, 634
Aśmakūṭa 521
aśman 382
Aśmaśāyana 343
Aśoka 22, 48, 51, 57, 66, 90, 104, 154, 211, 235, 300, 324, 381, 384, 412, 452, 533, 593, 596, 604, 639
象堅山 226
Aśoka's queen 159
Aśokārāma 154
Aśu-dharā 381
aśva 382
aśvagarbha 382
Aśvaghoṣa 5, 25, 69, 71, 98, 103, 127, 205, 382, 468, 486, 587
four suns 255
佛所行讚經 218
切勝 525
Aśvajit 127, 382, 389, 419
Aśvaka 460
Aśvakarṇa 51, 66, 127, 361, 382, 389, 636
aśvakāya 247
aśvamedha 127, 382
aśvattha 197, 381
aśvattha-vṛkṣa 382
Aśvayuj 486
Aśvayuja 382, 388, 389, 572
Aśvin 107, 284, 382
Aśvinī 382, 486
Aśīti 607
aḥ 431
Aṁśuvarman 390
aṅga 390, 471
aṅgajāta 304, 390
Aṅgiras 383
aṅguli-parvan 550
Aṅgulimālya 390, 550
Aṅguttara Nikāya 547
Aṅgāraka 53, 373, 390, 586, 631, 639
aṅgāraka 390
aṅgūṣa 390
aṇiman 89
aṇu 374, 375, 583
aṇḍaja 74, 250
Aṇḍīra 365, 388
aṣṭa 389, 601
Aṣṭa-mahāsiddhi 89
aṣṭa-mārga 285
Aṣṭa-vimokṣa 611
Aṣṭa-śatam 502
Aṣṭadaśa 370
Aṣṭama-hāśrī-caitya-saṁskṛta-stotra 342
Aṭali 114
aṭaṭa 2, 385, 389, 554, 610
Aṭāli 385

(Ā)
Ābhāsvara 40, 60, 89, 250, 301
Ābhāsvara palace 40
Ābhāsvara(-vimāna) 386
Ābhāsvara-vimāna 40
Ācāra 384
Ādarśana-jñāna 430
Ādi 218
Ādi-Buddha 97, 210, 221, 381, 431, 580
Ādi-buddha 384
Ādikarmika 384
Āditya 53, 375, 436, 586
Ādityas 107, 284
Ādyanutpanna 384
Ādyanutpāda 384
Āgama 546
Āgama sūtras 484
Āgamas 58, 98, 282, 324, 386, 415, 423, 456
四阿含 253
Āgantu-kleśa 14
Āgantuka 373
Āhāra 386
Āhāra āharaṇam āyuḥ-saṁtāraṇe 372
Ājñendriya 475
Ājñāta 383
Ājñāta-Kauṇḍinya 14, 42, 383, 419, 437
Ājñātṛ 383
Ājīvaka 374
Ājīvika 374
Ākarṣaṇī 419
Ākrośa 373

Ākāśa 373, 627
Ākāśagarbha 431, 627
Ākāśagarbha Bodhisattva 103
Ākāśagarbha sūtra 626
Ākāśapratiṣṭhita 105
Ākāśānantyāyatana 35, 152
Ālambana 320
Ālambana-pratyaya 476
Ālaya 187, 403
Ālaya vijñāna 433
Ālaya-soul 186
Ālaya-vijñāna 179, 202, 376, 476, 484, 532
 四相 249
 集起心, the totality of mind, the source of mental activity 351
Ālayavijñāna 52, 497, 520
Ālāra-Kālāma 376
Āmalaka 377
Āmla 390
Āmra 72, 377, 390
Āmradārikā 75, 341, 389
Āmrapālī 67, 75, 389, 390
Āmravana 390
Āmravana garden 389
Āmrāta 377
Āmrātaka 389
Āmrāvatī 390
Āna 374
Ānanda 24, 83, 88, 137, 140, 158, 225, 242, 263, 357, 374, 392, 400, 419, 486
 an attendant 340
Ānanda as Buddha 147
Ānandabhadra 374
Ānandapura 374
Ānandasāgara 374
Ānanda's 583
Ānāpāna 329, 374, 389, 549
Āpattivyutthāna 380
Āptanetravana 115
Āraṇya 620
Ārdrā 486
Ārya 100, 372, 377, 538
Ārya Sthavira 5
Ārya-tārā 377
Āryadeva 2, 317, 534, 540, 569
Āryadeśa 316
Āryadāsa 377
Āryamārga 609
Āryan 377
Āryasatyāni 534
Āryasena 377
Āryasiṁha 256, 486
Āryasthāvirāḥ 299, 324, 325
Āryavarman 377
Āryaśūra 100
Āryācalanātha 205, 385
Āryācalanātha Rāja 431
Āryāmogha-pūrṇamaṇi 213
Āryāsaṅga 382
Āryāvalokiteśvara 374, 377, 379
Ārāḍa Kālāma 376
Ārāḍa-Kālāma 376
Ārṣa 377
Ātharvaṇa 385
Ātman 85, 348, 515
Āvantikās 94
Āvantikāḥ 275
Āveṇika-buddhadharma 214
Āveṇikadharma 370
Āviddhakarṇa 380
Āvāhana 380
Āyatana 383
Āyurveda 328, 383
Āyuṣmant 44
Āśaya 381
Āśraya 320
Āśu-cittā 382
Āḥ-vi-ra-hūm-kham 380
Āṣāḍhā 254, 381, 389, 572
Āṭavika 101, 385

(ā)
ābhās 386
ābhāsvara 66, 386
ācārin 381, 624
ācārya 43, 59, 234, 367, 381, 385, 473, 606, 635
ācāryas 427
ādara 375
ādarśa 24
ādāna 52, 82, 385, 607
ādāna-vijñāna 562
ādānavijñāna 385
āgama 42, 119, 386
āgamas 282
āgata 119
āgāra 373
āhāra 344, 588
ājñendriya 485
ājñātāvīndriya 485
ākarṣaṇī 429
ākhu 304
ākiñcanyāyatana 55, 239
ākulakara 373
ākāśa 154, 373, 552
ākāśānantyāyatana 239
ākāśānantyāyatanam 55
ālambana 295
ālambana-pratyaya 120
ālaya 52, 120, 282, 376, 377
ālaya heresy 376
ālaya-vijñāna 36, 77, 82, 344, 385, 430, 457, 482, 490, 524, 562, 575, 576, 607, 628
 分別事識 209
ālaya-vijñāna mind 283
ālayavijñāna 61, 252, 320, 539, 562, 629
ālaya식 ālaya識 282
āliṅgī 377
āmantraṇa 609
āmra 75, 525
āmraka 209
āmrapālī 398
āmravana 475
ānanda 648
ānantarya 148
āpatti-pratideśanā 379
āraṇya 376
āraṇyaka 376
ārdraka 375
ārogya 372
ārya 314, 317
ārya-jñāna 318
āryabhāṣā 317
āryastūpamahāśrī 88
ārāma 49, 375, 447
ārūpyadhātu 266
āsana 541
āsrava 123, 456
āsravakṣaya 123
āsravakṣaya-jñāna 150, 468
ātharvaṇa 375

ātma-grāha 385
ātma-mada 377
ātmahitam 515
ātmakatva 575
ātman 53, 372, 415, 477, 491, 518
ātmane 587
ātyantika 384
āvaraṇa 520
āveśa 379
āya 383
āyatana 2, 470, 594
āyāna 383
āśaya 381
āścarya 69, 381
āśrama 182
āśvāsa-apānaka 381

(B)

Bactria 3, 166, 451
Badakchan 108
Badakshan 50, 172, 379, 451
Baghcheba 606
Baghelān 165
bahirātman 76
bahu 82
Bahu-śruta 83
bahujanya 199
Bahularatna 614
bahuvrīhi 462
Bahuśrutīyāḥ 325, 509
Baibhargiri 232
Baktra 75, 165
bala 120, 162, 163, 170, 318, 359, 461
bali 136, 165, 598
balin 163
Balkh 19, 635
Baltistan 171
balāhaka 162
bamboo 543
bamboo garden 92
bamboo-grove 543, 610
Bamian 19, 181
Bamyam 306
band 80
bandha 165, 246
bandhi 165
Bandhiasura 165
Bannu 179
banquet 401
banyan 80
baptism 290, 489
  with five vases of perfumed water 418
Baragong 72, 341
barber-monk 142
barren 79
Basarh 229
Baschpa 169
Bashpa 598, 606
Basiasita 164, 486
basket 617
Bassahar 229
Bassia latifolia 136
Bauhinia variegata 51
Bayana 181
Bbhadrapāla 169
beat 591
begging bowl 462
beginning 203, 446
Behar 86, 128
bells 427
belt 87
ben-zai-ten 94
Benares 48, 89, 161, 162, 380, 604
  deer park 308
  四塔 260
benevolence 493
Bengal 271, 326
benten 94, 147
Benzaiten 147
betel-nut 525
betel-nut tree 232
Betik 179
bhadanta 90, 162
bhadra 308, 627
bhadra-kalpa 48, 49, 165, 169, 170, 309, 625, 627, 630
bhadra-kumbha 627
Bhadradatta 169
Bhadrakapilā 170
Bhadrapāla 170, 627
Bhadraruci 170
Bhadravihāra 228
Bhadrayānīyāḥ 170, 325
Bhadrika 11, 165, 170, 379, 419
Bhaga 170
Bhagai 169, 611
Bhagava 170
Bhagavaddharma 2
Bhagavan 166
Bhagavat 162, 163, 166, 218, 320, 508
  six characteristics 461
Bhagavān 2, 162, 371
Bhagārāma 49
Bhairava 174
Bhaiṣajya 145, 193, 223, 277, 289, 357, 388, 431, 496, 500, 592, 600
Bhaiṣajya-guru-vaiḍūrya-prabhāsa 394
Bhaiṣajya-rāja 225, 373, 510
Bhaiṣajya-rāja Bodhisattva 394
Bhaiṣajya-samudgata 393
Bhaiṣajyaguruvaiḍūrya-prabhāsa 530
Bhallika 535
Bharaṇī 486
Bharukaccha 170
Bhauma 438
Bhava 206
bhava 286, 365
bhavarāga 459
bhaṅga 164
bhikṣu 17, 76, 95, 97, 588, 614, 616, 617
  bala, power 120
  great assembly 463
  regulations 293
  six common-herd 460
  四衆 four orders 259
  四輩 four grades 246
  四部衆 248
  比丘 225
bhikṣuṇī 79, 225, 398, 399, 588, 617
  四衆 four orders 259
  四輩 four grades 246
  四部衆 248
bhikṣuṇī-khaṇḍa 80
Bhikṣuṇī-sāṁghika-vinaya-prātimokṣa sūtra 226
Bhiḍa 227

bhojanīya 487, 614
Bhramaragiri 170
bhrāmara 169
bhrāmyati 453, 454
bhrānti 137
Bhrūkuṭī 226
Bhrūṁ 506
bhuvanatraya 266
bhuvaḥ 196, 266
Bhādrapada 167, 170, 572
Bhādrapadamāsa 599
Bhādrapadā 170
bhāga 162, 451
Bhāgalpur 574
Bhāgya 209
Bhāradvāja 598
Bhārata 94
Bhāratavarṣa 264
Bhāratī 94
Bhārgava 170
bhāryā 163
bhāva 80, 433, 454, 459, 498
Bhāvaviveka 164, 167, 232, 575
bhāvābhāva 457
bhāṣā 611
Bhīmā 102, 112, 226, 228
Bhīśma-garjita-ghoṣa-svara-rāja 96, 453
Bhū 595
Bhū-kampa 17
bhūdeva = Brahman 551
bhūmi 104, 550, 595
bhūpadī 211
bhūr 196, 266
bhūri 82
bhūrom 196
bhūta 203, 475, 515, 614, 638
bhūtatathatā 34, 105, 111, 139, 145, 147, 150, 152, 187, 189, 193, 201, 203, 207, 208, 217, 218, 219, 230, 231, 258, 268, 269, 274, 283, 292, 293, 315, 318, 345, 350, 351, 366, 367, 370, 394, 398, 400, 404, 408, 416, 421, 439, 446, 449, 473, 482, 486, 495, 502, 503, 504, 505, 507, 528, 532, 535, 537, 559, 560, 561, 569, 571, 588, 613, 646
    bhūtatathatā as absolute 525
    bhūtatathatā dharma-nature 202
    bhūtatathatā in limitations 520
    bhūtatathatā mind 351
    bhūtatathatā mind, by nature 355
    bhūtatathatā reality 561
    bhūtatathatā wisdom 428
    phenomenal bhūtatathatā 261
    resemblances between a mirror and the bhūtatathatā 238
    四信五行, faith and behavior 252
Bhṛkuṭī 213
Bihār 494
Bimba 232
Bimbasāra 232
Bimbisāra 4, 66, 67, 70, 159, 194, 232, 341, 381, 389, 409, 452, 497, 543, 613, 624
    王舍城, capital 436
Bingheul 566
biographical narratives 489
Biographies of famous pilgrims 305
Birat 600
birds 250
birth
    four functioning forms 255
    four fundamental states 248
birth and death 303
Bishamon 56
black 420
Black Udāyin 4
blind men 44
Blo-gros-rgyal-mtshan 606
Block-head 144
blue 420
Blue River 165
Blyxa octandra 525
boa-demons 143
boat i.e. pāramitā 467
bodhi 143, 275, 589
    five bodhi 410, 417
bodhi pakṣika dharma 422
bodhi tree 278
Bodhi-body 214
Bodhi-tree 218
bodhi-tree 446
Bodhi-vihāra 196
bodhicitta 143
Bodhidharma 79, 86, 171, 192, 486, 540, 631
    six brief treatises 321
    six patriarchs 466
    北宗 208
    少林寺 321
    胡子, nickname 633
Bodhidharma School 74
bodhidruma 7, 109, 132, 197, 218, 224, 232, 313, 485
Bodhila 221
Bodhimaṇḍa 65, 196
bodhimaṇḍala 109
bodhipākṣika 7
bodhipākṣika-dharma 254, 285, 414
Bodhiruci 79, 94, 124, 196, 418, 505, 540
bodhisattv
    four holy ways of rebirth 461
bodhisattva 143, 195, 196, 205, 242, 281, 286, 287, 288, 289, 292, 293, 295, 300, 360, 361, 366, 421, 489, 506, 509, 587, 589, 602, 603, 619, 622
    world from four points of view 255
    四聖 251
Bodhisattva Beautiful 648
bodhisattva canon 488
bodhisattva development 619
bodhisattva method 435
bodhisattva-cum-pratyeka-buddha 207
bodhisattva-cum-śrāvaka 207
bodhisattva-knowledge 292
bodhisattva-kṣānti 425
bodhisattva-mahāsattva 90, 94, 198
bodhisattva-merits 283
bodhisattva-mind 125

bodhisattva-realm 183
bodhisattva-stages 466
bodhisattva-wisdom 368
Bodhisattvabhūmi sūtra 466
bodhisattvahood 355, 369
ten fields of meditation 551
Bodhitara 86, 196
Bodhitaru 197
Bodhivṛkṣa 197, 485
bodhyaṅga 7, 77, 196, 237, 526, 589, 595, 648
body 6, 345
Bogdo gegen Hutuktu 94
Bokhara 181, 614
Bolor 171
bond 80
the mind of the six bonds 468
book 202
Borassus flabelliformis 82, 611
Boswellia thurifera 57, 455
bow 58
bowl 208
Brahma 159, 164, 180
Brahma-deva 180
Brahma-heaven 276, 606, 610
Brahma-loka 621
Brahma-maṇi 180
Brahma-net 181
Brahma-purohita 93, 250, 276
Brahma-pāriṣadya 93, 250, 276
Brahma-staff 180
Brahma-wheel 180
Brahmacārin 182
Brahmacārī 182
四梵志 247
Brahmadatta 97, 181
Brahmadatta's daughters 31
Brahmadaṇḍa 156, 180
Brahmadeva 182
Brahmadeva heretics 182
Brahmadevas 182
Brahmadhvaja 105, 181
Brahmajāla 181, 573
Brahmajāla sūtra 137, 181
Brahmakāyika 180, 181, 182, 301
Brahmakṣetra 182
Brahmaloka 35, 39, 93, 150, 152, 181, 182, 200, 266, 301, 344, 370, 371, 386, 401, 456, 468
梵住 258
Brahman 93, 162, 170, 180, 212
brahman 180
Brahmanic Vulcan 366
Brahmapura 162, 398
Brahmapurohita 181, 182, 301
Brahmaputra 271, 350, 375
Brahmapāriṣadya 182, 301
Brahmapārṣadya 182
Brahmavastu 182
brahmayāna 181
Brahma's net 573
Brahmin 163
Brahminic mythology 284
Brahminical temples 569
Brahminical Trimūrti 93, 181
Brahmā 71, 93, 94, 122, 162, 163, 171, 180, 181, 182, 276, 293, 366, 436, 452, 492, 496, 508, 509, 510, 528
a day, kalpa 17
female energy or wife 158
Brahmā-sahāṁpati 180
Braj 170
branch 548
breathe out 580
brethren 631
Broken fingers 381
brown 420
Brāhmanical 162
Brāhmany duck 518
Brāhmaṇa 92, 117, 162, 170
four castes 251
Brāhmaṇapura 162
Brāhmaṇarāṣṭra 162
Brāhmaṇas 461
Brāhmī 464
Buddha 208, 210
birthday 254
four holy ways of rebirth 461
meaning, completely conscious 210
thirty-two marks 261
world from four points of view 255
world hero 320
三品四善根 251
四聖 251
牛王 444
Buddha alive 303
Buddha field 220
Buddha incarnate 214
Buddha of the Tripiṭaka 210
Buddha realm 212, 221
Buddha Samantaprabhāsa 443
Buddha stage 221
Buddha thesaurus 220
Buddha vehicle 506
Buddha-abode 258
Buddha-aeon 103
Buddha-bhadra 92, 222
Buddha-bhūmi 221
Buddha-body 399
Buddha-carita-kāvya-sūtra 127
Buddha-cause 220
Buddha-centre 500
Buddha-charity 215
Buddha-clan 221
Buddha-cosmos 503
Buddha-dharmakāya 200, 529
Buddha-domain 503, 516
Buddha-dāna 215
Buddha-enlightenment 94
Buddha-fruition 469
Buddha-gayā
eight famous Caityas 548
Buddha-heart 219
Buddha-illumination 559
Buddha-kalpa 137
Buddha-knowledge 292
Buddha-kṣetra 65, 261, 350, 420, 516
Buddha-land 182
Buddha-lokanātha 371
Buddha-medicine 270
Buddha-mind 125
Buddha-nature 394
to behold the Buddha-nature, 見性 20
佛性 218
Buddha-omniscience 400
Buddha-parinirvāṇa 222
Buddha-pāla 222

Buddha-realm 183, 507
四不可思議 248
Buddha-realm seed 430
Buddha-samādhi 639
Buddha-seal 220
Buddha-seed nature 466
Buddha-son 561
Buddha-stage 467
Buddha-universe 211, 430, 501
Buddha-universe ocean 430
Buddha-vehicle 219, 223, 281
Buddha-vision 423
Buddha-wisdom 147, 221, 510
Buddha-wisdom mind 510
Buddha-world 293
Buddha-Yāna 504
Buddhabhadra 92, 132, 191, 222, 255
比丘尼僧祇律...經 226
Buddhabhāṣita-aṣṭāṅga-samyaṅ-mārga sūtra 609
Buddhacarita 217
Buddhacarita-kāvya-sūtra 218
Buddhachāyā 219
Buddhacinga 215
Buddhadeva 222, 261
Buddhadharma 216, 370
Buddhadāsa 222
Buddhagayā 2
Buddhaghoṣa 216, 380
Buddhagupta 222
Buddhahood 369
Buddhajīva 160, 222, 255, 303
Buddhakāya 68, 200, 219, 362
Buddhakṣetra 215, 221, 222, 277, 296, 592
Buddhamitra 222, 486
Buddhanandi 222, 486
Buddhaphala 214
Buddhasena 222
Buddhasiṁha 215, 222
Buddhatrāta 222
Buddhatā 218
Buddhavanagiri 222
Buddhavaṁsa 58
Buddhaveda 220
Buddhayaśas 222, 248, 255, 521
Buddhaśānta 222
Buddhaṁ śaraṇaṁ gacchāmi 268
Buddha's birthday 218
Buddha's canopy 567
Buddha's eyebrows 40, 434
Buddha's hand 496
Buddha's image 217
Buddha's nāda 223
Buddha's preaching 223
Buddha's relic 220
Buddha's teaching 214
Buddhism 214, 216, 267, 520
Buddhist canonical literature 212
Buddhist library 90
Buddhochinga 215
Buddhoṣingha 106
Buddhoṣṇīṣa 221
Buddhvaca 222
Buddhāvataṁsaka-mahāvaipulya-sūtra 92
Buddhāvataṁsaka-sūtra 540
Buddhāya 222
Budha 53, 586
Bukhara 9, 166, 614
bull 441
bullock 441
bullock cart 442
bullock carts 293
Bunghee 165
Burma 324
Burmese 271
burning house 642
bushel 113
Bāhu 486
Bāhya 436
Bāhya-āyatana 301
bāla 162, 441
Bālapṛthagjana 162
bālapṛthagjana 142, 162, 179, 476
bālukā 235
Bālāditya 643
Bārnagar 374
Bārāṇasī 363
Bāṣpa 164, 170
bīja 430, 514, 539
bījaka 224, 499
Bījapūra 53
Bījapūraka 53, 160
bō-tree 294
Bṛhad-araṇyaka 444
Bṛhaspati 53, 144, 158, 586
Bṛhatphala 39, 250, 301, 456

(C)

Cabool 71, 215, 634
Caitra 532, 572
Caitra-māsa 85
Caitrarathavana 254
caitya 145, 532, 548, 549, 562, 564
Buddha's Caitya 221
caitya-vandana 532
Caityaśaila 548
Caityaśailāḥ 325
Cakoka 525
cakra 47, 124, 517, 564
cakravartin 65, 124, 196, 584
cakravartin kings 243
cakravartī 18, 104, 285, 287, 296, 524, 527, 564, 567
cakravartī's troops 247
six kinds of 461
cakravartī kings 426
cakravartī(-rāja) 517
Cakravāka 518
cakravāla 51, 124, 407, 518, 574
Cakravāḍa 51, 361, 518, 574
Cakrāhva 518
cakṣu(s) 143, 388, 517
cakṣur-vijñāna 607
cakṣurdhātu 517
cakṣurindriya 485
cakṣurvijñāna-dhātu 388
calamities 288
call 60, 321
Calmadana 77, 592
Campa 574
Campaka 574
camphor 434
Campā 363, 574
can 2
Cancer 211, 364
Cancri 169
Candana 84, 522
Candra 345, 436, 450, 451, 485, 523

Candra-dīpa-samādhi 450
Candra-garbha 72
candra-maṇḍala 273
Candra-sūrya-pradīpa 458, 499
Candra-vimala-sūrya-prabhāsa-śrī 499
Candrabhāgā 451, 522
Candradeva 196, 452, 522
Candragupta 384
Candrakānta 451
Candraprabha 289, 450, 523
Candravarma 451
Candravaṁśa 451
Candrottarā-dārikā-vyākaraṇa-sūtra 451
Candrārkadīpa 499
Candī 543
cannot 598
Canogyza 10, 52
canon 469, 522
Canopus 373
Canton 86, 599
Capricornus 364
card 611
Caritra 525
caryā 335, 563
case-record 32
Cashmere 169
Caspian 165
cassia 83
cassock 5, 472
cassock and almsbowl 473
Castor 382
Catalpa Bungei 107
catastrophe
  the three final catastrophes 335
category 499
catty 61
catur 235
catur arūpa dhātu 55
catur ārūpya brahmaloka 345
Catur-aṅgabalakāya 247
catur-dvīpa
  四洲 258
Catur-lābha-sūtra
  四不可得 248
Catur-mahārāja 570
Catur-mahārāja-kāyikas 254, 260
catur-mahārāja-kāyikas 260
Catur-mahārājās 260
Catur-yoni 250
Catur-ārūpya (brahma)lokas 239
Catura 365
Caturdaśa 361
caturdiśaḥ 576
Caturdāraka-samādhi-sūtra 406
Caturmahārājakāyika 438
Catuḥ-parāmarśa 260
catuḥ-parāmarśa 28
Catuḥ-saṁgraha-vastu 251
Catuḥśataka-[śāstrakārikā] 175
Catuṣ-kuśala-mūla 250
Catvārahsūryās 255
Catvāri apramāṇāni 245
Catvāri ārya-satyāni 257
Catvāriṁśat 252
Catūrūpabrahmaloka 152
Caula 542
caura 542
caurī 542
causal force 496
cause 427
  active 465
  conditional or environmental 465
  cooperative 465
  empowering 465
  five causes 425
  non-resistant 465
  passive 465
  primary 465
  universal or omnipresent 465
cause and effect 35, 428, 446, 495, 584
cause and origin 498
Cauveri 591
cavern genii 308
Caṁścā 48
caṅkramaṇa 25
Caṇḍa-Kaniṣka 25
Caṇḍāla 522
caṇḍāla 108, 522
cease 551
Ceka 643
central 544
Central North India 544, 545, 546
certainly 616
certificate of ordination 28
cessation 81
Cetiya 306
Ceylon 79, 124, 186, 256, 305, 324, 338, 525, 562
Ceṭaka 206
Chagayana 521
chagrin 520
Chakoka 517
Chan-jan 86, 446, 631
  天台九祖 572
Chanda 460
chanda-ṛddhi-pādaḥ 254
Chandaka 563, 567
Chandas 232
  six śāstras 461
Chang Ch'ien 451
Chang Hsüeh-fêng 445
Chang Sui 511
Chang-an
  止觀論 551
change
  four functioning forms 255
  four fundamental states 248
chants 50
Chao Fa-shih 241
Chao-chou 537
chaplet of finger-bones 390
Charaka 243
Charekoor 634
charity 341, 461, 529
Charkhlik 75
chaste 233, 526
chastity 527
Chavannes 342
Chaḍâyatana 135
Chekiang 23, 402, 555, 572, 628
Chenab 522
Chenab river 451
chi 200
Chi-chou 635

ㄱ ㄴ ㄷ ㄹ ㅁ ㅂ ㅅ ㅇ ㅈ ㅊ ㅋ ㅌ ㅍ ㅎ 찾아보기

Chi-pin 6
chia tree 107
Chia-hsiang 271, 276
chief 541
Chien-chên 181
Chighnān 342
Chih 止 551
Chih-chao 498
Chih-chê 天台九祖 572
Chih-chên 502
Chih-ch'an 549
Chih-ch'ien 548, 549
Chih-i 146, 215, 434, 501, 555
四教儀 239
天台九祖 572
天台山 572
方等 173
Chih-i's works 573
Chih-kuan Tsung 551
Chih-k'ai 631
Chih-lang 549
Chih-li 244, 552
Chih-liang 549
Chih-lou-chia-ch'an 548
Chih-shêng 13
Chih-yen 550
Chihli 305, 537
Chikdha 566
child-killing 349
chiliocosm 102, 430, 501, 507
middling 546
chiliocosmos 500
Chin dynasty 325, 422
Chin Ling 419
Chin-i 304
Ching Shan 419
Ching-chou 574
Ching-ch'i 86, 360, 479, 572, 631
Ching-t'o 261
Ching-t'u 587
Ching-ying 258, 598
Chinkiang 12
Chitor 566
Chittagong 5
Chittore 566
Chiu-hua 241
Chiu-hua-shan 555
Cho-chou 305
chop 61
chos-kyi-daṅ-poḥi-saṅs-rgyas 384
Chos-kyi-od-zer 606
Chosŏn 537
Chou 103, 274
chrysalis 250
Chu 571
Chu Fa-lan 5
Chu Fo-nien 248
Chuang Tzŭ 401
Chuang Yen 146
Chuang Yen Lun 257
chung 398
Chung-nan Shan 538
chên-ju 193, 366, 370, 399, 400, 575
Chên-ting fu 126
chāyā 563, 565
ch'a 564
Ch'an 311, 507
ch'an-ting 311
Ch'ang-an 102, 104, 107, 630
Ch'ang-chia Fo 413
Ch'ang-shui 516
Ch'ang-t'ing-tzŭ 614
Ch'i dynasty 78
Ch'ien Lung 96
Ch'ien Shu 573
Ch'in-kuang 558
Ch'ing dynasty 520
Ch'ing-liang Ch'êng-kuan 639
Ch'ing-yang 555
Ch'ing-yüan 278, 312
Ch'iu-ming 46
Ch'u state 576
Ch'ung-hsüan temple 305
Ch'ên 555, 630
Ch'ên Chên-ti 545
Ch'ên dynasty 97
Ch'ên Shih 103
Ch'êng Tsu 208
Ch'êng-kuan 112, 562
ch'ün 389
cikitsā 415
cintāmaṇi 106, 400, 558
citra 562
Citrabhānu 638
Citral 294
Citraratha 16
citron tree 525
Citrā 419, 485, 562
citta(m) 549, 562, 585
質多, the heart as the seat of thought or intelligence 351
citta-caitta
心心, mind and mental conditions 354
citta-smṛtyupasthāna 315
citta-ṛddhi-pādaḥ 254
cittamātra 454
Cittasamprayuktasaṁskārāḥ 585
Cittaviprayuktasaṁskārāḥ 586
cittotpāda 518
Ciñcā-Māṇavikā 522
clause 44
claws 536
cleansing 318, 395
cow-dung 443
clerk 76
clever 42
Cloth-bag monk 614
cloves 434
cognition-mind 248
Cola 542
colours
compound 420
five primary 420
comet 53
commandment 342, 359, 481
commandments for the laity, 俗戒 326
complete commandments 481
fifth 220
first 217
five commandments 326
Five Commandments for Laymen 319
fourth 216
keeping the commandments 461
ninth 208
perfume of the commandments 28
second 219
seventh 212

sixth 219
tenth 221
third 220
沙彌尼戒 246
沙彌戒 246
commandment-keeping 416
commit suicide 515
common 613
世俗 319
common people 203, 617
compare 225
complete 522, 541
complete bodhi 355
complete commandments 89, 339, 429, 481
complete deliverance 492
complete nirvāṇa 54, 458
complete teaching 478
complete without lack 202
conflagration catastrophe 641
Confucian 453
Confucianism 267, 520
Confucius 31, 453
丘, personal name 44
Conjevaram 16
consequence 446
constant 621
constellations 331
contemplation 461
coordination 446
copulation 242
corpus 201
correct 526
correct law 529
correlation 446
Corvus 381
country 56
Cow-bezoar aid 445
cow-dung 14, 443
cow-faced 444
Crane-garden 620
Creator 93, 436
cremation 640
crimson 420
crocodile 349
crore 55
crosslegged 591
Crown-prince 594
crutch 541
cry 60
crystal 335
cubit 58
Cugopa 517
Culya 542
Cunda 91, 522
Cundi 543
Cundā 363, 541, 582
Cundī 104, 460
Cutch 25
Cuṇḍī 582
Cuṇḍī-Kuanyin 582
cypress 175
Cyrene 384
cyuti 235
Cāmara 525, 563, 610
Cāmuṇḍā 563, 583
Cārvāka school 401
Cārvāka system 122
Cātaka 563
cāturdiśa 576
Cāṇḍāśoka 522
Cīna 548, 550, 558
Cīna-deva-gotra 549
Cīnapati 550
Cīnarājaputra 550
Cīnasthāna 558
Cīnānī 550
cīvara 542, 548, 558
Cūlaka 328
cūrṇa 337
Cūḍa 328
Cūḍapanthaka 542
cūḍā 411, 541

(D)

dadhi 118, 415
dagoba 513, 593
dahara 323, 592
Dai-nichi-nyorai 101
Daiken 105
Daikoku 107
Dakṣiṇakosala 42
dakṣiṇā 74, 83, 86, 105, 441, 574, 582
dakṣiṇāgāthā 82, 597
dakṣiṇāyana 75
Dalai Lama 85, 117, 195, 537, 614, 644
Damila 591
danta 71, 592
danta-kāṣṭha 395, 582, 592
Dantaloka 83
Dantalokagiri 592
Darada 591
Dardu 591
darśana 19, 28, 85, 552
Dasyu 86
daurmanasyendriya 485
dauṣṭhulya 36
Dawn 84
day 253
日 498
Daśa 355
daśabala 162, 358
Daśabala-Kāśyapa 5, 164, 358, 419
Daśabhūmi 368
Daśabhūmikā sect 540
Daśabhūmipratiṣṭhite 87
Daśabhūmivibhāṣā śāstra 368
daśalakṣa 108
Daśākuśala 362
daṇḍa 73, 83, 84, 85, 496
Daṇḍaka 84, 592
Daṇḍaka-araṇyaka 84
Daṇḍaka-āraṇyaka. 376
death 136
four fundamental states 248
death-māra 604
debt 648
decadence 529
Deccan 83, 85, 86, 131, 136, 376, 593
deer cart 41, 293
deer park 308, 524
deficient 648
defilers 267
deha 345, 536, 610
deliverance 611
Delphinus Gangeticus 349
delusions 295
Demon-realm 183
Dengyō 244, 571, 624
depart 14
desire-heavens 107
desire-realm 55
desire-world 223, 586

desires, four 四欲 254
deteriorators 281
determination 81
deva 50, 360, 361, 366, 498, 534, 536, 569, 573, 587, 589, 606
sixteen devas 363
under-world 414
天仙 569
deva drum 567
deva genii 308
deva language 570
Deva Māra 568
deva son 57
Deva Subhūti 569
deva vision 357
Deva Ārya 224
Deva-arm city 568
deva-bow 568
deva-flowers 211
deva-foot ubiquity 348
deva-gati 468, 568
deva-king 54, 476, 574
Deva-māra-pāpīyān 534
Deva-realm 183
deva-vision 422
Deva-Ārya 211
Deva-ṛṣis 569
Devabodhisattva 3, 175, 243, 317, 534, 569
four suns 255
Devadarśita 568
Devadatta 47, 48, 73, 85, 91, 107, 176, 286, 331, 374, 417, 424, 462, 534, 553, 569, 604
Devadiṣṭa 568
Devakanyā 568
Devakṣema 534
devaloka 33, 301, 464, 556, 567, 605, 606
copulation 242
eight devalokas 610
six 468
six devalokas 569
天住 258
devaloka heaven 606
devalokas and purgatories 570
Devanāgarī 567
Devanāgarī alphabet 182
Devapati 571
Devaprajña 535
Devapura 567
devapuṣpa 211
Devarāja 534
Devarāja-tathāgata 570
devas 498
devas-and-men 421
Devasena 534
Devasopāna 568, 570
devatā 93, 569
Devatāgāra 569
Devatāgṛha 569
Devayāna 569
Devaśarman 534
developments 426
Devendra-samaya 571
devotion 137
Devālaya 569
devānām 307
Devānāṁpriya 570
Devātideva 534, 571
Devāvatāra 363
devī 203, 346, 535
deśanā 565
deśanīya 535
Dgah-ldan 11
Dhana-kaṭaka 305
Dhanada 260, 438, 485, 570
Dhanakaṭaka 113, 216, 379
Dhaniṣṭhā 485
Dhanus 58
dhara 86, 549
Dharaṇiṁdhara 549
dharma 292, 300, 605
一法, a law 502
三寶 283
三寶, Triratna 276, 508
三歸 268
大染法 dharma of defilement 100
大法, great Law 94
法 182
法住 Dharma abode 190
法威德力 august power 414
答哩磨 87
達磨 86
Dharma sect 86
dharma-bell 185
dharma-cakra 185, 524
dharma-court 623
dharma-gate 185
dharma-jñāna-mudrā 259
dharma-kāya 301
Dharma-lakṣaṇa school 456, 471
Dharma-lord 190
Dharma-nature 187
Dharma-shining 190
Dharma-state 189
Dharma-store 190
dharma-talk 185
Dharma-treasure 186
dharma-truth 287
Dharma-āraṇyaka. 376
dharma-śarīra 243
Dharmabala 579
Dharmabhadra 191
Dharmadeva 191
dharmadhātu 86, 102, 183, 427, 430, 508, 541, 544, 605
Dharmadhātu Buddha 183
dharmadhātu-palace 183
Dharmadhātu-prakṛti-jñāna 430
Dharmadhātu-reality 183
Dharmagahanābhyudgata-rāja 34
Dharmagupta 86, 186, 417, 419, 483
Dharmagupta school
four-division discipline 248
Dharmagupta-bhikṣuṇī-karman 248
Dharmagupta-vinaya 248
Dharmagupta's version 255
Dharmaguptāḥ 325, 457, 482, 509
Dharmajātayaśas 86
Dharmakoṣa 222
Dharmakāla 86
dharmakāya 7, 36, 45, 78, 90, 102, 148, 152, 181, 183, 185, 186, 187, 188, 207, 213, 214, 227, 230, 269, 274, 275, 282, 283, 290, 291, 296, 303, 316, 318, 350, 404, 418, 431, 448, 472, 475, 476, 481, 482, 483, 484, 490, 507, 517, 526, 535,

541, 559, 560, 561, 595, 612, 622, 623, 632
五種法身 five kinds 428
四身 four bodies 252
平等法身 universalized dharmakāya 613
心是法身 the mind is dharmakāya 353
Dharmakāya and Nirmāṇakāya 561
Dharmakāya as absolute being 481
Dharmakāya as wisdom 481
Dharmakāya Buddha 188
dharmakāya gāthā 403
Dharmakāya Mahāsattva 188
Dharmakāya of meditation 529
dharmakāya of the Tathāgata 242
dharmakāya of Vairocana 203
Dharmakāya Tathāgata 188
dharmakāya-kṣetra 420
Dharmakāya-Samantabhadra 384
dharmakṣetra 187, 484
Dharmalakṣaṇa 99, 367, 434, 602, 608
六部大乘經 462
Dharmalakṣaṇa School 33, 105, 152, 202, 207, 248, 259, 282, 429, 454, 546, 576, 609, 616, 622, 630
火辨, Citrabhānu 638
Dharmalakṣaṇa sect 158, 186, 223, 252, 420, 454, 540
Dharmamegha 189, 369
Dharmamitra 86
dharmanairātmya 185
Dharmanandi 86, 191
Dharmapada 58, 184
dharmaparyāya 185
Dharmaprabhāsa 185
Dharmaprabhāsa Buddha 206
Dharmaprajñā 95
dharmapravicaya-saṁbodhyaṅga 584
Dharmapriya 86
Dharmapāla 86, 302, 413, 431, 628
Dharmapālas 413
Dharmapūjā 184
Dharmarakṣa 5, 12, 79, 86, 93, 127, 378, 405, 528, 540, 578, 594
佛所行讚經 218
Dharmaratna 102, 186
Dharmaruci 86, 196
Dharmarāja 189, 431
Dharmasamatā 191
Dharmasatya 86
dharmasthititā 190
Dharmatrāta 86, 184, 261
Dharmatrāta Sūtra 207
dharmatā 187, 575
Dharmaviraja 574
Dharmavivardhana 16, 48, 51, 86, 147
Dharmayaśas 86
Dharmaṁ śaraṇaṁ gacchāmi 268
Dharmottarīyāḥ 325
Dharmādharma 186
Dharmāhāra 188
Dharmākara 86, 190
Dharmāraṇya 579
Dharmāśoka 188, 384
dhruva 205
Dhruvapaṭu 114
dhvaja 87, 593
Dhvajāgrakeyūra 145
dhyāna 55, 163, 212, 272, 276, 278, 295, 355, 416, 461, 593
definition 308
pure 257
ten fields of meditation 551
八定 609
八解脫 611
定 273
dhyāna devalokas 610
dhyāna heaven 50, 53, 279, 361, 544
fourth 426
dhyāna liberation 358
dhyāna pāramitā 310
dhyāna regions 309
Dhyāna sect 540
dhyāna stage 544
dhyāna-concentration 250
dhyāna-contemplation 309
dhyāna-meditation 623
dhyāni-bodhisattva 102, 205, 555
dhyāni-buddha 101, 142, 213, 276, 378, 417, 424, 427
四佛 248
dhyāni-buddhas 546
Dhānyakaṭaka (Amarāvatī) 211
dhāra 269
dhāraṇī 40, 82, 90, 95, 104, 140, 141, 146, 156, 161, 224, 225, 264, 269, 275, 294, 348, 502, 519, 542, 549, 560, 577, 608
四種總持 258
火界 636
dhāraṇī illuminant 549
Dhāraṇī-bodhisattva 82
dhāraṇī-sūtras 93
Dhāraṇīpiṭaka 62, 82
dhātu 25, 371, 594
dhātu-śarīra 243
Dhītika 556
dhūpa 112
dhūta 17, 114, 500, 504, 506
dhṛ 549
Dhṛtaka 486, 534, 556
Dhṛtarāṣtra 16, 229, 260, 438, 485, 532, 534, 549, 570, 626
Dhṛtiparipūrṇa 19
Diamond 278
Diamond Court 383
Diamond maṇḍala 63, 64
Diamond Ruler 278
Diamond samādhi 509
diamond sceptre 600
Diamond Sūtra 62, 79, 384, 464
diamond vehicle 64
diamond-kings 603
diamond-realm 213, 214, 363, 430
diamond-realm group 418
diamond-realm lotus 76
diamond-realm maṇḍala 56, 285
dictionary 522
Differentiated School 469
Differentiating School 194
Hua-yen school 193

Dignāga 100, 401, 484, 496, 497, 557
Dinabha 534
Dineśvara 534
direct way 479
direction 343
disc samādhi 273
discernment 137
Discipline sect 540
dismiss 14
distress 291
distressed 107
distresses 286
divide 209
divine 525
divyacakṣus 422, 569
Divyadundubhimeghanirghoṣa 567
divyaśrotra 422, 570
Divyāvadāna 311
Divākara 103, 173, 553
Diṅnāga 401, 557
Djaghing-gol 236
Djambalā 86
do not 211
Doab 227
Docetism 230
dogs, which vomit fire on sinners in hell 636
dollar 446
don-grub 213
Dong-hwa-sa 113
Double Three Samādhi 279
dragon 71
dragon king 335, 400, 440
Dragon King of the Ocean 622
dragon-arjuna tree 71
dragon-daughter 251
dragon-fierce 71
dragon-king 413
dragon-pearl 440
Dragon's palace 567
Dravila 591
Draviḍa 16, 85, 591
dravya 82, 466, 552
Dravya Mallaputra 87
droṇa 31
突路拏 a Brahman 112
Droṇastūpa 194
Droṇodana 31, 49, 107, 256
Droṇodana-rāja 374, 534
Druma 113, 114, 184
Drāvira 591
dual adornment 486
Dual powers 479
dual reward 481
duck 518
Dukkaṭa 112
dukūla 111, 114
dull 415
Dundubhiṣvara-rāja 567
Durdharṣa 78
durgati 260
Durgā 106, 112, 160, 228, 482, 543
dust 135
duḥkha 28, 31, 114, 266, 274, 291, 355
四諦 257
duḥkha-duḥkhatā 30
duḥkha-āryā-satyam 30
duḥkhendriya 485
duṣkara-caryā 31
duṣkṛta 70, 112, 177, 193, 343, 399, 478, 612
dvandva 462
dvau 475
dveṣa 474, 532, 535, 593
dvigu 462
dvitīya 475
Dviyāna 483
Dvā 475
Dvādaśa 364
Dvādaśa-nikāya(-mukha)-śāstra 243
Dvādaśa-nikāya-śāstra 270, 364, 540
Dvādaśaviharaṇa sūtra 365
Dvādaśāṅga pratītyasamutpāda 365
Dvārapati 591
Dvāravatī 591
Dvātriṁśadvaralakṣaṇa 285
Dvātriṁśat 285
dvīpa 535
dāha 591
dāna 82, 84, 85, 163, 198, 251, 269, 341, 357, 416, 461, 478
five kinds 428
dāna-pāramitā 249
Dānagāthā 82
dānapati 83, 84, 341
Dānapāla 341
Dānapāramitā 83
Dānavat 82
dāsaka 419, 593
dāsikā 593
dīnāra 558
dīpa 115
dīpapradīpa 115
Dīpaṃkara 92, 106, 147, 360, 527, 535, 536
Dīpaṃkara Buddha 402
Dīrgha 551
Dīrghabhavana-saṁghārāma 551
Dīrghāgama 386, 423, 519
dīrghāgamas
四阿含 253
Dūraṁgamā 369
dūta 114
dūtī 114
dṛḍha 19
dṛṣṭiparāmarśa 21, 410
dṛṣṭi 19, 85
dṛṣṭi-kaṣāya 21
dṛṣṭānta 455

(Ḍ)
Ḍākinī 82, 360

(ḍ)
ḍamara 71

(E)

each 7
earth 552
四大 241
earth genii 308
earth-devī 553, 556
earth-immortals 551
earth-prison 434
Earth-store 555
Earth-treasury 555
Earth-womb 555
earthen vessel 435
earthquake 552

east 113
Eastern Peak 113
Eastern Tsin 271
ecchantika 276
Ecclesia 276
effect 427
egg-born 594
ego 518
ego within 76
ego-infatuation 385
egoism 482
Egypt 384
eight 601
eight commandments 610
Eight Diagrams 425
eight inexpressibles 601
eight negations 601
eight seas 51
eight sections 610
eight sects 54
eight teachers 606
eight śāstras 371
eight-arm deva 606
eighteen 271, 370
eighty 607
eighty-four marks 587
eighty-one 607
eighty-one grades 56
Eka 498
Eka-jāti-prati-baddha 503
Ekabyohāra 503
Ekasmin samaye 504
ekatva 503
ekatva-anyatva 505
Ekavyāvahārika 223, 325, 503
Ekavīcika 499
Ekayāna 504
Ekaśṛṅga-ṛṣi 111, 499
ekaṃ samayaṃ 504
Ekottara-āgama 386, 547
ekottarikāgama 423
　增一阿含 253
Ekādaśa 366
ekādaśamukha 366
Ekāgra 503
elbow 58
elder 299
elder brother 631
element water 332
Eleocarpus 385
elephant's eyeball 482
Elephant's Head Mountain 2
eleven 366
eleven faces 363
elixir 84
Elāpattra 408, 474, 479, 496
emancipation 611
　symbol of emancipation, 木馬 144
embryo-initiation 425
employ 439
Empress Wu 103, 351
empty 32
empyrean 213
end 135
endurance 287
enemy 447
enlarge 635
epidemics 429
Epirus 384
Eros 100
Erythina Indica 600
Erāpattra 479
Erāvarṇa 479
Erāvati 479
Erāvaṇa 479
escape 611
esoteric doctrine 512
eternal 408
Eternal Buddha 210
eva 454
evam 399
Evam mayā śrutam 332
even 613
everlasting 408
every 7
Everywhere 510
evil by nature 316
Evil One 600
evolutions 426
exaggeration 460
Excalibur 581
excommunication 592
　四棄 240
expedient method 174
external 436
external Ego 436
extinction 80, 81, 83, 611
　four functioning forms 255
　four fundamental states 248
extinguishing 31
eye 143
eḍa 372
eḍamūka 372
Eḍavarṇa 479

(F)

Fa-chao 434
Fa-hsiang 186, 491
Fa-hsiang School 187
Fa-hsien 9, 79, 95, 132, 191, 378, 599, 604
　比丘尼僧祇律...經 226
Fa-hsien's version 92
fa-hsing 398
Fa-hua 281
　天台九祖 572
Fa-jung
　牛頭 442
Fa-li 91
Fa-pao 40, 422
Fa-tsang 69, 412, 625, 628
Fa-yen sect 188
Fa-yün 40, 239
Fan Wei Chih 550
Fan-i-ming-i 46, 80, 158, 222, 342
　five regular articles of food 167
Fan-i-ming-i dictionary 140
Farakhabad 10
fast 615
fasting 615
father 204
father and mother 204
feather
　毛 142
Fei-lai peak 546
Ferghana 37, 57, 128, 160, 614
ferry 461
Ficus Indica 80
Ficus pyrifolia 80
Ficus religiosa 80, 382, 446
fiery way 637
fifteen 363
finality 529
finger-joint 58

finger-prints 328
fire 552, 635
丙 194
四大 241
fire altar 637
fire dhyāna 342, 641
fire heaven 605
fire service 638
fire sign 640
fire wheel 637
fire-bell 637
fire-board 642
fire-chariot 641
fire-court 640
fire-pearl 334, 641
fire-rat 640
fire-spirits 366
fire-tender 638
fire-tongs 642
Fire-worship 294
fires 295
first 446
first dhyāna 55, 370
first samādhi 55
five 409
five commandments 356
Five Dynasties 419
five elements 552
five planets 53
Five Schools 412
Five Seas 370
five skandhas 463
Five Tastes 511
five vehicles 497
Five Wisdom 205
flame 636
flame dhyāna 636
flame samādhi 636
flattery 460
flavour 462, 502
flesh 288
flesh unclean 278
flood 335
flourishing 148
flower-eater 211
flower-plucker 211
Fo-lung monastery 624
Fo-t'u-ch'êng 106, 215
food
clean food 536
made clean by fire, or cooking 641
forbidden 211
foretell 200
form-realm 55, 223
formless realm 223
Fortune's womb 350
forty 252
forty arms 566
forty-ninth day 252
forty-two messengers 252
foundation books 202
four 235
Four Axioms 363, 608, 609
four dhyānas 55
four dogmas 475
世間經 319
四優檀那 254
four elements 241
four māras 604
Four Noble Truths 324, 421
Four Sufferings 235
Four Truths 274
four-character line 503
four-division Vinaya 248
fourteen 361
fragrance 625
Fragrance-land 626
fraternity members 631
Fraudulent 235
free bhūtatathatā 580
freedom 611
frog samādhi 618
Fudo 205
Fukien 452, 629, 644
Fukū 213
fundamental 200, 464
fundamental cause 446
fundamental doctrine 201
furnaces 243
Futtihpoor 171
future 159

(G)

Gacchati 2
Gachi 19
Gadgadasvara 146
gagana 3, 626
Gaganagarbha 627
Gaganaprekṣaṇa 2
Gahan 9
gaja 2, 295
Gajapati 296
Gajaśīrṣa 2
Gamini 2
Gandak 648
gandha 16, 625
Gandha-mādana 97, 375
Gandha-vyūha 16, 540
Gandhahastī 16, 625
gandhakuṭī 16, 396, 626
Gandhamādana 16, 31, 154, 361, 625, 626
gandhamādanamāla 16
gandharva 15, 16, 86, 113, 135, 158, 273, 386, 395, 568, 606, 626
gandharva city 15, 164, 363
Gandharva Kāyikās 16
Gandharāja 363, 626
Gandhāra 3, 15, 16, 206, 234, 382, 432, 519, 599, 615
gandhāri 16
Ganges 12, 235, 271, 375, 511, 607, 618, 621
four rivers 261
Gangpoor 9
Ganjam 32
Garana 57
garbha 396, 594
Garbhadhātu 50, 54, 62, 63, 86, 95, 102, 133, 142, 161, 206, 213, 217, 224, 225, 266, 332, 347, 371, 373, 379, 380, 383, 395, 401, 407, 413, 418, 430, 450, 467, 480, 494, 496, 500, 508, 509, 510, 544, 594, 628
eastern 305
inner Garbhadhātu 77
representation 133
seven northern constellations 208
thirteenth group 241
世間天院, the third court 319
水曜 334
火天 642

火曜 640
六大 461
Garbhadhātu group 71, 91, 213, 399, 419, 436, 556, 557
Garbhadhātu Kuan-yin group 90, 91
Garbhadhātu maṇḍala 63, 95, 137, 212, 213, 278, 364, 413, 432, 509, 546
四重曼荼羅 259
天鼓雷音佛, 鼓音如來 567
文殊 157
木曜 144
Garbhakośadhātu 102, 594
Gardabha 372
Garhwal 162
gariman 89
garjita 123
garuḍa 4, 19, 55, 66, 67, 91, 99, 101, 213, 372, 396, 400, 440, 568, 606
garuḍa-bird 71, 286
gata 2
Gatayaḥ 373
gati 19, 55, 108, 109, 110, 270, 278, 285, 300, 432, 475, 589, 619
six 461
Gaurī 583
gaus 441
Gautama 41, 42, 44, 48, 220
king of bulls 441
Gautama, the philosopher 496
Gautama-dharmajñāna 48
Gautama-prajñāruci 48
Gautama-saṅghadeva 48
Gautama's aunt 100
Gautamī 41, 42, 48, 54, 79, 96, 100
Gavāṁpati 2, 41, 67, 444
Gavāṁpati, 牛跡比丘 444
Gayaśāta 2, 486
Gayā 2, 80, 143, 521
Gayākāśyapa 2, 5
Gayāśīrṣa 296
Gayāśīrṣa sūtra
文殊師利 157
Gaṅgā 67, 621
Gaṅgā-nadī-vālukā 621
Gaṅgādatta 621
Gaṅgādevī 621
Gaṅgādvāra 67
Gaṇa 2
Gaṇapati 372, 373
Gaṇendra 212
Gaṇeśa 227, 233, 372, 643
Gaṇḍakī 342
gem 434
Gemini 364
generality 466
generation
世 318
世代 319
genii 347
人仙 307
germ-nature
bodhi-rank 429
five germ-natures 429
middle way 429
of study 429
saint 429
Germanai 245
geya 2, 50, 364, 471, 544
ghana 2, 16, 425, 608
Ghats 136
Ghazna 25, 620
Ghazni 620
ghaṇṭā 15, 538
ghola 416
Ghoree 165
Ghori 644
ghost genii 308
Ghoṣa 51, 147, 261
Ghoṣira 44, 47, 51
Ghoṣiravana park 44
ghrāṇa 2, 224
ghrāṇa-vijñāna 607
ghrāṇendriya 485
Ghuznee 536, 620
Ghāts 75
Ghūr 644
ghṛta 325
girdle 87
givings 249
go away 14
Go-rajas 443
Go-vratika 442
Goa 32
goat cart 41, 293
Gobharana 5, 115, 185, 314
四十二章經 253
Gobharaṇa 175
Gobi 592
goblins 429
gocara 24
God of Heaven 566
Godavery 100, 131, 216
Goddess of Mercy 38
Godhanya 47
gods in general 569
godāna 47, 379
Godāniya 47
Godānīya 305, 445
Godāvarī 388
Gokulika 25, 325, 645
Gokālī 47
gold and silver 303
Golden Clan 323
Golden Island 12
golden mean 503
golden vessel 435
golden-winged birds 525
gomatī 49
gomaya 14, 49, 443
gomūtra 49
gone 14
good by nature 316
Good Law Hall 567
good-fortune devīs 90
goose 518, 621
Gopikā 53
Gopsahasa 51
Gopā 47, 53, 393
水藏, Water-store 335
Gopāla 55
Gopī 393
Gorakhpur 17
gorocanā 48, 633
Gossypium Herbaceum 18
Gotamī 100
gourd 35
Gośīrṣa-candana 442
Gośṛṅga 52
ox-head 442
grabh 562
grades of saintship 239
gradual direct way 479

grah 562
graha 396, 562
grammar and composition 415
Grand Canal 536
Grantha 2
gravel 235
great 14, 635
great black deva 106
Great Brahmā 276
Great Law conch 94
Great Law drum 94
Great Master 341
great pity 510
Great Sun Tathāgata 227
Great-Light Ming-wang 89
green 420
grievance 447
grieved 107
Grosapam 49
Grīṣma 572
guardians
in a monastery 241
of the world 260
Guhyapati 485
guhā 57
Gujarat 54, 74, 130, 457
gully 31
Gumti 49
Gunduck 648
Gundwana 9
Gurjara 54
Gurupada 25
guṇa 44, 46, 77, 298, 439, 465, 466, 557, 615
six 467
Guṇabhadra 46, 79, 94, 101, 170, 518
guṇakṣetra 557
Guṇamati 48
Guṇanirdeśa-śāstra 324
Guṇaprabha 48
Guṇarata 48, 561, 599
Guṇavarman 46, 248
Guṇavṛddhi 46, 177
Gyeong-heo 135
gātha 2
gāthā 2, 19, 50, 68, 327, 364, 503, 537
Gītamitra 68
gṛdhra 68, 70
Gṛdhrakūṭa 68, 70, 92, 121, 234, 419, 463, 572, 580
Rājagṛha 436
Gṛdhrakūṭa mountain 118
Gṛha 396
gṛhapati 19, 519
gṛhastha 326

(H)

Hades 140
Hades-realm 183
Hae-in-sa 622
Hahava 2, 46, 376, 386, 610, 634
Hai-tung 446, 450
曉公四敎 239
Hail 508
Haimaka 618
Haimavatāḥ 104, 132, 313, 325, 631
hair 毛 142
Haklena 486
Haklenayaśas 620
half 166
Halfdeva brahman 166
hall 87
halo 40, 214, 301, 346, 567
halt 551
Halāhala 1
Hami 621
Han dynasty 56, 399, 424
Han Ming Ti 172, 212
Han Yü 213
handing down, transmission of the teaching 204
Hangchow 402, 419, 546, 549, 572, 573
Hangchow master 106
Hanging 628
Hangzhou 402
hao 111
Hao-chien 598
harali 9
hare in the moon 452
Haridrā 2
Haridwar 67
Harikeśa 1
Harita 2
Harivarman 1, 256, 324, 367, 456
hariṇa 618, 620
harmony 469
Harshavardhana 436
Harītakī 1, 510
Harṣavardhana 620
Hasara 620
Hasaurah 234
hasta 1, 328, 542
haste 67
Hastigarta 295
hastikāya 247, 296
hastin 295
Hastā 381, 486
hate 620
hatred 460
Haya 618
Hayagrīva 127, 213, 383, 431, 618
Hayamukha 222, 383
Hazāra 414
Haṁ 106
haṁsa 388, 618, 621
Haṁsa saṁghārāma 633
Haṇsarāja 595
head 446
healing 101
heart chaste as ice 353
Heart Sūtra 心經 352
heart within 76
heat 丙 194
heaven 292, 566
天堂 568
heavenly halls 568
heavens of desire 464
hell
scorching hell 638
三種地獄 the three kinds of hells 292
叫喚, fourth and fifth hot hells 60
hell-gati 555
hemanta 113, 572
heresy 436
heretics 436
hermaphrodites 168
heterodox 609
heterodox teaches 463
hetu 119, 235, 284, 292, 402,

415, 431, 493
hetu-viruddha 498
hetupratyaya 497, 631
hetuvidyā 496, 631
Hetuvidyā-śāstra 496
Hetuvādapūrva Sthavira 631
Hetuvādinaḥ 313
hima, 冬 113
Himatala 306, 648
Himālaya 361
Himālaya school 313
Himālayas 93, 494
hindrances 366, 368, 426
Hindu 494
Hindu mythology 107
Hindu philosophy 159
Hindukush 6, 294, 648
Hiouen Tsang 630
hiraṇya 61, 648
Hiraṇya-parvata 479
Hiraṇyavatī 66, 67, 118, 169, 170, 342, 345, 377, 383, 394, 607, 648
Hiuentsang 236
Hiyei 244
Hiüen-tsang 630
Hiḍḍa 631
hiṁsā 622
Hiṅgu 648
Hiṅgulā 161
Ho-ho-p'o 643
Ho-hsi 550
Ho-shan 635
Ho-shang 433
Hoangho 236
hole 31
Homa 294, 605, 620, 633, 634
四方 246
水壇 332
homa worship, burnt offerings 639
homa-spirits 366
Honan 96, 175
Honanfu 321
Hongwanji sect 561
Hooghly 85
hook 44
Hoosum Abdaul 85
horse 244, 365
horse-head 363, 618
Horse-master 127
Horse-neck 618
Horā 637
Hosna 620
Hossō 186, 367, 540, 587, 609
Hotei Oshō 614
hrada 618
Hrosminkan 647
hrīḥ 378, 431, 647
Hsi-an-fu 570
Hsi-ho 305
Hsi-lin 648
Hsi-ming 305
Hsi-yün 644
hsiang 316
Hsiang-chi 626
Hsiang-yen 625
Hsieh Ling-yün 406
Hsien 434
Hsien Shou Tsung 628
Hsien Tsung 213
Hsien-shou 298, 412, 516, 562
Hsien-shou Fa-tsang 190, 639
Hsin-hsing 266
hsing 316
Hsing-man 624
Hsining 539
Hsü 虛, one of the seven northern constellations 208
Hsü-chung 435
Hsü-t'ang 626
Hsüan Chuang 630
Hsüan Tsung 13, 173, 213, 378
Hsüan-ching 628
Hsüan-chio 628
Hsüan-ch'ang 630
Hsüan-fan 629
Hsüan-i 630
Hsüan-kao 628
Hsüan-lang 541, 628
Hsüan-sha 629
Hsüan-tsang 45, 51, 53, 79, 90, 92, 98, 99, 102, 110, 132, 136, 144, 158, 176, 222, 267, 276, 288, 305, 342, 345, 378, 379, 380, 388, 413, 416, 420, 424, 428, 431, 434, 455, 456, 497, 514, 540, 545, 546, 556, 567, 628, 629, 630, 632
Mokṣadeva 623
monastery where studied 341
唐三藏 87
Hsüan-tsang's translation 90, 362
Hsüan-ying 629, 632
Hsüan-yüan 629
hsün-tzǔ 210
hua-t'u 642
Hua-yen 24, 56, 92, 267, 280, 281, 283, 361, 367, 368, 412, 427, 478, 489, 503, 506, 587, 589, 607
Hua-yen ching 60, 455, 464
Hua-yen school 190, 292, 412, 479, 487, 516
Hua-yen sect 539
Hua-yen sūtra 207, 212, 280, 353, 363, 423, 430, 478, 479, 491, 611, 639
四勝身 252
Hua-yen yāna 639
Huang Ti 70
Huang-lung 644
Huang-po 644
Huch'iu Shan 634
Hugli 83
Huhuva 554
Hui Tsung 398
Hui-ching 633
Hui-ch'ao 633
Hui-ch'in 278
Hui-jih 378, 632
Hui-kuan 406, 632
Hui-kuang 41
Hui-k'ai 631
Hui-k'o 30, 86, 312, 339, 489, 631
six patriarchs 466
Hui-lin 632
Hui-lin-yin-i 648
Hui-ming 628
Hui-nan 644
Hui-ning 406
Hui-nêng 74, 88, 113, 121, 197, 312, 332, 410, 536, 538, 632
six patriarchs 466

北宗 208
Hui-ssŭ 555, 631, 632
台衡 594
天台九祖 572
Hui-wên
天台九祖 572
Hui-yen 406
Hui-yuan 120
Hui-yüan 120, 175, 325, 389, 531, 598, 632, 640
苑公四教 239
Hujikan 633
human corpse 142
human genii 308
human stage 498
Human-realm 183
Hun 633
Hunan 631, 633
hundred 175
Hung Fu monastery 630
Hung-chih 41
Hung-chou 177
Hung-fa 635
Hung-jên 312, 635
six patriarchs 466
北宗 208
Hunza-Nagar 171
Hupeh 434
Hupian 25, 634
Hurdwar 31
hut 389
Hutuktu 633, 644
Hydra 314, 383
hymns 182
Hêng mountains 631
Hêng-yo 628
Hêng-yo monastery 594
Hāhādhara 554
Hālāhala 1
Hāritī 1, 2, 59, 70, 166, 233, 305, 485
Hāva 639
Hāṭaka 2
Hīna 618
Hīnayāna 52, 281, 293, 323, 326, 339, 369, 478, 484, 488, 490, 504, 589, 602, 609, 619
Southern Buddhism 208
半字, half a character 167
Hīnayāna bodhisattva 41
Hīnayāna canon 488
Hīnayāna criteria 502
Hīnayāna nirvāṇa 276, 286
Hīnayāna philosophy 299
Hīnayāna rules 520
Hīnayāna saint 323
Hīnayāna salvation 357
Hīnayāna sanctity 261
Hīnayāna schools 280
Hīnayāna sūtra 287, 324, 325, 437
Hīnayāna to Mahāyāna 644
Hīnayāna śrāvakas 581
Hīnayāna śāstras 324
Hūna 643
Hūna king 103
hūṁ 106, 205, 386, 431
Hūṁkāra 647
Hṛd 620
hṛd 8, 124, 409, 472
心 351
hṛdaya 8, 15, 124, 409, 459, 620, 647
心 351
心經 Hṛdaya Sūtra 352

(I)

I 372
I-ching 305, 324, 424, 473, 497, 604, 633
王法經 436
I-chou 487
I-ch'ing 597
I-hsing 106, 511, 569, 637
I-hsüan 126
I-hsün 75
I-ju 398, 505
I-ning 500, 503
I-shan 503
I-tao 501
I-wu 621
I-wu Chün 487
I-wu(-lu) 487
icchanti 46, 84, 155, 272, 288, 457
icchantika 95, 276, 287, 292, 489, 498, 507, 567, 588
ice 233
ignorance, referred to as father 204
Ikṣvāku 11, 220, 228, 306, 499
Ikṣvāku Virūḍhaka 11, 507
Ili 644
illusion 643
immortal 216, 217, 307
immortality 408
仙經 308
immutable 217
immutable bhūtatathatā 217
Imperial Teacher 573
impermanence 464, 502
impure 409
in such a manner, tathā 83
In the Li 520
incantation 231
incarnations 186
Buddha's previous incarnations 202
incarnations of Amitābha 190
incarnations of vairocana represented with twelve arms 98
incarnations of Śākyamuni 144
previous incarnations 本事 80
incense 573, 625
incense kṣetra 626
incense-yielding tree 144
inch 577
incomplete nirvāṇa 458
increase 1
Indarab 167
independence 604
India 568, 571
Indian year 572
Indo-Scythian 3, 112, 451
Indra 41, 49, 54, 91, 101, 107, 163, 307, 333, 363, 365, 366, 492, 494, 496, 562, 566
四方 246
天主 571
天帝 571
Indra as General 496
Indra heaven 284, 606
Indra-altar 101

Indra-dhvaja 533
Indra-hasta 496
Indrabhavana 496, 572
Indraceṭa 496
Indradhanus 533
Indradhvaja 105, 496
Indraketu 496
Indranīla 131, 496, 533
Indranīla-(muktā) 105, 496
Indranīlaka 496
Indravadana 496, 572
Indravatī 496
Indraśailaguhā 419, 496, 533, 572, 633
Indra's attendants 496
Indra's banner 496
Indra's cave 496
Indra's city 496
Indra's hand 496
Indra's musicians 97, 135
indriya 78, 295, 474, 475
five indriyas 431
six indriyas 460
Indrākṣa 387
Indrāṇī 571, 583
Indu 571
Indu-dharmarakṣa 579
Indu-dharmāraṇya 579
Indus 346, 607
four rivers 261
inference in logic, 四宗 258
inferior 224, 404
infrangible-diamond rules 505
Ingachar 642
inherence 466
initial knowledge 200
inner 75, 436
inspect 314
instant 251
intellection 235
interaction 446
interdependence 446
intermediate existence 545
Intermediate school 205, 318, 515
internal and external 76
intoxicating liquor 136
Intuitional school 86, 539
intuitive certainty 354
intuitive principle 以心傳心 475
Invakā 486
inverted 108
invisibles 248
invite 321
inviter 321
Irawaddy 591
Irāvatī 479
Isfijab 176
Iskardu 9
Issar 648
Issikoul 85
Itivṛttaka 58, 143, 202, 364, 488, 502
itivṛttaka 50
ityukta 50, 202, 488
Iṣīkā 482

(Ī)
Īkṣaṇa 491
Īkṣaṇi 491
Īriṇa-parvata 479
Īrṣyā(paṇḍaka) 168
Īrṣyāpaṇḍaka 428, 480
Īśa 482
Īśvara 89, 102, 379, 483, 517
Īśvaradeva 517
Īśāna 246, 363, 482, 605
Īśānapura 482, 483
Īśānī 482
Īṣādhara 51, 66, 482, 549

(ī)
īrṣyā 562
īrṣyāpaṇḍaka 597
īśitva 90

(J)
jack-fruit 599
jade 434
jade Buddha 434
Jade-fountain and Jade-flower 434
jagat 235
Jaimini 159
Jaina 234
Jaina religion 68
jaka 599
jala 234
jalacandra 334
Jalandar 234
Jalavāhana 333, 335
Jalāmbara 333
Jamadagni 407
Jambhala 525
Jambhīra 525
Jambu 406
Jambu timber 15
Jambudvipa 165
Jambudvīpa 74, 89, 296, 313, 375, 406, 407, 563, 574, 610
四洲, four continents 258
Jambū 313
Jambūnadī 314
Jambūnadī river 314
Jamna 407
Janma-maraṇa 308
jantu 308
Japan 271, 324, 511
日域 499
日本 499
Japanese Buddhist sects 370
Japanese sects 609
jarā 78
Jarā-maraṇa 80
jarā-maraṇa 78, 365
jarāyu 234
jarāyuja 250
Jasminum Zambac 136
Jasminum Zambæ 211
jaundice 5
Java 31, 392, 393
Jaxartes 37
jaya 234, 418
Jayagupta 234
Jayanta 234
Jayapura 234
Jayasena 234, 274
Jayata 2, 234, 486
Jayendra 234
jaḍatā 82
Je-gwan 534
Jellalabad 71
Jellālabad 631
Jeta 29, 68, 304
Jeta grove 338
Jeta, Mount 550
Jetaka 340

Jetavana 29, 66, 68, 255, 338, 374, 446, 523, 604
eight famous Caityas 548
牛頭大王, guardian of the monastery 442
Jetavana vihāra 329, 463, 644
Jetavanīyāḥ 299, 325, 532, 550, 591
Jetā 68
Jetīyaśailāḥ 550
Jetṛ 68, 304
Jetṛvana 523
Jetṛvana School 550
Jhánas(Jñānas) 309
jhāpita 82, 234, 251, 392, 640
Ji-nul 112
Ji-shū 502
Jih-chao 553
jihvendriya 485
jihvā 312, 341
jihvā-vijñāna 607
jina 67, 100, 101, 557, 578
Jina Dignāga 604
Jinabandhu 558
Jinamitra 338
Jinaputra 345, 455, 558
Jinatrāta 558
Jinayaśas 67
Jizō 555
Jogye Order 113
Ma-gok-sa 128
Jonesia aśoka 384
Joseon 537
joy-born heaven 637
Joy-view city 284
Jshtrakh 634
ju 398, 505
Ju-ch'ü 83
ju-i pearl 4
Ju-lai 83, 399
Ju-t'ung Bodhisattva 527
Jui-chou 113
Jumna 15, 42, 52, 131, 607
junior monk 325
junior teacher 325
Jupiter 53, 144, 158, 383, 420
木星 144
Jupiter-lord 158
just 526
jvala 234
jvāla 234, 512
Jyaiṣṭha 304, 531, 572
Jyeṣṭhaghnī 485
Jyeṣṭhā 304, 485
Jyotiṣa 314
six śāstras 461
Jyotiṣa śāstra 331
Jyotiṣka 314, 329, 331
Jyotiṣprabha 40
Jyotīrasa 15, 329
Jên Wang Ching 119
jñapticaturthin 583
Jñaptidvitīyā karmavācanā 177
jñeya 476
jñāna 359, 393, 461, 550, 607, 608, 631
Jñāna-prasthāna-ṣaṭpādābhidharma 466
Jñānabhadra 92, 406
Jñānacandra 555, 632
Jñānagupta 93, 406
Jñānaguptā 217, 234
jñānakāya 553, 622
Jñānaprabha 552
Jñānayaśas 234
Jñānākara 385, 556
Jñāti 80
Jñāti Nirgrantha 264
Jñātīputra 393
Jñātṛ 72, 293, 436
Jñātṛ clan 293
Jñātṛputra 234
jāla 137, 316
Jālandhara 87, 234
Jālinīprabhakumāra 40
Jāmbūnada 314
Jāmbūnada-suvarṇa 314, 406
Jāta-rūpa 303
jātaka 50, 58, 234, 235, 364
Jātaka stories 489
Jātaka sūtras 202
jātakamālā 235
jātarūpa-rajata-paṭīggahaṇā-veramaṇī 356
jātarūpa-rajata-pratigrahaṇād vairamaṇī (virati) 221
jāti 80, 234, 302, 365, 647
jātijarā 234
Jātipaṇḍaka 168
Jātiṁdhara 549
Jātiṣenā 234, 274, 308
Jāuman 647
Jīva 67
jīva 67, 328, 644
Jīvajīvaka 140, 341
jīvaka 67, 341, 389, 644
Jīvakahrada 121
jīvaṁjīva 140
jīvita 140, 328
jīvitendriya 485
Jīvitākāra 341
Jōdō 54, 367, 540, 587
Jōdō sect 325, 547
Jōdō Shin-shu 215, 531, 538
Jōjitsu 367, 540, 609
Jōjitsu-shū 316

(K)

Kabul 6, 211, 224
Kach 25
Kacha 25
kadamba 3
Kadjéri 10
Kaifeng 96
Kajangala 10
Kajinghara 10
Kajūghira 10
Kakuda-Kātyāyana 4, 6, 436, 463
Kakṣa 25
Kalahu 9
kalala 3, 9, 608
kalalaṁ 425
kalandaka 4, 9
Kalaviṅka 1, 3, 4, 10, 55, 147, 232, 633
kalaviṅka pitcher 232
kalaśa 9
kali 3, 4
Kalingapatnam 10
Kalirāja 3, 4, 10, 494, 597
Kaliṅga 10
Kaliṅgarāja 4
kalmāṣapāda 167, 568
kalpa 17, 18, 47, 89, 265, 279, 280, 363, 504, 506, 584, 604

1,000th part, 世 318
illustration of the length 570
middling 544
six śāstras 461
四劫 238
kalpa of destruction 18, 250
kalpa of existence 18
kalpa of formation 18
kalpa of utter annihilation 18
kalpa-ash 19
Kalpa-kalpāyati 19
Kalpataru 18
kalyāṇamitra 311
kalā 3, 4
kambala 11, 396, 647
Kamboja 11
Kampa 17
Kampilla 18, 66
Kamrup 5
kan 442
Kan-lu-wang 586
kanaka 3, 9
Kanakamuni 3, 35, 47, 205, 360, 584
Kanauj 25, 52, 339, 604
Kandahar 16, 25, 620
Kandat 634
Kangra 58
kanika 3
Kaniṣka 3, 6, 22, 87, 179, 416, 451, 636, 647
Kanjur 11
Kansu 11, 29, 112, 539
kanthā 16
kanyā-ratna 196
Kanyākubja 10, 25, 31, 52, 97, 181, 342, 436, 604, 620
eight famous Caityas 548
Kanyākūbdja 75
Kao Tsung 40, 305, 630
Kao-ch'ang 29
kaparda 19
Kapila 5, 17, 169, 280, 339, 436, 492
Kapilavastu 2, 4, 5, 17, 119, 126, 176, 222, 228, 254, 256, 307, 328, 331, 363, 604
meaning 妙德 145
四塔 260
父城 204
Kapimala 5, 486
Kapittha 18, 339
Kapiñjala 4
Kapiñjalarāja 4
Kapiśa 243
Kapiśā 6, 46, 49, 170, 179, 226, 295, 388, 495
kapotaka 6, 621
Kapotaka-saṁghārāma 6, 621
Kapotana 19
Kapphiṇa 18, 47, 89
kapāla 18, 123
kapālī 123
kara 328
Karachi 384
Karakhodjo 29
Karakoram 9
Karaphu 9
Karashahr 29, 43, 44, 144, 225, 381, 412, 551, 555
Karavīka 15
Karavīra 4, 9
Karaṇḍa(ka) 4, 543, 633
Karaṇḍa-veṅuvana 4, 91, 224
Karaṇḍa-veṇuvana 543
Karghalik 517, 525
karma 9, 10, 282, 361, 365, 396, 505, 515, 586, 587, 588, 624
correct karma, 正報 319
karma forms, one of ten fields of meditation 551
karma of suffering 30
Karma school 341
karma-bondage 396
karma-bonds 396, 397
karma-cause 397, 505
karma-circumstance 397
karma-fetters 396
karma-hetu 476
karma-jñāna-mudrā 259
karma-māras 396
karma-seed 397
karmabīja 397
karmadhāraya 462
Karmadāna 10
karmadāna 265, 329, 404, 453, 553
karmaic reward 362
karman 140, 300, 396, 418, 466
karmasthāna 397
Karmavajra 431
Karmavācā 582
karmāvaraṇa 397
karpūra 10, 19
Karsana 49
Karsanah 227
Kartchou 9, 19
kartṛ 518
kartṛkaraṇa 609
karuṇā 4, 224, 242
Karāla 4
Karṇasuvarṇa 9, 313, 451
Karṣa 4
Karṣaṇa 4
karṣaṇīya 5
Kashanian 58
Kashgar 15, 57, 92, 186, 320, 517
Kashgaria 320
Kashmir 6, 18, 22, 137, 495
Kashmiri-Ghār 84, 592
Kasia 15
Kasiah 52, 343
Kasioi 9
kastūrī 136
Kathāvatthu 419
Kaukkuṭikas 25
Kaukkuṭikāḥ 47, 325
Kaumārī 583
Kaurava 610
Kaurukullakāḥ 275
kausīdya 622
kauśeya 29, 41
Kauśika 41, 308
Kauśāmbī 14, 42, 44, 52, 304, 363, 413, 441, 444, 523, 537
Kauṇḍinya 10, 42, 49, 241, 383, 635
Kauṣṭhila 52
Kaśanna 10
kaṅkara 12
Kaṇabhuj 9, 16
Kaṇāda 9, 16, 230, 280, 338, 452, 646
Kaṇṭhaka 15, 16
Kaṇṭhaka-aśvarāja 66

kaṣāya 1, 4, 5, 16, 125, 181, 288, 408, 432, 494, 521, 592
Kaṭapūtana 6, 10
kaṭhina 6, 579
Kebud 19
Kebudhana 19
keen 415
Kegon 283, 367, 427, 489, 540, 587, 609
Kegon sūtra 92
Kekaya 70
kele-yin iikin tegri 94
Kelikila 550
Kenshin 174
kerchief 598
Kermina 58
kesara 26
Keshbūd 19
ketu 26, 53, 87
Ketumatī 361
keyūra 70, 340
Keśakambala 340
Keśinī 83, 357, 419
khadira 6, 9, 18
Khadiraka 6, 10, 15, 16, 51, 66
khakkhara 60, 70, 305
Khan 2
khapuṣpa 35
khara 15, 120
Kharakaṇṭha 15
Kharismiga 10
Kharizm 635
kharjūra 9
Kharoṣṭha 120
Kharoṣṭhī 15, 373, 464
Kharādīya 2
Khatun 2
Khavakan 379
Khavandha 19, 549
Khawak 167
Khaśa 9
khaḍga 9, 15, 16
khaḍga-viṣāṇa 16
Khaṁ 106
Khaṅga 9
khaṇḍa 15, 16
khaṭaka 15
khaṭvā 15
Khaṭṭika 10
Khchara 236
khelā 648
Kheṭa 69
Khnora 236
Khojend 78
Khost 644
Khotan 51, 102, 169, 228, 342, 351, 409, 434, 442, 517, 551, 611, 635, 636
Khoten 644
Khri-srong-lde-btsan 17
Khro-bo 360
Khuddakāgama 58
Khulm 635, 647
Khusta 644
khādanīya 3, 15, 487
khāra 15
khāri 15
Khārismiga 635
khārī 15
khārīka 15
Kiang-nan 267
Kiangning 442
Kiangsi 12, 113, 127, 644
Kiangsu 12, 29, 442, 536
Kikaṇa 25
kill 217
Kilāsa 550
Kin 96
kindness 493
king 435
King Aśoka Shan 419
king of bulls 441, 444
King of the sugar-cane 11
King Udayana 14
King Yama 21
king-goose 383
kinnara 3, 20, 69, 97, 113, 114, 184, 365, 440, 497, 568, 606, 625
Kirāta 25
Kiṁkara 20, 67, 206
kiṁśuka 20, 69, 392
kleśa 78, 178, 237, 333, 409, 456, 481, 581, 623, 647
 ninety-eight kleśas 53
 six great 412, 461
 the seven messengers 585
kleśa-afflictions 165
kliṣṭa-mano-vijñāna 607
kliṣṭamano-vijñāna 532
klṛp 19
knowledge 231
knowledge-conduct-perfect 142
Koeppen's hypothesis 284
Kojend 327
Kokila 4, 43, 47, 55, 633
Kokyar 517
Kokāli 47
Kokālika 47
Kokāliya 47
Kolita 49, 143
Konkan 32
Konnāda 32
Konyodha 32
Koondooz 165
Kophen 6
Korea 25, 29, 43, 120, 161, 537
Korean canon 103
Korean canon of Buddhism 29
Korean monk
 incarnation of 地藏 555
Korean Tripiṭaka 120
Kosala 42, 129, 136, 171, 340
Kosam 15, 42, 51, 52
Kosambi 14
Kotlan 3
kovidāra 51
kośa 51, 324, 367
Kośa school 589
Kośa sect 540
Kośala 29, 42, 228, 363, 384
 prince 沙多婆漢那 495
Koṅkaṇapura 32
koṭī 35, 49, 55, 96, 175, 484, 582
Krakucchanda 4, 9, 35, 49, 360, 584
Krishna 388, 647
krodha 360, 558
krośa 44, 48, 100, 121, 454
krīḍā 648
Ku-tsang 29
Ku-wa-wa 31
kuan 37
 觀, compared to 止 551
Kuan Ti 37
Kuan-ting 173

Kuan-yin 38, 53, 57, 70, 89, 93, 95, 104, 213, 219, 226, 272, 284, 285, 366, 377, 408, 433, 465, 483, 484, 493, 505, 517, 566, 599, 603, 608
gazing at the moon in the water 334
half-opened lotus 159
horse-head 618
six kinds of 460
six words, six forms 465
with the thousand hands 433
日天子 499
Kuan-yin symbol 285
Kuan-yin's images 363
Kuang the general supervisor 41
Kuang-chai 40, 239
Kuang-ming ssŭ 40
Kuang-t'ung 267, 448
Kubera 17, 51, 56, 229
Kubhā 6, 25, 46
Kubhāna 25
Kublai 446
Kublai Khan 169, 606
Kucha 57
Kuche 44
Kuei-fêng 187, 412, 504
Kuei-fêng Tsung-mi 639
Kuei-shan 452
Kuei-yang 452
Kukejar 517
Kukkulikas 25
Kukkura 538
kukkura-vratika 442
kukkuṭa 43, 44, 46, 47
Kukkuṭa-ārāma 57
Kukkuṭapāda 25
Kukkuṭapādagiri 57
Kukkuṭeśvara 25, 43
Kukkuṭikas 25
Kukura 538
Kukyar 517
kula 48
Kulanātha 48, 561
kulapati 1, 4, 14, 48
Kulika 49, 307
Kulu 58
Kulun 58
Kulūta 58
Kumarata 44
kumbha 435
kumbhāṇḍa 32, 44, 46, 70, 228, 606
kumbhāṇḍa demons 58
kumbhāṇḍka 435
kumbhīra 17, 51, 58, 65, 349, 365, 387
Kumidha 50
kumuda 50, 120, 262
Kumuda-pati 450
kumāra 43, 44, 46, 49, 113, 436, 514
kumāra-bhūta 44
Kumārajīva 1, 43, 44, 47, 62, 97, 103, 104, 105, 118, 146, 175, 177, 181, 211, 225, 270, 303, 312, 355, 364, 368, 406, 453, 493, 505, 540, 545
九轍法師, nine division of the Lotus Sūtra 55
四聖, the four chief disciples 251
kumāraka 44
kumāraka-stage 44
Kumārakadeva 49
Kumāralabdha 44
four suns 255
Kumārarāja 594
Kumārata 49, 486
Kumārāyaṇa 44
Kunda 57
Kundoot 634, 648
Kunduruka 455, 646
Kunduz 634, 635, 647
Kunlun range 625
Kunti 60
Kunti Kuan-yin 53
Kuntu-bzan-po 384
Kuntī 28, 357
Kupana 43
Kuravaḥ 43, 610
Kuraṇṭa 48
Kurrah 15, 42
Kurrategeen 57
Kurree 374
Kuru 49, 265
Kurudvīpa 49
Kuryana 57
Kusha 367, 540, 609
Kusia 42
Kustana 51, 155, 351, 409, 442, 535, 636, 644
kusuma 44, 52, 636
kusuma-mālā 52, 637
Kusumapura 44, 52, 601, 639
kusumavatī 52
kusumbha 52
Kutche 57
Kuvayana 57
Kuvera 51, 56, 69, 94, 129, 229, 260, 363, 393, 520
Kuveradeva 293
Kuñjara 8, 442
kuśa 29, 70
kuśa-grass 52, 298
kuśala 308
kuśala-mūla 309
Kuśanābha 10
Kuśigrāmaka 343
Kuśika 41
Kuśinagara 46, 51, 52, 119, 136, 343, 363, 401, 405, 543, 604, 648
四塔 260
Kuśāgrapura 43, 52, 70, 229, 298, 436
kuśūla 52
Kuḍikā 57
kuṅkuma 82, 446
Kuṇāla 43, 48, 51, 442, 533
kuṇḍa 57
Kuṇḍali-rāja 431
Kuṇḍalin 57
Kuṇḍi 57
kuṇḍikā 57, 197, 537
kuṭaṅgaka 55
Kwangtung 197, 445, 536, 538
Kykānān 25
Kêng-shên 23
kāca 6
Kācalindikāka 6
Kācamaṇi 6
Kācilindi 6
Kāka 3
Kākala 3

ㄱ ㄴ ㄷ ㄹ ㅁ ㅂ ㅅ ㅇ ㅈ ㅊ ㅋ ㅌ ㅍ ㅎ 찾아보기

Kākaruta 3
kāla 4, 484, 647
Kālaka 2, 4
Kālaka and tinduka 4
Kālapināka 4
Kālarātri 647
Kālasūtra 327, 554, 647
kālasūtra 603
Kālikā 5
Kālodaka 365
Kālodayin 460
Kālodāyin 4
Kālāśoka 384
Kālī 106
kālīyaka 5
kāma 5, 17, 391, 438
kāma-bhava-dṛṣṭi-avidyā 439
Kāmadhātu 5, 113, 127, 266, 438, 439, 568
Kāmadhātu realms 438
Kāmalaṅkā 5
kāmalā 5
Kāmarūpa 5, 222
Kāpālikas 6, 123
Kāra(ka) 4
kāraṇa 518
Kāraṇahetu 465
Kārmikāḥ 341
kārpāsa 18
Kārpāsī 18
Kārttika 3, 572
Kārttika-māsa 6
Kārttikeya 583
Kārṣāpaṇa 4, 10, 25
Kātyāyana 6, 88, 357, 522, 602
Kātyāyanīputra 228
kāya 2, 6, 9, 345
four bodies 252
kāya-vijñāna 347, 607
kāyendriya 346, 485
Kāñcana-mālā 442
Kāñcīpura 16
Kāśa 1, 5
Kāśapura 5
Kāśmīra 6
Kāśyapa 5, 22, 25, 35, 57, 181, 265, 280, 293, 312, 316, 360, 471, 584
Buddha held up a flower and ~ smiled 406
Kāśyapa brothers: 12
Kāśyapa Buddha 5
Kāśyapa Mātaṅga 5, 115, 129, 314, 579
四十二章經 253
Kāśyapa-dhātu 131
Kāśyapa's radiant body 471
Kāśyapīyāḥ 5, 325, 417, 457, 482
Kāśyapīyāḥ school 1
Kāśī 6, 363, 610
Kāṇa 3
Kāṇadeva 2, 3, 273, 486, 534
Kāṣyapīyāḥ 509
kāṣāya 65, 287
kāṣṭha 144
Kāṭhmāṇḍū 81
kōan 480
Kōbō Daishi 133, 161, 595
Kōhō 368
Kōphēn 25
kūla 48, 388
Kūrān 57
Kūṭadantī 31, 357
Kūṭaśālmali 55
kṛpā 224
Kṛsara 5
kṛta 70, 647
Kṛttikā 486
kṛtya 393, 647
Kṛtyā 70, 647
Kṛtyānuṣṭhāna-jñāna 430
Kṛṣṇa 5, 71, 131, 164, 167, 350, 647
Kṛṣṇapakṣa 647
kṛṣṇapakṣa 177
Kṛṣṇapura 31, 131
kṣamayati 565
kṣamā 563, 565
kṣatriya 93, 342, 368, 451, 564
four castes 251
Kṣatriya
the founder of the Kṣatriya caste 613
kṣauma 565, 578
kṣaumaka 578
Kṣaya 17, 563
kṣaṇa 12, 78, 85, 251, 268, 329, 341, 500, 507, 563, 564, 576
kṣema 564
Kṣemadarśin 381
kṣetra 187, 304, 507, 531, 563, 564, 647
Kṣitigarbha 40, 357, 378, 555, 556
Kṣudra 541
Kṣudrakāgama 423
Kṣudrapanthaka 541
kṣumā 578
kṣānti 28, 163, 287, 416, 461, 493, 564, 608
kṣānti pāramitā 494
Kṣānti-ṛṣi 10
Kṣāntyṛṣi 494, 564
kṣārapāṇīya 563, 565
kṣīra 415
kṣīriṇikā 563
Kṣīṇāśrava 263
K'ai-yüan 13, 378
K'ai-yüan Catalogue 520
K'o-ch'in 278
K'u-ch'ê 29
K'uei-chi 98, 176, 186, 514, 632
K'un-lun 31
K'urun 29

(L)

lacking 617
Ladakh 395
ladder-to-heaven hill 571
laghiman 89
laghu 117
laguḍa 117
Lahore 171
laisser-faire 458
laity 77, 326
lakh 118, 358
lakṣa 270
lakṣaṇa 117, 285, 296, 459, 561, 611
lakṣaṇa-vyañjana 300
lakṣaṇāni 169, 421
Lakṣmī 70, 118, 350, 452, 485
Lalitavistara 306
Lama 117
Lamaistic branch 390
Lamaistic charm, oṁ maṇi

padme hūṁ 465
Lamaistic sect 635
Lambana 108, 119, 442
Lambhara 119
Lambinī 119
Lambura 119
Lambā 119, 357
Lamghan 119
Lampā(ka) 119
Lao Tzŭ 78, 644
convert Huns to Buddhism 226
Laocius 78
lapis lazuli 57, 227, 613
latārka 627
Laukika 319
Laurus Cassia 83
lava 119, 251
Lavinī 119
Law 94
correct Law, 正法 251
decadence of the Law, 末法 251
semblance of the Law, 像法 251
laḍḍuka 117
Laṅgala 327
Laṅkā 75, 79, 124
Laṅkā mountain 79
Laṅkāvatāra-sūtra 64, 79, 86, 106, 125, 127, 135, 183, 216, 310, 312, 344, 454, 507, 582
four bodies 252
leave 14
lekha 304
Lentil Monastery 114
Leo 364
letter 158
level 613
Lhasa 96, 195, 614
Lhasa Potala 195
li 58, 359
Li Po 56
Li-chou 631
Li-i 400
Liang dynasty 97
festival of water and land 333
Liang Wu Ti 323, 395, 443, 520
Liang-chou 199
Liang-pên 119
Liangchow 29
Liberation 611
Libra 364
Licchavi 120, 124, 125, 126, 229, 333, 390, 401
lie 216
Lien-shê sect 427
life 302
life and death 303
life-star 201
lifetime 319
Lignum Aloes 387
likh 304
likṣā 67, 500
Limbinī 119
lime 645
Limestone hill dwellers 645
Lin-chi 533
lineage 111
Ling Miao monastery 211
Ling-an Hsien 23
Ling-chi school
school 243
Ling-chih monastery 549
lion king 256
lion-flag 256
lion-throne 408
lion's roar 256
liquid 331
liquid fire 642
literalist 158
Little Bukharia 517
Liu Ch'iu 422
Liu Sung dynasty 101
Liṅga 129, 304
Lo-yang 73, 175, 379
lobha 8, 474
Locana 120, 124, 227, 276, 566
Locana Buddha 567
lofty 592
logic 415
Logos 108
loha 122
lohan 375
500 lohans 416
lohita(ka) 122
Lohita-mukta 121
loka 122
世 318
loka-geya 122
Lokajyeṣṭha 122, 320
Lokanātha 122, 320, 437
Lokapāla 224, 277, 407, 634
Lokavid 2, 122, 319, 371, 553
Lokaviruddha 319
Lokavit 122
Lokeśvara 437
Lokeśvara-rāja 121, 123, 320
Lokottaravādinaḥ 104, 121, 132, 325, 580
Lokottaravādinaḥ school 313
lokāntarika 29, 554
lokāntarika hells 192, 554
Lokāyata 401
lokāyatika 122
Lokāyatika teachings
世論 319
looseness 216
Lop 75
Lop Nor 412
lord 482, 541
lose 349
Lotus 278, 602
Lotus group 278
Lotus sect 190, 191, 499
Lotus Sūtra 120, 191, 212, 266, 416, 421, 428, 504, 546
burning house 642
six auspicious indications 463
twenty-eight chapters 260
Lotus-brilliance Bodhisattva 637
Lotus-kṣetra 120
Lotus-radiance 636
lotus-samādhi 509
Loyang 12, 86
Lu Hsüan-jih 577
Lu-chang 158
Lucknow 5
Lumbinī 119, 122, 123, 124, 126, 440, 479, 606
eight famous Caityas 548
Lumbinī deer park 288
Lumbinī garden 289
Luminous Religion 23

Lung Hsing monastery 440
Lung-shu 435
lust 276
Lythrum fructicosum 160
lākṣā 124
Lāra 74, 117, 130
Lāḍa 117
Lāṭa 117, 130, 179

(M)
Ma-gok-sa 128
Ma-tsu 12, 74, 127, 312
Macedonia 384
Madana 136
madhu 129, 131
madhugola 127
Madhurā 131, 158
madhya 136, 147, 532, 544
Madhyadeśa 137, 534, 544
Madhyama 282
Madhyamayāna 167, 281, 292, 293
Madhyamāgama 386, 423
 四阿含 253
Madhyānta-vibhāga-śāstra 545
Madhyāntika 137, 419, 495
Madhūka 136
Madya 136, 542
Magadha 4, 11, 42, 45, 49, 57, 70, 128, 156, 171, 229, 233, 234, 363, 374, 379, 381, 382, 390, 437, 482, 494, 523, 533, 604, 643
 language, Pali 598
 四塔 260
magha 133
Maghā 128, 486
Maghīn 159
Magic City 276
magical formula 502
Maha-maudgalyāyana 143
mahallakas 131
Maharddhiprāpta 400
Maharṣi 96
Mahendra 100, 130, 132, 133, 381, 494
Mahendrī 100
Maheśvara 93, 99, 102, 103, 104, 130, 132, 133, 168, 224, 273, 274, 320, 366, 400, 482, 485, 492, 508, 517, 566, 570
 他化自在天 592
 天中天 571
Maheśvara, wife of 112
Maheśvarapura 133
Maheśvarites 436
Maheśvarī 130
mahiman 89
Mahopāya 93
mahoraga 133, 137, 143, 365, 440, 568, 606
Mahratta 131
Mahā 88
Mahā-cundī 104
Mahā-cīna 548
Mahā-Dignāga 100
Mahā-kapphiṇa 18
Mahā-Kāśyapa 74, 122, 164, 617
mahā-nirvāṇa 431
Mahā-parinirvāṇa sūtras 92
Mahā-prajñā-pāramitā sūtra 92
Mahā-prajñā-pāramitā-sūtra 92, 326
mahā-prajñāpāramitā 132
mahā-śrāvaka 315
mahābali 106
Mahābherī-hāraka-parivarta 94
Mahābhijñā 83, 181, 256, 328, 556, 626
Mahābhijñā-jñānābhibhu 22, 96, 105, 108, 205, 533
Mahābhijñābhibhū 149, 293, 385, 445, 496
Mahābhārata 17
 reference of China 548
Mahābhūta
 四大 241
Mahābodhi-saṅghārāma 132
Mahābrahman 93, 182, 485
Mahābrahmā 250, 276, 301, 342
Mahābrahmā devarāja 93
Mahābrahmā Sahāṁpati 236
Mahābrahmā-sahāṁpati 180
Mahābrahmāṇas 93
Mahābrahmā's dharmakāya 93
Mahācakravāla 105
mahācittasattva 132
Mahādeva 99, 104, 106, 132, 299, 306, 324, 325, 419
Mahādevī 132
Mahādhyānaguru 200
mahādruma 97
Mahāgautamī 131
mahājñāna-mudrā 259
Mahākalpa 89
mahākalpa 18, 301
Mahākapphiṇa 89
Mahākaruṇā 95
Mahākaruṇā-puṇḍarīka sūtra 95
Mahākauṣṭhila 90, 131
Mahākāla 99, 106, 107, 131, 273, 647
Mahākātyanīputra 6
Mahākātyāyana 6, 88, 131
Mahākāya 99
Mahākāśyapa 2, 5, 40, 66, 73, 88, 101, 103, 131, 132, 241, 288, 299, 357, 419, 486
Mahākāśyapīyāḥ 471
Mahāmaheśvara 301
mahāmandāra 262
mahāmandāras 573
mahāmandārava 132
Mahāmati 104, 106, 127
Mahāmaudgalyāyana 49, 83, 91, 132, 142, 158, 241, 384, 416
Mahāmañjūṣaka 103
mahāmañjūṣaka 132, 262
mahāmañjūṣakas 573
Mahāmucilinda 132, 143
Mahāmuni 143
Mahāmāyā 130, 131, 216, 328
mahānagna 131
mahānirvāṇa 167
Mahānāga 71, 131
Mahānāma 49, 107
Mahānāma-Kulika 419
Mahānāman 131
Mahānīla 100, 105
mahānīla 131
Mahāpadma 132, 554

Mahāparinirvāṇa 92, 98
mahāparinirvāṇa 132
Mahāparinirvāṇa Sūtra 216, 405, 435
Mahāparinirvāṇa sūtra 187, 405
Mahāparinirvāṇa-sūtra 405, 540
Mahāprajñā 417
mahāprajñā 132
Mahāprajñā-pāramitā sūtra 105, 434
Mahāprajñāparāmitā-śāstra 243
Mahāprajñāpāramitā-sūtra 175
Mahāprajāpatī 41, 48, 79, 96, 100, 132, 133, 171, 510
the first 比丘尼 225
Mahāpralaya 97
Mahāpratibhāna 100
mahāpūrṇa 91
Mahāratna-dharma-rāja 94
Mahāratnakūṭa 94, 241
Mahāratnakūṭa-sūtra 94
Mahāraurava 90, 106, 554
mahāraurava 603
Mahāroṣaṇa 131
Mahārāja 100, 170, 548
mahārāja 131
mahārāja bodhisattva 32
Mahārāja-devas 570
mahārāja-devas 160
Mahārājas 107, 181, 502
mahārājas 208, 320, 363, 486, 606
四金剛 240
Mahārāṣṭra 131
Mahārūpa 96, 105
Mahāsamudra-sāgara 105
Mahāsattva 95, 127, 132, 198
Mahāsattva-kumāra-rāja 132
Mahāsatya-nirgrantha 95
Mahāsaṁbhava 96
Mahāsaṁmata 96, 306
Mahāsaṁnipāta 104
Mahāsaṅgha 104
Mahāsaṅghanikāya 132, 324
Mahāsaṅghāta 417
Mahāsaṅghāta-sūtra 104
Mahāsthavira 57, 299
Mahāsthavira school 132
Mahāsthavirāḥ 104
Mahāsthāma 96
Mahāsthāma-prāpta 280
Mahāsthāmaprāpta 96, 115, 119, 131, 132, 144, 161, 196, 224, 267, 277, 289, 318, 378, 450, 452, 493, 500, 603
Mahāsāra 132
Mahāsāṅghika 5, 57, 324, 377, 379, 641
Mahāsāṅghika-nikāya 133
Mahāsāṅghikas 313
分別 209
Mahāsāṅghikāḥ 104, 132, 223, 299, 300, 313, 325, 471, 631
Mahāsāṅghikāḥ division 580
Mahāsāṅghikāḥ school 113, 121, 211, 216, 221, 305, 339
Mahāsāṅghikāḥ-version 255
Mahāsāṅghikāḥs 25
mahātantra 89
Mahātantra(dhāraṇī) 131
Mahātejas 101
Mahātāpana 60, 100
Mahāvaipulya 92, 93
Mahāvaipulya-mahāsaṁnipāta-sūtra 93
Mahāvairocana 95, 101, 132
Mahāvana-saṅghārāma 91
Mahāvihāra 95, 132
Mahāvihāravāsinaḥ 132, 299, 591
Mahāvyūha 103
Mahāvādin 91
Mahāvīra 80
Mahāvṛkṣa 10, 31
Mahāvṛkṣa ṛṣi 97
Mahāyāna 88, 90, 94, 132, 151, 281, 293, 299, 316, 323, 339, 356, 403, 416, 448, 478, 480, 484, 488, 490, 492, 501, 503, 504, 510, 602, 609
Northern Buddhism 208
滿字, complete word 167
別教 416
Mahāyāna altar 27
Mahāyāna bodhisattva 41
Mahāyāna bodhisattva development 369
Mahāyāna Buddhism 43
Mahāyāna bugle 94
Mahāyāna canon 364, 488
Mahāyāna Ch'an 299
Mahāyāna doctrine 159, 502
Mahāyāna nirvāṇa 286
Mahāyāna sūtra 287
Mahāyāna sūtras 98
Mahāyāna way 294
Mahāyāna-cum-Hīnayāna 448
mahāyāna-cum-hīnayāna 421
Mahāyāna-deva 99
Mahāyāna-enlightenment 94
Mahāyāna-fundament 98
Mahāyāna-saṁparigraha-śāstra 314, 540
Mahāyāna-yoga 299
Mahāyāna-śraddhotpāda-śāstra 98, 127
Mahāyānadeva 132, 144, 630
Mahāyānasūtrālaṁkāra-ṭīkā 99
Mahāyānists 504
Mahāśramaṇa 95
Mahāśrāvaka 242
Mahāśrī 70, 586
Mahāśāsakāḥ 160
Mahī 607
Mahīśāsaka 5, 46, 133, 212, 325, 417, 457, 482, 531, 641
Mahīśāsaka school 286, 382
Mahīśāsaka Vinaya 417
Mahīśāsaka-version 255
Mahīśāsakanikāya-pañcavargavinaya 255
Mahīśāsakāḥ 509
Mahīśāsikāḥ 509
Maina 578
maina 243
Maireya 159, 160, 542
Maitreya 46, 47, 48, 71, 95, 102, 137, 138, 149, 160, 195, 206, 210, 213, 241, 280, 357, 378, 382, 384, 431, 455, 482, 503, 544, 545, 555, 601, 633

dwelling 77
four chief bodhisattvas 247
오부대론 五部大論 417
Maitreya group 278
Maitrāyaṇīputra 206
maitrī 242
Maitrībala-rāja 514
Maitrīmanas 138
maji 131
Makara 100, 128, 400
makara 23, 129
Makuṭadantī 357
mala 45
Malabar 75, 127, 130, 135, 136
Malakūṭa 135, 136, 195
Malasa 135, 294
Malava 385
Malay peninsula 136
Malaya 127, 130, 136, 343
Malaya mountains 75
Malaya-deśa 129
Malayagiri 75
male 74
male organ 304
malice 460
Malla 136
Mallas 52
Mallikā 136
mallikā 130
Malobathrum 83
Malwa 74, 385
mama-kāra 128
mammalia 250
man 615
Man-gong 135
Man-hae Yong-un 135
manas 53, 282
Manasarovar 154
Manasvatī 128
manaïndriya 485
Manaḥ 135
mandāra 262
Mandāra(va) 134
mandāra-flower 323
mandāras 573
mandārava 133
Manglavor 145
mango 75
Manichaean sect 104
Manichean missionary 136
Manichean monastery 566
Manichean religion 136, 566
Manicheans 566
manifest 580
mankind 615
mano-ayatana 86
mano-vijñāna 344, 484, 607
mano-vijñāna mind 283
Manobhirāma 474
Manodhātu 474
manojña 129
Manojña-śabdābhigarjita 147, 263
Manojñaghoṣa 135
Manojñasvara 135
manomaya 129, 474
Manoratha 135, 400
Manorhata 128
Manorhita 128, 135, 486
Manovijñāna 474
manovijñāna 430
mantle 587
mantra 269, 542
Mantra sect 540
Mantra-Vehicle 560
mantras 141
Manu 71
Manu laws
assert that Chinese were degenerate Kṣatriya 548
manual signs 418
Manuṣya 129, 135, 494
manuṣya 129, 458, 459, 589
manuṣya-gati 468
Mao Tzŭ-yüan 175
Marakata 136
marakata 129
Maraṇa 136
maraṇa 235
March-April 532
Marco Polo 75
Mardala 143
Marica 136
Maritchi 130
Markab 126
Markaṭa 128
markaṭa 158
Markaṭa-hrada 135
marmacchid 84
married monks 642
Mars 53, 373, 376, 390, 420, 586, 631
火星 639
火曜 640
martial 308
Marīci 112, 113, 130, 363, 460, 485, 543, 582
Maskari Gośālīputra 135
Maskari-Gośālīputra 436
Maskarin 463
master 482, 541
Master of Healing 364, 365
Masūra Saṅghārāma 114, 130
Mathai 129
Mathurā 31, 127, 129, 131, 135, 277, 297, 363, 600
Mati 137
mati 131, 458
Mati-siṁha 137
matimant 458
Matipura 31, 129, 135
matricide 424
Matsara 8, 137
matsya 127, 395
matta 634
Maudgalaputra 142, 143, 145, 158
Maudgalyāyana 47, 96, 132, 143, 145, 158, 243, 262, 322, 357, 443, 474, 565, 575
Mauriya 31
Maurya 31
Mayūra 31
mayūra 89, 130
Mayūrarāja 486
Mazdeism 136
mañju 134, 145
Mañjudeva 157
Mañjughoṣa 157
Mañjunātha 157
Mañjuśrī 7, 17, 40, 45, 57, 63, 65, 66, 79, 88, 94, 96, 102, 104, 134, 145, 157, 195, 205, 206, 212, 219, 241, 270, 277, 280, 289, 316, 343, 350, 357, 361, 400, 408, 411, 413, 419, 431, 440, 465, 488, 493, 500,

506, 539, 544, 562, 603, 608, 639
a sharp sword 125
four chief bodhisattvas 247
four groups 259
meaning wonderful and auspicious, 妙吉祥 145
messengers 557
red 426
six-word dhāraṇī 465
妙德 145
六足尊 466
Mañjuśrī court 450
Mañjuṣvara 157
Mañjūṣaka 133, 326
mañjūṣaka 262
mañjūṣakas 573
Maṅgala 145
Maṇi 136, 252
maṇi 94, 129, 499, 542
Maṇi-bhadra 129
Maṇiskandhanāga 129
maṇḍa 134
maṇḍaka 134
Maṇḍala 134
maṇḍala 84, 95, 133, 142, 156, 158, 201, 272, 419, 480, 508, 566, 585
central group 77
central heart 76
maṇḍala-king 91
maṇḍalas 89, 141, 272, 371, 508, 529
Maṭutacaṇḍī 647
meal
midday 545
Mean 544
mean 544
means 461
meanwhile
且 563
medial 390
Medicine 493
medicine 415
Medicine King 346, 474
Medicine of immortality 217
meditation 416, 461
Meditative School 410
medium 544
medium capacity 546
Megasthenes 129
megha 160, 445
Megha-dundubhi-ṣvara-rāja 445
Meghasvara 105
Meghasvara-rāja 445
Meghasvararāja 105
Mekhalā 160
Mekā 160
melon 35
Mencius 138
mendicant
比丘 225
Mercury 53, 420
水曜 334
Meru 113, 160, 338, 435, 549
Merudhvaja 328
Merukalpa 105, 328
Merukūṭa 105, 328
Messiah 71, 138, 441
metamorphic 250
metempsychosis 211
meteor 567
method 173
methods of dealing with questions 240
meum 319
meum and tuum 613
mi-bskyod-pa 205
Mi-tsang 208
Mi-t'o 280
mi-'khrugs-pa(mintug-pa) 205
Miao Chien 208
Miao-sê-shên 586
Miao-yo 146
Miccaka 486
Micchaka 160, 179, 486, 534
mice, night and day 249
microcosm 502
the mind 353
Middha 331
middle 390, 530, 544
middle kingdom 544
Middle School 271, 545, 601
middle school 401
middle vehicle 545
middle way 217, 469, 503
Mihira 365
Mihirakula 103, 133, 237, 643
Mikkaka 160, 486
Milinda, King 160
Milindapaṅha 72
Milindapaṅha sūtra 439
Mimaha 159
mind
as a microcosm 353
as a restless monkey 354
as a sea or ocean 355
mind in bondage 353
mind vehicle 353
minds 283
Ming 96, 502
ming 141
Ming dynasty 91, 103, 419
Ming Wang 11, 83, 205, 451
火頭金剛 637
Ming-tao 628
Ming-wang 97, 618
ming-wang 141
Mingbulak 566
minute 507
minutest, four 245
mirror 88
greates perfect 416
mirror and the bhūtatathatā 238
Mithyā 137
mithyā 410
mithyāmāna 244
miti 160
Mitraśānta 161
Miśrakāvana 254
Mleccha 161
mleccha 139, 160
mlecchas 138, 225
moca 148
Moggaliputta Tissa 419
moha 143, 474, 593
moisture 250
moktak 144
Mokṣa 144
mokṣa 171, 293, 492, 611, 622, 623
mokṣa mahā pariṣad 412
Mokṣa-deva 99
Mokṣa-mahā-pariṣad 99

Mokṣa-mahāpariṣad 169
Mokṣadeva 144, 623, 630
Mokṣagupta 144
Mokṣala 155
molecule 584
moment 507
monastic year 298
Monghir 479
Mongol 145
Mongol (dynasty) 446
Mongol language 606
Mongolia 145
Mongolian Buddhism 106, 633
monistic doctrine 220
monk
four necessaries: clothing, victuals, bedding, medicine 249
four offerings 249
in a burning house 642
monk-king 143
monkey 441
monkey, the active mind 468
monkeys 286
monk's outer 300
moon 53
reflected in the water 334
moon contemplation 451
moon rat 451
moon-black 451
Moon-deva 492
Moon-effulgence 451
moon-face Buddha 451
Moon-king 451
moon-love pearl 451
moon-love samādhi 451
moon-palace 450
Moon-shining 451
moon-spots 451
moon-wheel 273
Moonlight 498
moonlight 493
Moonlight king 450
Moonlight prince 450
moonstone 451
moreover
且 563
morning 537
mother-lord 142
motion 466
Mou 148
Moughian 159
mound
丘 44
Mount Fearless 154, 379
Mount Sumeru 546
Moṅgali 91, 114, 145
Mt. Omi in Szechwan 372
Mucilinda 143, 549
文池 158
mucira 144
Mudga 143, 158
Mudgara 144
muditā 242
Mudo 205
Mudrā 142, 144, 328
mudrā 143, 418, 494
Mudrā(-bala) 142
Mudrābala 170
muhūrta 133, 143
Mukha 45, 143
Mukhaproñchana 144
Mukta 143
Mukti 144
mukti 143, 273, 492, 611, 622, 623
muktā 143, 496
Multan 148, 171
Mungo 158
Muni 143, 157
muni 274, 306
Muniśrī 143
Munjeeth 133
munjeeth 326
Murderer 600
Muryangsujeon 149
Musala 436
muscæ 363
Muscæ volitantes 39
Muscœ volitantes 35
Muse of India 158
must 616
mustard-seed kalpa 13
Musālagarbha 142, 564
Musāragalva 130, 143, 564
musāragalva 130, 584
Musāvādā-veramaṇī 216
musāvādā-veramaṇī 356
Muttra 31, 127, 129, 131
Myrobalan 1
Myō-hō-ren-gwe kyō 499
Mêng family 138
Mādhava 129
Mādhyamaka-śāstra 270
Mādhyamika 99, 270, 271, 283, 367, 401, 506, 540, 601, 602
founder, 龍樹 71
Mādhyamika doctrine 601
Mādhyamika School 32
Mādhyamika school 122, 151, 175, 302, 304, 456, 457, 535, 545
Mādhyamika tradition 540
Mādhyamika śāstra 544
Mādhyamika-śāstra 152, 302, 540
Māgadhī Prākrit 45, 598
Māgha 128, 572
Māhendrī 583
Mālava 25, 74, 130, 162, 426
Mālyaśrī 130, 136, 338
mālā 127, 129
Mālā-gandha-vilepana-dhāraṇa-maṇḍana- 221
Māladharī 357, 549
Mālākuṭadantī 31
Māmakī 63, 127, 137
Māmukhī 137
māna 134, 604
Mānasa 128
Mānasa-saro-vara 154
Mānasarovara 154
Mānatta 128
Māndhātṛ 158
Mānuṣa 129, 135
Mānuṣa-kṛtya 495
Mānuṣi-Buddha 213, 276, 430
mānātimāna 375
Māra 68, 127, 164, 181, 184, 287, 355, 356, 411, 413, 414, 424, 467, 468, 534, 598, 600, 606
māra 129
death 254
five-skandhas 254
passions-and-delusion 254
Māra-attacks 603

māra-deeds
ten fields of meditation 551
Māra-dhyāna 130
Māra-giving 215
Māra-hindrances 281
māra-king 604
Māra-kings 426
Māra-pāpīyān 128
māra-subjugation 369
Mārakāyikās 130
Māras 604
māras 50, 244, 273, 387, 414, 604
Māras and heretics 568
Māra's 489
Mārga 135
mārga 31, 108, 111, 257, 589
Mārgaśīrṣa 572
māsa 598
Mātaṅga 115, 175, 185
mātaṅga 129
mātaṅga-araṅyaka 129
Mātaṅga-āraṇyaka. 376
Mātaṅgī 129
mātaṅgī 129
Māthava 129, 231
Mātratā 454
mātā 128
Mātṛ 142
mātṛ 128, 129
Mātṛgrāma 142
Mātṛkā 129, 130, 142, 216, 553, 562, 624
mātṛkā 201
Mātṛs 583
Māyā 90, 130, 216, 643
māyā 127
Māyā
father of 568
māyādṛṣṭi 145
Māyā's womb 12
māṁsa 130, 459, 496
māṁsabhakṣaṇa 459
māṁsacakṣus 459
Māṇava 128
Māṇavaka 147
māṇavaka 129
māṣa 114, 127, 128
Mīmāṁsā 159
mīmāṁsā-ṛddhi-pādaḥ 254
Mūla 485
mūla 61, 143
Mūla-sarvāstivādāḥ 143
Mūlabarhaṇī 485
Mūlagrantha 201
mūlagrantha 61, 143
Mūlasarvāstivādaḥ 509
Mūlasarvāstivādāḥ 300, 324, 457, 482
Mūlasthānapura 148, 171
Mūrdhaja 306
Mūrdhaja-rāja 527
Mūrdhajāta 158
mūrdhābhiṣikta 37
Mūḍha 581
mūḍha 441
mūṣa 304
Mṛdaṅga 143
mṛdu 144, 284
mṛdukā 464
mṛga 122, 161
mṛga-rāja 161
Mṛgadāva 121, 122, 161, 308
Mṛgadāva park 162
Mṛgala 158
Mṛgasthāpana 161
Mṛgaśiras 486
Mṛgānandi 158
Mṛgāṅka 450
mṛta 235
Mṛta-manuṣya 142
mṛtyu 144

(N)

Na-fu-po 75
Na-mo A-mi-to-Fo 378
nada 73
Nadī 73, 615
Nadī-Kāśyapa 5, 74
Nadī-kāśyapa 12
Nadīkāśyapa 73
Nag-po c'en-po 107
naga 71
Nagara 71, 75
Nagarahāra 71, 75
nail, cleaned 536
Nairañjanā 80, 296, 312, 345, 394, 440, 648
Nairañjanā river 121
nairātmya 153
naivasaṁjñānā-saṁjñānāyatana 55
Naivasaṁjñānāsaṁjñānāyatana 152
naivasaṁjñānāsaṁjñānāyatana 231, 239
Naiḥsargika-prāyaścittika 81
naiḥsargikāḥ-pāyattikāḥ 481
Nakshatra 211
Nakshatras 382
nakshatras 445
Nakṣatra 383
nakṣatra 331, 381, 435, 631
Nakṣatra Phālgunī 598
Nakṣatra-rāja-saṅkusumitābhijña 336
Nakṣatra-rāja-vikrīḍita 336
Nakṣatranātha 450
Nakṣatras 374, 599
nakṣatras 314, 485
Nakṣatratārā-rājāditya 499
namas 60
Namaḥ 72, 75, 201
namaḥ 60, 75
Namaḥ Amitābha 72
Namaḥ sarva-tathāgatebhyaḥ 106
name-form 140
Namo 72
namo 60
Namo Amitābha 357, 465, 619
Nan Shan 419
Nan-ch'üan 74
Nan-shan 454
Nan-shan sects 315
Nan-yang 74
Nan-yo 312, 572
Nanda 460
nanda 643
Nanda Upananda 73
Nandana-vana 643
Nandanavana 254
nandi 73
Nandika 73, 176, 331
nandikāvarta 73
nandyāvarta 73
Nandā 160

Nanking 74, 338, 525
Nara 71, 101
nara 494
Nara-nārī 71
Naraka 554
naraka 72, 74, 79, 80, 118, 603
naraka-gati 468
narakas 610
Naramānava 71
Narasaṁghārāma 495
Narbudda 170
Narendrayaśas 72, 95
Narmadā 75
narration 337
Narya 71
Narādhāra 71
nation 56
native place 203
natural and similar 303
Nauclea cadamba 3
Nava 72
nava 45
Navadevakula 75
Navagraha 53
Navamālikā 72
Navan 45
navanīta 415
Navasaṁjñā 51
Navasaṅghārāma 75
naya 71, 72
Nayuta 622
nayuta 72
Naśaśata 164
Naṭa 32, 71, 73
necessary 616
nectar 569
nectar city 11
nectar of nirvāṇa 11
needle 589
negations 601
Neither unity nor diversity 220
Nemindhara 361
Nemiṁdhara 51, 66, 81, 549
neophyte 539
Nepal 81, 324, 342, 381
Nepāla 81, 381
Nerbudda 75
Nestorian Christianity 23
Nestorian monastery 104
New Rājagṛha 70
New Year's eve 210
Nichiren 300, 499, 540
Nichiren sect 201, 499
四要品 254
Nichiren trinity 300
Nidhi 81
Nidhāpana 405
Nidāna 80
nidāna 125, 191, 364
老死 78
Nidāna-mātṛkā 80
nidāna-pollution 408
nidānas 140, 286, 288, 331, 365, 459, 495, 607
twelve 497
nigamana 431
night 253
nihilism 544
sophistic 545
Niladyan 312
Nimat 77, 592
Nimba 511
nimbus of rays 567
Nimindhara 81
nimitta 296
Nine 45
nine character maṇḍala 54
Nine classes 56
nine founders 54
nine grades 50
nine graha 55
nine honoured 54
nine karma 56
nine lands 55
nine luminaries 53
nine magical characters 54
nine orifices 47
nine realities 53
nine realms 55
nine similes 53
nine truths 54
ninety-eight tempters 52
Ningpo 41, 195, 244, 419, 568, 572
Nirarbuda 80, 554
nirarbuda 610
Niraya 75, 554
niraya 79
Nirdahana 405
nirdeśa 609
Nirgrantha 72, 80, 122, 135, 293, 444, 463
Nirgrantha sect 4, 136
Nirgrantha-Jñātiputra 436
Nirgrantha-putra 80, 436
Nirgranthajñāti 393
四仙 250
Nirgranthajñātiputra 80, 436
Nirgranthas 71, 280
nirgranthas 50
nirlakṣaṇa-buddha 151
nirmāṇa 472
Nirmāṇa sūtra 411
nirmāṇa-kāya 472, 519
Nirmāṇabuddha 638
Nirmāṇakāya 186, 214, 282, 283, 304, 350, 471, 472, 639
nirmāṇakāya 8, 20, 93, 99, 191, 192, 227, 290, 351, 399, 404, 418, 421, 428, 483, 484, 519, 559, 561, 642
four bodies 252
manifest, 出現 580
Nirmāṇakāya and Dharmakāya 303
nirmāṇakāya Buddha 638
Nirmāṇarati 80, 438, 637
Nirmāṇarati heaven 439
nirmāṇarati heaven 606
Nirodha 80, 81
nirodha 31, 138, 257
nirodha and mārga 139
nirodha-āryasatya 139
Nirukta
six śāstras 461
nirupadhiśeṣa-nirvāṇa 458
nirvikalpa 150
Nirvāṇa 104, 283, 325, 502, 587
nirvāṇa 36, 50, 54, 83, 107, 139, 206, 218, 222, 269, 273, 276, 278, 279, 281, 286, 287, 292, 293, 294, 324, 358, 405, 408, 411, 412, 463, 482, 488, 490, 495, 499, 502, 512, 585, 588, 589, 601, 604, 605, 606, 608, 609, 611
final 286, 483

great 103
incomplete 458
remnantless 490
yonder shore, 彼岸 616
出離 579
彼岸, the other shore 388
Nirvāṇa assembly 405
nirvāṇa emancipation 274
nirvāṇa mind 362
Nirvāṇa School 421
Nirvāṇa sect 540
Nirvāṇa Sūtra 204, 216, 361, 425, 586
Nirvāṇa sūtra 400, 421, 423, 434, 478, 608, 613
place where Buddha preached the Nirvāṇa sūtra 442
Nirvāṇa sūtras 478, 602
Nirvāṇa-Buddha 276
Nirvāṇa-buddha 276
nirvāṇa-deliverance 492
Nirvāṇa-ego 384
nirvāṇa-enlightenment 524
nirvāṇa-form 405
nirvāṇa-joy 281
nirvāṇa-method 521
nirvāṇa-mind 174
nirvāṇa-patience 521
nirvāṇa-realm 242
nirvāṇa-seed 529
Nirvāṇadhātu 405
Nirvāṇas 487
nirvāṇas 490
Nirābhāsa 154
nirābhasa 151
Nirṛti 77, 79, 605
四方 246
nitya 296
Nityaparivṛtta 105
Niu-t'ou shan fa 442
Nivartana-stūpa 645
Nivāsana 81
nivāsana 57, 79, 405
nivṛtti 138, 154
Niyama 81
Niyanti 81
Niyantr 81
niścala 205
Niśākara 450
niṣad 541
niṣaṇṇa 541
niṣkala 79, 405
Niṣkaṇṭaka 80
niṣkāla 405
niṣyanda 116
niṣyanda-phala 476
Niṣīdana 81
niṣīdana 462, 541, 585
niṣṭapana 77
Niṣṭyā 485
no 211
Nob 75
Nobatgang 75
non-abandonment 217
non-Buddhist doctrines 436
non-Buddhist scriptures 77
non-duality 220
non-personality 502
non-void 205
non-ālaya maṇḍala 72
north 208
Northern Buddhism 208, 324
Northern Bushel 208
Northern chou dynasty 629
Northern History 519
Northern Lāṭa 208
noumena and phenomena 482
Nujkend 78
Nujketh 78
numberless 621
nun 79
比丘尼 225
Nyagrodha 80
Nyāya 144, 159, 338, 538
Nyāya philosophy 82, 452
Nyāya-vaiśeṣika 338
Nyāyadvāratāraka-śāstra 497
Nyāyapraveśa 496
nābhi 72
nāga 71, 143, 295, 363, 479, 606
Nāga king 236
nāga meditation 71
nāga-guardian 479
nāga-king 143
nāga-puṣpa 440
Nāgakanyā 440
Nāgakrośana 71
Nāgarāja 440
nāgas 55, 91, 96, 211, 212, 414, 429, 568, 606
Nāgasena 72, 439
Nāgavadana monastery 451
Nāgavajra 436
Nāgārjuna 2, 3, 5, 60, 71, 97, 99, 104, 151, 222, 232, 236, 271, 273, 317, 340, 364, 368, 378, 382, 440, 456, 483, 486, 534, 540, 544, 560, 567, 575, 587, 601
and a prince of Kośala 495
four suns 255
Vasubandhu 572
天台九祖 572
Nāgārjuna's division 239
Nālandā 49, 72, 338, 342, 496, 521, 533
Nālandā monastery 473
Nālandā-saṁghārāma 191
Nālandā-saṅghārāma 341
Nālandāgrāṃa 243
Nālaya-maṇḍala 72
Nāma-rūpa 80
nāmamātra 454
Nāman 140
nāmarūpa 140, 365
nāraka 74
nārakagati 589
Nārakas 407
Nārikela 72
Nārikeladvīpa 72
Nārikera 72
nārāca 72
Nārāyaṇa 70, 71, 93, 102, 182, 206, 436, 508, 567, 615
Nārāyaṇa-deva 71, 160
Nārāyaṇadeva 606
Nāya 72
Nāṭya-gīta-vāditra-viśūkadarśanād vairamaṇī (virati) 212
Nīla 80
nīla 575
Nīla-udumbara 80
nīla-utpala 79
Nīlacakṣus 544
Nīladaṇḍa 360
Nīlanetra 569

Nīlapiṭa 80
Nīlavajra 80
Nīlotpala 80, 120, 554
Nīlājan 80
Nṛsiṁha 497

(Ñ)
Ña-khri-btsan-po 381

(ṅ)
ṅag-gi-lha-mo 94

(ṇ)
ṇacca-gīta-vādita-visūkadass anā-veramaṇī 356

(O)
O-mei 241
O-mei Shan 372
O-mei shan 272
objective 76
obscure 628
observance 59
obstacles 426
ocean symbol 622
Ocean-nāga 622
oceans 261
offering to Buddha 214
old 28
Olympus 160
Om 423
om 390
Om maṇi padme hūṁ. 390
Om-maṇi-padme-hūṁ 389
omen 536
Omniscience 210
omniscience 423, 510, 528
Omniscient 195
on every side 541
One Vehicle 193, 219, 367, 645
One Vehicle teaching 531
one Yāna 506
one-Buddha region 503
one-Buddha vehicle 503
one-tenth bodhisattva 503
One-Vehicle 281
one-yāna 97
one's own 200
onions 422
only 550
order 499
ordinary 613
ordinary man 617
organ
six organs of sense 465
original 200, 446
original Master 201
Originant 516
Orissa 32, 413
orthodoxy 609
Ortospana of Ptolemy 215
Osrushna 327
other cults 76
Oude 42
Oudh 5
Oujein 426, 441, 443
outside 436
oviparous 250
owe 648
ox 441
ox-cart 41
ox-head lictors 442
ox-head sandal-wood 442
Ox-horns 442
Ox-horns śāla grove 442
ox-pictures 363
ox-tracks 444
Oxus 165, 375, 607, 648
four rivers 261
Ozēnē 426
Oḍivisa 413
Oḍra 413
Oṁ maṇi padme hūṁ 465
Oṁ-maṇi-padme-hūṁ 136

(Ō)
Ōsh 642

(P)
Pa-ling 598
pada 165, 171, 172, 194
Padakāya 44
Padma 70, 120, 171, 172, 360, 554, 635
padma 262, 599, 610, 636
Padma-saṁbhava 102
Padma-vṛṣabha-vikramin 19
Padmaprabha 19, 636
Padmaprabha Buddha 243
Padmapāṇi 121, 390, 599
Padmaratna 620
padmarāga 171
Padmasaṁbhava 17
Padmavimāna 120
Padmaśrī 637
Padmottara 329
Padmāntaka 360
padmāsana 121
pagoda 221, 593
Pai Chang Shan 177
Pai Tai Shan 305
pain 31
Pajra 365
pakṣa 166
Pakṣa(pāṇḍaka) 168
Pakṣapaṇḍaka 428
Pakṣapaṇḍakās 166
pala 171
palace 58
Pali 598
Pali being 324
Pali Canon 228
palmyra 603
palāda 171
palāśa 599
Pamir 171
Pamira 600
Pamirs 342, 600
pan-Buddha 428, 448
Pan-Buddhist 210
panasa 599
Pancaśirsha 413
Panchen Lama 117
Pandus 265
Panthaka 167
pantheism 68
pantheon 278
Pao-shêng 586
Pao-t'ung 103
Pao-yün 199
Papaya forest 144
parables 177
paracitta-jñāna 422
Paracittajñāna
他心通 592
Paradise 56, 305
Paradise of Amitābha 40

parahita 125
parama 163, 171
parama-bodhi 171
Paramartha 540
Paramiti 79, 168
Paramārtha 48, 51, 69, 98, 127, 276, 420, 561
paramārtha 599
paramārtha-satya 488
Paramārtha-satya-śāstra 338
Paranirmita Vaśavartin 127
Paranirmita-vaśavartin 162, 568, 592
paranirmita-vaśavartin 606
Paranirmitavaśavartin 92, 164, 438
parasmai 587
parasmaipada 168
parents 204
pari 600
pari-nirvāṇa 89
pariccheda 563
paricitra 600
Parijñāna 438
parijñāna 607
parijñānas 422
parikalpana 209
Parikalpita 612
parikara 600
Parinirvāṇa 103, 167
parinirvāṇa 36, 103, 152, 167, 223, 278, 298, 418, 428, 504, 545, 600
parisrāvaṇa 171, 321
Parivrājaka 168, 598
parivāsa 600
pariśuddhi 574
pariṇāma 524
Pariṇāmanā 644
Paropamisus 9, 167
parricide 424
Parthia 9, 148, 388
particle 507
particularity 466
Parturition 210
Parvata 48
parvata 171
Paryayaṇa 600
paryaṅka-bandha 21
Parīttaśubha 250, 301
Parīttaśubhas 321
Parīttābha 250, 301, 621
Parīttābhās 321
Parūṣaka(vana) 163
Parūṣakavana 254
parṇa 408
passion
  ten fields of meditation 551
passion-māra 127
past 14, 159
paste pagoda 79
Patañjali 455
patch robe 462
patch-robe 5, 522
path 135
pati 600
patience 287, 416
patience pāramitā 494
patience under insult 461
Patna 5, 44, 52, 172, 229, 343, 601
patnī 165
patriarch
  fourth, Upagupta 433
  six patriarchs 466
  twenty-sixth 219
  Vasubandhu, 21st 572
patriarchs 486
  five 427
Pattala 195
pattikāya 247
pattra 82, 408, 611
patākā 178, 601
paulkasa 195
Pauṣa 194, 195, 572, 615
Pauṣamāsa 197
Pauṣṭika 634
pauṣṭika 195, 429
payas 164, 600
pañca 169, 409
Pañca (vārṣika) pariṣad 412
pañca balāni 162, 285
pañca indriyāṇi 285
Pañca veramaṇī 411
Pañca(vārṣika) pariṣad 155
Pañca-dharmakāya 418
pañca-gavya 426
pañca-indryāṇi 125
Pañca-kleśa 414
pañca-kleśa 593
Pañca-nada 227
Pañca-pariṣad 169
Pañca-vārṣika 169
pañca-śīla 342, 414
Pañcabala 120
pañcabalāni 414
Pañcabhojanīya 167, 427
Pañcadaśa 363
Pañcadharma 416
Pañcadvāra-dhyāna-sūtra-mahārtha-dharm 200
Pañcakhādanīya 167
pañcaphalāni 476
Pañcapiṭaka 57
Pañcarāṣṭra 166
Pañcasaptati 585
Pañcasattra 166
Pañcaskandha 424
pañcaskandha 300
Pañcatanmātrāṇi 425
Pañcavidyā 415
pañcavidyā-śāstras 496
Pañcaśata 416
Pañcaśikha 413, 426
Pañcendriyāṇi 412
Pañcābhijñā 421, 422
Pañcābhijñāna 169
Pañcāla 363
Pañcānantarya 424
Pañjara 167
paścima 304
paśu 600
Paśupati 327
Paṇḍaka 167, 428
paṇḍaka 15, 166, 168
paṇḍakas 428, 644
paṭa 172
paṭu 125
peacock 31, 89
Peacock City 131
Peacock king 32, 486
pearl 542
Pearl palace 252
pedant 158
Pegasus 126, 170
Pei Shan 419
pei-to 82

Pei-tu 174
penis 304
penitential service 434
pepper 136
perfect knowledge 510
perfect number 355
Perfect School 194
perfume 625
permanence 464
permanent 296
perpetual 408
perseverance 621
Persia 388, 600
Persian 600
persimmon-leaves 80
persistence 621
perverted 108
Peshawar 206, 519, 572, 644
Peshāwar 615
pettifogging 144
Peśī 613
peśī 425, 608, 614
peṭa 616
Phags-pa 169
Phagspa 606
phala 35, 598
四果 239
phalaśas 162
Phalgu 80
phallic emblem 568
phenomenal world
T'ien-tai's interpretation 320
phenomenon and noumenon 296
philosophy 231
philosophy (adhyātma) 415
phoenix-kṣetra 203
phrase 44
Phālguna 572, 598
Phālgunamāsa 598
phāṇita 598
Pi-chang 192
Pidjan 192
Pien-ch'êng Wang 192
Pig-head monk 520
Pilindavatsa 617
pint 113
pious vows 461
Pippala 22, 224, 601, 617
pippala 225, 232
pippala-vṛkṣa 232
Pipīla(ka) 225
Pisces 364
Pitāśilā 225
Pitṛ 204
pitṛ 224
Pitṛ mātṛ 204
Piśuna 68, 580
Piśāca 102
piśāca 225, 617
Piśāca-maheśvara 102
piśācas 606
piśācāḥ 229
Piśācī 229
Piṅgala 232, 233, 436
piṇḍa 84
Piṇḍada 232
Piṇḍala 232
Piṇḍapāta 210
piṇḍapātika 210
Piṇḍola 241
Piṇḍola-bhāradvāja 232
Piṇḍāra 232
Piṭaka 617, 638
piṭaka 31, 228, 519, 616
Piṭaka school 520, 596
Piṭaka-kośa 226
piṭakas 488
place 223
placenta 614
placenta tank 630
planets 432
plateau 594
platform 594
Pliny 83
plot
丘 44
plum 138
Pluto 106, 229
Pluto heaven 605
Po Chü-i 305
Poa cynosuroides 70
poison 111
poisons 270
Pollux 382
Polulo 171
Pootoo 195
pore 142
portfolio 158
position 222
possible and impossible 268
postulates of a universe 352
Potala 40, 195, 507, 614, 615
Potalaka 195, 199, 614
Potaraka 195
Potaraka monastery 195
pottery 435
power 120
Power-body 214
poṣa 394
Poṣadha 615
poṣadha 311, 465, 614
Prabhadvaja 342
Prabhu 171
prabhu 163
Prabhā 39
Prabhā(kara)mitra 601
Prabhā-maṇḍala 40
Prabhākaramitra 99, 599
Prabhākārī 369
Prabhāpāla 634
prabhāsa 65, 165
prabhāva 452
Prabhāvatī 599
Prabhū 446
prabhū 163
Prabhūta 598
Prabhūtaratna 83, 171, 199, 357, 431, 482, 483, 556, 586, 614
prabāla 262
pradakṣiṇa 171, 337, 441
Pradhāna 338, 516
pradhāna 314
Pradhānaśūra 439
Prajñapti 265
prajñapti 3, 280, 294
Prajñapti-vādinaḥ 104
Prajñaptivādin 325
Prajñaptivādinaḥ 132
Prajñaptivādinaḥ school 313
Prajñaptiśāstra 313
prajñendriya 485
Prajñā 416
prajñā 141, 163, 168, 269, 271, 274, 283, 288, 368, 421, 461,

475, 480, 559, 595, 631
contrast with 方便 174
referred to as mother of all knowledge and virtue 204
Prajñā Bodhisattva 524
Prajñā Pāramitā 98
Prajñā school 288
prajñā sūtras 282
Prajñā-pāramitā 169, 216, 363, 524
prajñā-pāramitā 552, 553
Prajñā-pāramitā sūtra 104, 607
Prajñā-pāramitā Sūtra
天地鏡 571
Prajñā-pāramitā-sūtra 168
prajñābala 414, 632
Prajñāgupta 168
Prajñākūṭa 556
Prajñāpāramitā 62, 329, 398, 456, 480, 519, 551, 552, 557
prajñāpāramitā 168, 417
Prajñāpāramitā Sūtra 33, 205
Prajñāpāramitā sūtra 120
Prajñāpāramitā sūtras 187
Prajñāpāramitā-sūtra 79
prajñās 275
Prajñātāra 168, 486
Prajāpati 5, 164, 171, 600
prakaraṇa 171
Prakṛti 170, 516
prakṛti 314
Pralambā 227
Pramiti 168
Pramuditā 369, 643
pramāṇa 119, 125
prapañca 648
Prasenajit 68, 130, 171, 224, 228, 338, 600
prastha 171
prati 144
pratibhāna 386
pratibimba 408
pratideśanā 171
pratigha 286, 456, 558
pratijñā 119, 234, 235, 284, 292, 431
Pratijñākāraka-vinaya 583
pratikrānta 171
Pratimokṣa 162
pratimokṣa 144, 163, 171, 469
pratimā 217, 631
pratirūpa 296
pratirūpaka 296, 646
pratisaṁkhyā-nirodha 154
pratisaṁkhyānirodha 595
Pratisaṁvid
四無礙智 245
pratisaṁvids 386
pratiśrut 625
pratyakṣa 629, 630
Pratyavekṣaṇa-jñāna 430
pratyaya 171, 402, 493
pratyaya-bala 403
pratyeka 191, 464, 483, 611
Pratyeka(-buddha) 617
Pratyeka-buddha 242, 281, 394
pratyeka-buddha 37, 41, 97, 111, 191, 229, 239, 281, 292, 300, 360, 403, 545, 548, 622
four holy ways of rebirth 461
world from four points of view 255
三品四善根 251
pratyeka-buddha knowledge 292
pratyeka-buddhahood 420
pratyeka-buddhas 93, 97, 205, 214, 270, 277, 282, 289, 290, 293, 360, 361, 415, 420, 421, 424, 529, 531, 545, 566, 581, 584, 587, 588
abiding in the fruit 542
四聖 251
Pratyekabuddha 281, 483
pratyekabuddha 286, 480, 506, 596, 602
Pratyekabuddha-realm 183
pratyekabuddhahood 324, 368, 369
pratyekabuddhas 286, 602, 604
pratyekas 483
pratyutpanna 169
pratyutpannasamādhi 169
Pratyātmāryajñāna 517
Pratāpana 60, 97, 100, 554, 576
pratāpana 603
Pratāpāditya 342
Pratītya-samutpāda 403
Pratītya-samutpāda śāstra 366
pravacana 42
pravara 601
Pravarasenapura 234
pravari 601
pravartana 523
praveśa 171
pravicaya 39
pravicāra 595
Pravraj 579
pravāraṇa 172, 516, 518
pravāḍa 262
pravṛtti-vijñāna 524
prayer 69
prayer-beads 240
Prayoga 1
Prayuta 171
Prayāga 171
praśaka 171
praśama 521
praśrabdhi-saṁbodhyaṅga 584
praśākhā 162, 171, 425, 608
Praṇidhāna 81
praṇidhāna 163, 359, 447, 461
praṇihita 447
present 159
preta 59, 225, 347, 589, 613, 617
preta-gati 468
Pretas 6
pretas 360, 606, 610, 619
primary cause 80
primordial 446
prince 435
principal 200
principle and gnosis 491
principle and practice 482
Priyadarśana 648
priyavacana 251
production and annihilation 302
Professor Vogel 52
prognosticate 525
Prāgbodhi 171, 523
Prājña 640
Prākrit 182

prākāmya 90
Prākāra 599
prāp 115
prāpta 115
prāpti 90
prāsaka 20
Prāsāda 170
prāsāda 87
Prātideśanīya 163, 535
prātideśanīya 171, 481, 612, 615, 625
Prātimokṣa 27
prātimokṣa 163, 171
Prātimokṣa sūtra 615
Prātipadika 44
Prātiśākhya sūtras 42
Prāyaścitta 591
prāyaścitta 164, 612
prāyaścittikāḥ 481
Prāñnyāya-mūla-śāstra-ṭīkā 544
prāṇa 167
Prāṇyamūla-śāstra-ṭīkā 544
Prāṇyamūla-śāstraṭīkā 243
Prāṇātipātād vairamaṇī (virati) 217
prīti 648
prīti-saṁbodhyaṅga 584
Pu-k'o 211
Pu-tai Ho-shang 614
publish 337
Pudgala 205, 211, 329
pudgala 195, 494
puggala 211
Pukkaśa 200
Pulo Condore 58
Pulo Condore Island 31, 615
Punaca 166
Punar 205
Punarvasu 205, 460, 486
Punjab 103, 294, 327, 342, 376, 522
Purandara 206
pure 175
Pure Land 56, 303, 367, 503, 619
Pure Land of Amitābha 528
Pure Land sect 223, 540
Pure Reward-Land 101
Pure Sanskrit 574
Pure-land 357, 511
Pure-land School 587
Pure-land sect 280, 500, 540
Pure-land sūtras 94
purgatives 204, 614
purgatories 360
purgatory 554
purities 292
Purity-path 541
purple 420
Purusha 71, 339
purusha 516
Purushapura 215
Puruṣa 348, 614, 615
puruṣa 195, 206, 494
Puruṣa-damya-sārathi 371, 537
puruṣakāra-phala 476
puruṣam 195
Puruṣapura 206, 519, 572, 615
puruṣasya 195
puruṣe 195
puruṣendriya 485
puruṣeṇa 195
puruṣāt 195
puruṣāya 195
Puryamitra 219
purāṇas 206
pustaka 304
putchuck 82
putchuk 61, 144
Puṇya 205
puṇya 199
Puṇya-prasava 370
Puṇyamitra 486
Puṇyaprasava 200, 250, 301
Puṇyatara 211, 255
Puṇyavardhana 363
Puṇyayaśas 205, 486
puṇyaśālā 209
Puṇyopāya 73, 615
Puṇyādarśa 211
Puṇḍarīka 91, 120, 175, 201, 208, 209
puṇḍarīka 209, 262, 610
Puṇḍra-vardhana 209
Puṣpa 615
puṣpa 195, 635, 636
Puṣpadantī 357, 642
Puṣpanāga 209
puṣpanāga 440
Puṣpapura 639
Puṣpāhara 211
Puṣya 169, 195, 206, 211, 360, 486
puṣya 195
Puṣyamitra 211
Puṣṭikarman 634
Pākhaṇḍa 170
pāla 162
Pāli 45
pāna 599
pānila 599
Pāpakārin 163
Pāpīmā 600
Pāpīmān 600
Pāpīyān 127, 411, 568, 600
pāra 616
Pāraga 599
pāraka 599
pāramitā 50, 107, 108, 109, 141, 163, 200, 342, 528, 607, 616
  six 461
  sixth, 布施 198
pāramitā boat 599
Pāramitā Bodhisattva 524
Pāramitā Bodhisattvas 186
pāramitās 92, 163, 342, 357, 359, 362, 461, 463
  five 413, 416
pāramitās seriatim 463
Pārasī 600
Pārijāta 163, 600
pārijāta tree 569
Pārijātaka 163
Pāriyātra 600
Pārvatī 543
Pārājika 163
pārājika 368, 481, 605, 612
  six 464
pārājika sins 240
pārājikas 258, 359
  他勝罪 592
  四波羅夷 246
  四重罪 259
pārāvata 599, 621
Pārśva 486, 599, 631
Pārśvika 486

pātaka 164
pātra 169, 171, 462, 471
Pātāla 434
Pāvā 136, 601
Pāñcika 166, 169, 262, 485
pāśa 20, 599
pāśakamālā 171
Pāśupata 79, 164, 599
Pāśupatas 109
Pāṁśupatas 109
Pāṇi 328
pāṇi 599
Pāṇini 226, 600
pāṇātipātā-veramaṇī 356
Pāṇḍaka and Lohitaka rule 168
Pāṇḍaravāsinī 93, 166, 167, 177
Pāṇḍu 166
Pāṣaṇḍa 170
Pāṣaṇḍin 170
Pāṭaliputra 22, 44, 52, 154, 172, 205, 363, 534, 598, 601, 639
pāṭalī 601
pāṭha 611
pāṭhaka 611
Pīlusāra-stūpa 295
Pīlusāragiri 226, 295
pūga 232
pūjā 32
Pūraṇa 203
Pūraṇa Kāśyapa 206
Pūraṇa-Kāśyapa 436, 463, 615
Pūraṇa-kāśyapa 215
Pūrikā 615
Pūrva 195, 599
pūrva 29, 113, 523
Pūrva-Aṣādhā 485
Pūrva-aṣādhā 381
pūrva-dvitīya 29
Pūrva-mīmāṁsā 159
Pūrva-Phalgunī 486
Pūrva-Proṣṭhapada 485
Pūrva-Videha 211, 615
Pūrva-videha 195
四洲, four continents 258
pūrvanivāsana 336
Pūrvanivāsānusmṛti-(jñāna) 336
pūrvanivāsānusmṛti-jñāna 345, 422
Pūrvapraṇidhāna 202
Pūrvavideha 216, 220, 231, 338, 610, 614
pūrvavideha 113
Pūrvaśaila 132, 211
Pūrvaśaila-saṅghārāma 113, 211
Pūrvaśailāḥ 104, 113, 216
Pūrṇa 22, 205, 206, 357, 615
pūrṇa 134, 195
Pūrṇabhadra 205, 615
Pūrṇaghaṭa 201
Pūrṇaka 209
Pūrṇamaitrāyaṇīputra 206, 232
Pūrṇeccha 205
Pūtana 205, 614
pūtanas 606
Pūti-agada 614
Pṛkkā 617
Pṛthagjana 617
pṛthagjana 476
pṛthak 475, 617
Pṛthivī 485, 550, 553, 556
pṛthivī 171, 595, 599
P'i-mo 226
p'i-p'a 231
p'ien 612
P'u Hsien 363, 368
十大願 357
P'u-hsien 63, 64, 100, 102, 223, 272, 285, 355, 372, 384, 433, 556, 559, 617, 647
四法 247
P'u-kuang 40
P'u-t'o 38, 241

(Q)

quality 466
queen 203
Queen of Heaven 543

(R)

rabbit's horns 596
rainbow
天弓 568
Raivata 125
Rajaori 620
Rajputana 54, 133
Rakas-tal 154
rakta 635
Raktapadma 172
raktikā 13
rakṣa 393
rakṣa-kings 79
Rakṣalevatā 436
rakṣas 284, 285, 366, 583
rakṣaḥ 500
Rakṣaḥ heaven 605
rancid 537
Rapetmapet 254
Rapti River 254
rasa 159, 405
rathakāya 247
ratna 117, 118, 194
Ratna-garbha 199
Ratnadhvaja 196
Ratnadvīpa 199
ratnagarbha 620
Ratnakaraṇḍaka 199
Ratnaketu 198
four regions 246
平等性智 259
ratnakūṭa 199
Ratnamati 124
ratnamudra samādhi 199
Ratnapiṭaka 199
ratnarāśi 199
Ratnasaṁbhava 62, 142, 198, 243, 586, 613
Ratnasaṃbhava 205, 418, 424, 430, 544
Ratnasaṃbhava's three forms 431
Ratnatraya 276
Ratnaśikhin 25, 117, 342
Ratnākara 117
Ratnāvabhāsa-kalpa 185
Raudrī 583
Raurava 60, 554
raurava 60, 603, 633, 634
Raurava hell 122
Ravi 479
Raśmi-śata-sahasra-pari-pūrṇa-dhvaja 393
Raśmiprabhāsa 40
realism 544
realm 499
noumenal 428

phenomenal 427
unimpeded 428
reasoning 235
receptacle 617
recluse 274
recompense 319
recompenses 276
Record of Western Countries 90
Record of Western Lands 31, 550
Records of Western countries 305
red 420, 635
加沙野 1
red lotus 635
red sandal-wood 442
Red sect 539
red sect 635
Regarder of the world's sounds 38
region 499
regular 621
reincarnations 502
rejoicing 434
relative
six immediate relatives 468
release 611
reliquary 221
remove 14
repa 126
repent 644
repentance 434
repentance of Mañjuśrī 158
repha 126
representation-consciousness 629
resentment 447
resolve 81
restrain 81
restraint 81
retreat 388, 516
winter retreat 113
return 644, 645
Revata 9, 125
Revatī 351, 486
reveal 580
revolve 644
rice 160
right 441, 526
Rigveda 564
riktamuṣṭi 33
Risshū 587
Ritsu 181, 367, 540, 587, 609
River Jumna 309, 408
River Sutlej 313
River-kāśyapa 12
robe
方服 173
Robusta 242
Rocana 121, 227
rock kalpa 14
rock-salt 241
Rohilcund 129, 135
Rohilkhand 135
rohita(ka) 121
Rohita(ka)-mukta 121
rohita-mukta 584
rohitaka 366
Rohiṇī 485, 486
Rohu 620
Roman empire 86
rosary 171, 177, 409
rosary-beads 144
royal 435
royal bull 444
royal ṛṣi 435
royal-stag Genius 308
Rubia cordifolia 326
rubia cordifolia 103
ruby 641
火珠 334
Rucika 121, 123
Ruciraketu 145
Rudhirāhāra 75
Rudra 123
Rudras 107, 284
Rudrākṣa 387
rudrākṣa 64, 409
ruffian 594
Rugṇa 168
Rui 19
rule 59
ruminating 444
ruta 122
Rutārtha 395
Ruṇḍa 428
Ruṇḍa paṇḍaka 168
Ruṇṇapaṇḍakas 124
rvalokabhayastambhitatva-vidhvaṁsanakār 105
Ryōnin 119
rāga 117, 375, 391, 593
rāgadveṣamoha 593
Rāhu 53, 118
Rāhu-asura 118
Rāhula 90, 109, 118, 161, 241, 357, 450, 509, 618, 620
水滿 333
Rāhulata 118, 338, 486
Rāja 117
rāja 117
王 435
Rāja-dhātu 376
rāja-haṁsa 383
water and milk 334
Rājabalendraketu 571
Rājagṛha 1, 22, 59, 68, 72, 91, 92, 117, 118, 175, 222, 224, 232, 233, 324, 329, 331, 341, 342, 343, 482, 543, 572, 580, 586, 601, 604, 620
eight famous Caityas 548
王舍城 436
Rājamahendrī 100
Rājamundry 100
Rājan 117
Rājapura 620
rājas 141, 360
Rājyavardhana 342, 435
rājñī 117
rākṣasa 73, 171, 376
Rākṣasas 4
rākṣasas 440, 606
Rākṣasī 106, 510
rākṣasī 31, 59, 73, 83, 119, 154, 356, 376, 603, 642, 647
Rāma 119
Rāmacandra 117
Rāmagaṅgā 135
Rāmagrāma 119
Rāmāyaṇa 117
Rāvaṇa 117
rāvaṇa 118
rāśi 314
rāṣṭrapāla 123
Rāṣṭrapālas 634

Rūpa 300
rūpa 140, 279, 291, 300, 374, 418, 424, 459, 463, 503
rūpa-kāya 301
rūpa-skandha 86
Rūpadhātu 113, 266, 301
rūpadhātu 370
rūpakāya 483
rūpaloka 301
rūpalokas 33, 569
rūpya 376, 470, 584
Rūpāvacara 631
rūpāvacara 301
Rūpāṇi 585

(Ṛ)
Ṛddhipāda 254
Ṛgveda 164, 272, 452, 618
Ṛṣabha 124, 280, 436, 492
Ṛṣigiri 482
Ṛṣi's city 308

(ṛ)
ṛddhi 254, 400
ṛddhi-mantra 348
ṛddhi-sākṣātkriyā 348, 422
ṛddhipāda 285, 348, 400
ṛddhividhi-jñāna 348
ṛṣi 88, 277, 347, 492, 535, 551, 589
仙 307
ṛṣi jina 497
ṛṣis 280, 429, 486
天仙 569

(S)
Sabhāgahetu 465
saddharma 146, 264
Saddharma Puṇḍarīka 98
saddharma-pratirūpaka 296
Saddharma-puṇḍarīka 93, 209, 264, 398
Saddharmapuṇḍarīka 146
Saddharmapuṇḍarīka Sūtra 540
Saddharmapuṇḍarīka-sūtra 191, 381
Sadvaha 170
Sadvāhana 236, 340
Sadāparibhūta 296
Sadāpralāpa 264
saffron 434
Sagala of Ptolemy 237
Sagittarii 130
Sagittarius 349, 364, 381
Sahabhūhetu 465
sahabhūhetu 53, 476
sahaja 113
Saharanpur 326
Sahasra 507
Sahasrabhujasahasranetra 566
Sahasrāra 567
Sahā 494
sahā 11, 236, 261
Sahā-world 492
Sahāloka 494
Sahālokadhātu 236, 494
Saindhava 241, 308
Sainika 308
sainika 304
Sakṛdāgāmin 222, 232, 236, 368, 477, 501, 576
sakṛdāgāmin 98, 343, 369
four stages 242
四向 261
四部 248
sakṛdāgāmin-phala
四果 239
Sal-tree 264
Sala-tree 234
Sama 271, 274, 613
Samakan 263, 295
Samanaioi 245
Samanantaram 272
Samanta 272, 510
Samanta-bhadra 102
Samanta-Prabhāsa 437
Samanta-prabhāsa 74, 125, 442
Samantabhadra 63, 64, 89, 194, 195, 223, 241, 272, 280, 289, 357, 363, 372, 377, 431, 434, 493, 531, 544, 559, 612, 617, 639, 647
four chief bodhisattvas 247
四法 247
Samantagandha 272
Samantaprabhāsa 195, 374, 580
Samantaprabhāsa Buddha 2, 18, 73
Samantarāja 407
Samarcand 327
Samarkand 9, 12, 19, 159, 263, 295
Samataṭa 271
Samatikram 577
samatā 613
Samatā-jñāna 430
Samatājñāna 613
Samavāya 271
samavāya 466
Samaya 272
samaya 202, 224, 258, 341, 484
Samaya assembly 272
Samaya commandments 272
Samaya wisdom 272
Samaya world 272
samaya-jñāna-mudrā 259
Samaya-maṇḍala 272
samaya-sign 202
Sambhoga 277
Sambhogakāya 120, 186, 214, 218, 277, 282, 283, 331
sambhogakāya 7, 20, 93, 121, 194, 227, 273, 283, 290, 351, 370, 404, 428, 471, 483, 484, 516, 559, 561, 641
four bodies 252
寂光淨土 499
sambhogakāya realm 421
sambhāra 514
Sambhūta 277
Sambodhi 277, 527
Sambuddha 278
same 113
Samkassam 339
Sampadi 48
Sampaha 294
Sampatti 275
sampradāna 609
Samprayuktahetu 465
samprayuktahetu 476
Samprāpta 275
Sampuṭa 277
Samudaya 274
samudaya 31, 562, 581

四諦 257
Samudra 274
samudra-sāgara 274
samudāya 562
Samyag-dṛṣṭi 609
Samyag-vyāyāma 609
Samyag-vāc 609
Samyag-ājīva 609
Samyagbodhi 528
Samyagbuddhi 528
Samyagdṛṣṭi 527
Samyagjñāna 531
Samyagvyāyāma 530
Samyagvāk 529
Samyagājīva 528
Samyak-karmānta 609
Samyak-sambodhi 115, 116, 273
Samyak-sambuddha 371
Samyak-samādhi 609
Samyak-saṁkalpa 609
Samyak-smṛti 609
Samyakkarmānta 530
Samyakprahāṇa 257
samyakprahāṇa 285
Samyaksambuddha 273, 528
Samyaksamādhi 530
Samyaksaṁkalpa 529
Samyaksmṛti 527
Samādhi 271, 273
samādhi 103, 116, 120, 214, 216, 270, 271, 272, 273, 279, 342, 355, 358, 418, 503, 508, 509, 511, 526, 551
great pity 95
Samādhi
referred to as father of all knowledge and virtue 204
Samādhi body 214
Samādhi Buddha 273
samādhi, unpropped 153
samādhi-equilibrium 116
Samādhi-māra 273
samādhi-saṁbodhyaṅga 584
samādhibala 414, 528
samādhis 89
king of 435
samādhīndriya 485, 527
Samāhita 271
samāhita 116
Samānārthatā 113
samānārthatā 251
Samāpanna 271, 272
Samāpatti 272
samāpatti 116, 273
samāpattis 272
Samāpta 294
Samāsa 271
samāsa 581
Samīkṣā 274
San Lun Sect 316
san-kuei 268
San-lun 122, 151, 271
sand 235
sandalwood 434
Sandhi-nirmocana-sūtra 622
Sandhinirmocana 262
Sandhinirmocana sūtra 546
Sandhinirmocana-sūtra 456
Sandrokottos 384
Sandānikā 263
sannāha(-sannaddha) 339
Sanron 122, 271, 367, 540, 587, 609
Sanskrit 54, 182, 324, 587, 609
Sanskrit alphabet 181
santati 298
santras- 614
Sapindus 643
sapratigha 456
Sapta 582
sapta 264
Sapta bodhyaṅga 78, 527
sapta bodhyaṅga 285
Sapta Buddha 117, 584
Sapta ratna 584
sapta ratna 143
Sapta Tathāgatāḥ 586
Sapta-anitya 587
Saptabodhyaṅga 584
Saptakoṭibuddha-mātṛ 582
Saptamātṛ 583
Saptaparṇaguhā 419, 563, 572
Saptaratna 62
saptaratna 179, 264, 524, 564, 634
Saptaratna Padmavikramin 109
saptaratna realm 196
Saptati 585
Saptādhikaraṇa-śamatha 583
Sarasvatī 94, 147, 158, 192, 264, 350, 485, 607
Sarikkol 236
Sarjarasa 264
Sarmanai 245
sarpa 236
sarpauṣadhi 264
Sarpauṣadhi monastery 236
sarpirmaṇḍa 416
Sarpiṣkuṇḍaika-pravara 419
Sarpiṣkuṇḍikā-prāgbhāra 572
Sarva 507
sarva 264, 533
Sarva-ruta-kauśalya 623
Sarva-tathāgata-puṇyo nirjāti 106
Sarvabhāva 509
sarvabhāva 534
Sarvadharma 508
sarvadharma 534
Sarvadharma-śūnyatā 508
Sarvadā 264, 508
Sarvajña 264, 510
Sarvajñadeva 264, 510
Sarvajñatā 510
sarvajñatā 221
sarvakleśa 264
sarvakāma 264
Sarvalokadhātūpadravodvega-pratyuttīrṇa 105, 108
Sarvasattva-priya-darśana 133, 509
Sarvasattva-pāpa-prahāṇa 510
Sarvasattvapriyadarśana 96
Sarvasattvāujohārī 357, 510
Sarvasiddhārtha 264
Sarvatathāgata 509
Sarvathā 106
Sarvatraga 612
sarvatraga 20, 612
Sarvatraga-hetu 20
Sarvatragahetu 465, 612
Sarvārthasiddha 264, 307, 349, 509
Sarvāstivāda 186, 228, 258,

264, 313, 325, 417, 457, 584, 631
Sarvāstivāda School 485
Sarvāstivāda school 6, 112, 133, 160, 280, 329, 338, 641
Sarvāstivāda Vinaya 432
Sarvāstivāda-version 255
Sarvāstivāda-vinaya 211
Sarvāstivāda-vinaya-saṅgraha 338
Sarvāstivādaḥ 509
Sarvāstivādin 5, 325, 367, 509, 586
Sarvāstivādin school 1, 377
Sarvāstivādin view 156
Sarvāstivādins 26, 61, 154, 165, 250, 325, 333, 419
Sarvāstivādāḥ school 136
sarṣapa 13, 243, 264
sat 145
satchel 158
satkāyadarśana 263
satkāyadṛṣṭi 346, 410
Satruṣṇa 327
sattva 264, 458
sattvakaṣāya 543
Sattvavajra 431
Saturn 53, 236, 420
Satya 236
satya 264
Satya-siddhi 504
Satya-siddhi school 456
Satya-siddhi sect 367
Satya-siddhi śāstra 287, 602
Satya-siddhi-śāstra 298
Satyadevatā 202
satyadevatā 236
Satyasiddhi 34, 258, 324
Satyasiddhi School 26
Satyasiddhi school 1
Satyasiddhi sect 316, 540
Satyasiddhi śāstra 1, 316
Satyasiddhi-śāstra 191, 540
ascribed to Harivarman 256
satyrs 429
saumanasyendriya 485
Sautrāntika 24, 504
Sautrāntikāḥ 325
Sautrāntikāḥ school 226, 313
Sautrāntikāḥ sect 44
Sauvastika 134
sauvastika 134
Sañjaya 262
sañjaya 565
Sañjaya-Vairāṭī 262
Sañjaya-Vairāṭīputra 262, 436
Sañjayin 463
Sañjayin Vairadīputra 262
Sañjayin Vairāṭīputra 218
Sañjñā 297, 300
sañjñā 262, 340, 424
sañjīva 297, 603
Saṁbhava 96, 105
Saṁgha 23, 576, 577
saṁgha 635
Saṁghārāma 543
Saṁghāta 543, 554
saṁjñā 140, 331, 340, 418, 611
Saṁjīv 554
saṁjīv 116
Saṁmata 272, 275
Saṁmatīya 160, 244, 274, 324, 325, 528
Saṁmatīyas 94
Saṁmiti 275
Saṁmitīya 300, 528
Saṁmitīyanikāya 275
Saṁmitīyas 275
Saṁmukha-vinaya 583
saṁnidhānārtha 609
Saṁskāra 80, 300
saṁskāra 331, 340, 365, 424, 623, 624
saṁskāra skandha 624
Saṁskṛtam 182
saṁskṛtam 339
saṁsthānarūpa 631
saṁsvedaja 250
saṁsāra 12, 124, 262, 281, 293, 303, 461
saṁsāra states 50
Saṁvaji 211, 276
Saṁvara 275
saṁvarta 18, 41
Saṁvarta kalpa 315
saṁvarta-kalpa 139
saṁvarta-siddha 41
Saṁvarta-siddha kalpa 315
saṁvartasiddha 18
saṁvartatthāhi 89
Saṁvṛti-satya 488
saṁyojana 238
Saṁyuktapiṭaka 518
Saṁyuktābhidharma-hṛdaya-śāstra 483
Saṁyuktāgama 386, 423, 518, 609
Saṁyuktāgamas 299
saṁyuktāgamas 四阿含 253
Saṅgha 268, 276, 277, 283, 300, 339, 360, 508, 566, 604
saṅgha 105, 337, 424, 493
Saṅghabheda 598
Saṅghabhūti 228
Saṅghanandi 486
Saṅghapāla 12, 338
Saṅghavarman 12, 218, 338
Saṅghaṁ śaraṇaṁ gacchāmi 268
Saṅghādiśeṣa 340
Saṅghāgāra 2
Saṅghānandi 118, 338
Saṅghārāma 2, 237, 338
saṅghārāma 119, 339, 375
saṅghāta 338, 603
Saṅghāvaśeṣa 340
saṅghāvaśeṣa 481, 612
Saṅghāṭī 2, 338
saṅghāṭī 2, 56, 75, 287, 338, 462, 472
Saṅgraha-vastu 125
Saṅgīti 22
Saṅgītiparyāya śāstra 90
Saṅkakṣikā 339
saṅkleśa 283, 339
sbyaṅs-can-ma 94
scarlet 420
scavenger 81
scent 292
scented ocean 625
Scheat 126
School of Presbyters 325
science 231
Scinde 346, 403, 571
Scorpio 172, 364, 374

scriptures 77, 332
Scythian king 25
Scythians 232
sea of incarnate life 461
seal 142, 506
six seals 466
seals 328
seasons of an Indian year 572
second 475
second synod 584
seed-word 514
seedless 79
self 76, 372
self-control 287
self-development 287
self-examination 615
self-existing 483
self-love 516
self-nature 516
self-progress 517
self-purification 287, 517
self-release 517
self-substance 516
semblance law 137, 529
semblance period 528
Semenghān 647
Semnoi 245
Senika 308
sense-organs 460
sentence 44
sentient 319
sentient beings 458
Senā 160
senā 308
separate 209
Separate school 467
Separatist 194
seriatim 304
Serpent 365
sesamum 549
seven 582
seven atoms 583
seven emotions 587
seven perfections 589
seven pretensions 583
seven vinaya 584
seventy 585
seventy-five 585
seventy-two 586
sexual intercourse 439
Shadumān 635
Shaman 245
shaman 95
Shamar 635
Shan-shan 75
Shan-tao 40, 77, 321, 540, 641
Shan-wai 263
Shansi 413, 451, 574
文殊 157
Shantung 113, 520
Shao Chou 197
Shao-chou 536, 538
Shao-k'ang 321
Shao-lin monastery 321
Shao-lung 634
Shao-shih 321
sharp 415
sheep 394
Shensi 232
Shensi monk 629
shield 8
shih 359
Shih Tsu 446
shih-shen-ma 480
Shih-t'ou 312
Shin 540
Shin Sect 511, 561
Shin sect 185, 332, 426
Shingon 64, 217, 265, 290, 299, 361, 367, 466, 502, 540, 587, 603, 609
Shingon custom 166
Shingon School 430, 477, 508, 510
Shingon sect 63, 160, 368, 434
Shinran 511, 561
四法 247
Shinran-Shōnin 538
Shinto 267, 608
Shintō 346
Shorea 242
shortcoming 617
shout 510
Shu-chou 597
Shun Chih 96
Shun, the Emperor 336
Shun-t'ien-fu 305
Shên Tsung 142
Shên-hsiu 74, 105, 312, 332, 410
北宗 208
shêng 339
Siam 324, 555
Sianfu 104
sickness
ten fields of meditation 551
Siddha 414
siddha(m) 349
Siddham 372, 514, 583
Siddhavastu 349
Siddhi 89
siddhi 187, 294, 316, 349
Siddhānta 532
siddhānta 125, 252, 319, 349, 538
Siddhārtha 84, 131, 307, 349, 509
天中天 571
Siggava 419
sign 142, 506, 549
signet-rings 328
Sikhs 2
Silhet 350
Simla 338
sin
six sins that smother the six pāramitās 468
五惡 five sins 423
Sindh 231, 345, 346
Sindhu 345, 346, 403, 494, 571
four rivers 261
sindhupāra 346
sindhuvāra 346
Sindūra 346
Sinkiang 435
Sir Aurel Stein 589
Sirikol 236, 536
Sirikol lake 600
Sitātapatra 418
sitātapatra 349
Sitātapatroṣṇīṣa-dhāraṇī 221
six entries 511
six gati 498
six inherent qualities 465
six objects 465
six organs 465
six pāramitās 421, 466

六種印 466
six schools 466
six senses 605
Six Ti-tsang 555
six śāstras 371
Six-legged Honoured One 413
six-word dhāraṇī 465
sixteen 492
sixty 463
Siṁha 256
siṁha 255, 340
Siṁha-bhikṣu 256
Siṁhadhvaja 105, 256
Siṁhaghoṣa 105, 256
Siṁhahanu 176, 256
Siṁhala 256, 338, 562
siṁhanāda 256
Siṁhapura 338
Siṁharaśmi 256
siṁhāsana 256
Skanda 485, 583
skandha 15, 300, 301
skandha of rūpa 302
skandha-māra 127
skandha-māras 604
skandhas 140, 279, 286, 355, 361, 400, 414, 416, 420, 421, 423, 424, 485, 495, 498, 602, 607, 609
five 424, 463
skillful 42
skirt 462
slackness 216
slave 78
slice 611
slip 611
smaller sūtra 89
smallest
水塵, atom of dust wandering freely in water 335
smṛti 77
smṛti-saṁbodhyaṅga 584
Smṛti-vinaya 583
smṛtibala 77, 414
Smṛtyupasthāna 240
smṛtyupasthāna 78, 228, 285
smṛtīndriya 78, 485
snake god 496
snigdha 464
so-come 398
so-gone 398
So-ho 217
Sogdiana 12
Soghdiana 12
Soma 53, 586
soma 11, 322
月 450
Somadeva 452
sombre 628
Son of Buddha 220
Son of Heaven 57, 219
Soo-chow 305
Soochow 634
sopādhiśeṣa-nirvāṇa 458
Soul of the universe 195
south
丙 194
Southern Buddhism 208, 324
Southern Collection 74
Southern Hill school 305
Southern Peak monastery 631
Southern Sung dynasty 419
Sovereign beholder 379
Sovereign Regarder 38
sovereign ruler 517
Sovereign Śakra 533
space 552
Sparśa 80
sparśa 365, 577
spawn-born 594
Sphaṭika 295, 334, 335, 600
sphaṭika 300, 499, 584, 598, 601
spirit 516
spirit genii 308
Spirit Vulture Peak 121
Spiritual Vulture Peak 580
spread abroad 635
Spṛkkā 617
spṛkkā 300
squat 591
Srinagar 234, 326
Srughna 234, 326
Ssang-gye-sa 371
Ssŭ-ch'uan province 566
Ssŭ-ming 244, 263, 552, 573
Ssŭ-ming school 244
Ssŭ-ming Shan 402
staff 541
Stage-struck 104
stamp 142
star-group 201
states of all phenomena 249
staunch 112
stay
four functioning forms 255
four fundamental states 248
Sthavira 5, 103, 297, 299, 300, 324, 325, 349, 457, 591
sthavira 78, 104, 265, 324
Sthavira school 250
Sthaviranikāya 299, 349
Sthaviras
分別 209
Sthaviravādin 300, 325
Sthavirāḥ 104, 299, 379, 485
sthira 19
Sthiramati 19, 349, 388
Sthitamati 388
sthiti 287, 542
sthāman 318, 591
Sthāna 591
sthāna 591
Sthāṇvīśvara 265
sthūla 578
Sthūlātyaya 596, 597
sthūlātyaya 612
stole 462
stone 305
stool 462
stop 79, 551
stop breathing 551
stotra 564
strike 591
strīndriya 485
stupid 415
stupid person 144
stupidity 276
Styx 555
Stūpa 221
stūpa 49, 79, 114, 221, 272, 326, 327, 424, 511, 593, 597
stūpas 105, 342, 604
su 145, 308
Su Tsung 74, 213, 378
Su-lo 320
Suastene 426
Subanta 609

subanta 323, 587
Subhadra 147, 323, 329
Subhūti 34, 140, 198, 241, 312, 316, 323, 329, 357
subjective 76
submission 434
subordinations 289
substance 203, 466
Subāhu-kumāra 146
Subāhu-paripṛcchā 594
Sucinti 329
Sucintā 329
Sucitti 329
Sudanta 329
Sudarśana 51, 66, 86, 107, 250, 284, 301, 322, 327, 329, 332, 648
四苑 254
sudarśana 250, 309
Sudarśana city 571
Sudarśanas 426
Sudatta 322, 329, 374, 386
suddenly 647
Sudhana 311
Sudhana-Kumāra 213
Sudharma Kinnaras 94
Sudharma-rāja 94
Sudhā 569
sudhā 11
Sudhāman 329
Sudhīra 158, 590
Sudurjayā 369
Sudāna 84, 90, 322, 328, 592
Sudṛśa 250, 301, 312, 329
sudṛśa 250, 391
Sudṛśas 426
suffering 114
five forms 411
to have to meet the hateful 447
Sugandhara 409
sugar-cane 11
Sugar-cane garden 443
Sugar-cane king 507
Sugata 310, 321, 322, 371
Sugatacetana 81
Sughoṣa 147
Sui dynasty 95, 104, 105, 107, 266, 325
Sujāta 160, 310, 342
sukha 327
sukhendriya 485
Sukhāvatī 60, 305, 378, 499, 531
Sukhāvatī sect 540
Sukhāvatī-vyūha 579
Sukhāvatīvyūha 378
Sukhāvatīvyūha-sūtra 149
Sumanā 328
sumanā 322, 325
Sumati 328
Sumatikīrti 539, 644
Sumatra 31
Sumeru 16, 47, 51, 62, 105, 160, 211, 263, 284, 322, 328, 361, 414, 468, 482, 501, 503, 582, 607
devalokas 464
scented ocean 625
Sumitra 158
summer 618
summer retreat 285, 510, 618
summon 321
Sumāgadhā 272
Sun 382
sun 53
日 498
Sun Yen 167
Sun-Buddha 544
Sun-buddha 63
Sun-deva 492
sun-deva 236
sun-face Buddha 451
sun-god 534
sun-ruler 499
Sunanda 326
Sundarananda 73, 326
Sundari 326
Sundarā 48
Sundarī 326, 522
Sung dynasty 88, 106, 263, 398, 469, 498, 516
Sung shan 321
Sunirmita 328
sunirmita 387
Sunlight 498
sunlight 493
supernatural beings 606
Suprabuddha 568
Supratiṣṭhita-cāritra 389
Supratiṣṭhitacāritra 241
Supreme Being 201
Supreme Buddha 210
Supreme Enlightenment 210
Supreme Soul 348
sura 333, 566
Surasthāna 600
surata 322
Sureśvara 517
Suri 327
Surā 327, 542
surā 333
Surā-maireya-madya-pramād asthānād vairamaṇī (virati) 220
surāmerayamajjapamādaṭṭhān ā-veramaṇī 356
Surāṣṭra 457
surūpa 146, 322
Surūpakāya Tathāgata 146
Susambhava 310
susiddhi 325
Susiddhikāra sūtras 325
susvara-nakṣatra-rāja-saṅku sumitā-bhij 445
Sutlej 87, 154, 375
Sutriṣṇa 327
suvarṇa 61, 65, 321, 323, 333, 584
Suvarṇa-prabhāsa-uttamarāja sūtra 65
Suvarṇabhūmi 66
Suvarṇagotra 323, 398
Suvarṣakāḥ 509
Suviśuddha 185
Suyata 328
Suyāma 328
Suyāma heavens 606
Suśānta 328
suṣvāgata 310, 327
sva 515
Svabhāva 615
svabhāva 235, 314, 516
svacitta 516
svalakṣaṇa 515
svar 196, 266
Svarga 107, 284
Svastika 409

svastika 70, 107, 179, 219, 239, 300
svayam 515
Svayambhuvaḥ 516
svayambhū 516
Svādi-devatā 201
Svāgata 322, 332
svāgata 234, 310
Svāhā 322, 336
svāhā 106, 246, 261
svāmivacana 609
svārtha-viruddha 516
Svāti 485
Swat 17, 145
sweet 11
sweet dew 11
syllabary 182
syllogism 214
symbol 506
synod
  Rājagṛha 436
Syria 558
Sêng-chao 303, 355, 537
  四聖 251
Sêng-jui 303
  四聖 251
Sêng-ts'an 312
  six patriarchs 466
sādhu 308, 311, 314
Sādhumatī 369
sādhumatī 312
sādhāraṇa 577
Sāgara 236, 485
sāgara 274, 622
Sāgara-nāgarāja 440
Sāgara-varadhara-buddhi-vikrīḍitābhijñ 263
Sāhet-Māhet 254
Sāl tree 242
Sāla 242
  eight famous Caityas 548
Sālva 264
Sāma-veda-saṁhitā 271
Sāmaveda 236, 452
Sāmānya 272
sāmānya 466
Sārasa 236
Sārnāth 122, 161
  deer park 308
Sātavāhana 236, 495
Sāṁghika-version 255
Sāṁkhya 179
Sāṅghika 339
sāṅghika 339
sāṅghikavinaya 339
Sāṅkhya 79, 91, 159, 274, 339
sāṅkhya 339
Sāṅkhya Kapila 236
Sāṅkhya philosophy 5, 17, 280, 436, 452, 516
Sāṅkhya principles 274
Sāṅkhya school 442
Sāṅkāśya 18, 125, 339
Sīmā 244
sūci 589
sūkṣma 145, 159
Sūnurīśvara 327
Sūrya 25, 130, 236, 328, 333, 485, 498
  日天子 499
sūrya 322
Sūrya-deva 196
Sūrya-garbha 72
Sūrya-prabhāsana 498
Sūryamitra 328
Sūryaraśmi 145
Sūryavaṁśa 220, 499, 507
Sūryāvarta samādhi 499
sūtra 322, 332, 364, 505, 583
Sūtra of Brahma's Net 26
Sūtra School 485
Sūtra school 250
Sūtra-piṭaka 98, 332
sūtra-piṭaka 24
sūtrapiṭaka 104
sūtras 266
Sūtrālaṅkāra-śāstra 103

(Ś)
Śabdavidyā 315
Śabdavidyā śāstra 315
Śacī 107, 259, 284, 313
Śacīpati 259
Śaila 318, 319
Śaivas 452
Śakra 165, 181, 262, 306, 307, 436, 496
  天帝 571
Śakra devānām Indra 485
Śakra heaven 605
Śakra-devendra 306
Śakro-devānām-indra 533
Śakro-devānāmindra 306, 307
Śakrāditya 72, 222, 262, 341
Śakti 213, 259, 313, 363
Śal tree 242
Śamatha 237
Śamatha-vipaśyanā 551
Śambara 360
Śamī 237
Śanaiścara 53, 236, 586, 595
Śani 595
Śanirājā 262
Śaraṇa-gamana 59, 268
Śarāvatī 350
Śarīra(m) 243
Śarīra-stūpa 243
Śata 502
Śata-śāstra 243, 271, 540
Śatabhiṣā 241, 485
Śatadru 87, 313, 375, 600
Śatakri 236
Śataparṇa 563
Śataśāstra 175
Śatru 313
Śayanāsana 319
Śaśa 259
Śaśa-viṣāṇa 596
Śaśa-śṛṅga 596
Śaśaka 249
Śaśin 259
Śaśāṅka 313, 451
Śaśī 259, 450
Śaṅkara 31, 297
Śaṅkarasvāmin 496
Śaṅkarācārya 297
Śaṅkha 184, 297
Śaṇavāsa 297, 419
Śaṇḍila 365, 564
Śikhin 35, 164, 342, 360, 584, 635
Śikhin Buddha 517
Śikṣamāṇa 343, 620
Śikṣā 343
  six śāstras 461
Śikṣākaraṇīya 14, 177, 343
Śikṣānanda 69, 79, 98, 127, 351,

473, 607, 640
Śikṣāpada 356
Śilpasthāna-vidyā 32
Śirīṣa 343, 621
Śirīṣaka 343
Śiva 93, 99, 102, 106, 133, 159, 163, 181, 273, 274, 276, 280, 293, 343, 366, 406, 452, 482, 496, 508, 510, 517, 520, 583
Creator or ruler of the world 436
Śiva heaven 605
Śiva-Rudra 482
Śivaism 17
Śivaites 129, 164, 436, 517
Śiva's ear 621
Śiva's wife 228
Śivi 343
Śiśumāra 349
Śloka 328, 331
Śmaśāna 234, 343, 351
Śobhanavatī 48
Śoṇaka 419
Śraddhotpāda 346
Śraddhotpāda Śāstra 69
Śraiṇya 308
Śramaṇa 296, 535
Śravaṇā 349, 383, 485
Śraviṣṭhā 485
Śreṇika 308
Śrota-āpanna 222, 329, 401, 512, 576
Śrota-āpanna stage 212
Śrotra 237
Śroṇakoṭīviṁśa 484
Śrāmaṇera 350
Śrāvaka 242, 281, 394, 483, 488
Śrāvaka-realm 183
Śrāvakas 270, 282
Śrāvakayāna 315
Śrāvastī 66, 68, 92, 118, 254, 272, 285, 338, 342, 350, 363, 445, 600, 617
Śrāvaṇa 388, 572
Śrāvaṇa(-māsa) 350
Śrī 270, 342, 452
Śrī-vatsa 70
Śrībhadra 452
Śrībhoja 136
Śrībhuja 343
Śrīdeva 350
Śrīgarbha 115, 350
Śrīgupta 343, 350
Śrīguṇa 343
Śrīhatta 350
Śrīkrītati 15, 350
Śrīkṣetra 350
Śrīlabdha 350
Śrīmatī-brāhmaṇī-paripṛcchā 456
Śrīmitra 343, 350
Śrīmālā-devī-siṁhanāda 338
Śrīvatsa 350
Śrīyaśas 343
Śubha-vyūha 89, 637
Śubhakara 337
Śubhakṛtsna 250, 301, 328
Śubhavastu 323, 386, 426
Śubhavyūha 38, 147, 236, 519, 529, 530
Śubhākarasiṁha 102, 211, 331, 337
Śuddha 342
Śuddhacandra 337
Śuddhipanthaka 541
Śuddhodana 131, 256, 328, 331, 404, 528, 549
Śuddhodana-maheśvara 102
Śuddhāvāsa 102, 328
Śuddhāvāsa-deva 537
Śuddhāvāsa-maheśvara 102
Śuddhāvāsadeva 527
Śudhyanti 337
Śuka 337, 537
Śuklapakṣa 177, 337
Śuklodana 256, 331, 550
Śuklodana-rāja 176
Śukra 53, 66, 337, 586
Śvetavājin 450
Śāka 220
Śākala 237
Śākya 220, 255, 507
Śākya clan 17, 96, 220
Śākya Mahānāma Kulika 307
Śākya-bodhisattva 307
Śākya-seed
比丘 225
Śākya-Tathāgata 45
Śākyamuni 47, 201, 276, 280, 283, 289, 342, 424, 482, 483, 489, 497, 584
four Buddhas of the four regions 246
life narration 218
life of 217
the first image was made of red sandal-wood 442
Śākyamuni Buddha 210
Śākyamuni's assemblies 276
Śākyamuni's austerities 460
Śākyamuni's eyebrows 177
Śākyamuni's relics 435
Śākyapaṇḍita 606
Śākyaputrīya 307
Śākyasiṁha 307
Śākyeṣu 307
Śāla 242
Śāla trees 19
Śālarāja 242
Śālavana 236
Śālendra-rāja 236
Śālva 264
Śālāturīya 600
Śāmaka 313
Śāmbī 294, 306
Śāntika 262, 634
Śāraṅganātha
deer park 308
Śāraṇa 242
Śārdūlakarṇa 242
Śārikā 243
Śāriputra 17, 47, 52, 90, 132, 199, 241, 243, 262, 313, 357, 441, 444, 550, 578, 636
four groups 259
Śāriputra's eyes 17
Śāriputra's mother 243
Śārī 243, 578
Śāstra 237
Śāstra school 122
Śāstras 91
Śāstā Devamanuṣyāṇām 570
Śāstā devamanuṣyāṇām 371
Śāstādevamanuṣyāṇām 241
Śāṇakavāsa 137, 297, 486
Śāṇḍilya 262
Śāṭaka 243

Śāṭhya 237
Śāṭhā 610
Śīghrabodhi 141
Śīla 26, 28, 342
Śīla-dharma 342
Śīlabhadra 28, 342, 552
Śīlaprabha 342
Śīlapāramitā 342
Śīlāditya 114, 313, 342, 451
Śīta 620
Śītamarīci 450
Śītavana 342
Śītā 77, 154, 235, 236, 375, 607, 642
Śītāṁśu 450
Śūdra 148, 337
Śūla 331
Śūnya 282, 336, 626
Śūnya sects 35
Śūnyapuṣpa 35
Śūnyasamādhi 509
Śūnyatā 337
Śūra 103, 331
Śūraṁgama 328, 516
Śūraṁgama dhyāna 328
Śūraṅgama sūtra 79, 168, 240, 449
Śṛgāla 349, 393

(ś)
śabda 314, 415, 557
śabda-vidyā 314
śaikṣa 459, 620
śakti 38, 71, 102, 262, 418, 430, 595
śalākā 242
śama 244
śamatha 551
śamī 313
śarad 572
śarāva 237
śarīra 160, 217, 221, 314, 350, 594
  spiritual relics 188
śata 175
śava 314
śaya 331
śayana 435
śaśa 596
śaśa-dhara 645
śaśin 596
śaśorṇa 510
śaṅkha 611
śikṣ 620
śikṣamāṇa 588
śikṣākaraṇīya 481
śilpakarmasthāna 415
śilā 342
śiśira 572
śiśumāra 336, 351
śiṣya 351
śmaśāna 244, 342, 577, 620
śraddhendriya 346, 485
śraddhā 237, 346
śraddhābala 347, 414
śramaṇa 61, 97, 140, 158, 242, 245, 342, 343, 351, 483, 553, 606
  Chih-lou-chia-ch'an 548
śramaṇa of Kashmir 102
śramaṇa of Kubhā 211
śramaṇas
  four grades, four titles 239
śrota-āpanna 98, 322, 327, 368, 369, 408
  four stages 242
  四向 261
  四部 248
śrota-āpanna-phala
  四果 239
śrota-āpannas 531
śrotra 337, 476
śrotra-vijñāna 607
śrotravijñāna 476
śrotrendriya 476, 485
śrāmaṇera 245, 294, 588, 624
śrāmaṇerikā 246, 588
śrāvaka 20, 41, 76, 94, 95, 97, 191, 239, 281, 286, 292, 300, 315, 360, 394, 401, 408, 425, 464, 480, 483, 506, 517, 596, 602, 622
  accepted four noble dogmas 257
  four holy ways of rebirth 461
  world from four points of view 255
  三品四善根 251
  聖住 258
śrāvaka method 435
śrāvaka vehicle 315
śrāvaka-cum-pratyeka-buddha 207
śrāvakas 93, 96, 97, 205, 214, 272, 277, 286, 287, 288, 289, 290, 293, 360, 414, 415, 420, 421, 422, 424, 429, 483, 529, 545, 566, 584, 587, 588, 602, 604, 607
  abiding in the fruit 542
  四聖 251
śrāvakas and pratyeka-buddhas 315
śrāvakas-cum-pratyeka-buddhas 421
śrī 70, 305, 350
śrīmitra 340
śrīpada 201
śrīvatsa 134
śrīvatsa-lakṣaṇa 134
śrīvāsas 350
śuka 336, 392
śukla 336
śukra 336
śyena 341
śāla trees
  四枯四榮, when the Buddha died 239
śāla-trees 371
śāli 160
śāluka 250
śānta 236
śānti 521
śāntika 308, 429
śārikā 242
śārī 242
śāsana 222
śāstra 104, 122, 266, 420, 482, 502
śāstra-writers 122
śāstras 23, 270, 295, 419, 604
  four śāstras 255
śāśana 42
śāśvata 296
śīla 109, 163, 342, 416, 461, 469
śīla-vrata-parāmarśa 410

śīlas 342
śītavana 105, 340, 620
śūdra 331
four castes 251
śūdra caste 78
śūdras 93
śūnya 32, 289, 350, 398, 602, 607
śūnya is rūpa 35
śūnya principle 33
śūnyatā 32, 34, 532

(Ṣ)
Ṣaḍ-āyatana 80
Ṣaḍakṣara-vidyāmantra 465
Ṣaḍāyatana 465, 468
Ṣaṅghabhadra 338
Ṣaṇḍha 168, 428, 522
Ṣaṇḍha(paṇḍaka) 168
Ṣaṇḍhaka 522
Ṣaṣṭi 463
Ṣaṭ 459
少, transliteration 321
Ṣaṭ-samāsa 271, 462
Ṣaṭsamāsa 263
Ṣoḍaśa 363
Ṣāṇṇagarika 240, 325, 463

(ṣ)
ṣaḍ 459
ṣaḍ-varṣa 261
ṣaḍabhijñā 468
ṣaḍāyatana 365, 511, 577, 625
ṣaḍāyatana-vijñāna mind 283
ṣaḍāyatanas 383
ṣaṇḍhaka 308
ṣaṇḍhila 534
ṣaṇḍhilas 432

(T)
ta 85
Ta Chuang Yen 253
Ta Shih Chih 161
Ta Tien 103
Ta-chih 104
Ta-hsien 105
Ta-mo 196
Ta-T'zŭ-En-Ssŭ 102
Tabernæmontana coronaria 82, 144
tabu 67
tabu day 67
tadyathā 85
Tae-go Bo-u 198
Tagara 144
tagara 2, 82
Tai Tsung 74, 142, 173, 213, 378
taints 464
Tajiks 536
Takṣaka 85, 107
Takṣaśilā 1, 85, 107, 579
Talas 85
Talekān 85
Talikhan 85, 644
Talima 550
talisman-pearl 400
talismanic pearl 568
talismanic vase 400
talismanic wheel 400
Tallakṣaṇa 170
talons 536
Tamasthiti 634
Tamlook 593
Tamluk 85, 593
Tamo 86
Tamāla 37
Tamāla-patra-candana-gandha 143
Tamāla-pattra-candana-gandha 105
Tamālapattra 83
Tamālapattra-candana-gandha 83
Tang and Ran 115
Tang-yang 434
tanmātra 88, 434
Tantra 347
Tantra School 275
Tantrayāna 89
Tantric 455
Tantric school 378, 382, 390
Tantric sects 577
Tantric trinity 276
tanu 345
Tao of Heaven 568
Tao-an 389
Tao-ch'o 77, 305
Tao-hsi 350
Tao-hsin 110, 312
six patriarchs 466
Tao-hsüan 74, 110, 305, 454, 469
Tao-jung 303
四聖 251
Tao-shêng 303, 406, 525
四聖 251
Tao-sui 551, 571, 572
Tao-wu 574
Taoism 267, 520, 628
Taoist 110
Taoist genii 66
Tapana 554
tapana 85, 404, 407, 576, 603
Tapas 31
tapas 404
Tara 82
Taras 78, 85
taraṅga 598, 600
tarka 26
Tashkend 514
tastes 462
tathā 83, 398
Tathāgata 32, 50, 66, 83, 85, 102, 103, 120, 212, 213, 217, 218, 270, 275, 368, 371, 399, 450, 471, 472, 476, 480, 505, 508, 509, 528, 553, 560, 561, 612, 632
tathāgata 622
Tathāgata apostle 399
Tathāgata day 399
Tathāgata in bonds 399
Tathāgata meditation 509
Tathāgata nature 275
Tathāgata vehicle 399
Tathāgata Worshipful Omniscient 399
Tathāgata, son of 113
Tathāgata-dharmakāya 504
Tathāgata-dhyānas 310
Tathāgata-dūta 399
Tathāgata-eye 509
Tathāgata-garbha 264, 282, 283, 289, 316, 403, 447
tathāgata-garbha 353
Tathāgata-garbha-sūtra 92

tathāgata-heart 647
Tathāgata-nature 429
tathāgata-power 270
Tathāgata-preṣya 399
Tathāgata-wisdom 491
Tathāgatagarbha 187, 198, 399, 520
tathāgatagarbha 278
Tathāgatakāya 399
Tathāgatas 424, 509, 586
Tathāgatayāna 399
Tathāgata's 280, 370
tatkṣaṇa 85
tatpuruṣa 462
Tatsvabhāvaiṣīya-vinaya 583
tattva 559
 mind-organ, one of the twenty five tattva 352
tattvajñāna 559
Tattvas 339
tattvas 274
Taurus 364
Taxila 1, 85, 107, 474
Tchadj 514
Tchakravālas 554
Tchañśuna 525
Tchundi 130
Tchāseh 514
Tchīnapati 87
teeth 373
Teitaro Suzuki 69, 127
Tejorāśi 418, 534
Tejorāśi-cakravartī 642
temple 217
temples in the palace 76
ten 355
ten armies 356
ten chief 357
ten commandments 361
ten dhātu 54
ten directions 343
ten evils 361, 588
ten kalpas 355
ten kings 343
ten monks 361
ten negations 601
ten objects 355
ten precious things 360
ten prohibitions 356
ten pāramitās 357, 411
ten schools 367
ten stages 368
ten virtues 357
ten vows 357
Tendai 367, 466, 540, 573, 587, 609
Termed 85
Tetsugen 208
Thanesar 265
the 418
Thelari 521
theories
 ten fields of meditation 551
Theravāda 5
thesaurus 617
Thesaurus of Wisdom 213
Thirty 283
thirty years, 世 318
thirty-five 284
thirty-seven conditions 285
thirty-three 284
thirty-three devas 107
thirty-two 285
thirty-two lakṣaṇa 296
thirty-two marks 261, 459
thirty-two signs 158, 587
thought 222
thoughts 279
thousand 507
thousand arms 566
thousand eyes 566
thousand hands 363
thousand-hand Kuan-yin 566
three 265
three doubts 505
three kalpas 265, 280
three meditations 544
three postulates 546
Three Precious Ones 268, 606
three samādhis 279
three vehicles 281, 292, 506
Three Śāstra School 270
three-vehicle 281
three-yānas 97
three-śāstra sect 540
throatless 80
thumb-mark 549
thunderbolt 80, 179, 496
Thus 463
Thus have I heard 399, 483, 504
thus have I heard 332
Ti Tsang group 467
Ti-hsin Tu-shun 639
Ti-tsang 2, 56, 95, 555
 six 461
Ti-tsang's court 213
Tibet 606
Tibetan 606
Tibetan Buddhism 85, 305
Tibetan canon 11
Tibetan Lamaism 305
Tibetans 360
Tien-chiang Hsien 197
ties 265
Tiladaka 521
Tiladhāka 521
Tilaśākya 521
tiles 435
time
 four short divisions 251
Timi 548
Timiṅgila 548
Tinduka 558
Tirmez 85
Tirmidh 85
Tiryagyoni 520
tiryagyoni 172, 579, 589
tiryagyoni-gati 468, 533
Tishya 211
Tissa 360
Titilambha 556
Tiṅanta 520
tiṅanta 478, 587
Tiṣya 176, 195, 243, 331, 360, 486, 520, 533, 550, 562
Tiṣya-rakṣitā 533
Tiṣyarakṣitā 159
Tiṭibha 556
to-lo 80
Tocharoi 107, 108
toe-nail 536
toga 339, 587
Tokharestan 107, 108, 451
Tokhari 2
Tokhāra 57
Toksun 112

tolerance 287
topknot 500
tortoise 227
torture 415
track 135
traidhātuka 207
Trailokya 115, 266, 277, 301
trailokya 50, 207, 266, 286, 430, 454, 619
trailokya-garbha 266
Trailokya-vijaya 533
Trailokya-vijaya-rāja 621
Trailokyavijaya 83
Trailokyavijayarāja 431
trance 509
tranquil 613
transformation body 519, 544
transformation realm of Amitābha 642
transformation-born 594
transforming method 640
transforming truth 640
transliterated 428
transmigration 490
Transmigration after transmigration 319
transmigration-world 524
Trapuṣa 535
traya 85
trayas 265
Trayastriṁśas 533
Trayastriṁśās 107, 284
Trayastriṁśāḥ 82, 85, 163, 284, 438, 600, 648
trayastriṁśāḥ
四王天 254
Trayastriṁśāḥ gods
四塔 260
Trayastriṁśāḥ heaven 146
Trayastriṁśāḥs heavens 567
Trayodaśa 361
tree 144
Tri 265
Tri-sahasra-mahā-sahasra-loka-dhātu 293, 430
tricīvaraka 85
Tridaśa 283
trijāti 562
Trikoṇa 508
Trikāya 6, 186, 188, 194, 219, 276, 277, 278, 282, 331, 378, 499, 505, 508, 639
trikāya 291, 357, 505
Triloka 266
Trimūrti 159, 181, 276, 452
trimūrti 93, 293, 571
Trinity 216, 217, 265
trinity 283, 430, 505, 508
Tripiṭaka 22, 57, 62, 88, 89, 91, 102, 103, 220, 227, 231, 267, 275, 277, 295, 317, 332, 415, 469, 483, 508, 519, 599, 602, 607, 617, 633
in Pali 598
of the esoteric sect 161
tripiṭaka 288, 295, 364
Tripiṭaka doctrine
천태삼교 573
Tripiṭaka school 324, 519
Tripiṭaka teacher of Dharma 630
tripiṭakas 488
triple-power verse 270
Triratna 26, 50, 59, 61, 85, 183, 186, 188, 210, 244, 276, 277, 294, 315, 318, 337, 346, 361, 368, 429, 501, 508, 516, 626
triratna 430
四不壞淨 248
Triratna forms 638
Trisahasra 293
Trisamaya 520
Trividha-dvāra 274, 286
Trividyā 273
trividyā 151
Triyāna 281, 282, 293
triyāna 97, 281
Triyāna
四車 the four vehicles 238
Triśaraṇa 268
triśaraṇa 429
trouble 114
True One 561
True Sect 561
True Word 560
trusts of dharma 186
truth dhāraṇī 473
truth-plot 109
Truth-wisdom 559
Tryanta 520
Trāta 106
Tsai-li secret society 520
Tsan-ning 564
Tsaukūṭa 536, 620
Tso-ch'i 541, 628
天台九祖 572
Tson-kha-pa 117
Tsong-kha-pa 94
Tsoṅ-kha-pa 11, 539, 644
Tsung-kao 106
Tsung-ling 3
Tsung-ling mountains 600
Tsung-mi 539
Ts'an-po 96
Ts'ao-ch'i 536, 538
Ts'ao-shan 536
Ts'ao-tung sect 536
tu 571
Tu Shun 114, 533, 538
Tu-shun 412
Tukhāra 3, 107, 108, 161, 171, 172, 377, 451, 579, 620, 635
tumburu 114
Tumluk 83
Tung-shan 536
Tungusian Saman 245
Turfān 192
Turk 633
Turkestan 15, 159, 327, 514
turn 644, 645
turn back 645
turtle 227
Turuṣka 112
turuṣka 114
Turuṣka olibanum 114
tuum 319
Tuṣita 114, 147, 438, 556, 637
Tuṣita heaven 12, 77, 103, 107, 108, 160, 214, 304, 382, 455, 578, 606, 642
Tuṣita Heaven
天宮寶藏 the treasury of all the sutras 567
Tuṣita heavens 137
Tuṣita-heaven 439
tuṣāra 114
tvam 85

Twelve 480
twelve animals 365
twelve causes 80
twelve devas 366
Twelve Nidānas 282, 421
twelve nidānas 365, 421, 465
twelve vows 480
twelve-nidānas 324
Twenty 484
twenty-eight yakṣas 486
twenty-five bodhisattvas 484
twenty-five guardian 484
twenty-one 294
twig 135
Two 475
two Vehicles
  ten fields of meditation 551
two-footed beings 395
Tyāgīhrada 121
tzŭ hour 341
Tzŭ-hsüan 516
Tzŭ-ên 429
Tz'ŭ-ming 514
Tz'ŭ-yün 514
Tz'ŭ-ên
  四部經 248
  六部大乘經 462
Tz'ŭ-ên sect 186
T'ien-t'ai School 54
Tê Shan 619
Tê-an 555, 572
Têng-fêng hsien 321
Têng-lu 414
Tāla 82
tāla 603
Tāla tree 82
Tāmasavana 87
tāmasavana 390
Tāmbūla 86
tāmra 113
Tāmralipti 83, 85, 593
Tāmraliptī 83, 85
Tāmraṣāṭīyāḥ 509
Tārā 82, 213, 314, 363, 603
tārā 38
Tārā Bodhisattva 82
Tārānāth 591
Tārīm
  four rivers 261
Tārīm River 154
tīkṣṇa 125
tīrthika
  six 463
Tīrthikas 135, 436
Tīrthyas 215, 262, 374, 436
tūla 114
tṛṇa 85
Tṛṇastāraka-vinaya 583
Tṛṣṇā 80
tṛṣṇā 9, 365, 391
T'ang dynasty 512, 607
T'ien-t'ai 608
T'ien-t'ai classifications 602
T'ien-t'ai division 477, 480
T'ien-t'ai school 480
T'ai Po Shan 419
T'ai Shan 113, 586, 594
T'ai Tsu 74, 142, 471
T'ai Tsung 102, 104, 630
T'ai-Hêng School 594
T'aichow 572
T'an Wu-ti 388
T'ang 274
T'ang dynasty 90, 102, 103, 104, 211, 271, 288, 299, 412, 424, 434, 446, 450
T'ang Tripiṭaka 87
T'ien-huang monastery 574
T'ien-kung
  天台九祖 572
T'ien-shan 15
T'ien-tu 568
T'ien-t'ai 24, 41, 93, 267, 280, 289, 324, 355, 361, 362, 367, 434, 478, 499, 501, 504, 506, 511, 531, 540, 584
  six kinds of Kuan-yin 460
  世諦, worldly postulates 320
  四土 261
  四教儀 239
  육즉 六即 210
  천태종 573
T'ien-t'ai doctrines 263
T'ien-t'ai laws 573
T'ien-t'ai meditation 207
T'ien-t'ai meditations 613
T'ien-t'ai mountain 263, 594
  天悌山 571
T'ien-t'ai patriarch 146, 541
T'ien-t'ai School 244, 263, 269, 434, 446, 463
T'ien-t'ai school 546
T'ien-t'ai School
  四身 252
T'ien-t'ai scriptures 624
T'ien-t'ai stages 423
T'ien-t'ai 삼관 544
T'ien-t'ai-Shao-Kuo-Shih 573
T'ien-t'ung monastery 41
T'ou-tzŭ 597
T'zŭ En monastery 630
T'zŭ-en monastery 40
T'zŭ-ên monastery 176

(Ṭ)
Ṭakka 171, 237
Ṭhaṭṭha 195

(U)
uccheda 84, 290
ucchedadarśana 85
Ucchuṣma 207, 432, 581
uccāsayanā-mahāsayanā-vera maṇī 356
Uch-Turfān 642
udaka 441, 446
Udakacandra 334
Udayana 211, 242, 304, 413, 441, 442, 444, 523
Udayana Vatsa 444
Uddāna 442
Udjyana 226
Udra(ka) Rāmaputra 446
Udraka Rāmaputra 376
Udumbara flower 304
udumbara tree 442
Udyāna 72, 145, 228, 236, 262, 264, 306, 341, 389, 426, 435
  優禪尼 452
udāharaṇa 119, 235, 284, 292, 431
Udāna 150, 324
udāna 254, 364, 432, 435, 441
Udāna(ya) 442
udānas 50

Udāyi 381
出現 580
Udāyin 4, 442, 460
Ugra 445
Ugra-bhaga 412
Ui-cheon 475
Ui-sang 474
Uighurs 645
Uigur 414
Uigur Manichaeans 100
Uigur tribe 647
Ujjain 48, 426, 561
Ujjayanta 457
Ujjayinī 426, 441, 443
Ukkacela 445
Ulag 414
Ulak 414
Ulkā 567
Ulkā-mukha 407
Ullambana 108, 119, 442
Ullambana festival 378
Ullambanapātra-sūtra 443
Ulūka 280, 338, 436, 443, 492
ulūka 646
umbrella 567
Umā 415
unable 211
unamāna 383
unattainables 248
unceasing 205
unchastity 220
unclean 207
uncreated 218
understanding 137
unenlightened 203
unfettered 580
unhindered 508
Unicorn 111
unicorn ṛṣi 499
unison 621
unitary 193
unite 621
unity 469, 506
universal 510
Universal Wise Sovereign 221
Universally Shining Vajrasattva 431
universe 430
Unmada 415
unobtainable 211
unpermissible 211
Upadeśa 201, 433, 444
upadeśa 122, 123, 364
upadeśana 609
Upagupta 57, 67, 151, 419, 433, 444, 486, 534
Upakeśinī 158, 419, 433
Upakleśabhūmikāh 323
upalakṣa 469
upalakṣaṇa 444
upamā 599
Upananda 433, 444, 460
upanaya 431
Upanishads 441
Upaniṣad 81, 441, 444
upaniṣad 81
Upasena 389
Upatiṣya 243, 441, 444
Upavasatha 433, 615
upavasatha 311, 533, 614
upavāsa 444
Upaśānti 599
Upaśūnya 99, 452
upekṣaka 584
upekṣendriya 485
Upekṣā 441
upekṣā 237, 242, 445, 551
upekṣā-saṁbodhyaṅga 584
Uposatha 433, 615
uposatha 533
Upoṣaṇa 615
upside down 108
upādhi 433
upādhi-nirvāṇa 433
Upādhyāya 201, 444, 459, 635
upādhyāya 169, 234, 433, 606
Upādāna 80, 581
upādāna 365, 433
Upāli 22, 27, 227, 357, 419, 444, 469, 600, 607
Upāsaka 492, 574, 614
upāsaka 61, 268, 347, 433, 444, 588
四衆 four orders 259
四輩 four grades 246
四部衆 248
upāsaka-upāsikā 165
Upāsikā 327, 574
upāsikā 61, 268, 346, 433, 444, 588
四衆 four orders 259
四輩 four grades 246
四部衆 248
Upāya 461
upāya 163, 359
Upāya
the seventh 波羅蜜 174
方便 173
upāya-kauśalya 207
upāya-pāramitā 441
Upāyajñāna
方便智 174
upāyakauśalya 441, 444
Ura-tepe 327
Uraga 414
Uraga(sāra)-candana 414
Uraśā 414
Uraśī 414
Urddhasthāna 215
Urga 29
urgency 67
Urgyan 17
urination 326
Ursa Major 145, 201, 385, 446, 572
妙見菩薩 208
Ursa major 208, 585
Urumuṇḍa 443
Uruvilvā 144, 446
Uruvilvā forest 443
Uruvilvā Kāśyapa 144, 443
Uruvilvā-Kāśyapa 5
Uruvilvā-kāśyapa 31
use 439
usual 613
Utkuṭukāsana 435
utkuṭukāsana 21
Utpala 120, 441, 443, 444, 554, 575
utpala 262, 435, 610
Utpāda 302
utpāda 69, 287
Utpādanirodha 302
utsaṅga 435
uttama 65, 445
Uttara 297, 435, 599
uttara 208, 435, 442, 445

uttara saṅghāṭī 299, 300
Uttara-Aṣāḍhā 485
Uttara-Phalgunī 486
Uttara-Proṣṭhapada 486
uttara-saṅghāṭī 462, 544
Uttaraka 93
Uttarakosala 42
Uttarakuru 43, 48, 49, 208, 338, 435, 445, 603, 610
四洲, four continents 258
uttarakuru 445
Uttaramantriṇaḥ 610
uttaramanuṣyadharmapralāpa
四波羅夷 246
Uttarasaṅghāṭī 339
Uttarasena 435
Uttaraśailāḥ 208, 325
Uttarāsaṅga 445, 587
uttarāsaṅga 287, 445, 472
Uttarāyaṇa 208
Uttarāṣāḍhā 435
uttras- 614
Uśīra 363
uśīra 435
Uḍa 413, 525
Uḍakhāṇḍa 432
Uḍradeśa 413
Uṣa 363
Uṣas 419
Uṣṇīṣa 446
uṣṇīṣa 148, 221, 421, 435, 459
Uṭabhāṇḍa 432

(ü)
ülü küdelükci 205

(Ū)
Ūrdhvasrotas 298
Ūrdvasthāna 215
Ūsh 642

(ū)
ūrṇā 41, 158, 321, 434

(V)
vadha(hiṁsā)
四波羅夷 246
Vadi 179
Vaibhāra 572
Vaibhāra cave 374
Vaibhāra cavern 232
Vaibhāra-vana 419
Vaibhāṣika 132, 509
Vaibhāṣika philosophy 377
Vaibhāṣika School 591
Vaibhāṣika school 112, 349
Vaibhāṣika schools 170
Vaibhāṣika śāstra 591
Vaibhāṣikas 228, 465
Vaidehī 409, 452
Vaidharī 361
Vaijayanta 107, 284
Vaipulya 92, 93, 98, 324
方廣 172
方等 173
vaipulya 39, 174, 229, 364
vaipulya period 421
Vaipulya sūtra 39
Vaipulya sūtras 324
Vaipulya-mahāvyūha-sūtra 103
Vaipulyas 415
vaipulyas 50, 92
Vairambha 613
vairambha 227
Vairambhavāta 119
Vairocana 39, 40, 54, 62, 63, 64, 86, 90, 93, 95, 101, 102, 103, 106, 142, 160, 175, 205, 206, 211, 214, 224, 227, 272, 276, 278, 280, 283, 289, 350, 357, 366, 386, 415, 418, 424, 431, 448, 484, 508, 509, 515, 517, 544, 546, 560, 563, 566, 594, 595, 603, 607, 608, 612, 613, 627, 639, 640
four female attendants 254
four-faced 244
yellow 426
四波羅蜜菩薩 246
心王 353
vairocana 102, 546
Vairocana Buddhahood 420
Vairocana germ-word 379
Vairocana group 278, 420
Vairocana maṇḍala 504
Vairocana Pure-land 294
Vairocana Schools 221
Vairocana sūtra 102, 588
Vairocana trinity 205
Vairocana-body 265
Vairocana-raśmi-pratimaṇḍita 147
Vairocana-raśmi-pratimaṇḍita-dhvaja 40
Vairocana-samādhi 509
Vairocana-Tathāgata 399
Vairocana's 508
Vairocana's maṇḍala 78
Vairocana's wrath 141
vaivartika 224
Vaiśeṣika 91, 452, 613
Vaiśeṣika philosophy 280, 466
founder 443
Vaiśeṣika school 9, 223, 230
founder 16
Vaiśeṣika sect 53
Vaiśeṣika-nikāya-daśapadārtha-śāstra 632
Vaiśeṣika-śāstra 338
Vaiśramaṇa 363, 366, 371, 438, 605
四方 246
火聚仙 642
Vaiśravaṇa 51, 56, 73, 223, 224, 229, 230, 236, 260, 262, 273, 313, 385, 393, 436, 485, 520, 570, 592, 613, 631
Vaiśvānara 510
Vaiśya 200, 229
vaiśya 613
four castes 251
vaiśyas 93
Vaiśākha 224, 572, 613
vaiśākha 229
Vaiśālī 22, 39, 117, 125, 126, 135, 170, 228, 229, 231, 313, 333, 361, 363, 407, 429, 450, 453, 544, 584, 604, 613, 646
eight famous Caityas 548
Vaiḍūrya 123, 224, 613
vaiḍūrya 227, 584, 600
Vaiṣṇavas 452
Vaiṣṇavī 583
Vajjiputtakas 112
Vajra 179, 278, 365, 636
vajra 62, 71, 80, 89, 213, 284,

285, 389, 411, 431, 496, 600
five-armed 411
vajra group 127
vajra representative 206
vajra wisdom 91
Vajra-bodhisattva 63, 400
Vajra-buddha 63
Vajra-hall 482
vajra-holder 549
vajra-king 64, 194
vajra-kings 413
Vajra-mahārāja 91
vajra-messenger 63
vajra-power 63
Vajra-pāramitā Bodhisattva 431
Vajra-rulers 260
vajra-śṛṅkhalā 64
Vajrabodhi 90, 213
Vajracchedikā-prajñāpāramitā-sūtra 62
Vajracchedikā-sūtra 79
Vajradeva 472
Vajradevas 65
Vajradhara 179, 328, 384, 549
vajradhara 562
Vajradharma 63
Vajradhātrī 224
Vajradhātu 62, 86, 95, 102, 133, 142, 161, 177, 214, 217, 225, 251, 285, 371, 379, 395, 417, 418, 427, 430, 450, 496, 500, 508, 510, 594, 628
four bodhisattvas associated with the five dhyāni-buddhas 260
representation 133
western 305
四波羅蜜菩薩 246
牙菩薩 373
vajradhātu 224, 364, 411
六大 461
Vajradhātu group 65, 70, 436, 472, 482, 556, 631
Vajradhātu groups 317, 506
Vajradhātu maṇḍala 10, 40, 63, 64, 417, 480, 517
vajradhātu maṇḍala 102
Vajradhūpa 63
Vajragarbha 63, 64
Vajraghaṇṭā 63
Vajragoḍa 436
Vajrahetu 63
Vajrahāsa 97
Vajrajaya 436
Vajrajvāla 179
vajraketu 63
Vajraketu Bodhisattva 63
Vajrakumāra 63
vajrakṣetra 65
Vajramati 377, 560
vajramati 65
Vajramāha 436
Vajraputra 179
Vajrapāla 95
Vajrapāśa 63
vajrapāśa 63
Vajrapāśa-bodhisattva 63
Vajrapāṇi 19, 63, 170, 205, 328, 359, 493, 549, 595, 636
vajrapāṇi 64, 161, 562
Vajrapāṇi Bodhisattva 64
Vajrapāṇibalin 165
Vajrapāṇis 26
Vajraratna 63
Vajrasamādhi 509
vajrasamādhi 65
Vajrasattva 63, 225, 384, 386, 419, 431, 560
Vajrasattva(-mahāsattva) 63
Vajrasena 63
Vajrasūci 63
Vajratejaḥ 63
Vajratīkṣṇa 63
Vajravāsin 436
Vajrayakṣa 64, 431, 487
Vajrayāna 64
Vajrāsana 65
Vajrāṅkuśa 63, 436
Vajrāṭṭahāsa 170
Vakhan 379
Vakrī 163
Vakula 166
Valabhī 48, 74, 114, 117, 179, 208
Valeria 242
valiant 647
Validśa 163
vallis Comedorum 50
Valour-sun 232
Vana 165
vana 167
Vanavāsin 179
Vandana 121, 135, 166, 635
vandana 25, 166, 179
vandanī 23, 166
vande 134
Vangueria spinosa 144
vara-padma-jāla-mūla-tantra-nāma-dhāraṇ 566
Varacāmara 610
Varanāda 162
Varaprabha 46, 106, 145
Varasena 167
Varaṅgala 194
Varaṇa 170, 179
varaṇa 520
Vardaks 215
Vardhasthāna 215
Varga 179, 510
varga 259, 616
vartana 523
Varucha 84
Varuṇa 147, 162, 163, 335, 375, 571, 605
四方 246
Varuṣa 170, 592
Varāṅga 179
Varṣa 179, 388
varṣa 441
Varṣipālī 164
varṣya 442
varṣā 285, 541
Varṣākāla 164, 572
varṣākāla 572
Varṣākāra 624
Varṣās 163, 388
varṣās 441, 618
Varṣāvasāna 388
varṣāvasāna 441
Vasanta 572
vasanta-vayantī 164
vases 417
Vasiṣṭha 96, 164, 165, 235
vast 635
vastra 165
Vasu 164

vasu 164, 520
Vasu-deva 167
Vasubandhu 48, 92, 98, 128, 135, 155, 164, 175, 179, 206, 234, 329, 338, 380, 382, 400, 420, 424, 440, 456, 486, 502, 519, 540, 545, 567, 572, 587
世親 320
俱舍論 51
Vasubandhu's 362
Vasubandhu's work 540
Vasudeva 164
Vasumatī 419
Vasumitra 3, 160, 164, 179, 261, 320, 486, 636
Vasus 107, 284
Vati 179, 479
vati 169
Vatsa 165, 211, 413
vatsa 112, 169
Vatsa-pattana 14
Vatsanābha 165
Vatsapattana 52
vatsara 318
Vatsarāja 211
Vatsch 235
vaśavartin 164
vaśitva 90
vaśitā 517
Vaśīkaraṇa 44, 634
vaśīkaraṇa 429
Vaḍiśa 163
vaṁ 379
Vaṅkṣu 165, 166, 575
Veda 226, 452, 453, 613
four Vedas and six śāstras 461
육론 六論 461
Veda śāstras 244
Vedanā 80, 281, 300
vedanā 140, 331, 365, 418, 424, 611
vedanās 463
five 421
Vedas 393, 415, 550
four Vedas 255
Vedic mythology 107, 284
Vedānta philosophy 230
Vedāṅgas 433, 459
vedāṅgas 461
vehicle 339
supreme 416
Vehicles
five 424
vehicles
five 421
Veluvana 92
velācakra 313
venerable
world's most venerable, 世尊 320
Venus 53, 66, 141, 337, 419, 420
Venus-planet mountain 568
Vetulla sect 92
Vetāla 224, 407, 452
vetāla 231, 391, 542
vetāla method 343
vexation 460
Veśa 229
Veṅgī 388
Veṅuvana 92, 224, 517
Veṅuvana monastery 91
Veṅuvana park 233
Veṅuvana vihāra 91
veṇu 543
Veṇuvana 543
Veṣṭana 193, 613
Vibhajya 209
Vibhajyavādinaḥ 509
Vibhajyavādinaḥs 209, 228
Vibhā 160
vibhāga 209
Vibhārakṣita 159
Vibhāvana 193
vibhāvana 39, 312
Vibhāṣā 164, 222, 223, 224, 521
vibhāṣā 228
Vibhāṣā school 380
Vibhāṣā śāstra 128, 135, 280
Vibhāṣā-śāstra 150, 228, 261
Vichavapura 231, 346
vicikitsā 474
vicāra 227, 231, 237, 351
vidagdhakasaṁjñā 51
vidarśanā 37
Videha 211, 231, 338, 610, 615
Videhaka 507
vidhu 599
Vidyā 226
vidyā 141, 231, 550
vidyā-caraṅa-saṁpanna 142
Vidyā-mātra-siddhi śāstra 315
Vidyācaraṅa-saṁpanna 223, 371
vidyādhara-piṭaka 549
Vidyādharapiṭaka 62, 231
Vidyāmātrasiddhi-tridaśakārikā-śāstra 454
Vidyāmātrasiddhi-viṃśakakārikā-śāstra 454
views
five wrong 410
vigama 232
vigata 232
Vigatāśoka 452
vighna 288
Vighnāntaka 360
vihiṁsā 622
Vihāra 237
vihāra 68, 89, 206, 229, 232, 339, 447, 543
Vihāragrāma 72
vihāragrāma 341
Vihārapāla 634
vihārapāla 232, 265
Vihārasvāmin 541
vihārasvāmin 232, 265
Vijaya 160, 418
vijaya 578
Vijaya Saṁbhava 102
vijitavat 231
vijñapti 230
Vijñaptimātra 230
Vijñaptimātratāsiddhi-śāstra 388, 454
vijñā 550
Vijñāna 80, 300
vijñāna 52, 140, 202, 231, 275, 295, 331, 344, 365, 418, 424, 524, 551, 552, 585, 634
seventh, intellection, reasoning 235
Vijñāna dhātu 344
vijñāna-skandha 345
Vijñāna-vāda School 99
Vijñānamātra-(vāda) 454

ㄱ ㄴ ㄷ ㄹ ㅁ ㅂ ㅅ ㅇ ㅈ ㅊ ㅋ ㅌ ㅍ ㅎ 찾아보기

Vijñānamātrasiddhi 316
vijñānas 320, 576
Vijñānavāda 283, 455
Vijñānānantyāyatana 152
vijñānānantyāyatana 239
vijñānānantyāyatanam 55
vikalpa 209
Vikarāla 365
vikhāditakasaṁjñā 51
Vikramāditya 232, 577, 617
Vikrītavana 138
vikrīḍita 454
Vikāla-bhojanād vairamaṇī (virati) 217
Vikālabhojanā 219
vikālabhojanā-veramaṇī 356
Vikāra 226
Vikīrṇa 418
vikṣiptakasaṁjñā 51
Vilamba 357
vile 207
vilepana-dhāraṇa-maṇḍana-vibhūṣanaṭṭhān 356
vilohitakasaṁjñā 51
Vimala 148, 228
vimala 527
Vimalacitra 228, 613
Vimaladattā 40
Vimalagarbha 530
Vimalakīrti 26, 66, 147, 156, 228, 453
方丈 173
Vimalakīrti sūtra 212
Vimalakīrti-nirdeśa sūtra 453
Vimalakīrti-nirdeśa-sūtra 93, 99
Vimalakīrtisūtra
月蓋 450
Vimalanetra 115, 529
Vimalā 369
Vimalākṣa 224
Vimba 232
Vimbara 232, 616
Vimokṣa 228
vimokṣa 475, 595, 622, 623
Vimuktaghoṣa 228
Vimukti 228
vimukti 611, 622, 623
Vimuni 143
Vinata 226
Vinataka 51, 66, 227
Vinaya 22, 23, 27, 28, 62, 80, 90, 163, 170, 227, 419, 478, 583, 591, 607, 615
vinaya 227, 277, 295, 333, 419, 469, 481
four vinaya 255
vinaya discipline 624
Vinaya Piṭaka 28
Vinaya piṭaka 163
Vinaya School 641
Vinaya school 324, 469
Vinaya sect 540
Vinaya-discipline 367
Vinaya-piṭaka 332, 469
Vinaya-vehicle 469
Vinayapiṭaka 227
Vināyaka 227, 233, 436
vinīlakasaṁjñā 51
Vinītaprabha 424
viparyaya 242, 523, 587
Vipaśyanā 228
vipaśyanā 37
Vipaśyanā-vipaśyanā 228
Vipaśyi 360
Vipaśyin 35, 101, 166, 228, 453, 584
vipaḍumakasaṁjñā 51
viprakṛ 262
vipula 39, 229
Vipulamati 39
Vipulaprajña 39
Vipāka 231
vipāka 476
vipāka-phala 476
Vipākahetu 465
vipākahetu 476
Vipāśā 87, 231
vipūyakasaṁjñā 51
Virgo 364, 532
virtue 493
virtues 269
Viruddha 226
Virūpākṣa 51, 160, 224, 225, 228, 260, 438, 485, 570, 578
virūpākṣa 39, 600
Virūḍhaka 160, 224, 228, 260, 306, 438, 485, 548, 570, 600
Visarj 210
visaṁyoga-phala 476
Vishnuites 452
vitarka 26, 227, 351
vitarka and vicāra 351
vitasti 17
Vitatha 626
vivaras 385
vivarjana 446
vivarta 18, 41
Vivarta kalpa 96, 315
Vivarta siddha kalpa 542
vivarta-siddha 41, 89
Vivarta-siddha kalpa 315
Vivartakalpa 306
vivartasiddha 18
Viveka 209
viveka 232
vivikta 521
viviparous 250
vivṛj 446
Viśeṣa 230
viśeṣa 193, 466
Viśiṣṭa-cāritra Bodhisattva 300
Viśiṣṭacāritra 241
Viśravas 229
viśru 229
viśuddha 159
Viśuddhacāritra 241
Viśuddhasiṁha 226
viśuddhi 574
Viśva 230
viśva 195
Viśvabhadra 195, 272, 617
Viśvabhū 35, 223, 229, 360, 509, 584
Viśvakarman 157, 230, 366
Viśvamitra 229, 308
Viśākhā 230, 374, 485
viśākhā 229
Viśāla 229
Viṁśati 484
Viṁśatikā-vijñaptimātratāsiddhi-śāstra 98
Viṅgila 194
Viṅkila 194
viṣaya 24
viṣāṇa 7, 229

Viṣṇu 4, 70, 71, 91, 93, 102, 134, 159, 163, 164, 171, 179, 181, 193, 276, 280, 293, 343, 350, 446, 452, 492, 496, 508, 510, 534
Horse-neck 618
vehicle 4
Viṣṇuites 436
Void 201
void 32
vow 81, 202
four universal vows of a Buddha or bodhisattva 261
Vow-body 214
vows of Amitābha 468
Vraja 170
vrata 145
Vulcan 157, 230
Vulture Peak 2, 22, 70, 92, 491, 580
Vulture Peak gāthā 580
vyañjana 612
vyādhmātakasaṁjñā 51
vyāghra 634
Vyākaraṇa 69, 226, 324, 329, 635
six śāstras 461
vyākaraṇa 69, 315, 364
Vyākaraṇa-Kauṇḍinya 42, 635
Vyākaraṇas 226
vyākaraṇas 50
Vyākāra 329
Vyāsa 230
Vyāvahārika 223
Vyūharāja 519
Vyūharāja sūtra 519
vāha 165
vāhana 165
vākya 165
Vākṣu 14, 165, 166, 236, 575
four rivers 261
vāma 165
Vāma-lokāyata 401
Vāna 172
vāri 163
Vārāhī 583
vārāhī 523
Vārāṇaśī 66, 122, 161, 162, 181, 227, 494, 600
deer park 308
eight famous Caityas 548
Vārṣagaṇya 165, 179
vārṣagaṇya 442
Vārṣika 164
vārṣika 135
vāsanā 207, 646
Vāsi-Asita 164
Vāsuki 179, 636
Vāta 274
Vātsīputra 165, 170, 179
Vātsīputrīyāḥ 112, 216, 275, 325, 417, 457, 463, 482, 536
Vātsīputrīyāḥ school 165, 380, 528
Vātsīputrīyāḥs 112, 325
Vātyā 163, 166
Vāyavī 165
Vāyu 10, 97, 436, 605
vāyu 164, 165, 616
Vāṣpa 164
vīja 539
Vīra 154, 401
Vīrabhadra 360
Vīradatta 154
Vīrasana 227
vīraṇakacchapa 227
Vīrya 557
vīrya 61, 163, 228, 416, 461, 526
vīrya-pāramitā 401
vīrya-saṁbodhyaṅga 584
vīrya-ṛddhi-pādaḥ 254
vīryabala 414, 526
Vīryasena 228
vīryendriya 485
Vītaśoka 227
Vītāśoka 452
Vīṇā 226
vīṇā 224
Vṛji 18, 170, 211, 276, 525
Vṛjiputra 170
Vṛjisthāna 215, 634
vṛka 228
Vṛkṣa 384, 617
vṛkṣa 228

(W)

wail 60
Wakhan 379, 635
wall-gazing Brahman 86
Wan Li 142
Wang Jih-hsiu 435
Wang Ku 435
Wang Tsêng 436
water 331, 504, 552
calamity 335
realm 332
water and wave 335
四大 241
water altar 332
water dhyāna 335
water heaven 605
water-bag 332
water-born 250
water-burial 335
water-deva 335
water-globule 334
water-lantern festival 332
Water-store 335
waterman 332
Wauneh 179
way 31, 135
ways of sentient existence 467
Wei 630
seven northern constellations 208
Wei dynasty 267, 274
wei-shih 429
Wei-to 452, 453
well 525
Wenchow monk 628
west 304
Western Paradise 540
Western Pure Land 305
What is this? 480
wheel 517
wheel-king 285, 564
wheel-kings 461
white 175, 420
White Cloud monastery 176
White Cloud vegetarians 176
white curl 434
White Heron Lake 175
White Horse Monastery 127
White Horse Temple 12, 175
White Lily Secret Society 120
White Lily Society 175, 520
white lotus 209

White Lotus sect 120
White Teeth 374
white-bullock cart 251, 442
white-clothed 167
white-clothed Kuan-yin 167
White-curled One 177
white-foot monk 177
white-umbrella dhāraṇī 221
Who am I? 480
whole 522
Wi-ta-cheon 453
wife 203
Wild Goose pagoda 388
wind 552
  四大 241
wind heaven 605
wine 169, 333, 542
winter 113
winter solstice 113
Wisdom 168
wisdom 137, 290, 461
  six kinds 469
wisdom of hearing 469
wisdom of neither extreme 469
wisdom of observance 469
wisdom of thought 469
wisdom of understanding 469
Wisdom-body 214
Wisdom-Tathāgatas 430
within 436
woman 400
womb-born 594
womb-palace 594
Won-gwang 319
Won-hyo 64, 359, 488
Wonderful Light 145
Wonderful-Law Lotus-Flower Sūtra 201
wooden fish 144
wooden horse 144
world
  世 318
world hero 320
world-devas 319
World-honoured 166, 320
world-honoured 162
world-kalpa 272
world-kalpa's end 111
world-law 319
world-state 319
worldly
  世俗 319
worldly dāna 319
worldly knowledge 319
worldly truth 320
Wu 148, 274
Wu Ti 219, 628
Wu Tsung 173
Wu Yüeh 573
Wu Ên 263
Wu-hsing 420
Wu-i 321
Wu-kuan Wang 409
Wu-liang-shou-ching 641
Wu-pên 113
Wu-ssŭ 409
Wu-ti 97
Wu-t'ai 241
Wu-t'ai Shan 413, 426
Wu-t'ai shan 574
  文殊 157
Wu-t'ai-shan 208
Wu-ên 573
WuTi
  festival of water and land 333
Wên Ti 95, 97, 105
Wên-shu 65, 66
Wên-su 435
Wên-yen 445
Wālā 179
Wŏn-hyo 450

(X)

Xanthochymus pictorius 83

(Y)

Yadbhūyasikīya-vinaya 583
Yajurveda 393, 452, 533
Yajñadatta 402
Yakṣa 393
yakṣa 70, 80, 209, 211, 297, 404, 515, 606, 615
Yakṣa-kṛtya 393
Yakṣa-rāja 363
yakṣas 568, 606
Yama 55, 94, 235, 363, 366, 367, 393, 406, 407, 408, 409, 417, 436, 526, 555
  四方 246
yama 364
Yama heaven 605
Yama heavens 114
Yama-devaloka 439
Yama-maṇḍala 407
Yama-rāja 485
Yamadevaloka 407
Yamaloka 393, 408
Yamana 406
Yamani 393
Yama's symbols 496
Yamuna 227
Yamunā 326, 406, 407, 408
Yamāntaka 360, 406, 413, 622
Yamī 407
Yang Ti 104
Yang-chou 46
Yang-shan 390
Yangishahr 642
Yangtsze 12, 525
Yao Ch'in 241
Yao Shih 365, 493, 530
Yao Shih Fo 193
Yao-shih 592, 600
Yarkand 517
Yarkand daria 236
yathā 398
yathābhūtam 400
Yathāvat 393
yava 138, 392
Yavadvīpa 392
Yavana 392, 406
Yaśas 392
yaśas 140
Yaśaskāma 46
Yaśodharā 47, 53, 393, 450
Yaśodā 392
Yaśogupta 234
yaṣṭi 117, 564
Yaṣṭi-vana 346
Yaṣṭivana 313, 409, 520
Yeke-gara 107
yellow 420
Yellow Dragon monastery 644
Yellow River 235, 375, 618
Yellow Sect 539
yellow-faced Buddha 644

Yellow-robe sect 85
Yen Ti
  the ruler over the fire-star, Mars. 637
Yen-ch'ing ssŭ 402
Yen-ming Ti-tsang 556
Yen-shou 402
Yen-Ts'ung 305
Yen-ts'ung 395
Yerkiang 517
yet
  且 563
Yin Fa-shih 613
Yin-tu 568
yin-yang 32
Ying Hsien 471
Ying Nêng 471
Ying Wên 471
Ying-ch'uan 555
Yo-chou 598
Yodhapatipura 380
Yoga 37, 99, 273, 359, 370, 445, 542
yoga 89
Yoga School 604
  in Japan 595
Yoga school 161, 272
yogin 455
Yogācāra 65, 213, 347, 455
Yogācāra school 213, 417, 433, 560
  天親 Vasubandhu 572
Yogācārya 82, 187, 191, 377, 382, 540, 602
yogācārya 89
Yogācārya School 443
Yogācārya school 32, 577
Yogācārya works 540
Yogācārya-bhūmi-śāstra 90
Yogācāryabhūmi-śāstra 382, 455
Yogācāryabhūmi-śāstra-kārikā 345
Yojana 454
yojana 58, 100, 284, 500, 510, 584
  16,000th part 542
yojanas 276, 500
yoke 455
Yoni 398
Young Lo 471
Yu-k'uei 556
Yu-t'an-na 254
Yuga 318
Yugas 17
Yugaṁdhara 16, 51, 66, 361, 371, 454, 455, 456, 549
Yugaṅdhara 456
yukta 299
yuktabodhi 459
yukti 459
yuktā 459
Yung Ho Kung 160
Yung Lo 91
Yung-ming 538, 598
Yü 442
Yü Hua Kung 630
Yü-ch'üan 434
Yü-hua 434
Yü-hua kung 434
Yüan 96
Yüan Addenda 123
Yüan Chwang 630
Yüan dynasty 419, 446, 469
Yüan Tripiṭaka 446
Yüan Tsang 630
Yüan-chao 121, 549
Yüan-hsiao 446, 450, 646
  曉公四教 239
Yüan-ts'ê 305
Yüeh-chih 3, 451
Yüeh-chih country 107
Yüeh-chih monk 548
Yüeh-chih people 51
Yün Wên 471
Yün-chou 113
Yün-hua 554
Yün-hua Chih-yen 639
Yün-jo 469
Yün-kung 632
Yün-k'an 469
Yün-mên 267, 598
Yün-mên Ch'an School 267
yācñā 69
Yāmī 409
Yāna 504
yāna 97, 286, 339, 619
Yānas
  five 424
yāvat 77
Yūsufzai 426

(Z)
zeal 416
zeal and progress 461
Zen 367, 507, 540, 587
Zend-Avesta 167
Zodiac 382
zodiacal mansions 314, 364
Zoroastrians 566
Zva-dmar 635

(ɣ)
ɣδηθ 211

(ν)
ν Leonis 128

(π)
πατάλα 195

(ㄱ)
가 伽 2
가 假 2, 32, 265, 269, 289, 290, 292, 302, 304, 477, 499, 505, 545, 546
가 加 1
가 可 2
가 呵 2, 15
가 哥 1
가 嘉 2
가 家 1
가 柯 1
가 榎 107
가 歌 3
가 珂 3, 15
가 街 1
가 袈 484
가 訶 1
가 謌 3
가 跏 3
가 迦 2, 3, 88, 101, 492
가(라)사야 迦(羅)沙野 4
가(라)사예 迦(羅)沙曳 4
가(라)사예 迦(邏)沙曳 5
가(라)사이 迦(羅)沙異 4
가(리)왕 哥(利)王 1

가가 迦迦 3
가가가 迦迦迦 3
가가나 伽謌那 16
가가나 迦迦那 3
가가나비려차나 伽伽那卑麗叉那 2
가가나필리기나 伽伽那必利綺那 2
가가라 迦迦羅 3
가가라충 迦迦羅蟲 3
가가루다 迦迦婁多 3
가가바가빈사라 迦迦婆迦頻闍邏 3
가게 歌偈 3
가관 假觀 3, 267, 412, 613
가구 家狗 1
가나 伽那 2
가나가모니 迦那伽牟尼 3
가나복력인 伽那馥力刃 2
가나제바 伽那提婆 2
가나제바 迦那提婆 3, 486
가낙가모니 迦諾迦牟尼 q.v. 47
가날지가마세 迦剌底迦麽洗 6
가니(색)가 迦膩(色)伽 3
가니가 迦尼迦 3
가다연나 迦多衍那 6
가다연니자 迦多衍尼子 or 迦多演尼子 6
가단니 珂但尼 3, 15
가담파 迦曇波 or 迦曇婆 3
가대 哥大 1
가돌라 珂咄羅 3
가등류 假等流 270
가라 伽羅 2
가라 哥羅 4
가라 歌羅 4
가라 迦羅 4, 17, 484, 558
가라(분) 歌羅(分) 3
가라가 迦羅迦 4, 5, 49
가라가 迦邏迦 4
가라가타 迦羅迦吒 4
가라구찬타 迦羅鳩飡陀 49
가라구촌타 迦羅鳩村馱 49
가라구타 迦羅鳩馱 4
가라니 伽羅尼 2
가라라 呵羅羅 2
가라라 哥羅羅 1
가라라 歌羅邏 3, 9
가라라 迦羅邏 4
가라부 迦羅富 4
가라비가 迦羅毘迦 4
가라비나가 迦羅臂拏迦 4
가라비라 迦羅毘囉 4
가라빈가 歌羅頻迦 3
가라사 迦羅舍 9
가라야차 伽羅夜叉 2
가라월 迦羅越 4, 14
가라진두 迦羅鎭頭 4
가라타 伽羅陀 2
가란(빈)가 迦蘭(頻)伽 4
가란가 加蘭伽 1
가란다 迦蘭陀 4
가란다가 迦蘭多迦 4
가란다이 迦蘭陀夷 4
가란비가 迦蘭毘伽 4
가란타 伽蘭他 2
가란타 迦蘭馱 4
가람 伽藍 2, 338
가람부 迦藍浮 4
가람신 伽藍神 2
가람타 迦藍陀 4
가력 加力 1
가로나 迦盧拏 4
가루(자) 可漏(子) 2
가루나 迦樓那 4
가루다 迦嘍嗏 67
가루다 迦嘍荼 4
가루라 伽樓羅 4
가루라 迦婁羅 4
가루라 迦樓羅 4, 66, 568, 606
가루라염 迦樓羅炎 4
가루자 可漏子 7
가류다이 迦留陀夷 4
가류라 迦留羅 4
가률지가월 迦慄底迦月 6
가릉(빈)가 迦陵(頻)伽 4
가릉가왕 迦陵伽王 4
가리 伽梨 2
가리 哥利 or 歌利 4
가리 歌利 3
가리 軻梨 6
가리 迦利 4
가리 迦梨 4
가리가 加梨加 49
가리가 迦梨迦 5
가리라 可梨羅 15
가리라 軻梨羅 6, 15
가리사(나) 迦利沙(那) 4
가리사바나 迦利沙婆拏 4
가리사바나 迦利沙波拏 4
가리사반나 迦利沙般拏 4
가리사발나 迦利沙鉢拏 4
가리사사니 迦梨沙舍尼 5
가리왕 歌利王 3
가리제 呵利帝 1
가리지 呵利底 1
가리지가마세 迦哩底迦麽洗 6
가리지가월 迦利邸迦月 6
가리타 呵利陀 1, 2
가린 伽隣 4
가린제 迦鄰提 6
가린타 迦鄰陀 6
가림마 伽林摩 284
가마 迦摩 5
가마라 迦摩羅 5, 209
가마랑가 迦摩浪迦 5
가마루파 迦摩縷波 5
가마타도 迦摩馱都 5
가말라 迦末羅 5
가명 假名 3
가명보살 假名菩薩 3
가명상 假名相 291
가명세간 假名世間 3
가명유 假名有 3, 291
가명종 假名宗 258
가무 歌舞 3
가무 謌舞 3
가문 伽文 306
가문 假門 3
가미니 伽彌尼 2
가미라 迦尾羅 4
가바 伽婆 2
가방 街方 1
가방파제 伽傍簸帝 2
가범 伽梵 2
가범달마 伽梵達摩 2
가범바제 迦梵波提 41
가범파제 伽梵波提 2
가부좌 跏趺坐 3
가불매조 訶佛罵祖 1
가비 伽憊 2
가비 加備 1
가비가(라) 迦毘伽(羅) 4
가비라 迦比羅 or 迦毗羅 17
가비라 迦比羅 or 迦毘羅 5
가비라 迦毘羅 4, 280
가비라(파) 迦毘羅(婆) or 迦比羅

(婆) 5
가비라소도 迦毗羅蘇都 17
가비라위 迦毘羅衛 17
가비라파솔도 伽毗羅皤窣都 17
가비라파솔도 迦毘羅皤率都 5
가비려 伽毗黎 2, 17
가비리 迦毘梨 5
가비마라 迦毘摩羅 5, 486
가빈자라 迦頻闍羅 or 迦賓闍羅 4
가빈자라왕 迦頻闍羅王 or 迦賓闍羅王 4
가사 伽邪 2
가사 伽闍 2
가사 加沙 1
가사 加私 1
가사 袈娑 472
가사 袈裟 1, 5, 173, 287
가사 迦奢 5
가사 迦師 5
가사 迦沙 1
가사 迦私 6
가사사다 伽邪舍多 2
가사야 加沙野 1
가사야 袈沙野 521
가사포라 迦奢布羅 5
가상 嘉祥 271, 276
가색 假色 3
가설 假設 3
가설 珂雪 3
가섭 迦葉 584
가섭(두타) 迦葉(頭陀) 131
가섭(파) 迦攝(波) 5
가섭(파) 迦葉(波) 5
가섭마등 迦葉摩騰 5, 579
가섭미라 迦葉彌羅 6
가섭비 迦葉毘 5
가섭비야 迦葉臂耶 5
가섭비유 迦葉毘維 509
가섭유 迦葉維 5
가섭유 迦葉遺 5
가섭유 迦葉遺 482
가섭파 迦葉波 5
가성 歌聲 3
가세국 家世國 1
가송 歌頌 3
가습미라 迦濕彌羅 6
가시 加尸 1
가시 迦尸 1, 6
가시비여 柯尸悲與 1, 5
가실 假實 3
가아 假我 3, 326, 351
가야 伽耶 2
가야 迦耶 6
가야 迦若 365
가야가섭 伽耶迦葉 2
가야달나 呵也怛那 2
가야사다 伽耶舍多 2, 486
가야산 伽耶山 2
가연 迦延 88
가염 可厭 554
가염 可染 303
가영 歌咏 3
가영 歌詠 271
가우 加祐 1
가우 謌友 68
가월 珂月 3
가유 假有 3
가유 迦維 17
가유(라열) 迦維(羅閱) 5
가유(라월) 迦維(羅越) 5
가율지가 歌栗底迦 3
가이 迦夷 17
가이립일체법 假以立一切法 32
가이파 迦肄婆 284
가자 迦柘 6
가자말니 迦柘末尼 6
가전 迦旃 4
가전(연자) 迦旃(延子) 6
가전린제 迦旃鄰提 6
가전린타 迦旃鄰陀 6
가전연(니자) 迦氈延(尼子) 6
가전연경 迦旃延經 325
가제 假諦 302
가제 迦提 6
가제월 迦提月 6
가주 家主 1
가지 伽胝 2
가지 加持 1
가지공물 加持供物 1
가지라 珂地羅 6
가지라 軻地羅 6
가지라산 軻地羅山 6
가지성불 加持成佛 1
가지신 加持身 1
가지야야나 迦底耶夜那 6
가지율나 迦止栗那 6
가지장 加持杖 1
가진린지가 迦眞鄰底迦 6
가집 嘉集 2
가차린지 迦遮鄰地 6
가차린지가 迦遮鄰底迦 6
가차말니 迦遮末尼 6
가차제 伽車提 2
가책건도 呵責犍度 2
가치나 伽絺那 10
가치나 迦絺那 6
가치나월 迦絺那月 6
가타 伽他 2
가타 伽陀 2, 19, 68, 327, 364
가타가 呵咜迦 2
가타부단나 迦咤富單那 6
가탄 歌嘆 3
가파리 迦波釐 6
가파제 伽婆帝 284
가파제 呵婆帝 284
가파파 呵婆婆 2
가패 歌唄 3
가패 珂貝 3
가포 迦布 6
가포당 迦逋唐 6
가포덕가 迦佈德迦 621
가포덕가 迦布德迦 6
가포덕가가람 迦布德迦伽藍 6
가피 加被 1
가필시 迦畢試 6
가하돈 可賀敦 2
가한 可汗 2
가합 假合 2
가합지신 假合之身 2
가행 加行 1, 251
가행도 加行道 242
가행선 加行善 1
가행위 加行位 1, 425
가호 加護 1
가화합 假和合 2
가회 嘉會 2
각 刻 7
각 却 7
각 各 7
각 恪 15
각 觳 7
각 脚 7
각 覺 7, 37, 210, 217, 288, 516
각 角 7, 428, 485, 532
각 閣 6
각각위인실단 各各爲人悉檀 252

각견 覺堅 7
각관 覺觀 7
각도 覺道 7
각도(지) 覺道(支) 7
각로 覺路 7
각료 覺了 7
각루 殼漏 2
각루자 殼漏子 7
각모 覺母 7, 157
각분 覺分 7, 595
각산 覺山 7
각상 覺相 7
각성 覺城 7
각성 覺性 7
각수 覺樹 7
각시 覺時 8
각심 覺心 7
각안 覺岸 7
각애 覺愛 196
각여 覺如 7
각오 覺悟 7, 409
각오지 覺悟智 7
각왕 覺王 8
각용 覺用 8
각웅 覺雄 8
각원 覺苑 8
각위 覺位 8
각인 覺人 8
각일 覺日 8
각입생사 却入生死 7
각자 覺者 8
각장 刻藏 7
각제 覺帝 8
각종 各種 7
각지 覺支 8
각진여 覺眞如 7
각책 覺策 8
각천 覺天 261
각타 覺他 8, 265, 477
각타 角馱 7
각포 脚布 7
각해 覺海 8
각행 覺行 8
각행궁만 覺行窮滿 265
각행원만 覺行圓滿 265
각화 覺華 8
각훈 覺訓 622
간 干 8, 442
간 慳 8, 137, 323, 410, 582
간 揀 8
간 看 8
간 簡 8
간 諫 8
간 間 8
간격 間隔 8
간경 看經 9
간경파 看經派 9, 112
간단 間斷 8
간률타 干栗馱 8
간률태 干栗太 8
간방편 看方便 8
간법 慳法 8
간별 簡別 8
간병 看病 8
간빈 慳貧 8
간사 奸詐 235
간사 揀師 8
간사나 干闍那 8
간색 間色 8
간석 慳惜 8
간시궐 乾屎橛 15
간심 慳心 8
간왕 諫王 8
간율대 肝栗大 647
간율타 干栗馱 620
간택 揀擇 8
간혜지 乾慧地 15, 369
갈 喝 9
갈 渴 9
갈 竭 9
갈 羯 9, 97, 265
갈 葛 9
갈 蝎 364
갈 褐 9
갈가 渴伽 9, 15
갈가타가 羯迦吒迦 365
갈구촌나 羯句忖那 49
갈나복 羯拏僕 9
갈남 羯南 16
갈니(가) 羯尼(迦) 9
갈달라 羯達羅 9
갈등 葛藤 9
갈라(빈)가 羯羅(頻)伽 4
갈라가촌지 羯羅迦寸地 49
갈라나 羯羅拏 2
갈라나소벌랄나 羯羅拏蘇伐刺那 9
갈라다 曷攞多 382
갈라람 羯羅藍 9, 608
갈라람 羯邏藍 9
갈라미 羯攞微 639
갈라미 羯羅微 366
갈라빈가 羯羅頻迦 9, 10
갈라사 羯攞賖 9
갈라사 羯羅舍 9
갈락가손타 羯洛迦孫馱 9, 49
갈란타가 羯蘭馱迦 4
갈란탁가 羯蘭鐸迦 4, 9
갈랄리 褐刺縭 9
갈랄예 曷刺羪 376
갈랍바 羯臘婆 9
갈랍박 羯臘縛 9
갈려(벌다) 褐麗(伐多) 9
갈록 渴鹿 9
갈뢰리 褐賴褵 9
갈률지가월 羯慄底迦月 6
갈릉가 羯餧伽 10
갈릉가 羯陵伽 10
갈리 羯利 4
갈리마 葛哩麻 9
갈리사발 羯利沙鉢 10
갈리사발나 羯利沙鉢那 or 羯利沙鉢拏 4
갈리왕 羯利王 10
갈마 羯摩 10
갈마 羯磨 10, 394
갈마륜 羯磨輪 243
갈마바라밀 羯磨波羅蜜 142
갈마승 羯磨僧 10
갈마신 羯磨身 10
갈마아차리 羯磨阿遮利 385
갈마인 羯磨印 10
갈마지인 羯摩智印 259
갈마타나 羯磨陀那 10, 453
갈마회 羯磨會 10, 317
갈법 渴法 9
갈비(가라) 羯毘(迦羅) 10
갈비가라 羯毘伽羅 4
갈상나 羯霜那 10
갈수라 渴樹羅 9
갈수올기라 羯殊嗢祇羅 10
갈습미라 羯濕弭羅 6
갈승게라 羯蠅揭羅 10
갈아 竭誐 9
갈앙 渴仰 9
갈애 渴愛 9, 391
갈야 葛耶 9

갈야국사 羯若鞠闍 10
갈지 竭支 9, 339
갈지라 羯地羅 15
갈지락가 羯地洛迦 10
갈지옥 渴地獄 9
갈차 竭叉 9
갈차 葛叉 17
갈치나 羯絺那 6
갈치나 羯耻那 10
갈치라 羯耻羅 10
갈타라 竭陀羅 9
갈타라 羯陀羅 9
갈타포달나 羯吒布怛那 10
갈타포달나 羯咤布怛那 6
갈포라 羯布羅 10
갈필가라 鶡鵯伽羅 4
갈한 喝捍 9
갈호라 曷估羅 118
감 减 10
감 勘 11
감 堪 11
감 感 11
감 敢 11
감 減 10, 11
kalpa 18
감 甘 11
감 監 11
감 紺 11
감 轗 15
감 鑑 10
감 龕 11
감겁 減劫 10
감겁 減劫 547
감과 感果 11
감능 堪能 11
감단 甘丹 11
감로 甘露 11
감로(왕) 甘露(王) 378
감로(왕)존 甘露(王)尊 11
감로경 甘露經 11
감로계 甘露界 11
감로고 甘露鼓 11
감로군다리명왕 甘露軍荼利明王 11
감로다라니주 甘露陀羅尼咒 11
감로멸 甘露滅 11
감로문 甘露門 11
감로반 甘露飯 11
감로반왕 甘露飯王 586
감로법 甘露法 11
감로법문 甘露法門 11
감로성 甘露城 11
감로왕 甘露王 11, 379
감로우 甘露雨 11
감로주 甘露咒 11
감만 敢曼 11
감발 紺髮 11
감방 紺坊 11
감변 勘辨 11
감보(자) 甘菩(遮) 11
감비 減費 10
감사 監寺 11, 541, 542
감수 監收 11
감우 紺宇 11
감원 監院 11
감원 紺園 11
감유리 紺瑠璃 11
감응 感應 11
감응묘 感應妙 358, 359
감이니연천상 甘伊泥延䏝相 478
감이니연천상 甘伊泥延腨相 478
감인 堪忍 11
감인세계 堪忍世界 11
감인지 堪忍地 11
감자 甘蔗 11, 220
감자왕 甘蔗王 11, 507
감전 紺殿 11
감정 紺頂 11
감주이 甘珠爾 11
감진 感進 11
감진 鑑眞 181
감찰 鑑察 10
감천궁 甘泉宮 646
감첩 紺睫 11
감청 紺靑 11
감탑 龕塔 11
감포 紺蒲 11
감포국 紺蒲國 11
갑 甲 11
갑마 甲馬 11
갑주인 甲胄印 11
강 僵 12
강 康 12
강 强 12
강 彊 12
강 江 12
강 綱 12
강 薑 12
강 講 12
강 降 12
강가 强伽 12, 621
강가섭 江迦葉 12
강갈라 薑羯羅 12
강거 康居 12
강경 講經 12
강당 講堂 12, 184
강림 降臨 12
강사 講師 12, 585
강사락 僵娑洛 12
강생 降生 12
강서 江西 12
강서도일 江西道一 127
강설 講說 12
강세 降世 12
강승개 康僧鎧 12
강승회 康僧會 12
강신 降神 12
강연 講演 12
강원 講院 9, 112, 240
강유 綱維 12
강적 强賊 108
강종 講宗 12
강천사 江天寺 12
강탄 降誕 12
강태 降胎 12
강하 講下 12
강호 江湖 12
개 介 12
개 改 13
개 疥 12
개 皆 12
개 箇 12
개 蓋 12
개 鎧 12
개 開 13
개각 開覺 13
개감로문 開甘露門 13
개갑 鎧甲 12
개개원상도 箇箇圓常道 12
개공 皆空 12
개광 開光 13
개구 開具 13
개권현실 開權顯實 14
개도자 開道者 13
개라야간 疥癩野干 12
개발 開發 13
개발기본유지덕 開發其本有之德

202
개백 開白 13
개법 開法 13
개본 開本 13
개사 開士 13, 95
개산 開山 13
개삼현일 開三顯一 13
개석 芥石 14
개소 開素 14
개시오입 開示悟入 13, 248
개심 開心 13
개안 開眼 13
개연 開演 13
개오 開悟 13
개원 開元 13
개원석교록 開元釋教錄 13
개원석교록약출 開元釋教錄略出 13
개이 介爾 12
개자 芥子 13, 243
개자겁 芥子劫 13
개재 開齋 14
개전 蓋纏 12
개정 開靜 14
개조 開祖 14
개종 改宗 13
개차 開遮 14
개침 開枕 14
개폐 開廢 14
개해 開解 14
개현 開顯 14
개현원 開顯圓 487
개혜 開慧 295
개화 開化 14
개황 開皇 508
개회 改悔 13
개훈 開葷 14
객 喀 15
객 客 14
객사 客司 14
객산 客山 14
객진 客塵 14
갱활 更活 116, 554
갹차 噱叉 14
거 佉 15, 487
거 去 14, 605
거 呿 15
거 居 14
거 巨 14, 46
거 據 15
거 擧 15
거 踞 15
거가 佉加 15
거가 擧家 15
거구 炬口 47
거다라 佉陀羅 6
거달라 佉達羅 6
거동 擧動 15
거득라가 佉得羅柯 15
거라건타 佉羅騫馱 15
거라제 佉羅帝 2
거라제야 佉羅提耶 2
거라타 佉羅陀 2, 15
거래 去來 14
거래금 去來今 14
거래실유종 去來實有宗 14, 30
거로 佉盧 15
거로(풍타) 佉盧(風吒) 15
거로슬타 佉路瑟吒 15
거루 佉樓 15
거륜 居倫 14, 49
거륵 佉勒 15
거륵가 佉勒迦 15
거리 佉梨 15
거린 居隣 14, 49
거마 巨磨 14
거사 佉沙 15
거사 居士 14, 229
거사 據事 15
거사니 佉闍尼 15
거사전 居士傳 14
거살라 居薩羅 42
거상미 巨賞彌 14
거익 巨益 14
거인 擧人 15
거일폐제 擧一蔽諸 15
거자니 佉闍尼 3
거제가 佉提迦 6
거제라(가) 佉提羅(迦) 15
거조라 佉啁羅 15
거지사자 踞地獅子 15
거차가라니시차계라니 去叉迦羅尼尸叉罽羅尼 14
거타 佉陀 3
거타가 佉吒迦 15
거타니 佉陀尼 15
거타라 佉陀羅 15
거타사마리 居吒奢摩利 or 居吒奢摩離 55
거하라부아 佉訶囉嚩阿 15
건 毽 265
건 乾 15
건 健 16
건 建 16
건 揵 15
건 蹇 16
건 鍵 16
건(달)성 乾(達)城 15
건국 建國 96
건나복 蹇拏僕 16
건나표하 健拏驃訶 16
건남 健南 16, 608
건남 健男 16
건남 鍵南 16
건남 鍵南 or 蹇南 16
건니타 蹇尼陀 9, 16
건다 乾陀 16
건다 乾馱 16
건다 健陀 16
건다 揵陀 15
건다 蹇荼 16
건다구지 健陀俱知 16
건다라 乾陀羅 16
건다라 健馱羅 16
건다라 揵馱邏 15
건다라 揵陀羅 15, 16
건다리 健馱梨 16
건다마다마라 健陀摩陀摩羅 16
건다바나 乾陀婆那 16
건다아 揵陀衙 15
건다월 乾陀越 16
건다위 乾陀衛 16
건다하 揵陀訶 15
건달 健達 16
건달바 乾闥婆 16, 158, 568, 606
건달바 健達婆 or 健闥婆 16
건달바 揵達婆 16
건달바성 乾闥婆城 16
건달바왕 乾闥婆王 16
건달박 健達縛 16
건달박 揵達縛 16
건달하제 乾闥訶提 16
건답 揵沓 15
건답파 乾沓婆 16
건답화 乾沓和 16
건덕 揵德 15
건도 揵度 15

건두 健杜 16
건두 巾斗 61
건률타 乾栗馱 8
건립 建立 16
건불남 犍不男 15
건상 健相 328
건섭구 犍涉駒 66
건용 鍵鎔 16
건용좌 健勇座 16
건율타 乾栗馱 620
건율타 乾栗馱 15
건율타야 乾栗陀耶 15
건자 建鎡 16
건자 犍茨 16
건자 鍵鎡 210
건자 鍵鎡 16
건절나 建折那 8
건지 健支 16
건지 犍地 15
건지 犍遲 15
건지보라 建志補羅 16
건지성 建志城 16
건척(마) 犍陟(馬) 15
건추 犍椎 15
건치 犍稚 15, 538
건타가 建佗歌 16
건퇴 犍槌 15
건황문 犍黃門 15
걸 乞 17, 563
걸 朅 16
걸 桀 17
걸가 朅伽 16
걸가비사나 朅伽毘沙拏 16
걸가파사 朅伽婆沙 16
걸나리고 朅那里酤 15
걸달라 朅達羅 6, 16
걸달락(가) 朅達洛(迦) 15
걸달락가 朅達洛迦 6
걸망 17
걸면 乞丏 17
걸사 乞士 17, 225
걸쇄 乞灑 17, 564
걸식 乞食 17
걸식사분 乞食四分 17
걸아 朅諏 16
걸안바라문 乞眼婆羅門 17
걸율쌍제찬 乞嘌雙提贊 17
걸지라 朅地羅 6
걸지락(가) 朅地洛(迦) 15
걸지락가 朅地洛迦 6, 16
걸차 乞叉 17, 564
걸차저벽사 乞叉底蘖沙 555
걸찰 乞察 17
검 劍 17
검 撿 17
검 檢 17
검교 撿挍 17
검교 檢校 17
검륜법 劍輪法 17
검림지옥 劍林地獄 17
검마사제 劍摩舍帝 17
검산 劍山 17
검수지옥 劍樹地獄 17
검엽림 劍葉林 493
검파 劍波 17
검포 劍蒲 11
겁 劫 504
　住劫 542
겁 劫 or 刦 17
겁구 劫具 17, 19
겁구(사) 劫具(娑) 18
겁박건 劫薄健 379
겁박나 劫縛拏 19
겁비(라) 劫比(羅) 17
겁비(라)천 劫比(羅)天 17
겁비나 劫庀那 or 劫比那 or 劫譬那 18
겁비나 劫比拏 17
겁비나왕 劫比拏王 18
겁비라 劫毘羅 5, 236
겁비라국 劫比羅國 17
겁비라벌솔도 劫比羅伐窣堵 or 劫比羅伐窣都 17
겁비사야 劫比舍也 18
겁비타 劫比他 18
겁빈나 劫貧那 172
겁빈나 劫賓那 17, 18, 89
겁사파사 劫沙波娑 19
겁소 劫燒 18, 19
겁수 劫水 18
겁염 劫焰 18, 19
겁재 劫災 18
겁지라 劫地羅 18
겁진화 劫盡火 19
겁초 劫初 18
겁탁 劫濁 18, 432
겁파 劫波 17, 18, 211, 315
겁파 劫簸 18
겁파 劫跛 18
겁파겁파야제 劫跛劫跛夜帝 19
겁파라 劫婆羅 18
겁파라 劫波羅 18
겁파라수 劫婆羅樹 19
겁파라천 劫波羅天 18
겁파배 劫波杯 18
겁파사 劫波娑 17, 18
겁파살 劫波薩 18
겁파수 劫波樹 18, 19
겁파육 劫波育 18
겁파타 劫婆吒 19
겁파파 劫波婆 18
겁포달나 劫布怛那 or 劫布咀那 19
겁포라 劫布羅 19
겁포저나 劫布咀那 19
겁포조나 劫布俎那 19
겁필라 劫畢羅 17
겁해 劫海 19
겁화 劫火 18, 19
겁회 劫灰 19
게 偈 19
게 揭 19
게로다 揭路茶 19
게로다 揭路荼 4
게리가발지 揭利呵跋底 19, 519
게리타라구지 揭梨馱羅鳩胝 68
게반타 揭盤陀 19
게송 偈頌 19
게지 揭底 19
게직 揭職 19
게찬 偈讚 19
게타 偈他 19
게타 偈陀 19
격 格 19
격 隔 19
격력 隔歷 19
격력삼제 隔歷三諦 19
격생 隔生 19
격숙 隔宿 19
격외 格外 19
견 堅 19
견 牽 20
견 甄 20
견 羂 20
견 肩 20
견 見 19, 50, 51, 85, 88, 177, 295, 361, 463, 481, 552, 582, 583,

585, 587
to the visible world 20
四流 243
견 遣 20
견(고)림 堅(固)林 19
견가라 甄迦羅 20
견결 見結 20, 265
견고 堅固 19, 71, 170
견고의 堅固意 19
견고혜 堅固慧 19
견나라 堅那羅 568
견다라 甄陀羅 69
견대 見大 20, 583
견도 見道 20, 104, 238, 363, 369, 417, 589, 608, 627
견도위 見道位 558
견도팔도행성 牽道八道行城 20
견독 見毒 20
견뢰 堅牢 19, 553
견뢰지기 堅牢地祇 19
견뢰지신 堅牢地神 19, 485
견뢰지천 堅牢地天 19
견루 見漏 20
견류 見流 457
견만보살 堅滿菩薩 19
견망 見網 20
견문 見聞 20
견문생 見聞生 279
견박 見縛 20
견법 堅法 19
견분 見分 248, 476
견불 見佛 20
견비견 見非見 20
견사 見思 20, 53, 261, 318, 448, 493, 505
견상 見相 20
견색 羂索 20
견서사자 堅誓師子 19
견성 見性 20
견성성불 見性成佛 603
견소단 見所斷 269, 290
견수 見修 20
견숙가 甄叔迦 20
견술 犬戌 365
견실 堅實 19
견실심 堅實心 19, 351
견애 見愛 21
견왕재 見王齋 21
견의 堅意 19
견인업 牽引業 495
견인인 牽引因 20
견일체주지 見一切住地 258
견자 肩茨 20
견장 見障 21
견쟁 見諍 21
견전도 見顚倒 21
견정 見正 21
견정경 見正經 21
견제 見諦 21
견지 堅智 19
견지 見地 21, 369
견진 見眞 21, 174
견처 見處 21
견취 見取 21, 581
견취견 見取見 21, 361, 410, 415
견취사 見取使 21
견타 甄陀 20
견탁 見濁 21, 432
견하 肩下 20
견행 見行 392
견혜 堅慧 19
견혜 見慧 21
견혹 見惑 20, 265, 493, 608
견혹사혹 見惑思惑 20
견화 見和 469
견환 遣喚 20
결 決 21
결 潔 21
결 結 21, 431
결 缺 21
결가 結跏 435
결가(부좌) 結跏(趺坐) 21
결강 結講 21
결경 結經 21
결계 結戒 22
결계 結界 22
결료 決了 21
결루 結漏 22
결루 缺漏 21
결박 結縛 22
결병 結病 22
결사 結使 22
결생 結生 22
결업 結業 22
결연 結緣 22
결연중 結緣衆 22, 259
결원 結願 22
결의 決疑 21
결인 結印 22
결재 潔齋 21
결적 結賊 22
결정 決定 21, 431
결정심 決定心 422
결정주 決定住 466
결제 結制 22
결주 結胄 22
결집 結集 22
결탄 結嘆 22
결택 決擇 21
결하 結夏 22
결하 結河 22
결해 結解 22
겸 兼 23
겸 鎌 23
겸단대대 兼但對帶 23
겸리 兼利 23
겸자 鎌子 23
경 境 24, 295, 373, 500
경 庚 23
경 徑 23
경 慶 23
경 敬 23
경 景 23
경 更 23, 485
경 硬 23
경 磬 23, 495
경 經 23, 101, 277, 295, 332, 594
경 謦 23
경 警 23
경 輕 23
경 鏡 24
경 驚 23
경 鯨 23
경(량)부 經(量)部 24, 313
경가 競伽 67
경가 經家 24
경가하문 競伽河門 67
경각 警覺 23
경각 驚覺 23, 272
경계 境界 24
경계 經戒 24
경계반야 境界般若 24
경계상 境界相 24, 281, 629
경곡 鏡谷 24
경교 景教 23
경교 經教 24
경궤 經軌 24

경도 經道 24
경량부 經量部 24, 226, 325
경량부 輕量部 300
경례 敬禮 23
경론 經論 24
경만 輕慢 23
경명일 景命日 23
경모 輕毛 23
경묘 境妙 358
경법 經法 24
경본 經本 23
경부 經部 485
경부종 經部宗 499
경사 經師 24
경사 經笥 24
경산 徑山 23, 419
경상 經箱 24
경상 鏡像 24
경생 經生 24
경수 敬首 157
경수 經手 24
경신회 庚申會 23
경안 輕安 23, 584
경애 敬愛 23
경약 更藥 23
경어 鯨魚 23
경연 硬軟 23
경유식 境唯識 429
경유자 經帷子 24
경율론 經律論 24
경음 鯨音 23
경의 經衣 24
경자 經者 24
경장 經藏 24
경전 敬田 23, 481, 606
경전 經典 24
경제 境諦 427
경종 經宗 24
경중 輕重 23
경지 境智 24
경찬 慶讚 23
경참 慶懺 23
경책 警策 23
경탈 敬脫 261
경탑 經塔 24
경패 經唄 24
경행 經行 25
경허 鏡虛 135
경협 經夾 182
경흥 憬興 25
계 係 25
계 啓 26
계 契 25
계 戒 26, 188, 274, 295, 342, 359, 362, 418, 479, 584, 585, 602
四不壞淨 248
四自在 256
계 界 25, 267, 361, 594, 607
ten fields of meditation 551
계 稽 25
계 繫 26
계 繼 25
계 罽 25, 97
계 薊 25
계 計 26
계 誡 25
계 雞 25
계 髻 26, 83
계 鷄 26, 645
계강나 稽薑那 25
계경 契經 23, 25, 332
계계 界繫 27
계구 戒垢 26
계구계 雞狗戒 25
계권 誡勸 25
계귀 雞貴 25
계금 戒禁 26
계금견 戒禁見 361
계금취견 戒禁取見 26, 28, 410, 415
계급승완 戒急乘緩 26
계기 戒器 26
계나시기 罽那尸棄 342
계나시기불 罽那尸棄佛 25
계내 界內 27
계내교 界內教 27, 478
계내리교 界內理教 27
계내사교 界內事教 27, 240
계내혹 界內惑 27
계념 係念 25
계념 繫念 26
계니타왕 罽膩吒王 25
계단 戒壇 27, 499
계단 谿丹 442
계덕 戒德 27
계도 繼道 541
계도 計都 26, 53
계도 鷄都 26
계도견 戒盜見 582
계독 雞毒 25
계두 鷄兜 26
계두마 鷄頭摩 433
계두마사 雞頭摩寺 25
계두마사 鷄頭摩寺 423
계두말사 雞頭末寺 25
계라다 罽羅多 25
계랍 戒臘 27, 119, 185
계랍 戒蠟 or 戒臘 27
계력 戒力 27
계령랑적산 雞嶺狼跡山 25
계류복 戒類福 277
계리계라 計里計羅 26
계리길라 髻利吉羅 26
계리길라 髻離吉羅 70
계리사반 罽利沙盤 4, 25
계리야 薊利耶 25
계리지라 計利枳攞 26
계명 戒名 185, 191
계명자상 計名字相 26, 468
계문 戒門 27
계바라밀 戒波羅蜜 27
계바리 戒婆離 27
계박 繫縛 26
계백 啓白 26
계벌 誡罰 25
계범 契範 25
계보 髻寶 26
계복 戒福 277
계본 戒本 27
계본경 戒本經 27
계봉 雞峯 25
계부 計部 26
계분 界分 27
계분별관 界分別觀 426
계빈 罽賓 6, 18, 25, 137
계빈국 罽賓國 211
계사 戒師 27
계사 繼嗣 25
계사라 計捨羅 26
계사오덕 戒師五德 27
계살라 計薩羅 or 鷄薩羅 26
계살라 雞薩羅 25
계상 戒相 27
계선 契線 25
계선 戒善 27
계설니 髻設尼 157, 158
계설니 髻設尼 or 計設尼 419

계수 稽首 25
계슬 戒膝 28
계실니 繼室尼 419
계아실유종 計我實有宗 26
계여 界如 27
계연 繫緣 26
계외 界外 27
계외교 界外教 27, 478
계외사교 界外事教 27, 240
계요이 罽饒夷 25
계원 雞園 25
계위 階位 116
계유 鷄酉 365
계윤부 雞胤部 25, 325
계율 戒律 28
계율장 戒律藏 28
계인 契印 494
계인 戒忍 28
계작사 雞雀寺 25
계장 戒場 28
계장 戒藏 28
계정혜 戒定慧 28, 150, 318
계족산 雞足山 25
계족산 鷄足山 119
계주 戒珠 28
계주 繫珠 26
계주 髻珠 26
계착 繫著 26
계착 計着 26
계첩 戒牒 28, 111, 574
계체 戒體 28
계촉 戒躅 28
계취 戒取 28
계취 界趣 27
계취견 戒取見 28
계취결 戒取結 265
계취사 戒取使 28
계타 契吒 25
계탁 計度 26, 227
계탁분별 計度分別 209
계품 戒品 28
계학 戒學 28, 294
계합 契合 299
계해 戒海 28
계향 戒香 28, 418
계험 戒驗 28
계현 戒賢 28
계현 戒賢(b 342
계화 戒和 469
계화상 戒和尚 27
계회 契會 25
고 估 29
고 古 28
고 告 29
고 姑 29
고 孤 29
고 庫 29
고 故 29
고 敲 29
고 枯 29
고 皐 28
고 膏 29
고 苦 28, 207, 271, 274, 281, 302, 427, 469
世間法 319
四諦 257
고 藁 29
고 酤 29
고 高 29
고 鼓 28, 428
고(독)원 孤(獨)園 29
고(독)지옥 孤(獨)地獄 29, 554
고간 藁幹 29
고고 故苦 29
고고 苦苦 30, 266
고골 故骨 29
고공 苦空 30
고공 高空 452
고과 苦果 30
고구 苦具 554
고구리하 高拘梨訶 25
고근 苦根 485
고금 古今 28
고기 苦器 554
고기송 孤起頌 2
고깔 29
고뇌 苦惱 30
고당지 苦當知 288
고도 苦道 30, 270
고독원 孤獨園 29
고동 苦楝 511
고락 苦樂 587
고락가 孤落迦 29
고락현가 鼓樂絃歌 28
고래실유종 古來實有宗 30
고려 高麗 29, 120
고려장 高麗藏 29
고력가 古力迦 49
고류(지)인 苦類(智)忍 30
고류지 苦類智 30, 608
고륜 庫倫 29
고륜 苦輪 30
고망 苦網 30
고명 膏明 29
고목 枯木 29
고목당 枯木堂 29
고박 苦縛 30
고벌라사 枯筏羅闍 29
고법인 苦法忍 608
고법지 苦法智 30, 608
고법지인 苦法智忍 30
고본 苦本 30
고불정 高佛頂 418
고사 高士 29
고사업 故思業 29
고산 孤山 29
고살라 高薩羅 29
고상작 高上作 445
고성 苦性 30
고성제 苦聖諦 30
고세야 高世耶 29, 41
고승 高僧 29
고승전 高僧傳 30
고시 告示 341
고시초 姑尸草 29
고액 苦厄 30
고언 苦言 30
고업 苦業 30
고여 苦餘 30
고역 苦域 30
고온 苦蘊 30
고운사 孤雲寺 30
고음 苦陰 30
고음 鼓音 28
고음성다라니경 鼓音聲陀羅尼經 248
고음성삼다라니경 鼓音聲三陀羅尼經 531
고음여래 鼓音如來 567
四佛 248
고의 估衣 29
고의 故意 29
고의방행위 故意方行位 29
고이 故二 29
고인 苦因 30
고작업 故作業 29
고장 姑藏 29

고적기 古迹記 105
고제 皐帝 357
고제 皐諦 28
고제 苦諦 30, 490
고제 苦際 30
고조 孤調 29
고조 高祖 29
고족 高足 29
고주계 酤酒戒 29
고지 故紙 29
고지 苦智 31, 370
고진 苦津 31
고집 苦集 31
고집멸 苦集滅
世間經 319
고집멸도 苦集滅道 31
고차 庫車 29, 47, 57, 551
고차 高車 29, 645
고참 古參 31
고창 估唱 29
고창 高昌 29, 645
고천 鼓天 28
고청 苦淸
四家 238
고타나 固陀那 284
고하 苦河 31
고해 苦海 31, 216
고행 苦行 31
고행림 苦行林 31, 144
고향 告香 29
고환전 顧歡傳 78
곡 哭 31
곡 斛 15, 31, 165
곡 曲 31
곡 穀 31
곡 谷 31
곡고고 谷呱呱 31
곡녀성 曲女城 31
곡두 穀頭 31
곡록 曲䌙 31
곡록 曲彔 31
곡록 曲祿 31
곡록 曲錄 31
곡반 斛飯 31
곡반왕 斛飯王 534
곡읍 哭泣 31
곡제 哭啼 31
곡치 曲齒 31, 357
곤륜 崑崙 31, 58
곤륜국 崑崙國 31
곤륜노 崑崙奴 31
곤륜산 崑崙山 31, 615
곤륜자 崑崙子 31
곤륵 蜫勒 31
곤륵 昆勒 31
골 骨 31
골목 骨目 31
골불 骨佛 31
골쇄 骨鏁 297
골쇄천 骨鏁天 31
골신 骨身 31
골인 骨人 31
골탑 骨塔 31
공 供 32
공 共 272
공 孔 31, 267
공 工 32
공 恭 32
공 空 27, 32, 88, 173, 211, 220, 266, 269, 271, 279, 282, 286, 289, 290, 292, 294, 303, 367, 398, 421, 429, 430, 454, 477, 499, 505, 544, 545, 546, 552, 582, 583, 607, 609
invisible to the enlightened 248
공 貢 32
공(무변)처정 空(無邊)處定 35
공가중 空假中 2, 19, 32, 191, 193, 230, 448, 449
공거천 空居天 33, 551
공건나보라 恭建那補羅 32
공겁 空劫 18, 33, 238, 315
공견 空見 33
공경 恭敬 32
공경 空經 33
공경시 恭敬施 32
공계 公界 32
공계 空界 33, 255
공계색 空界色 33
공고 貢高 32
공공 空空 33, 34, 279
공공적적 空空寂寂 33
공과 空果 33
공관 空觀 33, 267, 412, 613
공교 空敎 33, 456
공교론 功巧論 42
공교명 工巧明 32
공구 供具 32
공권 空拳 33
공기아 工伎兒 32
공대 空大 33
공덕 功德 478
공덕개 功德鎧 46
공덕법신 功德法身 428
공덕불 功德佛 252
공덕의 功德衣 579
공덕천 功德天 70, 90
공덕화 功德華 211
공로 功勞 245
공륜 空輪 33, 49
공리 空理 33
공마 空魔 33
공명조 共命鳥 140
공무 空無 33
공무변처 空無邊處 33, 35, 50, 53, 152, 239
공무변처지 空無邊處地 55
공무변처해탈 空無邊處解脫 611
공무아 空無我 33
공문 空門 33, 325
공문자 空門子 33
공물 供物 32
공반다 恭畔茶 32
공반야 共般若 480
공법 空法 33
공변처 空徧處 33, 34
공봉 供奉 32, 76
공부 功夫 32
공부 工夫 32
공불 供佛 32
공비림 恐毘林 342
공삼매 空三昧 33
공상 共相 515
공상 空想 33
공상 空相 33
공색 空色 34
공생 空生 34
공성 空性 34, 187, 337
공성 空聖 34
공성무경심 空性無境心 501
공시교 空始敎 34, 340, 412
공심 空心 34
공양 供養 32
공양제불문 供養諸佛門 360
공어타 恭御陀 32
공여래장 空如來藏 34

공왕 空王 34
공왕불 空王佛 34
공유 空有 33, 34, 271
공유이견 空有二見 34
공유이관 空有二觀 33, 34
공유이종 空有二宗 34
공유이집 空有二執 34, 35
공이파일체법 空以破一切法 32
공인 共因 240
공인 空忍 34
공일체처 空一切處 33, 34
공작 孔雀 31, 130
공작명왕 孔雀明王 32
공작불모 孔雀佛母 216
공작성 孔雀城 31, 131
공작왕 孔雀王 32, 89, 486
공장 供帳 32
공장운 供帳雲 32
공적 空寂 34, 376
공점 空點 34
공정 空定 34
공제 空諦 34
공제 空際 34
공조 空鳥 34
공종 空宗 35, 282, 489
공중가 空中假 571
공즉시색 空卽是色 35
공진 空塵 35
공진여 空眞如 487, 558
공집 空執 35
공처 空處 33, 35
공천 供天 32
공취 空聚 35
공파 空破 15
공한처 空閑處 35
공해 空海 35
공해 空解 35
공해탈 空解脫 295
공해탈문 空解脫門 35
공행 空行 35
공허 共許 272
공혜 空慧 35
공화 空華 or 空花 35
공화외도 空華外道 35
과 戈 35
과 果 35, 135, 425, 490, 493, 605, 608
과 瓜 35
과 科 35
과 跨 36
과 過 35, 159, 280
과 鍋 35
과거 過去 35, 280, 475, 630
과거성령 過去聖靈 35
과거세 過去世 35
과거칠불 過去七佛 35
과계원현 果界圓現 36
과과 果果 36
과과불성 果果佛性 36, 418
과극 果極 36
과극법신 果極法身 36, 481
과기 過期 67
과단 果斷 36
과덕 果德 36
과도 過度 35
과도견 果盜見 582
과두 果頭 36
과두 鍋頭 35
과두불 果頭佛 36
과만 果滿 36
과만 過慢 35, 583
과명 果名 36
과목교 過木橋 35
과문 科文 35
과박 果縛 36
과박단 果縛斷 36
과법 果法
四法 247
과보 果報 36
과보사상 果報四相 36, 249
과보토 果報土 36
과분 果分 36, 497
과불성 果佛性 36, 418
과상 果上 36
과상 果相 36
과수 果遂 36
과수원 果遂願 36
과숙식 果熟識 36
과숙인 果熟因 488
과순 果脣 36
과어 果語 588
과여 果如 362
과여 果餘 286
과오 過惡 36
과원 果圓 36
과원덕 果圓德 269
과위 果位 37
과유식 果唯識 37, 429
과의 科儀 35
과인 果人 37
과자 果子 515
과절 跨節 36
과제 果諦 427
과지 果地 37, 498
과천비구 寡淺比丘 489
과추 戈追 35
과피 瓜皮 35
과하 過夏 35
과해 果海 37
과현미 過現未 36
과호 果號 36
곽 or 확 廓 37
곽 藿 37
곽 霍 37
곽엽향 藿葉香 83
곽한 霍罕 37, 614
곽향 藿香 37
관 官 37
관 棺 37
관 灌 37, 489
관 管 37
관 觀 37, 355, 359, 492, 512
止 551
관 貫 37
관 關 37
관(세)자재 觀(世)自在 38
관경 觀經 38, 133
관경소 觀經疏 641
관공 觀空 38
관난 官難 37
관념 觀念 38
관달 觀達 38
관도 觀道 38
관랍 灌臘 37
관무량수경 觀無量壽經 38, 149, 248, 278, 427, 531, 641
관무량수경 觀無量壽經 499
관문 觀門 38
관문사 觀門寺 38
관문십법계 觀門十法界 38
관미륵보살상생도솔천경 觀彌勒菩薩上生兜率天經 278
관법 觀法 38
관보현보살행법경 觀普賢菩薩行法經 278
관불 灌佛 37
관불 觀佛 38

관불삼매 觀佛三昧 38
관상 觀想 38
관상 觀象 38
관상염불 觀像念佛 38
관상염불 觀想念佛 38
관선 觀禪 38
관세 灌洗 37
관세음 觀世音 38, 40, 278, 379, 431
관세음모 觀世音母 38
관세음보살 觀世音菩薩 38
관수 觀樹 38
관수 貫首 37
관신족 觀神足 254
관실 灌室 37
관심 觀心 39
관윤 觀尹 38
관음 觀音 38, 39, 163, 267, 357, 361, 367, 392, 402, 484, 493, 586, 614
관음사 觀音寺 39
관음전 觀音殿 39
관음현의기 觀音玄義記 315
관자재 觀自在 2, 379, 603
四佛 248
四無量心 245
관재 棺材 37
관재살타 觀在薩埵 39
관정 灌頂 37, 343
天台九祖 572
方等 173
관정 貫頂 37
관정...주경 灌頂...咒經 284
관정경 觀頂經 89
관정삼매 觀頂三昧 39
관정주 灌頂住 37, 368
관정지 灌頂智 613
관제 關帝 37
관조 觀照 39
관조궤 觀照軌 268
관조반야 觀照般若 39
관조반야 觀照般若 275, 480
관지 觀智 39
관찰 觀察 39, 274
관찰문 觀察門 39
관찰법인 觀察法忍 488
관해 觀解 39
관행 觀行 39
관행불 觀行佛 39
관행오품위 觀行五品位 636
관행즉 觀行卽 39, 467, 608
관현강 管絃講 37
관혜 觀慧 39
관화 貫花 37
광 光 39
광 廣 39, 92
광 曠 39
광 狂 39
광 誑 39, 323, 460
광강 光降 40
광겁 曠劫 39
광과 廣果 250, 456
광과천 廣果天 39, 301, 370
광교 廣敎 39
광구 狂狗 39
광기 光記 40
광난왕생 狂亂往生 39
광대 廣大 39
광대불정 廣大佛頂 221
광대지 廣大智 39
광대지혜관 廣大智慧觀 412
광대회 廣大會 39
광덕국 光德國 40
광등록 廣燈錄 414
광망 光網 158
광망동자 光網童子 40
광명 光明 39, 40
광명단 光明壇 40
광명대범 光明大梵 40
광명대사 光明大師 40
광명사 光明寺 40
광명산 光明山 40
광명심전 光明心殿 40
광명안 光明眼 362
광명왕 光明王 40, 485
광명진언 光明眞言 40
광명토 光明土 40
광명화상 光明和尙 40
광목 廣目 224
광목녀 光目女 40
광목천 廣目天 39, 260, 438
광목천왕 廣目天王 485, 570
광미 光味 329
광박 廣博 39
方廣 172
광박신 廣博身 39, 586
광백론본 廣百論本 175
광보 光寶 40
광부 光趺 40
광상 狂象 39
광상사 光相寺 372
광상성 光相城 342
광서 光瑞 40
광세음 光世音 38, 40, 379
광야 曠野 39
광엄성 廣嚴城 39
광염왕불 光談王佛 40
광왕 光王 600
광음 光音 40
광음궁 光音宮 40
광음천 光音天 40, 66, 267, 301, 370, 386
광장설 廣長舌 39
광조여래상 光照如來相 40
광좌 光座 40, 541
광찬반야 光讚般若 168
광천효원룡 光天曉苑龍 239
광취불정 光聚佛頂 40, 418, 642
광택 光宅 40, 41, 239
광택사교 光宅四敎 239
광택소 光宅疏 41
광통 光統 41, 267, 448
광해 廣解 228
광협 廣狹 39
광혜 廣慧 39
광혜 狂慧 39
광호 光毫 41
광화 狂華 39
괘 掛 41, 325
괘 罣 41
괘념 罣念 41
괘단 掛單 41
괘답 掛褡 41
괘라 掛羅 41
괘락 掛絡 41
괘락 掛落 41
괘석 掛錫 41
괘애 罣礙 41
괘자 掛子 41
괘진 掛眞 41
괘탑 掛搭 41
괴 傀 41
괴 壞 41
괴 愧 41, 359, 585
괴겁 壞劫 18, 41, 89, 238, 250, 315
괴견 壞見 41

ㄱ ㄴ ㄷ ㄹ ㅁ ㅂ ㅅ ㅇ ㅈ ㅊ ㅋ ㅌ ㅍ ㅎ 찾아보기

괴고 壞苦 41
괴납 壞納 41
괴도 壞道 41
괴려거 壞驢車 41
괴뢰자 傀儡子 41
괴법 壞法 41
괴산 壞山 41
괴상 壞相 41
괴색 壞色 41
괴색의 壞色依 41
괴제포결호 壞諸怖結護 241
굉 宏 41
굉지 宏智 41
교 交 42
교 喬 42
교 巧 42
교 憍 41, 46, 323, 460, 582
교 敎 42, 605, 608
교 校 42
교 橋 41
교 絞 42
교 膠 42
교 較 42
교갱 憍坑 41
교계 敎誡 637
교계륜 敎誡輪 271
교관 敎觀 42
교관이문 敎觀二門 42
교구지 僑矩胝 25
교내 敎內 42
교담미 憍曇彌 41
교답마 喬答摩 42, 48
교답미 喬答彌 42
교답미 憍答彌 41
교당 交堂 42
교대 交代 42
교도 敎導 42
교도 敎道 42, 479, 637
교량 校量 42
교량 橋梁 41
교령 敎令 42
교로 交蘆 42
교로 交露 42
교룡 蛟龍 65
교리 敎理 42
교리행과 敎理行果 42, 605
교마리 嬌麼哩 583
교만 憍慢 41, 604
교망 敎網 42
교명 巧明 42
교묘지 巧妙智 42
교문 敎門 42, 539, 604
교범(바제) 憍梵(波提) 41
교범바제 憍梵婆提 444
교범바제 憍梵波提 67, 444
교범발제 憍梵鉢提 41
교법 敎法 276
四法 247
교부 交付 42
교분자 膠盆子 42
교사야 憍奢耶 29, 41
교사야 憍舍耶 41
교살라 憍薩羅 42
교상 敎相 43
교상미 憍賞彌 14, 42, 52
교상부 敎相部 249
교섬미 憍閃彌 14, 52
교섬미 憍閃彌 or 憍睒彌 42
교수 敎授 43
교수사 敎授師 43
교수아사리 敎授阿闍梨 43
교수아차리 敎授阿遮利 385
교시 憍尸 29, 41
교시가 憍尸迦 41
교식 校飾 42
교식 絞飾 42
교어 敎語 43
교업명 巧業明 32
교외 敎外 42, 43
교외별전 敎外別傳 603
교원 敎圓 487
교유식 敎唯識 429
교의 敎義 43
교일 敎一 255
교적 敎迹 43, 641
교전 敎典 43
교점 交點 42
교주 敎主 43
교중 交衆 513
교증 敎證 43, 548
교지가 憍支迦 41
교지혜 巧智慧 42
교진나 憍陳那 42
교진여 憍陳如 42, 419
교체 敎體 43
교칙 敎勅 43
교판 敎判 43
교편최승 巧便最勝 589
교페리 嬌吠哩 583
교행 敎行 43
교행신증 敎行信證 247
교행증 敎行證 43
교향 膠香 42
교화 敎化 43
교회 敎會 43
교훈 敎訓 646
구 丘 44
구 久 44
구 九 45
구 俱 44, 46
구 具 44, 507
구 劬 47
구 勾 44
구 口 45, 270, 271, 274, 278, 279, 286, 291, 412, 431, 637
구 句 44
구 嘔 46
구 垢 45
구 懼 44
구 拘 46, 51
구 救 46
구 枸 44
구 求 46
구 漚 46, 441, 586
구 狗 43
구 瞿 46
구 矩 43, 46
구 究 46
구 窶 45
구 舊 45
구 衢 44
구 鉤 44, 244
구 驅 46
구 鬮 44
구 鳩 43, 58
구 龜 47
구가니 劬伽尼 47
구가니 瞿伽尼 47, 48, 445
구가리 仇伽離 47
구가리 俱伽離 47
구가리 俱迦利 47
구가리 瞿伽離 47
구가리 瞿迦離 47
구갈라 拘羯羅 47
구거 九居 47, 53
구걸라 俱乞羅 56
구겁 九劫 47

구결 九結 47
구결 口訣 45
구결 垢結 45
구경 九經 47
구경 究竟 46, 163
구경 舊經 45, 640
구경각 究竟覺 46, 238, 265, 410
구경락 究竟樂 46
구경법신 究竟法身 46
구경불 究竟佛 46
구경위 究竟位 46, 425
구경주 究竟住 466
구경즉 究竟卽 46, 467, 608
구계 九界 53
구계 具戒 44
구계 狗戒 43
구계(정집) 九界(情執) 47
구계방편 具戒方便 44
구계지 具戒地 44
구고 救苦 46
구공 九孔 47, 49, 54, 55
구공 俱空 47, 266
구구 句句 44
구구라 俱俱羅 47
구구라 求求羅 538
구구라 窶具羅 538
구구라부 俱俱羅部 47
구구인 九句因 47
구구타 矩矩吒 43
구구타 究究吒 46
구구타 鳩鳩吒 44
구구타예설라 矩矩吒醫設羅 43
구국라천 俱鞠羅天 17
구귀 九鬼 47
구규 九竅 47
구기(나라) 拘耆(那羅) 47
구나 求那 46, 615
구나(함)모니 拘那(含)牟尼 47
구나두 拘那頭 50
구나라 拘拏羅 48
구나라 拘那羅 48
구나라 鳩那羅 43, 48
구나라타 拘那羅陀 561
구나라타 拘那羅陀 or 拘那羅他 48
구나말지 瞿那末底 48
구나발라바 瞿拏鉢剌婆 48
구나발마 求那跋摩 46
구나발타라 求那跋陀羅 46
구나비지 求那毘地 46
구나함 拘那含 584
구나함모니 俱那含牟尼 584
구나합 拘那合 47
구난 九難 48
구낭 懼曩 44
구뇌 九惱 48, 55, 56
구다 具多 82
구다니 瞿陀尼 48, 445
구담 俱譚 48
구담 具譚 44, 48
구담 瞿曇 48, 220
구담(반야)류지 瞿曇(般若)流支 48
구담(반야)류지 瞿曇(般若)留支 48
구담달마사나 瞿曇達磨闍那 48
구담미 俱曇彌 41
구담미 瞿曇彌 48
구담법지 瞿曇法智 48
구담선 瞿曇仙 48
구담승가제바 瞿曇僧伽提婆 48
구당 勾當 44
구도 九道 48
구도 求道 218
구두선 口頭禪 45
구라 俱攞 48
구라구 拘羅瞿 14, 52
구라발저 俱欏鉢底 14
구라발지 俱攞鉢底 48
구라사 拘羅舍 454
구란난타 拘蘭難陀 48
구란타 俱蘭吒 48
구랍파 矩拉婆 43
구랑나 拘浪拏 48
구력가(라) 俱力迦(羅) 49
구력논사 口力論師 45
구력외도 口力外道 45
구련 九蓮 48
구례 九例 587
구로 拘盧 48
구로 狗盧 100
구로 瞿盧
四洲 258
구로(사) 拘盧(舍) 48
구로가 嘔盧伽 443
구로륭방 瞿盧隆謗 49
구로사 俱盧舍 48
구로사 枸盧舍 44
구로자나 瞿嚧者那 48
구로절나 瞿盧折那 48
구로주 俱盧洲 49
구로파타산 窶盧播陀山 57
구룡 驅龍 46
구루 九漏 47, 49
구루 拘屢 48
구루 漚樓 443
구루빈라 漚樓頻螺 443
구루사 拘樓賖 48
구루손 拘樓孫 584
구루손 鳩樓孫 49
구루진 拘樓秦 49
구류 九流 47, 49
구류사 拘流沙 49
구류생 九類生 49
구류손 俱留孫 49
구류손 拘留孫 4
구류손불 拘留孫佛 49
구류진불 拘留秦佛 49
구륜 九輪 49, 124
구륜 口輪 45
구륜 拘輪 14
구륜 拘輪 or 俱輪 49
구률 拘栗 49, 143
구리 俱利 49
구리 拘利 49
구리가 俱哩迦 49
구리가 拘理迦 49
구리가라 俱利伽羅 49
구리검 俱哩劍 49
구리태자 俱利太子 49
구린 俱隣 14, 49
구린 拘隣 49
구린린 拘鄰隣 437
구림정폐 狗臨井吠 43
구마(라) 鳩摩(羅) 43
구마(이) 瞿摩(夷) 49
구마라 俱摩羅 49
구마라 拘摩羅 49
구마라 矩摩羅 or 鳩摩羅 49
구마라 究磨羅 46
구마라 鳩摩羅 43, 293
구마라가 鳩摩羅伽 44
구마라가지 鳩摩羅伽地 44
구마라가천 鳩摩羅伽天 49
구마라기바 鳩摩羅耆婆 43
구마라다 鳩摩羅多 486
구마라다 鳩摩邏多 44

구마라다 鳩摩邏陀 44
구마라부다 鳩摩羅浮多 44
구마라시바 鳩摩羅時婆 43
구마라염 鳩摩羅炎 44
구마라존 拘摩羅尊 49
구마라집(바) 鳩摩羅什(婆) 43
구마라천 俱摩羅天 49
구마라천 拘摩羅天 49
구마제 瞿摩帝 49
구만 九慢 49, 375, 382, 383
구만나 鳩滿拏 44
구명보살 求名菩薩 46
구모 龜毛 47
구모다라 瞿摸怛羅 49
구모두 拘牟頭 or 拘某頭 50
구모타 拘母陀 50
구모타 究牟陀 50
구무간도 九無間道 50, 56
구무두 拘貿頭 50
구무애 九無礙 50
구무위 九無爲 50
구무학 九無學 50
구문 九門 50, 53
구문라 句文羅 50
구물도 拘物度 50
구물두 俱勿頭 50
구물두 拘勿頭 50
구물두 拘物頭 50
구물타 拘物陀 50
구물투 拘勿投 50
구미라 俱尾羅 51
구미타 拘謎陀 50
구밀 口密 45
구박 具縛 44
구박일탈 九縛一脫 50
구반 鳩槃 365
구반다 究槃茶 46
구반다 鳩槃茶 44, 70
구발 救拔 46
구발라 漚鉢羅 443
구발염구아귀다라니경 救拔燄口餓鬼陀羅尼經 407
구방편 九方便 50, 645
구방편십바라밀보살 九方便十波羅蜜菩薩 50
구범 九梵 50
구법 狗法 43
구변지 九徧知 50
구보살 鉤菩薩 44
구부 九部 98
구부(경) 九部(經) 50
구부경 九部經 47, 364
구부득고 求不得苦 46
구불(극)성 俱不(極)成 50
구불견 俱不遣 51
구비가 瞿比迦 54
구비다라 俱毘陀羅 51
구비다라 拘鞞陀羅 51
구비라 俱毘羅 51
구비라 鳩鞞羅 51
구비류바차 俱毘留波叉 51
구비야 劬毗耶 47
구비야 劬毘耶 393
구비야 瞿毘耶 54
구비타라 拘鞞陀羅 51
구빈(타) 劬嬪(陀) 47
구사 俱舍 34, 51, 99, 251, 324, 367, 370, 466, 589, 609
구사 口四 45, 588
구사 句捨 51
구사 拘沙 51
구사 瞿沙 51, 147
구사 矩奢 29, 70
구사게라보라 矩奢揭羅補羅 43, 70, 298
구사경 瞿沙經 51
구사라 具史羅 51
구사라 具史羅 or 瞿史羅 or 劬師羅 44
구사라 劬史羅 51
구사라 劬師羅 47
구사라 拘娑羅 42
구사라 瞿師羅 51
구사라 瞿私羅 51
구사론 俱舍論 51, 88, 93, 96, 104, 268, 269, 273, 274, 277, 280, 281, 287, 288, 316, 322, 358, 370, 425, 459, 540, 589
四劫 238
구사론 俱舍論 18 198
구사론 俱舍論 8 464
구사론기 俱舍論記 40
구사론세간품 俱舍論世間品 266
구사미 俱舍彌 14, 52
구사생지 九士生地 51, 343
구사종 俱舍宗 51, 367, 456, 540
四善根 251
구산팔해 九山八海 51, 241, 583, 611
구살달나 瞿薩怛那 51, 442
구살라 拘薩羅 42
구상 九想 207
구상 九相 51
구상(관) 九想(觀) 51
구상미 俱賞彌 14, 52
구상연혹 九上緣惑 51
구색 具色
육도과보 461
구생 俱生 51
구생(법) 俱生(法) 52
구생기 俱生起 52, 209
구생기번뇌 俱生起煩惱 481
구생법집 俱生法執 481
구생신 俱生神 52
구생아집 具生我執 486
구생혹 俱生惑 51
구선 九禪 52
구설 具說 44
구섬 拘暹 52
구섬미 俱睒彌 14, 42, 52
구섬미 拘睒彌 52
구섬미 拘睒彌 or 拘剡彌 14
구성정각 久成正覺 45
구세 九世 52
구세 救世 46
구세간 九世間 52
구세관세음 救世觀世音 46
구세륜 救世輪 46
구세보살 救世菩薩 46
구세원만 救世圓滿 46
구세자 救世者 46
구세존 救世尊 46
구세천제 救世闡提 46
구소 口疏 45
구소락(가) 俱蘇洛(迦) 52
구소마 俱蘇摩 52
구소마 拘蘇摩 52
구소마 枸蘇摩 44
구소마마라 俱蘇摩摩羅 52
구소마발저 俱蘇摩跋低 52
구소마보라 拘蘇摩補羅 52
구소마보라 枸蘇摩補羅 44
구소법 鉤召法 44
구손바 俱孫婆 52
구수 具壽 44
구수 口授 45
구수라 瞿修羅 52

구수라 瞿脩羅 52
구슬지라 俱瑟祉羅 52
구슬치라 拘瑟耻羅 52
구습 垢習 45
구시 究施 46, 52
구시나 俱尸那 52
구시나 拘尸那 46, 52
구시나갈 拘尸那竭 52
구시나게라 拘尸那揭羅 52, 343
구시나성 拘尸那城 343
구시라 拘翅羅 47
구시성 拘尸城 343
구식 九識 52
구식 垢識 45
구신 句身 44
구실릉가 瞿室餕伽 52, 442
구심 拘深 14, 52
구심 狗心 43
구심륜 九心輪 52
구십바일제 九十波逸提 481
구십오종외도 九十五種外道 52
구십육술 九十六術 52
구십육종외도 九十六種外道 52
구십팔사 九十八使 52
구십팔수면 九十八隨眠 52
구야니 瞿耶尼 47, 445
구야라 俱夜羅 53
구언 舊言 45
구업 九業 53
구업 口業 45, 431
구업공양 口業供養 45
구역 九域 53
구역 舊譯 45
구연과 俱緣果 53
구열반적 求涅槃寂 246
구염 垢染 45
구염 拘鹽 14
구염유 拘鹽惟 52
구오 垢汙 45
구오 軀烏 246
구오 驅烏 46
구오사미 駈烏沙彌 294
구요 九曜 53, 55
木曜 144
구원 久遠 44
구원 鳩垣 43
구원 鳩洹 43
구원실성 久遠實成 45
구유 九喩 53
구유 九有 53, 55
구유 俱有 53
구유 垢有 45
구유 鉤鈕 44
구유근 俱有根 53
구유법 俱有法 53
구유의 俱有依 53
구유인 俱有因 53, 465
구유정거 九有情居 47, 48, 50, 53, 55, 458, 585
구유정처 九有情處 50, 53
구음 九陰 53, 452
구의 九儀 53
구이 瞿夷 53, 55
구이나갈 拘夷那竭 343
구이나갈 拘夷那竭 or 俱夷那竭 52
구이다 拘肄多 49
구이라 鳩夷羅 43
구익 拘翼 14, 52
구인 口印 45
구인 口忍 45
구인사 救仁寺 54
구인일과 九因一果 54
구입 九入 47, 54
구자 丘慈 44
구자 丘茲 47, 57
구자 九字 54
구자 龜茲 44, 47, 57
구자만다라 九字曼荼羅 54
구자산 九子山 56
구장육 龜藏六 47
구재일 九齋日 54
구저사자피 狗箸獅子皮 43
구적 求寂 46, 246
구전 口傳 45
구절라 瞿折羅 54
구정 丘井 44
구제 九諦 54
구조(상승) 九祖(相承) 54
구조가사 九條袈裟 54
구조니 俱助尼 445
구조의 九條衣 54
구족 具足 44, 585
구족계 具足戒 26, 44, 477, 481
구족덕본원 具足德本願 44
구족무결 具足無缺 202
구존 九尊 54, 55, 354
구존 俱存 191
구종 九宗 54
구종대선 九種大禪 54
구죄보 九罪報 48, 55
구주 舊住 45
구주심 九住心 55
구주자 久住者 44
구중 九衆 55, 619
구중생거 九衆生居 53, 55
구지 九地 53, 55, 266, 425, 464, 619
구지 俱支 47
구지 俱胝 35, 49, 55
구지 拘胝 49
구지관정 具支灌頂 44
구지근 具知根 485
구지라 瞿枳羅 55
구집 九執 53, 55
구차제정 九次第定 55
구참상당 九參上堂 55
구창 九瘡 47, 55
구처 九處 56
구철 九徹 55
구철 九轍 55
구철법사 九轍法師 55
구치 俱致 55
구치 拘致 55
구칭 口稱 45
구칭삼매 口稱三昧 45
구타가 拘吒迦 55
구타니 瞿陀尼 47
구타단저 矩吒檀底 31
구타사마리 拘吒賒摩利 55
구탈 救脫 46
구파 瞿婆 54
구파 瞿波 47, 54, 55, 335, 393
구파라 瞿波羅 55
구폐라 俱吠羅 56
구품 九品 56, 300
구품각왕 九品覺王 56
구품대의 九品大衣 54, 56
구품미타 九品彌陀 56
구품번뇌 九品煩惱 56
구품상 九品上 56
구품안양 九品安養 56
구품안양지화생 九品安養之化生 56
구품연대 九品蓮臺 56
구품연대 九品蓮臺 48
구품왕생 九品往生 56

ㄱ ㄴ ㄷ ㄹ ㅁ ㅂ ㅅ ㅇ ㅈ ㅊ ㅋ ㅌ ㅍ ㅎ 찾아보기

구품왕생아미타…경 九品往生阿彌陀…經 364
구품정찰 九品淨刹 56
구품정토 九品淨土 56
구품행업 九品行業 56
구품혹 九品惑 56
구해탈 俱解脫 56
구해탈 具解脫 492
구해탈도 九解脫道 50, 56
구호 救護 46
구호혜 救護慧 158
구화 九華
四大名山 241
구화 口和 45, 469
구화산 九華山 56, 638
구화엄경 舊華嚴經 433
구환 仇桓 43
구회(만다라) 九會(曼陀羅) 56
구회(설) 九會(說) 56
구횡 九橫 48
구횡(사) 九橫(死) 56
구횡경 九橫經 56
구후후 嘔侯侯 46, 610
국 國 56
국 菊 57
국 鞠 57
국다 鞠多 57
국등 菊燈 57
국리연나 鞠利衍娜 57
국사 國師 57
국승정 國僧正 56
국왕 國王 57
국토 國土 56, 280
국토묘 國土妙 359
국토세간 國土世間 56
국토신 國土身 56
국화연나 鞠和衍娜 57
군 君 57
군 捃 57
군 群 57
군 裙 57, 389
군 軍 57
군나 軍那 57
군다 君茶 or 軍茶 57
군다 軍茶 57
군다리 軍茶利 57
군다리 軍茶梨 413
군다리명왕 軍茶利明王 57, 431
군류 群類 57
군맹 群萌 57
군미 群迷 57
군생 群生 57
군수교 捃收敎 478
군유 群有 57
군지 君持 57
군지 君遲 57
군지 軍持 57
군지 軍遲 57
군치가 君稚迦 or 捃稚迦 57
군치가 捃稺迦 or 捃稚迦 57
굴 屈 57
굴 崛 57
굴 掘 58
굴 窟 57
굴거 窟居 25
굴곡교 屈曲敎 478
굴구라 掘具羅 58
굴굴타파타 屈屈咤播陀 or 屈屈咤波陀 57
굴내 窟內 57
굴다 崛多 57
굴단 屈丹 442
굴랑나 屈浪那 or 屈浪拏 57
굴로다 屈露多 58
굴륜 掘倫 58
굴마라 屈摩羅 50, 58, 209
굴만라 屈滿囉 58
굴산 崛山 57
굴상니가 屈想儞迦 58
굴외 窟外 57
굴자 屈茨 47, 57
굴지 屈支 44, 47, 57
굴타가아함 屈陀伽阿含 423
굴타가아합 屈陀迦阿合 58
굴타아람마 屈吒阿濫摩 57
굴현 屈眴 58
궁 宮 58
궁 弓 58, 364
궁 窮 58
궁반다 弓槃茶 58
궁비라 宮毘羅 58, 65, 365
궁생사온 窮生死蘊 58, 286
궁자 窮子 58
궁태 宮胎 58
권 勸 58, 288
권 權 58, 268, 491
권 眷 58
권계 勸誡 58
권교 權敎 58, 155, 478, 612
권대승 權大乘 58
권도지 權道智 174
권모 權謀 58
권문 勸門 59
권문 權門 58
권발 勸發 58
권방편 權方便 58
권법 權法 146
권불 權佛 360
권비 權悲 58
권속 眷屬 58
권속묘 眷屬妙 358, 359
권실 權實 58, 360
권실불이문 權實不二門 58
권이 權理 58
권자 權者 58
권적 權迹 58
권전 勸轉 59, 288
권지 權智 58, 491
권지품 勸持品
四要品 254
권청 勸請 50
권편지 權便智 491
권현 權現 58
권화 勸化 58
권화 權化 58, 351
궐 厥 59
궐문 厥文 59
궐소락가 厥蘇洛迦 52
궐수라 厥修羅 52
궤 樻 59
궤 跪 59
궤 軌 59
궤경 軌經 566
궤두 樻頭 59
궤로 跪爐 59
궤배 跪拜 59
궤범 軌範 59
궤범사 軌範師 59
궤의 軌儀 59
궤지 軌持 59
귀 歸 59
귀 皈 59
귀 貴 59
귀 鬼 31, 59, 211, 486, 537
귀(법)계 鬼(法)界 59
귀견 鬼見 59
귀경 歸敬 60

귀도 鬼道 59
귀록 鬼錄 59
귀매 鬼魅 59
귀명 歸命 60, 201, 434
귀문 鬼門 59
귀병 鬼病 59
귀본 歸本 60
귀선 鬼仙 308, 347, 569
귀성 歸性 60
귀성 鬼城 59
귀속 歸俗 60
귀숙 鬼宿 520
귀신 鬼神 59
귀신식시 鬼神食時 59
귀신중 鬼神衆 486
귀앙 歸仰 59
귀원 歸元 60
귀의 歸依 50, 59
귀의 皈依 59
귀의법 歸依法 59, 268
귀의불 歸依佛 59, 268
귀의승 歸依僧 59, 268
귀입 歸入 60
귀자모 鬼子母 59, 70, 166
귀자모신 鬼子母神 59, 305, 485
귀적 歸寂 60
귀진 歸眞 60
귀천 貴賤 59
귀취 鬼趣 59
귀화 歸化 60
귀화 鬼火 59
규 叫 60
규 奎 486
규 窺 60
규궁 糾宮 60
규기 窺基 98, 176, 186, 514, 632
규봉 圭峯 187, 412, 504
규봉 종밀 圭峯宗密 427, 639
규환 叫喚 60, 554
규환 呌喚 또는 叫喚 60
균 均 60
균여 均如 640
균제 均提 60
극 亟 60
극 剋 60
극 極 60
극 隙 60
극각 極覺 60
극과 剋果 60
극과 極果 60
극광대불정 極廣大佛頂 221
극광음천 極光音天 60
극광정 極光淨 250
극광정천 極光淨天 40, 53, 60
극근 克勤 278
극기라 隙棄羅 60
극난승지 極難勝地 60, 369
극락 極樂 60
극락세계 極樂世界 60
극락화생 極樂化生 638
극랍 極臘 60
극략색 極略色 60
극묘 極妙 60
극미 極微 60, 159
극박사 亟縛屣 60
극성 剋聖 61
극성 極聖 60
극식 剋識 61
극실 剋實 60
극열지옥 極熱地獄 60
극위 極位 60
극유진 隙遊塵 60
극정 極靜 60
극존 極尊 60
극종 剋終 61
극증 剋證 61
극지 極地 60
극치 極致 60
극희지 極喜地 60
근 勤 61
근 斤 61
근 根 61, 88, 224, 295, 485
근 筋 428
근 近 61
근결 根缺 61
근경 根境 61
근고 勤苦 61
근구 勤求 61
근궐 根闕 61
근기 根器 61
근기 根機 61, 70
근념력 勤念力 414
근동 近童 61
근두 斤斗 61
근두 筋斗 61
근둔 根鈍 61
근력 根力 61
근리 根利 61
근문 根門 61
근변지옥 近邊地獄 554
근본 根本 61, 150, 491, 514
근본경 根本經 61
근본등지 根本等至 61
근본무명 根本無明 61, 152, 446, 549
근본번뇌 根本煩惱 61, 203, 481
근본법륜 根本法輪 271
근본살바다부율섭 根本薩婆多部律攝 457
근본살바유부율섭 根本薩婆有部律攝 457
근본선 根本禪 61
근본설일체유부 根本說一切有部 61, 324
근본설일체유부니다나 根本說一切有部尼陀那 457
근본설일체유부목득가 根本說一切有部目得迦 457
근본설일체유부비나야 根本說一切有部毘那耶 457
근본심 根本心 61, 283
근본업불상응염 根本業不相應染 464
근본정 根本定 61
근본지 根本智 61, 491, 646
근본지교 根本之教 201
근본지옥 根本地獄 554
근본혹 根本惑 61, 203
근본회 根本會 317
근사 近事 61
근사남 近事男 61
근사녀 近事女 61
근상하지력 根上下智力 61
근성 根性 61
근수 勤授 154
근식 勤息 61, 245
근신족 勤神足 254
근연 根緣 61
근연 近緣 286
근원 近圓 61
근인 近因 488
근정 根淨 61
근주 近住 61
근주율의 近住律儀 61
근진 根塵 61
근책남 勤策男 246
근책녀 勤策女 246

근패 根敗 61
근행 勤行 61
근향 根香 61, 82, 144
글쇄 走乞灑 17
금 今 62
금 禁 62
금 金 53, 61, 278, 584, 618
금(강)침 金(剛)針 62
금가 今家 62
금가라 金伽羅 67
금강 金剛 62, 64, 71, 305, 609
four degrees 242
금강(륜)산 金剛(輪)山 62
금강(위)산 金剛(圍)山 62
금강(저) 金剛(杵) 165, 179
금강경 金剛經 62
금강경석의 金剛經釋義 103
금강계 金剛界 62, 63, 66, 102, 103, 278, 395, 430, 508, 595
금강계오부 金剛界五部 62
금강관 金剛觀 62
금강광 金剛光 179
금강광보살 金剛光菩薩 63
금강구 金剛口 62, 65
금강구보살 金剛鉤菩薩 63
금강구왕 金剛鉤王 64
금강권 金剛拳 62
금강권보살 金剛拳菩薩 62
금강능단반야바라밀경 金剛能斷般若波羅蜜經 62
금강동자 金剛童子 63, 237
금강력 金剛力 63
금강력(사) 金剛力(士) 63
금강령 金剛鈴 63
금강령 金剛鈴 427
금강령보살 金剛鈴菩薩 63
금강륜 金剛輪 63, 243
금강륜좌 金剛輪座 101
금강리보살 金剛利菩薩 63
금강만다라 金剛曼荼羅 63
금강멸정 金剛滅定 65
금강모 金剛母 137
금강무승결호 金剛無勝結護 241
금강문 金剛門 63
금강밀적 金剛密迹 63, 485
금강바라밀 金剛波羅蜜 142
금강반야 金剛般若 168
금강반야론 金剛般若論 417
금강번 金剛幡 63
금강번보살 金剛幡菩薩 63
금강법계궁 金剛法界宮 63
금강법보살 金剛法菩薩 63
금강보계 金剛寶戒 63
금강보보살 金剛寶菩薩 63
금강보살 金剛菩薩 62, 63
금강보장 金剛寶藏 63
금강부 金剛部 63, 64, 127
금강부모 金剛部母 63
금강불 金剛佛 63
금강불괴(신) 金剛不壞(身) 63
금강불자 金剛佛子 63
금강사자 金剛使者 63
금강삭 金剛索 63
금강삭보살 金剛索菩薩 63
금강살타 金剛薩埵 63, 100, 225, 363, 402
금강삼매 金剛三昧 65, 509
금강삼매경 金剛三昧經 159
금강삼매경론 金剛三昧經論 64
금강상 金剛床 65
금강쇄 金剛鏁 64
금강쇄보살 金剛鏁菩薩 64
금강수 金剛手 63, 64, 90, 91, 98, 496, 603, 636
금강수 金剛水 64
금강수(보살) 金剛手(菩薩) 64
금강수(비밀왕) 金剛手(秘密王) 64
금강수보살 金剛手菩薩 63, 64
금강수살타 金剛手薩埵 64
금강승 金剛乘 64
금강신 金剛神 63, 64, 65, 174, 487, 636
금강신 金剛身 64
금강심 金剛心 64
금강심전 金剛心殿 64
금강야차 金剛夜叉 64, 431, 487
금강약차 金剛藥叉 64, 373
금강어언 金剛語言 64
금강역사 金剛力士 63, 64
금강염 金剛炎 64
火院 640
금강염송 金剛念誦 64
금강왕 金剛王 64
금강왕보각 金剛王寶覺 64
금강왕보살 金剛王菩薩 64
금강유정 金剛喩定 65
금강인보살 金剛因菩薩 63
금강자 金剛子 64, 387
금강장 金剛杖 64
금강장 金剛藏 64, 363, 484
금강장보살 金剛將菩薩 63
금강장보살 金剛藏菩薩 63
금강장왕 金剛藏王 64
금강저 金剛杵 62, 64, 600
금강정 金剛定 65
금강정 金剛頂 64
금강정경 金剛頂經 64, 102, 161, 278, 560
四佛 248
금강정유가천수...의궤경 金剛頂瑜伽千手...儀軌經 566
금강정종 金剛頂宗 64
금강좌 金剛座 65
금강중 金剛衆 65
금강지 金剛智 65, 90, 213, 377, 515, 609
금강지삼장 金剛智三藏 65
금강찰 金剛刹 65, 237
금강천 金剛天 65
금강체 金剛體 65
금강침보살 金剛針菩薩 63
금강향보살 金剛香菩薩 63
금강혜 金剛慧 65
금강혜인 金剛慧印 411
금강호보살 金剛護菩薩 95
금계 禁戒 62
금계 金界 62
금계 金鷄 65
금골 金骨 65
금광(명) 金光(明) 65
금광명 金光明 173
금광명경 金光明經 65, 471
四佛 248
금광명고 金光明鼓 65
금광명녀 金光明女 65
금광명최승왕경 金光明最勝王經 65
금광불찰 金光佛刹 65
금구 金口 65
금구 金軀 66
금구 金龜 65
금구상승 金口相承 65
금구조승 金口祖承 65
금니 金泥 66
금당 金堂 65
금대왕 金大王 65

금란가사 金襴袈裟 65
금란의 金襴衣 65
금륜 金輪 65, 271
금륜불정 金輪佛頂 98, 418, 527
금륜불정존 金輪佛頂尊 105
금륜왕 金輪王 65
금릉 金陵 419
금모사자 金毛獅子 65
금불 金佛 66
금비라 禁毘羅 65
금비라 金毗羅 18
금비라 金毘羅 58, 65, 349, 365
금비라 金毘邏 65
금비라대장 金毘羅大將 66
금비라비구 金毘羅比丘 66
금비라신 金毘羅神 66
금비라천 金比羅天 17
금비라타(가비라) 金毘羅陀(迦毘羅) 66
금사 金沙 66
금산 金山 62, 66, 574
금산사 金山寺 66
금산왕 金山王 66
금살 金薩 63
금색 金色 66
금색가섭 金色迦葉 66
금색공작왕 金色孔雀王 66
금색녀 金色女 66
금색두타 金色頭陀 66
금색세계 金色世界 66
금색왕 金色王 66
금색의 金色衣 65
금색존자 金色尊者 66
금선 金仙 48, 66
금성 金星 66, 337, 586
금속여래 金粟如來 66
금수 金水 66
금시조(왕) 金翅鳥(王) 66
금신 金身 66
금언 金言 66
금염 金炎 64
금원 今圓 62, 487
금인 金人 66
금장 金杖 66
금장 金藏 66, 484
금장운 金藏雲 66
금적 金寂 47
금전 金田 66
금제 金蹄 66
금주장 禁呪藏 62
금지 金地 66, 137
금지국 金地國 66, 494
금찰 金刹 66, 564
금천동자 金天童子 65
금출 金出 66
금태 金胎 66
금파라 金波羅 65
금하 金河 67
급 急 67
급 汲 67
급 笈 67
급 給 67
급고(독) 給孤(獨) 67
급다 笈多 67
급독 給獨 329
급방발지 笈房鉢底 41, 67
급시 急施 67
급시여률령 急施如律令 67
급원 給園 29
급정륜 汲井輪 67
긍 矜 67
긍가 兢伽 621
긍가 殑伽 67, 621
긍갈나 矜羯羅 206
긍갈라 矜羯羅 603
긍갈라 矜蝎羅 67
긍기 殑耆 67
긍사 亘娑 621
긍애 矜哀 67
긍하 殑河 67
기 伎 68
기 嗜 67
기 器 67, 280
기 奇 69
기 妓 67
기 寄 69
기 岐 278
기 己 68
기 忌 67
기 期 67
기 棄 68
기 機 68, 500
기 氣 283
기 祇 68
기 祈 69
기 箕 381, 485
기 紀 69
기 綺 67
기 耆 67
기 蟣 67
기 記 69, 156
기 譏 68
기 起 69
기 饑 67
기 騎 69
기감 機感 68
기강료 紀綱寮 69
기견 機見 68
기계 器界 67
기계 己界 68
기계설 器界說 67
기고 寄庫 69
기관 機關 68
기교 伎巧 68
기교 機教 68
기귀전 寄歸傳 604
기근 機根 68
기근재 饑饉災 67
기나 耆那 67, 341
기나야사 嗜那耶舍 67
기념 祈念 69
기다라 旂陀羅 450
기다밀 祇多蜜 68
기달(라) 旂達(羅) 450
기도 祈禱 69
기량 器量 67
기려멱려 騎驢覓驢 69
기론 記論 69
기리 己利 68
기리타 紀哩馱 351
기린 麒麟 494
기망 期望 67
기멸 起滅 69
기묘 奇妙 69
기바 耆婆 67, 328
기바기바(가) 耆婆耆婆(迦) 67
기바기바가 耆婆耆婆迦 140
기바조 耆婆鳥 67
기바천 耆婆天 67
기번 旗旛 178
기별 記別 69
기별 記莂 69
기별경 記別經 69
기사 耆闍 68
기사굴 耆闍崛 68, 419
기사굴산 耆闍崛山 57, 580
기사심 起事心 283

기사인 起死人 69
기성 機性 68
기세 棄世 68
기세간 器世間 67, 483
기세경 起世經 91
기세계 器世界 67, 319
기수급고독원 祇樹給孤獨園 68
기수라 祇修羅 52
기수원 祇樹園 68
기수화림굴 祇樹花林窟 68
기시귀 起尸鬼 69, 70
기신 起信 69
기신론 起信論 20, 46, 69, 77, 88, 97, 105, 150, 201, 207, 217, 238, 265, 267, 269, 275, 281, 298, 333, 344, 346, 350, 353, 394, 410, 433, 446, 464, 471, 476, 477, 482, 511, 524, 553, 558, 575, 578, 606, 629
mind as bhūtatathatā 355
分別 209
四覺 four intelligences 238
육추 六麤 468
기신론 起身論 422
기신론의기 起信論義記 69
기신미타유심정토 己身彌陀唯心淨土 68
기신이문 起信二門 69
기실 記室 69
기심 己心 68
기심 記心 69, 637
기심륜 記心輪 271
기심법문 己心法門 68
기심중소행법문 己心中所行法門 68
기아 伎兒 68
기아지옥 饑餓地獄 67
기악 妓樂 67
기야 祇夜 68, 364, 544
기어 機語 68
기어 綺語 67
기업상 起業相 468
기역 耆域 67
기연 機緣 68
기예 伎藝 68
기예천녀 伎藝天女 68
기요 機要 68
기우 祈雨 69
기우래우 騎牛來牛 441
기우멱우 騎牛覓牛 441
기원 祇園 255
기원 祇洹 29
기원 祈願 69
기원(정사) 祇園(精舍) 68
기원림 祇洹林 68
기원정사 祇園精舍 68
기유라 革奇由羅 70
기응 機應 68
기의 機宜 68
기이 奇異 69
기인 技人 69
기일 忌日 67
기자 起者 69
기재 奇哉 386
기증 己證 68
기지 祇支 68, 339
기지처 起止處 69, 581
기진 起盡 69
기청 祈請 69
기청 起請 69
기치반나 祇哆槃那 68
기치반림 祇哆槃林 68
기타 唫吒 69
기타 祇陀 68
기타림 祇陀林 68
기타원 祇陀園 68
기특 奇特 69
기평 譏評 613
기행 起行 69
기허신랑 氣虛神朗 273
기혐 譏嫌 68
기화 己和 69
기환림 祇桓林 68
기희 伎戲 71
긴 緊 69
긴나라 緊那羅 69, 606
긴날라 緊捺羅 69
긴다라 緊陀羅 69
긴요 緊要 69
긴축가 緊祝迦 69
길 吉 70, 393
길 姞 70
길가야 吉迦夜 70
길경 吉慶 70
길라 吉羅 70, 112
길률다(라구다) 姞栗陀(羅矩吒) 70
길률타 姞栗陀 70
길률타라구타 姞栗陀羅矩吒 68
길리 吉利 70
길리다 吉利多 70
길리라 吉利羅 70
길반다 吉槃茶 70
길상 吉祥 43, 70, 195
길상과 吉祥果 70
길상모 吉祥茅 70
길상모국 吉祥茅國 70, 298
길상병 吉祥瓶 533
길상천녀 吉祥天女 70
길상초 吉祥草 70
길상해운 吉祥海雲 70
길서 吉庶 70
길유라 吉由擢 340
길유라 吉由羅 70
길일 吉日 119
길일양진 吉日良辰 70
길자 吉蔗 70
길제라 佶提羅 51
길주 吉州 635
길차 吉遮 70
길하 吉河 70
깜냥 70
깨달음 70
꿇어앉기 70
끽 喫 70
끽기라 喫棄羅 70
끽소 喫素 70

(ㄴ)

나 娜 71
나 拏 71
나 那 71
나 裸 71
나가 娜伽 71
나가 那伽 71
나가서나 那伽犀那 72, 439
나가알갈수나 那伽閼曷樹那 71
나가알랄수나 那伽閼剌樹那 71, 382
나가정 那伽定 71
나게(라할라) 那揭(羅喝羅) 71
나계 螺髻 117, 342
나계범(지) 螺髻梵(志) 117
나계선인 螺髻仙人 117
나금함 那金含 73
나길니 拏吉儞 82
나다 娜多 71

나단납단라야 羅担納担羅耶 586
나도차 羅闍遮 284
나라 那羅 71
나라나리 那羅那里 71
나라마나 那羅摩那 71, 129
나라마납 那羅摩納 71
나라야나 那羅野拏 71
나라연 那羅延 508, 567
나라연(나) 那羅延(那) 71
나라연금강 那羅延金剛 493
나라연천 那羅延天 71, 606
나라연천후 那羅延天后 71
나라타 那羅陀 71
나락가 那洛迦 72
나락가 那落迦 74, 554
나란다 那爛陀 341
나란타 那爛陁 72
나랄차 那辣遮 72
나련(제여)야사 那連(提黎)耶舍 72
나리(계)라 那利(薊)羅 72
나마 娜麽 72
나마 娜麽 or 娜摩 140
나마 那摩 72
나마 那麻 72
나마가 羅摩伽 117
나마인도 羅摩印度 117
나모 娜母 72
나모 那謨 72
나모 那謨 or 那模 72
나무 南無 60, 72, 75, 201
나무불 南無佛 72
나무사 南無師 72
나무삼보 南無三寶 72
나무아미타불 南無阿彌陀佛 465
나바(마리) 那婆(摩利) 72
나바나 羅婆那 117
나발 螺髮 117
나비 那鞞 72
나사라 那闍羅 8
나선 那先 72
나선(비구)경 那先(比丘)經 72
나선비구경 那先比丘經 439
나술 那術 or 那述 72
나아뢰야만다라 那阿賴耶曼荼羅 72
나야 娜耶 71
나야 那耶 72
나야수마 那耶修摩 72
나열 羅閱 118
나열성 羅閱城 620
나예 羅預 117
나옹 혜근懶翁惠勤 72
나유다 那庾多 or 那由多 72
나유타 那由他 72, 622
나율 那律 73
나의 蘿衣 117
나제 那提 73, 74, 615
나제가섭 那提迦葉 73
나차사 羅叉娑 73
나차사 羅叉私 73
나찰(사) 羅刹(娑) 73
나찰국 羅刹國 73
나찰녀 羅刹女 73
나찰라 羅刹羅 73
나찰사 羅刹斯 73
나찰사 羅刹私 73
나찰천 羅刹天 73
나타 那他 73
나타 那吒 71
나타 那咤 73
나파나 羅婆那 284
나한 羅漢 375
나한전 羅漢殿 73
나함 那含 73, 428
나형외도 裸形外道 71
낙 諾 73
낙 洛 73
낙 樂 269, 281
four inverted beliefs 242
낙가 落迦 118
낙가나 諾伽那 73
낙거라 諾詎羅 73
낙건나 諾健那 73
낙경 酪經 118
낙과 樂果 386
낙구라 諾矩羅 73
낙구타 諾瞿陀 73, 80
낙근 樂根 485
낙근 樂根 386
낙미 酪味 118, 415
낙바라밀 樂波羅蜜 386
낙발 落髮 118
낙발염의 落髮染衣 118
낙방 樂邦 387
낙법 樂法 386
낙변화천 樂變化天 81, 387, 468, 637
낙사 洛沙 73, 330
낙수 樂受 386
낙시 樂施 386
낙식 樂食 252
낙양 洛陽 73
낙염 落染 118
낙욕 樂欲 386
낙욕대장 樂欲大將 246
낙잠 落賺 118
낙차 洛叉 358
낙차 落叉 118
낙차 洛叉 73, 330
낙착 樂著 386
낙토 樂土 386
낙흘삽미 落吃澁弭 118
난 暖 74
난 煖 74
난 難 73
난 欄 73
난국 蘭菊 119
난국 難國 272
난나 難拏 73
난도 難度 73
난도해 難度海 73
난동 暖洞 74
난료 暖寮 74
난법 煖法 74
四善根 251
난복 難伏 73
난분(회) 蘭盆(會) 119
난사 暖寺 74
난사 蘭闍 119
난사 難思 73
난사(대) 蘭奢(待) 119
난사광불 難思光佛 378
난상 亂想 118
난생 卵生 74, 250
난석 暖席 74
난석석열 難石石裂 305
난선 亂善 118
난선 難禪 54
난순 欄楯 73
난승 亂僧 118
난승 難勝 73, 212
난실 蘭室 118
난심 亂心 118
난야 蘭若 118
난어 爛魚 118
난위 煖位 141

난유 難有 73
난입 難入 73
난제 難提 73
난제가 難提迦 73, 176
난제가물다 難提迦物多 73
난지 難持 212
난타 難陀 73
난타 難陁 73
난타발난타 難陀跋難陀 73
난항복결호 難降伏結護 241
난행 亂行 118
난행도 難行道 479
난향 蘭香 119
난화 難化 73
날 捺 74
날나사낭 捺喇捨囊 19
날락가 捺落迦 74, 79, 554
날리라길리 捺喇羅吉喇 72
날마 捺麻 72, 74
날모 捺謨 72, 74
날지가섭파 捺地迦葉波 73, 74
남 南 74
남 男 74
남(방)무구(세계) 南(方)無垢(世界) 74
남근 男根 74, 485
남녀 男女 74
남능북수 南能北秀 74
남돈북점 南頓北漸 74
남라 南羅 74, 117
남락 嚂嗒 270
남마 藍摩 119
남막 藍莫 119
남망 南忙 72
남모 南牟 72
남모 南謨 72
남바 藍婆 119
남발라 藍勃羅 119
남방 南方 74
남방불교 南方佛教 74
남본대반열반경 南本大般涅槃經 406
남본열반경 南本涅槃經 361
남부 南浮 74
남부 南部 74
남산 南山 74, 267, 315, 419
남산종 南山宗 367
남섬부주 南贍部洲 74
남악 南岳 572, 631
남악 南嶽 312
남악대사 南嶽大師 632
남양 南陽 74
남염부제 南閻浮提 74
남우 藍宇 119
남장 南藏 74
남전 南泉 74
남종 南宗 74
남주 南洲 74
남중 南中 267
남중삼교 南中三教 74
남천(축) 南天(竺) 75
남파 濫波 119
남파 藍婆 357
남풍 藍風 119
남해마라야산 南海摩羅耶山 75
남행 南行 75
납 納 75
납 臘 27, 318
납 衲 75
납 蠟 75
납가리 納加梨 75
납가리 衲伽梨 75
납가사 衲袈裟 75
납계 納戒 75
납골 納骨 75
납구 納具 75
납득 納得 75
납막 納莫 72, 75
납모 納帽 75
납모 納慕 72, 75
납모 納謨 75
납박 臘縛 119
납박승가람 納縛僧伽藍 75
납박제반구라 納縛提嬖矩羅 75
납박파 納縛波 75
납벌니 臘伐尼 119, 126
납병 臘餅 119
납불 臘佛 119
납사어통 納蛇於筒 75
납살 拉薩 11
납수 納受 75
납의 納衣 75
납의 衲衣 209
납의 衲衣 or 納衣 75
납인 蠟印 75
납자 衲子 75
납중 衲衆 75
납차 臘次 119
납파 納播 75
납팔 臘八 119, 317
낭 囊 75
낭 娘 75
낭 曩 75
낭막 曩莫 72, 75
낭모 囊莫 75
낭모 囊謨 75
낭모 曩謨 72
낭아라하라 囊哦羅賀羅 75
낭아라하라 曩哦囉賀囉 71
낭적산 狼跡山 119
내 內 75, 395, 436
내 柰 75, 136
내 耐 75
내 또는 나 奈 75
내걸 內乞 76, 225, 436
내계 內界 76
내공 內空 76
내공(봉) 內供(奉) 76
내과 來果 119
내교 內教 76
내기 內記 76
내녀 柰女 75
내도 內道 34
내도량 內道場 76, 77
내리 奈利 75
내말타 耐抹陀 75
내명 內明 76, 415, 495
내무색상관외색해탈 內無色想觀外色解脫 611
내무위 內無爲 76
내문전 內門轉 76
내범 內凡 76, 467, 481
내범부지 內凡夫地 369
내범위 內凡位 76
내법 內法 76
내비 內秘 76
내사 內史 76
내사 內寺 76
내생 來生 119
내세 來世 119
내숙식 內宿食 76, 77
내식 內識 76
내심 內心 76
내심만다라 內心曼荼羅 76
내씨 柰氏 75
내아 內我 76
내연 內緣 76

내영 來迎 119
내왕 乃往 77
내외 內外 76
내외겸명 內外兼明 76
내외공 內外空 76
내외도 內外道 76
四執 260
내원 內院 77
내원 柰苑 or 柰園 75
내원해인 耐怨害忍 75
내유색상관외색해탈 內有色想觀外色解脫 611
내응 來應 119
내의 內衣 77
내자 內煮 76, 77
내장 內障 77
내재 內齋 76, 77
내전 內典 77
내종 內種 77
내중 內衆 77
내증 內證 77, 436
내지 乃至 77
내지일념 乃至一念 77
내진 內塵 77
내진 內陣 77
내치라하라 奈耻羅訶羅 75
내태 內胎 77
내하 奈河 75
내하교 奈河橋 75
내학 內學 77
내훈 內熏 140
내훈 內薰 77
냉 冷 77
냉광신 冷光神 450
냉난 冷暖 77
냉도 冷淘 77
냉면 冷麪 77
냉하 冷河 77
녈 涅 77
녈리지 涅哩底 77, 246
녈리지방 涅哩底方 77
녈말 涅末 77, 592
녈첩반나 涅疊般那 77
념 念 77, 104, 584
녕사나낭 甯史娜囊 81
노 奴 78
노 弩 78
노 老 78, 267
노가비 路伽憊 2
노가위사제 盧迦委斯諦 121
노결 勞結 122
노고 老苦 78
노고추 老古錐 78
노구다바타부 盧俱多婆拖部 121
노구다바타부 盧俱多婆拖部 580
노다 嚕多 122
노다라야 盧陀羅耶 121
노단 爐壇 122, 637
노달라쇄 弩達囉灑 78
노라바 嚕羅婆 122
노려 勞侶 122
노명 露命 122
노목랑 老木郞 96
노벽제 弩蘗帝 78
노복 奴僕 78
노비 奴婢 78
노사 盧舍 121
노사 老死 365
노사 老死 78, 80
노사나 盧舍那 121
노숙 老宿 78, 591
노신 露身 122
노엽달마 蘆葉達磨 122
노예 奴隸 78
노우 露牛 122
노원 勞怨 122
노자 老子 78
노자나 盧遮那 121
노자불 盧遮佛 121
노적건 皴赤建 78
노지 露地 122
노지나 盧脂那 121
노지불 盧至佛 121
노파 老婆 78
노행자 盧行者 121
노형 露形 122
노혜다 盧醯多 639
노혜다가 盧慧多迦 121
노혜달가 盧慧呾迦 121
노호 老胡 633
노히지가목다 盧吘胝訶目多 121
녹 漉 78
녹 綠 420
녹(왕) 鹿(王) 478
녹거 鹿車 122
녹계 鹿戒 122
녹두 綠豆 158
녹모 鹿母 229
녹선 鹿仙 122
녹수낭 漉水囊 78
녹수대 漉水袋 78
녹야원 鹿野園 122
녹원 鹿苑 122, 288
녹원시 鹿苑時 421
녹장 鹿杖 158
녹형신 鹿形神 450
논 論 23, 295
논가 論家 122
논민 論民 122, 126
논사 論師 122, 338
논소 論疏 122
논외도 論外道 338
논용 論用 629
논의 論議 123
논의 論議 50
논장 論藏 122
논종 論宗 122
농 膿 78
농 農 78
농 籠 78
농두 籠頭 78
농혈지옥 膿血地獄 78
뇌 惱 78, 323, 460
뇌관 牢關 123
뇌야 賴耶 123
뇌제 賴提 13
뇌총 牢寵 123
뇌타 瀨惰 123
뇌타(화라) 賴吒(啝羅) 123
뇨 尿 78
누겁 累劫 123
누계 漏戒 123
누려왕 樓黎王 228
누륵왕 婁勒王 228
누만 髏鬘 123
누무루 漏無漏 123
누업 漏業 123, 286
누영진무소외 漏永盡無所畏 123
누장 累障 123
누진 漏盡 123
누진(지증)통 漏盡(智證)通 468
누진명 漏盡明 123, 273
누진비구 漏盡比丘 123
누진의해 漏盡意解 123
누진증명 漏盡證明 123
누진지 漏盡智 123
누진지증명 漏盡智證明 273

누진통 漏盡通 123
누칠제 累七齊 123
누타 淚墮 123
누탄 樓炭 91
누탄 樓炭 123
누형 累形 123
늑 勒 492
능 能 79
능가 餧伽 79
능가 駿伽 79
능가 駿迦 124
능가 楞伽 79
능가경 楞伽經 79, 98, 292, 507, 587
六部大乘經 462
능가경 楞伽經 5 459, 469
능가아발다라보경 楞伽阿跋多羅寶經 79
능견상 能見相 281
능견심불상응염 能見心不相應染 464
능단금강경 能斷金剛經 79
능대사 能大師 79
능립 能立 79, 605
능변 能變 532
능별 能別 320, 539
능생 能生 550
능생인 能生因 488
능소 能所 79
능시보살 能施菩薩 99
능시태자 能施太子 79, 99
능신 能信 79
능엄 楞嚴 232
능엄경 楞嚴經 79, 88, 125, 308, 449, 493, 516, 627
능엄주 楞嚴呪 221
능연 能緣 79, 402
능의 能依 79
능인 能人 79
능인 能仁 79, 493
능작인 能作因 465
능지 能持 79
능지제 能知諦 427
능천제 能天帝 533
능파 能破 605
능행자 能行者 79
니 尼 79, 365, 398, 399
니 泥 79
니(사)타 尼(師)吒 373
니가라 尼迦羅 79
니건 尼健 80
니건 尼犍 80
니건 尼虔 80
니건(타) 尼乾(陀) 80
니건도 尼犍度 80
니건타가 尼建他迦 80
니건타불저라 尼犍陀弗呾羅 80
니건타야제자 尼乾陀若提子 80
니계 尼戒 79
니고 尼姑 79, 225, 238
니구니타 尼拘尼陀 80
니구다 尼拘陀 80
니구로타 尼拘盧陀 80
니구루타 尼拘婁陀 80
니구루타 尼拘屢陀 80
니구류 尼俱類 80
니구류타 尼拘類陀 80
니구율 尼拘律 80
니구타 尼俱陀 80
니구타 尼瞿陀 80
니근저 尼近底 80
니근지 尼近底 81
니다나 尼陀那 80, 364
니다나목득가 尼陀那目得迦 80
니단 尼壇 79
니대사 尼大師 79
니라 尼羅 80
니라구발라 尼羅漚鉢羅 80, 554
니라난나 儞羅難拏 360
니라바다라 尼羅婆陀羅 80
니라부다 尼羅浮陀 80
니라부타 尼羅浮陀 80
니라부타 泥羅浮陀 610
니라야 泥囉耶 79
니라오발라 尼羅烏鉢羅 80, 554
니라우담발라 尼羅優曇鉢羅 80
니라폐다 尼羅蔽荼 80
니랄부다 尼剌部陀 80
니랄부타 尼剌部陀 554
니랄부타 尼剌部陀 or 尼剌浮陀 80
니람바 尼藍婆 80
니려 泥黎 79
니련선 尼連禪 312
니련선(나) 尼連禪(那) 80
니련선하 尼連禪河 346
니련하 尼連河 80
니로도 泥盧都 79
니로발라 泥盧鉢羅 79
니루다 尼樓陀 80, 81
니루타 尼樓陀 257
니리 泥梨 75
니리 泥犁 79, 554
니리(야) 泥梨(耶) 79
니리가 泥梨迦 79
니리저 泥哩底 79
니마라 尼摩羅 80
니미유다 尼彌留陀 80, 81
니민다(라) 尼民陀(羅) 81
니민다라 尼民陀羅 51
니민달라 尼民達羅 81
니바라 尼波羅 81
니박사나 泥縛些那 79
니반 泥畔 79, 405
니벌산나 泥伐散娜 79
니법사 尼法師 79
니비구 尼比丘 79
니사 尼寺 79
니사다 尼沙陀 81
니사단 尼師壇 81
니사단나 尼師但那 81
니사불 尼思佛 81
니살기바일제 尼薩耆波逸提 81, 284
니살담 尼薩曇 81
니야마 尼夜摩 81
니연저 尼延底 80
니연지 尼延底 81
니연타가 尼延他柯 80
니왈 泥曰 79
니원 泥洹 79, 405
니위 尼衛 81
니인 泥人 79
니일 泥日 405
니저 泥底 79
니제 尼提 81
니중주 尼衆主 79
니지 尼低 81
니지 尼抵 81
니타 尼陀 81
니탑 泥塔 79
니파사 泥婆娑 79
니환 泥丸 79
니환 泥桓 79
님의 침묵 81

(ㄷ)

다 多 82, 88
다 茶 82
다 荼 82
다(라)장 多(羅)掌 82
다가라 多伽羅 2, 82, 144
다가루 多伽婁 82
다가류 多伽留 82
다건나 茶健那 73
다게라 多揭羅 82
다구마 茶矩磨 82
다구마 荼矩磨 82
다길니 茶吉尼 82
다나 陀那 82, 84
다나가타 陀那伽他 82
다나바 陀那婆 82
다나발지 陀那鉢底 83
다다갈다 陀多竭多 591
다라 多羅 82
다라 陀羅 82
다라과 多羅果 82
다라나 陀羅那 82
다라니 陀羅尼 82, 156, 484, 542
四種總持 258
다라니보살 陀羅尼菩薩 82
다라니집경 陀羅尼集經 82, 393
다라니품 陀羅尼品 356
다라라 陀羅羅 82
다라보살 多羅菩薩 82
다라수 多羅樹 82
다라야등릉사 多羅夜登陵舍 107, 284
다라야등육사 多羅夜登陸舍 82
다라엽 多羅葉 82
다라표 陀羅驃 82, 158
다력 陀歷 591
다령(로가야폐사야) 多齡(路迦也吠闍也) 83
다륵 多勒 80
다린니 陀隣尼 82
다마 多摩 593
다마 陀摩 591
다마라(발) 多摩羅(跋) 37
다마라발전단향 多摩羅跋旃檀香 83
다마리제 多摩梨帝 83, 85
다문 多聞 83, 229, 374
다문력 多聞力 361
다문부 多聞部 325, 509
다문비구 多聞比丘 489
다문제일 多聞第一 83
다문천 多聞天 260, 438
다문천왕 多聞天王 485, 570
다발 多髮 83, 357
다보 多寶 171, 199, 357, 431, 483, 586, 614
다보(여래) 多寶(如來) 83
다비 茶毘 82, 234, 640
다비 荼毘 82, 392
다비다 陀毘荼 591
다비라 陀毘羅 591
다생 多生 83
다아갈 多阿竭 83
다아마라발타라 多阿摩羅跋陀羅 83
다어비니 多語毘尼 583
다자타 茶闍他 82
다자탑 多子塔 293
다재귀 多財鬼 83
다재석 多財釋 462
다족 多足 83
다지니 茶枳尼 82
다체 多體 83
다타 多他 83
다타 多咃 83
다타 多陀 83, 398
다타 多陀 or 多他 398
다타아가도 多他阿伽度 83
다타아가타 多他阿伽馱 83
다타아가타 多陀阿伽陀 83, 399
다타아가타(야) 多他阿伽陀(耶) 83
다탐 多貪 83
다탕 茶湯 82
다하 陀呵 591
단 丹 84
단 但 84
단 單 84
단 團 84
단 壇 84
단 揣 83
단 斷 84, 200, 363, 464, 605, 608
단 旦 84
단 檀 83
단 段 84
단 煅 84
단 端 84
단 袒 616
단가 檀家 83
단견 斷見 85, 477, 582, 601
단결 斷結 84
단공 但空 84, 477
단공 單空 612
단과료 旦過寮 84
단과승 旦過僧 84
단규 檀圭 83
단나 單拏 84
단나 壇那 478
단나 檀拏 73, 83, 85, 496
단나 檀那 84, 85, 198, 341
단나발지 檀那鉢底 84
단나파 檀那波 284
단니비 檀尼毘 365
단다 但茶 83
단다 檀茶 496
단다 檀陀 83
단다가아란야 檀陁迦阿蘭若 84
단덕 斷德 84, 269, 479
단도 但茶 84
단도 斷屠 84
단도 斷道 85
단도 檀度 83
단두죄 斷頭罪 85
단림 檀林 83
단마 單痲 84
단말마 斷末摩 84
단망 旦望 84
단멸 斷滅 84
단바라밀 檀波羅蜜 83
단발 煅髮 84
단배 團拜 84
단번뇌습 斷煩惱習 176
단변견 斷邊見 481
단복 斷伏 84
단사 檀捨 83
단삼의 單三衣 287
단상 斷常 84
단선근 斷善根 84
단선근자 斷善根者 507
단선천제 斷善闡提 84
단시 檀施 83
단식 團食 83, 84
단식 揣食 83
단식 摶食 252
단식 斷食 85
단식 段食 252
단신 檀信 83

단심정의 端心正意 84
단악 斷惡 84
단엄 端嚴 84
단월 檀越 84
단위 單位 84
단육 斷肉 84
단의 褍衣 84
단이 檀耳 84
단장 斷障 587
단전 丹田 84
단전 單傳 193
단전 單前 84
단정 端正 84
단제 單提 416
단제대장 檀帝大將 246
단좌 端坐 84
단중 檀中 83
단청 丹靑 85
단친 檀嚫 83, 86
단칠 斷七 84
단타 但他 398
단타 團墮 210
단타 檀陀 83
단타아란야가 檀陀阿蘭若迦 376
단특 檀特 83
단혹 斷惑 84
단혹문 斷惑門 360
단화 斷和 84
달 呾 85
달 怛 85
달 達 85, 141
달 闥 85
달가 達架 86
달나 怛那 85
달니야타 呾你也他 or 呾儞也他 85
달다 怛茶 85
달다 達多 85
달달아갈 怛闥阿竭 83, 85
달도 達兜 534
달라 呾囉 82
달라건 呾喇健 85
달라마세 怛囉麼洗 85
달라미다 達羅弭茶 591
달라비다 達羅毘茶 85
달라비다 達羅毘荼 591
달라사 呾羅斯 85
달라야야 怛羅夜耶 85
달뢰라마 達賴喇嘛 85
달리사야 達梨舍耶 85
달리슬치 達利瑟致 85
달리야달라사 怛利耶怛喇舍 or 怛利耶怛喇奢 85
달리야달리사 怛利耶怛利奢 284
달리야달리사 怛唎耶怛唎奢 107
달리야등릉사 怛利夜登陵奢 284
달리지벌리가 怛哩支伐離迦 85
달리천 怛利天 284
달마 怛麼 85
달마 達摩 86, 183
six patriarchs 466
달마 達磨 86, 87, 183, 587
北宗 208
달마 達麼 86
달마구제 達摩瞿諦 86
달마기 達磨忌 86
달마다도 達磨馱都 86
달마류지 達磨流支 196
달마률저 呾摩栗底 83
달마률지 呾摩栗底 85
달마아란야가 達磨阿蘭若迦 376
달마종 達磨宗 86
달마타도 達磨馱都 183
달모 達謨 183
달밀 呾蜜 85
달바 達婆 86
달바 闥婆 85
달박 怛縛 85
달발나 怛鉢那 85
달삭가 怛索迦 85
달살아갈 怛薩阿竭 83, 85
달수 達水 86
달수 達須 86
달수 達首 86
달이마야 達而麻耶 86
달지 達池 86
달차시라 呾叉始羅 85
달찰나 呾剎那 85
달찰나 怛剎那 85
달친 噠嚫 86
달친 達瞡 or 達親 86
달친 達嚫 105
달친(나) 達嚫(拏) 86
달타 怛他 85, 398
달타갈다 怛陀竭多 85
달타게다 怛他揭多 85, 399
달타벽다 怛他蘖多 85
달타얼다 怛他蘖多 83
달타얼다모예저다 怛他蘖多母隸底多 399
달타의다 怛佗議多 85
담 噉 86
담 儋 87
담 擔 86
담 曇 86
담 湛 86
담 潭 86
담 談 87
담 譚 86
담공설유 談空說有 87
담난 曇鸞 427
담란 曇鸞 587
담림 談林 87
담마 曇摩 86, 183
담마 曇磨 86
담마 曇麼 72
담마국다 曇磨鞠多 86
담마률저 耽摩栗底 83
담마률지 耽摩栗底 85
담목(수) 擔木(樹) 583
담무 曇無 86, 183
담무덕 曇無德 86, 482
담무덕부 曇無德部 86
담무제 曇無諦 388
담바 譚婆 86
담박 憺怕 87
담발경 曇鉢經 184
담보라 擔步羅 86, 525
담월 噉月 86
담은 曇隱 258
담은 潭恩 86
담의 談義 87
담의 談議 87
담화 曇花 86
답 沓 87
답 答 87
답 荅 87
답 踏 87
답리마 答哩磨 87
답마 答摩 87
답말소벌나 答秣蘇伐那 87
답말소벌나 荅秣蘇伐那 87
답상 踏床 87
답섭포밀복라첩슬타제 荅攝蒲密卜羅牒瑟吒諦 87
답파 沓婆 87
답파마라 沓婆摩羅 87

답향 答香 87
당 唐 87
당 堂 87
당 幢 87
당 當 87
당경 唐經 640
당기 當機 87
당기중 當機衆 87, 259
당달 堂達 87, 585
당두 堂頭 87
당래 當來 87, 159, 628
당번 幢幡 87
당분 當分 87
당사 堂司 87
당삼장 唐三藏 87
당상 堂上 87
당상 幢相 87
당승 唐僧 87
당양 當陽 87, 434
당연 唐捐 87
당위즉묘 當位卽妙 87
당유 當有 280, 286, 454
당주 堂主 87
당체 當體 87
당체즉공 當體卽空 87
당탑 堂塔 87
당화엄경 唐華嚴經 361
대 代 88
대 大 88, 281, 415, 583
대 對 88
대 帶 87
대 待 88
대 戴 88
대 臺 88
대가다연나 大迦多衍那 88
대가섭 大迦葉 88
대각 大覺 88
대각금선 大覺金仙 88
대각모 大覺母 88
대각세존 大覺世尊 88
대각유정 大覺有情 197
대갈랍파 大羯臘婆 9
대갈인 大羯印 411
대감(선사) 大鑑(禪師) 88
대강 大綱 88
대거 大車 88
대겁 大劫 18, 89
대겁보녕 大劫寶寧 89
대게지 大揭底 19
대견고바라문 大堅固婆羅門 92
대경 大經 89, 92
대경권 大經卷 89
대계 大戒 89
대계 大界 89
대계외상 大界外相 89
대고왕 大高王 89
대고중 對告衆 88
대고해 大苦海 89
대공 大空 89
대공덕천 大功德天 485
대공불가득 大空不可得 648
대공삼매 大空三昧 509
대공작왕 大孔雀王 89
대공작주왕경 大孔雀咒王經 下 308
대관정 大灌頂 89
대광명왕 大光明王 89
대광명왕관음 大光明王觀音 89
대광보조 大光普照 89, 460
대광음천 大光音天 89
대광지삼장 大廣智三藏 89, 378
대교 大教 65, 89, 97, 400, 455
대교경 大教經 90
대교과 大教科 90
대교망 大教網 90
대구치나 大拘絺那 90
대권 大權 58, 90
대권선경 大權善經 90
대권수리보살 大權修利菩薩 90
대규 大叫 554
대규 大呌 90, 106
대규환지옥 大叫喚地獄 90
대근용 大勤勇 90
대근용변각화개부 大勤勇遍覺華開敷
四佛 248
대금강정경 大金剛頂經 90
대기 大機 90
대기 對機 88
대길대명보살 大吉大明菩薩 90
대길상금강 大吉祥金剛 90
대길상명보살 大吉祥明菩薩 90
대길상변보살 大吉祥變菩薩 90
대길상천 大吉祥天 90, 586
대나 大拏 90
대념 大念 322
대논사 大論師 91
대단 大壇 90
대당내전록 大唐內典錄 90
대당서역기 大唐西域記 90, 305, 630
대대 待對 88
대덕 大德 90, 162
대도사 大導師 90
대도사 大度師 90
대도수 帶刀睡 87
대도심 大道心 90
대도심중생 大道心衆生 197
대도와 帶刀臥 87
대둔사 大芚寺 91
대력 大力 248, 360
대력금강 大力金剛 91
대력왕 大力王 91
대련화 大蓮華 91
대련화법장계 大蓮華法藏界 91
대련화지혜삼마지지 大蓮華智慧三摩地智 91
대로변생 大路邊生 91
대론 大論 91
대룡권현 大龍權現 91
대루탄경 大樓炭經 91
대륜 大輪 603
대륜금강 大輪金剛 91
대륜명왕 大輪明王 91
대림사 大林寺 91
대림정사 大林精舍 91
대만 大慢 604
대만 大滿 91
대만(다라) 大曼(荼羅) 91
대만원의 大滿願義 91
대멸도 大滅度 92
대멸제금강지 大滅諦金剛智 91
대명 大命 91
대명백신보살 大明白身菩薩 91
대명삼장성교목록 大明三藏聖教目錄 91
대명속입장제집 大明續入藏諸集 91
대명왕 大明王 64, 91, 96
대모달라 大姥達羅 142
대목건련 大目乾連 91, 143
대목건련 大目犍連 143
대몽 大夢 91
대무량수경 大無量壽經 92
대바라문 大婆羅門 92
대바라문경 大婆羅門經 92
대바라밀 大波羅蜜 92

대바할나 大婆喝那 165
대반니원경 大般泥洹經 92, 406
대반니원경론 大般泥洹經論 92
대반니원경소 大般泥洹經疏 92
대반니원경후분 大般泥洹經後分 92
대반야(경) 大般若(經) 92
대반야(바라밀다)경 大般若(波羅蜜多)經 92
대반야경 大般若經 175, 260
대반야경 大般若經 434, 607
대반야공양 大般若供養 92
대반야바라밀다경 大般若波羅蜜多經 168
대반열반 大般涅槃 92
대반열반경 大般涅槃經 92, 405, 406
대반열반경후분 大般涅槃經後分 406
대발라유타 大鉢羅由他 171
대발라참 大跋羅攙 170
대발람 大跋藍 170
대방광 大方廣 92, 93
대방광불 大方廣佛 92
대방광불화엄경 大方廣佛華嚴經 92, 640
六部大乘經 462
대방광여래비밀장경 大方廣如來秘密藏經 92
대방등 大方等 92, 93
대방등다라니경 大方等陀羅尼經 173
대방등대집경 大方等大集經 93, 104
대방등대집현호경 大方等大集賢護經 93
대방등여래장경 大方等如來藏經 92
대방등정왕설경 大方等頂王說經 93
대방편 大方便 93
대백광신 大白光神 93, 450
대백단화 大白團華 93
대백산개불모 大白傘蓋佛母 93
대백우거 大白牛車 93
대백의 大白衣 93
대백화 大白華 93
대번뇌지법 大煩惱地法 93, 481
대범 大梵 93, 276
대범심원 大梵深遠 460
대범여의천 大梵如意天 93
대범천 大梵天 93, 182, 250, 301, 370
대범천왕 大梵天王 93, 485
대법 大法 94
대법 對法 88, 380
대법고 大法鼓 94
대법고경 大法鼓經 94
대법라 大法螺 94
대법만 大法慢 94
대법왕 大法王 94
대법우 大法雨 94
대법장 對法藏 88
대법종 對法宗 88
대변(재)공덕천 大辯(才)功德天 94
대변재천 大辯才天 192, 485
대변재천(녀) 大辯才天(女) 94
대변재천녀 大辯才天女 158
대변천 大辯天 94
대보 大寶 94
대보령사대장경목록 大普寧寺大藏經目錄 446
대보리(심) 大菩提(心) 94
대보리당 大菩提幢 94
대보마니 大寶摩尼 94
대보방 大寶坊 94, 197
대보법왕 大寶法王 94
대보살 大菩薩 94
대보장 大寶藏 94
대보적경 大寶積經 47, 94, 199
대보해 大寶海 94
대보화 大寶華 94
대보화왕 大寶華王 94
대보화왕좌 大寶華王座 94
대본 大本 89, 94
대불가기자부 大不可棄子部 94
대불선지법 大不善地法 94
대불정 大佛頂 95, 328
대불정경 大佛頂經 95
대비 大悲 95, 104, 176, 214, 460, 510
대비(태장)만다라 大悲(胎藏)曼荼羅 95
대비개주문 大悲鎧冑門 95
대비경 大悲經 95
대비관(세)음 大悲觀(世)音 95
대비구 大比丘 95
대비궁 大悲弓 95
대비단 大悲壇 95
대비대수고 大悲代受苦 95
대비로사나금강정경 大毘盧舍那金剛頂經 161
대비로자나 大毘盧遮那 95
대비바사론 大毗婆沙論 222
대비보살 大悲菩薩 95
대비보현 大悲普現 95
대비삼매 大悲三昧 95
대비생심삼매야 大悲生心三昧耶 95
대비자 大悲者 95
대비주 大悲呪 95
대비천수(지)옥 大悲千手(地)獄 95
대비천제 大悲闡提 95, 292, 507
대비태장 大悲胎藏 95
대비태장삼매 大悲胎藏三昧 95
대빈바라 大頻婆羅 232
대사 大士 95
대사 大寺 95
대사 大師 95
대사(인연) 大事(因緣) 95
대사문 大沙門 95
대사문통 大沙門統 95
대사저인 大死底人 95
대사첨 大士籖 95
대산야 大珊若 262
대살차니건자 大薩遮尼犍子 95
대삼말다 大三末多 96, 306
대상 大相 96
대상간 大相看 96
대상국사 大相國寺 96
대상기 大祥忌 96
대상장 大象藏 96
대생주 大生主 96
대선 大仙 96, 308
대선 大船 96
대선계 大仙戒 96
대선대리 大善大利 96
대선리 大善利 96
대선사 大船師 96
대선중 大仙衆 486
대선지법 大善地法 96
대선지식 大善知識 96
대섭수 大攝受 96
대성 大成 96
대성 大聖 96

대성금강야차 大聖金剛夜叉 96
대성만수실리 大聖曼殊室利 96
대성묘길상 大聖妙吉祥 96
대성문수 大聖文殊 96
대성세존 大聖世尊 96
대성주 大聖主 96
대성천 大聖天 96
대성환희천 大聖歡喜天 96, 643
대세(지보살) 大勢(至菩薩) 96
대세불 大勢佛 96
대세지 大勢至 115, 131, 267, 318, 484, 493, 603
대소 大召 96
대소 大笑 603
대소(명왕) 大笑(明王) 97
대소이승 大小二乘 97
대소자 大燒炙 554
대소자옥 大燒炙獄 97
대솔파인 大率婆印 411
대수 大樹 97, 293
대수 對首 88
대수긴나라 大樹緊那羅 97
대수긴나라왕소문경 大樹緊那羅王所問經 97
대수석 帶數釋 462
대수선 大樹仙 10
대수선인 大樹仙人 97
대수화(재) 大水火(災) 97
대승 大乘 97, 98, 132, 281, 286, 299, 339, 422, 504
대승 大僧 97
대승경 大乘經 98
대승계 大乘戒 98
대승계경 大乘戒經 98
대승교 大乘敎 98
대승교구부 大乘敎九部 98
대승금강 大勝金剛 98, 103
대승기 大乘基 98
대승기신론 大乘起信論 98, 127
대승기신론소 大乘起信論疏 98
대승능가경유식론 大乘楞伽經唯識論 98
대승대집지장십륜경 大乘大集地藏十輪經 556
대승론 大乘論 98, 123, 380
대승률종 大乘律宗 367
대승묘경 大乘妙經 98
대승무상법 大乘無上法 98
대승무작대계 大乘無作大戒 98
대승무작원돈계 大乘無作圓頓戒 98
대승밀엄경 大乘密嚴經 六部大乘經 462
대승방등경전 大乘方等經典 98
대승법사 大乘法師 98
대승법상교 大乘法相敎 98, 187, 412
대승보살십지 大乘菩薩十地 369
대승사과 大乘四果 98
대승선근계 大乘善根界 99
대승순계 大乘純界 99
대승시 大乘始 448
대승시교 大乘始敎 412
대승심 大乘心 99
대승심 大勝心 369
대승오온론 大乘五蘊論 424
대승원돈계 大乘圓頓戒 573
대승유식론 大乘唯識論 98
대승율종 大乘律宗 367
대승의장 大乘義章 273
대승이종성불 大乘二種成佛 99
대승인 大乘因 99
대승입릉가경 大乘入楞伽經 79
대승장엄경론 大乘莊嚴經論 99, 417
대승장엄론 大乘莊嚴論 466
대승정 大僧正 97, 105
대승정왕경 大乘頂王經 99
대승종 大乘宗 99
대승종 大乘終 448
대승종교 大乘終敎 412
대승천 大乘天 99
대승통 大僧統 97
대승파상교 大乘破相敎 98
대시 大時 106
대시보살 大施菩薩 99
대시절 大時節 17
대시태자 大施太子 99
대시회 大施會 99
대신 大神 335
대신 大身 99
대신(심) 大信(心) 99
대신력 大神力 99
대신불 大身佛 157
대신심해 大信心海 99
대신왕 大神王 99
대신주 大神呪 99
대심력 大心力 99
대심해 大心海 99
대아 大我 99
대아미타경 大阿彌陀經 435, 531
대아유다 大阿由多 383
대아촉비 大阿閦鞞 385
대악상 大惡象 99
대안달라 大安達羅 100
대안달라 大案達羅 388
대안반수의경 大安般守意經 389
대안위 大安慰 100
대애 大愛 100
대애도 大愛道 96, 100
대야 大夜 100
대양 對揚 88
대어 大魚 100
대역룡 大域龍 100
대연 大衍 258
대열 大熱 554, 603
대열반경 大涅槃經 431
대염(불) 大念(佛) 100
대염법 大染法 100
대염열 大炎熱 97, 100, 554
대오 탄문 大悟坦文 190
대올층가 大嗢蹭伽 435
대왕 大王 100
대요금강(살타) 大樂金剛(薩埵) 100
대요불공 大樂不空 100
대요설 大樂說 100
대용 大勇 100
대용맹보살 大勇猛菩薩 100
대우 大愚 100
대우거 大牛車 100
대우음 大牛音 100
대운광명사 大雲光明寺 100
대웅 大雄 100
대웅(보)전 大雄(寶)殿 100
대웅봉 大雄峯 100
대원 大院 595
대원 大願 101
대원각 大圓覺 101
대원경지 大圓鏡智 259, 416, 430
대원경지 大圓鏡知 101
대원경지관 大圓鏡知觀 101
대원력 大願力 414
대원선 大願船 101
대원수명왕 大元帥明王 101
대원업력 大願業力 101
대원적입 大圓寂入 92

대원청정보토 大願淸淨報土 101
대위덕 大威德 101, 603
대위덕 大威悳 466
대위덕명왕 大威德明王 101
대위덕왕 大威德王 485
대위덕자 大威德者 101
대위덕존 大威德尊 101
대은교주 大恩敎主 101
대음계입 大陰界入 101
대음광 大飮光 101
대응공 大應供 101
대의 大意 101
대의 大衣 101, 338
대의성 大義城 101
대의왕 大義王 101
대의왕 大醫王 101
대의왕불 大醫王佛 394
대인다라 大因陀羅 639
대인다라단 大因陀羅壇 101
대인다라좌 大因陀羅座 101
대인달라 大印達羅 494
대인법계 大忍法界 101
대인상인 大人相印 101
대인팔념 大人八念 603
대일 大日 62, 63, 95, 101, 214, 272, 357, 361, 415, 430, 431, 499, 544, 560, 595, 603, 609
대일각왕 大日覺王 101, 102
대일경 大日經 44, 50, 76, 88, 89, 99, 102, 161, 278, 294, 359, 368, 376, 477
四佛 248
대일경구연품 大日經具緣品 239
대일경부사의소 大日經不思議疏 102
대일경소 大日經疏 102, 275, 357, 362, 363, 366, 567
대일경십심품 大日經十心品 368
대일경의궤 大日經義軌 102
대일경의석 大日經義釋 102
대일경의소 大日經義疏 102
대일경주심품 大日經住心品 464
대일공 大日供 102
대일대성부동명왕 大日大聖不動明王 102
대일여래 大日如來 101, 225, 227
대일여석가동일불 大日與釋迦同一佛 102
대입멸식 大入滅息 92
대자 大姉 102
대자 大慈 102, 460
대자기 大慈起 102
대자대비 大慈大悲 102
대자생보살 大慈生菩薩 102
대자은 大慈恩 40
대자은사 大慈恩寺 102
대자은사삼장 大慈恩寺三藏 102
대자재 大自在 102, 570
대자재궁 大自在宮 103
대자재왕 大自在王 485
대자재천 大自在天 102, 133, 301, 320, 517
대자재천부 大自在天婦 102
대자존 大慈尊 102
대장 大將 363
대장(경) 大藏(經) 103
대장경 大藏經 508
대장목록 大藏目錄 103
대장법수 大藏法數 428
대장엄 大莊嚴 103, 253
대장엄경 大莊嚴經 103
대장엄경론 大莊嚴經論 103
대장엄논경 大莊嚴論經 103
대장엄론 大莊嚴論 370
대장엄세계 大莊嚴世界 103
대장음의 大藏音義 632
대장일람 大藏一覽 103
대재(회) 大齋(會) 103
대재해탈복 大哉解脫服 103
대적멸 大寂滅 103
대적법왕 大寂法王 103
대적실삼매 大寂室三昧 103
대적정 大寂定 103
대적정삼마지 大寂靜三摩地 103
대적화 大赤華 103
대전 大顚 103
대전륜불정 大轉輪佛頂 103
대전륜왕 大轉輪王 98, 103
대정지비 大定智悲 103
대정진 大精進 363
대정진보살 大精進菩薩 103
대제자 大弟子 103
대족왕 大族王 103
대종 代宗 100, 173
대종 大種 103
대종 大鍾 103
대좌 臺座 88
대주 大洲 49, 103
대주간정중경목록 大周刊定衆經目錄 103
대준제 大准提 104
대중 大衆 104, 105, 299, 482
대중부 大衆部 57, 104, 132, 299, 324, 325, 339, 641
대중위덕외 大衆威德畏 104
대중인 大衆印 104
대지 大地 91, 104
대지 大智 104
대지(법) 大地(法) 104
대지관정지 大智灌頂地 104
대지도론 大智度論 91, 104, 243, 552
대지법 大地法 96
대지분신 大志焚身 104
대지사륜 大地四輪 243
대지인 大智印 259
대지장 大智藏 104
대지치바 大地致婆 556
대지혜문 大智慧門 104
대진 大秦 136, 558
대진국 大秦國 86
대진사 大秦寺 104
대집 大集 98, 417
대집 大集 sūtra 94
대집(경)현호 大集(經)賢護 104
대집경 大集經 104, 197, 365, 601
대집부 大集部 104
대집비유왕경 大集譬喩王經 104
대집수미장경 大集須彌藏經 104
대집월장경 大集月藏經 104, 424
대집일장경 大集日藏經 104
대집회정법경 大集會正法經 104
대척경 大隻經 103
대천 大千 501
대천 大天 104, 299, 306, 324
대천(세계) 大千(世界) 105
대천계 大千界 250
대천세계 大千世界 293, 343
대철위(산) 大鐵圍(山) 105
대청주 大靑珠 105
대초 大草 293
대촉례 對觸禮 88
대총상법문 大總相法門 105
대치 對治 88
대치성광 大熾盛光 105
대치실단 對治悉檀 252
대친 大嚫 86, 105

대탑 戴塔 88
대탑길상 戴搭吉祥 88
대탑덕보살 帶塔德菩薩 87
대탑존 帶塔尊 87
대통 大統 105
대통(지승) 大通(智勝) 105
대통결연 大通結緣 22
대통지 大通智 293
대통지승 大通智勝 385, 496
대통지승불 大通智勝佛 22
대통화상 大通和尙 105
대품(경) 大品(經) 105
대품반야 大品般若 417, 422
대품반야경 大品般若經 463
대품반야경 大品般若經 1 467
대품반야경 大品般若經 105
대풍재 大風災 105
대하 大夏 451
대한림 大寒林 105
대해 大海 105, 601
대해십상 大海十相 105
대해인 大海印 105
대해중 大海衆 105
대해팔부사의 大海八不思議 105
대향 代香 88
대현 大賢 105
대혜 大慧 104, 106, 127
대혜 종고 大慧宗杲 106
대혜도인 大慧刀印 106
대혜무고 大慧武庫 106
대혜서 大慧書 106
대혜선사 大慧禪師 511
대혜어록 大慧語錄 106
대호 大呼 90, 106, 554
대호규 大號叫 554, 603
대호규 大號叫 90, 106
대호인 大護印 106
대홍련 大紅蓮 106
대화 大化 106
대화갈라 大和竭羅 106, 402
대화상 大和尙 95, 106
대화소인시유가근 大火燒人是猶可近 400
대환사 大幻師 106
대회 大會 106
대회중 大會衆 106
대휴사저 大休死底 106
대휴헐저 大休歇底 95, 106
대흑 大黑 131
대흑비력법 大黑飛礫法 107
대흑신 大黑神 106
대흑천 大黑天 106
대흥선사 大興善寺 107
덕 德 107, 479
덕(차)시라 德(叉)尸羅 107
덕모 德母 107
덕병 德瓶 107
덕본 德本 107
덕사 德士 107
덕산 德山 619
덕상병 德祥瓶 533
덕안 德安 555, 572
덕자 德字 107
덕전 德田 107
덕진 德進 46
덕차가 德叉迦 107, 166
덕풍 德風 107
덕해 德海 107
덕행 德行 107
덕향 德香 107
덕현 德賢 46
도 倒 108
도 到 107
도 圖 107
도 塗 109, 270
도 導 108
도 屠 108
도 度 108, 141, 163, 425, 571, 607
도 徒 108
도 忉 107
도 掉 109
도 淘 108
도 盜 108
도 稻 107
도 覩 108
도 謟 323
도 蹈 109
도 逃 108
도 途 107
도 道 108, 135, 267, 427, 587, 603
도 都 107
도 陶 108
도(거) 掉(擧) 109
도가륜 陶家輪 108
도가지 度伽地 284
도간 稻稈 107
도감 都監 109
도감사 都監寺 107
도검 道檢 109
도견 倒見 108
도고 屠沽 108
도과 度科 108
도과 道果 109
도관 道觀 109
도광 道光 109
도교 道交 109
도교 道敎 109
도구 道具 109
도구 道舊 109
도금 道禁 109
도기 道器 109
도기 道氣 109
도덕 道德 109
도도 刀塗 270
도도 刀途 109
도독고 塗毒鼓 109
도두 到頭 107
도등 道等
四等, four virtues 242
도라 堵羅 114
도락 道樂 109
도락차 度洛叉 108
도량 道場 72, 109, 185, 518
도량수 道場樹 109
도량신 道場神 109
도력 道力 109
도로(낙)단나 途盧(諾)檀那 107
도류 道流 109
도류지 道類智 110, 608
도륜 道倫 110
도리 倒離 108
도리 忉利 242, 496
도리 道理 110, 290
도리천 忉利天 107, 284, 438, 468, 571
도리타 闍利馱 284
도무극 度無極 108, 163
도문 道門 110
도반 道伴 110
도범 倒凡 108
도법 道法 110
도법인 道法忍 608
도법지 道法智 110, 608
도사 導師 108, 585
도사 道士 110

도사(다) 都史(多) 107
도사(천) 都史(天) 107
도사다천 覩史多天 108
도산 刀山 110
도산 掉散 109
도생 度生 108, 270
도생 道生 303, 406, 525
四聖 251
도선 逃禪 108
도선 道宣 74, 110, 305, 469
도세 度世 108
도속 道俗 110
도솔(치) 兜率(哆) 114
도솔(타) 兜率(陀) 114
도솔천 兜率天 438, 468
도솔천 都率天 107
도솔천자 兜率天子 114, 252
도수 道樹 110, 218, 446
도수 道水 110
도수 道邃 551, 571
十祖 572
도술 道術 110
도승 度僧 108
도시왕 都市王 107
도식 道識 110
도신 道信 110, 312, 587
six patriarchs 466
도심 道心 110
도아 倒我 108
도아 道芽 110
도안 道安 389
도안 道眼 110
도업 道業 110
도오 道悟 574
도옥초 度沃焦 108
도요 道要 110
도원 道元 110
도위 道位 110
도융 道融 303
四聖 251
도의 道意 110
도인 導引 108
도인 道人 110
도인로 刀刃路 17
도일체세간고뇌 度一切世間苦腦 108
도자 度者 108
도자 道子 278
도자 道者 110
도작 道綽 77, 305, 427, 587
도적 盜賊 108
도전의 稻田衣 335
도제 徒弟 108
도제 道諦 110, 490
四諦 257
도족유 塗足油 109
도종성 道種性 111, 429
도종지 道種智 111, 292
도중 徒衆 108
도중 道衆 111
도지 道智 111
도차 道次 111
도첩 度牒 28, 111
도체 道體 111
도총 都總 107
도칠보화 蹈七寶華 109
도타가 都吒迦 107
도탈 度脫 108
도태 淘汰 108
도통 道統 111
도통 道通 429
도품 道品 111, 196
도풍 刀風 111
도풍 道風 111
도피안 到彼岸 107, 163
도할 塗割 109
도합 倒合 108
도행 道行 111
도향 塗香 109
도현 倒懸 108
도호 道號 111
도화 導化 108
도화 道化 111
도화라 覩貨羅 108
도화라 都貨羅 107, 451
도회 掉悔 109
도회외도 塗灰外道 109
도희 道希 196, 350
독 毒 111
독 犢 112
독 獨 111
독 禿 111
독 篤 112
天竺 571
독 讀 112
독가다 獨柯多 111
독각 獨覺 111, 191, 403, 494, 617
독각선인 獨角仙人 111, 499
독거 獨居 111
독거사 禿居士 111
독경 讀經 9, 112
독고 毒鼓 111
독고 獨股 62
독고(저) 獨鈷(杵) 111
독고락가 獨孤洛加 111
독고저 獨股杵 111
독공 獨空 111
독기 毒器 111
독기 毒氣 111
독노 禿奴 111
독두무명 獨頭無明 111, 214
독룡 毒龍 111
독법 獨法 585
독사 毒蛇 111, 236
독사 讀師 112, 585
독생 獨生 617
독생독사독거독래 獨生獨死獨去獨來 111
독서파 讀書派 112
독송 讀誦 112
독수 毒樹 111
독약 毒藥 111
독영경 獨影境 111
독원 獨園 111
독인 禿人 111
독일법계 獨一法界 111
독자 犢子 112, 165, 170, 300
독자부 犢子部 112, 179, 216, 325, 380, 463
독전 毒箭 111
독존 獨尊 111
독진 篤進 112
독천이고 毒天二鼓 111
돈 敦 112
돈 頓 112, 145, 267, 290, 422, 448, 487, 640
돈각 頓覺 112
돈경 頓經 112
돈교 頓敎 75, 112, 412, 477, 525, 531, 602
천태삼교 573
돈기 頓機 112
돈단 頓斷 112, 525
돈대 頓大 112
돈돈돈원 頓頓頓圓 479
돈돈원 頓頓圓 112
돈법 頓法 112

돈사 頓寫 112, 506
돈성제행 頓成諸行 112
돈오 頓悟 112
돈오보살 頓悟菩薩 112
돈오점수 頓悟漸修 112
돈원 頓圓 112, 487
돈점 頓漸 112
돈지 頓旨 112
돈황 敦煌 or 燉煌 112
돌 突 112, 177
돌가 突迦 112
돌길라 突吉羅 14, 70, 112, 399, 478
돌로나 突路拏 112
돌로슬검 咄嚕瑟劍 112
돌바 突婆 112
돌슬궤리다 突瑟几理多 112
돌슬길률다 突膝吉栗多 112
돌실길률다 突悉吉栗多 112
동 冬 113
동 動 113
동 同 113
동 東 113
동 洞 113
동 童 113
동 銅 113
동가 洞家 113
동거지국토 同居之國土 222
동교일승 同敎一乘 193
동국임제종 東國臨濟宗 198
동귀교 同歸敎 422
동농마 童籠磨 113
동라 銅鑼 113
동류 同類 113
동류인 同類因 465, 488
동만다라 東曼陀羅 113
동명 同名 277, 394
동명천 同名天 113, 492
동밀 東密 113
동방 東方 113
동부동법 動不動法 113
동분 同分 113
동비제하 東毘提訶 四洲 258
동사 同事 113, 251
동사 東司 113, 581
동산 東山 113
동산 洞山 113, 536
동산부 東山部 113
동산사 東山寺 113
동상 同相 482
동상 洞上 113
동생 同生 277
동생신 同生神 113
동생천 同生天 113, 492
동성경 同性經 471
동세 同世 419
동세오사 同世五師 419
동수 童授 557
동승신주 東勝身洲 113
동안거 冬安居 113
동안국 東安國 9
동암 東庵 113
동야 冬夜 113
동옥 東獄 113
동의석 同依釋 462
동자 童子 49, 113
동재 冬齋 113
동전 銅錢 113
동정 東淨 113, 581
동조 冬朝 113
동좌신 同坐神 394
동지 冬至 113
동진 童眞 113
동진주 童眞住 113, 368
동청이문 同聽異聞 113
동체 同體 113
동체방편 同體方便 174
동체삼보 同體三寶 113
동체삼혹 同體三惑 505
동체자비 同體慈悲 113
동측 東厠 113
동토 東土 113
동품 同品 113
동하 洞下 113
동학 同學 113
동해 東海 213
동행 同行 113
동화사 桐華寺 113
두 兜 114
두 抖 114
두 斗 15, 113, 485
두 杜 114
두 豆 114
두 逗 114
두 頭 114
두가람 豆伽藍 114
두거 豆佉 28, 114
두구 四諦 257
두광 頭光 114
두구 杜口 114
두구라 頭鳩羅 114
두기 逗機 114
두다 杜多 114
두다 杜荼 114
두라 兜羅 114, 365
두라 蠹羅 114
두라면 兜羅綿 114
두라이 兜羅毦 114
두로 杜嚕 114
두로파발타 杜魯婆跋吒 114
두뢰타 頭賴吒 534
두루파 兜樓婆 114
두면작례 頭面作禮 114
두모 斗姥 113, 130
두모로 兜牟盧 114
두부천존 斗父天尊 113
두북면서 頭北面西 114
두사 兜沙 114
두수 抖擻 114
두수 斗藪 114
두수 頭袖 114
두수 頭首 114
두순 杜順 114, 412, 533, 538, 587
두술 兜術 114
두야 兜夜 114
두장 斗帳 113
두저 杜底 114
두타 頭陀 114
두파 兜婆 114, 593
두회 逗會 114
둔 屯 114
둔 遁 115
둔 鈍 115, 415
둔근 鈍根 115, 334, 349, 478
둔기 鈍機 115
둔륜마 屯崙摩 114
둔사 鈍使 115, 361
둔세 遁世 115
득 得 115, 349
득계 得戒 115
득계사미 得戒沙彌 115
득과 得果 115
득구 得求 478
득대세 得大勢 115
득도 得度 115
득도 得道 115

득라로가 得羅盧迦 115
득불지상신 得佛之常身 458
득수 得髓 115
득승 得勝 115
득승 得繩 115
득안림 得眼林 115
득어망전 得魚忘筌 522
득의 得意 115
득입 得入 115
득장 得藏 115
득탈 得脫 115
등 橙 115
등 燈 115
등 登 115
등 等 92, 115, 272, 274
方等 173
등 藤 115
등 騰 115
등각 等覺 115, 116, 366, 368, 423, 429, 457, 462, 477, 608
등각위 等覺位 464, 467
등각종성 等覺種性 429
등각혜 等覺慧 469
등공 等供 115
등공 等空 115
등관 等觀 115
등광 燈光 115
등득 等得 115
등란 騰蘭 115
등려 等侶 116
등로 燈爐 115
등롱 燈籠 115
등류 等流 116
등류과 等流果 116, 411, 476
등류상속 等流相續 116
등류신 等流身 567
등류심 等流心 422
등멸 燈滅 115
등명 燈明 115
등명불 燈明佛 115, 608
등묘 等妙 116
등묘각왕 等妙覺王 116
등무간연 等無間緣 116, 272
등미 等味 116
등봉 登封 321
등사 藤蛇 115
등시 登時 115
등시 等施 275
등신 等身 116
등심 等心 116
등원 等願 116
등인 等引 116
등일대거 等一大車 116
등일체제불 等一切諸佛 116
등자 等慈 116
등정각 等正覺 116
등제 等諦 116
등좌 登座 115
등주 登住 115
등중생계 等衆生界 116
등지 登地 115
등지 等持 116, 272, 273
등지 等智 116
등지 等至 116, 272
등지옥 等地獄 297
등화 燈火 115
등활 等活 116, 554, 603
등활지옥 等活地獄 116

(ㄹ)
라 攞 117
라 剌 117
라 囉 117
라 羅 117, 393
라 蘿 117
라 螺 117, 428
라 邏 117
라갈절 剌竭節 117
라걸주 邏乞酒 117
라걸첨나 攞乞尖拏 117, 296
라곡 羅縠 117
라구 邏求 117
라나 剌那 117
라나가라 剌那伽羅 117
라나시기 剌那尸棄 117
라달나 羅怛那 118
라달낭 羅怛囊 118
라달낭 羅怛曩 118
라도 邏闍 117
라도가 攞都迦 117
라륵가람 羅勒迦藍 376
라마 喇嘛 117
라마 羅摩 117
라문 羅門 117
라바 羅婆 117
라사 剌闍 117
라서 囉逝 117
라슬지 剌瑟胝 117
라아 羅誐 117
라야 囉惹 117
라야 羅惹 117
라야흘리희 囉惹訖哩呬 118
라열 羅閱 117
라열게려혜 羅閱揭黎醯 117
라열기 羅閱耆 117
라열저(가라) 羅閱衹(迦羅) 117
라예 羅預 251
라운 羅云 118
라운 羅雲 118
라월 羅越 118
라제 羅齊 118
라집 118
라집 羅什 43
라집 羅十 118
라차파 羅叉婆 376
라타(나) 羅陀(那) 118
라피나 羅被那 118
라하 羅呵 375
라한 羅漢 118
라호 羅虎 118
라호 羅護 118
라호라 羅怙羅 118
라후 羅睺 53, 118
라후라 羅吼羅 118
라후라 羅睺羅 118
라후라다 羅睺羅多 118, 486
라후아수라 羅睺阿修羅 118
라흘쇄 邏吃灑 117
락 絡 118
락 落 118
락 酪 118, 320
락 樂
四德 241
락자 絡子 389
란 亂 118
란 爛 118
란 蘭 118
랄나시기 剌那尸棄 342
람 嵐 119
람 攬 119
람 濫 119
람 藍 119
람 覽 119
람분니 藍傘尼 119
람비니 嵐毘尼 119, 126
람비니 嵐鞞尼 119
람비니 藍毘尼 119

랍 臈 119
랍 臘 119
랍벌니 臘伐尼 119
랑 狼 119
랑탕 莨菪 344
래 來 119, 605
략교 略教 39
량 良 119
량 量 119
比量 226
려 廬 120
려 濾 120
려 驢 120
려 麗 120
려 黎 120
려갈절 糲竭節 117
려사나 廬舍那 120
려차 黎車 125
력 力 120, 401, 461
육도과보 461
력 歷 120
련 憐 120
련 練 121
련 蓮 120
련 連 121
련사 蓮社 427
렬 烈 121
렵 獵 121
령 鈴 121, 244
령 靈 121
령 寧 121
례 禮 121, 135
례 隷 121
로 勞 122
로 嚕 122, 158
로 嚧 122
로 爐 122
로 盧 121
로 蘆 122
로 路 122
로 露 122
로 魯 122
로가 路伽 122
로가 路迦 122
世論 319
로가기야 路伽祇夜 122
로가나타 路迦那他 122, 320
로가다 路伽多 122
로가비 路迦憊 319
로가비 路迦憊 or 路伽憊 122
로가야(타) 路伽耶(陀) 122
로가야지가 路柯耶胝柯 122
로가야지가 路迦耶底迦 122
로가위사제 盧迦委斯諦 320
로날라 嚕捺羅 122
로날리 勞捺哩 583
로달라 澇達羅 122
로달라 魯達羅 122
로지 盧至 123
로차 盧遮 123
로하 路賀 122
록 鹿 122
록(사) 錄(司) 339
론 論 122, 277
론민니 論民尼 119
롱 礱 123
뢰 瀨 123
뢰 牢 123
뢰 賴 123
뢰 雷 123
뢰야연기 賴耶緣起 403
료 寮 123
료 料 123
료 療 123
룡미니 龍彌你 126
룡미니 龍彌你 119
루 婁 486
루 淚 123
루 漏 123
루 累 123
루 髏 123
루 樓 123
루다(라) 樓陀(羅) 123
루려 樓黎 123
루비 樓毘 123
루비니 樓毘尼 119
루유 樓由 123
루이환라 樓夷亘羅 123
루지 樓至 123
류 柳 383
류 流 124
류 留 124
류 類 124
류나 留拏 168
류미니 流彌你 126
류미니 流彌尼 119, 124
류비니 流毘尼 119, 124
류비니 留毘尼 119
륜 輪 124
률 栗 124
률첩반 栗呫嫳 125
륵 勒 124
륵나마제 勒那摩提 124
륵나바제 勒那婆提 124
륵사 勒沙 124
륵사바 勒沙婆 124
륵사파 勒沙婆 280
릉 駿 124
릉 棱 125
릉 陵 125
리 利 125, 415
리 梨 125
리 理 125, 201, 358, 359, 398, 416, 493, 608
佛性 218
리 里 125
리 離 125
리 魑 125
리 理 605
리계 理界 552
리단 離壇 621
리법신 理法身 481
리시 哩始 307
리야 梨耶 125, 377
리의 離意 400
리차 梨車 125
리차 離車 125
리포외 離怖畏 586
린 隣 126
림 林 126
림 淋 126
림 臨 126
림미니 林微尼 119, 126
림비니 林毘尼 119, 126
립 立 126

(ㅁ)
마 媽 127
마 摩 88, 128, 273
마 瑪 127
마 磨 127, 128, 531
마 馬 127
마 魔 127
마 麻 127
마 麽 127
마(파)순 魔(波)旬 128
마가 摩伽 128

마가다 摩伽陀 128
마가다 摩訶陀 128
마가라 摩伽羅 128
마가라 摩伽羅 or 摩迦羅 128
마가라 摩迦羅 131, 365
마가라대흑 摩迦羅大黑 107
마가타 摩迦吒 128
마갈 摩竭 128
마갈(나) 摩竭(羅) 100
마갈(라) 摩竭(羅) 128
마갈라 摩竭羅 129
마갈마니 馬曷摩尼 143
마갈제 摩竭提 128
마갈타 摩竭陀 128
마거 摩佉 128
마거 摩袪 128
마게 摩揭 128
마게다 摩揭陀 128
마경 魔境 128
마계 魔戒 128
마계 魔界 128
마계 魔繫 130
마곡사 麻谷寺 128
마광 魔光 489
마군 魔軍 128
마기 摩祇 128
마나 摩拏 128
마나라 摩拏羅 128, 486
마나바 摩那婆 128
마나반 摩那槃 129
마나사 摩拏赦 135
마나사 摩那斯 128
마나소바제 摩那蘇婆帝 128
마나타 摩那埵 128
마남구리 摩男拘利 419
마납 摩納 128
마납 磨納 128
마납(바가) 摩納(婆迦) 129
마납박(가) 摩納縛(迦) 129
마납선 摩納仙 129
마녀 魔女 129
마노 瑪瑙 127, 143, 584
마노라 摩奴羅 128
마노말야 摩奴末耶 129
마노사 摩奴史 135
마노사 摩奴娑 or 摩努娑 135
마노사 摩奴沙 129
마노사 摩奴沙 or 摩奴闍 129
마노사 摩奴闍 135
마노쇄 摩奴曬 135
마노시야 摩奴是若 129
마뇌 馬腦 382
마누사 摩雀沙 129, 135
마니 摩尼 129, 136, 142
마니건대룡왕 摩尼犍大龍王 129
마니발타(라) 摩尼跋陀(羅) 129
마다 摩多 129, 514
마다 磨多 128
마다나 摩陀那 136
마다라 摩陀羅 136
마다라가 摩多羅迦 129
마단 魔檀 129
마달 摩怛 129
마달나 摩達那 136
마달리 摩怛里 129
마달리가 摩咀里迦 129
마달리가 摩怛履迦 129
마달리가 摩怛理迦 142
마달리가 摩怛里迦 129
마달리가라마 摩咀理伽羅摩 142
마답반 摩沓婆 129
마덕륵가 摩德勒伽 129
마덕리가 摩德理迦 624
마도 摩度 131
마도 魔道 128, 129
마도라 摩度羅 31, 129, 131
마도라 麽度羅 127
마돌라 摩突羅 32, 131
마두 摩頭 136
마두 磨頭 128
마두 馬頭 127, 603
마두관음 馬頭觀音 127
마두구라 麻豆瞿羅 127
마두나찰 馬頭羅刹 127
마두대사 馬頭大士 127
마두라 摩頭羅 32, 131
마두명왕 馬頭明王 127, 431
마득륵가 摩得勒伽 129
마득륵가론 摩得勒伽論 255
마등 摩騰 129
마등가 摩登伽 or 摩燈伽 129
마등가 摩鄧伽 129
마등가경 摩登伽經 129
마등가아란야 摩登伽阿蘭若 129
마등가주 摩鄧伽咒 129
마등지 摩鄧祇 129
마라 摩羅 129
마라 魔羅 127, 130, 136, 568
마라 麽攞 127, 136
마라 麽羅 127, 130
마라가타 摩羅伽陀 or 摩羅迦陀 129
마라가타 摩羅迦陀 136
마라야 摩羅耶 129, 130, 136
마라야 魔羅耶 130
마라야저수 摩羅耶底數 129
마라야제수 摩羅耶提數 129
마라유 麽羅庾 127
마라정 摩羅廷 129
마라제 摩羅提 129
마랍바 摩臘婆 130
마래반도 馬來半島 136
마로다 摩嚕多 639
마뢰야 摩賴耶 129, 130
마리 摩利 130, 136
마리 摩梨 129
마리 摩離 129
마리가라야 摩利伽羅耶 129, 130
마리실라 摩利室羅 130
마리지 摩利支 113, 574, 582
마리지 摩利支 or 摩梨支 or 摩里支 130
마리지 摩里支 543
마리지천 摩利支天 485
마마 麽麽 127
마마가라 磨磨迦羅 128
마마계 麽麽鷄 127, 137
마막지 摩莫枳 127
마막지 麽莫枳 137
마망 魔網 130
마맥 馬麥 127
마명 馬鳴 5, 98, 127, 382, 587 佛所行讚經 218
마명대사 馬鳴大士 127, 486
마명보살 馬鳴菩薩 127
마명비구 馬鳴比丘 127
마민 魔民 130
마박 魔縛 130
마범 魔梵 130
마사 摩娑 130
마사 摩沙 114, 128
마사 摩蛇 128
마사 磨司 128
마사 馬師 127
마사 馬祀 127
마사 魔事 130
마사(라) 摩娑(羅) 143

마사경 摩事境 355
마사라 摩娑羅 130
마사라 摩沙羅 130, 143
마사타 摩斯吒 128
마선 魔禪 130
마세 麽洗 127
마쇄 磨灑 114, 128
마수라 摩庾囉 130
마승 馬勝 127, 382
마신타 摩哂陀 130
마실리가 摩室里迦 129
마야 摩耶 130, 216
마야 麽也 127
마연 魔緣 130
마오 馬午 365
마왕 魔王 130
마우 磨牛 128
마원 磨院 128
마원 馬苑 127
마원 魔怨 130
마유라 摩由羅 130
마유라 摩裕羅 31, 130
마유라가람 摩愉羅伽藍 130
마음장 馬陰藏 127
마이 摩夷 129, 130
마이 馬耳 382, 583
마이산 馬耳山 127
마인 魔忍 130
마자마녀 魔子魔女 130
마장 魔障 130
마전 磨磚 128
마정 摩頂 131
마정관정 摩頂灌頂 290
마제 摩提 131, 137
마제아란야가 摩祭阿蘭若迦 376
마조 馬祖 12, 74, 127, 312, 621
마주 馬主 258
마지 摩旨 131
마지 摩牴 128
마질리가 摩侄梨迦 129
마질리가 摩咥哩迦 562
마차 麻蹉 127
마천 魔天 131
마투 摩偸 129, 131
마투라 摩偸羅 32, 131
마하 摩河 607
마하 摩訶 88, 131
마하 磨下 128
마하 磨訶 128
마하 麽賀 88
마하가라 摩訶謌羅 106
마하가라 摩訶迦羅 106, 131
마하가라대흑녀 摩訶迦羅大黑女 106
마하가섭 摩訶迦葉 88
마하가섭(파) 摩訶迦葉(波) 131
마하가섭(파) 摩訶迦葉(波) 486
마하가전연 摩訶迦旃延 88, 131
마하교담미 摩訶憍曇彌 131
마하구슬치라 摩訶俱瑟耻羅 131
마하구지라 摩訶俱祉羅 90
마하구치라 摩訶俱絺羅 90
마하구치라 摩訶拘絺羅 131
마하기야물다라 摩訶岐若勿他羅 259
마하나가 摩訶那伽 131
마하나마 摩訶那摩 131
마하나발 摩訶那鉢 96, 131
마하낙가나 摩訶諾伽那 131
마하남 摩訶男 131
마하니라 摩訶尼羅 105
마하니라 摩訶尼羅 or 摩訶泥羅 131
마하단특 摩訶袒特 131
마하라 摩訶羅 131
마하라사 摩訶羅闍 131
마하라야 摩賀羅惹 100
마하라야나 摩訶羅夜那 143
마하랄타 摩訶剌佗 131
마하로슬나 摩訶盧瑟拏 131
마하마야 摩訶摩耶 131
마하마지 摩訶摩底 106, 127
마하만다라화 摩訶曼陀羅華 132
마하만수사화 摩訶曼殊沙華 132
마하만주사 摩訶曼珠沙 103
마하목건련 摩訶目犍連 91, 143
마하목건련 摩訶目犍連 132
마하목지린타 摩訶目脂隣陀 132
마하목진린타 摩訶目眞隣陀 132
마하문진린다 摩訶文眞隣陀 143
마하바라 摩訶婆羅 132
마하반야 摩訶般若 132
마하반야 摩訶般若 168
마하반야바라밀 摩訶般若波羅蜜 132
마하반야바라밀경 摩訶般若波羅蜜經 105
마하반열반나 摩訶般涅槃那 132
마하발랄사발저 摩訶鉢刺闍鉢底 133
마하발특마 摩訶鉢特摩 132, 554
마하벌나가람마 摩訶伐那伽藍摩 91
마하보리사 摩訶菩提寺 132
마하보리질제살타 摩訶菩提質帝薩埵 132
마하부인 摩訶夫人 132
마하비로자나 摩訶毘盧遮那 101, 132
마하비하라 摩訶毘訶羅 132
마하비하라주부 摩訶毘訶羅住部 132
마하사라 摩訶娑羅 132
마하살(타) 摩訶薩(埵) 132
마하살타 摩訶薩埵 128
마하살타왕자 摩訶薩埵王子 132
마하삼모날라사아나 摩訶三母捺羅娑誐羅 105
마하승기부 摩訶僧祇部 104, 132
마하승기율 摩訶僧祇律 132
마하실리 摩訶室利 70
마하야나 摩訶夜那 132
마하야나제바 摩訶耶那提婆 132
마하야나제파 摩訶耶那提婆 630
마하야니 摩訶夜泥 132
마하연 摩訶衍 97, 402
마하연(나) 摩訶衍(那) 132
마하인다라 摩訶因陀羅 132, 133
마하제바 摩訶提婆 104, 132
마하제비 摩訶第脾 132
마하지관 摩訶止觀 247, 448
마하지관론 摩訶止觀論 551
마하지나 摩訶至那
China 548
마하질제살타 摩訶質帝薩埵 132
마하찰두 摩訶刹頭 132
마하파사파제 摩訶波闍婆提 96
마하파사파제 摩訶波闍波提 100, 133
마할마제 馬曷麻諦 127
마합살독하 媽哈薩督呀 127
마향 魔鄕 133
마혜 摩醯 128, 131
마혜 磨醯 128
마혜 魔醯 133
마혜경벌라 摩醯徑伐羅 133
마혜라구라 摩醯羅矩羅 103

ㄱ ㄴ ㄷ ㄹ ㅁ ㅂ ㅅ ㅇ ㅈ ㅊ ㅋ ㅌ ㅍ ㅎ 찾아보기

마혜라구라 魔醯邏矩羅 133
마혜사바가부 摩醯奢婆迦部 509
마혜사사가 摩醯奢娑迦 133
마혜사사가부 磨醯奢娑迦部 641
마혜수라 摩醯首羅 485, 508, 570
마혜수라 魔醯首羅 133
마혜수습벌라 摩醯首濕伐羅 102
마혜습라보라 魔醯濕羅補羅 133
마혜인다라 摩醯因陀羅 133
마혜인다라 魔醯因陀羅 133
마호라 摩虎羅 365
마호라아 摩護囉誐 133
마호락가 摩呼洛迦 133
마후 摩睺 143
마후라 摩睺羅 133
마후라가 摩睺羅伽 133
마후라가 摩睺羅迦 568, 606
마후륵 摩睺勒 133
마휴륵 摩休勒 133
막 膜 133
막 莫 133
막가 莫伽 133
막갈락가 莫喝洛迦 131
막기 莫耆 128
막배 膜拜 133
막하 莫訶 131, 133
막하락가 莫訶洛迦 131
막하승기니가야 莫訶僧祇尼迦耶 133
막하연적 莫訶衍磧 133
막하정 莫賀廷 133
막하파가 莫訶婆伽 133
막혜 莫醯 133
막호락가(마) 莫呼洛迦(摩) 133
만 svastika 134
만 万 134
만 卍 134
만 慢 134, 355, 410, 414, 419, 582, 583, 585
만 晚 135
만 曼 133, 323
만 滿 134, 209
만 漫 134
만 萬 134
만 鬘 133
만감 慢感 134
만갱 慢坑 134
만거 慢擧 134
만견 慢見 134
만견자 滿見子 134
만결 慢結 134
만경 慢境 355
만경 萬境 134
만공 曼供 133
만공 월면 滿空月面 135
만과 滿果 134
만과견 慢過見 134
만기 滿期 67
만나라 曼拏羅 133
만니 滿泥 134
만다 滿茶 134
만다가 漫茶迦 134
만다라 曼茶羅 133
만다라 曼陀羅 93, 133
만다라 滿茶羅 134
만다라 滿荼邏 133
만다라 漫茶羅 134
만다라 漫陀羅 134
만다라 蔓陀囉 133
만다라교 曼茶羅敎 134
만달라 曼怛羅 133
만달라 滿怛羅 133, 134
만달라 漫怛羅 134
만당 慢幢 134
만만 慢慢 604
만물 萬物 134
만물여아일체 萬物與我一體 507
만법 萬法 134
만법성상 萬法性相 187
만법일심 萬法一心 134
만법일여 萬法一如 134
만분계 滿分戒 134
만사 慢使 134
만산 慢山 134
만상 慢想 134
만선 萬善 134
만성 滿成 134
만수 曼殊 134
만수사 曼殊沙 133
만수사화 曼殊沙華 326
만수시리 曼殊尸利 133
만수시리 滿殊尸利 134, 157
만수실리 曼殊室利 133, 157
만수실리경 曼殊室利經 133
만수안 曼殊顔 133, 326
만승존 曼勝尊 133
만업 滿業 134, 486
만원자 滿願子 134
만월존 滿月尊 134
만유 曼乳 134
만유 滿濡 134
만인 滿引 495
만자 滿字 134
만자 萬字 134
만자교 滿字敎 478
만자자 滿慈子 134
만제 漫提 134
만족 滿足 134
만좌 滿座 134
만죽 晩粥 135
만참 晩參 135, 565
만축자 滿祝子 134
만특라 曼特羅 133
만팔천세계 萬八千世界 134
만해 萬海 81
만해 용운 萬海龍雲 135
만행 萬行 134, 425
만화 鬘花 136
말 抹 135
말 末 135, 282
말 秣 135
말 襪 135
말 韈 135
말가 末伽 135
말가 末加 257
말가려구사려 末伽黎拘賒黎 135
말가리 末伽梨 135
말가리구사리 末伽梨拘賒梨 135
말가시라 末伽始羅 135
말가타하라타 末迦吒賀邏馱 135
말거리구사리 末佉梨劬奢離 135
말나 末那 135, 607
말나남 末捺南 135
말나식 末那識 135, 585, 607
말노갈랄타 末笯曷剌他 135, 400
말노갈리타 末笯曷利他 128
말노사 末奴沙 129, 135
말노시야삽바라 末奴是若颯縛羅 135
말노야구사 秣奴若瞿沙 135
말니 末尼 129, 136
말니교 末尼敎 136, 566
말다 末陀 136
말다리 末多利 136
말다마 末陀摩 136
말달나 末達那 136
말대 末代 137

말도가 末度迦 136
말두가 末杜迦 136
말득라 末得羅 142
말라 末羅 136
말라갈다 末羅羯多 136
말라구타 秣羅矩吒 135
말라구타 秣羅矩咤 136
말라사 秣羅娑 135
말라왕경 末羅王經 136
말라유 末羅遊 136
말라희미 末羅呬弭 583
말랄남 末剌諵 136, 235
말려낭 末麗曩 136
말률사가 靺嘌沙迦 135
말률자 末栗者 136
말리 末利 133, 136, 165
말리 末梨 136
말리부인 末利夫人 136
말리실라 末利室羅 136
말리지 末利支 130
말리화 茉莉花 136
말마 末摩 136
말법 末法 136, 251, 282
말법시 末法時 528
말사 末寺 136
말사가 靺師迦 135
말상 末上 137
말세 末世 137
말저승하 末底僧訶 137
말전 末田 137
말전제 末田提 137
말전지(나) 末田地(那) 137
말전지가 末田底加 137
말전탁가 末田鐸迦 137
말제마 末提摩 137
말제제사 末睇提舍 137
말지 末底 137
말지보라 秣底補羅 135
말차라 末嗟羅 137
말천지 末闡地 137
말탄지 末彈地 137
말토라 秣菟羅 131
말토라 秣□羅 32, 135
말향 抹香 135
말화 末化 137
망 亡 137
망 妄 137
망 忙 137
망 望 138
망 網 137
망 莽 137
망 蟒 137
망견 妄見 137
망경계 妄境界 137
망념 妄念 137
망망계 忙忙鷄 137
망망계 忙忙鷄 or 忙莽鷄 or 忙莽計 127
망망계 忙莽鷄 63
망망계금강 忙莽鷄金剛 or 忙莽計金剛 137
망망육도 忙忙六道 137
망명 網明 363
망목 網目 137
망법 妄法 137
망상 妄想 137, 416
망상 妄相 402
망설 妄說 137
망심 妄心 137, 146, 484
망어 妄語 137
망언 妄言 137
망연 妄緣 137
망염 妄染 137
망오중물 亡五衆物 137
망운 妄雲 137
망자 亡者 137
망진 妄塵 137
망집 妄執 137
망풍 妄風 137
망혼 亡魂 137
매 媒 465
매 梅 138
매 每 138
매 罵 138, 373
매 買 138
매 賣 138
매 魅 125, 138
매녀 魅女 138
매달라예니 梅呾囉曳尼 138
매달려 梅呾黎 138
매달려(사) 梅怛麗(邪) 160
매달려(야) 梅怛麗(藥) 160
매달려약 梅呾麗藥 138
매달리 每怛哩 160
매달리 每怛里 138
매달리(야) 梅呾利(耶) 138
매달리말나 每怛里末那 138
매달리야비수나얼다 昧怛利也毘庾拏蘖多 102
매달리예 昧怛𠼪曳 160
매달리예 昧怛履曳 138
매달리예나 梅呾利曳那 138
매득 買得 70
매롱 賣弄 138
매림 買林 138
매저리 梅低梨 160
맥 脉 428
맥 麥 58, 138
맹 孟 138
맹 猛 138
맹 盲 138
맹구 盲龜 138
맹란분 孟蘭盆 545
맹룡 盲龍 138
맹리 猛利 138
맹리번뇌 猛利煩惱 481
맹명 盲冥 138
맹파 盲跛 138
맹파신 孟婆神 138
맹파탕 孟婆湯 138
맹팔랑 孟八郞 138
맹화 猛火 138
면 免 138
면 眠 138
면 面 138
면목 面目 138
면문 面門 138
면벽 面壁 138
면수 面授 138
면승 免僧 138
면장 眠藏 138
멸 滅 55, 80, 81, 83, 138, 427, 605
four functioning forms 255
四諦 257
멸 篾 138
멸 蔑 139
멸갈마 滅羯磨 139
멸겁 滅劫 41, 89, 139
멸과 滅果 139
멸관 滅觀 139
멸도 滅度 139, 405
멸도 滅道 139
멸려차 蔑戾車 139, 225
멸례거 篾隸車 138
멸류지 滅類智 608
멸리 滅理 139

멸문 滅門 124
멸법 滅法 139
멸법계 滅法界 139
멸법인 滅法忍 608
멸법지 滅法智 139, 608
멸법지인 滅法智忍 139
멸병 滅病 139, 247
멸빈 滅擯 139, 232
멸상 滅相 139, 279
멸수상정 滅受想定 55, 139
멸수상정해탈 滅受想定解脫 611
멸업 滅業 139
멸장 滅場 139
멸쟁 滅諍 416
멸정 滅定 139
멸정지통 滅定智通 139
멸제 滅諦 139, 490
멸종 滅種 139
멸지 滅智 139
멸진삼매 滅盡三昧 139
멸진정 滅盡定 139
멸후 滅後 139
명 冥 140
명 名 72, 140, 265, 416
四尋思觀 252
명 命 140, 265
명 明 141, 288, 495
명 銘 141
명 鳴 139
명가 冥加 140, 476
명가 名假 140
명가시설 名假施設 280
명감 明鑑 10
명거 明炬 141
명계 冥界 140
명관 冥官 140
명광 命光 140
명광심 明光心 369
명광조 命光鳥 140
명구 命求 478
명근 命根 140, 249, 485
명난 命難 140
명납 名衲 141
명달 明達 141
명덕 名德 140
명도 冥途 140
명도 冥道 140
명도 明道 141, 628
명도무극 明度無極 141
명도사문 命道沙門 140
명득(정) 明得(定) 141
명득보살 明得菩薩 141
명등 命藤 140
명랍 名臘 140
명려 冥慮 140
명료 明了 141
명료론 明了論 255
명리 冥利 140
명리 名利 140
명리 明利 141
명명 明冥 141
명명조 命命鳥 67
명목 名目 140
명문 名聞 140
명민 明敏 141
명범 命梵 140
명법 明法 141
명별의통 名別義通 140
명보 命寶 140
명복 冥福 140
명부 冥府 140, 554
명부전 冥府殿 141
명분 明分 452
명비 明妃 141
명사 冥使 140
명사 冥思 140
명상 名相 140
명상 明相 141
명색 名色 80, 140, 365, 411
명석 鳴錫 139
명성 冥性 140, 516
명성 名聲 140
명성 明星 141, 627
명성천자 明星天子 267
명신 名身 141
명신 明神 141
명신불지 明信佛智 141
명심 明心 141
명심보리 明心菩提 417
명양회 冥陽會 140
명어 鳴魚 139
명언종자 名言種子 490
명왕 冥往 140
명왕 名王 618
명왕 明王 11, 83, 89, 91, 97, 101, 141, 144, 194, 392, 406, 431, 432, 451, 466, 546, 595, 621
火頭金剛 637
명월 明月 142
명월주 明月珠 142
명월천자 明月天子 142
명위 名爲 453
명응 冥應 140
명의 名義 140
명의불리 名義不離 140, 141
명의집 名義集 140
명익 冥益 140
명일 冥一 140
명자 冥資 140
명자 名字 140
명자 命者 140
명자보살 名字菩薩 140
명자불 名字佛 467
명자비구 名字比丘 140
명자사미 名字沙彌 140, 294
명자상 名字相 464
명자즉 名字卽 467
명장 明藏 142
명적 名籍 140
명정 明靜
止觀 551
명제 冥諦 140
명종 命終 140
명종 明宗 629
명주 明呪 231
명주 明珠 142
명중 冥衆 140
명지 明地 142
명지 明智 452
명진사 命盡死 490
명처 明處 142
명천 名天 566
명체 名體 141
명초 冥初 140
명총 茗葱 627
명탁 命濁 140, 432
명탈 明脫 142
명토 冥土 140
명통 冥通 140
명행족 明行足 142, 223, 371
명현양계 冥顯兩界 140
명혜 明慧 142
명호 名號 140
명훈 冥熏 140
명훈 明熏 142
모 冒 143
모 募 143

모 姥 142
모 慕 143
모 摸 143
모 母 142
모 毛 142
모 牟 143
모 茅 143
모 謨 142
모개두 茅蓋頭 143
모경 母經 142
모공 毛孔 142
모나라 慕捺囉 143
모나라 母捺羅 or 慕捺羅 142
모나마노사 母那摩奴沙 142
모니 牟尼 148, 157
모니(선) 牟尼(仙) 143
모니실리 牟尼室利 143
모니왕 牟尼王 143
모다라 母陀羅 142
모다라 牟陀羅 143
모다라수 母陀羅手 142
모다마노사 母陀摩奴沙 142
모달라 姥達羅 142
모도 毛道 142
모도범부 毛道凡夫 142
모도생 毛道生 142
모두 毛頭 142
모라 慕羅 143
모백 募魄 144
모병 毛病 142
모사(라) 牟娑(羅) 143
모사락(게파) 牟娑洛(揭婆) 143
모살라 牟薩羅 143
모살라 謨薩羅 142, 143
모상 摸象 38, 143
모승 毛繩 142
모연 募緣 143
모음 母音 514
모읍 母邑 142
모자원 茅子元 175
모주 母主 142
모지 冒地 143
모지린나 母止隣那 143
모지살달부 冒地薩怛嚩 143
모지질다 冒地質多 143
모진린나 母眞隣那 143
모진린다 牟眞隣陀 143
모진린타 牟眞鄰陀 143
모친 母親 582
모타 母馱 210
모타 母陀 210, 235
모타 母馱 142
모타가라자 毛馱伽羅子 142
모하 慕何 143
모하 謨賀 142
모하나 謨賀那 366, 639
모향 茅香 112
모호락 牟呼洛 143
모호률다 牟呼栗多 143
모화 募化 143
모환 茅環 576
목 木 53, 144
목 沐 144
목 牧 144
목 目 143, 322
목 睦 143
목(건)련 目(犍)連 145
목가략 目伽略 143
목갈람 目竭嵐 144
목거 目佉 143
목거포절나 木佉褒折娜 144
목건련 目犍連 143
목과림 木瓜林 31, 144
목기수양 目機銖兩 143
목다 目多 143
목다가 目多伽 143
목다라 目陀羅 142
목두 木頭 144
목득라 木得羅 143, 144
목란색 木蘭色 144
목란자 木欒子 144
목련 目連 143, 158, 384
목련 目連
毛馱伽羅子 142
목린 目隣 143
목마 木馬 144
목백태자 沐魄太子 144
목불 木佛 144
목사 木蛇 144
목사(라) 目娑(羅) 143
목상좌 木上座 144
목성 木星 144, 158, 586
목식 木食 144
목어 木魚 144
목요 木曜 144
목우 牧牛 144
목율승 木律僧 144
목제라 目帝羅 143, 144
목족 目足 144
목족선 目足仙 144
목지 木底 144
목지린다 目支隣陀 143
목지린다 目脂隣陀 143
목진린다 目眞隣陀 143
목진린타 目眞鄰陀 158
목차 木叉 144, 163
목차국다 木叉鞠多 144
목차제바 木叉提婆 99, 144
목차제파 木叉提婆 630
목탁 木鐸 144
목향 木香 61, 82, 144
목환자 木槵子 144, 377
몰 沒 144
몰겁 沒劫 144
몰교섭 沒交涉 144
몰도 沒度 144
몰도가라자 沒刀伽羅子 145
몰라감마 沒囉憾摩 162
몰라감마 沒羅憾摩 180
몰력가라자 沒力伽羅子 143
몰록 145
몰률나 沒嘌拏 366, 639
몰률다 沒栗多 145
몰률도 沒栗度 144
몰리지야폐 沒哩底野吠 144
몰예달리슬치 沒曳達利瑟致 145
몰자미 沒滋味 145
몰타 沒馱 145, 210
몰특가라자 沒特伽羅子 143, 145
몰파비 沒巴鼻 144
몽 夢 145
몽 蒙 145
몽갈리 夢揭釐 145
몽감 蒙感 145
몽견 夢見 145
몽고 蒙古 145
몽상 夢想 145
몽환 夢幻 145
묘 妙 88, 145, 469
묘 廟 145, 548
묘가 妙假 145
묘각 妙覺 115, 116, 145, 366, 410, 423, 425, 477, 608
묘각성 妙覺性 145, 466
묘각위 妙覺位 467
묘각지 妙覺地 145
묘거 妙車 145

묘견 妙見 145, 208
묘견대사 妙見大士 145
묘견보살 妙見菩薩 145, 585
묘고 妙高 328
묘고산(왕) 妙高山(王) 145
묘과 妙果 145
묘관 妙觀 145
묘관찰지 妙觀察智 259, 416, 430
묘광 妙光 145, 328
묘광불 妙光佛 145
묘교 妙教 145
묘길상 妙吉祥 145, 157, 603
묘당 妙幢 145
묘당상삼매 妙幢相三昧 145
묘덕 妙德 145, 157
묘두 妙頭 157
묘락화천 妙樂化天 387
묘명 妙明 146
묘무 妙無 146
묘문 妙門 76, 146, 643
묘법 妙法 146, 264
묘법궁 妙法宮 146
묘법당 妙法堂 146
묘법등 妙法燈 146
묘법륜 妙法輪 146
묘법선 妙法船 146
묘법연화 妙法蓮華 146
묘법연화경 妙法蓮華經
분다리가 209
묘법연화경 妙法蓮華經 97, 146, 191, 201, 278, 499
묘법연화경문구 妙法蓮華經文句 157
묘법연화경문구 妙法蓮華經文句 146
묘법연화경현의 妙法蓮華經玄義 147
묘법일승 妙法一乘 146
묘법장 妙法藏 146
묘법화 妙法華 146
묘비보살 妙臂菩薩 146
묘색 妙色 146
묘색신 妙色身 586
묘색신여래 妙色身如來 146
묘선공주 妙善公主 146
묘수 妙首 157
묘승 妙乘 97
묘시 妙翅 66
묘심 妙心 146
묘악 妙樂 146
묘어장 妙語藏 146
묘연화 妙蓮華 146
묘유 妙有 146
묘음 妙音 51, 146, 261
묘음(악)천 妙音(樂)天 147
묘음대사 妙音大士 146
묘음락천 妙音樂天 94
묘음변만 妙音徧滿 147
묘음보살 妙音菩薩 146
묘음불모 妙音佛母 94
묘음조 妙音鳥 147
묘음천 妙音天 94, 158
묘응 妙應 147
묘의보살 妙意菩薩 147
묘인 妙因 147
묘장(엄)왕 妙莊(嚴)王 147
묘장엄왕 妙莊嚴王 89
묘장왕 妙莊王 38, 396
묘전 妙典 147
묘종 妙宗 147
묘중 妙中 147
묘지 妙智 147
묘진여성 妙眞如性 147
묘취 妙趣 147
묘토 妙土 147
묘행 妙行 147
묘현 妙玄 147
묘현 妙賢 147
묘현산 妙顯山 147
묘희 妙喜 205
묘희국 妙喜國 643
묘희세계 妙喜世界 147
묘희족천 妙喜足天 147
무 戊 148
무 無 148, 454, 544, 586
무 舞 148
무 茂 148
무간 無間 8, 148, 380, 456, 554, 603
무간도 無間道 242, 479
무간업 無間業 148
무간연 無間緣 563
무간지옥 無間地獄 148, 155
무감 無減 148
무개 無蓋 148
무개대비 無蓋大悲 148
무개대회 無蓋大會 153
무거무래 無去無來 148
무견 無見 456, 477, 601
무견정상 無見頂相 148
무결 無結 80
무공덕 無功德 148
무공용 無功用 148
무공용결정 無功用決定 466
무광불 無光佛 148
무구 無垢 148
무구광 無垢光 158
무구식 無垢識 148, 282, 377
무구의 無垢衣 148
무구인 無垢忍 148
무구지 無垢地 148
무구진여 無垢眞如 487
무궁지명 無窮之命 265
무극 無極 148
무극지신 無極之身 265
무극지체 無極之體 148
무근 無根 148
무근신 無根信 148
무기 無記 148, 280, 476
무기 無起 279
무기법인 無起法忍 215
무기법진여 無記法眞如 293
무내무외 無內無外 507
무념 無念 149
무노 無怒 385
무능 無能 149
무능승 無能勝 149, 360, 384
무능승명 無能勝明 603
무니 茂尼 148, 157
무니 茂泥 143
무달라 戊達羅 148
무대광불 無對光佛 378
무도 無倒 149
무도대적 無刀大賊 149
무동 無動 149, 205, 385
무동불 無動佛 149
무동존 無動尊 149, 205
무동행 無動行 295
무등 無等 149
무등각 無等覺 149
무등등 無等等 149, 381, 385
무등등승 無等等乘 97, 149
무등승 無等乘 97
무라삼부로 茂羅三部盧 148
무라차 無羅叉 155
무락 無樂 604
무량 無量 149, 378, 456

무량각 無量覺 149
무량광 無量光 40, 149, 250, 363, 378, 386
무량광명 無量光明 149
무량광명토 無量光明土 149
무량광불 無量光佛 149, 364, 378
무량광천 無量光天 149, 267, 301, 370
무량력신통무동자 無量力神通無動者 206
무량수 無量壽 149, 246, 253, 378, 415
　四佛 248
무량수경 無量壽經 12, 94, 95, 149, 248, 277, 278, 285, 287, 323, 328, 427, 527, 531, 545, 618, 619
무량수경상 無量壽經上 364
무량수불 無量壽佛 149
무량수여래 無量壽如來 149
무량수왕 無量壽王 149
무량수전 無量壽殿 149
무량식 無量識 344
무량심 無量心 422
무량의 無量意 149
무량의 無量義 149, 501
무량의(문수) 無量意(文殊 363
무량의경 無量義經 93, 173, 278, 285
무량의경경 無量義經經 285
무량의경경원 無量義經經願 285
무량의처삼매 無量義處三昧 149
무량정 無量淨 250
무량정(천) 無量淨(天) 149
무량정천 無量淨天 301, 370
무량존 無量尊 149
무량청정불 無量清淨佛 149
무량청정평등각경 無量清淨平等覺經 531
무량혜 無量慧 149
무력 無力 479
무루 無漏 148, 149, 279, 294, 457, 479
무루(최)후신 無漏(最)後身 149
무루과 無漏果 149
무루근 無漏根 149, 485
무루도 無漏道 150, 457, 479
무루문 無漏門 150
무루법 無漏法 149
무루법성 無漏法性 149
무루실상 無漏實相 149
무루업 無漏業 286
무루인 無漏因 149
무루지 無漏智 149
무루혜 無漏慧 149
무멸 無滅 374
무명 無名 141
무명 無明 20, 80, 150, 201, 207, 271, 323, 355, 365, 422, 448, 464, 505, 581, 585, 619
　ignorance as father 204
　四流 243
　육추 六麤 468
무명견 無明見 150
무명결 無明結 150
무명루 無明漏 150
무명류 無明流 150
무명망 無明網 150
무명법성일체 無明法性一體 150
무명부 無明父 150
무명사 無明使 150
무명업상 無明業相 281
무명업애 無明業愛 150
무명염연 無明染緣 561
무명장 無明藏 150
무명주지 無明住地 150, 259
무명초 無明草 150
무명혹 無明惑 150, 295
무명훈습 無明熏習 150
무몰 無沒 151, 344, 376
무몰식 無沒識 376
무문 無問 150
무문비구 無聞比丘 150
무문자설 無問自說 50, 150
무문종 無門宗 150
무방 無方 150
무번 無煩 150, 250
무번천 無煩天 301, 370, 426
무법 無法 457
무법공 無法空 582
무법유법공 無法有法空 582
무변 無邊 150, 457, 481
무변광불 無邊光佛 378
무변법계 無邊法界 150
무변세계 無邊世界 150
무변신 無邊身 150
무변신보살 無邊身菩薩 485
무변음성불정 無邊音聲佛頂 221
무변행 無邊行 241
　本化四菩薩 247
무별진여 無別眞如 370
무분별 無分別 19, 150, 457
무분별법 無分別法 151
무분별심 無分別心 150
무분별지 無分別智 151, 209, 491
무불 無不 151
무비 無比 145, 151
무비 無非 151
무비법 無比法 151, 380, 386
무비신 無比身 151
무사지 無師智 151
무상 無上 151, 379
무상 無常 151, 207, 230, 249, 263, 273, 604
무상 無想 151, 457
무상 無相 151, 187, 266, 279, 286, 294, 350, 422, 560
무상(양족)존 無上(兩足)尊 151
무상가행장 無相加行障 367
무상각 無上覺 151
무상견 無常鵑 151
무상경 無常磬 151
무상계 無想界 151
무상계 無相戒 126
무상고공비아 無常苦空非我 230
무상공교 無相空敎 151
무상과 無想果 152
무상관 無相觀 477
무상교 無相敎 151
무상당 無常堂 151
무상대승 無相大乘 151
무상도 無上道 151
무상등 無上燈 151
무상묘각 無上妙覺 151
무상묘혜 無相妙慧 157
무상무량 無相無量 456
무상무상 無相無相 279
무상문 無想門 152
무상법 無上法 151
무상법륜 無上法輪 151
무상법왕 無上法王 151
무상보리 無上菩提 151, 417
무상보리 無相菩提 151
무상복전의 無上福田衣 151
무상복전의 無相福田衣 151
무상불 無相佛 151
무상사 無上士 151, 371

무상상 無上上 151
무상상 無相相 291
무상상승 無上上乘 97, 151
무상수 無常修 281
무상승 無上乘 97
무상신 無常身 484
무상안 無上眼 151
무상열반 無上涅槃 151
무상원 無常院 151
무상의 無常依 151
무상인 無上忍 151
무상정 無想定 152
무상정등정각 無上正等正覺 375
무상정변각 無上正徧覺 151
무상정변도 無上正徧道 151
무상정변지 無上正徧智 151
무상정변지 無上正徧知 375
무상종 無常鐘 151
무상종 無相宗 151
무상진여 無相眞如 292
무상참괴의 無上慚愧衣 151
무상처 無想處 151
무상천 無想天 53, 151, 250, 301, 370
무상해탈 無相解脫 295
무상해탈문 無相解脫門 151
무상혜 無上慧 151
무상혜 無相慧 469
무상호불 無相好佛 151
무색 無色 152, 310
무색계 無色界 35, 55, 152, 223, 266, 454, 484, 485, 569
무색무형 無色無形 353
무색유 無色有 152
무색정 無色定 422
무색탐 無色貪 152
무생 無生 152, 560
무생(법)인 無生(法)忍 487
무생관 無生觀 477
무생문 無生門 152
무생법 無生法 152
무생법인 無生法忍 152, 215
무생보국 無生寶國 152
무생신 無生身 152
무생심 無生心 352, 369
무생인 無生忍 152, 425
무생장 無生藏 152
무생제 無生際 152
무생지 無生智 152, 370
무생지생 無生之生 152
무생진여 無生眞如 292
무생회 無生悔 292
무섭수진여 無攝受眞如 370
무성 無性 152, 420, 457, 560
무성루 無聲漏 152
무성유정 無性有情 152
무성진여 無性眞如 293
무성천제 無性闡提 292
무소 無所 152
무소관 無所觀 152
무소득 無所得 152
무소부지 無所不至 152
무소불능 無所不能 152
무소연 無所緣 457
무소외 無所畏 401
무소유 無所有 152
무소유처 無所有處 50, 53, 152, 239
무소유처정 無所有處定 152
무소유처지 無所有處地 55, 619
무소유처해탈 無所有處解脫 611
무소주 無所住 152
무소착 無所著 152
무수 無數 152, 382
무승 無勝 152, 383
무승국 無勝國 152
무시 無始 152
무시간격 無始間隔 153
무시공 無始空 153
무시광겁 無始曠劫 152
무시무명 無始無明 61, 150, 152, 446
무시무변 無始無邊 153
무시무종 無始無終 153
무시이래 無始以來 201
무심 無心 153
무심도인 無心道人 153
무심삼매 無心三昧 153
무심정 無心定 153
무아 無我 153, 274, 372, 385, 604
무아성 無我性 187
무아수 無我修 281
무앙수겁 無央數劫 153
무애 無愛 153
무애 無礙 153, 183
무애광 無礙光 153
무애광불 無礙光佛 378
무애대회 無礙大會 153
무애도 無礙道 479
무애안 無碍眼 362
무애인 無礙人 153
무애지 無礙智 153, 386
무언 無言 153
무언설도 無言說道 153
무여 無餘 153, 154, 303
무여(의)열반 無餘(依)涅槃 153
무여기 無餘記 153
무여수기 無餘授記 490
무여열반 無餘涅槃 286, 458, 490
무여의 無餘依 490
무여회단 無餘灰斷 153
무연 無緣 153
무연삼매 無緣三昧 153
무연승 無緣乘 153
무연승심 無緣乘心 153
무연총 無緣塚 153
무연탑 無緣搭 153
무열 無熱 153, 250
무열지 無熱池 154
무열천 無熱天 153, 301, 370, 426
무염정진여 無染淨眞如 370
무염족 無厭足 154, 357
무영상 無影像 154
무외 無畏 154
무외결호 無畏結護 241
무외산 無畏山 154
무외수 無畏授 154
무외시 無畏施 154, 357
무외장 無畏藏 154
무우 無憂 154
무우가람 無憂伽藍 154
무우수 無憂樹 154
무우왕 無憂王 154
무운 無雲 250, 370
무운천 無雲天 301, 370
무원 無願 266, 279, 294
무원무원 無願無願 279
무위 無爲 50, 154, 176, 206, 316, 350, 362, 405, 435, 453, 458
무위계 無爲戒 280
무위공 無爲空 154
무위법 無爲法 154, 416, 425, 586
무위법계 無爲法界 427
무위법신 無爲法身 154
무위사 無爲舍 154
무위생사 無爲生死 154, 458
무위열반(계) 無爲涅槃(界) 154

무위이위 無爲而爲 223
무위자연 無爲自然 154
무위해탈 無爲解脫 492
무유 無有 154
무의 無依 154
무의 無意 154
무의 無疑 154
무의열반 無依涅槃 154
무의처 無依處 72
무이무삼 無二無三 148
무이홀기 無而忽起 636
무인 無咽 80
무인 無因 240
무인무과 無因無果 260
무인유과 無因有果 259
무일 無一 148
무자성 無自性 154
무자연성 無自然性 274
무작 無作 154, 279, 286
무작계 無作戒 155, 518
무작색 無作色 156
무작업 無作業 156
무작해탈 無作解脫 295
무장애법계 無障礙法界 428
무쟁 無諍 155
무쟁삼매 無諍三昧 155
무쟁성 無諍聲 376
무정 無淨 604
무제 武帝 274
무제 無際 155, 531
무종 武宗 173, 274
무종성 無種城 155
무종천제 無種闡提 155
무죄수 無罪樹 381
무주 無住 155
무주삼매 無住三昧 155
무지 戊地 148
무지 無智 561
무지 無知 140, 155, 383
무진 無塵 155
무진 無盡 155
무진 無瞋 279
무진등 無盡燈 155
무진법계 無塵法界 155
무진에 無瞋恚 205, 385
무진연기 無盡緣起 155
무진의 無盡意 155, 219
무진장 無盡藏 155
무진재 無盡財 236
무진지재 無盡之財 265
무진해 無盡海 155
무차 無遮 155
무차 茂遮 148
무차(대)회 無遮(大)會 155
무차대회 無遮大會 99
무차라 無叉羅 155
무착 無着 420, 604
무착 無著 155
무착 無著 또는 無着 382
무착천친종 無著天親宗 155
무착행 無著行 155
무참 無慚 155
무참무괴 無慚無愧 94
무체 無體 119
무체수정가 無體隨情假 476
무치 無痴 279
무치대충 無齒大蟲 155
무칭광불 無稱光佛 378
무타 毋馱 142
무탐 無貪 279
무택지옥 無擇地獄 155
무표 無表 28, 156
무표계 無表戒 155, 156
무표대계 無表大戒 98
무표색 無表色 156, 518, 585
무표업 無表業 156, 459
무학 無學 50, 156, 223, 459, 620
무학 자초 無學自超 156
무학도 無學道 20, 156
무학인전 無學人田 481
무해 無解 344, 459
무행공 無行空 582
무행반 無行般 428
무환자 無患子 144
무후 無厚 373
무후생사 無後生死 156
무희 舞戲 148
묵 墨 156
묵 默 156
묵갈제 墨竭提 156
묵리 默理 156
묵빈 默擯 156, 180, 232
묵언 默言 156
묵연 默然 156
묵의 墨衣 156
묵전 默傳 156
묵치기 默置記 156
문 問 156
문 文 156, 477
문 聞 156, 584, 585
문 門 156, 371
문(지)다라니 聞(持)陀羅尼 156
문경 門經 156
문광력 聞光力 156
문구 文句 156, 269, 400
　天台三部 573
문니 文尼 143, 148, 157
문다갈 文陀竭 158
문다갈왕경 文陀竭王經 158
문다라니 聞陀羅尼 184
문도 門徒 156
문려 門侶 156
문류 門流 156
문리 文理 157
문명 聞名 156
문물 聞物 254
문법 聞法 156
문법인 問法印 156
문사 門師 156
문수 文殊 133, 157, 280, 357, 361, 493
　meaning wonderful and auspicious, 妙吉祥 145
문수 門首 156
문수(사리) 文殊(師利) 157
문수문경 文殊問經 212
문수문경자모품 文殊問經字母品 514
문수사리문보리경 文殊師利問菩提經 157
문수삼매 文殊三昧 157
문수오사자 文殊五使者 157, 419
문수원 文殊院 158
문수팔대동자 文殊八大童子 158
문수회과 文殊悔過 158
문승 門丞 156
문신 問訊 156
문신 門神 156
문아 원측 文雅圓測 158, 305
문언 文偃 445
문여시 聞如是 399
문엽 門葉 156
문자 文字 158
문자반야 文字般若 275
문자법사 文字法師 158
문자인 文字人 158
문장 門狀 156

문적 門跡 156
문주 門主 156
문증 文證 158
문지 文池 158
문지 聞持 156
문지다라니 聞持陀羅尼 269
문진린다 文眞隣陀 143
문타륵 捫打勒 158
문태랄 門答辣 156
문파 門派 156
문협 文夾 158
문혜 聞慧 156, 469
물 勿 158
물 物 158
물가 勿伽 158
물가라자 勿伽羅子 158
물기 物機 158
물력가난제 勿力伽難提 158
물리가사파저 勿哩訶娑跛底 586
물리하사파지 勿哩訶娑跛底 144, 158
물시 物施 158
미 味 159
미 尾 160, 485
미 弭 159
미 彌 160
미 微 159
미 未 159, 280
미 獼 158
미 眉 158
미 米 160
미 美 158
미 迷 159, 220
미가 彌伽 160
미가 彌迦 160
미가라 彌呵羅 160
미가라 彌迦羅 160
미간광 眉間光 158
미간백호상 眉間白毫相 158
미개현 未開顯 159
미계 迷界 159
미과 美果 136
미관나득가 尾觀那得迦 360
미기라 迷企羅 365
미나 彌那 365
미념 未念 254
미니야 尾儞也 160
미도 味道 159
미도 未到 159
미도 迷倒 159
미두 米頭 160
미라 彌羅 160
미란 彌蘭 160
미래 未來 159, 280, 475, 630
미래세 未來世 159
미려거 彌戾車 160
미려마라 迷黎麻羅 159
미려야 米麗耶 160
미려야 迷麗耶 159
미례야 迷隸耶 159
미로 迷盧 159
미로단걸차 尾嚕愽乞叉 160
미로도가 尾嚕荼迦 160
미료인 未了因 159
미루 彌樓 160, 328
미륜나 彌倫那 365
미륵 彌勒 138, 160, 357, 361, 363, 431
미륵대성불경 彌勒大成佛經 278
미륵하생경 彌勒下生經 278, 619
미리 迷理 159
미리거 彌離車 160
미리야 尾唎也 228
미리지 彌離底 274
미만차 弭曼差 159
미말하 弭秣賀 159
미망 迷妄 159
미몰 迷沒 159
미묘 微妙 159
미묘법문 微妙法門 603
미묘성 微妙聲 246, 253
四佛 248
미밀 微密 159
미발사 微鉢沙 228
미부연화 未敷蓮華 159
미사 彌沙 365
미사 迷事 159
미사락기다 微沙落起多 159
미사새부 彌沙塞部 509
미사색 彌沙塞 482
미사색(부) 彌沙塞(部) 160
미사색부 彌娑塞部 641
미생 未生 280
미생 迷生 159
미생선 未生善 483
미생원 未生怨 159, 381
미서야 微誓耶 160
미세 微細 160
미세신 微細身 160
미수구인 未受具人 159
미수타 微戍陀 159
미슬뉴 微瑟紐 159
미심 迷心 159
미안 迷岸 159
미야갈라 弭也竭羅 634
미야야 微惹耶 160
미약포뇌가 微若布雷迦 160
미오 迷悟 159
미오불이 迷悟不二 159
미오인과 迷悟因果 159
미오일여 迷悟一如 159
미욕 味慾 159
미율두 彌栗頭 284
미음 美音 51, 158
미음(천녀) 美音(天女) 158
미음천 美音天 94
미인주 迷人咒 159
미자 迷子 159
미제례 迷諦隸 160
미제이 彌帝肄 160
미증유 未曾有 159
미증유경 未曾有經 159
미증유정법경 未曾有正法經 159
미지 彌底 160, 274, 528
미지 未至 159
미지당지근 未知當知根 485
미지리 迷底履 159
미지아 尾底牙 231
미지욕지근 未知欲知根 274
미진 味塵 159
미진 微塵 60, 159
미진 迷津 159
미진수 微塵數 159
미차가 彌遮迦 160, 486
미착 味著 159
미취 微聚 160
미타 彌陀 161, 280, 431
미타 未陀 159
미타산 彌陀山 161
미타삼성 彌陀三聖 161
미타삼존 彌陀三尊 161
미하라 尾賀羅 232
미행 微行 160
미현진실 未顯眞實 159
미혹 迷惑 159
미후 獼猴 158, 646
미후강 獼猴江 159

미후지 獼猴地 159
미희사바아부 彌喜捨婆阿部 509
미희사사아 彌喜捨娑阿 160, 641
민 悶 161
민 愍 161
민 敏 161
민 泯 161
민구리 敏俱理 161
민권귀실 泯權歸實 161
민기 愍忌 161
밀 密 161
밀 蜜 161
밀가 密家 161
밀경 密經 161
밀관 密灌 161
밀교 密教 82, 161, 213, 225, 363, 477, 512
밀교삼장 密教三藏 161
밀기 密機 161
밀률가실타발나 蜜栗伽悉他鉢娜 161
밀리가라 蜜利伽羅 158, 161
밀리차 蜜利車 161
밀림산 密林山 300
밀림산부 密林山部 325, 463
밀법 密法 161
밀부 密付 161
밀사두 密奢兜 161
밀수역사 密修力士 493
밀어 密語 161
밀엄국 密嚴國 161, 294
밀엄정토 密嚴淨土 161
밀우 密牛 364
밀의 密義 161
밀인 密印 161
밀인 密因 161
밀자 密字 161
밀장 密藏 161, 208
밀적 密跡 161
밀적 密迹 161
밀적금강력사 密迹金剛力士 161
밀적보살 密跡菩薩 493
밀적역사 密迹力士 63
밀종 密宗 161, 367
밀주 密咒 161
밀중 密衆 161
밀행 密行 161
밀호 密號 161

(ㅂ)

바 嚩 162
바 婆 162
바가 婆伽 162, 164
바가바(제) 婆伽婆(帝) 162
바가반 婆伽伴 162
바가범 婆伽梵 2, 162
바나 婆那 162
바나사 波那娑 166
바나화제 婆那和提 592
바니 嚩泥 162
바다 婆陀 162
바단타 婆檀陀 90, 162
바달라발다 婆達羅鉢陀 599
바라 婆羅 162
바라 波羅 171
바라(하) 婆羅(訶) 162
바라나(사) 波羅奈(斯) 162
바라나타 婆羅那馱 162
바라날(사) 波羅捺(寫) 162
바라날사 婆羅捺寫 162
바라날사 婆羅痆斯 162
바라날사 波羅痆斯 162
바라니밀바사발제 婆羅尼蜜婆舍跋提 164
바라니밀바사발제천 波羅尼密婆舍跋提天 162
바라니밀파사발제천 婆羅尼蜜婆舍跋提天 592
바라문 婆羅門 117, 162, 170
바라문 波羅門 163
바라문국 婆羅門國 162
바라문서 婆羅門書 162
바라문성 婆羅門城 162
바라문읍 婆羅門邑 162
바라밀 波羅蜜 108, 375, 468
바라밀(다) 波羅蜜(多) 461
바라밀다 波羅蜜多 163
바라부 波羅赴 163
바라사 婆羅奢 162
바라사거 婆羅捨佉 162
바라사이가 波羅闍已迦 163
바라사이가 波螺闍已迦 368
바라시가 波羅市迦 163
바라이 波羅夷 163, 416, 464
바라이사유 波羅夷四喩 163
바라제(제)사니 波羅提(提)舍尼 163
바라제목차 婆羅提木叉 162
바라제목차 波羅提木叉 144, 163
바라제목차 波羅提木叉 or 婆羅提木叉 27
바라제제사니 波羅提提舍尼 625
바라필리타가자나 婆羅必利他伽闍那 162
바라필리타흘나 婆羅必哩他仡那 162
바라필율탁흘나 婆羅必栗託仡那 162
바라하마 婆羅賀摩 180
바라하마 婆羅賀磨 or 婆羅賀摩 162
바라하마나 婆羅賀磨拏 162
바라합말나 婆羅欱末拏 162
바라흡마보라 婆羅吸摩補羅 162
바랄나사 波剌那斯 162
바랑 163
바로기제 嚩盧枳諦 162
바로기지습벌라 婆盧枳底濕伐羅 163
바로나 嚩嚕拏 162
바루나 婆樓那 163
바루나 波樓那 163
바리 婆利 163
바리 婆梨 163, 165
바리 波利 163
바리달라구가 波利咀羅拘迦 168
바리사 婆利師 163
바리사(가) 婆利師(迦) 163, 164
바리사가라 婆利史迦羅 163, 164
바리야 婆利耶 163
바리야 婆利耶 or 婆梨耶 163
바리야 婆哩野 163
바리자다가 婆利闍多迦 163
바리질(다)라 婆利質(多)羅 163
바리한 婆里旱 163, 165
바바가리 婆婆伽利 163
바부아제 婆嚩誐帝 163
바비베가 婆毘吠伽 164
바사 婆師 611
바사 婆槎 165
바사 婆沙 164
바사(가) 婆師(迦) 164
바사(타) 婆私(吒) 164
바사가 婆使迦 164
바사가 婆師迦 163
바사라 波闍羅 165, 179, 600
바사바 婆師婆 164

바사바 婆師波 164
바사바 婆沙波 164
바사바 波沙波 164
바사바리 婆師波利 164
바사바제 波闍波提 164
바사발제 婆舍跋提 164
바사발제 波舍跋提 592
바사사 波斯寺 104
바사사다 婆舍斯多 164
바사선 婆斯仙 164
바사슬체 婆私瑟摭 164
바사슬타 婆私瑟侘 164
바산바연지 婆珊婆演底 164
바성 婆城 164
바소밀다라 婆蘇蜜多羅 179
바소밀달라 婆蘇蜜呾羅 179
바수 婆數 164
바수 婆藪 164
바수 婆輸 165
바수루다가 婆收婁多柯 509
바수밀 婆須蜜 179
바수밀(다) 婆須蜜(多) 164
바수반두 婆修盤頭 164, 486
바수반두 婆藪槃豆 164, 179
바수반두 婆藪盤豆 164
바수반타 婆藪槃陀 164
바수발다 波輸鉢多 164
바습바 婆濕婆 164
바아 婆誐 164
바아종 婆誐鑁 162
바야 婆耶 164
바왈라 嚩曰囉 165
바왈라 嚩曰羅 162
바유 婆庾 163
바유 婆牖 164
바유 婆瘐 164
바유 婆萸 164
바일라 嚩馹囉 165
바일제 波逸提 164
바일지가 波逸底迦 164
바자라파니바리한 婆闍羅波尼婆里旱 165
바자자부 婆雌子部 165
바제 婆帝 170
바제 婆提 165, 170
바차 婆叉 165
바차 婆蹉 165
바차나바 婆蹉那婆 165
바차바 婆蹉婆 165
바차부(다)라 婆蹉富(多)羅 165
바차우바차 婆差優婆差 165
바척 婆陟 611
바추 婆芻 165
바추부라 婆麤富羅 165, 482
바치 婆稚 165
바타 婆吒 164
바타 波陀 165
바파사 婆頗娑 165
바하 婆訶 165
바하마 婆訶摩 165
바할나 婆喝那 165
박 剝 166
박 博 166
박 搏 83
박 簙 166
박 縛 165
박 薄 166
박가 縛迦 165
박가 薄伽 164
박가(범) 薄伽(梵) 166
박가(범) 薄迦(梵) 166
박가낭 縛伽浪 165
박가범 薄伽梵 162
박갈(라) 縛喝(羅) 165
박거라 薄佉羅 166
박건 薄健 166
박구라 簙句羅 166
박구라 簙拘羅 166
박구라 縛矩羅 166
박구라 薄俱羅 166
박구라 薄拘羅 166
박구라 薄矩羅 166
박니 縛尼 165
박라파구라 薄羅婆拘羅 166
박로나 縛嚕拏 335
박리사건나 縛利沙鍵拏 165
박마 縛摩 165
박마답 縛馬答 165
박복 薄福 166
박사선 縛斯仙 165
박살달라 縛薩怛羅 165
박수 拍手 166
박수 縛叟 164
박아범 薄阿梵 162
박야폐 縛野吠 165
박왈라 縛曰羅 62, 165, 179
박유 縛臾 165
박유방 縛臾方 165
박일라 縛日羅 62
박일라파다라 縛日羅播多羅 360
박장 拍掌 166
박저 縛底 165
박증 薄證 166
박지 薄地 166, 369
박차 博叉 165, 166, 168, 428
박차 薄叉 165
박차반다가 博叉般荼迦 166
박차반택가 博叉半擇迦 166
박추 縛芻 165
박타 縛馱 162
박탈 縛脫 165
박피 剝皮 166
박흘추 博吃蒭 166
반 伴 166
반 半 166
반 反 167
반 槃 167
반 攀 167
반 斑 167
반 槃 166
반 班 166
반 畔 166
반 盤 166
반 磐 166
반 般 166, 283, 412, 428
반 飯 167
반(뢰)야 般(賴)若 168
반가(부)좌 半跏(趺)坐 167
반각 攀覺 167
반경 飯磬 167
반나 般那 167
반나 飯那 162, 167
반나(사) 半娜(娑) 166
반나라부실녕 半拏囉嚩悉寧 177
반나라부실령 半拏囉嚩悉寧 167
반나마 般那摩 167
반나매 槃那寐 635
반나사 半那娑 599
반날바 般捺婆 166
반녈반(나) 般涅般(那 167
반녈반(나) 般涅般(那) 167
반노차 半篋嗟 166
반뇨사 半櫝娑 166
반니원 般尼洹 167
반니원 般泥洹 167
반니원경 般泥洹經 406
반다가 般茶迦 168

반다가 般荼迦 167, 428
반다라바자니 伴陀羅縛子尼 or 伴陀羅縛字尼 166
반다라박자니 伴陀羅縛子尼 167
반다로가법 般荼盧伽法 168
반다미 盤荼味 635
반다미 盤荼味 166
반달라발타 槃達羅鉢陀 167
반담 伴談 166, 635
반담 槃淡 166, 635
반대자 飯袋子 167
반두 槃頭 166
반두 飯頭 167
반라삽미 般羅颯迷 168
반라서나 鞶羅犀那 167
반라야 般羅若 168
반랄밀제 般剌蜜帝 168
반령 伴靈 166
반뢰야 般頼若 168
반리벌라구가 般利伐羅句迦 168
반리열반나 般利涅般那 167
반만교 半滿教 167
반망 盼望 138
반배 半拜 168
반비폐가 鞶毗吠伽 167
반비폐가 鞶毘吠伽 232
반사가 般闍迦 166
반석겁 槃石劫 211
반석겁 磐石劫 166
반선라마 班禪喇嘛 166
반선알이덕니 班禪頞爾德尼 166
반수천 鞶藪天 167
반시 半尸 343
반야 伴夜 166
반야 班若 168
반야 般若 34, 168, 304, 422, 475, 499
四大部經 241
四家 238
天地鏡 571
반야 般若 33, 98, 271, 283, 288, 368, 456, 501, 511, 551, 603
반야경 般若經 214, 416, 422, 467
반야경 般若經 168, 282
반야국다 般若鞠多 168
반야다라 般若多羅 168, 486
반야덕 般若德 269
반야두 般若頭 168
반야등론석대승중관석론 般若燈論釋大乘中觀釋論 545
반야바라밀(다) 般若波羅蜜(多) 168
반야바라밀다심경 般若波羅蜜多心經 352
반야바라밀다심경 般若波羅蜜多心經 103
반야보살 般若菩薩 168
반야봉 般若鋒 169
반야불모 般若佛母 169
반야선 般若船 169
반야시 般若時 421
반야시 般若時 169
반야심경 般若心經 305, 352
반야심경 般若心經 169
반야심밀경 般若深密經 239
반야지 般若智
contrast with 方便 174
반야탕 般若湯 169
반연 攀緣 167
반자 半字 134, 166
반자 半者 169
반자가단니 半者珂但尼 167
반자거단니 半者佉但尼 167
반자거사니 半者佉闍尼 167
반자교 半字教 167, 478
반자라 半遮羅 167
반자우슬 般闍于瑟 169
반자포사니 半者蒲闍尼 167
반자포선니 半者蒲膳尼 167, 427
반재 半齋 167
반절 反切 167, 525
반정왕 斑定王 568
반제 伴題 635
반제 畔睇 166, 635
반족왕 斑足王 167
반종 半鐘 or 飯鐘 643
반좌 盤坐 166
반주 般舟 169
반주(삼매) 般舟(三昧) 169
반주삼매경 般舟三昧經 169
반지가 半只迦 or 半支迦 166, 262
반지가 般止柯 166
반차 槃遮 166
반차 般遮 169
반차노 半嗟簸 166
반차발리사 般遮跋利沙 169
반차발슬가 般遮跋瑟迦 169
반차순 般遮旬 169
반차우슬 般遮于瑟 169
반차월사 般遮越師 169
반차자순 般遮子旬 169
반차파슬 般遮婆瑟 169
반차파율가사 般遮婆栗迦史 169
반차합장 反叉合掌 167
반천바라문 半天婆羅門 166
반첩바 畔喋婆 166
반초 半超 167
반출생사 反出生死 167
반타 槃陀 166
반타 般吒 168
반타(가) 槃陀(迦) 167
반타가 半他迦 167
반탁 半托 168
반탁가 半託迦 167
반탄남 畔彈南 166, 635
반택가 半擇迦 167, 168, 428
반특 槃特 166, 167
발 勃 169
발 拔 169
발 撥 170
발 發 169
발 跋 170, 285
발 鈸 169
발 鉢 169, 172
발 颰 169
발 髮 169
발가바 跋伽婆 170
발가선 跋伽仙 170
발가이 勃伽夷 169
발강 發講 170
발거 跋渠 170, 179, 510, 616
발건제 鉢健提 170
발계 發戒 170
발고여락 拔苦與樂 169
발광 發光 169
발광지 發光地 142, 369
발기 發起 170
발기중 發起衆 259
발길제 鉢吉帝 170
발나 跋那 170
발난다 跋難陀 170
발날라바나 跋捺囉婆娜 599
발날라파나 跋捺羅婆娜 170
발남마 跋濫摩 170
발납마 鉢納摩 172
발납만득가 鉢納鬘得迦 360

ㄱ ㄴ ㄷ ㄹ ㅁ ㅂ ㅅ ㅇ ㅈ ㅊ ㅋ ㅌ ㅍ ㅎ 찾아보기

발노마 鉢弩摩 172
발다 跋陀 170
발다(라) 鉢多(羅) 171
발다가비라 跋陀迦毘羅 170
발다나바나 跋陀娜婆娜 599
발다라 跋陀羅 170
발다라가비리야 跋陀羅迦卑梨耶 170
발다라루지 跋陀羅樓支 170
발다라야니 跋陀羅耶尼 170
발다파 跋陀婆 170
발달라 跋達羅 170
발달라 鉢咀羅 171
발달라 鉢怛羅 601
발달라겁 跋達羅劫 165
발담 鉢曇 171, 172
발담마 鉢曇摩 172
발담마라가 鉢曇摩羅伽 171
발두마 鉢頭摩 171, 172
발라 鉢羅 171
발라가라 鉢剌迦羅 171
발라가라 鉢囉迦羅 599
발라급보리 鉢羅笈菩提 171
발라루지 跋羅縷支 170
발라마라 拔羅魔囉 169
발라마보리 鉢羅摩菩提 171
발라말라기리 跋邏末羅耆釐 170
발라미 鉢羅弭 171
발라바라나 鉢刺婆刺拏 172
발라벌다 鉢羅伐多 171
발라보다라달낭야 鉢羅步多囉怛囊野 171
발라부다라달낭야 鉢羅部多囉怛囊野 171
발라사거 鉢羅奢佉 608
발라사거 鉢羅奢佉 or 鉢羅賒佉 171
발라사나시다 鉢邏斯那時多 600
발라사나특다 鉢羅斯那特多 171
발라사타 跋羅娑馱 170
발라살타 鉢羅薩他 171
발라서나시다 鉢邏犀那恃多 600
발라서나특다 鉢羅犀那特多 171
발라야 鉢羅若 171
발라야(발다예) 鉢囉惹(鉢多曳) 171
발라야가 鉢羅耶伽 171
발라예가불타 鉢刺翳迦佛陀 171
발라유타 鉢羅庾他 171
발라유타 鉢羅由他 171
발라제제사야매 鉢囉帝提舍耶寐 615
발라지가불 鉢攞底迦佛 617
발라지갈란다 鉢刺底羯爛多 171
발라지목차 鉢喇底木叉 171
발라지야 鉢羅底也 171
발라지양 鉢羅枳孃 168, 171
발라지제사나 鉢喇底提舍那 171
발라지제사니 鉢喇底提舍尼 171
발라참 跋羅攙 170
발라특기나 鉢喇特崎拏 171
발라폐사 鉢羅吠奢 171
발라현양 鉢羅賢禳 171
발라흡마 跋羅吸摩 93
발랄예가(불)타 鉢刺翳伽(佛)陀 403
발랄저라사니 鉢刺底羅舍尼 163
발람 跋藍 170
발람마 勃嚂摩 180
발람마 跋濫摩 162
발로 發露 170
발로라 鉢露羅 171
발로사 跋盧沙 170
발로사다 跋路娑陀 170
발로아 鉢露兒 171
발로파다 跋路婆陀 170
발록가 跋祿迦 170
발록갈첩파 跋祿羯呫婆 170
발론 髮論 169
발리부 鉢利部 446
발리부 鉢唎部 163, 171
발리사 跋利沙 170
발리사거 鉢李奢佉 162
발리살라벌나 鉢里薩囉伐拏 171
발리체미 鉢里體尾 550, 599
발리체폐 鉢哩體吠 171
발마 跋摩 170
발마라가 鉢摩羅伽 171
발무인과 撥無因果 170
발발 颰跋 627
발벌다 鉢伐多 171
발보리심 發菩提心 50
발사 勃沙 169, 211
발사 跋私 112
발사 跋闍 170
발사라 跋闍羅 62, 165, 170, 179
발사라 髮闍羅 179
발사라파니 跋闍羅波膩 170, 636
발사발 拔思發 169
발사불다라 跋私弗多羅 170
발사파 發思巴 606
발사팔 發思八 170
발색모 鉢塞莫 171
발생 發生 170
발설지옥 拔舌地獄 169
발솔도 跋窣堵 170
발신양 鉢腎禳 168
발심 發心 169, 170
四等, four virtues 242
발심공양 發心供養 169
발심보리 發心菩提 417
발심주 發心住 368
발야 鉢若 168
발왈라 跋曰囉 179
발우 169, 172
발원 發願 170
발위 鉢位 172
발의 發意 170
발이 跋移 165
발일라 跋日羅 165, 170
발자야 鉢刺若 168
발저야 拔底耶 169
발절다 跋折多 179
발절라 跋折羅 62, 165, 170, 179
발절라타가파 跋折羅咤訶婆 97
발절라타하사 跋折羅吒訶沙 170
발제 拔提 169, 419
발제 拔濟 169
발제 跋提 170, 479
발제달다 拔提達多 169
발제리가 跋提梨迦 or 跋提唎迦 170
발지 跋墀 165
발지 鉢底 600
발지육족론 發智六足論 325
발진 發眞 170
발초참현 撥草參玄 170
발초첨풍 撥草瞻風 170
발치 跋稚 165
발타 勃馱 210
발타 勃陀 169, 210
발타 勃馱 169
발타 鉢吒 172
발타 鉢陀 172
발타 颰陀 169
발타 馞陀 169
발타겁 颰陀劫 169

발타라파리 颰陀羅波梨 169
발타바라 颰陀波羅 169
발타보달라 鉢吒補怛囉 172
발타화(라) 颰陀和(羅) 169
발탁창나 鉢鐸創那 172
발탑 髮塔 169
발탑야 勃塔耶 169
발특 鉢特 171
발특(마) 鉢特(摩) 172
발특마 鉢特摩 554
발특망 鉢特忙 172
발파 拔婆 169
발파 拔波 169
발파타 鉢婆馱 284
발피 跋陂 170
발합사파 拔合思巴 169
발행성 發行城 525
발화라 盋和羅 172
발화라 鉢和羅 171, 172
발화란 鉢和蘭 171, 172
방 傍 172
방 坊 172
방 房 172, 374, 485
방 放 172
방 方 172
　方便 173
방 旁 172
방 榜 172
방 謗 172, 276
방 防 172
방광 放光 172, 642
방광 方廣 39, 50, 92, 172, 174, 229
　方等 173
방광관정 放光灌頂 290
방광대장엄경 方廣大莊嚴經 173
방광도인 方廣道人 173
방광불정 放光佛頂 418, 642
방광삼매 放光三昧 172
방광서 放光瑞 172
방구식 方口食 173
방규 方規 173
방나 防那 172
방난 防難 172
방등 放燈 172
방등 方等 92, 93, 98, 173, 174, 288, 501, 511, 603
방등 方等 sūtras 289
방등(계)단 方等(戒)壇 173
방등경 方等經 415
방등경전 方等經典 173
방등계단 方等戒壇 27
방등부 方等部 173
방등삼매 方等三昧 173
방등삼매행법 方等三昧行法 173
방등시 方等時 173, 421
방등참(회) 方等懺(悔) 173
방라 防羅 or 防邏 172
방법 方法
　方便 173
방법 謗法 172
방복 方服 173
방삼보계 謗三寶戒 172
방상 方相 173
방생 傍生 172, 579
방생 放生 172
방생 旁生 172
방생취 傍生趣 172
방수 房宿 18
방숙 房宿 172
방예 方詣 173
방외 方外 173
방일 放逸 172
방장 方丈 173
방장 스님 173
방전 方典 173
방정 方正 98
　方廣 172
방편 方便 58, 93, 97, 173, 207, 282, 359, 362, 432, 437, 461, 510, 575
　方等 173
방편가문 方便假門 174
방편구족주 方便具足住 368
방편력 方便力 361
방편문 方便門 174, 360
방편바라밀 方便波羅蜜 174
방편바라밀보살 方便波羅蜜菩薩 174
방편반야 方便般若 275
방편법 方便法 146
방편법신 方便法身 481
방편살생 方便殺生 174
방편선 方便善 1
방편선교 方便善巧 441
방편유여토 方便有餘土 174, 222, 261, 458
방편인 方便因 488
방편지 方便智 174, 491
방편토 方便土 174
방편품 方便品 174, 255
　four purpose of Buddha's appearing 248
　四要品 254
방편현열반 方便現涅槃 174
방편화신토 方便化身土 174
방포 方袍 173
방하 放下 172
방할 棒喝 203
방해 螃蟹 364
방행 傍行 533
배 倍 174
배 拜 174
배 杯 174
배 背 174
배 裴 174
배 陪 174
배념 背念 174
배도 杯度 174
배라부 陪囉嚩 174
배려 陪臚 174
배리 倍離 174
배불 拜佛 174
배불략 裴佛略 229
배불략 裴弗略 174
배사 背捨 174, 422
배식 陪食 174
배정 背正 174
배회경병 背繪經屏 174
백 柏 175
백 白 175, 420
백 百 175
백개불정 白蓋佛頂 176
백계 百界 175, 176
백계천여 百界千如 175
백고좌회 百高座會 175
백골관 白骨觀 214
백광변조왕 百光扁照王 101
백광변조왕 百光遍照王 175
백구지 百俱胝 175
백납의 百衲衣 175
백념(적) 白拈(賊) 175
백단 白檀 175
백대산 白帶山 305
백련(화) 白蓮(華) 175
백련(화)사 白蓮(華)社 175
백련교 白蓮教 175

백련사 白蓮社 427
백련지 白蓮池 120
백련지교 白蓮之交 175
백련채 白蓮菜 175
백련화 白蓮花 209
백련화좌 白蓮華座 175
백로지 白鷺池 175
백로지경 白鷺池經 175
백론 百論 175, 243, 270, 540
백마사 白馬寺 127, 175
백마주 白馬主 450
백만편 百萬遍 176
백목 百目 176
백미 百味 176
백반왕 白飯王 176
백법 百法 176
백법(명문)론 百法(明門)論 176
백법계 百法界 176
백법론 百法論 370
백법명문 百法明門 176
백보 白報 176
백복 百福 176
백본논사 百本論師 176
백본소주 百本疏主 176
백부지 百不知 176
백분 白分 177
백불 白佛 176
백불회 百不會 176
백비경 百譬經 177
백사 白四 583
백사(갈마) 白四(羯磨 502
백사갈마 白四羯磨 177
백사십불공법 百四十不共法 176
백산불정 白傘佛頂 176
백산불정 白繖佛頂 418
백상 白象 176
백상왕 白象王 485
백속 白俗 177
백솔(개)불정륜왕 白率(蓋)佛頂輪王 418
백수성 白水城 176
백심 白心 176
백양사 白羊寺 176
백엽화 百葉華 209
백우 白牛 176
백우거 白牛車 442
백우무각 白牛無角 176
백운 경한 白雲景閑 176
백운(종) 白雲(宗) 176
백운종 白雲宗 445
백운채 白雲菜 176
백월 白月 177
백유경 百喩經 177
백의 白衣 177
백의관음 白衣觀音 93, 177
백의대사 白衣大士 177
백이갈마 白二羯磨 177
백이십팔근본번뇌 百二十八根本煩惱 177
백이십팔사 百二十八使 177
백일 百一 175
백일갈마 白一羯磨 177
백일갈마 百一羯磨 23
백장 百丈 177
백장산 百丈山 177
백전 白戰 175
백절 白折 175
백족(화상) 白足(和尙) 177
백족아련 白足阿練 177
백중학 百衆學 177, 481
백즉백생 百卽百生 177
백진 白眞 177
백찬 白贊 177
백처관음 白處觀音 93, 177
백추 白槌 ; 白椎 177
백파 긍선 白坡亘璇 177
백팔 百八 177, 502
백팔결업 百八結業 177
백팔마니 百八摩尼 143
백팔모니 百八牟尼 177
백팔번뇌 百八煩惱 177
백팔수주 百八數珠 177
백팔존 百八尊 177
백팔종 百八鍾 177
백팔종 百八鐘 538
백팔환 百八丸 177
백호 白毫 177
백호지사 白毫之賜 177
백회 百會 177
백흑 白黑 177
백흑업 白黑業 177
백흑이서 白黑二鼠 304
백흑포살 白黑布薩 177
번 鑁 177
번 幡 178
번 旛 178
번 樊 178
번 煩 178
번 番 178
번 繙 178
번 翻 178
번경 翻經 178
번뇌 煩惱 14, 78, 115, 123, 178, 237, 352, 355, 394, 399, 430, 456, 479, 502, 523, 546, 581, 604
번뇌경 煩惱境 355
번뇌니 煩惱泥 178
번뇌도 煩惱道 178, 270
번뇌림 煩惱林 178
번뇌마 煩惱魔 178, 272, 604
번뇌무수서원단 煩惱無數誓願斷 261
번뇌병 煩惱病 178
번뇌빙 煩惱冰 178
번뇌습 煩惱習 178
번뇌신 煩惱薪 178
번뇌애 煩惱礙 178
번뇌업고 煩惱業苦 178
번뇌여 煩惱餘 178, 286
번뇌장 煩惱藏 178
번뇌장 煩惱障 178, 288, 488
번뇌적 煩惱賊 178
번뇌즉보리 煩惱卽菩提 179
번뇌진 煩惱陣 179
번뇌탁 煩惱濁 179, 432
번뇌하 煩惱河 179
번뇌해 煩惱海 179
번담 煩淡 635
번담 煩談 179
번롱 樊籠 178
번롱 煩籠 179
번범 翻梵 178
번사 翻邪 429
번승 番僧 178
번역 繙譯 401
번역 翻譯 178, 401
번역명의 繙譯名義
five regular articles of food 167
번역명의 翻譯名義 46, 140, 222, 273
번역명의집 翻譯名義集 178, 356
번유질 蕃維質 550
벌 伐 179
벌 筏 179
벌가 伐伽 179

벌나바사 伐那婆斯 179
벌납비 伐臘毗 179
벌랄나 伐刺拏 179
벌랑가 伐浪伽 179
벌리사 伐里沙 179, 442
벌사라 伐闍羅 62, 165, 179
벌사라불다라 伐闍羅弗多羅 179
벌소밀다라 筏蘇蜜多羅 or 伐蘇蜜多羅 179
벌소밀달라 伐蘇蜜呾羅 179
벌소밀달라 筏蘇蜜呾羅 164, 320, 636
벌소밀달라 筏蘇蜜呾羅 or 伐蘇蜜呾羅 179
벌소반도 伐蘇槃度 179
벌소반도 伐蘇畔度 179, 572
벌소반도 伐蘇畔徒 164
벌소반도 筏蘇畔徒 164
벌소반두 筏蘇盤豆 164, 179
벌소지 筏蘇枳 179
벌시가라궤 伐施迦囉軌 429
벌유 筏喩 179
벌절라 伐折羅 165, 179, 365
벌절라다라 伐折羅陀羅 179
벌절사부라 伐折闍嚩羅 179
벌지 伐地 179
벌차자 筏蹉子 179
범 凡 179
범 梵 93, 180
범 犯 180
범 範 180
범(부)성 凡(夫)性 180
범가이 梵迦夷 180
범계 犯戒 180
범궁 梵宮 180
범난 梵難 180
범녀 梵女 180
범단 梵壇 156, 180
범달 梵怛 180
범덕 梵德 180
범도 梵道 180
범람마 梵覽摩 93
범람마 梵覽摩 or 梵覽磨 180
범려 凡慮 180
범륜 梵輪 180
범마 梵摩 180
범마 梵魔 181
범마니 梵摩尼 180
범마달 梵摩達 181
범마라 梵摩羅 181
범마삼발 梵摩三鉢 180
범망 梵網 63, 181
범망경 梵網經 27, 98, 137, 181, 198, 371, 416, 423, 505, 573, 641
一乘分敎 239
四十位 253
범망경심지품 梵網經心地品 356, 360, 367
범망경하 梵網經下 586
범망계본 梵網戒本 181
범망계품 梵網戒品 181
범망종 梵網宗 181
범면불 梵面佛 181
범보 梵輔 181, 250, 276
범보천 梵輔天 182, 301, 370
범복 凡福 180
범복 梵服 181
범복 梵福 316, 362
범본 梵本 181
범부 凡夫 142, 179, 617
범부루 梵富樓 181
범부십중망 凡夫十重妄 179
범사 凡師 180
범상 梵相 181
범서 梵書 182
범석 梵釋 181
범석사천 梵釋四天 181
범성 凡聖 180
범성 梵聲 181
범성거동토 凡聖居同土 261
범성동거토 凡聖同居土 180
범성불이 凡聖不二 180
범성일여 凡聖一如 180, 303
범세계 梵世界 181
범세천 梵世天 181
범소 凡小 180
범소팔도 凡小八倒 180
범습 凡習 180
범승 凡僧 179
범승 梵乘 181
범승 梵僧 181
범식 凡識 180
범신 凡身 180
범신 梵身 181
범신천 梵身天 181
범실 梵室 181
범심 梵心 181
범어 梵語 181
범어사 梵魚寺 181
범연나 梵衍那 181
범왕 梵王 93, 181, 182, 509
범왕경 梵王經 465
범왕궁 梵王宮 181
범우 凡愚 180
범우 梵宇 181
범원 梵苑 182
범위 範衛 180
범음 梵音 182
범음사 梵音師 585
범인 凡人 203, 314
범자 梵字 182, 567
범장 梵杖 180
범장 梵章 182
범전 梵典 182
범정 凡情 180
범정 梵廷 182
범종 凡種 180
범종 梵鐘 182
범주 梵住 258
범중 梵衆 182, 250, 276
범중 犯重 180
범중천 梵衆天 53, 182, 301, 370
범지 梵志 182, 531
범찰 梵刹 182
범천 梵天 180, 181, 182, 320, 492, 508
범천계 梵天界 182
범천녀 梵天女 182
범천왕 梵天王 93, 182
범천외도 梵天外道 182
범천인 梵天人 534
범천후 梵天后 182
범토 梵土 182
범패 梵唄 182, 546
범학 梵學 182
범행 梵行 180, 182, 585
범향 梵響 182
범협 梵夾 182
범협 梵挾 182
범협 梵篋 182
범협 梵莢 182
범황 梵皇 182
법 法 86, 102, 182, 215, 265, 268, 276, 280, 283, 294, 425, 428, 480, 487, 505, 539
四等 242

법(신)사리 法(身)舍利 188
법가 法家 183
법간 法慳 183
법거 法炬 183
법검 法劍 183
법견 法見 183
법경 法鏡 183, 211
법계 法界 86, 183, 187, 366, 507, 541, 544, 560, 605
법계(체성)지 法界(體性)智 515
법계가지 法界加持 183
법계궁 法界宮 183
법계등류 法界等流 183
법계무변지 法界無邊智 370
법계무애지 法界無礙智 183, 370
법계불 法界佛 183
법계불변지 法界佛邊智 183
법계성 法界性 183
법계신 法界身 184, 428
법계실상 法界實相 183
법계연기 法界緣起 155, 183, 403
법계원융 法界圓融 183
법계유심 法界唯心 183
법계일상 法界一相 183
법계장 法界藏 183, 429
법계정 法界定 183
법계체성지 法界體性智 184, 430
법고 法鼓 184
법공 法公 184
법공 法空 33, 88, 184, 266, 477
법공관 法空觀 184, 477
법공양 法供養 184, 489
법공좌 法空座 268
법공진여 法空眞如 184
법광정 法光定 184
법교 法敎 184
법교 法橋 184
법구 法救 261
법구경 法句經 184, 263
법귀 法歸 386
법금강 法金剛 431
법기 法器 184
법긴나라왕 法緊那羅王 184
법념처 法念處 184
법니 法尼 184
법다라니 法陀羅尼 184
법당 法堂 184
법당 法幢 184
법도 法度 184
법동사 法同舍 184, 237
법등 法燈 184
법라 法螺 184
법락 法樂 185
법란 法蘭 185
법랍 法噶 501
법랍 法臘 119, 185, 191, 618
법려 法侶 185
법력 法力 185
법령 法鈴 185
법뢰 法雷 185
법륜 法輪 185, 243
법률 法律 185
법리 法利 185
법립 法立 91
법마 法魔 185
법멸 法滅 185
법명 法名 185
법명 法命 185
법명 法明 185
법명도 法明道 185
법명문 法明門 185
법명여래 法明如來 206
법무거래 法無去來 367
법무거래종 法無去來宗 641
법무별진여 法無別眞如 370
법무성 法無性 274
법무아 法無我 185, 480
법무아지 法無我智 185
법무애(지) 法無礙(智) 185
법무애(해) 法無礙(解) 185
법문 法文 186
법문 法門 183, 185, 604
법문무진서원학 法門無盡誓願學 261
법문신 法門身 185, 291
법문해 法門海 185
법미 法味 186
법미자재장 法未自在障 367
법밀 法密 186
법밀부 法密部 509
법바라밀 法波羅蜜 142, 186
법박 法縛 186
법보 法寶 40, 102, 186, 199, 422
법보승보 法寶僧寶 217
법보시 法布施 188
법보응 法報應 283
법보장 法寶藏 186
법보화삼신 法報化三身 186
법보화신 法報化身 378
법복 法服 186
법본 法本 186
법불 法佛 186
법비 法臂 186
법비량 法比量 186
법비법 法非法 186
법사 法事 186
법사 法師 186, 635
법사 法沙 186
법사십덕 法師十德 357
법사의 法四依 186, 255
법사품 法師品 268, 428, 472
법산 法山 186
법상 法上 300
법상 法相 34, 99, 105, 186, 187, 188, 223, 248, 259, 276, 291, 344, 370, 427, 434, 454, 466, 482, 491, 514, 587, 608, 609, 612, 630
법상 法相 School 544
법상 法相 school 419
법상교 法相敎 98, 187
법상부 法上部 325
법상종 法相宗 33, 120, 152, 158, 186, 188, 202, 207, 252, 282, 290, 299, 367, 420, 429, 454, 456, 457, 471, 489, 529, 534, 538, 540, 544, 546, 576, 615, 622
四善根 251
火辨, Citrabhānu 638
總相念住 251
六部大乘經 462
법서 法誓 187
법선 法船 190
법성 法城 187
법성 法性 183, 187, 188, 293, 366, 367, 398, 505, 560
법성법신 法性法身 188, 481
법성불 法性佛 186, 316
법성산 法性山 187
법성상락 法性常樂 187
법성생신 法性生身 428
법성수 法性水 187
법성수망 法性隨妄 187
법성수연 法性隨緣 187
법성신 法性身 187
법성종 法性宗 187, 290, 317,

489, 538
법성지리 法性之理 492
법성진여 法性眞如 187
법성취 法成就 187
법성토 法性土 187, 189, 318, 420
법성해 法性海 187
법세 法歲 501
법수 法數 187
법수 法樹 187
법수 法水 187
법순 法順 587
법시 法施 188, 357
법식 法食 188
법식시 法食時 188
법신 法臣 188
법신 法身 102, 181, 183, 186, 187, 188, 213, 214, 227, 270, 282, 283, 301, 303, 316, 350, 379, 438, 475, 476, 483, 484, 505, 526, 559, 560
四身 252
법신게 法身偈 188, 403
법신관 法身觀 188
법신대사 法身大士 188
법신덕 法身德 269
법신보살 法身菩薩 188
법신불 法身佛 186, 188
법신여래 法身如來 188
법신유전 法身流轉 188
법신장 法身藏 188, 429
법신체성 法身體性 188
법신탑 法身塔 188
법신혜명 法身慧命 185
법신화생 法身化生 638
법아 法我 34, 85, 153, 188
법아 法芽 188
법아견 法我見 188, 486
법아육 法阿育 188
법안 法眼 188, 362
법안정 法眼淨 188
법안종 法眼宗 188, 310, 410
법애 法愛 189, 439, 486
법약 法藥 189
법어 法語 189
법역 法域 189
법연 法然 189, 587
법연 法緣 189
법열 法悅 189
법온 法蘊 189, 604
법왕 法王 189
법왕자 法王子 157, 189
법왕자주 法王子住 368
법요 法要 189
법우 法宇 189
법우 法雨 189
법운 法雲 40, 178, 189, 239
법운등각 法雲等覺 189
법운지 法雲地 189, 369
법원 法苑 189
법원주림 法苑珠林 68
법위 法位 189, 350
법위덕력 法威德力 414
법유 法乳 189
법유 法有 33, 189, 291
법유아무 法有我無 367
법유아무종 法有我無宗 189
법융 法融
牛頭 442
법은 法恩 189
법음 法音 189
법응 法應 472
법의 法依 189
법의 法衣 186
법이 法爾 189, 516
법인 法印 190
법인 法忍 189
법인 탄문 法印坦文 190
법입 法入 190
법자 法子 190
법자상상위인 法自相相違因 190
법자재 法自在 190, 484
법장 法匠 190
법장 法場 185
법장 法將 190
법장 法藏 69, 189, 190, 300, 412, 587, 604, 625, 628
법장부 法藏部 325, 509
법재 法財 190
법재일 法齋日 190
법전 法典 190
법전 法殿 190
법전 法電 185
법정 法定 187, 190, 366
법제 法帝 190
법제 法弟 190
법조 法照 190, 427, 434
법주 法主 190
법주 法住 187, 190, 366
법주 法舟 190
법주사 法住寺 190
법중 法衆 190
법증 法證 350
법지 法智 190, 370
법지인 法智印 259
법진 法塵 191
법집 法執 186, 191, 491
법집 法集 191
법처 法處 190
법천 法天 191
법체 法體 191
법평등 法平等 191
법하 法夏 191
법하 法河 187
법해 法海 187
법행 法行 349
법현 法顯 191
법호 法號 191
법호부 法護部 509
법화 法化 191
법화 法華 92, 98, 120, 146, 191, 281, 282, 305, 416, 417, 422, 501
天台九祖 572
법화강 法華講 191
법화경 法華經 98, 191, 263, 264, 271, 504, 540
천태삼교 573
법화경묘음품 法華經妙音品 499
법화경방편품 法華經方便品 294, 508
법화경서품 法華經序品 463, 499
법화경수량품 法華經壽量品 45
법화경현찬 法華經玄贊 630
법화법 法華法 191
법화삼매 法華三昧 191
법화삼매경 法華三昧經 191
법화생신 法化生身 191
법화열반 法華涅槃 511
법화열반시 法華涅槃時 421
법화일실 法華一實 191
법화종 法華宗 191, 367, 499
법화팔년 法華八年 191
법화화성품 法華化城品 276
법화회 法華會 191
법회 法會 189, 191
법회사 法會社 191
법흥 法興 184

법희 法喜 191
법희식 法喜食 191
벽 僻 192
벽 劈 192
벽 壁 192, 486
벽 碧 192
벽 辟 191
벽 闢 192
벽 霹 192
벽견 僻見 192
벽관 壁觀 192
벽관바라문 壁觀婆羅門 86
벽귀 辟鬼 192
벽력 霹靂 192
벽로나 蘗嚕拏 4
벽뢰 辟雷 192
벽망 闢妄 192
벽안호 碧眼胡 192
벽여다 薜荔多 59
벽전 闢展 192
벽전급 劈箭急 192
벽정 壁定 192
벽제 辟除 192
벽지(가) 辟支(迦) 191
벽지(가)불(타) 辟支(迦)佛(陀) 191
벽지가 辟支迦 611
벽지가불 辟支迦佛 403
벽지불 辟支佛 403, 548, 617
벽지불승 辟支佛乘 192
벽지불지 辟支佛地 369
벽추 煏芻 617
벽타 薜陀 452
변 變 167, 192
변 辨 192
변 辮 192
변 辯 192
육도과보 461
변 邊 192
변견 邊見 192, 361, 410, 415
변계 偏界 612
변계 偏計 612
변계 遍計 612
변계 邊界 192
변계소집성 偏計所執性 613
변계소집성 遍計所執性 612
변괴 變壞 192
변무애 辯無礙 192
변발 辮髮 192
변법계신 遍法界身 612
변사나 便社那 612
변선 便旋 612
변선나 便膳那 or 便善那 612
변성 變成 192
변성남자 變成男子 192
변성왕 變成王 192
변역 變易 192, 401
변역생사 變易生死 192, 209
변역신 變易身 192, 484
변역토 變易土 222
변옥 邊獄 192
변의원삼성 徧依圓三性 280, 282
변인 辯因 431
변일체처 徧一切處 227, 612
변재 辯才 192
변재문 辯才門 249
변재천 辨才天 192
변재천 辯才天 192
변재천(녀) 辨才天(女) 147
변적 辨積 363
변정 徧淨 250, 612
변정천 徧淨天 301, 370
변정천 遍淨天 53, 612
변제 邊際 192
변제지 邊際智 192
변조 徧照 612
변조금강 遍照金剛 431
변조여래 遍照如來 101, 612
변죄 邊罪 192
변주 遍周 612
변주 邊州 192
변중변론 辨中邊論 370
변중변론송 辨中邊論頌 417, 545
변지 遍智 612
변지 遍至 612
변지 邊地 192
변집견 邊執見 192
변처 遍處 612
변체 辨體 629
변출외도 遍出外道 612
변행 遍行 612
변행인 徧行因 612
변행인 遍行因 465
변행진여 遍行眞如 370
변화 變化 192, 282
변화법신 變化法身 192, 428
변화생 變化生 192
변화신 變化身 192, 252, 639
변화인 變化人 192
변화토 變化土 192, 421
별 別 193, 268, 280, 477, 478, 487, 544, 584, 638
별 瞥 192
별 鼈 193
별겁 別劫 193
별견 別見 193, 194
별경 別境 193
별경심소 別境心所 193
별교 別敎 23, 27, 146, 147, 150, 183, 193, 194, 239, 240, 245, 267, 289, 318, 332, 348, 368, 370, 416, 425, 460, 467, 469, 478, 485, 505, 584, 587, 602
천태삼교 573
별교일승 別敎一乘 193
별리수연 別理隨緣 193
별보 別報 193, 486, 577
별불 別佛 210
별불신구 鼈不愼口 193
별상 別相 193, 483, 577
별상계 別相戒 577
별상념처 別相念處 241
별상삼관 別相三觀 193
별시염불 別時念佛 193
별업 別業 193
별염불 別念佛 193
별원 別圓 193
별원 別願 193, 577
별의 別依 193
별전 別傳 193
별중 別衆 193
별지 瞥地 192
별청 別請 193
별타나 別他那 193
별해탈계 別解脫戒 194
별해탈율의 別解脫律儀 194
별향원수 別向圓修 194
별혹 別惑 194
병 丙 194
병 屛 194
병 柄 194
병 甁 194, 364
병 病 194
병 竝 194
병기 竝起 194
병기라 甁耆羅 194
병사 屛莎 194

병사 洴沙 232
병사 洴舍 194
병사 瓶沙 232
병사 萍沙 233
병사왕 洴沙王 194
병사왕 瓶沙王 194
병솔도파 瓶窣都波 194
병어 柄語 194
병율 屛律 566
병자 病子 194
병정 丙丁
junior or so-and-so 194
병정동자 丙丁童子 194
병환경 病患境 355
보 保 194
보 報 194, 283
보 寶 194
보 普 195, 272, 507, 615
보 步 194
보 煲 195
보 菩 194, 270, 281
보 補 195, 615
보가라 補伽羅 195
보갈사 補羯娑 200
보갈파 補羯婆 195
보개 寶蓋 196
보거 寶車 196
보거 普去 373
보경장군 保境將軍 194
보계 寶界 196
보과 報果 194, 477
보관 寶冠 418
보관금강 普觀金剛 213
보광 普光 40, 195
보광명지 寶光明池 196
보광천자 寶光天子 196, 499
보국 寶國 196
보길상 寶吉祥 452
보길상천 寶吉祥天 196
보녀 寶女 196
보노사 補盧沙 234
보다라 普陀羅 614
보단락가 補但落迦 195
보달락가 補怛落迦 195
보달락가 補怛洛迦 195
보당 寶幢 196, 499
四佛 248
보도 普渡 195
보도중생 普渡衆生 195
보득 報得 570
보등 普等 195
보등록 普燈錄 414
보라부 補囉嚩 195
보랄나 補剌拏 195
보령 寶鈴 427
보례 普禮 195
보로사 補盧沙 195, 615
보로사나 補盧沙拏 195
보로사다 補盧沙 195
보로사야 補盧沙耶 195
보로살사 補盧殺沙 195
보로삼 補盧衫 195
보로쇄 補盧鎩 195
보륜 寶輪 243
보륭 嚧嚨 196
보리 菩提 7, 143, 196, 277, 546
보리골로지 菩提鶻露支 196
보리다라 菩提多羅 196
보리달마 菩提達磨 196, 486, 587
보리도 菩提道 580
보리도량 菩提道場 196
보리량 菩提場 196, 518
보리류지 菩提流志 196
보리류지 菩提留支 196
보리문 菩提門 196
보리분 菩提分 7, 196
보리분법 菩提分法 196
보리사 菩提寺 196
보리살 菩提薩 284
보리살타 菩提薩埵 196
보리색다 菩提索多 196
보리소 菩提所 196
보리수 菩提樹 197, 382, 446
보리수신 菩提樹神 197, 485
보리신 菩提身 214
보리심 菩提心 99, 143, 197
보리심계 菩提心戒 280
보리심론 菩提心論 275
보리심마 菩提心魔 272
보리심의 菩提心義 560
보리자 菩提者 197
보리자량론 菩提資糧論 483
보림 保任 197
보림 寶林 197
보림전 寶林傳 197
보망 寶網 197
보명 報命 194
보명 普明 195
보문 普聞 229
보문 普門 195
보문 普門 chapter 284
보문 菩門 111
보문품 普門品
四要品 254
보미 550
보바라밀 寶波羅蜜 142
보방 寶坊 197
보벌 寶筏 197
보법 普法 195
보병 寶瓶 197
보병인 寶瓶印 106
보불 報佛 194
보사 報沙 194
보사 報謝 194
보사 普莎 195
보사 補沙 195, 211
보사마세 寶沙麽洗 197
보사타 褒沙陀 615
보살 菩薩 97, 196, 197, 204, 281, 300
보살경 菩薩境 355
보살계 菩薩戒 98, 198
보살계경 菩薩戒經 181
보살대사 菩薩大士 198
보살도 菩薩道 198
보살마하살 菩薩摩訶薩 198
보살성 菩薩性 198
보살성중 菩薩聖衆 198
보살승 菩薩乘 197, 421
보살승 菩薩僧 197
보살십주 菩薩十住 198
보살십지 菩薩十地 198
보살오지 菩薩五智 197
보살장 菩薩藏 198, 488
보살장경하 菩薩藏經下 91
보살지 菩薩地 369
보살지지경 菩薩地持經 54, 466
보살지지경 菩薩地持經 8 466
보살행 菩薩行 198
보삽파 補澀波 615
보삽파 補澁波 195
보상 寶相 198, 246, 253
四佛 248
보상여래 寶相如來 157
보상일 寶相日 399
보생 寶生 62, 198, 415, 431
四佛 248

보생삼매 報生三昧 194
보성 寶城 198
보성 寶性 198
보소 寶所 198
보수 寶手 198
보수 寶樹 198
보수 普首 157
보슬가 補瑟迦 195
보슬징가 補瑟徵迦 429
보슬치 補瑟置 195
보승 寶乘 198
보승 寶勝 198, 586
보시 布施 198, 251, 461
보신 報身 186, 194, 227, 273, 277, 282, 283, 331, 351, 483, 505
四身 252
보실저가 寶悉低迦 198
보씨 寶氏 157
보여 報如 362
보연 報緣 194
보왕 寶王 198
보왕 普王 195, 407
보왕삼매 寶王三昧 198
보요경 普曜經 173
보우 普愚 198
보운 寶雲 199
보은 報恩 194
보은시 報恩施 194
보은전 報恩田 194
보응 報應 194
보인 報因 194, 488
보인 寶印 199
보인삼매 寶印三昧 199
보임 保任 199
보자나 補刺拏 206
보자나 補刺那 206
보장 報障 195, 288
보장 寶藏 199
보장 菩藏 484
보장엄동자 普莊嚴童子 252
보장여래 寶藏如來 199
보저 寶渚 199
보적 寶積 98, 199
四大部經 241
보적경 寶積經 199
보적불 寶積佛 199
보적삼매 寶積三昧 199
보적장자자 寶積長者子 199
보전 寶典 199
보전수 寶殿手 636
보조일체세간지 普照一切世間智 370
보주 寶主 198, 258
보주 寶住 157
보주 寶州 199
보주 寶珠 199
보지 寶池 199
보지 普知 195
보지자 普知者 195
보찰 寶刹 199
보처 補處 195
보처삼매 寶處三昧 199
보척 步擲 603
보척금강 步擲金剛 194
보첩살독하 僕牒薩督呀 195
보취 寶聚 199
보타 普陀 195
四大名山 241
보타 步他 194
보타 補陀 195
보타 補陁 195
보타낙가산 普陀洛伽山 195
보타락(가) 補陀落(迦) 195
보타암 寶陀巖 199
보탁 寶鐸 199
보탑 寶塔 199
보탑품 寶塔品 83
보토 報土 194, 492
보통 報通 195, 398, 429
보통 寶通 103
보통 普通 195
보특가라 補特伽羅 195, 211
보편 普徧 195
보편 普遍 195
보현 普現 195
보현 普賢 64, 194, 195, 272, 357, 361, 363, 367, 368, 402, 431, 484, 493, 531, 603, 612, 647
四無量心 245
보현 普顯 157, 434, 617
보현관 普賢觀 501
보현불 普現佛 157
보현행법 普顯行法 305
보협 寶篋 199
보호 寶號 199
보화 寶華 199
보화 普化 195, 371
보훈 普熏 272
복 伏 55, 200
복 僕 199
복 卜 200
복 服 200
복 福 199, 481, 489
복 腹 200
복 複 200
복 覆 200, 323
복가라 福伽羅 211
복갈사 卜羯娑 200
복강 覆講 200
복개 福蓋 200
복견 覆肩 200
복경 福慶 200
복과 福果 200
복관 福觀 200
복기 覆器 200
복나 僕拏 199
복덕 福德 199, 486
복덕문 福德門 200
복덕신 福德身 200, 214
복덕자량 福德資糧 200
복덕장엄 福德莊嚴 200
복록 福祿 200
복면 覆面 200
복묘 覆墓 200
복발 覆鉢 200
복백 覆帛 200
복보 福報 199
복상법신 福相法身 200
복생 福生 200, 250, 370
복생 腹生 250
복생천 福生天 200, 301, 304, 370
복속제 覆俗諦 488
복수론사 服水論師 200
복심보리 伏心菩提 417
복업 福業 200
복인 伏忍 200, 425
복인 福因 199
복인복보 福因福報 287
복장 伏藏 200
복전 福田 200, 522
복전의 福田衣 200
복정 福庭 199
복제 覆諦 488
복족 福足 200, 633
복중 腹中 200
복지 福地 199

복지 福智 200
복타 伏陀 200
복타밀다 伏馱密多 486
복타밀다 伏馱蜜多 200
복행 福行 200
복혜 福慧 200
복호선나 僕呼繕那 199
본 本 200, 202
본(래)공 本(來)空 201
본각 本覺 200, 201, 238, 265, 340, 410, 447, 476, 595
본각진여 本覺眞如 201
본거 本據 201
본고적하 本高迹下 201
본과묘 本果妙 359
본교 本敎 201
본나리가 本拏哩迦 201, 209
본낭가타 本囊伽吒 201
본래 本來 201, 297
본래무일물 本來無一物 201
본래법이 本來法爾 201
본래성불 本來成佛 201
본말 本末 201
본말구경등 本末究竟等 362
본명 本明 201, 446
본명도량 本命道場 201
본명성 本命星 201
본명수 本命宿 201
본명원진 本命元辰 201
본모 本母 201
본문 本門 201, 202, 358
본문본존 本門本尊 201
본문사관 本門事觀 201
본문십묘 本門十妙 359
본법신 本法身 203
본불 本佛 201
본불생제 本不生際 201
본사 本事 80, 489
본사 本寺 202
본사 本師 201
본사경 本事經 202
본사화상 本師和尙 201
본산 本山 202
본삼매야인 本三昧耶印 202
본생경 本生經 202
본생설 本生說 202
본서 本書 202
본서 本誓 202
본성 本性 202
본성상 本性常 290
본성주종성 本性住種性 490
본시 本時 202
본식 本識 202, 376
본신 本身 202, 203
본심 本心 202
본연 本緣 202
본원 本願 202
본원일실대도 本願一實大道 202
본유 本有 202, 454
본유가 本有家 202
본유수생 本有修生 202
본유종자 本有種子 490
본이 本二 202
본인 本因 359
본적 本迹 201, 202
본적이문 本迹二門 202
본정무루 本淨(無漏) 202
본존 本尊 92, 202, 236, 270, 499
본지 本地 203
본지문 本地門 203
본지수적 本地垂迹 202
본지신 本地身 203
본질 本質 203
본체 本體 359
본초 本初 203
본초불생 本初不生 384
본행 本行 203
본행(집)경 本行(集)經 203
본행경 本行經 342
본형 本形 203
본혹 本惑 203
본화 本化 522
본화사보살 本化四菩薩 247
봉 奉 203
봉 封 203
봉 捧 203
봉 棒 203
봉 鋒 203
봉 鳳 203
봉가 奉加 203
봉납 奉納 203
봉물 捧物 203
봉사 奉事 203
봉선사 奉先寺 203
봉원사 奉元寺 203
봉찰 鳳刹 203
봉청법신 奉請法身 50
봉체 封體 203
봉행 奉行 203
부 付 204
부 俯 390
부 傅 205
부 副 204
부 夫 203
부 婦 203
부 富 204, 615
육도과보 461
부 復 204
부 扶 204
부 敷 204
부 棓 203
부 浮 204
부 溥 205
부 父 204
부 腐 204
부 負 204
부 賻 204
부 赴 204
부 趺 204
부 部 179, 203
부 附 203
부(속)제 覆(俗)諦 200
부(진)근 扶(塵)根 204
부(진)근 浮(塵)根 204
부(특)가라 富(特)伽羅 205
부가라 富伽羅 211
부공 浮孔 204
부교 部敎 203
부구 敷具 204
부근 扶根 478
부기 赴機 204
부나 富那 205
부나(야)사 富那(夜)奢 205
부나기 富那奇 205
부나바소 富那婆蘇 205
부나발타 富那跋陀 205
부나야사 富那耶舍 205, 486
부남국 扶南國 338
부낭 浮囊 204
부니 嚩泥 162
부다 部多 203, 475, 515, 638
부다나 富多那 614
부다나 富陀那 614
부다다타다 部多多他多 560
부단 不斷 205
부단(독)경 不斷(讀)經 205
부단공 不但空 84, 205, 477

부단광 不斷光 205
부단광불 不斷光佛 205
부단광불 不斷光佛 378
부단나 富單那 205, 614
부단륜 不斷輪 205
부단상 不斷常 205
부단상 不斷常 290, 298
부단상응염 不斷相應染 205
부단상응염 不斷相應染 464
부단염불 不斷念佛 205
부도 浮圖 204, 210
부도 浮屠 204, 646
부동 不動 113
부동 不動 205, 286, 385, 413, 605
부동강 不動講 206
부동공 不動供 205
부동금강명왕 不動金剛明王 206
부동다라니 不動陀羅尼 205
부동명왕 不動明王 207, 253, 337
부동명왕 不動明王 49, 55, 63, 149, 205, 206, 361, 385, 412, 431, 603
부동무위 不動無爲 206
부동법 不動法 206
부동분노왕 不動忿怒王 206
부동불 不動佛 149, 206
부동사자 不動使者 205
부동사자(다라니)비밀법 不動使者(陀羅尼)秘密法 205
부동생사 不動生死 206
부동아라한 不動阿羅漢 206
부동안진법 不動安鎭法 205
부동업 不動業 295
부동여래 不動如來 205
부동의 不動義 206
부동자구주 不動慈救呪 205
부동자호주 不動慈護呪 205
부동정 不動定 205
부동존 不動尊 252
부동존 不動尊 205, 206, 234, 360, 567, 603
火生三昧 638
火界 636
부동주 不動呪 205
부동지 不動地 205, 369
부동해탈 不動解脫 206
부두 浮頭 204, 210
부득착전금은보물 不得捉錢金銀寶物 356
부라 富羅 206
부란 不蘭 206
부란나 富蘭那 206
부란나가섭 富蘭那迦葉 206, 215
부란다라 富蘭陀羅 206
부란약 腐爛藥 204, 557
부랄나 棓剌拏 203
부료 副寮 204
부루나 富樓那 206
부루나미다라니자 富樓那彌多羅尼子 206
부루사 富樓沙 206
부루사부라 富婁沙富羅 206, 519
부류사부라 富留沙富羅 206
부만다라 敷曼荼羅 204
부모 父母 204
부모 部母 142
부모소생지육신즉위불신야 父母所生之肉身卽爲佛身也 275
부목 浮木 204
부문 負門 204
부법장(인연전) 付法藏(因緣傳) 204
부법장경 付法藏經 204
부법장전 付法藏傳 204
부부 夫婦 364
부불법외도 附佛法外道 203
부사 富沙 206, 211
부사 浮舍 229
부사의 不思議 206, 211
부사의 不思議 385
부사의(해탈)경 不思議(解脫)經 207
부사의계 不思議界 187, 207, 366
부사의공 不思議空 207
부사의공지 不思議空智 207
부사의변 不思議變 207
부사의변역생사 不思義變易生死 303
부사의변역생사 不思議變易生死 207
부사의승 不思議乘 206
부사의심 不思議心 369
부사의업상 不思議業相 207
부사의용상 不思議用相 482
부사의지 不思議智 206
부사의진언상도법 不思議眞言相道法 207
부사의혜동자 不思議慧童子 206
부사의훈 不思議薰 207
부살 扶薩 204
부상 浮想 204
부성 父城 204
부소 扶疏 204
부소마지 嚩蘇摩底 419
부속 付屬 204
부속제 覆俗諦
世諦 320
부수 溥首 205
부식 復飾 204
부왈라 嚩曰羅 179
부운 浮雲 204
부원 部圓 487
부유 嚩庾 246
부유발타라 富維跋陀羅 206
부율담상(교) 扶律談常(敎) 204
부율담상교 扶律談常敎 478
부의 賻儀 204
부인 夫人 203
부인 婦人 203
부인타 部引陀 or 部引陁 203
부일라 嚩馹囉 179
부자나 棓剌拏 or 棓剌那 206
부자재 不自在 207
부장인 不障因 465
부재정 不才淨 207
부정 不定 207
부정 不淨 207
부정 不定 267, 290, 291, 640
천태삼교 573
부정(종)성 不定(種)性 207
부정(지)관 不定(止)觀 207
부정관 不淨觀 207, 276
부정관 不淨觀 426
부정관경 不淨觀經 207
부정교 不定敎 207
부정교 不定敎 75, 603
부정금강 不淨金剛 207
부정륜 不淨輪 207
부정분노 不淨忿怒 207
부정설법 不淨說法 207
부정성취 不定性聚 207
부정수업 不定受業 207
부정시 不淨施 207
부정식 不正食 207
부정육 不淨肉 207, 220
부정인 不定因 214
부정지법 不定地法 207

부정취 不定聚 207
부정취 不定聚 294
부정행 不淨行 207
부좌 趺佐 204
부좌고광대상 不坐高廣大牀 208
부좌고광대상 不坐高廣大牀 356
부주 部主 142, 203
부중명왕 不重明王 67
부중존 不重尊 45
부즉류 不喞嚁 208
부즉불리 不卽不離 208
부증감진여 不增減眞如 208
부증감진여 不增減眞如 370
부증불감 不增不減 208
부진 浮塵 204
부진근 扶塵根 204, 478
부진근 浮塵根 478
부진종 不眞宗 258
부집 部執 203
부처(님) 佛 208
부척귀 埠惕鬼 597
부청 赴請 204
부촉 付囑 204
부친 父親 582
부타 浮陀 204, 210
부타 部陀 210, 586
부타나 富陀那 205
부탑 浮塔 210
부화 赴火 469
부화외도 赴火外道 204
부활 復活 204
부훈 傅訓 205
북 北 208
북교살라 北憍薩羅 254
북구로주 北拘盧洲 or 北俱盧洲 208
북대 北臺 208
북도 北度 208
북두(칠성) 北斗(七星) 208
북두당 北斗堂 208
북라 北羅 74, 117, 179, 208
북방 北方 74
북방불교 北方佛敎 208
북방칠요중 北方七曜衆 208
북본 北本 406
북본열반경 北本涅槃經 208
북사 北史 519
북산 北山 419
북산부 北山部 136
북산주부 北山住部 208, 325
북장 北藏 208
북종 北宗 208
북주 北周 629
북주 北洲 208
북진 北辰 208
북진보살 北辰菩薩 208
북침 北枕 208
북행 北行 208
분 分 209
분 墳 208
분 奔 201, 209
분 奮 209
분 忿 208, 323
분 焚 209
분 盆 208
분 粉 208
분 糞 209
분 芬 208
분결 忿結 208
분골쇄신 粉骨碎身 208
분과 糞果 209
분나가 分那柯 209
분나가 奔那伽 209, 440
분나벌전나 奔那伐戰那 209
분노 忿怒 208, 366, 639
분노(명)왕 忿怒(明)王 208
분노구 忿怒鉤 208
분다 奔茶 91
분다(리가) 奔茶(利迦) 209
분다리 分陀利 91, 175, 610
분다리 芬陀利 or 芬陁利 208
분다리(가) 分陀利(迦) 209
분다리가 分茶利迦 209
분다리화 奔茶利華 209
분단 分段 209
분단동거 分段同居 209
분단변역 分段變易 209
분단사 分段死 209
분단삼도 分段三道 209
분단생사 分斷生死 303
분단생사 分段生死 209
분단신 分段身 209, 484
분단윤회 分段輪廻 209
분리 芬利 91
분묘 墳墓 208
분별 分別 209, 416
분별경 分別經 209
분별공덕론 分別功德論 324
분별기 分別起 209
분별기번뇌 分別起煩惱 481
분별다라니 分別陀羅尼 269
분별명 分別明 569
분별법집 分別法執 481
분별사식 分別事識 209, 484
분별설 分別說 228
분별설부 分別說部 209, 509
분별설삼 分別說三 209
분별식 分別識 209, 282
분별아집 分別我執 486
분별유가론 分別瑜伽論 370, 417
분별지 分別智 209, 646
분별지상응염 分別智相應染 209, 464
분산 分散 210
분상문 分相門 210
분석 分析 210, 306
분세 分歲 210
분소 糞掃 209
분소의 糞掃衣 209
분신 分身 210
분신 奮迅 209
분양사라 奔攘舍羅 209
분왕 忿王 208
분용 分用 548
분위 分位 210
분위 分衛 210
분위등류 分位等流 270
분유 分喩 210
분자 鐼子 210
분제 糞除 209
분증(즉) 分證(卽) 210
분증즉 分證卽 210, 467
분진(즉) 分眞(卽) 210
분진즉 分眞卽 210, 608
분타 芬陀 209
분향 焚香 209
분회 盆會 208
불 不 211, 278
불 佛 210, 267, 268, 274, 276, 278, 294
불 弗 211
불 拂 211
불가 不可 211, 212
불가 佛家 212
불가견무대색 不可見無對色 212
불가견유대색 不可見有對色 212
불가기 不可棄 212

불가득 不可得 211
불가득공 不可得空 211, 582
불가라 弗伽羅 211
불가무창기부주관청 不歌舞倡伎不住觀聽 356
불가무창기불왕관청 不歌舞倡伎不往觀聽 212
불가사의 不可思議 88, 145, 211, 418, 507
불가사의(해탈)경 不可思議(解脫)經 212
불가사의광여래 不可思議光如來 212
불가사의삼관 不可思議三觀 505
불가사의존 不可思議尊 212
불가사의해탈법문 不可思議解脫法門 212
불가설 不可說 212
불가설불 不可說佛 212
불가월수호 不可越守護 212
불가유 不可有 212
불가칭지 不可稱智 212
불각 不覺 212
불각현행위 不覺現行位 212
불갱악취원 不更惡趣願 212
불견 佛見 212
불경 不輕 212
불경 佛境 212
불경 佛經 212
불경행 不輕行 212
불계 佛戒 213
불계 佛界 212
불고 不高 226
불고론종 不顧論宗 213
불고불락수 不苦不樂受 213
불골 佛骨 213
불공 不共 214
불공 不空 213, 363, 415, 493, 570, 609, 632
불공 佛供 214
불공 不空 431
불공(금강) 不空(金剛) 377
불공가 不空假 290
불공견보살 不空見菩薩 213
불공견삭(관음) 不空羂索(觀音) 213
불공견삭(보살) 不空羂索(菩薩) 213
불공견삭(왕) 不空羂索(王) 213
불공견삭구사 不空羂索俱捨 213
불공공양보살 不空供養菩薩 213
불공구관음 不空鉤觀音 213
불공금강 不空金剛 233
불공금강보살 不空金剛菩薩 213
불공무명 不共無明 111, 214
불공반야 不共般若 214
불공반야 不共般若 480
불공법 不共法 214
불공변 不共變 214
불공부정 不共不定 214
불공삼매 不共三昧 214
불공삼장 不空三藏 213
불공상 不共相 214
불공성취 不空成就 62
불공성취여래 不空成就如來 213 四佛 248
불공업 不共業 214
불공여래장 不空如來藏 213
불공중공 不共中共 214
불공진여 不空眞如 213, 487
불과 佛果 214, 469
불광 佛光 214, 489
불괴 不壞 214
불괴구 不壞句 214
불괴금강 不壞金剛 214
불괴금강광명심전 不壞金剛光明心殿 64
불괴금강광명필전 不壞金剛光明必殿 214
불괴법 不壞法 214
불괴사선 不壞四禪 214
불교 佛敎 214, 494
불구 不久 214
불구 佛具 214
불구사심 佛口蛇心 236
불구십신 佛具十身 214, 542
불구예도량 不久詣道場 214
불국 佛國 215, 221, 222
불국기 佛國記 191, 215, 624
불국사 佛國寺 215
불근 不勤
四佛 248
불근존 不勤尊 546
불기 佛記 215
불기법인 不起法忍 215
불기어 不綺語 215
불납차 不臘次 215
불단 佛檀 215
불덕 佛德 215
불도 佛圖 646
불도 佛道 215
불도등 佛圖磴 or 佛圖橙 215
불도무상서원성 佛道無上誓願成 261
불도징 佛圖澄 106, 215, 222
불라파 不羅婆 284
불락 不樂 554
불란가섭 不蘭迦葉 215
불랍일 佛臘日 215
불랍차 不臘次 215
불래 不來 215, 374
불래불거 不來不去 215
불래영 不來迎 215
불로 不老 605
불롱 佛隴 215
불료 不了 215
불료불지 不了佛智 215
불료의 不了義 437
불료의경 不了義經 215, 437
불료의교 不了義敎 478
불룡사 佛龍寺 624
불루사 佛樓沙 215, 615
불률지살당나 佛栗持薩儻那 215
불률특 弗栗特 211
불리 不離 546
불리무시자 不釐務侍者 216
불립문자 不立文字 603
불립문자(교) 不立文字(敎) 216
불립삼매 佛立三昧 216
불망선 不忘禪 216
불망어 不妄語 216, 356, 411
불멸 不滅 216, 218, 408
불멸(도) 佛滅(度) 216
불멸불생 不滅不生 216
불명 佛鳴 216
불모 佛母 7, 216
불모대금요공작명왕 佛母大金曜孔雀明王 32
불모신 佛母身 219
불모존 佛母尊 219
불모진삼매 佛母眞三昧 216
불모품 佛母品 463
불무애혜 佛無礙慧 216
불무차별 佛無差別 216
불문악명원 不聞惡名願 216
불바 佛婆 220
불바(비)제(하) 弗婆(毗)提(訶)

615
불바라부 佛婆羅部 216
불바비다제 弗婆鞞陀提 211
불바비제하 佛婆毘提訶 113
불바비제하 弗婆毘提訶 231
불바세라 弗婆勢羅 211
불바세라승가람 弗婆勢羅僧伽藍 211
불바제 佛婆提 113
불바제 弗婆提 211
불바제 弗把提 211
불바제 弗波提 211
불바제(하) 佛婆提(訶) 216
불바하라 弗婆呵羅 211
불반니원경 佛般泥洹經 216, 405
불반세라 佛槃勢羅 216
불반세라부 佛婆勢羅部 113
불반세라승가람 佛槃勢羅僧伽藍 211
불방일 不放逸 216
불배 不拜 216
불범일체 佛凡一體 216
불법 不法 217, 218
불법 佛法 216, 488
불법수명 佛法壽命 216
불법승 佛法僧 183, 216
불법장 佛法藏 190, 217
불변불개 不變不改 560
불변수연 不變隨緣 217
불변역성 不變易性 217
불변이성 不變異性 187, 366
불변진여 不變眞如 217, 334, 486
불보 佛寶 217
불보살화생 佛菩薩化生 638
불본행집경 佛本行集經 217
불부 佛部 217
불분별 不分別 217
불비시식 不非時食 217, 219, 356
불비제하 佛毗提訶 216
불비제하 弗毘提訶 211
불사 不死 217, 605
불사 佛事 186, 217
불사 佛使 217
불사 佛舍 217
불사 弗沙 169, 211, 228
불사가왕경 弗沙迦王經 211
불사각 不死覺 217
불사감로 不死甘露 217
불사리 佛舍利 217
불사문 不死門 217
불사밀다 弗沙蜜多 211
불사밀다라 弗沙蜜多羅 211
불사불 弗沙佛 211
불사서약 不捨誓約 217
불사약 不死藥 217
불사왕 弗沙王 211, 444
불사음 不邪婬 411
불사의 不思議 217
불사혜 不思慧 158
불살생 不殺生 217, 356, 411
불상 佛像 217
불상리법 不相離法 425
불상응법 不相應法 416
불상응심 不相應心 217
불상응행 不相應行 176, 217
불상인법 不相因法 425
불생 不生 216, 217, 218, 375, 405, 408
불생단 不生斷 218, 269, 290
불생불멸 不生不滅 201, 218, 353, 488
불생일 佛生日 218
불석 拂石 211
불석신명 不惜身命 218
불선 不善 218
불선법진여 不善法眞如 293
불선율의 不善律儀 218
불설 佛說 218
불설관무량수경 佛說觀無量壽經 266
불설관무량수불경 佛說觀無量壽佛經 38
불설무량수경 佛說無量壽經 89, 218, 266, 394
불설방등반니원경 佛說方等般泥洹經 406
불설사중과죄계 不說四衆過罪戒 218
불설산개불모총지다라니경 佛說傘蓋佛母總持陀羅尼經 93
불설아미타경 佛說阿彌陀經 266
불설아함정행경 佛說阿含正行經 531
불설인왕반야바라밀경 佛說仁王般若波羅蜜經 493
불성 佛性 187, 218, 560
불성계 佛性戒 218
불성교 佛性教 422
불성불수라 佛性不受羅 218
불성상주 佛性常住 218
불성진여 佛性眞如 218
불세 佛世 218
불세계 佛世界 218
불세존 佛世尊 218, 371
불소행찬경 佛所行讚經 127, 218
불수 不受 samādhi 219
불수 佛壽 218
불수 佛手 496
불수 佛樹 218, 446
불수삼매 不受三昧 219
불수외도 不修外道 218
불수일체법 不受一切法 219
불수현 不須現 492
불숙 弗宿 205
불승 佛乘 219, 282
불승계 佛乘戒 219
불승십지 佛乘十地 369
불시해탈 不時解脫 219, 492
불식육 不食肉 217, 219
불신 佛身 219, 362, 639
불심 不審 219
불심 佛心 219
불심인 佛心印 70, 219, 220
불심종 佛心宗 219, 354
불심천자 佛心天子 219
불악승 不惡乘 97
불안 佛眼 216, 219, 362
불안부모 佛眼部母 219
불안불모 佛眼佛母 219
불안존 佛眼尊 219
불야다라 弗若多羅 211
불약라 不若羅 284
불어 佛語 219
불어심 佛語心 219
불여단 弗如檀 211
불여만 不如慢 604
불여밀다 不如密多 486
불여밀다 不如蜜多 219
불여취 不與取 219
불열 不悅 219
불염세간법 不染世間法 219
불염오무지 不染汚無知 219
불염착제법삼매 不染著諸法三昧 219
불영 佛影 219
불오성 佛五姓 220
불욕행장 不欲行障 367

불우비바제하 弗于毗婆提訶 615
불우비바제하 弗于毘婆提訶 211
불우체 佛于逮 113, 216, 220
불우체 弗于逮 211
불원 佛願 220
불월 佛月 220
불위 佛位 220
불위위 佛位位 425
불위타 佛圍陀 220
불율의 不律儀 220
불음욕 不婬慾 220, 356
불음주 不飮酒 220, 356, 411
불응설어 不應說語 588
불의살 不疑殺 220
불이 不二 220, 546
불이법문 不二法門 220
불이불이 不二不異 220
불이지법 不二之法 220
불인 佛印 220
불인 佛因 220
불일 佛日 220
불일불이 不一不異 208, 220
불임열반기법주경 佛臨涅槃記法住經 216
불자 佛子 220
불자 拂子 211
불장 佛藏 220, 484
불장경왕고품 佛藏經往古品 253
불적 佛跡 220
불적 佛迹 220
불적입현 拂迹入玄 211
불전 佛田 220
불전함 佛殿函 221
불정 佛頂 40, 221, 421, 534, 538, 642
불정골 佛頂骨 221
불정산개불모 佛頂傘蓋佛母 93
불정인 佛頂印 221
불정존 佛頂尊 103, 221
불정주 佛頂呪 221
불제반 佛提婆 216
불제반 弗提婆 231
불제자 佛弟子 221
불조 佛祖 221
불조(역대)통재 佛祖(歷代)通載 221
불조통기 佛祖統紀 175, 221
불종 佛宗 221
불종 佛種 221
불종성 佛種姓 221
불주 佛住 258
불지 佛地 221, 369
불지 佛智 221, 510
불지견 佛知見 221
불지라 佛地羅 221
불지위 佛地位 464
불지제 佛支提 221
불착지생상금은보물 不捉持生像金銀寶物 221
불착향화만불향도신 不著香華鬘不香塗身 221
불착화만호향도신 不著華鬘好香塗身 356
불찰 佛刹 221, 222
불참거 不懺擧 221
불천 佛天 222
불청 不請 222
불청법 不請法 222
불청지우 不請之友 222
불취정각원 不取正覺願 222
불치비니 不痴毘尼 583
불칙 佛敕 또는 佛勅 222
불타 佛馱 222
불타 佛陀 142, 169, 210, 222
불타 佛駄 222
불타국다 佛陀鞠多 222
불타급다 佛馱笈多 222
불타난제 佛陀難提 222, 486
불타다라(다) 佛陀多羅(多) 222
불타밀다라 佛陀蜜多羅 222
불타반차 佛陀槃遮 222
불타발타라 佛陀跋陀羅 191, 222
불타발타라 佛馱跋陀羅 222
불타벌나산 佛陀伐那山 222
불타사나 佛馱斯那 222
불타선다 佛陀扇多 222
불타승하 佛陀僧訶 215, 222
불타십 佛陀什 222
불타야 佛馱耶 222
불타야사 佛陀耶舍 222, 521
불타야사 佛馱耶舍 222
불타제바 佛陀提婆 222
불타집 佛馱什 222
불타타사 佛陀馱沙 222
불타파리 佛陀波利 222
불토 佛土 221, 222, 277, 278, 516
불토경계 佛土境界
四不可思議 248
불퇴 不退 362, 380
불퇴(전) 不退(轉) 222
불퇴(전법)륜 不退(轉法)輪 223
불퇴결정 不退決定 466
불퇴보살 不退菩薩 223
불퇴불환향 不退不還向 223
불퇴상 不退相 223
불퇴전 不退轉 380, 616
불퇴주 不退住 223, 368
불퇴지 不退地 223
불퇴토 不退土 223
불투도 不偸盜 223, 356, 411
불학 不學 223, 375
불학대사전 佛學大辭典 314
불해 不害 223
불해 佛海 223
불행이행 不行而行 223
불허망성 不虛妄性 187, 223, 366
불혜 佛慧 223
불화합성 不和合城 223
불환 不還 223, 374, 545, 588
불환과 不還果 223
불환희일 佛歡喜日 223
불활외 不活畏 223
불회 不廻 223
불회 佛會 191
불후 佛吼 223
불후보현 佛後普賢 223
불흘차달라 佛紇差怛羅 221
비 俾 225
비 卑 224
비 妃 224
비 婢 226
비 悲 224
비 批 224
비 比 225
比量 226
비 毘 224, 265, 615
비 痺 225
비 碑 224
비 秘 225
비 緋 420
비 羆 223
비 肥 224
비 臂 225
비 蜱 224
비 誹 225
비 譬 226
비 費 226

비 非 225
비 鞞 53, 223, 224
비 飛 226
비 髀 225
비 鼻 224
비(밀)경 秘(密)經 225
비(밀)교 秘(密)敎 225
비(밀)장 秘(密)藏 225
비(지) 毘(至) 380
비(하)만 卑(下)慢 224
비(행)선 飛(行)仙 226
비(행황)제 飛(行皇)帝 226
비가라 毘伽羅 226
비가라론 毘伽羅論 69
비갈라 毘羯羅 365
비거라 毘佉羅 226
비격선사 鼻隔禪師 224
비결 秘決 225
비결 秘訣 225
비고가 鼻鼓迦 224
비공 非空 231
비공비유 非空非有 507
비공지공 非空之空 558
비관 悲觀 412
비관자관 悲觀慈觀 224
비구 比丘 225, 588, 617
비구니 比丘尼 79, 225, 399, 588
비구니계 比丘尼戒 226
비구니계본 比丘尼戒本 226
비구니승기율바라제목차계경 比丘尼僧祇律波羅提木叉戒經 226
비구대흑 比丘大黑 106
비구지 毘俱胝 or 毘俱知 226
비구회 比丘會 226
비근 鼻根 224, 485
비급마 毘笈摩 232
비기 非器 227
비기타선나 比耆陀羨那 226
비나 批那 224
비나 毗那 226
비나(다) 比那(多) 226
비나다가 毘那多迦 51
비나달가 毘那怛迦 227
비나야 毘那耶 227
비나야 毘奈耶 227, 469
비나야 鼻那夜 224, 227
비나야가 毘那夜加 227
비나야가 毘那耶加 227
비나야달가 毘那耶怛加 227
비나야잡사 毘奈耶雜事 321
비나야장 毘奈耶藏 227
비남파 毘藍婆 357
비뉴 毘紐 159, 452
비뉴바나 鞞紐婆那 224
비니 毘尼 227
비니 毘尼 or 鞞尼 227
비니 肥膩 224
비니가 毘泥迦 or 鞞泥迦 227
비니모론 毘尼母論 255
비니타가 毘泥吒迦 227
비다 比多 204
비다 毘荼 227
비다라 毘陀羅 340, 343
비다세라 臂多勢羅 225
비다수 毘多輸 227
비다차라나(삼반나) 毘多遮羅那(三般那) 223
비달가 毘怛迦 227, 231, 351
비담 毘曇 227
비덕 悲德 479
비도 非道 227
비두리 毘頭利 227
비두리 毘頭梨 600
비두리 鞞頭梨 224
비라나갈차바 毘囉拏羯車婆 227
비라사락(산) 比羅娑落(山) 226
비라산나 毘羅删拏 227
비라시 蜱羅尸 614
비락수 非樂修 281
비람 毘嵐 230
비람 鞞嵐 227
비람(바) 毘藍(婆) or 鞞藍婆 227
비람바 毘藍婆 227
비람풍 毘嵐風 227
비래 飛來 546
비량 比量 119, 226, 479, 605
비량상위 比量相違 226
비려야 毘黎耶 228
비례다 俾禮多 225
비례야 鞞隸夜 229
비로 毘盧 227
비로두나 鞞嚧杜那 223, 227
비로바아흘 鞞路波阿迄 228
비로사야 毘盧舍耶 227
비로석가왕 毘盧釋迦王 228
비로자나 毘盧遮那 563
비로자나 毘盧遮那 367
비로자나성불경 毘盧遮那成佛經 161
비로자나성불신변가지경 毘盧遮那成佛神變加持經 102
비로절야 毘盧折耶 227
비로차야 毘盧遮耶 227
비로택가왕 毘盧宅迦王 228
비로파아차 鼻路波阿叉 224
비로파아흘 髀路波阿迄 225
비루나 毘樓那 227
비루륵왕 毘婁勒王 228
비루박차 毘樓博叉 228
비루비무루업 非漏非無漏業 286
비류다가 鼻溜茶迦 228
비류다가 鼻溜茶迦 224
비류단차 毘留博叉 600
비류리 毘瑠璃 160, 227, 228
비류바아차 鼻溜波阿叉 228
비류바차 毘流波叉 228
비류박차 毘流博叉 228
비류왕 毘瑠王 228
비류파아차 鼻溜波阿叉 600
비류파차 毘流波叉 160
비률차 卑栗蹉 225
비륵 蜫勒 228
비륵 毘勒 31, 228
비륵론 毘勒論 325
비리사 毘利沙 365
비리야 毘利耶 228
비리야 毘梨耶 228
비리야 毘離耶 228
비리야서나 毘離耶犀那 228
비리지가 毘梨支迦 365
비리차 毘利差 228
비리타 毘梨馱 284
비마 媲摩 226
비마 毘摩 228
비마라 毘摩羅 228
비마라계리제 鼻磨羅鷄利帝 228
비마라차 卑摩羅叉 224
비마라힐 毘摩羅詰 228, 453
비마사 比摩寺 226
비마질다 毘摩質多 228
비만 卑慢 583
비멸 非滅 228
비목구사 毘目瞿沙 228
비목다라 毘目多羅 228
비목지 毘木底 228
비목차 毘木叉 228

비목차 毘目叉 228
비무량심 悲無量心 224, 245
비밀 秘密 225, 640
비밀(상)승 秘密(上)乘 225
비밀결집 秘密結集 225
비밀계 秘密戒 225
비밀교 秘密教 603
비밀단 秘密壇 225
비밀만다라 秘密曼荼羅 76
비밀유가 秘密瑜伽 225
비밀종 秘密宗 225
비밀주 秘密主 225
비밀주 秘密咒 225
비밀호 秘密號 225
비바 毘婆 228
비바사 毘婆沙 228
비바사 毘頗沙 228
비바사 鞞婆沙 223
비바사 鞞婆沙 or 鼻婆沙 228
비바사나 毘婆舍那 228
비바사론 毘婆沙論 135
비바사론사 毘婆沙論師 228
비바사바제 毘婆闍婆提 228
비바시 毘婆尸 228, 584
비바시 鞞婆尸 223
비바하라 鞞婆訶羅 223, 503
비발라 卑鉢羅 224
비발라 痺鉢羅 225
비발사 毘鉢沙 228
비발사나 毘鉢舍那 228
비발야사 毘跋耶斯 228
비발치 鞞跋致 224
비방 誹謗 16, 172, 225
비방정법 誹謗正法 225
비범행 非梵行 207
비법 秘法 225
비보살 鼊菩薩 223
비보살 非菩薩 229
비부라 毘富羅 229
비불략 毗佛畧 93
비불략 毘佛略 172, 229, 364
비불략 鞞佛略 229
비비리야 臂卑履也 225
비비상처 非非想處 229
비비상천 非非想天 229
비사 毘舍 229
비사 毘邪 646
비사 鞞舍 229
비사(려야) 鞞舍(隸夜) 224
비사(리) 鞞舍(離) 224
비사가 鼻奢迦 613
비사거 毘舍佉 229, 374
비사거 鼻奢佉 224, 229
비사거모 毘舍佉母 229
비사나 毘沙拏 229
비사나오동자 毘沙拏五童子 229
비사라 毘舍羅 229
비사라바나 鞞舍羅婆拏 224, 229
비사량저 非思量底 229
비사례야 鞞奢隸夜 223
비사리 毘舍離 229
비사명 毗捨明 229
비사문 毘沙門 51, 56, 485, 592
비사문 鞞沙門 223
비사문(천왕) 毘沙門(天王) 229
비사밀다라 毘奢蜜多羅 229
비사바 毘舍婆 229, 584
비사부 毘舍浮 229
비사부 毘舍符 229
비사사 毘舍闍 102, 229
비사야 毘社耶 160
비사연 毘闍延 107
비사자 毘舍闍 617
비사자 臂奢柘 225, 617
비사자 辟舍柘 or 譬舍柘 229
비사자라소 俾沙闍羅所 225
비사지 毘舍支 229
비사차 毘舍遮 229, 617
비삭가 鞞索迦 224
비살사 鞞殺社 223
비삼비일 非三非一 230
비상 非常 230
비상 非想 230
비상고공비아 非常苦空非我 230
비상비비상 非想非非想 53
비상비비상처 非想非非想處 50, 152, 230, 231, 239
비상비비상처지 非想非非想處地 55
비상비비상처해탈 非想非非想處解脫 611
비상비비상천 非想非非想天 230, 231
비상천 非想天 304
비새가 鞞崽迦 223
비색 非色 230
비색비심 非色非心 230, 231, 287, 458
비색사온 非色四蘊 230
비생비멸 非生非滅 230
비서바부 鞞恕婆附 223, 229
비서사부 毘恕沙付 229
비석 飛錫 226
비선계 非善戒 218
비선닉 卑先匿 224
비선연 毘禪延 107
비선자 毘詵遮 308
비섭라 毘攝羅 229
비성 毘城 229
비세사 鞞世師 223, 452
비세사가 鞞世思迦 452
비소단 非所斷 230, 269, 290
비쇄가 毘灑迦 230
비수 悲手 224
비수(갈마) 毘首(羯磨) 230
비수갈마 毘守羯磨 230
비수뉴 毘搜紐 or 毘瘦紐 159
비수니 比壽尼 386
비수타승하 毗戍陀僧訶 226
비슬노 毘瑟怒 or 毘瑟紱 452
비슬노 毘瑟紱 or 毘瑟怒 159
비슬뉴 毘瑟紐 159, 452
비습바 毘濕婆 or 毘濕波 230
비습바부 毘濕婆部 229
비습박갈마 毘濕縛羯磨 230
비시 篳尸 614
비시 非時 230
비시사 毘尸沙 230
비시식 非時食 230
비식 非食 230
비식 鼻息 224
비식 鼻識 224
비실라만낭 鞞室羅懣囊 223, 229
비심 悲心 224
비심 非心 230
비심비불 非心非佛 230, 547
비안립 非安立 230
비안립제 非安立諦 230
비안립진여 非安立眞如 230, 487
비야(사) 毘耶(舍) 229
비야갈랄남 毘耶羯剌諵 226
비야남 毘若南 230, 231
비야사 毘耶娑 230, 586
비야사 鞞耶舍 229
비야지 毘若底 230
비야지마달랄다 毘若底摩呾剌多 230

비업 非業 231
비여 譬如 431
비예산 比叡山 244
비오 秘奧 225
비요 秘要 225
비원 悲願 224
비원반 悲願般 224
비유 譬喩 50, 226
비유 非喩 231
비유 非有 229, 231
비유(론)사 譬喩(論)師 226
비유량 譬喩量 119, 226
비유비공 非有非空 231, 239, 325
비유비무지중도 非有非無之中道 279
비유상 非有想 230
비유상비무상 非有想非無想 239
비유상비무상처 非有想非無想處 231
비유상비무상천 非有想非無想天 231
비유위비무위법계 非有爲非無爲法界 428
비유품 譬喩品
四車 238
비육생 非六生 231
비율의 非律儀 218
비이취 非二聚 231
비인 秘印 225
비인 非人 231
비인지조작자 非人之造作者 571
비입 鼻入 224
비자나 毘闍那 230, 231
비자야 肥者耶 224
비저라 毘低羅 226
비적가 比摘迦 617
비전 悲田 224, 481, 606
비점반보라 毘苫婆補羅 231
비정 非情 231, 302, 460
비정성불 非情成佛 231
비제 毘睇 231
비제리 卑帝利 224
비제하 毗提訶 216
비제하 毘提訶 113, 231
비제하 鼻提賀 113
비제희 毘提希 452
비조리야 鞞稠利夜 224, 227
비종 秘宗 225
비증보살 悲增菩薩 491
비지 悲智 224
비지 比智 226
비지다바다 毘指多婆多 231
비차라 毘遮羅 227, 231, 237, 351
비천 非天 231
비충작불 蜱蟲作佛 224
비치가 鼻致迦 224, 499
비치차라나(삼반나) 鞞侈遮羅那(三般那) 223
비치차라나삼반나 婢侈遮羅那三般那 142
비타 毘陀 231, 452
비타 鞞陀 224, 452
비타가구사 比吒迦俱舍 226
비타라 毘陀羅 231
비타로바 鞞陀路婆 224
비택멸 非擇滅 50
비파 琵琶 231
비파가 毘播迦 231
비파라발노 鞞婆羅跋怒 419
비파사 毘播奢 231
비파사 鼻婆沙 224
비폐 鞞吠 or 毘吠 613
비폐가 毘吠伽 232
비포라 毘布羅 229
비하갈리나 毘何羯唎拏 226
비하라 毘訶羅 95, 232
비하라 毘訶羅 or 鼻訶羅 237
비하라 鞞訶羅 232
비하라 鼻訶羅 224, 232
비하라바라 毘訶羅波羅 232
비하라사미 毘訶羅莎弭 232
비학세자 非學世者 232
비학자 非學者 232
비행 飛行 226
비행야차 飛行夜叉 226
비호 比呼 225
비화 飛化 226
비흑비백업 非黑非白業 232
비흘라마아질다 毘訖羅摩阿迭多 232
빈 擯 232
빈 檳 232
빈 貧 232
빈 賓 232
빈 邠 232
빈 頻 232
빈가 頻伽 232
빈가라 賓伽羅 232
빈가타 頻伽陀 232
빈궁 貧窮 232
빈기문타불 邠祁文陀弗 232
빈나야가 頻那也加 227
빈나야가 頻那夜迦 233
빈녀 貧女 232
빈녀보장 貧女寶藏 232
빈다야 賓茶夜 210
빈다파다 賓茶波多 210
빈도 貧道 232, 245
빈두 賓頭 232
빈두로파라타 賓頭盧頗羅墮 232
빈랑 檳榔 232
빈래과 頻來果 232
빈바 頻婆 232
빈바(라) 頻婆(羅) 232
빈바라 頻婆羅 616
빈바사라 頻婆娑羅 232
빈발라 賓鉢羅 232
빈발리력차 賓撥利力叉 232
빈비사라 頻毘娑羅 232
빈지 賓坻 232
빈출 擯出 232
빈치 擯治 232
빈타라 賓吒羅 232
빈파라굴 賓波羅窟 232
빙 冰 233
빙 氷 233
빙가라 冰伽羅 233
빙가라 氷伽羅 233
빙게라 氷揭羅 233
빙게라천동자경 氷揭羅天童子經 233

(ㅅ)

사 事 235, 359, 416, 493
사 伺 227, 237
사 似 234
사 使 237, 278, 414
사 嗣 237
사 四 235, 276, 425
사 士 234
사 奢 237
사 娑 166, 236, 477
사 寫 237
사 寺 237
사 師 234, 268
사 徙 236
사 思 104, 177, 235, 295, 417

to the mental and moral world 20
사 捨 81, 237, 281, 445, 584, 585
사 斯 236, 477
사 死 136, 235
사 沙 235
사 瀉 237
사 獅 234
사 砂 235
사 社 235, 595
사 祠 236
사 私 235
사 舍 234
사 莎 234
사 蛇 236
사 詐 235
사 詞 234
사 謝 237
사 賒 236
사 赦 236
사 辭 234
사 邪 235, 265, 609
사 闍 234
사(대)천왕 四(大)天王 260
사(미)니 沙(彌)尼 246
사(성)제 四(聖)諦 259
사가 四家 238
사가 娑呵 236
사가 思假 235
사가 社伽 235
사가(타) 莎伽(陀) 332
사가기욕 捨家棄欲 237
사가라 娑伽羅 236
사가만낭 沙迦懣囊 245
사가만낭 沙迦滿囊 242
사가타 沙伽陀 234
사가타 莎迦陀 or 莎伽陀 234
사가행 四加行 1, 141, 238
사가행위 四加行位 74, 253, 320
사각 四覺 238, 333
사갈라 奢羯羅 237
사갈라 娑竭羅 236
사갈라 賒羯羅 517
사갈라인다라 賒羯羅因陀羅 307
사갈용왕 娑竭龍王 485
사갈타 沙竭陀 234
사개대승 四箇大乘 238
사거 四車 238, 251
사거가 四車家 238
사겁 四劫 238, 432
사겁 沙劫 238
사게치 莎揭哆 234
사견 邪見 19, 238, 361, 410, 415, 582
사견승 邪見乘 238
사견신 四堅信 238
사견조림 邪見稠林 238
사결 四結 238
사경 四鏡 238
사경 寫經 237
사계 四戒 238
사계 四界 238, 241, 481
사계 娑界 236
사계 沙界 238
사계 莎髻 234
사계 謝戒 237
사계 邪戒 433, 477
사계섭지 四界攝持 238
사계성도 四階成道 238
사계성불 四階成佛 238
사고 四股 239
사고 四苦 238, 302
사고 師姑 238
사고 死苦 235
사고사영 四枯四榮 239
사공(처) 四空(處) 239
사공(천) 四空(天) 239
사공정 四空定 34, 239, 245
사공처 四空處 245, 266, 344, 610
사공천 四空天 152, 231, 344, 611
사과 四果 239, 267, 374, 605, 607
사관 事觀 477
사교 事教 240
사교 四教 193, 239, 446
四家 238
四門 245
사교과 四教科 240
사교삼관 四教三觀 239
사교삼밀 四教三密 239
사교오시 四教五時 239
사교의 四教儀 239
사교의 四教義 606
사교지 四教地 239
사구 四句 240
사구 死句 240
사구분별 四句分別 240
사구성도 四句成道 240
사구집 四句執 240
사구추검 四句推撿 240, 249
사굴산 闍堀山 234
사궐 死闕 235
사극중감타죄 四極重感墮罪
四波羅夷 246
사근 師筋 261
사근 捨根 485
사근본극악 四根本極惡 481
사근본성죄 四根本性罪 240
사근본중죄 四根本重罪 240
사금강 四金剛 240
사기 四棄 240
四波羅夷 246
사기 四記 240
사나 斯那
China 548
사나 舍那 240
사나 舍那 or 奢那 243
사나 闍那 550
사나굴다 闍那崛多 234
사나리가 沙那利迦 240
사나바사 舍那波私 297
사나신 舍那身 240
사나야사 闍那耶舍 234
사나존특 舍那尊特 240
사나화수 舍那和修 297
사낭 師娘 75
사내이실절라 賒乃以室折羅 236, 586
사내이실탁라 賒乃以室拆羅 595
사념주 四念住 240
사념주 四念珠 240
사념처 四念處 78, 184, 228, 240, 285, 315, 426, 485
사념처(관) 四念處(觀) 240
사념처관 四念處觀 487
사념청정지 捨念清淨地 55
사눌로 娑訥嚕 313
사능립 似能立 605
사능파 似能破 235, 605
사니사 赦儞娑 236
사다 奢多 236
사다 徙多 236
사다 私多 77, 235, 349
사다 賒多 236
사다(사)바 私陀(娑)婆 328
사다가 闍多伽 234, 364
사다가 闍陀伽 234
사다길리 娑多吉哩 236

사다바(한)나 娑多婆(漢)那 236
사다비사 舍多毘沙 241
사다제바마누사남 舍多提婆摩㝹舍喃 570
사다제바마누사남 舍多提婆魔㝹舍諵 241
사다파한나 娑多婆漢那 340
사다파한나 沙多婆漢那 495
사다함 斯陀含 98, 222, 236
四果 239
사다함지 斯陀含地 369
사단 師檀 241
사달 四達 241
사답 四答 240
사당 祠堂 236
사당은 祠堂銀 236
사대 四大 88, 101, 103, 238, 241, 245, 465, 511, 552, 605, 616, 637
四蛇 249
水大 332
사대(부)주 四大(部)洲 241
사대계 四大界 241
사대명산 四大名山 241
사대명왕 四大明王 241
사대보살 四大菩薩 241
사대부경 四大部經 241
사대부조 四大不調 241
사대불호원 四大佛護院 241
사대사 四大師 241, 495
사대성문 四大聲聞 241
사대원무주 四大元無主 241
사대제자 四大弟子 241
사대종 四大種 241
사대주 四大洲 614
사대천왕 四大天王 100, 241
사대해 四大海 241
사대호 四大護 241
사덕 四德 180, 241
사덕락방 四德樂邦 242
사덕바라밀 四德波羅蜜 242, 386
사도 事度 235
사도 四倒 242
사도 四道 242, 248
사도 娑度 236
사도 死刀 235
사도 邪道 242
사도가행 四度加行 242
사도견 邪倒見 242
사도로 捨覩嚧 313
사도리교형 四忉利交形 242
사독사 四毒蛇 242, 249
사동자삼매경 四童子三昧經 406
사두 舍頭 634
사두간 舍頭諫 242
사득가 社得迦 235
사득가마라 社得迦摩羅 235
사등 四等 242, 245
사라 娑羅 236, 242
사라 沙羅 236, 242
사라 舍羅 242
사라(수)왕 娑羅(樹)王 236
사라나 沙羅那 or 沙羅拏 242
사라리불 娑羅梨弗 237
사라림 娑羅林 236, 242
사라마나 舍囉摩拏 242
사라마나 舍羅磨拏 245
사라바가 舍羅婆迦 242
사라바실제야 舍羅婆悉帝耶 254
사라범 捨囉梵 237
사라사 娑羅娑 236
사라수 娑羅樹 236
사라수 沙羅樹 343
사라수 莎羅樹 234
사라쌍수 沙羅雙樹 242
사라왕 沙羅王 242
사라타 捨攞馱 237
사락가 沙洛迦 243
사란달라 闍爛達羅 234
사랄라왕 娑剌拏王 242
사량 思量 135, 235, 607
사량(능변)식 思量(能變)識 235
사량심 思量心 351
사려 闍黎 234, 385
사력 四力 243
사령 死靈 235
사로 四爐 243
사로다라 娑路多羅 237
사론 事論 243
사론 四論 243
사론종 四論宗 243
사료간 四料簡 243
사루 四漏 20
사루 闍樓 234
사루가 舍樓伽 250
사류 四流 243
사류인 四類忍 608
사류지 四類智 610
사륜 四輪 243
사륜왕 四輪王 243, 574
사륵 舍勒 243
사리 事理 243, 291
사리 奢利 237
사리 師利 342
사리 舍利 160, 221, 242, 243
火葬 640
사리 闍利 234
사리 闍梨 234, 385
사리(무애)법계 事理(無礙)法界 244
사리무애법계 事理無礙法界 428
사리보단라 奢利補担羅 237
사리보단라 奢利補袒羅 243
사리부(다)라 奢利富(多)羅 243
사리부다라 奢利富多羅 237
사리불 舍利佛 243
사리불(다)라 奢利佛(多)羅 243
사리불다라 奢利弗多羅 237
사리사 舍利沙 343
사리사파 舍利娑婆 243
사리사파 舍利沙婆 13
사리삼천 事理三千 244
사리선 事理善 483
사리수나 闍提首那 274, 308
사리아 斯哩牙 236
사리오법 事理五法 244, 416
사리자 舍利子 243
사리탑 舍利塔 243
사립종 似立宗 234
사마 四馬 244
사마 娑磨 236
사마 死魔 272, 604
사마 沙磨 271
사마 舍摩 244
사마 邪魔 244
사마(실) 四摩(室) 244
사마라 娑麽囉 237
사마사나 奢磨奢那 244
사마사나 舍磨奢那 244
사마외도 邪魔外道 244
사마제 沙摩帝 244
사마지 奢摩地 273
사마타 奢摩他 551
사마타 奢摩他 or 奢摩陀 237
사마타 舍摩他 237
사마타 舍摩陀 244
사마타비바사나 奢摩他毗婆舍那

551
사마타비발사나 奢摩他毗鉢舍那 551
사만 邪慢 244, 583, 604
사만두 土饅頭 234, 596
사망 四忘 244
사망 死亡 235
사망 邪網 244
사맹월 四孟月 244
사면비로자나 四面毘盧遮那 244
사명 四明 244, 263, 552, 573
사명 邪命 17, 374
사명 유정 四溟惟政 244
사명(식) 邪命(食) 244
사명가 四明家 244
사명산 四明山 244, 402
사명설법 邪命說法 207, 244
사명존자 四明尊者 244
사무(소)외 四無(所)畏 244
사무량 四無量 242
사무량(심) 四無量(心) 245
사무량심 四無量心 180, 252, 369
사무량심 捨無量心 237, 245
사무상게 四無常偈 244
사무색 四無色 55, 245, 266
사무색계 四無色界 239
사무색정 四無色定 239
사무애변 四無礙辯 245, 262
사무애지 四無礙智 245
사무애지 詞無礙智 234
사무애지 辭無礙智 234
사무애해 四無礙解 245
사무외 四無畏 176, 214
사문 四門 245, 448
사문 娑門 245
사문 死門 235
사문 沙門 242, 245, 349
사문과 沙門果 245
사문나 沙門那 245
사문유관 四門遊觀 245
사문통 沙門統 245
사물 四物 245
사미 四味 245
사미 四微 245, 605
사미 四迷 245, 259
사미 奢弭 237
사미 奢彌 237
사미 沙彌 245, 350, 588, 624
사미계 沙彌戒 246
사미과 沙彌科 246
사미니 沙彌尼 588
사미니계 沙彌尼戒 246
사밀 事密 480
사바 四波 246
사바 娑婆 236
사바갈다 娑婆羯多 234
사바라밀(보살) 四波羅蜜(菩薩) 246
사바라이 四波羅夷 163, 240, 246, 255, 260, 481, 605
사바바슬 沙婆婆瑟 261
사바세계 娑婆世界 236
사바제 舍婆提 246, 254
사바하 娑婆訶 236
사바하 沙波訶 246, 261
사박 四縛 246, 523
사박하 娑縛賀 236
사반 娑槃 236
사발 四鉢 246
사발알 莎發斡 516
사방 四方 246
사방대장 四方大將 246
사방사불 四方四佛 246
사배 四輩 246
사백 四百 246
사백계 四百戒 246
사백사병 四百四病 246
사번뇌 四煩惱 247, 261
사번뇌 捨煩惱
四家 238
사범당 四梵堂 247
사범주 四梵住 247
사범지 四梵志 247
사범행 四梵行 245
사법 嗣法 237
사법 四法 247, 349, 605
사법 邪法 247
사법계 事法界 247, 427
사법계 四法界 244, 247, 258
사법본말 四法本末 247
사법불괴 四法不壞 247
사법삼원 四法三願 247
사법성취 四法成就 247
사법시 四法施 247
사법신 事法身 247, 481
사법인 四法印 247
사법인 四法忍 608
사법지 四法智 610
사변 四變 214
사병 四兵 247
사병 四病 139, 247, 511
사보살 四菩薩 247
사본상 四本相 248, 606
사본지관 四本止觀 247
사부 四部 248
사부 士夫 234, 615
사부견 士夫見 234, 601
사부경 四部經 248
사부라 闍嚩囉 234
사부승 四部僧 248
사부율 四部律 248
사부제자 四部弟子 248
사부중 四部衆 248
사분 四分 248
사분가 四分家 248
사분비구니갈마법 四分比丘尼羯磨法 248
사분승계본 四分僧戒本 248
사분율 四分律 255, 485, 540
사분율 四分律 74, 248, 602
사분율장 四分律藏 248
사분종 四分宗 248
사불 四佛 248
사불가경 四不可輕 248
사불가득 四不可得 248
사불가사의 四不可思議 248
사불견 四不見 248
사불괴신 四不壞信 238, 248
사불괴정 四不壞淨 248
사불기부 四不寄附 248
사불생 四不生 218, 249
사불성 四不成 249
사불지견 四佛知見 248
사불토 四佛土 248
사불퇴 四不退 222
사비 闍毘 82, 234
사비가라 娑毘迦羅 236
사비구 四比丘 249
사비다 闍鼻多 82, 234
사비량 似比量 605
사비상게 四非常偈 244
사사 事事 291
사사 四事 249
사사 四捨 249
사사 四蛇 249, 254
사사 四邪 249, 259
사사 蛇巳 365

사사 邪私 249
사사가 舍舍迦 249
사사경 四事經 249
사사공양 四事供養 249
사사명 四邪命 173
사사명식 四邪命食 618
사사무애법계 事事無礙法界 247, 292, 428
사사법문 四事法門 249
사사불가사의 四事不可思議 249
사사유 邪思惟 249
사사타 私私吒 164
사산 四山 249
사산 死山 235
사산 邪山 249
사살달라 奢薩怛羅 237
사살달라 舍薩怛羅 237
사상 事相 249
사상 四上 249
사상 四相 249, 606
四有爲相 255
사상 死相 235
사상부 事相部 249
사상선사 事相禪師 249
사생 四生 74, 250, 302, 304, 337, 638
사생 死生 235, 303
사생백겁 四生百劫 250
사생지증명 死生智證明 273
사선 四仙 250
사선 四禪 55
사선 邪扇 250
사선(천) 四禪(天) 250, 257
사선근 四善根 238, 242, 250, 369
사선근위 四善根位 76
사선정 四禪定 250
사선천 四禪天 89, 250, 266, 301, 610
사선팔정 四禪八定 250
사선피사 四仙避死 250
사선화자 死禪和子 235
사섭금강 四攝金剛 251
사섭법 四攝法 113, 125, 251
사섭보살 四攝菩薩 251
사섭사 四攝事 251
사섭중 四攝衆 251
사성 四姓 251
사성 四聖 251
사성정(취) 邪性定(聚) 251
사성제 四聖諦 251, 257, 317
사성종 四聖種 251, 255
사성행 四性行 251
사성행 四聖行 251, 253
사세 四世 251
사세 闍世 234
사손 師孫 251
사수 捨受 213, 237
사수상 四隨相 606
사수유 四須臾 251
사순 邪旬 251
사술 四術 251, 259
사승 四乘 238, 251, 254, 369
사승마 蛇繩麻 236
사승신 四勝身 251, 311
사승의제 四勝義諦 251
사시 四施 252
사시 死屍 235
사식 四食 252
사식 思食 235, 252
사식시 四食時 252
사신 四信 252
사신 四身 252, 516
사신 捨身 237
사신산 蛇神山 496
사신오행 四信五行 252
사신족 四神足 252, 254
사실 四實 241
사실단 四悉檀 252
사심 四心 252
사심 師心 353
사심 捨心 237
사심 沙心 252
사심사관 四尋思觀 252
사십 四十 252
사십구등 四十九燈 252
사십구승 四十九僧 252
사십구일 四十九日 252
사십구중마니전 四十九重摩尼殿 252
사십구중여의전 四十九重如意殿 252
사십여년미현진실 四十餘年未顯眞實 253
사십위 四十位 253
사십이사자 四十二使者 252
사십이위 四十二位 252
사십이자문 四十二字門 252
사십이장경 四十二章經 212, 253
사십이품무명 四十二品無明 252
사십일위 四十一位 252
사십일지 四十一地 252
사십팔년 四十八年 253
사십팔사자 四十八使者 253
사십팔원 四十八願 253
사십화엄경 四十華嚴經 289
사아 絲阿 365
사아급마 四阿笈摩 253
사아함 四阿含 239, 253
사아함경 四阿含經 261, 282, 386
사악(도) 四惡(道) 253
사악(취) 四惡(趣) 253
사악비구 四惡比丘 249, 253
사안 四眼 253
사안락(행) 四安樂(行) 253
사안락행 四安樂行 474
사애기 四愛起 253
사애생 四愛生 253
사액 四軛 253
사야 闍夜 234
사야국다 闍耶麴多 234
사야다 闍夜多 234, 486
사야보라 闍耶補羅 234
사야서나 闍耶犀那 234, 274
사야인다라 闍耶因陀羅 234
사야재나 闍耶宰那 234
사야지제바다 娑也地提嚩多 236
사야지제박다 娑也地提縛多 202
사야팔주 四夜八晝 253
사약 瀉藥 237
사약 蛇藥 236
사양약 四良藥 251, 253
사업최승 事業最勝 589
사여리 事如理 359
사여실관 四如實觀 253
사여의 四如意 485
사여의족 四如意足 252, 253, 285
사연 四緣 320
사연 四衍 254
사연제 闍演帝 234
사연지 闍演底 234
사예 四翳 238, 254
사왕 四王 242
사왕 死王 235
사왕 闍王 234
사왕(천) 四王(天) 254
사왕도리 四王忉利 254
사왕천 四王天 468

사요품 四要品 254
사욕 四欲 254
사용과 士用果 411, 476
사우단나 四優檀那 254
사우사행살타 四隅四行薩埵 254
사운 邪雲 254
사운(심) 四運(心) 254
사원 四園 254
사원 四怨 254
사원 四苑 254
사원 寺院 237
사원사 四蚖蛇 254
사월 四月 254
사월파일 四月八日 254
사위 舍衛 246, 254, 342
사위(타) 四韋(陀) 255
사위국 舍衛國 350
사위의 四威儀 255
사유 255
사유 四喩 255
사유 四有 545
사유 思惟 235, 310
사유 闍維 82, 234, 640
사유위상 四有爲相 249, 255, 458
사유파 私鍮簸 593
사율오론 四律五論 255
사율오론 四律五論 248
사음 邪婬 255
사의 四依 255
사의단 四意斷 255, 257
사의입정 四依入正 255
사이 舍夷 220, 255
사이(계) 四夷(戒) 255
사이(죄) 四夷(罪) 255
사이나 闍伊那 234
사익범천소문경 思益梵天所問經 422
사인 私印 235
사인관세 四人觀世 255
사인사과 邪因邪果 259
사일 四一 255
사일 四日 255
사자 師子 234, 255
사자 獅子 255, 364
사자개 師子鎧 1, 256
사자광 師子光 256
사자국 師子國 256
사자무외 師子無畏 460
사자분신 師子奮迅 256
사자비구 師子比丘 256
사자상 師子牀 256
사자상 師子相 256
사자신중충 師子身中蟲 256
사자왕 師子王 256
사자유 獅子乳 256
사자유희삼매 師子遊戲三昧 256
사자음 師子音 256
사자재 四自在 256
사자존자 師子尊者 256, 486
사자좌 師子座 256
사자주 師子冑 256
사자침 四自侵 256
사자협옥 師子頰玉 256
사자후 師子吼 256, 484
사장 事障 256, 488
사장 四藏 519
사재일 四齋日 256
사적 事迹 256
사적 死賊 235
사전 四田 257
사전 思專 273
사전 辭典 522
사전도 四顚倒 384
사절 四節 257
사절 四絶 257
사정 四定 55, 257
사정 四淨 176
사정구품사혹 四定九品思惑 55
사정근 四正勤 255, 257, 285, 485
사정기 四定記 257
사정단 四正斷 257
사정려(천) 四靜慮(天 250
사정려(천) 四靜慮(天) 257
사정성취 邪定性聚 207
사정정 四淨定 257
사정취 邪定聚 294
사제 四諦 28, 31, 80, 135, 139, 190, 251, 257, 261, 271, 288, 324, 363, 417, 421, 427, 480, 490, 534, 552, 608, 609
suffering 114
사제 捨帝 306
사제 闍提 234
사제경 四諦經 257
사제불정 捨除佛頂 418
사제사니 四提舍尼 481
사제사라 闍提闍羅 234
사제수나 闍提首那 234
사제연기경 四諦緣起經 239
사제일게 四第一偈 257
사조 事造 257, 478
사조 師祖 258
사족 蛇足 236
사종 四宗 258
사종 四種 258
사종관행 四種觀行 258
사종근본죄 四種根本罪 258
사종단법 四種壇法 247, 258
사종법계 四種法界 247, 258
사종사생 四種死生 258
사종삼매(야) 四種三昧(耶) 258
사종선정 四種禪定 254
사종성취법 四種成就法 258
사종승물 四種僧物 343
사종신심 四種信心 252, 258
사종실지 四種悉地 258
사종연기 四種緣起 155
사종천 四種天 566
사종총지 四種總持 258, 259
사종행인 四種行人 258
사주 四主 258
사주 四住 258
사주 四洲 103, 241, 258, 535, 610
사주 寺主 173, 265
사주(지) 四住(地) 258
사주지 四住地 260
사중 四衆 87, 248, 259
사중 四重
四波羅夷 246
사중(금) 四重(禁) 259
사중(죄) 四重(罪) 467
사중만다라 四重曼荼羅 259
사중성중 四重聖衆 259
사중원단 四重圓壇 259
사중죄 四重罪 259
사중팔중 四重八重 259
사지 四地 425
사지 四持 259
사지 四智 259
사지 四知 259
사지 舍支 249, 259
사지 舍脂 259
사지발저 舍脂鉢低 259
사지야 娑底也 236
사지인 四智印 259
사지찬 四智讚 259
사진 四鎭 259

사진(제) 四眞(諦) 259
사진제 四眞諦 257
사집 四執 245, 249, 251, 259
사집 邪執 259
사집과 四集科 260
사집금강 四執金剛 260
사창 四唱 260
사처문신 四處問訊 260
사처십육회 四處十六會 260
사천상하 四天上下 260
사천왕 四天王 304, 320, 465, 486, 570
四方大將 246
四金剛 240
사천왕천 四天王天 260, 438
사천하 四天下 260
사천하경 四天下經 260
사취 四取 28, 260, 383
사취 四趣 260
사취 邪聚 260
사친근 四親近 260
사칠품 四七品 260
사타 奢陀 237
사타 捨墮 416
사타 私陀 235
사타(락법) 四墮(落法) 260
사타가 舍吒迦 243
사타가 闍陀伽 202
사타라 闍吒羅 366, 639
사탑 四塔 260
사택력 思擇力 235, 479
사토 四土 36, 174, 180, 248, 261, 267
사파게다 沙婆揭多 332
사파례 闍婆隸 234
사파파 私婆婆 235
사판 事判 261, 492
사팔상 四八相 261
사팔지응 四八之應 95
사평가 四評家 261
사풍 死風 235
사피다육론 四皮陀六論 461
사하 四河 261
사하 娑訶 217, 236, 246, 261, 336
사하 沙訶 236, 261
사하루타 娑訶樓陀 236
사함 四含 261
사항 四恒 261
사해 四海 261
사해 死海 235
사해론주 四海論主 261
사행 四行 261
사행 蛇行 236
사행 邪行 261, 531
사행상 四行相 261
사행장 邪行障 366
사행진여 邪行眞如 261, 588
사향 四向 223, 261, 605, 607
사현 師鉉 261
사현량 似現量 234, 605
사혜 四慧 261
사혜 思慧 235, 295, 469
사혹 事惑 493
사혹 四惑 261
사혹 思惑 20, 235, 335, 493
사홍서 四弘誓 434
사홍서원 四弘誓願 261
사화 事火 262, 318
사화 四花 262
사화법 四化法 262
사회 四悔 262
삭 爍 262
삭 鑠 262
삭 索 244, 262
삭가라 爍迦羅 262
삭가라아일다 鑠迦羅阿逸多 262
삭갈라 爍羯囉 262
삭계모니 鑠雞謀儞 262
삭도로 爍覩嚧 262, 313
삭발 削髮 262
삭사 索訶 261
삭아 索阿 262
삭어 索語 262
삭지저 鑠枳底 262
삭치 索哆 262
삭하 索訶 236, 262
삭화 索話 262
삭흘저 鑠訖底 262
산 刪 262
산 刪 218, 262
산 山 262
산 散 262
산 珊 262
산 算 262
산 訕 262
산가 山家 263, 573
산가종 山家宗 263
산공 散供 262
산근 山斤 255, 263
산내 山內 school 289
산니 霰尼 308
산니라자 珊尼羅闍 262
산도사다 珊都史多 or 珊覩史多 114
산란 散亂 262
산문 山門 263
산사야 刪闍夜 262
산사야비라지 珊闍邪毘羅胝 or 珊闍夜毘羅胝 262
산사야비라지자 刪闍耶毗羅胝子 262
산생재 散生齋 263
산서이비랄지자 刪逝移毗剌知子 262
산선 散善 262, 483
산성 山城 298
산세 山世 263
산수 算數 262
산수납 山水衲 263
산승 山僧 263
산신 山神 263
산신각 山神閣 263
산심 散心 262, 484
산야 珊若 262
산야 訕若 262, 565
산야바 珊若婆 262
산업 散業 262
산업염불 散業念佛 263
산왕 山王 263
산외 山外 409, 573
산외 山外 school 289
산외종 山外宗 263
산의삼매 散疑三昧 263
산일 散日 262
산전 散錢 263
산정 散定 526
산제람 刪提嵐 262
산지 散地 262
산지 散支 262
산지 訕底 262
산지(가) 散支(迦) 166
산지(가) 散脂(迦) 262
산지(가)대장 散脂(迦)大將 485
산지대장 散脂大將 246
산지라 珊底羅 365
산지열모절나 刪地涅暮折那 262
산타나 散陀那 263

산타나가리가부 山拖那伽梨柯部 463
산탁라 散拓羅 262
산해공시 山海空市 263
산해여래 山海如來 263
산해혜 山海慧 484
산해혜자재통왕여래 山海慧自在通王如來 or 山海惠自在通王如來 263
산호 山毫 263
산호 珊瑚 262
산화 散花 263
산화 散華 263
산화사 散花師 585
살 撒 263
살 殺 263
살 薩 263
살가야견 薩迦耶見 263
살귀 殺鬼 263
살다기리 薩多琦梨 264
살다바 薩多婆 264
살다바륜 薩陀波崙 264
살다반나구가 薩多般那求呵 419
살다야 薩跢也 264
살달(라)마 薩達(剌)摩 146
살달다반달라 薩怛多般怛羅 264
살달라마 薩達喇摩 264
살달마분다리(가) 薩達磨芬陀利(迦) 264
살달마분다리가 薩達磨奔茶利迦 264
살달박 薩怛縛 264
살담분다리 薩曇分陀利 264
살담분다리경 薩曇芬陀利經 146
살라 薩羅 264, 607
살라릉벌지 薩羅隆伐底 264
살라바박지 薩羅婆縛底 264
살라사박지 薩羅娑縛底 94
살라산지 薩羅酸底 94, 264
살라살벌지 薩囉薩筏底 158
살리살파 薩利殺跛 264
살리찰파 薩利刹跛 13
살마아한 撒馬兒罕 263
살바 薩婆 264
살바가마 薩婆迦摩 264
살바갈라타실타 薩婆曷刺他悉陀 264
살바다 薩婆多 457, 482
살바다(부) 薩婆多(部) 264
살바다론 薩婆多論 255
살바다부 薩婆多部 485, 509
살바달 薩縛達 264
살바신야제바 薩婆愼若提婆 264
살바신야제바 薩婆愼若提婆 510
살바실다 薩婆悉多 264
살바실달다 薩婆悉達多 264
살바아사저바타부 薩婆阿私底婆拖部 509
살바아사지바타 薩婆阿私底婆拖 264
살바알타실타 薩婆頞他悉陀 264
살바야 薩婆若 264
살바야나 薩婆若那 264
살바야낭 薩婆若囊 264
살바야다 薩婆若多 264
살바흘예사 薩婆吃隸奢 264
살박달 薩縛達 508
살박알타실지 薩縛頞他悉地 264
살벌야 薩伐若 264
살벌야 薩栰若 264
살부살지 薩裒煞地 264
살부시살 薩裒施殺 264
살불답 薩不荅 264
살불답라적날 薩不荅羅的捺 264, 584
살사라사 薩闍羅娑 264
살삼마사 殺三摩娑 263
살삼마사 煞三摩娑 271
살생 殺生 263
살업 殺業 263
살운야 薩云若 264
살운야 薩雲若 264
살운연 薩云然 264
살자 殺者 263, 568, 600
살적 殺賊 263, 375
살절라사 薩折羅娑 264
살지야 薩底也 264
살차니건(련타) 薩遮尼乾(連陀) 264
살타 薩埵 264, 431, 458
살타 薩陀 296, 600
살타니습벌라 薩他泥濕伐羅 265
살투라 薩偸羅 597
살파서혼직가발파라 薩簸恕魂直迦鉢婆羅 419
삼 三 265
삼 參 565
삼 森 265
삼 參 486
삼가 三假 140, 265, 294
삼가관 三假觀 265
삼가섭 三迦葉 12
삼가섭 三迦葉 265
삼가시설 三假施設 265, 280
삼각 三覺 265
삼각단 三角壇 265
삼감 三監 265
삼강 三綱 265, 297
삼거 三擧 221, 265
삼건 三愆 265
삼겁 三劫 265
삼겁삼천불 三劫三千佛 265
삼견 三堅 265
삼결 三結 265, 295
삼경 三境 266
삼경일론 三經一論 266
삼계 三契 266
삼계 三季 266
삼계 三戒 266
삼계 三界 27, 50, 56, 115, 207, 236, 266, 286, 301, 303, 430, 454, 478
삼계(불)법 三階(佛)法 266
삼계교 三階敎 266
삼계구지 三界九地 266
삼계만영패 三界萬靈牌 266
삼계상 三界牀 266
삼계안 三界眼 266
삼계웅 三界雄 266
삼계원 三階院 266
삼계유일심 三界唯一心 266
삼계자부 三界慈父 266
삼계장 三界藏 266
삼계존 三界尊 266
삼계화택 三界火宅 266
삼고 三古 266
삼고 三股 62, 266
삼고 三苦 266
삼고 三鈷 266
삼고령 三鈷鈴 427
삼공 三空 266, 279, 295
삼공(관)문 三空(觀)門 267
삼과 三果 267
삼과 三科 267
삼과 三過 267
삼관 三觀 145, 267, 544, 546
삼관등 三觀等 266

삼광(천) 三光(天) 267
삼광사 三光寺 267
삼교 三敎 267, 280, 282
삼구 三句 267
삼구 三垢 267, 295
삼구족 三具足 267
삼국토 三國土 267
삼권일실 三權一實 268
삼궤 三軌 266, 268, 276
삼궤홍경 三軌弘經 268
삼귀 三歸 59, 268
삼귀 三皈 268
삼귀(오)계 三歸(五)戒 268
삼귀수법 三歸受法 268
삼귀의 三歸依 268
삼극소 三極少 268
삼근 三根 268, 270
삼금 三金 268
삼기 三機 268
삼나삼불 三那三佛 268
삼난 三難 268
삼념주 三念住 214, 268
삼념처 三念處 176, 268
삼능 三能 278
삼능삼불능 三能三不能 268
삼다 三多 269
삼다라니 三陀羅尼 269
삼단 三斷 218, 269
삼단 三檀 269
삼달 三達 269, 273, 294
삼대 三大 88, 269
삼대부 三大部 269, 464
삼대비법 三大秘法 499
삼덕 三德 91, 103, 230, 269, 283, 553
삼도 三倒 270
삼도 三塗 270
삼도 三道 178, 270, 271
삼도진언 三道眞言 270
삼독 三毒 267, 268, 270, 275, 276, 278, 279, 281, 288, 291, 292, 295, 535
삼독룡 三毒龍 249
삼독시리 三毒尸利 270
삼등 三等 270
삼등류 三等流 270
삼등지 三等持 279
삼라만상 森羅萬象 265
삼라만상즉법신 森羅萬象卽法身 265
삼라만상지원 森羅萬象之元 446
삼락 三樂 270
삼락차 三落叉 270
삼력 三力 120, 270, 637
삼력게 三力偈 270
삼례 三禮 270
삼례사 三禮師 585
삼론 三論 34, 99, 122, 175, 187, 270, 276, 302, 304, 316, 364, 370, 395, 427, 466, 544, 545, 587, 609, 610, 612
삼론 三論 School 544
삼론종 三論宗 188, 270, 271, 367, 456, 534, 540, 544, 601, 605
삼론현의 三論玄義 271, 544
삼루 三漏 271, 295, 438
삼류경 三類境 266
삼륙 三六 271
삼륙구 三六九 271
삼륜 三輪 45, 178, 270, 271
삼륜교 三輪敎 271, 290
삼륜상 三輪相 271
삼륜세계 三輪世界 271
삼륜화도 三輪化導 271, 637
삼마 三摩 271
삼마 三馬 272
삼마 三魔 272
삼마갈 三摩竭 272
삼마근리 三摩近離 272
삼마난달라 三摩難呾囉 272
삼마달타 三摩咀吒 271
삼마바야 三摩婆夜 271
삼마반나 三摩半那 271, 272
삼마발제 三摩拔提 272
삼마발제 三摩跋提 272
삼마발제 三摩鉢提 272
삼마발지 三摩鉢底 116, 272, 273
삼마사 三摩娑 271
삼마야 三摩耶 272
삼마야 三摩若 272
삼마야도 三摩耶道 272
삼마예 三摩曳 272
삼마월 三摩越 272
삼마제 三摩帝 271
삼마제 三摩提 271, 526
삼마지 三摩既 271
삼마지 三摩地 104, 271, 551
삼마지 三摩底 271
삼마지(제) 三摩地(帝) 273
삼마지(제) 三摩地(提) 273
삼마지(지) 三摩地(既) 273
삼마지(지) 三摩地(底) 273
삼마지염송 三摩地念誦 271
삼마착 三摩捉 284
삼마피타 三摩皮陀 271
삼마희다 三摩呬多 271
삼만 三曼 195, 272
삼만 三滿 272
삼만(다)발다(라) 三曼(陀)颰陀(羅) 272
삼만다 三曼多 272
삼만다 三曼陀 272
삼만다 三滿多 272
삼만다건다 三曼陀犍陀 272
삼만다건제 三萬陀犍提 272
삼만다발날라 三滿多跋捺囉 272
삼만발다 三曼跋陀 272
삼말다 三末多 272
삼매 三昧 271, 328
삼매(야) 三昧(耶) 271, 272
삼매(지) 三昧(地) 273
삼매마 三昧魔 272, 273
삼매문 三昧門 273
삼매불 三昧佛 273
삼매상응 三昧相應 273
삼매신 三昧身 214
삼매야 三昧耶 272, 484
삼매야계 三昧耶戒 272, 280, 294
삼매야계 三昧耶界 272
삼매야만다라 三昧耶曼荼羅 272
삼매야신 三昧耶身 272
삼매야인 三昧耶印 259
삼매야지 三昧耶智 272
삼매야형 三昧耶形 272, 295
삼매야회 三昧耶會 272
삼매왕 三昧王 435, 485
삼매왕삼매 三昧王三昧 435
삼매월륜상 三昧月輪相 273
삼매화 三昧火 273
삼먁 三藐 116
삼먁삼모지 三貌糝帽地 273
삼먁삼보리 三藐三菩提 273, 285
삼먁삼불타 三藐三佛陀 268, 273, 285, 528
삼면대흑 三面大黑 273
삼명 三明 142, 151, 269, 273,

ㄱ ㄴ ㄷ ㄹ ㅁ ㅂ ㅅ ㅇ ㅈ ㅊ ㅋ ㅌ ㅍ ㅎ 찾아보기

294, 570
삼명(지) 三明(智) 273
삼명경 三明經 273
삼모날라사아라 三母捺羅娑誐羅 274
삼모니 三牟尼 274
삼모다 三暮多 274
삼모달라 三慕達羅 274
삼모제야 三牟提耶 274
四諦 257
삼모지 糝帽地 277
삼목 三目 274
삼묘행 三妙行 274
삼무 三武 274
삼무루근 三無漏根 149, 268, 274, 475
삼무루학 三無漏學 274
삼무성 三無性 152, 274, 298
삼무위법 三無爲法 405
삼무진장엄장 三無盡莊嚴藏 274
삼무차(별) 三無差(別) 274
삼무차별 三無差別 276
삼묵당 三默堂 274
삼문 三門 274
삼문삼대시자 三門三大侍者 274
삼미 三味 274
삼미 三迷 274
삼미제 三彌提 275
삼미지 三彌底 94, 160, 274, 275, 528
삼미지부론 三彌底部論 275
삼미지여량제자 三眉底與量弟子 275
삼미지여부 三眉底與部 274
삼미차 三彌叉 274
삼밀 三密 45, 239, 275, 294
삼밀 三蜜 160
삼밀상응 三密相應 275
삼밀육대 三密六大 275
삼밀율지니가야 三密栗底尼迦耶 274, 275
삼밀율지니가야 三蜜栗底尼迦耶 274
삼바라 三婆羅 275
삼박 三縛 275
삼반야 三般若 275
삼발라 三跋羅 275
삼발라거치 三鉢羅佉哆 275
삼발심 三發心 275
삼발제 三拔諦 275
삼발제 三跋諦 275
삼발치 三拔致 275
삼발치 三跋致 275
삼방편 三方便 275
삼배 三拜 276
삼배 三輩 275, 545
삼백법 三白法 276
삼백사십일계 三百四十一戒 276
삼백사십팔계 三百四十八戒 276
삼백식 三白食 276
삼백유순 三百由旬 276
삼백육십회 三百六十會 276
삼번뇌 三煩惱 276, 295
삼벌시 三伐恃 211
삼벌업 三罰業 276
삼벌지 三伐持 276
삼범 三梵 276
삼법 三法 276, 366
삼법(묘) 三法(妙) 268
삼법계 三法界 369
삼법륜 三法輪 276
삼법묘 三法妙 276, 353, 358
삼법무차 三法無差 276
삼법신 三法身 188
삼법인 三法印 199, 276, 287
삼법인 三法忍 276
삼변(토전) 三變(土田) 276
삼병 三病 276, 292
삼보 三報 276
삼보 三寶 7, 186, 210, 217, 268, 276, 277, 283, 349
四信五行 252
삼보가 三菩伽 277
삼보가가야 三菩伽迦耶 277
삼보리 三菩提 277
삼보물 三寶物 277
삼보불 三寶佛 210
삼보신 三寶身 277, 282
삼보의 三寶衣 277
삼보장 三寶藏 277
삼보종찰 三寶宗刹 277
삼보타 三補吒 277
삼복 三福 277, 291
世福 319
삼복 三覆 277
삼복업 三福業 277
삼복전 三福田 470
삼복팔교 三覆八校 277
삼부 三部 266, 595
삼부(대법) 三部(大法) 278
삼부경 三部經 278
삼부라 三嚩羅 275
삼부비경 三部秘經 278
삼부정육 三不淨肉 278
삼부주색 三部主色 278
삼분과경 三分科經 278
삼분별 三分別 209
삼불 三佛 278
삼불견법 三不堅法 278
삼불능 三不能 278
삼불보리 三佛菩提 278
삼불삼신 三不三信 278
삼불선근 三不善根 278
삼불성 三佛性 278, 495
삼불신 三佛身 278
삼불실 三不失 278
삼불어 三佛語 278
삼불율지 三佛栗底 278
삼불자 三佛子 278
삼불타 三佛陀 278
삼불토 三佛土 278, 294
삼불퇴 三不退 222, 278, 452
삼불호 三不護 176, 278
삼비밀 三秘密 278
삼비밀신 三秘密身 278
삼사 三使 278, 293
삼사 三思 278
삼사계 三事戒 279
삼사납 三事衲 279
삼사련마 三事練磨 279
삼사연마 三事練磨 294
삼사의 三事衣 279
삼사칠증 三師七證 279, 361, 588
삼삼마(지) 三三摩(地) 279
삼삼매 三三昧 33, 34, 151, 266, 279, 292, 294, 295, 422
삼삼매(지) 三三昧(地) 279
삼삼매관 三三昧觀 294
삼삼매문 三三昧門 294
삼삼매지 三三昧地 294
삼상 三想 279
삼상 三相 126, 279
삼상속 三相續 279
삼색 三色 279
삼생 三生 279, 280
삼생과수 三生果遂 503
삼생성불 三生成佛 279

삼선 三仙 276
삼선 三善 279
삼선 三禪 55, 279
삼선근 三善根 279
삼선도 三善道 279
삼선이천 三仙二天 280
삼선지식 三善知識 279
삼선천 三禪天 250, 301
삼선취 三善趣 279
삼섭제 三攝提 265, 280
삼성 三性 148, 280, 282, 419, 473, 608, 612
삼성 三聖 280
삼성분별 三性分別 280
삼세 三世 159, 280, 289, 293, 533
삼세 三細 280, 629
육추 六麤 468
삼세가실 三世假實 280
삼세각모 三世覺母 280
삼세간 三世間 280, 291
삼세무장애지계 三世無障礙智戒 280, 294
삼세불 三世佛 280
삼세불가득 三世不可得 280
삼세삼천불 三世三千佛 280
삼세성불 三世成佛 280
삼세실유법체항유 三世實有法體恒有 280
삼세심 三世心 280
삼세심불가득 三世心不可得 211
삼세요달 三世了達 280
삼세지 三世智 280, 370
삼세항(명왕) 三世降(明王) 83
삼세항강(명왕) 三世降(明王) 83
삼소단 三所斷 230
삼쇠 三衰 281
삼수 三修 281
삼수 三受 213, 281
삼수 三獸 281
삼수 三銖 281
삼수업 三受業 281
삼술 三術 281
삼승 三乘 270, 281, 282, 286, 293, 369, 422
방편 方便 174
삼승가 三乘家 282, 293
삼승기 三僧祇 282
삼승법 三乘法 281
삼승법문 三乘法門 293
삼승별교 三乘別教 239, 421
삼승진실일승방편 三乘眞實一乘方便 282
삼승통교 三乘通教 239, 421
삼시 三施 269, 282
삼시 三時 282
삼시교 三時教 267, 279
삼시교(판) 三時教(判) 282
삼시년한 三時年限 282
삼시성 三時性 282
삼시업 三時業 282
삼시좌선 三時坐禪 282
삼식 三識 282, 344
삼신 三身 7, 186, 188, 194, 276, 277, 278, 282, 283, 291, 331, 370, 471, 505, 639
삼신불성 三身佛性 283
삼신삼덕 三身三德 283
삼신업 三身業 283
삼신여래 三身如來 283
삼심 三心 283, 645
삼십 三十 283
삼십사수 三十捨隨 481
삼십사타 三十捨墮 284
삼십삼 三十三 284
삼십삼(존)관음 三十三(尊)觀音 284
삼십삼과 三十三過 284
삼십삼신 三十三身 284
삼십삼천 三十三天 82, 107, 284, 533
삼십생 三十生 284
삼십오불 三十五佛 284
삼십유식론 三十唯識論 370
삼십육(부)신 三十六(部)神 284
삼십육물 三十六物 285
삼십이 三十二 285
삼십이대인상 三十二大人相 285
삼십이상 三十二相 176, 285, 607
삼십이상경 三十二相經 285
삼십이신 三十二身 285
삼십이응 三十二應 285
삼십칠(보리)분법 三十七(菩提)分法 285
삼십칠(조)도품 三十七(助)道品 285
삼십칠과도품 三十七科道品 254
삼십칠도품 三十七道品 7, 257, 485
삼십칠보리분 三十七菩提分 584
삼십칠조도품 三十七助道品 414
삼십칠존 三十七尊 285
삼십칠존사대륜 三十七尊四大輪 285
삼십칠품 三十七品 285, 422
삼아 三阿 292
삼아승기겁 三阿僧祇劫 282, 285
삼악 三惡 285
삼악각 三惡覺 285
삼악도 三惡道 253, 268, 279, 285, 642
삼악취 三惡趣 270, 285
삼안거 三安居 285
삼애 三礙 319
삼야삼보 三耶三菩 273, 285
삼야삼불(단) 三耶三佛(壇 273
삼야삼불(단) 三耶三佛(壇) 285
삼어 三語 285
삼억가 三億家 285
삼업 三業 45, 142, 274, 286, 360, 396, 409, 474
삼업공양 三業供養 286
삼업상응 三業相應 286
삼여 三餘 286, 397
삼역 三逆 286
삼연 三緣 286
삼연 三衍 286
삼연마 三練磨 286
삼열 三熱 286
삼열반문 三涅槃門 295
삼열반문 三列槃門 286
삼온 三蘊 286
삼욕 三欲 286
삼원 三猿 286
삼위일진 三僞一眞 286
삼유 三有 266, 286, 439, 454
삼유대 三有對 286
삼유위법 三有爲法 286, 458
삼유위상 三有爲相 287
삼응공양 三應供養 287
삼의 三疑 287
삼의 三衣 277, 287, 462, 472
삼의 三醫 287
삼의육물 三衣六物 462
삼인 三印 276, 287
삼인 三因 287
삼인 三忍 276, 287, 648
삼인불성 三因佛性 418

삼인삼과 三因三果 287
삼일 三一 265
삼일이승 三一二乘 483
삼일재 三日齋 287
삼자 三子 287
삼자 三字 287
삼자 三慈 287
삼자 三自 287
삼잡 三帀 287
삼잡염 三雜染 288
삼장 三藏 23, 288, 295, 448, 485, 519, 520, 617
삼장 三障 288, 460
삼장(재)월 三長(齋)月 288
삼장교 三藏敎 245, 267, 288, 602
천태삼교 573
삼장법사 三藏法師 168, 267, 288, 630
삼장법수 三藏法數 285, 507
삼장불 三藏佛 210
삼장엄 三莊嚴 288
삼장전 三藏傳 382
삼장학자 三藏學者 288
삼재 三災 18, 19, 288
水災 335
水風火災 335
火災 641
삼재월 三齋月 288
삼전 三田 288
삼전(법륜) 三轉(法輪) 288
삼전도 三顚倒 270, 288
삼전법륜 三轉法輪 59
삼전법륜십이행(상) 三轉法輪十二行(相) 288
삼절 三節 288
삼점 三漸 288
삼점 三點 288
삼정 三定 55, 257, 279
삼정기 三精氣 288
삼정육 三淨肉 278, 288
삼정취 三定聚 288
삼제 三諦 2, 20, 145, 269, 289, 290, 499, 544, 546
삼제 三際 280, 289
삼제상즉 三諦相卽 289
삼제시 三際時 289
삼조 三照 289
삼조연하 三條椽下 289
삼존 三尊 289
삼존내영 三尊來迎 289
삼존불 三尊佛 289
삼종 三宗 290
삼종 三從 265, 289
삼종 三種 290
삼종견혹 三種見惑 290
삼종공양 三種供養 290
삼종관정 三種灌頂 290
삼종광명 三種光明 290
삼종교상 三種敎相 290
삼종단 三種斷 290
삼종대지 三種大智 290
삼종바라밀 三種波羅蜜 290, 291
삼종법륜 三種法輪 290
삼종삼관 三種三觀 290
삼종삼세 三種三世 290
삼종상 三種常 290
삼종상 三種相 290
삼종색 三種色 279, 291
삼종생 三種生 291
삼종선근 三種善根 291
삼종세간 三種世間 291
삼종시도 三種示導 271, 291
삼종신 三種身 291
삼종신고 三種身苦 291
삼종심고 三種心苦 291
삼종연자 三種緣慈 291
삼종욕 三種欲 291
삼종원융 三種圓融 291
삼종유 三種有 291
삼종인행 三種忍行 291
삼종자비 三種慈悲 287, 291
삼종정업 三種淨業 277, 291
삼종지 三種智 290, 291
삼종지관 三種止觀 291
삼종지옥 三種地獄 292
삼종참법 三種懺法 292
삼종천 三種天 292, 566
삼종천제 三種闡提 292
삼종청정 三種淸淨 292
삼종향 三種香 292
삼종회법 三種悔法 292, 293
삼주 三株 270, 292
삼주관월 三舟觀月 292
삼중등지 三重等持 279, 292
삼중법계 三重法界 292
삼중삼매 三重三昧 279, 292
삼중장 三重障 288
삼즉일 三卽一 292
삼지 三地 425
삼지 三智 111, 266, 292, 509
삼지(비량) 三支(比量) 292
삼지백(대)겁 三祇百(大)劫 292
삼진여 三眞如 292
삼차 三車 281, 293
삼차가 三車家 293
삼참 三懺 293
삼처목차 三處木叉 293
삼처아란야 三處阿蘭若 293
삼처전심 三處傳心 293
삼천 三千 293
삼천 三天 293
삼천(세)계 三千(世)界 293
삼천년일현 三千年一現 293
삼천대천 三千大千 105
삼천대천세계 三千大千世界 293, 326, 430, 478, 501, 546
삼천불 三千佛 293
삼천불명경 三千佛名經 280
삼천사 三天使 278, 293, 569
삼천사선 三天四仙 293
삼천세계경 三千世界經 293
삼천실상 三千實相 293
삼천위의 三千威儀 293
삼천진점겁 三千塵點劫 293
삼첨 三舌甘 293
삼청 三請 293
삼초 三草 97, 546
삼초이목 三草二木 293, 323, 326
삼취 三聚 251, 260, 268, 288, 294, 531
삼취(정)계 三聚(淨)戒 294
삼취원계 三聚圓戒 294
삼취정계 三聚淨戒 98
삼치 三治 279, 294
삼칠일사유 三七日思惟 294
삼탈문 三脫門 294
삼태 三台 572
삼토 三土 294, 642
삼통력 三通力 294
삼퇴굴 三退屈 121, 279, 286, 294
삼파다 三波多 294
삼파라섭제 三波羅攝提 294
삼파하 三波訶 294
삼팔일 三八日 294
삼평등 三平等 272, 294
삼평등계 三平等戒 280, 294
삼평등관 三平等觀 294

삼평등지 三平等地 294
삼평등호마단 三平等護摩壇 294
삼품 三品 294
삼품사미 三品沙彌 294
삼품사선근 三品四善根 251
삼품성취 三品成就 294
삼품실지 三品悉地 294
삼품청법 三品廳法 294
삼학 三學 28, 294, 369, 531
삼학위 三學位 242
삼해탈 三解脫 279, 294
삼해탈(문) 三解脫(門 294
삼해탈(문) 三解脫(門) 295
삼해탈문 三解脫門 267, 274, 286
삼행 三行 295
삼현 三賢 242, 423
삼현십성 三賢十聖 295
삼현십지 三賢十地 295
삼현위 三賢位 76, 318
삼협 三篋 295
삼형 三形 295
삼혜 三慧 142, 295
삼호 三胡 266
삼혹 三惑 20, 150, 276, 295
삼화 三和 295
삼화 三火 295
삽 挿 295
삽 澁 295
삽 颯 295
삽 馺 295
삽단 挿單 295
삽말건 颯秣建 295
삽촉 澁觸 295
삽파치가 颯破椒迦 295
상 上 268, 294, 297, 544, 618
상 傷 297
상 像 282, 296
상 償 297
상 商 296
상 喪 296
상 常 269, 296, 463, 464, 605
four inverted beliefs 242
四德 241
상 想 104, 140, 297, 417, 423, 424, 587
상 桑 296
상 相 88, 201, 292, 296, 300, 416, 428
상 祥 295
상 象 71, 295
four snakes 249
상가 商迦 296
상가 象駕 296
상간 上間 297
상갈라 商羯羅 31, 297
상갈라아사리 商羯羅阿闍梨 297
상갈라주 商羯羅主 496
상갈야 桑渴耶 296
상강 上綱 297
상거 傷佉 297
상거 商佉 184, 296
상거 霜佉 297
상견 上肩 297
상견 常見 85, 296, 477, 582, 601
상견산 象堅山 226, 295
상견순전 上肩順轉 297
상경 像經 296
상경 常境 296
상계 像季 296
상계 相繼 25
상계천 上界天 297, 414
상고 商賈 229, 297
상공 上供 297
상공 相空 267, 297, 477, 582
상공관 相空觀 267
상광 常光 296, 477, 489
상교 像敎 296
상교 象敎 296
상구보리 上求菩提 619
상구보리하화중생 上求菩提下化衆生 297
상구본래 上求本來 297
상군 象軍 296
상근 上根 297
상기라 償起羅 297
상기라 商企羅 297
상나화수 商那和修 137, 297, 486
상낙(가)박사 商諾(迦)縛娑 297
상념 常念 296
상념 想念 297
상당 上堂 297
상당패 上堂牌 297
상대 相大 269, 298
상대 相對 297
상대 相待 297, 487
상대묘 相待妙 480
상대원 相待圓 487
상대유 相待有 291
상도 常途 296
상도 常道 296
상두산 象頭山 296
상락아정 常樂我淨 36, 187, 296, 372, 405, 528, 604, 609
상랍 上臘 298, 618
상량 商量 297
상력 常力 296, 361
상류(반) 上流(般) 298
상류반 上流般 428
상류반열반 上流般涅槃 298
상륜 相輪 298
상립승번 常立勝幡 296
상말 像末 296
상명 傷命 297
상명오법 相名五法 298, 416
상모(궁)성 上茅(宮)城 298
상몰 常沒 296
상무상 常無常 587
상무성 相無性 274, 298
상무아 常無我 153
상문 喪門 245
상문 桑門 242, 245, 296
상바라밀 常波羅蜜 296
상박 相縛 298
상방 上方 298
상배 上輩 298
상배관 上輩觀 298
상번뇌 上煩惱 298
상법 像法 136, 251, 282, 296, 646
상법 象法 or 像法 646
상법시 像法時 528
상변견 常邊見 481
상분 相分 248, 298, 476
상불경 常不輕 81, 296
상불경보살 常不經菩薩 212
상불망실 常不忘失 176
상비 象鼻 296, 583
상사 上士 298, 545
상사 相似 298
상사각 相似覺 238, 298, 410
상사불 相似佛 298
상사즉 相似卽 76, 460, 467, 608
상사즉(불) 相似卽(佛) 298
상삼도 上三途 461
상상 上上 56
상상구절종 相想俱絶宗 298
상상인 上上人 299
상색 相色 287

상생 想生 291
상생 相生 291
상서 祥瑞 295
상성 相性 296
상속 相續 298
상속가 相續假 298
상속무상 相續無常 480
상속상 相續常 290, 298
상속상 相續相 298, 464, 468
상속식 相續識 298, 344, 422
상속심 相續心 298
상수 上手 298
상수 上首 298
상승 上乘 97, 299
상승 相承 299
상승밀종 上乘密宗 299
상승선 上乘禪 299
상승유가 上乘瑜伽 299
상시 像始 296
상시교 相始教 34, 340, 412
상신 常身 296, 484
상아 常我 372
상아 象牙 296
상안 常眼 296
상애 想愛 297
상여 相如 362
상연 上衍 299
상온 想蘊 297
상왕 象王 296
상운 像運 296
상원 上元 545
상원소등 上元燒燈 299
상월 祥月 295
상위석 相違釋 462
상위인 相違因 299
상응 相應 299
상응박 相應縛 298, 299
상응법 相應法 299
상응아급마 相應阿笈摩 299
상응인 相應因 299, 465
상응종 相應宗 299
상의 上衣 299
상이계 上二界 370
상인 上人 299
상일주재 常一主宰 497
상일지체 常一之體 153
상입 相入 299
상적 常寂 296
상적 想寂 273
상적광토 常寂光土 222, 261, 296
상전 上轉 299, 619
상전도 想顚倒 297
상제 上祭 299
상제보살 常啼菩薩 296
상제불 常啼佛 264
상족 上足 299
상존국 象尊國 295
상종 相宗 299, 489
상좌 上坐 5, 103, 591
상좌 上座 265, 297, 299, 482, 541
상좌부 上坐部 104, 324, 325, 349
상좌부 上座部 57, 299, 300, 324, 325, 485
상주 常住 218, 296, 605
상주 象主 258, 295
상주교 常住教 422
상주일상 常住一相 296
상중 上中 56
상중하법 上中下法 300
상중하품 上中下品 616
상즉 相卽 300
상지 上地 469
상지 常智 296
상지 相智 300
상지옥 想地獄 297
상착의 上著衣 300
상초 祥草 295
상취 上趣 300
상친 喪櫬 296
상타갱 象墮阬 295
상토 相土 492
상품 上品 240, 294, 298, 300
상품상생 上品上生 56, 300
상품연대 上品蓮臺 300
상품중생 上品中生 300
상품하생 上品下生 300
상하 上下 56
상항 常恒 296
상행 上行 241
本化四菩薩 247
상행 常行 296
상행도 常行道 169
상행보살 上行菩薩 300
상행삼매 常行三昧 169
상호 相好 300
상호장엄신 相好莊嚴身 214
상화 像化 296
상화기 傷和氣 297
새 塞 300
새 賽 300
새건나 塞健那 300
새건다(라) 塞建陀(羅) 300
새건타 塞健陀 300
새박실지가 塞縛悉底迦 300
새전 賽錢 300
새파지가 塞頗胝加 300
새파치가 塞頗致迦 600
새필력가 塞畢力迦 300
색 色 140, 266, 297, 300, 423, 424, 458, 503, 607, 615
색 索 262
색개 色蓋 301
색경 色境 301
색계 色界 55, 223, 266, 301, 401, 426, 454, 456, 484, 485
색공외도 色空外道 301
색광 色光 301, 477
색광명 色光明 489
색구 色具 301
색구경 色究竟 250
색구경천 色究竟天 301, 426, 458
색구의천 色究意天 370
색미 色味 301
색미 色微 301
색박실저가 塞縛悉底迦 134
색법 色法 176, 416, 425, 585
색불이공 色不異空 35
색상 色相 301
색상토 色相土 301, 421
색성 色聲 301
색신 色身 291, 301
색심 色心 302
색애주지 色愛住地 258
색염 色焰 302
색온 色蘊 302
색욕 色欲 302
색유 色有 302
색음 色陰 302
색입 色入 302
색정 色頂 301
색제 色諦 302
색중 色衆 302
색진 色塵 302
색처 色處 302
색취지미 色聚之微 60
색타 索埵 264
색파지가 塞頗胝迦 334

색포 色泡 302
생 生 80, 302, 365, 605
four functioning forms 255
four methods, egg, womb, water, transmigration 647
생경 生經 302
생공 生空 302, 373, 497
생귀주 生貴住 368
생기 生起 302
생념처보살 生念處菩薩 302
생대 生臺 302
생도 生途 302
생득 生得 315
생득선 生得善 1
생령 生靈 302
생로병사 生老病死 302
생맹 生盲 302
생멸 生滅 302
생멸거래 生滅去來 302
생멸멸이적멸위락 生滅滅已寂滅爲樂 608
생무성 生無性 274
생반 生盤 302
생반 生般 428
생반 生飯 302, 579
생법 生法 302
생법이신 生法二身 303
생보 生報 276, 303
생불 生佛 303
생불가명 生佛假名 303
생불부증불멸 生佛不增不滅 303
생불불이 生佛不二 303
생불일여 生佛一如 303
생불일체 生佛一體 303
생사 生似 303
생사 生死 80, 153, 267, 303, 308, 545
생사(대)해 生死(大)海 303
생사니 生死泥 303
생사류 生死流 303
생사륜 生死輪 303
생사안 生死岸 303
생사야 生死野 303
생사연 生死淵 303
생사운 生死雲 303
생사원 生死園 303
생사장야 生死長夜 303
생사제 生死際 303
생사즉열반 生死卽涅槃 303
생사지제 生死之際 531
생사해탈 生死解脫 303
생상 生像 303
생색 生色 303
생생 生生 303
생생사사 生生死死 303
생생조 生生鳥 140
생소 生酥 320
생소미 生酥味 415
생승결정 生勝決定 466
생신 生身 303, 484
생신공 生身供 303
생신사리 生身舍利 303
생유 生有 303
생인 生因 287, 425, 437, 488
생인 生忍 303
생전 生田 303
생조융예 生肇融叡 303
생주 生主 171
생주멸 生住滅 542
생주이멸 生住異滅 249, 296, 303, 318, 458
생즉무생, 무생즉생 生卽無生, 無生卽生 304
생지 生支 304
생진 生津 304
생천 生天 304, 566
생취 生趣 304
생화 生化 304
생화이신 生化二身 304
서 序 304
서 庶 304
서 書 304
서 棲 304
서 瑞 304
서 西 90, 304
서 誓 305
서 逝 66, 68, 304
서 鼠 304
서가행 西加行 493
서건 西乾 304
서광 棲光 304
서광 西光 304
서구다니 西瞿陀尼 305
서구야니 西瞿耶尼 305
서궁 逝宮 304
서기 書記 69, 304
서니가 西儞迦 304, 308
서다 誓多 68
서다 逝多 304
서다림 逝多林 29, 550
서다원 逝多苑 550
서류 庶類 304
서만다라 西曼陀羅 305
서명 西明 305
서명사 西明寺 305
서반 西班 305
서방 西方 304, 305
서방극락세계 西方極樂世界 305
서방접인 西方接引 305
서방정토 西方淨土 305
서분 序分 278, 501
서사 書寫 304
서산대사 西山大師 305
서산사 西山寺 379
서산주부 西山住部 305, 325
서상 瑞像 304
서상 瑞相 304
서서 西序 305
서수 誓水 64
서슬타 逝瑟吒 304
서신 棲神 304
서신 棲身 304
서안국 西安國 148
서약 誓約 305
서역구법고승전 西域求法高僧傳 305
서역기 西域記 17, 31, 80, 91, 97, 103, 104, 147, 157, 304, 305, 432, 442, 546, 550
the first image was made of red sandal-wood 442
서역기 西域記 10 495
서역기 西域記 12 549
서역기 西域記 5 14
서역기주 西域記主 258
서역전 西域傳 305
서왕 序王 304
서우화주 西牛貨洲 305
서원 誓願 305
서응 瑞應 304
서자 庶子 220, 278
서자 鼠子 365
서장 西藏 305
서장라마교 西藏喇嘛教 305
서장불교 西藏佛教 305
서장신지 西藏新志 539
서정 西淨 305, 581

서주 舒州 597
서주 西主 304
서즉조공 鼠喞鳥空 304
서찰 西刹 304
서천 西天 304
서천교주 西天敎主 304
서품 序品 157
서하 西河 305
서행 西行 305
석 夕 305
석 惜 306
석 昔 305
석 析 210, 306
석 石 305
석 釋 267, 306
석 錫 305
석가 釋家 306
석가 釋迦 220, 306, 361, 367, 584
석가(파) 釋迦(婆) 306, 307
석가모니 釋迦牟尼 306
석가문(니) 釋迦文(尼) 306
석가보살 釋迦菩薩 307
석가사자 釋迦獅子 307
석가여래성도기 釋迦如來成道記 306
석가제바인(다라) 釋迦提婆因(陀羅) 306
석가제바인달라 釋迦提婆因達羅 533
석가제환인(다라) 釋迦提桓因(陀羅) 306
석가제환인다라 釋迦提桓因陀羅 533
석가존 釋迦尊 306
석경산 石經山 305
석교 釋敎 214, 307
석궁 釋宮 307
석낭 惜囊 306
석녀 石女 305
석녀 釋女 307
석녀아 石女兒 305
석두 石頭 312
석등 石燈 307
석라 釋羅 307
석란 錫蘭 79
석려 釋侶 307
석론 釋論 307
석류 石榴 305
석륜 釋輪 307
석륜 錫崙 305
석리 昔哩 305, 342
석마남 釋摩男 307
석명 釋名 629
석문 釋門 307
석문정통 釋門正統
水陸齋, festival of water and land 333
석문정통 釋門正統 4 204
석미진 析微塵 306
석밀 石蜜 305
석발 石鉢 305
석범 釋梵 307
석벽경 石壁經 305
석비바소론 釋毘婆少論 615
석사 釋師 307
석사자 釋師子 307
석상고목 石霜枯木 29
석소 析小 306
석수 析水 306
석시(수) 釋翅(搜) 307
석씨 釋氏 307
석씨수 釋氏庾 307
석씨요람 釋氏要覽 299
석웅 釋雄 307
석원 昔圓 62, 487
석의 釋疑 307
석자 釋子 307
석자룡 石子龍 106
석장 石藏 382
석장 釋藏 307
석장 錫丈 305
석장사 錫杖師 585
석전 釋典 307
석제 釋帝 307
석제환인 釋帝桓因 533
석제환인 釋提桓因 307, 643
석종 釋種 225, 307
석좌 夕座 305
석지 析智 306
석풍 釋風 307
석화 石火 305
선 仙 307
선 僊 307
선 先 308
선 善 280, 284, 308
선 宣 308
선 扇 262, 308
선 旋 308
선 禪 37, 53, 54, 55, 88, 99, 196, 216, 359, 410, 422, 425, 489, 498, 587, 609
mental impression, intuitive certainty 354
선 線 307
선 線 308
선 繕 308
선 羨 308
선 船 308
선 詵 308
선 選 308
선가 禪家 309
선가귀감 禪家龜鑑 309
선각 善覺 284
선각장자 善覺長者 568
선거 禪居 309, 311
선겁 善劫 309, 627
선견 善見 250, 284, 309, 332, 583
선견론 善見論 103, 255
선견성 善見城 107, 571, 648
四苑 254
선견천 善見天 301, 370, 426
선결 善結 284
선경 仙經 308
선경 善敬 284
선경 線經 402
선고 善固 284
선공 善供 284
선과 善果 309
선관 禪觀 309
선광 善光 284
선교 善巧 309
선교 禪敎 309
선구 禪毬 309
선굴 禪窟 309
선권 禪卷 309
선귀신 善鬼神 311
선근 善根 309
선길 善吉 284
선나 禪那 308, 309
선나 羨那 308
선남신녀 善男信女 309
선남자 善男子 309
선니 先尼 304, 308
선니 禪尼 310
선다라니 旋陀羅尼 308
선다바 先陀婆 241
선달 先達 308

선당 禪堂 310, 311
선도 善導 40, 321, 427, 540, 587, 641
선도 善道 77
선도 繕都 308
선두 禪豆 308
선두 繕兜 308
선두 繕頭 308
선락 禪樂 310
선람 旋嵐 308
선래 善來 234, 310
선려 禪侶 310
선력 善力 284, 361
선록 禪錄 310
선록왕 仙鹿王 308
선류 宣流 308
선림 禪林 310
선마 繕摩 647
선마말라남 繕摩末剌諵 308
선명 善明 284
선묘 善妙 285
선무외 善無畏 102
선무외삼장 善無畏三藏 331
선문 禪門 309, 310, 312
선문답 禪問答 310
선문오종 禪門五宗 310
선문정로 禪門正路 310
선미 禪味 310
선바라밀 禪波羅密 312
선바라밀 禪波羅蜜 248
선반다가 扇般荼迦 308
선반택가 扇半擇迦 308
선방 禪房 310, 311
선배 先輩 308
선벌 船筏 308
선범천 禪梵天 310
선법 善法 567
선법 禪法 310
선법당 善法堂 77, 146
선법진여 善法眞如 293
선병 禪病 310
선복 善福 284
선본 善本 310
선비 善備 284
선사 善思 284
선사 善捨 284
선사 禪師 310, 433, 636
선사 禪思 310
선사 船師 308
선사유 善思惟 384
선산 仙山 482
선산 善山 284
선삼매 禪三昧 310
선생 先生 308
선생 善生 284, 310
선생경 善生經 462
선서 善逝 234, 284, 310, 371
선선 鄯善 75
선설 宣設 308
선성 仙城 308
선성 善性 310
선세 先世 308
선세부 善歲部 509
선수 善壽 284
선수 禪髓 311
선숙 善宿 311, 615
선술 善術 284
선습 禪習 311
선승 禪僧 311
선시 善施 284
선시분 善時分 393
선신 善神 311, 363
선실 禪室 311, 312
선심 善心 311
선아 善牙 329
선악 善惡 311
선악불이 善惡不二 220
선암사 仙巖寺 311
선업 先業 308
선업 善業 486
선연 禪延 107
선열 禪悅 311
선열식 禪悅食 311
선옥 禪屋 311
선우 善友 311
선우 選友 308
선운사 禪雲寺 311
선원 仙苑 308
선원 善願 284
선원 禪苑 310
선원 禪院 311
선월 善月 284, 311
선율 禪律 311
선음 仙音 308
선음 善音 284
선의 善意 284
선인 仙人 307
선인 善人 311
선인 善因 309, 311
선인 禪人 311
선인녹야원 仙人鹿野苑 308
선인녹원 仙人鹿園 308
선인선 善人禪 54
선인원 仙人園 122
선자 詵遮 308
선장 善藏 284
선장 禪杖 311
선재 善哉 311
선재동자 善財童子 252, 311
선적 善寂 284
선정 善淨 185, 284
선정 禪定 309, 311, 461, 526, 551
선정 禪靜 312
선정경 禪定境 355
선제 善帝 284
선제 禪齊 312
선조 善照 284
선조 善調 284
선조고산 先照高山 308
선종 宣宗 173
선종 禪宗 86, 309, 312, 354, 367, 507, 540, 603
patriarchs 466
선좌 禪坐 312
선주 善主 284
선주 善住 284
선지 善知 312
선지 善至 275
선지 禪智 312
선지가 扇底迦 308, 429
선지식 善知識 312
선지식마 善知識魔 272
선진 先進 308
선진 禪鎭 312
선천 善天 284
선천 禪天 312
선철 先哲 308
선체 扇搋 168, 308, 428
선쾌 善快 205
선타(바) 先陀(婆) 308
선타객 先陀客 308
선파 禪波 312
선판 禪版 473
선품 善品 284
선하 禪河 312
선합 線合 554
선행 禪行 312

선향 善香 284
선향 線香 308
선현 善現 250, 312, 391
선현 善賢 147
선현대장 善現大將 246
선현색 善現色 312
선현천 善現天 301, 312, 329, 370, 426
선혜 禪慧 312
선혜지 善慧地 312, 369
선화 禪化 312
선화 禪和 312
선화륜 旋火輪 308
선화자 禪和子 312
선화자 禪和者 312
설 泄 313
설 舌 312
설 薛 313
설 設 313
설 說 313
설 雪 313
설가부 說假部 313, 325
설경 說經 313
설계 說戒 313
설근 舌根 312, 485
설다도로 設多圖盧 313
설도로 設覩嚕 313
설도로 設都嚧 313
설돌로 設咄嚕 313
설라작갈라 薛攞斫羯羅 313
설려(다) 薛荔(多) 313
설령 雪嶺 313
설리(라) 設利(羅) 313
설리라 設利羅 243
설리불달라 設利弗怛羅 313
설묵 說默 313
설법 說法 313
설법륜 說法輪 271
설법묘 說法妙 358, 359
설법문 說法門 360
설법전 說法殿 313
설복 薛服 313
설불란 舌不爛 312
설사(리) 薛舍(離) 313
설사거 薛舍佉 613
설사달라 設婆怛羅 237
설산 雪山 217, 300, 313, 494
설산대사 雪山大士 313
설산동자 雪山童子 313
설산부 雪山部 313, 325
설산하 雪山下 648
설상 舌相 312
설상가 設賞迦 313, 451
설슬지림 洩瑟知林 520
설시 設施 259, 313
설시 說示 313
설식 舌識 312
설실라말나 薛室羅末拏 313
설은 雪隱 581
설인부 說因部 313
설일체유부 說一切有部 300, 313, 325, 509, 641
설전부 說轉部 313
설죄 說罪 313
설출세부 說出世部 313, 325
설타 薛陀 313
설통 說通 313
섬 睒 313
섬 譫 313
섬 贍 313
섬 閃 313
섬다 閃多 313
섬라 暹羅 555
섬마 睒摩 313
섬미 睒彌 313
섬부 剡浮 313, 406
섬부 譫浮 313
섬부 贍部 313
섬부(금) 贍部(金) 314
섬부광상 贍部光像 314
섬부날타금 贍部捺陀金 314
섬부제 贍部提 313
섬부주 贍部州 554
섬부주 譫浮洲 313
섬부주 贍部洲 313
四洲 258
섬전광 閃電光 313
섬파 睒婆 574
섭 攝 55, 314
섭 鍱 314
섭념산림 攝念山林 314
섭대승론 攝大乘論 314, 370, 420, 540
섭론 攝論 314
섭론석 攝論釋 362
섭론종 攝論宗 314, 540
섭리람 攝哩藍 314
섭마등 攝摩騰 314
섭말귀본법륜 攝末歸本法輪 271
섭박 攝縛 314
섭복 鍱腹 314
섭수 攝受 314
섭수기특 攝受奇特 69
섭실람 攝嗘藍 243
섭심 攝心 314, 528
섭의음악 攝意音樂 314
섭중생계 攝衆生戒 314
섭취 攝取 314
섭타필다 攝拖苾馱 314
성 城 314
성 性 55, 314, 429, 594
identified with 心 353
성 成 314
성 星 314, 486
성 省 314
성 聖 295, 314, 423, 429, 481
성 聲 270, 281, 314
성 誠 314
성각 性覺 315
성각이승 聲覺二乘 483
성겁 成劫 18, 41, 89, 238, 315
성겁오왕 成劫五王 96
성계 性戒 277, 315, 317, 563
성공 性空 267, 315, 477, 582
성공 星供 314
성공 聖供 315
성공관 性空觀 267, 315
성공교 性空教 315
성공종 性空宗 367
성과 聖果 315, 467
성교 聖教 315
성교 聲教 315
성교량 聖教量 119, 315
比量 226
성구 性具 183, 315
성근 聲根 315
성기 性起 315
성념송 聲念誦 315
성념처 性念處 315
성덕 性德 315, 479
성도 成道 317
성도 聖道 315, 317
성도문 聖道門 315, 492
성도지성 聖道支性 50
성도회 成道會 317
성독 聲獨 315
성득 性得 315

성등정각 成等正覺 317
성력 星曆 314
성령 聖靈 316
성론 聲論 315
성망 聖網 316
성명 性命 316
성명 聖明 316
성명 聲明 315
성명기론 聲明記論 226
성명론 聲明論 315, 390
성문 聲聞 191, 242, 281, 300, 315, 329, 483
성문승 聲聞乘 315, 421
성문승 聲聞僧 315
성문승십지 聲聞乘十地 369
성문장 聲聞藏 315, 488
성방 聖方 316
성법 聖法 316
성보장신 聖寶藏神 316
성복 聖福 316
성분 性分 316
성불 性佛 214, 316
성불 成佛 316
성불득탈 成佛得脫 316
성사자 聖師子 316
성상 性相 316
성상 省常 427
성상용 性相用 439
성상이종 性相二宗 316
성상학 性相學 316
성색 性色 316
성선 性善 316, 342
성선 聖仙 316
성성 聖性 316, 368
성성리생 聖性離生 316
성세 聖世 251
성소작지 成所作智 259, 416, 430
성수 星宿 280, 314
성수겁 星宿劫 265, 314, 627
성수왕 星宿王 450
성숙자 成熟者 317
성승 聖僧 179, 316
성식 性識 316
성신 誠信 314
성신회 成身會 317, 517
성실 成實 34, 99, 251, 316, 324, 370, 466, 609
성실론 成實論 1, 53, 191, 256, 287, 298, 316, 325, 540
성실종 成實宗 26, 258, 316, 367, 456, 540
四善根 251
성심 性心 317
성심 聖心 317
성아 性我 317
성악 性惡 316
성어 聖語 317
성언 聖言 317
성여 性如 362
성연 聖緣 317
성연 聲緣 315
성욕 性慾 317
성용 聖勇 100
성위 聖位 317
성유식론 成唯識論 315, 368, 454
성유식론소 成唯識論疏 317
성유식요결 成唯識要決 110
성응 聖應 317
성의 聖儀 317
성인 聖人 314
성인 聖因 467
성입 聲入 315
성자 聖者 317, 462, 475
성자성공 性自性空 582
성자연각 成自然覺 317
성장 聲杖 315
성전 聖典 317
성점법 星占法 314
성정 聖淨 317
성정해탈 性淨解脫 492
성제 星祭 314
성제 聖諦 317
성제 誠諦 314
성제바 聖提婆 317
성존 聖尊 317
성종 性宗 317, 489
성종 聖種 317
성종계 性種戒 317
성종성 性種性 317, 429
성종성 聖種性 429, 490
성종자 性種子 490
성죄 性罪 317, 491
성주 聖住 258
성주괴공 成住壞空 18
성주사자 聖主師子 318
성주천중천 聖主天中天 318
성중 聖衆 318
성중래영 聖衆來迎 318
성즉시심심즉시불 性即是心心即是佛 353
성지 性地 318, 369
성지 聖智 318, 531, 561
성진 聲塵 315
성차 性遮 318
성천 聖天 569, 643
성취 成就 316, 349, 360
성취중생 成就衆生 317
성취중생문 成就衆生門 360
성태 聖胎 318
성토 性土 318, 492
성패 成敗 91
성해 性海 318
성행 聖行 318, 608
성행당 省行堂 314
성화 性火 262, 318
성황신 城隍神 314
성횡수종 性橫修縱 318
세 世 318
세 勢 318
세 歲 318
세 洗 318
세 細 318, 456
세(속)지 世(俗)智 318
세간 世間 122, 318, 319
세간경 世間經 319
세간교 世間敎 478
세간난신첩경 世間難信捷徑 319
세간단 世間壇 478
세간단 世間檀 319
세간바라밀 世間波羅蜜 290
세간반야 世間般若 480
세간법 世間法 319
세간상상주 世間相常住 319
세간상위 世間相違 319
세간승 世間乘 318
세간안 世間眼 319
세간인과 世間因果 490
세간지 世間智 291, 292, 319
세간천 世間天 319
세간천원 世間天院 319
세간해 世間解 319, 371
세계 世界 319
世間 318
四不可思議 248
세계류어 世界流語 588
세계실단 世界悉檀 252, 319
세계주 世界主 319

세골욕 細骨欲 318
세대 世代 88, 319
세라 世羅 319
세라 勢羅 318, 319
세력귀 勢力鬼 318
세력신 勢力身 214
세로 世路 319
세론 世論 319
세법 世法 319
세복 世福 277, 319
세사상 細四相 318
세상 世相 319
세상현행장 細相現行障 367
세색 細色 318
세선 世善 319
세성 歲星 586
세세생생 世世生生 319
세속 世俗 319
세속오계 世俗五戒 319
세속제 世俗諦 278, 488
世諦 320
세속지 世俗智 369
세심 細心 318
세안 世眼 319
세야 歲夜 210
세야나살남 世耶那薩喃 319
세영 世英 320
세요왕 世饒王 320
세요왕(불) 世饒王(佛 437
세우 世友 3, 179, 261, 320
세웅 世雄 8, 307, 320
세웅양족존 世雄兩足尊 320
세의 世依 320
세의식 細意識 318
세인 細人 578
세자재왕 世自在王 320
세전 世典 320
세정 洗淨 318
세제 世諦 320, 326, 488
세제불생멸 世諦不生滅 320
세제일법 世第一法 320
四善根 251
세존 世尊 122, 162, 166, 320, 571
세지 勢至 96, 115, 318, 361, 367, 450, 452
세촉 細觸 286
세친 世親 164, 320, 572, 587
세혹현행장 細惑現行障 366
소 召 321
소 塑 321
소 小 281, 321
소 少 321
소 所 320
소 掃 321
소 消 321
소 燒 321
소 疎 320
소 疏 156, 320, 629
소 素 321
소 紹 321
소 蔬 320
소 蘇 321, 398
소 逍 321
소 酥 320
소 銷 321
소 騷 321
소가 蘇呵 322
소가다 蘇伽多 322
소가타 蘇伽陀 322
소가타 騷伽陀 321
소강 小康 427
소강 少康 321
소겁 小劫 18, 322
소게다 蘇揭多 234, 322, 332
소게다 騷揭多 321
소견 素絹 321
소경 小經 322
소계 小界 322
소고석산 小孤石山 496
소공 小空 322
소광 少光 40, 250
소광(천) 少光(天) 321
소광천 少光天 267, 301, 370
소교 小敎 97
소구 素具 321
소구가 所句迦 517, 525
소구지옥 燒炙地獄 321
소근 小根 322
소기 小機 322
소념 小念 322
소다라 素多羅 332
소달나 蘇達拏 90, 322, 329
소달다 蘇達多 322, 329
소달라 素呾羅 332
소달라 蘇怛羅 322
소달람 素呾纜 or 素怛纜 332
소달람 素怛纜 321
소달리사나 蘇達梨舍那 51
소달이사나 蘇達梨舍那 322
소도파 素覩波 593
소두 疏頭 320
소등 蘇燈 322
소등 酥燈 320, 322
소라 素羅 566
소라다 蘇囉多 322
소량 所量 320
소로 小路 541
소로다파나 蘇盧多波那 322
소루파 蘇樓波 146, 322
소륭 紹隆 321, 634
소륵 疎勒 186
소륵 疏勒 15, 320
소리사부 蘇梨沙部 509
소리야 蘇利耶 322, 333, 498, 499
소리야 蘇哩耶 322
소리야바라피자나 蘇利也波羅皮遮那 498
소림무예 少林武藝 321
소림사 少林寺 321
소립 所立 320
소마 蘇摩 11, 322, 450, 578, 586
소마나 蘇摩那 322, 328
소마사 蘇摩蛇 322
소마제바 蘇摩提婆 322, 452
소만 蘇漫 587
소만나 蘇蔓那 322
소만다 蘇漫多 323, 609
소말나 蘇末那 322
소멸 消滅 321
소목련 小目連 322
소미(로) 蘇迷(盧) 322
소미경 小彌經 322
소미로 蘇迷盧 328
소미루 蘇彌樓 322, 328
소바리나 素嚩哩拏 321
소바살도 蘇婆薩都 323
소바하 蘇婆訶 322
소바하 蘇波訶 322
소반다 蘇槃多 323, 587
소반벌솔다 蘇槃伐率多 323
소발다라 蘇跋陀羅 323
소발리가부 蘇跋梨柯部 509
소백화 小白華 323
소번뇌지법 小煩惱地法 323, 481
소벌라 蘇伐剌 323
소벌라 蘇伐羅 321, 323
소벌라나구달라 蘇伐剌拏瞿怛羅

323
소벌랄 蘇伐剌 61, 333
소법 小法 323
소법신 素法身 321, 482
소변계 所遍計 320
소별 所別 320, 539
소보지 蘇補底 323, 329
소본 小本 89, 94, 322, 323
소부라 蘇嚩囉 323
소부지 蘇部底 323, 329
소비라 騷毗羅 321
소사 小使 323
소사 小師 323
소사 蕭寺 323
소삼 小參 323
소삼두 小參頭 323
소상 塑像 321
소상기 小祥忌 323
소석 消釋 321
소석 銷釋 321
소성 小聖 323
소소연연 疏所緣緣 320
소수 小樹 293, 323
소수복 消瘦服 321
소수천석 小水穿石 323
소승 小乘 97, 104, 278, 281, 282, 286, 323, 339, 371, 422, 448
소승경 小乘經 324
소승계 小乘戒 324
소승교 小乘敎 412
소승구부 小乘九部 324
소승론 小乘論 123, 324, 380
소승사문 小乘四門 324
소승삼인 小乘三印 325
소승십팔부 小乘十八部 325
소승아비달마 小乘阿毗達磨 324
소승외도 小乘外道 325
소승율종 小乘律宗 367
소승이부 小乘二部 325
소승파상교 小乘破相敎 412
소승편점계 小乘偏漸戒 325
소식 小食 325
소식 素食 321
소신 所信 79
소실 少室 321
소실육문집 少室六門集 321
소실지 蘇悉地 213, 325
소실지갈라경 蘇悉地羯羅經 325
소실지경 蘇悉地經 161, 278, 325, 560
소실지법 蘇悉地法 278
소아사 小阿師 325
소야마 蘇夜摩 393
소연 所緣 320, 402, 404
소연연 所緣緣 320, 404
소오조 小五條 325
소왕 小王 325
소요자재 逍遙自在 321
소욕지족 少欲知足 321
소원 小遠 325
소원 小院 325
소위 所謂 85
소유 所有 320
소유 蘇油 325
소율의 小律儀 326
소의 所依 79, 320, 550
소의 素意 321
소인 所引 320
소자 燒炙 554
소작 所作 320
소재 消災 321
소재귀 少財鬼 321
소적화 小赤華 326
소전 所詮 320
소정 少淨 250
소정(천) 少淨(天) 321
소정천 少淨天 301, 370
소제 消除 321
소종 小宗 326
소주전강현 韶州典江縣 197
소지 掃地 321
소지의 所知依 320
소지의식 所知依識 376
소지장 所知障 320, 488
소지제 所知諦 427
소질리사나 蘇跌里舍那 322
소찬 素饌 321
소참 小參 565
소천(세계) 小千(世界) 326
소천계 小千界 250
소천세계 小千世界 293
소청 召請 158, 321
소청동자 召請童子 321
소초 小草 326
소타 蘇陀 11
소투파 蘇偸婆 326
소파호경근본부 蘇婆呼經根本部 161
소품 小品 326
소품(반야바라밀)경 小品(般若波羅蜜)經 326
소행 小行 323, 326
소향 燒香 321
소향산아녹달 小香山阿耨達 494
소호 素豪 321
소화 所化 320
소화하 蘇和訶 322
소회 素懷 321
속 俗 289, 326
속 粟 326
속 續 326
속 贖 326
속 速 326
속계 俗戒 326
속득 速得 326
속등록 續燈錄 414
속려 束慮 326
속로 束蘆 42
속류 俗流 326
속망진실 俗妄眞實 367
속명 續命 326
속명 贖命 326
속명신번 續命神幡 326
속산 粟散 326
속산국 粟散國 326
속산왕 粟散王 325, 326
속성 速成 326
속아 俗我 326
속인 俗人 326
속제 俗諦 304, 326, 488, 561, 601 世諦 320
속지 俗智 326, 491
속진 俗塵 326
속질귀 速疾鬼 326
속향 速香 326
속형 俗形 326
손 孫 326
손 損 326
손 遜 326
손다라난다 孫陀羅難陀 326
손다리 孫陀利 326
손멸변 損滅邊 481
손복단 損伏斷 326
손염 孫炎 167
손파 孫婆 431
솔 率 326
솔 窣 327

솔누려습벌라 窣㲉黎濕伐羅 327
솔도리혜나 窣都利慧那 327
솔도파 率都婆 326, 593
솔도파 窣堵波 327, 593
솔도환 窣覩喚 313
솔라 窣羅 327
솔로다아반나 窣路多阿半那 327, 329
솔로타아발낭 窣路陀阿鉢囊 329
솔록근나 率祿勤那 326
솔리 窣利 327
솔리 窣唎 327
솔사게치 窣莎揭哆 327
송 宋 327
송 誦 327
송 送 327
송 頌 327
송경 誦經 327
송고승전 宋高僧傳 564
송광사 松廣寺 327
송망 送亡 327
송원속입장제론 宋元續入藏諸論 123
송원입장제대소승경 宋元入藏諸大小乘經 327
송장 送葬 327, 519
송제왕 宋帝王 327
송파 送婆 360
쇄 曬 327
쇄 灑 327
쇄 碎 327
쇄 鎖 327
쇄 鏁 244
쇄계 曬罽 327
쇄수 灑水 327
쇄시 鎖匙 327
쇄신사리 碎身舍利 327
쇄약 鎖鑰 327
쇄정 灑淨 327
쇠 衰 327
쇠상 衰相 327
쇠환 衰患 327
수 修 50, 331
수 受 80, 104, 140, 265, 280, 331, 365, 411, 417, 423, 424, 487
수 嗽 327
수 垂 327
수 壽 328
육도과보 461
수 守 328
수 宿 331
수 手 328
수 授 329
수 收 331
수 數 329
수 樹 331
수 殊 329
수 水 53, 271, 331, 552, 583
수 獸 327
수 睡 331
수 竪 331
수 繡 328
수 藪 327
수 豎 492
수 輸 331
수 遂 579
수 酬 328
수 銖 327
수 隨 327
수 須 328
수 首 328
수(식)문 數(息)門 329
수가다 修伽多 332
수가도 修伽度 332
수가타 修伽陀 331
수갈라 戍羯羅 586
수건타 須乾陀 284
수게다 修揭多 332
수견 修堅 332
수결 受決 331
수결 授決 329
수경 手磬 328, 495
수경 樹經 331
수경률 隨經律 332
수경아차리 授經阿遮利 385
수계 受戒 331
수계 水界 332
수계건도 受戒犍度 485
수골 收骨 331
수관 水冠 332
수관 水觀 332
수구 受具 331
수구 隨求 332
수구로나 輸拘盧那 331
수구보살 隨求菩薩 332
수구의상응 手口意相應 328
수구즉득천자 隨求卽得天子 332
수구천자 隨求天子 332
수기 受記 331
수기 授記 50, 69, 329, 635
수기 水器 332
수기 隨機 332
수기관정 授記灌頂 290
수나 輸那 331
수날라 戍捺羅 328
수낭 水囊 332
수념분별 隨念分別 209
수능 秀能 332
수능엄 首楞嚴 328
수능엄경 首楞嚴經 79, 168, 221, 328
수능엄정 首楞嚴定 328
수다 須陀 329
수다(라) 首陀(羅) 328
수다(사)바 首陀(娑)婆 328
수다(수)마 須陀(須)摩 329
수다라 修多羅 332, 364
수다라 戍陀羅 328
수다란 修多蘭 332
수다리사나 修陀里舍那 332
수다반나 須陀般那 329
수다원 須陀洹 98, 222, 329, 512
四果 239
수다원지 須陀洹地 369
수단 水壇 332
수단라 修單羅 332
수단란다 修單蘭多 332
수달(다) 須達(多) 329
수달나 須達拏 90, 329
수달다 須達多 374
수달라 戍達羅 148, 328
수달라 輸達羅 331
수달리사나 須達梨舍那 329
수달리사누 藪達梨舍菟 327
수달천 須達天 329
수대 水大 332
수대 須帶 329
수대나 須大拏 90, 328, 329
수덕 修德 315, 479
수덕사 修德寺 332
수도 修道 20, 332, 417
수도다나 首圖馱那 328
수두 水頭 332
수두단 輸頭檀 328
수두파 藪斗婆 327
수두파 藪斗波 593
수득 修得 570

수득선 修得善 1
수등 水燈 332
수라 修羅 333, 382
수라 水羅 332
수라 輸羅 331
수라 首羅 541
수라(발) 首羅(髮) 328
수라군 修羅軍 333
수라궁 修羅宮 294
수라도 修羅道 333
수라장 修羅場 333, 382
수라주 修羅酒 333
수라취 修羅趣 333
수라항 修羅巷 382
수량품 壽量品 218, 328
四要品 254
수로 手爐 328
수로(가) 首盧(迦) or 首盧(柯) 328
수로가(바) 輸盧迦(波) 328, 331
수로학 水老鶴 333
수론 壽論 328
수론 數論 329
수론사 數論師 329
수론외도 數論外道 329
수루다 戍縷多 237, 337
수류 隨類 333
수류복 修類福 277
수류생 隨類生 333
수류응동 隨類應同 333
수륙재 水陸齋 333
수륙회 水陸會 333
수륜 手輪 328
수륜 水輪 333
수륜삼매 水輪三昧 333
수릉가마 首楞伽摩 328
수릉엄정 首楞嚴定 435
수리 修利 333, 342, 499
수리밀다 繡利蜜多 328
수리야 須梨耶 328
수리야 須梨耶 322
수림 樹林 331
수마 須摩 578
수마(가) 須摩(迦) 578
수마나 修摩那 328
수마나 須摩那 322, 328
수마제 須摩提 or 須摩題 328
수만 水滿 333
수만나 須曼那 328
수말포염 水沫泡焰 333
수면 睡眠 331
수면 隨眠 333, 582
수면개 睡眠蓋 331
수면욕 睡眠欲 331
수멸무위 數滅無爲 329
수명 壽命 328
수명견 壽命見 601
수명묘 壽命妙 359
수명무수겁 壽命無數劫 328
수명무유량 壽命無有量 328
수묘신 殊妙身 329
수문존 守門尊 328
수문천 守門天 328
수미 須彌 51, 328
수미가 殊微伽 329
수미단 須彌壇 328
수미등왕불 須彌燈王佛 328
수미루 修迷樓 328
수미루 須彌樓 328
수미상 須彌相 328
수미정 須彌頂 328
수미좌 須彌座 328
수민 愁悶 161
수밀다천 須密陀天 80
수밀라천 須蜜羅天 328
수바가라 輸婆迦羅 331
수바가라 輸波迦羅 331
수발나 修跋拏 321, 333
수발다(라) 須跋陀(羅) 329
수방 隨方 333
수방비니 隨方毘尼 333
수백로 水白鷺 333
수백학 水白鶴 333
수번뇌 隨煩惱 333, 481
수법 守法 328
수법인 數法人 329
수법행 隨法行 333
수별 受別 331
수보리 須菩提 329
수부리 須扶提 329
수부제 須浮帝 329
수분 隨分 333
수분각 隨分覺 238, 333, 410
수불 繡佛 328
수비 嗽卑 327
수사 守寺 328
수사 授事 329
수사리 隨舍利 333
수사리 隨邪利 333
수사화 水梭花 333
수삼귀지 受三歸地 369
수상 壽像 328
수상 壽相 381, 384
四相 249
수상 水想 332
수상 隨相 333
수상계 隨相戒 333
수상관 水相觀 332
수상론 隨相論 48
수상포 水上泡 333
수상행식 受想行識 331
수색마니 隨色摩尼 334
수색화 隨色花 209
수생 修生 202, 334
수선 修善 334
수선다 須扇多 328
수선육묘문 修禪六妙門 334
수성 修性 334
수성 水星 586
수성불이문 修性不二門 334
수세 受歲 331
수소단 修所斷 269, 334
수수 受隨 331
수수 授手 329
수순 隨順 334
수습결정 修習決定 466
수습력 修習力 334, 479
수습위 修習位 425
수승 殊勝 284, 329
수승불정 殊勝佛頂 418
수승전 殊勝殿 329
수승지 殊勝池 329
수시 垂示 327
수식 數息 329
수식관 數息觀 329, 426
수신 水神 335
수신행 隨信行 333, 334
수심 隨心 334
수심결 修心訣 334
수아기나 首阿旣那 328
수악 修惡 334
수야마 須夜摩 328, 393
수야천자 修野天子 499
수어 垂語 327
수업 受業 331
수연 隨緣 334
수연두 須延頭 328

ㄱ ㄴ ㄷ ㄹ ㅁ ㅂ ㅅ ㅇ ㅈ ㅊ ㅋ ㅌ ㅍ ㅎ 찾아보기

수연불변 隨緣不變 334
수연진 數緣盡 329
수연진여 隨緣眞如 217, 334, 486
수연화물 隨緣化物 334
수열밀타 須涅蜜陀 328
수염마 須炎摩 or 須燄摩 328
수엽 隧葉 229
수옥 水玉 334, 335, 601
수온 受蘊 331
수요 宿曜 331
수요 水曜 334
수용 受用 282, 331
수용신 受用身 331
수용토 受用土 331
수원 水圓 334
火珠 641
수월 水月 334, 335
수월관음 水月觀音 334
수월나 修越拏 333
수위심 受位心 369
수유 水乳 334
수유 須臾 251, 329
수율경 隨律經 332
수의 授衣 329
수의 竪義 331
수의 銖衣 327
수의 隨宜 334
수의 隨意 334, 516
수의 隨義 334
수의과 隨意科 334
수의천자 修意天子 499
수인 手印 328
수인 數人 329
수자 受者 331
수자 竪者 331
수자 隨自 335
수자의어 隨自意語 335
수자타 須闍陀 342
수장 水葬 335
수장 水藏 335
수재 水災 335
수적 垂迹 327
수적 竪敵 331
수전(리문) 隨轉(理門) 335
수전의 水田衣 335
수정 水定 332, 335
수정 水淨 335
수정 水精 335
수정 隨情 335
수제 樹提 342
수제 首題 328
수제(가) 樹提(伽) 331
수제가 樹提迦 329
수제리나 須提梨拏 329
수조국 修造局 335
수좌 首座 328, 541
수주 數珠 329
수주 獸主 327
수중월 水中月 335
수중하중 水中河中 137
수증 修證 360
수지 受持 331
수지(색)가 殊底(色)迦 329
수지사론 竪底沙論 331
수지색가 殊底穡迦 329
수지색가 殊底色迦 314, 331
수진 水塵 335
수진 須眞 329
수집금강저 手執金剛杵 328
수참 修懺 335
수천 水天 163, 335
수천공 水天供 335
수천권속 水天眷屬 335
수천덕불 水天德佛 147, 335
수천법 水天法 335
수천비 水天妃 335
수체수행 受體隨行 331
수초 收鈔 331
수축 隨逐 335
수출 竪出 492
수취취 數取趣 211, 329
수치아라바 殊致阿羅婆 329
수타 首陁 148
수투로 修妬路 332
수파 水波 335
수파축랑 隨波逐浪 267
수풍화재 水風火災 335
수하기나 首訶旣那 328
수학 水涸 333
수행 修行 270, 335
수행단 修行斷 290
수행문 修行門 360
수행번뇌 數行煩惱 329, 481
수행주 修行住 335, 368
수험종 修驗宗 371
수현 須現 492
수형호 隨形好 335
수혜 修慧 295, 469
수호 守護 328
수혹 修惑 56, 335, 493
수혹 隨惑 333
수환 酬還 328
수회 首悔 328
수희 隋喜 50
수희 隨喜 335
숙 叔 336
숙 宿 336
숙 熟 279, 336, 619
숙가 叔迦 537
숙가(파) 叔迦(婆) or 㖃迦(婆) 336
숙근 宿根 336
숙기 宿忌 336
숙리 叔離 336
숙명 宿命 336
숙명(지)통 宿命(智)通 336
숙명(지증)통 宿命(智證)通 422
숙명력 宿命力 336
숙명명 宿命明 273, 336
숙보 宿報 336
숙복 宿福 336
숙선 宿善 336
숙세 宿世 336
숙소 熟酥 320
숙소경 熟酥經 336
숙소미 熟酥味 416
숙숙(마)라 叔叔(摩)羅 336
숙습 宿習 336
숙식 宿植 336
숙야 宿夜 100, 336
숙업 宿業 336, 396
숙연 宿緣 336
숙왕화 宿王華 336
숙왕희 宿王戲 336
숙원 宿願 336
숙원력 宿願力 336
숙의 宿意 336
숙인 宿因 336
숙작 宿作 336
숙작외도 宿作外道 336
숙주 宿住 336
숙주(수념지증)통 宿住(隨念智證)通 336
숙주지증명 宿住智證明 273
숙집 宿執 336
숙집개발 宿執開發 336
숙채 宿債 336

숙합 宿哈 336
순 巡 337
순 循 337
순 旬 336
순 純 336
순 舜 336
순 順 336
순경 巡更 337
순나 諄那 337
순다 純陀 336
순단 旬單 336
순당 巡當 337
순류 順流 336, 479
순리 順理 311
순분 順分 336
순상분결 順上分結 336
순석 巡錫 337
순세 順世 122, 336
순순 淳純 336
순신관 循身觀 337
순아 順牙 336
순안 巡案 337
순야 舜若 336
순야다 舜若多 32, 337
순역 順逆 336
순요 巡寮 337
순인 順忍 336, 425
순일 純一 336
순중론 順中論 545
순진 純眞 336
순차 順次 336
순타 純陀 91, 522, 541, 543
순하분결 順下分結 336
순화 巡火 337
순화 順化 336
순환 循環 337
술 戌 337
술 術 337
술 述 337
술가 戌迦 337
술가라박걸사 戌迦羅博乞史 337
술갈라 戌羯羅 337
술날라 戌捺羅 337
술달 戌達 337
술달라 戌怛羅 337
술로달라 述嚕怛羅 337
술루다 戌縷多 337
술륜율제 戌輪聿提 337
술바가 術婆迦 337
술의 述義 156
술타 戌陀 337
술타라 戌陀羅 337
술타전달라 戌陀戰達羅 337
술파게라승하 戌婆揭羅僧訶 337
숭 崇 337
숭경 崇敬 337
숭산 嵩山 321
숭신 崇信 337
스님 337
스승 337
슬 瑟 337
슬닉 瑟匿 342
슬석 瑟石 337
슬슬 瑟瑟 337
습 拾 337
습 溼 337
습 濕 337
습 習 337
습기 習氣 337, 398
습기과 習氣果 477
습득 拾得 337
습멸 習滅 337
습박건 濕薄健 379
습비 濕鞞 343
습생 濕生 250, 337
습소성종성 習所成種性 490
습인 習因 287, 488
습인습과 習因習果 337
습종성 習種性 317, 429
습종자 習種子 490
승 乘 339
승 僧 166, 262, 268, 276, 294, 337
승 勝 88, 338
승 承 338
승 繩 338
승 陞 338
승가 僧伽 337, 340, 635
　比丘會 226
승가 僧加 338
승가 僧可 339
승가 僧迦 339
승가 勝伽 297
승가난제 僧伽難提 338, 486
승가다 僧伽多 338
승가라 僧伽羅 338
승가람 僧伽藍 237
승가람(마) 僧伽藍(摩) 338
승가람마 僧伽藍摩 2
승가려 僧伽黎 338
승가리 僧伽梨 2, 287, 338
승가리 僧加梨 56
승가리의 僧伽梨衣 472
승가바라 僧伽婆羅 338
승가바시사 僧伽婆尸沙 338
승가발다라 僧伽跋陀羅 338
승가발마 僧伽跋摩 338
승가사 僧迦舍 339
승가시 僧伽施 339
승가자 僧柯者 339
승가지 僧伽胝 2, 338
승가지 僧伽胝 338
승가타 僧伽吒 338
승가타 僧伽陀 338
승가타경 僧伽吒經 452
승가표다미 僧柯慓多弭 339
승각기 僧却崎 339
승각기가 僧脚崎迦 339
승갈지 僧竭支 339
승거 乘炬 339
승거 僧佉 339
승거 勝佉 297
승거시 僧佉尸 18
승겁 僧劫 5
승계 僧戒 339
승계구급 乘戒俱急 26
승계구완 乘戒俱緩 26
승과 勝果 338
승관 僧官 339
승광왕 勝光王 600
승군 勝軍 338
승군지장 勝軍地藏 556
승급계완 乘急戒緩 26
승기 僧祇 339, 382
승기물 僧祇物 339
승기부 僧祇部 339
승기야 僧企耶 338, 339
승기율 僧祇律 191, 255, 339, 540
승기지 僧祇支 68, 339
승길이삭 僧吉肄鑠 339
승나승열 僧那(僧涅) 339
승니 僧尼 339
승람 僧藍 2
승랍 僧臘 27
승랑 僧朗 339
승려 僧侶 339
승로반 承露盤 or 承露槃 338

승론종 勝論宗 280, 338, 452, 534
승류진여 勝流眞如 370
승림 勝林 338
승림부 勝林部 550
승만경 勝鬘經 338
승만부인 勝鬘夫人 338
승만회 勝鬘會 338
승무 僧舞 339
승발 僧跋 275
승방 僧坊 339
승방 僧房 339
승법 僧法 338
승법 勝法 380
승보 僧寶 339
승보과 僧寶果 339
승보라 僧補羅 338
승불 乘拂 339
승불 勝佛 293
승사 僧詞 340
승사 勝士 338
승사 承事 338
승상 繩床 338
승색가라 僧塞迦羅 340
승생 勝生 445
승속 僧俗 340
승승 勝乘 97, 338
승신주 勝神州 338
승신주 勝神洲 216
승심 勝心 338
승야 僧若 340
승업 勝業 338
승예 僧叡 303
四聖 251
승오 僧伍 340
승우 勝友 338
승육다아함 僧育多阿含 423
승응신 勝應身 338, 472, 487
승의 僧儀 340
승의 勝義 274, 338
승의공 勝義空 338
승의근 勝義根 204, 338, 478
승의무성 勝義無性 274
승의법 勝義法 338
승의제 勝義諦 338, 488
승의제론 勝義諦論 338
승자 勝者 338
승자수 勝子樹 338
승자자일 僧自恣日 340
승잔 僧殘 340, 416
승정 僧正 339
승제 勝諦 427
승조 乘潮 537
승조 僧肇 303, 355, 537
四聖 251
승종 乘種 339
승종 勝宗 338
승종십구의론 勝宗十句義論 632
승좌 陞座 338
승주 勝州 338
승중 僧衆 340
승지 乘持 339
승지지 僧祇支 9
승진 乘津 339
승진도 勝進道 242
승차 僧次 340
승찬 僧璨 312, 587
six patriarchs 466
승처 勝處 422
승통 僧統 339
승해 勝解 104
시 侍 340
시 廝 340
시 嘶 341
시 始 340
시 尸 340, 342, 343
시 屍 340
시 屎 341
시 市 340
시 施 279, 341, 357, 359, 382
시 是 341
시 時 272, 341, 371, 585
시 柴 341
시 矢 340
시 示 288, 341
시 翅 340
시 視 341
시 試 342
시(산)외도 時(散)外道 341
시가 枲伽 255
시가라월 尸迦羅越 342
시각 始覺 200, 265, 340, 410, 476, 595
시개폐 施開廢 341
시걸바 時乞縛 312
시걸박 時乞縛 341
시걸차난타 施乞叉難陀 351
시경 試經 342
시교 始敎 340
시교 示敎 341
시귀 屍鬼 340
시기 尸棄 25, 93, 342, 584, 635
시기나 尸棄那 342
시기니 尸棄尼 342
시기불 尸棄佛 342
시기비 尸棄毘 342
시나 視那 341
시다 枲多 235
시다(림) 尸陀(林) 342
시다림 尸陀林 342, 343
시다림 屍陀林 340
시다바나 尸多婆那 342
시다파나 尸多婆那 342
시달나 尸怛羅 342
시담자 屎擔子 341
시두 柴頭 341
시라 尸羅 26, 340, 342, 414
시라 施羅 319
시라 試羅 342
시라달마 尸羅達磨 342
시라당 尸羅幢 342
시라바라밀 尸羅波羅蜜 342
시라발다제 尸羅拔陀提 342
시라발제 尸羅跋提 254, 342
시라발타라 尸羅拔陀羅 342
시라발타라 尸羅跋陀羅 342
시라발파 尸羅鉢頗 342
시라불청정 尸羅不清淨 342
시라아질다 尸羅阿迭多 342
시라청정 尸羅清淨 342
시랑 豺狼 342
시랑지옥 豺狼地獄 342
시려밀 屍黎密 340, 343
시뢰 尸賴 345
시뢰나벌지 尸賴拏伐底 342
시류복 施類福 277
시리 尸利 305, 342
시리 尸里 70
시리가나 尸梨伽那 343
시리국다 尸利鞠多 343
시리국다장자경 尸利鞠多長者經 343
시리굴다 尸利崛多 343
시리랄나벌지 尸離刺拏伐底 342
시리밀다라 尸利蜜多羅 343
시리불서 尸利佛逝 136, 343
시리사 尸利沙 343, 621
시리사 尸利駛 343

시리사가 尸利沙迦 343
시리쇄 尸利灑 343, 621
시리야 尸利夜 343
시림 尸林 342
시림 施林 341
시마사나 尸摩舍那 343
시마사나 尸摩賖那 342
시명일진법계 是名一眞法界 507
시무염 施無厭 72
시무염(사) 施無厭(寺) 341
시무외 施無畏 341
시미귀 時媚鬼 341
시바시바가 時婆時婆迦 341
시박가 時縛迦 67, 341
시반시 尸半尸 343
시방 十方 104, 343
시방불토 十方佛土 343
시방상주승물 十方常住僧物 343
시방세계 十方世界 343
시방십불 十方十佛 343
시방중회 十方衆會 443
시방현전승물 十方現前僧物 343
시변처정 十遍處定 366
시분 時分 210, 341, 393
시분지옥 屎糞地獄 341
시분천 時分天 18
시비가 尸毘伽 343
시비가 尸毘迦 343
시비다가라 時毘多迦羅 341
시비략 尸毘略 343
시사 始士 340
시사흠바라 翅舍欽婆羅 340
시삼무차별 是三無差別 266, 274, 353
시석 矢石 340
시설 施設 341
시설론부 施設論部 341
시성 尸城 343
시성취 時成就 341
시승 施僧 341
시식 施食 341
시식 時食 341
시신 施身 50
시심시불 是心是佛 230, 341
시심마 是甚磨 480
시야나 澌夜那 341
시연득가 市演得迦 340
시왕 十王 343, 367, 411
시유라 翅由邏 340
시의 時衣 341
시이라 翅夷羅 340
시자 侍者 340
시적 示寂 341
시전 示轉 288
시제불교 是諸佛敎 535
시종 始終 340
시종 時宗 341, 502
시주 施主 83, 341
시중 時衆 341
시지 時至 275
시처비처력 是處非處力 341
시처제연 時處諸緣 341
시타 屍陀 342
시타벌나 尸陀伐那 342
시타파 尸陀婆 342
시해 豕亥 365
시해탈 時解脫 219, 492
시행 施行 341
시행인 始行人 340
시혜 施惠 631
시호 施護 341
시화 施化 341
시화 施和 469
식 式 343
식 息 55, 343
식 植 343
식 識 88, 140, 202, 230, 268, 275, 282, 295, 344, 365, 411, 415, 423, 424, 430, 484, 488, 490, 511, 552, 583, 641
　eighth 77, 231
　four divisions of the function 248
　육대 六大 460
식 食 266, 344, 480
식 飾 343
식(무변)처 識(無邊)處 239
식경 食頃 344
식계 識界 344
식고 息苦 343
식기 式棄 342, 343, 635
식기가미 息忌伽彌 343
식기다가미 息忌陀伽迷 343
식닉 式匿 342
식닉 識匿 342
식당 食堂 344
식대 識大 583
식랑 識浪 344
식랑탕 食莨菪 344
식려응심 息慮凝心 273
식무변처 識無邊處 50, 53, 152, 344
식무변처정 識無邊處定 344
식무변처지 識無邊處地 55
식무변처해탈 識無邊處解脫 344, 611
식물오과 食物五果 344
식밀 食蜜 344
식변 識變 344
식숙명통 識宿命通 345
식시 食時 344
식식 識食 252, 345
식심 息心 343
식심 識心 248, 345
식악행자 息惡行慈 246
식엽 式葉 343
식온 識蘊 345
식외무법 識外無法 454
식욕 食欲 344
식우 識牛 345
식자 息慈 343
식장 識藏 345
식재 息災 343
식전 食前 344
식정 識精 345
식주 識主 345
식주 識住 345
식중덕본 植衆德本 343
식차 式叉 343
식차(마나)니 式叉(摩那)尼 343
식차가라니 式叉迦羅尼 343
식차가라니시차계라니 式叉迦羅尼尸叉罽羅尼 14
식차마나 式叉摩那 588
식처정 識處定 345
식처천 識處天 344, 345
식해 識海 345
식화 息化 343
식화 食花 211
식환 識幻 345
식후 食後 344
식힐 式詰 342
신 信 223, 278, 346, 359, 362, 412, 423, 584, 585
　四分 248
신 愼 345
신 新 345

신 晨 345
신 申 345
신 神 294, 345, 347, 463
신 薪 345
신 蜃 345
신 身 45, 265, 270, 271, 273, 274, 278, 279, 286, 291, 345, 412, 431, 483, 487, 587
　四等 242
신거 身車 346
신견 身見 346, 361, 373, 410, 415
신경 新經 640
신경지통 神境智通 348
신계 信戒 346
신계 新戒 345
신계심혜 身戒心慧 355
신고 信鼓 346
신공 神供 346
신광 神光 346
신광 身光 346
신교 神敎 267
신구양역 新舊兩譯 345
신구의 新舊醫 345
신구의 身口意 239, 459, 512
신근 信根 346, 485
신근 愼謹 345
신근 神根 346
신근 身根 346, 485
신기 身器 346
신나불달라 愼那弗怛羅 345
신녀 信女 346
신녀 神女 346
신노(파)림 申恕(波)林 346
신단 神丹 558
신단 神旦 558
신덕 信德 346
신도 信度 346, 494
신도 信徒 346
신도 神道 346
신도하 信度河 346
신독 申毒 345
신두 辛頭 346
신두라 申頭羅 346
신두파라향 辛頭波羅香 346
신등 身燈 346
신등지오근 信等之五根 485
신라 新羅 555
신락 信樂 346
신력 信力 347, 414
신력 神力 347, 587, 596
신력품 神力品
　四要品 254
신련 身蓮 347
신루대 蜃樓臺 345
신명 神明 347
신명 身命 347
신모상미상 身毛上靡相 347
신묘 神妙 347
신밀 身密 268
신발의 新發意 345
신법 信法
　四法 247
신법지 信法地 369
신변 神變 271, 347, 637
신복 信伏 347
신분심경 神分心經 352
신사 信士 347
신사남 信事男 347
신삼 身三 588
신삼구사의삼 身三口四意三 347
신상 身相 347
신선 神仙 308, 347, 361, 569
신선 神僊 347
신선불 神仙佛 157
신성 身城 347
신성취발심 信成就發心 275
신세 新歲 345
신수 信受 347
신수 信手 347
신수 信水 347
신수 信首 347
신수 神秀 74, 105, 312, 332, 410
　北宗 208
신수봉행 信受奉行 347
신순 信順 347
신슬지림 申瑟知林 346
신시 信施 347
신식 神識 347
신식 身識 347
신심 信心 347
신심 身心 347
신아 神我 206, 348, 615
신안심락 身安心樂 388
신암 神闇 348
신앙 信仰 348
신업 身業 348, 431
신업공양 身業供養 45
신여의통 神如意通 422
신여의통 身如意通 348
신역 神域 348
신운 身雲 348
신인 信忍 348, 425
신인 神人 348
신인 身忍 45
신일 申日 345
신입 身入 345
신자 神字 567
신장 信藏 348
신전 身田 348
신조 晨朝 345
신족 神足 90, 400
신족(통) 神足(通) 348
신족륜 神足輪 271
신족월 神足月 348
신족통 神足通 422
신족통 身足通 348
신종 信種 348
신좌 神坐 348
신좌 身座 348
신주 信珠 348
신주 神咒 348
신주 神酒 322
신지 信地 369
신지 神智 348
신진(화멸) 薪盡(火滅) 345
신출가 身出家 579
신토 身土 348
신통 神通 271, 290, 429, 596
　四自在 256
신통 身通 348
신통(력) 神通(力) 348
신통(지증)통 神通(智證)通 422
신통광 神通光 477
신통금강 神通金剛 642
신통기특 神通奇特 69
신통력 神通力 638
신통묘 神通妙 358, 359
신통문 神通門 360
신통승 神通乘 348
신통월 神通月 348
신통유희경 神通遊戲經 또는 神通遊戲經 306
신하 申河 345
신해 信海 349
신해 信解 349
신해행증 信解行證 349
　四法 247

신행 信行 266, 349
신향 信向 349
신현관 信現觀 349
신혜 信慧 349
신화 身和 469
신회 神會 587
신훈종자 新薰種子 490
신흥사 神興寺 349
실 失 349
실 室 349, 485
실 實 58, 268, 289, 302, 349, 394, 491
실 悉 349
실가라 悉伽羅 349
실경 實經 349
실공 實空 350
실공무 實空無 289
실교 實敎 155, 350, 478
실나 室拏 242
실념 失念 349
실다(알타) 悉多(頞他) 349
실다알타 悉多頞他 349
실단 悉檀 349
실달(다) 悉達(多) 349
실달다반달라 悉怛多般怛羅 349
실담 悉曇 252, 349, 414, 514, 583
실담 悉談 349
실담장 悉曇章 349
실대승 實大乘 58
실대승교 實大乘敎 350
실도 實道 350
실라마나락가 室羅摩拏洛迦 245, 350
실라마나리가 室羅摩拏理迦 246, 350
실라마니라 室羅摩尼羅 245
실라말니라 室羅末尼羅 350
실라바 失羅婆 349
실라바나(마세) 室羅縛拏(磨洗) 350
실라벌 室羅伐 350
실라벌(실지) 室羅伐(悉底) 254
실라벌나(마세) 室羅筏拏(磨洗) 350
실라벌실지 室羅筏悉底 350
실로가 室路迦 328
실로가(바) 室盧迦(波) 328
실리 室利 70, 305, 342, 349, 350
실리 室哩 342
실리 室離 342
실리 實利 243, 350
실리 悉利 342, 349
실리게바 室利揭婆 350
실리국 室利鞠 350
실리국다 室利鞠多 343
실리라 室利羅 243, 350
실리라다 室利羅多 or 室利邏多 350
실리말차 室利靺瑳 134
실리말차 室利靺蹉 350
실리밀다라 室利蜜多羅 350
실리바새가 室利嚩塞迦 350
실리제바 室利提婆 350
실리차달라 室利差呾羅 350
실리흘률다저 室利訖栗多底 15
실리흘률다지 室利訖栗多底 350
실마 室摩 349
실마나라 室摩那拏 245
실말나이낙가 室末那伊洛迦 245
실망 失望 138
실법 實法 146, 282, 476
실보무장애 實報無障礙 222
실보무장애토 實報無障礙土 36, 261
실보토 實報土 350, 421
실본 實本 350
실불 實佛 360
실상 實相 183, 187, 317, 350, 398, 544, 560, 561
실상관 實相觀 350
실상무상 實相無相 350, 603
실상반야 實相般若 275, 480
실상법계 實相法界 350
실상법밀 實相法密 305
실상법신 實相法身 428
실상삼매 實相三昧 350
실상신 實相身 291, 484
실상위물이신 實相爲物二身 350
실상인 實相印 350
실상지공리 實相之公理 208
실상지신 實相智身 350
실상진여 實相眞如 588
실상풍 實相風 350
실상혜 實相慧 350
실상화 實相花 350
실색신 實色身 351
실성 室星 351
실성 實性 350, 351
실쇄 室灑 351
실수마라 失守摩羅 or 失收摩羅 349
실수마라 失收摩羅 351
실수마라 室獸摩羅 351
실신 實身 484
실아 實我 282, 326, 351, 476
실안 實眼 351
실어 實語 351
실유 實有 282
실저치 悉抵哆 284
실제 實諦 350, 351
실제 實際 34, 187, 350, 351, 366, 398
실제리지 實際理地 351
실지 實智 58, 351, 491
실지 悉地 187, 213, 275, 349
실지 悉底 349
실차난타 實叉難陀 351
실창 實唱 351
실체야 悉替耶 349
실치라말지 悉耻羅末底 349, 388
실타 悉陁 349
실타 悉陀 235, 349
실타벽라 悉他薜攞 349
실타폐라니가야 悉他陛攞尼迦耶 349
실화 實化 351
실화이신 實化二身 351
심 審 352
심 尋 227, 351
심 心 274, 294, 351, 409, 458, 483, 485, 487, 587, 607
심 深 351
심 甚 352
심갱 深坑 351
심경 心經 169, 352
심경 心鏡 352
심경 深經 351
심공 心空 352
심관 心觀 352, 353
심광 心光 301, 352, 477
심광명 心光明 489
심구 心垢 352
심구심 尋求心 422
심귀 心鬼 352
심극 心極 352
심근 心根 352
심기 心器 352

심기 心機 352
심념불공과 心念不空過 352
심등 心燈 352
심량 心量 352
심려사 審慮思 352
심련 心蓮 352
심령 心靈 352
심로 心路 352
심리 深理 351
심마 心馬 352
심마 甚麽 355
심마(적) 心魔(賊) 352
심마사나 深摩舍那 342, 351
심명 心命 352
심목 心目 352
심묘 深妙 351
심무소주 心無所住 352
심밀 深密 34, 351, 422
심밀경 深密經 239, 282, 546
심밀반야 深密般若 282
심박 心縛 353
심번뇌장 心煩惱障 288
심법 心法 176, 353, 416, 425, 585
심법(문) 深法(門) 351
심법신 心法身 353
심법인 深法忍 351
심불 心佛 214, 353
심불급중생 心佛及衆生 266, 274, 353
심불급중생시삼무차별 心佛及衆生是三無差別 508
심불상응(행) 心不相應(行) 353
심불상응(행법) 心不相應(行法) 353
심불상응행법 心不相應行法 586
심비 深秘 351
심빙 心冰 353
심사 尋伺 7, 351
심사 心師 353
심상 心想 353
심상 心相 353
심상염불 尋常念佛 351
심상응행 心相應行 353
심생멸문 心生滅門 353
심성 心城 353, 354
심성 心性 317, 353
심성삼천 心性三千 353
심소 心所 353, 354, 424
심소(법) 心所(法) 353
심소법 心所法 235, 416, 425
심소유법 心所有法 176, 353, 585
심수 心數 329, 353, 354
심수 心水 353
심승 心乘 353
심시법신 心是法身 353
심식 心識 76, 282, 354, 377
심식지일분설 心識之一分說 502
심신 心神 354
심신 深信 351
심신족 心神足 254
심심 心心 354
심심 深心 283, 351
심심 甚深 352
심심수 心心數 354
심안 心眼 354
심약 心藥 354
심연 心緣 354
심오 深奧 351
심왕 心王 353, 354, 424
심왕심소 心王心所 354
심왕여래 心王如來 354
심외무별법 心外無別法 266
심요 心要 354
심원 心源 354
심원 心猿 352, 354
심원 心願 354
심월 心月 354
심월륜 心月輪 354
심의식 心意識 354
심인 心印 354
심일경성 心一境性 354
심입 深入 81, 351
심자재자 心自在者 354
심작 心作 354
심장 深藏 351
심적 心跡 354
심전 心田 354
심정 心亭 353, 354
심정 深淨 351
심정지어일처 心定止於一處 551
심종 心宗 354, 367
심주 心咒 354
심주 心珠 354
심증 心證 355
심지 心地 355
심지 心志 551
심지 心智 355
심지 深智 351
심지관경 心地觀經 204
심진 心塵 355
심진 心眞 355
심진여 心眞如 105
심진여문 心眞如門 355
심출가 心出家 579
심취 心趣 355
심파 心波 355
심해 心海 355
심해탈 心解脫 492
심행 心行 355
심행 深行 351
심행불리 心行不離 355
심향 心香 355
심현 深玄 351
심혜 心慧 355
심화 心華 355
심회연모 心懷戀慕 355
십 什 355
십 十 355
십감로명 十甘露明 11
십감로왕 十甘露王 355
십감로주 十甘露咒 11
십겁 十劫 355
십겁미타 十劫彌陀 355
십겁수유 十劫須臾 355
십겁정각 十劫正覺 355
십견 十見 355
십경 十境 355
십계 十戒 246, 342, 355, 356, 362, 477
십계 十界 27, 54, 356, 566
육도사성 六道四聖 461
십계 十誡 355
십계개성불 十界皆成佛 356
십계능화보살 十界能化菩薩 356
십공덕(론) 十功德(論) 356
십과 十科 356
십과 十過 356
십교 十教 356
십구계 十九界 532
십군 十軍 356, 368
십근본번뇌 十根本煩惱 356, 361
십금강 十金剛
四十位 253
십금강심 十金剛心 356
십금강심향과 十金剛心向果 356
십나찰녀 十羅刹女 356
십념 十念 357

십념성취 十念成就 357
십념왕생 十念往生 357
십념처 十念處 357
십념혈맥 十念血脈 357
십뇌란 十惱亂 357
십대명왕 十大明王 371
십대원 十大願 357
십대제자 十大弟子 357
십대혹 十大惑 357, 361
십덕 十德 357
십도 十度 163, 357, 359
십도 十道 357
십도삼행 十度三行 357
십락 十樂 357
십락 十樂 370
십래(게) 十來(偈) 357
십력 十力 120, 162, 176, 214, 358, 368, 369
십력(무등)존 十力(無等)尊 358
십력가섭 十力迦葉 419
십력가섭 十力迦葉 358
십력교 十力敎 358
십력명 十力明 358
십륜 十輪 358
십리 十利 358
십마 什麽 355
십만 十萬 358
십만억불토 十萬億佛土 358
십명 十名 358
십명품 十明品 368
십묘 十妙 358, 522
십무애 十無礙 359
십무이 十無二 359
십무진계 十無盡戒 359
십무진장 十無盡藏 359
십문 十問 359
십문 十門 359, 482
십문화쟁론 十門和諍論 359
십물 什物 355
십바라밀 十波羅蜜 357, 359
십바라밀다 十波羅密多 359
십바라이 十波羅夷 359, 368
십발취 十發趣
四十位 253
십발취심 十發趣心 360
십법 十法 360
십법계 十法界 356, 360
십법행 十法行 360
십변처정 十遍處定 360
십보 十寶 360
십보문 十普門 360
십보산 十寶山 360
십분로명왕 十忿怒明王 360
십불 十不 601
십불 十佛 360
십불선 十不善 368
십불선도 十不善道 360
십불선업 十不善業 360
십불이문 十不二門 58, 360, 407
십불회계 十不悔戒 360
십사 十使 356, 357, 361, 371
십사 十四 361
십사 十師 361
십사경 十事經 361
십사공덕 十事功德 361
십사난 十四難 361
십사변화 十四變化 361
십사불국왕생 十四佛國往生 361
십사비법 十事非法 361
십사신구왕 十四神九王 361
십사향 十四向 368
십산왕 十山王 361
십삼 十三 361
십삼력 十三力 361
십삼불 十三佛 361
십삼입 十三入 532
십삼잔 十三殘 481
십삼종 十三宗 361
십상 十相 279
십선 十善 27, 360, 362, 412, 571
십선(정법) 十善(正法) 361
십선계 十善戒 361, 520
십선계력 十善戒力 361
십선교 十善巧 361
십선보살 十善菩薩 361
십선심 十善心 369
십선십악 十善十惡 311
십선업(도) 十善業(道) 361
십선왕 十善王 360, 361
십선위 十善位 361
십선지 十禪支 361, 366
십성 十成 361
십성 十聲 357
십송율 十誦律 255
십송율 十誦律 211, 225, 457, 540
십수승어 十殊勝語 362
십승(관) 十乘(觀) 362
십승관법 十乘觀法 368
십승상 十乘床 362
십승풍 十乘風 362
십승행 十勝行 362
십신 十信 3, 252, 298, 362, 371, 410, 467, 481
십신 十身 362
십신위 十信位 361, 460, 461, 464, 467
십심 十心 362
십악 十惡 45, 361, 362, 368, 588, 592, 618
십악(업) 十惡(業) 360
십악업 十惡業 395
십악업(도) 十惡業(道) 362
십안 十眼 362, 423
십야(염불) 十夜(念佛) 362
십여 十如 27
십여(시) 十如(是) 362
십여래지 十如來地 362
십여시 十如是 370
십연관 十緣觀 363
십연생구 十緣生句 363
십오 十五 363
십오존 十五尊 363
십오존관음 十五尊觀音 363
십오지단 十五智斷 363
십우도(서) 十牛圖(序) 363
십원왕 十願王 363
십유관 十喩觀 363
십육 十六 363
십육(대)천 十六(大)天 363
십육(심)행 十六(心)行 363
십육관 十六觀 363
십육관 十六觀 492
십육국왕 十六國王 363
십육대국 十六大國 363
십육대력 十六大力 363
십육대사 十六大士 363
십육보살 十六菩薩 363
십육사 十六師 363
십육사미 十六沙彌 363
십육상관 十六想觀 363
십육선신 十六善神 363
십육소지옥 十六小地獄 554
십육신아 十六神我 363
십육심 十六心 363, 608
십육왕자(불) 十六王子(佛) 363
십육유증지옥 十六遊增地獄 554
십육자구 十六資具 363

ㄱ ㄴ ㄷ ㄹ ㅁ ㅂ ㅅ ㅇ ㅈ ㅊ ㅋ ㅌ ㅍ ㅎ 찾아보기

십육정사 十六正士 363
십육제관 十六諦觀 363
십육행상 十六行相 363
십육회 十六會 363
십은 十恩 364
십이 十二 364
십이(대)원 十二(大)願 364
십이(상)원 十二(上)願 364
십이(유)지 十二(有)支 365
십이공 十二空 364, 366
십이광불 十二光佛 364
십이궁 十二宮 314, 364
십이극원 十二棘園 365
십이금 十二禽 364
십이대천중 十二大天衆 366
십이등 十二燈 364
십이륜 十二輪 365
십이무위 十二無爲 364, 366
십이문 十二門 364, 365
십이문론 十二門論 243, 270, 364, 540
십이법인 十二法人 364
십이부 十二部 324
십이부경 十二部經 50, 159, 229, 364, 489, 604
십이부교 十二部敎 415
십이분경 十二分經 364
십이분교 十二分敎 364
십이불 十二佛 364
십이불율의 十二不律儀 365
십이솔련 十二率連 365
십이수 十二獸 364, 365
십이신 十二神 93, 365
십이신(명왕) 十二神(明王) 365
십이신장 十二神將 365
십이악률의 十二惡律儀 365
십이악율의 十二惡律儀 365
십이약차대장 十二藥叉大將 365
십이연기 十二緣起 365, 403
십이연생 十二緣生 404
십이외상 十二外相 436
십이원왕 十二願王 365
십이유경 十二遊經 365
십이인연 十二因緣 80, 288, 302, 324, 364, 365, 403, 421, 465, 468, 480, 497, 511, 581, 617
십이인연론 十二因緣論 366
십이입 十二入 101, 190, 267, 315
십이종화법 十二種火法 366
십이중성 十二重城 365
십이지 十二地 366
십이지 十二支 581
십이진여 十二眞如 364, 366
십이처 十二處 190, 267, 565
십이천 十二天 366
십이화존 十二火尊 366
십이화천 十二火天 366
십인 十因 299
  引發因 495
십인 十忍 34
십인십과 十因十果 493
십일 十一 366
십일면관음 十一面觀音 366
십일체처 十一切處 360, 361, 366
십장 十障 366, 368, 370
십장양 十長養
  四十位 253
십장양심 十長養心 367
십재(일) 十齋(日) 367
십재(일)불 十齋(日)佛 367
십전 十纏 523
십전염왕 十殿閻王 367
십제자 十弟子 367
십조 什肇 355
십조 十條 356
십종 十宗 356, 367, 412
십종관법 十種觀法 368
십종마군 十種魔軍 368
십종방편 十種方便 368
십종부정 十種不淨 367
십종소관법 十種所觀法 367
십종지력 十種智力 358, 368
십종지명 十種智明 368
십종행원 十種行願 368
십주 十住 76, 223, 258, 295, 298, 318, 358, 362, 367, 368, 371, 380, 410, 425, 429, 461, 464, 466, 467, 469, 542, 550, 566, 582, 608
  四十位 253
십주경 十住經 368
십주비바사론 十住毘婆沙論 368
십주심 十住心 368
십주위 十住位 464
십중(금)계 十重(禁)戒 359, 368
십중금계 十重禁戒 359
십중장 十重障 368
십중죄 十重罪 368
십지 十地 29, 60, 142, 208, 212, 223, 258, 284, 295, 318, 358, 362, 366, 367, 368, 369, 370, 425, 429, 462, 464, 467, 469, 542, 550, 576, 608, 619
  四十位 253
십지 十智 368, 369
  他心通 592
십지경 十地經 368
십지경론 十地經論 41, 552
십지론 十支論 370
십지심 十地心 369
십지십심 十地十心 369
십지원행 十地願行 369
십지위 十地位 464
십지품 十地品 155, 369
십진구퇴 十進九退 370
십진여 十眞如 366, 370
십칠존만다라 十七尊曼荼羅 419
십쾌 十快 357, 370
십통 十通 370
십팔 十八 370
십팔(대)경 十八(大)經 371
십팔경계 十八境界 371
십팔계 十八界 101, 371, 485
십팔니리경 十八泥梨經 554
십팔도 十八道 371
  four degrees 242
십팔명처 十八明處 371
십팔물 十八物 371
십팔부 十八部 371
십팔불공법 十八不共法 214, 370
십팔생처 十八生處 371
십팔원만 十八圓滿 370
십팔원정 十八圓淨 370
십팔유학 十八有學 371
십팔응진 十八應眞 371
십팔종 十八宗 370
십팔중지옥 十八重地獄 371
십팔천 十八天 370
십팔현(성) 十八賢(聖) 371
십팔현(중) 十八賢(衆) 371
십행 十行 258, 295, 298, 317, 318, 367, 371, 410, 425, 429, 461, 466, 467, 469, 608
  四十位 253
십현(연기) 十玄(緣起) 371
십현문 十玄門 371, 629
십현연기 十玄緣起 629

십호 十號 358, 371
십호 十護 371
십혹 十惑 371
십회향 十回向 194
십회향 十廻向 251, 258, 295, 298, 318, 367, 410, 425, 429, 461, 466, 467, 469, 608, 645
四十位 253
십회향 十迴向 116
십회향위 十廻向位 464
십희 十喜 569
쌍 雙 371
쌍계사 雙溪寺 371
쌍녀 雙女 364
쌍류 雙流 371
쌍림 雙林 371
쌍목 雙木 371
쌍수 雙樹 371
쌍신 雙身 371
쌍왕 雙王 371
쌍지 雙持 371
씨 氏 485

(ㅇ)

아 譌 372
아 亞 372
아 俄 373
아 哦 373
아 啞 372
아 峨 372
아 我 269, 372, 433
four inverted beliefs 242
四德 241
四相 249
아 牙 373
아 痾 372
아 蛾 372
아 阿 2, 91, 214, 217, 372, 437, 493, 501, 514, 586
아 餓 372
아(왕)안 鵝(王)眼 383
아가 阿伽 373
아가 阿迦 373
아가 阿迦 or 阿伽 375
아가낭 阿迦嚢 373
아가니(슬)긔 阿迦尼(瑟)挩 373
아가니(슬)타 阿迦尼(瑟)吒 373
아가니사타 阿迦尼沙吒 or 아가니사탁 373
아가니사탁 阿迦尼師託 373
아가다 阿伽陀 373
아가담 阿伽曇 373
아가담 阿迦曇 373
아가라가 阿伽羅伽 373
아가로 阿伽嚧 373
아가루 阿伽樓 373
아가마 阿伽摩 373, 386
아가배 阿伽坏 373
아가사 阿迦奢 373
아가색 阿迦色 373
아가운 阿迦雲 373
아가이타 阿迦貳吒 373
아가타 阿伽陀 385
아가타 阿伽馱 284
아가파 阿訶婆 284
아갈다 阿竭多 373
아갈다 阿竭陀 373
아갈다선 阿竭多仙 373
아갈라 阿羯羅 373
아갈라쇄 阿羯囉灑 321
아갈사니 阿羯沙尼 419, 429
아건다 阿犍多 or 阿揵多 373
아걸사라 阿乞使囉 514
아걸사라 阿乞史羅 387
아게(다) 阿揭(陀) 373
아게다 阿揭多 373
아견 我見 85, 145, 373, 410, 463, 482, 497, 582, 601
四煩惱 247
아공 我空 266, 302, 373, 477, 497
아공진여 我空眞如 373
아구 阿傴 373
아구 阿嘔 373
아구 阿歐 373
아구 阿漚 373
아구라가라 阿鳩羅加羅 373
아구로사 阿拘盧奢 373
아구차국 阿拘遮國 494
아귀 餓鬼 59, 372
아귀계 餓鬼界 372
아귀도 餓鬼道 372
아귀성 餓鬼城 372
아귀애 餓鬼愛 372
아귀취 餓鬼趣 372, 468
아급마 阿笈摩 386
아기(다)달 阿耆(多)達 374
아기(다)타 阿耆(多)陀 374
아기니 阿祇儞 374
아기니 阿祇儞 or 阿祇尼 374
아기니 阿耆尼 374, 412
아기다 阿嗜多 384
아기다 阿耆多 374, 384
아기다경사감바라 阿耆多頸舍甘婆羅 374
아기다시사흠바라 阿耆多翅舍欽婆羅 374
아기비가 阿耆毘伽 374
아나 阿拏 60, 374, 375, 583
아나 阿那 167, 374, 375, 549
아나(아)바나 阿那(阿)波那 374
아나(아)파나 阿那(阿)波那 389
아나가미 阿那伽迷 or 阿那伽彌 374
아나기지라 阿那耆智羅 374
아나리라바 阿那籬攞嚩 374
아나바나 阿那波那 374, 381
아나바달다 阿那波達多 375
아나바루길저수 阿那婆婁吉低輸 379
아나바태다 阿那婆答多 375
아나반나 阿那般那 374
아나발씨 譏那鉢氏 372
아나발저 俄那鉢底 373
아나빈저 阿那邠抵 232
아나수라바 阿那藪囉嚩 374
아나율 阿那律 374
아나율 阿那律 375
아나율도 阿那律徒 374
아나율타 阿那律陀 374
아나타 阿那他 374
아나타빈저 阿那他賓低 374
아나파루길지수 阿那婆婁吉低輸 374
아나함 阿那含 98, 215, 222, 223
사과 239
아나함 阿那含 or 阿那鋡 374
아나함과 阿那含果 374
아나함지 阿那含地 369
아나함향 阿那含向 374
아난 阿難 374, 486
아난사사경 阿難四事經 249
아난타 阿難陀 374
아난타보라 阿難陀補羅 374
아난타야차 阿難陀夜叉 374
아날마 阿捺摩 385
아노라타 阿奴邏陀 374
아노모다 阿奴謨柁 374

ㄱ ㄴ ㄷ ㄹ ㅁ ㅂ ㅅ ㅇ ㅈ ㅊ ㅋ ㅌ ㅍ ㅎ 찾아보기

아뇩 阿耨 583
아뇩달다 阿耨達多 603
아뇩달지 阿耨達池 235
아누 阿耄 60, 374
아누 阿耨 374, 375
아누(다라삼먁삼)보리 阿耨(多羅三藐三)菩提 375
아누관음 阿耨觀音 375
아누달 阿耨達 375
아누달산 阿耨達山 375
아누라다보라 阿耄羅陀補羅 375
아누루타 阿耄樓馱 374, 375
아누루타 阿耨樓陀 375
아누률타 阿耄律陀 374
아누솔도파 阿耨窣都婆 374, 375
아누타천제 阿耄吒闡提 374
아니라가 阿儞囉迦 375
아니로두 阿尼盧豆 374
아니지야 阿泥底耶 375
아다나식 阿陀那識 607
아다나식 阿陁那識 52
아다라 阿陀囉 375
아다라 阿馱囉 375
아단 阿檀 385
아달마 阿怛摩 515
아달바나 阿闥婆那 or 阿達婆那 375
아달바다 阿達波陀 375
아달바비타 阿達婆鞞陀 385
아달바타 阿闥婆陀 385
아덕 我德 375
아도 我倒 375
아등만 我等慢 375
아라 阿羅 375, 379
아라가 阿羅伽 375
아라가 阿羅歌 375, 386
아라가계 阿羅伽界 376
아라가과 阿羅伽果 375
아라가하 阿羅伽訶 375
아라가향 阿羅伽向 375
아라나 誐囉娜 372
아라다가라마 阿羅茶迦邏摩 376
아라라 阿羅邏 376
아라라가라마 阿羅邏迦羅摩 376
아라라가람 阿羅邏迦藍 376
아라마 阿羅磨 375
아라미 阿羅彌 375
아라사 阿羅闍 376
아라야 阿羅耶 376
아라파루 阿羅波樓 386
아라파자나 阿羅派遮那 or 阿羅婆遮那 375
아라하 阿羅訶 or 阿羅呵 375
아라한 阿羅漢 98, 222, 375, 377, 384
四果 239
아라한지 阿羅漢地 369
아락가파 阿落迦婆 376
아락찰파 阿落刹婆 376
아란가란 阿蘭迦蘭 376
아란나 阿蘭那 376
아란야 阿蘭若 35, 293, 376
아란야가 阿蘭若迦 376
아란양 阿蘭攘 376
아란타 阿蘭陀 or 阿蘭陁 376
아람 阿藍 376
아람(가람) 阿藍(伽藍) 376
아람가 阿藍迦 376
아람마 阿藍麼 or 阿藍摩 376
아략 亞略 372
아략 阿略 377
아략 阿畧 or 阿略 375
아려사 阿黎沙 377
아려야 阿黎耶 376
아려의 阿黎宜 377
아려하 阿黎呵 375
아련야 阿練若 376
아련여 阿練茹 376
아로 誐嚕 372
아로가 阿盧伽 375
아로기 痾略祇 372
아로나 誐嚕拏 4
아로나 阿盧那 376
아로나발저 阿盧那跋底 376
아로나화 阿盧那花 376
아로노 阿路猱 376
아로파 阿路巴 376
아록록지 阿轆轆地 376
아뢰야 阿賴耶 376, 377
아뢰야식 阿賴耶識 52, 344, 376, 607
아뢰야외도 阿賴耶外道 376
아루가 阿婁呵 284
아루나 阿樓那 376
아류나 阿留那 376
아리(슬)타 阿梨(瑟)吒 377
아리(야)다라 阿唎(耶)多羅 377
아리(의)사나 阿梨(宜)斯那 377
아리니 阿利尼 377
아리라발제 阿利羅跋提 377, 383
아리라벌지 阿利羅伐底 342
아리사 阿利沙 377
아리사게 阿利沙偈 377
아리사주처 阿利沙住處 377
아리수 阿梨樹 377
아리슬가자 阿梨瑟迦紫 144
아리야 阿利耶 377
아리야 阿利耶 or 阿梨耶 376
아리야 阿哩夜 377
아리야 阿梨耶 377
아리야바로갈제삭발라야 阿唎耶婆盧羯帝爍鉢囉耶 377
아리야바루길호세 阿梨耶婆樓吉弖稅 379
아리야벌마 阿梨耶伐摩 377
아리야식 阿梨耶識 484
아리의 阿利宜 377
아리의 阿犁宜 377
아리의 阿離宜 377
아리의타사 阿梨宜馱娑 377
아리저 阿利底 233
아리지 阿利底 1
아리타 阿梨陀 2
아리하 阿梨呵 375, 377
아마 阿摩 377
아마다다 阿摩爹爹 377
아마라 阿摩羅 377
아마라식 阿摩羅識 52
아마락가 阿摩洛迦 377
아마제 阿摩提 or 阿麼提 377
아마채 阿摩齡 377
아만 我慢 288, 377, 583, 604
四煩惱 247
아만 我曼 482
아말다 阿末多 374
아말라 阿末羅 377, 390
아모가 阿牟伽 377
아모가 阿牟伽 or 阿謨伽 377
아모가파사 阿牟伽皤賒 213, 377
아목 阿目 90
아목가 阿穆伽 377
아목거 阿目佉 89, 377
아목거(발절라) 阿目佉(跋折羅) 377
아목거발절라 阿目佉跋折羅 213
아목길발절라 阿目佶跋折羅 213
아몰률도 阿沒嘌都 379

아무아 我無我 587
아미 峨眉
四大名山 241
아미 蛾眉 372
아미(타) 阿彌(陀) 378
아미도단나 阿彌都檀那 11
아미라흠흠 阿味囉吽欠 380
아미비라검 阿尾卑羅劍 380
아미사 阿尾奢 379
아미사 阿尾捨 379
아미사 阿尾舍 379
아미사 阿尾賒 379
아미산 峨眉山 or 峩眉山 372
아미저야 阿彌底耶 586
아미타 阿彌陀 62, 287, 305, 361, 367, 586
아미타경 阿彌陀經 94, 248, 278, 323, 378, 427, 531
아미타단나 阿彌陀檀那 379
아미타바 阿彌陀婆 378
아미타불 阿彌陀佛 378
아미타불오십보살상 阿彌陀佛五十菩薩像 423
아미타삼마지집다라니경 阿彌陀三摩地集陀羅尼經 56
아미타성 阿彌陀聖 378
아미타유사 阿彌陀庾斯 378
아밀률제 阿密嘌帝 379
아밀리다 阿密哩多 11, 379
아밀리다군다리 阿密哩多軍荼利 379
아밀리달 啞密哩達 11, 372
아바다나 阿波陀那 162, 165, 364, 580
아바라길제사바라 阿婆羅吉帝舍婆羅 379
아바라밀 我波羅蜜 379
아바라하거 阿縛羅訶佉 379
아바로기제습벌라 阿縛盧枳帝濕伐邏 379
아바로기지습벌라 阿縛盧枳低濕伐邏 379
아바로길지사바라 阿婆盧吉低舍婆羅 385
아바로다이습벌라 阿縛盧多伊濕伐邏 379
아바잉가라 阿婆孕迦羅 385
아박 阿縛 374
아박건 阿薄健 379
아반 阿潘 379
아반다라 阿槃陀羅 379
아발 阿跋 375
아발다라 阿跋多羅 379
아발라지하제 阿鉢羅呧訶諦 379
아발리구다니 阿鉢利瞿陀尼 445
아발리구타니 阿鉢唎瞿陀尼 379
아발리시다 阿鉢唎市多 379
아발리이다 阿跋唎爾多 379
아발마 阿鉢摩 386
아발마라 阿跋摩羅 386
아발야기리 阿跋耶祇釐 379
아발지발라지제사나 阿鉢底鉢喇底提舍那 379
아방 阿傍 379
아방 阿防 379
아방라찰 阿傍羅刹 379
아번 阿鑁 379
아번람함흠 阿鑁覽唅欠 379
아벌라세라 阿伐羅勢羅 379
아벌라숙라 阿伐羅塾羅 305
아법 啞法 372
아법 我法 34, 302, 380
아법구유 我法俱有 367
아법구유종 我法俱有宗 380
아별석해이 啞撇釋該而 372
아보살 牙菩薩 373
아부(타)달마 阿浮(陀)達摩 380
아부달마 阿浮達摩 364
아부담 阿部曇 380
아부타 阿浮陀 159
아부하나 阿浮呵那 or 阿浮訶那 380
아비 阿卑 379
아비 阿毗 380, 554
아비 阿鼻 380, 554
아비(지)지옥 阿鼻(旨)地獄 380
아비다갈라나 阿避陀羯刺拏 380
아비달마 阿毗達磨 380
아비달마 阿毘達摩 364
아비달마 阿毘達磨 227
아비달마 阿鼻達磨 380
아비달마경 阿毘達磨經
六部大乘經 462
아비달마구사론 阿毗達磨俱舍論 380
아비달마논장 阿毗達磨論藏 380
아비달마대비바사론 阿毗達磨大毗婆娑論 416
아비달마식신족론 阿毘達磨識身足論 534
아비달마장 阿毗達磨藏 380
아비담 阿毗曇 380
아비대성 阿鼻大城 380
아비라제 阿比羅提 383
아비라흠흠 阿卑羅吽欠 380
아비목거 阿毗目佉 or 阿比目佉 380
아비목지 阿毗目底 380
아비발치 阿毗跋致 380
아비발치 阿毘跋致 380
아비발치 阿鞞跋致 380, 616
아비비라흠 阿毘卑羅吽 380
아비사 阿毘舍 379
아비사도 阿毗私度 380
아비삼불(타) 阿毗三佛(陀) 380
아비좌라 阿毗左囉 380
아비좌류가 阿毗左嚠迦 380
아비지 阿毗至 554
아비지 阿鼻旨 380
아비지 阿鼻脂 380
아비지 阿鼻至 380
아비차라 阿毗遮羅 380
아비차로가 阿毗遮嚕迦 380
아비척류가 阿毗拓嚠迦 380
아비초열지옥 阿鼻焦熱地獄 380
아비환지옥 阿鼻喚地獄 380
아사 我事 380
아사가 阿賒迦 380
아사갈갈파 阿舍喝竭波 382
아사나 阿闍那 382
아사다 阿沙荼 381
아사다설돌로 阿闍多設咄路 381
아사라 阿奢羅 385
아사라 阿娑羅 381
아사라낭 阿奢羅曩 205
아사라서타 阿奢囉逝咤 205
아사려 阿闍黎 385
아사리 阿舍梨 385
아사리 阿闍梨 381, 385
아사리아 阿奢理兒 381
아사리이 阿奢理貳 381
아사마보다 阿娑摩補多 380
아사마사마 阿娑磨娑摩 or 阿娑摩娑摩 381
아사미 阿娑弭 381
아사바 阿娑嚩 380
아사선 阿私仙 381

아사세 阿闍世 381
아사세 阿闍貰 381
아사세왕 阿闍世王 159
아사세왕경 阿闍世王經 159
아사야 阿奢也 381
아사타 阿沙陀 381
아사타 阿私陀 384
아사타 阿私陀 or 阿斯陀 381
아사파나가 阿娑頗那伽 381
아사파타 阿舍波他 381
아살다 阿薩多 381
아살사 阿薩闍 381
아상 我相 381, 384
아서 阿誓 383
아서가 阿恕伽 384
아서가 阿舒迦 384
아서단사나 阿誓單闍那 381
아설라부 阿設羅部 381
아설시 阿說示 382
아설지 阿說旨 382
아설타 阿設他 381
아섬지하라 阿剡底訶羅 381
아세야 阿世耶 381
아소 我所 381
아소견 我所見 381, 410
아소라 阿蘇羅 or 阿素羅 382
아소락 阿素洛 382
아소사 我所事 381
아소심 我所心 381
아소유 我所有 381
아수가 阿輸柯 381
아수가 阿輸迦 384
아수갈게파 阿輸喝揭波 382
아수라 阿修羅 231, 279, 333, 382, 568, 606
아수라 阿須羅 382
아수라금 阿修羅琴 382
아수라도 阿修羅道 382
아수라취 阿修羅趣 468
아수륜 阿修倫 or 阿須倫 or 阿須輪 382
아수사 阿輸闍 384
아수실 阿輸實 382
아수타 阿輸他 381
아수할나 阿輸割那 382
아숙가 阿叔迦 384
아순나 阿順那 382, 384
아술달 阿術達 382
아습 阿濕 389
아습갈갈파 阿濕喝碣波 382
아습갈게파 阿濕喝揭婆 382
아습갈미타 阿濕喝迷陀 382
아습갈타파력차 阿濕喝咃波力叉 382
아습마 阿濕摩 or 阿濕麽 or 阿濕魔 382
아습바 阿濕波 382
아습바게바 阿濕嚩揭波 382
아습바유야 阿濕嚩喩若 382
아습박갈나 阿濕縛羯拏 382
아습박구사 阿濕縛窶沙 127
아습박구사 阿濕縛窶沙 or 阿溼縛窶沙 382
아습박벌다 阿濕縛伐多 382
아습박유사 阿濕縛庾闍 382
아습비니 阿濕毘儞 382
아습파 阿濕婆 382
아습파(씨다) 阿濕婆(氏多) 382
아습파시 阿濕婆恃 382
아습파지 阿濕波持 382
아습파타 阿濕婆他 381
아승(가) 阿僧(伽) 382
아승기 阿僧祇 382
아승기야 阿僧企耶 18, 382
아승만 我勝慢 382
아승지 阿僧祗 292
아시 阿恃 381, 384
아시 阿施 382
아시다 阿恃多 383
아시다벌지 阿恃多伐底 383, 648
아시단사나 阿恃單闍那 381
아시라바나 阿尸羅婆那 383
아실 我室 383
아실려사 阿失麗沙 383
아씨다 阿氏多 381, 384
아아소 我我所 383
아애 我愛 383
四煩惱 247
아야 阿耶 383
아야(다) 阿若(多) 383
아야건다 阿夜健多 383
아야게리바 阿耶揭哩婆 or 阿耶揭唎婆 383
아야교진나 阿若憍陳那 42
아야교진여 阿若憍陳如 383
아야구린 阿若拘隣 42
아야달나 阿耶怛那 565
아야달나 阿耶怛那 or 阿也怛那 383
아야라 阿耶羅 383
아야목거 阿耶穆佉 222, 383
아야새건나 阿夜塞健那 383
아양(승) 啞羊(僧) 372
아어취 我語取 383
아여륵과 阿黎勒果 510
아열만 我劣慢 383
아예라 阿詣羅 383
아와나고답니야 啞呱囉孤答尼耶 379
아와라고답니야 啞呱囉孤答尼耶 372
아왕 鵝王 383
아왕별유 鵝王別乳 383
아외자로가 阿畏遮嚕迦 429
아우 我愚 383
아우 阿優 373
아우루타 阿㝹樓馱 374
아위 阿魏 648
아위화라 阿衛貨羅 386
아유 我有 383
아유 阿由 328, 383
아유가 阿留伽 284
아유다 阿庾多 383
아유다 阿由多 383
아유다 阿由多 or 阿庾多 383
아유라제 阿維羅提 383
아유사 阿踰闍 384
아유삼불 阿惟三佛 380
아유월치 阿惟越致 380, 554
아유타 阿由他 622
아유타 阿踰陀 384
아육 阿育 188, 384
아육가경 阿育伽經 384
아육가수 阿育伽樹 384
아육가전 阿育伽傳 384
아육왕산 阿育王山 419
아의니 阿擬尼 374
아이 阿夷 375, 377, 381, 384
아이 阿姨 226
아이념 阿夷恬 384
아이다부지 阿爾多嚩底 383
아이두 阿夷頭 384
아이라바제 阿夷羅婆帝 384
아이라바지 阿夷羅婆底 383, 384
아이라발제 阿夷羅拔提 383
아이라발제 阿夷羅跋提 384
아이라화제 阿夷羅和帝 384

아인라바지 阿寅羅婆底 383
아인사상 我人四相 249, 384
아일(다) 阿逸(多) 384
아일다 阿逸多 149, 160, 374, 384
아자득몽 啞子得夢 372
아전도 我顚倒 384
아전저가 阿顚底迦 292
아전지가 阿顚底迦 384
아절라 阿折羅 384
아점바시라국 阿點婆翅羅國 384
아제 阿提 385
아제다 阿喇多 384
아제다 阿制多 384
아제목다(가) 阿提目多(伽) 384
아제불타 阿提佛陀 384
아제아녹바다 阿提阿耨波陀 384
아주다 阿周陀 384
아주다나 阿周陀那 382, 384
아지다 阿底多 384
아지라바지 阿脂羅婆底 383
아지리 阿底哩 385
아지리 阿祇利 or 阿祇梨 385
아지목다(가) 阿地目多(伽) 384
아지목득가 阿地目得迦 385
아진제야 阿軫帝也 206
아진타 阿軫馳 385
아질리 阿跌哩 385
아집 我執 385, 491, 498
아차 阿差 382
아차 阿遮 381
아차라 阿遮(羅) or 阿遮攞 385
아차루 阿遮樓 385
아차리야 阿遮利耶 385
아차마라 阿叉摩羅 385
아차말 阿差末 385
아찰라 阿刹羅 514
아천 阿擅 385
아천 阿闡 384
아천제가 阿闡提迦 292
아천지(가) 阿闡底(迦) 385
아천지가 阿闡底迦 507
아촉 阿閦 62, 246, 253, 361, 385, 415, 431
四佛 248
아촉(바) 阿閦(婆) 205
아촉(비) 阿閦(鞞) 205
아촉바 阿閦婆 149, 385
아촉비 阿閦鞞 385
아추비야 阿芻鞞耶 385
아치 我痴 385
四煩惱 247
아치야 哦哆也 373
아타 阿他 375
아타 阿陀 385
아타나 阿陀那 376, 385
아타나식 阿陀那識 385
아타리 阿吒利 385
아타리 阿吒釐 385
아타바폐타 阿他婆吠陀 385
아타박가 阿咤薄迦 101
아타박개 阿咤薄皆 101
아타박구 阿吒薄俱 385
아타박구 阿咤薄俱 101
아타벌저 阿吒筏底 385
아타부가 阿吒嚩迦 385
아타타 阿吒吒 385, 554, 610
아타파구 阿吒婆拘 385
아토색 阿菟色 583
아특다벌지 阿特多伐底 377
아파 阿婆 385
아파 阿波 226
아파(라)마나(아)파 阿波(羅)摩那(阿)婆 386
아파(사)마라 阿婆(娑)摩羅 385
아파나가지 阿波那伽低 386
아파다나 阿波陀那 386
아파라 阿波羅 386
아파라라 阿波羅囉 386
아파라라 阿波邏囉 386
아파라리 阿波邏利 386
아파라실다 阿波羅實多 379
아파라질다 阿波羅質多 379
아파마 阿婆磨 385
아파마나 阿波摩那 386
아파마나파 阿婆摩那婆 386
아파마라 阿婆摩羅 386
아파마라 阿波摩羅 386
아파마라아 阿波麼羅誐 386
아파말가 阿波末加 or 阿婆末加 386
아파사마라 阿跛娑摩囉 386
아파최라(서) 阿波嘬羅(庶) 386
아파타라 阿波他羅 386
아파타라 阿波陁羅 386
아파파 阿波波 386, 554, 610, 643
아파회 阿婆論 386
아파회 阿波會 386
아하라 阿賀羅 344, 386
아하하 阿呵呵 386
아할라아할라마마애유이솔탑라니 啞曷囉啞曷囉馬麻藹由而率塔囉尼 372
아함 阿含 98, 373, 386, 406, 421, 456, 484, 501, 511, 519, 603
아함 阿鋡 386
아함경 阿含經 275, 282, 285, 324, 415, 546
아함모 阿含暮 386
아함부 阿含部 386
아함시 阿含時 386
아호 阿呼 386
아호지옥 阿呼地獄 386
아회긍수 阿會亘修 386
아회긍차 阿會亘差 386
아흠 阿吽 386
악 惡 280, 387
악 鰐 349, 387
악 樂 386
악각 惡覺 387
악건달바 樂乾闥婆 386
악게로 惡揭嚕 373, 387
악견 惡見 178, 387
악견처 惡見處 387
악과 惡果 387
악구 惡口 387
악귀신 惡鬼神 387
악기니 惡祁尼 387
악나야간심 惡癩野干心 387
악도 惡道 387
악로 惡露 387
악론 惡論 319
악마 惡魔 387
악무과 惡無過 387
악보 惡報 387
악사 惡師 387
악생왕 惡生王 228
악세계 惡世界 387
악신 樂神 386
악애 惡愛 568
악어 鰐魚 387
악업 惡業 387, 486
악연 惡緣 387
악율의 惡律儀 387
악음 樂音 135
악음 樂音 387
악음수 樂音樹 387
악인 惡因 387

악일 惡日 465
악자 惡者 600
악작 惡作 387
악주 岳州 598
악지식 惡知識 387
악차 惡叉 387
악차취 惡叉聚 387
악찰나 惡察那 387
악찰라 惡刹羅 387
악찰라 惡察羅 387
악천 樂天 386
악촉 惡觸 388
악취 惡趣 388
악취공 惡取空 388
안 安 55, 388
  육도과보 461
안 岸 388
안 按 389
안 案 388
안 眼 288, 388
안 雁 388
안 鴈 388
안거 安居 388, 442
안계 眼界 388, 517
안근 眼根 388, 485
안나 安那 374
안나 頞那 389
안나반나 安那般那 374, 389
안다리반다리 安荼詈般荼詈 465
안다바사 安多婆沙 389
안다바삼 安多婆參 389
안다발살 安多跋薩 389
안다예반다예 安荼隸般荼隸 465
안달라 案達羅 388
안달라바 安呾羅縛 388
안달바사 安怛婆沙 389
안달바삼 安怛婆參 389
안두 岸頭 388
안두가 頞杜迦 389
안락 安樂 246, 388, 405
안락국 安樂國 388
안락정토 安樂淨土 388
안락행품 安樂行品
  四要品 254
안름 安廩 388
안립 安立 389, 458, 487
안립진여 安立眞如 588
안립행 安立行 241, 389
  本化四菩薩 247
안명 安名 388
안명(유)산 安明(由)山 388
안목 眼目 388
안문 鴈門 388
안반 安般 374, 389
안법흠 安法欽 388
안사나 安闍那 389
안서국 安西國 148
안선 安禪 388
안선나 安膳那 or 安繕那 or 安禪那 389
안세고 安世高 56, 388, 424
  四諦經 257
안수 岸樹 388
안수고인 安受苦忍 488
안습박갈나 安濕縛竭拏 51
안식 安息 388
안식 眼識 388
안식(국) 安息(國) 388
안식계 眼識界 388
안식향 安息香 388
안심 安心 388
안양 安養 56
안양정토 安養淨土 388
안온 安穩 388
안왕 鴈王 388
안원 安遠 389
안은 安隱 388
안입 眼入 388
안자 雁字 388
안제 安帝 271
안주최승 安住最勝 589
안지 按指 389
안지 眼智 388
안지라 安底羅 365, 388
안청 安淸 388
안타림 安陀林 342
안타발살 安陀跋薩 389
안타회 安陀會 287
안타회 安陁會 389
안타회의 安陀會衣 472
안탑 雁塔 388
안토지 安土地 388
안하 安下 388
안하처 安下處 388
안행 雁行 388
안현 安玄 388
안혜 安慧 388, 502
알 斡 389
알 遏 389
알 閼 389
알 頞 389
알가 遏伽 373
알가 遏迦 373
알가 閼伽 373, 389
알가배 閼伽杯 389
알가화 閼伽花 389
알니라 頞儞羅 365
알두가만절리 頞杜迦曼折利 377
알반저 頞飯底 389
알부다 遏部多 389
알부담 頞部曇 389
알부타 頞浮陀 389, 610
알부타 頞部陀 389
알부타지옥 頞浮陀地獄 554
알비 頞鞞 382, 389
알사다 頞沙茶 381, 389
알순나 頞順那 382, 389
알슬타 頞瑟吒 389
알습갈타파 遏濕喝咃波 382
알습바유사 頞濕婆瘐闍 389
알습박갈나 頞濕縛羯拏 389
알실다 頞悉多 389
알자라 斡資羅 389
알찰타 頞哳吒 389, 554
알타박구 遏吒薄俱 385
암 唵 389, 390, 423
암 巖 389
암 庵 389
암 暗 389
암 菴 389
암 闇 390
암곡 巖谷 389
암둔 闇鈍 390
암둔장 暗鈍障 366
암라 菴羅 75, 389, 390
암라녀 菴羅女 390
암라원 菴羅園 390
암림 闇林 390
암마니발눌명우 唵麽抳鉢訥銘吽 390
암마니발두미우 唵嚩呢鉢頭迷吽 390
암마니팔미우 唵嚩呢叭㘑吽 465
암마니팔이우 唵嚩呢叭㘑吽 390
암마라 菴摩羅 377, 390
암마라가 菴摩羅迦 377
암마라식 菴摩羅識 390

암마락가 菴摩洛迦 377
암마륵 菴摩勒 390
암마륵가 菴摩勒迦 377
암먀니필멸감 菴乜呢必滅堪 389
암몰라 菴沒羅 377, 390
암미라 菴弭羅 390
암밀리제다리 闇密里帝茶利 390
암바(라)녀 菴婆(羅)女 389
암바라다가 菴婆羅多迦 389
암바리사 菴婆利沙 390
암박계담납막 唵縛鷄淡納莫 465
암사 庵寺 389
암선 暗禪 389
암수원 菴樹園 390
암실 庵室 389
암실 闇室 390
암심 闇心 390
암야천 闇夜天 647
암원 菴園 389
암위원 菴衛園 390
암자 庵子 390
암장 闇障 390
암주 庵主 389
암증 暗證 389
암증선사 暗證禪師 389
암파계타나마 闇婆髻馱那麼 or 闇婆計陀那麼 465
암파라 菴婆羅 377
암폐 暗蔽 389
암화 菴華 390
압 壓 390
압사유 壓沙油 390
압유 壓油 390
압유륜죄 壓油輪罪 390
앙 仰 390
앙 央 390
앙 昂 486
앙 盎 390
앙 鴦 390
앙가 鴦伽 390
앙가사치 鴦伽社哆 390
앙구리마라 盎窶利摩羅 or 鴦窶利摩羅 390
앙구리마라 盎窶利魔羅 390
앙구리마라 鴦窶利摩羅 390
앙구마라 央仇魔羅 390
앙구사 央俱捨 213
앙구사 鴦俱舍 390
앙구식 仰口食 618
앙굴(리)마라 鴦崛(利)摩羅 390
앙굴(마라) 央掘(摩羅) 390
앙굴다라 鴦掘多羅 390
앙굴다라아함 鴦掘多羅阿含 423
앙굴리마라 盎崛利摩羅 or 鴦崛利摩羅 390
앙굴마라 鴦堀摩羅 390
앙굴마라 鴦掘摩羅 390
앙굴만 央崛鬘 390
앙산 仰山 390
앙수벌마 鴦輸伐摩 390
앙아라가 盎哦囉迦 390, 586
앙아라가 鴦哦囉迦 390, 639
앙월점 仰月點 390
애 哀 391
애 愛 80, 365, 391, 419
애 礙 391
애 藹 391
애가 愛假 391
애갈 愛渴 391
애견 愛繭 391
애견 愛羂 391
애견 愛見 391
애결 愛結 391
애계 愛界 391
애계 愛繫 391
애과 愛果 391
애귀 愛鬼 391
애근 愛根 391
애길(지) 藹吉(支) 391
애독 愛毒 391
애라벌나 藹羅筏拏 391
애라찰녀 愛羅刹女 391
애락 愛樂 391
애련 哀憐 391
애론 愛論 391
애류 愛流 391
애륜 愛輪 391
애민 哀愍 391
애법 愛法 391
애별리고 愛別離苦 391
애석 愛惜 391
애수 愛水 391
애신천 愛身天 391
애심 愛心 391
애아 哀雅 391
애안 愛眼 392
애어 愛語 251, 392
애업 愛業 392
애에 愛恚 392
애연 愛涎 392
애연 愛緣 392
애염 愛染 392
애염명왕 愛染明王 100
애염왕 愛染王 392
애옥 愛獄 392
애욕 愛欲 392
애욕해 愛欲海 392
애윤 愛潤 392
애자 愛刺 392
애종 愛種 392
애증 愛憎 392
애집 愛執 392
애착 愛著 392
애착미 愛著迷 392
애착생사 愛著生死 392
애하 愛河 392
애해 愛海 392
애행 愛行 392
애혹 愛惑 392
애화 愛火 392
액 額 392
액부담 額部曇 608
액비 額鞞 419
액상주 額上珠 392
앵 鸚 392
앵무 鸚鵡 392
앵무보 鸚鵡寶 392
야 冶 393
야 夜 393
야 惹 393
야 耶 392
야 野 393
야간 野干 349, 393
야걸차 夜乞叉 393
야나 惹那 393
야나 若那 393, 550
야나 野那 339
야남 若南 393
야다 惹多 302
야마 夜摩 393
야마려가 夜摩廬迦 393
야마천 夜摩天 393, 468
야마천궁품 夜摩天宮品 353
야매니 野寐尼 393
야바 耶婆 138, 392
야바로길제 耶婆盧吉帝 392
야바제 耶婆提 392

야반승 野盤僧 393
야보시 野布施 393
야사 耶舍 392
야사다 耶舍陀 392
야수 夜殊 393
야수다(라) 耶輸陀(羅) 393
야수다라 耶輸多羅 393
야수달라 耶戍達羅 393
야수피타 冶受皮陀 393
야순 耶旬 82, 392
야유 耶維 82, 392
야장 野葬 393
야제 若提 80
야제자 若提子 250, 293, 393
야차 夜叉 57, 393, 515, 568, 606
야차대흑 夜叉大黑 107
야차신 夜叉神 487
야타발 夜他跋 393
야토형신 野兎形神 450
야합수 夜合樹 343
야호선 野狐禪 393
약 略 393
약 約 393
약 若 393
약 藥 268, 393
약걸차 藥乞叉 393
약계 略戒 393
약교 約敎 393
약기 約機 393
약능견사제즉득단생사 若能見四諦則得斷生死 257
약리영발라바구마라 惹哩寧鉢囉婆俱摩羅 40
약법 約法 393
약부 約部 393
약사 藥師 145, 202, 225, 252, 277, 357, 361, 364, 365, 367, 388, 394, 431, 450, 480, 496, 530
日 499
牛頭大王 442
약사경 藥師經 604
약사불 藥師佛 193
약사유리광여래 藥師琉璃光如來 394
약상 藥上 484, 500
약상보살 藥上菩薩 393
약수왕 藥樹王 394
약수왕신 藥樹王身 394
약왕 藥王 367, 393, 431, 484, 500, 510, 648
약왕보살 藥王菩薩 394
약왕삼존 藥王三尊 394
약왕수 藥王樹 394
약왕십이서원 藥王十二誓願 394
약왕십이신장 藥王十二神將 394
약왕유리광 藥王瑠璃光 394
약왕칠불 藥王七佛 394
약유문법자무일불성불 若有聞法者無一不成佛 508
약차 藥叉 393
약초 藥草 394
양 楊 395
양 癢 394
양 禳 394
양 羊 364, 394
양 陽 394
양 養 394
양 兩 394
양각 羊角 394
양거 贜佉 297
양거 儴佉 297
양거 羊車 394
양견신 兩肩神 394
양계 兩界 394, 395
양고 壤苦 266
양과 量果 119
양광 陽光 394
양구(여여) 兩垢(如如) 394
양권 兩權 394
양권경 兩卷經 394
양기 楊岐 278, 310
양기 楊岐 or 揚岐 410
양등신 量等身 120
양류 楊柳 80
양류관음 楊柳觀音 395
양모진 羊毛塵 394
양미 羊未 365
양복전 良福田 119
양부 兩部 394, 395, 595
양부만다라 兩部曼荼羅 395
양분 良賁 119
양서 兩鼠 395
양석 羊石 394
양설 兩舌 394
양승 羊乘 394
양시 兩翅 394
양염 陽炎 404
양염 陽餤 394
양엽 楊葉 395
양월식 禳月蝕 394
양인 良忍 119
양인 養因 425
양일 良日 119
양일식 禳日蝕 394
양재 禳災 394
양재 兩財 395
양족 兩足 489
양족존 兩足尊 395
양주 揚州 46
양주 涼州 199
양지 楊枝 395
양척촉 羊躑躅 4
양하 兩河 394
양화자 癢和子 394
양황참 梁皇懺 395
어 於 395, 442
어 語 270, 395, 585
四等 242
어 醧 395
어 魚 364, 395
어고 魚鼓 395
어망대 醧忘臺 395
어모 魚母 395
어밀 語密 45, 268
어사리결단야 於事理決斷也 550
어언 語言 395
어업 語業 45, 395
어의 語義 395
어자 魚子 395
어제 於諦 395
어토 魚兎 395
어판 魚板 395
어휘 於麾 395
억 億 49, 270, 358, 395
억 憶 395
억 抑 395
억념 憶念 395
억념륜 憶念輪 271
억념비니 憶念毘尼 583
억양 抑揚 422
억양교 抑揚敎 395, 422
억지 憶持 395
억지 抑止 395
억지섭취 抑止攝取 395
억지악사 抑止惡事 395
언 彦 395

언 言 396
언교 言敎 396
언구 言句 396
언달박 彦達縛 16, 395
언망려절지공 言亡慮絶之空 211
언설 言說 396
언어 言語 396
언의 言依 396
언전 言詮 396
언종 彦悰 395
언종 彦琮 305, 395
언진 言陳 396
언행 言行 396
얼 孼 396
얼 蘖 396
얼다타구타 蘖多馱矩吒 396
얼라바 蘖喇婆 396
얼라하 蘖羅訶 396
얼로나 蘖嚕拏 396
얼리하 蘖哩訶 396
엄 嚴 396
엄 掩 396
엄 頗 396
엄발라 頗鉢羅 396
엄색 掩色 396
엄식 嚴飾 396
엄실 掩室 396
엄왕 嚴王 396
엄정 嚴淨 396
엄토 掩土 396
업 業 271, 396, 428, 586
업감 業感 396
업감연기 業感緣起 403
업견 業羂 396
업결 業結 396
업경 業鏡 396
업계 業繫 396
업계고상 業繫苦相 396, 468
업고 業苦 396
업과 業果 396
업구 業垢 396
업금강 業金剛 431
업뇌 業惱 396
업도 業道 270, 396
업도(신) 業道(神) 396
업력 業力 396, 596
업륜 業輪 396
업마 業魔 396
업망 業網 397
업박 業縛 397
업병 業病 397
업보 業報 397
업보신 業報身 397
업부 業簿 397
업상 業相 397, 464
업상경 業相境 355
업성 業性 397, 398
업수 業受 397
업수 業壽 397
업승 業繩 397
업식 業識 397, 422
업식 業食 397
업액 業厄 397
업여 業餘 286, 397
업연 業緣 397
업영 業影 397
업유 業有 397
업인 業因 397, 505
업자재등소의진여 業自在等所依眞如 370
업장 業障 288, 397
업장제 業障除 397
업적 業賊 397
업전 業田 397
업종 業種 397
업종자 業種子 490
업진 業塵 397
업처 業處 397
업천 業天 397
업체 業體 397, 398
업칭 業秤 398
업통 業通 398, 429
업풍 業風 398
업해 業海 398
업행 業行 398
업화 業火 398
에 恚 398, 410
에결 恚結 398
에로 恚怒 398
여 女 398
여 如 83, 289, 398
여 汝 398
여 與 398
여 餘 398, 486
여 女 485
여감자 餘甘子 398
여거 如去 83, 398
여거사 女居士 14
여거사 女居士 398
여과 與果 581
여국 女國 162, 398
여근 女根 398, 485
여기 餘氣 398
여년 驢年 120
여념 餘念 398
여덕 女德 398
여라 濾羅 120
여래 如來 83, 371, 398, 399, 564
천상천하유아독존 569
여래광명출이환입 如來光明出已還入 399
여래무 如來舞 399
여래민보살 如來愍菩薩 399
여래법신 如來法身 504
여래부 如來部 399
여래사 如來使 399
여래상주 如來常住 399
여래선 如來禪 310
여래수량품 如來壽量品 399
여래승 如來乘 399
여래신 如來身 399
여래신력품 如來神力品 399
여래실 如來室 399
여래응공정변지 如來應供正徧智 399
여래일 如來日 399
여래장 如來藏 187, 190, 289, 399, 429, 560
여래장경 如來藏經 399
여래장론 如來藏論 399
여래장성 如來藏性 399
여래장심 如來藏心 353, 399, 484
여래장연기 如來藏緣起 403
여래지 如來地 399
여래청정선 如來淸淨禪 416
여래출현공덕장엄경 如來出現功德莊嚴經
六部大乘經 462
여량 如量 491
여량지 如量智 491
여력 與力 398
여력인 與力因 465
여리 如理 491
여리사 如理師 399
여리지 如理智 416, 491
여만 如慢 604
여몽 如夢 398

여범 女犯 399
여법 如法 399
여법염불 如法念佛 193
여법조복제중생력 如法調伏諸衆生力 361
여법치 如法治 399
여병 女病 399
여사 餘師 458
여상 如常 560
여색 女色 399
여쇄 女鎖 399
여수낭 濾水囊 120
여숙 女宿 380
여순 驢脣 120
여습 餘習 398
여승 女僧 399
여승 餘乘 398
여시 如是 176, 373, 399
여시아문 如是我聞 23, 332, 399, 597
여실 如實 400
여실공 如實空 400, 477
여실불공 如實不空 400
여실불공 如實不空 477
여실일도심 如實一道心 501
여실지 如實智 400
여실지견 如實知見 400
여실지자 如實知者 400
여실지자심 如實知自心 400, 501
여아취등화 如蛾趣燈火 372
여앙가라화 與盎伽羅和 383
여야 黎耶 120
여어 如語 400
여여 如如 400, 416, 543
여여경 如如境 400
여여불 如如佛 252
여여지 如如智 400
여여지법신 如如智法身 428
여염 如焰 398
여영 如影 398
여운 如雲 398
여원 與願 398
여의 如意 135, 363, 400, 431
여의금강 如意金剛 213
여의륜 如意輪 400
여의륜관음 如意輪觀音 400
여의마니 如意摩尼 400
여의무탐 如意無貪 374
여의병 如意瓶 400
여의보 如意寶 418
여의보(주) 如意寶(珠) 400
여의신 如意身 90, 214, 400
여의어 如意語 588
여의음 如意音 135
여의족 如意足 400
여의주 如意珠 400, 568
여의통 如意通 348
여인 女人 400
여인권속론사 女人眷屬論師 400
여인금제 女人禁制 400
여인배 女人拜 400
여인성불원 女人成佛願 400
여인왕생원 女人往生願 400
여인육욕 女人六欲 400
여인정 女人定 400
여인지심불가득실 女人之心不可得實 400
여자출정 女子出定 400
여장 麗藏 120
여적 女賊 401
여전 如電 398
여정 女情 401
여종 餘宗 398
여지심 慮知心 351, 403
여차 黎車 401
여창 黎昌 126
여천 女天 401
여체비 麗掣毘 120
여체타 戾禘馱 284
여탑 麗塔 120
여파다 黎波多 125
여포 如泡 398
여향 如響 398
여화 如化 398
여환 如幻 398
역 亦 401
역 力 359
역 域 401
역 易 401
역 譯 401
역 逆 401
역겁 歷劫 120
역관 譯官 401
역관 逆觀 401
역로가야타 逆路伽耶陀 401
역룡 域龍 401, 557
역류 逆流 329, 362, 401, 479
역무(소)외 力無(所)畏 401
역바라밀 力波羅蜜 401
역바라밀보살 力波羅蜜菩薩 401
역방 逆謗 401
역사 力士 71, 163, 401
역사생지 力士生地 401
역사성 力士城 401
역생 力生 401, 635
역수 逆修 401
역순 逆順 401
역심 域心 401
역여 力如 362
역연 歷然 120
역연 逆緣 401
역연대경 歷緣對境 120
역유 逆喩 401
역유역공 亦有亦空 239
역유역공문 亦有亦空門 325, 401
역유위역무위법계 亦有爲亦無爲法界 428
역자 力者 401
역자(법사) 力者(法師) 401
역화 逆化 401
역회 域懷 401
연 宴 401
연 延 402
연 椽 402
연 演 402
연 烟 402
연 然 402
연 煙 402
연 燃 106, 402
연 緁 402
연 緣 270, 272, 281, 402, 465, 493
environmental, or secondary cause 497
연 蓮 278
연 蠕 402
연 衍 339, 402
연 軟 402
연 輭 402
연 年 401
연 戀 402
연(화)종 蓮(花)宗 531
연각 緣覺 191, 229, 281, 300, 315, 403, 483, 617
연각법계 緣覺法界 403
연각보리 緣覺菩提 403
연각승 緣覺乘 403, 421

연각승십지 緣覺乘十地 369
연각신 緣覺身 403
연개 烟蓋 402
연개 煙蓋 402
연경 綖經 402
연경 蓮經 120
연경사 延慶寺 402
연계 年戒 401
연관 緣觀 403
연궁 蓮宮 120
연기 緣機 403
연기 緣起 50, 315, 403, 561
연기 年忌 401
연기(법)송 緣起(法)頌 403
연기게 緣起偈 403
연기법 緣起法 403
연기제법지근본자위심법 緣起諸法之根本者爲心法 353
연기지성 緣起支性 50
연날리 燕捺利 583
연년 延年 402
연년전수 延年轉壽 402
연념 憐念 120
연념 緣念 403
연담 유일 蓮潭有一 403
연대 蓮臺 501
연독 身毒 25, 345, 403, 494, 571
연동 蠕動 402
연등 然燈 92, 115, 536
연등록 聯燈錄 414
연등불 然燈佛 147, 402, 527
연락 聯絡 118
연랍 年臘 402
연려심 緣慮心 351, 403
연력 緣力 361, 403, 496
연리 緣理 403, 404
연리 蓮理 120
연리단구 緣理斷九 403
연마 練磨 121
연만수구 年滿受具 402
연명 延命 402
연명법 延命法 402
연명보살 延命菩薩 402
연명지장 延命地藏 556
연모 戀慕 402
연묵 宴默 401
연문 蓮門 121
연문 衍門 402
연민 憐愍 120
연박 緣縛 269
연박단 緣縛斷 290
연방 蓮邦 121
연불 緣佛 404
연비 燃臂 404
연사 緣事 403, 404
연사 蓮社 120, 175
연상 緣想 403
연상 緣相 404
연생 緣生 403, 404
연설 演說 402
연성 緣成 404
연성 年星 401
연소정행 年少淨行 402
연수 延壽 402
연수 緣修 483
연수당 延壽堂 151, 314, 402
연심 緣心 404
연안 蓮眼 120
연애 憐愛 120
연야 練若 121
연약(달다) 演若(達多) 402
연어 軟語 402
연여 緣如 362
연연 緣緣 402, 404
연우 蓮祐 120
연인 緣因 404, 488, 530
연인불성 緣因佛性 404, 438
연일 緣日 404
연자 蓮子 120
연적 宴寂 401
연적 輭賊 402
연정 緣正 404
연종 蓮宗 120, 121, 146, 190, 367
연좌 宴坐 401
연좌 蓮座 120
연중 緣中 404
연진 緣塵 404
연찰 蓮刹 120
연창 演暢 402
연촉겁지 延促劫智 402
연태 蓮胎 120
연하 連河 121
연행 練行 121
연화 緣化 404
연화 蓮華 or 蓮花 120
연화경 蓮華經
분다리가 209
연화국 蓮華國 120
연화대 蓮華臺 121
연화복 蓮華服 121
연화부 蓮華部 121
연화생상사 蓮華生上師 17
연화수보살 蓮華手菩薩 121
연화안 蓮華眼 121, 499
연화왕 蓮華王 450
연화의 蓮華衣 121
연화자 蓮華子 121
연화장세계 蓮華藏世界 121
연화장엄 蓮華莊嚴 246
연화좌 蓮華坐 121
연화지 蓮華智 121
열 悅 313, 404
열 涅 404
열 熱 289, 404
열 閱 404
열 劣 404
열 裂 404
열가라 涅迦羅 405
열나파나 咥那婆那 479
열뇌 404
열뇌 熱惱 154
열니연 咥尼延 478
열두단 閱頭檀 328, 404
열라파나 咥羅婆那 479
열반 涅槃 77, 79, 98, 167, 350, 405, 422, 501
四大部經 241
열반(적정)인 涅槃(寂靜)印 405
열반경 涅槃經 92, 99, 269, 271, 274, 281, 285, 287, 288, 289, 400, 405, 416, 417, 419, 486, 501, 540, 604
열반경 涅槃經 23 566
열반경 涅般經 434
열반계 涅槃界 405
열반궁 涅槃宮 405
열반기 涅槃忌 405
열반나 涅槃那 405
열반당 涅槃堂 151, 405
열반락 涅槃樂 405
열반묘 涅槃妙 359
열반묘심 涅槃妙心 603
열반문 涅槃門 406
열반박 涅槃縛 406
열반분 涅槃分 405
열반불 涅槃佛 405
열반산 涅槃山 405

열반상 涅槃像 405
열반상 涅槃相 405
열반색 涅槃色 406
열반성 涅槃城 405
열반성 涅槃聖 406
열반승 涅槃僧 79, 405
열반식 涅槃食 406
열반월일 涅槃月日 405
열반제 涅槃際 406
열반종 涅槃宗 204, 395, 405, 540
열반주 涅槃洲 405
열반첩나 涅槃疊那 405
열반팔미 涅槃八味 405
열반풍 涅槃風 406
열반회 涅槃會 405
열병 熱病 404
열사지 烈士池 121
열상 裂裳 404
열시염 熱時炎 404
열응신 劣應身 472
열응신 劣應身 487
열장 閱藏 404
열중 悅衆 404
열지 劣智 404
열차 閱叉 393, 404
열철지옥 熱鐵地獄 404
염 剡 406
염 厭 407
염 念 222, 362, 412
염 拈 406
염 染 407, 641
염 炎 407
염 焰 407
염 燄 407
염 閻 406
염 鹽 407
염(색)의 染(色)衣 408
염각지 念覺支 78
염경 念經 78
염경 炎經 407
염계 染界 407
염구 厭求 407
염구 染垢 407
염구 燄口 407
염근 念根 78, 485
염념 念念 78
염념무상 念念無常 78, 480
염념상속 念念相續 78
염도귀 厭禱鬼 407
염라 閻羅 406
염라왕 閻羅王 406
염력 念力 77, 414
염로 閻老 406
염루 念漏 78
염리 厭離 407
염마 焰魔 235
염마 琰魔 408
염마 閻摩 393, 406
염마(왕) 閻魔(王) 406
염마계 琰魔界 408
염마나주국 閻摩那洲國 406
염마대화선 焰摩大火仙 407
염마라 閻摩羅 406
염마라왕 閻摩羅王 485
염마모나 琰魔母那 408
염마사 琰魔使 408
염마왕청 琰魔王廳 408
염마졸 琰魔卒 408
염마천 焰摩天 407
염마천비 焰摩天妃 407
염만덕가 閻曼德迦 406
염만득가 焰鬘得迦 360
염망 焰網 407
염매 厭魅 407
염모(니)나 鹽牟(尼)那 407
염모나 閻牟那 406, 408
염법 染法 407
염부 閻浮 313, 406, 494
염부나제금 閻浮那提金 406
염부단금 閻浮檀金 406
염부제 閻浮提 406
염불 念佛 77
염불문 念佛門 77
염불삼매 念佛三昧 77
염불왕생 念佛往生 78
염불왕생원 念佛往生願 78
염불위본 念佛爲本 78
염불위선 念佛爲先 78
염불자 念佛者 77
염불종 念佛宗 77
염불종 念佛宗 540
염불회향 念佛廻向 78
염세 厭世 407
염송 念誦 78
염습 染習 408
염식 念食 252
염심 染心 209, 407
염애 染愛 407
염애진 染愛塵 438
염어 拈語 406
염언 念言 78
염에치 染恚痴 407
염연 染緣 408
염열 炎熱 554, 603
염열지옥 炎熱地獄 407
염오 染汚 407
염오의 染汚意 407
염왕 閻王 406
염왕광불 焰王光佛 407
염왕광불 燄王光佛 378
염우 拈右 406
염의 拈衣 406
염이 念已 254
염점 炎點 407
염정 念定 78
염정 染淨 407
염정불이문 染淨不二門 407
염정심 染淨心 422
염정진여 染淨眞如 407
염제 拈提 406
염제 炎帝 637
염주 念珠 78
염주 念珠 408
염지 念持 78
염착 念著 78
염착 染著 391, 408
염처 念處 78
염천 念天 78
염천 鹽天 407
염청정지 念淸淨地 237
염태 焰胎 407
염파도 閻婆度 406
염향 拈香 406
염향 鹽香 407
염혜심 焰慧心 369
염혜지 焰慧地 369, 407
염화미소 拈花微笑 406
염흔 厭欣 407
염흔관 厭欣觀 469
엽 葉 408
엽개 葉蓋 408
엽사 獵師 121
엽의관음 葉衣觀音 408
엽이강 葉爾羌 517
영 嬰 408
영 影 408
영 榮 408

영 永 408
영 瓔 408
영 迎 408
영 領 408
영감 靈感 121
영감 靈龕 121
영겁 永劫 408
영계 靈界 121
영골 靈骨 121
영공 影供 408
영공 靈供 121
영길사이 英吉沙爾 642
영납 領納 408
영당 影堂 408
영동 嬰童 408
영락 瓔珞 408
영명 永明 538, 598
영묘 靈妙 121
영묘사 靈妙寺 211
영사 影事 408
영사 靈祠 121
영산 靈山 121, 293, 580
영상 影像 408
영상 靈像 121
영생 永生 408
영서 榮西 408
영서화 靈瑞華 121
영성비구 鈴聲比丘 611
영신 靈神 121
영악 靈嶽 121
영안 寧安 121
영응 靈應 121
영적 永寂 247
영접 迎接 408
영지 靈芝 121, 549
영천 穎川 555
영취산 靈鷲山 121, 580
영해 領解 408
영향 影向 408
영향 影響 625
영향중 影向衆 259, 408
영향중 影嚮衆 408
영현 影現 408
영호 影護 408
영혼 靈魂 121, 347
영화 榮華 408
예 曳 409
예 猊 408
예 瘞 409
예 瞖 409
예 穢 409
예 翳 408
예 豫 408
예 預 408
예가 翳迦 408
예가비치가 翳迦鼻致迦 499
예거 隸車 121
예거아실지가 穢佉阿悉底迦 409
예경 禮敬 121
예국 穢國 409
예니야 瞖尼耶 478
예니야 翳尼耶 478
예니연 黳尼延 478
예라발달라 翳羅鉢呾羅 408
예라엽 黳羅葉 479
예류 預流 401, 408
예류과 預流果 21
예미국 預彌國 409
예배 禮拜 121
예불 禮佛 409
예수 豫修 401
예슬지림 曳瑟知林 409
예슬지림 洩瑟知林 313
예식 穢食 409
예신 穢身 409
예신약 翳身藥 408
예업 穢業 409
예이 翳呬 475
예적금강 穢迹金剛 409
예전 瘞錢 409
예좌 猊座 408
예주 澧州 631
예찰 穢刹 409
예참 禮懺 121
예토 穢土 409, 492
예하 猊下 408
오 五 409, 520
오 伍 409
오 午 409
오 嗚 409
오 塢 409
오 奧 409
오 悟 220, 409
오 懊 409
오 晤 409
오 汙 또는 汚 409
오 汚 409
오 澳 409
오 烏 409
오 鄔 81, 441
오(종)잡행 五(種)雜行 427
오(종)증상연 五(種)增上緣 410
오(포)외 五(怖)畏 410
오가 汚家 409
오가(칠종) 五家(七宗) 410
오가소공 五家所共 410
오각 五覺 410
오간 五慳 410
오간색 五間色 410, 420
오개 五蓋 126, 410
오거 五居 410
오겁사유 五劫思惟 410
오견 五見 21, 28, 346, 355, 410, 423
오견고 五堅固 410
오견십악 五見十惡 238
오결 五結 410
오결악자 五結樂子 410
오경 五境 411, 432, 585
오경 五更 410
오계 五戒 412, 423, 433, 477
오계 五界 76
오계 五繫 411
오계 五髻 411
오계(법) 五戒(法) 411
오계관 五髻冠 411
오계문수 五髻文殊 411
오계이십오신 五戒二十五神 26, 411
오고 五股 411
오고 五古 411
오고 五苦 411
오고 五鈷 411
오고(금강) 五股(金剛) 411
오고(저) 五股(杵) 411
오고금강(저) 五股金剛(杵) 411
오고금강(저) 五鈷金剛(杵) 411
오고령 五鈷鈴 427
오고인 五股印 411
오공 午供 409
오공덕문 五功德門 411
오공양 五供養 411
오과 五果 411
오관 五官 411
오관 五觀 412, 426
오관왕 五官王 411
오관왕 伍官王 409

오교 五敎 412, 498, 504, 538
오교장 五敎章 412
오구륜 五俱倫 412
오구린 五拘隣 412
오구족 五具足 412
오구파가 烏俱婆迦 603
오구파아 烏俱婆誐 412
오근 五根 78, 125, 162, 285, 347, 349, 412, 426, 431, 478, 527, 585
오근본 五根本 412
오근색 五根色 412, 420
오금 五禁 412
오금강 五金剛 431
오기 烏耆 412
오기연나 烏耆延那 426
오나 澳那 409, 442
오나가 烏娜迦 446
오나한 五羅漢 460
오나함천 五那含天 412
오나함천자 五那含天子 432
오납의 五納衣 412
오년대회 五年大會 155, 412
오념문 五念門 39, 412
오뇌 懊惱 78, 409
오니야낭 烏儞也曩 426
오다 烏荼 413
오다연나 烏陀衍那 413
오다이 烏陀夷 4
오단법 五壇法 413
오담발라 烏曇跋羅 442
오대 五大 88, 413, 415, 416, 434, 552, 583
오대 五臺 426
四大名山 241
오대관 五大觀 413
오대력보살 五大力菩薩 413
오대명왕 五大明王 413, 414, 418
오대사 五大使 411, 569
오대사자 五大使者 413
오대산 五臺山 413
오대색 五大色 413
오대색색 五大色色 420
오대시 五大施 413
오대용왕 五大龍王 413
오대원 五大院 413
오대월륜 五大月輪 433
오대인 五大印 411
오대존 五大尊 413
오대형 五大形 413
오덕 五德 413
오도 五刀 414, 416
오도 五度 413
오도 五道 413, 423, 432
오도 悟道 409
오도명관 五道冥官 413
오도사문 汚道沙門 409
오도육도 五道六道 413
오도장군 五道將軍 413
오도전륜왕 五道轉輪王 413
오독 五讀 426
오동연의식 五同緣意識 414
오둔사 五鈍使 61, 414, 430, 434, 593
오등록 五燈錄 414
오등엄통 五燈嚴統 414
오등회원 五燈會元 414
오라가 烏羅伽 414
오락 五樂 414
오락 烏落 414
오락가 烏洛迦 414
오락가전단 烏洛迦旃檀 414
오랄시 烏剌尸 414
오력 五力 120, 162, 285, 412, 414, 485, 528
오력명왕 五力明王 414
오로날라차 嗚嚕捺囉叉 409
오로빈라 烏盧頻羅 443
오로빈라 烏盧頻螺 443
오론 五論 414
오류설법 五類說法 414, 429
오류성 五類聲 414
오류용왕 五類龍王 413
오류천 五類天 414
오륜 五輪 413, 414, 432, 553
오륜(솔)탑파 五輪(率)塔婆 415
오륜관 五輪觀 415
오륜삼마지 五輪三摩地 415
오륜삼매 五輪三昧 333
오륜성신 五輪成身 415
오륜육대 五輪六大 415
오륜제 五輪際 415
오륜탑파 五輪塔婆 433
오률타 汙栗馱 409
오리사 五利使 61, 115, 410, 415
오마 烏摩 415
오마비 烏摩妃 415
오명 五名 426
오명 五明 76, 415
오명(처) 五明(處 142
오명론 五明論 496
오몽 五夢 415
오묘 五妙 415
오묘(욕) 五妙(欲) 415
오묘경계락 五妙境界樂 415
오무간 五無間 415
오무간업 五無間業 424
오무량 五無量 415
오무량업 五無量業 415
오무량죄 五無量罪 415
오문선 五門禪 415
오문선경요용법 五門禪經要用法 200
오미 五味 415, 511
오미선 五味禪 416
오미죽 五味粥 416
오바국다 烏波鞠多 444
오바라밀 五波羅密 416
오바라밀 五波羅蜜 413
오발도적 五拔刀賊 416
오발라 烏鉢羅 441
오방오념불문 五方五念佛門 416
오방오지 五方五智 416
오방편 五方便 416
오백 五百 416
오백(대)나한 五百(大)羅漢 416
오백계 五百戒 79, 226, 416
오백문(사) 五百問(事) 416
오백부 五百部 416
오백생 五百生 416
오백생무수 五百生無手 416
오백세 五百世 416
오백소승 五百小乘 416
오백수기품 五百授記品 472
오백유순 五百由旬 416
오백이부 五百異部 416
오법 五法 223, 353, 416, 419, 608
오법성신 五法成身 417, 420
오법신 五法身 417
오법인 五法人 417
오변 五邊 417
오변행 五遍行 417
오병 五甁 417
오병관정 五甁灌頂 417
오병지수 五甁智水 417
오보 五寶 417
오보리 五菩提 410, 417

오보천관 五寶天冠 418
오본 悟本 113
오봉광명 五峯光明 411
오봉금강저 五峯金剛杵 411
오봉인 五峯印 411
오부 五部 411, 417, 419, 425
오부교주 五部敎主 417
오부대론 五部大論 414, 417
오부대승경 五部大乘經 417
오부법 五部法 417
오부비장 五部秘藏 417
오부율 五部律 255, 324, 417
오부정(거염마라) 五部淨(居炎摩羅) 417
오부정식 五不正食 418
오부존법 五部尊法 417, 427, 429
오부좌 五部座 417
오부합단 五部合斷 417
오분 五分 188, 417
오분계본 五分戒本 417
오분노 五忿怒 418, 431
오분률 五分律 160
오분법신 五分法身 26, 417, 418, 428, 529, 623
오분율 五分律 417
오분작법 五分作法 431
오분향 五分香 418, 434
오불 五佛 54, 62, 354, 378, 411, 413, 418, 430
오불가과 五不可果 418
오불가사의 五不可思議 418
오불갈마인 五佛羯磨印 418
오불관 五佛冠 418
오불관정 五佛灌頂 418
오불보관 五佛寶冠 418, 431
오불생오보살 五佛生五菩薩 431
오불성 五佛性 36, 418
오불오신 五佛五身 418
오불자 五佛子 418, 419
오불정(존) 五佛頂(尊) 221, 418
오불정경 五佛頂經 418
오불정법 五佛頂法 418
오불정삼매다라니경 五佛頂三昧陀羅尼經 418
오불정존 五佛頂尊 426
오불환천 五不還天 418, 426
오비(밀) 五秘(密) 418
오비(밀)만다라 五秘(密)曼荼羅 419
오비가 奧箄迦 409
오비구 五比丘 412, 418, 419
오사 五師 417, 419
오사 烏社 635
오사(명) 五邪(命) 419
오사망어 五事妄語 419
오사사 烏沙斯 419
오사자 五使者 157, 419
오사자 五師子 419
오산 五山 419
오삼팔이 五三八二 419
오상 五相 419
오상분결 五上分結 420
오상성신 五相成身 417, 419, 426
오상성신(관) 五相成身(觀) 419
오색 五色 410, 412, 420, 427
오색건타 五塞犍陀 424
오색루 五色縷 420
오색선 五色線 420
오색승 五色繩 420
오색정 五色綎 420
오생 五生 420
오선 五善 420
오선제라 五扇提羅 420, 432
오설 五說 420, 429
오섭론 五攝論 420
오성 五性 420
오성 五星 420, 432
오성 五聖 433
오성 五聲 420, 425
오성음고 五盛陰苦 420, 425
오성종 五性宗 420
오소 五燒 420, 433
오소 奧疏 45
오소사마 烏素沙摩 432
오소의토 五所依土 420
오손 烏孫 426
오쇄 烏鎩 642
오쇠 五衰 419, 421, 571
오수 五受 421, 485
오순 五旬 421
오슬(니사) 塢瑟(膩沙) 421
오슬(니사) 烏瑟(膩沙) 421
오슬니사 烏瑟膩沙 459
오승 五乘 293, 339, 421, 424, 425, 497, 498, 569
오승제입 五乘齊入 421
오시(교) 五時(敎) 421
오시교 五時敎 173, 239, 412, 416, 422, 455
오시팔교 五時八敎 421
오식 五識 344, 422, 553, 629
오식 五食 422
오신 五身 422
오신 五辛 422, 434
오신변 五神變 422
오신통 五神通 370, 421, 422, 433, 468
오실니사 烏失尼沙 421, 459
오심 五心 422
오십공덕 五十功德 422
오십법 五十法 422, 610
오십삼불 五十三佛 423
오십삼삼 五十三參 423
오십삼존 五十三尊 423
오십삼지식 五十三智識 423
오십소겁 五十小劫 423
오십악 五十惡 423
오십오선지식 五十五善知識 423
오십육억칠천만세 五十六億七千萬歲 423
오십이류 五十二類 423
오십이신상 五十二身像 423
오십이위 五十二位 423
오십이존 五十二尊 423
오십이종공물 五十二種供物 423
오십이중 五十二衆 423
오십자문 五十字門 423
오십전 五十轉 422
오십전전 五十展轉 422, 423
오십천공 五十天供 423
오십팔계 五十八戒 423
오아급마 五阿笈摩 423
오아함 五阿含 423
오악 五惡 423
오악견 五惡見 423
오악취 五惡趣 423, 432
오안 五眼 423, 429
오암 烏菴 423
오애 五礙 423, 426
오약 五藥 341
오업 五業 423
오여래 五如來 424, 430
오역 五逆 415, 424, 618
오역십악 五逆十惡 218
오역죄 五逆罪 276
오연 五緣 410
오연 五衍 424

오염 汚染 409
오예 五翳 424
오오백년 五五百年 410, 424
오오보살 五五菩薩 424
오오재편 五五才便 416
오온 五蘊 10, 140, 267, 301, 417, 424, 425, 430
오온개공경 五蘊皆空經 424
오온론 五蘊論 370, 424
오온론석 五蘊論釋 424
오온마 五蘊魔 424, 425, 427
오온비유경 五蘊譬喩經 424
오온세간 五蘊世間 424, 425
오온택 五蘊宅 424
오외 五畏 425
오욕 五欲 414, 425, 426, 636
四蛇 four snakes 249
오운 五雲 425, 426
오월 吳越 573
오위 五位 425
오위군신 五位君臣 425
오위백법 五位百法 176
오위삼매 五位三昧 425
오유(량) 五唯(量) 425
오율 五律 425
오은 悟恩 573
오은 晤恩 263, 409
오음 五陰 30, 101, 280, 420, 424, 425, 470, 604, 607
오음 五音 420, 425, 427
오음(성)고 五陰(盛)苦 425
오음마 五陰魔 425, 427
오음성(고) 五陰盛(苦) 420
오음세간 五陰世間 424, 425
오의 五衣 425
오이 偽夷 412
오인 五印 546
오인 五因 425
오인 五忍 200, 425
오인 悟忍 409
오인(도) 五印(度) 425
오인설경 五人說經 426, 429
오입 五入 302
오입 悟入 409
오자 烏闍 443
오자연나 烏闍衍那 426
오작업근 五作業根 426
오장 五藏 57, 519
오장 五障 414, 423, 425, 426, 430
오장 烏場 426
오장 烏萇 426
오장나 烏仗那 426
오장나 烏杖那 426
오장삼종 五障三從 426
오재 五滓 432
오전 五專 426
오전 五箭 426
오전 五轉 426
오전색 五轉色 426
오전성신 五轉成身 420, 426
오정 五情 426
오정 五淨 426
오정 五頂 426
오정(거천) 五淨(居天 426
오정거중 五淨居衆 432
오정거천 五淨居天 410, 412, 418, 432
오정륜왕 五頂輪王 418, 426
오정사념 五停四念 426
오정산 五頂山 426
오정색 五正色 427
오정색색 五正色色 420
오정식 五正食 426, 427
오정식 五淨食 426
오정심관 五停心觀 240, 369, 415, 426, 526
오정천 五淨天 154
오정행 五正行 427, 429
오제 五諦 427
오조 五祖 427
오조(가사) 五條(袈裟) 427
오조자 五調子 425, 427
오족여래 五族如來 427
오종 五宗 427
오종 五種 427
오종관정 五種灌頂 427, 429, 432
오종금강사 五種金剛使 419
오종나함 五種那含 427, 428
오종단법 五種壇法 417, 427
오종령 五種鈴 427
오종마 五種魔 424, 427
오종반 五種般 427, 428
오종법계 五種法界 427
오종법사 五種法師 428, 429
오종법신 五種法身 418, 422, 428
오종보시 五種布施 428
오종불남 五種不男 428
오종불녀 五種不女 428
오종불번 五種不翻 428
오종불퇴(전) 五種不退(轉) 223
오종불환 五種不還 427, 428
오종비량 五種比量 428
오종산란 五種散亂 428
오종삼귀 五種三歸 268, 429
오종삼매 五種三昧 425
오종설인 五種說人 414, 420, 426, 429
오종성 五種性 429, 466, 529
오종수법 五種修法 417, 427, 429
오종실지 五種悉地 417
오종아나함 五種阿那含 418
오종악병 五種惡病 429
오종유식 五種唯識 37, 429
오종인 五種印 429
오종잡행 五種雜行 429
오종장 五種藏 429
오종정색 五種正色 427
오종정식 五種正食 427
오종정식 五種淨食 426
오종정행 五種正行 466
오종천 五種天 566
오종통 五種通 429, 437
오종행 五種行 429
오종호마 五種護摩 417
오주(지) 五住(地) 430
오주지 五住地 259, 549
오주지혹 五住地惑 430
오중 五衆 424, 425, 430
오중마 五衆魔 427
오중세간 五衆世間 424
오중세계 五重世界 430
오중운 五重雲 430
오중체 五重滯 414, 430
오지 五智 157, 245, 411, 415, 416, 420, 430, 613
文殊 157
오지(보)관 五智(寶)冠 418
오지계 五支戒 431
오지근 五知根 431
오지금강저 五智金剛杵 411
오지다 烏地多 431
오지보관 五智寶冠 431
오지소생삼신 五智所生三身 431
오지여래 五智如來 205, 411, 417, 418, 424, 430, 433, 567
四佛 248
오지오불 五智五佛 430

오지인 五智印 411
오지작법 五支作法 431
오진 五塵 432
오집 五執 420, 432
오차지옥 五叉地獄 432
오찬탄 五讚嘆 426
오찰 悟刹 409
오참상당 五參上堂 432
오참일 五參日 432
오처가지 五處加持 432
오처공양 五處供養 432
오처진언 五處眞言 432
오천 五天 432
오천(자) 五天(子) 432
오천사 五天使 569
오천사자 五天使者 413
오천상만 五千上慢 432
오천제라 五闡提羅 420, 432
오천축 五天竺 425, 432
오체 五體 414, 432
오체투지 五體投地 432
오추사마 烏樞沙摩 432
오추사마 烏芻沙摩 432
오추사마명왕 烏樞沙摩明王 or 烏芻沙摩明王 207
오추삽마 烏芻澁摩 432
오추슬마 烏樞瑟摩 432
오추슬마 烏芻瑟摩 432
火頭金剛 637
오취 五趣 413, 423, 432, 518
오취생사륜 五趣生死輪 432
오취온 五取蘊 432
오침남 烏枕南 432
오탁 五濁 140, 432, 592
오탁가한다 烏鐸迦漢茶 432
오탁증시 五濁增時 432
오통 五痛 420, 433
오통 五通 433, 473, 596
오통(력) 五通(力) 422
오통만다라 五通曼荼羅 423
오통보살 五通菩薩 423, 433
오통선 五通仙 433
오통신 五通神 433
오파 烏波 433
오파계사자 烏波髻使者 433
오파계설니 烏婆計設尼 433
오파계시니 烏波髻施儞 or 烏波髻施尼 419
오파국다 烏波鞠多 433
오파난다 烏波難陀 or 塢波難陀 433
오파다야 烏波陀耶 201, 433, 459
오파사가 烏波娑迦 433
오파사가 烏波斯迦 433
오파삭가 烏波索迦 433
오파제 烏波提 433
오파제삭 烏波第鑠 433
오파타야 烏波陀耶 635
오팔 五八 433
오팔식 五八識 433
오팔십구 五八十具 433
오팔존 五八尊 433
오편 五篇 612
오포사타 烏浦沙他 433
오포외 五怖畏 425
오품 五品 39, 433
오품관행 五品觀行 467
오품제자위 五品弟子位 467
오하분결 五下分結 433
오학처 五學處 433
오해 五海 370, 433
오해탈륜 五解脫輪 415, 433
오행 五行 413, 433, 573
오향 五香 434
오현 五顯 433
오호금강(저) 五胡金剛(杵) 411
오혹 五惑 414, 434
오혼 五渾 432
오회 五悔 434, 645
오회법사 五會法師 434
오회법사찬 五會法師讚 434
오회염불 五會念佛 434
오훈 五葷 422, 434
옥 屋 434
옥 沃 434
옥 獄 434
옥 玉 434
옥녀 玉女 196
옥리인 屋裏人 434
옥불 玉佛 434
옥야 玉耶 434
옥야(녀)경 玉耶(女)經 434
옥유 玉柔 434
옥천 玉泉 434
옥천옥화양종 玉泉玉花兩宗 434
옥초산 沃焦山 434
옥초석 沃焦石 434
옥초해 沃焦海 434
옥호 玉毫 434
옥호 玉豪 434
옥화 玉花 434
옥화궁 玉花宮 434
옥화궁 玉華宮 630
옥환 玉環 434
온 溫 435
온 蘊 434
온다라 溫陀羅 435
온락 蘊落 435
온마 蘊魔 435
온숙 溫宿 435
온식 蘊識 435
온실 溫室 435
온처계 蘊處界 435
온타남 蘊馱南 435
올 嗢 435
올구타 嗢俱吒 435
올굴죽가 嗢屈竹迦 435
올다연나벌차 嗢陀演那伐蹉 444
올달라 嗢呾羅 297
올달라 嗢咀羅 or 嗢怛羅 435
올달라구로 嗢呾羅矩嚕 435
올달라서나 嗢呾羅犀那 435
올달라알사다 嗢呾羅頞沙茶 435
올로가 嗢露迦 443
올발(라) 嗢鉢(羅) 435
올발라 嗢鉢羅 441, 554
올슬니사 嗢瑟尼沙 435
올슬니사 嗢瑟膩沙 421
올시라 嗢尸羅 435
올층가 嗢蹭伽 435
옹 擁 435
옹 甕 435
옹 癰 435
옹창 癰瘡 435
옹형 甕形 435
옹호 擁護 435
와 卧 435
와 瓦 435
와 臥 435
와구 臥具 435
와기금기 瓦器金器 435
와발 瓦鉢 435
와불사 臥佛寺 435
와사 瓦師 435
완 剜 435
완 頑 435
완공 頑空 594

완등 剜燈 435
완석점두 頑石點頭 435
왈가타 曰迦他 235
왕 往 436
왕 枉 435
왕 王 435
왕갈라사벌탄나 王曷邏闍伐彈那 435
왕고 王古 435
왕법 王法 436, 488
왕법경 王法經 436
왕사 枉死 435
왕사 王師 436
왕사(성) 王舍(城) 436
왕사성 王舍城 70, 620
왕삼매 王三昧 435
왕상회향 往相回向 436
왕생 往生 436
왕선 王仙 435
왕선 王膳 436
왕일 王日 435
왕일휴 王日休 435
왕자가라대흑 王子迦羅大黑 106
왕종 王種 564
왕증 王增 435
외 外 395, 436
외걸 外乞 76, 225, 436
외계 外界 76
외교 外教 76, 436
외금강부 外金剛部 436
외금강부원 外金剛部院 436
외도 外道 34, 436, 463
四執 259
외도론 外道論 461
외도육사 外道六師 135, 436
외무위 外無爲 436
외범 外凡 76, 467, 481
외법 外法 436
외상 外相 436
외속 外俗 77
외아 外我 76, 436
외연사 外緣死 490
외외도 外外道 436
외용 外用 436
외자 外子 220, 278
외전 外典 77, 436
외진 外塵 436
외집 外執 436
외타라 畏陀羅 542
외탐욕 外貪欲 436
외학 外學 436
외해 外海 436
외호 外護 436
요 了 436
요 妖 437
요 曜 437
요 澆 437
요 瑤 437
요 繞 437
요 腰 437
요 要 437
요 遶 437
요 鐃 436
요 饒 437
요간 料簡 123
요계 澆季 437
요교 了教 437
요달 了達 437
요달 尿闥 78
요도 要道 437
요령 鐃鈴 or 搖鈴 437
요로 要路 437
요료견 了了見 437
요묘 要妙 437
요문 要文 437
요문 要門 437
요백 腰白 437
요별 了別 344
요별심 了別心 351
요병 療病 123
요본제 了本際 437
요불 繞佛 437
요불 遶佛 437
요상귀자 尿牀鬼子 78
요설 樂說
四無礙智 245
요설 饒舌 437
요설 樂說 386
요설변재 樂說辯才 386
요숙 曜宿 437
요약 要略 393
요언 要言 437
요오 了悟 437
요왕(불) 饒王(佛) 437
요우나 搖尤那 407
요원 寮元 123
요의 了義 437
요의 腰衣 437
요의경 了義經 437
요의교 了義教 437, 478
요익 饒益 437
요인 了因 437, 488
요인불성 了因佛性 437, 438
요장 寮長 123
요주 寮主 123
요지 了知 438
요지 要旨 437
요진 姚秦 241
요진 要津 437
요철선정 了徹禪定 438
요탑 遶塔 437
요통 妖通 429, 437
요행 要行 437
요화궁 瑤花宮 437
욕 慾 438
욕 欲 104, 266, 271, 285, 419, 438, 582
四流 243
욕 浴 438
욕각 欲覺 438
욕계 欲界 55, 114, 266, 438, 454, 484, 485, 586
욕계오취지 欲界五趣地 55
욕계지인천 欲界之人天 53
욕고 欲苦 438
욕고 浴鼓 438
욕구 欲鉤 438
욕금강 欲金剛 439
욕기 欲氣 438
욕념 欲念 254
욕니 欲泥 438
욕두 浴頭 438
욕락 欲樂 438
욕루 欲漏 438
욕류 欲流 438
욕마 欲魔 438
욕불 浴佛 37, 438
욕불식 浴佛式 438
욕사행 欲邪行 438
욕상 浴像 438
욕색 欲色 438
욕성 欲性 439
욕신족 欲神足 254
욕실 浴室 438
욕심 欲心 439
욕애 慾愛 438
욕애 欲愛 189, 439, 486, 585

욕애주지 欲愛住地 258, 439
욕염 欲染 439
욕유 欲有 123, 439
욕유견무명 欲有見無明 439
욕자 欲刺 439
욕전 欲箭 439
욕주 浴主 438
욕진 欲塵 439
욕천 欲天 439
욕천오음 欲天五婬 439
욕탐 欲貪 439
욕하 欲河 439
욕해 欲海 439
욕화 欲火 439
용 勇 439
용 容 439
용 涌 439
용 用 88, 269, 439, 505
용 龍 71, 439, 568
용 龍 606
四不可思議 248
용감 龍龕 439
용군 龍軍 439
용궁 龍宮 440, 567
용녀 龍女 440
용녀 龍女 251
용뇌향 龍腦香 19
용대 用大 269, 439
용맹 龍猛 71, 440
용맹 龍猛 609
용맹정진 勇猛精進 439, 440
용멸 用滅 439
용미니 龍彌你 440
용발 龍鉢 440
용방 龍方 440
용분신삼매 龍奮迅三昧 440
용상 龍象 440
용서 龍舒 435
용수 榕樹 80
용수 龍樹 71, 440
용수 龍樹 97, 486, 587
天台九祖 572
용수사교 龍樹四教 239
용시보살 勇施菩薩 439
용신 龍神 440
용신팔부 龍神八部 606
용왕 龍王 440
용유석 容有釋 439
용유설 容有說 439
용장 龍章 440
용장 龍藏 440
용종(상)존(왕불) 龍種(上)尊(王佛) 440
용종상불 龍種上佛 157
용주 龍珠 440
용주사 龍珠寺 440
용지 龍智 609
용진 龍辰 365
용천 涌泉 439
용천 龍天 440
용천팔부 龍天八部 440
용출 涌出 439
용탕 龍湯 440
용하 龍河 440
용호 龍戶 440
용화수 龍華樹 440
용화회 龍華會 440
용흥 龍興 440
우 于 442
우 偶 441
우 優 80, 293, 441, 492
우 友 268
우 右 441
우 吽 493
우 寓 441
우 愚 441
우 憂 441
우 漚 441
우 牛 364, 441, 485
우 禺 441
우 藕 441
우 鄔 441
우 雨 289, 441
우각 牛角 442
우각사라림 牛角娑羅林 442
우각산 牛角山 442
우각일촉 牛角一觸 442
우거 牛車 442
우걸 雨乞 441
우계 牛戒 442
우구 牛狗 469
우구외도 牛狗外道 442
우근 憂根 485
우기 雨期 441
우다가 優陀伽 446
우다가 憂陀伽 441
우다나 優陀那 364, 442
우다나 憂陀那 441
우다라 優多羅 442
우다라승 漚多羅僧 441
우다연 優陀延 442, 444
우다연 鄔陀延 441, 442
우다연나 烏陀衍那 441
우다연나 鄔陀衍那 444
우다이 優陀夷 442
出現 580
우단나 優檀那 442
우단전단 牛檀栴檀 442
우담(발) 優曇(鉢) 442
우담바라 優曇婆羅 442
우담발라 鄔曇跋羅 442
우두 牛頭 442
우두대왕 牛頭大王 442
우두산 牛頭山 442
우두산법 牛頭山法 442
우두선 牛頭禪 442
우두전단 牛頭旃檀 522
우두전단 牛頭栴檀 442
우두종 牛頭宗 442
우두향 牛頭香 442
우둔 于遁 442
우둔 愚鈍 441
우란 盂蘭 266, 442
우란(분) 盂蘭(盆) 442
우란(분)경 盂蘭(盆)經 443
우란(분)재 盂蘭(盆)齋 443
우란(분)회 盂蘭(盆)會 443
우란승회 盂蘭勝會 213
우람락 吽噉嚂 270
우람바(나) 烏藍婆(拏) 442
우려이유 牛驢二乳 443
우루(가) 優樓(迦) 443
우루거 優婁佉 443
우루거 優樓佉 280
우루비려 優樓毘蠡 443
우루빈라 優樓頻螺 144, 443
우루빈라가섭 優樓頻螺迦葉 443
우루빈려 優樓頻蠡 443
우류가 憂流迦 443, 567
우류만타 優流漫陀 443
우마타 優摩陀 415
우모진 牛毛塵 443
우민 憂悶 161
우바교사라 優波憍舍羅 444
우바국다 優婆鞠多 444
우바국다 優婆鞠多 444
우바국다 優波鞠多 444

우바국다 鄔波鞠多 444
우바굴다 優婆掘多 444
우바굴다 鄔波屈多 444
우바급다 優波笈多 444
우바급다 鄔波級多 444
우바난다 優波難陀 444
우바다 優波陀 444
우바다야 優婆馱耶 444
우바라차 優婆羅叉 444
우바라참 優波羅懺 444
우바리 優婆利 444
우바리 優婆離 27, 444
우바리 優波利 444
우바리 優波離 444
우바리 鄔波離 444
우바바사 優波婆娑 444
우바사 優婆斯 444
우바사가 優婆娑柯 444
우바사가 優婆私柯 444
우바사가 優波娑迦 433, 444
우바사가 優波賜迦 444
우바사가 鄔婆斯迦 444
우바사가 鄔波斯迦 444
우바삭가 鄔波索迦 444
우바새 優婆塞 433, 444
우바새 優婆塞 268, 588
우바색(가) 鄔波塞(加) 444
우바소가 鄔波素迦 444
우바실사 優婆室沙 444
우바이 優婆夷 268, 444, 588
우바이 優波夷 444
우바이(사가) 優波夷(賜迦) 433
우바제사 優婆提舍 364, 444
우바제사 優婆題舍 444
우바제사 優波提舍 433, 444
우바제사 憂婆提舍 441
우바제삭 鄔波弟鑠 444
우바제삭 鄔波提鑠 433
우바제삭 鄔波題鑠 444
우바지사 優婆至沙 444
우바체(사) 優波替(舍) 444
우바체사 優波替舍 444
우발라 優鉢剌 443
우발라 優鉢羅 441, 443, 444, 554, 610
우발라 漚鉢羅 441
우발라 鄔鉢羅 443
우법 愚法 441
우보타파 優補陀婆 615
우부 愚夫 441
우부니 遇嚩柅 445
우부종성 愚夫種性 490
우분 牛糞 443
우분종 牛糞種 443
우사 牛司 444
우사 藕絲 441
우사나 于闍那 442
우사라 于闍羅 8, 442
우상 441
우상 牛相 444
우선 右旋 441
우선나 優禪那 426
우선니 優禪尼 443, 452
우세 憂世 441
우수 右手 441
우수 憂受 441
우슬초 牛膝草 386
우승 愚僧 441
우시 雨時 441
우안거 雨安居 441
우양(심)안 牛羊(心)眼 443
우왕 牛王 441, 444
the teaching of a Buddha 444
우왕(존자) 牛王(尊者) 444
우왕가지 牛王加持 445
우왕존자 牛王尊者 444
우요 右繞 287, 441
우육 牛肉 434
우이생 愚異生 179
우자연나 鄔闍衍那 441
우적 牛跡 444
우적비구 牛跡比丘 444
우전 于塡 442
우전 于殿 442
우전 于闐 442, 444
우전 優塡 211, 444, 523
우전 寓錢 441
우종 寓宗 441
우주 牛主 2
우중 禺中 441
우중 雨衆 442
우차나마라 于遮那摩羅 442
우축 牛丑 365
우치 愚痴 441
우파 優婆 444
우파 優波 444
우파가루다 憂波迦嘍嗏 67
우파계설니 優婆計設尼 419
우파계설니 優波髻設尼 158
우파계설니 鄔波計設尼 419
우파계설니 鄔波髻設尼 158
우파국다 優婆鞠多 486
우파나하 優波那訶 444
우파니사담 優婆尼沙曇 444
우파니사타 優婆尼沙陀 444
우파니사타 優波尼沙陀 444
우파니사토 優波尼沙土 444
우파니살담 鄔波尼殺曇 441
우파니살담분 優波尼薩曇分 81
우파야바라밀 漚婆耶婆羅蜜 441
우피 牛皮 444
우필사 優畢捨 445
우필차 優畢叉 445
우필차 憂畢叉 441
우혹 愚惑 441
우화 憂火 441
우화 漚和 174
우화 牛貨
四洲 258
우화 雨花 442
우화 雨華 442
우화구사라 漚和俱舍羅 or 傴和拘舍羅 441
우화주 牛貨洲 445
우황가지 牛黃加持 445
욱 郁 445
욱가 郁伽 445
욱가 郁迦 445
욱가지라 郁伽支羅 445
욱다(라승가) 郁多(羅僧伽) 445
욱다라구루 郁多羅拘樓 445
운 云 445
운 殞 445
운 運 445
운 雲 445
운고 雲鼓 445
운공 雲公 632
운납 雲納 445
운납 雲衲 445
운당 雲堂 445
운뢰음숙왕화지 雲雷音宿王華智 445
운뢰음왕 雲雷音王 445
운문 雲門 267, 445, 598
운문(선)종 雲門(禪)宗 445
운문종 雲門宗 310, 410

운수 雲水 445
운심 運心 445
운심 雲心 445
운운 云云 445
운자재등왕 雲自在燈王 567
운자재왕 雲自在王 445
운종 雲宗 445
운중수중 雲衆水衆 445
운지 運攎 57
운집 雲集 445
운판 雲板 445
운하 云何 445
운하패 云何唄 445
운해 雲海 445
운형수제 雲兄水弟 445
운화 雲華 554
운화 지엄 雲華智儼 427
운화 지엄 雲華智嚴 639
울 鬱 208, 338, 445, 587
울금 鬱金 82, 446
울다나 鬱陀那 446
울다라 鬱多羅 445
울다라가신 鬱多羅迦神 93
울다라구루 鬱多羅拘樓 445
울다라구루 鬱多羅鳩婁 445
울다라구류 鬱多羅究留 445
울다라마자 鬱陀羅摩子 446
울다라승 鬱多羅僧 287
울다라승(가) 鬱多羅僧(伽) 445
울다라승의 鬱多羅僧衣 472
울다마 鬱多摩 445
울다세라부 鬱多世羅部 208
울단월 鬱單越 445
울달라 鬱怛羅 445
울달라구류 鬱怛羅拘瑠 445
울달라월 鬱怛羅越 445
울두 鬱頭 446
울두람(불) 鬱頭藍(佛) 446
울두람자 鬱頭藍子 446
울력 446
울발라 鬱鉢羅 446, 554
울비라 鬱鞞羅 446
울슬니사 鬱瑟尼沙 446, 459
울슬니사 鬱瑟膩沙 421
울실니사 鬱失尼沙 446
울지 鬱持 446
울지가 鬱持迦 446
울타 鬱陀 446
웅 熊 446
웅이산 熊耳山 446
원 元 446
원 原 447
원 園 447
원 圓 267, 268, 447, 448, 477, 478, 544, 638
원 寃 447
원 怨 447
원 源 447
원 苑 446
원 遠 446
원 院 447
원 願 81, 359, 362, 447, 461
원 鴛 446
원가 怨家 447
원각 圓覺 447, 617
원각경 圓覺經 420, 447
원결 怨結 447
원계 圓戒 447
원공 圓空 447
원공 源空 587
원공사교 苑公四教 239, 446
원과 圓果 447
원관 園觀 447
원광 圓光 319, 447
원교 圓交 150
원교 圓教 23, 58, 146, 183, 194, 219, 225, 231, 239, 245, 280, 289, 318, 370, 412, 416, 448, 449, 460, 467, 478, 485, 499, 560, 602, 608
원교사문 圓教四門 448
원교지이보살 圓教之二菩薩 584
원구 圓具 448
원극 圓極 448
원기 圓機 448
원길수 元吉樹 446
원내도행잡작의 院內道行雜作衣 427
원단 圓壇 448
원단 圓斷 448
원도 圓道 448
원도 願度 447
원돈 圓頓 291, 448
원돈(지)관 圓頓(止)觀 448
원돈계 圓頓戒 98, 447, 448, 505
원돈교 圓頓教 448
원돈무작대계 圓頓無作大戒 448
원돈보살대계 圓頓菩薩大戒 448
원돈일승 圓頓一乘 448
원돈종 圓頓宗 448
원두 園頭 447
원력 願力 361, 447
원령 怨靈 447
원륜 願輪 447
원리 遠離 376, 446
원리락 遠離樂 447
원리처 遠離處 237
원만 圓滿 448
원만경 圓滿經 448
원명 元明 201, 446
원묘 元妙 446
원묘 圓妙 448
원밀 圓密 448
원바라밀 願波羅蜜 447
원반 鴛班 446
원불 圓佛 211, 448
원불 願佛 447
원사 遠師 446
원사함독유역가촉 蚖蛇含毒猶亦可觸 400
원상 圓常 422
원상 怨想 279
원선 願船 447
원성 圓成 449, 612
원성실성 圓成實性 449, 560
원수 圓修 449
원승 圓乘 449
원시 元始 446
원시무명 元始無明 61
원식 願食 447
원신 圓信 449
원신 源信 587
원신 願身 214, 447
원신성 元神星 446
원실 圓實 449
원심 元心 446
원심 圓心 449
원심 願心 360, 447
원오 圓悟 449
원위 圓位 449
원융 圓融 449
원융삼관 圓融三觀 505
원융삼제 圓融三諦 449
원응 圓凝 449
원인 元因 446
원인 原因 446
원인 遠因 425, 488

원인론 原人論 373, 447
원작 願作 447
원장 元藏 446
원장목록 元藏目錄 446
원저 源底 447
원적 圓寂 449
원적 怨敵 447
원적 怨賊 447
원전 圓詮 449
원조 元照 121, 446, 549
원조 元祖 446
원종 圓宗 449
원종문류 圓宗文類 449
원주 院主 447, 449
원주 願主 447
원주실 院主室 449
원증회고 怨憎會苦 447
원지 願智 447
원지구만족 願志求滿足 81
원진리구 遠塵離垢 446
원진성 元辰星 446
원측 圓測 305, 449
원친 寃親 447
원친 怨親 447
원친평등심 寃親平等心 447
원토 願土 447
원통 圓通 449
원통대사 圓通大士 449
원통삼매 圓通三昧 449
원품무명 元品無明 152, 446
원한 怨恨 620
원합 圓合 450
원해 圓海 450
원해 願海 447
원행 圓行 450
원행 願行 447
원행지 遠行地 369, 446
원효 元曉 446, 450, 646
曉公四敎 64, 239
월 月 53, 450, 572
월 越 450
월개 月蓋 450
월광 月光 363, 450, 493
월광(보살) 月光(菩薩) 498
월광동자 月光童子 450
월광동자경 月光童子經 450
월광변조 月光邊照 394
월광보살 月光菩薩 450, 451
월광보살경 月光菩薩經 450
월광아 月光兒 450
월광왕 月光王 450, 485
월광태자 月光太子 450
월궁 月宮 450
월궁천자 月宮天子 485
월기 月忌 450
월단 月壇 450
월등삼매 月燈三昧 450
월륜 月輪 451
월륜관 月輪觀 451
월륜삼매 月輪三昧 273, 451
월마니 月摩尼 143
월면불 月面佛 451
월명동남 月明童男 451
월명동자 月明童子 451
월명보살 月明菩薩 451
월명보살경 月明菩薩經 451
월미 月眉 451
월분 月分 451, 522
월사 越闍 450
월상녀경 月上女經 451
월서 月鼠 451
월씨(국) 月氏(國) 451
월애삼매 月愛三昧 451
월애주 月愛珠 451
월연 月輦 451
월염존 月黶尊 451
월왕 月王 451
월요 月曜 451
월정(마니) 月精(摩尼) 451
월정사 月精寺 451
월정수 月精手 451
월종 月種 451
월죄 越罪 450
월주 月胄 451
월지 月支 3, 107, 108
월지(국) 月支(國) 451
월천 月天 452, 492
월천비 月天妃 452
월천자 月天子 267, 450, 451, 452
월토 月兎 452
월파수나 月婆首那 452
월희삼매 越喜三昧 450
위 位 222, 223, 362, 452, 481, 605, 608
위 僞 452
위 危 452, 485
위 圍 453
위 委 453
위 威 452
위 潙 452
위 爲 453
위 胃 486
seven northern constellations 208
위 衛 452
위 違 453
위 韋 452
위(천)장군 韋(天)將軍 452
위경 違境 453
위기 爲己 453
위노 威怒 453
위노왕 威怒王 453
위뉴 違紐 452
위뉴 韋紐 159
위뉴천 韋紐天 452
위다라 韋陀羅 285
위덕 威德 453
위력 威力 452
위리 爲利 453
위리 違理 311
위묘 位妙 358
위물신 爲物身 484
위불퇴 位不退 452
위산 潙山 452
위선 爲善 453
위성 危城 452
위세사 衛世師 452
위수뉴 韋廋紐 452
위수뉴 韋搜紐 452
위순 委順 453
위순 違順 453
위신 威神 453
위신력 威神力 452
위앙 潙仰 452
위앙종 潙仰宗 310, 410
위연 違緣 453
위요 圍繞 453
위유 韋糅 452
위음왕 威音王 453
위의 威儀 452
위의(법)사 威儀(法)師 453
위의승 威儀僧 453
위자순타 違自順他 453
위제(희) 韋提(希) 452
위타 圍陀 231, 452
위타 違陀 453
위타 韋陀 231, 452

위타(천) 韋馱(天) 452
위타라 韋陀羅 452
위타수 韋陀輸 or 韋馱輸 452
위타순자 違他順自 453
위타천 韋陀天 or 韋馱天 453
위타천신 韋馱天神 485
위패 位牌 452
유 乳 455
유 儒 267, 453
유 唯 454
유 喩 119, 126, 284, 292, 455
유 幼 643
유 幽 455
유 惟 456
유 揄 455
유 有 80, 220, 271, 279, 282, 365, 433, 454, 484, 486, 544, 546, 586
 四流 243
유 柔 455
유 柳 453
유 油 455
유 流 362
유 游 453
유 濡 455
유 猶 453
유 瑜 90, 455
유 由 454
유 維 453, 605
유 踰 456
유 逾 456
유 遊 454
유 遺 455
유 柳 486
유가 瑜伽 34, 82, 99, 455
유가 遊迦 455
유가기 瑜伽祇 455
유가론 瑜伽論 187, 370, 420
유가사 瑜伽師 455
유가사지론 瑜伽師地論 82, 90, 382, 417, 455
유가사지론기 瑜伽師地論記 110
유가사지론석 瑜伽師地論釋 455
유가삼밀 瑜伽三密 455
유가아사리 瑜伽阿闍梨 455
유가종 瑜伽宗 455
유각경사 有脚經笥 24
유간 有間 456
유간파라 惟干頗羅 456
유건 由乾 454
유건다라 由乾陀羅 or 由乾陁羅 454
유건다라 遊乾陀羅 51
유건달라 踰健達羅 454, 456
유건달라 逾健達羅 456
유건타라 瑜乾馱羅 455
유건타라 踰乾陀羅 456
유견 有見 19, 456, 477, 601
유결 有結 456
유경 乳經 455
유경무식 唯境無識 454
유계 有界 456
유공 有空 456
유공불이 有空不二 456
유공중 有空中 456, 457
유공중삼시 有空中三時 456
유관 有觀 267
유관행지력 由觀行之力 202
유광수 有光壽 321
유괴 有愧 556
유교 有教 456
유교 遺教 455
유구식 維口食 453
유구진여 有垢眞如 487
유규 劉虬 or 劉虯 422
유근신 有根身 456
유기 瑜岐 455
유기 瑜祁 455
유기경 瑜祇經 363
유나 留拏 124
유나 維那 10, 265, 453, 541
유나 留拏 428
유난 留難 124
유대 有對 456
유대 有待 456
유덕녀 有德女 456
유덕녀소문대승경 有德女所問大乘經 456
유도 幽途 455
유동 儒童 527
유동보살 儒童菩薩 453
유람 游藍 453
유래 流來 124
유래생사 流來生死 124
유량 有量 456
유력 有力 479
유령 幽靈 455
유령 有靈 456
유루 有漏 279, 456, 479
유루도 有漏道 457, 479
유루려왕 維樓黎王 228
유루로 有漏路 457
유루삼계 有漏三界 457
유루선법 有漏善法 457
유루세계 有漏世界 457
유루악법 有漏惡法 457
유루정토 有漏淨土 457
유류 有流 457
유륜 有輪 457
유리 琉璃 584
유리사부 遊梨沙部 509
유리왕 流離王 228
유마 維摩 26, 66, 305, 453
 方丈 173
유마(라)힐 維摩(羅)詰 453
유마거사 維摩居士 147
유마경 維摩經 212, 422, 626
 方便 174
유마경보살품 維摩經菩薩品 265
유마사익 維摩思益 395
유마힐 維磨詰 228
유마힐경 維摩詰經 147, 453, 473
유마힐소설경 維摩詰所說經 453
유명 唯名 454
유명 幽冥 455
유목 乳木 455
유무사견 有無邪見 457
유무이견 有無二見 457
유무이변 有無二邊 457
유문 有門 324
유미 乳味 415, 455
유미정 猶未定 453
유발 油鉢 455
유방 遊方 454
유법 有法 457, 539
유법 遺法 455
유법공 有法空 582
유변 有邊 457, 481
유부 有部 457
유부니다나 有部尼陀那 457
유부목득가 有部目得迦 457
유부율 有部律 457
유분별 有分別 457
유분별지 有分別智 491
유분식 有分識 457
유불 濡佛 455
유사 有事 457

유사 流沙 124
유사 踰闍 456
유사(나) 踰闍(那) 456
유사나 流舍那 124
유사나 踰闍那 454
유산 遊山 454
유상 有想 457
유상 有相 422, 457
유상교 有相教 457
유상사 有上士 457
유상업 有相業 457
유상유량 有相有量 456
유상종 有相宗 457
유색 唯色 454
유색유형 有色有形 353
유선나 踰繕那 454, 456
유선다 有善多 457
유성 有性 457
유소연 有所緣 457
유수 有手 458
유수 流水 124, 333
유수 濡首 157, 455
유수안 乳水眼 455
유순 兪旬 454
유순 揄旬 454, 455
유순 由旬 13, 454
유순인 柔順忍 455
유시 逾時 456
유식 唯識 230, 290, 315, 320, 333, 337, 344, 416, 425, 454, 514, 544, 558, 607
유식 唯識 School 176
유식 有識 458
유식가 唯識家 454
유식관 唯識觀 267, 454
유식론 唯識論 187, 230, 231, 274, 280, 316, 340, 367, 370, 388, 421, 454, 461, 524, 560, 588, 589
Vasubandhu 572
四身 252
유식론 唯識論 2 495
유식론 唯識論 4 135
유식론 有識論 476
유식무경 唯識無境 454
유식삼성관 唯識三性觀 454
유식삼십론 唯識三十論 454
유식석론 唯識釋論 628
유식수도오위 唯識修道五位 454
유식심정 唯識心定 454
유식원 唯識圓 267
유식원교 唯識圓教 454
유식이십론 唯識二十論 98, 454, 485
유식종 唯識宗 1, 454, 456, 608
유식중도 唯識中道 454, 544
유식진여 唯識眞如 588
유심 唯心 454
유심게 唯心偈 454
유심법계 遊心法界 454
유아 瑜誐 455
유애 有愛 585
유애주지 有愛住地 258
유야(리) 維夜(離) 229
유야리 維耶離 453
유야무야 有耶無耶 458
유약 猶若 453
유어 喩語 588
유여 有餘 458
유여사 有餘師 458
유여사설 有餘師說 458
유여설 有餘說 458
유여수기 有餘授記 490
유여열반 有餘涅槃 458, 490
유여의 有餘依 490
유여의(열반) 有餘依(涅槃) 458
유여토 有餘土 458
유연 有緣 458
유연 柔軟 326
유연 柔輭 455
유연 由延 454
유연나 踰延那 454
유연성 柔軟聲 464
유연어 柔輭語 455
유월 維越 453
유월 逾越 456
유위 有爲 316, 453, 458
유위 維衛 228
유위(불) 維衛(佛) 453
유위공 有爲空 458
유위과 有爲果 458
유위무상 有爲無常 458
유위무위 有爲無爲 453
유위법 有爲法 296, 457
유위법계 有爲法界 427
유위생사 有爲生死 458
유위전변 有爲轉變 458
유위해탈 有爲解脫 492
유의 喩依 455
유의 幽儀 455
유의 有意 458, 459
유인 有人 458
유인무과 有因無果 260
유일진실 惟一眞實 507
유자파라 惟子頗羅 456
유작 有作 458
유장 流漿 124
유재석 有財釋 462
유적 遺跡 455
유전 流轉 124
유전문 流轉門 124
유전진여 流轉眞如 124, 588
유정 有情 195, 264, 302, 319, 435, 456, 458, 460, 526, 543
유정(천) 有頂(天) 458
유정거 有情居 458
유정근본지심식 有情根本之心識 376
유정세간 有情世間 483
유정수 有情數 458
유정연자 有情緣慈 458
유정천 有頂天 231
유정혹 有頂惑 458
유제 遺弟 455
유제사 有諸師 458
유종 有宗 367
유주 流注 124
유주물 有主物 459
유주생 流注生 291
유주재지용 有主宰之用 153
유증지옥 遊增地獄 454
유지 有支 459
유지 柳枝 453
유지 流支 124
유지 類智 124, 370
유지 類智 226
유지경 瑜祇經 418
유지혜 有智慧 459
유집수 有執受 459
유체 喩體 455
유체 有體 459
유체시설가 有體施設假 476
유탐 有貪 459
유택성 流澤聲 464
유통 流通 124
유통분 流通分 278, 501
유파제야야 有波弟耶夜 433

유파제야야 有波第耶夜 459
유표색 有表色 459
유표업 有表業 459
유학 有學 371, 459
유해 有海 459
유해 有解 459
유행 遊行 454
유행반 有行般 428
유행처 遊行處 232
유향 乳香 455
유허공천 遊虛空天 414, 454
유형 遺形 455
유화 柔和 455
유화 遊化 454
유화 遺化 455
유황 磂黃 420
유훈 遺訓 455
유희 遊戲 454
유희신통 遊戲神通 454
육 肉 459
육 育 459
육 六 459
육(신)통 六(神)通 336
육검 六劍 459
육결 六結 459, 469
육결정 六決定 459
육경 六境 287, 371, 583
육경 六境 459, 460, 465, 467, 468
육계 肉髻 421, 459
육계 六界 460, 461
육계취 六界聚 460
육고행 六苦行 460
육고행외도 六苦行外道 460
육공구 六供具 460
육관 六觀 466
육관(법) 六觀(法) 460
육관법 六觀法 38
육관음 六觀音 460, 461
육구(법) 六垢(法) 460
육군비구 六羣比丘 467
육군비구 六群比丘 460
육근 六根 287, 371, 583
육근 六根 312, 460, 463, 465, 467, 468, 476, 484, 485, 544
육근(청)정 六根(清)淨 460
육근공덕 六根功德 460
육근오용 六根五用 460
육근참회 六根懺悔 460
육근청정위 六根淸淨位 460, 467
육긍일 陸亘日 577
육나한 六羅漢 460
육난 六難 460
육년고행 六年苦行 460
육념 六念 462
육념(법) 六念(法) 460
육념처 六念處 460
육다바제 育多婆提 459
육단심 肉團心 351, 459
육대 六大 88, 430, 460
육대관 六大觀 461
육대무애 六大無礙 461
육대번뇌 六大煩惱 461, 462
육대법성 六大法性 461
육대신 六大神 461
육대적 六大賊 461
육대체대 六大體大 461
육덕 六德 461
육도 六度 282
육도 六道 619
육도 六度 83, 292, 421, 461, 466, 467, 489, 494
육행 六行 469
육도 六道 302, 461, 467, 468, 579
天道 568
육도가타경 六道伽陀經 461
육도과보 六度果報 461
육도능화보살 六道能化菩薩 461
육도무극 六度無極 461
육도불보살 六道佛菩薩 461
육도사생 六道四生 461
육도사성 六道四聖 461
육도집경 六道集經 461
육도피안 六到彼岸 461
육등 肉燈 459
육력 六力 120
육론 六論 461
육륜 六輪 461
육리합석 六離合釋 271
육리합석 六離合釋 462, 466, 468
육만장 六萬藏 462
육망 六妄 462
육면존 六面尊 462
육묘 六妙 528
육묘문 六妙門 38, 248
육묘행 六妙行 462, 469
육무상육비 六無常六譬 462
육물 六物 462
육미 六味 462
육반신족 六般神足 462
육방 六方 462
육방례 六方禮 462
육방증명 六方證明 462
육방증성 六方證誠 462
육방호념 六方護念 462
육번뇌 六煩惱 462
육번뇌장 肉煩惱障 288
육범 六凡 462
육법 六法 462
육법(계) 六法(戒) 462
육부대승경 六部大乘經 462
육비 六譬 463
육사 六師 463
육사가왕 六師迦王 463
육사성취 六事成就 463
육사자 六使者 555
육상 六相 193, 463
육색 肉色 459
육서 六瑞 462, 463
육성 六性 145
육성부 六城部 463
육성취 六成就 341, 463
육쇠 六衰 463
육수 六銖 284
육수 六受 463, 465
육수면 六隨眠 47
육술 六術 463, 466
육시 六時 463
육시부단 六時不斷 463
육시삼매 六時三昧 463
육시예찬 六時禮讚 463
육시왕생종 六時往生宗 341
육시참 六時懺 463
육식 六識 287, 371, 583, 605
육식 肉食 459
육식 六識 80, 252, 312, 344, 467, 484
육신 肉身 459
육신보살 肉身菩薩 459
육신통 六神通 188, 463
他心通 592
육심 肉心 459
육십 六十 463
육십권 六十卷 464
육십사범음 六十四梵音 464
육십사서 六十四書 464
육십사안 六十四眼 464
육십심 六十心 464

육십이견 六十二見 463
육십화엄경 六十華嚴經 289
육아야달나 六阿耶怛那 or 六阿也怛那 465
육안 肉眼 362, 459
육업 六業 396
육여 六如 464
육염심 六染心 205, 464
육욕 六慾 631
육욕 六欲 464
육욕(천) 六欲(天) 464
육욕사선 六欲四禪 464
육욕오진 六欲五塵 439
육욕천 六欲天 468, 569
육욕천음상 六欲天婬相 464
육위 六位 460, 461, 464, 465, 466, 469
육유 六喩 462, 464
육의 六依 464, 465
육이 六夷 464
육인 六因 465, 466
육입 六入 365
육입 六入 2, 80, 345, 460, 465, 467, 468, 511
육자 六字 465
육자공 六字供 465
육자명호 六字名號 465
육자문수 六字文殊 465
육자법 六字法 465
육자재왕 六自在王 465
육자하림법 六字河臨法 465
육자호마 六字護摩 465
육작 六作 463, 465
육재 六裁 465, 468
육재 六齋 277
육재일 六齋日 465
육저 育抵 459
육적 六賊 461, 463, 465
육전 六箭 459, 465
육정 六情 464, 465
육제 六諦 452, 466
육조 六祖 466
육족아비담마 六足阿毗曇摩 466
육족존 六足尊 413, 462, 466
육족존금강 六足尊金剛 413
육종 六宗 466
육종결정 六種決定 459, 466
육종고행외도 六種苦行外道 466
육종교방편 六種巧方便 466
육종구생혹 六種俱生惑 466
육종동상 六種動相 467
육종삼보 六種三寶 276
육종석 六種釋 462, 466
육종성 六種性 460, 466
육종외도 六種外道 463, 466
육종인 六種印 466
육종인 六種因 466
육종정행 六種正行 466
육종주 六種住 466
육종진 六種震 467
육종진동 六種震動 467
육죄인 六罪人 467
육주 六住 467
육주 六舟 467
육중 六衆 460, 467
육중생 六衆生 463, 467, 468
육즉 六卽 39, 46, 76, 210, 460, 467, 608
육즉불 六卽佛 467
육지 育坻 459
육지 六地 425
육지장 六地藏 461, 467, 555
육지화 育坻華 459
육진 六塵 183, 191, 301, 302, 459, 460, 463, 465, 467, 468, 484
육진 六震 467
육진설법 六塵說法 467
육착(심) 六著(心) or 六着(心) 468
육창일원 六窗一猿 468
육처 六處 411, 460, 465, 467, 468, 474, 475
육천 六天 464, 468
天女 568
육촉 六觸 465, 468
육추 六麤 26, 280, 281, 468, 562
육축 六畜 468
육취 六趣 304, 461, 468, 579
四諦 257
육취윤회경 六趣輪廻經 468
육친 六親 468
육통 六通 150, 463, 468, 570
天眼 569
육파 六波 468
육팔초세본원 六八超世本願 468
육팔홍서 六八弘誓 468
육폐 六蔽 468
육합석 六合釋 462, 468
육해일망 六解一亡 468
육행 六行 460, 463, 466, 469
육행관 六行觀 462, 469
육향 肉香 459
육현관 六現觀 349
육혜 六慧 469
육화(경) 六和(敬) 469
육화합 六和合 469
윤 允 469
윤 潤 469
윤 輪 207
윤(다리)화 輪(多梨)華 124
윤감 允堪 469
윤망 輪輞 124
윤문 允炆 471
윤번 輪番 124
윤보 輪寶 124
윤복 輪輻 124
윤상 輪相 124, 298
윤생 潤生 469
윤야 允若 469
윤업 潤業 469
윤연 輪緣 124
윤왕 輪王 124, 524
윤원(구족) 輪圓(具足) 124
윤위산 輪圍山 124
윤장 輪藏 124
윤전 輪轉 124
윤제 輪臍 124
윤좌 輪座 124
윤차 輪差 124
윤타 輪埵 124
윤회 輪廻 124, 303, 524
윤회삼도 輪廻三道 270
율 律 23, 99, 227, 277, 295, 324, 370, 466, 469, 478, 587, 609
율가 律迦 49
율법 律法 469
율사 律師 433, 469, 636
율상 律相 469
율서 律書 457
율선 律禪 469
율승 律乘 469
율의 律儀 469
율의계 律儀戒 469
율장 律藏 469
율종 律宗 181, 248, 367, 427, 469, 540, 635

율참 律懺 469
율창 栗唱 126
율첩(바)비 栗呫(婆)毘 124
율첩바 栗呫婆 126
율첩반 栗呫媻 401
율첩비 栗呫毘 126
율타 栗馱 124
율파 律派 469
율행 律行 469
융 融 470
융식 融識 470
융통 融通 470
융통염불 融通念佛 370
융통염불 融通念佛 119
은 恩 470
은 慇 470
은 銀 470, 584
은 隱 470
은근 慇懃 470
은덕 恩德 269
은도 恩度 470
은련 恩憐 470
은밀 隱密 470
은복 隱覆 470
은사 恩師 470
은색 銀色 470
은소 隱所 470
은신 隱身 470
은애 恩愛 470
은애옥 恩愛獄 470
은원덕 恩圓德 269
은전 恩田 470, 606
은하 恩河 470
은해 恩海 470
은해사 銀海寺 470
은형 隱形 470
은혜 恩惠 631
음 吟 470
음 婬 266, 470
음 淫 470
음 陰 425, 470, 563
ten fields of meditation 551
음 音 470
음 飮 471
음경 陰境 355, 470
음계 婬戒 470
음계 陰界 470
음광 飮光 66, 300, 471
음광부 飮光部 325, 471
음교 音敎 470
음노치 婬怒癡 470
음노치 婬怒痴 407
음라 淫羅 470
음라망 婬羅網 470
음마 陰魔 272, 470, 604
음망 陰妄 470
음망일념 陰妄一念 470
음목 音木 470
음성 音聲 470
음성불사 音聲佛事 470
음식 飮食 471
음악 音樂 470
음영 吟詠 470
음욕 婬欲 470
음욕 淫欲 470
음욕병 淫欲病 470
음욕화 淫欲火 470
음의 音義 470
음입계 陰入界 470
음장 陰藏 470
음전 陰錢 470
음주 飮酒 471
음탕 淫湯 470
음풍 吟諷 470
음향인 音響忍 470
음혈지옥 飮血地獄 471
음화 婬火 470
음환 陰幻 470
응 凝 471
응 應 471
응(화)신 應(化)身 639
응가 應伽 471
응감 應感 471
응공 應供 371, 375, 471
응과 應果 471
응기 應器 471
응능 膺能 471
응량기 應量器 471
응리(원실)종 應理(圓實)宗 471
응문 膺文 471
응법 應法 246, 471
응법묘복 應法妙服 471
응법사미 應法沙彌 294, 471
응병여약 應病與藥 471
응보 應報 471
응불 應佛 471
응송 應頌 471
응신 應身 194, 227, 283, 471, 472, 483, 505, 639
四身 252
응신토 應身土 472
응연상 凝然常 471
응용무변 應用無邊 472
응응 應應 472
응의 應儀 472
응인 應人 472
응작 應作 472
응적 應迹 472
응정변지 應正遍知 472
응진 應眞 472
응토 應土 472
응현 應現 472
응현 膺賢 471
응형 應形 472
응호 應護 472
응화 應化 472
응화법신 應化法身 188, 472, 481
응화성문 應化聲聞 472
응화신 應化身 283, 472, 544
응화이생 應化利生 472
의 依 473
의 儀 473
의 意 45, 135, 270, 271, 274, 278, 279, 286, 291, 412, 431, 473, 475, 607
心地 355
의 擬 473
의 疑 414, 433, 474, 582, 585
의 矣 472
의 禕 630
의 義 473, 477, 585
四尋思觀 252
의 蟻 472
의 衣 472
의 醫 474
의가비여바하리가 猗柯毘與婆訶利柯 503
의감 疑感 474
의개 疑蓋 474
의견 意見 474
의견 疑見 355, 474, 582
의결 疑結 265, 474
의계 意界 474
의계 衣裓 473
의과 依果 473, 481
의과최승 意果最勝 589
의궤 儀軌 473

의근 意根 474, 485, 585, 605
의나 衣那 473
의내 依耐 642
의념왕생 意念往生 474
의다라니 義陀羅尼 473
의라발달라 醫羅鉢呾邏 474
의라엽 翳羅葉 479
의락 意樂 474
의력 意力 361, 474
의력하발지 疑叻賀鉢底 519
의례 義例 473
의률타 矣栗馱 472
의마 意馬 474
의마심원 意馬心猿 474
의무애 義無礙 473
의문 義門 473
의밀 意密 268
의발 衣鉢 473
의방 醫方 474
의법 衣法 472
의법불의인 依法不依人 473
의변 義辯 473
의보 依報 473, 481
의보 衣寶 472
의복수념원 衣服隨念願 472
의복천 衣服天 472
의본심 依本心 283
의분천 意憤天 474
의사 疑使 474
의사마 懿師摩 11
의사석 依士釋 462
의삼 意三 474
의상 義湘 474, 640
의상 義相 473
의생 意生 366, 639
의생신 意生身 214, 474
의생화신 意生化身 474
의성 意成 474
의성신 意成身 474
의성천 意成天 474
의성태궁 疑城胎宮 58, 474
의소 義疏 473
의수 意水 474
의술 蟻術 472
의식 儀式 473
의식 意識 282, 344, 414, 430, 474
의신 依身 473
의신 疑神 69
의심 疑心 474
의안락행 意安樂行 474
의언 意言 474
의언진여 依言眞如 473, 487
의업 意業 354, 431, 474
의업공양 意業供養 45
의왕 醫王 474
의왕선서 醫王善逝 394
의원 依圓 473
의원 意猿 474
의의 義意 473
의인 依因 287, 425
의인 意忍 45
의자 疑刺 474
의자 醫子 474
의정 依正 473
의정 義淨 305, 473
의좌실 衣座室 472
의죄 擬罪 473
의주 衣珠 472
의주석 依主釋 462
의준 義准 119
의지 依地 473
의지 依止 473
의지 意地 475
의지사 依止師 473
의지심심 依止甚深 473
의지아사리 依止阿闍梨 473
의지아차리 依止阿遮利 385
의지최승 依止最勝 589
의집 疑執 474
의차 意車 475
의처 意處 475
의천 義天 475, 566
의청 義靑 597
의취 意趣 475
의취 義趣 473
의타 依他 473, 612
의타(기)성 依他(起)性 473
의타심 依他心 473
의타십유 依他十喩 473
의타자성 依他自性 473
의통 依通 429, 473
의판 依版 473
의학 意學 475
의해 意解 475
의현 義玄 126
의호 依怙 473
의화 意和 469
의회 疑悔 474
이 二 475, 489
이 以 475
이 伊 475
이 利 414
이 已 475
이 彝 475
이 爾 476
이 犛 475
이 理 283
이 異 475, 605
four functioning forms 255
이 移 476
이 耳 294, 476
이 貳 476
이 離 469
이 易 401
이 李 475
이가 二假 476
이가 二加 476
이가바제라나 伊迦波提羅那 476
이각 二覺 476
이간어 離間語 126
이감 移龕 476
이개 離蓋 126
이거 離佉 125
이검 利劍 125
이것이 무엇인고 480
이견 二見 477
이견 異見 476
이경체 二經體 477
이계 二戒 477
이계 理界 477
이계과 離繫果 411, 476
이계불계 離繫不繫 80
이계자 離繫子 126
이고 二苦 477
이공 二空 477, 495
이공관 二空觀 477
이과 二果 477
이관 二觀 477
이관 理觀 477
이광 二光 477
이교 二敎 477, 487
이구 二求 478
이구 理具 257, 315, 478
이구 離垢 125
이구동음 異口同音 475
이구범과 二俱犯過 478
이구삼천 理具三千 478

이구세계 離垢世界 125
이구안 離垢眼 125
이구오부 二九五部 478
이구운 二九韻 478, 587
이구지 離垢地 125, 369
이구청정 離垢淸淨 491
이근 二根 478
이근 利根 125, 349, 478, 598
이근 耳根 476, 485
이금당 已今當 475
이금당왕생 已今當往生 475
이기 二記 329
이길라 二吉羅 478
이나반파룡 伊那槃婆龍 479
이나발나 伊那鉢那 479
이녀 二女 478
이니연 伊尼延 478
이니연(타) 伊尼延(陀) 478
이단 二壇 478
이단 異端 476
이달대덕 已達大德 475
이답 二答 479
이덕 二德 479
이도 二道 479
이돈 二頓 479
이동자 二童子 206
이라 伊羅 479
이라다라 伊羅多羅 479
이라바나 伊羅婆拏 479
이라바나 伊羅婆那 479
이라바나용상왕 伊羅婆那龍象王 479
이라발(다라)용왕 伊羅鉢(多羅)龍王 479
이라발나 伊羅鉢那 479
이라발라 伊羅跋羅 479
이라발제하 伊羅跋提河 479
이락 利樂 125
이락유정 利樂有情 125
이란 伊蘭 479
이란나(발벌다) 伊爛拏(鉢伐多) 479
이량 二量 479
이력 二力 120, 479
이론 理論 243, 479
이루 二漏 479
이류 二流 479
이류각생 二類各生 480
이류종자 二類種子 480
이륙 二六 480
이륙시중 二六時中 480
이륙지연 二六之緣 480
이륙지원 二六之願 480
이륜 二輪 480
이륜 耳輪 476
이르다 道曰 480
이리 二利 480
이리 理理 291
이리사반다가 伊梨沙般茶迦 or 伊利沙般茶迦 480
이리사장나 伊梨沙掌拏 168, 428, 480
이리순나 夷離淳那 382
이리연(타) 伊梨延(陀) 478
이리욕자 已離欲者 475
이만다라 理曼陀羅 480
이명이상 離名離相 507
이묘 二妙 480
이무기 二無記 480
이무상 二無常 480
이무아 二無我 419, 480, 497, 608
이무아지 二無我智 480
이문 二門 480
mind as bhūtatathatā 355
이물 利物 125
이뭣고 480
이미 二美 480
이미 離微 126
이밀 二密 480
이밀 理密 480
이바다 梨婆多 125
이바다 離婆多 125
이바다 離波多 125
이박다 泥縛多 569
이반야 二般若 480
이방편 異方便 475
이백오십계 二百五十戒 81, 481
이번뇌 二煩惱 481
이범 二凡 481
이범 二犯 481
이법 理法
四法 247
이법계 理法界 247, 292, 427, 481
이법신 二法身 188, 481
이법신 理法身 247, 481
이법집 二法執 481, 486
이변 二邊 481
이변 利辯 125
이변지 已辨地 369
이보 二報 481
이복 二福 481
이복전 二福田 481
이부 異部 476
이부오부 二部五部 482
이부정법 二不定法 481
이분별 離分別 19
이불 理佛 467, 482
이불병좌 二佛竝坐 482
이불성 二佛性 482
이불성 理佛性 482
이불성 理佛性 482
이불신 二佛身 482
이불중문 二佛中門 482
이빈 二貧 482
이사 二師 482
이사 伊沙 482
이사 伊私 482
이사 利使 125
이사 理事 482
이사 離奢 126
이사 利使 361
이사가 伊師迦 482
이사굴 伊沙堀 68
이사기리 伊私耆梨 482
이사나 伊沙那 482, 483
이사나 伊舍那 482
이사나 伊邪那 or 伊賒那 482
이사나(천) 伊舍那(天) 482
이사나후 伊舍那后 482
이사니 伊舍尼 246
이사다라 伊沙馱羅 482
이사다라 伊沙陀羅 51
이사다라 伊沙陁羅 482
이사무애 理事無礙 482
이사무애관 理事無礙觀 267
이사무애법계 理事無礙法界 292
이사무애법계 理事無礙法界 247
이사무애십문 理事無礙十門 359
이사시불 以砂施佛 235
이산 移山 476
이삼 二三 482
이삼사도 二三邪徒 482
이상 二相 482
이상 伊賞 482
이상 異相 476, 482
이상 離相 126, 279
이상계 離相戒 126

이상나보라 伊賞那補羅 483
이색신 二色身 483, 484
이생 利生 125
이생 已生 280, 475
이생 異生 179, 475, 476, 617
이생 離生 126
이생선 已生善 483
이생성 異生性 180, 368
이생성 離生性 126, 187, 366
이생성장 異生性障 366
이생저양심 異生羝羊心 476
이생희락지 離生喜樂地 55, 126
이서 二序 483
이서 二鼠 483
이선 二善 483
이선 二禪 55
이선 理禪 483
이선묘락지 離善妙樂地 55
이선천 二禪天 250, 301
이설 二舌 486
이설 異說 228, 476
이섭파라 伊葉波羅 483
이성 二聖 483
이성 理性 483, 595
이성무별불 離性無別佛 126
이세 二世 483
이세간 二世間 483, 489
이세간품 離世間品 368
이세오사 異世五師 419
이세존 二世尊 482, 483, 489
이소목조 泥塑木雕 321
이쇠 離衰 453
이수 二修 483
이수 二受 483
이숙 異熟 36, 475
이숙(식) 異熟(識) 476
이숙과 異熟果 411, 476, 547
이숙등오과 異熟等五果 476
이숙생 異熟生 476
이숙식 異熟識 376
이숙인 異熟因 465, 476
이숙인이숙과 異熟因異熟果 287
이순 伊循 75
이습벌라 伊溼伐羅 483
이습벌라 伊濕伐羅 517
이승 二乘 324, 483
이승경 二乘境 355
이승과 二勝果 483
이승작불 二乘作佛 483
이시 二始 484
이시 二時 484
이식 二識 344, 484
이식 二食 484
이식 耳識 476
이신 二身 482, 484
이신이토 理身理土 484
이심 二心 484
이심 異心 475
이심전심 以心傳心 475
이십 二十 484
이십건도 二十犍度 485
이십구유 二十九有 486
이십부 二十部 485
이십억이 二十億耳 484
이십오방편 二十五方便 416, 484
이십오보살 二十五菩薩 424, 484
이십오신 二十五神 484
이십오원통 二十五圓通 484
이십오유 二十五有 484
이십오점 二十五點 485
이십오조 二十五條 5, 484
이십유식 二十唯識 485
이십유식론 二十唯識論 370
이십이근 二十二根 61, 274, 485
이십이문 二十二門 485
이십이품 二十二品 485
이십지 二十智 485
이십천 二十天 485
이십팔부 二十八部 566
이십팔부중 二十八部衆 486
이십팔생 二十八生 486
이십팔수 二十八宿 314, 485
이십팔약차 二十八藥叉 486
이십팔유 二十八有 486
이십팔조 二十八祖 131, 486, 537
이십팔천 二十八天 485
이아 二我 497
이아(견) 二我(見) 486
이아집 二我執 481, 486
이애 二愛 486
이애 二礙 486
이양 利養 125
이양박 利養縛 125
이어 二語 486
이어계 耳語戒 476
이언 離言 126
이언 離言 473
이언전 離言詮 396
이언진여 離言眞如 487
이엄 二嚴 486
이업 二業 486
이여 二如 486, 491
이여 二餘 486
이여사 理如事 359
이연 異緣 476
이열반 二涅槃 487
이염 爾炎 476
이염 爾燄 476
이염복 離染服 126
이오 二悟 487
이오 伊吾 621
이오(로) 伊吾(盧) 487
이오식 二五食 487
이왈 離曰 125
이왕 二往 487
이왕 二王 487
이욕 離欲 126
이욕지 離欲地 369
이욕청정 離欲淸淨 180
이우 伊優 492
이우 犛牛 475
이원 二圓 480, 487
이원 李園 475
이월 離越 125
이위 以爲 453
이유 已有 280
이유식 理唯識 429
이응신 二應身 487
이의 二義 487
이의 二衣 487
이이 伊伊 475
이이합연 二二合緣 487
이익 二益 487
이익 二翼 487
이익 利益 125
이익묘 利益妙 125, 359
이인 二因 437, 488
이인 二忍 487
이인 利人 125
이인 異人 475
이인 異因 475
이인구범 二人俱犯 478
이일 理一 255
이입 二入 488, 511
이입 理入 488
이입 耳入 476
이입 理入 488

이자 二字 488
이자문수 二字文殊 488
이자삼점 伊字三點 288, 475
이장 二藏 488, 519
이장 二障 486, 488
이장 理障 256, 488
이장의 二障義 488
이재절언 理在絶言 488
이전 二詮 488
이전 爾前 476, 641
이정 二定 55
이제 二諦 488
이제 二際 488
이제목다 伊帝目多 364
이제목다가 伊帝目多伽 488
이제목다가 伊提目多伽 143
이제왈다가 伊帝曰多伽 488
이제월다가 伊帝越多伽 488
이제허망지상 離諸虛妄之相 504
이조 二鳥 489
이조(단비) 二祖(斷臂) 489
이족 二足 489
이족존 二足尊 489
이존 二尊 483, 489
이존이교 二尊二教 489
이존일교 二尊一教 489
이존일치 二尊一致 489
이종 二宗 489
이종 二種 489
이종(보)시 二種(布)施 489
이종(일)천제 二種(一)闡提 489
이종공양 二種供養 489
이종관정 二種灌頂 489
이종광명 二種光明 489
이종병 二種病 489
이종보살 二種菩薩 489
이종보살신 二種菩薩身 489
이종보시 二種布施 198, 490
이종불경 二種佛境 489
이종비구 二種比丘 489
이종사 二種死 490
이종사견 二種邪見 490
이종사리 二種舍利 490
이종성 二種性 490
이종성 二種聖 490
이종세간 二種世間 489
이종수기 二種授記 490
이종시 二種施 490
이종심상 二種心相 490
이종열반 二種涅槃 487, 490
이종인과 二種因果 490
이종인욕 二種忍辱 490
이종자 二種子 480, 490
이종자량 二種資糧 490
이종적정 二種寂靜 491
이종청정 二種清淨 491
이죄 二罪 491
이중 二衆 491
이즉 理卽 467
이즉(불) 理卽(佛) 491
이증보살 二增菩薩 491
이지 二地 466
이지 二持 491
이지 二智 491, 550
이지 利智 125
이지 已知 383
이지 理智 62, 491
이지근 已知根 475, 485
이지오법 理智五法 491
이지오법 理智五法 416
이지원만 二智圓滿 491
이진복 離塵服 125
이진여 二眞如 45, 491
이집 二執 491
이집 異執 475
이차 利車 126
이차 梨車 401
이차 離車 401
이차(비) 離車(毘) 126
이차비 梨車毘 126
이찰니 伊刹尼 491
이처 耳處 476
이처삼회 二處三會 491
이천 二天 492
이천삼선 二天三仙 250, 293, 436, 492
이체 理體 492
이초 二超 492
이출 二出 492
이타 二吒 373
이타 利他 125, 269, 371, 595
이타 貳吒 476
이타 利他 480
이타일심 利他一心 125
이토 二土 492
이파다 離波多 125
이파파 利波波 125
이판 理判 261, 492
이팔 二八 492
이포새 伊蒲塞 444
이포색 伊蒲塞 492, 614
이품 異品 475
이하백도 二河白道 492
이학 二學 492
이학 異學 475
이합 利合 271
이해 異解 476
이해탈 二解脫 492
이행 二行 492
이행 易行 401
이행 利行 251
이행 離行 227
이행도 易行道 479
이행섭 利行攝 125
이현 二現 492
이혈세혈 以血洗血 630
이협사 二脇士 493
이협시 二挾侍 493
이혜 異慧 475
이호 二護 493
이혹 二惑 493
이혹 理惑 493
이화 二和 493
이화 利和 469
이환 已還 475
익 翼 486
인 人 135, 211, 279, 347, 494, 615
　四相 249
인 仁 493
인 刃 493
인 印 142, 270, 494, 496
인 因 119, 126, 135, 284, 292, 365, 402, 425, 431, 465, 490, 493, 494, 605, 608
　primary cause 497
인 引 495
인 忍 54, 493, 608
인 認 495
인 麟 494
인(욕)개 忍(辱)鎧 494
인(중)분다리화 人(中)分陀利華 498
인(중)사자 人(中)師子 498
인(중)수 人(中)樹 498
인가 印可 494, 495
인가대사 引駕大師 495

인가람 人伽藍 495
인가행 忍加行 493
인각 麟角 494
인견 人見 497
인계 人界 618
인계 印契 494
인계 忍界 494
인공 人空 88, 302, 373, 477, 495, 497
인공관 人空觀 477, 495
인과 因果 35, 428, 495
인과 引果 495
인과개공종 因果皆空宗 495
인과어 因果語 588
인과응보 因果應報 495
인광 印光 494
인귀 人鬼 495
인근 隣近 126
인근석 隣近釋 462
인길서 人吉庶 495
인나 堙那 479
인날리 印捺哩 583
인내(이명) 因內(二明) 495
인능변 因能變 495
인니연 因尼延 478, 496
인다(라)니라(목다) 因陀(羅)尼羅(目多) 496
인다라 因陀羅 107, 365, 496, 571
인다라가실다 因陀羅呵悉多 496
인다라갈실치 因陀羅喝悉哆 496
인다라굴 因陀羅窟 496
인다라니 忍陀羅尼 82
인다라달바문불 因陀囉達婆門佛 496
인다라대장 因陀羅大將 496
인다라망 因陀羅網 197
인다라바다나 因陀羅婆他那 496, 572
인다라발제 因陀羅跋帝 496
인다라서다 因陀囉誓多 496
인다라세라구가 因陀羅勢羅求呵 419
인다라세라구하 因陀羅世羅求訶 496
인다라세라구하 因陀羅勢羅寠訶 496
인다라하색다 因陀羅訶塞多 496
인단 隣單 126
인달라 印達羅 494
인달라 因達羅 496
인달라대장 因達羅大將 496
인도 人道 498
인도 印度 345, 403, 494, 568, 571
인도 因道 496
인도 引導 495
인도불교 印度佛教 494
인동품 因同品 496
인두당 人頭幢 496
인라 堙羅 479
인라나 堙羅那 496
인란 因蘭 597
인력 因力 361, 403, 496
인력론사 因力論師 45
인론 因論 496, 631
인마 人馬 364
인마사 人摩娑 496
인만다라 因曼陀羅 496
인망사 人莾娑 496
인명 因明 292, 495, 496, 631
인명론 因明論 496
인명사종 因明四宗 213
인명입정리론 因明入正理論 496
인명정리문론 因明正理門論 497
인명팔정리론 因明八正理論 605
인모 印母 494
인무아 人無我 480, 497
인무아지 人無我智 497
인바라밀 忍波羅蜜 494
인반대사 引飯大師 495
인발인 引發因 495
인법 人法 302, 497
인법 忍法
四善根 251
인법(위) 忍法(位) 494
인법사 印法師 613
인보 人寶 497
인분 因分 497
인분가설과분불가설 因分可說果分不可說 497
인불 印佛 494
인불작법 印佛作法 494
인불타악취 忍不墮惡趣 493
인비인 人非人 69, 497
인사 人師 497
인사구 因沙舊 496
인사자 人師子 497, 498
인사자 人獅子 497, 498
인상 人相 381, 384
인상 印相 494
인상 因相 497
인생본 人生本 71
인선 人仙 307, 308, 497, 569
인선 忍仙 493
인선 忍善 493
인섭 引攝 495
인수 因修 497
인수 忍水 494
인승 人乘 421, 497
인승 仁勝
四佛 248
인식 認識 495
인신 人身 497
인신우 人身牛 497
인십사과 因十四過 497
인아 人我 85, 153, 497
인아견 人我見 486, 497
인약왕자 人藥王子 497
인어 因語 588
인업 因業 497
인업 引業 134, 486, 495
인여 因如 362
인역 印域 494
인연 因緣 282, 361, 364, 402, 497, 584, 607
인연관 因緣觀 276, 365, 426, 497
인연생 因緣生 497
인연의 因緣依 497
인연종 因緣宗 258
인엽림 刃葉林 493
인왕 仁王 493
인왕강 仁王講 493
인왕경 仁王經 119, 363, 493, 568
四無常偈 244
인왕경수지품 仁王經受持品 583
인왕경중 仁王經中 201
인왕공 仁王供 493
인왕다라니 仁王陀羅尼 493
인왕반야 仁王般若 168
인왕반야경 仁王般若經 493
인왕존 仁王尊 493
인왕주 仁王咒 493
인왕호국반야 仁王護國般若 493
인왕회 仁王會 493
인욕 忍辱 359, 461, 494
인욕선 忍辱仙 494
인욕의 忍辱衣 268, 494
인욕지 忍辱地 494

인욕태자 忍辱太子 494
인웅사자 人雄師子 497, 498
인원 因源 498
인원 隣圓 126
인원과만 因圓果滿 498
인원덕 因圓德 269
인위 因位 498
인위 忍位 493
인유 人有 498
인유 引喩 431
인이품 因異品 498
인인 人因 498
인인 因人 498
인인 引因 495
인인본구 人人本具 498
인일 人一 255
인입 引入 495
인자 仁者 493
인접 引接 495
인정 人定 498
인정태자 引正太子 495
인제 因提 496
인제 因諦 427
인제리 因提梨 496
인조 忍調 494
인존 人尊 498
인존 仁尊 493
인좌 引座 495
인죄 認罪 495
인주 人主 258
인중사자 人中師子 497
인중삼악 人中三惡 498
인중우왕 人中牛王 498
인중존 人中尊 498
인지 因地 498
인지 因坻 496
인지 忍地 493
인지 忍智 493
인지 隣智 126
인지가라 印持伽羅 572
인지동시 印紙同時 494
인지화 人持花 71
인진 隣珍 126
인집 人執 385, 491, 497, 498
인천 人天 498
인천교 人天教 412, 498
인천승 人天乘 498
인천승묘선과 人天勝妙善果 498
인천안목 人天眼目 498
인청사리 引請闍梨 495
인출불성 引出佛性 278, 495
인취 人趣 468, 498
인치 印治 494
인토 印土 494
인토 忍土 493
인특가 印特伽 494
인행과 因行果 498
인허 隣虛 126
인화 引化 495
일 一 498, 605
일 壹 475
일 日 53, 498
일 逸 499
일가연 一家宴 499
일각선인 一角仙人 499
일간 一間 499
일간성자 一間聖者 499
일개반개 一個半個 499
일경 一境 499
일경사심 一境四心 499, 504
일경삼제 一境三諦 499
일경초 一莖草 500
일계 一髻 500
일계나찰녀 一髻羅刹女 500
일계나찰왕보살 一髻羅刹王菩薩 500
일계문수 一髻文殊 500, 506
일고령 一鈷鈴 427
일공 一空 500
일광 日光 493
일광(보살) 日光(菩薩) 498
일광변조 日光邊照 394
일광삼존 一光三尊 500
일구 一九 500
일구 一句 500
일구도진 一句道盡 500
일구자 一句子 500
일구지생 一九之生 500
일구투화 一句投火 500
일궁 日宮 499
일궁천자 日宮天子 485
일극 一極 500
일기 一期 500, 511
일기 一蟣 500
일기온 一期蘊 286
일기일경 一機一境 500
일념 一念 500, 564
일념만년 一念萬年 500
일념불생 一念不生 500
일념삼천 一念三千 500
일념삼천(지관법) 一念三千(之觀法) 175
일념업성 一念業成 500
일념온 一念蘊 286
일녕 一寧 500, 503
일다 逸多 499
일단구 一壇構 500
일단구 一檀構 500
일단사 一段事 500
일단식 一揣食 500
일단식 一摶食 500
일당화안고 日幢華眼鼓 499
일대 一代 501
일대교 一代教 501
일대사 一大事 501
일대삼단 一代三段 501
일대삼천세계 一大三千世界 501
일대오시불법 一代五時佛法 501
일대차 一大車 501
일대택 一大宅 501
일도 一道 501
일도무위심 一道無爲心 501
일도법문 一道法門 501
일도삼례 一刀三禮 501, 510
일도신광 一道神光 501
일독승 一禿乘 501
일등 一等 501
일랍 一臘 501
일랍 一臘 501
일래(향) 一來(向) 501
일래과 一來果 501
일련 一蓮 501
일련 日蓮 371, 499
일련종 日蓮宗 499
일련지실 一蓮之實 501
일련탁생 一蓮托生 501
일루 一縷 510
일루일촉 一縷一觸 501
일류 一流 501
일륜 日輪 499
일륜삼매 日輪三昧 499
일마만전 一魔萬箭 502
일마일미 一麻一米 502
일명 一明 502
일모단 一毛端 502
일목다가 一目多伽 502
일무애도 一無礙道 502

일문 一門 502
일문보문 一門普門 502, 505
일물부장래 一物不將來 502
일미 一味 502, 503
일미사병 一味瀉瓶 502
일미진 一微塵 502
일백 一百 502
일백삼갈마 一白三羯磨 502
일백팔 一百八 502
일법 一法 502
일법계 一法界 502
일법계심 一法界心 502
일법구 一法句 502
일법인 一法印 502
일변 一遍 502
일보 一寶 502
일보 一普 502, 506
일본 日本 499
일부구 一浮漚 502
일분가 一分家 502
일분보살 一分菩薩 503
일불(국)토 一佛(國)土 503
일불다불 一佛多佛 503
일불세계 一佛世界 503
일불승 一佛乘 219, 503, 504
일불정토 一佛淨土 503
일사구게 一四句偈 503
일사천하 一四天下 503
일산 一山 503
일살다생 一殺多生 503
일삼매 一三昧 503
일상 一相 350, 503
일상관 日想觀 499
일상무상 一相無相 503
일상법문 一相法門 503
일상삼매 一相三昧 503, 511
일상일미 一相一味 503
일상지 一相智 503
일색 一色 503
일색일향무비중도 一色一香無非中道 503
일생 一生 503
일생과수 一生果遂 503
일생보처 一生補處 503
일생보처보살 一生補處菩薩 503
일생보처보살상 一生補處菩薩像 503
일생불범 一生不犯 503
일생소계보살 一生所繫菩薩 503
일생애 一生涯 511
일생입묘각 一生入妙覺 503
일선삼매 日旋三昧 499
일설부 一說部 223, 325, 503
일성수 日星宿 499
일성일체성 一成一切成 503
일성종 一性宗 504
일소겁 一小劫 504
일수사견 一水四見 500, 504
일숙각 一宿覺 628
일승 一乘 193, 219, 281, 422, 504
일승가 一乘家 504
일승경 一乘經 504
일승구경교 一乘究竟敎 504
일승만교 一乘滿敎 239
일승묘문 一乘妙文 504
일승묘전 一乘妙典 504
일승법(문) 一乘法(門) 504
일승보리 一乘菩提 504
일승분교 一乘分敎 239
일승원종 一乘圓宗 504
일승지주 一乘之珠 504
일승현성교 一乘顯性敎 412, 504
일시 一時 341, 504
일식 一息 504
일식 一識 344, 504
일식 一食 504
일식반보 一息半步 504
일식외도 一識外道 504
일실 一實 268, 287, 349, 350, 487, 500, 502, 504, 507, 512
일실경계 一實境界 504
일실무상 一實無相 504
일실상 一實相 504
일실승 一實乘 504
일실원승 一實圓乘 504
일실원종 一實圓宗 504
일실제 一實諦 506
일심 一心 267, 446, 447, 504
일심금강보계 一心金剛寶戒 505
일심삼관 一心三觀 352, 505, 571
일심삼지 一心三智 292, 505
일심삼혹 一心三惑 505
일심즉일체심 一心卽一切心 506
일심칭명 一心稱名 504
일안지귀 一眼之龜 505
일업 一業 505
일여 一如 350, 398, 502, 504, 505, 507
일여관음 一如觀音 505
일여돈증 一如頓證 505
일여본정심 一如本淨心 501
일역 日域 499
일엽 一葉 505
일엽관음 一葉觀音 505
일예 一翳 505
일왈다가 一曰多伽 502
일왕 一往 505
일요 日曜 499
일우 一雨 505
일우중 日禺中 499
일원건립 一願建立 505
일월등명불 日月燈明佛 115, 499
일월삼신 一月三身 505
일월삼주 一月三舟 292, 505
일월정명덕 日月淨明德 499
일위일체위 一位一切位 505
일음교 一音敎 505
일이 一異 503, 505
일이단상 一異斷常 302
일이유무 一異有無 244
일인 一印 506
일인 一因 505
일인작허만인전실 一人作虛萬人傳實 506
일인회 一印會 506
일일 一一 498
일일 一日 506
일일경 一日經 112, 506
일일불 一日佛 506
일일삼시 一日三時 506
일일일야 一日一夜 506
일자 一字 506
일자금륜(정)법 一字金輪(頂)法 506
일자금륜불정법 一字金輪佛頂法 506
일자문수 一字文殊 500, 506
일자불정륜왕경 一字佛頂輪王經 418
일자삼례 一字三禮 501, 506
일자선 一字禪 506
일자주 一字呪 354
일자최승불정(륜왕) 一字最勝佛頂(輪王) 418
일장육상 一丈六像 506
일전가 一顚迦 506, 507
일전도 一箭道 506

일전어 一轉語 506
일정마니 日精摩尼 499
일제 一諦 506
일제 一際 506
일조 日照 553
일조왕 日照王 485
일종 一種 499
일종 日種 220, 499
일종선생 日種善生 507
일좌식 一坐食 506
일주 一炷 506
일주관 一周關 506
일주기 一周忌 506, 511
일주문 一柱門 506
일중 一中 506
일중 日中 137
일중일체중 一中一切中 506
일즉삼 一卽三 506
일즉십 一卽十 506
일즉일체일체즉일 一卽一切一切卽一 506
일증일감 一增一減 504, 506
일지 一地 507
일지 一持 507
일지 一智 550
일지두선 一指頭禪 507
일진 一塵 507
일진 一眞 504, 507
일진무위 一眞無爲 507
일진법계 一塵法界 507
일진법계 一眞法界 507
일진법계一眞法界 one 507
일진지 一眞地 507
일차구왕 一叉鳩王 11, 507
일찰 一刹 507
일찰 一拶 507
일찰나 一刹那 507
일천 一千 501, 507
일천 日天 492, 499
일천(자) 日天(子) 499
일천만만만만만만만만조 一千萬萬萬萬萬萬萬萬兆 382
일천이백 一千二百 507
일천이백공덕 一千二百功德 507
일천자 日天子 267, 499
일천제 一闡提 498, 567
일천제(가) 一闡提(迦) 507
일천제가 一闡提迦 292, 506
일천중 日天衆 499
일체 一體 507
일체 一切 183, 507
일체개공종 一切皆空宗 508
일체개성불 一切皆成佛 508
일체경 一切經 508, 520
일체경음의 一切經音義 629
일체남녀아부모 一切男女我父母 204
일체만법 一切萬法 508
일체무장법인명 一切無障法印明 508
일체무장애 一切無障礙 508
일체문선 一切門禪 54
일체물 一切物 508
일체법 一切法 508
일체법계결정지인 一切法界決定智印 508
일체법계생인 一切法界生印 508
일체법계자신표 一切法界自身表 508
일체법공 一切法空 508
일체법리언설공 一切法離言說空 582
일체변지인 一切徧智印 508
일체변지인 一切遍智印 508
일체보문신 一切普門身 508
일체불심인 一切佛心印 508
일체불회 一切佛會 508
일체삼보 一體三寶 113, 508
일체삼분 一體三分 508
일체삼신자성불 一體三身自性佛 508
일체선 一切禪 54
일체세존최존특신 一切世尊最尊特身 508
일체속질력삼매 一體速疾力三昧 508
일체시 一切施 508
일체어언부 一切語言部 508, 509
일체여래 一切如來 509
일체여래금강서계 一切如來金剛誓誡 509
일체여래보 一切如來寶 509
일체여래안색여명조삼마지 一切如來眼色如明照三摩地 509
일체여래정 一切如來定 509
일체여래제법본성청정연화삼매 一切如來諸法本性淸淨蓮華三昧 509
일체여래지인 一切如來智印 509
일체여래필정인 一切如來必定印 509
일체여인개시중악지소주처 一切女人皆是衆惡之所住處 400
일체유 一切有 264, 509
일체유근본 一切有根本 509
일체유근본부 一切有根本部 509
일체유근본식 一切有根本識 61
일체유부 一切有部 417, 457, 508, 509
일체유위 一切有爲 509
일체유정 一切有情 509
일체의성 一切義成 509
일체인중존 一切人仲尊 509
일체일심식 一切一心識 509
일체제법 一切諸法 293, 508, 521
일체제불 一切諸佛 509
일체종묘삼매 一切種妙三昧 509
일체종식 一切種識 509
일체종지 一切種智 292, 491, 509
일체중생 一切衆生 509
일체중생개실성불 一切衆生皆悉成佛 508
일체중생이제악취 一切衆生離諸惡趣 510
일체중생정기 一切衆生精氣 510
일체중생지부 一切衆生之父 93, 509
일체중생평등성불 一切衆生平等成佛 613
일체중생희견불 一切衆生喜見佛 509
일체즉일 一切卽一 510
일체지 一切智 176, 292, 491, 510
일체지경 一切智經 510
일체지구 一切智句 510
일체지상 一切智相 510
일체지선 一切智船 510
일체지심 一切智心 510
일체지안 一切智眼 362
일체지인 一切智人 510
일체지자 一切智者 510
일체지장 一切智藏 510
일체지주 一切智舟 510
일체지지 一切智地 510
일체지지 一切智智 42, 510
일체지천 一切智天 510
일체지혜자 一切智慧者 510

일체진언심 一切眞言心 510
일체진언주 一切眞言主 510
일체처 一切處 510
일체처무불상응진언 一切處無不相應眞言 510
일체행선 一切行禪 54
일촉 一觸 510
일출론자 日出論者 226, 499
일취 一吹 510
일타 一唾 510
일타일취 一唾一吹 510
일토모진 一兎毛塵 510
일품(경) 一品(經) 510
일필구(소) 一筆勾(銷) 510
일필삼례 一筆三禮 501, 510
일하 一夏 501, 510
일하자 一訶子 510
일할 一喝 510
일합상 一合相 511
일항(하사) 一恒(河沙) 511
일행 一行 106, 511, 569, 637
일행삼매 一行三昧 416, 503, 511
일행일체행 一行一切行 147
일행일체행 一行一切行 511
일향 一向 511
일향기 一向記 511
일향대승사 一向大乘寺 511
일향소승사 一向小乘寺 511
일향종 一向宗 511
일향청정무유여인 一向淸淨無有女人 511
일협사사 一篋四蛇 511
일형 一形 511
일화 一化 511
일화오미지교 一化五味之敎 511
일회기 一回忌 506, 511
임 任 511
임 紝 511
임등 林藤 126
임바 任婆 511
임바 紝婆 511
임병 任病 247
임병투자개진열재전 臨兵鬪者皆陳列在前 54
임비 林毘 126
임섭 林燮 126
임운 任運 511
임장 林葬 126
임재 臨齋 126
임제 臨濟 126, 371, 533, 621
summary 243
임제종 臨濟宗 310, 410
임종 臨終 126
임한 淋汗 126
입 入 284, 379, 511, 607
ten fields of meditation 551
입감 入龕 511
입골 入骨 511, 513
입관 入觀 512
입교 立敎 126
입교개종 立敎開宗 126
입단 入壇 512
입당(오법) 入堂(五法) 512
입당팔가 入唐八家 512
입도 入道 512
입량 立量 126
입류 入流 322, 327, 329, 512
입릉가경 入楞伽經 79
입멸 入滅 512
입문해석 入文解釋 512
입법 立法 126
입법계 入法界 117, 423
입법문문 入法門門 360
입부라 入嚩羅 512
입불 入佛 512
입불공양 入佛供養 512
입불이문 入不二門 512
입불평등계 入佛平等戒 512
입산 入山 512
입성 入聖 512
입성종 立性宗 258
입승 立繩 512
입승수좌 立僧首座 126
입식 入識 320
입신 入信 512
입실 入室 512
입심 入心 283, 512
입아아입 入我我入 101, 275, 294, 512
입왕궁취락의 入王宮聚落衣 512
입음성다라니 入音聲陀羅尼 269
입의 立義 331, 431
입인 立因 425
입적 入寂 512
입적멸 入寂滅 512
입정 入定 512, 580
입제 立題 532
입종 立宗 431
입주출 入住出 512
입주출삼심 入住出三心 512
입중 入衆 512, 513
입중오법 入衆五法 513
입중현문 入重玄門 513
입지 入地 512
입출이문 入出二門 513
입탑 入塔 513
입파 立播 126
입파 立破 126

(ㅈ)

자 子 341, 514
자 字 270, 514
四等 242
자 慈 279, 514
자 炙 521
자 煮 515
자 磁 515
자 紫 420, 515
자 自 515
자 藉 515
자 觜 486
자 資 514
자 赭 514
자 鷓 514
자가 紫袈 515
자가라 柘迦羅 517
자가회 炙茄會 521
자각 自覺 265, 477
자각각타 自覺覺他 8
자각성지 自覺聖智 515
자각오심 自覺悟心 515
자갈 赭羯 514
자경 慈敬 514
자계 字界 514
자고 紫姑 515
자고 鷓鴣 4, 514
자고반 鷓鴣斑 514
자과 子果 515
자관 慈觀 412
자관조리 自觀照理 512
자광 慈光 514
자기 自棄 68
자내증 自內證 515
자념금강 慈念金剛 102
자단 子斷 515
자도 自度 287, 517
자량 資糧 514

자량위 資糧位 425
자력 自力 479, 515
자력교 自力敎 492
자력왕 慈力王 514
자력종 自力宗 591
자류인과 自類因果 515
자륜 字輪 514
자리 自利 97, 269, 371, 480, 515, 595
자리이타 自利利他 125, 515
자리이타 自利利他 95, 97, 197, 198, 516, 517
자마 紫磨 515
자마금 紫磨金 515
자마인욕 紫磨忍辱 515
자만과 子滿果 515
자명 慈明 514
자모 字母 514
자모표 字母表 514
자모품 字母品 514
자무량심 慈無量心 245
자문 慈門 514
자민삼장 慈愍三藏 633
자민혜 慈愍慧 102
자바기바(기) 闍婆耆婆(耆) 67
자박 子縛 36, 515
자발생 慈發生 102
자법신 自法身 428
자변 慈辯 514
자복 紫服 515
자비 慈悲 138, 392, 399, 514
　四等, four virtues 242
자비관 慈悲觀 276, 426, 514
자비만행 慈悲萬行 514
자비보 慈悲普 360
자비실 慈悲室 268, 514
자비의 慈悲衣 514
자비희사 慈悲喜捨 149, 242, 247
자사 煮沙 515
자살 自殺 515
자상 自相 287, 515
자상공 自相空 582
자상자의 字相字義 514
자생 自生 515
자생 資生 514
자서수계 自誓受戒 515
자석 磁石 515
자선 子璿 516
자성 自性 140, 282, 516, 539, 588, 615
　四尋思觀 252
자성계 自性戒 516
자성궤 資成軌 268
자성단 自性斷 269, 290
자성법신 自性法身 481
자성본원계 自性本源戒 280
자성분별 自性分別 209
자성삼보 自性三寶 516
자성선 自性善 516
자성선 自性禪 54
자성성 者性性 235
자성신 自性身 252
자성주불성 自性住佛性 278
자성청정 自性淸淨 491
자성청정심 自性淸淨心 187, 353, 560
자성청정장 自性淸淨藏 429
자손손타 自損損他 516
자수 慈水 514
자수법락 自受法樂 516
자수용 自受用 331
자수용신 自受用身 252, 283, 516
자수용토 自受用土 421, 516, 592
자시 赭時 514
자시자연 自始自然 201
자신자불 自身自佛 516
자신지 自信智 370
자심 慈心 514
자심 自心 516
자심지적정 自心之寂靜 512
자씨 慈氏 160, 514, 603
자아 自我 469
자안 慈眼 514
자애 自愛 516
자어법신 字語法身
　四等 242
자어상위 自語相違 516
자언비니 自言毘尼 583
자엄 慈嚴 514
자업자득 自業自得 517
자연 字緣 514
자연 自然 189, 507, 511, 516
　無因有果 259
자연 資緣 514
자연석가 自然釋迦 516
자연성 自然性 154
자연성불도 自然成佛道 516
자연오도 自然悟道 516
자연외도 自然外道 516
자연자 自然慈 516
자연지 自然智 516
자연허무신 自然虛無身 516
자용 自用 287
자운 慈雲 514
자원 子院 516
자은 慈恩 186, 267, 429, 514
　四部經 248
　六部大乘經 462
자은사 慈恩寺 176, 630
자은종 慈恩宗 186, 367
자의 慈意 514
자의 紫衣 515
자이 自爾 516
자인 慈忍 514
자인 自因 240
자자 慈子 514
자자 自恣 516
자자일 自恣日 516
자작자수 自作自受 517
자재 自在 171, 375, 379, 483, 517
자재등인종 自在等因宗 517
자재왕 自在王 517
자재장 資財帳 514
자재지 自在持 482
자재천 自在天 517
자재천외도 自在天外道 517
자정 自淨 287, 517
자정기의 自淨其意 535
자조 自調 287, 517
자조자정자도 自調自淨自度 517
자존 慈尊 514
자좌 自坐 469
자주 慈霔 514
자증 自證 68, 517
자증단 自證壇 517
자증분 自證分 248
자증성지 自證聖智 517
자증신 自證身 517
자증회 自證會 517
자체 自體 287
자체체 自體體 235
자태 姿態 286
자통개도 藉通開導 515
자합국 子合國 517
자항 慈航 514
자행화타 自行化他 517
작 作 518

작 嚼 517
작 斫 517
작 鵲 517
작(걸)추 斫(乞)芻 517
작가 作家 518
작가라 斫迦羅 51, 517
작거 作擧 518
작계 作戒 518
작구가 斫句迦 517, 525
작납 嚼蠟 517
작례 作禮 50, 518
작마(생) 作麽(生) 518
작범 作犯 481, 518, 549
작범(패) 作梵(唄) 518
작법 作法 518
작법계 作法界 518
작법득 作法得 518
작법참 作法懺 292
작법참(회) 作法懺(悔) 518
작병 作病 247
작병천자 作甁天子 537
작불 作佛 518
작불사 作佛事 518
작선 作善 518
작소 鵲巢 517
작악 作惡 518
작업 作業 518
작여 作如 362
작용 作用 518
작원 鵲園 517
작원문 作願門 518
작의 作意 104, 417, 518
작일체물 作一切物 615
작자 作者 518, 615
작지 作持 491, 549
작지계 作持戒 518
작흘라 斫訖羅 517
작흘라바(가) 斫訖羅婆(迦) 518
작흘라벌랄지 斫訖羅伐辣底 517
작흘라산 斫訖羅山 518
잔 殘 518
잔과 殘果 518
잔습 殘習 398
잠 暫 518
잠 蠶 518
잠가 暫假 575
잠가 暫暇 518
잠견 蠶繭 518
잠시 暫時 405
잠연 湛然 86, 446, 631
天台九祖 572
잡 雜 483, 518
잡건도 雜犍度 485
잡림원 雜林苑 254
잡생세계 雜生世界 518
잡쇄의 雜碎衣 542
잡아함 雜阿含 253, 386
잡아함경 雜阿含經 424, 609
잡아함경 雜阿含經 25 211
잡업 雜業 518
잡염 雜染 518
잡장 雜藏 518, 563
잡주계 雜住界 518
잡집론 雜集論 370
잡함 雜含 518
잡화(경) 雜華(經) 518
장 丈 519
장 場 518
장 張 486
장 掌 518
장 章 156, 171, 518
장 莊 519
장 葬 519
장 藏 51, 268, 280, 288, 376, 477, 478, 487, 519, 584, 587, 638
장 裝 519
장 長 519
장 障 469, 520
장걸식 長乞食 519
장경 藏經 508, 520
장과 掌果 518
장교 藏敎 228, 239, 519, 575
장교지성연이인 藏敎之聲緣二人 584
장궤 長跪 519
장로 長老 519
장륙 丈六 519
장륙금신 丈六金身 506, 519
장리 藏理 520
장림 杖林 346, 409, 520
장물 長物 519
장발 長鉢 519
장복 章服 518
장부 丈夫 195, 519, 615
장부국 丈夫國 519
장부지간 丈夫志幹 519
장사 藏司 519
장상 裝像 519
장생 長生 519
장생부 長生符 519
장생불로 長生不老 519
장생불사 長生不死 519
장생은 長生銀 236
장선 掌善 556
장설봉 張雪峯 445
장송 葬送 519
장수 張遂 511
장수 長壽 519
장수 長水 516
장수천 長壽天 519
장식 藏識 520
장식 裝飾 343
장식 長食 519
장식사상 藏識四相 249
장아함 長阿含 253, 273, 386
장아함경 長阿含經 53, 423, 519
장아함대연방변경 長阿含大緣方便經 49
장아함유행경 長阿含遊行經 92
장악 掌惡 556
장안 章安
四家 238
止觀論 551
장안 長安 630
장애 障礙 520, 583
장야 長夜 519
장양 長養 615
장엄 莊嚴 35, 146, 280, 519
장엄겁 莊嚴劫 265, 519, 627
장엄경 莊嚴經 463
장엄대승론 莊嚴大乘論 382
장엄론 莊嚴論 257
장엄문 莊嚴門 519
장엄보리심경 莊嚴菩提心經 161
장엄왕 莊嚴王 519
장엄왕경 莊嚴王經 519
장왕 莊王 519
장의 長衣 519
장일 長日 519
장자 長者 519
장전 藏殿 520
장정자 長汀子 614
장제론 藏諸論 380
장주 藏主 519
장진 藏塵 519
장진해탈 障盡解脫 492, 520
장통 藏通 520

장통별원 藏通別圓 519
장편 章篇 485
장향 裝香 519
재 再 520
재 在 520
재 財 265, 520
재 齋 602
재가 在家 520
재가계 在家戒 520
재가이계 在家二戒 520
재가출가 在家出家 520
재간 財慳 520
재공양 財供養 489, 520
재당 齋堂 344
재리교 在理敎 520
재색 財色 520
재성결정 財成決定 466
재세 在世 520
재속 在俗 520
재시 財施 357, 520
재신 財神 520
재왕 再往 487, 520
재욕 財欲 520
재재처처 在在處處 520
재전 在纏 399, 520
재전공양 在纏供養 489
재전여래 在纏如來 353
재전진여 在纏眞如 487, 520, 580
재주 財主 520
재혜 財慧 419
재혜동자 財慧童子 557
쟁 諍 520
쟁론 諍論 520
저 低 521
저 底 520
저 豬 520
저 著 521
저 這 521
저개 這箇 521
저돌 觝突 521
저두화상 豬頭和尙 520
저라석가 低羅釋迦 521
저라택가 低羅擇迦 521
저률차 底栗車 520
저리 底哩 520
저리 底理 520
저리 這裏 521
저미 抵彌 548
저사 底沙 211, 520, 535, 562
저사불 底沙佛 211
저언다 底彦多 520
저하 底下 520
적 寂 143, 521
적 敵 521
적 積 521
적 賊 521
적 赤 420, 521
加沙野 1
적 蹟 200
적 迹 202, 358, 522
적 適 521
적 炙 521
적(멸도)량 寂(滅道)場 521
적공루덕 積功累德 521
적광 寂光 521
적광(토) 寂光(土) 521
적광정토 寂光淨土 499
적광토 寂光土 267
적귀 赤鬼 522
적념 寂念 521
적동엽 赤銅葉 83
적루 積累 521
적막 適莫 521
적매단 赤梅檀 521
적멸 寂滅 405, 521, 605
적멸도량 寂滅道場 237
적멸무이 寂滅無二 521
적멸법 寂滅法 521
적멸상 寂滅相 521
적멸인 寂滅忍 425, 521
적명지 寂命智 521
적묵 寂默 306, 469
적묵외도 寂默外道 521
적문 迹門 202
적문십묘 迹門十妙 358
적백이제 赤白二渧 521
적상 寂常 521
적석산 積石山 521
적악연나 赤鄂衍那 521
적안 寂岸 521
적안 赤眼 521
적업사자 寂業師子 521
적연 寂然 521
적연계 寂然界 521
적용담연 寂用湛然 521
적육(단) 赤內(團) 521
적인 寂忍 521
적자비바사 赤髭毘婆沙 521
적재 寂災 521
적전단 赤栴檀 442
적정 寂定 521
적정 寂靜 521
적정문 寂靜門 521
적정법 寂靜法 521
적정행 寂靜行 521
적조 寂照 521
止觀 551
적조혜 寂照慧 469, 521
적종 寂種 521
적주 賊住 521
적주 赤珠 584
적증 敵證 521
적취정요심 積聚精要心 351
적화 迹化 522
적화 適化 521
적화십묘 迹化十妙 522
전 傳 523
전 全 522
전 典 522
전 前 523
전 囀 523
전 塡 523
전 奠 523
전 專 483, 523
전 展 523
전 戰 523
전 旃 522
전 殿 522
전 煎 523
전 田 522
전 筌 522
전 箋 522
전 箭 522
전 纏 523
전 詮 522
전 轉 55, 523
전 電 522
전 顚 523
전(상)의 田(相)衣 522
전가부좌 全跏趺坐 522
전객 典客 522
전격란 轉格欄 523
전경 轉經 523
전계 傳戒 523
전광석화 電光石火 522
전교 傳敎 244, 523, 571
전교 轉敎 524

전나라 戰捺羅 523
전날라 戰捺羅 450
전녀성남 轉女成男 524
전념 專念 523
전다 奠茶 523
전다라 旃茶羅 522
전다라 旃陀羅 522
전다리 旃陀利 522
전다아수가 旃陀阿輸柯 522
전단 旃丹 522
China 548
전단(나) 旃檀(娜) 522
전단이 旃檀耳 84, 336, 522
전단지림 旃檀之林 83
전달라 戰達羅 450, 523
전달라 旃達羅 522
전달라바가 旃達羅婆伽 522
전달라발랄바 戰達羅鉢剌婆 450, 523
전달라벌마 旃達羅伐摩 451
전달라파가 旃達羅婆伽 451
전달제바 旃達提婆 452, 522
전당 前堂 523
전대반야경 轉大般若經 524
전도 箭道 522
전도 顚倒 523, 587
전도 顚到 241
전도망상 顚倒妄想 523
전독 轉讀 523
전등 傳燈 523
전등록 傳燈錄 414, 524
전라희 囀羅呬 523
전람 典攬 522
전례 專禮 426
전록록지 轉轆轆地 376
전륜 轉輪 524
전륜(성)왕 轉輪(聖)王 524
전륜(왕) 轉輪(王) 517
전륜성제 轉輪聖帝 524
전륜왕불정 轉輪王佛頂 418
전릉 塡陵 523
전무명 纏無明 523
전물 轉物 524
전미개오 轉迷開悟 524
전박 纏縛 523
전범륜 轉梵輪 524
전법 傳法 237, 523, 524
전법 轉法 524
전법륜 轉法輪 185, 271, 524
전법륜보살 轉法輪菩薩 431, 524
전법륜상 轉法輪相 524
전법륜일 轉法輪日 524
전변 詮辯 522
전변 轉變 524, 615
전변무상 轉變無常 524
전보 纏報 523
전분계 全分戒 522
전분수 全分受 522
전불 前佛 523
전빈 典賓 522
전사 殿司 522
전상 專想 523
전상 轉相 20, 464
전생 前生 523
전서 箋書 522
전세 前世 523
전세 轉世 524
전숙 錢俶 573
전승림 戰勝林 523
전시가 旃簛迦 522
전식 轉識 422, 524
전신 前身 523
전심 傳心 523
전심 專心 523
전어 筌魚 522
전역 傳譯 401
전연 旃延 522
전영 電影 522
전왕 塡王 523
전의 傳衣 523
전자 旃闍 522
전장 轉藏 523
전전력 展轉力 523
전점 煎點 523
전정 專精 523
전정각 前正覺 171
전정각산 前正覺山 523
전제라 旃提羅 522
전좌 典坐 541
전좌 典座 265, 522
전주 殿主 522
전주 田主 564
전중후 前中後 523
전지 傳持 523
전지 詮旨 522
전진 前塵 523
전진 前陳 539
전차 戰遮 522
전차 旃遮 522
전취 轉趣 644
전통 傳通 523
전파가 旃坡迦 574
전회 轉廻 524
전후제단 前後際斷 523
절 切 525
절 寺 524
절 截 524
절 折 525
절 拜 524
절 絶 525
절구가 折句迦 525
절단중류 截斷衆流 267
절대 絶大 525
절대 絶對 525
절대 絶待 145, 525
절대묘 絶待妙 480
절대원 絶待圓 487
절대진여 絶待眞如 525
절량식 節量食 500
절로 折蘆 525
절리단라 折利但羅 525
절리달라 折利咀羅 413
절리달라 折利怛羅 525
절복섭수 折伏攝受 525
절석 折石 525
절승 切勝 525
절식 絶食 525
절우주 截雨呪 524
절처 切處 422
절학 絶學 525
점 占 525
점 漸 112, 267, 290, 422, 487, 525, 640
점 苫 525
점 點 525
점교 漸教 74, 477, 525, 531, 602
천태삼교 573
점단 漸斷 525
점돈점원 漸頓漸圓 479
점등 點燈 525
점말라 苫末羅 525
점바라 苫婆羅 525
점석 點石 525
점수나 占戍拏 525
점심 點心 325, 525
점열 漸熱 525
점원 漸圓 487

점점수습이차제개현불덕야 漸漸修習而次第開顯佛德也 202
점차 漸次 291, 525
점찰 占察 525
점파 占婆 574
점화 點化 525
접 接 525
접대 接待 525
접생 接生 525
접생계 接生戒 314
접인 接引 525
접족작례 接足作禮 525
정 井 486, 525
정 停 526
정 定 53, 55, 188, 230, 273, 274, 295, 354, 358, 362, 394, 412, 418, 425, 479, 480, 492, 494, 512, 526, 584
정 庭 526
정 情 264, 526
정 政 526
정 正 235, 282, 516, 526, 609
정 淨 269, 516, 527
four inverted beliefs 242
四德 241
정 精 526
정 貞 526
정 鉦 525
정 靜 469, 526
정 頂 527
정가 淨家 527
정각 正覺 527
정각 淨覺 527
정각지 定覺支 527
정거 淨居 102
정거천 淨居天 103, 527
정견 情見 526
정견 政見 228
정견 正見 527, 609
정결오욕 淨潔五欲 527
정계 正戒 477
정계 淨戒 527
정계 頂髻 342
정고 鉦鼓 525
정과 正果 481, 528
정관 淨觀 527
정광 定光 123, 367, 527
정광 錠光 402
정광 頂光 527
정교 政教 526
정교륜 正教輪 45, 271
정국 淨國 527
정근 定根 485, 527
정근 正根 204, 478
정기 正忌 527
정기 精氣 526
정념 正念 254, 527, 609
정념정관제통명력 正念正觀諸通明力 361
정념정지 正念正智 268
정당임마시 正當恁麽時 527
정도 正道 123
정도 淨道 527
정두 淨頭 528
정등각 正等覺 273, 277, 528, 531
정등정각 正等正覺 273, 528
정량 正量 300
정량부 正量部 244, 275, 324, 325, 528
정려 定侶 528
정려 淨呂 528
정려 精廬 526
정려 靜慮 309, 526
정력 定力 361, 414, 528
정력 靜力 526
정령붕 精靈棚 526
정례 頂禮 527
정륜 頂輪 527
정리 正理 72
정만 淨滿 227
정명 定命 528
정명 正命 17, 528, 609
정명 淨命 528
정문 淨門 528
정문안 頂門眼 527
정미귀 精媚鬼 341
정미심원 精微深遠 145
정바라밀 淨波羅密 528
정반 淨飯 328
정반왕 淨飯王 528
정발 淨髮 528
정방 淨方 528
정방 淨邦 528
정범왕 淨梵王 528
정법 正法 136, 251, 282, 528, 529
정법 頂法
四善根 251
정법거 正法炬 528
정법계 淨法界 528
정법명여래 正法明如來 528
정법수 正法壽 528
정법시 正法時 528
정법안장 正法眼藏 603
정법의 正法依 528
정법장 正法藏 429
정법화경 正法華經 146, 528
정변각 正偏覺 273, 528
정변지 正偏智 528
정변지 正偏知 273, 371
정변지(도) 正偏知(道 273
정변해 正偏海 528
정보 定報 473
정보 正報 319, 481, 528
정보리심 淨菩提心 529
정부정 淨不淨 587
정불 淨佛 529
정비 定妃 529
정사 正士 529
정사 正思 609
정사 精舍 237, 526
정사 靜思 526
정사유 正思惟 529
정사자 淨師子 226
정산 定散 529
정산이선 定散二善 529
정상 定相 529
정상 頂相 527
정상말 政像末 185
정상말 正像末 296, 529
정생왕 頂生王 158, 306, 527
정생희락지 定生喜樂地 55
정석 頂石 527
정선 定善 262, 483
정성 定性 529
정성 正性 402
정성 淨聖 529
정성이승 定性二乘 529
정성희락지 定性喜樂地 529
정소 頂巢 527
정수 定水 529
정수 正受 273
정시 淨施 489, 529
정식 靜息 526
정식동심 靜息動心 551
정신 定身 529
정신 淨信 529
정신 淨身 413

정신 精神 526
정신작증구족주해탈 淨身作證具足住解脫 611
정실 精室 526
정실 貞實 526
정실 靜室 526
정심 停心 526
정심 定心 484, 529
정심 淨心 529
정심 頂心 360
정심삼매 定心三昧 529
정심주 正心住 368
정심주 淨心住 466, 529
정심행처 正心行處 273
정안 淨眼 115, 529
정안치 丁岸哆 478, 520
정어 正語 529, 609
정어 淨語 529
정언다 丁彦多 587
정업 定業 207, 530
정업 正業 486, 530, 537, 609
정업 淨業 530
정업결정 定業決定 466
정업역능전 定業亦能轉 530
정역 淨域 530
정영 淨影 258, 598
정예 淨裔 530
정옥 淨屋 530
정욕 情欲 526
정원 情猿 526
정원각심 淨圓覺心 530
정월 正月 85
정월 淨月 337
정유 情有 526
정유리무 情有理無 526
정유리세계 淨瑠璃世界 530
정육 淨肉 530
정의 定意 529
정의 庭儀 526
정의경 正依經 530
정인 定忍 530
정인 正因 488, 530
정인불성 正因佛性 404, 437
정일 正日 530
정자재왕 定自在王 485
정장 淨藏 530
정정 正定 273, 414, 530, 609
정정성취 正定性聚 207
정정업 正定業 530
정정진 正精進 530, 609
정정취 正定聚 294
정제근 淨諸根 530
정종 淨宗 530
정종분 正宗分 278, 501
정주 淨主 530
정주 淨住 237, 530, 615
정주 靜主 526
정주 頂珠 527
정중 正中 530
정중 淨衆 530
정중로월 井中撈月 525
정중종 淨衆宗 151
정지 定智 530
정지 正地 641
정지 正智 416, 531
정지 正至 275
정지 淨地 531
정지 淨志 245
정지 靜智 526
정지부 正地部 509, 531, 641
정지상 淨智相 482
정직 正直 531
정직사방편 正直捨方便 531
정진 情塵 526
정진 精眞 526
정진 精進 61, 228, 359, 362, 412, 461, 526, 557, 584
정진각 正盡覺 531
정진궁지혜전 精進弓智慧箭 526
정진근 精進根 485
정진력 精進力 414, 526
정진바라밀 精進波羅蜜 526
정찰 淨刹 388, 531
정천 淨天 531, 566
정천안 淨天眼 531
정체지 正體智 491
정취 定聚 531
정토 淨土 99, 370, 378, 492, 528, 531, 587
정토론 淨土論 519
정토삼부 淨土三部 278
정토종 淨土宗 325, 367, 530, 531, 540
정토진종 淨土眞宗 215, 531, 538
정판 定判 531
정하 井河 526
정학 定學 295, 531
정행 正行 385, 531
정행 淨行 162, 241
本化四菩薩 247
정행경 正行經 531
정행자 淨行者 531
정행진여 正行眞如 588
정향 定香 418
정혜 定慧 531, 584
止觀 551
정혜 靜慧 526
정혜결사문 定慧結社文 177
정화 井華 526
정화중 淨華衆 531
제 制 532
제 劑 533
제 啼 534
제 帝 533
제 弟 534
제 提 106, 533, 565
제 梯 531
제 濟 533
제 祭 533
제 第 532
제 諦 425, 534, 607
四家 238
心根, one of the twenty-five 諦 352
제 諸 533
제 醍 532
제 除 532, 584
제 際 531
제 題 532
제 齊 531
제(석)궁 帝(釋)弓 533
제(석)망 帝(釋)網 533
제가 濟家 533
제각지 除覺支 532
제강 提綱 536
제개장 除蓋障 102, 532, 603
제개장불정 除蓋障佛頂 418
제거 帝居 533
제견 諸見 534
제견경 諸見境 355
제계 制戒 532
제계 劑戒 533
제고 劑鼓 533
제곡 啼哭 534
제곡불 啼哭佛 534
제관 諦觀 534
제교 制教 478, 532, 642

제구장 除垢障 272
제근 諸根 534
제근 除饉 225, 532
제나바 提那婆 534
제다 制多 532, 548
제다가 提多迦 486, 534
제다라 制多羅 564
제다라타 提多羅吒 534
제다산 制多山 208
제다산부 制多山部 325, 532, 548, 550
제단 除斷 532
제달라 制怛羅 532
제담타야나 提曇陀若那 535
제당 劑堂 533
제도 濟度 533
제등 梯隥 531
제라 提羅 534
제려다갈라살타라 第黎多曷羅殺吒羅 534
제려다할라살타라 第黎多曷羅殺吒羅 532
제리야구유니가 帝利耶瞿榆泥伽 533
제망 帝網 197
제명 諸冥 534
제목 題目 499, 532
제문 制門 532
제문 祭文 533
제문 齊文 533
제바 提婆 227, 534, 536, 566, 569
제바 提波 534
제바달 提婆達 534
제바달다 提婆達多 534
제바달도 提婆達兜 534
제바달도 諦婆達兜 534
제바마라파패 提婆魔囉播稗 534
제바보살 提婆菩薩 534, 569
제바서나 提婆犀那 534
제바설마 提婆設摩 534
제바오법 提婆五法 416
제바종 提婆宗 534
제바지제바 提婆地提婆 534
제번뇌선 除煩惱禪 54
제법 劑法 533
제법 諸法 534
四等 242
제법개공 諸法皆空 535
제법공 諸法空 582
제법단명종 諸法但名宗 503
제법무아 諸法無我 535
제법실상 諸法實相 99, 293, 535
제법오위 諸法五位 535
제법적멸상 諸法寂滅相 535
제법지성 諸法之性 398
제불가 諸佛家 535
제불모보살 諸佛母菩薩 535
제불심인 諸佛心印 508
제불지실상 諸佛之實相 398
제불평등법신 諸佛平等法身 507
제비 提鞞 535
제비리 梯毘利 591
제비사 提鞞沙 535
제비사 醍鞞沙 532
제비파 提鞞波 535
제사 帝沙 176, 533, 550
제사 提舍 535, 612
제사나 提舍那 535
제사니 提捨尼 416
제사니 提舍尼 163, 535
제사론 祭祠論 533
제사선 第四禪 532
제사타 際史吒 531
제산 除散 532
제삼능변 第三能變 532
제삼선 第三禪 532
제상 帝相 533
제상 諸相 535
제색 諸色 535
제서 齊書 78
제석 劑席 533
제석 帝釋 307, 533, 566
天帝 571
제석굴 帝釋窟 533
제석법왕 諸釋法王 535
제석병 帝釋甁 533
제석석굴 帝釋石窟 496
제석암 帝釋巖 533
제석존천 帝釋尊天 485
제석천 帝釋天 492, 496
제선 諸仙 535
제선봉행 諸善奉行 535
제설제문 齊說齊聞 531
제수 提樹 535
제수 諸數 535
제승 劑僧 533
제시 劑時 533
제시 提撕 535
제식 劑食 533
제실라차 帝失羅叉 533
제심 帝心 533
제심 두순 帝心杜順 639
제십팔원 第十八願 532
제악 除惡 363
제악무작 諸惡無作 535
제야나 第耶那 532
제업불정 除業佛頂 418
제업신 齊業身 531
제연 劑筵 533
제연 諸緣 535
제예로가야폐사야 帝隸路迦也吠闍耶 533
제오대 第五大 532
제온 諸蘊 535
제요 提要 536
제우 除憂 363
제운반야 提雲般若 535
제원갈 提洹竭 402, 535
제원갈 提洹羯 527
제월 劑月 533
제위파리 提謂波利 535
제유 諸有 535
제육음 第六陰 532
제의 制衣 487
제의 除疑 532
제이 帝肄 83
제이능변 第二能變 532
제이선 第二禪 532
제이월 第二月 532
제일 劑日 533
제일 帝日 262
제일 第一 532
제일구 第一句 532
제일승 第一乘 532
제일식 第一識 376
제일의 第一義 532
제일의공 第一義空 207, 532
제일의관 第一義觀 532
제일의락 第一義樂 532
제일의성지대공 第一義聖智大空 582
제일의실단 第一義悉檀 252, 532
제일의제 第一義諦 532
제일의지 第一義智 532
제일의천 第一義天 566
제일적멸 第一寂滅 532
제일정 第一定 55

제일제 第一諦 488
제일체악 除一切惡 532
제자 弟子 534
제자십덕 弟子十德 357
제장 劑場 533
제장불정 除障佛頂 418, 538
제재 除災 532
제저 制底 532
제저(야) 制底(耶) 548
제저반제 制底畔睇 532
제저반탄나 制底畔彈那 532
제조 提調 535
제존 諸尊 535
제종 劑鐘 533
제주 劑主 533
제죽 劑粥 533
제지 制地 548
제지 劑持 533
제진 諸塵 535
제착 諸著 535
제창 提唱 536
제천 諸天 536
제청 帝青 533
제체 制體 532
제취 諸趣 536
제취라작갈라박리지 帝聚羅斫羯羅縛哩底 642
제칠 劑七 533
제칠선 第七仙 532
제칠정 第七情 532
제타가 制吒迦 206, 603
제통 諸通 536
제퇴 劑退 533
제파 劑罷 533
제파라 提婆羅 284
제팔식 第八識 377, 532
제하 提訶 536
제하 濟下 533
제한불한 諸閑不閑 536
제행 諸行 536
제행무상 諸行無常 536
제호 醍醐 320, 532
제호미 醍醐味 416
제화 提和 534, 536
제화갈 提和竭 402
제화갈라 提和竭羅 536
제환 提桓 307, 534, 536
제회 劑會 533
조 兆 536
조 助 537
조 早 537
조 曹 536
조 朝 537
조 條 536
조 槽 536
조 漕 536
조 潮 537
조 澡 537
조 照 536, 537
조 爪 536
조 祖 537
조 稠 537
조 竈 536
조 肇 537
조 臊 537
조 調 537
조 趙 537
조 造 537
조 釣 537
조 鳥 536
조(바)달(다) 調(婆)達(多) 537
조(상)토 爪(上)土 536
조강 糟糠 538
조경 照鏡 538
조계 曹溪 536
조계사 曹溪寺 538
조계산 曹溪山 538
조관 澡罐 537
조구타 漕矩吒 536
조달 調達 73, 176
조도 助道 537
조도 調度 537
조도 鳥道 536
조독 爪犢 536
조동 曹洞 113, 371
조동종 曹洞宗 310, 410, 536
조람 照覽 538
조로 朝露 537
조림 稠林 537
조모 朝暮 537
조바달다 調婆達多 534
조법륜 照法輪 271
조법사 肇法師 241, 537
조병 澡瓶 537
조병천자 澡瓶天子 537
조복 調伏 227, 537
조불 照拂 537
조사 祖師 537
조사선 祖師禪 310
조산 曹山 536
조산 朝山 537
조상 造像 537
조상현행장 粗相現行障 367
조서승 鳥鼠僧 536
조서천 造書天 537
조석 朝夕 537
조선 朝鮮 537
조선불교유신론 朝鮮佛教維新論 538
조소 釣召 419
조송 調頌 537
조신 竈神 536
조실 祖室 538
조실스님 祖室- 538
조어 調御 537
조어 釣語 537
조어사 調御師 537
조어장부 調御丈夫 371, 537
조업 助業 486, 537
조음 助音 537
조의 條衣 536
조의 調意 537
조작 造作 458
조장발론 爪章髮論 536
조재영겁 兆載永劫 536
조적 照寂 537
조적 鳥迹 536
조적혜 照寂慧 469
조정 爪淨 536
조제리 早帝梨 537
조좌 朝座 305
조주 趙州 537
조지 條支 536
조직정 調直定 273, 537
조참 早參 537, 565
조창 槽廠 536
조타 臊陀 537
조탑 爪塔 536
조패 照牌 538
조하 漕河 536
조현사 照玄寺 536
조화 造化 537
조화 造花 537
족 足 538
족목 足目 538
족오근 足五根 485
족하 足下 408

존 存 538
존 尊 538
존견 存見 538
존귀 尊貴 538
존기 尊記 538
존명 存命 538
존생(명) 存生(命) 538
존숙 尊宿 538
존승 尊勝 418, 538
존승다라니 尊勝陀羅尼 305
존자 尊者 538
존제 尊提 543
존족 尊足 57
존족산 尊足山 25
존중 尊重 538
존칙 尊勅 538
졸 拙 538
졸구라 拙具羅 538
졸도 拙度 538
졸이심 卒爾心 422
종 宗 102, 119, 126, 269, 272, 284, 292, 410, 538
종 從 539
종 種 279, 427, 539, 619
종 終 538
종 縱 318
종 鐘 538
종가 宗家 540
종각 種覺 539
종각 鐘閣 539
종객파 宗喀巴 94, 644
종객파 宗客巴 539
종경록 宗鏡錄 359
종고 宗杲 106
종고루 鐘鼓樓 539
종골 宗骨 539
종교 終敎 538
종귀어공 終歸於空 538
종극 宗極 539
종근기 種根器 539
종남 두순 終南杜順 427
종남산 終南山 538
종루 鐘樓 538
종륜론 宗輪論 325
종무소 宗務所 539
종문 宗門 539
종밀 宗密 447, 539, 587
종법 宗法 539, 540
종본이래불생불멸 從本以來不生不滅 507
종색 宗賾 427
종설구통 宗說俱通 539
종성 種性 539
종성주 種性住 466
종숙탈 種熟脫 539
종승 宗乘 539
종승 從僧 539
종식 種識 539
종요 宗要 539
종용 宗用 539
종용 從容 539
종원 宗元 539
종의 宗依 539
종의 宗儀 539
종의 宗義 540
종인유 宗因喩 455, 540
종자 種子 15, 199, 376, 413, 430, 514, 515, 539
종자식 種子識 376, 539
종장 宗匠 540
종정 宗正 540
종조 宗祖 540
종종색세계 種種色世界 539
종지 宗旨 540
종지 種智 539
종지용출 從地踊出 539
종체 宗體 539, 540
종치 宗致 540
종파 宗派 361, 538, 540
종풍 宗風 540
종학 宗學 540
좌 坐 541
좌 左 541
좌 座 541
좌계 左溪 541, 628
天台九祖 572
좌광 座光 541
좌구 坐具 541
좌구성로 坐久成勞 541
좌당 坐堂 541
좌랍 坐臘 388, 541
좌랍 座臘 541
좌문나 左問拏 583
좌선 坐禪 541
좌선당 坐禪堂 541
좌선법요 坐禪法要 248
좌원 座元 541
좌주 座主 541
좌증 坐證 541
좌참 坐參 541
좌하 坐夏 388, 541, 618
좌하유 坐夏由 541
죄 罪 541
죄구 罪垢 541
죄근 罪根 541
죄기 罪器 415
죄보 罪報 541
죄복 罪福 541
죄복무주 罪福無主 541
죄성 罪性 541
죄악 罪惡 541
죄얼 罪孽 396
죄업 罪業 541
죄장 罪障 541
죄처소비니 罪處所毘尼 583
죄행 罪行 541
주 主 142, 541
주 住 284, 423, 542, 550, 576, 587
four functioning forms 255
주 周 541
주 呪 542
주 廚 541
주 拄 541
주 晝 542
주 朱 542
주 柱 542
주 注 542
주 洲 541
주 珠 542
주 籌 543
주 肘 58, 542
주 註 542
주 走 543
주 酒 542
주 麈 541
주겁 住劫 18, 41, 89, 238, 315, 432, 542
주과 住果 542
주과나한 住果羅漢 542
주과연각 住果緣覺 542
주관 周關 541
주기 周忌 541
주기사귀 呪起死鬼 542
주기시귀 呪起屍鬼 542
주기재 周忌齋 541
주나 周那 91, 336, 541

주다반탁가 朱荼半託迦 541
주다반탁가 注荼半托迦 542
주라(발) 周羅(髮) 328, 541
주라파리가라 朱羅波梨迦羅 542
주량 籌量 543
주리 周利 541
주리 朱利 542
주리반타가 周利槃陀加 or 周梨槃陀加 541
주리반토 周利般兎 541
주리반특(가) 周利槃特(迦) 541
주리야 珠利耶 542
주리초 朱利草 542
주매 呪罵 138
주반 主伴 541
주방신 主方神 542
주변 周遍 541
주변법계 周遍法界 541
주변함용관 周遍含容觀 267
주변함용관십문 周遍含容觀十門 359
주사 主事 541
주산 主山 14
주살 咒殺 542
주상 住相 542
주상 周祥 541
주소 註疏 542
주수 主首 542
주술 咒術 542
주심 住心 283, 376
주심 咒心 542
주암림 晝暗林 342, 542
주원 咒願 542
주원 珠圓 334
주원사 咒願師 585
주위 住位 542, 550
주인 住因 425
주장 咒藏 542
주장(자) 拄杖(子) 541
주재 主宰 541
주저 咒咀 542
주저 洲渚 541
주정 住定 542
주정보살 住定菩薩 542
주지 住地 150, 178, 542
주지 住持 542, 543
주지신 住持身 214, 542
주지일체세계지 住持一切世界智 370
주지제산부 住支提山部 550
주치반타가 周稚般他迦 541
주타 周陀 541
주탑 柱塔 542
주해 走海 543
죽 竹 543
天竺 571
죽 粥 543
죽림 竹林 224, 517
죽림(정사) 竹林(精舍) or 竹林(精寺) 543
죽림정사 竹林精寺 91
죽림정사 竹林精舍 91
죽반승 粥飯僧 543
죽비 竹篦 543
죽원 竹園 543
죽원 竹苑 91, 543
준 准 543
준 準 543
준 遵 543
준수 遵守 543
준순 准純 336
준제 準提 543, 582
준제관음 準提觀音 582
준제불모 准提佛母 216
준지 准胝 543
준타 準陀 543
중 中 32, 56, 137, 268, 269, 281, 282, 289, 290, 292, 294, 398, 477, 499, 505, 544, 545, 546
중 衆 543
중 重 543
중가의 中價衣 544
중각강당 重閣講堂 544
중간삼매 中間三昧 544
중간선 中間禪 544
중간정 中間定 351, 544
중간정려 中間靜慮 544
중개 衆磕 543
중겁 中劫 507, 544
중고 衆苦 543
중공 重空 543
중관 中觀 99, 267, 412, 544
중관 重關 543
중관론 中觀論 243, 540, 544
중국 中國 544, 545, 546
Central India 137
중근 中根 544
중대 中臺 544
중대팔엽원 中臺八葉院 544
중도 中道 217, 457, 469, 503, 544, 545
중도 衆徒 543
중도 衆道 543
중도공 中道空 205
중도관 中道觀 544
중도교 中道敎 33, 544
중도실상 中道實相 255, 544, 545
중도응본 中道應本 544
중도제일의 中道第一義 544
중도종 中道宗 544
중도즉법계 中道卽法界 544
중론 中論 152, 218, 220, 270, 302, 544, 545, 605
founder, 龍樹 71
四絶 257
중론성교 中論性敎 222, 545
중론소 中論疏 545
중료 衆寮 543
중류 中流 545, 616
중반 中般 428, 545
중배 中輩 545
중배관 中輩觀 545
중배생 中輩生 545
중범 中梵 544, 545
중변론 中邊論 545
중변분별론 中邊分別論 382
중보왕 衆寶王 485
중사 中士 298, 545
중산 重山 543
중삼삼매 重三三昧 279
중생 衆生 125, 195, 199, 211, 264, 274, 280, 294, 303, 308, 458, 543
四不可思議 248
四相 249
중생견 衆生見 543, 601
중생계 衆生界 543
중생공 衆生空 373
중생구 衆生垢 543
중생근 衆生根 543
중생무변서원도 衆生無邊誓願度 261
중생무시무종 衆生無始無終 543
중생무아 衆生無我 497
중생본성 衆生本性 543
중생상 衆生想 543
중생상 衆生相 381, 384, 543

중생세간 衆生世間 543
중생세계 衆生世界 319
중생심지체성 衆生心之體性 269
중생인 衆生忍 487, 543
중생지심체 衆生之心體 200
중생탁 衆生濁 432, 543
중성 衆聖 543
중송 重頌 2, 471, 544
중숙의 中宿衣 545
중승 中乘 191, 278, 281, 286, 545
중승 衆僧 543
중식 中食 545
중실 中實 544, 545
중심 中心 396
중심경 中心經 545
중아함 中阿含 253, 386, 423
중아함경 中阿含經 285, 410, 510
중여 重如 543
중우 衆祐 543
중원 中元 545
중원 衆園 543
중유 中有 286, 454, 545, 589
중유지려 中有之旅 545
중음 中陰 545, 589
중음법사 中陰法事 545
중이묘일체법 中以妙一切法 32
중인 中印 544, 546
중인 中因 546
중인상 中人想 279
중잡의 重雜衣 338
중장 重障 544
중제 中諦 546
중존 中尊 546
중종 中宗 546
중좌 中座 299
중주 中洲 546
중주 衆主 96
중중 重重 543
중중제강 重重帝綱 543
중차원 衆車苑 254
중착의 中着衣 545
중천 中千 501
중천(세)계 中千(世)界 546
중천(축) 中天(竺) 544, 546
중천계 中千界 250
중천세계 中千世界 293
중천축사 中天竺寺 546
중체 中體 546
중초 中草 546
중태(장) 中胎(藏) 546
중패 中唄 546
중품 中品 240, 294, 300, 546
중학 衆學 416
중학법 衆學法 14
중함 中含 546
중합 衆合 554, 603
중합(지옥) 衆合(地獄) 543
중합지옥 衆合地獄 597
중향국토 衆香國土 543
중현사 重玄寺 305
중화 重火 543
중회 中悔 546
중회 衆會 543
즉 則 582
즉 卽 303, 546
즉가 卽假 289
즉공 卽空 289
즉공즉가즉중 卽空卽假卽中 33, 546
즉득 卽得 547
즉리 卽離 547
즉비 卽非 547
즉사이진 卽事而眞 547
즉사즉리 卽事卽理 547
즉상즉심 卽相卽心 547
즉시 卽時 547
즉신 卽身 547
즉신보리 卽身菩提 547
즉신성불 卽身成佛 547
즉심 卽心 547
즉심념불 卽心念佛 547
즉심성불 卽心成佛 547
즉심시불 卽心是佛 547
즉심즉불 卽心卽佛 547
즉유즉공 卽有卽空 547
즉중 卽中 289, 547
즘 怎 547
즘생 怎生 547
증 增 547
kalpa 18
증 憎 547
증 烝 548
증 蒸 548
증 證 223, 288, 548
四分 248
증 贈 547
증각 證覺 548
증겁 增劫 10, 547
증경 證境 489
증계학 增戒學 547
증과 證果 548
증대보리 證大菩提 548
증덕 證德 548
증도 證道 479, 548
증도손생 增道損生 548
증득 證得 548
증멸겁 增滅劫 18, 89
증명 證明 548
증발심 證發心 275
증법 證法 276
四法 247
증별야 贈別夜 547
증비 增悲 547
증사 蒸沙 548
증사작반 烝砂作飯 548
증상 增上 547
증상과 增上果 411, 476, 547
증상만 增上慢 547, 583, 604
증상심 增上心 547
증상심학 增上心學 547
증상연 增上緣 286, 402, 547
증식 增息 547
증애 憎愛 547
증오 證悟 548
증오중 贈五重 547
증익 增益 548
증익변 增益邊 481
증일아함 增一阿含 253, 386
증일아함경 增一阿含經 211, 547
증입 證入 548
증입생 證入生 279
증자증 證自證 248
증장 增長 548
증장광목 增長廣目 548
증장인 增長因 425
증장천 增長天 260, 438, 548
증장천왕 增長天王 485, 570
증전 增轉 288
증지 增智 547
증지 證智 548
증진 增進 548
지 只 550
지 地 347, 423, 466, 467, 542, 550, 552, 576, 583
지 志 551
지 抵 548
지 持 549

加 1
지 指 549
지 支 548
지 旨 550
지 智 95, 201, 210, 273, 288, 359, 363, 366, 393, 461, 485, 489, 505, 550, 551, 587, 605, 607, 608, 631
四自在 256
지 枝 549
지 枳 550
지 止 361, 551
지 知 550
지 祇 551
지 紙 550
지 脂 549
지 至 550
지 芝 549
지 誌 551
지(주심) 持(住心) 55
지(행)선 地(行)仙 551
지(혜)검 智(慧)劍 556
지(혜)광명 智(慧)光明 489
지가 地珂 551
지가반바나승가람 地迦嫛縛那僧伽藍 551
지개 智愷 631
지객 知客 522, 551
지거 地居 438
지거 智炬 551
지거천 地居天 414, 551
지견 知見 188, 363, 551
지견각조 知見覺照 488
지견바라밀 知見波羅蜜 551
지겸 支謙 548, 549
지경 智境 552
지경 智鏡 552
지경사상 智境四相 249
지계 地界 552
지계 持戒 444, 461, 549
지계 智界 477, 552
지계바라밀 持戒波羅蜜 549
지계인욕정진선정력 持戒忍辱精進禪定力 361
지고 知庫 552
지고단집 知苦斷集 552
지과 智果 552
지관 止觀 37, 38, 68, 247, 269, 273, 292, 355, 362, 394, 480, 484, 506, 551, 610
四信五行 252
天台三部 573
지관 紙冠 550
지관론 止觀論 551
지관사 止觀捨 551
지관십문 止觀十門 359
지관의례 止觀義例 473
지관종 止觀宗 551
지관현문 止觀玄文 551
지관화상 止觀和尙 551
지광 智光 552
지교 至敎 550
지구 持句 549
지구 支具 548
지국자 持國者 549
지국천 持國天 229, 260, 438, 549, 582
지국천왕 持國天王 485, 570
지귀 旨歸 550
지극 至極 46
지근 知根 274, 552
지금강 持金剛 179, 549
지기 地祇 569
지나 指那
China 548
지나 支那 550
China 548
지나 脂那 549
지나 至那 550
China 548
지나니 至那儞 550
지나라사불달라 至那羅闍弗呾羅 550
지나복지 至那僕底 550
지나제바구항라 支那提婆瞿恒羅 549
지난 指難 550
지내 地內 556
지념 持念 549
지눌 知訥 112, 552
지다 指多 549
지다나 支多那 284
지단 地壇 552
지단 智斷 552
지달(나) 枳怛(那) 550
지당 智幢 363
지대 地大 552
지덕 指德 603
지덕 智德 269, 479
지도 支度 548
지도 智度 552
지도론 智度論 47, 48, 137, 142, 166, 169, 212, 258, 270, 273, 274, 279, 282, 285, 292, 322, 343, 358, 363, 369, 370, 399, 400, 401, 403, 416, 422, 430, 483, 484, 490, 552, 582, 603, 618
육재일 六齋日 465
지도론 智度論 12 450
지도론 智度論 22 566
지도론 智度論 7 566
지도론 智度論 78 352
지도론 智度論 9 464
지도자 知道者 552
지동 地動 552
지득과불성 至得果佛性 278
지라소 枳羅蘇 550
지라파 枳羅婆 550
지란 脂難
China 548
지랍비 地臘脾 552
지랑 支郞 549
지량 支亮 549
지력 智力 552
지례 知禮 244, 552
지론 地論 552
지론 知論 552
지론종 地論宗 540
지료 知寮 552
지루가참 支樓迦讖 548
지륜 地輪 553
지륜단 地輪壇 553
지률가 地口栗伽 551
지률거 底栗車 579
지리 至理 550
지리지리 枳哩枳哩 550
지린 支隣 143
지린타 支隣陀 549
지만 指鬘 390, 550
지만다라 智曼陀羅 480
지말 枝末 150
지말무명 枝末無明 549
지말법륜 枝末法輪 271
지말혹 枝末惑 549
지명 持名 549
지명 持明 549

지명선 持明仙 549
지명원 持明院 413
지명장 持明藏 549
지모 智母 553
지묘 智妙 358, 553
지무변제불지 知無邊諸佛智 370, 553
지문 智門 553
지미 支微 548
지바달다 地婆達多 534, 553
지바달도 地婆達兜 534
지바달두 地婆達兜 553
지바라밀 智波羅蜜 553
지바하라 地婆訶羅 553
지박라 至縛羅 548
지방립상 指方立相 550
지벌라 支伐羅 548
지범 持犯 518, 549
지범 止犯 481, 549, 551
지법 知法 553
지법륜 持法輪 271
지법신 智法身 481
지법자 持法者 549
지변 智辯 553
지변산 持邊山 549, 583
지병 止病 247
지보금강 持寶金剛 400
지복친 指腹親 550
지본 持本 549
지본제 知本際 437
지불 支佛 548
지불관 支佛觀 365
지불지 支佛地 369, 548
지비 智悲 553
지사 底沙 228
지사 知事 404, 553
지사 至沙 550
지산 智山 553
지상 地上 553
지상 智相 464, 468, 553
지상 智象 553
지상존자 至相尊者 550
지선 地仙 308, 569
지성 智城 553
지성심 至誠心 283
지세간 知世間 319, 553
지소 持素 549
지수 持水 549
지수 智手 553
지슬미낭 地瑟娓囊 1
지승 智昇 13
지식 止息 273, 551
지식 知識 422, 553
지식념 持息念 549
지식중 知識衆 553
지신 地神 553, 556
지신 智身 214, 553
지심 智心 553
지심 至心 550
지쌍 持雙 583
지쌍산 持雙山 549
지악문 止惡門 551
지안 智眼 362, 554
지애 智礙 554
지언 至言 550
지엄 智儼 550, 554
지엄 智嚴 587
지업석 持業釋 462
지엽 紙葉 550
지영락 持瓔珞 357, 549
지옥 地獄 72, 74, 209, 434, 493, 554, 603, 610
지옥도 地獄道 555
지옥천자 地獄天子 114, 555
지옥취 地獄趣 468, 555
지욕 知浴 438
지용 地涌 555
지용 支用 548
지우계 持牛戒 549
지원 芝苑 549
지월 指月 549, 550
지월 智月 555, 632
지위 地位 210, 555
지유라 枳由羅 340
지유라 枳由邏 70
지유발 持油鉢 455
지유죄지무죄 知有罪知無罪 635
지율 持律 549
지의 志意 551
지의 智顗 146, 215, 501, 551, 555
　台衡 594
　四教儀 239
　天台 572
　天台九祖 572
지의 紙衣 550
지이근 知已根 274
지인 持因 425
지인 指印 549
지인 智刃 555
지인 至人 550
지인지과 智因智果 287
지일불분 志一不分 273
지일체법지 知一切法智 370, 555
지일체중생지 知一切衆生智 370, 555
지자 智者 555
　天台九祖 572
지자 知者 555
지자재소의 智自在所依 370
지장 地藏 40, 56, 357, 361, 367, 402, 555, 556, 603
　Korean monk, an incarnation 555
지장 智藏 213, 555
지장 智障 488
지장(보살)본원경 地藏(菩薩)本願經 556
지장십륜경 地藏十輪經 2, 556
지장전 地藏殿 556
지재 持齋 549
지저 智杵 556
지저가부 只底舸部 548, 550
지저여세라부 只底與世羅部 550
지적 智積 385, 556
지전 地前 556
지전 知殿 556
지전 紙錢 550
지절 指節 58, 550
지정각 智正覺 280
지정상 智淨相 556
지제 支帝 548
지제 支提 221, 548
지제 支提 or 支帝 532
지제 智諦 427
지제 脂帝 548
지제 至諦 427
지제가부 支提加部 548, 550
지제부도 脂帝浮圖 549
지제산부 支提山部 548, 550
지조 智照 498
지족 知足 556
지족(천) 知足(天) 556
지족원 知足院 556
지종 地種 556
지중 地中 556
지즙 智楫 556
지증 智證 556

지증보살 智增菩薩 491
지지 持地 549
지지 指底 235
지지 智智 556
지지 止持 491, 549, 551
지지가 地底迦 556
지지계 止持戒 518, 551
지지문 止持門 551
지지산 地持山 81
지지산 持地山 583
지지작범 止持作犯 551
지진 地塵 255, 556
지진 智眞 502
지진 至眞 550
지참 支讖 548, 549
지천 地天 553, 556
지천 指釧 550
지천후 地天后 556
지축 持軸 482, 583
지축산 持軸山 549
지치바 地致婆 556
지타 支陀 548
지타 枳吒 550
지타나 支陀那 284
지타심통 知他心通 592
지토 指兎 549
지하천 地下天 414
지향 枝香 549
지혜 地慧 158
지혜 智慧 141, 157, 168, 461, 486, 556
지혜관 智慧觀 556
지혜광불 智慧光佛 378, 556
지혜금강 智慧金剛 168
지혜동자 地慧童子 or 持慧童子 557
지혜력 智慧力 556
지혜문 智慧門 556
지혜불 智慧佛 252
지혜수 智慧水 556
지혜해 智慧海 556
지혹 智惑 557
지화 智火 557
지환 指環 550
지환 祇桓 550
직 直 557
직 職 557
직당 直堂 557
직도 直道 557
직분 職分 557
직설 直說 557
직세 直歲 541, 557
직심 直心 557
직전 直傳 557
직지사 直指寺 557
직지인심 直指人心 603
직철 直掇 557
직철 直裰 557
진 嗔 414
진 塵 77, 467, 557
진 振 557
진 晉 325, 422, 576
derivation of China 548
진 津 557
진 珍 558
진 盡 557
진 眞 289, 371, 426, 558
진 瞋 265, 270, 276, 278, 285, 433, 558
진 秦 558
derivation of China 548
진 軫 381, 486
진 辰 558
진 進 557, 584
진 鎭 558
진 陳 557, 630
derivation of China 548
진 震 558
진(점)겁 塵(點)劫 557
진각 眞覺 558
진견도 眞見道 558
진경 塵境 557
진경 晉經 640
진경 眞境 558
진공 眞空 350, 558
진공관 眞空觀 267
진공묘유 眞空妙有 558
진관 眞觀 412
진광왕 秦廣王 558
진구 塵垢 557
진구 進具 557
진금 眞金 558
진금산 眞金山 558
진금상 眞金像 558
진기약 陳棄藥 557
진나 眞那
China 548
진나 辰那 558
진나 陳那 100, 401, 497, 557, 604
진나달라다 辰那呾邏多 558
진나라 塵那羅 558
진나반다 辰那飯茶 558
진나불다라 辰那弗多羅 558
진다라 眞陀羅 69
진다말니 震多末尼 558
진단 振丹
China 548
진단 振旦 558
China 548
진단 眞丹 558
China 548
진단 眞旦 558
진단 震旦 494, 558
China 548
진달라 眞達羅 365
진도 塵道 558
진도 眞道 559
진동 震動 558
진두 鎭頭 558
진두가 鎭頭迦 558
진두가라 鎭頭迦羅 558
진등류 眞等流 270
진량 津梁 557
진령 振鈴 557
진령 震嶺 558
진로 塵勞 557, 604
진루 塵累 558
진리 眞理 559
진망 塵妄 557
진망 塵網 558
진망 眞妄 559
진망이심 眞妄二心 559
진맥 診脈 287
진명 眞明 559
진묘 塵妙 505
진묘 眞妙 559
진무루지 眞無漏智 559
진문 眞文 559
진문 眞門 559
진미래제 盡未來際 557
진발명성 眞發明性 559
진번뇌 瞋煩惱 558
진법 眞法 559
진법계 眞法戒 280
진법계 眞法界 559
진보 珍寶 558
진보현 眞普賢 559

진불 眞佛 559
진불자 眞佛子 559
진사 塵沙 20, 448, 557
진사 進士 435
진사혹 塵沙惑 295
진상 眞常 559
진색 眞色 316, 559
진설 眞設 559
진성 眞性 350, 559
진성 辰星 586
진성궤 眞性軌 268
진속 眞俗 559
진송 津送 557
진수 眞修 483
진수 鎭守 558
진승 眞乘 559
진시방 盡十方 557
진식 眞識 282, 559
진신 眞身 227, 484, 559, 561
진실 眞實 398, 559, 560
진실 陳實 103
진실(리문) 眞實(理門) 335
진실명 眞實明 559
진실성 眞實性 223
진실제 眞實際 559, 561
진실지 眞實智 559
진실지제극 眞實之際極 398
진심 眞心 146, 447, 484
진심 瞋心 558
진심직설 眞心直說 560
진아 眞我 99, 326, 560
진어 眞語 560
진언 眞言 64, 82, 99, 141, 187, 205, 211, 214, 217, 225, 275, 299, 348, 362, 363, 368, 370, 430, 431, 434, 466, 477, 560, 587, 609, 628
진언구세자 眞言救世者 560
진언비밀 眞言秘密 560
진언승 眞言乘 560
진언종 眞言宗 63, 367, 540, 560
진언지 眞言智 560
진에 瞋恚 558, 585
진에사 瞋恚使 558
진에심 瞋恚心 558
진여 眞如 88, 152, 170, 187, 193, 201, 203, 207, 208, 213, 244, 267, 268, 269, 274, 283, 292, 293, 350, 351, 390, 398, 399, 400, 412, 416, 421, 427, 438, 439, 446, 477, 482, 486, 491, 505, 507, 560, 561, 569, 575, 588, 613
四信五行 252
四種信心 258
진여내훈 眞如內熏 560
진여법성지덕 眞如法性之德 202
진여법신 眞如法身 560
진여삼매 眞如三昧 416, 511, 560
진여수연 眞如隨緣 187, 561
진여식 眞如識 344
진여실상 眞如實相 561
진여심 眞如心 399
진여연기 眞如緣起 561
진여일실 眞如一實 561
진여지리무이무별 眞如之理無二無別 504
진여해 眞如海 561
진역 珍域 558
진연 塵緣 558
진영 眞影 561
진욕 塵欲 557
진월 震越 558
진유식관 眞唯識觀 251
진응이신 眞應二身 484, 561
진인 眞人 561
진인 眞因 561
진자 眞子 220, 561
진적 眞寂 561
진전 眞詮 561
진정 眞淨 561
진정부 眞定俯 126
진정허융 盡淨虛融 557
진제 眞諦 304, 350, 488, 561, 599, 601
世諦 320
진제 眞際 561
진제삼장 眞諦三藏 48, 561, 599
진종 眞宗 258, 332, 511, 561
진주 塵洲 557
진중 珍重 558
진증 眞證 561
진지 振地 557
진지 盡智 370
진지 眞智 491, 561
진진삼매 塵塵三昧 557
진진제 陳眞諦 545
진진찰토 塵塵刹土 557
진찰 塵刹 557
진칠일 盡七日 557
진타대흑 眞陀大黑 106
진표 塵表 558
진해탈 眞解脫 561
진향 塵鄕 558
진화 眞化 561
진화 瞋火 558
진화이신 眞化二身 561
진흥 眞興 189
질 咥 562
질 嫉 323, 410, 562
질 疾 562
질 蒺 562
질 蛭 562
질 質 562
질다 質多 351, 549
질다(야) 質多(耶) 562
질다나 質多羅 419
질다라 質多羅 158, 562
질달나 質怛羅 419
질달라바나 質咀羅婆拏 638
질락희염 叱洛呬談 506
질려 蒺藜 562
질리가 咥哩迦 562
질리약지 咥哩若底 562
질서 疾書 562
질수 蛭數 562
질애 質礙 266, 353
질저 質底 532, 562
질제 質帝 562
질직 質直 562
질투 嫉妬 288
집 執 562
집 集 427, 562
世間法 319
四諦 257
집견 執見 562
집금강 執金剛 179, 549
집금강신 執金剛神 493, 562
집기 集起 562
집기심 集起心 351
집류지 集類智 608
집법인 集法忍 608
집법지 集法智 608
집사 執事 562
집사자국 執師子國 562
집상응염 執相應染 464
집수 執受 562

집심 執心 562
집요 執曜 562
집장 執障 562
집정 執情 562
집제 集諦 274, 490, 562
집중 集衆 562
집지 執持 385, 562
집지식 執持識 376, 562
집진론 集眞論 221
집착 執著 562
집취 執取 81
집취상 執取相 464, 468, 562
집회 集會 562
집회소 集會所 562
징 澄 562
징관 澄觀 112, 562, 587

(ㅊ)
차 且 563
차 借 563
차 叉 17, 563
차 嗟 564
차 嵯 563
차 差 17, 563
차 次 563
차 此 563, 616
차 磋 563
차 遮 488, 563
차 또는 거 車 563
차가(라) 遮迦(羅) 564
차가라 遮伽羅 or 遮迦羅 517
차가월라 遮迦越羅 517
차거 硨磲 143, 564, 584
차계 遮戒 277, 563
차나 叉拏 563
차나 遮那 563
차난 遮難 563
차닉 車匿 567
차다라 差多羅 222, 563, 564
차단 遮斷 563
차라파니 差羅波尼 563
차리니가 差利尼迦 563
차리야 遮唎耶 563
차리야 遮梨夜 563
차마 叉磨 563, 565
차마라 遮摩羅 563
차말라 遮末邏 563
차문다 遮文荼 583
차문다 遮文茶 563
차발라파 車鉢羅婆 563
차별 差別 539, 563
四尋思觀 252
차생 此生 563
차성 遮性 563
차세 此世 563
차세타세락선 此世他世樂禪 54
차수 叉手 563
차식력 借識力 414
차악 遮惡 563
차안 此岸 563, 616
차야 叉耶 563
차야 車也 563
차유 遮遺 563
차익 車匿 563
차전 遮銓 615
차정 遮情 615
차제 次第 563
차제 車帝 563
차제 遮制 563
차제연 次第緣 402, 563
차제정 次第定 422
차조 遮照 563, 598
차죄 遮罪 491, 563
차축 車軸 482, 563
차타가 遮吒迦 563
차탄 嗟嘆 564
차토이근리 此土耳根利 563
차토저술 此土著述 563
차화헌불 借花獻佛 563
차희 且喜 563
착 着 564
착 著 521, 564
착개 著鎧 564
착락 著樂 564
착마폐타 縒摩吠陀 271
착법 著法 564
착상 著想 564
착심 著心 564
착아 著我 564
착의 著衣 564
착의끽반 著衣喫飯 564
착주 涿州 305
찬 撰 564
찬 羼 564
찬 讚 564
찬 贊 564
찬 鑽 564
찬나낭 贊那曩 564
찬녕 贊寧 564
찬두 讚頭 564
찬례 讚禮 564
찬불 讚佛 564
찬송 讚誦 564
찬수구소 鑽水求酥 564
찬저라 羼底羅 564
찬제 羼提 493, 564
찬제라 羼提羅 564
찬제바라밀다 羼提波羅蜜多 494
찬제선인 羼提仙人 564
찬중 讚衆 564
찬지 羼底 493, 564
찬지바라밀다 羼底波羅蜜多 494
찬탄 讚嘆 564
찬탄 讚歎 564
찬패 讚唄 564
찬호 撰號 564
찰 刹 12, 17, 548, 564
찰 擦 564
찰(제)리 刹(帝)利 564
찰간 刹竿 564
찰나 刹那 563, 564
찰나무상 刹那無常 564
찰나삼세 刹那三世 564
찰나생멸 刹那生滅 564
찰다라 刹多羅 564
찰달리야 刹怛利耶 222, 564
찰마 刹摩 564
찰주 刹柱 564
찰진 刹塵 564
찰토 刹土 564
찰한 擦汗 564
찰해 刹海 564
참 參 565
참 慙 585
참 慙 또는 慚 565
참 慚 359
참 懺 565
참 讖 565
참괴 慚愧 584
참당 參堂 565
참두 參頭 565
참라반니 讖羅半尼 565
참마 懺摩 565
참마 讖摩 578
참마의 懺摩衣 565
참문 參問 565
참방 參榜 156

참법 懺法 565
참상 參狀 156
참선 參禪 565
참예 參詣 565
참의 懺儀 565
참전 參前 565
참제 懺除 565
참청 參請 565
참퇴 參退 565
참회 懺悔 379, 563, 565
참후 參後 565
창 唱 565
창 彰 565
창 瘡 565
창 蒼 565
창도 唱導 565
창도사 唱道師 565
창례 唱禮 565
창룡굴 蒼龍窟 565
창명 唱名 565
창문 瘡門 565
창색 蒼色 233
창소지론 彰所知論 606
창식 唱食 565
창야신 創夜神 450
창의 唱衣 565
창적 唱寂 565
채 採 565
채 菜 565
채 蔡 565
채두 菜頭 565
채소 菜蔬 565
채숙씨 採菽氏 565
채화 採花 565
채화 採華 565
채화 蔡華 565
책 柵 565
책 策 565
책가 磔迦 643
책문나 柵門那 565
책수 策修 565
처 處 223, 361, 565
처불퇴 處不退 565
처중 處中 565
척 擲 566
척 蹋 566
척다 徙多 235
척도 蹋倒 566
척악인 擲惡人 566
척지다 擲枳多 566
천 千 566
천 天 279, 347, 534, 566, 568, 606
천 川 566
천 淺 567
천 祆 566
천 穿 567
천 遷 567
천 闡 567
천(계)역사 天(界)力士 567
천가로 天迦盧 567
천개 天蓋 567
천계 天界 567
천계대룡상척경사 天界大龍翔隻慶寺 419
천계역사 天界力士 71
천고 天鼓 567
천고뇌음 天鼓雷音 499
천고뢰음불 天鼓雷音佛 567
천고음 天鼓音 567
천공 天供 32
천관 天冠 567
천교 祆教 566
천구 天口 567
천구 天狗 567
천궁 天宮 566, 567
天台九祖 572
천궁 天弓 533, 568
천궁보장 天宮寶藏 567
천귀 天鬼 568
천근 天根 568
천기 天機 568
천나 闡那 567
천녀 天女 568
천당 天堂 568
천당래자 天堂來者 568
천당지옥 天堂地獄 568
천덕병 天德甁 194, 568
천도 天道 567, 568, 570, 572
천독 天督 568
천동 天童 41, 568
천동산 天潼山 568
천동산 天童山 568
천라국 天羅國 568
천랍 淺臘 567
천략 淺略 567
천룡 天龍 568
천룡야차 天龍夜叉 568
천룡팔부 天龍八部 568, 606
천리구 千里駒 567
천마 天魔 272, 568
천마외도 天魔外道 568
천명 天命 250
천백억신 千百億身 566
천법명문 千法明門 566
천부 天部 568
천부론사 千部論師 567
천부론주 千部論主 567
천부선신 天部善神 568
천불 千佛 566
천불동 千佛洞 112
천불명경 千佛名經 566
천비성 天臂城 568
천사 天使 569
천사 天師 569
천사 天祠 569
천사 祆寺 566
천사나 千闍那 8
천상 天上 569
천상옥녀 天上玉女 158
천상천하유아독존 天上天下唯我獨尊 569
천석가 闡釋迦 567
천선 天仙 569
classification 308
천수 天授 569
천수(천안) 千手(千眼) 566
천수경 千手經 95, 566
천수관음 千手觀音 566
천수궤 千手軌 566
천수다라니 千手陀羅尼 95, 566
천수보리 天須菩提 569
천수왕 天樹王 569
천수천비다라니신주 千手千臂陀羅尼神咒 566
천수천안관세음보살대...다라니경 千手千眼觀世音菩薩大...陀羅尼經 566
천수천안관세음보살모다라니신경 千手千眼觀世音菩薩姥陀羅尼身經 566
천수천안관음 千手千眼觀音 566
천수천안광대원만무애대비심다라니경 千手千眼廣大圓滿無礙大悲心陀羅尼經 566
천수천안대자대비관음보살 千手千眼大慈大悲觀音菩薩 566

천수천안의궤경 千手千眼儀軌經 566
천승 天乘 421, 569
천시아귀 川施餓鬼 566
천식 天識 569
천식 天食 569
천신 天神 534, 566, 569
천신지기 天神地祇 569
천악 天樂 569
천안 天眼 357, 362, 374, 569, 570
천안(지증)통 天眼(智證)通 422
천안력 天眼力 570
천안명 天眼明 273, 570
천안지 天眼智 570
천안지(증)통 天眼智(證)通 570
천안지통원 天眼智通願 570
천안천 千眼天 566
천안천비관세음 千眼千臂觀世音 566
천안통 天眼通 570
천애 天愛 570
천어 天語 570
천여시 千如是 566
천연지진리 天然之眞理 571
천엽대 千葉臺 566
천옥 天獄 570
천왕 天王 133, 566, 570, 571
천왕당 天王堂 570
천왕문반야 天王問般若 168
천왕여래 天王如來 570
천유 天有 570
천의 天衣 570
천의불천세 天衣拂千歲 570
천의수 天意樹 568, 570
천이(지증)통 天耳(智證)通 422
천이(통) 天耳(通) 570
천이객 穿耳客 567
천이백설공덕 千二百舌功德 566
천이백오십인 千二百五十人 566
천이백의공덕 千二百意功德 566
천이백이공덕 千二百耳功德 566
천이승 穿耳僧 567
천이지(통) 天耳智(通) 570
천이지증통 天耳智證通 570
천이지통원 天耳智通願 570
천인 天人 570
천인 賤人 647
천인도사 天人道師 108, 570
천인사 天人師 241, 371, 570
천인산화신상 天人散花身上 570
천인장부 天人丈夫 460
천자 天子 57, 141, 566, 571
천자(업)마 天子(業)魔 571
천제 天帝 496, 571
천제 闡提 457, 567
천제산 天悌山 571
천제생려태 天帝生驢胎 571
천제석성 天帝釋城 571
천존 天尊 211, 224, 571
천주 天主 571
천주 天住 258
천주 天酒 11
천주교법 天主教法 571
천주제 天主帝 496
천중 天衆 571
천중오상 天衆五相 571
천중천 天中天 571
천지경 天地鏡 571
천지여아동근 天地與我同根 507
천진 天眞 571
천진독랑 天眞獨朗 571
천진불 天眞佛 571
천천 千泉 566
천축 天竺 494, 568, 578
천축(국) 天竺(國) 571
천축구의 天竺九儀 572
천축국 天竺國 304
천축삼시 天竺三時 572
천축삼제 天竺三際 572
천축오산 天竺五山 572
천취 天趣 468, 568, 572
천친 天親 164, 179, 382, 519, 572, 587
世親 320
천친정토론 天親淨土論 266
천타 闡陀 567
천탁가 闡鐸迦 563, 567
천태 天台 99, 187, 370, 427, 434, 466, 572, 587, 609
천태(대사) 天台(大師) 555
천태구조 天台九祖 572
천태구종 天台九宗 54
천태대사 天台大師 572
천태덕소국사 天台德韶國師 573
천태사교 天台四教 239, 573
천태사교의 天台四教儀 534, 573
천태산 天台山 572
天悌山 571
천태삼교 天台三教 573
천태삼부 天台三部 573
천태율 天台律 573
천태종 天台宗 188, 367, 475, 540, 544, 573
천태팔교 天台八教 573
천택가 闡擇迦 567
천폭륜상 千輻輪相 567
천행 天行 573
천향 天香 573
천화 千化 566
천화 天畫 574
천화 天華 211, 573
천화 遷化 567
천황 天皇 574
천후 天后 113, 130, 543, 574
철 徹 574
철 鐵 574
철륜 鐵輪 574
철륜왕 鐵輪王 574
철발 鐵鉢 574
철성 鐵城 574
철심 徹心 574
철안 鐵眼 208
철위산 鐵圍山 574
철제 鐵際 574
철찰 鐵札 574
첨 檐 574
첨 添 574
첨 瞻 574
첨 諂 460, 574
첨곡 諂曲 574
첨박 瞻博 522
첨박(가) 瞻博(迦) 574
첨병 瞻病 574
첨복 瞻蔔 522
첨복(가) 瞻匐(迦) 574
첨부 瞻部 406, 574
첨앙 瞻仰 574
첨탁 簷鐸 199
첨파 瞻婆 574
첨파 瞻波 522, 574
첨파국 瞻波國 574
첨파성 瞻婆城 574
첨품 添品 574
첨품묘법연화경 添品妙法蓮華經 146
첨풍 瞻風 574
첩 牒 574

첩 貼 574
첩친 貼嚫 574
청 淸 574
청 聽 575
청 請 575
청 靑 420, 575
청가 請假 575
청경관음 靑頸觀音 575
청교 聽敎 575
청귀 靑鬼 575
청덕 淸德 603
청두 靑頭 575
청량 淸凉 342
청량 淸凉 or 淸涼 574
청량 징관 淸凉澄觀 427, 639
청량국사 淸凉國師 574
청량금강 淸凉金剛 450
청량사 淸凉寺 574
청량산 淸凉山 157, 413, 574
청량월 淸凉月 574
청량지 淸凉地 574
청련 靑蓮 575
청룡 靑龍 575
청면금강 靑面金剛 575
청명 淸明 574
청목 靑木 569
청목 靑目 575
청문 聽聞 575
청백 淸白 575
청범 淸梵 574
청변 淸辯 232, 575
청불 請佛 575
청성 聽聲 287
청소 請召 158, 419
청신남 淸信男 574
청신녀 淸信女 574
청신사 淸身士 574
청심 靑心 575
청양 淸揚 574
청우 請雨 575
청원 淸遠 278
청원 靑原 312
청의 聽衣 487
청익 請益 575
청재 淸齋 575
청절 請折 575
청정 淸淨 574, 605
청정각해 淸淨覺海 575
청정관 淸淨觀 412
청정광명신 淸淨光明身 574
청정광불 淸淨光佛 378
청정법 淸淨法 574
청정법계 淸淨法界 574
청정법안 淸淨法眼 574
청정본연 淸淨本然 574
청정식 淸淨識 575
청정심 淸淨心 574
청정업처 淸淨業處 574
청정연화명왕앙구사 淸淨蓮華明王央俱捨 213
청정원 淸淨園 574
청정원 淸淨遠 237
청정인 淸淨人 574
청정정선 淸淨淨禪 54
청정조유 淸淨調柔 585
청정지 淸淨智 574
청정진여 淸淨眞如 575, 588
청정최승 淸淨最勝 589
청정해탈삼매 淸淨解脫三昧 575
청제녀 靑提女 575
청풍무형시역가착 淸風無形是亦可捉 400
청하 淸河 575
청하 靑河 165, 575
체 剃 575
체 替 575
체 逮 575
체 體 88, 201, 269, 281, 428, 439, 505, 575, 594
체공 體空 87, 575
체구 體具 315
체내방편 體內方便 174, 575
체달 體達 575
체대 體大 269, 575
체도 剃刀 575
체두 剃頭 575
체로 體露 575
체리희음 體哩呬淫 506
체무부재 體無不在 88
체문 體文 514
체바달다 禘婆達多 534
체발 剃髮 575
체법 體法 575
체비리 體毘履 575
체비리 體毘履 or 體毘裏 591
체상 體相 291, 575
체상용 體相用 575
체성 體性 575
체수라시 諦殊羅施 534
체승 替僧 575
체야 逮夜 575
체여 體如 362
체외방편 體外方便 174, 575
체용 體用 575
체지 體智 575
초 初 546, 576
초 招 576
초 楚 576
초 焦 576
초 草 576
초 超 577
초 醮 576
초 鈔 576
초 鞘 51
초 麨 576
초강왕 楚江王 576
초경 初更 576
초과 初果 576
초과 超過 577
초과향 初果向 576
초능변 初能變 576
초당 草堂 576
초당사 草堂寺 576
초두라 招杜羅 365
초목 草木 576
초목성불 草木成佛 576
초반 草飯 576
초발심 初發心 576
초발심시변성정각 初發心時便成正覺 576
초복지비니 草覆地毘尼 583
초선 初禪 55
초선범천 初禪梵天 576
초선정 初禪定 576
초선천 初禪天 250, 301, 576
초세 超世 577
초소 招召 419
초수음 超受陰 526
초승기 初僧祇 576
초시교 初時敎 576
초심 初心 576
초암 草庵 576
초야 初夜 576
초열대초열 焦熱大焦熱 576
초열지옥 576
초월 超越 577
초위 初位 576

ㄱ ㄴ ㄷ ㄹ ㅁ ㅂ ㅅ ㅇ ㅈ ㅊ ㅋ ㅌ ㅍ ㅎ 찾아보기

초일분 初日分 576
초일왕 超日王 577
초일월광불 超日月光佛 378
초자 草子 13
초제 招提 576
초좌 草座 576
초주 初住 188, 576
초중후 初中後 576
초지 初地 188, 356, 425, 464, 556, 576
초지 草指 550
초지견도 初地見道 466
초지이상 初地以上 553
초찰나식 初刹那識 576
초창 草創 576
초천 草釧 550
초팔 超八 577
초혜 草鞋 576
초혼 招魂 576
초환 草環 576
초환희지 初歡喜地 576
촉 囑 577
촉 觸 80, 104, 365, 411, 417, 419, 511, 577
촉 髑 577
촉금강 觸金剛 207
촉독 觸毒 577
촉락 觸樂 577
촉례 觸禮 577
촉루 囑累 577
촉루 髑髏 577
촉병 觸瓶 577
촉식 觸食 252, 577
촉예 觸穢 577
촉욕 觸欲 577
촉인 觸因 577
촉종 觸鐘 577
촉지 觸指 577
촉진 觸塵 577
촉통 觸桶 577
촌 寸 577
촌사불괘 寸絲不掛 577
총 叢 577
총 塚 577
총 總 577
총 聰 577
총공 總供 577
총규 叢規 577
총림 叢林 173, 327, 577
총명 聰明 141, 577
총명론 總明論 577
총민 聰敏 161
총별 總別 577
총보 總報 486
총보업 總報業 495, 577
총상 總相 483, 577
총상계 總相戒 577
총상념주 總相念住 251
총상념처 總相念處 241
총업 總業 193
총원 總願 577
총의 總依 193
총지 總持 577
총지문 總持門 577
최 最 578
최(말)후 最(末)後 578
최고현광안장여래 最高顯廣眼藏如來 102
최상 最上 578
최상대실지 最上大悉地 578
최상승 最上乘 416, 578
최상천왕 最上天王 476
최쇄불정 摧碎佛頂 418
최승 最勝 240, 578
최승승 最勝乘 578
최승존 最勝尊 578
최승진여 最勝眞如 370
최정각 最正覺 578
최후념 最後念 578
최후생 最後生 578
최후신 最後身 578
최후심 最後心 578
최후십념 最後十念 578
추 墜 578
추 抽 578
추 推 578
추 椎 578
추 樞 578
추 芻 578
추 蒭 578
추 追 578
추 醜 578
추 錐 72
추 雛 578
추 鶖 578
추 麤 456, 469, 578
추(로)자 鶖(鷺)子 578
추각 推却 578
추개 墜芥 578
추공귀본 推功歸本 578
추구 推究 578
추로자 秋露子 578
추루 醜陋 578
추마 芻摩 or 蒭摩 578
추마 菆摩 578
추마 蒭摩 578
추마가 芻摩迦 578
추목 醜目 578
추복 追福 578
추상 麤相 578
추선 追善 578
추수 追修 578
추승 雛僧 578
추악어 麤惡語 578
추악원 麤惡苑 254, 578
추안 醜眼 578
추언 麤言 578
추엄 追嚴 578
추요 樞要 578
추인 麤人 578
추천 追薦 578
추첨 抽籤 578
추탈 抽脫 578
축 畜 579
축 祝 579
축 竺 578
축 逐 579
축건 竺乾 578
축경 竺經 578
축기돈 逐機頓 579
축담마라찰 竺曇摩羅察 578
축법란 竺法蘭 5, 185, 579
축법력 竺法力 579
축법호 竺法護 578
축불념 竺佛念 248
축불도징 竺佛圖澄 215
축생 畜生 579
축생계 畜生界 579
축생도 畜生道 579
축생인 畜生因 579
축생취 畜生趣 468, 579
축섭마등 竺葉摩騰 579
축성 祝聖 579
축찰시라 竺刹尸羅 85, 579
축토 竺土 578
출 出 284, 513, 579
출가 出家 520, 579

출가아차리 出家阿遮利 385
출가인 出家人 579
출가입도 出家入道 512
출가행 出假行 579
출기 出期 579
출대 出隊 579
출대가제 出隊迦提 579
출도 出道 579
출도보리 出到菩提 417
출리 出離 579
출리번뇌 出離煩惱 579
출반 出飯 302, 579
출불신혈 出佛身血 579
출생 出生 579
출생사안 出生死眼 362
출성 出聖 579
출세 出世 579
출세(간)설부 出世(間)說部 580
출세(간)어언부 出世(間)語言部 580
출세간 出世間 580
　四諦 257
출세간교 出世間教 478
출세간단 出世間壇 478
출세간도 出世間道 580
출세간바라밀 出世間波羅蜜 290
출세간반야 出世間般若 480
출세간법 出世間法 580
출세간상상바라밀 出世間上上波羅蜜 290
출세간상상장 出世間上上藏 429
출세간상상지 出世間上上智 291, 292
출세간승 出世間乘 319
출세간인과 出世間因果 490
출세간지 出世間智 291, 292
출세과 出世果 579
출세대사 出世大事 579
출세복 出世服 580
출세본회 出世本懷 579
출세부 出世部 580
출세사 出世舍 237, 580
출세심 出世心 579
출세업 出世業 580
출세장 出世藏 429
출식 出息 580
출식부대입 出息不待入 580
출심 出心 283
출요경 出曜經 580
출전 出纏 399
출전공양 出纏供養 489
출전진여 出纏眞如 487, 580
출정 出定 580
출죄 出罪 50
출진 出塵 580
출진 出陣 580
출체 出體 580
출출세간 出出世間 580
출현 出現 580
출혜 出慧 580
충 忠 580
충 虫 580
충 蟲 580
충만일체지 充滿一切智 370
충식 蟲食 580
충심 忠心 580
충심경 忠心經 545
췌 揣 83
취 取 21, 80, 365, 581
취 吹 581
취 毳 580
취 聚 581
　四諦 257
취 臭 581
취 趣 580
취 醉 580
취 鷲 580
취계 聚戒 469
취과 取果 581
취과 醉果 136
취광 吹光 581
취구 臭口 47
취구귀 臭口鬼 581
취대 鷲臺 580
취두(산) 鷲頭(山) 580
취락 聚落 482
취말 聚沫 581
취모 吹毛 581
취모귀 臭毛鬼 581
취무 趣無 386
취법나 吹法螺 581
취봉 鷲峯 580
취봉게 鷲峯偈 580
취산 鷲山 580
취상 取相 581
취상 醉象 580
취상참 取相懺 581
취상회 取相悔 292
취시 就是 546
취시공 就是空 289
취악 鷲嶽 580
취암 鷲巖 580
취여 取與 581
취온 取蘊 581
취의 毳衣 580
취적 趣寂 580
취제 聚諦 274, 581
취지색가 聚底色迦 329
취집 聚集 581
취차어 取次語 581
취착 取著 581
취향 趣向 195
측 厠 581
치 値 582
치 治 582
치 熾 581
치 痴 270, 278, 581
치 癡 276, 414, 582
치 緇 581
치 置 582
치 耻 581
치 雉 581
치 齒 582
치구 痴狗 581
치구림화 雉救林火 581
치국천 治國天 549, 582
치답 置答 582
치도 緇徒 581
치독 痴毒 581
치등 痴燈 581
치류 緇流 581
치림 緇林 581
치림 齒臨 506
치만 痴慢 581
치망 痴網 582
치목 齒木 582
치문 緇門 581
치문반 緇文班 582
치미 痴迷 582
치박 痴縛 582
치범 痴凡 581
치사 痴使 581
치생 治生 582
치성광불 熾盛光佛 581
치소모대 耻小慕大 581
치수 痴水 581
치심 痴心 581

치암 痴闇 582
치애 痴愛 581
치우 値遇 582
치의 緇衣 581
치인 齒印 582
치자 痴子 581
치정 痴定 581
치지주 治地住 368, 582
치취 痴取 581
치혹 痴惑 581
치효 鴟梟 602
치후 痴猴 581
칙 則 582
칙 勅 582
칙극 則劇 582
칙명 勅命 582
친 嚫 582
친 親 582
친교(사) 親教(師) 582
친권 親眷 582
친근처 親近處 237
친금 嚫金 582
친리 親里 602
친물 嚫物 582
친상 親想 279
친시 嚫施 582
친애 親愛 582
친연 親緣 286
친우 親友 582
친자 嚫資 582
친재 嚫財 582
친전 嚫錢 582
친척 親戚 582
칠 七 425, 582
칠 漆 582
칠가행 七加行 582
칠가행(위) 七加行(位) 584
칠가행위 七加行位 589
칠각 七覺 7
칠각분 七覺分 582, 584
칠각지 七覺支 78, 196, 285, 582, 584
칠갈마 七羯磨 582, 589
칠견 七見 582
칠공 七空 582
칠과도품 七科道品 584
칠과만 七過慢 583
칠구 七垢 582
칠구지불모존 七俱胝佛母尊 582
칠궁의왕 七躬醫王 582, 584
칠금산 七金山 51, 66, 582
칠난 七難 583, 587
칠담 七曇 583
칠대 七大 88, 484, 583
칠대부 七大夫 589
칠등각지 七等覺支 583, 584
칠례 七例 587
칠마달리 七摩怛里 583
칠만 七慢 224, 583
칠멸쟁 七滅諍 481
칠멸쟁법 七滅諍法 583, 584
칠모천 七母天 583
칠몽(경) 七夢(經) 583
칠무상도 七無上道 583
칠미 七微 374, 583
칠방편 七方便 582
칠방편(위) 七方便(位) 584
칠방편위 七方便位 589
칠백결집 七白結集 584
칠백현성 七百賢聖 584
칠법 七法 584
칠법재 七法財 584, 587
칠보 七寶 62, 143, 264, 524, 564, 584, 588
칠보리보 七菩提寶 584
칠보리분 七菩提分 8, 77, 527, 582, 583, 584, 585, 589
칠보사 七步蛇 584
칠보수림 七寶樹林 584
칠불 七佛 584
칠불가피 七不可避 584
칠불약사 七佛藥師 582, 584
칠비니 七毘尼 584
칠사 七使 582, 585
칠사부 七士夫 589
칠사부취 七士夫趣 587
칠사수신 七事隨身 585
칠생 七生 585, 586
칠선 七善 585
칠성 七星 585
칠성 七聖 589
칠성 七聲 585, 587
칠성(위) 七聖(位 584
칠성(위) 七聖(位) 589
칠성각 七星閣 585
칠성각 七聖覺 585
칠성인 七聖人 589
칠승 七僧 585
칠승법회 七僧法會 585
칠승사 七勝事 585, 587
칠승재 七僧齋 585
칠식십명 七識十名 585
칠식주 七識住 53, 585
칠심계 七心界 585
칠심신 七深信 459
칠십 七十 585
칠십삼존 七十三尊 585
칠십오 七十五 585
칠십오법 七十五法 287, 585
칠십이세 七十二歲 586
칠십이자 七十二字 586
칠십이천 七十二天 586
칠여래 七如來 586
칠여래보탑 七如來寶塔 586
칠역 七逆 588
칠역(죄) 七逆(罪) 586
칠엽암 七葉巖 586
칠예구 七例句 586
칠요 七曜 314, 437, 586
칠유 七喩 586
칠유 七有 498, 585, 586, 587
칠유의복업 七有依福業 586
칠자 七子 586
칠자매 七姉妹 583
칠장부 七丈夫 587
칠재 七財 587
칠재난 七災難 587
칠전구례 七轉九例 585, 587
칠전구예 七轉九例 586
칠전도 七顚倒 523, 587
칠정 七情 587
칠정화 七淨華 587
칠조 七祖 587
칠조(가사) 七條(袈裟) 587
칠조(의) 七條(衣) 587
칠조성교 七祖聖教 587
칠종 七宗 587
칠종무상 七種無上 583, 585, 587
칠종무상 七種無常 587
칠종반 七種般 588
칠종변 七種辯 125, 588
칠종보시 七種布施 587
칠종부정 七種不淨 587
칠종사 七種捨 587
칠종생사 七種生死 587
칠종식 七種食 588
칠종어 七種語 588

칠종예불 七種禮佛 587
칠종의 七種衣 588
칠종자성 七種自性 588
칠종참회심 七種懺悔心 587
칠중 七衆 55, 588
칠중익수 七衆溺水 588
칠중인 七衆人 588
칠중행수 七重行樹 588
칠증(사) 七證(師) 588
칠지 七地 425, 464, 466
칠지 七支 588
칠지 七知 588
칠지업 七支業 588
칠지염송 七支念誦 588
칠지염송수행법 七支念誦隨行法 588
칠진 七珍 588
칠진여 七眞如 588
칠차죄 七遮罪 588
칠처 七處 285
칠처구회 七處九會 588
칠처팔회 七處八會 588
칠처평만상 七處平滿相 588
칠최승 七最勝 589
칠취 七趣 589
칠치 七治 582, 589
칠칠 七七 589
칠칠기 七七忌 589
칠칠재 七七齋 589
칠통 漆桶 582
칠팔행 七八行 589
칠현(위) 七賢(位) 584, 589
칠현칠성 七賢七聖 587, 589
칠화 七華 587, 589
침 寝 589
침 沈 589
침 沉 589
침 針 589
침(수)향 沈(水)香 589
침개 針芥 589
침공 沈空 589
침공 針孔 589
침구 鍼口 47
침구귀 針口鬼 589
침단 沈檀 589
침당 寝堂 589
침명 沈冥 589
침모귀 針毛鬼 589
침봉 針鋒 589
침수향 沉水香 387
침향 沈香 373
칭 秤 364
칭 稱 589
칭명 稱名 589
칭명잡행 稱名雜行 589
칭불 稱佛 589
칭의화 稱意華 589
칭찬 稱讚 589
칭찬정토불섭수경 稱讚淨土拂攝受經 531

(ㅋ)

쾌 快 590
쾌락 快樂 590, 605
쾌목왕 快目王 590
큰방 590
큰스님 590

(ㅌ)

타 591
타 馱 593
타 他 591
타 佗 591
타 咃 591
타 咤 591
타 墮 81, 591
타 打 591
타 拖 591
타 陀 591
타 陁 591
타(나)연나 馱(那)演那 593
타공 打供 591
타기 他己 591
타기니 馱器尼 593
타길니 吒吉尼 82
타나 他那 591
타나 吒那 591
타나갈책가 馱那羯磔迦 594
타남 馱南 593
타니대수 拖泥帶水 591
타도 馱都 594
타도 馱都 25
타라 陀羅 603
타라 陀羅 or 陁羅 134
타라발지 墮羅鉢底 591
타력 他力 479, 515, 591
타력교 他力敎 492
타력염불 他力念佛 591
타력종 他力宗 591
타리사 陀利奢 284
타마 馱摩 593
타마 馱摩 86
타면의 打眠衣 591
타박야 馱縛若 593
타반 打飯 591
타보 他寶 591
타비라부 他鞞羅部 299, 591
타비리 他毘利 591
타비리여부 他毘梨與部 299, 591
타삭가 馱索迦 593
타생 他生 591
타성일편 打成一片 591
타세 他世 591
타수용 他受用 331
타수용신 他受用身 252, 283, 338
타수용토 他受用土 421, 592
타승죄 他勝罪 592
타심(지증)통 他心(智證)通 422
타심지 他心智 370, 592
타심지통 他心智通 592
타심통 他心通 592
타연나 馱衍那 593
타왕 吒王 25
타인 他因 240
타정 打靜 591
타좌 打坐 591
타지 吒枳 360
타청 打聽 591
타파 咤婆 591
타판 打板 591
타포 打包 591
타화 他化 606
타화(자재)천 他化(自在)天 592
타화자재천 他化自在天 127, 162, 164, 438, 468
타화자재천마 他化自在天魔 604
타화자재천자마 他化自在天子魔 272
탁 卓 592
탁 托 592
탁 拆 592
탁 濁 432, 592
탁 鐸 323, 592
탁 拓 592
탁갈라 鐸曷攞 592
탁겁 濁劫 592
탁구가 拆句迦 517

탁난 濁亂 592
탁리마 託吏麼 550
탁림라 拓林羅 592
탁마타나 拆摩馱那 592
탁발 托鉢 592, 624
탁사마 託史麼 550
탁생 托生 592
탁석 卓錫 592
탁세 濁世 592
탁악세 濁惡世 592
탁악처 濁惡處 592
탁업 濁業 592
탁탑천왕 托塔天王 592
탁태 托胎 592
탁투제사 拓鬪提舍 576
탄 嘆 593
탄 彈 592
탄 憚 592
탄 歎 592
탄 炭 592
탄 誕 592
탄다 彈多 592
탄다 憚哆 592
탄다가슬다 憚哆家瑟多 592
탄다니슬체 彈多抳瑟搋 592
탄다락가 彈多落迦 83, 592
탄덕 嘆德 593
탄두 炭頭 592
탄령 嘆靈 593
탄불 嘆佛 593
탄생회 誕生會 592
탄지 彈指 592
탄택가 彈宅迦 592
탄택가림 彈宅迦林 592
탄파나 歎波那 592
탈 奪 593
탈 脫 279, 593, 619
탈사 脫闍 593
탈일체중생정기 奪一切衆生精氣 357
탈정귀 奪精鬼 593
탈진착폐 脫珍著幣 593
탈체 脫體 593
탈혼귀 奪魂鬼 593
탐 探 593
탐 貪 81, 207, 265, 270, 276, 278, 355, 410, 414, 433, 593
탐(욕)사 貪(欲)使 593
탐견 貪見 593
탐결 貪結 593
탐독 貪毒 593
탐랑 貪狼 593
탐마율저 耽摩栗底 593
탐마율지 耽摩栗底 593
탐박 貪縛 593
탐번뇌 貪煩惱 593
탐석 貪惜 593
탐수 探水 593
탐수 貪水 593
탐습 貪習 593
탐습인 貪習因 593
탐애 貪愛 593
desire referred to as mother 204
탐에치 貪恚痴 593
탐염 貪染 593
탐욕 貪欲 288, 593
탐욕개 貪欲蓋 593
탐욕즉시도 貪欲卽是道 593
탐욕진에우치 貪欲瞋恚愚痴 593
탐진치 貪瞋痴 111, 143, 165, 178, 407, 593
탐진치만의 貪瞋痴慢疑 178
탐착 貪著 593
탐탁 貪濁 593
탐포라 耽餔羅 86
탑 塔 548, 593
탑령 塔鈴 427
탑묘 塔廟 593
탑상 塔像 593
탑인 塔印 106
탑파 塔婆 221, 593
탕 湯 593
탕두 湯頭 593
태 台 594
태 太 594
태 泰 594
태 胎 413, 594
태 駄 593
태가 台家 594
태고 太古 594
태고사 太古寺 594
태고위생 太孤危生 594
태고집 太古集 594
태교 台敎 594
태궁 胎宮 192, 594
태금 胎金 594
태내오위 胎內五位 594
태대일 胎大日 594
태도 台徒 594
태도 台道 594
태란습화 胎卵濕化 594
태무 太武 274
태백 太白 141, 586
태백산 太白山 419, 568
태산 泰山 594
태생 胎生 250, 594, 614
태악 台岳 594
태야 迨夜 100
태양 太陽 586
태옥 胎獄 594
태외오위 胎外五位 594
태자 太子 594
태자쇄호경 太子刷護經 594
태자화휴경 太子和休經 594
태장 胎臟
four degrees 242
태장 胎藏 496
태장계 胎藏界 62, 66, 102, 278, 395, 430, 508, 594, 607
태종 台宗 594
태추생 太麤生 594
태허공 太虛空 594
태현 太賢 or 大賢 595
태형 台衡 594
택 擇 595
택 宅 595
택력 擇力 595
택멸 擇滅 50, 329, 595
택법각지 擇法覺支 584
택법보리분 擇法菩提分 584
택법안 擇法眼 595
택법학지 擇法學支 595
택식 宅識 377
택유안 擇乳眼 595
택지 擇地 595
토 兎 596
토 吐 596
토 土 53, 595
토각 兎角 596
토라차 土羅遮 596
토루 吐淚 596
토만두 土饅頭 234, 596
토모진 兎毛塵 596
토묘 兎卯 365
토사가지 土砂加持 596
토사공양 土砂供養 596

토성 土星 236, 586, 595
토지 土地 550
토지당 土地堂 595
토지신 土地神 595
토지풍경 土地諷經 595
토초 土麨 596
토파 土波 596
통 桶 596
통 通 268, 477, 478, 487, 584, 587, 596, 638
통교 通教 27, 84, 98, 205, 215, 239, 245, 267, 318, 416, 485, 575, 596, 602, 621
　천태삼교 573
통교지성연보삼인 通教之聲緣菩三人 584
통달 通達 596
통달보리심 通達菩提心 596
통달심 通達心 596
통달위 通達位 425
통도 通途 596
통도사 通度寺 596
통두 桶頭 596
통력 通力 414, 596, 636
통리 通利 596
통리원 統理院 597
통명혜 通明慧 597
통별이서 通別二序 597
통불 通佛 210
통서 通序 597
통야 通夜 597
통염불 通念佛 597
통출 通出 423
통행 通行 597
통혜 通慧 597
통혹 通惑 597
통화 通化 597
통회 通會 597
퇴 堆 597
퇴 槌 597
퇴 退 597
퇴굴 退屈 597
퇴대 退大 597
퇴돈 槌敦 597
퇴몰 退沒 597
퇴압 堆壓 554
퇴압지옥 堆壓地獄 597
퇴전 退轉 597
퇴좌 退座 597
퇴척귀 槌惕鬼 597
퇴척귀 堆惕鬼 597
퇴침 槌砧 597
투 偸 597
투 妬 597
투 投 597
투 鬪 597
투기 投機 597
투도 偸盜 597
투라 妬羅 114
투란(차야) 偸蘭(遮耶) 597
투란차 偸蘭遮 118, 596
투로파 妬路婆 114
투불남 妬不男 597
투슬다 鬪瑟多 114
투승 鬪勝 597
투신 投身 597
투연 投淵 469, 597
투자 投子 597
투쟁 鬪諍 597
투쟁왕 鬪諍王 597
투파 偸婆 593, 597
투화 投華 597
특 特 597
특승 特勝 597
특의나가타 特欹拏伽陀 597
특존 特尊 597

(ㅍ)

파 叵 598
파 婆 166, 398
파 巴 598
파 帕 598
파 播 599
파 波 598
파 皤 598
파 破 598
파 簸 598
파 罷 598
파 頗 598
파(라)사발제 波(邏)闍鉢提 600
파(라야)질지가 波(羅夜)質胝迦 164
파(뢰)야 波(賴)若 168
파(률)습바 波(栗)濕縛 599
파(리)가라 波利伽羅 600
파(사)현(정) 破(邪)顯(正) 599
파가파 婆呵婆 284
파계 破戒 598
파괴 破壞 598
파괴선 破壞善 598
파구려 波鳩蠡 166
파극사파 帕克斯巴 598
파나사 波那娑 599
파날라파날마세 婆捺囉婆捺麽洗 599
파남 婆南 635
파노 波奴 599
파능삼전어 巴陵三轉語 598
파니 播尼 599
파니 波尼 599
파니 波抳 599
파니니 波你尼 600
파니다 頗尼多 598
파니람 波尼藍 599
파달극산 巴達克山 172
파달라 波怛囉 or 播怛囉 171
파담마 波曇摩 599
파두마 波頭摩 599, 610
파두마색니 波頭摩色尼 599
파라 波羅 179, 612, 616
파라 頗羅 35, 598
파라가 波羅伽 599
파라가 波羅迦 599
파라가라 波羅伽羅 599
파라리불다라 波羅利弗多羅 601
파라말타 波羅末陀 561, 599
파라미다 播囉弭多 163
파라부 波羅赴 446
파라사니 波羅舍尼 163
파라사화 波羅奢華 599
파라새 波羅塞 20
파라실 波羅悉 600
파라아질다 婆羅阿迭多 643
파라양 波羅孃 168
파라우나마세 叵囉虞那麽洗 598
파라우니 頗攞遇抳 598
파라월 波羅越 599
파라일니가 波羅逸尼柯 164
파라제비 波羅提毘 or 波羅梯毘 599
파라타 頗羅墮 or 頗羅陀 598
파라파 婆邏婆 284
파라파가라밀다라 波羅頗迦羅蜜多羅 599
파라파바지 波羅頗婆底 599
파라필리타가사나 婆羅必利他伽闍那 179

파라필율탁흘나 婆羅必栗託仡那 179
파라하마 波羅賀磨 93
파랍부다 簸臘復多 598
파랑 波浪 600
파려 玻瓈 584
파려 頗黎 598, 600
파련불 巴蓮弗 601
파련불 巴連佛 598
파뢰타 波賴他 171
파루나 婆樓那 335
파루사가 波樓沙迦 163
파륜 波崙 600
파륵구나 頗勒具那 or 頗勒窶拏 598
파륵구나 頗勒窶拏 598
파륵나 叵勒拏 598
파리 巴利 45, 598
파리 波利 600
파리 波離 600
파리 玻璃 600
파리 皤利 598
파리 頗梨 598, 600
파리나 波利那 284
파리나 波夷羅 600
파리닐박남 波利暱縛喃 600
파리바라사가 簸利婆羅闍迦 598
파리바자가 簸利婆闍迦 168
파리수 波利樹 600
파리열박남 波利涅縛南 600
파리열반나 波利涅般那 167
파리왕 玻璃王 600
파리의다라 波里衣多羅 600
파리질(다)라 波利質(多)羅 600
파리질다 波利質多 569
파리타 波利陀 284
파리파사 波利婆娑 600
파립 破立 598
파마 播磨 599
파마 破魔 599
파마나 波摩那 386
파모 波暮 599
파문 破門 599
파미니 波彌尼 600
파미라 波謎羅 600
파반낭결사파 播般曩結使波 194
파발라유 波鉢羅由 171
파법 破法 598
파비 巴鼻 or 把鼻 or 巴臂 598
파비 波卑 600
파비 波鞞 600
파비(야) 波卑(夜) 568
파비면 波卑面 600
파비연 波卑椽 600
파비연 波卑緣 600
파사 播捨 599
파사 波奢 599
파사 波斯 388, 600
파사(닉) 波斯(匿) 600
파사닉 波斯匿 171
파사론 婆沙論 104, 280
파사사다 婆舍斯多 486
파사슬차 婆私瑟侘 96
파사파 巴思巴 598
파사파제 波闍波提 600
파살제 破薩提 599
파상종 破相宗 258, 290, 538, 598
파성종 破性宗 258
파수밀 婆須蜜 486
파수반두 婆藪槃豆 or 婆修槃豆 572
파수반타 婆藪槃陀 572
파수발다 播輸鉢多 599
파수발다 波輸鉢多 599
파순 波旬 568, 600
파순(유) 波旬(踰) 600
파술 波戍 600
파승 破僧 598
파시 波嘶 600
파실제마 跛室制麼 304
파안미소 破顔微笑 599
파암만원 破闇滿願 599
파야 波耶 600
파야제 波夜提 164
파약치 波藥致 164
파연나 波演那 or 波衍那 600
파유 破有 598
파율습박 波栗溼縛 486
파의질구 波疑質姤 600
파이라 波夷羅 365
파일 波逸 612
파자사 波刺斯 600
파자사 波刺私 600
파자자부 皤雌子部 598
파재 破齋 599
파정 破正 598
파정명 破正命 598
파제 波帝 600
파지 婆志 162
파지가 頗胝迦 598
파지라사니 波胝羅舍尼 163
파지옥 破地獄 598
파집 破執 598
파차 波叉 600
파참 罷參 598
파치가 婆致迦 334, 601
파치가 波哆迦 601
파치가 頗置迦 598
파타 婆吒 235
파타 播陀 172
파타 波陀 172
파타겁 波陀劫 165
파타라 波吒羅 601
파타리 波吒釐 598
파타리(자) 波吒釐(子) 601
파타리불 波吒利弗 601
파타리야 波吒梨耶 601
파파 波波 601
파파 波頗 599, 601
파파겁겁 波波劫劫 601
파파라 波波羅 601
파파리 波波利 601
파파리 波波梨 601
파파리 波波離 601
파파리엄파 波波梨奄婆 601
파하 破夏 598
파화나 婆和邏 284
파화리 波和利 601
파화합승 破和合僧 598
판 判 601
판 板 601
판 瓣 601
판 辦 601
판교 判教 601, 629
판도 辦道 601
판사 辦事 601
판석 判釋 601
판향 瓣香 601
팔 八 601
팔가 八家 609
팔가구종 八家九宗 609
팔각 八覺 602
팔건 八乾 602
팔건도 八犍度 602
팔건도론 八犍度論 15
팔건론 八犍論 602
팔경계 八敬戒 226, 601, 602, 609

팔경법 八敬法 602
팔계 八戒 477, 520, 603, 610
팔계 八計 601
팔계(재) 八戒(齋) 602
팔계재 八戒齋 602, 609
팔고 八苦 230, 602, 604
팔곡사두 八斛四斗 243
팔관재 八關齋 602
팔괘 八卦 425
팔교 八憍 602
팔교 八教 573, 602
팔교 八校 277
팔교도 八交道 603
팔구의 八句義 603
팔금 八禁 603
팔기 八棄 603
팔기 八記 329
팔난 八難 603
팔난무가애 八難無暇礙 605
팔념(문) 八念(門) 603
팔념(법) 八念(法) 603
팔념경 八念經 603
팔다라수 八多羅樹 603
팔대(지옥) 八大(地獄) 603
팔대관음 八大觀音 603
팔대금강동자 八大金剛童子 603, 604
팔대금강명왕 八大金剛明王 603
팔대동자 八大童子 206, 603
팔대명왕 八大明王 603, 604
팔대보살 八大菩薩 604, 606
팔대보살경 八大菩薩經 604
팔대보살만다라경 八大菩薩曼荼羅經 604
팔대신고 八大辛苦 604
팔대영탑 八大靈塔 604
팔대영탑 八大靈塔 610
팔대영탑범찬 八大靈塔梵讚 342
팔대자재 八大自在 608
팔대자재아 八大自在我 326, 517, 604
팔대장 八大將 393
팔대지옥 八大地獄 607, 610
팔도 八倒 604, 609
팔도(선) 八道(船) 604
팔도(지) 八道(支) 604
팔도(행) 八道(行) 604
팔도선 八道船 609
팔도행 八道行 609
팔동자 八童子 157, 604
팔론 八論 604
팔륜 八輪 604
팔마 八魔 604
팔만 八慢 604
팔만 八萬 604
팔만사(천) 八萬四(千) 604
팔만사천법장 八萬四千法藏 604
팔만십이 八萬十二 604
팔만위의 八萬威儀 604
팔무가 八無暇 603, 605
팔문(양익) 八門(兩益) 605
팔문(이오) 八門(二悟) 605
팔미 八味 605
팔미 八迷 601, 605
팔바라이 八波羅夷 603, 605, 610
팔발(사) 八發(思) 169
팔방상하 八方上下 605
팔방천 八方天 605
팔배 八輩 605
팔배사 八背捨 605, 611
팔벌 八筏 605
팔법 八法 605, 610
팔변 八辯 605
팔변화 八變化 605, 607, 608
팔보살 八菩薩 606
팔복생처 八福生處 606
팔복전 八福田 606
팔부(중) 八部(衆) 606
팔부귀중 八部鬼衆 606
팔부사의 八不思議 601
팔부정 八不淨 601
팔불 八不 220, 544
팔불 八佛 606
팔불(중도) 八不(中道) 601
팔불가과법 八不可過法 602
팔불가월 八不可越 601
팔불가월법 八不可越法 602
팔불정견 八不正見 601
팔불정관 八不正觀 601
팔불중관 八不中觀 601
팔불중도 八不中道 605, 610
팔불현실 八不顯實 601
팔비천 八臂天 606
팔사 八師 606
팔사 八邪 606
팔사경 八師經 606
팔사수신 八事隨身 606
팔사파 八思巴 169, 598, 606
팔상 八相 639
팔상(성도) 八相(成道) 606
팔상성도 八相成道 607
팔상시현 八相示現 606
팔색번 八色幡 607
팔선 八仙 307
팔성 八成 607
팔성 八聖 607
팔성(도지) 八聖(道支) 607
팔성도 八聖道 108, 135, 405, 534
팔성도지 八聖道支 609
팔성립인 八成立因 607
팔수 八水 607
팔승처 八勝處 607, 611
팔시 八時 607
팔식 八識 76, 135, 252, 275, 419, 509, 607, 608
waves in mind sea 355
팔식심소 八識心所 607
팔식심왕 八識心王 607
팔식체별 八識體別 607
팔식체일 八識體一 607
팔신변 八神變 605, 607
팔십 八十 607
팔십송률 八十誦律 607
팔십수형호 八十隨形好 607
팔십일과 八十一科 607
팔십일법 八十一法 607
팔십일품사혹 八十一品思惑 55, 607
팔십종호 八十種好 176, 607
팔십화엄경 八十華嚴經 607
팔억사천만념 八億四千萬念 607
팔열지옥 八熱地獄 607
팔엽 八葉 607
팔엽연대 八葉蓮臺 607
팔엽연좌 八葉蓮座 607
팔엽원 八葉院 607
팔엽화 八葉華 209
팔예 八穢 608
팔오삼이 八五三二 608
팔왕일 八王日 435, 608
팔왕자 八王子 608
팔원 八圓 608
팔위 八位 467, 608
팔위태장 八位胎藏 608, 613
팔유 八喩 231
팔유행 八由行 608, 609
팔유행 八遊行 608, 609

팔음 八音 608
팔인 八忍 30, 139, 363, 608, 610
팔인지 八人地 369
팔인지 八忍地 369
팔인팔관 八忍八觀 608
팔인팔지 八忍八智 608
팔자 八字 608
팔자문수법 八字文殊法 608
팔자재 八自在 605, 608
팔자포자 八字布字 608
팔재(계) 八齋(戒) 609
팔재계 八齋戒 602
팔전 八纏 609
팔전(성) 八囀(聲) 609
팔전도 八顚倒 523, 604, 609
팔전성 八轉聲 587
팔정 八定 609
팔정도 八正道 7, 135, 285, 527, 528, 529, 530, 589, 604, 605, 606, 607, 608, 610
四依入正 255
四諦 257
팔정도(분) 八正道(分) 609
팔정도경 八正道經 609
팔정문 八正門 135, 609
팔제 八諦 609
팔조상승 八組相承 609
팔존중법 八尊重法 602, 609
팔종 八宗 54, 609
팔종(보)시 八種(布)施 610
팔종구종 八宗九宗 609
팔종법 八種法 610
팔종별해탈계 八種別解脫戒 609
팔종보시 八種布施 648
팔종수기 八種授記 610
팔종승법 八種勝法 602, 610
팔종죽 八種粥 610
팔종청풍 八種淸風 610
팔중무가 八重無價 610
팔중죄 八重罪 605
팔중주 八中洲 610
팔중진보 八重眞寶 610
팔지 八地 92, 464, 613
팔지 八支 610
팔지 八智 30, 110, 139, 363, 608, 610
팔지재 八支齋 602
팔직도 八直道 608, 609
팔직행 八直行 608, 609
팔차 八遮 610
팔천 八天 610
팔촉 八觸 610
팔타 八墮 610
팔탑 八塔 610
팔풍 八風 605, 610
팔한(빙)지옥 八寒(冰)地獄 610
팔한지옥 八寒地獄 554, 603
팔한팔열 八寒八熱 611
팔해 八海 611
팔해탈 八解脫 605, 607, 611, 623
팔회 八會 611
패 唄 611
패 孛 611
패 敗 611
패 梖 611
패 稗 611
패 貝 611
패가이 孛伽夷 611
패괴보살 敗壞菩薩 611
패근 敗根 611
패기 唄器 611
패닉 唄匿 611
패다 貝多 611
패다라(엽) 貝多羅(葉) 611
패다수 梖多樹 611
패다엽 梖多葉 611
패문 貝文 611
패비구 唄比丘 611
패사 唄士 611
패사 唄師 585, 611
패사문 稗沙門 611
패엽 貝葉 611
패제 稗稊 611
패종 敗種 611
패종 貝鐘 611
패지가 貝支迦 611
패찬 唄讚 611
패첩 貝牒 611
편 便 612
方便 173
편 偏 612
편 徧 또는 遍 612
편 片 611
편 篇 611
편 編 612
편 蝙 612
편 遍 272, 507, 612
편각 徧覺 612
편공 偏空 594, 612
편교 偏教 478, 612
편길 徧吉 272, 612
편단 偏袒 612
편리 便利 612
편목 篇目 611
편문 偏門 612
편발 編髮 612
편복승 蝙蝠僧 612
편삼 偏衫 612
편선 片禪 611
편선나 甂膳那 612
편성 徧成 612
편소 偏小 612
편소정 偏小情 612
편용 便用
方便 173
편원 偏圓 612
편지 徧智 491
편진 偏眞 612
편집 偏執 612
편취 篇聚 611
평 平 613
평 苹 613
평 評 613
평가사 平袈裟 613
평도교 平道教 478
평등 平等 98, 237, 271, 272, 563, 613
평등각 平等覺 613
평등관 平等觀 613
평등교 平等教 613
평등대혜 平等大慧 613
평등력 平等力 613
평등법 平等法 613
평등법신 平等法身 613
평등불이 平等不二 400
평등성 平等性 187, 366, 613
평등성지 平等性智 259, 416, 430, 613
평등심 平等心 613
평등왕 平等王 613
평등의 平等義 613
평등지 平等智 613
평론 平論 271
평론 評論 613
평사 萍沙 613
평사왕 萍沙王 194
평사왕오원경 萍沙王五願經 211

평상 平常 613
평생 平生 613
평주 評註 613
폐 吠 224, 613
폐 廢 613
폐 弊 614
폐 閉 613
폐관 閉關 613
폐권립실 廢權立實 613
폐나야달가 吠那野怛加 227
폐노리야 吠努璃耶 613
폐람 吠嵐 613
폐람(바) 吠藍(婆) 227
폐람바 吠嵐婆 227
폐람승가 吠嵐僧伽 227
폐려다 閉黎多 613
폐로 閉爐 613
폐로자나 吠路者那 613
폐로차나 吠嚧遮那 227, 613
폐류리 吠瑠璃 227
폐류리(야) 吠瑠璃(耶) 613
폐마질달리 吠摩質呾利 228
폐마질달리 吠摩質怛利 613
폐사 吠奢 613
폐사 吠舍 613
폐사거 吠舍佉 229, 613
폐사리 吠舍釐 or 吠舍離 613
폐사리 吠舍離 or 吠舍釐 229
폐세사 吠世師 613
폐세사가 吠世史迦 452, 613
폐솔노 吠率怒 613
폐솔노천 吠率怒天 193
폐슬나미 吠瑟拏微 583
폐시 蔽尸 614
폐시 閉尸 608, 613, 614
폐실라말나 吠室囉末拏 613
폐악수선 廢惡修善 613
폐욕 弊欲 614
폐적현본 廢迹顯本 613
폐전교 廢前教 613
폐제희 吠提希 452
폐제희불다라 吠題呬弗多羅 452
폐타 吠陀 613
폐타 吠陀 or 吠馱 452
폐파리(야) 吠玻璃(耶) 600
포 布 614
포 怖 614
포 抱 614
포 捕 614
포 泡 614
포 胞 614
포 蒲 487, 614
포 袍 614
포 褒 614
포 逋 614
포 飽 614
포갈 捕喝 614
포게 捕揭 614
포교 布教 614
포니아게 布儞阿偈 614
포다 鋪多 614
포다(라) 逋多(羅) 195, 614
포단 蒲團 614
포단나 布單那 614
포달나 布怛那 614
포달납 布達拉 614
포달락가 布呾洛加 195
포대화상 布袋和尙 614
포랄나 布剌拏 615
포로갈지섭벌라 逋盧羯底攝伐羅 614
포로나발다라 布嚕那跋陀羅 615
포로바 布嚕婆 113
포로바 布嚕波 211
포로바비제하 布嚕婆毗提訶 216, 615
포로사 布嚕沙 615
포로사 布路沙 615
포로사포라 布路沙布羅 615
포리가 布利迦 615
포리바 逋利婆 113
포리바비제하 逋利婆鼻提賀 216, 614, 615
포마 怖魔 614
포복 袍服 614
포불각 抱佛脚 614
포사 布史 615
포사 逋沙 211, 614
포사니 蒲闍尼 614
포사타 布沙他 615
포사타 逋沙他 614
포살 布薩 615
포살건도 布薩犍度 615
포살일 布薩日 615
포살타파 布薩陀婆 615
포살호 布薩護 615
포상 袍裳 614
포새 蒲塞 614
포선니 蒲膳尼 614
포쇄타 布灑他 615
포슬징가 布瑟徵迦 429
포슬파 布瑟波 615
포언벌야 布焉伐耶 73
포여나제 布如那提 73
포여조벌야 布如鳥伐耶 615
포열 疱裂 610
포영 泡影 614
포외 怖畏 104
포외시 怖畏施 614
포자관 布字觀 615
포자나 布刺拏 206
포자나 布刺拏 or 布刺那 or 晡刺拏 or 晡刺那 206
포저락가 布咀洛迦 615
포태 胞胎 614
포포 捕哺 614
포학 飽學 614
포한 怖悍 37
포한 怖捍 614
포휴라란 袍休羅蘭 614
폭 瀑 615
폭류 瀑流 615
표 幖 615
표 標 616
표 表 488, 615
표덕 表德 615
표령 標領 616
표무표계 表無表戒 615
표백 表白 26, 615
표상 標相 291
표색 表色 301, 518, 615
표시 表示 615
표월 標月 616
표전 表詮 615
표찰 表刹 564, 615
표치 幖幟 615
표치 標幟 616
품 品 616
품 稟 616
품교 稟敎 616
품구 稟具 616
풍 諷 616
풍 豐 616
풍 風 271, 430, 552, 583, 616
풍(륜)제 風(輪)際 616
풍(전)등 風(前)燈 616
풍(전)촉 風(前)燭 616

풍(중)등 風(中)燈 616
풍(중)촉 風(中)燭 616
풍경 諷經 616
풍경 風磬 616
풍계 風界 616
풍대 風大 616
풍도 風刀 616
풍륜 風輪 616
풍분삼매 風奮三昧 616
풍삼매 風三昧 616
풍색 風色 616
풍송 諷誦 616
풍송 諷頌 616
풍재 豊財 616
풍재 風災 616
풍천 風天 616
풍탁 風鐸 199
피 彼 616
피 披 616
피 皮 616
피 被 616
피 避 616
피가루자 皮可漏子 616
피각루자 皮殼漏子 616
피다 彼茶 616
피대 皮袋 616
피라 避羅 616
피박 皮薄 126
피번뇌장 皮煩惱障 288
피사 避死 616
피안 彼岸 388, 616
피엽의관음 被葉衣觀音 616
피위 被位 616
피의 皮衣 616
피체 披剃 616
피타 皮陀 231, 452
피피공 彼彼空 582
피혁 皮革 616
픽 煏 616
픽추 煏芻 225, 616
필 必 616
필 畢 486, 617
필 筆 616
필 苾 617
필가 鞞柯 617
필가라마아질다 鞞柯羅摩阿迭多 232
필경 畢境 617
필경 畢竟 384
필경각 畢境覺 617
필경공 畢境空 617
필경공 畢竟空 219
필경무 畢境無 617
필경의 畢境依 617
필경지 畢境智 617
필도가 苾闍伽 284
필락차 畢洛叉 617
필랄차 畢剌叉 617
필력가 畢力迦 617
필률가 畢栗迦 617
필률탁흘나 必栗託仡那 617
필륵지지가(불) 畢勒支底迦(佛) 617
필릉 畢陵 125
필릉(가바차) 畢陵(伽婆蹉) 617
필리다 畢利多 617
필리잉가 畢哩孕迦 233
필리차 畢利叉 384, 617
필발(라) 畢鉢(羅) 617
필사지 畢舍支 229
필사차 畢舍遮 617
필수 筆受 616
필수발타 邲輸跋陀 617
필적가 必棏家 617
필정 必定 616
필지 必至 617
필지불 畢支佛 617
필추 苾芻 225, 617
필추니 苾芻尼 225, 617
필추율의 苾芻律儀 617
핍 乏 617
핍 逼 617
핍뇌 逼惱 114
핍도 乏道 617
핍박 逼迫 617

(ㅎ)

하 下 56, 268, 294, 544, 618
하 何 618
하 夏 618
하 河 618
하 荷 618
하 蝦 618
하 訶 1, 2
하 賀 618
하간 下間 297, 618
하거 下炬 619
하견 下肩 20
하경 夏竟 618
하계 下界 618
하구식 下口食 618
하근 下根 618
하날파 賀捺婆 618
하담 荷擔 618
하당 下堂 618
하라타 賀羅馱 or 賀邏馱 618
하라하라 訶羅訶羅 1
하라학 訶囉鶴 270
하라호라 何羅怙羅 618
하랍 下臘 298
하랍 下蠟 618
하랍 夏臘 119, 185, 618
하력피타 荷力皮陀 618
하리 訶利 1
하리 訶梨 1
하리기사 訶利枳舍 1
하리나 何履那 618
하리달계 訶梨怛鷄 1
하리득지 訶梨得枳 1
하리륵 訶梨勒 1
하리발마 訶梨跋摩 1
하리제 訶利帝 or 訶哩帝 1
하리제 訶梨帝 59
하리지 訶利底 1
하리지남 訶利底南 1
하리지모 訶利底母 1
하마선 蝦蟆禪 618
하만 夏滿 618
하말 夏末 618
하바 訶婆 639
하배관 下輩觀 618
하배하생관 下輩下生觀 618
하봉 下棒 619
하비지 河鼻旨 554, 618
하사 下士 298, 545
하사 河沙 618
하사생 何似生 618
하삼도 下三途 461, 619
하생경 下生經 619
하서 河西 550
하수 夏首 618
하승 下乘 619
하승열반장 下乘涅槃障 367
하실다 訶悉多 1
하안거 夏安居 618
하야 何耶 618
하야게리바 何耶揭唎婆 618

하야홀리부 賀野紇哩嚩 618
하어 下語 619
하여륵과 訶黎勒果 510
하연흘리부 賀演屹哩嚩 618
하열승 下劣乘 619
하원 下元 545
하의 下衣 427, 619
하이마가 何夷摩柯 618
하자 訶子 1
하전 下轉 299, 619
하제 下祭 299
하제중생 下濟衆生 619
하종 下種 619
하좌 下座 299
하좌 夏坐 618
하중 下衆 619
하중 夏中 618
하중 夏衆 618
하지 下地 469, 619
하지추고장 下地麤苦障 619
하진 下塵 619
하타가 訶咤迦 2
하택 荷澤 587
하팔지 下八地 619
하품 下品 240, 294, 300, 618, 619
하품상생 下品上生 619
하품중생 下品中生 619
하품하생 下品下生 56, 619
하해 夏解 618
하호라 何怙羅 118
하화 下化 619
하화 下火 619
하화(중생) 下化(衆生) 619
학 學 620
학 瘧 620
학 鶴 620
학가지 瘧加持 620
학교성미 學敎成迷 620
학귀 瘧鬼 620
학도 學徒 620
학려 學侶 620
학륵나 鶴勒那 486
학륵나야사 鶴勒那夜奢 620
학림 鶴林 620
학말 鶴秣 620
학무학 學無學 620
학법녀 學法女 620
학병법 瘧病法 620
학살라 鶴薩羅 620
학생 學生 620
학수 鶴樹 620
학신계 學信戒 369
학실나 鶴悉那 620
학원 鶴苑 620
학인 學人 620
학인전 學人田 481
학자 學者 620
학장 學匠 620
학학파 嚯嚯婆 643
학학파 矐矐婆 554
학화 學和 469
학회 學悔 620
한 寒 620
한 恨 323, 460, 620
한 汗 620
한 漢 620
한 閑 620
한 限 620
한거십덕 閑居十德 620
한노 恨怒. 620
한도인 閑道人 620
한률타 汗栗馱 351
한률태 汗栗太 351
한림 寒林 342, 620
한무고사 漢武故事 646
한문자 閑文字 620
한분 限分 620
한서 寒暑 620
한심 恨心 620
한열화합생 寒熱和合生 250
한옥 寒獄 620
한왕자 漢王子 550
한율타 汗栗馱 647
한율타 汗栗馱 620
한정 閑靜 376
한제시 寒際時 289
한진경 閑塵境 620
한처 閑處 620
한천종 漢天種 549
할 割 621
할 喝 9, 621
할 曷 620
할 瞎 621
할 訶 1
할단 割斷 621
할라사길리희 曷羅闍姞利呬 620
할라사보라 曷羅闍補羅 620
할라호 曷羅胡 620
할라호라 曷羅怙羅 620
할랄달나게파 曷剌怛那揭婆 620
할랄예 曷剌羠 620
할려 瞎驢 621
할루생 瞎屢生 621
할리 嗽里 1
할리계사 嗽里鷄舍 1
할리나 曷利拏 620
할리사벌탄나 曷利沙伐彈那 620
할부다 曷部多 620
함 函 621
함 含 621
함 咸 621
함 鹹 621
함개건곤 函蓋乾坤 267
함개상응 函蓋相應 621
함동 咸同 621
함령 含靈 621
함류 含類 621
함생 含生 621
함수 鹹水 621
함식 含識 621
함정 含情 621
함중교 含中敎 621
함화 含華 621
합 合 431, 621
합 盍 621
합 蛤 621
합 鴿 621
합단 合壇 621
합련화 合蓮華 621
합루긍 盍樓亘 621
합리관음 蛤唎觀音 621
합밀 哈密 621
합발마나파 盍鉢摩那婆 386
합비 合譬 431
합살 合殺 621
합십 合十 621
합용 合用 621
합원 鴿園 6, 621
합장 合掌 621
합장차수 合掌叉手 621
합조 合爪 621
합천 盍天 321, 621
합파(마나) 盍波(摩那) 621
합혼수 合婚樹 343
합혼수 合昏(樹) 621
합환 合歡 621
항 亢 485

항 恒 12, 621
항 降 621
항가 恒伽 621
항가달 恒伽達 621
항가사 恒伽沙 621
항가제바 恒伽提婆 621
항가하 恒伽河 621
항다라 抗陀羅 284
항마 降魔 622
항복 降伏 622
항사 恒娑 621
항사 恒沙 621
항삼세 降三世 413
항삼세 降三世 603, 621
항삼세금강 降三世金剛 431
항삼세명왕 降三世明王 451
항삼세명왕 降三世明王 431, 621
항상 恒常 621
항수 恒水 621
항염마존 降焰魔尊 622
항용 降龍 622
항용발 降龍鉢 622
항용복호 降龍伏虎 622
항하 恒河 235, 618, 621
해 姟 622
해 害 285, 323, 460, 622
해 廨 622
해 懈 622
해 海 255, 622
해 解 55, 283, 622
　四分 248
해 該 622
해각 害覺 622
해경십불 解境十佛 622
해계 解界 622
해공 解空 622
해공제일 解空第一 329
해덕 海德 622
해동 海東
　曉公四敎 239
해동고승전 海東高僧傳 622
해동사 海東師 446, 450
해라 該羅 622
해람초 解纜鈔 604
해룡왕 海龍王 622
해룡왕경 海龍王經 622
해만 懈慢 192
해만계 懈慢界 622
해만국 懈慢國 622
해상 害想 622
해섭 該攝 622
해섭문 該攝門 210
해심밀경 解深密經 187, 262, 282, 456
　六部大乘經 462
해심밀경 解深蜜經 622
해오 解悟 622
해운 海雲 134
해원주 廨院主 622
해인 海印 622
해인사 海印寺 29, 622
해인삼매 海印三昧 105
해일체중생언어 解一切衆生言語 623
해적 解賊 108
해제 解制 623
해조음 海潮音 622
해주 海珠 622
해중 海衆 622
해지견 解知見 623
해탈 解脫 143, 188, 228, 269, 273, 405, 418, 475, 593, 611, 622, 623
　木底 144
해탈계 解脫戒 623
해탈관 解脫冠 623
해탈당상의 解脫幢相衣 623
해탈덕 解脫德 283
해탈도 解脫道 242, 479, 623
해탈문 解脫門 279, 623
해탈미 解脫味 623
해탈복 解脫服 623
해탈상 解脫相 279, 623
해탈신 解脫身 623
해탈의 解脫衣 623
해탈이 解脫耳 623
해탈장 解脫障 488
해탈지견 解脫知見 418, 623
해탈처 解脫處 623
해탈천 解脫天 623
해탈청정법전 解脫淸淨法殿 623
해탈풍 解脫風 623
해탈해 解脫海 623
해태 懈怠 622
해태적 懈怠賊 622
해하 解夏 623
해행 解行 623
해행발심 解行發心 275
해행생 解行生 279
해행신 解行身 251
해행주 解行住 466
해행지 解行地 623
해회 海會 622
행 行 80, 140, 222, 223, 288, 361, 365, 423, 424, 605, 608, 623
　佛性 218
　四分 248
행각(승) 行脚(僧) 624
행건도 行犍度 624
행걸 行乞 624
행고 行苦 266, 624
행공 行空 582
행공양 行供養 624
행과 行果 624
행교 行敎 624, 642
행교화 行敎化 625
행덕 行德 624
행도 行道 624
행도적주 行道迹住 466
행리 行履 624
행만 行滿 366, 624, 639
행모 行母 624
행묘 行妙 358
행발 行鉢 624
행법 行法 276
　四法 247
행복 行福 277
행불성 行佛性 482
행사 行捨 584
행사의 行四依 251, 255
행사초중 行事鈔中 267
행상 行像 624
행상 行相 363, 624
행선 行善 624
행수 行樹 624
행신 行信 624
행업 行業 624
행온 行蘊 624
행요 行要 624
행우 行雨 624
행원 行願 624
행위 行位 477
행유 行有 397
행유식 行唯識 429
행의 行儀 624
행인 行人 624
행일 行一 255

행입 行入 488
행자 行者 624
행자기간 行者期間 624
행족 行足 624
행주 行籌 625
행주좌와 行住坐臥 625
행증 行證 625
행측 行厠 625
행향 行香 625
행화 行化 625
행화 行和 469
행화 行華 625
향 享 625
향 向 625
향 鄕 625
향 響 625
향 餉 625
향 香 625
향(광장)엄 香(光莊)嚴 625
향(복)의 香(複)衣 626
향(수)해 香(水)海 625
향거 餉佉 297
향계 香界 625
향공 餉供 625
향국 香國 626
향당 享堂 625
향로 香爐 625
향룡뇌 香龍腦 625
향루 香樓 625
향반 香盤 626
향법 向法 380
향산 香山 16, 31, 375, 625
향상 向上 625
향상 香象 363, 625, 626
향상대사 香象大師 625
향상지문 香象之文 625
향색 香色 626
향수 香水 625
향수전 香水錢 625
향식 香食 625
향신 香神 626
향실 香室 626
향염 香染 626
향왕 香王 626
향욕 香欲 626
향유 香油 322
향음신 香音神 626
향인 鄕人 625
향인 香印 626
향입 香入 626
향적 香積 246, 625, 626
향전 香殿 626
향전 香篆 626
향주 香廚 626
향주 香炷 626
향진 香塵 626
향집 香集 625, 626
향찰 香刹 626
향취산 香聚山 or 香醉山 625
향탕 香湯 626
향풍산 香風山 626
향피회 向彼悔 625
향피회죄 向彼悔罪 163
향하 向下 625
향화 香火 626
향화 香華 626
향환 香丸 626
허 虛 485, 626
seven northern constellations 208
허 許 626
허가 虛假 626
허가 許可 626
허공 虛空 15, 50, 626
허공계 虛空界 366, 627
허공고 虛空庫
四無量心 245
허공무위 虛空無爲 627
허공법신 虛空法身 428, 627
허공불 虛空佛 219
허공신 虛空神 627
허공신 虛空身 627
허공안 虛空眼 535, 627
허공잉 虛空孕 627
허공장 虛空藏 302, 361, 363, 431, 484, 603, 627
四無量心 245
허공장보살 虛空藏菩薩 103, 267
허공장보살경 虛空藏菩薩經 626
허공주 虛空住 626
허공처 虛空處 239
허공천 虛空天 414, 438, 627
허공화 虛空華 627
허광어 虛誑語 627
허당 虛堂 626
허망 虛妄 350, 560, 626
허망륜 虛妄輪 626
허망법 虛妄法 626
허망부실 虛妄不實 265
허무 虛無 626
허무신 虛無身 626
허심 虛心 626
허언 虛言 627
허위 虛僞 626
허정계 虛定界 187
허중 虛中 435
허통 虛通 605
헌 獻 627
헌신 獻身 627
헌향 獻香 627
험 驗 627
험생인중 驗生人中 627
험생지옥 驗生地獄 627
혁 革 627
혁총 革蔥 627
현 懸 628
현 玄 628
현 現 159, 280, 627
현 賢 280, 363, 429, 627
현 顯 301, 615, 628
T'ien-t'ai four schools 239
현가 顯加 476
현가 顯家 628
현각 玄覺 628
현감거사 玄鑑居士 628
현겁 賢劫 165, 170, 212, 265, 627
현겁경 賢劫經 627
현경 玄景 628
현경 玄鏡 628
현경 顯經 628
현고 玄高 628
현과당 現過當 628
현과미 現過未 628
현관 現觀 628
현광 懸曠 628
현교 顯敎 161, 363, 477, 628
현기 懸記 628
현기광 現起光 489, 628
현담 懸談 628
현담 玄談 628
현당 現當 628
현도 玄道 628
현도만다라 現圖曼陀羅 628
현두 賢豆 494, 572, 627
현두 賢頭 345
현랑 玄朗 541, 628
현량 現量 119, 479, 605, 629

比量 226
현량상위 現量相違 629
현로 顯露 628
현료 顯了 470
현류 玄流 629
현명 顯冥 628
현명 顯明 628
현문 玄門 371, 629
현밀 顯蜜 628
현범 玄範 629
현병 賢甁 107, 627
현보 現報 276, 629
현본 顯本 628
현사 玄沙 629
현상 現相 464, 629
현상 現象 359
현상병 賢祥甁 533
현색 顯色 628
현색불상응염 現色不相應染 464
현생 現生 629
현생이익 現生利益 629
현성 現成 629
현성 賢聖 627
현세 現世 629
현소 玄疏 629
현수 賢首 412, 516, 562, 627
현수 법장 賢首法藏 427, 639
현수경 賢首經 628
현수법장 賢首法藏 190
현수종 賢首宗 367, 628
현시 顯示 628
현식 現識 282, 376, 422, 629
현식 顯識 628
현신 現身 629
현실종 顯實宗 258
현양론 顯揚論 370
현업 現業 396
현완 玄琬 629
현우경 賢愚經 342, 590
현유 現喩 629
현유 現有 286
현응 玄應 629, 632
현응음의 玄應音義 629
현의 玄義 146, 269, 629
天台三部 573
현익 現益 629
현인 賢人 627
현일 玄一 630
현자 賢者 627
현장 玄奘 99, 144, 267, 276, 288, 305, 630
현재 現在 280, 475, 630
현재세 現在世 630
현재현겁 現在賢劫 630
현재현겁천불경 現在賢劫千佛經 627
현전 現前 380, 630
현전 顯典 628
현전비니 現前毘尼 583
현전심 現前心 369
현전지 現前地 369, 630
현정 顯正 628
현종 玄宗 630
현종 顯宗 628
현주 賢胄 300
현주부 賢胄部 325
현증 現證 630
현찬 玄贊 630
현창 玄暢 630
현통가실 現通假實 367
현행 現行 630
현행법 現行法 630
현호 賢護 170, 363, 627
혈 血 630
혈도 血塗 270
혈도 血途 630
혈맥 血脈 630
혈분경 血盆經 630
혈분지 血盆池 555
혈서 血書 630
혈오지 血汚池 630
혈해 血海 630
협 夾 631
협 挾 631
협 脇 631
협 頰 630
협사 脇士 631
협산 夾山 631
협시 挾侍 631
협시 脇侍 631
협존 脇尊 631
협존자 脇尊者 486, 599
협차 頰車 630
형 兄 631
형 形 273, 301, 615, 631
형 熒 631
형 荊 631
형 衡 631
형감심 熒感心 631
형감천 熒感天 631
형계 荊溪 86, 360, 479, 572, 631
형구 刑具 648
형량 衡量 631
형모 形貌 286, 631
형모욕 形貌欲 631
형산 形山 631
형산 衡山 631
형상 形像 631
형상 形相 291
형색 形色 631
형악 衡岳 628
台衡 594
형제 兄弟 631
형주 荊州 574
형혹성 熒惑星 631
혜 惠 631
혜 慧 104, 137, 188, 274, 279, 295, 355, 358, 359, 362, 366, 393, 394, 412, 418, 419, 479, 480, 492, 494, 585, 631
四自在 256
혜 醯 631
혜가 慧可 86, 312, 339, 489, 587, 631
six patriarchs 466
혜개 慧愷 631
혜거 慧炬 632
혜검 慧劍 632
혜견 慧見 632
혜경 慧鏡 632
혜과 惠果 609
혜관 慧觀 632
혜광 慧光 41, 603
혜광심 慧光心 369
혜근 慧勤 278
혜근 慧根 485, 632
혜남 慧南 644
혜능 慧能 57, 74, 79, 88, 113, 121, 312, 332, 410, 536, 538, 587, 632
six patriarchs 466
南宗 208
혜도 醯都 631
혜도발라지야 醯都鉢羅底也 631
혜도비타 醯都費陀 496, 631
혜두파타부 醯兜婆拖部 631
혜등 慧燈 632
혜등왕 慧燈王 632
혜라 醯羅 631
혜력 慧力 361, 414, 632

혜류 慧流 632
혜리 惠利 631
혜림 慧琳 632
혜림음의 慧琳音義 632, 648
혜마발다부 醯摩跋多部 631
혜마발타 醯摩跋陀 631
혜마부다 醯摩嚩多 631
혜명 慧命 352, 632
혜명 慧明 628
혜목 慧目 632
혜문 慧文
천台九祖 572
혜박 慧縛 632
혜사 慧思 555, 572, 631, 632
teacher of Chih-i 594
台衡 594
天台九祖 572
혜상보살문대권선경 慧上菩薩問大權善經 90
혜수 慧壽 632
혜수 慧數 632
혜신 慧身 632
혜심기특 慧心奇特 69
혜안 慧眼 362, 632
혜업 慧業 632
혜운 慧雲 632
혜원 慧苑 632, 640
苑公四敎 239
혜원 慧遠 120, 175, 325, 389, 446, 531, 598
혜원음의 慧苑音義 632
혜월 慧月 632
혜의 慧義 632
혜인 慧印 632
혜인 慧忍 632
혜일 慧日 378, 632
혜장 慧藏 633
혜정 慧淨 633
혜족 慧足 633
혜초 慧超 633
혜학 慧學 295, 633
혜해 慧解 633
혜해탈 慧解脫 492, 633
혜환 慧幻 633
혜희 慧喜 603
호 互 633
호 呼 633
호 好 300, 633
호 毫 633
호 浩 634
호 湖 633
호 狐 633
호 瑚 633
호 胡 633
호 虎 634
호 號 634
호 護 634
四梵堂 247
四等, 慈悲喜捨 242
호감 顥鑑 598
호경 胡經 633
호계신 護戒神 634
호구산 虎丘山 634
호국 護國 634
호궤 互跪 633
호궤 胡跪 633
호규 號叫 554, 603
호규 號叫 60
호규지옥 號叫地獄 634
호남 湖南 633
호념 護念 634
호도극도 呼圖克圖 633
호도인 胡道人 633
호동자법 護童子法 634
호두 胡豆 143, 158
호란 胡亂 633
호로차나 胡嚧遮那 633
호마 呼摩 633
호마 呼麼 634
호마 護摩 246, 567, 633, 634
four degrees 242
호마 護磨 634
호명 護命 634
호명대사 護明大士 634
호묘 浩妙 634
호미 毫眉 633
호박 琥珀 634
호법 護法 362, 634
호법신 護法神 634
호부 護符 634
호사 護寺 634
호사가람 互娑伽藍 633
호상 好相 633
호상 毫相 633
호생 好生 633
호성조 好聲鳥 633
호세사천왕 護世四天王 260
호세자 護世者 634
호소다 胡蘇多 633
호신 護身 634
호실건 胡實健 633
호심 護心 360
호연 瑚璉 633
호용죄 互用罪 633
호음조 好音鳥 633
호이 虎耳 242, 634
호인 虎寅 365
호자 胡子 633
호조 好照 633
호종족 胡種族 633
호토극도 胡土克圖 633
호필나 護苾那 25, 634
호호 633
호호 呼呼 60, 554
호호파 虎虎婆 554, 634
호흡 呼吸 648
혹 惑 269, 271, 295, 608, 634
혹도 惑道 270
혹업고 惑業苦 124, 178, 634
혹염 惑染 634
혹인 惑人 634
혹장 惑障 634
혹착 惑著 634
혹취 惑趣 634
혹행고 惑行苦 387
혼 惛 634
혼 昏 634
혼 混 635
혼 魂 634
혼고 昏鼓 634
혼돈 混沌 635
혼묵다 昏默多 634
혼백 魂魄 634
혼성 昏城 634
혼식 昏識 634
혼신 魂神 634
혼종 昏鐘 634
혼취 昏醉 634
혼침 惛沈 634
혼회 昏晦 645
홀 忽 635
홀로마 忽露摩 635
홀름 忽懍 635
홍 弘 635
홍 紅 420, 635
홍(서)원 弘(誓)願 635
홍교 弘敎 635
홍교 紅敎 635
홍련지옥 紅蓮地獄 635
홍련화 紅蓮花 635

홍법 弘法 368, 609, 635
홍복사 弘福寺 630
홍서 弘誓 635
홍서문 弘誓門 360
홍선 弘宣 635
홍의파 紅衣派 635
홍인 弘忍 312, 587, 635
six patriarchs 466
北宗 208
홍주 洪州 177
홍통 弘通 635
화 化 283, 636
화 和 635
화 火 342, 552, 583, 635
화 畫 635
화 禍 636
화 禾 635
화 花 635
화 華 635, 636
화 話 636
화 貨 635
화(자)락천 化(自)樂天 387
화(합)승 和(合)僧 635
화(합)중 和(合)衆 635
화가나 和伽那 635
화가라 和伽羅 226, 329, 364
화가라(나) 和伽羅(那) 635
화가라나 和伽羅那 69
화개 華蓋 636
화개부 華開敷 499
화객 火客 636
화갱 火坑 636
화거 花筥 635
화경 化境 489, 636
화계 火界 636
火院 640
화계정 火界定 636
화계주 火界咒 636
화공귀기 化功歸己 636
화광 火光 636
화광 華光 636
화광대제 華光大帝 636
화광불 華光佛 243
화광불정 火光佛頂 418
화광삼매 火光三昧 636, 640
화광정 火光定 636
화광존 火光尊 636
화교 化教 478, 636
화구 火狗 636
화궁전 化宮殿 636
화궁전수 化宮殿手 636
화남 和南 166, 635
화녀 化女 640
화니 化尼 637
화니합수 和泥合水 591
화다 化茶 637
화단 化壇 637
화단 火壇 637
화대 火大 637
화대 華臺 637
화덕보살 華德菩薩 637
화덕성군 火德星君 637
화도 化導 637
화도 化度 637
화도 化道 637
화도 火塗 270
화도 火塗 or 火道 637
화도력 化導力 637
화두 火頭 637
화두 話頭 637
화두금강 火頭金剛 637
화라 火羅 637
화라나 和羅那 635
화락 化樂 606
화락천 化樂天 81, 438, 637
화려 火鑪 637
화령 火鈴 637
화로 火爐 637
화룡 花龍 635
화륜 火輪 124, 637
화륜인 火輪印 637
화리 化理 637
화리습미가 貨利習彌迦 635
화만 華鬘 637
화목 和睦 143
화목 華目 637
화문 化門 533
화미 化米 637
화반 火伴 636, 638
화방 華方 638
화범 華梵 638
화법 化法 603, 638, 640
화법 火法 638
화법교 化法教 602
화법사교 化法四教 421, 573, 602, 638
화변 火辨 638
화병 畫餅 635
화보 華報 638
화보살 化菩薩 638
화분지옥 火焚地獄 638
화불 化佛 252, 638
화사 和社 635
화사 和闍 635
화사 火舍 638
화사 火蛇 638
화사법 火祠法 638
화산 禾山 635
화산 華山 638
화상 化相 638
화상 和上 635
화상 和尙 169, 433, 459, 635
화상 畫像 635
화상삼보 化相三寶 638
화색(신) 化色(身) 638
화생 化生 250, 304, 515, 638, 639
화생 火生
火定 641
화생삼매 火生三昧 638, 640
화서 火鼠 640
화석 畫石 305, 635
화성 化城 639
화성 火星 53, 586, 639
화소 化疏 639
화속 化屬 639
화속결연 化俗結緣 639
화수 火首 342
화수 畫水 635
화수 華手 639
화수길 和修吉 636
화수길 和須吉 179, 636
화수밀(다) 和須蜜(多) 636
화수밀다 和須蜜多 179
화순 和順 635
화식 火食 639
화신 化身 99, 186, 214, 282, 283, 351, 471, 472, 484, 519, 561, 639
四身 252
화신 火神 387, 639, 641, 642
화신팔상 化身八相 639
화심 化心 639
화씨 華氏 639
화씨성 華氏城 639
화암 和闇 433
화야 火夜 639
화엄 504
화엄 華嚴 16, 56, 98, 99, 187, 280, 281, 368, 370, 417, 427, 454, 466, 484, 501, 508, 511,

516, 555, 558, 587, 589, 602, 609, 629, 639
四勝身 252
四大部經 241
화엄 華嚴 sūtra 266, 271
화엄경 華嚴經 60, 92, 207, 212, 267, 273, 274, 280, 353, 356, 359, 370, 415, 455, 540, 588, 602, 607, 611, 639
一乘滿教 239
화엄경법계관 華嚴經法界觀 267
화엄경십지품 華嚴經十地品 357
화엄대소 華嚴大疏 359
화엄법계현경 華嚴法界玄鏡 628
화엄부 華嚴部 640
화엄사 華嚴寺 640
화엄삼매 華嚴三昧 639
화엄삼왕 華嚴三王 639
화엄석경십문 華嚴釋經十門 359
화엄시 華嚴時 421, 639
화엄왕 華嚴王 485
화엄원인론 華嚴原人論 447
화엄음의 華嚴音義 640
화엄일승 華嚴一乘 639
화엄일승교분기원통초 華嚴一乘教分記圓通抄 640
화엄일승법계도기 華嚴一乘法界圖記 640
화엄일승법계도원통기 華嚴一乘法界圖圓通記 640
화엄종 華嚴宗 188, 292, 359, 367, 507, 540, 615, 639
別教 193
화연 化緣 640
화염삼매 火燄三昧 640
화예 華翳 640
화완포가사 火浣布袈裟 640
화왕세계 華王世界 640
화요 火曜 640
화요교 火祆教 136
화요일 火曜日 631
화원 化源 640
화원 火院 636, 640
화원(계인) 火院(界印) 64
화원(밀봉인) 火院(密縫印) 64
화유 化誘 640
화융 和融 546
화음천 和音天 301
화의 化儀 602, 638, 640
화의사교 化儀四教 421, 573, 602, 640
화이라 和夷羅 636
화이라원열차 和夷羅洹閱叉 636
화인 化人 640
화인 火印 640
화일체처 火一切處 640
화자 化者 58
화자 和闍 433
화작 化作 640
화장 火帳 641
화장 火葬 640
화장 華藏 161, 641
화장(세)계 華藏(世)界 641
화장여극락 華藏與極樂 641
화장팔엽 華藏八葉 641
화재 火災 641
화재정 火災頂 342
화적 化迹 641
화전 化前 641
화전 化轉 641
화전 和闐 442, 636
화전 火佃 636
화전방편 化前方便 641
화전서 化前序 641
화정 火定 342, 641
화정 火淨 641
화정산 火頂山 641
화제 化制 642
화제이교 化制二教 641
화제이문 化制二門 533
화존 火尊 639, 641
화종거사 火種居士 641
화좌 花座 635
화좌 華座 641
화주 化主 641
화주 火珠 334, 641
화중지병 畫中之餅 635
화지 化地 212, 286, 300
화지부 化地部 325, 509, 641
화차 火車 641
화차지옥 火車地獄 641
화천 火天 636, 639, 642
화천 華天 642
화첨 火栝 642
화취 火聚 642
화취불정 火聚佛頂 418, 642
화취선 火聚仙 642
화치 華齒 357, 642
화칙 話則 636
화타 化他 251, 642
화타수 化他壽 642
화탄 化炭 637
화탕 火湯 642
화태 華胎 642
화택 火宅 442, 501, 642
화택승 火宅僧 642
화토 化土 472, 492, 636, 642
화판 火版 642
화합 和合 635
화합인 和合因 425
화합해 和合海 635
화행 化行 641
화행(이교) 化行(二教) 642
화행이교 化行二教 636
화향환 和香丸 636
화현 化現 642
화혈 花血 635
화혈도 火血刀 642
화회 和會 635
확 鑊 642
확 廓 37
확사 鑊沙 642
확연대오 廓然大悟 37
확탕지옥 鑊湯地獄 642
확확파 臛臛婆 643
환 喚 643
환 幻 643
환 桓 643
환 槵 643
환 歡 643
환 還 643
환 鐶 643
환감 幻感 643
환구 幻垢 643
환년약 還年藥 643
환락원 歡樂園 643
환력 幻力 643
환례 還禮 643
환멸 還滅 643
환문 幻門 643
환문 還門 643
환배 還拜 643
환법 幻法 643
환사 幻士 643
환사 幻師 643
환상 幻相 643
환상 還相 643
환상회향 還相回向 436
환생 還生 643
환속 還俗 643

환신 幻身 643
환심 幻心 643
환야 幻野 643
환원 還源 643
환유 幻有 643
환인 幻人 643
환인 桓因 643
환일왕 幻日王 643
환자 幻者 643
환자 槵子 643
환종 喚鐘 643
환천 鐶釧 643
환향 丸香 643
환향 還香 643
환화 幻化 643
환희 歡喜 246, 372, 374, 643
환희광불 歡喜光佛 378, 643
환희국 歡喜國 643
환희단 歡喜團 643
환희원 歡喜苑 643
환희일 歡喜日 643
환희장마니보정불 歡喜藏摩尼寶精佛 157
환희지 歡喜地 369, 643
환희천 歡喜天 96, 643
환희환 歡喜丸 117, 643
환희회 歡喜會 643
활 活 644
활 豁 644
활 闊 644
활구 活句 240, 644
활국 活國 644
활단 豁旦 551, 644
활명 活命 644
활불 活佛 644
활실다 闊悉多 644
활아자 活兒子 644
황 荒 644
황 黃 420, 644
황공 荒空 644
황교 荒郊 644
황교 黃敎 644
황금 黃金 644
황금택 黃金宅 644
황답 黃沓 644
황로 黃壚 644
황룡 黃龍 310, 410
황룡사 黃龍寺 644
황룡탕 黃龍湯 440
황매동산 黃梅東山 113
황면 黃面 644
황모교 黃帽敎 539, 644
황문 黃門 168, 644
황번 黃幡 644
황벽 黃檗 371, 644
황야 荒野 644
황양목선 黃楊木禪 644
황엽 黃葉 644
황의 黃衣 644
황천 黃泉 644
황혼 黃昏 644
회 回 644, 645
회 廻 645
회 悔 434, 645
회 懷 645
회 晦 645
회 會 272, 645
회 灰 645
회 繪 645
회 迴 645
회가솔탑파 回駕窣塔婆 645
회감 懷感 427
회개 繪蓋 645
회골 回鶻 645
회과 悔過 565, 645
회광반조 回光返照 644
회기 回忌 645
회대입일 廻大入一 645
회두토면 灰頭土面 645
회득 會得 645
회령 懷靈 645
회례 回禮 644
회사 灰沙 645
회사향리 回事向理 644
회산주부 灰山住部 645
회삼귀일 會三歸一 422, 645
회세이향출세 回世而向出世 644
회소향대 回小向大 644
회시 廻施 645
회식 會式 645
회신멸지 灰身滅智 645
회심 回心 644
회심 廻心 645
회심계 回心戒 644
회심참회 回心懺悔 644
회역 會繹 645
회오 回悟 644
회이 僞彝 645
회인 灰人 645
회인향과 回因向果 644
회자향타 回自向他 644
회재 回財 645
회제 回祭 645
회중 會衆 645
회참법 悔懺法 645
회취 回趣 645
회토 懷兎 645
회토자 懷兎者 596
회통 會通 645
회하 會下 645
회하 灰河 645
회향 回向 644, 645
회향 廻向 362, 423, 434, 643, 644, 645
회향 迴向 50
회향발원심 廻向發願心 283
회향최승 廻向最勝 589
회호 僞胡 645
회호 回互 644
획 獲 645
획득 獲得 645
횡 橫 318, 492, 646
횡수 橫竪 646
횡절 橫截 646
횡종 橫縱 646
횡초 橫超 646
횡출 橫出 492, 646
효 孝 646
효 曉 646
효고 曉鼓 646
효공 曉公 646
효공사교 曉公四教 239
효료 曉了 646
효복 孝服 646
효순 孝順 646
효자 孝子 646
후 後 546, 646
후 猴 646
후가 後架 581
후광 後光 646
후덕 厚德 343
후득 後得 491
후득지 後得智 491, 646
후멸 後滅 280
후법 後法 646
후보 後報 276, 646
후생 後生 646
후설 後設 646
후세 後世 646
후신 後身 646

후신 猴申 365
후야 後夜 646
후엄경 厚嚴經
六部大乘經 462
후오(백년) 後五(百年) 646
후오(백세) 後五(百歲) 646
후유 後有 646
후진 後陳 539
후토 后土 595
후패 後唄 646
훈 焄 646
훈 葷 646
훈 薰 340, 646
훈 訓 646
훈습 熏習 646
훈습 薰習 646
훈신 葷辛 646
훈육향 薰陸香 144, 646
훈주 葷酒 646
훈회 訓誨 646
훼 毀 646
훼석 毀釋 646
훼자 毀呰 646
휘일 諱日 67
휴 休 646
휴 鵂 646
휴도 休屠 210, 646
휴류 鵂鶹 280, 646
휴정 休靜 244, 647
흉 胸 647
흉자 胸字 647
흉행 胸行 647
흑 黑 420, 647
흑가 黑袈 647
흑백 黑白 647
흑분 黑分 177, 647
흑승 黑繩 554, 603, 647
흑암 黑闇 647
흑암녀 黑闇女 478
흑암천 黑闇天 647
흑야신 黑夜神 647
흑야천 黑夜天 647
흑업 黑業 647
흑원 黑蚖 647
흑월 黑月 647
흑의 黑衣 647
흑천 黑天 647
흑치 黑齒 357, 647
흑칠통 黑漆桶 647
흑풍 黑風 647
흔 忻 647
흔 欣 647
흔계 欣界 647
흔구 欣求 647
흘 仡 647
흘 吃 15, 647
흘 紇 647
흘 訖 647
흘나 仡那 647
흘로실니 紇露悉泥 647
흘률다 吃栗多 647
흘률저 訖栗著 70
흘리(구) 紇哩(俱) or 紇利(俱) 647
흘리구 紇利俱 647
흘리나야 紇哩娜耶 647
흘리내야 紇哩乃耶 647
흘리다 訖利多 8, 70, 647
흘리다야 紇利陀耶 459
흘리다왕 訖利多王 647
흘리슬나 訖里瑟拏 647
흘리타 鈙利陀 647
흘리타야 紇利陀耶 647
흘리타야 紇哩陀耶 620, 647
흘리타야 訖利馱耶 647
흘쇄 吃灑 17
흘쇄야 吃灑耶 639
흘쇄야 迄灑耶 366
흘차달라 紇差怛羅 222, 564, 647
흠 吽 or 㕳 647
흠 欠 648
흠 欽 647
흠가라신 吽迦囉身 647
흠바라 欽婆羅 647
흠흠 吽吽 647
흡 吸 648
흥 興 648
흥거 興渠 648
흥구 興舊 648
흥기행경하 興起行經下 522
흥성 興盛 648
흥세 興世 648
흥의 興宜 648
흥행 興行 648
희 喜 584, 648
희 嬉 648
희 希 648
희 戲 648
희 煕 648
희각지 喜覺支 648
희견 喜見 648
희견보살 喜見菩薩 648
희견성 喜見城 284, 571, 648
희견천 喜見天 648
희구시 希求施 648
희근 喜根 485
희기 希奇 648
희나연 希那衍 323
희능 悕能 225
희락 喜樂 648
희랄나벌지 呬剌拏伐底 648
희련 熙連 648
희련선 希連禪 80, 648
희련하 希連河 80, 648
희론 戲論 648
희린음의 希麟音義 648
희림원 喜林苑 254, 643, 648
희마달라 呬摩怛羅 648
희망(염)천 戲忘(念)天 648
희무량심 喜無量心 245
희법 希法 648
희사 喜捨 648
희사귀 希祀鬼 648
희수 喜受 648
희심 喜心 360
희열 喜悅 648
희운 希運 644
희유 希有 73, 159, 648
희유인 希有人 648
희인 喜忍 648
희천시 希天施 648
희환 喜歡 648
희회지두식 喜懷之頭飾 450
희희 嬉戲 648
힐 黠 648
힐리 纈利 647
힐예벌다 頡隷伐多 125
힐혜 黠慧 648

편저자 : 고영섭

동국대학교 불교학과 및 동 대학원 석・박사과정 졸업
고려대학교 대학원 철학과 박사과정 수료
불교방송 인터넷 텔레비젼에서 <파워특강 : 고영섭의 한국불교사> 강의
인터넷신문 『불교저널』에 <고영섭 교수의 원효에세이> 연재
현재 동국대학교 불교학과 교수

저서 : 『한국불학사』 1, 2, 3, 4, 『한국불교사』,
『나는 오늘도 길을 간다 : 원효, 한국사상의 새벽』,
『원효탐색』, 『한국의 사상가 10인 : 원효』,
『한국철학자 15인 이후 : 원효 이후』,
『원효, 중생의 마음속에 심은 부처의 가르침』,
『불교적 인간』, 『인문적 인간』, 『불경이야기』 등 20여권이 있다.
1998년~1999년 월간 『문학과 창작』 2회 추천을 완료(신인상)하였으며
시집으로는 『몸이라는 화두』, 『흐르는 물의 선정』, 『황금똥에 대한 삼매』,
『바람과 달빛 아래 흘러간 시』(근간) 등이 있다.

황남주

서울대학교 자연대학 물리학과(1992년) 및
동 대학원 석사과정 졸업(1994년)
원광대학교 한의과대학 한의예과 재학 중
이비즈파트너(주) 대표(2000년~2001년)
(주)지오텔 및 (주)씨디네트웍스 이사 역임(2002년~2008년)
IT멘토협의회장(2007년~2009년)

역서 : 莊子의 길(고려원미디어, 1991년),
명상의 씨앗(늘푸름, 1993년)

한영불교사전
韓英佛教辭典

1판 1쇄 찍음 • 2010년 7월 20일
1판 1쇄 펴냄 • 2010년 7월 30일

편저자 • 고영섭, 황남주
발행인 • 정 현 걸
발 행 • 신 아 사
인 쇄 • 인덕인쇄

출판등록 • 1956년 1월 5일 (제9-52호)
서울특별시 은평구 녹번동 28-36번지(2F)
전화 (02)382－6411 • 팩스 (02)382－6401
홈페이지 • www.shinasa.co.kr
E－mail • shinasa@chol.com

ISBN : 978-89-8396-702-2

정가 40,000원